Peterson's
Two-Year
Colleges
2008

PETERSON'S

A **nelnet** COMPANY

PETERSON'S

A ⓝelnet COMPANY

About Peterson's, a Nelnet company

Peterson's (www.petersons.com) is a leading provider of education information and advice, with books and online resources focusing on education search, test preparation, and financial aid. Its Web site offers searchable databases and interactive tools for contacting educational institutions, online practice tests and instruction, and planning tools for securing financial aid. Peterson's serves 110 million education consumers annually.

For more information, contact Peterson's, 2000 Lenox Drive, Lawrenceville, NJ 08648; 800-338-3282; or find us on the World Wide Web at www.petersons.com/about.

Previous editions published as *Peterson's Annual Guide to Undergraduate Study,* © 1970, 1971, 1972, 1973, 1974, 1975, 1976, 1977, 1978, 1979, 1980, 1981, 1982, and as *Peterson's Guide to Two-Year Colleges,* © 1983, 1984, 1985, 1986, 1987, 1988, 1989, 1990, 1991, 1992, 1993, 1994, 1995, 1996, 1997, 1998, 1999, 2000, 2001, 2002, 2003, 2004, 2005, 2006

Editor: Fern A. Oram; Production Editor: Jill C. Schwartz; Copy Editors: Bret Bollmann, Michael Haines, Brooke James, Sally Ross, Pam Sullivan, and Valerie Bolus Vaughan; Research Project Manager: Daniel Margolin; Research Associate: Mary Meyer-Penniston; Programmers: Phyllis Johnson and Alex Lin; Manufacturing Manager: Ivona Skibicki; Composition Manager: Gary Rozmierski; Client Relations Representatives: Janet Clements-Garwo, Mimi Kaufman, Karen Mount, and Danielle Vreeland; Contributing Editors: Kitty M. Villa and Richard Woodland

ISSN 0894-9328
ISBN-13: 978-0-7689-2401-5
ISBN-10: 0-7689-2401-4

Printed in the United States of America

10   9   8   7   6   5   4   3   2   1   09 08 07

Thirty-eighth Edition

Contents

INDEXES

A Note from the Peterson's Editors

For nearly 40 years, Peterson's has given students and parents the most comprehensive, up-to-date information on undergraduate institutions in the United States. Peterson's researches the data published in *Peterson's Two-Year Colleges* each year. The information is furnished by the colleges and is accurate at the time of publishing.

This guide also features advice and tips on the college search and selection process, such as how to decide if a two-year college is right for you, how to approach transferring between colleges, and what's in store for adults returning to college. If you seem to be getting more, not less, anxious about choosing and getting into the right college, *Peterson's Two-Year Colleges* provides just the right help, giving you the information you need to make important college decisions and ace the admission process.

Opportunities abound for students, and this guide can help you find what you want in a number of ways:

- In "What You Need to Know About Two-Year Colleges," David R. Pierce, former President of the American Association of Community Colleges, outlines the basic features and advantages of two-year colleges. "Surviving Standardized Tests" gives an overview of the common examinations students take prior to attending college. "Who's Paying for This? Financial Aid Basics" provides guidelines for financing your college education. "Frequently Asked Questions About Transferring" takes a look at the two-year college scene from the perspective of a student who is looking toward the day when he or she may pursue additional education at a four-year institution. "Returning to School: Advice for Adult Students" is an analysis of the pros and cons (mostly pros) of returning to college after already having begun a professional career. "What International Students Need to Know About Admission to U.S. Colleges and Universities" is an article written particularly for students overseas who are considering a U.S. college education. "Searching for Two-Year Colleges Online" outlines why you'll want to visit Petersons.com for even more college search and selection resources. Finally, "How to Use This Guide" gives details on the data in this guide: what terms mean and why they're here.

- If you already have specifics in mind, such as a particular institution or major, turn to the easy-to-use **Quick-Reference Chart** or **Indexes**. You can look up a particular feature—location and programs offered—or use the alphabetical index and immediately find the colleges that meet your criteria.

- For information about particular colleges, turn to the **Profiles of Two-Year Colleges** section. Here, our comprehensive college descriptions are arranged alphabetically by state. They provide a complete picture of need-to-know information about every accredited two-year college—from admission to graduation, including expenses, financial aid, majors, and campus safety. All the information you need to apply is placed together at the conclusion of each college **Profile.** In addition, for nearly 100 colleges, two-page narrative descriptions appear in the **College Close-Ups** section. These descriptions are paid for and written by college officials and offer great detail about each college. They are edited to provide a consistent format across entries for your ease of comparison.

Peterson's publishes a full line of resources to help you and your family with any information you need to guide you through the admissions process. Peterson's publications can be found at your local bookstore, library, and high school guidance office—or visit us on the Web at www.petersons.com.

We welcome any comments or suggestions you may have about this publication and invite you to complete our online survey at **www.petersons.com/booksurvey.**

Your feedback will help us make your educational dreams possible.

Colleges will be pleased to know that Peterson's helped you in your selection. Admissions staff members are more than happy to answer questions, address specific problems and help in any way they can. The editors at Peterson's wish you great success in your college search.

The College Admissions Process:

An Overview

What You Need to Know About Two-Year Colleges

David R. Pierce

Two-year colleges—better known as community colleges—are often called "the people's colleges." With their open-door policies (admission is open to individuals with a high school diploma or its equivalent), community colleges provide access to higher education for millions of Americans who might otherwise be excluded from higher education. Community college students are diverse and of all ages, races, and economic backgrounds. While many community college students enroll full-time, an equally large number attend on a part-time basis so they can fulfill employment and family commitments as they advance their education.

Community colleges can also be referred to as either technical or junior colleges, and they may either be under public or independent control. What unites two-year colleges is that they are regionally accredited, postsecondary institutions, whose highest credential awarded is the associate degree. With few exceptions, community colleges offer a comprehensive curriculum, which includes transfer, technical, and continuing education programs.

IMPORTANT FACTORS IN A COMMUNITY COLLEGE EDUCATION

The student who attends a community college can count on receiving high-quality instruction in a supportive learning community. This setting frees the student to pursue his or her own goals, nurture special talents, explore new fields of learning, and develop the capacity for lifelong learning.

From the student's perspective, four characteristics capture the essence of community colleges:

1. They are community-based institutions that work in close partnership with high schools, community groups, and employers in extending high-quality programs at convenient times and places.

2. Community colleges are cost effective. Annual tuition and fees at public community colleges average approximately half those at public four-year colleges and less than 15 percent of private four-year institutions. In addition, since most community colleges are generally close to their students' homes, these students can also save a significant amount of money on the room, board, and transportation expenses traditionally associated with a college education.

3. They provide a caring environment, with faculty members who are expert instructors, known for excellent teaching and meeting students at the point of their individual needs, regardless of age, sex, race, current job status, or previous academic preparation. Community colleges join a strong curriculum with a broad range of counseling and career services that are intended to assist students in making the most of their educational opportunities.

4. Many offer comprehensive programs, including transfer curricula in such liberal arts programs as chemistry, psychology, and business management, that lead directly to a baccalaureate degree and career programs that prepare students for employment or assist those already employed in upgrading their skills. For those students who need to strengthen their academic skills, community colleges also offer a wide range of developmental programs in mathematics, languages, and learning skills, designed to prepare the student for success in college studies.

GETTING TO KNOW YOUR TWO-YEAR COLLEGE

The first step in determining the quality of a community college is to check the status of its accreditation. Once you have established that a community college is appropriately accredited, find out as much as you can about the programs and services it has to offer. Much of that information can be found in materials the college provides. However, the best way to learn about a college is to visit in person.

During a campus visit, be prepared to ask a lot of questions. Talk to students, faculty members, administrators, and counselors about the college and its programs, particularly those in which you have a special interest. Ask about available certificates and associate degrees. Don't be shy. Do what you can to dig below the surface. Ask college officials about the transfer

rate to four-year colleges. If a college emphasizes student services, find out what particular assistance is offered, such as educational or career guidance. Colleges are eager to provide you with the information you need to make informed decisions.

COMMUNITY COLLEGES CAN SAVE YOU MONEY

If you are able to live at home while you attend college, you will certainly save money on room and board, but it does cost something to commute. Many two-year colleges offer you instruction in your own home through cable television or public broadcast stations or through home study courses that can save both time and money. Look into all the options, and be sure to add up all the costs of attending various colleges before deciding which is best for you.

FINANCIAL AID

Many students who attend community colleges are eligible for a range of financial aid programs, including Federal Pell Grants, Perkins and Stafford Loans, state aid, and on-campus jobs. Your high school counselor or the financial aid officer at a community college will also be able to help you. It is in your interest to apply for financial aid months in advance of the date you intend to start your college program, so find out early what assistance is available to you. While many community colleges are able to help students who make a last-minute decision to attend college, either through short-term loans or emergency grants, if you are considering entering college and think you might need financial aid, it is best to find out as much as you can as early as you can.

WORKING AND GOING TO SCHOOL

Many two-year college students maintain full-time or part-time employment while they earn their degrees. Over the years, a steadily growing number of students have chosen to attend community colleges while they fulfill family and employment responsibilities. To enable these students to balance the demands of home, work, and school, most community colleges offer classes at night and on weekends.

For the full-time student, the usual length of time it takes to obtain an associate degree is two years. However, your length of study will depend on the course load you take: the fewer credits you earn each term, the longer it will take you to earn a degree. To assist you in moving more quickly toward earning your degree, many community colleges now award credit through examination or for equivalent knowledge gained through relevant life experiences. Be certain to find out the credit options that are available to you at the college in which you are interested. You may discover that it will take less time to earn a degree than you first thought.

PREPARATION FOR TRANSFER

Studies have repeatedly shown that students who first attend a community college and then transfer to a four-year college or university do at least as well academically as the students who entered the four-year institutions as freshmen. Most community colleges have agreements with nearby four-year institutions to make transfer of credits easier. If you are thinking of transferring, be sure to meet with a counselor or faculty adviser before choosing your courses. You will want to map out a course of study with transfer in mind. Make sure you also find out the credit-transfer requirements of the four-year institution you might want to attend.

ATTENDING A TWO-YEAR COLLEGE IN ANOTHER REGION

Although many community colleges serve a specific county or district, they are committed (to the extent of their ability) to the goal of equal educational opportunity without regard to economic status, race, creed, color, sex, or national origin. Independent two-year colleges recruit from a much broader geographical area—throughout the United States and, increasingly, around the world.

Although some community colleges do provide on-campus housing for their students, most do not. However, even if on-campus housing is not available, most colleges do have housing referral services.

NEW CAREER OPPORTUNITIES

Community colleges realize that many entering students are not sure about the field in which they want to focus their studies or the career they would like to pursue. Often, students discover fields and careers they never knew existed. Community colleges have the resources to help students identify areas of career interest and to set challenging occupational goals.

Once a career goal is set, you can be confident that a community college will provide job-relevant, technical education. About half of the students who take courses for credit at community colleges do so to prepare for employment or to acquire or upgrade skills for their current job. Especially helpful in charting a career path is the assistance of a counselor or a faculty adviser, who can discuss job opportunities in your chosen field and help you map out your course of study.

In addition, since community colleges have close ties to their communities, they are in constant contact with leaders in business, industry, organized labor, and public life. Community colleges work with these individuals and their organizations to prepare students for direct entry into the world of work. For example, some community colleges have established partnerships with local businesses and industries to provide specialized training programs. Some also provide the academic portion of apprenticeship training, while others offer extensive job-shadowing and cooperative education opportunities. Be sure to examine all of the career-preparation opportunities offered by the community colleges in which you are interested.

David R. Pierce is the former President of the American Association of Community Colleges.

Surviving Standardized Tests

WHAT ARE STANDARDIZED TESTS?

Colleges and universities in the United States use tests to help evaluate applicants' readiness for admission or to place them in appropriate courses. The tests that are most frequently used by colleges are the ACT of American College Testing, Inc., and the College Board's SAT. In addition, the Educational Testing Service (ETS) offers the TOEFL test, which evaluates the English-language proficiency of nonnative speakers. The tests are offered at designated testing centers located at high schools and colleges throughout the United States and U.S. territories and at testing centers in various countries throughout the world. The ACT and SAT are each taken by more than a million students each year. The TOEFL test is taken by more than 800,000 students each year.

Upon request, special accommodations for students with documented visual, hearing, physical, or learning disabilities are available. Examples of special accommodations include tests in Braille or large print and such aids as a reader, recorder, magnifying glass, or sign language interpreter. Additional testing time may be allowed in some instances. Contact the appropriate testing program or your guidance counselor for details on how to request special accommodations.

College Board SAT Program

Currently, the SAT Program consists of the SAT and the SAT Subject Tests. The SAT is a 3-hour 45-minute test made up of ten sections, primarily multiple-choice, that focuses on college success skills of writing, critical reading, and mathematics. The writing component measures grammar and usage and includes a short, student-written essay. The critical reading sections test verbal reasoning and critical reading skills. Emphasis is placed on reading passages, which are 400–850 words in length. Some reading passages are paired; the second opposes, supports, or in some way complements the point of view expressed in the first. The three mathematics sections test a student's ability to solve problems involving arithmetic, Algebra I and II, and geometry. They include questions that require students to produce their own responses, in addition to questions with four or five answer choices from which students can choose. Calculators may be used on the SAT mathematics sections.

The SAT Subject Tests are 1-hour tests, primarily multiple-choice, in specific subjects that measure students' knowledge of these subjects and their ability to apply that knowledge. Some colleges may require or recommend these tests for placement, or even admission. The Subject Tests measure a student's academic achievement in high school and may indicate readiness for certain college programs. Tests offered include Literature, U.S. History, World History, Mathematics Level 1, Mathematics Level 2, Biology E/M (Ecological/Molecular), Chemistry, Physics, French, German, Modern Hebrew, Italian, Latin, and Spanish, as well as Foreign Language Tests with Listening in Chinese, French, German, Japanese, Korean, and Spanish. The Mathematics Level 1 and 2 tests require the use of a scientific calculator.

SAT scores are automatically sent to each student who has taken the test. On average, they are mailed about three weeks after the test. Students may request that the scores be reported to their high schools or to the colleges to which they are applying.

ACT Program

The ACT Program is a comprehensive data collection, processing, and reporting service designed to assist in educational and career planning. The ACT instrument consists of four academic tests, taken under timed conditions, and a Student Profile Section and Interest Inventory, completed when students register for the ACT.

The academic tests cover four areas—English, mathematics, reading, and science reasoning. The ACT consists of 215

Don't Forget To . . .

- Take the SAT or ACT before application deadlines.

- Note that test registration deadlines precede test dates by about six weeks.

- Register to take the TOEFL test if English is not your native language and you are planning on studying at a North American college.

- Practice your test-taking skills with **Peterson's Master the SAT, Peterson's Ultimate ACT Tool Kit, The Real ACT Prep Guide** (published by Peterson's), and **Peterson's Master TOEFL Reading Skills, Peterson's Master TOEFL Vocabulary,** and **Peterson's Master TOEFL Writing Skills.**

- Contact the College Board or American College Testing, Inc., in advance if you need special accommodations when taking tests.

2007–08 ACT and SAT Test Dates

ACT

September 15, 2007*
October 27, 2007
December 8, 2007
February 9, 2008**
April 12, 2008
June 14, 2008

All test dates fall on a Saturday. Tests are also given on the Sundays following the Saturday test dates for students who cannot take the test on Saturday because of religious reasons. The basic ACT registration fee for 2006–07 was $29 ($49 outside of the U.S.). The optional writing test is $14 and is refundable for students who are absent on test day.

---

  * The September test is available only in Arizona, California, Florida, Georgia, Illinois, Indiana, Maryland, Nevada, North Carolina, Pennsylvania, South Carolina, Texas, and Washington.

** The February test date is not available in New York.

SAT

October 16, 2007 (SAT and SAT Subject Tests)
November 3, 2007 (SAT, SAT Subject Tests, and Language Tests with Listening)
December 1, 2007 (SAT and SAT Subject Tests)
January 26, 2008 (SAT, SAT Subject Tests, and ELPT)
March 1, 2008 (SAT only)**
May 3, 2008 (SAT and SAT Subject Tests)
June 7, 2008 (SAT and SAT Subject Tests)

For the 2006–07 academic year, the basic fee for the SAT was $41.50. The basic fee for the SAT Subject Tests was $18, $19 for the Language Tests with Listening, and $8 each for all other Subject Tests. Students can take up to three SAT Subject Tests on a single date, and an $18 basic registration and reporting fee should be added for each test date. Tests are also given on the Sundays following the Saturday test dates for students who cannot take the test on Saturday because of religious reasons. Fee waivers are available to juniors and seniors who cannot afford test fees.

---

  * Language Tests with Listening are only offered in November. See the Registration Bulletin for details.

** The March test date is only available in the U.S. and its territories.

---

multiple-choice questions and takes approximately 3 hours and 30 minutes to complete with breaks (testing time is actually 2 hours and 55 minutes). They are designed to assess the student's educational development and readiness to handle college-level work. The minimum standard score is 1, the maximum is 36, and the national average is 21. Students should note that an optional writing test is also offered.

The Student Profile Section requests information about each student's admission and enrollment plans, academic and out-of-class high school achievements and aspirations, and high school course work. The student is also asked to supply biographical data and self-reported high school grades in the four subject-matter areas covered by the academic tests.

The ACT has a number of career planning services, including the ACT Interest Inventory, which is designed to measure six major dimensions of student interests–business contact, business operations, technical, science, arts, and social service. Results are used to compare the student's interests with those of college-bound students who later majored in each of a wide variety of areas. Inventory results are also used to help students compare their work-activity preferences with work activities that characterize twenty-three "job families."

Because the information resulting from the ACT Program is used in a variety of educational settings, American College Testing, Inc., prepares three reports for each student: the Student Report, the High School Report, and the College

Report. The Student Report normally is sent to the student's high school, except after the June test date, when it is sent directly to the student's home address. The College Report is sent to the colleges the student designates.

Early in the school year, American College Testing, Inc., sends registration packets to high schools across the country that contain all the information a student needs to register for the ACT. High school guidance offices also receive a supply of *Preparing for the ACT,* a booklet that contains a complete practice test, an answer key, and general information about preparing for the test.

Test of English as a Foreign Language (TOEFL)

The TOEFL is used by various organizations, such as colleges and universities, to determine English proficiency. The test is offered in different formats depending on the test taker's location. The TOEFL iBT tests students in the areas of speaking, listening, reading, and writing in an Internet-based format.

The TOEFL PBT (paper-based test) tests students in the areas of listening, structure, reading comprehension, and writing. Score requirements are set by individual institutions. For more information on TOEFL, and to obtain a copy of the Information Bulletin, contact the Educational Testing Service.

Who's Paying for This?
Financial Aid Basics

A college education can be expensive—costing more than $150,000 for four years at some of the higher priced private colleges and universities. Even at the lower cost state colleges and universities, the cost of a four-year education can approach $60,000. Determining how you and your family will come up with the necessary funds to pay for your education requires planning, perseverance, and learning as much as you can about the options that are available to you. But before you get discouraged, recent College Board statistics show that 42 percent of full-time students attend four-year public and private colleges with tuition and fees less than $6000, while 13 percent attend colleges that have tuition and fees more than $24,000. College costs tend to be less in the western states and higher in New England.

Paying for college should not be looked at as a four-year financial commitment. For many families, paying the total cost of a student's college education out of current income and savings is usually not realistic. For families that have planned ahead and have financial savings established for higher education, the burden is a lot easier. But for most, meeting the cost of college requires the pooling of current income and assets and investing in longer-term loan options. These family resources, together with financial assistance from state, federal, and institutional sources, enable millions of students each year to attend the institution of their choice.

FINANCIAL AID PROGRAMS

There are three types of financial aid:

1. Gift-aid—Scholarships and grants are funds that do not have to be repaid.

2. Loans—Loans must be repaid, usually after graduation; the amount you have to pay back is the total you've borrowed plus any accrued interest. This is considered a source of self-help aid.

3. Student employment—Student employment is a job arranged for you by the financial aid office. This is another source of self-help aid.

The federal government has four major grant programs—the Federal Pell Grant, the Federal Supplemental Educational Opportunity Grant, Academic Competitiveness Grants (ACG), and SMART grants. ACG and SMART grants are limited to students who qualify for a Pell grant and are awarded to a select group of students. Overall, these grants are targeted to low-to-moderate income families with significant financial need. The federal government also sponsors a student employment program called the Federal Work-Study Program, which offers jobs both on and off campus; and several loan programs, including those for students and for parents of undergraduate students.

There are two types of student loan programs: subsidized and unsubsidized. The subsidized Federal Stafford Student Loan and the Federal Perkins Loan are need-based, government-subsidized loans. Students who borrow through these programs do not have to pay interest on the loan until after they graduate or leave school. The unsubsidized Federal Stafford Student Loan and the Parent Loan Program are not based on need, and borrowers are responsible for the interest while the student is in school. There are different methods on how these loans are administered. Once you choose your college, the financial aid office will guide you through this process.

After you've submitted your financial aid application and you've been accepted for admission, each college will send you a letter describing your financial aid award. Most award letters show estimated college costs, how much you and your family are expected to contribute, and the amount and types of aid you have been awarded. Most students are awarded aid from a combination of sources and programs. Hence, your award is often called a financial aid "package."

SOURCES OF FINANCIAL AID

More than 12 million students and family apply for financial aid each year. Financial aid from all sources exceeds $152 billion per year. The largest single source of aid is the federal government, which awarded more than $94 billion during 2005–06.

The next largest source of financial aid is found in the college and university community. Institutions award an estimated $24.4 billion to students each year. Most of this aid is awarded to students who have a demonstrated need based on the Federal Methodology. Some institutions use a different formula, the Institutional Methodology (IM), to award their

own funds in conjunction with other forms of aid. Institutional aid may be either need-based or non-need based. Aid that is not based on need is usually awarded for a student's academic performance (merit awards), specific talents or abilities, or to attract the type of students a college seeks to enroll.

Another source of financial aid is from state government, awarding more than $6.8 billion per year. All states offer grant and/or scholarship aid, most of which is need-based. However, more and more states are offering substantial merit-based aid programs. Most state programs award aid only to students attending college in their home state.

Other sources of financial aid include:

- Private agencies

- Foundations

- Corporations

- Clubs

- Fraternal and service organizations

- Civic associations

- Unions

- Religious groups that award grants, scholarships, and low-interest loans

- Employers that provide tuition reimbursement benefits for employees and their children

More information about these different sources of aid is available from high school guidance offices, public libraries, college financial aid offices, directly from the sponsoring organizations, and on the Web at www.petersons.com and www.finaid.org.

HOW NEED-BASED FINANCIAL AID IS AWARDED

When you apply for aid, your family's financial situation is analyzed using a government-approved formula called the Federal Methodology. This formula looks at five items:

1. Demographic information of the family

2. Income of the parents

3. Assets of the parents

4. Income of the student

5. Assets of the student

This analysis determines the amount you and your family are expected to contribute toward your college expenses, called your Expected Family Contribution or EFC. If the EFC is equal to or more than the cost of attendance at a particular college, then you do not demonstrate financial need. However, even if you don't have financial need, you may still qualify for aid, as there are grants, scholarships, and loan programs that are not need-based.

If the cost of your education is greater than your EFC, then you do demonstrate financial need and qualify for assistance. The amount of your financial need that can be met varies from school to school. Some are able to meet your full need, while others can only cover a certain percentage of need. Here's the formula:

Cost of Attendance
− Expected Family Contribution
= Financial Need

The EFC remains constant, but your need will vary according to the costs of attendance at a particular college. In general, the higher the tuition and fees at a particular college, the higher the cost of attendance will be. Expenses for books and supplies, room and board, transportation, and other miscellaneous items are included in the overall cost of attendance. It is important to remember that you do not have to be "needy" to qualify for financial aid. Many middle and upper-middle income families qualify for need-based financial aid.

APPLYING FOR FINANCIAL AID

Every student must complete the Free Application for Federal Student Aid (FAFSA) to be considered for financial aid. The FAFSA is available from your high school guidance office, many public libraries, colleges in your area, or directly from the U.S. Department of Education.

Students are encouraged to apply for federal student aid on the Web. The electronic version of the FAFSA can be accessed at http://www.fafsa.ed.gov. Both the student and at least one parent must apply for a federal pin number at http://www.pin.ed.gov. The pin number serves as your electronic signature when applying for aid on the Web.

To award their own funds, some colleges require an additional application, the Financial Aid PROFILE® form. The PROFILE asks supplemental questions that some colleges and awarding agencies feel provide a more accurate assessment of the family's ability to pay for college. It is up to the college to decide whether it will use only the FAFSA or both the FAFSA and the PROFILE. PROFILE applications are available from the high school guidance office and on the Web. Both the paper application and the Web site list those colleges and programs that require the PROFILE application.

If Every College You're Applying to for Fall 2008 Requires the FAFSA

. . . then it's pretty simple: Complete the FAFSA after January 1, 2008, being certain to send it in before any college-imposed deadlines. (You are not permitted to send in the 2008–09 FAFSA before January 1, 2008.) Most college FAFSA application deadlines are in February or early March. It is easier if you have all your financial records for the previous year available, but if that is not possible, you are strongly encouraged to use estimated figures.

After you send in your FAFSA, either with the paper application or electronically, you'll receive a Student Aid

Report (SAR) that includes all of the information you reported and shows your EFC. If you provided an e-mail address, the SAR is sent to you electronically; otherwise, you will receive a paper copy in the mail. Be sure to review the SAR, checking to see if the information you reported is accurately represented. If you used estimated numbers to complete the FAFSA, you may have to resubmit the SAR with any corrections to the data. The college(s) you have designated on the FAFSA will receive the information you reported and will use that data to make their decision. In many instances, the colleges you've applied to will ask you to send copies of your and your parents' federal income tax returns for 2007, plus any other documents needed to verify the information you reported.

If a College Requires the PROFILE

Step 1: Register for the Financial Aid PROFILE in the fall of your senior year in high school.

You can apply for the PROFILE online at http://profileonline.collegeboard.com/index.jsp. Registration information with a list of the colleges that require the PROFILE are available in most high school guidance offices. There is a fee for using the Financial Aid PROFILE application ($23 for the first college and $18 for each additional college). You must pay for the service by credit card when you register. If you do not have a credit card, you will be billed. A limited number of fee waivers are automatically granted to first-time applicants based on the financial information provided on the PROFILE.

Step 2: Fill out your customized Financial Aid PROFILE.

Once you register, your application will be immediately available online and will have questions which all students must complete, questions which must be completed by the student's parents (unless the student is independent and the colleges or programs selected do not require parental information), and *may* have supplemental questions needed by one or more of your schools or programs. If required, those will be found in Section Q of the application.

In addition to the PROFILE Application you complete online, you may also be required to complete a Business/Farm Supplement via traditional paper format. Completion of this form is not a part of the online process. If this form is required, instructions on how to download and print the supplemental form are provided. If your biological or adoptive parents are separated or divorced and your colleges and programs require it, your noncustodial parent may be asked to complete the Noncustodial PROFILE.

Once you complete and submit your PROFILE Application, it will be processed and sent directly to your requested colleges and programs.

IF YOU DON'T QUALIFY FOR NEED-BASED AID

If you are not eligible for need-based aid, you can still find ways to lessen the burden on your parents.

Here are some suggestions:

- Search for merit scholarships. You can start at the initial stages of your application process. College merit awards are becoming increasingly important as more and more colleges award these grants to students they especially want to attract. As a result, applying to a college at which your qualifications put you at the top of the entering class may give you a larger merit award. Another source of aid to look for is private scholarships that are given for special skills and talents. Additional information can be found at www.petersons.com and at www.finaid.org.

- Seek employment during the summer and the academic year. The student employment office at your college can help you locate a school-year job. Many colleges and local businesses have vacancies remaining after they have hired students who are receiving Federal Work-Study Program financial aid.

- Borrow through the unsubsidized Federal Stafford Student Loan programs. These are generally available to all students. The terms and conditions are similar to the subsidized loans. The biggest difference is that the borrower is responsible for the interest while still in college, although most lenders permit students to delay paying the interest right away and add the accrued interest to the total amount owed. You must file the FAFSA to be considered.

After you've secured what you can through scholarships, working, and borrowing, your parents will be expected to meet their share of the college bill (the Expected Family Contribution). Many colleges offer monthly payment plans that spread the cost over the academic year. If the monthly payments are too high, parents can borrow through the Federal Parent Loan for Undergraduate Students (Federal PLUS Program), through one of the many private education loan programs available, or through home equity loans and lines of credit. Families seeking assistance in financing college expenses should inquire at the financial aid office about what programs are available at the college. Some families seek the advice of professional financial advisers and tax consultants.

HOW IS YOUR EXPECTED FAMILY CONTRIBUTION CALCULATED?

The chart on the next page makes the following assumptions:

- two parent family where age of older parent is 45

- lower income families (under $30,000) will file the 1040A or 1040EZ tax form

- student income is less than $2300

- there are no student assets

- there is only one family member attending college

All figures are estimates and may vary when the complete FAFSA or PROFILE application is submitted.

APPROXIMATE EXPECTED FAMILY CONTRIBUTION

		INCOME BEFORE TAXES								
ASSETS		**$20,000**	**30,000**	**40,000**	**50,000**	**60,000**	**70,000**	**80,000**	**90,000**	**100,000**
$ 20,000										
FAMILY SIZE	3	$ 0	160	1,800	3,500	5,800	9,100	12,600	14,100	17,400
	4	0	0	850	2,500	4,400	7,100	10,600	12,000	15,300
	5	0	0	0	1,600	3,300	5,500	8,600	10,100	13,400
	6	0	0	0	600	2,200	4,100	6,600	7,900	11,200
$ 30,000										
FAMILY SIZE	3	$ 0	160	1,800	3,500	5,800	9,100	12,600	14,100	17,400
	4	0	0	850	2,500	4,400	7,100	10,600	12,000	15,300
	5	0	0	0	1,600	3,300	5,500	8,600	10,100	13,400
	6	0	0	0	600	2,200	4,100	6,600	7,900	11,200
$ 40,000										
FAMILY SIZE	3	$ 0	160	1,800	3,500	5,800	9,100	12,600	14,100	17,400
	4	0	0	850	2,500	4,400	7,100	10,600	12,000	15,300
	5	0	0	0	1,600	3,300	5,500	8,600	10,100	13,400
	6	0	0	0	600	2,200	4,100	6,600	7,900	11,200
$ 50,000										
FAMILY SIZE	3	$ 0	340	2,000	3,800	6,200	9,500	13,000	14,500	17,800
	4	0	0	1,100	2,700	4,700	7,400	11,000	12,400	15,700
	5	0	0	0	1,800	3,500	5,800	9,000	10,400	13,750
	6	0	0	0	800	2,400	4,300	6,900	8,300	11,600
$ 60,000										
FAMILY SIZE	3	$ 0	600	2,300	4,100	6,600	10,000	13,600	15,000	18,300
	4	0	0	1,300	3,000	5,000	8,000	11,500	13,000	16,300
	5	0	0	400	2,050	3,800	6,200	9,600	11,000	14,300
	6	0	0	0	1,000	2,700	4,600	7,400	8,800	12,150
$ 80,000										
FAMILY SIZE	3	$ 0	1,130	2,800	4,800	7,600	11,200	14,700	16,150	19,500
	4	0	170	1,800	3,600	5,900	9,100	9,600	14,100	17,400
	5	0	0	900	2,600	4,500	7,200	10,700	12,100	15,450
	6	0	0	0	1,600	3,200	5,400	8,500	10,000	13,300
$ 100,000										
FAMILY SIZE	3	$ 0	1,660	3,400	5,600	8,800	12,300	15,900	17,300	20,600
	4	0	700	2,400	4,200	6,800	10,250	13,800	15,200	18,500
	5	0	0	1,400	3,100	5,300	8,300	11,800	13,300	16,600
	6	0	0	400	2,100	3,900	6,300	9,700	11,100	14,400
$ 120,000										
FAMILY SIZE	3	$ 0	2,190	4,000	6,500	9,900	13,400	17,000	18,400	21,700
	4	0	1,220	3,000	4,900	7,800	11,400	14,900	16,350	19,650
	5	0	310	2,000	3,700	6,100	9,500	13,000	14,400	17,700
	6	0	0	1,000	2,600	4,600	7,300	10,800	12,200	15,550
$ 140,000										
FAMILY SIZE	3	$ 0	2,700	4,700	7,500	11,000	13,400	18,100	19,500	22,850
	4	0	1,750	3,500	5,700	9,000	12,500	16,000	17,750	20,800
	5	0	850	2,500	4,400	7,100	10,500	14,100	15,500	18,850
	6	0	0	1,500	3,200	5,300	8,400	11,900	13,350	16,650

This chart makes the following assumptions:

- two parent family where age of older parent is 45
- lower income families will file the 1040A or 1040EZ tax form
- student income is less than $2300
- there are no student assets
- there is only one family member in college
- All figures are estimates and may vary when the complete FAFSA or PROFILE application is submitted.

Frequently Asked Questions About Transferring

Muriel M. Shishkoff

Among the students attending two-year colleges are a large number who began their higher education knowing they would eventually transfer to a four-year school to obtain their bachelor's degree. There are many reasons why students go this route. Upon graduating from high school, some simply do not have definite career goals. Although they don't want to put their education on hold, they prefer not to pay exorbitant amounts in tuition while trying to "find themselves." As the cost of a university education escalates—even in public institutions—the option of spending the freshman and sophomore years at a two-year college looks attractive to many students. Others attend a two-year college because they are unable to meet the initial entrance standards—a specified grade point average (GPA), standardized test scores, or knowledge of specific academic subjects—required by the four-year school of their choice. Many such students praise the community college system for giving them the chance to be, academically speaking, "born again." In addition, students from other countries often find that they can adapt more easily to language and cultural changes at a two-year school before transferring to a larger, more diverse four-year college.

If your plan is to attend a two-year college with the ultimate goal of transferring to a four-year school, you will be pleased to know that the increased importance of the community college route to a bachelor's degree is recognized by all segments of higher education. As a result, many two-year schools have revised their course outlines and established new courses in order to comply with the programs and curricular offerings of the universities. Institutional improvements to make transferring easier have also proliferated at both the two- and four-year levels. The generous transfer policies of the Pennsylvania, New York, and Florida state university systems, among others, reflect this attitude; these systems accept *all* credits from students who have graduated from accredited community colleges.

If you are interested in moving from a two-year college to a four-year school, the sooner you make up your mind that you are going to make the switch, the better position you will be in to transfer successfully (that is, without having wasted valuable time and credits). The ideal point at which to make such a decision is **before** you register for classes at your two-year school; a counselor can help you plan your course work with an eye toward fulfilling the requirements needed for your major course of study.

Naturally, it is not always possible to plan your transferring strategy that far in advance, but keep in mind that the key to a successful transfer is **preparation,** and preparation takes time—time to think through your objectives and time to plan the right classes to take.

As students face the prospect of transferring from a two-year to a four-year school, many thoughts and concerns about this complicated and often frustrating process race through their minds. Here are answers to the questions that are most frequently asked by transferring students.

Q Does every college and university accept transfer students?

A Most four-year institutions accept transfer students, but some do so more enthusiastically than others. Graduating from a community college is an advantage at, for example, Arizona State University and the University of Massachusetts Boston; both accept more community college transfer students than traditional freshmen. At the State University of New York at Albany, graduates of two-year transfer programs within the State University of New York System are given priority for upper-division (i.e., junior- and senior-level) vacancies.

Schools offering undergraduate work at the upper division only are especially receptive to transfer applications. On the other hand, some schools accept only a few transfer students; others refuse entrance to sophomores or those in their final year. Princeton University requires an "excellent academic record and particularly compelling reasons to transfer." Check the catalogs of several colleges for their transfer requirements before you make your final choice.

Q Do students who go directly from high school to a four-year college do better academically than transfer students from community colleges?

A On the contrary: some institutions report that transfers from two-year schools who persevere until graduation do *better* than those who started as freshmen in a four-year college.

Q Why is it so important that my two-year college be accredited?

A Four-year colleges and universities accept transfer credits only from schools formally recognized by a regional, national, or professional educational agency. This accreditation signifies that an institution or program of study meets or exceeds a minimum level of educational quality necessary for meeting stated educational objectives.

Q After enrolling at a four-year school, may I still make up necessary courses at a community college?

A Some institutions restrict credit after transfer to their own facilities. Others allow students to take a limited number of transfer courses after matriculation, depending on the subject matter. A few provide opportunities for cross-registration or dual enrollment, which means taking classes on more than one campus.

Q What do I need to do to transfer?

A First, send for your high school and college transcripts. Having chosen the school you wish to transfer to, check its admission requirements against your transcripts. If you find that you are admissible, file an application as early as possible before the deadline. Part of the process will be asking your former schools to send official transcripts to the admission office, i.e., not the copies you used in determining your admissibility.

Plan your transfer program with the head of your new department as soon as you have decided to transfer. Determine the recommended general education pattern and necessary preparation for your major. At your present school, take the courses you will need to meet transfer requirements for the new school.

Q What qualifies me for admission as a transfer student?

A Admission requirements for most four-year institutions vary. Depending on the reputation or popularity of the school and program you wish to enter, requirements may be quite selective and competitive. Usually, you will need to show satisfactory test scores, an academic record up to a certain standard, and completion of specific subject matter.

Transfer students can be eligible to enter a four-year school in a number of ways: by having been eligible for admission directly upon graduation from high school, by making up shortcomings in grades (or in subject matter not covered in high school) at a community college, or by satisfactory completion of necessary courses or credit hours at another postsecondary institution. Ordinarily, students coming from a community college or from another four-year institution must meet or exceed the receiving institution's standards for freshmen and show appropriate college-level course work taken since high school. Students who did not graduate from high school can present proof of proficiency through results on the General Educational Development (GED) test.

Q Are exceptions ever made for students who don't meet all the requirements for transfer?

A Extenuating circumstances, such as disability, low family income, refugee or veteran status, or athletic talent, may permit the special enrollment of students who would not otherwise be eligible but who demonstrate the potential for academic success. Consult the appropriate office—the Educational Opportunity Program, the disabled students' office, the athletic department, or the academic dean—to see whether an exception can be made in your case.

Q How far in advance do I need to apply for transfer?

A Some schools have a rolling admission policy, which means that they process transfer applications as they are received, all year long. With other schools, you must apply during the priority filing period, which can be up to a year before you wish to enter. Check the date with the admission office at your prospective campus.

Q Is it possible to transfer courses from several different institutions?

A Institutions ordinarily accept the courses that they consider transferable, regardless of the number of accredited schools involved. However, there is the danger of exceeding the maximum number of credit hours that can be transferred from all other schools or earned through credit by examination, extension courses, or correspondence courses. The limit placed on transfer credits varies from school to school, so read the catalog carefully to avoid taking courses you won't be able to use. To avoid duplicating courses, keep attendance at different campuses to a minimum.

Q What is involved in transferring from a semester system to a quarter or trimester system?

A In the semester system, the academic calendar is divided into two equal parts. The quarter system is more aptly named trimester, since the academic calendar is divided into three equal terms (not counting a summer session). To convert semester units into

quarter units or credit hours, simply multiply the semester units by one and a half. Conversely, multiply quarter units by two thirds to come up with semester units. If you are used to a semester system of fifteen- to sixteen-week courses, the ten-week courses of the quarter system may seem to fly by.

Q Why might a course be approved for transfer credit by one four-year school but not by another?

A The beauty of postsecondary education in the United States lies in its variety. Entrance policies and graduation requirements are designed to reflect and serve each institution's mission. Because institutional policies vary so widely, schools may interpret the subject matter of a course from quite different points of view. Given that the granting of transfer credit indicates that a course is viewed as being, in effect, parallel to one offered by the receiving institution, it is easy to see how this might be the case at one university and not another.

Q Must I take a foreign language to transfer?

A Foreign language proficiency is often required for admission to a four-year institution; such proficiency also often figures in certain majors or in the general education pattern. Often, two or three years of a single language in high school will do the trick. Find out if scores received on Advanced Placement (AP) examinations, placement examinations given by the foreign language department, or SAT Subject Tests will be accepted in lieu of college course work.

Q Will the school to which I'm transferring accept pass/no pass, pass/fail, or credit/no credit grades in lieu of letter grades?

A Usually, a limit is placed on the number of these courses you can transfer, and there may be other restrictions as well. If you want to use other-than-letter grades for the fulfillment of general education requirements or lower-division (freshman and sophomore) preparation for the major, check with the receiving institution.

Q Which is more important for transfer—my grade point average or my course completion pattern?

A Some schools believe that your past grades indicate academic potential and overshadow prior preparation for a specific degree program. Others require completion of certain introductory courses before transfer to prepare you for upper-division work in your major. In any case, appropriate course selection will cut down the time to graduation and increase your chances of making a successful transfer.

Q What happens to my credits if I change majors?

A If you change majors after admission, your transferable course credit should remain fairly intact. However, because you may need extra or different preparation for your new major, some of the courses you've taken may now be useful only as electives. The need for additional lower-level preparation may mean you're staying longer at your new school than you originally planned. On the other hand, you may already have taken courses that count toward your new major as part of the university's general education pattern.

Excerpted from *Transferring Made Easy: A Guide to Changing Colleges Successfully,* by Muriel M. Shishkoff, © 1991 by Muriel M. Shishkoff (published by Peterson's).

Returning to School: Advice for Adult Students

Sandra Cook, Ph.D.
Director, University Advising Center, San Diego State University

Many adults think for a long time about returning to school without taking any action. One purpose of this article is to help the "thinkers" finally make some decisions by examining what is keeping them from action. Another purpose is to describe not only some of the difficulties and obstacles that adult students may face when returning to school but also tactics for coping with them.

If you have been thinking about going back to college, and believing that you are the only person your age contemplating college, you should know that approximately 7 million adult students are currently enrolled in higher education institutions. This number represents 50 percent of total higher education enrollments. The majority of adult students are enrolled at two-year colleges.

There are many reasons why adult students choose to attend a two-year college. Studies have shown that the three most important criteria that adult students consider when choosing a college are location, cost, and availability of the major or program desired. Most two-year colleges are public institutions that serve a geographic district, making them readily accessible to the community. Costs at most two-year colleges are far less than at other types of higher education institutions. For many students who plan to pursue a bachelor's degree, completing their first two years of college at a community college is an affordable means to that end. If you are interested in an academic program that will transfer to a four-year institution, most two-year colleges offer the "general education" courses that comprise most freshman and sophomore years. If you are interested in a vocational or technical program, two-year colleges excel in providing this type of training.

SETTING THE STAGE

There are three different "stages" in the process of adults returning to school. The first stage is uncertainty. Do I really want to go back to school? What will my friends or family think? Can I compete with those 18-year-old whiz kids? Am I too old? The second stage is choice. Once the decision to return has been made, you must choose where you will attend. There are many criteria to use in making this decision. The third stage is support. You have just added another role to your already-too-busy life. There are, however, strategies that will help you accomplish your goals—perhaps not without struggle, but with grace and humor nonetheless. Let's look at each of these stages.

UNCERTAINTY

Why are you thinking about returning to school? Is it to:

- fulfill a dream that had to be delayed?
- become more educationally well-rounded?
- fill an intellectual void in your life?

These reasons focus on *personal growth*.

If you are returning to school to:

- meet people and make friends
- attain and enjoy higher social status and prestige among friends, relatives, and associates
- understand/study a cultural heritage
- have a medium in which to exchange ideas

you are interested in *social and cultural opportunities*.

If you are like most adult students, you want to:

- qualify for a new occupation
- enter or reenter the job market
- increase earnings potential
- qualify for a more challenging position in the same field of work

You are seeking *career growth*.

Understanding the reasons why you want to go back to school is an important step in setting your educational goals and will help you to establish some criteria for selecting a college.

However, don't delay your decision because you have not been able to clearly define your motives. Many times, these aren't clear until you have already begun the process, and they may change as you move through your college experience.

Assuming you agree that additional education will benefit you, what is it that keeps you from returning to school? You may have a litany of excuses running through your mind:

- I don't have time.

- I can't afford it.

- I'm too old to learn.

- My friends will think I'm crazy.

- The teachers will be younger than I.

- My family can't survive without me to take care of them every minute.

- I'll be X years old when I finish.

- I'm afraid.

- I don't know what to expect.

And that is just what these are—excuses. You can make school, like anything else in your life, a priority or not. If you really want to return, you can. The more you understand your motivation for returning to school and the more you understand what excuses are keeping you from taking action, the easier your task will be.

If you think you don't have time: The best way to decide how attending class and studying can fit into your schedule is to keep track of what you do with your time each day for several weeks. Completing a standard time-management grid (each day is plotted out by the half hour) is helpful for visualizing how your time is spent. For each 3-credit-hour class you take, you will need to find 3 hours for class plus 6 to 9 hours for reading-studying-library time. This study time should be spaced evenly throughout the week, not loaded up on one day. It is not possible to learn or retain the material that way. When you examine your grid, see where there are activities that could be replaced with school and study time. You may decide to give up your bowling league or some time in front of the TV. Try not to give up sleeping, and don't cut out every moment of free time. Here are some suggestions that have come from adults who have returned to school:

- Enroll in a time-management workshop. It helps you rethink how you use your time.

- Don't think you have to take more than one course at a time. You may eventually want to work up to taking more, but consider starting with one. (It is more than you are taking now!)

- If you have a family, start assigning to them those household chores that you usually do—and don't redo what they do.

- Use your lunch hour or commuting time for reading.

If you think you cannot afford it: As mentioned earlier, two-year colleges are extremely affordable. If you cannot afford the tuition, look into the various financial aid options. Most federal and state funds are available to full- and part-time students. Loans are also available. While many people prefer not to accumulate a debt for school, these same people will think nothing of taking out a loan to buy a car. After five or six years, which is the better investment? Adult students who work should look into whether their company has a tuition-reimbursement policy. There are also private scholarships, available through foundations, service organizations, and clubs, that are focused on adult learners. Your public library, the Web, and a college financial aid adviser are three excellent sources for reference materials regarding financial aid.

If you think you are too old to learn: This is pure myth. A number of studies have shown that adult learners perform as well as, or better than, traditional-age students.

If you are afraid your friends will think you're crazy: Who cares? Maybe they will, maybe they won't. Usually, they will admire your courage and be just a little jealous of your ambition (although they'll never tell you that). Follow your dreams, not theirs.

If you are concerned because the teachers or students will be younger than you: Don't be. The age differences that may be apparent in other settings evaporate in the classroom. If anything, an adult in the classroom strikes fear into the hearts of some 18-year-olds because adults have been known to be prepared, ask questions, be truly motivated, and be there to learn!

If you think your family will have a difficult time surviving while you are in school: If you have done everything for them up to now, they might struggle. Consider this an opportunity to help them become independent and self-sufficient. Your family can only make you feel guilty if you let them. You are not abandoning them; you are becoming an educational role model. When you are happy and working toward your goals, everyone benefits. Admittedly, it sometimes takes time for them to realize this. For single parents, there are schools that offer support groups, child care, and cooperative babysitting.

If you're appalled at the thought of being X years old when you graduate in Y years: How old will you be in Y years if you don't go back to school?

If you are afraid or don't know what to expect: Know that these are natural feelings when one encounters any new situation. Adult students find that their fears usually dissipate once they begin classes. Fear of trying is usually the biggest roadblock to the reentry process.

No doubt you have dreamed up a few more reasons for not making the decision to return to school. Keep in mind that what you are doing is making up excuses, and you are using these excuses to release you from the obligation to make a decision about your life. The thought of returning to college can be scary. Anytime anyone ventures into unknown territory, there is a risk, but taking risks is a necessary component of personal

and professional growth. It is your life, and you alone are responsible for making the decisions that determine its course. Education is an investment in your future.

CHOICE

Once you have decided to go back to school, your next task is to decide where to go. If your educational goals are well defined (e.g., you want to pursue a degree in order to change careers), then your task is a bit easier. But even if your educational goals are still evolving, do not defer your return. Many students who enter higher education with a specific major in mind change that major at least once.

Most students who attend a public two-year college choose the community college in the district in which they live. This is generally the closest and least expensive option if the school offers the programs you want. If you are planning to begin your education at a two-year college and then transfer to a four-year school, there are distinct advantages to choosing your four-year school early. Many community and four-year colleges have "articulation" agreements that designate what credits from the two-year school will transfer to the four-year college and how. Some four-year institutions accept an associate degree as equivalent to the freshman and sophomore years, regardless of the courses you have taken. Some four-year schools accept two-year college work only on a course-by-course basis. If you can identify which school you will transfer to, you can know in advance exactly how your two-year credits will apply, preventing an unexpected loss of credit or time.

Each institution of higher education is distinctive. Your goal in choosing a college is to come up with the best student-institution fit—matching your needs with the offerings and characteristics of the school. The first step in choosing a college is to determine what criteria are most important to you in attaining your educational goals. Location, cost, and program availability are the three main factors that influence an adult student's college choice. In considering location, don't forget that some colleges have conveniently located branch campuses. In considering cost, remember to explore your financial aid options before ruling out an institution because of its tuition. Program availability should include not only the major in which you are interested, but also whether or not classes in that major are available when you can take them.

Some additional considerations beyond location, cost, and programs are:

- Does the school have a commitment to adult students and offer appropriate services, such as child care, tutoring, and advising?

- Are classes offered at times when you can take them?

- Are there academic options for adults, such as credit for life or work experience, credit by examination (including CLEP and PEP), credit for military service, or accelerated programs?

- Is the faculty sensitive to the needs of adult learners?

Once you determine which criteria are vital in your choice of an institution, you can begin to narrow your choices. There are myriad ways for you to locate the information you desire. Many urban newspapers publish a "School Guide" several times a year in which colleges and universities advertise to an adult student market. In addition, schools themselves publish catalogs, class schedules, and promotional materials that contain much of the information you need, and they are yours for the asking. Many colleges sponsor information sessions and open houses that allow you to visit the campus and ask questions. An appointment with an adviser is a good way to assess the fit between you and the institution. Be sure to bring your questions with you to your interview.

SUPPORT

Once you have made the decision to return to school and have chosen the institution that best meets your needs, take some additional steps to ensure your success during your crucial first semester. Take advantage of institutional support and build some social support systems of your own. Here are some ways of doing just that:

- Plan to participate in any orientation programs. These serve the threefold purpose of providing you with a great deal of important information, familiarizing you with the campus and its facilities, and giving you the opportunity to meet and begin networking with other students.

- Take steps to deal with any academic weaknesses. Take mathematics and writing placement tests if you have reason to believe you may need some extra help in these areas. It is not uncommon for adult students to need a math refresher course or a program to help alleviate math anxiety. Ignoring a weakness won't make it go away.

- Look into adult reentry programs. Many institutions offer adults workshops focusing on ways to improve study skills, textbook reading, test-taking, and time-management skills.

- Build new support networks by joining an adult student organization, making a point of meeting other adult students through workshops, or actively seeking out a "study buddy" in each class—that invaluable friend who shares and understands your experience.

- Incorporate your new status as "student" into your family life. Doing your homework with your children at a designated "homework time" is a valuable family activity and reinforces the importance of education.

- Make sure you take a reasonable course load in your first semester. It is far better to have some extra time on your hands and to succeed magnificently than to spend the entire semester on the brink of a breakdown. Also,

whenever possible, try to focus your first courses not only on requirements, but also on areas of personal interest.

- ■ Faculty members, advisers, and student affairs personnel are there to help you during difficult times—let them assist you as often as necessary.

After completing your first semester, you will probably look back in wonder at why you thought going back to school was so imposing. Certainly, it's not without its occasional exasperations. But, as with life, keeping things in perspective and maintaining your sense of humor make the difference between just coping and succeeding brilliantly.

What International Students Need to Know About Admission to U.S. Colleges and Universities

Kitty M. Villa

There are two principles to remember about admission to a university in the United States. First, applying is almost never a one-time request for admission but an ongoing process that may involve several exchanges of information between applicant and institution. "Admission process" or "application process" means that a "yes" or "no" is usually not immediate, and requests for additional information are to be expected. To successfully manage this process, you must be prepared to send additional information when requested and then wait for replies. You need a thoughtful balance of persistence to communicate regularly and effectively with your selected universities and patience to endure what can be a very long process.

The second principle involves a marketplace analogy. The most successful applicants are alert to opportunities to create a positive impression that sets them apart from other applicants. They are able to market themselves to their target institution. Institutions are also trying to attract the highest-quality student that they can. The admissions process presents you with the opportunity to analyze your strengths and weaknesses as a student and to look for ways to present yourself in the most marketable manner.

FIRST STEP—SELECTING INSTITUTIONS

With thousands of institutions of higher education in the U.S., how do you begin to narrow your choices down to the institutions that are best for you? There are many factors to consider, and you must ultimately decide which factors are most important to you.

Location

You may spend several years studying in the U.S. Do you prefer an urban or rural campus? Large or small metropolitan

area? If you need to live on campus, will you be unhappy at a university where most students commute from off-campus housing? How do you feel about extremely hot summers or cold winters? Eliminating institutions that do not match your preferences in terms of location will narrow your choices.

Recommendations from Friends, Professors, or Others

There are valid academic reasons to consider the recommendations of people who know you well and have firsthand knowledge about particular institutions. Friends and contacts may be able to provide you with "inside information" about the campus or its academic programs to which published sources have no access. You should carefully balance anecdotal information with your own research and your own impressions. However, current and former students, professors, and others may provide excellent information during the application process.

Your Own Academic and Career Goals

Consideration of your academic goals is more complex than it may seem at first glance. All institutions do not offer the same academic programs. The application form usually provides a definitive listing of the academic programs offered by an institution. A course catalog describes the degree program and all the courses offered. In addition to printed sources, there is a tremendous amount of institutional information available on the Web. Program descriptions, even course descriptions and course syllabi, are often available to peruse online.

You may be interested in the rankings of either the university or of a program of study. Keep in mind, however, that rankings usually assume that quality is quantifiable. Rankings are usually based on presumptions about how data

relate to quality that are likely to be unproven. It is important to carefully consider the source and the criteria of any ranking information before believing and acting upon it.

Your Own Educational Background

You may be concerned about the interpretation of your educational credentials, since your country's degree nomenclature and the grading scale may differ from those in the U.S. Universities use reference books about the educational systems of other countries to help them understand specific educational credentials. Generally, these credentials are interpreted by each institution; there is not a single interpretation that applies to every institution. The lack of uniformity is good news for most students, since it means that students from a wide variety of educational backgrounds can find a U.S. university that is appropriate to their needs.

To choose an appropriate institution, you can and should do an informal self-evaluation of your educational background. This self-analysis involves three important questions:

1. How Many Years of Study Have You Completed?

Completion of secondary school with at least twelve total years of education usually qualifies students to apply for undergraduate (bachelor's) degree programs. Completion of a university degree program that involves at least sixteen years of total education qualifies one to apply for admission to graduate (master's) degree programs in the U.S.

2. Does the Education That You Have Completed in Your Country Provide Access to Further Study in the U.S.?

Consider the kind of institution where you completed your previous studies. If educational opportunities in your country are limited, it may be necessary to investigate many U.S. institutions and programs in order to find a match.

3. Are Your Previous Marks or Grades Excellent, Average, or Poor?

Your educational record influences your choice of U.S. institutions. If your grades are average or poor, it may be advisable to apply to several institutions with minimally difficult or noncompetitive entrance levels.

YOU are one of the best sources of information about the level and quality of your previous studies. Awareness of your educational assets and liabilities will serve you well throughout the application process.

SECOND STEP—PLANNING AND ASSEMBLING THE APPLICATION

Planning and assembling a university application can be compared to the construction of a building. First, you must start with a solid foundation, which is the application form itself.

The application, often available online as well as in paper form, usually contains a wealth of useful information, such as deadlines, fees, and degree programs available at that institution. To build a solid application, it is best to begin well in advance of the application deadline.

How to Obtain the Application Form

Application forms and links to institutional Web sites may also be available at a U.S. educational advising center associated with the American Embassy or Consulate in your country. These centers are excellent resources for international students and provide information about standardized test administration, scholarships, and other matters to students who are interested in studying in the U.S. Your local U.S. Embassy or Consulate can guide you to the nearest educational advising center.

What Are the Key Components of a Complete Application?

Institutional requirements vary, but the standard components of a complete application include:

- Transcript
- Required standardized examination scores
- Evidence of financial support
- Letters of recommendation
- Application fee

Transcript

A complete academic record or transcript includes all courses completed, grades earned, and degrees awarded. Most universities require an official transcript to be sent directly from the school or university. In many other countries, however, the practice is to issue official transcripts and degree certificates directly to the student. If you have only one official copy of your transcript, it may be a challenge to get additional certified copies that are acceptable to U.S. universities. Some institutions will issue additional official copies for application purposes.

If your institution does not provide this service, you may have to seek an alternate source of certification. As a last resort, you may send a photocopy of your official transcript, explain that you have only one original, and ask the university for advice on how to deal with this situation.

Required Standardized Examination Scores

Arranging to take standardized examinations and earning the required scores seem to cause the most anxiety for international students.

The university application form usually indicates which examinations are required. The standardized examination required most often for undergraduate admission is the Test of English as a Foreign Language (TOEFL). In most countries,

TOEFL has changed from a paper-and-pencil test to an Internet-based test. Institutions may also require the SAT of undergraduate applicants. These standardized examinations are administered by the Educational Testing Service (ETS).

These examinations are offered in almost every country of the world. It is advisable to begin planning for standardized examinations at least six months prior to the application deadline of your desired institutions. Test centers fill up quickly, so it is important to register as soon as possible. Information about the examinations is available at U.S. educational advising centers associated with embassies or consulates.

Most universities require that the original test scores, not a student copy, be sent directly by the testing service. When you register for the test, be sure to indicate that the testing service should send the test scores directly to the universities.

You should begin your application process before you receive your test scores. Delaying submission of your application until the test scores arrive may cause you to miss deadlines and negatively affect the outcome of your application. If you want to know your scores in order to assess your chances of admission to an institution with rigorous admission standards, you should take the tests early.

Many universities in the U.S. set minimum required scores on the TOEFL or other standardized examinations. Test scores are an important factor, but most institutions also look at a number of other factors in their consideration of a candidate for admission.

Evidence of Financial Support

Evidence of financial support is required to issue immigration documents to admitted students. This is part of a complete application package but usually plays no role in determining admission. Most institutions make admissions decisions without regard to the source and amount of financial support.

Letters of Recommendation

Most institutions require one or more letters of recommendation. The best letters are written by former professors, employers, or others who can comment on your academic achievements or professional potential.

Some universities provide a special form for the letters of recommendation. If possible, use the forms provided. If you are applying to a large number of universities, however, or if your recommenders are not available to complete several forms, it may be necessary for you to duplicate a general recommendation letter.

Application Fee

Most universities also require an application fee, ranging from $25 to $100, which must be paid to initiate consideration of the application.

FOR MORE INFORMATION

Questions about test formats, locations, dates, and registration may be addressed to:

Educational Testing Service
Rosedale Road
Princeton, New Jersey 08541
Web sites: http://www.ets.org
　　　　　http://www.toefl.org
Telephone: 609-921-9000
Fax: 609-734-5410

Completing the Application Form

Whether sent by mail or electronically, the application form must be neat and thoroughly filled out. Although parts of the application may not seem to apply to you or your situation, do your best to answer all the questions.

Remember that this is a process. You provide information, and your proposed university then requests clarification and further information. If you have questions, it is better to initiate the entire process by submitting the application form rather than asking questions before you apply. The university will be better able to respond to you after it has your application. Always complete as much as you can. Do not permit uncertainty about the completion of the application form to cause unnecessary delays.

THIRD STEP—DISTINGUISH YOUR APPLICATION

To distinguish your application—to market yourself successfully—is ultimately the most important part of the application process. As you select your prospective universities, you begin to analyze your strengths and weaknesses as a prospective student. As you complete your application, you should strive to create a positive impression and set yourself apart from other applicants, to highlight your assets and bring these qualities to the attention of the appropriate university administrators and professors. Applying early is a very easy way to distinguish your application.

Deadline or Guideline?

The application deadline is the last date that an application for a given semester will be accepted. Often, the application will specify that all required documents and information be submitted before the deadline date. To meet the deadlines, start the application process early. This also gives you more time to take—and perhaps retake and improve—the required standardized tests.

Admissions deliberations may take several weeks or months. In the meantime, most institutions accept additional information, including improved test scores, after the posted deadline.

Even if your application is initially rejected, you may be able to provide additional information to change the decision. You can request reconsideration based on additional information, such as improved test scores, strong letters of recommendation, or information about your class rank. Applying early allows more time to improve your application. Also, some students may decide not to accept their offers of admission, leaving room for offers to students on a waiting list. Reconsideration of the admission decisions can occur well beyond the application deadline.

Think of the deadline as a guideline rather than an impermeable barrier. Many factors—the strength of the application, your research interests, the number of spaces available at the proposed institution—can override the enforcement of an application deadline. So, if you lack a test score or transcript by the official deadline, you may still be able to apply and be accepted.

Statement of Purpose

The statement of purpose is your first and perhaps best opportunity to present yourself as an excellent candidate for admission. Whether or not a personal history essay or statement of purpose is required, always include a carefully written statement of purpose with your applications. A compelling statement of purpose does not have to be lengthy, but it should include some basic components:

- Part One—Introduce yourself and describe your educational background. This is your opportunity to describe any facet of your educational experience that you wish to emphasize. Perhaps you attended a highly ranked secondary school or university in your home country. Mention the name and any noteworthy characteristics of the secondary school or university from which you graduated. Explain the grading scale used at your university. Do not forget to mention your rank in your graduating class and any honors you may have received. This is not the time to be modest.

- Part Two—Describe your current academic and career interests and goals. Think about how these will fit into those of the institution to which you are applying, and mention the reasons why you have selected that institution.

- Part Three—Describe your long-term goals. When you finish your program of study, what do you plan to do next? If you already have a job offer or a career plan, describe it. Give some thought to how you'll demonstrate that studying in the U.S. will ultimately benefit others.

Use Personal Contacts When Possible

Appropriate and judicious use of your own network of contacts can be very helpful. Friends, former professors, former students of your selected institutions, and others may be willing to advise you during the application process and provide you with introductions to key administrators or professors. If suggested, you may wish to contact certain professors or administrators by mail, telephone, or e-mail. A personal visit to discuss your interest in the institution may be appropriate. Whatever your choice of communication, try to make the encounter pleasant and personal. Your goal is to make a positive impression, not to rush the admission decision.

There is no single right way to be admitted to U.S. universities. The same characteristics that make the educational choice in the U.S. so difficult—the number of institutions and the variety of programs of study—are the same attributes that allow so many international students to find the institution that's right for them.

Kitty M. Villa is the former Assistant Director, International Office, at the University of Texas at Austin.

Searching for Two-Year Colleges Online

The Internet can be a great tool for gathering information about two-year colleges and universities. There are many worthwhile sites that are ready to help guide you through the various aspects of the selection process, including Peterson's College Search at www.petersons.com.

HOW PETERSON'S COLLEGE SEARCH CAN HELP

Peterson's College Search is a comprehensive information resource that will help you make sense of the college admissions process and is a great place to start your college search-and-selection journey—it's as easy as:

1. Decide What's Important

2. Define Your Criteria

3. Get Results

Decide What's Important

There's no such thing as a best college—there's only the best college *for you*! Peterson's College Search site is organized into various sections and offers you enhanced search criteria—and it's easy to use! You can find colleges by name or keyword for starters, or do a detailed search based on the following:

- The Basics (location, setting, size, cost, type, religious and ethnic affiliation)

- Student Body (male-female ratio, diversity, in-state vs. out-of-state)

- Getting In (selectivity, GPA)

- Academics (degree type, majors, special programs)

- Campus Life (sports, clubs, fraternities and sororities)

Define Your Criteria

Now it's time to take to define your criteria by taking a closer look at some more specific details. Here you are able to answer questions about what is important to you, skip questions that aren't important, and click for instant results. You'll be prompted to think about criteria such as:

- Where do you want to study?

- What range of tuition are you willing to consider?

- How many people do you want to got to school with?

- What kinds of clubs and activities are you looking for?

Get Results

Once you have gotten your results, simply click on any school to get information about the institution, including school type, setting, degrees offered, comprehensive cost, entrance difficulty, application deadline, undergraduate student population, minority breakdown, international population, housing information, freshman, faculty, majors, academic programs, student life, athletics, facilities/endowment, costs, financial aid, and applying. Keep reading but take a peek at all the great info you'll see on Petersons.com on the next page!

Get Free Info

If, after looking at the information provided on Peterson's College Search, you still have questions, you can send an e-mail directly to the admissions department of the school. Just click on the "Get Free Info" button and send your message!

Visit School Site

For institutions that have provided information about their Web sites, simply click on the "Visit School Site" button and you will be taken directly to that institution's Web page. Once you arrive at the school's Web site, look around and get a feel for the place. Often, schools offer virtual tours of the campus, complete with photos and commentary.

College Close-Up

If the schools you are interested in have provided Peterson's with a **College Close-Up,** you can do a keyword search on that description. Here, schools are given the opportunity to communicate unique features of their programs to prospective students.

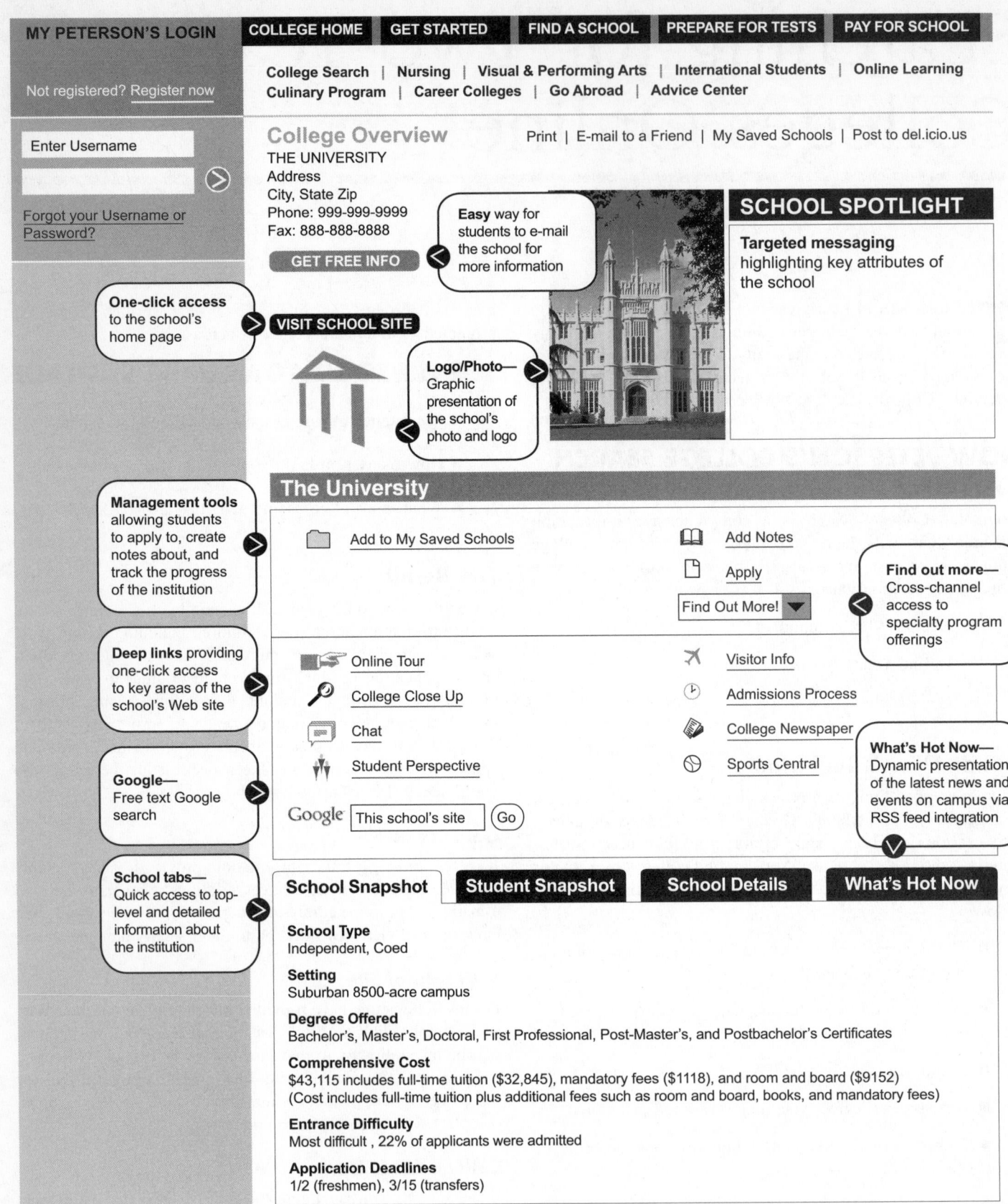

The University

School Snapshot | Student Snapshot | School Details | What's Hot Now

School Type
Independent, Coed

Setting
Suburban 8500-acre campus

Degrees Offered
Bachelor's, Master's, Doctoral, First Professional, Post-Master's, and Postbachelor's Certificates

Comprehensive Cost
$43,115 includes full-time tuition ($32,845), mandatory fees ($1118), and room and board ($9152)
(Cost includes full-time tuition plus additional fees such as room and board, books, and mandatory fees)

Entrance Difficulty
Most difficult , 22% of applicants were admitted

Application Deadlines
1/2 (freshmen), 3/15 (transfers)

Add to My Saved Schools/Add Notes/Apply

The "Add to My Saved Schools" features are designed to help you with your college planning with management tools to create notes about and track the school. The Apply link gives you the ability to directly apply to the school online.

WRITE ADMISSIONS ESSAYS

This year, 500,000 college applicants will write 500,000 different admissions essays. Half will be rejected by their first-choice school, while only 11 percent will gain admission to the nation's most selective colleges. With acceptance rates at all-time lows, setting yourself apart requires more than just blockbuster SAT scores and impeccable transcripts—it requires the perfect application essay. Named "the world's premier application essay editing service" by the *New York Times* Learning Network and "one of the best essay services on the Internet" by the *Washington Post*, EssayEdge (www.essayedge.com) has helped more applicants write successful personal statements than any other

company in the world. Learn more about EssayEdge and how it can give you an edge over hundreds of applicants with comparable academic credentials.

PRACTICE FOR YOUR TEST

At Peterson's, we understand that the college admissions process can be very stressful. With the stakes so high and the competition getting tighter every year, it's easy to feel like the process is out of your control. Fortunately, preparing for college admissions tests, like the PSAT/NMSQT, SAT, and ACT, helps you exert some control over the options you will have available to you. You can visit Peterson's Prep Central to learn more about how Peterson's can help you maximize your scores—and your options.

USE THE TOOLS TO YOUR ADVANTAGE

Choosing a college is an involved and complicated process. The tools available to you on www.petersons.com can help you to be more productive in this process. So, what are you waiting for? Fire up your computer; your future alma mater may be just a click away!

How to Use This Guide

*P*eterson's *Two-Year Colleges 2008* contains a wealth of information for anyone interested in colleges offering associate degrees. This section details the criteria that institutions must meet to be included in this guide and provides information about research procedures used by Peterson's.

QUICK-REFERENCE CHART

The **Quick-Reference Chart** is a geographically arranged table that lists colleges by name and city within the state, territory, or country in which they are located. Areas listed include the United States and its territories and other countries; the institutions in these countries are included because they are accredited by recognized U.S. accrediting bodies (see **Criteria for Inclusion** section).

The At-a-Glance chart contains basic information that enables you to compare institutions quickly according to broad characteristics such as enrollment, application requirements, financial aid availability, and numbers of sports and majors offered. An asterisk (*) after an institution's name denotes that a **Special Message** is included in the college's profile, and a dagger (†) indicates that an institution has one or more entries in the **College Close-Ups** section.

Column 1: Degrees Awarded

C = *college transfer associate degree:* the degree awarded after a "university-parallel" program, equivalent to the first two years of a bachelor's degree.

T = *terminal associate degree:* the degree resulting from a one- to three-year program providing training for a specific occupation.

B = *bachelor's degree (baccalaureate):* the degree resulting from a liberal arts, science, professional, or preprofessional program normally lasting four years, although in some cases an accelerated program can be completed in three years.

M = *master's degree:* the first graduate (postbaccalaureate) degree in the liberal arts and sciences and certain professional fields, usually requiring one to two years of full-time study.

D = *doctoral degree (doctorate):* the highest degree awarded in research-oriented academic disciplines, usually requiring from three to six years of full-time study beyond the baccalaureate and intended as preparation for university-level teaching and research.

F = *first professional degree:* the degree required to be academically qualified to practice in certain professions, such as law and medicine, having as a prerequisite at least two years of college credit and usually requiring a total of at least six years of study including prior college-level work.

Column 2: Institutional Control

Private institutions are designated as one of the following:

Ind = *independent* (nonprofit)

I-R = *independent-religious:* nonprofit; sponsored by or affiliated with a particular religious group or having a nondenominational or interdenominational religious orientation.

Prop = *proprietary* (profit-making)

Public institutions are designated by the source of funding, as follows:

Fed = *federal*

St = *state*

Comm = *commonwealth* (Puerto Rico)

Terr = *territory* (U.S. territories)

Cou = *county*

Dist = *district:* an administrative unit of public education, often having boundaries different from units of local government.

City = *city*

St-L = *state and local:* local may refer to county, district, or city.

St-R = *state-related:* funded primarily by the state but administratively autonomous.

Column 3: Student Body

M = *men only* (100% of student body)

PM = *coed, primarily men*

W = *women only* (100% of student body)

PW = *coed, primarily women*

M/W = *coeducational*

Column 4: Undergraduate Enrollment

The figure shown represents the number of full-time and part-time students enrolled in undergraduate degree programs as of fall 2006.

Columns 5–7: Enrollment Percentages

Figures are shown for the percentages of the fall 2006 undergraduate enrollment made up of students attending part-time (column 5) and students 25 years of age or older (column 6). Also listed is the percentage of students in the last graduating class who completed a college-transfer associate program and went directly on to four-year colleges (column 7).

For columns 8 through 15, the following letter codes are used: Y = yes; N = no; R = recommended; S = for some.

Columns 8–10: Admission Policies

The information in these columns shows whether the college has an open admission policy (column 8) whereby virtually all applicants are accepted without regard to standardized test scores, grade average, or class rank; whether a high school equivalency certificate is accepted in place of a high school diploma for admission consideration (column 9); and whether a high school transcript (column 10) is required as part of the application process. In column 10, the combination of the codes R and S indicates that a high school transcript is recommended for all applicants (R) or required for some (S).

Columns 11–12: Financial Aid

These columns show which colleges offer the following types of financial aid: need-based aid (column 11) and part-time jobs (column 12), including those offered through the federal government's Federal Work-Study program.

Columns 13–15: Services and Facilities

These columns show which colleges offer the following: career counseling (column 13) on either an individual or group basis, job placement services (column 14) for individual students, and college-owned or -operated housing facilities (column 16) for noncommuting students.

Column 16: Sports

This figure indicates the number of sports that a college offers at the intramural and/or intercollegiate levels.

Column 17: Majors

This figure indicates the number of major fields of study in which a college offers degree programs.

PROFILES OF TWO-YEAR COLLEGES AND SPECIAL MESSAGES

The **Profiles of Two-Year Colleges** contain basic data in capsule form for quick review and comparison. The following outline of the **Profile** format shows the section headings and the items that each section covers. Any item that does not apply to a particular college or for which no information was supplied is omitted from that college's **Profile. Special Messages,** which appear in the **Profiles** just below the bulleted highlights, have been written by those colleges that chose to supplement their **Profile** data with additional information.

Bulleted Highlights

The bulleted highlights section features important information, including the institution's Web site, for quick reference and comparison. The number of possible bulleted highlights that an ideal **Profile** would have if all questions were answered in a timely manner follow. However, not every institution provides all of the information necessary to fill out every bulleted line. In such instances, the line will not appear.

First Bullet

Institutional control: Private institutions are designated as independent (nonprofit), proprietary (profit-making), or independent, with a specific religious denomination or affiliation. Nondenominational or interdenominational religious orientation is possible and would be indicated.

Public institutions are designated by the source of funding. Designations include federal, state, province, commonwealth (Puerto Rico), territory (U.S. territories), county, district (an administrative unit of public education, often having boundaries different from units of local government), city, state and local (local may refer to county, district, or city), or state-related (funded primarily by the state but administratively autonomous).

Religious affiliation is also noted here.

Institutional type: Each institution is classified as one of the following:

> *Primarily two-year college:* Awards baccalaureate degrees, but the vast majority of students are enrolled in two-year programs.

> *Four-year college:* Awards baccalaureate degrees; may also award associate degrees; does not award graduate (postbaccalaureate) degrees.

> *Five-year college:* Awards a five-year baccalaureate in a professional field such as architecture or pharmacy; does not award graduate degrees.

> *Upper-level institution:* Awards baccalaureate degrees, but entering students must have at least two years of previous college-level credit; may also offer graduate degrees.

Comprehensive institution: Awards baccalaureate degrees; may also award associate degrees; offers graduate degree programs, primarily at the master's, specialist's, or professional level, although one or two doctoral programs may be offered.

University: Offers four years of undergraduate work plus graduate degrees through the doctorate in more than two academic or professional fields.

Founding date: If the year an institution was chartered differs from the year when instruction actually began, the earlier date is given.

System or administrative affiliation: Any coordinate institutions or system affiliations are indicated. An institution that has separate colleges or campuses for men and women but shares facilities and courses is termed a coordinate institution. A formal administrative grouping of institutions, either private or public, of which the college is a part, or the name of a single institution with which the college is administratively affiliated, is a system.

Second Bullet

Setting: Schools are designated as urban (located within a major city), suburban (a residential area within commuting distance of a major city), small-town (a small but compactly settled area not within commuting distance of a major city), or rural (a remote and sparsely populated area). The phrase *easy access to . . .* indicates that the campus is within an hour's drive of the nearest major metropolitan area that has a population greater than 500,000.

Third Bullet

Endowment: The total dollar value of donations to the institution or the multicampus educational system of which the institution is a part.

Fourth Bullet

Student body: An institution is coed (coeducational—admits men and women), primarily (80 percent or more) women, primarily men, women only, or men only. A few schools are designated as undergraduate: women only; graduate: coed or undergraduate: men only; graduate: coed.

Undergraduate students: Represents the number of full-time and part-time students enrolled in undergraduate degree programs as of fall 2006. The percentage of full-time undergraduates and the percentages of men and women are given.

Special Messages

These messages have been written by those colleges that chose to supplement their **Profile** data with additional, timely, important information.

Category Overviews

Undergraduates

For fall 2006, the number of full- and part-time undergraduate students is listed. This list provides the number of states and U.S. territories, including the District of Columbia and Puerto Rico (or, for Canadian institutions, provinces and territories), and other countries from which undergraduates come. Percentages are given of undergraduates who are from out of state; Native American, African American, and Asian American or Pacific Islander; international students; transfer students; and living on campus.

Retention: The percentage of freshmen (or, for upper-level institutions, entering students) who returned the following year for the fall term.

Freshmen

Admission: Figures are given for the number of students who applied for fall 2006 admission, the number of those who were admitted, and the number who enrolled. Freshman statistics include the average high school GPA; the percentage of freshmen who took the SAT and received critical reading and math scores above 500, above 600, and above 700; as well as the percentage of freshmen taking the ACT who received a composite score of 18 or higher.

Faculty

Total: The total number of faculty members; the percentage of full-time faculty members as of fall 2006; and the percentage of full-time faculty members who hold doctoral/first professional/terminal degrees.

Student-faculty ratio: The school's estimate of the ratio of matriculated undergraduate students to faculty members teaching undergraduate courses.

Majors

This section lists the major fields of study offered by the college.

Academics

Calendar: Most colleges indicate one of the following: 4-1-4, 4-4-1, or a similar arrangement (two terms of equal length plus an abbreviated winter or spring term, with the numbers referring to months); semesters; trimesters; quarters; 3-3 (three courses for each of three terms); modular (the academic year is divided into small blocks of time; courses of varying lengths are assembled according to individual programs); or standard year (for most Canadian institutions).

Degrees: This names the full range of levels of certificates, diplomas, and degrees, including prebaccalaureate, graduate, and professional, that are offered by this institution:

Associate degree: Normally requires at least two but fewer than four years of full-time college work or its equivalent.

Bachelor's degree (baccalaureate): Requires at least four years but not more than five years of full-time college-level work or its equivalent. This includes all bachelor's degrees in which the normal four years of work are completed in three years and bachelor's degrees conferred in a five-year cooperative (work-study plan) program. A cooperative plan provides for alternate class attendance and employment in business, industry, or government. This allows students to combine actual work experience with their college studies.

Master's degree: Requires the successful completion of a program of study of at least the full-time equivalent of one but not more than two years of work beyond the bachelor's degree.

Doctoral degree (doctorate): The highest degree in graduate study. The doctoral degree classification includes Doctor of Education, Doctor of Juridical Science, Doctor of Public Health, and the Doctor of Philosophy in any nonprofessional field.

First professional degree: The first postbaccalaureate degree in one of the following fields: chiropractic (DC, DCM), dentistry (DDS, DMD), medicine (MD), optometry (OD), osteopathic medicine (DO), rabbinical and Talmudic studies (MHL, Rav), pharmacy (BPharm, PharmD), podiatry (PodD, DP, DPM), veterinary medicine (DVM), law (JD), or divinity/ministry (BD, MDiv).

First professional certificate (postdegree): Requires completion of an organized program of study after completion of the first professional degree. Examples are refresher courses or additional units of study in a specialty or subspecialty.

Post-master's certificate: Requires completion of an organized program of study of 24 credit hours beyond the master's degree but does not meet the requirements of academic degrees at the doctoral level.

Special study options: Details are next given here on study options available at each college:

Accelerated degree program: Students may earn a bachelor's degree in three academic years.

Academic remediation for entering students: Instructional courses designed for students deficient in the general competencies necessary for a regular postsecondary curriculum and educational setting.

Adult/continuing education programs: Courses offered for nontraditional students who are currently working or are returning to formal education.

Advanced placement: Credit toward a degree awarded for acceptable scores on College Board Advanced Placement (AP) tests.

Cooperative (co-op) education programs: Formal arrangements with off-campus employers allowing students to combine work and study in order to gain degree-related experience, usually extending the time required to complete a degree.

Distance learning: For-credit courses that can be accessed off-campus via cable television, the Internet, satellite, videotape, correspondence course, or other media.

Double major: A program of study in which a student concurrently completes the requirements of two majors.

English as a second language (ESL): A course of study designed specifically for students whose native language is not English.

External degree programs: A program of study in which students earn credits toward a degree through a combination of independent study, college courses, proficiency examinations, and personal experience. External degree programs require minimal or no classroom attendance.

Freshmen honors college: A separate academic program for talented freshmen.

Honors programs: Any special program for very able students offering the opportunity for educational enrichment, independent study, acceleration, or some combination of these.

Independent study: Academic work, usually undertaken outside the regular classroom structure, chosen or designed by the student with departmental approval and instructor supervision.

Internships: Any short-term, supervised work experience usually related to a student's major field, for which the student earns academic credit. The work can be full- or part-time, on or off-campus, paid or unpaid.

Off-campus study: A formal arrangement with one or more domestic institutions under which students may take courses at the other institution(s) for credit.

Part-time degree program: Students may earn a degree through part-time enrollment in regular session (daytime) classes or evening, weekend, or summer classes.

Self-designed major: Program of study based on individual interests, designed by the student with the assistance of an adviser.

Services for LD students: Special help for learning-disabled students with resolvable difficulties, such as dyslexia.

Study abroad: An arrangement by which a student completes part of the academic program studying in another country. A college may operate a campus abroad or it may have a cooperative agreement with other U.S. institutions or institutions in other countries.

Summer session for credit: Summer courses through which students may make up degree work or accelerate their program.

Tutorials: Undergraduates can arrange for special in-depth academic assignments (not for remediation) working with faculty members one-on-one or in small groups.

ROTC: Army, Naval, or Air Force Reserve Officers' Training Corps programs offered either on campus, at a branch campus [designated by a (b)], or at a cooperating host institution [designated by (c)].

Unusual degree programs: Nontraditional programs such as a 3-2 degree program, in which 3 years of liberal arts study is followed by 2 years of study in a professional field at another institution (or in a professional division of the same institution), resulting in two bachelor's degrees or a bachelor's and a master's degree.

Student Life

Housing options: The institution's policy about whether students are permitted to live off-campus or are required to live on campus for a specified period; whether freshmen-only, coed, single-sex, cooperative, and disabled student housing options are available; whether campus housing is leased by the school and/or provided by a third party; whether freshman applicants are given priority for college housing. The phrase *college housing not available* indicates that no college-owned or -operated housing facilities are provided for undergraduates and that noncommuting students must arrange for their own accommodations.

Activities and organizations: Lists information on drama-theater groups, choral groups, marching bands, student-run campus newspapers, student-run radio stations, and social organizations (sororities, fraternities, eating clubs, etc.) and how many are represented on campus.

Campus security: Campus safety measures including 24-hour emergency response devices (telephones and alarms) and patrols by trained security personnel, student patrols, late-night transport-escort service, and controlled dormitory access (key, security card, etc.).

Student services: Information provided indicates services offered to students by the college, such as legal services, health clinics, personal-psychological counseling, and women's centers.

Athletics

Membership in one or more of the following athletic associations is indicated by initials.

NCAA: National Collegiate Athletic Association

NAIA: National Association of Intercollegiate Athletics

NCCAA: National Christian College Athletic Association

NSCAA: National Small College Athletic Association

NJCAA: National Junior College Athletic Association

CIS: Canadian Interuniversity Sports

The overall NCAA division in which all or most intercollegiate teams compete is designated by a roman numeral I, II, or III. All teams that do not compete in this division are listed as exceptions.

Sports offered by the college are divided into two groups: intercollegiate (**M** or **W** following the name of each sport indicates that it is offered for men or women) and intramural. An **s** in parentheses following an **M** or **W** for an intercollegiate sport indicates that athletic scholarships (or grants-in-aid) are offered for men or women in that sport, and a c indicates a club team as opposed to a varsity team.

Standardized Tests

The most commonly required standardized tests are the ACT, SAT, and SAT Subject Tests. These and other standardized tests may be used for selective admission, as a basis for counseling or course placement, or for both purposes. This section notes if a test is used for admission or placement and whether it is required, required for some, or recommended.

In addition to the ACT and SAT, the following standardized entrance and placement examinations are referred to by their initials:

ABLE: Adult Basic Learning Examination

ACT ASSET: ACT Assessment of Skills for Successful Entry and Transfer

ACT PEP: ACT Proficiency Examination Program

CAT: California Achievement Tests

CELT: Comprehensive English Language Test

CPAt: Career Programs Assessment

CPT: Computerized Placement Test

DAT: Differential Aptitude Test

LSAT: Law School Admission Test

MAPS: Multiple Assessment Program Service

MCAT: Medical College Admission Test

MMPI: Minnesota Multiphasic Personality Inventory

OAT: Optometry Admission Test

PAA: Prueba de Aptitude Académica (Spanish-language version of the SAT)

PCAT: Pharmacy College Admission Test

PSAT/NMSQT: Preliminary SAT National Merit Scholarship Qualifying Test

SCAT: Scholastic College Aptitude Test

SRA: Scientific Research Association (administers verbal, arithmetical, and achievement tests)

TABE: Test of Adult Basic Education

TASP: Texas Academic Skills Program

TOEFL: Test of English as a Foreign Language (for international students whose native language is not English)

WPCT: Washington Pre-College Test

Costs

Costs are given for the 2007–08 academic year or for the 2006–07 academic year if 2007–08 figures were not yet available. Annual expenses may be expressed as a comprehensive fee (including full-time tuition, mandatory fees, and college room and board) or as separate figures for full-time tuition, fees, room and board, or room only. For public institutions where tuition differs according to residence, separate figures are given for area or state residents and for nonresidents. Part-time tuition is expressed in terms of a per-unit rate (per credit, per semester hour, etc.) as specified by the institution.

The tuition structure at some institutions is complex in that freshmen and sophomores may be charged a different rate from that for juniors and seniors, a professional or vocational division may have a different fee structure from the liberal arts division of the same institution, or part-time tuition may be prorated on a sliding scale according to the number of credit hours taken. Tuition and fees may vary according to academic program, campus/location, class time (day, evening, weekend), course/credit load, course level, degree level, reciprocity agreements, and student level. Room and board charges are reported as an average for one academic year and may vary according to the board plan selected, campus/location, type of housing facility, or student level. If no college-owned or -operated housing facilities are offered, the phrase *college housing not available* will appear in the Housing section of the Student Life paragraph.

Tuition payment plans that may be offered to undergraduates include tuition prepayment, installment payments, and deferred payment. A tuition prepayment plan gives a student the option of locking in the current tuition rate for the entire term of enrollment by paying the full amount in advance rather than year by year. Colleges that offer such a prepayment plan may also help the student to arrange financing.

The availability of full or partial undergraduate tuition waivers to minority students, children of alumni, employees or their children, adult students, and senior citizens may be listed.

Financial Aid

The number of Federal Work Study and/or part-time jobs and average earnings are listed. Financial aid deadlines are given as well.

Applying

Application and admission options include the following:

Early admission: Highly qualified students may matriculate before graduating from high school.

Early action plan: An admission plan that allows students to apply and be notified of an admission decision well in advance of the regular notification dates. If accepted, the candidate is not committed to enroll; students may reply to the offer under the college's regular reply policy.

Early decision plan: A plan that permits students to apply and be notified of an admission decision (and financial aid offer, if applicable) well in advance of the regular notification date. Applicants agree to accept an offer of admission and to withdraw their applications from other colleges. Candidates who are not accepted under early decision are automatically considered with the regular applicant pool, without prejudice.

Deferred entrance: The practice of permitting accepted students to postpone enrollment, usually for a period of one academic term or year.

Application fee: The fee required with an application is noted. This is typically nonrefundable, although under certain specified conditions it may be waived or returned.

Requirements: Other application requirements are grouped into three categories: required for all, required for some, and recommended. They may include an essay, standardized test scores, a high school transcript, a minimum high school grade point average (expressed as a number on a scale of 0 to 4.0, where 4.0 equals A, 3.0 equals B, etc.), letters of recommendation, an interview on campus or with local alumni, and, for certain types of schools or programs, special requirements such as a musical audition or an art portfolio.

Application deadlines and notification dates: Admission application deadlines and dates for notification of acceptance or rejection are given either as specific dates or as **rolling** and **continuous.** Rolling means that applications are processed as they are received, and qualified students are accepted as long as there are openings. Continuous means that applicants are notified of acceptance or rejection as applications are processed up until the date indicated or the actual beginning of classes. The application deadline and the notification date for transfers are given if they differ from the dates for freshmen. Early decision and early action application deadlines and notification dates are also indicated when relevant.

Admissions Contact

The name, title, and telephone number of the person to contact for application information are given at the end of the Profile. The admission office address is listed. Toll-free telephone numbers may also be included. The admission office fax number and e-mail address, if available, are listed, provided the school wanted them printed for use by prospective students.

Additional Information

Each college that has a **College Close-Up** in the guide will have a cross-reference appended to the Profile, referring you directly to that **College Close-Up.**

COLLEGE CLOSE-UPS

Nearly 100 two-page narrative descriptions provide an inside look at colleges and universities appearing in this section, shifting the focus to a variety of other factors, some of them intangible, that should also be considered. The descriptions presented in this section provide a wealth of statistics that are crucial components in the college decision-making equation—components such as tuition, financial aid, and major fields of study. Prepared exclusively by college officials, the descriptions are designed to help give students a better sense of the individuality of each institution, in terms that include campus environment, student activities, and lifestyle. Such quality-of-life intangibles can be the deciding factors in the college selection process. The absence from this section of any college or university does not constitute an editorial decision on the part of Peterson's. In essence, this section is an open forum for colleges and universities, on a voluntary basis, to communicate their particular message to prospective college students. The colleges included have paid a fee to Peterson's to provide this information. The **College Close-Ups** are edited to provide a consistent format across entries for your ease of comparison and are presented alphabetically by the official name of the institution.

INDEXES

Associate Degree Programs at Two- and Four-Year Colleges

These indexes present hundreds of undergraduate fields of study that are currently offered most widely according to the colleges' responses on *Peterson's Annual Survey of Undergraduate Institutions*. The majors appear in alphabetical order, each followed by an alphabetical list of the schools that offer an associate-level program in that field. Liberal Arts and Studies indicates a general program with no specified major. The terms used for the majors are those of the U.S. Department of Education Classification of Instructional Programs (CIPs). Many institutions, however, use different terms. Readers should visit www.petersons.com in order to contact a college and ask for its catalog or refer to the **College Close-Up** in this book for the school's exact terminology. In addition, although the term "major" is used in this guide, some colleges may use other terms, such as "concentration," "program of study," or "field."

DATA COLLECTION PROCEDURES

The data contained in the **Profiles of Two-Year Colleges** and **Indexes** were researched between fall 2006 and spring 2007 through *Peterson's Annual Survey of Undergraduate Institutions*. Questionnaires were sent to the more than 1,800 colleges that meet the outlined inclusion criteria. All data included in this edition have been submitted by officials (usually admission and financial aid officers, registrars, or institutional research personnel) at the colleges themselves. In addition, the great majority of institutions that submitted data were contacted directly by Peterson's research staff to verify unusual figures, resolve discrepancies, and obtain additional data. All usable information received in time for publication has been included. The omission of any particular item from the **Profiles of Two-Year Colleges** and **Indexes** listing signifies either that the item is not applicable to that institution or that data were not available. Because of the comprehensive editorial review that takes place in our offices and because all material comes directly from college officials, Peterson's has every reason to believe that the information presented in this guide is accurate at the time of printing. However, students should check with a specific college or university at the time of application to verify such figures as tuition and fees, which may have changed since the publication of this volume.

CRITERIA FOR INCLUSION IN THIS BOOK

Peterson's Two-Year Colleges 2008 covers accredited institutions in the United States, U.S. territories, and other countries that award the associate degree as their most popular undergraduate offering (a few also offer bachelor's, master's, or doctoral degrees). The term two-year college is the commonly used designation for institutions that grant the associate degree, since two years is the normal duration of the traditional associate degree program. However, some programs may be completed in one year, others require three years, and, of course, part-time programs may take a considerably longer period. Therefore, "two-year college" should be understood as a conventional term that accurately describes most of the institutions included in this guide but which should not be taken literally in all cases. Also included are some non-degree-granting institutions, usually branch campuses of a multicampus system, which offer the equivalent of the first two years of a bachelor's degree, transferable to a bachelor's degree–granting institution.

To be included in this guide, an institution must have full accreditation or be a candidate for accreditation (preaccreditation) status by an institutional or specialized accrediting body recognized by the U.S. Department of Education or the Council for Higher Education Accreditation (CHEA). Institutional accrediting bodies, which review each institution as a whole, include the six regional associations of schools and colleges (Middle States, New England, North Central, Northwest, Southern, and Western), each of which is responsible for a specified portion of the United States and its territories. Other institutional accrediting bodies are national in scope and accredit specific kinds of institutions (e.g., Bible colleges, independent colleges, and rabbinical and Talmudic schools). Program registration by the New York State Board of Regents is considered to be the equivalent of institutional accreditation, since the board requires that all programs offered by an institution meet its standards before recognition is granted.

This guide also includes institutions outside the United States that are accredited by these U.S. accrediting bodies. There are recognized specialized or professional accrediting bodies in more than forty different fields, each of which is authorized to accredit institutions or specific programs in its particular field. For specialized institutions that offer programs in one field only, we designate this to be the equivalent of institutional accreditation. A full explanation of the accrediting process and complete information on recognized, institutional (regional and national), and specialized accrediting bodies can be found online at www.chea.org or at www.ed.gov//admins/finaid/accred/index.html.

Quick-Reference CHART

Two-Year Colleges At-a-Glance

This chart includes the names and locations of accredited two-year colleges in the United States and U.S. territories and shows institutions' responses to the *Peterson's Annual Survey of Undergraduate Institutions*. If an institution submitted incomplete data, one or more columns opposite the institution's name is blank.

An asterisk after the school name denotes a *Special Message* following the college's profile, and a dagger indicates that the institution has one or more entries in the *College Close-Ups* section. If a school does not appear, it did not report any of the information.

Y—Yes; N—No; R—Recommended; S—For Some

Column headings (left to right): Institution · City · Degrees Awarded (College Transfer Associate (C), Terminal Associate (T), Bachelor's (B), Master's (M), Doctoral (D), First Professional (F)) · Institutional Control (Federal, State, Commonwealth, Territory; County District City, State and Local State-Related; Independent-Religious, Proprietary) · Student Body (Men, Primarily Men, Women, Primarily Women, Coed) · Undergraduate Enrollment · Percent Attending Part-Time · Percent 25 Years of Age or Older · Percent of Grads Going on to Four-Year Colleges · High School Equivalency Certificate Accepted · High School Transcript Required · Open Admissions · Need-Based Aid Available · Part-Time Jobs Available · Career Counseling Available · Job Placement Services Available · College Housing Available · Number of Sports Offered · Number of Majors Offered

Institution	City	Degrees	Control	Student Body	Undergrad Enrollment	% Part-Time	% 25+	% to 4-Yr	HS Equiv	HS Transcript	Open Adm	Need-Based Aid	PT Jobs	Career Counsel	Job Placement	College Housing	Sports	Majors
UNITED STATES																		
Alabama																		
Bishop State Community College	Mobile	C,T	St	M/W	4,070	50	45		Y	Y	Y	S	Y	Y	Y	N	3	16
Calhoun Community College	Decatur	C,T	St	M/W	8,549		38		Y	Y	S	Y	Y			N		46
Chattahoochee Valley Community College	Phenix City	C,T	St	M/W	2,034													
Community College of the Air Force	Maxwell Air Force Base	T	Fed	PM	351,715													
Gadsden State Community College	Gadsden	C,T	St	M/W	5,204	45	34		Y	Y	Y	Y	Y	Y	Y	Y	7	21
George C. Wallace Community College	Dothan	C,T	St	M/W	3,316	46	35		Y	Y	Y	Y	Y	Y	Y	N	3	26
H. Councill Trenholm State Technical College	Montgomery	T	St	M/W	1,311	50	50		Y	Y	Y	Y	Y	Y	Y	N		31
ITT Technical Institute	Birmingham	T,B	Prop	M/W					N	Y	Y	Y	Y	Y	Y	N		14
James H. Faulkner State Community College*	Bay Minette	C,T	St	M/W	3,323	36	39		Y	Y	Y	Y	Y	Y	Y	Y	6	18
Jefferson State Community College	Birmingham	C,T	St	M/W	7,173	56												
J. F. Drake State Technical College	Huntsville	T	St	M/W	764	41	55		Y		Y		Y	Y	Y	N		7
Lawson State Community College	Birmingham	C,T	St	M/W	3,141	46	39	9	Y	Y	Y	Y	Y	Y	Y	Y	11	44
Marion Military Institute	Marion	C,T	Ind	PM	165		0	100	N	Y	Y	Y	Y	Y	Y	Y	14	3
Northwest-Shoals Community College	Muscle Shoals	C	St	M/W	2,077	31	55		Y	Y	Y	Y	Y	Y	Y	Y	9	41
Prince Institute of Professional Studies	Montgomery	T	Ind	PW	94	40												
Reid State Technical College	Evergreen	T	St	M/W	545	40	13		Y		Y	Y	Y	Y	Y	N		2
Remington College–Mobile Campus	Mobile	C,T,B	Prop	M/W	433													
Shelton State Community College	Tuscaloosa	C,T	St	M/W	5,754	42												
Snead State Community College	Boaz	C,T	St	M/W														
Wallace Community College	Hanceville	C,T	St	M/W	6,028		40	79	Y	Y	Y	Y	Y	Y	Y	Y	9	59
Alaska																		
Ilisagvik College	Barrow	C	St	M/W	263	81												
University of Alaska Anchorage, Kodiak College	Kodiak	C,T	St	M/W	786		72		Y	Y	R		Y		N			3
University of Alaska Anchorage, Matanuska-Susitna College	Palmer	C,T	St	M/W	1,326	71												
University of Alaska, Prince William Sound Community College	Valdez	C,T	St	M/W	823		76		Y			Y	Y	Y		Y		5
University of Alaska Southeast, Sitka Campus	Sitka	C,T	St	M/W	1,552		65	40	Y	Y	Y			Y		N		9
Arizona																		
Arizona College of Allied Health	Glendale		Prop	M/W	197													2
Arizona Western College	Yuma	C,T	St-L	M/W	6,579	61	38	36	Y	Y		Y	Y	Y	Y	Y	9	43
Central Arizona College	Coolidge	C,T	Cou	M/W	6,471		71		Y			Y	Y	Y	Y	Y	7	26
Chandler-Gilbert Community College	Chandler	C,T	St-L	M/W	9,420	73	29		Y			Y	Y	Y	Y	N		7
Cochise College	Douglas	C,T	St-L	M/W	4,436	65	50	23	Y		R	Y	Y	Y	Y	Y	3	49
Cochise College	Sierra Vista	C,T	St-L	M/W	4,446	72	50		Y		R	Y	Y	Y	Y	Y	4	34
Coconino Community College	Flagstaff	C,T	St	M/W	3,883	79	41		Y	Y	R	Y	Y	Y	N			7
Diné College	Tsaile	C,T	Fed	M/W	1,825	54												
Eastern Arizona College	Thatcher	C,T	St-L	M/W	5,520	71	22		Y		R	Y	Y	Y	Y	Y	10	50
Everest College	Phoenix	C,T,B	Prop	M/W	1,187	47	41	7	N	Y	Y	Y		Y	Y	N		5
GateWay Community College	Phoenix	C,T	St-L	M/W	9,377	90												
Glendale Community College	Glendale	C,T	St-L	M/W	20,070	70												
International Institute of the Americas	Mesa	T,B	Ind	M/W	145		57							Y	Y	N		5
International Institute of the Americas	Phoenix	T,B	Ind	M/W	424		61		Y	Y				Y	Y	N		5
International Institute of the Americas	Tucson	T,B	Ind	M/W	267		55							Y	Y	N		5
ITT Technical Institute	Tucson	T,B	Prop	M/W					N	Y	Y	Y	Y	Y	Y	N		15
Long Technical College	Phoenix	T	Prop	M/W	388													3
Mesa Community College	Mesa	C,T	St-L	M/W	28,000		44	5	Y			Y	Y	Y	N	11	36	
Mohave Community College	Kingman	C,T	St	M/W	5,307	76	55		Y			Y	Y	Y	N		23	
Paradise Valley Community College	Phoenix	C,T	St-L	M/W	8,406				Y			Y	Y	Y	N	6	7	
The Paralegal Institute, Inc.	Phoenix	T	Prop	M/W	400													
Phoenix College	Phoenix	C,T	St-L	M/W	12,549													
Pima Community College	Tucson	C,T	St-L	M/W	32,532	71	43	15	Y			Y	Y	Y	N	16	48	
The Refrigeration School	Phoenix	T	Prop	M/W	350							Y		Y	Y	N		1
Rio Salado College	Tempe	C,T	St-L	M/W	6,000		43		Y			Y	Y	Y	N	1	15	
Scottsdale Community College	Scottsdale	C,T	St-L	M/W	10,884	70	26		Y			Y	Y	Y	N	14	25	
Southwest Institute of Healing Arts	Tempe	T	Prop	M/W	1,752													1
Yavapai College	Prescott	C,T	St-L	M/W	7,422	82												
Arkansas																		
Arkansas Northeastern College	Blytheville	C,T	St	M/W	1,830	47												
Arkansas State University–Beebe	Beebe	C,T	St	M/W	3,976	47												
Arkansas State University–Mountain Home	Mountain Home	T	St	M/W	960	40	39		Y	Y		Y	Y	Y	Y	N		11
Arkansas State University–Newport	Newport	C,T	St	M/W	896		38		Y	Y		Y	Y					13

This chart includes the names and locations of accredited two-year colleges in the United States and U.S. territories and shows institutions' responses to the *Peterson's Annual Survey of Undergraduate Institutions.* If an institution submitted incomplete data, one or more columns opposite the institution's name is blank. An asterisk after the school name denotes a *Special Message* following the college's profile, and a dagger indicates that the institution has one or more entries in the *College Close-Ups* section. If a school does not appear, it did not report any of the information.

Y—Yes; N—No; R—Recommended; S—For Some

Degrees Awarded: College Transfer Associate (C), Terminal Associate (T), Bachelor's (B), Master's (M), Doctoral (D), First Professional (P)

College	City	Degrees Awarded	Institutional Control	Student Body	Undergraduate Enrollment	Percent Attending Part-Time	Percent 25 or Older	Percent of Grads to 4-Year	HS Equivalency Accepted	Open Admissions	HS Transcript Required	Need-Based Aid Available	Part-Time Jobs Available	Career Counseling Available	Job Placement Services Available	College Housing Available	Number of Sports Offered	Number of Majors Offered
Cossatot Community College of the University of Arkansas	De Queen	C,T	St	M/W	1,133			39	Y	Y	R	Y	Y	Y	Y	N		12
East Arkansas Community College	Forrest City	C,T	St	M/W	1,477	50												
ITT Technical Institute	Little Rock	T,B	Prop	M/W					N	Y	Y	Y	Y	Y	Y	N		14
Mid-South Community College	West Memphis	C,T	St	M/W	1,467	69												
National Park Community College	Hot Springs	C,T	St-L	M/W	2,996	59		63	Y	Y	S	Y	Y	Y	Y	N	5	31
North Arkansas College	Harrison	C,T	St-L	M/W	2,047	47		42	Y	Y	S	Y	Y	Y	Y	N	11	24
NorthWest Arkansas Community College	Bentonville	C,T	St-L	M/W	5,732	67	39	37	Y	Y	Y	Y	Y	Y	Y	N	11	17
Ouachita Technical College	Malvern	C,T	St	M/W	1,590	65		45	Y	Y	Y	Y	Y	Y	Y	N		16
Ozarka College	Melbourne	C,T	St	M/W	885	43		52	Y	Y	Y	Y	Y	Y		N		10
Pulaski Technical College	North Little Rock	C,T	St	M/W	8,455	52		59	Y	Y		Y	Y	Y		N	8	8
Remington College–Little Rock Campus	Little Rock	T	Prop	M/W	456													5
South Arkansas Community College	El Dorado	C,T	St	M/W	1,368	55												
Southern Arkansas University Tech	Camden	C,T	St	M/W	1,767	69												
University of Arkansas Community College at Batesville	Batesville	C,T	St	M/W	1,288	41		48	Y	Y	Y	Y	Y	Y	Y	N		13
University of Arkansas Community College at Morrilton	Morrilton	C,T	St	M/W	1,763	35		36	Y	Y	Y	Y	Y	Y	Y	N		17
California																		
Allan Hancock College	Santa Maria	C,T	St-L	M/W	10,387	71												
Antelope Valley College	Lancaster	C,T	St-L	M/W	12,570	69		30	Y			Y	Y	Y	Y	N	12	45
Aviation & Electronic Schools of America	Colfax	T	Prop	M/W														1
Bakersfield College	Bakersfield	C,T	St-L	M/W	15,001	50				Y		Y	Y	Y	Y	N	11	77
Barstow College	Barstow	C,T	St-L	M/W	3,000	60				Y	R	Y	Y	Y	Y	N	3	17
Berkeley City College	Berkeley	C,T	St-L	M/W	5,100	65		90	Y		R	Y	Y	Y	Y	N		21
Brooks College	Long Beach	T	Prop	M/W	826	8												
Brooks College	Sunnyvale	T	Prop	M/W	370									Y				5
Bryan College	Gold River	T	Prop	M/W	129									Y				3
Cabrillo College	Aptos	C,T	Dist	M/W	14,094	50				Y		S	Y	Y	Y	Y	N	17	38
California School of Culinary Arts	Pasadena	T	Prop	M/W	1,726													2
Cañada College	Redwood City	C,T	St-L	M/W	6,230	65			Y	Y		Y	Y	Y	Y	N	5	49
Cerritos College	Norwalk	C,T	St-L	M/W	24,000	46				Y		Y	Y	Y	Y	Y	13	67
Chaffey College	Rancho Cucamonga	C,T	Dist	M/W	17,930	40						Y	Y	Y	Y	N	10	63
Citrus College	Glendora	C,T	St-L	M/W	11,576	57		25	Y	Y	Y		Y	Y	Y	N	12	43
City College of San Francisco	San Francisco	C,T	St-L	M/W	106,480	62			Y			Y	Y	Y	Y	N	16	69
College of Alameda	Alameda	C,T	St-L	M/W	5,500	44			Y	Y		Y	Y	Y	Y	N	6	31
College of Marin	Kentfield	C,T	St-L	M/W	6,607	50			Y			Y	Y	Y	Y	N	10	56
College of San Mateo	San Mateo	C,T	St-L	M/W	10,872	51		85	Y			Y	Y	Y	Y	N	7	60
College of the Canyons	Santa Clarita	C,T	St-L	M/W	19,023	65		18	Y		R	Y	Y	Y	Y	N	11	46
College of the Desert	Palm Desert	C,T	St-L	M/W	9,946	40			Y	Y		Y	Y	Y	Y	N	14	64
College of the Redwoods	Eureka	C,T	St-L	M/W	7,708	51			Y	Y		Y	Y	Y	Y	Y	9	29
College of the Siskiyous	Weed	C,T	St-L	M/W	3,400	39	30		Y			Y	Y	Y	Y	Y	11	30
Columbia College	Sonora	C,T	St-L	M/W	2,670	66			Y	Y	S	Y	Y	Y	Y	Y	4	32
Concorde Career Colleges, Inc.	Garden Grove	T	Prop	M/W	527								S	Y				1
Concorde Career Institute	North Hollywood	T	Prop	M/W	487									Y				1
Contra Costa College	San Pablo	C,T	St-L	M/W	8,834	55	67	69		Y		Y	Y	Y	Y	N	7	46
Cosumnes River College	Sacramento	C,T	Dist	M/W	19,284	52			Y	Y		Y	Y	Y	Y	N	12	61
Crafton Hills College	Yucaipa	C,T	St-L	M/W	5,300	47			Y	Y	S	Y	Y	Y	Y	N	4	42
Cuesta College	San Luis Obispo	C,T	Dist	M/W	11,150	33				Y		Y	Y	Y	Y	N	11	50
Cypress College	Cypress	C,T	St-L	M/W	15,347	45				Y	R	Y	Y	Y	Y	N	11	68
De Anza College	Cupertino	C,T	St-L	M/W	23,344	62	52	13	Y	Y		Y	Y	Y	Y	N	13	65
Deep Springs College	Deep Springs	C	Ind	M	27													1
Diablo Valley College	Pleasant Hill	C,T	St-L	M/W	20,145	38				Y	R	Y	Y	Y	Y	N	10	1
Don Bosco Technical Institute	Rosemead	C,T	I-R	PM	1,208	0	85		N	Y		Y	Y	Y	Y	N	8	8
El Camino College	Torrance	C	St	M/W	24,000	42	40		Y			Y	Y	Y	Y	N	16	73
Everest College	Ontario	T	Prop	M/W	1,031													3
Evergreen Valley College	San Jose	C,T	St-L	M/W	11,751													
Fashion Careers College	San Diego	C,T	Prop	PW	101													
Feather River College	Quincy	C,T	St-L	M/W	1,714	57												
FIDM/The Fashion Institute of Design & Merchandising, Los Angeles Campus†	Los Angeles	C,T,B	Prop	M/W	4,143	16		15	N	Y	Y	Y	Y	Y	Y	N		9
FIDM/The Fashion Institute of Design & Merchandising, San Diego Campus	San Diego	C,T	Prop	M/W	288	19		10	N	Y			Y	Y	Y	N		7
FIDM/The Fashion Institute of Design & Merchandising, San Francisco Campus	San Francisco	C,T	Prop	PW	983	18		25	N	Y	Y			Y	Y	N		8
Folsom Lake College	Folsom	C,T	Cou	M/W	6,337	47												22
Foothill College	Los Altos Hills	C,T	St-L	M/W	18,342	80	43	31	Y		R	Y	Y	Y	Y	N	9	52
Fresno City College	Fresno	C,T	Dist	M/W	22,812	7	85		Y		Y	Y	Y	Y	Y	N	16	62
Fullerton College	Fullerton	C,T	St-L	M/W	19,862		40		Y				Y	Y	Y	N	10	68
Gavilan College	Gilroy	C,T	St-L	M/W	6,064													
Glendale Community College	Glendale	C,T	St-L	M/W	14,265	67												
Golden West College	Huntington Beach	C,T	St-L	M/W	13,091	44		80	Y	Y	R	Y	Y	Y	Y	N	13	35
Grossmont College	El Cajon	C,T	St-L	M/W	16,829	38			Y			Y	Y	Y	Y	N	12	54
Hartnell College	Salinas	C,T	Dist	M/W	10,074				Y	Y	S	Y	Y	Y	Y	N	12	52
Heald College-Concord	Concord	C,T	Ind	M/W	639	18												
Heald College-Fresno	Fresno	C,T	Ind	M/W	729	25												
Heald College-Hayward	Hayward	C,T	Ind	M/W	864	26												
Heald College-Rancho Cordova	Rancho Cordova	C,T	Ind	M/W	471	26												
Heald College-Roseville	Roseville	C,T	Ind	M/W	528	29												
Heald College-Salinas	Salinas	C,T	Ind	M/W	414	21												

This chart includes the names and locations of accredited two-year colleges in the United States and U.S. territories and shows institutions' responses to the *Peterson's Annual Survey of Undergraduate Institutions*. If an institution submitted incomplete data, one or more columns opposite the institution's name is blank.
An asterisk after the school name denotes a *Special Message* following the college's profile, and a dagger indicates that the institution has one or more entries in the *College Close-Ups* section. If a school does not appear, it did not report any of the information.

Y—Yes; N—No; R—Recommended; S—For Some

Institution	Location	Degrees Awarded	Institutional Control	Student Body	Undergraduate Enrollment	Percent Attending Part-Time	Percent 25 Years of Age or Older	Percent of Grads Going on to Four-Year Colleges	Open Admissions	HS Equivalency Certificate Accepted	HS Transcript Required	Need-Based Aid Available	Part-Time Jobs Available	Job Placement Services Available	Career Counseling Available	College Housing Available	Number of Sports Offered	Number of Majors Offered
Heald College-San Francisco	San Francisco	C,T	Ind	M/W	389	30												
Heald College-San Jose	Milpitas	C,T	Ind	M/W	639	21												
Heald College-Stockton	Stockton	C,T	Ind	M/W	530	25												
High-Tech Institute	Sacramento	T	Prop	M/W	716													1
Imperial Valley College	Imperial	C,T	St-L	M/W	7,413			12	Y		R,S	Y	Y	Y	Y	N	5	35
Irvine Valley College	Irvine	C,T	St-L	M/W	10,511		55		Y			Y	Y	Y	Y	N	5	21
ITT Technical Institute	Anaheim	T,B	Prop	M/W					N	Y	Y	Y	Y	Y	Y	N		11
ITT Technical Institute	Lathrop	T,B	Prop	M/W					N	Y	Y	Y	Y	Y	Y	N		14
ITT Technical Institute	Oxnard	C,T,B	Prop	M/W					N	Y	Y	Y	Y	Y	Y	N		12
ITT Technical Institute	Rancho Cordova	T,B	Prop	M/W					N	Y	Y	Y	Y	Y	Y	N		13
ITT Technical Institute	San Bernardino	T,B	Prop	M/W					N	Y	Y	Y	Y	Y	Y	N		11
ITT Technical Institute	San Diego	T,B	Prop	M/W					N	Y	Y	Y	Y	Y	Y	N		11
ITT Technical Institute	San Dimas	T,B	Prop	M/W					N	Y	Y	Y	Y	Y	Y	N		13
ITT Technical Institute	Sylmar	T,B	Prop	M/W					N	Y	Y	Y	Y	Y	Y	N		12
ITT Technical Institute	Torrance	T,B	Prop	M/W					N	Y	Y	Y	Y	Y	Y	N		14
Lake Tahoe Community College	South Lake Tahoe	C,T	St-L	M/W	3,000		68		Y		R	Y	Y	Y	Y	N	2	27
Laney College	Oakland	C,T	St-L	M/W	13,463	82	57		Y	Y		Y	Y	Y	Y	N	5	42
Las Positas College	Livermore	C,T	St	M/W	8,044		50		Y		R	Y	Y	Y	Y	N	7	23
Lassen Community College District	Susanville	C,T	St-L	M/W	2,161		58		Y		R	Y	Y	Y	Y	Y	18	59
Long Beach City College	Long Beach	C,T	St	M/W	26,296	64												
Los Angeles City College	Los Angeles	C,T	Dist	M/W	25,000		62		Y			Y	Y	Y	Y	N	16	84
Los Angeles Harbor College	Wilmington	C,T	St-L	M/W	9,469	76	49	18	Y			Y	Y	Y	Y	N	7	23
Los Angeles Mission College	Sylmar	C,T	St-L	M/W	7,617		55	8	Y			Y	Y	Y	Y	N		38
Los Angeles Pierce College	Woodland Hills	C,T	St-L	M/W	16,255		48		Y			Y	Y	Y	Y	N	16	34
Los Angeles Southwest College	Los Angeles	C,T	St-L	M/W	6,000		63		Y			S	Y	Y	Y	N	9	34
Los Medanos College	Pittsburg	C,T	Dist	M/W	7,152		56		Y	Y		S	Y	Y	Y	N	6	29
Maric College	Panorama City	T	Prop	M/W	529													4
Maric College	San Diego	C,T	Prop	M/W	298		60			Y	Y	Y	Y	Y	Y	N		1
Marymount College, Palos Verdes, California	Rancho Palos Verdes	C,T	I-R	M/W	652	4	1		N	Y	Y	Y	Y	Y	Y	Y	8	1
Mendocino College	Ukiah	C,T	St-L	M/W	5,400		65	25	Y			Y	Y	Y	Y	N	9	38
Merced College	Merced	C,T	St-L	M/W	12,525		51		Y		R	Y	Y	Y	Y	N	14	58
MiraCosta College*	Oceanside	C,T	St	M/W	10,252													
Mission College	Santa Clara	C,T	St-L	M/W	10,500	62	60	32	Y			Y	Y	Y	Y	N	6	24
Modesto Junior College	Modesto	C,T	St-L	M/W	18,240													
Monterey Peninsula College	Monterey	C,T	St	M/W	14,074				Y			Y	Y	Y	Y	N	10	70
Moorpark College	Moorpark	C,T	Cou	M/W	15,266		42		Y	Y	R,S	Y	Y	Y	Y	N	10	38
Mt. San Antonio College	Walnut	C,T	Dist	M/W	29,079	69			Y		S	Y	Y	Y	Y	N	14	72
MTI College of Business & Technology	Sacramento	C,T	Prop	M/W	600													
Napa Valley College	Napa	C,T	St-L	M/W	6,908	72			Y		S	Y	Y	Y	Y	N	20	37
National Institute of Technology	Long Beach	T	Prop	M/W	1,144													2
Ohlone College	Fremont	C,T	St-L	M/W	10,867	68	49		Y	Y	Y	Y	Y	Y	Y	N	8	39
Orange Coast College	Costa Mesa	C,T	St-L	M/W	22,412	59	34		Y			Y	Y	Y	Y	N	14	102
Oxnard College	Oxnard	C	St	M/W	6,379	70	42		Y	Y	Y	Y	Y	Y	Y	N	6	44
Palo Verde College	Blythe	C,T	St-L	M/W	3,648													
Pasadena City College	Pasadena	C,T	St-L	M/W	29,618		42		Y			Y	Y	Y	Y	N	11	105
Platt College San Diego*	San Diego	C,T,B	Prop	M/W	264		44	90	N	Y	Y		Y	Y	Y	N		9
Porterville College	Porterville	C,T	St	M/W	5,024		48		Y		Y	Y	Y	Y	Y	N	6	34
Quality College of Culinary Careers	Fresno	C,T	Prop	M/W	34													2
Queen of the Holy Rosary College	Mission San Jose	C,T	I-R	PW	195		100		Y	Y	Y					N		1
Reedley College	Reedley	C,T	St-L	M/W	11,782	62	39		Y	Y	Y	Y	Y	Y	Y	Y	9	39
Rio Hondo College	Whittier	C,T	St-L	M/W	15,000		40		Y			Y	Y	Y	Y	N	10	4
Riverside Community College District	Riverside	T	St-L	M/W	30,709	71	40		Y		Y	Y	Y	Y	Y	N	16	22
Sacramento City College	Sacramento	C,T	St-L	M/W	21,890		50		Y			Y	Y	Y	Y	N	18	49
Saddleback College	Mission Viejo	C	St-L	M/W	18,351													
Sage College	Moreno Valley	T	Prop	M/W	387													2
The Salvation Army College for Officer Training at Crestmont	Rancho Palos Verdes	C,T	I-R	M/W	27													
San Bernardino Valley College	San Bernardino	C,T	St-L	M/W	1,540		55		Y	Y		Y	Y	Y	Y	N	9	64
San Diego City College	San Diego	C	St-L	M/W	15,475		44		Y		S	Y	Y	Y	Y	N	16	68
San Diego Mesa College	San Diego	C	St-L	M/W	21,198													
San Joaquin Delta College	Stockton	C,T	Dist	M/W	18,800		40		Y			Y	Y	Y	Y	N	18	82
San Joaquin Valley College	Visalia	C,T	Ind	M/W	3,352													
Santa Ana College	Santa Ana	C,T	St	M/W	22,189		63		Y	Y		Y	Y	Y	Y	N	13	74
Santa Barbara City College	Santa Barbara	T	St-L	M/W	16,043	59	25		Y	Y	R	Y	Y	Y	Y	N	10	79
Santa Rosa Junior College†	Santa Rosa	C,T	St-L	M/W	25,031		56		Y			Y	Y	Y	Y	N	15	83
Santiago Canyon College	Orange	C,T	St	M/W	10,214		50		Y	Y		Y	Y	Y		N		45
Shasta College	Redding	C,T	St-L	M/W	10,240	58	56	16	Y		Y	Y	Y	Y	Y	Y	11	36
Skyline College	San Bruno	C,T	St-L	M/W	8,147													
South Coast College	Orange	T	Prop	M/W	368													1
Stanbridge College	Irvine	T	Prop	M/W	28													1
Taft College	Taft	C	St-L	M/W	9,500	95	47		Y		S	Y	Y	Y	Y	Y	5	24
Ventura College	Ventura	C,T	St-L	M/W	11,757	67	47		Y	Y	Y	Y	Y	Y	Y	N	12	29
Victor Valley College	Victorville	C,T	St	M/W	10,580	65			Y			Y	Y	Y	Y	N	12	41
Western Career College	Pleasant Hill	T	Prop	M/W	397													8
Western Career College	Sacramento	T	Prop	M/W	1,053													7
Western Career College	San Leandro	T	Prop	M/W														5
West Hills Community College	Coalinga	C,T	St	M/W	6,088	68	48	22	Y		R	Y	Y	Y	Y	Y	7	29
West Los Angeles College	Culver City	C,T	St-L	M/W	9,800		76		Y		R	Y	Y	Y	Y	N	5	45
West Valley College	Saratoga	C,T	St-L	M/W	11,000		58		Y			Y	Y	Y	Y	N	13	40
Westwood College—Anaheim†	Anaheim	T,B	Prop	M/W	674	15												

This chart includes the names and locations of accredited two-year colleges in the United States and U.S. territories and shows institutions' responses to the *Peterson's Annual Survey of Undergraduate Institutions*. If an institution submitted incomplete data, one or more columns opposite the institution's name is blank. An asterisk after the school name denotes a *Special Message* following the college's profile, and a dagger indicates that the institution has one or more entries in the *College Close-Ups* section. If a school does not appear, it did not report any of the information.

Y—Yes; N—No; R—Recommended; S—For Some

Column legend: Deg = Degrees Awarded (Bachelor's (B), Master's (M), Doctoral (D), First Professional (F), College Transfer Associate (C), Terminal Associate (T)); Ctrl = Institutional Control; Body = Student Body; Enroll = Undergraduate Enrollment; PT% = Percent Attending Part-Time; 25+% = Percent 25 Years of Age or Older; Grad% = Percent of Grads Going on to Four-Year Colleges; HSEq = High School Equivalency Certificate Accepted; HSTr = High School Transcript Required; Open = Open Admissions; Need = Need-Based Aid Available; PTJob = Part-Time Jobs Available; Care = Career Counseling Available; JobP = Job Placement Services Available; Hous = College Housing Available; Sport = Number of Sports Offered; Maj = Number of Majors Offered

College	Location	Deg	Ctrl	Body	Enroll	PT%	25+%	Grad%	HSEq	HSTr	Open	Need	PTJob	Care	JobP	Hous	Sport	Maj
Westwood College–Inland Empire†	Upland	T,B	Prop	M/W	803	19												
Westwood College–Los Angeles†	Los Angeles	T,B	Prop	M/W	679	15												
Westwood College–South Bay Campus†	Long Beach	T,B	Prop	M/W	265									Y	Y	Y		3
WyoTech	Fremont	T	Prop	PM	1,554								Y	Y	Y	Y		
Yuba College	Marysville	C	St-L	M/W	6,623			48	Y	Y	Y	Y	Y	Y			9	58
Colorado																		
Aims Community College	Greeley	C,T	Dist	M/W	5,098	56		60		Y		Y	Y	Y	Y	N	2	18
Arapahoe Community College	Littleton	C,T	St	M/W	7,560	69												
Boulder College of Massage Therapy	Boulder	T	Ind	M/W	220													
Cambridge College	Aurora	T	Ind		578													7
CollegeAmerica–Colorado Springs	Colorado Spring	T,B	Prop	M/W														7
CollegeAmerica–Denver	Denver	T,B	Prop	M/W	444							Y						7
Colorado Mountain College*†	Glenwood Springs	C,T	Dist	M/W	1,393			70	Y	Y	Y	Y	Y	Y	Y	Y	7	24
Colorado Mountain College, Alpine Campus	Steamboat Springs	C,T	Dist	M/W	1,093			59	Y	Y	Y	Y	Y	Y	Y	Y	6	21
Colorado Mountain College, Timberline Campus	Leadville	C,T	Dist	M/W	470			60	Y	Y	Y	Y	Y	Y	Y	Y	6	12
Colorado School of Healing Arts	Lakewood	T	Prop	M/W	240	38												
Colorado School of Trades	Lakewood	T	Prop	M/W	125													
Community College of Aurora	Aurora	C,T	St	M/W	5,477	74												
Community College of Denver	Denver	C,T	St	M/W	8,909	77												
Front Range Community College	Westminster	C,T	St	M/W	14,749	65		38		Y			Y	Y	Y	N		25
Heritage College	Denver	T	Prop	M/W	496						R							3
IntelliTec College	Grand Junction	C	Prop	M/W	486													14
ITT Technical Institute	Thornton	T,B	Prop	M/W					N	Y	Y	Y	Y	Y	Y	N		50
Lamar Community College	Lamar	C,T	St	M/W	1,021			43	Y	Y		Y	Y	Y	Y	Y	7	50
Morgan Community College	Fort Morgan	C,T	St	M/W	1,647			46		Y		Y	Y	Y	Y	N		10
Northeastern Junior College	Sterling	C,T	St	M/W	3,633	75	3	75	Y	Y	Y	Y	Y	Y	Y	Y	14	67
Otero Junior College	La Junta	C,T	St	M/W	1,636	53												36
Pueblo Community College	Pueblo	C,T	St	M/W	5,393	62		38	Y			Y	Y	Y	Y	N	1	40
Red Rocks Community College	Lakewood	C,T	St	M/W	6,727	69		46	Y			Y	Y	Y	Y	N	1	40
Trinidad State Junior College	Trinidad	C,T	St	M/W	1,732	58		59	Y	Y	Y	Y	Y	Y	Y	Y	13	46
Westwood College–Denver North†	Denver	T,B	Prop	M/W	1,423	24												
Westwood College–Denver South†	Denver	T,B	Prop	M/W	429	31												
Connecticut																		
Asnuntuck Community College	Enfield	C,T	St	M/W	1,638	65		42	Y	Y	Y	Y	Y	Y	Y	N		21
Briarwood College†	Southington	C,T,B	Prop	M/W	647	40	38	7	N	Y	Y	Y	Y	Y	Y	Y	3	22
Capital Community College	Hartford	C,T	St	M/W	3,550	75			Y	Y	R	Y	Y	Y	N			20
Gateway Community College	New Haven	C,T	St	M/W	5,824	66	43	40	Y	Y	Y	Y	Y	Y	N		4	33
Goodwin College	East Hartford	C,T	Prop	M/W	1,219	89												
Housatonic Community College	Bridgeport	C,T	St	M/W	4,343		46		Y	Y	Y	Y	Y	Y	N			24
International College of Hospitality Management†	Suffield	C,T	Prop	M/W	116													
Manchester Community College	Manchester	C,T	St	M/W	6,135	56												
Middlesex Community College	Middletown	C,T	St	M/W	2,474	62	42	45	Y	Y	Y	Y	Y	Y	N	N		25
Naugatuck Valley Community College	Waterbury	C,T	St	M/W	5,659	60	39		Y	Y	Y	Y	Y	Y	N			50
Northwestern Connecticut Community College	Winsted	C,T	St	M/W	1,544	66	35	30	Y	Y		Y	Y	Y	N			35
Norwalk Community College	Norwalk	C,T	St	M/W	6,040													
Quinebaug Valley Community College	Danielson	C,T	St	M/W	1,779	62	41		Y	Y	R,S	Y	Y	Y	Y	N		18
Three Rivers Community College	Norwich	C,T	St	M/W	3,793	66	45		Y	Y	R	Y	Y	Y	Y	N	1	41
Tunxis Community College	Farmington	C,T	St	M/W	3,663	60	47		Y	Y	R		Y	Y	Y	N		23
Delaware																		
Delaware College of Art and Design	Wilmington	C,T	Ind	M/W	194	24												
Delaware Technical & Community College, Jack F. Owens Campus	Georgetown	T	St	M/W	3,936	59												
Delaware Technical & Community College, Stanton/Wilmington Campus	Newark	T	St	M/W	7,473	63												
Delaware Technical & Community College, Terry Campus	Dover	T	St	M/W	2,569	66												
Federated States of Micronesia																		
College of Micronesia–FSM	Kolonia Pohnpei	C,T	Terr	M/W	2,283			8	N	Y	Y	Y	Y	Y	Y	Y	7	18
Florida																		
Angley College	Deland	T,B	Prop		94													5
ATI Career Training Center	Oakland Park	T	Prop		591													2
Brevard Community College	Cocoa	C,T	St	M/W	13,670	64	34	65	Y	Y	Y	Y	Y	Y	Y	N	5	37
Broward Community College	Fort Lauderdale	C,T	St	M/W	31,030	68	37	39	Y		S	Y	Y	Y	Y	N	8	48
Brown Mackie College–Miami†	Miami	T	Prop	M/W	311							Y						6
Central Florida College	Winter Park	T	Prop	M/W	453													2
Central Florida Community College	Ocala	C,T	St-L	M/W	5,825	59	31	33	Y	Y	Y	Y	Y	Y	Y	N	4	19
Chipola College	Marianna	C,T,B	St	M/W	2,104		27	45	Y	Y		Y	Y	Y	Y	N	3	19
City College	Fort Lauderdale	T,B	Ind	M/W	712							Y						
City College	Gainesville	T,B	Ind	M/W	352							Y						11
City College	Miami	T,B	Ind	M/W	291							Y						9
College of Business and Technology	Miami	C	Prop	M/W	250													2
Florida College of Natural Health	Bradenton	T	Prop	M/W	160													
Florida College of Natural Health	Maitland	T	Prop	M/W	376													2
Florida College of Natural Health	Miami	T	Prop	M/W	166													2

This chart includes the names and locations of accredited two-year colleges in the United States and U.S. territories and shows institutions' responses to the *Peterson's Annual Survey of Undergraduate Institutions.* If an institution submitted incomplete data, one or more columns opposite the institution's name is blank. An asterisk after the school name denotes a *Special Message* following the college's profile, and a dagger indicates that the institution has one or more entries in the *College Close-Ups* section. If a school does not appear, it did not report any of the information.

Column key (diagonal headers): **Degrees Awarded** — Bachelor's (B), Master's (M), Doctoral (D), First Professional (F), College Transfer Associate (C), Terminal Associate (T); **Institutional Control**; **Student Body** — Men, Primarily Men, Women, Primarily Women, Coed; **Percent Attending Part-Time**; **Undergraduate Enrollment**; **Percent 25 Years of Age or Older**; **Percent of Grads Going on to Four-Year Colleges**; **Y—Yes; N—No; R—Recommended; S—For Some**: High School Equivalency Certificate Accepted; High School Transcript Required; Open Admissions; Need-Based Aid Required; Part-Time Jobs Available; Career Counseling Available; Job Placement Services Available; College Housing Available; Number of Sports Offered; Number of Majors Offered.

Institution	Location	Degrees	Control	Body	Enroll	%PT	%25+	%→4yr	HS Equiv	HS Transcr	Open Adm	Need Aid	PT Jobs	Career	Job Place	Housing	Sports	Majors
Florida College of Natural Health	Pompano Beach	T	Prop	M/W	275													2
Florida Community College at Jacksonville	Jacksonville	C,T	St	M/W	29,831	75												
Florida Metropolitan University–Orange Park Campus	Orange Park	T	Prop	M/W	457													5
Florida National College	Hialeah	C,T	Prop	M/W	1,884	18	60	24	Y	Y	Y	Y	Y	Y	Y	N		34
Florida Technical College	DeLand	C,T	Prop	M/W	260													
Full Sail Real World Education†	Winter Park	T,B	Prop	PM	5,219													
Gulf Coast College	Tampa	T	Priv	PW	152		35		Y	Y			Y	Y	Y	N		6
High-Tech Institute	Orlando	T	Prop	M/W	1,066													10
Hillsborough Community College	Tampa	C,T	St	M/W	21,445	74	36		Y	Y	Y	Y	Y	Y	Y	N	5	63
ITT Technical Institute	Fort Lauderdale	T,B	Prop	M/W					N	Y	Y	Y	Y	Y	Y	N		13
ITT Technical Institute	Jacksonville	T,B	Prop	M/W					N	Y	Y	Y	Y	Y	Y	N		12
ITT Technical Institute	Lake Mary	T,B	Prop	M/W					N	Y	Y	Y	Y	Y	Y	N		13
ITT Technical Institute	Miami	T,B	Prop	M/W					N	Y	Y	Y	Y	Y	Y	N		13
ITT Technical Institute	Tampa	T,B	Prop	M/W					N	Y	Y	Y	Y	Y	Y	N		12
Keiser Career College - Greenacres	Greenacres	T	Prop	M/W	433									Y				15
Keiser University	Miami	C,T,B	Prop	M/W	812		65	43						Y	Y	N		10
Lake City Community College	Lake City	C,T	St	M/W	2,736	60												
Lake-Sumter Community College	Leesburg	C,T	St-L	M/W	3,641	65	37		Y		Y	Y	Y	Y	Y	N	4	14
Manatee Community College	Bradenton	C,T	St	M/W	9,080	55	39		Y	Y	Y	Y	Y	Y	Y	N	5	96
Miami Dade College*†	Miami	C,T,B	St-L	M/W	51,329	64	36	78	Y	Y	Y	Y	Y	Y	Y	N	10	136
National School of Technology, Inc.	Hialeah	T	Prop	M/W	801													1
Okaloosa-Walton College	Niceville	C,T,B	St-L	M/W	8,728													
Orlando Culinary Academy	Orlando	T	Prop	M/W	951													4
Palm Beach Community College	Lake Worth	C,T	St	M/W	21,938	68	37	90	Y	Y	Y	Y	Y	Y	Y	N	9	67
Pasco-Hernando Community College	New Port Richey	C,T	St	M/W	7,547	63	65		Y	Y	Y	Y	Y	Y	Y	N	5	19
Polk Community College	Winter Haven	C,T	St	M/W	6,964	70	36		Y	Y	Y	Y	Y	Y	Y	N	5	21
Remington College–Jacksonville Campus	Jacksonville	T,B	Prop	M/W	94													5
Remington College–Tampa Campus	Tampa	C,B	Prop	M/W	685													
St. Petersburg College	St. Petersburg	C,T,B	St-L	M/W	24,102	67												
Sanford-Brown Institute	Lauderdale Lakes		Prop	M/W	303		46	10						Y	Y	N		
Sanford-Brown Institute	Tampa	T	Prop	M/W	473													1
Seminole Community College	Sanford	C,T	St-L	M/W	11,747	65	37		Y	Y	Y	Y	Y	Y	Y	N	6	50
South Florida Community College	Avon Park	C,T	St	M/W	2,076	61	33		Y	Y	Y	Y	Y	Y	Y	N	3	20
Southwest Florida College	Fort Myers	T,B	Ind	M/W	1,263													
Tallahassee Community College	Tallahassee	C,T	St-L	M/W	13,493	50	22	85	Y	Y	Y	Y	Y	Y	Y	N	15	30
Valencia Community College	Orlando	C,T	St	M/W	30,245	59	27	75	Y	Y	Y	Y	Y	Y	Y	N		41

Georgia

Institution	Location	Degrees	Control	Body	Enroll	%PT	%25+	%→4yr	HS Equiv	HS Transcr	Open Adm	Need Aid	PT Jobs	Career	Job Place	Housing	Sports	Majors
Abraham Baldwin Agricultural College	Tifton	C,T	St	M/W	3,423	35												
Albany Technical College	Albany	T	St	M/W	2,580	52			Y					Y	Y	N		17
Altamaha Technical College	Jesup	T	St	M/W	957	59			Y					Y		N		9
Appalachian Technical College	Jasper	T	St	M/W	1,089	63			Y					Y		N		9
Athens Technical College	Athens	T	St	M/W	3,961	63	40		Y					Y	Y	N		28
Atlanta Metropolitan College	Atlanta	C,T	St	M/W	1,748	51												
Atlanta Technical College	Atlanta	T	St	M/W	3,172	51			Y					Y		N		11
Augusta Technical College	Augusta	T	St	M/W	4,445	51	49		Y					Y		N		24
Bainbridge College	Bainbridge	C,T	St	M/W	2,784		48	30	Y	S	Y	Y	Y	Y	Y	N	2	34
Brown Mackie College–Atlanta†	Norcross	T	Prop	M/W	325					Y		Y	Y	Y	Y	N		9
Central Georgia Technical College	Macon	T	St	M/W	4,898	54	59		Y					Y		N		28
Chattahoochee Technical College	Marietta	T	St	M/W	5,994	60	52		Y					Y		N		23
Coastal Georgia Community College	Brunswick	C,T	St	M/W	3,054	66	44			Y		Y	Y	Y	Y	N	6	35
Columbus Technical College	Columbus	T	St	M/W	3,327	62			Y					Y	Y	N		24
Coosa Valley Technical College	Rome	T	St	M/W	2,797	57			Y					Y		N		13
DeKalb Technical College	Clarkston	T	St	M/W	3,641	60	64		Y					Y	Y	N		28
East Central Technical College	Fitzgerald	T	St	M/W	1,096	54			Y					Y		N		5
East Georgia College	Swainsboro	C,T	St	M/W	1,318	33	18	86	N	Y	Y	Y	Y	Y	Y	Y	13	23
Emory University, Oxford College	Oxford	C,T	I-R	M/W	554		0	99	N	Y	Y	N	Y	Y	Y	Y	11	1
Flint River Technical College	Thomaston	T	St	M/W	890	49			Y					Y		N		11
Gainesville College	Oakwood	C,T,B	St	M/W	6,717													
Georgia Aviation & Technical College	Eastman	T	St	M/W	248	35			Y					Y		N		3
Georgia Highlands College	Rome	C,T	St	M/W	3,933	45	27		N	Y	Y	Y	Y	Y	Y	N	12	40
Georgia Military College	Milledgeville	C,T	St-L	M/W	4,062	39	27		N	Y	Y	Y	Y	Y	Y		9	10
Gordon College	Barnesville	C,T	St	M/W	3,595	34	19	50	Y	Y	Y	Y	Y	Y	Y	Y	13	25
Griffin Technical College	Griffin	T	St	M/W	3,287	56	49		Y					Y	Y	N		23
Gwinnett Technical College	Lawrenceville	T	St	M/W	4,253	58	80		Y					Y		N		27
Heart of Georgia Technical College	Dublin	T	St	M/W	1,588	64			Y					Y		N		9
Herzing College	Atlanta	T,B	Prop	M/W	276													
Interactive College of Technology	Chamblee	T	Prop	M/W	1,069	1												
ITT Technical Institute	Duluth	T,B	Prop	M/W					N	Y	Y	Y	Y	Y	Y	N		8
ITT Technical Institute	Kennesaw	T,B	Prop	M/W										Y				5
Lanier Technical College	Oakwood	T	St	M/W	3,145	63			Y					Y		N		22
Le Cordon Bleu College of Culinary Arts, Atlanta	Tucker	T	Prop	M/W	763													1
Middle Georgia College*	Cochran	C,T	St	M/W	3,051	33	21		Y	Y	Y	Y	Y	Y	Y	Y	9	15
Middle Georgia Technical College	Warner Robbins	T	St	M/W	2,577	47			Y					Y	Y			11
Moultrie Technical College	Moultrie	T	St	M/W	2,020	57			Y					Y		N		10
North Georgia Technical College	Clarkesville	T	St	M/W	1,905	41			Y					Y		Y		11
North Metro Technical College	Acworth	T	St	M/W	1,928	61			Y					Y		Y		10
Northwestern Technical College	Rock Springs	T	St	M/W	2,350	59	60		Y					Y	Y	N		17
Ogeechee Technical College	Statesboro	T	St	M/W	1,951	53	39		Y					Y				24

This chart includes the names and locations of accredited two-year colleges in the United States and U.S. territories and shows institutions' responses to the *Peterson's Annual Survey of Undergraduate Institutions.* If an institution submitted incomplete data, one or more columns opposite the institution's name is blank. An asterisk after the school name denotes a *Special Message* following the college's profile, and a dagger indicates that the institution has one or more entries in the *College Close-Ups* section. If a school does not appear, it did not report any of the information.

Column headings (left to right): **Degrees Awarded** — College Transfer Associate (C), Terminal Associate (T), Bachelor's (B), Master's (M), Doctoral (D), First Professional (P); **Institutional Control** — County, District, City, State and Local, State-Related, Federal, State, Commonwealth, Territory, Independent, Independent-Religious, Proprietary; **Student Body** — Men, Primarily Men, Women, Primarily Women, Coed; Undergraduate Enrollment; Percent Attending Part-Time; Percent 25 Years of Age or Older; Percent of Grads Going on to Four-Year Colleges; High School Equivalency Certificate Accepted; High School Transcript Required; Open Admissions; Need-Based Aid Available; Part-Time Jobs Available; Career Counseling Available; Job Placement Services Available; College Housing Available; Number of Sports Offered; Number of Majors Offered.

Y—Yes; N—No; R—Recommended; S—For Some

Institution	Location	Deg	Ctrl	Body	Enroll	PT%	25+%	Grads4yr%	OpenAdm	HSEquiv	HSTrans	NeedAid	PTJobs	Career	JobPlace	Housing	Sports	Majors
Okefenokee Technical College	Waycross	T	St	M/W	1,453	67				Y				Y		N		11
Sandersville Technical College	Sandersville	T	St	M/W	719	63				Y				Y				5
Savannah River College	Augusta	T	Prop	M/W	254													6
Savannah Technical College	Savannah	T	St	M/W	3,965	57	59			Y				Y	Y	N		16
Southeastern Technical College	Vidalia	T	St	M/W	912	54				Y				Y		N		14
South Georgia College	Douglas	C,T	St	M/W	1,504	31	34		N	Y	Y	Y	Y	Y	Y	Y	8	53
South Georgia Technical College	Americus	T	St	M/W	1,711	50				Y				Y		Y	1	15
Southwest Georgia Technical College	Thomasville	T	St	M/W	1,453	65	74			Y		Y	Y	Y	Y	N		12
Swainsboro Technical College	Swainsboro	T	St	M/W	718	62				Y				Y		N		10
Truett-McConnell College	Cleveland	C,T,B	I-R	M/W	375	9												16
Valdosta Technical College	Valdosta	T	St	M/W	2,483	60	29			Y				Y	Y	N		16
West Central Technical College	Waco	T	St	M/W	3,010	69	13			Y		Y	Y	Y	Y	N		21
West Georgia Technical College	LaGrange	T	St	M/W	1,779	60	60			Y		Y	Y	Y		N		17
Young Harris College	Young Harris	C	I-R	M/W	606	6	1	93	N	Y	Y	Y	Y	Y	Y	Y	14	36

Guam

Institution	Location	Deg	Ctrl	Body	Enroll	PT%	25+%	Grads4yr%	OpenAdm	HSEquiv	HSTrans	NeedAid	PTJobs	Career	JobPlace	Housing	Sports	Majors
Guam Community College	Barrigada	T	Terr	M/W	2,841	82												

Hawaii

Institution	Location	Deg	Ctrl	Body	Enroll	PT%	25+%	Grads4yr%	OpenAdm	HSEquiv	HSTrans	NeedAid	PTJobs	Career	JobPlace	Housing	Sports	Majors
Hawaii Tokai International College	Honolulu	C	Ind	M/W	54													
Heald College-Honolulu	Honolulu	C,T	Ind	M/W	807	27												
Kapiolani Community College	Honolulu	C,T	St	M/W	7,174	61												
Kauai Community College	Lihue	C	St	M/W	1,210													
Leeward Community College	Pearl City	C,T	St	M/W	6,201		35		Y	Y	S	Y	Y	Y	Y	Y	4	12
Maui Community College	Kahului	C,T	St	M/W	2,779		43		Y		S	Y	Y	Y	Y	Y	4	17
TransPacific Hawaii College	Honolulu	C	Ind	PW	240													

Idaho

Institution	Location	Deg	Ctrl	Body	Enroll	PT%	25+%	Grads4yr%	OpenAdm	HSEquiv	HSTrans	NeedAid	PTJobs	Career	JobPlace	Housing	Sports	Majors
Brigham Young University –Idaho	Rexburg	C,T	I-R	M/W	11,443		2	90	N	Y	Y	Y	Y	Y	Y	Y	19	112
College of Southern Idaho	Twin Falls	C,T	St-L	M/W	7,543		49		Y	Y	Y	Y	Y	Y		Y	13	73
Eastern Idaho Technical College	Idaho Falls	T	St	M/W	755	70												
ITT Technical Institute	Boise	T,B	Prop	M/W					N	Y	Y	Y	Y	Y	Y	N		14
North Idaho College	Coeur d'Alene	C,T	St-L	M/W	4,293	43	35		N	Y	S	Y	Y	Y	Y	Y	18	68

Illinois

Institution	Location	Deg	Ctrl	Body	Enroll	PT%	25+%	Grads4yr%	OpenAdm	HSEquiv	HSTrans	NeedAid	PTJobs	Career	JobPlace	Housing	Sports	Majors
Black Hawk College	Moline	C,T	St-L	M/W	6,600	52	43		Y		Y	Y	Y	Y	Y	N	6	70
City Colleges of Chicago, Harold Washington College	Chicago	C,T	St-L	M/W	8,434	69	57	58	Y	Y		Y	Y	Y	Y	N		50
City Colleges of Chicago, Harry S. Truman College	Chicago	C,T	St-L	M/W	12,518		70		Y	Y		Y	Y	Y	Y	N	6	23
City Colleges of Chicago, Kennedy-King College	Chicago	C,T	St-L	M/W	3,054		48		Y		Y	Y	Y	Y	Y	N	5	33
City Colleges of Chicago, Olive-Harvey College	Chicago	C,T	St-L	M/W	2,188		54		Y	Y	R	Y	Y	Y	Y	N	9	22
City Colleges of Chicago, Richard J. Daley College	Chicago	C,T	St-L	M/W	10,654	67	47		Y	Y	Y	Y	Y	Y	Y	N		38
City Colleges of Chicago, Wilbur Wright College	Chicago	C,T	St-L	M/W	6,980		45	25	Y	Y		Y	Y	Y	Y	N	6	30
College of DuPage	Glen Ellyn	C,T	St-L	M/W	26,032	66	34	76	Y		Y	Y	Y	Y	Y	N	16	84
College of Lake County	Grayslake	C,T	Dist	M/W	15,558	70	44		Y		S	Y	Y	Y	Y	N	9	40
The College of Office Technology	Chicago	T	Priv		388							Y						1
The Cooking and Hospitality Institute of Chicago†	Chicago	C,T	Prop	M/W	898	20	36		Y		R	Y		Y	Y	N		2
Elgin Community College	Elgin	C,T	St-L	M/W	10,072	68	42		Y		S	Y	Y	Y	Y	N	7	49
Harper College	Palatine	C,T	St-L	M/W	15,053	58	38	50	Y	Y	Y	Y	Y	Y	Y	N	15	70
Heartland Community College	Normal	C,T	St-L	M/W	4,667													
Highland Community College	Freeport	C,T	St-L	M/W	2,406	53												
Illinois Central College	East Peoria	C,T	St-L	M/W	12,343													
Illinois Eastern Community Colleges, Frontier Community College	Fairfield	C,T	St-L	M/W	2,453	89	50		Y	Y		Y	Y	Y	Y	N		8
Illinois Eastern Community Colleges, Lincoln Trail College	Robinson	C,T	St-L	M/W	1,504	64	49		Y	Y		Y	Y	Y	Y	N	4	14
Illinois Eastern Community Colleges, Olney Central College	Olney	C,T	St-L	M/W	1,737	54	42		Y	Y		Y	Y	Y	Y	N	4	19
Illinois Eastern Community Colleges, Wabash Valley College	Mount Carmel	C,T	St-L	M/W	4,840	87	45		Y	Y		Y	Y	Y	Y	N	6	19
Illinois Valley Community College	Oglesby	C,T	Dist	M/W	3,939	56	25		Y		Y	Y	Y	Y	Y	N	4	26
ITT Technical Institute	Burr Ridge	T,B	Prop	M/W					N	Y	Y	Y	Y	Y	Y			6
ITT Technical Institute	Mount Prospect	T,B,M	Prop	M/W					N	Y	Y	Y	Y	Y	Y	N		7
ITT Technical Institute	Orland Park	T,B	Prop	M/W					N	Y	Y	Y	Y	Y	Y	N		9
John Wood Community College	Quincy	C,T	Dist	M/W	2,516	51	32		Y	Y		Y	Y	Y	Y	N	5	35
Joliet Junior College	Joliet	C,T	St-L	M/W	12,924	61	40		Y		Y	Y	Y	Y	Y	Y	6	51
Kankakee Community College	Kankakee	C,T	St-L	M/W	3,353	60			Y	Y		Y	Y	Y	Y	N	4	28
Kaskaskia College	Centralia	C,T	St-L	M/W	4,742	60												
Lake Land College	Mattoon	C,T	St-L	M/W	7,431		36		Y		R	Y	Y	Y	Y	N	8	37
Lincoln College	Lincoln	C	Ind	M/W	758	8												
Lincoln College–Normal	Normal	C,T,B	Ind	M/W	520	33												
Lincoln Land Community College	Springfield	C,T	Dist	M/W	6,532	59	39		Y		R	Y	Y	Y	Y	N	6	29
Moraine Valley Community College	Palos Hills	C,T	St-L	M/W	15,693	58	29	91	Y	Y	Y	Y	Y	Y	Y	N	9	28
Morrison Institute of Technology†	Morrison	C,T	Ind	PM	126													
Morton College	Cicero	C,T	St-L	M/W	5,049	75	46	7	Y	Y		Y	Y	Y	Y	N	7	20
Parkland College	Champaign	C,T	Dist	M/W	9,336	53			Y		R	Y	Y	Y	Y	N	7	60
Prairie State College	Chicago Heights	C,T	St-L	M/W	5,083	66												
Richland Community College	Decatur	C,T	Dist	M/W	3,152	68	40	37	Y	Y		Y	Y	Y	Y	Y		27
Rockford Business College	Rockford	T	Ind	PW	428	43	65		Y	Y		Y	Y	Y	Y			9
Rock Valley College	Rockford	C,T	Dist	M/W	8,145	57												

This chart includes the names and locations of accredited two-year colleges in the United States and U.S. territories and shows institutions' responses to the *Peterson's Annual Survey of Undergraduate Institutions*. If an institution submitted incomplete data, one or more columns opposite the institution's name is blank.

An asterisk after the school name denotes a *Special Message* following the college's profile, and a dagger indicates that the institution has one or more entries in the *College Close-Ups* section. If a school does not appear, it did not report any of the information.

Y—Yes; N—No; R—Recommended; S—For Some

Name	Location	Degrees Awarded	Institutional Control	Student Body	Undergraduate Enrollment	Percent Attending Part-Time	Percent 25 Years of Age or Older	Percent of Grads Going on to Four-Year Colleges	Open Admissions	High School Equivalency Certificate Accepted	High School Transcript Required	Need-Based Aid Available	Part-Time Jobs Available	Career Counseling Available	Job Placement Services Available	College Housing Available	Number of Sports Offered	Number of Majors Offered
Sauk Valley Community College	Dixon	C,T	Dist	M/W	2,745	58												
Southeastern Illinois College	Harrisburg	C,T	St	M/W	2,559													
Southwestern Illinois College	Belleville	C,T	Dist	M/W	14,479	63												
Spoon River College	Canton	C,T	St	M/W	2,333													
Springfield College in Illinois	Springfield	C	I-R	M/W	552	51												
Taylor Business Institute	Chicago	T	Prop	M/W	95													5
Triton College	River Grove	C,T	St	M/W	11,021	65												
Waubonsee Community College	Sugar Grove	C,T	Dist	M/W	8,834	70												
Indiana																		
Ancilla College	Donaldson	C,T	I-R	M/W	624	36												
Aviation Institute of Maintenance–Indianapolis	Indianapolis		Prop															
Brown Mackie College–Fort Wayne†	Fort Wayne	T	Prop	M/W	872				Y	Y	Y	Y	Y					9
Brown Mackie College–Merrillville†	Merrillville	T	Prop	M/W	615		40		Y	Y	Y	Y	Y	Y	Y	N		9
Brown Mackie College–Michigan City†	Michigan City	C,T	Prop	M/W	461													
Brown Mackie College–South Bend†	South Bend	C,T	Prop	PW	661		65	60	N	Y	Y			Y	Y			13
College of Court Reporting	Hobart	C,T	Prop	PW	156	43	60		N	Y	Y			Y	Y			13
Holy Cross College	Notre Dame	C,B	I-R	M/W	430	10	0.04	85	N	Y	Y	Y	Y	Y	Y	Y	14	1
Indiana Business College	Anderson	T	Prop	M/W	214				N		Y			Y	Y			9
Indiana Business College	Columbus	T	Prop	M/W	295				N	Y	Y	Y	Y	Y	Y	N		8
Indiana Business College	Evansville	T	Prop	M/W	325				N		Y	Y	Y	Y	Y			7
Indiana Business College	Fort Wayne	T	Prop	M/W	480				N	Y	Y	Y	Y	Y	Y	N		6
Indiana Business College†	Indianapolis	T	Prop	M/W	1,227				N	Y	Y			Y	Y	N		14
Indiana Business College	Indianapolis	T	Prop	M/W	191						Y			Y	Y	N		6
Indiana Business College	Lafayette	T	Prop	M/W	319				N	Y	Y	Y	Y	Y	Y	N		9
Indiana Business College	Marion	T	Prop	M/W	131				N	Y	Y			Y	Y			5
Indiana Business College	Muncie	T	Prop	M/W	379				N	Y	Y	Y	Y	Y	Y	N		11
Indiana Business College	Terre Haute	T	Prop	M/W	246				N	Y	Y			Y	Y			8
Indiana Business College-Medical	Indianapolis	T	Prop	M/W	592				N	Y	Y			Y	Y	N		6
International Business College	Fort Wayne	T,B	Prop	PW	758	8			N	Y	Y			Y	Y	Y		14
International Business College	Indianapolis	T	Prop	M/W	289													
ITT Technical Institute	Fort Wayne	T,B	Prop	M/W					N	Y	Y	Y	Y	Y	Y	N		14
ITT Technical Institute	Indianapolis	T,B	Prop	M/W					N	Y	Y	Y	Y	Y	Y	N	N	16
ITT Technical Institute	Newburgh	T,B	Prop	M/W					N	Y	Y	Y	Y	Y	Y	N		15
Ivy Tech Community College–Bloomington	Bloomington	C,T	St	M/W	3,565	54												
Ivy Tech Community College–Central Indiana	Indianapolis	C,T	St	M/W	11,590	69												
Ivy Tech Community College–Columbus	Columbus	C,T	St	M/W	2,216	65												
Ivy Tech Community College–East Central	Muncie	C,T	St	M/W	5,943	57												
Ivy Tech Community College–Kokomo	Kokomo	C,T	St	M/W	3,248	68												
Ivy Tech Community College–Lafayette	Lafayette	C,T	St	M/W	5,970	60												
Ivy Tech Community College–North Central	South Bend	C,T	St	M/W	5,228	77												
Ivy Tech Community College–Northeast	Fort Wayne	C,T	St	M/W	6,082	65												
Ivy Tech Community College–Northwest	Gary	C,T,B	St	M/W	4,815	71												
Ivy Tech Community College–Southeast	Madison	C,T	St	M/W	1,766	64												
Ivy Tech Community College–Southern Indiana	Sellersburg	C,T	St	M/W	3,112	71												
Ivy Tech Community College–Southwest	Evansville	C,T	St	M/W	4,858	69												
Ivy Tech Community College–Wabash Valley	Terre Haute	C,T	St	M/W	4,992	57												
Ivy Tech Community College–Whitewater	Richmond	C,T	St	M/W	1,832	69												
Kaplan College–Indianapolis	Indianapolis	T	Ind	PW	469								Y	Y	Y		Y	Y		2
Mid-America College of Funeral Service	Jeffersonville	T,B	Ind	PM	120		13		Y	Y	Y	Y		Y	Y	N	1	1
Vincennes University Jasper Campus	Jasper	C,T	St	M/W	835		50		Y	Y	Y	Y	Y	Y		N		25
Iowa																		
AIB College of Business	Des Moines	T	Ind	M/W	909		24		N	Y	Y	Y	Y	Y	Y	Y	8	18
Clinton Community College	Clinton	C,T	St-L	M/W	1,285	56	29	59	Y		Y		Y	Y	Y	N	11	14
Hamilton College	Cedar Falls	C,T,B	Prop	M/W	695	22												
Hamilton College	Cedar Rapids	C,T,B	Prop	M/W	511	14												
Hamilton College	Council Bluffs	T	Prop	M/W	297													3
Hawkeye Community College	Waterloo	C,T	St-L	M/W	5,663	57	30		Y	Y	Y	Y	Y	Y	Y	N	5	55
Iowa Lakes Community College	Estherville	C,T	St-L	M/W	3,052	57	20		Y	Y	Y	Y	Y	Y	Y	Y	16	195
Kaplan University	Davenport	C,T,B	Prop	M/W	22,529	80	84		N	Y	Y	Y	Y	Y	Y	N		13
Kirkwood Community College	Cedar Rapids	C,T	St-L	M/W	15,064	43	27		Y	Y	Y	Y	Y	Y	Y	N	10	108
Muscatine Community College	Muscatine	C,T	St	M/W	1,470	59	28	45	Y		Y	Y	Y	Y	Y	Y	6	15
Northeast Iowa Community College	Calmar	C,T	St-L	M/W	4,764	57	16		Y	Y	R	Y	Y	Y	Y	N	9	13
North Iowa Area Community College	Mason City	C,T	St-L	M/W	3,022	44	25	70	Y	Y	Y	Y	Y	Y	Y	Y	15	29
Northwest Iowa Community College	Sheldon	C,T	St	M/W	1,224	56	17	62	Y	Y	Y	Y	Y	Y	Y	Y	4	22
St. Luke's College	Sioux City	T	Ind	M/W	179	26	29	65	N	Y	Y	Y	Y	Y	Y	N		3
Scott Community College	Bettendorf	C,T	St-L	M/W	4,434	52	39	47	Y		Y	Y	Y	Y	Y	N	2	30
Southeastern Community College, North Campus	West Burlington	C,T	St-L	M/W	2,045		34		Y	Y	Y	Y	Y	Y		N	6	29
Southeastern Community College, South Campus	Keokuk	C,T	St-L	M/W	548				Y		R	Y	Y	Y		N	2	11
Vatterott College	Des Moines	T,B	Prop	M/W														
Western Iowa Tech Community College	Sioux City	C,T	St	M/W	5,334	61												
Kansas																		
Allen County Community College	Iola	C,T	St-L	M/W	2,814		35	60	Y	Y		Y	Y	Y	Y	Y	11	69
Barton County Community College	Great Bend	C,T	St-L	M/W	4,263	79	46		Y	Y	R	Y	Y	Y	Y	Y	14	84
Brown Mackie College–Kansas City†	Lenexa	T	Prop	M/W	370		60		Y	Y	Y	Y	Y	Y	Y	N		10

Two-Year Colleges At-a-Glance

This chart includes the names and locations of accredited two-year colleges in the United States and U.S. territories and shows institutions' responses to the *Peterson's Annual Survey of Undergraduate Institutions*. If an institution submitted incomplete data, one or more columns opposite the institution's name is blank.

An asterisk after the school name denotes a *Special Message* following the college's profile, and a dagger indicates that the institution has one or more entries in the *College Close-Ups* section. If a school does not appear, it did not report any of the information.

Key: Y—Yes; N—No; R—Recommended; S—For Some

Name	Location	Degrees Awarded	Institutional Control	Student Body	Undergraduate Enrollment	Percent Attending Part-Time	Percent 25 Years of Age or Older	Percent of Grads Going on to Four-Year Colleges	High School Equivalency Certificate Accepted	Open Admissions	High School Transcript Required	Need-Based Aid Available	Part-Time Jobs Available	Career Counseling Available	Job Placement Services Available	College Housing Available	Number of Sports Offered	Number of Majors Offered
Brown Mackie College–Salina†	Salina	C,T	Prop	M/W	429		38	27	Y	Y	Y	Y	Y	Y	Y	N	3	13
Butler Community College	El Dorado	C,T	St-L	M/W	8,863	59												
Colby Community College	Colby	C,T	St-L	M/W	1,690	53	22	60	Y	Y	Y	Y	Y	Y	Y		10	58
Cowley County Community College and Area Vocational–Technical School	Arkansas City	C,T	St-L	M/W	4,679	49												
Dodge City Community College	Dodge City	C,T	St-L	M/W	1,766		67	92	Y		Y	Y	Y	Y	Y		11	71
Flint Hills Technical College	Emporia	T	St	M/W	424													15
Hesston College	Hesston	C,T	I-R	M/W	462	13	20	60	Y	Y	Y	Y	Y	Y			7	8
Hutchinson Community College and Area Vocational School	Hutchinson	C,T	St-L	M/W	4,790	56	35	71	Y	Y	R	Y	Y	Y	Y	Y	14	40
Independence Community College	Independence	C,T	St	M/W	906	47												
Kansas City Kansas Community College	Kansas City	C,T	St-L	M/W	5,547	65	50		Y	Y	Y	Y	Y	Y	Y	N	8	22
Labette Community College	Parsons	C,T	St-L	M/W	1,401	67	40	30	Y	Y	R	Y	Y	Y			7	33
Manhattan Area Technical College	Manhattan	T	St-L	M/W	401	19												
National American University	Overland Park	T	Ind	M/W	156													4
Neosho County Community College	Chanute	C,T	St-L	M/W	1,826	66	58	60	Y	Y	Y	Y	Y	Y			6	24
North Central Kansas Technical College	Beloit	T	St	M/W	513													8
Northwest Kansas Technical College	Goodland	T	St	M/W	281													15
Pratt Community College	Pratt	C,T	St-L	M/W	1,546	60												4
Wichita Area Technical College	Wichita	C,T	Dist	M/W	693	54	53					S		Y	Y	N		4
Kentucky																		
Ashland Community and Technical College	Ashland	C,T	St	M/W	4,120		41	40	Y	Y	Y	Y	Y	Y	Y	N	2	12
Brown Mackie College–Hopkinsville†	Hopkinsville	C	Prop	PW	150					Y			Y	Y	Y			9
Brown Mackie College–Louisville†	Louisville	T	Prop	M/W	300		63		N	Y	Y	Y	Y	Y	Y	N		12
Brown Mackie College–Northern Kentucky†	Fort Mitchell	C,T	Prop	M/W	500		59		Y	Y	Y	Y	Y	Y	Y	N		11
Draughons Junior College	Bowling Green	C	Prop	PW	510	44	35	6	Y	Y	Y	S	Y	Y	Y	N		8
Elizabethtown Technical College	Elizabethtown	C,T	St	M/W	4,980	53	49					S		Y	Y	N		21
Hopkinsville Community College	Hopkinsville	C,T	St	M/W	3,353	63	52		Y	Y	R	Y	Y	Y	Y	N	5	17
ITT Technical Institute	Louisville	T,B	Prop	M/W					N	Y	Y	Y	Y	Y	Y	N		11
Jefferson Community and Technical College	Louisville	C,T	St	M/W	14,710	68	40		Y	Y	Y	Y	Y	Y		N		18
Madisonville Community College	Madisonville	C,T	St	M/W	3,500		42		Y	Y	Y	Y	Y	Y	Y	N	2	18
Owensboro Community and Technical College	Owensboro	C,T	St	M/W	5,188	69	37	26	Y	Y	Y	Y	Y	Y		N	2	17
St. Catharine College	St. Catharine	C,T	I-R	M/W	751		32		N	Y	S	Y	Y	Y	Y	Y	9	49
Southeast Kentucky Community and Technical College	Cumberland	C,T	St	M/W	4,578				Y	Y	Y	Y	Y	Y	Y	Y	5	14
Spencerian College	Louisville	C,T	Prop	M/W	1,180				Y	Y	Y	Y	Y					3
Louisiana																		
Baton Rouge School of Computers	Baton Rouge	T	Prop	M/W	83									Y	Y			2
Camelot College	Baton Rouge	T	Prop	M/W	336										Y			19
Career Technical College	Monroe	T	Prop	M/W	549													9
Delgado Community College	New Orleans	C,T	St	M/W	16,501	55								Y	Y			6
Delta School of Business & Technology	Lake Charles	T	Priv	M/W	362													
Elaine P. Nunez Community College	Chalmette	C,T	St	M/W	1,064	56	40	31	Y	S	Y	Y	Y	Y	Y	N	4	21
Gretna Career College	Gretna	T	Prop	M/W	96													5
ITI Technical College	Baton Rouge	T	Prop	M/W	351	36												
ITT Technical Institute	St. Rose	T,B	Prop	M/W	541				N	Y	Y	Y	Y	Y	Y	N		13
Louisiana State University at Alexandria	Alexandria	C,T,B	St	M/W	2,988	47												
Louisiana State University at Eunice	Eunice	C,T	St	M/W	2,833		40	40	Y	Y	Y	Y	Y	Y	Y		6	11
Louisiana Technical College	Baton Rouge	C	St	M/W	13,414	46												
Remington College–Baton Rouge Campus	Baton Rouge	T	Prop	M/W	607													5
Remington College–Lafayette Campus	Lafayette	T	Prop	M/W	367													
Southern University at Shreveport	Shreveport	C,T	St	M/W	1,324	30	41	25	Y	Y	Y	Y	Y	Y	Y	N	2	32
Maine																		
Beal College	Bangor	T	Prop	M/W	373	36												
Central Maine Community College	Auburn	C,T	St	M/W	2,200		46		N	Y	Y	Y	Y	Y	Y	Y	11	23
Kennebec Valley Community College	Fairfield	C,T	St	M/W	1,926	69	55		Y	Y	Y	Y	Y	Y	Y	N	4	36
Northern Maine Community College	Presque Isle	C,T	St-R	M/W	901	32	42	10	Y	Y	Y	Y	Y	Y	Y	Y	13	20
Southern Maine Community College	South Portland	C,T	St	M/W	4,785		39		Y	Y	Y	Y	Y	Y	Y	Y	7	46
Washington County Community College	Calais	C,T	St	M/W	350	59		4	Y	Y	Y	Y	Y	Y	Y		1	4
York County Community College	Wells	C,T	St	M/W	949						Y	Y	Y	Y	Y	N		11
Maryland																		
Allegany College of Maryland	Cumberland	C,T	St-L	M/W	3,538	42	33		Y	Y	Y	Y	Y	Y	Y	N	6	26
Anne Arundel Community College	Arnold	C,T	St-L	M/W	14,699		43		Y	Y	Y	Y	Y	Y		N	8	69
Baltimore City Community College	Baltimore	C,T	St-L	M/W	7,097		57		Y	Y	Y	Y	Y	Y		N	3	35
Baltimore International College†	Baltimore	C,T,B,M	Ind	M/W	516	6												15
Carroll Community College	Westminster	C,T	St-L	M/W	3,216	55	28		Y	Y	Y	Y	Y	Y		N		15
Cecil Community College	North East	C	Cou	M/W	1,945	63	42		Y	Y	Y	Y	Y	Y		N	6	34
Chesapeake College	Wye Mills	C,T	St-L	M/W	2,579		45	45	Y	Y	Y	Y	Y	Y		N	6	29
College of Southern Maryland	La Plata	C,T	St-L	M/W	7,504	63			Y		R	Y	Y	Y	Y	N	7	28
The Community College of Baltimore County	Baltimore	C,T	Cou	M/W	19,446	65	44		Y	Y	Y	Y	Y		N	N		
Frederick Community College	Frederick	C,T	St-L	M/W	4,825	62	37	47	Y	Y	Y	Y	Y	Y	N	N	6	44
Garrett College	McHenry	C,T	St-L	M/W	734	39	21		Y	Y	Y	Y	Y	Y	Y		6	24
Hagerstown Business College	Hagerstown	T	Prop	M/W	932													
Hagerstown Community College	Hagerstown	C,T	St-L	M/W	3,629	66	37		Y	S	S	Y	Y	Y	Y	N	12	24
Howard Community College	Columbia	C,T	St-L	M/W	7,161				Y	S	S	Y	Y	Y	Y	N	9	55

This chart includes the names and locations of accredited two-year colleges in the United States and U.S. territories and shows institutions' responses to the *Peterson's Annual Survey of Undergraduate Institutions.* If an institution submitted incomplete data, one or more columns opposite the institution's name is blank. An asterisk after the school name denotes a *Special Message* following the college's profile, and a dagger indicates that the institution has one or more entries in the *College Close-Ups* section. If a school does not appear, it did not report any of the information.

Legend: Y—Yes; N—No; R—Recommended; S—For Some

Institution	Location	Degrees Awarded	Institutional Control	Student Body	Undergrad Enrollment	% Part-Time	% 25+	% Grads to 4-Yr	HS Equiv Cert Accepted	HS Transcript Required	Open Admissions	Need-Based Aid	Part-Time Jobs	Career Counseling	Job Placement	College Housing	# Sports	# Majors
ITT Technical Institute	Owings Mills	T,B	Prop	M/W											Y			8
Montgomery College	Rockville	C,T	St-L	M/W	22,893	62	34	54			R	Y	Y	Y	Y	N	12	31
TESST College of Technology	Baltimore	T	Prop	M/W	1,282													2
TESST College of Technology	Beltsville	T	Prop	M/W	695													3
TESST College of Technology	Towson	T	Prop	M/W														
Wor-Wic Community College	Salisbury	C,T	St-L	M/W	3,036	68	41	68	Y		R	Y	Y	Y	Y	N		17
Massachusetts																		
Bay State College†	Boston	C,T,B	Ind	M/W	757													
Benjamin Franklin Institute of Technology†	Boston	C,T,B	Ind	PM	386													
Berkshire Community College	Pittsfield	C,T	St	M/W	2,225	58	38	64	Y	Y	Y	Y	Y	Y	Y			28
Bristol Community College	Fall River	C,T	St	M/W	6,873	55												
Bunker Hill Community College†	Boston	C,T	St	M/W	7,837	70												
Cape Cod Community College	West Barnstable	C,T	St	M/W	4,212	65			Y	Y	Y	Y	Y	Y	Y	N	12	41
Dean College	Franklin	C,T,B	Ind	M/W	1,106	12	0	92	N	Y		Y	Y	Y	Y	Y	11	12
FINE Mortuary College, LLC	Norwood	T	Prop	M/W	73													1
Fisher College	Boston	C,T,B	Ind	M/W	507		47	50	N	Y		Y	Y	Y	Y	Y	3	11
Greenfield Community College	Greenfield	C,T	St	M/W	2,217	55												
Holyoke Community College	Holyoke	C,T	St	M/W	6,297	48	35		Y		Y	Y	Y	Y	Y	N	8	40
ITT Technical Institute	Norwood	T	Prop	M/W					Y	Y		Y	Y	Y	Y	N		6
ITT Technical Institute	Woburn	T	Prop	M/W					Y			Y	Y	Y	Y	N		5
Marian Court College	Swampscott	C,T	I-R	PW	281		45	25	N	Y		Y	Y	Y	Y	Y		12
Massachusetts Bay Community College†	Wellesley Hills	C,T	St	M/W	5,040	60	43		Y	Y		Y	Y	Y	Y	N	9	30
Massasoit Community College	Brockton	C,T	St	M/W	6,975	53	39	32	Y	Y		Y	Y	Y	Y	N	4	38
Mount Wachusett Community College*	Gardner	C,T	St	M/W	3,937	56	45	20	Y	Y	Y	Y		Y	Y	N		35
New England College of Finance	Boston	T	Ind	PW	412													
Northern Essex Community College*	Haverhill	C,T	St	M/W	6,362		51	40	Y		Y	Y		Y	Y	N	10	59
North Shore Community College	Danvers	C,T	St	M/W	6,910	58	42	62	Y	Y	S	Y	Y	Y	Y	N		42
Quincy College	Quincy	C,T	City	M/W	4,000		45		Y	Y		Y	Y	Y	Y	N		29
Quinsigamond Community College	Worcester	C,T	St	M/W	5,970	54												
Roxbury Community College	Roxbury Crossing	C,T	St	M/W	2,382	53	61		Y	Y		Y	Y	Y	Y	N	5	22
Springfield Technical Community College	Springfield	C,T	St	M/W	5,992	58	41		Y	Y		Y	Y	Y	Y	N	9	57
Michigan																		
Alpena Community College	Alpena	C,T	St-L	M/W	1,903		40	42	Y			Y		Y	Y	Y	7	29
Delta College	University Center	C,T	Dist	M/W	10,210	61												
Grand Rapids Community College	Grand Rapids	C,T	Dist	M/W	15,224	56	29	50	Y	Y	Y	Y	Y	Y	Y	N	14	30
Henry Ford Community College	Dearborn	C,T	Dist	M/W	13,000		44		Y	Y	R	Y	Y	Y	Y	N	12	53
ITT Technical Institute	Canton	T	Prop	M/W					N		Y	Y		Y	Y	N		8
ITT Technical Institute	Flint	C	Prop	M/W														8
ITT Technical Institute	Grand Rapids	T	Prop	M/W					N		Y	Y		Y	Y	N		7
ITT Technical Institute	Troy	T	Prop	M/W					N		Y	Y		Y	Y	N		6
Jackson Community College	Jackson	C,T	Cou	M/W	5,870	64												
Kellogg Community College	Battle Creek	C,T	St-L	M/W	5,326	67	47		Y			S	Y		Y	Y	N	5	73
Kirtland Community College	Roscommon	C,T	Dist	M/W	1,624	57	52		Y	Y			Y		Y	Y			20
Lake Michigan College	Benton Harbor	C,T	Dist	M/W	4,043	69												
Lansing Community College	Lansing	C,T	St-L	M/W	20,394	67	24		Y		S	Y		Y	Y	N	9	104
Lewis College of Business	Detroit	C,T	Ind	M/W	324				Y	Y		Y	Y	Y	Y	N	1	11
Macomb Community College	Warren	C,T	Dist	M/W	21,131	62	45		Y			Y	Y	Y	Y	N	11	73
Montcalm Community College	Sidney	C,T	St-L	M/W	2,451	55	58		Y	Y	R		Y	Y	Y	N	1	22
Mott Community College	Flint	C,T	Dist	M/W	10,038	63	46		Y		R			Y	Y	N	6	50
Muskegon Community College	Muskegon	C,T	St-L	M/W	5,000				Y		Y	Y		Y	Y	N	8	45
North Central Michigan College	Petoskey	C,T	Cou	M/W	2,738		55	85	Y			Y		Y	Y	Y	1	21
Oakland Community College	Bloomfield Hills	C,T	St-L	M/W	24,123	67	42		Y			R		Y	Y	N	8	90
Saginaw Chippewa Tribal College	Mount Pleasant	C,T	Ind	M/W	123	65	74					Y						3
Schoolcraft College	Livonia	C,T	Dist	M/W	11,105	64	36		Y	Y	R,S	Y	Y	Y	Y	N	5	36
Southwestern Michigan College	Dowagiac	C,T	St-L	M/W	2,500	61	42		Y	Y	Y	Y	Y	Y	Y	N	14	27
West Shore Community College	Scottville	C,T	Dist	M/W	1,372		43		Y			Y	Y	Y	Y	N	8	14
Minnesota																		
Academy College	Minneapolis	C,T,B	Prop	M/W	210	2	56		Y	Y		Y		Y	Y	N		25
Alexandria Technical College	Alexandria	C,T	St	M/W	2,015		19		Y	Y		Y		Y	Y	N	5	50
Anoka-Ramsey Community College	Coon Rapids	C,T	St	M/W	6,009		31		Y	Y		Y		Y	Y	N	10	16
Anoka-Ramsey Community College, Cambridge Campus	Cambridge	C,T	St	M/W	1,785		42		Y	Y	S			Y	Y	N	5	13
Brown College	Mendota Heights	C,T,B	Prop	M/W	2,054	8												
Central Lakes College	Brainerd	C,T	St	M/W	2,831		33		Y			Y		Y	Y	N	9	10
Century College	White Bear Lake	C,T	St	M/W	8,323	52	37		Y	Y		Y		Y	Y	N	5	36
Fond du Lac Tribal and Community College	Cloquet	C,T	St	M/W	1,735		32		Y		S	Y		Y	Y	Y	4	10
Globe College	Oakdale	T,B	Prop	M/W	845													
Hennepin Technical College	Brooklyn Park	C,T	St	M/W	8,623				Y	Y	R	Y			Y	N		18
Herzing College	Minneapolis	T,B	Prop	PW	270	10	43		Y	Y		Y			Y	N		8
Hibbing Community College	Hibbing	C,T	St	M/W	1,176													
High-Tech Institute	St. Louis Park	T	Prop	M/W	795													7
Inver Hills Community College	Inver Grove Heights	C,T	St	M/W	4,325		56		Y	Y	R,S	Y		Y	Y	N	9	23
Itasca Community College	Grand Rapids	C,T	St	M/W	1,185		22	80	Y	Y		Y		Y	Y	Y	9	30
ITT Technical Institute	Eden Prairie	T,B	Prop	M/W										Y				10
Lake Superior College	Duluth	C,T	St	M/W	4,200													
Leech Lake Tribal College	Cass Lake	T	Ind	M/W	189													4

This chart includes the names and locations of accredited two-year colleges in the United States and U.S. territories and shows institutions' responses to the *Peterson's Annual Survey of Undergraduate Institutions.* If an institution submitted incomplete data, one or more columns opposite the institution's name is blank. An asterisk after the school name denotes a *Special Message* following the college's profile, and a dagger indicates that the institution has one or more entries in the *College Close-Ups* section. If a school does not appear, it did not report any of the information.

Y—Yes; N—No; R—Recommended; S—For Some

Name	Location	Degrees Awarded	Institutional Control	Student Body	Undergraduate Enrollment	Percent Attending Part-Time	Percent 25 Years of Age or Older	Percent of Grads Going on to Four-Year Colleges	High School Equivalency Certificate Accepted	High School Transcript Required	Open Admissions	Need-Based Aid Available	Part-Time Jobs Available	Career Counseling Available	Job Placement Services Available	College Housing Available	Number of Sports Available	Number of Majors Offered
McNally Smith College of Music	Saint Paul	C,T,B	Prop	M/W	474	12	11		Y	Y				Y	Y	N		4
Mesabi Range Community and Technical College	Virginia	C,T	St	M/W	1,467	23	80		Y	Y		Y	Y	Y	Y	N	13	16
Minneapolis Business College	Roseville	T	Prop	PW	350													
Minneapolis Community and Technical College	Minneapolis	C,T	St	M/W	7,618	58	47		Y			Y	Y	Y	Y	N	3	25
Minnesota School of Business–Brooklyn Center	Brooklyn Center	T,B,M	Prop	M/W	551				Y	Y	Y			Y	Y	N		16
Minnesota School of Business–Plymouth	Minneapolis	T,B,M	Prop	M/W	445				Y	Y	Y			Y	Y	N		15
Minnesota School of Business–Richfield	Richfield	T,B,M	Prop	M/W	763		40		Y	Y	Y			Y	Y	N		15
Minnesota School of Business–St. Cloud	Waite Park	T,B,M	Prop	M/W	724				Y	Y	Y			Y	Y	N		15
Minnesota School of Business–Shakopee	Shakopee	T,B,M	Prop	M/W	381				Y	Y	Y			Y	Y	N		12
Minnesota State College–Southeast Technical	Winona	C,T	St	M/W	1,900	39	39		Y	Y		Y	Y	Y	Y			28
Minnesota State Community and Technical College–Fergus Falls	Fergus Falls	C,T	St	M/W	6,093	42	20	81	Y	Y	Y	Y	Y	Y	Y	Y	13	40
Minnesota West Community and Technical College	Pipestone	C,T	St	M/W	2,783	48												
National American University	Bloomington	T	Prop	M/W	474	34	51				R,S			Y	Y	Y		10
Normandale Community College	Bloomington	C,T	St	M/W	8,261													
North Hennepin Community College	Brooklyn Park	C,T	St	M/W	6,292	61	40	39	Y		R	Y	Y	Y	Y	N	7	16
Northland Community and Technical College–Thief River Falls	Thief River Falls	C,T	St	M/W	4,120		40	75	Y	Y	Y	Y	Y	Y	Y	N	8	46
Pine Technical College	Pine City	C,T	St	M/W	770	66	45		Y	Y		Y	Y	Y	Y			6
Rainy River Community College	International Falls	C,T	St	M/W	399	54	62		Y	Y	Y	Y	Y	Y	Y	Y	11	6
Rasmussen College Brooklyn Park	Brooklyn Park	T	Prop		213													19
Rasmussen College Eden Prairie	Eden Prairie	T	Prop	M/W	363	42												
Rasmussen College Mankato	Mankato	T	Prop	PW	463													
Ridgewater College	Willmar	C,T	St	M/W	3,918	39			Y	Y		Y	Y	Y	Y	N	9	73
Riverland Community College	Austin	C,T	St	M/W	3,477	54	45	63	Y	Y		Y	Y	Y	Y	Y	5	28
St. Cloud Technical College	St. Cloud	T	St	M/W	3,405	33	22		Y	Y		Y	Y	Y	Y	N		52
Saint Paul College–A Community & Technical College	St. Paul	C,T	St-R	M/W	5,259				Y	Y	S	Y	Y	Y	Y	N		13
Vermilion Community College	Ely	C,T	St	M/W	745													
Mississippi																		
Antonelli College	Hattiesburg	C	Prop	M/W	354													10
Coahoma Community College	Clarksdale	C,T	St-L	M/W	1,838	7	44		Y	Y	Y	Y	Y	Y	Y	Y	3	28
Copiah-Lincoln Community College	Wesson	C,T	St-L	M/W	2,161													
Jones County Junior College	Ellisville	C,T	St-L	M/W	5,640		22		Y	Y	Y	Y	Y	Y	Y	Y	9	31
Meridian Community College	Meridian	C,T	St-L	M/W	3,572		30	75	Y	Y	Y	Y	Y	Y	Y	Y	11	21
Mississippi Delta Community College	Moorhead	C,T	Dist	M/W	4,000		19		N	Y	Y	Y	Y	Y	Y	Y	9	44
Mississippi Gulf Coast Community College	Perkinston	C,T	Dist	M/W	8,822	37	0		Y	Y	Y	Y	Y	Y	Y	Y	9	46
Northwest Mississippi Community College	Senatobia	C,T	St-L	M/W	6,300				Y	Y	Y	Y	Y	Y	Y	Y	7	48
Pearl River Community College	Poplarville	C,T	St-L	M/W	3,700		27		Y	Y	Y	Y	Y	Y	Y	Y	10	9
Southwest Mississippi Community College	Summit	C,T	St-L	M/W	1,752	21	31		Y	Y	Y	Y	Y	Y	Y	Y	6	38
Missouri																		
Allied College	Maryland Heights	T	Prop	M/W	732													7
Aviation Institute of Maintenance–Kansas City	Kansas City	T	Prop															1
Concorde Career Institute	Kansas City	T	Prop	M/W	524									Y				1
Cottey College†	Nevada	C	Ind	W	318	1	95		N	Y		Y	Y	Y		Y	12	2
Crowder College	Neosho	C,T	St-L	M/W	2,930	52	23		Y	Y	Y	Y	Y	Y	Y	N	3	35
East Central College	Union	C,T	Dist	M/W	3,474	55	32		Y	Y	Y	Y	Y	Y	Y	N	2	46
Everest College	Springfield	T,B	Prop	M/W	548													4
Hickey College*	St. Louis	T,B	Prop	M/W	610													
High-Tech Institute	Kansas City	T	Prop	M/W	687													6
ITT Technical Institute	Arnold	T,B	Prop	M/W					N	Y	Y	Y	Y	Y	Y	N		16
ITT Technical Institute	Earth City	T,B	Prop	M/W					N	Y	Y	Y	Y	Y	Y	N		13
ITT Technical Institute	Kansas City	T,B	Prop	M/W							Y							9
Linn State Technical College	Linn	T	St	PM	877	11	13			Y		Y	Y	Y	Y	Y	8	16
Metro Business College	Jefferson City	T	Prop	M/W	155	10												
Metropolitan Community College–Blue River	Independence	C,T	St-L	M/W	2,662	60	32		Y	Y			Y	Y	Y	N		9
Metropolitan Community College–Business & Technology Campus	Kansas City	C,T	St-L	PM	602	80	64							Y	Y	N		43
Metropolitan Community College–Longview	Lee's Summit	C,T	St-L	M/W	5,667	57	29		Y	Y			Y	Y	Y	N	5	25
Metropolitan Community College–Maple Woods	Kansas City	C,T	St-L	M/W	4,442	59	26		Y	Y			Y	Y	Y	N	3	19
Metropolitan Community College–Penn Valley	Kansas City	C,T	St-L	M/W	4,627	69	54		Y	Y		Y	Y	Y	Y	N	1	31
Midwest Institute	Kirkwood	T	Prop	M/W	162						R			Y	Y	N		2
Missouri State University–West Plains	West Plains	C,T	St	M/W	1,592	50	10		Y	Y	S	Y	Y	Y	Y	Y	2	18
Moberly Area Community College	Moberly	C,T	St-L	M/W	3,710	49	23		Y	Y	Y	Y	Y	Y	Y	Y	3	15
North Central Missouri College	Trenton	C,T	Dist	M/W	1,458	48	20		Y	Y	Y	Y	Y	Y	Y	Y	3	21
Ozarks Technical Community College	Springfield	C,T	Dist	M/W	8,488	50	25		Y	Y	Y	Y	Y	Y	Y	N	1	34
Saint Charles Community College	St. Peters	C,T	St	M/W	6,844	50	31		Y	Y	R,S	Y	Y	Y	Y	N	6	22
St. Louis Community College at Florissant Valley	St. Louis	C,T	Dist	M/W			53			Y		Y	Y	Y	Y	N	7	48
Southeast Missouri Hospital College of Nursing and Health Sciences	Cape Girardeau	T	Ind	M/W	221	7	57	50				Y			Y	N		2
State Fair Community College	Sedalia	C,T	Dist	M/W	3,391	50	54		Y	Y		Y	Y	Y	Y	Y	3	31
Three Rivers Community College	Poplar Bluff	C,T	St-L	M/W	2,996	44	37	40	Y	Y	Y	Y	Y	Y	Y	Y	5	24
Vatterott College	Kansas City	T	Prop	M/W	702													11
Wentworth Military Academy and Junior College	Lexington	C	Ind	M/W	561	58												
Montana																		
Chief Dull Knife College	Lame Deer	C,T	Ind	M/W	460		60	50	Y	Y		Y	Y	Y	Y	N	2	8

This chart includes the names and locations of accredited two-year colleges in the United States and U.S. territories and shows institutions' responses to the *Peterson's Annual Survey of Undergraduate Institutions*. If an institution submitted incomplete data, one or more columns opposite the institution's name is blank. An asterisk after the school name denotes a *Special Message* following the college's profile, and a dagger indicates that the institution has one or more entries in the *College Close-Ups* section. If a school does not appear, it did not report any of the information.

Y—Yes; N—No; R—Recommended; S—For Some

Column headers: Degrees Awarded / Institutional Control / Student Body (Men, Women, Coed) / Undergraduate Enrollment / Percent Attending Part-Time / Percent 25 Years of Age or Older / Percent of Grads Going on to Four-Year Colleges / High School Equivalency Certificate Accepted / High School Transcript Required / Open Admissions / Need-Based Aid Available / Part-Time Jobs Available / Career Counseling Available / Job Placement Services Available / College Housing Available / Number of Sports Offered / Number of Majors Offered

Institution	Location	Degrees	Control	Body	Enroll	PT%	25+%	4yr%	HS Equiv	HS Trans	Open Adm	Need Aid	PT Jobs	Career	Job Place	Housing	Sports	Majors
Fort Belknap College	Harlem	C,T	Fed	M/W	158	26	67	29	Y	Y		Y	Y	Y	Y	N	3	9
Little Big Horn College	Crow Agency	C,T	Ind	M/W	317		50		Y		Y		Y	Y	Y	N	1	7
Salish Kootenai College	Pablo	C,T,B	Ind	M/W	1,088	46	48		Y	Y	Y	Y	Y	Y	Y	N	8	15
Stone Child College	Box Elder	C,T	Ind	M/W	240				Y	Y		Y	Y	Y	Y	N		5
The University of Montana-Helena College of Technology	Helena	C,T	St	M/W	850				Y	Y		Y	Y	Y	Y	N	2	18
Nebraska																		
Central Community College–Columbus Campus	Columbus	C,T	St-L	M/W	2,091	79	50		Y	Y	Y	Y	Y	Y	Y	Y	5	22
Central Community College–Grand Island Campus	Grand Island	C,T	St-L	M/W	2,890	84	57		Y	Y	Y	Y	Y	Y	Y	Y	3	22
Central Community College–Hastings Campus	Hastings	C,T	St-L	M/W	2,485	63	44		Y	Y	Y	Y	Y	Y	Y	Y	6	36
The Creative Center	Omaha	T	Prop	M/W	100						Y			Y	Y	N		3
ITT Technical Institute	Omaha	T,B	Prop	M/W					N	Y	Y	Y		Y	Y	N		14
Metropolitan Community College*	Omaha	C,T	St-L	M/W	14,098	61	44	39	Y		R		Y	Y	Y	Y		33
Mid-Plains Community College	North Platte	C,T	Dist	M/W	3,030	65	67		Y	Y		R	Y		Y	Y	5	18
Myotherapy Institute	Lincoln	T	Prop	M/W	52													1
Nebraska College of Technical Agriculture	Curtis	C,T	St	M/W	272	3			Y	Y	Y	Y	Y	Y	Y	Y	6	10
Nebraska Indian Community College	Macy	C,T	Fed	M/W	115	52	75		Y	Y	Y	Y	Y	Y	Y	N		11
Northeast Community College	Norfolk	C,T	St-L	M/W	5,261	59	38	21	Y	Y		R	Y	Y	Y	Y	8	76
Western Nebraska Community College	Sidney	C,T	St-L	M/W	3,151		43		Y	Y		R	Y	Y	Y	Y	10	48
Nevada																		
Career College of Northern Nevada	Reno	T	Prop	M/W	283													
Community College of Southern Nevada	North Las Vegas	C	St	M/W	34,204	77	60		Y			Y	Y	Y	Y	N	6	82
Great Basin College	Elko	C,T,B	St	M/W	3,349	75	54		Y		Y	Y	Y	Y	Y	Y	4	27
Heritage College	Las Vegas	T	Prop		227													8
High-Tech Institute	Las Vegas	T	Prop		589													7
ITT Technical Institute	Henderson	T,B	Prop	M/W					N	Y	Y	Y	Y	Y	Y	N		13
Le Cordon Bleu College of Culinary Arts, Las Vegas	Las Vegas	T	Prop	M/W	892													1
Western Nevada Community College	Carson City	C,T	St	M/W	5,531	82	55	21	Y		S	Y	Y	Y	Y	N	3	42
New Hampshire																		
Hesser College†	Manchester	C,T,B	Prop	M/W	3,398	38	25	65	N		Y	Y	Y	Y	Y	Y	8	33
New Hampshire Community Technical College, Manchester/Stratham	Manchester	C,T	St	M/W	3,122		40	9	N	Y		Y	Y	Y	Y	N	8	23
New Hampshire Community Technical College, Nashua/Claremont	Nashua	C,T	St	M/W	1,725				N	Y	Y	Y	Y	Y	Y	N	4	31
New Hampshire Technical Institute	Concord	C	St	M/W	3,700		50	18		Y	Y	Y	Y	Y	Y	Y	5	32
New Jersey																		
Assumption College for Sisters	Mendham	C	I-R	W	37	19												1
Atlantic Cape Community College	Mays Landing	C,T	Cou	M/W	6,845	55												
Bergen Community College	Paramus	C,T	Cou	M/W	14,608		31	80	Y	Y		Y	Y	Y	Y	N	10	55
Berkeley College	West Paterson	C,T,B	Prop	M/W	2,729	15	23		N	Y	Y	Y	Y	Y	Y	Y	5	11
Burlington County College	Pemberton	C,T	Cou	M/W	7,797	48	27	60	Y	Y	Y	Y	Y	Y	Y	N	5	49
Essex County College	Newark	C,T	Cou	M/W	10,972	43	50	68	Y		Y	Y	Y	Y	Y	N	6	48
Gloucester County College	Sewell	C,T	Cou	M/W	5,863				Y	Y	Y	Y	Y	Y	Y	N	9	43
Mercer County Community College	Trenton	C,T	St-L	M/W	8,928	62												
Middlesex County College†	Edison	C,T	Cou	M/W	11,276													
Ocean County College	Toms River	C,T	Cou	M/W	8,449	52												
Passaic County Community College	Paterson	C,T	Cou	M/W	6,308		41		Y			Y	Y	Y	Y	N	4	27
Raritan Valley Community College	Somerville	C,T	Cou	M/W	6,408	57	36	48	Y	Y	Y	Y	Y	Y	Y	N	4	46
Salem Community College	Carneys Point	C,T	Cou	M/W	1,251	52												
Somerset Christian College	Zarephath	C,T	I-R	M/W	142	95	0		N	Y	S		Y		Y	N		1
Sussex County Community College	Newton	C,T	St-L	M/W	3,566		41			Y		Y	Y	Y	Y	N	6	20
Union County College	Cranford	C,T	St-L	M/W	11,166	52	44	77	Y		Y	Y	Y	Y	Y	N	6	35
Warren County Community College	Washington	C,T	St-L	M/W	1,801		57		Y			Y	Y	Y	Y	N		13
New Mexico																		
Central New Mexico Community College	Albuquerque	C,T	St	M/W	22,615	70	51		Y		R	Y	Y	Y	Y	N		35
Clovis Community College	Clovis	C,T	St	M/W	3,522	74	51		Y	Y	Y	Y	Y	Y	Y	N	5	36
Eastern New Mexico University–Roswell	Roswell	C,T	St	M/W	3,522		55		Y	Y		Y	Y	Y	Y	Y	7	21
International Institute of the Americas	Albuquerque	T,B	Ind	M/W	185		42						Y	Y	Y	N		4
ITT Technical Institute	Albuquerque	T,B	Prop	M/W					N	Y	Y	Y	Y	Y	Y	N		12
National American University	Rio Rancho	T	Prop	M/W	231													9
New Mexico Junior College	Hobbs	C,T	St-L	M/W	3,222		52	67				Y	Y	Y	Y	Y	10	53
New Mexico Military Institute	Roswell	C	St	PM	480		0	96	N	Y		Y	Y	Y	Y	Y	17	28
New Mexico State University–Alamogordo	Alamogordo	C,T	St	M/W	1,897	62	64		Y	Y	Y	Y	Y	Y	Y	N	2	16
Northern New Mexico College	Española	C,T,B	St	M/W	2,272		60		Y	Y	Y							13
Pima Medical Institute	Albuquerque	T	Prop	M/W	420													
San Juan College	Farmington	C,T	St	M/W	6,366	62	34		Y	Y	Y	Y	Y	Y	Y	N	16	52
Southwestern Indian Polytechnic Institute	Albuquerque	C,T	Fed	M/W	818		35		Y	Y	Y	Y	Y	Y	Y	N	1	15
University of New Mexico–Gallup	Gallup	C,T,B	St	M/W	2,858		50	10	Y	Y		S	Y	Y	Y	N		26
University of New Mexico–Los Alamos Branch	Los Alamos	C,T	St	M/W	890		40		Y			Y	Y	Y	Y	Y		14
University of New Mexico–Taos	Taos	T	St	M/W	1,186													15
University of New Mexico–Valencia Campus	Los Lunas	C,T	St	M/W	1,544		76	50	Y	Y	R	Y	Y	Y	Y	N		14
New York																		

This chart includes the names and locations of accredited two-year colleges in the United States and U.S. territories and shows institutions' responses to the *Peterson's Annual Survey of Undergraduate Institutions*. If an institution submitted incomplete data, one or more columns opposite the institution's name is blank.

An asterisk after the school name denotes a *Special Message* following the college's profile, and a dagger indicates that the institution has one or more entries in the *College Close-Ups* section. If a school does not appear, it did not report any of the information.

Y—Yes; N—No; R—Recommended; S—For Some

Institution	Location	Degrees Awarded	Institutional Control	Student Body	Undergraduate Enrollment	Percent Attending Part-Time	Percent 25 Years of Age or Older	Percent of Grads Going on to Four-Year Colleges	High School Equivalency Certificate Accepted	High School Transcript Required	Open Admissions	Need-Based Aid Required	Part-Time Jobs Available	Job Placement Services Available	Career Counseling Available	College Housing Available	Number of Sports Offered	Number of Majors Offered
American Academy McAllister Institute of Funeral Service	New York	T	Ind	M/W	130		29		Y	Y	Y	Y		Y		N		1
American Academy of Dramatic Arts†	New York	T	Ind	M/W	248		12		N	Y	Y	Y	Y	Y	Y	Y	N	1
The Art Institute of New York City†	New York	C,T	Prop	M/W	1,519		40		Y	Y	Y	Y	Y	Y	Y	Y	N	5
Berkeley College-New York City Campus	New York	C,T,B	Prop	M/W	2,412	9	29		N	Y	Y	Y	Y	Y	Y	N		12
Berkeley College-Westchester Campus	White Plains	C,T,B	Prop	M/W	640	8	17		N	Y	Y	Y	Y	Y	Y			11
Borough of Manhattan Community College of the City University of New York	New York	C,T	St-L	M/W	18,776	42												
Bramson ORT College	Forest Hills	T	Ind	M/W	600		80		Y	Y	Y	Y	Y	Y	Y	N		14
Bronx Community College of the City University of New York	Bronx	C,T	St-L	M/W	8,556	42												
Broome Community College	Binghamton	C,T	St-L	M/W	6,282	36	31		Y	Y	Y	Y	Y	Y	Y	N	10	35
Bryant and Stratton College	Albany	T	Prop	M/W	470	25												
Bryant and Stratton College	Rochester	T	Prop	M/W	297	20												
Bryant and Stratton College	Rochester	T	Prop	M/W	194	22												
Bryant and Stratton College	Syracuse	T	Prop	M/W	636	22												
Bryant and Stratton College, Amherst Campus	Clarence	T,B	Prop	M/W	403	40												
Bryant and Stratton College, Buffalo Campus	Buffalo	T	Prop	M/W	603	18												
Bryant and Stratton College, Lackawanna Campus	Lackawanna	T	Prop	M/W	269	30												
Business Informatics Center, Inc.	Valley Stream	T	Prop	M/W	108									Y				2
The College of Westchester†	White Plains	C,T	Prop	M/W	1,039	20												
Columbia-Greene Community College	Hudson	C,T	St-L	M/W	1,771	43	30	39	Y		Y	Y	Y	Y		N	11	23
Corning Community College	Corning	C,T	St-L	M/W	5,310	50												
Dorothea Hopfer School of Nursing at The Mount Vernon Hospital	Mount Vernon	T	Ind		120													1
Ellis Hospital School of Nursing	Schenectady	C,T	Ind	PW	69		80						Y	Y				1
Elmira Business Institute	Elmira	C,T	Priv	PW	280	31	70		Y	Y	Y	Y		Y	Y	N		5
Erie Community College	Buffalo	C,T	St-L	M/W	2,993	28	45	47	Y	Y	Y	Y	Y	Y	Y	N	14	19
Erie Community College, North Campus	Williamsville	C,T	St-L	M/W	5,859	34	30	43	Y	Y	Y	Y	Y	Y	Y	N	14	26
Erie Community College, South Campus	Orchard Park	C,T	St-L	M/W	4,160	39	20	58	Y	Y	Y	Y	Y	Y	Y	N	14	20
Eugenio María de Hostos Community College of the City University of New York	Bronx	C,T	St-L	M/W	4,697		54	25	Y		Y	Y	Y	Y	Y	N	4	17
Finger Lakes Community College	Canandaigua	C,T	St-L	M/W	5,150		32		Y	Y	Y	Y	Y	Y	Y	N	8	49
Fiorello H. LaGuardia Community College of the City University of New York*	Long Island City	C,T	St-L	M/W	14,185	45	43	37	Y		Y	Y	Y	Y	Y	N	6	33
Fulton-Montgomery Community College	Johnstown	C,T	St-L	M/W	2,157	35	28		Y		Y		Y	Y	Y	N	7	44
Genesee Community College	Batavia	C,T	St-L	M/W	6,503	53	30	60	Y	Y	Y	Y	Y	Y	Y	Y	15	37
Helene Fuld College of Nursing of North General Hospital	New York	C,T	Ind	PW	363		96		N	Y	Y	Y		Y		N		1
Hudson Valley Community College	Troy	C,T	St-L	M/W	12,205													
Institute of Design and Construction	Brooklyn	C,T	Ind	PM	246		59	20	Y	Y		Y	Y	Y		N		4
Island Drafting and Technical Institute	Amityville	C,T	Prop	PM	143		45		Y	Y	R	Y	Y	Y	Y	N		8
ITT Technical Institute	Albany	T	Prop	M/W					N	Y	Y	Y	Y	Y	Y	N		5
ITT Technical Institute	Getzville	T	Prop	M/W					N	Y	Y	Y	Y	Y	Y	N		6
ITT Technical Institute	Liverpool	T	Prop	M/W					N	Y	Y	Y	Y	Y	Y	N		5
Jamestown Community College	Jamestown	C,T	St-L	M/W	3,721	34	27		Y	Y	Y	Y	Y	Y	Y	N	10	22
Jefferson Community College	Watertown	C,T	St-L	M/W	3,545	49												
Kingsborough Community College of the City University of New York	Brooklyn	C,T	St-L	M/W	14,687	47	29	75	Y	Y	Y	Y	Y	Y	Y	N	7	38
Long Island Business Institute	Commack	C	Prop	PW	880	24	75	0	Y	Y	Y			Y	Y	N		4
Long Island College Hospital School of Nursing	Brooklyn	C,T	Ind	PW	140	49	84		N	Y	Y	Y	Y			N		1
Maria College	Albany	C,T	Ind	M/W	788	65												
Memorial Hospital School of Nursing	Albany	T	Ind	M/W	113						R							
Mohawk Valley Community College†	Utica	C,T	St-L	M/W	5,895	37	25	84	Y	Y	Y	Y	Y	Y	Y	Y	17	73
Monroe Community College	Rochester	C,T	St-L	M/W	16,596	43	35	52	Y	Y	Y	Y	Y	Y	Y		16	67
Nassau Community College	Garden City	C,T	St-L	M/W	21,229	35	20	65	Y	Y	Y	Y	Y	Y	Y	N	19	55
New York Career Institute	New York	T	Prop	M/W	564				N	Y	Y	Y	Y	Y	Y	N		2
New York City College of Technology of the City University of New York	Brooklyn	C,T,B	St-L	M/W	13,368	43	34		Y	Y	Y	Y	Y	Y	Y	N	5	29
New York College of Health Professions†	Syosset	T,B,M	Ind	M/W	801	59			N	Y	Y	Y	Y	Y	N			2
Niagara County Community College	Sanborn	C,T	St-L	M/W	5,944	40	27	62	Y	Y	Y	Y	Y	Y	Y	N	10	36
North Country Community College	Saranac Lake	C,T	St-L	M/W	1,636	41	26	34	Y	Y	Y	Y	Y	Y	Y	Y	12	14
Onondaga Community College	Syracuse	C,T	St-L	M/W	9,394	44	48	73	Y	Y	Y	Y	Y	Y	Y	Y	7	58
Orange County Community College	Middletown	C,T	St-L	M/W	6,441	48												
Phillips Beth Israel School of Nursing	New York	C,T	Ind	PW	200													
Queensborough Community College of the City University of New York	Bayside	C,T	St-L	M/W	13,008		32		Y	Y	Y	Y	Y	Y	Y	N	14	21
St. Elizabeth College of Nursing	Utica	T	Ind	M/W	208													
St. Joseph's College of Nursing	Syracuse	T	Ind	PW	293													
Saint Vincent Catholic Medical Centers School of Nursing	Fresh Meadows	T	Ind	M/W	106		50		N	Y	Y	Y	Y	Y	Y	N		1
Samaritan Hospital School of Nursing	Troy	C,T	Ind		70		60						Y					1
State University of New York College of Agriculture and Technology at Morrisville	Morrisville	C,T,B	St	M/W	3,288	16	21	54	N	Y	Y	Y	Y	Y	Y	Y	19	61
State University of New York College of Environmental Science & Forestry, Ranger School†	Wanakena	C,T	St	PM	43		20	38	N	N	R	Y	Y	Y	Y	Y	7	2
State University of New York College of Technology at Alfred	Alfred	C,T,B	St	M/W	3,231	6	7	83	N	Y	Y	Y	Y	Y	Y	Y	22	57
State University of New York College of Technology at Canton	Canton	C,T,B	St	M/W	2,584	16	21		N	Y	Y	Y	Y	Y	Y	Y	11	36
State University of New York College of Technology at Delhi	Delhi	C,T,B	St	M/W	2,557													
Suffolk County Community College	Selden	C,T	St-L	M/W	20,280	46	33	75	Y	Y	Y	Y	Y	Y	Y	N	11	60

This chart includes the names and locations of accredited two-year colleges in the United States and U.S. territories and shows institutions' responses to the *Peterson's Annual Survey of Undergraduate Institutions*. If an institution submitted incomplete data, one or more columns opposite the institution's name is blank. An asterisk after the school name denotes a *Special Message* following the college's profile, and a dagger indicates that the institution has one or more entries in the *College Close-Ups* section. If a school does not appear, it did not report any of the information.

Y—Yes; N—No; R—Recommended; S—For Some

Institution	City	Degrees Awarded	Institutional Control	Student Body	Undergraduate Enrollment	% Attending Part-Time	% 25 or Older	% Grads to 4-Year	HS Equiv. Cert. Accepted	HS Transcript Required	Open Admissions	Need-Based Aid Available	Part-Time Jobs Available	Career Counseling Available	Job Placement Services Available	College Housing Available	No. of Sports Offered	No. of Majors Offered
Sullivan County Community College	Loch Sheldrake	C,T	St-L	M/W	1,684	37												
Tompkins Cortland Community College	Dryden	C,T	St-L	M/W	3,009	30	31		Y		Y	Y	Y	Y	Y	Y	16	45
Trocaire College	Buffalo	C,T	Ind	PW	780		51	17	N	Y		Y	Y	Y	Y	Y			15
Ulster County Community College	Stone Ridge	C,T	St-L	M/W	3,105		40	15	N	Y		Y	Y	Y	Y	Y	N	7	28
Villa Maria College of Buffalo	Buffalo	C,T,B	I-R	M/W	514	20	30	59	N	Y	Y	Y		Y	Y	Y	N		12
Westchester Community College	Valhalla	C,T	St-L	M/W	11,579	52	30		Y	Y		Y	Y	Y	Y	Y	N	11	52
Wood Tobe–Coburn School	New York	T	Prop	PW	269														
North Carolina																		
Alamance Community College	Graham	C,T	St	M/W	4,637	60	49	1	Y	Y		Y	Y	Y	Y	Y	N	4	33
The Art Institute of Charlotte†	Charlotte	T,B	Prop	M/W	880	29			N	Y		Y				Y			
Asheville-Buncombe Technical Community College	Asheville	C,T	St	M/W	6,449		47		Y	Y		Y	Y	Y	Y	Y	N	3	27
Beaufort County Community College	Washington	C,T	St	M/W	1,433		58	75	Y	Y		Y	Y	Y	Y	Y	N		21
Bladen Community College	Dublin	C,T	St-L	M/W	1,407	40	62	81	Y	Y		Y	Y	Y	Y	Y	N		15
Brunswick Community College	Supply	C,T	St	M/W	1,011	57	46		Y	Y		Y		Y	Y	Y	N	4	17
Caldwell Community College and Technical Institute	Hudson	C,T	St	M/W	3,878	66	47		Y	Y		Y	Y	Y	Y	Y	N	4	25
Cape Fear Community College	Wilmington	C,T	St	M/W	7,473	59	40	85	Y	Y	S	Y	Y	Y	Y	Y	N	7	31
Carteret Community College	Morehead City	C,T	St	M/W	1,659	61													
Catawba Valley Community College	Hickory	C,T	St-L	M/W	4,869	59	27		Y	Y		Y	Y	Y	Y	Y	N	2	42
Central Carolina Community College	Sanford	C,T	St-L	M/W	4,857	62	50		Y	Y		Y	Y	Y	Y	Y	N	5	29
Central Piedmont Community College	Charlotte	C,T	St-L	M/W	16,631	63	50	46	Y	Y		Y	Y	Y	Y	Y	N	1	69
Cleveland Community College	Shelby	C,T	St	M/W	3,341	59	48		Y	Y		Y	Y	Y	Y	Y	N		31
Coastal Carolina Community College	Jacksonville	C,T	St-L	M/W	4,111	50	45		Y	Y		Y	Y	Y	Y	Y	N		19
College of The Albemarle	Elizabeth City	C,T	St	M/W	2,071	59	56	84	Y	Y		Y	Y	Y	Y	Y	N	14	26
Davidson County Community College	Lexington	C,T	St-L	M/W	2,303	64	55	79	Y			Y	Y	Y	Y	Y	N		20
ECPI Technical College	Raleigh	T	Prop	M/W	550														
Fayetteville Technical Community College	Fayetteville	C,T	St	M/W	10,290	69	58		Y	Y	S	Y	Y	Y	Y	Y	N	3	53
Forsyth Technical Community College	Winston-Salem	C,T	St	M/W	6,978	64	51		Y	Y		Y	Y	Y	Y	Y	N	4	38
Gaston College	Dallas	C,T	St-L	M/W	5,048	51													
Guilford Technical Community College	Jamestown	C,T	St-L	M/W	9,802	49	43	64	Y	Y		Y	Y	Y	Y	Y	N		52
Isothermal Community College	Spindale	C,T	St	M/W	2,005	51	49		Y	Y		Y	Y	Y	Y	Y	N	3	34
James Sprunt Community College	Kenansville	C,T	St	M/W	1,192	50	51	65	Y	Y		Y	Y	Y	Y	Y	N	2	13
Johnston Community College	Smithfield	C,T	St	M/W	4,011	68	43		Y	Y		Y	Y	Y	Y	Y	N	4	19
King's College	Charlotte	C,T	Prop	M/W	515						Y								8
Lenoir Community College	Kinston	C,T	St	M/W	3,771				Y	Y		Y	Y	Y	Y	Y	N	4	44
Louisburg College	Louisburg	C,T	I-R	M/W	730	2	4		N	Y		Y	Y	Y	Y	Y	Y	9	42
Martin Community College	Williamston	C,T	St	M/W	834	66	37	50	Y	Y		Y	Y	Y	Y	Y	N		20
Montgomery Community College	Troy	C,T	St	M/W	850	54													
Pamlico Community College	Grantsboro	C,T	St	M/W	300		58		Y	Y		Y	Y	Y	Y	Y	N	2	11
Richmond Community College	Hamlet	C,T	St	M/W	1,472	53													
Robeson Community College	Lumberton	C,T	St	M/W	2,313				Y	Y			Y	Y	Y	N			12
Rockingham Community College	Wentworth	C,T	St	M/W	2,036	70													
Sampson Community College	Clinton	C,T	St-L	M/W	1,579	57	52	23	Y	Y		Y	Y	Y	Y	Y	N	2	15
Sandhills Community College	Pinehurst	C,T	St-L	M/W	3,535	44			Y	Y		Y	Y	Y	Y	Y	N		48
School of Communication Arts	Raleigh	T	Prop	M/W	298														3
Southeastern Community College	Whiteville	C,T	St	M/W	1,949		45		Y	Y		Y	Y	Y	Y	Y	N	4	21
South Piedmont Community College	Polkton	C,T	St	M/W	2,075		62	32	Y	Y		Y	Y	Y	Y				23
Southwestern Community College	Sylva	C,T	St	M/W	2,065	59	43	80	Y	Y		Y	Y	Y	Y	Y	N		32
Stanly Community College	Albemarle	C,T	St	M/W	2,000		48		Y	Y		Y	Y	Y	Y	Y	N		31
Surry Community College	Dobson	C,T	St	M/W	3,600		42	81	Y	Y		Y	Y	Y	Y	Y	N	4	29
Tri-County Community College	Murphy	C,T	St	M/W	1,155		65	40	Y	Y		Y	Y	Y	Y	Y	N		11
Vance-Granville Community College	Henderson	C,T	St	M/W	4,057	58													
Wayne Community College	Goldsboro	C,T	St-L	M/W	3,181		33		Y	Y		Y	Y	Y	Y	Y	N	8	29
Western Piedmont Community College	Morganton	C,T	St	M/W	2,897				Y	Y		Y	Y	Y	Y	Y	N	2	26
Wilkes Community College	Wilkesboro	C,T	St	M/W	2,617	49													
Wilson Technical Community College	Wilson	C,T	St	M/W	1,849	54	59	80	Y	Y		Y	Y	Y	Y	Y	N		18
North Dakota																		
Aakers College	Fargo	C,T,B	Prop	M/W	577	45													
Bismarck State College	Bismarck	C,T	St	M/W	3,477	37	34		Y	Y		Y		Y	Y	Y	Y	6	23
Cankdeska Cikana Community College	Fort Totten	C,T	Fed	M/W	168		30	10	Y	Y				Y	Y		N	4	19
Fort Berthold Community College	New Town	C,T	Ind	M/W	416		40	42	Y	Y			Y	Y		N	7		16
Lake Region State College	Devils Lake	C,T	St	M/W	1,471	72													
Minot State University–Bottineau Campus	Bottineau	C,T	St	M/W	605	49	35	60	Y	Y		Y	Y	Y	Y	Y	Y	8	36
North Dakota State College of Science	Wahpeton	C,T	St	M/W	2,468	21													
Sitting Bull College	Fort Yates	C,T	Ind	M/W	214		35		Y	Y		Y	Y	Y			N	1	15
Turtle Mountain Community College	Belcourt	C,T	Ind	M/W	579	35	75		Y	Y		Y	Y	Y			N	4	33
United Tribes Technical College	Bismarck	C,T	Fed	M/W	885	28													
Williston State College	Williston	C,T	St	M/W	947	41													
Northern Mariana Islands																		
Northern Marianas College	Saipan	C,T,B	Terr	M/W	1,299	40	40		Y			Y			Y	Y	N	5	13
Ohio																		
Academy of Court Reporting	Cleveland	T	Prop	M/W	448														3
The Art Institute of Ohio–Cincinnati†	Cincinnati	C,T	Prop	M/W	329		29	19	Y	Y	Y				Y	Y			2
ATS Institute of Technology	Highland Heights	C,T	Prop	M/W	353														1
Bowling Green State University–Firelands College	Huron	C,T,B	St	M/W	1,984	45	33		Y	Y		Y	Y	Y	Y	Y	N	6	28

This chart includes the names and locations of accredited two-year colleges in the United States and U.S. territories and shows institutions' responses to the *Peterson's Annual Survey of Undergraduate Institutions*. If an institution submitted incomplete data, one or more columns opposite the institution's name is blank.

An asterisk after the school name denotes a *Special Message* following the college's profile, and a dagger indicates that the institution has one or more entries in the *College Close-Ups* section. If a school does not appear, it did not report any of the information.

Legend: Y—Yes; N—No; R—Recommended; S—For Some

Degrees Awarded: College Transfer Associate (C), Terminal Associate (T), Bachelor's (B), Master's (M), Doctoral (D), First Professional (F)

Institution	Location	Degrees Awarded	Institutional Control	Student Body	Undergraduate Enrollment	Percent Attending Part-Time	Percent 25 or Older	Percent of Grads Going on to Four-Year Colleges	Open Admissions	HS Equivalency Cert. Accepted	HS Transcript Required	Need-Based Aid Available	Part-Time Jobs Available	Career Counseling Available	Job Placement Services Available	College Housing Available	Number of Sports Offered	Number of Majors Offered
Brown Mackie College–Akron†	Akron	T	Prop	M/W	681		70	9	N	Y		Y		Y	Y	N		13
Brown Mackie College–Cincinnati†	Cincinnati	T	Prop	M/W	1,322		55		Y	Y	Y	Y		Y	Y	N		15
Brown Mackie College–Findlay†	Findlay	T	Prop	M/W	615		80		Y	Y	Y	Y			Y	N		10
Brown Mackie College–North Canton†	North Canton	T	Prop	M/W	930					N	Y	Y			Y	N		12
Bryant and Stratton College	Parma	T,B	Prop	M/W	329	44												
Central Ohio Technical College	Newark	T	St	M/W	2,592	56	76		Y	Y	Y	Y	Y	Y	Y	Y	13	18
Chatfield College	St. Martin	C,T	I-R	PW	230													
Cincinnati College of Mortuary Science	Cincinnati	T,B	Ind	M/W	133													
Cincinnati State Technical and Community College	Cincinnati	C,T	St	M/W	8,277	60	45	33	Y	Y	Y	Y	Y	Y	Y	N	4	65
Clark State Community College	Springfield	C,T	St	M/W	3,352				Y	Y	Y	Y	Y	Y	Y	N	4	37
Cleveland Institute of Electronics	Cleveland	T	Prop	PM	2,317		85		Y	Y	Y	Y			Y	N		
Cuyahoga Community College	Cleveland	C,T	St-L	M/W	24,796	59	50	63	Y			S	Y	Y	Y	N	8	32
Davis College	Toledo	T	Prop	M/W	451	50												
Gallipolis Career College	Gallipolis	T	Ind	PW	154	6												
Hocking College	Nelsonville	C,T	St	M/W	5,250		37	9	Y	Y	Y	Y	Y	Y	Y	Y	10	45
ITT Technical Institute	Dayton	T	Prop	M/W					N	Y		Y		Y	Y	N		10
ITT Technical Institute	Hilliard	T	Prop	M/W							Y							8
ITT Technical Institute	Norwood	C	Prop	M/W					N	Y		Y		Y	Y	N		9
ITT Technical Institute	Strongsville	T	Prop	M/W					N	Y		Y		Y	Y	N		10
ITT Technical Institute	Warrensville Heights	T	Prop	M/W							Y							7
ITT Technical Institute	Youngstown	T	Prop	M/W					N	Y		Y		Y	Y	N		9
Jefferson Community College	Steubenville	C,T	St-L	M/W	1,600		43		Y	Y	S		Y	Y	Y	N	6	25
Kent State University, Ashtabula Campus	Ashtabula	C,T,B	St	M/W	1,396				Y	Y			Y	Y	Y	N		20
Kent State University, East Liverpool Campus	East Liverpool	C,T	St	M/W	657		47		Y	Y	Y	Y	Y	Y	Y	N		10
Kent State University, Geauga Campus	Burton	C,B	St	M/W	1,057	67	73		Y	Y	Y	Y	Y	Y	Y	N	4	8
Kent State University, Trumbull Campus	Warren	C,T,B	St	M/W	1,996	54	43		Y	Y	Y	Y	Y	Y	Y	N	4	12
Kent State University, Tuscarawas Campus	New Philadelphia	C,T,B,M	St	M/W	1,977	49	37		Y	Y	Y	Y	Y	Y	Y	Y	2	16
Kettering College of Medical Arts	Kettering	C,T,B	I-R	PW	773	46	50		N	Y		Y	Y	Y	Y	Y	3	7
Lorain County Community College	Elyria	C,T	St-L	M/W	10,521	61	42		Y	Y	S	Y	Y	Y	Y	N	6	74
Mercy College of Northwest Ohio	Toledo	C,B	I-R	PW	780	47	51		N	Y		Y	Y	Y	Y	N		6
Miami University Hamilton	Hamilton	C,T,B,M	St	M/W	3,189	55	25		Y	Y	Y	Y	Y	Y	Y	N	11	99
Miami University–Middletown Campus	Middletown	C,T,B	St	M/W	2,660		28		Y	Y	Y	Y	Y	Y	Y	N	13	51
National Institute of Technology	Cuyahoga Falls	T	Prop	M/W	375													6
Ohio Business College	Sandusky	C	Prop	M/W	192	18												1
Ohio College of Massotherapy	Akron	T	Ind	M/W	282													
Ohio Institute of Photography and Technology	Dayton	T	Prop	M/W	740													
The Ohio State University Agricultural Technical Institute	Wooster	C,T	St	M/W	747			10	Y	Y			Y	Y	Y	Y	5	36
Ohio Technical College	Cleveland	T	Prop	M/W	654													3
Owens Community College	Toledo	C,T	St	M/W	19,141	63	53		Y	Y	R	Y	Y	Y	Y	N	11	25
Remington College–Cleveland West Campus	North Olmsted	T	Prop	M/W	399											Y		1
Rosedale Bible College	Irwin	T	I-R	M/W	89													1
School of Advertising Art	Kettering	C,T	Prop	M/W	146													
Sinclair Community College	Dayton	C,T	St-L	M/W	19,563	61												
Southeastern Business College	Jackson	T	Prop	M/W	76													7
Southeastern Business College	Lancaster	T	Prop	M/W	71													5
Southeastern Business College	New Boston	T	Prop	M/W	78													5
Southern State Community College	Hillsboro	C,T	St	M/W	2,363		49		Y	Y	R	Y	Y	Y	Y	N	5	15
Stark State College of Technology	North Canton	C,T	St-L	M/W	7,611	67	49		Y	Y	Y	Y		Y	Y	N		49
Technology Education College	Columbus	T	Priv	PW	491								Y					7
Terra State Community College	Fremont	C,T	St	M/W	2,314	65	45		Y	Y	Y	Y	Y	Y	Y	N	7	37
Trumbull Business College	Warren	T	Prop	PW	321	9	51					Y	Y	Y	Y	Y		
The University of Akron–Wayne College	Orrville	C,T	St	M/W	1,737	47	41	75	Y	Y	S	Y	Y	Y	Y	N	4	20
University of Cincinnati Clermont College	Batavia	C,T	St	M/W	2,408		50		Y	Y	Y	Y	Y	Y	Y	N	5	19
University of Northwestern Ohio*	Lima	C,B	Ind	M/W	2,915	10												5
Vatterott College	Broadview Heights	T	Prop	M/W	236													
Washington State Community College	Marietta	C,T	St	M/W	2,086	44	50	90			R,S		Y	Y	Y	N	3	27
Wright State University, Lake Campus	Celina	C,T	St	M/W	828		52		Y	Y	Y		Y	Y	Y	N	1	34
Zane State College	Zanesville	C,T	St-L	M/W	1,915		49	6	Y	Y	Y	Y	Y	Y	Y	N	4	27
Oklahoma																		
Carl Albert State College	Poteau	C,T	St	M/W	2,501	41												
Community Care College	Tulsa	T	Prop	M/W	525	2												
ITT Technical Institute	Tulsa	T,B	Prop	M/W							Y							9
Murray State College	Tishomingo	C,T	St	M/W	1,958				Y	Y	Y	Y	Y	Y	Y	Y	7	32
Northern Oklahoma College	Tonkawa	C,T	St	M/W	3,050		40		Y	Y	Y	Y	Y	Y	Y	Y	11	17
Oklahoma City Community College	Oklahoma City	C,T	St	M/W	12,516	62		27	Y			Y	Y	Y	Y	N	6	44
Oklahoma State University, Oklahoma City	Oklahoma City	C,T	St	M/W	5,704	69	50	30	Y			Y	Y	Y	Y	N	2	29
Oklahoma State University, Okmulgee	Okmulgee	C,T	St	M/W	2,329	26	37		Y			Y	Y	Y	Y	Y	8	29
Platt College	Moore	T	Prop	M/W	71													1
Platt College	Tulsa	T	Prop	M/W	415													2
Redlands Community College	El Reno	C,T	St	M/W	2,323	75	36	59	Y	Y	Y	Y	Y	Y	Y	N	3	32
Rose State College	Midwest City	C,T	St-L	M/W	7,000		60		Y	Y	Y	Y	Y	Y	Y	N	7	49
Seminole State College	Seminole	C,T	St	M/W	2,534		47		Y	Y	Y	Y	Y	Y	Y	Y	5	18
Southwestern Oklahoma State University at Sayre	Sayre	C,T	St-L	M/W	549	40												
Tulsa Community College	Tulsa	C,T	St	M/W	16,632	64	49	53	Y	Y	Y	Y	Y	Y	Y	N	10	158
Tulsa Welding School	Tulsa	T	Prop	PM	604		37							Y	Y	Y		1
Vatterott College	Oklahoma City	T,F	Prop	M/W	267							Y			Y	Y		5
Vatterott College	Tulsa	T	Prop	PW	226													
Western Oklahoma State College	Altus	C,T	St	M/W	2,061	58												

This chart includes the names and locations of accredited two-year colleges in the United States and U.S. territories and shows institutions' responses to the *Peterson's Annual Survey of Undergraduate Institutions*. If an institution submitted incomplete data, one or more columns opposite the institution's name is blank.
An asterisk after the school name denotes a *Special Message* following the college's profile, and a dagger indicates that the institution has one or more entries in the *College Close-Ups* section. If a school does not appear, it did not report any of the information.

Y—Yes; N—No; R—Recommended; S—For Some

Column key (left to right): Degrees Awarded — College Transfer Associate (C), Terminal Associate (T), Bachelor's (B), Master's (M), Doctoral (D), First Professional (F); Institutional Control; Student Body; Undergraduate Enrollment; Percent Attending Part-Time; Percent 25 Years of Age or Older; Percent of Grads Going on to Four-Year Colleges; High School Equivalency Certificate Accepted; High School Transcript Required; Open Admissions; Need-Based Aid Available; Part-Time Jobs Available; Career Counseling Available; Job Placement Services Available; College Housing Available; Number of Sports Offered; Number of Majors Offered.

Institution	Location	Degrees	Control	Body	Enroll	PT%	25+%	Grads%	HS Equiv	HS Trans	Open Adm	Need Aid	PT Jobs	Career Couns	Job Place	Housing	Sports	Majors
Oregon																		
Central Oregon Community College*	Bend	C,T	Dist	M/W	4,200	68	36	60	Y				Y	Y	Y	Y	13	38
Chemeketa Community College	Salem	C,T	St-L	M/W	15,000													
Clackamas Community College	Oregon City	C,T	Dist	M/W	5,976	67	3	92	Y			Y	Y	Y	Y	N	10	15
Clatsop Community College	Astoria	C,T	Cou	M/W	3,002		50	30	Y		R	Y	Y	Y		N		12
Everest College	Portland	T	Prop	M/W	827								Y	Y				1
Heald College-Portland	Portland	C,T	Ind	M/W	206	28												
ITT Technical Institute	Portland	T,B	Prop	M/W					N	Y	Y	Y	Y	Y	Y	N		14
Klamath Community College	Klamath Falls	T	St	M/W	918											N		12
Linn-Benton Community College	Albany	C,T	St-L	M/W	4,983	47			Y		S	Y	Y	Y	Y	N	5	61
Mt. Hood Community College	Gresham	C,T	St-L	M/W	8,771	64	56		Y		S	Y	Y	Y	Y	N	19	40
Oregon Coast Community College	Newport	C	Pub	M/W	479	75	62		Y					Y		N		4
Pioneer Pacific College†	Wilsonville	C,B	Prop	M/W	986	27	67		Y	Y	Y	Y	Y	Y	Y	N		10
Rogue Community College	Grants Pass	C,T	St-L	M/W	4,341	65	52	9	Y			Y	Y	Y	Y	N	4	19
Southwestern Oregon Community College	Coos Bay	C,T	St-L	M/W	1,980	51												
Tillamook Bay Community College	Tillamook	C,T	Dist	M/W	299	76												
Treasure Valley Community College	Ontario	C,T	St-L	M/W	1,912	47	37		Y			Y	Y	Y	Y	Y	6	40
Umpqua Community College	Roseburg	C,T	St-L	M/W	2,190	65	52	35			R	Y	Y	Y	Y	N	1	53
Western Culinary Institute	Portland	T	Prop	M/W	1,025													4
Pennsylvania																		
Antonelli Institute	Erdenheim	T	Prop	M/W	189	3												
The Art Institute of Philadelphia	Philadelphia	T,B	Prop	M/W	3,600	28	20		N	Y	Y	Y	Y	Y	Y	Y	2	13
Berks Technical Institute	Wyomissing	C,T	Prop	M/W	650													
Bidwell Training Center	Pittsburgh	T	Ind	M/W	143													1
Bradford School	Pittsburgh	T	Priv		441						Y	Y	Y					9
Bradley Academy for the Visual Arts†	York	T	Prop	M/W	596	7	8		N	Y	Y	Y	Y	Y	Y	N		10
Bucks County Community College	Newtown	C,T	Cou	M/W	9,572	57	34	29	Y	Y	Y	Y	Y	Y	Y	N	8	55
Business Institute of Pennsylvania	Meadville	T	Prop	PW	68													
Business Institute of Pennsylvania	Sharon	T	Prop	PW	106	8	71			Y	Y		Y	Y	N			9
Butler County Community College	Butler	C,T	Cou	M/W	3,809	48												
Cambria-Rowe Business College	Johnstown	C,T	Prop	PW	230		51	3	N	Y	Y		Y	Y	N			5
Career Training Academy	Monroeville	T	Prop	M/W	35													3
Career Training Academy	New Kensington	D,C,T	Prop	M/W														
Career Training Academy	Pittsburgh	T	Prop	M/W	54													2
Commonwealth Technical Institute	Johnstown	T	St	M/W	275				Y	Y	R,S	Y	Y	Y		Y		7
Community College of Allegheny County	Pittsburgh	C,T	Cou	M/W	18,036	59	46	39	Y		R	Y	Y	Y	Y		15	116
Community College of Beaver County	Monaca	C,T	St	M/W	2,530		56		Y		R	Y	Y	Y	Y	N	6	30
Community College of Philadelphia	Philadelphia	C,T	St-L	M/W	23,230		53	73	Y	Y	Y		Y	Y		N	8	54
Consolidated School of Business	Lancaster	T	Prop	PW	173													
Consolidated School of Business	York	T	Prop	PW	176													
Erie Business Center, Main	Erie	T	Prop	M/W	393	29												
Harcum College†	Bryn Mawr	C,T	Ind	PW	573	33												
Harrisburg Area Community College	Harrisburg	C,T	St-L	M/W	18,082	61	42	67	Y		Y	Y	Y	Y	Y	N	11	85
JNA Institute of Culinary Arts	Philadelphia	T	Prop	M/W	65													1
Johnson College†	Scranton	T	Ind	M/W	405													
Katharine Gibbs School	Norristown	T	Prop	M/W	386													7
Keystone College†	La Plume	C,T,B	Ind	M/W	1,708	24	28	71	N		Y	Y	Y	Y	Y	Y	16	65
Lackawanna College	Scranton	C,T	Ind	M/W	1,197	37												
Lancaster General College of Nursing & Health Sciences	Lancaster	T	Ind	M/W	299							Y						5
Laurel Business Institute	Uniontown	C,T	Prop	M/W	305		50		Y		Y	Y	Y	Y	Y	N		28
Lehigh Carbon Community College	Schnecksville	C,T	St-L	M/W	7,076	62	36	49	Y		S	Y	Y	Y	Y	N	18	71
Lehigh Valley College†	Center Valley	T	Prop	M/W	711	29	29		Y	Y	Y		Y	Y	Y	N		14
Luzerne County Community College	Nanticoke	C,T	Cou	M/W	6,170	52												
Manor College*†	Jenkintown	C,T	I-R	M/W	865	50												
Montgomery County Community College	Blue Bell	C,T	Cou	M/W	11,174	56	38	68	Y		S	Y	Y	Y	Y	N	12	53
Newport Business Institute	Lower Burrell	T	Prop	M/W	79													
Newport Business Institute	Williamsport	T	Prop	PW	104	1												
Northampton County Area Community College	Bethlehem	C,T	St-L	M/W	9,488	57	39	72	Y	Y	Y	Y	Y	Y	Y	Y	12	57
North Central Industrial Technical Education Center	Ridgway	T	Prop	M/W	22													2
Oakbridge Academy of Arts	Lower Burrell	C,T	Prop	M/W	66													
Pace Institute	Reading	C,T	Priv	M/W	274		95					Y	Y			N		9
Penn Foster Career School	Scranton	T	Prop	M/W	18,881													
Penn State Beaver	Monaca	C,T,B	St-R	M/W	721	17	10		N		Y		Y	Y	Y	Y	10	118
Penn State Delaware County	Media	T,B	St-R	M/W	1,631	15	10		N	Y	Y	Y	Y	Y	Y	N	10	120
Penn State DuBois	DuBois	C,T,B	St-R	M/W	808	25	32		N	Y	Y	Y	Y	Y	Y	N	7	127
Penn State Fayette, The Eberly Campus	Uniontown	C,T,B	St-R	M/W	1,139	30	38		N	Y	Y	Y	Y	Y	Y	N	11	124
Penn State Hazleton	Hazleton	C,T,B	St-R	M/W	1,142	5	5		N	Y	Y	Y	Y	Y	Y	Y	8	125
Penn State Lehigh Valley	Fogelsville	T,B	St-R	M/W	730	24	14		N		Y	Y	Y	Y	Y	N	13	119
Penn State McKeesport	McKeesport	T,B	St-R	M/W	761	15	8		N	Y	Y	Y	Y	Y	Y	Y	12	119
Penn State Mont Alto	Mont Alto	T,B	St-R	M/W	1,032	25	19		N	Y	Y	Y	Y	Y	Y	Y	10	124
Penn State New Kensington	New Kensington	C,T,B	St-R	M/W	840	26	22		N		Y	Y	Y	Y	Y	N	13	124
Penn State Schuylkill	Schuylkill Haven	C,T,B	St-R	M/W	899	16	15		N		Y	Y	Y	Y	Y	N	8	124
Penn State Shenango	Sharon	C,T,B	St-R	M/W	893	45	51		N		Y	Y	Y	Y	Y	N	7	124
Penn State Wilkes-Barre	Lehman	C,T,B	St-R	M/W	698	17	13		N		Y	Y	Y	Y	Y	Y	11	122
Penn State Worthington Scranton	Dunmore	T,B	St-R	M/W	1,291	19	23		N		Y	Y	Y	Y	Y	N	10	119
Penn State York	York	C,T,B	St-R	M/W	1,437	43	30		N		Y	Y	Y	Y	Y	N	10	126
Pennsylvania Highland Community College	Johnstown	C,T	St-L	M/W	1,300		66		Y		R	Y	Y	Y	Y			22
Pennsylvania Institute of Technology	Media	C,T	Ind	M/W	384	30												

Two-Year Colleges At-a-Glance

This chart includes the names and locations of accredited two-year colleges in the United States and U.S. territories and shows institutions' responses to the *Peterson's Annual Survey of Undergraduate Institutions*. If an institution submitted incomplete data, one or more columns opposite the institution's name is blank. An asterisk after the school name denotes a *Special Message* following the college's profile, and a dagger indicates that the institution has one or more entries in the *College Close-Ups* section. If a school does not appear, it did not report any of the information.

Y—Yes; N—No; R—Recommended; S—For Some

Name	City	Degrees Awarded	Institutional Control	Student Body	Undergraduate Enrollment	Percent Attending Part-Time	Percent 25 Years of Age or Older	Percent of Grads Going on to Four-Year Colleges	Open Admissions	High School Equivalency Certificate Accepted	High School Transcript Required	Need-Based Aid Available	Part-Time Jobs Available	Career Counseling Available	Job Placement Services Available	College Housing Available	Number of Sports Offered	Number of Majors Offered
Pittsburgh Institute of Aeronautics	Pittsburgh	C,T	Ind	PM	571		30		Y	Y	R			Y	Y	N		4
Pittsburgh Institute of Mortuary Science, Incorporated	Pittsburgh	C,T	Ind	M/W	192	6												
The PJA School	Upper Darby	T	Prop	M/W	230	54								Y	Y	N		3
Rosedale Technical Institute	Pittsburgh	T	Ind	PM	200													
Schuylkill Institute of Business and Technology	Pottsville	C,T	Prop	M/W	136													
South Hills School of Business & Technology	State College	C,T	Prop	M/W	663	8												
Triangle Tech, Inc.–DuBois School	DuBois	T	Prop	PM	246													
Triangle Tech, Inc.–Greensburg School	Greensburg	T	Prop	PM	271													
Triangle Tech, Inc.–Sunbury School	Sunbury	T	Prop	M/W	155													1
Tri-State Business Institute	Erie	T	Priv		475													10
University of Pittsburgh at Titusville	Titusville	C,T	St-R	M/W	541			100	N	Y	Y	Y	Y	Y	Y	Y	11	8
Valley Forge Military College*†	Wayne	C	Ind	M/W	165													
Westmoreland County Community College	Youngwood	C,T	Cou	M/W	5,986	56	44			Y	Y			Y	Y	Y	N	12	53
The Williamson Free School of Mechanical Trades	Media	T	Ind	M	251	0	12		N	Y	Y	Y		Y	Y	Y	N	14	8
Winner Institute of Arts & Sciences	Transfer	T	Ind	M/W	61													1
WyoTech	Blairsville	T	Prop	PM														

Puerto Rico

Name	City	Degrees Awarded	Institutional Control	Student Body	Undergraduate Enrollment	Percent Attending Part-Time	Percent 25 Years of Age or Older	Percent of Grads Going on to Four-Year Colleges	Open Admissions	High School Equivalency Certificate Accepted	High School Transcript Required	Need-Based Aid Available	Part-Time Jobs Available	Career Counseling Available	Job Placement Services Available	College Housing Available	Number of Sports Offered	Number of Majors Offered
Centro de Estudios Multidisciplinarios	San Juan	T	Ind	M/W	1,687													3
Colegio Universitario de San Juan	San Juan	T	City	M/W	961													10
Colegio Universitario de San Juan	San Juan	C,T,B	City	M/W	777	24	40		Y	Y	Y	Y	Y	Y	Y		7	7
ICPR Junior College–Hato Rey Campus	San Juan	T	Prop	M/W	371													9
International Junior College	Santurce	T	Prop		207					Y		Y	Y					5
Puerto Rico Technical Junior College	San Juan	T	Prop	M/W	137					Y								1
Universidad Central del Caribe	Bayamón	T,M,F	Ind	M/W	81													1
University of Puerto Rico at Carolina	Carolina	C,T,B	Com	M/W	3,879	30	5		N	Y	Y		Y	Y	Y		6	15

Rhode Island

Name	City	Degrees Awarded	Institutional Control	Student Body	Undergraduate Enrollment	Percent Attending Part-Time	Percent 25 Years of Age or Older	Percent of Grads Going on to Four-Year Colleges	Open Admissions	High School Equivalency Certificate Accepted	High School Transcript Required	Need-Based Aid Available	Part-Time Jobs Available	Career Counseling Available	Job Placement Services Available	College Housing Available	Number of Sports Offered	Number of Majors Offered
Community College of Rhode Island	Warwick	C,T	St	M/W	16,373	63	38		Y	Y		Y	Y	Y	Y	N	10	43
New England Institute of Technology	Warwick	C,T,B	Ind	M/W	3,009	13			Y	Y		Y	Y	Y	Y	N		17

South Carolina

Name	City	Degrees Awarded	Institutional Control	Student Body	Undergraduate Enrollment	Percent Attending Part-Time	Percent 25 Years of Age or Older	Percent of Grads Going on to Four-Year Colleges	Open Admissions	High School Equivalency Certificate Accepted	High School Transcript Required	Need-Based Aid Available	Part-Time Jobs Available	Career Counseling Available	Job Placement Services Available	College Housing Available	Number of Sports Offered	Number of Majors Offered
Aiken Technical College	Aiken	C,T	St-L	M/W	2,516	44			Y		Y	Y	Y	Y	Y	N		17
Central Carolina Technical College	Sumter	C,T	St	M/W	3,244	71	46	11	Y	Y	Y	Y	Y	Y	Y	N		
Clinton Junior College	Rock Hill	T	I-R	M/W	123													2
Denmark Technical College	Denmark	C,T	St	M/W	1,408	31												
Florence-Darlington Technical College	Florence	C,T	St	M/W	4,041	47			Y		S	Y	Y	Y	Y	N		29
Forrest Junior College	Anderson	C,T	Prop	PW	231		35	2		Y	Y	Y	Y	Y	Y	N		10
Greenville Technical College	Greenville	C,T	St	M/W	13,000		42		Y	Y	Y	Y	Y	Y	N	4	33
Horry-Georgetown Technical College	Conway	C,T	St-L	M/W	5,362	54												
ITT Technical Institute	Greenville	T,B	Prop	M/W					N	Y	Y	Y	Y	Y	N		9
Midlands Technical College	Columbia	C,T	St-L	M/W	10,849	55	36	50	Y	Y	R	Y	Y	Y	N	4	49
Northeastern Technical College	Cheraw	C,T	St-L	M/W	964	51	45	5	Y	Y	Y	Y	Y	Y	N		11
Piedmont Technical College	Greenwood	C,T	St	M/W	4,911		38		Y	Y	Y	Y	Y	Y	N	4	35
Spartanburg Methodist College	Spartanburg	C,T	I-R	M/W	779	8												
Spartanburg Technical College	Spartanburg	C,T	St	M/W	4,409													
Trident Technical College	Charleston	C,T	St-L	M/W	11,808	56	13		Y	Y	S	Y	Y	Y	N		40
University of South Carolina Lancaster	Lancaster	C,T	St	M/W	1,202		19	42	Y	Y	Y	Y	Y	Y	N	5	6
University of South Carolina Sumter	Sumter	C	St	M/W	1,098	47												
University of South Carolina Union	Union	C	St	M/W	321	50												
York Technical College	Rock Hill	C,T	St	M/W	4,263	52	39		Y		S	Y	Y	Y	N		35

South Dakota

Name	City	Degrees Awarded	Institutional Control	Student Body	Undergraduate Enrollment	Percent Attending Part-Time	Percent 25 Years of Age or Older	Percent of Grads Going on to Four-Year Colleges	Open Admissions	High School Equivalency Certificate Accepted	High School Transcript Required	Need-Based Aid Available	Part-Time Jobs Available	Career Counseling Available	Job Placement Services Available	College Housing Available	Number of Sports Offered	Number of Majors Offered
Kilian Community College	Sioux Falls	C,T	Ind	M/W	477	81	60		Y	Y		Y	Y	Y	Y	N		13
National American University	Ellsworth AFB	T	Prop	M/W	209													2
Southeast Technical Institute	Sioux Falls	T	St	M/W	2,115	17	21		N	Y	Y	Y	Y	Y	Y	Y	2	50

Tennessee

Name	City	Degrees Awarded	Institutional Control	Student Body	Undergraduate Enrollment	Percent Attending Part-Time	Percent 25 Years of Age or Older	Percent of Grads Going on to Four-Year Colleges	Open Admissions	High School Equivalency Certificate Accepted	High School Transcript Required	Need-Based Aid Available	Part-Time Jobs Available	Career Counseling Available	Job Placement Services Available	College Housing Available	Number of Sports Offered	Number of Majors Offered
Chattanooga State Technical Community College	Chattanooga	C,T	St	M/W	8,060	56	41		Y	Y	Y	Y	Y	Y	Y	N	3	63
Cleveland State Community College	Cleveland	C,T	St	M/W	2,947	47	42	44	Y	Y	Y	Y	Y	Y	Y	N	10	11
Concorde Career College	Memphis	T	Prop	M/W	1,049						Y							1
Dyersburg State Community College	Dyersburg	C,T	St	M/W	2,586	49	39		Y	Y	Y	Y	Y	Y	Y	N	4	8
Fountainhead College of Technology	Knoxville	C,T,B	Prop	M/W	120		20		Y	Y	R	Y		Y	Y	N		6
High-Tech Institute	Memphis	T	Prop	M/W	1,101													5
High-Tech Institute	Nashville	T	Prop	M/W	1,319													8
ITT Technical Institute	Cordova	T,B	Prop	M/W					N	Y	Y		Y	Y	Y	N		13
ITT Technical Institute	Knoxville	T,B	Prop	M/W					N	Y	Y	Y	Y	Y	Y	N		15
ITT Technical Institute	Nashville	T,B	Prop	M/W					N	Y	Y	Y	Y	Y	Y	N		15
Jackson State Community College	Jackson	C,T	St	M/W	4,106	45	41	43	Y	Y	S	Y	Y	Y	Y	Y	8	15
John A. Gupton College	Nashville	C,T	Ind	M/W	97	6	22	8	N	Y		Y		Y	Y	Y		1
Mid-America Baptist Theological Seminary	Cordova	T,M,D,F	I-R	PM	51	43			Y	Y	S		Y					1
Miller-Motte Technical College	Clarksville	T	Prop	M/W	516							Y	Y					12
Motlow State Community College	Tullahoma	C,T	St	M/W	3,833	46	30	64	Y	Y	Y	Y	Y	Y	N	9	4
Nashville Auto Diesel College	Nashville	T	Prop	PM	1,306													
North Central Institute	Clarksville	T	Prop	PM	130	60												
Northeast State Technical Community College	Blountville	C,T	St	M/W	5,154	46	47	90	Y	Y		Y	Y	Y	Y	N	3	22
Nossi College of Art	Goodlettsville	T	Ind	M/W	250		70		N	Y		Y						2
Pellissippi State Technical Community College	Knoxville	C,T	St	M/W	7,686	49												

This chart includes the names and locations of accredited two-year colleges in the United States and U.S. territories and shows institutions' responses to the *Peterson's Annual Survey of Undergraduate Institutions*. If an institution submitted incomplete data, one or more columns opposite the institution's name is blank.
An asterisk after the school name denotes a *Special Message* following the college's profile, and a dagger indicates that the institution has one or more entries in the *College Close-Ups* section. If a school does not appear, it did not report any of the information.

Y—Yes; N—No; R—Recommended; S—For Some

Institution	Location	Degrees Awarded	Institutional Control	Student Body	Undergrad Enrollment	% Attending Part-Time	% 25 Yrs or Older	% Grads to 4-Yr	HS Equiv Cert Accepted	Open Admissions	HS Transcript Required	Need-Based Aid Required	Part-Time Jobs Available	Career Counseling Available	Job Placement Services Available	College Housing Available	Number of Sports Offered	Number of Majors Offered
Remington College–Nashville Campus	Nashville	T	Prop	M/W	276													4
Roane State Community College	Harriman	C,T	St	M/W	5,353	44	39		Y	Y	Y		Y	Y	Y	N	9	39
Southwest Tennessee Community College	Memphis	C,T	St	M/W	11,556	51												
Vatterott College	Memphis	T	Prop	M/W	233													5
Volunteer State Community College	Gallatin	C,T	St	M/W	7,370	52	36	14	Y	Y		Y	Y	Y	Y	N	3	11
Texas																		
Amarillo College	Amarillo	C,T	St-L	M/W	10,354		38	52	Y		Y	Y	Y	Y	Y	Y	3	83
Angelina College	Lufkin	C,T	St-L	M/W	4,976		33		Y		Y	Y	Y	Y	Y	Y	8	58
Austin Community College	Austin	C,T	Dist	M/W	31,908	72												
Blinn College	Brenham	C,T	St-L	M/W	14,016	46		14	Y		Y	Y	Y	Y	Y	Y	10	34
Brazosport College	Lake Jackson	C,T	St-L	M/W	3,503	52												
Brookhaven College	Farmers Branch	C,T	Cou	M/W	10,269	91	46		Y		Y		Y	Y	Y	N	9	10
Cedar Valley College	Lancaster	C,T	St	M/W	4,504		41		Y		R	Y	Y	Y	Y	N	5	16
Center for Advanced Legal Studies	Houston	T	Prop		53							Y						1
Central Texas College	Killeen	C,T	St-L	M/W	17,726	82	50	30	Y		Y	Y	Y	Y	Y	Y	10	48
Cisco Junior College	Cisco	C,T	St-L	M/W	3,525		45		Y		Y	Y	Y	Y	Y	Y	7	35
Clarendon College	Clarendon	C,T	St-L	M/W	1,102	48	20		Y		Y	Y	Y	Y		Y	6	42
Coastal Bend College	Beeville	C,T	Cou	M/W	3,267	63	31		Y	Y	Y	Y	Y	Y	Y	Y	13	67
College of the Mainland	Texas City	C,T	St-L	M/W	3,849		41		Y	Y		S	Y	Y	Y	N	11	25
Collin County Community College District	Plano	C,T	St-L	M/W	19,332	61	35		Y		Y	Y	Y	Y	Y	N	3	31
Culinary Institute Alain & Marie LeNotre	Houston	T	Prop	M/W	22													3
Dallas Institute of Funeral Service	Dallas	C,T	Ind	M/W	247													
Eastfield College	Mesquite	C,T	St-L	M/W	12,111	81												
El Centro College	Dallas	C,T	Cou	M/W	6,281	77	56	40	Y	Y		S	Y	Y	Y	N	4	46
Everest College	Arlington	T	Prop	M/W	838							Y						1
Everest College	Dallas	T	Prop	M/W	748													1
Everest College	Fort Worth	T	Prop	M/W	381													1
Galveston College	Galveston	C,T	St-L	M/W	2,230	62												
Grayson County College	Denison	C,T	St-L	M/W	3,344		53		Y	Y			Y	Y	Y		Y	5	39
Hallmark Institute of Aeronautics	San Antonio	T	Priv	M/W					Y			Y						2
Houston Community College System	Houston	C,T	St-L	M/W	42,526	69		25	Y			S	Y	Y	Y	N		65
Howard College	Big Spring	C,T	St-L	M/W	2,725	57												
ITT Technical Institute	Arlington	T	Prop	M/W					N	Y	Y	Y	Y	Y	Y	N		4
ITT Technical Institute	Austin	T	Prop	M/W					N	Y	Y	Y	Y	Y	Y	N		5
ITT Technical Institute	Houston	T	Prop	M/W					N	Y	Y	Y	Y	Y	Y	N		6
ITT Technical Institute	Houston	T	Prop	M/W	585				N	Y	Y	Y	Y	Y	Y	N		3
ITT Technical Institute	Richardson	T	Prop	M/W					N	Y	Y	Y	Y	Y	Y	N		6
ITT Technical Institute	San Antonio	T	Prop	M/W					N	Y	Y	Y	Y	Y	Y	N		5
ITT Technical Institute	Webster	T	Prop	M/W					N	Y	Y	Y	Y	Y	Y	N		6
Jacksonville College	Jacksonville	C,T	I-R	M/W	300	27												
KD Studio	Dallas	T	Prop	M/W	152													
Kingwood College	Kingwood	C,T	St-L	M/W	6,842	81												
Lamar Institute of Technology	Beaumont	T	St	M/W	2,711									Y	Y				26
Lamar State College–Orange	Orange	C,T	St	M/W	2,143	57												
Lamar State College–Port Arthur	Port Arthur	C,T	St	M/W	2,530	61												
Laredo Community College	Laredo	C,T	St-L	M/W	8,152	63	34		Y		Y	Y	Y	Y	Y	Y	7	29
Lee College	Baytown	C,T	Dist	M/W	5,347	66	50		Y		S	Y	Y	Y	N	7	60
McLennan Community College	Waco	C,T	Cou	M/W	7,794	56	45		Y	Y	Y	Y	Y	Y	Y	N	7	26
Midland College	Midland	C,T,B	St-L	M/W	5,531	63												
Montgomery College	Conroe	C,T	St-L	M/W	8,306	64												
Mountain View College	Dallas	C,T	St-L	M/W	6,496													
Navarro College	Corsicana	C,T	St-L	M/W	4,411	43	35		Y	Y	Y	Y	Y	Y	Y	Y	9	56
North Central Texas College	Gainesville	C,T	Cou	M/W	6,183		33		Y	Y	Y	Y	Y		Y	Y	8	43
North Lake College	Irving	C,T	Cou	M/W	9,397	69	37		Y	Y		R	Y		Y	N	4	15
Northwest Vista College	San Antonio	C,T	St-L	M/W	8,519		74					R		Y	Y	N		16
Odessa College	Odessa	C,T	St-L	M/W	4,647	66	40	42	Y		Y	Y	Y	Y	Y	Y	10	60
Palo Alto College	San Antonio	C,T	St-L	M/W	8,038		33		Y	Y		Y	Y	Y	Y	N	4	38
Panola College	Carthage	C,T	St-L	M/W	1,871	54	22		Y		R,S	Y	Y	Y	Y	Y	7	5
Paris Junior College	Paris	C,T	St-L	M/W	4,118	65												
Ranger College	Ranger	C,T	St-R	M/W	843							Y	Y				Y	8	6
Remington College–Dallas Campus	Garland	T	Prop	M/W	861													6
Remington College–Fort Worth Campus	Fort Worth	T	Prop	M/W	922													8
Richland College	Dallas	C,T	St-L	M/W	14,128		47		Y		S	Y	Y	Y	Y	N	13	16
St. Philip's College	San Antonio	C,T	Dist	M/W	9,264	58	47		Y	Y	Y	Y	Y	Y	Y	N	6	73
San Antonio College	San Antonio	C,T	St-L	M/W	21,800	62	36		Y	Y	R,S		Y	Y	Y	N	5	44
San Jacinto College District	Pasadena		St-L	M/W	23,753		24				Y			Y	Y	N		
South Plains College	Levelland	C,T	St-L	M/W	9,045	52	39	90	Y		Y	Y	Y	Y	Y	Y	10	59
South Texas College	McAllen	C,T,B	Dist	M/W	18,460	64	37		Y	Y	Y	Y	Y	Y	Y	N	10	26
Southwest Texas Junior College	Uvalde	C,T	St-L	M/W	4,350		34	80	Y	Y		Y	Y	Y	Y	Y	7	14
Tarrant County College District	Fort Worth	C,T	Cou	M/W	34,892	65												
Temple College	Temple	C,T	Dist	M/W	4,279	61	33		Y	Y	S	Y	Y	Y	Y	Y	8	20
Texarkana College	Texarkana	C,T	St-L	M/W	3,895	60	42	25	Y	Y	Y	Y	Y	Y	Y	Y	7	34
Texas State Technical College–Marshall	Marshall	T	St		565													
Texas State Technical College Waco	Waco	C,T	St	M/W	4,452	33												12
Texas State Technical College West Texas	Sweetwater	T	St	M/W	1,537	42	33		Y		Y	Y	Y	Y	Y	Y	11	13
Tomball College	Tomball	C,T	St-L	M/W	7,787	82	32		Y		Y	R,S	Y	Y	Y	Y		10
Trinity Valley Community College	Athens	C,T	St-L	M/W	5,821	58										N		10
Tyler Junior College	Tyler	C,T	St-L	M/W	9,591		50		Y		Y	Y	Y	Y	Y	Y	9	59

This chart includes the names and locations of accredited two-year colleges in the United States and U.S. territories and shows institutions' responses to the *Peterson's Annual Survey of Undergraduate Institutions*. If an institution submitted incomplete data, one or more columns opposite the institution's name is blank.

An asterisk after the school name denotes a *Special Message* following the college's profile, and a dagger indicates that the institution has one or more entries in the *College Close-Ups* section. If a school does not appear, it did not report any of the information.

Column key:
- **Degrees Awarded:** College Transfer Associate (C), Terminal Associate (T), Bachelor's (B), Master's (M), Doctoral (D), First Professional (P)
- **Institutional Control:** County, District, City; Federal; Independent; Independent-Religious; Proprietary; State; State and Local; State-Commonwealth; State-Related; Territory
- **Student Body:** Men, Primarily Men, Women, Primarily Women, Coed

Y—Yes; N—No; R—Recommended; S—For Some

College	Location	Degrees Awarded	Institutional Control	Student Body	Undergraduate Enrollment	% Attending Part-Time	% 25 Years of Age or Older	% of Grads Going on to Four-Year Colleges	HS Equivalency Certificate Accepted	HS Transcript Required	Open Admissions	Need-Based Aid Available	Part-Time Jobs Available	Career Counseling Available	Job Placement Services Available	College Housing Available	Number of Sports Offered	Number of Majors Offered
Vernon College	Vernon	C,T	St-L	M/W	2,270	47			Y	Y	Y	Y	Y	Y	Y	N	9	16
Victoria College	Victoria	C,T	Cou	M/W	4,244	49			Y	Y	Y	Y	Y	Y	Y	N	2	16
Virginia College at Austin	Austin	T	Prop	M/W	769													15
Weatherford College	Weatherford	C,T	St-L	M/W	4,552													
Western Technical College	El Paso	C,T	Priv	M/W	825													
Western Texas College	Snyder	C,T	St-L	M/W	1,685	39			Y	Y	Y	Y	Y	Y	Y	Y	11	22
Westwood College–Dallas†	Dallas	T	Prop	M/W	404	2												
Westwood College–Fort Worth†	Euless	T	Prop	M/W	472	21												
Westwood College–Houston South Campus†	Houston	T	Prop	M/W	16													
Wharton County Junior College	Wharton	C,T	St-L	M/W	6,029													
Utah																		
College of Eastern Utah	Price	C,T	St	M/W	2,294	43												
Dixie State College of Utah	St. George	C,T,B	St	M/W	5,704	43	22		Y	Y	Y	Y	Y	Y	Y	Y	9	79
ITT Technical Institute	Murray	T,B	Prop	M/W					N	Y	Y	Y	Y	Y	Y	N		13
LDS Business College	Salt Lake City	C,T	I-R	M/W	1,317	23			Y	Y	Y		Y	Y	Y	Y		20
Provo College	Provo	T	Prop	M/W	656													13
Salt Lake Community College	Salt Lake City	C,T	St	M/W	24,241	67	40		Y			Y	Y	Y	Y	N	6	63
Snow College	Ephraim	C,T	St	M/W	3,333	26												
Utah Career College	West Jordan	C	Prop	M/W	570	73												
Vermont																		
Community College of Vermont	Waterbury	C,T	St	M/W	6,048	60	45		Y	Y		Y			Y	N		15
Landmark College†	Putney	C,T	Ind	M/W	460	33	4		N	Y		Y	Y			Y	13	1
New England Culinary Institute	Montpelier	T,B	Prop	M/W	569	32			N	Y	Y	Y	Y	Y	Y	Y		4
New England Culinary Institute at Essex	Essex Junction	C,T,B	Prop	M/W	501													
Virginia																		
ACT College	Arlington	T	Prop	M/W	482													3
Advanced Technology Institute	Virginia Beach	T	Prop	M/W	697													2
Aviation Institute of Maintenance–Manassas	Manassas	T	Prop															
Aviation Institute of Maintenance–Virginia Beach	Virginia Beach	T	Prop															
Beta Tech	Richmond	T	Prop		306													3
Blue Ridge Community College	Weyers Cave	C,T	St	M/W	3,804	60												
Bryant and Stratton College, Richmond	Richmond	T,B	Prop	M/W	421	67												
Central Virginia Community College	Lynchburg	C,T	St	M/W	4,741	42	24		Y		S	Y	Y	Y	Y	N		23
Dabney S. Lancaster Community College	Clifton Forge	C,T	St	M/W	1,453	59	60		Y	Y		Y	Y	Y	Y	N	9	17
Danville Community College	Danville	C,T	St	M/W	3,884	58			Y	Y	Y	Y	Y	Y	Y	N	6	9
Eastern Shore Community College	Melfa	C,T	St	M/W	807	45	50		Y	Y	Y	Y	Y	Y	Y	Y		9
ECPI College of Technology	Virginia Beach	T,B	Prop	M/W	6,501	3	50		N	Y		Y	Y	Y	Y			20
ECPI Technical College	Richmond	T,B	Prop	M/W	869		46		N	Y	Y	Y	Y	Y	Y	N		25
ECPI Technical College	Roanoke	T,B	Prop	M/W	358		47		N	Y		Y	Y	Y	Y	N		21
Germanna Community College	Locust Grove	C,T	St	M/W	5,167	69	35	27	Y		S	Y	Y	Y	Y	N	7	9
ITT Technical Institute	Chantilly	T,B	Prop	M/W					N	Y	Y	Y	Y	Y	Y	N		13
ITT Technical Institute	Norfolk	T,B	Prop	M/W					N	Y	Y	Y	Y	Y	Y	N		12
ITT Technical Institute	Richmond	T,B	Prop	M/W					N	Y	Y	Y	Y	Y	Y	N		11
ITT Technical Institute	Springfield	T,B	Prop	M/W					N	Y	Y	Y	Y	Y	Y	N		10
John Tyler Community College	Chester	C,T	St	M/W	7,165	75	41	12	Y		R	Y	Y	Y	Y	N	4	14
Lord Fairfax Community College	Middletown	C,T	St	M/W	5,492	72												
Medical Careers Institute	Newport News	T	Prop	M/W	1,891													
New River Community College	Dublin	C,T	St	M/W	4,345	54	40		Y		S	Y	Y	Y	Y	N	10	30
Paul D. Camp Community College	Franklin	C,T	St	M/W	1,560	55	45		Y	Y	Y	Y	Y	Y	Y	N		6
Piedmont Virginia Community College	Charlottesville	C,T	St	M/W	4,451	77	38	45	Y	Y	S	Y	Y	Y	Y	N	11	30
Rappahannock Community College	Glenns	C,T	St-R	M/W	2,824	36			Y			Y	Y	Y	Y	N	4	9
Richard Bland College of The College of William and Mary	Petersburg	C	St	M/W	1,437	43												
Southside Virginia Community College	Alberta	C,T	St	M/W	4,686	71	46		Y	Y		Y	Y	Y	Y	N	5	14
Southwest Virginia Community College	Richlands	C,T	St	M/W	3,580	64	56		Y	Y	Y	Y	Y	Y	Y	N	10	18
TESST College of Technology	Alexandria	T	Prop	M/W	324													3
Thomas Nelson Community College	Hampton	C,T	St	M/W	8,595	69			Y			Y	Y	Y	Y	N		
Tidewater Community College	Norfolk	C,T	St	M/W	24,938	48	41		Y			Y	Y	Y	Y	N	5	26
Tidewater Tech	Virginia Beach	T	Prop	M/W	1,192													8
Virginia Highlands Community College	Abingdon	C,T	St	M/W	2,452	52	65		Y		Y	Y	Y	Y	Y	N	7	19
Virginia Western Community College	Roanoke	C,T	St	M/W	7,636	46			Y	Y	R,S	Y	Y	Y	Y	N	2	25
Wytheville Community College	Wytheville	C,T	St	M/W	2,450	54			Y			Y	Y	Y	Y	N	6	22
Washington																		
Bellingham Technical College	Bellingham	T	St	M/W	4,159	52			Y			Y	Y	Y	Y			6
Big Bend Community College	Moses Lake	C,T	St	M/W	2,697	30			Y		S	Y	Y	Y	Y	Y	4	14
Cascadia Community College	Bothell	C,T	St	M/W	1,950	52	24		Y							N		3
Centralia College	Centralia	C,T	St	M/W	3,808	60	64		Y	Y	Y	Y	Y	Y	Y	N	5	66
Clark College	Vancouver	C,T	St	M/W	9,906	57	71	67	Y		S	Y	Y	Y	Y	N	9	35
Columbia Basin College	Pasco	C,T	St	M/W	5,837	58	57	50	Y	Y		Y	Y	Y	Y	N	9	27
Crown College	Tacoma	C,T,B	Prop	M/W	218													
Edmonds Community College	Lynnwood	C,T	St-L	M/W	7,581	55												
Everett Community College	Everett	C,T	St	M/W	5,780	47	38		Y		R	Y	Y	Y	Y	N	12	71
Grays Harbor College	Aberdeen	C,T	St	M/W	2,156	52	51	40	Y	Y	R	Y	Y	Y	Y	N	5	18
Highline Community College*	Des Moines	C,T	St	M/W	6,372	49												
ITT Technical Institute	Bothell	T,B	Prop	M/W					N	Y	Y	Y	Y	Y	Y	N		14

This chart includes the names and locations of accredited two-year colleges in the United States and U.S. territories and shows institutions' responses to the *Peterson's Annual Survey of Undergraduate Institutions*. If an institution submitted incomplete data, one or more columns opposite the institution's name is blank. An asterisk after the school name denotes a *Special Message* following the college's profile, and a dagger indicates that the institution has one or more entries in the *College Close-Ups* section. If a school does not appear, it did not report any of the information.

Column legend — Degrees Awarded: College Transfer Associate (C), Terminal Associate (T), Bachelor's (B), Master's (M), Doctoral (D), First Professional (P). Institutional Control: County, District City, Federal, State and Local, State-Related, Independent, Independent-Religious, State, Commonwealth, Proprietary, Territory. Student Body: Men, Primarily Men, Women, Primarily Women, Coed. Service columns: Y—Yes; N—No; R—Recommended; S—For Some.

Institution	Location	Degrees Awarded	Institutional Control	Student Body	Undergrad Enrollment	% Attending Part-Time	% 25 or Older	% Grads to Four-Year	HS Equiv. Accepted	HS Transcript Required	Open Admissions	Need-Based Aid	Part-Time Jobs	Career Counseling	Job Placement	College Housing	Sports Offered	Majors Offered
ITT Technical Institute	Seattle	T,B	Prop	M/W					N	Y		Y	Y	Y	Y	N			13
ITT Technical Institute	Spokane	T,B	Prop	M/W					N	Y		Y	Y	Y	Y	N			11
Lower Columbia College	Longview	C,T	St	M/W	3,268	46	59		Y			R		Y	Y	N		5	79
North Seattle Community College	Seattle	C,T	St	M/W	6,210	70	54	40	Y				Y	Y	Y	N	1	27
Northwest Aviation College	Auburn	C,T	Priv	M/W	50					Y			Y	Y	Y			1
Northwest Indian College	Bellingham	C,T	Fed	M/W	1,189													
Olympic College	Bremerton	C,T	St	M/W	6,765	49	49	31	Y			S		Y	Y	N	5	46
Peninsula College	Port Angeles	C,T	St	M/W	3,948		41		Y			S		Y	Y	N	11	19
Pierce College	Puyallup	C,T	St	M/W	13,294		56		Y					Y	Y	N	5	20
Renton Technical College	Renton	T	St	M/W	9,301		71		Y			S		Y	Y	N		19
Seattle Central Community College	Seattle	C,T	St	M/W	9,418				Y					Y	Y	N		
Skagit Valley College	Mount Vernon	C,T	St	M/W	6,858		68		Y			S		Y	Y	Y	12	65
South Seattle Community College	Seattle	C,T	St	M/W	6,769		54		Y					Y	Y	N	2	28
Spokane Community College	Spokane	C,T	St	M/W	5,874	27	40		Y	Y		R		Y	Y	N	12	53
Spokane Falls Community College	Spokane	C,T	St	M/W	5,445	30	19		Y	Y		R		Y	Y	N	11	31
Wenatchee Valley College	Wenatchee	C,T	St-L	M/W	4,046		54		Y			S		Y	Y	Y	13	34
Yakima Valley Community College	Yakima	C,T	St	M/W	6,225													
West Virginia																		
Blue Ridge Community and Technical College	Martinsburg	C,T	Cou	M/W	1,953													
Eastern West Virginia Community and Technical College	Moorefield	C,T	St	M/W	786	91	0	50						Y		N		8
Marshall Community and Technical College	Huntington	T	Cou	M/W	2,579	51	55		Y	Y	Y			Y	Y	Y		23
Mountain State College	Parkersburg	T	Prop	PW	166		55		N	Y		Y	Y	Y	Y	Y		6
Potomac State College of West Virginia University	Keyser	C,T	St	M/W	1,330		13	80	Y	Y		Y	Y	Y	Y	Y	9	53
Southern West Virginia Community and Technical College	Mount Gay	C,T	St	M/W	1,982	37												
Valley College	Martinsburg	T	Prop	PW	47													
West Virginia Business College	Wheeling	T	Prop	PW	78													
West Virginia Northern Community College	Wheeling	C,T	St	M/W	2,842	50												
West Virginia State Community and Technical College	Institute	C,T	Cou	M/W	1,717	38	51					Y		Y	Y	Y		20
West Virginia University at Parkersburg	Parkersburg	C,T,B	St	M/W	3,884	43	45	18	Y	Y		S		Y	Y	N	10	22
Wisconsin																		
Bryant and Stratton College	Milwaukee	T,B	Prop	M/W	488													
Chippewa Valley Technical College	Eau Claire	T	Dist	M/W	16,100		50		Y	Y		Y	Y	Y	Y	N		34
College of Menominee Nation	Keshena	C,T	Ind	M/W	499				Y	Y				Y	Y	N		8
Fox Valley Technical College	Appleton	C,T	St-L	M/W	7,462	71	50		Y			Y	Y	Y	Y	N	7	35
Gateway Technical College	Kenosha	T	St-L	M/W	6,816	81	50		Y			S	Y	Y	Y	N		41
Herzing College	Madison	C,T,B	Prop	PM	650			20	Y	Y		Y	Y	Y	Y	N		5
ITT Technical Institute	Green Bay	T,B	Prop	M/W					N	Y		Y	Y	Y	Y	N		14
ITT Technical Institute	Greenfield	T,B	Prop	M/W	548				N	Y		Y	Y	Y	Y	N		11
Lac Courte Oreilles Ojibwa Community College	Hayward	C,T	Fed	M/W	505	42												
Lakeshore Technical College	Cleveland	C,T	St-L	M/W	2,789	75	54		Y			S	Y	Y	Y	N		21
Madison Area Technical College	Madison	C,T	Dist	M/W	13,479		50		Y			S	Y	Y	Y	N	9	47
Madison Media Institute	Madison	T	Prop	M/W	133													4
Mid-State Technical College	Wisconsin Rapids	C,T	St-L	M/W	10,737		51		Y			Y	Y	Y	Y	N	5	21
Moraine Park Technical College	Fond du Lac	C,T	St-L	M/W	7,509	84												
Nicolet Area Technical College	Rhinelander	C,T	St-L	M/W	1,600		64	50	Y	Y		Y	Y	Y	Y	N	6	21
University of Wisconsin–Baraboo/Sauk County	Baraboo	C,T	St	M/W	553	16		80	N		Y	Y	Y	Y		N	9	1
University of Wisconsin–Fond du Lac	Fond du Lac	C	St	M/W	716	37	16		N		Y	Y	Y	Y		N	7	1
University of Wisconsin–Fox Valley	Menasha	C,T	St	M/W	1,797				N		Y	Y	Y	Y	Y	N	4	1
University of Wisconsin–Manitowoc	Manitowoc	C,T	St	M/W	588		26	90	N		Y	Y	Y	Y	Y	N	5	1
University of Wisconsin–Marshfield/Wood County	Marshfield	C,T	St	M/W	643		25	98	N		Y	Y	Y	Y		N	9	1
University of Wisconsin–Richland	Richland Center	C	St	M/W	464	33										N		1
University of Wisconsin–Washington County	West Bend	C	St	M/W	951	30	16	55	N		Y	Y		Y	Y	N	7	1
University of Wisconsin–Waukesha	Waukesha	C	St	M/W	2,020		16	95	N		Y	Y	Y	Y	Y	N	9	1
Waukesha County Technical College	Pewaukee	T	St-L	M/W	7,123	75	48		Y					Y		N	7	34
Western Technical College	La Crosse	C,T	Dist	M/W	4,765													
Wisconsin Indianhead Technical College	Shell Lake	T	Dist	M/W	3,533	56												
Wyoming																		
Casper College	Casper	C,T	Dist	M/W	4,285	56												
Central Wyoming College	Riverton	C,T	St-L	M/W	1,711	60	26	17	Y	Y		R	Y	Y	Y	Y	12	41
Eastern Wyoming College	Torrington	C,T	St-L	M/W	1,346	61												
Laramie County Community College	Cheyenne	C,T	St	M/W	4,584	61	39	54	Y	Y		Y	Y	Y	Y	Y	10	78
Sheridan College–Sheridan and Gillette	Sheridan	C,T	St-L	M/W	3,136	67	37		Y	Y		R,S	Y	Y	Y	Y	8	42
Western Wyoming Community College	Rock Springs	C,T	St-L	M/W	2,698	61	48	66	Y	Y		Y	Y	Y	Y	Y	15	86
OTHER COUNTRIES																		
Marshall Islands																		
College of the Marshall Islands	Majuro	T	St		634									Y	Y	Y		5
Federated States of Micronesia																		
College of Micronesia–FSM	Kolonia Pohnpei	C,T	Terr	M/W	2,283		8		N	Y		Y	Y	Y	Y	Y	7	18
Palau																		
Palau Community College	Koror	C,T	Terr	M/W	731	34	33		Y			Y	Y	Y	Y	Y	7	14

Profiles of Two-Year

COLLEGES

U.S. AND U.S. TERRITORIES

ALABAMA

ALABAMA SOUTHERN COMMUNITY COLLEGE
Monroeville, Alabama   www.ascc.edu/

Director of Admissions Ms. Jana S. Horton, Registrar, Alabama Southern Community College, PO Box 2000, Monroeville, AL 36461. *Phone:* 251-575-3156 Ext. 252. *E-mail:* jhorton@ascc.edu.

BEVILL STATE COMMUNITY COLLEGE
Sumiton, Alabama   www.bscc.edu/

Director of Admissions Ms. Melissa Stowe, Enrollment Supervisor, Bevill State Community College, PO Box 800, Sumiton, AL 35148. *Phone:* 205-932-3221 Ext. 5101.

BISHOP STATE COMMUNITY COLLEGE
Mobile, Alabama   www.bscc.cc.al.us/

- **State-supported** 2-year, founded 1965, part of Alabama College System
- **Urban** 9-acre campus
- **Endowment** $583,017
- **Coed,** 4,070 undergraduate students, 50% full-time, 68% women, 32% men

Undergraduates 2,035 full-time, 2,035 part-time. Students come from 5 states and territories, 1% are from out of state, 68% African American, 0.7% Asian American or Pacific Islander, 0.5% Hispanic American, 0.3% Native American, 36% transferred in.

Freshmen *Admission:* 590 enrolled.

Faculty *Total:* 209, 58% full-time, 11% with terminal degrees. *Student/faculty ratio:* 17:1.

Majors Accounting technology and bookkeeping; administrative assistant and secretarial science; civil engineering technology; computer and information sciences; drafting and design technology; electrical, electronic and communications engineering technology; engineering technology; funeral service and mortuary science; general studies; graphic and printing equipment operation/production; health information/medical records technology; instrumentation technology; liberal arts and sciences/liberal studies; nursing (registered nurse training); physical therapist assistant; special education (hearing impaired).

Academics *Calendar:* semesters. *Degree:* certificates and associate. *Special study options:* academic remediation for entering students, adult/continuing education programs, cooperative education, distance learning, internships, part-time degree program, services for LD students, summer session for credit.

Library Minnie Slade Bishop Library with 53,883 titles, 207 serial subscriptions, 461 audiovisual materials.

Student Life *Housing:* college housing not available. *Activities and Organizations:* drama/theater group, student-run radio station, choral group, Student Government Association, Health Occupations Students of America, Phi Beta Lambda, Phi Theta Kappa, Vocational Industrial Clubs of America. *Campus security:* 24-hour emergency response devices and patrols. *Student services:* health clinic.

Athletics Member NJCAA. *Intercollegiate sports:* baseball M, basketball M(s)/W(s), softball W(s).

Costs (2007–08) *Tuition:* state resident $1728 full-time; nonresident $3456 full-time. *Required fees:* $432 full-time.

Financial Aid Of all full-time matriculated undergraduates, 299 Federal Work-Study jobs (averaging $2400).

Applying *Options:* early admission, deferred entrance. *Required:* high school transcript. *Application deadlines:* rolling (freshmen), rolling (transfers). *Notification:* continuous until 9/17 (freshmen), continuous until 9/17 (transfers).

Freshmen Application Contact Dr. Terry Hazzard, Dean of Students, Bishop State Community College, 351 North Broad Street, Mobile, AL 36603-5898. *Phone:* 251-405-7089. *Fax:* 251-438-5403. *E-mail:* info@bishop.edu.

CALHOUN COMMUNITY COLLEGE
Decatur, Alabama   www.calhoun.edu/

- **State-supported** 2-year, founded 1965, part of Alabama College System
- **Suburban** campus
- **Coed,** 8,549 undergraduate students, 36% full-time, 56% women, 44% men

Undergraduates 3,063 full-time, 5,486 part-time. Students come from 9 states and territories, 16 other countries, 1% are from out of state, 19% African American, 2% Asian American or Pacific Islander, 2% Hispanic American, 3% Native American.

Freshmen *Admission:* 6,037 applied, 6,028 admitted.

Faculty *Total:* 424, 28% full-time, 13% with terminal degrees. *Student/faculty ratio:* 21:1.

Majors Accounting; aeronautical/aerospace engineering technology; agriculture; biology/biological sciences; business administration and management; child care and support services management; computer and information sciences; computer graphics; criminal justice/police science; dental assisting; drafting and design technology; dramatic/theater arts; education; electrical and power transmission installation related; electrical, electronic and communications engineering technology; electromechanical and instrumentation and maintenance technologies related; elementary education; emergency medical technology (EMT paramedic); English; entrepreneurship; family resource management; fire services administration; general studies; graphic design; heating, air conditioning and refrigeration technology; heating, air conditioning, ventilation and refrigeration maintenance technology; industrial mechanics and maintenance technology; legal assistant/paralegal; liberal arts and sciences/liberal studies; machine tool technology; mathematics; military technologies; music; nursing (registered nurse training); office management; photographic and film/video technology; pre-dentistry studies; pre-law studies; pre-medical studies; pre-pharmacy studies; pre-veterinary studies; real estate; secondary education; special education (early childhood); transportation management; visual and performing arts.

Academics *Calendar:* semesters. *Degree:* certificates and associate. *Special study options:* academic remediation for entering students, accelerated degree program, adult/continuing education programs, advanced placement credit, cooperative education, distance learning, English as a second language, independent study, part-time degree program, services for LD students, summer session for credit.

Library Brewer Library plus 2 others with 36,699 titles, 202 serial subscriptions, 23,948 audiovisual materials, an OPAC, a Web page.

Student Life *Housing:* college housing not available. *Activities and Organizations:* drama/theater group, student-run newspaper, television station, choral group, Student Government Association, Black Students Alliance, Phi Theta Kappa, BACCHUS/SADD, VICA. *Campus security:* 24-hour patrols. *Student services:* personal/psychological counseling.

Standardized Tests *Required for some:* SAT or ACT (for admission).

Costs (2007–08) *Tuition:* state resident $3040 full-time; nonresident $3040 full-time.

Financial Aid Of all full-time matriculated undergraduates, 50 Federal Work-Study jobs (averaging $3000).

Applying *Required for some:* high school transcript. *Application deadlines:* rolling (freshmen), rolling (transfers). *Notification:* continuous (freshmen), continuous (transfers).

Freshmen Application Contact Ms. Patricia Landers, Admissions Receptionist, Calhoun Community College, PO Box 2216, 6250 Highway 31 North, Decatur, AL 35609-2216. *Phone:* 256-306-2593. *Toll-free phone:* 800-626-3628 Ext. 2594. *Fax:* 256-306-2941. *E-mail:* pml@calhoun.edu.

CENTRAL ALABAMA COMMUNITY COLLEGE
Alexander City, Alabama   www.cacc.cc.al.us/

Freshmen Application Contact Ms. Bettie Macmillan, Admission, Central Alabama Community College, PO Box 699, Alexander City, AL 35011-0699. *Phone:* 256-234-6346 Ext. 6232. *Toll-free phone:* 800-643-2657 Ext. 6232.

CHATTAHOOCHEE VALLEY COMMUNITY COLLEGE

Phenix City, Alabama **www.cv.edu/**

- **State-supported** 2-year, founded 1974
- **Small-town** 103-acre campus
- **Endowment** $42,791
- **Coed**

Undergraduates 972 full-time, 1,062 part-time. Students come from 6 states and territories, 10 other countries, 43% African American, 0.6% Asian American or Pacific Islander, 2% Hispanic American, 0.0% Native American. *Retention:* 66% of 2003 full-time freshmen returned.

Academics *Calendar:* semesters. *Degree:* certificates and associate. *Special study options:* academic remediation for entering students, adult/continuing education programs, advanced placement credit, distance learning, honors programs, off-campus study, part-time degree program, services for LD students, student-designed majors, summer session for credit.

Student Life *Campus security:* 24-hour emergency response devices and patrols.

Athletics Member NJCAA.

Costs (2006–07) *Tuition:* state resident $2160 full-time, $90 per credit hour part-time; nonresident $3864 full-time, $161 per credit hour part-time. Full-time tuition and fees vary according to course load. Part-time tuition and fees vary according to course load.

Financial Aid Of all full-time matriculated undergraduates, 40 Federal Work-Study jobs (averaging $2000). 10 state and other part-time jobs (averaging $2000).

Applying *Options:* early admission. *Required:* high school transcript.

Freshmen Application Contact Ms. Rita Cherry, Admissions Clerk, Chattahoochee Valley Community College, PO Box 1000, Phenix City, AL 36869. *Phone:* 334-291-4995. *Toll-free phone:* 800-842-2822. *Fax:* 334-291-4994. *E-mail:* information@cv.edu.

COMMUNITY COLLEGE OF THE AIR FORCE

Maxwell Air Force Base, Alabama **www.au.af.mil/au/ccaf/**

- **Federally supported** 2-year, founded 1972
- **Suburban** campus
- **Coed, primarily men**

Undergraduates 351,715 full-time. 15% African American, 4% Asian American or Pacific Islander, 1% Native American.

Faculty *Student/faculty ratio:* 28:1.

Academics *Calendar:* continuous. *Degrees:* certificates and associate (courses conducted at 125 branch locations worldwide for members of the U.S. Air Force). *Special study options:* academic remediation for entering students, adult/continuing education programs, advanced placement credit, distance learning, independent study, internships.

Student Life *Campus security:* 24-hour emergency response devices and patrols.

Standardized Tests *Required:* Armed Services Vocational Aptitude Battery (for admission).

Costs (2006–07) *Tuition:* Tuition, room and board, and medical and dental care are provided by the U.S. government. Each student receives a salary from which to pay for uniforms, supplies, and personal expenses.

Applying *Options:* electronic application. *Required:* high school transcript, letters of recommendation, interview, pass military physical, be of good character, no criminal record.

Freshmen Application Contact C.M. Sgt. Robert McAlexander, Director of Admissions/Registrar, Community College of the Air Force, 130 West Maxwell Boulevard, Building 836, Maxwell Air Force Base, Maxwell AFB, AL 36112-6613. *Phone:* 334-953-6436. *Fax:* 334-953-8211. *E-mail:* ronald.hall@maxwell.af.mil.

ENTERPRISE-OZARK COMMUNITY COLLEGE

Enterprise, Alabama **www.eocc.edu/**

Director of Admissions Mr. Gary Deas, Associate Dean of Students/Registrar, Enterprise-Ozark Community College, PO Box 1300, Enterprise, AL 36331. *Phone:* 334-347-2623 Ext. 2233. *E-mail:* gdeas@eocc.edu.

GADSDEN STATE COMMUNITY COLLEGE

Gadsden, Alabama **www.gadsdenstate.edu/**

- **State-supported** 2-year, founded 1965, part of Alabama College System
- **Small-town** 275-acre campus with easy access to Birmingham
- **Endowment** $2.4 million
- **Coed,** 5,204 undergraduate students, 55% full-time, 61% women, 39% men

Undergraduates 2,839 full-time, 2,365 part-time. Students come from 4 states and territories, 32 other countries, 4% are from out of state, 19% African American, 0.4% Asian American or Pacific Islander, 1% Hispanic American, 0.3% Native American, 4% international.

Freshmen *Admission:* 1,895 applied, 1,895 admitted, 1,407 enrolled.

Faculty *Total:* 263, 54% full-time, 5% with terminal degrees. *Student/faculty ratio:* 20:1.

Majors Administrative assistant and secretarial science; child care and support services management; civil engineering technology; clinical/medical laboratory technology; computer and information sciences; court reporting; criminal justice/police science; emergency medical technology (EMT paramedic); general retailing/wholesaling; general studies; heating, air conditioning and refrigeration technology; legal assistant/paralegal; liberal arts and sciences/liberal studies; mechanical engineering/mechanical technology; medical radiologic technology; nursing (registered nurse training); physical education teaching and coaching; radio and television broadcasting technology; substance abuse/addiction counseling; telecommunications; tool and die technology.

Academics *Calendar:* semesters. *Degree:* certificates and associate. *Special study options:* academic remediation for entering students, adult/continuing education programs, advanced placement credit, cooperative education, English as a second language, external degree program, part-time degree program, services for LD students, summer session for credit.

Library Meadows Library with 109,568 titles, 234 serial subscriptions, 12,030 audiovisual materials, an OPAC, a Web page.

Student Life *Housing Options:* coed. *Activities and Organizations:* drama/theater group, student-run newspaper, radio station, choral group, Science, Math, and Engineering Club, Student Government Association, Circle K, Phi Beta Lambda, VICA. *Campus security:* 24-hour patrols. *Student services:* women's center.

Athletics Member NJCAA. *Intercollegiate sports:* baseball M(s), basketball M(s)/W(s), cross-country running W(s), golf M(s), softball W(s), tennis M(s), volleyball W(s). *Intramural sports:* basketball M/W, volleyball M/W.

Costs (2006–07) *Tuition:* state resident $2160 full-time, $90 per credit hour part-time; nonresident $3864 full-time, $161 per credit hour part-time. Full-time tuition and fees vary according to reciprocity agreements. Part-time tuition and fees vary according to reciprocity agreements. *Room and board:* $3750. *Waivers:* minority students, adult students, senior citizens, and employees or children of employees.

Financial Aid Of all full-time matriculated undergraduates, 95 Federal Work-Study jobs (averaging $1364).

Applying *Options:* early admission, deferred entrance. *Required:* high school transcript. *Application deadlines:* rolling (freshmen), rolling (transfers).

Freshmen Application Contact Dr. Teresa Rhea, Admissions and Records, Gadsden State Community College, Admissions, Allen Hall, PO Box 227, Gadsden, AL 35902-0227. *Phone:* 256-549-8210. *Toll-free phone:* 800-226-5563. *Fax:* 256-549-8205. *E-mail:* info@gadsdenstate.edu.

GEORGE CORLEY WALLACE STATE COMMUNITY COLLEGE

Selma, Alabama **www.wccs.edu/**

Director of Admissions Ms. Sunette Newman, Registrar, George Corley Wallace State Community College, 3000 Earl Goodwin Parkway, Selma, AL 36702-2530. *Phone:* 334-876-9305.

GEORGE C. WALLACE COMMUNITY COLLEGE

Dothan, Alabama **www.wallace.edu/**

- **State-supported** 2-year, founded 1949, part of The Alabama College System
- **Rural** 200-acre campus
- **Coed,** 3,316 undergraduate students, 54% full-time, 66% women, 34% men

George C. Wallace Community College (continued)

Undergraduates 1,786 full-time, 1,530 part-time. Students come from 31 states and territories, 4 other countries, 4% are from out of state, 28% African American, 0.5% Asian American or Pacific Islander, 1% Hispanic American, 0.3% Native American.

Freshmen *Admission:* 812 enrolled.

Faculty *Total:* 241, 52% full-time. *Student/faculty ratio:* 7:1.

Majors Accounting; administrative assistant and secretarial science; automobile/automotive mechanics technology; business administration and management; carpentry; clinical/medical laboratory technology; commercial and advertising art; computer science; criminal justice/police science; data processing and data processing technology; drafting and design technology; electrical, electronic and communications engineering technology; emergency medical technology (EMT paramedic); heating, air conditioning, ventilation and refrigeration maintenance technology; industrial mechanics and maintenance technology; laser and optical technology; liberal arts and sciences/liberal studies; machine tool technology; medical administrative assistant and medical secretary; medical/clinical assistant; nursing (licensed practical/vocational nurse training); nursing (registered nurse training); physical therapist assistant; radiologic technology/science; respiratory care therapy; welding technology.

Academics *Calendar:* semesters. *Degree:* associate. *Special study options:* academic remediation for entering students, adult/continuing education programs, advanced placement credit, cooperative education, distance learning, English as a second language, independent study, off-campus study, part-time degree program.

Library Learning Resource Center with 45,353 titles, 399 serial subscriptions.

Student Life *Housing:* college housing not available. *Activities and Organizations:* drama/theater group, student-run newspaper. *Campus security:* 24-hour patrols. *Student services:* personal/psychological counseling.

Athletics Member NJCAA. *Intercollegiate sports:* basketball M(s)/W(s), tennis M(s)/W(s). *Intramural sports:* basketball M/W, tennis M/W, volleyball M/W.

Standardized Tests *Recommended:* SAT or ACT (for admission).

Costs (2007–08) *Tuition:* state resident $2160 full-time, $72 per hour part-time; nonresident $4320 full-time, $144 per hour part-time. *Required fees:* $540 full-time, $18 per credit hour part-time.

Financial Aid Of all full-time matriculated undergraduates, 83 Federal Work-Study jobs (averaging $2217).

Applying *Options:* early admission. *Required:* high school transcript. *Application deadlines:* rolling (freshmen), rolling (transfers).

Freshmen Application Contact Dr. Brenda Barnes, Assistant Dean of Student Affairs, George C. Wallace Community College, 1141 Wallace Drive, Dothan, AL 36303-9234. *Phone:* 334-983-3521 Ext. 2470. *Toll-free phone:* 800-543-2426. *Fax:* 334-983-3600. *E-mail:* bbarnes@wallace.edu.

H. COUNCILL TRENHOLM STATE TECHNICAL COLLEGE

Montgomery, Alabama   www.trenholmtech.cc.al.us/

- **State-supported** 2-year, founded 1962, part of Alabama Department of Post Secondary Education
- **Urban** 78-acre campus
- **Coed,** 1,311 undergraduate students, 50% full-time, 50% women, 50% men

Undergraduates 661 full-time, 650 part-time. Students come from 2 states and territories, 60% African American, 0.5% Asian American or Pacific Islander, 0.3% Hispanic American, 10% transferred in. *Retention:* 40% of 2003 full-time freshmen returned.

Freshmen *Admission:* 1,057 applied, 1,057 admitted, 358 enrolled.

Faculty *Total:* 131, 49% full-time. *Student/faculty ratio:* 10:1.

Majors Accounting technology and bookkeeping; administrative assistant and secretarial science; automobile/automotive mechanics technology; automotive engineering technology; carpentry; child care and support services management; clothing/textiles; computer and information sciences; construction engineering technology; cosmetology; culinary arts; dental assisting; dental laboratory technology; drafting and design technology; electrical, electronic and communications engineering technology; electrician; emergency medical technology (EMT paramedic); graphic and printing equipment operation/production; graphic communications related; heating, air conditioning, ventilation and refrigeration maintenance technology; heavy equipment maintenance technology; industrial electronics technology; industrial mechanics and maintenance technology; information science/studies; instrumentation technology; machine tool technology; massage therapy; medical/clinical assistant; pipefitting and sprinkler fitting; tool and die technology; welding technology.

Academics *Calendar:* semesters. *Degree:* certificates, diplomas, and associate. *Special study options:* academic remediation for entering students, adult/

---

continuing education programs, advanced placement credit, cooperative education, external degree program, internships, part-time degree program, services for LD students, summer session for credit.

Library Main Library plus 1 other with 6,377 titles, 192 serial subscriptions, 496 audiovisual materials, an OPAC, a Web page.

Student Life *Housing:* college housing not available. *Campus security:* 24-hour emergency response devices and patrols, late-night transport/escort service.

Standardized Tests *Required for some:* ACT (for admission).

Costs (2007–08) *Tuition:* state resident $1727 full-time, $71 per hour part-time; nonresident $3456 full-time, $142 per hour part-time. *Required fees:* $456 full-time, $19 per hour part-time.

Applying *Options:* early admission. *Required:* high school transcript. *Application deadlines:* rolling (freshmen), rolling (transfers).

Freshmen Application Contact Ms. Tennie McBryde, Registrar, H. Councill Trenholm State Technical College, 1225 Air Base Boulevard, Montgomery, AL 36108. *Phone:* 334-420-4306. *Fax:* 334-420-4201. *E-mail:* tmcbryde@trenholmtech.cc.al.us.

HERZING COLLEGE

Birmingham, Alabama   www.herzing.edu/birmingham/

Director of Admissions Ms. Tess Anderson, Admissions Coordinator, Herzing College, 280 West Valley Avenue, Birmingham, AL 35209. *Phone:* 205-916-2800. *E-mail:* admiss@bhm.herzing.edu.

ITT TECHNICAL INSTITUTE

Birmingham, Alabama   www.itt-tech.edu/

- **Proprietary** primarily 2-year, founded 1994, part of ITT Educational Services, Inc
- **Suburban** campus
- **Coed**

Majors Animation, interactive technology, video graphics and special effects; business administration and management; CAD/CADD drafting/design technology; communications technology; computer and information systems security; computer engineering technology; computer software engineering; computer software technology; computer systems networking and telecommunications; construction management; criminal justice/law enforcement administration; electrical, electronic and communications engineering technology; web/multimedia management and webmaster; web page, digital/multimedia and information resources design.

Academics *Calendar:* quarters. *Degrees:* associate and bachelor's.

Library a Web page.

Student Life *Housing:* college housing not available. *Activities and Organizations:* student-run newspaper. *Campus security:* 24-hour emergency response devices.

Standardized Tests *Required:* Wonderlic aptitude test (for admission).

Costs (2006–07) *Tuition:* Contact school for program costs.

Applying *Options:* deferred entrance. *Application fee:* $100. *Required:* high school transcript, interview. *Recommended:* letters of recommendation. *Application deadlines:* rolling (freshmen), rolling (transfers). *Notification:* continuous (freshmen), continuous (transfers).

Freshmen Application Contact Mr. Jesse L. Johnson, Director of Recruitment, ITT Technical Institute, 6270 Park South Drive, Bessemer, AL 35022. *Phone:* 205-497-5700. *Toll-free phone:* 800-488-7033. *Fax:* 205-497-5799.

JAMES H. FAULKNER STATE COMMUNITY COLLEGE

Bay Minette, Alabama   www.faulknerstate.edu/

- **State-supported** 2-year, founded 1965, part of Alabama College System
- **Small-town** 105-acre campus
- **Coed,** 3,323 undergraduate students, 64% full-time, 63% women, 37% men

Faulkner State Community College (FSCC), which is accredited by the Southern Association of Colleges and Schools, offers transfer, technical, and certificate programs. The main campus is located in Bay Minette, Alabama, with branches in Fairhope and Gulf Shores, Alabama. FSCC

---

serves the entire Gulf Coast area. For information, prospective students should call 800-231-3752 (toll-free).

Undergraduates 2,139 full-time, 1,184 part-time. 3% are from out of state, 13% African American, 0.5% Asian American or Pacific Islander, 0.6% Hispanic American, 1% Native American, 9% live on campus.

Freshmen *Admission:* 988 enrolled.

Faculty *Total:* 193, 33% full-time. *Student/faculty ratio:* 15:1.

Majors Administrative assistant and secretarial science; agricultural economics; business administration and management; commercial and advertising art; computer and information sciences; criminal justice/law enforcement administration; dental assisting; environmental engineering technology; general studies; hospitality administration; landscaping and groundskeeping; legal assistant/paralegal; liberal arts and sciences/liberal studies; mass communications; nursing (licensed practical/vocational nurse training); nursing (registered nurse training); parks, recreation and leisure facilities management; surgical technology.

Academics *Calendar:* semesters. *Degree:* certificates and associate. *Special study options:* academic remediation for entering students, adult/continuing education programs, advanced placement credit, cooperative education, honors programs, internships, part-time degree program, services for LD students.

Library Austin R. Meadows Library with 53,100 titles, 200 serial subscriptions, an OPAC.

Student Life *Housing Options:* men-only, women-only. Campus housing is university owned. *Activities and Organizations:* drama/theater group, student-run newspaper, choral group, Student Government Association, Pow-Wow Leadership Society, Phi Theta Kappa, Association of Computational Machinery, Phi Beta Lambda, national fraternities. *Campus security:* 24-hour emergency response devices and patrols, controlled dormitory access. *Student services:* personal/psychological counseling.

Athletics Member NJCAA. *Intercollegiate sports:* baseball M(s), basketball M(s)/W(s), golf M(s), softball W(s), tennis M(s)/W(s), volleyball W(s). *Intramural sports:* basketball M, tennis M/W, volleyball M/W.

Costs (2007–08) *Tuition:* state resident $2790 full-time, $93 per credit hour part-time; nonresident $4920 full-time, $164 per credit hour part-time. *Required fees:* $71 full-time. *Room and board:* $4050.

Applying *Options:* early admission, deferred entrance. *Required:* high school transcript. *Application deadlines:* rolling (freshmen), rolling (transfers). *Notification:* continuous until 8/18 (freshmen), continuous until 8/18 (transfers).

Freshmen Application Contact Ms. Carmelita Mikkelsen, Director of Admissions and High School Relations, James H. Faulkner State Community College, 1900 Highway 31 South, Bay Minette, AL 36507. *Phone:* 251-580-2213. *Toll-free phone:* 800-231-3752 Ext. 2111. *Fax:* 251-580-2285. *E-mail:* cmikkelsen@faulknerstate.edu.

JEFFERSON DAVIS COMMUNITY COLLEGE

Brewton, Alabama www.jdcc.edu/

Director of Admissions Ms. Robin Sessions, Registrar, Jefferson Davis Community College, PO Box 958, Brewton, AL 36427. *Phone:* 251-867-4832.

JEFFERSON STATE COMMUNITY COLLEGE

Birmingham, Alabama www.jeffstateonline.com

- **State-supported** 2-year, founded 1965, part of Alabama College System
- **Suburban** 234-acre campus
- **Coed**

Undergraduates 3,129 full-time, 4,044 part-time. Students come from 28 states and territories, 61 other countries, 1% are from out of state, 21% African American, 2% Asian American or Pacific Islander, 1% Hispanic American, 0.3% Native American, 2% international, 8% transferred in.

Faculty *Student/faculty ratio:* 21:1.

Academics *Calendar:* semesters. *Degree:* certificates and associate. *Special study options:* academic remediation for entering students, adult/continuing education programs, advanced placement credit, distance learning, honors programs, independent study, internships, part-time degree program, services for LD students, summer session for credit. *ROTC:* Army (c), Air Force (c).

Student Life *Campus security:* 24-hour patrols.

Athletics Member NJCAA.

Financial Aid Of all full-time matriculated undergraduates, 189 Federal Work-Study jobs (averaging $1926).

Applying *Options:* electronic application, early admission, deferred entrance. *Required for some:* high school transcript.

Freshmen Application Contact Mr. Michael Hobbs, Director of Enrollment Services, Jefferson State Community College, 2601 Carson Road, Birmingham, AL 35215-3098. *Phone:* 205-853-1200 Ext. 7991. *Toll-free phone:* 800-239-5900. *Fax:* 205-856-6070.

J. F. DRAKE STATE TECHNICAL COLLEGE

Huntsville, Alabama www.drakestate.edu/

- **State-supported** 2-year, founded 1961, part of Alabama Department of Postsecondary Education
- **Urban** 6-acre campus with easy access to Huntsville
- **Coed,** 764 undergraduate students, 59% full-time, 49% women, 51% men

Undergraduates 454 full-time, 310 part-time. Students come from 1 other state, 4% are from out of state, 57% African American, 0.9% Asian American or Pacific Islander, 2% Hispanic American, 0.3% Native American.

Freshmen *Admission:* 628 applied, 378 admitted, 212 enrolled.

Faculty *Total:* 67, 37% full-time, 6% with terminal degrees. *Student/faculty ratio:* 21:1.

Majors Accounting; administrative assistant and secretarial science; commercial and advertising art; drafting and design technology; electrical, electronic and communications engineering technology; information science/studies; machine tool technology.

Academics *Calendar:* semesters. *Degree:* certificates, diplomas, and associate. *Special study options:* academic remediation for entering students, cooperative education, internships, part-time degree program, services for LD students.

Library S.C. O'Neal Library Technology Center.

Student Life *Housing:* college housing not available. *Activities and Organizations:* student-run newspaper, Phi Beta Lambda, Vocational Industrial Clubs of America. *Campus security:* 24-hour patrols.

Costs (2007–08) *Tuition:* state resident $2160 full-time.

Applying *Options:* deferred entrance. *Required:* high school transcript. *Application deadline:* rolling (freshmen).

Freshmen Application Contact Mrs. Monica Sudeall, Registrar, J. F. Drake State Technical College, 3421 Meridian Street, Huntsville, AL 35811. *Phone:* 256-539-8161. *Toll-free phone:* 888-413-7253. *Fax:* 256-551-3142. *E-mail:* sudeall@drakestate.edu.

LAWSON STATE COMMUNITY COLLEGE

Birmingham, Alabama www.lawsonstate.edu/

- **State-supported** 2-year, founded 1949, part of Alabama College System
- **Urban** 30-acre campus
- **Coed,** 3,141 undergraduate students, 54% full-time, 63% women, 37% men

Undergraduates 1,710 full-time, 1,431 part-time. Students come from 2 states and territories, 1% are from out of state, 82% African American, 0.4% Asian American or Pacific Islander, 0.4% Hispanic American, 0.1% Native American, 9% transferred in. *Retention:* 66% of 2003 full-time freshmen returned.

Freshmen *Admission:* 1,557 applied, 700 admitted, 700 enrolled.

Faculty *Total:* 222, 45% full-time. *Student/faculty ratio:* 16:1.

Majors Accounting; administrative assistant and secretarial science; art; biology/biological sciences; business administration and management; business teacher education; carpentry; chemistry; clinical laboratory science/medical technology; clothing/textiles; computer and information sciences related; cosmetology; crafts, folk art and artisanry; criminal justice/law enforcement administration; criminal justice/police science; dietetics; drafting and design technology; education; electrical, electronic and communications engineering technology; English; fire science; health and physical education; heavy equipment maintenance technology; history; hydrology and water resources science; information science/studies; legal administrative assistant/secretary; liberal arts and sciences/liberal studies; library science; mathematics; music; nursing (registered nurse training); parks, recreation and leisure; physical sciences; physical therapy; political science and government; pre-engineering; pre-law studies; psychology; radio and television; social sciences; social work; sociology; urban studies/affairs.

Academics *Calendar:* semesters. *Degree:* certificates and associate. *Special study options:* academic remediation for entering students, adult/continuing

Lawson State Community College (continued)

education programs, cooperative education, distance learning, freshman honors college, honors programs, internships, part-time degree program, services for LD students, summer session for credit.

Library Lawson State Library with 48,903 titles, 243 serial subscriptions, an OPAC.

Student Life *Housing Options:* coed. Campus housing is university owned. *Activities and Organizations:* choral group. *Campus security:* 24-hour emergency response devices and patrols, student patrols.

Athletics Member NJCAA. *Intercollegiate sports:* baseball W, basketball M/W, cross-country running M(s), equestrian sports M, volleyball W(s). *Intramural sports:* basketball M/W, softball M/W, swimming and diving M/W, table tennis M/W, tennis M/W, track and field M/W, volleyball W, weight lifting M.

Costs (2007–08) *Tuition:* state resident $2160 full-time, $72 per credit part-time; nonresident $4320 full-time, $144 per credit part-time. *Required fees:* $540 full-time, $9 per credit part-time. *Room and board:* $3000; room only: $2000.

Financial Aid Of all full-time matriculated undergraduates, 91 Federal Work-Study jobs (averaging $3000).

Applying *Options:* early admission, deferred entrance. *Required:* high school transcript. *Application deadlines:* rolling (freshmen), rolling (transfers). *Notification:* continuous (freshmen), continuous (transfers).

Freshmen Application Contact Mr. Jeff Shelley, Director of Admissions and Records, Lawson State Community College, 3060 Wilson Road, SW, Birmingham, AL 35221-1798. *Phone:* 205-929-6361. *Fax:* 205-923-7106. *E-mail:* jshelley@lawsonstate.edu.

LURLEEN B. WALLACE COMMUNITY COLLEGE

Andalusia, Alabama   www.lbwcc.edu/

Director of Admissions Mrs. Judy Hall, Director of Student Services, Lurleen B. Wallace Community College, PO Box 1418, Andalusia, AL 36420. *Phone:* 334-222-6591 Ext. 271.

MARION MILITARY INSTITUTE

Marion, Alabama   www.marionmilitary.org/

- **Independent** 2-year, founded 1842
- **Small-town** 130-acre campus
- **Endowment** $1.2 million
- **Coed, primarily men,** 165 undergraduate students

Undergraduates Students come from 35 states and territories, 3 other countries, 8% are from out of state, 97% live on campus.

Freshmen *Admission:* 269 applied, 226 admitted. *Average high school GPA:* 3.0.

Faculty *Total:* 44, 91% full-time, 82% with terminal degrees. *Student/faculty ratio:* 6:1.

Majors Biological and physical sciences; engineering; liberal arts and sciences/liberal studies.

Academics *Calendar:* semesters. *Degree:* associate. *Special study options:* academic remediation for entering students, off-campus study, part-time degree program. *ROTC:* Army (b), Air Force (b).

Library Baer Memorial Library with 36,000 titles, 140 serial subscriptions, 8,471 audiovisual materials.

Student Life *Housing Options:* men-only, women-only. *Activities and Organizations:* drama/theater group, student-run newspaper, choral group, marching band, Swamp Foxes, White Knights, marching band, Drama Club, Scabbard and Blade. *Campus security:* night patrols by trained security personnel. *Student services:* health clinic, personal/psychological counseling.

Athletics Member NJCAA. *Intercollegiate sports:* golf M/W, soccer M/W, tennis M/W. *Intramural sports:* baseball M/W, basketball M/W, football M/W, golf M/W, lacrosse M/W, racquetball M/W, soccer M/W, softball M/W, swimming and diving M/W, table tennis M/W, tennis M/W, volleyball M/W, water polo M/W, weight lifting M/W.

Standardized Tests *Required:* SAT or ACT (for admission).

Costs (2006–07) *Tuition:* state resident $8646 full-time; nonresident $14,646 full-time.

Financial Aid Of all full-time matriculated undergraduates, 21 Federal Work-Study jobs (averaging $339).

Applying *Options:* deferred entrance. *Application fee:* $35. *Required:* high school transcript, minimum 2.0 GPA, 2 letters of recommendation. *Recommended:* interview, minimum SAT score of 920 or ACT score of 19. *Application deadlines:* 8/30 (freshmen), 8/30 (transfers).

Director of Admissions Director of Admissions, Marion Military Institute, 1101 Washington Street, Marion, AL 36756. *Phone:* 800-664-1842 Ext. 306. *Toll-free phone:* 800-664-1842 Ext. 307.

NORTHEAST ALABAMA COMMUNITY COLLEGE

Rainsville, Alabama   www.nacc.edu/

Freshmen Application Contact Dr. Joe Burke, Director of Admissions, Northeast Alabama Community College, PO Box 159, Rainsville, AL 35986. *Phone:* 256-228-6001. *Fax:* 256-638-6043. *E-mail:* burkej@nacc.edu.

NORTHWEST-SHOALS COMMUNITY COLLEGE

Muscle Shoals, Alabama   www.nwscc.edu/

- **State-supported** 2-year, founded 1963, part of Alabama Department of Postsecondary Education
- **Small-town** 210-acre campus
- **Coed,** 2,077 undergraduate students, 69% full-time, 60% women, 40% men

Undergraduates 1,432 full-time, 645 part-time. Students come from 6 states and territories, 1 other country, 1% are from out of state, 11% African American, 0.3% Asian American or Pacific Islander, 1% Hispanic American, 1% Native American, 8% transferred in, 2% live on campus.

Freshmen *Admission:* 2,110 applied, 1,053 admitted, 887 enrolled.

Faculty *Total:* 217, 35% full-time, 7% with terminal degrees. *Student/faculty ratio:* 20:1.

Majors Accounting; administrative assistant and secretarial science; agricultural teacher education; art; business administration and management; child development; clinical laboratory science/medical technology; computer and information sciences; computer engineering technology; computer programming; computer science; computer typography and composition equipment operation; criminal justice/law enforcement administration; criminal justice/police science; drafting and design technology; education; electrical, electronic and communications engineering technology; elementary education; environmental biology; environmental science; fire science; forestry; general studies; industrial electronics technology; industrial mechanics and maintenance technology; information science/studies; liberal arts and sciences/liberal studies; medical laboratory technology; multi-/interdisciplinary studies related; nursing (licensed practical/vocational nurse training); nursing (registered nurse training); pre-dentistry studies; pre-engineering; pre-law studies; pre-nursing studies; pre-pharmacy studies; pre-veterinary studies; secondary education; veterinary sciences; water quality and wastewater treatment management and recycling technology; welding technology.

Academics *Calendar:* semesters. *Degree:* certificates, diplomas, and associate. *Special study options:* academic remediation for entering students, accelerated degree program, adult/continuing education programs, advanced placement credit, cooperative education, distance learning, honors programs, independent study, part-time degree program, study abroad, summer session for credit.

Library Larry W. McCoy Learning Resource Center and James Glasgow Library with 66,986 titles, 262 serial subscriptions, 1,401 audiovisual materials.

Student Life *Housing Options:* coed. Campus housing is university owned. *Activities and Organizations:* choral group, Student Government Association, Science Club, Phi Theta Kappa, Baptist Campus Ministry, Northwest-Shoals Singers. *Campus security:* 24-hour emergency response devices and patrols. *Student services:* personal/psychological counseling.

Athletics Member NJCAA. *Intercollegiate sports:* baseball M(s), basketball M(s)/W(s), cheerleading M(s)/W(s), cross-country running M(s), golf M(s), softball W(s), tennis W(s), volleyball W(s). *Intramural sports:* basketball M/W, softball M/W, table tennis M/W, tennis M/W, volleyball M/W.

Costs (2007–08) *Tuition:* state resident $2130 full-time, $71 per credit hour part-time; nonresident $4260 full-time, $142 per credit hour part-time. *Required fees:* $750 full-time, $25 per credit hour part-time. *Room and board:* room only: $1675.

Financial Aid *Financial aid deadline:* 6/1.

Applying *Required:* high school transcript. *Application deadlines:* rolling (freshmen), rolling (transfers). *Notification:* continuous (transfers).

Freshmen Application Contact Dr. Karen Berryhill, Vice President of Student Development Services, Northwest-Shoals Community College, PO Box 2545, Muscle Shoals, AL 35662. *Phone:* 256-331-5261. *Toll-free phone:* 800-645-8967. *Fax:* 256-331-5366. *E-mail:* berryk@nwscc.edu.

PRINCE INSTITUTE OF PROFESSIONAL STUDIES

Montgomery, Alabama   www.princeinstitute.edu/

- **Independent** 2-year, founded 1976
- **Suburban** campus
- **Endowment** $6040
- **Coed, primarily women**

Undergraduates 56 full-time, 38 part-time. 1% are from out of state, 17% African American.

Faculty *Student/faculty ratio:* 15:1.

Academics *Calendar:* quarters. *Degree:* certificates and associate.

Costs (2006–07) *Tuition:* $8448 full-time. *Required fees:* $340 full-time.

Applying *Application fee:* $90. *Required:* high school transcript, interview.

Freshmen Application Contact Ms. Sherry Hill, Director of Admissions, Prince Institute of Professional Studies, 7735 Atlanta Highway, Montgomery, AL 36117. *Phone:* 334-271-1670. *Toll-free phone:* 877-853-5569. *Fax:* 334-271-1671. *E-mail:* admissions@princeinstitute.edu.

REID STATE TECHNICAL COLLEGE

Evergreen, Alabama   www.rstc.cc.al.us/

- **State-supported** 2-year, founded 1966, part of Alabama College System
- **Rural** 26-acre campus
- **Coed,** 545 undergraduate students, 60% full-time, 70% women, 30% men

Undergraduates 326 full-time, 219 part-time. Students come from 2 states and territories, 1% are from out of state, 54% African American, 0.2% Asian American or Pacific Islander, 0.2% Hispanic American, 0.4% Native American.

Freshmen *Admission:* 115 applied, 115 admitted, 115 enrolled.

Faculty *Total:* 41, 59% full-time, 5% with terminal degrees. *Student/faculty ratio:* 12:1.

Majors Administrative assistant and secretarial science; electrical, electronic and communications engineering technology.

Academics *Calendar:* semesters. *Degree:* certificates, diplomas, and associate. *Special study options:* academic remediation for entering students, adult/continuing education programs, double majors, independent study, internships, part-time degree program, services for LD students, summer session for credit.

Library Edith A. Gray with 3,800 titles, 17,236 serial subscriptions, 356 audiovisual materials, a Web page.

Student Life *Housing:* college housing not available. *Activities and Organizations:* student-run newspaper, Student Government Association. *Campus security:* 24-hour emergency response devices, day and evening security guard. *Student services:* personal/psychological counseling.

Costs (2006–07) *Tuition:* state resident $2592 full-time, $72 per credit hour part-time; nonresident $5184 full-time, $144 per credit hour part-time. *Required fees:* $81 full-time, $27 per credit hour part-time. *Waivers:* senior citizens and employees or children of employees.

Financial Aid Of all full-time matriculated undergraduates, 35 Federal Work-Study jobs (averaging $1500).

Applying *Options:* early admission. *Required:* high school transcript. *Application deadlines:* rolling (freshmen), rolling (transfers).

Freshmen Application Contact Ms. Alesia Stuart, Public Relations/Marketing, Reid State Technical College, PO Box 588, Intersection of I-95 and Highway 83, Evergreen, AL 36401-0588. *Phone:* 251-578-1313 Ext. 108.

REMINGTON COLLEGE—MOBILE CAMPUS

Mobile, Alabama   www.remingtoncollege.edu/

- **Proprietary** primarily 2-year, part of Education America, Inc
- **Suburban** 5-acre campus
- **Coed**

Undergraduates 433 full-time. Students come from 3 states and territories, 4% are from out of state, 47% African American, 0.9% Asian American or Pacific Islander, 1% Hispanic American, 1% Native American. *Retention:* 90% of 2003 full-time freshmen returned.

Faculty *Student/faculty ratio:* 16:1.

Academics *Calendar:* quarters. *Degrees:* diplomas, associate, and bachelor's. *Special study options:* adult/continuing education programs, cooperative education, services for LD students.

Standardized Tests *Required:* Wonderlic aptitude test (for admission).

Costs (2006–07) *Tuition:* $34,200 full-time. *Required fees:* $50 full-time.

Financial Aid Of all full-time matriculated undergraduates, 500 applied for aid, 500 were judged to have need. *Average percent of need met:* 45. *Average financial aid package:* $7043. *Average need-based loan:* $3000. *Average need-based gift aid:* $7043. *Average indebtedness upon graduation:* $14,000.

Applying *Application fee:* $50. *Required:* high school transcript, interview.

Freshmen Application Contact Mr. Chris Jones, Director of Recruitment, Remington College–Mobile Campus, 828 Downtowner Loop West, Mobile, AL 36609. *Phone:* 251-343-8200 Ext. 208. *Toll-free phone:* 800-866-0850. *Fax:* 251-343-0577.

SHELTON STATE COMMUNITY COLLEGE

Tuscaloosa, Alabama   www.sheltonstate.edu/

- **State-supported** 2-year, founded 1979, part of Alabama College System
- **Small-town** 30-acre campus with easy access to Birmingham
- **Coed**

Undergraduates 3,363 full-time, 2,391 part-time. Students come from 11 states and territories, 2% are from out of state, 29% African American, 1% Asian American or Pacific Islander, 0.9% Hispanic American, 0.4% Native American, 35% transferred in.

Faculty *Student/faculty ratio:* 30:1.

Academics *Calendar:* semesters. *Degree:* certificates, diplomas, and associate. *Special study options:* academic remediation for entering students, accelerated degree program, adult/continuing education programs, advanced placement credit, distance learning, honors programs, part-time degree program, services for LD students, summer session for credit. *ROTC:* Army (c), Air Force (c).

Student Life *Campus security:* 24-hour emergency response devices and patrols.

Athletics Member NJCAA.

Costs (2006–07) *Tuition:* state resident $2160 full-time, $72 per credit hour part-time; nonresident $4290 full-time, $143 per credit hour part-time. *Required fees:* $570 full-time, $18 per credit hour part-time, $8 per term part-time.

Financial Aid Of all full-time matriculated undergraduates, 95 Federal Work-Study jobs (averaging $3807). 35 state and other part-time jobs (averaging $3477).

Applying *Options:* electronic application. *Required:* high school transcript.

Freshmen Application Contact Ms. Loretta Jones, Assistant to the Dean of Students, Shelton State Community College, Shelton State Community College, 9500 Old Greensboro Road, Tuscaloosa, AL 35405. *Phone:* 205-391-2236. *Fax:* 205-391-3910.

SNEAD STATE COMMUNITY COLLEGE

Boaz, Alabama   www.snead.edu/

- **State-supported** 2-year, founded 1898, part of Alabama College System
- **Small-town** 42-acre campus with easy access to Birmingham
- **Endowment** $1.6 million
- **Coed**

Undergraduates Students come from 6 states and territories, 1% are from out of state, 2% live on campus.

Academics *Calendar:* semesters. *Degree:* certificates and associate. *Special study options:* academic remediation for entering students, accelerated degree program, adult/continuing education programs, advanced placement credit, distance learning, independent study, internships, part-time degree program, services for LD students, student-designed majors, summer session for credit.

Student Life *Campus security:* 24-hour patrols, student patrols.

Athletics Member NJCAA.

Financial Aid Of all full-time matriculated undergraduates, 45 Federal Work-Study jobs.

Applying *Options:* early admission, deferred entrance. *Required:* high school transcript. *Required for some:* interview.

Freshmen Application Contact Dr. Greg Chapman, Director of Instruction, Snead State Community College, PO Box 734, Boaz, AL 35957-0734. *Phone:* 256-840-4111. *Fax:* 256-593-7180. *E-mail:* gchapman@snead.edu.

SOUTHERN UNION STATE COMMUNITY COLLEGE

Wadley, Alabama www.suscc.cc.al.us/

Director of Admissions Mrs. Susan Salatto, Director of Student Development, Southern Union State Community College, PO Box 1000, Roberts Street, Wadley, AL 36276. *Phone:* 256-395-2211.

VIRGINIA COLLEGE AT HUNTSVILLE

Huntsville, Alabama www.vc.edu/

Director of Admissions Ms. Pat Foster, Director of Admissions, Virginia College at Huntsville, 2800-A Bob Wallace Avenue, Huntsville, AL 35805. *Phone:* 205-533-7387.

WALLACE STATE COMMUNITY COLLEGE

Hanceville, Alabama www.wallacestate.edu/

- **State-supported** 2-year, founded 1966
- **Rural** 216-acre campus with easy access to Birmingham
- **Coed,** 6,028 undergraduate students

Undergraduates Students come from 15 states and territories, 6% are from out of state, 3% live on campus.

Freshmen *Admission:* 1,219 applied, 1,219 admitted. *Test scores:* ACT scores over 18: 72%; ACT scores over 24: 14%; ACT scores over 30: 1%.

Faculty *Total:* 612, 37% full-time. *Student/faculty ratio:* 30:1.

Majors Accounting; administrative assistant and secretarial science; agriculture; airline pilot and flight crew; art teacher education; automobile/automotive mechanics technology; avionics maintenance technology; business administration and management; business teacher education; carpentry; child development; clinical/medical laboratory technology; computer programming; computer science; construction engineering technology; cosmetology; criminal justice/law enforcement administration; criminal justice/police science; dental assisting; dental hygiene; drafting and design technology; education; electrical, electronic and communications engineering technology; elementary education; emergency medical technology (EMT paramedic); engineering; farm and ranch management; fashion merchandising; finance; fire science; health information/medical records administration; heating, air conditioning, ventilation and refrigeration maintenance technology; horticultural science; industrial radiologic technology; interior design; kindergarten/preschool education; labor and industrial relations; legal administrative assistant/secretary; legal assistant/paralegal; liberal arts and sciences/liberal studies; library science; machine tool technology; marketing/marketing management; medical administrative assistant and medical secretary; medical/clinical assistant; mental health/rehabilitation; music; nursing (licensed practical/vocational nurse training); nursing (registered nurse training); occupational safety and health technology; occupational therapy; physical therapy; postal management; poultry science; real estate; religious studies; respiratory care therapy; special products marketing; welding technology.

Academics *Calendar:* semesters. *Degree:* diplomas and associate. *Special study options:* academic remediation for entering students, advanced placement credit, cooperative education, part-time degree program, summer session for credit.

Library Wallace State College Library with 41,500 titles, 425 serial subscriptions, an OPAC.

Student Life *Housing Options:* men-only, women-only. Campus housing is university owned. *Activities and Organizations:* choral group, Student Government Association, Vocational Industrial Clubs of America. *Student services:* personal/psychological counseling.

Athletics Member NJCAA. *Intercollegiate sports:* baseball M(s), basketball M(s)/W(s), cross-country running M(s)/W(s), golf M(s), soccer M(s)/W(s), softball W(s), tennis M/W, track and field M(s)/W(s), volleyball W(s). *Intramural sports:* basketball M/W, softball M/W, tennis M/W, volleyball M/W.

Standardized Tests *Required for some:* ACT (for placement), nursing exam. *Recommended:* ACT (for placement).

Costs (2006–07) *Tuition:* state resident $2700 full-time; nonresident $4830 full-time.

Financial Aid Of all full-time matriculated undergraduates, 70 Federal Work-Study jobs. *Financial aid deadline:* 5/1.

Applying *Options:* early admission, deferred entrance. *Required:* high school transcript. *Application deadlines:* rolling (freshmen), rolling (transfers). *Notification:* continuous (freshmen), continuous (transfers).

Director of Admissions Ms. Linda Sperling, Director of Admissions, Wallace State Community College, PO Box 2000, 801 Main Street, Hanceville, AL 35077-2000. *Phone:* 256-352-8278. *Toll-free phone:* 866-350-9722.

ALASKA

CHARTER COLLEGE

Anchorage, Alaska www.chartercollege.org/

Director of Admissions Ms. Lily Sirianni, Vice President, Charter College, 2221 East Northern Lights Boulevard, Suite 120, Anchorage, AK 99508-4157. *Phone:* 907-277-1000. *Toll-free phone:* 800-279-1008.

ILISAGVIK COLLEGE

Barrow, Alaska www.ilisagvik.cc/

- **State-supported** 2-year, founded 1995
- **Endowment** $155,880
- **Coed**
- 100% of applicants were admitted

Undergraduates 49 full-time, 214 part-time. 0.4% African American, 3% Asian American or Pacific Islander, 0.8% Hispanic American, 90% Native American.

Faculty *Student/faculty ratio:* 10:1.

Academics *Calendar:* semesters. *Degree:* certificates, diplomas, and associate.

Standardized Tests *Required:* ACT ASSET (for admission).

Costs (2006–07) *Tuition:* area resident $1440 full-time, $60 per credit hour part-time; state resident $2880 full-time, $120 per credit hour part-time; nonresident $2880 full-time, $120 per credit hour part-time. *Required fees:* $100 full-time, $50 per term part-time. *Room and board:* room only: $4000.

Applying *Required:* essay or personal statement, high school transcript, minimum 2.0 GPA.

Freshmen Application Contact Ms. Beverly Patkotak Grinage, President, Ilisagvik College, UIC/Narl, Barrow, AK 99723. *Phone:* 907-852-1820. *Toll-free phone:* 800-478-7337. *Fax:* 907-852-1821. *E-mail:* beverly.grinage@ilisagvik.cc.

UNIVERSITY OF ALASKA ANCHORAGE, KENAI PENINSULA COLLEGE

Soldotna, Alaska www.kpc.alaska.edu/

Freshmen Application Contact Ms. Shelly Love, Admission and Registration Coordinator, University of Alaska Anchorage, Kenai Peninsula College, 34820 College Drive, Soldotna, AK 99669-9798. *Phone:* 907-262-0311.

UNIVERSITY OF ALASKA ANCHORAGE, KODIAK COLLEGE

Kodiak, Alaska www.koc.alaska.edu/

- **State-supported** 2-year, founded 1968, part of University of Alaska System
- **Rural** 68-acre campus
- **Coed,** 786 undergraduate students

Undergraduates Students come from 1 other state, 2% African American, 6% Asian American or Pacific Islander, 4% Hispanic American, 10% Native American.

Freshmen *Admission:* 64 applied, 64 admitted.

Faculty *Total:* 40, 25% full-time. *Student/faculty ratio:* 19:1.

Majors Administrative assistant and secretarial science; business administration and management; liberal arts and sciences/liberal studies.

Academics *Calendar:* semesters. *Degree:* certificates and associate. *Special study options:* academic remediation for entering students, adult/continuing education programs, advanced placement credit, double majors, part-time degree program.

Library Carolyn Floyd Library with 21,000 titles, 39 serial subscriptions, 2,400 audiovisual materials, an OPAC, a Web page.

Student Life *Housing:* college housing not available.

Standardized Tests *Required:* ACT ASSET (for placement).

Applying *Application fee:* $35. *Recommended:* high school transcript. *Application deadline:* rolling (freshmen).

Director of Admissions Ms. Karen Hamer, Registrar, University of Alaska Anchorage, Kodiak College, 117 Benny Benson Drive, Kodiak, AK 99615. *Phone:* 907-486-1235. *Toll-free phone:* 800-486-7660.

UNIVERSITY OF ALASKA ANCHORAGE, MATANUSKA-SUSITNA COLLEGE

Palmer, Alaska   **www.matsu.alaska.edu/**

- **State-supported** 2-year, founded 1958, part of University of Alaska System
- **Small-town** 950-acre campus with easy access to Anchorage
- **Coed**

Undergraduates 384 full-time, 942 part-time. Students come from 51 states and territories, 18 other countries, 2% African American, 0.8% Asian American or Pacific Islander, 3% Hispanic American, 4% Native American, 0.2% international. *Retention:* 67% of 2003 full-time freshmen returned.

Faculty *Student/faculty ratio:* 14:1.

Academics *Calendar:* semesters. *Degree:* certificates and associate. *Special study options:* academic remediation for entering students, adult/continuing education programs, advanced placement credit, cooperative education, distance learning, double majors, independent study, internships, off-campus study, part-time degree program, summer session for credit.

Student Life *Campus security:* 24-hour patrols.

Costs (2006–07) *Tuition:* state resident $2880 full-time; nonresident $9576 full-time. Full-time tuition and fees vary according to course level and course load. Part-time tuition and fees vary according to course level and course load. *Required fees:* $250 full-time.

Financial Aid Of all full-time matriculated undergraduates, 8 Federal Work-Study jobs (averaging $3000).

Applying *Application fee:* $40. *Required:* high school transcript.

Freshmen Application Contact Ms. Sandra Gravley, Student Services Manager, University of Alaska Anchorage, Matanuska-Susitna College, PO Box 2889, Palmer, AK 99645-2889. *Phone:* 907-745-9712. *Fax:* 907-745-9747. *E-mail:* info@matsu.alaska.edu.

UNIVERSITY OF ALASKA, PRINCE WILLIAM SOUND COMMUNITY COLLEGE

Valdez, Alaska   **www.pwscc.edu/**

- **State-supported** 2-year, founded 1978, part of University of Alaska System
- **Small-town** campus
- **Endowment** $62,630
- **Coed,** 823 undergraduate students

Undergraduates Students come from 1 other state, 1 other country, 4% are from out of state, 2% live on campus.

Freshmen *Admission:* 107 applied, 95 admitted. *Average high school GPA:* 2.75.

Faculty *Total:* 52, 12% full-time.

Majors Administrative assistant and secretarial science; broadcast journalism; business administration and management; liberal arts and sciences/liberal studies; mental health/rehabilitation.

Academics *Calendar:* semesters. *Degree:* certificates, diplomas, and associate. *Special study options:* academic remediation for entering students, adult/continuing education programs, advanced placement credit, cooperative education, distance learning, double majors, English as a second language, independent study, internships, summer session for credit.

Library Valdez Consortium Library with 40,870 titles, 137 serial subscriptions, an OPAC, a Web page.

Student Life *Housing Options:* coed. *Campus security:* student patrols, housing manager supervision. *Student services:* personal/psychological counseling.

Standardized Tests *Recommended:* SAT or ACT (for admission).

Costs (2006–07) *Tuition:* state resident $3206 full-time.

Applying *Options:* early admission. *Application fee:* $10. *Application deadlines:* rolling (freshmen), rolling (transfers).

Freshmen Application Contact Mr. Nathan J. Platt, Director of Student Services, University of Alaska, Prince William Sound Community College, PO Box 97, Valdez, AK 99686-0097. *Phone:* 907-834-1631. *Toll-free phone:* 800-478-8800 Ext. 1600. *E-mail:* studentservices@pwscc.edu.

UNIVERSITY OF ALASKA SOUTHEAST, KETCHIKAN CAMPUS

Ketchikan, Alaska   **www.ketch.alaska.edu/**

Director of Admissions Mrs. Gail Klein, Student Services Coordinator, University of Alaska Southeast, Ketchikan Campus, 2600 7th Avenue, Ketchikan, AK 99901-5798. *Phone:* 907-228-4508. *Fax:* 907-225-3624. *E-mail:* knblj@acad1.alaska.edu.

UNIVERSITY OF ALASKA SOUTHEAST, SITKA CAMPUS

Sitka, Alaska   **www.uas.alaska.edu/**

- **State-supported** 2-year, founded 1962, part of University of Alaska System
- **Small-town** campus
- **Coed,** 1,552 undergraduate students

Undergraduates Students come from 10 states and territories, 2 other countries.

Faculty *Total:* 105. *Student/faculty ratio:* 13:1.

Majors Business administration and management; computer and information sciences; computer engineering technology; computer systems analysis; environmental engineering technology; health/health care administration; liberal arts and sciences/liberal studies; medical/clinical assistant; water quality and wastewater treatment management and recycling technology.

Academics *Calendar:* semesters. *Degree:* certificates, diplomas, and associate. *Special study options:* academic remediation for entering students, adult/continuing education programs, cooperative education, English as a second language, internships, off-campus study, part-time degree program, summer session for credit.

Library Stratton Library with 80,050 titles, 306 serial subscriptions, an OPAC, a Web page.

Student Life *Housing:* college housing not available. *Options:* coed. *Activities and Organizations:* Student Government Association, Tai Chi Club. *Campus security:* 24-hour emergency response devices.

Costs (2006–07) *Tuition:* $6120 full-time, $128 per credit part-time. Full-time tuition and fees vary according to course level. Part-time tuition and fees vary according to course level. *Required fees:* $1590 full-time, $796 per term part-time. *Payment plan:* deferred payment. *Waivers:* senior citizens and employees or children of employees.

Applying *Options:* early admission. *Application fee:* $35. *Required:* high school transcript, minimum 2.0 GPA. *Required for some:* essay or personal statement. *Application deadlines:* rolling (freshmen), rolling (transfers). *Notification:* continuous (freshmen), continuous (transfers).

Freshmen Application Contact Cynthia Rogers, Coordinator of Admissions, University of Alaska Southeast, Sitka Campus, 1332 Seward Avenue, Sitka, AK 99835-9418. *Phone:* 907-747-7705. *Toll-free phone:* 800-478-6653. *Fax:* 907-747-7793. *E-mail:* cynthia.rogers@uas.alaska.edu.

AMERICAN SAMOA

AMERICAN SAMOA COMMUNITY COLLEGE

Pago Pago, American Samoa   **www.ascc.as/**

Director of Admissions Mrs. Sina P. Ward, Registrar, American Samoa Community College, PO Box 2609, Pago Pago, AS 96799. *Phone:* 684-699-1141.

ARIZONA

APOLLO COLLEGE—PHOENIX, INC.

Phoenix, Arizona www.apollocollege.com/

Director of Admissions Mr. Randy Utley, Campus Director, Apollo College–Phoenix, Inc., 2701 West Bethany Home Road, Phoenix, AZ 85051. *Phone:* 602-864-1571. *Toll-free phone:* 800-36-TRAIN. *Fax:* 602-864-8207. *E-mail:* rutley@apollocollege.com.

APOLLO COLLEGE—TRI-CITY, INC.

Mesa, Arizona www.apollocollege.com/

Director of Admissions Mr. James Norris Miller, Campus Director, Apollo College–Tri-City, Inc., 630 West Southern Avenue, Mesa, AZ 85210-5004. *Phone:* 480-831-6585. *Toll-free phone:* 800-36-TRAIN. *E-mail:* jmiller@apollocollege.com.

APOLLO COLLEGE—TUCSON, INC.

Tucson, Arizona www.apollocollege.com/

Director of Admissions Ms. Jenell McKinney, Campus Director, Apollo College–Tucson, Inc., 3870 North Oracle Road, Tucson, AZ 85705-3227. *Phone:* 520-888-5885. *Toll-free phone:* 800-36-TRAIN. *Fax:* 520-887-3005. *E-mail:* jmckinney@apollocollege.com.

APOLLO COLLEGE—WESTSIDE, INC.

Phoenix, Arizona www.apollocollege.com/

Director of Admissions Ms. Cindy Nestor, Vice President, Apollo College–Westside, Inc., 2701 West Bethany Home Road, Phoenix, AZ 85017. *Phone:* 602-433-1222 Ext. 251. *Toll-free phone:* 800-36-TRAIN. *Fax:* 602-433-1222. *E-mail:* cnestor@apollocollege.com.

ARIZONA AUTOMOTIVE INSTITUTE

Glendale, Arizona www.aai.edu/

Director of Admissions Mr. Mark LaCara, Director of Admissions, Arizona Automotive Institute, 6829 North 46th Avenue, Glendale, AZ 85301-3597. *Phone:* 623-934-7273 Ext. 211. *Fax:* 623-937-5000.

ARIZONA COLLEGE OF ALLIED HEALTH

Glendale, Arizona www.arizonacollege.edu/

- **Proprietary** 2-year, founded 1992
- **Coed,** 197 undergraduate students

Majors Allied health and medical assisting services related; health information/medical records technology.

Academics *Calendar:* quarters.

Costs (2006–07) *Tuition:* $10,500 full-time.

Applying *Application fee:* $25.

Freshmen Application Contact Admissions Department, Arizona College of Allied Health, 4425 West Olive Avenue, Suite 300, Glendale, AZ 85302. *E-mail:* lhicks@arizonacollege.edu.

ARIZONA WESTERN COLLEGE

Yuma, Arizona www.azwestern.edu/

- **State and locally supported** 2-year, founded 1962, part of Arizona State Community College System
- **Rural** 640-acre campus
- **Coed,** 6,579 undergraduate students, 39% full-time, 61% women, 39% men

Undergraduates 2,593 full-time, 3,986 part-time. Students come from 22 states and territories, 27 other countries, 10% are from out of state, 3% African American, 2% Asian American or Pacific Islander, 50% Hispanic American, 2% Native American, 12% international, 0.8% transferred in, 5% live on campus. *Retention:* 65% of 2003 full-time freshmen returned.

Freshmen *Admission:* 1,132 enrolled.

Faculty *Total:* 349, 33% full-time, 5% with terminal degrees. *Student/faculty ratio:* 18:1.

Majors Administrative assistant and secretarial science; agricultural business and management; agriculture; art; automobile/automotive mechanics technology; biological and physical sciences; biology/biological sciences; broadcast journalism; business administration and management; chemistry; computer science; criminal justice/law enforcement administration; criminal justice/police science; developmental and child psychology; drafting and design technology; dramatic/theater arts; education; electrical, electronic and communications engineering technology; engineering technology; English; environmental studies; family and consumer economics related; fire science; geology/earth science; health science; heating, air conditioning, ventilation and refrigeration maintenance technology; hospitality administration; hospitality administration related; human services; information science/studies; marketing/marketing management; massage therapy; mathematics; music; nursing (licensed practical/vocational nurse training); nursing (registered nurse training); physical education teaching and coaching; physics; radiologic technology/science; social sciences; Spanish; water quality and wastewater treatment management and recycling technology; welding technology.

Academics *Calendar:* semesters. *Degree:* certificates and associate. *Special study options:* academic remediation for entering students, adult/continuing education programs, advanced placement credit, cooperative education, distance learning, English as a second language, honors programs, independent study, part-time degree program, summer session for credit.

Library Arizona Western College Library with 94,116 titles, 402 serial subscriptions, 4,486 audiovisual materials, an OPAC, a Web page.

Student Life *Housing Options:* coed. Campus housing is university owned. *Activities and Organizations:* drama/theater group, student-run newspaper, radio and television station, choral group, Associated Students Governing Board, MECHA, Umoja, Honors Club, UVU. *Campus security:* 24-hour emergency response devices and patrols, student patrols, late-night transport/escort service. *Student services:* health clinic, personal/psychological counseling.

Athletics Member NJCAA. *Intercollegiate sports:* baseball M(s), basketball M(s), football M(s), soccer M(s), softball W(s), volleyball W(s). *Intramural sports:* badminton M/W, basketball M/W, football M, soccer M, softball M/W, swimming and diving M/W, table tennis M/W, volleyball M/W.

Costs (2006–07) *Tuition:* state resident $1200 full-time, $40 per credit hour part-time; nonresident $5760 full-time, $46 per credit hour part-time. *Room and board:* $4468; room only: $1790.

Financial Aid Of all full-time matriculated undergraduates, 350 Federal Work-Study jobs (averaging $1500). 100 state and other part-time jobs (averaging $1800).

Applying *Options:* early admission, deferred entrance. *Application deadlines:* rolling (freshmen), rolling (transfers).

Freshmen Application Contact Mr. Bryan Doak, Dean of Enrollment Services, Arizona Western College, PO Box 929, Yuma, AZ 85366. *Phone:* 928-317-7617. *Toll-free phone:* 888-293-0392. *Fax:* 928-344-7730. *E-mail:* bryan.doak@azwestern.edu.

THE BRYMAN SCHOOL

Phoenix, Arizona www.brymanschool.edu/

Director of Admissions Ms. Vicki Maurer, Admission Manager, The Bryman School, 2250 W. Peoria Avenue, Phoenix, AZ 85029. *Phone:* 602-274-4300. *Toll-free phone:* 800-729-4819.

CENTRAL ARIZONA COLLEGE

Coolidge, Arizona   www.centralaz.edu/

- **County-supported** 2-year, founded 1961
- **Rural** 709-acre campus with easy access to Phoenix
- **Coed,** 6,471 undergraduate students, 27% full-time, 56% women, 44% men

Undergraduates 1,730 full-time, 4,741 part-time. Students come from 6 other countries, 6% African American, 2% Asian American or Pacific Islander, 33% Hispanic American, 6% Native American, 0.4% international, 17% live on campus.

Freshmen *Admission:* 2,469 applied, 1,801 admitted.

Faculty *Total:* 332, 29% full-time. *Student/faculty ratio:* 17:1.

Majors Accounting; administrative assistant and secretarial science; agriculture; automobile/automotive mechanics technology; business administration and management; child development; civil engineering technology; computer and information sciences; computer science; corrections; criminal justice/law enforcement administration; dietetics; emergency medical technology (EMT paramedic); engineering; health aide; hotel/motel administration; industrial technology; kindergarten/preschool education; legal administrative assistant/secretary; liberal arts and sciences/liberal studies; marketing/marketing management; materials science; medical administrative assistant and medical secretary; medical transcription; nursing (licensed practical/vocational nurse training); nursing (registered nurse training).

Academics *Calendar:* semesters. *Degree:* certificates and associate. *Special study options:* academic remediation for entering students, adult/continuing education programs, distance learning, honors programs, independent study, part-time degree program, services for LD students, student-designed majors, summer session for credit.

Library Learning Resource Center with 99,480 titles, 494 serial subscriptions, a Web page.

Student Life *Housing Options:* coed, men-only, women-only. Campus housing is university owned. *Activities and Organizations:* drama/theater group, student-run newspaper, choral group. *Campus security:* 24-hour emergency response devices and patrols. *Student services:* personal/psychological counseling.

Athletics Member NJCAA. *Intercollegiate sports:* baseball M(s), basketball M(s)/W(s), cross-country running M(s)/W(s), equestrian sports M(s)/W(s), golf M(s), softball W(s), track and field M(s)/W(s).

Costs (2007–08) *Tuition:* state resident $1596 full-time; nonresident $7112 full-time. *Room and board:* $4670.

Financial Aid Of all full-time matriculated undergraduates, 68 Federal Work-Study jobs (averaging $1310).

Applying *Options:* early admission, deferred entrance. *Application deadlines:* rolling (freshmen), rolling (transfers). *Notification:* continuous (freshmen), continuous (transfers).

Freshmen Application Contact Ms. Doris Helmich, Associate Vice President of Student Development, Central Arizona College, 8470 North Overfield Road, Coolidge, AZ 85228. *Phone:* 520-426-4406. *Toll-free phone:* 800-237-9814. *Fax:* 520-426-4271. *E-mail:* leonor_verduzoo@centralaz.edu.

CHANDLER-GILBERT COMMUNITY COLLEGE

Chandler, Arizona   www.cgc.maricopa.edu/

- **State and locally supported** 2-year, founded 1985, part of Maricopa County Community College District System
- **Rural** 80-acre campus with easy access to Phoenix
- **Endowment** $315,961
- **Coed,** 9,420 undergraduate students, 27% full-time, 56% women, 44% men

Undergraduates 2,589 full-time, 6,831 part-time. Students come from 38 states and territories, 5 other countries, 4% are from out of state, 4% African American, 5% Asian American or Pacific Islander, 15% Hispanic American, 0.1% Native American, 0.9% international, 4% transferred in.

Freshmen *Admission:* 357 enrolled.

Faculty *Total:* 412, 22% full-time. *Student/faculty ratio:* 19:1.

Majors Accounting; airframe mechanics and aircraft maintenance technology; avionics maintenance technology; business administration and management; computer engineering technology; liberal arts and sciences/liberal studies; management information systems.

Academics *Calendar:* semesters. *Degree:* certificates, diplomas, and associate. *Special study options:* academic remediation for entering students, advanced placement credit, English as a second language, freshman honors college, honors programs, part-time degree program, summer session for credit.

Library Chandler-Gilbert Community College Library with 26,060 titles, 170 serial subscriptions, an OPAC.

Student Life *Activities and Organizations:* student-run newspaper, choral group. *Campus security:* 24-hour emergency response devices and patrols, late-night transport/escort service. *Student services:* personal/psychological counseling.

Costs (2007–08) *Tuition:* area resident $795 full-time; state resident $3012 full-time; nonresident $3360 full-time.

Applying *Options:* electronic application.

Director of Admissions Ms. Irene Pearl, Supervisor of Admissions and Records, Chandler-Gilbert Community College, 2626 East Pecos Road, Chandler, AZ 85225-2479. *Phone:* 480-732-7307.

CHAPARRAL COLLEGE

Tucson, Arizona   www.chap-col.edu/

Director of Admissions Ms. Becki Rossini, Director of Admissions, Chaparral College, 4585 East Speedway, # 204, Tucson, AZ 85712. *Phone:* 520-327-6866.

COCHISE COLLEGE

Douglas, Arizona   www.cochise.edu/

- **State and locally supported** 2-year, founded 1962
- **Rural** 500-acre campus
- **Endowment** $1.8 million
- **Coed,** 4,436 undergraduate students, 35% full-time, 61% women, 39% men

Undergraduates 1,535 full-time, 2,901 part-time. Students come from 40 states and territories, 3 other countries, 5% are from out of state, 6% African American, 3% Asian American or Pacific Islander, 41% Hispanic American, 1% Native American, 6% transferred in, 2% live on campus. *Retention:* 57% of 2003 full-time freshmen returned.

Freshmen *Admission:* 1,901 applied, 1,901 admitted, 794 enrolled. *Average high school GPA:* 3.3.

Faculty *Total:* 381, 27% full-time. *Student/faculty ratio:* 13:1.

Majors Administrative assistant and secretarial science; agricultural business and management; airframe mechanics and aircraft maintenance technology; airline pilot and flight crew; anthropology; art; avionics maintenance technology; biology/biological sciences; business administration and management; chemistry; communication/speech communication and rhetoric; computer and information systems security; computer programming; computer science; computer systems networking and telecommunications; criminal justice/police science; culinary arts; data processing and data processing technology; early childhood education; economics; education; electrical, electronic and communications engineering technology; emergency medical technology (EMT paramedic); English; family psychology; fire science; foreign languages and literatures; general studies; health and physical education; health services/allied health/health sciences; history; hospitality administration; humanities; human services; information science/studies; journalism; language interpretation and translation; liberal arts and sciences/liberal studies; manufacturing engineering; mathematics; military technologies; nursing (registered nurse training); physical education teaching and coaching; political science and government; pre-nursing studies; psychology; social work; sociology; welding technology.

Academics *Calendar:* semesters. *Degree:* certificates and associate. *Special study options:* academic remediation for entering students, accelerated degree program, adult/continuing education programs, advanced placement credit, cooperative education, distance learning, English as a second language, honors programs, independent study, internships, part-time degree program, services for LD students, summer session for credit.

Library Charles DePeso plus 2 others with 65,000 titles, 7,000 serial subscriptions, 4,000 audiovisual materials, an OPAC, a Web page.

Student Life *Housing Options:* men-only, women-only, disabled students. Campus housing is university owned. *Activities and Organizations:* choral group, student government, Phi Theta Kappa. *Campus security:* 24-hour emergency response devices and patrols, controlled dormitory access. *Student services:* health clinic, personal/psychological counseling.

Athletics Member NJCAA. *Intercollegiate sports:* baseball M(s), basketball M(s)/W(s), soccer W(s). *Intramural sports:* basketball M.

Costs (2007–08) *Tuition:* state resident $1410 full-time, $47 per credit hour part-time; nonresident $6960 full-time, $68 per credit hour part-time. *Required fees:* $60 full-time, $30 per term part-time. *Room and board:* $3910.

Financial Aid Of all full-time matriculated undergraduates, 137 Federal Work-Study jobs (averaging $1070).

Cochise College (continued)

Applying *Options:* early admission, deferred entrance. *Recommended:* high school transcript. *Application deadlines:* rolling (freshmen), rolling (out-of-state freshmen), rolling (transfers). *Notification:* continuous (freshmen), continuous (out-of-state freshmen), continuous (transfers).

Freshmen Application Contact Deb Munson, Admissions Counselor, Cochise College, 4190 West Highway 80, Douglas, AZ 85607-9724. *Phone:* 520-515-5411. *Toll-free phone:* 800-966-7946. *Fax:* 520-515-5452. *E-mail:* admissions@cochise.edu.

COCHISE COLLEGE

Sierra Vista, Arizona   **www.cochise.edu**

- **State and locally supported** 2-year, founded 1977, part of Cochise College
- **Small-town** 200-acre campus with easy access to Tucson
- **Coed,** 4,446 undergraduate students, 28% full-time, 57% women, 43% men

Undergraduates 1,257 full-time, 3,189 part-time. Students come from 27 states and territories, 8 other countries, 5% are from out of state, 7% African American, 4% Asian American or Pacific Islander, 31% Hispanic American, 1% Native American, 0.5% international, 6% transferred in.

Freshmen *Admission:* 1,088 applied, 688 admitted, 688 enrolled. *Average high school GPA:* 2.93.

Faculty *Total:* 394, 23% full-time. *Student/faculty ratio:* 14:1.

Majors Administrative assistant and secretarial science; anthropology; art; behavioral sciences; biology/biological sciences; business administration and management; chemistry; computer programming; computer science; criminal justice/law enforcement administration; criminal justice/police science; drafting and design technology; education; electrical, electronic and communications engineering technology; English; film/cinema studies; fire science; history; hotel/motel administration; information science/studies; international relations and affairs; journalism; legal administrative assistant/secretary; liberal arts and sciences/liberal studies; mass communication/media; medical administrative assistant and medical secretary; nursing (registered nurse training); physical education teaching and coaching; political science and government; psychology; social sciences; social work; teacher assistant/aide; welding technology.

Academics *Calendar:* semesters. *Degree:* certificates and associate. *Special study options:* academic remediation for entering students, accelerated degree program, adult/continuing education programs, cooperative education, distance learning, double majors, English as a second language, external degree program, honors programs, independent study, internships, part-time degree program, services for LD students, summer session for credit.

Library Charles DiPeso Main Library plus 1 other with 67,317 titles, 305 serial subscriptions, 3,124 audiovisual materials, an OPAC, a Web page.

Student Life *Housing Options:* Campus housing is university owned. Freshman campus housing is guaranteed. *Activities and Organizations:* drama/theater group, choral group, student government, Phi Theta Kappa. *Campus security:* 24-hour emergency response devices and patrols. *Student services:* personal/psychological counseling.

Athletics Member NJCAA. *Intercollegiate sports:* baseball M, basketball M/W, equestrian sports M/W, soccer W.

Standardized Tests *Required for some:* ACCUPLACER. *Recommended:* SAT (for admission), ACT (for admission), SAT or ACT (for admission), SAT and SAT Subject Tests or ACT (for admission), SAT Subject Tests (for admission), SAT or ACT (for placement).

Costs (2006–07) *Tuition:* state resident $1350 full-time, $45 per credit hour part-time; nonresident $6300 full-time, $65 per credit hour part-time. Full-time tuition and fees vary according to location and reciprocity agreements. Part-time tuition and fees vary according to course load and location. *Required fees:* $60 full-time, $30 per term part-time. *Room and board:* $3562. Room and board charges vary according to board plan and housing facility. *Payment plan:* installment. *Waivers:* senior citizens and employees or children of employees.

Applying *Options:* electronic application, early admission, deferred entrance. *Recommended:* high school transcript. *Application deadlines:* rolling (freshmen), rolling (transfers). *Notification:* continuous (freshmen), continuous (transfers).

Freshmen Application Contact Ms. Debbie Quick, Director of Admissions and Records, Cochise College, 901 North Columbo, Sierra Vista, AZ 85635-2317. *Phone:* 520-515-5412. *Toll-free phone:* 800-593-9567. *Fax:* 520-515-4006. *E-mail:* quickd@cochise.edu.

COCONINO COMMUNITY COLLEGE

Flagstaff, Arizona   **www.coconino.edu/**

- **State-supported** 2-year, founded 1991
- **Small-town** 5-acre campus
- **Endowment** $568,934
- **Coed,** 3,883 undergraduate students, 21% full-time, 57% women, 43% men

Undergraduates 832 full-time, 3,051 part-time. Students come from 8 states and territories, 2% are from out of state, 1% African American, 1% Asian American or Pacific Islander, 10% Hispanic American, 25% Native American, 23% transferred in.

Freshmen *Admission:* 879 enrolled.

Faculty *Total:* 270, 15% full-time. *Student/faculty ratio:* 16:1.

Majors Accounting; biological and physical sciences; business administration and management; criminal justice/law enforcement administration; fire science; information science/studies; liberal arts and sciences/liberal studies.

Academics *Calendar:* semesters. *Degree:* certificates and associate. *Special study options:* academic remediation for entering students, adult/continuing education programs, distance learning, honors programs, independent study, internships, part-time degree program, study abroad.

Library IRLS with 3,026 titles, 45 serial subscriptions, 1,598 audiovisual materials, an OPAC, a Web page.

Student Life *Housing:* college housing not available. *Activities and Organizations:* choral group. *Campus security:* 24-hour patrols.

Costs (2006–07) *Tuition:* state resident $1344 full-time, $61 per credit part-time; nonresident $5376 full-time.

Financial Aid Of all full-time matriculated undergraduates, 25 Federal Work-Study jobs (averaging $4000).

Applying *Required for some:* essay or personal statement, interview. *Recommended:* high school transcript. *Application deadlines:* rolling (freshmen), rolling (transfers).

Freshmen Application Contact Marrianna Dougherty, Coconino Community College, 2800 South Lone Tree Road, Flagstaff, AZ 86001. *Phone:* 928-527-1222. *Toll-free phone:* 800-350-7122. *E-mail:* marrianna.dougherty@coconino.edu.

COLLEGEAMERICA–FLAGSTAFF

Flagstaff, Arizona   **www.collegeamerica.com/**

Freshmen Application Contact Admissions Office, CollegeAmerica–Flagstaff, 5200 East Cortland Boulevard, Suite A-19, Flagstaff, AZ 86004. *Phone:* 928-526-0763 Ext. 1402. *Toll-free phone:* 800-622-2894.

DINÉ COLLEGE

Tsaile, Arizona   **www.dinecollege.edu/**

- **Federally supported** 2-year, founded 1968
- **Rural** 1200-acre campus
- **Endowment** $3.5 million
- **Coed**

Undergraduates 843 full-time, 982 part-time. Students come from 1 other state, 3 other countries, 0.2% African American, 0.3% Asian American or Pacific Islander, 98% Native American, 12% transferred in, 8% live on campus.

Academics *Calendar:* semesters. *Degree:* certificates and associate. *Special study options:* academic remediation for entering students, adult/continuing education programs, off-campus study, part-time degree program, services for LD students, summer session for credit.

Student Life *Campus security:* 24-hour emergency response devices and patrols, student patrols, late-night transport/escort service.

Athletics Member NSCAA, NJCAA.

Costs (2006–07) *Tuition:* state resident $720 full-time, $30 per hour part-time; nonresident $720 full-time, $30 per hour part-time. *Room and board:* $3764; room only: $1180.

Financial Aid Of all full-time matriculated undergraduates, 100 Federal Work-Study jobs (averaging $650).

Applying *Options:* early admission. *Required:* high school transcript, certificate of Indian Blood form for Native American Students.

Freshmen Application Contact Mrs. Louise Litzin, Registrar, Diné College, PO Box 67, Tsaile, AZ 86556. *Phone:* 928-724-6633. *Fax:* 928-724-3349. *E-mail:* louise@dinecollege.edu.

EASTERN ARIZONA COLLEGE
Thatcher, Arizona
www.eac.edu/

- **State and locally supported** 2-year, founded 1888, part of Arizona State Community College System
- **Small-town** campus
- **Endowment** $1.8 million
- **Coed,** 5,520 undergraduate students, 29% full-time, 60% women, 40% men

Undergraduates 1,585 full-time, 3,935 part-time. Students come from 27 states and territories, 5% are from out of state, 2% African American, 1% Asian American or Pacific Islander, 18% Hispanic American, 4% Native American, 0.5% international, 2% transferred in, 5% live on campus. *Retention:* 43% of 2003 full-time freshmen returned.

Freshmen *Admission:* 2,800 applied, 2,800 admitted, 623 enrolled.

Faculty *Total:* 292, 31% full-time, 5% with terminal degrees. *Student/faculty ratio:* 18:1.

Majors Agribusiness; agriculture; anthropology; art; art teacher education; automobile/automotive mechanics technology; biology/biological sciences; business administration and management; business, management, and marketing related; business operations support and secretarial services related; business teacher education; chemistry; child care provision; civil engineering technology; commercial and advertising art; corrections; criminal justice/law enforcement administration; criminal justice/police science; data entry/microcomputer applications; drafting and design technology; dramatic/theater arts; elementary education; emergency medical technology (EMT paramedic); English; entrepreneurship; foreign languages and literatures; forestry; geology/earth science; health and physical education; health/medical preparatory programs related; history; information science/studies; liberal arts and sciences/liberal studies; machine shop technology; management information systems and services related; mathematics; mining technology; music; nursing (registered nurse training); physics; political science and government; pre-law studies; pre-medical studies; pre-pharmacy studies; psychology; secondary education; sociology; technology/industrial arts teacher education; welding technology; wildlife biology.

Academics *Calendar:* semesters. *Degree:* certificates and associate. *Special study options:* academic remediation for entering students, adult/continuing education programs, advanced placement credit, cooperative education, double majors, independent study, part-time degree program, services for LD students, study abroad, summer session for credit.

Library Alumni Library plus 1 other with an OPAC, a Web page.

Student Life *Housing Options:* men-only, women-only. Campus housing is university owned. *Activities and Organizations:* drama/theater group, choral group, marching band, Latter-Day Saints Student Association, Criminal Justice Student Association, Multicultural Council, Phi Theta Kappa, Mark Allen Dorm Club. *Campus security:* late-night transport/escort service, controlled dormitory access, 20-hour patrols by trained security personnel. *Student services:* personal/psychological counseling.

Athletics Member NJCAA. *Intercollegiate sports:* baseball M(s), basketball M(s)/W(s), football M(s), golf M/W, softball W(s), volleyball W(s). *Intramural sports:* basketball M/W, racquetball M/W, swimming and diving M/W, table tennis M/W, tennis M/W, volleyball M/W.

Costs (2007–08) *Tuition:* state resident $1300 full-time, $55 per credit hour part-time; nonresident $6540 full-time, $105 per credit hour part-time. *Room and board:* $4230; room only: $2108.

Financial Aid Of all full-time matriculated undergraduates, 314 Federal Work-Study jobs (averaging $1800). 145 state and other part-time jobs (averaging $1800).

Applying *Options:* electronic application, early admission, deferred entrance. *Recommended:* high school transcript. *Application deadlines:* rolling (freshmen), rolling (transfers). *Notification:* continuous (freshmen).

Freshmen Application Contact Dr. Gary Sorenson, Director of Recruitment, Eastern Arizona College, 615 North Stadium Avenue, Thatcher, AZ 85552-0769. *Phone:* 928-426-8247. *Toll-free phone:* 800-678-3808. *Fax:* 928-428-8462. *E-mail:* admissions@eac.edu.

ESTRELLA MOUNTAIN COMMUNITY COLLEGE
Avondale, Arizona
www.emc.maricopa.edu/

Director of Admissions Dr. Ernesto Laura, Dean of Student Services, Estrella Mountain Community College, 3000 North Dysart Road, Avondale, AZ 85323-1000. *Phone:* 623-935-8808.

EVEREST COLLEGE
Phoenix, Arizona
www.everest-college.com/

- **Proprietary** primarily 2-year, founded 1982, part of Corinthian Colleges, Inc.
- **Urban** campus
- **Coed,** 1,187 undergraduate students, 53% full-time, 83% women, 17% men

Undergraduates 624 full-time, 563 part-time. Students come from 29 states and territories, 24% are from out of state, 13% African American, 2% Asian American or Pacific Islander, 17% Hispanic American, 4% Native American, 0.3% international. *Retention:* 65% of 2003 full-time freshmen returned.

Freshmen *Admission:* 672 applied, 527 admitted, 527 enrolled.

Faculty *Total:* 77, 19% full-time, 32% with terminal degrees. *Student/faculty ratio:* 23:1.

Majors Accounting; business/commerce; criminal justice/police science; legal assistant/paralegal; medical/clinical assistant.

Academics *Calendar:* 6 or 12 week terms. *Degrees:* diplomas, associate, and bachelor's. *Special study options:* academic remediation for entering students, adult/continuing education programs, distance learning, double majors, independent study, services for LD students, study abroad.

Library Everest College Library with 17,515 titles, 48 serial subscriptions, 514 audiovisual materials, a Web page.

Student Life *Housing:* college housing not available. *Activities and Organizations:* Collegiate Secretaries International, Toastmasters. *Campus security:* 24-hour emergency response devices and patrols. *Student services:* personal/psychological counseling.

Costs (2007–08) *Tuition:* $13,056 full-time, $272 per quarter hour part-time. *Required fees:* $100 full-time, $25 per term part-time.

Applying *Options:* deferred entrance. *Required:* high school transcript, minimum 2.0 GPA, interview. *Required for some:* essay or personal statement. *Application deadline:* rolling (freshmen). *Notification:* continuous (freshmen).

Freshmen Application Contact Mr. Jim Askins, Director of Admissions, Everest College, 10400 North 25th Avenue, Suite 190, Phoenix, AZ 85021. *Phone:* 602-942-4141. *Fax:* 602-943-0960. *E-mail:* jaskins@cci.edu.

GATEWAY COMMUNITY COLLEGE
Phoenix, Arizona
www.gwc.maricopa.edu/

- **State and locally supported** 2-year, founded 1968, part of Maricopa County Community College District System
- **Urban** 20-acre campus
- **Coed**

Undergraduates 976 full-time, 8,401 part-time. Students come from 50 states and territories, 26 other countries, 3% are from out of state, 8% African American, 2% Asian American or Pacific Islander, 21% Hispanic American, 4% Native American.

Faculty *Student/faculty ratio:* 25:1.

Academics *Calendar:* semesters. *Degree:* certificates and associate. *Special study options:* academic remediation for entering students, accelerated degree program, adult/continuing education programs, advanced placement credit, cooperative education, distance learning, English as a second language, honors programs, independent study, internships, part-time degree program, services for LD students, summer session for credit. *ROTC:* Army (c), Air Force (c).

Student Life *Campus security:* 24-hour emergency response devices and patrols, student patrols, late-night transport/escort service.

Athletics Member NJCAA.

Costs (2006–07) *Tuition:* area resident $1560 full-time, $65 per credit part-time; state resident $6720 full-time, $85 per credit part-time; nonresident $6720 full-time, $85 per credit part-time. *Required fees:* $30 full-time.

Applying *Options:* electronic application, early admission, deferred entrance. *Required for some:* high school transcript.

Freshmen Application Contact Ms. Cathy Gibson, Director of Admissions and Records, GateWay Community College, 108 North 40th Street, Phoenix, AZ 85034. *Phone:* 602-286-8052. *Fax:* 602-286-8200. *E-mail:* cathy.gibson@gwmail.maricopa.edu.

GLENDALE COMMUNITY COLLEGE
Glendale, Arizona
www.gc.maricopa.edu/

- **State and locally supported** 2-year, founded 1965, part of Maricopa County Community College District System
- **Suburban** 160-acre campus with easy access to Phoenix
- **Endowment** $353,507
- **Coed**

Glendale Community College (continued)

Undergraduates 6,108 full-time, 13,962 part-time. Students come from 50 states and territories, 3% are from out of state, 7% African American, 4% Asian American or Pacific Islander, 22% Hispanic American, 2% Native American, 1% international, 28% transferred in. *Retention:* 60% of 2003 full-time freshmen returned.

Faculty *Student/faculty ratio:* 22:1.

Academics *Calendar:* semesters. *Degree:* certificates and associate. *Special study options:* academic remediation for entering students, adult/continuing education programs, advanced placement credit, cooperative education, distance learning, double majors, English as a second language, freshman honors college, honors programs, internships, off-campus study, part-time degree program, services for LD students, summer session for credit. *ROTC:* Army (c), Air Force (c).

Student Life *Campus security:* 24-hour patrols, student patrols, late-night transport/escort service.

Athletics Member NJCAA.

Costs (2006–07) *Tuition:* area resident $1560 full-time, $65 per credit hour part-time; state resident $6720 full-time, $280 per credit hour part-time; nonresident $6720 full-time, $280 per credit hour part-time. *Required fees:* $30 full-time, $15 per term part-time.

Financial Aid Of all full-time matriculated undergraduates, 350 Federal Work-Study jobs (averaging $1700).

Applying *Options:* electronic application. *Required for some:* high school transcript.

Freshmen Application Contact Ms. Mary Lou Massal, Dean of Enrollment Services, Glendale Community College, 6000 West Olive Avenue, Glendale, AZ 85302. *Phone:* 623-435-3305. *Toll-free phone:* 623-845-3000. *Fax:* 623-845-3303. *E-mail:* info@gc.maricopa.edu.

HIGH-TECH INSTITUTE
Phoenix, Arizona   www.high-techinstitute.com/

Freshmen Application Contact Mr. Glen Husband, Vice President of Admissions, High-Tech Institute, 1515 East Indian School Road, Phoenix, AZ 85014-4901. *Phone:* 602-279-9700.

INTERNATIONAL INSTITUTE OF THE AMERICAS
Mesa, Arizona   www.iia-online.com/site/

- **Independent** primarily 2-year, founded 1982
- **Urban** campus
- **Coed,** 145 undergraduate students, 100% full-time, 88% women, 12% men

Undergraduates 145 full-time. 5% African American, 26% Hispanic American, 19% Native American.

Faculty *Total:* 15, 40% full-time, 20% with terminal degrees. *Student/faculty ratio:* 10:1.

Majors Accounting; business administration and management; criminal justice/law enforcement administration; health/health care administration; legal assistant/paralegal.

Academics *Calendar:* semesters. *Degrees:* diplomas, associate, and bachelor's. *Special study options:* distance learning, part-time degree program.

Library Learning Resource Center with an OPAC.

Student Life *Housing:* college housing not available. *Campus security:* 24-hour emergency response devices.

Costs (2007–08) *Tuition:* $9850 full-time. *Required fees:* $200 full-time.

Applying *Application fee:* $200. *Required:* interview. *Application deadlines:* rolling (freshmen), rolling (out-of-state freshmen), rolling (transfers). *Notification:* continuous (freshmen), continuous (out-of-state freshmen), continuous (transfers).

Freshmen Application Contact Mr. Todd Olehausen, Campus Director, International Institute of the Americas, 925 South Gilbert Road, Suite 201, Mesa, AZ 85204-4448. *Phone:* 480-545-8755. *Toll-free phone:* 888-886-2428. *Fax:* 480-926-1371. *E-mail:* wging@iia.edu.

INTERNATIONAL INSTITUTE OF THE AMERICAS
Phoenix, Arizona   www.iia-online.com/site/

- **Independent** primarily 2-year, founded 1979
- **Urban** campus
- **Coed,** 424 undergraduate students, 100% full-time, 88% women, 12% men

Undergraduates 424 full-time. 17% African American, 3% Asian American or Pacific Islander, 32% Hispanic American, 7% Native American.

Faculty *Total:* 34, 56% full-time, 21% with terminal degrees. *Student/faculty ratio:* 12:1.

Majors Accounting; business administration and management; health/health care administration; legal assistant/paralegal; nursing (registered nurse training).

Academics *Calendar:* semesters. *Degrees:* diplomas, associate, and bachelor's. *Special study options:* distance learning, part-time degree program.

Library Learning Resource Center with an OPAC.

Student Life *Housing:* college housing not available. *Campus security:* 24-hour emergency response devices.

Costs (2007–08) *Tuition:* $9850 full-time. *Required fees:* $200 full-time.

Applying *Options:* electronic application, early admission, deferred entrance. *Application fee:* $200. *Required:* interview. *Application deadlines:* rolling (freshmen), rolling (out-of-state freshmen), rolling (transfers). *Notification:* continuous (freshmen), continuous (out-of-state freshmen), continuous (transfers).

Freshmen Application Contact Mr. Lynn McConnell, Campus Director, International Institute of the Americas, 6049 North 43 Avenue, Phoenix, AZ 85019. *Phone:* 602-242-6265. *Toll-free phone:* 800-793-2428. *Fax:* 602-973-2572. *E-mail:* lmcconnell@iia.edu.

INTERNATIONAL INSTITUTE OF THE AMERICAS
Tucson, Arizona   www.iia-online.com/site/

- **Independent** primarily 2-year, founded 1979
- **Urban** campus
- **Coed,** 267 undergraduate students, 100% full-time, 88% women, 12% men

Undergraduates 267 full-time. 16% African American, 0.4% Asian American or Pacific Islander, 43% Hispanic American, 9% Native American.

Faculty *Total:* 26, 54% full-time, 12% with terminal degrees. *Student/faculty ratio:* 10:1.

Majors Accounting; business administration and management; criminal justice/law enforcement administration; health/health care administration; legal assistant/paralegal.

Academics *Calendar:* semesters. *Degrees:* diplomas, associate, and bachelor's. *Special study options:* distance learning, part-time degree program.

Library Learning Resource Center with an OPAC.

Student Life *Housing:* college housing not available. *Campus security:* 24-hour emergency response devices.

Costs (2007–08) *Tuition:* $9850 full-time. *Required fees:* $200 full-time.

Applying *Application fee:* $200. *Required:* interview. *Application deadlines:* rolling (freshmen), rolling (out-of-state freshmen), rolling (transfers). *Notification:* continuous (freshmen), continuous (out-of-state freshmen), continuous (transfers).

Freshmen Application Contact Ms. Leigh Anne Pechota, Campus Director, International Institute of the Americas, 5441 East 22nd Street, Suite 125, Tucson, AZ 85711-5444. *Phone:* 520-748-9799. *Toll-free phone:* 888-292-2428. *Fax:* 520-748-9355. *E-mail:* lpechota@iia.edu.

ITT TECHNICAL INSTITUTE
Phoenix, Arizona   www.itt-tech.edu/

Freshmen Application Contact Mr. Gene McWhorter, Director of Recruitment, ITT Technical Institute, 4837 East McDowell Road, Phoenix, AZ 85008. *Phone:* 602-252-2331. *Toll-free phone:* 800-879-4881.

ITT TECHNICAL INSTITUTE

Tucson, Arizona **www.itt-tech.edu/**

- **Proprietary** primarily 2-year, founded 1984, part of ITT Educational Services, Inc
- **Urban** 3-acre campus
- **Coed**

Majors Animation, interactive technology, video graphics and special effects; business administration and management; CAD/CADD drafting/design technology; communications technology; computer and information systems security; computer engineering technology; computer software engineering; computer software technology; computer systems networking and telecommunications; criminal justice/law enforcement administration; electrical, electronic and communications engineering technology; medical laboratory technology; system, networking, and LAN/WAN management; web/multimedia management and webmaster; web page, digital/multimedia and information resources design.

Academics *Calendar:* quarters. *Degrees:* associate and bachelor's.

Library a Web page.

Student Life *Housing:* college housing not available.

Standardized Tests *Required:* Wonderlic aptitude test (for admission).

Costs (2006–07) *Tuition:* Contact school for program costs.

Applying *Options:* deferred entrance. *Application fee:* $100. *Required:* high school transcript, interview. *Recommended:* letters of recommendation. *Application deadlines:* rolling (freshmen), rolling (transfers). *Notification:* continuous (freshmen), continuous (transfers).

Freshmen Application Contact Ms. Linda Lemken, Director of Recruitment, ITT Technical Institute, 1455 West River Road, Tucson, AZ 85704. *Phone:* 520-408-7488. *Toll-free phone:* 800-870-9730.

LAMSON COLLEGE

Tempe, Arizona **www.lamsoncollege.com/**

Director of Admissions Mr. Chico Chavez, Director of Admissions, Lamson College, 1126 North Scottsdale Road, Suite 17, Tempe, AZ 85281. *Phone:* 480-898-7000. *Toll-free phone:* 800-898-7017.

LONG TECHNICAL COLLEGE

Phoenix, Arizona **www.longtechnicalcollege.com/**

- **Proprietary** 2-year, founded 1972
- **Coed,** 388 undergraduate students

Majors Respiratory care therapy; veterinary/animal health technology; veterinary technology.

Academics *Calendar:* continuous. *Degree:* associate.

Costs (2006–07) *Tuition:* $28,674 per degree program part-time.

Freshmen Application Contact Admissions Office, Long Technical College, 13610 North Black Canyon Highway, Suite 104, Phoenix, AZ 85029. *Phone:* 602-548-1955. *Toll-free phone:* 877-548-1955.

MESA COMMUNITY COLLEGE

Mesa, Arizona **www.mc.maricopa.edu/**

- **State and locally supported** 2-year, founded 1965, part of Maricopa County Community College District System
- **Urban** 160-acre campus with easy access to Phoenix
- **Coed,** 28,000 undergraduate students

Undergraduates Students come from 18 states and territories, 4% are from out of state, 3% African American, 5% Asian American or Pacific Islander, 14% Hispanic American, 3% Native American.

Freshmen *Average high school GPA:* 2.0.

Faculty *Total:* 1,065, 25% full-time.

Majors Accounting; administrative assistant and secretarial science; agricultural business and management; agricultural mechanization; agronomy and crop science; art; automobile/automotive mechanics technology; biology/biological sciences; business administration and management; child development; criminal justice/law enforcement administration; data processing and data processing technology; drafting and design technology; electrical, electronic and communications engineering technology; engineering technology; family and consumer sciences/human sciences; fashion merchandising; finance; fire science; heavy equipment maintenance technology; horticultural science; industrial technology; insurance; interior design; liberal arts and sciences/liberal studies; library science; marketing/marketing management; mathematics; medical administrative assistant and medical secretary; music; nursing (registered nurse training); ornamental horticulture; pre-engineering; quality control technology; real estate; teacher assistant/aide.

Academics *Calendar:* semesters. *Degree:* certificates and associate. *Special study options:* academic remediation for entering students, adult/continuing education programs, advanced placement credit, cooperative education, distance learning, English as a second language, freshman honors college, honors programs, independent study, off-campus study, part-time degree program, services for LD students, student-designed majors, study abroad, summer session for credit. *ROTC:* Army (c), Air Force (c).

Library Information Commons with 56,224 titles, 794 serial subscriptions, an OPAC, a Web page.

Student Life *Housing:* college housing not available. *Activities and Organizations:* drama/theater group, student-run newspaper, radio station, choral group, MECHA, International Student Association, American Indian Association, Asian/Pacific Islander Club. *Campus security:* 24-hour emergency response devices and patrols, student patrols. *Student services:* personal/psychological counseling, legal services.

Athletics Member NJCAA. *Intercollegiate sports:* baseball M, basketball M/W, cross-country running M, football M, golf M/W, soccer M/W, softball W, tennis M/W, track and field M/W, volleyball W, wrestling M. *Intramural sports:* basketball M/W, cross-country running M, football M/W, tennis M/W, track and field M/W, volleyball M/W, wrestling M/W.

Costs (2006–07) *Tuition:* area resident $1590 full-time, $65 per credit part-time; state resident $6054 full-time, $251 per credit part-time; nonresident $6750 full-time, $280 per credit part-time. Full-time tuition and fees vary according to course load and reciprocity agreements. Part-time tuition and fees vary according to course load and reciprocity agreements. *Required fees:* $15 per term part-time. *Payment plan:* installment. *Waivers:* employees or children of employees.

Applying *Options:* electronic application, early admission, deferred entrance. *Application deadlines:* 8/22 (freshmen), 8/22 (transfers). *Notification:* continuous (freshmen).

Freshmen Application Contact Ms. Kathleen Perales, Manager, Recruitment, Mesa Community College, 1833 West Southern Avenue, Mesa, AZ 85202-4866. *Phone:* 480-461-7751. *Fax:* 480-654-7379. *E-mail:* admissions@mc.maricopa.edu.

MOHAVE COMMUNITY COLLEGE

Kingman, Arizona **www.mohave.edu/**

- **State-supported** 2-year, founded 1971
- **Small-town** 160-acre campus
- **Coed,** 5,307 undergraduate students, 24% full-time, 66% women, 34% men

Undergraduates 1,250 full-time, 4,057 part-time. Students come from 17 states and territories, 5% are from out of state, 1% African American, 2% Asian American or Pacific Islander, 17% Hispanic American, 2% Native American.

Freshmen *Admission:* 1,355 applied, 1,355 admitted, 1,355 enrolled.

Faculty *Total:* 376, 16% full-time, 6% with terminal degrees. *Student/faculty ratio:* 16:1.

Majors Accounting; art; automobile/automotive mechanics technology; business administration and management; ceramic arts and ceramics; computer and information sciences related; computer programming (specific applications); computer science; criminal justice/police science; English; fire science; health science; history; information technology; liberal arts and sciences/liberal studies; marketing/marketing management; mathematics; metal and jewelry arts; music; nursing (registered nurse training); psychology; sociology; word processing.

Academics *Calendar:* semesters. *Degree:* certificates and associate. *Special study options:* academic remediation for entering students, adult/continuing education programs, cooperative education, distance learning, English as a second language, independent study, part-time degree program, summer session for credit.

Library Mohave Community College Library with 45,849 titles, 476 serial subscriptions, an OPAC, a Web page.

Student Life *Housing:* college housing not available. *Activities and Organizations:* drama/theater group, student-run newspaper, choral group, Art Club, Pottery Club, Astronomy Club, Phi Theta Kappa, national fraternities, national sororities. *Campus security:* late-night transport/escort service.

Costs (2007–08) *Tuition:* state resident $1200 full-time, $50 per credit hour part-time; nonresident $3600 full-time, $150 per credit hour part-time. *Required fees:* $80 full-time, $40 per term part-time.

Applying *Options:* early admission, deferred entrance. *Application deadlines:* rolling (freshmen), rolling (transfers). *Notification:* continuous (freshmen), continuous (transfers).

Mohave Community College (continued)

Freshmen Application Contact Ms. RuthAnn Wilson, Assistant to the Chancellor for Institutional Effectiveness, Mohave Community College, 1971 Jagerson Avenue, Kingman, AZ 86401. *Phone:* 928-757-0840. *Toll-free phone:* 888-664-2832. *Fax:* 928-757-0890. *E-mail:* rwilson@mohave.edu.

NORTHLAND PIONEER COLLEGE

Holbrook, Arizona   **www.npc.edu/**

Freshmen Application Contact Ms. Suzette Willis, Coordinator of Admissions, Northland Pioneer College, PO Box 610, Holbrook, AZ 86025-0610. *Phone:* 928-536-6271. *Toll-free phone:* 800-266-7845. *Fax:* 928-536-6212.

PARADISE VALLEY COMMUNITY COLLEGE

Phoenix, Arizona   **www.pvc.maricopa.edu/**

- **State and locally supported** 2-year, founded 1985, part of Maricopa County Community College District System
- **Urban** campus
- **Coed,** 8,406 undergraduate students, 26% full-time, 60% women, 40% men

Undergraduates 2,187 full-time, 6,219 part-time. 4% are from out of state, 3% African American, 3% Asian American or Pacific Islander, 9% Hispanic American, 2% Native American.

Faculty *Total:* 486, 21% full-time.

Majors Accounting; administrative assistant and secretarial science; business administration and management; computer typography and composition equipment operation; international business/trade/commerce; liberal arts and sciences/liberal studies; occupational safety and health technology.

Academics *Calendar:* semesters. *Degree:* certificates and associate. *Special study options:* academic remediation for entering students, adult/continuing education programs, advanced placement credit, cooperative education, distance learning, English as a second language, freshman honors college, honors programs, independent study, internships, off-campus study, services for LD students, study abroad.

Library Paradise Valley Community College Library plus 1 other with an OPAC, a Web page.

Student Life *Housing:* college housing not available. *Activities and Organizations:* drama/theater group, student-run newspaper, choral group, Phi Theta Kappa, International Student Club, Recreational Outing Club, AWARE, Student Christian Association. *Campus security:* 24-hour emergency response devices and patrols, late-night transport/escort service. *Student services:* personal/psychological counseling.

Athletics Member NJCAA. *Intercollegiate sports:* cross-country running M/W, golf M/W, soccer M/W, softball W, tennis M/W, track and field M/W.

Costs (2006–07) *Tuition:* area resident $1950 full-time, $65 per credit hour part-time; state resident $7740 full-time, $85 per credit hour part-time; nonresident $8400 full-time, $280 per credit hour part-time.

Financial Aid Of all full-time matriculated undergraduates, 50 Federal Work-Study jobs (averaging $2500).

Applying *Options:* early admission. *Application deadlines:* rolling (freshmen), rolling (transfers).

Freshmen Application Contact Ms. Donna Simon, Paradise Valley Community College, 18401 North 32nd Street, Phoenix, AZ 85032. *Phone:* 602-787-7063. *Fax:* 602-787-6545. *E-mail:* donna.simon@pvmail.maricopa.edu.

THE PARALEGAL INSTITUTE, INC.

Phoenix, Arizona   **www.theparalegalinstitute.com/**

- **Proprietary** 2-year, founded 1974
- 400 undergraduate students
- 25% of applicants were admitted

Academics *Degree:* diplomas and associate.

Costs (2006–07) *Tuition:* Full-time tuition and fees vary according to program. Part-time tuition and fees vary according to program. No tuition increase for student's term of enrollment. Contact school as tuition and fees vary according to program.

Freshmen Application Contact Patricia Yancy, Director of Admissions, The Paralegal Institute, Inc., 2933 West Indian School Road, Drawer 11408, Phoenix,

AZ 85061-1408. *Phone:* 602-212-0501. *Toll-free phone:* 800-354-1254. *Fax:* 602-212-0502. *E-mail:* paralegalinst@mindspring.com.

PHOENIX COLLEGE

Phoenix, Arizona   **www.pc.maricopa.edu/**

- **State and locally supported** 2-year, founded 1920, part of Maricopa County Community College District System
- **Urban** 52-acre campus
- **Coed**

Undergraduates Students come from 42 states and territories, 2% are from out of state, 8% African American, 2% Asian American or Pacific Islander, 32% Hispanic American, 4% Native American.

Academics *Calendar:* semesters. *Degree:* certificates, diplomas, and associate. *Special study options:* academic remediation for entering students, adult/continuing education programs, advanced placement credit, cooperative education, English as a second language, freshman honors college, honors programs, internships, part-time degree program, services for LD students, study abroad, summer session for credit. *ROTC:* Army (c), Air Force (c).

Student Life *Campus security:* 24-hour emergency response devices, student patrols, late-night transport/escort service.

Athletics Member NJCAA.

Costs (2006–07) *Tuition:* state resident $1560 full-time, $65 per credit hour part-time; nonresident $6720 full-time, $280 per credit hour part-time. *Required fees:* $30 full-time, $15 per term part-time.

Financial Aid Of all full-time matriculated undergraduates, 350 Federal Work-Study jobs (averaging $2800).

Applying *Options:* electronic application, early admission, deferred entrance.

Freshmen Application Contact Ms. Mary Blackwell, Director of Admissions, Registration and Records, Phoenix College, Phoenix, AZ 85013. *Phone:* 602-285-7500. *Fax:* 602-285-7813. *E-mail:* mblackwell@pcmail.maricopa.edu.

PIMA COMMUNITY COLLEGE

Tucson, Arizona   **www.pima.edu/**

- **State and locally supported** 2-year, founded 1966
- **Urban** 483-acre campus
- **Endowment** $2.8 million
- **Coed,** 32,532 undergraduate students, 29% full-time, 56% women, 44% men

Undergraduates 9,280 full-time, 23,252 part-time. Students come from 40 states and territories, 52 other countries, 7% are from out of state, 4% African American, 3% Asian American or Pacific Islander, 30% Hispanic American, 3% Native American, 1% international, 10% transferred in.

Freshmen *Admission:* 5,574 applied, 5,574 admitted, 5,574 enrolled. *Test scores:* ACT scores over 18: 52%; ACT scores over 24: 14%; ACT scores over 30: 2%.

Faculty *Total:* 1,471, 21% full-time. *Student/faculty ratio:* 24:1.

Majors Accounting; administrative assistant and secretarial science; aircraft powerplant technology; American Indian/Native American studies; anthropology; architectural drafting and CAD/CADD; automobile/automotive mechanics technology; building/construction finishing, management, and inspection related; building/property maintenance and management; business administration and management; child care and support services management; child care provision; computer and information sciences; computer engineering technology; computer systems analysis; computer systems networking and telecommunications; computer technology/computer systems technology; construction engineering technology; criminal justice/police science; criminal justice/safety; dental hygiene; dental laboratory technology; design and visual communications; dramatic/theater arts; electrical, electronic and communications engineering technology; elementary education; emergency medical technology (EMT paramedic); environmental engineering technology; fire science; general studies; hospitality administration; industrial technology; international business/trade/commerce; legal assistant/paralegal; liberal arts and sciences/liberal studies; machine shop technology; medical radiologic technology; music; nursing (registered nurse training); pharmacy technician; political science and government; real estate; respiratory care therapy; restaurant, culinary, and catering management; security and protective services related; sign language interpretation and translation; sociology; veterinary/animal health technology; welding technology.

Academics *Calendar:* semesters. *Degrees:* certificates, associate, and post-bachelor's certificates. *Special study options:* academic remediation for entering students, accelerated degree program, adult/continuing education programs, advanced placement credit, cooperative education, distance learning, double majors, English as a second language, freshman honors college, honors pro-

grams, independent study, internships, part-time degree program, services for LD students, student-designed majors, summer session for credit. *ROTC:* Army (c), Navy (c), Air Force (c).

Library Pima College Library with 219,346 titles, 984 serial subscriptions, an OPAC, a Web page.

Student Life *Housing:* college housing not available. *Activities and Organizations:* drama/theater group, student-run newspaper, choral group. *Campus security:* 24-hour emergency response devices and patrols, late-night transport/escort service. *Student services:* personal/psychological counseling, women's center.

Athletics Member NJCAA. *Intercollegiate sports:* baseball M(s), basketball M(s)/W(s), cheerleading W, cross-country running M(s)/W(s), football M(s), golf M(s)/W(s), soccer M(s)/W(s), softball W(s), tennis M(s)/W(s), track and field M(s)/W(s), volleyball W(s). *Intramural sports:* badminton M/W, basketball M/W, cross-country running M/W, equestrian sports M(c)/W(c), football M, golf M/W, ice hockey M(c), racquetball M/W, tennis M/W, track and field M/W, volleyball M/W, wrestling M(c).

Costs (2007–08) *Tuition:* state resident $1410 full-time, $47 per credit part-time; nonresident $7080 full-time, $80 per credit part-time. *Required fees:* $150 full-time, $5 per credit part-time, $10 per term part-time.

Applying *Options:* early admission. *Application fee:* $5. *Application deadlines:* rolling (freshmen), rolling (transfers).

Freshmen Application Contact Dr. Wendy Kilgore, Director of Enrollment Services and Registration, Pima Community College, 4905B East Broadway Boulevard, Tucson, AZ 85709-1120. *Phone:* 520-206-4640. *Fax:* 520-206-4790. *E-mail:* wendy.kilgore@pima.edu.

PIMA MEDICAL INSTITUTE

Mesa, Arizona   **www.pmi.edu/**

Freshmen Application Contact Admissions Office, Pima Medical Institute, Pima Medical Institute, 957 South Dobson Road, Mesa, AZ 85202. *Phone:* 480-644-0267 Ext. 225. *Toll-free phone:* 888-898-9048.

PIMA MEDICAL INSTITUTE

Tucson, Arizona   **www.pmi.edu/**

Freshmen Application Contact Admissions Office, Pima Medical Institute, Pima Medical Institute, 3350 East Grant Road, Tucson, AZ 85716-2800. *Phone:* 520-326-1600 Ext. 5112. *Toll-free phone:* 888-898-9048.

THE REFRIGERATION SCHOOL

Phoenix, Arizona   **www.refrigerationschool.com/**

- **Proprietary** 2-year, founded 1965
- **Urban** campus
- **Coed,** 350 undergraduate students

Faculty *Total:* 22, 55% full-time. *Student/faculty ratio:* 38:1.

Majors Mechanical engineering/mechanical technology.

Academics *Calendar:* continuous. *Degree:* certificates, diplomas, and associate.

Student Life *Housing:* college housing not available.

Costs (2007–08) *Tuition:* $12,200 full-time.

Freshmen Application Contact Ms. Heather Haskell, The Refrigeration School, 4210 East Washington Street, Phoenix, AZ 85034-1816. *Phone:* 602-275-7133. *Fax:* 602-267-4811. *E-mail:* heather@rsiaz.edu.

RIO SALADO COLLEGE

Tempe, Arizona   **www.rio.maricopa.edu/**

- **State and locally supported** 2-year, founded 1978, part of Maricopa County Community College District System
- **Urban** campus
- **Coed,** 6,000 undergraduate students

Undergraduates Students come from 44 states and territories, 38 other countries, 4% are from out of state.

Faculty *Total:* 1,004, 1% full-time. *Student/faculty ratio:* 25:1.

Majors Business administration and management; computer and information sciences related; computer programming related; computer science; computer/

technical support; consumer services and advocacy; data entry/microcomputer applications; dental hygiene; information science/studies; information technology; public administration; substance abuse/addiction counseling; system administration; web/multimedia management and webmaster; web page, digital/multimedia and information resources design.

Academics *Calendar:* semesters. *Degree:* certificates and associate. *Special study options:* academic remediation for entering students, accelerated degree program, adult/continuing education programs, advanced placement credit, cooperative education, distance learning, double majors, English as a second language, external degree program, honors programs, independent study, internships, part-time degree program, services for LD students, summer session for credit.

Library Rio Salado Library and Information Center with 16,000 titles, 125 serial subscriptions, 8,000 audiovisual materials, an OPAC, a Web page.

Student Life *Housing:* college housing not available. *Campus security:* 24-hour emergency response devices, late-night transport/escort service. *Student services:* personal/psychological counseling.

Athletics *Intramural sports:* cheerleading M/W.

Standardized Tests *Required for some:* ACT ASSET.

Costs (2006–07) *Tuition:* area resident $1950 full-time, $65 per credit part-time; state resident $2700 full-time, $90 per credit part-time; nonresident $4770 full-time, $159 per credit part-time. *Required fees:* $30 full-time, $15 per semester part-time. *Payment plans:* installment, deferred payment.

Applying *Options:* electronic application, early admission, deferred entrance. *Application deadlines:* rolling (freshmen), rolling (transfers).

Freshmen Application Contact Laurel Thomas, Supervisor of Admissions and Records, Rio Salado College, 2323 West 14th Street, Tempe, AZ 85281-6950. *Phone:* 480-517-8563. *Toll-free phone:* 800-729-1197. *Fax:* 480-517-8199. *E-mail:* admission@riomail.maricopa.edu.

SCOTTSDALE COMMUNITY COLLEGE

Scottsdale, Arizona   **www.sc.maricopa.edu/**

- **State and locally supported** 2-year, founded 1969, part of Maricopa County Community College District System
- **Urban** 160-acre campus with easy access to Phoenix
- **Coed,** 10,884 undergraduate students, 30% full-time, 55% women, 45% men

Undergraduates 3,303 full-time, 7,581 part-time. Students come from 36 states and territories, 48 other countries, 6% are from out of state, 4% African American, 2% Asian American or Pacific Islander, 10% Hispanic American, 5% Native American, 1% international.

Freshmen *Admission:* 502 applied, 502 admitted, 502 enrolled.

Faculty *Total:* 629, 27% full-time, 10% with terminal degrees. *Student/faculty ratio:* 17:1.

Majors Accounting; administrative assistant and secretarial science; business administration and management; criminal justice/law enforcement administration; culinary arts; dramatic/theater arts; electrical, electronic and communications engineering technology; emergency medical technology (EMT paramedic); environmental design/architecture; equestrian studies; fashion merchandising; finance; fire science; hospitality administration; hotel/motel administration; information science/studies; interior design; kindergarten/preschool education; mathematics; medical administrative assistant and medical secretary; nursing (registered nurse training); photography; public administration; real estate; special products marketing.

Academics *Calendar:* semesters. *Degree:* certificates, diplomas, and associate. *Special study options:* academic remediation for entering students, adult/continuing education programs, advanced placement credit, cooperative education, English as a second language, honors programs, internships, off-campus study, part-time degree program, services for LD students, study abroad, summer session for credit.

Library an OPAC, a Web page.

Student Life *Housing:* college housing not available. *Activities and Organizations:* drama/theater group, student-run newspaper, radio station, choral group. *Campus security:* 24-hour emergency response devices and patrols, student patrols, late-night transport/escort service, 24-hour automatic surveillance cameras. *Student services:* personal/psychological counseling.

Athletics Member NJCAA. *Intercollegiate sports:* baseball M, basketball M/W, cross-country running M/W, football M, golf M/W, soccer M/W, softball W, tennis M/W, track and field M/W, volleyball W. *Intramural sports:* archery M/W, badminton M/W, basketball M/W, bowling M/W, racquetball M/W, track and field M/W, volleyball M/W.

Costs (2007–08) *Tuition:* area resident $1950 full-time, $65 per credit hour part-time; state resident $7530 full-time, $90 per credit hour part-time; nonresident $8400 full-time, $90 per credit hour part-time. *Required fees:* $30 full-time, $15 per term part-time.

Scottsdale Community College (continued)

Financial Aid Of all full-time matriculated undergraduates, 75 Federal Work-Study jobs (averaging $2000). *Financial aid deadline:* 7/15.

Applying *Options:* early admission. *Application deadline:* rolling (freshmen). *Notification:* continuous (freshmen).

Freshmen Application Contact Ms. Fran Watkins, Director of Admissions and Records, Scottsdale Community College, 9000 East Chaparral Road, Scottsdale, AZ 85256. *Phone:* 602-423-6133. *Fax:* 480-423-6200. *E-mail:* fran.watkins@sccmail.maricopa.edu.

SCOTTSDALE CULINARY INSTITUTE

Scottsdale, Arizona　　　　**www.scichefs.com/**

Director of Admissions Mr. Jon Alberts, President, Scottsdale Culinary Institute, 8100 East Camelback Road, Suite 1001, Scottsdale, AZ 85251-3940. *Toll-free phone:* 800-848-2433.

SOUTH MOUNTAIN COMMUNITY COLLEGE

Phoenix, Arizona　　　　**www.smc.maricopa.edu/**

Director of Admissions Mr. Tony Bracamonte, Senior Associate Dean of Enrollment Services, South Mountain Community College, 7050 South 24th Street, Phoenix, AZ 85042. *Phone:* 602-243-8120.

SOUTHWEST INSTITUTE OF HEALING ARTS

Tempe, Arizona　　　　**www.swiha.org/**

- **Proprietary** 2-year, founded 1992
- **Coed**, 1,752 undergraduate students

Majors Alternative and complementary medical support services related.

Academics *Calendar:* quarters. *Degree:* associate.

Costs (2006–07) *Tuition:* $15,500 per degree program part-time.

Applying *Application fee:* $75.

Director of Admissions Katie Yearous, Student Advisor, Southwest Institute of Healing Arts, 1100 East Apache Boulevard, Tempe, AZ 85281. *Phone:* 480-994-9244. *Toll-free phone:* 888-504-9106. *E-mail:* joannl@swiha.net.

TOHONO O'ODHAM COMMUNITY COLLEGE

Sells, Arizona　　　　**www.tocc.cc.az.us/**

Director of Admissions Tohono O'odham Community College, PO Box 3129, Sells, AZ 85634. *Phone:* 520-383-8401. *Fax:* 520-383-8403. *E-mail:* tocc@tocc.cc.az.us.

UNIVERSAL TECHNICAL INSTITUTE

Avondale, Arizona　　　　**www.uticorp.com/**

Admissions Office Contact Universal Technical Institute, 10695 W. Pierce Street, Avondale, AZ 85323-7946. *Toll-free phone:* 800-859-1202.

YAVAPAI COLLEGE

Prescott, Arizona　　　　**www2.yc.edu/**

- **State and locally supported** 2-year, founded 1966, part of Arizona State Community College System
- **Small-town** 100-acre campus
- **Coed**

Undergraduates 1,322 full-time, 6,100 part-time. Students come from 30 states and territories, 18% are from out of state, 1% African American, 1% Asian American or Pacific Islander, 7% Hispanic American, 4% Native American, 5% live on campus.

Faculty *Student/faculty ratio:* 15:1.

Academics *Calendar:* semesters. *Degree:* certificates and associate. *Special study options:* academic remediation for entering students, adult/continuing education programs, advanced placement credit, cooperative education, distance learning, English as a second language, honors programs, independent study, internships, off-campus study, part-time degree program, services for LD students, summer session for credit. *ROTC:* Army (c), Air Force (c).

Student Life *Campus security:* 24-hour emergency response devices and patrols, student patrols, late-night transport/escort service, controlled dormitory access.

Athletics Member NJCAA.

Costs (2006–07) *Tuition:* state resident $1080 full-time, $45 per credit part-time; nonresident $6880 full-time, $56 per credit part-time.

Applying *Options:* early admission, deferred entrance. *Required:* high school transcript. *Required for some:* essay or personal statement, letters of recommendation.

Freshmen Application Contact Mr. David Vanness, Admissions, Registration, and Records Manager, Yavapai College, 1100 East Sheldon Street, Prescott, AZ 86301-3297. *Phone:* 928-776-2188. *Toll-free phone:* 800-922-6787. *Fax:* 520-776-2151. *E-mail:* registration@yc.edu.

ARKANSAS

ARKANSAS NORTHEASTERN COLLEGE

Blytheville, Arkansas　　　　**www.anc.edu/**

- **State-supported** 2-year, founded 1975
- **Rural** 80-acre campus with easy access to Memphis
- **Endowment** $187,500
- **Coed**

Undergraduates 962 full-time, 868 part-time. Students come from 3 states and territories, 17% are from out of state, 29% African American, 1% Asian American or Pacific Islander, 0.9% Hispanic American, 0.2% Native American, 5% transferred in. *Retention:* 50% of 2003 full-time freshmen returned.

Faculty *Student/faculty ratio:* 18:1.

Academics *Calendar:* semesters. *Degree:* certificates and associate. *Special study options:* academic remediation for entering students, adult/continuing education programs, advanced placement credit, distance learning, double majors, part-time degree program, summer session for credit.

Student Life *Campus security:* 24-hour patrols.

Costs (2006–07) *Tuition:* area resident $1440 full-time, $48 per semester hour part-time; state resident $1740 full-time, $58 per semester hour part-time; nonresident $3240 full-time, $108 per semester hour part-time. *Required fees:* $220 full-time, $6 per semester hour part-time, $20 per term part-time. *Payment plans:* installment, deferred payment.

Financial Aid Of all full-time matriculated undergraduates, 42 Federal Work-Study jobs (averaging $2500).

Applying *Options:* deferred entrance. *Recommended:* high school transcript.

Freshmen Application Contact Mrs. Leslie Wells, Admissions Counselor, Arkansas Northeastern College, PO Box 1109, Blytheville, AR 72316. *Phone:* 870-762-1020 Ext. 1118. *Fax:* 870-763-1654. *E-mail:* lwells@anc.edu.

ARKANSAS STATE UNIVERSITY—BEEBE

Beebe, Arkansas　　　　**www.asub.edu/**

- **State-supported** 2-year, founded 1927, part of Arkansas State University System
- **Small-town** 320-acre campus with easy access to Memphis
- **Coed**

Undergraduates 2,124 full-time, 1,852 part-time. Students come from 25 states and territories, 5% African American, 1% Asian American or Pacific Islander, 2% Hispanic American, 1% Native American, 0.1% international, 2% transferred in, 12% live on campus.

Faculty *Student/faculty ratio:* 30:1.

Academics *Calendar:* semesters. *Degree:* certificates and associate. *Special study options:* academic remediation for entering students, adult/continuing education programs, advanced placement credit, distance learning, honors programs, part-time degree program, summer session for credit.

Student Life *Campus security:* 24-hour emergency response devices and patrols.

Standardized Tests *Recommended:* ACT (for placement).

Financial Aid Of all full-time matriculated undergraduates, 36 Federal Work-Study jobs (averaging $1800). 112 state and other part-time jobs (averaging $750).

Applying *Options:* deferred entrance. *Required:* high school transcript.

Director of Admissions Mr. James Washburn, Director of Admissions, Arkansas State University–Beebe, PO Box 1000, Beebe, AR 72012-1000. *Phone:* 501-882-8280. *Toll-free phone:* 800-632-9985.

ARKANSAS STATE UNIVERSITY– MOUNTAIN HOME

Mountain Home, Arkansas　　　　**www.asumh.edu/**

- **State-supported** 2-year, founded 2000, part of Arkansas State University System
- **Small-town** 136-acre campus
- **Endowment** $3.3 million
- **Coed,** 960 undergraduate students, 60% full-time, 65% women, 35% men

Undergraduates 572 full-time, 388 part-time. Students come from 12 states and territories, 0.3% African American, 0.3% Asian American or Pacific Islander, 2% Hispanic American, 0.8% Native American, 0.1% international, 18% transferred in. *Retention:* 43% of 2003 full-time freshmen returned.

Freshmen *Admission:* 830 applied, 381 admitted, 207 enrolled. *Average high school GPA:* 2.44. *Test scores:* ACT scores over 18: 60%; ACT scores over 24: 20%.

Faculty *Total:* 57, 67% full-time, 23% with terminal degrees. *Student/faculty ratio:* 21:1.

Majors Audiology and hearing sciences; business automation/technology/data entry; criminal justice/law enforcement administration; criminal justice/safety; emergency medical technology (EMT paramedic); forensic science and technology; funeral service and mortuary science; information science/studies; liberal arts and sciences/liberal studies; middle school education; opticianry.

Academics *Calendar:* semesters. *Degree:* certificates and associate. *Special study options:* academic remediation for entering students, advanced placement credit, cooperative education, distance learning, independent study, part-time degree program, services for LD students, summer session for credit.

Library Norma Wood Library with 33,573 titles, 15,360 serial subscriptions, 2,212 audiovisual materials, an OPAC, a Web page.

Student Life *Housing:* college housing not available. *Activities and Organizations:* choral group, Phi Theta Kappa, Circle K, Criminal Justice Club, Mortuary Science Club, Student Ambassadors.

Standardized Tests *Recommended:* SAT or ACT (for admission), COMPASS, ASSET.

Costs (2007–08) *Tuition:* state resident $2130 full-time, $71 per credit hour part-time; nonresident $3660 full-time, $122 per credit hour part-time. *Required fees:* $240 full-time, $8 per credit hour part-time.

Financial Aid Of all full-time matriculated undergraduates, 14 Federal Work-Study jobs (averaging $3200).

Applying *Required:* high school transcript. *Recommended:* placement scores. *Notification:* continuous (freshmen).

Freshmen Application Contact Mr. Scott Raney, Director of Student Services, Arkansas State University–Mountain Home, 1600 South College Street, Mountain Home, AR 72653. *Phone:* 870-508-6168. *Fax:* 870-508-6287. *E-mail:* araney@asumh.edu.

ARKANSAS STATE UNIVERSITY– NEWPORT

Newport, Arkansas　　　　**www.asun.edu/**

- **State-supported** 2-year, founded 1989, part of Arkansas State University System
- **Coed,** 896 undergraduate students

Undergraduates 16% African American, 2% Asian American or Pacific Islander, 2% Hispanic American, 0.8% Native American, 0.6% international.

Faculty *Total:* 50, 46% full-time. *Student/faculty ratio:* 12:1.

Majors Business/commerce; computer technology/computer systems technology; criminal justice/law enforcement administration; early childhood education; emergency medical technology (EMT paramedic); forensic science and technology; general studies; health/medical preparatory programs related; liberal arts and sciences/liberal studies; management information systems and services related; middle school education; multi-/interdisciplinary studies related; nursing (registered nurse training).

Academics *Calendar:* semesters. *Degree:* certificates, diplomas, and associate. *Special study options:* academic remediation for entering students, adult/continuing education programs, English as a second language, external degree program, independent study, internships, off-campus study, services for LD students.

Standardized Tests *Required:* ACT (for admission).

Costs (2006–07) *Tuition:* state resident $1824 full-time; nonresident $3048 full-time.

Financial Aid Of all full-time matriculated undergraduates, 19 Federal Work-Study jobs (averaging $4500).

Applying *Required:* interview.

Director of Admissions Ms. Tara Byrd, Registrar, Director of Admissions, Arkansas State University–Newport, 7648 Victory Boulevard, Newport, AR 72112. *Phone:* 870-512-7800. *Toll-free phone:* 800-976-1676.

BLACK RIVER TECHNICAL COLLEGE

Pocahontas, Arkansas　　　　**www.blackrivertech.edu/**

Director of Admissions Mr. Jim Ulmer, Director of Admissions, Black River Technical College, 1410 Highway 304 East, Pocahontas, AR 72455. *Phone:* 870-892-4565. *Toll-free phone:* 800-919-3086.

COSSATOT COMMUNITY COLLEGE OF THE UNIVERSITY OF ARKANSAS

De Queen, Arkansas　　　　**www.cccua.edu/**

- **State-supported** 2-year, founded 1991, part of University of Arkansas System
- **Rural** campus
- **Endowment** $110,096
- **Coed,** 1,133 undergraduate students

Undergraduates Students come from 5 states and territories, 2% are from out of state, 13% African American, 0.8% Asian American or Pacific Islander, 10% Hispanic American, 2% Native American.

Freshmen *Admission:* 361 applied, 301 admitted.

Faculty *Total:* 74, 46% full-time, 3% with terminal degrees. *Student/faculty ratio:* 12:1.

Majors Automobile/automotive mechanics technology; business administration and management; carpentry; computer management; emergency medical technology (EMT paramedic); environmental studies; industrial technology; liberal arts and sciences/liberal studies; medical/clinical assistant; occupational safety and health technology; welding technology; wood science and wood products/pulp and paper technology.

Academics *Calendar:* semesters. *Degree:* certificates and associate. *Special study options:* academic remediation for entering students, adult/continuing education programs, advanced placement credit, cooperative education, distance learning, double majors, English as a second language, external degree program, independent study, internships, off-campus study, part-time degree program, services for LD students, summer session for credit.

Library Kimbell Library.

Student Life *Housing:* college housing not available.

Costs (2006–07) *Tuition:* area resident $1350 full-time, $45 per credit hour part-time; state resident $1650 full-time, $55 per credit hour part-time; nonresident $4950 full-time, $165 per credit hour part-time. Full-time tuition and fees vary according to course load and program. Part-time tuition and fees vary according to course load and program. *Required fees:* $250 full-time, $15 per course part-time, $53 per term part-time. *Payment plan:* installment. *Waivers:* senior citizens and employees or children of employees.

Financial Aid Of all full-time matriculated undergraduates, 14 Federal Work-Study jobs (averaging $2700).

Applying *Options:* electronic application. *Recommended:* high school transcript.

Freshmen Application Contact Ms. Nancy Cowling, Admissions Advisor, Cossatot Community College of the University of Arkansas, PO Box 960, DeQueen, AR 71832. *Phone:* 870-584-4471. *Toll-free phone:* 800-844-4471. *Fax:* 870-642-8766. *E-mail:* ncowling@cccua.edu.

CROWLEY'S RIDGE COLLEGE
Paragould, Arkansas   www.crowleysridgecollege.edu/

Freshmen Application Contact Mrs. Nancy Joneshill, Director of Admissions, Crowley's Ridge College, 100 College Drive, Paragould, AR 72450. *Phone:* 870-236-6901. *Toll-free phone:* 800-264-1096. *Fax:* 870-236-7748. *E-mail:* njoneshi@crc.pioneer.paragould.ar.us.

EAST ARKANSAS COMMUNITY COLLEGE
Forrest City, Arkansas   www.eacc.edu/

- **State-supported** 2-year, founded 1974
- **Small-town** 40-acre campus with easy access to Memphis
- **Endowment** $217,500
- **Coed**

Undergraduates 745 full-time, 732 part-time. Students come from 4 states and territories, 1% are from out of state, 41% African American, 0.7% Asian American or Pacific Islander, 1% Hispanic American, 0.2% Native American, 0.1% international.

Faculty *Student/faculty ratio:* 17:1.

Academics *Calendar:* semesters. *Degree:* certificates and associate. *Special study options:* academic remediation for entering students, adult/continuing education programs, advanced placement credit, honors programs, part-time degree program, services for LD students, summer session for credit.

Student Life *Campus security:* 24-hour emergency response devices, 16-hour patrols by trained security personnel.

Costs (2006–07) *Tuition:* area resident $1470 full-time, $49 per credit hour part-time; state resident $1710 full-time, $57 per credit hour part-time; nonresident $2070 full-time, $69 per credit hour part-time. *Required fees:* $150 full-time, $5 per credit hour part-time.

Financial Aid Of all full-time matriculated undergraduates, 74 Federal Work-Study jobs (averaging $1104).

Applying *Options:* early admission, deferred entrance. *Required:* high school transcript.

Freshmen Application Contact Ms. DeAnna Adams, Director of Enrollment Management/Institutional Research, East Arkansas Community College, 1700 Newcastle Road, Forrest City, AR 72335-2204. *Phone:* 870-633-4480. *Toll-free phone:* 877-797-3222. *Fax:* 870-633-3840. *E-mail:* dadams@eacc.edu.

ITT TECHNICAL INSTITUTE
Little Rock, Arkansas   www.itt-tech.edu/

- **Proprietary** primarily 2-year, founded 1993, part of ITT Educational Services, Inc
- **Urban** campus
- **Coed**

Majors Accounting technology and bookkeeping; animation, interactive technology, video graphics and special effects; business administration and management; CAD/CADD drafting/design technology; communications technology; computer and information systems security; computer engineering technology; computer software engineering; computer software technology; computer systems networking and telecommunications; criminal justice/law enforcement administration; electrical, electronic and communications engineering technology; web/multimedia management and webmaster; web page, digital/multimedia and information resources design.

Academics *Calendar:* quarters. *Degrees:* associate and bachelor's.

Library a Web page.

Student Life *Housing:* college housing not available.

Standardized Tests *Required:* Wonderlic aptitude test (for admission).

Costs (2006–07) *Tuition:* Contact school for program costs.

Applying *Options:* deferred entrance. *Application fee:* $100. *Required:* high school transcript, interview. *Recommended:* letters of recommendation. *Application deadlines:* rolling (freshmen), rolling (transfers). *Notification:* continuous (freshmen), continuous (transfers).

Freshmen Application Contact Ms. Terri Lowery, Director of Recruitment, ITT Technical Institute, 4520 South University Avenue, Little Rock, AR 72204. *Phone:* 501-565-5550. *Toll-free phone:* 800-359-4429.

MID-SOUTH COMMUNITY COLLEGE
West Memphis, Arkansas   www.midsouthcc.edu/

- **State-supported** 2-year, founded 1993
- **Suburban** 80-acre campus with easy access to Memphis
- **Endowment** $894,155
- **Coed**

Undergraduates 457 full-time, 1,010 part-time. Students come from 2 other countries, 5% are from out of state, 49% African American, 0.7% Asian American or Pacific Islander, 1% Hispanic American, 0.2% Native American, 0.4% international, 5% transferred in. *Retention:* 41% of 2003 full-time freshmen returned.

Faculty *Student/faculty ratio:* 15:1.

Academics *Calendar:* semesters. *Degree:* certificates and associate. *Special study options:* academic remediation for entering students, adult/continuing education programs, distance learning, independent study, internships, part-time degree program, summer session for credit.

Student Life *Campus security:* 24-hour emergency response devices, security during class hours.

Standardized Tests *Required for some:* ACT (for admission), ASSET, COMPASS.

Costs (2006–07) *Tuition:* area resident $1410 full-time, $47 per credit part-time; state resident $1740 full-time, $58 per credit part-time; nonresident $3150 full-time, $105 per credit part-time. Full-time tuition and fees vary according to course load and reciprocity agreements. Part-time tuition and fees vary according to course load and reciprocity agreements. *Required fees:* $210 full-time, $7 per credit part-time.

Financial Aid Of all full-time matriculated undergraduates, 29 Federal Work-Study jobs (averaging $1914).

Applying *Options:* electronic application, early admission. *Required:* high school transcript.

Freshmen Application Contact Ms. Leslie Anderson, Registrar, Mid-South Community College, 2000 West Broadway, West Memphis, AR 72301. *Phone:* 870-733-6732. *Fax:* 870-733-6719. *E-mail:* landerson@midsouthcc.edu.

NATIONAL PARK COMMUNITY COLLEGE
Hot Springs, Arkansas   www.npcc.edu/

- **State and locally supported** 2-year, founded 1973, part of Arkansas Department of Higher Education
- **Suburban** 50-acre campus with easy access to Little Rock
- **Endowment** $11.3 million
- **Coed,** 2,996 undergraduate students, 41% full-time, 60% women, 40% men

Undergraduates 1,237 full-time, 1,759 part-time. Students come from 1 other state, 2% are from out of state, 6% African American, 1% Asian American or Pacific Islander, 1% Hispanic American, 1% Native American, 17% transferred in. *Retention:* 100% of 2003 full-time freshmen returned.

Freshmen *Admission:* 4,969 applied, 4,969 admitted, 345 enrolled.

Faculty *Total:* 147, 44% full-time, 12% with terminal degrees. *Student/faculty ratio:* 21:1.

Majors Accounting; administrative assistant and secretarial science; art; business administration and management; child development; clinical laboratory science/medical technology; clinical/medical laboratory technology; commercial and advertising art; computer graphics; criminal justice/law enforcement administration; data processing and data processing technology; education; electrical, electronic and communications engineering technology; elementary education; emergency medical technology (EMT paramedic); finance; fire science; health/health care administration; health information/medical records administration; health science; industrial radiologic technology; information science/studies; liberal arts and sciences/liberal studies; medical administrative assistant and medical secretary; nursing (registered nurse training); parks, recreation and leisure; parks, recreation and leisure facilities management; physical sciences; public administration; radiologic technology/science; trade and industrial teacher education.

Academics *Calendar:* semesters. *Degree:* certificates, diplomas, and associate. *Special study options:* academic remediation for entering students, adult/continuing education programs, advanced placement credit, cooperative education, distance learning, double majors, external degree program, honors programs, independent study, internships, part-time degree program, services for LD students, student-designed majors, study abroad, summer session for credit.

Library Garland County Community College Library with 17,800 titles, 290 serial subscriptions, an OPAC.

Student Life *Housing:* college housing not available. *Activities and Organizations:* student-run newspaper, choral group, student newspaper, choral group.

Campus security: 24-hour emergency response devices and patrols. *Student services:* health clinic, personal/psychological counseling, women's center.

Athletics *Intramural sports:* basketball M/W, bowling M/W, golf M/W, swimming and diving M/W, tennis M/W.

Standardized Tests *Required:* SAT and SAT Subject Tests or ACT (for admission). *Recommended:* ACT ASSET.

Costs (2006–07) *Tuition:* area resident $1740 full-time; state resident $2040 full-time; nonresident $3960 full-time.

Applying *Options:* early admission, deferred entrance. *Required:* high school transcript. *Application deadlines:* rolling (freshmen), rolling (transfers).

Director of Admissions Dr. Allen B. Moody, Director of Institutional Services/Registrar, National Park Community College, 101 College Drive, Hot Springs, AR 71913. *Phone:* 501-760-4222. *Toll-free phone:* 800-760-1825. *E-mail:* bmoody@npcc.edu.

NORTH ARKANSAS COLLEGE

Harrison, Arkansas   **www.northark.edu/**

- **State and locally supported** 2-year, founded 1974
- **Small-town** 40-acre campus
- **Endowment** $337,290
- **Coed,** 2,047 undergraduate students, 53% full-time, 61% women, 39% men

Undergraduates 1,084 full-time, 963 part-time. Students come from 20 states and territories, 1 other country, 3% are from out of state, 0.3% African American, 0.7% Asian American or Pacific Islander, 2% Hispanic American, 1% Native American, 0.1% international, 7% transferred in. *Retention:* 49% of 2003 full-time freshmen returned.

Freshmen *Admission:* 631 applied, 631 admitted, 417 enrolled. *Average high school GPA:* 2.91. *Test scores:* ACT scores over 18: 74%; ACT scores over 24: 20%; ACT scores over 30: 1%.

Faculty *Total:* 148, 44% full-time, 3% with terminal degrees. *Student/faculty ratio:* 15:1.

Majors Administrative assistant and secretarial science; agricultural business and management; agriculture; automobile/automotive mechanics technology; biomedical technology; business/commerce; clinical/medical laboratory assistant; clinical/medical laboratory technology; computer and information sciences; criminal justice/law enforcement administration; criminal justice/police science; drafting/design technology; electrical, electronic and communications engineering technology; electromechanical and instrumentation and maintenance technologies related; electromechanical technology; emergency medical technology (EMT paramedic); forensic science and technology; industrial technology; institutional food workers; liberal arts and sciences/liberal studies; medical radiologic technology; middle school education; nursing (registered nurse training); surgical technology.

Academics *Calendar:* semesters. *Degree:* certificates and associate. *Special study options:* academic remediation for entering students, adult/continuing education programs, advanced placement credit, distance learning, freshman honors college, honors programs, independent study, internships, part-time degree program, services for LD students, summer session for credit.

Library North Arkansas College Library plus 1 other with 28,751 titles, 219 serial subscriptions, 1,235 audiovisual materials, an OPAC, a Web page.

Student Life *Housing:* college housing not available. *Activities and Organizations:* drama/theater group, choral group, Phi Beta Lambda, Phi Theta Kappa, Student Nurses Association, Vocational Industrial Clubs, Baptist Student Union. *Campus security:* 24-hour patrols. *Student services:* personal/psychological counseling.

Athletics Member NJCAA. *Intercollegiate sports:* baseball M, basketball M(s)/W(s), softball W. *Intramural sports:* archery M/W, badminton M/W, baseball M/W, football M/W, golf M/W, racquetball M/W, softball W, table tennis M/W, tennis M/W, volleyball M/W.

Costs (2007–08) *Tuition:* area resident $1560 full-time, $52 per credit hour part-time; state resident $2190 full-time, $73 per credit hour part-time; nonresident $4320 full-time, $144 per credit hour part-time. *Required fees:* $150 full-time, $5 per credit hour part-time.

Financial Aid Of all full-time matriculated undergraduates, 107 Federal Work-Study jobs (averaging $1103).

Applying *Options:* deferred entrance. *Required for some:* high school transcript. *Application deadlines:* rolling (freshmen), rolling (transfers). *Notification:* continuous (freshmen), continuous (transfers).

Freshmen Application Contact Ms. Charla McDonald, Director of Admissions, North Arkansas College, 1515 Pioneer Drive, Harrison, AR 72601. *Phone:* 870-391-3221. *Toll-free phone:* 800-679-6622. *Fax:* 870-391-3339. *E-mail:* charlam@northark.edu.

NORTHWEST ARKANSAS COMMUNITY COLLEGE

Bentonville, Arkansas   **www.nwacc.edu/**

- **State and locally supported** 2-year, founded 1989
- **Urban** 77-acre campus
- **Coed,** 5,732 undergraduate students, 33% full-time, 60% women, 40% men

Undergraduates 1,889 full-time, 3,843 part-time. Students come from 17 states and territories, 2% are from out of state, 2% African American, 4% Asian American or Pacific Islander, 9% Hispanic American, 2% Native American, 14% transferred in.

Freshmen *Admission:* 924 enrolled. *Average high school GPA:* 3.0. *Test scores:* ACT scores over 18: 72%; ACT scores over 24: 14%.

Faculty *Total:* 400, 31% full-time. *Student/faculty ratio:* 14:1.

Majors Accounting; administrative assistant and secretarial science; business administration and management; computer programming; criminal justice/law enforcement administration; data processing and data processing technology; drafting and design technology; education; electrical, electronic and communications engineering technology; emergency medical technology (EMT paramedic); finance; industrial radiologic technology; liberal arts and sciences/liberal studies; nursing (registered nurse training); occupational safety and health technology; physical therapy; respiratory care therapy.

Academics *Calendar:* semesters. *Degree:* certificates and associate. *Special study options:* academic remediation for entering students, accelerated degree program, adult/continuing education programs, advanced placement credit, cooperative education, distance learning, double majors, English as a second language, freshman honors college, honors programs, independent study, internships, part-time degree program, services for LD students, student-designed majors, summer session for credit. *ROTC:* Air Force (c).

Library Library Resource Center plus 1 other with 15,500 titles, 159 serial subscriptions, an OPAC.

Student Life *Housing:* college housing not available. *Activities and Organizations:* drama/theater group, choral group, Student Advisory Activity Council, Gamma Beta Phi, Phi Beta Lambda, Student Nurses Association, Students in Free Enterprise. *Campus security:* 24-hour emergency response devices and patrols.

Athletics *Intramural sports:* basketball M/W, bowling M/W, football M/W, golf M, racquetball M/W, softball M/W, swimming and diving M/W, table tennis M/W, tennis M/W, volleyball W, weight lifting M/W.

Costs (2007–08) *Tuition:* area resident $1740 full-time, $58 per credit hour part-time; state resident $2700 full-time, $90 per credit hour part-time; nonresident $3810 full-time, $127 per credit hour part-time. *Required fees:* $385 full-time, $10 per credit hour part-time, $50 per term part-time.

Applying *Application fee:* $10. *Required:* high school transcript. *Application deadline:* rolling (freshmen). *Notification:* continuous (freshmen).

Freshmen Application Contact Mr. John Honey, Director, NorthWest Arkansas Community College, One College Drive, Bentonville, AR 72712. *Phone:* 479-636-9222. *Toll-free phone:* 800-995-6922. *Fax:* 479-619-4116. *E-mail:* admissions@nwacc.edu.

OUACHITA TECHNICAL COLLEGE

Malvern, Arkansas   **www.otcweb.edu/**

- **State-supported** 2-year, founded 1972
- **Small-town** 11-acre campus
- **Coed,** 1,590 undergraduate students, 35% full-time, 51% women, 49% men

Undergraduates 556 full-time, 1,034 part-time. Students come from 2 states and territories, 2 other countries, 0.1% are from out of state, 12% African American, 0.9% Asian American or Pacific Islander, 1% Hispanic American, 0.6% Native American, 0.3% international, 6% transferred in. *Retention:* 50% of 2003 full-time freshmen returned.

Freshmen *Admission:* 325 applied, 325 admitted, 210 enrolled. *Average high school GPA:* 2.67. *Test scores:* ACT scores over 18: 62%; ACT scores over 24: 9%.

Faculty *Total:* 99, 33% full-time, 12% with terminal degrees. *Student/faculty ratio:* 16:1.

Majors Accounting; administrative assistant and secretarial science; automobile/automotive mechanics technology; business administration and management; child care and support services management; computer and information sciences; criminal justice/law enforcement administration; general studies; industrial arts; industrial technology; legal administrative assistant/secretary; legal assistant/paralegal; liberal arts and sciences/liberal studies; machine tool technology;

Ouachita Technical College (continued)

management information systems; marketing/marketing management; medical administrative assistant and medical secretary; nursing (licensed practical/vocational nurse training).

Academics *Calendar:* semesters. *Degree:* certificates and associate. *Special study options:* academic remediation for entering students, accelerated degree program, advanced placement credit, cooperative education, distance learning, double majors, independent study, internships, part-time degree program, services for LD students, summer session for credit.

Library Ouachita Technical College Library/Learning Resource Center with 8,000 titles, 100 serial subscriptions, 1,200 audiovisual materials, an OPAC, a Web page.

Student Life *Housing:* college housing not available. *Campus security:* 24-hour patrols. *Student services:* personal/psychological counseling.

Standardized Tests *Recommended:* SAT or ACT (for admission), ACT COMPASS or ASSET.

Costs (2007–08) *Tuition:* state resident $1590 full-time, $53 per credit hour part-time; nonresident $3180 full-time, $106 per credit hour part-time. *Required fees:* $450 full-time, $15 per credit hour part-time.

Financial Aid Of all full-time matriculated undergraduates, 18 Federal Work-Study jobs (averaging $2400).

Applying *Options:* electronic application, early admission, deferred entrance. *Required:* high school transcript. *Application deadlines:* rolling (freshmen), rolling (transfers).

Freshmen Application Contact Mr. Vaughn Kesterson, Counselor, Ouachita Technical College, One College Circle, Malvern, AR 72104. *Phone:* 501-337-5000 Ext. 1117. *Toll-free phone:* 800-337-0266. *Fax:* 501-337-9382. *E-mail:* vkesterson@otcweb.edu.

OZARKA COLLEGE

Melbourne, Arkansas www.ozarka.edu/

- **State-supported** 2-year, founded 1973
- **Rural** 40-acre campus
- **Coed,** 885 undergraduate students

Undergraduates 1% are from out of state, 1% African American.

Faculty *Total:* 71, 44% full-time, 4% with terminal degrees. *Student/faculty ratio:* 20:1.

Majors Administrative assistant and secretarial science; automobile/automotive mechanics technology; banking and financial support services; business administration and management; criminal justice/law enforcement administration; culinary arts; health information/medical records technology; information science/studies; liberal arts and sciences/liberal studies; middle school education.

Academics *Calendar:* semesters. *Degree:* certificates and associate. *Special study options:* academic remediation for entering students, advanced placement credit, distance learning, external degree program, internships, services for LD students, summer session for credit.

Library Ozarka College Library with 10,500 titles, 4,000 serial subscriptions, an OPAC.

Student Life *Housing:* college housing not available. *Activities and Organizations:* drama/theater group, VICA, Phi Beta Lambda, Drama Club, HOSA, Phi Theta Kappa. *Campus security:* security patrols after business hours. *Student services:* personal/psychological counseling.

Costs (2006–07) *Tuition:* state resident $1950 full-time; nonresident $5040 full-time. *Required fees:* $330 full-time.

Financial Aid Of all full-time matriculated undergraduates, 50 Federal Work-Study jobs, 40 state and other part-time jobs.

Applying *Options:* deferred entrance. *Required:* high school transcript. *Required for some:* essay or personal statement, letters of recommendation, interview. *Recommended:* minimum 2.0 GPA. *Application deadlines:* 8/19 (freshmen), 8/15 (transfers).

Freshmen Application Contact Ms. Zeda Wilkerson, Director of Admissions, Ozarka College, PO Box 12, 218 College Drive, Melbourne, AR 72556. *Phone:* 870-368-7371 Ext. 2028. *Toll-free phone:* 800-821-4335. *E-mail:* zwilkerson@ozarka.edu.

PHILLIPS COMMUNITY COLLEGE OF THE UNIVERSITY OF ARKANSAS

Helena, Arkansas www.pccua.edu/

Director of Admissions Mr. Lynn Boone, Registrar, Phillips Community College of the University of Arkansas, PO Box 785, Helena, AR 72342-0785. *Phone:* 870-338-6474.

PULASKI TECHNICAL COLLEGE

North Little Rock, Arkansas www.pulaskitech.edu/

- **State-supported** 2-year, founded 1945
- **Urban** 40-acre campus with easy access to Little Rock
- **Coed,** 8,455 undergraduate students, 48% full-time, 69% women, 31% men

Undergraduates 4,064 full-time, 4,391 part-time. Students come from 5 states and territories, 1% are from out of state, 53% African American, 1% Asian American or Pacific Islander, 2% Hispanic American, 0.6% Native American, 0.1% international, 11% transferred in.

Freshmen *Admission:* 2,156 applied, 2,156 admitted, 1,202 enrolled. *Average high school GPA:* 2.5.

Faculty *Total:* 477, 25% full-time, 10% with terminal degrees. *Student/faculty ratio:* 23:1.

Majors Administrative assistant and secretarial science; computer engineering technology; drafting and design technology; electromechanical technology; industrial technology; information science/studies; occupational therapist assistant; respiratory care therapy.

Academics *Calendar:* semesters. *Degree:* certificates and associate. *Special study options:* academic remediation for entering students, advanced placement credit, distance learning, part-time degree program, services for LD students, summer session for credit.

Library Ottenheimer Library with 35,406 titles, 276 serial subscriptions, 1,994 audiovisual materials, an OPAC, a Web page.

Student Life *Housing:* college housing not available. *Activities and Organizations:* drama/theater group. *Campus security:* certified law enforcement personnel 7 a.m. to 11 p.m.

Costs (2007–08) *Tuition:* state resident $1776 full-time, $74 per credit hour part-time; nonresident $2952 full-time, $123 per credit hour part-time. *Required fees:* $216 full-time, $9 per credit hour part-time, $10 per semester part-time.

Applying *Options:* electronic application. *Required:* high school transcript. *Application deadline:* rolling (freshmen).

Freshmen Application Contact Ms. Danita Ormand, Records and Enrollment Services, Pulaski Technical College, 3000 West Scenic Drive, North Little Rock, AR 72118. *Phone:* 501-812-2233. *Fax:* 501-812-2316. *E-mail:* dormand@pulaskitech.edu.

REMINGTON COLLEGE–LITTLE ROCK CAMPUS

Little Rock, Arkansas www.remingtoncollege.edu/

- **Proprietary** 2-year
- **Coed,** 456 undergraduate students
- **100%** of applicants were admitted

Freshmen *Admission:* 234 applied, 234 admitted.

Majors Business administration, management and operations related; computer and information sciences related; computer systems networking and telecommunications; criminal justice/law enforcement administration; criminal justice/safety.

Academics *Degree:* associate.

Costs (2006–07) *Tuition:* $12,825 full-time.

Applying *Application fee:* $50.

Director of Admissions Mr. David Caldwell, Campus President, Remington College–Little Rock Campus, 19 Remington Drive, Little Rock, AR 72204. *Phone:* 501-312-0007. *Fax:* 501-225-3819. *E-mail:* david.caldwell@remingtoncollege.edu.

RICH MOUNTAIN COMMUNITY COLLEGE

Mena, Arkansas www.rmcc.edu/

Director of Admissions Dr. Steve Rook, Dean of Students, Rich Mountain Community College, 1100 College Drive, Mena, AR 71953. *Phone:* 479-394-7622 Ext. 1400.

SOUTH ARKANSAS COMMUNITY COLLEGE

El Dorado, Arkansas www.southark.edu/

- **State-supported** 2-year, founded 1975, part of Arkansas Department of Higher Education
- **Small-town** 4-acre campus
- **Coed**

Undergraduates 612 full-time, 756 part-time. Students come from 2 states and territories, 6% are from out of state, 32% African American, 0.3% Asian American or Pacific Islander, 1% Hispanic American, 0.5% Native American. *Retention:* 46% of 2003 full-time freshmen returned.

Faculty *Student/faculty ratio:* 13:1.

Academics *Calendar:* semesters. *Degree:* certificates and associate. *Special study options:* academic remediation for entering students, adult/continuing education programs, advanced placement credit, internships, part-time degree program, services for LD students, summer session for credit.

Student Life *Campus security:* security guard.

Standardized Tests *Required for some:* ACT COMPASS. *Recommended:* SAT or ACT (for admission).

Costs (2006–07) *Tuition:* area resident $1710 full-time; state resident $1950 full-time; nonresident $3600 full-time.

Financial Aid Of all full-time matriculated undergraduates, 45 Federal Work-Study jobs (averaging $1300).

Applying *Options:* early admission, deferred entrance. *Required:* high school transcript.

Freshmen Application Contact Dean Inman, Director of Enrollment Services, South Arkansas Community College, PO Box 7010, El Dorado, AR 71731-7010. *Phone:* 870-864-7142. *Toll-free phone:* 800-955-2289 Ext. 142. *Fax:* 870-864-7109. *E-mail:* dinman@southark.edu.

SOUTHEAST ARKANSAS COLLEGE

Pine Bluff, Arkansas www.seark.edu/

Freshmen Application Contact Ms. Barbara Dunn, Coordinator of Admissions and Enrollment Management, Southeast Arkansas College, 1900 Hazel Street, Pine Bluff, AR 71603. *Phone:* 870-543-5957. *Toll-free phone:* 888-SEARK TC. *Fax:* 870-543-5956. *E-mail:* bdunn@seark.edu.

SOUTHERN ARKANSAS UNIVERSITY TECH

Camden, Arkansas www.sautech.edu/

- **State-supported** 2-year, founded 1967, part of Arkansas Department of Higher Education
- **Rural** 96-acre campus
- **Coed**

Undergraduates 554 full-time, 1,213 part-time. Students come from 6 states and territories, 1% are from out of state, 25% African American, 0.3% Asian American or Pacific Islander, 0.7% Hispanic American, 0.5% Native American, 2% transferred in.

Faculty *Student/faculty ratio:* 21:1.

Academics *Calendar:* semesters. *Degree:* certificates and associate. *Special study options:* academic remediation for entering students, adult/continuing education programs, advanced placement credit, distance learning, double majors, honors programs, independent study, internships, off-campus study, part-time degree program, summer session for credit.

Student Life *Campus security:* 24-hour emergency response devices, patrols by trained security personnel.

Costs (2006–07) *Tuition:* state resident $1638 full-time, $63 per hour part-time; nonresident $2184 full-time, $84 per hour part-time. Full-time tuition and fees vary according to course load. Part-time tuition and fees vary according to course load. *Required fees:* $574 full-time, $21 per credit hour part-time. *Room and board:* $3413; room only: $2100. Room and board charges vary according to housing facility.

Financial Aid Of all full-time matriculated undergraduates, 21 Federal Work-Study jobs (averaging $1274).

Applying *Options:* deferred entrance. *Required for some:* high school transcript.

Freshmen Application Contact Mrs. Beverly Clark, Admissions Secretary, Southern Arkansas University Tech, PO Box 3499, East Camden, AR 71711. *Phone:* 870-574-4558. *Fax:* 870-574-4478. *E-mail:* bclark@sautech.edu.

UNIVERSITY OF ARKANSAS COMMUNITY COLLEGE AT BATESVILLE

Batesville, Arkansas www.uaccb.edu/

- **State-supported** 2-year, part of University of Arkansas System
- **Small-town** campus
- **Endowment** $412,000
- **Coed**, 1,288 undergraduate students, 59% full-time, 71% women, 29% men

Undergraduates 757 full-time, 531 part-time. Students come from 2 states and territories, 3% African American, 0.7% Asian American or Pacific Islander, 2% Hispanic American, 0.7% Native American, 9% transferred in.

Freshmen *Admission:* 403 applied, 403 admitted, 256 enrolled.

Faculty *Total:* 117, 38% full-time. *Student/faculty ratio:* 15:1.

Majors Business/commerce; computer systems networking and telecommunications; criminal justice/safety; data entry/microcomputer applications; education; emergency medical technology (EMT paramedic); industrial technology; information technology; kindergarten/preschool education; medical office management; nursing (registered nurse training); system administration; web page, digital/multimedia and information resources design.

Academics *Calendar:* semesters. *Degree:* certificates and associate. *Special study options:* academic remediation for entering students, adult/continuing education programs, advanced placement credit, cooperative education, distance learning, double majors, English as a second language, external degree program, independent study, internships, off-campus study, part-time degree program, services for LD students, student-designed majors, summer session for credit.

Library University of Arkansas Community College at Batesville Library with 8,000 titles, 149 serial subscriptions, an OPAC, a Web page.

Student Life *Housing:* college housing not available. *Campus security:* student patrols, security cameras, County Deputy Sherriff Patrol. *Student services:* personal/psychological counseling.

Costs (2007–08) *Tuition:* area resident $1400 full-time, $50 per credit hour part-time; state resident $1680 full-time, $60 per credit hour part-time; nonresident $3360 full-time, $120 per credit hour part-time. *Required fees:* $448 full-time, $16 per credit hour part-time, $5 per term part-time.

Financial Aid Of all full-time matriculated undergraduates, 49 Federal Work-Study jobs (averaging $1311).

Applying *Required:* high school transcript, immunization records. *Application deadlines:* rolling (freshmen), rolling (transfers). *Notification:* continuous (freshmen), continuous (transfers).

Freshmen Application Contact Ms. Sharon Gage, Admissions Coordinator, University of Arkansas Community College at Batesville, PO Box 3350, Batesville, AR 72503. *Phone:* 870-612-2042. *Toll-free phone:* 800-508-7878. *Fax:* 870-612-2129. *E-mail:* sgage@uaccb.edu.

UNIVERSITY OF ARKANSAS COMMUNITY COLLEGE AT HOPE

Hope, Arkansas www.uacch.edu/

Freshmen Application Contact Ms. Danita Ormand, Director of Enrollment Services, University of Arkansas Community College at Hope, AR 71802-0140. *Phone:* 870-777-5722. *Fax:* 870-722-6630. *E-mail:* danita.ormand@uacch.edu.

UNIVERSITY OF ARKANSAS COMMUNITY COLLEGE AT MORRILTON

Morrilton, Arkansas www.uaccm.edu/

- **State-supported** 2-year, founded 1961, part of University of Arkansas System
- **Rural** 63-acre campus
- **Endowment** $65,879
- **Coed,** 1,763 undergraduate students, 65% full-time, 61% women, 39% men

University of Arkansas Community College at Morrilton *(continued)*

Undergraduates 1,140 full-time, 623 part-time. Students come from 2 states and territories, 1 other country, 6% African American, 0.7% Asian American or Pacific Islander, 3% Hispanic American, 0.8% Native American, 0.1% international, 11% transferred in.

Freshmen *Admission:* 886 applied, 688 admitted, 501 enrolled. *Average high school GPA:* 2.81. *Test scores:* ACT scores over 18: 71%; ACT scores over 24: 16%.

Faculty *Total:* 105, 48% full-time, 7% with terminal degrees.

Majors Administrative assistant and secretarial science; automobile/automotive mechanics technology; child development; commercial and advertising art; computer systems networking and telecommunications; computer typography and composition equipment operation; drafting and design technology; heating, air conditioning, ventilation and refrigeration maintenance technology; horticultural science; information science/studies; liberal arts and sciences/liberal studies; machine tool technology; marketing/marketing management; nursing (licensed practical/vocational nurse training); ornamental horticulture; survey technology; welding technology.

Academics *Calendar:* semesters. *Degree:* certificates and associate. *Special study options:* academic remediation for entering students, advanced placement credit, distance learning, double majors, internships, off-campus study, part-time degree program, services for LD students, student-designed majors, summer session for credit.

Library Gordon Library with 15,621 titles, 45 serial subscriptions, 197 audiovisual materials, an OPAC, a Web page.

Student Life *Housing:* college housing not available. *Activities and Organizations:* Business Students' Organization, Student Activity Board, Early Childhood Development Organization, Graphic Design Club, Student Practical Nurses Organization. *Campus security:* 24-hour emergency response devices. *Student services:* personal/psychological counseling.

Costs (2007–08) *Tuition:* area resident $1920 full-time, $64 per credit hour part-time; state resident $2100 full-time, $70 per credit hour part-time; nonresident $3060 full-time, $102 per credit hour part-time. *Required fees:* $414 full-time, $18 per credit hour part-time, $15 per term part-time.

Financial Aid Of all full-time matriculated undergraduates, 20 Federal Work-Study jobs (averaging $1000). *Financial aid deadline:* 7/23.

Applying *Options:* early admission, deferred entrance. *Required:* high school transcript. *Required for some:* immunization records. *Application deadlines:* rolling (freshmen), rolling (transfers). *Notification:* continuous (freshmen), continuous (transfers).

Freshmen Application Contact Ms. Wanda Hensley, Registrar, University of Arkansas Community College at Morrilton, One Bruce Street, Morrilton, AR 72110. *Phone:* 501-997-2028. *Toll-free phone:* 800-264-1094. *Fax:* 501-977-2123. *E-mail:* hensley@uaccm.edu.

CALIFORNIA

ALLAN HANCOCK COLLEGE

Santa Maria, California www.hancockcollege.edu/

- **State and locally supported** 2-year, founded 1920
- **Small-town** 120-acre campus
- **Endowment** $1.1 million
- **Coed**

Undergraduates 2,996 full-time, 7,391 part-time. Students come from 27 states and territories, 12 other countries, 4% African American, 3% Asian American or Pacific Islander, 33% Hispanic American, 1% Native American, 0.1% international.

Faculty *Student/faculty ratio:* 17:1.

Academics *Calendar:* semesters. *Degree:* certificates and associate. *Special study options:* adult/continuing education programs, advanced placement credit, cooperative education, distance learning, English as a second language, part-time degree program, services for LD students, study abroad, summer session for credit.

Student Life *Campus security:* 24-hour emergency response devices and patrols, student patrols, late-night transport/escort service.

Costs (2006–07) *Tuition:* state resident $0 full-time; nonresident $4956 full-time, $177 per unit part-time. *Required fees:* $792 full-time, $27 per unit part-time.

Financial Aid Of all full-time matriculated undergraduates, 250 Federal Work-Study jobs (averaging $3000).

Applying *Options:* early admission. *Required:* high school transcript.

Freshmen Application Contact Ms. Marian Quaid Maltagliati, Interim Director of Admissions and Records, Allan Hancock College, 800 South College Drive, Santa Maria, CA 93454-6399. *Phone:* 805-922-6966 Ext. 3272. *Toll-free phone:* 866-342-5242. *Fax:* 805-922-3477.

AMERICAN ACADEMY OF DRAMATIC ARTS/HOLLYWOOD

Hollywood, California www.aada.org/

Freshmen Application Contact Mr. Dan Justin, Director of Admissions, American Academy of Dramatic Arts/Hollywood, 1336 North LaBrea Avenue, Hollywood, CA 90028. *Phone:* 323-464-2777. *Toll-free phone:* 800-222-2867. *Fax:* 323-464-1250. *E-mail:* djustin@ca.aada.org.

▶See page 472 for the College Close-Up.

AMERICAN RIVER COLLEGE

Sacramento, California www.arc.losrios.edu/

Freshmen Application Contact Ms. Robin Neal, Dean of Enrollment Services, American River College, 4700 College Oak Drive, Sacramento, CA 95841-4286. *Phone:* 916-484-8171. *E-mail:* recadmiss@mail.arc.losrios.cc.ca.us.

ANTELOPE VALLEY COLLEGE

Lancaster, California www.avc.edu/

- **State and locally supported** 2-year, founded 1929, part of California Community College System
- **Suburban** 135-acre campus with easy access to Los Angeles
- **Endowment** $299,569
- **Coed**, 12,570 undergraduate students, 31% full-time, 62% women, 38% men

Undergraduates 3,924 full-time, 8,646 part-time. Students come from 7 states and territories, 1% are from out of state, 19% African American, 6% Asian American or Pacific Islander, 29% Hispanic American, 1% Native American, 19% transferred in.

Freshmen *Admission:* 1,852 applied, 1,852 admitted, 307 enrolled.

Faculty *Total:* 605, 31% full-time. *Student/faculty ratio:* 12:1.

Majors Administrative assistant and secretarial science; aircraft powerplant technology; airframe mechanics and aircraft maintenance technology; autobody/collision and repair technology; automobile/automotive mechanics technology; avionics maintenance technology; biology/biological sciences; business administration and management; business/commerce; child care and support services management; child guidance; cinematography and film/video production; clothing/textiles; computer and information sciences; computer graphics; computer programming; construction engineering technology; consumer education; corrections; criminal justice/law enforcement administration; criminal justice/police science; data processing and data processing technology; drafting and design technology; electrical, electronic and communications engineering technology; engineering; engineering technology; family living/parenthood; fiber, textile and weaving arts; fire protection and safety technology; foods, nutrition, and wellness; health and physical education; heating, air conditioning, ventilation and refrigeration maintenance technology; interior design; liberal arts and sciences/liberal studies; marketing/marketing management; mathematics; medical administrative assistant and medical secretary; music; nursing (registered nurse training); ornamental horticulture; photography; physical sciences; real estate; teacher assistant/aide; welding technology.

Academics *Calendar:* semesters. *Degree:* certificates and associate. *Special study options:* academic remediation for entering students, adult/continuing education programs, advanced placement credit, cooperative education, English as a second language, honors programs, part-time degree program, services for LD students, student-designed majors, summer session for credit. *ROTC:* Air Force (c).

Library Antelope Valley College Library with 43,000 titles, 175 serial subscriptions, an OPAC.

Student Life *Housing:* college housing not available. *Activities and Organizations:* drama/theater group, student-run newspaper, choral group. *Campus security:* 24-hour emergency response devices and patrols, late-night transport/escort service. *Student services:* personal/psychological counseling.

Athletics *Intercollegiate sports:* baseball M, basketball M/W, cross-country running M/W, football M, soccer W, softball W, tennis W, track and field M/W,

volleyball W. *Intramural sports:* basketball M/W, golf M/W, swimming and diving M/W, tennis M/W, volleyball M/W, weight lifting M/W.

Applying *Options:* early admission. *Required:* high school transcript. *Recommended:* assessment. *Application deadlines:* rolling (freshmen), rolling (transfers). *Notification:* continuous (freshmen), continuous (transfers).

Freshmen Application Contact Welcome Center, Antelope Valley College, 3041 West Avenue K, Lancaster, CA 93536-5426. *Phone:* 661-722-6331.

AVIATION & ELECTRONIC SCHOOLS OF AMERICA

Colfax, California **www.aesa.com/**

- **Proprietary** 2-year, founded 1988
- **Coed**

Majors Computer science.

Academics *Calendar:* continuous. *Degree:* certificates and associate.

Costs (2006–07) *Tuition:* $24,101 per degree program part-time.

Admissions Office Contact Aviation & Electronic Schools of America, P.O. Box 1810, 111 South Railroad Street, Colfax, CA 95713. *Toll-free phone:* 800-345-2742.

BAKERSFIELD COLLEGE

Bakersfield, California **www.bakersfieldcollege.edu/**

- **State and locally supported** 2-year, founded 1913, part of California Community College System
- **Urban** 175-acre campus
- **Coed,** 15,001 undergraduate students

Majors Accounting; administrative assistant and secretarial science; agricultural business and management; agriculture; animal sciences; anthropology; architectural engineering technology; art; art teacher education; automobile/automotive mechanics technology; biology/biological sciences; broadcast journalism; business administration and management; carpentry; chemistry; child development; computer science; corrections; cosmetology; criminal justice/law enforcement administration; criminal justice/police science; culinary arts; data processing and data processing technology; dental hygiene; developmental and child psychology; dietetics; drafting and design technology; dramatic/theater arts; economics; electrical, electronic and communications engineering technology; emergency medical technology (EMT paramedic); engineering; English; environmental engineering technology; family and consumer economics related; finance; fire science; foods, nutrition, and wellness; forestry; French; geography; geology/earth science; German; history; horticultural science; hotel/motel administration; human services; industrial arts; industrial radiologic technology; industrial technology; information science/studies; interior design; journalism; legal administrative assistant/secretary; liberal arts and sciences/liberal studies; machine tool technology; marketing/marketing management; mathematics; music; nursing (registered nurse training); ornamental horticulture; parks, recreation and leisure; petroleum technology; philosophy; photography; physical education teaching and coaching; physics; pipefitting and sprinkler fitting; political science and government; psychology; real estate; sociology; Spanish; speech and rhetoric; survey technology; welding technology; wood science and wood products/pulp and paper technology.

Academics *Calendar:* semesters. *Degree:* associate. *Special study options:* academic remediation for entering students, accelerated degree program, adult/continuing education programs, advanced placement credit, cooperative education, English as a second language, internships, part-time degree program, services for LD students, summer session for credit.

Library Grace Van Dyke Bird Library with 93,500 titles, 298 serial subscriptions, an OPAC, a Web page.

Student Life *Housing:* college housing not available. *Activities and Organizations:* drama/theater group, student-run newspaper, radio station, choral group. *Campus security:* 24-hour patrols, late-night transport/escort service. *Student services:* health clinic, women's center.

Athletics *Intercollegiate sports:* baseball M, basketball M/W, cross-country running M/W, football M, golf M, soccer W, softball W, tennis M/W, track and field M/W, volleyball W, wrestling M.

Costs (2006–07) *Tuition:* state resident $682 full-time; nonresident $5582 full-time.

Financial Aid Of all full-time matriculated undergraduates, 300 Federal Work-Study jobs (averaging $2500). 15 state and other part-time jobs (averaging $2500).

Applying *Application deadline:* rolling (freshmen).

Director of Admissions Ms. Sue Vaughn, Director of Enrollment Services, Bakersfield College, 1801 Panorama Drive, Bakersfield, CA 93305-1299. *Phone:* 661-395-4301. *E-mail:* svaughn@bakersfieldcollege.edu.

BARSTOW COLLEGE

Barstow, California **www.barstow.edu/**

- **State and locally supported** 2-year, founded 1959, part of California Community College System
- **Small-town** 50-acre campus
- **Coed,** 3,000 undergraduate students

Undergraduates Students come from 43 states and territories, 8 other countries.

Faculty *Total:* 127, 28% full-time. *Student/faculty ratio:* 20:1.

Majors Accounting; administrative assistant and secretarial science; automobile/automotive mechanics technology; business administration and management; child development; computer science; cosmetology; drafting and design technology; education; electrical, electronic and communications engineering technology; humanities; kindergarten/preschool education; liberal arts and sciences/liberal studies; mathematics; medical/clinical assistant; physical education teaching and coaching; social sciences.

Academics *Calendar:* semesters. *Degree:* associate. *Special study options:* academic remediation for entering students, adult/continuing education programs, cooperative education, English as a second language, external degree program, part-time degree program, services for LD students, student-designed majors, summer session for credit.

Library Thomas Kimball Library with 38,000 titles, 110 serial subscriptions, an OPAC, a Web page.

Student Life *Housing:* college housing not available. *Activities and Organizations:* drama/theater group, student-run newspaper. *Campus security:* evening security personnel. *Student services:* personal/psychological counseling.

Athletics Member NJCAA. *Intercollegiate sports:* baseball M, basketball M, volleyball W. *Intramural sports:* basketball M.

Standardized Tests *Required:* assessment test approved by the Chancellor's office (for placement).

Applying *Options:* early admission, deferred entrance. *Recommended:* high school transcript. *Application deadlines:* rolling (freshmen), rolling (transfers).

Director of Admissions Mr. Don Low, Interim Vice President, Barstow College, 2700 Barstow Road, Barstow, CA 92311-6699.

BERKELEY CITY COLLEGE

Berkeley, California **www.berkeleycitycollege.edu/**

- **State and locally supported** 2-year, founded 1974
- **Urban** campus with easy access to San Francisco
- **Coed,** 5,100 undergraduate students

Undergraduates 1% are from out of state, 22% African American, 15% Asian American or Pacific Islander, 11% Hispanic American, 0.7% Native American, 5% international.

Faculty *Total:* 164, 21% full-time. *Student/faculty ratio:* 25:1.

Majors Accounting; art; biology/biotechnology laboratory technician; business administration and management; business/commerce; computer and information sciences; computer and information sciences related; computer and information systems security; computer graphics; computer software and media applications related; creative writing; data entry/microcomputer applications related; English; English composition; fine/studio arts; general studies; liberal arts and sciences/liberal studies; medical administrative assistant and medical secretary; office management; Spanish; web page, digital/multimedia and information resources design.

Academics *Calendar:* semesters. *Degree:* certificates and associate. *Special study options:* academic remediation for entering students, adult/continuing education programs, cooperative education, English as a second language, independent study, internships, off-campus study, part-time degree program, services for LD students, student-designed majors, study abroad, summer session for credit.

Library Vista Community College Library with an OPAC, a Web page.

Student Life *Housing:* college housing not available. *Activities and Organizations:* drama/theater group, student-run newspaper. *Campus security:* 24-hour patrols. *Student services:* personal/psychological counseling.

Costs (2007–08) *Tuition:* state resident $0 full-time; nonresident $5160 full-time, $172 per unit part-time. *Required fees:* $784 full-time, $26 per unit part-time, $2 per term part-time.

Berkeley City College (continued)

Financial Aid Of all full-time matriculated undergraduates, 50 Federal Work-Study jobs (averaging $3000). 20 state and other part-time jobs (averaging $2000).

Applying *Options:* electronic application, early admission, deferred entrance. *Recommended:* high school transcript. *Application deadline:* rolling (freshmen). *Notification:* continuous (freshmen).

Freshmen Application Contact Dr. Mario Rivas, Vice President of Student Services, Berkeley City College, 2020 Milvia Street, Berkeley, CA 94704. *Phone:* 510-981-2820. *Fax:* 510-841-7333. *E-mail:* mrivas@peralta.edu.

BROOKS COLLEGE

Long Beach, California   **www.brookscollege.edu/**

- **Proprietary** 2-year, founded 1971
- **Suburban** 7-acre campus with easy access to Los Angeles
- **Coed**

Undergraduates 757 full-time, 69 part-time. Students come from 17 other countries, 39% are from out of state, 6% African American, 5% Asian American or Pacific Islander, 18% Hispanic American, 0.5% Native American, 60% live on campus.

Academics *Calendar:* quarters. *Degree:* diplomas and associate. *Special study options:* academic remediation for entering students, cooperative education, internships, services for LD students, summer session for credit.

Student Life *Campus security:* 24-hour emergency response devices and patrols, controlled dormitory access.

Costs (2006–07) *Comprehensive fee:* $23,564 includes full-time tuition ($15,075), mandatory fees ($50), and room and board ($8439). Part-time tuition: $335 per unit. Part-time tuition and fees vary according to course load. *Room and board:* Room and board charges vary according to housing facility.

Applying *Options:* deferred entrance. *Application fee:* $50. *Required:* essay or personal statement, high school transcript, minimum 2.0 GPA, letters of recommendation, interview. *Recommended:* portfolio.

Freshmen Application Contact Ms. Christina Varon, Director of Admissions, Brooks College, 4825 East Pacific Coast Highway, Long Beach, CA 90804-3291. *Phone:* 562-498-2441 Ext. 265. *Toll-free phone:* 800-421-3775. *Fax:* 562-597-7412. *E-mail:* info@brookscollege.edu.

BROOKS COLLEGE

Sunnyvale, California   **www.brookssv.com/**

- **Proprietary** 2-year
- **Coed,** 370 undergraduate students

Majors Animation, interactive technology, video graphics and special effects; design and visual communications; fashion/apparel design; fashion merchandising; system administration.

Academics *Calendar:* quarters. *Degree:* associate.

Costs (2006–07) *Tuition:* $16,425 full-time.

Applying *Application fee:* $50.

Freshmen Application Contact Admissions Office, Brooks College, 1120 Kifer Road, Sunnyvale, CA 94086.

BRYAN COLLEGE

Gold River, California   **www.bryancollege.edu/**

- **Proprietary** 2-year, founded 1995
- **Coed,** 129 undergraduate students
- **51% of applicants were admitted**

Freshmen *Admission:* 134 applied, 69 admitted.

Majors Computer and information sciences; health and physical education related; massage therapy.

Academics *Degree:* associate.

Applying *Application fee:* $35.

Freshmen Application Contact Admissions Office, Bryan College, 2317 Gold Meadow Way, Gold River, CA 95670-4443. *Phone:* 916-649-2400. *Toll-free phone:* 866-649-2400.

BRYMAN COLLEGE

City of Industry, California   **www.everest.edu/**

Freshmen Application Contact Admissions Office, Bryman College, 12801 Crossroads Parkway South, City of Industry, CA 91746-1023.

BRYMAN COLLEGE

Ontario, California   **www.everest.edu/**

Freshmen Application Contact Admissions Office, Bryman College, Ontario, CA 91761.

BUTTE COLLEGE

Oroville, California   **www.butte.edu/**

Freshmen Application Contact Ms. Nancy Jenson, Registrar, Butte College, 3536 Butte Campus Drive, Oroville, CA 95965. *Phone:* 530-895-2361.

CABRILLO COLLEGE

Aptos, California   **www.cabrillo.edu/**

- **District-supported** 2-year, founded 1959, part of California Community College System
- **Small-town** 120-acre campus with easy access to San Jose
- **Coed,** 14,094 undergraduate students, 28% full-time, 58% women, 42% men

Undergraduates 3,993 full-time, 10,101 part-time. Students come from 21 states and territories, 21 other countries, 2% are from out of state, 1% African American, 4% Asian American or Pacific Islander, 27% Hispanic American, 0.9% Native American, 1% international.

Faculty *Total:* 651, 18% full-time, 29% with terminal degrees.

Majors Accounting; biological and physical sciences; business administration and management; business machine repair; cartography; ceramic arts and ceramics; child development; computer programming; computer science; construction management; consumer merchandising/retailing management; data processing and data processing technology; dental hygiene; drafting and design technology; electrical, electronic and communications engineering technology; energy management and systems technology; fire science; food science; food services technology; health information/medical records administration; health science; horticultural science; industrial design; kindergarten/preschool education; liberal arts and sciences/liberal studies; medical administrative assistant and medical secretary; natural sciences; nursing (registered nurse training); parks, recreation and leisure; physical education teaching and coaching; pre-engineering; real estate; solar energy technology; Spanish; special products marketing; welding technology; wildlife and wildlands science and management; women's studies.

Academics *Calendar:* semesters. *Degree:* certificates and associate. *Special study options:* academic remediation for entering students, adult/continuing education programs, advanced placement credit, cooperative education, distance learning, double majors, English as a second language, honors programs, independent study, internships, part-time degree program, services for LD students, study abroad, summer session for credit.

Library Cabrillo College Library with 60,000 titles, 300 serial subscriptions, an OPAC, a Web page.

Student Life *Housing:* college housing not available. *Activities and Organizations:* drama/theater group, student-run newspaper. *Campus security:* 24-hour emergency response devices and patrols, late-night transport/escort service. *Student services:* health clinic, personal/psychological counseling, women's center.

Athletics *Intercollegiate sports:* baseball M, basketball M/W, cross-country running M/W, football M, golf M/W, soccer M/W, softball W, swimming and diving M/W, tennis M/W, track and field M/W, volleyball M/W, water polo M/W, wrestling M. *Intramural sports:* basketball M/W, cheerleading W, sailing M/W, skiing (cross-country) M/W, skiing (downhill) M/W, volleyball W.

Costs (2007–08) *Tuition:* area resident $480 full-time, $20 per unit part-time; state resident $480 full-time, $20 per unit part-time; nonresident $4656 full-time, $194 per unit part-time.

Financial Aid Of all full-time matriculated undergraduates, 50 Federal Work-Study jobs (averaging $4000).

Applying *Options:* early admission. *Required for some:* high school transcript. *Application deadlines:* rolling (freshmen), rolling (transfers).

Freshmen Application Contact Ms. Esperanza Nee, Interim Director of Admissions and Records, Cabrillo College, 6500 Soquel Drive, Aptos, CA 95003. *Phone:* 831-479-6213. *Fax:* 831-479-5782. *E-mail:* esnee@cabrillo.edu.

CALIFORNIA CULINARY ACADEMY
San Francisco, California **www.baychef.com/**

Director of Admissions Ms. Nancy Seyfert, Vice President of Admissions, California Culinary Academy, 625 Polk Street, San Francisco, CA 94102-3368. *Phone:* 800-229-2433 Ext. 275. *Toll-free phone:* 800-229-2433 (in-state); 800-BAYCHEF (out-of-state).

CALIFORNIA SCHOOL OF CULINARY ARTS
Pasadena, California **www.csca.edu/**

- **Proprietary** 2-year, founded 1994
- **Coed,** 1,726 undergraduate students

Majors Culinary arts; restaurant/food services management.
Academics *Degree:* diplomas and associate.
Applying *Application fee:* $75.
Director of Admissions Admissions Office, California School of Culinary Arts, 521 East Green Street, Pasadena, CA 91101.

CAÑADA COLLEGE
Redwood City, California **www.canadacollege.net/**

- **State and locally supported** 2-year, founded 1968, part of San Mateo County Community College District System
- **Suburban** 131-acre campus with easy access to San Francisco and San Jose
- **Coed,** 6,230 undergraduate students

Undergraduates Students come from 32 other countries, 3% African American, 8% Asian American or Pacific Islander, 41% Hispanic American, 0.3% Native American, 0.7% international. *Retention:* 65% of 2003 full-time freshmen returned.
Freshmen *Admission:* 1,020 applied, 1,020 admitted.
Faculty *Total:* 250.
Majors Accounting; administrative assistant and secretarial science; anatomy; anthropology; art; art history, criticism and conservation; biological and physical sciences; biology/biological sciences; business administration and management; business machine repair; chemistry; computer engineering technology; computer programming; computer science; dance; data processing and data processing technology; dramatic/theater arts; drawing; economics; engineering; English; environmental studies; fashion/apparel design; French; geography; geology/earth science; German; health science; health teacher education; history; humanities; industrial radiologic technology; information science/studies; interior design; journalism; kindergarten/preschool education; kinesiology and exercise science; legal assistant/paralegal; liberal arts and sciences/liberal studies; mathematics; music; philosophy; physical education teaching and coaching; political science and government; psychology; sociology; Spanish; speech and rhetoric; tourism and travel services management.
Academics *Calendar:* semesters. *Degree:* certificates and associate. *Special study options:* academic remediation for entering students, accelerated degree program, adult/continuing education programs, advanced placement credit, cooperative education, English as a second language, internships, part-time degree program, services for LD students, study abroad, summer session for credit.
Library 53,417 titles, 414 serial subscriptions, an OPAC.
Student Life *Housing:* college housing not available. *Activities and Organizations:* drama/theater group, choral group, Latin-American Club, student government, Environmental Club, athletics, Interior Design Club. *Campus security:* 12-hour patrols by trained security personnel. *Student services:* health clinic, personal/psychological counseling.
Athletics *Intercollegiate sports:* baseball M. *Intramural sports:* basketball M/W, soccer M, tennis M/W, volleyball M/W.
Costs (2007–08) *Tuition:* state resident $0 full-time; nonresident $5520 full-time, $184 per unit part-time. *Required fees:* $648 full-time, $20 per unit part-time, $24 per term part-time.
Financial Aid Of all full-time matriculated undergraduates, 25 Federal Work-Study jobs (averaging $4000).

Applying *Options:* early admission. *Application deadlines:* rolling (freshmen), rolling (transfers).
Freshmen Application Contact Cañada College, 4200 Farm Hill Boulevard, Redwood City, CA 94061. *Phone:* 650-306-3118.

CERRITOS COLLEGE
Norwalk, California **www.cerritos.edu/**

- **State and locally supported** 2-year, founded 1956, part of California Community College System
- **Suburban** 140-acre campus with easy access to Los Angeles
- **Coed,** 24,000 undergraduate students

Undergraduates Students come from 32 other countries.
Faculty *Total:* 690, 36% full-time.
Majors Accounting; administrative assistant and secretarial science; agriculture; anthropology; architectural engineering technology; art; automobile/automotive mechanics technology; biology/biological sciences; biomedical technology; botany/plant biology; business administration and management; chemistry; computer programming; computer science; cosmetology; court reporting; criminal justice/police science; data processing and data processing technology; dental hygiene; drafting and design technology; dramatic/theater arts; economics; electrical, electronic and communications engineering technology; English; family and consumer sciences/human sciences; fashion/apparel design; food services technology; forestry; French; geography; geology/earth science; German; Hispanic-American, Puerto Rican, and Mexican-American/Chicano studies; history; industrial arts; industrial technology; journalism; kindergarten/preschool education; legal administrative assistant/secretary; liberal arts and sciences/liberal studies; machine tool technology; marketing/marketing management; mathematics; medical administrative assistant and medical secretary; medical/clinical assistant; music; nursing (registered nurse training); ornamental horticulture; parks, recreation and leisure; pharmacy; philosophy; photography; physical education teaching and coaching; physical sciences related; physical therapy; physics; plastics engineering technology; political science and government; pre-engineering; psychology; real estate; sociology; Spanish; speech and rhetoric; welding technology; wildlife and wildlands science and management; zoology/animal biology.
Academics *Calendar:* semesters. *Degree:* associate. *Special study options:* academic remediation for entering students, adult/continuing education programs, advanced placement credit, English as a second language, part-time degree program, services for LD students, study abroad, summer session for credit.
Library Wilford Michael Library with 74,502 titles, 396 serial subscriptions.
Student Life *Housing:* college housing not available. *Activities and Organizations:* drama/theater group, student-run newspaper, radio station. *Student services:* health clinic, personal/psychological counseling, women's center, legal services.
Athletics Member NJCAA. *Intercollegiate sports:* baseball M, basketball M/W, cross-country running M/W, football M, golf M, soccer M, softball W, swimming and diving M/W, tennis M/W, track and field M/W, volleyball W, water polo M, wrestling M.
Costs (2006–07) *Tuition:* state resident $580 full-time; nonresident $4420 full-time.
Financial Aid Of all full-time matriculated undergraduates, 180 Federal Work-Study jobs (averaging $3000). 89 state and other part-time jobs (averaging $2734).
Applying *Options:* early admission, deferred entrance. *Application deadlines:* rolling (freshmen), rolling (transfers).
Director of Admissions Ms. Stephanie Murguia, Director of Admissions and Records, Cerritos College, 11110 Alondra Boulevard, Norwalk, CA 90650-6298. *Phone:* 562-860-2451. *E-mail:* smurguia@cerritos.edu.

CERRO COSO COMMUNITY COLLEGE
Ridgecrest, California **www.cerrocoso.edu/**

Freshmen Application Contact Mrs. Heather Ootash, Counseling/Matriculation Coordinator, Cerro Coso Community College, 3000 College Heights Boulevard, Ridgecrest, CA 93555. *Phone:* 760-384-6291. *Fax:* 760-375-4776. *E-mail:* hostash@cerrocoso.edu.

CHABOT COLLEGE
Hayward, California **www.chabotcollege.edu/**

Director of Admissions Ms. Judy Young, Director of Admissions and Records, Chabot College, 25555 Hesperian Boulevard, Hayward, CA 94545. *Phone:* 510-723-6700.

CHAFFEY COLLEGE

Rancho Cucamonga, California   **www.chaffey.edu/**

- **District-supported** 2-year, founded 1883, part of California Community College System
- **Suburban** 200-acre campus with easy access to Los Angeles
- **Coed,** 17,930 undergraduate students

Undergraduates 2% are from out of state.

Faculty *Total:* 683, 27% full-time.

Majors Accounting; administrative assistant and secretarial science; anthropology; art; automobile/automotive mechanics technology; biology/biological sciences; broadcast journalism; business administration and management; business teacher education; ceramic arts and ceramics; chemistry; child development; computer typography and composition equipment operation; corrections; court reporting; dance; developmental and child psychology; dietetics; drafting and design technology; dramatic/theater arts; economics; electrical, electronic and communications engineering technology; engineering; English; environmental engineering technology; family and consumer sciences/human sciences; fashion/apparel design; French; geology/earth science; German; gerontology; history; hotel/motel administration; humanities; industrial design; information science/studies; interior design; journalism; kindergarten/preschool education; legal administrative assistant/secretary; liberal arts and sciences/liberal studies; marketing/marketing management; mathematics; medical administrative assistant and medical secretary; medical radiologic technology; music; nursing (registered nurse training); philosophy; photography; physical education teaching and coaching; physical sciences; physics; political science and government; psychology; quality control technology; real estate; religious studies; social sciences; sociology; Spanish; special products marketing; speech and rhetoric; telecommunications.

Academics *Calendar:* semesters. *Degree:* certificates and associate. *Special study options:* academic remediation for entering students, adult/continuing education programs, advanced placement credit, cooperative education, English as a second language, honors programs, internships, part-time degree program, services for LD students, study abroad, summer session for credit. *ROTC:* Army (c).

Library Chaffey College Library with 72,000 titles, 232 serial subscriptions.

Student Life *Housing:* college housing not available. *Activities and Organizations:* drama/theater group, student-run newspaper, radio station, choral group, The Associated Students of Chaffey College, Multicultural Club, Style Club. *Campus security:* 24-hour emergency response devices, late-night transport/escort service. *Student services:* health clinic, personal/psychological counseling.

Athletics Member NJCAA. *Intercollegiate sports:* baseball M, basketball M/W, football M, soccer M/W, softball W, swimming and diving M/W, tennis M/W, track and field M/W, volleyball W, water polo M/W.

Costs (2006–07) *Tuition:* state resident $714 full-time; nonresident $4668 full-time.

Financial Aid Of all full-time matriculated undergraduates, 700 Federal Work-Study jobs (averaging $3000).

Applying *Options:* early admission. *Application deadlines:* rolling (freshmen), rolling (transfers). *Notification:* continuous (freshmen), continuous (transfers).

Director of Admissions Ms. Cecilia Carerra, Director of Admissions, Registration, and Records, Chaffey College, 5885 Haven Avenue, Rancho Cucamonga, CA 91737-3002. *Phone:* 909-941-2631. *Fax:* 909-466-2820.

CITRUS COLLEGE

Glendora, California   **www.citruscollege.edu/**

- **State and locally supported** 2-year, founded 1915, part of California Community College System
- **Small-town** 104-acre campus with easy access to Los Angeles
- **Coed,** 11,576 undergraduate students, 43% full-time, 57% women, 43% men

Undergraduates 4,957 full-time, 6,619 part-time. 17% are from out of state, 5% African American, 10% Asian American or Pacific Islander, 43% Hispanic American, 0.7% Native American, 4% international.

Freshmen *Admission:* 2,069 enrolled.

Faculty *Total:* 447, 38% full-time. *Student/faculty ratio:* 26:1.

Majors Administrative assistant and secretarial science; art; automobile/automotive mechanics technology; behavioral sciences; biology/biological sciences; business administration and management; computer and information sciences related; computer science; cosmetology; criminal justice/law enforcement administration; criminal justice/police science; dance; data processing and data processing technology; dental assisting; drafting and design technology; dramatic/theater arts; electrical, electronic and communications engineering

technology; engineering; engineering technology; English; French; German; health and physical education; hydrology and water resources science; Japanese; journalism; liberal arts and sciences/liberal studies; library assistant; library science; mathematics; mechanical engineering/mechanical technology; modern languages; music; natural sciences; nursing (licensed practical/vocational nurse training); photography; physical education teaching and coaching; physical sciences; public administration; real estate; social sciences; Spanish; visual and performing arts.

Academics *Calendar:* semesters. *Degree:* certificates, diplomas, and associate. *Special study options:* academic remediation for entering students, advanced placement credit, cooperative education, distance learning, English as a second language, honors programs, part-time degree program, services for LD students, study abroad, summer session for credit.

Library Hayden Library with 45,091 titles, 133 serial subscriptions, an OPAC, a Web page.

Student Life *Housing:* college housing not available. *Activities and Organizations:* drama/theater group, student-run newspaper, choral group, Student Government, AGS Honor Society, International Student Association, Cosmetology Club. *Campus security:* 24-hour patrols, student patrols, late-night transport/escort service. *Student services:* health clinic, personal/psychological counseling, legal services.

Athletics *Intercollegiate sports:* baseball M, basketball M/W, cross-country running M/W, football M, golf M/W, soccer M/W, softball W, swimming and diving M/W, tennis M/W, track and field M/W, volleyball W, water polo M/W.

Costs (2006–07) *Tuition:* state resident $0 full-time; nonresident $4480 full-time, $160 per unit part-time. *Required fees:* $684 full-time, $20 per unit part-time, $55 per term part-time.

Financial Aid Of all full-time matriculated undergraduates, 141 Federal Work-Study jobs (averaging $5500).

Applying *Required:* high school transcript.

Freshmen Application Contact Admissions and Records, Citrus College, 1000 West Foothill Boulevard, Glendora, CA 91741-1899. *Phone:* 626-914-8511. *Fax:* 626-914-8613. *E-mail:* admissions@citruscollege.edu.

CITY COLLEGE OF SAN FRANCISCO

San Francisco, California   **www.ccsf.edu/**

- **State and locally supported** 2-year, founded 1935, part of California Community College System
- **Urban** 56-acre campus
- **Coed,** 106,480 undergraduate students

Undergraduates Students come from 51 states and territories, 3% are from out of state, 9% African American, 40% Asian American or Pacific Islander, 16% Hispanic American, 0.6% Native American, 3% international. *Retention:* 75% of 2003 full-time freshmen returned.

Faculty *Total:* 2,317, 33% full-time.

Majors Accounting; African-American/Black studies; agricultural business and management; airframe mechanics and aircraft maintenance technology; art; Asian studies; atmospheric sciences and meteorology; automobile/automotive mechanics technology; avionics maintenance technology; botany/plant biology; broadcast journalism; business administration and management; chemical engineering; chemistry; cinematography and film/video production; civil engineering technology; computer programming; computer science; construction management; consumer services and advocacy; court reporting; criminal justice/law enforcement administration; criminal justice/police science; dental hygiene; developmental and child psychology; dietetics; educational/instructional media design; electrical, electronic and communications engineering technology; English; fashion merchandising; finance; fire science; forestry; geology/earth science; graphic and printing equipment operation/production; health information/medical records administration; horticultural science; hotel/motel administration; industrial radiologic technology; industrial technology; insurance; interior design; journalism; labor and industrial relations; landscape architecture; Latin American studies; legal administrative assistant/secretary; library science; marketing/marketing management; mathematics; mechanical engineering/mechanical technology; music; nursing (licensed practical/vocational nurse training); nursing (registered nurse training); ornamental horticulture; parks, recreation and leisure; photography; physical therapy; pre-engineering; psychology; public administration; public health; real estate; respiratory care therapy; social sciences; social work; transportation technology; wildlife and wildlands science and management; women's studies.

Academics *Calendar:* semesters. *Degree:* certificates, diplomas, and associate. *Special study options:* academic remediation for entering students, adult/continuing education programs, advanced placement credit, English as a second language, internships, off-campus study, part-time degree program, services for LD students, study abroad, summer session for credit.

Library Louise and Claude Rosenberg, Jr. Library plus 2 others with 93,518 titles, 774 serial subscriptions, a Web page.

Student Life *Housing:* college housing not available. *Activities and Organizations:* drama/theater group, student-run newspaper. *Campus security:* 24-hour emergency response devices and patrols, late-night transport/escort service. *Student services:* health clinic, personal/psychological counseling, women's center.

Athletics *Intercollegiate sports:* archery W, basketball M, cross-country running M/W, fencing W, football M, golf M, gymnastics W, soccer M, swimming and diving M, tennis M/W, track and field M/W, volleyball M/W, water polo M. *Intramural sports:* archery M/W, badminton M/W, basketball M/W, bowling M/W, fencing M/W, football M, golf M, gymnastics M/W, soccer M/W, swimming and diving M/W, tennis M/W, track and field M/W, volleyball M/W, wrestling M.

Costs (2007–08) *Tuition:* state resident $0 full-time; nonresident $4320 full-time, $144 per unit part-time. *Required fees:* $646 full-time, $20 per unit part-time, $23 per term part-time.

Financial Aid Of all full-time matriculated undergraduates, 3,000 Federal Work-Study jobs (averaging $3000). *Financial aid deadline:* 6/11.

Applying *Options:* early admission. *Application deadlines:* 8/9 (freshmen), 8/9 (out-of-state freshmen), 8/9 (transfers). *Notification:* continuous (freshmen), continuous (out-of-state freshmen), continuous (transfers).

Freshmen Application Contact Ms. Mary Lou Leyba-Frank, Dean of Admissions and Records, City College of San Francisco, 50 Phelan Avenue, San Francisco, CA 94112-1821. *Phone:* 415-239-3860. *Fax:* 415-239-3936. *E-mail:* mleyba@ccsf.edu.

COASTLINE COMMUNITY COLLEGE
Fountain Valley, California   coastline.cccd.edu/

Freshmen Application Contact Jennifer McDonald, Director of Admissions and Records, Coastline Community College, 11460 Warner Avenue, Fountain Valley, CA 92708. *Phone:* 714-241-6163.

COLEMAN COLLEGE
San Marcos, California   www.coleman.edu/

Director of Admissions Mr. James Warner, Senior Admissions Officer, Coleman College, 1284 West San Marcos Boulevard, San Marcos, CA 92078. *Phone:* 760-747-3990. *Fax:* 760-752-9808.

COLLEGE OF ALAMEDA
Alameda, California   www.peralta.cc.ca.us/

- **State and locally supported** 2-year, founded 1970, part of Peralta Community College District System
- **Urban** 62-acre campus with easy access to San Francisco
- **Coed,** 5,500 undergraduate students

Undergraduates Students come from 18 states and territories, 9 other countries.

Faculty *Total:* 166, 48% full-time.

Majors Accounting; administrative assistant and secretarial science; African-American/Black studies; anthropology; art; automobile/automotive mechanics technology; avionics maintenance technology; biological and physical sciences; biology/biological sciences; business administration and management; business teacher education; dental hygiene; English; fashion/apparel design; fashion merchandising; general studies; geography; Hispanic-American, Puerto Rican, and Mexican-American/Chicano studies; history; human development and family studies; humanities; information science/studies; liberal arts and sciences/liberal studies; marketing/marketing management; mathematics; philosophy; political science and government; psychology; social sciences; sociology; Spanish.

Academics *Calendar:* semesters. *Degree:* certificates and associate. *Special study options:* academic remediation for entering students, adult/continuing education programs, cooperative education, off-campus study, part-time degree program, services for LD students, summer session for credit.

Library Learning Resources Center with 40,000 titles, 200 serial subscriptions.

Student Life *Housing:* college housing not available. *Activities and Organizations:* student-run newspaper. *Student services:* women's center.

Athletics *Intercollegiate sports:* basketball M/W, bowling M/W. *Intramural sports:* soccer M/W, tennis M/W, track and field M/W, volleyball M/W.

Costs (2006–07) *Tuition:* state resident $648 full-time; nonresident $5460 full-time.

Financial Aid Of all full-time matriculated undergraduates, 90 Federal Work-Study jobs (averaging $2500).

Applying *Application deadlines:* rolling (freshmen), rolling (transfers).

Freshmen Application Contact Ms. Barbara Simmons, District Admissions Officer, College of Alameda, 555 Ralph Appezzato Memorial Parkway, Alameda, CA 94501-2109. *Phone:* 510-466-7370. *E-mail:* hperdue@peralta.cc.ca.us.

COLLEGE OF MARIN
Kentfield, California   www.marin.edu/

- **State and locally supported** 2-year, founded 1926, part of California Community College System
- **Small-town** 410-acre campus with easy access to San Francisco
- **Coed,** 6,607 undergraduate students, 21% full-time, 59% women, 41% men

Undergraduates 1,419 full-time, 5,188 part-time.

Faculty *Total:* 489, 30% full-time.

Majors Accounting; administrative assistant and secretarial science; applied art; architectural engineering technology; art; automobile/automotive mechanics technology; behavioral sciences; biology/biological sciences; business administration and management; chemistry; computer science; consumer merchandising/retailing management; corrections; court reporting; criminal justice/police science; cultural studies; dance; data processing and data processing technology; dental hygiene; dramatic/theater arts; ecology; electrical, electronic and communications engineering technology; engineering; engineering technology; fire science; French; geology/earth science; German; history; humanities; information science/studies; interior design; journalism; kindergarten/preschool education; landscape architecture; landscaping and groundskeeping; liberal arts and sciences/liberal studies; machine tool technology; marine technology; marketing/marketing management; mass communication/media; mathematics; medical administrative assistant and medical secretary; medical/clinical assistant; music; natural sciences; nursing (registered nurse training); philosophy; physical education teaching and coaching; physics; political science and government; psychology; real estate; sociology; Spanish; speech and rhetoric.

Academics *Calendar:* semesters. *Degree:* associate. *Special study options:* academic remediation for entering students, adult/continuing education programs, cooperative education, distance learning, English as a second language, part-time degree program, services for LD students, student-designed majors, summer session for credit.

Library 85,000 titles, 500 serial subscriptions.

Student Life *Housing:* college housing not available. *Activities and Organizations:* drama/theater group, student-run newspaper. *Campus security:* 24-hour patrols. *Student services:* health clinic, personal/psychological counseling.

Athletics *Intercollegiate sports:* basketball M/W, cross-country running M/W, football M/W, golf M/W, soccer M/W, swimming and diving M/W, tennis M/W, track and field M/W, volleyball M/W, water polo M/W.

Costs (2007–08) *Tuition:* state resident $0 full-time; nonresident $4776 full-time, $175 per unit part-time. *Required fees:* $516 full-time, $20 per unit part-time, $15 per term part-time.

Financial Aid Of all full-time matriculated undergraduates, 100 Federal Work-Study jobs (averaging $2500).

Applying *Options:* early admission. *Application deadline:* rolling (freshmen). *Notification:* continuous (freshmen).

Freshmen Application Contact Ms. Gina Longo, Administrative Assistant to the Dean of Enrollment Services, College of Marin, 835 College Avenue, Kentfield, CA 94904. *Phone:* 415-485-9417. *Fax:* 415-460-0773. *E-mail:* gina.longo@marin.edu.

COLLEGE OF SAN MATEO
San Mateo, California   www.collegeofsanmateo.edu/

- **State and locally supported** 2-year, founded 1922, part of California Community College System
- **Suburban** 150-acre campus
- **Coed,** 10,872 undergraduate students

Undergraduates Students come from 35 other countries.

Faculty *Total:* 476, 39% full-time. *Student/faculty ratio:* 15:1.

Majors Accounting; administrative assistant and secretarial science; airframe mechanics and aircraft maintenance technology; airline pilot and flight crew; architectural engineering technology; art; avionics maintenance technology; biology/biological sciences; biology/biotechnology laboratory technician; broadcast journalism; business administration and management; chemistry; cinematography and film/video production; commercial and advertising art; computer science; construction engineering technology; consumer merchandising/retailing

College of San Mateo (continued)

management; cosmetology; criminal justice/police science; cultural studies; dental hygiene; drafting and design technology; drawing; electrical, electronic and communications engineering technology; engineering; engineering technology; English; environmental studies; fire science; French; geology/earth science; German; horticultural science; humanities; information science/studies; journalism; landscape architecture; landscaping and groundskeeping; liberal arts and sciences/liberal studies; machine tool technology; management information systems; marketing/marketing management; mathematics; medical administrative assistant and medical secretary; medical/clinical assistant; music; nursing (registered nurse training); ornamental horticulture; photography; physical sciences; physics; pipefitting and sprinkler fitting; printmaking; radio and television; real estate; social sciences; Spanish; speech and rhetoric; substance abuse/addiction counseling; welding technology.

Academics *Calendar:* semesters. *Degree:* certificates and associate. *Special study options:* academic remediation for entering students, accelerated degree program, adult/continuing education programs, advanced placement credit, cooperative education, English as a second language, honors programs, internships, part-time degree program, services for LD students, study abroad, summer session for credit. *ROTC:* Army (c), Navy (c), Air Force (c).

Library College of San Mateo Library with 85,085 titles, 300 serial subscriptions, an OPAC, a Web page.

Student Life *Housing:* college housing not available. *Activities and Organizations:* student-run newspaper. *Campus security:* 24-hour emergency response devices and patrols. *Student services:* health clinic, personal/psychological counseling.

Athletics *Intercollegiate sports:* basketball M/W, cross-country running M/W, football M, golf M, soccer W, tennis W, track and field M/W.

Costs (2006–07) *Tuition:* state resident $508 full-time; nonresident $5216 full-time.

Applying *Options:* early admission. *Application deadline:* rolling (freshmen).

Director of Admissions Mr. Henry Villareal, Dean of Admissions and Records, College of San Mateo, 1700 West Hillsdale Boulevard, San Mateo, CA 94402-3784. *Phone:* 650-574-6594. *E-mail:* csmadmission@smcccd.cc.ca.us.

COLLEGE OF THE CANYONS

Santa Clarita, California   www.canyons.edu/

- **State and locally supported** 2-year, founded 1969, part of California Community College System
- **Suburban** 158-acre campus with easy access to Los Angeles
- **Coed,** 19,023 undergraduate students, 35% full-time, 41% women, 59% men

Undergraduates 6,649 full-time, 12,374 part-time. 2% are from out of state, 5% African American, 9% Asian American or Pacific Islander, 25% Hispanic American, 0.7% Native American, 1% international, 21% transferred in.

Freshmen *Admission:* 1,231 enrolled.

Faculty *Total:* 597, 27% full-time. *Student/faculty ratio:* 27:1.

Majors Accounting; administrative assistant and secretarial science; art; biological and physical sciences; biology/biological sciences; business administration and management; chemistry; child development; cinematography and film/video production; computer and information sciences related; computer engineering related; computer science; criminal justice/law enforcement administration; criminal justice/police science; developmental and child psychology; drafting and design technology; electrical, electronic and communications engineering technology; English; French; geography; geology/earth science; German; health science; history; hotel/motel administration; humanities; hydrology and water resources science; information science/studies; interior design; journalism; kindergarten/preschool education; liberal arts and sciences/liberal studies; mathematics; natural sciences; nursing (licensed practical/vocational nurse training); nursing (registered nurse training); physical education teaching and coaching; physical sciences; political science and government; pre-engineering; psychology; quality control technology; real estate; social sciences; Spanish; welding technology.

Academics *Calendar:* semesters. *Degree:* certificates and associate. *Special study options:* academic remediation for entering students, adult/continuing education programs, advanced placement credit, cooperative education, distance learning, double majors, English as a second language, honors programs, independent study, internships, off-campus study, part-time degree program, services for LD students, study abroad, summer session for credit.

Library College of the Canyons Library with 55,559 titles, 160 serial subscriptions, 20,436 audiovisual materials, an OPAC, a Web page.

Student Life *Housing:* college housing not available. *Activities and Organizations:* drama/theater group, student-run newspaper, choral group, HITE, Phi Theta Kappa, Alpha Gamma Sigma, MECHA, Biology Club. *Campus security:* student patrols, late-night transport/escort service. *Student services:* health clinic, personal/psychological counseling.

Athletics *Intercollegiate sports:* baseball M, basketball M/W, cross-country running M/W, football M, golf M, soccer W, softball W, swimming and diving M/W, track and field M/W, volleyball W, water polo M.

Costs (2007–08) *Tuition:* state resident $0 full-time; nonresident $4500 full-time, $150 per unit part-time. *Required fees:* $638 full-time, $20 per unit part-time, $38 per year part-time.

Applying *Options:* electronic application, early admission. *Recommended:* high school transcript. *Application deadlines:* 8/22 (freshmen), 8/22 (transfers). *Notification:* continuous until 8/22 (freshmen), continuous until 8/22 (transfers).

Freshmen Application Contact Ms. Jasmine Ruys, Director, Admissions and Records and Online Services, College of the Canyons, 26455 Rockwell Canyon Road, Santa Clara, CA 91355. *Phone:* 661-362-3280. *Toll-free phone:* 888-206-7827. *Fax:* 661-254-7996. *E-mail:* jasimine.ruys@canyons.edu.

COLLEGE OF THE DESERT

Palm Desert, California   www.collegeofthedesert.edu

- **State and locally supported** 2-year, founded 1959, part of California Community College System
- **Small-town** 160-acre campus
- **Coed,** 9,946 undergraduate students

Undergraduates Students come from 23 states and territories, 1% are from out of state, 3% African American, 6% Asian American or Pacific Islander, 52% Hispanic American, 0.6% Native American.

Freshmen *Average high school GPA:* 2.72.

Faculty *Total:* 338, 30% full-time.

Majors Administrative assistant and secretarial science; agricultural business and management; anthropology; architectural engineering technology; art; automobile/automotive mechanics technology; biology/biological sciences; business administration and management; business/managerial economics; chemistry; computer and information sciences related; computer graphics; computer programming related; computer science; computer/technical support; computer typography and composition equipment operation; construction management; criminal justice/law enforcement administration; criminal justice/police science; culinary arts; drafting and design technology; dramatic/theater arts; economics; education; engineering technology; English; environmental studies; fire science; French; geography; geology/earth science; heating, air conditioning, ventilation and refrigeration maintenance technology; history; horticultural science; interior design; Italian; journalism; kindergarten/preschool education; liberal arts and sciences/liberal studies; marketing/marketing management; mass communication/media; mathematics; medical/clinical assistant; music; natural resources management and policy; nursing (registered nurse training); ornamental horticulture; parks, recreation and leisure; parks, recreation and leisure facilities management; philosophy; physical education teaching and coaching; physics; political science and government; pre-engineering; psychology; real estate; respiratory care therapy; Romance languages; social sciences; sociology; speech and rhetoric; teacher assistant/aide; welding technology; word processing.

Academics *Calendar:* semesters. *Degree:* certificates, diplomas, and associate. *Special study options:* academic remediation for entering students, adult/continuing education programs, English as a second language, honors programs, part-time degree program, services for LD students, summer session for credit.

Library College of the Desert Library with 58,000 titles, 260 serial subscriptions.

Student Life *Housing:* college housing not available. *Activities and Organizations:* drama/theater group, student-run newspaper, choral group, student association, International Club, African-Americans for College Education. *Campus security:* 24-hour emergency response devices, late-night transport/escort service. *Student services:* health clinic, personal/psychological counseling.

Athletics *Intercollegiate sports:* baseball M, basketball M/W, cross-country running M/W, football M, golf M/W, soccer M, softball W, tennis M/W, track and field M/W, volleyball W. *Intramural sports:* badminton M/W, basketball M/W, fencing M/W, golf M/W, soccer M, softball M/W, swimming and diving M/W, table tennis M/W, tennis M/W, volleyball M/W.

Costs (2007–08) *Tuition:* state resident $0 full-time; nonresident $4860 full-time, $162 per unit part-time. *Required fees:* $638 full-time, $0 per unit part-time, $15 per term part-time.

Financial Aid Of all full-time matriculated undergraduates, 125 Federal Work-Study jobs (averaging $750). 50 state and other part-time jobs (averaging $750).

Applying *Options:* early admission. *Application deadlines:* rolling (freshmen), rolling (transfers). *Notification:* continuous (freshmen), continuous (transfers).

Freshmen Application Contact Ms. Kathi Westerfield, Registrar, College of the Desert, 43-500 Monterey Avenue, Palm Desert, CA 92260-9305. *Phone:* 760-773-2519. *Toll-free phone:* 760-773-2516.

COLLEGE OF THE REDWOODS

Eureka, California   www.redwoods.edu/

- **State and locally supported** 2-year, founded 1964, part of California Community College System
- **Small-town** 322-acre campus
- **Endowment** $1.8 million
- **Coed**, 7,708 undergraduate students

Undergraduates Students come from 52 states and territories, 2% live on campus.

Freshmen *Admission:* 717 applied, 717 admitted.

Faculty *Total:* 414, 25% full-time. *Student/faculty ratio:* 21:1.

Majors Administrative assistant and secretarial science; agricultural business and management; agronomy and crop science; architectural engineering technology; automobile/automotive mechanics technology; business administration and management; child care provision; commercial and advertising art; computer and information sciences; computer engineering technology; computer programming; computer typography and composition equipment operation; construction engineering technology; criminal justice/law enforcement administration; dental assisting; diesel mechanics technology; drafting and design technology; electrical, electronic and communications engineering technology; forestry; kindergarten/preschool education; legal administrative assistant/secretary; legal assistant/paralegal; machine tool technology; marine science/merchant marine officer; medical/clinical assistant; nursing (registered nurse training); real estate; web page, digital/multimedia and information resources design; welding technology.

Academics *Calendar:* semesters. *Degree:* certificates and associate. *Special study options:* academic remediation for entering students, adult/continuing education programs, advanced placement credit, cooperative education, distance learning, English as a second language, honors programs, off-campus study, part-time degree program, services for LD students, summer session for credit.

Library College of the Redwoods Library with 50,266 titles, 969 serial subscriptions, an OPAC, a Web page.

Student Life *Housing Options:* coed. Campus housing is provided by a third party. *Activities and Organizations:* Associated Students College of the Redwoods, Spanish Club, Computer Information Systems Club, Math/Science Club, International Student Club. *Campus security:* 24-hour emergency response devices and patrols, late-night transport/escort service. *Student services:* health clinic, personal/psychological counseling.

Athletics *Intercollegiate sports:* baseball M, basketball M/W, cross-country running M/W, football M, golf M, soccer W, softball W, track and field M/W, volleyball W.

Costs (2006–07) *Tuition:* state resident $654 full-time; nonresident $5864 full-time.

Financial Aid Of all full-time matriculated undergraduates, 50 Federal Work-Study jobs (averaging $4000). 20 state and other part-time jobs (averaging $4000).

Applying *Options:* early admission. *Application deadlines:* rolling (freshmen), rolling (transfers).

Freshmen Application Contact Kathy Goodlive, Director of Enrollment Management, College of the Redwoods, 7351 Tompkins Hill Road, Eureka, CA 95501-9300. *Phone:* 707-476-4168. *Toll-free phone:* 800-641-0400.

COLLEGE OF THE SEQUOIAS

Visalia, California   www.cos.edu/

Freshmen Application Contact Mr. Don Mast, Associate Dean of Admissions/Registrar, College of the Sequoias, 915 South Mooney Boulevard, Visalia, CA 93277-2234. *Phone:* 559-737-4844. *Fax:* 559-737-4820.

COLLEGE OF THE SISKIYOUS

Weed, California   www.siskiyous.edu/

- **State and locally supported** 2-year, founded 1957, part of California Community College System
- **Rural** 260-acre campus
- **Coed,** 3,400 undergraduate students

Undergraduates Students come from 18 states and territories, 6 other countries, 27% are from out of state, 3% African American, 3% Asian American or Pacific Islander, 7% Hispanic American, 4% Native American, 0.5% international, 10% live on campus.

Freshmen *Admission:* 389 applied, 389 admitted.

Faculty *Total:* 152, 33% full-time. *Student/faculty ratio:* 21:1.

Majors Accounting; biology/biological sciences; biology teacher education; business administration and management; chemistry; chemistry teacher education; computer graphics; computer programming; computer science; computer/technical support; criminal justice/law enforcement administration; English; English language and literature related; English/language arts teacher education; fire science; geology/earth science; history; history related; information technology; intermedia/multimedia; kindergarten/preschool education; legal assistant/paralegal; legal studies; mathematics; philosophy; physical sciences; physics; physics teacher education; web/multimedia management and webmaster; web page, digital/multimedia and information resources design.

Academics *Calendar:* semesters. *Degree:* certificates and associate. *Special study options:* academic remediation for entering students, adult/continuing education programs, advanced placement credit, cooperative education, distance learning, double majors, English as a second language, honors programs, independent study, internships, part-time degree program, services for LD students, student-designed majors, summer session for credit.

Library College of the Siskiyous Library with 34,708 titles, 148 serial subscriptions, 9,433 audiovisual materials, an OPAC, a Web page.

Student Life *Housing Options:* coed, men-only. Campus housing is university owned. *Activities and Organizations:* drama/theater group, student-run newspaper, television station, choral group, Associated Student Body, Latino Student Union, Phi Theta Kappa, Black Student Union, American Indian Alliance. *Campus security:* 24-hour emergency response devices, controlled dormitory access. *Student services:* health clinic, personal/psychological counseling, women's center, legal services.

Athletics Member NJCAA. *Intercollegiate sports:* baseball M, basketball M/W, cross-country running M/W, football M, softball W, track and field M/W, volleyball W. *Intramural sports:* basketball M/W, cheerleading M/W, skiing (cross-country) M/W, skiing (downhill) M/W, tennis M/W, volleyball W.

Costs (2007–08) *Tuition:* state resident $0 full-time; nonresident $4440 full-time, $185 per unit part-time. *Required fees:* $264 full-time, $20 per unit part-time, $9 per unit part-time.

Financial Aid Of all full-time matriculated undergraduates, 51 Federal Work-Study jobs (averaging $1897). 30 state and other part-time jobs (averaging $2000).

Applying *Options:* early admission, deferred entrance. *Application deadlines:* rolling (freshmen), rolling (transfers). *Notification:* continuous (freshmen), continuous (transfers).

Freshmen Application Contact Ms. Christina Bruck, Recruitment and Outreach Coordinator, College of the Siskiyous, 800 College Avenue, Weed, CA 96094. *Phone:* 530-938-5847. *Toll-free phone:* 888-397-4339 Ext. 5847.

COLUMBIA COLLEGE

Sonora, California   www.gocolumbia.org/

- **State and locally supported** 2-year, founded 1968, part of Yosemite Community College District System
- **Rural** 200-acre campus
- **Coed,** 2,670 undergraduate students, 34% full-time, 58% women, 42% men

Undergraduates 903 full-time, 1,767 part-time. 1% African American, 2% Asian American or Pacific Islander, 7% Hispanic American, 2% Native American, 7% live on campus.

Freshmen *Admission:* 344 applied, 344 admitted, 344 enrolled.

Faculty *Total:* 163, 33% full-time.

Majors Administrative assistant and secretarial science; anthropology; art; automobile/automotive mechanics technology; biology/biological sciences; business administration and management; chemistry; computer science; culinary arts; developmental and child psychology; dramatic/theater arts; English; environmental studies; fire science; food services technology; forestry technology; geology/earth science; health teacher education; history; hotel/motel administration; humanities; liberal arts and sciences/liberal studies; mathematics; music; natural resources management and policy; photography; physical education teaching and coaching; physical sciences; physics; psychology; sociology; special products marketing.

Academics *Calendar:* semesters. *Degree:* certificates and associate. *Special study options:* academic remediation for entering students, adult/continuing education programs, advanced placement credit, cooperative education, distance learning, double majors, English as a second language, independent study, internships, off-campus study, part-time degree program, services for LD students, summer session for credit.

Library Columbia College Library with 34,892 titles, 320 serial subscriptions, an OPAC, a Web page.

Student Life *Housing Options:* coed. Campus housing is provided by a third party. *Activities and Organizations:* drama/theater group, student-run newspaper, choral group, International Club, Jazz Club, Ecology Action Club, Christian

Columbia College (continued)

Club. *Campus security:* 24-hour emergency response devices and patrols, late-night transport/escort service. *Student services:* health clinic, personal/psychological counseling.

Athletics Member NJCAA. *Intercollegiate sports:* basketball M, cross-country running M/W, tennis M/W, volleyball W.

Costs (2007–08) *Tuition:* state resident $0 full-time; nonresident $4320 full-time, $160 per credit part-time. *Required fees:* $520 full-time, $20 per unit part-time, $20 per term part-time. *Room and board:* room only: $7550.

Financial Aid Of all full-time matriculated undergraduates, 42 Federal Work-Study jobs (averaging $2350).

Applying *Options:* electronic application, early admission. *Required for some:* high school transcript. *Application deadlines:* rolling (freshmen), rolling (transfers). *Notification:* continuous (freshmen), continuous (transfers).

Freshmen Application Contact Dr. Kathleen Smith, Director Student Success/Matriculation, Columbia College, Columbia College, 11600 Columbia College Drive, Sonora, CA 95370. *Phone:* 209-588-5234. *Fax:* 209-588-5337. *E-mail:* smithk@yosemite.edu.

CONCORDE CAREER COLLEGES, INC.

Garden Grove, California   www.concorde.edu/

- **Proprietary** 2-year
- **Coed,** 527 undergraduate students
- 100% of applicants were admitted

Freshmen *Admission:* 371 applied, 371 admitted.

Majors Respiratory care therapy.

Academics *Degree:* associate.

Costs (2006–07) *Tuition:* $24,009 per degree program part-time.

Applying *Required:* high school transcript.

Freshmen Application Contact Admissions Office, Concorde Career Colleges, Inc., 12951 Euclid Street, Suite 101, Garden Grove, CA 92840-9201.

CONCORDE CAREER INSTITUTE

North Hollywood, California   www.concordecareercolleges.com/

- **Proprietary** 2-year, founded 1955
- **Coed,** 487 undergraduate students
- 100% of applicants were admitted

Freshmen *Admission:* 358 applied, 358 admitted.

Majors Respiratory care therapy.

Academics *Degree:* associate.

Applying *Required:* high school transcript.

Freshmen Application Contact Admissions Office, Concorde Career Institute, 12412 Victory Boulevard, North Hollywood, CA 91606.

CONTRA COSTA COLLEGE

San Pablo, California   www.contracosta.edu/

- **State and locally supported** 2-year, founded 1948, part of Contra Costa Community College District and California Community College System
- **Small-town** 83-acre campus with easy access to San Francisco
- **Coed,** 8,834 undergraduate students, 45% full-time, 62% women, 38% men

Undergraduates 3,973 full-time, 4,861 part-time. Students come from 9 states and territories, 21 other countries, 10% are from out of state, 28% African American, 15% Asian American or Pacific Islander, 28% Hispanic American, 0.6% Native American, 2% international, 41% transferred in. *Retention:* 45% of 2003 full-time freshmen returned.

Freshmen *Admission:* 6,517 applied, 4,126 enrolled. *Average high school GPA:* 2.5.

Faculty *Total:* 415, 28% full-time, 22% with terminal degrees.

Majors Administrative assistant and secretarial science; African-American/Black studies; anthropology; art; automobile/automotive mechanics technology; biology/biological sciences; biology/biotechnology laboratory technician; business administration and management; chemistry; computer programming; computer science; criminal justice/law enforcement administration; criminal justice/

police science; culinary arts; dental hygiene; drafting and design technology; electrical, electronic and communications engineering technology; emergency medical technology (EMT paramedic); engineering; English; family and consumer sciences/human sciences; French; geography; geology/earth science; German; Hispanic-American, Puerto Rican, and Mexican-American/Chicano studies; history; humanities; industrial arts; Italian; journalism; kindergarten/preschool education; liberal arts and sciences/liberal studies; materials science; mathematics; music; nursing (licensed practical/vocational nurse training); nursing (registered nurse training); philosophy; physics; political science and government; quality control technology; real estate; sociology; Spanish; welding technology.

Academics *Calendar:* semesters. *Degree:* certificates and associate. *Special study options:* academic remediation for entering students, accelerated degree program, adult/continuing education programs, cooperative education, distance learning, English as a second language, honors programs, independent study, internships, off-campus study, part-time degree program, services for LD students, student-designed majors, study abroad, summer session for credit.

Library Contra Costa College Library with 57,017 titles, 333 serial subscriptions, 4,976 audiovisual materials, a Web page.

Student Life *Housing:* college housing not available. *Activities and Organizations:* drama/theater group, student-run newspaper. *Campus security:* 24-hour emergency response devices and patrols, student patrols, late-night transport/escort service. *Student services:* personal/psychological counseling, women's center.

Athletics *Intercollegiate sports:* baseball M, basketball M/W, cross-country running M/W, football M, softball W, track and field M/W, volleyball W.

Costs (2006–07) *Tuition:* state resident $0 full-time; nonresident $3912 full-time, $163 per unit part-time. *Required fees:* $600 full-time, $20 per unit part-time.

Financial Aid Of all full-time matriculated undergraduates, 100 Federal Work-Study jobs (averaging $3000).

Applying *Options:* early admission. *Application deadline:* rolling (freshmen).

Freshmen Application Contact Ken Blustajn, Admissions and Records Manager, Contra Costa College, 2600 Mission Bell Drive, San Pablo, CA 94806-3195. *Phone:* 510-235-7800.

COPPER MOUNTAIN COLLEGE

Joshua Tree, California   www.cmccd.cc.ca.us/

Freshmen Application Contact Dr. Laraine Turk, Associate Dean of Student Services, Copper Mountain College, 6162 Rotary Way, Joshua Tree, CA 92252. *Phone:* 760-366-5290.

COSUMNES RIVER COLLEGE

Sacramento, California   www.crc.losrios.edu/

- **District-supported** 2-year, founded 1970, part of Los Rios Community College District System
- **Rural** 180-acre campus
- **Coed,** 19,284 undergraduate students

Undergraduates Students come from 15 states and territories, 30 other countries.

Faculty *Total:* 550, 27% full-time.

Majors Accounting; advertising; agricultural business and management; agricultural mechanization; agronomy and crop science; American studies; animal sciences; applied art; architectural engineering technology; art; automobile/automotive mechanics technology; biological and physical sciences; biology/biological sciences; broadcast journalism; business administration and management; child development; computer management; computer programming; construction engineering technology; construction management; criminal justice/law enforcement administration; cultural studies; drafting and design technology; dramatic/theater arts; electrical, electronic and communications engineering technology; emergency medical technology (EMT paramedic); environmental design/architecture; environmental engineering technology; environmental studies; family and consumer economics related; farm and ranch management; finance; fire science; geology/earth science; gerontology; health information/medical records administration; horticultural science; humanities; human services; information science/studies; interior design; journalism; kindergarten/preschool education; landscaping and groundskeeping; liberal arts and sciences/liberal studies; management information systems; marketing/marketing management; mass communication/media; mathematics; medical administrative assistant and medical secretary; medical/clinical assistant; music; photography; pre-engineering; public relations/image management; radio and television; real estate; social sciences; special products marketing; veterinary technology; women's studies.

Academics *Calendar:* semesters. *Degree:* certificates and associate. *Special study options:* academic remediation for entering students, adult/continuing education programs, advanced placement credit, cooperative education, English as a second language, honors programs, part-time degree program, services for LD students, study abroad, summer session for credit.

Library Cosumnes River College Library with 55,447 titles, 375 serial subscriptions.

Student Life *Housing:* college housing not available. *Activities and Organizations:* drama/theater group, student-run newspaper, radio station, choral group, Latino/Hispanic Scholars Club, Animal Health Technology Club, Christian Club, Club Mesa, Writers' Workshop. *Campus security:* 24-hour emergency response devices and patrols, student patrols, late-night transport/escort service. *Student services:* health clinic, personal/psychological counseling, women's center.

Athletics *Intercollegiate sports:* baseball M/W, basketball M/W, soccer M/W, softball W, swimming and diving M/W, tennis M/W, track and field M/W, volleyball W, water polo M/W. *Intramural sports:* badminton M/W, basketball M/W, bowling M/W, soccer M/W, table tennis M/W, tennis M/W, track and field M/W, volleyball M/W.

Standardized Tests *Recommended:* SAT or ACT (for placement).

Costs (2006–07) *Tuition:* state resident $674 full-time; nonresident $5154 full-time.

Financial Aid Of all full-time matriculated undergraduates, 139 Federal Work-Study jobs (averaging $2000).

Applying *Options:* early admission. *Application deadlines:* 8/1 (freshmen), 8/15 (transfers). *Notification:* continuous until 8/15 (freshmen), continuous until 8/15 (transfers).

Freshmen Application Contact Ms. Dianna L. Moore, Supervisor of Admissions Records, Cosumnes River College, 8401 Center Parkway, Sacramento, CA 95823-5799. *Phone:* 916-688-7423.

CRAFTON HILLS COLLEGE
Yucaipa, California   www.craftonhills.edu/

- **State and locally supported** 2-year, founded 1972, part of California Community College System
- **Small-town** 526-acre campus with easy access to Los Angeles
- **Coed,** 5,300 undergraduate students

Undergraduates Students come from 19 states and territories, 12 other countries.

Faculty *Total:* 208, 37% full-time.

Majors Accounting; administrative assistant and secretarial science; anthropology; art; astronomy; biological and physical sciences; biology/biological sciences; business administration and management; chemistry; child care provision; child development; community organization and advocacy; computer science; criminal justice/law enforcement administration; dramatic/theater arts; economics; emergency medical technology (EMT paramedic); English; fire science; French; geology/earth science; history; humanities; human services; industrial radiologic technology; liberal arts and sciences/liberal studies; marketing/marketing management; mathematics; medical administrative assistant and medical secretary; music; philosophy; physical education teaching and coaching; physics; political science and government; pre-engineering; psychology; religious studies; respiratory care therapy; sociology; Spanish; speech and rhetoric; speech-language pathology.

Academics *Calendar:* semesters. *Degree:* certificates and associate. *Special study options:* academic remediation for entering students, adult/continuing education programs, advanced placement credit, cooperative education, distance learning, part-time degree program, services for LD students, student-designed majors, summer session for credit.

Library Crafton Hills College Library with 65,731 titles, 425 serial subscriptions.

Student Life *Housing:* college housing not available. *Activities and Organizations:* drama/theater group. *Campus security:* 24-hour patrols, late-night transport/escort service. *Student services:* health clinic, personal/psychological counseling, women's center.

Athletics *Intramural sports:* golf M/W, tennis M/W, volleyball M/W, weight lifting M/W.

Costs (2006–07) *Tuition:* state resident $762 full-time; nonresident $4934 full-time.

Financial Aid Of all full-time matriculated undergraduates, 60 Federal Work-Study jobs (averaging $3000).

Applying *Options:* early admission, deferred entrance. *Required for some:* high school transcript. *Application deadline:* rolling (freshmen). *Notification:* continuous (freshmen), continuous (transfers).

Director of Admissions Mr. Joe Caabrales, Director of Admissions, Crafton Hills College, 11711 Sand Canyon Road, Yucaipa, CA 92399. *Phone:* 909-389-3355.

CUESTA COLLEGE
San Luis Obispo, California   www.cuesta.edu/

- **District-supported** 2-year, founded 1964, administratively affiliated with San Luis Obispo County Community College District
- **Rural** 129-acre campus
- **Endowment** $5.0 million
- **Coed,** 11,150 undergraduate students

Undergraduates Students come from 19 other countries, 10% are from out of state, 1% African American, 4% Asian American or Pacific Islander, 17% Hispanic American, 1% Native American.

Faculty *Total:* 555, 25% full-time, 12% with terminal degrees. *Student/faculty ratio:* 24:1.

Majors Administrative assistant and secretarial science; agricultural mechanization; applied art; art; artificial intelligence and robotics; arts management; automobile/automotive mechanics technology; biology/biological sciences; business administration and management; chemistry; child development; computer engineering technology; computer hardware engineering; computer science; computer systems networking and telecommunications; computer/technical support; construction engineering technology; data processing and data processing technology; electrical, electronic and communications engineering technology; engineering; family and consumer economics related; fashion merchandising; foods, nutrition, and wellness; geology/earth science; human development and family studies; human services; industrial technology; information technology; interior design; journalism; kindergarten/preschool education; liberal arts and sciences/liberal studies; library science; marketing/marketing management; mass communication/media; mathematics; medical/clinical assistant; nursing (registered nurse training); parks, recreation and leisure facilities management; physical education teaching and coaching; physics; pre-engineering; psychology; radio and television; real estate; system administration; telecommunications; therapeutic recreation; web page, digital/multimedia and information resources design; welding technology.

Academics *Calendar:* semesters. *Degree:* certificates and associate. *Special study options:* academic remediation for entering students, adult/continuing education programs, advanced placement credit, cooperative education, distance learning, double majors, English as a second language, honors programs, independent study, internships, off-campus study, part-time degree program, services for LD students, study abroad, summer session for credit. *ROTC:* Army (c).

Library Cuesta College Library with 67,018 titles, 5,551 serial subscriptions, 1,593 audiovisual materials, an OPAC, a Web page.

Student Life *Housing:* college housing not available. *Activities and Organizations:* drama/theater group, student-run newspaper, radio station, choral group, Associated Students of Cuesta College, Alpha Gamma Sigma, Student Nurses Association, Latina Leadership Network, MECHA. *Campus security:* 24-hour emergency response devices and patrols, late-night transport/escort service. *Student services:* health clinic, personal/psychological counseling, legal services.

Athletics *Intercollegiate sports:* baseball M, basketball M/W, cross-country running M/W, soccer W, softball W, swimming and diving M/W, tennis W, track and field M/W, volleyball W, water polo M/W, wrestling M.

Costs (2006–07) *Tuition:* state resident $658 full-time, $26 per unit part-time; nonresident $4760 full-time, $170 per unit part-time. *Required fees:* $86 full-time, $43 per term part-time.

Applying *Options:* electronic application, early admission, deferred entrance. *Required:* high school transcript. *Recommended:* essay or personal statement. *Application deadlines:* rolling (freshmen), rolling (transfers). *Notification:* continuous (freshmen), continuous (transfers).

Freshmen Application Contact Ms. Juileta Siu, Admissions Clerk, Cuesta College, PO Box 8106, Highway 1, San Luis Obispo, CA 93403-8106. *Phone:* 805-546-3140. *E-mail:* jsiu@cuesta.edu.

CUYAMACA COLLEGE
El Cajon, California   www.cuyamaca.net/

Freshmen Application Contact Dr. Beth Appenzeller, Dean of Admissions and Records, Cuyamaca College, 900 Rancho San Diego Parkway, El Cajon, CA 92019-4304. *Phone:* 619-660-4302. *Fax:* 619-660-4575. *E-mail:* beth.appenzeller@gcccd.edu.

CYPRESS COLLEGE

Cypress, California   www.cypress.cc.ca.us/

- **State and locally supported** 2-year, founded 1966, part of California Community College System
- **Suburban** 108-acre campus with easy access to Los Angeles
- **Coed,** 15,347 undergraduate students

Undergraduates Students come from 41 states and territories, 22 other countries, 1% are from out of state.

Faculty *Total:* 590, 39% full-time.

Majors Accounting; administrative assistant and secretarial science; advertising; airline flight attendant; airline pilot and flight crew; anthropology; applied art; art; autobody/collision and repair technology; automobile/automotive mechanics technology; aviation/airway management; biological and physical sciences; biology/biological sciences; business administration and management; chemistry; computer and information sciences related; computer graphics; computer/information technology services administration related; computer programming related; computer programming (specific applications); computer science; computer software and media applications related; computer systems networking and telecommunications; court reporting; culinary arts; dance; data entry/microcomputer applications; data entry/microcomputer applications related; dental assisting; dental hygiene; dramatic/theater arts; economics; engineering; English; funeral service and mortuary science; geography; geology/earth science; health information/medical records administration; health science; heating, air conditioning, ventilation and refrigeration maintenance technology; history; hotel/motel administration; human services; industrial radiologic technology; information science/studies; legal administrative assistant/secretary; liberal arts and sciences/liberal studies; marketing/marketing management; mathematics; medical administrative assistant and medical secretary; music; natural sciences; nursing (registered nurse training); philosophy; photography; physical education teaching and coaching; physics; political science and government; psychiatric/mental health services technology; psychology; social sciences; sociology; special products marketing; speech and rhetoric; system administration; tourism and travel services management; web page, digital/multimedia and information resources design; word processing.

Academics *Calendar:* semesters. *Degree:* certificates and associate. *Special study options:* academic remediation for entering students, adult/continuing education programs, advanced placement credit, cooperative education, distance learning, double majors, English as a second language, freshman honors college, honors programs, independent study, internships, off-campus study, part-time degree program, services for LD students, study abroad, summer session for credit.

Library Cypress College Library plus 1 other with 76,696 titles, 255 serial subscriptions, 1,113 audiovisual materials, an OPAC, a Web page.

Student Life *Housing:* college housing not available. *Activities and Organizations:* drama/theater group, student-run newspaper, choral group, Alpha Gamma Sigma, California Student Nurses Association, Court Reporting Club, MECHA. *Campus security:* 24-hour emergency response devices. *Student services:* health clinic, personal/psychological counseling, women's center, legal services.

Athletics *Intercollegiate sports:* baseball M, basketball M/W, golf M/W, soccer M/W, softball W, swimming and diving M/W, tennis M/W, volleyball W, water polo M/W, wrestling M. *Intramural sports:* football M(c).

Costs (2006–07) *Tuition:* state resident $552 full-time; nonresident $3744 full-time.

Financial Aid Of all full-time matriculated undergraduates, 100 Federal Work-Study jobs (averaging $4000).

Applying *Recommended:* high school transcript. *Application deadlines:* 8/25 (freshmen), 1/25 (transfers).

Director of Admissions Mr. David Wassenaar, Dean of Admissions and Records, Cypress College, 9200 Valley View, Cypress, CA 90630. *Phone:* 714-484-7435. *E-mail:* dwassenaar@cypresscollege.edu.

DE ANZA COLLEGE

Cupertino, California   www.deanza.fhda.edu/

- **State and locally supported** 2-year, founded 1967, part of California Community College System
- **Suburban** 112-acre campus with easy access to San Francisco and San Jose
- **Coed,** 23,344 undergraduate students, 38% full-time, 53% women, 47% men

Undergraduates 8,860 full-time, 14,484 part-time. Students come from 48 states and territories, 79 other countries, 6% African American, 33% Asian American or Pacific Islander, 15% Hispanic American, 0.5% Native American, 6% international.

Freshmen *Admission:* 2,411 enrolled. *Average high school GPA:* 2.86.

Faculty *Total:* 812, 63% full-time.

Majors Accounting; administrative assistant and secretarial science; art; art history, criticism and conservation; automobile/automotive mechanics technology; behavioral sciences; biology/biological sciences; business administration and management; business machine repair; ceramic arts and ceramics; child development; commercial and advertising art; computer graphics; computer management; computer programming; computer science; construction engineering technology; corrections; criminal justice/law enforcement administration; criminal justice/police science; cultural studies; developmental and child psychology; dramatic/theater arts; drawing; economics; engineering; engineering technology; English; environmental studies; film/cinema studies; history; humanities; industrial technology; information science/studies; international relations and affairs; journalism; legal assistant/paralegal; liberal arts and sciences/liberal studies; machine tool technology; marketing/marketing management; mass communication/media; mathematics; mechanical design technology; medical/clinical assistant; music; nursing (licensed practical/vocational nurse training); nursing (registered nurse training); philosophy; photography; physical education teaching and coaching; physical therapy; physics; political science and government; pre-engineering; printmaking; psychology; purchasing, procurement/acquisitions and contracts management; radio and television; real estate; sculpture; social sciences; sociology; Spanish; speech and rhetoric; technical and business writing.

Academics *Calendar:* quarters. *Degree:* certificates, diplomas, and associate. *Special study options:* academic remediation for entering students, adult/continuing education programs, advanced placement credit, cooperative education, distance learning, English as a second language, external degree program, honors programs, independent study, internships, part-time degree program, services for LD students, student-designed majors, study abroad, summer session for credit. *ROTC:* Army (c), Air Force (c).

Library A. Robert DeHart Learning Center with 80,000 titles, 927 serial subscriptions.

Student Life *Housing:* college housing not available. *Activities and Organizations:* drama/theater group, student-run newspaper, choral group, Student Nurses Association, Phi Theta Kappa, Automotive Club, Vietnamese Club, Filipino Club. *Campus security:* 24-hour emergency response devices, student patrols, late-night transport/escort service. *Student services:* health clinic, personal/psychological counseling, legal services.

Athletics *Intercollegiate sports:* baseball M, basketball M/W, cross-country running M/W, football M, golf M/W, soccer M/W, softball W, swimming and diving M/W, tennis M/W, track and field M/W, volleyball M/W, water polo M. *Intramural sports:* badminton M/W, basketball M, soccer M/W, swimming and diving M/W, volleyball M/W.

Costs (2006–07) *Tuition:* state resident $0 full-time; nonresident $3636 full-time, $101 per unit part-time. *Required fees:* $818 full-time. *Payment plans:* installment, deferred payment.

Applying *Options:* early admission. *Application fee:* $22. *Application deadlines:* rolling (freshmen), rolling (transfers). *Notification:* continuous (freshmen), continuous (transfers).

Director of Admissions Ms. Kathleen Moberg, Director of Records and Admissions, De Anza College, 21250 Stevens Creek Boulevard, Cupertino, CA 95014. *Phone:* 408-864-8292. *E-mail:* webregda@mercury.fhda.edu.

DEEP SPRINGS COLLEGE

Deep Springs, California   www.deepsprings.edu/

- **Independent** 2-year, founded 1917
- **Rural** 3000-acre campus
- **Endowment** $9.0 million
- **Men only**

Undergraduates 27 full-time. Students come from 14 states and territories, 3 other countries, 85% are from out of state, 4% international, 100% live on campus. *Retention:* 87% of 2003 full-time freshmen returned.

Faculty *Student/faculty ratio:* 3:1.

Academics *Calendar:* 6 seven-week terms. *Degree:* associate. *Special study options:* accelerated degree program, cooperative education, freshman honors college, honors programs, independent study, internships, student-designed majors, summer session for credit.

Standardized Tests *Required:* SAT and SAT Subject Tests or ACT (for admission).

Costs (2006–07) *Tuition:* Contact the college directly for admission/tuition details.

Applying *Required:* essay or personal statement, high school transcript, letters of recommendation, interview.

Freshmen Application Contact Dr. F. Ross Peterson, President, Deep Springs College, HC 72, Box 45001, Dyer, NV 89010-9803. *Phone:* 760-872-2000. *Fax:* 760-872-4466. *E-mail:* apcom@deepsprings.edu.

DIABLO VALLEY COLLEGE
Pleasant Hill, California   www.dvc.edu/

- **State and locally supported** 2-year, founded 1949, part of Contra Costa Community College District
- **Suburban** 100-acre campus with easy access to San Francisco
- **Coed**, 20,145 undergraduate students, 33% full-time, 54% women, 46% men

Undergraduates 6,661 full-time, 13,484 part-time. Students come from 16 states and territories, 0.2% are from out of state, 6% African American, 18% Asian American or Pacific Islander, 13% Hispanic American, 0.7% Native American.

Faculty *Total:* 831, 31% full-time. *Student/faculty ratio:* 15:1.

Majors Liberal arts and sciences/liberal studies.

Academics *Calendar:* semesters. *Degree:* certificates and associate. *Special study options:* academic remediation for entering students, adult/continuing education programs, advanced placement credit, cooperative education, part-time degree program, services for LD students, student-designed majors, study abroad, summer session for credit. *ROTC:* Air Force (c).

Library 88,286 titles, 298 serial subscriptions.

Student Life *Housing:* college housing not available. *Activities and Organizations:* drama/theater group, student-run newspaper, choral group. *Campus security:* 24-hour emergency response devices and patrols, student patrols. *Student services:* women's center.

Athletics *Intercollegiate sports:* basketball M/W, cross-country running M/W, football M, soccer W, softball W, swimming and diving M/W, tennis M/W, track and field M/W, volleyball W, water polo M/W.

Costs (2006–07) *Tuition:* state resident $0 full-time; nonresident $4890 full-time, $163 per unit part-time. Full-time tuition and fees vary according to course load. Part-time tuition and fees vary according to course load. *Required fees:* $600 full-time, $20 per unit part-time.

Financial Aid Of all full-time matriculated undergraduates, 67 Federal Work-Study jobs (averaging $3000). *Financial aid deadline:* 5/23.

Applying *Options:* early admission. *Recommended:* high school transcript. *Application deadlines:* 8/15 (freshmen), rolling (transfers).

Freshmen Application Contact Judith Watkins, Supervisor of Admissions and Records, Diablo Valley College, 321 Golf Club Road, Pleasant Hill, CA 94523-1529. *Phone:* 925-685-1230 Ext. 2561. *Fax:* 925-609-8085. *E-mail:* jwatkins@dvc.edu.

DON BOSCO TECHNICAL INSTITUTE
Rosemead, California   www.boscotech.edu/

- **Independent** 2-year, founded 1955, affiliated with Roman Catholic Church
- **Suburban** 30-acre campus with easy access to Los Angeles
- **Coed, primarily men,** 1,208 undergraduate students

Undergraduates Students come from 1 other state.

Faculty *Total:* 80.

Majors Automobile/automotive mechanics technology; commercial and advertising art; construction engineering technology; drafting and design technology; electrical, electronic and communications engineering technology; graphic and printing equipment operation/production; industrial technology; metallurgical technology.

Academics *Calendar:* semesters. *Degree:* associate. *Special study options:* advanced placement credit, cooperative education, independent study.

Library 16,400 titles, 70 serial subscriptions.

Student Life *Housing:* college housing not available. *Activities and Organizations:* marching band. *Campus security:* 24-hour emergency response devices. *Student services:* personal/psychological counseling.

Athletics *Intramural sports:* baseball M, basketball M, cross-country running M, football M, golf M, soccer M, volleyball M, weight lifting M.

Standardized Tests *Required for some:* SAT or ACT (for admission).

Financial Aid Of all full-time matriculated undergraduates, 2 Federal Work-Study jobs (averaging $2400).

Applying *Application fee:* $25. *Required:* high school transcript, minimum 2.0 GPA, 2 letters of recommendation. *Application deadlines:* 2/15 (freshmen), 8/1 (transfers).

Director of Admissions Director of College Admissions, Don Bosco Technical Institute, 1151 San Gabriel Boulevard, Rosemead, CA 91770-4299. *Phone:* 626-940-2036. *E-mail:* gr8piper@aol.com.

EAST LOS ANGELES COLLEGE
Monterey Park, California   www.elac.edu/

Freshmen Application Contact Mr. Jeremy Allred, Associate Dean of Admissions, East Los Angeles College, 1301 Avenida Cesar Chavez, Monterey Park, CA 91754-6001. *Phone:* 323-265-8801. *Fax:* 323-265-8688. *E-mail:* allredjp@elac.edu.

EL CAMINO COLLEGE
Torrance, California   www.elcamino.edu/

- **State-supported** 2-year, founded 1947, part of California Community College System
- **Urban** 15-acre campus with easy access to Los Angeles
- **Coed**, 24,000 undergraduate students

Undergraduates Students come from 17 states and territories, 30 other countries, 10% are from out of state, 21% African American, 21% Asian American or Pacific Islander, 33% Hispanic American, 0.5% Native American. *Retention:* 81% of 2003 full-time freshmen returned.

Faculty *Total:* 645, 51% full-time. *Student/faculty ratio:* 20:1.

Majors Accounting; administrative assistant and secretarial science; advertising; African-American/Black studies; American studies; anthropology; architectural engineering technology; art; art history, criticism and conservation; Asian studies; astronomy; automobile/automotive mechanics technology; biology/biological sciences; botany/plant biology; business administration and management; chemistry; construction engineering technology; cosmetology; criminal justice/police science; culinary arts; data processing and data processing technology; drafting and design technology; dramatic/theater arts; economics; electrical, electronic and communications engineering technology; engineering; English; family and consumer sciences/human sciences; fashion/apparel design; finance; fire science; forestry technology; geography; geology/earth science; German; gerontology; heating, air conditioning, ventilation and refrigeration maintenance technology; history; horticultural science; industrial arts; interior design; Italian; Japanese; journalism; kindergarten/preschool education; labor and industrial relations; legal assistant/paralegal; liberal arts and sciences/liberal studies; marketing/marketing management; mathematics; medical/clinical assistant; music; nursing (licensed practical/vocational nurse training); nursing (registered nurse training); ornamental horticulture; philosophy; photography; physical education teaching and coaching; physical sciences; physics; political science and government; psychology; real estate; respiratory care therapy; Russian; social work; sociology; Spanish; special products marketing; speech and rhetoric; technical and business writing; welding technology; zoology/animal biology.

Academics *Calendar:* semesters. *Degree:* certificates, diplomas, and associate. *Special study options:* academic remediation for entering students, advanced placement credit, cooperative education, distance learning, English as a second language, freshman honors college, honors programs, independent study, internships, part-time degree program, services for LD students, study abroad, summer session for credit.

Library El Camino College Schauerman Library with 116,051 titles, 864 serial subscriptions.

Student Life *Housing:* college housing not available. *Activities and Organizations:* drama/theater group, student-run newspaper. *Campus security:* 24-hour emergency response devices and patrols, late-night transport/escort service. *Student services:* health clinic, personal/psychological counseling, women's center.

Athletics *Intercollegiate sports:* baseball M, basketball M/W, cross-country running M/W, football M, golf M, gymnastics W, soccer M, swimming and diving M/W, tennis M/W, track and field M/W, volleyball M/W, water polo M, wrestling M. *Intramural sports:* archery M/W, badminton M/W, bowling M/W.

Costs (2007–08) *Tuition:* state resident $0 full-time; nonresident $4152 full-time, $173 per unit part-time. *Required fees:* $558 full-time, $20 per unit part-time, $25 per term part-time.

Applying *Options:* early admission. *Required:* high school transcript. *Recommended:* high school transcript. *Application deadlines:* rolling (freshmen), rolling (transfers). *Notification:* continuous (freshmen), continuous (transfers).

Director of Admissions Mr. William Mulrooney, Director of Admissions, El Camino College, 16007 Crenshaw Boulevard, Torrance, CA 90506. *Phone:* 310-660-3418. *Toll-free phone:* 866-ELCAMINO. *Fax:* 310-660-6779.

EMPIRE COLLEGE
Santa Rosa, California   www.empcol.com/

Freshmen Application Contact Ms. Dahnja Barker, Admissions Officer, Empire College, 3035 Cleveland Avenue, Santa Rosa, CA 95403. *Phone:* 707-546-4000.

EVEREST COLLEGE

Ontario, California　www.everest-college.com/about.php?schoolLocation=Ontario%20Metro

- **Proprietary** 2-year
- 1,031 undergraduate students
- 87% of applicants were admitted

Freshmen *Admission:* 143 applied, 125 admitted.
Majors Business/commerce; business, management, and marketing related; criminal justice/law enforcement administration.
Academics *Degree:* associate.
Costs (2006–07) *Tuition:* $9978 full-time.
Applying *Application fee:* $25.
Freshmen Application Contact Admissions Office, Everest College, 1819 South Excise Avenue, Ontario, CA 91761.

EVEREST COLLEGE

Rancho Cucamonga, California　www.everest-college.com/
Admissions Office Contact Everest College, 9616 Archibald Avenue, Suite 100, Rancho Cucamonga, CA 91730.

EVERGREEN VALLEY COLLEGE

San Jose, California　www.evc.edu/

- **State and locally supported** 2-year, founded 1975, part of California Community College System
- **Urban** 175-acre campus
- **Coed**

Undergraduates 11,751 full-time. Students come from 23 states and territories, 11 other countries, 1% are from out of state, 5% African American, 40% Asian American or Pacific Islander, 29% Hispanic American, 0.8% Native American, 1% international.
Academics *Calendar:* semesters. *Degree:* certificates and associate. *Special study options:* academic remediation for entering students, accelerated degree program, adult/continuing education programs, advanced placement credit, cooperative education, distance learning, English as a second language, freshman honors college, honors programs, independent study, off-campus study, part-time degree program, services for LD students, summer session for credit. *ROTC:* Army (c).
Student Life *Campus security:* 24-hour emergency response devices, late-night transport/escort service, patrols by trained security personnel.
Costs (2006–07) *Tuition:* state resident $0 full-time; nonresident $4872 full-time, $177 per unit part-time. *Required fees:* $664 full-time, $26 per unit part-time.
Financial Aid Of all full-time matriculated undergraduates, 107 Federal Work-Study jobs (averaging $3000). 6 state and other part-time jobs (averaging $1500).
Applying *Options:* early admission.
Freshmen Application Contact Ms. Cindy Tayag, Admissions and Records, Evergreen Valley College, 3095 Yerba Buena Road, San Jose, CA 95135-1598. *Phone:* 408-274-7900 Ext. 6443. *Fax:* 408-223-9351.

FASHION CAREERS COLLEGE

San Diego, California　www.fashioncollege.com/

- **Proprietary** 2-year, founded 1979
- **Urban** campus
- **Coed, primarily women**

Undergraduates 101 full-time. Students come from 18 states and territories, 3 other countries, 27% are from out of state, 7% African American, 4% Asian American or Pacific Islander, 31% Hispanic American, 2% international. *Retention:* 75% of 2003 full-time freshmen returned.
Faculty *Student/faculty ratio:* 32:1.
Academics *Calendar:* quarters. *Degree:* certificates and associate. *Special study options:* adult/continuing education programs, cooperative education, double majors, internships.
Student Life *Campus security:* 24-hour emergency response devices.
Standardized Tests *Required:* Wonderlic aptitude test (for admission).

Costs (2006–07) *Tuition:* $15,900 full-time. *Required fees:* $325 full-time.
Financial Aid Of all full-time matriculated undergraduates, 10 Federal Work-Study jobs (averaging $1200).
Applying *Options:* electronic application. *Application fee:* $25. *Required:* essay or personal statement, high school transcript, interview.
Freshmen Application Contact Ms. Karen Rogue, Admissions Representative, Fashion Careers College, 1923 Morena Boulevard, San Diego, CA 92110. *Phone:* 619-275-4700 Ext. 314. *Toll-free phone:* 888-FCCC999. *Fax:* 619-275-0635. *E-mail:* karen@fashioncareerscollege.com.

FEATHER RIVER COLLEGE

Quincy, California　www.frc.edu/

- **State and locally supported** 2-year, founded 1968, part of California Community College System
- **Rural** 150-acre campus
- **Coed**

Undergraduates 732 full-time, 982 part-time. Students come from 24 states and territories, 6 other countries, 23% are from out of state, 7% African American, 3% Asian American or Pacific Islander, 9% Hispanic American, 3% Native American, 1% international, 4% transferred in, 24% live on campus. *Retention:* 62% of 2003 full-time freshmen returned.
Faculty *Student/faculty ratio:* 18:1.
Academics *Calendar:* semesters. *Degree:* certificates, diplomas, and associate. *Special study options:* academic remediation for entering students, adult/continuing education programs, advanced placement credit, cooperative education, distance learning, double majors, honors programs, independent study, part-time degree program, services for LD students, summer session for credit.
Student Life *Campus security:* student patrols.
Costs (2006–07) *Tuition:* state resident $0 full-time; nonresident $5768 full-time, $180 per unit part-time. *Required fees:* $806 full-time, $26 per unit part-time, $13 per unit part-time. *Room and board:* room only: $3920. Room and board charges vary according to housing facility.
Financial Aid Of all full-time matriculated undergraduates, 22 Federal Work-Study jobs (averaging $750). 103 state and other part-time jobs (averaging $1504).
Applying *Options:* electronic application.
Freshmen Application Contact Ms. Karen Sue Hayden, Registrar, Feather River College, 570 Golden Eagle Avenue, Quincy, CA 95971. *Phone:* 530-283-0202 Ext. 285. *Toll-free phone:* 800-442-9799 Ext. 286. *Fax:* 530-283-9961. *E-mail:* info@frc.edu.

FIDM/THE FASHION INSTITUTE OF DESIGN & MERCHANDISING, LOS ANGELES CAMPUS

Los Angeles, California　www.fidm.edu/

- **Proprietary** primarily 2-year, founded 1969, part of Fashion Institute of Design and Merchandising
- **Urban** campus
- **Coed**, 4,143 undergraduate students, 84% full-time, 90% women, 10% men

Undergraduates 3,461 full-time, 682 part-time. Students come from 4 states and territories, 25 other countries, 19% are from out of state, 5% African American, 16% Asian American or Pacific Islander, 23% Hispanic American, 0.5% Native American, 7% international, 15% transferred in. *Retention:* 100% of 2003 full-time freshmen returned.
Freshmen *Admission:* 1,149 admitted, 1,045 enrolled.
Faculty *Total:* 292, 21% full-time. *Student/faculty ratio:* 14:1.
Majors Apparel and accessories marketing; apparel and textiles; business administration and management; commercial and advertising art; consumer merchandising/retailing management; design and visual communications; fashion/apparel design; fashion merchandising; interior design.
Academics *Calendar:* quarters. *Degrees:* associate and bachelor's (also includes Orange County Campus). *Special study options:* academic remediation for entering students, adult/continuing education programs, advanced placement credit, cooperative education, distance learning, English as a second language, independent study, internships, part-time degree program, services for LD students, study abroad, summer session for credit.
Library FIDM Los Angeles Campus Library with 21,099 titles, 462 serial subscriptions, an OPAC.

Student Life *Housing:* college housing not available. *Activities and Organizations:* student-run newspaper, ASID (student chapter), International Club, DECA, Association of Manufacturing Students, Honor Society. *Campus security:* 24-hour emergency response devices and patrols, late-night transport/escort service. *Student services:* personal/psychological counseling.

Standardized Tests *Required:* Wonderlic Aptitude Test (for admission).

Costs (2007–08) *Tuition:* $18,285 full-time. *Required fees:* $500 full-time.

Financial Aid Of all full-time matriculated undergraduates, 88 Federal Work-Study jobs (averaging $2935).

Applying *Options:* electronic application, deferred entrance. *Application fee:* $225. *Required:* essay or personal statement, high school transcript, 3 letters of recommendation, interview, major-determined project. *Required for some:* 3 letters of recommendation, major-determined project. *Application deadlines:* rolling (freshmen), rolling (transfers).

Freshmen Application Contact Ms. Susan Aronson, Director of Admissions, FIDM/The Fashion Institute of Design & Merchandising, Los Angeles Campus, FIDM LA, 919 South Grand Avenue, Los Angeles, CA 90015. *Phone:* 213-624-1200 Ext. 5400. *Toll-free phone:* 800-624-1200. *Fax:* 213-624-4799. *E-mail:* info@fidm.com.

▶See page 540 for the College Close-Up.

FIDM/THE FASHION INSTITUTE OF DESIGN & MERCHANDISING, ORANGE COUNTY CAMPUS

Irvine, California   **www.fidm.com/**

Freshmen Application Contact Admissions, FIDM/The Fashion Institute of Design & Merchandising, Orange County Campus, 17590 Gillette Avenue, Irvine, CA 92614-5610. *Phone:* 949-851-6200. *Toll-free phone:* 888-974-3436. *Fax:* 949-851-6808.

FIDM/THE FASHION INSTITUTE OF DESIGN & MERCHANDISING, SAN DIEGO CAMPUS

San Diego, California   **www.fidm.com/**

- **Proprietary** 2-year, founded 1985, part of Fashion Institute of Design and Merchandising
- **Urban** campus
- **Coed,** 288 undergraduate students, 81% full-time, 94% women, 6% men

Undergraduates 234 full-time, 54 part-time. Students come from 2 other countries, 19% are from out of state, 3% African American, 10% Asian American or Pacific Islander, 25% Hispanic American, 0.7% Native American, 1% international, 20% transferred in.

Freshmen *Admission:* 120 admitted, 120 enrolled.

Faculty *Total:* 27, 11% full-time. *Student/faculty ratio:* 11:1.

Majors Apparel and accessories marketing; commercial and advertising art; consumer merchandising/retailing management; design and visual communications; fashion/apparel design; fashion merchandising; interior design.

Academics *Calendar:* quarters. *Degree:* associate. *Special study options:* academic remediation for entering students, adult/continuing education programs, advanced placement credit, cooperative education, distance learning, English as a second language, independent study, internships, part-time degree program, services for LD students, study abroad, summer session for credit.

Library FIDM San Diego Campus Library with 2,959 titles, 178 serial subscriptions, 58 audiovisual materials, an OPAC.

Student Life *Housing:* college housing not available. *Options:* Campus housing is provided by a third party. *Activities and Organizations:* ASID (student chapter), DECA, Honor Society, Phi Theta Kappa. *Campus security:* 24-hour emergency response devices and patrols. *Student services:* personal/psychological counseling.

Costs (2007–08) *Tuition:* $18,285 full-time, $406 per unit part-time. *Required fees:* $500 full-time.

Applying *Options:* electronic application, deferred entrance. *Application fee:* $225. *Required:* essay or personal statement, 3 letters of recommendation, interview, major-determined project. *Required for some:* 3 letters of recommendation, major-determined project. *Recommended:* minimum 2.0 GPA. *Application deadlines:* rolling (freshmen), rolling (transfers).

Freshmen Application Contact Ms. Susan Aronson, Director of Admissions, FIDM/The Fashion Institute of Design & Merchandising, San Diego Campus,

FIDM San Diego, 1010 2nd Avenue, San Diego, CA 92101. *Phone:* 213-624-1200 Ext. 5400. *Toll-free phone:* 800-243-3436. *Fax:* 619-232-4322. *E-mail:* info@fidm.com.

FIDM/THE FASHION INSTITUTE OF DESIGN & MERCHANDISING, SAN FRANCISCO CAMPUS

San Francisco, California   **www.fidm.edu/**

- **Proprietary** 2-year, founded 1973, part of Fashion Institute of Design and Merchandising
- **Urban** campus
- **Coed, primarily women,** 983 undergraduate students, 82% full-time, 93% women, 7% men

Undergraduates 807 full-time, 176 part-time. Students come from 15 states and territories, 20 other countries, 6% are from out of state, 6% African American, 18% Asian American or Pacific Islander, 15% Hispanic American, 0.9% Native American, 3% international, 18% transferred in.

Freshmen *Admission:* 303 admitted, 280 enrolled.

Faculty *Total:* 90, 12% full-time.

Majors Apparel and accessories marketing; apparel and textiles; commercial and advertising art; consumer merchandising/retailing management; design and visual communications; fashion/apparel design; fashion merchandising; interior design.

Academics *Calendar:* quarters. *Degree:* associate. *Special study options:* academic remediation for entering students, adult/continuing education programs, advanced placement credit, cooperative education, distance learning, English as a second language, honors programs, independent study, internships, off-campus study, part-time degree program, services for LD students, study abroad, summer session for credit.

Library FIDM San Francisco Library with 5,592 titles, 252 serial subscriptions, 328 audiovisual materials, an OPAC.

Student Life *Housing:* college housing not available. *Options:* Campus housing is provided by a third party. *Activities and Organizations:* ASID (student chapter), DECA, Visual Design Form, Honor Society. *Campus security:* 24-hour emergency response devices and patrols. *Student services:* personal/psychological counseling.

Standardized Tests *Required:* Wonderlic aptitude test (for admission).

Costs (2007–08) *Tuition:* $18,285 full-time, $406 per unit part-time. *Required fees:* $500 full-time.

Applying *Options:* electronic application, deferred entrance. *Application fee:* $225. *Required:* essay or personal statement, high school transcript, 3 letters of recommendation, interview, major-determined project. *Required for some:* 3 letters of recommendation. *Recommended:* minimum 2.0 GPA. *Application deadlines:* rolling (freshmen), rolling (transfers).

Freshmen Application Contact Ms. Susan Aronson, Director of Admissions, FIDM/The Fashion Institute of Design & Merchandising, San Francisco Campus, 55 Stockton Street, San Francisco, CA 94108. *Phone:* 213-624-1200 Ext. 5400. *Toll-free phone:* 800-711-7175. *Fax:* 415-296-7299. *E-mail:* info@fidm.com.

FOLSOM LAKE COLLEGE

Folsom, California   **www.flc.losrios.edu/**

- **County-supported** 2-year, founded 2004, part of Los Rios Community College District System
- **Coed,** 6,337 undergraduate students

Undergraduates 2% African American, 8% Asian American or Pacific Islander, 9% Hispanic American, 1% Native American.

Faculty *Total:* 253, 29% full-time.

Majors Accounting; art; biology/biological sciences; business administration and management; communication and journalism related; computer and information sciences; criminal justice/law enforcement administration; early childhood education; education; English; finance; geology/earth science; human services; interdisciplinary studies; liberal arts and sciences/liberal studies; marketing/marketing management; mathematics; physical sciences related; physics; psychology; real estate; social sciences.

Academics *Degree:* associate.

Costs (2006–07) *Tuition:* state resident $0 full-time; nonresident $5154 full-time. *Required fees:* $674 full-time.

Freshmen Application Contact Admissions Office, Folsom Lake College, 10 College Parkway, Folsom, CA 95630. *Phone:* 916-608-6500.

FOOTHILL COLLEGE

Los Altos Hills, California   www.foothill.edu/

- **State and locally supported** 2-year, founded 1958, part of Foothill-DeAnza Community College District
- **Suburban** 122-acre campus with easy access to San Jose
- **Coed,** 18,342 undergraduate students, 20% full-time, 51% women, 49% men

Undergraduates 3,728 full-time, 14,614 part-time. Students come from 16 states and territories, 74 other countries, 7% are from out of state, 5% African American, 17% Asian American or Pacific Islander, 19% Hispanic American, 0.5% Native American, 7% international, 25% transferred in.

Freshmen *Admission:* 5,697 applied, 5,697 admitted, 1,266 enrolled.

Faculty *Total:* 633, 32% full-time. *Student/faculty ratio:* 34:1.

Majors Accounting; American studies; anthropology; art; art history, criticism and conservation; athletic training; avionics maintenance technology; biology/biological sciences; biology/biotechnology laboratory technician; business administration and management; chemistry; child development; classics and languages, literatures and linguistics; creative writing; cultural studies; dental assisting; dental hygiene; diagnostic medical sonography and ultrasound technology; economics; electrical, electronic and communications engineering technology; emergency medical technology (EMT paramedic); English; fine/studio arts; history; international business/trade/commerce; landscape architecture; legal studies; linguistics; literature; mathematics; medical radiologic technology; music; ornamental horticulture; philosophy; photography; physical education teaching and coaching; physician assistant; physics; plant nursery management; political science and government; psychology; radio and television; radiologic technology/science; real estate; respiratory care therapy; social sciences; sociology; Spanish; speech and rhetoric; tourism and travel services management; veterinary technology; women's studies.

Academics *Calendar:* quarters. *Degree:* certificates and associate. *Special study options:* academic remediation for entering students, accelerated degree program, adult/continuing education programs, advanced placement credit, cooperative education, distance learning, English as a second language, honors programs, independent study, internships, off-campus study, part-time degree program, services for LD students, student-designed majors, study abroad, summer session for credit. *ROTC:* Army (c), Air Force (c).

Library Hubert H. Semans Library with 70,000 titles, 450 serial subscriptions, an OPAC, a Web page.

Student Life *Housing:* college housing not available. *Activities and Organizations:* drama/theater group, student-run newspaper, radio station, choral group, Alpha Gamma Sigma, student government. *Campus security:* 24-hour emergency response devices and patrols, late-night transport/escort service. *Student services:* health clinic, personal/psychological counseling, legal services.

Athletics Member NJCAA. *Intercollegiate sports:* basketball M/W, football M, golf M/W, soccer M/W, softball W, swimming and diving M/W, tennis M, volleyball W, water polo M/W.

Costs (2007–08) *Tuition:* state resident $0 full-time; nonresident $4600 full-time, $108 per unit part-time. *Required fees:* $908 full-time, $17 per unit part-time, $41 per term part-time.

Financial Aid Of all full-time matriculated undergraduates, 80 Federal Work-Study jobs (averaging $1300). 210 state and other part-time jobs.

Applying *Options:* electronic application. *Recommended:* high school transcript. *Application deadlines:* 9/15 (freshmen), rolling (transfers). *Notification:* continuous (freshmen), continuous (transfers).

Freshmen Application Contact Ms. Penny Johnson, Dean, Counseling and Student Services, Foothill College, Admissions and Records, 12345 El Monte Road, Los Altos Hills, CA 94022. *Phone:* 650-949-7326. *Fax:* 650-949-7375.

FOUNDATION COLLEGE

San Diego, California

Director of Admissions Peggy Aplin, Admissions Manager, Foundation College, 5353 Mission Center Road, Suite 100, San Diego, CA 92108-1306. *Phone:* 619-683-3273 Ext. 105. *Toll-free phone:* 888-707-3273.

FRESNO CITY COLLEGE

Fresno, California   www.fresnocitycollege.edu

- **District-supported** 2-year, founded 1910, part of California Community College System
- **Urban** 103-acre campus
- **Endowment** $853,060
- **Coed,** 22,812 undergraduate students

Undergraduates Students come from 1 other state, 8% African American, 14% Asian American or Pacific Islander, 32% Hispanic American, 1% Native American, 0.9% international. *Retention:* 85% of 2003 full-time freshmen returned.

Freshmen *Admission:* 2,996 applied, 2,996 admitted.

Faculty *Total:* 1,476, 19% full-time. *Student/faculty ratio:* 16:1.

Majors Administrative assistant and secretarial science; African-American/Black studies; American Indian/Native American studies; anthropology; art; autobody/collision and repair technology; automobile/automotive mechanics technology; business administration and management; carpentry; commercial and advertising art; computer typography and composition equipment operation; construction engineering technology; construction management; corrections; criminal justice/law enforcement administration; criminal justice/police science; cultural studies; dental hygiene; design and visual communications; dietetics; drafting and design technology; dramatic/theater arts; engineering; family and consumer sciences/human sciences; fashion merchandising; fire science; food services technology; graphic and printing equipment operation/production; health information/medical records administration; heating, air conditioning, ventilation and refrigeration maintenance technology; Hispanic-American, Puerto Rican, and Mexican-American/Chicano studies; humanities; human services; industrial arts; industrial radiologic technology; industrial technology; journalism; legal administrative assistant/secretary; legal assistant/paralegal; liberal arts and sciences/liberal studies; library science; machine tool technology; mathematics and computer science; medical administrative assistant and medical secretary; medical/clinical assistant; music performance; nursing (licensed practical/vocational nurse training); nursing (registered nurse training); parks, recreation and leisure; photography; physical sciences; piano and organ; real estate; respiratory care therapy; social sciences; Spanish; speech and rhetoric; substance abuse/addiction counseling; teacher assistant/aide; theater design and technology; voice and opera; women's studies.

Academics *Calendar:* semesters. *Degree:* certificates and associate. *Special study options:* academic remediation for entering students, advanced placement credit, cooperative education, English as a second language, freshman honors college, honors programs, off-campus study, part-time degree program, services for LD students, study abroad, summer session for credit. *ROTC:* Army (c), Air Force (c).

Library Fresno City College Library with 67,500 titles, an OPAC, a Web page.

Student Life *Housing:* college housing not available. *Activities and Organizations:* drama/theater group, student-run newspaper, choral group, marching band, MECHA, HMONG Club, Rotaract, Students in Free Enterprise, Latter Day Saints Student Association. *Campus security:* 24-hour emergency response devices and patrols, late-night transport/escort service. *Student services:* health clinic, personal/psychological counseling.

Athletics Member NJCAA. *Intercollegiate sports:* baseball M(s), basketball M/W, cross-country running M(s)/W(s), football M(s), golf M(s)/W(s), soccer M(s)/W(s), softball W(s), tennis M(s)/W(s), track and field M(s)/W(s), volleyball W(s), wrestling M(s). *Intramural sports:* badminton M/W, basketball M/W, cross-country running M/W, football M, golf M/W, gymnastics M/W, soccer M/W, softball M/W, swimming and diving M/W, table tennis M/W, tennis M/W, track and field M/W, volleyball M/W, weight lifting M/W, wrestling M.

Costs (2006–07) *Tuition:* state resident $508 full-time; nonresident $4320 full-time.

Financial Aid Of all full-time matriculated undergraduates, 350 Federal Work-Study jobs (averaging $3000).

Applying *Options:* early admission, deferred entrance. *Required:* high school transcript. *Application deadlines:* rolling (freshmen), rolling (transfers). *Notification:* continuous (freshmen), continuous (transfers).

Freshmen Application Contact Ms. Stephanie Pauhi, Office Assistant, Fresno City College, 1101 East University Avenue, Fresno, CA 93741. *Phone:* 559-442-8225. *Toll-free phone:* 866-245-3276.

FULLERTON COLLEGE

Fullerton, California   www.fullcoll.edu/

- **State and locally supported** 2-year, founded 1913, part of California Community College System
- **Suburban** 79-acre campus with easy access to Los Angeles
- **Coed,** 19,862 undergraduate students

Undergraduates Students come from 21 other countries. *Retention:* 50% of 2003 full-time freshmen returned.

Faculty *Total:* 835, 39% full-time.

Majors Accounting; agriculture; anthropology; architectural engineering technology; art; astronomy; automobile/automotive mechanics technology; biology/biological sciences; business administration and management; carpentry; chemistry; civil engineering technology; computer science; construction engineering technology; cosmetology; criminal justice/police science; cultural studies; dance; data processing and data processing technology; developmental and child psychology; drafting and design technology; dramatic/theater arts; econom-

ics; English; environmental studies; family and consumer sciences/human sciences; fashion/apparel design; fashion merchandising; fish/game management; forestry; geology/earth science; graphic and printing equipment operation/production; history; horticultural science; industrial arts; industrial technology; information science/studies; interior design; international business/trade/commerce; journalism; kindergarten/preschool education; land use planning and management; Latin American studies; legal administrative assistant/secretary; legal assistant/paralegal; liberal arts and sciences/liberal studies; library science; marketing/marketing management; mass communication/media; mathematics; music; oceanography (chemical and physical); ornamental horticulture; parks, recreation and leisure; philosophy; physical education teaching and coaching; physics; political science and government; psychology; purchasing, procurement/acquisitions and contracts management; radio and television; real estate; religious studies; sociology; speech and rhetoric; tourism and travel services management; wildlife and wildlands science and management; zoology/animal biology.

Academics *Calendar:* semesters. *Degree:* certificates and associate. *Special study options:* academic remediation for entering students, adult/continuing education programs, advanced placement credit, cooperative education, English as a second language, honors programs, part-time degree program, services for LD students, study abroad, summer session for credit. *ROTC:* Army (c), Navy (c), Air Force (c).

Library William T. Boyce Library with 113,236 titles, 600 serial subscriptions.

Student Life *Housing:* college housing not available. *Activities and Organizations:* drama/theater group, student-run newspaper, radio station. *Student services:* health clinic, personal/psychological counseling, women's center, legal services.

Athletics *Intercollegiate sports:* basketball M/W, cross-country running M/W, football M, golf M/W, soccer M, swimming and diving M/W, tennis M/W, track and field M/W, volleyball W, water polo M.

Costs (2006–07) *Tuition:* state resident $580 full-time; nonresident $4296 full-time.

Financial Aid Of all full-time matriculated undergraduates, 200 Federal Work-Study jobs (averaging $3000). *Financial aid deadline:* 6/30.

Applying *Options:* early admission. *Application deadlines:* rolling (freshmen), rolling (transfers).

Director of Admissions Mr. Peter Fong, Dean of Admissions and Records, Fullerton College, 321 East Chapman Avenue, Fullerton, CA 92832-2095. *Phone:* 714-992-7582.

GAVILAN COLLEGE
Gilroy, California   www.gavilan.edu/

- **State and locally supported** 2-year, founded 1919, part of California Community College System
- **Rural** 150-acre campus with easy access to San Jose
- **Coed**

Undergraduates 1,212 full-time, 4,852 part-time. Students come from 6 states and territories, 11 other countries, 4% are from out of state, 2% African American, 6% Asian American or Pacific Islander, 41% Hispanic American, 0.7% Native American, 0.1% international.

Academics *Calendar:* semesters. *Degree:* certificates, diplomas, and associate. *Special study options:* academic remediation for entering students, adult/continuing education programs, advanced placement credit, cooperative education, distance learning, English as a second language, honors programs, independent study, internships, part-time degree program, services for LD students, study abroad, summer session for credit.

Student Life *Campus security:* 24-hour emergency response devices and patrols, late-night transport/escort service.

Costs (2006–07) *Tuition:* state resident $0 full-time; nonresident $4800 full-time. *Required fees:* $676 full-time, $26 per semester part-time.

Financial Aid Of all full-time matriculated undergraduates, 50 Federal Work-Study jobs (averaging $2000). *Financial aid deadline:* 6/30.

Freshmen Application Contact Ms. Joy Parker, Director of Admissions, Gavilan College, 5055 Santa Teresa Boulevard, Gilroy, CA 95020. *Phone:* 408-848-4735. *Fax:* 408-846-4940.

GLENDALE COMMUNITY COLLEGE
Glendale, California   www.glendale.edu/

- **State and locally supported** 2-year, founded 1927, part of California Community College System
- **Urban** 119-acre campus with easy access to Los Angeles
- **Endowment** $5.3 million
- **Coed**

Undergraduates 4,730 full-time, 9,535 part-time. Students come from 56 states and territories, 121 other countries, 1% are from out of state, 3% African American, 10% Asian American or Pacific Islander, 22% Hispanic American, 0.4% Native American, 26% international, 6% transferred in.

Academics *Calendar:* semesters. *Degree:* certificates and associate. *Special study options:* academic remediation for entering students, adult/continuing education programs, advanced placement credit, cooperative education, distance learning, English as a second language, honors programs, independent study, internships, part-time degree program, services for LD students, study abroad, summer session for credit.

Student Life *Campus security:* student patrols, late-night transport/escort service.

Standardized Tests *Recommended:* CPT.

Costs (2006–07) *Tuition:* state resident $0 full-time; nonresident $4280 full-time, $150 per unit part-time. Full-time tuition and fees vary according to course load. Part-time tuition and fees vary according to course load. *Required fees:* $680 full-time, $26 per unit part-time, $170 per term part-time.

Financial Aid Of all full-time matriculated undergraduates, 300 Federal Work-Study jobs (averaging $2500).

Applying *Options:* electronic application, early admission, deferred entrance. *Recommended:* high school transcript.

Freshmen Application Contact Ms. Sharon Combs, Dean, Admissions, and Records, Glendale Community College, 1500 North Verdugo Road, Glendale, CA 91208. *Phone:* 818-551-5115. *Fax:* 818-551-5255. *E-mail:* scombs@glendale.edu.

GOLDEN WEST COLLEGE
Huntington Beach, California   www.gwc.cccd.edu/

- **State and locally supported** 2-year, founded 1966, part of Coast Community College District System
- **Suburban** 122-acre campus with easy access to Los Angeles
- **Endowment** $880,684
- **Coed,** 13,091 undergraduate students, 32% full-time, 54% women, 46% men

Undergraduates 4,244 full-time, 8,847 part-time. Students come from 28 other countries.

Faculty *Total:* 440, 44% full-time. *Student/faculty ratio:* 32:1.

Majors Accounting; administrative assistant and secretarial science; architectural engineering technology; art; automobile/automotive mechanics technology; biological and physical sciences; biology/biological sciences; business administration and management; commercial and advertising art; consumer merchandising/retailing management; cosmetology; criminal justice/law enforcement administration; criminal justice/police science; drafting and design technology; electrical, electronic and communications engineering technology; engineering technology; graphic and printing equipment operation/production; humanities; journalism; legal administrative assistant/secretary; liberal arts and sciences/liberal studies; marketing/marketing management; mathematics; music; natural sciences; nursing (registered nurse training); ornamental horticulture; physical sciences; pre-engineering; public relations/image management; radio and television; real estate; sign language interpretation and translation; technical and business writing; telecommunications.

Academics *Calendar:* semesters (summer session). *Degree:* certificates and associate. *Special study options:* academic remediation for entering students, adult/continuing education programs, advanced placement credit, cooperative education, English as a second language, external degree program, internships, part-time degree program, student-designed majors, study abroad, summer session for credit. *ROTC:* Air Force (c).

Library Golden West College Library plus 1 other with 95,000 titles, 410 serial subscriptions, an OPAC, a Web page.

Student Life *Housing:* college housing not available. *Activities and Organizations:* drama/theater group, student-run newspaper, radio station, choral group. *Campus security:* 24-hour emergency response devices and patrols, late-night transport/escort service. *Student services:* health clinic, personal/psychological counseling, legal services.

Athletics Member NJCAA. *Intercollegiate sports:* baseball M, basketball M/W, cross-country running M/W, football M, golf M/W, soccer M/W, softball W, swimming and diving M/W, tennis M/W, track and field M/W, volleyball M/W, water polo M/W, wrestling M.

Standardized Tests *Required for some:* ACT COMPASS. *Recommended:* ACT COMPASS.

Costs (2006–07) *Tuition:* state resident $638 full-time; nonresident $4286 full-time.

Applying *Options:* early admission. *Required for some:* essay or personal statement. *Recommended:* high school transcript. *Application deadlines:* rolling (freshmen), rolling (transfers). *Notification:* continuous (freshmen), continuous (transfers).

Golden West College (continued)

Director of Admissions Ms. Shirley Donnelly, Director of Enrollment Services, Golden West College, 15744 Golden West Street, PO Box 2748, Huntington Beach, CA 92647. *Phone:* 714-892-7711 Ext. 58196.

GROSSMONT COLLEGE

El Cajon, California   www.grossmont.edu/

- **State and locally supported** 2-year, founded 1961, part of California Community College System
- **Suburban** 135-acre campus with easy access to San Diego
- **Coed**, 16,829 undergraduate students

Undergraduates Students come from 52 other countries.
Faculty *Total:* 794, 28% full-time. *Student/faculty ratio:* 17:1.
Majors Accounting; administrative assistant and secretarial science; advertising; art; art history, criticism and conservation; biology/biological sciences; business administration and management; ceramic arts and ceramics; chemistry; child development; clinical laboratory science/medical technology; computer management; computer programming; computer science; consumer merchandising/retailing management; corrections; creative writing; criminal justice/law enforcement administration; criminal justice/police science; cultural studies; dance; developmental and child psychology; dietetics; dramatic/theater arts; drawing; economics; English; family and consumer economics related; French; geography; geology/earth science; German; history; information science/studies; international business/trade/commerce; legal administrative assistant/secretary; liberal arts and sciences/liberal studies; marketing/marketing management; mathematics; medical administrative assistant and medical secretary; medical/clinical assistant; music; nursing (registered nurse training); occupational therapy; philosophy; photography; physics; political science and government; radio and television; respiratory care therapy; sculpture; Spanish; speech and rhetoric; telecommunications.
Academics *Calendar:* semesters. *Degree:* certificates and associate. *Special study options:* academic remediation for entering students, adult/continuing education programs, advanced placement credit, cooperative education, English as a second language, honors programs, internships, part-time degree program, services for LD students, student-designed majors, summer session for credit. *ROTC:* Army (c), Air Force (c).
Library Lewis F. Smith Learning Resource Center with 105,000 titles, 759 serial subscriptions, an OPAC, a Web page.
Student Life *Housing:* college housing not available. *Activities and Organizations:* drama/theater group, student-run newspaper, radio station, choral group. *Campus security:* 24-hour emergency response devices, student patrols, late-night transport/escort service. *Student services:* health clinic, personal/psychological counseling, legal services.
Athletics Member NJCAA. *Intercollegiate sports:* baseball M, basketball M/W, cross-country running M, football M, golf M, soccer W, softball W, swimming and diving M/W, tennis M/W, track and field M, volleyball M/W, water polo M/W.
Costs (2006–07) *Tuition:* state resident $754 full-time; nonresident $5133 full-time.
Financial Aid Of all full-time matriculated undergraduates, 289 Federal Work-Study jobs (averaging $1802).
Applying *Options:* early admission. *Application deadlines:* 8/12 (freshmen), 8/12 (transfers). *Notification:* continuous until 8/12 (freshmen), continuous until 8/12 (transfers).
Freshmen Application Contact Ms. Sharon Clark, Registrar, Grossmont College, 8800 Grossmont College Drive, El Cajon, CA 92020-1799. *Phone:* 619-644-7170.

HARTNELL COLLEGE

Salinas, California   www.hartnell.edu/

- **District-supported** 2-year, founded 1920, part of California Community College System
- **Small-town** 50-acre campus with easy access to San Jose
- **Coed,** 10,074 undergraduate students

Undergraduates Students come from 16 states and territories, 14 other countries.
Faculty *Total:* 378, 28% full-time.
Majors Administrative assistant and secretarial science; agricultural business and management; agronomy and crop science; animal sciences; anthropology; architectural engineering technology; art; automobile/automotive mechanics technology; behavioral sciences; business administration and management; business machine repair; carpentry; child development; commercial and adver-

tising art; computer graphics; computer science; construction engineering technology; corrections; criminal justice/law enforcement administration; criminology; data processing and data processing technology; developmental and child psychology; drafting and design technology; economics; electrical, electronic and communications engineering technology; English; family and consumer economics related; fire science; forestry technology; health teacher education; history; horticultural science; human services; hydrology and water resources science; industrial technology; kindergarten/preschool education; liberal arts and sciences/liberal studies; library science; machine tool technology; marketing/marketing management; mathematics; mechanical design technology; musical instrument fabrication and repair; nursing (registered nurse training); parks, recreation and leisure; photography; physical education teaching and coaching; physician assistant; real estate; substance abuse/addiction counseling; veterinary technology; welding technology.
Academics *Calendar:* semesters. *Degree:* certificates and associate. *Special study options:* academic remediation for entering students, adult/continuing education programs, cooperative education, English as a second language, honors programs, part-time degree program, services for LD students, student-designed majors, study abroad, summer session for credit.
Library Hartnell College Library plus 1 other with 70,000 titles, 480 serial subscriptions.
Student Life *Housing:* college housing not available. *Activities and Organizations:* drama/theater group, student-run newspaper, choral group, Chicano Students Club, Alpha Gamma Sigma. *Campus security:* 24-hour emergency response devices, student patrols, late-night transport/escort service. *Student services:* women's center.
Athletics *Intercollegiate sports:* baseball M, basketball M/W, cross-country running M/W, football M, golf M, soccer M/W, softball W, swimming and diving M/W, tennis M/W, track and field M/W, volleyball W, water polo M.
Costs (2006–07) *Tuition:* state resident $698 full-time; nonresident $5468 full-time.
Financial Aid Of all full-time matriculated undergraduates, 50 Federal Work-Study jobs (averaging $3000).
Applying *Options:* early admission, deferred entrance. *Required for some:* high school transcript. *Application deadlines:* rolling (freshmen), rolling (transfers). *Notification:* continuous (freshmen), continuous (transfers).
Director of Admissions Ms. Mary Dominguez, Director of Admissions, Hartnell College, 156 Homestead Avenue, Salinas, CA 93901-1697. *Phone:* 831-755-6711.

HEALD COLLEGE-CONCORD

Concord, California   www.heald.edu/

- **Independent** 2-year, founded 1863
- **Small-town** 5-acre campus with easy access to San Francisco
- **Coed**

Undergraduates 524 full-time, 115 part-time. 5% African American, 3% Asian American or Pacific Islander, 5% Hispanic American.
Faculty *Student/faculty ratio:* 18:1.
Academics *Calendar:* quarters. *Degree:* certificates, diplomas, and associate. *Special study options:* academic remediation for entering students, advanced placement credit, internships, part-time degree program, summer session for credit.
Student Life *Campus security:* 24-hour emergency response devices.
Standardized Tests *Required:* COMPASS (for admission).
Costs (2006–07) *Tuition:* $10,275 full-time.
Applying *Options:* electronic application, early admission, deferred entrance. *Application fee:* $40. *Required:* high school transcript, interview.
Freshmen Application Contact Keith Woodman, Director of Admissions, Heald College-Concord, 5130 Commercial Circle, Concord, CA 94520. *Phone:* 925-288-5800. *Toll-free phone:* 800-755-3550. *Fax:* 925-288-5896. *E-mail:* kwoodman@heald.edu.

HEALD COLLEGE-FRESNO

Fresno, California   www.heald.edu/

- **Independent** 2-year, founded 1863
- **Suburban** 3-acre campus
- **Coed**

Undergraduates 547 full-time, 182 part-time. 2% African American, 3% Asian American or Pacific Islander, 11% Hispanic American, 0.1% Native American.
Faculty *Student/faculty ratio:* 20:1.

Academics *Calendar:* quarters. *Degree:* certificates, diplomas, and associate. *Special study options:* academic remediation for entering students, advanced placement credit, internships, part-time degree program, summer session for credit.

Standardized Tests *Required:* COMPASS (for admission).

Costs (2006–07) *Tuition:* $10,275 full-time.

Applying *Options:* electronic application, early admission, deferred entrance. *Application fee:* $40. *Required:* high school transcript, interview.

Freshmen Application Contact Ms. Tina Mathis, Director of Admissions, Heald College-Fresno, 255 West Bullard Avenue, Fresno, CA 93704-1706. *Phone:* 559-438-4222. *Toll-free phone:* 800-755-3550. *E-mail:* tmathis@heald.edu.

HEALD COLLEGE-HAYWARD

Hayward, California www.heald.edu/

- **Independent** 2-year, founded 1863
- **Urban** campus with easy access to San Francisco
- **Coed**

Undergraduates 637 full-time, 227 part-time. 6% African American, 6% Asian American or Pacific Islander, 9% Hispanic American, 0.3% Native American.

Faculty *Student/faculty ratio:* 26:1.

Academics *Calendar:* quarters. *Degree:* certificates, diplomas, and associate. *Special study options:* academic remediation for entering students, advanced placement credit, internships, part-time degree program, summer session for credit.

Student Life *Campus security:* 24-hour emergency response devices and patrols.

Standardized Tests *Required:* COMPASS (for admission).

Costs (2006–07) *Tuition:* $10,275 full-time. Full-time tuition and fees vary according to class time, course load, and program. Part-time tuition and fees vary according to class time, course load, and program. No tuition increase for student's term of enrollment. *Payment plans:* tuition prepayment, installment.

Applying *Options:* electronic application, early admission, deferred entrance. *Application fee:* $40. *Required:* high school transcript, interview.

Freshmen Application Contact Mrs. Barbara Gordon, Director of Admissions, Heald College-Hayward, 25500 Industrial Boulevard, Hayward, CA 94545. *Phone:* 510-783-2100. *Toll-free phone:* 800-755-3550. *Fax:* 510-783-3287. *E-mail:* bgordon@heald.edu.

HEALD COLLEGE-RANCHO CORDOVA

Rancho Cordova, California www.heald.edu/

- **Independent** 2-year, founded 1863
- **Suburban** 1-acre campus with easy access to Sacramento
- **Coed**

Undergraduates 349 full-time, 122 part-time. 12% African American, 9% Asian American or Pacific Islander, 13% Hispanic American, 0.2% Native American.

Faculty *Student/faculty ratio:* 20:1.

Academics *Calendar:* quarters. *Degree:* certificates, diplomas, and associate. *Special study options:* academic remediation for entering students, advanced placement credit, internships, part-time degree program, summer session for credit.

Student Life *Campus security:* late-night transport/escort service.

Standardized Tests *Required:* COMPASS (for admission).

Costs (2006–07) *Tuition:* $10,275 full-time.

Applying *Options:* electronic application, early admission, deferred entrance. *Application fee:* $40. *Required:* high school transcript, interview.

Freshmen Application Contact Director of Admissions, Heald College-Rancho Cordova, 2910 Prospect Park Drive, Rancho Cordova, CA 95670-6005. *Phone:* 916-638-1616. *Toll-free phone:* 800-755-3550. *Fax:* 916-853-8282. *E-mail:* info@heald.edu.

HEALD COLLEGE-ROSEVILLE

Roseville, California www.heald.edu/

- **Independent** 2-year, founded 1863
- **Urban** 5-acre campus
- **Coed**

Undergraduates 376 full-time, 152 part-time. 1% African American, 2% Asian American or Pacific Islander, 7% Hispanic American, 0.8% Native American.

Faculty *Student/faculty ratio:* 19:1.

Academics *Calendar:* quarters. *Degree:* certificates, diplomas, and associate. *Special study options:* academic remediation for entering students, advanced placement credit, internships, part-time degree program, summer session for credit.

Student Life *Campus security:* 24-hour emergency response devices, evening security guard.

Standardized Tests *Required:* COMPASS (for admission).

Costs (2006–07) *Tuition:* $10,275 full-time.

Financial Aid Of all full-time matriculated undergraduates, 35 Federal Work-Study jobs.

Applying *Options:* electronic application, early admission, deferred entrance. *Application fee:* $40. *Required:* high school transcript, interview.

Freshmen Application Contact Kristi Culpepper, Director of Admissions, Heald College-Roseville, 7 Sierra Gate Plaza, Roseville, CA 95678. *Phone:* 916-789-8600. *Toll-free phone:* 800-755-3550. *E-mail:* kculpepp@heald.edu.

HEALD COLLEGE-SALINAS

Salinas, California www.heald.edu/

- **Independent** 2-year, founded 1863
- **Small-town** campus with easy access to San Jose
- **Coed**

Undergraduates 329 full-time, 85 part-time. 3% African American, 0.5% Asian American or Pacific Islander, 18% Hispanic American.

Faculty *Student/faculty ratio:* 24:1.

Academics *Calendar:* quarters. *Degree:* certificates, diplomas, and associate. *Special study options:* academic remediation for entering students, advanced placement credit, internships, part-time degree program, summer session for credit.

Student Life *Campus security:* 24-hour emergency response devices, evening security personnel.

Standardized Tests *Required:* COMPASS (for admission).

Costs (2006–07) *Tuition:* $10,275 full-time.

Applying *Options:* electronic application, early admission, deferred entrance. *Application fee:* $40. *Required:* high school transcript, interview.

Freshmen Application Contact Mr. Jason Ferguson, Director of Admissions, Heald College-Salinas, 1450 North Main Street, Salinas, CA 93906. *Phone:* 831-443-1700. *Toll-free phone:* 800-755-3550. *Fax:* 831-443-1050. *E-mail:* jferguso@heald.edu.

HEALD COLLEGE-SAN FRANCISCO

San Francisco, California www.heald.edu/

- **Independent** 2-year, founded 1863
- **Urban** campus
- **Coed**

Undergraduates 273 full-time, 116 part-time. 5% African American, 5% Asian American or Pacific Islander, 5% Hispanic American, 0.3% Native American.

Faculty *Student/faculty ratio:* 16:1.

Academics *Calendar:* quarters. *Degree:* certificates, diplomas, and associate. *Special study options:* academic remediation for entering students, advanced placement credit, internships, part-time degree program, summer session for credit.

Standardized Tests *Required:* COMPASS (for admission).

Costs (2006–07) *Tuition:* $10,275 full-time.

Applying *Options:* electronic application, early admission, deferred entrance. *Application fee:* $40. *Required:* high school transcript, interview.

Freshmen Application Contact Ms. Jennifer Dunckel, Director of Admissions, Heald College-San Francisco, 350 Mission Street, San Francisco, CA 94105. *Phone:* 415-808-3000. *Toll-free phone:* 800-755-3550. *Fax:* 415-808-3003. *E-mail:* jennifer_dunckel@heald.edu.

HEALD COLLEGE-SAN JOSE

Milpitas, California   www.heald.edu/

- **Independent** 2-year, founded 1863
- **Small-town** 5-acre campus with easy access to San Jose
- **Coed**

Undergraduates 502 full-time, 137 part-time. 11% African American, 19% Asian American or Pacific Islander, 39% Hispanic American, 0.3% Native American.

Faculty *Student/faculty ratio:* 20:1.

Academics *Calendar:* quarters. *Degree:* certificates, diplomas, and associate. *Special study options:* academic remediation for entering students, advanced placement credit, internships, part-time degree program, summer session for credit.

Standardized Tests *Required:* COMPASS (for admission).

Costs (2006–07) *Tuition:* $10,275 full-time.

Financial Aid Of all full-time matriculated undergraduates, 20 Federal Work-Study jobs.

Applying *Options:* electronic application, early admission, deferred entrance. *Application fee:* $40. *Required:* high school transcript, interview.

Freshmen Application Contact Clarence Hardiman, Director of Admissions, Heald College-San Jose, 341 Great Mall Parkway, Milpitas, CA 95035. *Phone:* 408-934-4900. *Toll-free phone:* 800-755-3550. *Fax:* 408-934-7777. *E-mail:* chardima@heald.edu.

HEALD COLLEGE-STOCKTON

Stockton, California   www.heald.edu/

- **Independent** 2-year, founded 1863
- **Coed**

Undergraduates 398 full-time, 132 part-time. 4% African American, 8% Asian American or Pacific Islander, 17% Hispanic American, 0.2% Native American.

Faculty *Student/faculty ratio:* 17:1.

Academics *Calendar:* quarters. *Degree:* certificates, diplomas, and associate. *Special study options:* academic remediation for entering students, advanced placement credit, internships, part-time degree program, summer session for credit.

Standardized Tests *Required:* COMPASS (for admission).

Costs (2006–07) *Tuition:* $10,275 full-time.

Applying *Options:* electronic application, early admission, deferred entrance. *Application fee:* $40. *Required:* high school transcript, interview.

Freshmen Application Contact Director of Admissions, Heald College-Stockton, 1605 East March Lane, Stockton, CA 95210. *Phone:* 209-473-5200. *Toll-free phone:* 800-755-3550. *Fax:* 209-477-2739. *E-mail:* info@heald.edu.

HIGH-TECH INSTITUTE

Sacramento, California   www.high-techinstitute.com/

- **Proprietary** 2-year, founded 1992
- **Coed,** 716 undergraduate students

Majors Computer and information sciences related.

Academics *Degree:* associate.

Applying *Application fee:* $50.

Freshmen Application Contact Admissions Office, High-Tech Institute, Suite 100, Sacramento, CA 95827. *Phone:* 916-929-9700. *Toll-free phone:* 800-322-4128.

IMPERIAL VALLEY COLLEGE

Imperial, California   www.imperial.cc.ca.us/

- **State and locally supported** 2-year, founded 1922, part of California Community College System
- **Rural** 160-acre campus
- **Endowment** $832,061
- **Coed,** 7,413 undergraduate students

Undergraduates Students come from 12 states and territories, 3% are from out of state, 1% African American, 1% Asian American or Pacific Islander, 86% Hispanic American, 0.4% Native American.

Majors Accounting; administrative assistant and secretarial science; agricultural business and management; agricultural mechanization; agriculture; anthropology; art; automobile/automotive mechanics technology; behavioral sciences; biological and physical sciences; business administration and management; criminal justice/law enforcement administration; English; fire science; French; human development and family studies; humanities; hydrology and water resources science; information science/studies; journalism; kindergarten/preschool education; liberal arts and sciences/liberal studies; marketing/marketing management; mathematics; modern languages; music; nursing (licensed practical/vocational nurse training); nursing (registered nurse training); physical education teaching and coaching; physical sciences; pre-engineering; psychology; social sciences; Spanish; welding technology.

Academics *Calendar:* semesters. *Degree:* certificates and associate. *Special study options:* academic remediation for entering students, accelerated degree program, adult/continuing education programs, advanced placement credit, double majors, English as a second language, part-time degree program, services for LD students, student-designed majors, summer session for credit.

Library Spencer Library with 55,875 titles, 425 serial subscriptions, 3,383 audiovisual materials, an OPAC, a Web page.

Student Life *Housing:* college housing not available. *Activities and Organizations:* drama/theater group, student-run newspaper, choral group, Student Support Services Club, Pre-School Mothers, Care Club, Christian Club, Nursing Club. *Campus security:* student patrols. *Student services:* personal/psychological counseling, women's center.

Athletics *Intercollegiate sports:* baseball M, basketball M/W, soccer M/W, softball W, tennis M/W.

Costs (2006–07) *Tuition:* state resident $802 full-time; nonresident $6002 full-time.

Financial Aid Of all full-time matriculated undergraduates, 400 Federal Work-Study jobs (averaging $2500). 80 state and other part-time jobs (averaging $2500).

Applying *Application fee:* $23. *Required for some:* high school transcript. *Recommended:* high school transcript. *Application deadlines:* rolling (freshmen), rolling (transfers). *Notification:* continuous (freshmen), continuous (transfers).

Director of Admissions Kathie C. Westerfield, Associate Dean of Admissions and Records, Imperial Valley College, 380 East Aten Road, PO Box 158, Imperial, CA 92251. *Phone:* 760-352-8320 Ext. 200.

IRVINE VALLEY COLLEGE

Irvine, California   www.ivc.edu/

- **State and locally supported** 2-year, founded 1979, part of Saddleback Community College District
- **Suburban** 20-acre campus with easy access to Los Angeles
- **Coed,** 10,511 undergraduate students

Faculty *Total:* 344, 27% full-time.

Majors Accounting; administrative assistant and secretarial science; art; behavioral sciences; biological and physical sciences; biology/biological sciences; business administration and management; business machine repair; computer engineering technology; creative writing; criminal justice/law enforcement administration; data processing and data processing technology; electromechanical technology; English; history; humanities; liberal arts and sciences/liberal studies; literature; mathematics; social sciences; speech and rhetoric.

Academics *Calendar:* semesters. *Degree:* certificates and associate. *Special study options:* academic remediation for entering students, adult/continuing education programs, advanced placement credit, cooperative education, English as a second language, part-time degree program, services for LD students, summer session for credit.

Library Irvine Valley College Library with 24,000 titles, 250 serial subscriptions.

Student Life *Housing:* college housing not available. *Activities and Organizations:* drama/theater group, student-run newspaper. *Campus security:* late-night transport/escort service. *Student services:* health clinic, personal/psychological counseling, women's center.

Athletics *Intercollegiate sports:* basketball M/W, cross-country running M/W, soccer M/W, tennis M/W, volleyball M.

Costs (2006–07) *Tuition:* state resident $770 full-time; nonresident $4972 full-time.

Financial Aid Of all full-time matriculated undergraduates, 100 Federal Work-Study jobs (averaging $3000).

Applying *Options:* early admission. *Application deadline:* rolling (freshmen). *Notification:* continuous (freshmen), continuous (transfers).

Director of Admissions Mr. John Edwards, Director of Admissions, Records and Enrollment Services, Irvine Valley College, 5500 Irvine Center Drive, Irvine, CA 92618. *Phone:* 949-451-5416.

ITT TECHNICAL INSTITUTE

Anaheim, California   www.itt-tech.edu/

- **Proprietary** primarily 2-year, founded 1982, part of ITT Educational Services, Inc
- **Suburban** 5-acre campus with easy access to Los Angeles
- **Coed**

Majors Animation, interactive technology, video graphics and special effects; business administration and management; communications technology; computer and information systems security; computer engineering technology; computer systems networking and telecommunications; construction management; criminal justice/law enforcement administration; electrical, electronic and communications engineering technology; medical laboratory technology; web page, digital/multimedia and information resources design.

Academics *Calendar:* quarters. *Degrees:* associate and bachelor's.

Library a Web page.

Student Life *Housing:* college housing not available. *Activities and Organizations:* student-run newspaper.

Standardized Tests *Required:* Wonderlic aptitude test (for admission).

Costs (2006–07) *Tuition:* Contact school for program costs.

Financial Aid Of all full-time matriculated undergraduates, 20 Federal Work-Study jobs (averaging $5000).

Applying *Options:* deferred entrance. *Application fee:* $100. *Required:* high school transcript, interview. *Recommended:* letters of recommendation. *Application deadlines:* rolling (freshmen), rolling (transfers). *Notification:* continuous (freshmen), continuous (transfers).

Freshmen Application Contact Ms. Sheryl Schulgen, Director of Recruitment, ITT Technical Institute, 525 North Muller Avenue, Anaheim, CA 92801. *Phone:* 714-535-3700. *Fax:* 714-535-1802.

ITT TECHNICAL INSTITUTE

Lathrop, California   www.itt-tech.edu/

- **Proprietary** primarily 2-year, founded 1997, part of ITT Educational Services, Inc
- **Coed**

Majors Animation, interactive technology, video graphics and special effects; business administration and management; CAD/CADD drafting/design technology; communications technology; computer and information systems security; computer engineering technology; computer software engineering; computer software technology; computer systems networking and telecommunications; construction management; criminal justice/law enforcement administration; electrical, electronic and communications engineering technology; medical laboratory technology; web page, digital/multimedia and information resources design.

Academics *Calendar:* quarters. *Degrees:* associate and bachelor's.

Library a Web page.

Student Life *Housing:* college housing not available.

Standardized Tests *Required:* Wonderlic aptitude test (for admission).

Costs (2006–07) *Tuition:* Contact school for program costs.

Applying *Options:* deferred entrance. *Application fee:* $100. *Required:* high school transcript, interview. *Recommended:* letters of recommendation. *Application deadlines:* rolling (freshmen), rolling (transfers). *Notification:* continuous (freshmen), continuous (transfers).

Freshmen Application Contact Ms. Kathy Paradis, Director of Recruitment, ITT Technical Institute, 16916 South Harlan Road, Lathrop, CA 95330. *Phone:* 209-858-0077. *Toll-free phone:* 800-346-1786.

ITT TECHNICAL INSTITUTE

Oxnard, California   www.itt-tech.edu/

- **Proprietary** primarily 2-year, founded 1993, part of ITT Educational Services, Inc
- **Urban** campus with easy access to Los Angeles
- **Coed**

Majors Animation, interactive technology, video graphics and special effects; business administration and management; CAD/CADD drafting/design technol-

ogy; computer and information systems security; computer engineering technology; computer software technology; computer systems networking and telecommunications; construction management; criminal justice/law enforcement administration; electrical, electronic and communications engineering technology; medical laboratory technology; web page, digital/multimedia and information resources design.

Academics *Calendar:* quarters. *Degrees:* associate and bachelor's.

Library a Web page.

Student Life *Housing:* college housing not available. *Campus security:* 24-hour emergency response devices and patrols.

Standardized Tests *Required:* Wonderlic aptitude test (for admission).

Costs (2006–07) *Tuition:* Contact school for program costs.

Applying *Options:* deferred entrance. *Application fee:* $100. *Required:* high school transcript, interview. *Recommended:* letters of recommendation. *Application deadlines:* rolling (freshmen), rolling (transfers). *Notification:* continuous (freshmen), continuous (transfers).

Freshmen Application Contact Milo Hager, Director of Recruitment, ITT Technical Institute, 2051 Solar Drive, Building B, Oxnard, CA 93036. *Phone:* 805-988-0143. *Toll-free phone:* 800-530-1582.

ITT TECHNICAL INSTITUTE

Rancho Cordova, California   www.itt-tech.edu/

- **Proprietary** primarily 2-year, founded 1954, part of ITT Educational Services, Inc
- **Urban** 5-acre campus
- **Coed**

Majors Animation, interactive technology, video graphics and special effects; business administration and management; CAD/CADD drafting/design technology; communications technology; computer and information systems security; computer engineering technology; computer systems networking and telecommunications; construction management; criminal justice/law enforcement administration; electrical, electronic and communications engineering technology; health information/medical records technology; web/multimedia management and webmaster; web page, digital/multimedia and information resources design.

Academics *Calendar:* quarters. *Degrees:* associate and bachelor's.

Library a Web page.

Student Life *Housing:* college housing not available.

Standardized Tests *Required:* Wonderlic aptitude test (for admission).

Costs (2006–07) *Tuition:* Contact school for program costs.

Applying *Options:* deferred entrance. *Application fee:* $100. *Required:* high school transcript, interview. *Recommended:* letters of recommendation. *Application deadlines:* rolling (freshmen), rolling (transfers). *Notification:* continuous (freshmen), continuous (transfers).

Freshmen Application Contact Mr. Vance Klinke, Director of Recruitment, ITT Technical Institute, 10863 Gold Center Drive, Rancho Cordova, CA 95670. *Phone:* 916-851-3900. *Toll-free phone:* 800-488-8466.

ITT TECHNICAL INSTITUTE

San Bernardino, California   www.itt-tech.edu/

- **Proprietary** primarily 2-year, founded 1987, part of ITT Educational Services, Inc
- **Urban** campus with easy access to Los Angeles
- **Coed**

Majors Animation, interactive technology, video graphics and special effects; business administration and management; CAD/CADD drafting/design technology; computer and information systems security; computer engineering technology; computer systems networking and telecommunications; construction management; criminal justice/law enforcement administration; electrical, electronic and communications engineering technology; health information/medical records technology; web page, digital/multimedia and information resources design.

Academics *Calendar:* quarters. *Degrees:* associate and bachelor's.

Library a Web page.

Student Life *Housing:* college housing not available.

Standardized Tests *Required:* Wonderlic aptitude test (for admission).

Costs (2006–07) *Tuition:* Contact school for program costs.

Applying *Options:* deferred entrance. *Application fee:* $100. *Required:* high school transcript, interview. *Recommended:* letters of recommendation. *Application deadlines:* rolling (freshmen), rolling (transfers). *Notification:* continuous (freshmen), continuous (transfers).

ITT Technical Institute (continued)

Freshmen Application Contact Director of Recruitment, ITT Technical Institute, 670 East Carnegie Drive, San Bernardino, CA 92408. *Phone:* 909-806-4600. *Toll-free phone:* 800-888-3801.

ITT TECHNICAL INSTITUTE
San Diego, California
www.itt-tech.edu/

- **Proprietary** primarily 2-year, founded 1981, part of ITT Educational Services, Inc
- **Suburban** campus
- **Coed**

Majors Animation, interactive technology, video graphics and special effects; business administration and management; CAD/CADD drafting/design technology; computer and information systems security; computer engineering technology; computer systems networking and telecommunications; construction management; criminal justice/law enforcement administration; electrical, electronic and communications engineering technology; health information/medical records technology; web page, digital/multimedia and information resources design.

Academics *Calendar:* quarters. *Degrees:* associate and bachelor's.

Library a Web page.

Student Life *Housing:* college housing not available.

Standardized Tests *Required:* Wonderlic aptitude test (for admission).

Costs (2006–07) *Tuition:* Contact school for program costs.

Applying *Options:* deferred entrance. *Application fee:* $100. *Required:* high school transcript, interview. *Recommended:* letters of recommendation. *Application deadlines:* rolling (freshmen), rolling (transfers). *Notification:* continuous (freshmen), continuous (transfers).

Freshmen Application Contact Ron Begora, Director of Recruitment, ITT Technical Institute, 9680 Granite Ridge Drive, San Diego, CA 92123. *Phone:* 858-571-8500. *Toll-free phone:* 800-883-0380.

ITT TECHNICAL INSTITUTE
San Dimas, California
www.itt-tech.edu/

- **Proprietary** primarily 2-year, founded 1982, part of ITT Educational Services, Inc
- **Suburban** 4-acre campus with easy access to Los Angeles
- **Coed**

Majors Animation, interactive technology, video graphics and special effects; business administration and management; CAD/CADD drafting/design technology; computer and information systems security; computer engineering technology; construction management; criminal justice/law enforcement administration; e-commerce; electrical, electronic and communications engineering technology; health information/medical records technology; robotics technology; system, networking, and LAN/WAN management; web page, digital/multimedia and information resources design.

Academics *Calendar:* quarters. *Degrees:* associate and bachelor's.

Library a Web page.

Student Life *Housing:* college housing not available.

Standardized Tests *Required:* Wonderlic aptitude test (for admission).

Costs (2006–07) *Tuition:* Contact school for program costs.

Financial Aid Of all full-time matriculated undergraduates, 20 Federal Work-Study jobs (averaging $4500).

Applying *Options:* deferred entrance. *Application fee:* $100. *Required:* high school transcript, interview. *Recommended:* letters of recommendation. *Application deadlines:* rolling (freshmen), rolling (transfers). *Notification:* continuous (freshmen), continuous (transfers).

Freshmen Application Contact Ms. Laura Brozeck, Director of Recruitment, ITT Technical Institute, 650 West Cienega Avenue, San Dimas, CA 91773. *Phone:* 909-971-2300. *Toll-free phone:* 800-414-6522.

ITT TECHNICAL INSTITUTE
Sylmar, California
www.itt-tech.edu/

- **Proprietary** primarily 2-year, founded 1982, part of ITT Educational Services, Inc
- **Urban** campus with easy access to Los Angeles
- **Coed**

Majors Animation, interactive technology, video graphics and special effects; business administration and management; CAD/CADD drafting/design technology; communications technology; computer and information systems security; computer engineering technology; computer systems networking and telecommunications; construction management; criminal justice/law enforcement administration; electrical, electronic and communications engineering technology; health information/medical records technology; web page, digital/multimedia and information resources design.

Academics *Calendar:* quarters. *Degrees:* associate and bachelor's.

Library a Web page.

Student Life *Housing:* college housing not available.

Standardized Tests *Required:* Wonderlic aptitude test (for admission).

Costs (2006–07) *Tuition:* Contact school for program costs.

Applying *Options:* deferred entrance. *Application fee:* $100. *Required:* high school transcript, interview. *Recommended:* letters of recommendation. *Application deadlines:* rolling (freshmen), rolling (transfers). *Notification:* continuous (freshmen), continuous (transfers).

Freshmen Application Contact Ms. Kelly Christensen, Director of Recruitment, ITT Technical Institute, 12669 Encinitas Avenue, Sylmar, CA 91342. *Phone:* 818-364-5151. *Toll-free phone:* 800-363-2086.

ITT TECHNICAL INSTITUTE
Torrance, California
www.itt-tech.edu/

- **Proprietary** primarily 2-year, founded 1987, part of ITT Educational Services, Inc
- **Urban** campus with easy access to Los Angeles
- **Coed**

Majors Animation, interactive technology, video graphics and special effects; business administration and management; CAD/CADD drafting/design technology; communications technology; computer and information systems security; computer engineering technology; computer software engineering; computer software technology; computer systems networking and telecommunications; construction management; criminal justice/law enforcement administration; electrical, electronic and communications engineering technology; health information/medical records technology; web page, digital/multimedia and information resources design.

Academics *Calendar:* quarters. *Degrees:* associate and bachelor's.

Library a Web page.

Student Life *Housing:* college housing not available.

Standardized Tests *Required:* Wonderlic aptitude test (for admission).

Costs (2006–07) *Tuition:* Contact school for program costs.

Financial Aid Of all full-time matriculated undergraduates, 6 Federal Work-Study jobs (averaging $4000).

Applying *Options:* deferred entrance. *Application fee:* $100. *Required:* high school transcript, interview. *Recommended:* letters of recommendation. *Application deadlines:* rolling (freshmen), rolling (transfers). *Notification:* continuous (freshmen), continuous (transfers).

Freshmen Application Contact Mr. Freddie Polk, Director of Recruitment, ITT Technical Institute, 20050 South Vermont Avenue, Torrance, CA 90502. *Phone:* 310-380-1555.

LAKE TAHOE COMMUNITY COLLEGE
South Lake Tahoe, California
www.ltcc.edu/

- **State and locally supported** 2-year, founded 1975, part of California Community College System
- **Small-town** 164-acre campus
- **Coed,** 3,000 undergraduate students

Freshmen *Admission:* 450 applied, 450 admitted.

Faculty *Total:* 200, 21% full-time.

Majors Accounting; administrative assistant and secretarial science; art; biological and physical sciences; business administration and management; computer science; criminal justice/law enforcement administration; criminal justice/police science; dance; dramatic/theater arts; finance; fire science; hotel/motel administration; humanities; kindergarten/preschool education; liberal arts and sciences/liberal studies; marketing/marketing management; mathematics; medical administrative assistant and medical secretary; medical/clinical assistant; music; natural sciences; physical education teaching and coaching; psychology; real estate; social sciences; Spanish.

Academics *Calendar:* quarters. *Degree:* associate. *Special study options:* academic remediation for entering students, advanced placement credit, cooperative education, distance learning, double majors, English as a second lan-

guage, independent study, internships, part-time degree program, services for LD students, study abroad, summer session for credit.

Library Lake Tahoe Community College Library with 20,000 titles, 10,000 serial subscriptions, 5,000 audiovisual materials, an OPAC, a Web page.

Student Life *Housing:* college housing not available. *Activities and Organizations:* drama/theater group, choral group, Associated Student Council, Alpha Gamma Sigma, Foreign Language Club, Art Club, Performing Arts League. *Campus security:* 24-hour emergency response devices, late-night transport/ escort service. *Student services:* personal/psychological counseling.

Athletics *Intercollegiate sports:* skiing (cross-country) M/W, volleyball W.

Costs (2007–08) *Tuition:* state resident $0 full-time; nonresident $6210 full-time, $138 per unit part-time. *Required fees:* $597 full-time, $13 per unit part-time, $4 per term part-time.

Financial Aid Of all full-time matriculated undergraduates, 15 Federal Work-Study jobs (averaging $1500).

Applying *Options:* early admission. *Recommended:* high school transcript. *Application deadlines:* rolling (freshmen), rolling (transfers). *Notification:* continuous (freshmen), continuous (transfers).

Freshmen Application Contact Office of Admissions and Records, Lake Tahoe Community College, One College Drive, South Lake Tahoe, CA 96150-4524. *Phone:* 530-541-4660 Ext. 211. *Fax:* 530-541-7852. *E-mail:* admissions@ ltcc.edu.

LANEY COLLEGE

Oakland, California **www.peralta.cc.ca.us/**

- **State and locally supported** 2-year, founded 1953, part of Peralta Community College District System
- **Urban** campus with easy access to San Francisco
- **Coed,** 13,463 undergraduate students, 18% full-time, 58% women, 42% men

Undergraduates 2,424 full-time, 11,039 part-time.

Freshmen *Admission:* 776 admitted, 776 enrolled.

Faculty *Total:* 451, 26% full-time.

Majors Accounting; administrative assistant and secretarial science; African-American/Black studies; architectural engineering technology; art; Asian studies; biological and physical sciences; broadcast journalism; business administration and management; carpentry; ceramic arts and ceramics; commercial and advertising art; computer programming; computer typography and composition equipment operation; construction management; cosmetology; culinary arts; cultural studies; dance; dramatic/theater arts; engineering; engineering technology; finance; graphic and printing equipment operation/production; heating, air conditioning, ventilation and refrigeration maintenance technology; Hispanic-American, Puerto Rican, and Mexican-American/Chicano studies; humanities; information science/ studies; journalism; labor and industrial relations; liberal arts and sciences/liberal studies; machine tool technology; management information systems; marketing/ marketing management; mathematics; music; photography; radio and television; reading teacher education; social sciences; welding technology; wood science and wood products/pulp and paper technology.

Academics *Calendar:* semesters. *Degree:* certificates and associate. *Special study options:* academic remediation for entering students, adult/continuing education programs, part-time degree program, services for LD students, summer session for credit.

Library Laney Library with 78,054 titles, 209 serial subscriptions.

Student Life *Housing:* college housing not available. *Activities and Organizations:* drama/theater group, student-run newspaper, La Raza Club, African Student Union, Vision Christian Society, Asian/Pacific Islander Club, Vietnamese Student Club.

Athletics *Intercollegiate sports:* baseball M, football M, golf M, softball W, volleyball W.

Costs (2006–07) *Tuition:* state resident $648 full-time; nonresident $5460 full-time.

Financial Aid Of all full-time matriculated undergraduates, 120 Federal Work-Study jobs (averaging $2500).

Applying *Options:* early admission. *Application deadline:* rolling (freshmen).

Freshmen Application Contact Mrs. Barbara Simmons, District Admissions Officer, Laney College, 900 Fallon Street, Oakland, CA 94607-4893. *Phone:* 510-466-7369.

LAS POSITAS COLLEGE

Livermore, California **www.laspositascollege.edu/**

- **State-supported** 2-year, founded 1988, part of California Community College System
- **Suburban** 150-acre campus with easy access to Oakland and San Francisco
- **Coed,** 8,044 undergraduate students

Majors Accounting; administrative assistant and secretarial science; automobile/ automotive mechanics technology; business administration and management; computer science; criminal justice/police science; drafting and design technology; education; electrical, electronic and communications engineering technology; environmental studies; fashion merchandising; fire science; horticultural science; industrial design; industrial radiologic technology; information science/ studies; interior design; kindergarten/preschool education; liberal arts and sciences/ liberal studies; marketing/marketing management; occupational safety and health technology; real estate; welding technology.

Academics *Calendar:* semesters. *Degree:* certificates, diplomas, and associate. *Special study options:* academic remediation for entering students, advanced placement credit, English as a second language, internships, part-time degree program, services for LD students, student-designed majors, summer session for credit.

Library Learning Resource Center.

Student Life *Housing:* college housing not available. *Activities and Organizations:* drama/theater group, student-run newspaper, choral group. *Campus security:* 24-hour emergency response devices, late-night transport/escort service. *Student services:* health clinic, personal/psychological counseling.

Athletics *Intercollegiate sports:* cross-country running M/W, soccer M/W. *Intramural sports:* basketball M/W, fencing M/W, racquetball M/W, soccer M/W, softball M/W, volleyball M/W.

Costs (2006–07) *Tuition:* state resident $754 full-time; nonresident $4929 full-time.

Financial Aid Of all full-time matriculated undergraduates, 28 Federal Work-Study jobs (averaging $1500).

Applying *Recommended:* high school transcript.

Director of Admissions Mrs. Sylvia R. Rodriguez, Director of Admissions and Records, Las Positas College, 3033 Collier Canyon Road, Livermore, CA 94551-7650. *Phone:* 925-373-4942.

LASSEN COMMUNITY COLLEGE DISTRICT

Susanville, California **www.lassencollege.edu/**

- **State and locally supported** 2-year, founded 1925, part of California Community College System
- **Rural** 100-acre campus
- **Coed,** 2,161 undergraduate students

Undergraduates Students come from 12 states and territories, 3 other countries.

Faculty *Total:* 204, 22% full-time.

Majors Accounting; administrative assistant and secretarial science; agricultural business and management; agricultural economics; agricultural mechanization; agriculture; agronomy and crop science; applied art; art; automobile/ automotive mechanics technology; biological and physical sciences; biology/ biological sciences; botany/plant biology; business administration and management; business machine repair; carpentry; ceramic arts and ceramics; chemistry; child guidance; commercial and advertising art; communications technology; computer science; construction engineering technology; construction trades; corrections; cosmetology; criminal justice/police science; drafting and design technology; drawing; energy management and systems technology; engineering technology; farm and ranch management; health and physical education; history; humanities; human services; information technology; journalism; kindergarten/preschool education; legal administrative assistant/secretary; liberal arts and sciences/ liberal studies; mass communication/media; mathematics; mathematics related; mechanical engineering/mechanical technology; medical administrative assistant and medical secretary; natural sciences; nursing (licensed practical/ vocational nurse training); nursing (registered nurse training); photography; physical education teaching and coaching; physical sciences; pre-engineering; psychology; radio and television; real estate; social sciences; substance abuse/ addiction counseling; welding technology.

Academics *Calendar:* semesters. *Degree:* certificates and associate. *Special study options:* academic remediation for entering students, adult/continuing education programs, advanced placement credit, cooperative education, English as a second language, internships, off-campus study, part-time degree program, services for LD students, summer session for credit.

Library Lassen College Library with 15,000 titles, 100 serial subscriptions.

Student Life *Housing Options:* coed. *Activities and Organizations:* drama/ theater group, student-run newspaper, Lassen Student Union. *Student services:* health clinic, legal services.

Athletics Member NJCAA. *Intercollegiate sports:* basketball M/W, cross-country running M/W, golf M/W, riflery M/W, softball W, track and field M/W, volleyball W, wrestling M. *Intramural sports:* basketball M/W, cross-country running M/W, equestrian sports M/W, football M, golf M/W, gymnastics M/W, racquetball M/W, riflery M/W, sailing M/W, skiing (cross-country) M/W, skiing

Lassen Community College District (continued)

(downhill) M/W, softball W, swimming and diving M/W, tennis M/W, track and field M/W, volleyball M/W, weight lifting M, wrestling M.

Standardized Tests *Recommended:* ACT (for placement).

Costs (2006–07) *Tuition:* state resident $567 full-time; nonresident $4944 full-time, $42 per unit part-time. Full-time tuition and fees vary according to reciprocity agreements. Part-time tuition and fees vary according to reciprocity agreements. *Required fees:* $26 per unit part-time, $5 per term part-time. *Room and board:* Room and board charges vary according to board plan. *Payment plan:* installment.

Financial Aid Of all full-time matriculated undergraduates, 165 Federal Work-Study jobs (averaging $3000). 35 state and other part-time jobs (averaging $1500).

Applying *Options:* early admission. *Recommended:* high school transcript. *Application deadlines:* rolling (freshmen), rolling (transfers). *Notification:* continuous (freshmen), continuous (transfers).

Freshmen Application Contact Mr. Chris J. Alberico, Registrar, Lassen Community College District, Highway 139, PO Box 3000, Susanville, CA 96130. *Phone:* 530-257-6181.

LONG BEACH CITY COLLEGE

Long Beach, California   www.lbcc.edu/

- **State-supported** 2-year, founded 1927, part of California Community College System
- **Urban** 40-acre campus with easy access to Los Angeles
- **Coed**

Undergraduates 9,580 full-time, 16,716 part-time. 1% are from out of state, 14% African American, 15% Asian American or Pacific Islander, 37% Hispanic American, 0.8% Native American, 3% transferred in.

Faculty *Student/faculty ratio:* 24:1.

Academics *Calendar:* semesters. *Degree:* certificates and associate. *Special study options:* academic remediation for entering students, adult/continuing education programs, advanced placement credit, distance learning, English as a second language, honors programs, internships, part-time degree program, services for LD students, summer session for credit.

Student Life *Campus security:* 24-hour emergency response devices and patrols, student patrols, late-night transport/escort service.

Athletics Member NJCAA.

Costs (2006–07) *Tuition:* state resident $0 full-time; nonresident $3840 full-time, $160 per unit part-time. *Required fees:* $692 full-time, $26 per unit part-time, $34 per term part-time.

Financial Aid Of all full-time matriculated undergraduates, 275 Federal Work-Study jobs (averaging $4400). 225 state and other part-time jobs (averaging $4400).

Applying *Options:* early admission. *Recommended:* high school transcript.

Director of Admissions Mr. Ross Miyashiro, Dean of Admissions and Records, Long Beach City College, 4901 East Carson Boulevard, Long Beach, CA 90808. *Phone:* 562-938-4130.

LOS ANGELES CITY COLLEGE

Los Angeles, California   www.lacitycollege.edu/

- **District-supported** 2-year, founded 1929, part of Los Angeles Community College District System
- **Urban** 42-acre campus
- **Coed,** 25,000 undergraduate students

Undergraduates Students come from 52 states and territories, 12% African American, 19% Asian American or Pacific Islander, 43% Hispanic American.

Faculty *Total:* 572, 44% full-time.

Majors Accounting; administrative assistant and secretarial science; advertising; African-American/Black studies; American studies; applied art; architectural engineering technology; art; biological and physical sciences; biology/biological sciences; broadcast journalism; business administration and management; ceramic arts and ceramics; chemistry; child development; clothing/textiles; computer and information sciences related; computer and information systems security; computer engineering technology; computer/information technology services administration related; computer programming; computer programming related; computer programming (specific applications); computer programming (vendor/product certification); computer software and media applications related; computer systems networking and telecommunications; computer/technical support; consumer merchandising/retailing management; corrections; criminal justice/law enforcement administration; criminal justice/police science; data entry/

microcomputer applications; data entry/microcomputer applications related; data processing and data processing technology; dental hygiene; developmental and child psychology; dietetics; drafting and design technology; dramatic/theater arts; electrical, electronic and communications engineering technology; engineering; English; family and consumer economics related; family and consumer sciences/human sciences; finance; food science; food services technology; French; German; Hispanic-American, Puerto Rican, and Mexican-American/Chicano studies; history; human services; industrial radiologic technology; information technology; journalism; legal administrative assistant/secretary; liberal arts and sciences/liberal studies; marketing/marketing management; mass communication/media; mathematics; medical administrative assistant and medical secretary; mental health/rehabilitation; music; nuclear medical technology; ophthalmic laboratory technology; photography; physics; psychology; public administration; public relations/image management; radio and television; radiologic technology/science; real estate; sociology; Spanish; special products marketing; speech and rhetoric; system administration; teacher assistant/aide; telecommunications; tourism and travel services management; web/multimedia management and webmaster; web page, digital/multimedia and information resources design; word processing.

Academics *Calendar:* semesters. *Degree:* certificates, diplomas, and associate. *Special study options:* academic remediation for entering students, adult/continuing education programs, advanced placement credit, English as a second language, honors programs, part-time degree program, services for LD students, study abroad, summer session for credit. *ROTC:* Army (c), Air Force (c).

Library 150,000 titles, 150 serial subscriptions.

Student Life *Housing:* college housing not available. *Activities and Organizations:* drama/theater group, student-run newspaper, choral group, marching band. *Campus security:* 24-hour emergency response devices and patrols, student patrols, late-night transport/escort service. *Student services:* health clinic, personal/psychological counseling.

Athletics *Intercollegiate sports:* basketball M, cross-country running M, football M, gymnastics M, track and field M/W, volleyball M/W. *Intramural sports:* archery M/W, badminton M/W, basketball W, bowling M/W, golf M/W, gymnastics W, soccer M/W, swimming and diving M/W, table tennis M/W, tennis M/W, weight lifting M/W, wrestling M.

Costs (2006–07) *Tuition:* area resident $698 full-time; state resident $698 full-time; nonresident $4832 full-time.

Applying *Application deadlines:* 9/5 (freshmen), 9/5 (transfers). *Notification:* continuous until 9/5 (freshmen), continuous until 9/5 (transfers).

Freshmen Application Contact Elaine Geismar, Director of Student Assistance Center, Los Angeles City College, 855 North Vermont Avenue, Los Angeles, CA 90029. *Phone:* 323-953-4340.

LOS ANGELES COUNTY COLLEGE OF NURSING AND ALLIED HEALTH

Los Angeles, California   www.ladhs.org/lacusc/lacnah/

Freshmen Application Contact Admissions Office, Los Angeles County College of Nursing and Allied Health, 1237 North Mission Road, Los Angeles, CA 90033. *Phone:* 323-226-4911.

LOS ANGELES HARBOR COLLEGE

Wilmington, California   www.lahc.edu/

- **State and locally supported** 2-year, founded 1949, part of Los Angeles Community College District System
- **Suburban** 80-acre campus
- **Coed,** 9,469 undergraduate students, 24% full-time, 61% women, 39% men

Undergraduates 2,311 full-time, 7,158 part-time. Students come from 14 states and territories, 15% African American, 17% Asian American or Pacific Islander, 43% Hispanic American.

Freshmen *Admission:* 1,970 applied, 1,970 admitted, 1,970 enrolled. *Average high school GPA:* 2.5.

Faculty *Total:* 270, 41% full-time. *Student/faculty ratio:* 40:1.

Majors Accounting; administrative assistant and secretarial science; architectural engineering technology; automobile/automotive mechanics technology; biology/biological sciences; business administration and management; computer engineering technology; criminal justice/police science; data processing and data processing technology; developmental and child psychology; drafting and design technology; electrical, electronic and communications engineering technology; electromechanical technology; engineering technology; fire science; information science/studies; legal administrative assistant/secretary; liberal arts and sciences/

liberal studies; medical administrative assistant and medical secretary; nursing (registered nurse training); physics; pre-engineering; real estate.

Academics *Calendar:* semesters. *Degree:* certificates and associate. *Special study options:* academic remediation for entering students, adult/continuing education programs, advanced placement credit, cooperative education, distance learning, double majors, English as a second language, freshman honors college, honors programs, independent study, off-campus study, part-time degree program, services for LD students, study abroad, summer session for credit.

Library Harbor College Library with 82,790 titles, 302 serial subscriptions, an OPAC, a Web page.

Student Life *Housing:* college housing not available. *Activities and Organizations:* drama/theater group, student-run radio and television station, choral group, Alpha Gamma Sigma, Abilities Unlimited, Students in Free Enterprise, Association of Future Firefighters. *Campus security:* 24-hour emergency response devices and patrols, late-night transport/escort service. *Student services:* health clinic, personal/psychological counseling, legal services.

Athletics *Intercollegiate sports:* baseball M, basketball M/W, football M, golf M, soccer M, tennis W, volleyball W.

Costs (2007–08) *Tuition:* state resident $0 full-time; nonresident $3816 full-time, $159 per unit part-time. *Required fees:* $504 full-time, $20 per unit part-time, $12 per term part-time.

Financial Aid Of all full-time matriculated undergraduates, 122 Federal Work-Study jobs (averaging $1800).

Applying *Options:* early admission, deferred entrance. *Application deadlines:* 9/3 (freshmen), 9/3 (out-of-state freshmen), 9/3 (transfers).

Director of Admissions Mr. David Ching, Dean of Admissions and Records, Los Angeles Harbor College, 1111 Figueroa Place, Wilmington, CA 90744-2397. *Phone:* 310-233-4091.

LOS ANGELES MISSION COLLEGE

Sylmar, California   www.lamission.edu/

- **State and locally supported** 2-year, founded 1974, part of Los Angeles Community College District System
- **Small-town** 22-acre campus with easy access to Los Angeles
- **Coed,** 7,617 undergraduate students

Undergraduates Students come from 8 other countries.

Faculty *Total:* 270, 31% full-time. *Student/faculty ratio:* 33:1.

Majors Accounting; administrative assistant and secretarial science; art teacher education; avionics maintenance technology; biology/biological sciences; business administration and management; chemistry; computer programming; consumer services and advocacy; criminal justice/police science; culinary arts; developmental and child psychology; dramatic/theater arts; economics; English; family and consumer economics related; family and consumer sciences/home economics teacher education; finance; French; geography; health teacher education; history; humanities; Italian; journalism; liberal arts and sciences/liberal studies; mathematics; music; philosophy; physical education teaching and coaching; physical sciences; psychology; real estate; social sciences; sociology; Spanish; speech and rhetoric; teacher assistant/aide.

Academics *Calendar:* semesters. *Degree:* associate. *Special study options:* academic remediation for entering students, adult/continuing education programs, advanced placement credit, cooperative education, English as a second language, external degree program, part-time degree program, services for LD students, summer session for credit.

Library Los Angeles Mission College with 40,000 titles, 450 serial subscriptions, an OPAC, a Web page.

Student Life *Housing:* college housing not available. *Activities and Organizations:* drama/theater group, student-run newspaper. *Campus security:* 24-hour emergency response devices and patrols, student patrols. *Student services:* personal/psychological counseling, women's center.

Costs (2006–07) *Tuition:* state resident $624 full-time; nonresident $4644 full-time.

Financial Aid Of all full-time matriculated undergraduates, 35 Federal Work-Study jobs (averaging $4000).

Applying *Options:* early admission. *Notification:* continuous until 9/25 (freshmen).

Freshmen Application Contact Ms. Angela Merrill, Admissions Supervisor, Los Angeles Mission College, 13356 Eldridge Avenue, Sylmar, CA 91342-3245. *Phone:* 818-364-7658.

LOS ANGELES PIERCE COLLEGE

Woodland Hills, California   www.lapc.cc.ca.us/

- **State and locally supported** 2-year, founded 1947, part of Los Angeles Community College District System
- **Suburban** 425-acre campus with easy access to Los Angeles
- **Coed,** 16,255 undergraduate students

Undergraduates Students come from 2 states and territories, 48 other countries.

Freshmen *Admission:* 26,070 applied, 26,070 admitted.

Faculty *Total:* 558.

Majors Accounting; agriculture; animal sciences; architectural engineering technology; art; automobile/automotive mechanics technology; computer engineering technology; computer programming; computer science; construction engineering technology; data processing and data processing technology; drafting and design technology; dramatic/theater arts; electrical, electronic and communications engineering technology; equestrian studies; horticultural science; industrial arts; industrial technology; journalism; landscape architecture; landscaping and groundskeeping; liberal arts and sciences/liberal studies; machine tool technology; music; nursing (registered nurse training); ornamental horticulture; photography; plant protection and integrated pest management; pre-engineering; quality control technology; real estate; sign language interpretation and translation; veterinary technology; welding technology.

Academics *Calendar:* semesters. *Degree:* certificates and associate. *Special study options:* academic remediation for entering students, adult/continuing education programs, advanced placement credit, cooperative education, distance learning, English as a second language, honors programs, independent study, internships, part-time degree program, services for LD students, study abroad, summer session for credit.

Library Pierce College Library plus 1 other with 106,122 titles, 395 serial subscriptions.

Student Life *Housing:* college housing not available. *Activities and Organizations:* drama/theater group, student-run newspaper, choral group, Alpha Gamma Sigma, Club Latino United for Education, United African-American Student Association, Hillel Club, Filipino Club. *Campus security:* 24-hour patrols, late-night transport/escort service. *Student services:* health clinic, personal/psychological counseling, women's center.

Athletics Member NJCAA. *Intercollegiate sports:* baseball M, basketball W, football M, softball W, swimming and diving M/W, tennis M/W, volleyball M/W, water polo M. *Intramural sports:* cross-country running M/W, equestrian sports M/W, fencing M/W, golf M/W, racquetball M/W, skiing (downhill) M/W, soccer M/W, swimming and diving M/W, tennis M/W, volleyball M/W, weight lifting M/W.

Costs (2007–08) *Tuition:* state resident $0 full-time; nonresident $4770 full-time, $159 per unit part-time. *Required fees:* $612 full-time, $20 per unit part-time, $12 per term part-time.

Financial Aid Of all full-time matriculated undergraduates, 124 Federal Work-Study jobs (averaging $3000). 28 state and other part-time jobs (averaging $3000).

Applying *Options:* electronic application, early admission. *Application deadline:* 8/20 (freshmen).

Director of Admissions Ms. Shelley L. Gerstl, Dean of Admissions and Records, Los Angeles Pierce College, 6201 Winnetka Avenue, Woodland Hills, CA 91371-0001. *Phone:* 818-719-6448.

LOS ANGELES SOUTHWEST COLLEGE

Los Angeles, California   www.lasc.cc.ca.us/

- **State and locally supported** 2-year, founded 1967, part of Los Angeles Community College District System
- **Urban** 69-acre campus
- **Coed,** 6,000 undergraduate students

Undergraduates Students come from 20 states and territories, 4 other countries.

Faculty *Total:* 223, 34% full-time.

Majors Accounting; administrative assistant and secretarial science; African studies; anthropology; behavioral sciences; biology/biological sciences; business administration and management; child development; computer science; criminal justice/law enforcement administration; criminal justice/police science; data processing and data processing technology; developmental and child psychology; drafting and design technology; dramatic/theater arts; economics; education; electrical, electronic and communications engineering technology; engineering; English; family and consumer economics related; finance; humanities; kindergarten/preschool education; marketing/marketing management; music; nursing (registered nurse training); quality control technology; radio and television; real estate; sign language interpretation and translation; social sciences; Spanish; teacher assistant/aide.

Academics *Calendar:* semesters. *Degree:* certificates, diplomas, and associate. *Special study options:* academic remediation for entering students, accelerated degree program, adult/continuing education programs, cooperative education, English as a second language, freshman honors college, honors programs, internships, part-time degree program, services for LD students, summer session for credit.

Los Angeles Southwest College (continued)

Library Main Library plus 1 other with 60,000 titles, 600 serial subscriptions, an OPAC, a Web page.

Student Life *Housing:* college housing not available. *Activities and Organizations:* student-run newspaper, choral group. *Campus security:* 24-hour emergency response devices and patrols, student patrols, late-night transport/escort service.

Athletics *Intercollegiate sports:* basketball M/W, cross-country running M/W, football M, track and field M/W. *Intramural sports:* archery M/W, badminton M/W, basketball M/W, bowling M/W, cross-country running M/W, golf M/W, volleyball M/W.

Costs (2006–07) *Tuition:* state resident $698 full-time; nonresident $4832 full-time.

Applying *Options:* early admission. *Required for some:* high school transcript. *Recommended:* essay or personal statement, minimum 2.0 GPA. *Application deadline:* 9/9 (freshmen). *Notification:* continuous until 9/9 (freshmen).

Director of Admissions Dan W. Walden, Dean of Academic Affairs, Los Angeles Southwest College, 1600 West Imperial Highway, Los Angeles, CA 90047-4810. *Phone:* 323-242-5511.

LOS ANGELES TRADE-TECHNICAL COLLEGE

Los Angeles, California   www.lattc.edu/

Director of Admissions Mrs. Rosemary Royal, Dean of Enrollment Management, Los Angeles Trade-Technical College, 400 West Washington Boulevard, Los Angeles, CA 90015. *Phone:* 213-763-5301.

LOS ANGELES VALLEY COLLEGE

Van Nuys, California   www.lavc.cc.ca.us/

Director of Admissions Mr. Florentino Manzano, Associate Dean, Los Angeles Valley College, 5800 Fulton Avenue, Valley Glen, CA 91401. *Phone:* 818-947-2353. *E-mail:* manzanf@lavc.edu.

LOS MEDANOS COLLEGE

Pittsburg, California   www.losmedanos.net/

- **District-supported** 2-year, founded 1974, part of California Community College System
- **Suburban** 120-acre campus with easy access to San Francisco
- **Coed,** 7,152 undergraduate students

Undergraduates Students come from 3 states and territories, 15 other countries, 0.2% are from out of state.

Faculty *Total:* 244, 43% full-time.

Majors Accounting; administrative assistant and secretarial science; anthropology; art; automobile/automotive mechanics technology; behavioral sciences; biology/biological sciences; business administration and management; business/managerial economics; chemistry; commercial and advertising art; developmental and child psychology; drafting and design technology; electrical, electronic and communications engineering technology; emergency medical technology (EMT paramedic); fire science; heating, air conditioning, ventilation and refrigeration maintenance technology; journalism; liberal arts and sciences/liberal studies; mathematics; music; music management and merchandising; nursing (registered nurse training); psychology; real estate; small engine mechanics and repair technology; sociology; tourism and travel services management; welding technology.

Academics *Calendar:* semesters. *Degree:* certificates and associate. *Special study options:* academic remediation for entering students, advanced placement credit, cooperative education, double majors, English as a second language, honors programs, independent study, part-time degree program, services for LD students, study abroad, summer session for credit.

Library Learning Resource Center with 15,439 titles, 205 serial subscriptions.

Student Life *Housing:* college housing not available. *Activities and Organizations:* student-run newspaper, choral group, Alpha Gamma Sigma, Christian Fellowship Club, Student Nurses Association, La Raza Club. *Campus security:* 24-hour patrols, student patrols, late-night transport/escort service. *Student services:* women's center.

Athletics *Intercollegiate sports:* baseball M, basketball M/W, football M, soccer M, softball W, volleyball W.

Standardized Tests *Required for some:* Assessment and Placement Services for Community Colleges.

Costs (2006–07) *Tuition:* state resident $732 full-time; nonresident $4526 full-time.

Financial Aid Of all full-time matriculated undergraduates, 150 Federal Work-Study jobs (averaging $800).

Applying *Required for some:* high school transcript. *Application deadlines:* 8/29 (freshmen), 8/29 (transfers). *Notification:* continuous until 8/29 (freshmen), continuous until 8/29 (transfers).

Freshmen Application Contact Ms. Gail Newman, Director of Admissions and Records, Los Medanos College, 2700 East Leland Road, Pittsburg, CA 94565-5197. *Phone:* 925-439-2181 Ext. 7500.

MARIC COLLEGE

Anaheim, California   www.mariccollege.edu/

Freshmen Application Contact Renee Codner, Director of Admissions, Maric College, 1360 South Anaheim Boulevard, Anaheim, CA 92805. *Toll-free phone:* 800-206-0095. *E-mail:* rcodner@mariccollege.edu.

MARIC COLLEGE

North Hollywood, California   www.mariccollege.edu/

Freshmen Application Contact Ms. Renee Codner, Director of Admissions, Maric College, 6180 Laurel Canyon Boulevard, Suite 101, North Hollywood, CA 91606. *Phone:* 818-763-2563 Ext. 240. *Toll-free phone:* 800-404-9729. *E-mail:* rcodner@mariccollege.edu.

MARIC COLLEGE

Panorama City, California   www.mariccollege.edu/

- **Proprietary** 2-year, founded 1996
- **Coed,** 529 undergraduate students

Majors Business administration, management and operations related; computer and information sciences related; court reporting; legal assistant/paralegal.

Academics *Degree:* associate.

Costs (2006–07) *Tuition:* $11,340 full-time. *Required fees:* $45 full-time. *Payment plan:* installment. *Waivers:* employees or children of employees.

Freshmen Application Contact Linda King, Director of Admissions, Maric College, 14355 Roscoe Boulevard, Panorama City, PA 91402. *Phone:* 818-672-3005. *Toll-free phone:* 800-206-0095. *E-mail:* lking@mariccollege.edu.

MARIC COLLEGE

Sacramento, California   www.mariccollege.edu/maric_sacramento.html

Freshmen Application Contact Charlie Reese, Director of Admissions, Maric College, 4330 Watt Avenue, Suite 400, Sacramento, CA 95821. *Phone:* 916-649-8168. *Toll-free phone:* 800-955-8168. *Fax:* 916-649-8344.

MARIC COLLEGE

Salida, California   www.mariccollege.edu/

Freshmen Application Contact Ms. Renee Codner, Director of Admissions, Maric College, 5172 Kiernan Court, Salida, CA 95368. *Phone:* 209-543-7000. *E-mail:* rcodner@mariccollege.edu.

MARIC COLLEGE

San Diego, California   **www.mariccollege.edu/**

- **Proprietary** 2-year, founded 1976
- **Urban** 4-acre campus
- **Coed,** 298 undergraduate students, 100% full-time, 90% women, 10% men

Undergraduates 298 full-time. 9% African American, 3% Asian American or Pacific Islander, 40% Hispanic American, 4% Native American.

Freshmen *Admission:* 5 enrolled.

Faculty *Total:* 65, 69% full-time.

Majors Nursing (registered nurse training).

Academics *Calendar:* semesters. *Degrees:* certificates and associate (also includes Vista campus). *Special study options:* academic remediation for entering students, adult/continuing education programs, internships, summer session for credit.

Library Student Resource Center.

Student Life *Housing:* college housing not available. *Campus security:* 24-hour patrols.

Costs (2006–07) *Tuition:* Contact college directly as tuition varies by program.

Applying *Required:* essay or personal statement, high school transcript, interview. *Notification:* continuous (freshmen).

Freshmen Application Contact Ms. Renee Codner, Director of Admissions, Maric College, 3666 Kearny Villa Road, Suite 100, San Diego, CA 92123-1995. *Phone:* 858-654-3601. *Toll-free phone:* 800-400-8232. *E-mail:* rcodner@ mariccollege.edu.

MARYMOUNT COLLEGE, PALOS VERDES, CALIFORNIA

Rancho Palos Verdes, California   **www.marymountpv.edu/**

- **Independent Roman Catholic** 2-year, founded 1932
- **Suburban** 26-acre campus with easy access to Los Angeles
- **Coed,** 652 undergraduate students, 96% full-time, 54% women, 46% men

Undergraduates 627 full-time, 25 part-time. Students come from 26 states and territories, 21 other countries, 23% are from out of state, 4% African American, 8% Asian American or Pacific Islander, 19% Hispanic American, 0.8% Native American, 10% international, 68% live on campus. *Retention:* 53% of 2003 full-time freshmen returned.

Freshmen *Admission:* 1,224 applied, 806 admitted, 305 enrolled. *Average high school GPA:* 2.63.

Faculty *Total:* 91, 46% full-time, 35% with terminal degrees. *Student/faculty ratio:* 16:1.

Majors Liberal arts and sciences/liberal studies.

Academics *Calendar:* semesters. *Degree:* associate. *Special study options:* academic remediation for entering students, adult/continuing education programs, advanced placement credit, English as a second language, honors programs, independent study, internships, part-time degree program, services for LD students, study abroad, summer session for credit.

Library College Library plus 1 other with 42,104 titles, 328 serial subscriptions, an OPAC.

Student Life *Housing Options:* coed. Campus housing is university owned. *Activities and Organizations:* drama/theater group, student-run newspaper, choral group, Socratic Circle, Hawaii Club, Ski Club, African-American Student Union, MOVE (Marymount Opportunities for Volunteer Experiences). *Campus security:* 24-hour patrols, late-night transport/escort service, controlled dormitory access. *Student services:* health clinic, personal/psychological counseling.

Athletics Member NJCAA. *Intercollegiate sports:* golf M/W, tennis M(s)/ W(s). *Intramural sports:* archery M, basketball M/W, golf M/W, soccer M/W, softball M/W, swimming and diving M/W, tennis M/W, volleyball M/W.

Standardized Tests *Recommended:* SAT or ACT (for admission).

Costs (2007–08) *Comprehensive fee:* $31,445 includes full-time tuition ($21,230), mandatory fees ($321), and room and board ($9894). Part-time tuition: $700 per unit.

Financial Aid Of all full-time matriculated undergraduates, 40 Federal Work-Study jobs (averaging $1500).

Applying *Options:* electronic application, early admission. *Application fee:* $35. *Required:* high school transcript. *Required for some:* essay or personal statement, letters of recommendation, interview. *Recommended:* minimum 2.0 GPA. *Application deadlines:* 7/1 (freshmen), 8/15 (transfers). *Notification:* continuous until 9/1 (freshmen), continuous until 9/1 (transfers).

Freshmen Application Contact Ms. Nina Lococo, Dean of Admission and Financial Aid, Marymount College, Palos Verdes, California, 30800 Palos Verdes Drive East, Rancho Palos Verdes, CA 90815. *Phone:* 310-377-5501. *Fax:* 310-265-0962. *E-mail:* admissions@marymountpv.edu.

MENDOCINO COLLEGE

Ukiah, California   **www.mendocino.cc.ca.us/**

- **State and locally supported** 2-year, founded 1973, part of California Community College System
- **Rural** 127-acre campus
- **Coed,** 5,400 undergraduate students

Undergraduates Students come from 16 states and territories, 1% African American, 2% Asian American or Pacific Islander, 12% Hispanic American, 4% Native American.

Freshmen *Admission:* 459 applied, 459 admitted.

Faculty *Total:* 240, 22% full-time, 4% with terminal degrees. *Student/faculty ratio:* 12:1.

Majors Accounting; administrative assistant and secretarial science; agriculture; animal sciences; art; automobile/automotive mechanics technology; biology/ biological sciences; business administration and management; chemistry; child development; criminal justice/law enforcement administration; criminal justice/ police science; cultural studies; data processing and data processing technology; developmental and child psychology; dramatic/theater arts; electrical, electronic and communications engineering technology; English; fiber, textile and weaving arts; finance; French; health science; human services; information science/ studies; kindergarten/preschool education; liberal arts and sciences/liberal studies; mathematics; music; ornamental horticulture; physical education teaching and coaching; physical sciences; psychology; real estate; social sciences; Spanish; speech and rhetoric; substance abuse/addiction counseling; welding technology.

Academics *Calendar:* semesters. *Degree:* certificates and associate. *Special study options:* academic remediation for entering students, adult/continuing education programs, advanced placement credit, cooperative education, English as a second language, honors programs, internships, part-time degree program, services for LD students, summer session for credit.

Library Lowery Library with 27,441 titles, 275 serial subscriptions.

Student Life *Housing:* college housing not available. *Activities and Organizations:* drama/theater group, student-run newspaper. *Campus security:* late-night transport/escort service, security patrols 6 p.m. to 10 p.m. *Student services:* personal/psychological counseling.

Athletics *Intercollegiate sports:* baseball M, basketball M/W, football M, golf M, track and field M/W, volleyball W. *Intramural sports:* bowling M/W, table tennis M/W, tennis M/W.

Costs (2006–07) *Tuition:* state resident $658 full-time; nonresident $4234 full-time.

Financial Aid *Financial aid deadline:* 5/20.

Applying *Options:* early admission, deferred entrance. *Application deadlines:* rolling (freshmen), rolling (transfers). *Notification:* continuous (freshmen), continuous (transfers).

Director of Admissions Ms. Kristie Anderson, Director of Admissions and Records, Mendocino College, 1000 Hensley Creek Road, Ukiah, CA 95482-0300. *Phone:* 707-468-3103. *Fax:* 707-468-3430. *E-mail:* kanderson@ mendocino.edu.

MERCED COLLEGE

Merced, California   **www.mccd.edu/**

- **State and locally supported** 2-year, founded 1962, part of California Community College System
- **Small-town** 269-acre campus
- **Coed,** 12,525 undergraduate students, 37% full-time, 69% women, 31% men

Undergraduates 4,598 full-time, 7,927 part-time. Students come from 30 states and territories, 2% are from out of state, 5% African American, 10% Asian American or Pacific Islander, 37% Hispanic American, 1% Native American.

Freshmen *Admission:* 2,593 applied, 2,593 admitted.

Faculty *Total:* 421, 34% full-time.

Majors Accounting; administrative assistant and secretarial science; agricultural business and management; agriculture; agronomy and crop science; airframe mechanics and aircraft maintenance technology; animal sciences; applied art; art; automobile/automotive mechanics technology; biological and physical sciences; business administration and management; carpentry; computer engineering technology; computer science; construction engineering technology; consumer

Merced College (continued)

merchandising/retailing management; criminal justice/police science; data processing and data processing technology; dental hygiene; developmental and child psychology; dietetics; dramatic/theater arts; electrical, electronic and communications engineering technology; environmental engineering technology; family and consumer sciences/human sciences; fashion/apparel design; fashion merchandising; finance; fire science; humanities; human services; industrial arts; industrial radiologic technology; insurance; kindergarten/preschool education; landscape architecture; legal administrative assistant/secretary; liberal arts and sciences/liberal studies; library science; management information systems; marketing/marketing management; mathematics; medical administrative assistant and medical secretary; medical/clinical assistant; music; natural sciences; nursing (licensed practical/vocational nurse training); nursing (registered nurse training); ornamental horticulture; physical education teaching and coaching; physical sciences; political science and government; pre-engineering; real estate; social sciences; special products marketing; teacher assistant/aide.

Academics *Calendar:* semesters. *Degree:* certificates and associate. *Special study options:* academic remediation for entering students, adult/continuing education programs, advanced placement credit, cooperative education, English as a second language, honors programs, internships, off-campus study, part-time degree program, student-designed majors, study abroad, summer session for credit. *ROTC:* Army (c).

Library Lesher Library with 45,000 titles, 200 serial subscriptions, 300 audiovisual materials, an OPAC.

Student Life *Housing:* college housing not available. *Activities and Organizations:* drama/theater group, student-run newspaper, choral group. *Campus security:* 24-hour patrols, late-night transport/escort service. *Student services:* health clinic, personal/psychological counseling, women's center, legal services.

Athletics *Intercollegiate sports:* baseball M, basketball M/W, bowling M/W, cross-country running M, equestrian sports M/W, football M, golf M/W, soccer M, softball W, swimming and diving M/W, tennis M/W, track and field M/W, volleyball M/W, water polo M.

Costs (2007–08) *Tuition:* state resident $0 full-time; nonresident $4152 full-time, $173 per unit part-time. *Required fees:* $548 full-time, $20 per unit part-time, $34 per term part-time.

Financial Aid Of all full-time matriculated undergraduates, 329 Federal Work-Study jobs (averaging $3545). 231 state and other part-time jobs (averaging $3545).

Applying *Options:* early admission. *Recommended:* high school transcript. *Application deadlines:* rolling (freshmen), rolling (transfers). *Notification:* continuous (freshmen), continuous (transfers).

Freshmen Application Contact Ms. Sherry Elms, Associate Registrar, Merced College, 3600 M Street, Merced, CA 95348-2898. *Phone:* 209-384-6188. *Fax:* 209-384-6339.

MERRITT COLLEGE
Oakland, California **www.merritt.edu/**

Freshmen Application Contact Ms. Barbara Simmons, District Admissions Officer, Merritt College, 12500 Campus Drive, Oakland, CA 94619-3196. *Phone:* 510-466-7369. *E-mail:* hperdue@peralta.cc.ca.us.

MIRACOSTA COLLEGE
Oceanside, California **www.miracosta.edu/**

- **State-supported** 2-year, founded 1934, part of California Community College System
- **Suburban** 131-acre campus with easy access to San Diego
- **Endowment** $894,495
- **Coed**

MiraCosta College's campuses in Oceanside and Cardiff are minutes from the beach. MiraCosta offers a strong university transfer program, including transfer admission guarantees. Courses of special interest include computer science, horticulture, multimedia, and music technology. Facilities include technology hubs at both campuses and a wellness center at the Oceanside campus.

Undergraduates Students come from 37 states and territories, 44 other countries, 2% are from out of state.

Faculty *Student/faculty ratio:* 23:1.

Academics *Calendar:* semesters. *Degree:* certificates, diplomas, and associate. *Special study options:* academic remediation for entering students, accelerated degree program, adult/continuing education programs, advanced placement credit, cooperative education, distance learning, double majors, English as a

second language, freshman honors college, honors programs, independent study, internships, part-time degree program, services for LD students, student-designed majors, study abroad, summer session for credit.

Student Life *Campus security:* 24-hour emergency response devices, student patrols, late-night transport/escort service, trained security personnel during class hours.

Athletics Member NJCAA.

Costs (2006–07) *Tuition:* state resident $0 full-time; nonresident $4800 full-time, $160 per unit part-time. *Required fees:* $804 full-time, $26 per unit part-time.

Financial Aid Of all full-time matriculated undergraduates, 83 Federal Work-Study jobs (averaging $1315).

Applying *Options:* early admission, deferred entrance.

Freshmen Application Contact Admissions and Records Assistant, MiraCosta College, One Barnard Drive, Oceanside, CA 92056. *Phone:* 760-795-6620. *Toll-free phone:* 888-201-8480.

MISSION COLLEGE
Santa Clara, California **www.missioncollege.org/**

- **State and locally supported** 2-year, founded 1977, part of California Community College System
- **Urban** 167-acre campus with easy access to San Francisco and San Jose
- **Coed,** 10,500 undergraduate students, 38% full-time, 52% women, 48% men

Undergraduates 4,000 full-time, 6,500 part-time. Students come from 18 other countries, 0.3% are from out of state, 8% African American, 52% Asian American or Pacific Islander, 14% Hispanic American, 0.2% Native American, 3% international, 0.5% transferred in.

Freshmen *Admission:* 1,260 enrolled.

Faculty *Total:* 390, 46% full-time, 26% with terminal degrees. *Student/faculty ratio:* 26:1.

Majors Accounting; administrative assistant and secretarial science; art; business administration and management; commercial and advertising art; computer engineering technology; computer programming; data processing and data processing technology; drafting and design technology; electrical, electronic and communications engineering technology; electrical/electronics drafting and CAD/CADD; fire science; food services technology; graphic and printing equipment operation/production; health science; information science/studies; liberal arts and sciences/liberal studies; marketing/marketing management; mathematics; nursing (licensed practical/vocational nurse training); pre-engineering; real estate; social sciences; special products marketing.

Academics *Calendar:* semesters. *Degree:* certificates, diplomas, and associate. *Special study options:* academic remediation for entering students, adult/continuing education programs, cooperative education, distance learning, double majors, English as a second language, independent study, internships, part-time degree program, services for LD students, summer session for credit. *ROTC:* Army (c), Air Force (c).

Library 43,456 titles, 323 serial subscriptions.

Student Life *Housing:* college housing not available. *Campus security:* 24-hour emergency response devices, late-night transport/escort service. *Student services:* personal/psychological counseling.

Athletics *Intercollegiate sports:* badminton M/W(s), baseball M, basketball W, soccer M/W, softball W, tennis M/W.

Standardized Tests *Recommended:* SAT (for placement).

Costs (2006–07) *Tuition:* state resident $552 full-time; nonresident $3840 full-time.

Financial Aid Of all full-time matriculated undergraduates, 75 Federal Work-Study jobs (averaging $2000). *Financial aid deadline:* 5/15.

Applying *Options:* electronic application, early admission. *Application deadline:* rolling (freshmen). *Notification:* continuous (freshmen), continuous (transfers).

Director of Admissions Daniel Sanidad, Dean of Student Services, Mission College, 3000 Mission College Boulevard, Santa Clara, CA 95054-1897. *Phone:* 408-855-5139.

MODESTO JUNIOR COLLEGE
Modesto, California **www.mjc.edu/**

- **State and locally supported** 2-year, founded 1921, part of Yosemite Community College District System
- **Urban** 229-acre campus
- **Endowment** $817,811
- **Coed**

Faculty *Student/faculty ratio:* 40:1.

Academics *Calendar:* semesters. *Degree:* certificates and associate. *Special study options:* academic remediation for entering students, adult/continuing education programs, advanced placement credit, cooperative education, distance learning, English as a second language, honors programs, independent study, part-time degree program, services for LD students, study abroad, summer session for credit.

Student Life *Campus security:* 24-hour emergency response devices and patrols, late-night transport/escort service.

Costs (2006–07) *Tuition:* state resident $0 full-time; nonresident $3840 full-time, $160 per unit part-time. *Required fees:* $664 full-time, $26 per unit part-time, $40 per year part-time.

Financial Aid Of all full-time matriculated undergraduates, 152 Federal Work-Study jobs (averaging $2732). 62 state and other part-time jobs (averaging $1655).

Applying *Options:* electronic application. *Recommended:* high school transcript.

Freshmen Application Contact Ms. Susie Agostini, Dean of Matriculation, Admissions, and Records, Modesto Junior College, 435 College Avenue, Modesto, CA 95350. *Phone:* 209-575-6470. *Fax:* 209-575-6859. *E-mail:* mjcadmissions@mail.yosemite.cc.ca.us.

MONTEREY PENINSULA COLLEGE
Monterey, California www.mpc.edu/

- **State-supported** 2-year, founded 1947, part of California Community College System
- **Small-town** 87-acre campus
- **Coed,** 14,074 undergraduate students

Undergraduates Students come from 29 states and territories, 47 other countries.

Faculty *Total:* 317, 43% full-time.

Majors Accounting; administrative assistant and secretarial science; anthropology; art; art history, criticism and conservation; automobile/automotive mechanics technology; biology/biological sciences; business administration and management; ceramic arts and ceramics; chemistry; child development; clothing/textiles; commercial and advertising art; computer engineering technology; computer science; computer typography and composition equipment operation; criminal justice/law enforcement administration; criminal justice/police science; cultural studies; dance; data processing and data processing technology; dental hygiene; dramatic/theater arts; drawing; economics; engineering; English; family and consumer economics related; fashion merchandising; fiber, textile and weaving arts; fine/studio arts; fire science; fish/game management; French; geology/earth science; German; history; hospitality administration; hotel/motel administration; information science/studies; interior design; international business/trade/commerce; kindergarten/preschool education; kinesiology and exercise science; legal administrative assistant/secretary; liberal arts and sciences/liberal studies; marketing/marketing management; mass communication/media; mathematics; medical administrative assistant and medical secretary; medical/clinical assistant; metal and jewelry arts; music; nursing (registered nurse training); occupational therapy; ornamental horticulture; parks, recreation and leisure facilities management; philosophy; photography; physical education teaching and coaching; physical therapy; physics; political science and government; psychology; real estate; sculpture; sociology; Spanish; wildlife and wildlands science and management; women's studies.

Academics *Calendar:* semesters. *Degree:* certificates and associate. *Special study options:* academic remediation for entering students, adult/continuing education programs, advanced placement credit, cooperative education, English as a second language, part-time degree program, services for LD students, summer session for credit.

Library Monterey Peninsula College Library with 52,000 titles, 281 serial subscriptions, 2,623 audiovisual materials, an OPAC, a Web page.

Student Life *Housing:* college housing not available. *Activities and Organizations:* drama/theater group, student-run newspaper, choral group. *Campus security:* 24-hour emergency response devices, late-night transport/escort service. *Student services:* health clinic, personal/psychological counseling, women's center.

Athletics *Intercollegiate sports:* baseball M, basketball M, cross-country running M/W, football M, golf M/W, softball W, swimming and diving M/W, tennis M/W, track and field M/W, volleyball W.

Costs (2006–07) *Tuition:* state resident $674 full-time; nonresident $4298 full-time.

Financial Aid Of all full-time matriculated undergraduates, 167 Federal Work-Study jobs.

Applying *Options:* early admission. *Application deadlines:* rolling (freshmen), rolling (transfers). *Notification:* continuous (freshmen), continuous (transfers).

Director of Admissions Ms. Vera Coleman, Registrar, Monterey Peninsula College, 980 Fremont Street, Monterey, CA 93940. *Phone:* 831-646-4007. *E-mail:* vcoleman@mpc.edu.

MOORPARK COLLEGE
Moorpark, California www.moorpark.cc.ca.us/

- **County-supported** 2-year, founded 1967, part of Ventura County Community College District System
- **Small-town** 121-acre campus with easy access to Los Angeles
- **Coed,** 15,266 undergraduate students, 41% full-time, 56% women, 44% men

Undergraduates 6,183 full-time, 9,083 part-time. Students come from 45 states and territories, 50 other countries, 2% African American, 11% Asian American or Pacific Islander, 15% Hispanic American, 1% Native American.

Freshmen *Admission:* 2,000 applied, 2,000 admitted.

Faculty *Total:* 590, 29% full-time. *Student/faculty ratio:* 30:1.

Majors Accounting; animal sciences; anthropology; art; behavioral sciences; biology/biological sciences; broadcast journalism; business administration and management; business machine repair; chemistry; commercial and advertising art; computer science; corrections; criminal justice/law enforcement administration; criminal justice/police science; data processing and data processing technology; dramatic/theater arts; electrical, electronic and communications engineering technology; engineering; engineering technology; fashion/apparel design; film/cinema studies; geology/earth science; graphic and printing equipment operation/production; information science/studies; journalism; kindergarten/preschool education; laser and optical technology; liberal arts and sciences/liberal studies; marketing/marketing management; mathematics; music; natural sciences; nursing (registered nurse training); photography; teacher assistant/aide; telecommunications; wildlife and wildlands science and management.

Academics *Calendar:* semesters. *Degree:* certificates and associate. *Special study options:* academic remediation for entering students, adult/continuing education programs, advanced placement credit, cooperative education, distance learning, English as a second language, honors programs, independent study, internships, part-time degree program, services for LD students, summer session for credit.

Library 50,000 titles, 100 serial subscriptions.

Student Life *Housing:* college housing not available. *Activities and Organizations:* student-run newspaper. *Campus security:* 24-hour patrols. *Student services:* health clinic, personal/psychological counseling, women's center.

Athletics *Intercollegiate sports:* baseball M, basketball M/W, cross-country running M/W, football M, golf M/W, soccer M/W, softball W, track and field M/W, volleyball M/W, wrestling M.

Costs (2006–07) *Tuition:* state resident $822 full-time; nonresident $5892 full-time.

Financial Aid Of all full-time matriculated undergraduates, 70 Federal Work-Study jobs (averaging $2000).

Applying *Options:* electronic application, early admission, deferred entrance. *Required for some:* high school transcript. *Recommended:* high school transcript. *Application deadlines:* rolling (freshmen), rolling (transfers). *Notification:* continuous (freshmen), continuous (transfers).

Freshmen Application Contact Ms. Kathy Colborn, Registrar, Moorpark College, 7075 Campus Road, Moorpark, CA 93021-2899. *Phone:* 805-378-1415.

MT. SAN ANTONIO COLLEGE
Walnut, California www.mtsac.edu/

- **District-supported** 2-year, founded 1946, part of California Community College System
- **Suburban** 421-acre campus with easy access to Los Angeles
- **Coed,** 29,079 undergraduate students, 31% full-time, 54% women, 46% men

Undergraduates 9,147 full-time, 19,932 part-time. Students come from 51 states and territories, 6% African American, 24% Asian American or Pacific Islander, 45% Hispanic American, 0.5% Native American, 1% international.

Freshmen *Admission:* 3,757 enrolled.

Faculty *Total:* 1,330, 29% full-time.

Majors Accounting; administrative assistant and secretarial science; advertising; agricultural business and management; agricultural mechanization; agriculture; agronomy and crop science; airframe mechanics and aircraft maintenance technology; airline pilot and flight crew; air traffic control; animal sciences; apparel and textiles; architectural engineering technology; avionics maintenance technology; business administration and management; business teacher educa-

Mt. San Antonio College (continued)

tion; child development; civil engineering technology; commercial and advertising art; computer engineering technology; computer graphics; computer science; construction management; corrections; criminal justice/police science; dairy science; data processing and data processing technology; drafting and design technology; electrical, electronic and communications engineering technology; emergency medical technology (EMT paramedic); engineering technology; family and consumer sciences/human sciences; fashion merchandising; finance; fire science; forestry technology; heating, air conditioning, ventilation and refrigeration maintenance technology; horticultural science; hotel/motel administration; industrial arts; industrial design; industrial radiologic technology; interior design; journalism; kindergarten/preschool education; landscape architecture; legal administrative assistant/secretary; legal assistant/paralegal; liberal arts and sciences/liberal studies; machine tool technology; marketing/marketing management; materials science; mechanical design technology; medical administrative assistant and medical secretary; mental health/rehabilitation; nursing (registered nurse training); occupational safety and health technology; ornamental horticulture; parks, recreation and leisure; parks, recreation and leisure facilities management; photography; physical sciences related; pre-engineering; quality control technology; radio and television; real estate; respiratory care therapy; sign language interpretation and translation; survey technology; transportation technology; welding technology; wildlife and wildlands science and management.

Academics *Calendar:* semesters. *Degree:* certificates, diplomas, and associate. *Special study options:* academic remediation for entering students, adult/continuing education programs, cooperative education, distance learning, English as a second language, honors programs, part-time degree program, services for LD students, study abroad, summer session for credit.

Library Learning Resources Center with 64,291 titles, 753 serial subscriptions, an OPAC, a Web page.

Student Life *Housing:* college housing not available. *Activities and Organizations:* drama/theater group, student-run radio station, choral group, Alpha Gamma Sigma, Muslim Student Association, student government, Asian Student Association, Kasama-Filipino Student Organization. *Campus security:* 24-hour emergency response devices and patrols, late-night transport/escort service. *Student services:* health clinic, personal/psychological counseling, women's center, legal services.

Athletics *Intercollegiate sports:* badminton W, baseball M, basketball M/W, cross-country running M/W, football M, golf M/W, soccer M/W, softball W, swimming and diving M/W, tennis M/W, track and field M/W, volleyball M/W, water polo M/W, wrestling M.

Costs (2006–07) *Tuition:* state resident $0 full-time; nonresident $4320 full-time, $186 per unit part-time. Full-time tuition and fees vary according to course load. Part-time tuition and fees vary according to course load. *Required fees:* $532 full-time, $26 per unit part-time, $25 per term part-time.

Financial Aid Of all full-time matriculated undergraduates, 250 Federal Work-Study jobs (averaging $2898).

Applying *Options:* early admission, deferred entrance. *Required for some:* high school transcript. *Notification:* continuous (freshmen), continuous (transfers).

Freshmen Application Contact Mr. James Ocampo, Interim Director of Admissions and Records, Mt. San Antonio College, 1100 North Grand Avenue, Walnut, CA 91789. *Phone:* 909-594-5611 Ext. 4415. *Toll-free phone:* 800-672-2463 Ext. 4415. *Fax:* 909-468-4068. *E-mail:* admissions@mtsac.edu.

Mt. San Jacinto College

San Jacinto, California   www.msjc.edu/

Freshmen Application Contact Ms. Susan Loomis, Supervisor, Enrollment Services, Mt. San Jacinto College, 1499 North State Street, San Jacinto, CA 92583-2399. *Phone:* 909-672-6752 Ext. 2401. *Toll-free phone:* 800-624-5561 Ext. 1410.

MTI College of Business & Technology

Sacramento, California   www.mticollege.com/

- **Proprietary** 2-year, founded 1965
- **Coed**

Academics *Calendar:* continuous. *Degree:* diplomas and associate.

Standardized Tests *Required:* MTI Assessment (for admission).

Financial Aid Of all full-time matriculated undergraduates, 35 Federal Work-Study jobs (averaging $1722).

Applying *Application fee:* $75.

Freshmen Application Contact Ms. Marije Miller, Director of Admissions, MTI College of Business & Technology, 5221 Madison Avenue, Sacramento, CA 95841. *Phone:* 916-339-1500. *Fax:* 916-339-0305. *E-mail:* mmiller@mticollege.edu.

Napa Valley College

Napa, California   www.napavalley.edu/

- **State and locally supported** 2-year, founded 1942, part of California Community College System
- **Suburban** 188-acre campus with easy access to San Francisco
- **Coed,** 6,908 undergraduate students, 28% full-time, 61% women, 39% men

Undergraduates 1,909 full-time, 4,999 part-time. 8% African American, 18% Asian American or Pacific Islander, 20% Hispanic American, 1% Native American. *Retention:* 66% of 2003 full-time freshmen returned.

Freshmen *Admission:* 2,000 applied, 2,000 admitted, 525 enrolled.

Faculty *Total:* 311, 32% full-time. *Student/faculty ratio:* 22:1.

Majors Accounting; administrative assistant and secretarial science; agriculture; art; behavioral sciences; biological and physical sciences; biomedical technology; business administration and management; child development; communications technology; computer science; corrections; cosmetology; criminal justice/law enforcement administration; criminal justice/police science; data processing and data processing technology; drafting and design technology; electrical, electronic and communications engineering technology; emergency medical technology (EMT paramedic); engineering; environmental engineering technology; environmental studies; humanities; kindergarten/preschool education; legal administrative assistant/secretary; legal assistant/paralegal; machine tool technology; management information systems; marketing/marketing management; music; nursing (registered nurse training); photography; radio and television; real estate; respiratory care therapy; telecommunications; welding technology.

Academics *Calendar:* semesters. *Degree:* certificates and associate. *Special study options:* academic remediation for entering students, advanced placement credit, cooperative education, distance learning, English as a second language, part-time degree program, services for LD students, study abroad, summer session for credit.

Library Napa Valley College Library plus 1 other with 42,000 titles, 250 serial subscriptions, an OPAC.

Student Life *Housing:* college housing not available. *Activities and Organizations:* drama/theater group, student-run newspaper, choral group, Hispano-Americano Club, African-American Club, Environmental Action Coalition, International Student Club, Phi Theta Kappa. *Campus security:* late-night transport/escort service. *Student services:* personal/psychological counseling, women's center.

Athletics Member NJCAA. *Intercollegiate sports:* baseball M, basketball M/W, cross-country running M/W, soccer M, softball W, swimming and diving M/W, tennis M/W, volleyball W, wrestling M. *Intramural sports:* archery M/W, badminton M/W, basketball M/W, bowling M/W, fencing M/W, gymnastics M/W, racquetball M/W, rugby M, skiing (cross-country) M/W, skiing (downhill) M/W, soccer M/W, swimming and diving M/W, tennis M/W, volleyball M/W, water polo M/W, weight lifting M/W, wrestling M.

Costs (2007–08) *Tuition:* state resident $0 full-time; nonresident $3840 full-time, $160 per unit part-time. *Required fees:* $516 full-time, $20 per unit part-time, $18 per term part-time.

Financial Aid *Financial aid deadline:* 3/2.

Applying *Required for some:* high school transcript. *Application deadlines:* rolling (freshmen), rolling (out-of-state freshmen), rolling (transfers).

Director of Admissions Mr. Oscar De Haro, Vice President of Student Services, Napa Valley College, 2277 Napa-Vallejo Highway, Napa, CA 94558-6236. *Phone:* 707-253-3000. *E-mail:* odeharo@napavalley.edu.

National Institute of Technology

Long Beach, California   www.nitschools.com/

- **Proprietary** 2-year, founded 1969
- **Coed,** 1,144 undergraduate students
- 63% of applicants were admitted

Freshmen *Admission:* 683 applied, 428 admitted.

Majors Electrical/electronics maintenance and repair technology related; electrician.

Academics *Calendar:* quarters. *Degree:* associate.

Costs (2006–07) *Tuition:* $15,855 per degree program part-time.

Admissions Office Contact National Institute of Technology, 2161 Technology Place, Long Beach, CA 90810.

NATIONAL POLYTECHNIC COLLEGE OF ENGINEERING AND OCEANEERING

Wilmington, California   **www.coo.edu/**

Director of Admissions Tony Rodriguez, Director of Admissions, National Polytechnic College of Engineering and Oceaneering, 272 South Fries Avenue, Wilmington, CA 90744-6399. *Phone:* 310-834-2501 Ext. 237. *Toll-free phone:* 800-432-DIVE Ext. 237.

NORTHROP RICE AVIATION INSTITUTE OF TECHNOLOGY

Inglewood, California   **www.nrait.edu/**

Director of Admissions Mr. James Michael Rice, Chief Administrative Officer, Northrop Rice Aviation Institute of Technology, 1155 West Arbor Vitae Street, Suite 115, Inglewood, CA 90301-2904. *Phone:* 310-568-8541. *Fax:* 310-568-8542. *E-mail:* info@nrait.edu.

OHLONE COLLEGE

Fremont, California   **www.ohlone.edu/**

- **State and locally supported** 2-year, founded 1967, part of California Community College System
- **Suburban** 530-acre campus with easy access to San Francisco
- **Coed,** 10,867 undergraduate students, 32% full-time, 52% women, 48% men

Undergraduates 3,473 full-time, 7,394 part-time. Students come from 54 states and territories, 4% African American, 41% Asian American or Pacific Islander, 12% Hispanic American, 0.4% Native American.

Freshmen *Admission:* 968 enrolled.

Faculty *Total:* 430, 33% full-time. *Student/faculty ratio:* 24:1.

Majors Accounting; administrative assistant and secretarial science; art; biology/biological sciences; broadcast journalism; business administration and management; child development; commercial and advertising art; computer programming; computer science; computer typography and composition equipment operation; consumer services and advocacy; criminal justice/law enforcement administration; criminal justice/police science; drafting and design technology; electrical, electronic and communications engineering technology; family and consumer sciences/human sciences; fashion merchandising; food science; foods, nutrition, and wellness; health science; interior design; journalism; kindergarten/preschool education; liberal arts and sciences/liberal studies; marketing/marketing management; mass communication/media; medical administrative assistant and medical secretary; medical/clinical assistant; natural sciences; nursing (registered nurse training); physical sciences; physical therapist assistant; pre-engineering; radio and television; real estate; respiratory care therapy; sign language interpretation and translation; social sciences.

Academics *Calendar:* semesters. *Degree:* associate. *Special study options:* academic remediation for entering students, adult/continuing education programs, cooperative education, English as a second language, honors programs, off-campus study, part-time degree program, services for LD students, student-designed majors, study abroad, summer session for credit. *ROTC:* Army (c), Air Force (c).

Library Ohlone College Library with 65,000 titles, 410 serial subscriptions.

Student Life *Housing:* college housing not available. *Activities and Organizations:* drama/theater group, student-run newspaper, choral group. *Campus security:* 24-hour emergency response devices and patrols, late-night transport/escort service.

Athletics Member NJCAA. *Intercollegiate sports:* baseball M, basketball M/W, soccer M/W, softball W, swimming and diving M/W, track and field M/W, volleyball M/W, water polo M.

Standardized Tests *Required for some:* ACT ASSET.

Costs (2006–07) *Tuition:* state resident $0 full-time; nonresident $4860 full-time, $162 per unit part-time. *Required fees:* $830 full-time, $26 per unit part-time, $46 per year part-time.

Financial Aid Of all full-time matriculated undergraduates, 35 Federal Work-Study jobs (averaging $1800).

Applying *Options:* early admission. *Required:* high school transcript. *Application deadlines:* rolling (freshmen), rolling (transfers). *Notification:* continuous (freshmen), continuous (transfers).

Freshmen Application Contact Kimberly Robbie, Registrar, Ohlone College, 43600 Mission Boulevard, Fremont, CA 94539-5884. *Phone:* 510-659-6165. *Fax:* 510-659-7321. *E-mail:* krobbie@ohlone.edu.

ORANGE COAST COLLEGE

Costa Mesa, California   **www.orangecoastcollege.com/**

- **State and locally supported** 2-year, founded 1947, part of Coast Community College District System
- **Suburban** 162-acre campus with easy access to Los Angeles
- **Endowment** $8.0 million
- **Coed,** 22,412 undergraduate students, 41% full-time, 50% women, 50% men

Undergraduates 9,296 full-time, 13,116 part-time. Students come from 52 states and territories, 76 other countries, 2% are from out of state, 2% African American, 26% Asian American or Pacific Islander, 19% Hispanic American, 0.6% Native American, 2% international, 9% transferred in. *Retention:* 79% of 2003 full-time freshmen returned.

Freshmen *Admission:* 3,040 enrolled.

Faculty *Total:* 940, 32% full-time. *Student/faculty ratio:* 20:1.

Majors Accounting; administrative assistant and secretarial science; aeronautics/aviation/aerospace science and technology; airline pilot and flight crew; anthropology; architectural engineering technology; art; athletic training; avionics maintenance technology; behavioral sciences; biology/biological sciences; building/home/construction inspection; business administration and management; cardiovascular technology; chemistry; child care and support services management; child care provision; cinematography and film/video production; clinical laboratory science/medical technology; commercial and advertising art; communications technology; computer engineering technology; computer graphics; computer programming; computer programming (specific applications); computer typography and composition equipment operation; construction engineering technology; culinary arts; cultural studies; dance; data entry/microcomputer applications related; data processing and data processing technology; dental hygiene; dietetics; drafting and design technology; dramatic/theater arts; economics; electrical and power transmission installation; electrical, electronic and communications engineering technology; electrical/electronics equipment installation and repair; emergency medical technology (EMT paramedic); engineering; English; family and consumer economics related; family and consumer sciences/human sciences; fashion merchandising; film/cinema studies; food science; food services technology; foods, nutrition, and wellness; French; general retailing/wholesaling; geography; geology/earth science; German; health science; heating, air conditioning, ventilation and refrigeration maintenance technology; history; horticultural science; hotel/motel administration; housing and human environments; human development and family studies; humanities; industrial design; industrial radiologic technology; information science/studies; interior design; journalism; kindergarten/preschool education; kinesiology and exercise science; legal administrative assistant/secretary; liberal arts and sciences/liberal studies; machine shop technology; machine tool technology; marine technology; marketing/marketing management; mass communication/media; mathematics; medical administrative assistant and medical secretary; medical/clinical assistant; music; musical instrument fabrication and repair; music management and merchandising; natural sciences; nuclear medical technology; ornamental horticulture; philosophy; photography; physical education teaching and coaching; physics; political science and government; religious studies; respiratory care therapy; restaurant, culinary, and catering management; retailing; selling skills and sales; social sciences; sociology; Spanish; special products marketing; welding technology; word processing.

Academics *Calendar:* semesters plus summer session. *Degree:* certificates and associate. *Special study options:* academic remediation for entering students, adult/continuing education programs, advanced placement credit, cooperative education, distance learning, double majors, English as a second language, external degree program, freshman honors college, honors programs, internships, off-campus study, part-time degree program, services for LD students, student-designed majors, study abroad, summer session for credit. *ROTC:* Army (c), Air Force (c).

Library Norman E. Watson Library with 84,447 titles, 420 serial subscriptions, an OPAC, a Web page.

Student Life *Housing:* college housing not available. *Activities and Organizations:* drama/theater group, student-run newspaper, choral group, Vietnamese Student Association, International Club, Adventurist Souls, Muslim Student Association. *Campus security:* 24-hour emergency response devices and patrols, student patrols, late-night transport/escort service. *Student services:* health clinic, personal/psychological counseling, legal services.

Orange Coast College (continued)

Athletics *Intercollegiate sports:* baseball M, basketball M/W, bowling M(c)/W(c), crew M/W, cross-country running M/W, football M, golf M/W, soccer M/W, softball W, swimming and diving M/W, tennis M/W, track and field M/W, volleyball M/W, water polo M/W.

Costs (2007–08) *Tuition:* state resident $0 full-time; nonresident $4680 full-time, $156 per unit part-time. *Required fees:* $658 full-time, $20 per unit part-time, $28 per term part-time.

Financial Aid Of all full-time matriculated undergraduates, 108 Federal Work-Study jobs (averaging $3000). *Financial aid deadline:* 5/28.

Applying *Application deadlines:* rolling (freshmen), rolling (transfers). *Notification:* continuous (freshmen), continuous (transfers).

Freshmen Application Contact Ms. Nancy Kidder, Administrative Dean, Enrollment Services, Orange Coast College, 2701 Fairview Road, Costa Mesa, CA 92626. *Phone:* 714-432-5788. *Fax:* 714-432-5072. *E-mail:* nkidder@mail.occ.cccd.edu.

OXNARD COLLEGE

Oxnard, California　　　　　**www.oxnardcollege.edu/**

- **State-supported** 2-year, founded 1975, part of Ventura County Community College District System
- **Urban** 119-acre campus
- **Coed,** 6,379 undergraduate students, 30% full-time, 58% women, 42% men

Undergraduates 1,940 full-time, 4,439 part-time. Students come from 10 states and territories, 30 other countries, 4% African American, 10% Asian American or Pacific Islander, 61% Hispanic American, 0.7% Native American, 0.4% international.

Freshmen *Admission:* 1,262 applied, 1,262 admitted, 598 enrolled.

Faculty *Total:* 267, 35% full-time. *Student/faculty ratio:* 23:1.

Majors Accounting; administrative assistant and secretarial science; agricultural business and management; agricultural mechanization; anthropology; art teacher education; automobile/automotive mechanics technology; behavioral sciences; biology/biological sciences; business administration and management; child development; culinary arts; dental assisting; dental hygiene; dramatic/theater arts; economics; electrical, electronic and communications engineering technology; English; family and community services; family and consumer sciences/human sciences; fashion merchandising; fire science; heating, air conditioning, ventilation and refrigeration maintenance technology; history; hotel/motel administration; information science/studies; journalism; kindergarten/preschool education; legal studies; liberal arts and sciences/liberal studies; library science; machine tool technology; marketing/marketing management; mathematics; mental health/rehabilitation; philosophy; physical education teaching and coaching; radio and television; real estate; sociology; Spanish; telecommunications; transportation technology; welding technology.

Academics *Calendar:* semesters. *Degree:* certificates, diplomas, and associate. *Special study options:* academic remediation for entering students, accelerated degree program, adult/continuing education programs, advanced placement credit, distance learning, double majors, English as a second language, honors programs, independent study, part-time degree program, services for LD students, summer session for credit.

Library Oxnard College Library with 31,500 titles, 107 serial subscriptions, an OPAC, a Web page.

Student Life *Housing:* college housing not available. *Activities and Organizations:* drama/theater group, student-run newspaper, television station, choral group. *Campus security:* 24-hour patrols. *Student services:* health clinic, personal/psychological counseling, women's center.

Athletics *Intercollegiate sports:* baseball M, basketball M/W, cross-country running M/W, soccer M/W, track and field M/W, volleyball W.

Costs (2007–08) *Tuition:* state resident $0 full-time; nonresident $4200 full-time, $195 per unit part-time. *Required fees:* $522 full-time, $20 per unit part-time, $21 per term part-time.

Financial Aid Of all full-time matriculated undergraduates, 80 Federal Work-Study jobs (averaging $3000).

Applying *Options:* electronic application, early admission. *Recommended:* high school transcript. *Application deadlines:* rolling (freshmen), rolling (transfers). *Notification:* continuous (freshmen), continuous (transfers).

Freshmen Application Contact Ms. Susan Cabral, Registrar, Oxnard College, 4000 South Rose Avenue, Oxnard, CA 93033-6699. *Phone:* 805-986-5843. *Fax:* 805-986-5943.

PALOMAR COLLEGE

San Marcos, California　　　　**www.palomar.edu/**

Freshmen Application Contact Mr. Herman Lee, Director of Enrollment Services, Palomar College, 1140 West Mission Road, San Marcos, CA 92069-1487. *Phone:* 760-744-1150 Ext. 2171. *Fax:* 760-744-2932. *E-mail:* admissions@palomar.edu.

PALO VERDE COLLEGE

Blythe, California　　　　**www.paloverde.edu/**

- **State and locally supported** 2-year, founded 1947, part of California Community College System
- **Small-town** 10-acre campus
- **Coed**

Undergraduates 3,648 full-time. Students come from 4 states and territories, 3 other countries, 9% African American, 4% Asian American or Pacific Islander, 30% Hispanic American, 2% Native American.

Academics *Calendar:* semesters. *Degree:* associate. *Special study options:* academic remediation for entering students, adult/continuing education programs, advanced placement credit, English as a second language, internships, part-time degree program, services for LD students, summer session for credit.

Student Life *Campus security:* student patrols, security personnel during open hours.

Financial Aid Of all full-time matriculated undergraduates, 30 Federal Work-Study jobs (averaging $1000).

Applying *Options:* early admission. *Recommended:* high school transcript.

Freshmen Application Contact Ms. Pat Koester, Vice President of Student Services, Palo Verde College, 1 College Drive, Blythe, CA 92225. *Phone:* 760-921-5409. *Fax:* 760-921-3608.

PASADENA CITY COLLEGE

Pasadena, California　　　　**www.pasadena.edu/**

- **State and locally supported** 2-year, founded 1924, part of California Community College System
- **Urban** 55-acre campus with easy access to Los Angeles
- **Coed,** 29,618 undergraduate students, 100% full-time, 56% women, 44% men

Undergraduates 29,618 full-time. Students come from 15 states and territories, 6% African American, 31% Asian American or Pacific Islander, 34% Hispanic American, 0.5% Native American.

Faculty *Total:* 1,345, 31% full-time. *Student/faculty ratio:* 20:1.

Majors Accounting; administrative assistant and secretarial science; advertising; African-American/Black studies; African studies; airline pilot and flight crew; anthropology; architectural engineering technology; art; art history, criticism and conservation; astronomy; automobile/automotive mechanics technology; aviation/airway management; avionics maintenance technology; biological and physical sciences; biology/biological sciences; broadcast journalism; business administration and management; business teacher education; carpentry; ceramic arts and ceramics; ceramic sciences and engineering; chemistry; civil engineering technology; communications technology; computer engineering technology; computer programming; computer science; computer typography and composition equipment operation; construction engineering technology; cosmetology; criminal justice/law enforcement administration; cultural studies; data processing and data processing technology; dental hygiene; developmental and child psychology; drafting and design technology; dramatic/theater arts; drawing; economics; electrical, electronic and communications engineering technology; engineering; engineering technology; English; fashion merchandising; fiber, textile and weaving arts; finance; fire science; forestry technology; French; geography; geology/earth science; German; Hispanic-American, Puerto Rican, and Mexican-American/Chicano studies; history; human services; industrial radiologic technology; information science/studies; interdisciplinary studies; interior design; journalism; kindergarten/preschool education; landscape architecture; Latin American studies; legal administrative assistant/secretary; legal studies; liberal arts and sciences/liberal studies; library science; machine tool technology; marketing/marketing management; mass communication/media; mathematics; mechanical engineering/mechanical technology; medical/clinical assistant; metal and jewelry arts; Mexican-American studies; modern languages; music; music therapy; nursing (licensed practical/vocational nurse training); nursing (registered nurse training); occupational therapy; parks, recreation and leisure; pharmacy; philosophy; photography; physical education teaching and coaching; physical sciences; physics; political science and government;

psychology; radio and television; real estate; religious studies; sign language interpretation and translation; social sciences; sociology; Spanish; speech and rhetoric; statistics; teacher assistant/aide; telecommunications; tourism and travel services management; veterinary sciences; welding technology.

Academics *Calendar:* semesters. *Degree:* certificates and associate. *Special study options:* academic remediation for entering students, adult/continuing education programs, advanced placement credit, English as a second language, honors programs, part-time degree program, services for LD students, student-designed majors, study abroad, summer session for credit.

Library Pasadena City College Library plus 1 other with 120,000 titles, 350 serial subscriptions, an OPAC.

Student Life *Housing:* college housing not available. *Activities and Organizations:* drama/theater group, student-run newspaper, radio station, choral group, marching band. *Campus security:* 24-hour emergency response devices and patrols, late-night transport/escort service, cadet patrols. *Student services:* health clinic, personal/psychological counseling, women's center.

Athletics *Intercollegiate sports:* baseball M, basketball M/W, cross-country running M/W, football M, soccer M/W, softball W, swimming and diving M/W, tennis M/W, track and field M/W, volleyball W, water polo M.

Costs (2006–07) *Tuition:* state resident $0 full-time; nonresident $4530 full-time, $160 per unit part-time. *Required fees:* $780 full-time, $26 per unit part-time.

Applying *Options:* early admission, deferred entrance. *Application deadlines:* rolling (freshmen), rolling (transfers). *Notification:* continuous (freshmen), continuous (transfers).

Freshmen Application Contact Ms. Carol Kaser, Supervisor of Admissions and Records, Pasadena City College, 1570 East Colorado Boulevard, Pasadena, CA 91106. *Phone:* 626-585-7397. *Fax:* 626-585-7915.

PIMA MEDICAL INSTITUTE

Chula Vista, California   www.pmi.edu/

Freshmen Application Contact Admissions Office, Pima Medical Institute, Pima Medical Institute, 780 Bay Boulevard, Suite 101, Chula Vista, CA 91910. *Phone:* 619-425-3200. *Toll-free phone:* 888-898-9048.

PLATT COLLEGE

Cerritos, California   www.platt.edu/

Freshmen Application Contact Ms. Ilene Holt, Dean of Student Services, Platt College, 10900 East 183rd Street, Suite 290, Cerritos, CA 90703-5342. *Phone:* 562-809-5100. *Toll-free phone:* 800-807-5288.

PLATT COLLEGE

Huntington Beach, California   www.plattcollege.edu/

Director of Admissions Ms. Lisa Rhodes, President, Platt College, 3901 MacArthur Boulevard, Suite 101, Newport Beach, CA 92660. *Phone:* 949-833-2300 Ext. 222. *Toll-free phone:* 888-866-6697 Ext. 230.

PLATT COLLEGE

Ontario, California   www.plattcollege.edu/

Director of Admissions Ms. Jennifer Abandonato, Director of Admissions, Platt College, 3700 Inland Empire Boulevard, Ontario, CA 91764. *Phone:* 909-941-9410. *Toll-free phone:* 888-866-6697.

PLATT COLLEGE–LOS ANGELES, INC

Alhambra, California   www.plattcollege.edu/

Director of Admissions Mr. Detroit Whiteside, Director of Admissions, Platt College–Los Angeles, Inc, 7470 North Figueroa Street, Los Angeles, CA 90041-1717. *Phone:* 323-258-8050. *Toll-free phone:* 888-866-6697.

PLATT COLLEGE SAN DIEGO

San Diego, California   www.platt.edu/

- **Proprietary** primarily 2-year, founded 1879
- **Suburban** campus with easy access to San Diego
- **Coed,** 264 undergraduate students, 100% full-time, 27% women, 73% men

Since 1980, Platt College (media arts) has been the only campus in San Diego, California, to focus solely on 3-D animation, digital video production, graphic design, and Web design. Bachelor's and associate degrees are offered. Job placement assistance and financial aid (for those who qualify) are available. For further information, students should call 866-PLATTCOLLEGE (toll-free) or visit http://www.platt.edu.

Undergraduates 264 full-time. Students come from 4 states and territories, 5% are from out of state, 6% African American, 10% Asian American or Pacific Islander, 16% Hispanic American, 51% transferred in. *Retention:* 98% of 2003 full-time freshmen returned.

Freshmen *Admission:* 130 admitted, 130 enrolled.

Faculty *Total:* 37, 19% full-time, 3% with terminal degrees. *Student/faculty ratio:* 15:1.

Majors Animation, interactive technology, video graphics and special effects; commercial and advertising art; computer graphics; computer software and media applications related; digital communication and media/multimedia; graphic design; intermedia/multimedia; web/multimedia management and webmaster; Web page, digital/multimedia and information resources design.

Academics *Calendar:* continuous. *Degrees:* certificates, diplomas, associate, and bachelor's. *Special study options:* academic remediation for entering students, adult/continuing education programs, cooperative education.

Library Platt College San Diego Library with 750 titles, 27 serial subscriptions, 403 audiovisual materials.

Student Life *Housing:* college housing not available. *Campus security:* 24-hour emergency response devices, surveillance cameras. *Student services:* personal/psychological counseling.

Costs (2007–08) *Tuition:* $19,214 full-time. *Required fees:* $110 full-time.

Applying *Application fee:* $110. *Required:* high school transcript, interview, Wonderlic aptitude test. *Recommended:* essay or personal statement.

Freshmen Application Contact Mr. Craig Hinson, Admissions Representative, Platt College San Diego, 6250 El Cajon Boulevard, San Diego, CA 92115-3919. *Phone:* 619-265-0107. *Toll-free phone:* 866-752-8826. *Fax:* 619-265-8655. *E-mail:* chinson@platt.edu.

PORTERVILLE COLLEGE

Porterville, California   www.pc.cc.ca.us/

- **State-supported** 2-year, founded 1927, part of Kern Community College District System
- **Rural** 60-acre campus
- **Endowment** $1.3 million
- **Coed,** 5,024 undergraduate students

Undergraduates Students come from 1 other state, 4 other countries.

Freshmen *Admission:* 3,586 applied, 3,586 admitted.

Faculty *Total:* 140, 43% full-time.

Majors Administrative assistant and secretarial science; agricultural business and management; applied art; art; automobile/automotive mechanics technology; biological and physical sciences; biology/biological sciences; business administration and management; business teacher education; carpentry; child development; commercial and advertising art; computer science; criminal justice/law enforcement administration; criminal justice/police science; drafting and design technology; education; English; finance; fire science; history; human services; industrial arts; liberal arts and sciences/liberal studies; mathematics; mental health/rehabilitation; music; natural sciences; nursing (licensed practical/vocational nurse training); photography; physical education teaching and coaching; pre-engineering; social sciences; welding technology.

Academics *Calendar:* semesters. *Degree:* certificates and associate. *Special study options:* academic remediation for entering students, adult/continuing education programs, advanced placement credit, distance learning, part-time degree program, services for LD students, summer session for credit.

Library Porterville College Library/Media Center with 31,557 titles, 297 serial subscriptions, an OPAC.

Student Life *Housing:* college housing not available. *Activities and Organizations:* drama/theater group, choral group. *Campus security:* 24-hour emergency response devices, student patrols. *Student services:* health clinic, personal/psychological counseling.

Porterville College (continued)

Athletics *Intercollegiate sports:* baseball M, basketball M/W, soccer M/W, softball W, tennis M/W, volleyball W.

Costs (2006–07) *Tuition:* state resident $678 full-time; nonresident $5578 full-time.

Applying *Options:* electronic application, early admission. *Required:* high school transcript. *Application deadlines:* rolling (freshmen), rolling (transfers).

Director of Admissions Ms. Judy Pope, Director of Admissions and Records/Registrar, Porterville College, 100 East College Avenue, Porterville, CA 93257-6058. *Phone:* 559-791-2222.

PROFESSIONAL GOLFERS CAREER COLLEGE

Temecula, California www.golfcollege.edu/

Freshmen Application Contact Mr. Arnold Maravilla, Director of Admissions, Professional Golfers Career College, PO Box 892319, 261 Ynez Road, Temecula, CA 92589-2319. *Phone:* 951-693-2963. *Toll-free phone:* 800-877-4380. *Fax:* 951-719-1643. *E-mail:* arnold@golfcollege.edu.

QUALITY COLLEGE OF CULINARY CAREERS

Fresno, California www.qualityschool.com/

- **Proprietary** 2-year, founded 1994
- **Coed,** 34 undergraduate students

Majors Baking and pastry arts; culinary arts.

Academics *Calendar:* continuous. *Degree:* certificates and associate.

Costs (2006–07) *Tuition:* $12,600 full-time.

Applying *Application fee:* $75.

Freshmen Application Contact Admissions Office, Quality College of Culinary Careers, 1776 North Fine Avenue, Fresno, CA 93727. *Toll-free phone:* 866-373-2433. *Fax:* 559-264-4454. *E-mail:* lonney.edwards@qualitycollege.edu.

QUEEN OF THE HOLY ROSARY COLLEGE

Mission San Jose, California www.msjdominicans.org/QHRC/index.html

- **Independent Roman Catholic** 2-year, founded 1930
- **Suburban** 37-acre campus with easy access to San Jose
- **Coed, primarily women,** 195 undergraduate students, 3% full-time, 97% women, 3% men

Undergraduates 5 full-time, 190 part-time.

Freshmen *Admission:* 2 applied, 2 admitted.

Faculty *Total:* 17, 12% with terminal degrees. *Student/faculty ratio:* 5:1.

Majors Religious studies.

Academics *Calendar:* semesters. *Degree:* associate. *Special study options:* academic remediation for entering students, adult/continuing education programs, English as a second language, part-time degree program, summer session for credit.

Library Karcher Library with 24,937 titles, 150 serial subscriptions, 502 audiovisual materials, an OPAC.

Student Life *Housing:* college housing not available. *Activities and Organizations:* choral group. *Campus security:* 24-hour emergency response devices. *Student services:* health clinic, personal/psychological counseling.

Standardized Tests *Recommended:* SAT (for admission).

Applying *Application fee:* $15. *Required:* essay or personal statement, high school transcript, minimum 2.0 GPA. *Recommended:* minimum 3.0 GPA, interview. *Application deadlines:* 7/1 (freshmen), 7/1 (transfers).

Director of Admissions Sr. Mary Paul Mehegan, Dean of the College, Queen of the Holy Rosary College, 43326 Mission Boulevard, PO Box 3908, Mission San Jose, CA 94539. *Phone:* 510-657-2468 Ext. 322.

REEDLEY COLLEGE

Reedley, California www.reedleycollege.com/

- **State and locally supported** 2-year, founded 1926, part of State Center Community College District System
- **Rural** 350-acre campus
- **Endowment** $1.2 million
- **Coed,** 11,782 undergraduate students, 38% full-time, 61% women, 39% men

Undergraduates 4,423 full-time, 7,359 part-time. Students come from 15 states and territories, 1% are from out of state, 3% African American, 5% Asian American or Pacific Islander, 43% Hispanic American, 1% Native American.

Freshmen *Admission:* 1,224 applied, 1,224 admitted, 1,089 enrolled. *Average high school GPA:* 2.5.

Faculty *Total:* 534, 34% full-time. *Student/faculty ratio:* 14:1.

Majors Accounting; administrative assistant and secretarial science; agricultural business and management; agricultural mechanization related; agriculture; animal sciences; art; automobile/automotive mechanics technology; avionics maintenance technology; biology/biological sciences; business/commerce; child care and support services management; commercial and advertising art; computer and information sciences; corrections and criminal justice related; criminal justice/police science; dental assisting; English; entrepreneurship; fine arts related; foreign languages and literatures; general studies; health and physical education; horticultural science; hospitality administration; information science/studies; liberal arts and sciences/liberal studies; machine tool technology; management science; mathematics; music performance; natural resources management; office occupations and clerical services; physical sciences; plant sciences; precision metal working related; social sciences; voice and opera; welding technology.

Academics *Calendar:* semesters. *Degree:* certificates, diplomas, and associate. *Special study options:* academic remediation for entering students, adult/continuing education programs, advanced placement credit, cooperative education, distance learning, English as a second language, freshman honors college, honors programs, independent study, part-time degree program, services for LD students, study abroad, summer session for credit. *ROTC:* Air Force (c).

Library Reedley College Library with 36,000 titles, 217 serial subscriptions, an OPAC.

Student Life *Housing Options:* coed. Campus housing is university owned. *Activities and Organizations:* drama/theater group, student-run newspaper, choral group. *Campus security:* 24-hour emergency response devices, late-night transport/escort service, 24-hour on-campus police dispatcher. *Student services:* personal/psychological counseling.

Athletics *Intercollegiate sports:* baseball M, basketball M/W, football M, golf M, softball W, tennis M/W, track and field M/W, volleyball W. *Intramural sports:* basketball M/W, football M/W, swimming and diving M/W, tennis M/W, track and field M/W, volleyball M/W.

Costs (2007–08) *Tuition:* state resident $0 full-time; nonresident $4348 full-time, $173 per unit part-time. *Required fees:* $508 full-time, $20 per unit part-time, $18 per term part-time.

Financial Aid Of all full-time matriculated undergraduates, 200 Federal Work-Study jobs (averaging $3500).

Applying *Required:* high school transcript. *Application deadlines:* rolling (freshmen), rolling (transfers). *Notification:* continuous until 8/1 (freshmen), continuous until 8/1 (transfers).

Freshmen Application Contact Admissions and Records Office, Reedley College, 995 North Reed Avenue, Reedley, CA 93654. *Phone:* 559-638-0323. *Fax:* 599-637-2523.

RIO HONDO COLLEGE

Whittier, California www.riohondo.edu

- **State and locally supported** 2-year, founded 1960, part of California Community College System
- **Suburban** 128-acre campus with easy access to Los Angeles
- **Coed,** 15,000 undergraduate students

Undergraduates Students come from 5 states and territories, 40 other countries.

Faculty *Total:* 710, 30% full-time.

Majors Business teacher education; criminal justice/law enforcement administration; liberal arts and sciences/liberal studies; nursing (registered nurse training).

Academics *Calendar:* semesters. *Degree:* certificates and associate. *Special study options:* academic remediation for entering students, adult/continuing education programs, advanced placement credit, English as a second language,

honors programs, part-time degree program, services for LD students, study abroad, summer session for credit. *ROTC:* Army (c), Navy (c), Air Force (c).

Library Main Library plus 1 other with 94,143 titles, 479 serial subscriptions, a Web page.

Student Life *Housing:* college housing not available. *Activities and Organizations:* drama/theater group, student-run newspaper, radio station, choral group. *Campus security:* 24-hour patrols, late-night transport/escort service. *Student services:* health clinic, personal/psychological counseling, women's center, legal services.

Athletics *Intercollegiate sports:* baseball M, basketball M/W, cross-country running M/W, softball W, swimming and diving M/W, tennis M/W, volleyball W, water polo M/W, wrestling M. *Intramural sports:* field hockey W, volleyball M/W.

Costs (2006–07) *Tuition:* state resident $650 full-time; nonresident $3626 full-time.

Financial Aid Of all full-time matriculated undergraduates, 150 Federal Work-Study jobs (averaging $3200). 35 state and other part-time jobs (averaging $3200). *Financial aid deadline:* 5/1.

Applying *Options:* early admission. *Application deadlines:* 7/10 (freshmen), 7/10 (transfers). *Notification:* continuous (freshmen), continuous (transfers).

Director of Admissions Ms. Judy G. Pearson, Director of Admissions and Records, Rio Hondo College, 3600 Workman Mill Road, Whittier, CA 90601-1699. *Phone:* 562-692-0921 Ext. 3153.

RIVERSIDE COMMUNITY COLLEGE DISTRICT
Riverside, California **www.rcc.edu/**

- **State and locally supported** 2-year, founded 1916, part of California Community College System
- **Suburban** 108-acre campus with easy access to Los Angeles
- **Coed,** 30,709 undergraduate students, 29% full-time, 57% women, 43% men

Undergraduates 8,847 full-time, 21,862 part-time. Students come from 23 states and territories, 13% African American, 11% Asian American or Pacific Islander, 37% Hispanic American, 0.6% Native American, 1% transferred in.

Freshmen *Admission:* 890 applied, 890 admitted, 890 enrolled.

Faculty *Total:* 1,453, 18% full-time. *Student/faculty ratio:* 21:1.

Majors Autobody/collision and repair technology; automobile/automotive mechanics technology; business administration and management; cinematography and film/video production; computer programming; computer programming related; construction engineering technology; cosmetology; criminal justice/law enforcement administration; culinary arts; fire science; graphic and printing equipment operation/production; heating, air conditioning and refrigeration technology; liberal arts and sciences/liberal studies; nursing (licensed practical/vocational nurse training); nursing (registered nurse training); office management; paralegal/legal assistant; photography; retail management; sign language interpretation and translation; welding technology.

Academics *Calendar:* semesters. *Degree:* certificates and associate. *Special study options:* academic remediation for entering students, adult/continuing education programs, advanced placement credit, distance learning, double majors, English as a second language, internships, part-time degree program, services for LD students, study abroad, summer session for credit. *ROTC:* Army (c), Air Force (c).

Library Digital Library Learning Resource Center with 101,243 titles, 911 serial subscriptions, an OPAC, a Web page.

Student Life *Housing:* college housing not available. *Activities and Organizations:* drama/theater group, student-run newspaper, radio station, choral group, marching band, Marching Tigers Band, Wind Ensemble, Student Nurses Organization, Gospel Singers, Alpha Gamma Sigma. *Campus security:* 24-hour patrols, late-night transport/escort service. *Student services:* health clinic, personal/psychological counseling.

Athletics *Intercollegiate sports:* baseball M, basketball M/W, cross-country running M/W, football M, golf M, soccer M/W, softball W, swimming and diving M/W, tennis M/W, track and field M/W, volleyball W, water polo M/W. *Intramural sports:* badminton M/W, basketball M/W, bowling M/W, football M, golf M/W, racquetball M/W, soccer M/W, tennis M/W, volleyball M/W, weight lifting M/W.

Costs (2006–07) *Tuition:* state resident $0 full-time; nonresident $3840 full-time, $160 per unit part-time. *Required fees:* $480 full-time, $20 per unit part-time, $20 per term part-time.

Applying *Required:* high school transcript. *Application deadlines:* rolling (freshmen), rolling (transfers). *Notification:* continuous (freshmen), continuous (transfers).

Freshmen Application Contact Ms. Lorraine Anderson, District Dean of Admissions and Records, Riverside Community College District, 4800 Magnolia Avenue, Riverside, CA 92506. *Phone:* 951-222-8600. *Fax:* 951-222-8037. *E-mail:* admissions@rcc.edu.

SACRAMENTO CITY COLLEGE
Sacramento, California **www.scc.losrios.edu/**

- **State and locally supported** 2-year, founded 1916, part of California Community College System
- **Urban** 60-acre campus
- **Coed,** 21,890 undergraduate students

Undergraduates Students come from 35 states and territories, 13% African American, 24% Asian American or Pacific Islander, 14% Hispanic American, 2% Native American.

Faculty *Total:* 554. *Student/faculty ratio:* 30:1.

Majors Accounting; administrative assistant and secretarial science; advertising; airframe mechanics and aircraft maintenance technology; Army R.O.T.C./military science; art; avionics maintenance technology; biological and physical sciences; business administration and management; computer science; cosmetology; criminal justice/law enforcement administration; cultural studies; data processing and data processing technology; dental assisting; dental hygiene; drafting and design technology; dramatic/theater arts; electrical, electronic and communications engineering technology; engineering; family and consumer economics related; graphic and printing equipment operation/production; humanities; human services; kindergarten/preschool education; legal administrative assistant/secretary; liberal arts and sciences/liberal studies; library science; literature; mass communication/media; mathematics; medical administrative assistant and medical secretary; music; natural resources management and policy; natural sciences; nursing (licensed practical/vocational nurse training); nursing (registered nurse training); occupational therapy; physical education teaching and coaching; physical sciences; physical therapist assistant; psychology; real estate; social sciences; social work; speech and rhetoric; survey technology; transportation technology; women's studies.

Academics *Calendar:* semesters. *Degree:* certificates, diplomas, and associate. *Special study options:* academic remediation for entering students, adult/continuing education programs, advanced placement credit, cooperative education, English as a second language, honors programs, off-campus study, part-time degree program, services for LD students, student-designed majors, study abroad, summer session for credit.

Library Sacramento City College Library with 68,462 titles, 415 serial subscriptions, an OPAC, a Web page.

Student Life *Housing:* college housing not available. *Activities and Organizations:* drama/theater group, student-run newspaper, choral group, BOSS, African Student Alliance, Asian Pacific Club, MECHA, SMEC. *Campus security:* 24-hour emergency response devices and patrols, student patrols, late-night transport/escort service. *Student services:* personal/psychological counseling, women's center.

Athletics *Intercollegiate sports:* baseball M, basketball M/W, cross-country running M/W, football M, golf M/W, soccer W, softball W, swimming and diving M/W, tennis M/W, track and field M/W, volleyball W, water polo W, wrestling M. *Intramural sports:* badminton M/W, baseball M/W, basketball M/W, bowling M/W, cross-country running M/W, fencing M/W, football M/W, golf M/W, soccer M/W, softball W, swimming and diving M/W, table tennis M/W, tennis M/W, volleyball M/W, weight lifting M/W.

Costs (2006–07) *Tuition:* state resident $674 full-time; nonresident $5154 full-time.

Financial Aid Of all full-time matriculated undergraduates, 201 Federal Work-Study jobs (averaging $1425).

Applying *Application deadlines:* rolling (freshmen), rolling (transfers). *Notification:* continuous (freshmen), continuous (transfers).

Director of Admissions Mr. Sam T. Sandusky, Dean, Student Services, Sacramento City College, 3835 Freeport Boulevard, Sacramento, CA 95822-1386. *Phone:* 916-558-2438.

SADDLEBACK COLLEGE
Mission Viejo, California **www.saddleback.cc.ca.us/**

- **State and locally supported** 2-year, founded 1967
- **Suburban** 200-acre campus with easy access to Los Angeles and San Diego
- **Coed**

Saddleback College (continued)

Undergraduates 6,337 full-time, 12,014 part-time. Students come from 37 states and territories, 23 other countries, 2% African American, 11% Asian American or Pacific Islander, 14% Hispanic American, 0.6% Native American, 1% international.

Academics *Calendar:* semesters. *Degree:* certificates and associate. *Special study options:* academic remediation for entering students, adult/continuing education programs, advanced placement credit, cooperative education, distance learning, English as a second language, honors programs, off-campus study, part-time degree program, services for LD students, study abroad, summer session for credit.

Student Life *Campus security:* 24-hour emergency response devices and patrols, late-night transport/escort service.

Costs (2006–07) *Tuition:* nonresident $178 per unit part-time. *Required fees:* $26 per unit part-time, $14 per term part-time.

Financial Aid Of all full-time matriculated undergraduates, 125 Federal Work-Study jobs (averaging $4000). 125 state and other part-time jobs.

Applying *Options:* early admission.

Freshmen Application Contact Admissions Office, Saddleback College, 28000 Marguerite Parkway, Mission Viejo, CA 92692-3635. *Phone:* 949-582-4555. *Fax:* 949-347-8315. *E-mail:* earaiza@saddleback.edu.

SAGE COLLEGE

Moreno Valley, California   **www.sagecollege.edu/**

- **Proprietary** 2-year, founded 1973
- **Coed,** 387 undergraduate students
- 100% of applicants were admitted

Freshmen *Admission:* 12 applied, 12 admitted.

Majors Court reporting; legal administrative assistant.

Academics *Calendar:* quarters. *Degree:* associate.

Costs (2006–07) *Tuition:* $9725 full-time.

Applying *Application fee:* $100.

Admissions Office Contact Sage College, 12125 Day Street, Building L, Moreno Valley, CA 92557-6720. *Toll-free phone:* 888-781-2727.

THE SALVATION ARMY COLLEGE FOR OFFICER TRAINING AT CRESTMONT

Rancho Palos Verdes, California   **www.crestmont.edu/**

- **Independent religious** 2-year, founded 1878, administratively affiliated with The Salvation Army
- **Suburban** 44-acre campus with easy access to Los Angeles
- **Endowment** $85.5 million
- **Coed**

Undergraduates 27 full-time. Students come from 14 states and territories, 1 other country, 67% are from out of state, 7% African American, 15% Asian American or Pacific Islander, 30% Hispanic American, 7% international, 100% live on campus. *Retention:* 98% of 2003 full-time freshmen returned.

Faculty *Student/faculty ratio:* 1:1.

Academics *Calendar:* quarters. *Degree:* associate. *Special study options:* academic remediation for entering students, accelerated degree program, cooperative education, distance learning, English as a second language, external degree program, independent study, internships, off-campus study, student-designed majors.

Student Life *Campus security:* 24-hour emergency response devices and patrols.

Costs (2006–07) *Comprehensive fee:* $10,600 includes full-time tuition ($1500), mandatory fees ($850), and room and board ($8250).

Applying *Application fee:* $15. *Required:* essay or personal statement, high school transcript, 2 letters of recommendation, interview.

Freshmen Application Contact Capt. Kevin Jackson, Director of Curriculum, The Salvation Army College for Officer Training at Crestmont, 30840 Hawthorne Boulevard, Rancho Palos Verdes, CA 90275. *Phone:* 310-544-6442. *Toll-free phone:* 310-544-6440. *Fax:* 310-265-6520.

SAN BERNARDINO VALLEY COLLEGE

San Bernardino, California   **www.valleycollege.edu/**

- **State and locally supported** 2-year, founded 1926, part of San Bernardino Community College District System
- 82-acre campus with easy access to Los Angeles
- **Coed,** 1,540 undergraduate students

Undergraduates Students come from 2 states and territories.

Faculty *Total:* 375, 47% full-time.

Majors Accounting; administrative assistant and secretarial science; aeronautics/aviation/aerospace science and technology; anthropology; architectural engineering technology; art; astronomy; automobile/automotive mechanics technology; biology/biological sciences; botany/plant biology; business administration and management; chemical engineering; chemistry; civil engineering technology; clinical/medical laboratory technology; commercial and advertising art; computer engineering technology; computer science; corrections; criminal justice/police science; data processing and data processing technology; dental hygiene; developmental and child psychology; drafting and design technology; economics; electrical, electronic and communications engineering technology; English; environmental studies; family and consumer economics related; finance; French; geography; geology/earth science; German; heating, air conditioning, ventilation and refrigeration maintenance technology; history; hotel/motel administration; human services; interior design; journalism; liberal arts and sciences/liberal studies; machine tool technology; marketing/marketing management; mathematics; mental health/rehabilitation; music; nursing (registered nurse training); parks, recreation and leisure; philosophy; photography; physical education teaching and coaching; physical sciences; physics; political science and government; pre-engineering; psychology; radio and television; real estate; religious studies; sociology; Spanish; telecommunications; welding technology; zoology/animal biology.

Academics *Calendar:* semesters. *Degree:* certificates, diplomas, and associate. *Special study options:* academic remediation for entering students, cooperative education, part-time degree program, services for LD students, summer session for credit.

Library 122,802 titles, 657 serial subscriptions.

Student Life *Housing:* college housing not available. *Activities and Organizations:* drama/theater group, student-run newspaper, radio station. *Student services:* health clinic, personal/psychological counseling, women's center.

Athletics *Intercollegiate sports:* basketball M/W, cross-country running M/W, football M, golf M, soccer M/W, tennis M/W, track and field M/W, volleyball W, wrestling M. *Intramural sports:* basketball M/W, soccer M/W.

Standardized Tests *Required:* CGP (for placement).

Costs (2006–07) *Tuition:* state resident $806 full-time.

Financial Aid Of all full-time matriculated undergraduates, 100 Federal Work-Study jobs (averaging $3000).

Applying *Application deadline:* 8/29 (freshmen).

Director of Admissions Ms. Helena Johnson, Director of Admissions and Records, San Bernardino Valley College, 701 South Mount Vernon Avenue, San Bernardino, CA 92410-2748. *Phone:* 909-384-4401.

SAN DIEGO CITY COLLEGE

San Diego, California   **www.sdcity.edu/**

- **State and locally supported** 2-year, founded 1914, part of San Diego Community College District System
- **Urban** 56-acre campus
- **Coed,** 15,475 undergraduate students

Undergraduates 13% African American, 12% Asian American or Pacific Islander, 31% Hispanic American, 1% Native American.

Faculty *Total:* 485, 33% full-time, 26% with terminal degrees. *Student/faculty ratio:* 35:1.

Majors Accounting; administrative assistant and secretarial science; African-American/Black studies; anthropology; art; artificial intelligence and robotics; automobile/automotive mechanics technology; behavioral sciences; biology/biological sciences; business administration and management; carpentry; commercial and advertising art; computer engineering technology; consumer services and advocacy; cosmetology; court reporting; data processing and data processing technology; developmental and child psychology; drafting and design technology; dramatic/theater arts; electrical, electronic and communications engineering technology; emergency medical technology (EMT paramedic); engineering technology; English; environmental engineering technology; fashion merchandising; finance; graphic and printing equipment operation/production; Hispanic-American, Puerto Rican, and Mexican-American/Chicano studies; hospitality administration; industrial arts; industrial technology; insurance; interior design; journalism; labor and industrial relations; Latin American studies; legal administrative assistant/secretary; legal assistant/paralegal; liberal arts and sciences/liberal studies; machine tool technology; marketing/marketing management; mathematics; modern languages; music; nursing (licensed practical/vocational nurse training); nursing (registered nurse training); occupational safety and health technology; parks, recreation and leisure; photography; physical education teaching and coaching; physical sciences; political science and government; postal management; pre-engineering; psychology; radio and television; real estate; social sciences; social work; sociology; special products marketing; speech and rhetoric; teacher assistant/aide; telecommunications; tourism and travel services management; transportation technology; welding technology.

Academics *Calendar:* semesters. *Degree:* certificates and associate. *Special study options:* academic remediation for entering students, adult/continuing education programs, cooperative education, distance learning, English as a second language, external degree program, honors programs, independent study, off-campus study, part-time degree program, services for LD students, student-designed majors, summer session for credit. *ROTC:* Air Force (c).

Library San Diego City College Library with 73,000 titles, 337 serial subscriptions, an OPAC.

Student Life *Housing:* college housing not available. *Activities and Organizations:* drama/theater group, student-run newspaper, radio station, choral group, Alpha Gamma Sigma, Association of United Latin American Students, MECHA, Afrikan Student Union, Student Nurses Association. *Campus security:* 24-hour emergency response devices and patrols, late-night transport/escort service. *Student services:* health clinic, personal/psychological counseling.

Athletics Member NJCAA. *Intercollegiate sports:* baseball M, basketball M/W, cross-country running M/W, football M, golf M/W, soccer M/W, softball W, tennis M/W, track and field M/W, volleyball M/W. *Intramural sports:* archery M/W, badminton M/W, baseball M, basketball M/W, bowling M/W, racquetball M/W, soccer M/W, softball W, swimming and diving M/W, tennis M/W, track and field M/W, volleyball M/W, weight lifting M/W.

Costs (2007–08) *Tuition:* state resident $0 full-time; nonresident $4392 full-time, $183 per unit part-time. *Required fees:* $480 full-time, $20 per unit part-time, $13 per term part-time.

Financial Aid Of all full-time matriculated undergraduates, 100 Federal Work-Study jobs (averaging $4000).

Applying *Options:* electronic application. *Required for some:* high school transcript. *Application deadlines:* rolling (freshmen), rolling (transfers).

Freshmen Application Contact Ms. Lou Humphries, Supervisor of Admissions and Records, San Diego City College, 1313 Twelfth Avenue, San Diego, CA 92101-4787. *Phone:* 619-388-3474. *Fax:* 619-388-3505. *E-mail:* lhumphri@sdccd.edu.

SAN DIEGO GOLF ACADEMY

Vista, California   www.sdgagolf.com/

Director of Admissions Ms. Deborah Wells, Admissions Coordinator, San Diego Golf Academy, 1910 Shadowridge Drive, Suite 111, Vista, CA 92083. *Phone:* 760-414-1501. *Toll-free phone:* 800-342-7342. *E-mail:* sdga@sdgagolf.com.

SAN DIEGO MESA COLLEGE

San Diego, California   www.sandiegomesacollege.net/

- **State and locally supported** 2-year, founded 1964, part of San Diego Community College District System
- **Suburban** 104-acre campus
- **Coed**

Undergraduates 21,198 full-time. 6% African American, 16% Asian American or Pacific Islander, 17% Hispanic American, 0.9% Native American.

Academics *Calendar:* semesters. *Degree:* certificates, diplomas, and associate. *Special study options:* academic remediation for entering students, adult/continuing education programs, English as a second language, external degree program, honors programs, independent study, part-time degree program, services for LD students, summer session for credit.

Student Life *Campus security:* 24-hour emergency response devices and patrols, late-night transport/escort service.

Financial Aid Of all full-time matriculated undergraduates, 237 Federal Work-Study jobs (averaging $5000). *Financial aid deadline:* 6/30.

Applying *Options:* early admission.

Freshmen Application Contact Ms. Dominga Arellano, Senior Student Services Assistant, San Diego Mesa College, 7250 Mesa College Drive, San Diego, CA 92111. *Phone:* 619-388-2686. *Fax:* 619-388-3960. *E-mail:* darellano@sdccd.edu.

SAN DIEGO MIRAMAR COLLEGE

San Diego, California   www.miramar.sdccd.cc.ca.us/

Freshmen Application Contact Ms. Dana Andras, Admissions Supervisor, San Diego Miramar College, 10440 Black Mountain Road, San Diego, CA 92126-2999. *Phone:* 619-536-7854. *E-mail:* dmaxwell@sdccd.cc.ca.us.

SAN JOAQUIN DELTA COLLEGE

Stockton, California   www.deltacollege.edu/

- **District-supported** 2-year, founded 1935, part of California Community College System
- **Urban** 165-acre campus with easy access to Sacramento
- **Coed,** 18,800 undergraduate students, 38% full-time, 58% women, 42% men

Undergraduates 7,135 full-time, 11,665 part-time. Students come from 15 states and territories, 10% African American, 20% Asian American or Pacific Islander, 28% Hispanic American, 1% Native American, 1% international. *Retention:* 25% of 2003 full-time freshmen returned.

Freshmen *Admission:* 12,712 applied, 12,712 admitted.

Faculty *Total:* 633, 33% full-time. *Student/faculty ratio:* 33:1.

Majors Accounting; agricultural business and management; agricultural mechanization; agriculture; animal sciences; anthropology; art; automobile/automotive mechanics technology; behavioral sciences; biology/biological sciences; botany/plant biology; broadcast journalism; business administration and management; business/managerial economics; carpentry; chemistry; child development; civil engineering technology; commercial and advertising art; computer engineering technology; computer programming; computer science; construction engineering technology; corrections; criminal justice/police science; culinary arts; dance; developmental and child psychology; drafting and design technology; dramatic/theater arts; drawing; economics; electrical, electronic and communications engineering technology; emergency medical technology (EMT paramedic); engineering; engineering related; engineering technology; English; family and consumer sciences/human sciences; fashion merchandising; fire science; food services technology; French; geology/earth science; German; graphic and printing equipment operation/production; health science; heating, air conditioning, ventilation and refrigeration maintenance technology; history; humanities; industrial radiologic technology; interior design; Italian; Japanese; journalism; kindergarten/preschool education; liberal arts and sciences/liberal studies; literature; machine tool technology; marketing/marketing management; mathematics; mechanical engineering/mechanical technology; music; natural resources management and policy; natural sciences; nursing (licensed practical/vocational nurse training); nursing (registered nurse training); ornamental horticulture; philosophy; photography; physical education teaching and coaching; physical sciences; political science and government; psychiatric/mental health services technology; psychology; public administration; religious studies; social sciences; sociology; Spanish; special products marketing; speech and rhetoric.

Academics *Calendar:* semesters. *Degree:* certificates and associate. *Special study options:* academic remediation for entering students, adult/continuing education programs, advanced placement credit, cooperative education, distance learning, English as a second language, honors programs, independent study, part-time degree program, services for LD students, summer session for credit.

Library Goleman Library plus 1 other with 92,398 titles, 605 serial subscriptions, an OPAC, a Web page.

Student Life *Housing:* college housing not available. *Activities and Organizations:* drama/theater group, student-run newspaper, radio station, choral group, Alpha Gamma Sigma, Fashion Club, International Club, Badminton Club. *Campus security:* 24-hour emergency response devices and patrols, late-night transport/escort service. *Student services:* personal/psychological counseling, legal services.

Athletics Member NJCAA. *Intercollegiate sports:* baseball M, basketball M/W, cross-country running M/W, fencing M/W, football M, golf M/W, soccer M/W, softball W, swimming and diving M/W, tennis M/W, track and field M/W, volleyball W, water polo M/W, wrestling M. *Intramural sports:* badminton M/W, basketball M/W, bowling M/W, soccer M/W, swimming and diving M/W, tennis M/W, ultimate Frisbee M/W, volleyball M/W, weight lifting M/W.

Costs (2007–08) *Tuition:* state resident $0 full-time; nonresident $5190 full-time, $173 per unit part-time. *Required fees:* $600 full-time, $20 per unit part-time.

Financial Aid Of all full-time matriculated undergraduates, 315 Federal Work-Study jobs (averaging $3100). 210 state and other part-time jobs (averaging $1172).

Applying *Options:* electronic application, early admission. *Application deadlines:* rolling (freshmen), rolling (transfers). *Notification:* continuous (freshmen), continuous (transfers).

Freshmen Application Contact Ms. Catherine Mooney, Registrar, San Joaquin Delta College, 5151 Pacific Avenue, Stockton, CA 95207. *Phone:* 209-954-5635. *Fax:* 209-954-5769. *E-mail:* admissions@deltacollege.edu.

SAN JOAQUIN VALLEY COLLEGE

Visalia, California   www.sjvc.edu

- **Independent** 2-year, founded 1977
- **Small-town** campus
- **Coed**

San Joaquin Valley College (continued)

Undergraduates 3,351 full-time, 1 part-time. 6% are from out of state, 8% African American, 6% Asian American or Pacific Islander, 46% Hispanic American, 1% Native American.

Faculty *Student/faculty ratio:* 10:1.

Academics *Calendar:* semesters. *Degree:* certificates and associate. *Special study options:* academic remediation for entering students.

Student Life *Campus security:* late-night transport/escort service, full-time security personnel.

Costs (2006–07) *Tuition:* $11,475 full-time, $348 per unit part-time.

Applying *Required:* high school transcript. *Required for some:* essay or personal statement, minimum X GPA, letters of recommendation, interview.

Freshmen Application Contact Mr. Joseph Holt, Director of Marketing and Admissions, San Joaquin Valley College, 8400 West Mineral King Avenue, Visalia, CA 93291. *Fax:* 559-734-9048. *E-mail:* josephh@sjvc.edu.

SAN JOSE CITY COLLEGE

San Jose, California www.sjcc.edu/

Freshmen Application Contact Mr. Carlo Santos, Director of Admissions/Registrar, San Jose City College, 2100 Moorpark Avenue, San Jose, CA 95128-2799. *Phone:* 408-288-3707. *Fax:* 408-298-1935.

SANTA ANA COLLEGE

Santa Ana, California www.sac.edu/

- **State-supported** 2-year, founded 1915, part of California Community College System
- **Urban** 58-acre campus with easy access to Los Angeles
- **Coed,** 22,189 undergraduate students

Undergraduates Students come from 50 states and territories, 4% are from out of state.

Faculty *Total:* 1,296, 19% full-time. *Student/faculty ratio:* 20:1.

Majors Accounting; administrative assistant and secretarial science; African-American/Black studies; anthropology; art; automobile/automotive mechanics technology; biological and physical sciences; biology/biological sciences; business administration and management; chemistry; commercial and advertising art; communication/speech communication and rhetoric; computer and information sciences related; computer programming related; computer science; cosmetology; criminal justice/law enforcement administration; criminal justice/police science; cultural studies; dance; data entry/microcomputer applications; data entry/microcomputer applications related; diesel mechanics technology; drafting and design technology; dramatic/theater arts; economics; electrical, electronic and communications engineering technology; engineering; engineering technology; English; environmental studies; family and consumer economics related; fashion/apparel design; fashion merchandising; fire science; foods, nutrition, and wellness; geography; geology/earth science; Hispanic-American, Puerto Rican, and Mexican-American/Chicano studies; history; industrial technology; information science/studies; information technology; journalism; kindergarten/preschool education; kinesiology and exercise science; legal studies; liberal arts and sciences/liberal studies; library science; management science; marketing/marketing management; mathematics; medical/clinical assistant; modern languages; music; nursing (registered nurse training); occupational therapy; pharmacy technician; philosophy; photography; physics; political science and government; psychology; quality control technology; real estate; sales, distribution and marketing; social sciences; sociology; telecommunications; tourism and travel services management; water resources engineering; welding technology; women's studies; word processing.

Academics *Calendar:* semesters. *Degree:* certificates and associate. *Special study options:* academic remediation for entering students, accelerated degree program, adult/continuing education programs, advanced placement credit, cooperative education, distance learning, English as a second language, external degree program, freshman honors college, honors programs, part-time degree program, services for LD students, study abroad, summer session for credit. *ROTC:* Air Force (c).

Library McNeally Library with 99,473 titles, 7,690 audiovisual materials.

Student Life *Housing:* college housing not available. *Activities and Organizations:* drama/theater group, student-run newspaper, television station, choral group, Students of Diverse Cultures, Students United for Better Education, Phi Beta Kappa, Alpha Gamma Sigma, Puente. *Campus security:* late-night transport/escort service. *Student services:* health clinic, personal/psychological counseling, women's center, legal services.

Athletics *Intercollegiate sports:* baseball M, basketball M/W, cross-country running M/W, football M, golf M, soccer M, softball W, swimming and diving M, tennis M/W, track and field M/W, volleyball W, water polo M, wrestling M.

Costs (2006–07) *Tuition:* state resident $552 full-time; nonresident $4488 full-time.

Financial Aid Of all full-time matriculated undergraduates, 259 Federal Work-Study jobs (averaging $1600).

Applying *Options:* early admission. *Application deadlines:* 8/21 (freshmen), 8/21 (transfers).

Freshmen Application Contact Mrs. Christie Steward, Admissions Clerk, Santa Ana College, 1530 West 17th Street, Santa Ana, CA 92704. *Phone:* 714-564-6053.

SANTA BARBARA CITY COLLEGE

Santa Barbara, California www.sbcc.edu/

- **State and locally supported** 2-year, founded 1908, part of California Community College System
- **Small-town** 65-acre campus
- **Endowment** $21.8 million
- **Coed,** 16,043 undergraduate students, 41% full-time, 54% women, 46% men

Undergraduates 6,643 full-time, 9,400 part-time. Students come from 46 states and territories, 58 other countries, 6% are from out of state, 3% African American, 6% Asian American or Pacific Islander, 23% Hispanic American, 1% Native American, 7% international, 5% transferred in.

Freshmen *Admission:* 3,093 applied, 3,093 admitted, 1,642 enrolled.

Faculty *Total:* 751, 35% full-time. *Student/faculty ratio:* 28:1.

Majors Accounting; acting; administrative assistant and secretarial science; African-American/Black studies; American Indian/Native American studies; anthropology; applied horticulture; art history, criticism and conservation; athletic training; automobile/automotive mechanics technology; biology/biological sciences; biomedical technology; biotechnology; business administration and management; chemistry; child care and support services management; commercial and advertising art; communication/speech communication and rhetoric; computer engineering; computer science; cosmetology; criminal justice/law enforcement administration; culinary arts related; cultural studies; drafting and design technology; dramatic/theater arts; economics; electrical, electronic and communications engineering technology; electrical/electronics equipment installation and repair; engineering; engineering technology; English; environmental/environmental health engineering; environmental studies; film/cinema studies; finance; fine/studio arts; foodservice systems administration; French; geography; geology/earth science; health information/medical records technology; Hispanic-American, Puerto Rican, and Mexican-American/Chicano studies; history; hotel/motel administration; industrial engineering; industrial technology; information science/studies; information technology; institutional food workers; interior design; international relations and affairs; kindergarten/preschool education; kinesiology and exercise science; landscaping and groundskeeping; legal studies; liberal arts and sciences/liberal studies; marine technology; marketing/marketing management; mathematics; medical radiologic technology; music; nursing (licensed practical/vocational nurse training); nursing (registered nurse training); ornamental horticulture; parks, recreation and leisure; philosophy; physical education teaching and coaching; physics; political science and government; psychology; real estate; sales, distribution and marketing; selling skills and sales; sociology; Spanish; system administration; theater design and technology; therapeutic recreation.

Academics *Calendar:* semesters. *Degree:* certificates and associate. *Special study options:* academic remediation for entering students, adult/continuing education programs, advanced placement credit, cooperative education, distance learning, double majors, English as a second language, honors programs, independent study, internships, part-time degree program, services for LD students, study abroad, summer session for credit. *ROTC:* Army (c).

Library Eli Luria Library with 131,918 titles, 6,832 serial subscriptions, 40 audiovisual materials, an OPAC, a Web page.

Student Life *Housing:* college housing not available. *Activities and Organizations:* drama/theater group, student-run newspaper, choral group, MECHA, International-Cultural Exchange Club, Geology Club, Computer Club, Future Teachers Club. *Campus security:* 24-hour emergency response devices and patrols, late-night transport/escort service. *Student services:* health clinic, personal/psychological counseling.

Athletics *Intercollegiate sports:* baseball M, basketball M/W, cross-country running M/W, football M, golf M/W, soccer M/W, softball W, tennis M/W, track and field M/W, volleyball M/W.

Costs (2007–08) *Tuition:* state resident $0 full-time, $153 per unit part-time; nonresident $4590 full-time, $159 per unit part-time. *Required fees:* $653 full-time, $20 per unit part-time, $53 per year part-time.

Applying *Options:* early admission. *Recommended:* high school transcript. *Application deadlines:* 8/22 (freshmen), 8/22 (transfers). *Notification:* continuous (freshmen), continuous (transfers).

Freshmen Application Contact Ms. Allison Curtis, Director of Admissions and Records, Santa Barbara City College, 721 Cliff Drive, Santa Barbara, CA 93109. *Phone:* 805-965-0581 Ext. 2352. *Fax:* 805-962-0497. *E-mail:* admissions@ sbcc.edu.

SANTA MONICA COLLEGE

Santa Monica, California   www.smc.edu/

Director of Admissions Ms. Teresita Rodriguez, Dean of Enrollment Services, Santa Monica College, 1900 Pico Boulevard, Santa Monica, CA 90405-1628. *Phone:* 207-786-6000 Ext. 4774. *Fax:* 207-786-6025.

►See page 584 for the College Close-Up.

SANTA ROSA JUNIOR COLLEGE

Santa Rosa, California   www.santarosa.edu/

- **State and locally supported** 2-year, founded 1918, part of California Community College System
- **Urban** 93-acre campus with easy access to San Francisco
- **Endowment** $16.5 million
- **Coed,** 25,031 undergraduate students, 28% full-time, 57% women, 43% men

Undergraduates 6,953 full-time, 18,078 part-time. 2% are from out of state, 0.4% African American, 0.8% Asian American or Pacific Islander, 19% Hispanic American, 0.2% Native American, 0.3% international.

Freshmen *Admission:* 4,714 applied, 4,714 admitted.

Faculty *Total:* 1,486, 20% full-time, 10% with terminal degrees. *Student/faculty ratio:* 22:1.

Majors Advertising; aeronautical/aerospace engineering technology; agricultural business and management; agricultural mechanization; agriculture; animal health; animal physiology; animal sciences; anthropology; art; astronomy; athletic training; atmospheric sciences and meteorology; behavioral sciences; biology/biological sciences; botany/plant biology; business administration and management; chemistry; child guidance; civil engineering; communication/speech communication and rhetoric; computer science; construction management; criminal justice/law enforcement administration; culinary arts; cultural studies; dance; dental hygiene; dietetics; dramatic/theater arts; economics; education; electrical, electronic and communications engineering technology; emergency medical technology (EMT paramedic); engineering; engineering technology; English; environmental science; environmental studies; ethnic, cultural minority, and gender studies related; family and consumer sciences/human sciences; film/cinema studies; fire science; fishing and fisheries sciences and management; floriculture/floristry management; geography; geology/earth science; gerontological services; graphic design; health and physical education related; history; horse husbandry/equine science and management; hotel/motel administration; human services; industrial design; interior design; journalism; landscape architecture; Latin American studies; liberal arts and sciences/liberal studies; mathematics; mechanics and repair; music; natural resources/conservation; natural resources management and policy; nursing (registered nurse training); oceanography (chemical and physical); ophthalmic laboratory technology; philosophy; physical education teaching and coaching; physical sciences; physician assistant; physics; political science and government; precision production trades; pre-pharmacy studies; psychology; social sciences; sociology; speech-language pathology; surveying engineering; wildlife and wildlands science and management; women's studies.

Academics *Calendar:* semesters. *Degree:* certificates and associate. *Special study options:* academic remediation for entering students, adult/continuing education programs, advanced placement credit, cooperative education, distance learning, English as a second language, independent study, internships, off-campus study, part-time degree program, services for LD students, study abroad, summer session for credit.

Library Plover Library with 123,068 titles, 389 serial subscriptions, 10,600 audiovisual materials, an OPAC, a Web page.

Student Life *Housing:* college housing not available. *Activities and Organizations:* drama/theater group, student-run newspaper, choral group, International Club, MECHA, Alpha Gamma Sigma, Asian/Pacific Island Association, Phi Theta Kappa. *Campus security:* 24-hour emergency response devices and patrols. *Student services:* health clinic, personal/psychological counseling.

Athletics Member NJCAA. *Intercollegiate sports:* baseball M, basketball M/W, cross-country running M/W, football M, golf M, ice hockey M(c), rugby M(c), soccer M/W, softball W, swimming and diving M/W, tennis M/W, track and field M/W, volleyball W, water polo M/W, wrestling M.

Costs (2007–08) *Tuition:* state resident $0 full-time; nonresident $4152 full-time, $173 per unit part-time. *Required fees:* $508 full-time, $20 per unit part-time, $14 per term part-time.

Financial Aid Of all full-time matriculated undergraduates, 228 Federal Work-Study jobs (averaging $3500).

Applying *Options:* electronic application, early admission. *Application deadlines:* rolling (freshmen), rolling (transfers). *Notification:* continuous (freshmen), continuous (transfers).

Freshmen Application Contact Ms. Diane Traversi, Director of Enrollment Services, Santa Rosa Junior College, 1501 Mendocino Avenue, Santa Rosa, CA 95401. *Phone:* 707-527-4685. *Fax:* 707-527-4798. *E-mail:* admininfo@ santarosa.edu.

►See page 586 for the College Close-Up.

SANTIAGO CANYON COLLEGE

Orange, California   www.sccollege.edu/

- **State-supported** 2-year, founded 2000, part of California Community College System
- **Coed,** 10,214 undergraduate students

Faculty *Total:* 417, 22% full-time. *Student/faculty ratio:* 23:1.

Majors Accounting; anthropology; art; biology/biological sciences; business administration and management; business administration, management and operations related; business automation/technology/data entry; carpentry; cartography; chemistry; communication/speech communication and rhetoric; computer and information sciences; computer science; cosmetology; cultural studies; dramatic/theater arts; economics; electrician; English; geography; geology/earth science; history; human development and family studies; kinesiology and exercise science; liberal arts and sciences/liberal studies; management science; marketing/marketing management; mathematics; modern languages; music; natural sciences; philosophy; physics; political science and government; psychology; public administration; radio, television, and digital communication related; real estate; sheet metal technology; social sciences; sociology; survey technology; tourism and travel services management; water quality and wastewater treatment management and recycling technology; women's studies.

Academics *Calendar:* semesters. *Degree:* certificates and associate. *Special study options:* academic remediation for entering students, adult/continuing education programs, advanced placement credit, cooperative education, distance learning, English as a second language, external degree program, freshman honors college, honors programs, part-time degree program, services for LD students, summer session for credit.

Library Santiago Canyon College Library with 31,000 titles, 2,260 serial subscriptions, 4,082 audiovisual materials, an OPAC, a Web page.

Student Life *Housing:* college housing not available.

Costs (2006–07) *Tuition:* state resident $580 full-time; nonresident $4516 full-time.

Applying *Options:* early admission. *Application deadlines:* 8/21 (freshmen), 8/21 (transfers).

Freshmen Application Contact Denise Pennock, Admissions and Records, Santiago Canyon College, 8045 East Chapman, Orange, CA 92669. *Phone:* 714-564-4000.

SHASTA COLLEGE

Redding, California   www.shastacollege.edu/

- **State and locally supported** 2-year, founded 1948, part of California Community College System
- **Rural** 336-acre campus
- **Endowment** $1.3 million
- **Coed,** 10,240 undergraduate students, 42% full-time, 61% women, 39% men

Undergraduates 4,336 full-time, 5,904 part-time. 2% are from out of state, 1% African American, 3% Asian American or Pacific Islander, 6% Hispanic American, 4% Native American, 0.3% international.

Freshmen *Admission:* 3,586 applied, 3,586 admitted, 2,891 enrolled.

Faculty *Total:* 491, 30% full-time.

Majors Accounting; administrative assistant and secretarial science; agricultural business and management; animal sciences; art; automobile/automotive mechanics technology; avionics maintenance technology; business administration and management; civil engineering technology; computer management; construction engineering technology; criminal justice/law enforcement administration; culinary arts; dental hygiene; design and visual communications; diesel mechanics technology; drafting and design technology; dramatic/theater arts; electrical, electronic and communications engineering technology; family and

Shasta College (continued)

consumer sciences/human sciences; fire science; horticultural science; journalism; kindergarten/preschool education; legal administrative assistant/secretary; legal assistant/paralegal; management information systems; medical administrative assistant and medical secretary; medical/clinical assistant; music; natural resources management and policy; nursing (registered nurse training); ornamental horticulture; real estate; speech and rhetoric; welding technology.

Academics *Calendar:* semesters. *Degree:* certificates and associate. *Special study options:* academic remediation for entering students, adult/continuing education programs, advanced placement credit, cooperative education, distance learning, double majors, English as a second language, honors programs, internships, part-time degree program, services for LD students, summer session for credit.

Library Shasta College Learning Resource Center with 67,500 titles, 1,700 serial subscriptions, 4,859 audiovisual materials, an OPAC, a Web page.

Student Life *Housing Options:* coed. *Activities and Organizations:* drama/theater group, student-run newspaper, choral group, Associated Student Body, Environmental Resource Leadership Club, Intercultural Club, Inter-Varsity Christian Fellowship, Music Education National Conference. *Campus security:* 24-hour emergency response devices, student patrols, late-night transport/escort service, 16-hour patrols by trained security personnel. *Student services:* health clinic, personal/psychological counseling.

Athletics *Intercollegiate sports:* baseball M, basketball M/W, cross-country running M/W, football M, golf M/W, soccer M/W, softball W, swimming and diving M/W, tennis M/W, track and field M/W, volleyball W. *Intramural sports:* cross-country running M/W.

Standardized Tests *Required:* Assessment and Placement Services for Community Colleges (for placement). *Recommended:* SAT or ACT (for placement).

Costs (2006–07) *Tuition:* state resident $552 full-time; nonresident $4536 full-time.

Financial Aid Of all full-time matriculated undergraduates, 1,000 Federal Work-Study jobs (averaging $2500).

Applying *Options:* early admission. *Required:* high school transcript. *Application deadline:* rolling (freshmen). *Notification:* continuous (freshmen).

Director of Admissions Ms. Cassandra Ryan, Admissions and Records Office Director, Shasta College, PO Box 496006, 11555 Old Oregon Trail, Redding, CA 96049-6006. *Phone:* 530-225-4841.

SIERRA COLLEGE

Rocklin, California   www.sierracollege.edu/

Director of Admissions Ms. Gail Modder, Program Manager, Admissions and Records, Sierra College, 5000 Rocklin Road, Rocklin, CA 93677-3397. *Phone:* 916-781-0599.

SKYLINE COLLEGE

San Bruno, California   skylinecollege.net/

- **State and locally supported** 2-year, founded 1969, part of San Mateo County Community College District System
- **Suburban** 125-acre campus with easy access to San Francisco
- **Coed**

Undergraduates Students come from 9 other countries, 2% are from out of state.

Faculty *Student/faculty ratio:* 27:1.

Academics *Calendar:* semesters. *Degree:* certificates and associate. *Special study options:* academic remediation for entering students, adult/continuing education programs, advanced placement credit, cooperative education, distance learning, English as a second language, honors programs, part-time degree program, services for LD students, study abroad, summer session for credit.

Student Life *Campus security:* security guards during open hours.

Athletics Member NJCAA.

Costs (2006–07) *Tuition:* state resident $0 full-time; nonresident $5628 full-time, $175 per unit part-time. *Required fees:* $768 full-time, $26 per unit part-time, $24 per term part-time.

Financial Aid Of all full-time matriculated undergraduates, 125 Federal Work-Study jobs (averaging $4000).

Applying *Required for some:* high school transcript.

Freshmen Application Contact Terry Stats, Admissions Office, Skyline College, 3300 College Drive, San Bruno, CA 94066-1698. *Phone:* 650-738-4251. *E-mail:* stats@smccd.net.

SOLANO COMMUNITY COLLEGE

Suisun City, California   www.solano.edu/

Director of Admissions Mr. Gerald Fisher, Dean of Admissions and Records, Solano Community College, 4000 Suisun Valley Road, Fairfield, CA 94534. *Phone:* 707-864-7113. *E-mail:* admissions@solano.cc.ca.us.

SONOMA COLLEGE

Petaluma, California   www.sonomacollege.com/

Director of Admissions Ms. Delores Ford, Chief Operating Officer/Campus Director, Sonoma College, 130 Avram Avenue, Rhonert Park, CA 94928. *Phone:* 707-664-9267 Ext. 12. *Toll-free phone:* 800-437-9474. *Fax:* 707-664-9237.

SONOMA COLLEGE

San Francisco, California   www.sonomacollege.com/

Director of Admissions Sonoma College, 301 Howard Street, Suite 510, San Francisco, CA 94105. *Toll-free phone:* 888-649-7801.

SOUTH COAST COLLEGE

Orange, California   www.southcoastcollege.com/

- **Proprietary** 2-year, founded 1961
- **Coed,** 368 undergraduate students

Majors Medical transcription.

Academics *Degree:* associate.

Costs (2006–07) *Tuition:* $16,200 per degree program part-time.

Applying *Application fee:* $99.

Director of Admissions South Coast College, 2011 West Chapman Avenue, Orange, CA 92868. *Toll-free phone:* 800-337-8366.

SOUTHERN CALIFORNIA INSTITUTE OF TECHNOLOGY

Anaheim, California   www.scitcollege.com/

Freshmen Application Contact Ms. Soheila Saboury, Director of Admissions, Southern California Institute of Technology, 1900 West Crescent Avenue, Building B, Anaheim, CA 92801. *Phone:* 714-520-5552. *Fax:* 714-520-4520. *E-mail:* ssaboury@scit-scu.edu.

SOUTHWESTERN COLLEGE

Chula Vista, California   www.swc.cc.ca.us/

Freshmen Application Contact Director of Admissions and Records, Southwestern College, 900 Otay Lakes Road, Chula Vista, CA 91910. *Phone:* 619-482-6550. *Fax:* 619-482-6489.

STANBRIDGE COLLEGE

Irvine, California   www.stanbridge.edu/

- **Proprietary** 2-year
- **28 undergraduate students**
- **95% of applicants were admitted**

Freshmen *Admission:* 65 applied, 62 admitted.

Majors Computer and information systems security.

Academics *Degree:* associate.

Costs (2006–07) *Tuition:* $22,482 per degree program part-time.

Admissions Office Contact Stanbridge College, 2041 Business Center Drive, Irvine, CA 92612.

TAFT COLLEGE

Taft, California   www.taftcollege.edu/

- **State and locally supported** 2-year, founded 1922, part of California Community College System
- **Small-town** 15-acre campus
- **Endowment** $14,405
- **Coed,** 9,500 undergraduate students, 5% full-time, 20% women, 80% men

Undergraduates 505 full-time, 8,995 part-time. Students come from 10 states and territories, 1 other country, 5% are from out of state, 8% African American, 5% Asian American or Pacific Islander, 32% Hispanic American, 2% Native American, 3% transferred in, 6% live on campus.

Freshmen *Admission:* 812 applied, 812 admitted, 324 enrolled.

Faculty *Total:* 91, 41% full-time, 9% with terminal degrees. *Student/faculty ratio:* 18:1.

Majors Accounting; administrative assistant and secretarial science; art; automobile/automotive mechanics technology; biology/biological sciences; business administration and management; computer science; criminal justice/law enforcement administration; data processing and data processing technology; dental hygiene; drafting and design technology; electrical, electronic and communications engineering technology; English; general studies; industrial arts; journalism; kindergarten/preschool education; liberal arts and sciences/liberal studies; mathematics; parks, recreation and leisure; physical education teaching and coaching; physical sciences; pre-engineering; social sciences.

Academics *Calendar:* semesters. *Degree:* certificates and associate. *Special study options:* academic remediation for entering students, adult/continuing education programs, advanced placement credit, distance learning, English as a second language, honors programs, independent study, part-time degree program, services for LD students, summer session for credit.

Library Taft College Library with 28,500 titles, 150 serial subscriptions, 1,500 audiovisual materials, an OPAC, a Web page.

Student Life *Housing Options:* coed, disabled students. Campus housing is university owned. *Activities and Organizations:* student-run newspaper, International Club, Alpha Gamma Sigma, Rotoract Club, ASB Club. *Campus security:* controlled dormitory access, parking lot security. *Student services:* personal/psychological counseling.

Athletics *Intercollegiate sports:* baseball M, basketball W, soccer M, softball W, volleyball W.

Costs (2007–08) *Tuition:* state resident $0 full-time; nonresident $5790 full-time. *Required fees:* $600 full-time, $20 per unit part-time. *Room and board:* $3372; room only: $1428.

Financial Aid Of all full-time matriculated undergraduates, 63 Federal Work-Study jobs (averaging $1500).

Applying *Options:* electronic application. *Required for some:* high school transcript. *Application deadlines:* rolling (freshmen), 8/1 (transfers).

Freshmen Application Contact Harold Russell III, Director of Financial Aid and Admissions, Taft College, 29 Emmons Park Drive, Taft, CA 93268. *Phone:* 661-763-7763. *Fax:* 661-763-7758. *E-mail:* hrussell@taft.org.

VENTURA COLLEGE

Ventura, California   www.venturacollege.edu/

- **State and locally supported** 2-year, founded 1925, part of California Community College System
- **Suburban** 103-acre campus with easy access to Los Angeles
- **Coed,** 11,757 undergraduate students, 33% full-time, 58% women, 42% men

Undergraduates 3,869 full-time, 7,888 part-time. Students come from 25 states and territories, 11% are from out of state, 3% African American, 7% Asian American or Pacific Islander, 37% Hispanic American, 1% Native American, 0.9% international, 20% transferred in.

Freshmen *Admission:* 2,652 applied, 864 enrolled.

Faculty *Total:* 504, 27% full-time. *Student/faculty ratio:* 26:1.

Majors Accounting; agriculture; automobile/automotive mechanics technology; biology/biological sciences; business administration and management; ceramic arts and ceramics; commercial and advertising art; computer and information sciences; construction engineering technology; criminal justice/law enforcement administration; dramatic/theater arts; engineering; fashion/apparel design; fine/studio arts; hydrology and water resources science; journalism; liberal arts and sciences/liberal studies; machine tool technology; medical/clinical assistant; medical transcription; music; natural resources management and policy; nursing (registered nurse training); parks, recreation and leisure; physical sciences; plant sciences; real estate; tool and die technology; welding technology.

Academics *Calendar:* semesters. *Degree:* certificates, diplomas, and associate. *Special study options:* academic remediation for entering students, adult/continuing education programs, advanced placement credit, English as a second language, independent study, internships, part-time degree program, services for LD students, summer session for credit.

Library Ventura College Library with 63,529 titles, 341 serial subscriptions, an OPAC, a Web page.

Student Life *Housing:* college housing not available. *Activities and Organizations:* drama/theater group, student-run newspaper, choral group, Pan American Student Union, MECHA, Automotive Technology Club, Campus Christian Fellowship, Asian-American Club. *Campus security:* 24-hour emergency response devices and patrols, student patrols. *Student services:* health clinic, personal/psychological counseling, women's center.

Athletics *Intercollegiate sports:* baseball M, basketball M/W, cross-country running M/W, football M, golf M, soccer M/W, softball W, swimming and diving M/W, tennis M/W, track and field M/W, volleyball W, water polo M/W.

Costs (2006–07) *Tuition:* state resident $0 full-time; nonresident $4650 full-time. *Required fees:* $816 full-time. *Payment plan:* installment.

Financial Aid Of all full-time matriculated undergraduates, 70 Federal Work-Study jobs.

Applying *Required:* high school transcript.

Freshmen Application Contact Ms. Susan Bricker, Registrar, Ventura College, 4667 Telegraph Road, Ventura, CA 93003-3899. *Phone:* 805-654-6456. *Fax:* 805-654-6466. *E-mail:* sbricker@vcccd.net.

VICTOR VALLEY COLLEGE

Victorville, California   www.vvc.edu/

- **State-supported** 2-year, founded 1961, part of California Community College System
- **Small-town** 253-acre campus with easy access to Los Angeles
- **Coed,** 10,580 undergraduate students, 35% full-time, 62% women, 38% men

Undergraduates 3,663 full-time, 6,917 part-time. 10% African American, 4% Asian American or Pacific Islander, 24% Hispanic American, 1% Native American.

Freshmen *Admission:* 1,226 enrolled.

Faculty *Total:* 460, 30% full-time.

Majors Administrative assistant and secretarial science; agricultural teacher education; art; automobile/automotive mechanics technology; biological and physical sciences; biology/biological sciences; business administration and management; business/commerce; child care and support services management; child development; computer and information sciences; computer programming (specific applications); computer science; construction engineering technology; construction management; criminal justice/police science; dramatic/theater arts; electrical, electronic and communications engineering technology; fire protection and safety technology; fire science; food services technology; horticultural science; humanities; information science/studies; kindergarten/preschool education; liberal arts and sciences/liberal studies; management information systems; mathematics; music; natural sciences; nursing (registered nurse training); ornamental horticulture; physical sciences; real estate; respiratory care therapy; science technologies related; social sciences; teacher assistant/aide; trade and industrial teacher education; vehicle maintenance and repair technologies related; welding technology.

Academics *Calendar:* semesters. *Degree:* certificates and associate. *Special study options:* academic remediation for entering students, advanced placement credit, cooperative education, distance learning, English as a second language, honors programs, off-campus study, part-time degree program, services for LD students, study abroad, summer session for credit.

Library Learning Resource Center with 41,789 titles, 534 serial subscriptions, an OPAC, a Web page.

Student Life *Housing:* college housing not available. *Activities and Organizations:* drama/theater group, student-run newspaper, choral group, Black Student Union, Drama Club, rugby, Phi Theta Kappa. *Campus security:* 24-hour emergency response devices and patrols, late-night transport/escort service, part-time trained security personnel. *Student services:* health clinic, personal/psychological counseling.

Athletics Member NCAA, NJCAA. *Intercollegiate sports:* baseball M, basketball M/W, cross-country running M/W, football M, golf M, soccer M/W, softball W, tennis M/W, track and field M/W, volleyball W, wrestling M. *Intramural sports:* rock climbing M/W.

Standardized Tests *Recommended:* ACCUPLACER.

Costs (2006–07) *Tuition:* state resident $0 full-time; nonresident $3840 full-time, $157 per unit part-time. *Required fees:* $624 full-time, $26 per unit part-time. *Payment plan:* installment.

Victor Valley College (continued)

Financial Aid Of all full-time matriculated undergraduates, 300 Federal Work-Study jobs (averaging $5000). 50 state and other part-time jobs (averaging $5000).

Applying *Options:* early admission. *Application deadline:* rolling (freshmen). *Notification:* continuous (freshmen), continuous (transfers).

Freshmen Application Contact Ms. Greta Moon, Director of Admissions and Records (Interim), Victor Valley College, 18422 Bear Valley Road, Victorville, CA 92392. *Phone:* 760-245-4271. *Fax:* 760-843-7707. *E-mail:* moong@vvc.edu.

WESTERN CAREER COLLEGE

Emeryville, California   www.westerncollege.edu/

Director of Admissions Ms. Marianne Dulay, Admissions Representative, Western Career College, 1400 65th Street, Suite 200, Emeryville, CA 94608. *Phone:* 510-601-0133 Ext. 14. *Toll-free phone:* 800-750-5627.

WESTERN CAREER COLLEGE

Fremont, California   www.westerncollege.edu/

Director of Admissions Mr. Anton Croos, Admissions Director, Western Career College, 41350 Christy Street, Fremont, CA 94538. *Phone:* 510-623-9966 Ext. 212. *Toll-free phone:* 800-750-5627.

WESTERN CAREER COLLEGE

Pleasant Hill, California   www.westerncollege.edu/

- **Proprietary** 2-year, founded 1997
- **Coed,** 397 undergraduate students
- 90% of applicants were admitted

Freshmen *Admission:* 142 applied, 128 admitted.

Majors Dental assisting; graphic communications related; health and medical administrative services related; massage therapy; medical/clinical assistant; medical insurance/medical billing; pharmacy technician; veterinary/animal health technology.

Academics *Calendar:* semesters. *Degree:* associate.

Costs (2006–07) *Tuition:* $14,760 full-time.

Applying *Application fee:* $100.

Admissions Office Contact Western Career College, 380 Civic Drive, Suite 300, Pleasant Hill, CA 94523. *Toll-free phone:* 888-203-9947.

WESTERN CAREER COLLEGE

Sacramento, California   www.westerncollege.edu/

- **Proprietary** 2-year, founded 1967
- **Coed,** 1,053 undergraduate students
- 79% of applicants were admitted

Freshmen *Admission:* 434 applied, 344 admitted.

Majors Dental assisting; massage therapy; medical/clinical assistant; medical office management; nursing (registered nurse training); pharmacy technician; veterinary/animal health technology.

Academics *Calendar:* semesters. *Degree:* associate.

Costs (2006–07) *Tuition:* $14,760 full-time.

Applying *Application fee:* $100.

Admissions Office Contact Western Career College, 8909 Folsom Boulevard, Sacramento, CA 95826. *Toll-free phone:* 888-203-9947.

WESTERN CAREER COLLEGE

San Jose, California   www.westerncollege.edu/

Director of Admissions Ms. Patricia Fraser, Admissions Director, Western Career College, 6201 San Ignacio Avenue, San Jose, CA 95119. *Phone:* 408-360-0840 Ext. 247. *Toll-free phone:* 800-750-5627.

WESTERN CAREER COLLEGE

San Leandro, California   www.westerncollege.edu/

- **Proprietary** 2-year, founded 1986
- **Coed**
- 75% of applicants were admitted

Freshmen *Admission:* 249 applied, 187 admitted.

Majors Health and medical administrative services related; medical/clinical assistant; nursing related; pharmacy technician; veterinary/animal health technology.

Academics *Calendar:* semesters. *Degree:* associate.

Costs (2006–07) *Tuition:* $14,760 full-time.

Applying *Application fee:* $100.

Admissions Office Contact Western Career College, 15555 E. 14th Street, Suite 500, San Leandro, CA 94578. *Toll-free phone:* 888-203-9947.

WESTERN CAREER COLLEGE

Walnut Creek, California   www.westerncollege.edu/campus_locations/antioch_campus.html

Director of Admissions Mr. Mark Millen, Admissions Director, Western Career College, 2800 Mitchell Drive, Walnut Creek, CA 94598. *Phone:* 925-280-0235 Ext. 37. *Toll-free phone:* 888-203-9947.

WEST HILLS COMMUNITY COLLEGE

Coalinga, California   www.westhillscollege.com/

- **State-supported** 2-year, founded 1932, part of California Community College System
- **Small-town** 193-acre campus
- **Coed,** 6,088 undergraduate students, 32% full-time, 61% women, 39% men

Undergraduates 1,956 full-time, 4,132 part-time. Students come from 25 states and territories, 5 other countries, 2% are from out of state, 6% African American, 6% Asian American or Pacific Islander, 46% Hispanic American, 1% Native American, 2% international, 20% live on campus.

Freshmen *Admission:* 2,523 enrolled. *Average high school GPA:* 2.75.

Faculty *Total:* 263, 33% full-time, 5% with terminal degrees. *Student/faculty ratio:* 20:1.

Majors Accounting; administrative assistant and secretarial science; agricultural business and management; agricultural mechanization; agronomy and crop science; animal sciences; art; automobile/automotive mechanics technology; biology/biological sciences; business administration and management; chemistry; child development; criminal justice/law enforcement administration; equestrian studies; geography; geology/earth science; health science; humanities; information science/studies; kindergarten/preschool education; liberal arts and sciences/liberal studies; mathematics; physical education teaching and coaching; physics; pre-engineering; psychology; social sciences; transportation technology; welding technology.

Academics *Calendar:* semesters. *Degree:* certificates, diplomas, and associate. *Special study options:* academic remediation for entering students, adult/continuing education programs, advanced placement credit, cooperative education, distance learning, English as a second language, independent study, off-campus study, part-time degree program, services for LD students, study abroad, summer session for credit.

Library West Hills Community College Library with 32,000 titles, 210 serial subscriptions.

Student Life *Housing Options:* men-only, women-only. Campus housing is university owned. *Activities and Organizations:* drama/theater group. *Student services:* personal/psychological counseling.

Athletics *Intercollegiate sports:* baseball M, basketball M, equestrian sports M/W, football M, softball W, tennis W, volleyball W.

Costs (2007–08) *Tuition:* state resident $0 full-time; nonresident $3840 full-time, $160 per unit part-time. *Required fees:* $480 full-time, $20 per unit part-time. *Room and board:* $5296.

Financial Aid Of all full-time matriculated undergraduates, 253 Federal Work-Study jobs (averaging $1351). 42 state and other part-time jobs (averaging $1669).

Applying *Options:* early admission. *Recommended:* high school transcript. *Application deadlines:* rolling (freshmen), rolling (transfers). *Notification:* continuous (freshmen), continuous (transfers).

Freshmen Application Contact Sandra Dagnino, West Hills Community College, 300 Cherry Lane, Coalinga, CA 93210-1399. *Phone:* 559-934-3203. *Toll-free phone:* 800-266-1114. *Fax:* 559-934-2830. *E-mail:* sandradagnino@westhillscollege.com.

WEST LOS ANGELES COLLEGE

Culver City, California   www.wlac.cc.ca.us/

- **State and locally supported** 2-year, founded 1969, part of Los Angeles Community College District System
- **Urban** 69-acre campus with easy access to Los Angeles
- **Coed,** 9,800 undergraduate students

Undergraduates Students come from 20 states and territories.

Faculty *Total:* 320, 38% full-time.

Majors Accounting; administrative assistant and secretarial science; airframe mechanics and aircraft maintenance technology; anthropology; art; avionics maintenance technology; biology/biological sciences; business administration and management; chemistry; computer programming; consumer merchandising/retailing management; criminal justice/law enforcement administration; criminal justice/police science; data processing and data processing technology; dental hygiene; developmental and child psychology; drafting and design technology; economics; education; electrical, electronic and communications engineering technology; engineering; English; family and consumer economics related; French; geography; geology/earth science; history; journalism; legal administrative assistant/secretary; legal assistant/paralegal; liberal arts and sciences/liberal studies; marketing/marketing management; mathematics; medical administrative assistant and medical secretary; music; philosophy; physical education teaching and coaching; physics; political science and government; psychology; real estate; sociology; Spanish; speech and rhetoric; tourism and travel services management.

Academics *Calendar:* semesters. *Degree:* associate. *Special study options:* academic remediation for entering students, adult/continuing education programs, advanced placement credit, cooperative education, English as a second language, honors programs, part-time degree program, services for LD students, summer session for credit. *ROTC:* Army (c), Air Force (c).

Library 51,000 titles, 400 serial subscriptions.

Student Life *Housing:* college housing not available. *Activities and Organizations:* choral group. *Campus security:* 24-hour patrols. *Student services:* health clinic, personal/psychological counseling.

Athletics *Intercollegiate sports:* basketball M, football M, golf M, track and field M/W, volleyball W.

Costs (2006–07) *Tuition:* state resident $698 full-time; nonresident $4832 full-time.

Financial Aid Of all full-time matriculated undergraduates, 40 Federal Work-Study jobs (averaging $2500). 20 state and other part-time jobs (averaging $2500).

Applying *Options:* early admission. *Recommended:* high school transcript. *Application deadlines:* 8/16 (freshmen), 8/16 (transfers).

Director of Admissions Mr. Len Isaksen, Director of Admissions, West Los Angeles College, 9000 Overland Avenue, Culver City, CA 90230-3519. *Phone:* 310-287-4255.

WEST VALLEY COLLEGE

Saratoga, California   www.westvalley.edu/

- **State and locally supported** 2-year, founded 1963, part of California Community College System
- **Small-town** 143-acre campus with easy access to San Francisco and San Jose
- **Coed,** 11,000 undergraduate students

Undergraduates Students come from 2 states and territories, 20 other countries.

Faculty *Total:* 560, 38% full-time.

Majors Accounting; administrative assistant and secretarial science; art; biology/biological sciences; business administration and management; chemistry; court reporting; criminal justice/law enforcement administration; criminal justice/police science; data processing and data processing technology; drafting and design technology; dramatic/theater arts; economics; English; fashion/apparel design; French; German; health information/medical records administration; history; information science/studies; interior design; Italian; kindergarten/preschool education; landscape architecture; legal administrative assistant/

secretary; liberal arts and sciences/liberal studies; marketing/marketing management; mathematics; medical administrative assistant and medical secretary; medical/clinical assistant; music; parks, recreation and leisure facilities management; physical education teaching and coaching; physics; psychology; social sciences; sociology; Spanish; speech and rhetoric; women's studies.

Academics *Calendar:* semesters. *Degree:* certificates and associate. *Special study options:* academic remediation for entering students, adult/continuing education programs, cooperative education, English as a second language, honors programs, internships, part-time degree program, services for LD students, summer session for credit. *ROTC:* Army (c), Air Force (c).

Library West Valley College Library with 82,959 titles, 491 serial subscriptions.

Student Life *Housing:* college housing not available. *Activities and Organizations:* drama/theater group, student-run newspaper. *Student services:* health clinic, personal/psychological counseling.

Athletics *Intercollegiate sports:* basketball M/W, cross-country running M/W, football M, golf M, soccer M, swimming and diving M/W, tennis M/W, track and field M, volleyball M/W, water polo M, wrestling M. *Intramural sports:* badminton M/W, basketball M, bowling M/W, swimming and diving M/W, tennis M/W, track and field W, volleyball M/W.

Costs (2006–07) *Tuition:* state resident $688 full-time; nonresident $3624 full-time.

Financial Aid Of all full-time matriculated undergraduates, 125 Federal Work-Study jobs (averaging $2000).

Applying *Options:* early admission. *Application deadlines:* rolling (freshmen), rolling (transfers). *Notification:* continuous (freshmen), continuous (transfers).

Freshmen Application Contact Mr. Albert Moore, Admissions and Records Supervisor, West Valley College, 14000 Fruitvale Avenue, Saratoga, CA 95070-5698. *Phone:* 408-741-2533.

WESTWOOD COLLEGE—ANAHEIM

Anaheim, California   www.westwood.edu/

- **Proprietary** primarily 2-year
- **Suburban** campus with easy access to Los Angeles
- **Coed**
- 37% of applicants were admitted

Undergraduates 570 full-time, 104 part-time. 2% African American, 11% Asian American or Pacific Islander, 41% Hispanic American, 0.4% Native American, 0.1% international.

Academics *Calendar:* continuous. *Degrees:* associate and bachelor's.

Applying *Required:* interview, high school diploma or GED and passing scores on SAT/ACT or Accuplacer test.

Director of Admissions Mr. Paul Sallenbach, Director of Admissions, Westwood College–Anaheim, 1551 South Douglass Road, Anaheim, CA 92806. *Phone:* 714-226-9990. *Toll-free phone:* 877-650-6050.

▶See page 592 for the College Close-Up.

WESTWOOD COLLEGE—INLAND EMPIRE

Upland, California   www.westwood.edu/

- **Proprietary** primarily 2-year
- **Suburban** campus with easy access to Los Angeles
- **Coed**

Undergraduates 647 full-time, 156 part-time. 7% African American, 4% Asian American or Pacific Islander, 50% Hispanic American, 1% Native American.

Academics *Calendar:* continuous. *Degrees:* associate and bachelor's.

Applying *Required:* interview, high school diploma or GED, pass entrance exam (or provide acceptable SAT/ACT scores).

Director of Admissions Mr. Lyle Seavers, Director of Admissions, Westwood College–Inland Empire, 20 West 7th Street, Upland, CA 91786-7148. *Phone:* 909-931-7550. *Toll-free phone:* 866-288-9488.

▶See page 620 for the College Close-Up.

WESTWOOD COLLEGE—LOS ANGELES

Los Angeles, California   www.westwood.edu/

- **Proprietary** primarily 2-year
- **Urban** campus with easy access to Los Angeles
- **Coed**

Westwood College–Los Angeles (continued)

Undergraduates 577 full-time, 102 part-time. 13% African American, 10% Asian American or Pacific Islander, 66% Hispanic American.

Academics *Calendar:* continuous. *Degrees:* associate and bachelor's.

Applying *Application fee:* $100. *Required:* interview, high school diploma/GED and passing scores on ACT/SAT or Accuplacer.

Director of Admissions Mr. Ron Milman, Director of Admissions, Westwood College–Los Angeles, 3250 Wilshire Boulevard, 4th Floor, Los Angeles, CA 90010. *Phone:* 213-739-9999. *Toll-free phone:* 877-377-4600.

▶See page 622 for the College Close-Up.

WESTWOOD COLLEGE–SOUTH BAY CAMPUS

Long Beach, California　　　www.westwood.edu

- **Proprietary** primarily 2-year, founded 2002, part of AITU Colleges
- **Urban** 1-acre campus with easy access to Los Angeles
- **Coed**

Undergraduates 265 full-time. Students come from 4 states and territories, 2% are from out of state, 14% African American, 8% Asian American or Pacific Islander, 48% Hispanic American, 0.4% Native American, 0.4% international.

Faculty *Student/faculty ratio:* 15:1.

Academics *Calendar:* continuous. *Degrees:* associate and bachelor's. *Special study options:* accelerated degree program, adult/continuing education programs, advanced placement credit, cooperative education, external degree program, freshman honors college, honors programs, independent study, internships, off-campus study, part-time degree program, services for LD students, student-designed majors.

Student Life *Campus security:* 24-hour emergency response devices and patrols, late-night transport/escort service.

Standardized Tests *Required:* ACCUPLACER (for admission). *Recommended:* SAT or ACT (for admission).

Applying *Options:* electronic application. *Application fee:* $100. *Required:* high school transcript, interview.

Director of Admissions Jesse Kamekona, Director of Admissions, Westwood College–South Bay Campus, 19700 South Vermont Avenue, Suite 100, Torrance, CA 90502. *Phone:* 310-522-2088 Ext. 100. *Toll-free phone:* 888-403-3308.

▶See page 624 for the College Close-Up.

WYOTECH

Fremont, California　　　www.wyotech.com/

- **Proprietary** 2-year, founded 1966, administratively affiliated with Corinthian Colleges, Inc
- **Urban** campus
- **Coed, primarily men,** 1,554 undergraduate students, 100% full-time, 3% women, 97% men
- 97% of applicants were admitted

Undergraduates 1,554 full-time. 8% African American, 25% Asian American or Pacific Islander, 34% Hispanic American, 0.8% Native American, 0.1% international, 1% live on campus.

Freshmen *Admission:* 416 applied, 405 admitted.

Faculty *Total:* 62, 100% full-time. *Student/faculty ratio:* 25:1.

Majors Automobile/automotive mechanics technology; automotive engineering technology; heating, air conditioning, ventilation and refrigeration maintenance technology.

Academics *Calendar:* continuous. *Degree:* certificates, diplomas, and associate. *Special study options:* academic remediation for entering students.

Library Learning Resource Center with 1,000 audiovisual materials.

Student Life *Housing Options:* Campus housing is leased by the school. *Campus security:* late-night transport/escort service, security personnel.

Standardized Tests *Required:* SRA or ATB Entrance Exam (for admission).

Costs (2007–08) *Tuition:* $25,016 full-time. *Required fees:* $50 full-time.

Applying *Required:* successful completion of school's admission requirements as outlined in catalog.

Freshmen Application Contact Admissions Department, WyoTech, 200 Whitney Place, Fremont, CA 94539-7663. *Phone:* 510-580-3507. *Toll-free phone:* 800-248-8585. *Fax:* 510-490-8599.

WYOTECH

West Sacramento, California　　　www.wyotech.com/

Admissions Office Contact WyoTech, 980 Riverside Parkway, West Sacramento, CA 95605-1507.

YUBA COLLEGE

Marysville, California　　　www.yccd.edu/

- **State and locally supported** 2-year, founded 1927, part of California Community College System
- **Rural** 160-acre campus with easy access to Sacramento
- **Endowment** $3.7 million
- **Coed,** 6,623 undergraduate students

Faculty *Total:* 510, 26% full-time.

Majors Accounting; administrative assistant and secretarial science; advertising; African-American/Black studies; agricultural business and management; agricultural mechanization; agriculture; agronomy and crop science; animal sciences; art; automobile/automotive mechanics technology; biological and physical sciences; biology/biological sciences; business administration and management; chemistry; child development; communication/speech communication and rhetoric; computer and information sciences related; computer science; corrections; cosmetology; criminal justice/law enforcement administration; criminal justice/police science; cultural studies; dramatic/theater arts; education; electrical, electronic and communications engineering technology; elementary education; English; family and consumer economics related; family and consumer sciences/human sciences; fire science; health teacher education; Hispanic-American, Puerto Rican, and Mexican-American/Chicano studies; history; human services; industrial radiologic technology; industrial technology; kindergarten/preschool education; machine tool technology; mass communication/media; mathematics; music; nursing (licensed practical/vocational nurse training); nursing (registered nurse training); philosophy; photography; physical education teaching and coaching; pre-engineering; psychiatric/mental health services technology; psychology; robotics technology; social sciences; substance abuse/addiction counseling; veterinary technology; welding technology; women's studies; word processing.

Academics *Calendar:* semesters. *Degree:* certificates and associate. *Special study options:* academic remediation for entering students, advanced placement credit, distance learning, double majors, English as a second language, part-time degree program, services for LD students, summer session for credit.

Library Learning Resource Center and Library plus 1 other with 65,000 titles, 1,300 serial subscriptions, 9,419 audiovisual materials, an OPAC.

Student Life *Activities and Organizations:* drama/theater group, choral group. *Campus security:* 24-hour patrols, student patrols. *Student services:* health clinic, personal/psychological counseling, women's center.

Athletics Member NCAA. *Intercollegiate sports:* baseball M(s), basketball M/W, cross-country running M/W, football M, soccer M/W, softball W, tennis M/W, track and field M/W, volleyball W.

Costs (2006–07) *Tuition:* state resident $0 full-time; nonresident $5280 full-time, $176 per unit part-time. *Required fees:* $610 full-time, $20 per unit part-time, $5 per semester part-time.

Financial Aid Of all full-time matriculated undergraduates, 290 Federal Work-Study jobs (averaging $2400). 50 state and other part-time jobs (averaging $1000).

Applying *Options:* electronic application. *Required:* high school transcript. *Application deadlines:* rolling (freshmen), rolling (transfers).

Director of Admissions Dr. David Farrell, Dean of Student Development, Yuba College, 2088 North Beale Road, Marysville, CA 95901. *Phone:* 530-741-6705.

COLORADO

AIMS COMMUNITY COLLEGE

Greeley, Colorado　　　www.aims.edu/

- **District-supported** 2-year, founded 1967
- **Urban** 185-acre campus with easy access to Denver
- **Endowment** $71,813
- **Coed,** 5,098 undergraduate students, 44% full-time, 55% women, 45% men

Undergraduates 2,252 full-time, 2,846 part-time. Students come from 8 states and territories. *Retention:* 45% of 2003 full-time freshmen returned.

Freshmen *Admission:* 849 enrolled.

Faculty *Total:* 321, 32% full-time, 5% with terminal degrees. *Student/faculty ratio:* 16:1.

Majors Accounting; administrative assistant and secretarial science; agricultural mechanization; automobile/automotive mechanics technology; avionics maintenance technology; child development; commercial and advertising art; criminal justice/law enforcement administration; criminal justice/police science; electrical, electronic and communications engineering technology; engineering technology; fire science; industrial radiologic technology; information science/studies; kindergarten/preschool education; liberal arts and sciences/liberal studies; marketing/marketing management; welding technology.

Academics *Calendar:* semesters. *Degree:* certificates, diplomas, and associate. *Special study options:* academic remediation for entering students, adult/continuing education programs, advanced placement credit, cooperative education, English as a second language, external degree program, freshman honors college, honors programs, part-time degree program, student-designed majors, summer session for credit. *ROTC:* Air Force (c).

Library Aims Community College Library with 39,129 titles, 258 serial subscriptions, an OPAC.

Student Life *Housing:* college housing not available. *Activities and Organizations:* drama/theater group, student-run newspaper, radio station, choral group. *Campus security:* 24-hour emergency response devices, day and evening patrols by trained security personnel. *Student services:* personal/psychological counseling, women's center.

Athletics *Intramural sports:* basketball M/W, volleyball M/W.

Standardized Tests *Required:* CPT (for placement).

Costs (2006–07) *Tuition:* area resident $1518 full-time; state resident $2118 full-time; nonresident $7518 full-time.

Financial Aid Of all full-time matriculated undergraduates, 26 Federal Work-Study jobs (averaging $1800). 185 state and other part-time jobs (averaging $1800).

Applying *Options:* early admission, deferred entrance. *Application deadlines:* rolling (freshmen), rolling (transfers).

Freshmen Application Contact Ms. Susie Gallardo, Admissions Technician, Aims Community College, Box 69, 5401 West 20th Street, Greeley, CO 80632-0069. *Phone:* 970-330-8008 Ext. 6624. *E-mail:* wgreen@chiron.aims.edu.

ARAPAHOE COMMUNITY COLLEGE

Littleton, Colorado   www.arapahoe.edu/

- **State-supported** 2-year, founded 1965, part of Colorado Community College and Occupational Education System
- **Suburban** 52-acre campus with easy access to Denver
- **Coed**

Undergraduates 2,312 full-time, 5,248 part-time. Students come from 35 other countries, 3% African American, 3% Asian American or Pacific Islander, 9% Hispanic American, 1% Native American, 1% international.

Faculty *Student/faculty ratio:* 19:1.

Academics *Calendar:* semesters. *Degree:* certificates, diplomas, and associate. *Special study options:* academic remediation for entering students, accelerated degree program, adult/continuing education programs, advanced placement credit, cooperative education, distance learning, double majors, English as a second language, honors programs, independent study, internships, off-campus study, part-time degree program, services for LD students, student-designed majors, study abroad, summer session for credit. *ROTC:* Army (c), Air Force (c).

Student Life *Campus security:* 24-hour emergency response devices and patrols, late-night transport/escort service.

Athletics Member NJCAA.

Costs (2006–07) *Tuition:* state resident $1619 full-time, $90 per credit hour part-time; nonresident $8000 full-time, $369 per credit hour part-time. *Required fees:* $81 full-time.

Financial Aid Of all full-time matriculated undergraduates, 100 Federal Work-Study jobs (averaging $4200). 200 state and other part-time jobs (averaging $4200).

Applying *Options:* electronic application, early admission, deferred entrance.

Freshmen Application Contact Mr. Howard Fukaye, Admissions Specialist, Arapahoe Community College, 5900 South Santa Fe Drive, PO Box 9002, Littleton, CO 80160-9002. *Phone:* 303-797-5622. *Fax:* 303-797-5970. *E-mail:* hfukaye@arapahoe.edu.

BEL–REA INSTITUTE OF ANIMAL TECHNOLOGY

Denver, Colorado   www.bel-rea.com/

Director of Admissions Ms. Paulette Kaufman, Director, Bel–Rea Institute of Animal Technology, 1681 South Dayton Street, Denver, CO 80247. *Phone:* 303-751-8700. *Toll-free phone:* 800-950-8001.

BOULDER COLLEGE OF MASSAGE THERAPY

Boulder, Colorado   www.bcmt.org/

- **Independent** 2-year, founded 1975
- **Coed,** 220 undergraduate students

Majors Massage therapy.

Academics *Calendar:* quarters. *Degree:* certificates and associate.

Costs (2006–07) *Tuition:* $13,860 full-time.

Applying *Application fee:* $75.

Freshmen Application Contact Admissions Office, Boulder College of Massage Therapy, Boulder, CO 80301-3295. *Toll-free phone:* 800-442-5131.

CAMBRIDGE COLLEGE

Aurora, Colorado   www.cambridgecollege.com/

- **Independent** 2-year
- 578 undergraduate students

Majors Criminal justice/safety; information science/studies; massage therapy; medical/clinical assistant; medical insurance coding; medical radiologic technology; surgical technology.

Academics *Degree:* certificates and associate.

Costs (2006–07) *Tuition:* $26,224 per degree program part-time.

Applying *Application fee:* $50.

Director of Admissions Admissions Office, Cambridge College, 350 Blackhawk Street, Aurora, CO 80011. *Toll-free phone:* 800-322-4132.

COLLEGEAMERICA–COLORADO SPRINGS

Colorado Spring, Colorado   www.collegeamerica.com/

- **Proprietary** primarily 2-year
- **Coed**

Majors Accounting; business administration and management; computer programming; computer science; computer systems networking and telecommunications; graphic design; health/health care administration.

Academics *Degrees:* associate and bachelor's.

Freshmen Application Contact Admissions Office, CollegeAmerica–Colorado Springs, 3645 Citadel Drive South, Colorado Springs, CO 80909.

COLLEGEAMERICA–DENVER

Denver, Colorado   www.collegeamerica.com/

- **Proprietary** primarily 2-year, founded 1962
- **Urban** campus
- **Coed,** 444 undergraduate students

Majors Accounting; business administration and management; computer programming; computer science; computer systems networking and telecommunications; graphic design; health/health care administration.

Academics *Degrees:* certificates, associate, and bachelor's.

Freshmen Application Contact Admissions Office, CollegeAmerica–Denver, 1385 South Colorado Boulevard, Denver, CO 80222. *Phone:* 303-691-9756. *Toll-free phone:* 800-97-SKILLS.

COLLEGEAMERICA—FORT COLLINS

Fort Collins, Colorado   www.collegeamerica.edu/

Director of Admissions Ms. Anna DiTorrice-Mull, Director of Admissions, CollegeAmerica–Fort Collins, 4601 South Mason Street, Fort Collins, CO 80525. *Phone:* 970-223-6060 Ext. 8002. *Toll-free phone:* 800-97-SKILLS.

COLORADO MOUNTAIN COLLEGE

Glenwood Springs, Colorado   www.coloradomtn.edu/

- **District-supported** 2-year, founded 1965, part of Colorado Mountain College District System
- **Rural** 680-acre campus
- **Coed,** 1,393 undergraduate students

Colorado Mountain College (CMC) offers high-quality instruction in a centered environment. Degree choices range from occupational to transfer options. CMC's Associate of Arts and Associate of Science degrees are part of the State Transfer Guarantee to any four-year public college/university in Colorado. CMC also offers specialized occupational programs in culinary arts, graphic design, natural resources, outdoor leadership, photography, ski industry, the resort industry, and veterinary technology.

Undergraduates Students come from 49 states and territories, 34% are from out of state, 0.4% African American, 0.9% Asian American or Pacific Islander, 23% Hispanic American, 0.6% Native American, 0.4% international, 44% live on campus.

Freshmen *Admission:* 2,237 applied, 2,237 admitted. *Average high school GPA:* 2.4.

Faculty *Total:* 22. *Student/faculty ratio:* 12:1.

Majors Accounting; behavioral sciences; biological and physical sciences; biology/biological sciences; business administration and management; commercial and advertising art; computer engineering technology; computer systems networking and telecommunications; computer/technical support; criminal justice/law enforcement administration; data entry/microcomputer applications related; dramatic/theater arts; English; humanities; liberal arts and sciences/liberal studies; mathematics; natural sciences; nursing (licensed practical/vocational nurse training); nursing (registered nurse training); photography; psychology; social sciences; therapeutic recreation; veterinary technology.

Academics *Calendar:* semesters. *Degree:* certificates and associate. *Special study options:* academic remediation for entering students, adult/continuing education programs, advanced placement credit, cooperative education, distance learning, double majors, English as a second language, honors programs, independent study, internships, part-time degree program, services for LD students, study abroad, summer session for credit.

Library Quigley Library with 36,000 titles, 186 serial subscriptions, an OPAC, a Web page.

Student Life *Housing:* on-campus residence required for freshman year. *Options:* coed, disabled students. Campus housing is university owned. Freshman applicants given priority for college housing. *Activities and Organizations:* drama/theater group, student-run newspaper, student government, outdoor activities, World Awareness Society, Peer Mentors, Student Activities Board. *Campus security:* 24-hour emergency response devices, student patrols, controlled dormitory access. *Student services:* health clinic, personal/psychological counseling.

Athletics Member NJCAA. *Intercollegiate sports:* soccer M/W. *Intramural sports:* basketball M/W, rock climbing M/W, skiing (cross-country) M/W, skiing (downhill) M/W, ultimate Frisbee M/W, volleyball M/W.

Standardized Tests *Recommended:* SAT or ACT (for admission).

Costs (2007–08) *Tuition:* area resident $1290 full-time, $42 per credit part-time; state resident $2160 full-time, $72 per credit part-time; nonresident $6930 full-time, $231 per credit part-time. *Required fees:* $180 full-time. *Room and board:* $6866; room only: $3570.

Applying *Options:* early admission, deferred entrance. *Required:* high school transcript. *Application deadlines:* rolling (freshmen), rolling (transfers).

Freshmen Application Contact Vicky Butler, Admissions Assistant, Colorado Mountain College, PO Box 10001, Department PG, Glenwood Springs, CO 81601. *Phone:* 970-947-8276. *Toll-free phone:* 800-621-8559. *E-mail:* joinus@coloradomtn.edu.

▶See page 532 for the College Close-Up.

COLORADO MOUNTAIN COLLEGE, ALPINE CAMPUS

Steamboat Springs, Colorado   www.coloradomtn.edu/

- **District-supported** 2-year, founded 1965, part of Colorado Mountain College District System
- **Rural** 10-acre campus
- **Coed,** 1,093 undergraduate students

Undergraduates Students come from 49 states and territories, 15% are from out of state, 0.6% African American, 0.7% Asian American or Pacific Islander, 0.4% Hispanic American, 0.7% Native American, 0.2% international, 44% live on campus.

Freshmen *Admission:* 1,824 applied, 1,824 admitted. *Average high school GPA:* 2.4.

Faculty *Total:* 19. *Student/faculty ratio:* 12:1.

Majors Accounting; behavioral sciences; biological and physical sciences; biology/biological sciences; business administration and management; computer engineering technology; consumer merchandising/retailing management; data entry/microcomputer applications related; English; fine/studio arts; geology/earth science; hospitality administration; hotel/motel administration; humanities; liberal arts and sciences/liberal studies; marketing/marketing management; mathematics; parks, recreation and leisure facilities management; physical sciences; pre-engineering; social sciences.

Academics *Calendar:* semesters. *Degree:* certificates and associate. *Special study options:* academic remediation for entering students, adult/continuing education programs, advanced placement credit, cooperative education, distance learning, double majors, English as a second language, honors programs, independent study, internships, part-time degree program, services for LD students, study abroad, summer session for credit.

Library 17,000 titles, 192 serial subscriptions, an OPAC, a Web page.

Student Life *Housing:* on-campus residence required for freshman year. *Options:* coed, disabled students. Campus housing is university owned. *Activities and Organizations:* student-run newspaper, student government, Forensics Team, Ski Club, International Club, Phi Theta Kappa. *Campus security:* 24-hour emergency response devices, student patrols, controlled dormitory access. *Student services:* health clinic, personal/psychological counseling.

Athletics *Intercollegiate sports:* skiing (downhill) M/W. *Intramural sports:* basketball M/W, skiing (cross-country) M/W, skiing (downhill) M/W, soccer M/W, ultimate Frisbee M/W, volleyball M/W.

Standardized Tests *Recommended:* SAT or ACT (for admission).

Costs (2007–08) *Tuition:* area resident $1290 full-time, $43 per credit part-time; state resident $2160 full-time, $72 per credit part-time; nonresident $6930 full-time, $231 per credit part-time. *Required fees:* $180 full-time. *Room and board:* $6866; room only: $3570.

Applying *Options:* early admission, deferred entrance. *Required:* high school transcript. *Application deadlines:* rolling (freshmen), rolling (transfers).

Freshmen Application Contact Ms. Janice Bell, Admissions Assistant, Colorado Mountain College, Alpine Campus, PO Box 10001, Department PG, Glenwood Springs, CO 81602. *Phone:* 970-870-4417 Ext. 4417. *Toll-free phone:* 800-621-8559. *E-mail:* joinus@coloradomtn.edu.

COLORADO MOUNTAIN COLLEGE, TIMBERLINE CAMPUS

Leadville, Colorado   www.coloradomtn.edu/

- **District-supported** 2-year, founded 1965, part of Colorado Mountain College District System
- **Rural** 200-acre campus
- **Coed,** 470 undergraduate students

Undergraduates Students come from 49 states and territories, 20% are from out of state, 0.7% Asian American or Pacific Islander, 16% Hispanic American, 0.4% Native American, 30% live on campus.

Freshmen *Admission:* 1,242 applied, 1,242 admitted. *Average high school GPA:* 2.4.

Faculty *Total:* 14. *Student/faculty ratio:* 12:1.

Majors Accounting; business/commerce; corrections; criminal justice/law enforcement administration; early childhood education; environmental studies; general studies; historic preservation and conservation; land use planning and management; liberal arts and sciences/liberal studies; parks, recreation and leisure; parks, recreation and leisure facilities management.

Academics *Calendar:* semesters. *Degree:* certificates and associate. *Special study options:* academic remediation for entering students, adult/continuing education programs, advanced placement credit, cooperative education, distance

learning, double majors, English as a second language, honors programs, independent study, internships, part-time degree program, services for LD students, study abroad, summer session for credit.

Library 25,000 titles, 185 serial subscriptions, an OPAC, a Web page.

Student Life *Housing:* on-campus residence required for freshman year. *Options:* coed, disabled students. Freshman applicants given priority for college housing. *Activities and Organizations:* Environmental Club, Outdoor Club, Student Activities Board. *Campus security:* 24-hour emergency response devices, student patrols, controlled dormitory access. *Student services:* health clinic, personal/psychological counseling.

Athletics *Intramural sports:* basketball M, rock climbing M/W, skiing (cross-country) M/W, skiing (downhill) M/W, soccer M/W, volleyball M/W.

Standardized Tests *Recommended:* SAT or ACT (for admission).

Costs (2007–08) *Tuition:* area resident $1290 full-time, $43 per credit part-time; state resident $2160 full-time, $72 per credit part-time; nonresident $6930 full-time, $231 per credit part-time. *Required fees:* $180 full-time. *Room and board:* $6866; room only: $3570.

Applying *Options:* early admission, deferred entrance. *Required:* high school transcript. *Application deadlines:* rolling (freshmen), rolling (transfers).

Freshmen Application Contact Ms. Virginia Espinoza, Admissions Assistant, Colorado Mountain College, Timberline Campus, PO Box 10001, Department PG, Glenwood Springs, CO 81602. *Phone:* 719-486-4291. *Toll-free phone:* 800-621-8559. *E-mail:* joinus@coloradomtn.edu.

COLORADO NORTHWESTERN COMMUNITY COLLEGE

Rangely, Colorado　　　　　　　　　**www.cncc.edu/**

Colorado Northwestern Community College's residential campus in Rangely provides athletics and outdoor recreation opportunities. The Rangely and Craig campuses offer A.A. and A.S. degrees and vocational programs, such as aviation, construction technology, criminal justice, dental hygiene, nursing, and power plant and petroleum technology. Prospective students can check for new programs at http://www.cncc.edu or call 800-562-1105 (toll-free) for more information.

Director of Admissions Mr. Gene Bilodeau, Registrar, Colorado Northwestern Community College, 500 Kennedy Drive, Rangely, CO 81648. *Phone:* 970-824-1103. *Toll-free phone:* 970-675-3221 Ext. 218 (in-state); 800-562-1105 Ext. 218 (out-of-state). *E-mail:* gene.bilodeau@cncc.edu.

COLORADO SCHOOL OF HEALING ARTS

Lakewood, Colorado　　　　　　　　　**www.csha.net/**

- **Proprietary** 2-year, founded 1986
- **Coed**

Undergraduates 149 full-time, 91 part-time. 3% African American, 0.8% Asian American or Pacific Islander, 9% Hispanic American, 2% Native American, 1% international.

Faculty *Student/faculty ratio:* 13:1.

Academics *Calendar:* quarters. *Degree:* certificates and associate.

Costs (2006–07) *Tuition:* $8925 full-time. *Required fees:* $1236 full-time.

Applying *Application fee:* $50. *Required:* high school transcript, interview.

Freshmen Application Contact Ms. Chris Smith, Colorado School of Healing Arts, 7655 West Mississippi Avenue, Suite 100, Lakewood, CO 80226. *Phone:* 303-986-2320. *Toll-free phone:* 800-233-7114. *Fax:* 303-980-6594.

COLORADO SCHOOL OF TRADES

Lakewood, Colorado　　　　　　　**www.schooloftrades.com/**

- **Proprietary** 2-year, founded 1947
- **Coed**
- 87% of applicants were admitted

Undergraduates 125 full-time. 88% are from out of state.

Faculty *Student/faculty ratio:* 12:1.

Academics *Degree:* associate.

Costs (2006–07) *Tuition:* $16,200 full-time. *Required fees:* $154 full-time.

Applying *Application fee:* $25. *Required:* essay or personal statement, high school transcript, interview.

Director of Admissions Mr. Robert Martin, Director, Colorado School of Trades, 1575 Hoyt Street, Lakewood, CO 80215-2996. *Toll-free phone:* 800-234-4594.

COMMUNITY COLLEGE OF AURORA

Aurora, Colorado　　　　　　　　　**www.ccaurora.edu/**

- **State-supported** 2-year, founded 1983
- **Suburban** campus with easy access to Denver
- **Endowment** $3.3 million
- **Coed**

Undergraduates 1,412 full-time, 4,065 part-time. 0.1% are from out of state, 24% African American, 6% Asian American or Pacific Islander, 13% Hispanic American, 0.9% Native American, 2% international, 1% transferred in.

Faculty *Student/faculty ratio:* 21:1.

Academics *Calendar:* semesters. *Degree:* certificates and associate. *Special study options:* academic remediation for entering students, adult/continuing education programs, distance learning, English as a second language, external degree program, independent study, internships, off-campus study, part-time degree program, services for LD students, summer session for credit.

Student Life *Campus security:* late-night transport/escort service.

Costs (2006–07) *Tuition:* state resident $2236 full-time, $75 per credit hour part-time; nonresident $10,354 full-time, $345 per credit hour part-time. *Required fees:* $126 full-time, $3 per credit hour part-time, $21 per credit hour part-time.

Financial Aid Of all full-time matriculated undergraduates, 61 Federal Work-Study jobs (averaging $2357). 91 state and other part-time jobs (averaging $2431).

Applying *Options:* early admission. *Required for some:* high school transcript.

Freshmen Application Contact Ms. Connie Simpson, Director of Registrations, Records, and Admission, Community College of Aurora, 16000 East CentreTech Parkway, Aurora, CO 80011-9036. *Phone:* 303-360-4700.

COMMUNITY COLLEGE OF DENVER

Denver, Colorado　　　　　　　　　**www.ccd.edu/**

- **State-supported** 2-year, founded 1970, part of Colorado Community College and Occupational Education System
- **Urban** 171-acre campus
- **Coed**

Undergraduates 2,041 full-time, 6,868 part-time. Students come from 35 states and territories, 0.4% are from out of state, 17% African American, 6% Asian American or Pacific Islander, 26% Hispanic American, 2% Native American, 6% international, 2% transferred in.

Faculty *Student/faculty ratio:* 23:1.

Academics *Calendar:* semesters. *Degree:* certificates and associate. *Special study options:* academic remediation for entering students, accelerated degree program, adult/continuing education programs, advanced placement credit, cooperative education, distance learning, double majors, English as a second language, freshman honors college, honors programs, independent study, internships, off-campus study, part-time degree program, services for LD students, study abroad, summer session for credit. *ROTC:* Army (c).

Student Life *Campus security:* 24-hour emergency response devices and patrols, late-night transport/escort service.

Costs (2006–07) *Tuition:* state resident $2237 full-time, $75 per credit part-time; nonresident $10,355 full-time, $345 per credit part-time. Full-time tuition and fees vary according to location and program. Part-time tuition and fees vary according to location and program. *Required fees:* $636 full-time.

Financial Aid Of all full-time matriculated undergraduates, 95 Federal Work-Study jobs (averaging $2442). 305 state and other part-time jobs (averaging $2156).

Applying *Options:* electronic application, early admission, deferred entrance.

Freshmen Application Contact Ms. Emita Samuels, Dean of Enrollment Services, Community College of Denver, PO Box 173363, 1111 West Colfax Avenue, Denver, CO 80217-3363. *Phone:* 303-556-6325. *E-mail:* enrollment_services@ccd.edu.

DENVER ACADEMY OF COURT REPORTING

Westminster, Colorado　　　　　　　　　**www.dacr.org/**

Director of Admissions Mr. Howard Brookner, Director of Admissions, Denver Academy of Court Reporting, 7290 Samuel Drive, Suite 200, Denver, CO 80221-2792. *Phone:* 303-427-5292 Ext. 14. *Toll-free phone:* 800-574-2087.

DENVER AUTOMOTIVE AND DIESEL COLLEGE

Denver, Colorado   **www.dadc.com/**

Director of Admissions Jennifer Hash, Assistant Director of Admissions, Denver Automotive and Diesel College, 460 South Lipan Street, Denver, CO 80223-2025. *Phone:* 800-347-3232 Ext. 43032. *Toll-free phone:* 800-347-3232.

DENVER CAREER COLLEGE

Thornton, Colorado   **www.denvercareercollege.com/**

Freshmen Application Contact Admissions Office, Denver Career College, 500 East 84th Avenue, Suite W-200, Thornton, CO 80229.

EVEREST COLLEGE

Aurora, Colorado   **www.everest.edu/**

Freshmen Application Contact Admissions Office, Everest College, Suite 100, Aurora, CO 80012. *Phone:* 303-745-6244.

EVEREST COLLEGE

Colorado Springs, Colorado   **blair-college.com/**

Director of Admissions Don Webb, Director of Admissions, Everest College, 1815 Jet Wing Drive, Colorado Springs, CO 80916. *Phone:* 719-630-6580. *Toll-free phone:* 888-741-4271. *Fax:* 719-574-4493. *E-mail:* dwebb@cci.edu.

EVEREST COLLEGE

Denver, Colorado   **www.parks-college.com/**

Director of Admissions Ms. JoAnn Q. Navarro, Director of Admissions, Everest College, 9065 Grant Street, Denver, CO 80229-4339. *Phone:* 303-457-2757. *Fax:* 303-457-4030. *E-mail:* jqnira@cci.edu.

FRONT RANGE COMMUNITY COLLEGE

Westminster, Colorado   **frcc.cc.co.us/**

- **State-supported** 2-year, founded 1968, part of Community Colleges of Colorado System
- **Suburban** 90-acre campus with easy access to Denver
- **Coed,** 14,749 undergraduate students, 35% full-time, 59% women, 41% men

Undergraduates 5,182 full-time, 9,567 part-time. Students come from 49 states and territories, 2% are from out of state, 1% African American, 4% Asian American or Pacific Islander, 12% Hispanic American, 1% Native American, 0.2% international, 10% transferred in.

Freshmen *Admission:* 13,440 applied, 13,440 admitted, 4,143 enrolled.

Faculty *Total:* 991, 20% full-time, 2% with terminal degrees. *Student/faculty ratio:* 18:1.

Majors Accounting; architectural engineering technology; automotive engineering technology; business administration and management; business automation/technology/data entry; computer and information sciences; construction trades; dietetic technician; drafting/design engineering technologies related; early childhood education; electrical/electronics maintenance and repair technology related; general studies; heating, air conditioning and refrigeration technology; intermedia/multimedia; landscaping and groundskeeping; language interpretation and translation; liberal arts and sciences/liberal studies; machine tool technology; medical staff services technology; nursing assistant/aide and patient care assistant; nursing (registered nurse training); paralegal/legal assistant; restaurant/food services management; veterinary technology; welding technology.

Academics *Calendar:* semesters. *Degree:* certificates and associate. *Special study options:* academic remediation for entering students, advanced placement credit, cooperative education, distance learning, double majors, English as a second language, external degree program, freshman honors college, honors programs, independent study, internships, off-campus study, part-time degree program, services for LD students, student-designed majors, study abroad, summer session for credit. *ROTC:* Army (c), Air Force (c).

Library College Hill Library with an OPAC, a Web page.

Student Life *Housing:* college housing not available. *Activities and Organizations:* drama/theater group, student-run newspaper, Student Government Association, Student Colorado Registry of Interpreters for the Deaf, Alpha Mu Psi, Alpha Tau Kappa, Hispanic Club. *Campus security:* 24-hour patrols, late-night transport/escort service. *Student services:* personal/psychological counseling.

Costs (2006–07) *Tuition:* state resident $1800 full-time, $75 per credit part-time; nonresident $8250 full-time, $345 per credit part-time. *Required fees:* $312 full-time, $10 per credit part-time, $156 per term part-time. *Payment plan:* deferred payment.

Financial Aid Of all full-time matriculated undergraduates, 165 Federal Work-Study jobs (averaging $1316). 277 state and other part-time jobs (averaging $1635).

Applying *Options:* electronic application, early admission, deferred entrance. *Application deadlines:* rolling (freshmen), rolling (transfers).

Freshmen Application Contact Ms. Yolanda Espinoza, Registrar, Front Range Community College, 3645 West 112th Avenue, Westminster, CO 80031. *Phone:* 303-404-5000. *Fax:* 303-439-2614. *E-mail:* yolanda.espinoza@frontrange.edu.

HERITAGE COLLEGE

Denver, Colorado   **www.heritage-education.com/**

- **Proprietary** 2-year, founded 1986
- **Coed,** 496 undergraduate students
- 53% of applicants were admitted

Freshmen *Admission:* 329 applied, 175 admitted.

Majors Allied health and medical assisting services related; massage therapy; rehabilitation and therapeutic professions related.

Academics *Degree:* associate.

Costs (2006–07) *Tuition:* $16,790 per degree program part-time.

Applying *Recommended:* high school transcript.

Freshmen Application Contact Admissions Office, Heritage College, 12 Lakeside Lane, Denver, CO 80212.

INSTITUTE OF BUSINESS & MEDICAL CAREERS

Fort Collins, Colorado   **www.ibmcedu.com/**

Freshmen Application Contact Mr. Steve Steele, Vice President of Operations, Institute of Business & Medical Careers, 1609 Oakridge Drive, Fort Collins, CO 80525. *Phone:* 970-223-2669. *Toll-free phone:* 800-495-2669. *Fax:* 970-223-2796. *E-mail:* info@ibmcedu.com.

INTELLITEC COLLEGE

Colorado Springs, Colorado   **www.intelliteccollege.edu/**

Director of Admissions Ms. Ellen Pitrone, Director of Admissions, IntelliTec College, 2315 East Pikes Peak Avenue, Colorado Springs, CO 80909-6030. *Phone:* 719-632-7626. *Toll-free phone:* 800-748-2282.

INTELLITEC COLLEGE

Grand Junction, Colorado   **www.intelliteccollege.edu/**

- **Proprietary** 2-year
- **Small-town** campus
- **Coed**

Undergraduates 486 full-time. 2% African American, 28% Hispanic American, 0.6% Native American.

Academics *Calendar:* continuous. *Degree:* certificates, diplomas, and associate.

Costs (2006–07) *Tuition:* $5940 full-time.

Applying *Required:* high school transcript, interview.

Freshmen Application Contact Admissions, IntelliTec College, 772 Horizon Drive, Grand Junction, CO 81506. *Phone:* 970-245-8101. *Fax:* 970-243-8074.

INTELLITEC MEDICAL INSTITUTE

Colorado Springs, Colorado   www.intelliteccollege.edu/

Director of Admissions Michelle Squibb, Admissions Representative, IntelliTec Medical Institute, 2345 North Academy Boulevard, Colorado Springs, CO 80909. *Phone:* 719-596-7400.

ITT TECHNICAL INSTITUTE

Thornton, Colorado   www.itt-tech.edu/

- **Proprietary** primarily 2-year, founded 1984, part of ITT Educational Services, Inc
- **Suburban** 2-acre campus with easy access to Denver
- **Coed**

Majors Animation, interactive technology, video graphics and special effects; business administration and management; CAD/CADD drafting/design technology; computer and information systems security; computer engineering technology; computer programming; computer software engineering; computer systems networking and telecommunications; criminal justice/law enforcement administration; electrical, electronic and communications engineering technology; medical laboratory technology; system, networking, and LAN/WAN management; web/multimedia management and webmaster; web page, digital/multimedia and information resources design.

Academics *Calendar:* quarters. *Degrees:* associate and bachelor's.

Library a Web page.

Student Life *Housing:* college housing not available. *Activities and Organizations:* student-run newspaper.

Standardized Tests *Required:* Wonderlic aptitude test (for admission).

Costs (2006–07) *Tuition:* Contact school for program costs.

Applying *Options:* deferred entrance. *Application fee:* $100. *Required:* high school transcript, interview. *Recommended:* letters of recommendation. *Application deadlines:* rolling (freshmen), rolling (transfers). *Notification:* continuous (freshmen), continuous (transfers).

Freshmen Application Contact Ms. Tracy Arnett, Director of Recruitment, ITT Technical Institute, 500 East 84th Avenue, Thornton, CO 80229. *Phone:* 303-288-4488. *Toll-free phone:* 800-395-4488.

LAMAR COMMUNITY COLLEGE

Lamar, Colorado   www.lamarcc.edu/

- **State-supported** 2-year, founded 1937, part of Colorado Community College and Occupational Education System
- **Small-town** 125-acre campus
- **Endowment** $200,000
- **Coed,** 1,021 undergraduate students

Undergraduates Students come from 25 states and territories, 12 other countries.

Freshmen *Admission:* 414 applied, 414 admitted.

Faculty *Total:* 48, 50% full-time.

Majors Accounting; administrative assistant and secretarial science; agricultural business and management; agricultural teacher education; agriculture; agronomy and crop science; animal sciences; art; behavioral sciences; biological and physical sciences; biology/biological sciences; business administration and management; business teacher education; community organization and advocacy; computer engineering technology; computer management; computer programming; computer science; computer typography and composition equipment operation; cosmetology; criminal justice/safety; data processing and data processing technology; emergency medical technology (EMT paramedic); engineering; English; equestrian studies; farm and ranch management; history; humanities; information science/studies; legal administrative assistant/secretary; liberal arts and sciences/liberal studies; literature; management information systems; marketing/marketing management; mass communication/media; mathematics; medical administrative assistant and medical secretary; medical office management; nursing (licensed practical/vocational nurse training); nursing (registered nurse training); physical sciences; physics; pre-engineering; quality control technology; range science and management; social sciences; social work; teacher assistant/aide; western civilization.

Academics *Calendar:* semesters. *Degree:* certificates, diplomas, and associate. *Special study options:* academic remediation for entering students, adult/continuing education programs, advanced placement credit, cooperative education, English as a second language, internships, part-time degree program, services for LD students, student-designed majors, summer session for credit.

Library Learning Resources Center with 27,729 titles, 172 serial subscriptions.

Student Life *Housing:* on-campus residence required for freshman year. *Options:* coed. *Activities and Organizations:* drama/theater group, student-run newspaper, choral group. *Campus security:* 24-hour emergency response devices and patrols, student patrols, late-night transport/escort service, controlled dormitory access. *Student services:* health clinic, personal/psychological counseling.

Athletics Member NJCAA. *Intercollegiate sports:* baseball M(s), basketball M(s), cross-country running W, equestrian sports M/W, golf M, softball W, volleyball W(s).

Standardized Tests *Recommended:* SAT or ACT (for placement).

Costs (2006–07) *Tuition:* state resident $2610 full-time; nonresident $5190 full-time.

Financial Aid Of all full-time matriculated undergraduates, 32 Federal Work-Study jobs (averaging $1000). 89 state and other part-time jobs (averaging $1000).

Applying *Options:* early admission. *Application deadlines:* 9/16 (freshmen), 9/16 (transfers).

Freshmen Application Contact Director of Admissions, Lamar Community College, 2401 South Main Street, Lamar, CO 81052-3999. *Phone:* 719-336-1590. *Toll-free phone:* 800-968-6920.

MORGAN COMMUNITY COLLEGE

Fort Morgan, Colorado   www.morgancc.edu/

- **State-supported** 2-year, founded 1967, part of Colorado Community College and Occupational Education System
- **Rural** 20-acre campus with easy access to Denver
- **Coed,** 1,647 undergraduate students, 25% full-time, 72% women, 28% men

Undergraduates 408 full-time, 1,239 part-time. Students come from 3 states and territories, 3% are from out of state, 1% African American, 0.7% Asian American or Pacific Islander, 16% Hispanic American, 2% Native American, 0.1% international, 5% transferred in.

Freshmen *Admission:* 177 applied, 177 admitted, 164 enrolled.

Faculty *Total:* 149, 23% full-time, 6% with terminal degrees. *Student/faculty ratio:* 11:1.

Majors Accounting; administrative assistant and secretarial science; automobile/automotive mechanics technology; biological and physical sciences; business administration and management; business/managerial economics; business teacher education; liberal arts and sciences/liberal studies; occupational therapy; physical therapy.

Academics *Calendar:* semesters. *Degree:* certificates and associate. *Special study options:* academic remediation for entering students, adult/continuing education programs, advanced placement credit, internships, part-time degree program, services for LD students, summer session for credit.

Library Learning Resource Center with 13,800 titles, 80 serial subscriptions, 1,096 audiovisual materials, an OPAC, a Web page.

Student Life *Housing:* college housing not available. *Activities and Organizations:* student-run newspaper.

Costs (2006–07) *Tuition:* state resident $1789 full-time, $75 per credit hour part-time; nonresident $8284 full-time, $345 per credit hour part-time. *Required fees:* $310 full-time.

Financial Aid Of all full-time matriculated undergraduates, 20 Federal Work-Study jobs (averaging $1700). 50 state and other part-time jobs (averaging $2000).

Applying *Options:* early admission, deferred entrance. *Required:* high school transcript. *Application deadlines:* rolling (freshmen), rolling (transfers).

Freshmen Application Contact Mr. Kent Bauer, Student Services, Morgan Community College, Student Services, 17800 Road 20, Fort Morgan, CO 80701. *Phone:* 970-542-3111. *Toll-free phone:* 800-622-0216. *Fax:* 970-867-6608. *E-mail:* kent.bauer@mcc.cccoes.edu.

NORTHEASTERN JUNIOR COLLEGE

Sterling, Colorado   www.njc.edu/

- **State-supported** 2-year, founded 1941, part of Colorado Community College and Occupational Education System
- **Small-town** 65-acre campus
- **Endowment** $800,000
- **Coed,** 3,633 undergraduate students, 25% full-time, 57% women, 43% men

Northeastern Junior College (continued)

Undergraduates 910 full-time, 2,723 part-time. Students come from 21 states and territories, 10% are from out of state, 1% transferred in.

Freshmen *Admission:* 941 applied, 941 admitted, 479 enrolled. *Average high school GPA:* 2.95.

Faculty *Total:* 286, 20% full-time, 2% with terminal degrees. *Student/faculty ratio:* 4:1.

Majors Accounting; administrative assistant and secretarial science; agricultural business and management; agricultural economics; agricultural mechanization; agricultural teacher education; agriculture; agronomy and crop science; anatomy; animal sciences; applied mathematics; art; art teacher education; automobile/automotive mechanics technology; biological and physical sciences; biology/biological sciences; business administration and management; business teacher education; child development; clinical laboratory science/medical technology; computer engineering technology; computer science; corrections; cosmetology; criminal justice/police science; data processing and data processing technology; dramatic/theater arts; drawing; economics; education; elementary education; emergency medical technology (EMT paramedic); English; equestrian studies; family and consumer sciences/human sciences; farm and ranch management; fashion merchandising; fine/studio arts; forestry; health science; history; horticultural science; humanities; journalism; kindergarten/preschool education; landscaping and groundskeeping; legal administrative assistant/secretary; liberal arts and sciences/liberal studies; marine technology; marketing/marketing management; mathematics; medical administrative assistant and medical secretary; music; music teacher education; natural sciences; nursing (licensed practical/vocational nurse training); nursing (registered nurse training); physical education teaching and coaching; physical sciences; pre-engineering; psychology; radio and television; social sciences; social work; trade and industrial teacher education; veterinary sciences; zoology/animal biology.

Academics *Calendar:* semesters. *Degree:* certificates and associate. *Special study options:* academic remediation for entering students, accelerated degree program, adult/continuing education programs, advanced placement credit, cooperative education, distance learning, double majors, English as a second language, honors programs, independent study, internships, part-time degree program, services for LD students, summer session for credit.

Library Monahan Library with 45,260 titles, 414 serial subscriptions, an OPAC, a Web page.

Student Life *Housing:* on-campus residence required for freshman year. *Options:* coed. *Activities and Organizations:* drama/theater group, student-run newspaper, radio station, choral group, Associated Student Government, Post Secondary Agriculture (PAS), Rodeo Team and Club, Students in Free Enterprise (SIFE), Campus Christian Fellowship. *Campus security:* 24-hour emergency response devices, controlled dormitory access, night patrols by trained security personnel. *Student services:* health clinic, personal/psychological counseling, women's center.

Athletics Member NJCAA. *Intercollegiate sports:* baseball M(s), basketball M(s)/W(s), equestrian sports M(s)/W(s), softball W(s), volleyball W(s). *Intramural sports:* badminton M/W, basketball M/W, cross-country running M/W, football M, golf M/W, racquetball M/W, soccer M/W, tennis M/W, track and field M/W, volleyball M/W, weight lifting M/W.

Standardized Tests *Required for some:* SAT or ACT (for placement). *Recommended:* ACT (for placement).

Costs (2006–07) *Tuition:* state resident $2382 full-time; nonresident $7219 full-time.

Applying *Options:* electronic application, early admission, deferred entrance. *Required:* high school transcript. *Application deadlines:* 8/1 (freshmen), 8/1 (transfers). *Notification:* continuous until 8/1 (freshmen), continuous until 8/1 (transfers).

Freshmen Application Contact Ms. Tina Joyce, Director of Admissions, Northeastern Junior College, 100 College Avenue, Sterling, CO 80751. *Phone:* 970-521-7000. *Toll-free phone:* 800-626-4637.

OTERO JUNIOR COLLEGE

La Junta, Colorado www.ojc.edu/

- **State-supported** 2-year, founded 1941, part of Colorado Community College and Occupational Education System
- **Rural** 50-acre campus
- **Coed**

Undergraduates 771 full-time, 865 part-time. Students come from 12 states and territories, 2% are from out of state, 2% African American, 0.7% Asian American or Pacific Islander, 30% Hispanic American, 2% Native American, 0.4% international, 15% transferred in, 14% live on campus.

Academics *Calendar:* semesters. *Degree:* certificates and associate. *Special study options:* academic remediation for entering students, adult/continuing

education programs, advanced placement credit, distance learning, external degree program, internships, part-time degree program, summer session for credit.

Student Life *Campus security:* 24-hour patrols, late-night transport/escort service.

Athletics Member NJCAA.

Costs (2006–07) *Tuition:* state resident $1788 full-time, $75 per credit part-time; nonresident $6626 full-time, $276 per credit part-time. *Required fees:* $184 full-time. *Room and board:* $4512.

Financial Aid Of all full-time matriculated undergraduates, 30 Federal Work-Study jobs (averaging $2000). 100 state and other part-time jobs (averaging $2000).

Applying *Options:* electronic application, early admission. *Recommended:* high school transcript.

Freshmen Application Contact Mr. Brad Franz, Vice President for Student Services, Otero Junior College, 1802 Colorado Avenue, La Junta, CO 81050-3415. *Phone:* 719-384-6833. *Fax:* 719-384-6933. *E-mail:* j_schiro@ojc.cccoes.edu.

PIKES PEAK COMMUNITY COLLEGE

Colorado Springs, Colorado www.ppcc.edu/

Director of Admissions Mr. Troy Nelson, Associate Director, Enrollment Services, Admissions, Pikes Peak Community College, 5675 South Academy Boulevard, Colorado Springs, CO 80906-5498. *Phone:* 719-540-7041. *Toll-free phone:* 866-411-7722.

PIMA MEDICAL INSTITUTE

Denver, Colorado www.pmi.edu/

Freshmen Application Contact Admissions Office, Pima Medical Institute, Pima Medical Institute, 1701 West 72nd Avenue, Suite 130, Denver, CO 80221. *Phone:* 303-426-1800. *Toll-free phone:* 888-898-9048.

PLATT COLLEGE

Aurora, Colorado www.plattcolorado.edu/

Freshmen Application Contact Admissions Office, Platt College, 3100 South Parker Road, Suite 200, Aurora, CO 80014-3141. *Phone:* 303-369-5151.

PUEBLO COMMUNITY COLLEGE

Pueblo, Colorado www.pueblocc.edu/

- **State-supported** 2-year, founded 1933, part of Colorado Community College and Occupational Education System
- **Urban** 35-acre campus
- **Coed,** 5,393 undergraduate students, 38% full-time, 64% women, 36% men

Undergraduates 2,049 full-time, 3,344 part-time. 1% are from out of state, 2% African American, 0.9% Asian American or Pacific Islander, 36% Hispanic American, 3% Native American, 0.2% international, 3% transferred in.

Freshmen *Admission:* 1,218 applied, 1,218 admitted, 749 enrolled. *Test scores:* SAT verbal scores over 500: 75%; SAT math scores over 500: 100%; ACT scores over 18: 53%; ACT scores over 24: 7%.

Faculty *Total:* 78, 95% full-time, 5% with terminal degrees. *Student/faculty ratio:* 42:1.

Majors Accounting; administrative assistant and secretarial science; autobody/collision and repair technology; automobile/automotive mechanics technology; business administration and management; business/commerce; civil engineering technology; computer graphics; corrections; criminal justice/law enforcement administration; criminal justice/police science; culinary arts; dental assisting; dental hygiene; design and visual communications; electrical, electronic and communications engineering technology; engineering technology; general studies; health information/medical records administration; information science/studies; kindergarten/preschool education; legal administrative assistant/secretary; legal assistant/paralegal; liberal arts and sciences/liberal studies; library assistant; machine tool technology; management information systems; medical administrative assistant and medical secretary; medical radiologic technology; metal and jewelry arts; nursing (registered nurse training); occupational therapist

assistant; occupational therapy; ophthalmic laboratory technology; physical therapist assistant; psychiatric/mental health services technology; respiratory care therapy; welding technology.

Academics *Calendar:* semesters. *Degree:* certificates and associate. *Special study options:* academic remediation for entering students, accelerated degree program, advanced placement credit, cooperative education, distance learning, double majors, independent study, internships, part-time degree program, services for LD students, summer session for credit.

Library Pueblo Community College Learning Resources Center with 23,755 titles, 286 serial subscriptions, 14,626 audiovisual materials, an OPAC.

Student Life *Housing:* college housing not available. *Activities and Organizations:* drama/theater group, choral group, Criminal Justice Club, Phi Beta Lambda, Automotive Society, Nursing Club, Business and Office Technology Club. *Campus security:* 24-hour emergency response devices, late-night transport/escort service. *Student services:* personal/psychological counseling.

Costs (2006–07) *One-time required fee:* $10. *Tuition:* state resident $2183 full-time, $73 per credit part-time; nonresident $10,355 full-time, $345 per credit part-time. *Required fees:* $233 full-time, $8 per credit part-time, $19 per term part-time.

Financial Aid Of all full-time matriculated undergraduates, 116 Federal Work-Study jobs (averaging $1450). 207 state and other part-time jobs (averaging $2235).

Applying *Options:* electronic application, early admission, deferred entrance. *Application deadlines:* rolling (freshmen), rolling (out-of-state freshmen), rolling (transfers). *Notification:* continuous until 9/1 (freshmen), continuous until 9/1 (out-of-state freshmen), continuous until 9/1 (transfers).

Freshmen Application Contact Maija Kurtz, Assistant Director of Admissions and Records, Pueblo Community College, 900 West Orman Avenue, Pueblo, CO 81004. *Phone:* 719-549-3085. *Toll-free phone:* 800-642-6017. *Fax:* 719-549-3012. *E-mail:* maija.kurtz@pueblocc.edu.

RED ROCKS COMMUNITY COLLEGE

Lakewood, Colorado www.rrcc.edu/

- **State-supported** 2-year, founded 1969, part of Colorado Community College and Occupational Education System
- **Urban** 120-acre campus with easy access to Denver
- **Coed,** 6,727 undergraduate students, 31% full-time, 51% women, 49% men

Undergraduates 2,068 full-time, 4,659 part-time. Students come from 27 states and territories, 20 other countries, 4% are from out of state, 2% African American, 3% Asian American or Pacific Islander, 12% Hispanic American, 2% Native American, 0.3% international, 8% transferred in.

Freshmen *Admission:* 2,633 applied, 2,633 admitted, 1,865 enrolled.

Faculty *Total:* 414, 14% full-time. *Student/faculty ratio:* 8:1.

Majors Accounting; administrative assistant and secretarial science; art; biological and physical sciences; biology/biological sciences; business administration and management; carpentry; chemistry; computer engineering technology; computer programming; computer science; criminal justice/law enforcement administration; drafting and design technology; economics; electrical, electronic and communications engineering technology; English; fire science; French; geology/earth science; German; heavy equipment maintenance technology; history; humanities; hydrology and water resources science; liberal arts and sciences/liberal studies; marketing/marketing management; mass communication/media; mathematics; mechanical engineering/mechanical technology; physics; political science and government; psychology; public administration; real estate; sanitation technology; sociology; solar energy technology; Spanish; survey technology; welding technology.

Academics *Calendar:* semesters. *Degree:* certificates and associate. *Special study options:* academic remediation for entering students, adult/continuing education programs, cooperative education, English as a second language, off-campus study, part-time degree program, study abroad, summer session for credit.

Library Marvin Buckels Library with 55,188 titles, 350 serial subscriptions, 5,434 audiovisual materials, an OPAC, a Web page.

Student Life *Housing:* college housing not available. *Activities and Organizations:* drama/theater group, student-run newspaper. *Campus security:* 24-hour emergency response devices and patrols. *Student services:* personal/psychological counseling, women's center.

Athletics *Intramural sports:* volleyball M/W.

Costs (2007–08) *Tuition:* area resident $2315 full-time, $77 per credit hour part-time; state resident $2315 full-time, $77 per credit hour part-time; nonresident $10,718 full-time, $357 per credit hour part-time. *Required fees:* $272 full-time, $8 per credit hour part-time, $10 per credit hour part-time.

Financial Aid Of all full-time matriculated undergraduates, 21 Federal Work-Study jobs (averaging $2600). 65 state and other part-time jobs (averaging $3600).

Applying *Options:* early admission. *Application deadlines:* rolling (freshmen), rolling (transfers). *Notification:* continuous (freshmen), continuous (transfers).

Freshmen Application Contact RRCC Admissions Office, Red Rocks Community College, 13300 West 6th Avenue Box 5, Lakewood, CO 80228-1255. *Phone:* 303-914-6360. *Fax:* 303-914-6457. *E-mail:* admissions@rrcc.edu.

TRINIDAD STATE JUNIOR COLLEGE

Trinidad, Colorado www.trinidadstate.edu/

- **State-supported** 2-year, founded 1925, part of Colorado Community College and Occupational Education System
- **Small-town** 17-acre campus
- **Endowment** $4.7 million
- **Coed,** 1,732 undergraduate students, 42% full-time, 56% women, 44% men

Undergraduates 720 full-time, 1,012 part-time. Students come from 17 states and territories, 1 other country, 8% are from out of state, 2% African American, 0.8% Asian American or Pacific Islander, 38% Hispanic American, 2% Native American, 0.1% international, 5% transferred in, 30% live on campus. *Retention:* 54% of 2003 full-time freshmen returned.

Freshmen *Admission:* 1,633 applied, 1,633 admitted, 472 enrolled.

Faculty *Total:* 154, 24% full-time, 100% with terminal degrees. *Student/faculty ratio:* 14:1.

Majors Accounting; administrative assistant and secretarial science; aquaculture; art teacher education; automobile/automotive mechanics technology; biological and physical sciences; biology/biological sciences; business administration and management; carpentry; chemistry; civil engineering technology; commercial and advertising art; computer and information sciences related; computer science; computer systems networking and telecommunications; construction engineering technology; corrections; cosmetology; criminal justice/police science; data processing and data processing technology; design and visual communications; digital communication and media/multimedia; drafting and design technology; dramatic/theater arts; education; engineering; English; farm and ranch management; forestry; gunsmithing; heavy equipment maintenance technology; industrial technology; information science/studies; information technology; kindergarten/preschool education; liberal arts and sciences/liberal studies; management information systems; music; natural resources management and policy; nursing assistant/aide and patient care assistant; nursing (licensed practical/vocational nurse training); nursing (registered nurse training); occupational safety and health technology; physical education teaching and coaching; pre-engineering; psychology.

Academics *Calendar:* semesters. *Degree:* certificates, diplomas, and associate. *Special study options:* academic remediation for entering students, accelerated degree program, adult/continuing education programs, advanced placement credit, cooperative education, distance learning, double majors, English as a second language, honors programs, independent study, internships, part-time degree program, services for LD students, student-designed majors, summer session for credit.

Library Frendenthal Library plus 1 other with 54,255 titles, 105 serial subscriptions, 1,574 audiovisual materials, an OPAC.

Student Life *Housing Options:* coed, men-only, women-only. Campus housing is university owned. *Activities and Organizations:* drama/theater group, student-run newspaper, choral group, student association, International Club, Gunsmithing Club, Nursing Club, Cosmetology Club. *Campus security:* 24-hour emergency response devices and patrols, late-night transport/escort service.

Athletics Member NJCAA. *Intercollegiate sports:* baseball M(s), basketball M(s), softball W, volleyball W(s). *Intramural sports:* badminton M/W, basketball M, bowling M/W, football M/W, riflery M/W, skiing (cross-country) M/W, skiing (downhill) M/W, softball M/W, table tennis M/W, tennis M/W, volleyball M/W, weight lifting M/W.

Costs (2006–07) *Tuition:* state resident $2250 full-time, $75 per credit part-time; nonresident $8280 full-time, $276 per credit part-time. *Required fees:* $460 full-time, $14 per credit part-time. *Room and board:* $4298; room only: $1048. Room and board charges vary according to board plan. *Payment plan:* installment. *Waivers:* senior citizens and employees or children of employees.

Financial Aid Of all full-time matriculated undergraduates, 30 Federal Work-Study jobs (averaging $2040). 40 state and other part-time jobs (averaging $2040).

Applying *Options:* electronic application, deferred entrance. *Required:* high school transcript. *Application deadlines:* rolling (freshmen), rolling (transfers). *Notification:* continuous (freshmen), continuous (transfers).

Freshmen Application Contact Dr. Sandra Veltri, Dean of Students, Trinidad State Junior College, 600 Prospect, Trinidad, CO 81082-2396. *Phone:* 719-5559. *Toll-free phone:* 800-621-8752. *Fax:* 719-846-5620. *E-mail:* sandy.veltri@trinidadstate.edu.

WESTWOOD COLLEGE–DENVER NORTH

Denver, Colorado   www.westwood.edu/

- **Proprietary** primarily 2-year, founded 1953
- **Suburban** 11-acre campus
- **Coed**

Undergraduates 1,086 full-time, 337 part-time. Students come from 38 states and territories, 2 other countries, 16% are from out of state, 3% African American, 3% Asian American or Pacific Islander, 16% Hispanic American, 2% Native American, 0.1% international, 0.2% transferred in. *Retention:* 28% of 2003 full-time freshmen returned.

Faculty *Student/faculty ratio:* 13:1.

Academics *Calendar:* 5 terms. *Degrees:* diplomas, associate, and bachelor's. *Special study options:* academic remediation for entering students, accelerated degree program, advanced placement credit, distance learning, independent study, internships, part-time degree program, services for LD students, summer session for credit.

Student Life *Campus security:* 24-hour emergency response devices.

Standardized Tests *Required for some:* ACCUPLACER. *Recommended:* SAT or ACT (for admission), SAT and SAT Subject Tests or ACT (for admission).

Costs (2006–07) *Tuition:* $12,300 full-time, $467 per credit part-time. Full-time tuition and fees vary according to course load and program. Part-time tuition and fees vary according to course load and program. *Required fees:* $510 full-time, $120 per term part-time.

Applying *Options:* deferred entrance. *Application fee:* $100. *Required:* high school transcript, interview.

Freshmen Application Contact Ms. Dianne Hopkins, New Student Coordinator, Westwood College–Denver North, 7350 North Broadway, Denver, CO 80221-3653. *Phone:* 303-650-5050 Ext. 325. *Toll-free phone:* 800-992-5050. *Fax:* 303-487-0214.

►**See page 612 for the College Close-Up.**

WESTWOOD COLLEGE–DENVER SOUTH

Denver, Colorado   www.westwood.edu/

- **Proprietary** primarily 2-year
- **Urban** campus with easy access to Denver, CO
- **Coed**
- **58% of applicants were admitted**

Undergraduates 294 full-time, 135 part-time. 4% African American, 4% Asian American or Pacific Islander, 17% Hispanic American.

Academics *Calendar:* continuous. *Degrees:* associate and bachelor's.

Applying *Required:* interview, high school diploma or GED and entrance exam (SAT/ACT or Accuplacer).

Director of Admissions Mr. Ron DeJong, Director of Admissions, Westwood College–Denver South, 3150 South Sheridan Boulevard, Denver, CO 80227-5548. *Phone:* 303-934-2790. *Toll-free phone:* 800-281-2978.

►**See page 614 for the College Close-Up.**

CONNECTICUT

ASNUNTUCK COMMUNITY COLLEGE

Enfield, Connecticut   www.acc.commnet.edu/

- **State-supported** 2-year, founded 1972, part of Connecticut Community College System
- **Suburban** 4-acre campus
- **Coed,** 1,638 undergraduate students, 35% full-time, 55% women, 45% men

Undergraduates 568 full-time, 1,070 part-time. Students come from 2 states and territories, 7% are from out of state, 8% African American, 2% Asian American or Pacific Islander, 5% Hispanic American, 0.2% Native American, 7% transferred in. *Retention:* 55% of 2003 full-time freshmen returned.

Freshmen *Admission:* 272 applied, 272 admitted, 255 enrolled.

Faculty *Total:* 120, 22% full-time. *Student/faculty ratio:* 15:1.

Majors Accounting; administrative assistant and secretarial science; banking and financial support services; business administration and management; business automation/technology/data entry; communication and media related; computer and information sciences; criminal justice/safety; early childhood education; engineering science; fine/studio arts; general studies; human services; industrial technology; legal administrative assistant; liberal arts and sciences/liberal studies; machine tool technology; mass communication/media; medical office assistant; radio and television; special products marketing.

Academics *Calendar:* semesters. *Degree:* certificates and associate. *Special study options:* academic remediation for entering students, adult/continuing education programs, advanced placement credit, cooperative education, distance learning, double majors, English as a second language, independent study, internships, part-time degree program, services for LD students, student-designed majors, summer session for credit.

Library ACTC Learning Resource Center with 31,700 titles, 257 serial subscriptions, an OPAC.

Student Life *Housing:* college housing not available. *Activities and Organizations:* drama/theater group, student-run newspaper, radio station, Phi Theta Kappa, Drama Club, Outdoor Club, Poetry Club, Ski Club. *Campus security:* 24-hour patrols, late-night transport/escort service. *Student services:* women's center.

Costs (2007–08) *Tuition:* state resident $2496 full-time, $104 per credit part-time; nonresident $7488 full-time, $312 per credit part-time. *Required fees:* $332 full-time, $59 per credit part-time.

Financial Aid Of all full-time matriculated undergraduates, 23 Federal Work-Study jobs (averaging $3000). 5 state and other part-time jobs (averaging $3000).

Applying *Options:* deferred entrance. *Application fee:* $20. *Required:* high school transcript. *Application deadlines:* rolling (freshmen), rolling (transfers). *Notification:* continuous (freshmen), continuous (transfers).

Freshmen Application Contact Ms. Donna Shaw, Director of Admissions, Asnuntuck Community College, 170 Elm Street, Enfield, CT 06082-3800. *Phone:* 860-253-3018. *Toll-free phone:* 800-501-3967. *Fax:* 860-253-3014. *E-mail:* dshaw@acc.commnet.edu.

BRIARWOOD COLLEGE

Southington, Connecticut   www.briarwood.edu/

- **Proprietary** primarily 2-year, founded 1966
- **Small-town** 32-acre campus with easy access to Boston and Hartford
- **Endowment** $27,595
- **Coed,** 647 undergraduate students, 60% full-time, 74% women, 26% men

Undergraduates 389 full-time, 258 part-time. Students come from 11 states and territories, 2 other countries, 7% are from out of state, 22% African American, 0.8% Asian American or Pacific Islander, 11% Hispanic American, 0.2% Native American, 1% international, 13% transferred in, 21% live on campus.

Freshmen *Admission:* 607 applied, 442 admitted, 165 enrolled. *Test scores:* SAT verbal scores over 500: 16%; SAT math scores over 500: 19%; SAT verbal scores over 600: 3%; SAT math scores over 600: 16%; SAT verbal scores over 700: 3%; SAT math scores over 700: 16%.

Faculty *Total:* 95, 31% full-time. *Student/faculty ratio:* 10:1.

Majors Accounting; administrative assistant and secretarial science; biotechnology; business administration and management; child development; communication/speech communication and rhetoric; criminal justice/law enforcement administration; dental assisting; dietetics; fashion merchandising; funeral service and mortuary science; general studies; health information/medical records administration; hotel/motel administration; legal administrative assistant/secretary; legal assistant/paralegal; medical administrative assistant and medical secretary; medical/clinical assistant; medical office management; occupational therapist assistant; radio and television broadcasting technology; tourism and travel services management.

Academics *Calendar:* semesters. *Degrees:* certificates, diplomas, associate, and bachelor's. *Special study options:* academic remediation for entering students, accelerated degree program, adult/continuing education programs, advanced placement credit, double majors, English as a second language, independent study, internships, part-time degree program, services for LD students, summer session for credit.

Library Pupillo Library with 11,500 titles, 154 serial subscriptions, a Web page.

Student Life *Housing Options:* coed. Freshman applicants given priority for college housing. *Activities and Organizations:* student-run radio station, student government, Yearbook Committee, Student Ambassador Club, F.A.M.E. (Fashion Merchandising Club). *Campus security:* 24-hour patrols, late-night transport/escort service. *Student services:* personal/psychological counseling.

Athletics *Intramural sports:* basketball M, soccer W, softball M/W.

Costs (2007–08) *Tuition:* $16,400 full-time, $540 per credit part-time. *Required fees:* $220 full-time. *Room only:* $3600.

Financial Aid Of all full-time matriculated undergraduates, 33 Federal Work-Study jobs (averaging $600). 30 state and other part-time jobs.

Applying *Options:* electronic application. *Application fee:* $25. *Required:* high school transcript. *Required for some:* essay or personal statement, letters of recommendation, interview. *Application deadlines:* rolling (freshmen), rolling (transfers).

Freshmen Application Contact Mr. Jack LeConche, Chief Administrative Officer, Briarwood College, 2279 Mount Vernon Road, Southington, CT 06489. *Phone:* 860-628-4751 Ext. 131. *Toll-free phone:* 800-952-2444. *Fax:* 860-628-6444. *E-mail:* leconchej@briarwood.edu.

▶See page 494 for the College Close-Up.

CAPITAL COMMUNITY COLLEGE

Hartford, Connecticut   www.ccc.commnet.edu/

- **State-supported** 2-year, founded 1946, part of Connecticut Community–Technical College System
- **Urban** 10-acre campus
- **Coed**, 3,550 undergraduate students, 25% full-time, 72% women, 28% men

Undergraduates 896 full-time, 2,654 part-time. 39% African American, 3% Asian American or Pacific Islander, 30% Hispanic American, 0.2% Native American, 0.7% international.

Freshmen *Admission:* 533 enrolled.

Faculty *Total:* 209.

Majors Accounting; administrative assistant and secretarial science; business administration and management; computer and information sciences; computer and information sciences related; computer engineering technology; data entry/microcomputer applications related; electrical, electronic and communications engineering technology; emergency medical technology (EMT paramedic); fire protection and safety technology; fire services administration; information technology; kindergarten/preschool education; liberal arts and sciences/liberal studies; medical/clinical assistant; medical radiologic technology; nursing (registered nurse training); physical therapist assistant; social work; web page, digital/multimedia and information resources design.

Academics *Calendar:* semesters. *Degree:* certificates and associate. *Special study options:* academic remediation for entering students, accelerated degree program, adult/continuing education programs, advanced placement credit, distance learning, double majors, English as a second language, independent study, internships, part-time degree program, services for LD students, summer session for credit.

Library Arthur C. Banks, Jr. Library plus 1 other with 46,760 titles, 359 serial subscriptions, an OPAC, a Web page.

Student Life *Housing:* college housing not available. *Activities and Organizations:* drama/theater group, student-run television station, choral group, Latin American Student Association, Student Senate, Senior Renewal Club, Early Childhood Club, Pre-Professional Club. *Campus security:* late-night transport/escort service, security staff during hours of operation, emergency telephones 7 a.m. - 11 p.m. *Student services:* personal/psychological counseling.

Costs (2007–08) *Tuition:* state resident $2496 full-time; nonresident $7488 full-time. *Required fees:* $332 full-time.

Financial Aid Of all full-time matriculated undergraduates, 87 Federal Work-Study jobs (averaging $3000). 160 state and other part-time jobs (averaging $3000).

Applying *Application fee:* $20. *Recommended:* high school transcript. *Application deadlines:* rolling (freshmen), rolling (transfers). *Notification:* continuous until 9/1 (freshmen), continuous until 9/1 (transfers).

Freshmen Application Contact Ms. Jackie Phillips, Director of the Welcome and Advising Center, Capital Community College, 950 Main Street, Hartford, CT 06103. *Phone:* 860-906-5078. *Toll-free phone:* 800-894-6126. *E-mail:* mballj-davis@ccc.commnet.edu.

GATEWAY COMMUNITY COLLEGE

New Haven, Connecticut   www.gwcc.commnet.edu/

- **State-supported** 2-year, founded 1992, part of Connecticut Community College System
- **Urban** 5-acre campus with easy access to New York City
- **Coed,** 5,824 undergraduate students, 34% full-time, 64% women, 36% men

Undergraduates 1,961 full-time, 3,863 part-time. Students come from 15 states and territories, 38 other countries, 26% African American, 3% Asian American or Pacific Islander, 14% Hispanic American, 0.2% Native American, 1% international, 10% transferred in.

Freshmen *Admission:* 3,800 applied, 3,651 admitted, 1,045 enrolled.

Faculty *Total:* 329, 28% full-time, 5% with terminal degrees. *Student/faculty ratio:* 18:1.

Majors Accounting; automobile/automotive mechanics technology; avionics maintenance technology; biomedical technology; business administration and management; computer and information sciences related; computer engineering related; computer engineering technology; computer graphics; computer typography and composition equipment operation; consumer merchandising/retailing management; data entry/microcomputer applications; data processing and data processing technology; dietetics; electrical, electronic and communications engineering technology; engineering technology; fashion merchandising; fire science; gerontology; hotel/motel administration; human services; industrial radiologic technology; industrial technology; kindergarten/preschool education; legal administrative assistant/secretary; liberal arts and sciences/liberal studies; mechanical engineering/mechanical technology; medical administrative assistant and medical secretary; mental health/rehabilitation; nuclear medical technology; special products marketing; substance abuse/addiction counseling; word processing.

Academics *Calendar:* semesters. *Degree:* certificates and associate. *Special study options:* academic remediation for entering students, adult/continuing education programs, advanced placement credit, distance learning, English as a second language, external degree program, independent study, internships, off-campus study, part-time degree program, services for LD students, summer session for credit.

Library Gateway Community College Library plus 1 other with 54,802 titles, 532 serial subscriptions, an OPAC.

Student Life *Housing:* college housing not available. *Campus security:* late-night transport/escort service.

Athletics Member NJCAA. *Intercollegiate sports:* baseball M, basketball M/W, soccer M, softball W.

Costs (2007–08) *Tuition:* state resident $2496 full-time, $104 per credit part-time; nonresident $7488 full-time, $312 per credit part-time. *Required fees:* $332 full-time.

Financial Aid Of all full-time matriculated undergraduates, 60 Federal Work-Study jobs (averaging $6000).

Applying *Options:* early admission, deferred entrance. *Application fee:* $20. *Required:* high school transcript. *Required for some:* essay or personal statement, interview. *Application deadlines:* 9/1 (freshmen), 9/1 (transfers). *Notification:* continuous until 9/1 (freshmen), continuous until 9/1 (transfers).

Freshmen Application Contact Ms. Kim Shea, Director of Admissions, Gateway Community College, 60 Sargent Drive, New Haven, CT 06511. *Phone:* 203-789-7043. *Toll-free phone:* 800-390-7723. *Fax:* 203-285-2018. *E-mail:* gateway_ctc@commnet.edu.

GIBBS COLLEGE

Norwalk, Connecticut   www.gibbscollege.com/

Director of Admissions Mr. Ted Havelka, Vice President of Admissions/Marketing, Gibbs College, 148 East Avenue, Norwalk, CT 06851. *Phone:* 203-633-2311. *Toll-free phone:* 800-845-5333.

GOODWIN COLLEGE

East Hartford, Connecticut   www.goodwin.edu/

- **Proprietary** 2-year, founded 1999
- **Urban** campus with easy access to Hartford
- **Endowment** $1.0 million
- **Coed**

Undergraduates 132 full-time, 1,087 part-time. Students come from 1 other state, 1% are from out of state, 30% African American, 1% Asian American or Pacific Islander, 14% Hispanic American, 0.4% Native American, 10% transferred in.

Faculty *Student/faculty ratio:* 10:1.

Academics *Calendar:* semesters. *Degree:* certificates, diplomas, and associate. *Special study options:* academic remediation for entering students, accelerated degree program, adult/continuing education programs, advanced placement credit, cooperative education, distance learning, double majors, English as a second language, external degree program, honors programs, independent study, internships, off-campus study, part-time degree program, services for LD students, summer session for credit.

Goodwin College (continued)

Student Life *Campus security:* evening security patrolman.

Costs (2006–07) *Tuition:* $13,570 full-time, $425 per credit part-time. *Required fees:* $300 full-time.

Applying *Options:* electronic application, deferred entrance. *Application fee:* $50. *Required:* essay or personal statement, high school transcript, minimum 2.0 GPA, medical exam. *Recommended:* 2 letters of recommendation, interview.

Freshmen Application Contact Mr. Daniel P. Noonan, Director of Enrollment, Goodwin College, 745 Burnside Avenue, East Hartford, CT 06108. *Phone:* 860-528-4111 Ext. 6902. *Toll-free phone:* 800-889-3282. *Fax:* 860-291-8285. *E-mail:* dnoonan@goodwin.edu.

HOUSATONIC COMMUNITY COLLEGE

Bridgeport, Connecticut   www.hctc.commnet.edu/

- **State-supported** 2-year, founded 1965, part of Connecticut Community–Technical College System
- **Urban** 4-acre campus with easy access to New York City
- **Coed,** 4,343 undergraduate students

Undergraduates 30% African American, 3% Asian American or Pacific Islander, 21% Hispanic American, 0.2% Native American. *Retention:* 55% of 2003 full-time freshmen returned.

Freshmen *Admission:* 2,252 applied, 2,014 admitted.

Faculty *Total:* 243, 27% full-time. *Student/faculty ratio:* 17:1.

Majors Accounting; administrative assistant and secretarial science; art; avionics maintenance technology; business administration and management; child development; clinical/medical laboratory technology; commercial and advertising art; computer typography and composition equipment operation; criminal justice/law enforcement administration; data processing and data processing technology; environmental studies; humanities; human services; journalism; liberal arts and sciences/liberal studies; mathematics; mental health/rehabilitation; nursing (registered nurse training); physical therapy; pre-engineering; public administration; social sciences; substance abuse/addiction counseling.

Academics *Calendar:* semesters. *Degree:* certificates and associate. *Special study options:* academic remediation for entering students, adult/continuing education programs, advanced placement credit, cooperative education, double majors, English as a second language, honors programs, independent study, internships, part-time degree program, services for LD students, summer session for credit. *ROTC:* Army (c).

Library 30,000 titles, 280 serial subscriptions, an OPAC, a Web page.

Student Life *Housing:* college housing not available. *Activities and Organizations:* student-run newspaper, Student Senate, Association of Latin American Students, African-American Cultural Society, Art Club. *Campus security:* 24-hour emergency response devices, late-night transport/escort service. *Student services:* personal/psychological counseling.

Standardized Tests *Required for some:* ACCUPLACER.

Costs (2006–07) *Tuition:* area resident $2352 full-time, $98 per credit part-time; state resident $3528 full-time, $147 per credit part-time; nonresident $7056 full-time, $294 per credit part-time. Full-time tuition and fees vary according to course load and program. Part-time tuition and fees vary according to course load and program. *Required fees:* $320 full-time. *Payment plans:* installment, deferred payment. *Waivers:* senior citizens and employees or children of employees.

Financial Aid Of all full-time matriculated undergraduates, 70 Federal Work-Study jobs (averaging $2850).

Applying *Options:* deferred entrance. *Application fee:* $20. *Required:* high school transcript. *Required for some:* letters of recommendation, interview. *Application deadlines:* rolling (freshmen), rolling (transfers).

Freshmen Application Contact Ms. Delores Y. Curtis, Director of Admissions, Housatonic Community College, 900 Lafayette Boulevard, Bridgeport, CT 06604-4704. *Phone:* 203-332-5102.

INTERNATIONAL COLLEGE OF HOSPITALITY MANAGEMENT

Suffield, Connecticut   www.ichm.edu/

- **Proprietary** 2-year, founded 1992
- **Small-town** 56-acre campus with easy access to New York City or Boston, MA
- **Coed**

Undergraduates 116 full-time. Students come from 6 states and territories, 34 other countries, 50% are from out of state, 6% African American, 16% Asian American or Pacific Islander, 7% Hispanic American, 51% international, 16% transferred in, 90% live on campus.

Academics *Calendar:* continuous. *Degree:* certificates and associate. *Special study options:* academic remediation for entering students, accelerated degree program, adult/continuing education programs, advanced placement credit, cooperative education, distance learning, English as a second language, independent study, internships, part-time degree program, services for LD students, study abroad.

Student Life *Campus security:* 24-hour emergency response devices, student patrols, late-night transport/escort service, controlled dormitory access, weekend patrols by trained security personnel.

Standardized Tests *Recommended:* SAT (for admission).

Costs (2006–07) *Comprehensive fee:* $20,878 includes full-time tuition ($15,900) and room and board ($4978). Part-time tuition: $650 per credit. *Room and board:* Room and board charges vary according to board plan.

Applying *Options:* electronic application, deferred entrance. *Application fee:* $100. *Required:* high school transcript, 2 letters of recommendation. *Required for some:* essay or personal statement, interview. *Recommended:* interview.

Freshmen Application Contact Mrs. Jolie Swanson, Director of Admissions, International College of Hospitality Management, 1760 Mapleton Avenue, Suffield, CT 06078. *Phone:* 860-668-3515 Ext. 126. *Toll-free phone:* 800-955-0809. *Fax:* 860-668-7369. *E-mail:* admissions@ichm.edu.

▶See page 550 for the College Close-Up.

MANCHESTER COMMUNITY COLLEGE

Manchester, Connecticut   www.mcc.commnet.edu/

- **State-supported** 2-year, founded 1963, part of Connecticut Community–Technical College System
- **Small-town** 160-acre campus with easy access to Hartford
- **Coed**

Undergraduates 2,713 full-time, 3,422 part-time. Students come from 5 states and territories, 12% African American, 4% Asian American or Pacific Islander, 10% Hispanic American, 0.2% Native American, 0.7% international, 11% transferred in. *Retention:* 60% of 2003 full-time freshmen returned.

Faculty *Student/faculty ratio:* 21:1.

Academics *Calendar:* semesters. *Degree:* certificates and associate. *Special study options:* academic remediation for entering students, adult/continuing education programs, cooperative education, distance learning, double majors, English as a second language, independent study, internships, off-campus study, part-time degree program, services for LD students, student-designed majors, summer session for credit.

Athletics Member NJCAA.

Costs (2006–07) *Tuition:* state resident $2352 full-time, $98 per credit hour part-time; nonresident $7056 full-time, $294 per credit hour part-time.

Financial Aid Of all full-time matriculated undergraduates, 100 Federal Work-Study jobs (averaging $2000). 25 state and other part-time jobs (averaging $2000).

Applying *Options:* electronic application, deferred entrance. *Application fee:* $20. *Required:* high school transcript.

Freshmen Application Contact Mr. Peter Harris, Director of Admissions, Manchester Community College, PO Box 1046, MS #12, Manchester, CT 06045-1046. *Phone:* 860-512-3210. *Fax:* 860-512-3221.

MIDDLESEX COMMUNITY COLLEGE

Middletown, Connecticut   www.mxcc.commnet.edu/

- **State-supported** 2-year, founded 1966, part of Connecticut Community–Technical College System
- **Suburban** 38-acre campus with easy access to Hartford
- **Endowment** $207,000
- **Coed,** 2,474 undergraduate students, 38% full-time, 63% women, 37% men

Undergraduates 943 full-time, 1,531 part-time. Students come from 4 states and territories, 1% are from out of state, 8% African American, 3% Asian American or Pacific Islander, 9% Hispanic American, 0.2% Native American, 0.3% international, 15% transferred in. *Retention:* 55% of 2003 full-time freshmen returned.

Freshmen *Admission:* 834 applied, 620 admitted, 455 enrolled.

Faculty *Total:* 178, 22% full-time. *Student/faculty ratio:* 17:1.

Majors Accounting; administrative assistant and secretarial science; biological and physical sciences; biology/biotechnology laboratory technician; broadcast journalism; business administration and management; commercial and advertising art; computer programming; engineering science; engineering technology; environmental studies; fine/studio arts; human services; industrial radiologic

technology; intermedia/multimedia; legal administrative assistant/secretary; liberal arts and sciences/liberal studies; marketing/marketing management; mass communication/media; medical administrative assistant and medical secretary; mental health/rehabilitation; ophthalmic laboratory technology; pre-engineering; radio and television; substance abuse/addiction counseling.

Academics *Calendar:* semesters. *Degree:* certificates and associate. *Special study options:* academic remediation for entering students, advanced placement credit, cooperative education, distance learning, double majors, English as a second language, honors programs, independent study, internships, off-campus study, part-time degree program, services for LD students, summer session for credit.

Library Jean Burr Smith Library with 45,000 titles, 180 serial subscriptions, an OPAC, a Web page.

Student Life *Housing:* college housing not available. *Activities and Organizations:* Collegiate Secretaries International, Minority Opportunities in Education, Radio Club. *Campus security:* 24-hour patrols. *Student services:* personal/psychological counseling.

Costs (2007–08) *Tuition:* state resident $2352 full-time, $98 per credit part-time; nonresident $7056 full-time, $294 per credit part-time. *Required fees:* $320 full-time, $3 per credit part-time.

Financial Aid Of all full-time matriculated undergraduates, 50 Federal Work-Study jobs (averaging $5000). 2 state and other part-time jobs (averaging $5000).

Applying *Options:* early admission, deferred entrance. *Application fee:* $20. *Required:* high school transcript, CPT. *Application deadlines:* rolling (freshmen), rolling (transfers).

Freshmen Application Contact Mensimah Shabazz, Director of Admissions, Middlesex Community College, 100 Training Hill Road, Middletown, CT 06457-4889. *Phone:* 860-343-5742. *Fax:* 860-344-3055. *E-mail:* mshabazz@mxcc.commnet.edu.

Naugatuck Valley Community College

Waterbury, Connecticut www.nvcc.commnet.edu/

- **State-supported** 2-year, founded 1992, part of Connecticut Community–Technical College System
- **Urban** 110-acre campus
- **Coed**, 5,659 undergraduate students, 40% full-time, 61% women, 39% men

Undergraduates 2,266 full-time, 3,393 part-time. 6% are from out of state, 8% African American, 3% Asian American or Pacific Islander, 11% Hispanic American, 0.3% Native American, 0.2% transferred in.

Freshmen *Admission:* 3,499 applied, 1,369 admitted, 1,136 enrolled.

Faculty *Total:* 210. *Student/faculty ratio:* 5:1.

Majors Accounting; administrative assistant and secretarial science; American studies; automobile/automotive mechanics technology; biological and physical sciences; business administration and management; chemical engineering; computer/information technology services administration related; computer programming; computer programming (specific applications); criminal justice/law enforcement administration; drafting and design technology; electrical, electronic and communications engineering technology; engineering technology; environmental studies; finance; fire science; gerontology; history; horticultural science; hospitality administration; hotel/motel administration; human services; industrial radiologic technology; industrial technology; information science/studies; information technology; international relations and affairs; kindergarten/preschool education; kinesiology and exercise science; legal administrative assistant/secretary; legal assistant/paralegal; liberal arts and sciences/liberal studies; marketing/marketing management; mathematics; mechanical engineering/mechanical technology; medical administrative assistant and medical secretary; mental health/rehabilitation; music; natural sciences; nursing (registered nurse training); physical sciences; physical therapist assistant; pre-engineering; quality control technology; social work; special products marketing; substance abuse/addiction counseling; system administration; word processing.

Academics *Calendar:* semesters. *Degree:* certificates and associate. *Special study options:* academic remediation for entering students, accelerated degree program, adult/continuing education programs, advanced placement credit, cooperative education, English as a second language, external degree program, independent study, internships, off-campus study, part-time degree program, services for LD students, student-designed majors, study abroad, summer session for credit.

Library Max R. Traurig Learning Resource Center with 35,000 titles, 520 serial subscriptions, an OPAC, a Web page.

Student Life *Housing:* college housing not available. *Activities and Organizations:* drama/theater group, student-run newspaper, choral group, Student Senate, Choral Society, Automotive Technician Club, Human Service Club, Legal Assistant Club. *Campus security:* 24-hour emergency response devices and patrols, late-night transport/escort service, security escort service. *Student services:* health clinic, personal/psychological counseling.

Athletics Member NJCAA.

Standardized Tests *Required:* ACCUPLACER (for admission).

Costs (2006–07) *Tuition:* state resident $2826 full-time; nonresident $8444 full-time.

Financial Aid Of all full-time matriculated undergraduates, 70 Federal Work-Study jobs (averaging $1942). 16 state and other part-time jobs (averaging $1660).

Applying *Options:* deferred entrance. *Application fee:* $20. *Required:* high school transcript. *Required for some:* interview. *Application deadlines:* rolling (freshmen), rolling (transfers). *Notification:* continuous (freshmen), continuous (transfers).

Freshmen Application Contact Ms. Lucretia Sveda, Director of Enrollment Services, Naugatuck Valley Community College, Waterbury, CT 06708. *Phone:* 203-575-8016. *Fax:* 203-596-8766. *E-mail:* lsveda@nvcc.commnet.edu.

Northwestern Connecticut Community College

Winsted, Connecticut www.nwctc.commnet.edu/

- **State-supported** 2-year, founded 1965, part of Connecticut Community–Technical College System
- **Small-town** 5-acre campus with easy access to Hartford
- **Coed**, 1,544 undergraduate students, 34% full-time, 64% women, 36% men

Undergraduates 521 full-time, 1,023 part-time. Students come from 6 states and territories, 1% are from out of state, 1% African American, 2% Asian American or Pacific Islander, 3% Hispanic American, 0.1% Native American, 6% transferred in. *Retention:* 56% of 2003 full-time freshmen returned.

Freshmen *Admission:* 384 applied, 384 admitted, 284 enrolled.

Faculty *Total:* 154, 19% full-time. *Student/faculty ratio:* 12:1.

Majors Accounting; administrative assistant and secretarial science; art; behavioral sciences; biology/biological sciences; business administration and management; child development; commercial and advertising art; communications technology; computer engineering technology; computer graphics; computer programming; computer science; criminal justice/law enforcement administration; criminal justice/police science; electrical, electronic and communications engineering technology; engineering; English; health science; human services; information science/studies; kindergarten/preschool education; legal assistant/paralegal; liberal arts and sciences/liberal studies; mathematics; medical/clinical assistant; parks, recreation and leisure; parks, recreation and leisure facilities management; physical sciences; pre-engineering; sign language interpretation and translation; social sciences; substance abuse/addiction counseling; therapeutic recreation; veterinary technology.

Academics *Calendar:* semesters. *Degree:* certificates and associate. *Special study options:* academic remediation for entering students, adult/continuing education programs, advanced placement credit, cooperative education, distance learning, double majors, English as a second language, independent study, internships, part-time degree program, services for LD students, summer session for credit.

Library Northwestern Connecticut Community–Technical College Learning Center with 37,666 titles, 267 serial subscriptions, 1,599 audiovisual materials, an OPAC.

Student Life *Housing:* college housing not available. *Activities and Organizations:* student-run newspaper, Ski Club, Student Senate, Deaf Club, Recreation Club, Early Childhood Educational Club. *Campus security:* evening security patrols.

Costs (2007–08) *Tuition:* state resident $2828 full-time, $163 per semester hour part-time; nonresident $8444 full-time, $478 per semester hour part-time.

Applying *Options:* deferred entrance. *Application fee:* $20. *Application deadlines:* rolling (freshmen), rolling (transfers). *Notification:* continuous (freshmen), continuous (transfers).

Freshmen Application Contact Admissions Office, Northwestern Connecticut Community College, Park Place East, Winsted, CT 06098. *Phone:* 860-738-6330. *Fax:* 860-738-6437. *E-mail:* admissions@nwcc.commnet.edu.

Norwalk Community College

Norwalk, Connecticut www.ncc.commnet.edu/

- **State-supported** 2-year, founded 1961, part of Connecticut Community–Technical College System
- **Suburban** 30-acre campus with easy access to New York City
- **Endowment** $11.0 million
- **Coed**

Norwalk Community College (continued)

Undergraduates Students come from 4 states and territories, 30 other countries, 1% are from out of state, 19% African American, 5% Asian American or Pacific Islander, 19% Hispanic American, 0.2% Native American.

Faculty *Student/faculty ratio:* 20:1.

Academics *Calendar:* semesters. *Degree:* certificates and associate. *Special study options:* academic remediation for entering students, adult/continuing education programs, advanced placement credit, cooperative education, distance learning, English as a second language, freshman honors college, honors programs, independent study, internships, part-time degree program, services for LD students, summer session for credit.

Student Life *Campus security:* 24-hour emergency response devices and patrols, student patrols, late-night transport/escort service, patrols by security.

Costs (2007–08) *Tuition:* state resident $2496 full-time, $104 per credit part-time; nonresident $8112 full-time, $312 per credit part-time. *Required fees:* $332 full-time, $166 per term part-time.

Financial Aid Of all full-time matriculated undergraduates, 42 Federal Work-Study jobs (averaging $2581). 60 state and other part-time jobs (averaging $2046).

Applying *Options:* deferred entrance. *Application fee:* $20. *Required:* high school transcript.

Freshmen Application Contact Mr. Curtis Antrum, Admissions Counselor, Norwalk Community College, 188 Richards Avenue, Norwalk, CT 06854-1655. *Phone:* 203-857-7060. *Toll-free phone:* 888-462-6282. *Fax:* 203-857-3335. *E-mail:* admissions@commnet.edu.

QUINEBAUG VALLEY COMMUNITY COLLEGE

Danielson, Connecticut   www.qvcc.commnet.edu/

- **State-supported** 2-year, founded 1971, part of Connecticut Community and Technical College System
- **Rural** 60-acre campus
- **Coed,** 1,779 undergraduate students, 38% full-time, 68% women, 32% men

Undergraduates 669 full-time, 1,110 part-time. Students come from 3 states and territories, 1% are from out of state, 2% African American, 1% Asian American or Pacific Islander, 10% Hispanic American, 0.8% Native American, 9% transferred in.

Freshmen *Admission:* 586 applied, 576 admitted, 375 enrolled.

Faculty *Total:* 126, 23% full-time. *Student/faculty ratio:* 18:1.

Majors Accounting; administrative assistant and secretarial science; art; avionics maintenance technology; business administration and management; computer and information sciences related; computer graphics; computer systems networking and telecommunications; data entry/microcomputer applications; engineering technology; human services; liberal arts and sciences/liberal studies; medical/clinical assistant; plastics engineering technology; pre-engineering; substance abuse/addiction counseling; system administration; word processing.

Academics *Calendar:* semesters. *Degree:* certificates and associate. *Special study options:* academic remediation for entering students, adult/continuing education programs, advanced placement credit, distance learning, English as a second language, external degree program, independent study, internships, part-time degree program, study abroad, summer session for credit.

Library Audrey Beck Library with 31,000 titles, 130 serial subscriptions, an OPAC.

Student Life *Housing:* college housing not available. *Campus security:* evening security guard.

Costs (2007–08) *Tuition:* state resident $2496 full-time, $104 per credit part-time; nonresident $7488 full-time, $312 per credit part-time. *Required fees:* $320 full-time.

Financial Aid Of all full-time matriculated undergraduates, 38 Federal Work-Study jobs (averaging $1400). 24 state and other part-time jobs (averaging $1350).

Applying *Options:* electronic application, early admission, deferred entrance. *Application fee:* $20. *Required for some:* high school transcript. *Recommended:* high school transcript. *Application deadlines:* 9/1 (freshmen), 9/1 (transfers). *Notification:* continuous until 9/1 (freshmen), continuous until 9/1 (transfers).

Freshmen Application Contact Dr. Toni Moumouris, Director of Admissions, Quinebaug Valley Community College, 742 Upper Maple Street, Danielson, CT 06239. *Phone:* 860-774-1130 Ext. 318. *Fax:* 860-774-7768. *E-mail:* qu_isd@commnet.edu.

ST. VINCENT'S COLLEGE

Bridgeport, Connecticut   www.stvincentscollege.edu/

Freshmen Application Contact Mr. Joseph Marrone, Director of Admissions and Recruitment Marketing, St. Vincent's College, 2800 Main Street, Bridgeport, CT 06606-4292. *Phone:* 203-576-5515. *Fax:* 203-576-5893. *E-mail:* jmarrone@stvincentscollege.edu.

THREE RIVERS COMMUNITY COLLEGE

Norwich, Connecticut   www.trcc.commnet.edu/

- **State-supported** 2-year, founded 1963, part of Connecticut Community–Technical College System
- **Small-town** 40-acre campus with easy access to Hartford
- **Coed,** 3,793 undergraduate students, 34% full-time, 62% women, 38% men

Undergraduates 1,279 full-time, 2,514 part-time. Students come from 6 states and territories, 1% are from out of state, 7% African American, 4% Asian American or Pacific Islander, 8% Hispanic American, 1% Native American, 0.5% international, 12% transferred in.

Freshmen *Admission:* 810 enrolled.

Faculty *Total:* 212, 36% full-time.

Majors Accounting; administrative assistant and secretarial science; architectural engineering technology; avionics maintenance technology; business administration and management; civil engineering technology; computer engineering technology; computer programming; computer typography and composition equipment operation; consumer merchandising/retailing management; corrections; criminal justice/law enforcement administration; data processing and data processing technology; drafting and design technology; dramatic/theater arts; electrical, electronic and communications engineering technology; engineering; engineering science; engineering technology; environmental engineering technology; fire science; hospitality administration; hotel/motel administration; human services; hydrology and water resources science; industrial technology; kindergarten/preschool education; laser and optical technology; legal administrative assistant/secretary; liberal arts and sciences/liberal studies; marketing; marketing management; mechanical engineering/mechanical technology; medical administrative assistant and medical secretary; nuclear/nuclear power technology; nursing (registered nurse training); pre-engineering; public administration; special products marketing; substance abuse/addiction counseling; technical and business writing; tourism and travel services management.

Academics *Calendar:* semesters. *Degrees:* certificates and associate (engineering technology programs are offered on the Thames Valley Campus; liberal arts, transfer and career programs are offered on the Mohegan Campus). *Special study options:* academic remediation for entering students, adult/continuing education programs, advanced placement credit, cooperative education, double majors, English as a second language, external degree program, independent study, internships, part-time degree program, services for LD students, student-designed majors, study abroad, summer session for credit.

Library Three Rivers Community College Learning Resource Center plus 2 others with 53,768 titles, 549 serial subscriptions, an OPAC.

Student Life *Housing:* college housing not available. *Activities and Organizations:* drama/theater group, student-run newspaper, Student Senate/Student Government Association, Theater Guild, Phi Theta Kappa, Student Nurses Association, African-American Organization, national fraternities. *Campus security:* late-night transport/escort service, 14 hour patrols by trained security personnel. *Student services:* personal/psychological counseling.

Athletics *Intramural sports:* bowling M/W.

Costs (2007–08) *Tuition:* state resident $2496 full-time, $104 per credit hour part-time; nonresident $7488 full-time, $312 per credit hour part-time. *Required fees:* $332 full-time, $40 per course part-time.

Financial Aid Of all full-time matriculated undergraduates, 40 Federal Work-Study jobs (averaging $3000). 80 state and other part-time jobs (averaging $3000).

Applying *Options:* early admission, deferred entrance. *Application fee:* $20. *Required for some:* minimum 3.0 GPA. *Recommended:* high school transcript. *Application deadlines:* rolling (freshmen), rolling (transfers). *Notification:* continuous (freshmen), continuous (transfers).

Freshmen Application Contact Ms. Aida Garcia, Admissions and Recruitment Counselor, Mohegan Campus, Three Rivers Community College, Mahan Drive, Norwich, CT 06360. *Phone:* 860-383-5260. *Fax:* 860-885-1684. *E-mail:* admissions@trcc.commnet.edu.

TUNXIS COMMUNITY COLLEGE

Farmington, Connecticut   **www.tunxis.commnet.edu/**

- **State-supported** 2-year, founded 1969, part of Connecticut Community–Technical College System
- **Suburban** 12-acre campus with easy access to Hartford
- **Coed,** 3,663 undergraduate students, 40% full-time, 62% women, 38% men

Undergraduates 1,455 full-time, 2,208 part-time. Students come from 6 states and territories, 2% are from out of state, 5% African American, 3% Asian American or Pacific Islander, 9% Hispanic American, 0.2% Native American, 0.7% international.

Freshmen *Admission:* 587 enrolled.

Faculty *Total:* 239, 28% full-time, 12% with terminal degrees. *Student/faculty ratio:* 19:1.

Majors Accounting; administrative assistant and secretarial science; applied art; art; business administration and management; commercial and advertising art; corrections; criminal justice/law enforcement administration; data processing and data processing technology; dental hygiene; engineering; engineering technology; fashion merchandising; forensic science and technology; human services; information science/studies; kindergarten/preschool education; legal administrative assistant/secretary; liberal arts and sciences/liberal studies; marketing/marketing management; medical administrative assistant and medical secretary; physical therapy; substance abuse/addiction counseling.

Academics *Calendar:* semesters. *Degree:* certificates and associate. *Special study options:* academic remediation for entering students, adult/continuing education programs, English as a second language, part-time degree program, summer session for credit.

Library Tunxis Community College Library with 33,866 titles, 285 serial subscriptions, an OPAC.

Student Life *Housing:* college housing not available. *Activities and Organizations:* student-run newspaper, Phi Theta Kappa, Student American Dental Hygiene Association (SADHA), Human Services Club, student newspaper, Bible Club. *Campus security:* 24-hour patrols. *Student services:* health clinic.

Costs (2007–08) *Tuition:* state resident $2496 full-time, $105 per hour part-time; nonresident $7488 full-time, $312 per hour part-time. *Required fees:* $332 full-time.

Applying *Options:* deferred entrance. *Application fee:* $20. *Required:* high school transcript. *Application deadlines:* rolling (freshmen), rolling (transfers).

Freshmen Application Contact Kelly Pittman, Academic Advisor, Tunxis Community College, 271 Scott Swamp Road, Farmington, CT 06032. *Phone:* 860-255-3544. *Fax:* 860-255-3559. *E-mail:* kpittman@txcc.commnet.edu.

DELAWARE

DELAWARE COLLEGE OF ART AND DESIGN

Wilmington, Delaware   **www.dcad.edu/**

- **Independent** 2-year, founded 1997, administratively affiliated with Corcoran College of Art and Design
- **Urban** 1-acre campus
- **Endowment** $65,295
- **Coed**

Undergraduates 148 full-time, 46 part-time. Students come from 9 states and territories, 45% are from out of state, 9% African American, 1% Asian American or Pacific Islander, 4% Hispanic American, 0.5% Native American, 1% international, 11% transferred in, 50% live on campus.

Faculty *Student/faculty ratio:* 5:1.

Academics *Calendar:* semesters. *Degree:* associate. *Special study options:* academic remediation for entering students, adult/continuing education programs, advanced placement credit, double majors, off-campus study, part-time degree program, services for LD students, study abroad, summer session for credit.

Costs (2006–07) *Tuition:* $14,070 full-time, $595 per credit part-time. *Required fees:* $200 per term part-time. *Room only:* $5490.

Applying *Options:* electronic application, deferred entrance. *Application fee:* $25. *Required:* essay or personal statement, high school transcript, minimum 2 GPA, interview, portfolio. *Required for some:* letters of recommendation.

Freshmen Application Contact Krista Rothwell, Admissions Recruiter, Delaware College of Art and Design, 600 North Market Street, Wilmington, DE 19801. *Phone:* 302-622-8000 Ext. 111. *Fax:* 302-622-8870. *E-mail:* admissions@dcad.edu.

DELAWARE TECHNICAL & COMMUNITY COLLEGE, JACK F. OWENS CAMPUS

Georgetown, Delaware   **www.dtcc.edu/**

- **State-supported** 2-year, founded 1967, part of Delaware Technical and Community College System
- **Small-town** 120-acre campus
- **Coed**

Undergraduates 1,600 full-time, 2,336 part-time. Students come from 3 states and territories, 9 other countries, 6% are from out of state, 15% African American, 0.9% Asian American or Pacific Islander, 3% Hispanic American, 0.3% Native American, 6% international.

Faculty *Student/faculty ratio:* 15:1.

Academics *Calendar:* semesters. *Degree:* certificates, diplomas, and associate. *Special study options:* academic remediation for entering students, adult/continuing education programs, cooperative education, distance learning, English as a second language, external degree program, internships, part-time degree program, services for LD students, student-designed majors, summer session for credit.

Student Life *Campus security:* 24-hour patrols, late-night transport/escort service.

Athletics Member NJCAA.

Costs (2006–07) *Tuition:* state resident $2070 full-time, $86 per credit hour part-time; nonresident $5176 full-time, $216 per credit hour part-time. *Required fees:* $216 full-time, $6 per credit hour part-time, $21 per term part-time.

Financial Aid Of all full-time matriculated undergraduates, 250 Federal Work-Study jobs (averaging $2000).

Applying *Options:* early admission. *Application fee:* $10. *Required:* high school transcript.

Freshmen Application Contact Ms. Claire McDonald, Admissions Counselor, Delaware Technical & Community College, Jack F. Owens Campus, PO Box 610, Georgetown, DE 19947. *Phone:* 302-856-5400. *Fax:* 302-856-9461.

DELAWARE TECHNICAL & COMMUNITY COLLEGE, STANTON/WILMINGTON CAMPUS

Newark, Delaware   **www.dtcc.edu/**

- **State-supported** 2-year, founded 1968, part of Delaware Technical and Community College System
- **Coed**

Undergraduates 2,767 full-time, 4,706 part-time. Students come from 13 states and territories, 45 other countries, 8% are from out of state, 23% African American, 3% Asian American or Pacific Islander, 5% Hispanic American, 0.4% Native American, 2% international.

Faculty *Student/faculty ratio:* 15:1.

Academics *Calendar:* semesters. *Degree:* certificates, diplomas, and associate. *Special study options:* academic remediation for entering students, adult/continuing education programs, cooperative education, English as a second language, external degree program, part-time degree program, services for LD students, summer session for credit.

Student Life *Campus security:* 24-hour patrols, late-night transport/escort service.

Athletics Member NJCAA.

Costs (2006–07) *Tuition:* state resident $2070 full-time, $86 per credit hour part-time; nonresident $5176 full-time, $216 per credit hour part-time. *Required fees:* $216 full-time, $6 per credit hour part-time, $21 per term part-time.

Applying *Options:* early admission. *Application fee:* $10. *Required:* high school transcript.

Freshmen Application Contact Ms. Rebecca Bailey, Admissions Coordinator, Wilmington, Delaware Technical & Community College, Stanton/Wilmington Campus, 333 Shipley Street, Wilmington, DE 19713. *Phone:* 302-571-5366. *Fax:* 302-577-2548.

DELAWARE TECHNICAL & COMMUNITY COLLEGE, TERRY CAMPUS

Dover, Delaware www.dtcc.edu/terry/

- **State-supported** 2-year, founded 1972, part of Delaware Technical and Community College System
- **Small-town** 70-acre campus with easy access to Philadelphia
- **Coed**

Undergraduates 875 full-time, 1,694 part-time. Students come from 10 states and territories, 10 other countries, 3% are from out of state, 24% African American, 2% Asian American or Pacific Islander, 3% Hispanic American, 0.4% Native American, 1% international, 10% transferred in.

Faculty *Student/faculty ratio:* 14:1.

Academics *Calendar:* semesters. *Degree:* certificates, diplomas, and associate. *Special study options:* academic remediation for entering students, adult/continuing education programs, cooperative education, English as a second language, internships, part-time degree program, services for LD students, summer session for credit.

Student Life *Campus security:* late-night transport/escort service.

Costs (2006–07) *Tuition:* state resident $2070 full-time, $86 per credit hour part-time; nonresident $5176 full-time, $216 per credit hour part-time. *Required fees:* $216 full-time, $6 per credit hour part-time, $21 per term part-time.

Financial Aid Of all full-time matriculated undergraduates, 50 Federal Work-Study jobs (averaging $1500).

Applying *Options:* early admission. *Application fee:* $10. *Required:* high school transcript.

Freshmen Application Contact Mrs. Maria Harris, Admissions Officer, Delaware Technical & Community College, Terry Campus, 100 Campus Drive, Dover, DE 19904. *Phone:* 302-857-1020. *Fax:* 302-857-1296. *E-mail:* mharris@outland.dtcc.edu.

FLORIDA

ANGLEY COLLEGE

Deland, Florida www.angley.edu

- **Proprietary** primarily 2-year
- 94 undergraduate students
- 97% of applicants were admitted

Freshmen *Admission:* 117 applied, 113 admitted.

Majors Business administration and management; business operations support and secretarial services related; health services administration; medical administrative assistant and medical secretary; medical/clinical assistant.

Academics *Calendar:* continuous. *Degrees:* diplomas, associate, and bachelor's.

Costs (2006–07) *Tuition:* $4350 full-time.

Applying *Application fee:* $25.

Freshmen Application Contact Admissions Office, Angley College, 230 North Woodland Boulevard, Suite 310, Deland, FL 32720. *Phone:* 386-740-1215 Ext. 125. *Toll-free phone:* 866-639-1215. *E-mail:* admissions@angley.edu.

ATI CAREER TRAINING CENTER

Fort Lauderdale, Florida www.aticareertraining.com/

Director of Admissions Ms. Wendy Hopkins Goffinet, Director of Admissions, ATI Career Training Center, 2880 NW 62nd Street, Fort Lauderdale, FL 33309-9731. *Phone:* 954-973-4760.

ATI CAREER TRAINING CENTER

Miami, Florida www.aticareertraining.com/

Director of Admissions Ms. Mary Fernandez, Director of Admissions, ATI Career Training Center, 1 NE 19th Street, Miami, FL 33132. *Phone:* 305-573-1600.

ATI CAREER TRAINING CENTER

Oakland Park, Florida www.aticareertraining.edu/

- **Proprietary** 2-year
- 591 undergraduate students

Majors Automobile/automotive mechanics technology; heating, air conditioning, ventilation and refrigeration maintenance technology.

Academics *Degree:* certificates and associate.

Costs (2006–07) *Tuition:* $24,010 per degree program part-time.

Applying *Application fee:* $100.

Freshmen Application Contact Admissions Office, ATI Career Training Center, 3501 Northwest 9th Avenue, Oakland Park, FL 33309. *Phone:* 954-563-5899.

ATI HEALTH EDUCATION CENTER

Miami, Florida www.aticareertraining.com/

Director of Admissions Mrs. Barbara Woosley, Director, ATI Health Education Center, 1395 NW 167th Street, Suite 200, Miami, FL 33169-5742. *Phone:* 305-628-1000. *Fax:* 305-628-1461. *E-mail:* bwoolsey@atienterprises.edu.

BREVARD COMMUNITY COLLEGE

Cocoa, Florida www.brevardcc.edu/

- **State-supported** 2-year, founded 1960, part of Florida Community College System
- **Suburban** 100-acre campus with easy access to Orlando
- **Coed**, 13,670 undergraduate students, 36% full-time, 60% women, 40% men

Undergraduates 4,953 full-time, 8,717 part-time. Students come from 47 states and territories, 79 other countries, 9% African American, 3% Asian American or Pacific Islander, 7% Hispanic American, 0.6% Native American, 0.9% international.

Freshmen *Admission:* 5,366 applied, 5,366 admitted, 2,467 enrolled.

Faculty *Total:* 1,016, 19% full-time. *Student/faculty ratio:* 22:1.

Majors Accounting; business administration and management; chemical engineering; clinical/medical laboratory technology; computer engineering technology; computer/information technology services administration related; computer programming; computer programming (specific applications); computer software and media applications related; computer systems analysis; computer systems networking and telecommunications; corrections; criminal justice/law enforcement administration; criminal justice/police science; culinary arts; dental hygiene; digital communication and media/multimedia; drafting and design technology; early childhood education; electrical, electronic and communications engineering technology; electrical/electronics drafting and CAD/CADD; emergency medical technology (EMT paramedic); fire science; international business/trade/commerce; legal assistant/paralegal; liberal arts and sciences/liberal studies; manufacturing technology; medical administrative assistant and medical secretary; medical/clinical assistant; nursing (registered nurse training); radio and television; radiologic technology/science; surgical technology; system administration; system, networking, and LAN/WAN management; veterinary technology; web page, digital/multimedia and information resources design.

Academics *Calendar:* semesters. *Degree:* certificates and associate. *Special study options:* academic remediation for entering students, accelerated degree program, adult/continuing education programs, advanced placement credit, cooperative education, distance learning, double majors, English as a second language, external degree program, honors programs, independent study, internships, part-time degree program, services for LD students, study abroad, summer session for credit. *ROTC:* Army (b), Air Force (b).

Library UCF Library with 213,873 titles, 904 serial subscriptions, an OPAC, a Web page.

Student Life *Housing:* college housing not available. *Activities and Organizations:* drama/theater group, student-run newspaper, television station, choral

group, Phi Theta Kappa, ROTORACT, African-American Student Union, Student Government Association, Psi Beta. *Campus security:* 24-hour emergency response devices and patrols. *Student services:* women's center.

Athletics Member NJCAA. *Intercollegiate sports:* baseball M(s), basketball M(s)/W(s), golf M(s), softball W(s), volleyball W(s).

Costs (2006–07) *Tuition:* state resident $1626 full-time, $68 per credit hour part-time; nonresident $5928 full-time, $247 per credit hour part-time. *Waivers:* senior citizens and employees or children of employees.

Financial Aid Of all full-time matriculated undergraduates, 200 Federal Work-Study jobs (averaging $2244). 200 state and other part-time jobs (averaging $2000).

Applying *Options:* electronic application. *Application fee:* $30. *Required:* high school transcript. *Application deadlines:* rolling (freshmen), rolling (transfers). *Notification:* continuous (freshmen), continuous (transfers).

Freshmen Application Contact Ms. Stephanie Burnette, Registrar, Brevard Community College, 1519 Clearlake Road, Cocoa, FL 32922-6597. *Phone:* 321-433-7271. *Fax:* 321-433-7172. *E-mail:* cocoaadmissions@brevardcc.edu.

BROWARD COMMUNITY COLLEGE

Fort Lauderdale, Florida   www.broward.edu/

- **State-supported** 2-year, founded 1960, part of Florida Community College System
- **Urban** campus with easy access to Miami
- **Coed,** 31,030 undergraduate students, 32% full-time, 60% women, 40% men

Undergraduates 10,006 full-time, 21,024 part-time. Students come from 14 states and territories, 4 other countries, 18% are from out of state, 28% African American, 3% Asian American or Pacific Islander, 26% Hispanic American, 0.3% Native American, 8% international, 10% transferred in.

Freshmen *Admission:* 4,653 applied, 4,653 admitted, 4,653 enrolled. *Test scores:* SAT verbal scores over 500: 22%; SAT math scores over 500: 28%; SAT verbal scores over 600: 3%; SAT math scores over 600: 4%.

Faculty *Total:* 1,561, 28% full-time, 24% with terminal degrees.

Majors Accounting; administrative assistant and secretarial science; airline pilot and flight crew; architectural engineering technology; automobile/automotive mechanics technology; aviation/airway management; avionics maintenance technology; business administration and management; child development; civil engineering technology; clinical laboratory science/medical technology; clinical/medical laboratory technology; computer engineering technology; computer programming; computer science; construction management; corrections; criminal justice/law enforcement administration; criminal justice/police science; data processing and data processing technology; dental hygiene; electrical, electronic and communications engineering technology; elementary education; emergency medical technology (EMT paramedic); engineering science; environmental engineering technology; finance; fire science; hotel/motel administration; industrial radiologic technology; information science/studies; insurance; interior design; kindergarten/preschool education; legal administrative assistant/secretary; legal assistant/paralegal; liberal arts and sciences/liberal studies; marketing/marketing management; mechanical engineering/mechanical technology; medical administrative assistant and medical secretary; medical/clinical assistant; nuclear medical technology; nursing (registered nurse training); physical therapy; pre-engineering; respiratory care therapy; special products marketing; tourism and travel services management.

Academics *Calendar:* trimesters. *Degree:* certificates, diplomas, and associate. *Special study options:* academic remediation for entering students, adult/continuing education programs, advanced placement credit, cooperative education, English as a second language, honors programs, part-time degree program, services for LD students, student-designed majors, study abroad, summer session for credit. *ROTC:* Army (b).

Library South Regional/Broward Community College Library with 200,000 titles, 600 serial subscriptions, an OPAC.

Student Life *Housing:* college housing not available. *Activities and Organizations:* drama/theater group, student-run newspaper, choral group. *Campus security:* 24-hour emergency response devices and patrols, late-night transport/escort service. *Student services:* personal/psychological counseling, women's center.

Athletics Member NJCAA. *Intercollegiate sports:* baseball M(s), basketball M(s)/W(s), soccer W, softball W(s), swimming and diving M(s)/W(s), tennis W(s), volleyball W(s), wrestling M(s). *Intramural sports:* baseball M, basketball M/W, tennis W.

Costs (2006–07) *Tuition:* state resident $1614 full-time, $70 per credit hour part-time; nonresident $6458 full-time, $243 per credit hour part-time. *Required fees:* $480 full-time, $16 per credit hour part-time.

Financial Aid *Financial aid deadline:* 7/1.

Applying *Options:* early admission, deferred entrance. *Application fee:* $35. *Required for some:* high school transcript, minimum 2.75 GPA.

Freshmen Application Contact Willie J. Alexander, Associate Vice President for Student Affairs/College Registrar, Broward Community College, 225 East Las Olas Boulevard, Fort Lauderdale, FL 33301-2298. *Phone:* 954-201-7471. *Fax:* 954-201-7466.

BROWN MACKIE COLLEGE—MIAMI

Miami, Florida   www.brownmackie.edu/locations.asp?locid=25

- **Proprietary** 2-year
- **Coed,** 311 undergraduate students

Faculty *Total:* 19. *Student/faculty ratio:* 18:1.

Majors Accounting technology and bookkeeping; business administration and management; computer software technology; criminal justice/law enforcement administration; medical/clinical assistant; paralegal/legal assistant.

Academics *Degree:* diplomas and associate.

Library 19,750 titles.

Student Life *Activities and Organizations:* national sororities. *Student services:* personal/psychological counseling.

Costs (2006–07) *Comprehensive fee:* $19,752 includes full-time tuition ($11,472), mandatory fees ($480), and room and board ($7800). Full-time tuition and fees vary according to student level. Part-time tuition: $239 per credit hour. *Room and board:* Room and board charges vary according to housing facility. *Payment plans:* installment, deferred payment. *Waivers:* employees or children of employees.

Applying *Required:* high school transcript, interview. *Application deadlines:* rolling (freshmen), rolling (transfers). *Notification:* continuous (freshmen), continuous (transfers).

Freshmen Application Contact Director of Admissions, Brown Mackie College–Miami, 1501 Biscayne Boulevard, Miami, FL 33132. *Phone:* 305-341-6600. *Toll-free phone:* 866-505-0335. *Fax:* 305-373-8814. *E-mail:* mkoontz@brownmackie.edu.

▶**See page 514 for the College Close-Up.**

CENTRAL FLORIDA COLLEGE

Winter Park, Florida   www.centralfloridacollege.edu/

- **Proprietary** 2-year, founded 1984
- **Coed,** 453 undergraduate students

Majors Medical administrative assistant and medical secretary; medical insurance/medical billing.

Academics *Degree:* associate.

Costs (2006–07) *Tuition:* $12,045 full-time.

Applying *Application fee:* $50.

Freshmen Application Contact Admissions Office, Central Florida College, 1573 West Fairbanks Avenue, Suite 100, Winter Park, FL 32789. *Toll-free phone:* 800-442-7610.

CENTRAL FLORIDA COMMUNITY COLLEGE

Ocala, Florida   www.cf.edu/

- **State and locally supported** 2-year, founded 1957, part of Florida Community College System
- **Small-town** 139-acre campus
- **Endowment** $29.1 million
- **Coed,** 5,825 undergraduate students, 41% full-time, 63% women, 37% men

Undergraduates 2,379 full-time, 3,446 part-time. 10% African American, 2% Asian American or Pacific Islander, 8% Hispanic American, 0.6% Native American, 0.4% international.

Freshmen *Admission:* 1,205 admitted, 1,106 enrolled.

Faculty *Total:* 485, 25% full-time, 9% with terminal degrees. *Student/faculty ratio:* 15:1.

Majors Accounting technology and bookkeeping; automobile/automotive mechanics technology; business/commerce; drafting and design technology; early childhood education; emergency medical technology (EMT paramedic); fire science; health information/medical records technology; human services; information technology; landscaping and groundskeeping; liberal arts and sciences/

Central Florida Community College (continued)

liberal studies; marketing/marketing management; nursing (registered nurse training); office management; parks, recreation and leisure; physical therapist assistant; restaurant, culinary, and catering management; veterinary/animal health technology.

Academics *Calendar:* semesters. *Degree:* certificates and associate. *Special study options:* academic remediation for entering students, adult/continuing education programs, advanced placement credit, cooperative education, distance learning, English as a second language, freshman honors college, honors programs, independent study, internships, part-time degree program, services for LD students, summer session for credit.

Library Learning Resources Center plus 1 other with 82,112 titles, 412 serial subscriptions, 6,244 audiovisual materials, an OPAC, a Web page.

Student Life *Housing:* college housing not available. *Options:* Campus housing is provided by a third party. *Activities and Organizations:* drama/theater group, student-run newspaper, choral group, Student Activities Board, African-American Student Union, ROC (Realizing Our Cause), Gay Straight Alliance, Musagettas. *Campus security:* 24-hour emergency response devices and patrols, student patrols, late-night transport/escort service. *Student services:* personal/psychological counseling.

Athletics Member NJCAA. *Intercollegiate sports:* baseball M(s), basketball M(s)/W(s), softball W(s), tennis W(s).

Costs (2006–07) *Tuition:* state resident $2038 full-time, $68 per credit hour part-time; nonresident $7382 full-time, $246 per credit hour part-time. *Room and board:* $5562. *Waivers:* employees or children of employees.

Financial Aid Of all full-time matriculated undergraduates, 103 Federal Work-Study jobs (averaging $1500).

Applying *Options:* early admission. *Application fee:* $20. *Required:* high school transcript. *Application deadlines:* rolling (freshmen), rolling (transfers). *Notification:* continuous (freshmen), continuous (transfers).

Freshmen Application Contact Ms. Christy Jones, Registrar, Central Florida Community College, PO Box 1388, 3001 SW College Road, Ocala, FL 34474-1388. *Phone:* 352-237-2111 Ext. 1398. *Fax:* 352-873-5882. *E-mail:* jonesch@cf.edu.

CENTRAL FLORIDA INSTITUTE

Palm Harbor, Florida   www.cfinstitute.com/

Director of Admissions Carol Bruno, Director of Admissions, Central Florida Institute, 60522 US Highway 19 North, Suite 200, Palm Harbor, FL 34684. *Phone:* 727-786-4707.

CHIPOLA COLLEGE

Marianna, Florida   www.chipola.edu/

- **State-supported** primarily 2-year, founded 1947
- **Rural** 105-acre campus
- **Coed,** 2,104 undergraduate students

Undergraduates Students come from 13 states and territories, 7 other countries, 3% are from out of state.

Freshmen *Admission:* 798 applied, 755 admitted. *Average high school GPA:* 2.5. *Test scores:* SAT verbal scores over 500: 16%; SAT math scores over 500: 36%; ACT scores over 18: 81%; SAT verbal scores over 600: 4%; SAT math scores over 600: 12%; ACT scores over 24: 25%; ACT scores over 30: 3%.

Faculty *Total:* 69, 78% full-time, 12% with terminal degrees. *Student/faculty ratio:* 24:1.

Majors Accounting; agriculture; agronomy and crop science; art; biological and physical sciences; business administration and management; clinical laboratory science/medical technology; computer and information sciences related; computer science; education; finance; liberal arts and sciences/liberal studies; mass communication/media; mathematics teacher education; nursing (registered nurse training); pre-engineering; science teacher education; secondary education; social work.

Academics *Calendar:* semesters. *Degrees:* certificates, associate, and bachelor's. *Special study options:* academic remediation for entering students, adult/continuing education programs, advanced placement credit, distance learning, honors programs, independent study, part-time degree program, services for LD students, summer session for credit.

Library Chipola Library with 37,740 titles, 226 serial subscriptions.

Student Life *Housing:* college housing not available. *Activities and Organizations:* drama/theater group, student-run newspaper, choral group, Drama/Theater Group. *Campus security:* night security personnel.

Athletics Member NJCAA. *Intercollegiate sports:* baseball M(s), basketball M(s)/W(s), softball W(s).

Standardized Tests *Required:* SAT or ACT (for placement).

Costs (2007–08) *Tuition:* state resident $2200 full-time, $68 per hour part-time; nonresident $6000 full-time, $200 per hour part-time.

Applying *Options:* early admission. *Required:* high school transcript. *Application deadlines:* rolling (freshmen), rolling (transfers). *Notification:* continuous (freshmen), continuous (transfers).

Freshmen Application Contact Dr. Jayne Roberts, Dean of Enrollment Services and Registrar, Chipola College, Marianna, FL 32446. *Phone:* 850-718-2209. *Fax:* 850-718-2287. *E-mail:* robertsj@chipola.edu.

CITY COLLEGE

Casselberry, Florida   www.citycollegeorlando.edu/

Director of Admissions Ms. Yvonne C. Hunter, Director of Admissions, City College, 853 Semoran Boulevard, Suite 200, Casselberry, FL 32707-5342. *Phone:* 407-831-9816. *Fax:* 407-831-1147. *E-mail:* yhunter@citycollege.edu.

CITY COLLEGE

Fort Lauderdale, Florida   www.citycollege.edu/

- **Independent** primarily 2-year, founded 1984
- **Coed,** 712 undergraduate students
- 77% of applicants were admitted

Freshmen *Admission:* 227 applied, 175 admitted.

Faculty *Total:* 61, 23% full-time.

Majors Accounting; business administration, management and operations related; computer programming (specific applications); emergency medical technology (EMT paramedic); hospitality administration related; medical administrative assistant and medical secretary; medical office assistant; paralegal/legal assistant; radio and television.

Academics *Calendar:* semesters. *Degrees:* certificates, associate, and bachelor's.

Costs (2006–07) *Tuition:* $8640 full-time.

Financial Aid Of all full-time matriculated undergraduates, 6 Federal Work-Study jobs.

Applying *Application fee:* $25.

Freshmen Application Contact Admissions Office, City College, 2000 West Commercial Boulevard, Suite 200, Fort Lauderdale, FL 33309. *Phone:* 954-492-5353.

CITY COLLEGE

Gainesville, Florida   www.citycollege.edu/

- **Independent** primarily 2-year, founded 1986
- **Coed,** 352 undergraduate students
- 100% of applicants were admitted

Freshmen *Admission:* 24 applied, 24 admitted.

Majors Accounting; business administration, management and operations related; computer programming (specific applications); emergency medical technology (EMT paramedic); hospitality administration related; medical administrative assistant and medical secretary; medical office assistant; mental health/rehabilitation; paralegal/legal assistant; phlebotomy; radio and television.

Academics *Calendar:* semesters. *Degrees:* certificates, associate, and bachelor's.

Costs (2006–07) *Tuition:* $8559 full-time.

Applying *Application fee:* $25. *Required:* high school transcript.

Freshmen Application Contact Admissions Office, City College, 2400 S.W. 13th Street, Gainesville, FL 32608.

CITY COLLEGE

Miami, Florida   www.citycollege.edu/

- **Independent** primarily 2-year, founded 1997
- **Coed,** 291 undergraduate students
- 79% of applicants were admitted

Freshmen *Admission:* 101 applied, 80 admitted.

Majors Accounting; business administration, management and operations related; computer programming (specific applications); emergency medical technology (EMT paramedic); hospitality administration related; medical administrative assistant and medical secretary; medical office assistant; paralegal/legal assistant; radio and television.
Academics *Calendar:* semesters. *Degrees:* certificates, associate, and bachelor's.
Costs (2006–07) *Tuition:* $9840 full-time.
Applying *Application fee:* $25. *Required:* high school transcript.
Freshmen Application Contact Admissions Office, City College, 9300 South Dadeland Boulevard, Suite PH, Miami, FL 33156. *Phone:* 305-666-9242. *Fax:* 305-666-9243.

COLLEGE OF BUSINESS AND TECHNOLOGY
Miami, Florida www.cbt.edu/

- **Proprietary** 2-year, founded 1988
- **Endowment** $3.5 million
- **Coed**

Undergraduates Students come from 7 states and territories, 90% Hispanic American.
Faculty *Student/faculty ratio:* 10:1.
Academics *Calendar:* semesters. *Degree:* certificates, diplomas, and associate. *Special study options:* academic remediation for entering students, accelerated degree program, adult/continuing education programs, advanced placement credit, cooperative education, distance learning, double majors, English as a second language, honors programs, independent study, internships, off-campus study, part-time degree program, services for LD students, summer session for credit.
Costs (2006–07) *Tuition:* $10,500 full-time, $278 per semester hour part-time. *Required fees:* $200 full-time. *Room only:* $6000.
Applying *Options:* electronic application. *Application fee:* $100. *Required:* essay or personal statement, high school transcript, minimum 2.6 GPA, 2 letters of recommendation, interview.
Freshmen Application Contact Ms. Ivis Delgado, Admissions Representative, College of Business and Technology, 8991 Southwest 107 Avenue, Suite 200, Miami, FL 33176. *Phone:* 305-273-4499 Ext. 2204. *Fax:* 305-485-4411. *E-mail:* admissions@cbt.edu.

DAYTONA BEACH COMMUNITY COLLEGE
Daytona Beach, Florida www.dbcc.edu/

Director of Admissions Mr. Thomas LoBasso, Dean of Enrollment Development, Daytona Beach Community College, PO Box 2811, Daytona Beach, FL 32120-2811. *Phone:* 386-506-3732.

EDISON COLLEGE
Fort Myers, Florida www.edison.edu/

Freshmen Application Contact Ms. Pat Armstrong, Admissions Specialist, Edison College, PO Box 60210, Fort Myers, FL 33906-6210. *Phone:* 941-489-9121. *Toll-free phone:* 800-749-2ECC. *Fax:* 941-489-9094. *E-mail:* inquiry@eccrs.edison.cc.fl.us.

FLORIDA CAREER COLLEGE
Miami, Florida www.careercollege.edu/

Director of Admissions Mr. David Knobel, President, Florida Career College, 1321 Southwest 107 Avenue, Miami, FL 33174. *Phone:* 305-553-6065.

FLORIDA COLLEGE OF NATURAL HEALTH
Bradenton, Florida www.fcnh.com/

- **Proprietary** 2-year, founded 1998
- **Coed,** 160 undergraduate students

Majors Aesthetician/esthetician and skin care; massage therapy.
Academics *Degree:* associate.
Costs (2006–07) *Tuition:* $34,343 per degree program part-time.
Freshmen Application Contact Admissions Office, Florida College of Natural Health, 616 67th Street Circle East, Bradenton, FL 34208. *Phone:* 941-954-8999. *Toll-free phone:* 800-966-7117.

FLORIDA COLLEGE OF NATURAL HEALTH
Maitland, Florida www.fcnh.com/

- **Proprietary** 2-year, founded 1995
- **Coed,** 376 undergraduate students

Majors Aesthetician/esthetician and skin care; massage therapy.
Academics *Degree:* associate.
Costs (2006–07) *Tuition:* $34,343 per degree program part-time.
Freshmen Application Contact Admissions Office, Florida College of Natural Health, 2600 Lake Lucien Drive, Suite 140, Maitland, FL 32751. *Phone:* 407-261-0319. *Toll-free phone:* 800-393-7337.

FLORIDA COLLEGE OF NATURAL HEALTH
Miami, Florida www.fcnh.com/

- **Proprietary** 2-year, founded 1993
- **Coed,** 166 undergraduate students

Majors Aesthetician/esthetician and skin care; massage therapy.
Academics *Degree:* associate.
Costs (2006–07) *Tuition:* $34,343 per degree program part-time.
Director of Admissions Ms. Lissette Vidal, Admissions Coordinator, Florida College of Natural Health, 7925 Northwest 12th Street, Suite 201, Miami, FL 33126. *Phone:* 305-597-9599. *Toll-free phone:* 800-599-9599. *Fax:* 305-597-9110. *E-mail:* miami@fcnh.com.

FLORIDA COLLEGE OF NATURAL HEALTH
Pompano Beach, Florida www.fcnh.com/

- **Proprietary** 2-year, founded 1986
- **Coed,** 275 undergraduate students

Majors Aesthetician/esthetician and skin care; massage therapy.
Academics *Degree:* associate.
Costs (2006–07) *Tuition:* $34,343 per degree program part-time.
Freshmen Application Contact Admissions Office, Florida College of Natural Health, 2001 West Sample Road, Suite 100, Pompano Beach, FL 33064. *Phone:* 954-975-6400. *Toll-free phone:* 800-541-9299.

FLORIDA COMMUNITY COLLEGE AT JACKSONVILLE
Jacksonville, Florida www.fccj.edu/

- **State-supported** 2-year, founded 1963, part of Florida Community College System
- **Urban** 656-acre campus
- **Endowment** $3.9 million
- **Coed**

Florida Community College at Jacksonville (continued)

Undergraduates 7,462 full-time, 22,369 part-time. Students come from 19 states and territories, 108 other countries, 23% are from out of state, 28% African American, 4% Asian American or Pacific Islander, 6% Hispanic American, 0.3% Native American, 20% transferred in.

Faculty *Student/faculty ratio:* 21:1.

Academics *Calendar:* semesters. *Degree:* certificates, diplomas, and associate. *Special study options:* academic remediation for entering students, accelerated degree program, adult/continuing education programs, advanced placement credit, cooperative education, distance learning, double majors, English as a second language, honors programs, independent study, internships, off-campus study, part-time degree program, services for LD students, study abroad, summer session for credit. *ROTC:* Navy (c).

Student Life *Campus security:* 24-hour emergency response devices and patrols, student patrols, late-night transport/escort service.

Athletics Member NJCAA.

Applying *Options:* early admission, deferred entrance. *Application fee:* $15. *Required:* high school transcript.

Freshmen Application Contact Mr. Peter Biegel, District Director of Enrollment Services and Registrar, Florida Community College at Jacksonville, 501 West State Street, Jacksonville, FL 32202. *Phone:* 904-632-3131. *Fax:* 904-632-5105. *E-mail:* admissions@fccj.edu.

FLORIDA CULINARY INSTITUTE

West Palm Beach, Florida   www.floridaculinary.com/

Director of Admissions Mr. David Conway, Associate Director of Admissions, Florida Culinary Institute, 2400 Metrocentre Boulevard, West Palm Beach, FL 33407. *Phone:* 561-842-8324 Ext. 202. *Toll-free phone:* 800-826-9986. *E-mail:* info@floridaculinary.com.

FLORIDA HOSPITAL COLLEGE OF HEALTH SCIENCES

Orlando, Florida   www.fhchs.edu/

Freshmen Application Contact Ms. Katie Shaw, Director of Recruiting, Florida Hospital College of Health Sciences, 800 Lake Estelle Drive, Orlando, FL 32803. *Phone:* 407-303-1878. *Toll-free phone:* 800-500-7747. *Fax:* 407-303-5671. *E-mail:* katie.shaw@fhchs.edu.

FLORIDA KEYS COMMUNITY COLLEGE

Key West, Florida   www.fkcc.edu/

Director of Admissions Ms. Cheryl A. Malsheimer, Director of Admissions and Records, Florida Keys Community College, 5901 College Road, Key West, FL 33040. *Phone:* 305-296-9081 Ext. 201.

FLORIDA METROPOLITAN UNIVERSITY— ORANGE PARK CAMPUS

Orange Park, Florida   www.fmu.edu/

- **Proprietary** 2-year, founded 2003
- **Coed,** 457 undergraduate students
- 69% of applicants were admitted

Freshmen *Admission:* 236 applied, 162 admitted.

Majors Business administration and management; criminalistics and criminal science; criminal justice/law enforcement administration; management science; medical/clinical assistant.

Academics *Calendar:* quarters. *Degree:* associate.

Costs (2006–07) *Tuition:* $10,320 full-time.

Freshmen Application Contact Admissions Office, Florida Metropolitan University–Orange Park Campus, 805 Wells Road, Orange Park, FL 32073.

FLORIDA NATIONAL COLLEGE

Hialeah, Florida   www.fnc.edu/

- **Proprietary** 2-year, founded 1982
- **Urban** campus with easy access to Miami
- **Coed,** 1,884 undergraduate students, 82% full-time, 67% women, 33% men

Undergraduates 1,549 full-time, 335 part-time. Students come from 1 other state, 2% African American, 1% Asian American or Pacific Islander, 93% Hispanic American, 0.2% Native American, 2% international.

Freshmen *Admission:* 520 applied, 454 admitted, 443 enrolled.

Faculty *Total:* 69, 41% full-time, 25% with terminal degrees. *Student/faculty ratio:* 24:1.

Majors Accounting; administrative assistant and secretarial science; allied health and medical assisting services related; business administration and management; computer and information systems security; computer graphics; computer programming; computer programming related; computer programming (specific applications); computer science; computer systems networking and telecommunications; computer/technical support; data entry/microcomputer applications; data entry/microcomputer applications related; data processing and data processing technology; dental hygiene; diagnostic medical sonography and ultrasound technology; education; health services/allied health/health sciences; hospitality administration; legal administrative assistant/secretary; legal assistant/paralegal; legal professions and studies related; legal studies; liberal arts and sciences/liberal studies; medical administrative assistant and medical secretary; medical/clinical assistant; radiologic technology/science; system administration; technical and business writing; tourism and travel services management; tourism promotion; web page, digital/multimedia and information resources design; word processing.

Academics *Calendar:* semesters. *Degree:* certificates, diplomas, and associate. *Special study options:* academic remediation for entering students, adult/continuing education programs, cooperative education, distance learning, English as a second language, services for LD students, student-designed majors, summer session for credit.

Library Hialeah Campus Library with 28,754 titles, 123 serial subscriptions, 2,348 audiovisual materials, an OPAC, a Web page.

Student Life *Housing:* college housing not available. *Activities and Organizations:* student-run newspaper, Student Government Association. *Campus security:* 24-hour emergency response devices.

Costs (2007–08) *Tuition:* $10,800 full-time, $360 per credit part-time. *Required fees:* $645 full-time.

Financial Aid Of all full-time matriculated undergraduates, 20 Federal Work-Study jobs (averaging $8050).

Applying *Options:* deferred entrance. *Required:* high school transcript. *Application deadlines:* rolling (freshmen), rolling (transfers). *Notification:* continuous (freshmen).

Freshmen Application Contact Ms. Maria C. Reguerio, Vice President, Florida National College, 4425 West 20 Avenue, Hialeah, FL 33012. *Phone:* 305-821-3333. *Fax:* 305-362-0595. *E-mail:* admissions@fnc.edu.

THE FLORIDA SCHOOL OF MIDWIFERY

Gainseville, Florida   www.midwiferyschool.org/

Director of Admissions Ms. Gloria Huffman, Director of Finance, The Florida School of Midwifery, PO Box 5505, Gainseville, FL 32627-5505. *Phone:* 352-338-0766.

FLORIDA TECHNICAL COLLEGE

Auburndale, Florida   www.flatech.edu/

Director of Admissions Mr. Charles Owens, Admissions Office, Florida Technical College, 298 Havendale Boulevard, Auburndale, FL 33823. *Phone:* 863-967-8822.

FLORIDA TECHNICAL COLLEGE

DeLand, Florida   www.flatech.edu/

- **Proprietary** 2-year
- **Coed**

Undergraduates 260 full-time.

Faculty *Student/faculty ratio:* 22:1.

Academics *Calendar:* quarters. *Degree:* associate.

Applying *Application fee:* $25.

Freshmen Application Contact Mr. Bill Atkinson, Director, Florida Technical College, 1450 South Woodland Boulevard, 3rd Floor, DeLand, FL 32720. *Phone:* 386-734-3303. *Fax:* 386-734-5150.

FLORIDA TECHNICAL COLLEGE

Jacksonville, Florida www.flatech.edu/

Director of Admissions Mr. Bryan Gulebiam, Director of Admissions, Florida Technical College, 8711 Lone Star Road, Jacksonville, FL 32211. *Phone:* 407-678-5600.

FLORIDA TECHNICAL COLLEGE

Orlando, Florida www.flatech.edu/

Director of Admissions Ms. Jeanette E. Muschlitz, Director of Admissions, Florida Technical College, 1819 North Semoran Boulevard, Orlando, FL 32807-3546. *Phone:* 407-678-5600.

FULL SAIL REAL WORLD EDUCATION

Winter Park, Florida www.fullsail.com/

- **Proprietary** primarily 2-year, founded 1979
- **Suburban** campus with easy access to Orlando
- **Coed, primarily men**

Undergraduates 5,219 full-time. Students come from 47 states and territories, 6 other countries, 70% are from out of state, 11% African American, 3% Asian American or Pacific Islander, 10% Hispanic American, 0.7% Native American, 1% international.

Faculty *Student/faculty ratio:* 10:1.

Academics *Calendar:* modular. *Degrees:* associate and bachelor's. *Special study options:* academic remediation for entering students, cooperative education, internships, services for LD students, summer session for credit.

Student Life *Campus security:* 24-hour patrols.

Financial Aid Of all full-time matriculated undergraduates, 212 Federal Work-Study jobs (averaging $561).

Applying *Options:* electronic application. *Application fee:* $150. *Required:* high school transcript. *Required for some:* minimum "A" average in Algebra II.

Freshmen Application Contact Ms. Mary Beth Plank, Director of Admissions, Full Sail Real World Education, 3300 University Boulevard, Winter Park, FL 32792. *Phone:* 407-679-6333 Ext. 2122. *Toll-free phone:* 800-226-7625. *E-mail:* admissions@fullsail.com.

▶**See page 542 for the College Close-Up.**

GULF COAST COLLEGE

Tampa, Florida gulfcoastcollege.com/

- **Private** 2-year, founded 1978
- **Urban** 2-acre campus
- **Coed, primarily women,** 152 undergraduate students

Undergraduates Students come from 1 other state, 21% African American, 21% Hispanic American.

Faculty *Total:* 17, 6% with terminal degrees. *Student/faculty ratio:* 12:1.

Majors Computer science; computer systems analysis; information technology; medical/clinical assistant; nursing (licensed practical/vocational nurse training); system administration.

Academics *Calendar:* quarters. *Degree:* diplomas and associate. *Special study options:* accelerated degree program, advanced placement credit, internships.

Library Webster Tech Library with 2,063 titles, 14 serial subscriptions, 65 audiovisual materials.

Student Life *Housing:* college housing not available. *Campus security:* 24-hour emergency response devices, evening security guard. *Student services:* personal/psychological counseling.

Costs (2006–07) *Tuition:* $10,860 full-time.

Financial Aid Of all full-time matriculated undergraduates, 5 Federal Work-Study jobs.

Applying *Options:* electronic application. *Application fee:* $75. *Required:* interview.

Director of Admissions Mr. Todd A. Matthews Sr., Regional Vice President, Gulf Coast College, 3910 US Hwy 301 North, Suite 200, Tampa, FL 33619. *Phone:* 813-620-1446. *Toll-free phone:* 888-729-7247.

GULF COAST COMMUNITY COLLEGE

Panama City, Florida www.gulfcoast.edu/

Freshmen Application Contact Mrs. Jackie Kuczenski, Administrative Secretary of Admissions, Gulf Coast Community College, 5230 West Highway 98, Panama City, FL 32401. *Phone:* 850-769-1551 Ext. 4892. *Toll-free phone:* 800-311-3628. *Fax:* 850-913-3308.

HERZING COLLEGE

Winter Park, Florida www.herzing.edu/

Director of Admissions Ms. Karen Mohamad, Director of Admissions, Herzing College, 1595 South Semoran Boulevard, Suite 1501, Winter Park, FL 32792-5509. *Phone:* 407-478-0500. *Fax:* 407-380-0269.

HIGH-TECH INSTITUTE

Orlando, Florida www.high-techinstitute.com/

- **Proprietary** 2-year, founded 1998
- **Coed,** 1,066 undergraduate students

Majors Computer and information systems security; criminal justice/law enforcement administration; dental assisting; massage therapy; medical/clinical assistant; medical insurance/medical billing; medical radiologic technology; pharmacy technician; surgical technology; web page, digital/multimedia and information resources design.

Academics *Degree:* associate.

Costs (2006–07) *Tuition:* $23,256 per degree program part-time.

Applying *Application fee:* $50.

Freshmen Application Contact Admissions Office, High-Tech Institute, 3710 Maguire Boulevard, Orlando, FL 32803. *Toll-free phone:* 866-326-1985.

HILLSBOROUGH COMMUNITY COLLEGE

Tampa, Florida www.hccfl.edu/

- **State-supported** 2-year, founded 1968, part of Florida Community College System
- **Urban** campus
- **Endowment** $1.7 million
- **Coed,** 21,445 undergraduate students, 26% full-time, 60% women, 40% men

Undergraduates 5,469 full-time, 15,976 part-time. Students come from 38 states and territories, 101 other countries, 5% are from out of state, 19% African American, 4% Asian American or Pacific Islander, 21% Hispanic American, 0.4% Native American, 2% international, 18% transferred in. *Retention:* 60% of 2003 full-time freshmen returned.

Freshmen *Admission:* 10,212 applied, 10,212 admitted, 2,827 enrolled.

Faculty *Total:* 1,166, 24% full-time. *Student/faculty ratio:* 20:1.

Majors Accounting; administrative assistant and secretarial science; agricultural production; aquaculture; architectural engineering technology; art; biomedical technology; business administration and management; business operations support and secretarial services related; child development; commercial and advertising art; computer engineering technology; computer programming; computer systems networking and telecommunications; construction engineering technology; corrections; criminal justice/law enforcement administration; criminal justice/police science; culinary arts; culinary arts related; dance; dental hygiene; diagnostic medical sonography and ultrasound technology; digital communication and media/multimedia; dramatic/theater arts; education; electrical, electronic and communications engineering technology; elementary education; emergency medical technology (EMT paramedic); engineering; environmental studies; finance; fire science; hospitality administration; hotel/motel administration; human services; industrial radiologic technology; information

Hillsborough Community College (continued)

science/studies; interior design; intermedia/multimedia; legal administrative assistant/secretary; legal studies; liberal arts and sciences/liberal studies; marketing/marketing management; mass communication/media; medical administrative assistant and medical secretary; music; nuclear medical technology; nursing (registered nurse training); occupational therapy; office occupations and clerical services; ophthalmic laboratory technology; ornamental horticulture; pharmacy technician; physical education teaching and coaching; physical therapy; radio and television; radio and television broadcasting technology; radiologic technology/science; radio, television, and digital communication related; respiratory care therapy; restaurant, culinary, and catering management; sign language interpretation and translation.

Academics *Calendar:* semesters. *Degree:* certificates and associate. *Special study options:* academic remediation for entering students, adult/continuing education programs, advanced placement credit, cooperative education, distance learning, English as a second language, honors programs, off-campus study, part-time degree program, services for LD students, summer session for credit. *ROTC:* Army (c), Air Force (c).

Library Main Library plus 4 others with 170,615 titles, 1,283 serial subscriptions, 50,000 audiovisual materials, an OPAC, a Web page.

Student Life *Housing:* college housing not available. *Activities and Organizations:* drama/theater group, student-run newspaper, radio station, Student Government Association, Student Nursing Association, Phi Theta Kappa, Disabled Students Association, Radiography Club, national fraternities. *Campus security:* 24-hour emergency response devices and patrols. *Student services:* personal/psychological counseling.

Athletics Member NJCAA. *Intercollegiate sports:* baseball M(s), basketball M(s)/W(s), softball W(s), tennis W(s), volleyball W(s).

Costs (2006–07) *Tuition:* state resident $1587 full-time, $66 per credit hour part-time; nonresident $5785 full-time, $241 per credit hour part-time.

Applying *Options:* early admission. *Application fee:* $20. *Required:* high school transcript, high school diploma or equivalent. *Application deadlines:* rolling (freshmen), rolling (transfers).

Director of Admissions Ms. Kathy G. Cecil, Admissions, Registration, and Records Officer, Hillsborough Community College, PO Box 31127, Tampa, FL 33631-3127. *Phone:* 813-253-7027.

INDIAN RIVER COMMUNITY COLLEGE
Fort Pierce, Florida   www.ircc.edu/

Freshmen Application Contact Mr. Steven Payne, Dean of Educational Services, Indian River Community College, 3209 Virginia Avenue, Fort Pierce, FL 34981-5596. *Phone:* 772-462-7805. *E-mail:* spayne@ircc.edu.

ITT TECHNICAL INSTITUTE
Fort Lauderdale, Florida   www.itt-tech.edu/

- **Proprietary** primarily 2-year, founded 1991, part of ITT Educational Services, Inc
- **Suburban** campus with easy access to Miami
- **Coed**

Majors Animation, interactive technology, video graphics and special effects; business administration and management; CAD/CADD drafting/design technology; computer and information systems security; computer engineering technology; computer software technology; computer systems networking and telecommunications; construction management; criminal justice/law enforcement administration; electrical, electronic and communications engineering technology; medical laboratory technology; web/multimedia management and webmaster; web page, digital/multimedia and information resources design.

Academics *Calendar:* quarters. *Degrees:* associate and bachelor's.

Library a Web page.

Student Life *Housing:* college housing not available.

Standardized Tests *Required:* Wonderlic aptitude test (for admission).

Costs (2006–07) *Tuition:* Contact school for program costs.

Applying *Options:* deferred entrance. *Application fee:* $100. *Required:* high school transcript, interview. *Recommended:* letters of recommendation. *Application deadlines:* rolling (freshmen), rolling (transfers). *Notification:* continuous (freshmen), continuous (transfers).

Freshmen Application Contact Ms. Lori Glaser, Director of Recruitment, ITT Technical Institute, 3401 South University Drive, Fort Lauderdale, FL 33328. *Phone:* 954-476-9300. *Toll-free phone:* 800-488-7797.

ITT TECHNICAL INSTITUTE
Jacksonville, Florida   www.itt-tech.edu/

- **Proprietary** primarily 2-year, founded 1991, part of ITT Educational Services, Inc
- **Urban** 1-acre campus
- **Coed**

Majors Animation, interactive technology, video graphics and special effects; business administration and management; CAD/CADD drafting/design technology; computer and information systems security; computer engineering technology; computer software technology; computer systems networking and telecommunications; construction management; criminal justice/law enforcement administration; electrical, electronic and communications engineering technology; web/multimedia management and webmaster; web page, digital/multimedia and information resources design.

Academics *Calendar:* quarters. *Degrees:* associate and bachelor's.

Library a Web page.

Student Life *Housing:* college housing not available.

Standardized Tests *Required:* Wonderlic aptitude test (for admission).

Costs (2006–07) *Tuition:* Contact school for program costs.

Financial Aid Of all full-time matriculated undergraduates, 5 Federal Work-Study jobs.

Applying *Options:* deferred entrance. *Application fee:* $100. *Required:* high school transcript, interview. *Recommended:* letters of recommendation. *Application deadlines:* rolling (freshmen), rolling (transfers). *Notification:* continuous (freshmen), continuous (transfers).

Freshmen Application Contact Mr. Jorge Torres, Director of Recruitment, ITT Technical Institute, 6600-10 Youngerman Circle, Jacksonville, FL 32244. *Phone:* 904-573-9100. *Toll-free phone:* 800-318-1264.

ITT TECHNICAL INSTITUTE
Lake Mary, Florida   www.itt-tech.edu/

- **Proprietary** primarily 2-year, founded 1989, part of ITT Educational Services, Inc
- **Suburban** 1-acre campus with easy access to Orlando
- **Coed**

Majors Animation, interactive technology, video graphics and special effects; business administration and management; CAD/CADD drafting/design technology; communications technology; computer and information systems security; computer engineering technology; computer systems networking and telecommunications; construction management; criminal justice/law enforcement administration; electrical, electronic and communications engineering technology; health information/medical records technology; web/multimedia management and webmaster; web page, digital/multimedia and information resources design.

Academics *Calendar:* quarters. *Degrees:* associate and bachelor's.

Library a Web page.

Student Life *Housing:* college housing not available. *Activities and Organizations:* student-run newspaper.

Standardized Tests *Required:* Wonderlic aptitude test (for admission).

Costs (2006–07) *Tuition:* Contact school for program costs.

Applying *Options:* deferred entrance. *Application fee:* $100. *Required:* high school transcript, interview. *Recommended:* letters of recommendation. *Application deadlines:* rolling (freshmen), rolling (transfers). *Notification:* continuous (freshmen), continuous (transfers).

Freshmen Application Contact Gabe Garces, Director of Recruitment, ITT Technical Institute, 1400 International Pkwy South, Lake Mary, FL 32746. *Phone:* 407-660-2900. *Toll-free phone:* 866-489-8441. *Fax:* 407-660-2566.

ITT TECHNICAL INSTITUTE
Miami, Florida   www.itt-tech.edu/

- **Proprietary** primarily 2-year, founded 1996, part of ITT Educational Services, Inc
- **Coed**

Majors Accounting technology and bookkeeping; animation, interactive technology, video graphics and special effects; business administration and management; communications technology; computer and information systems security; computer engineering technology; computer systems networking and telecommunications; construction management; criminal justice/law enforcement administration; electrical, electronic and communications engineering technology;

medical laboratory technology; web/multimedia management and webmaster; web page, digital/multimedia and information resources design.

Academics *Calendar:* quarters. *Degrees:* associate and bachelor's.

Library a Web page.

Student Life *Housing:* college housing not available.

Standardized Tests *Required:* Wonderlic aptitude test (for admission).

Costs (2006–07) *Tuition:* Contact school for program costs.

Applying *Options:* deferred entrance. *Application fee:* $100. *Required:* high school transcript, interview. *Recommended:* letters of recommendation. *Application deadlines:* rolling (freshmen), rolling (transfers). *Notification:* continuous (freshmen), continuous (transfers).

Freshmen Application Contact Mr. Alan Arellano, Director of Recruitment, ITT Technical Institute, 7955 NW 12th Street, Suite 119, Miami, FL 33126. *Phone:* 305-477-3080.

ITT TECHNICAL INSTITUTE

Tampa, Florida www.itt-tech.edu/

- **Proprietary** primarily 2-year, founded 1981, part of ITT Educational Services, Inc
- **Suburban** campus with easy access to St. Petersburg
- **Coed**

Majors Animation, interactive technology, video graphics and special effects; business administration and management; CAD/CADD drafting/design technology; computer and information systems security; computer engineering technology; computer systems networking and telecommunications; construction management; criminal justice/law enforcement administration; electrical, electronic and communications engineering technology; health information/medical records technology; web/multimedia management and webmaster; web page, digital/multimedia and information resources design.

Academics *Calendar:* quarters. *Degrees:* associate and bachelor's.

Library a Web page.

Student Life *Housing:* college housing not available.

Standardized Tests *Required:* Wonderlic aptitude test (for admission).

Costs (2006–07) *Tuition:* Contact school for program costs.

Applying *Options:* deferred entrance. *Application fee:* $100. *Required:* high school transcript, interview. *Recommended:* letters of recommendation. *Application deadlines:* rolling (freshmen), rolling (transfers). *Notification:* continuous (freshmen), continuous (transfers).

Freshmen Application Contact Mr. Joseph E. Rostkowski, Director of Recruitment, ITT Technical Institute, 4809 Memorial Highway, Tampa, FL 33634. *Phone:* 813-885-2244. *Toll-free phone:* 800-825-2831.

KEISER CAREER COLLEGE - GREENACRES

Greenacres, Florida www.keisercareer.edu/kcc2005/ga_campus.htm

- **Proprietary** 2-year
- **Coed,** 433 undergraduate students
- 98% of applicants were admitted

Freshmen *Admission:* 536 applied, 526 admitted.

Majors Aesthetician/esthetician and skin care; business, management, and marketing related; computer and information sciences and support services related; computer systems networking and telecommunications; emergency medical technology (EMT paramedic); health professions related; massage therapy; medical/clinical assistant; medical insurance coding; medical insurance/medical billing; nursing (licensed practical/vocational nurse training); parks, recreation and leisure facilities management; pharmacy technician; salon/beauty salon management; surgical technology.

Academics *Degree:* certificates and associate.

Costs (2006–07) *Tuition:* $12,440 full-time.

Applying *Application fee:* $55. *Required:* high school transcript.

Freshmen Application Contact Admissions Office, Keiser Career College - Greenacres, 6812 Forest Hill Boulevard, Suite D-1, Greenacres, FL 33413.

KEISER UNIVERSITY

Daytona Beach, Florida www.keisercollege.edu/

Director of Admissions Ms. Heather Armstrong, Director of Admissions, Keiser University, 1800 West International Speedway, Building 3, Daytona Beach, FL 32114. *Phone:* 386-274-5060. *Toll-free phone:* 800-749-4456. *Fax:* 386-274-2725.

KEISER UNIVERSITY

Jacksonville, Florida www.keiseruniversity.edu

Admissions Office Contact Keiser University, 6700 Southpoint Parkway, Suite 400, Jacksonville, FL 32216.

KEISER UNIVERSITY

Lakeland, Florida www.keisercollege.edu/

Freshmen Application Contact Admissions Office, Keiser University, 2400 Interstate Drive, Lakeland, FL 33805. *Phone:* 863-701-7789.

KEISER UNIVERSITY

Melbourne, Florida www.keisercollege.edu/

Director of Admissions Ms. Susan Zeigelhofer, Director of Admissions, Keiser University, 900 South Babcock Street, Melbourne, FL 32901-1461. *Phone:* 954-776-4456. *Toll-free phone:* 800-749-4456. *Fax:* 954-771-4894.

KEISER UNIVERSITY

Miami, Florida www.keisercollege.edu/

- **Proprietary** primarily 2-year
- **Suburban** campus
- **Coed,** 812 undergraduate students, 100% full-time, 64% women, 36% men

Undergraduates 812 full-time. Students come from 3 states and territories, 2 other countries, 10% African American, 2% Asian American or Pacific Islander, 79% Hispanic American, 0.2% international. *Retention:* 100% of 2003 full-time freshmen returned.

Freshmen *Admission:* 650 enrolled.

Faculty *Total:* 49, 88% full-time, 27% with terminal degrees. *Student/faculty ratio:* 18:1.

Majors Accounting; business administration and management; computer and information sciences; health and medical administrative services related; health science; health services/allied health/health sciences; legal assistant/paralegal; medical office assistant; nuclear medical technology; nursing (registered nurse training); occupational therapist assistant; radiologic technology/science.

Academics *Calendar:* 3 semesters per year. *Degrees:* associate and bachelor's. *Special study options:* academic remediation for entering students, accelerated degree program, adult/continuing education programs, distance learning, part-time degree program.

Library an OPAC.

Student Life *Housing:* college housing not available. *Activities and Organizations:* Student Ambassador Program. *Campus security:* 24-hour patrols.

Standardized Tests *Recommended:* SAT or ACT (for admission).

Costs (2007–08) *Tuition:* $11,640 full-time, $1455 per course part-time. *Required fees:* $400 full-time, $100 per course part-time.

Applying *Application fee:* $55. *Required:* high school transcript, interview. *Required for some:* essay or personal statement, letters of recommendation, interview.

Freshmen Application Contact Mr. Ted Weiner, Director of Admissions, Keiser University, 8505 Mills Drive, Miami, FL 33183. *Phone:* 305-596-2226. *Fax:* 305-596-7077. *E-mail:* tedw@keisercollege.edu.

KEISER UNIVERSITY

Orlando, Florida   www.keisercollege.edu/

Freshmen Application Contact Admissions Office, Keiser University, 5600 Lake Underhill Road, Orlando, FL 32807.

KEISER UNIVERSITY

Pembroke Pines, Florida   www.keisercollege.edu/

Admissions Office Contact Keiser University, 12520 Pines Boulevard, Pembroke Pines, FL 33027. *Toll-free phone:* 954-431-4300.

KEISER UNIVERSITY

Port St. Lucie, Florida   www.keisercollege.edu/

Admissions Office Contact Keiser University, 9468 South US 1, Port St. Lucie, FL 34952. *Toll-free phone:* 772-398-9990.

KEISER UNIVERSITY

Sarasota, Florida   www.keisercollege.edu/

Director of Admissions Brandon Barnhill, Director of Admissions, Keiser University, 6151 Lake Osprey Drive, Sarasota, FL 34240. *Phone:* 941-907-3900. *Toll-free phone:* 866-KEISER2. *Fax:* 941-907-2016.

KEISER UNIVERSITY

Tallahassee, Florida   www.keisercollege.edu/

Director of Admissions Phil Hooks, Director of Admissions, Keiser University, 1700 Halstead Boulevard, Tallahassee, FL 32308. *Phone:* 850-906-9494. *Toll-free phone:* 800-749-4456. *Fax:* 850-906-9497.

KEISER UNIVERSITY

Tampa, Florida   www.keiseruniversity.edu/tampa.htm

Admissions Office Contact Keiser University, 5225 Memorial Highway, Tampa, FL 33634.

KEISER UNIVERSITY

West Palm Beach, Florida   www.keisercollege.edu/

Admissions Office Contact Keiser University, 2085 Vista Parkway, West Palm Beach, FL 33411. *Toll-free phone:* 561-471-6000.

KEY COLLEGE

Fort Lauderdale, Florida   www.keycollege.edu/

Director of Admissions Mr. Ronald H. Dooley, President and Director of Admissions, Key College, 5225 West Broward Boulevard, Ft. Lauderdale, FL 33317. *Phone:* 954-581-2223 Ext. 23. *Toll-free phone:* 800-581-8292.

LAKE CITY COMMUNITY COLLEGE

Lake City, Florida   www.lakecity.cc.fl.us/

- **State-supported** 2-year, founded 1962, part of Florida Community College System
- **Small-town** 132-acre campus with easy access to Jacksonville
- **Endowment** $3.3 million
- **Coed**

Undergraduates 1,084 full-time, 1,652 part-time. Students come from 18 states and territories, 7 other countries, 11% African American, 2% Asian American or Pacific Islander, 2% Hispanic American, 0.2% Native American, 0.5% international, 2% live on campus.

Faculty *Student/faculty ratio:* 18:1.

Academics *Calendar:* semesters. *Degree:* certificates, diplomas, and associate. *Special study options:* academic remediation for entering students, adult/continuing education programs, advanced placement credit, cooperative education, distance learning, English as a second language, independent study, internships, part-time degree program, services for LD students, study abroad, summer session for credit.

Student Life *Campus security:* 24-hour patrols.

Athletics Member NJCAA.

Costs (2006–07) *Tuition:* state resident $2037 full-time; nonresident $7290 full-time. *Room and board:* $4535.

Financial Aid Of all full-time matriculated undergraduates, 58 Federal Work-Study jobs (averaging $975).

Applying *Options:* early admission, deferred entrance. *Application fee:* $15. *Required for some:* high school transcript.

Freshmen Application Contact Vince Rice, Director of Postsecondary Transition, Lake City Community College, Route 19, Box 1030, Lake City, FL 32025-8703. *Phone:* 386-754-4288. *Fax:* 386-755-1521. *E-mail:* admissions@mail.lakecity.cc.fl.us.

LAKE-SUMTER COMMUNITY COLLEGE

Leesburg, Florida   www.lscc.edu/

- **State and locally supported** 2-year, founded 1962, part of Florida Department of Education
- **Suburban** 110-acre campus with easy access to Orlando
- **Endowment** $3.5 million
- **Coed,** 3,641 undergraduate students, 35% full-time, 66% women, 34% men

Undergraduates 1,282 full-time, 2,359 part-time. Students come from 4 states and territories, 1% are from out of state, 10% African American, 2% Asian American or Pacific Islander, 9% Hispanic American, 0.5% Native American, 0.9% international, 35% transferred in.

Freshmen *Admission:* 971 applied, 971 admitted, 540 enrolled.

Faculty *Total:* 183, 33% full-time, 18% with terminal degrees. *Student/faculty ratio:* 20:1.

Majors Business administration and management; commercial and advertising art; computer and information sciences related; computer science; criminal justice/law enforcement administration; emergency medical technology (EMT paramedic); fire science; health information/medical records administration; legal assistant/paralegal; liberal arts and sciences/liberal studies; nursing (registered nurse training); office management; sport and fitness administration/management; theater design and technology.

Academics *Calendar:* semesters. *Degree:* certificates, diplomas, and associate. *Special study options:* academic remediation for entering students, adult/continuing education programs, advanced placement credit, cooperative education, distance learning, double majors, independent study, off-campus study, part-time degree program, services for LD students, summer session for credit.

Library Lake-Sumter Community College Library with 74,858 titles, 284 serial subscriptions, 980 audiovisual materials, an OPAC, a Web page.

Student Life *Housing:* college housing not available. *Activities and Organizations:* drama/theater group, student-run newspaper, television station, choral group, Phi Theta Kappa, Baptist Collegiate Ministry, Environmental Society, Nursing Students' Association. *Campus security:* 24-hour emergency response devices. *Student services:* women's center.

Athletics Member NJCAA. *Intercollegiate sports:* baseball M(s), softball W(s), volleyball W(s). *Intramural sports:* basketball M/W, softball W, volleyball W.

Costs (2006–07) *Tuition:* state resident $2008 full-time, $67 per credit hour part-time; nonresident $7552 full-time, $252 per credit hour part-time. Full-time tuition and fees vary according to course load. Part-time tuition and fees vary according to course load. *Required fees:* $30 full-time, $1 per credit hour part-time. *Waivers:* employees or children of employees.

Applying *Application fee:* $25. *Required:* high school transcript. *Application deadlines:* rolling (freshmen), rolling (transfers). *Notification:* continuous (freshmen), continuous (transfers).

Freshmen Application Contact Ms. Bonnie Yanick, Enrollment Specialist, Lake-Sumter Community College, 9501 US Highway 441, Leesburg, FL 34788-8751. *Phone:* 352-365-3561. *Fax:* 352-365-3553. *E-mail:* admissinquiry@lscc.edu.

MANATEE COMMUNITY COLLEGE

Bradenton, Florida
www.mccfl.edu/

- **State-supported** 2-year, founded 1957, part of Florida Community College System
- **Suburban** 100-acre campus with easy access to Tampa–St. Petersburg
- **Endowment** $38.2 million
- **Coed,** 9,080 undergraduate students, 45% full-time, 63% women, 37% men

Undergraduates 4,116 full-time, 4,964 part-time. Students come from 22 states and territories, 40 other countries, 3% are from out of state, 11% African American, 2% Asian American or Pacific Islander, 8% Hispanic American, 0.2% Native American, 2% international, 7% transferred in. *Retention:* 67% of 2003 full-time freshmen returned.

Freshmen *Admission:* 1,867 applied, 1,867 admitted, 1,683 enrolled. *Test scores:* SAT verbal scores over 500: 36%; SAT math scores over 500: 36%; ACT scores over 18: 57%; SAT verbal scores over 600: 8%; SAT math scores over 600: 8%; ACT scores over 24: 18%; SAT verbal scores over 700: 1%; SAT math scores over 700: 1%; ACT scores over 30: 3%.

Faculty *Total:* 463, 27% full-time, 11% with terminal degrees. *Student/faculty ratio:* 23:1.

Majors Accounting; administrative assistant and secretarial science; advertising; African-American/Black studies; American government and politics; American studies; art; art history, criticism and conservation; Asian studies; astronomy; biology/biological sciences; biology teacher education; business administration and management; business/commerce; business/managerial economics; chemistry; chemistry teacher education; child guidance; civil engineering technology; commercial and advertising art; community health services counseling; computer and information sciences; computer and information sciences related; computer engineering technology; computer graphics; computer programming; computer programming related; construction engineering technology; criminal justice/safety; dietetics; drafting and design technology; dramatic/theater arts; economics; electrical, electronic and communications engineering technology; engineering; English; English/language arts teacher education; European studies (Central and Eastern); family and consumer sciences/home economics teacher education; finance; fine/studio arts; fire science; foreign language teacher education; French; German; health/health care administration; health teacher education; history; hospital and health care facilities administration; humanities; information science/studies; jazz/jazz studies; Jewish/Judaic studies; journalism; kindergarten/preschool education; Latin American studies; legal assistant/paralegal; liberal arts and sciences/liberal studies; mass communication/media; mathematics teacher education; medical radiologic technology; music; music performance; music teacher education; music theory and composition; nursing (registered nurse training); occupational therapist assistant; occupational therapy; philosophy; physical education teaching and coaching; physical therapist assistant; physical therapy; physician assistant; physics; physics teacher education; pre-pharmacy studies; psychology; public administration; radio and television; radio and television broadcasting technology; radiologic technology/science; religious studies; respiratory care therapy; Russian studies; science teacher education; social psychology; social sciences; social studies teacher education; social work; Spanish; speech and rhetoric; statistics; technology/industrial arts teacher education; trade and industrial teacher education; vocational rehabilitation counseling; women's studies.

Academics *Calendar:* semesters. *Degree:* certificates and associate. *Special study options:* academic remediation for entering students, advanced placement credit, cooperative education, distance learning, English as a second language, honors programs, independent study, part-time degree program, services for LD students, summer session for credit.

Library Sara Harlee Library plus 1 other with 65,386 titles, 378 serial subscriptions, an OPAC, a Web page.

Student Life *Housing:* college housing not available. *Activities and Organizations:* drama/theater group, student-run newspaper, choral group, Student Government Association, Phi Theta Kappa, American Chemical Society Student Affiliate, Campus Ministry, Medical Community Club. *Campus security:* 24-hour emergency response devices and patrols, late-night transport/escort service.

Athletics Member NJCAA. *Intercollegiate sports:* baseball M(s), basketball M(s), softball W(s), volleyball W(s). *Intramural sports:* basketball M/W, softball M/W, volleyball M/W, weight lifting M/W.

Costs (2007–08) *Tuition:* state resident $2195 full-time, $73 per credit part-time; nonresident $9052 full-time, $302 per credit part-time.

Financial Aid Of all full-time matriculated undergraduates, 82 Federal Work-Study jobs (averaging $2800). *Financial aid deadline:* 8/15.

Applying *Options:* early admission. *Application fee:* $40. *Required:* high school transcript. *Application deadlines:* 8/20 (freshmen), 8/20 (transfers). *Notification:* continuous (freshmen), continuous (transfers).

Freshmen Application Contact Ms. MariLynn Lewy, Registrar, Manatee Community College, PO Box 1849, Bradenton, FL 34206. *Phone:* 941-752-5384. *Fax:* 941-727-6380. *E-mail:* lewym@mccfl.edu.

MEDVANCE INSTITUTE

Atlantis, Florida
www.medvance.org/

Director of Admissions Ms. Brenda Cortez, Campus Director, MedVance Institute, 170 JFK Drive, Atlantis, FL 33462. *Phone:* 561-304-3466. *Toll-free phone:* 888-86-GO-MED. *Fax:* 561-304-3471. *E-mail:* bcortez@medvance.org.

MIAMI DADE COLLEGE

Miami, Florida
www.mdc.edu/

- **State and locally supported** primarily 2-year, founded 1960, part of Florida Community College System
- **Urban** campus
- **Endowment** $110.0 million
- **Coed,** 51,329 undergraduate students, 36% full-time, 61% women, 39% men

Miami Dade College offers undergraduate study in more than 200 academic areas and professions. The College is internationally recognized as an educational leader in undergraduate programs that are innovative and diverse within a multicultural, multiethnic environment. Annually, more than 165,000 credit- and noncredit-seeking students are enrolled at eight major campuses and numerous outreach centers.

Undergraduates 18,291 full-time, 33,038 part-time. Students come from 41 states and territories, 156 other countries, 9% are from out of state, 20% African American, 1% Asian American or Pacific Islander, 65% Hispanic American, 3% international, 2% transferred in.

Freshmen *Admission:* 20,445 applied, 20,445 admitted, 10,067 enrolled.

Faculty *Total:* 2,052, 35% full-time, 15% with terminal degrees. *Student/faculty ratio:* 26:1.

Majors Accounting technology and bookkeeping; administrative assistant and secretarial science; aeronautics/aviation/aerospace science and technology; agriculture; airline pilot and flight crew; air traffic control; American studies; anthropology; architectural drafting and CAD/CADD; architectural engineering technology; art; Asian studies; audiology and speech-language pathology; aviation/airway management; behavioral sciences; biology/biological sciences; biology teacher education; biomedical technology; business administration and management; chemistry; chemistry teacher education; child development; cinematography and film/video production; civil engineering technology; clinical/medical laboratory technology; commercial and advertising art; computer engineering technology; computer graphics; computer programming; computer science; computer software technology; computer technology/computer systems technology; construction engineering technology; court reporting; criminal justice/law enforcement administration; criminal justice/police science; dance; data processing and data processing technology; dental hygiene; diagnostic medical sonography and ultrasound technology; dietetics; dietetic technician; drafting and design technology; dramatic/theater arts; economics; education; education (specific subject areas) related; electrical and electronic engineering technologies related; electrical, electronic and communications engineering technology; elementary education; emergency medical technology (EMT paramedic); engineering; engineering related; engineering technology; English; environmental engineering technology; finance; fire science; food science; forestry; French; funeral service and mortuary science; general studies; geology/earth science; German; health information/medical records administration; health/medical preparatory programs related; health professions related; heating, air conditioning and refrigeration technology; heating, air conditioning, ventilation and refrigeration maintenance technology; histologic technician; history; horticultural science; hospitality administration; humanities; human services; industrial technology; information science/studies; interior design; international relations and affairs; Italian; journalism; kindergarten/preschool education; landscaping and groundskeeping; Latin American studies; legal administrative assistant/secretary; legal assistant/paralegal; literature; management information systems; marketing/marketing management; mass communication/media; mathematics; mathematics teacher education; medical/clinical assistant; middle school education; music; music

Miami Dade College (continued)

performance; music teacher education; natural sciences; non-profit management; nuclear medical technology; nursing (registered nurse training); ophthalmic technology; ornamental horticulture; parks, recreation and leisure; philosophy; photographic and film/video technology; photography; physical education teaching and coaching; physical sciences; physical therapist assistant; physics; physics teacher education; plant nursery management; political science and government; Portuguese; pre-engineering; psychology; public administration; radio and television; radio and television broadcasting technology; radiologic technology/science; recording arts technology; respiratory care therapy; respiratory therapy technician; science teacher education; sign language interpretation and translation; social sciences; social work; sociology; Spanish; special education; substance abuse/addiction counseling; teacher assistant/aide; telecommunications technology; tourism and travel services management.

Academics *Calendar:* 16-16-6-6. *Degrees:* certificates, associate, and bachelor's. *Special study options:* academic remediation for entering students, adult/continuing education programs, advanced placement credit, cooperative education, distance learning, English as a second language, freshman honors college, honors programs, independent study, internships, part-time degree program, services for LD students, study abroad, summer session for credit. *ROTC:* Army (c), Air Force (c).

Library Main Library plus 8 others with 342,933 titles, 4,201 serial subscriptions, 25,427 audiovisual materials, an OPAC, a Web page.

Student Life *Housing:* college housing not available. *Activities and Organizations:* drama/theater group, student-run newspaper, radio station, choral group, Welcome Back, Hispanic Heritage Month, Black History Month, Paella Festival. *Campus security:* 24-hour patrols. *Student services:* personal/psychological counseling.

Athletics Member NJCAA. *Intercollegiate sports:* baseball M(s), basketball M(s)/W(s), softball W(s), volleyball W(s). *Intramural sports:* basketball M/W, racquetball M/W, soccer M/W, softball M/W, swimming and diving M/W, tennis M/W, track and field M/W, volleyball M/W, weight lifting M/W.

Costs (2006–07) *Tuition:* state resident $1668 full-time, $56 per credit part-time; nonresident $6177 full-time, $206 per credit part-time. Full-time tuition and fees vary according to degree level. Part-time tuition and fees vary according to degree level. *Required fees:* $302 full-time, $13 per credit part-time. *Waivers:* employees or children of employees.

Financial Aid Of all full-time matriculated undergraduates, 800 Federal Work-Study jobs (averaging $5000). 125 state and other part-time jobs (averaging $5000).

Applying *Options:* electronic application, early admission. *Application fee:* $20. *Required:* high school transcript. *Application deadline:* rolling (freshmen). *Notification:* continuous (freshmen), continuous (transfers).

Freshmen Application Contact Mr. Steven Kelly, College Registrar, Miami Dade College, 11011 SW 104th Street, Miami, FL 33176. *Phone:* 305-237-0633. *Fax:* 305-237-2964. *E-mail:* skelly@mdc.edu.

▶See page 566 for the College Close-Up.

NATIONAL SCHOOL OF TECHNOLOGY, INC.
Fort Lauderdale, Florida
www.nst.cc/

Director of Admissions Ashly Miller, Director of Admissions, National School of Technology, Inc., 1040 Bayview Drive, Fort Lauderdale, FL 33304. *Phone:* 954-630-0066. *Fax:* 954-630-0076. *E-mail:* amiller@cci.edu.

NATIONAL SCHOOL OF TECHNOLOGY, INC.
Hialeah, Florida
www.nst.cc/

- **Proprietary** 2-year, founded 1977
- **Coed,** 801 undergraduate students
- 67% of applicants were admitted

Freshmen *Admission:* 300 applied, 201 admitted.

Majors Criminal justice/law enforcement administration.

Academics *Calendar:* continuous. *Degree:* associate.

Costs (2006–07) *Tuition:* $18,377 per degree program part-time.

Director of Admissions Mr. Daniel Alonso, Director of Admissions, National School of Technology, Inc., 4410 West 16th Avenue, Suite 52, Hialeah, FL 33012. *Phone:* 305-558-9500. *Toll-free phone:* 888-741-4270. *Fax:* 305-558-4419. *E-mail:* dalonso@cci.edu.

NATIONAL SCHOOL OF TECHNOLOGY, INC.
Miami, Florida
www.nst.cc/

Director of Admissions Ms. Amber Stenbeck, Director of Admissions, National School of Technology, Inc., 111 Northwest 183rd Street, 2nd Floor, Miami, FL 33169. *Phone:* 305-386-9900.

NATIONAL SCHOOL OF TECHNOLOGY, INC.
North Miami Beach, Florida
www.nst.cc/

Director of Admissions Mr. Walter McQuade, Director of Admissions, National School of Technology, Inc., 16150 Northeast 17th Avenue, North Miami Beach, FL 33162-4744. *Phone:* 305-949-9500.

NEW ENGLAND INSTITUTE OF TECHNOLOGY AT PALM BEACH
West Palm Beach, Florida
newenglandtech.com/

Director of Admissions Mr. Kevin Cassidy, Director of Admissions, New England Institute of Technology at Palm Beach, 1126 53rd Court, West Palm Beach, FL 33407-2384. *Phone:* 561-842-8324 Ext. 117. *Toll-free phone:* 800-826-9986. *Fax:* 561-842-9503.

NORTH FLORIDA COMMUNITY COLLEGE
Madison, Florida
www.nfcc.edu/

Freshmen Application Contact Mr. Bobby Scott, North Florida Community College, 1000 Turner Davis Drive, Madison, FL 32340-1602. *Phone:* 850-973-9450. *Fax:* 850-973-1697.

OKALOOSA-WALTON COLLEGE
Niceville, Florida
www.owc.edu/

- **State and locally supported** primarily 2-year, founded 1963, part of Florida Community College System
- **Small-town** 264-acre campus
- **Endowment** $21.0 million
- **Coed**

Undergraduates Students come from 18 states and territories, 10% African American.

Faculty *Student/faculty ratio:* 20:1.

Academics *Calendar:* semesters plus summer sessions. *Degrees:* certificates, associate, and bachelor's. *Special study options:* academic remediation for entering students, adult/continuing education programs, advanced placement credit, distance learning, English as a second language, independent study, part-time degree program, services for LD students, summer session for credit. *ROTC:* Army (c).

Student Life *Campus security:* 24-hour patrols.

Athletics Member NJCAA.

Standardized Tests *Required:* ACT, SAT I, ACT ASSET, MAPS, or Florida College Entry Placement Test (for admission).

Costs (2006–07) *Tuition:* state resident $1774 full-time, $59 per credit part-time; nonresident $6730 full-time, $224 per credit part-time. Full-time tuition and fees vary according to degree level and student level. Part-time tuition and fees vary according to degree level and student level. *Payment plans:* installment, deferred payment.

Financial Aid Of all full-time matriculated undergraduates, 81 Federal Work-Study jobs (averaging $1500). 11 state and other part-time jobs (averaging $1460).

Applying *Options:* early admission, deferred entrance. *Required:* high school transcript.

Freshmen Application Contact Ms. Christine Bishop, Registrar/Division Director Enrollment Services, Okaloosa-Walton College, 100 College Boulevard, Niceville, FL 32578. *Phone:* 850-729-5373. *Fax:* 850-729-5323. *E-mail:* registrar@owc.edu.

ORLANDO CULINARY ACADEMY

Orlando, Florida   www.orlandoculinary.com/

- **Proprietary** 2-year, founded 2002
- **Coed,** 951 undergraduate students

Majors Baking and pastry arts; cooking and related culinary arts; hospitality administration related; hotel and restaurant management.

Academics *Degree:* associate.

Costs (2006–07) *Tuition:* $39,500 per degree program part-time.

Applying *Application fee:* $50.

Admissions Office Contact Orlando Culinary Academy, 8511 Commodity Circle, Suite 100, Orlando, FL 32819. *Toll-free phone:* 888-793-3222.

PALM BEACH COMMUNITY COLLEGE

Lake Worth, Florida   www.pbcc.edu/

- **State-supported** 2-year, founded 1933, part of Florida Community College System
- **Urban** 150-acre campus with easy access to West Palm Beach
- **Endowment** $14.4 million
- **Coed,** 21,938 undergraduate students, 32% full-time, 62% women, 38% men

Undergraduates 6,923 full-time, 15,015 part-time. Students come from 49 states and territories, 138 other countries, 5% are from out of state, 22% African American, 3% Asian American or Pacific Islander, 17% Hispanic American, 0.3% Native American, 3% international, 10% transferred in.

Freshmen *Admission:* 21,938 applied, 21,938 admitted, 2,519 enrolled.

Faculty *Total:* 1,272, 23% full-time, 14% with terminal degrees. *Student/faculty ratio:* 22:1.

Majors Accounting; administrative assistant and secretarial science; airline pilot and flight crew; art; art history, criticism and conservation; biology/biological sciences; botany/plant biology; business administration and management; ceramic arts and ceramics; chemistry; clothing/textiles; commercial and advertising art; computer programming; computer programming (specific applications); computer science; computer/technical support; construction management; criminal justice/law enforcement administration; criminal justice/police science; data processing and data processing technology; dental hygiene; drafting and design technology; dramatic/theater arts; economics; education; electrical, electronic and communications engineering technology; elementary education; English; family and consumer sciences/human sciences; fashion/apparel design; fashion merchandising; finance; fire science; foods, nutrition, and wellness; health teacher education; history; hotel/motel administration; industrial radiologic technology; interior design; journalism; kindergarten/preschool education; legal administrative assistant/secretary; liberal arts and sciences/liberal studies; literature; marketing/marketing management; mass communication/media; mathematics; music; nursing (registered nurse training); occupational therapy; philosophy; photography; physical education teaching and coaching; physical sciences; physical therapy; political science and government; pre-engineering; psychology; religious studies; social sciences; social work; special products marketing; survey technology; system administration; web page, digital/multimedia and information resources design; word processing; zoology/animal biology.

Academics *Calendar:* semesters. *Degree:* certificates and associate. *Special study options:* academic remediation for entering students, adult/continuing education programs, advanced placement credit, cooperative education, distance learning, double majors, English as a second language, freshman honors college, honors programs, independent study, internships, off-campus study, part-time degree program, services for LD students, student-designed majors, study abroad, summer session for credit.

Library Harold C. Manor Library plus 3 others with 151,000 titles, 1,474 serial subscriptions, an OPAC, a Web page.

Student Life *Housing:* college housing not available. *Activities and Organizations:* drama/theater group, student-run newspaper, choral group, student government, Phi Theta Kappa, Students for International Understanding, Black Student Union, Drama Club, national fraternities. *Campus security:* 24-hour emergency response devices and patrols. *Student services:* health clinic, women's center.

Athletics Member NJCAA. *Intercollegiate sports:* baseball M(s), basketball M(s)/W(s), softball W(s), volleyball M(s)/W(s). *Intramural sports:* basketball M/W, bowling M/W, football M/W, racquetball M/W, soccer M, tennis M/W, volleyball M/W.

Costs (2006–07) *Tuition:* state resident $1596 full-time, $67 per credit hour part-time; nonresident $5688 full-time, $237 per credit hour part-time. Full-time tuition and fees vary according to course load. Part-time tuition and fees vary according to course load. *Required fees:* $20 full-time, $10 per term part-time. *Waivers:* employees or children of employees.

Applying *Options:* electronic application, early admission, deferred entrance. *Application fee:* $20. *Application deadlines:* 8/20 (freshmen), 8/20 (transfers). *Notification:* continuous until 8/20 (freshmen), continuous until 8/20 (transfers).

Freshmen Application Contact Ms. Anne Guiler, Coordinator of Distance Learning, Palm Beach Community College, 4200 Congress Avenue, Lake Worth, FL 33461. *Phone:* 561-868-3032. *Fax:* 561-868-3584. *E-mail:* enrollmt@pbcc.edu.

PASCO-HERNANDO COMMUNITY COLLEGE

New Port Richey, Florida   www.phcc.edu/

- **State-supported** 2-year, founded 1972, part of Florida Community College System
- **Small-town** 142-acre campus with easy access to Tampa
- **Endowment** $20.3 million
- **Coed,** 7,547 undergraduate students, 37% full-time, 65% women, 35% men

Undergraduates 2,794 full-time, 4,753 part-time. Students come from 10 states and territories, 9 other countries, 1% are from out of state, 5% African American, 2% Asian American or Pacific Islander, 9% Hispanic American, 0.5% Native American, 0.5% international, 6% transferred in.

Freshmen *Admission:* 3,027 admitted, 1,134 enrolled.

Faculty *Total:* 350, 30% full-time, 13% with terminal degrees. *Student/faculty ratio:* 28:1.

Majors Business administration and management; computer programming related; computer programming (specific applications); computer systems networking and telecommunications; computer technology/computer systems technology; criminal justice/law enforcement administration; dental hygiene; drafting and design technology; e-commerce; emergency medical technology (EMT paramedic); human services; information technology; legal assistant/paralegal; liberal arts and sciences/liberal studies; marketing/marketing management; nursing (registered nurse training); physical therapist assistant; radiologic technology/science; web page, digital/multimedia and information resources design.

Academics *Calendar:* semesters. *Degree:* certificates, diplomas, and associate. *Special study options:* academic remediation for entering students, accelerated degree program, adult/continuing education programs, advanced placement credit, cooperative education, distance learning, double majors, honors programs, independent study, internships, off-campus study, part-time degree program, services for LD students, summer session for credit. *ROTC:* Army (c).

Library Pottberg Library plus 2 others with 69,903 titles, 231 serial subscriptions, an OPAC, a Web page.

Student Life *Housing:* college housing not available. *Activities and Organizations:* drama/theater group, choral group, Student Government Association, Phi Theta Kappa, Phi Beta Lambda, Human Services, PHCC Cares. *Campus security:* 24-hour patrols.

Athletics Member NJCAA. *Intercollegiate sports:* baseball M(s), basketball M(s), softball W(s), tennis W(s), volleyball W(s).

Standardized Tests *Recommended:* SAT and SAT Subject Tests or ACT (for admission), CPT.

Costs (2006–07) *Tuition:* state resident $1967 full-time, $66 per credit part-time; nonresident $7368 full-time, $242 per credit part-time. *Required fees:* $20 full-time. *Payment plan:* installment.

Financial Aid Of all full-time matriculated undergraduates, 45 Federal Work-Study jobs (averaging $2133).

Applying *Options:* electronic application. *Application fee:* $20. *Required:* high school transcript. *Application deadlines:* rolling (freshmen), rolling (transfers). *Notification:* continuous (freshmen), continuous (transfers).

Freshmen Application Contact Ms. Debra Bullard, Director of Admissions and Student Records, Pasco-Hernando Community College, 10230 Ridge Road, New Port Richey, FL 34654-5199. *Phone:* 727-816-3261. *Fax:* 727-816-3389. *E-mail:* bullard@phcc.edu.

PENSACOLA JUNIOR COLLEGE

Pensacola, Florida www.pjc.edu/

Freshmen Application Contact Ms. Martha Caughey, Registrar, Pensacola Junior College, 1000 College Boulevard, Pensacola, FL 32504-8998. *Phone:* 850-484-1600. *Fax:* 850-484-1829.

POLK COMMUNITY COLLEGE

Winter Haven, Florida www.polk.edu/

- **State-supported** 2-year, founded 1964, part of Florida Community College System
- **Suburban** 98-acre campus with easy access to Orlando and Tampa
- **Endowment** $14.0 million
- **Coed,** 6,964 undergraduate students, 30% full-time, 65% women, 35% men

Undergraduates 2,081 full-time, 4,883 part-time. Students come from 16 states and territories, 49 other countries, 1% are from out of state, 15% African American, 3% Asian American or Pacific Islander, 10% Hispanic American, 0.3% Native American, 0.8% international, 20% transferred in.

Freshmen *Admission:* 1,002 admitted, 1,002 enrolled.

Faculty *Total:* 534, 27% full-time, 9% with terminal degrees. *Student/faculty ratio:* 13:1.

Majors Accounting technology and bookkeeping; business administration and management; child development; corrections; criminal justice/law enforcement administration; data processing and data processing technology; emergency medical technology (EMT paramedic); finance; fire science; health information/medical records administration; information science/studies; legal administrative assistant/secretary; liberal arts and sciences/liberal studies; marketing/marketing management; medical administrative assistant and medical secretary; nursing (registered nurse training); occupational therapist assistant; physical therapist assistant; pre-engineering; radiologic technology/science; respiratory care therapy.

Academics *Calendar:* semesters 16-16-6-6. *Degree:* certificates and associate. *Special study options:* academic remediation for entering students, accelerated degree program, adult/continuing education programs, advanced placement credit, cooperative education, distance learning, double majors, English as a second language, honors programs, independent study, part-time degree program, services for LD students, student-designed majors, study abroad, summer session for credit. *ROTC:* Army (c).

Library Polk Community College Library with 181,000 titles, 325 serial subscriptions, 2,500 audiovisual materials, an OPAC, a Web page.

Student Life *Housing:* college housing not available. *Activities and Organizations:* drama/theater group, student-run newspaper, choral group. *Campus security:* 24-hour emergency response devices and patrols.

Athletics Member NJCAA. *Intercollegiate sports:* baseball M(s), basketball M(s), soccer W(s), softball W(s), volleyball W(s).

Costs (2006–07) *Tuition:* state resident $2006 full-time, $67 per credit hour part-time; nonresident $7393 full-time, $246 per credit hour part-time. *Waivers:* employees or children of employees.

Financial Aid Of all full-time matriculated undergraduates, 16 Federal Work-Study jobs (averaging $400).

Applying *Options:* early admission, deferred entrance. *Application fee:* $20. *Required:* high school transcript. *Application deadlines:* rolling (freshmen), rolling (transfers). *Notification:* continuous (freshmen), continuous (transfers).

Freshmen Application Contact Polk Community College, 999 Avenue H, Northeast, Winter Haven, FL 33881. *Phone:* 863-297-1010 Ext. 5282.

REMINGTON COLLEGE–JACKSONVILLE CAMPUS

Jacksonville, Florida www.remingtoncollege.edu/

- **Proprietary** primarily 2-year
- **Coed,** 94 undergraduate students

Undergraduates 40% African American, 7% Asian American or Pacific Islander, 10% Hispanic American.

Freshmen *Admission:* 163 applied, 160 admitted.

Faculty *Total:* 24, 58% full-time, 21% with terminal degrees. *Student/faculty ratio:* 15:1.

Majors Business administration, management and operations related; computer and information sciences and support services related; computer and information sciences related; corrections and criminal justice related; operations management.

Academics *Degrees:* diplomas, associate, and bachelor's.

Costs (2006–07) *Tuition:* $12,825 full-time.

Applying *Application fee:* $50.

Director of Admissions Mr. Tony Galang, Campus President, Remington College–Jacksonville Campus, 7011 A.C. Skinner Parkway, Jacksonville, FL 32256. *Phone:* 904-296-3435 Ext. 218. *Fax:* 904-296-9097. *E-mail:* tony.galang@ remingtoncollege.edu.

REMINGTON COLLEGE–PINELLAS CAMPUS

Largo, Florida www.remingtoncollege.edu/

Director of Admissions Ms. Edna Higgins, Campus President, Remington College–Pinellas Campus, 8550 Ulmerton Road, Largo, FL 33771. *Phone:* 727-532-1999. *Toll-free phone:* 888-900-2343. *Fax:* 727-530-7710.

REMINGTON COLLEGE–TAMPA CAMPUS

Tampa, Florida www.remingtoncollege.edu/

- **Proprietary** primarily 2-year, founded 1948
- **Urban** 10-acre campus
- **Coed**

Undergraduates 685 full-time. 36% African American, 1% Asian American or Pacific Islander, 18% Hispanic American, 0.9% Native American, 3% international.

Faculty *Student/faculty ratio:* 15:1.

Academics *Calendar:* quarters. *Degrees:* diplomas, associate, and bachelor's. *Special study options:* academic remediation for entering students, accelerated degree program, internships.

Student Life *Campus security:* late-night transport/escort service.

Standardized Tests *Required:* Wonderlic aptitude test (for admission).

Financial Aid Of all full-time matriculated undergraduates, 12 Federal Work-Study jobs (averaging $8000).

Applying *Options:* deferred entrance. *Application fee:* $50. *Required:* high school transcript, interview.

Freshmen Application Contact Mr. James Royster, Director of Admissions, Remington College–Tampa Campus, 2410 East Busch Boulevard, Tampa, FL 33612. *Phone:* 813-935-5700. *Toll-free phone:* 800-992-4850. *Fax:* 813-935-7415.

ST. JOHNS RIVER COMMUNITY COLLEGE

Palatka, Florida www.sjrcc.cc.fl.us/

Director of Admissions Mr. O'Neal Williams, Dean of Admissions and Records, St. Johns River Community College, 5001 Saint Johns Avenue, Palatka, FL 32177-3897. *Phone:* 386-312-4032. *Fax:* 386-312-4289.

ST. PETERSBURG COLLEGE

St. Petersburg, Florida www.spjc.edu/

- **State and locally supported** primarily 2-year, founded 1927
- **Suburban** campus
- **Endowment** $13.4 million
- **Coed**

Undergraduates 8,012 full-time, 16,090 part-time. Students come from 45 states and territories, 30 other countries, 4% are from out of state, 11% African American, 3% Asian American or Pacific Islander, 6% Hispanic American, 0.7% Native American, 1% international.

Academics *Calendar:* semesters. *Degrees:* certificates, diplomas, associate, and bachelor's. *Special study options:* academic remediation for entering students, adult/continuing education programs, advanced placement credit, cooperative education, distance learning, English as a second language, freshman

honors college, honors programs, internships, part-time degree program, services for LD students, summer session for credit.

Student Life *Campus security:* late-night transport/escort service.

Athletics Member NJCAA.

Financial Aid Of all full-time matriculated undergraduates, 350 Federal Work-Study jobs (averaging $2500).

Applying *Options:* electronic application, early admission, deferred entrance. *Application fee:* $35. *Required:* high school transcript.

Freshmen Application Contact Mr. Martyn Clay, Admissions Director/Registrar, St. Petersburg College, PO Box 13489, St. Petersburg, FL 33733-3489. *Phone:* 727-712-5892. *Fax:* 727-712-5872. *E-mail:* information@spcollege.edu.

SANFORD-BROWN INSTITUTE

Jacksonville, Florida   www.sbjacksonville.com/

Admissions Office Contact Sanford-Brown Institute, 10255 Fortune Parkway, Suite 501, Jacksonville, FL 32256.

SANFORD-BROWN INSTITUTE

Lauderdale Lakes, Florida   www.sbftlauderdale.com/

- **Proprietary** 2-year, part of Career Education Corporation
- **Urban** campus
- **Coed,** 303 undergraduate students
- 29% of applicants were admitted

Undergraduates Students come from 6 states and territories, 3 other countries, 16% are from out of state, 25% African American, 6% Asian American or Pacific Islander, 14% Hispanic American. *Retention:* 29% of 2003 full-time freshmen returned.

Freshmen *Admission:* 1,028 applied, 303 admitted. *Average high school GPA:* 3.1.

Faculty *Total:* 30, 83% full-time, 13% with terminal degrees. *Student/faculty ratio:* 10:1.

Academics *Special study options:* academic remediation for entering students, adult/continuing education programs, advanced placement credit, internships, services for LD students.

Library SBI plus 1 other with 4,000 titles, 67 serial subscriptions, 34 audiovisual materials, an OPAC, a Web page.

Student Life *Housing:* college housing not available. *Campus security:* 24-hour emergency response devices and patrols, late-night transport/escort service, controlled dormitory access.

Applying *Required:* high school transcript, interview. *Application deadlines:* rolling (freshmen), rolling (transfers). *Notification:* continuous (freshmen), continuous (transfers).

Director of Admissions Scott Nelowet, Sanford-Brown Institute, 1201 West Cypress Creek Road, Ft. Lauderdale, FL 33309. *Phone:* 904-363-6221. *Fax:* 904-363-6824. *E-mail:* snelowet@sbjacksonville.com.

SANFORD-BROWN INSTITUTE

Tampa, Florida   www.sbtampa.com/

- **Proprietary** 2-year
- **Coed,** 473 undergraduate students

Majors Cardiovascular technology.

Academics *Degree:* associate.

Costs (2006–07) *Tuition:* $13,175 per degree program part-time.

Applying *Application fee:* $25.

Admissions Office Contact Sanford-Brown Institute, 5701 East Hillsborough Avenue, Tampa, FL 33610. *Toll-free phone:* 888-450-0333.

SANTA FE COMMUNITY COLLEGE

Gainesville, Florida   www.sfcc.edu/

Director of Admissions Ms. Margaret Karrh, Registrar, Santa Fe Community College, 3000 Northwest 83rd Street, Gainesville, FL 32606-6200. *Phone:* 352-395-5857. *Fax:* 352-395-4118. *E-mail:* information@santafe.cc.fl.us.

SEMINOLE COMMUNITY COLLEGE

Sanford, Florida   www.scc-fl.edu/

- **State and locally supported** 2-year, founded 1966
- **Small-town** 200-acre campus with easy access to Orlando
- **Endowment** $5.6 million
- **Coed,** 11,747 undergraduate students, 35% full-time, 59% women, 41% men

Undergraduates 4,068 full-time, 7,679 part-time. Students come from 96 other countries, 4% are from out of state, 13% African American, 3% Asian American or Pacific Islander, 15% Hispanic American, 0.4% Native American, 5% international, 9% transferred in. *Retention:* 60% of 2003 full-time freshmen returned.

Freshmen *Admission:* 1,928 enrolled.

Faculty *Total:* 807, 24% full-time, 9% with terminal degrees. *Student/faculty ratio:* 11:1.

Majors Accounting; administrative assistant and secretarial science; architectural engineering technology; automobile/automotive mechanics technology; banking and financial support services; business administration and management; child development; civil engineering technology; computer and information sciences related; computer and information systems security; computer engineering related; computer engineering technology; computer graphics; computer hardware engineering; computer/information technology services administration related; computer programming; computer programming related; computer programming (specific applications); computer programming (vendor/product certification); computer software and media applications related; computer software engineering; computer systems networking and telecommunications; computer/technical support; construction engineering technology; construction management; criminal justice/law enforcement administration; data entry/microcomputer applications; data entry/microcomputer applications related; data modeling/warehousing and database administration; data processing and data processing technology; drafting and design technology; electrical, electronic and communications engineering technology; emergency medical technology (EMT paramedic); finance; fire science; industrial technology; information science/studies; information technology; interior design; legal assistant/paralegal; liberal arts and sciences/liberal studies; marketing/marketing management; nursing (registered nurse training); physical therapy; respiratory care therapy; system administration; telecommunications; web/multimedia management and webmaster; web page, digital/multimedia and information resources design; word processing.

Academics *Calendar:* semesters. *Degree:* certificates, diplomas, and associate. *Special study options:* academic remediation for entering students, accelerated degree program, adult/continuing education programs, advanced placement credit, cooperative education, distance learning, double majors, English as a second language, external degree program, honors programs, independent study, internships, part-time degree program, services for LD students, study abroad, summer session for credit. *ROTC:* Army (b).

Library Seminole Community College Library plus 2 others with 112,000 titles, 373 serial subscriptions, 6,550 audiovisual materials, an OPAC, a Web page.

Student Life *Housing:* college housing not available. *Activities and Organizations:* drama/theater group, student-run newspaper, choral group, Phi Beta Lambda, Phi Theta Kappa, Student Government Association, International Student Organization. *Campus security:* 24-hour emergency response devices and patrols. *Student services:* personal/psychological counseling.

Athletics Member NJCAA. *Intercollegiate sports:* baseball M(s), basketball M(s)/W(s), softball W(s). *Intramural sports:* basketball M/W, golf M, tennis M/W, volleyball M/W.

Costs (2006–07) *Tuition:* state resident $1592 full-time, $54 per credit hour part-time; nonresident $6125 full-time, $220 per credit hour part-time. *Required fees:* $488 full-time, $18 per credit hour part-time. *Payment plan:* deferred payment. *Waivers:* senior citizens and employees or children of employees.

Applying *Options:* early admission, deferred entrance. *Required:* high school transcript, minimum 2.0 GPA. *Application deadlines:* rolling (freshmen), rolling (transfers). *Notification:* continuous (freshmen), continuous (transfers).

Freshmen Application Contact Ms. Pamela Mennechey, Director of Admissions, Seminole Community College, 100 Weldon Boulevard, Sanford, FL 32773-6199. *Phone:* 407-708-2050. *Fax:* 407-708-2395. *E-mail:* admissions@scc-fl.edu.

SOUTH FLORIDA COMMUNITY COLLEGE
Avon Park, Florida   **www.sfcc.cc.fl.us/**

- **State-supported** 2-year, founded 1965, part of Florida Community College System
- **Rural** 80-acre campus with easy access to Tampa–St. Petersburg and Orlando
- **Endowment** $3.3 million
- **Coed,** 2,076 undergraduate students, 39% full-time, 59% women, 41% men

Undergraduates 813 full-time, 1,263 part-time. Students come from 12 states and territories, 4 other countries.

Freshmen *Admission:* 286 enrolled.

Faculty *Total:* 203, 23% full-time, 9% with terminal degrees. *Student/faculty ratio:* 15:1.

Majors Accounting; administrative assistant and secretarial science; agricultural business and management; agricultural mechanization; business administration and management; business/commerce; child development; computer programming; construction engineering technology; criminal justice/law enforcement administration; drafting and design technology; education; electrical, electronic and communications engineering technology; finance; hospitality administration; liberal arts and sciences/liberal studies; marketing/marketing management; medical administrative assistant and medical secretary; nursing (registered nurse training); ornamental horticulture.

Academics *Calendar:* semesters. *Degree:* certificates, diplomas, and associate. *Special study options:* academic remediation for entering students, accelerated degree program, adult/continuing education programs, advanced placement credit, cooperative education, English as a second language, internships, part-time degree program, services for LD students, summer session for credit.

Library Learning Resource Center with 42,000 titles, 237 serial subscriptions, an OPAC.

Student Life *Activities and Organizations:* student-run newspaper, choral group, Phi Theta Kappa, Student Activities Board, Cheerleaders Club, African-American Association, Future Educators. *Campus security:* 24-hour patrols. *Student services:* personal/psychological counseling, women's center.

Athletics Member NJCAA. *Intercollegiate sports:* baseball M(s), tennis W(s), volleyball W(s).

Standardized Tests *Required:* SAT, ACT or Florida College Entry-Level Placement Test, CPT (for placement).

Costs (2006–07) *Tuition:* state resident $2048 full-time; nonresident $7692 full-time.

Applying *Options:* early admission, deferred entrance. *Required:* high school transcript. *Application deadline:* rolling (freshmen). *Notification:* continuous (freshmen).

Director of Admissions Ms. Annie Alexander-Harvey, Dean of Student Services, South Florida Community College, 600 West College Drive, Avon Park, FL 33825-9356. *Phone:* 863-453-6661 Ext. 7107.

SOUTHWEST FLORIDA COLLEGE
Fort Myers, Florida   **www.swfc.edu/**

- **Independent** primarily 2-year, founded 1940
- **Urban** campus
- **Coed**

Academics *Calendar:* quarters. *Degrees:* diplomas, associate, and bachelor's. *Special study options:* academic remediation for entering students, cooperative education, internships.

Student Life *Campus security:* day and evening security guards.

Financial Aid Of all full-time matriculated undergraduates, 10 Federal Work-Study jobs (averaging $5000).

Applying *Recommended:* high school transcript.

Freshmen Application Contact Ms. Carmen King, Director of Admissions, Southwest Florida College, 1685 Medical Lane, Fort Myers, FL 33907. *Phone:* 239-939-4766. *Toll-free phone:* 866-SWFC-NOW. *Fax:* 239-936-4040.

SOUTHWEST FLORIDA COLLEGE
Tampa, Florida   **www.swfc.edu/**

Director of Admissions Admissions, Southwest Florida College, 3910 Riga Boulevard, Tampa, FL 33619. *Phone:* 813-630-4401. *Toll-free phone:* 877-907-2456.

TALLAHASSEE COMMUNITY COLLEGE
Tallahassee, Florida   **www.tcc.fl.edu/**

- **State and locally supported** 2-year, founded 1966, part of Florida Community College System
- **Suburban** 258-acre campus
- **Coed,** 13,493 undergraduate students, 50% full-time, 56% women, 44% men

Undergraduates 6,766 full-time, 6,727 part-time. Students come from 40 states and territories, 37 other countries, 8% are from out of state, 32% African American, 1% Asian American or Pacific Islander, 6% Hispanic American, 0.4% Native American, 0.9% international, 29% transferred in.

Freshmen *Admission:* 2,138 enrolled.

Faculty *Total:* 581, 31% full-time, 24% with terminal degrees. *Student/faculty ratio:* 30:1.

Majors Accounting technology and bookkeeping; administrative assistant and secretarial science; business administration and management; civil engineering technology; computer and information sciences; computer graphics; computer programming; computer programming (specific applications); computer systems networking and telecommunications; construction engineering technology; criminal justice/law enforcement administration; data processing and data processing technology; dental hygiene; emergency medical technology (EMT paramedic); engineering; film/cinema studies; finance; health information/medical records technology; kindergarten/preschool education; legal administrative assistant/secretary; legal assistant/paralegal; liberal arts and sciences/liberal studies; management information systems; marketing/marketing management; nursing (registered nurse training); parks, recreation and leisure; public administration; respiratory care therapy; system administration; word processing.

Academics *Calendar:* semesters. *Degree:* certificates and associate. *Special study options:* academic remediation for entering students, accelerated degree program, adult/continuing education programs, advanced placement credit, distance learning, English as a second language, external degree program, honors programs, independent study, off-campus study, part-time degree program, services for LD students, study abroad, summer session for credit. *ROTC:* Army (c), Navy (c), Air Force (c).

Library Tallahassee Community College Library with 108,282 titles, 179 serial subscriptions, 9,283 audiovisual materials, an OPAC.

Student Life *Housing:* college housing not available. *Activities and Organizations:* drama/theater group, student-run newspaper, choral group, Phi Theta Kappa, student government, International Student Organization, Black Student Union, Returning Adults Valuing Education. *Campus security:* 24-hour emergency response devices and patrols, late-night transport/escort service. *Student services:* personal/psychological counseling.

Athletics Member NJCAA. *Intercollegiate sports:* baseball M(s), basketball M(s)/W(s), softball W(s). *Intramural sports:* basketball M/W, bowling M/W, cross-country running M/W, football M/W, golf M/W, racquetball M/W, soccer M/W, softball M/W, swimming and diving M/W, table tennis M/W, tennis M/W, track and field M/W, volleyball M/W, weight lifting M/W.

Costs (2006–07) *Tuition:* state resident $1875 full-time, $63 per credit hour part-time; nonresident $6705 full-time, $224 per credit hour part-time.

Financial Aid Of all full-time matriculated undergraduates, 226 Federal Work-Study jobs (averaging $2000).

Applying *Options:* electronic application, early admission, deferred entrance. *Required:* high school transcript. *Application deadlines:* 8/1 (freshmen), 8/1 (transfers).

Freshmen Application Contact TCC Student Success Center, Tallahassee Community College, 444 Appleyard Drive, Tallahassee, FL 32304-2895. *Phone:* 850-201-8555. *E-mail:* enroll@mail.tallahassee.cc.fl.us.

VALENCIA COMMUNITY COLLEGE
Orlando, Florida   **www.valencia.cc.fl.us/**

- **State-supported** 2-year, founded 1967, part of Florida Community College System
- **Urban** campus
- **Endowment** $14.4 million
- **Coed,** 30,245 undergraduate students, 41% full-time, 58% women, 42% men

Undergraduates 12,522 full-time, 17,723 part-time. Students come from 23 states and territories, 84 other countries, 4% are from out of state, 16% African American, 5% Asian American or Pacific Islander, 24% Hispanic American, 0.5% Native American, 3% international, 6% transferred in.

Freshmen *Admission:* 9,141 applied, 9,115 admitted, 5,393 enrolled. *Test scores:* SAT verbal scores over 500: 34%; SAT math scores over 500: 34%; SAT

writing scores over 500: 34; SAT verbal scores over 600: 6%; SAT math scores over 600: 6%; SAT writing scores over 600: 6.

Faculty *Total:* 1,215, 32% full-time, 17% with terminal degrees. *Student/faculty ratio:* 24:1.

Majors Accounting; administrative assistant and secretarial science; business administration and management; cardiovascular technology; cinematography and film/video production; civil engineering technology; commercial and advertising art; computer programming; computer programming related; computer programming (specific applications); construction engineering technology; criminal justice/law enforcement administration; culinary arts; data entry/microcomputer applications; dental hygiene; diagnostic medical sonography and ultrasound technology; drafting and design technology; dramatic/theater arts; electrical, electronic and communications engineering technology; emergency medical technology (EMT paramedic); environmental engineering technology; fire science; hospitality administration; human resources management; industrial technology; information technology; legal administrative assistant/secretary; legal assistant/paralegal; liberal arts and sciences/liberal studies; marketing/marketing management; medical administrative assistant and medical secretary; medical radiologic technology; nursing (registered nurse training); office management; ornamental horticulture; physical education teaching and coaching; pre-engineering; respiratory care therapy; survey technology; tourism and travel services management; word processing.

Academics *Calendar:* semesters. *Degree:* certificates, diplomas, and associate. *Special study options:* academic remediation for entering students, accelerated degree program, adult/continuing education programs, advanced placement credit, cooperative education, distance learning, double majors, English as a second language, honors programs, independent study, internships, part-time degree program, services for LD students, student-designed majors, summer session for credit. *ROTC:* Army (c).

Library Learning Resources Center plus 4 others with 183,264 titles, 2,196 serial subscriptions, 23,140 audiovisual materials, an OPAC, a Web page.

Student Life *Housing:* college housing not available. *Activities and Organizations:* drama/theater group, student-run newspaper, choral group, Phi Theta Kappa, Valencia Intercultural Student Association, Student Government Association, Latin American Student Association, Valencia Student Nurses Association. *Campus security:* 24-hour emergency response devices and patrols, student patrols, late-night transport/escort service. *Student services:* personal/psychological counseling.

Costs (2006–07) *Tuition:* state resident $1673 full-time, $70 per credit part-time; nonresident $6287 full-time, $262 per credit part-time.

Financial Aid Of all full-time matriculated undergraduates, 238 Federal Work-Study jobs (averaging $2400).

Applying *Options:* early admission. *Application fee:* $25. *Required:* high school transcript. *Application deadlines:* 8/10 (freshmen), 8/10 (transfers).

Freshmen Application Contact Dr. Renee Simpson, Assistant Vice President of Admissions and Records, Valencia Community College, PO Box 3028, Orlando, FL 32802-3028. *Phone:* 407-582-1511. *Fax:* 407-582-1866. *E-mail:* rsimpson@valenciacc.edu.

WEBSTER COLLEGE

Holiday, Florida   www.webstercollege.com/

Director of Admissions Ms. Claire L. Walker, Senior Admissions Representative, Webster College, 2127 Grand Boulevard, Holiday, FL 34690. *Phone:* 727-942-0069. *Toll-free phone:* 888-729-7247.

WEBSTER COLLEGE

Ocala, Florida   www.webstercollege.com/

Freshmen Application Contact Admissions Office, Webster College, 1530 SW Third Avenue, Ocala, FL 34474. *Phone:* 352-629-1941.

GEORGIA

ABRAHAM BALDWIN AGRICULTURAL COLLEGE

Tifton, Georgia   www.abac.edu/

- **State-supported** 2-year, founded 1933, part of University System of Georgia
- **Small-town** 390-acre campus
- **Endowment** $4.3 million
- **Coed**

Undergraduates 2,237 full-time, 1,186 part-time. Students come from 10 states and territories, 17% African American, 0.6% Asian American or Pacific Islander, 3% Hispanic American, 0.1% Native American, 1% international, 28% live on campus.

Faculty *Student/faculty ratio:* 22:1.

Academics *Calendar:* semesters. *Degree:* certificates and associate. *Special study options:* academic remediation for entering students, adult/continuing education programs, advanced placement credit, English as a second language, honors programs, internships, off-campus study, part-time degree program, services for LD students, summer session for credit.

Student Life *Campus security:* 24-hour emergency response devices and patrols, late-night transport/escort service.

Athletics Member NJCAA.

Financial Aid Of all full-time matriculated undergraduates, 158 Federal Work-Study jobs (averaging $1675).

Applying *Options:* early admission, deferred entrance. *Application fee:* $20. *Required:* high school transcript, minimum 2.0 GPA, college prep curriculum. *Required for some:* minimum 2.2 GPA.

Freshmen Application Contact Ms. Beth Saxon, Director of Enrollment Services, Abraham Baldwin Agricultural College, 2802 Moore Highway, Tifton, GA 31793. *Phone:* 229-391-5001. *Toll-free phone:* 800-733-3653. *Fax:* 229-386-7181. *E-mail:* esaxon@abac.edu.

ALBANY TECHNICAL COLLEGE

Albany, Georgia   www.albanytech.edu/

- **State-supported** 2-year, founded 1961, part of Georgia Department of Technical and Adult Education
- **Coed**, 2,580 undergraduate students, 48% full-time, 64% women, 36% men

Undergraduates 1,242 full-time, 1,338 part-time. 68% African American, 0.4% Asian American or Pacific Islander, 0.7% Hispanic American, 0.2% Native American.

Freshmen *Admission:* 407 enrolled.

Faculty *Total:* 91, 100% full-time.

Majors Accounting; child care and guidance related; child development; computer and information sciences; corrections and criminal justice related; culinary arts; drafting and design technology; electrical and electronic engineering technologies related; forestry technology; gerontological services; hotel and restaurant management; industrial technology; manufacturing technology; marketing/marketing management; medical radiologic technology; pharmacy technician; tourism and travel services management.

Academics *Calendar:* quarters. *Degree:* certificates, diplomas, and associate. *Special study options:* academic remediation for entering students, adult/continuing education programs, advanced placement credit, distance learning, internships, part-time degree program, services for LD students.

Library Albany Technical College Library and Media Center plus 1 other with 42,000 titles, 40 serial subscriptions, 520 audiovisual materials, an OPAC, a Web page.

Student Life *Housing:* college housing not available.

Standardized Tests *Required:* ACT COMPASS or ASSET (for admission).

Costs (2006–07) *Tuition:* state resident $1116 full-time, $31 per credit hour part-time; nonresident $2232 full-time, $62 per credit hour part-time. Full-time tuition and fees vary according to course load and program. Part-time tuition and fees vary according to course load and program. *Required fees:* $243 full-time. *Waivers:* senior citizens.

Applying *Options:* electronic application, deferred entrance. *Application fee:* $15. *Required:* high school transcript.

Director of Admissions Ms. Lynderia S. Cheevers, Director of Admissions, Albany Technical College, 1704 South Slappey Boulevard, Albany, GA 31701. *Phone:* 229-430-3520. *Fax:* 229-430-6180. *E-mail:* lcheevers@albanytech.edu.

ALTAMAHA TECHNICAL COLLEGE

Jesup, Georgia   www.altamahatech.edu/

- **State-supported** 2-year, part of Georgia Department of Technical and Adult Education
- **Coed,** 957 undergraduate students, 41% full-time, 50% women, 50% men

Undergraduates 393 full-time, 564 part-time. 33% African American, 0.5% Asian American or Pacific Islander, 4% Hispanic American, 0.2% Native American.

Freshmen *Admission:* 278 enrolled.

Altamaha Technical College (continued)

Faculty *Total:* 106, 39% full-time.

Majors Administrative assistant and secretarial science; child development; computer programming; computer systems networking and telecommunications; criminal justice/safety; information science/studies; machine tool technology; manufacturing technology; marketing/marketing management.

Academics *Calendar:* quarters. *Degree:* certificates, diplomas, and associate. *Special study options:* academic remediation for entering students, advanced placement credit, distance learning, internships, services for LD students.

Library 4,435 titles, 90 serial subscriptions, 292 audiovisual materials.

Student Life *Housing:* college housing not available.

Costs (2006–07) *Tuition:* state resident $1116 full-time, $31 per credit hour part-time; nonresident $2232 full-time, $62 per credit hour part-time. Full-time tuition and fees vary according to course load and program. Part-time tuition and fees vary according to course load and program. *Required fees:* $243 full-time. *Waivers:* senior citizens.

Applying *Options:* deferred entrance. *Application fee:* $15. *Required:* high school transcript.

Director of Admissions Lillian Burns, Admissions Director, Altamaha Technical College, 1777 West Cherry Street, Jesup, GA 31545. *Phone:* 912-427-5817. *Fax:* 912-427-5823. *E-mail:* lburns@altamahatech.edu.

ANDREW COLLEGE

Cuthbert, Georgia　　　　**www.andrewcollege.edu/**

Freshmen Application Contact Ms. Bridget Kurkowski, Director of Admission, Andrew College, 413 College Street, Cuthbert, GA 39840. *Phone:* 229-732-5986. *Toll-free phone:* 800-664-9250. *Fax:* 229-732-2176. *E-mail:* admissions@andrewcollege.edu.

▶See page 474 for the College Close-Up.

APPALACHIAN TECHNICAL COLLEGE

Jasper, Georgia　　　　**www.appalachiantech.edu/**

- **State-supported** 2-year, founded 1965, part of Georgia Department of Technical and Adult Education
- **Coed,** 1,089 undergraduate students, 37% full-time, 66% women, 34% men

Undergraduates 401 full-time, 688 part-time. 2% African American, 0.9% Asian American or Pacific Islander, 0.7% Hispanic American, 0.4% Native American.

Freshmen *Admission:* 326 enrolled.

Faculty *Total:* 77, 40% full-time.

Majors Accounting; administrative assistant and secretarial science; business administration and management; child development; computer systems networking and telecommunications; criminal justice/safety; forensic science and technology; information science/studies; paralegal/legal assistant.

Academics *Calendar:* quarters. *Degree:* certificates, diplomas, and associate. *Special study options:* academic remediation for entering students, advanced placement credit, distance learning, double majors, internships, services for LD students.

Student Life *Housing:* college housing not available.

Standardized Tests *Required:* ACT COMPASS or ASSET (for admission).

Costs (2006–07) *Tuition:* state resident $1116 full-time, $31 per credit hour part-time; nonresident $2232 full-time, $62 per credit hour part-time. Full-time tuition and fees vary according to course load and program. Part-time tuition and fees vary according to course load and program. *Required fees:* $243 full-time. *Waivers:* senior citizens.

Applying *Options:* deferred entrance. *Application fee:* $15. *Required:* high school transcript.

Director of Admissions Nina Faix, Admissions Officer, Appalachian Technical College, 100 Campus Drive, Jasper, GA 30143-1253. *Phone:* 706-253-4537. *Fax:* 706-253-4433. *E-mail:* nfaix@appalachiantech.edu.

ASHWORTH COLLEGE

Norcross, Georgia　　　　**www.ashworthcollege.com/**

Director of Admissions Mr. John Graves, Dean of Undergraduate Studies, Ashworth College, 430 Technology Parkway, Norcross, GA 30092. *Toll-free phone:* 800-223-4542.

ATHENS TECHNICAL COLLEGE

Athens, Georgia　　　　**www.athenstech.edu/**

- **State-supported** 2-year, founded 1958, part of Georgia Department of Technical and Adult Education
- **Suburban** 41-acre campus with easy access to Atlanta
- **Coed,** 3,961 undergraduate students, 37% full-time, 68% women, 32% men

Undergraduates 1,474 full-time, 2,487 part-time. Students come from 2 states and territories, 24% African American, 5% Asian American or Pacific Islander, 2% Hispanic American.

Freshmen *Admission:* 521 enrolled.

Faculty *Total:* 289, 28% full-time.

Majors Accounting; administrative assistant and secretarial science; biology/biotechnology laboratory technician; child development; clinical laboratory science/medical technology; communications technology; computer programming; computer systems networking and telecommunications; criminal justice/law enforcement administration; dental assisting; dental hygiene; diagnostic medical sonography and ultrasound technology; electrical, electronic and communications engineering technology; emergency medical technology (EMT paramedic); hotel and restaurant management; information science/studies; legal assistant/paralegal; logistics and materials management; marketing/marketing management; medical laboratory technology; medical radiologic technology; nursing (licensed practical/vocational nurse training); nursing (registered nurse training); physical therapy; respiratory care therapy; surgical technology; tourism and travel services management; veterinary technology.

Academics *Calendar:* quarters. *Degree:* certificates, diplomas, and associate. *Special study options:* academic remediation for entering students, adult/continuing education programs, advanced placement credit, distance learning, internships, part-time degree program, services for LD students, summer session for credit.

Library 33,891 titles, 538 serial subscriptions, 3,279 audiovisual materials.

Student Life *Housing:* college housing not available. *Activities and Organizations:* Athens Technical Student Advisory Council, Phi Theta Kappa, Delta Epsilon Chi, Radiological Technology Society, Organized Black Students Encouraging Unity and Excellence. *Campus security:* 24-hour patrols.

Standardized Tests *Required:* ACT COMPASS or ASSET (for admission).

Costs (2006–07) *Tuition:* state resident $1116 full-time, $31 per credit hour part-time; nonresident $2232 full-time, $62 per credit hour part-time. Full-time tuition and fees vary according to course load and program. Part-time tuition and fees vary according to course load and program. *Required fees:* $243 full-time. *Waivers:* senior citizens.

Financial Aid Of all full-time matriculated undergraduates, 34 Federal Work-Study jobs (averaging $3090).

Applying *Options:* deferred entrance. *Application fee:* $15. *Required:* high school transcript.

Director of Admissions Mr. Lenzy Reid, Director of Admissions, Athens Technical College, 800 US Highway 29 North, Athens, GA 30601-1500. *Phone:* 706-355-5124. *Fax:* 706-369-5756. *E-mail:* lreid@athenstech.org.

ATLANTA METROPOLITAN COLLEGE

Atlanta, Georgia　　　　**www.atlm.edu/**

- **State-supported** 2-year, founded 1974, part of University System of Georgia
- **Urban** 68-acre campus
- **Coed**

Undergraduates 860 full-time, 888 part-time. Students come from 33 states and territories, 39 other countries, 8% are from out of state, 94% African American, 0.7% Asian American or Pacific Islander, 0.6% Hispanic American, 0.1% Native American, 3% international, 8% transferred in.

Faculty *Student/faculty ratio:* 23:1.

Academics *Calendar:* semesters. *Degree:* certificates and associate. *Special study options:* academic remediation for entering students, adult/continuing education programs, cooperative education, part-time degree program, services for LD students, study abroad, summer session for credit.

Student Life *Campus security:* 24-hour emergency response devices and patrols.

Athletics Member NJCAA.

Costs (2006–07) *Tuition:* state resident $1588 full-time, $67 per credit part-time; nonresident $6350 full-time, $265 per credit part-time. No tuition increase for student's term of enrollment. *Required fees:* $250 full-time, $120 per term part-time.

Applying *Options:* electronic application. *Application fee:* $20. *Required:* high school transcript.

Freshmen Application Contact Ms. Audrey Reid, Director, Office of Admissions, Atlanta Metropolitan College, 1630 Metropolitan Parkway, SW, Atlanta, GA 30310-4498. *Phone:* 404-756-4004. *Fax:* 404-756-4407. *E-mail:* admissions@atlm.edu.

ATLANTA TECHNICAL COLLEGE

Atlanta, Georgia www.atlantatech.org/

- **State-supported** 2-year, founded 1945, part of Georgia Department of Technical and Adult Education
- **Coed,** 3,172 undergraduate students, 49% full-time, 61% women, 39% men

Undergraduates 1,545 full-time, 1,627 part-time. 93% African American, 1% Asian American or Pacific Islander, 1% Hispanic American, 0.1% Native American.

Freshmen *Admission:* 633 enrolled.

Faculty *Total:* 188, 46% full-time.

Majors Accounting; child development; computer programming; culinary arts; dental hygiene; health information/medical records technology; hotel and restaurant management; information technology; marketing/marketing management; paralegal/legal assistant; tourism and travel services management.

Academics *Calendar:* quarters. *Degree:* certificates, diplomas, and associate. *Special study options:* academic remediation for entering students, advanced placement credit, distance learning, internships, services for LD students.

Student Life *Housing:* college housing not available.

Standardized Tests *Required:* ACT COMPASS or ASSET (for admission).

Costs (2006–07) *Tuition:* state resident $1116 full-time, $31 per credit hour part-time; nonresident $2232 full-time, $62 per credit hour part-time. Full-time tuition and fees vary according to course load and program. Part-time tuition and fees vary according to course load and program. *Required fees:* $246 full-time. *Waivers:* senior citizens.

Applying *Options:* deferred entrance. *Application fee:* $15. *Required:* high school transcript.

Director of Admissions Ms. Jill Triplett, Admissions Officer, Atlanta Technical College, 1560 Metropolitan Parkway SW, Atlanta, GA 30310-4446. *Phone:* 404-225-4446. *Fax:* 404-225-4721. *E-mail:* jtriplet@atlantatech.edu.

AUGUSTA TECHNICAL COLLEGE

Augusta, Georgia www.augustatech.edu/

- **State-supported** 2-year, founded 1961, part of Georgia Department of Technical and Adult Education
- **Urban** 70-acre campus
- **Coed,** 4,445 undergraduate students, 49% full-time, 63% women, 37% men

Undergraduates 2,169 full-time, 2,276 part-time. Students come from 2 states and territories, 52% African American, 1% Asian American or Pacific Islander, 2% Hispanic American, 0.3% Native American, 0.1% international.

Freshmen *Admission:* 757 enrolled.

Faculty *Total:* 376, 36% full-time.

Majors Accounting; administrative assistant and secretarial science; biotechnology; business administration and management; cardiovascular technology; child development; computer programming; computer systems networking and telecommunications; criminal justice/safety; culinary arts; e-commerce; electrical, electronic and communications engineering technology; emergency medical technology (EMT paramedic); fire science; information science/studies; marketing/marketing management; mechanical engineering/mechanical technology; medical radiologic technology; occupational therapist assistant; parks, recreation and leisure facilities management; pharmacy technician; respiratory care therapy; respiratory therapy technician; surgical technology.

Academics *Calendar:* quarters. *Degree:* certificates, diplomas, and associate. *Special study options:* academic remediation for entering students, advanced placement credit, cooperative education, distance learning, internships, part-time degree program, services for LD students, summer session for credit.

Library Information Technology Center with 70,816 titles, 445 serial subscriptions, 7,733 audiovisual materials, an OPAC, a Web page.

Student Life *Housing:* college housing not available. *Activities and Organizations:* VICA, professional organizations. *Campus security:* 24-hour emergency response devices, 12-hour patrols by trained security personnel.

Standardized Tests *Required:* ACT COMPASS or ASSET (for admission).

Costs (2006–07) *Tuition:* state resident $1116 full-time, $31 per credit hour part-time; nonresident $2232 full-time, $62 per credit hour part-time. Full-time tuition and fees vary according to course load and program. Part-time tuition and fees vary according to course load and program. *Required fees:* $255 full-time. *Waivers:* senior citizens.

Applying *Options:* deferred entrance. *Application fee:* $15. *Required:* high school transcript.

Director of Admissions Mr. Brian Roberts, Director of Admissions and Counseling, Augusta Technical College, 3200 Augusta Tech Drive, Augusta, GA 30906. *Phone:* 706-771-4027. *Fax:* 706-771-4034. *E-mail:* bcrobert@augustatech.edu.

BAINBRIDGE COLLEGE

Bainbridge, Georgia www.bainbridge.edu/

- **State-supported** 2-year, founded 1972, part of University System of Georgia
- **Small-town** 160-acre campus
- **Coed,** 2,784 undergraduate students, 38% full-time, 72% women, 28% men

Undergraduates 1,057 full-time, 1,727 part-time. Students come from 6 states and territories, 1% are from out of state, 54% African American, 1% Asian American or Pacific Islander, 0.8% Hispanic American, 0.4% Native American.

Freshmen *Admission:* 1,707 applied, 1,362 admitted.

Faculty *Total:* 156, 40% full-time, 14% with terminal degrees.

Majors Accounting; administrative assistant and secretarial science; agriculture; art; automobile/automotive mechanics technology; biology/biological sciences; business administration and management; business teacher education; chemistry; criminal justice/law enforcement administration; data processing and data processing technology; drafting and design technology; dramatic/theater arts; education; electrical, electronic and communications engineering technology; elementary education; English; family and consumer sciences/human sciences; forestry; health teacher education; history; information science/studies; journalism; kindergarten/preschool education; liberal arts and sciences/liberal studies; marketing/marketing management; mathematics; nursing (licensed practical/vocational nurse training); nursing (registered nurse training); political science and government; psychology; sociology; speech and rhetoric; welding technology.

Academics *Calendar:* semesters. *Degree:* certificates and associate. *Special study options:* academic remediation for entering students, adult/continuing education programs, advanced placement credit, distance learning, double majors, independent study, part-time degree program, services for LD students, study abroad, summer session for credit.

Library Bainbridge College Library with 37,387 titles, 180 serial subscriptions, an OPAC.

Student Life *Housing:* college housing not available. *Activities and Organizations:* drama/theater group, Phi Theta Kappa, Alpha Beta Gamma, Drama Club, Delta Club, Sigma Kappa Delta. *Campus security:* 24-hour patrols.

Athletics *Intramural sports:* table tennis M/W, volleyball M/W.

Standardized Tests *Required for some:* SAT or ACT (for admission), ACT COMPASS.

Costs (2006–07) *Tuition:* state resident $1542 full-time, $67 per credit hour part-time; nonresident $6166 full-time, $265 per credit hour part-time. No tuition increase for student's term of enrollment. *Required fees:* $124 full-time. *Waivers:* senior citizens.

Applying *Options:* electronic application, early admission. *Required for some:* high school transcript, minimum 1.8 GPA, 3 letters of recommendation, interview, immunizations, or waivers; medical records and criminal background checks. *Application deadlines:* 8/1 (freshmen), 8/1 (transfers). *Notification:* continuous (freshmen), continuous (transfers).

Freshmen Application Contact Mrs. Connie Snyder, Director of Admissions and Records, Bainbridge College, 2500 East Shotwell Street, Bainbridge, GA 39819. *Phone:* 229-248-2504. *Fax:* 229-248-2525. *E-mail:* csnyder@bainbridge.edu.

BAUDER COLLEGE

Atlanta, Georgia www.bauder.edu/

Freshmen Application Contact Ms. Lillie Lanier, Admissions Representative, Bauder College, Phipps Plaza, 3500 Peachtree Road NE, Atlanta, GA 30326. *Phone:* 404-237-7573. *Toll-free phone:* 404-237-7573 (in-state); 800-241-3797 (out-of-state).

BROWN MACKIE COLLEGE—ATLANTA

**Norcross,
Georgia**   www.brownmackie.edu/locations.asp?locid=3

- **Proprietary** 2-year
- **Urban** campus
- **Coed,** 325 undergraduate students, 100% full-time, 62% women, 38% men

Undergraduates 325 full-time. 35% are from out of state, 77% African American, 3% Hispanic American.

Freshmen *Admission:* 250 enrolled.

Faculty *Total:* 12, 50% full-time, 50% with terminal degrees. *Student/faculty ratio:* 19:1.

Majors Accounting technology and bookkeeping; business administration and management; CAD/CADD drafting/design technology; computer programming (specific applications); computer software technology; criminal justice/law enforcement administration; electrical, electronic and communications engineering technology; medical/clinical assistant; paralegal/legal assistant.

Academics *Degree:* diplomas and associate.

Student Life *Activities and Organizations:* student-run newspaper. *Student services:* health clinic, personal/psychological counseling.

Costs (2006–07) *Tuition:* $5760 full-time, $160 per credit hour part-time. *Required fees:* $360 full-time.

Applying *Required:* high school transcript, interview. *Application deadlines:* rolling (freshmen), rolling (transfers). *Notification:* continuous (freshmen), continuous (transfers).

Freshmen Application Contact Mr. Abul Hussain, Brown Mackie College–Atlanta, 4975 Jimmy Carter Boulevard, Suite 600, Norcross, GA 30093. *Phone:* 770-510-2318. *Fax:* 770-638-0479. *E-mail:* bmcatadm@brownmackie.edu.

▶**See page 498 for the College Close-Up.**

CENTRAL GEORGIA TECHNICAL COLLEGE

Macon, Georgia   www.cgtcollege.org/

- **State-supported** 2-year, founded 1966, part of Georgia Department of Technical and Adult Education
- **Suburban** 152-acre campus
- **Coed,** 4,898 undergraduate students, 46% full-time, 66% women, 34% men

Undergraduates 2,254 full-time, 2,644 part-time. Students come from 5 states and territories, 1 other country, 53% African American, 0.9% Asian American or Pacific Islander, 1% Hispanic American, 0.4% Native American, 26% transferred in.

Freshmen *Admission:* 691 enrolled.

Faculty *Total:* 484, 23% full-time.

Majors Accounting; administrative assistant and secretarial science; banking and financial support services; business administration and management; cabinetmaking and millwork; cardiovascular technology; carpentry; child care and support services management; child development; clinical/medical laboratory technology; computer programming; computer systems networking and telecommunications; criminal justice/safety; dental hygiene; drafting and design technology; e-commerce; electrical, electronic and communications engineering technology; gerontological services; hotel and restaurant management; industrial technology; information science/studies; marketing/marketing management; medical laboratory technology; medical radiologic technology; paralegal/legal assistant; tourism and travel services management; veterinary technology; web page, digital/multimedia and information resources design.

Academics *Calendar:* quarters. *Degree:* certificates, diplomas, and associate. *Special study options:* academic remediation for entering students, advanced placement credit, distance learning, external degree program, internships, off-campus study, part-time degree program, services for LD students.

Library 16,500 titles, 300 serial subscriptions, 1,800 audiovisual materials, an OPAC, a Web page.

Student Life *Housing:* college housing not available. *Activities and Organizations:* Skills USA-VICA, student government. *Campus security:* 24-hour patrols.

Standardized Tests *Required:* ACT COMPASS or ASSET (for admission).

Costs (2006–07) *Tuition:* state resident $1116 full-time, $61 per credit hour part-time; nonresident $2232 full-time, $62 per credit hour part-time. Full-time tuition and fees vary according to course load and program. Part-time tuition and fees vary according to course load and program. *Required fees:* $243 full-time. *Waivers:* senior citizens.

Financial Aid Of all full-time matriculated undergraduates, 175 Federal Work-Study jobs (averaging $2000). *Financial aid deadline:* 9/1.

Applying *Options:* deferred entrance. *Application fee:* $15. *Required:* high school transcript.

Freshmen Application Contact Admissions Director, Central Georgia Technical College, 3300 Macon Tech Drive, Macon, GA 31206. *Phone:* 478-757-3403. *Fax:* 478-757-3454.

CHATTAHOOCHEE TECHNICAL COLLEGE

Marietta, Georgia   www.chattcollege.com

- **State-supported** 2-year, founded 1961, part of Georgia Department of Technical and Adult Education
- **Suburban** campus with easy access to Atlanta
- **Coed,** 5,994 undergraduate students, 40% full-time, 54% women, 46% men

Undergraduates 2,397 full-time, 3,597 part-time. 39% African American, 2% Asian American or Pacific Islander, 4% Hispanic American, 0.4% Native American, 2% international.

Freshmen *Admission:* 937 enrolled.

Faculty *Total:* 300, 22% full-time.

Majors Accounting; administrative assistant and secretarial science; automobile/automotive mechanics technology; biomedical technology; business administration and management; child development; civil engineering technology; computer and information systems security; computer programming; computer systems networking and telecommunications; criminal justice/safety; culinary arts; drafting and design technology; electrical, electronic and communications engineering technology; fire science; horticultural science; information science/studies; logistics and materials management; marketing/marketing management; medical laboratory technology; medical radiologic technology; parks, recreation and leisure facilities management; web page, digital/multimedia and information resources design.

Academics *Calendar:* quarters. *Degree:* certificates, diplomas, and associate. *Special study options:* academic remediation for entering students, advanced placement credit, distance learning, internships, part-time degree program, services for LD students, study abroad.

Library 22,127 titles, 292 serial subscriptions, 1,826 audiovisual materials, a Web page.

Student Life *Housing:* college housing not available. *Activities and Organizations:* student government, Vocational Industrial Clubs of America, Institute for Electrical and Electronic Engineers, National Technical-Vocational Honor Society, Phi Beta Lambda. *Campus security:* full-time day and evening security.

Standardized Tests *Required:* ACT COMPASS or ASSET (for admission).

Costs (2006–07) *Tuition:* state resident $1116 full-time, $31 per credit hour part-time; nonresident $2232 full-time, $62 per credit hour part-time. Full-time tuition and fees vary according to course load and program. Part-time tuition and fees vary according to course load and program. *Required fees:* $264 full-time. *Waivers:* senior citizens.

Financial Aid Of all full-time matriculated undergraduates, 40 Federal Work-Study jobs (averaging $2500).

Applying *Options:* deferred entrance. *Application fee:* $15. *Required:* high school transcript.

Freshmen Application Contact Admissions Director, Chattahoochee Technical College, 980 South Cobb Drive, Marietta, GA 30060-3398. *Phone:* 770-528-4465. *Fax:* 770-528-4580.

COASTAL GEORGIA COMMUNITY COLLEGE

Brunswick, Georgia   www.cgcc.edu/

- **State-supported** 2-year, founded 1961, part of University System of Georgia
- **Small-town** 193-acre campus with easy access to Jacksonville
- **Endowment** $88,604
- **Coed,** 3,054 undergraduate students, 34% full-time, 67% women, 33% men

Undergraduates 1,027 full-time, 2,027 part-time. Students come from 36 states and territories, 11 other countries, 5% are from out of state, 28% African American, 1% Asian American or Pacific Islander, 2% Hispanic American, 0.4% Native American, 0.5% international, 39% transferred in. *Retention:* 55% of 2003 full-time freshmen returned.

Freshmen *Admission:* 1,432 applied, 1,027 admitted, 657 enrolled.

Faculty *Total:* 148, 50% full-time, 11% with terminal degrees. *Student/faculty ratio:* 18:1.

Majors Agricultural business and management; art; biology/biological sciences; business administration and management; chemistry; clinical/medical laboratory technology; computer science; criminal justice/law enforcement administration; dental hygiene; education (multiple levels); English; foreign languages and literatures; forestry; geology/earth science; health and physical education; history; liberal arts and sciences/liberal studies; mathematics; medical radiologic technology; nursing (registered nurse training); occupational therapy; parks, recreation and leisure facilities management; philosophy; physical therapy; physician assistant; physics; political science and government; pre-dentistry studies; pre-engineering; pre-medical studies; pre-pharmacy studies; pre-veterinary studies; psychology; respiratory care therapy; sociology.

Academics *Calendar:* semesters. *Degree:* certificates and associate. *Special study options:* academic remediation for entering students, adult/continuing education programs, advanced placement credit, distance learning, double majors, part-time degree program, services for LD students, study abroad, summer session for credit.

Library Clara Wood Gould Memorial Library with 535 serial subscriptions, 1,151 audiovisual materials, an OPAC.

Student Life *Housing:* college housing not available. *Activities and Organizations:* student-run newspaper, Association of Nursing Students, Minority Advisement and Social Development Association, Student Government Association, Baptist Student Union, Phi Theta Kappa. *Campus security:* 24-hour patrols, late-night transport/escort service. *Student services:* personal/psychological counseling.

Athletics Member NJCAA. *Intercollegiate sports:* basketball M(s), softball W(s). *Intramural sports:* basketball M/W, soccer M/W, swimming and diving M/W, tennis M/W, volleyball M/W.

Costs (2006–07) *Tuition:* state resident $1588 full-time, $67 per credit hour part-time; nonresident $6560 full-time, $266 per credit hour part-time. Full-time tuition and fees vary according to student level. Part-time tuition and fees vary according to student level. No tuition increase for student's term of enrollment. *Required fees:* $212 full-time, $52 per term part-time. *Waivers:* senior citizens and employees or children of employees.

Financial Aid Of all full-time matriculated undergraduates, 80 Federal Work-Study jobs (averaging $1500).

Applying *Options:* electronic application, deferred entrance. *Application fee:* $20. *Required:* high school transcript, minimum 2.0 GPA, immunization records. *Application deadlines:* 8/15 (freshmen), 8/15 (transfers). *Notification:* continuous (freshmen), continuous (transfers).

Freshmen Application Contact Ms. Lisa Lessig, Director of Admissions/Registrar, Coastal Georgia Community College, 3700 Altama Avenue, Brunswick, GA 31525. *Phone:* 912-264-7253. *Toll-free phone:* 800-675-7235. *Fax:* 912-262-3072. *E-mail:* admiss@cgcc.edu.

COLUMBUS TECHNICAL COLLEGE
Columbus, Georgia   **www.columbustech.edu**

- **State-supported** 2-year, founded 1961, part of Georgia Department of Technical and Adult Education
- **Urban** campus with easy access to Atlanta
- **Coed,** 3,327 undergraduate students, 38% full-time, 64% women, 36% men

Undergraduates 1,267 full-time, 2,060 part-time. Students come from 9 states and territories, 46% African American, 2% Asian American or Pacific Islander, 3% Hispanic American, 0.6% Native American, 0.1% international.

Freshmen *Admission:* 623 enrolled.

Faculty *Total:* 230, 33% full-time.

Majors Accounting; administrative assistant and secretarial science; automobile/automotive mechanics technology; child development; computer engineering related; computer systems networking and telecommunications; dental hygiene; diagnostic medical sonography and ultrasound technology; drafting and design technology; electrical, electronic and communications engineering technology; emergency medical technology (EMT paramedic); health information/medical records technology; horticultural science; industrial technology; information science/studies; machine tool technology; mechanical engineering/mechanical technology; medical office management; medical radiologic technology; nursing (registered nurse training); pharmacy technician; respiratory therapy technician; surgical technology; web page, digital/multimedia and information resources design.

Academics *Calendar:* quarters. *Degree:* certificates, diplomas, and associate. *Special study options:* academic remediation for entering students, adult/continuing education programs, advanced placement credit, distance learning, internships, part-time degree program, services for LD students.

Library Columbus Technical College Library with 26,072 titles, 49 serial subscriptions, 533 audiovisual materials.

Student Life *Housing:* college housing not available. *Campus security:* security patrols during class hours.

Standardized Tests *Required:* ACT COMPASS or ASSET (for admission).

Costs (2006–07) *Tuition:* state resident $1116 full-time, $31 per credit hour part-time; nonresident $2232 full-time, $62 per credit hour part-time. Full-time tuition and fees vary according to course load and program. Part-time tuition and fees vary according to course load and program. *Required fees:* $246 full-time. *Waivers:* senior citizens.

Financial Aid Of all full-time matriculated undergraduates, 6 Federal Work-Study jobs (averaging $2000).

Applying *Options:* deferred entrance. *Application fee:* $20. *Required:* high school transcript.

Director of Admissions Ms. Nichole Kennedy, Admissions Director, Columbus Technical College, 928 Manchester Expressway, Columbus, GA 31904-6572. *Phone:* 706-649-1174. *Fax:* 706-649-1804. *E-mail:* nkennedy@columbustech.edu.

COOSA VALLEY TECHNICAL COLLEGE
Rome, Georgia   **www.coosavalleytech.edu/**

- **State-supported** 2-year, founded 1962, part of Georgia Department of Technical and Adult Education
- **Coed,** 2,797 undergraduate students, 43% full-time, 64% women, 36% men

Undergraduates 1,200 full-time, 1,597 part-time. 13% African American, 0.7% Asian American or Pacific Islander, 2% Hispanic American, 0.5% Native American.

Freshmen *Admission:* 634 enrolled.

Faculty *Total:* 191, 38% full-time.

Majors Accounting; child development; computer programming; criminal justice/safety; environmental engineering technology; fire science; information science/studies; marketing/marketing management; medical office management; paralegal/legal assistant; respiratory therapy technician; surgical technology; web page, digital/multimedia and information resources design.

Academics *Calendar:* quarters. *Degree:* certificates, diplomas, and associate. *Special study options:* academic remediation for entering students, advanced placement credit, distance learning, internships, services for LD students.

Student Life *Housing:* college housing not available.

Standardized Tests *Required:* ACT COMPASS or ASSET (for admission).

Costs (2006–07) *Tuition:* state resident $1116 full-time, $31 per credit hour part-time; nonresident $2232 full-time, $62 per credit hour part-time. Full-time tuition and fees vary according to course load and program. Part-time tuition and fees vary according to course load and program. *Required fees:* $243 full-time. *Waivers:* senior citizens.

Applying *Options:* deferred entrance. *Application fee:* $15. *Required:* high school transcript.

Director of Admissions Stuart Phillips, Admissions Director, Coosa Valley Technical College, One Maurice Culberson Drive, Rome, GA 30161. *Phone:* 706-624-1117. *Fax:* 706-624-1120. *E-mail:* sphillip@coosavalleytech.edu.

DARTON COLLEGE
Albany, Georgia   **www.darton.edu/**

Freshmen Application Contact Assistant Director, Admissions, Darton College, 2400 Gillionville Road, Albany, GA 31707. *Phone:* 229-430-6740. *E-mail:* darton@cavalier.dartnet.peachnet.edu.

DeKALB TECHNICAL COLLEGE
Clarkston, Georgia   **www.dekalbtech.edu/**

- **State-supported** 2-year, founded 1961, part of Georgia Department of Technical and Adult Education
- **Suburban** 17-acre campus with easy access to Atlanta
- **Coed,** 3,641 undergraduate students, 40% full-time, 63% women, 37% men

Undergraduates 1,471 full-time, 2,170 part-time. Students come from 2 states and territories, 72% African American, 4% Asian American or Pacific Islander, 2% Hispanic American, 0.3% Native American.

Freshmen *Admission:* 615 enrolled.

DeKalb Technical College (continued)

Faculty *Total:* 459, 21% full-time, 0.2% with terminal degrees. *Student/faculty ratio:* 15:1.

Majors Accounting; administrative assistant and secretarial science; automobile/automotive mechanics technology; business/commerce; clinical/medical laboratory technology; computer engineering technology; computer programming; computer systems networking and telecommunications; criminal justice/safety; drafting and design technology; electrical, electronic and communications engineering technology; electromechanical technology; engineering technology; heating, air conditioning and refrigeration technology; industrial technology; information science/studies; instrumentation technology; legal administrative assistant/secretary; machine tool technology; marketing/marketing management; medical/clinical assistant; medical laboratory technology; operations management; ophthalmic laboratory technology; opticianry; paralegal/legal assistant; surgical technology; telecommunications.

Academics *Calendar:* quarters. *Degree:* certificates, diplomas, and associate. *Special study options:* academic remediation for entering students, adult/continuing education programs, advanced placement credit, distance learning, internships, part-time degree program, services for LD students, summer session for credit.

Library an OPAC, a Web page.

Student Life *Housing:* college housing not available. *Activities and Organizations:* Student Government Association, Phi Beta Lambda, National Vocational-Technical Honor Society, Collegiate Secretaries International, Epsilon Delta Phi. *Campus security:* security during class hours.

Standardized Tests *Required:* ACT COMPASS or ASSET (for admission).

Costs (2006–07) *Tuition:* state resident $1116 full-time, $31 per credit hour part-time; nonresident $2232 full-time, $62 per credit hour part-time. Full-time tuition and fees vary according to course load and program. Part-time tuition and fees vary according to course load and program. *Required fees:* $291 full-time. *Waivers:* senior citizens.

Financial Aid Of all full-time matriculated undergraduates, 50 Federal Work-Study jobs (averaging $4000).

Applying *Options:* deferred entrance. *Application fee:* $15. *Required:* high school transcript.

Freshmen Application Contact Mr. Terry Richardson, Coordinator of Admissions, DeKalb Technical College, 495 North Indian Creek Drive, Clarkston, GA 30021-2397. *Phone:* 404-297-9522 Ext. 1229. *Fax:* 404-294-4234. *E-mail:* admissonsclark@dekalbtech.org.

EAST CENTRAL TECHNICAL COLLEGE

Fitzgerald, Georgia   **www.eastcentraltech.edu/**

- **State-supported** 2-year, founded 1968, part of Georgia Department of Technical and Adult Education
- **Rural** 30-acre campus
- **Coed,** 1,096 undergraduate students, 46% full-time, 66% women, 34% men

Undergraduates 508 full-time, 588 part-time. 36% African American, 1% Hispanic American, 0.1% Native American.

Freshmen *Admission:* 238 enrolled.

Faculty *Total:* 90, 52% full-time.

Majors Administrative assistant and secretarial science; child development; computer systems networking and telecommunications; criminal justice/safety; information science/studies.

Academics *Calendar:* quarters. *Degree:* certificates, diplomas, and associate. *Special study options:* academic remediation for entering students, cooperative education, distance learning, internships, services for LD students.

Student Life *Housing:* college housing not available.

Standardized Tests *Required:* ACT COMPASS or ASSET (for admission).

Costs (2006–07) *Tuition:* state resident $1116 full-time, $31 per credit hour part-time; nonresident $2232 full-time, $62 per credit hour part-time. Full-time tuition and fees vary according to course load and program. Part-time tuition and fees vary according to course load and program. *Required fees:* $264 full-time. *Waivers:* senior citizens.

Applying *Options:* deferred entrance. *Application fee:* $15. *Required:* high school transcript.

Director of Admissions Ms. Connie Coffey, Admissions Director, East Central Technical College, 667 Perry House Road, Fitzgerald, GA 31750. *Phone:* 229-468-2033. *Fax:* 229-468-2110. *E-mail:* ccoffey@ectcollege.org.

EAST GEORGIA COLLEGE

Swainsboro, Georgia   **www.ega.edu/**

- **State-supported** 2-year, founded 1973, part of University System of Georgia
- **Rural** 207-acre campus
- **Endowment** $32,500
- **Coed,** 1,318 undergraduate students, 67% full-time, 60% women, 40% men

Undergraduates 887 full-time, 431 part-time. Students come from 12 states and territories, 3 other countries, 1% are from out of state, 32% African American, 0.8% Asian American or Pacific Islander, 1% Hispanic American, 0.3% Native American, 1% transferred in.

Freshmen *Admission:* 758 applied, 493 admitted, 479 enrolled. *Average high school GPA:* 2.5. *Test scores:* SAT verbal scores over 500: 27%; SAT math scores over 500: 21%; SAT verbal scores over 600: 5%; SAT math scores over 600: 3%; SAT verbal scores over 700: 1%.

Faculty *Total:* 61, 54% full-time, 21% with terminal degrees. *Student/faculty ratio:* 23:1.

Majors Agriculture; anthropology; art; biology/biological sciences; business administration and management; business teacher education; chemistry; criminal justice/law enforcement administration; education; elementary education; English; family and consumer sciences/home economics teacher education; geology/earth science; health teacher education; history; liberal arts and sciences/liberal studies; mathematics; nursing (registered nurse training); parks, recreation and leisure; physical education teaching and coaching; political science and government; psychology; sociology.

Academics *Calendar:* semesters. *Degree:* certificates and associate. *Special study options:* academic remediation for entering students, adult/continuing education programs, advanced placement credit, distance learning, honors programs, independent study, off-campus study, part-time degree program, services for LD students, study abroad, summer session for credit.

Library East Georgia College Library with 43,780 titles, 203 serial subscriptions, an OPAC, a Web page.

Student Life *Housing:* college housing not available. *Activities and Organizations:* drama/theater group, student-run newspaper, choral group, Hoopee Bird, student government, yearbook, Gamma Beta Phi, Wiregrass. *Campus security:* 24-hour patrols. *Student services:* personal/psychological counseling.

Athletics *Intramural sports:* archery M/W, badminton M/W, basketball M/W, cheerleading M/W, cross-country running M/W, football M/W, golf M/W, softball M/W, table tennis M/W, tennis M/W, volleyball M/W, weight lifting M/W, wrestling M.

Costs (2006–07) *Tuition:* state resident $1756 full-time; nonresident $6564 full-time.

Financial Aid Of all full-time matriculated undergraduates, 43 Federal Work-Study jobs (averaging $1560).

Applying *Options:* early admission, deferred entrance. *Application fee:* $20. *Required:* high school transcript. *Application deadlines:* rolling (freshmen), rolling (transfers). *Notification:* continuous (freshmen), continuous (transfers).

Freshmen Application Contact Ms. Linda Connelly, Office Coordinator, East Georgia College, 131 College Circle, Swainsboro, GA 30401. *Phone:* 478-289-2019.

EMORY UNIVERSITY, OXFORD COLLEGE

Oxford, Georgia   **www.emory.edu/OXFORD/**

- **Independent Methodist** 2-year, founded 1836, part of Emory University
- **Small-town** 150-acre campus with easy access to Atlanta
- **Endowment** $26.0 million
- **Coed,** 554 undergraduate students, 100% full-time, 59% women, 41% men

Undergraduates 554 full-time. Students come from 29 states and territories, 7 other countries, 45% are from out of state, 12% African American, 21% Asian American or Pacific Islander, 4% Hispanic American, 0.4% Native American, 3% international, 0.5% transferred in, 95% live on campus. *Retention:* 83% of 2003 full-time freshmen returned.

Freshmen *Admission:* 1,421 applied, 1,030 admitted, 248 enrolled. *Average high school GPA:* 3.5. *Test scores:* SAT verbal scores over 500: 93%; SAT math scores over 500: 98%; ACT scores over 18: 99%; SAT verbal scores over 600: 54%; SAT math scores over 600: 63%; ACT scores over 24: 75%; SAT verbal scores over 700: 15%; SAT math scores over 700: 13%; ACT scores over 30: 13%.

Faculty *Total:* 54, 80% full-time, 81% with terminal degrees. *Student/faculty ratio:* 10:1.

Majors Liberal arts and sciences/liberal studies.

Academics *Calendar:* semesters. *Degree:* associate. *Special study options:* advanced placement credit, distance learning, double majors, independent study, internships, off-campus study, services for LD students, study abroad, summer session for credit.

Library Hoke O'Kelly Library with 80,099 titles, 240 serial subscriptions, 656 audiovisual materials, an OPAC, a Web page.

Student Life *Housing:* on-campus residence required through sophomore year. *Options:* coed, women-only. Campus housing is university owned. Freshman campus housing is guaranteed. *Activities and Organizations:* drama/theater group, student-run newspaper, choral group, Residence Hall Association, intramurals/junior varsity sports, Student Government Association, Student Admissions Association, Volunteer Oxford. *Campus security:* 24-hour emergency response devices and patrols, student patrols, late-night transport/escort service, controlled dormitory access. *Student services:* health clinic, personal/psychological counseling.

Athletics Member NJCAA. *Intercollegiate sports:* basketball M, soccer W, tennis M/W. *Intramural sports:* badminton M/W, basketball M/W, cross-country running M/W, football M/W, soccer M/W, softball M/W, swimming and diving M/W, tennis M/W, ultimate Frisbee M/W, volleyball M/W, water polo M/W.

Standardized Tests *Required:* SAT or ACT (for admission). *Required for some:* SAT Subject Tests (for admission).

Financial Aid Of all full-time matriculated undergraduates, 225 Federal Work-Study jobs (averaging $1600).

Applying *Options:* electronic application, early admission, early action, deferred entrance. *Application fee:* $40. *Required:* essay or personal statement, high school transcript, 1 letter of recommendation, level of interest. *Required for some:* interview. *Recommended:* minimum 3.0 GPA, 2 letters of recommendation. *Application deadlines:* 2/1 (freshmen), rolling (transfers), 11/15 (early action). *Notification:* continuous (freshmen), continuous (transfers), 1/3 (early action).

Director of Admissions Ms. Jennifer B. Taylor, Dean of Admission and Financial Aid, Emory University, Oxford College, 100 Hamill Street, PO Box 1418, Oxford, GA 30054. *Phone:* 770-784-8328. *Toll-free phone:* 800-723-8328.

FLINT RIVER TECHNICAL COLLEGE

Thomaston, Georgia   www.flintrivertech.edu/

- **State-supported** 2-year, founded 1961, part of Georgia Department of Technical and Adult Education
- **Coed,** 890 undergraduate students, 51% full-time, 73% women, 27% men

Undergraduates 455 full-time, 435 part-time. 52% African American, 0.4% Asian American or Pacific Islander, 0.1% Hispanic American.

Freshmen *Admission:* 227 enrolled.

Faculty *Total:* 88, 33% full-time.

Majors Accounting; administrative assistant and secretarial science; child development; computer and information systems security; computer systems networking and telecommunications; criminal justice/safety; electrical, electronic and communications engineering technology; information science/studies; manufacturing technology; medical laboratory technology; web page, digital/multimedia and information resources design.

Academics *Calendar:* quarters. *Degree:* certificates, diplomas, and associate. *Special study options:* academic remediation for entering students, advanced placement credit, cooperative education, distance learning, internships, services for LD students.

Library 2,653 titles, 82 serial subscriptions, 202 audiovisual materials.

Student Life *Housing:* college housing not available.

Standardized Tests *Required:* ACT COMPASS or ASSET (for admission).

Costs (2006–07) *Tuition:* state resident $1116 full-time, $31 per credit hour part-time; nonresident $2232 full-time, $62 per credit hour part-time. Full-time tuition and fees vary according to course load and program. Part-time tuition and fees vary according to course load and program. *Required fees:* $243 full-time. *Waivers:* senior citizens.

Applying *Options:* deferred entrance. *Application fee:* $15. *Required:* high school transcript.

Director of Admissions Mr. Gary Williams, Admissions Director, Flint River Technical College, 1533 US Highway 19 South, Thomaston, GA 30286-4752. *Phone:* 706-646-6148. *Toll-free phone:* 800-752-9681. *Fax:* 706-646-6152. *E-mail:* gwilliams@flintrivertech.edu.

GAINESVILLE COLLEGE

Oakwood, Georgia   www.gc.peachnet.edu/

- **State-supported** primarily 2-year, founded 1964, part of University System of Georgia
- **Small-town** 220-acre campus with easy access to Atlanta
- **Endowment** $9.2 million
- **Coed**

Undergraduates Students come from 22 states and territories, 12 other countries, 4% are from out of state, 4% African American, 2% Asian American or Pacific Islander, 4% Hispanic American, 0.4% Native American, 2% international.

Faculty *Student/faculty ratio:* 24:1.

Academics *Calendar:* semesters. *Degrees:* associate and bachelor's. *Special study options:* academic remediation for entering students, adult/continuing education programs, advanced placement credit, distance learning, double majors, English as a second language, honors programs, internships, off-campus study, part-time degree program, services for LD students, summer session for credit.

Student Life *Campus security:* 24-hour patrols.

Standardized Tests *Recommended:* SAT or ACT (for admission).

Costs (2007–08) *Tuition:* state resident $1872 full-time, $78 per credit hour part-time; nonresident $7488 full-time, $312 per credit hour part-time. *Required fees:* $180 full-time, $80 per term part-time.

Financial Aid Of all full-time matriculated undergraduates, 40 Federal Work-Study jobs (averaging $2000). *Financial aid deadline:* 6/1.

Applying *Options:* early admission. *Application fee:* $35. *Required:* high school transcript.

Freshmen Application Contact Mr. W. Mack Palmour, Director of Admissions, Gainesville College, PO Box 1358, Gainesville, GA 30503. *Phone:* 678-717-3641. *Fax:* 678-717-3751. *E-mail:* mpalmour@gsc.edu.

GEORGIA AVIATION & TECHNICAL COLLEGE

Eastman, Georgia   www.gavtc.org/

- **State-supported** 2-year, founded 1995, part of Georgia Department of Technical and Adult Education
- **Coed,** 248 undergraduate students, 65% full-time, 12% women, 88% men

Undergraduates 161 full-time, 87 part-time. 14% African American, 1% Hispanic American, 2% Native American.

Freshmen *Admission:* 51 enrolled.

Faculty *Total:* 23, 100% full-time.

Majors Airline pilot and flight crew; air traffic control; aviation/airway management.

Academics *Calendar:* quarters. *Degree:* certificates, diplomas, and associate. *Special study options:* academic remediation for entering students, advanced placement credit, cooperative education, distance learning, internships, services for LD students.

Student Life *Housing:* college housing not available.

Standardized Tests *Required:* ACT COMPASS or ASSET (for admission).

Costs (2006–07) *Tuition:* state resident $1116 full-time, $31 per credit hour part-time; nonresident $2232 full-time, $62 per credit hour part-time. Full-time tuition and fees vary according to course load and program. Part-time tuition and fees vary according to course load and program. *Required fees:* $293 full-time. *Waivers:* senior citizens.

Applying *Options:* deferred entrance. *Application fee:* $15. *Required:* high school transcript.

Director of Admissions Teresa Spires, Georgia Aviation & Technical College, 71 Airport Road - Heart of Georgia Regional Airport, Eastman, GA 31023. *Phone:* 478-374-6980. *Fax:* 478-374-6641. *E-mail:* tspires@gaaviationtech.edu.

GEORGIA HIGHLANDS COLLEGE

Rome, Georgia   www.highlands.edu/

- **State-supported** 2-year, founded 1970, part of University System of Georgia
- **Small-town** 226-acre campus with easy access to Atlanta
- **Endowment** $469,616
- **Coed,** 3,933 undergraduate students, 55% full-time, 64% women, 36% men

Georgia Highlands College (continued)

Undergraduates 2,175 full-time, 1,758 part-time. Students come from 27 states and territories, 4% are from out of state, 11% African American, 2% Asian American or Pacific Islander, 3% Hispanic American, 0.3% Native American, 1% international, 7% transferred in.

Freshmen *Admission:* 2,079 applied, 1,739 admitted, 1,076 enrolled. *Average high school GPA:* 2.7.

Faculty *Total:* 251, 34% full-time, 17% with terminal degrees. *Student/faculty ratio:* 25:1.

Majors Accounting; agriculture; art; automobile/automotive mechanics technology; biological and physical sciences; business administration and management; clinical laboratory science/medical technology; computer programming; criminal justice/police science; criminal justice/safety; dental hygiene; economics; electrical, electronic and communications engineering technology; emergency medical technology (EMT paramedic); English; foreign languages and literatures; forestry; geology/earth science; history; horticultural science; hotel/motel administration; human services; information science/studies; journalism; kindergarten/preschool education; legal assistant/paralegal; liberal arts and sciences/liberal studies; marketing/marketing management; nursing (registered nurse training); occupational therapy; philosophy; physical therapist assistant; physical therapy; physician assistant; political science and government; psychology; radiologic technology/science; respiratory care therapy; secondary education; sociology.

Academics *Calendar:* semesters. *Degree:* certificates, diplomas, and associate. *Special study options:* academic remediation for entering students, advanced placement credit, cooperative education, distance learning, double majors, honors programs, independent study, part-time degree program, services for LD students, study abroad, summer session for credit.

Library Georgia Highlands Library plus 2 others with 65,090 titles, 267 serial subscriptions, 9,964 audiovisual materials, an OPAC, a Web page.

Student Life *Housing:* college housing not available. *Activities and Organizations:* student-run newspaper, Floyd Association of Nursing Students, Health, Physical Education, and Recreation Club, Black Awareness Society, Political Science Association. *Campus security:* 24-hour patrols. *Student services:* personal/psychological counseling.

Athletics *Intramural sports:* basketball M/W, bowling M/W, football M/W, golf M/W, sailing M/W, soccer M/W, softball M/W, table tennis M/W, tennis M/W, ultimate Frisbee M/W, volleyball M/W, weight lifting M/W.

Costs (2006–07) *Tuition:* state resident $3208 full-time, $68 per credit hour part-time; nonresident $6416 full-time, $272 per credit hour part-time. Part-time tuition and fees vary according to course load. *Required fees:* $198 full-time, $69 per term part-time. *Waivers:* senior citizens.

Financial Aid Of all full-time matriculated undergraduates, 50 Federal Work-Study jobs (averaging $3500).

Applying *Options:* electronic application, early admission, deferred entrance. *Application fee:* $20. *Required:* high school transcript, minimum 2.0 GPA. *Required for some:* minimum 2.2 GPA, freshman index of 1830. *Application deadlines:* rolling (freshmen), rolling (transfers). *Notification:* continuous (freshmen), continuous (out-of-state freshmen), continuous (transfers).

Freshmen Application Contact Mr. Todd Jones, Director of Admissions, Georgia Highlands College, 3175 Cedartown Highway, Rome, GA 30162. *Phone:* 706-295-6339. *Toll-free phone:* 800-332-2406. *Fax:* 706-295-6610. *E-mail:* tjones@highlands.edu.

GEORGIA MEDICAL INSTITUTE–DEKALB

Atlanta, Georgia　　　　www.georgia-med.com/

Freshmen Application Contact Admissions Office, Georgia Medical Institute–DeKalb, 1706 Northeast Expressway, Atlanta, GA 30329. *Phone:* 404-327-8787.

GEORGIA MILITARY COLLEGE

Milledgeville, Georgia　　　　www.gmc.cc.ga.us/

- **State and locally supported** 2-year, founded 1879
- **Small-town** 40-acre campus
- **Coed,** 4,062 undergraduate students, 61% full-time, 58% women, 42% men

Undergraduates 2,471 full-time, 1,591 part-time. Students come from 29 states and territories, 40% African American, 2% Asian American or Pacific Islander, 3% Hispanic American, 0.4% Native American.

Freshmen *Admission:* 2,258 applied, 2,258 admitted, 984 enrolled.

Faculty *Total:* 231, 35% full-time, 3% with terminal degrees. *Student/faculty ratio:* 20:1.

Majors Army R.O.T.C./military science; biological and physical sciences; business administration and management; criminal justice/law enforcement administration; engineering; fire science; liberal arts and sciences/liberal studies; mass communication/media; nuclear/nuclear power technology; pre-engineering.

Academics *Calendar:* quarters. *Degree:* associate. *Special study options:* academic remediation for entering students, advanced placement credit, external degree program, off-campus study, part-time degree program, summer session for credit. *ROTC:* Army (b).

Library Sibley-Cone Library with 20,000 titles, 150 serial subscriptions.

Student Life *Housing:* on-campus residence required through sophomore year. *Options:* coed. *Activities and Organizations:* student-run newspaper, marching band. *Campus security:* 24-hour emergency response devices and patrols. *Student services:* personal/psychological counseling.

Athletics Member NSCAA. *Intercollegiate sports:* football M(s), riflery M(s)/W(s). *Intramural sports:* basketball M, cross-country running M/W, football M, golf M, soccer M/W, tennis M/W, track and field M/W, volleyball M/W.

Standardized Tests *Required for some:* SAT or ACT (for admission). *Recommended:* SAT or ACT (for admission).

Costs (2006–07) *Tuition:* state resident $4990 full-time.

Financial Aid Of all full-time matriculated undergraduates, 50 Federal Work-Study jobs (averaging $1421).

Applying *Options:* early admission, deferred entrance. *Application fee:* $25. *Required:* high school transcript. *Application deadlines:* rolling (freshmen), rolling (transfers).

Director of Admissions Mrs. Donna W. Findley, Director of Admissions, Georgia Military College, 201 East Greene Street, Milledgeville, GA 31061-3398. *Phone:* 478-445-2751. *Toll-free phone:* 800-342-0413.

GEORGIA PERIMETER COLLEGE

Decatur, Georgia　　　　www.gpc.edu/

Director of Admissions Doug Ruch, Director of Enrollment Management, Georgia Perimeter College, 555 North Indian Creek Drive, Clarkston, GA 30021-2396. *Phone:* 678-891-3250. *Toll-free phone:* 888-696-2780.

GORDON COLLEGE

Barnesville, Georgia　　　　www.gdn.edu/

- **State-supported** 2-year, founded 1852, part of University System of Georgia
- **Small-town** 125-acre campus with easy access to Atlanta
- **Endowment** $4.5 million
- **Coed,** 3,595 undergraduate students, 66% full-time, 64% women, 36% men

Undergraduates 2,365 full-time, 1,230 part-time. Students come from 6 states and territories, 19 other countries, 1% are from out of state, 33% African American, 2% Asian American or Pacific Islander, 2% Hispanic American, 0.1% Native American, 0.7% international, 5% transferred in, 20% live on campus.

Freshmen *Admission:* 4,117 applied, 3,738 admitted, 1,289 enrolled. *Average high school GPA:* 2.74. *Test scores:* SAT verbal scores over 500: 36%; SAT math scores over 500: 18%; ACT scores over 18: 66%; ACT scores over 24: 33%.

Faculty *Total:* 161, 60% full-time, 46% with terminal degrees. *Student/faculty ratio:* 24:1.

Majors Administrative assistant and secretarial science; agriculture; art; behavioral sciences; biological and physical sciences; biology/biological sciences; business administration and management; computer and information sciences related; computer science; dramatic/theater arts; education; English; general studies; history; information technology; journalism; mathematics; nursing (licensed practical/vocational nurse training); nursing (registered nurse training); parks, recreation and leisure; physical sciences; political science and government; psychology; sociology; Spanish.

Academics *Calendar:* semesters. *Degree:* certificates and associate. *Special study options:* academic remediation for entering students, accelerated degree program, adult/continuing education programs, advanced placement credit, cooperative education, honors programs, internships, off-campus study, part-time degree program, study abroad, summer session for credit.

Library Hightower Library with 122,918 titles, 6,682 serial subscriptions, 5,463 audiovisual materials, an OPAC, a Web page.

Student Life *Housing Options:* coed, men-only, women-only. Campus housing is university owned. *Activities and Organizations:* drama/theater group, student-run newspaper, choral group, Explorers, Minority Advisement Program, Georgia Association of Nursing Students, Baptist Student Union, Phi Beta Lambda. *Campus security:* 24-hour patrols, late-night transport/escort service. *Student services:* personal/psychological counseling.

Athletics Member NJCAA. *Intercollegiate sports:* baseball M(s), soccer M(s)/W(s), softball W(s), tennis W(s). *Intramural sports:* badminton M/W, basketball M/W, cheerleading W, football M/W, golf M/W, racquetball M/W, table tennis M/W, tennis M, volleyball M/W, wrestling M.

Standardized Tests *Required:* SAT or ACT (for admission).

Costs (2007–08) *Tuition:* state resident $1643 full-time, $71 per credit hour part-time; nonresident $6572 full-time, $264 per credit hour part-time. *Required fees:* $245 full-time, $149 per term part-time. *Room and board:* room only: $2300.

Financial Aid Of all full-time matriculated undergraduates, 75 Federal Work-Study jobs (averaging $1850).

Applying *Options:* electronic application, early admission, deferred entrance. *Application fee:* $20. *Required:* high school transcript, minimum 1.8 GPA, minimum SAT score of 830 and 15 CPC credits. *Application deadlines:* rolling (freshmen), rolling (transfers).

Freshmen Application Contact Gordon College, 419 College Drive, Barnesville, GA 30204. *Phone:* 770-358-5023. *Toll-free phone:* 800-282-6504. *Fax:* 770-358-3031. *E-mail:* gordon@gdn.edu.

GRIFFIN TECHNICAL COLLEGE

Griffin, Georgia   **www.griffintech.edu**

- **State-supported** 2-year, founded 1965, part of Georgia Department of Technical and Adult Education
- **Small-town** 10-acre campus with easy access to Atlanta
- **Coed,** 3,287 undergraduate students, 44% full-time, 65% women, 35% men

Undergraduates 1,462 full-time, 1,825 part-time. Students come from 1 other country, 38% African American, 2% Asian American or Pacific Islander, 2% Hispanic American, 0.4% Native American.

Freshmen *Admission:* 568 enrolled.

Faculty *Total:* 240, 28% full-time.

Majors Accounting; administrative assistant and secretarial science; automobile/automotive mechanics technology; business administration and management; child development; computer and information systems security; computer programming; computer systems networking and telecommunications; criminal justice/safety; drafting and design technology; electrical, electronic and communications engineering technology; emergency medical technology (EMT paramedic); heating, air conditioning and refrigeration technology; horticultural science; industrial technology; manufacturing technology; marketing/marketing management; medical radiologic technology; paralegal/legal assistant; pharmacy technician; respiratory therapy technician; surgical technology; web page, digital/multimedia and information resources design.

Academics *Calendar:* quarters. *Degree:* certificates, diplomas, and associate. *Special study options:* academic remediation for entering students, adult/continuing education programs, advanced placement credit, distance learning, honors programs, internships, part-time degree program, services for LD students.

Library Griffin Technical College Library with 12,493 titles, 188 serial subscriptions, 1,326 audiovisual materials, an OPAC, a Web page.

Student Life *Housing:* college housing not available. *Activities and Organizations:* Phi Beta Lambda, Vocational Industrial Clubs of America, student government.

Standardized Tests *Required:* ACT COMPASS or ASSET (for admission).

Costs (2006–07) *Tuition:* state resident $1116 full-time, $31 per credit hour part-time; nonresident $2232 full-time, $62 per credit hour part-time. Full-time tuition and fees vary according to course load and program. Part-time tuition and fees vary according to course load and program. *Required fees:* $243 full-time. *Waivers:* senior citizens.

Applying *Options:* deferred entrance. *Application fee:* $15. *Required:* high school transcript.

Director of Admissions Christine James-Brown, Admissions Officer, Griffin Technical College, 501 Varsity Road, Griffin, GA 30223-2042. *Phone:* 770-228-7371. *Fax:* 770-229-3227. *E-mail:* cbrown@griftec.org.

GUPTON-JONES COLLEGE OF FUNERAL SERVICE

Decatur, Georgia   **www.gupton-jones.edu/**

Freshmen Application Contact Ms. Beverly Wheaton, Registrar, Gupton-Jones College of Funeral Service, 5141 Snapfinger Woods Drive, Decatur, GA 30035. *Phone:* 770-593-2257. *Toll-free phone:* 800-848-5352.

GWINNETT TECHNICAL COLLEGE

Lawrenceville, Georgia   **www.gwinnetttech.edu/**

- **State-supported** 2-year, founded 1984, part of Georgia Department of Technical and Adult Education
- **Suburban** 93-acre campus with easy access to Atlanta
- **Coed,** 4,253 undergraduate students, 42% full-time, 56% women, 44% men

Undergraduates 1,769 full-time, 2,484 part-time. 28% African American, 6% Asian American or Pacific Islander, 6% Hispanic American, 0.3% Native American.

Freshmen *Admission:* 607 enrolled.

Faculty *Total:* 206, 34% full-time.

Majors Accounting; administrative assistant and secretarial science; automobile/automotive mechanics technology; business administration and management; computer programming; computer science; computer systems networking and telecommunications; construction management; drafting and design technology; electrical, electronic and communications engineering technology; emergency medical technology (EMT paramedic); horticultural science; hotel/motel administration; information science/studies; interior design; machine tool technology; management information systems; marketing/marketing management; medical/clinical assistant; medical radiologic technology; ornamental horticulture; photography; physical therapist assistant; physical therapy; respiratory care therapy; tourism and travel services management; veterinary/animal health technology.

Academics *Calendar:* quarters. *Degree:* certificates, diplomas, and associate. *Special study options:* academic remediation for entering students, adult/continuing education programs, advanced placement credit, distance learning, internships, part-time degree program, services for LD students, summer session for credit.

Library Gwinnett Technical Institute Media Center with 19,547 titles, 246 serial subscriptions, 2,289 audiovisual materials.

Student Life *Housing:* college housing not available. *Campus security:* patrols by campus police.

Standardized Tests *Required:* ACT COMPASS or ASSET (for admission), ACT COMPASS or ASSET (for placement).

Costs (2006–07) *Tuition:* state resident $1116 full-time, $31 per credit hour part-time; nonresident $2232 full-time, $62 per credit hour part-time. Full-time tuition and fees vary according to course load and program. Part-time tuition and fees vary according to course load and program. *Required fees:* $309 full-time. *Waivers:* senior citizens.

Financial Aid Of all full-time matriculated undergraduates, 20 Federal Work-Study jobs (averaging $2100).

Applying *Options:* deferred entrance. *Application fee:* $20. *Required:* high school transcript.

Director of Admissions Michelle McIntire, Admissions Director, Gwinnett Technical College, PO Box 1505, 5150 Sugarloaf Parkway, Lawrenceville, GA 30043-5702. *Phone:* 770-962-7580 Ext. 434. *Fax:* 770-685-1267. *E-mail:* mmcintire@gwinnett.tec.ga.us.

HEART OF GEORGIA TECHNICAL COLLEGE

Dublin, Georgia   **www.hgtc.org/**

- **State-supported** 2-year, founded 1984, part of Georgia Department of Technical and Adult Education
- **Small-town** campus with easy access to Atlanta
- **Coed,** 1,588 undergraduate students, 36% full-time, 55% women, 45% men

Undergraduates 568 full-time, 1,020 part-time. 43% African American, 0.4% Asian American or Pacific Islander, 0.7% Hispanic American, 0.6% Native American, 0.1% international.

Freshmen *Admission:* 362 enrolled.

Faculty *Total:* 186, 34% full-time.

Majors Business, management, and marketing related; child development; criminal justice/safety; electrical, electronic and communications engineering technology; health information/medical records technology; machine tool technology; marketing/marketing management; medical radiologic technology; respiratory therapy technician.

Academics *Calendar:* quarters. *Degree:* certificates, diplomas, and associate. *Special study options:* academic remediation for entering students, advanced placement credit, cooperative education, distance learning, internships, services for LD students.

Student Life *Housing:* college housing not available.

Standardized Tests *Required:* ACT COMPASS or ASSET (for admission).

Heart of Georgia Technical College (continued)

Costs (2006–07) *Tuition:* state resident $1116 full-time, $31 per credit hour part-time; nonresident $2232 full-time, $62 per credit hour part-time. Full-time tuition and fees vary according to course load and program. Part-time tuition and fees vary according to course load and program. *Required fees:* $255 full-time. *Waivers:* senior citizens.

Applying *Options:* deferred entrance. *Application fee:* $15. *Required:* high school transcript.

Director of Admissions Ms. Lisa Kelly, Director of Admissions, Heart of Georgia Technical College, 560 Pinehill Road, Dublin, GA 31021. *Phone:* 478-274-7837. *Fax:* 478-296-6113. *E-mail:* lisak@hgtc.org.

HERZING COLLEGE

Atlanta, Georgia
www.herzing.edu/atlanta/

- **Proprietary** primarily 2-year, founded 1949, part of Herzing Institutes, Inc
- **Urban** campus
- **Coed**

Undergraduates 161 full-time, 115 part-time. Students come from 5 states and territories, 73% African American, 4% Asian American or Pacific Islander, 3% Hispanic American, 0.7% Native American.

Faculty *Student/faculty ratio:* 8:1.

Academics *Calendar:* semesters. *Degrees:* certificates, diplomas, associate, and bachelor's. *Special study options:* academic remediation for entering students, English as a second language, honors programs, internships.

Student Life *Campus security:* 24-hour patrols.

Standardized Tests *Required:* Wonderlic aptitude test (for admission).

Costs (2006–07) *Tuition:* $11,200 full-time, $350 per credit hour part-time. *Required fees:* $125 full-time, $30 per credit hour part-time, $25 per term part-time.

Applying *Application fee:* $25. *Required:* high school transcript, interview.

Freshmen Application Contact Mrs. Rose White, Director of Admissions, Herzing College, 3355 Lenox Road, Suite 100, Atlanta, GA 30326. *Phone:* 404-816-4533. *Toll-free phone:* 800-573-4533. *Fax:* 404-816-5576. *E-mail:* info@ath.herzing.edu.

HIGH-TECH INSTITUTE

Marietta, Georgia
www.high-techinstitute.com/

Director of Admissions Frank Webster, Office Manager, High-Tech Institute, 1090 Northchase Parkway, Suite 150, Marietta, GA 30067. *Phone:* 770-988-9877. *Toll-free phone:* 800-987-0110. *Fax:* 770-988-8824. *E-mail:* ckusema@hightechschools.com.

INTERACTIVE COLLEGE OF TECHNOLOGY

Chamblee, Georgia
www.ict-ils.edu/

- **Proprietary** 2-year, part of Interactive Learning Systems
- **Coed**

Undergraduates 1,063 full-time, 6 part-time. Students come from 3 states and territories, 80 other countries.

Faculty *Student/faculty ratio:* 18:1.

Academics *Degree:* certificates, diplomas, and associate. *Special study options:* academic remediation for entering students, accelerated degree program, adult/continuing education programs, advanced placement credit, double majors, English as a second language, independent study, internships, part-time degree program.

Costs (2006–07) *Tuition:* $6480 full-time.

Applying *Application fee:* $50. *Required:* high school transcript. *Recommended:* high school transcript, interview.

Freshmen Application Contact Ms. Nicole Caruso, Associate Dean of Admissions, Interactive College of Technology, 5303 New Peachtree Road, Chamblee, GA 30341. *Phone:* 770-216-2960. *Toll-free phone:* 800-550-3475. *Fax:* 770-216-2989.

ITT TECHNICAL INSTITUTE

Duluth, Georgia
www.itt-tech.edu/

- **Proprietary** primarily 2-year, founded 2003, part of ITT Educational Services, Inc
- **Coed**

Majors Animation, interactive technology, video graphics and special effects; CAD/CADD drafting/design technology; computer and information systems security; computer engineering technology; computer systems networking and telecommunications; criminal justice/law enforcement administration; electrical, electronic and communications engineering technology; web page, digital/multimedia and information resources design.

Academics *Calendar:* quarters. *Degrees:* associate and bachelor's.

Library a Web page.

Student Life *Housing:* college housing not available.

Standardized Tests *Required:* Wonderlic aptitude test (for admission).

Costs (2006–07) *Tuition:* Contact school for program costs.

Applying *Options:* deferred entrance. *Application fee:* $100. *Required:* high school transcript, interview. *Recommended:* letters of recommendation. *Application deadlines:* rolling (freshmen), rolling (transfers). *Notification:* continuous (freshmen), continuous (transfers).

Freshmen Application Contact Mr. Paul Curry, Director of Recruitment, ITT Technical Institute, 10700 Abbotts Bridge Road, Suite 190, Duluth, GA 30097. *Phone:* 678-957-8510. *Toll-free phone:* 866-489-8818.

ITT TECHNICAL INSTITUTE

Kennesaw, Georgia
www.itt-tech.edu/

- **Proprietary** primarily 2-year, founded 2004, part of ITT Educational Services, Inc
- **Coed**

Majors CAD/CADD drafting/design technology; computer engineering technology; computer systems networking and telecommunications; criminal justice/law enforcement administration; web page, digital/multimedia and information resources design.

Academics *Calendar:* quarters. *Degrees:* associate and bachelor's.

Standardized Tests *Required:* Wonderlic aptitude test (for admission).

Costs (2006–07) *Tuition:* Contact school for program costs.

Applying *Application fee:* $100. *Required:* high school transcript, interview. *Recommended:* letters of recommendation. *Application deadlines:* rolling (freshmen), rolling (transfers). *Notification:* continuous (freshmen), continuous (transfers).

Freshmen Application Contact Mr. Carmichael James, Director of Recruitment, ITT Technical Institute, 1000 Cobb Place Boulevard NW, Kennesaw, GA 30144. *Phone:* 770-426-2300.

LANIER TECHNICAL COLLEGE

Oakwood, Georgia
www.laniertech.edu/

- **State-supported** 2-year, founded 1964, part of Georgia Department of Technical and Adult Education
- **Coed**, 3,145 undergraduate students, 37% full-time, 66% women, 34% men

Undergraduates 1,157 full-time, 1,988 part-time. 11% African American, 2% Asian American or Pacific Islander, 5% Hispanic American, 0.2% Native American.

Freshmen *Admission:* 769 enrolled.

Faculty *Total:* 262, 27% full-time.

Majors Accounting; administrative assistant and secretarial science; banking and financial support services; child development; computer and information systems security; computer programming; computer science; computer systems networking and telecommunications; criminal justice/safety; drafting and design technology; electrical, electronic and communications engineering technology; fire science; health professions related; industrial technology; information science/studies; interior design; marketing/marketing management; medical laboratory technology; medical radiologic technology; occupational safety and health technology; surgical technology; web page, digital/multimedia and information resources design.

Academics *Calendar:* quarters. *Degree:* certificates, diplomas, and associate. *Special study options:* academic remediation for entering students, advanced placement credit, distance learning, services for LD students.

Library 7,096 titles, 154 serial subscriptions, 570 audiovisual materials.

Student Life *Housing:* college housing not available.

Standardized Tests *Required:* ACT COMPASS or ASSET (for admission).

Costs (2006–07) *Tuition:* state resident $1116 full-time, $31 per credit hour part-time; nonresident $2232 full-time, $62 per credit hour part-time. Full-time tuition and fees vary according to course load and program. Part-time tuition and fees vary according to course load and program. *Required fees:* $270 full-time. *Waivers:* senior citizens.

Applying *Options:* deferred entrance. *Application fee:* $15. *Required:* high school transcript.

Freshmen Application Contact Mr. Mike Marlowe, Admissions Director, Lanier Technical College, 2990 Landrum Education Drive, Oakwood, GA 30566. *Phone:* -531-6333. *Fax:* 770-531-6328.

LE CORDON BLEU COLLEGE OF CULINARY ARTS, ATLANTA

Tucker, Georgia www.atlantaculinary.com/

- **Proprietary** 2-year
- **Coed,** 763 undergraduate students

Majors Cooking and related culinary arts.

Academics *Degree:* associate.

Costs (2006–07) *Tuition:* $36,000 per degree program part-time.

Applying *Application fee:* $50.

Freshmen Application Contact Admissions Office, Le Cordon Bleu College of Culinary Arts, Atlanta, 1957 Lakeside Parkway, Tucker, GA 30084. *Toll-free phone:* 888-549-8222.

MIDDLE GEORGIA COLLEGE

Cochran, Georgia www.mgc.edu/

- **State-supported** 2-year, founded 1884, part of University System of Georgia
- **Small-town** 165-acre campus
- **Endowment** $951,987
- **Coed,** 3,051 undergraduate students, 67% full-time, 59% women, 41% men

Middle Georgia College is a small, residential public college with a student population of approximately 3,000. Transfer programs are offered in more than 100 academic disciplines, including business, education, engineering, and nursing. A Bachelor of Science degree is offered in aviation management. Numerous clubs and organizations enrich student life.

Undergraduates 2,050 full-time, 1,001 part-time. Students come from 19 states and territories, 9 other countries, 3% are from out of state, 38% African American, 0.6% Asian American or Pacific Islander, 1% Hispanic American, 0.1% Native American, 0.5% international, 5% transferred in, 33% live on campus.

Freshmen *Admission:* 2,642 applied, 2,199 admitted, 1,162 enrolled. *Average high school GPA:* 2.77.

Faculty *Total:* 131, 61% full-time, 26% with terminal degrees. *Student/faculty ratio:* 25:1.

Majors Business administration and management; computer and information sciences related; computer engineering related; computer/information technology services administration related; computer science; criminal justice/police science; data processing and data processing technology; fashion merchandising; information science/studies; liberal arts and sciences/liberal studies; nursing (registered nurse training); occupational therapist assistant; physical therapist assistant; public administration; survey technology.

Academics *Calendar:* semesters. *Degree:* certificates and associate. *Special study options:* academic remediation for entering students, accelerated degree program, advanced placement credit, cooperative education, distance learning, honors programs, internships, part-time degree program, student-designed majors, study abroad, summer session for credit.

Library Roberts Memorial Library with 105,568 titles, 220 serial subscriptions, 1,000 audiovisual materials, an OPAC, a Web page.

Student Life *Housing:* on-campus residence required through sophomore year. *Options:* men-only, women-only. Campus housing is university owned. Freshman campus housing is guaranteed. *Activities and Organizations:* drama/theater group, student-run newspaper, choral group, marching band, Baptist Student Union, Student Government Association, MGC Ambassadors, Encore Productions, United Voices of Praise. *Campus security:* 24-hour emergency response

devices and patrols, late-night transport/escort service, controlled dormitory access, patrols by police officers. *Student services:* health clinic, personal/psychological counseling.

Athletics Member NJCAA. *Intercollegiate sports:* baseball M(s), basketball M(s)/W(s), soccer M(s)/W(s), softball W(s). *Intramural sports:* badminton M/W, basketball M/W, football M/W, golf M/W, softball M/W, swimming and diving M/W, tennis M/W.

Costs (2007–08) *Tuition:* state resident $1604 full-time, $68 per credit hour part-time; nonresident $6412 full-time, $268 per credit hour part-time. *Required fees:* $374 full-time. *Room and board:* $4500; room only: $2200.

Financial Aid Of all full-time matriculated undergraduates, 91 Federal Work-Study jobs (averaging $692).

Applying *Options:* electronic application, early admission, deferred entrance. *Application fee:* $20. *Required:* high school transcript, minimum 2.0 GPA. *Required for some:* essay or personal statement, minimum 3.5 GPA, letters of recommendation, interview. *Application deadlines:* rolling (freshmen), rolling (transfers). *Notification:* continuous (freshmen), continuous (transfers).

Freshmen Application Contact Ms. Jennifer Brannon, Director of Admissions, Middle Georgia College, 1100 2nd Street, SE, Cochran, GA 31014. *Phone:* 478-934-3103. *Fax:* 478-934-3403. *E-mail:* admissions@mgc.edu.

MIDDLE GEORGIA TECHNICAL COLLEGE

Warner Robbins, Georgia www.middlegatech.edu/

- **State-supported** 2-year, founded 1973, part of Georgia Department of Technical and Adult Education
- **Coed,** 2,577 undergraduate students, 53% full-time, 54% women, 46% men

Undergraduates 1,361 full-time, 1,216 part-time. 34% African American, 2% Asian American or Pacific Islander, 2% Hispanic American, 0.1% Native American.

Freshmen *Admission:* 816 enrolled.

Faculty *Total:* 235, 47% full-time.

Majors Accounting; administrative assistant and secretarial science; airframe mechanics and aircraft maintenance technology; child development; computer systems networking and telecommunications; dental hygiene; drafting and design technology; information science/studies; marketing/marketing management; medical radiologic technology; web page, digital/multimedia and information resources design.

Academics *Calendar:* quarters. *Degree:* certificates, diplomas, and associate. *Special study options:* academic remediation for entering students, advanced placement credit, cooperative education, distance learning, internships, services for LD students.

Library 2,124 titles, 69 serial subscriptions, 211 audiovisual materials.

Student Life *Housing:* college housing not available.

Standardized Tests *Required:* ACT COMPASS or ASSET (for admission).

Costs (2006–07) *Tuition:* state resident $1116 full-time, $31 per credit hour part-time; nonresident $2232 full-time, $62 per credit hour part-time. Full-time tuition and fees vary according to course load and program. Part-time tuition and fees vary according to course load and program. *Required fees:* $243 full-time. *Waivers:* senior citizens.

Applying *Options:* deferred entrance. *Application fee:* $15. *Required:* high school transcript.

Director of Admissions Craig B. Jackson, Director of Admissions, Middle Georgia Technical College, 80 Cohen Walker Drive, Warner Robins, GA 31088. *Phone:* 478-988-6843. *Toll-free phone:* 800-474-1031. *Fax:* 478-988-6813. *E-mail:* cjackson@middlegatech.edu.

MOULTRIE TECHNICAL COLLEGE

Moultrie, Georgia www.moultrietech.edu/

- **State-supported** 2-year, founded 1964, part of Georgia Department of Technical and Adult Education
- **Coed,** 2,020 undergraduate students, 43% full-time, 64% women, 36% men

Undergraduates 878 full-time, 1,142 part-time. 33% African American, 0.2% Asian American or Pacific Islander, 3% Hispanic American, 0.2% Native American.

Freshmen *Admission:* 419 enrolled.

Faculty *Total:* 96, 49% full-time.

Majors Accounting; administrative assistant and secretarial science; child development; civil engineering technology; computer systems networking and telecommunications; criminal justice/safety; electrical, electronic and communi-

Moultrie Technical College (continued)

cations engineering technology; information science/studies; marketing/marketing management; web page, digital/multimedia and information resources design.

Academics *Calendar:* quarters. *Degree:* certificates, diplomas, and associate. *Special study options:* academic remediation for entering students, advanced placement credit, distance learning, internships, services for LD students.

Student Life *Housing:* college housing not available.

Standardized Tests *Required:* ACT COMPASS or ASSET (for admission).

Costs (2006–07) *Tuition:* state resident $1116 full-time, $31 per credit hour part-time; nonresident $2232 full-time, $62 per credit hour part-time. Full-time tuition and fees vary according to course load and program. Part-time tuition and fees vary according to course load and program. *Required fees:* $243 full-time. *Waivers:* senior citizens.

Applying *Options:* deferred entrance. *Application fee:* $15. *Required:* high school transcript.

Director of Admissions Leigh Wallace, Admissions Director, Moultrie Technical College, 800 Veterans Parkway North, Moultrie, GA 31788. *Phone:* 229-217-4144. *Fax:* 229-891-7010. *E-mail:* lwallace@moultrietech.edu.

NORTH GEORGIA TECHNICAL COLLEGE

Clarkesville, Georgia   www.northgatech.edu/

- **State-supported** 2-year, founded 1943, part of Georgia Department of Technical and Adult Education
- **Coed,** 1,905 undergraduate students, 59% full-time, 62% women, 38% men

Undergraduates 1,127 full-time, 778 part-time. 6% African American, 1% Asian American or Pacific Islander, 1% Hispanic American, 0.2% Native American.

Freshmen *Admission:* 532 enrolled.

Faculty *Total:* 189, 36% full-time.

Majors Administrative assistant and secretarial science; computer systems networking and telecommunications; criminal justice/safety; culinary arts; heating, air conditioning and refrigeration technology; horticultural science; industrial technology; medical laboratory technology; parks, recreation and leisure facilities management; turf and turfgrass management; web page, digital/multimedia and information resources design.

Academics *Calendar:* quarters. *Degree:* certificates, diplomas, and associate. *Special study options:* academic remediation for entering students, advanced placement credit, distance learning, internships, services for LD students.

Library 15,684 titles, 162 serial subscriptions, 990 audiovisual materials.

Standardized Tests *Required:* ACT COMPASS or ASSET (for admission).

Costs (2006–07) *Tuition:* state resident $1116 full-time, $31 per credit hour part-time; nonresident $2232 full-time, $62 per credit hour part-time. Full-time tuition and fees vary according to course load and program. Part-time tuition and fees vary according to course load and program. *Required fees:* $285 full-time. *Room and board:* $2925; room only: $645. *Waivers:* senior citizens.

Applying *Options:* deferred entrance. *Application fee:* $15. *Required:* high school transcript.

Director of Admissions Gail Taylor, Admissions Director, North Georgia Technical College, PO Box 65, 1500 Georgia Highway 197, Clarkesville, GA 30523. *Phone:* 706-754-7724. *Fax:* 706-754-7777. *E-mail:* gtaylor@northgatech.edu.

NORTH METRO TECHNICAL COLLEGE

Acworth, Georgia   www.northmetrotech.edu/

- **State-supported** 2-year, founded 1989, part of Georgia Department of Technical and Adult Education
- **Coed,** 1,928 undergraduate students, 39% full-time, 65% women, 35% men

Undergraduates 754 full-time, 1,174 part-time. 19% African American, 1% Asian American or Pacific Islander, 3% Hispanic American, 0.5% Native American, 0.1% international.

Freshmen *Admission:* 368 enrolled.

Faculty *Total:* 110, 31% full-time.

Majors Accounting; administrative assistant and secretarial science; child development; computer systems networking and telecommunications; design and visual communications; electrical, electronic and communications engineering technology; horticultural science; marketing/marketing management; medical radiologic technology; web page, digital/multimedia and information resources design.

Academics *Calendar:* quarters. *Degree:* certificates, diplomas, and associate. *Special study options:* academic remediation for entering students, advanced placement credit, distance learning, internships, services for LD students.

Student Life *Housing:* college housing not available.

Standardized Tests *Required:* ACT COMPASS or ASSET (for admission).

Costs (2006–07) *Tuition:* state resident $1116 full-time, $31 per credit hour part-time; nonresident $2232 full-time, $62 per credit hour part-time. Full-time tuition and fees vary according to course load and program. Part-time tuition and fees vary according to course load and program. *Required fees:* $243 full-time. *Waivers:* senior citizens.

Applying *Options:* deferred entrance. *Application fee:* $15. *Required:* high school transcript.

Director of Admissions Missy Cusack, Admissions Director, North Metro Technical College, 5198 Ross Road, Acworth, GA 30102-3012. *Phone:* 770-975-4079. *Fax:* 770-975-4142. *E-mail:* mcusack@northmetrotech.edu.

NORTHWESTERN TECHNICAL COLLEGE

Rock Springs, Georgia   www.northwesterntech.edu/

- **State-supported** 2-year, founded 1966, part of Georgia Department of Technical and Adult Education
- **Rural** campus
- **Coed,** 2,350 undergraduate students, 41% full-time, 69% women, 31% men

Undergraduates 965 full-time, 1,385 part-time. Students come from 3 states and territories, 4% African American, 0.5% Asian American or Pacific Islander, 0.9% Hispanic American, 0.7% Native American.

Freshmen *Admission:* 320 enrolled.

Faculty *Total:* 110, 45% full-time.

Majors Accounting; administrative assistant and secretarial science; automobile/automotive mechanics technology; cardiovascular technology; child development; computer systems networking and telecommunications; criminal justice/safety; drafting and design technology; electrical, electronic and communications engineering technology; health information/medical records technology; information science/studies; nursing (registered nurse training); occupational therapist assistant; pharmacy technician; social work; surgical technology; web page, digital/multimedia and information resources design.

Academics *Calendar:* quarters. *Degree:* certificates, diplomas, and associate. *Special study options:* academic remediation for entering students, adult/continuing education programs, advanced placement credit, distance learning, internships, part-time degree program, services for LD students, summer session for credit.

Library Northwestern Technical Institute Library with 350,000 titles, 180 serial subscriptions, 20,000 audiovisual materials, an OPAC, a Web page.

Student Life *Housing:* college housing not available.

Standardized Tests *Required:* ACT COMPASS or ASSET (for admission).

Costs (2006–07) *Tuition:* state resident $1116 full-time, $31 per credit hour part-time; nonresident $2232 full-time, $62 per credit hour part-time. Full-time tuition and fees vary according to course load and program. Part-time tuition and fees vary according to course load and program. *Required fees:* $243 full-time. *Waivers:* senior citizens.

Financial Aid Of all full-time matriculated undergraduates, 30 Federal Work-Study jobs (averaging $4800).

Applying *Options:* deferred entrance. *Application fee:* $15. *Required:* high school transcript.

Director of Admissions Mrs. Carolyn Solmon, Director of Admissions and Career Planning, Northwestern Technical College, 265 Bicentennial Trail, PO Box 569, Rock Spring, GA 30739. *Phone:* 706-764-3511. *Toll-free phone:* 800-735-5726. *Fax:* 706-764-3707. *E-mail:* csolmon@northwesterntech.edu.

OGEECHEE TECHNICAL COLLEGE

Statesboro, Georgia   www.ogeecheetech.edu

- **State-supported** 2-year, founded 1989, part of Georgia Department of Technical and Adult Education
- **Small-town** campus
- **Coed,** 1,951 undergraduate students, 47% full-time, 67% women, 33% men

Undergraduates 923 full-time, 1,028 part-time. 32% African American, 0.8% Asian American or Pacific Islander, 1% Hispanic American, 0.4% Native American.

Freshmen *Admission:* 374 enrolled.

Faculty *Total:* 142, 51% full-time.

Majors Accounting; administrative assistant and secretarial science; agribusiness; automobile/automotive mechanics technology; banking and financial support services; child development; computer systems networking and telecommunications; construction trades; culinary arts; dental hygiene; forestry technology; funeral service and mortuary science; health information/medical records technology; hotel and restaurant management; information science/studies; interior design; marketing/marketing management; opticianry; paralegal/legal assistant; tourism and travel services management; veterinary technology; water quality and wastewater treatment management and recycling technology; wildlife and wildlands science and management; wood science and wood products/pulp and paper technology.

Academics *Calendar:* quarters. *Degree:* certificates, diplomas, and associate. *Special study options:* academic remediation for entering students, advanced placement credit, distance learning, internships, services for LD students.

Library 2,477 titles, 109 serial subscriptions, 276 audiovisual materials.

Student Life *Housing:* college housing not available.

Standardized Tests *Required:* ACT COMPASS or ASSET (for admission).

Costs (2006–07) *Tuition:* state resident $1116 full-time, $31 per credit hour part-time; nonresident $2232 full-time, $62 per credit hour part-time. Full-time tuition and fees vary according to course load and program. Part-time tuition and fees vary according to course load and program. *Required fees:* $258 full-time. *Waivers:* senior citizens.

Applying *Options:* deferred entrance. *Application fee:* $15. *Required:* high school transcript.

Director of Admissions Mr. Ryan Foley, Admissions Director, Ogeechee Technical College, 1 Joe Kennedy Boulevard, Statesboro, GA 30458. *Phone:* 912-871-1600. *Toll-free phone:* 800-646-1316. *Fax:* 912-486-7413. *E-mail:* rfoley@ogeecheetech.edu.

OKEFENOKEE TECHNICAL COLLEGE

Waycross, Georgia   www.okefenokeetech.edu/

- **State-supported** 2-year, part of Georgia Department of Technical and Adult Education
- **Small-town** campus
- **Coed,** 1,453 undergraduate students, 33% full-time, 66% women, 34% men

Undergraduates 484 full-time, 969 part-time. 25% African American, 0.8% Asian American or Pacific Islander, 1% Hispanic American, 0.8% Native American.

Freshmen *Admission:* 274 enrolled.

Faculty *Total:* 113, 42% full-time.

Majors Administrative assistant and secretarial science; child development; clinical/medical laboratory technology; computer systems networking and telecommunications; computer technology/computer systems technology; criminal justice/police science; forestry technology; information science/studies; occupational safety and health technology; respiratory therapy technician; surgical technology.

Academics *Calendar:* quarters. *Degree:* certificates, diplomas, and associate. *Special study options:* academic remediation for entering students, advanced placement credit, distance learning, internships, services for LD students.

Library 1,714 titles.

Student Life *Housing:* college housing not available.

Standardized Tests *Required:* ACT COMPASS or ASSET (for admission).

Costs (2006–07) *Tuition:* state resident $1116 full-time, $31 per credit hour part-time; nonresident $2232 full-time, $62 per credit hour part-time. Full-time tuition and fees vary according to course load and program. Part-time tuition and fees vary according to course load and program. *Required fees:* $243 full-time. *Waivers:* senior citizens.

Applying *Options:* deferred entrance. *Application fee:* $15. *Required:* high school transcript.

Director of Admissions Reba Smith, Director of Admissions, Okefenokee Technical College, 1701 Carswell Avenue, Waycross, GA 31503. *Phone:* 912-287-5806. *Fax:* 912-284-2508. *E-mail:* reba@okefenokeetech.org.

SANDERSVILLE TECHNICAL COLLEGE

Sandersville, Georgia   www.sandersvilletech.edu/

- **State-supported** 2-year, part of Georgia Department of Technical and Adult Education
- **Coed,** 719 undergraduate students, 37% full-time, 58% women, 42% men

Undergraduates 264 full-time, 455 part-time. 65% African American, 0.2% Native American.

Freshmen *Admission:* 165 enrolled.

Faculty *Total:* 100, 30% full-time.

Majors Accounting; administrative assistant and secretarial science; child development; computer systems networking and telecommunications; information science/studies.

Academics *Calendar:* quarters. *Degree:* certificates, diplomas, and associate. *Special study options:* academic remediation for entering students, advanced placement credit, distance learning, internships, services for LD students.

Student Life *Housing:* college housing not available.

Standardized Tests *Required:* ACT COMPASS or ASSET (for admission).

Costs (2006–07) *Tuition:* state resident $1116 full-time, $31 per credit hour part-time; nonresident $2232 full-time, $62 per credit hour part-time. Full-time tuition and fees vary according to course load and program. Part-time tuition and fees vary according to course load and program. *Required fees:* $243 full-time. *Waivers:* senior citizens.

Applying *Options:* deferred entrance. *Application fee:* $15. *Required:* high school transcript.

Director of Admissions Patrick Wilson, Admissions Director, Sandersville Technical College, 1189 Deepstep Road, Sandersville, GA 31082. *Phone:* 478-553-2065. *Fax:* 478-553-2118. *E-mail:* pwilson@sandervilletech.edu.

SAVANNAH RIVER COLLEGE

Augusta, Georgia   www.savannahrivercollege.edu/

- **Proprietary** 2-year, founded 1983
- **Coed,** 254 undergraduate students
- 86% of applicants were admitted

Freshmen *Admission:* 66 applied, 57 admitted.

Majors Business administration, management and operations related; computer programming related; executive assistant/executive secretary; medical/health management and clinical assistant; medical insurance/medical billing; medical office management.

Academics *Degree:* associate.

Costs (2006–07) *Tuition:* $7999 full-time.

Applying *Application fee:* $50.

Admissions Office Contact Savannah River College, 2528 Center West Parkway, Augusta, GA 30909.

SAVANNAH TECHNICAL COLLEGE

Savannah, Georgia   www.savannahtech.edu/

- **State-supported** 2-year, founded 1929, part of Georgia Department of Technical and Adult Education
- **Urban** 15-acre campus
- **Coed,** 3,965 undergraduate students, 43% full-time, 67% women, 33% men

Undergraduates 1,699 full-time, 2,266 part-time. Students come from 4 states and territories, 56% African American, 2% Asian American or Pacific Islander, 4% Hispanic American, 0.5% Native American, 1% international, 3% transferred in.

Freshmen *Admission:* 953 enrolled.

Faculty *Total:* 290, 21% full-time.

Majors Accounting; administrative assistant and secretarial science; automobile/automotive mechanics technology; child development; computer systems networking and telecommunications; criminal justice/safety; culinary arts; electrical, electronic and communications engineering technology; fire science; heating, air conditioning and refrigeration technology; hotel and restaurant management; industrial technology; information technology; marketing/marketing management; surgical technology; tourism and travel services management.

Academics *Calendar:* quarters. *Degree:* certificates, diplomas, and associate. *Special study options:* academic remediation for entering students, advanced placement credit, distance learning, internships, part-time degree program, services for LD students, summer session for credit.

Library 20,804 titles, 160 serial subscriptions, 3,150 audiovisual materials, an OPAC, a Web page.

Student Life *Housing:* college housing not available. *Activities and Organizations:* Phi Beta Lambda, Vocational Industrial Clubs of America (VICA).

Standardized Tests *Required:* ACT COMPASS or ASSET (for admission).

Costs (2006–07) *Tuition:* state resident $1116 full-time, $31 per credit hour part-time; nonresident $2232 full-time, $62 per credit hour part-time. Full-time

Savannah Technical College (continued)

tuition and fees vary according to course load and program. Part-time tuition and fees vary according to course load and program. *Required fees:* $243 full-time. *Waivers:* senior citizens.

Applying *Options:* deferred entrance. *Application fee:* $15. *Required:* high school transcript.

Director of Admissions Angela Southerland, Admissions Director, Savannah Technical College, 5717 White Bluff Road, Savannah, GA 31405-5594. *Phone:* 912-303-1772. *Toll-free phone:* 800-769-6362. *Fax:* 912-303-1781. *E-mail:* asoutherland@savannahtech.edu.

SOUTHEASTERN TECHNICAL COLLEGE
Vidalia, Georgia   **www.southeasterntech.edu/**

- **State-supported** 2-year, founded 1989, part of Georgia Department of Technical and Adult Education
- **Coed,** 912 undergraduate students, 46% full-time, 74% women, 26% men

Undergraduates 418 full-time, 494 part-time. 29% African American, 0.5% Asian American or Pacific Islander, 2% Hispanic American, 0.1% Native American.

Freshmen *Admission:* 166 enrolled.

Faculty *Total:* 102, 39% full-time.

Majors Accounting; administrative assistant and secretarial science; child development; computer systems networking and telecommunications; criminal justice/safety; dental hygiene; design and visual communications; electrical, electronic and communications engineering technology; information science/studies; marketing/marketing management; medical laboratory technology; medical radiologic technology; respiratory therapy technician; web page, digital/multimedia and information resources design.

Academics *Calendar:* quarters. *Degree:* certificates, diplomas, and associate. *Special study options:* academic remediation for entering students, advanced placement credit, distance learning, internships, services for LD students.

Student Life *Housing:* college housing not available.

Standardized Tests *Required:* ACT COMPASS or ASSET (for admission).

Costs (2006–07) *Tuition:* state resident $1116 full-time, $31 per credit hour part-time; nonresident $2232 full-time, $62 per credit hour part-time. Full-time tuition and fees vary according to course load and program. Part-time tuition and fees vary according to course load and program. *Required fees:* $243 full-time. *Waivers:* senior citizens.

Applying *Options:* deferred entrance. *Application fee:* $15. *Required:* high school transcript.

Director of Admissions Christopher P. Carroll, Admissions Director, Southeastern Technical College, 3001 East First Street, Vidalia, GA 30474. *Phone:* 912-538-3121. *Fax:* 912-538-3156. *E-mail:* ccarroll@southeasterntech.edu.

SOUTH GEORGIA COLLEGE
Douglas, Georgia   **www.sga.edu/**

- **State-supported** 2-year, founded 1906, part of University System of Georgia
- **Small-town** 250-acre campus
- **Endowment** $150,321
- **Coed,** 1,504 undergraduate students, 69% full-time, 64% women, 36% men

Undergraduates 1,037 full-time, 467 part-time. Students come from 3 states and territories, 2 other countries, 25% African American, 1% Asian American or Pacific Islander, 2% Hispanic American, 0.2% Native American, 0.7% international, 11% live on campus.

Freshmen *Admission:* 610 applied, 608 admitted, 542 enrolled. *Average high school GPA:* 2.83. *Test scores:* SAT verbal scores over 500: 9%; SAT math scores over 500: 21%; SAT verbal scores over 600: 2%; SAT math scores over 600: 7%; SAT math scores over 700: 1%.

Faculty *Total:* 60, 53% full-time.

Majors Accounting; administrative assistant and secretarial science; agricultural business and management; agricultural teacher education; agriculture; animal sciences; applied mathematics; biological and physical sciences; biology/biological sciences; business administration and management; business/managerial economics; business teacher education; chemistry; computer and information sciences; computer programming; computer science; creative writing; criminal justice/law enforcement administration; criminology; dramatic/theater arts; economics; education; elementary education; English; finance; French; German; health teacher education; history; humanities; information science/studies; jour-

nalism; kindergarten/preschool education; kinesiology and exercise science; liberal arts and sciences/liberal studies; mass communication/media; mathematics; middle school education; nursing (registered nurse training); parks, recreation and leisure; parks, recreation and leisure facilities management; philosophy; physical education teaching and coaching; physical sciences; physics; political science and government; pre-engineering; psychology; science teacher education; sociology; Spanish; speech and rhetoric; sport and fitness administration/management.

Academics *Calendar:* semesters. *Degree:* certificates and associate. *Special study options:* academic remediation for entering students, adult/continuing education programs, advanced placement credit, part-time degree program, services for LD students, study abroad, summer session for credit.

Library William S. Smith Library with 79,190 titles, 327 serial subscriptions, an OPAC, a Web page.

Student Life *Housing:* on-campus residence required for freshman year. *Options:* Campus housing is university owned. *Activities and Organizations:* drama/theater group, student-run newspaper, Georgia Association of Student Nurses, Baptist Student Union, Agricultural Club, Residents Assistants Club, Student Organization for Black Unity. *Campus security:* 24-hour emergency response devices and patrols, controlled dormitory access. *Student services:* personal/psychological counseling.

Athletics Member NJCAA. *Intercollegiate sports:* baseball M(s), soccer M, softball W(s). *Intramural sports:* basketball M/W, football M, golf M/W, soccer M, tennis M/W, volleyball M/W.

Standardized Tests *Required:* SAT or ACT (for placement). *Required for some:* SAT Subject Tests (for placement).

Costs (2006–07) *Tuition:* state resident $2406 full-time, $68 per credit hour part-time; nonresident $9618 full-time, $268 per credit hour part-time. *Required fees:* $429 full-time. *Room and board:* $8475; room only: $3900.

Applying *Options:* electronic application, early admission, deferred entrance. *Required:* high school transcript. *Notification:* continuous (freshmen), continuous (transfers).

Director of Admissions Dr. Randy L. Braswell, Director of Admissions, Records, and Research, South Georgia College, 100 West College Park Drive, Douglas, GA 31533-5098. *Phone:* 912-389-4200. *Toll-free phone:* 800-342-6364. *E-mail:* rbraswell@sga.edu.

SOUTH GEORGIA TECHNICAL COLLEGE
Americus, Georgia   **www.southgatech.edu/**

- **State-supported** 2-year, founded 1948, part of Georgia Department of Technical and Adult Education
- **Coed,** 1,711 undergraduate students, 50% full-time, 50% women, 50% men

Undergraduates 862 full-time, 849 part-time. 58% African American, 0.3% Asian American or Pacific Islander, 1% Hispanic American, 0.1% Native American.

Freshmen *Admission:* 481 enrolled.

Faculty *Total:* 143, 48% full-time.

Majors Accounting; administrative assistant and secretarial science; child development; computer systems networking and telecommunications; criminal justice/safety; culinary arts; drafting and design technology; electrical, electronic and communications engineering technology; heating, air conditioning and refrigeration technology; horticultural science; industrial technology; information science/studies; manufacturing technology; marketing/marketing management; paralegal/legal assistant.

Academics *Calendar:* quarters. *Degree:* certificates, diplomas, and associate. *Special study options:* academic remediation for entering students, advanced placement credit, cooperative education, distance learning, internships, services for LD students.

Student Life *Housing Options:* men-only, women-only.

Athletics Member NJCAA. *Intercollegiate sports:* basketball M/W.

Standardized Tests *Required:* ACT COMPASS or ASSET (for admission).

Costs (2006–07) *Tuition:* state resident $1116 full-time, $31 per credit hour part-time; nonresident $2232 full-time, $62 per credit hour part-time. Full-time tuition and fees vary according to course load and program. Part-time tuition and fees vary according to course load and program. *Required fees:* $270 full-time. *Room and board:* $3600. *Waivers:* senior citizens.

Applying *Options:* deferred entrance. *Application fee:* $15. *Required:* high school transcript.

Director of Admissions Karen Werling, Admissions Director, South Georgia Technical College, 900 South Georgia Tech Parkway, Americus, GA 31709-8104. *Phone:* 229-931-2299. *Fax:* 229-931-5001. *E-mail:* kwerling@southgatech.edu.

SOUTHWEST GEORGIA TECHNICAL COLLEGE

Thomasville, Georgia　　www.southwestgatech.edu/

- **State-supported** 2-year, founded 1963, part of Georgia Department of Technical and Adult Education
- **Coed**, 1,453 undergraduate students, 35% full-time, 70% women, 30% men

Undergraduates 511 full-time, 942 part-time. 39% African American, 0.2% Asian American or Pacific Islander, 0.9% Hispanic American, 0.5% Native American.

Freshmen *Admission:* 269 enrolled.

Faculty *Total:* 62, 100% full-time.

Majors Accounting; administrative assistant and secretarial science; agricultural mechanization; child development; computer systems networking and telecommunications; criminal justice/safety; information science/studies; medical laboratory technology; medical radiologic technology; nursing (registered nurse training); respiratory care therapy; surgical technology.

Academics *Calendar:* quarters. *Degree:* certificates, diplomas, and associate. *Special study options:* academic remediation for entering students, advanced placement credit, cooperative education, distance learning, internships, part-time degree program, services for LD students, summer session for credit.

Library 19,767 titles, 113 serial subscriptions, 920 audiovisual materials, an OPAC, a Web page.

Student Life *Housing:* college housing not available.

Standardized Tests *Required:* ACT COMPASS or ASSET (for admission).

Costs (2006–07) *Tuition:* state resident $1116 full-time, $31 per credit hour part-time; nonresident $2232 full-time, $62 per credit hour part-time. Full-time tuition and fees vary according to course load and program. Part-time tuition and fees vary according to course load and program. *Required fees:* $243 full-time. *Waivers:* senior citizens.

Applying *Options:* electronic application, deferred entrance. *Application fee:* $20. *Required:* high school transcript.

Freshmen Application Contact Admissions Office, Southwest Georgia Technical College, 15689 US Highway 19 N, Thomasville, GA 31792. *Phone:* 229-225-5060. *Fax:* 229-225-4330. *E-mail:* info@southwestgatech.edu.

SWAINSBORO TECHNICAL COLLEGE

Swainsboro, Georgia　　www.swainsborotech.edu/

- **State-supported** 2-year, founded 1963, part of Georgia Department of Technical and Adult Education
- **Coed**, 718 undergraduate students, 38% full-time, 73% women, 27% men

Undergraduates 275 full-time, 443 part-time. 44% African American, 0.2% Asian American or Pacific Islander, 0.2% Hispanic American, 0.2% Native American.

Freshmen *Admission:* 124 enrolled.

Faculty *Total:* 79, 52% full-time.

Majors Accounting; administrative assistant and secretarial science; child development; computer systems networking and telecommunications; criminal justice/safety; drafting and design technology; electrical, electronic and communications engineering technology; fish/game management; forestry technology; information science/studies.

Academics *Calendar:* quarters. *Degree:* certificates, diplomas, and associate. *Special study options:* advanced placement credit, cooperative education, distance learning, internships, services for LD students.

Student Life *Housing:* college housing not available.

Standardized Tests *Required:* ACT COMPASS or ASSET (for admission).

Costs (2006–07) *Tuition:* state resident $1116 full-time, $31 per credit hour part-time; nonresident $2232 full-time, $62 per credit hour part-time. Full-time tuition and fees vary according to course load and program. Part-time tuition and fees vary according to course load and program. *Required fees:* $243 full-time. *Waivers:* senior citizens.

Applying *Options:* deferred entrance. *Application fee:* $15. *Required:* high school transcript.

Director of Admissions Mitchell Fagler, Admissions Director, Swainsboro Technical College, 346 Kite Road, Swainsboro, GA 30401. *Phone:* 478-289-2259. *Fax:* 478-289-2263. *E-mail:* mfagler@swainsborotech.edu.

TRUETT-MCCONNELL COLLEGE

Cleveland, Georgia　　www.truett.edu/

- **Independent Baptist** primarily 2-year, founded 1946
- **Rural** 310-acre campus with easy access to Atlanta
- **Coed**

Undergraduates 340 full-time, 35 part-time. Students come from 4 states and territories, 4 other countries, 3% are from out of state, 11% African American, 2% Asian American or Pacific Islander, 3% Hispanic American, 0.3% Native American, 5% transferred in, 73% live on campus. *Retention:* 55% of 2003 full-time freshmen returned.

Faculty *Student/faculty ratio:* 11:1.

Academics *Calendar:* semesters. *Degrees:* associate and bachelor's. *Special study options:* academic remediation for entering students, accelerated degree program, advanced placement credit, double majors, honors programs, part-time degree program, services for LD students, study abroad, summer session for credit.

Student Life *Campus security:* 24-hour weekday patrols, 10-hour weekend patrols by trained security personnel.

Athletics Member NJCAA.

Standardized Tests *Required:* SAT or ACT (for admission).

Costs (2006–07) *Comprehensive fee:* $17,450 includes full-time tuition ($11,950), mandatory fees ($500), and room and board ($5000). Part-time tuition: $398 per credit hour. *Required fees:* $250 per term part-time. *Room and board:* college room only: $2300.

Applying *Options:* early admission, deferred entrance. *Application fee:* $25. *Required:* high school transcript, minimum 2.0 GPA, minimum SAT score of 720 or ACT score of 15. *Required for some:* letters of recommendation, interview.

Freshmen Application Contact Ms. Penny Loggins, Dean for Admissions, Truett-McConnell College, 100 Alumni Drive, Cleveland, GA 30528-9799. *Phone:* 706-865-2134 Ext. 210. *Toll-free phone:* 800-226-8621. *Fax:* 706-865-7615. *E-mail:* admissions@truett.edu.

VALDOSTA TECHNICAL COLLEGE

Valdosta, Georgia　　www.valdostatech.edu/

- **State-supported** 2-year, founded 1963, part of Georgia Department of Technical and Adult Education
- **Suburban** 18-acre campus
- **Coed**, 2,483 undergraduate students, 40% full-time, 63% women, 37% men

Undergraduates 996 full-time, 1,487 part-time. Students come from 2 states and territories, 38% African American, 0.8% Asian American or Pacific Islander, 1% Hispanic American, 0.3% Native American, 4% transferred in.

Freshmen *Admission:* 480 enrolled.

Faculty *Total:* 186, 36% full-time.

Majors Accounting; administrative assistant and secretarial science; banking and financial support services; child development; computer and information systems security; computer programming; computer systems networking and telecommunications; criminal justice/safety; drafting and design technology; e-commerce; fire science; machine tool technology; marketing/marketing management; medical laboratory technology; medical radiologic technology; web page, digital/multimedia and information resources design.

Academics *Calendar:* quarters. *Degree:* certificates, diplomas, and associate. *Special study options:* academic remediation for entering students, advanced placement credit, distance learning, external degree program, internships, services for LD students.

Library Valdosta Technical College Library plus 1 other with 3,373 titles, 109 serial subscriptions, 225 audiovisual materials, an OPAC.

Student Life *Housing:* college housing not available.

Standardized Tests *Required:* ACT COMPASS or ASSET (for admission).

Costs (2006–07) *Tuition:* state resident $1116 full-time, $31 per credit hour part-time; nonresident $2232 full-time, $62 per credit hour part-time. Full-time tuition and fees vary according to course load and program. Part-time tuition and fees vary according to course load and program. *Required fees:* $276 full-time. *Waivers:* senior citizens.

Applying *Options:* deferred entrance. *Application fee:* $15. *Required:* high school transcript.

Director of Admissions Amanda Leavy, Admissions Director, Valdosta Technical College, Student Customer Services, PO Box 928, 4089 Valtech Road, Valdosta, GA 31602. *Phone:* 229-333-1394. *Fax:* 229-333-5368. *E-mail:* aleavy@valdostatech.edu.

WAYCROSS COLLEGE

Waycross, Georgia　　　www.waycross.edu/

Freshmen Application Contact Mrs. Susan Dukes, Assistant Director for Admissions, Waycross College, 2001 South Georgia Parkway, Waycross, GA 31503. *Phone:* 912-285-6133.

WEST CENTRAL TECHNICAL COLLEGE

Waco, Georgia　　　www.westcentraltech.edu/

- **State-supported** 2-year, founded 1968, part of Georgia Department of Technical and Adult Education
- **Coed,** 3,010 undergraduate students, 31% full-time, 72% women, 28% men

Undergraduates 941 full-time, 2,069 part-time. 47% are from out of state, 23% African American, 0.8% Asian American or Pacific Islander, 1% Hispanic American, 0.5% Native American.

Freshmen *Admission:* 555 enrolled.

Faculty *Total:* 310, 27% full-time.

Majors Accounting; administrative assistant and secretarial science; business administration and management; child development; computer and information sciences related; computer programming (specific applications); computer systems networking and telecommunications; criminal justice/safety; data entry/microcomputer applications; dental hygiene; electrical, electronic and communications engineering technology; heavy equipment maintenance technology; industrial radiologic technology; information science/studies; manufacturing technology; marketing/marketing management; medical laboratory technology; medical radiologic technology; nursing (registered nurse training); web page, digital/multimedia and information resources design; word processing.

Academics *Calendar:* quarters. *Degree:* certificates, diplomas, and associate. *Special study options:* academic remediation for entering students, adult/continuing education programs, advanced placement credit, distance learning, external degree program, internships, part-time degree program, services for LD students.

Library 18,462 titles, 1,635 audiovisual materials.

Student Life *Housing:* college housing not available.

Standardized Tests *Required:* ACT COMPASS or ASSET (for admission).

Costs (2006–07) *Tuition:* state resident $1116 full-time, $31 per credit hour part-time; nonresident $2232 full-time, $62 per credit hour part-time. Full-time tuition and fees vary according to course load and program. Part-time tuition and fees vary according to course load and program. *Required fees:* $255 full-time. *Waivers:* senior citizens.

Financial Aid Of all full-time matriculated undergraduates, 45 Federal Work-Study jobs (averaging $1000).

Applying *Options:* electronic application, deferred entrance. *Application fee:* $25. *Required:* high school transcript.

Director of Admissions Mrs. Mary Alderhold, Director of Student Services, West Central Technical College, 176 Murphy Campus Boulevard, Waco, GA 30182. *Phone:* 770-537-5712. *Fax:* 770-537-7995. *E-mail:* malderhold@westcentral.edu.

WEST GEORGIA TECHNICAL COLLEGE

LaGrange, Georgia　　　www.westgatech.edu/

- **State-supported** 2-year, founded 1966, part of Georgia Department of Technical and Adult Education
- **Coed,** 1,779 undergraduate students, 40% full-time, 60% women, 40% men

Undergraduates 706 full-time, 1,073 part-time. Students come from 2 states and territories, 38% African American, 0.4% Asian American or Pacific Islander, 1% Hispanic American, 0.2% Native American, 7% transferred in.

Freshmen *Admission:* 339 enrolled.

Faculty *Total:* 142, 32% full-time.

Majors Accounting; administrative assistant and secretarial science; automobile/automotive mechanics technology; child development; computer systems networking and telecommunications; criminal justice/safety; electrical, electronic and communications engineering technology; fire science; health information/medical records technology; industrial technology; information science/studies; marketing/marketing management; medical radiologic technology; pharmacy technician; plastics engineering technology; social work; web page, digital/multimedia and information resources design.

Academics *Calendar:* quarters. *Degree:* certificates, diplomas, and associate. *Special study options:* academic remediation for entering students, advanced placement credit, distance learning, internships, services for LD students.

Library 19,683 titles, 218 serial subscriptions, 525 audiovisual materials.

Student Life *Housing:* college housing not available. *Activities and Organizations:* Student Government Association, Vocational Industrial Clubs of America, Phi Beta Lambda. *Campus security:* 24-hour emergency response devices.

Standardized Tests *Required:* ACT COMPASS or ASSET (for admission).

Costs (2006–07) *Tuition:* state resident $1116 full-time, $31 per credit hour part-time; nonresident $2232 full-time, $62 per credit hour part-time. Full-time tuition and fees vary according to course load and program. Part-time tuition and fees vary according to course load and program. *Required fees:* $243 full-time. *Waivers:* senior citizens.

Financial Aid Of all full-time matriculated undergraduates, 68 Federal Work-Study jobs (averaging $800).

Applying *Options:* deferred entrance. *Application fee:* $15. *Required:* high school transcript.

Director of Admissions Lori Basham, Admissions Director, West Georgia Technical College, 303 Fort Drive, LaGrange, GA 30240. *Phone:* 706-837-4244. *Fax:* 706-845-4340. *E-mail:* lbasham@westgatech.edu.

WESTWOOD COLLEGE–ATLANTA MIDTOWN

Atlanta, Georgia　　　www.westwood.edu/

Director of Admissions Rory Laney, Director of Admissions, Westwood College–Atlanta Midtown, 1100 Spring Street, Ste. 101A, Atlanta, GA 30309. *Phone:* 404-870-8982.

▶**See page 598 for the College Close-Up.**

YOUNG HARRIS COLLEGE

Young Harris, Georgia　　　www.yhc.edu/

- **Independent United Methodist** 2-year, founded 1886
- **Rural** 30-acre campus
- **Endowment** $118.5 million
- **Coed,** 606 undergraduate students, 94% full-time, 48% women, 52% men

Undergraduates 570 full-time, 36 part-time. Students come from 10 states and territories, 9 other countries, 6% are from out of state, 2% African American, 0.5% Asian American or Pacific Islander, 3% Hispanic American, 0.2% Native American, 2% international, 3% transferred in, 90% live on campus. *Retention:* 60% of 2003 full-time freshmen returned.

Freshmen *Admission:* 1,505 applied, 872 admitted, 387 enrolled. *Average high school GPA:* 3.3. *Test scores:* SAT verbal scores over 500: 54%; SAT math scores over 500: 54%; SAT verbal scores over 600: 13%; SAT math scores over 600: 17%; SAT verbal scores over 700: 1%; SAT math scores over 700: 2%.

Faculty *Total:* 53, 68% full-time, 49% with terminal degrees. *Student/faculty ratio:* 14:1.

Majors Agriculture; art; art teacher education; biological and physical sciences; biology/biological sciences; business administration and management; chemistry; clinical laboratory science/medical technology; computer science; criminal justice/law enforcement administration; dramatic/theater arts; education; English; French; geology/earth science; health teacher education; history; hospitality administration; international business/trade/commerce; journalism; liberal arts and sciences/liberal studies; mathematics; music; music related; music teacher education; natural sciences; nursing (registered nurse training); parks, recreation and leisure; physical therapy; physics; political science and government; pre-engineering; psychology; religious studies; sociology; Spanish.

Academics *Calendar:* semesters. *Degree:* associate. *Special study options:* academic remediation for entering students, accelerated degree program, advanced placement credit, double majors, internships, part-time degree program, summer session for credit.

Library J. Lon Duckworth Library with 90,000 titles, 130 serial subscriptions, 3,000 audiovisual materials, an OPAC, a Web page.

Student Life *Housing:* on-campus residence required through sophomore year. *Options:* coed, men-only, women-only. Campus housing is university owned. *Activities and Organizations:* drama/theater group, student-run newspaper, choral group, Wesley Fellowship, BSU, Quantrek (outdoor club), intramurals. *Campus security:* 24-hour emergency response devices and patrols. *Student services:* health clinic, personal/psychological counseling.

Athletics Member NJCAA. *Intercollegiate sports:* baseball M(s), soccer M(s)/W(s), softball W(s), tennis W(s). *Intramural sports:* badminton M/W, basketball

M/W, bowling M/W, football M/W, golf M/W, skiing (downhill) M/W, softball M/W, swimming and diving M/W, tennis M/W, ultimate Frisbee M/W, volleyball M/W, weight lifting M/W.

Standardized Tests *Required:* SAT or ACT (for admission).

Costs (2007–08) *Comprehensive fee:* $20,500 includes full-time tuition ($15,636) and room and board ($4864). Part-time tuition: $500 per hour. *Room and board:* college room only: $1870.

Financial Aid Of all full-time matriculated undergraduates, 89 Federal Work-Study jobs (averaging $1000). 242 state and other part-time jobs (averaging $1000).

Applying *Options:* electronic application, early admission, deferred entrance. *Application fee:* $30. *Required:* high school transcript, minimum 2.5 GPA. *Required for some:* letters of recommendation. *Recommended:* interview. *Application deadlines:* rolling (freshmen), rolling (transfers). *Notification:* continuous (freshmen), continuous (transfers).

Freshmen Application Contact Mr. Clinton G. Hobbs, Vice President for Enrollment Management, Young Harris College, PO Box 116, Young Harris, GA 30582-0098. *Phone:* 706-379-3111 Ext. 5147. *Toll-free phone:* 800-241-3754. *Fax:* 706-379-3108. *E-mail:* admissions@yhc.edu.

GUAM

GUAM COMMUNITY COLLEGE
Barrigada, Guam　　　　　**www.guamcc.net/**

- **Territory-supported** 2-year, founded 1977
- **Suburban** 22-acre campus
- **Endowment** $6.4 million
- **Coed**

Undergraduates 504 full-time, 2,337 part-time. Students come from 10 other countries, 0.7% African American, 90% Asian American or Pacific Islander, 0.6% Hispanic American, 0.1% Native American, 2% international.

Academics *Calendar:* semesters. *Degree:* certificates, diplomas, and associate. *Special study options:* academic remediation for entering students, adult/continuing education programs, cooperative education, double majors, English as a second language, honors programs, independent study, internships, off-campus study, part-time degree program, services for LD students, summer session for credit. *ROTC:* Army (c).

Student Life *Campus security:* 12-hour patrols by trained security personnel.

Costs (2006–07) *Tuition:* area resident $2100 full-time; nonresident $2850 full-time. *Required fees:* $244 full-time.

Financial Aid Of all full-time matriculated undergraduates, 83 Federal Work-Study jobs (averaging $940).

Applying *Options:* early admission. *Required:* high school transcript.

Freshmen Application Contact Mr. Patrick L. Clymer, Registrar, Guam Community College, PO Box 23069, Sesame Street, Barrigada, GU 96921, Guam. *Phone:* 671-735-5531. *Fax:* 671-735-5531. *E-mail:* pclymer@guamcc.edu.

HAWAII

HAWAII BUSINESS COLLEGE
Honolulu, Hawaii　　　　　**www.hbc.edu/**

Director of Admissions Seira Puletasi, Registrar, Hawaii Business College, 33 South King Street, Fourth Floor, Honolulu, HI 96813. *Phone:* 808-524-4014 Ext. 136.

HAWAII COMMUNITY COLLEGE
Hilo, Hawaii　　　　　**www.hawcc.hawaii.edu/**

Director of Admissions Mrs. Tammy M. Tanaka, Admissions Specialist, Hawaii Community College, 200 West Kawili Street, Hilo, HI 96720-4091. *Phone:* 808-974-7661.

HAWAII TOKAI INTERNATIONAL COLLEGE
Honolulu, Hawaii　　　　　**www.tokai.edu/**

- **Independent** 2-year, founded 1992, part of Tokai University Educational System (Japan)
- **Urban** campus
- **Coed**

Undergraduates 54 full-time. Students come from 1 other state, 3 other countries, 100% Asian American or Pacific Islander, 60% live on campus. *Retention:* 83% of 2003 full-time freshmen returned.

Faculty *Student/faculty ratio:* 4:1.

Academics *Calendar:* quarters. *Degree:* certificates, diplomas, and associate. *Special study options:* English as a second language, summer session for credit.

Student Life *Campus security:* 24-hour patrols.

Costs (2006–07) *Tuition:* $375 per credit part-time.

Applying *Options:* deferred entrance. *Application fee:* $50. *Required:* essay or personal statement, high school transcript, interview.

Freshmen Application Contact Mr. Derrick Kerr, Director, Student Services, Hawaii Tokai International College, 2241 Kapiolani Boulevard, Honolulu, HI 96826. *Phone:* 808-983-4154. *Fax:* 808-983-4107. *E-mail:* htic@tokai.edu.

HEALD COLLEGE-HONOLULU
Honolulu, Hawaii　　　　　**www.heald.edu/**

- **Independent** 2-year, founded 1863
- **Urban** campus
- **Coed**

Undergraduates 591 full-time, 216 part-time. 3% African American, 80% Asian American or Pacific Islander, 2% Hispanic American, 0.2% Native American.

Faculty *Student/faculty ratio:* 17:1.

Academics *Calendar:* quarters. *Degree:* certificates, diplomas, and associate. *Special study options:* academic remediation for entering students, advanced placement credit, internships, part-time degree program, summer session for credit.

Standardized Tests *Required:* COMPASS (for admission).

Costs (2006–07) *Tuition:* $10,275 full-time.

Applying *Options:* electronic application, early admission, deferred entrance. *Application fee:* $40. *Required:* high school transcript, interview.

Freshmen Application Contact Wendy Nishimura, Director of Admissions, Heald College-Honolulu, 1500 Kapiolani Boulevard, Suite 201, Honolulu, HI 96814. *Phone:* 808-955-1500. *Toll-free phone:* 800-755-3550. *Fax:* 808-955-6964. *E-mail:* wnishimu@heald.edu.

HONOLULU COMMUNITY COLLEGE
Honolulu, Hawaii　　　　　**www.honolulu.hawaii.edu/**

Freshmen Application Contact Admissions Office, Honolulu Community College, 874 Dillingham Boulevard, Honolulu, HI 96817. *Phone:* 808-845-9129. *E-mail:* admission@hccadb.hcc.hawaii.edu.

KAPIOLANI COMMUNITY COLLEGE
Honolulu, Hawaii　　　　　**www.kcc.hawaii.edu/**

- **State-supported** 2-year, founded 1957, part of University of Hawaii System
- **Urban** 52-acre campus
- **Coed**

Kapiolani Community College (continued)

Undergraduates 2,833 full-time, 4,341 part-time. Students come from 27 states and territories, 59 other countries, 0.9% African American, 75% Asian American or Pacific Islander, 2% Hispanic American, 0.2% Native American, 7% international, 18% transferred in.

Academics *Calendar:* semesters. *Degree:* certificates and associate. *Special study options:* academic remediation for entering students, adult/continuing education programs, advanced placement credit, cooperative education, distance learning, English as a second language, honors programs, internships, off-campus study, part-time degree program, services for LD students, student-designed majors, summer session for credit. *ROTC:* Army (c), Air Force (c).

Student Life *Campus security:* 24-hour patrols.

Costs (2006–07) *Tuition:* state resident $1344 full-time, $56 per credit hour part-time; nonresident $5976 full-time, $249 per credit hour part-time. *Required fees:* $60 full-time, $2 per credit hour part-time, $10 per term part-time.

Financial Aid Of all full-time matriculated undergraduates, 30 Federal Work-Study jobs (averaging $2275). 440 state and other part-time jobs (averaging $1762).

Applying *Options:* early admission.

Freshmen Application Contact Ms. Jerilynn Lorenzo, Chief Admissions Officer, Kapiolani Community College, 4303 Diamond Head Road, Honolulu, HI 96816-4421. *Phone:* 808-734-9587. *E-mail:* jilorenz@hawaii.edu.

KAUAI COMMUNITY COLLEGE
Lihue, Hawaii kauai.hawaii.edu/

- **State-supported** 2-year, founded 1965, part of University of Hawaii System
- **Small-town** 100-acre campus
- **Coed**

Academics *Calendar:* semesters. *Degree:* certificates and associate. *Special study options:* accelerated degree program, advanced placement credit, cooperative education, distance learning, English as a second language, internships, part-time degree program, services for LD students, summer session for credit.

Student Life *Campus security:* student patrols, 6-hour evening patrols by trained security personnel.

Financial Aid Of all full-time matriculated undergraduates, 10 Federal Work-Study jobs (averaging $3000). 30 state and other part-time jobs (averaging $3000).

Applying *Options:* early admission. *Required for some:* high school transcript. *Recommended:* high school transcript.

Freshmen Application Contact Mr. Leighton Oride, Admissions Officer and Registrar, Kauai Community College, 3-1901 Kaumualii Highway, Lihue, HI 96766. *Phone:* 808-245-8225. *Fax:* 808-245-8297. *E-mail:* arkauai@hawaii.edu.

LEEWARD COMMUNITY COLLEGE
Pearl City, Hawaii www.lcc.hawaii.edu/

- **State-supported** 2-year, founded 1968, part of University of Hawaii System
- **Suburban** 49-acre campus with easy access to Honolulu
- **Coed,** 6,201 undergraduate students

Undergraduates Students come from 25 states and territories.

Faculty *Total:* 236, 76% full-time.

Majors Accounting; administrative assistant and secretarial science; automobile/automotive mechanics technology; business administration and management; commercial and advertising art; computer science; consumer merchandising/retailing management; drafting and design technology; food services technology; human services; liberal arts and sciences/liberal studies; parks, recreation and leisure.

Academics *Calendar:* semesters. *Degree:* associate. *Special study options:* academic remediation for entering students, adult/continuing education programs, advanced placement credit, cooperative education, distance learning, English as a second language, honors programs, independent study, internships, off-campus study, part-time degree program, services for LD students, summer session for credit. *ROTC:* Army (b), Air Force (c).

Library 62,000 titles, 358 serial subscriptions, 1,009 audiovisual materials, an OPAC, a Web page.

Student Life *Housing:* college housing not available. *Activities and Organizations:* drama/theater group, student-run newspaper, choral group. *Campus security:* 24-hour patrols, late-night transport/escort service. *Student services:* health clinic, personal/psychological counseling.

Athletics *Intramural sports:* basketball M/W, bowling M/W, tennis M/W, volleyball M/W.

Costs (2006–07) *Tuition:* state resident $1369 full-time; nonresident $6001 full-time.

Financial Aid Of all full-time matriculated undergraduates, 40 Federal Work-Study jobs (averaging $2000).

Applying *Options:* early admission. *Application fee:* $25. *Required for some:* high school transcript, letters of recommendation. *Application deadlines:* 8/15 (freshmen), 8/15 (transfers). *Notification:* continuous until 8/19 (freshmen), continuous until 8/19 (transfers).

Freshmen Application Contact Ms. Veda Tokashiki, Clerk, Leeward Community College, 96-045 Ala Ike, Pearl City, HI 96782-3393. *Phone:* 808-455-0217.

MAUI COMMUNITY COLLEGE
Kahului, Hawaii mauicc.hawaii.edu/

- **State-supported** 2-year, founded 1967, part of University of Hawaii System
- **Rural** 77-acre campus
- **Coed,** 2,779 undergraduate students

Undergraduates Students come from 15 other countries, 0.3% African American, 60% Asian American or Pacific Islander, 2% Hispanic American, 0.5% Native American, 4% international, 1% live on campus.

Faculty *Total:* 92.

Majors Accounting; administrative assistant and secretarial science; agricultural mechanization; automobile/automotive mechanics technology; carpentry; construction engineering technology; criminal justice/law enforcement administration; fashion/apparel design; fire science; food services technology; horticultural science; hotel/motel administration; human services; liberal arts and sciences/liberal studies; marketing/marketing management; nursing (registered nurse training); welding technology.

Academics *Calendar:* semesters. *Degree:* certificates and associate. *Special study options:* academic remediation for entering students, adult/continuing education programs, cooperative education, English as a second language, external degree program, part-time degree program, services for LD students, summer session for credit.

Library Maui Community College Library plus 1 other with 49,812 titles, 631 serial subscriptions, 1,333 audiovisual materials, an OPAC, a Web page.

Student Life *Housing Options:* coed. *Activities and Organizations:* student-run newspaper. *Campus security:* 24-hour emergency response devices and patrols. *Student services:* health clinic, personal/psychological counseling.

Athletics *Intramural sports:* basketball M/W, table tennis M/W, tennis M/W, volleyball M/W.

Standardized Tests *Required:* CTBS (for placement).

Costs (2007–08) *Tuition:* state resident $1512 full-time, $63 per credit part-time; nonresident $7680 full-time, $320 per credit part-time. *Required fees:* $76 full-time, $5 per credit part-time, $10 per term part-time. *Room and board:* room only: $3210.

Financial Aid Of all full-time matriculated undergraduates, 40 Federal Work-Study jobs (averaging $2500).

Applying *Options:* electronic application, early admission. *Application fee:* $25. *Required for some:* high school transcript. *Application deadlines:* rolling (freshmen), rolling (transfers).

Freshmen Application Contact Mr. Stephen Kameda, Director of Admissions and Records, Maui Community College, 310 Kaahumanu Avenue, Kahului, HI 96732. *Phone:* 808-984-3267. *Toll-free phone:* 800-479-6692. *Fax:* 808-242-9618. *E-mail:* kameda@hawaii.edu.

TRANSPACIFIC HAWAII COLLEGE
Honolulu, Hawaii www.transpacific.org/

- **Independent** 2-year, founded 1977
- **Suburban** campus
- **Endowment** $1.0 million
- **Coed, primarily women**

Undergraduates 240 full-time. Students come from 3 other countries, 100% international, 2% transferred in.

Faculty *Student/faculty ratio:* 5:1.

Academics *Calendar:* quarters. *Degrees:* associate (majority of students are from outside of U.S. and participate in intensive ESL program in preparation for

transfer to a 4-year institution). *Special study options:* academic remediation for entering students, accelerated degree program, English as a second language, independent study.

Student Life *Campus security:* 24-hour emergency response devices.

Costs (2006–07) *Tuition:* $16,250 full-time. No tuition increase for student's term of enrollment.

Applying *Options:* electronic application, early admission, deferred entrance. *Application fee:* $50. *Required:* essay or personal statement, high school transcript. *Required for some:* interview.

Freshmen Application Contact Dr. John Norris, President, TransPacific Hawaii College, 5257 Kalanianaole Highway, Honolulu, HI 96821. *Phone:* 808-377-5402 Ext. 313. *Fax:* 808-373-4754. *E-mail:* jnorris@transpacific.org.

WINDWARD COMMUNITY COLLEGE

Kaneohe, Hawaii www.wcc.hawaii.edu/

Director of Admissions Mr. Russell Chan, Registrar, Windward Community College, 45-720 Keaahala Road, Kaneohe, HI 96744. *Phone:* 808-235-7400.

IDAHO

APOLLO COLLEGE

Boise, Idaho www.apolloboise.com/

Director of Admissions Kevin Price, Director of Admissions, Apollo College, 1200 North Liberty, Boise, ID 83704. *Phone:* 208-377-8080 Ext. 35. *Toll-free phone:* 800-473-4365.

BRIGHAM YOUNG UNIVERSITY —IDAHO

Rexburg, Idaho www.byui.edu/

- **Independent** 2-year, founded 1888, affiliated with The Church of Jesus Christ of Latter-day Saints
- **Small-town** 255-acre campus
- **Coed,** 11,443 undergraduate students

Undergraduates Students come from 50 states and territories, 64% are from out of state, 20% live on campus.

Freshmen *Admission:* 6,500 applied, 6,200 admitted. *Average high school GPA:* 3.5. *Test scores:* ACT scores over 18: 94%; ACT scores over 24: 45%; ACT scores over 30: 3%.

Faculty *Total:* 420. *Student/faculty ratio:* 25:1.

Majors Accounting; administrative assistant and secretarial science; advertising; agricultural business and management; agricultural economics; agriculture; agronomy and crop science; animal sciences; architectural engineering technology; Army R.O.T.C./military science; art; athletic training; automobile/automotive mechanics technology; biology/biological sciences; botany/plant biology; broadcast journalism; business administration and management; business teacher education; carpentry; chemical engineering; chemistry; child development; Chinese; civil engineering technology; clinical/medical laboratory technology; clothing/textiles; commercial and advertising art; computer programming; computer science; construction engineering technology; criminal justice/law enforcement administration; criminal justice/police science; dairy science; dance; data processing and data processing technology; dental hygiene; dietetics; drafting and design technology; dramatic/theater arts; ecology; economics; education; electrical, electronic and communications engineering technology; elementary education; emergency medical technology (EMT paramedic); engineering; engineering related; engineering technology; English; family and community services; family and consumer sciences/home economics teacher education; family and consumer sciences/human sciences; farm and ranch management; fashion/apparel design; fashion merchandising; finance; foods, nutrition, and wellness; forestry; French; geography; geology/earth science; German; health science; history; horticultural science; humanities; industrial arts; industrial design; industrial technology; information science/studies; interior design; journalism; kindergarten/preschool education; landscape architecture; liberal arts and sciences/liberal studies; machine tool technology; marine biology and biological oceanography; marketing/marketing management; mass communication/media; mathematics; mechanical design technology; mechanical engineering/mechanical technology; metallurgical technology; music; music teacher education; nursing

(registered nurse training); occupational therapy; ornamental horticulture; parks, recreation and leisure; photography; physical education teaching and coaching; physical sciences; physical therapy; physics; piano and organ; plastics engineering technology; political science and government; pre-engineering; psychology; radio and television; radiologic technology/science; range science and management; Russian; social work; sociology; Spanish; special products marketing; speech therapy; trade and industrial teacher education; welding technology; wildlife and wildlands science and management; zoology/animal biology.

Academics *Calendar:* semesters. *Degree:* associate. *Special study options:* academic remediation for entering students, accelerated degree program, adult/continuing education programs, advanced placement credit, honors programs, internships, part-time degree program, services for LD students, summer session for credit. *ROTC:* Army (b).

Library David O. McKay Library with 134,423 titles, 889 serial subscriptions, 34,556 audiovisual materials, an OPAC.

Student Life *Housing Options:* men-only, women-only. Campus housing is university owned. *Activities and Organizations:* drama/theater group, student-run newspaper, radio station, choral group, R Friends, Dance Committee, Student Activities Committee, national fraternities, national sororities. *Campus security:* 24-hour emergency response devices and patrols, late-night transport/escort service. *Student services:* health clinic, personal/psychological counseling, legal services.

Athletics Member NJCAA. *Intramural sports:* archery M/W, badminton M/W, basketball M/W, bowling M/W, cross-country running M/W, fencing M/W, football M/W, golf M/W, racquetball M/W, skiing (cross-country) M/W, skiing (downhill) M/W, soccer M/W, softball M/W, swimming and diving M/W, table tennis M/W, tennis M/W, volleyball M/W, water polo M/W, wrestling M.

Standardized Tests *Required:* SAT or ACT (for admission).

Costs (2006–07) *Comprehensive fee:* $7440 includes full-time tuition ($2890) and room and board ($4550). Full-time tuition and fees vary according to program. Part-time tuition: $1440 per term. Part-time tuition and fees vary according to course load. Non-Latter Day Saints' full year tuition is $5,780. *Room and board:* Room and board charges vary according to board plan, housing facility, and location. *Waivers:* employees or children of employees.

Financial Aid Of all full-time matriculated undergraduates, 2,400 state and other part-time jobs.

Applying *Options:* electronic application. *Application fee:* $30. *Required:* essay or personal statement, high school transcript, interview. *Application deadlines:* 2/15 (freshmen), 3/15 (transfers). *Notification:* 4/1 (freshmen), 3/15 (transfers).

Freshmen Application Contact Mr. Steven Davis, Assistant Director of Admissions, Brigham Young University –Idaho, 120 Kimball, Rexburg, ID 83460-1615. *Phone:* 208-356-1026. *E-mail:* daviss@byui.edu.

COLLEGE OF SOUTHERN IDAHO

Twin Falls, Idaho www.csi.edu/

- **State and locally supported** 2-year, founded 1964
- **Small-town** 287-acre campus
- **Endowment** $15.0 million
- **Coed,** 7,543 undergraduate students

Undergraduates Students come from 29 states and territories, 27 other countries, 3% are from out of state, 0.5% African American, 0.9% Asian American or Pacific Islander, 9% Hispanic American, 0.8% Native American, 4% international, 10% live on campus.

Faculty *Total:* 338, 48% full-time. *Student/faculty ratio:* 26:1.

Majors Accounting; agricultural business and management; agriculture; anthropology; art; autobody/collision and repair technology; automobile/automotive mechanics technology; biology/biological sciences; botany/plant biology; business administration and management; business/commerce; cabinetmaking and millwork; chemistry; child development; clinical laboratory science/medical technology; commercial and advertising art; communication/speech communication and rhetoric; computer science; criminal justice/law enforcement administration; criminal justice/police science; culinary arts; dental assisting; dental hygiene; diesel mechanics technology; dietetics; drafting and design technology; dramatic/theater arts; education; electrical, electronic and communications engineering technology; elementary education; engineering; English; environmental studies; equestrian studies; finance; fish/game management; foreign languages and literatures; forestry; geography; geology/earth science; health/health care administration; heating, air conditioning, ventilation and refrigeration maintenance technology; history; hotel/motel administration; human services; hydrology and water resources science; liberal arts and sciences/liberal studies; library science; marketing/marketing management; mathematics; medical radiologic technology; music; natural sciences; nursing (registered nurse training); occupational therapy; photography; physical education teaching and coaching; physical therapy; physician assistant; physics; political science and government; pre-pharmacy studies; psychology; public health education and promotion; range

College of Southern Idaho *(continued)*

science and management; real estate; respiratory care therapy; sociology; surgical technology; veterinary technology; welding technology; woodworking; zoology/animal biology.

Academics *Calendar:* semesters. *Degree:* certificates, diplomas, and associate. *Special study options:* academic remediation for entering students, adult/continuing education programs, advanced placement credit, cooperative education, distance learning, English as a second language, honors programs, independent study, internships, part-time degree program, services for LD students, summer session for credit.

Library College of Southern Idaho Library with 62,556 titles, 374 serial subscriptions, 4,216 audiovisual materials, an OPAC, a Web page.

Student Life *Housing Options:* coed. Campus housing is university owned. *Activities and Organizations:* drama/theater group, student-run newspaper, radio station, choral group, BPA, Dex, Chi Alpha (Christian Group), Vet Tech Club, Equine Club. *Campus security:* 24-hour emergency response devices and patrols, controlled dormitory access. *Student services:* health clinic, personal/psychological counseling, women's center, legal services.

Athletics Member NJCAA. *Intercollegiate sports:* baseball M(s)/W, basketball M(s)/W(s), cheerleading M(s)/W(s), equestrian sports M(s)(c)/W(s)(c), volleyball M/W(s). *Intramural sports:* badminton M/W, basketball M/W, football M/W, racquetball M/W, rock climbing M/W, soccer M/W, softball M/W, tennis M/W, ultimate Frisbee M/W, volleyball M/W.

Standardized Tests *Required:* ACT COMPASS (for admission). *Required for some:* ACT (for admission).

Costs (2007–08) *Tuition:* state resident $2100 full-time, $105 per credit part-time; nonresident $5900 full-time, $295 per credit part-time.

Financial Aid Of all full-time matriculated undergraduates, 250 Federal Work-Study jobs (averaging $2000). 100 state and other part-time jobs (averaging $2000).

Applying *Required:* high school transcript. *Required for some:* letters of recommendation, interview. *Application deadlines:* rolling (freshmen), rolling (transfers).

Freshmen Application Contact Ms. Gail G. Schull, Director of Admissions, Registration, and Records, College of Southern Idaho, PO Box 1238, 315 Falls Avenue, Twin Falls, ID 83303. *Phone:* 208-732-6232. *Toll-free phone:* 800-680-0274. *Fax:* 208-736-3014.

EASTERN IDAHO TECHNICAL COLLEGE

Idaho Falls, Idaho　　　　www.eitc.edu/

- **State-supported** 2-year, founded 1970
- **Small-town** 40-acre campus
- **Endowment** $1.4 million
- **Coed**

Undergraduates 229 full-time, 526 part-time. Students come from 5 states and territories, 0.9% African American, 0.6% Asian American or Pacific Islander, 6% Hispanic American, 0.5% Native American, 11% transferred in. *Retention:* 50% of 2003 full-time freshmen returned.

Faculty *Student/faculty ratio:* 12:1.

Academics *Calendar:* semesters. *Degree:* certificates and associate. *Special study options:* academic remediation for entering students, adult/continuing education programs, cooperative education, distance learning, internships, part-time degree program, services for LD students, summer session for credit.

Student Life *Campus security:* 24-hour patrols.

Costs (2006–07) *Tuition:* state resident $1578 full-time, $79 per credit part-time; nonresident $5784 full-time, $158 per credit part-time. Full-time tuition and fees vary according to course load and reciprocity agreements. Part-time tuition and fees vary according to class time and reciprocity agreements. *Required fees:* $124 full-time, $15 per term part-time.

Financial Aid Of all full-time matriculated undergraduates, 37 Federal Work-Study jobs (averaging $1176). 11 state and other part-time jobs (averaging $1619).

Applying *Options:* deferred entrance. *Application fee:* $10. *Required:* high school transcript, interview, COMPASS. *Required for some:* essay or personal statement.

Freshmen Application Contact Dr. Steve Albiston, Dean of Students, Eastern Idaho Technical College, 1600 South 25th East, Idaho Falls, ID 83404. *Phone:* 208-524-3000 Ext. 3366. *Toll-free phone:* 800-662-0261 Ext. 3371. *Fax:* 208-525-7026. *E-mail:* salbisto@eitc.edu.

ITT TECHNICAL INSTITUTE

Boise, Idaho　　　　www.itt-tech.edu/

- **Proprietary** primarily 2-year, founded 1906, part of ITT Educational Services, Inc
- **Urban** 1-acre campus
- **Coed**

Majors Animation, interactive technology, video graphics and special effects; business administration and management; CAD/CADD drafting/design technology; communications technology; computer and information systems security; computer engineering technology; computer software engineering; computer systems networking and telecommunications; construction management; criminal justice/law enforcement administration; electrical, electronic and communications engineering technology; health information/medical records technology; web/multimedia management and webmaster; web page, digital/multimedia and information resources design.

Academics *Calendar:* quarters. *Degrees:* associate and bachelor's.

Library a Web page.

Student Life *Housing:* college housing not available.

Standardized Tests *Required:* Wonderlic aptitude test (for admission).

Costs (2006–07) *Tuition:* Contact school for program costs.

Financial Aid Of all full-time matriculated undergraduates, 9 Federal Work-Study jobs (averaging $5500).

Applying *Options:* deferred entrance. *Application fee:* $100. *Required:* high school transcript, interview. *Recommended:* letters of recommendation. *Application deadlines:* rolling (freshmen), rolling (transfers). *Notification:* continuous (freshmen), continuous (transfers).

Freshmen Application Contact Ms. Jennifer Kandler, Director of Recruitment, ITT Technical Institute, 12302 West Explorer Drive, Boise, ID 83713. *Phone:* 208-322-8844. *Toll-free phone:* 800-666-4888. *Fax:* 208-322-0173.

NORTH IDAHO COLLEGE

Coeur d'Alene, Idaho　　　　www.nic.edu/

- **State and locally supported** 2-year, founded 1933
- **Small-town** 42-acre campus
- **Endowment** $5.7 million
- **Coed,** 4,293 undergraduate students, 57% full-time, 61% women, 39% men

Undergraduates 2,457 full-time, 1,836 part-time. Students come from 34 states and territories, 9 other countries, 10% are from out of state, 0.2% African American, 0.8% Asian American or Pacific Islander, 2% Hispanic American, 2% Native American, 13% transferred in.

Freshmen *Admission:* 1,472 applied, 1,472 admitted, 996 enrolled.

Faculty *Total:* 294, 51% full-time, 4% with terminal degrees. *Student/faculty ratio:* 16:1.

Majors Administrative assistant and secretarial science; agriculture; American Indian/Native American studies; anthropology; art; astronomy; athletic training; automobile/automotive mechanics technology; biological and physical sciences; biology/biological sciences; botany/plant biology; business administration and management; business teacher education; carpentry; chemistry; clinical laboratory science/medical technology; commercial and advertising art; computer and information sciences related; computer programming; computer science; computer/technical support; criminal justice/law enforcement administration; criminal justice/police science; culinary arts; developmental and child psychology; drafting and design technology; dramatic/theater arts; education; electrical, electronic and communications engineering technology; elementary education; engineering; English; environmental health; fish/game management; forestry; French; geology/earth science; German; health/health care administration; heating, air conditioning, ventilation and refrigeration maintenance technology; heavy equipment maintenance technology; history; hospitality administration; human services; journalism; legal administrative assistant/secretary; legal assistant/paralegal; liberal arts and sciences/liberal studies; machine tool technology; marine technology; mass communication/media; mathematics; medical administrative assistant and medical secretary; music; music teacher education; nursing (licensed practical/vocational nurse training); nursing (registered nurse training); physical sciences; physics; political science and government; psychology; social sciences; sociology; Spanish; welding technology; wildlife and wildlands science and management; wildlife biology; zoology/animal biology.

Academics *Calendar:* semesters. *Degree:* certificates and associate. *Special study options:* academic remediation for entering students, adult/continuing education programs, advanced placement credit, cooperative education, distance learning, English as a second language, independent study, internships, off-campus study, part-time degree program, services for LD students, summer session for credit.

Library Molstead Library Computer Center with 60,893 titles, 751 serial subscriptions, an OPAC, a Web page.

Student Life *Housing Options:* Campus housing is university owned. *Activities and Organizations:* drama/theater group, student-run newspaper, choral group, Ski Club, Fusion, Baptist student ministries, Journalism Club, Phi Theta Kappa. *Campus security:* 24-hour emergency response devices and patrols, late-night transport/escort service. *Student services:* health clinic, personal/psychological counseling, women's center, legal services.

Athletics Member NJCAA. *Intercollegiate sports:* basketball M(s)/W(s), cheerleading M(s)/W(s), soccer M(s)/W(s), softball W(s), volleyball W(s), wrestling M(s). *Intramural sports:* basketball M/W, bowling M/W, cheerleading M/W, crew M(c)/W(c), cross-country running M(c)/W(c), football M/W, golf M/W, racquetball M/W, sailing M(c)/W(c), skiing (cross-country) M(c)/W(c), skiing (downhill) M(c)/W(c), soccer M(c)/W(c), softball M/W, table tennis M/W, tennis M/W, track and field M(c)/W(c), volleyball M/W.

Costs (2007–08) *Tuition:* area resident $1234 full-time, $140 per credit part-time; state resident $2234 full-time, $203 per credit part-time; nonresident $5786 full-time, $425 per credit part-time. *Required fees:* $876 full-time. *Room and board:* $5620.

Financial Aid Of all full-time matriculated undergraduates, 142 Federal Work-Study jobs (averaging $1425). 106 state and other part-time jobs (averaging $1327).

Applying *Options:* electronic application, early admission, deferred entrance. *Application fee:* $25. *Required for some:* essay or personal statement, high school transcript, county residency certificate. *Application deadlines:* 8/20 (freshmen), 8/20 (transfers).

Freshmen Application Contact Dr. Candace Wheeler, Director of Distance Education, North Idaho College, 1000 West Garden Avenue, Coeur d'Alene, ID 83814-2199. *Phone:* 208-769-3436. *Toll-free phone:* 877-404-4536 Ext. 3311. *Fax:* 208-769-3399. *E-mail:* admit@nic.edu.

ILLINOIS

BLACK HAWK COLLEGE
Moline, Illinois   **www.bhc.edu/**

- **State and locally supported** 2-year, founded 1946, part of Black Hawk College District System
- **Urban** 161-acre campus
- **Coed,** 6,600 undergraduate students, 48% full-time, 61% women, 39% men

Undergraduates 3,138 full-time, 3,462 part-time. Students come from 5 states and territories, 3% are from out of state, 7% African American, 0.8% Asian American or Pacific Islander, 7% Hispanic American, 0.5% Native American, 0.1% transferred in. *Retention:* 62% of 2003 full-time freshmen returned.

Freshmen *Admission:* 944 admitted, 944 enrolled. *Test scores:* ACT scores over 18: 64%; ACT scores over 24: 15%; ACT scores over 30: 1%.

Faculty *Total:* 364, 38% full-time, 13% with terminal degrees. *Student/faculty ratio:* 18:1.

Majors Accounting; administrative assistant and secretarial science; agribusiness; agricultural mechanics and equipment technology; agricultural mechanization; agricultural production related; animal/livestock husbandry and production; animal sciences; autobody/collision and repair technology; banking and financial support services; business administration and management; CAD/CADD drafting/design technology; carpentry; child development; civil engineering technology; communications technology; computer/information technology services administration related; computer installation and repair technology; computer programming; computer systems networking and telecommunications; computer/technical support; criminal justice/law enforcement administration; culinary arts; data processing and data processing technology; dental assisting; design and visual communications; diesel mechanics technology; electrical, electronics and communications engineering; electrician; electromechanical technology; electroneurodiagnostic/electroencephalographic technology; engine machinist; environmental control technologies related; environmental health; equestrian studies; finance; finance and financial management services related; fire services administration; health information/medical records administration; heating, air conditioning, ventilation and refrigeration maintenance technology; horse husbandry/equine science and management; horticultural science; information technology; interior design; international business/trade/commerce; legal administrative assistant/secretary; legal assistant/paralegal; library assistant; machine tool technology; management science; manufacturing technology; marketing related; mechanics and repair; medical transcription; nursing (licensed practical/vocational nurse training); nursing (registered nurse training); physical

therapist assistant; radio and television broadcasting technology; radiologic technology/science; retailing; security and protective services related; sheet metal technology; sign language interpretation; small business administration; teacher assistant/aide; tool and die technology; truck and bus driver/commercial vehicle operation; vehicle maintenance and repair technologies related; web/multimedia management and webmaster; welding technology.

Academics *Calendar:* semesters. *Degree:* certificates and associate. *Special study options:* academic remediation for entering students, accelerated degree program, adult/continuing education programs, advanced placement credit, cooperative education, distance learning, English as a second language, independent study, internships, off-campus study, part-time degree program, services for LD students, study abroad, summer session for credit.

Library Quad City Campus Library plus 1 other with 59,840 titles, 612 serial subscriptions, 140 audiovisual materials, an OPAC.

Student Life *Housing:* college housing not available. *Activities and Organizations:* drama/theater group, student-run newspaper, television station, choral group. *Campus security:* 24-hour patrols. *Student services:* personal/psychological counseling.

Athletics Member NJCAA. *Intercollegiate sports:* baseball M(s), basketball M(s)/W(s), golf M(s), softball W(s), volleyball W(s). *Intramural sports:* soccer M.

Standardized Tests *Required for some:* ACT (for placement), COMPASS.

Costs (2006–07) *Tuition:* area resident $1860 full-time, $62 per credit hour part-time; state resident $4200 full-time, $140 per credit hour part-time; nonresident $7770 full-time, $259 per credit hour part-time. *Required fees:* $210 full-time, $7 per credit hour part-time.

Financial Aid Of all full-time matriculated undergraduates, 173 Federal Work-Study jobs (averaging $1531). 196 state and other part-time jobs (averaging $1228).

Applying *Options:* early admission, deferred entrance. *Required:* high school transcript. *Application deadline:* rolling (freshmen). *Notification:* continuous (freshmen).

Freshmen Application Contact Ms. Rose Hernandez, Coordinator of Recruitment, Black Hawk College, 6600 34th Avenue, Moline, IL 61265. *Phone:* 309-796-5342.

CARL SANDBURG COLLEGE
Galesburg, Illinois   **www.sandburg.edu/**

Director of Admissions Ms. Carol Kreider, Dean of Student Support Services, Carl Sandburg College, 2400 Tom L. Wilson Boulevard, Galesburg, IL 61401-9576. *Phone:* 309-341-5234.

CITY COLLEGES OF CHICAGO, HAROLD WASHINGTON COLLEGE
Chicago, Illinois   **hwashington.ccc.edu/**

- **State and locally supported** 2-year, founded 1962, part of City Colleges of Chicago
- **Urban** 1-acre campus
- **Coed,** 8,434 undergraduate students, 31% full-time, 58% women, 42% men

Undergraduates 2,608 full-time, 5,826 part-time. Students come from 3 states and territories, 47% African American, 11% Asian American or Pacific Islander, 19% Hispanic American, 0.7% Native American, 6% transferred in.

Freshmen *Admission:* 1,653 enrolled.

Faculty *Total:* 231, 51% full-time. *Student/faculty ratio:* 23:1.

Majors Accounting; administrative assistant and secretarial science; architectural engineering technology; art; biology/biological sciences; business administration and management; chemistry; child development; commercial and advertising art; corrections; criminal justice/law enforcement administration; criminal justice/police science; data processing and data processing technology; developmental and child psychology; dramatic/theater arts; elementary education; emergency medical technology (EMT paramedic); engineering; engineering technology; English; finance; fire science; French; German; hospitality administration; hotel/motel administration; humanities; information science/studies; international business/trade/commerce; Italian; Japanese; journalism; kindergarten/preschool education; legal studies; liberal arts and sciences/liberal studies; marketing/marketing management; mathematics; mental health/rehabilitation; music; philosophy; physical sciences; physics; pre-engineering; social sciences; social work; Spanish; speech and rhetoric; substance abuse/addiction counseling; teacher assistant/aide; tourism and travel services management.

City Colleges of Chicago, Harold Washington College (continued)

Academics *Calendar:* semesters. *Degree:* certificates and associate. *Special study options:* academic remediation for entering students, accelerated degree program, adult/continuing education programs, advanced placement credit, cooperative education, distance learning, double majors, English as a second language, independent study, internships, off-campus study, part-time degree program, services for LD students, summer session for credit.

Library Harold Washington College Library plus 1 other with 65,926 titles, 360 serial subscriptions, 2,695 audiovisual materials.

Student Life *Housing:* college housing not available. *Activities and Organizations:* drama/theater group, student-run newspaper, choral group, Phi Theta Kappa, Organization of Latin American Students, Black Student Union, Student Government Association, Global Friendship. *Campus security:* 24-hour emergency response devices and patrols. *Student services:* personal/psychological counseling, women's center.

Standardized Tests *Required:* DTLS, DTMS (for placement).

Costs (2006–07) *Tuition:* area resident $2410 full-time; state resident $5675 full-time; nonresident $8998 full-time.

Financial Aid Of all full-time matriculated undergraduates, 100 Federal Work-Study jobs (averaging $3500).

Applying *Options:* early admission, deferred entrance. *Application deadlines:* rolling (freshmen), rolling (transfers). *Notification:* continuous (freshmen), continuous (transfers).

Director of Admissions Mr. Terry Pendleton, Admissions Coordinator, City Colleges of Chicago, Harold Washington College, 30 East Lake Street, Chicago, IL 60601. *Phone:* 312-553-6006.

CITY COLLEGES OF CHICAGO, HARRY S. TRUMAN COLLEGE

Chicago, Illinois   **www.trumancollege.cc/**

- **State and locally supported** 2-year, founded 1956, part of City Colleges of Chicago
- **Urban** 5-acre campus
- **Coed,** 12,518 undergraduate students

Undergraduates *Retention:* 25% of 2003 full-time freshmen returned.

Faculty *Total:* 503, 23% full-time. *Student/faculty ratio:* 61:1.

Majors Accounting; art; business administration and management; chemical engineering; clinical laboratory science/medical technology; criminal justice/police science; developmental and child psychology; drafting and design technology; education; elementary education; health information/medical records administration; information science/studies; journalism; legal studies; liberal arts and sciences/liberal studies; marketing/marketing management; medical administrative assistant and medical secretary; modern languages; nursing (registered nurse training); physical education teaching and coaching; pre-engineering; speech and rhetoric; teacher assistant/aide.

Academics *Calendar:* semesters. *Degree:* certificates, diplomas, and associate. *Special study options:* academic remediation for entering students, adult/continuing education programs, advanced placement credit, cooperative education, distance learning, English as a second language, honors programs, internships, part-time degree program, services for LD students, summer session for credit.

Library 59,750 titles, 250 serial subscriptions.

Student Life *Housing:* college housing not available. *Activities and Organizations:* drama/theater group. *Campus security:* 24-hour patrols, late-night transport/escort service. *Student services:* personal/psychological counseling.

Athletics Member NJCAA. *Intercollegiate sports:* baseball M, basketball M/W, tennis M/W, wrestling M. *Intramural sports:* basketball M/W, swimming and diving M/W, tennis M/W, volleyball M/W.

Standardized Tests *Required:* ACT (for placement).

Costs (2006–07) *Tuition:* area resident $2410 full-time; state resident $5675 full-time; nonresident $8998 full-time.

Financial Aid Of all full-time matriculated undergraduates, 150 Federal Work-Study jobs (averaging $3000).

Applying *Options:* early admission, deferred entrance. *Application deadlines:* rolling (freshmen), rolling (transfers). *Notification:* continuous until 9/8 (freshmen), continuous until 9/8 (transfers).

Director of Admissions Mrs. Kelly O'Malley, Assistant Dean, Student Services, City Colleges of Chicago, Harry S. Truman College, 1145 West Wilson Avenue, Chicago, IL 60640-5616. *Phone:* 773-907-4720.

CITY COLLEGES OF CHICAGO, KENNEDY-KING COLLEGE

Chicago, Illinois   **kennedyking.ccc.edu/**

- **State and locally supported** 2-year, founded 1935, part of City Colleges of Chicago
- **Urban** 18-acre campus
- **Endowment** $14.1 million
- **Coed,** 3,054 undergraduate students

Undergraduates Students come from 51 states and territories.

Faculty *Total:* 147, 41% full-time, 12% with terminal degrees.

Majors Accounting; administrative assistant and secretarial science; architectural engineering technology; automobile/automotive mechanics technology; biology/biological sciences; broadcast journalism; business administration and management; chemistry; child development; clinical laboratory science/medical technology; commercial and advertising art; data processing and data processing technology; education; engineering; family and consumer sciences/human sciences; graphic and printing equipment operation/production; health science; heating, air conditioning, ventilation and refrigeration maintenance technology; kindergarten/preschool education; legal studies; liberal arts and sciences/liberal studies; marketing/marketing management; mathematics; mental health/rehabilitation; nursing (registered nurse training); parks, recreation and leisure; pharmacy; physics; pre-engineering; radio and television; social work; special products marketing; teacher assistant/aide.

Academics *Calendar:* semesters. *Degree:* certificates and associate. *Special study options:* academic remediation for entering students, adult/continuing education programs, advanced placement credit, cooperative education, distance learning, English as a second language, honors programs, internships, part-time degree program, summer session for credit.

Library Harold Washington College Library with 45,000 titles, 200 serial subscriptions, 2,500 audiovisual materials, an OPAC, a Web page.

Student Life *Housing:* college housing not available. *Activities and Organizations:* drama/theater group, student-run newspaper, radio station, choral group, Phi Theta Kappa, Phi Beta Lambda, Herman Bryant Auto Club, Communication Art Guild, POP (print club), national fraternities. *Campus security:* late-night transport/escort service. *Student services:* personal/psychological counseling.

Athletics Member NJCAA. *Intercollegiate sports:* basketball M(s)/W(s), soccer M, track and field M/W, wrestling M. *Intramural sports:* basketball M, volleyball M/W.

Standardized Tests *Recommended:* SAT or ACT (for placement).

Costs (2006–07) *Tuition:* area resident $2410 full-time; state resident $5675 full-time; nonresident $8998 full-time.

Financial Aid Of all full-time matriculated undergraduates, 148 Federal Work-Study jobs (averaging $1539).

Applying *Options:* electronic application. *Required:* high school transcript. *Application deadlines:* rolling (freshmen), rolling (transfers).

Freshmen Application Contact Ms. Joyce Collins, Clerical Supervisor for Admissions and Records, City Colleges of Chicago, Kennedy-King College, 6800 South Wentworth Avenue, Chicago, IL 60621. *Phone:* 773-602-5000 Ext. 5055.

CITY COLLEGES OF CHICAGO, MALCOLM X COLLEGE

Chicago, Illinois   **malcolmx.ccc.edu/**

Freshmen Application Contact Mr. Ghingo Brooks, Vice President of Enrollment Management and Student Services, City Colleges of Chicago, Malcolm X College, 1900 West Van Buren Street, Chicago, IL 60612. *Phone:* 312-850-7120. *Fax:* 312-850-7092. *E-mail:* gbrooks@ccc.edu.

CITY COLLEGES OF CHICAGO, OLIVE-HARVEY COLLEGE

Chicago, Illinois   **oliveharvey.ccc.edu/**

- **State and locally supported** 2-year, founded 1970, part of City Colleges of Chicago
- **Urban** 67-acre campus
- **Coed,** 2,188 undergraduate students, 36% full-time, 76% women, 24% men

Undergraduates 795 full-time, 1,393 part-time. 89% African American, 0.6% Asian American or Pacific Islander, 8% Hispanic American, 0.4% Native American.

Freshmen *Admission:* 384 applied, 384 admitted.

Faculty *Total:* 130, 62% full-time. *Student/faculty ratio:* 19:1.

Majors Accounting; African-American/Black studies; art; biology/biological sciences; business administration and management; chemistry; computer engineering technology; developmental and child psychology; electrical, electronic and communications engineering technology; engineering; geology/earth science; kindergarten/preschool education; liberal arts and sciences/liberal studies; marketing/marketing management; mathematics; music; nursing (registered nurse training); philosophy; photography; physics; respiratory therapy technician; social sciences.

Academics *Calendar:* semesters. *Degree:* certificates and associate. *Special study options:* academic remediation for entering students, accelerated degree program, adult/continuing education programs, advanced placement credit, cooperative education, distance learning, part-time degree program, services for LD students, student-designed majors, study abroad, summer session for credit.

Library Library with 56,318 titles, 325 serial subscriptions, an OPAC, a Web page.

Student Life *Housing:* college housing not available. *Activities and Organizations:* drama/theater group, Student Government Association, Club Tech, African-American Club, Phi Theta Kappa, Panther Dena. *Campus security:* 24-hour emergency response devices and patrols. *Student services:* personal/psychological counseling, women's center.

Athletics Member NJCAA. *Intercollegiate sports:* baseball M, basketball M(s), volleyball W(s). *Intramural sports:* basketball M/W, gymnastics M/W, soccer M/W, swimming and diving M/W, tennis M/W, track and field M/W, volleyball M/W, wrestling M.

Costs (2007–08) *Tuition:* area resident $864 full-time, $72 per credit part-time; state resident $2279 full-time, $190 per credit part-time; nonresident $3717 full-time, $310 per credit part-time. *Required fees:* $200 full-time, $72 per credit part-time, $75 per term part-time.

Financial Aid Of all full-time matriculated undergraduates, 150 Federal Work-Study jobs (averaging $3900).

Applying *Options:* early admission, deferred entrance. *Recommended:* high school transcript, minimum 2.0 GPA. *Application deadlines:* rolling (freshmen), rolling (transfers).

Freshmen Application Contact Michelle Adams, Assistant Dean of Student Services, City Colleges of Chicago, Olive-Harvey College, 10001 South Woodlawn, Chicago, IL 60628-1696. *Phone:* 773-291-6349. *Fax:* 773-291-6304. *E-mail:* OH_admissions@ccc.edu.

CITY COLLEGES OF CHICAGO, RICHARD J. DALEY COLLEGE

Chicago, Illinois   daley.ccc.edu/

- **State and locally supported** 2-year, founded 1960, part of City Colleges of Chicago
- **Urban** 25-acre campus
- **Coed,** 10,654 undergraduate students, 33% full-time, 63% women, 37% men

Undergraduates 3,545 full-time, 7,109 part-time. Students come from 29 states and territories, 71 other countries, 37% African American, 2% Asian American or Pacific Islander, 42% Hispanic American, 0.3% Native American.

Freshmen *Admission:* 1,174 admitted, 1,174 enrolled.

Majors Accounting; administrative assistant and secretarial science; architectural engineering technology; art; avionics maintenance technology; business administration and management; child development; clinical laboratory science/medical technology; criminal justice/police science; data processing and data processing technology; dental hygiene; developmental and child psychology; drafting and design technology; dramatic/theater arts; education; electrical, electronic and communications engineering technology; elementary education; fire science; horticultural science; humanities; journalism; legal studies; liberal arts and sciences/liberal studies; machine tool technology; marketing/marketing management; mass communication/media; medical administrative assistant and medical secretary; modern languages; music; nursing (registered nurse training); pharmacy; photography; pre-engineering; social work; speech and rhetoric; teacher assistant/aide; telecommunications; transportation technology.

Academics *Calendar:* semesters. *Degree:* certificates and associate. *Special study options:* academic remediation for entering students, adult/continuing education programs, advanced placement credit, English as a second language, honors programs, off-campus study, part-time degree program, services for LD students, summer session for credit. *ROTC:* Air Force (c).

Library Learning Resource Center plus 1 other with 53,201 titles, 275 serial subscriptions, an OPAC.

Student Life *Housing:* college housing not available. *Activities and Organizations:* drama/theater group, student-run newspaper, Latin Student Organization, Student Government Association, African-American Culture Club. *Campus security:* 24-hour patrols. *Student services:* personal/psychological counseling.

Standardized Tests *Required for some:* ACT (for placement). *Recommended:* ACT (for placement).

Costs (2006–07) *Tuition:* area resident $2410 full-time; state resident $5675 full-time; nonresident $8998 full-time.

Financial Aid Of all full-time matriculated undergraduates, 250 Federal Work-Study jobs (averaging $2500).

Applying *Options:* early admission, deferred entrance. *Required:* high school transcript. *Required for some:* essay or personal statement, letters of recommendation. *Recommended:* interview. *Application deadlines:* rolling (freshmen), rolling (transfers).

Freshmen Application Contact Ms. Karla Reynolds, Registrar, City Colleges of Chicago, Richard J. Daley College, 7500 South Pulaski Road, Chicago, IL 60652-1242. *Phone:* 773-838-7599. *E-mail:* kreynolds@ccc.edu.

CITY COLLEGES OF CHICAGO, WILBUR WRIGHT COLLEGE

Chicago, Illinois   wright.ccc.edu/

- **State and locally supported** 2-year, founded 1934, part of City Colleges of Chicago
- **Urban** 20-acre campus with easy access to Chicago, Illinois
- **Coed,** 6,980 undergraduate students, 37% full-time, 59% women, 41% men

Undergraduates 2,559 full-time, 4,421 part-time. 11% African American, 10% Asian American or Pacific Islander, 41% Hispanic American, 0.5% Native American.

Freshmen *Admission:* 2,680 applied, 2,680 admitted. *Average high school GPA:* 2.5.

Faculty *Total:* 258, 42% full-time, 28% with terminal degrees. *Student/faculty ratio:* 26:1.

Majors Accounting; architectural engineering technology; architectural technology; art; biological and physical sciences; business administration and management; computer and information sciences; computer and information systems security; criminal justice/police science; data processing and data processing technology; elementary education; engineering; English; environmental engineering technology; environmental science; general studies; gerontology; Hispanic-American, Puerto Rican, and Mexican-American/Chicano studies; journalism; liberal arts and sciences/liberal studies; library science; machine tool technology; marketing/marketing management; medical radiologic technology; modern languages; music; occupational therapy; physical sciences; pre-engineering; speech and rhetoric.

Academics *Calendar:* semesters. *Degree:* certificates and associate. *Special study options:* academic remediation for entering students, accelerated degree program, adult/continuing education programs, distance learning, English as a second language, part-time degree program, summer session for credit.

Library Learning Resource Center plus 1 other with 60,000 titles, 350 serial subscriptions.

Student Life *Housing:* college housing not available. *Activities and Organizations:* drama/theater group, student-run newspaper, choral group, student government, Circle K, Phi Theta Kappa, Black Student Union. *Campus security:* 24-hour emergency response devices and patrols, student patrols, late-night transport/escort service. *Student services:* legal services.

Athletics Member NJCAA. *Intercollegiate sports:* basketball M(s)/W(s), wrestling M(s). *Intramural sports:* basketball M, cross-country running M/W, golf M/W, volleyball M/W, weight lifting M/W, wrestling M/W.

Costs (2007–08) *Tuition:* area resident $2010 full-time, $72 per credit hour part-time; state resident $5595 full-time, $181 per credit hour part-time; nonresident $7929 full-time, $292 per credit hour part-time. *Required fees:* $250 full-time, $70 per term part-time.

Financial Aid Of all full-time matriculated undergraduates, 67 Federal Work-Study jobs (averaging $1000).

Applying *Options:* early admission, deferred entrance. *Application deadlines:* rolling (freshmen), rolling (transfers). *Notification:* continuous (freshmen), continuous (transfers).

Freshmen Application Contact Ms. Amy Aiello, Assistant Dean of Student Services, City Colleges of Chicago, Wilbur Wright College, 4300 North Narragansett, Chicago, IL 60634. *Phone:* 773-481-8207. *Fax:* 773-481-8185. *E-mail:* aaiello@ccc.edu.

COLLEGE OF DUPAGE
Glen Ellyn, Illinois
www.cod.edu/

- **State and locally supported** 2-year, founded 1967
- **Suburban** 297-acre campus with easy access to Chicago
- **Endowment** $10.5 million
- **Coed,** 26,032 undergraduate students, 34% full-time, 55% women, 45% men

Undergraduates 8,909 full-time, 17,123 part-time. Students come from 19 states and territories, 6% African American, 11% Asian American or Pacific Islander, 8% Hispanic American, 0.3% Native American, 8% transferred in. *Retention:* 64% of 2003 full-time freshmen returned.

Freshmen *Admission:* 3,158 admitted, 2,732 enrolled.

Faculty *Total:* 1,167, 26% full-time, 25% with terminal degrees. *Student/faculty ratio:* 21:1.

Majors Accounting; administrative assistant and secretarial science; automobile/automotive mechanics technology; baking and pastry arts; biological and physical sciences; building/property maintenance and management; business administration and management; child care and support services management; child care provision; child development; cinematography and film/video production; commercial and advertising art; communications systems installation and repair technology; communications technology; computer installation and repair technology; computer programming (specific applications); computer typography and composition equipment operation; corrections; criminal justice/law enforcement administration; criminal justice/police science; culinary arts; data entry/microcomputer applications related; dental hygiene; design and visual communications; desktop publishing and digital imaging design; drafting and design technology; electrical, electronic and communications engineering technology; electrical/electronics equipment installation and repair; electromechanical technology; emergency medical technology (EMT paramedic); engineering; fashion and fabric consulting; fashion/apparel design; fashion merchandising; fire science; graphic and printing equipment operation/production; health/health care administration; health information/medical records administration; health information/medical records technology; heating, air conditioning, ventilation and refrigeration maintenance technology; hospital and health care facilities administration; hospitality administration; hotel/motel administration; human services; industrial electronics technology; industrial technology; interior design; landscaping and groundskeeping; legal administrative assistant/secretary; liberal arts and sciences/liberal studies; library assistant; library science; machine tool technology; manufacturing technology; marketing/marketing management; massage therapy; mechanical design technology; medical radiologic technology; merchandising; nuclear medical technology; nursing (registered nurse training); occupational therapist assistant; occupational therapy; office management; ornamental horticulture; photography; physical therapist assistant; plastics engineering technology; precision production trades; real estate; respiratory care therapy; restaurant, culinary, and catering management; retailing; robotics technology; sales, distribution and marketing; selling skills and sales; speech-language pathology; substance abuse/addiction counseling; surgical technology; tourism and travel services management; tourism and travel services marketing; tourism promotion; transportation technology; welding technology.

Academics *Calendar:* quarters. *Degree:* certificates and associate. *Special study options:* academic remediation for entering students, accelerated degree program, adult/continuing education programs, advanced placement credit, cooperative education, distance learning, double majors, English as a second language, external degree program, honors programs, independent study, internships, off-campus study, part-time degree program, services for LD students, student-designed majors, study abroad, summer session for credit.

Library College of DuPage Library with 203,300 titles, 6,005 serial subscriptions, an OPAC, a Web page.

Student Life *Housing:* college housing not available. *Activities and Organizations:* drama/theater group, student-run newspaper, choral group, Latino Ethnic Awareness Association, The Christian Group, Phi Theta Kappa, International Students Organization, Muslim Student Association. *Campus security:* 24-hour emergency response devices and patrols, student patrols, late-night transport/escort service. *Student services:* health clinic, personal/psychological counseling.

Athletics Member NJCAA. *Intercollegiate sports:* baseball M, basketball M/W, cheerleading M/W, cross-country running M/W, football M, golf M, soccer M/W, softball W, swimming and diving M/W, tennis M/W, track and field M/W, volleyball W. *Intramural sports:* basketball M/W, bowling M/W, golf M/W, ice hockey M(c), racquetball M/W, soccer M/W, softball M/W, swimming and diving M/W, tennis M/W, volleyball M/W, weight lifting M/W.

Costs (2007–08) *Tuition:* area resident $2467 full-time; state resident $8760 full-time; nonresident $10,500 full-time. *Required fees:* $622 full-time.

Applying *Options:* early admission, deferred entrance. *Application fee:* $10. *Application deadlines:* rolling (freshmen), rolling (transfers). *Notification:* continuous (freshmen), continuous (transfers).

Freshmen Application Contact Mrs. Christine A. Legner, Coordinator of Admission Services, College of DuPage, SRC 2046, 425 Fawell Boulevard, Glen Ellyn, IL 60137-6599. *Phone:* 630-942-2442. *Fax:* 630-790-2686. *E-mail:* protis@cdnet.cod.edu.

COLLEGE OF LAKE COUNTY
Grayslake, Illinois
www.clcillinois.edu/

- **District-supported** 2-year, founded 1967, part of Illinois Community College Board
- **Suburban** 226-acre campus with easy access to Chicago and Milwaukee
- **Endowment** $2.6 million
- **Coed,** 15,558 undergraduate students, 30% full-time, 57% women, 43% men

Undergraduates 4,608 full-time, 10,950 part-time. Students come from 18 states and territories, 31 other countries, 1% are from out of state, 9% African American, 5% Asian American or Pacific Islander, 17% Hispanic American, 0.2% Native American, 0.6% international, 8% transferred in. *Retention:* 60% of 2003 full-time freshmen returned.

Freshmen *Admission:* 3,461 applied, 3,461 admitted, 1,949 enrolled.

Faculty *Total:* 832, 22% full-time, 12% with terminal degrees. *Student/faculty ratio:* 21:1.

Majors Accounting technology and bookkeeping; administrative assistant and secretarial science; architectural drafting; art; automobile/automotive mechanics technology; biological and physical sciences; business administration and management; business automation/technology/data entry; business computer programming; business systems networking/ telecommunications; chemical technology; child care provision; civil engineering technology; computer installation and repair technology; construction engineering technology; criminal justice/police science; dental hygiene; electrical, electronic and communications engineering technology; electrician; engineering; fire protection and safety technology; heating, air conditioning, ventilation and refrigeration maintenance technology; industrial mechanics and maintenance technology; landscaping and groundskeeping; liberal arts and sciences/liberal studies; machine shop technology; mechanical engineering/mechanical technology; medical office management; medical radiologic technology; music; music teacher education; natural resources management and policy; nursing (registered nurse training); ornamental horticulture; restaurant, culinary, and catering management; sales operations; social work; substance abuse/addiction counseling; technical and business writing; turf and turfgrass management.

Academics *Calendar:* semesters. *Degree:* certificates and associate. *Special study options:* academic remediation for entering students, adult/continuing education programs, advanced placement credit, cooperative education, distance learning, double majors, English as a second language, honors programs, independent study, internships, off-campus study, part-time degree program, services for LD students, student-designed majors, study abroad, summer session for credit.

Library College of Lake County Library plus 1 other with 106,842 titles, 766 serial subscriptions, an OPAC, a Web page.

Student Life *Housing:* college housing not available. *Activities and Organizations:* drama/theater group, student-run newspaper, radio station, choral group, Latino Alliance, Asian Student Alliance, Black Student Union, International Student Council, Phi Theta Kappa. *Campus security:* 24-hour emergency response devices and patrols, late-night transport/escort service. *Student services:* health clinic, personal/psychological counseling, women's center.

Athletics Member NJCAA. *Intercollegiate sports:* baseball M(s), basketball M(s)/W(s), cross-country running M(s)/W(s), golf M(s), soccer M(s)/W(s), softball W(s), tennis M(s)/W(s), volleyball W(s). *Intramural sports:* cheerleading W, golf M/W.

Costs (2007–08) *Tuition:* area resident $2130 full-time, $71 per credit hour part-time; state resident $5880 full-time, $196 per credit hour part-time; nonresident $8010 full-time, $267 per credit hour part-time. *Required fees:* $270 full-time, $9 per credit hour part-time.

Financial Aid Of all full-time matriculated undergraduates, 68 Federal Work-Study jobs (averaging $1856). 178 state and other part-time jobs (averaging $1937).

Applying *Options:* electronic application, early admission, deferred entrance. *Required for some:* high school transcript, interview. *Application deadlines:* rolling (freshmen), rolling (transfers). *Notification:* continuous (freshmen), continuous (transfers).

Freshmen Application Contact Director, Student Recruitment, College of Lake County, 19351 West Washington Street, Grayslake, IL 60030-1198. *Phone:* 847-543-2383. *Fax:* 847-543-3061.

THE COLLEGE OF OFFICE TECHNOLOGY

Chicago, Illinois   www.cotedu.com/

- **Private** 2-year
- 388 undergraduate students

Majors Data entry/microcomputer applications related.

Academics *Degree:* associate.

Costs (2006–07) *Tuition:* $8650 per degree program part-time.

Applying *Application fee:* $50.

Director of Admissions Mr. William Bolton, Director of Admissions, The College of Office Technology, 1520 West Division Street, Chicago, IL 60622. *Phone:* 773-278-0042. *Toll-free phone:* 800-953-6161. *E-mail:* bbolton@cotedu.com.

THE COOKING AND HOSPITALITY INSTITUTE OF CHICAGO

Chicago, Illinois   www.chicnet.org/

- **Proprietary** 2-year, founded 1983, part of Career Education Corporation
- **Urban** campus
- **Endowment** $35,000
- **Coed,** 898 undergraduate students, 80% full-time, 42% women, 58% men

Undergraduates 721 full-time, 177 part-time. Students come from 13 states and territories, 26% are from out of state, 16% African American, 5% Asian American or Pacific Islander, 16% Hispanic American, 0.4% Native American.

Freshmen *Admission:* 152 enrolled.

Faculty *Total:* 68, 41% full-time. *Student/faculty ratio:* 19:1.

Majors Baking and pastry arts; culinary arts.

Academics *Calendar:* continuous. *Degree:* associate. *Special study options:* academic remediation for entering students, advanced placement credit, internships, services for LD students.

Library Learning Resource Center with 11,000 titles, 40 serial subscriptions, 150 audiovisual materials, an OPAC.

Student Life *Housing:* college housing not available. *Activities and Organizations:* student-run newspaper, The Student Board, Culinary Competition Club, Recipe Development Association, The Cellar Club, Pastry Display Club. *Campus security:* 24-hour emergency response devices and patrols.

Costs (2007–08) *Tuition:* $39,950 full-time. *Required fees:* $400 full-time.

Financial Aid Of all full-time matriculated undergraduates, 10 Federal Work-Study jobs.

Applying *Options:* electronic application, deferred entrance. *Application fee:* $100. *Recommended:* essay or personal statement, high school transcript, interview.

Freshmen Application Contact Mr. Matthew Verratti, Vice President of Admissions and Marketing, The Cooking and Hospitality Institute of Chicago, 361 West Chestnut, Chicago, IL 60610. *Phone:* 312-873-2064. *Toll-free phone:* 877-828-7772. *Fax:* 312-798-2903. *E-mail:* mverratti@chicnet.org.

▶**See page 534 for the College Close-Up.**

DANVILLE AREA COMMUNITY COLLEGE

Danville, Illinois   www.dacc.cc.il.us/

Director of Admissions Ms. Stacy L. Ehmen, Director of Admissions of Records/Registrar, Danville Area Community College, 2000 East Main Street, Danville, IL 61832-5199. *Phone:* 217-443-8800.

ELGIN COMMUNITY COLLEGE

Elgin, Illinois   www.elgin.edu/

- **State and locally supported** 2-year, founded 1949, part of Illinois Community College Board
- **Suburban** 145-acre campus with easy access to Chicago
- **Coed,** 10,072 undergraduate students, 32% full-time, 56% women, 44% men

Undergraduates 3,184 full-time, 6,888 part-time. Students come from 1 other state, 2 other countries, 6% African American, 7% Asian American or Pacific Islander, 18% Hispanic American, 0.3% Native American, 42% transferred in.

Freshmen *Admission:* 716 admitted, 716 enrolled.

Faculty *Total:* 476, 25% full-time, 10% with terminal degrees. *Student/faculty ratio:* 33:1.

Majors Accounting; accounting technology and bookkeeping; administrative assistant and secretarial science; art; automobile/automotive mechanics technology; biological and physical sciences; business administration and management; clinical/medical laboratory technology; commercial and advertising art; computer graphics; computer programming (specific applications); computer typography and composition equipment operation; consumer merchandising/retailing management; corrections; criminal justice/law enforcement administration; criminal justice/police science; culinary arts; design and visual communications; drafting and design technology; electrical, electronic and communications engineering technology; emergency medical technology (EMT paramedic); executive assistant/executive secretary; fire protection and safety technology; fire science; general retailing/wholesaling; gerontology; health information/medical records administration; heating, air conditioning, ventilation and refrigeration maintenance technology; hotel/motel administration; human services; industrial technology; information science/studies; kindergarten/preschool education; legal administrative assistant/secretary; legal assistant/paralegal; liberal arts and sciences/liberal studies; machine tool technology; marketing/marketing management; medical administrative assistant and medical secretary; medical transcription; mental health/rehabilitation; metallurgical technology; nursing (licensed practical/vocational nurse training); nursing (registered nurse training); pre-engineering; social work; substance abuse/addiction counseling; tourism and travel services management; welding technology.

Academics *Calendar:* semesters. *Degree:* certificates, diplomas, and associate. *Special study options:* academic remediation for entering students, accelerated degree program, adult/continuing education programs, advanced placement credit, cooperative education, distance learning, double majors, English as a second language, honors programs, independent study, internships, off-campus study, part-time degree program, services for LD students, student-designed majors, summer session for credit.

Library Renner Learning Resource Center with 58,413 titles, 458 serial subscriptions, an OPAC, a Web page.

Student Life *Housing:* college housing not available. *Activities and Organizations:* drama/theater group, student-run newspaper, choral group, Phi Theta Kappa, United Students of All Cultures, Organization of Latin American Students, Black Student Association, Office Administration Association. *Campus security:* 24-hour patrols. *Student services:* personal/psychological counseling, legal services.

Athletics Member NJCAA. *Intercollegiate sports:* baseball M(s)/W, basketball M(s)/W(s), cross-country running M/W, golf M(s), softball W, tennis W(s), volleyball W(s).

Costs (2007–08) *Tuition:* area resident $2730 full-time, $91 per credit hour part-time; state resident $10,779 full-time, $359 per credit hour part-time; nonresident $13,117 full-time, $437 per credit hour part-time.

Applying *Options:* early admission. *Required for some:* high school transcript. *Application deadlines:* rolling (freshmen), rolling (transfers). *Notification:* continuous (freshmen), continuous (transfers).

Freshmen Application Contact Admissions, Recruitment, and Student Life, Elgin Community College, 1700 Spartan Drive, Elgin, IL 60123. *Phone:* 847-214-7414. *E-mail:* admissions@elgin.edu.

FOX COLLEGE

Oak Lawn, Illinois   www.foxcollege.com/

Director of Admissions Ms. Susan Szala, Director of Admissions, Fox College, 4201 West 93rd Street, Oak Lawn, IL 60453. *Phone:* 708-636-7700. *Toll-free phone:* 866-636-7711. *Fax:* 708-636-8078. *E-mail:* sszala@foxcollege.edu.

GEM CITY COLLEGE

Quincy, Illinois   www.gemcitycollege.com/

Director of Admissions Admissions Director, Gem City College, PO Box 179, Quincy, IL 62306-0179. *Phone:* 217-222-0391.

HARPER COLLEGE

Palatine, Illinois   www.harpercollege.edu/

- **State and locally supported** 2-year, founded 1965, part of Illinois Community College Board
- **Suburban** 200-acre campus with easy access to Chicago
- **Coed,** 15,053 undergraduate students, 42% full-time, 56% women, 44% men

Undergraduates 6,267 full-time, 8,786 part-time. Students come from 5 states and territories, 17 other countries, 1% are from out of state, 4% African American, 12% Asian American or Pacific Islander, 16% Hispanic American, 0.3% Native American, 0.8% international, 7% transferred in. *Retention:* 66% of 2003 full-time freshmen returned.

Freshmen *Admission:* 4,663 applied, 4,663 admitted, 2,309 enrolled.

Faculty *Total:* 843, 23% full-time. *Student/faculty ratio:* 23:1.

Majors Accounting; administrative assistant and secretarial science; architectural engineering technology; art; biological and physical sciences; biology/biological sciences; botany/plant biology; business administration and management; child development; computer and information sciences; computer engineering technology; computer management; computer programming; computer science; computer typography and composition equipment operation; criminal justice/law enforcement administration; criminal justice/police science; culinary arts; data processing and data processing technology; dental hygiene; dietetics; drafting and design technology; electrical, electronic and communications engineering technology; engineering; fashion/apparel design; fashion merchandising; finance; fire science; health teacher education; heating, air conditioning, ventilation and refrigeration maintenance technology; horticultural science; hospitality administration; hotel/motel administration; humanities; human resources management; industrial technology; information science/studies; insurance; interior design; international business/trade/commerce; journalism; kindergarten/preschool education; kinesiology and exercise science; landscape architecture; landscaping and groundskeeping; legal administrative assistant/secretary; legal assistant/paralegal; liberal arts and sciences/liberal studies; machine tool technology; management information systems; marketing/marketing management; materials science; mathematics; mechanical design technology; mechanical engineering/mechanical technology; medical administrative assistant and medical secretary; medical/clinical assistant; music; nursing (licensed practical/vocational nurse training); nursing (registered nurse training); parks, recreation and leisure facilities management; physical education teaching and coaching; physical sciences; pre-engineering; purchasing, procurement/acquisitions and contracts management; quality control technology; real estate; rehabilitation therapy; sign language interpretation and translation; social sciences.

Academics *Calendar:* semesters. *Degree:* certificates and associate. *Special study options:* academic remediation for entering students, accelerated degree program, adult/continuing education programs, advanced placement credit, cooperative education, distance learning, English as a second language, honors programs, independent study, internships, part-time degree program, services for LD students, study abroad, summer session for credit.

Library Harper College Library with 141,124 titles, 6,606 serial subscriptions, 37,973 audiovisual materials, an OPAC, a Web page.

Student Life *Housing:* college housing not available. *Activities and Organizations:* drama/theater group, student-run newspaper, radio station, choral group, student radio station, Program Board, Student Senate, Nursing Club, Phi Theta Kappa. *Campus security:* 24-hour emergency response devices and patrols, late-night transport/escort service. *Student services:* health clinic, personal/psychological counseling, women's center, legal services.

Athletics Member NJCAA. *Intercollegiate sports:* baseball M, basketball M/W, cross-country running M/W, football M, soccer M/W, softball W, track and field M/W, volleyball W, wrestling M. *Intramural sports:* baseball M, basketball M/W, bowling M, racquetball M/W, skiing (cross-country) M/W, skiing (downhill) M/W, softball M/W, table tennis M/W, tennis M/W, volleyball M/W.

Costs (2006–07) *Tuition:* area resident $1944 full-time, $81 per credit hour part-time; state resident $6912 full-time, $288 per credit hour part-time; nonresident $8688 full-time, $362 per credit hour part-time. *Required fees:* $450 full-time.

Financial Aid Of all full-time matriculated undergraduates, 85 Federal Work-Study jobs (averaging $1210).

Applying *Options:* electronic application, early admission, deferred entrance. *Application fee:* $25. *Required:* high school transcript. *Application deadlines:* rolling (freshmen), rolling (transfers). *Notification:* continuous (freshmen), continuous (transfers).

Freshmen Application Contact Admissions Office, Harper College, 1200 West Algonquin Road, Palatine, IL 60067. *Phone:* 847-925-6700. *Fax:* 847-925-6044. *E-mail:* admissions@harpercollege.edu.

HEARTLAND COMMUNITY COLLEGE

Normal, Illinois   www.heartland.edu/

- **State and locally supported** 2-year, founded 1990, part of Illinois Community College Board
- **Urban** campus
- **Coed**

Undergraduates Students come from 5 states and territories, 2 other countries, 1% are from out of state. *Retention:* 55% of 2003 full-time freshmen returned.

Faculty *Student/faculty ratio:* 19:1.

Academics *Calendar:* semesters. *Degree:* certificates and associate. *Special study options:* academic remediation for entering students, adult/continuing education programs, advanced placement credit, cooperative education, distance learning, double majors, English as a second language, independent study, internships, part-time degree program, services for LD students, study abroad, summer session for credit. *ROTC:* Army (c).

Student Life *Campus security:* 24-hour emergency response devices and patrols.

Standardized Tests *Required for some:* ACT COMPASS. *Recommended:* SAT (for placement), ACT (for placement).

Costs (2006–07) *Tuition:* area resident $2010 full-time, $67 per semester hour part-time; state resident $4020 full-time, $134 per semester hour part-time; nonresident $6030 full-time, $201 per semester hour part-time. *Required fees:* $90 full-time, $3 per semester hour part-time.

Financial Aid Of all full-time matriculated undergraduates, 65 Federal Work-Study jobs (averaging $1500).

Applying *Recommended:* high school transcript.

Freshmen Application Contact Ms. Candace Brownlee, Director of Student Recruitment, Heartland Community College, 1500 West Raab Road, Normal, IL 61761. *Phone:* 309-268-8041. *Fax:* 309-268-7992. *E-mail:* candace.brownlee@heartland.edu.

HIGHLAND COMMUNITY COLLEGE

Freeport, Illinois   www.highland.edu/

- **State and locally supported** 2-year, founded 1962, part of Illinois Community College Board
- **Rural** 240-acre campus
- **Endowment** $5.6 million
- **Coed**

Undergraduates 1,134 full-time, 1,272 part-time. Students come from 8 states and territories, 2% are from out of state, 9% African American, 1% Asian American or Pacific Islander, 2% Hispanic American, 0.1% Native American, 0.2% international. *Retention:* 65% of 2003 full-time freshmen returned.

Faculty *Student/faculty ratio:* 16:1.

Academics *Calendar:* semesters. *Degree:* certificates and associate. *Special study options:* academic remediation for entering students, adult/continuing education programs, advanced placement credit, distance learning, English as a second language, external degree program, independent study, internships, part-time degree program, services for LD students, student-designed majors, summer session for credit.

Student Life *Campus security:* 24-hour patrols.

Athletics Member NJCAA.

Costs (2006–07) *Tuition:* area resident $1608 full-time, $67 per credit part-time; state resident $2880 full-time, $120 per credit part-time; nonresident $2880 full-time, $120 per credit part-time. *Required fees:* $120 full-time, $5 per credit part-time.

Financial Aid Of all full-time matriculated undergraduates, 50 Federal Work-Study jobs (averaging $2000). 50 state and other part-time jobs (averaging $2000).

Applying *Options:* early admission, deferred entrance. *Required for some:* high school transcript.

Freshmen Application Contact Mr. Karl Richards, Dean of Enrollment Services, Highland Community College, 2998 West Pearl City Road, Freeport, IL 61032. *Phone:* 815-235-6121 Ext. 3486. *Fax:* 815-235-6130.

ILLINOIS CENTRAL COLLEGE

East Peoria, Illinois   www.icc.edu/

- **State and locally supported** 2-year, founded 1967, part of Illinois Community College Board
- **Suburban** 430-acre campus
- **Coed**

Undergraduates 4,907 full-time, 7,436 part-time. Students come from 20 other countries, 10% African American, 2% Asian American or Pacific Islander, 2% Hispanic American, 0.4% Native American, 0.6% international.

Academics *Calendar:* semesters. *Degree:* certificates and associate. *Special study options:* academic remediation for entering students, adult/continuing education programs, advanced placement credit, English as a second language, honors programs, internships, part-time degree program, services for LD students, summer session for credit.

Athletics Member NJCAA.

Costs (2006–07) *Tuition:* area resident $2240 full-time, $70 per semester hour part-time; state resident $4960 full-time, $155 per semester hour part-time; nonresident $4960 full-time, $155 per semester hour part-time. *Room and board:* room only: $3978.

Applying *Options:* early admission. *Required:* high school transcript.

Freshmen Application Contact Mr. John Avendano, Vice President of Academic Affairs and Student Development, Illinois Central College, One College Drive, East Peoria, IL 61635-0001. *Phone:* 309-694-5784. *Toll-free phone:* 800-422-2293. *Fax:* 309-694-5450. *E-mail:* info@icc.edu.

ILLINOIS EASTERN COMMUNITY COLLEGES, FRONTIER COMMUNITY COLLEGE

Fairfield, Illinois   www.iecc.edu/fcc/

- **State and locally supported** 2-year, founded 1976, part of Illinois Eastern Community College System
- **Rural** 8-acre campus
- **Coed,** 2,453 undergraduate students, 11% full-time, 62% women, 38% men

Undergraduates 277 full-time, 2,176 part-time. 1% are from out of state, 0.3% African American, 0.6% Asian American or Pacific Islander, 0.3% Hispanic American, 0.1% Native American.

Freshmen *Admission:* 21 enrolled.

Faculty *Total:* 235, 2% full-time.

Majors Administrative assistant and secretarial science; biological and physical sciences; business automation/technology/data entry; corrections; general studies; liberal arts and sciences/liberal studies; nursing (registered nurse training); quality control technology.

Academics *Calendar:* semesters. *Degree:* certificates and associate. *Special study options:* academic remediation for entering students, adult/continuing education programs, advanced placement credit, cooperative education, distance learning, double majors, English as a second language, external degree program, independent study, part-time degree program, services for LD students, student-designed majors, summer session for credit.

Library 20,993 titles, 6,749 serial subscriptions, 2,679 audiovisual materials.

Student Life *Housing:* college housing not available.

Costs (2007–08) *Tuition:* area resident $1824 full-time, $57 per credit hour part-time; state resident $5849 full-time, $183 per credit hour part-time; nonresident $7259 full-time, $227 per credit hour part-time. *Required fees:* $106 full-time, $3 per credit hour part-time, $5 per term part-time.

Applying *Options:* early admission, deferred entrance. *Application fee:* $10. *Required:* high school transcript. *Application deadlines:* rolling (freshmen), rolling (transfers). *Notification:* continuous (freshmen), continuous (transfers).

Freshmen Application Contact Mrs. Suzanne Brooks, Coordinator of Registration and Records, Illinois Eastern Community Colleges, Frontier Community College, 2 Frontier Drive, Fairfield, IL 62837. *Phone:* 618-842-3711 Ext. 4111. *Fax:* 618-842-6340. *E-mail:* brookss@iecc.edu.

ILLINOIS EASTERN COMMUNITY COLLEGES, LINCOLN TRAIL COLLEGE

Robinson, Illinois   www.iecc.edu/ltc/

- **State and locally supported** 2-year, founded 1969, part of Illinois Eastern Community College System
- **Rural** 120-acre campus
- **Coed,** 1,504 undergraduate students, 36% full-time, 48% women, 52% men

Undergraduates 542 full-time, 962 part-time. 1% are from out of state, 17% African American, 2% Asian American or Pacific Islander, 3% Hispanic American, 0.1% Native American.

Freshmen *Admission:* 153 enrolled.

Faculty *Total:* 88, 31% full-time.

Majors Biological and physical sciences; building/property maintenance and management; business automation/technology/data entry; corrections; culinary arts; general studies; heating, air conditioning, ventilation and refrigeration maintenance technology; liberal arts and sciences/liberal studies; mechanical engineering/mechanical technology; music; music teacher education; quality control technology; teacher assistant/aide; telecommunications.

Academics *Calendar:* semesters. *Degree:* certificates and associate. *Special study options:* academic remediation for entering students, adult/continuing education programs, advanced placement credit, cooperative education, distance learning, double majors, English as a second language, external degree program, independent study, internships, part-time degree program, services for LD students, student-designed majors, summer session for credit.

Library Eagleton Learning Resource Center with 16,954 titles, 76 serial subscriptions, 1,447 audiovisual materials.

Student Life *Housing:* college housing not available. *Activities and Organizations:* drama/theater group, choral group, national fraternities. *Student services:* personal/psychological counseling.

Athletics Member NJCAA. *Intercollegiate sports:* baseball M(s), basketball M(s)/W(s), softball W(s), volleyball W(s). *Intramural sports:* baseball M, basketball M, softball W, volleyball M/W.

Costs (2007–08) *Tuition:* area resident $1824 full-time, $57 per credit hour part-time; state resident $5849 full-time, $183 per credit hour part-time; nonresident $7259 full-time, $227 per credit hour part-time. *Required fees:* $106 full-time, $3 per credit hour part-time, $5 per term part-time.

Applying *Options:* early admission, deferred entrance. *Application fee:* $10. *Required:* high school transcript. *Application deadlines:* rolling (freshmen), rolling (transfers). *Notification:* continuous (freshmen), continuous (transfers).

Freshmen Application Contact Ms. Becky Mikeworth, Director of Admissions, Illinois Eastern Community Colleges, Lincoln Trail College, 11220 State Highway 1, Robinson, IL 62454. *Phone:* 618-544-8657 Ext. 1137. *Fax:* 618-544-7423. *E-mail:* mikeworthb@iecc.edu.

ILLINOIS EASTERN COMMUNITY COLLEGES, OLNEY CENTRAL COLLEGE

Olney, Illinois   www.iecc.edu/occ/

- **State and locally supported** 2-year, founded 1962, part of Illinois Eastern Community College System
- **Rural** 128-acre campus
- **Coed,** 1,737 undergraduate students, 46% full-time, 62% women, 38% men

Undergraduates 805 full-time, 932 part-time. 0.9% African American, 1% Asian American or Pacific Islander, 0.6% Hispanic American, 0.1% Native American, 0.1% international.

Freshmen *Admission:* 89 enrolled.

Faculty *Total:* 122, 39% full-time.

Majors Accounting; administrative assistant and secretarial science; autobody/collision and repair technology; automobile/automotive mechanics technology; biological and physical sciences; business automation/technology/data entry; cabinetmaking and millwork; corrections; criminal justice/police science; general studies; heavy equipment maintenance technology; industrial mechanics and maintenance technology; liberal arts and sciences/liberal studies; medical administrative assistant and medical secretary; medical radiologic technology; music; music teacher education; nursing (licensed practical/vocational nurse training); nursing (registered nurse training).

Academics *Calendar:* semesters. *Degree:* certificates and associate. *Special study options:* academic remediation for entering students, adult/continuing education programs, advanced placement credit, cooperative education, distance learning, double majors, English as a second language, external degree program, independent study, internships, part-time degree program, services for LD students, student-designed majors, summer session for credit.

Library Anderson Learning Resources Center with 22,917 titles, 28,036 serial subscriptions, 1,081 audiovisual materials.

Student Life *Housing:* college housing not available. *Activities and Organizations:* drama/theater group, student-run newspaper, choral group. *Student services:* personal/psychological counseling, women's center.

Athletics Member NJCAA. *Intercollegiate sports:* baseball M(s), basketball M(s)/W(s), softball W(s), volleyball W(s). *Intramural sports:* baseball M, basketball M/W, softball W.

Costs (2007–08) *Tuition:* area resident $1824 full-time, $57 per credit hour part-time; state resident $5849 full-time, $183 per credit hour part-time; nonresident $7259 full-time, $227 per credit hour part-time. *Required fees:* $106 full-time, $3 per credit hour part-time, $5 per term part-time.

Illinois Eastern Community Colleges, Olney Central College (continued)

Applying *Options:* early admission, deferred entrance. *Application fee:* $10. *Required:* high school transcript. *Application deadlines:* rolling (freshmen), rolling (transfers). *Notification:* continuous (freshmen), continuous (transfers).

Freshmen Application Contact Ms. Chris Webber, Assistant Dean for Student Services, Illinois Eastern Community Colleges, Olney Central College, 305 North West Street, Olney, IL 62450. *Phone:* 618-395-7777 Ext. 2005. *Fax:* 618-392-5212. *E-mail:* webberc@iecc.edu.

ILLINOIS EASTERN COMMUNITY COLLEGES, WABASH VALLEY COLLEGE

Mount Carmel, Illinois   **www.iecc.edu/wvc/**

- **State and locally supported** 2-year, founded 1960, part of Illinois Eastern Community College System
- **Rural** 40-acre campus
- **Coed,** 4,840 undergraduate students, 13% full-time, 47% women, 53% men

Undergraduates 620 full-time, 4,220 part-time. 1% are from out of state, 3% African American, 1% Asian American or Pacific Islander, 0.9% Hispanic American, 0.2% Native American, 0.1% international.

Freshmen *Admission:* 62 enrolled.

Faculty *Total:* 168, 23% full-time.

Majors Administrative assistant and secretarial science; agricultural business and management; agricultural production; biological and physical sciences; business administration and management; business automation/technology/data entry; child development; corrections; court reporting; diesel mechanics technology; electrical, electronic and communications engineering technology; general studies; industrial technology; liberal arts and sciences/liberal studies; machine shop technology; manufacturing technology; mining technology; radio and television; social work.

Academics *Calendar:* semesters. *Degree:* certificates and associate. *Special study options:* academic remediation for entering students, adult/continuing education programs, advanced placement credit, cooperative education, distance learning, double majors, English as a second language, external degree program, independent study, internships, part-time degree program, services for LD students, student-designed majors, summer session for credit.

Library Bauer Media Center with 31,988 titles, 85 serial subscriptions, 1,374 audiovisual materials.

Student Life *Housing:* college housing not available. *Activities and Organizations:* drama/theater group, student-run newspaper, radio and television station, choral group.

Athletics Member NJCAA. *Intercollegiate sports:* baseball M(s), basketball M(s)/W(s), softball W(s), tennis M, volleyball W(s). *Intramural sports:* baseball M, basketball M/W, cross-country running M/W, softball W, volleyball M/W.

Costs (2007–08) *Tuition:* area resident $1824 full-time, $57 per credit hour part-time; state resident $5849 full-time, $183 per credit hour part-time; nonresident $7259 full-time, $227 per credit hour part-time. *Required fees:* $106 full-time, $3 per credit hour part-time, $5 per term part-time.

Applying *Options:* early admission, deferred entrance. *Application fee:* $10. *Required:* high school transcript. *Application deadlines:* rolling (freshmen), rolling (transfers). *Notification:* continuous (freshmen), continuous (transfers).

Freshmen Application Contact Mrs. Diana Spear, Assistant Dean for Student Services, Illinois Eastern Community Colleges, Wabash Valley College, 2200 College Drive, Mt. Carmel, IL 62863. *Phone:* 618-262-8641 Ext. 3101. *Fax:* 618-262-8641. *E-mail:* speard@iecc.edu.

ILLINOIS VALLEY COMMUNITY COLLEGE

Oglesby, Illinois   **www.ivcc.edu/**

- **District-supported** 2-year, founded 1924, part of Illinois Community College Board
- **Rural** 410-acre campus with easy access to Chicago
- **Coed,** 3,939 undergraduate students, 44% full-time, 56% women, 44% men

Undergraduates 1,732 full-time, 2,207 part-time. Students come from 4 states and territories, 4% African American, 1% Asian American or Pacific Islander, 7% Hispanic American, 0.2% Native American, 4% transferred in.

Freshmen *Admission:* 406 enrolled.

Faculty *Total:* 233, 39% full-time.

Majors Accounting; administrative assistant and secretarial science; agricultural business and management; agriculture; automobile/automotive mechanics technology; business administration and management; carpentry; child develop-

ment; computer programming; computer systems networking and telecommunications; criminal justice/law enforcement administration; criminal justice/police science; data processing and data processing technology; drafting and design technology; education; electrical, electronic and communications engineering technology; elementary education; English; industrial technology; journalism; liberal arts and sciences/liberal studies; marketing/marketing management; mechanical design technology; mechanical engineering/mechanical technology; nursing (registered nurse training); pre-engineering.

Academics *Calendar:* semesters. *Degree:* associate. *Special study options:* academic remediation for entering students, adult/continuing education programs, advanced placement credit, distance learning, English as a second language, honors programs, independent study, internships, off-campus study, part-time degree program, services for LD students, student-designed majors, study abroad, summer session for credit.

Library Jacobs Library with 58,250 titles, 504 serial subscriptions.

Student Life *Housing:* college housing not available. *Activities and Organizations:* drama/theater group, student-run newspaper, choral group. *Campus security:* 24-hour patrols. *Student services:* personal/psychological counseling.

Athletics *Intercollegiate sports:* basketball M/W, golf M, tennis M/W. *Intramural sports:* basketball M, volleyball W.

Costs (2007–08) *Tuition:* area resident $2104 full-time, $66 per credit hour part-time; state resident $6841 full-time, $214 per credit hour part-time; nonresident $7900 full-time, $247 per credit hour part-time.

Financial Aid Of all full-time matriculated undergraduates, 81 Federal Work-Study jobs (averaging $955).

Applying *Options:* early admission, deferred entrance. *Required:* high school transcript. *Application deadlines:* rolling (freshmen), rolling (transfers). *Notification:* continuous (freshmen), continuous (transfers).

Freshmen Application Contact Ms. Tracy Morris, Director of Admissions and Records, Illinois Valley Community College, 815 North Orlando Smith Avenue Oglesby, Oglesby, IL 61348. *Phone:* 815-224-0437. *Fax:* 815-224-3033. *E-mail:* tracy_morris@ivcc.edu.

ITT TECHNICAL INSTITUTE

Burr Ridge, Illinois   **www.itt-tech.edu/**

- **Proprietary** primarily 2-year, founded 1998, part of ITT Educational Services, Inc
- **Coed**

Majors Computer and information systems security; computer engineering technology; computer software technology; system, networking, and LAN/WAN management; web/multimedia management and webmaster; web page, digital/multimedia and information resources design.

Academics *Calendar:* quarters. *Degrees:* associate and bachelor's.

Library a Web page.

Student Life *Housing:* college housing not available.

Standardized Tests *Required:* Wonderlic aptitude test (for admission).

Costs (2006–07) *Tuition:* Contact school for program costs.

Applying *Options:* deferred entrance. *Application fee:* $100. *Required:* high school transcript, interview. *Recommended:* letters of recommendation. *Application deadlines:* rolling (freshmen), rolling (transfers). *Notification:* continuous (freshmen), continuous (transfers).

Freshmen Application Contact Mr. Andrew Mical, Director of Recruitment, ITT Technical Institute, 7040 High Grove Boulevard, Burr Ridge, IL 60527. *Phone:* 630-455-6470. *Toll-free phone:* 877-488-0001. *Fax:* 630-455-6476.

ITT TECHNICAL INSTITUTE

Mount Prospect, Illinois   **www.itt-tech.edu/**

- **Proprietary** primarily 2-year, founded 1986, part of ITT Educational Services, Inc
- **Suburban** 1-acre campus with easy access to Chicago
- **Coed**

Majors CAD/CADD drafting/design technology; computer and information systems security; computer engineering technology; computer programming; electrical, electronic and communications engineering technology; system, networking, and LAN/WAN management; web page, digital/multimedia and information resources design.

Academics *Calendar:* quarters. *Degrees:* associate, bachelor's, and master's.

Library a Web page.

Student Life *Housing:* college housing not available.

Standardized Tests *Required:* Wonderlic aptitude test (for admission).

Costs (2006–07) *Tuition:* Contact school for program costs.

Applying *Options:* deferred entrance. *Application fee:* $100. *Required:* high school transcript, interview. *Recommended:* letters of recommendation. *Application deadlines:* rolling (freshmen), rolling (transfers). *Notification:* continuous (freshmen), continuous (transfers).

Freshmen Application Contact Mr. Cesar Rodriguez Jr., Director of Recruitment, ITT Technical Institute, 1401 Feehanville Drive, Mount Prospect, IL 60056. *Phone:* 847-375-8800.

ITT TECHNICAL INSTITUTE
Orland Park, Illinois
www.itt-tech.edu/

- **Proprietary** primarily 2-year, founded 1993, part of ITT Educational Services, Inc
- **Suburban** campus with easy access to Chicago
- **Coed**

Majors CAD/CADD drafting/design technology; computer engineering technology; computer programming; computer systems networking and telecommunications; e-commerce; electrical, electronic and communications engineering technology; system, networking, and LAN/WAN management; web/multimedia management and webmaster; web page, digital/multimedia and information resources design.

Academics *Calendar:* quarters. *Degrees:* associate and bachelor's.

Library a Web page.

Student Life *Housing:* college housing not available.

Standardized Tests *Required:* Wonderlic aptitude test (for admission).

Costs (2006–07) *Tuition:* Contact school for program costs.

Financial Aid Of all full-time matriculated undergraduates, 6 Federal Work-Study jobs (averaging $4000).

Applying *Options:* deferred entrance. *Application fee:* $100. *Required:* high school transcript, interview. *Recommended:* letters of recommendation. *Application deadlines:* rolling (freshmen), rolling (transfers). *Notification:* continuous (freshmen), continuous (transfers).

Freshmen Application Contact Mr. James Tannheimer, ITT Technical Institute, 11551 184th Place, Orland Park, IL 60467. *Phone:* 708-326-3200.

JOHN A. LOGAN COLLEGE
Carterville, Illinois
www.jalc.edu/

Director of Admissions Mr. Terry Crain, Dean of Student Services, John A. Logan College, 700 Logan College Road, Carterville, IL 62918-9900. *Phone:* 618-985-3741 Ext. 8382. *E-mail:* terry.crain@jalc.edu.

JOHN WOOD COMMUNITY COLLEGE
Quincy, Illinois
www.jwcc.edu/

- **District-supported** 2-year, founded 1974, part of Illinois Community College Board
- **Small-town** campus
- **Coed,** 2,516 undergraduate students, 49% full-time, 63% women, 37% men

Undergraduates 1,222 full-time, 1,294 part-time. Students come from 4 states and territories, 3 other countries, 9% are from out of state, 3% African American, 1% Asian American or Pacific Islander, 0.7% Hispanic American, 0.2% Native American, 0.5% international, 7% transferred in.

Freshmen *Admission:* 498 applied, 498 admitted, 498 enrolled. *Test scores:* ACT scores over 18: 64%; ACT scores over 24: 11%; ACT scores over 30: 1%.

Faculty *Total:* 192, 29% full-time, 7% with terminal degrees. *Student/faculty ratio:* 16:1.

Majors Accounting; accounting technology and bookkeeping; administrative assistant and secretarial science; agricultural business and management; agricultural production; animal/livestock husbandry and production; applied horticulture; biological and physical sciences; business administration and management; business/commerce; child guidance; clinical/medical laboratory technology; computer programming (specific applications); criminal justice/police science; early childhood education; electrical, electronic and communications engineering technology; electrician; emergency medical technology (EMT paramedic); executive assistant/executive secretary; fire protection and safety technology; general studies; health and physical education; hotel/motel administration; industrial electronics technology; industrial mechanics and maintenance technology; legal administrative assistant/secretary; liberal arts and sciences/liberal studies; mechanical drafting and CAD/CADD; medical administrative assistant

and medical secretary; medical radiologic technology; nursing (registered nurse training); psychology; restaurant, culinary, and catering management; sales, distribution and marketing; sociology.

Academics *Calendar:* semesters. *Degree:* certificates and associate. *Special study options:* academic remediation for entering students, adult/continuing education programs, advanced placement credit, cooperative education, distance learning, English as a second language, external degree program, independent study, internships, off-campus study, part-time degree program, services for LD students, student-designed majors, study abroad, summer session for credit.

Library 18,000 titles, 160 serial subscriptions, an OPAC, a Web page.

Student Life *Housing:* college housing not available. *Activities and Organizations:* choral group. *Campus security:* 24-hour emergency response devices, late-night transport/escort service.

Athletics Member NJCAA. *Intercollegiate sports:* baseball M(s), basketball M(s)/W(s), golf M(s), softball W(s), volleyball W(s). *Intramural sports:* basketball M/W, volleyball M/W.

Standardized Tests *Recommended:* ACT (for admission).

Costs (2007–08) *Tuition:* area resident $2640 full-time, $88 per credit hour part-time; state resident $5640 full-time, $188 per credit hour part-time; nonresident $5640 full-time, $188 per credit hour part-time. *Required fees:* $240 full-time, $8 per credit hour part-time.

Financial Aid Of all full-time matriculated undergraduates, 360 Federal Work-Study jobs (averaging $364).

Applying *Options:* early admission. *Required:* high school transcript. *Application deadlines:* rolling (freshmen), rolling (transfers). *Notification:* continuous (freshmen), continuous (transfers).

Freshmen Application Contact Mr. Mark McNett, Director of Admissions, John Wood Community College, 1301 South 48th Street, Quincy, IL 62305-8736. *Phone:* 217-641-4339. *Fax:* 217-224-4208. *E-mail:* admissions@jwcc.edu.

JOLIET JUNIOR COLLEGE
Joliet, Illinois
www.jjc.edu/

- **State and locally supported** 2-year, founded 1901, part of Illinois Community College Board
- **Suburban** 463-acre campus with easy access to Chicago
- **Endowment** $9.6 million
- **Coed,** 12,924 undergraduate students, 39% full-time, 59% women, 41% men

Undergraduates 5,103 full-time, 7,821 part-time. Students come from 14 states and territories, 0.3% are from out of state, 10% African American, 2% Asian American or Pacific Islander, 10% Hispanic American, 0.2% Native American, 0.1% international, 1% transferred in.

Freshmen *Admission:* 4,484 applied, 4,484 admitted, 2,263 enrolled.

Faculty *Total:* 554, 34% full-time, 9% with terminal degrees. *Student/faculty ratio:* 25:1.

Majors Accounting; administrative assistant and secretarial science; agricultural business and management; animal physiology; art; automobile/automotive mechanics technology; biology/biological sciences; business administration and management; business automation/technology/data entry; business/managerial economics; chemistry; clinical laboratory science/medical technology; computer and information sciences; computer programming; computer programming (specific applications); computer systems networking and telecommunications; computer/technical support; construction engineering technology; corrections; criminal justice/law enforcement administration; criminal justice/police science; culinary arts; ecology; education; electrical, electronic and communications engineering technology; electrical/electronics drafting and CAD/CADD; emergency medical technology (EMT paramedic); fashion merchandising; fire science; geography; greenhouse management; horticultural science; hospitality administration; industrial technology; interior design; landscaping and groundskeeping; marketing/marketing management; massage therapy; mathematics; mechanical design technology; medical administrative assistant and medical secretary; nuclear/nuclear power technology; nursing (registered nurse training); plant nursery management; real estate; special products marketing; teacher assistant/aide; turf and turfgrass management; veterinary/animal health technology; web page, digital/multimedia and information resources design; welding technology.

Academics *Calendar:* semesters. *Degree:* certificates, diplomas, and associate. *Special study options:* academic remediation for entering students, adult/continuing education programs, advanced placement credit, distance learning, English as a second language, honors programs, independent study, internships, part-time degree program, services for LD students, summer session for credit.

Library Learning Resource Center with 60,364 titles, 360 serial subscriptions, an OPAC.

Student Life *Housing Options:* Campus housing is provided by a third party. *Activities and Organizations:* drama/theater group, student-run newspaper, choral group, Phi Theta Kappa, JC Players, Nursing Student Association, Student

Joliet Junior College (continued)

Agricultural Association, Inter-Varsity Christian Fellowship, national fraternities. *Campus security:* 24-hour emergency response devices and patrols, student patrols, late-night transport/escort service. *Student services:* personal/psychological counseling, women's center.

Athletics Member NJCAA. *Intercollegiate sports:* basketball M/W, football M, golf M, softball W, tennis M/W, volleyball W.

Costs (2007–08) *Tuition:* area resident $1860 full-time, $62 per credit hour part-time; state resident $6990 full-time, $233 per credit hour part-time; nonresident $7860 full-time, $262 per credit hour part-time. *Required fees:* $420 full-time, $14 part-time, $420 per year part-time.

Financial Aid Of all full-time matriculated undergraduates, 96 Federal Work-Study jobs (averaging $1168). 254 state and other part-time jobs (averaging $1778).

Applying *Options:* early admission, deferred entrance. *Required:* high school transcript. *Application deadlines:* rolling (freshmen), rolling (transfers).

Freshmen Application Contact Ms. Jennifer Kloberdanz, Dean of Admissions and Financial Aid, Joliet Junior College, 1215 Houbolt Road, Joliet, IL 60431. *Phone:* 815-280-2493. *Fax:* 815-280-6740. *E-mail:* admission@jjc.edu.

KANKAKEE COMMUNITY COLLEGE

Kankakee, Illinois   www.kcc.cc.il.us/

- **State and locally supported** 2-year, founded 1966, part of Illinois Community College Board
- **Small-town** 178-acre campus with easy access to Chicago
- **Endowment** $3.1 million
- **Coed,** 3,353 undergraduate students, 40% full-time, 65% women, 35% men

Undergraduates 1,340 full-time, 2,013 part-time. Students come from 5 other countries, 14% African American, 1% Asian American or Pacific Islander, 5% Hispanic American, 0.3% Native American, 0.1% international, 36% transferred in.

Freshmen *Admission:* 260 admitted, 260 enrolled.

Faculty *Total:* 193, 28% full-time, 4% with terminal degrees. *Student/faculty ratio:* 20:1.

Majors Accounting; administrative assistant and secretarial science; automobile/automotive mechanics technology; avionics maintenance technology; biological and physical sciences; business/commerce; child development; clinical/medical laboratory technology; criminal justice/law enforcement administration; criminal justice/police science; drafting and design technology; electrical, electronic and communications engineering technology; elementary education; emergency medical technology (EMT paramedic); engineering; fine/studio arts; heating, air conditioning, ventilation and refrigeration maintenance technology; industrial radiologic technology; information science/studies; liberal arts and sciences/liberal studies; machine tool technology; marketing/marketing management; nursing (registered nurse training); physical therapist assistant; psychology; real estate; respiratory care therapy; welding technology.

Academics *Calendar:* semesters. *Degrees:* certificates, diplomas, and associate (also offers continuing education program with significant enrollment not reflected in profile). *Special study options:* academic remediation for entering students, adult/continuing education programs, advanced placement credit, cooperative education, distance learning, English as a second language, honors programs, independent study, internships, off-campus study, part-time degree program, services for LD students, student-designed majors, study abroad, summer session for credit.

Library Kankakee Community College Learning Resource Center with 48,239 titles, 245 serial subscriptions, 2,308 audiovisual materials.

Student Life *Housing:* college housing not available. *Campus security:* 24-hour patrols.

Athletics Member NJCAA. *Intercollegiate sports:* baseball M(s), basketball M(s)/W(s), softball W(s), volleyball W(s). *Intramural sports:* basketball M.

Standardized Tests *Required for some:* ACT ASSET or ACT COMPASS.

Costs (2007–08) *Tuition:* area resident $1890 full-time; state resident $4963 full-time; nonresident $9095 full-time. *Required fees:* $180 full-time.

Financial Aid Of all full-time matriculated undergraduates, 70 Federal Work-Study jobs (averaging $1100). *Financial aid deadline:* 10/1.

Applying *Options:* early admission. *Required:* high school transcript. *Application deadlines:* rolling (freshmen), rolling (transfers). *Notification:* continuous (freshmen), continuous (transfers).

Freshmen Application Contact Ms. Michelle Driscoll, Kankakee Community College, Box 888, Kankakee, IL 60901. *Phone:* 815-802-8520. *Fax:* 815-802-8101. *E-mail:* mdriscoll@kcc.edu.

KASKASKIA COLLEGE

Centralia, Illinois   www.kaskaskia.edu/

- **State and locally supported** 2-year, founded 1966, part of Illinois Community College Board
- **Rural** 195-acre campus with easy access to St. Louis
- **Endowment** $606,505
- **Coed**

Undergraduates 1,908 full-time, 2,834 part-time. Students come from 23 states and territories, 2 other countries, 1% are from out of state, 7% African American, 0.4% Asian American or Pacific Islander, 2% Hispanic American, 0.3% Native American, 0.2% international, 21% transferred in.

Faculty *Student/faculty ratio:* 22:1.

Academics *Calendar:* semesters. *Degree:* certificates and associate. *Special study options:* academic remediation for entering students, accelerated degree program, adult/continuing education programs, cooperative education, distance learning, double majors, English as a second language, honors programs, independent study, internships, off-campus study, part-time degree program, services for LD students, study abroad, summer session for credit.

Student Life *Campus security:* 24-hour patrols, late-night transport/escort service.

Athletics Member NJCAA.

Standardized Tests *Recommended:* ACT (for admission), ASSET.

Costs (2006–07) *Tuition:* area resident $1792 full-time, $56 per credit hour part-time; state resident $3408 full-time, $107 per credit hour part-time; nonresident $8125 full-time, $254 per credit hour part-time. Full-time tuition and fees vary according to location and program. Part-time tuition and fees vary according to location and program. *Required fees:* $224 full-time, $7 per credit hour part-time.

Applying *Options:* early admission, deferred entrance. *Required:* high school transcript. *Required for some:* interview.

Freshmen Application Contact Jan Ripperda, Coordinator of Student Records, Kaskaskia College, 27210 College Road, Centralia, IL 62801. *Phone:* 618-545-3041. *Toll-free phone:* 800-642-0859. *Fax:* 618-532-1990.

KISHWAUKEE COLLEGE

Malta, Illinois   www.kishwaukeecollege.edu/

Freshmen Application Contact Ms. Sally Misciasci, Admission Analyst, Kishwaukee College, 21193 Malta Road, Malta, IL 60150-9699. *Phone:* 815-825-2086 Ext. 400.

LAKE LAND COLLEGE

Mattoon, Illinois   www.lakelandcollege.edu/

- **State and locally supported** 2-year, founded 1966, part of Illinois Community College Board
- **Rural** 308-acre campus
- **Endowment** $2.7 million
- **Coed,** 7,431 undergraduate students, 43% full-time, 47% women, 53% men

Undergraduates 3,160 full-time, 4,271 part-time. Students come from 14 other countries, 1% are from out of state, 10% African American, 0.7% Asian American or Pacific Islander, 3% Hispanic American, 0.3% Native American, 0.6% international.

Freshmen *Admission:* 2,830 applied, 2,830 admitted.

Faculty *Total:* 191, 61% full-time, 5% with terminal degrees. *Student/faculty ratio:* 21:1.

Majors Accounting technology and bookkeeping; administrative assistant and secretarial science; agricultural business and management; agricultural mechanization; agricultural production; architectural engineering technology; automobile/automotive mechanics technology; biological and physical sciences; business administration and management; child care and support services management; civil engineering technology; computer programming (specific applications); computer systems networking and telecommunications; corrections; criminal justice/police science; dental hygiene; desktop publishing and digital imaging design; drafting and design technology; electrical, electronic and communications engineering technology; electromechanical technology; executive assistant/executive secretary; general studies; graphic and printing equipment operation/production; human services; industrial technology; information technology; legal administrative assistant/secretary; liberal arts and sciences/liberal studies; marketing/marketing management; medical administrative assistant and medical

secretary; nursing (registered nurse training); office management; physical therapist assistant; printing press operation; radio and television; social work; telecommunications.

Academics *Calendar:* semesters. *Degree:* certificates and associate. *Special study options:* academic remediation for entering students, accelerated degree program, adult/continuing education programs, cooperative education, distance learning, English as a second language, external degree program, honors programs, internships, part-time degree program, services for LD students, summer session for credit.

Library Virgil H. Judge Learning Resource Center with 28,000 titles, 225 serial subscriptions, 1,939 audiovisual materials, an OPAC.

Student Life *Housing:* college housing not available. *Activities and Organizations:* student-run newspaper, radio station, choral group, Agriculture Production and Management Club, Cosmetology Club, Agriculture Transfer Club, Phi Theta Kappa, Civil Engineering Technology Club. *Campus security:* 24-hour patrols. *Student services:* personal/psychological counseling.

Athletics Member NJCAA. *Intercollegiate sports:* baseball M(s), basketball M(s)/W(s), cheerleading W, softball W(s), tennis M(s)/W, volleyball W(s). *Intramural sports:* basketball M/W, bowling M/W, golf M/W, softball M/W, volleyball M/W.

Costs (2007–08) *Tuition:* area resident $1755 full-time, $59 per semester hour part-time; state resident $4235 full-time, $141 per semester hour part-time; nonresident $8896 full-time, $297 per semester hour part-time. *Required fees:* $459 full-time, $15 per semester hour part-time.

Financial Aid Of all full-time matriculated undergraduates, 120 Federal Work-Study jobs (averaging $1400).

Applying *Options:* electronic application, early admission. *Required for some:* letters of recommendation. *Recommended:* high school transcript. *Application deadlines:* rolling (freshmen), rolling (transfers). *Notification:* continuous (freshmen), continuous (transfers).

Freshmen Application Contact Mr. Jon VanDyke, Dean of Admission Services, Lake Land College, Mattoon, IL 61938-9366. *Phone:* 217-234-5378. *Toll-free phone:* 800-252-4121. *E-mail:* admissions@lakeland.cc.il.us.

LEWIS AND CLARK COMMUNITY COLLEGE

Godfrey, Illinois www.lc.edu/

Director of Admissions Ms. Peggy Hudson, Director of Enrollment Center for Admissions Services, Lewis and Clark Community College, Enrollment Center, 5800 Godfrey Road, Godfrey, IL 62035. *Phone:* 618-468-5100. *Toll-free phone:* 800-500-LCCC.

LINCOLN COLLEGE

Lincoln, Illinois www.lincolncollege.edu/

- **Independent** 2-year, founded 1865
- **Small-town** 42-acre campus
- **Endowment** $14.0 million
- **Coed**

Undergraduates 700 full-time, 58 part-time. Students come from 15 states and territories, 9% are from out of state, 2% transferred in, 90% live on campus.

Faculty *Student/faculty ratio:* 16:1.

Academics *Calendar:* semesters. *Degree:* associate. *Special study options:* academic remediation for entering students, accelerated degree program, freshman honors college, honors programs, independent study, part-time degree program, summer session for credit.

Student Life *Campus security:* 24-hour emergency response devices and patrols, controlled dormitory access.

Athletics Member NJCAA.

Standardized Tests *Required:* SAT or ACT (for admission).

Costs (2006–07) *Comprehensive fee:* $21,370 includes full-time tuition ($15,000), mandatory fees ($570), and room and board ($5800). Part-time tuition: $500 per credit. *Required fees:* $19 per credit part-time. *Room and board:* college room only: $2200.

Financial Aid Of all full-time matriculated undergraduates, 200 Federal Work-Study jobs (averaging $900).

Applying *Options:* early admission, deferred entrance. *Application fee:* $25. *Required:* high school transcript. *Required for some:* 1 letter of recommendation. *Recommended:* interview.

Director of Admissions Mr. Tony Schilling, Director of Admissions, Lincoln College, 300 Keokuk Street, Lincoln, IL 62656-1699. *Toll-free phone:* 800-569-0556.

LINCOLN COLLEGE–NORMAL

Normal, Illinois www.lincolncollege.edu/normal/

- **Independent** primarily 2-year, founded 1865
- **Suburban** 10-acre campus
- **Endowment** $14.0 million
- **Coed**

Undergraduates 350 full-time, 170 part-time. Students come from 6 states and territories, 3 other countries, 6% are from out of state, 17% African American, 2% Hispanic American, 1% international, 10% transferred in, 40% live on campus.

Faculty *Student/faculty ratio:* 14:1.

Academics *Calendar:* semesters. *Degrees:* certificates, associate, and bachelor's. *Special study options:* academic remediation for entering students, adult/continuing education programs, cooperative education, honors programs, internships, part-time degree program, summer session for credit.

Student Life *Campus security:* 24-hour emergency response devices and patrols, student patrols, late-night transport/escort service, controlled dormitory access.

Athletics Member NJCAA.

Standardized Tests *Required for some:* SAT or ACT (for admission).

Costs (2006–07) *Tuition:* $15,000 full-time. No tuition increase for student's term of enrollment. *Required fees:* $810 full-time. *Room only:* $3200.

Applying *Options:* electronic application, deferred entrance. *Application fee:* $25. *Required:* high school transcript.

Freshmen Application Contact Mr. Joe Hendrix, Dean of Student Affairs, Lincoln College–Normal, 715 West Raab Road, Normal, IL 61761. *Phone:* 309-454-0500. *Toll-free phone:* 800-569-0558. *Fax:* 309-454-5652. *E-mail:* ncadmissionsinfo@lincolncollege.edu.

LINCOLN LAND COMMUNITY COLLEGE

Springfield, Illinois www.llcc.edu/

- **District-supported** 2-year, founded 1967, part of Illinois Community College Board
- **Suburban** 441-acre campus with easy access to St. Louis
- **Endowment** $1.7 million
- **Coed,** 6,532 undergraduate students, 41% full-time, 59% women, 41% men

Undergraduates 2,675 full-time, 3,857 part-time. Students come from 2 states and territories, 0.1% are from out of state, 8% African American, 1% Asian American or Pacific Islander, 2% Hispanic American, 0.4% Native American, 0.2% international, 1% transferred in. *Retention:* 54% of 2003 full-time freshmen returned.

Freshmen *Admission:* 865 applied, 865 admitted, 865 enrolled. *Average high school GPA:* 2.89. *Test scores:* ACT scores over 18: 65%; ACT scores over 24: 30%; ACT scores over 30: 4%.

Faculty *Total:* 372, 34% full-time, 9% with terminal degrees. *Student/faculty ratio:* 17:1.

Majors Administrative assistant and secretarial science; agricultural production; architectural drafting and CAD/CADD; art; automobile/automotive mechanics technology; biological and physical sciences; business administration and management; business automation/technology/data entry; child care provision; child guidance; computer programming (specific applications); computer systems networking and telecommunications; criminal justice/police science; electrical, electronic and communications engineering technology; fire protection and safety technology; general studies; hotel/motel administration; landscaping and groundskeeping; legal administrative assistant/secretary; liberal arts and sciences/liberal studies; literature; medical radiologic technology; music; nursing (registered nurse training); occupational therapist assistant; physical therapist assistant; pre-engineering; respiratory care therapy; selling skills and sales.

Academics *Calendar:* semesters. *Degree:* certificates and associate. *Special study options:* academic remediation for entering students, accelerated degree program, adult/continuing education programs, advanced placement credit, distance learning, English as a second language, external degree program, honors programs, independent study, internships, off-campus study, part-time degree program, services for LD students, study abroad, summer session for credit.

Library Learning Resource Center with 65,000 titles, 10,000 serial subscriptions, an OPAC, a Web page.

Student Life *Housing:* college housing not available. *Activities and Organizations:* drama/theater group, student-run newspaper, choral group, Student Senate, Phi Theta Kappa, Model Illinois Government, student newspaper, Madrigals. *Campus security:* 24-hour emergency response devices and patrols, late-night transport/escort service. *Student services:* health clinic, personal/psychological counseling, women's center.

Lincoln Land Community College (continued)

Athletics Member NJCAA. *Intercollegiate sports:* baseball M(s), basketball M(s)/W(s), soccer M(s), softball W(s), volleyball W(s). *Intramural sports:* basketball M/W, tennis M/W.

Costs (2007–08) *Tuition:* area resident $2160 full-time, $72 per credit hour part-time; state resident $4320 full-time, $144 per credit hour part-time; nonresident $6480 full-time, $216 per credit hour part-time. *Required fees:* $300 full-time, $10 per credit hour part-time.

Applying *Options:* early admission, deferred entrance. *Recommended:* high school transcript. *Application deadlines:* rolling (freshmen), rolling (transfers). *Notification:* continuous (freshmen), continuous (transfers).

Freshmen Application Contact Mr. Ron Gregoire, Executive Director of Admissions and Records, Lincoln Land Community College, 5250 Shepherd Road, PO Box 19256, Springfield, IL 62794-9256. *Phone:* 217-786-2243. *Toll-free phone:* 800-727-4161 Ext. 298. *Fax:* 217-786-2492. *E-mail:* ron.gregoire@llcc.edu.

MacCormac College

Chicago, Illinois　　　　**www.maccormac.edu/**

Director of Admissions Ms. Rosa Medina, Coordinator of Admissions, MacCormac College, 506 South Wabash Avenue, Chicago, IL 60605-1667. *Phone:* 312-922-1884 Ext. 106.

McHenry County College

Crystal Lake, Illinois　　　　**www.mchenry.edu/**

Freshmen Application Contact Fran Duwaldt, Coordinator of Admissions, McHenry County College, 8900 US Highway 14, Crystal Lake, IL 60012. *Phone:* 815-479-7620. *Toll-free phone:* 815-455-8530. *E-mail:* admissions@mchenry.edu.

Moraine Valley Community College

Palos Hills, Illinois　　　　**www.morainevalley.edu/**

- **State and locally supported** 2-year, founded 1967, part of Illinois Community College Board
- **Suburban** 294-acre campus with easy access to Chicago
- **Endowment** $12.3 million
- **Coed,** 15,693 undergraduate students, 42% full-time, 58% women, 42% men

Undergraduates 6,660 full-time, 9,033 part-time. Students come from 6 states and territories, 36 other countries, 9% African American, 3% Asian American or Pacific Islander, 11% Hispanic American, 0.2% Native American, 2% international, 4% transferred in. *Retention:* 65% of 2003 full-time freshmen returned.

Freshmen *Admission:* 4,252 applied, 4,252 admitted, 1,821 enrolled. *Test scores:* ACT scores over 18: 69%; ACT scores over 24: 13%.

Faculty *Total:* 749, 22% full-time, 8% with terminal degrees. *Student/faculty ratio:* 27:1.

Majors Administrative assistant and secretarial science; automobile/automotive mechanics technology; biological and physical sciences; business administration and management; business/commerce; child care provision; computer programming (specific applications); computer systems networking and telecommunications; corrections; criminal justice/police science; design and visual communications; entrepreneurship; fire protection and safety technology; health information/medical records technology; human resources management; instrumentation technology; liberal arts and sciences/liberal studies; mechanical engineering/mechanical technology; medical radiologic technology; nursing (registered nurse training); parks, recreation and leisure facilities management; respiratory care therapy; restaurant, culinary, and catering management; retailing; selling skills and sales; therapeutic recreation; tourism and travel services marketing; visual and performing arts.

Academics *Calendar:* semesters. *Degree:* certificates and associate. *Special study options:* academic remediation for entering students, accelerated degree program, adult/continuing education programs, advanced placement credit, cooperative education, distance learning, double majors, English as a second language, external degree program, freshman honors college, honors programs, independent study, internships, off-campus study, part-time degree program, services for LD students, study abroad, summer session for credit.

Library Robert E. Turner Learning Resources Center/Library plus 1 other with 74,091 titles, 464 serial subscriptions, an OPAC, a Web page.

Student Life *Housing:* college housing not available. *Activities and Organizations:* drama/theater group, student-run newspaper, choral group, student newspaper, Speech Team, Alliance of Latin American Students, Phi Theta Kappa, Arab Student Union. *Campus security:* 24-hour emergency response devices and patrols, late-night transport/escort service, safety and security programs. *Student services:* personal/psychological counseling, women's center.

Athletics Member NJCAA. *Intercollegiate sports:* baseball M(s), basketball M(s)/W(s), cross-country running M(s)/W(s), golf M(s), soccer M(s)/W(s), softball W, tennis M/W(s), volleyball W(s). *Intramural sports:* badminton M/W, basketball M/W, softball W, volleyball W.

Standardized Tests *Recommended:* ACT (for admission).

Costs (2006–07) *Tuition:* area resident $2010 full-time, $67 per credit hour part-time; state resident $5970 full-time, $199 per credit hour part-time; nonresident $7260 full-time, $242 per credit hour part-time. *Required fees:* $152 full-time, $5 per credit hour part-time, $1 per term part-time. *Payment plan:* installment. *Waivers:* senior citizens and employees or children of employees.

Financial Aid Of all full-time matriculated undergraduates, 84 Federal Work-Study jobs (averaging $1900). 150 state and other part-time jobs (averaging $800).

Applying *Options:* electronic application, early admission, deferred entrance. *Required:* high school transcript. *Application deadlines:* rolling (freshmen), rolling (transfers). *Notification:* continuous (freshmen), continuous (transfers).

Freshmen Application Contact Ms. Claudia Roselli, Director, Admissions and Recruitment, Moraine Valley Community College, 9000 West College Parkway, Palos Hills, IL 60465-0937. *Phone:* 708-974-5357. *Fax:* 708-974-0681. *E-mail:* roselli@morainevalley.edu.

Morrison Institute of Technology

Morrison, Illinois　　　　**www.morrison.tec.il.us/**

- **Independent** 2-year, founded 1973
- **Small-town** 17-acre campus
- **Endowment** $76,000
- **Coed, primarily men**

Undergraduates Students come from 4 states and territories, 6% are from out of state, 4% African American, 3% Hispanic American, 55% live on campus.

Faculty *Student/faculty ratio:* 12:1.

Academics *Calendar:* semesters. *Degree:* associate. *Special study options:* academic remediation for entering students, double majors, internships, part-time degree program.

Student Life *Campus security:* late-night transport/escort service, controlled dormitory access.

Standardized Tests *Recommended:* SAT or ACT (for admission).

Costs (2006–07) *Tuition:* $12,100 full-time, $504 per credit part-time. *Required fees:* $560 full-time, $125 per term part-time. *Room only:* $2600. *Payment plans:* installment, deferred payment.

Financial Aid Of all full-time matriculated undergraduates, 25 Federal Work-Study jobs (averaging $2000).

Applying *Options:* deferred entrance. *Application fee:* $100. *Required:* high school transcript, proof of immunization.

Freshmen Application Contact Mrs. Tammy Pruis, Admission Secretary, Morrison Institute of Technology, 701 Portland Avenue, Morrison, IL 61270. *Phone:* 815-772-7218. *Fax:* 815-772-7584. *E-mail:* admissions@morrison.tec.il.us.

▶**See page 572 for the College Close-Up.**

Morton College

Cicero, Illinois　　　　**www.morton.edu/**

- **State and locally supported** 2-year, founded 1924, part of Illinois Community College Board
- **Suburban** 25-acre campus with easy access to Chicago
- **Coed,** 5,049 undergraduate students, 25% full-time, 61% women, 39% men

Undergraduates 1,278 full-time, 3,771 part-time. Students come from 3 states and territories, 0.1% are from out of state, 4% African American, 2% Asian American or Pacific Islander, 77% Hispanic American, 0.1% Native American, 2% international, 2% transferred in. *Retention:* 55% of 2003 full-time freshmen returned.

Freshmen *Admission:* 365 enrolled. *Average high school GPA:* 2.66.

Faculty *Total:* 228, 23% full-time, 11% with terminal degrees. *Student/faculty ratio:* 21:1.

Majors Accounting; administrative assistant and secretarial science; art; automobile/automotive mechanics technology; biological and physical sciences; business administration and management; criminal justice/police science; data processing and data processing technology; drafting and design technology; finance; fine/studio arts; heating, air conditioning, ventilation and refrigeration maintenance technology; legal administrative assistant/secretary; liberal arts and sciences/liberal studies; marketing/marketing management; medical administrative assistant and medical secretary; music; nursing (registered nurse training); physical therapy; real estate.

Academics *Calendar:* semesters. *Degree:* certificates and associate. *Special study options:* academic remediation for entering students, adult/continuing education programs, advanced placement credit, English as a second language, internships, part-time degree program, services for LD students, student-designed majors, summer session for credit.

Library Learning Resource Center with 40,972 titles, 327 serial subscriptions.

Student Life *Housing:* college housing not available. *Activities and Organizations:* drama/theater group, student-run newspaper, choral group, Hispanic Heritage Club, Program Board, Student Senate, Law Enforcement Association, Nursing Club. *Campus security:* 24-hour patrols, security cameras.

Athletics Member NJCAA. *Intercollegiate sports:* baseball M(s), basketball M(s)/W(s), cross-country running M(s)/W(s), soccer M, softball W(s), volleyball W(s). *Intramural sports:* basketball M/W, cross-country running M/W, volleyball M/W, weight lifting M/W.

Costs (2007–08) *Tuition:* $61 per credit hour part-time; state resident $183 per credit hour part-time; nonresident $244 per credit hour part-time.

Financial Aid Of all full-time matriculated undergraduates, 15 Federal Work-Study jobs (averaging $2000).

Applying *Application fee:* $10. *Required:* high school transcript. *Application deadlines:* rolling (freshmen), rolling (transfers).

Director of Admissions Roslyn Castro, Director of Admissions, Morton College, 3801 South Central Avenue, Cicero, IL 60804. *Phone:* 708-656-8000 Ext. 400.

NORTHWESTERN BUSINESS COLLEGE

Chicago, Illinois　　　　　**www.northwesternbc.edu/**

Director of Admissions Mr. Mark Sliz, Director of Admissions, Northwestern Business College, 4839 North Milwaukee Avenue, Chicago, IL 60630. *Phone:* 773-481-3730. *Toll-free phone:* 800-396-5613.

OAKTON COMMUNITY COLLEGE

Des Plaines, Illinois　　　　　**www.oakton.edu/**

Freshmen Application Contact Mr. Dale Cohen, Admissions Specialist, Oakton Community College, 1600 East Golf Road, Des Plaines, IL 60016. *Phone:* 847-635-1703. *Fax:* 847-635-1890. *E-mail:* dcohen@oakton.edu.

PARKLAND COLLEGE

Champaign, Illinois　　　　　**www.parkland.edu/**

- **District-supported** 2-year, founded 1967, part of Illinois Community College Board
- **Suburban** 233-acre campus
- **Coed,** 9,336 undergraduate students, 47% full-time, 53% women, 47% men

Undergraduates 4,431 full-time, 4,905 part-time. 1% are from out of state, 6% transferred in. *Retention:* 59% of 2003 full-time freshmen returned.

Freshmen *Admission:* 6,399 applied, 2,911 admitted, 1,621 enrolled. *Test scores:* ACT scores over 18: 61%; ACT scores over 24: 17%; ACT scores over 30: 1%.

Faculty *Total:* 535, 31% full-time, 12% with terminal degrees. *Student/faculty ratio:* 20:1.

Majors Accounting technology and bookkeeping; administrative assistant and secretarial science; advertising; agricultural business and management; agricultural mechanization; art; art teacher education; autobody/collision and repair technology; automobile/automotive mechanics technology; biological and physical sciences; biomedical technology; business administration and management; business automation/technology/data entry; child care provision; computer and information sciences; computer graphics; computer/information technology services administration related; computer programming; computer programming (specific applications); computer programming (vendor/product certification); computer science; computer software and media applications related; computer

systems networking and telecommunications; computer/technical support; construction management; consumer merchandising/retailing management; criminal justice/safety; data entry/microcomputer applications; dental hygiene; design and visual communications; early childhood education; electroneurodiagnostic/electroencephalographic technology; elementary education; engineering science; English; general studies; graphic design; history; human services; industrial technology; information science/studies; landscaping and groundskeeping; liberal arts and sciences/liberal studies; mass communication/media; medical radiologic technology; music performance; music teacher education; nursing (registered nurse training); occupational therapist assistant; radio and television; radio and television broadcasting technology; respiratory care therapy; sales and marketing/marketing and distribution teacher education; secondary education; speech-language pathology; surgical technology; system administration; theater/theater arts management; veterinary/animal health technology; web page, digital/multimedia and information resources design.

Academics *Calendar:* semesters. *Degree:* certificates and associate. *Special study options:* academic remediation for entering students, accelerated degree program, adult/continuing education programs, advanced placement credit, cooperative education, distance learning, double majors, English as a second language, honors programs, independent study, internships, off-campus study, part-time degree program, services for LD students, student-designed majors, study abroad, summer session for credit. *ROTC:* Army (c), Navy (c), Air Force (c).

Library Parkland College Library with an OPAC, a Web page.

Student Life *Housing:* college housing not available. *Activities and Organizations:* drama/theater group, student-run newspaper, radio and television station, choral group. *Campus security:* 24-hour emergency response devices and patrols, late-night transport/escort service. *Student services:* personal/psychological counseling.

Athletics Member NJCAA. *Intercollegiate sports:* baseball M(s), basketball M(s)/W(s), golf M(s), soccer M(s)/W(s), softball W(s), volleyball W(s). *Intramural sports:* basketball M/W, bowling M/W, softball M/W, volleyball M/W.

Standardized Tests *Required for some:* ACT (for admission).

Costs (2006–07) *Tuition:* area resident $3179 full-time, $77 per credit hour part-time; state resident $7319 full-time, $215 per credit hour part-time; nonresident $9450 full-time, $318 per credit hour part-time.

Financial Aid Of all full-time matriculated undergraduates, 100 Federal Work-Study jobs (averaging $2000).

Applying *Options:* deferred entrance. *Recommended:* high school transcript. *Application deadlines:* rolling (freshmen), rolling (transfers). *Notification:* continuous (freshmen), continuous (transfers).

Freshmen Application Contact Admissions Representative, Parkland College, 2400 West Bradley Avenue, Champaign, IL 61821-1899. *Phone:* 217-351-2482. *Toll-free phone:* 800-346-8089. *Fax:* 217-351-2640. *E-mail:* mhenry@parkland.edu.

PRAIRIE STATE COLLEGE

Chicago Heights, Illinois　　　　　**www.prairiestate.edu/**

- **State and locally supported** 2-year, founded 1958, part of Illinois Community College Board
- **Suburban** 68-acre campus with easy access to Chicago
- **Endowment** $573,000
- **Coed**

Undergraduates 1,714 full-time, 3,369 part-time. Students come from 4 states and territories, 4% are from out of state, 47% African American, 1% Asian American or Pacific Islander, 10% Hispanic American, 0.6% Native American, 0.2% international, 0.4% transferred in. *Retention:* 48% of 2003 full-time freshmen returned.

Faculty *Student/faculty ratio:* 16:1.

Academics *Calendar:* semesters. *Degree:* certificates and associate. *Special study options:* academic remediation for entering students, adult/continuing education programs, advanced placement credit, distance learning, English as a second language, honors programs, internships, part-time degree program, services for LD students, student-designed majors, summer session for credit.

Student Life *Campus security:* 24-hour emergency response devices and patrols, student patrols, late-night transport/escort service.

Athletics Member NJCAA.

Costs (2006–07) *Tuition:* area resident $1968 full-time, $82 per credit hour part-time; state resident $5736 full-time, $239 per credit hour part-time; nonresident $7848 full-time, $327 per credit hour part-time. Full-time tuition and fees vary according to course load. Part-time tuition and fees vary according to course load. *Required fees:* $236 full-time, $9 per credit hour part-time, $10 per term part-time. *Room and board:* Room and board charges vary according to location. *Payment plans:* installment, deferred payment.

Financial Aid Of all full-time matriculated undergraduates, 60 Federal Work-Study jobs (averaging $2500).

Prairie State College (continued)

Applying *Options:* deferred entrance. *Application fee:* $10. *Required:* high school transcript.

Freshmen Application Contact Ms. Marietta Turner, Director, Admissions, Enrollment and Career Development Services, Prairie State College, 202 South Halsted Street, Chicago Heights, IL 60411. *Phone:* 708-709-3513. *Toll-free phone:* 708-709-3516. *E-mail:* webmaster@prairiestate.edu.

REND LAKE COLLEGE

Ina, Illinois　　　www.rlc.edu/

Freshmen Application Contact Mr. Jason Swann, Recruiter, Rend Lake College, 468 North Ken Gray Parkway, Ina, IL 62846-9801. *Phone:* 618-437-5321 Ext. 1265. *Toll-free phone:* 800-369-5321. *Fax:* 618-437-5677. *E-mail:* swannj@rlc.edu.

RICHLAND COMMUNITY COLLEGE

Decatur, Illinois　　　www.richland.edu/

- **District-supported** 2-year, founded 1971, part of Illinois Community College Board
- **Small-town** 117-acre campus
- **Endowment** $4.8 million
- **Coed,** 3,152 undergraduate students, 32% full-time, 63% women, 37% men

Undergraduates 1,003 full-time, 2,149 part-time. Students come from 1 other state, 16% African American, 0.8% Asian American or Pacific Islander, 2% Hispanic American, 0.5% Native American, 0.2% international, 43% transferred in. *Retention:* 53% of 2003 full-time freshmen returned.

Freshmen *Admission:* 769 applied, 769 admitted, 491 enrolled. *Test scores:* ACT scores over 18: 74%; ACT scores over 24: 22%; ACT scores over 30: 2%.

Faculty *Total:* 217, 31% full-time, 5% with terminal degrees. *Student/faculty ratio:* 14:1.

Majors Accounting; administrative assistant and secretarial science; agricultural business and management; automobile/automotive mechanics technology; biological and physical sciences; business administration and management; child development; computer and information sciences related; computer graphics; computer programming (specific applications); construction engineering technology; criminal justice/police science; data entry/microcomputer applications; data entry/microcomputer applications related; drafting and design technology; electrical, electronic and communications engineering technology; fire science; food services technology; industrial technology; information science/studies; insurance; legal administrative assistant/secretary; liberal arts and sciences/liberal studies; medical administrative assistant and medical secretary; nursing (registered nurse training); pre-engineering; word processing.

Academics *Calendar:* semesters. *Degree:* certificates and associate. *Special study options:* academic remediation for entering students, adult/continuing education programs, advanced placement credit, distance learning, English as a second language, freshman honors college, honors programs, part-time degree program, services for LD students, student-designed majors, summer session for credit.

Library Kitty Lindsay Library with 39,452 titles, 275 serial subscriptions, an OPAC, a Web page.

Student Life *Housing:* college housing not available. *Activities and Organizations:* student-run newspaper, Student Senate, Forensics Club, Drama Club, Black Student Association, Student Activities Board. *Campus security:* 24-hour emergency response devices and patrols. *Student services:* personal/psychological counseling.

Standardized Tests *Recommended:* ACT (for admission).

Costs (2006–07) *Tuition:* area resident $1725 full-time, $60 per credit hour part-time; state resident $6955 full-time, $258 per credit hour part-time; nonresident $10,222 full-time, $383 per credit hour part-time. *Required fees:* $155 full-time, $5 per credit hour part-time, $10 per term part-time.

Financial Aid Of all full-time matriculated undergraduates, 43 Federal Work-Study jobs (averaging $1339). 129 state and other part-time jobs (averaging $578).

Applying *Options:* early admission. *Required:* high school transcript. *Application deadlines:* rolling (freshmen), rolling (transfers).

Freshmen Application Contact Ms. JoAnn Wirey, Director of Admissions and Records, Richland Community College, One College Park, Decatur, IL 62521. *Phone:* 217-875-7200 Ext. 284. *Fax:* 217-875-7783. *E-mail:* jwirey@richland.edu.

ROCKFORD BUSINESS COLLEGE

Rockford, Illinois　　　www.rbcsuccess.com/

- **Independent** 2-year, founded 1862
- **Urban** campus with easy access to Chicago
- **Coed, primarily women,** 428 undergraduate students, 57% full-time, 89% women, 11% men

Undergraduates 243 full-time, 185 part-time. Students come from 2 states and territories, 1% are from out of state, 34% African American, 0.2% Asian American or Pacific Islander, 7% Hispanic American, 0.2% Native American, 8% transferred in.

Freshmen *Admission:* 125 applied, 90 enrolled.

Faculty *Total:* 26, 31% full-time. *Student/faculty ratio:* 15:1.

Majors Accounting; business administration and management; computer and information sciences; executive assistant/executive secretary; legal administrative assistant/secretary; legal assistant/paralegal; marketing/marketing management; medical/clinical assistant; medical transcription.

Academics *Calendar:* quarters. *Degree:* certificates, diplomas, and associate. *Special study options:* academic remediation for entering students, adult/continuing education programs, advanced placement credit, cooperative education, honors programs, independent study, internships, part-time degree program, services for LD students, summer session for credit.

Library Rockford Business College Library plus 1 other with 1,823 titles, 161 serial subscriptions, 50 audiovisual materials.

Student Life *Activities and Organizations:* student-run newspaper, International Students Club. *Campus security:* 24-hour patrols, late-night transport/escort service. *Student services:* personal/psychological counseling.

Costs (2006–07) *Tuition:* $10,131 full-time.

Applying *Options:* electronic application, early admission. *Application fee:* $50. *Required:* high school transcript, interview. *Required for some:* essay or personal statement. *Application deadlines:* 9/4 (freshmen), 9/4 (transfers).

Director of Admissions Ms. Barbara Holliman, Director of Admissions, Rockford Business College, 730 North Church Street, Rockford, IL 61103. *Phone:* 815-965-8616 Ext. 16.

ROCK VALLEY COLLEGE

Rockford, Illinois　　　www.rockvalleycollege.edu/

- **District-supported** 2-year, founded 1964, part of Illinois Community College Board
- **Suburban** 217-acre campus with easy access to Chicago
- **Coed**

Undergraduates 3,508 full-time, 4,637 part-time. Students come from 2 states and territories, 3 other countries, 1% are from out of state, 9% African American, 3% Asian American or Pacific Islander, 6% Hispanic American, 0.4% Native American, 0.3% international.

Faculty *Student/faculty ratio:* 21:1.

Academics *Calendar:* semesters. *Degree:* certificates and associate. *Special study options:* academic remediation for entering students, adult/continuing education programs, advanced placement credit, cooperative education, distance learning, English as a second language, honors programs, independent study, internships, part-time degree program, services for LD students, student-designed majors, study abroad, summer session for credit.

Student Life *Campus security:* 24-hour emergency response devices and patrols, late-night transport/escort service.

Athletics Member NJCAA.

Costs (2006–07) *Tuition:* area resident $1830 full-time, $61 per credit part-time; state resident $7350 full-time, $245 per credit part-time; nonresident $12,030 full-time, $401 per credit part-time. Full-time tuition and fees vary according to course load. Part-time tuition and fees vary according to course load. *Required fees:* $274 full-time, $9 per credit part-time, $2 per term part-time. *Payment plans:* installment, deferred payment.

Financial Aid Of all full-time matriculated undergraduates, 120 Federal Work-Study jobs (averaging $1800).

Applying *Required:* high school transcript.

Freshmen Application Contact Registrar, Rock Valley College, 3301 North Mulford Road, Rockford, IL 61114-5699. *Phone:* 815-921-4267. *Toll-free phone:* 800-973-7821. *Fax:* 815-921-4269. *E-mail:* j.hinton-rivera@rvc.cc.il.us.

SAUK VALLEY COMMUNITY COLLEGE

Dixon, Illinois   www.svcc.edu/

- **District-supported** 2-year, founded 1965, part of Illinois Community College Board
- **Rural** 165-acre campus
- **Coed**

Undergraduates 1,154 full-time, 1,591 part-time. 2% African American, 0.9% Asian American or Pacific Islander, 7% Hispanic American, 0.2% Native American.

Faculty *Student/faculty ratio:* 19:1.

Academics *Calendar:* semesters. *Degree:* certificates and associate. *Special study options:* academic remediation for entering students, accelerated degree program, adult/continuing education programs, cooperative education, distance learning, English as a second language, honors programs, independent study, internships, off-campus study, part-time degree program, services for LD students, student-designed majors.

Student Life *Campus security:* 24-hour emergency response devices and patrols, late-night transport/escort service.

Athletics Member NJCAA.

Standardized Tests *Recommended:* ACT (for admission).

Costs (2006–07) *Tuition:* area resident $2560 full-time, $80 per credit hour part-time; state resident $9632 full-time, $301 per credit hour part-time; nonresident $10,688 full-time, $334 per credit hour part-time.

Financial Aid Of all full-time matriculated undergraduates, 150 Federal Work-Study jobs (averaging $3000).

Applying *Options:* early admission, deferred entrance. *Recommended:* high school transcript.

Freshmen Application Contact Ms. Pamela Clodfelter, Director of Admissions, Records, and Placement, Sauk Valley Community College, 173 Illinois Route 2, Dixon, IL 61021. *Phone:* 815-288-5511 Ext. 310. *Fax:* 815-288-3190. *E-mail:* skyhawk@svcc.edu.

SHAWNEE COMMUNITY COLLEGE

Ullin, Illinois   www.shawneecc.edu/

Director of Admissions Ms. Dee Blakely, Director of Admissions, Shawnee Community College, 8364 Shawnee College Road, Ullin, IL 62992-2206. *Phone:* 618-634-3200 Ext. 3247. *Toll-free phone:* 800-481-2242.

SOUTHEASTERN ILLINOIS COLLEGE

Harrisburg, Illinois   www.sic.edu/

- **State-supported** 2-year, founded 1960, part of Illinois Community College Board
- **Rural** 140-acre campus
- **Coed**

Undergraduates 795 full-time, 1,764 part-time. Students come from 5 states and territories, 2 other countries, 17% are from out of state, 7% African American, 1% Hispanic American, 0.3% international.

Faculty *Student/faculty ratio:* 12:1.

Academics *Calendar:* semesters. *Degree:* certificates and associate. *Special study options:* academic remediation for entering students, adult/continuing education programs, advanced placement credit, distance learning, independent study, internships, off-campus study, part-time degree program, services for LD students, student-designed majors, summer session for credit.

Student Life *Campus security:* student patrols, evening security guard.

Athletics Member NJCAA.

Costs (2006–07) *Tuition:* area resident $1920 full-time, $64 per hour part-time; state resident $2790 full-time, $93 per hour part-time; nonresident $3210 full-time, $107 per hour part-time. *Required fees:* $60 full-time, $2 per hour part-time. *Room and board:* $3655.

Financial Aid Of all full-time matriculated undergraduates, 57 Federal Work-Study jobs (averaging $1152). 68 state and other part-time jobs (averaging $1152).

Applying *Options:* electronic application, early admission, deferred entrance. *Required:* high school transcript.

Freshmen Application Contact Dr. David Nudo, Director of Counseling, Southeastern Illinois College, 3575 College Road, Harrisburg, IL 62946-4925. *Phone:* 618-252-5400 Ext. 2430. *Toll-free phone:* 866-338-2742.

SOUTH SUBURBAN COLLEGE

South Holland, Illinois   www.southsuburbancollege.edu/

Freshmen Application Contact Ms. Jazaer Farrar, Director of New Student Services, South Suburban College, 15800 South State Street, South Holland, IL 60473-1270. *Phone:* 708-596-2000 Ext. 2291. *Fax:* 708-225-5823. *E-mail:* jfarrar@southsuburbancollege.edu.

SOUTHWESTERN ILLINOIS COLLEGE

Belleville, Illinois   www.southwestern.cc.il.us/

- **District-supported** 2-year, founded 1946, part of Illinois Community College Board
- **Suburban** 150-acre campus with easy access to St. Louis
- **Endowment** $3.1 million
- **Coed**

Undergraduates 5,296 full-time, 9,183 part-time. Students come from 6 states and territories, 19 other countries, 18% African American, 2% Asian American or Pacific Islander, 3% Hispanic American, 0.6% Native American, 0.1% international, 43% transferred in.

Faculty *Student/faculty ratio:* 17:1.

Academics *Calendar:* semesters. *Degree:* certificates, diplomas, and associate. *Special study options:* academic remediation for entering students, accelerated degree program, adult/continuing education programs, advanced placement credit, cooperative education, distance learning, double majors, English as a second language, internships, off-campus study, part-time degree program, services for LD students, study abroad, summer session for credit. *ROTC:* Army (c), Air Force (c).

Student Life *Campus security:* 24-hour emergency response devices and patrols, student patrols, late-night transport/escort service.

Athletics Member NJCAA.

Standardized Tests *Required for some:* ACT ASSET or ACT COMPASS, ACT ASSET or ACT COMPASS.

Costs (2006–07) *Tuition:* area resident $1890 full-time, $63 per credit hour part-time; state resident $5220 full-time, $174 per credit hour part-time; nonresident $8070 full-time, $269 per credit hour part-time.

Financial Aid Of all full-time matriculated undergraduates, 170 Federal Work-Study jobs (averaging $1537). 179 state and other part-time jobs (averaging $1004).

Applying *Options:* early admission, deferred entrance. *Application fee:* $10. *Required:* high school transcript.

Freshmen Application Contact Mike Leiker, Director of Admissions, Southwestern Illinois College, 2500 Carlyle Road, Belleville, IL 62221-5899. *Phone:* 618-235-2700 Ext. 5400. *Toll-free phone:* 800-222-5131. *Fax:* 618-277-0631.

SPOON RIVER COLLEGE

Canton, Illinois   www.spoonrivercollege.net/

- **State-supported** 2-year, founded 1959, part of Illinois Community College Board
- **Rural** 160-acre campus
- **Endowment** $98,726
- **Coed**

Undergraduates 1,053 full-time, 1,280 part-time. Students come from 6 states and territories, 0.5% are from out of state, 5% African American, 1% Asian American or Pacific Islander, 0.9% Hispanic American, 0.5% Native American, 0.1% international.

Faculty *Student/faculty ratio:* 20:1.

Academics *Calendar:* semesters. *Degree:* certificates and associate. *Special study options:* accelerated degree program, adult/continuing education programs, advanced placement credit, distance learning, English as a second language, freshman honors college, honors programs, internships, part-time degree program, services for LD students, summer session for credit. *ROTC:* Army (b).

Student Life *Campus security:* 24-hour emergency response devices.

Athletics Member NJCAA.

Costs (2006–07) *Tuition:* area resident $1935 full-time, $65 per credit hour part-time; state resident $3735 full-time, $125 per credit hour part-time; nonresident $4845 full-time, $162 per credit hour part-time. Full-time tuition and fees vary according to course load. Part-time tuition and fees vary according to course load. *Required fees:* $315 full-time, $11 per credit hour part-time.

Applying *Options:* early admission. *Required:* high school transcript.

Spoon River College (continued)

Freshmen Application Contact Ms. Missy Wilkinson, Director of Admissions and Records, Spoon River College, 23235 North County 22, Canton, IL 61520-9801. *Phone:* 309-649-6305. *Toll-free phone:* 800-334-7337. *Fax:* 309-649-6235. *E-mail:* info@spoonrivercollege.edu.

SPRINGFIELD COLLEGE IN ILLINOIS

Springfield, Illinois www.sci.edu/

- **Independent** 2-year, founded 1929, affiliated with Roman Catholic Church
- **Urban** 8-acre campus
- **Endowment** $694,388
- **Coed**

Undergraduates 271 full-time, 281 part-time. Students come from 13 states and territories, 8 other countries, 3% are from out of state, 15% African American, 0.2% Asian American or Pacific Islander, 0.7% Hispanic American, 0.2% Native American, 0.9% international, 6% transferred in.
Faculty *Student/faculty ratio:* 12:1.
Academics *Calendar:* semesters. *Degrees:* associate (the college partners with Benedictine University, offering baccalaureate and master degree programs at Springfield College's campus). *Special study options:* academic remediation for entering students, adult/continuing education programs, advanced placement credit, off-campus study, part-time degree program, student-designed majors, summer session for credit.
Student Life *Campus security:* 24-hour emergency response devices.
Athletics Member NJCAA.
Standardized Tests *Required:* SAT and SAT Subject Tests or ACT (for admission).
Costs (2006–07) *Comprehensive fee:* $15,400 includes full-time tuition ($7490), mandatory fees ($1990), and room and board ($5920). Part-time tuition: $312 per hour.
Financial Aid Of all full-time matriculated undergraduates, 30 Federal Work-Study jobs (averaging $1700).
Applying *Application fee:* $20. *Required:* high school transcript. *Required for some:* interview. *Recommended:* minimum 2.0 GPA.
Director of Admissions Ms. Kim Fontana, Director of Admissions, Springfield College in Illinois, 1500 North Fifth Street, Springfield, IL 62702-2694. *Phone:* 217-525-1420 Ext. 241. *Toll-free phone:* 800-635-7289.

TAYLOR BUSINESS INSTITUTE

Chicago, Illinois www.tbiil.edu/

- **Proprietary** 2-year, founded 1964
- **Coed,** 95 undergraduate students
- **78% of applicants were admitted**

Freshmen *Admission:* 131 applied, 102 admitted.
Majors Accounting technology and bookkeeping; criminal justice/law enforcement administration; electrical, electronic and communications engineering technology; health information/medical records technology; medical insurance/medical billing.
Academics *Degree:* associate.
Costs (2006–07) *Tuition:* $10,800 full-time.
Applying *Application fee:* $25.
Director of Admissions Mr. Rashed Jahangir, Taylor Business Institute, 318 West Adams, Chicago, IL 60007.

TRITON COLLEGE

River Grove, Illinois www.triton.cc.il.us/

- **State-supported** 2-year, founded 1964, part of Illinois Community College Board
- **Suburban** 100-acre campus with easy access to Chicago
- **Coed**

Undergraduates 3,831 full-time, 7,190 part-time. Students come from 26 other countries, 2% are from out of state, 21% African American, 5% Asian American or Pacific Islander, 17% Hispanic American, 0.3% Native American, 0.2% international.
Faculty *Student/faculty ratio:* 22:1.

Academics *Calendar:* semesters. *Degree:* certificates and associate. *Special study options:* academic remediation for entering students, adult/continuing education programs, advanced placement credit, cooperative education, distance learning, English as a second language, freshman honors college, honors programs, internships, part-time degree program, student-designed majors, summer session for credit.
Student Life *Campus security:* 24-hour emergency response devices and patrols.
Athletics Member NJCAA.
Costs (2006–07) *Tuition:* area resident $1680 full-time, $56 per semester hour part-time; state resident $5244 full-time, $175 per semester hour part-time; nonresident $6670 full-time, $222 per semester hour part-time. *Required fees:* $250 full-time, $5 per credit hour part-time, $30 per term part-time.
Financial Aid Of all full-time matriculated undergraduates, 250 Federal Work-Study jobs (averaging $2000).
Applying *Options:* deferred entrance. *Required:* high school transcript.
Freshmen Application Contact Mr. Doug Olson, Dean of Student Services, Triton College, 2000 Fifth Avenue, River Grove, IL 60171. *Phone:* 708-456-0300 Ext. 3230. *Toll-free phone:* 800-942-7404. *Fax:* 708-583-3121. *E-mail:* dolson@triton.edu.

WAUBONSEE COMMUNITY COLLEGE

Sugar Grove, Illinois www.waubonsee.edu/

- **District-supported** 2-year, founded 1966, part of Illinois Community College Board
- **Rural** 243-acre campus with easy access to Chicago
- **Endowment** $1.6 million
- **Coed**

Undergraduates 2,624 full-time, 6,210 part-time. Students come from 1 other state, 2 other countries, 7% African American, 2% Asian American or Pacific Islander, 17% Hispanic American, 0.3% Native American, 0.0% international, 2% transferred in. *Retention:* 63% of 2003 full-time freshmen returned.
Faculty *Student/faculty ratio:* 17:1.
Academics *Calendar:* semesters. *Degree:* certificates and associate. *Special study options:* academic remediation for entering students, accelerated degree program, advanced placement credit, distance learning, honors programs, independent study, internships, part-time degree program, services for LD students, study abroad, summer session for credit. *ROTC:* Army (c).
Student Life *Campus security:* 24-hour emergency response devices and patrols, late-night transport/escort service.
Athletics Member NJCAA.
Costs (2006–07) *Tuition:* area resident $2010 full-time, $67 per semester hour part-time; state resident $6300 full-time, $210 per semester hour part-time; nonresident $7110 full-time, $237 per semester hour part-time. Full-time tuition and fees vary according to course load. Part-time tuition and fees vary according to course load. *Required fees:* $90 full-time, $3 per semester hour part-time.
Financial Aid Of all full-time matriculated undergraduates, 23 Federal Work-Study jobs (averaging $2000).
Freshmen Application Contact Recruitment and Retention Office, Waubonsee Community College, Route 47 at Waubonsee Drive, Sugar Grove, IL 60554. *Phone:* 630-466-7900 Ext. 5756. *Fax:* 630-466-4964. *E-mail:* recruitment@waubonsee.edu.

WESTWOOD COLLEGE—CHICAGO DU PAGE

Woodridge, Illinois www.westwood.edu/

Director of Admissions Mr. Scott Kawall, Director of Admissions, Westwood College–Chicago Du Page, 7155 James Avenue, Woodridge, IL 60517-2321. *Phone:* 630-434-8244. *Toll-free phone:* 888-721-7646.

▶See page 602 for the College Close-Up.

WESTWOOD COLLEGE—CHICAGO LOOP CAMPUS

Chicago, Illinois www.westwood.edu/

Director of Admissions Gus Pyrolis, Acting Director of Admissions, Westwood College–Chicago Loop Campus, 17 North State Street, Suite 1500, Chicago, IL 60602. *Phone:* 312-739-0850.

▶See page 604 for the College Close-Up.

Westwood College—Chicago O'Hare Airport

Schiller Park, Illinois www.westwood.edu/

Director of Admissions Mr. David Traub, Director of Admissions, Westwood College–Chicago O'Hare Airport, 4825 North Scott Street, Suite 100, Schiller Park, IL 60176-1209. *Phone:* 847-928-0200 Ext. 100. *Toll-free phone:* 877-877-8857.

▶**See page 606 for the College Close-Up.**

Westwood College—Chicago River Oaks

Calumet City, Illinois www.westwood.edu/

Director of Admissions Tash Uray, Director of Admissions, Westwood College–Chicago River Oaks, 80 River Oaks Drive, Suite D-49, Calumet City, IL 60409-5820. *Phone:* 708-832-1988. *Toll-free phone:* 888-549-6873.

▶**See page 608 for the College Close-Up.**

Worsham College of Mortuary Science

Wheeling, Illinois www.worshamcollege.com/

Director of Admissions Ms. Stephanie Kann, President, Worsham College of Mortuary Science, 495 Northgate Parkway, Wheeling, IL 60090-2646. *Phone:* 847-808-8444.

INDIANA

American Trans Air Aviation Training Academy

Indianapolis, Indiana www.aviationmaintenance.edu/

Freshmen Application Contact Admissions Office, American Trans Air Aviation Training Academy, 7251 West McCarty Street, Indianapolis, IN 46241. *Toll-free phone:* 888-349-5387.

Ancilla College

Donaldson, Indiana www.ancilla.edu/

- **Independent Roman Catholic** 2-year, founded 1937
- **Rural** 63-acre campus with easy access to Chicago
- **Endowment** $1.9 million
- **Coed**

Undergraduates 397 full-time, 227 part-time. Students come from 10 states and territories, 1% are from out of state, 6% African American, 0.2% Asian American or Pacific Islander, 3% Hispanic American, 1% Native American, 0.2% international, 9% transferred in. *Retention:* 55% of 2003 full-time freshmen returned.

Faculty *Student/faculty ratio:* 15:1.

Academics *Calendar:* semesters. *Degree:* certificates and associate. *Special study options:* academic remediation for entering students, accelerated degree program, adult/continuing education programs, advanced placement credit, cooperative education, double majors, independent study, internships, part-time degree program, services for LD students, student-designed majors, summer session for credit.

Student Life *Campus security:* 24-hour patrols, late-night transport/escort service.

Athletics Member NJCAA.

Standardized Tests *Required:* SAT and SAT Subject Tests or ACT (for admission). *Recommended:* SAT (for admission), SAT or ACT (for admission).

Costs (2006–07) *Tuition:* $10,800 full-time, $360 per credit hour part-time. Full-time tuition and fees vary according to course load and program. Part-time tuition and fees vary according to course load and program. *Required fees:* $230 full-time, $55 per term part-time.

Financial Aid Of all full-time matriculated undergraduates, 28 Federal Work-Study jobs (averaging $1820). 16 state and other part-time jobs (averaging $1000). *Financial aid deadline:* 3/1.

Applying *Options:* electronic application. *Application fee:* $25. *Required:* high school transcript. *Recommended:* interview.

Freshmen Application Contact Erin Wittmeyer, Director of Admissions, Ancilla College, 9601 Union Road, Donaldson, IN 46513. *Phone:* 574-936-8898 Ext. 350. *Toll-free phone:* 866-262-4552 Ext. 350. *Fax:* 574-935-1773. *E-mail:* admissions@ancilla.edu.

Aviation Institute of Maintenance—Indianapolis

Indianapolis, Indiana www.aviationmaintenance.edu/aviation-indianapolis.asp

- **Proprietary** 2-year

Academics *Calendar:* quarters.

Applying *Application fee:* $25. *Required:* High school diploma or GED.

Director of Admissions Mr. Andrew Duncan, School Director, Aviation Institute of Maintenance–Indianapolis, 7251 W. McCarty Street, Indianapolis, IN 46241. *Phone:* 317-243-4519. *Toll-free phone:* 888-349-5387. *E-mail:* directorami@aviationmaintenance.edu.

Brown Mackie College—Fort Wayne

Fort Wayne, Indiana www.brownmackie.edu/locations.asp?locid=1

- **Proprietary** 2-year
- **Coed,** 872 undergraduate students

Faculty *Total:* 53, 34% full-time. *Student/faculty ratio:* 16:1.

Majors Accounting technology and bookkeeping; business administration and management; CAD/CADD drafting/design technology; computer software technology; criminal justice/law enforcement administration; electrical, electronic and communications engineering technology; legal assistant/paralegal; medical/clinical assistant; occupational therapist assistant.

Academics *Calendar:* quarters. *Degree:* certificates, diplomas, and associate.

Student Life *Student services:* personal/psychological counseling.

Costs (2006–07) *Tuition:* $9072 full-time, $179 per credit hour part-time. Full-time tuition and fees vary according to location and program. (Contact school directly for practical nursing and occupational therapy). *Required fees:* $480 full-time, $10 per credit hour part-time. *Payment plans:* installment, deferred payment. *Waivers:* employees or children of employees.

Applying *Required:* high school transcript, interview, Verify High School Grad or Equivalent. *Application deadlines:* rolling (freshmen), rolling (transfers). *Notification:* continuous (freshmen), continuous (transfers).

Freshmen Application Contact Director of Admissions, Brown Mackie College–Fort Wayne, 4422 East State Boulevard, Fort Wayne, IN 46815. *Phone:* 260-484-4400. *Fax:* 260-484-2678. *E-mail:* ktaboh@brownmackie.edu.

▶**See page 504 for the College Close-Up.**

Brown Mackie College—Merrillville

Merrillville, Indiana www.brownmackie.edu/locations.asp?locid=19

- **Proprietary** 2-year, founded 1890, part of American Education Centers, Inc
- **Small-town** 2-acre campus with easy access to Chicago
- **Coed,** 615 undergraduate students

Brown Mackie College–Merrillville (continued)

Undergraduates 4% are from out of state, 42% African American, 0.2% Asian American or Pacific Islander, 8% Hispanic American, 0.2% Native American.

Faculty *Total:* 40, 28% full-time. *Student/faculty ratio:* 17:1.

Majors Accounting technology and bookkeeping; business administration and management; computer software technology; criminal justice/safety; gerontology; health services administration; legal assistant/paralegal; medical office management; surgical technology.

Academics *Calendar:* quarters. *Degree:* certificates and associate. *Special study options:* internships, student-designed majors, summer session for credit.

Student Life *Housing:* college housing not available. *Campus security:* 24-hour emergency response devices.

Costs (2006–07) *Tuition:* $8592 full-time, $179 per credit hour part-time.

Financial Aid Of all full-time matriculated undergraduates, 2 Federal Work-Study jobs.

Applying *Options:* early admission, deferred entrance. *Required:* high school transcript, interview. *Application deadlines:* rolling (freshmen), rolling (transfers). *Notification:* continuous (freshmen), continuous (transfers).

Freshmen Application Contact Director of Admissions, Brown Mackie College–Merrillville, 1000 East 80th Place, Suite 101, N, Merrillville, IN 46410. *Phone:* 800-258-3321. *Fax:* 219-738-1076. *E-mail:* bmcmeadm@brownmackie.edu.

▶See page 512 for the College Close-Up.

BROWN MACKIE COLLEGE–MICHIGAN CITY

Michigan City, Indiana   www.brownmackie.edu/locations.asp?locid=20

- **Proprietary** 2-year, founded 1890, part of Commonwealth Business College, Inc
- **Rural** 2-acre campus with easy access to Chicago
- **Coed**

Undergraduates 461 full-time. Students come from 2 states and territories, 2% are from out of state, 18% African American, 0.4% Asian American or Pacific Islander, 3% Hispanic American.

Faculty *Student/faculty ratio:* 13:1.

Academics *Calendar:* quarters. *Degree:* diplomas and associate. *Special study options:* adult/continuing education programs, advanced placement credit, internships, part-time degree program, student-designed majors, summer session for credit.

Student Life *Campus security:* 24-hour emergency response devices.

Applying *Options:* early admission, deferred entrance. *Required:* high school transcript.

Director of Admissions Ms. Sheryl Elston, Director of Admissions, Brown Mackie College–Michigan City, 325 East US Highway 20, Michigan City, IN 46360. *Phone:* 219-877-3100. *Toll-free phone:* 800-519-2416. *Fax:* 219-877-3110. *E-mail:* selston@brownmackie.edu.

▶See page 516 for the College Close-Up.

BROWN MACKIE COLLEGE–SOUTH BEND

South Bend, Indiana   www.brownmackie.edu/locations.asp?locid=2

- **Proprietary** 2-year, founded 1882, part of American Education Centers, Inc
- **Urban** 5-acre campus with easy access to Chicago
- **Coed, primarily women,** 661 undergraduate students

Undergraduates Students come from 2 states and territories, 10% are from out of state, 29% African American, 0.8% Asian American or Pacific Islander, 4% Hispanic American.

Freshmen *Average high school GPA:* 2.0.

Faculty *Total:* 42, 45% full-time. *Student/faculty ratio:* 12:1.

Majors Accounting technology and bookkeeping; business administration and management; CAD/CADD drafting/design technology; computer programming; computer software technology; computer systems networking and telecommunications; criminal justice/law enforcement administration; electrical, electronic and communications engineering technology; health/health care administration; legal assistant/paralegal; medical/clinical assistant; occupational therapist assistant; physical therapist assistant.

Academics *Calendar:* quarters. *Degree:* certificates and associate. *Special study options:* academic remediation for entering students, accelerated degree program, adult/continuing education programs, double majors, summer session for credit.

Library Michiana College Library with 1,409 titles, 65 serial subscriptions, 65 audiovisual materials.

Student Life *Activities and Organizations:* Business Club, Medical Assisting Club, Legal Club, Physical Therapy Assistant Club, Occupational Therapy Assistant Club. *Campus security:* 24-hour emergency response devices. *Student services:* personal/psychological counseling.

Costs (2006–07) *Tuition:* $9072 full-time, $189 per credit hour part-time. Full-time tuition and fees vary according to program. *Required fees:* $480 full-time, $10 per credit hour part-time. *Payment plan:* installment. *Waivers:* employees or children of employees.

Applying *Options:* deferred entrance. *Required:* essay or personal statement, high school transcript, interview. *Required for some:* minimum 2.0 GPA, 2 letters of recommendation. *Application deadlines:* rolling (freshmen), rolling (transfers). *Notification:* continuous (freshmen), continuous (transfers).

Freshmen Application Contact Director of Admissions, Brown Mackie College–South Bend, 1030 East Jefferson Boulevard, South Bend, IN 46617-3123. *Phone:* 574-237-0774. *Toll-free phone:* 800-743-2447. *Fax:* 574-237-3585. *E-mail:* phooks@brownmackie.edu.

▶See page 526 for the College Close-Up.

COLLEGE OF COURT REPORTING

Hobart, Indiana   www.ccredu.com/

- **Proprietary** 2-year
- **Coed, primarily women,** 156 undergraduate students, 57% full-time, 99% women, 1% men
- 88% of applicants were admitted

Undergraduates 89 full-time, 67 part-time. Students come from 3 states and territories, 5% are from out of state, 2% transferred in.

Freshmen *Admission:* 33 applied, 29 admitted.

Faculty *Total:* 16, 50% full-time. *Student/faculty ratio:* 8:1.

Majors Court reporting.

Academics *Degree:* certificates, diplomas, and associate.

Costs (2006–07) *Tuition:* $8640 full-time, $240 per credit hour part-time. No tuition increase for student's term of enrollment. *Required fees:* $75 full-time. *Payment plan:* installment.

Freshmen Application Contact Ms. Nicky Rodriquez, Director of Admissions, College of Court Reporting, 111 West Tenth Street, Suite 111, Hobart, IN 46342. *Phone:* 219-942-1459 Ext. 226. *Toll-free phone:* 866-294-3974. *Fax:* 219-942-1631. *E-mail:* nrodriquez@ccredu.com.

DAVENPORT UNIVERSITY

Granger, Indiana   www.davenport.edu/

Freshmen Application Contact Admissions Office, Davenport University, 415 East Fulton Street, Grand Rapids, MI 49503. *Phone:* 616-698-7111. *Toll-free phone:* 800-632-9569. *Fax:* 616-698-0333. *E-mail:* gradmiss@davenport.edu.

DAVENPORT UNIVERSITY

Hammond, Indiana   www.davenport.edu/

Director of Admissions Admissions, Davenport University, 415 East Fulton Street, Grand Rapids, MI 49503. *Toll-free phone:* 800-632-9569.

DAVENPORT UNIVERSITY

Merrillville, Indiana   www.davenport.edu/

Freshmen Application Contact Admissions, Davenport University, 415 East Fulton Street, Grand Rapids, MI 49503. *Phone:* 616-698-7111. *Toll-free phone:* 800-632-9569. *Fax:* 616-698-0333. *E-mail:* gradmisss@davenport.edu.

HOLY CROSS COLLEGE

Notre Dame, Indiana   **www.hcc-nd.edu/**

- **Independent Roman Catholic** primarily 2-year, founded 1966
- **Urban** 150-acre campus
- **Coed,** 430 undergraduate students, 90% full-time, 36% women, 64% men

Undergraduates 386 full-time, 44 part-time. Students come from 31 states and territories, 7 other countries, 64% are from out of state, 3% African American, 3% Asian American or Pacific Islander, 8% Hispanic American, 0.2% Native American, 2% international, 8% transferred in, 54% live on campus. *Retention:* 55% of 2003 full-time freshmen returned.

Freshmen *Admission:* 500 applied, 486 admitted, 202 enrolled. *Average high school GPA:* 3.2.

Faculty *Total:* 38, 68% full-time, 32% with terminal degrees. *Student/faculty ratio:* 12:1.

Majors Liberal arts and sciences/liberal studies.

Academics *Calendar:* semesters. *Degrees:* associate and bachelor's. *Special study options:* academic remediation for entering students, accelerated degree program, advanced placement credit, double majors, English as a second language, freshman honors college, honors programs, independent study, internships, off-campus study, student-designed majors, study abroad, summer session for credit. *ROTC:* Army (c), Air Force (c).

Library Holy Cross Library with 15,000 titles, 160 serial subscriptions, an OPAC.

Student Life *Housing Options:* coed, men-only, women-only, cooperative. Campus housing is university owned. *Activities and Organizations:* drama/theater group, student-run newspaper, choral group, marching band, Student Advisory Committee, Campus Ministry, Volunteers in Support of Admissions, intramural athletics. *Campus security:* 24-hour emergency response devices and patrols, 24-hour patrols by trained personnel on certain days. *Student services:* personal/psychological counseling.

Athletics *Intercollegiate sports:* basketball M, crew M/W, cross-country running M/W, lacrosse M, soccer M/W. *Intramural sports:* basketball M/W, football M/W, golf M/W, lacrosse M, rugby M, skiing (downhill) M, soccer M, softball M/W, table tennis M/W, tennis M/W, ultimate Frisbee M/W, volleyball M/W.

Standardized Tests *Required:* SAT or ACT (for admission).

Costs (2007–08) *Comprehensive fee:* $24,660 includes full-time tuition ($15,660), mandatory fees ($1000), and room and board ($8000). Part-time tuition: $520 per credit hour. *Required fees:* $565 per year part-time.

Financial Aid Of all full-time matriculated undergraduates, 54 Federal Work-Study jobs (averaging $857).

Applying *Options:* electronic application, deferred entrance. *Application fee:* $50. *Required:* essay or personal statement, high school transcript, minimum 2.5 GPA, College Success Program (2.0). *Required for some:* letters of recommendation. *Recommended:* interview. *Application deadlines:* rolling (freshmen), rolling (transfers).

Freshmen Application Contact Office of Admissions, Holy Cross College, PO Box 308, Notre Dame, IN 46556. *Phone:* 574-239-8400. *Fax:* 574-239-8323. *E-mail:* vduke@hcc-nd.edu.

INDIANA BUSINESS COLLEGE

Anderson, Indiana   **www.ibcschools.edu/**

- **Proprietary** 2-year, founded 1902
- **Small-town** campus
- **Coed,** 214 undergraduate students

Faculty *Student/faculty ratio:* 16:1.

Majors Accounting; administrative assistant and secretarial science; business administration and management; business administration, management and operations related; criminal justice/safety; health information/medical records technology; human resources management; medical/clinical assistant; medical insurance/medical billing.

Academics *Calendar:* quarters. *Degree:* certificates, diplomas, and associate. *Special study options:* adult/continuing education programs, cooperative education, distance learning, double majors, independent study, internships, part-time degree program.

Standardized Tests *Required:* Wonderlic Scholastic Level Exam (SLE) (for admission).

Costs (2006–07) *Tuition:* Contact campus as full and part-time tuition depends on program.

Applying *Options:* electronic application, early admission. *Application fee:* $50. *Required:* high school transcript, interview. *Application deadlines:* rolling

(freshmen), rolling (out-of-state freshmen), rolling (transfers). *Notification:* continuous (freshmen), continuous (out-of-state freshmen), continuous (transfers).

Freshmen Application Contact Ms. Charlene Stacy, Executive Director, Indiana Business College, 140 East 53rd Street, Anderson, IN 46013. *Phone:* 765-644-7514. *Toll-free phone:* 800-IBC-GRAD. *Fax:* 765-664-5724. *E-mail:* charlene.stacy@ibcschools.edu.

INDIANA BUSINESS COLLEGE

Columbus, Indiana   **www.ibcschools.edu/**

- **Proprietary** 2-year
- **Rural** campus
- **Coed,** 295 undergraduate students

Faculty *Student/faculty ratio:* 16:1.

Majors Accounting; administrative assistant and secretarial science; business administration and management; business administration, management and operations related; criminal justice/safety; human resources management; medical/clinical assistant; medical insurance/medical billing.

Academics *Calendar:* quarters. *Degree:* certificates, diplomas, and associate. *Special study options:* adult/continuing education programs, cooperative education, distance learning, double majors, independent study, internships, part-time degree program.

Student Life *Housing:* college housing not available.

Standardized Tests *Required:* Wonderlic Scholastic Level Exam (SLE) (for admission).

Costs (2006–07) *Tuition:* Contact campus as full and part-time tuition depends on program.

Applying *Options:* electronic application. *Application fee:* $50. *Required:* high school transcript, interview. *Application deadlines:* rolling (freshmen), rolling (out-of-state freshmen), rolling (transfers). *Notification:* continuous (freshmen), continuous (out-of-state freshmen), continuous (transfers).

Freshmen Application Contact Ms. Gina Pate, Director of Admissions, Indiana Business College, 2222 Poshard Drive, Columbus, IN 47203. *Phone:* 812-379-9000. *Toll-free phone:* 800-IBC-GRAD. *Fax:* 812-375-0414. *E-mail:* gina.pate@ibcschools.edu.

INDIANA BUSINESS COLLEGE

Evansville, Indiana   **www.ibcschools.edu/**

- **Proprietary** 2-year
- **Urban** campus
- **Coed,** 325 undergraduate students

Faculty *Student/faculty ratio:* 16:1.

Majors Accounting; administrative assistant and secretarial science; business administration and management; criminal justice/safety; human resources management; information technology; medical/clinical assistant; medical insurance coding; medical insurance/medical billing.

Academics *Calendar:* quarters. *Degree:* certificates, diplomas, and associate. *Special study options:* adult/continuing education programs, cooperative education, distance learning, double majors, independent study, internships, part-time degree program.

Standardized Tests *Required:* Wonderlic Scholastic Level Exam (SLE) (for admission).

Costs (2006–07) *Tuition:* Contact campus as full and part-time tuition depends on program.

Applying *Options:* electronic application. *Application fee:* $50. *Required:* high school transcript, interview. *Application deadlines:* rolling (freshmen), rolling (out-of-state freshmen), rolling (transfers). *Notification:* continuous (freshmen), continuous (out-of-state freshmen), continuous (transfers).

Freshmen Application Contact Ms. Starlet Gupton, Indiana Business College, 4601 Theater Drive, Evansville, IN 47715. *Phone:* 812-476-6000. *Toll-free phone:* 800-IBC-GRAD. *Fax:* 812-471-8576.

INDIANA BUSINESS COLLEGE

Fort Wayne, Indiana   **www.ibcschools.edu/**

- **Proprietary** 2-year
- **Urban** campus
- **Coed,** 480 undergraduate students

Faculty *Student/faculty ratio:* 16:1.

Indiana Business College (continued)

Majors Accounting; administrative assistant and secretarial science; business administration and management; criminal justice/safety; human resources management; medical/clinical assistant; medical insurance/medical billing; surgical technology.

Academics *Calendar:* quarters. *Degree:* certificates, diplomas, and associate. *Special study options:* adult/continuing education programs, cooperative education, distance learning, double majors, independent study, internships, part-time degree program.

Student Life *Housing:* college housing not available.

Standardized Tests *Required:* Wonderlic Scholastic Level Exam (SLE) (for admission).

Costs (2006–07) *Tuition:* Contact campus as full and part-time tuition depends on program.

Applying *Options:* electronic application. *Application fee:* $50. *Required:* high school transcript, interview. *Application deadlines:* rolling (freshmen), rolling (out-of-state freshmen), rolling (transfers). *Notification:* continuous (freshmen), continuous (out-of-state freshmen), continuous (transfers).

Freshmen Application Contact Ms. Kim Yates, Associate Director of Admissions, Indiana Business College, 6413 North Clinton Street, Fort Wayne, IN 46825. *Phone:* 260-471-7667. *Toll-free phone:* 260-471-6918. *Fax:* 260-471-6918. *E-mail:* kim.yates@ibcschools.edu.

INDIANA BUSINESS COLLEGE

Indianapolis, Indiana www.ibcschools.edu/

- **Proprietary** 2-year, founded 1902
- **Urban** 1-acre campus
- **Coed,** 1,227 undergraduate students

Faculty *Student/faculty ratio:* 16:1.

Majors Accounting; administrative assistant and secretarial science; business administration and management; business administration, management and operations related; computer and information sciences; computer and information sciences and support services related; computer programming; computer programming (specific applications); criminal justice/safety; fashion merchandising; human resources management; information technology; legal administrative assistant/secretary; management information systems and services related; medical/clinical assistant.

Academics *Calendar:* quarters. *Degree:* certificates, diplomas, and associate. *Special study options:* adult/continuing education programs, cooperative education, distance learning, double majors, internships, part-time degree program, summer session for credit.

Student Life *Housing:* college housing not available. *Activities and Organizations:* Student Advisory Board, Student Ambassadors, Phi Beta Lambda. *Campus security:* 24-hour patrols.

Standardized Tests *Required:* Wonderlic Scholastic Level Exam (SLE) (for admission).

Costs (2006–07) *Tuition:* Contact campus as full and part-time tuition depends on program.

Applying *Options:* electronic application. *Application fee:* $50. *Required:* high school transcript, interview. *Application deadlines:* rolling (freshmen), rolling (transfers). *Notification:* continuous (freshmen), continuous (transfers).

Freshmen Application Contact Ms. Laura Hale, Regional Director, Indiana Business College, 550 East Washington Street, Indianapolis, IN 46204. *Phone:* 317-264-5656. *Toll-free phone:* 800-IBC-GRAD. *Fax:* 317-264-5650. *E-mail:* laura.hale@ibcschools.edu.

▶See page 548 for the College Close-Up.

INDIANA BUSINESS COLLEGE

Indianapolis, Indiana www.ibcschools.edu/campuses/northwest.asp

- **Proprietary** 2-year
- **Urban** campus
- **Coed,** 191 undergraduate students

Faculty *Student/faculty ratio:* 16:1.

Majors Accounting; administrative assistant and secretarial science; business administration and management; criminal justice/safety; human resources management; massage therapy; medical/clinical assistant; medical insurance coding; medical insurance/medical billing; medical laboratory technology; surgical technology.

Academics *Calendar:* quarters. *Degree:* certificates, diplomas, and associate. *Special study options:* adult/continuing education programs.

Student Life *Housing:* college housing not available.

Standardized Tests *Required:* Wonderlic Scholastic Level Exam (for admission).

Costs (2006–07) *Tuition:* Contact campus as full and part-time tuition depends on program.

Applying *Application fee:* $50. *Required:* high school transcript, interview. *Application deadlines:* rolling (freshmen), rolling (out-of-state freshmen), rolling (transfers). *Notification:* continuous (freshmen), continuous (out-of-state freshmen), continuous (transfers).

Freshmen Application Contact Mr. Rod Allee, Executive Director, Indiana Business College, 6300 Technology Center Drive, Indianapolis, IN 46278. *Phone:* 317-873-6500. *Fax:* 317-733-6266. *E-mail:* rod.allee@ibcschools.edu.

INDIANA BUSINESS COLLEGE

Lafayette, Indiana www.ibcschools.edu/

- **Proprietary** 2-year
- **Small-town** campus
- **Coed,** 319 undergraduate students

Faculty *Student/faculty ratio:* 20:1.

Majors Accounting; administrative assistant and secretarial science; business administration and management; business administration, management and operations related; computer and information sciences and support services related; criminal justice/safety; human resources management; information technology; medical/clinical assistant; medical insurance coding; medical insurance/medical billing.

Academics *Calendar:* quarters. *Degree:* certificates, diplomas, and associate. *Special study options:* adult/continuing education programs, cooperative education, distance learning, double majors, independent study, internships, part-time degree program.

Student Life *Housing:* college housing not available.

Standardized Tests *Required:* Wonderlic Scholastic Level Exam (SLE) (for admission).

Costs (2006–07) *Tuition:* Contact campus as full and part-time tuition depends on program.

Applying *Options:* electronic application. *Application fee:* $50. *Required:* high school transcript, interview. *Application deadlines:* rolling (freshmen), rolling (out-of-state freshmen), rolling (transfers). *Notification:* continuous (freshmen), continuous (out-of-state freshmen), continuous (transfers).

Freshmen Application Contact Ms. Stacy Golleher, Associate Director of Admissions, Indiana Business College, 2 Executive Drive, Lafayette, IN 47905. *Phone:* 765-447-9550. *Toll-free phone:* 800-IBC-GRAD. *Fax:* 765-447-0868. *E-mail:* stacy.golleher@ibcschools.edu.

INDIANA BUSINESS COLLEGE

Marion, Indiana www.ibcschools.edu/

- **Proprietary** 2-year
- **Coed,** 131 undergraduate students

Faculty *Student/faculty ratio:* 20:1.

Majors Accounting; administrative assistant and secretarial science; business administration and management; criminal justice/safety; human resources management; medical/clinical assistant; medical insurance coding.

Academics *Calendar:* quarters. *Degree:* certificates, diplomas, and associate. *Special study options:* adult/continuing education programs, cooperative education, distance learning, double majors, internships, part-time degree program.

Standardized Tests *Required:* Wonderlic Scholastic Level Exam (SLE) (for admission).

Costs (2006–07) *Tuition:* Contact campus as full and part-time tuition depends on program.

Applying *Options:* electronic application. *Application fee:* $50. *Required:* high school transcript, interview. *Application deadlines:* rolling (freshmen), rolling (transfers). *Notification:* continuous (freshmen), continuous (transfers).

Freshmen Application Contact Mr. Richard Herman, Executive Director, Indiana Business College, 830 North Miller Avenue, Marion, IN 46952. *Phone:* 765-662-7497. *Toll-free phone:* 800-IBC-GRAD. *Fax:* 765-651-9421. *E-mail:* richard.herman@ibcschools.edu.

INDIANA BUSINESS COLLEGE

Muncie, Indiana   www.ibcschools.edu/

- **Proprietary** 2-year
- **Small-town** campus
- **Coed,** 379 undergraduate students

Faculty *Student/faculty ratio:* 16:1.

Majors Accounting; administrative assistant and secretarial science; business administration and management; business administration, management and operations related; computer and information sciences and support services related; computer programming (specific applications); criminal justice/safety; health information/medical records technology; human resources management; information technology; management information systems and services related; medical office assistant.

Academics *Calendar:* quarters. *Degree:* certificates, diplomas, and associate. *Special study options:* adult/continuing education programs, cooperative education, distance learning, double majors, independent study, part-time degree program.

Student Life *Housing:* college housing not available. *Activities and Organizations:* Phi Beta Lambda.

Standardized Tests *Required:* Wonderlic Scholastic Level Exam (SLE) (for admission).

Costs (2006–07) *Tuition:* Contact campus as full and part-time tuition depends on program.

Applying *Options:* electronic application. *Application fee:* $50. *Required:* high school transcript, interview. *Application deadlines:* rolling (freshmen), rolling (out-of-state freshmen), rolling (transfers). *Notification:* continuous (freshmen), continuous (out-of-state freshmen), continuous (transfers).

Freshmen Application Contact Mr. Gregory Bond, Indiana Business College, 411 West Riggin Road, Muncie, IN 47303. *Phone:* 765-288-8681. *Toll-free phone:* 800-IBC-GRAD. *Fax:* 765-288-8797.

INDIANA BUSINESS COLLEGE

Terre Haute, Indiana   www.ibcschools.edu/

- **Proprietary** 2-year, founded 1902
- **Small-town** campus
- **Coed,** 246 undergraduate students

Faculty *Student/faculty ratio:* 16:1.

Majors Accounting; administrative assistant and secretarial science; business administration and management; business administration, management and operations related; criminal justice/safety; human resources management; medical/clinical assistant; medical insurance/medical billing.

Academics *Calendar:* quarters. *Degree:* certificates, diplomas, and associate. *Special study options:* adult/continuing education programs, cooperative education, distance learning, double majors, independent study, internships, part-time degree program.

Standardized Tests *Required:* Wonderlic Scholastic Level Exam (SLE) (for admission).

Costs (2006–07) *Tuition:* Contact campus as full and part-time tuition depends on program.

Applying *Options:* electronic application. *Application fee:* $50. *Required:* high school transcript, interview, Wonderlic Scholastic Level Exam. *Application deadlines:* rolling (freshmen), rolling (out-of-state freshmen), rolling (transfers). *Notification:* continuous (freshmen), continuous (out-of-state freshmen), continuous (transfers).

Freshmen Application Contact Ms. Catherine Davee, Associate Director of Admissions, Indiana Business College, 3175 South Third Place, Terre Haute, IN 47802. *Phone:* 812-877-2100. *Toll-free phone:* 800-IBC-GRAD. *Fax:* 812-877-4440. *E-mail:* Catherine.Davee@ibcschools.edu.

INDIANA BUSINESS COLLEGE-MEDICAL

Indianapolis, Indiana   www.ibcschools.edu/

- **Proprietary** 2-year
- **Urban** campus
- **Coed,** 592 undergraduate students

Faculty *Student/faculty ratio:* 16:1.

Majors Clinical/medical laboratory technology; massage therapy; medical/clinical assistant; medical insurance coding; medical insurance/medical billing; surgical technology.

Academics *Calendar:* quarters. *Degree:* certificates, diplomas, and associate. *Special study options:* adult/continuing education programs, cooperative education, distance learning, double majors, independent study, internships, part-time degree program.

Student Life *Housing:* college housing not available.

Standardized Tests *Required:* Wonderlic Scholastic Level Exam (SLE) (for admission).

Costs (2006–07) *Tuition:* Contact campus as full and part-time tuition depends on program.

Applying *Options:* electronic application. *Application fee:* $50. *Required:* high school transcript, interview. *Application deadlines:* rolling (freshmen), rolling (out-of-state freshmen), rolling (transfers). *Notification:* continuous (freshmen), continuous (out-of-state freshmen), continuous (transfers).

Freshmen Application Contact Mr. Gary McGee, Senior Regional Director, Indiana Business College-Medical, 8150 Brookville Road, Indianapolis, IN 46239. *Phone:* 317-375-8000. *Toll-free phone:* 800-IBC-6611. *Fax:* 317-351-1871. *E-mail:* gary.mcgee@ibcschools.edu.

INTERNATIONAL BUSINESS COLLEGE

Fort Wayne, Indiana   www.ibcfortwayne.edu/

- **Proprietary** primarily 2-year, founded 1889, part of Bradford Schools, Inc
- **Suburban** 2-acre campus
- **Coed, primarily women,** 758 undergraduate students, 92% full-time, 78% women, 22% men

Undergraduates 700 full-time, 58 part-time. 14% are from out of state, 20% live on campus.

Freshmen *Admission:* 980 applied, 924 admitted, 443 enrolled.

Faculty *Total:* 68, 18% full-time. *Student/faculty ratio:* 22:1.

Majors Accounting; administrative assistant and secretarial science; business administration and management; commercial and advertising art; computer engineering technology; computer programming; consumer merchandising/retailing management; engineering/industrial management; finance; hospitality administration; legal administrative assistant/secretary; legal assistant/paralegal; medical/clinical assistant; tourism and travel services management.

Academics *Calendar:* semesters. *Degrees:* diplomas, associate, and bachelor's. *Special study options:* adult/continuing education programs, independent study, internships, part-time degree program.

Library 2,100 titles, 100 serial subscriptions.

Student Life *Housing Options:* Campus housing is leased by the school. Freshman applicants given priority for college housing. *Activities and Organizations:* Student Senate, Collegiate Secretarial Institute, Accounting Club. *Campus security:* controlled dormitory access.

Costs (2007–08) *Tuition:* $12,240 full-time.

Applying *Options:* deferred entrance. *Application fee:* $50. *Required:* high school transcript. *Application deadline:* 9/4 (freshmen).

Director of Admissions Mr. Steve Kinzer, School Director, International Business College, 5699 Coventry Lane, Fort Wayne, IN 46804. *Phone:* 219-459-4513. *Toll-free phone:* 800-589-6363.

INTERNATIONAL BUSINESS COLLEGE

Indianapolis, Indiana   www.intlbusinesscollege.com/

- **Proprietary** 2-year, administratively affiliated with Bradford Schools, Charlotte, NC
- **Coed**

Undergraduates 289 full-time. 14% African American, 0.7% Asian American or Pacific Islander, 3% Hispanic American.

Faculty *Student/faculty ratio:* 20:1.

Academics *Calendar:* semesters. *Degree:* diplomas and associate. *Special study options:* academic remediation for entering students, internships.

Costs (2006–07) *Tuition:* $11,960 full-time. Full-time tuition and fees vary according to class time and program. No tuition increase for student's term of enrollment. *Room only:* $6100.

Applying *Options:* electronic application. *Application fee:* $50. *Required:* high school transcript. *Required for some:* paralegal test.

Freshmen Application Contact Ms. Kathy Chiudioni, Director of Admissions, International Business College, 7205 Shadeland Station, Indianapolis, IN 46256. *Phone:* 317-213-2320. *Fax:* 317-841-6419. *E-mail:* info@intlbusinesscollege.com.

ITT TECHNICAL INSTITUTE

Fort Wayne, Indiana   www.itt-tech.edu/

- **Proprietary** primarily 2-year, founded 1967, part of ITT Educational Services, Inc
- **Coed**

Majors Accounting technology and bookkeeping; animation, interactive technology, video graphics and special effects; business administration and management; CAD/CADD drafting/design technology; communications technology; computer and information systems security; computer engineering technology; computer software technology; computer systems networking and telecommunications; criminal justice/law enforcement administration; electrical, electronic and communications engineering technology; health information/medical records technology; industrial technology; web page, digital/multimedia and information resources design.

Academics *Calendar:* quarters. *Degrees:* associate and bachelor's.

Library a Web page.

Student Life *Housing:* college housing not available.

Standardized Tests *Required:* Wonderlic aptitude test (for admission).

Costs (2006–07) *Tuition:* Contact school for program costs.

Applying *Options:* deferred entrance. *Application fee:* $100. *Required:* high school transcript, interview. *Recommended:* letters of recommendation. *Application deadlines:* rolling (freshmen), rolling (transfers). *Notification:* continuous (freshmen), continuous (transfers).

Freshmen Application Contact Mr. Mike Cavins, Director of Recruitment, ITT Technical Institute, 2810 Dupont Commerce Court, Fort Wayne, IN 46825. *Phone:* 260-497-6200. *Toll-free phone:* 800-866-4488. *Fax:* 260-497-6299.

ITT TECHNICAL INSTITUTE

Indianapolis, Indiana   www.itt-tech.edu/

- **Proprietary** founded 1966, part of ITT Educational Services, Inc
- **Suburban** 10-acre campus
- **Coed**

Majors Accounting technology and bookkeeping; business administration and management; CAD/CADD drafting/design technology; computer and information systems security; computer engineering technology; computer software engineering; computer software technology; computer systems networking and telecommunications; construction management; criminal justice/law enforcement administration; electrical, electronic and communications engineering technology; health information/medical records technology; industrial technology; information technology; web/multimedia management and webmaster; web page, digital/multimedia and information resources design.

Academics *Calendar:* quarters. *Degrees:* diplomas, associate, and bachelor's. *Special study options:* distance learning.

Library a Web page.

Student Life *Housing:* college housing not available. *Activities and Organizations:* student-run newspaper.

Standardized Tests *Required:* Wonderlic aptitude test (for admission).

Costs (2006–07) *Tuition:* Contact school for program costs.

Applying *Options:* deferred entrance. *Application fee:* $100. *Required:* high school transcript, interview. *Recommended:* letters of recommendation. *Application deadlines:* rolling (freshmen), rolling (transfers). *Notification:* continuous (freshmen), continuous (transfers).

Freshmen Application Contact Mr. James Mills, Director of Recruitment, ITT Technical Institute, 9511 Angola Court, Indianapolis, IN 46268. *Phone:* 317-875-8640. *Toll-free phone:* 800-937-4488.

ITT TECHNICAL INSTITUTE

Newburgh, Indiana   www.itt-tech.edu/

- **Proprietary** primarily 2-year, founded 1966, part of ITT Educational Services, Inc
- **Coed**

Majors Animation, interactive technology, video graphics and special effects; business administration and management; CAD/CADD drafting/design technology; computer and information systems security; computer engineering technology; computer software technology; computer systems networking and telecommunications; criminal justice/law enforcement administration; electrical, electronic and communications engineering technology; health information/medical records technology; industrial technology;

web/multimedia management and webmaster; Web page, digital/multimedia and information resources design; web page, digital/multimedia and information resources design.

Academics *Calendar:* quarters. *Degrees:* associate and bachelor's.

Library a Web page.

Student Life *Housing:* college housing not available.

Standardized Tests *Required:* Wonderlic aptitude test (for admission).

Costs (2006–07) *Tuition:* Contact school for program costs.

Applying *Options:* deferred entrance. *Application fee:* $100. *Required:* high school transcript, interview. *Recommended:* letters of recommendation. *Application deadlines:* rolling (freshmen), rolling (transfers). *Notification:* continuous (freshmen), continuous (transfers).

Freshmen Application Contact Mr. Thomas Montgomery, Director of Recruitment, ITT Technical Institute, 10999 Stahl Road, Newburgh, IN 47630. *Phone:* 812-858-1600. *Toll-free phone:* 800-832-4488.

IVY TECH COMMUNITY COLLEGE– BLOOMINGTON

Bloomington, Indiana   www.ivytech.edu/

- **State-supported** 2-year, founded 2001, part of Ivy Tech State College System
- **Endowment** $15.9 million
- **Coed**

Undergraduates 1,639 full-time, 1,926 part-time. 3% African American, 0.7% Asian American or Pacific Islander, 1% Hispanic American, 0.3% Native American, 0.1% international, 4% transferred in.

Academics *Calendar:* semesters. *Degree:* certificates and associate. *Special study options:* academic remediation for entering students, adult/continuing education programs, advanced placement credit, distance learning, external degree program, internships, part-time degree program, services for LD students, summer session for credit.

Student Life *Campus security:* late-night transport/escort service.

Costs (2006–07) *Tuition:* state resident $2633 full-time, $88 per credit part-time; nonresident $5355 full-time, $179 per credit part-time. *Required fees:* $80 full-time. *Payment plans:* installment, deferred payment.

Financial Aid Of all full-time matriculated undergraduates, 51 Federal Work-Study jobs (averaging $3259).

Applying *Options:* deferred entrance. *Required:* high school transcript. *Required for some:* interview.

Freshmen Application Contact Mr. Neil Frederick, Assistant Director of Admissions, Ivy Tech Community College–Bloomington, 200 Daniels Way, Bloomington, IN 47404-1511. *Phone:* 812-330-6026. *Fax:* 812-332-8147. *E-mail:* nfrederi@ivytech.edu.

IVY TECH COMMUNITY COLLEGE– CENTRAL INDIANA

Indianapolis, Indiana   www.ivytech.edu/

- **State-supported** 2-year, founded 1963
- **Urban** 10-acre campus
- **Endowment** $15,900
- **Coed**

Undergraduates 3,581 full-time, 8,009 part-time. 25% African American, 1% Asian American or Pacific Islander, 2% Hispanic American, 0.5% Native American, 0.2% international, 6% transferred in.

Academics *Calendar:* semesters. *Degree:* certificates and associate. *Special study options:* academic remediation for entering students, adult/continuing education programs, advanced placement credit, cooperative education, distance learning, English as a second language, internships, off-campus study, part-time degree program, services for LD students, summer session for credit.

Student Life *Campus security:* 24-hour emergency response devices and patrols, late-night transport/escort service.

Costs (2006–07) *Tuition:* state resident $2633 full-time, $88 per credit part-time; nonresident $5355 full-time, $179 per credit part-time. *Required fees:* $80 full-time. *Payment plans:* installment, deferred payment.

Financial Aid Of all full-time matriculated undergraduates, 92 Federal Work-Study jobs (averaging $3766).

Applying *Options:* early admission, deferred entrance. *Required:* high school transcript. *Required for some:* interview.

Freshmen Application Contact Ms. Tracy Funk, Director of Admissions, Ivy Tech Community College–Central Indiana, One West 26th Street, Indianapolis,

IN 46208-4777. *Phone:* 317-921-4371. *Toll-free phone:* 888-IVYLINE. *Fax:* 317-917-5919. *E-mail:* tfunk@ivytech.edu.

IVY TECH COMMUNITY COLLEGE–COLUMBUS

Columbus, Indiana www.ivytech.edu/

- **State-supported** 2-year, founded 1963, part of Ivy Tech State College System
- **Small-town** campus with easy access to Indianapolis
- **Endowment** $15.9 million
- **Coed**

Undergraduates 777 full-time, 1,439 part-time. 2% African American, 0.7% Asian American or Pacific Islander, 0.8% Hispanic American, 0.2% Native American, 0.1% international, 8% transferred in.
Academics *Calendar:* semesters. *Degree:* certificates and associate. *Special study options:* academic remediation for entering students, adult/continuing education programs, advanced placement credit, distance learning, internships, part-time degree program, services for LD students, summer session for credit.
Student Life *Campus security:* late-night transport/escort service, trained evening security personnel, escort service.
Costs (2006–07) *Tuition:* state resident $2633 full-time, $88 per credit part-time; nonresident $5355 full-time, $179 per credit part-time. *Required fees:* $80 full-time. *Payment plans:* installment, deferred payment.
Financial Aid Of all full-time matriculated undergraduates, 26 Federal Work-Study jobs (averaging $1694).
Applying *Options:* early admission, deferred entrance. *Required:* high school transcript. *Required for some:* interview.
Freshmen Application Contact Mr. Neil Bagadiong, Assistant Director of Student Affairs, Ivy Tech Community College–Columbus, 4475 Central Avenue, Columbus, IN 47203-1868. *Phone:* 812-374-5129. *Toll-free phone:* 800-922-4838. *Fax:* 812-372-0331. *E-mail:* nbagadio@ivytech.edu.

IVY TECH COMMUNITY COLLEGE–EAST CENTRAL

Muncie, Indiana www.ivytech.edu/

- **State-supported** 2-year, founded 1968, part of Ivy Tech State College System
- **Suburban** 15-acre campus with easy access to Indianapolis
- **Endowment** $15.9 million
- **Coed**

Undergraduates 2,551 full-time, 3,392 part-time. 8% African American, 0.3% Asian American or Pacific Islander, 1% Hispanic American, 0.3% Native American, 4% transferred in.
Academics *Calendar:* semesters. *Degree:* certificates and associate. *Special study options:* academic remediation for entering students, adult/continuing education programs, advanced placement credit, distance learning, internships, part-time degree program, services for LD students.
Costs (2006–07) *Tuition:* state resident $2633 full-time, $88 per credit part-time; nonresident $5355 full-time, $179 per credit part-time. *Required fees:* $80 full-time. *Payment plans:* installment, deferred payment.
Financial Aid Of all full-time matriculated undergraduates, 65 Federal Work-Study jobs (averaging $2666).
Applying *Options:* early admission, deferred entrance. *Required:* high school transcript. *Required for some:* interview.
Freshmen Application Contact Ms. Mary Lewellen, Ivy Tech Community College–East Central, 4301 South Cowan Road, Muncie, IN 47302-9448. *Phone:* 765-289-2291 Ext. 391. *Toll-free phone:* 800-589-8324. *Fax:* 765-289-2292. *E-mail:* mlewelle@ivytech.edu.

IVY TECH COMMUNITY COLLEGE–KOKOMO

Kokomo, Indiana www.ivytech.edu/

- **State-supported** 2-year, founded 1968, part of Ivy Tech State College System
- **Small-town** 20-acre campus with easy access to Indianapolis
- **Endowment** $15.9 million
- **Coed**

Undergraduates 1,031 full-time, 2,217 part-time. 4% African American, 0.4% Asian American or Pacific Islander, 2% Hispanic American, 0.9% Native American, 0.2% transferred in.
Academics *Calendar:* semesters. *Degree:* certificates and associate. *Special study options:* academic remediation for entering students, adult/continuing education programs, advanced placement credit, distance learning, internships, part-time degree program, services for LD students, summer session for credit.
Student Life *Campus security:* 24-hour emergency response devices, late-night transport/escort service.
Costs (2006–07) *Tuition:* state resident $2633 full-time, $88 per credit part-time; nonresident $5355 full-time, $179 per credit part-time. *Required fees:* $80 full-time. *Payment plans:* installment, deferred payment.
Financial Aid Of all full-time matriculated undergraduates, 45 Federal Work-Study jobs (averaging $1829).
Applying *Options:* early admission. *Required:* high school transcript. *Required for some:* interview.
Freshmen Application Contact Ms. Suzanne Dillman, Director of Admissions, Ivy Tech Community College–Kokomo, 1815 East Morgan Street, Kokomo, IN 46903-1373. *Phone:* 765-459-0561 Ext. 318. *Toll-free phone:* 800-459-0561. *Fax:* 765-454-5111. *E-mail:* sdillman@ivytech.edu.

IVY TECH COMMUNITY COLLEGE–LAFAYETTE

Lafayette, Indiana www.ivytech.edu/

- **State-supported** 2-year, founded 1968, part of Ivy Tech State College System
- **Suburban** campus with easy access to Indianapolis
- **Endowment** $15.9 million
- **Coed**

Undergraduates 2,374 full-time, 3,596 part-time. 3% African American, 1% Asian American or Pacific Islander, 4% Hispanic American, 0.3% Native American, 0.1% international, 4% transferred in.
Academics *Calendar:* semesters. *Degree:* certificates and associate. *Special study options:* academic remediation for entering students, advanced placement credit, distance learning, internships, part-time degree program, services for LD students, summer session for credit.
Costs (2006–07) *Tuition:* state resident $2633 full-time, $88 per credit part-time; nonresident $5355 full-time, $179 per credit part-time. *Required fees:* $80 full-time. *Payment plans:* installment, deferred payment.
Financial Aid Of all full-time matriculated undergraduates, 65 Federal Work-Study jobs (averaging $2222). 1 state and other part-time job (averaging $2436).
Applying *Required:* high school transcript. *Required for some:* interview.
Freshmen Application Contact Ms. Judy Doppelfeld, Director of Admissions, Ivy Tech Community College–Lafayette, 3101 South Creagy Lane, PO Box 6299, Lafayette, IN 47903. *Phone:* 765-269-5116. *Toll-free phone:* 800-669-4882. *Fax:* 765-772-9293. *E-mail:* jdopplef@ivytech.edu.

IVY TECH COMMUNITY COLLEGE–NORTH CENTRAL

South Bend, Indiana www.ivytech.edu/

- **State-supported** 2-year, founded 1968, part of Ivy Tech State College System
- **Suburban** 4-acre campus
- **Endowment** $15.9 million
- **Coed**

Undergraduates 1,225 full-time, 4,003 part-time. 2% are from out of state, 14% African American, 0.9% Asian American or Pacific Islander, 5% Hispanic American, 0.5% Native American, 0.3% international, 2% transferred in.
Academics *Calendar:* semesters. *Degree:* certificates and associate. *Special study options:* academic remediation for entering students, adult/continuing education programs, advanced placement credit, distance learning, English as a second language, internships, off-campus study, part-time degree program, services for LD students, summer session for credit.
Student Life *Campus security:* 24-hour emergency response devices and patrols, late-night transport/escort service, security during open hours.
Costs (2006–07) *Tuition:* state resident $2633 full-time, $88 per credit part-time; nonresident $5355 full-time, $179 per credit part-time. *Required fees:* $80 full-time. *Payment plans:* installment, deferred payment.
Financial Aid Of all full-time matriculated undergraduates, 100 Federal Work-Study jobs (averaging $1538).

Ivy Tech Community College–North Central (continued)

Applying *Options:* early admission, deferred entrance. *Required:* high school transcript. *Required for some:* interview.

Freshmen Application Contact Ms. Pam Decker, Director of Admissions, Ivy Tech Community College–North Central, 220 Dean Johnson Boulevard, South Bend, IN 46601-3415. *Phone:* 574-289-7001. *Fax:* 574-236-7177. *E-mail:* pdecker@ivytech.edu.

IVY TECH COMMUNITY COLLEGE–NORTHEAST

Fort Wayne, Indiana   www.ivytech.edu/

- **State-supported** 2-year, founded 1969, part of Ivy Tech State College System
- **Urban** 22-acre campus
- **Endowment** $15.9 million
- **Coed**

Undergraduates 2,120 full-time, 3,962 part-time. 1% are from out of state, 15% African American, 1% Asian American or Pacific Islander, 2% Hispanic American, 0.5% Native American, 0.1% international, 3% transferred in.

Academics *Calendar:* semesters. *Degree:* certificates and associate. *Special study options:* adult/continuing education programs, advanced placement credit, distance learning, English as a second language, internships, part-time degree program, services for LD students, summer session for credit.

Student Life *Campus security:* 24-hour emergency response devices and patrols, late-night transport/escort service.

Costs (2006–07) *Tuition:* state resident $2633 full-time, $88 per credit part-time; nonresident $5355 full-time, $179 per credit part-time. *Required fees:* $80 full-time. *Payment plans:* installment, deferred payment.

Financial Aid Of all full-time matriculated undergraduates, 40 Federal Work-Study jobs (averaging $4041).

Applying *Options:* early admission. *Required:* high school transcript. *Required for some:* interview.

Freshmen Application Contact Mr. Steve Scheer, Director of Admissions, Ivy Tech Community College–Northeast, 3800 North Anthony Boulevard, Ft. Wayne, IN 46805-1489. *Phone:* 260-480-4221. *Toll-free phone:* 800-859-4882. *Fax:* 260-480-2053. *E-mail:* sscheer@ivytech.edu.

IVY TECH COMMUNITY COLLEGE–NORTHWEST

Gary, Indiana   www.ivytech.edu/

- **State-supported** primarily 2-year, founded 1963, part of Ivy Tech State College System
- **Urban** 13-acre campus with easy access to Chicago
- **Endowment** $15.9 million
- **Coed**

Undergraduates 1,395 full-time, 3,420 part-time. 30% African American, 0.7% Asian American or Pacific Islander, 9% Hispanic American, 0.2% Native American, 0.1% international, 5% transferred in.

Academics *Calendar:* semesters. *Degrees:* certificates, associate, and bachelor's. *Special study options:* academic remediation for entering students, adult/continuing education programs, advanced placement credit, distance learning, internships, part-time degree program, services for LD students, summer session for credit.

Student Life *Campus security:* 24-hour emergency response devices, late-night transport/escort service.

Costs (2006–07) *Tuition:* state resident $2633 full-time, $88 per credit part-time; nonresident $5355 full-time, $179 per credit part-time. *Required fees:* $80 full-time. *Payment plans:* installment, deferred payment.

Financial Aid Of all full-time matriculated undergraduates, 74 Federal Work-Study jobs (averaging $2131).

Applying *Options:* deferred entrance. *Required:* high school transcript. *Required for some:* interview.

Freshmen Application Contact Ms. Twilla Lewis, Associate Dean of Student Affairs, Ivy Tech Community College–Northwest, 1440 East 35th Avenue, Gary, IN 46409-1499. *Phone:* 219-981-1111 Ext. 2273. *Toll-free phone:* 800-843-4882. *Fax:* 219-981-4415. *E-mail:* tlewis@ivytech.edu.

IVY TECH COMMUNITY COLLEGE–SOUTHEAST

Madison, Indiana   www.ivytech.edu/

- **State-supported** 2-year, founded 1963, part of Ivy Tech State College System
- **Small-town** 5-acre campus with easy access to Louisville
- **Endowment** $15.9 million
- **Coed**

Undergraduates 630 full-time, 1,136 part-time. 2% are from out of state, 0.9% African American, 0.3% Asian American or Pacific Islander, 0.6% Hispanic American, 0.1% Native American, 0.1% international, 2% transferred in.

Academics *Calendar:* semesters. *Degree:* certificates and associate. *Special study options:* academic remediation for entering students, advanced placement credit, distance learning, internships, part-time degree program, services for LD students, summer session for credit.

Student Life *Campus security:* 24-hour emergency response devices.

Costs (2006–07) *Tuition:* state resident $2633 full-time, $88 per credit part-time; nonresident $5355 full-time, $179 per credit part-time. *Required fees:* $80 full-time. *Payment plans:* installment, deferred payment.

Financial Aid Of all full-time matriculated undergraduates, 26 Federal Work-Study jobs (averaging $1696).

Applying *Required:* high school transcript. *Required for some:* interview.

Freshmen Application Contact Ms. Cindy Hutcherson, Assistant Director of Admission/Career Counselor, Ivy Tech Community College–Southeast, 590 Ivy Tech Drive, Madison, IN 47250-1881. *Phone:* 812-265-2580 Ext. 4142. *Toll-free phone:* 800-403-2190. *Fax:* 812-265-4028. *E-mail:* chutcher@ivytech.edu.

IVY TECH COMMUNITY COLLEGE–SOUTHERN INDIANA

Sellersburg, Indiana   www.ivytech.edu/

- **State-supported** 2-year, founded 1968, part of Ivy Tech State College System
- **Small-town** 63-acre campus with easy access to Louisville
- **Endowment** $15.9 million
- **Coed**

Undergraduates 904 full-time, 2,208 part-time. 25% are from out of state, 5% African American, 0.5% Asian American or Pacific Islander, 0.5% Hispanic American, 0.6% Native American, 5% transferred in.

Academics *Calendar:* semesters. *Degree:* certificates and associate. *Special study options:* academic remediation for entering students, adult/continuing education programs, advanced placement credit, cooperative education, distance learning, internships, part-time degree program, services for LD students, summer session for credit.

Student Life *Campus security:* late-night transport/escort service.

Costs (2006–07) *Tuition:* state resident $2633 full-time, $88 per credit part-time; nonresident $5355 full-time, $179 per credit part-time. *Required fees:* $80 full-time. *Payment plans:* installment, deferred payment.

Financial Aid Of all full-time matriculated undergraduates, 20 Federal Work-Study jobs (averaging $5007). 1 state and other part-time job (averaging $6080).

Applying *Options:* early admission, deferred entrance. *Required:* high school transcript. *Required for some:* interview.

Freshmen Application Contact Ms. Mindy Steinberg, Director of Admissions, Ivy Tech Community College–Southern Indiana, 8204 Highway 311, Sellersburg, IN 47172-1897. *Phone:* 812-246-3301. *Toll-free phone:* 800-321-9021. *Fax:* 812-246-9905. *E-mail:* msteinbe@ivytech.edu.

IVY TECH COMMUNITY COLLEGE–SOUTHWEST

Evansville, Indiana   www.ivytech.edu/

- **State-supported** 2-year, founded 1963, part of Ivy Tech State College System
- **Suburban** 15-acre campus
- **Endowment** $15.9 million
- **Coed**

Undergraduates 1,526 full-time, 3,332 part-time. 2% are from out of state, 8% African American, 0.5% Asian American or Pacific Islander, 1% Hispanic American, 0.3% Native American, 4% transferred in.

Academics *Calendar:* semesters. *Degree:* certificates and associate. *Special study options:* academic remediation for entering students, advanced placement credit, cooperative education, distance learning, independent study, internships, part-time degree program, services for LD students, summer session for credit.

Student Life *Campus security:* late-night transport/escort service.

Costs (2006–07) *Tuition:* state resident $2633 full-time, $88 per credit part-time; nonresident $5355 full-time, $179 per credit part-time. *Required fees:* $80 full-time. *Payment plans:* installment, deferred payment.

Financial Aid Of all full-time matriculated undergraduates, 65 Federal Work-Study jobs (averaging $2264).

Applying *Options:* early admission, deferred entrance. *Required:* high school transcript. *Required for some:* interview.

Freshmen Application Contact Ms. Denise Johnson-Kincade, Director of Admissions, Ivy Tech Community College–Southwest, 3501 First Avenue, Evansville, IN 47710-3398. *Phone:* 812-429-1430. *Fax:* 812-429-9878. *E-mail:* ajohnson@ivytech.edu.

IVY TECH COMMUNITY COLLEGE–WABASH VALLEY

Terre Haute, Indiana　　　　　**www.ivytech.edu/**

- **State-supported** 2-year, founded 1966, part of Ivy Tech State College System
- **Suburban** 55-acre campus with easy access to Indianapolis
- **Endowment** $15.9 million
- **Coed**

Undergraduates 2,169 full-time, 2,823 part-time. 2% are from out of state, 3% African American, 0.4% Asian American or Pacific Islander, 0.3% Hispanic American, 0.6% Native American, 3% transferred in.

Academics *Calendar:* semesters. *Degree:* certificates and associate. *Special study options:* academic remediation for entering students, adult/continuing education programs, advanced placement credit, distance learning, internships, part-time degree program, services for LD students, summer session for credit.

Student Life *Campus security:* 24-hour emergency response devices.

Costs (2006–07) *Tuition:* state resident $2633 full-time, $88 per credit part-time; nonresident $5355 full-time, $179 per credit part-time. *Required fees:* $80 full-time. *Payment plans:* installment, deferred payment.

Financial Aid Of all full-time matriculated undergraduates, 51 Federal Work-Study jobs (averaging $2110). 1 state and other part-time job (averaging $2963).

Applying *Options:* early admission, deferred entrance. *Required:* high school transcript. *Required for some:* interview.

Freshmen Application Contact Mr. Michael Fisher, Director of Admissions, Ivy Tech Community College–Wabash Valley, 7999 U.S. Highway 41 South, Terre Haute, IN 47802-4898. *Phone:* 812-298-2300. *Toll-free phone:* 800-377-4882. *Fax:* 812-298-2291. *E-mail:* mfisher@ivytech.edu.

IVY TECH COMMUNITY COLLEGE–WHITEWATER

Richmond, Indiana　　　　　**www.ivytech.edu/**

- **State-supported** 2-year, founded 1963, part of Ivy Tech State College System
- **Small-town** 23-acre campus with easy access to Indianapolis
- **Endowment** $15.9 million
- **Coed**

Undergraduates 570 full-time, 1,262 part-time. 4% are from out of state, 5% African American, 0.2% Asian American or Pacific Islander, 0.8% Hispanic American, 0.3% Native American, 2% transferred in.

Academics *Calendar:* semesters. *Degree:* certificates and associate. *Special study options:* academic remediation for entering students, adult/continuing education programs, advanced placement credit, distance learning, independent study, internships, off-campus study, part-time degree program, services for LD students, summer session for credit.

Student Life *Campus security:* 24-hour emergency response devices, late-night transport/escort service.

Costs (2006–07) *Tuition:* state resident $2633 full-time, $88 per credit part-time; nonresident $5355 full-time, $179 per credit part-time. *Required fees:* $80 full-time. *Payment plans:* installment, deferred payment.

Financial Aid Of all full-time matriculated undergraduates, 14 Federal Work-Study jobs (averaging $3106). 1 state and other part-time job (averaging $3380).

Applying *Options:* early admission. *Required:* high school transcript. *Required for some:* interview.

Freshmen Application Contact Mr. Jeff Plasterer, Director of Admissions, Ivy Tech Community College–Whitewater, 2325 Chester Boulevard, Richmond, IN 47374-1298. *Phone:* 765-966-2656 Ext. 1212. *Toll-free phone:* 800-659-4562. *Fax:* 765-962-8741. *E-mail:* jplaster@ivytech.edu.

KAPLAN COLLEGE–INDIANAPOLIS

Indianapolis, Indiana　　getinfo.kaplancollege.com/KaplanCollegePortal/KaplanCollegeCampuses/Indiana/Indianapolis/

- **Independent** 2-year
- **Coed, primarily women,** 469 undergraduate students, 100% full-time, 90% women, 10% men

Undergraduates 469 full-time.

Freshmen *Admission:* 107 applied, 71 admitted. *Average high school GPA:* 2.0.

Faculty *Total:* 39, 74% full-time. *Student/faculty ratio:* 12:1.

Majors Computer programming (specific applications); computer software and media applications related.

Academics *Degree:* certificates and associate. *Special study options:* internships, part-time degree program.

Applying *Application fee:* $100. *Required:* essay or personal statement, high school transcript, minimum 1.7 GPA, 2 letters of recommendation. *Required for some:* interview, CPAt, health exam, keyboard test.

Director of Admissions Ms. Paulette M. Clay, Director of Admissions, Kaplan College–Indianapolis, 7302 Woodland Drive, Indianapolis, IN 46217. *Phone:* 317-299-6001 Ext. 320. *Toll-free phone:* 800-849-4995.

LINCOLN TECHNICAL INSTITUTE

Indianapolis, Indiana　　　　　**www.lincolntech.com/**

Director of Admissions Ms. Cindy Ryan, Director of Admissions, Lincoln Technical Institute, 1201 Stadium Drive, Indianapolis, IN 46202-2194. *Phone:* 317-632-5553. *Toll-free phone:* 800-554-4465.

MID-AMERICA COLLEGE OF FUNERAL SERVICE

Jeffersonville, Indiana　　　　　**www.mid-america.edu/**

- **Independent** primarily 2-year, founded 1905
- **Small-town** 3-acre campus with easy access to Louisville
- **Coed, primarily men,** 120 undergraduate students, 100% full-time, 45% women, 55% men

Undergraduates 120 full-time. Students come from 6 states and territories.

Faculty *Total:* 7, 86% full-time. *Student/faculty ratio:* 13:1.

Majors Funeral service and mortuary science.

Academics *Calendar:* quarters. *Degrees:* associate and bachelor's. *Special study options:* academic remediation for entering students.

Library 1,500 titles, 20 serial subscriptions.

Student Life *Housing:* college housing not available.

Athletics *Intercollegiate sports:* softball M/W.

Costs (2006–07) *Tuition:* $11,400 full-time, $200 per credit hour part-time. Full-time tuition and fees vary according to course load and program. No tuition increase for student's term of enrollment. *Payment plan:* installment.

Applying *Options:* deferred entrance. *Application fee:* $25. *Required:* high school transcript. *Application deadline:* rolling (freshmen).

Freshmen Application Contact Mr. Richard Nelson, Dean of Students, Mid-America College of Funeral Service, 3111 Hamburg Pike, Jeffersonville, IN 47130-9630. *Phone:* 812-288-8878. *Toll-free phone:* 800-221-6158. *Fax:* 812-288-5942. *E-mail:* macfs@mindspring.com.

SAWYER COLLEGE
Hammond, Indiana   www.sawyercollege.edu/

Director of Admissions Director, Sawyer College, 6040 Hohman Avenue, Hammond, IN 46320. *Phone:* 219-844-0100.

SAWYER COLLEGE
Merrillville, Indiana   www.sawyercollege.edu/

Admissions Office Contact Sawyer College, 3803 East Lincoln Highway, Merrillville, IN 46410.

VINCENNES UNIVERSITY
Vincennes, Indiana   www.vinu.edu/

Director of Admissions Mr. Chris M. Crews, Director of Admissions, Vincennes University, 1002 North First Street, Vincennes, IN 47591. *Phone:* 812-888-4313. *Toll-free phone:* 800-742-9198.

VINCENNES UNIVERSITY JASPER CAMPUS
Jasper, Indiana   vujc.vinu.edu/

- **State-supported** 2-year, founded 1970, part of Vincennes University
- **Small-town** 120-acre campus
- **Coed,** 835 undergraduate students, 41% full-time, 73% women, 27% men

Undergraduates 339 full-time, 496 part-time. Students come from 1 other state, 1 other country, 0.1% African American, 0.1% Asian American or Pacific Islander, 0.2% Hispanic American, 0.1% international.

Freshmen *Admission:* 247 applied, 245 admitted.

Faculty *Total:* 51, 39% full-time. *Student/faculty ratio:* 16:1.

Majors Accounting; administrative assistant and secretarial science; behavioral sciences; business administration and management; business teacher education; computer programming; computer programming related; computer systems networking and telecommunications; criminal justice/police science; drafting and design technology; education; education (K-12); elementary education; finance; furniture design and manufacturing; industrial technology; legal administrative assistant/secretary; liberal arts and sciences/liberal studies; management information systems; medical administrative assistant and medical secretary; psychology; social sciences; social work; sociology; word processing.

Academics *Calendar:* semesters. *Degree:* certificates and associate. *Special study options:* academic remediation for entering students, adult/continuing education programs, advanced placement credit, distance learning, part-time degree program, summer session for credit.

Library Vincennes University Jasper Library with 14,000 titles, 180 serial subscriptions, an OPAC.

Student Life *Housing:* college housing not available. *Activities and Organizations:* student-run newspaper. *Student services:* personal/psychological counseling.

Standardized Tests *Required for some:* SAT or ACT (for placement). *Recommended:* SAT or ACT (for placement).

Costs (2006–07) *Tuition:* state resident $3575 full-time, $119 per credit hour part-time; nonresident $8684 full-time, $289 per credit hour part-time. *Required fees:* $174 full-time. *Payment plan:* installment. *Waivers:* senior citizens and employees or children of employees.

Financial Aid Of all full-time matriculated undergraduates, 3 Federal Work-Study jobs (averaging $3200).

Applying *Application fee:* $20. *Required:* high school transcript. *Application deadlines:* rolling (freshmen), rolling (transfers).

Freshmen Application Contact Ms. Louann Gilbert, Director, Vincennes University Jasper Campus, 850 College Avenue, Jasper, IN 47546. *Phone:* 812-482-3030. *Toll-free phone:* 800-809-VUJC. *Fax:* 812-481-5960. *E-mail:* lagilbert@vinu.edu.

IOWA

AIB COLLEGE OF BUSINESS
Des Moines, Iowa   www.aib.edu/

- **Independent** 2-year, founded 1921
- **Urban** 20-acre campus
- **Coed,** 909 undergraduate students, 65% full-time, 71% women, 29% men

Undergraduates 592 full-time, 317 part-time. Students come from 5 states and territories, 1% are from out of state, 2% African American, 3% Asian American or Pacific Islander, 2% Hispanic American, 0.3% Native American, 48% live on campus. *Retention:* 59% of 2003 full-time freshmen returned.

Freshmen *Admission:* 546 applied, 405 admitted. *Average high school GPA:* 3.34. *Test scores:* ACT scores over 18: 77%; ACT scores over 24: 20%.

Faculty *Total:* 67, 42% full-time, 7% with terminal degrees. *Student/faculty ratio:* 17:1.

Majors Accounting; administrative assistant and secretarial science; business administration and management; computer management; computer programming (specific applications); computer software and media applications related; computer systems networking and telecommunications; court reporting; data entry/microcomputer applications related; finance; hospitality and recreation marketing; legal administrative assistant/secretary; marketing/marketing management; medical administrative assistant and medical secretary; system administration; tourism and travel services management; tourism and travel services marketing; tourism promotion.

Academics *Calendar:* continuous. *Degree:* diplomas and associate. *Special study options:* academic remediation for entering students, adult/continuing education programs, distance learning, double majors, internships, part-time degree program, summer session for credit.

Library 5,400 titles, 185 serial subscriptions.

Student Life *Housing:* on-campus residence required through sophomore year. *Options:* coed. Campus housing is university owned. *Activities and Organizations:* Business Management Association, Institute of Management Accountants, International Association of Administrative Professionals, Association of Information Technology Professionals, Student Court Reporters Association, national fraternities, national sororities. *Campus security:* 24-hour emergency response devices, late-night transport/escort service, controlled dormitory access, video security. *Student services:* personal/psychological counseling.

Athletics *Intramural sports:* badminton M/W, basketball M/W, bowling M/W, football M/W, golf M/W, softball M/W, table tennis M/W, volleyball M/W.

Standardized Tests *Recommended:* ACT (for admission).

Costs (2006–07) *Comprehensive fee:* $15,837 includes full-time tuition ($11,880) and room and board ($3957). Part-time tuition: $330 per credit hour. *Room and board:* college room only: $2895. *Payment plans:* installment, deferred payment. *Waivers:* employees or children of employees.

Financial Aid Of all full-time matriculated undergraduates, 104 Federal Work-Study jobs (averaging $1135). 1 state and other part-time job (averaging $457).

Applying *Options:* electronic application. *Application fee:* $25. *Required:* high school transcript. *Recommended:* interview. *Application deadlines:* rolling (freshmen), rolling (transfers).

Freshmen Application Contact Mr. Tim Hauber, Dean of Enrollment, AIB College of Business, Keith Fenton Administration Building, 2500 Fleur Drive, Des Moines, IA 50321-1799. *Phone:* 515-244-4221. *Toll-free phone:* 800-444-1921. *Fax:* 515-244-6773. *E-mail:* haubert@aib.edu.

CLINTON COMMUNITY COLLEGE
Clinton, Iowa   www.eicc.edu/ccc/

- **State and locally supported** 2-year, founded 1946, part of Eastern Iowa Community College District
- **Small-town** 20-acre campus
- **Coed,** 1,285 undergraduate students, 44% full-time, 65% women, 35% men

Undergraduates 562 full-time, 723 part-time. Students come from 9 states and territories, 10% are from out of state, 5% African American, 0.4% Asian American or Pacific Islander, 2% Hispanic American, 0.9% Native American, 0.1% international. *Retention:* 1% of 2003 full-time freshmen returned.

Freshmen *Admission:* 378 applied, 378 admitted, 378 enrolled.

Faculty *Total:* 76, 42% full-time.

Majors Administrative assistant and secretarial science; architectural drafting and CAD/CADD; business administration and management; computer/

information technology services administration related; electrical, electronic and communications engineering technology; emergency medical technology (EMT paramedic); environmental engineering technology; graphic and printing equipment operation/production; liberal arts and sciences/liberal studies; machine tool technology; nursing (licensed practical/vocational nurse training); nursing (registered nurse training); occupational safety and health technology; pharmacy technician.

Academics *Calendar:* semesters. *Degree:* certificates, diplomas, and associate. *Special study options:* academic remediation for entering students, adult/continuing education programs, advanced placement credit, cooperative education, distance learning, double majors, English as a second language, independent study, internships, part-time degree program, services for LD students, study abroad, summer session for credit.

Library Clinton Community College Library with 18,701 titles, 155 serial subscriptions, an OPAC.

Student Life *Housing:* college housing not available. *Activities and Organizations:* drama/theater group. *Student services:* personal/psychological counseling.

Athletics Member NJCAA. *Intercollegiate sports:* basketball M(s), cheerleading M/W, soccer M/W, softball W(s), volleyball W(s). *Intramural sports:* basketball M, bowling M/W, football M/W, racquetball M/W, skiing (downhill) M/W, tennis M/W, volleyball M/W, weight lifting M/W.

Costs (2006–07) *Tuition:* area resident $2910 full-time, $97 per credit hour part-time; state resident $4365 full-time, $145 per credit hour part-time. *Payment plan:* installment.

Financial Aid Of all full-time matriculated undergraduates, 31 Federal Work-Study jobs (averaging $3000). 3 state and other part-time jobs (averaging $3000).

Applying *Options:* early admission, deferred entrance. *Required:* high school transcript. *Application deadlines:* rolling (freshmen), rolling (transfers). *Notification:* continuous (freshmen), continuous (transfers).

Freshmen Application Contact Mr. Gary Mohr, Executive Director of Enrollment Management and Marketing, Clinton Community College, 1000 Lincoln Boulevard, Clinton, IA 52732-6299. *Phone:* 563-336-3322. *Fax:* 563-336-3350. *E-mail:* gmohr@eicc.edu.

DES MOINES AREA COMMUNITY COLLEGE
Ankeny, Iowa — www.dmacc.edu/

Freshmen Application Contact Mr. Michael Lentsch, Director of Enrollment Management, Des Moines Area Community College, Building 1, 2006 South Ankeny Boulevard, Ankeny, IA 50021. *Phone:* 515-964-6216. *Toll-free phone:* 800-362-2127. *Fax:* 515-964-6391. *E-mail:* mjleutsch@dmacc.edu.

ELLSWORTH COMMUNITY COLLEGE
Iowa Falls, Iowa — www.iavalley.cc.ia.us/ecc/

Director of Admissions Mrs. Nancy Walters, Registrar, Ellsworth Community College, 1100 College Avenue, Iowa Falls, IA 50126-1199. *Phone:* 641-648-4611. *Toll-free phone:* 800-ECC-9235.

HAMILTON COLLEGE
Cedar Falls, Iowa — www.hamiltoncf.com/

- **Proprietary** primarily 2-year, founded 2000
- **Coed**

Undergraduates 541 full-time, 154 part-time. 10% African American, 1% Hispanic American, 0.3% Native American.

Faculty *Student/faculty ratio:* 25:1.

Academics *Calendar:* quarters. *Degrees:* associate and bachelor's.

Standardized Tests *Required:* Wonderlic aptitude test (for admission).

Costs (2006–07) *One-time required fee:* $25. *Tuition:* Contact school as costs vary with program selected. Tuition includes books.

Applying *Application fee:* $20. *Required:* essay or personal statement, high school transcript, letters of recommendation, interview.

Freshmen Application Contact Ms. Jill Lines, Director of Admissions, Hamilton College, 7009 Nordic Drive, Cedar Falls, IA 50613. *Phone:* 319-277-0220. *Toll-free phone:* 800-728-1220. *Fax:* 319-268-0978. *E-mail:* jilines@hamiltoncf.com.

HAMILTON COLLEGE
Cedar Rapids, Iowa — www.hamiltonia.edu/

- **Proprietary** primarily 2-year, founded 1900
- **Suburban** 4-acre campus
- **Coed**

Undergraduates 440 full-time, 71 part-time. Students come from 1 other state, 3% African American, 2% Asian American or Pacific Islander, 1% Hispanic American, 0.6% Native American. *Retention:* 52% of 2003 full-time freshmen returned.

Faculty *Student/faculty ratio:* 25:1.

Academics *Calendar:* quarters. *Degrees:* certificates, diplomas, associate, and bachelor's (branch locations in Des Moines, Mason City, and Cedar Falls with significant enrollment not reflected in profile). *Special study options:* academic remediation for entering students, adult/continuing education programs, cooperative education, distance learning, internships, part-time degree program.

Student Life *Campus security:* 24-hour emergency response devices.

Standardized Tests *Required:* Wonderlic aptitude test (for admission).

Costs (2006–07) *Tuition:* $17,040 full-time, $355 per credit hour part-time.

Financial Aid Of all full-time matriculated undergraduates, 10 Federal Work-Study jobs (averaging $889). 3 state and other part-time jobs (averaging $1885).

Applying *Options:* early admission, deferred entrance. *Application fee:* $50. *Required:* high school transcript, interview.

Freshmen Application Contact Ms. Niki Donahue, Director of Admissions, Hamilton College, 1924 D Street SW, Cedar Rapids, IA 52404. *Phone:* 319-363-0481. *Toll-free phone:* 800-728-0481. *Fax:* 319-363-3812.

HAMILTON COLLEGE
Council Bluffs, Iowa — www.hamiltoncb.com/

- **Proprietary** 2-year, founded 2004
- **Coed,** 297 undergraduate students

Majors Business administration and management; criminal justice/law enforcement administration; medical/clinical assistant.

Academics *Degree:* associate.

Costs (2006–07) *Tuition:* $12,325 full-time.

Applying *Application fee:* $25.

Freshmen Application Contact Admissions Office, Hamilton College, 1751 Madison Avenue, Council Bluffs, IA 51503. *Toll-free phone:* 800-518-4212.

HAWKEYE COMMUNITY COLLEGE
Waterloo, Iowa — www.hawkeyecollege.edu/

- **State and locally supported** 2-year, founded 1966
- **Rural** 320-acre campus
- **Endowment** $847,924
- **Coed,** 5,663 undergraduate students, 43% full-time, 57% women, 43% men

Undergraduates 2,436 full-time, 3,227 part-time. Students come from 11 states and territories, 11 other countries, 1% are from out of state, 8% African American, 1% Asian American or Pacific Islander, 2% Hispanic American, 0.3% Native American, 0.3% international.

Freshmen *Admission:* 3,798 applied, 1,729 admitted, 1,177 enrolled.

Faculty *Total:* 348, 34% full-time, 6% with terminal degrees. *Student/faculty ratio:* 21:1.

Majors Accounting; administrative assistant and secretarial science; agricultural business and management; agricultural mechanization; agronomy and crop science; animal sciences; architectural engineering technology; autobody/collision and repair technology; automobile/automotive mechanics technology; avionics maintenance technology; biology/biological sciences; business administration and management; business/commerce; child development; civil engineering technology; clinical/medical laboratory technology; commercial and advertising art; computer engineering technology; computer/information technology services administration related; computer systems networking and telecommunications; computer/technical support; corrections; criminal justice/law enforcement administration; criminal justice/police science; data entry/microcomputer applications related; dental hygiene; drafting and design technology; education; engineering technology; farm and ranch management; fire science; food science; heavy equipment maintenance technology; horticultural science; information technology; interdisciplinary studies; interior design; liberal arts and sciences/liberal studies; machine tool technology; marketing/

Hawkeye Community College (continued)

marketing management; mechanical design technology; mechanical engineering/mechanical technology; medical administrative assistant and medical secretary; natural resources management and policy; nursing (registered nurse training); ornamental horticulture; parks, recreation and leisure facilities management; photography; respiratory care therapy; survey technology; system administration; tool and die technology; web/multimedia management and webmaster; web page, digital/multimedia and information resources design; word processing.

Academics *Calendar:* semesters. *Degree:* certificates, diplomas, and associate. *Special study options:* academic remediation for entering students, adult/continuing education programs, advanced placement credit, cooperative education, distance learning, English as a second language, external degree program, part-time degree program, services for LD students, study abroad, summer session for credit. *ROTC:* Army (c).

Library Hawkeye Community College Library with 42,327 titles, 337 serial subscriptions, 2,599 audiovisual materials, an OPAC, a Web page.

Student Life *Housing:* college housing not available. *Options:* Campus housing is provided by a third party. *Activities and Organizations:* Student Senate, Phi Theta Kappa, Environmental Conservation Club/Ag Club, Law Enforcement/Criminal Justice, Fashion Merchandising. *Campus security:* 24-hour patrols. *Student services:* personal/psychological counseling, women's center.

Athletics *Intramural sports:* basketball M/W, bowling M/W, golf M/W, softball M/W, volleyball M/W.

Standardized Tests *Required for some:* ACT (for admission).

Costs (2006–07) *Tuition:* state resident $3090 full-time, $103 per credit part-time; nonresident $6180 full-time, $206 per credit part-time. Full-time tuition and fees vary according to course load and program. Part-time tuition and fees vary according to course load and program. *Required fees:* $315 full-time, $11 per credit part-time. *Payment plans:* installment, deferred payment. *Waivers:* employees or children of employees.

Applying *Options:* electronic application, deferred entrance. *Required:* high school transcript. *Application deadlines:* rolling (freshmen), rolling (transfers). *Notification:* continuous (freshmen), continuous (transfers).

Freshmen Application Contact Ms. Holly Grimm, Admissions Coordinator, Hawkeye Community College, PO Box 8015, Waterloo, IA 50704-8015. *Phone:* 319-296-4277. *Toll-free phone:* 800-670-4769. *Fax:* 319-296-2505. *E-mail:* admission@hawkeyecollege.edu.

INDIAN HILLS COMMUNITY COLLEGE

Ottumwa, Iowa   www.ihcc.cc.ia.us/

Freshmen Application Contact Mrs. Jane Sapp, Admissions Officer, Indian Hills Community College, 525 Grandview Avenue, Building #1, Ottumwa, IA 52501-1398. *Phone:* 641-683-5155. *Toll-free phone:* 800-726-2585.

IOWA CENTRAL COMMUNITY COLLEGE

Fort Dodge, Iowa   www.iccc.cc.ia.us/

Freshmen Application Contact Mrs. Deb Bahis, Coordinator of Admissions, Iowa Central Community College, 330 Avenue M, Ft. Dodge, IA 50501. *Phone:* 515-576-0099 Ext. 2402. *Toll-free phone:* 800-362-2793. *Fax:* 515-576-7724. *E-mail:* bahls@iowacentral.com.

IOWA LAKES COMMUNITY COLLEGE

Estherville, Iowa   www.iowalakes.edu/

- **State and locally supported** 2-year, founded 1967, part of Iowa Area Community College System
- **Small-town** 20-acre campus
- **Endowment** $2.0 million
- **Coed,** 3,052 undergraduate students, 43% full-time, 55% women, 45% men

Undergraduates 1,299 full-time, 1,753 part-time. Students come from 19 states and territories, 2 other countries, 8% are from out of state, 0.8% African American, 0.6% Asian American or Pacific Islander, 1% Hispanic American, 0.1% Native American, 0.3% international, 4% transferred in, 24% live on campus.

Freshmen *Admission:* 1,897 applied, 1,541 admitted, 699 enrolled. *Test scores:* ACT scores over 18: 70%; ACT scores over 24: 16%; ACT scores over 30: 1%.

Faculty *Total:* 224, 42% full-time. *Student/faculty ratio:* 20:1.

Majors Accounting; accounting technology and bookkeeping; administrative assistant and secretarial science; agribusiness; agricultural business and management; agricultural business and management related; agricultural business technology; agricultural economics; agricultural/farm supplies retailing and wholesaling; agricultural mechanics and equipment technology; agricultural mechanization; agricultural power machinery operation; agricultural production; agricultural production related; agricultural teacher education; agriculture; agronomy and crop science; airline pilot and flight crew; animal/livestock husbandry and production; animal sciences; applied art; art; art history, criticism and conservation; art teacher education; astronomy; athletic training; autobody/collision and repair technology; automobile/automotive mechanics technology; aviation/airway management; behavioral sciences; biological and physical sciences; biology/biological sciences; botany/plant biology; broadcast journalism; business administration and management; business automation/technology/data entry; business machine repair; business teacher education; carpentry; ceramic arts and ceramics; chemistry; child care provision; child development; chiropractic assistant; commercial and advertising art; communication and journalism related; computer and information sciences related; computer graphics; computer/information technology services administration related; computer programming; computer science; computer software technology; computer systems networking and telecommunications; construction engineering technology; construction management; construction trades; consumer merchandising/retailing management; cooking and related culinary arts; corrections; criminal justice/law enforcement administration; criminal justice/police science; crop production; culinary arts related; data entry/microcomputer applications; data processing and data processing technology; desktop publishing and digital imaging design; developmental and child psychology; drafting and design technology; drawing; early childhood education; ecology; economics; education; elementary education; emergency care attendant (EMT ambulance); emergency medical technology (EMT paramedic); energy management and systems technology; engineering; English; environmental design/architecture; environmental education; environmental engineering technology; environmental studies; family and consumer sciences/human sciences; farm and ranch management; fashion merchandising; finance; fine/studio arts; fish/game management; fishing and fisheries sciences and management; flight instruction; food preparation; foods and nutrition related; food service and dining room management; foreign languages and literatures; forestry; general studies; geology/earth science; graphic and printing equipment operation/production; graphic communications; graphic design; health and physical education; health/health care administration; history; hospitality administration; hotel/motel administration; humanities; human resources management and services related; hydrology and water resources science; information technology; institutional food workers; jazz/jazz studies; journalism; kindergarten/preschool education; landscaping and groundskeeping; legal administrative assistant/secretary; legal assistant/paralegal; legal studies; liberal arts and sciences and humanities related; liberal arts and sciences/liberal studies; literature; marine maintenance and ship repair technology; marketing/marketing management; massage therapy; mass communication/media; mathematics; medical administrative assistant and medical secretary; medical/clinical assistant; medical laboratory technology; medical office assistant; medical office computer specialist; medical reception; medical transcription; merchandising, sales, and marketing operations related (general); motorcycle maintenance and repair technology; music; music teacher education; natural resources/conservation; natural sciences; nursing (registered nurse training); office management; office occupations and clerical services; parks, recreation and leisure; pharmacy; philosophy; photography; physical education teaching and coaching; physical sciences; piano and organ; political science and government; pre-dentistry studies; pre-engineering; pre-law studies; pre-medical studies; pre-nursing studies; pre-pharmacy studies; pre-veterinary studies; printing press operation; psychology; radio and television; radio and television broadcasting technology; real estate; receptionist; rehabilitation therapy; restaurant, culinary, and catering management; restaurant/food services management; retailing; sales, distribution and marketing; science teacher education; selling skills and sales; small business administration; small engine mechanics and repair technology; social sciences; social work; sociology; soil science and agronomy; Spanish; speech and rhetoric; sport and fitness administration/management; surgical technology; system administration; system, networking, and LAN/WAN management; technology/industrial arts teacher education; tourism and travel services management; tourism and travel services marketing; tourism promotion; trade and industrial teacher education; turf and turfgrass management; voice and opera; water, wetlands, and marine resources management; welding technology; wildlife and wildlands science and management; wildlife biology; wind/percussion instruments; word processing.

Academics *Calendar:* semesters. *Degree:* certificates, diplomas, and associate. *Special study options:* academic remediation for entering students, accelerated degree program, adult/continuing education programs, advanced placement credit, cooperative education, distance learning, honors programs, independent study, internships, part-time degree program, services for LD students, study abroad, summer session for credit.

Library Iowa Lakes Community College Library plus 2 others with 36,881 titles, 353 serial subscriptions, an OPAC.

Student Life *Housing Options:* coed. Campus housing is university owned. Freshman campus housing is guaranteed. *Activities and Organizations:* drama/theater group, student-run newspaper, radio and television station, choral group, Criminal Justice Club, Ecology Club, Nursing Club, Student Senate, BPA,

---

Campus security: 24-hour emergency response devices, student patrols. *Student services:* personal/psychological counseling, women's center.

Athletics Member NJCAA. *Intercollegiate sports:* baseball M(s), basketball M(s)/W(s), cross-country running M/W, golf M(s)/W(s), softball W(s), volleyball W(s), weight lifting M/W. *Intramural sports:* basketball M/W, football M/W, golf M/W, racquetball M/W, skiing (cross-country) M/W, skiing (downhill) M/W, soccer M/W, softball M/W, swimming and diving M/W, table tennis M/W, tennis M/W, volleyball M/W, weight lifting M/W, wrestling M.

Costs (2007–08) *Tuition:* state resident $3616 full-time, $113 per credit hour part-time; nonresident $3616 full-time, $115 per credit hour part-time.

Financial Aid Of all full-time matriculated undergraduates, 210 Federal Work-Study jobs (averaging $800).

Applying *Options:* deferred entrance. *Required:* high school transcript. *Required for some:* letters of recommendation, interview. *Application deadlines:* rolling (freshmen), rolling (transfers).

Freshmen Application Contact Ms. Anne Stansbury, Assistant Director Admissions, Iowa Lakes Community College, 3200 College Drive, Emmetsburg, IA 50536. *Phone:* 712-852-5254. *Toll-free phone:* 800-521-5054. *Fax:* 712-362-3639. *E-mail:* info@iowalakes.edu.

IOWA WESTERN COMMUNITY COLLEGE
Council Bluffs, Iowa www.iwcc.edu/

Freshmen Application Contact Ms. Tori Christie, Director of Admissions, Iowa Western Community College, 2700 College Road, Box 4-C, Council Bluffs, IA 51502. *Phone:* 712-325-3288. *Toll-free phone:* 800-432-5852. *E-mail:* admissions@iwcc.edu.

KAPLAN UNIVERSITY
Davenport, Iowa www.kaplancollegeia.com/

- **Proprietary** primarily 2-year, founded 1937, part of Kaplan Higher Education
- **Suburban** campus
- **Coed,** 22,529 undergraduate students, 20% full-time, 74% women, 26% men

Undergraduates 4,432 full-time, 18,097 part-time. Students come from 54 states and territories, 96% are from out of state, 0.5% African American, 0.1% Hispanic American, 38% transferred in.

Freshmen *Admission:* 4,953 applied, 4,302 admitted, 4,211 enrolled.

Faculty *Total:* 1,692, 6% full-time, 6% with terminal degrees. *Student/faculty ratio:* 11:1.

Majors Accounting; business administration and management; business/commerce; computer and information sciences; court reporting; criminal justice/safety; information technology; legal assistant/paralegal; management information systems; medical/clinical assistant; medical transcription; multi-/interdisciplinary studies related; tourism and travel services management.

Academics *Calendar:* quarters. *Degrees:* certificates, diplomas, associate, and bachelor's (profile includes both traditional and on-line students). *Special study options:* academic remediation for entering students, adult/continuing education programs, cooperative education, distance learning, double majors, independent study, internships, part-time degree program, summer session for credit.

Library Academic Resource Center with 7,000 titles, 120 serial subscriptions, an OPAC.

Student Life *Housing:* college housing not available. *Activities and Organizations:* academic department clubs. *Student services:* personal/psychological counseling.

Costs (2007–08) *Tuition:* $13,680 full-time, $380 per credit hour part-time.

Applying *Options:* early admission, deferred entrance. *Application fee:* $25. *Required:* high school transcript, interview. *Application deadlines:* rolling (freshmen), rolling (transfers).

Freshmen Application Contact Ms. Carla Batchelor, Director of Admissions, Kaplan University, 1801 East Kimberly Road, Suite 1, Davenport, IA 52807. *Phone:* 563-441-2496. *Toll-free phone:* 800-747-1035. *Fax:* 563-355-1320. *E-mail:* cbatchelor@kucampus.edu.

KIRKWOOD COMMUNITY COLLEGE
Cedar Rapids, Iowa www.kirkwood.cc.ia.us/

- **State and locally supported** 2-year, founded 1966, part of Iowa Department of Education Division of Community Colleges
- **Suburban** 630-acre campus
- **Endowment** $4.4 million
- **Coed,** 15,064 undergraduate students, 57% full-time, 54% women, 46% men

Undergraduates 8,590 full-time, 6,474 part-time. Students come from 21 states and territories, 27 other countries, 2% are from out of state, 5% African American, 1% Asian American or Pacific Islander, 2% Hispanic American, 1% Native American, 1% international, 3% transferred in.

Freshmen *Admission:* 3,587 enrolled.

Faculty *Total:* 832, 34% full-time. *Student/faculty ratio:* 20:1.

Majors Accounting; administrative assistant and secretarial science; agricultural business and management; agricultural teacher education; agriculture; agronomy and crop science; animal sciences; applied art; art; artificial intelligence and robotics; art teacher education; automobile/automotive mechanics technology; biological and physical sciences; biology/biological sciences; biology/biotechnology laboratory technician; broadcast journalism; business administration and management; business teacher education; ceramic arts and ceramics; child development; communications technology; computer programming; computer science; construction engineering technology; consumer merchandising/retailing management; corrections; criminal justice/law enforcement administration; criminal justice/police science; culinary arts; data processing and data processing technology; developmental and child psychology; drafting and design technology; dramatic/theater arts; education; electrical, electronic and communications engineering technology; electromechanical technology; elementary education; engineering; English; equestrian studies; farm and ranch management; fashion/apparel design; fashion merchandising; finance; fire science; fish/game management; food services technology; forestry; French; graphic and printing equipment operation/production; health information/medical records administration; heating, air conditioning, ventilation and refrigeration maintenance technology; history; horticultural science; hospitality and recreation marketing; hotel/motel administration; humanities; human services; hydrology and water resources science; industrial technology; interior design; international business/trade/commerce; jazz/jazz studies; journalism; kindergarten/preschool education; landscape architecture; legal administrative assistant/secretary; legal assistant/paralegal; legal studies; liberal arts and sciences/liberal studies; management information systems; marketing/marketing management; mass communication/media; mathematics; mechanical design technology; mechanical engineering/mechanical technology; medical administrative assistant and medical secretary; medical/clinical assistant; music; natural resources/conservation; nursing (licensed practical/vocational nurse training); nursing (registered nurse training); occupational therapy; ornamental horticulture; parks, recreation and leisure; parks, recreation and leisure facilities management; physical education teaching and coaching; political science and government; pre-engineering; psychology; public relations/image management; radio and television; respiratory care therapy; sanitation technology; social sciences; social work; sociology; Spanish; special products marketing; teacher assistant/aide; telecommunications; veterinary sciences; veterinary technology; voice and opera; welding technology; wildlife and wildlands science and management; wildlife biology; wind/percussion instruments.

Academics *Calendar:* semesters. *Degree:* certificates, diplomas, and associate. *Special study options:* academic remediation for entering students, accelerated degree program, adult/continuing education programs, advanced placement credit, cooperative education, distance learning, English as a second language, external degree program, honors programs, independent study, internships, off-campus study, part-time degree program, services for LD students, student-designed majors, summer session for credit.

Library Library with 60,622 titles, 565 serial subscriptions, an OPAC.

Student Life *Housing:* college housing not available. *Activities and Organizations:* drama/theater group, student-run newspaper, choral group. *Campus security:* 24-hour patrols. *Student services:* health clinic, personal/psychological counseling, legal services.

Athletics Member NJCAA. *Intercollegiate sports:* baseball M(s), basketball M(s)/W(s), golf M(s), soccer M/W, softball W(s), volleyball W(s). *Intramural sports:* basketball M/W, football M/W, golf M/W, racquetball M/W, soccer M/W, softball W, tennis M/W, volleyball M/W, weight lifting M/W.

Costs (2007–08) *Tuition:* state resident $3090 full-time, $103 per credit hour part-time; nonresident $6180 full-time, $206 per credit hour part-time.

Applying *Options:* electronic application, early admission. *Required:* high school transcript. *Application deadlines:* rolling (freshmen), rolling (transfers). *Notification:* continuous (freshmen), continuous (transfers).

Director of Admissions Mr. Doug Bannon, Director of Admissions, Kirkwood Community College, PO Box 2068, Cedar Rapids, IA 52406-2068. *Phone:* 319-398-5517. *Toll-free phone:* 800-332-2055. *E-mail:* dbannon@kirkwood.cc.ia.us.

MARSHALLTOWN COMMUNITY COLLEGE
Marshalltown,
Iowa www.marshalltowncommunitycollege.com/

Freshmen Application Contact Ms. Deana Inman, Director of Admissions, Marshalltown Community College, 3700 South Center Street, Marshalltown, IA 50158. *Phone:* 641-752-7106. *Toll-free phone:* 866-622-4748. *Fax:* 641-752-8149.

MUSCATINE COMMUNITY COLLEGE

Muscatine, Iowa   **www.eicc.edu/**

- **State-supported** 2-year, founded 1929, part of Eastern Iowa Community College District
- **Small-town** 25-acre campus
- **Coed,** 1,470 undergraduate students, 41% full-time, 55% women, 45% men

Undergraduates 604 full-time, 866 part-time. Students come from 6 states and territories, 5% are from out of state, 0.9% African American, 0.9% Asian American or Pacific Islander, 10% Hispanic American, 2% Native American, 0.2% international, 5% live on campus. *Retention:* 16% of 2003 full-time freshmen returned.

Freshmen *Admission:* 528 applied, 528 admitted, 528 enrolled. *Test scores:* ACT scores over 18: 80%; ACT scores over 24: 24%; ACT scores over 30: 1%.

Faculty *Total:* 91, 35% full-time.

Majors Accounting; administrative assistant and secretarial science; agricultural/farm supplies retailing and wholesaling; agricultural production; business administration and management; child care and support services management; computer/information technology services administration related; emergency medical technology (EMT paramedic); environmental engineering technology; liberal arts and sciences/liberal studies; machine tool technology; natural resources/conservation; nursing (licensed practical/vocational nurse training); occupational safety and health technology; pharmacy technician.

Academics *Calendar:* semesters. *Degree:* certificates, diplomas, and associate. *Special study options:* academic remediation for entering students, adult/continuing education programs, advanced placement credit, cooperative education, distance learning, double majors, English as a second language, honors programs, independent study, internships, part-time degree program, services for LD students, study abroad, summer session for credit.

Library Muscatine Community College Library with 19,588 titles, 176 serial subscriptions, an OPAC.

Student Life *Housing Options:* coed. Campus housing is university owned. *Activities and Organizations:* drama/theater group, student-run newspaper, choral group. *Student services:* personal/psychological counseling.

Athletics Member NJCAA. *Intercollegiate sports:* baseball M(s), softball W(s). *Intramural sports:* golf M/W, skiing (downhill) M/W, softball M/W, table tennis M/W, tennis M/W.

Costs (2006–07) *Tuition:* $97 per credit hour part-time; state resident $2910 full-time, $149 per credit hour part-time; nonresident $4365 full-time. *Room and board:* room only: $3390. *Payment plan:* installment.

Financial Aid Of all full-time matriculated undergraduates, 39 Federal Work-Study jobs (averaging $3000). 1 state and other part-time job (averaging $3000).

Applying *Options:* early admission, deferred entrance. *Required:* high school transcript. *Application deadlines:* rolling (freshmen), rolling (transfers). *Notification:* continuous (freshmen), continuous (transfers).

Freshmen Application Contact Gary Mohr, Executive Director of Enrollment Management and Marketing, Muscatine Community College, 152 Colorado Street, Muscatine, IA 52761-5396. *Phone:* 563-336-3322. *Toll-free phone:* 800-351-4669. *Fax:* 563-336-3350. *E-mail:* gmohr@eicc.edu.

NORTHEAST IOWA COMMUNITY COLLEGE

Calmar, Iowa   **www.nicc.edu/**

- **State and locally supported** 2-year, founded 1966, part of Iowa Area Community Colleges System
- **Small-town** 210-acre campus
- **Coed,** 4,764 undergraduate students, 43% full-time, 60% women, 40% men

Undergraduates 2,051 full-time, 2,713 part-time. 1% African American, 0.6% Asian American or Pacific Islander, 0.9% Hispanic American, 0.2% Native American, 0.2% international.

Freshmen *Admission:* 2,533 applied, 1,177 admitted, 648 enrolled.

Faculty *Total:* 192, 66% full-time, 5% with terminal degrees. *Student/faculty ratio:* 15:1.

Majors Accounting; agricultural business and management; clinical/medical laboratory technology; computer engineering technology; construction engineering technology; dairy science; electrical, electronic and communications engineering technology; health information/medical records administration; liberal arts and sciences/liberal studies; marketing/marketing management; mechanical design technology; nursing (registered nurse training); trade and industrial teacher education.

Academics *Calendar:* semesters. *Degree:* certificates, diplomas, and associate. *Special study options:* academic remediation for entering students, adult/continuing education programs, cooperative education, distance learning, double majors, English as a second language, independent study, internships, off-campus study, services for LD students, student-designed majors, study abroad, summer session for credit.

Library Wilder Resource Center plus 1 other with 21,337 titles, 294 serial subscriptions, 4,813 audiovisual materials, an OPAC.

Student Life *Housing:* college housing not available. *Activities and Organizations:* student-run newspaper. *Campus security:* security personnel on weeknights. *Student services:* personal/psychological counseling.

Athletics *Intramural sports:* basketball M/W, bowling M/W, football M/W, golf M/W, skiing (cross-country) M/W, skiing (downhill) M/W, swimming and diving M/W, tennis M/W, volleyball M/W.

Costs (2007–08) *Tuition:* state resident $3910 full-time, $115 per credit part-time; nonresident $3910 full-time, $115 per credit part-time. *Required fees:* $442 full-time, $13 per credit part-time.

Financial Aid Of all full-time matriculated undergraduates, 154 Federal Work-Study jobs (averaging $1248). 45 state and other part-time jobs (averaging $980).

Applying *Recommended:* high school transcript. *Application deadlines:* rolling (freshmen), rolling (transfers). *Notification:* continuous (freshmen), continuous (transfers).

Freshmen Application Contact Ms. Martha Keune, Admissions Representative, Northeast Iowa Community College, PO Box 400, Calmar, IA 52132. *Phone:* 563-562-3263 Ext. 307. *Toll-free phone:* 800-728-CALMAR. *Fax:* 563-562-4369. *E-mail:* keunem@nicc.edu.

NORTH IOWA AREA COMMUNITY COLLEGE

Mason City, Iowa   **www.niacc.edu/**

- **State and locally supported** 2-year, founded 1918, part of Iowa Area Community Colleges System
- **Rural** 320-acre campus
- **Coed,** 3,022 undergraduate students, 56% full-time, 53% women, 47% men

Undergraduates 1,691 full-time, 1,331 part-time. Students come from 25 states and territories, 10 other countries, 6% are from out of state, 4% African American, 1% Asian American or Pacific Islander, 2% Hispanic American, 0.2% Native American, 0.7% international, 63% transferred in, 15% live on campus. *Retention:* 58% of 2003 full-time freshmen returned.

Freshmen *Admission:* 1,914 applied, 1,914 admitted, 841 enrolled. *Average high school GPA:* 2.68. *Test scores:* ACT scores over 18: 76%; ACT scores over 24: 17%; ACT scores over 30: 1%.

Faculty *Total:* 160, 52% full-time, 5% with terminal degrees. *Student/faculty ratio:* 20:1.

Majors Accounting; accounting technology and bookkeeping; administrative assistant and secretarial science; agricultural business technology; agricultural economics; agricultural production; automobile/automotive mechanics technology; business administration and management; carpentry; clinical/medical laboratory technology; computer and information sciences; criminal justice/police science; electrical, electronic and communications engineering technology; emergency medical technology (EMT paramedic); entrepreneurship; fire services administration; heating, air conditioning, ventilation and refrigeration maintenance technology; industrial electronics technology; liberal arts and sciences/liberal studies; machine shop technology; machine tool technology; medical/clinical assistant; nursing assistant/aide and patient care assistant; nursing (licensed practical/vocational nurse training); nursing (registered nurse training); physical therapist assistant; sport and fitness administration/management; tool and die technology; welding technology.

Academics *Calendar:* semesters. *Degree:* certificates, diplomas, and associate. *Special study options:* academic remediation for entering students, advanced placement credit, cooperative education, distance learning, double majors, English as a second language, external degree program, honors programs, independent study, internships, off-campus study, part-time degree program, services for LD students, student-designed majors, summer session for credit.

Library North Iowa Area Community College Library with 29,540 titles, 413 serial subscriptions, 7,773 audiovisual materials, an OPAC, a Web page.

Student Life *Housing:* on-campus residence required for freshman year. *Options:* coed. Campus housing is university owned. Freshman applicants given priority for college housing. *Activities and Organizations:* student-run newspaper, choral group, Student Senate, school newspaper, intramurals, choral groups, band/orchestra. *Campus security:* 24-hour emergency response devices, controlled dormitory access. *Student services:* personal/psychological counseling.

Athletics Member NJCAA. *Intercollegiate sports:* baseball M(s), basketball M(s)/W(s), cross-country running W(s), football M(s), golf M(s)/W(s), soccer M(s)/W(s), softball W(s), track and field M(s)/W(s), volleyball W(s). *Intramural*

sports: basketball M/W, bowling M/W, cheerleading W, football M, skiing (downhill) M/W, soccer M/W, softball W, table tennis M/W, tennis M/W, volleyball M/W, weight lifting M/W.

Costs (2006–07) *Tuition:* state resident $2880 full-time, $96 per credit part-time; nonresident $4320 full-time, $144 per credit part-time. *Required fees:* $354 full-time, $11 per credit part-time. *Room and board:* $4076. *Payment plan:* installment. *Waivers:* employees or children of employees.

Financial Aid Of all full-time matriculated undergraduates, 125 Federal Work-Study jobs (averaging $2000).

Applying *Options:* electronic application. *Required:* high school transcript. *Application deadlines:* rolling (freshmen), rolling (transfers). *Notification:* continuous (freshmen), continuous (transfers).

Freshmen Application Contact Ms. Rachel McGuire, Director of Admissions, North Iowa Area Community College, 500 College Drive, Mason City, IA 50401. *Phone:* 641-422-4104. *Toll-free phone:* 888-GO NIACC Ext. 4245. *Fax:* 641-422-4385. *E-mail:* request@niacc.edu.

NORTHWEST IOWA COMMUNITY COLLEGE

Sheldon, Iowa
www.nwicc.edu/

- **State-supported** 2-year, founded 1966, part of Iowa Department of Education Division of Community Colleges
- **Small-town** 263-acre campus with easy access to Sioux City, IA; Sioux Falls, SD
- **Endowment** $1.0 million
- **Coed,** 1,224 undergraduate students, 44% full-time, 53% women, 47% men

Undergraduates 544 full-time, 680 part-time. Students come from 11 states and territories, 1 other country, 5% are from out of state, 0.3% African American, 0.2% Asian American or Pacific Islander, 1% Hispanic American, 0.1% Native American, 0.1% international, 5% transferred in, 5% live on campus. *Retention:* 71% of 2003 full-time freshmen returned.

Freshmen *Admission:* 776 applied, 639 admitted, 197 enrolled.

Faculty *Total:* 130, 32% full-time, 5% with terminal degrees. *Student/faculty ratio:* 11:1.

Majors Accounting; administrative assistant and secretarial science; autobody/collision and repair technology; automobile/automotive mechanics technology; business administration and management; computer programming; computer programming related; computer systems networking and telecommunications; construction/heavy equipment/earthmoving equipment operation; diesel mechanics technology; electrical, electronic and communications engineering technology; emergency medical technology (EMT paramedic); health information/medical records technology; industrial electronics technology; liberal arts and sciences/liberal studies; lineworker; machine shop technology; mechanical design technology; nursing (licensed practical/vocational nurse training); nursing (registered nurse training); tool and die technology; welding technology.

Academics *Calendar:* semesters. *Degree:* certificates, diplomas, and associate. *Special study options:* academic remediation for entering students, adult/continuing education programs, cooperative education, distance learning, double majors, English as a second language, off-campus study, part-time degree program, services for LD students, study abroad.

Library Northwest Iowa Community College Library plus 1 other with 16,300 titles, 170 serial subscriptions, 3,800 audiovisual materials, an OPAC, a Web page.

Student Life *Housing Options:* coed. Campus housing is university owned. *Activities and Organizations:* student-run newspaper. *Campus security:* 24-hour emergency response devices. *Student services:* personal/psychological counseling.

Athletics *Intramural sports:* basketball M/W, bowling M/W, football M, volleyball M/W.

Standardized Tests *Required:* ACT COMPASS (for placement). *Required for some:* ACT COMPASS.

Costs (2007–08) *Tuition:* state resident $3210 full-time; nonresident $4440 full-time. *Required fees:* $480 full-time. *Room and board:* $3200; room only: $2200.

Financial Aid Of all full-time matriculated undergraduates, 60 Federal Work-Study jobs (averaging $900).

Applying *Options:* electronic application. *Application fee:* $10. *Required:* high school transcript. *Required for some:* minimum 2.0 GPA. *Application deadlines:* rolling (freshmen), rolling (transfers). *Notification:* continuous (freshmen), continuous (transfers).

Director of Admissions Ms. Lisa Story, Director of Enrollment Management, Northwest Iowa Community College, 603 West Park Street, Sheldon, IA 51201-1046. *Phone:* 712-324-5061 Ext. 115. *Toll-free phone:* 800-352-4907. *E-mail:* lstory@nwicc.edu.

ST. LUKE'S COLLEGE

Sioux City, Iowa
stlukescollege.edu/

- **Independent** 2-year, founded 1967, part of St. Luke's Regional Medical Center
- **Rural** 3-acre campus
- **Endowment** $1.0 million
- **Coed,** 179 undergraduate students, 74% full-time, 91% women, 9% men

Undergraduates 133 full-time, 46 part-time. Students come from 10 states and territories, 27% are from out of state, 2% Asian American or Pacific Islander, 3% Hispanic American, 13% transferred in. *Retention:* 84% of 2003 full-time freshmen returned.

Freshmen *Admission:* 81 applied, 44 admitted, 7 enrolled. *Average high school GPA:* 3.02. *Test scores:* ACT scores over 18: 92%; ACT scores over 24: 33%; ACT scores over 30: 11%.

Faculty *Total:* 19, 68% full-time, 26% with terminal degrees. *Student/faculty ratio:* 12:1.

Majors Nursing (registered nurse training); radiologic technology/science; respiratory care therapy.

Academics *Calendar:* semesters. *Degree:* certificates and associate. *Special study options:* advanced placement credit, cooperative education, part-time degree program, summer session for credit.

Library St. Luke's Library with 2,713 titles, 108 serial subscriptions, 45 audiovisual materials, an OPAC, a Web page.

Student Life *Housing:* college housing not available. *Campus security:* 24-hour emergency response devices and patrols, late-night transport/escort service. *Student services:* health clinic, personal/psychological counseling.

Standardized Tests *Required:* ACT (for admission).

Costs (2007–08) *Tuition:* $12,852 full-time, $357 per credit part-time. *Required fees:* $600 full-time.

Financial Aid Of all full-time matriculated undergraduates, 16 Federal Work-Study jobs (averaging $1453).

Applying *Options:* electronic application, early admission, early action. *Application fee:* $25. *Required:* essay or personal statement, high school transcript, minimum 2.50 GPA, interview, minimum ACT score of 19. *Application deadline:* 8/1 (freshmen). *Notification:* continuous (transfers).

Freshmen Application Contact Ms. Sherry McCarthy, Admissions Coordinator, St. Luke's College, 2720 Stone Park Boulevard, Sioux City, IA 51104. *Phone:* 712-279-3149. *Toll-free phone:* 800-352-4660 Ext. 3149. *Fax:* 712-233-8017. *E-mail:* mccartsj@stlukes.org.

SCOTT COMMUNITY COLLEGE

Bettendorf, Iowa
www.eicc.edu/scc/

- **State and locally supported** 2-year, founded 1966, part of Eastern Iowa Community College District
- **Urban** campus
- **Coed,** 4,434 undergraduate students, 48% full-time, 63% women, 37% men

Undergraduates 2,138 full-time, 2,296 part-time. 10% are from out of state, 8% African American, 2% Asian American or Pacific Islander, 5% Hispanic American, 0.9% Native American, 0.2% international, 1% transferred in.

Freshmen *Admission:* 1,079 applied, 1,079 admitted, 1,079 enrolled.

Faculty *Total:* 310, 23% full-time. *Student/faculty ratio:* 20:1.

Majors Accounting; administrative assistant and secretarial science; airline pilot and flight crew; autobody/collision and repair technology; automobile/automotive mechanics technology; business administration and management; child care and support services management; clinical/medical laboratory technology; computer and information sciences; criminal justice/police science; culinary arts; diesel mechanics technology; electroneurodiagnostic/electroencephalographic technology; emergency medical technology (EMT paramedic); environmental engineering technology; equestrian studies; heating, air conditioning, ventilation and refrigeration maintenance technology; interior design; liberal arts and sciences/liberal studies; machine tool technology; medical radiologic technology; nursing (licensed practical/vocational nurse training); nursing (registered nurse training); occupational safety and health technology; occupational therapist assistant; pharmacy technician; physical therapy; radio and television broadcasting technology; respiratory care therapy; sign language interpretation and translation.

Academics *Calendar:* semesters. *Degree:* certificates, diplomas, and associate. *Special study options:* academic remediation for entering students, adult/continuing education programs, advanced placement credit, cooperative education, distance learning, double majors, English as a second language, honors pro-

Scott Community College (continued)

grams, independent study, internships, off-campus study, part-time degree program, services for LD students, study abroad, summer session for credit.

Library Scott Community College Library with 22,700 titles, 183 serial subscriptions, an OPAC.

Student Life *Housing:* college housing not available. *Activities and Organizations:* drama/theater group, student government, Campus Activities Board. *Campus security:* 24-hour emergency response devices. *Student services:* personal/psychological counseling.

Athletics Member NJCAA. *Intercollegiate sports:* golf M(s)/W(s), soccer M(s)/W(s).

Costs (2006–07) *Tuition:* $97 per credit hour part-time; state resident $3104 full-time, $145 per credit hour part-time; nonresident $4656 full-time. *Payment plan:* installment.

Financial Aid Of all full-time matriculated undergraduates, 72 Federal Work-Study jobs (averaging $3000).

Applying *Options:* early admission, deferred entrance. *Required:* high school transcript. *Application deadlines:* rolling (freshmen), rolling (transfers). *Notification:* continuous (freshmen), continuous (transfers).

Freshmen Application Contact Mr. Gary Mohr, Executive Director of Enrollment Management and Marketing, Scott Community College, 500 Belmont Road, Bettendorf, IA 52722-6804. *Phone:* 563-336-3322. *Toll-free phone:* 800-895-0811. *Fax:* 563-336-3350. *E-mail:* gmohr@eicc.edu.

SOUTHEASTERN COMMUNITY COLLEGE, NORTH CAMPUS

West Burlington, Iowa www.secc.cc.ia.us/

- **State and locally supported** 2-year, founded 1968, part of Iowa Department of Education Division of Community Colleges
- **Small-town** 160-acre campus
- **Coed,** 2,045 undergraduate students

Undergraduates Students come from 8 states and territories, 3% live on campus.

Faculty *Total:* 94, 13% full-time.

Majors Accounting; administrative assistant and secretarial science; agricultural business and management; agronomy and crop science; artificial intelligence and robotics; automobile/automotive mechanics technology; biomedical technology; business administration and management; child development; computer programming; construction engineering technology; cosmetology; criminal justice/law enforcement administration; drafting and design technology; electrical, electronic and communications engineering technology; emergency medical technology (EMT paramedic); engineering related; industrial radiologic technology; information science/studies; liberal arts and sciences/liberal studies; machine tool technology; mechanical engineering/mechanical technology; medical/clinical assistant; nursing (licensed practical/vocational nurse training); nursing (registered nurse training); respiratory care therapy; substance abuse/addiction counseling; trade and industrial teacher education; welding technology.

Academics *Calendar:* semesters. *Degree:* diplomas and associate. *Special study options:* academic remediation for entering students, adult/continuing education programs, advanced placement credit, cooperative education, distance learning, English as a second language, internships, part-time degree program, services for LD students, summer session for credit.

Library Yohe Memorial Library with 39,304 titles, 282 serial subscriptions.

Student Life *Housing Options:* men-only, women-only. *Activities and Organizations:* choral group, Student Senate, Criminal Justice Club, Art Club, Science Club. *Campus security:* controlled dormitory access, night patrols by trained security personnel.

Athletics Member NJCAA. *Intercollegiate sports:* baseball M(s), basketball M(s), softball W(s), volleyball W(s). *Intramural sports:* basketball M, bowling M/W, softball M/W, volleyball M/W, weight lifting M/W.

Standardized Tests *Required:* ACT ASSET (for placement). *Recommended:* ACT (for placement).

Costs (2006–07) *Tuition:* state resident $3060 full-time; nonresident $3420 full-time.

Applying *Options:* early admission, deferred entrance. *Application deadlines:* rolling (freshmen), rolling (transfers).

Freshmen Application Contact Ms. Stacy White, Admissions, Southeastern Community College, North Campus, 1500 West Agency Street, PO Box 180, West Burlington, IA 52655-0180. *Phone:* 319-752-2731 Ext. 8137. *Toll-free phone:* 866-722-4692.

SOUTHEASTERN COMMUNITY COLLEGE, SOUTH CAMPUS

Keokuk, Iowa www.secc.cc.ia.us/

- **State and locally supported** 2-year, founded 1967, part of Iowa Department of Education Division of Community Colleges
- **Small-town** 3-acre campus
- **Coed,** 548 undergraduate students

Faculty *Total:* 25, 72% full-time.

Majors Administrative assistant and secretarial science; business administration and management; cosmetology; criminal justice/safety; emergency medical technology (EMT paramedic); information science/studies; liberal arts and sciences/liberal studies; medical administrative assistant and medical secretary; nursing (licensed practical/vocational nurse training); nursing (registered nurse training); substance abuse/addiction counseling.

Academics *Calendar:* semesters. *Degree:* certificates, diplomas, and associate. *Special study options:* academic remediation for entering students, advanced placement credit, distance learning, independent study, off-campus study, part-time degree program, services for LD students, summer session for credit.

Library Fred Karre Memorial Library with 10,000 titles, 70 serial subscriptions, an OPAC.

Student Life *Housing:* college housing not available. *Activities and Organizations:* drama/theater group, student-run newspaper, choral group, Business Professionals of America, Art Club, Student Nurses Association, Computer Club, Student Board. *Student services:* personal/psychological counseling.

Athletics *Intramural sports:* basketball M, volleyball M/W.

Costs (2006–07) *Tuition:* $102 per credit hour part-time; state resident $2448 full-time; nonresident $2736 full-time, $114 per hour part-time. *Payment plan:* installment.

Applying *Options:* electronic application, early admission, deferred entrance. *Recommended:* high school transcript. *Application deadlines:* rolling (freshmen), rolling (transfers).

Freshmen Application Contact Ms. Kari Bevans, Admissions Coordinator, Southeastern Community College, South Campus, PO Box 6007, 335 Messenger Road, Keokuk, IA 52632. *Phone:* 319-524-3221. *Toll-free phone:* 866-722-4692 Ext. 8416. *Fax:* 319-524-8621. *E-mail:* kbevans@scciowa.edu.

SOUTHWESTERN COMMUNITY COLLEGE

Creston, Iowa www.swcc.cc.ia.us/

Freshmen Application Contact Ms. Lisa Carstens, Admissions Coordinator, Southwestern Community College, 1501 West Townline Street, Creston, IA 50801. *Phone:* 641-782-7081. *Toll-free phone:* 800-247-4023. *Fax:* 641-782-3312. *E-mail:* carstens@swcciowa.edu.

VATTEROTT COLLEGE

Des Moines, Iowa www.vatterott-college.edu/

- **Proprietary** primarily 2-year
- **Urban** 25-acre campus
- **Coed**

Undergraduates 6% African American, 3% Asian American or Pacific Islander, 3% Hispanic American.

Faculty *Student/faculty ratio:* 15:1.

Academics *Calendar:* ten week periods. *Degrees:* certificates, diplomas, associate, and bachelor's.

Applying *Required:* high school transcript, interview.

Freshmen Application Contact Mr. Henry Franken, Co-Director, Vatterott College, 6100 Thornton Avenue, Suite 290, Des Moines, IA 50321. *Phone:* 515-309-9000. *Toll-free phone:* 800-353-7264. *Fax:* 515-309-0366.

WESTERN IOWA TECH COMMUNITY COLLEGE

Sioux City, Iowa www.witcc.edu/

- **State-supported** 2-year, founded 1966, part of Iowa Department of Education Division of Community Colleges
- **Urban** 143-acre campus
- **Endowment** $337,763
- **Coed**

Undergraduates 2,086 full-time, 3,248 part-time. 10% are from out of state, 2% African American, 2% Asian American or Pacific Islander, 6% Hispanic American, 2% Native American, 0.1% international, 7% transferred in, 2% live on campus.

Faculty *Student/faculty ratio:* 20:1.

Academics *Calendar:* semesters. *Degree:* certificates, diplomas, and associate. *Special study options:* academic remediation for entering students, accelerated degree program, adult/continuing education programs, distance learning, double majors, English as a second language, honors programs, independent study, internships, part-time degree program, services for LD students, summer session for credit.

Student Life *Campus security:* 24-hour emergency response devices and patrols.

Costs (2006–07) *Tuition:* state resident $2910 full-time, $97 per credit hour part-time; nonresident $3990 full-time, $133 per credit hour part-time. *Required fees:* $450 full-time, $15 per credit hour part-time. *Room and board:* room only: $2160.

Applying *Options:* early admission, deferred entrance. *Application fee:* $20. *Required:* high school transcript.

Freshmen Application Contact Lora Vanderzwaag, Director of Admissions, Western Iowa Tech Community College, 4647 Stone Avenue, Sioux City, IA 51102-5199. *Phone:* 712-274-6400. *Toll-free phone:* 800-352-4649 Ext. 6403. *Fax:* 712-274-6441.

KANSAS

ALLEN COUNTY COMMUNITY COLLEGE

Iola, Kansas www.allencc.net/

- **State and locally supported** 2-year, founded 1923, part of Kansas State Board of Regents
- **Small-town** 88-acre campus
- **Coed,** 2,814 undergraduate students

Undergraduates Students come from 17 states and territories, 16 other countries, 4% are from out of state, 4% African American, 0.6% Asian American or Pacific Islander, 3% Hispanic American, 1% Native American, 1% international, 10% live on campus. *Retention:* 56% of 2003 full-time freshmen returned.

Freshmen *Admission:* 893 applied, 893 admitted. *Average high school GPA:* 2.97. *Test scores:* ACT scores over 18: 64%; ACT scores over 24: 14%; ACT scores over 30: 2%.

Faculty *Total:* 155, 23% full-time. *Student/faculty ratio:* 17:1.

Majors Accounting; administrative assistant and secretarial science; agricultural production; architecture; art; athletic training; banking and financial support services; biology/biological sciences; business administration and management; business/commerce; business teacher education; chemistry; child development; computer science; computer systems networking and telecommunications; criminal justice/law enforcement administration; data processing and data processing technology; drafting and design technology; dramatic/theater arts; economics; electrical, electronic and communications engineering technology; electrical, electronics and communications engineering; elementary education; emergency medical technology (EMT paramedic); engineering; engineering technology; English composition; equestrian studies; family and consumer sciences/human sciences; farm and ranch management; forestry; funeral service and mortuary science; general studies; geography; health aide; health and physical education; history; home health aide/home attendant; hospital and health care facilities administration; humanities; industrial arts; industrial technology; information science/studies; journalism; language interpretation and translation; library science; mathematics; music; nuclear/nuclear power technology; nursing assistant/aide and patient care assistant; parks, recreation and leisure facilities management; philosophy; physical therapy; physics; political science and government; postal management; pre-dentistry studies; pre-law studies; pre-medical studies; pre-pharmacy studies; pre-veterinary studies; psychology; religious studies; secondary education; social work; sociology; speech and rhetoric; technology/industrial arts teacher education; wood science and wood products/pulp and paper technology.

Academics *Calendar:* semesters. *Degree:* certificates and associate. *Special study options:* academic remediation for entering students, adult/continuing education programs, cooperative education, part-time degree program, services for LD students, student-designed majors, summer session for credit.

Library Learning Resource Center with 49,416 titles, 159 serial subscriptions, an OPAC.

Student Life *Housing:* on-campus residence required through sophomore year. *Options:* coed. Campus housing is university owned. *Activities and Organiza-tions:* drama/theater group, student-run newspaper, choral group, intramurals, Student Senate, Biology Club, student newspaper, Phi Theta Kappa. *Campus security:* controlled dormitory access. *Student services:* personal/psychological counseling.

Athletics Member NJCAA. *Intercollegiate sports:* baseball M(s), basketball M(s)/W(s), cross-country running M(s)/W(s), golf M(s), soccer M(s)/W(s), softball W(s), track and field M(s)/W(s), volleyball W(s). *Intramural sports:* basketball M/W, football M/W, soccer M/W, softball M/W, table tennis M/W, tennis M/W, volleyball M/W.

Costs (2007–08) *Tuition:* area resident $1260 full-time, $42 per hour part-time; state resident $1560 full-time, $52 per hour part-time; nonresident $1560 full-time, $52 per hour part-time. *Required fees:* $720 full-time, $16 per hour part-time.

Financial Aid Of all full-time matriculated undergraduates, 25 Federal Work-Study jobs (averaging $1650). 80 state and other part-time jobs (averaging $1650).

Applying *Options:* early admission, deferred entrance. *Required:* high school transcript. *Application deadlines:* 8/24 (freshmen), 8/24 (transfers). *Notification:* continuous (freshmen), continuous (transfers).

Freshmen Application Contact Mr. Dan Kinney, Dean of Student Affairs, Allen County Community College, 1801 North Cottonwood, Iola, KS 66749. *Phone:* 620-365-5116 Ext. 267. *Fax:* 620-365-7406.

BARTON COUNTY COMMUNITY COLLEGE

Great Bend, Kansas www.bartonccc.edu/

- **State and locally supported** 2-year, founded 1969, part of Kansas Board of Regents
- **Rural** 140-acre campus
- **Endowment** $4.6 million
- **Coed,** 4,263 undergraduate students, 21% full-time, 46% women, 54% men

Undergraduates 895 full-time, 3,368 part-time. Students come from 41 states and territories, 16 other countries, 7% are from out of state, 13% African American, 3% Asian American or Pacific Islander, 9% Hispanic American, 1% Native American, 0.6% international, 4% transferred in, 6% live on campus. *Retention:* 60% of 2003 full-time freshmen returned.

Freshmen *Admission:* 1,421 enrolled. *Average high school GPA:* 3.01. *Test scores:* ACT scores over 18: 72%; ACT scores over 24: 17%; ACT scores over 30: 1%.

Faculty *Total:* 190, 38% full-time, 4% with terminal degrees. *Student/faculty ratio:* 18:1.

Majors Accounting; administrative assistant and secretarial science; agricultural business and management; agriculture; anthropology; architecture; art; athletic training; automobile/automotive mechanics technology; banking and financial support services; biology/biological sciences; business administration and management; business computer programming; chemistry; child care and support services management; chiropractic assistant; clinical/medical laboratory technology; communication/speech communication and rhetoric; computer/information technology services administration related; computer science; computer systems networking and telecommunications; criminal justice/police science; crop production; cytotechnology; dance; dental hygiene; dietitian assistant; dramatic/theater arts; early childhood education; economics; elementary education; emergency medical technology (EMT paramedic); engineering technology; English; fire science; forestry; funeral service and mortuary science; general studies; geology/earth science; graphic design; hazardous materials management and waste technology; health information/medical records administration; history; home health aide; human resources management and services related; information science/studies; journalism; kinesiology and exercise science; liberal arts and sciences/liberal studies; livestock management; marketing/marketing management; mathematics; medical administrative assistant and medical secretary; medical/clinical assistant; military studies; modern languages; music; nursing (registered nurse training); occupational therapy; optometric technician; pharmacy; philosophy; physical education teaching and coaching; physical sciences; physical therapist assistant; physical therapy; physician assistant; physics; political science and government; pre-dentistry studies; pre-engineering; pre-law studies; pre-medical studies; pre-veterinary studies; psychology; public administration; radiologic technology/science; religious studies; respiratory care therapy; secondary education; social work; sociology; sport and fitness administration/management; wildlife and wildlands science and management.

Academics *Calendar:* semesters. *Degree:* certificates and associate. *Special study options:* academic remediation for entering students, accelerated degree program, adult/continuing education programs, advanced placement credit, cooperative education, distance learning, double majors, English as a second language, external degree program, honors programs, independent study, internships, part-time degree program, services for LD students, summer session for credit.

Barton County Community College (continued)

Library Barton County Community College Library with 41,380 titles, 66 serial subscriptions, 1,325 audiovisual materials, an OPAC, a Web page.

Student Life *Housing Options:* coed, disabled students. Campus housing is university owned. Freshman campus housing is guaranteed. *Activities and Organizations:* drama/theater group, student-run newspaper, choral group, Danceline, Business Professionals, Psychology Club, Agriculture Club, Cougarettes. *Campus security:* 24-hour emergency response devices and patrols. *Student services:* health clinic, personal/psychological counseling.

Athletics Member NJCAA. *Intercollegiate sports:* baseball M(s), basketball M(s)/W(s), cheerleading M(s)/W, cross-country running M(s)/W(s), golf M(s), soccer M(s)/W(s), softball W(s), tennis M(s)/W(s), track and field M(s)/W(s), volleyball W(s). *Intramural sports:* basketball M/W, bowling M/W, football M/W, golf M/W, swimming and diving M/W, table tennis M/W, tennis M/W, track and field M/W, volleyball M/W.

Costs (2007–08) *Tuition:* state resident $1470 full-time, $49 per credit hour part-time; nonresident $2040 full-time, $68 per credit hour part-time. *Required fees:* $540 full-time, $18 per credit hour part-time. *Room and board:* $3854.

Financial Aid Of all full-time matriculated undergraduates, 102 Federal Work-Study jobs (averaging $2400).

Applying *Options:* electronic application, early admission. *Recommended:* high school transcript. *Application deadlines:* rolling (freshmen), rolling (transfers).

Freshmen Application Contact Mr. Todd Moore, Director of Admissions and Marketing, Barton County Community College, 245 Northeast 30th Road, Great Bend, KS 67530. *Phone:* 620-792-9241. *Toll-free phone:* 800-722-6842. *Fax:* 620-786-1160. *E-mail:* admissions@bartoncc.edu.

BROWN MACKIE COLLEGE–KANSAS CITY

Lenexa, Kansas　　　　　**www.bmcaec.com/**

- **Proprietary** 2-year, founded 1892, part of Education Management Corporation
- **Suburban** 3-acre campus with easy access to Kansas City
- **Coed,** 370 undergraduate students, 100% full-time, 77% women, 23% men

Undergraduates 370 full-time. Students come from 2 states and territories, 35% are from out of state, 26% African American, 1% Asian American or Pacific Islander, 8% Hispanic American, 2% Native American.

Freshmen *Admission:* 111 enrolled.

Faculty *Total:* 21, 38% full-time, 33% with terminal degrees.

Majors Accounting technology and bookkeeping; business administration and management; CAD/CADD drafting/design technology; computer software and media applications related; computer systems networking and telecommunications; electrical, electronic and communications engineering technology; legal assistant/paralegal; medical/clinical assistant; medical office management; sales, distribution and marketing.

Academics *Calendar:* quarters. *Degree:* certificates, diplomas, and associate. *Special study options:* academic remediation for entering students, adult/continuing education programs, cooperative education.

Library Brown Mackie College Library with 9,600 titles, 48 serial subscriptions, 200 audiovisual materials, an OPAC, a Web page.

Student Life *Housing:* college housing not available. *Activities and Organizations:* Coffee Club (service and social organization). *Campus security:* 24-hour emergency response devices. *Student services:* personal/psychological counseling.

Costs (2006–07) *Tuition:* $9360 full-time. *Required fees:* $576 full-time.

Applying *Options:* deferred entrance. *Required:* high school transcript, interview. *Recommended:* minimum 2.0 GPA. *Application deadlines:* rolling (freshmen), rolling (transfers). *Notification:* continuous (freshmen), continuous (transfers).

Freshmen Application Contact Ms. Mary Lou Whitton, Brown Mackie College–Kansas City, 9705 Lenexa Drive, Lenexa, KS 66215. *Phone:* 913-768-1900. *Toll-free phone:* 800-635-9101. *Fax:* 913-495-9555. *E-mail:* mwhitton@brownmackie.edu.

►See page 508 for the College Close-Up.

BROWN MACKIE COLLEGE–SALINA

Salina, Kansas　　**www.brownmackie.edu/locations.asp?locid=13**

- **Proprietary** 2-year, founded 1892
- **Small-town** 10-acre campus with easy access to Wichita
- **Coed,** 429 undergraduate students

Undergraduates Students come from 10 states and territories, 2 other countries, 26% are from out of state.

Faculty *Total:* 34, 44% full-time. *Student/faculty ratio:* 13:1.

Majors Accounting technology and bookkeeping; business administration and management; CAD/CADD drafting/design technology; computer and information sciences; computer software and media applications related; computer systems networking and telecommunications; criminal justice/law enforcement administration; electrical, electronic and communications engineering technology; legal assistant/paralegal; medical/clinical assistant; medical office management; nursing (registered nurse training); sales, distribution and marketing.

Academics *Calendar:* modular. *Degree:* certificates, diplomas, and associate. *Special study options:* academic remediation for entering students, adult/continuing education programs, advanced placement credit, cooperative education, independent study, services for LD students, summer session for credit.

Library Brown Mackie College Library plus 1 other with 14,788 titles, 45 serial subscriptions, 195 audiovisual materials, an OPAC, a Web page.

Student Life *Housing:* college housing not available. *Activities and Organizations:* student-run newspaper, Student Senate, Athletic Booster Club.

Athletics Member NJCAA. *Intercollegiate sports:* baseball M(s), basketball M(s)/W(s), softball W(s).

Costs (2007–08) *Tuition:* $9360 full-time, $195 per credit hour part-time.

Financial Aid Of all full-time matriculated undergraduates, 10 Federal Work-Study jobs (averaging $1500).

Applying *Options:* deferred entrance. *Required:* high school transcript, interview. *Application deadlines:* rolling (freshmen), rolling (transfers). *Notification:* continuous (freshmen), continuous (transfers).

Freshmen Application Contact Director of Admissions, Brown Mackie College–Salina, 2106 South 9th Street, Salina, KS 67401. *Phone:* 785-825-5422. *Toll-free phone:* 800-365-0433. *Fax:* 785-827-7623. *E-mail:* dheath@brownmackie.edu.

►See page 524 for the College Close-Up.

BUTLER COMMUNITY COLLEGE

El Dorado, Kansas　　　　**www.butlercc.edu/**

- **State and locally supported** 2-year, founded 1927, part of Kansas State Board of Education
- **Small-town** 80-acre campus
- **Coed**

Undergraduates 3,658 full-time, 5,205 part-time. Students come from 28 states and territories, 21 other countries, 5% are from out of state, 12% African American, 2% Asian American or Pacific Islander, 6% Hispanic American, 2% Native American, 3% international, 5% transferred in, 4% live on campus. *Retention:* 57% of 2003 full-time freshmen returned.

Faculty *Student/faculty ratio:* 18:1.

Academics *Calendar:* semesters. *Degree:* certificates and associate. *Special study options:* academic remediation for entering students, accelerated degree program, adult/continuing education programs, advanced placement credit, cooperative education, distance learning, double majors, English as a second language, honors programs, independent study, part-time degree program, services for LD students, student-designed majors, summer session for credit.

Student Life *Campus security:* 24-hour emergency response devices and patrols, controlled dormitory access, video cameras at dormitory entrances and parking lot.

Athletics Member NJCAA.

Costs (2006–07) *Tuition:* state resident $1808 full-time, $57 per credit hour part-time; nonresident $3248 full-time, $116 per credit hour part-time. Full-time tuition and fees vary according to course load. Part-time tuition and fees vary according to course load. *Required fees:* $462 full-time, $14 per credit hour part-time. *Room and board:* $4420. Room and board charges vary according to housing facility.

Financial Aid Of all full-time matriculated undergraduates, 210 Federal Work-Study jobs (averaging $1800).

Applying *Options:* early admission, deferred entrance. *Required:* high school transcript.

Freshmen Application Contact Mr. Paul Kyle, Director of Enrollment Management, Butler Community College, 901 South Haverhill Road, El Dorado, KS 67042. *Phone:* 316-321-2222. *Fax:* 316-322-3109. *E-mail:* admissions@butlercc.edu.

CLOUD COUNTY COMMUNITY COLLEGE

Concordia, Kansas　　　　**www.cloud.edu/**

Director of Admissions Kim Reynolds, Director of Admissions, Cloud County Community College, 2221 Campus Drive, PO Box 1002, Concordia, KS 66901-1002. *Phone:* 785-243-1435 Ext. 214. *Toll-free phone:* 800-729-5101.

COFFEYVILLE COMMUNITY COLLEGE
Coffeyville, Kansas www.coffeyville.edu/

Freshmen Application Contact Ms. Kim Lay, Coordinator/Advisor of Enrollment Services, Coffeyville Community College, 400 West 11th, Coffeyville, KS 67337. *Phone:* 620-252-7155.

COLBY COMMUNITY COLLEGE
Colby, Kansas www.colbycc.edu/
- **State and locally supported** 2-year, founded 1964, part of Kansas State Board of Education
- **Small-town** 80-acre campus
- **Endowment** $3.2 million
- **Coed,** 1,690 undergraduate students, 47% full-time, 63% women, 37% men

Undergraduates 789 full-time, 901 part-time. Students come from 14 states and territories, 5 other countries, 13% are from out of state, 9% transferred in, 30% live on campus.

Freshmen *Admission:* 647 applied, 647 admitted, 221 enrolled. *Average high school GPA:* 3.28.

Faculty *Total:* 60, 100% full-time, 28% with terminal degrees. *Student/faculty ratio:* 19:1.

Majors Accounting; agricultural business and management; agricultural economics; agricultural teacher education; agriculture; agronomy and crop science; animal sciences; behavioral sciences; biological and physical sciences; biology/biological sciences; broadcast journalism; business administration and management; business/managerial economics; business teacher education; chemistry; child development; commercial and advertising art; computer and information sciences related; computer science; criminal justice/law enforcement administration; dental hygiene; dramatic/theater arts; education; English; family and consumer sciences/human sciences; farm and ranch management; foods, nutrition, and wellness; forestry; geology/earth science; history; humanities; journalism; kindergarten/preschool education; liberal arts and sciences/liberal studies; library science; marketing/marketing management; mass communication/media; mathematics; music; music teacher education; nursing (licensed practical/vocational nurse training); nursing (registered nurse training); pharmacy; physical education teaching and coaching; physical therapist assistant; physical therapy; political science and government; pre-engineering; psychology; radio and television; range science and management; science teacher education; social work; sociology; veterinary sciences; veterinary technology; wildlife biology; zoology/animal biology.

Academics *Calendar:* semesters. *Degree:* certificates, diplomas, and associate. *Special study options:* academic remediation for entering students, adult/continuing education programs, advanced placement credit, cooperative education, distance learning, double majors, honors programs, internships, part-time degree program, services for LD students, student-designed majors, summer session for credit.

Library Davis Library with 32,000 titles, 350 serial subscriptions, an OPAC.

Student Life *Housing:* on-campus residence required for freshman year. *Options:* men-only, women-only. Campus housing is university owned. *Activities and Organizations:* drama/theater group, student-run newspaper, radio and television station, choral group, marching band, KSNEA, Physical Therapist Assistants Club, Block and Bridle, SVTA, COPNS. *Campus security:* 24-hour emergency response devices and patrols. *Student services:* health clinic, personal/psychological counseling.

Athletics Member NJCAA. *Intercollegiate sports:* baseball M(s), basketball M(s)/W(s), cheerleading W, cross-country running M(s)/W(s), equestrian sports M/W, golf M(s)/W(s), softball W(s), track and field M(s)/W(s), volleyball W(s), wrestling M(s). *Intramural sports:* basketball M/W, softball M/W, volleyball M/W.

Costs (2006–07) *Tuition:* state resident $1372 full-time; nonresident $2620 full-time. *Required fees:* $640 full-time. *Room and board:* $3542. Room and board charges vary according to board plan. *Payment plan:* installment. *Waivers:* senior citizens and employees or children of employees.

Financial Aid Of all full-time matriculated undergraduates, 95 Federal Work-Study jobs (averaging $1500). 30 state and other part-time jobs (averaging $2000).

Applying *Options:* early admission, deferred entrance. *Required:* high school transcript. *Application deadlines:* rolling (freshmen), rolling (transfers). *Notification:* continuous (freshmen), continuous (transfers).

Freshmen Application Contact Ms. Nikol Nolan, Admissions Director, Colby Community College, 1255 South Range, Colby, KS 67701-4099. *Phone:* 785-462-3984 Ext. 5496. *Toll-free phone:* 888-634-9350 Ext. 690. *Fax:* 785-460-4691. *E-mail:* admissions@colbycc.edu.

COWLEY COUNTY COMMUNITY COLLEGE AND AREA VOCATIONAL–TECHNICAL SCHOOL
Arkansas City, Kansas www.cowley.cc.ks.us/
- **State and locally supported** 2-year, founded 1922, part of Kansas State Board of Education
- **Small-town** 19-acre campus
- **Endowment** $3.0 million
- **Coed**

Undergraduates 2,386 full-time, 2,293 part-time. Students come from 16 states and territories, 12 other countries, 6% are from out of state, 8% African American, 5% Asian American or Pacific Islander, 4% Hispanic American, 0.9% Native American, 0.9% international, 7% live on campus.

Faculty *Student/faculty ratio:* 31:1.

Academics *Calendar:* semesters. *Degree:* certificates, diplomas, and associate. *Special study options:* academic remediation for entering students, accelerated degree program, adult/continuing education programs, advanced placement credit, cooperative education, distance learning, external degree program, independent study, part-time degree program, student-designed majors, summer session for credit.

Student Life *Campus security:* student patrols, late-night transport/escort service, residence hall entrances are locked at night.

Athletics Member NJCAA.

Standardized Tests *Recommended:* ACT (for admission).

Costs (2006–07) *Tuition:* area resident $1290 full-time, $43 per credit hour part-time; state resident $1440 full-time, $48 per credit hour part-time; nonresident $3000 full-time, $100 per credit hour part-time. *Required fees:* $570 full-time, $19 per credit hour part-time. *Room and board:* $3530.

Financial Aid Of all full-time matriculated undergraduates, 50 Federal Work-Study jobs (averaging $1500). 75 state and other part-time jobs (averaging $2000).

Applying *Options:* early admission, deferred entrance. *Required:* high school transcript.

Freshmen Application Contact Ms. Sue Saia, Associate Dean of Admissions, Cowley County Community College and Area Vocational–Technical School, 125 South Second, PO Box 1147, Arkansas City, KS 67005-1147. *Phone:* 620-441-5245. *Toll-free phone:* 800-593-CCCC. *Fax:* 620-441-5264. *E-mail:* admissions@cowley.cc.ks.us.

DODGE CITY COMMUNITY COLLEGE
Dodge City, Kansas www.dccc.cc.ks.us/
- **State and locally supported** 2-year, founded 1935, part of Kansas State Board of Education
- **Small-town** 143-acre campus
- **Coed,** 1,766 undergraduate students, 100% full-time, 58% women, 42% men

Undergraduates 1,766 full-time. Students come from 20 states and territories, 6% African American, 2% Asian American or Pacific Islander, 24% Hispanic American, 2% Native American, 20% live on campus.

Faculty *Total:* 163, 34% full-time. *Student/faculty ratio:* 18:1.

Majors Accounting; administrative assistant and secretarial science; agricultural business and management; agricultural economics; agricultural mechanization; agronomy and crop science; animal sciences; art; athletic training; automobile/automotive mechanics technology; behavioral sciences; biological and physical sciences; biology/biological sciences; broadcast journalism; business administration and management; chemistry; child development; clinical laboratory science/medical technology; communications technology; computer programming; computer science; construction engineering technology; cosmetology; criminal justice/law enforcement administration; data processing and data processing technology; dramatic/theater arts; education; electrical, electronic and communications engineering technology; elementary education; engineering; engineering technology; English; equestrian studies; farm and ranch management; finance; fire science; forestry; health information/medical records administration; history; humanities; hydrology and water resources science; industrial arts; industrial technology; information science/studies; journalism; legal administrative assistant/secretary; liberal arts and sciences/liberal studies; marketing/marketing management; mass communication/media; mathematics; medical administrative assistant and medical secretary; music; music teacher education; nursing (licensed practical/vocational nurse training); nursing (registered nurse training); physical education teaching and coaching; physical sciences; physical therapy; physics; political science and government; pre-

Dodge City Community College (continued)

engineering; pre-pharmacy studies; psychology; radio and television; real estate; respiratory care therapy; social sciences; social work; speech and rhetoric; welding technology; wildlife biology.

Academics *Calendar:* semesters. *Degree:* certificates and associate. *Special study options:* academic remediation for entering students, adult/continuing education programs, advanced placement credit, cooperative education, English as a second language, external degree program, internships, part-time degree program, student-designed majors, summer session for credit.

Library Learning Resource Center with 30,000 titles, 225 serial subscriptions.

Student Life *Housing Options:* coed. Campus housing is university owned. *Activities and Organizations:* drama/theater group, student-run newspaper, radio station, choral group. *Student services:* health clinic, personal/psychological counseling.

Athletics Member NJCAA. *Intercollegiate sports:* baseball M(s), basketball M(s)/W(s), cross-country running M(s)/W(s), equestrian sports M/W, football M(s), golf M(s), softball W(s), volleyball W(s). *Intramural sports:* basketball M/W, bowling M/W, football M, golf M, racquetball M/W, volleyball M/W, weight lifting M/W.

Costs (2006–07) *Tuition:* state resident $1120 full-time, $35 per credit hour part-time; nonresident $1344 full-time, $42 per credit hour part-time. *Required fees:* $806 full-time, $23 per credit hour part-time, $35 per term part-time. *Room and board:* $4060.

Applying *Options:* early admission, deferred entrance. *Required:* high school transcript. *Application deadlines:* rolling (freshmen), rolling (transfers). *Notification:* continuous (freshmen), continuous (transfers).

Director of Admissions Mrs. Tammy Tabor, Director of Admissions, Placement, Testing and Student Services Marketing, Dodge City Community College, 2501 North 14th Street, Dodge City, KS 67801-2399. *Phone:* 620-225-1321. *Toll-free phone:* 800-742-9519. *E-mail:* admin@dc3.edu.

DONNELLY COLLEGE

Kansas City, Kansas   www.donnelly.edu/

Freshmen Application Contact Mr. Kevin Kelley, Vice President of Enrollment Management, Donnelly College, 608 North 18th Street, Kansas City, KS 66102. *Phone:* 913-621-8769. *Fax:* 913-621-8719. *E-mail:* admissions@donnelly.edu.

FLINT HILLS TECHNICAL COLLEGE

Emporia, Kansas   www.fhtc.net/

- **State-supported** 2-year, founded 1963
- **Coed,** 424 undergraduate students

Majors Administrative assistant and secretarial science; automobile/automotive mechanics technology; building/property maintenance and management; carpentry; commercial and advertising art; computer programming; computer systems networking and telecommunications; dental assisting; drafting/design technology; emergency medical technology (EMT paramedic); foodservice systems administration; graphic and printing equipment operation/production; manufacturing technology; nuclear engineering technology; nursing (licensed practical/vocational nurse training).

Academics *Calendar:* semesters. *Degree:* associate.

Costs (2006–07) *Tuition:* state resident $2888 full-time.

Freshmen Application Contact Admissions Office, Flint Hills Technical College, 3301 West 18th Avenue, Emporia, KS 66801. *Toll-free phone:* 800-711-6947.

FORT SCOTT COMMUNITY COLLEGE

Fort Scott, Kansas   www.fortscott.edu/

Director of Admissions Mrs. Mert Barrows, Director of Admissions, Fort Scott Community College, 2108 South Horton, Fort Scott, KS 66701. *Phone:* 620-223-2700 Ext. 353. *Toll-free phone:* 800-874-3722.

GARDEN CITY COMMUNITY COLLEGE

Garden City, Kansas   www.gcccks.edu/

Freshmen Application Contact Office of Admissions, Garden City Community College, 801 Campus Drive, Garden City, KS 67846. *Phone:* 620-276-9531. *Fax:* 620-276-9650. *E-mail:* admissions@gcccks.edu.

HESSTON COLLEGE

Hesston, Kansas   www.hesston.edu/

- **Independent Mennonite** 2-year, founded 1909
- **Small-town** 50-acre campus with easy access to Wichita
- **Coed,** 462 undergraduate students, 87% full-time, 55% women, 45% men

Undergraduates 401 full-time, 61 part-time. Students come from 29 states and territories, 14 other countries, 53% are from out of state, 6% African American, 1% Asian American or Pacific Islander, 2% Hispanic American, 1% Native American, 9% international, 9% transferred in, 74% live on campus. *Retention:* 71% of 2003 full-time freshmen returned.

Freshmen *Admission:* 579 applied, 579 admitted, 172 enrolled. *Average high school GPA:* 3.2.

Faculty *Total:* 44, 43% full-time, 18% with terminal degrees. *Student/faculty ratio:* 11:1.

Majors Aeronautics/aviation/aerospace science and technology; biblical studies; business administration and management; computer/information technology services administration related; kindergarten/preschool education; liberal arts and sciences/liberal studies; nursing (registered nurse training); pastoral studies/counseling.

Academics *Calendar:* semesters. *Degree:* associate. *Special study options:* academic remediation for entering students, advanced placement credit, cooperative education, double majors, English as a second language, independent study, internships, part-time degree program, services for LD students, summer session for credit.

Library Mary Miller Library with 35,000 titles, 234 serial subscriptions, 2,670 audiovisual materials, an OPAC, a Web page.

Student Life *Housing:* on-campus residence required through sophomore year. *Options:* men-only, women-only. Campus housing is university owned. Freshman campus housing is guaranteed. *Activities and Organizations:* drama/theater group, student-run newspaper, choral group. *Campus security:* 24-hour emergency response devices, controlled dormitory access. *Student services:* personal/psychological counseling.

Athletics Member NJCAA. *Intercollegiate sports:* baseball M(s), basketball M(s)/W(s), soccer M(s), softball W(s), tennis M(s)/W(s), volleyball W(s). *Intramural sports:* basketball M/W, golf M(c)/W(c), soccer M/W, softball W, tennis M/W, volleyball M/W.

Standardized Tests *Required:* SAT or ACT (for admission).

Costs (2007–08) *Comprehensive fee:* $23,600 includes full-time tuition ($17,140), mandatory fees ($280), and room and board ($6180). Part-time tuition: $714 per hour. *Required fees:* $70 per term part-time.

Financial Aid Of all full-time matriculated undergraduates, 120 Federal Work-Study jobs (averaging $800).

Applying *Options:* electronic application, early admission, deferred entrance. *Application fee:* $15. *Required:* high school transcript, 2 letters of recommendation. *Required for some:* interview. *Application deadlines:* rolling (freshmen), rolling (transfers).

Freshmen Application Contact Joel Kauffman, Vice President for Admissions, Hesston College, Box 3000, Hesston, KS 67062. *Phone:* 620-327-8222. *Toll-free phone:* 800-995-2757. *Fax:* 620-327-8300. *E-mail:* admissions@hesston.edu.

HIGHLAND COMMUNITY COLLEGE

Highland, Kansas   www.highlandcc.edu/

Director of Admissions Ms. Cheryl Rasmussen, Vice President of Student Services, Highland Community College, 606 West Main Street, Highland, KS 66035-4165. *Phone:* 785-442-6020. *Fax:* 785-442-6106.

HUTCHINSON COMMUNITY COLLEGE AND AREA VOCATIONAL SCHOOL

Hutchinson, Kansas www.hutchcc.edu/

- **State and locally supported** 2-year, founded 1928, part of Kansas State Board of Education
- **Small-town** 47-acre campus
- **Endowment** $3.9 million
- **Coed,** 4,790 undergraduate students, 44% full-time, 57% women, 43% men

Undergraduates 2,116 full-time, 2,674 part-time. Students come from 41 states and territories, 12 other countries, 7% are from out of state, 6% African American, 1% Asian American or Pacific Islander, 5% Hispanic American, 1% Native American, 0.5% international, 6% transferred in, 11% live on campus. *Retention:* 59% of 2003 full-time freshmen returned.

Freshmen *Admission:* 3,220 applied, 3,220 admitted, 1,034 enrolled. *Average high school GPA:* 2.85. *Test scores:* ACT scores over 18: 76%; ACT scores over 24: 20%; ACT scores over 30: 1%.

Faculty *Total:* 332, 34% full-time, 6% with terminal degrees. *Student/faculty ratio:* 16:1.

Majors Administrative assistant and secretarial science; agricultural mechanization; agriculture; autobody/collision and repair technology; automobile/automotive mechanics technology; biology/biological sciences; business and personal/financial services marketing; business/commerce; carpentry; child care and support services management; communication/speech communication and rhetoric; communications technology; computer and information sciences; criminal justice/police science; drafting and design technology; education; educational/instructional media design; electrical/electronics equipment installation and repair; emergency medical technology (EMT paramedic); engineering; English; family and consumer sciences/human sciences; farm and ranch management; fire science; foreign languages and literatures; health information/medical records technology; legal assistant/paralegal; liberal arts and sciences/liberal studies; machine tool technology; management information systems; manufacturing technology; mathematics; medical radiologic technology; nursing (registered nurse training); physical sciences; psychology; retailing; social sciences; visual and performing arts; welding technology.

Academics *Calendar:* semesters. *Degree:* certificates and associate. *Special study options:* academic remediation for entering students, adult/continuing education programs, advanced placement credit, cooperative education, distance learning, double majors, English as a second language, honors programs, independent study, internships, part-time degree program, services for LD students, student-designed majors, summer session for credit. *ROTC:* Army (c).

Library John F. Kennedy Library plus 1 other with 42,500 titles, 245 serial subscriptions, 3,150 audiovisual materials, an OPAC, a Web page.

Student Life *Housing Options:* men-only, women-only. Campus housing is university owned. *Activities and Organizations:* drama/theater group, student-run newspaper, choral group, Student Government Association, Black Cultural Society, Hispanic-American Leadership Organization, Hutchinson Christian Fellowship, Campus Crusade for Christ. *Campus security:* 24-hour emergency response devices and patrols, student patrols, late-night transport/escort service, controlled dormitory access. *Student services:* health clinic, personal/psychological counseling.

Athletics Member NJCAA. *Intercollegiate sports:* baseball M(s), basketball M(s)/W(s), cheerleading M(s)/W(s), cross-country running M(s)/W(s), football M(s), golf M(s), soccer W(s), softball W(s), tennis M(s)/W(s), track and field M(s)/W(s), volleyball W(s). *Intramural sports:* badminton M/W, basketball M/W, bowling M/W, football M/W, racquetball M/W, soccer M/W, tennis M/W, track and field M/W, volleyball M/W.

Costs (2007–08) *Tuition:* state resident $1664 full-time, $52 per hour part-time; nonresident $2816 full-time, $88 per hour part-time. *Required fees:* $480 full-time, $15 per hour part-time. *Room and board:* $4680.

Applying *Options:* electronic application, early admission, deferred entrance. *Required for some:* interview. *Recommended:* high school transcript. *Application deadlines:* rolling (freshmen), rolling (transfers).

Freshmen Application Contact Mr. Corbin Strobel, Director of Admissions, Hutchinson Community College and Area Vocational School, 1300 North Plum, Hutchinson, KS 67501. *Phone:* 620-665-3536. *Toll-free phone:* 800-289-3501 Ext. 3536. *Fax:* 620-665-3301. *E-mail:* strobelc@hutchcc.edu.

INDEPENDENCE COMMUNITY COLLEGE

Independence, Kansas www.indycc.edu/

- **State-supported** 2-year, founded 1925, part of Kansas State Board of Education
- **Small-town** 68-acre campus
- **Coed**

Undergraduates 478 full-time, 428 part-time. Students come from 18 states and territories, 17 other countries, 9% are from out of state, 2% African American, 4% Asian American or Pacific Islander, 2% Hispanic American, 2% Native American, 0.9% international, 10% live on campus.

Faculty *Student/faculty ratio:* 17:1.

Academics *Calendar:* semesters. *Degree:* certificates and associate. *Special study options:* academic remediation for entering students, adult/continuing education programs, advanced placement credit, cooperative education, English as a second language, honors programs, internships, part-time degree program, summer session for credit.

Student Life *Campus security:* night patrol.

Athletics Member NJCAA.

Standardized Tests *Recommended:* SAT or ACT (for placement).

Costs (2006–07) *Tuition:* state resident $800 full-time, $25 per credit hour part-time; nonresident $2080 full-time, $65 per credit hour part-time. *Required fees:* $800 full-time. *Room and board:* $4100.

Financial Aid Of all full-time matriculated undergraduates, 85 Federal Work-Study jobs (averaging $900).

Applying *Options:* electronic application, early admission. *Required:* high school transcript.

Freshmen Application Contact Ms. Sally A. Ciufulescu, Director of Admissions, Independence Community College, PO Box 708, Independence, KS 67301. *Phone:* 620-332-5400. *Toll-free phone:* 800-842-6063. *Fax:* 620-331-0946. *E-mail:* sciufulescu@indycc.edu.

JOHNSON COUNTY COMMUNITY COLLEGE

Overland Park, Kansas www.johnco.cc.ks.us/

Director of Admissions Dr. Charles J. Carlsen, President, Johnson County Community College, 12345 College Park Boulevard, Overland Park, KS 66210. *Phone:* 913-469-8500 Ext. 3806.

KANSAS CITY KANSAS COMMUNITY COLLEGE

Kansas City, Kansas www.kckcc.edu/

- **State and locally supported** 2-year, founded 1923
- **Urban** 148-acre campus
- **Coed,** 5,547 undergraduate students, 35% full-time, 66% women, 34% men

Undergraduates 1,931 full-time, 3,616 part-time. Students come from 25 states and territories, 27 other countries, 5% are from out of state, 27% African American, 2% Asian American or Pacific Islander, 7% Hispanic American, 0.8% Native American, 2% international, 6% transferred in.

Freshmen *Admission:* 668 admitted, 668 enrolled.

Faculty *Total:* 407, 28% full-time. *Student/faculty ratio:* 14:1.

Majors Administrative assistant and secretarial science; business administration and management; child care and support services management; computer engineering technology; criminal justice/police science; data processing and data processing technology; drafting and design technology; emergency medical technology (EMT paramedic); fire science; funeral service and mortuary science; hazardous materials management and waste technology; international business/trade/commerce; legal assistant/paralegal; liberal arts and sciences and humanities related; liberal arts and sciences/liberal studies; nursing (registered nurse training); physical therapist assistant; recording arts technology; respiratory care therapy; respiratory therapy technician; substance abuse/addiction counseling; web page, digital/multimedia and information resources design.

Academics *Calendar:* semesters. *Degree:* certificates, diplomas, and associate. *Special study options:* academic remediation for entering students, adult/continuing education programs, advanced placement credit, cooperative education, distance learning, English as a second language, external degree program, freshman honors college, honors programs, independent study, internships, part-time degree program, services for LD students, summer session for credit.

Library Kansas City Kansas Community College Library with 65,000 titles, 200 serial subscriptions, 7,000 audiovisual materials, an OPAC, a Web page.

Student Life *Housing:* college housing not available. *Activities and Organizations:* drama/theater group, student-run newspaper, choral group, Student Senate, Phi Theta Kappa, Drama Club, The African American Student Union, Christian Student Union. *Campus security:* 24-hour emergency response devices and patrols, student patrols, late-night transport/escort service. *Student services:* health clinic, personal/psychological counseling, women's center.

Kansas City Kansas Community College *(continued)*

Athletics Member NJCAA. *Intercollegiate sports:* baseball M(s), basketball M(s)/W(s), cross-country running M(s)/W(s), golf M(s), soccer M(s), softball W(s), track and field M(s)/W(s), volleyball W(s).

Costs (2006–07) *Tuition:* state resident $1470 full-time, $49 per credit hour part-time; nonresident $4410 full-time, $147 per credit hour part-time. Full-time tuition and fees vary according to course load. Part-time tuition and fees vary according to course load. *Required fees:* $300 full-time, $10 per credit hour part-time. *Payment plan:* installment. *Waivers:* employees or children of employees.

Financial Aid Of all full-time matriculated undergraduates, 125 Federal Work-Study jobs (averaging $3000).

Applying *Options:* electronic application. *Required:* high school transcript. *Application deadlines:* rolling (freshmen), rolling (transfers). *Notification:* continuous (freshmen), continuous (transfers).

Freshmen Application Contact Ms. Theresa Holliday, Admissions Counselor, Kansas City Kansas Community College, 7250 State Avenue, Kansas City, KS 66112. *Phone:* 913-288-7601. *Fax:* 913-288-7648. *E-mail:* admiss@kckcc.edu.

LABETTE COMMUNITY COLLEGE

Parsons, Kansas www.labette.edu/

- **State and locally supported** 2-year, founded 1923, part of Kansas State Board of Education
- **Small-town** 4-acre campus
- **Coed,** 1,401 undergraduate students, 33% full-time, 65% women, 35% men

Undergraduates 466 full-time, 935 part-time. Students come from 7 states and territories, 4 other countries, 4% African American, 0.4% Asian American or Pacific Islander, 4% Hispanic American, 1% Native American, 0.6% international.

Freshmen *Admission:* 212 applied, 212 admitted, 201 enrolled.

Faculty *Total:* 208, 15% full-time.

Majors Accounting; administrative assistant and secretarial science; art; behavioral sciences; biology/biological sciences; business administration and management; chemistry; child development; commercial and advertising art; computer science; criminal justice/law enforcement administration; criminal justice/police science; data processing and data processing technology; drafting and design technology; education; elementary education; English; fire science; heating, air conditioning, ventilation and refrigeration maintenance technology; history; industrial radiologic technology; industrial technology; kindergarten/preschool education; legal administrative assistant/secretary; liberal arts and sciences/liberal studies; mathematics; medical administrative assistant and medical secretary; music; nursing (registered nurse training); physical education teaching and coaching; pre-engineering; respiratory care therapy; social sciences.

Academics *Calendar:* semesters. *Degree:* certificates and associate. *Special study options:* academic remediation for entering students, accelerated degree program, adult/continuing education programs, advanced placement credit, cooperative education, distance learning, double majors, independent study, internships, off-campus study, part-time degree program, services for LD students, summer session for credit. *ROTC:* Army (c).

Library Labette Community College Library with 26,000 titles, 235 serial subscriptions, 542 audiovisual materials, an OPAC, a Web page.

Student Life *Housing Options:* coed. *Activities and Organizations:* choral group, Adult Women Who Are Returning to Education (AWARE), Phi Beta Lambda. *Student services:* personal/psychological counseling.

Athletics Member NJCAA. *Intercollegiate sports:* baseball M(s), basketball M(s)/W(s), cheerleading W(s), softball W(s), tennis W(s), volleyball W(s), wrestling M(s).

Standardized Tests *Required:* ACT COMPASS (for placement). *Recommended:* ACT (for placement).

Costs (2006–07) *Tuition:* state resident $984 full-time, $41 per credit hour part-time; nonresident $2280 full-time, $95 per credit hour part-time. *Required fees:* $672 full-time, $28 per credit hour part-time. *Payment plan:* installment. *Waivers:* senior citizens and employees or children of employees.

Financial Aid Of all full-time matriculated undergraduates, 17 Federal Work-Study jobs (averaging $1172).

Applying *Options:* early admission. *Required for some:* letters of recommendation, interview. *Recommended:* high school transcript. *Application deadlines:* rolling (freshmen), rolling (transfers). *Notification:* continuous (freshmen), continuous (transfers).

Freshmen Application Contact Ms. Tammy Fuentez, Director of Admission, Labette Community College, 200 South 14th Street, Parsons, KS 67357. *Phone:* 620-421-6700. *Toll-free phone:* 888-522-3883. *Fax:* 620-421-0180.

MANHATTAN AREA TECHNICAL COLLEGE

Manhattan, Kansas www.matc.net/

- **State and locally supported** 2-year, founded 1965
- **Suburban** 19-acre campus
- **Coed**

Undergraduates 324 full-time, 77 part-time. 4% African American, 1% Asian American or Pacific Islander, 4% Hispanic American, 2% Native American, 37% transferred in.

Faculty *Student/faculty ratio:* 11:1.

Academics *Calendar:* semesters. *Degree:* certificates, diplomas, and associate.

Costs (2006–07) *Tuition:* state resident $2035 full-time, $55 per credit hour part-time. *Required fees:* $400 full-time, $10 per credit hour part-time.

Applying *Application fee:* $40. *Required for some:* high school transcript. *Recommended:* high school transcript.

Freshmen Application Contact Mr. Rick Smith, Coordinator of Admissions and Recruitment, Manhattan Area Technical College, 3136 Dickens Avenue, Manhattan, KS 66503-2499. *Phone:* 785-587-2800 Ext. 104. *Toll-free phone:* 800-352-7575. *Fax:* 913-587-2804.

NATIONAL AMERICAN UNIVERSITY

Overland Park, Kansas www.national.edu/

- **Independent** 2-year
- **Coed,** 156 undergraduate students

Majors Business administration, management and operations related; computer and information sciences related; information technology; legal assistant/paralegal.

Academics *Degree:* associate.

Costs (2006–07) *Tuition:* $13,322 full-time.

Applying *Application fee:* $25.

Freshmen Application Contact Admissions Office, National American University, 10310 Mastin, Overland Park, KS 66212.

NEOSHO COUNTY COMMUNITY COLLEGE

Chanute, Kansas www.neosho.edu/

- **State and locally supported** 2-year, founded 1936, part of Kansas State Board of Education
- **Small-town** 50-acre campus
- **Endowment** $370,000
- **Coed,** 1,826 undergraduate students, 34% full-time, 67% women, 33% men

Undergraduates 615 full-time, 1,211 part-time. Students come from 15 states and territories, 5% African American, 2% Asian American or Pacific Islander, 3% Hispanic American, 1% Native American, 5% live on campus.

Freshmen *Admission:* 573 applied, 573 admitted, 244 enrolled.

Faculty *Total:* 126, 32% full-time.

Majors Accounting; administrative assistant and secretarial science; athletic training; biological and physical sciences; business administration and management; business machine repair; carpentry; computer science; construction engineering technology; criminal justice/law enforcement administration; criminal justice/police science; electrical, electronic and communications engineering technology; finance; information science/studies; liberal arts and sciences/liberal studies; marketing/marketing management; materials science; nursing (licensed practical/vocational nurse training); nursing (registered nurse training); physical sciences; pre-engineering; teacher assistant/aide; trade and industrial teacher education; welding technology.

Academics *Calendar:* semesters. *Degree:* certificates, diplomas, and associate. *Special study options:* academic remediation for entering students, adult/continuing education programs, advanced placement credit, part-time degree program, services for LD students, student-designed majors, summer session for credit.

Library Chapman Library with 33,000 titles, 200 serial subscriptions.

Student Life *Housing:* on-campus residence required for freshman year. *Options:* coed. *Activities and Organizations:* drama/theater group, student-run newspaper, choral group, Business Club, Science Club, Student Nurses Association, Fellow-

ship of Christian Athletes, Nontraditional Student Organization. *Campus security:* controlled dormitory access. *Student services:* personal/psychological counseling.

Athletics Member NJCAA. *Intercollegiate sports:* baseball M(s), basketball M(s)/W(s), cross-country running M(s)/W(s), softball W(s), track and field M(s), volleyball W(s). *Intramural sports:* basketball M/W, cross-country running M/W, softball M/W, track and field M/W, volleyball M/W.

Standardized Tests *Required:* ACT (for placement).

Costs (2006–07) *Tuition:* state resident $640 full-time, $40 per credit hour part-time; nonresident $640 full-time, $40 per credit hour part-time. Full-time tuition and fees vary according to location. Part-time tuition and fees vary according to location. *Required fees:* $656 full-time, $41 per credit hour part-time. *Room and board:* Room and board charges vary according to housing facility. *Payment plan:* installment. *Waivers:* senior citizens and employees or children of employees.

Financial Aid Of all full-time matriculated undergraduates, 73 Federal Work-Study jobs (averaging $800).

Applying *Options:* early admission. *Required:* high school transcript. *Application deadlines:* 9/15 (freshmen), 9/15 (transfers). *Notification:* continuous (freshmen), continuous (transfers).

Freshmen Application Contact Ms. Lisa Last, Dean of Student Development, Neosho County Community College, 800 West 14th Street, Chanute, KS 66720-2699. *Phone:* 620-431-2820 Ext. 213. *Toll-free phone:* 800-729-6222. *Fax:* 620-431-0082. *E-mail:* llast@neosho.edu.

NORTH CENTRAL KANSAS TECHNICAL COLLEGE

Beloit, Kansas www.ncktc.edu

- **State-supported** 2-year, founded 1963
- **Coed,** 513 undergraduate students

Majors Administrative assistant and secretarial science; agricultural power machinery operation; automobile/automotive mechanics technology; communications systems installation and repair technology; diesel mechanics technology; electrical, electronic and communications engineering technology; electrician; nursing (registered nurse training).

Academics *Calendar:* semesters. *Degree:* associate.

Costs (2006–07) *Tuition:* area resident $2628 full-time; state resident $2830 per degree program part-time. Full-time tuition and fees vary according to program. *Required fees:* $325 full-time. *Room and board:* $3847. *Payment plan:* installment.

Applying *Application fee:* $50.

Freshmen Application Contact Ms. Judy Heidrick, Director of Admissions, North Central Kansas Technical College, PO Box 507, 3033 US Highway 24, Beloit, KS 67420. *Toll-free phone:* 800-658-4655. *E-mail:* jheidrick@ncktc.tec.ks.us.

NORTHEAST KANSAS TECHNICAL COLLEGE

Atchison, Kansas www.nektc.net/

Admissions Office Contact Northeast Kansas Technical College, 1501 West Riley Street, Atchison, KS 66002. *Toll-free phone:* 800-567-4890.

NORTHWEST KANSASTECHNICAL COLLEGE

Goodland, Kansas www.nwktc.org/

- **State-supported** 2-year, founded 1964
- **Coed,** 281 undergraduate students

Majors Administrative assistant and secretarial science; autobody/collision and repair technology; automobile/automotive mechanics technology; carpentry; civil engineering technology; communications systems installation and repair technology; cosmetology; desktop publishing and digital imaging design; diesel mechanics technology; electrical/electronics equipment installation and repair; electrician; heating, air conditioning, ventilation and refrigeration maintenance technology; industrial electronics technology; medical/clinical assistant; welding technology.

Academics *Calendar:* semesters. *Degree:* associate.

Costs (2006–07) *Tuition:* state resident $4859 per degree program part-time.

Applying *Application fee:* $50.

Admissions Office Contact Northwest KansasTechnical College, PO Box 668, 1209 Harrison Street, Goodland, KS 67735. *Toll-free phone:* 800-316-4127.

PRATT COMMUNITY COLLEGE

Pratt, Kansas www.prattcc.edu/

- **State and locally supported** 2-year, founded 1938, part of Kansas State Board of Education
- **Rural** 80-acre campus with easy access to Wichita
- **Coed**

Undergraduates 625 full-time, 921 part-time. Students come from 21 states and territories, 16% are from out of state, 5% African American, 0.8% Asian American or Pacific Islander, 5% Hispanic American, 0.8% Native American, 2% international, 22% live on campus. *Retention:* 51% of 2003 full-time freshmen returned.

Faculty *Student/faculty ratio:* 14:1.

Academics *Calendar:* semesters. *Degree:* certificates and associate. *Special study options:* academic remediation for entering students, adult/continuing education programs, advanced placement credit, cooperative education, distance learning, internships, part-time degree program, summer session for credit.

Student Life *Campus security:* 24-hour patrols, late-night transport/escort service, controlled dormitory access.

Athletics Member NJCAA.

Standardized Tests *Required for some:* ASSET.

Costs (2006–07) *Tuition:* state resident $1344 full-time, $42 per credit hour part-time; nonresident $1344 full-time, $42 per credit hour part-time. *Required fees:* $928 full-time, $29 per credit hour part-time. *Room and board:* $3768.

Financial Aid Of all full-time matriculated undergraduates, 77 Federal Work-Study jobs (averaging $800). 13 state and other part-time jobs (averaging $800). *Financial aid deadline:* 8/1.

Applying *Options:* early admission. *Required:* high school transcript.

Freshmen Application Contact Ms. Yolanda Mendoza, Student Services, Pratt Community College, 348 Northeast State Road 61, Pratt, KS 67124. *Phone:* 620-450-2217. *Toll-free phone:* 800-794-3091. *Fax:* 620-672-5288. *E-mail:* yolandam@prattcc.edu.

SEWARD COUNTY COMMUNITY COLLEGE

Liberal, Kansas www.sccc.edu/

Director of Admissions Dr. Gerald Harris, Dean of Student Services, Seward County Community College, PO Box 1137, Liberal, KS 67905-1137. *Phone:* 620-624-1951 Ext. 617. *Toll-free phone:* 800-373-9951 Ext. 710.

WICHITA AREA TECHNICAL COLLEGE

Wichita, Kansas www.wichitatech.com/

- **District-supported** 2-year, founded 1963
- **Urban** campus
- **Coed,** 693 undergraduate students, 46% full-time, 50% women, 50% men

Undergraduates 317 full-time, 376 part-time. Students come from 1 other state, 14% African American, 4% Asian American or Pacific Islander, 9% Hispanic American, 2% Native American, 0.2% international, 13% transferred in.

Freshmen *Admission:* 208 enrolled.

Faculty *Total:* 58, 76% full-time. *Student/faculty ratio:* 12:1.

Majors Automobile/automotive mechanics technology; clinical/medical laboratory technology; interior design; mechanical engineering/mechanical technology.

Academics *Calendar:* semesters. *Degree:* certificates, diplomas, and associate. *Special study options:* academic remediation for entering students, internships, part-time degree program.

Library Library and Learning Resource Center plus 1 other with 3,696 titles, 57 serial subscriptions, 1,611 audiovisual materials, an OPAC, a Web page.

Student Life *Housing:* college housing not available. *Campus security:* 24-hour emergency response devices.

Wichita Area Technical College (continued)

Standardized Tests *Required for some:* WorkKeys, COMPASS & TEAS.

Costs (2006–07) *Tuition:* area resident $2970 full-time, $99 per credit hour part-time; nonresident $11,730 full-time, $345 per credit part-time. *Required fees:* $216 full-time, $80 per term part-time.

Applying *Application fee:* $16. *Required for some:* high school transcript. *Application deadlines:* rolling (freshmen), rolling (transfers).

Freshmen Application Contact Ms. Jessica Ross, Dean, Enrollment Management, Wichita Area Technical College, 301 South Grove Street, Wichita, KS 67211. *Phone:* 316-677-9400. *Fax:* 316-677-9555. *E-mail:* info@watc.edu.

KENTUCKY

ASHLAND COMMUNITY AND TECHNICAL COLLEGE

Ashland, Kentucky www.ashland.kctcs.edu/

- **State-supported** 2-year, founded 1937, part of Kentucky Community and Technical College System
- **Small-town** 47-acre campus
- **Endowment** $870,926
- **Coed,** 4,120 undergraduate students

Undergraduates Students come from 6 states and territories, 10% are from out of state. *Retention:* 44% of 2003 full-time freshmen returned.

Freshmen *Admission:* 404 applied, 404 admitted. *Test scores:* ACT scores over 18: 53%; ACT scores over 24: 7%.

Faculty *Total:* 97. *Student/faculty ratio:* 19:1.

Majors Accounting; administrative assistant and secretarial science; business administration and management; criminal justice/police science; engineering technology; information science/studies; liberal arts and sciences/liberal studies; management information systems; nursing (registered nurse training); physical therapist assistant; real estate; respiratory care therapy.

Academics *Calendar:* semesters. *Degree:* certificates, diplomas, and associate. *Special study options:* academic remediation for entering students, adult/continuing education programs, advanced placement credit, cooperative education, distance learning, honors programs, internships, off-campus study, part-time degree program, services for LD students, summer session for credit.

Library Joseph and Sylvia Mansbach Memorial Library with 41,379 titles, 391 serial subscriptions, an OPAC.

Student Life *Housing:* college housing not available. *Activities and Organizations:* drama/theater group, student-run newspaper, choral group, Phi Theta Kappa, Phi Beta Lambda, Kentucky Association of Nursing Students, Baptist Student Union/Students for Christ, Circle K. *Campus security:* 24-hour emergency response devices and patrols, late-night transport/escort service, electronic surveillance of bookstore and business office. *Student services:* personal/psychological counseling.

Athletics *Intramural sports:* fencing M/W, tennis M/W.

Standardized Tests *Required:* ACT COMPASS (for placement). *Recommended:* ACT (for placement).

Costs (2007–08) *Tuition:* state resident $3450 full-time, $115 per credit hour part-time; nonresident $10,350 full-time, $345 per credit hour part-time.

Financial Aid Of all full-time matriculated undergraduates, 12 Federal Work-Study jobs (averaging $2500). 1 state and other part-time job (averaging $1000).

Applying *Options:* early admission, deferred entrance. *Required:* high school transcript. *Application deadlines:* 8/20 (freshmen), 8/20 (transfers).

Freshmen Application Contact Mrs. Willie G. McCullough, Dean of Student Affairs, Ashland Community and Technical College, 1400 College Drive, Ashland, KY 41101. *Phone:* 660-326-2114. *Toll-free phone:* 800-370-7191. *E-mail:* willie.mccullough@kctcs.net.

BECKFIELD COLLEGE

Florence, Kentucky www.beckfield.edu/

Freshmen Application Contact Mrs. Leah Boerger, Director of Admissions, Beckfield College, 16 Spiral Drive, Florence, KY 41042. *Phone:* 859-371-9393. *E-mail:* lboerger@beckfield.edu.

BIG SANDY COMMUNITY AND TECHNICAL COLLEGE

Prestonsburg, Kentucky www.bigsandy.kctcs.edu/

Director of Admissions Mr. Jim Glover, Director of Admissions, Big Sandy Community and Technical College, One Bert T. Combs Drive, Prestonsburg, KY 41653-1815. *Phone:* 606-886-3863 Ext. 220. *Toll-free phone:* 888-641-4132. *E-mail:* ccsprerg@kctcs.edu.

BOWLING GREEN TECHNICAL COLLEGE

Bowling Green, Kentucky www.bowlinggreen.kctcs.edu/

Admissions Office Contact Bowling Green Technical College, 1845 Loop Drive, Bowling Green, KY 42101.

BROWN MACKIE COLLEGE—HOPKINSVILLE

Hopkinsville, Kentucky www.brownmackie.edu/locations.asp?locid=17

- **Proprietary** 2-year
- **Small-town** campus
- **Coed, primarily women,** 150 undergraduate students

Undergraduates 25% African American, 0.7% Asian American or Pacific Islander, 3% Hispanic American, 0.7% Native American.

Faculty *Total:* 11, 27% full-time. *Student/faculty ratio:* 12:1.

Majors Accounting technology and bookkeeping; business administration and management; computer programming; computer programming (specific applications); criminal justice/law enforcement administration; electrical, electronic and communications engineering technology; medical/clinical assistant; medical office management; paralegal/legal assistant.

Academics *Calendar:* quarters. *Degree:* diplomas and associate.

Costs (2006–07) *Tuition:* $8592 full-time, $179 per credit hour part-time.

Financial Aid Of all full-time matriculated undergraduates, 12 Federal Work-Study jobs.

Applying *Required:* high school transcript. *Recommended:* interview. *Application deadlines:* rolling (freshmen), rolling (transfers). *Notification:* continuous (freshmen), continuous (transfers).

Freshmen Application Contact Director of Admissions, Brown Mackie College–Hopkinsville, 4001 Fort Campbell Boulevard, Hopkinsville, KY 42240-4962. *Phone:* 270-886-1302. *Toll-free phone:* 800-359-4753. *Fax:* 270-886-3544. *E-mail:* bmchoadm@brownmackie.edu.

▶See page 506 for the College Close-Up.

BROWN MACKIE COLLEGE—LOUISVILLE

Louisville, Kentucky www.brownmackie.edu/locations.asp?locid=18

- **Proprietary** 2-year, founded 1972
- **Suburban** campus
- **Coed,** 300 undergraduate students

Undergraduates Students come from 3 states and territories, 1 other country.

Faculty *Total:* 26, 23% full-time. *Student/faculty ratio:* 11:1.

Majors Accounting technology and bookkeeping; business administration and management; computer software and media applications related; computer systems networking and telecommunications; criminal justice/law enforcement administration; electrical, electronic and communications engineering technology; gerontology; graphic design; health/health care administration; medical/clinical assistant; paralegal/legal assistant; pharmacy technician.

Academics *Calendar:* quarters. *Degree:* associate. *Special study options:* academic remediation for entering students.

Library Main Library plus 1 other with 1,210 titles, 23 serial subscriptions.

Student Life *Housing:* college housing not available. *Campus security:* 24-hour emergency response devices, evening security guards, electronically operated building access. *Student services:* personal/psychological counseling.

Costs (2006–07) *Tuition:* $8592 full-time, $179 per credit part-time. *Required fees:* $480 full-time.

Applying *Options:* early admission, deferred entrance. *Required:* high school transcript, interview. *Application deadlines:* rolling (freshmen), rolling (transfers). *Notification:* continuous (freshmen), continuous (transfers).

Freshmen Application Contact Director of Admissions, Brown Mackie College–Louisville, 300 Highrise Drive, Louisville, KY 40213. *Phone:* 502-968-7191. *Toll-free phone:* 800-999-7387. *Fax:* 502-968-9956. *E-mail:* mdonahue@brownmackie.edu.

▶See page 510 for the College Close-Up.

BROWN MACKIE COLLEGE–NORTHERN KENTUCKY

Fort Mitchell, Kentucky   www.brownmackie.edu

- **Proprietary** 2-year, founded 1927, part of American Education Centers, Inc
- **Suburban** 5-acre campus with easy access to Cincinnati
- **Coed,** 500 undergraduate students

Undergraduates Students come from 3 states and territories, 12% are from out of state, 8% African American, 0.9% Asian American or Pacific Islander, 1% Hispanic American. *Retention:* 81% of 2003 full-time freshmen returned.

Faculty *Total:* 29, 31% full-time. *Student/faculty ratio:* 17:1.

Majors Accounting technology and bookkeeping; business administration and management; CAD/CADD drafting/design technology; computer programming (specific applications); computer software technology; computer systems networking and telecommunications; criminal justice/law enforcement administration; health/health care administration; medical/clinical assistant; paralegal/legal assistant; pharmacy technician.

Academics *Calendar:* quarters. *Degree:* certificates, diplomas, and associate. *Special study options:* academic remediation for entering students, adult/continuing education programs, internships, part-time degree program, summer session for credit.

Library 1,500 titles, 50 serial subscriptions.

Student Life *Housing:* college housing not available. *Campus security:* 24-hour emergency response devices, late-night transport/escort service. *Student services:* personal/psychological counseling.

Costs (2006–07) *Tuition:* $9072 full-time, $189 per credit hour part-time.

Applying *Required:* interview. *Application deadlines:* rolling (freshmen), rolling (transfers). *Notification:* continuous (freshmen), continuous (transfers).

Freshmen Application Contact Director of Admissions, Brown Mackie College–Northern Kentucky, 309 Buttermilk Pike, Fort Mitchell, KY 41017. *Phone:* 859-341-5627. *Toll-free phone:* 800-888-1445. *Fax:* 859-341-6483. *E-mail:* jdellefield@brownmackie.edu.

▶See page 522 for the College Close-Up.

DAYMAR COLLEGE

Louisville, Kentucky   www.daymarcollege.edu/

Director of Admissions Mr. Patrick Carney, Director of Admissions, Daymar College, 4400 Breckenridge Lane, Suite 415, Louisville, KY 40218.

DAYMAR COLLEGE

Owensboro, Kentucky   www.daymarcollege.edu/

Freshmen Application Contact Ms. Vickie McDougal, Director of Admissions, Daymar College, 3361 Buckland Square, PO Box 22150, Owensboro, KY 42303. *Phone:* 270-926-4040. *Toll-free phone:* 800-960-4090. *Fax:* 270-685-4090. *E-mail:* info@daymarcollege.edu.

DRAUGHONS JUNIOR COLLEGE

Bowling Green, Kentucky   www.draughons.edu/

- **Proprietary** 2-year, founded 1989, administratively affiliated with Draughons Junior College, Inc
- **Suburban** campus with easy access to Nashville
- **Coed, primarily women,** 510 undergraduate students, 56% full-time, 84% women, 16% men

Undergraduates 285 full-time, 225 part-time. Students come from 2 states and territories, 1% are from out of state, 9% African American, 1% Hispanic American, 9% transferred in. *Retention:* 73% of 2003 full-time freshmen returned.

Freshmen *Admission:* 158 applied, 158 admitted, 158 enrolled. *Average high school GPA:* 3.0.

Faculty *Total:* 24, 42% full-time, 4% with terminal degrees. *Student/faculty ratio:* 13:1.

Majors Accounting; administrative assistant and secretarial science; business administration and management; health information/medical records administration; information science/studies; information technology; legal administrative assistant/secretary; medical/clinical assistant.

Academics *Calendar:* semesters. *Degree:* diplomas and associate. *Special study options:* adult/continuing education programs, part-time degree program.

Library Draughons Junior College Library with 5,000 titles, 30 serial subscriptions, a Web page.

Student Life *Housing:* college housing not available. *Activities and Organizations:* student-run newspaper, Student Council. *Campus security:* 24-hour emergency response devices. *Student services:* personal/psychological counseling.

Costs (2007–08) *Tuition:* $215 per quarter hour part-time.

Financial Aid Of all full-time matriculated undergraduates, 2 Federal Work-Study jobs (averaging $4950).

Applying *Required:* high school transcript.

Freshmen Application Contact Mrs. Traci Henderson, Admissions Director, Draughons Junior College, 2421 Fitzgerald Industrial Drive, Bowling Green, KY 42101. *Phone:* 270-843-6750.

ELIZABETHTOWN COMMUNITY AND TECHNICAL COLLEGE

Elizabethtown, Kentucky   www.elizabethtown.kctcs.edu/

Director of Admissions Dr. Dale Buckles, Dean of Student Affairs, Elizabethtown Community and Technical College, 600 College Street Road, Elizabethtown, KY 42701. *Phone:* 270-769-2371 Ext. 68431. *Toll-free phone:* 877-246-2322.

ELIZABETHTOWN TECHNICAL COLLEGE

Elizabethtown, Kentucky   www.elizabethtown.kctcs.edu/

- **State-supported** 2-year, founded 1966
- **Small-town** 80-acre campus
- **Coed,** 4,980 undergraduate students, 47% full-time, 61% women, 39% men

Undergraduates 2,317 full-time, 2,663 part-time. Students come from 9 states and territories, 3 other countries, 1% are from out of state, 8% African American, 2% Asian American or Pacific Islander, 2% Hispanic American, 0.6% Native American, 0.1% international, 4% transferred in.

Freshmen *Admission:* 957 enrolled.

Faculty *Total:* 284, 43% full-time. *Student/faculty ratio:* 19:1.

Majors Automobile/automotive mechanics technology; business administration and management; child care provider; computer and information sciences; criminal justice/law enforcement administration; data processing and data processing technology; diesel mechanics technology; electrician; engineering technology; executive assistant/executive secretary; industrial electronics technology; industrial mechanics and maintenance technology; interdisciplinary studies; liberal arts and sciences/liberal studies; medical administrative assistant; medical radiologic technology; nursing (registered nurse training); quality control and safety technologies related; social work; teacher assistant/aide; welding technology.

Academics *Calendar:* semesters. *Degree:* certificates and associate. *Special study options:* academic remediation for entering students, advanced placement credit, cooperative education, distance learning, internships, off-campus study, part-time degree program, services for LD students, summer session for credit.

Library ECTC Media Center.

Student Life *Housing:* college housing not available. *Campus security:* late-night transport/escort service.

Standardized Tests *Required for some:* COMPASS. *Recommended:* ACT (for admission).

Costs (2007–08) *Tuition:* area resident $2760 full-time, $115 per credit hour part-time; nonresident $8280 full-time, $345 per credit hour part-time.

Applying *Required for some:* high school transcript, letters of recommendation. *Application deadlines:* rolling (freshmen), rolling (transfers). *Notification:* continuous (freshmen), continuous (transfers).

Elizabethtown Technical College (continued)

Freshmen Application Contact Admissions Office, Elizabethtown Technical College, 600 College Street Road, Elizabethtown, KY 42701. *Phone:* 270-406-8800. *Toll-free phone:* 877-246-2322.

GATEWAY COMMUNITY AND TECHNICAL COLLEGE

Covington, Kentucky   www.gateway.kctcs.edu/

Director of Admissions Mr. Paul Brinkman, Dean of Student Affairs, Gateway Community and Technical College, 1025 Amsterdam Road, Covington, KY 41011.

HAZARD COMMUNITY AND TECHNICAL COLLEGE

Hazard, Kentucky   www.hazard.kctcs.edu/

Freshmen Application Contact Mr. Steve Jones, Director of Admissions, Hazard Community and Technical College, 1 Community College Drive, Hazard, KY 41701-2403. *Phone:* 606-436-5721 Ext. 8076. *Toll-free phone:* 800-246-7521.

HENDERSON COMMUNITY COLLEGE

Henderson, Kentucky   www.henderson.kctcs.edu/

Freshmen Application Contact Ms. Teresa Hamiton, Admissions Counselor, Henderson Community College, 2660 South Green Street, Henderson, KY 42420-4623. *Phone:* 270-827-1867 Ext. 354.

HOPKINSVILLE COMMUNITY COLLEGE

Hopkinsville, Kentucky   www.hopcc.kctcs.edu/

- **State-supported** 2-year, founded 1965, part of Kentucky Community and Technical College System (KCTCS)
- **Small-town** 69-acre campus with easy access to Nashville
- **Endowment** $1.6 million
- **Coed,** 3,353 undergraduate students, 37% full-time, 67% women, 33% men

Undergraduates 1,240 full-time, 2,113 part-time. Students come from 11 states and territories, 2 other countries, 31% are from out of state, 22% African American, 1% Asian American or Pacific Islander, 4% Hispanic American, 0.6% Native American, 6% transferred in. *Retention:* 38% of 2003 full-time freshmen returned.

Freshmen *Admission:* 445 enrolled. *Test scores:* ACT scores over 18: 53%; ACT scores over 24: 9%; ACT scores over 30: 1%.

Faculty *Total:* 156, 42% full-time. *Student/faculty ratio:* 21:1.

Majors Administrative assistant and secretarial science; animal/livestock husbandry and production; business administration and management; child care and support services management; criminal justice/police science; early childhood education; electrical, electronic and communications engineering technology; finance; human services; industrial technology; kindergarten/preschool education; liberal arts and sciences/liberal studies; management information systems; manufacturing technology; mental health/rehabilitation; nursing (licensed practical/vocational nurse training); nursing (registered nurse training).

Academics *Calendar:* semesters. *Degree:* certificates, diplomas, and associate. *Special study options:* academic remediation for entering students, advanced placement credit, cooperative education, distance learning, honors programs, independent study, part-time degree program, services for LD students, summer session for credit.

Library Learning Resource Center with an OPAC, a Web page.

Student Life *Housing:* college housing not available. *Activities and Organizations:* student-run newspaper, television station, Baptist Student Union, Circle K, Minority Student Union, Donovan Scholars, Nursing Club. *Campus security:* 24-hour emergency response devices, late-night transport/escort service, security provided by trained security personnel during hours of normal operation.

Athletics *Intramural sports:* basketball M, football M, golf M, table tennis M/W, volleyball M/W.

Costs (2007–08) *Tuition:* state resident $3450 full-time, $115 per credit hour part-time; nonresident $4140 full-time, $138 per credit hour part-time.

Financial Aid Of all full-time matriculated undergraduates, 30 Federal Work-Study jobs (averaging $1500). *Financial aid deadline:* 6/30.

Applying *Options:* early admission, deferred entrance. *Recommended:* high school transcript. *Application deadlines:* rolling (freshmen), rolling (transfers). *Notification:* continuous (freshmen), continuous (transfers).

Freshmen Application Contact Ms. Ruth Ann Rettie, Hopkinsville Community College, North Drive, PO Box 2100, Hopkinsville, KY 42241-2100. *Phone:* 270-707-3811. *Fax:* 270-886-0237. *E-mail:* admit.record@stu.kctcs.edu.

ITT TECHNICAL INSTITUTE

Louisville, Kentucky   www.itt-tech.edu/

- **Proprietary** primarily 2-year, founded 1993, part of ITT Educational Services, Inc
- **Suburban** campus
- **Coed**

Majors Animation, interactive technology, video graphics and special effects; CAD/CADD drafting/design technology; computer and information systems security; computer engineering technology; computer software technology; criminal justice/law enforcement administration; electrical, electronic and communications engineering technology; medical laboratory technology; system, networking, and LAN/WAN management; web/multimedia management and webmaster; web page, digital/multimedia and information resources design.

Academics *Calendar:* quarters. *Degrees:* associate and bachelor's.

Library a Web page.

Student Life *Housing:* college housing not available.

Standardized Tests *Required:* Wonderlic aptitude test (for admission).

Costs (2006–07) *Tuition:* Contact school for program costs.

Applying *Options:* deferred entrance. *Application fee:* $100. *Required:* high school transcript, interview. *Recommended:* letters of recommendation. *Application deadlines:* rolling (freshmen), rolling (transfers). *Notification:* continuous (freshmen), continuous (transfers).

Freshmen Application Contact Mr. Michael Alcorn, Director of Recruitment, ITT Technical Institute, 10509 Timberwood Circle, Louisville, KY 40223. *Phone:* 502-327-7424. *Toll-free phone:* 888-790-7427.

JEFFERSON COMMUNITY AND TECHNICAL COLLEGE

Louisville, Kentucky   www.jctc.kctcs.edu/

- **State-supported** 2-year, founded 1968, part of Kentucky Community and Technical College System
- **Urban** 10-acre campus
- **Endowment** $1.4 million
- **Coed,** 14,710 undergraduate students, 32% full-time, 52% women, 48% men

Undergraduates 4,697 full-time, 10,013 part-time. Students come from 17 states and territories, 9% are from out of state, 19% African American, 2% Asian American or Pacific Islander, 2% Hispanic American, 0.4% Native American, 0.5% international, 13% transferred in.

Freshmen *Admission:* 1,856 enrolled.

Faculty *Total:* 652, 45% full-time. *Student/faculty ratio:* 19:1.

Majors Accounting; business administration and management; child development; commercial and advertising art; culinary arts; data processing and data processing technology; electrical, electronic and communications engineering technology; health information/medical records technology; liberal arts and sciences/liberal studies; mechanical engineering/mechanical technology; medical radiologic technology; nuclear medical technology; nursing (registered nurse training); physical therapy; real estate; respiratory care therapy; social work; welding technology.

Academics *Calendar:* semesters. *Degree:* certificates, diplomas, and associate. *Special study options:* academic remediation for entering students, adult/continuing education programs, advanced placement credit, cooperative education, distance learning, English as a second language, external degree program, honors programs, independent study, internships, off-campus study, part-time degree program, services for LD students, summer session for credit. *ROTC:* Army (c).

Library John T. Smith Learning Resource Center plus 3 others with 76,578 titles, 391 serial subscriptions, an OPAC, a Web page.

Student Life *Housing:* college housing not available. *Activities and Organizations:* drama/theater group, student-run newspaper. *Campus security:* 24-hour

emergency response devices and patrols, late-night transport/escort service. *Student services:* personal/psychological counseling.
Costs (2007–08) *Tuition:* state resident $3450 full-time, $115 per credit hour part-time; nonresident $10,350 full-time, $345 per credit hour part-time. *Required fees:* $75 full-time, $25 per term part-time.
Financial Aid Of all full-time matriculated undergraduates, 50 Federal Work-Study jobs (averaging $4000).
Applying *Options:* early admission. *Application deadlines:* rolling (freshmen), rolling (transfers). *Notification:* continuous (freshmen), continuous (transfers).
Freshmen Application Contact Ms. Melanie Vaughan-Cooke, Admissions Coordinator, Jefferson Community and Technical College, 109 East Broadway, Louisville, KY 40202. *Phone:* 502-213-4000. *Fax:* 502-213-2540.

LEXINGTON COMMUNITY COLLEGE
Lexington, Kentucky   www.uky.edu/lcc/

Freshmen Application Contact Mrs. Shelbie Hugle, Director of Admission Services, Lexington Community College, 200 Oswald Building, Cooper Drive, Lexington, KY 40506-0235. *Phone:* 859-246-6216. *Toll-free phone:* 866-744-4872 Ext. 5111. *E-mail:* shelbie.hugle@kctcs.edu.

LOUISVILLE TECHNICAL INSTITUTE
Louisville, Kentucky   www.louisvilletech.com/

Freshmen Application Contact Director of Admissions, Louisville Technical Institute, 3901 Atkinson Square Drive, Louisville, KY 40218. *Phone:* 502-456-6509. *Toll-free phone:* 800-884-6528. *Fax:* 502-456-2351.

MADISONVILLE COMMUNITY COLLEGE
Madisonville, Kentucky   www.madcc.kctcs.edu/

- **State-supported** 2-year, founded 1968, part of Kentucky Community and Technical College System
- **Small-town** 150-acre campus
- **Endowment** $2.4 million
- **Coed,** 3,500 undergraduate students

Undergraduates 0.2% are from out of state.
Faculty *Total:* 184, 52% full-time, 8% with terminal degrees.
Majors Accounting; accounting technology and bookkeeping; administrative assistant and secretarial science; banking and financial support services; biomedical technology; business administration and management; computer technology/computer systems technology; consumer merchandising/retailing management; criminal justice/police science; electrical, electronic and communications engineering technology; information science/studies; mechanical engineering/mechanical technology; nursing (registered nurse training); occupational therapist assistant; physical therapist assistant; radiologic technology/science; real estate; respiratory care therapy.
Academics *Calendar:* semesters. *Degree:* certificates, diplomas, and associate. *Special study options:* academic remediation for entering students, adult/continuing education programs, advanced placement credit, cooperative education, distance learning, external degree program, independent study, internships, off-campus study, part-time degree program, services for LD students, summer session for credit.
Library Loman C. Trover Library plus 1 other with 26,793 titles, 227 serial subscriptions, 1,688 audiovisual materials, an OPAC, a Web page.
Student Life *Housing:* college housing not available. *Activities and Organizations:* drama/theater group, student-run newspaper, choral group, student government, Baptist Student Union, Socratic Society, Student Ambassadors, Academic Team. *Campus security:* 24-hour emergency response devices, late-night transport/escort service, evening patrols. *Student services:* personal/psychological counseling.
Athletics *Intramural sports:* basketball M/W, volleyball M/W.
Standardized Tests *Required:* ACT (for placement), ACT ASSET (for placement).
Costs (2006–07) *Tuition:* state resident $2616 full-time; nonresident $7848 full-time.
Financial Aid Of all full-time matriculated undergraduates, 50 Federal Work-Study jobs (averaging $2100). 15 state and other part-time jobs (averaging $1600).

Applying *Options:* electronic application, early admission, deferred entrance. *Required:* high school transcript. *Application deadlines:* rolling (freshmen), rolling (transfers). *Notification:* continuous (freshmen), continuous (transfers).
Director of Admissions Mr. Jay Parent, Registrar, Madisonville Community College, 2000 College Drive, Madisonville, KY 42431. *Phone:* 270-821-2250.

MAYSVILLE COMMUNITY AND TECHNICAL COLLEGE
Maysville, Kentucky   www.maycc.kctcs.net/

Director of Admissions Ms. Patee Massie, Registrar, Maysville Community and Technical College, 1755 US 68, Maysville, KY 41056. *Phone:* 606-759-7141. *Fax:* 606-759-5818. *E-mail:* ccsmayrg@ukcc.uky.edu.

NATIONAL COLLEGE
Danville, Kentucky   www.national-college.edu/

Director of Admissions Ms. Stacie Catlett, Campus Director, National College, 115 East Lexington Avenue, Danville, KY 40422. *Phone:* 859-236-6991. *Toll-free phone:* 800-664-1886.

NATIONAL COLLEGE
Florence, Kentucky   www.national-college.edu/

Director of Admissions Ron Thomas, Campus Director, National College, 7627 Ewing Boulevard, Florence, KY 41042. *Phone:* 859-525-6510. *Toll-free phone:* 800-664-1886.

NATIONAL COLLEGE
Lexington, Kentucky   www.national-college.edu/

Director of Admissions Kim Thomasson, Campus Director, National College, 628 East Main Street, Lexington, KY 40508-2312. *Phone:* 859-266-0401. *Toll-free phone:* 800-664-1886.

NATIONAL COLLEGE
Louisville, Kentucky   www.national-college.edu/

Director of Admissions Mike Fiore, Campus Director, National College, 3950 Dixie Highway, Louisville, KY 40216. *Phone:* 502-447-7634. *Toll-free phone:* 800-664-1886.

NATIONAL COLLEGE
Pikeville, Kentucky   www.national-college.edu/

Director of Admissions Mr. Jerry Lafferty, Campus Director, National College, 288 South Mayo Trail, Suite 2, Pikeville, KY 41501. *Phone:* 606-432-5477. *Toll-free phone:* 800-664-1886.

NATIONAL COLLEGE
Richmond, Kentucky   www.national-college.edu/

Director of Admissions Ms. Keeley Gadd, Campus Director, National College, 139 Killarney Lane, Richmond, KY 40475. *Phone:* 859-623-8956. *Toll-free phone:* 800-664-1886.

OWENSBORO COMMUNITY AND TECHNICAL COLLEGE

Owensboro, Kentucky　　　　www.octc.kctcs.edu/

- **State-supported** 2-year, founded 1986, part of Kentucky Community and Technical College System
- **Suburban** 102-acre campus
- **Endowment** $109,305
- **Coed,** 5,188 undergraduate students, 31% full-time, 62% women, 38% men

Undergraduates 1,604 full-time, 3,584 part-time. Students come from 6 states and territories, 2 other countries, 3% are from out of state, 3% African American, 0.3% Asian American or Pacific Islander, 0.7% Hispanic American, 0.2% Native American.

Freshmen *Admission:* 956 applied, 956 admitted, 655 enrolled. *Test scores:* ACT scores over 18: 72%; ACT scores over 24: 17%; ACT scores over 30: 1%.

Faculty *Total:* 242, 40% full-time. *Student/faculty ratio:* 21:1.

Majors Agriculture; business administration and management; computer and information sciences; computer/information technology services administration related; criminal justice/police science; data entry/microcomputer applications; electrical, electronic and communications engineering technology; executive assistant/executive secretary; human services; information technology; kindergarten/preschool education; liberal arts and sciences/liberal studies; medical radiologic technology; nursing (registered nurse training); social work; system administration; word processing.

Academics *Calendar:* semesters. *Degree:* certificates and associate. *Special study options:* academic remediation for entering students, adult/continuing education programs, advanced placement credit, cooperative education, distance learning, double majors, English as a second language, external degree program, honors programs, independent study, off-campus study, part-time degree program, services for LD students, student-designed majors, study abroad.

Library Learning Resource Center with 18,200 titles, 80 serial subscriptions, an OPAC, a Web page.

Student Life *Housing:* college housing not available. *Activities and Organizations:* drama/theater group, student-run newspaper, radio and television station, choral group, student government, Psychology Club, Nursing Club. *Campus security:* 24-hour emergency response devices, late-night transport/escort service.

Athletics *Intramural sports:* basketball M, softball M/W.

Standardized Tests *Recommended:* SAT or ACT (for admission).

Costs (2007–08) *Tuition:* area resident $3450 full-time; state resident $115 per credit hour part-time; nonresident $10,350 full-time, $345 per credit hour part-time.

Financial Aid Of all full-time matriculated undergraduates, 60 Federal Work-Study jobs (averaging $2500). *Financial aid deadline:* 4/1.

Applying *Required:* high school transcript. *Application deadlines:* rolling (freshmen), rolling (transfers). *Notification:* continuous (freshmen), continuous (transfers).

Freshmen Application Contact Ms. Barbara Tipmore, Admissions Counselor, Owensboro Community and Technical College, 4800 New Hartford Road, Owensboro, KY 42303. *Phone:* 270-686-4527. *Toll-free phone:* 866-755-6282.

PADUCAH TECHNICAL COLLEGE

Paducah, Kentucky　　　　www.paducahtech.edu/

Director of Admissions Mr. Arnold Harris, Director of Admissions, Paducah Technical College, 509 South 30th Street, PO Box 8252, Paducah, KY 42001. *Phone:* 502-444-9676. *Toll-free phone:* 800-995-4438.

ROWAN TECHNICAL COLLEGE

Morehead, Kentucky　　　　www.rowtc.kctcs.edu/

Director of Admissions Patee Massie, Registrar, Rowan Technical College, 609 Viking Drive, Morehead, KY 40351. *Phone:* 606-759-7141 Ext. 66184.

ST. CATHARINE COLLEGE

St. Catharine, Kentucky　　　　www.sccky.edu/

- **Independent Roman Catholic** 2-year, founded 1931
- **Rural** 643-acre campus with easy access to Louisville
- **Endowment** $300,000
- **Coed,** 751 undergraduate students

Undergraduates Students come from 45 other countries, 9% African American, 1% Asian American or Pacific Islander, 0.5% Hispanic American, 0.1% Native American, 0.5% international, 19% live on campus.

Freshmen *Admission:* 700 applied, 317 admitted.

Faculty *Total:* 49, 71% full-time. *Student/faculty ratio:* 15:1.

Majors Accounting; administrative assistant and secretarial science; agricultural business and management; agriculture; animal sciences; art; art history, criticism and conservation; art teacher education; biblical studies; biological and physical sciences; biology/biological sciences; business administration and management; business machine repair; business/managerial economics; business teacher education; ceramic arts and ceramics; chemistry; computer engineering technology; criminal justice/law enforcement administration; dance; education; elementary education; environmental studies; farm and ranch management; health teacher education; history; horticultural science; humanities; information science/studies; insurance; Japanese; journalism; kindergarten/preschool education; landscape architecture; landscaping and groundskeeping; land use planning and management; legal administrative assistant/secretary; liberal arts and sciences/liberal studies; mathematics; medical administrative assistant and medical secretary; music; nursing (registered nurse training); physical education teaching and coaching; piano and organ; range science and management; social sciences; social work; sociology; Spanish.

Academics *Calendar:* semesters. *Degree:* certificates and associate. *Special study options:* academic remediation for entering students, advanced placement credit, cooperative education, internships, part-time degree program, services for LD students, summer session for credit.

Library St. Catharine College Library with 25,000 titles, 110 serial subscriptions, an OPAC, a Web page.

Student Life *Housing Options:* coed. *Activities and Organizations:* drama/theater group, student-run newspaper, choral group, African-American Club, International Club, student government, Phi Theta Kappa. *Campus security:* 24-hour emergency response devices, night security guard. *Student services:* personal/psychological counseling.

Athletics Member NJCAA. *Intercollegiate sports:* baseball M(s)/W(s), basketball M(s)/W(s), softball W(s). *Intramural sports:* archery M/W, badminton M/W, table tennis M(c)/W(c), tennis M/W, volleyball M/W, weight lifting M/W.

Standardized Tests *Required:* ACT (for admission).

Costs (2006–07) *Tuition:* $11,800 full-time.

Financial Aid Of all full-time matriculated undergraduates, 45 Federal Work-Study jobs (averaging $1000).

Applying *Options:* electronic application, early admission. *Application fee:* $15. *Required:* minimum ACT score of 12. *Required for some:* high school transcript. *Application deadlines:* rolling (freshmen), rolling (transfers).

Director of Admissions Ms. Amy C. Carrico, Director of Admissions, St. Catharine College, 2735 Bardstown Road, St. Catharine, KY 40061. *Phone:* 859-336-5082. *Toll-free phone:* 800-599-2000 Ext. 1227.

SOMERSET COMMUNITY COLLEGE

Somerset, Kentucky　　　　www.somerset.kctcs.edu/

Freshmen Application Contact Mr. Sean Ayers, Recruiter, Somerset Community College, 808 Monticello Street, Somerset, KY 42501. *Phone:* 606-679-8501 Ext. 3778. *Toll-free phone:* 877-629-9722.

SOUTHEAST KENTUCKY COMMUNITY AND TECHNICAL COLLEGE

Cumberland, Kentucky　　　　www.soucc.kctcs.net/

- **State-supported** 2-year, founded 1960, part of Kentucky Community and Technical College System
- **Small-town** 150-acre campus
- **Endowment** $2.0 million
- **Coed,** 4,578 undergraduate students, 34% full-time, 47% women, 53% men

Undergraduates 1,535 full-time, 3,043 part-time. 2% African American, 0.2% Asian American or Pacific Islander, 0.3% Hispanic American, 0.3% Native American.

Faculty *Total:* 175, 63% full-time, 10% with terminal degrees. *Student/faculty ratio:* 19:1.

Majors Administrative assistant and secretarial science; business administration and management; clinical/medical laboratory technology; computer engineering technology; computer/information technology services administration related; criminal justice/police science; data processing and data processing technology; information technology; liberal arts and sciences/liberal studies;

management information systems; medical radiologic technology; nursing (registered nurse training); physical therapist assistant; respiratory care therapy.

Academics *Calendar:* semesters. *Degree:* certificates, diplomas, and associate. *Special study options:* academic remediation for entering students, accelerated degree program, adult/continuing education programs, advanced placement credit, distance learning, independent study, part-time degree program, study abroad, summer session for credit.

Library Gertrude Dale Library with 25,921 titles, 200 serial subscriptions, an OPAC, a Web page.

Student Life *Housing:* college housing not available. *Activities and Organizations:* drama/theater group, student-run newspaper, choral group, Professional Business Leaders, Student Government Association, Phi Theta Kappa, Black Student Union, Nursing Club.

Athletics *Intramural sports:* basketball M/W, football M/W, golf M/W, table tennis M/W, volleyball M/W.

Standardized Tests *Required:* ACT (for admission).

Costs (2007–08) *Tuition:* state resident $2760 full-time, $115 per credit hour part-time; nonresident $8280 full-time, $345 per credit hour part-time. *Required fees:* $144 full-time.

Financial Aid Of all full-time matriculated undergraduates, 90 Federal Work-Study jobs (averaging $635).

Applying *Required:* high school transcript. *Application deadline:* 8/20 (freshmen). *Notification:* continuous until 9/3 (freshmen), continuous until 9/3 (transfers).

Director of Admissions Ms. Cookie Baker, Director of Admissions, Southeast Kentucky Community and Technical College, 700 College Road, Cumberland, KY 40823. *Phone:* 606-589-2145 Ext. 13018. *Toll-free phone:* 888-274-SECC Ext. 2108.

SOUTHWESTERN COLLEGE OF BUSINESS

Florence, Kentucky   www.swcollege.net/

Director of Admissions Mr. Bruce Budesheim, Director, Southwestern College of Business, 8095 Connector Drive, Florence, KY 41042. *Phone:* 859-341-6633. *Fax:* 859-341-6749. *E-mail:* bbudesheim@swcollege.net.

SPENCERIAN COLLEGE

Louisville, Kentucky   www.spencerian.edu/

- **Proprietary** 2-year, founded 1892, part of The Sullivan University System
- **Urban** 10-acre campus
- **Coed,** 1,180 undergraduate students, 65% full-time, 90% women, 10% men

Undergraduates 766 full-time, 414 part-time. 20% African American, 0.4% Asian American or Pacific Islander, 0.6% Hispanic American, 0.3% Native American.

Freshmen *Admission:* 296 admitted.

Faculty *Total:* 91, 48% full-time, 4% with terminal degrees. *Student/faculty ratio:* 14:1.

Majors Accounting; business administration and management; medical office management.

Academics *Calendar:* quarters. *Degree:* certificates, diplomas, and associate. *Special study options:* academic remediation for entering students, accelerated degree program, advanced placement credit, cooperative education, distance learning, double majors, external degree program, honors programs, independent study, internships, part-time degree program, services for LD students.

Library Laura Diener with 140 titles, an OPAC, a Web page.

Student Life *Housing Options:* coed. Campus housing is leased by the school and is provided by a third party. *Activities and Organizations:* student-run newspaper, Spencerian Business Leaders. *Campus security:* 24-hour emergency response devices. *Student services:* personal/psychological counseling.

Standardized Tests *Recommended:* SAT or ACT (for admission).

Costs (2006–07) *Tuition:* $12,960 full-time, $216 per credit hour part-time. *Required fees:* $565 full-time, $35 per course part-time. *Room only:* $4320. *Payment plans:* installment, deferred payment.

Applying *Options:* electronic application. *Application fee:* $100. *Required:* high school transcript, interview. *Required for some:* essay or personal statement, letters of recommendation. *Notification:* continuous until 9/1 (freshmen), continuous until 9/1 (transfers).

Director of Admissions Terri D. Thomas, Director of Admissions, Spencerian College, 4627 Dixie Highway, Louisville, KY 40299. *Phone:* 502-447-1000 Ext. 7808. *Toll-free phone:* 800-264-1799.

SPENCERIAN COLLEGE—LEXINGTON

Lexington, Kentucky   www.spencerian.edu/

Freshmen Application Contact Ms. Georgia Mullins, Admissions Representative, Spencerian College–Lexington, 2355 Harrodsburg Road, Lexington, KY 40504. *Phone:* 800-456-3253 Ext. 8010. *Toll-free phone:* 800-456-3253. *Fax:* 859-224-7744. *E-mail:* admissions@spencerian.edu.

WEST KENTUCKY COMMUNITY AND TECHNICAL COLLEGE

Paducah, Kentucky   www.westkentucky.kctcs.edu/

Freshmen Application Contact Mr. Jerry Anderson, Admissions Counselor, West Kentucky Community and Technical College, 4810 Alben Barkley Drive, PO Box 7380, Paducah, KY 42002-7380. *Phone:* 270-554-9200.

LOUISIANA

BATON ROUGE COMMUNITY COLLEGE

Baton Rouge, Louisiana   www.brcc.cc.la.us/

Director of Admissions Ms. Michelle L. Hill, Associate Dean, Enrollment Services, Baton Rouge Community College, 5310 Florida Boulevard, Baton Rouge, LA 70806. *Phone:* 225-216-8700. *Toll-free phone:* 800-601-4558.

BATON ROUGE SCHOOL OF COMPUTERS

Baton Rouge, Louisiana   www.brsc.edu/

- **Proprietary** 2-year, founded 1979
- **Coed,** 83 undergraduate students

Majors Computer and information sciences and support services related; computer systems networking and telecommunications.

Academics *Degree:* certificates and associate.

Costs (2006–07) *Tuition:* $10,500 per degree program part-time. No tuition increase for student's term of enrollment. *Payment plan:* installment.

Freshmen Application Contact Brenda Boss, Baton Rouge School of Computers, 10425 Plaza Americana, Baton Rouge, LA 70816-8188. *Phone:* 225-923-2524. *Fax:* 225-923-2979. *E-mail:* admissions@brsc.net.

BLUE CLIFF COLLEGE—LAFAYETTE

Lafayette, Louisiana   www.bluecliffcollege.com/

Freshmen Application Contact Admissions Office, Blue Cliff College–Lafayette, 100 Asma Boulevard, Suite 350, Lafayette, LA 70508-3862. *Toll-free phone:* 800-514-2609.

BLUE CLIFF COLLEGE—SHREVEPORT

Shreveport, Louisiana   www.bluecliffcollege.com/

Admissions Office Contact Blue Cliff College–Shreveport, 200 North Thomas Drive, Suite A, Shreveport, LA 71107. *Toll-free phone:* 800-516-6597.

BOSSIER PARISH COMMUNITY COLLEGE

Bossier City, Louisiana　　　　**www.bpcc.edu/**

Freshmen Application Contact Ms. Ann Jampole, Director of Admissions, Bossier Parish Community College, 2719 Airline Drive North, Bossier City, LA 71111-5801. *Phone:* 318-678-6166. *Fax:* 318-742-8664.

CAMELOT COLLEGE

Baton Rouge, Louisiana　　　　**www.camelotcollege.com/**

- **Proprietary** 2-year, founded 1986
- **Coed,** 336 undergraduate students

Majors Paralegal/legal assistant.

Academics *Degree:* diplomas and associate.

Costs (2006–07) *Tuition:* $11,100 per degree program part-time.

Freshmen Application Contact Camelot College, 2618 Wooddale Boulevard, Suite A, Baton Rouge, LA 70805. *Phone:* 225-928-3005. *Toll-free phone:* 800-470-3320.

CAMERON COLLEGE

New Orleans, Louisiana　　　　**www.cameroncollege.com/**

Admissions Office Contact Cameron College, 2740 Canal Street, New Orleans, LA 70119.

CAREER TECHNICAL COLLEGE

Monroe, Louisiana　　　　**www.careertc.edu/**

- **Proprietary** 2-year, founded 1985
- **Coed,** 549 undergraduate students
- 84% of applicants were admitted

Freshmen *Admission:* 172 applied, 145 admitted.

Majors Criminal justice/safety; data processing and data processing technology; general studies; massage therapy; medical/clinical assistant; medical office management; office management; radiologic technology/science; surgical technology.

Academics *Calendar:* quarters. *Degree:* diplomas and associate.

Costs (2006–07) *Tuition:* $11,241 full-time.

Applying *Application fee:* $35.

Freshmen Application Contact Admissions Office, Career Technical College, 2319 Louisville Avenue, Monroe, LA 71201. *Toll-free phone:* 800-234-6766.

DELGADO COMMUNITY COLLEGE

New Orleans, Louisiana　　　　**www.dcc.edu/**

- **State-supported** 2-year, founded 1921, part of Louisiana Community and Technical College System
- **Urban** 57-acre campus
- **Endowment** $1.0 million
- **Coed**

Undergraduates 7,376 full-time, 9,125 part-time. Students come from 33 states and territories, 3 other countries, 0.3% are from out of state, 43% African American, 2% Asian American or Pacific Islander, 4% Hispanic American, 0.7% Native American. *Retention:* 53% of 2003 full-time freshmen returned.

Faculty *Student/faculty ratio:* 20:1.

Academics *Calendar:* semesters. *Degree:* certificates and associate. *Special study options:* academic remediation for entering students, advanced placement credit, cooperative education, distance learning, English as a second language, honors programs, off-campus study, part-time degree program, services for LD students, student-designed majors, summer session for credit. *ROTC:* Army (c), Air Force (c).

Student Life *Campus security:* 24-hour patrols, student patrols.

Athletics Member NJCAA.

Standardized Tests *Required for some:* ACT (for placement). *Recommended:* ACT (for placement).

Costs (2006–07) *Tuition:* state resident $1482 full-time, $420 per term part-time; nonresident $4462 full-time, $1275 per term part-time. Part-time tuition and fees vary according to course load. *Required fees:* $362 full-time, $5 per term part-time, $10 per term part-time.

Financial Aid Of all full-time matriculated undergraduates, 308 Federal Work-Study jobs (averaging $1375).

Applying *Application fee:* $15. *Required for some:* high school transcript. *Recommended:* high school transcript, proof of immunization.

Freshmen Application Contact Ms. Gwen Boute, Director of Admissions, Delgado Community College, 615 City Park Avenue, New Orleans, LA 70119. *Phone:* 504-483-4004. *Fax:* 504-483-1895. *E-mail:* enroll@dcc.edu.

DELTA COLLEGE OF ARTS AND TECHNOLOGY

Baton Rouge, Louisiana　　　　**www.deltacollege.com/**

Freshmen Application Contact Ms. Beulah Laverghe-Brown, Admissions Director, Delta College of Arts and Technology, 7380 Exchange Place, Baton Rouge, LA 70806. *Phone:* 225-928-7770. *Fax:* 225-927-9096. *E-mail:* bbrown@deltacollege.com.

DELTA SCHOOL OF BUSINESS & TECHNOLOGY

Lake Charles, Louisiana　　　　**www.deltatech.edu/**

- **Private** 2-year
- 362 undergraduate students

Majors Accounting; administrative assistant and secretarial science; business administration and management; CAD/CADD drafting/design technology; information technology; medical office assistant.

Academics *Calendar:* quarters. *Degree:* associate.

Costs (2006–07) *Tuition:* $10,090 full-time.

Director of Admissions Mr. Gary J. Holt, President, Delta School of Business & Technology, 517 Broad Street, Lake Charles, LA 70601. *Phone:* 337-439-5765. *Toll-free phone:* 800-259-5627. *Fax:* 337-436-5151. *E-mail:* gholt@deltatech.edu.

ELAINE P. NUNEZ COMMUNITY COLLEGE

Chalmette, Louisiana　　　　**www.nunez.edu/**

- **State-supported** 2-year, founded 1992, part of Louisiana Community and Technical College System
- **Suburban** 20-acre campus with easy access to New Orleans
- **Endowment** $770,000
- **Coed,** 1,064 undergraduate students, 44% full-time, 66% women, 34% men

Undergraduates 468 full-time, 596 part-time. Students come from 5 states and territories, 2% are from out of state, 31% African American, 2% Asian American or Pacific Islander, 3% Hispanic American, 2% Native American, 7% transferred in.

Freshmen *Admission:* 107 applied, 107 admitted, 107 enrolled.

Faculty *Total:* 62, 56% full-time, 8% with terminal degrees. *Student/faculty ratio:* 15:1.

Majors Accounting; administrative assistant and secretarial science; computer and information sciences related; computer engineering technology; computer/information technology services administration related; computer science; computer/technical support; drafting and design technology; electrical, electronic and communications engineering technology; emergency medical technology (EMT paramedic); environmental engineering technology; health information/medical records administration; heating, air conditioning, ventilation and refrigeration maintenance technology; information science/studies; institutional food workers; kindergarten/preschool education; laser and optical technology; legal assistant/paralegal; liberal arts and sciences/liberal studies; nursing (licensed practical/vocational nurse training); plastics engineering technology.

Academics *Calendar:* semesters. *Degree:* certificates and associate. *Special study options:* academic remediation for entering students, adult/continuing

education programs, advanced placement credit, cooperative education, distance learning, double majors, English as a second language, independent study, internships, off-campus study, part-time degree program, services for LD students, student-designed majors, summer session for credit.

Library Nunez Community College Library with 68,000 titles, 2,500 serial subscriptions, 750 audiovisual materials, an OPAC, a Web page.

Student Life *Housing:* college housing not available. *Activities and Organizations:* drama/theater group, student-run newspaper, choral group, Nunez Environmental Team, national fraternities. *Campus security:* 24-hour emergency response devices, late-night transport/escort service, security cameras. *Student services:* personal/psychological counseling.

Athletics *Intramural sports:* basketball M, football M/W, softball M/W, volleyball M/W.

Costs (2007–08) *Tuition:* area resident $1402 full-time; nonresident $2520 full-time. *Required fees:* $368 full-time.

Financial Aid Of all full-time matriculated undergraduates, 70 Federal Work-Study jobs (averaging $1452).

Applying *Options:* deferred entrance. *Application fee:* $10. *Required for some:* high school transcript. *Application deadlines:* rolling (freshmen), rolling (transfers).

Freshmen Application Contact Mrs. Becky Maillet, Elaine P. Nunez Community College, 3710 Paris Road, Chalmette, LA 70043. *Phone:* 504-278-7467. *E-mail:* bmaillet@nunez.edu.

GRETNA CAREER COLLEGE
Gretna, Louisiana   www.gretnacareercollege.com/
- **Proprietary** 2-year, founded 1991
- **Coed,** 96 undergraduate students

Majors Computer and information sciences and support services related; medical administrative assistant and medical secretary; medical/clinical assistant; medical insurance/medical billing; nursing assistant/aide and patient care assistant.

Academics *Degree:* associate.

Costs (2006–07) *Tuition:* $19,000 per degree program part-time.

Freshmen Application Contact Admissions Office, Gretna Career College, 1415 Whitney Avenue, Gretna, LA 70053.

HERZING COLLEGE
Kenner, Louisiana   www.herzing.edu/
Director of Admissions Genny Bordelon, Director of Admissions, Herzing College, 2400 Veterans Boulevard, Kenner, LA 70062. *Phone:* 504-733-0074. *Fax:* 504-733-0020.

ITI TECHNICAL COLLEGE
Baton Rouge, Louisiana   www.iticollege.edu/
- **Proprietary** 2-year, founded 1973
- **Suburban** 10-acre campus
- **Coed**
- 85% of applicants were admitted

Undergraduates 226 full-time, 125 part-time. 1% are from out of state, 32% African American, 0.4% Asian American or Pacific Islander, 2% Hispanic American, 0.4% Native American.

Faculty *Student/faculty ratio:* 10:1.

Academics *Calendar:* continuous. *Degree:* certificates and associate.

Applying *Required:* high school transcript, interview.

Freshmen Application Contact Mr. Joe Martin, President, ITI Technical College, 13944 Airline Highway, Baton Rouge, LA 70817. *Phone:* 225-752-4230 Ext. 213. *Toll-free phone:* 800-467-4484. *Fax:* 225-756-0903. *E-mail:* jmartin@iticollege.edu.

ITT TECHNICAL INSTITUTE
St. Rose, Louisiana   www.itt-tech.edu/
- **Proprietary** primarily 2-year, founded 1998, part of ITT Educational Services, Inc
- **Coed,** 541 undergraduate students

Majors Accounting technology and bookkeeping; animation, interactive technology, video graphics and special effects; business administration and management; CAD/CADD drafting/design technology; computer and information systems security; computer engineering technology; computer software technology; computer systems networking and telecommunications; construction management; criminal justice/law enforcement administration; electrical, electronic and communications engineering technology; web/multimedia management and webmaster; web page, digital/multimedia and information resources design.

Academics *Calendar:* quarters. *Degrees:* associate and bachelor's.

Library a Web page.

Student Life *Housing:* college housing not available.

Standardized Tests *Required:* Wonderlic aptitude test (for admission).

Costs (2006–07) *Tuition:* Contact school for program costs.

Applying *Options:* deferred entrance. *Application fee:* $100. *Required:* high school transcript, interview. *Recommended:* letters of recommendation. *Application deadlines:* rolling (freshmen), rolling (transfers). *Notification:* continuous (freshmen), continuous (transfers).

Freshmen Application Contact Mr. John Richard, Director of Recruitment, ITT Technical Institute, 140 James Drive East, Saint Rose, LA 70087. *Phone:* 504-463-0338. *Toll-free phone:* 866-463-0338.

LOUISIANA STATE UNIVERSITY AT ALEXANDRIA
Alexandria, Louisiana   www.lsua.edu/
- **State-supported** primarily 2-year, founded 1960, part of Louisiana State University System
- **Rural** 3114-acre campus
- **Endowment** $588,481
- **Coed**

Undergraduates 1,572 full-time, 1,416 part-time. Students come from 14 states and territories, 6 other countries, 0.7% are from out of state, 19% African American, 0.8% Asian American or Pacific Islander, 0.8% Hispanic American, 2% Native American, 0.5% international, 9% transferred in.

Faculty *Student/faculty ratio:* 16:1.

Academics *Calendar:* semesters. *Degrees:* certificates, associate, and bachelor's. *Special study options:* academic remediation for entering students, adult/continuing education programs, advanced placement credit, distance learning, part-time degree program, services for LD students, summer session for credit. *ROTC:* Army (c).

Student Life *Campus security:* 24-hour patrols.

Standardized Tests *Required:* ACT (for admission).

Costs (2006–07) *Tuition:* area resident $2364 full-time; state resident $99 per credit hour part-time; nonresident $4820 full-time, $200 per credit hour part-time. Part-time tuition and fees vary according to course load. *Required fees:* $750 full-time, $35 per credit hour part-time, $73 per term part-time.

Financial Aid Of all full-time matriculated undergraduates, 53 Federal Work-Study jobs (averaging $1226). 76 state and other part-time jobs (averaging $1261).

Applying *Options:* early admission. *Application fee:* $20. *Required:* high school transcript.

Freshmen Application Contact Ms. Shelly Kieffer, Recruiter/Admissions Counselor, Louisiana State University at Alexandria, 8100 Highway 71 South, Alexandria, LA 71302-9121. *Phone:* 318-473-6508. *Toll-free phone:* 888-473-6417. *Fax:* 318-473-6418. *E-mail:* skieffer@lsua.edu.

LOUISIANA STATE UNIVERSITY AT EUNICE
Eunice, Louisiana   www.lsue.edu/
- **State-supported** 2-year, founded 1967, part of Louisiana State University System
- **Small-town** 199-acre campus
- **Coed,** 2,833 undergraduate students

Undergraduates Students come from 4 states and territories, 0.4% are from out of state.

Freshmen *Admission:* 1,753 applied, 1,734 admitted. *Test scores:* ACT scores over 18: 76%; ACT scores over 24: 22%; ACT scores over 30: 2%.

Faculty *Total:* 131.

Majors Administrative assistant and secretarial science; business administration and management; computer programming; criminal justice/police science;

Louisiana State University at Eunice (continued)

criminal justice/safety; fire science; general studies; legal assistant/paralegal; nursing (registered nurse training); radiologic technology/science; respiratory care therapy.

Academics *Calendar:* semesters. *Degree:* certificates and associate. *Special study options:* academic remediation for entering students, adult/continuing education programs, advanced placement credit, cooperative education, distance learning, honors programs, part-time degree program, services for LD students, summer session for credit.

Library Arnold LeDoux Library with 100,000 titles, 253 serial subscriptions, an OPAC.

Student Life *Housing Options:* Campus housing is provided by a third party. *Activities and Organizations:* student-run newspaper, Student Government Association, Students in Free Enterprise, Criminal Justice Society, Student Nurses Association, Phi Theta Kappa. *Campus security:* 24-hour emergency response devices and patrols. *Student services:* personal/psychological counseling.

Athletics Member NJCAA. *Intercollegiate sports:* baseball M, basketball W. *Intramural sports:* basketball M/W, football M, softball M/W, tennis M/W, volleyball M/W.

Standardized Tests *Required for some:* ACT (for placement). *Recommended:* ACT (for placement).

Costs (2006–07) *Tuition:* state resident $2180 full-time; nonresident $5180 full-time.

Financial Aid Of all full-time matriculated undergraduates, 78 Federal Work-Study jobs (averaging $1525).

Applying *Options:* early admission. *Application fee:* $25. *Required:* high school transcript. *Application deadlines:* 8/7 (freshmen), 8/7 (transfers).

Freshmen Application Contact Ms. Gracie Guillory, Director of Financial Aid, Louisiana State University at Eunice, PO Box 1129, Eunice, LA 70535-1129. *Phone:* 337-550-1282. *Toll-free phone:* 888-367-5783.

LOUISIANA TECHNICAL COLLEGE

Baton Rouge, Louisiana   www.ltc.edu/

- **State-supported** 2-year, founded 1930
- **Endowment** $286,936
- **Coed**

Undergraduates 7,264 full-time, 6,150 part-time. 1% are from out of state, 37% African American, 0.9% Asian American or Pacific Islander, 1% Hispanic American, 0.7% Native American.

Faculty *Student/faculty ratio:* 10:1.

Academics *Degree:* certificates, diplomas, and associate.

Costs (2006–07) *Tuition:* state resident $552 full-time, $23 per credit hour part-time; nonresident $1104 full-time, $46 per credit hour part-time. *Required fees:* $214 full-time, $9 per credit hour part-time, $5 per term part-time.

Applying *Application fee:* $5. *Required:* high school transcript.

Freshmen Application Contact Ms. Janice M. Bolden, Vice Chancellor of Student Affairs, Enrollment Management, and College Registrar, Louisiana Technical College, 150 3rd Street, Baton Rouge, LA 70801. *Toll-free phone:* 800-351-7611.

LOUISIANA TECHNICAL COLLEGE— FLORIDA PARISHES CAMPUS

Greensburg, Louisiana   www.theltc.net/

Director of Admissions Mrs. Sharon G. Hornsby, Campus Dean, Louisiana Technical College–Florida Parishes Campus, Student Services, PO Box 1300, 100 College Street, Greensburg, LA 70441. *Phone:* 225-222-4251. *Toll-free phone:* 800-827-9750.

MEDVANCE INSTITUTE

Baton Rouge, Louisiana   www.medvance.org/

Director of Admissions Ms. Sheri Kirley, Associate Director of Admissions, MedVance Institute, 4173 Government Street, Baton Rouge, LA 70806. *Phone:* 225-248-1015.

METROPOLITAN COMMUNITY COLLEGE

Gretna, Louisiana   www.metrocc.us/

Admissions Office Contact Metropolitan Community College, 2550 Belle Chasse Highway, Gretna, LA 70053. *Toll-free phone:* 866-838-3159.

REMINGTON COLLEGE—BATON ROUGE CAMPUS

Baton Rouge, Louisiana   www.remingtoncollege.edu/

- **Proprietary** 2-year
- **Coed,** 607 undergraduate students
- 100% of applicants were admitted

Freshmen *Admission:* 289 applied, 289 admitted.

Majors Business administration and management; computer and information sciences and support services related; computer systems networking and telecommunications; criminal justice/law enforcement administration; electrical, electronics and communications engineering.

Academics *Calendar:* continuous. *Degree:* associate.

Costs (2006–07) *Tuition:* $12,520 per degree program part-time.

Applying *Application fee:* $50.

Director of Admissions Mr. Gregg Falcon, Campus President, Remington College–Baton Rouge Campus, 10551 Coursey Boulevard, Baton Rouge, LA 70816. *Phone:* 225-922-3990. *Fax:* 225-922-9569. *E-mail:* gregg.falcon@remingtoncollege.edu.

REMINGTON COLLEGE—LAFAYETTE CAMPUS

Lafayette, Louisiana   www.remingtoncollege.edu/

- **Proprietary** 2-year, founded 1940, part of Education America, Inc
- **Urban** 4-acre campus
- **Coed**

Undergraduates 367 full-time. 50% African American, 2% Asian American or Pacific Islander, 2% Hispanic American, 0.5% Native American.

Faculty *Student/faculty ratio:* 18:1.

Academics *Calendar:* continuous. *Degree:* diplomas and associate. *Special study options:* honors programs, independent study.

Student Life *Campus security:* 24-hour emergency response devices.

Costs (2006–07) *Tuition:* $12,825 full-time.

Applying *Options:* early admission, deferred entrance. *Application fee:* $50. *Required:* high school transcript, interview.

Freshmen Application Contact Mr. Gary Schwartz, Director of Recruiting, Remington College–Lafayette Campus, 303 Rue Louis XIV, Lafayette, LA 70508. *Phone:* 337-981-9010. *Toll-free phone:* 800-736-2687. *Fax:* 337-983-7130.

REMINGTON COLLEGE—NEW ORLEANS CAMPUS

Metairie, Louisiana   www.remingtoncollege.edu/

Director of Admissions Mr. Roy Kimble, Director of Recruitment, Remington College–New Orleans Campus, 321 Veterans Memorial Boulevard, Metairie, LA 70005. *Phone:* 504-831-8889.

RIVER PARISHES COMMUNITY COLLEGE

Sorrento, Louisiana   rpcc.cc.la.us/

Director of Admissions Ms. Allison Dauzat, Dean of Students and Enrollment Management, River Parishes Community College, PO Box 310, 7384 John LeBlanc Boulevard, Sorrento, LA 70778. *Phone:* 225-675-8270. *Fax:* 225-675-5478. *E-mail:* adauzat@rpcc.cc.la.us.

SCHOOL OF URBAN MISSIONS–NEW ORLEANS

New Orleans, Louisiana   www.sumonline.org/

Admissions Office Contact School of Urban Missions–New Orleans, PO Box 53344, New Orleans, LA 70153. *Toll-free phone:* 800-385-6364.

SOUTHERN UNIVERSITY AT SHREVEPORT

Shreveport, Louisiana   www.susla.edu/

- **State-supported** 2-year, founded 1964, part of Southern University System
- **Urban** 103-acre campus
- **Coed,** 1,324 undergraduate students, 70% full-time, 71% women, 29% men

Undergraduates 921 full-time, 403 part-time. Students come from 5 states and territories, 45% are from out of state, 92% African American, 0.2% Asian American or Pacific Islander, 0.2% Hispanic American, 0.2% Native American, 0.1% international, 10% transferred in.

Freshmen *Admission:* 420 enrolled. *Average high school GPA:* 2.0. *Test scores:* ACT scores over 18: 8%.

Faculty *Total:* 98, 50% full-time, 15% with terminal degrees. *Student/faculty ratio:* 16:1.

Majors Accounting; avionics maintenance technology; banking and financial support services; biology/biological sciences; business administration and management; cardiovascular technology; chemistry; clinical/medical laboratory technology; computer science; criminal justice/law enforcement administration; dental hygiene; electrical, electronic and communications engineering technology; general studies; health information/medical records administration; hospitality administration; hotel/motel administration; human services; kindergarten/preschool education; legal assistant/paralegal; mathematics; mechanical engineering/mechanical technology; medical radiologic technology; mental health/rehabilitation; physical therapist assistant; public administration; respiratory care therapy; robotics technology; sociology; substance abuse/addiction counseling; surgical technology; teacher assistant/aide; tourism and travel services management.

Academics *Calendar:* semesters. *Degree:* certificates and associate. *Special study options:* academic remediation for entering students, adult/continuing education programs, advanced placement credit, cooperative education, honors programs, internships, off-campus study, part-time degree program, student-designed majors, summer session for credit.

Library Library/Learning Resources Center with 380 serial subscriptions, 24,016 audiovisual materials, an OPAC.

Student Life *Housing:* college housing not available. *Activities and Organizations:* student-run newspaper, choral group, Afro-American Society, SUSBO Gospel Choir, Student Center Board, Allied Health, Engineering Club. *Campus security:* 24-hour patrols. *Student services:* personal/psychological counseling.

Athletics Member NJCAA. *Intercollegiate sports:* basketball M(s)/W. *Intramural sports:* basketball M/W, cheerleading M/W.

Standardized Tests *Recommended:* ACT (for admission).

Costs (2006–07) *Tuition:* state resident $2252 full-time; nonresident $3382 full-time.

Financial Aid Of all full-time matriculated undergraduates, 252 Federal Work-Study jobs (averaging $1500).

Applying *Options:* early admission. *Application fee:* $5. *Required:* high school transcript. *Application deadlines:* rolling (freshmen), rolling (transfers). *Notification:* continuous until 8/15 (freshmen), continuous until 8/15 (transfers).

Freshmen Application Contact Ms. Juanita Johnson, Acting Admissions Records Technician, Southern University at Shreveport, 3050 Martin Luther King, Jr. Drive, Shreveport, LA 71107. *Phone:* 318-674-3342. *Toll-free phone:* 800-458-1472 Ext. 342.

MAINE

ANDOVER COLLEGE

Portland, Maine   www.andovercollege.com/

Director of Admissions Wendy Burbank, Director of Admissions, Andover College, 901 Washington Avenue, Portland, ME 04103-2791. *Phone:* 207-774-6126. *Toll-free phone:* 800-639-3110 Ext. 240 (in-state); 800-639-3110 Ext. 242 (out-of-state).

BEAL COLLEGE

Bangor, Maine   www.bealcollege.edu/

- **Proprietary** 2-year, founded 1891
- **Small-town** 4-acre campus
- **Coed**

Undergraduates 239 full-time, 134 part-time. Students come from 2 states and territories, 1% African American, 0.8% Hispanic American, 0.8% Native American.

Faculty *Student/faculty ratio:* 16:1.

Academics *Calendar:* modular. *Degree:* certificates, diplomas, and associate. *Special study options:* academic remediation for entering students, accelerated degree program, adult/continuing education programs, advanced placement credit, double majors, internships, part-time degree program, summer session for credit.

Applying *Options:* deferred entrance. *Application fee:* $25. *Required:* high school transcript. *Recommended:* interview.

Freshmen Application Contact Ms. Susan Palmer, Admissions Assistant, Beal College, 629 Main Street, Bangor, ME 04401. *Phone:* 207-947-4591. *Toll-free phone:* 800-660-7351. *Fax:* 207-947-0208.

CENTRAL MAINE COMMUNITY COLLEGE

Auburn, Maine   www.cmcc.edu/

- **State-supported** 2-year, founded 1964, part of Maine Technical College System
- **Small-town** 135-acre campus
- **Coed,** 2,200 undergraduate students

Undergraduates Students come from 5 states and territories, 11% live on campus. *Retention:* 77% of 2003 full-time freshmen returned.

Freshmen *Admission:* 858 applied, 464 admitted. *Test scores:* SAT verbal scores over 500: 29%; SAT math scores over 500: 25%; SAT verbal scores over 600: 4%; SAT math scores over 600: 5%.

Faculty *Total:* 135, 39% full-time, 1% with terminal degrees. *Student/faculty ratio:* 18:1.

Majors Accounting; administrative assistant and secretarial science; architecture; automobile/automotive mechanics technology; business administration and management; civil engineering technology; clinical/medical laboratory technology; commercial and advertising art; computer science; construction engineering technology; electromechanical technology; general studies; graphic and printing equipment operation/production; hospitality administration; industrial radiologic technology; kindergarten/preschool education; machine tool technology; mechanical design technology; medical administrative assistant and medical secretary; medical laboratory technology; nursing (registered nurse training); occupational safety and health technology; telecommunications.

Academics *Calendar:* semesters. *Degree:* certificates, diplomas, and associate. *Special study options:* academic remediation for entering students, adult/continuing education programs, advanced placement credit, cooperative education, distance learning, English as a second language, independent study, internships, part-time degree program, services for LD students, summer session for credit.

Library Central Maine Technical College Library with 15,000 titles, 240 serial subscriptions, a Web page.

Student Life *Housing Options:* coed, men-only, women-only. Campus housing is university owned. Freshman applicants given priority for college housing. *Activities and Organizations:* drama/theater group, student-run television station, Student Senate, Drama Club, Outing Club, intramural sports, Phi Theta Kappa. *Campus security:* 24-hour emergency response devices, controlled dormitory access, night patrols by police. *Student services:* health clinic, personal/psychological counseling.

Athletics Member NSCAA. *Intercollegiate sports:* baseball M, basketball M/W, soccer M/W, softball W. *Intramural sports:* baseball M, basketball M/W, bowling M/W, cross-country running M/W, skiing (cross-country) M/W, skiing (downhill) M/W, soccer M/W, softball M/W, table tennis M/W, volleyball M/W, weight lifting M/W.

Costs (2007–08) *Tuition:* state resident $3516 full-time, $78 per credit hour part-time; nonresident $5946 full-time, $159 per credit hour part-time. *Required fees:* $640 full-time, $15 per credit hour part-time, $30 per year part-time.

Financial Aid Of all full-time matriculated undergraduates, 170 Federal Work-Study jobs (averaging $1200).

Applying *Options:* deferred entrance. *Application fee:* $20. *Required:* essay or personal statement, high school transcript. *Required for some:* 2 letters of recommendation, interview. *Recommended:* minimum 2.0 GPA. *Application deadlines:* rolling (freshmen), rolling (transfers). *Notification:* continuous (freshmen), continuous (transfers).

Central Maine Community College (continued)

Freshmen Application Contact Ms. Joan Nichols, Administrative Assistant, Admissions Department, Central Maine Community College, 1250 Turner Street, Auburn, ME 04210-6498. *Phone:* 207-755-5273. *Toll-free phone:* 800-891-2002. *Fax:* 207-755-5493. *E-mail:* jnichols@cmcc.edu.

CENTRAL MAINE MEDICAL CENTER SCHOOL OF NURSING

Lewiston, Maine　　　　　　　　**www.cmmcson.edu/**

Freshmen Application Contact Mrs. Kathleen C. Jacques, Registrar, Central Maine Medical Center School of Nursing, 70 Middle Street, Lewiston, ME 04240-0305. *Phone:* 207-795-2858. *Fax:* 207-795-2849. *E-mail:* jacqueka@cmhc.org.

EASTERN MAINE COMMUNITY COLLEGE

Bangor, Maine　　　　　　　　**www.emcc.edu/**

Freshmen Application Contact Mr. W. Gregory Swett, Director of Admissions, Eastern Maine Community College, 354 Hogan Road, Bangor, ME 04401. *Phone:* 207-974-4680. *Toll-free phone:* 800-286-9357. *Fax:* 207-974-4683. *E-mail:* admissions@emcc.edu.

KENNEBEC VALLEY COMMUNITY COLLEGE

Fairfield, Maine　　　　　　　　**www.kvcc.me.edu/**

- **State-supported** 2-year, founded 1970, part of Maine Community College System
- **Small-town** 58-acre campus
- **Endowment** $2.3 million
- **Coed,** 1,926 undergraduate students, 31% full-time, 68% women, 32% men

Undergraduates 604 full-time, 1,322 part-time. Students come from 4 states and territories, 0.5% African American, 0.7% Asian American or Pacific Islander, 1% Hispanic American, 0.9% Native American.

Freshmen *Admission:* 481 applied, 345 admitted, 345 enrolled.

Faculty *Total:* 216, 19% full-time. *Student/faculty ratio:* 22:1.

Majors Accounting; administrative assistant and secretarial science; biology/biological sciences; business administration and management; child care and support services management; child care provision; communications systems installation and repair technology; computer/information technology services administration related; computer installation and repair technology; computer management; computer programming related; computer science; computer software and media applications related; computer systems networking and telecommunications; data modeling/warehousing and database administration; drafting and design technology; education; electrical/electronics equipment installation and repair; emergency medical technology (EMT paramedic); executive assistant/executive secretary; general studies; health information/medical records administration; industrial electronics technology; industrial mechanics and maintenance technology; legal administrative assistant/secretary; liberal arts and sciences/liberal studies; machine tool technology; marketing/marketing management; medical/clinical assistant; nursing (registered nurse training); occupational therapist assistant; physical therapist assistant; respiratory care therapy; sales, distribution and marketing; web/multimedia management and webmaster; web page, digital/multimedia and information resources design; wood science and wood products/pulp and paper technology.

Academics *Calendar:* semesters. *Degree:* certificates, diplomas, and associate. *Special study options:* academic remediation for entering students, accelerated degree program, adult/continuing education programs, advanced placement credit, distance learning, external degree program, independent study, internships, part-time degree program, services for LD students, summer session for credit.

Library Lunder Library with 28,928 titles, 188 serial subscriptions, 1,480 audiovisual materials, an OPAC, a Web page.

Student Life *Housing:* college housing not available. *Activities and Organizations:* Vocational Industrial Clubs of America (VICA) Skills USA, Student Senate, Phi Theta Kappa, Glee Club. *Campus security:* evening security patrol. *Student services:* personal/psychological counseling.

Athletics *Intramural sports:* basketball M/W, bowling M/W, ultimate Frisbee M/W, volleyball M/W.

Standardized Tests *Required for some:* nursing exam, HOBET, ACCUPLACER. *Recommended:* SAT or ACT (for admission).

Costs (2007–08) *Tuition:* state resident $2340 full-time, $78 per credit part-time; nonresident $4770 full-time, $159 per credit part-time. *Required fees:* $450 full-time.

Financial Aid Of all full-time matriculated undergraduates, 34 Federal Work-Study jobs (averaging $1207).

Applying *Options:* electronic application, deferred entrance. *Application fee:* $20. *Required:* essay or personal statement, high school transcript. *Required for some:* letters of recommendation, interview. *Application deadlines:* rolling (freshmen), rolling (transfers). *Notification:* continuous (freshmen), continuous (transfers).

Freshmen Application Contact Mr. Jim Bourgoin, Director of Admissions, Kennebec Valley Community College, 92 Western Avenue, Fairfield, ME 04937-1367. *Phone:* 207-453-5035. *Toll-free phone:* 800-528-5882 Ext. 5035. *Fax:* 207-453-5011. *E-mail:* admissions@kvcc.me.edu.

NORTHERN MAINE COMMUNITY COLLEGE

Presque Isle, Maine　　　　　　　　**www.nmcc.edu/**

- **State-related** 2-year, founded 1963, part of Maine Community College System
- **Small-town** 86-acre campus
- **Coed,** 901 undergraduate students, 68% full-time, 52% women, 48% men

Undergraduates 611 full-time, 290 part-time. Students come from 6 states and territories, 7 other countries, 2% are from out of state, 0.4% African American, 0.8% Asian American or Pacific Islander, 1% Hispanic American, 3% Native American, 3% international, 63% live on campus. *Retention:* 61% of 2003 full-time freshmen returned.

Freshmen *Admission:* 783 applied, 494 admitted, 253 enrolled.

Faculty *Total:* 81, 48% full-time. *Student/faculty ratio:* 18:1.

Majors Accounting; administrative assistant and secretarial science; automobile/automotive mechanics technology; business administration and management; carpentry; computer engineering technology; computer programming; data processing and data processing technology; drafting and design technology; electrical, electronic and communications engineering technology; emergency medical technology (EMT paramedic); heating, air conditioning, ventilation and refrigeration maintenance technology; heavy equipment maintenance technology; industrial arts; instrumentation technology; kindergarten/preschool education; legal administrative assistant/secretary; medical administrative assistant and medical secretary; nursing (registered nurse training); pipefitting and sprinkler fitting.

Academics *Calendar:* semesters. *Degree:* certificates, diplomas, and associate. *Special study options:* academic remediation for entering students, adult/continuing education programs, advanced placement credit, cooperative education, double majors, independent study, internships, off-campus study, part-time degree program, services for LD students, summer session for credit.

Library Northern Maine Technical College Library with 14,600 titles, 125 serial subscriptions, 200 audiovisual materials, an OPAC, a Web page.

Student Life *Housing Options:* coed. Campus housing is university owned. *Campus security:* 24-hour emergency response devices and patrols, controlled dormitory access. *Student services:* health clinic.

Athletics Member NSCAA. *Intercollegiate sports:* basketball M/W, cross-country running M/W, golf M/W, ice hockey M/W, soccer M/W. *Intramural sports:* archery M/W, basketball M/W, football M/W, golf M, racquetball M/W, soccer M, softball M/W, table tennis M/W, tennis M/W, volleyball M/W, weight lifting M/W.

Standardized Tests *Required:* ACCUPLACER (for admission).

Costs (2007–08) *Tuition:* state resident $2340 full-time, $78 per credit hour part-time; nonresident $3510 full-time, $159 per credit hour part-time. *Required fees:* $678 full-time, $14 per credit hour part-time, $31 per term part-time. *Room and board:* $4930; room only: $1900.

Financial Aid Of all full-time matriculated undergraduates, 74 Federal Work-Study jobs (averaging $1950).

Applying *Options:* electronic application, early admission. *Application fee:* $20. *Required:* high school transcript, interview. *Required for some:* letters of recommendation, Net Test/RN. *Recommended:* essay or personal statement, minimum 2.0 GPA. *Application deadline:* rolling (freshmen). *Notification:* continuous (freshmen).

Freshmen Application Contact Ms. Nancy Gagnon, Admissions Secretary, Northern Maine Community College, 33 Edgemont Drive, Presque Isle, ME 04769-2016. *Phone:* 207-768-2785. *Toll-free phone:* 800-535-6682. *Fax:* 207-768-2848. *E-mail:* ngagnon@nmcc.edu.

SOUTHERN MAINE COMMUNITY COLLEGE

South Portland, Maine   www.smccme.edu/

- **State-supported** 2-year, founded 1946, part of Maine Community College System
- **Small-town** 65-acre campus
- **Endowment** $513,726
- **Coed,** 4,785 undergraduate students, 48% full-time, 51% women, 49% men

Undergraduates 2,320 full-time, 2,465 part-time. Students come from 16 states and territories, 25 other countries, 4% are from out of state, 3% African American, 1% Asian American or Pacific Islander, 1% Hispanic American, 1% Native American, 0.2% international, 5% live on campus.

Faculty *Total:* 259, 34% full-time. *Student/faculty ratio:* 18:1.

Majors Agronomy and crop science; architectural engineering technology; automobile/automotive mechanics technology; botany/plant biology; business administration and management; business machine repair; cardiovascular technology; carpentry; child development; cinematography and film/video production; communications technology; computer engineering technology; computer management; construction engineering technology; criminal justice/law enforcement administration; criminal justice/police science; culinary arts; dietetics; drafting and design technology; electrical, electronic and communications engineering technology; engineering related; environmental engineering technology; fire science; food services technology; general studies; heating, air conditioning, ventilation and refrigeration maintenance technology; horticultural science; hospitality administration; hotel/motel administration; industrial radiologic technology; information science/studies; kindergarten/preschool education; landscaping and groundskeeping; liberal arts and sciences/liberal studies; machine tool technology; management information systems; marine biology and biological oceanography; medical/clinical assistant; nursing (licensed practical/vocational nurse training); nursing (registered nurse training); oceanography (chemical and physical); pipefitting and sprinkler fitting; radiologic technology/science; respiratory care therapy; special products marketing; surgical technology.

Academics *Calendar:* semesters. *Degree:* certificates, diplomas, and associate. *Special study options:* academic remediation for entering students, advanced placement credit, cooperative education, distance learning, double majors, English as a second language, internships, off-campus study, part-time degree program, services for LD students, study abroad, summer session for credit.

Library Southern Maine Community College Library with 15,000 titles, 350 serial subscriptions, an OPAC, a Web page.

Student Life *Housing Options:* coed. Campus housing is university owned and is provided by a third party. *Activities and Organizations:* drama/theater group, student-run newspaper, choral group, SEA Club, student government, Phi Theta Kappa, VICA. *Campus security:* 24-hour emergency response devices, student patrols, late-night transport/escort service. *Student services:* health clinic, personal/psychological counseling, women's center.

Athletics Member NSCAA. *Intercollegiate sports:* baseball M, basketball M, golf M/W, soccer M/W, softball W, volleyball M/W. *Intramural sports:* basketball M/W, football M/W, golf M/W, soccer M/W, volleyball M/W.

Standardized Tests *Required for some:* ACCUPLACER.

Costs (2006–07) *Tuition:* area resident $3192 full-time, $78 per hour part-time; state resident $3192 full-time, $78 per hour part-time; nonresident $5692 full-time, $155 per hour part-time. *Required fees:* $827 full-time. *Room and board:* $6402; room only: $3602. Room and board charges vary according to board plan, housing facility, and location. *Payment plan:* installment. *Waivers:* senior citizens and employees or children of employees.

Financial Aid Of all full-time matriculated undergraduates, 130 Federal Work-Study jobs (averaging $1500).

Applying *Options:* electronic application. *Application fee:* $20. *Required:* high school transcript. *Application deadlines:* rolling (freshmen), rolling (transfers). *Notification:* continuous (freshmen), continuous (transfers).

Freshmen Application Contact Staci Grasky, Associate Dean for Enrollment Services, Southern Maine Community College, Admissions, 2 Fort Road, South Portland, ME 04106. *Phone:* 207-741-5515. *Toll-free phone:* 877-282-2182. *Fax:* 207-741-5760. *E-mail:* sgrasky@smccme.edu.

WASHINGTON COUNTY COMMUNITY COLLEGE

Calais, Maine   www.wccc.me.edu/

- **State-supported** 2-year, founded 1969, part of Maine Technical College System
- **Rural** 40-acre campus
- **Coed,** 350 undergraduate students

Undergraduates Students come from 12 states and territories, 1 other country, 4% are from out of state, 22% live on campus.

Freshmen *Admission:* 273 applied, 267 admitted.

Faculty *Total:* 39, 74% full-time, 3% with terminal degrees. *Student/faculty ratio:* 9:1.

Majors Automobile/automotive mechanics technology; construction engineering technology; engineering technology; marine technology.

Academics *Calendar:* semesters. *Degree:* certificates, diplomas, and associate. *Special study options:* academic remediation for entering students, adult/continuing education programs, advanced placement credit, cooperative education, distance learning, double majors, external degree program, independent study, internships, off-campus study, part-time degree program, services for LD students, study abroad.

Library Washington County Technical College Library with 26,370 titles, 232 serial subscriptions, 50 audiovisual materials.

Student Life *Housing Options:* coed. *Activities and Organizations:* choral group, Hiking Club, Native American Club. *Campus security:* 24-hour emergency response devices. *Student services:* personal/psychological counseling.

Athletics *Intramural sports:* basketball M/W.

Standardized Tests *Required:* ACT ASSET (for placement).

Financial Aid Of all full-time matriculated undergraduates, 42 Federal Work-Study jobs (averaging $562).

Applying *Options:* deferred entrance. *Application fee:* $20. *Required:* essay or personal statement, high school transcript, interview. *Recommended:* minimum 2.0 GPA, letters of recommendation. *Application deadline:* rolling (freshmen). *Notification:* continuous (freshmen).

Director of Admissions Mr. Kent Lyons, Admissions Counselor, Washington County Community College, One College Drive, Calais, ME 04619. *Phone:* 207-454-1000. *Toll-free phone:* 800-210-6932 Ext. 41049.

YORK COUNTY COMMUNITY COLLEGE

Wells, Maine   www.yccc.edu/

- **State-supported** 2-year, founded 1994, part of Maine Technical College System
- **Small-town** 84-acre campus with easy access to Boston
- **Coed,** 949 undergraduate students

Undergraduates Students come from 3 states and territories, 2 other countries, 2% are from out of state.

Freshmen *Admission:* 540 applied, 406 admitted.

Faculty *Total:* 71, 15% full-time, 7% with terminal degrees. *Student/faculty ratio:* 15:1.

Majors Accounting; business administration and management; computer engineering technology; computer/information technology services administration related; computer systems networking and telecommunications; culinary arts; drafting and design technology; general studies; hotel/motel administration; kindergarten/preschool education; web page, digital/multimedia and information resources design.

Academics *Calendar:* semesters. *Degree:* certificates and associate. *Special study options:* accelerated degree program, cooperative education, distance learning, double majors, independent study, internships, part-time degree program, summer session for credit.

Library Library and Learning Resource Center plus 1 other with 4,000 titles, 75 serial subscriptions, an OPAC, a Web page.

Student Life *Housing:* college housing not available. *Activities and Organizations:* student-run newspaper, Student Senate, Veteran's Club, Early Childhood Education Club, Skills-USA Club. *Campus security:* 24-hour emergency response devices.

Costs (2006–07) *Tuition:* state resident $4000 full-time, $78 per credit hour part-time; nonresident $6000 full-time, $159 per credit hour part-time.

Financial Aid Of all full-time matriculated undergraduates, 20 Federal Work-Study jobs (averaging $1200).

Applying *Application fee:* $20. *Required:* high school transcript, interview. *Application deadlines:* rolling (freshmen), rolling (transfers).

Director of Admissions Fred Quistgard, Director of Admissions, York County Community College, 112 College Drive, Wells, ME 04090. *Phone:* 207-646-9282 Ext. 311. *Toll-free phone:* 800-580-3820. *E-mail:* fquistgard@yccc.edu.

MARYLAND

ALLEGANY COLLEGE OF MARYLAND
Cumberland, Maryland   www.allegany.edu/

- **State and locally supported** 2-year, founded 1961, part of Maryland State Community Colleges System
- **Small-town** 311-acre campus
- **Endowment** $5.8 million
- **Coed,** 3,538 undergraduate students, 58% full-time, 65% women, 35% men

Undergraduates 2,048 full-time, 1,490 part-time. 41% are from out of state, 8% African American, 0.4% Asian American or Pacific Islander, 0.6% Hispanic American, 0.1% Native American, 5% transferred in, 7% live on campus. *Retention:* 52% of 2003 full-time freshmen returned.

Freshmen *Admission:* 2,124 applied, 1,937 admitted, 791 enrolled. *Test scores:* SAT verbal scores over 500: 25%; SAT math scores over 500: 31%; ACT scores over 18: 62%; SAT verbal scores over 600: 5%; SAT math scores over 600: 5%; ACT scores over 24: 10%; SAT verbal scores over 700: 1%.

Faculty *Total:* 236, 49% full-time, 10% with terminal degrees. *Student/faculty ratio:* 17:1.

Majors Accounting technology and bookkeeping; administrative assistant and secretarial science; automobile/automotive mechanics technology; business administration and management; clinical/medical laboratory assistant; clinical/medical laboratory technology; communications technology; computer engineering technology; cosmetology and personal grooming arts related; criminal justice/police science; culinary arts; dental hygiene; forest/forest resources management; health professions related; hospitality administration; legal assistant/paralegal; liberal arts and sciences/liberal studies; management information systems; marketing/marketing management; medical radiologic technology; nursing (registered nurse training); occupational therapist assistant; occupational therapy; physical therapist assistant; psychiatric/mental health services technology; respiratory care therapy.

Academics *Calendar:* semesters. *Degree:* certificates and associate. *Special study options:* academic remediation for entering students, adult/continuing education programs, advanced placement credit, distance learning, double majors, English as a second language, honors programs, independent study, internships, part-time degree program, summer session for credit. *ROTC:* Army (c).

Library Allegany College of Maryland Library with 86,636 titles, 313 serial subscriptions, an OPAC, a Web page.

Student Life *Housing:* college housing not available. *Options:* Campus housing is provided by a third party. *Activities and Organizations:* choral group, SAHDA, Honors Club, EMT Club, Forestry Club. *Campus security:* 24-hour emergency response devices and patrols, late-night transport/escort service. *Student services:* personal/psychological counseling, women's center.

Athletics Member NJCAA. *Intercollegiate sports:* baseball M, basketball M/W, soccer M/W, softball W, tennis M/W, volleyball W.

Standardized Tests *Required for some:* ACT (for admission).

Costs (2006–07) *Tuition:* area resident $2850 full-time, $95 per credit part-time; state resident $5310 full-time, $177 per credit part-time; nonresident $6210 full-time, $207 per credit part-time. Full-time tuition and fees vary according to course load and location. Part-time tuition and fees vary according to course load and location. *Required fees:* $194 full-time, $8 per credit part-time, $41 per term part-time. *Room and board:* room only: $4720. *Waivers:* employees or children of employees.

Applying *Options:* electronic application, early admission. *Required:* high school transcript. *Application deadlines:* rolling (freshmen), rolling (transfers). *Notification:* continuous (transfers).

Freshmen Application Contact Ms. Cathy Nolan, Director of Admissions and Registration, Allegany College of Maryland, 12401 Willowbrook Road, SE, Cumberland, MD 21502. *Phone:* 301-784-5000 Ext. 5202. *Fax:* 301-784-5220. *E-mail:* cnolan@allegany.edu.

ANNE ARUNDEL COMMUNITY COLLEGE
Arnold, Maryland   www.aacc.edu/

- **State and locally supported** 2-year, founded 1961
- **Suburban** 230-acre campus with easy access to Baltimore and Washington, DC
- **Endowment** $2.4 million
- **Coed,** 14,699 undergraduate students

Undergraduates Students come from 12 states and territories, 19 other countries, 0.8% are from out of state, 12% African American, 3% Asian American or Pacific Islander, 2% Hispanic American, 0.6% Native American, 0.7% international. *Retention:* 58% of 2003 full-time freshmen returned.

Freshmen *Admission:* 3,228 admitted.

Faculty *Total:* 899, 28% full-time. *Student/faculty ratio:* 18:1.

Majors Accounting; administrative assistant and secretarial science; American studies; applied art; architectural engineering technology; art; astronomy; behavioral sciences; biological and physical sciences; biology/biological sciences; botany/plant biology; broadcast journalism; business administration and management; business/managerial economics; chemistry; cinematography and film/video production; clinical laboratory science/medical technology; communications technology; computer and information sciences related; computer engineering technology; computer management; computer programming; computer science; computer/technical support; consumer merchandising/retailing management; corrections; criminal justice/law enforcement administration; criminal justice/police science; data entry/microcomputer applications; data processing and data processing technology; economics; education; electrical, electronic and communications engineering technology; elementary education; emergency medical technology (EMT paramedic); engineering technology; English; environmental studies; European studies; food services technology; health teacher education; horticultural science; hotel/motel administration; humanities; human services; industrial radiologic technology; industrial technology; information science/studies; kindergarten/preschool education; landscape architecture; legal assistant/paralegal; liberal arts and sciences/liberal studies; marine science/merchant marine officer; marketing/marketing management; mass communication/media; mathematics; mechanical engineering/mechanical technology; medical/clinical assistant; mental health/rehabilitation; music; nursing (registered nurse training); photography; physical education teaching and coaching; public administration; public policy analysis; real estate; social sciences; system administration; telecommunications.

Academics *Calendar:* semesters. *Degree:* certificates and associate. *Special study options:* academic remediation for entering students, accelerated degree program, adult/continuing education programs, advanced placement credit, cooperative education, distance learning, English as a second language, freshman honors college, honors programs, independent study, internships, part-time degree program, services for LD students, summer session for credit. *ROTC:* Army (c), Air Force (c).

Library Andrew G. Truxal Library with 144,694 titles, 403 serial subscriptions, 8,060 audiovisual materials, an OPAC, a Web page.

Student Life *Housing:* college housing not available. *Activities and Organizations:* drama/theater group, student-run newspaper, choral group, Drama Club, student association, Black Student Union, International Student Association, Chemistry Club. *Campus security:* 24-hour emergency response devices and patrols, student patrols, late-night transport/escort service. *Student services:* health clinic, personal/psychological counseling.

Athletics Member NJCAA. *Intercollegiate sports:* baseball M(s), basketball M/W, cross-country running M(s)/W(s), golf M, lacrosse M(s), soccer M(s)/W(s), softball W(s), volleyball W. *Intramural sports:* lacrosse W.

Standardized Tests *Recommended:* SAT or ACT (for placement).

Costs (2007–08) *Tuition:* area resident $2064 full-time, $86 per credit hour part-time; state resident $3960 full-time, $165 per credit hour part-time; nonresident $8760 full-time, $292 per credit hour part-time. *Required fees:* $232 full-time, $8 per credit hour part-time, $20 per term part-time.

Financial Aid Of all full-time matriculated undergraduates, 104 Federal Work-Study jobs (averaging $1900). 55 state and other part-time jobs (averaging $1740).

Applying *Options:* early admission, deferred entrance. *Application deadlines:* rolling (freshmen), rolling (transfers).

Freshmen Application Contact Mr. Thomas McGinn, Director of Enrollment Development and Admissions, Anne Arundel Community College, 101 College Parkway, Arnold, MD 21012-1895. *Phone:* 410-777-2240. *Fax:* 410-777-2246. *E-mail:* 4info@aacc.edu.

BALTIMORE CITY COMMUNITY COLLEGE
Baltimore, Maryland   www.bccc.state.md.us/

- **State-supported** 2-year, founded 1947
- **Urban** 19-acre campus
- **Endowment** $139,215
- **Coed,** 7,097 undergraduate students

Undergraduates Students come from 4 states and territories, 1% are from out of state.

Freshmen *Admission:* 1,380 applied.

Faculty *Total:* 436, 28% full-time. *Student/faculty ratio:* 17:1.

Majors Accounting; administrative assistant and secretarial science; biological and physical sciences; business administration and management; commercial and advertising art; computer graphics; computer science; computer/technical

support; corrections; criminal justice/police science; data processing and data processing technology; dental hygiene; dietetics; drafting and design technology; electrical, electronic and communications engineering technology; emergency medical technology (EMT paramedic); engineering; fashion/apparel design; fashion merchandising; gerontology; health information/medical records administration; hospitality administration; human services; information science/studies; kindergarten/preschool education; legal administrative assistant/secretary; legal assistant/paralegal; liberal arts and sciences/liberal studies; marketing/marketing management; medical administrative assistant and medical secretary; nursing (registered nurse training); physical therapy; respiratory care therapy; surgical technology; word processing.

Academics *Calendar:* semesters. *Degree:* certificates and associate. *Special study options:* academic remediation for entering students, adult/continuing education programs, advanced placement credit, cooperative education, distance learning, double majors, English as a second language, honors programs, internships, part-time degree program, services for LD students, study abroad, summer session for credit.

Library Bard Library with 72,413 titles, 150 serial subscriptions, 1,074 audiovisual materials, an OPAC, a Web page.

Student Life *Housing:* college housing not available. *Activities and Organizations:* student-run newspaper, radio station, choral group. *Student services:* health clinic, personal/psychological counseling.

Athletics *Intercollegiate sports:* basketball M/W, cross-country running M/W, track and field M/W.

Standardized Tests *Recommended:* SAT Subject Tests (for placement).

Costs (2007–08) *Tuition:* state resident $1872 full-time, $78 per credit hour part-time; nonresident $4032 full-time, $168 per credit hour part-time. *Required fees:* $168 full-time, $5 per credit hour part-time, $30 per term part-time.

Financial Aid Of all full-time matriculated undergraduates, 331 Federal Work-Study jobs (averaging $1879).

Applying *Options:* early admission, deferred entrance. *Application fee:* $10. *Required:* high school transcript. *Recommended:* interview. *Application deadlines:* 8/9 (freshmen), 8/9 (transfers). *Notification:* continuous (freshmen), continuous (transfers).

Freshmen Application Contact Mrs. Scheherazade Forman, Admissions Coordinator, Baltimore City Community College, 2901 Liberty Heights Avenue, Baltimore, MD 21215. *Phone:* 410-462-8300. *Toll-free phone:* 888-203-1261 Ext. 8300. *E-mail:* sforman@bccc.edu.

BALTIMORE INTERNATIONAL COLLEGE
Baltimore, Maryland   www.bic.edu/

- **Independent** primarily 2-year, founded 1972
- **Urban** 6-acre campus with easy access to Washington, DC
- **Endowment** $83,144
- **Coed**

Undergraduates 486 full-time, 30 part-time. Students come from 19 states and territories, 5 other countries, 12% are from out of state, 52% African American, 3% Asian American or Pacific Islander, 2% Hispanic American, 0.4% Native American, 1% international, 21% transferred in, 24% live on campus. *Retention:* 39% of 2003 full-time freshmen returned.

Academics *Calendar:* semesters. *Degrees:* certificates, associate, bachelor's, and master's. *Special study options:* academic remediation for entering students, accelerated degree program, adult/continuing education programs, advanced placement credit, cooperative education, double majors, honors programs, internships, off-campus study, study abroad.

Student Life *Campus security:* late-night transport/escort service, controlled dormitory access.

Standardized Tests *Required for some:* SAT or ACT (for admission), CPat or TOEFL.

Costs (2006–07) *Comprehensive fee:* $21,328 includes full-time tuition ($15,488), mandatory fees ($111), and room and board ($5729). *Room and board:* college room only: $3418. Room and board charges vary according to housing facility. *Payment plans:* tuition prepayment, installment.

Applying *Options:* electronic application, early action, deferred entrance. *Application fee:* $35. *Required:* high school transcript. *Required for some:* essay or personal statement. *Recommended:* letters of recommendation, interview.

Freshmen Application Contact Ms. Kristin Ciarlo, Director of Admissions, Baltimore International College, Commerce Exchange, 17 Commerce Street, Baltimore, MD 21202-3230. *Phone:* 410-752-4710 Ext. 239. *Toll-free phone:* 800-624-9926 Ext. 120. *Fax:* 410-752-3730. *E-mail:* admissions@bic.edu.

▶See page 486 for the College Close-Up.

CARROLL COMMUNITY COLLEGE
Westminster, Maryland   www.carrollcc.edu/

- **State and locally supported** 2-year, founded 1993, part of Maryland Higher Education Commission
- **Suburban** 80-acre campus with easy access to Baltimore
- **Endowment** $1.6 million
- **Coed,** 3,216 undergraduate students, 45% full-time, 64% women, 36% men

Undergraduates 1,441 full-time, 1,775 part-time. Students come from 4 states and territories, 8 other countries, 2% are from out of state, 3% African American, 1% Asian American or Pacific Islander, 2% Hispanic American, 0.5% Native American, 0.3% international, 9% transferred in.

Freshmen *Admission:* 795 applied, 795 admitted, 794 enrolled.

Faculty *Total:* 208, 30% full-time, 6% with terminal degrees. *Student/faculty ratio:* 18:1.

Majors Accounting; business administration and management; computer and information sciences; computer graphics; data processing and data processing technology; education (multiple levels); general studies; health science; human services; kindergarten/preschool education; liberal arts and sciences/liberal studies; mechanical design technology; music; nursing (registered nurse training); physical therapist assistant.

Academics *Calendar:* semesters plus winter session. *Degree:* certificates and associate. *Special study options:* academic remediation for entering students, advanced placement credit, distance learning, English as a second language, honors programs, independent study, internships, part-time degree program, services for LD students, summer session for credit.

Library Random House Learning Resources Center with 39,187 titles, 318 serial subscriptions, an OPAC, a Web page.

Student Life *Housing:* college housing not available. *Activities and Organizations:* drama/theater group, student-run newspaper, choral group, Student Government Organization, Carroll Community Chorus, Programming Board. *Campus security:* late-night transport/escort service. *Student services:* personal/psychological counseling.

Costs (2007–08) *Tuition:* area resident $3234 full-time, $92 per credit part-time; state resident $4476 full-time, $128 per credit part-time; nonresident $6788 full-time, $195 per credit part-time. *Required fees:* $16 per credit part-time.

Financial Aid Of all full-time matriculated undergraduates, 22 Federal Work-Study jobs (averaging $1772).

Applying *Options:* early admission. *Required:* high school transcript. *Application deadlines:* rolling (freshmen), rolling (transfers). *Notification:* continuous (freshmen), continuous (transfers).

Freshmen Application Contact Ms. Candace Edwards, Coordinator of Admissions, Carroll Community College, 1601 Washington Road, Westminster, MD 21157. *Phone:* 410-386-8430. *Toll-free phone:* 888-221-9748. *Fax:* 410-386-8446. *E-mail:* cedwards@carrollcc.edu.

CECIL COMMUNITY COLLEGE
North East, Maryland   www.cecilcc.edu/

- **County-supported** 2-year, founded 1968
- **Small-town** 100-acre campus with easy access to Baltimore
- **Coed,** 1,945 undergraduate students, 37% full-time, 65% women, 35% men

Undergraduates 725 full-time, 1,220 part-time. Students come from 6 states and territories, 4 other countries, 12% are from out of state, 8% African American, 2% Asian American or Pacific Islander, 2% Hispanic American, 0.5% Native American, 0.3% international, 0.4% transferred in.

Freshmen *Admission:* 462 applied, 462 admitted, 460 enrolled.

Faculty *Total:* 185, 23% full-time, 6% with terminal degrees. *Student/faculty ratio:* 10:1.

Majors Accounting; administrative assistant and secretarial science; air traffic control; art; artificial intelligence and robotics; biology/biological sciences; business administration and management; carpentry; computer engineering technology; computer graphics; computer programming; construction engineering technology; criminal justice/law enforcement administration; data processing and data processing technology; education; education (K-12); electrical, electronic and communications engineering technology; elementary education; general studies; hydrology and water resources science; information science/studies; information technology; kindergarten/preschool education; liberal arts and sciences/liberal studies; marketing/marketing management; mathematics; medical laboratory technology; nursing (registered nurse training); photography; physical sciences; physics; pipefitting and sprinkler fitting; transportation and materials moving related; welding technology.

Cecil Community College (continued)

Academics *Calendar:* semesters. *Degree:* certificates and associate. *Special study options:* academic remediation for entering students, accelerated degree program, adult/continuing education programs, advanced placement credit, cooperative education, distance learning, double majors, English as a second language, independent study, internships, part-time degree program, services for LD students, summer session for credit.

Library Cecil County Veteran's Memorial Library with 37,354 titles, 202 serial subscriptions, 1,205 audiovisual materials, an OPAC, a Web page.

Student Life *Housing:* college housing not available. *Activities and Organizations:* drama/theater group, student-run newspaper, student government, Nontraditional Student Organization, Student Nurses Association, student newspaper, national fraternities. *Campus security:* 24-hour emergency response devices, late-night transport/escort service. *Student services:* personal/psychological counseling, women's center.

Athletics Member NJCAA. *Intercollegiate sports:* baseball M(s), basketball M(s)/W(s), cheerleading W, softball W, volleyball W(s). *Intramural sports:* basketball M/W, tennis M/W.

Costs (2006–07) *Tuition:* area resident $2550 full-time, $85 per credit hour part-time; state resident $5250 full-time, $175 per credit hour part-time; nonresident $6600 full-time, $220 per credit hour part-time. *Required fees:* $345 full-time.

Financial Aid Of all full-time matriculated undergraduates, 59 Federal Work-Study jobs (averaging $1421).

Applying *Options:* electronic application, early admission, deferred entrance. *Required:* high school transcript. *Application deadlines:* rolling (freshmen), rolling (transfers). *Notification:* continuous (freshmen), continuous (transfers).

Freshmen Application Contact Ms. Sandra Rajaski, Cecil Community College, One Seahawk Drive, North East, MD 21901. *Phone:* 410-287-6060 Ext. 212. *Fax:* 410-287-1026. *E-mail:* srajaski@cecil.edu.

CHESAPEAKE COLLEGE

Wye Mills, Maryland   www.chesapeake.edu/

- **State and locally supported** 2-year, founded 1965
- **Rural** 170-acre campus with easy access to Baltimore and Washington, DC
- **Coed,** 2,579 undergraduate students

Undergraduates Students come from 2 states and territories, 1% are from out of state, 21% African American, 0.9% Asian American or Pacific Islander, 1% Hispanic American, 0.2% Native American, 0.1% international.

Faculty *Total:* 130, 42% full-time. *Student/faculty ratio:* 16:1.

Majors Accounting; administrative assistant and secretarial science; architectural engineering technology; art; biological and physical sciences; business administration and management; computer engineering technology; computer programming; computer science; corrections; criminal justice/law enforcement administration; data processing and data processing technology; electrical, electronic and communications engineering technology; elementary education; health teacher education; humanities; human services; kindergarten/preschool education; legal administrative assistant/secretary; liberal arts and sciences/liberal studies; mathematics; medical administrative assistant and medical secretary; medical radiologic technology; music; parks, recreation and leisure; physical education teaching and coaching; physical sciences; social sciences; sociology.

Academics *Calendar:* semesters. *Degree:* certificates and associate. *Special study options:* academic remediation for entering students, adult/continuing education programs, advanced placement credit, cooperative education, distance learning, English as a second language, honors programs, independent study, internships, part-time degree program, services for LD students, student-designed majors, summer session for credit.

Library Learning Resource Center plus 1 other with 44,049 titles, 132 serial subscriptions, 1,600 audiovisual materials, an OPAC, a Web page.

Student Life *Housing:* college housing not available. *Activities and Organizations:* drama/theater group, choral group, student government action teams, Phi Theta Kappa, UHURU, Chesapeake Players. *Campus security:* 24-hour patrols. *Student services:* personal/psychological counseling, women's center.

Athletics Member NJCAA. *Intercollegiate sports:* baseball M, basketball M/W, soccer M/W, softball W, tennis M/W, volleyball W. *Intramural sports:* soccer M/W, volleyball M/W.

Costs (2007–08) *Tuition:* area resident $2492 full-time, $89 per credit hour part-time; state resident $4816 full-time, $172 per credit hour part-time; nonresident $6972 full-time, $249 per credit hour part-time. *Required fees:* $384 full-time, $13 per credit hour part-time, $10 per term part-time.

Financial Aid Of all full-time matriculated undergraduates, 32 Federal Work-Study jobs (averaging $1482).

Applying *Options:* early admission, deferred entrance. *Required:* high school transcript. *Application deadlines:* rolling (freshmen), rolling (transfers). *Notification:* continuous (freshmen), continuous (transfers).

Freshmen Application Contact Ms. Kathy Petrichenko, Dean of Recruitment, Chesapeake College, PO Box 8, Wye Mills, MD 21679. *Phone:* 410-822-5400 Ext. 287. *E-mail:* kpetrichenko@chesapeake.edu.

COLLEGE OF SOUTHERN MARYLAND

La Plata, Maryland   www.csmd.edu/

- **State and locally supported** 2-year, founded 1958
- **Rural** 175-acre campus with easy access to Washington, DC
- **Coed,** 7,504 undergraduate students, 37% full-time, 65% women, 35% men

Undergraduates 2,761 full-time, 4,743 part-time. Students come from 19 other countries, 1% are from out of state, 19% African American, 3% Asian American or Pacific Islander, 3% Hispanic American, 0.8% Native American, 45% transferred in.

Freshmen *Admission:* 2,336 enrolled. *Average high school GPA:* 2.86.

Faculty *Total:* 503, 25% full-time. *Student/faculty ratio:* 20:1.

Majors Accounting; agribusiness; art; biology/biological sciences; biotechnology; business administration and management; communication/speech communication and rhetoric; computer programming; dramatic/theater arts; early childhood education; education; electrical, electronic and communications engineering technology; elementary education; emergency medical technology (EMT paramedic); English; fire protection and safety technology; history; human services; information science/studies; journalism; legal assistant/paralegal; liberal arts and sciences/liberal studies; massage therapy; music; nursing (licensed practical/vocational nurse training); nursing (registered nurse training); physical therapist assistant; social sciences.

Academics *Calendar:* semesters. *Degree:* certificates and associate. *Special study options:* academic remediation for entering students, accelerated degree program, adult/continuing education programs, advanced placement credit, cooperative education, distance learning, honors programs, internships, part-time degree program, services for LD students, study abroad, summer session for credit.

Library College of Southern Maryland Library with 44,896 titles, 166 serial subscriptions, an OPAC, a Web page.

Student Life *Housing:* college housing not available. *Activities and Organizations:* drama/theater group, student-run newspaper, choral group, Spanish Club, Nursing Student Association, Science Club, Black Student Union, BACCHUS. *Campus security:* 24-hour emergency response devices and patrols. *Student services:* personal/psychological counseling, women's center.

Athletics Member NJCAA. *Intercollegiate sports:* baseball M, basketball M/W, golf M/W, soccer M/W, softball W, tennis M/W, volleyball W.

Costs (2006–07) *Tuition:* area resident $2256 full-time, $94 per credit part-time; state resident $3936 full-time, $164 per credit part-time; nonresident $5016 full-time, $209 per credit part-time.

Financial Aid Of all full-time matriculated undergraduates, 25 Federal Work-Study jobs (averaging $1200).

Applying *Options:* electronic application, early admission, deferred entrance. *Recommended:* high school transcript. *Application deadlines:* rolling (freshmen), rolling (transfers). *Notification:* continuous (freshmen), continuous (transfers).

Freshmen Application Contact Information Center Coordinator, College of Southern Maryland, PO Box 910, La Plata, MD 20646-0910. *Phone:* 301-934-7520 Ext. 7765. *Toll-free phone:* 800-933-9177. *Fax:* 301-934-7698. *E-mail:* info@csmd.edu.

THE COMMUNITY COLLEGE OF BALTIMORE COUNTY

Baltimore, Maryland   www.ccbcmd.edu/

- **County-supported** 2-year, founded 1957
- **Suburban** 350-acre campus
- **Coed,** 19,446 undergraduate students, 35% full-time, 63% women, 37% men

Undergraduates 6,846 full-time, 12,600 part-time. 1% are from out of state, 31% African American, 5% Asian American or Pacific Islander, 2% Hispanic American, 0.4% Native American.

Freshmen *Admission:* 3,027 enrolled.

Faculty *Total:* 1,061, 34% full-time, 9% with terminal degrees.

Academics *Calendar:* semesters. *Degree:* certificates and associate. *Special study options:* academic remediation for entering students, advanced placement credit, cooperative education, distance learning, English as a second language, honors programs, independent study, internships, services for LD students, study abroad, summer session for credit.

Student Life *Housing:* college housing not available. *Activities and Organizations:* student-run newspaper.

Standardized Tests *Recommended:* SAT or ACT (for admission).

Costs (2007–08) *Tuition:* area resident $2700 full-time, $90 per hour part-time; state resident $5220 full-time, $174 per hour part-time; nonresident $7080 full-time, $236 per hour part-time. *Required fees:* $355 full-time, $10 per hour part-time, $30 per term part-time.

Applying *Application fee:* $15.

Freshmen Application Contact Ms. Diane Drake, Director of Admissions, The Community College of Baltimore County, 800 South Rolling Road, Baltimore, MD 21228-5381. *Phone:* 410-455-4392. *Fax:* 410-719-6546.

FREDERICK COMMUNITY COLLEGE

Frederick, Maryland   **www.frederick.edu/**

- **State and locally supported** 2-year, founded 1957
- **Small-town** 125-acre campus with easy access to Baltimore and Washington, DC
- **Endowment** $4.0 million
- **Coed,** 4,825 undergraduate students, 38% full-time, 62% women, 38% men

Undergraduates 1,856 full-time, 2,969 part-time. Students come from 9 states and territories, 10 other countries, 1% are from out of state, 9% African American, 4% Asian American or Pacific Islander, 5% Hispanic American, 0.6% Native American, 63% transferred in.

Freshmen *Admission:* 1,103 enrolled.

Faculty *Total:* 465, 19% full-time. *Student/faculty ratio:* 15:1.

Majors Accounting; art; biology/biological sciences; business administration and management; chemistry; child development; computer engineering technology; computer science; construction management; criminal justice/law enforcement administration; data processing and data processing technology; drafting and design technology; education; electrical, electronic and communications engineering technology; elementary education; emergency medical technology (EMT paramedic); engineering; English; finance; fire science; general studies; human services; information technology; international business/trade/commerce; kindergarten/preschool education; legal administrative assistant/secretary; legal assistant/paralegal; liberal arts and sciences/liberal studies; marketing/marketing management; mass communication/media; mathematics; mathematics teacher education; medical administrative assistant and medical secretary; medical laboratory technology; music teacher education; nuclear medical technology; nursing (registered nurse training); physical education teaching and coaching; physical sciences; political science and government; psychology; respiratory care therapy; Spanish language teacher education; surgical technology.

Academics *Calendar:* semesters. *Degree:* certificates and associate. *Special study options:* academic remediation for entering students, adult/continuing education programs, advanced placement credit, cooperative education, distance learning, external degree program, honors programs, independent study, off-campus study, part-time degree program, services for LD students, study abroad, summer session for credit. *ROTC:* Army (c).

Library FCC Library with 40,000 titles, 5,150 serial subscriptions, an OPAC, a Web page.

Student Life *Housing:* college housing not available. *Activities and Organizations:* drama/theater group, student-run newspaper. *Campus security:* 24-hour emergency response devices and patrols. *Student services:* personal/psychological counseling, women's center.

Athletics Member NJCAA. *Intercollegiate sports:* baseball M, basketball M/W, golf M/W, soccer M/W, softball W, volleyball W.

Costs (2006–07) *Tuition:* area resident $2040 full-time, $87 per credit hour part-time; state resident $4368 full-time, $190 per credit hour part-time; nonresident $6096 full-time, $259 per credit hour part-time. *Required fees:* $292 full-time, $11 per credit hour part-time, $19 per term part-time. *Payment plan:* installment. *Waivers:* senior citizens and employees or children of employees.

Financial Aid Of all full-time matriculated undergraduates, 25 Federal Work-Study jobs (averaging $1368). 14 state and other part-time jobs (averaging $2715).

Applying *Options:* early admission, deferred entrance. *Application deadlines:* 9/1 (freshmen), 9/1 (transfers). *Notification:* continuous (freshmen), continuous (transfers).

Freshmen Application Contact Ms. Lisa Freel, Coordinator of Recruitment and Outreach, Frederick Community College, Welcome and Registration Center, 7932 Opossumtown Pike, Frederick, MD 21702. *Phone:* 301-846-2466. *Fax:* 301-624-2799. *E-mail:* admissions@frederick.edu.

GARRETT COLLEGE

McHenry, Maryland   **www.garrettcollege.edu/**

- **State and locally supported** 2-year, founded 1966
- **Rural** 62-acre campus
- **Coed,** 734 undergraduate students, 61% full-time, 50% women, 50% men

Undergraduates 450 full-time, 284 part-time. Students come from 12 states and territories, 14 other countries, 22% are from out of state, 5% African American, 0.3% Asian American or Pacific Islander, 1% Hispanic American, 0.6% Native American, 3% international, 50% transferred in, 12% live on campus.

Freshmen *Admission:* 314 enrolled.

Faculty *Total:* 62, 27% full-time, 16% with terminal degrees. *Student/faculty ratio:* 10:1.

Majors Administrative assistant and secretarial science; agricultural mechanization; art; behavioral sciences; biology/biological sciences; business administration and management; criminal justice/safety; education; elementary education; fish/game management; general studies; hotel/motel administration; liberal arts and sciences/liberal studies; mathematics; music; natural resources management and policy; parks, recreation and leisure; parks, recreation and leisure facilities management; physical education teaching and coaching; psychology; social sciences; sociology; wildlife and wildlands science and management; wildlife biology.

Academics *Calendar:* semesters. *Degree:* certificates and associate. *Special study options:* academic remediation for entering students, adult/continuing education programs, advanced placement credit, cooperative education, distance learning, double majors, external degree program, honors programs, independent study, internships, part-time degree program, services for LD students, summer session for credit.

Library Learning Resource Center with 24,105 titles, 69 serial subscriptions, 2,535 audiovisual materials, an OPAC, a Web page.

Student Life *Housing Options:* coed. Campus housing is university owned and leased by the school. *Activities and Organizations:* drama/theater group, student-run newspaper, Wildlife Club, Raiders of the Lost Arts, student government, national fraternities. *Campus security:* 24-hour patrols, controlled dormitory access. *Student services:* personal/psychological counseling.

Athletics Member NJCAA. *Intercollegiate sports:* baseball M(s), basketball M(s)/W(s), golf M, skiing (downhill) M(c)/W(c), volleyball W(s). *Intramural sports:* softball W.

Costs (2007–08) *Tuition:* area resident $2340 full-time, $78 per credit hour part-time; state resident $5880 full-time, $196 per credit hour part-time; nonresident $6960 full-time, $232 per credit hour part-time. *Required fees:* $630 full-time, $20 per credit hour part-time, $15 per semester part-time. *Room and board:* $4992.

Financial Aid Of all full-time matriculated undergraduates, 55 Federal Work-Study jobs (averaging $1018). 75 state and other part-time jobs (averaging $954).

Applying *Options:* early admission, deferred entrance. *Application deadlines:* rolling (freshmen), rolling (out-of-state freshmen), rolling (transfers). *Notification:* continuous (freshmen), continuous (out-of-state freshmen), continuous (transfers).

Freshmen Application Contact Connie Meyers, Coordinator of Student Assistance Center, Garrett College, 687 Mosser Road, McHenry, MD 21541. *Phone:* 301-387-3044. *Fax:* 301-387-3038. *E-mail:* admissions@garrettcollege.edu.

HAGERSTOWN BUSINESS COLLEGE

Hagerstown, Maryland   **www.hagerstownbusinesscol.org/**

- **Proprietary** 2-year, founded 1938, part of Kaplan Higher Education
- **Small-town** 8-acre campus with easy access to Baltimore and Washington, DC
- **Coed**

Undergraduates 770 full-time, 162 part-time. 64% are from out of state, 10% African American, 1% Asian American or Pacific Islander, 2% Hispanic American, 0.1% Native American, 3% live on campus.

Faculty *Student/faculty ratio:* 18:1.

Academics *Calendar:* quarters. *Degree:* certificates and associate. *Special study options:* academic remediation for entering students, accelerated degree program, adult/continuing education programs, advanced placement credit, internships, summer session for credit.

Student Life *Campus security:* 24-hour emergency response devices.

Costs (2006–07) *Tuition:* Contact college for current tuition, fees, and room and board expenses.

Financial Aid Of all full-time matriculated undergraduates, 21 Federal Work-Study jobs (averaging $1343).

Hagerstown Business College (continued)

Applying *Options:* early admission, deferred entrance. *Required:* high school transcript, interview.

Freshmen Application Contact Mr. Steve Shinham, Director of Admissions, Hagerstown Business College, 18618 Crestwood Drive, Hagerstown, MD 21742-2797. *Phone:* 301-739-2680 Ext. 217. *Toll-free phone:* 800-422-2670. *Fax:* 301-791-7661. *E-mail:* info@hagerstownbusinesscol.org.

HAGERSTOWN COMMUNITY COLLEGE

Hagerstown, Maryland   **www.hagerstowncc.edu/**

- **State and locally supported** 2-year, founded 1946
- **Suburban** 187-acre campus with easy access to Baltimore and Washington, DC
- **Endowment** $5.7 million
- **Coed,** 3,629 undergraduate students, 34% full-time, 62% women, 38% men

Undergraduates 1,226 full-time, 2,403 part-time. Students come from 11 states and territories, 23% are from out of state, 9% African American, 1% Asian American or Pacific Islander, 3% Hispanic American, 0.4% Native American, 5% transferred in. *Retention:* 60% of 2003 full-time freshmen returned.

Freshmen *Admission:* 1,373 applied, 1,373 admitted, 815 enrolled.

Faculty *Total:* 237, 28% full-time, 6% with terminal degrees. *Student/faculty ratio:* 14:1.

Majors Accounting technology and bookkeeping; animation, interactive technology, video graphics and special effects; business administration and management; business/commerce; child care and support services management; commercial and advertising art; computer and information sciences; criminal justice/police science; early childhood education; education; electromechanical technology; elementary education; emergency medical technology (EMT paramedic); engineering; health information/medical records administration; industrial technology; liberal arts and sciences and humanities related; liberal arts and sciences/liberal studies; management information systems; mechanical engineering/mechanical technology; medical radiologic technology; nursing (registered nurse training); psychiatric/mental health services technology; web page, digital/multimedia and information resources design.

Academics *Calendar:* semesters. *Degree:* certificates and associate. *Special study options:* academic remediation for entering students, accelerated degree program, adult/continuing education programs, advanced placement credit, cooperative education, distance learning, English as a second language, honors programs, independent study, internships, off-campus study, part-time degree program, services for LD students, student-designed majors, summer session for credit.

Library William Brish Library with 45,705 titles, 228 serial subscriptions, an OPAC, a Web page.

Student Life *Housing:* college housing not available. *Activities and Organizations:* drama/theater group, student-run newspaper, choral group, Phi Theta Kappa, Robinwood Players, Association of Nursing Students, Theta Lambda Upsilon, Art Club. *Campus security:* 24-hour patrols. *Student services:* health clinic, personal/psychological counseling.

Athletics Member NJCAA. *Intercollegiate sports:* baseball M(s), basketball M(s)/W(s), cross-country running M(s)/W(s), golf M/W, soccer M(s)/W, softball W(s), track and field M(s)/W(s), volleyball W(s). *Intramural sports:* cheerleading M/W, golf M/W, lacrosse M/W, table tennis M/W, tennis M/W.

Costs (2007–08) *Tuition:* area resident $2820 full-time, $94 per credit hour part-time; state resident $4470 full-time, $149 per credit hour part-time; nonresident $5880 full-time, $196 per credit hour part-time. *Required fees:* $280 full-time, $8 per credit hour part-time, $20 per credit hour part-time.

Financial Aid Of all full-time matriculated undergraduates, 27 Federal Work-Study jobs (averaging $2955).

Applying *Options:* electronic application, early admission, deferred entrance. *Required for some:* high school transcript, ACT composite score of 21, 1 lab chemistry and algebra for admission into nursing and radiography programs. *Application deadlines:* rolling (freshmen), rolling (transfers). *Notification:* continuous (freshmen), continuous (transfers).

Freshmen Application Contact Dr. Daniel Bock, Assistant Director, Admissions, Records and Registration, Hagerstown Community College, 11400 Robinwood Drive, Hagerstown, MD 21742-6590. *Phone:* 301-790-2800. *Fax:* 301-791-4165. *E-mail:* bockd@hagerstowncc.edu.

HARFORD COMMUNITY COLLEGE

Bel Air, Maryland   **www.harford.edu/**

Freshmen Application Contact Ms. Donna Strasavich, Enrollment Specialist, Harford Community College, 401 Thomas Run Road, Bel Air, MD 21015-1698. *Phone:* 410-836-4311. *Fax:* 410-836-4169. *E-mail:* sendinfo@harford.edu.

HOWARD COMMUNITY COLLEGE

Columbia, Maryland   **www.howardcc.edu/**

- **State and locally supported** 2-year, founded 1966
- **Suburban** 122-acre campus with easy access to Baltimore and Washington, DC
- **Endowment** $2.0 million
- **Coed,** 7,161 undergraduate students, 39% full-time, 59% women, 41% men

Undergraduates 2,773 full-time, 4,388 part-time. 1% are from out of state, 21% African American, 11% Asian American or Pacific Islander, 4% Hispanic American, 0.6% Native American.

Faculty *Total:* 525, 24% full-time. *Student/faculty ratio:* 18:1.

Majors Accounting; administrative assistant and secretarial science; applied art; architecture; art; biological and physical sciences; biomedical technology; biotechnology; business administration and management; cardiovascular technology; child development; clinical laboratory science/medical technology; computer and information sciences related; computer graphics; computer/information technology services administration related; computer science; computer systems networking and telecommunications; consumer merchandising/retailing management; criminal justice/law enforcement administration; data entry/microcomputer applications; dramatic/theater arts; electrical, electronic and communications engineering technology; elementary education; emergency medical technology (EMT paramedic); engineering; environmental studies; fashion merchandising; financial planning and services; general studies; health teacher education; information science/studies; information technology; kindergarten/preschool education; legal administrative assistant/secretary; liberal arts and sciences/liberal studies; medical administrative assistant and medical secretary; music; nuclear medical technology; nursing (licensed practical/vocational nurse training); nursing (registered nurse training); office management; ophthalmic/optometric services; photography; physical sciences; pre-dentistry studies; pre-medical studies; pre-pharmacy studies; pre-veterinary studies; psychology; secondary education; social sciences; sport and fitness administration/management; substance abuse/addiction counseling; telecommunications; theater design and technology.

Academics *Calendar:* semesters. *Degree:* certificates and associate. *Special study options:* academic remediation for entering students, adult/continuing education programs, advanced placement credit, cooperative education, distance learning, double majors, English as a second language, external degree program, honors programs, off-campus study, part-time degree program, services for LD students, study abroad, summer session for credit.

Library Howard Community College Library with 40,380 titles, 1,201 serial subscriptions, an OPAC, a Web page.

Student Life *Housing:* college housing not available. *Activities and Organizations:* drama/theater group, student-run newspaper, choral group, Secretarial Club, Nursing Club, Black Leadership Organization, student newspaper, Student Government Association. *Campus security:* 24-hour emergency response devices and patrols, late-night transport/escort service. *Student services:* personal/psychological counseling.

Athletics Member NJCAA. *Intercollegiate sports:* basketball M/W, cross-country running M/W, lacrosse M, soccer M/W, tennis M/W, track and field M/W, volleyball W. *Intramural sports:* baseball M, basketball M/W, lacrosse M, softball W.

Standardized Tests *Required for some:* SAT or ACT (for admission).

Costs (2007–08) *Tuition:* area resident $3420 full-time, $114 per credit part-time; state resident $5910 full-time, $197 per credit part-time; nonresident $7260 full-time, $242 per credit part-time. *Required fees:* $572 full-time, $19 per credit part-time.

Applying *Options:* electronic application, early admission, deferred entrance. *Application fee:* $25. *Required for some:* essay or personal statement, high school transcript, 2 letters of recommendation. *Application deadlines:* rolling (freshmen), rolling (transfers). *Notification:* continuous (freshmen), continuous (transfers).

Freshmen Application Contact Ms. Christy Thomson, Assistant Director of Admissions, Howard Community College, 10901 Little Patuxent Parkway, Columbia, MD 21044-3197. *Phone:* 410-772-4856. *Fax:* 410-772-4589. *E-mail:* hsinfo@howardcc.edu.

ITT TECHNICAL INSTITUTE

Owings Mills, Maryland   **www.itt-tech.edu/**

- **Proprietary** primarily 2-year, founded 2005
- **Coed**

Majors CAD/CADD drafting/design technology; communications technology; computer and information systems security; computer engineering technology; computer systems networking and telecommunications; electrical, electronic and

communications engineering technology; web/multimedia management and webmaster; web page, digital/multimedia and information resources design.

Academics *Calendar:* quarters. *Degrees:* associate and bachelor's.

Standardized Tests *Required:* Wonderlic aptitude test (for admission).

Costs (2006–07) *Tuition:* Contact school for program costs.

Applying *Application fee:* $100. *Required:* high school transcript, interview. *Recommended:* letters of recommendation. *Application deadlines:* rolling (freshmen), rolling (transfers). *Notification:* continuous (freshmen), continuous (transfers).

Freshmen Application Contact Mr. Tony Owens, Director of Recruitment, ITT Technical Institute, 11301 Red Run Boulevard, Owings Mills, MD 21117. *Phone:* 443-394-7115.

MONTGOMERY COLLEGE

Rockville, Maryland   **www.montgomerycollege.edu/**

- **State and locally supported** 2-year, founded 1946
- **Suburban** 345-acre campus with easy access to Washington D.C.
- **Coed,** 22,893 undergraduate students, 38% full-time, 55% women, 45% men

Undergraduates 8,792 full-time, 14,101 part-time. Students come from 16 states and territories, 174 other countries, 6% are from out of state, 25% African American, 13% Asian American or Pacific Islander, 14% Hispanic American, 0.3% Native American, 8% international, 4% transferred in.

Freshmen *Admission:* 7,388 applied, 7,388 admitted, 3,955 enrolled.

Faculty *Total:* 1,347, 37% full-time, 26% with terminal degrees. *Student/faculty ratio:* 20:1.

Majors Accounting technology and bookkeeping; applied horticulture; architectural drafting and CAD/CADD; automobile/automotive mechanics technology; business administration and management; business/commerce; child care and support services management; civil engineering technology; commercial and advertising art; commercial photography; computer and information sciences; computer technology/computer systems technology; construction management; criminal justice/police science; diagnostic medical sonography and ultrasound technology; education; electrical, electronic and communications engineering technology; electromechanical technology; engineering; fire protection and safety technology; general studies; graphic and printing equipment operation/production; health information/medical records technology; hotel/motel administration; legal assistant/paralegal; liberal arts and sciences/liberal studies; management information systems; medical radiologic technology; nursing (registered nurse training); physical therapist assistant; psychiatric/mental health services technology.

Academics *Calendar:* semesters. *Degree:* certificates and associate. *Special study options:* academic remediation for entering students, accelerated degree program, adult/continuing education programs, advanced placement credit, cooperative education, distance learning, English as a second language, honors programs, off-campus study, part-time degree program, services for LD students, study abroad.

Student Life *Housing:* college housing not available. *Activities and Organizations:* drama/theater group, student-run newspaper, radio station, choral group. *Campus security:* 24-hour emergency response devices and patrols, late-night transport/escort service. *Student services:* personal/psychological counseling, women's center.

Athletics Member NJCAA. *Intercollegiate sports:* baseball M/W, basketball M/W, cross-country running M/W, golf M, soccer M/W, swimming and diving M/W, tennis M/W, track and field M/W, volleyball W. *Intramural sports:* baseball M/W, basketball M/W, bowling M/W, cross-country running M/W, fencing M/W, football M/W, golf M/W, soccer M/W, swimming and diving M/W, tennis M/W, volleyball M/W.

Standardized Tests *Recommended:* SAT or ACT (for admission).

Costs (2007–08) *Tuition:* area resident $2880 full-time, $96 per credit hour part-time; state resident $6516 full-time, $217 per credit hour part-time; nonresident $9000 full-time, $300 per credit hour part-time. *Required fees:* $996 full-time, $33 per credit hour part-time.

Financial Aid Of all full-time matriculated undergraduates, 216 Federal Work-Study jobs (averaging $3050). 250 state and other part-time jobs (averaging $2000).

Applying *Application fee:* $25. *Required for some:* letters of recommendation. *Recommended:* high school transcript, interview. *Application deadlines:* rolling (freshmen), rolling (transfers). *Notification:* continuous (freshmen), continuous (transfers).

Freshmen Application Contact Mr. Sherman Helberg, Director of Admissions and Enrollment, Montgomery College, 51 Mannakee Street, Rockville, MD 20850. *Phone:* 301-279-5034. *E-mail:* sherman.helberg@montgomerycollege.edu.

PRINCE GEORGE'S COMMUNITY COLLEGE

Largo, Maryland   **www.pgcc.edu/**

Freshmen Application Contact Ms. Vera Bagley, Director of Admissions and Records, Prince George's Community College, 301 Largo Road, Largo, MD 20774-2199. *Phone:* 301-322-0801. *Fax:* 301-322-0119.

TESST COLLEGE OF TECHNOLOGY

Baltimore, Maryland   **www.tesst.com/**

- **Proprietary** 2-year, founded 1956
- **Coed,** 1,282 undergraduate students

Majors Computer systems networking and telecommunications; electrical, electronic and communications engineering technology.

Academics *Calendar:* quarters. *Degree:* associate.

Costs (2006–07) *Tuition:* $11,900 per degree program part-time.

Director of Admissions Ms. Susan Sherwood, Director, TESST College of Technology, 1520 South Caton Avenue, Baltimore, MD 21227-1063. *Phone:* 410-644-6400. *Toll-free phone:* 800-833-0209. *Fax:* 410-644-6481. *E-mail:* ssherwood@tesst.com.

TESST COLLEGE OF TECHNOLOGY

Beltsville, Maryland   **www.tesst.com/**

- **Proprietary** 2-year, founded 1967
- **Coed,** 695 undergraduate students

Majors Computer systems networking and telecommunications; criminal justice/police science; electrical, electronic and communications engineering technology.

Academics *Calendar:* quarters. *Degree:* associate.

Costs (2006–07) *Tuition:* $11,320 per degree program part-time.

Applying *Application fee:* $20.

Director of Admissions Ms. Mary Colling, Director of Admissions, TESST College of Technology, 4600 Powder Mill Road, Beltsville, MD 20705. *Phone:* 301-937-8448. *Toll-free phone:* 800-833-0209. *Fax:* 301-937-5327. *E-mail:* mcolling@tesst.com.

TESST COLLEGE OF TECHNOLOGY

Towson, Maryland   **www.tesst.com/**

- **Proprietary** 2-year, founded 1992
- **Coed**

Academics *Calendar:* quarters. *Degree:* associate.

Applying *Required:* high school transcript, interview.

Freshmen Application Contact Ms. Diane McRae, President, TESST College of Technology, 803 Glen Eagles Court, Towson, MD 21286. *Phone:* 410-296-5350. *Toll-free phone:* 800-48-TESST. *Fax:* 410-296-5356. *E-mail:* dmcrae@tesst.com.

WOR-WIC COMMUNITY COLLEGE

Salisbury, Maryland   **www.worwic.edu/**

- **State and locally supported** 2-year, founded 1976
- **Small-town** 202-acre campus
- **Endowment** $4.9 million
- **Coed,** 3,036 undergraduate students, 32% full-time, 65% women, 35% men

Undergraduates 984 full-time, 2,052 part-time. Students come from 9 states and territories, 2% are from out of state, 22% African American, 1% Asian American or Pacific Islander, 2% Hispanic American, 0.2% Native American, 8% transferred in.

Freshmen *Admission:* 1,100 applied, 1,100 admitted, 694 enrolled.

Faculty *Total:* 169, 34% full-time, 14% with terminal degrees. *Student/faculty ratio:* 20:1.

Wor-Wic Community College (continued)

Majors Accounting technology and bookkeeping; administrative assistant and secretarial science; business administration and management; business/commerce; child care and support services management; computer and information sciences; computer systems analysis; criminal justice/police science; electrical, electronic and communications engineering technology; elementary education; emergency medical technology (EMT paramedic); engineering technologies related; hospitality administration; liberal arts and sciences and humanities related; medical radiologic technology; nursing (registered nurse training); substance abuse/addiction counseling.

Academics *Calendar:* semesters. *Degree:* certificates and associate. *Special study options:* academic remediation for entering students, accelerated degree program, adult/continuing education programs, advanced placement credit, distance learning, double majors, English as a second language, honors programs, independent study, internships, part-time degree program, services for LD students, summer session for credit.

Library Patricia M. Hazel Media Center plus 2 others with 44 serial subscriptions, 272 audiovisual materials, a Web page.

Student Life *Housing:* college housing not available. *Activities and Organizations:* drama/theater group, student-run newspaper, choral group, Student Government Association, Arts Club, Bioneer Club, Future Educators of America Club, student newspaper. *Campus security:* 24-hour emergency response devices, late-night transport/escort service, patrols by trained security personnel 9 a.m. to midnight. *Student services:* personal/psychological counseling.

Standardized Tests *Required for some:* ACT (for admission).

Costs (2007–08) *Tuition:* area resident $2280 full-time, $76 per credit hour part-time; state resident $5760 full-time, $192 per credit hour part-time; nonresident $6720 full-time, $224 per credit hour part-time. *Required fees:* $124 full-time, $3 per credit hour part-time, $17 per term part-time.

Applying *Options:* early admission. *Recommended:* high school transcript. *Application deadlines:* rolling (freshmen), rolling (transfers).

Freshmen Application Contact Mr. Richard Webster, Director of Admissions, Wor-Wic Community College, 32000 Campus Drive, Salisbury, MD 21804. *Phone:* 410-334-2895. *Fax:* 410-334-2954. *E-mail:* admissions@worwic.edu.

MASSACHUSETTS

BAY STATE COLLEGE
Boston, Massachusetts   www.baystate.edu/

- **Independent** primarily 2-year, founded 1946
- **Urban** campus
- **Coed**

Undergraduates 522 full-time, 235 part-time. Students come from 11 states and territories, 11 other countries, 11% are from out of state, 18% African American, 8% Asian American or Pacific Islander, 10% Hispanic American, 0.9% international, 21% live on campus. *Retention:* 50% of 2003 full-time freshmen returned.

Faculty *Student/faculty ratio:* 13:1.

Academics *Calendar:* semesters. *Degrees:* associate and bachelor's. *Special study options:* academic remediation for entering students, adult/continuing education programs, advanced placement credit, cooperative education, English as a second language, independent study, internships, part-time degree program.

Student Life *Campus security:* late-night transport/escort service, controlled dormitory access, 14-hour patrols by trained security personnel.

Costs (2006–07) *Comprehensive fee:* $26,325 includes full-time tuition ($15,900), mandatory fees ($350), and room and board ($10,075). Part-time tuition: $1530 per course.

Financial Aid Of all full-time matriculated undergraduates, 20 Federal Work-Study jobs (averaging $2600).

Applying *Options:* early admission. *Application fee:* $40. *Required:* essay or personal statement, high school transcript. *Recommended:* minimum 2.0 GPA, interview.

Freshmen Application Contact Stephen Lyons M.Ed., Director of Admissions, Bay State College, 122 Commonwealth Avenue, Boston, MA 02116. *Phone:* 617-217-9040. *Toll-free phone:* 800-81-LEARN. *Fax:* 617-536-1735. *E-mail:* admissions@baystate.edu.

▶**See page 488 for the College Close-Up.**

BENJAMIN FRANKLIN INSTITUTE OF TECHNOLOGY
Boston, Massachusetts   www.bfit.edu/

- **Independent** primarily 2-year, founded 1908
- **Urban** 3-acre campus
- **Endowment** $8.0 million
- **Coed, primarily men**

Undergraduates Students come from 12 states and territories, 38% African American, 12% Asian American or Pacific Islander, 13% Hispanic American, 0.3% Native American, 0.3% international.

Faculty *Student/faculty ratio:* 11:1.

Academics *Calendar:* semesters. *Degrees:* certificates, associate, and bachelor's. *Special study options:* academic remediation for entering students, adult/continuing education programs, advanced placement credit, English as a second language, internships, off-campus study, part-time degree program, summer session for credit.

Student Life *Campus security:* 24-hour emergency response devices, student patrols.

Athletics Member NJCAA.

Standardized Tests *Recommended:* SAT or ACT (for admission).

Costs (2006–07) *Tuition:* $12,750 full-time, $531 per credit part-time.

Applying *Options:* electronic application, deferred entrance. *Application fee:* $20. *Required:* high school transcript. *Recommended:* essay or personal statement, minimum 2.0 GPA, letters of recommendation, interview.

Freshmen Application Contact Ms. Andrea Dawes, Associate Director of Admissions, Benjamin Franklin Institute of Technology, 41 Berkeley Street, Boston, MA 02116-6296. *Phone:* 617-423-4630 Ext. 190. *Fax:* 617-482-3706. *E-mail:* adawes@bfit.edu.

▶**See page 490 for the College Close-Up.**

BERKSHIRE COMMUNITY COLLEGE
Pittsfield, Massachusetts   www.berkshirecc.edu/

- **State-supported** 2-year, founded 1960, part of Massachusetts Public Higher Education System
- **Suburban** 100-acre campus
- **Endowment** $3.6 million
- **Coed,** 2,225 undergraduate students, 42% full-time, 64% women, 36% men

Undergraduates 945 full-time, 1,280 part-time. Students come from 4 states and territories, 18 other countries, 5% are from out of state, 4% African American, 2% Asian American or Pacific Islander, 3% Hispanic American, 0.4% Native American, 2% international, 6% transferred in.

Freshmen *Admission:* 426 applied, 426 admitted, 426 enrolled.

Faculty *Total:* 176, 31% full-time, 64% with terminal degrees. *Student/faculty ratio:* 13:1.

Majors Banking and financial support services; biology/biological sciences; business administration and management; business automation/technology/data entry; business/commerce; computer and information sciences; criminal justice/safety; dramatic/theater arts; early childhood education; electrical, electronic and communications engineering technology; engineering; engineering technology; environmental science; fire science; health professions related; hospitality administration; human services; international/global studies; liberal arts and sciences/liberal studies; music; nursing (registered nurse training); peace studies and conflict resolution; physical therapist assistant; respiratory care therapy; social work; surgical technology; system, networking, and LAN/WAN management; visual and performing arts.

Academics *Calendar:* semesters. *Degree:* certificates and associate. *Special study options:* academic remediation for entering students, accelerated degree program, adult/continuing education programs, advanced placement credit, cooperative education, distance learning, double majors, English as a second language, honors programs, independent study, internships, off-campus study, part-time degree program, services for LD students, summer session for credit.

Library Jonathan Edwards Library plus 1 other with 72,325 titles, 319 serial subscriptions, 13,304 audiovisual materials, an OPAC, a Web page.

Student Life *Housing:* college housing not available. *Activities and Organizations:* drama/theater group, choral group, Mass PIRG, Student Nurse Organization, Student Senate, Diversity Club, LPN Organization. *Campus security:* 24-hour emergency response devices and patrols, late-night transport/escort service. *Student services:* personal/psychological counseling.

Athletics Member NJCAA.

Costs (2007–08) *Tuition:* state resident $624 full-time, $26 per credit part-time; nonresident $6240 full-time, $260 per credit part-time. *Required fees:* $2316 full-time, $97 per credit part-time.

Financial Aid Of all full-time matriculated undergraduates, 72 Federal Work-Study jobs (averaging $1600).

Applying *Options:* deferred entrance. *Application fee:* $10. *Required:* high school transcript. *Recommended:* interview. *Application deadlines:* rolling (freshmen), rolling (transfers). *Notification:* continuous (freshmen), continuous (transfers).

Freshmen Application Contact Ms. Margo J. Handschu, Coordinator of Admissions, Berkshire Community College, 1350 West Street, Pittsfield, MA 01201-5786. *Phone:* 413-236-1631. *Toll-free phone:* 800-816-1233 Ext. 242. *Fax:* 413-496-9511. *E-mail:* mhandsch@berkshirecc.edu.

BRISTOL COMMUNITY COLLEGE
Fall River, Massachusetts   www.bristol.mass.edu/

- **State-supported** 2-year, founded 1965
- **Urban** 105-acre campus with easy access to Boston
- **Endowment** $2.9 million
- **Coed**

Undergraduates 3,097 full-time, 3,776 part-time. Students come from 7 states and territories, 25 other countries, 7% are from out of state, 5% African American, 2% Asian American or Pacific Islander, 3% Hispanic American, 0.6% Native American, 0.2% international, 5% transferred in.

Faculty *Student/faculty ratio:* 19:1.

Academics *Calendar:* semesters. *Degree:* certificates and associate. *Special study options:* academic remediation for entering students, adult/continuing education programs, cooperative education, distance learning, English as a second language, honors programs, independent study, internships, off-campus study, part-time degree program, services for LD students, student-designed majors, summer session for credit.

Student Life *Campus security:* 24-hour emergency response devices and patrols, student patrols, late-night transport/escort service.

Costs (2006–07) *Tuition:* state resident $576 full-time, $24 per credit part-time; nonresident $5520 full-time, $230 per credit part-time. *Required fees:* $2544 full-time, $99 per credit part-time, $30 per term part-time.

Financial Aid Of all full-time matriculated undergraduates, 205 Federal Work-Study jobs (averaging $1627). 65 state and other part-time jobs (averaging $1478).

Applying *Application fee:* $10. *Required:* high school transcript.

Freshmen Application Contact Mr. Rodney Clark, Director of Admissions, Bristol Community College, 777 Elsbree Street, Hudnall Administration Building, Fall River, MA 02720. *Phone:* 508-678-2811 Ext. 2177. *Fax:* 508-730-3265. *E-mail:* rclark@bristol.mass.edu.

BUNKER HILL COMMUNITY COLLEGE
Boston, Massachusetts   www.bhcc.mass.edu/

- **State-supported** 2-year, founded 1973
- **Urban** 21-acre campus
- **Endowment** $2.1 million
- **Coed**

Undergraduates 2,388 full-time, 5,449 part-time. Students come from 18 states and territories, 93 other countries, 1% are from out of state, 29% African American, 14% Asian American or Pacific Islander, 14% Hispanic American, 0.8% Native American, 6% international, 3% transferred in.

Faculty *Student/faculty ratio:* 19:1.

Academics *Calendar:* semesters. *Degree:* certificates and associate. *Special study options:* academic remediation for entering students, advanced placement credit, cooperative education, distance learning, English as a second language, external degree program, honors programs, independent study, internships, part-time degree program, services for LD students, study abroad, summer session for credit.

Student Life *Campus security:* 24-hour emergency response devices and patrols, late-night transport/escort service.

Athletics Member NSCAA, NJCAA.

Costs (2006–07) *Tuition:* state resident $576 full-time, $24 per credit part-time; nonresident $5520 full-time, $230 per credit part-time. Full-time tuition and fees vary according to course load. Part-time tuition and fees vary according to course load. *Required fees:* $1824 full-time, $76 per credit part-time.

Financial Aid Of all full-time matriculated undergraduates, 116 Federal Work-Study jobs (averaging $1500).

Applying *Options:* deferred entrance. *Application fee:* $10. *Required:* high school transcript.

Freshmen Application Contact Ms. Debra Boyer, Registrar/Director of Enrollment Services, Bunker Hill Community College, BHCC Enrollment Services Center, 250 New Rutherford Avenue, Boston, MA 02129. *Phone:* 617-228-2420. *Fax:* 617-228-2082.

▶See page 528 for the College Close-Up.

CAPE COD COMMUNITY COLLEGE
West Barnstable, Massachusetts   www.capecod.mass.edu/

- **State-supported** 2-year, founded 1961, part of Massachusetts Public Higher Education System
- **Rural** 120-acre campus with easy access to Boston
- **Endowment** $3.2 million
- **Coed**, 4,212 undergraduate students, 35% full-time, 62% women, 38% men

Undergraduates 1,465 full-time, 2,747 part-time. 6% African American, 1% Asian American or Pacific Islander, 2% Hispanic American, 1% Native American, 0.9% international. *Retention:* 55% of 2003 full-time freshmen returned.

Freshmen *Admission:* 620 enrolled.

Faculty *Total:* 314, 21% full-time. *Student/faculty ratio:* 16:1.

Majors Accounting; administrative assistant and secretarial science; art; biological and physical sciences; business administration and management; computer and information sciences related; computer graphics; computer science; computer systems networking and telecommunications; criminal justice/law enforcement administration; dental hygiene; dramatic/theater arts; education; environmental engineering technology; environmental studies; executive assistant/executive secretary; fire science; history; hotel/motel administration; information science/studies; information technology; kindergarten/preschool education; legal administrative assistant/secretary; legal assistant/paralegal; liberal arts and sciences/liberal studies; management science; mass communication/media; mathematics; medical administrative assistant and medical secretary; modern languages; music; nursing (registered nurse training); parks, recreation and leisure; philosophy; physical education teaching and coaching; physical therapist assistant; pre-engineering; psychology; system administration; web/multimedia management and webmaster; web page, digital/multimedia and information resources design.

Academics *Calendar:* semesters. *Degree:* certificates and associate. *Special study options:* academic remediation for entering students, adult/continuing education programs, advanced placement credit, cooperative education, distance learning, English as a second language, freshman honors college, honors programs, independent study, internships, off-campus study, part-time degree program, services for LD students, study abroad, summer session for credit.

Library Cape Cod Community College Learning Resource Center with 54,342 titles, 705 serial subscriptions, an OPAC.

Student Life *Housing:* college housing not available. *Activities and Organizations:* drama/theater group, student-run newspaper, radio station, choral group, Innkeepers Club, Phi Theta Kappa, Student Senate, Learning Disabilities Support Group, Ethnic Diversity. *Campus security:* 24-hour patrols. *Student services:* health clinic, personal/psychological counseling, women's center.

Athletics *Intramural sports:* badminton M/W, baseball M, basketball M/W, crew M/W, racquetball M/W, sailing M/W, skiing (downhill) M/W, soccer M, softball M/W, tennis M/W, volleyball M/W, weight lifting M/W.

Costs (2006–07) *Tuition:* $24 per credit part-time; state resident $720 full-time, $24 per credit part-time; nonresident $6900 full-time, $230 per credit part-time. *Required fees:* $2940 full-time, $98 per credit part-time. *Payment plan:* installment. *Waivers:* senior citizens and employees or children of employees.

Financial Aid Of all full-time matriculated undergraduates, 50 Federal Work-Study jobs (averaging $1650).

Applying *Options:* deferred entrance. *Application fee:* $10. *Required:* high school transcript. *Required for some:* essay or personal statement, letters of recommendation. *Application deadlines:* 8/10 (freshmen), 8/10 (transfers). *Notification:* continuous (freshmen), continuous (transfers).

Freshmen Application Contact Ms. Susan Kline-Symington, Director of Admissions, Cape Cod Community College, 2240 Lyanough Road, West Barnstable, MA 02668-1599. *Phone:* 508-362-2131. *Toll-free phone:* 877-846-3672. *Fax:* 508-375-4089. *E-mail:* admiss@capecod.edu.

DEAN COLLEGE
Franklin, Massachusetts
www.dean.edu/

- **Independent** primarily 2-year, founded 1865
- **Small-town** 100-acre campus with easy access to Boston and Providence
- **Endowment** $22.8 million
- **Coed,** 1,106 undergraduate students, 88% full-time, 48% women, 52% men

Undergraduates 975 full-time, 131 part-time. Students come from 23 states and territories, 131 other countries, 48% are from out of state, 7% African American, 1% Asian American or Pacific Islander, 3% Hispanic American, 0.6% Native American, 10% international, 4% transferred in, 88% live on campus. *Retention:* 62% of 2003 full-time freshmen returned.

Freshmen *Admission:* 1,910 applied, 1,398 admitted, 551 enrolled. *Average high school GPA:* 2.2. *Test scores:* SAT verbal scores over 500: 24%; SAT math scores over 500: 23%; ACT scores over 18: 48%; SAT verbal scores over 600: 4%; SAT math scores over 600: 4%; ACT scores over 24: 7%.

Faculty *Total:* 112, 29% full-time, 20% with terminal degrees. *Student/faculty ratio:* 19:1.

Majors Athletic training; business administration and management; communication/speech communication and rhetoric; criminal justice/law enforcement administration; criminal justice/police science; dance; dramatic/theater arts; early childhood education; liberal arts and sciences/liberal studies; mathematics and computer science; physical education teaching and coaching; sport and fitness administration/management.

Academics *Calendar:* semesters. *Degrees:* certificates, associate, and bachelor's. *Special study options:* academic remediation for entering students, accelerated degree program, adult/continuing education programs, advanced placement credit, English as a second language, freshman honors college, honors programs, independent study, internships, off-campus study, part-time degree program, services for LD students, student-designed majors, summer session for credit.

Library E. Ross Anderson Library with 45,565 titles, 174 serial subscriptions, 1,203 audiovisual materials.

Student Life *Housing:* on-campus residence required through sophomore year. *Options:* coed, women-only, disabled students. Campus housing is university owned. Freshman campus housing is guaranteed. *Activities and Organizations:* drama/theater group, student-run radio station, choral group, Emerging Leaders, College Success Staff, Student Ambassadors, student government, Phi Theta Kappa. *Campus security:* 24-hour emergency response devices and patrols, late-night transport/escort service, controlled dormitory access. *Student services:* health clinic, personal/psychological counseling.

Athletics Member NJCAA. *Intercollegiate sports:* baseball M(s), basketball M(s)/W(s), football M(s), golf M, lacrosse M(s)/W(s), soccer M(s)/W(s), softball W(s), volleyball W(s). *Intramural sports:* basketball M, football M, golf M, lacrosse M, skiing (cross-country) M/W, skiing (downhill) M/W, tennis M/W, volleyball M/W.

Standardized Tests *Required:* SAT or ACT (for admission).

Costs (2007–08) *Comprehensive fee:* $36,380 includes full-time tuition ($25,420) and room and board ($10,960). Part-time tuition: $690 per course. *Room and board:* college room only: $6930.

Applying *Options:* electronic application, deferred entrance. *Application fee:* $35. *Required:* essay or personal statement, high school transcript, letters of recommendation. *Recommended:* minimum 2.0 GPA, interview. *Application deadlines:* rolling (freshmen), rolling (transfers). *Notification:* continuous (freshmen), continuous (transfers).

Freshmen Application Contact Mr. Paul Vaccaro, Assistant Vice President for Enrollment Services and Dean of Admission, Dean College, 99 Main Street, Franklin, MA 02038. *Phone:* 508-541-1508. *Toll-free phone:* 877-TRY-DEAN. *Fax:* 508-541-8726. *E-mail:* admission@dean.edu.

FINE MORTUARY COLLEGE, LLC
Norwood, Massachusetts
www.fine-ne.com/

- **Proprietary** 2-year, founded 1996
- **Coed,** 73 undergraduate students

Majors Funeral service and mortuary science.

Academics *Calendar:* continuous. *Degree:* associate.

Costs (2006–07) *Tuition:* $21,564 full-time.

Applying *Application fee:* $50.

Freshmen Application Contact Admissions Office, FINE Mortuary College, LLC, 150 Kerry Place, Norwood, MA 02062.

FISHER COLLEGE
Boston, Massachusetts
www.fisher.edu/

- **Independent** primarily 2-year, founded 1903
- **Urban** campus
- **Endowment** $12.9 million
- **Coed,** 507 undergraduate students, 100% full-time, 66% women, 34% men

Undergraduates 507 full-time. Students come from 14 states and territories, 21 other countries, 21% are from out of state, 19% African American, 4% Asian American or Pacific Islander, 16% Hispanic American, 0.2% Native American, 11% international, 18% transferred in, 50% live on campus.

Freshmen *Admission:* 1,700 applied, 1,060 admitted, 254 enrolled. *Average high school GPA:* 2.52.

Faculty *Total:* 48, 50% full-time, 21% with terminal degrees. *Student/faculty ratio:* 18:1.

Majors Accounting; business administration and management; fashion/apparel design; fashion merchandising; health science; hospitality administration; humanities; kindergarten/preschool education; liberal arts and sciences/liberal studies; psychology; tourism and travel services management.

Academics *Calendar:* semesters. *Degrees:* associate and bachelor's. *Special study options:* academic remediation for entering students, adult/continuing education programs, advanced placement credit, English as a second language, independent study, off-campus study, part-time degree program, study abroad, summer session for credit.

Library Fisher College Library plus 1 other with 30,000 titles, 160 serial subscriptions, an OPAC.

Student Life *Housing Options:* coed, women-only. Campus housing is university owned. *Activities and Organizations:* drama/theater group, choral group, Drama Club, student government, Student Activity Club, Inter-Cultural Club. *Campus security:* 24-hour emergency response devices and patrols, controlled dormitory access. *Student services:* health clinic, personal/psychological counseling, women's center.

Athletics Member NAIA. *Intercollegiate sports:* baseball M, basketball M/W, softball W.

Costs (2007–08) *Comprehensive fee:* $32,565 includes full-time tuition ($20,065), mandatory fees ($950), and room and board ($11,550). Part-time tuition: $668 per credit.

Applying *Options:* deferred entrance. *Application fee:* $25. *Required:* high school transcript. *Required for some:* essay or personal statement, letters of recommendation, interview. *Recommended:* minimum 2.0 GPA. *Application deadlines:* rolling (freshmen), rolling (transfers). *Notification:* continuous (freshmen), continuous (transfers).

Freshmen Application Contact Mr. Robert Melaragni, Director Admissions, Fisher College, 118 Beacon Street, Boston, MA 02116. *Phone:* 617-236-8800 Ext. 4401. *Toll-free phone:* 800-821-3050 (in-state); 800-446-1226 (out-of-state). *Fax:* 617-236-5473. *E-mail:* admissions@fisher.edu.

GIBBS COLLEGE
Boston, Massachusetts
www.katharinegibbs.com/

Director of Admissions Ms. Jaimee Tyler, Director of Admissions, Gibbs College, 126 Newbury Street, Boston, MA 02116-2904. *Phone:* 617-578-7150. *Toll-free phone:* 800-6SKILLS.

GREENFIELD COMMUNITY COLLEGE
Greenfield, Massachusetts
www.gcc.mass.edu/

- **State-supported** 2-year, founded 1962
- **Small-town** 120-acre campus
- **Coed**

Undergraduates 994 full-time, 1,223 part-time. Students come from 5 states and territories, 7 other countries, 5% are from out of state, 3% African American, 3% Asian American or Pacific Islander, 3% Hispanic American, 0.4% Native American, 12% transferred in.

Faculty *Student/faculty ratio:* 23:1.

Academics *Calendar:* semesters. *Degree:* certificates and associate. *Special study options:* academic remediation for entering students, adult/continuing education programs, advanced placement credit, cooperative education, distance learning, double majors, English as a second language, honors programs, independent study, internships, part-time degree program, services for LD students, summer session for credit.

Student Life *Campus security:* 24-hour emergency response devices and patrols, late-night transport/escort service.

Standardized Tests *Required for some:* Psychological Corporation Practical Nursing Entrance Examination.

Costs (2006–07) *Tuition:* state resident $780 full-time, $26 per credit part-time; nonresident $8430 full-time, $281 per credit part-time. Full-time tuition and fees vary according to class time. Part-time tuition and fees vary according to class time. *Required fees:* $3317 full-time, $107 per credit part-time, $61 per semester part-time.

Applying *Application fee:* $10. *Required for some:* high school transcript, interview.

Freshmen Application Contact Mr. Herbert Hentz, Assistant Director of Admission, Greenfield Community College, 1 College Drive, Greenfield, MA 01301-9739. *Phone:* 413-775-1000. *Fax:* 413-773-5129. *E-mail:* admission@gcc.mass.edu.

HOLYOKE COMMUNITY COLLEGE

Holyoke, Massachusetts　　　　　**www.hcc.mass.edu/**

- **State-supported** 2-year, founded 1946, part of Massachusetts Public Higher Education System
- **Small-town** 135-acre campus
- **Endowment** $6.3 million
- **Coed,** 6,297 undergraduate students, 52% full-time, 64% women, 36% men

Undergraduates 3,265 full-time, 3,032 part-time. Students come from 14 states and territories, 1% are from out of state, 6% African American, 2% Asian American or Pacific Islander, 15% Hispanic American, 0.5% Native American, 0.5% international, 7% transferred in.

Freshmen *Admission:* 1,660 admitted, 1,660 enrolled.

Faculty *Total:* 446, 26% full-time. *Student/faculty ratio:* 19:1.

Majors Accounting; administrative assistant and secretarial science; American studies; biology/biological sciences; business administration and management; business teacher education; chemistry; cinematography and film/video production; clinical laboratory science/medical technology; commercial and advertising art; computer typography and composition equipment operation; consumer merchandising/retailing management; criminal justice/police science; dramatic/theater arts; elementary education; engineering science; environmental studies; family and consumer sciences/human sciences; fine/studio arts; foods, nutrition, and wellness; general studies; health information/medical records administration; hospitality administration; hotel/motel administration; human services; information science/studies; international business/trade/commerce; kindergarten/preschool education; legal administrative assistant/secretary; liberal arts and sciences/liberal studies; mass communication/media; music; nursing (registered nurse training); photography; physics; pre-engineering; radiologic technology/science; sport and fitness administration/management; tourism and travel services management; veterinary sciences; veterinary technology; visual and performing arts.

Academics *Calendar:* semesters. *Degree:* certificates and associate. *Special study options:* academic remediation for entering students, adult/continuing education programs, advanced placement credit, cooperative education, English as a second language, honors programs, independent study, internships, off-campus study, part-time degree program, services for LD students, student-designed majors, study abroad, summer session for credit. *ROTC:* Army (c), Air Force (c).

Library Elaine Marieb Library with 76,322 titles, 284 serial subscriptions, 6,583 audiovisual materials, an OPAC, a Web page.

Student Life *Housing:* college housing not available. *Activities and Organizations:* drama/theater group, student-run newspaper, radio station, choral group, Drama Club, Music Club, Student Advisory Board. *Campus security:* 24-hour emergency response devices and patrols, student patrols, late-night transport/escort service. *Student services:* health clinic, personal/psychological counseling, women's center.

Athletics Member NJCAA. *Intercollegiate sports:* baseball M, basketball M/W, golf M/W, skiing (downhill) M(c)/W(c), soccer M/W, softball W, tennis M/W, volleyball W.

Costs (2007–08) *Tuition:* state resident $2640 full-time, $110 per credit part-time; nonresident $7584 full-time, $316 per credit part-time. *Required fees:* $128 full-time.

Applying *Options:* electronic application, early admission, deferred entrance. *Application fee:* $10. *Required:* high school transcript. *Recommended:* interview. *Application deadlines:* rolling (freshmen), rolling (transfers). *Notification:* continuous (freshmen), continuous (transfers).

Freshmen Application Contact Ms. Marcia Rosbury-Henne, Director of Admissions and Transfer Affairs, Holyoke Community College, Holyoke Community College, Attn: Admission Office, Holyoke, MA 01040. *Phone:* 413-552-

2000. *Toll-free phone:* 888-530-8855 (in-state); 413-552-2850 (out-of-state). *Fax:* 413-552-2045. *E-mail:* admissions@hcc.mass.edu.

ITT TECHNICAL INSTITUTE

Norwood, Massachusetts　　　　　**www.itt-tech.edu/**

- **Proprietary** 2-year, founded 1990, part of ITT Educational Services, Inc
- **Suburban** campus with easy access to Boston
- **Coed**

Majors CAD/CADD drafting/design technology; computer engineering technology; computer software engineering; computer systems networking and telecommunications; web/multimedia management and webmaster; web page, digital/multimedia and information resources design.

Academics *Calendar:* quarters. *Degree:* associate.

Library a Web page.

Student Life *Housing:* college housing not available.

Standardized Tests *Required:* Wonderlic aptitude test (for admission).

Costs (2006–07) *Tuition:* Contact school for program costs.

Applying *Options:* deferred entrance. *Application fee:* $100. *Required:* high school transcript, interview. *Recommended:* letters of recommendation. *Application deadlines:* rolling (freshmen), rolling (transfers). *Notification:* continuous (freshmen), continuous (transfers).

Freshmen Application Contact Mr. Thomas F. Ryan III, Director of Recruitment, ITT Technical Institute, 333 Providence Highway, Norwood, MA 02062. *Phone:* 781-278-7200. *Toll-free phone:* 800-879-8324.

ITT TECHNICAL INSTITUTE

Woburn, Massachusetts　　　　　**www.itt-tech.edu/**

- **Proprietary** 2-year, founded 2000, part of ITT Educational Services, Inc
- **Coed**

Majors CAD/CADD drafting/design technology; communications technology; computer engineering technology; web/multimedia management and webmaster; web page, digital/multimedia and information resources design.

Academics *Calendar:* quarters. *Degree:* associate.

Library a Web page.

Student Life *Housing:* college housing not available.

Standardized Tests *Required:* Wonderlic aptitude test (for admission).

Costs (2006–07) *Tuition:* Contact school for program costs.

Applying *Options:* deferred entrance. *Application fee:* $100. *Required:* high school transcript, interview. *Recommended:* letters of recommendation. *Application deadlines:* rolling (freshmen), rolling (transfers). *Notification:* continuous (freshmen), continuous (transfers).

Freshmen Application Contact Mr. Gordon Berridge, ITT Technical Institute, 10 Forbes Road, Woburn, MA 01801. *Phone:* 781-937-8324. *Toll-free phone:* 800-430-5097.

LABOURÉ COLLEGE

Boston, Massachusetts　　　　　**www.laboure.edu/**

Director of Admissions Ms. Gina M. Morrissette, Director of Admissions, Labouré College, 2120 Dorchester Avenue, Boston, MA 02124. *Phone:* 617-296-8300.

MARIAN COURT COLLEGE

Swampscott, Massachusetts　　　　　**www.mariancourt.edu/**

- **Independent Roman Catholic** 2-year, founded 1964
- **Suburban** 6-acre campus with easy access to Boston
- **Coed, primarily women,** 281 undergraduate students, 69% full-time, 93% women, 7% men

Undergraduates 194 full-time, 87 part-time. Students come from 1 other state, 5 other countries.

Freshmen *Admission:* 136 applied, 132 admitted. *Average high school GPA:* 2.4.

Marian Court College (continued)

Faculty *Total:* 25, 28% full-time. *Student/faculty ratio:* 10:1.

Majors Accounting; administrative assistant and secretarial science; business administration and management; clinical laboratory science/medical technology; criminal justice/safety; data processing and data processing technology; hospitality administration; human resources management; legal administrative assistant/secretary; liberal arts and sciences/liberal studies; medical administrative assistant and medical secretary; tourism and travel services management.

Academics *Calendar:* semesters. *Degree:* certificates and associate. *Special study options:* academic remediation for entering students, adult/continuing education programs, advanced placement credit, honors programs, independent study, internships, off-campus study, part-time degree program, summer session for credit.

Library Lindsay Library with 5,006 titles, 122 serial subscriptions, an OPAC.

Student Life *Housing:* college housing not available. *Activities and Organizations:* choral group, Travel Club, student government, Yearbook Committee, Theater Club. *Campus security:* well-lit parking lots. *Student services:* personal/psychological counseling.

Costs (2006–07) *Tuition:* $13,200 full-time.

Financial Aid Of all full-time matriculated undergraduates, 14 Federal Work-Study jobs (averaging $780).

Applying *Options:* electronic application, deferred entrance. *Required:* essay or personal statement, high school transcript, minimum 2.0 GPA, 2 letters of recommendation, interview. *Application deadlines:* rolling (freshmen), rolling (transfers).

Director of Admissions Mrs. Lisa Emerson Parker, Associate Director of Admissions, Marian Court College, 35 Little's Point Road, Swampscott, MA 01907-2840. *Phone:* 781-595-6768 Ext. 239. *Fax:* 781-595-3536. *E-mail:* lparker@mariancourt.edu.

MASSACHUSETTS BAY COMMUNITY COLLEGE

Wellesley Hills, Massachusetts **www.massbay.edu/**

- **State-supported** 2-year, founded 1961
- **Suburban** 84-acre campus with easy access to Boston
- **Coed,** 5,040 undergraduate students, 40% full-time, 61% women, 39% men

Undergraduates 2,035 full-time, 3,005 part-time. Students come from 4 states and territories, 51 other countries, 3% are from out of state, 12% African American, 4% Asian American or Pacific Islander, 8% Hispanic American, 0.3% Native American, 3% international, 27% transferred in. *Retention:* 52% of 2003 full-time freshmen returned.

Freshmen *Admission:* 2,517 applied, 2,492 admitted, 1,125 enrolled.

Faculty *Total:* 343, 23% full-time. *Student/faculty ratio:* 19:1.

Majors Accounting; automotive engineering technology; biological and physical sciences; biology/biotechnology laboratory technician; business administration and management; business/commerce; chemical technology; child care and support services management; communication/speech communication and rhetoric; computer and information sciences; computer engineering technology; computer science; criminal justice/law enforcement administration; drafting and design technology; engineering technology; environmental engineering technology; forensic science and technology; general studies; hospitality administration; human services; information science/studies; international relations and affairs; legal assistant/paralegal; liberal arts and sciences/liberal studies; mechanical engineering/mechanical technology; medical radiologic technology; nursing (registered nurse training); physical therapist assistant; respiratory care therapy; social sciences.

Academics *Calendar:* semesters. *Degree:* certificates and associate. *Special study options:* academic remediation for entering students, adult/continuing education programs, advanced placement credit, cooperative education, distance learning, honors programs, internships, part-time degree program, services for LD students, summer session for credit.

Library Perkins Library with 51,429 titles, 280 serial subscriptions, 4,780 audiovisual materials, an OPAC, a Web page.

Student Life *Housing:* college housing not available. *Activities and Organizations:* drama/theater group, student-run newspaper, Student Government Association, Latino Student Organization, New World Society Club, Mass Bay Players, Student Occupational Therapy Association. *Campus security:* 24-hour emergency response devices and patrols. *Student services:* health clinic, personal/psychological counseling.

Athletics Member NJCAA. *Intercollegiate sports:* baseball M, basketball M/W, cross-country running M/W, golf M/W, soccer M/W, softball W, tennis M/W, volleyball W. *Intramural sports:* ice hockey M, soccer M/W.

Costs (2006–07) *Tuition:* state resident $720 full-time, $24 per credit part-time; nonresident $6900 full-time, $230 per credit part-time. *Required fees:* $2890 full-time, $95 per credit part-time.

Financial Aid Of all full-time matriculated undergraduates, 30 Federal Work-Study jobs (averaging $3000).

Applying *Options:* electronic application, deferred entrance. *Application fee:* $20. *Application deadlines:* rolling (freshmen), rolling (transfers). *Notification:* continuous (freshmen), continuous (transfers).

Freshmen Application Contact Ms. Donna Raposa, Director of Admissions, Massachusetts Bay Community College, 50 Oakland Street, Wellesley Hills, MA 02481. *Phone:* 781-239-2500. *Fax:* 781-239-1047. *E-mail:* info@massbay.edu.

▶See page 562 for the College Close-Up.

MASSASOIT COMMUNITY COLLEGE

Brockton, Massachusetts **www.massasoit.mass.edu/**

- **State-supported** 2-year, founded 1966
- **Suburban** 100-acre campus with easy access to Boston
- **Coed,** 6,975 undergraduate students, 47% full-time, 58% women, 42% men

Undergraduates 3,311 full-time, 3,664 part-time. Students come from 8 states and territories, 3 other countries, 1% are from out of state, 17% African American, 2% Asian American or Pacific Islander, 3% Hispanic American, 0.6% Native American, 0.5% international, 5% transferred in.

Freshmen *Admission:* 1,527 admitted, 1,527 enrolled.

Faculty *Total:* 502, 24% full-time.

Majors Accounting; administrative assistant and secretarial science; architectural engineering technology; business administration and management; business administration, management and operations related; child care and support services management; child care provision; computer and information sciences; computer and information sciences and support services related; computer and information sciences related; computer programming; computer/technical support; criminal justice/police science; culinary arts; dental assisting; diesel mechanics technology; dramatic/theater arts; electrical and electronic engineering technologies related; electrical, electronic and communications engineering technology; engineering technologies related; fine/studio arts; fire science; graphic design; heating, air conditioning and refrigeration technology; hotel/motel administration; human services; liberal arts and sciences and humanities related; liberal arts and sciences/liberal studies; marketing/marketing management; medical/clinical assistant; nursing (registered nurse training); operations management; radiologic technology/science; respiratory care therapy; respiratory therapy technician; restaurant/food services management; tourism and travel services management; vehicle maintenance and repair technologies related.

Academics *Calendar:* semesters. *Degree:* certificates and associate. *Special study options:* academic remediation for entering students, accelerated degree program, adult/continuing education programs, cooperative education, distance learning, English as a second language, independent study, internships, off-campus study, part-time degree program, services for LD students, summer session for credit.

Library 75,000 titles, 396 serial subscriptions, a Web page.

Student Life *Housing:* college housing not available. *Activities and Organizations:* drama/theater group, student-run newspaper, radio station, Drama Club, student newspaper, Phi Theta Kappa, International Student Association, Student Senate. *Campus security:* 24-hour patrols. *Student services:* health clinic, personal/psychological counseling, women's center.

Athletics Member NJCAA. *Intercollegiate sports:* baseball M, basketball M(s)/W, soccer M(s)/W, softball W(s). *Intramural sports:* basketball M/W.

Costs (2007–08) *Tuition:* state resident $576 full-time, $24 per credit part-time; nonresident $5520 full-time, $230 per credit part-time. *Required fees:* $2088 full-time, $87 per credit part-time.

Financial Aid Of all full-time matriculated undergraduates, 45 Federal Work-Study jobs (averaging $3200).

Applying *Application deadlines:* rolling (freshmen), rolling (transfers). *Notification:* continuous (freshmen), continuous (transfers).

Freshmen Application Contact Ms. Michelle Hughes, Director of Admissions, Massasoit Community College, 1 Massasoit Boulevard, Brockton, MA 02302-3996. *Phone:* 508-588-9100. *Toll-free phone:* 800-CAREERS.

MIDDLESEX COMMUNITY COLLEGE

Bedford, Massachusetts **www.middlesex.mass.edu/**

Director of Admissions Ms. Laurie Dimitrov, Director, Admissions and Recruitment, Middlesex Community College, 33 Kearney Square, Lowell, MA 01852. *Phone:* 978-656-3207. *Toll-free phone:* 800-818-3434. *E-mail:* orellanad@middlesex.cc.ma.us.

MOUNT WACHUSETT COMMUNITY COLLEGE

Gardner, Massachusetts   www.mwcc.mass.edu/

- **State-supported** 2-year, founded 1963, part of Massachusetts Public Higher Education System
- **Small-town** 270-acre campus with easy access to Boston
- **Endowment** $1.7 million
- **Coed,** 3,937 undergraduate students, 44% full-time, 67% women, 33% men

Mount Wachusett Community College (MWCC) is a two-year public community college that offers more than forty associate degree and certificate programs and noncredit and professional development courses. At MWCC, students gain education and training to build new skills, start a career, or transfer to a four-year public or private college or university. Prospective students may visit the College's Web site at http://www.mwcc.edu.

Undergraduates 1,745 full-time, 2,192 part-time. Students come from 5 states and territories, 14 other countries, 4% are from out of state, 5% African American, 2% Asian American or Pacific Islander, 9% Hispanic American, 0.4% Native American, 0.8% international, 7% transferred in. *Retention:* 48% of 2003 full-time freshmen returned.

Freshmen *Admission:* 1,942 applied, 1,919 admitted, 859 enrolled.

Faculty *Total:* 221, 32% full-time. *Student/faculty ratio:* 21:1.

Majors Accounting; art; automobile/automotive mechanics technology; business administration and management; child development; computer graphics; computer technology/computer systems technology; criminal justice/law enforcement administration; dental hygiene; electrical, electronic and communications engineering technology; entrepreneurship; environmental studies; fine/studio arts; fire science; general studies; human services; industrial engineering; industrial technology; information science/studies; kinesiology and exercise science; legal assistant/paralegal; liberal arts and sciences/liberal studies; management information systems; manufacturing technology; massage therapy; medical/clinical assistant; nursing (licensed practical/vocational nurse training); nursing (registered nurse training); physical therapy; plastics engineering technology; radio/television broadcasting technology; sign language interpretation and translation; speech therapy; telecommunications; web page, digital/multimedia and information resources design.

Academics *Calendar:* semesters. *Degree:* certificates and associate. *Special study options:* academic remediation for entering students, adult/continuing education programs, advanced placement credit, cooperative education, distance learning, double majors, English as a second language, honors programs, independent study, internships, part-time degree program, services for LD students, study abroad, summer session for credit.

Library LaChance Library with 54,084 titles, 27,248 serial subscriptions, 2,509 audiovisual materials, an OPAC, a Web page.

Student Life *Housing:* college housing not available. *Activities and Organizations:* drama/theater group, student-run newspaper, choral group, Sophomore Nursing Club, Freshman Nursing Club, Alpha Beta Gamma, Physical Therapist Assistant Club, Multicultural Club. *Campus security:* 24-hour emergency response devices and patrols. *Student services:* health clinic, personal/psychological counseling, women's center.

Costs (2007–08) *Tuition:* state resident $750 full-time, $25 per credit part-time; nonresident $6900 full-time, $230 per credit part-time. *Required fees:* $3660 full-time, $117 per credit part-time, $55 per term part-time.

Financial Aid Of all full-time matriculated undergraduates, 47 Federal Work-Study jobs (averaging $2228).

Applying *Options:* early admission. *Application fee:* $10. *Required:* high school transcript. *Required for some:* essay or personal statement, 2 letters of recommendation. *Application deadlines:* rolling (freshmen), rolling (transfers). *Notification:* continuous (freshmen), continuous (transfers).

Freshmen Application Contact Mr. John D. Walsh, Director of Admissions, Mount Wachusett Community College, 444 Green Street, Gardner, MA 01440-1000. *Phone:* 978-632-6600 Ext. 110. *Fax:* 978-630-9554. *E-mail:* admissions@mwcc.mass.edu.

NEW ENGLAND COLLEGE OF FINANCE

Boston, Massachusetts   www.finance.edu/

- **Independent** 2-year, founded 1909
- **Urban** campus
- **Coed, primarily women**

Undergraduates 412 part-time. Students come from 4 states and territories, 5% are from out of state, 9% African American, 8% Asian American or Pacific Islander, 9% Hispanic American, 0.5% Native American.

Faculty *Student/faculty ratio:* 11:1.

Academics *Calendar:* 8 week terms (6 per academic year). *Degrees:* certificates and associate (offers primarily part-time evening degree programs; bachelor's degree offered jointly with Bentley College, Assumption College, Providence College, University of Hartford, and University System College for Lifelong Learning). *Special study options:* academic remediation for entering students, adult/continuing education programs, distance learning, independent study, internships, part-time degree program, summer session for credit.

Student Life *Campus security:* reception desk in lobby of building.

Applying *Required:* essay or personal statement, high school transcript, 1 letter of recommendation, interview.

Freshmen Application Contact Mr. Robert Wagstaff, Registrar, New England College of Finance, 10 High Street, Suite 204, Boston, MA 02111-2645. *Phone:* 617-951-2350 Ext. 230. *Toll-free phone:* 888-696-NECF. *Fax:* 617-951-2533.

NORTHERN ESSEX COMMUNITY COLLEGE

Haverhill, Massachusetts   www.necc.mass.edu/

- **State-supported** 2-year, founded 1960
- **Suburban** 106-acre campus with easy access to Boston
- **Endowment** $2.1 million
- **Coed,** 6,362 undergraduate students, 36% full-time, 65% women, 35% men

Northern Essex Community College is a two-year public community college with an open and rolling admission process, offering more than seventy degree and certificate programs in arts and sciences, business, computer information sciences, electronic technology and engineering science, health, human services, and paralegal studies. Students can prepare for a career or begin a bachelor's degree through the Joint Admissions Program or transfer agreements with four-year colleges and universities.

Undergraduates 2,300 full-time, 4,062 part-time. Students come from 4 states and territories, 16% are from out of state, 2% African American, 2% Asian American or Pacific Islander, 20% Hispanic American, 0.3% Native American, 0.9% international. *Retention:* 54% of 2003 full-time freshmen returned.

Freshmen *Admission:* 3,347 applied, 3,164 admitted.

Faculty *Total:* 497, 20% full-time. *Student/faculty ratio:* 20:1.

Majors Accounting; administrative assistant and secretarial science; biological and physical sciences; business administration and management; business teacher education; civil engineering technology; commercial and advertising art; computer and information sciences; computer engineering technology; computer graphics; computer programming; computer programming related; computer programming (specific applications); computer science; computer systems networking and telecommunications; computer typography and composition equipment operation; criminal justice/law enforcement administration; dance; data processing and data processing technology; dental assisting; dramatic/theater arts; education; electrical, electronic and communications engineering technology; elementary education; engineering science; finance; general studies; health information/medical records administration; history; hotel/motel administration; human services; industrial radiologic technology; international relations and affairs; journalism; kindergarten/preschool education; legal assistant/paralegal; liberal arts and sciences/liberal studies; machine tool technology; marketing/marketing management; materials science; medical administrative assistant and medical secretary; medical transcription; mental health/rehabilitation; music; nursing (registered nurse training); parks, recreation and leisure; physical education teaching and coaching; political science and government; radiologic technology/science; real estate; respiratory care therapy; respiratory therapy technician; sign language interpretation and translation; telecommunications technology; tourism and travel services management; web/multimedia management and webmaster; web page, digital/multimedia and information resources design; women's studies; word processing.

Academics *Calendar:* semesters. *Degree:* certificates and associate. *Special study options:* academic remediation for entering students, adult/continuing education programs, advanced placement credit, cooperative education, distance learning, double majors, English as a second language, freshman honors college, honors programs, independent study, internships, off-campus study, part-time degree program, services for LD students, study abroad, summer session for credit. *ROTC:* Air Force (c).

Library Bentley Library with 61,120 titles, 598 serial subscriptions, an OPAC.

Student Life *Housing:* college housing not available. *Activities and Organizations:* drama/theater group, student-run newspaper. *Campus security:* 24-hour emergency response devices and patrols. *Student services:* health clinic, personal/psychological counseling, women's center.

Northern Essex Community College (continued)

Athletics Member NJCAA. *Intercollegiate sports:* baseball M, basketball M/W, cross-country running M/W, volleyball M/W. *Intramural sports:* basketball M/W, cross-country running M/W, football M/W, golf M/W, racquetball M/W, skiing (cross-country) M/W, skiing (downhill) M/W, weight lifting M/W.

Standardized Tests *Required:* Psychological Corporation Aptitude Test for Practical Nursing (for admission).

Costs (2006–07) *Tuition:* state resident $3150 full-time, $105 per credit part-time; nonresident $3660 full-time, $346 per credit part-time.

Financial Aid Of all full-time matriculated undergraduates, 83 Federal Work-Study jobs (averaging $1393).

Applying *Options:* early admission. *Required:* high school transcript. *Application deadlines:* rolling (freshmen), rolling (transfers). *Notification:* continuous (freshmen), continuous (transfers).

Freshmen Application Contact Ms. Nora Sheridan, Director of Admissions, Northern Essex Community College, 100 Elliott Street, Haverhill,, MA 01830. *Phone:* 978-556-3616. *Toll-free phone:* 800-NECC-123. *Fax:* 978-556-3155.

NORTH SHORE COMMUNITY COLLEGE
Danvers, Massachusetts www.northshore.edu/

- **State-supported** 2-year, founded 1965
- **Suburban** campus with easy access to Boston
- **Endowment** $4.7 million
- **Coed,** 6,910 undergraduate students, 42% full-time, 61% women, 39% men

Undergraduates 2,873 full-time, 4,037 part-time. Students come from 5 states and territories, 8 other countries, 1% are from out of state, 8% African American, 3% Asian American or Pacific Islander, 13% Hispanic American, 0.5% Native American, 0.3% international, 9% transferred in.

Freshmen *Admission:* 3,089 applied, 2,501 admitted, 1,524 enrolled.

Faculty *Total:* 412, 33% full-time, 61% with terminal degrees. *Student/faculty ratio:* 18:1.

Majors Accounting; administrative assistant and secretarial science; airline pilot and flight crew; applied horticulture; biology/biotechnology laboratory technician; business administration and management; child development; computer and information sciences related; computer engineering technology; computer graphics; computer programming; computer programming (specific applications); computer science; criminal justice/law enforcement administration; culinary arts; data entry/microcomputer applications; engineering science; fire science; foods, nutrition, and wellness; forestry; gerontology; health science; hospitality administration; information science/studies; interdisciplinary studies; kindergarten/preschool education; landscaping and groundskeeping; legal administrative assistant/secretary; legal assistant/paralegal; liberal arts and sciences/liberal studies; marketing/marketing management; medical administrative assistant and medical secretary; medical radiologic technology; mental health/rehabilitation; nursing (registered nurse training); occupational therapy; physical therapist assistant; pre-engineering; respiratory care therapy; substance abuse/addiction counseling; tourism and travel services management; veterinary technology; Web page, digital/multimedia and information resources design.

Academics *Calendar:* semesters. *Degree:* certificates and associate. *Special study options:* academic remediation for entering students, accelerated degree program, adult/continuing education programs, advanced placement credit, cooperative education, distance learning, English as a second language, honors programs, independent study, internships, part-time degree program, services for LD students, summer session for credit.

Library Learning Resource Center plus 2 others with 71,548 titles, 403 serial subscriptions, 7,058 audiovisual materials, an OPAC.

Student Life *Housing:* college housing not available. *Activities and Organizations:* drama/theater group, student-run newspaper, Program Council, student government, performing arts, student newspaper, Phi Theta Kappa. *Campus security:* 24-hour emergency response devices and patrols, late-night transport/escort service. *Student services:* health clinic, personal/psychological counseling, women's center.

Costs (2007–08) *Tuition:* state resident $600 full-time, $25 per credit part-time; nonresident $6168 full-time, $257 per credit part-time. *Required fees:* $2184 full-time, $91 per credit part-time.

Applying *Options:* electronic application, early admission. *Required for some:* high school transcript, interview. *Application deadlines:* rolling (freshmen), rolling (transfers). *Notification:* continuous (freshmen), continuous (transfers).

Freshmen Application Contact Dr. Joanne Light, Dean of Enrollment Services, North Shore Community College, PO Box 3340, Danvers, MA 01923. *Phone:* 978-762-4000 Ext. 4337. *Fax:* 978-762-4015. *E-mail:* info@northshore.edu.

QUINCY COLLEGE
Quincy, Massachusetts www.quincycollege.edu/

- **City-supported** 2-year, founded 1958
- **Suburban** 2-acre campus with easy access to Boston
- **Endowment** $112,021
- **Coed,** 4,000 undergraduate students

Undergraduates Students come from 11 states and territories, 92 other countries, 20% African American, 13% Asian American or Pacific Islander, 3% Hispanic American, 0.1% Native American.

Faculty *Total:* 404, 5% full-time.

Majors Accounting; American government and politics; behavioral sciences; business administration and management; computer/technical support; criminal justice/law enforcement administration; criminal justice/police science; dramatic/theater arts; early childhood education; elementary education; emergency medical technology (EMT paramedic); English; fire science; general studies; history; humanities; human services; legal studies; liberal arts and sciences/liberal studies; mathematics; music; natural sciences; nursing (registered nurse training); political science and government; psychology; social sciences; social work; sociology; visual and performing arts.

Academics *Calendar:* semesters. *Degree:* certificates and associate. *Special study options:* academic remediation for entering students, adult/continuing education programs, advanced placement credit, English as a second language, internships, part-time degree program, summer session for credit.

Library Anselmo Library plus 1 other with 32,000 titles, 125 serial subscriptions.

Student Life *Housing:* college housing not available. *Activities and Organizations:* Student Government Association, Phi Theta Kappa, campus newspaper. *Campus security:* 24-hour emergency response devices and patrols.

Standardized Tests *Required:* CPT (for placement).

Costs (2006–07) *Tuition:* state resident $4625 full-time; nonresident $4625 full-time. *Waivers:* senior citizens and employees or children of employees.

Applying *Options:* early admission, deferred entrance. *Application fee:* $20. *Required:* high school transcript. *Application deadlines:* rolling (freshmen), rolling (transfers). *Notification:* continuous (freshmen).

Freshmen Application Contact Paula Smith, Dean Enrollment Services, Quincy College, 34 Coddington Street, Quincy, MA 02169. *Phone:* 617-984-1700. *Toll-free phone:* 800-698-1700. *Fax:* 617-984-1779. *E-mail:* psmith@quincycollege.edu.

QUINSIGAMOND COMMUNITY COLLEGE
Worcester, Massachusetts www.qcc.mass.edu/

- **State-supported** 2-year, founded 1963
- **Urban** 57-acre campus with easy access to Boston
- **Coed**

Undergraduates 2,761 full-time, 3,209 part-time. Students come from 3 states and territories, 13 other countries, 8% African American, 3% Asian American or Pacific Islander, 9% Hispanic American, 0.5% Native American, 0.5% international, 4% transferred in.

Academics *Calendar:* semesters. *Degree:* certificates and associate. *Special study options:* academic remediation for entering students, accelerated degree program, adult/continuing education programs, advanced placement credit, cooperative education, double majors, English as a second language, internships, off-campus study, part-time degree program, services for LD students, summer session for credit. *ROTC:* Army (c).

Student Life *Campus security:* 24-hour emergency response devices and patrols, late-night transport/escort service.

Athletics Member NJCAA.

Financial Aid Of all full-time matriculated undergraduates, 70 Federal Work-Study jobs (averaging $2350).

Applying *Application fee:* $20. *Required:* high school transcript. *Required for some:* interview.

Freshmen Application Contact Mr. Ronald C. Smith, Director of Admissions, Quinsigamond Community College, 670 West Boylston Street, Worcester, MA 01606-2092. *Phone:* 508-854-4262. *Fax:* 508-854-4357. *E-mail:* qccadm@qcc.mass.edu.

ROXBURY COMMUNITY COLLEGE

Roxbury Crossing, Massachusetts www.rcc.mass.edu/

- **State-supported** 2-year, founded 1973, part of Massachusetts Public Higher Education System
- **Urban** 12-acre campus with easy access to Boston
- **Coed,** 2,382 undergraduate students, 47% full-time, 64% women, 36% men

Undergraduates 1,124 full-time, 1,258 part-time. Students come from 14 states and territories, 48% African American, 4% Asian American or Pacific Islander, 16% Hispanic American, 0.1% Native American, 0.4% international, 0.5% transferred in.

Freshmen *Admission:* 1,290 applied, 1,076 admitted, 558 enrolled.

Faculty *Total:* 120, 54% full-time. *Student/faculty ratio:* 16:1.

Majors Accounting; administrative assistant and secretarial science; biology/biological sciences; business administration and management; criminal justice/law enforcement administration; data entry/microcomputer applications; English; environmental engineering technology; general studies; humanities; information science/studies; international business/trade/commerce; kindergarten/preschool education; legal administrative assistant/secretary; mathematics; medical administrative assistant and medical secretary; music; nursing (registered nurse training); physical sciences; pre-engineering; radio and television broadcasting technology; social sciences; visual and performing arts.

Academics *Calendar:* semesters. *Degree:* certificates and associate. *Special study options:* academic remediation for entering students, adult/continuing education programs, English as a second language, honors programs, internships, off-campus study, part-time degree program, services for LD students, student-designed majors, summer session for credit.

Library Roxbury Community College Library with 12,800 titles.

Student Life *Housing:* college housing not available. *Activities and Organizations:* drama/theater group, student-run newspaper, choral group. *Campus security:* 24-hour emergency response devices and patrols, late-night transport/escort service. *Student services:* personal/psychological counseling.

Athletics Member NJCAA. *Intercollegiate sports:* baseball M, basketball M/W, soccer M/W, tennis M/W. *Intramural sports:* basketball M/W, racquetball M/W.

Costs (2006–07) *Tuition:* state resident $2838 full-time; nonresident $8142 full-time.

Financial Aid Of all full-time matriculated undergraduates, 70 Federal Work-Study jobs (averaging $2200).

Applying *Options:* deferred entrance. *Application fee:* $10. *Required:* high school transcript. *Application deadlines:* rolling (freshmen), rolling (transfers). *Notification:* continuous (freshmen), continuous (transfers).

Director of Admissions Milton Samuels, Director/Admissions, Roxbury Community College, 1234 Columbus Avenue, Roxbury Crossing, MA 02120-3400. *Phone:* 617-541-5310.

SPRINGFIELD TECHNICAL COMMUNITY COLLEGE

Springfield, Massachusetts www.stcc.edu/

- **State-supported** 2-year, founded 1967
- **Urban** 34-acre campus
- **Endowment** $3.9 million
- **Coed,** 5,992 undergraduate students, 42% full-time, 59% women, 41% men

Undergraduates 2,545 full-time, 3,447 part-time. 4% are from out of state, 14% African American, 2% Asian American or Pacific Islander, 16% Hispanic American, 0.5% Native American, 0.7% international.

Freshmen *Admission:* 2,532 applied, 2,094 admitted, 1,259 enrolled.

Faculty *Total:* 341, 46% full-time. *Student/faculty ratio:* 19:1.

Majors Accounting; administrative assistant and secretarial science; architectural engineering technology; automotive engineering technology; biology/biological sciences; biotechnology; business administration and management; business/commerce; CAD/CADD drafting/design technology; chemistry; civil engineering technology; clinical/medical laboratory technology; commercial and advertising art; communications technologies and support services related; computer and information sciences and support services related; computer engineering technology; computer science; cosmetology; criminal justice/police science; dental hygiene; desktop publishing and digital imaging design; diagnostic medical sonography and ultrasound technology; electrical and electronic engineering technologies related; electrical, electronic and communications engineering technology; electromechanical technology; elementary education; engineering; entrepreneurship; finance; fine/studio arts; fire science; general studies; graphic design; health aide; heating, air conditioning and refrigeration technology; kindergarten/preschool education; landscaping and groundskeeping; laser and optical technology; liberal arts and sciences/liberal studies; logistics and materials management; marketing/marketing management; massage therapy; mathematics; mechanical engineering/mechanical technology; medical administrative assistant and medical secretary; medical/clinical assistant; medical insurance coding; medical radiologic technology; nuclear medical technology; nursing (registered nurse training); occupational therapist assistant; physical therapist assistant; quality control technology; rehabilitation and therapeutic professions related; respiratory care therapy; surgical technology; web/multimedia management and webmaster.

Academics *Calendar:* semesters. *Degree:* certificates and associate. *Special study options:* academic remediation for entering students, adult/continuing education programs, advanced placement credit, cooperative education, distance learning, English as a second language, honors programs, independent study, internships, off-campus study, part-time degree program, services for LD students, summer session for credit.

Library Springfield Technical Community College Library with 61,857 titles, 266 serial subscriptions, 16,810 audiovisual materials, an OPAC, a Web page.

Student Life *Housing:* college housing not available. *Activities and Organizations:* drama/theater group, student-run television station, Phi Theta Kappa Honor Society, Landscape Club, Dental Hygiene Club, Clinical Lab Club, Physical Therapist Assistant Club. *Campus security:* 24-hour emergency response devices and patrols, late-night transport/escort service. *Student services:* health clinic, personal/psychological counseling.

Athletics Member NJCAA. *Intercollegiate sports:* basketball M/W, golf M/W, soccer M/W, tennis M/W, wrestling M. *Intramural sports:* basketball M/W, cross-country running M/W, golf M/W, skiing (cross-country) M/W, volleyball M/W, weight lifting M/W.

Standardized Tests *Required for some:* SAT (for admission).

Costs (2007–08) *Tuition:* state resident $750 full-time, $25 per credit hour part-time; nonresident $7260 full-time, $242 per credit hour part-time. *Required fees:* $2706 full-time, $83 per credit hour part-time, $103 per term part-time.

Financial Aid Of all full-time matriculated undergraduates, 124 Federal Work-Study jobs (averaging $2400).

Applying *Application fee:* $10. *Required:* high school transcript. *Required for some:* interview. *Application deadlines:* rolling (freshmen), rolling (transfers).

Freshmen Application Contact Mr. Ray Blair, Springfield Technical Community College, One Armory Square, Springfield, MA 01105. *Phone:* 413-781-7822 Ext. 4868. *E-mail:* rblair@stcc.edu.

URBAN COLLEGE OF BOSTON

Boston, Massachusetts www.urbancollegeofboston.org/

Director of Admissions Dr. Henry J. Johnson, Director of Enrollment Services/Registrar, Urban College of Boston, 178 Tremont Street, Boston, MA 02111-1093. *Phone:* 617-292-4723 Ext. 6357.

MICHIGAN

ALPENA COMMUNITY COLLEGE

Alpena, Michigan www.alpenacc.edu/

- **State and locally supported** 2-year, founded 1952
- **Small-town** 700-acre campus
- **Endowment** $3.3 million
- **Coed,** 1,903 undergraduate students

Undergraduates Students come from 4 states and territories, 0.8% African American, 0.5% Asian American or Pacific Islander, 0.2% Hispanic American, 0.4% Native American, 2% live on campus. *Retention:* 55% of 2003 full-time freshmen returned.

Freshmen *Admission:* 1,163 applied, 1,163 admitted. *Average high school GPA:* 2.67.

Faculty *Total:* 125, 41% full-time, 2% with terminal degrees. *Student/faculty ratio:* 17:1.

Majors Accounting; administrative assistant and secretarial science; automobile/automotive mechanics technology; biology/biological sciences; business administration and management; business automation/technology/data entry; chemical engineering; chemistry; computer and information sciences; computer/information technology services administration related; computer systems networking and telecommunications; corrections; criminal justice/police science; data process-

Alpena Community College (continued)

ing and data processing technology; drafting and design technology; elementary education; English; general studies; information science/studies; liberal arts and sciences/liberal studies; manufacturing technology; mathematics; medical office assistant; nursing (licensed practical/vocational nurse training); nursing (registered nurse training); office management; operations management; pre-engineering; secondary education.

Academics *Calendar:* semesters. *Degree:* certificates and associate. *Special study options:* academic remediation for entering students, advanced placement credit, distance learning, double majors, internships, part-time degree program, services for LD students, summer session for credit.

Library Stephen Fletcher Library with 29,000 titles, 183 serial subscriptions, an OPAC, a Web page.

Student Life *Housing Options:* coed, men-only, women-only. Campus housing is provided by a third party. *Activities and Organizations:* drama/theater group, student-run newspaper, choral group, Nursing Association, Student Senate, Phi Theta Kappa, Lumberjack Newspaper, Law Enforcement Club. *Campus security:* 24-hour emergency response devices. *Student services:* personal/psychological counseling, women's center.

Athletics Member NJCAA. *Intercollegiate sports:* basketball M(s)/W(s), golf M, softball W(s), volleyball W(s). *Intramural sports:* basketball M/W, bowling M/W, football M, soccer M, softball M/W, volleyball M/W.

Standardized Tests *Required:* ACT COMPASS (for placement). *Recommended:* ACT (for placement).

Costs (2007–08) *Tuition:* area resident $2400 full-time, $80 per contact hour part-time; state resident $3600 full-time, $120 per contact hour part-time; nonresident $4800 full-time, $160 per contact hour part-time. *Required fees:* $520 full-time, $16 per contact hour part-time, $20 per term part-time. *Room and board:* room only: $3300.

Financial Aid Of all full-time matriculated undergraduates, 80 Federal Work-Study jobs (averaging $1200). 20 state and other part-time jobs (averaging $800).

Applying *Options:* electronic application, early admission, deferred entrance. *Required:* high school transcript. *Application deadlines:* rolling (freshmen), rolling (transfers). *Notification:* continuous (freshmen), continuous (transfers).

Freshmen Application Contact Mr. Mike Kollien, Admissions Technician, Alpena Community College, 666 Johnson Street, Alpena, MI 49707-1495. *Phone:* 989-358-7339. *Toll-free phone:* 888-468-6222. *Fax:* 989-358-7561. *E-mail:* kollienm@alpenacc.edu.

BAY DE NOC COMMUNITY COLLEGE
Escanaba, Michigan www.baydenoc.cc.mi.us/

Freshmen Application Contact Ms. Cynthia Carter, Director of Admissions, Bay de Noc Community College, Student Center, 2001 North Lincoln Road, Escanaba, MI 49829-2511. *Phone:* 906-786-5802 Ext. 1276. *Toll-free phone:* 800-221-2001 Ext. 1276. *Fax:* 906-786-8515. *E-mail:* carterc@baycollege.edu.

BAY MILLS COMMUNITY COLLEGE
Brimley, Michigan www.bmcc.edu/

Freshmen Application Contact Ms. Elaine Lehre, Admissions Officer, Bay Mills Community College, 12214 West Lakeshore Drive, Brimley, MI 49715. *Phone:* 906-248-3354. *Toll-free phone:* 800-844-BMCC. *Fax:* 906-248-3351.

DAVENPORT UNIVERSITY
Alma, Michigan www.davenport.edu/

Director of Admissions Admissions, Davenport University, 415 East Fulton Street, Grand Rapids, MI 49503. *Toll-free phone:* 800-632-9569.

DAVENPORT UNIVERSITY
Bad Axe, Michigan www.davenport.edu/

Director of Admissions Admissions, Davenport University, 415 East Fulton Street, Grand Rapids, MI 49503. *Toll-free phone:* 800-632-9569.

DAVENPORT UNIVERSITY
Bay City, Michigan www.davenport.edu/

Director of Admissions Admissions, Davenport University, 415 East Fulton Street, Grand Rapids, MI 49503. *Toll-free phone:* 800-632-9569.

DAVENPORT UNIVERSITY
Caro, Michigan www.davenport.edu/

Director of Admissions Admissions, Davenport University, 415 East Fulton Street, Grand Rapids, MI 49503. *Toll-free phone:* 800-632-9569.

DAVENPORT UNIVERSITY
Midland, Michigan www.davenport.edu/

Director of Admissions Admissions, Davenport University, 415 East Fulton Street, Grand Rapids, MI 49503. *Toll-free phone:* 800-632-9569.

DAVENPORT UNIVERSITY
Saginaw, Michigan www.davenport.edu/

Freshmen Application Contact Admissions, Davenport University, 415 East Fulton Street, Grand Rapids, MI 49503. *Phone:* 616-698-7111. *Toll-free phone:* 800-632-9569. *Fax:* 616-698-0333. *E-mail:* gradmiss@davenport.edu.

DELTA COLLEGE
University Center, Michigan www.delta.edu/

- **District-supported** 2-year, founded 1961
- **Rural** 640-acre campus
- **Endowment** $8.6 million
- **Coed**

Undergraduates 3,938 full-time, 6,272 part-time. Students come from 22 other countries, 7% African American, 0.8% Asian American or Pacific Islander, 4% Hispanic American, 0.8% Native American, 0.9% international, 4% transferred in.

Faculty *Student/faculty ratio:* 20:1.

Academics *Calendar:* semesters. *Degree:* certificates and associate. *Special study options:* academic remediation for entering students, adult/continuing education programs, advanced placement credit, cooperative education, distance learning, double majors, external degree program, freshman honors college, honors programs, independent study, internships, off-campus study, part-time degree program, services for LD students, student-designed majors, summer session for credit.

Student Life *Campus security:* 24-hour emergency response devices and patrols, student patrols, late-night transport/escort service.

Athletics Member NJCAA.

Costs (2006–07) *Tuition:* area resident $1824 full-time, $76 per credit hour part-time; state resident $2616 full-time, $109 per credit hour part-time; nonresident $3744 full-time, $156 per credit hour part-time. Full-time tuition and fees vary according to course load. Part-time tuition and fees vary according to course load. *Required fees:* $360 full-time, $6 per credit part-time, $30 per term part-time.

Financial Aid Of all full-time matriculated undergraduates, 154 Federal Work-Study jobs (averaging $1575). 382 state and other part-time jobs (averaging $1865).

Applying *Options:* electronic application, early admission, deferred entrance. *Application fee:* $20. *Required for some:* essay or personal statement. *Recommended:* high school transcript.

Freshmen Application Contact Mr. Duff Zube, Director of Admissions, Delta College, 1961 Delta Road, University Center, MI 48710. *Phone:* 989-686-9449. *Toll-free phone:* 800-285-1705. *Fax:* 989-667-2202. *E-mail:* admit@delta.edu.

GLEN OAKS COMMUNITY COLLEGE

Centreville, Michigan   www.glenoaks.edu/

Freshmen Application Contact Ms. Beverly M. Andrews, Director of Admissions/Registrar, Glen Oaks Community College, 62249 Shimmel Road, Centreville, MI 49032-9719. *Phone:* 269-467-9945 Ext. 248. *Toll-free phone:* 888-994-7818.

GOGEBIC COMMUNITY COLLEGE

Ironwood, Michigan   www.gogebic.edu/

Freshmen Application Contact Ms. Jeanne Graham, Director of Admissions, Gogebic Community College, E-4946 Jackson Road, Ironwood, MI 49938. *Phone:* 906-932-4231 Ext. 306. *Toll-free phone:* 800-682-5910 Ext. 207. *Fax:* 906-932-2339. *E-mail:* jeanneg@gogebic.edu.

GRAND RAPIDS COMMUNITY COLLEGE

Grand Rapids, Michigan   www.grcc.edu/

- **District-supported** 2-year, founded 1914, part of Michigan Department of Education
- **Urban** 35-acre campus
- **Endowment** $13.5 million
- **Coed,** 15,224 undergraduate students, 44% full-time, 52% women, 48% men

Undergraduates 6,630 full-time, 8,594 part-time. Students come from 20 states and territories, 6 other countries, 0.3% are from out of state, 10% African American, 2% Asian American or Pacific Islander, 6% Hispanic American, 1% Native American, 0.7% international, 44% transferred in. *Retention:* 61% of 2003 full-time freshmen returned.

Freshmen *Admission:* 6,802 applied, 3,642 admitted, 3,471 enrolled. *Average high school GPA:* 2.82.

Faculty *Total:* 672, 36% full-time, 7% with terminal degrees. *Student/faculty ratio:* 25:1.

Majors Administrative assistant and secretarial science; architectural engineering technology; art; automobile/automotive mechanics technology; business administration and management; computer engineering technology; computer programming; computer science; corrections; criminal justice/law enforcement administration; criminal justice/police science; culinary arts; dental hygiene; drafting and design technology; electrical, electronic and communications engineering technology; fashion merchandising; forestry; geology/earth science; heating, air conditioning, ventilation and refrigeration maintenance technology; industrial technology; legal administrative assistant/secretary; liberal arts and sciences/liberal studies; mass communication/media; medical administrative assistant and medical secretary; music; nursing (licensed practical/vocational nurse training); nursing (registered nurse training); plastics engineering technology; quality control technology; welding technology.

Academics *Calendar:* semesters. *Degree:* certificates and associate. *Special study options:* academic remediation for entering students, adult/continuing education programs, advanced placement credit, cooperative education, distance learning, English as a second language, honors programs, independent study, off-campus study, part-time degree program, services for LD students, study abroad, summer session for credit.

Library Arthur Andrews Memorial Library plus 1 other with 163,225 titles, 10,711 serial subscriptions, an OPAC, a Web page.

Student Life *Housing:* college housing not available. *Activities and Organizations:* drama/theater group, student-run newspaper, choral group, Student Congress, Phi Theta Kappa, Hispanic Student Organization, Asian Student Organization, Service Learning Advisory Board, national fraternities, national sororities. *Campus security:* 24-hour emergency response devices, late-night transport/escort service. *Student services:* personal/psychological counseling.

Athletics Member NJCAA. *Intercollegiate sports:* baseball M/W(s), basketball M(s)/W(s), football M(s), golf M(s), softball W(s), swimming and diving M(s)/W(s), tennis M(s)/W(s), track and field M(s), volleyball W(s), wrestling M(s). *Intramural sports:* badminton M/W, basketball M/W, skiing (cross-country) M/W, skiing (downhill) M/W, soccer M/W, swimming and diving M/W, tennis M/W, volleyball M/W.

Standardized Tests *Required for some:* ACT ASSET. *Recommended:* SAT or ACT (for admission).

Costs (2006–07) *Tuition:* area resident $2205 full-time, $74 per contact hour part-time; state resident $4260 full-time, $142 per contact hour part-time; nonresident $6060 full-time, $202 per contact hour part-time. Full-time tuition and fees vary according to course load. Part-time tuition and fees vary according

to course load. *Required fees:* $100 full-time, $100 per term part-time. *Payment plan:* installment. *Waivers:* employees or children of employees.

Financial Aid Of all full-time matriculated undergraduates, 196 Federal Work-Study jobs (averaging $1799). 66 state and other part-time jobs (averaging $1348).

Applying *Options:* early admission, deferred entrance. *Application fee:* $20. *Required:* high school transcript. *Application deadline:* 8/30 (freshmen). *Notification:* continuous (freshmen), continuous (transfers).

Freshmen Application Contact Ms. Diane Patrick, Director of Admissions, Grand Rapids Community College, 143 Bostwick Avenue, NE, Grand Rapids, MI 49503-3201. *Phone:* 616-234-4100. *Fax:* 616-234-4005. *E-mail:* dpatrick@grcc.edu.

HENRY FORD COMMUNITY COLLEGE

Dearborn, Michigan   www.hfcc.edu/

- **District-supported** 2-year, founded 1938
- **Suburban** 75-acre campus with easy access to Detroit
- **Coed,** 13,000 undergraduate students, 100% full-time, 57% women, 43% men

Undergraduates 13,000 full-time. Students come from 3 states and territories, 18 other countries, 2% are from out of state, 17% African American, 2% Asian American or Pacific Islander, 3% Hispanic American, 0.8% Native American, 0.2% international.

Freshmen *Admission:* 3,000 applied, 3,000 admitted.

Faculty *Total:* 770, 29% full-time.

Majors Accounting; administrative assistant and secretarial science; applied art; art; artificial intelligence and robotics; automobile/automotive mechanics technology; business administration and management; business machine repair; ceramic arts and ceramics; commercial and advertising art; computer and information sciences; computer science; construction engineering technology; corrections; criminal justice/law enforcement administration; criminal justice/police science; culinary arts; dance; data processing and data processing technology; drafting and design technology; dramatic/theater arts; drawing; electrical, electronic and communications engineering technology; emergency medical technology (EMT paramedic); energy management and systems technology; fire science; food services technology; health information/medical records administration; heating, air conditioning, ventilation and refrigeration maintenance technology; hospitality administration; hotel/motel administration; industrial radiologic technology; industrial technology; information science/studies; instrumentation technology; interior design; kinesiology and exercise science; legal administrative assistant/secretary; legal assistant/paralegal; liberal arts and sciences/liberal studies; marketing/marketing management; mass communication/media; materials science; medical administrative assistant and medical secretary; medical/clinical assistant; nursing (registered nurse training); pre-engineering; quality control technology; radiologic technology/science; real estate; respiratory care therapy; special products marketing; transportation technology.

Academics *Calendar:* semesters. *Degree:* certificates and associate. *Special study options:* academic remediation for entering students, adult/continuing education programs, advanced placement credit, cooperative education, distance learning, English as a second language, freshman honors college, honors programs, independent study, internships, part-time degree program, study abroad, summer session for credit.

Library Eshleman Library with 80,000 titles, 650 serial subscriptions, an OPAC, a Web page.

Student Life *Housing:* college housing not available. *Activities and Organizations:* drama/theater group, student-run newspaper, radio station, choral group, Phi Theta Kappa, Student Nurses, Future Teachers, ASAD (American Students of African Descent), Inter-Varsity Christian Fellowship. *Campus security:* 24-hour emergency response devices and patrols, late-night transport/escort service. *Student services:* personal/psychological counseling, women's center.

Athletics Member NJCAA. *Intercollegiate sports:* baseball M(s), basketball M(s)/W(s), golf M(s), softball W(s), tennis W(s), track and field M(s), volleyball W(s). *Intramural sports:* badminton M/W, basketball M/W, bowling M/W, racquetball M/W, sailing M/W, softball W, tennis M/W, volleyball M/W, weight lifting M/W.

Costs (2007–08) *Tuition:* area resident $1440 full-time, $60 per credit part-time; state resident $2760 full-time, $115 per credit part-time; nonresident $2880 full-time, $120 per credit part-time. *Required fees:* $384 full-time, $13 per credit part-time, $36 per term part-time.

Applying *Options:* early admission, deferred entrance. *Application fee:* $30. *Recommended:* high school transcript. *Application deadlines:* rolling (freshmen), rolling (transfers). *Notification:* continuous (freshmen), continuous (transfers).

Freshmen Application Contact Henry Ford Community College, 5101 Evergreen Road, Dearborn, MI 48128-1495. *Phone:* 313-845-9600.

ITT Technical Institute

Canton, Michigan   www.itt-tech.edu/

- **Proprietary** 2-year, founded 2002, part of ITT Educational Services, Inc
- **Coed**

Majors Business administration and management; CAD/CADD drafting/design technology; computer engineering technology; computer software technology; computer systems networking and telecommunications; criminal justice/law enforcement administration; web/multimedia management and webmaster; web page, digital/multimedia and information resources design.

Academics *Calendar:* quarters. *Degree:* associate.

Library a Web page.

Student Life *Housing:* college housing not available.

Standardized Tests *Required:* (for admission).

Costs (2006–07) *Tuition:* Contact school for program costs.

Applying *Options:* deferred entrance. *Application fee:* $100. *Required:* high school transcript, interview. *Recommended:* letters of recommendation. *Application deadlines:* rolling (freshmen), rolling (transfers). *Notification:* continuous (freshmen), continuous (transfers).

Freshmen Application Contact Mr. Rodney L. Cline, Director of Recruitment, ITT Technical Institute, 1905 South Haggerty Road, Canton, MI 48188. *Phone:* 784-397-7800. *Toll-free phone:* 800-247-4477.

ITT Technical Institute

Flint,

Michigan www.itt-tech.edu/campus/school.cfm?lloc_num=62

- **Proprietary** 2-year, founded 2005, part of ITT Educational Services, Inc
- **Coed**

Majors Business administration and management; CAD/CADD drafting/design technology; computer engineering technology; computer software technology; computer systems networking and telecommunications; criminal justice/law enforcement administration; web/multimedia management and webmaster; web page, digital/multimedia and information resources design.

Academics *Calendar:* quarters. *Degree:* associate.

Costs (2006–07) *Tuition:* Contact school directly for program costs.

Freshmen Application Contact Mr. Jeff Wright, Director of Recruitment, ITT Technical Institute, 5405 Gateway Centre Drive, Flint, MI 48507. *Phone:* 810-762-2500. *Toll-free phone:* 800-514-6564. *Fax:* 810-762-2599.

ITT Technical Institute

Grand Rapids, Michigan   www.itt-tech.edu/

- **Proprietary** 2-year, part of ITT Educational Services, Inc
- **Coed**

Majors Business administration and management; CAD/CADD drafting/design technology; computer engineering technology; computer systems networking and telecommunications; criminal justice/law enforcement administration; web/multimedia management and webmaster; web page, digital/multimedia and information resources design.

Academics *Calendar:* quarters. *Degree:* associate.

Library a Web page.

Student Life *Housing:* college housing not available.

Standardized Tests *Required:* Wonderlic aptitude test (for admission).

Costs (2006–07) *Tuition:* Contact school for program costs.

Applying *Options:* deferred entrance. *Application fee:* $100. *Required:* high school transcript, interview. *Recommended:* letters of recommendation. *Application deadlines:* rolling (freshmen), rolling (transfers). *Notification:* continuous (freshmen), continuous (transfers).

Freshmen Application Contact Mr. Todd Peuler, Director of Recruitment, ITT Technical Institute, 4020 Sparks Drive SE, Grand Rapids, MI 49546. *Phone:* 616-956-1060. *Toll-free phone:* 800-632-4676.

ITT Technical Institute

Troy, Michigan   www.itt-tech.edu/

- **Proprietary** 2-year, founded 1987, part of ITT Educational Services, Inc
- **Coed**

Majors Business administration and management; CAD/CADD drafting/design technology; computer engineering technology; criminal justice/law enforcement administration; web/multimedia management and webmaster; web page, digital/multimedia and information resources design.

Academics *Calendar:* quarters. *Degree:* associate.

Library a Web page.

Student Life *Housing:* college housing not available.

Standardized Tests *Required:* Wonderlic aptitude test (for admission).

Costs (2006–07) *Tuition:* Contact school for program costs.

Applying *Options:* deferred entrance. *Application fee:* $100. *Required:* high school transcript, interview. *Recommended:* letters of recommendation. *Application deadlines:* rolling (freshmen), rolling (transfers). *Notification:* continuous (freshmen), continuous (transfers).

Freshmen Application Contact Ms. Jennifer Alterman, ITT Technical Institute, 1522 East Big Beaver Road, Troy, MI 48083. *Phone:* 248-524-1800. *Toll-free phone:* 800-832-6817. *Fax:* 248-524-1965.

Jackson Community College

Jackson, Michigan   www.jccmi.edu

- **County-supported** 2-year, founded 1928
- **Suburban** 580-acre campus with easy access to Detroit
- **Endowment** $10.7 million
- **Coed**

Undergraduates 2,108 full-time, 3,762 part-time. 1% are from out of state, 5% African American, 0.8% Asian American or Pacific Islander, 4% Hispanic American, 0.7% Native American, 0.1% international. *Retention:* 65% of 2003 full-time freshmen returned.

Faculty *Student/faculty ratio:* 19:1.

Academics *Calendar:* semesters. *Degree:* certificates and associate. *Special study options:* academic remediation for entering students, adult/continuing education programs, advanced placement credit, cooperative education, distance learning, English as a second language, independent study, internships, part-time degree program, services for LD students, summer session for credit.

Student Life *Campus security:* 24-hour patrols.

Costs (2006–07) *Tuition:* area resident $1884 full-time, $79 per hour part-time; state resident $2832 full-time, $118 per hour part-time; nonresident $3768 full-time, $157 per hour part-time. *Required fees:* $17 per hour part-time.

Financial Aid Of all full-time matriculated undergraduates, 60 Federal Work-Study jobs (averaging $1304). 19 state and other part-time jobs (averaging $1192).

Applying *Options:* electronic application, early admission.

Freshmen Application Contact Ms. Julie Hand, Director of Enrollment Services, Jackson Community College, 2111 Emmons Road, Jackson, MI 49201. *Phone:* 517-796-8425. *Toll-free phone:* 888-522-7344. *Fax:* 517-796-8631. *E-mail:* admissions@jccmi.edu.

Kalamazoo Valley Community College

Kalamazoo, Michigan   www.kvcc.edu/

Director of Admissions Mr. Michael McCall, Director of Admissions, Registration and Records, Kalamazoo Valley Community College, PO Box 4070, Kalamazoo, MI 49003-4070. *Phone:* 269-488-4207.

Kellogg Community College

Battle Creek, Michigan   www.kellogg.edu/

- **State and locally supported** 2-year, founded 1956, part of Michigan Department of Education
- **Urban** 120-acre campus
- **Endowment** $91,005
- **Coed**, 5,326 undergraduate students, 33% full-time, 67% women, 33% men

Undergraduates 1,762 full-time, 3,564 part-time. Students come from 3 states and territories, 11 other countries, 1% are from out of state, 7% African American, 1% Asian American or Pacific Islander, 2% Hispanic American, 0.7% Native American, 0.5% international, 1% transferred in.

Freshmen *Admission:* 2,114 applied, 2,021 admitted, 908 enrolled.

Faculty *Total:* 380, 24% full-time, 7% with terminal degrees. *Student/faculty ratio:* 23:1.

Majors Accounting; accounting technology and bookkeeping; administrative assistant and secretarial science; anthropology; art; art teacher education; biology/biological sciences; business administration and management; chemical technology; chemistry; clinical/medical laboratory technology; commercial and advertising art; communication/speech communication and rhetoric; computer engineering technology; computer graphics; computer programming; computer programming (specific applications); computer software and media applications related; corrections; criminal justice/police science; criminal justice/safety; data entry/microcomputer applications related; dental hygiene; drafting and design technology; dramatic/theater arts; elementary education; emergency medical technology (EMT paramedic); engineering; English; executive assistant/executive secretary; fire protection and safety technology; general studies; heating, air conditioning, ventilation and refrigeration maintenance technology; history; human services; industrial technology; international relations and affairs; journalism; kindergarten/preschool education; legal administrative assistant/secretary; legal assistant/paralegal; liberal arts and sciences/liberal studies; machine tool technology; mathematics; medical administrative assistant and medical secretary; medical radiologic technology; music; nursing (licensed practical/vocational nurse training); nursing (registered nurse training); philosophy; physical education teaching and coaching; physical therapist assistant; physics; pipefitting and sprinkler fitting; plastics engineering technology; political science and government; pre-law studies; pre-medical studies; pre-pharmacy studies; pre-theology/pre-ministerial studies; pre-veterinary studies; psychology; public relations/image management; radio and television broadcasting technology; robotics technology; secondary education; sheet metal technology; social work; sociology; special education; technology/industrial arts teacher education; welding technology; word processing.

Academics *Calendar:* semesters. *Degree:* certificates and associate. *Special study options:* academic remediation for entering students, accelerated degree program, adult/continuing education programs, advanced placement credit, cooperative education, distance learning, double majors, freshman honors college, honors programs, independent study, internships, off-campus study, part-time degree program, services for LD students, summer session for credit.

Library Emory W. Morris Learning Resource Center with 42,131 titles, 172 serial subscriptions, an OPAC, a Web page.

Student Life *Housing:* college housing not available. *Activities and Organizations:* drama/theater group, student-run newspaper, choral group, Tech Club, Phi Theta Kappa, Student Nurses Association, Crude Arts Club, Art League. *Campus security:* 24-hour emergency response devices and patrols, late-night transport/escort service.

Athletics Member NJCAA. *Intercollegiate sports:* baseball M(s), basketball M(s)/W(s), soccer M, softball W(s), volleyball W(s).

Standardized Tests *Required for some:* ACT (for admission), SAT or ACT (for admission).

Costs (2007–08) *Tuition:* area resident $1950 full-time, $69 per credit hour part-time; state resident $3165 full-time, $110 per credit hour part-time; nonresident $4770 full-time, $159 per credit hour part-time. *Required fees:* $210 full-time, $7 per credit hour part-time.

Financial Aid Of all full-time matriculated undergraduates, 41 Federal Work-Study jobs (averaging $2251). 43 state and other part-time jobs (averaging $2058).

Applying *Options:* early admission, deferred entrance. *Required for some:* high school transcript, minimum 2.0 GPA. *Application deadlines:* 8/30 (freshmen), rolling (transfers). *Notification:* continuous (freshmen), continuous (transfers).

Freshmen Application Contact Mr. Sedgwick Harris, Director of Admissions, Kellogg Community College, 450 North Avenue, Battle Creek, MI 49017. *Phone:* 269-965-3931 Ext. 2641. *Fax:* 269-965-4133. *E-mail:* harriss@kellogg.edu.

KIRTLAND COMMUNITY COLLEGE
Roscommon, Michigan   **www.kirtland.edu/**

- **District-supported** 2-year, founded 1966, part of Michigan Department of Education
- **Rural** 180-acre campus
- **Endowment** $2.0 million
- **Coed,** 1,624 undergraduate students, 43% full-time, 61% women, 39% men

Undergraduates 693 full-time, 931 part-time. Students come from 13 states and territories, 2 other countries, 1% African American, 0.2% Asian American or Pacific Islander, 1% Hispanic American, 2% Native American, 0.1% international.

Freshmen *Admission:* 278 applied, 278 admitted, 278 enrolled.

Faculty *Total:* 82, 41% full-time. *Student/faculty ratio:* 20:1.

Majors Accounting; administrative assistant and secretarial science; art; automobile/automotive mechanics technology; biological and physical sciences; business administration and management; corrections; cosmetology; creative writing; criminal justice/law enforcement administration; drafting and design technology; industrial technology; information science/studies; legal administrative assistant/secretary; liberal arts and sciences/liberal studies; marketing/marketing management; medical administrative assistant and medical secretary; nursing (licensed practical/vocational nurse training); nursing (registered nurse training); welding technology.

Academics *Calendar:* semesters. *Degree:* certificates and associate. *Special study options:* academic remediation for entering students, adult/continuing education programs, advanced placement credit, cooperative education, distance learning, English as a second language, honors programs, independent study, internships, part-time degree program, summer session for credit.

Library Kirtland Community College Library with 35,000 titles, 317 serial subscriptions.

Student Life *Housing Options:* men-only, women-only. Campus housing is university owned. *Activities and Organizations:* drama/theater group, student-run newspaper, choral group. *Campus security:* student patrols, late-night transport/escort service. *Student services:* personal/psychological counseling.

Costs (2007–08) *Tuition:* area resident $2213 full-time, $74 per contact hour part-time; state resident $4056 full-time, $135 per contact hour part-time; nonresident $5013 full-time, $159 per contact hour part-time. *Required fees:* $270 full-time, $8 per contact hour part-time, $15 per term part-time. *Room and board:* room only: $2800.

Financial Aid Of all full-time matriculated undergraduates, 46 Federal Work-Study jobs (averaging $1282). 82 state and other part-time jobs (averaging $1578).

Applying *Options:* early admission, deferred entrance. *Required:* placement testing or ACT/SAT scores. *Application deadlines:* rolling (freshmen), rolling (transfers). *Notification:* continuous until 8/22 (freshmen), continuous until 8/22 (transfers).

Freshmen Application Contact Ms. Luann Beilfuss, Registrar, Kirtland Community College, 10775 North St Helen Road, Roscommon, MI 48653-9699. *Phone:* 989-275-5000. *Fax:* 989-275-6789. *E-mail:* registrar@kirtland.edu.

LAKE MICHIGAN COLLEGE
Benton Harbor, Michigan   **www.lmc.cc.mi.us/**

- **District-supported** 2-year, founded 1946, part of Michigan Department of Education
- **Small-town** 260-acre campus
- **Endowment** $5.0 million
- **Coed**

Undergraduates 1,235 full-time, 2,808 part-time. Students come from 5 states and territories, 2% are from out of state, 15% African American, 2% Asian American or Pacific Islander, 4% Hispanic American, 1% Native American, 0.9% international.

Faculty *Student/faculty ratio:* 18:1.

Academics *Calendar:* semesters. *Degree:* certificates and associate. *Special study options:* academic remediation for entering students, adult/continuing education programs, honors programs, part-time degree program, student-designed majors, summer session for credit.

Athletics Member NJCAA.

Costs (2006–07) *Tuition:* area resident $2175 full-time, $73 per credit hour part-time; state resident $3060 full-time, $102 per credit hour part-time; nonresident $4080 full-time, $136 per credit hour part-time. *Required fees:* $930 full-time, $31 per credit hour part-time.

Financial Aid Of all full-time matriculated undergraduates, 105 Federal Work-Study jobs (averaging $1200). 176 state and other part-time jobs (averaging $1200).

Applying *Options:* early admission, deferred entrance. *Required:* high school transcript. *Required for some:* interview.

Freshmen Application Contact Ms. Julie Bruns, Assistant Registrar, Lake Michigan College, 2755 East Napier, Benton Harbor, MI 49022-1899. *Phone:* 616-927-8100 Ext. 5083. *Toll-free phone:* 800-252-1LMC. *E-mail:* bruns@lakemichigancollege.edu.

LANSING COMMUNITY COLLEGE

Lansing, Michigan www.lcc.edu/

- **State and locally supported** 2-year, founded 1957, part of Michigan Department of Education
- **Urban** 28-acre campus
- **Endowment** $3.5 million
- **Coed,** 20,394 undergraduate students, 33% full-time, 54% women, 46% men

Undergraduates 6,712 full-time, 13,682 part-time. Students come from 29 states and territories, 54 other countries, 1% are from out of state, 9% African American, 2% Asian American or Pacific Islander, 5% Hispanic American, 1% Native American, 1% international.

Freshmen *Admission:* 3,609 applied, 3,609 admitted, 3,609 enrolled.

Faculty *Total:* 1,444, 16% full-time. *Student/faculty ratio:* 18:1.

Majors Accounting; administrative assistant and secretarial science; airline pilot and flight crew; architectural engineering technology; art; automobile/automotive mechanics technology; avionics maintenance technology; biological and physical sciences; biology/biological sciences; biology/biotechnology laboratory technician; broadcast journalism; business administration and management; carpentry; chemical engineering; chemistry; child development; cinematography and film/video production; civil engineering technology; clinical laboratory science/medical technology; commercial and advertising art; computer engineering technology; computer graphics; computer management; computer programming; computer typography and composition equipment operation; construction engineering technology; consumer merchandising/retailing management; corrections; court reporting; criminal justice/law enforcement administration; criminal justice/police science; dance; dental hygiene; developmental and child psychology; diagnostic medical sonography and ultrasound technology; drafting and design technology; dramatic/theater arts; education; electrical, electronic and communications engineering technology; electromechanical technology; elementary education; emergency medical technology (EMT paramedic); engineering; engineering technology; English; film/cinema studies; finance; fine/studio arts; fire science; geography; geology/earth science; gerontology; heating, air conditioning, ventilation and refrigeration maintenance technology; heavy equipment maintenance technology; horticultural science; hospitality administration; hotel/motel administration; human resources management; human services; industrial technology; information science/studies; international business/trade/commerce; journalism; kindergarten/preschool education; labor and industrial relations; landscape architecture; legal administrative assistant/secretary; legal assistant/paralegal; liberal arts and sciences/liberal studies; machine tool technology; management information systems; marketing/marketing management; mass communication/media; mathematics; mechanical design technology; mechanical engineering/mechanical technology; medical/clinical assistant; medical radiologic technology; music; nursing (licensed practical/vocational nurse training); nursing (registered nurse training); philosophy; photography; physical education teaching and coaching; pre-engineering; public administration; public relations/image management; quality control technology; radio and television; real estate; religious studies; respiratory care therapy; sign language interpretation and translation; social work; special products marketing; speech and rhetoric; surgical technology; survey technology; teacher assistant/aide; telecommunications; tourism and travel services management; veterinary technology; voice and opera; welding technology.

Academics *Calendar:* semesters. *Degree:* certificates and associate. *Special study options:* academic remediation for entering students, adult/continuing education programs, advanced placement credit, cooperative education, distance learning, double majors, English as a second language, external degree program, honors programs, independent study, internships, part-time degree program, services for LD students, study abroad, summer session for credit. *ROTC:* Army (c), Air Force (c).

Library Abel Sykes Technology and Learning Center plus 1 other with 98,125 titles, 600 serial subscriptions, an OPAC, a Web page.

Student Life *Housing:* college housing not available. *Activities and Organizations:* drama/theater group, student-run newspaper, radio station, choral group, Student Marketing, Legal Assistants Club, Student Nursing Club, Phi Theta Kappa, Student Advising Club, national fraternities, national sororities. *Campus security:* 24-hour emergency response devices and patrols, student patrols, late-night transport/escort service. *Student services:* personal/psychological counseling, women's center.

Athletics Member NJCAA. *Intercollegiate sports:* basketball M(s)/W(s), cross-country running M(s)/W(s), golf M(s), track and field M(s)/W(s), volleyball W(s). *Intramural sports:* baseball M, basketball M/W, cross-country running M/W, ice hockey M, soccer M/W, softball W, track and field M/W, volleyball W.

Costs (2007–08) *Tuition:* area resident $2010 full-time, $67 per contact hour part-time; state resident $3600 full-time, $120 per contact hour part-time; nonresident $5400 full-time, $180 per contact hour part-time. *Required fees:* $50 full-time, $25 per term part-time.

Financial Aid Of all full-time matriculated undergraduates, 125 Federal Work-Study jobs (averaging $2636). 122 state and other part-time jobs (averaging $2563).

Applying *Options:* electronic application, early admission, deferred entrance. *Required for some:* essay or personal statement, high school transcript, 2 letters of recommendation, interview. *Application deadlines:* rolling (freshmen), rolling (transfers).

Freshman Application Contact Ms. Tammy Grossbauer, Director of Admissions/Registrar, Lansing Community College, PO Box 40010, Lansing, MI 48901-7210. *Phone:* 517-483-9886. *Toll-free phone:* 800-644-4LCC. *Fax:* 517-483-1170. *E-mail:* grossbt@lcc.edu.

LEWIS COLLEGE OF BUSINESS

Detroit, Michigan www.lewiscollege.edu/

- **Independent** 2-year, founded 1929
- **Urban** 11-acre campus
- **Coed,** 324 undergraduate students

Undergraduates 99% African American, 0.6% Hispanic American.

Faculty *Total:* 36, 25% full-time. *Student/faculty ratio:* 15:1.

Majors Accounting; administrative assistant and secretarial science; business administration and management; computer management; computer programming; computer science; data processing and data processing technology; information science/studies; legal administrative assistant/secretary; liberal arts and sciences/liberal studies; medical administrative assistant and medical secretary.

Academics *Calendar:* semesters. *Degree:* associate. *Special study options:* academic remediation for entering students, cooperative education, part-time degree program, summer session for credit.

Library Main Library plus 1 other with 3,355 titles, 90 serial subscriptions.

Student Life *Housing:* college housing not available. *Activities and Organizations:* student-run newspaper, Sister to Sister, Brother to Brother, The Voice, Student Government Association, Business Club, national sororities. *Campus security:* parking lot security. *Student services:* personal/psychological counseling.

Athletics *Intercollegiate sports:* basketball M.

Costs (2006–07) *Tuition:* $8130 full-time. Contact college directly for program costs.

Financial Aid Of all full-time matriculated undergraduates, 80 Federal Work-Study jobs (averaging $2000). 40 state and other part-time jobs (averaging $1000).

Applying *Options:* early admission, deferred entrance. *Application fee:* $15. *Required:* high school transcript. *Application deadlines:* rolling (freshmen), 8/1 (transfers). *Notification:* continuous until 8/30 (freshmen), continuous until 8/30 (transfers).

Freshmen Application Contact Ms. Frances Ambrose, Admissions Secretary, Lewis College of Business, 17370 Meyers Road, Detroit, MI 48235-1423. *Phone:* 313-862-6300.

MACOMB COMMUNITY COLLEGE

Warren, Michigan www.macomb.edu/

- **District-supported** 2-year, founded 1954, part of Michigan Public Community College System
- **Suburban** 384-acre campus with easy access to Detroit
- **Endowment** $8.1 million
- **Coed,** 21,131 undergraduate students, 38% full-time, 52% women, 48% men

Undergraduates 7,986 full-time, 13,145 part-time. Students come from 5 states and territories, 6% African American, 3% Asian American or Pacific Islander, 1% Hispanic American, 0.4% Native American, 4% international. *Retention:* 54% of 2003 full-time freshmen returned.

Freshmen *Admission:* 1,638 enrolled.

Faculty *Total:* 1,016, 23% full-time, 10% with terminal degrees.

Majors Accounting; administrative assistant and secretarial science; agriculture; architectural drafting and CAD/CADD; automobile/automotive mechanics technology; automotive engineering technology; biology/biological sciences; business administration and management; business automation/technology/data entry; business/commerce; cabinetmaking and millwork; chemistry; child care and support services management; civil engineering technology; commercial and advertising art; communication/speech communication and rhetoric; computer programming; computer programming (specific applications); construction engineering technology; criminal justice/law enforcement administration; criminal justice/police science; culinary arts; drafting and design technology; electrical, electronic and communications engineering technology; electrical/electronics equipment installation and repair; electromechanical technology; emergency medical technology (EMT paramedic); energy management and systems tech-

nology; engineering related; finance; fire protection and safety technology; forensic science and technology; general studies; graphic and printing equipment operation/production; heating, air conditioning and refrigeration technology; heating, air conditioning, ventilation and refrigeration maintenance technology; industrial mechanics and maintenance technology; industrial technology; international/global studies; legal assistant/paralegal; legal studies; liberal arts and sciences/liberal studies; machine tool technology; manufacturing technology; marketing/marketing management; mathematics; mechanical design technology; mechanical drafting and CAD/CADD; mechanical engineering/mechanical technology; mechanic and repair technologies related; medical/clinical assistant; mental health/rehabilitation; metallurgical technology; music performance; nursing (registered nurse training); occupational therapist assistant; operations management; physical therapist assistant; plastics engineering technology; plumbing technology; pre-engineering; quality control technology; respiratory care therapy; robotics technology; safety/security technology; sheet metal technology; social psychology; surgical technology; survey technology; tool and die technology; veterinary/animal health technology; veterinary sciences; welding technology.

Academics *Calendar:* semesters. *Degree:* certificates and associate. *Special study options:* academic remediation for entering students, adult/continuing education programs, advanced placement credit, cooperative education, English as a second language, honors programs, internships, off-campus study, part-time degree program, services for LD students, student-designed majors, summer session for credit.

Library Library of South Campus, Library of Center Campus with 159,226 titles, 4,240 serial subscriptions, an OPAC.

Student Life *Housing:* college housing not available. *Activities and Organizations:* drama/theater group, Phi Beta Kappa, Adventure Unlimited, Alpha Rho Rho, SADD. *Campus security:* 24-hour emergency response devices and patrols, late-night transport/escort service, security phones in parking lots, surveillance cameras. *Student services:* health clinic, personal/psychological counseling.

Athletics Member NJCAA. *Intercollegiate sports:* baseball M(s), basketball M(s), cross-country running M(s)/W(s), soccer M(s), softball W(s), track and field M(s)/W(s), volleyball W(s). *Intramural sports:* baseball M, basketball M, bowling M/W, cross-country running M/W, football M/W, skiing (cross-country) M/W, skiing (downhill) M/W, volleyball M/W.

Costs (2006–07) *Tuition:* area resident $2108 full-time, $68 per credit hour part-time; state resident $3224 full-time, $104 per credit hour part-time; nonresident $4185 full-time, $135 per credit hour part-time. Full-time tuition and fees vary according to course load. Part-time tuition and fees vary according to course load. *Required fees:* $40 full-time, $20 per term part-time. *Waivers:* senior citizens and employees or children of employees.

Financial Aid Of all full-time matriculated undergraduates, 150 Federal Work-Study jobs (averaging $3600).

Applying *Options:* early admission, deferred entrance. *Application deadlines:* rolling (freshmen), rolling (transfers).

Freshmen Application Contact Mr. Richard P. Stevens, Coordinator of Admissions and Assessment, Macomb Community College, G312, 14500 East 12 Mile Road, Warren, MI 48088-3896. *Phone:* 586-445-7246. *Toll-free phone:* 866-622-6624. *Fax:* 586-445-7140. *E-mail:* stevensr@macomb.edu.

MID MICHIGAN COMMUNITY COLLEGE

Harrison, Michigan   www.midmich.cc.mi.us/

Freshmen Application Contact Ms. Brenda Mather, Admissions Specialist, Mid Michigan Community College, 1375 South Clare Avenue, Harrison, MI 48625. *Phone:* 989-386-6661. *E-mail:* apply@midmich.edu.

MONROE COUNTY COMMUNITY COLLEGE

Monroe, Michigan   www.monroeccc.edu/

Freshmen Application Contact Mr. Mark V. Hall, Director of Admissions and Guidance Services, Monroe County Community College, 155 South Raisinville Road, Monroe, MI 48161-9047. *Phone:* 734-384-4261. *Toll-free phone:* 877-YES MCCC. *Fax:* 734-242-9711. *E-mail:* mhall@monroeccc.edu.

MONTCALM COMMUNITY COLLEGE

Sidney, Michigan   www.montcalm.edu/

- **State and locally supported** 2-year, founded 1965, part of Michigan Department of Education
- **Rural** 240-acre campus with easy access to Grand Rapids
- **Endowment** $3.4 million
- **Coed,** 2,451 undergraduate students, 45% full-time, 70% women, 30% men

Undergraduates 1,107 full-time, 1,344 part-time. 0.1% African American, 0.5% Asian American or Pacific Islander, 1% Hispanic American, 0.7% Native American, 17% transferred in.

Freshmen *Admission:* 622 applied, 622 admitted, 381 enrolled. *Average high school GPA:* 2.28. *Test scores:* ACT scores over 18: 74%; ACT scores over 24: 15%.

Faculty *Total:* 133, 19% full-time, 9% with terminal degrees. *Student/faculty ratio:* 13:1.

Majors Accounting; administrative assistant and secretarial science; business administration and management; child care and support services management; child care provision; computer installation and repair technology; corrections; cosmetology; criminal justice/law enforcement administration; data processing and data processing technology; drafting and design technology; electrical, electronic and communications engineering technology; emergency medical technology (EMT paramedic); entrepreneurship; executive assistant/executive secretary; industrial radiologic technology; industrial technology; liberal arts and sciences/liberal studies; management information systems; medical administrative assistant and medical secretary; medical radiologic technology; nursing (registered nurse training).

Academics *Calendar:* semesters. *Degree:* certificates and associate. *Special study options:* academic remediation for entering students, adult/continuing education programs, advanced placement credit, cooperative education, distance learning, double majors, independent study, internships, off-campus study, part-time degree program, services for LD students, summer session for credit.

Library Montcalm Community College Library with 29,848 titles, 3,670 serial subscriptions, an OPAC, a Web page.

Student Life *Housing:* college housing not available. *Activities and Organizations:* drama/theater group, choral group, Nursing Club, Native American Club, Phi Theta Kappa, Business Club, Judo Club. *Student services:* personal/psychological counseling.

Athletics *Intramural sports:* volleyball M/W.

Costs (2007–08) *Tuition:* area resident $2100 full-time, $70 per credit hour part-time; state resident $3330 full-time, $111 per credit hour part-time; nonresident $4470 full-time, $149 per credit hour part-time. *Required fees:* $195 full-time, $7 per credit hour part-time.

Financial Aid Of all full-time matriculated undergraduates, 57 Federal Work-Study jobs (averaging $2000).

Applying *Options:* early admission, deferred entrance. *Recommended:* high school transcript. *Application deadlines:* rolling (freshmen), rolling (transfers). *Notification:* continuous (freshmen), continuous (transfers).

Freshmen Application Contact Ms. Debra Alexander, Director of Admissions, Montcalm Community College, 2800 College Drive, Sidney, MI 48885. *Phone:* 989-328-1276. *Toll-free phone:* 877-328-2111. *E-mail:* admissions@montcalm.edu.

MOTT COMMUNITY COLLEGE

Flint, Michigan   www.mcc.edu/

- **District-supported** 2-year, founded 1923, part of Michigan Labor and Economic Growth Department
- **Urban** 20-acre campus with easy access to Detroit
- **Endowment** $36.4 million
- **Coed,** 10,038 undergraduate students, 37% full-time, 61% women, 39% men

Undergraduates 3,666 full-time, 6,372 part-time. Students come from 10 states and territories, 33 other countries, 18% African American, 0.7% Asian American or Pacific Islander, 2% Hispanic American, 1% Native American, 0.3% international, 3% transferred in.

Freshmen *Admission:* 2,888 applied, 772 admitted, 772 enrolled.

Faculty *Total:* 472, 33% full-time, 10% with terminal degrees. *Student/faculty ratio:* 22:1.

Majors Accounting technology and bookkeeping; administrative assistant and secretarial science; architectural engineering technology; autobody/collision and repair technology; automobile/automotive mechanics technology; business administration and management; business/commerce; communications technology; community health services counseling; computer and information sciences and support services related; computer systems networking and telecommunications; criminal justice/police science; culinary arts; dental assisting; dental hygiene; drafting and design technology; early childhood education; electrical, electronic and communications engineering technology; emergency medical technology (EMT paramedic); engineering technologies related; entrepreneurship; fire protection and safety technology; foodservice systems administration; general studies; graphic design; heating, air conditioning and refrigeration technology; histologic technician; information resources management; international business/trade/commerce; legal administrative assistant/secretary; liberal arts and sciences/liberal studies; management information systems; manufacturing technology; marketing/marketing management; mechanical drafting and CAD/CADD;

Mott Community College (continued)

mechanical engineering/mechanical technology; medical administrative assistant and medical secretary; medical radiologic technology; nursing (registered nurse training); occupational therapist assistant; office management; photography; physical therapist assistant; precision production related; quality control technology; respiratory care therapy; salon/beauty salon management; sign language interpretation and translation; survey technology; teacher assistant/aide.

Academics *Calendar:* semesters. *Degree:* certificates and associate. *Special study options:* academic remediation for entering students, accelerated degree program, adult/continuing education programs, advanced placement credit, cooperative education, distance learning, double majors, English as a second language, honors programs, independent study, internships, part-time degree program, services for LD students, summer session for credit.

Library Charles Stewart Mott Library with 96,910 titles, 277 serial subscriptions, an OPAC, a Web page.

Student Life *Housing:* college housing not available. *Activities and Organizations:* choral group, Criminal Justice Association, Phi Theta Kappa, Dental Assisting Club, Connoisseur's Club, Social Work Club. *Campus security:* 24-hour emergency response devices and patrols, student patrols, late-night transport/escort service. *Student services:* health clinic, personal/psychological counseling.

Athletics Member NJCAA. *Intercollegiate sports:* baseball M(s), basketball M(s)/W(s), cross-country running M(s)/W(s), golf M(s), softball W(s), volleyball W(s).

Costs (2007–08) *Tuition:* area resident $2708 full-time, $82 per contact hour part-time; state resident $4054 full-time, $123 per contact hour part-time; nonresident $5410 full-time, $164 per contact hour part-time. *Required fees:* $111 full-time.

Financial Aid Of all full-time matriculated undergraduates, 258 Federal Work-Study jobs (averaging $1000). 300 state and other part-time jobs (averaging $1000).

Applying *Options:* electronic application, early admission, deferred entrance. *Required:* high school transcript. *Application deadline:* 8/31 (freshmen). *Notification:* continuous (transfers).

Freshmen Application Contact Ms. Delores Deen, Executive Dean of Student Services, Mott Community College, 1401 East Court Street, Flint, MI 48503. *Phone:* 810-762-0315. *Toll-free phone:* 800-852-8614. *Fax:* 810-232-9442.

MUSKEGON COMMUNITY COLLEGE

Muskegon, Michigan   www.muskegoncc.edu/

- **State and locally supported** 2-year, founded 1926, part of Michigan Department of Education
- **Small-town** 112-acre campus with easy access to Grand Rapids
- **Coed,** 5,000 undergraduate students

Faculty *Total:* 150, 67% full-time.

Majors Accounting; administrative assistant and secretarial science; advertising; anthropology; applied art; applied mathematics; art; art history, criticism and conservation; art teacher education; automobile/automotive mechanics technology; biology/biotechnology laboratory technician; biomedical technology; business administration and management; business machine repair; chemical engineering; child development; commercial and advertising art; criminal justice/law enforcement administration; data processing and data processing technology; developmental and child psychology; drafting and design technology; economics; education; electrical, electronic and communications engineering technology; electromechanical technology; elementary education; emergency medical technology (EMT paramedic); engineering technology; finance; hospitality administration; hospitality and recreation marketing; hotel/motel administration; industrial arts; industrial technology; information science/studies; legal administrative assistant/secretary; liberal arts and sciences/liberal studies; machine tool technology; marketing/marketing management; medical administrative assistant and medical secretary; nursing (registered nurse training); parks, recreation and leisure; special products marketing; transportation technology; welding technology.

Academics *Calendar:* semesters. *Degree:* associate. *Special study options:* academic remediation for entering students, adult/continuing education programs, cooperative education, honors programs, part-time degree program, student-designed majors, summer session for credit.

Library 48,597 titles, 450 serial subscriptions.

Student Life *Housing:* college housing not available. *Activities and Organizations:* drama/theater group, choral group. *Student services:* personal/psychological counseling.

Athletics Member NJCAA. *Intercollegiate sports:* baseball M, basketball M(s)/W(s), golf M/W, softball W, tennis M/W, volleyball W(s), wrestling M. *Intramural sports:* basketball M/W, skiing (downhill) M(c)/W(c).

Financial Aid Of all full-time matriculated undergraduates, 250 Federal Work-Study jobs (averaging $2500). 50 state and other part-time jobs (averaging $2500).

Applying *Options:* early admission, deferred entrance. *Application deadlines:* rolling (freshmen), rolling (transfers). *Notification:* continuous (freshmen), continuous (transfers).

Freshmen Application Contact Ms. Lynda Schwartz, Admissions Coordinator, Muskegon Community College, 221 South Quarterline Road, Muskegon, MI 49442-1493. *Phone:* 231-773-9131 Ext. 366.

NORTH CENTRAL MICHIGAN COLLEGE

Petoskey, Michigan   www.ncmich.edu/

- **County-supported** 2-year, founded 1958, part of Michigan Department of Education
- **Small-town** 270-acre campus
- **Coed,** 2,738 undergraduate students

Undergraduates Students come from 4 states and territories, 0.1% African American, 0.6% Asian American or Pacific Islander, 0.6% Hispanic American, 4% Native American, 3% live on campus.

Freshmen *Admission:* 424 applied, 424 admitted.

Faculty *Total:* 133, 23% full-time. *Student/faculty ratio:* 17:1.

Majors Accounting; administrative assistant and secretarial science; business administration and management; child guidance; computer and information sciences related; computer programming; computer systems networking and telecommunications; criminal justice/law enforcement administration; criminal justice/police science; data processing and data processing technology; drafting and design technology; emergency medical technology (EMT paramedic); engineering technology; finance; information technology; legal administrative assistant/secretary; legal assistant/paralegal; liberal arts and sciences/liberal studies; marketing/marketing management; nursing (registered nurse training); pre-engineering.

Academics *Calendar:* semesters. *Degree:* certificates and associate. *Special study options:* academic remediation for entering students, advanced placement credit, cooperative education, distance learning, double majors, independent study, internships, part-time degree program, services for LD students, summer session for credit.

Library North Central Michigan College Library with 29,249 titles, 325 serial subscriptions, an OPAC, a Web page.

Student Life *Housing Options:* coed. Campus housing is university owned. *Activities and Organizations:* choral group. *Campus security:* 24-hour emergency response devices. *Student services:* personal/psychological counseling.

Athletics *Intramural sports:* basketball M/W.

Standardized Tests *Required:* ACT (for placement).

Costs (2006–07) *Tuition:* area resident $1960 full-time; state resident $3000 full-time; nonresident $3690 full-time.

Financial Aid Of all full-time matriculated undergraduates, 25 Federal Work-Study jobs (averaging $2400). 20 state and other part-time jobs (averaging $2400).

Applying *Required:* high school transcript. *Application deadlines:* rolling (freshmen), rolling (transfers). *Notification:* continuous (freshmen), continuous (transfers).

Director of Admissions Ms. Julieanne Tobin, Director of Enrollment Management, North Central Michigan College, 1515 Howard Street, Petoskey, MI 49770-8717. *Phone:* 231-439-6511. *Toll-free phone:* 888-298-6605.

NORTHWESTERN MICHIGAN COLLEGE

Traverse City, Michigan   www.nmc.edu/

Freshmen Application Contact Mr. James Bensley, Coordinator of Admissions, Northwestern Michigan College, 1701 East Front Street, Traverse City, MI 49686. *Phone:* 231-995-1034. *Toll-free phone:* 800-748-0566. *Fax:* 616-955-1339. *E-mail:* welcome@nmc.edu.

OAKLAND COMMUNITY COLLEGE

Bloomfield Hills, Michigan   www.oaklandcc.edu/

- **State and locally supported** 2-year, founded 1964, part of Michigan Department of Career Development
- **Suburban** 540-acre campus with easy access to Detroit
- **Endowment** $1.6 million
- **Coed,** 24,123 undergraduate students, 33% full-time, 58% women, 42% men

Undergraduates 7,931 full-time, 16,192 part-time. Students come from 15 states and territories, 375 other countries, 0.3% are from out of state, 17% African American, 2% Asian American or Pacific Islander, 2% Hispanic American, 0.6% Native American, 8% international. *Retention:* 65% of 2003 full-time freshmen returned.

Freshmen *Admission:* 5,600 applied, 5,600 admitted, 1,861 enrolled.

Faculty *Total:* 960, 29% full-time. *Student/faculty ratio:* 27:1.

Majors Accounting; allied health diagnostic, intervention, and treatment professions related; applied horticulture; architectural engineering technology; architecture; automobile/automotive mechanics technology; aviation/airway management; business administration and management; business automation/technology/data entry; cabinetmaking and millwork; carpentry; ceramic arts and ceramics; child care and support services management; clinical/medical laboratory science and allied professions related; computer and information sciences; computer programming; computer technology/computer systems technology; construction management; consumer merchandising/retailing management; corrections and criminal justice related; cosmetology; court reporting; criminal justice/law enforcement administration; criminal justice/police science; culinary arts; dental hygiene; diagnostic medical sonography and ultrasound technology; electrical, electronic and communications engineering technology; electromechanical technology; electroneurodiagnostic/electroencephalographic technology; emergency medical technology (EMT paramedic); engineering; entrepreneurship; environmental control technologies related; fashion merchandising; fine arts related; fire science; foodservice systems administration; forensic science and technology; general studies; gerontology; graphic design; health and physical education related; health/health care administration; health professions related; heating, air conditioning and refrigeration technology; histologic technician; hotel/motel administration; industrial electronics technology; industrial technology; interior design; international business/trade/commerce; kinesiology and exercise science; landscape architecture; landscaping and groundskeeping; legal assistant/paralegal; liberal arts and sciences and humanities related; liberal arts and sciences/liberal studies; library assistant; machine tool technology; management information systems and services related; management science; manufacturing technology; marketing related; massage therapy; mechanical drafting and CAD/CADD; medical/clinical assistant; medical radiologic technology; medical transcription; mental and social health services and allied professions related; nuclear medical technology; nursing (licensed practical/vocational nurse training); nursing (registered nurse training); office management; operations management; ornamental horticulture; pharmacy technician; photography; precision metal working related; pre-engineering; radio and television broadcasting technology; respiratory care therapy; restaurant/food services management; robotics technology; salon/beauty salon management; sport and fitness administration/management; surgical technology; tool and die technology; welding technology; woodworking related.

Academics *Calendar:* semesters. *Degrees:* certificates, associate, and post-bachelor's certificates. *Special study options:* academic remediation for entering students, adult/continuing education programs, advanced placement credit, cooperative education, distance learning, English as a second language, internships, off-campus study, part-time degree program, services for LD students, study abroad, summer session for credit.

Library Main Library plus 5 others with 251,482 titles, 2,649 serial subscriptions, 10,393 audiovisual materials, an OPAC, a Web page.

Student Life *Housing:* college housing not available. *Activities and Organizations:* drama/theater group, choral group, Phi Theta Kappa, International Student Organization, organizations related to student majors. *Campus security:* 24-hour emergency response devices, late-night transport/escort service. *Student services:* personal/psychological counseling, women's center.

Athletics Member NJCAA. *Intercollegiate sports:* basketball M(s)/W(s), cross-country running M(s)/W(s), golf M(s), soccer M, softball W(s), tennis W(s), volleyball W(s). *Intramural sports:* basketball M/W, racquetball M/W, tennis W, volleyball M/W.

Costs (2006–07) *Tuition:* area resident $1704 full-time, $57 per credit hour part-time; state resident $2885 full-time, $96 per credit hour part-time; nonresident $4045 full-time, $135 per credit hour part-time. *Required fees:* $70 full-time, $35 per term part-time. *Waivers:* employees or children of employees.

Financial Aid Of all full-time matriculated undergraduates, 135 Federal Work-Study jobs (averaging $2800). 70 state and other part-time jobs (averaging $2800).

Applying *Options:* deferred entrance. *Recommended:* high school transcript, interview. *Application deadlines:* rolling (freshmen), rolling (transfers). *Notification:* continuous (freshmen), continuous (transfers).

Freshmen Application Contact Dr. Maurice McCall, Registrar and Director of Enrollment Services, Oakland Community College, METC Building, 2900 Featherstone Road, Auburn Hills, MI 48304-2845. *Phone:* 248-341-2186. *Fax:* 248-341-2099. *E-mail:* mhmccall@oaklandcc.edu.

SAGINAW CHIPPEWA TRIBAL COLLEGE
Mount Pleasant, Michigan　　www.sagchip.org/tribalcollege/

- **Independent** 2-year, founded 1998
- **Coed,** 123 undergraduate students, 35% full-time, 75% women, 25% men

Undergraduates 43 full-time, 80 part-time. 2% African American, 3% Hispanic American, 85% Native American.

Freshmen *Admission:* 36 applied, 36 admitted, 36 enrolled.

Faculty *Total:* 17, 24% full-time. *Student/faculty ratio:* 9:1.

Majors American Indian/Native American studies; business/commerce; liberal arts and sciences/liberal studies.

Academics *Calendar:* semesters. *Degree:* associate.

Student Life *Activities and Organizations:* student-run newspaper.

Costs (2007–08) *Tuition:* $1320 full-time, $55 per credit hour part-time. *Required fees:* $136 full-time, $68 per term part-time.

Applying *Required:* high school transcript.

Freshmen Application Contact Ms. Tracy Reed, Admissions Officer/Registrar/Financial Aid, Saginaw Chippewa Tribal College, 2274 Enterprise Drive, Mount Pleasant, MI 48858. *Phone:* 989-775-4123. *Fax:* 989-775-4528. *E-mail:* treed@sagchip.org.

ST. CLAIR COUNTY COMMUNITY COLLEGE
Port Huron, Michigan　　www.sc4.edu/

Director of Admissions Mr. Pete Lacey, Registrar, St. Clair County Community College, 323 Erie Street, PO Box 5015, PO Box 5015, Port Huron, MI 48061-5015. *Phone:* 810-989-5500. *Toll-free phone:* 800-553-2427.

SCHOOLCRAFT COLLEGE
Livonia, Michigan　　www.schoolcraft.edu/

- **District-supported** 2-year, founded 1961, part of Michigan Department of Education
- **Suburban** 183-acre campus with easy access to Detroit
- **Coed,** 11,105 undergraduate students, 36% full-time, 56% women, 44% men

Undergraduates 4,035 full-time, 7,070 part-time. 2% are from out of state, 8% African American, 2% Asian American or Pacific Islander, 2% Hispanic American, 0.6% Native American, 1% international. *Retention:* 62% of 2003 full-time freshmen returned.

Freshmen *Admission:* 1,918 enrolled.

Faculty *Total:* 429, 22% full-time. *Student/faculty ratio:* 30:1.

Majors Accounting; administrative assistant and secretarial science; biomedical technology; business administration and management; child care and support services management; commercial and advertising art; computer programming; computer technology/computer systems technology; corrections; criminal justice/police science; culinary arts; data processing and data processing technology; drafting and design technology; education; electrical, electronic and communications engineering technology; electromechanical technology; emergency medical technology (EMT paramedic); engineering; entrepreneurship; environmental engineering technology; fire science; health information/medical records technology; industrial technology; laser and optical technology; liberal arts and sciences/liberal studies; marketing/marketing management; mechanical engineering/mechanical technology; medical laboratory technology; metallurgical technology; music teacher education; nursing (registered nurse training); occupational therapist assistant; physical sciences related; radio and television broadcasting technology; robotics technology; welding technology.

Academics *Calendar:* semesters. *Degree:* certificates and associate. *Special study options:* academic remediation for entering students, adult/continuing education programs, advanced placement credit, distance learning, English as a second language, honors programs, internships, part-time degree program, services for LD students, study abroad, summer session for credit.

Library Bradner Library with an OPAC.

Student Life *Housing:* college housing not available. *Activities and Organizations:* drama/theater group, student-run newspaper, choral group, Student Activities Board, Ski Club, student newspaper, Music Club, Phi Theta Kappa, national fraternities. *Campus security:* 24-hour emergency response devices and patrols, late-night transport/escort service. *Student services:* health clinic, women's center, legal services.

Schoolcraft College (continued)

Athletics Member NJCAA. *Intercollegiate sports:* basketball M(s)/W(s), cross-country running W(s), golf M(s)/W(s), soccer M(s)/W(s), volleyball W(s).

Costs (2007–08) *Tuition:* area resident $2100 full-time, $70 per credit hour part-time; state resident $3090 full-time, $103 per credit hour part-time; nonresident $4620 full-time, $154 per credit hour part-time. *Required fees:* $190 full-time, $4 per credit hour part-time, $35 per term part-time.

Financial Aid Of all full-time matriculated undergraduates, 42 Federal Work-Study jobs (averaging $1722).

Applying *Options:* early admission, deferred entrance. *Required for some:* high school transcript. *Recommended:* high school transcript. *Application deadlines:* rolling (freshmen), rolling (transfers).

Freshmen Application Contact Ms. Cheryl Hagen, Dean of Student Services, Schoolcraft College, 18600 Hagerty Road, Livonia, MI 48152-2696. *Phone:* 734-462-4426. *Fax:* 734-462-4553. *E-mail:* admissions@schoolcraft.edu.

SOUTHWESTERN MICHIGAN COLLEGE
Dowagiac, Michigan   www.swmich.edu/

- **State and locally supported** 2-year, founded 1964, part of Michigan Department of Education
- **Rural** 240-acre campus
- **Coed,** 2,500 undergraduate students, 39% full-time, 65% women, 35% men

Undergraduates 964 full-time, 1,536 part-time. Students come from 4 states and territories, 27 other countries, 8% are from out of state, 8% African American, 1% Asian American or Pacific Islander, 5% Hispanic American, 0.7% Native American, 4% international, 39% transferred in. *Retention:* 53% of 2003 full-time freshmen returned.

Freshmen *Admission:* 438 applied, 438 admitted, 438 enrolled.

Faculty *Total:* 145, 33% full-time, 11% with terminal degrees. *Student/faculty ratio:* 19:1.

Majors Accounting technology and bookkeeping; administrative assistant and secretarial science; airframe mechanics and aircraft maintenance technology; automobile/automotive mechanics technology; business administration and management; business, management, and marketing related; child care and support services management; computer and information sciences related; computer programming; data entry/microcomputer applications related; drafting and design technology; electrical and electronic engineering technologies related; engineering technology; general studies; graphic and printing equipment operation/production; health professions related; heavy/industrial equipment maintenance technologies related; industrial mechanics and maintenance technology; legal assistant/paralegal; liberal arts and sciences and humanities related; liberal arts and sciences/liberal studies; machine shop technology; merchandising, sales, and marketing operations related (general); nursing (registered nurse training); precision production related; precision systems maintenance and repair technologies related; welding technology.

Academics *Calendar:* semesters. *Degree:* certificates and associate. *Special study options:* academic remediation for entering students, accelerated degree program, adult/continuing education programs, advanced placement credit, cooperative education, distance learning, double majors, English as a second language, independent study, internships, part-time degree program, services for LD students, student-designed majors, summer session for credit.

Library Fred L. Mathews Library with 36,877 titles, 127 serial subscriptions, 1,537 audiovisual materials, an OPAC, a Web page.

Student Life *Housing:* college housing not available. *Activities and Organizations:* drama/theater group, student-run newspaper, choral group, Phi Theta Kappa. *Campus security:* 24-hour emergency response devices, evening police patrols.

Athletics *Intramural sports:* archery M/W, badminton M/W, basketball M/W, cross-country running M/W, football M/W, golf M/W, racquetball M/W, skiing (cross-country) M/W, skiing (downhill) M/W, soccer M/W, softball M/W, track and field M/W, volleyball M/W, weight lifting M/W.

Costs (2007–08) *Tuition:* area resident $2426 full-time, $78 per contact hour part-time; state resident $3092 full-time, $100 per contact hour part-time; nonresident $3340 full-time, $108 per contact hour part-time. *Required fees:* $651 full-time, $21 per contact hour part-time.

Financial Aid Of all full-time matriculated undergraduates, 125 Federal Work-Study jobs (averaging $1000). 75 state and other part-time jobs (averaging $1000).

Applying *Options:* electronic application, deferred entrance. *Required:* high school transcript. *Required for some:* letters of recommendation, interview. *Application deadlines:* rolling (freshmen), rolling (transfers). *Notification:* continuous until 9/10 (freshmen), continuous until 9/10 (transfers).

Freshmen Application Contact Dr. Margaret Hay, Dean of Students and Academic Support, Southwestern Michigan College, 58900 Cherry Grove Road,

Dowagiac, MI 49047. *Phone:* 269-782-1000 Ext. 1306. *Toll-free phone:* 800-456-8675. *Fax:* 269-782-1331. *E-mail:* mhay@swmich.edu.

WASHTENAW COMMUNITY COLLEGE
Ann Arbor, Michigan   www.wccnet.edu/

Freshmen Application Contact Mr. Bradley D. Hoth, Admissions Representative, Washtenaw Community College, 4800 East Huron River Drive, PO Box D-1, Ann Arbor, MI 48106. *Phone:* 734-973-3676. *E-mail:* wccinfo@orchard.washtenaw.cc.mi.us.

WAYNE COUNTY COMMUNITY COLLEGE DISTRICT
Detroit, Michigan   www.wcccd.edu/

Freshmen Application Contact Office of Enrollment Management and Student Services, Wayne County Community College District, 801 West Fort Street, Detroit, MI 48226-2539. *Phone:* 313-496-2600. *E-mail:* caafjh@wccc.edu.

WEST SHORE COMMUNITY COLLEGE
Scottville, Michigan   www.westshore.edu/

- **District-supported** 2-year, founded 1967, part of Michigan Department of Education
- **Rural** 375-acre campus
- **Endowment** $291,972
- **Coed,** 1,372 undergraduate students

Undergraduates Students come from 3 states and territories, 1% are from out of state.

Freshmen *Admission:* 323 applied, 323 admitted. *Average high school GPA:* 2.94.

Faculty *Total:* 55, 45% full-time. *Student/faculty ratio:* 25:1.

Majors Accounting; corrections; criminal justice/police science; data entry/microcomputer applications related; data processing and data processing technology; electrical, electronic and communications engineering technology; emergency medical technology (EMT paramedic); information technology; liberal arts and sciences/liberal studies; machine tool technology; marketing/marketing management; nursing (licensed practical/vocational nurse training); nursing (registered nurse training); welding technology.

Academics *Calendar:* semesters. *Degree:* certificates and associate. *Special study options:* academic remediation for entering students, adult/continuing education programs, advanced placement credit, cooperative education, distance learning, independent study, internships, off-campus study, part-time degree program, services for LD students, student-designed majors, summer session for credit.

Library West Shore Library plus 1 other with 2,500 titles, 150 serial subscriptions, 1,100 audiovisual materials, an OPAC, a Web page.

Student Life *Housing:* college housing not available. *Activities and Organizations:* drama/theater group, student-run newspaper, choral group, Art Club, Student Senate, Phi Theta Kappa, Science Club, Law Enforcement Club. *Campus security:* 24-hour emergency response devices and patrols. *Student services:* personal/psychological counseling.

Athletics *Intramural sports:* basketball M/W, football M/W, racquetball M/W, softball M/W, swimming and diving M/W, table tennis M/W, volleyball M/W, weight lifting M/W.

Standardized Tests *Required for some:* ACT ASSET. *Recommended:* ACT (for placement).

Costs (2006–07) *Tuition:* area resident $1005 full-time, $67 per credit hour part-time; state resident $1650 full-time, $110 per credit hour part-time; nonresident $2190 full-time, $146 per credit hour part-time. Full-time tuition and fees vary according to course load and program. *Required fees:* $86 full-time, $45 per term part-time. *Payment plan:* installment. *Waivers:* senior citizens and employees or children of employees.

Financial Aid Of all full-time matriculated undergraduates, 80 Federal Work-Study jobs (averaging $3000). 40 state and other part-time jobs (averaging $3000).

Applying *Options:* early admission, deferred entrance. *Application fee:* $10. *Required:* high school transcript. *Application deadlines:* rolling (freshmen), rolling (transfers). *Notification:* continuous (freshmen), continuous (transfers).

Freshmen Application Contact Mr. Tom Bell, Director of Admissions, West Shore Community College, PO Box 277, 3000 North Stiles Road, Scottville, MI 49454-0277. *Phone:* 231-845-6211. *Fax:* 231-845-3944. *E-mail:* admissions@westshore.cc.mi.us.

MICRONESIA

COLLEGE OF MICRONESIA–FSM
Kolonia Pohnpei, Federated States of Micronesia, Micronesia   **www.comfsm.fm/**

- **Territory-supported** 2-year, founded 1963
- **Rural** 70-acre campus
- **Coed,** 2,283 undergraduate students

Undergraduates Students come from 1 other state, 4 other countries, 20% live on campus.
Freshmen *Admission:* 485 applied, 340 admitted.
Faculty *Total:* 42, 88% full-time.
Majors Accounting; agriculture; business administration and management; communication and media related; computer and information sciences; early childhood education; education; elementary education; health professions related; hospitality administration related; hotel and restaurant management; liberal arts and sciences/liberal studies; marine science/merchant marine officer; nursing (registered nurse training); social sciences; special education; teacher assistant/aide; telecommunications technology.
Academics *Calendar:* semesters. *Degree:* certificates and associate. *Special study options:* academic remediation for entering students, adult/continuing education programs, double majors, English as a second language, independent study, internships, summer session for credit.
Library Learning Resources Center plus 1 other with 25,390 titles, 121 serial subscriptions.
Student Life *Housing Options:* coed. *Activities and Organizations:* Pohnpei Student Organization, Kosrae Student Organization, Chuuk Student Organization, Yap Student Organization. *Student services:* health clinic, personal/psychological counseling.
Athletics *Intramural sports:* basketball M/W, softball M/W, swimming and diving M/W, table tennis M/W, tennis M/W, track and field M/W, volleyball M/W.
Costs (2006–07) *Tuition:* territory resident $3060 full-time.
Financial Aid Of all full-time matriculated undergraduates, 566 Federal Work-Study jobs (averaging $350).
Applying *Options:* deferred entrance. *Application fee:* $10. *Required:* high school transcript, minimum 2.0 GPA. *Application deadline:* 4/15 (freshmen). *Notification:* 6/30 (freshmen).
Director of Admissions Mr. Wilson J. Kalio, Coordinator of Admissions and Records, College of Micronesia–FSM, PO Box 159, Kolonia Pohnpei, FM 96941-0159, Micronesia. *Phone:* 691-320-2480 Ext. 6200.

MINNESOTA

ACADEMY COLLEGE
Minneapolis, Minnesota   **www.academycollege.edu/**

- **Proprietary** primarily 2-year, founded 1936
- **Urban** campus
- **Coed,** 210 undergraduate students, 98% full-time, 39% women, 61% men

Undergraduates 206 full-time, 4 part-time. Students come from 2 states and territories, 2% are from out of state, 18% African American, 8% Asian American or Pacific Islander, 3% Hispanic American, 2% Native American, 8% transferred in. *Retention:* 100% of 2003 full-time freshmen returned.
Freshmen *Admission:* 22 enrolled.
Faculty *Total:* 54, 7% full-time. *Student/faculty ratio:* 8:1.

Majors Accounting; airline pilot and flight crew; aviation/airway management; business administration and management; business/commerce; commercial and advertising art; computer and information sciences; computer and information sciences and support services related; computer and information systems security; computer graphics; computer programming; computer science; computer systems networking and telecommunications; data processing and data processing technology; design and visual communications; finance; graphic design; intermedia/multimedia; management information systems; office management; sales, distribution and marketing; system administration; system, networking, and LAN/WAN management; web/multimedia management and webmaster; web page, digital/multimedia and information resources design.
Academics *Calendar:* quarters. *Degrees:* certificates, associate, and bachelor's. *Special study options:* academic remediation for entering students, accelerated degree program, adult/continuing education programs, advanced placement credit, cooperative education, distance learning, double majors, English as a second language, honors programs, internships, part-time degree program, services for LD students, summer session for credit.
Library Learning Resource Center plus 1 other with 1,309 titles, 22 serial subscriptions, an OPAC, a Web page.
Student Life *Housing:* college housing not available.
Costs (2007–08) *Tuition:* $19,527 full-time, $305 per credit part-time. *Required fees:* $250 full-time.
Applying *Options:* electronic application, early admission, deferred entrance. *Application fee:* $30. *Required:* high school transcript, interview. *Notification:* continuous (freshmen), continuous (transfers).
Freshmen Application Contact Ms. Jacinda Miller, Director, Academy College, 1101 East 78th Street, Suite 100, Minneapolis, MN 55420. *Phone:* 952-851-0066. *Toll-free phone:* 800-292-9149. *Fax:* 952-851-0094. *E-mail:* admissions@academycollege.edu.

ALEXANDRIA TECHNICAL COLLEGE
Alexandria, Minnesota   **www.alextech.edu/**

- **State-supported** 2-year, founded 1961, part of Minnesota State Colleges and Universities System
- **Small-town** 106-acre campus
- **Coed,** 2,015 undergraduate students, 78% full-time, 44% women, 56% men

Undergraduates 1,573 full-time, 442 part-time. Students come from 14 states and territories, 1 other country, 4% are from out of state, 0.4% African American, 0.5% Asian American or Pacific Islander, 0.6% Hispanic American, 0.6% Native American.
Freshmen *Admission:* 2,001 applied, 1,312 admitted.
Faculty *Total:* 89, 84% full-time, 42% with terminal degrees. *Student/faculty ratio:* 21:1.
Majors Accounting; administrative assistant and secretarial science; banking and financial support services; business administration and management; CAD/CADD drafting/design technology; carpentry; cartography; child care and support services management; child care provision; clinical/medical laboratory technology; commercial and advertising art; computer and information sciences; computer programming (specific applications); computer systems networking and telecommunications; computer technology/computer systems technology; criminal justice/police science; diesel mechanics technology; farm and ranch management; fashion merchandising; health and physical education; hospitality administration; hotel/motel administration; human services; hydraulics and fluid power technology; industrial technology; interior design; legal administrative assistant/secretary; legal assistant/paralegal; machine tool technology; marine maintenance and ship repair technology; marketing/marketing management; masonry; mechanical drafting and CAD/CADD; medical administrative assistant and medical secretary; medical insurance coding; medical reception; medical transcription; nursing assistant/aide and patient care assistant; nursing (licensed practical/vocational nurse training); office management; office occupations and clerical services; operations management; phlebotomy; receptionist; selling skills and sales; small business administration; small engine mechanics and repair technology; truck and bus driver/commercial vehicle operation; web page, digital/multimedia and information resources design; welding technology.
Academics *Calendar:* semesters. *Degree:* certificates, diplomas, and associate. *Special study options:* academic remediation for entering students, advanced placement credit, distance learning, double majors, independent study, internships, part-time degree program, services for LD students, student-designed majors, summer session for credit.
Library Learning Resource Center with 15,600 titles, 110 serial subscriptions, 1,240 audiovisual materials, an OPAC, a Web page.
Student Life *Housing:* college housing not available. *Activities and Organizations:* VICA (Vocational Industrial Clubs of America) Skills USA, BPA (Business Professionals of America), DECA (Delta Epsilon Club), Student Senate, Phi

Alexandria Technical College (continued)

Theta Kappa. *Campus security:* student patrols, late-night transport/escort service, security cameras inside and outside. *Student services:* personal/psychological counseling.

Athletics *Intercollegiate sports:* basketball M, volleyball W. *Intramural sports:* basketball M/W, football M/W, golf M/W, softball M/W, volleyball M/W.

Costs (2007–08) *Tuition:* state resident $4491 full-time, $132 per credit part-time; nonresident $4491 full-time, $132 per credit part-time. *Required fees:* $521 full-time, $15 per credit part-time.

Financial Aid Of all full-time matriculated undergraduates, 94 Federal Work-Study jobs (averaging $1871).

Applying *Options:* electronic application, early admission. *Application fee:* $20. *Required:* high school transcript, interview. *Application deadlines:* rolling (freshmen), rolling (transfers).

Freshmen Application Contact Janet Dropik, Admissions Receptionist, Alexandria Technical College, 1601 Jefferson Street, Alexandria, MN 56308. *Phone:* 320-762-4520. *Toll-free phone:* 888-234-1222. *Fax:* 320-762-4603. *E-mail:* admissionsrep@alextech.edu.

ANOKA-RAMSEY COMMUNITY COLLEGE

Coon Rapids, Minnesota   www.anokaramsey.edu/

- **State-supported** 2-year, founded 1965, part of Minnesota State Colleges and Universities System
- **Suburban** 100-acre campus with easy access to Minneapolis–St. Paul
- **Coed,** 6,009 undergraduate students, 46% full-time, 63% women, 37% men

Undergraduates 2,752 full-time, 3,257 part-time. 2% are from out of state, 6% African American, 4% Asian American or Pacific Islander, 1% Hispanic American, 1% Native American, 0.5% international. *Retention:* 51% of 2003 full-time freshmen returned.

Freshmen *Admission:* 3,338 applied, 3,326 admitted.

Faculty *Total:* 247, 37% full-time. *Student/faculty ratio:* 27:1.

Majors Accounting; administrative assistant and secretarial science; art; biomedical science; business administration and management; cartography; clinical laboratory science/medical technology; computer science; computer systems networking and telecommunications; computer/technical support; liberal arts and sciences/liberal studies; marketing/marketing management; music; nursing (registered nurse training); physical therapist assistant; pre-engineering.

Academics *Calendar:* semesters. *Degree:* certificates and associate. *Special study options:* academic remediation for entering students, accelerated degree program, advanced placement credit, cooperative education, distance learning, honors programs, independent study, internships, off-campus study, part-time degree program, services for LD students, study abroad, summer session for credit. *ROTC:* Air Force (c).

Library Coon Rapids Campus Library with 41,300 titles, 235 serial subscriptions, 800 audiovisual materials, an OPAC, a Web page.

Student Life *Housing:* college housing not available. *Activities and Organizations:* drama/theater group, student-run newspaper, choral group, Phi Theta Kappa, Student Senate, student newspaper, International Student Club, Inter-Varsity Christian Fellowship. *Campus security:* 24-hour emergency response devices and patrols, late-night transport/escort service. *Student services:* personal/psychological counseling.

Athletics Member NJCAA. *Intercollegiate sports:* baseball M, basketball M/W, volleyball W. *Intramural sports:* basketball M/W, bowling M/W, football M/W, golf M/W, ice hockey M/W, soccer M/W, softball M/W, tennis M/W, volleyball M/W.

Costs (2006–07) *Tuition:* state resident $3390 full-time, $113 per credit part-time; nonresident $6780 full-time, $226 per credit part-time. Full-time tuition and fees vary according to course load and reciprocity agreements. Part-time tuition and fees vary according to course load and reciprocity agreements. *Required fees:* $414 full-time, $14 per credit part-time. *Waivers:* senior citizens and employees or children of employees.

Financial Aid Of all full-time matriculated undergraduates, 88 Federal Work-Study jobs (averaging $4000). 106 state and other part-time jobs (averaging $4000).

Applying *Options:* early admission, deferred entrance. *Application fee:* $20. *Required for some:* high school transcript. *Application deadlines:* rolling (freshmen), rolling (transfers). *Notification:* continuous (freshmen), continuous (transfers).

Freshmen Application Contact Admissions Department, Anoka-Ramsey Community College, 11200 Mississippi Boulevard NW, Coon Rapids, MN 55433. *Phone:* 763-433-1300. *Fax:* 763-433-1521. *E-mail:* admissions@anokaramsey.edu.

ANOKA-RAMSEY COMMUNITY COLLEGE, CAMBRIDGE CAMPUS

Cambridge, Minnesota   www.anokaramsey.edu/

- **State-supported** 2-year, founded 1965, part of Minnesota State Colleges and Universities System
- **Small-town** campus
- **Coed,** 1,785 undergraduate students, 37% full-time, 67% women, 33% men

Undergraduates 652 full-time, 1,133 part-time. 1% are from out of state, 2% African American, 0.8% Asian American or Pacific Islander, 2% Hispanic American, 1% Native American. *Retention:* 48% of 2003 full-time freshmen returned.

Freshmen *Admission:* 1,031 applied, 1,031 admitted.

Faculty *Total:* 61, 43% full-time. *Student/faculty ratio:* 27:1.

Majors Accounting; administrative assistant and secretarial science; art; biomedical science; business administration and management; cartography; computer science; computer systems networking and telecommunications; liberal arts and sciences/liberal studies; marketing/marketing management; music; nursing (registered nurse training); pre-engineering.

Academics *Calendar:* semesters. *Degree:* certificates and associate. *Special study options:* academic remediation for entering students, accelerated degree program, advanced placement credit, cooperative education, distance learning, honors programs, independent study, internships, off-campus study, part-time degree program, services for LD students, study abroad, summer session for credit. *ROTC:* Air Force (c).

Library Cambridge Campus Library with 18,927 titles, 122 serial subscriptions, 1,536 audiovisual materials, an OPAC, a Web page.

Student Life *Housing:* college housing not available. *Activities and Organizations:* drama/theater group, student-run newspaper, choral group. *Student services:* personal/psychological counseling.

Athletics Member NJCAA. *Intercollegiate sports:* baseball M, basketball M/W, volleyball W. *Intramural sports:* bowling M/W, golf M/W, volleyball M/W.

Costs (2006–07) *Tuition:* state resident $3390 full-time, $113 per credit part-time; nonresident $6780 full-time, $226 per credit part-time. Full-time tuition and fees vary according to course load and reciprocity agreements. Part-time tuition and fees vary according to course load and reciprocity agreements. *Required fees:* $414 full-time, $14 per credit part-time. *Waivers:* senior citizens and employees or children of employees.

Applying *Options:* early admission, deferred entrance. *Application fee:* $20. *Required for some:* high school transcript. *Application deadlines:* rolling (freshmen), rolling (transfers). *Notification:* continuous (freshmen), continuous (transfers).

Freshmen Application Contact Admissions Department, Anoka-Ramsey Community College, Cambridge Campus, 300 Polk Street South, Cambridge, MN 55008. *Phone:* 763-433-1300. *Fax:* 763-433-1841. *E-mail:* admissions@anokaramsey.edu.

ANOKA TECHNICAL COLLEGE

Anoka, Minnesota   www.ank.tec.mn.us/

Director of Admissions Mr. Robert Hoenie, Director of Admissions, Anoka Technical College, 1355 West Highway 10, Anoka, MN 55303. *Phone:* 763-576-4746.

BROWN COLLEGE

Mendota Heights, Minnesota   www.browncollege.edu/

- **Proprietary** primarily 2-year, founded 1946, part of Career Education Corporation
- **Suburban** 20-acre campus with easy access to Minneapolis–St. Paul
- **Endowment** $352,500
- **Coed**

Undergraduates 1,891 full-time, 163 part-time. Students come from 15 states and territories, 21% are from out of state, 6% African American, 4% Asian American or Pacific Islander, 2% Hispanic American, 0.7% Native American.

Faculty *Student/faculty ratio:* 21:1.

Academics *Calendar:* quarters. *Degrees:* certificates, associate, and bachelor's. *Special study options:* academic remediation for entering students, internships, part-time degree program, summer session for credit.

Student Life *Campus security:* 24-hour emergency response devices, student patrols, late-night transport/escort service.

Costs (2006–07) *Tuition:* $18,540 full-time. Full-time tuition and fees vary according to degree level and program. No tuition increase for student's term of enrollment. *Required fees:* $2200 full-time. *Payment plans:* tuition prepayment, installment.

Financial Aid Of all full-time matriculated undergraduates, 20 Federal Work-Study jobs (averaging $2000).

Applying *Options:* deferred entrance. *Application fee:* $50. *Required:* high school transcript, interview. *Required for some:* minimum 2.0 GPA. *Recommended:* letters of recommendation.

Freshmen Application Contact Mr. Mark Fredrichs, Registrar, Brown College, 1440 Northland Drive, Mendota Heights, MN 55120. *Phone:* 651-905-3400. *Toll-free phone:* 800-6BROWN6. *Fax:* 651-905-3550.

CENTRAL LAKES COLLEGE

Brainerd, Minnesota   **www.clcmn.edu/**

- **State-supported** 2-year, founded 1938, part of Minnesota State Colleges and Universities System
- **Small-town** 1-acre campus
- **Endowment** $3.7 million
- **Coed,** 2,831 undergraduate students, 64% full-time, 57% women, 43% men

Undergraduates 1,820 full-time, 1,011 part-time. Students come from 10 states and territories, 0.3% are from out of state, 2% African American, 0.8% Asian American or Pacific Islander, 1% Hispanic American, 2% Native American.

Faculty *Total:* 162, 57% full-time. *Student/faculty ratio:* 17:1.

Majors Accounting; administrative assistant and secretarial science; business administration and management; developmental and child psychology; horticultural science; legal administrative assistant/secretary; liberal arts and sciences/liberal studies; marketing/marketing management; medical administrative assistant and medical secretary; nursing (registered nurse training).

Academics *Calendar:* semesters. *Degree:* certificates, diplomas, and associate. *Special study options:* academic remediation for entering students, advanced placement credit, external degree program, off-campus study, part-time degree program, summer session for credit.

Library Learning Resource Center with 16,052 titles, 286 serial subscriptions, an OPAC.

Student Life *Housing:* college housing not available. *Activities and Organizations:* drama/theater group, student-run newspaper, choral group. *Campus security:* 24-hour emergency response devices, student patrols, late-night transport/escort service.

Athletics Member NJCAA. *Intercollegiate sports:* baseball M, basketball M/W, football M, golf M/W, soccer M/W, softball W, volleyball W. *Intramural sports:* basketball M/W, bowling M/W, football M, golf M/W, softball M/W, tennis M/W, volleyball M/W.

Costs (2006–07) *Tuition:* $116 per credit hour part-time; state resident $4010 full-time; nonresident $4010 full-time. Full-time tuition and fees vary according to course load and program. Part-time tuition and fees vary according to course load and program. *Required fees:* $511 full-time. *Room and board:* Room and board charges vary according to housing facility. *Payment plan:* installment. *Waivers:* senior citizens and employees or children of employees.

Applying *Options:* deferred entrance. *Application fee:* $20. *Required:* high school transcript. *Application deadlines:* rolling (freshmen), rolling (transfers).

Freshmen Application Contact Ms. Charlotte Daniels, Director of Admissions, Central Lakes College, 501 West College Drive, Brainerd, MN 56401-3904. *Phone:* 218-828-2525. *Toll-free phone:* 800-933-0346 Ext. 2586. *Fax:* 218-855-8220. *E-mail:* cdaniels@clcmn.edu.

CENTURY COLLEGE

White Bear Lake, Minnesota   **www.century.edu/**

- **State-supported** 2-year, founded 1970, part of Minnesota State Colleges and Universities System
- **Suburban** 150-acre campus with easy access to Minneapolis–St. Paul
- **Coed,** 8,323 undergraduate students, 48% full-time, 59% women, 41% men

Undergraduates 4,023 full-time, 4,300 part-time. Students come from 29 states and territories, 39 other countries, 6% are from out of state, 8% African American, 11% Asian American or Pacific Islander, 2% Hispanic American, 1% Native American, 1% international, 7% transferred in.

Freshmen *Admission:* 2,804 applied, 2,804 admitted, 1,439 enrolled.

Faculty *Total:* 323, 51% full-time. *Student/faculty ratio:* 25:1.

Majors Accounting; administrative assistant and secretarial science; autobody/collision and repair technology; automobile/automotive mechanics technology; business administration and management; computer engineering technology; cosmetology; criminal justice/police science; dental assisting; dental hygiene; dental laboratory technology; diesel mechanics technology; educational/instructional media design; emergency medical technology (EMT paramedic); environmental studies; fashion merchandising; general retailing/wholesaling; heating, air conditioning, ventilation and refrigeration maintenance technology; industrial technology; interior design; legal administrative assistant/secretary; liberal arts and sciences/liberal studies; machine tool technology; management information systems; medical administrative assistant and medical secretary; medical/clinical assistant; medical radiologic technology; music management and merchandising; nursing (registered nurse training); orthotics/prosthetics; pharmacy technician; quality control technology; selling skills and sales; small engine mechanics and repair technology; social work; substance abuse/addiction counseling.

Academics *Calendar:* semesters. *Degree:* certificates, diplomas, and associate. *Special study options:* academic remediation for entering students, adult/continuing education programs, advanced placement credit, distance learning, double majors, English as a second language, honors programs, internships, part-time degree program, services for LD students, summer session for credit. *ROTC:* Air Force (c).

Library Century College Main Library plus 1 other with 56,867 titles, 486 serial subscriptions, 3,569 audiovisual materials, an OPAC, a Web page.

Student Life *Housing:* college housing not available. *Activities and Organizations:* drama/theater group, student-run newspaper, choral group, Student Senate, Phi Theta Kappa, Dental Assistants Club, Creative Arts Alliance, Christian Club. *Campus security:* late-night transport/escort service, day patrols. *Student services:* personal/psychological counseling, women's center.

Athletics *Intercollegiate sports:* golf M/W. *Intramural sports:* badminton M/W, basketball M/W, golf M/W, soccer M/W, softball M/W.

Costs (2006–07) *Tuition:* state resident $3810 full-time, $127 per credit part-time; nonresident $7620 full-time, $254 per credit part-time. *Required fees:* $434 full-time, $14 per credit part-time.

Financial Aid Of all full-time matriculated undergraduates, 72 Federal Work-Study jobs (averaging $2544). 103 state and other part-time jobs (averaging $1360).

Applying *Application fee:* $20. *Required:* high school transcript. *Application deadlines:* rolling (freshmen), rolling (transfers).

Freshmen Application Contact Ms. Christine Paulos, Admissions Director, Century College, 3300 Century Avenue North, White Bear Lake, MN 55110. *Phone:* 651-779-2619. *Toll-free phone:* 800-228-1978. *Fax:* 651-779-5810. *E-mail:* admissions@century.edu.

DAKOTA COUNTY TECHNICAL COLLEGE

Rosemount, Minnesota   **www.dctc.edu/**

Freshmen Application Contact Mr. Patrick Lair, Admissions Director, Dakota County Technical College, 1300 145th Street East, Rosemount, MN 55068. *Phone:* 651-423-8399. *Toll-free phone:* 877-YES-DCTC Ext. 302 (in-state); 877-YES-DCTC (out-of-state). *Fax:* 651-423-8775. *E-mail:* admissions@dctc.mnscu.edu.

DULUTH BUSINESS UNIVERSITY

Duluth, Minnesota   **www.dbumn.edu/**

Freshmen Application Contact Mr. Mark Traux, Director of Admissions, Duluth Business University, 4724 Mike Colalillo Drive, Duluth, MN 55807. *Phone:* 218-722-4000. *Toll-free phone:* 800-777-8406. *Fax:* 218-628-2127. *E-mail:* markt@dbumn.edu.

DUNWOODY COLLEGE OF TECHNOLOGY

Minneapolis, Minnesota   **www.dunwoody.edu/**

Freshmen Application Contact Shaun Manning, Director of Admissions, Dunwoody College of Technology, 818 Dunwoody Boulevard, Minneapolis, MN 55403. *Phone:* 612-374-5800 Ext. 2010. *Toll-free phone:* 800-292-4625. *E-mail:* smanning@dunwoody.tec.mn.us.

FOND DU LAC TRIBAL AND COMMUNITY COLLEGE

Cloquet, Minnesota   www.fdltcc.edu/

- **State-supported** 2-year, founded 1987, part of Minnesota State Colleges and Universities System
- **Rural** 31-acre campus
- **Endowment** $270,000
- **Coed,** 1,735 undergraduate students, 41% full-time, 46% women, 54% men

Undergraduates 719 full-time, 1,016 part-time. 2% are from out of state, 1% African American, 1% Asian American or Pacific Islander, 0.5% Hispanic American, 20% Native American, 10% live on campus.

Freshmen *Admission:* 751 applied, 751 admitted.

Faculty *Total:* 80, 35% full-time. *Student/faculty ratio:* 21:1.

Majors American Indian/Native American studies; business/commerce; corrections; criminal justice/police science; environmental studies; finance; human services; insurance; liberal arts and sciences/liberal studies; real estate.

Academics *Calendar:* semesters. *Degree:* certificates and associate. *Special study options:* academic remediation for entering students, adult/continuing education programs, advanced placement credit, cooperative education, distance learning, double majors, external degree program, independent study, internships, off-campus study, part-time degree program, services for LD students, summer session for credit.

Library Ruth Meyers Library with 3,482 titles, 216 serial subscriptions, 307 audiovisual materials, an OPAC.

Student Life *Housing Options:* coed, disabled students. Campus housing is university owned. *Activities and Organizations:* drama/theater group, student-run newspaper, choral group, Human Services Club, Anishinaabe Club, Phi Theta Kappa, Law Enforcement Club, Student Senate. *Campus security:* 24-hour emergency response devices, late-night transport/escort service, controlled dormitory access, video surveillance system. *Student services:* personal/psychological counseling.

Athletics *Intramural sports:* basketball M/W, bowling M/W, softball M/W, weight lifting M/W.

Standardized Tests *Required:* ASAP (for placement).

Costs (2006–07) *Tuition:* state resident $4216 full-time; nonresident $7978 full-time.

Applying *Options:* electronic application, early admission, deferred entrance. *Application fee:* $20. *Required for some:* high school transcript. *Notification:* continuous until 8/20 (freshmen), continuous until 8/20 (transfers).

Freshmen Application Contact Ms. Nancy Gordon, Admissions Representative, Fond du Lac Tribal and Community College, 2101 14th Street, Cloquet, MN 55720. *Phone:* 218-879-0808. *Toll-free phone:* 800-657-3712. *E-mail:* darla@asab.fdl.cc.mn.us.

GLOBE COLLEGE

Oakdale, Minnesota   www.globecollege.com/

- **Proprietary** primarily 2-year, founded 1885
- **Suburban** campus
- **Coed**

Undergraduates 533 full-time, 312 part-time. Students come from 1 other country, 8% are from out of state.

Faculty *Student/faculty ratio:* 15:1.

Academics *Calendar:* quarters. *Degrees:* certificates, diplomas, associate, and bachelor's. *Special study options:* academic remediation for entering students, accelerated degree program, adult/continuing education programs, cooperative education, distance learning, internships, part-time degree program, summer session for credit.

Standardized Tests *Required:* CPAt (for admission).

Costs (2006–07) *Tuition:* $15,750 full-time, $350 per credit part-time. Full-time tuition and fees vary according to course load. Part-time tuition and fees vary according to course load. *Required fees:* $500 full-time.

Applying *Options:* electronic application. *Application fee:* $50. *Required:* high school transcript, interview. *Required for some:* essay or personal statement.

Freshmen Application Contact Ms. Christina Hilipipre, Director of Admissions, Globe College, 7166 10th Street North, Oakdale, MN 55128. *Phone:* 651-730-5100. *Fax:* 651-730-5151. *E-mail:* admissions@globecollege.edu.

HENNEPIN TECHNICAL COLLEGE

Brooklyn Park, Minnesota   www.hennepintech.edu/

- **State-supported** 2-year, founded 1972, part of Minnesota State Colleges and Universities System
- **Urban** 100-acre campus with easy access to Minneapolis–St. Paul
- **Coed,** 8,623 undergraduate students

Undergraduates 10% African American, 5% Asian American or Pacific Islander, 1% Hispanic American, 0.5% Native American, 0.2% international.

Freshmen *Admission:* 11,773 applied, 11,314 admitted.

Faculty *Total:* 452. *Student/faculty ratio:* 25:1.

Majors Architectural drafting and CAD/CADD; automobile/automotive mechanics technology; carpentry; child guidance; computer programming; computer systems networking and telecommunications; dental assisting; desktop publishing and digital imaging design; electrical, electronic and communications engineering technology; fire science; hydraulics and fluid power technology; legal administrative assistant/secretary; machine tool technology; mechanical design technology; medical administrative assistant and medical secretary; photography; plastics engineering technology; publishing.

Academics *Calendar:* semesters. *Degree:* certificates, diplomas, and associate. *Special study options:* academic remediation for entering students, advanced placement credit, cooperative education, distance learning, double majors, English as a second language, independent study, internships, services for LD students.

Student Life *Housing:* college housing not available. *Campus security:* late-night transport/escort service, security service. *Student services:* personal/psychological counseling, women's center.

Costs (2006–07) *Tuition:* state resident $3947 full-time; nonresident $7718 full-time.

Financial Aid Of all full-time matriculated undergraduates, 72 Federal Work-Study jobs (averaging $3000).

Applying *Application fee:* $20. *Recommended:* high school transcript, interview. *Application deadlines:* rolling (freshmen), rolling (transfers). *Notification:* continuous (freshmen), continuous (transfers).

Director of Admissions Mrs. Joy Bodin, Director of Marketing and Admissions, Hennepin Technical College, 9000 Brooklyn Boulevard, Brooklyn Park, MN 55445. *Phone:* 763-488-2415. *Toll-free phone:* 800-345-4655. *Fax:* 763-550-2113.

HERZING COLLEGE

Minneapolis, Minnesota   www.herzing.edu/

- **Proprietary** primarily 2-year, founded 1961, part of Herzing College
- **Suburban** 1-acre campus
- **Coed, primarily women,** 270 undergraduate students, 90% full-time, 92% women, 8% men

Undergraduates 242 full-time, 28 part-time. Students come from 3 states and territories, 1% are from out of state, 11% African American, 6% Asian American or Pacific Islander, 0.7% Hispanic American, 0.7% Native American.

Freshmen *Admission:* 128 applied, 96 admitted, 53 enrolled.

Faculty *Total:* 32, 66% full-time, 25% with terminal degrees. *Student/faculty ratio:* 14:1.

Majors Computer and information sciences; computer systems networking and telecommunications; dental assisting; dental hygiene; management information systems; massage therapy; medical/clinical assistant; medical insurance coding.

Academics *Calendar:* semesters. *Degrees:* certificates, diplomas, associate, and bachelor's. *Special study options:* adult/continuing education programs, distance learning, internships, part-time degree program.

Library Main Library plus 1 other.

Student Life *Housing:* college housing not available. *Campus security:* 24-hour emergency response devices. *Student services:* personal/psychological counseling.

Standardized Tests *Required:* ACCUPLACER (for admission).

Costs (2007–08) *Tuition:* $13,186 full-time, $440 per credit part-time. *Required fees:* $25 full-time.

Applying *Required:* high school transcript, interview.

Freshmen Application Contact Ms. Shelly Larson, Director of Admissions, Herzing College, 5700 West Broadway, Minneapolis, MN 55428. *Phone:* 763-231-3155. *Toll-free phone:* 800-878-DRAW. *Fax:* 763-535-9205. *E-mail:* info@mpls.herzing.edu.

HIBBING COMMUNITY COLLEGE

Hibbing, Minnesota   **www.hcc.mnscu.edu/**

- **State-supported** 2-year, founded 1916, part of Minnesota State Colleges and Universities System
- **Small-town** 100-acre campus
- **Coed**

Undergraduates Students come from 20 states and territories, 5% African American, 0.9% Asian American or Pacific Islander, 1% Hispanic American, 2% Native American, 10% live on campus.

Faculty *Student/faculty ratio:* 14:1.

Academics *Calendar:* semesters. *Degree:* certificates, diplomas, and associate. *Special study options:* academic remediation for entering students, adult/continuing education programs, advanced placement credit, cooperative education, distance learning, internships, off-campus study, part-time degree program, services for LD students, study abroad, summer session for credit.

Student Life *Campus security:* late-night transport/escort service.

Athletics Member NJCAA.

Costs (2006–07) *Tuition:* state resident $4252 full-time, $124 per credit part-time. Full-time tuition and fees vary according to course load and reciprocity agreements. Part-time tuition and fees vary according to course load and reciprocity agreements. *Required fees:* $474 full-time. *Room and board:* $4500; room only: $2900.

Applying *Options:* early admission, deferred entrance. *Application fee:* $20. *Required:* high school transcript.

Freshmen Application Contact Ms. Shelly Corradi, Admissions, Hibbing Community College, 1515 East 25th Street, Hibbing, MN 55746. *Phone:* 218-262-7207. *Toll-free phone:* 800-224-4HCC. *Fax:* 218-262-6717. *E-mail:* admissions@hibbing.edu.

HIGH-TECH INSTITUTE

St. Louis Park, Minnesota   **www.high-techinstitute.com/**

- **Proprietary** 2-year, founded 1996
- **Coed,** 795 undergraduate students

Majors Computer and information systems security; massage therapy; medical/clinical assistant; medical insurance/medical billing; medical radiologic technology; pharmacy technician; surgical technology.

Academics *Calendar:* semesters. *Degree:* associate.

Costs (2006–07) *Tuition:* $24,204 per degree program part-time.

Applying *Application fee:* $50.

Freshmen Application Contact Admissions Office, High-Tech Institute, 5100 Gamble Drive, St. Louis Park, MN 55416. *Toll-free phone:* 888-324-9700.

INVER HILLS COMMUNITY COLLEGE

Inver Grove Heights, Minnesota   **www.inverhills.edu/**

- **State-supported** 2-year, founded 1969, part of Minnesota State Colleges and Universities System
- **Suburban** 100-acre campus with easy access to Minneapolis–St. Paul
- **Coed,** 4,325 undergraduate students, 36% full-time, 59% women, 41% men

Undergraduates 1,566 full-time, 2,759 part-time. Students come from 13 states and territories.

Faculty *Total:* 210, 40% full-time.

Majors Accounting; administrative assistant and secretarial science; airline pilot and flight crew; air traffic control; aviation/airway management; business administration and management; computer programming (specific applications); computer programming (vendor/product certification); computer/technical support; construction engineering technology; construction management; criminal justice/police science; criminal justice/safety; emergency medical technology (EMT paramedic); health/health care administration; human services; legal administrative assistant/secretary; legal assistant/paralegal; liberal arts and sciences/liberal studies; marketing/marketing management; medical administrative assistant and medical secretary; nursing (registered nurse training); system administration.

Academics *Calendar:* semesters. *Degree:* certificates and associate. *Special study options:* academic remediation for entering students, advanced placement credit, cooperative education, English as a second language, external degree

program, honors programs, independent study, internships, off-campus study, part-time degree program, services for LD students, summer session for credit.

Library 42,073 titles, 300 serial subscriptions, an OPAC, a Web page.

Student Life *Housing:* college housing not available. *Activities and Organizations:* drama/theater group, student-run newspaper, choral group, PTK, Black Student Union, Student Senate, Biology Club. *Campus security:* late-night transport/escort service, evening police patrol. *Student services:* health clinic, personal/psychological counseling.

Athletics *Intramural sports:* basketball M/W, football M/W, golf M/W, ice hockey M/W, skiing (cross-country) M/W, soccer M/W, tennis M/W, volleyball M/W, weight lifting M/W.

Costs (2006–07) *Tuition:* state resident $3157 full-time, $132 per credit part-time; nonresident $6339 full-time, $264 per credit part-time. Full-time tuition and fees vary according to location, program, and reciprocity agreements. Part-time tuition and fees vary according to location, program, and reciprocity agreements. *Required fees:* $324 full-time, $14 per credit part-time. *Payment plan:* installment. *Waivers:* senior citizens and employees or children of employees.

Financial Aid Of all full-time matriculated undergraduates, 80 Federal Work-Study jobs (averaging $2000). 75 state and other part-time jobs (averaging $2000).

Applying *Application fee:* $20. *Required for some:* high school transcript. *Recommended:* high school transcript. *Application deadlines:* 8/15 (freshmen), rolling (transfers). *Notification:* continuous (freshmen), continuous (transfers).

Freshmen Application Contact Mr. LeAnn Huber, Assistant Director of Enrollment Services, Inver Hills Community College, 2500 East 80th Street, Inver Grove Heights, MN 55076-3224. *Phone:* 651-450-8501. *Fax:* 651-450-8677. *E-mail:* lhuber@inverhills.edu.

ITASCA COMMUNITY COLLEGE

Grand Rapids, Minnesota   **www.itascacc.edu/**

- **State-supported** 2-year, founded 1922, part of Minnesota State Colleges and Universities System
- **Rural** 24-acre campus
- **Endowment** $3.9 million
- **Coed,** 1,185 undergraduate students, 77% full-time, 51% women, 49% men

Undergraduates 909 full-time, 276 part-time. Students come from 10 states and territories, 2 other countries, 4% are from out of state, 2% African American, 0.7% Asian American or Pacific Islander, 0.2% Hispanic American, 3% Native American, 2% international, 10% live on campus. *Retention:* 59% of 2003 full-time freshmen returned.

Freshmen *Admission:* 725 applied, 725 admitted.

Faculty *Total:* 77, 56% full-time, 1% with terminal degrees. *Student/faculty ratio:* 15:1.

Majors Accounting; American Indian/Native American studies; business administration and management; chemical engineering; civil engineering; computer engineering; computer engineering related; education; education (K-12); engineering; engineering related; engineering science; engineering technology; environmental studies; fish/game management; forestry; forestry technology; general studies; geography; human services; liberal arts and sciences/liberal studies; mechanical engineering; natural resources/conservation; natural resources management and policy; nuclear engineering; nursing (licensed practical/vocational nurse training); pre-engineering; psychology; special education (early childhood); wildlife and wildlands science and management.

Academics *Calendar:* semesters. *Degree:* certificates, diplomas, and associate. *Special study options:* academic remediation for entering students, adult/continuing education programs, advanced placement credit, cooperative education, double majors, independent study, internships, off-campus study, part-time degree program, services for LD students, study abroad, summer session for credit.

Library Itasca Community College Library with 28,790 titles, 280 serial subscriptions, an OPAC, a Web page.

Student Life *Housing Options:* coed. Campus housing is university owned. *Activities and Organizations:* student association, Circle K, Student Ambassadors, Minority Student Club, Psychology Club. *Campus security:* student patrols, late-night transport/escort service, controlled dormitory access, evening patrols by trained security personnel. *Student services:* legal services.

Athletics Member NJCAA. *Intercollegiate sports:* baseball M, basketball M/W, football M, softball W, volleyball W, wrestling M. *Intramural sports:* basketball M, bowling M/W, golf W, softball M/W, table tennis M/W, volleyball M/W.

Costs (2006–07) *Tuition:* state resident $3942 full-time, $128 per credit part-time; nonresident $4424 full-time, $160 per credit part-time. *Required fees:* $482 full-time, $15 per credit part-time. *Room and board:* $3850; room only: $3000.

Itasca Community College (continued)

Financial Aid Of all full-time matriculated undergraduates, 63 Federal Work-Study jobs (averaging $1350). 155 state and other part-time jobs (averaging $910).

Applying *Options:* electronic application. *Application fee:* $20. *Required:* high school transcript. *Required for some:* 3 letters of recommendation. *Application deadlines:* 9/4 (freshmen), 9/4 (transfers). *Notification:* continuous (freshmen), continuous (transfers).

Freshmen Application Contact Ms. Candace Perry, Director of Enrollment Services, Itasca Community College, 1851 East Highway 169, Grand Rapids, MN 55744. *Phone:* 218-327-4464. *Toll-free phone:* 800-996-6422 Ext. 4464. *Fax:* 218-327-4350. *E-mail:* iccinfo@itascacc.edu.

ITT TECHNICAL INSTITUTE

Eden Prairie, Minnesota   www.itt-tech.edu/

- **Proprietary** primarily 2-year, founded 2003, part of ITT Educational Services, Inc
- **Coed**

Majors Animation, interactive technology, video graphics and special effects; CAD/CADD drafting/design technology; computer and information systems security; computer engineering technology; computer software engineering; computer software technology; computer systems networking and telecommunications; electrical and communications engineering technology; system, networking, and LAN/WAN management; web page, digital/multimedia and information resources design.

Academics *Calendar:* quarters. *Degrees:* associate and bachelor's.

Standardized Tests *Required:* Wonderlic aptitude test (for admission).

Costs (2006–07) *Tuition:* Contact school for program costs.

Applying *Application fee:* $100. *Required:* high school transcript, interview. *Recommended:* letters of recommendation. *Application deadlines:* rolling (freshmen), rolling (transfers). *Notification:* continuous (freshmen), continuous (transfers).

Freshmen Application Contact Mr. Paul Rozeski, ITT Technical Institute, 8911 Columbine Road, Eden Prairie, MN 55347. *Phone:* 952-914-5300. *Toll-free phone:* 888-488-9646.

LAKE SUPERIOR COLLEGE

Duluth, Minnesota   www.lsc.edu/

- **State-supported** 2-year, founded 1995, part of Minnesota State Colleges and Universities System
- **Urban** 105-acre campus
- **Endowment** $148,576
- **Coed**

Undergraduates 2,429 full-time, 1,771 part-time. 13% are from out of state, 2% African American, 1% Asian American or Pacific Islander, 0.7% Hispanic American, 2% Native American.

Faculty *Student/faculty ratio:* 20:1.

Academics *Calendar:* semesters. *Degree:* certificates, diplomas, and associate. *Special study options:* academic remediation for entering students, advanced placement credit, distance learning, double majors, English as a second language, independent study, internships, part-time degree program, services for LD students, summer session for credit.

Student Life *Campus security:* late-night transport/escort service, 15-hour patrols by trained security personnel.

Costs (2006–07) *Tuition:* state resident $3450 full-time, $115 per credit part-time; nonresident $6900 full-time, $230 per credit part-time. *Required fees:* $477 full-time, $16 per credit part-time.

Financial Aid Of all full-time matriculated undergraduates, 100 Federal Work-Study jobs (averaging $2380). 100 state and other part-time jobs (averaging $2380).

Applying *Options:* early admission, deferred entrance. *Application fee:* $20. *Required for some:* high school transcript.

Freshmen Application Contact Ms. Melissa Leno, Director of Admissions, Lake Superior College, 2101 Trinity Road, Duluth, MN 55811. *Phone:* 218-723-4895. *Toll-free phone:* 800-432-2884. *Fax:* 218-733-5945. *E-mail:* enroll@lsc.edu.

LEECH LAKE TRIBAL COLLEGE

Cass Lake, Minnesota   www.lltc.org/

- **Independent** 2-year, founded 1992
- **Coed,** 189 undergraduate students

Majors Business administration, management and operations related; early childhood education; foods, nutrition, and wellness; liberal arts and sciences/liberal studies.

Academics *Calendar:* semesters. *Degree:* associate.

Costs (2006–07) *Tuition:* state resident $3240 full-time.

Applying *Application fee:* $15.

Freshmen Application Contact Admissions Office, Leech Lake Tribal College, 6945 Littlewolf Road NW, Cass Lake, MN 56633. *Phone:* 218-335-4200.

McNALLY SMITH COLLEGE OF MUSIC

Saint Paul, Minnesota   www.mcnallysmith.edu/

- **Proprietary** primarily 2-year, founded 1985
- **Urban** campus
- **Coed,** 474 undergraduate students, 88% full-time, 15% women, 85% men

Undergraduates 418 full-time, 56 part-time. Students come from 36 states and territories, 6 other countries, 48% are from out of state, 7% African American, 3% Asian American or Pacific Islander, 3% Hispanic American, 1% Native American, 2% international, 13% transferred in.

Freshmen *Admission:* 162 applied, 146 admitted, 146 enrolled.

Faculty *Total:* 61, 54% full-time. *Student/faculty ratio:* 10:1.

Majors Engineering technologies related; music; music management and merchandising; music performance.

Academics *Calendar:* semesters. *Degrees:* certificates, diplomas, associate, and bachelor's. *Special study options:* advanced placement credit, cooperative education, independent study, internships, part-time degree program, summer session for credit.

Library McNally Smith College Learning Center plus 1 other with 4,500 titles, 50 serial subscriptions, 4,000 audiovisual materials, an OPAC.

Student Life *Housing:* college housing not available. *Activities and Organizations:* student-run newspaper, Student Advisory Board, Audio Engineering Society, Minnesota Songwriters Association. *Campus security:* 24-hour emergency response devices. *Student services:* personal/psychological counseling.

Standardized Tests *Required for some:* ACT (for admission). *Recommended:* ACT (for admission).

Costs (2007–08) *Tuition:* $16,770 full-time, $645 per credit part-time. *Required fees:* $2805 full-time, $1365 per term part-time.

Applying *Application fee:* $75. *Required:* essay or personal statement, high school transcript, 2 letters of recommendation, interview. *Required for some:* audition. *Application deadline:* 8/1 (freshmen). *Notification:* 8/1 (freshmen).

Freshmen Application Contact Mrs. Kathy Hawks, Director of Admissions, McNally Smith College of Music, 19 Exchange Street East, St. Paul, MN 55101. *Phone:* 651-291-0177 Ext. 2373. *Toll-free phone:* 800-594-9500. *Fax:* 651-291-0366. *E-mail:* khawks@mcnallysmith.edu.

MESABI RANGE COMMUNITY AND TECHNICAL COLLEGE

Virginia, Minnesota   www.mr.mnscu.edu/

- **State-supported** 2-year, founded 1918, part of Minnesota State Colleges and Universities System
- **Small-town** 30-acre campus
- **Coed,** 1,467 undergraduate students

Undergraduates Students come from 6 states and territories, 5% are from out of state, 5% African American, 0.3% Hispanic American, 1% Native American, 10% live on campus.

Faculty *Total:* 137. *Student/faculty ratio:* 24:1.

Majors Administrative assistant and secretarial science; business/commerce; computer graphics; computer/information technology services administration related; computer programming related; computer programming (specific applications); computer software and media applications related; computer systems networking and telecommunications; electrical/electronics equipment installation and repair; human services; information technology; instrumentation tech-

nology; liberal arts and sciences/liberal studies; pre-engineering; substance abuse/addiction counseling; web page, digital/multimedia and information resources design.

Academics *Calendar:* semesters. *Degree:* certificates, diplomas, and associate. *Special study options:* academic remediation for entering students, adult/continuing education programs, advanced placement credit, cooperative education, independent study, internships, off-campus study, part-time degree program, services for LD students, student-designed majors, summer session for credit.

Library Mesabi Library with 23,000 titles, 167 serial subscriptions.

Student Life *Housing Options:* coed. Campus housing is provided by a third party. *Activities and Organizations:* drama/theater group, student-run newspaper, choral group, Student Senate, Human Services Club, Native American Club, Student Life Club, Black Awareness Club. *Campus security:* late-night transport/escort service. *Student services:* personal/psychological counseling.

Athletics Member NJCAA. *Intercollegiate sports:* baseball M, basketball M/W, football M, softball W, volleyball W. *Intramural sports:* badminton M/W, basketball M/W, bowling M/W, field hockey M/W, football M/W, golf M/W, ice hockey M/W, skiing (cross-country) M/W, skiing (downhill) M/W, tennis M/W, volleyball M/W.

Costs (2006–07) *Tuition:* state resident $3779 full-time, $126 per credit part-time; nonresident $4724 full-time, $157 per credit part-time. *Required fees:* $474 full-time, $16 per credit part-time. *Room and board:* room only: $3352.

Financial Aid Of all full-time matriculated undergraduates, 117 Federal Work-Study jobs (averaging $1610). 77 state and other part-time jobs (averaging $1470).

Applying *Options:* early admission, deferred entrance. *Application fee:* $20. *Application deadlines:* rolling (freshmen), rolling (transfers). *Notification:* continuous (freshmen), continuous (transfers).

Freshmen Application Contact Ms. Brenda Kochevar, Enrollment Services Director, Mesabi Range Community and Technical College, 1001 Chestnut Street West, Virginia, MN 55792. *Phone:* 218-749-0314. *Toll-free phone:* 800-657-3860. *Fax:* 218-749-0318. *E-mail:* b.kochevar@mr.mnscu.edu.

MINNEAPOLIS BUSINESS COLLEGE

Roseville, Minnesota www.minneapolisbusinesscollege.edu/

- **Proprietary** 2-year, founded 1874, part of The Bradford School
- **Coed, primarily women**

Undergraduates Students come from 2 states and territories, 11% are from out of state.

Faculty *Student/faculty ratio:* 30:1.

Academics *Degree:* diplomas and associate.

Student Life *Campus security:* 24-hour emergency response devices.

Costs (2006–07) *Tuition:* $12,240 full-time. *Room only:* $6360.

Applying *Application fee:* $50. *Required:* high school transcript.

Freshmen Application Contact Mr. David Whitman, President, Minneapolis Business College, 1711 West County Road B, Roseville, MN 55113. *Phone:* 651-604-4118. *Toll-free phone:* 800-279-5200. *Fax:* 651-686-8185. *E-mail:* info@minneapolisbusinesscollege.edu.

MINNEAPOLIS COMMUNITY AND TECHNICAL COLLEGE

Minneapolis, Minnesota www.mctc.mnscu.edu/

- **State-supported** 2-year, founded 1965, part of Minnesota State Colleges and Universities System
- **Urban** 4-acre campus
- **Coed,** 7,618 undergraduate students, 42% full-time, 55% women, 45% men

Undergraduates 3,191 full-time, 4,427 part-time. Students come from 28 states and territories, 3% are from out of state, 31% African American, 6% Asian American or Pacific Islander, 4% Hispanic American, 2% Native American, 2% international. *Retention:* 55% of 2003 full-time freshmen returned.

Freshmen *Admission:* 6,627 applied, 6,252 admitted, 1,465 enrolled.

Faculty *Total:* 487, 30% full-time. *Student/faculty ratio:* 23:1.

Majors Accounting technology and bookkeeping; administrative assistant and secretarial science; aircraft powerplant technology; airframe mechanics and aircraft maintenance technology; automobile/automotive mechanics technology; avionics maintenance technology; business administration and management; business/commerce; child guidance; cinematography and film/video production; commercial and advertising art; computer and information sciences related; computer programming; criminal justice/police science; criminal justice/safety; culinary arts; human services; information science/studies; legal administrative

assistant/secretary; liberal arts and sciences/liberal studies; nursing (registered nurse training); parks, recreation and leisure; substance abuse/addiction counseling; web/multimedia management and webmaster; web page, digital/multimedia and information resources design.

Academics *Calendar:* semesters. *Degree:* certificates, diplomas, and associate. *Special study options:* academic remediation for entering students, adult/continuing education programs, advanced placement credit, distance learning, English as a second language, honors programs, independent study, internships, off-campus study, part-time degree program, services for LD students, student-designed majors, summer session for credit.

Library Minneapolis Community and Technical College Library with 65,865 titles, 600 serial subscriptions, an OPAC.

Student Life *Housing:* college housing not available. *Activities and Organizations:* drama/theater group, student-run newspaper, choral group, Student Senate, National Vocational-Technical Honor Society, Phi Theta Kappa, Association of Black Collegiates, Soccer Club. *Campus security:* 24-hour emergency response devices, late-night transport/escort service. *Student services:* personal/psychological counseling, women's center.

Athletics Member NJCAA. *Intercollegiate sports:* basketball M/W, golf M/W. *Intramural sports:* soccer M(c)/W(c).

Costs (2006–07) *Tuition:* state resident $3923 full-time, $131 per credit hour part-time; nonresident $7845 full-time, $262 per credit hour part-time. *Required fees:* $362 full-time.

Financial Aid Of all full-time matriculated undergraduates, 188 Federal Work-Study jobs (averaging $5000). 190 state and other part-time jobs (averaging $5000).

Applying *Options:* early admission, deferred entrance. *Application fee:* $20. *Required:* high school transcript. *Application deadlines:* 8/31 (freshmen), rolling (transfers). *Notification:* continuous (freshmen), continuous (transfers).

Freshmen Application Contact Minneapolis Community and Technical College, 1501 Hennepin Avenue, Minneapolis, MN 55403. *Phone:* 612-659-6200. *Toll-free phone:* 800-247-0911. *E-mail:* admissions.office@minneapolis.edu.

MINNESOTA SCHOOL OF BUSINESS—BROOKLYN CENTER

Brooklyn Center, Minnesota www.msbcollege.edu/

- **Proprietary** primarily 2-year, founded 1989
- **Suburban** campus
- **Coed,** 551 undergraduate students

Faculty *Student/faculty ratio:* 13:1.

Majors Accounting; administrative assistant and secretarial science; business administration and management; computer systems networking and telecommunications; information technology; intermedia/multimedia; legal administrative assistant/secretary; massage therapy; medical administrative assistant; music related; nursing science; paralegal/legal assistant; physician assistant; taxation; veterinary technology; web page, digital/multimedia and information resources design.

Academics *Calendar:* quarters. *Degrees:* certificates, diplomas, associate, bachelor's, and master's. *Special study options:* academic remediation for entering students, accelerated degree program, adult/continuing education programs, cooperative education, distance learning, internships, part-time degree program.

Library Minnesota School of Business – Brooklyn Center with 1,534 titles, 99 serial subscriptions, an OPAC, a Web page.

Student Life *Housing:* college housing not available.

Standardized Tests *Required:* CPAt (for admission).

Costs (2006–07) *Tuition:* $14,850 full-time, $350 per credit hour part-time.

Applying *Options:* electronic application. *Application fee:* $50. *Required:* high school transcript, interview. *Required for some:* essay or personal statement. *Application deadline:* 10/6 (freshmen).

Freshmen Application Contact Mr. Bruce Christman, Director of Admissions, Minnesota School of Business–Brooklyn Center, 5910 Shingle Creek Parkway, Brooklyn Center, MN 55430. *Phone:* 763-585-7777. *Fax:* 763-566-7030.

MINNESOTA SCHOOL OF BUSINESS—PLYMOUTH

Minneapolis, Minnesota www.msbcollege.edu/

- **Proprietary** primarily 2-year, founded 2002
- **Suburban** 3-acre campus
- **Coed,** 445 undergraduate students

Minnesota School of Business–Plymouth (continued)

Faculty *Student/faculty ratio:* 10:1.

Majors Accounting; administrative assistant and secretarial science; business administration and management; computer systems networking and telecommunications; information technology; intermedia/multimedia; massage therapy; medical administrative assistant; music related; nursing science; paralegal/legal assistant; physician assistant; taxation; veterinary technology; web page, digital/multimedia and information resources design.

Academics *Calendar:* quarters. *Degrees:* certificates, diplomas, associate, bachelor's, and master's. *Special study options:* academic remediation for entering students, accelerated degree program, adult/continuing education programs, cooperative education, distance learning, internships, part-time degree program, summer session for credit.

Library Minnesota School of Business-Plymouth with 1,189 titles, 106 serial subscriptions, an OPAC, a Web page.

Student Life *Housing:* college housing not available.

Standardized Tests *Required:* CPAt (for admission).

Costs (2006–07) *Tuition:* $14,850 full-time, $350 per credit part-time. Full-time tuition and fees vary according to course load. Part-time tuition and fees vary according to course load. *Payment plan:* installment. *Waivers:* senior citizens and employees or children of employees.

Applying *Options:* electronic application. *Application fee:* $50. *Required:* high school transcript, interview. *Required for some:* essay or personal statement. *Application deadline:* 10/6 (freshmen).

Freshmen Application Contact Stacy Severson, Minnesota School of Business–Plymouth, 1455 County Road 101 North, Plymouth, MN 55447. *Phone:* 763-476-2000. *Fax:* 763-476-1000.

MINNESOTA SCHOOL OF BUSINESS– RICHFIELD

Richfield, Minnesota　　　　**www.msbcollege.edu/**

- **Proprietary** primarily 2-year, founded 1877, administratively affiliated with Globe University
- **Urban** 3-acre campus with easy access to Minneapolis–St. Paul
- **Coed,** 763 undergraduate students

Undergraduates Students come from 5 states and territories.

Faculty *Student/faculty ratio:* 14:1.

Majors Accounting; administrative assistant and secretarial science; business administration and management; computer systems networking and telecommunications; information technology; intermedia/multimedia; legal assistant/paralegal; massage therapy; medical/clinical assistant; medical office management; music related; nursing science; taxation; veterinary technology; web page, digital/multimedia and information resources design.

Academics *Calendar:* quarters. *Degrees:* certificates, diplomas, associate, bachelor's, and master's. *Special study options:* academic remediation for entering students, accelerated degree program, adult/continuing education programs, cooperative education, distance learning, internships, part-time degree program, summer session for credit.

Library Minnesota School of Business-Richfield with 2,420 titles, 93 serial subscriptions, an OPAC, a Web page.

Student Life *Housing:* college housing not available.

Standardized Tests *Required:* CPAt (for admission).

Costs (2006–07) *Tuition:* $14,850 full-time, $350 per credit hour part-time.

Applying *Options:* electronic application. *Application fee:* $50. *Required:* high school transcript, interview. *Required for some:* essay or personal statement. *Application deadline:* 10/6 (freshmen).

Freshmen Application Contact Ms. Patricia Murray, Director of Admissions, Minnesota School of Business–Richfield, 1401 West 76th Street, Richfield, MN 55430. *Phone:* 612-861-2000 Ext. 720. *Toll-free phone:* 800-752-4223. *Fax:* 612-861-5548. *E-mail:* pmurray@msbcollege.com.

MINNESOTA SCHOOL OF BUSINESS– ST. CLOUD

Waite Park, Minnesota　　　　**www.msbcollege.edu/**

- **Proprietary** primarily 2-year, founded 2004
- **Small-town** campus
- **Coed,** 724 undergraduate students

Faculty *Student/faculty ratio:* 13:1.

Majors Accounting; administrative assistant and secretarial science; business administration and management; computer systems networking and telecommunications; information technology; intermedia/multimedia; massage therapy; medical administrative assistant; music related; nursing science; paralegal/legal assistant; physician assistant; taxation; veterinary technology; web page, digital/multimedia and information resources design.

Academics *Calendar:* quarters. *Degrees:* certificates, diplomas, associate, bachelor's, and master's. *Special study options:* academic remediation for entering students, accelerated degree program, adult/continuing education programs, cooperative education, distance learning, internships, part-time degree program, summer session for credit.

Library Minnesota School of Business-St. Cloud with 724 titles, 88 serial subscriptions, an OPAC, a Web page.

Student Life *Housing:* college housing not available.

Standardized Tests *Required:* CPAt (for admission).

Costs (2006–07) *Tuition:* $14,850 full-time, $350 per credit hour part-time.

Applying *Options:* electronic application. *Application fee:* $50. *Required:* high school transcript, interview. *Required for some:* essay or personal statement. *Application deadline:* 10/6 (freshmen).

Freshmen Application Contact Mr. Jim Beck, Director of Admissions, Minnesota School of Business–St. Cloud, 1201 2nd Street S, Waite Park, MN 56387. *Phone:* 320-257-2000. *Toll-free phone:* 866-403-3333. *Fax:* 320-257-0131. *E-mail:* jbeck@msbcollege.edu.

MINNESOTA SCHOOL OF BUSINESS– SHAKOPEE

Shakopee, Minnesota　　　　**www.msbcollege.edu/**

- **Proprietary** primarily 2-year, founded 2004
- **Suburban** campus
- **Coed,** 381 undergraduate students

Faculty *Student/faculty ratio:* 12:1.

Majors Accounting; administrative assistant and secretarial science; business administration and management; computer systems networking and telecommunications; information technology; intermedia/multimedia; massage therapy; medical administrative assistant; music related; nursing science; paralegal/legal assistant; physician assistant; veterinary technology; web page, digital/multimedia and information resources design.

Academics *Calendar:* quarters. *Degrees:* certificates, diplomas, associate, bachelor's, and master's. *Special study options:* academic remediation for entering students, accelerated degree program, adult/continuing education programs, cooperative education, distance learning, internships, part-time degree program, summer session for credit.

Library Minnesota School of Business-Shakopee with 919 titles, 95 serial subscriptions, an OPAC, a Web page.

Student Life *Housing:* college housing not available.

Standardized Tests *Required:* CPAt (for admission).

Costs (2006–07) *Tuition:* $14,850 full-time, $350 per credit part-time. Full-time tuition and fees vary according to course load. Part-time tuition and fees vary according to course load. *Payment plan:* installment. *Waivers:* senior citizens and employees or children of employees.

Applying *Options:* electronic application. *Application fee:* $50. *Required:* high school transcript, interview. *Required for some:* essay or personal statement. *Application deadline:* 10/6 (freshmen).

Freshmen Application Contact Ms. Gretchen Seifert, Director of Admissions, Minnesota School of Business–Shakopee, 1200 Shakopee Town Square, Shakopee, MN 55379. *Phone:* 952-516-7015. *Toll-free phone:* 866-766-1200. *Fax:* 952-345-1201.

MINNESOTA STATE COLLEGE– SOUTHEAST TECHNICAL

Winona, Minnesota　　　　**www.southeastmn.edu/**

- **State-supported** 2-year, founded 1992, part of Minnesota State Colleges and Universities System
- **Small-town** campus with easy access to Minneapolis–St. Paul
- **Endowment** $1.6 million
- **Coed,** 1,900 undergraduate students, 61% full-time, 58% women, 42% men

Undergraduates 1,158 full-time, 742 part-time. Students come from 29 states and territories, 28% are from out of state, 3% African American, 1% Asian

American or Pacific Islander, 0.7% Hispanic American, 1% Native American, 3% international, 40% transferred in. *Retention:* 40% of 2003 full-time freshmen returned.

Freshmen *Admission:* 1,263 applied, 1,104 admitted, 685 enrolled.

Faculty *Total:* 100. *Student/faculty ratio:* 19:1.

Majors Accounting; administrative assistant and secretarial science; automobile/automotive mechanics technology; avionics maintenance technology; business machine repair; carpentry; child development; computer engineering technology; computer programming; computer typography and composition equipment operation; consumer merchandising/retailing management; cosmetology; drafting and design technology; electrical, electronic and communications engineering technology; emergency medical technology (EMT paramedic); heating, air conditioning, ventilation and refrigeration maintenance technology; industrial technology; kindergarten/preschool education; legal administrative assistant/secretary; machine tool technology; marketing/marketing management; mechanical design technology; medical administrative assistant and medical secretary; musical instrument fabrication and repair; nursing (licensed practical/vocational nurse training); nursing (registered nurse training); violin, viola, guitar and other stringed instruments; welding technology.

Academics *Calendar:* semesters. *Degree:* certificates, diplomas, and associate. *Special study options:* academic remediation for entering students, advanced placement credit, distance learning, double majors, internships, off-campus study, part-time degree program, services for LD students, study abroad, summer session for credit.

Library Learning Resource Center plus 1 other with 8,000 titles, 150 serial subscriptions, 50 audiovisual materials, an OPAC, a Web page.

Student Life *Housing:* college housing not available. *Activities and Organizations:* Student Senate. *Campus security:* 24-hour emergency response devices, late-night transport/escort service.

Costs (2007–08) *Tuition:* state resident $4074 full-time, $136 per credit part-time; nonresident $8148 full-time, $272 per credit part-time. *Required fees:* $357 full-time, $15 per credit part-time.

Financial Aid Of all full-time matriculated undergraduates, 65 Federal Work-Study jobs (averaging $2500). 65 state and other part-time jobs (averaging $2500).

Applying *Options:* electronic application. *Application fee:* $20. *Required:* high school transcript. *Application deadlines:* rolling (freshmen), rolling (out-of-state freshmen), rolling (transfers). *Notification:* continuous (freshmen), continuous (out-of-state freshmen), continuous (transfers).

Freshmen Application Contact Ms. Christine Humble, Director of Enrollment Services, Minnesota State College–Southeast Technical, PO Box 409, Winona, MN 55987. *Phone:* 507-453-2732. *Toll-free phone:* 800-372-8164. *E-mail:* chumble@win.tec.mn.us.

MINNESOTA STATE COMMUNITY AND TECHNICAL COLLEGE–FERGUS FALLS

Fergus Falls, Minnesota www.minnesota.edu/

- **State-supported** 2-year, founded 1960, part of Minnesota State Colleges and Universities System
- **Rural** 146-acre campus
- **Endowment** $1.8 million
- **Coed,** 6,093 undergraduate students, 58% full-time, 58% women, 42% men

Undergraduates 3,512 full-time, 2,581 part-time. Students come from 15 states and territories, 2 other countries, 3% are from out of state, 2% African American, 1% Asian American or Pacific Islander, 1% Hispanic American, 2% Native American, 0.0% international, 10% transferred in, 2% live on campus. *Retention:* 52% of 2003 full-time freshmen returned.

Freshmen *Admission:* 3,320 applied, 2,703 admitted, 1,288 enrolled.

Faculty *Total:* 341, 52% full-time. *Student/faculty ratio:* 18:1.

Majors Accounting; administrative assistant and secretarial science; architectural engineering technology; automotive engineering technology; biological and physical sciences; business administration and management; clinical/medical laboratory assistant; clinical/medical laboratory technology; computer and information systems security; computer programming; computer systems networking and telecommunications; corrections; cosmetology; criminal justice/police science; dental hygiene; early childhood education; electrical and electronic engineering technologies related; electrical, electronic and communications engineering technology; financial planning and services; fire services administration; forensic science and technology; health information/medical records technology; heating, air conditioning and refrigeration technology; human resources management; industrial technology; legal administrative assistant; legal administrative assistant/secretary; liberal arts and sciences/liberal studies; manufacturing technology; marketing/marketing management; mechanical engineering/mechanical technology; medical administrative assistant and medical secretary; medical laboratory technology; merchandising, sales, and market-

ing operations related (general); nursing (licensed practical/vocational nurse training); nursing (registered nurse training); pharmacy technician; pre-engineering; radiologic technology/science; telecommunications technology; web page, digital/multimedia and information resources design.

Academics *Calendar:* semesters. *Degree:* certificates, diplomas, and associate. *Special study options:* academic remediation for entering students, advanced placement credit, distance learning, English as a second language, freshman honors college, honors programs, independent study, off-campus study, part-time degree program, services for LD students, study abroad, summer session for credit.

Library Fergus Falls Community College Library with 30,000 titles, 173 serial subscriptions, an OPAC.

Student Life *Housing Options:* coed. Campus housing is university owned. *Activities and Organizations:* drama/theater group, student-run newspaper, choral group, Student Senate, Students In Free Enterprise, Phi Theta Kappa. *Campus security:* late-night transport/escort service, security for special events. *Student services:* personal/psychological counseling, women's center.

Athletics Member NJCAA. *Intercollegiate sports:* baseball M, basketball M/W, football M, golf M/W, softball W, volleyball W. *Intramural sports:* badminton M/W, basketball M, bowling M/W, football M/W, golf M/W, skiing (cross-country) M/W, skiing (downhill) M/W, softball M/W, table tennis M/W, tennis M/W, volleyball M/W, weight lifting M/W.

Costs (2007–08) *Tuition:* state resident $4150 full-time, $138 per credit part-time; nonresident $4150 full-time, $138 per credit part-time. *Required fees:* $570 full-time, $19 per credit part-time. *Room and board:* room only: $3100.

Financial Aid Of all full-time matriculated undergraduates, 80 Federal Work-Study jobs (averaging $1900). 80 state and other part-time jobs (averaging $1900).

Applying *Options:* electronic application, early admission, deferred entrance. *Application fee:* $20. *Required:* high school transcript. *Application deadlines:* rolling (freshmen), rolling (transfers). *Notification:* continuous (freshmen), continuous (transfers).

Freshmen Application Contact Ms. Carrie Brimhall, Director of Enrollment Management, Minnesota State Community and Technical College–Fergus Falls, 1414 College Way, Fergus Falls, MN 56537-1009. *Phone:* 218-736-1528. *Toll-free phone:* 888-MY-MSCTC. *Fax:* 218-736-1510. *E-mail:* carrie.brimhall@minnesota.edu.

MINNESOTA WEST COMMUNITY AND TECHNICAL COLLEGE

Pipestone, Minnesota www.mnwest.edu/

- **State-supported** 2-year, founded 1967, part of Minnesota State Colleges and Universities System
- **Rural** 103-acre campus
- **Coed**

Undergraduates 1,439 full-time, 1,344 part-time. Students come from 25 states and territories, 3 other countries, 11% are from out of state, 3% African American, 1% Asian American or Pacific Islander, 3% Hispanic American, 0.6% Native American, 5% transferred in. *Retention:* 63% of 2003 full-time freshmen returned.

Faculty *Student/faculty ratio:* 13:1.

Academics *Calendar:* semesters. *Degrees:* certificates, diplomas, and associate (profile contains information from Canby, Granite Falls, Jackson, and Worthington campuses). *Special study options:* academic remediation for entering students, advanced placement credit, cooperative education, distance learning, double majors, external degree program, honors programs, independent study, internships, part-time degree program, services for LD students, summer session for credit.

Athletics Member NJCAA.

Costs (2006–07) *Tuition:* state resident $4085 full-time, $136 per credit part-time; nonresident $8171 full-time, $272 per credit part-time. *Required fees:* $377 full-time, $13 per credit part-time.

Applying *Options:* electronic application. *Application fee:* $20. *Required:* high school transcript.

Freshmen Application Contact Mr. Gary Gillin, Dean of Communication and Enrollment, Minnesota West Community and Technical College, 1314 North Hiawatha Avenue, Pipestone, MN 56164. *Phone:* 507-825-6804. *Toll-free phone:* 800-658-2330. *Fax:* 507-825-4656. *E-mail:* garygillin@mnwest.edu.

NATIONAL AMERICAN UNIVERSITY

Bloomington, Minnesota   www.national.edu/

- **Proprietary** 2-year
- **Urban** campus
- **Coed,** 474 undergraduate students, 66% full-time, 63% women, 37% men
- 100% of applicants were admitted

Undergraduates 311 full-time, 163 part-time. Students come from 25 states and territories, 7 other countries, 24% are from out of state, 2% African American, 3% Asian American or Pacific Islander, 0.8% Hispanic American, 4% Native American, 4% transferred in, 18% live on campus. *Retention:* 46% of 2003 full-time freshmen returned.

Freshmen *Admission:* 36 applied, 36 admitted, 35 enrolled. *Average high school GPA:* 2.85.

Faculty *Total:* 46, 33% full-time, 7% with terminal degrees. *Student/faculty ratio:* 19:1.

Majors Accounting; business administration and management; computer and information sciences; computer/information technology services administration related; finance and financial management services related; health/health care administration; international business/trade/commerce; management science; marketing/marketing management; paralegal/legal assistant.

Academics *Degree:* associate. *Special study options:* adult/continuing education programs, advanced placement credit, cooperative education, distance learning, double majors, English as a second language, external degree program, honors programs, independent study, internships, part-time degree program, services for LD students, summer session for credit. *ROTC:* Air Force (b).

Library Jefferson Library.

Student Life *Housing:* on-campus residence required through sophomore year. *Options:* coed. Campus housing is university owned.

Costs (2006–07) *Tuition:* $240 per credit hour part-time.

Applying *Application fee:* $25. *Required for some:* high school transcript, letters of recommendation. *Recommended:* high school transcript, interview.

Freshmen Application Contact Ms. Jennifer Michaelson, Admissions Assistant, National American University, 321 Kansas City Street, Rapid City, SD 57201. *Phone:* 605-394-4827. *Toll-free phone:* 800-209-0490. *E-mail:* jmichaelson@national.edu.

NATIONAL AMERICAN UNIVERSITY

Brooklyn Center, Minnesota   www.national.edu/

Freshmen Application Contact Admissions Office, National American University, 6120 Earle Brown Drive, Suite 100, Brooklyn Center, MN 55430.

NORMANDALE COMMUNITY COLLEGE

Bloomington, Minnesota   www.normandale.edu/

- **State-supported** 2-year, founded 1968, part of Minnesota State Colleges and Universities System
- **Suburban** 90-acre campus with easy access to Minneapolis–St. Paul
- **Endowment** $1.4 million
- **Coed**

Undergraduates 4,139 full-time, 4,122 part-time. Students come from 22 states and territories, 2% are from out of state, 10% African American, 7% Asian American or Pacific Islander, 2% Hispanic American, 0.8% Native American, 1% international.

Faculty *Student/faculty ratio:* 28:1.

Academics *Calendar:* semesters. *Degree:* certificates and associate. *Special study options:* academic remediation for entering students, accelerated degree program, adult/continuing education programs, advanced placement credit, cooperative education, distance learning, English as a second language, independent study, internships, off-campus study, part-time degree program, services for LD students, student-designed majors, study abroad, summer session for credit. *ROTC:* Army (c), Air Force (c).

Student Life *Campus security:* 24-hour emergency response devices, student patrols, late-night transport/escort service.

Costs (2006–07) *Tuition:* state resident $4608 full-time, $144 per credit part-time; nonresident $8734 full-time, $273 per credit part-time.

Financial Aid Of all full-time matriculated undergraduates, 480 Federal Work-Study jobs (averaging $4000). 1,200 state and other part-time jobs (averaging $4000).

Applying *Options:* early admission, deferred entrance. *Application fee:* $20. *Required for some:* high school transcript.

Freshmen Application Contact Admissions Office, Normandale Community College, 9700 France Avenue South, Bloomington, MN 55431. *Phone:* 952-487-8201. *Toll-free phone:* 866-880-8740. *Fax:* 952-487-8230. *E-mail:* information@normandale.edu.

NORTH HENNEPIN COMMUNITY COLLEGE

Brooklyn Park, Minnesota   www.nhcc.edu/

- **State-supported** 2-year, founded 1966, part of Minnesota State Colleges and Universities System
- **Suburban** 80-acre campus
- **Endowment** $811,377
- **Coed,** 6,292 undergraduate students, 39% full-time, 60% women, 40% men

Undergraduates 2,447 full-time, 3,845 part-time. Students come from 10 states and territories, 62 other countries, 2% are from out of state, 15% African American, 10% Asian American or Pacific Islander, 1% Hispanic American, 0.7% Native American, 1% international, 29% transferred in. *Retention:* 8% of 2003 full-time freshmen returned.

Freshmen *Admission:* 1,931 applied, 1,931 admitted, 1,611 enrolled.

Faculty *Total:* 231, 43% full-time. *Student/faculty ratio:* 28:1.

Majors Accounting; biology/biological sciences; chemistry; computer science; construction management; criminal justice/law enforcement administration; criminal justice/safety; finance; fine/studio arts; graphic design; histologic technology/histotechnologist; marketing/marketing management; medical laboratory technology; nursing (registered nurse training); paralegal/legal assistant; pre-engineering.

Academics *Calendar:* semesters. *Degree:* certificates and associate. *Special study options:* academic remediation for entering students, accelerated degree program, adult/continuing education programs, advanced placement credit, distance learning, double majors, English as a second language, external degree program, honors programs, independent study, internships, off-campus study, part-time degree program, services for LD students, student-designed majors, study abroad, summer session for credit.

Library Learning Resource Center plus 1 other with 70,776 titles, 2,500 serial subscriptions, 2,822 audiovisual materials, an OPAC, a Web page.

Student Life *Housing:* college housing not available. *Activities and Organizations:* drama/theater group, student-run newspaper, choral group. *Campus security:* 24-hour emergency response devices, student patrols, late-night transport/escort service. *Student services:* personal/psychological counseling.

Athletics Member NJCAA. *Intramural sports:* basketball M/W, bowling M/W, football M, golf M/W, soccer M, tennis M/W, volleyball M/W.

Costs (2007–08) *Tuition:* state resident $3158 full-time, $132 per credit part-time; nonresident $5848 full-time, $244 per credit part-time. *Required fees:* $247 full-time, $10 per credit part-time.

Applying *Options:* early admission, deferred entrance. *Application fee:* $20. *Recommended:* high school transcript. *Application deadlines:* rolling (freshmen), rolling (transfers). *Notification:* continuous (freshmen), continuous (transfers).

Freshmen Application Contact Ms. Jeneifer Lambrecht, Director of Campus Outreach, North Hennepin Community College, 7411 85th Avenue North, Brooklyn Park, MN 55445-2231. *Phone:* 763-424-0702. *Fax:* 763-424-0929. *E-mail:* jlsummer@nhcc.edu.

NORTHLAND COMMUNITY AND TECHNICAL COLLEGE—EAST GRAND FORKS

East Grand Forks, Minnesota   www.northlandcollege.edu/

Director of Admissions Ms. Rita Lealos, Enrollment Specialist, Northland Community and Technical College–East Grand Forks, 2022 Central Avenue, NW, East Grand Forks, MN 56721-2702. *Phone:* 218-773-4546. *Toll-free phone:* 800-451-3441. *Fax:* 218-773-4502.

NORTHLAND COMMUNITY AND TECHNICAL COLLEGE–THIEF RIVER FALLS

Thief River Falls, Minnesota   **www.northlandcollege.edu/**

- **State-supported** 2-year, founded 1965, part of Minnesota State Colleges and Universities System
- **Rural** campus
- **Coed,** 4,120 undergraduate students, 49% full-time, 55% women, 45% men

Undergraduates 2,008 full-time, 2,112 part-time. Students come from 16 states and territories, 3 other countries, 44% are from out of state, 3% African American, 0.8% Asian American or Pacific Islander, 2% Hispanic American, 4% Native American, 0.2% international.

Freshmen *Admission:* 2,202 applied, 2,202 admitted.

Faculty *Total:* 250, 50% full-time, 4% with terminal degrees. *Student/faculty ratio:* 17:1.

Majors Accounting; administrative assistant and secretarial science; aeronautics/aviation/aerospace science and technology; architectural engineering technology; athletic training; automobile/automotive mechanics technology; aviation/airway management; avionics maintenance technology; broadcast journalism; business administration and management; child care provision; child development; computer and information sciences related; computer graphics; computer science; computer software and media applications related; computer systems networking and telecommunications; computer/technical support; consumer merchandising/retailing management; cosmetology; criminal justice/law enforcement administration; criminal justice/police science; criminology; data entry/microcomputer applications; data entry/microcomputer applications related; data modeling/warehousing and database administration; drafting and design technology; electrical, electronic and communications engineering technology; farm and ranch management; industrial electronics technology; information technology; international business/trade/commerce; legal administrative assistant/secretary; legal assistant/paralegal; legal studies; liberal arts and sciences/liberal studies; marketing/marketing management; mass communication/media; nursing (licensed practical/vocational nurse training); nursing (registered nurse training); radio and television; system administration; web/multimedia management and webmaster; web page, digital/multimedia and information resources design; welding technology; word processing.

Academics *Calendar:* semesters. *Degree:* certificates, diplomas, and associate. *Special study options:* academic remediation for entering students, adult/continuing education programs, advanced placement credit, distance learning, internships, off-campus study, part-time degree program, services for LD students, summer session for credit.

Library Northland College Library.

Student Life *Housing:* college housing not available. *Activities and Organizations:* drama/theater group, student-run newspaper, radio and television station, choral group, Law Enforcement Club, All-Nations Club, Environmental Club, PAMA, VICA. *Campus security:* student patrols, late-night transport/escort service. *Student services:* personal/psychological counseling, women's center.

Athletics Member NJCAA. *Intercollegiate sports:* baseball M, basketball M/W, football M, golf M(s)/W(s), softball W, volleyball W. *Intramural sports:* basketball M/W, bowling M/W, golf M/W, softball M/W, tennis M/W, volleyball M/W.

Costs (2007–08) *Tuition:* state resident $4840 full-time, $145 per credit part-time; nonresident $4840 full-time, $145 per credit part-time. *Required fees:* $532 full-time, $17 per credit part-time.

Financial Aid Of all full-time matriculated undergraduates, 75 Federal Work-Study jobs (averaging $2500). 40 state and other part-time jobs (averaging $2500).

Applying *Options:* electronic application, early admission, deferred entrance. *Application fee:* $20. *Required:* high school transcript. *Application deadlines:* 8/31 (freshmen), 8/31 (transfers). *Notification:* continuous (freshmen), continuous (transfers).

Freshmen Application Contact Mr. Eugene Klinke, Director of Enrollment Management, Northland Community and Technical College–Thief River Falls, 1101 Highway #1 East, Thief River Falls, MN 56701. *Phone:* 218-681-0862. *Toll-free phone:* 800-959-6282. *Fax:* 218-681-0774. *E-mail:* eugene.klinke@northlandcollege.edu.

NORTHWEST TECHNICAL COLLEGE

Bemidji, Minnesota   **bemidji.ntcmn.edu/**

Freshmen Application Contact Admissions Office, Northwest Technical College, 905 Grant Avenue, SE, Bemidji, MN 56601. *Phone:* 218-846-7444. *Toll-free phone:* 800-942-8324.

NORTHWEST TECHNICAL INSTITUTE

Eden Prairie, Minnesota   **www.nti.edu/**

Director of Admissions Mr. John Hartman, Director of Admissions, Northwest Technical Institute, 11995 Singletree Lane, Eden Prairie, MN 55344-5351. *Phone:* 952-944-0080 Ext. 103. *Toll-free phone:* 800-443-4223.

PINE TECHNICAL COLLEGE

Pine City, Minnesota   **www.pinetech.edu/**

- **State-supported** 2-year, founded 1965, part of Minnesota State Colleges and Universities System
- **Small-town** 6-acre campus with easy access to Minneapolis–St. Paul
- **Coed,** 770 undergraduate students, 34% full-time, 71% women, 29% men

Undergraduates 258 full-time, 512 part-time. Students come from 5 states and territories, 10% are from out of state, 1% African American, 0.6% Asian American or Pacific Islander, 0.4% Hispanic American, 2% Native American, 3% transferred in.

Freshmen *Admission:* 349 enrolled.

Faculty *Total:* 65, 34% full-time. *Student/faculty ratio:* 16:1.

Majors Administrative assistant and secretarial science; automobile/automotive mechanics technology; business teacher education; human services; machine tool technology; safety/security technology.

Academics *Calendar:* semesters. *Degree:* certificates, diplomas, and associate. *Special study options:* academic remediation for entering students, advanced placement credit, distance learning, double majors, independent study, internships, part-time degree program, services for LD students, summer session for credit.

Library Media Center plus 1 other with 6,000 titles, 30 serial subscriptions, an OPAC, a Web page.

Student Life *Housing:* college housing not available. *Campus security:* late-night transport/escort service. *Student services:* personal/psychological counseling, women's center.

Standardized Tests *Required:* ASAP (for placement).

Costs (2006–07) *Tuition:* state resident $3257 full-time; nonresident $6173 full-time.

Financial Aid Of all full-time matriculated undergraduates, 6 Federal Work-Study jobs (averaging $2000). 10 state and other part-time jobs.

Applying *Options:* early admission. *Application fee:* $20. *Required:* high school transcript. *Required for some:* letters of recommendation. *Application deadlines:* rolling (freshmen), rolling (transfers).

Director of Admissions Mr. Phil Schroeder, Dean, Student Affairs, Pine Technical College, 900 Fourth Street, SE, Pine City, MN 55063. *Phone:* 320-629-5100. *Toll-free phone:* 800-521-7463.

RAINY RIVER COMMUNITY COLLEGE

International Falls, Minnesota   **www.rrcc.mnscu.edu/**

- **State-supported** 2-year, founded 1967, part of Minnesota State Colleges and Universities System
- **Small-town** 80-acre campus
- **Coed,** 399 undergraduate students, 76% full-time, 55% women, 45% men

Undergraduates 302 full-time, 97 part-time. Students come from 8 states and territories, 1 other country, 21% African American, 0.8% Asian American or Pacific Islander, 2% Hispanic American, 4% Native American, 10% live on campus.

Faculty *Total:* 33, 45% full-time.

Majors Administrative assistant and secretarial science; biological and physical sciences; business administration and management; liberal arts and sciences/liberal studies; pre-engineering; real estate.

Academics *Calendar:* semesters. *Degree:* certificates, diplomas, and associate. *Special study options:* academic remediation for entering students, adult/continuing education programs, advanced placement credit, cooperative education, English as a second language, honors programs, independent study, internships, part-time degree program, services for LD students, summer session for credit.

Library Rainy River Community College Library with 20,000 titles, an OPAC.

Student Life *Housing Options:* coed, disabled students. *Activities and Organizations:* drama/theater group, Anishinaabe Student Coalition, Student Senate,

Rainy River Community College (continued)

Black Student Association. *Campus security:* 24-hour emergency response devices, late-night transport/escort service, controlled dormitory access. *Student services:* personal/psychological counseling.

Athletics Member NJCAA. *Intercollegiate sports:* basketball M/W, softball W, volleyball W. *Intramural sports:* archery M/W, badminton M/W, bowling M/W, skiing (cross-country) M/W, skiing (downhill) M/W, swimming and diving M/W, tennis M/W, volleyball M/W, weight lifting M/W.

Costs (2006–07) *Tuition:* $127 per credit part-time; state resident $3912 full-time, $159 per credit part-time; nonresident $4891 full-time. *Required fees:* $544 full-time, $17 per credit part-time. *Room and board:* room only: $2190. *Payment plan:* installment. *Waivers:* employees or children of employees.

Financial Aid Of all full-time matriculated undergraduates, 110 Federal Work-Study jobs (averaging $2000). 55 state and other part-time jobs (averaging $2000).

Applying *Options:* early admission, deferred entrance. *Application fee:* $20. *Required:* high school transcript. *Application deadlines:* rolling (freshmen), rolling (transfers). *Notification:* continuous (freshmen), continuous (transfers).

Freshmen Application Contact Ms. Berta Hagen, Registrar, Rainy River Community College, 1501 Highway 71, International Falls, MN 56649. *Phone:* 218-285-2207. *Toll-free phone:* 800-456-3996. *Fax:* 218-285-2239. *E-mail:* bhagen@rrc.mnscu.edu.

RASMUSSEN COLLEGE BROOKLYN PARK

Brooklyn Park, Minnesota   **www.rasmussen.edu/**

- **Proprietary** 2-year
- **213 undergraduate students**

Majors Accounting; administrative assistant and secretarial science; business administration and management; child care and support services management; child development; commercial and advertising art; computer and information systems security; computer systems networking and telecommunications; criminal justice/law enforcement administration; health/health care administration; health information/medical records technology; massage therapy; medical administrative assistant and medical secretary; medical office assistant; medical transcription; nursing (licensed practical/vocational nurse training); pharmacy technician; surgical technology; Web page, digital/multimedia and information resources design.

Academics *Degree:* associate.

Costs (2006–07) *Tuition:* $17,640 full-time.

Applying *Application fee:* $60.

Admissions Office Contact Rasmussen College Brooklyn Park, 8301 93rd Avenue North, Brooklyn Park, MN 55445-1512. *Toll-free phone:* 877-495-4500.

RASMUSSEN COLLEGE EAGAN

Eagan, Minnesota   **www.rasmussen.edu/**

Director of Admissions Ms. Jacinda Miller, Admissions Coordinator, Rasmussen College Eagan, 3500 Federal Drive, Eagan, MN 55122-1346. *Phone:* 651-687-9000. *Toll-free phone:* 651-687-0507 (in-state); 800-852-6367 (out-of-state).

RASMUSSEN COLLEGE EDEN PRAIRIE

Eden Prairie, Minnesota   **www.rasmussen.edu/**

- **Proprietary** 2-year, founded 1904, part of Rasmussen College System
- **Suburban** 2-acre campus with easy access to Minneapolis–St. Paul
- **Coed**

Undergraduates 209 full-time, 154 part-time. Students come from 1 other state, 13% African American, 3% Asian American or Pacific Islander, 2% Hispanic American, 1% Native American.

Faculty *Student/faculty ratio:* 11:1.

Academics *Calendar:* quarters. *Degree:* certificates, diplomas, and associate. *Special study options:* academic remediation for entering students, internships, part-time degree program, summer session for credit.

Student Life *Campus security:* late-night transport/escort service.

Standardized Tests *Required:* COMPASS (for admission).

Costs (2006–07) *Tuition:* $18,900 full-time, $315 per credit part-time. Full-time tuition and fees vary according to program. Part-time tuition and fees vary according to program.

Financial Aid Of all full-time matriculated undergraduates, 3 state and other part-time jobs (averaging $4338).

Applying *Options:* early admission, deferred entrance. *Application fee:* $60. *Required:* high school transcript, interview.

Freshmen Application Contact Mr. Jeff Hagy, Director of Admissions, Rasmussen College Eden Prairie, 7905 Golden Triangle Drive, Suite 100, Eden Prairie, MN 55344. *Phone:* 952-545-2000. *Toll-free phone:* 800-852-0929.

RASMUSSEN COLLEGE MANKATO

Mankato, Minnesota   **www.rasmussen.edu/**

- **Proprietary** 2-year, founded 1904, part of Rasmussen College System
- **Suburban** campus with easy access to Minneapolis–St. Paul
- **Coed, primarily women**

Undergraduates 463 full-time. 1% African American, 1% Asian American or Pacific Islander, 4% Hispanic American.

Faculty *Student/faculty ratio:* 18:1.

Academics *Calendar:* quarters. *Degree:* certificates, diplomas, and associate. *Special study options:* academic remediation for entering students, advanced placement credit, cooperative education, internships, part-time degree program, services for LD students, summer session for credit.

Student Life *Campus security:* limited access to buildings after hours.

Standardized Tests *Required:* ACT COMPASS (for admission).

Costs (2006–07) *Tuition:* $295 per credit part-time.

Financial Aid Of all full-time matriculated undergraduates, 5 Federal Work-Study jobs (averaging $4000). 3 state and other part-time jobs (averaging $4000).

Applying *Options:* deferred entrance. *Application fee:* $60. *Required:* high school transcript, minimum 2.0 GPA, interview.

Freshmen Application Contact Ms. Kathy Clifford, Director of Admissions, Rasmussen College Mankato, 501 Holly Lane, Mankato, MN 56001-6803. *Phone:* 507-625-6556. *Toll-free phone:* 800-657-6767. *Fax:* 507-625-6557. *E-mail:* rascoll@ic.mankato.mn.us.

RASMUSSEN COLLEGE ST. CLOUD

St. Cloud, Minnesota   **www.rasmussen.edu/**

Freshmen Application Contact Ms. Andrea Peters, Director of Admissions, Rasmussen College St. Cloud, 226 Park Avenue South, St. Cloud, MN 56301. *Phone:* 320-251-5600. *Toll-free phone:* 800-852-0460. *Fax:* 320-251-3702. *E-mail:* admstc@rasmussen.edu.

RIDGEWATER COLLEGE

Willmar, Minnesota   **www.ridgewater.mnscu.edu/**

- **State-supported** 2-year, founded 1961, part of Minnesota State Colleges and Universities System
- **Small-town** 83-acre campus
- **Coed,** 3,918 undergraduate students, 61% full-time, 57% women, 43% men

Undergraduates 2,396 full-time, 1,522 part-time. 1% African American, 0.8% Asian American or Pacific Islander, 3% Hispanic American, 0.5% Native American.

Freshmen *Admission:* 978 enrolled.

Faculty *Total:* 224, 58% full-time.

Majors Accounting; administrative assistant and secretarial science; agricultural business and management; agricultural mechanization; animal/livestock husbandry and production; applied art; art; audio engineering; biological and physical sciences; broadcast journalism; business administration and management; child development; community organization and advocacy; computer and information sciences related; computer engineering technology; computer graphics; computer/information technology services administration related; computer installation and repair technology; computer management; computer programming (specific applications); computer systems networking and telecommunications; consumer merchandising/retailing management; criminal justice/law enforcement administration; criminal justice/police science; data processing and data processing technology; developmental and child psychology; drafting and design technology; dramatic/theater arts; electrical, electronic and communica-

tions engineering technology; electrical/electronics equipment installation and repair; engineering; family and community services; farm and ranch management; gerontology; health information/medical records administration; health unit management/ward supervision; history; humanities; human services; industrial radiologic technology; information science/studies; instrumentation technology; interdisciplinary studies; journalism; legal administrative assistant/secretary; liberal arts and sciences/liberal studies; machine shop technology; mass communication/media; mathematics; medical administrative assistant and medical secretary; mental health/rehabilitation; metallurgical technology; music; nursing (licensed practical/vocational nurse training); nursing (registered nurse training); photography; physical education teaching and coaching; physical sciences; pre-engineering; psychology; quality control technology; real estate; sales, distribution and marketing; social work; sociology; speech and rhetoric; substance abuse/addiction counseling; system administration; teacher assistant/aide; tourism and travel services management; veterinary technology; web/multimedia management and webmaster; web page, digital/multimedia and information resources design.

Academics *Calendar:* semesters. *Degree:* certificates, diplomas, and associate. *Special study options:* academic remediation for entering students, advanced placement credit, cooperative education, distance learning, internships, off-campus study, part-time degree program, services for LD students, student-designed majors, summer session for credit.

Library 30,000 titles, 401 serial subscriptions, an OPAC, a Web page.

Student Life *Housing:* college housing not available. *Activities and Organizations:* drama/theater group, student-run newspaper, choral group, Student Senate, Ski Club, Nontraditional Students Club, BACCHUS, Creative Writers, Unlimited. *Campus security:* 24-hour emergency response devices. *Student services:* personal/psychological counseling, women's center.

Athletics Member NJCAA. *Intercollegiate sports:* baseball M, basketball M/W, football M, softball W, tennis M/W, volleyball W, wrestling M. *Intramural sports:* basketball M/W, football M, golf M/W, softball M/W, weight lifting M/W.

Costs (2006–07) *Tuition:* state resident $4155 full-time, $130 per credit part-time; nonresident $4155 full-time, $130 per credit part-time. *Required fees:* $490 full-time, $15 per credit part-time.

Financial Aid Of all full-time matriculated undergraduates, 350 Federal Work-Study jobs (averaging $3000). 133 state and other part-time jobs (averaging $2400).

Applying *Options:* early admission, deferred entrance. *Application fee:* $20. *Required:* high school transcript. *Required for some:* letters of recommendation, interview.

Freshmen Application Contact Ms. Linda Barron, Admissions Assistant, Ridgewater College, PO Box 1097, Willmar, MN 56201-1097. *Phone:* 320-222-5976. *Toll-free phone:* 800-722-1151 Ext. 2906. *E-mail:* linda.barron@ridgewater.edu.

RIVERLAND COMMUNITY COLLEGE
Austin, Minnesota   www.riverland.edu/

- **State-supported** 2-year, founded 1940, part of Minnesota State Colleges and Universities System
- **Small-town** 187-acre campus with easy access to Minneapolis–St. Paul
- **Coed,** 3,477 undergraduate students, 46% full-time, 54% women, 46% men

Undergraduates 1,600 full-time, 1,877 part-time. Students come from 5 states and territories, 3% are from out of state, 3% African American, 2% Asian American or Pacific Islander, 4% Hispanic American, 0.3% Native American, 45% transferred in, 2% live on campus.

Freshmen *Admission:* 2,700 applied, 2,241 admitted, 1,333 enrolled. *Average high school GPA:* 3.1.

Faculty *Total:* 158, 64% full-time. *Student/faculty ratio:* 18:1.

Majors Administrative assistant and secretarial science; autobody/collision and repair technology; business administration and management; computer and information systems security; computer installation and repair technology; computer programming (specific applications); computer programming (vendor/product certification); computer software and media applications related; computer systems networking and telecommunications; computer/technical support; corrections; criminal justice/police science; data entry/microcomputer applications; data entry/microcomputer applications related; diesel mechanics technology; electrical/electronics equipment installation and repair; health unit coordinator/ward clerk; human services; industrial mechanics and maintenance technology; legal administrative assistant/secretary; liberal arts and sciences/liberal studies; machine shop technology; medical administrative assistant and medical secretary; medical radiologic technology; nursing (registered nurse training); web/multimedia management and webmaster; web page, digital/multimedia and information resources design; word processing.

Academics *Calendar:* semesters. *Degree:* certificates, diplomas, and associate. *Special study options:* academic remediation for entering students, adult/

continuing education programs, advanced placement credit, distance learning, double majors, English as a second language, independent study, internships, off-campus study, part-time degree program, services for LD students, study abroad, summer session for credit.

Library Riverland Community College Library plus 2 others with 33,500 titles, 278 serial subscriptions, an OPAC.

Student Life *Housing Options:* Campus housing is provided by a third party. *Activities and Organizations:* drama/theater group, student-run newspaper, choral group, College Choir, student newspaper, Student Activities Board, Phi Theta Kappa, Theater Club. *Campus security:* late-night transport/escort service. *Student services:* personal/psychological counseling, women's center.

Athletics Member NJCAA. *Intercollegiate sports:* baseball M, basketball M/W, golf M/W, softball W, volleyball W. *Intramural sports:* basketball M.

Costs (2007–08) *Tuition:* state resident $4080 full-time, $136 per credit part-time; nonresident $4080 full-time, $136 per credit part-time. *Required fees:* $525 full-time, $18 per credit part-time. *Room and board:* room only: $1320.

Applying *Options:* early admission. *Application fee:* $20. *Required:* high school transcript. *Application deadlines:* rolling (freshmen), rolling (transfers).

Freshmen Application Contact Ms. Renee Njos, Admission Secretary, Riverland Community College, 1900 8th Avenue NW, Austin, MN 55912. *Phone:* 507-433-0820. *Toll-free phone:* 800-247-5039. *Fax:* 507-433-0515. *E-mail:* admissions@riverland.edu.

ROCHESTER COMMUNITY AND TECHNICAL COLLEGE
Rochester, Minnesota   www.roch.edu/

Director of Admissions Mr. Troy Tynsky, Director of Admissions, Rochester Community and Technical College, 851 30th Avenue, SE, Rochester, MN 55904-4999. *Phone:* 507-280-3509.

ST. CLOUD TECHNICAL COLLEGE
St. Cloud, Minnesota   www.sctc.edu/

- **State-supported** 2-year, founded 1948, part of Minnesota State Colleges and Universities System
- **Urban** 35-acre campus with easy access to Minneapolis–St. Paul
- **Coed,** 3,405 undergraduate students, 67% full-time, 52% women, 48% men

Undergraduates 2,283 full-time, 1,122 part-time. Students come from 17 states and territories, 6 other countries, 3% are from out of state, 3% African American, 1% Asian American or Pacific Islander, 0.8% Hispanic American, 0.5% Native American, 0.2% international, 12% transferred in.

Freshmen *Admission:* 2,640 applied, 1,756 admitted, 912 enrolled. *Average high school GPA:* 3.16.

Faculty *Total:* 251, 45% full-time, 3% with terminal degrees. *Student/faculty ratio:* 17:1.

Majors Accounting; accounting technology and bookkeeping; administrative assistant and secretarial science; advertising; architectural drafting and CAD/CADD; architectural engineering technology; autobody/collision and repair technology; automobile/automotive mechanics technology; banking and financial support services; business administration and management; cardiovascular technology; carpentry; child care and support services management; child development; civil engineering technology; computer/information technology services administration related; computer programming; computer programming related; computer programming (specific applications); computer systems networking and telecommunications; computer/technical support; construction engineering technology; consumer merchandising/retailing management; dental assisting; dental hygiene; diagnostic medical sonography and ultrasound technology; diesel mechanics technology; electrical and power transmission installation; electrical, electronic and communications engineering technology; electrocardiograph technology; emergency medical technology (EMT paramedic); finance; general retailing/wholesaling; heating, air conditioning and refrigeration technology; heating, air conditioning, ventilation and refrigeration maintenance technology; information technology; instrumentation technology; kindergarten/preschool education; legal administrative assistant/secretary; machine tool technology; marketing/marketing management; mechanical design technology; mechanical drafting and CAD/CADD; medical administrative assistant and medical secretary; medical office management; nursing (licensed practical/vocational nurse training); office management; pipefitting and sprinkler fitting; surgical technology; teacher assistant/aide; water quality and wastewater treatment management and recycling technology; welding technology.

Academics *Calendar:* semesters. *Degree:* certificates, diplomas, and associate. *Special study options:* academic remediation for entering students, adult/

St. Cloud Technical College (continued)

continuing education programs, advanced placement credit, cooperative education, distance learning, English as a second language, independent study, internships, part-time degree program, services for LD students, summer session for credit.

Library Learning Resource Center plus 1 other with 10,000 titles, 600 serial subscriptions, an OPAC, a Web page.

Student Life *Housing:* college housing not available. *Activities and Organizations:* student-run newspaper, Student Senate, Distributive Education Club of America, Business Professionals of America, Child and Adult Care Education, Central Minnesota Builders Association. *Campus security:* late-night transport/escort service. *Student services:* personal/psychological counseling, women's center.

Athletics Member NJCAA. *Intercollegiate sports:* baseball M, basketball M/W, softball W, volleyball W. *Intramural sports:* golf M/W, volleyball M/W.

Costs (2006–07) *Tuition:* state resident $3678 full-time; nonresident $7356 full-time. Full-time tuition and fees vary according to program. Part-time tuition and fees vary according to program. *Required fees:* $302 full-time. *Waivers:* senior citizens and employees or children of employees.

Financial Aid Of all full-time matriculated undergraduates, 38 Federal Work-Study jobs (averaging $4000). 38 state and other part-time jobs (averaging $4000).

Applying *Options:* electronic application, early admission, deferred entrance. *Application fee:* $20. *Required:* high school transcript. *Required for some:* interview. *Application deadlines:* rolling (freshmen), rolling (transfers). *Notification:* continuous until 8/1 (freshmen), continuous until 8/1 (transfers).

Freshmen Application Contact Ms. Jodi Elness, Admissions Office, St. Cloud Technical College, 1540 Northway Drive, St. Cloud, MN 56303. *Phone:* 320-308-5089. *Toll-free phone:* 800-222-1009. *Fax:* 320-308-5981. *E-mail:* jelness@sctc.edu.

SAINT PAUL COLLEGE—A COMMUNITY & TECHNICAL COLLEGE

St. Paul, Minnesota   **www.saintpaul.edu/**

- **State-related** 2-year, founded 1919, part of Minnesota State Colleges and Universities System
- **Urban** campus
- **Coed,** 5,259 undergraduate students, 39% full-time, 55% women, 45% men

Undergraduates 2,048 full-time, 3,211 part-time. 2% are from out of state, 26% African American, 8% Asian American or Pacific Islander, 2% Hispanic American, 1% Native American.

Freshmen *Admission:* 3,424 applied, 3,424 admitted.

Faculty *Total:* 316, 34% full-time, 33% with terminal degrees. *Student/faculty ratio:* 18:1.

Majors Accounting; administrative assistant and secretarial science; child development; civil engineering technology; clinical/medical laboratory technology; computer programming; electrical, electronic and communications engineering technology; human resources management; industrial technology; international business/trade/commerce; medical administrative assistant and medical secretary; respiratory care therapy; sign language interpretation and translation.

Academics *Calendar:* semesters. *Degree:* certificates, diplomas, and associate. *Special study options:* academic remediation for entering students, adult/continuing education programs, distance learning, English as a second language, honors programs, internships, off-campus study, part-time degree program, summer session for credit.

Library Saint Paul College Library with 12,000 titles, 110 serial subscriptions, an OPAC, a Web page.

Student Life *Housing:* college housing not available. *Activities and Organizations:* Student Senate. *Campus security:* late-night transport/escort service. *Student services:* personal/psychological counseling, women's center.

Standardized Tests *Required:* ACCUPLACER (for admission).

Costs (2007–08) *Tuition:* state resident $4000 full-time, $133 per credit part-time; nonresident $8000 full-time, $266 per credit part-time. *Required fees:* $330 full-time, $11 per credit part-time.

Financial Aid Of all full-time matriculated undergraduates, 48 Federal Work-Study jobs (averaging $2500). 94 state and other part-time jobs (averaging $2500).

Applying *Options:* electronic application, early admission. *Application fee:* $20. *Required for some:* high school transcript, interview. *Application deadline:* rolling (freshmen).

Freshmen Application Contact Ms. Sarah Carrico, Saint Paul College—A Community & Technical College, 235 Marshall Avenue, Saint Paul, MN 55102. *Phone:* 651-846-1424. *Toll-free phone:* 800-227-6029. *Fax:* 651-846-1468. *E-mail:* admissions@saintpaul.edu.

SOUTH CENTRAL COLLEGE

North Mankato, Minnesota   **southcentral.edu/**

Freshmen Application Contact Ms. Beverly Herda, Director of Admissions, South Central College, 1920 Lee Boulevard, North Mankato, MN 56003. *Phone:* 507-389-7334. *Fax:* 507-388-9951.

VERMILION COMMUNITY COLLEGE

Ely, Minnesota   **www.vcc.edu/**

- **State-supported** 2-year, founded 1922, part of Minnesota State Colleges and Universities System
- **Rural** 5-acre campus
- **Coed**

Undergraduates 533 full-time, 212 part-time. Students come from 42 states and territories, 3 other countries, 9% African American, 0.8% Asian American or Pacific Islander, 3% Hispanic American, 1% Native American, 50% live on campus.

Faculty *Student/faculty ratio:* 13:1.

Academics *Calendar:* semesters. *Degree:* certificates, diplomas, and associate. *Special study options:* academic remediation for entering students, adult/continuing education programs, advanced placement credit, cooperative education, honors programs, internships, off-campus study, part-time degree program, services for LD students, summer session for credit.

Student Life *Campus security:* student patrols, late-night transport/escort service, controlled dormitory access.

Athletics Member NJCAA.

Costs (2006–07) *Tuition:* state resident $4190 full-time, $140 per credit part-time; nonresident $5120 full-time, $171 per credit part-time. *Room and board:* $4560; room only: $2900.

Financial Aid Of all full-time matriculated undergraduates, 150 Federal Work-Study jobs (averaging $1000). 30 state and other part-time jobs (averaging $1000).

Applying *Options:* electronic application, early admission, deferred entrance. *Application fee:* $20. *Required:* high school transcript.

Freshmen Application Contact Mr. Todd Heiman, Director of Enrollment Services, Vermilion Community College, 1900 East Camp Street, Ely, MN 55731-1996. *Phone:* 218-365-7224. *Toll-free phone:* 800-657-3608.

MISSISSIPPI

ANTONELLI COLLEGE

Hattiesburg, Mississippi   **antonellicollege.edu/**

- **Proprietary** 2-year
- **Coed,** 354 undergraduate students

Majors Accounting technology and bookkeeping; administrative assistant and secretarial science; allied health and medical assisting services related; business automation/technology/data entry; information technology; interior design; legal administrative assistant; massage therapy; medical insurance coding; medical transcription.

Academics *Calendar:* quarters. *Degree:* certificates and associate.

Costs (2006–07) *Tuition:* $12,400 full-time, $290 per credit hour part-time. Part-time tuition and fees vary according to course load. *Required fees:* $150 per term part-time. *Payment plan:* installment.

Applying *Application fee:* $75.

Freshmen Application Contact Mrs. Karen Gautreau, Director, Antonelli College, 1500 North 31st Avenue, Hattiesburg, MS 39401. *Phone:* 601-583-4100. *Fax:* 601-583-0839. *E-mail:* admissionsh@antonellicollege.edu.

ANTONELLI COLLEGE

Jackson, Mississippi   www.antonellic.com/

Director of Admissions Ms. Page McDaniel, Senior Admissions Officer, Antonelli College, 480 East Woodrow Wilson Drive, Jackson, MS 39216. *Phone:* 601-362-9991.

COAHOMA COMMUNITY COLLEGE

Clarksdale, Mississippi   www.ccc.cc.ms.us/

- **State and locally supported** 2-year, founded 1949, part of Mississippi State Board for Community and Junior Colleges
- **Rural** 29-acre campus with easy access to Memphis
- **Coed,** 1,838 undergraduate students, 93% full-time, 72% women, 28% men

Undergraduates 1,702 full-time, 136 part-time. Students come from 9 states and territories, 3% are from out of state, 96% African American, 0.2% Hispanic American, 22% live on campus. *Retention:* 44% of 2003 full-time freshmen returned.

Freshmen *Admission:* 1,176 enrolled.

Faculty *Total:* 95, 74% full-time. *Student/faculty ratio:* 22:1.

Majors Accounting; administrative assistant and secretarial science; art; autobody/collision and repair technology; barbering; biology/biological sciences; business administration and management; business machine repair; carpentry; chemistry; clinical laboratory science/medical technology; computer installation and repair technology; computer science; cosmetology; criminal justice/law enforcement administration; elementary education; English; health teacher education; industrial mechanics and maintenance technology; kindergarten/preschool education; liberal arts and sciences/liberal studies; nursing (licensed practical/vocational nurse training); radio and television; respiratory therapy technician; restaurant, culinary, and catering management; social work; sport and fitness administration/management; welding technology.

Academics *Calendar:* semesters. *Degree:* certificates and associate. *Special study options:* academic remediation for entering students, accelerated degree program, adult/continuing education programs, advanced placement credit, cooperative education, distance learning, off-campus study, part-time degree program, student-designed majors.

Library Dickerson-Johnson Library with a Web page.

Student Life *Housing Options:* men-only, women-only, disabled students. Campus housing is university owned. *Activities and Organizations:* drama/theater group, student-run newspaper, choral group, marching band, Student Government Association, VICA, Phi Theta Kappa Honor Society. *Campus security:* 24-hour patrols, controlled dormitory access. *Student services:* health clinic, personal/psychological counseling.

Athletics Member NJCAA. *Intercollegiate sports:* baseball M, basketball M(s)/W(s), football M.

Costs (2006–07) *Tuition:* state resident $1600 full-time, $90 per semester hour part-time; nonresident $3050 full-time. *Required fees:* $140 full-time, $65 per term part-time. *Room and board:* $2914.

Financial Aid Of all full-time matriculated undergraduates, 350 Federal Work-Study jobs (averaging $600). 45 state and other part-time jobs (averaging $1000).

Applying *Required:* high school transcript. *Required for some:* minimum X GPA, letters of recommendation, interview. *Application deadlines:* rolling (freshmen), rolling (transfers). *Notification:* continuous (freshmen), continuous (transfers).

Freshmen Application Contact Mrs. Wanda Holmes, Director of Admissions and Records, Coahoma Community College, Route 1, PO Box 616, Clarksdale, MS 38614-9799. *Phone:* 662-621-4205. *Toll-free phone:* 800-844-1222.

COPIAH-LINCOLN COMMUNITY COLLEGE

Wesson, Mississippi   www.colin.edu/

- **State and locally supported** 2-year, founded 1928, part of Mississippi State Board for Community and Junior Colleges
- **Rural** 525-acre campus with easy access to Jackson
- **Coed**

Undergraduates Students come from 7 states and territories, 2 other countries, 2% are from out of state, 30% live on campus.

Academics *Calendar:* semesters. *Degree:* certificates and associate. *Special study options:* academic remediation for entering students, adult/continuing

education programs, advanced placement credit, honors programs, part-time degree program, student-designed majors, summer session for credit.

Student Life *Campus security:* 24-hour patrols.

Athletics Member NJCAA.

Costs (2006–07) *Tuition:* state resident $1700 full-time, $105 per hour part-time; nonresident $3600 full-time, $180 per hour part-time. *Required fees:* $100 full-time. *Room and board:* $2800; room only: $1500. Room and board charges vary according to board plan.

Financial Aid Of all full-time matriculated undergraduates, 125 Federal Work-Study jobs (averaging $1000).

Applying *Options:* early admission. *Required:* high school transcript.

Freshmen Application Contact Laura Lofton, Director of Distance Learning, Copiah-Lincoln Community College, PO Box 371, Wesson, MS 39191-0457. *Phone:* 601-643-8307. *Fax:* 601-643-8222. *E-mail:* phil.broome@colin.edu.

COPIAH-LINCOLN COMMUNITY COLLEGE—NATCHEZ CAMPUS

Natchez, Mississippi   www.colin.edu/

Freshmen Application Contact Mrs. Gwen S. McCalip, Director of Admissions and Records, Copiah-Lincoln Community College–Natchez Campus, 11 Co-Lin Circle, Natchez, MS 39120. *Phone:* 601-442-9111. *Fax:* 601-446-1222. *E-mail:* gwen.mccalip@colin.edu.

EAST CENTRAL COMMUNITY COLLEGE

Decatur, Mississippi   www.eccc.cc.ms.us/

Director of Admissions Ms. Donna Luke, Director of Admissions, Records, and Research, East Central Community College, PO Box 129, Decatur, MS 39327-0129. *Phone:* 601-635-2111 Ext. 206. *Toll-free phone:* 877-462-3222.

EAST MISSISSIPPI COMMUNITY COLLEGE

Scooba, Mississippi   www.eastms.edu/

Director of Admissions Ms. Melinda Sciple, Admissions Officer, East Mississippi Community College, PO Box 158, Scooba, MS 39358-0158. *Phone:* 662-476-5041.

HINDS COMMUNITY COLLEGE

Raymond, Mississippi   www.hindscc.edu/

Director of Admissions Mr. Jay Allen, Director of Admissions and Records, Hinds Community College, PO Box 1100, Raymond, MS 39154-1100. *Phone:* 601-857-3280. *Toll-free phone:* 800-HINDSCC.

HOLMES COMMUNITY COLLEGE

Goodman, Mississippi   www.holmescc.edu/

Director of Admissions Dr. Lynn Wright, Dean of Admissions and Records, Holmes Community College, PO Box 369, Goodman, MS 39079-0369. *Phone:* 601-472-2312 Ext. 1023.

ITAWAMBA COMMUNITY COLLEGE

Fulton, Mississippi   www.icc.cc.ms.us/

Freshmen Application Contact Mr. Max Munn, Director of Recruiting, Itawamba Community College, 602 West Hill Street, Fulton, MS 38843. *Phone:* 601-862-8252.

JONES COUNTY JUNIOR COLLEGE
Ellisville, Mississippi
www.jcjc.edu/

- **State and locally supported** 2-year, founded 1928, part of Mississippi State Board for Community and Junior Colleges
- **Small-town** 360-acre campus
- **Coed,** 5,640 undergraduate students

Undergraduates Students come from 9 states and territories, 20% live on campus.

Faculty *Total:* 175, 97% full-time. *Student/faculty ratio:* 25:1.

Majors Accounting; agriculture; applied art; art teacher education; biological and physical sciences; biology/biological sciences; business administration and management; chemistry; child development; criminal justice/police science; data processing and data processing technology; drafting and design technology; economics; education; electrical, electronic and communications engineering technology; emergency medical technology (EMT paramedic); engineering science; English; family and consumer sciences/home economics teacher education; family and consumer sciences/human sciences; forestry technology; horticultural science; mathematics; music; music teacher education; nursing (licensed practical/vocational nurse training); nursing (registered nurse training); physical education teaching and coaching; physical sciences; science teacher education; voice and opera.

Academics *Calendar:* semesters. *Degree:* certificates and associate. *Special study options:* academic remediation for entering students, advanced placement credit, cooperative education, distance learning, honors programs, part-time degree program, summer session for credit. *ROTC:* Army (c), Air Force (c).

Library Memorial Library with 62,349 titles, 654 serial subscriptions.

Student Life *Housing Options:* men-only, women-only. Campus housing is university owned. *Activities and Organizations:* drama/theater group, student-run newspaper, choral group, marching band, student government. *Campus security:* 24-hour patrols. *Student services:* health clinic, personal/psychological counseling.

Athletics Member NJCAA. *Intercollegiate sports:* baseball M, basketball M(s)/W(s), football M(s), golf M, soccer M/W, softball W, tennis M/W, track and field M. *Intramural sports:* basketball M/W, tennis M/W, volleyball M/W.

Standardized Tests *Required:* SAT or ACT (for admission).

Costs (2006–07) *Tuition:* state resident $1588 full-time; nonresident $3488 full-time.

Financial Aid Of all full-time matriculated undergraduates, 325 Federal Work-Study jobs (averaging $1850).

Applying *Options:* early admission. *Required:* high school transcript. *Application deadlines:* 8/26 (freshmen), 8/25 (transfers). *Notification:* continuous (freshmen), continuous (transfers).

Director of Admissions Mrs. Dianne Speed, Director of Admissions and Records, Jones County Junior College, 900 South Court Street, Ellisville, MS 39437. *Phone:* 601-477-4025.

MERIDIAN COMMUNITY COLLEGE
Meridian, Mississippi
www.meridiancc.edu

- **State and locally supported** 2-year, founded 1937, part of Mississippi State Board for Community and Junior Colleges
- **Small-town** 62-acre campus
- **Endowment** $4.8 million
- **Coed,** 3,572 undergraduate students, 74% full-time, 70% women, 30% men

Undergraduates 2,649 full-time, 923 part-time. Students come from 16 states and territories, 3% are from out of state, 39% African American, 0.4% Asian American or Pacific Islander, 0.8% Hispanic American, 2% Native American, 0.1% international, 12% live on campus.

Freshmen *Admission:* 1,214 admitted.

Faculty *Total:* 256, 56% full-time, 3% with terminal degrees.

Majors Administrative assistant and secretarial science; athletic training; broadcast journalism; clinical/medical laboratory technology; computer engineering technology; computer graphics; dental hygiene; drafting and design technology; electrical, electronic and communications engineering technology; emergency medical technology (EMT paramedic); fire science; health information/medical records administration; horticultural science; hotel/motel administration; machine tool technology; marketing/marketing management; medical radiologic technology; nursing (registered nurse training); physical therapy; respiratory care therapy; telecommunications.

Academics *Calendar:* semesters. *Degree:* certificates and associate. *Special study options:* academic remediation for entering students, adult/continuing education programs, advanced placement credit, cooperative education, distance learning, English as a second language, external degree program, independent study, part-time degree program, services for LD students, summer session for credit.

Library L.O. Todd Library with 50,000 titles, 600 serial subscriptions.

Student Life *Housing Options:* coed, men-only, women-only. Campus housing is university owned and leased by the school. *Activities and Organizations:* drama/theater group, student-run newspaper, radio station, choral group, Phi Theta Kappa, Vocational Industrial Clubs of America, Health Occupations Students of America, Organization of Student Nurses, Distributive Education Clubs of America. *Campus security:* 24-hour patrols, student patrols. *Student services:* health clinic, personal/psychological counseling.

Athletics Member NJCAA. *Intercollegiate sports:* baseball M(s), basketball M(s)/W(s), cross-country running M(s)/W(s), golf M(s), soccer M(s), softball W(s), tennis M(s)/W(s), track and field M(s)/W(s). *Intramural sports:* basketball M/W, bowling M/W, cross-country running M/W, swimming and diving M/W, tennis M/W, volleyball M/W.

Standardized Tests *Required:* ACCUPLACER (for admission). *Recommended:* ACT (for admission).

Costs (2007–08) *Tuition:* state resident $1450 full-time, $80 per credit hour part-time; nonresident $2740 full-time, $137 per credit hour part-time. *Required fees:* $156 full-time, $4 per credit hour part-time, $20 per term part-time. *Room and board:* $2600.

Financial Aid Of all full-time matriculated undergraduates, 100 Federal Work-Study jobs (averaging $2100).

Applying *Options:* early admission. *Required:* high school transcript, minimum 2.0 GPA. *Required for some:* essay or personal statement. *Application deadlines:* rolling (freshmen), rolling (transfers).

Freshmen Application Contact Ms. Dianne Walton, Director of Enrollment Services, Meridian Community College, 910 Highway 19 North, Meridian, MS 39307. *Phone:* 601-484-8895. *Toll-free phone:* 800-622-8731. *E-mail:* dwalton@meridiancc.edu.

MISSISSIPPI DELTA COMMUNITY COLLEGE
Moorhead, Mississippi
www.msdelta.edu/

- **District-supported** 2-year, founded 1926, part of Mississippi State Board for Community and Junior Colleges
- **Small-town** 425-acre campus
- **Coed,** 4,000 undergraduate students

Undergraduates Students come from 6 states and territories, 25% live on campus.

Freshmen *Admission:* 909 applied, 909 admitted.

Faculty *Total:* 125.

Majors Accounting; administrative assistant and secretarial science; advertising; agricultural business and management; agricultural economics; American studies; applied art; architectural engineering technology; art teacher education; behavioral sciences; biology/biological sciences; business machine repair; civil engineering technology; clinical/medical laboratory technology; computer engineering technology; criminal justice/law enforcement administration; dental hygiene; developmental and child psychology; dramatic/theater arts; economics; education; electrical, electronic and communications engineering technology; elementary education; English; family and consumer sciences/human sciences; geography; graphic and printing equipment operation/production; health information/medical records administration; health teacher education; history; horticultural science; liberal arts and sciences/liberal studies; management information systems; masonry; mathematics; medical office computer specialist; medical radiologic technology; music; music teacher education; nursing (registered nurse training); physical education teaching and coaching; political science and government; science teacher education; social work.

Academics *Calendar:* semesters. *Degree:* certificates, diplomas, and associate. *Special study options:* academic remediation for entering students, adult/continuing education programs, advanced placement credit, part-time degree program, summer session for credit.

Library Stanny Sanders Library with 33,020 titles, 250 serial subscriptions, an OPAC.

Student Life *Housing Options:* Campus housing is university owned. *Activities and Organizations:* drama/theater group, student-run newspaper, choral group, marching band. *Campus security:* 24-hour emergency response devices and patrols, late-night transport/escort service. *Student services:* personal/psychological counseling.

Athletics Member NJCAA. *Intercollegiate sports:* baseball M(s), basketball M(s)/W(s), football M(s), golf M(s), soccer M, tennis M/W, track and field M. *Intramural sports:* badminton M/W, basketball M/W, football M/W, golf M/W, tennis M/W, track and field M/W, volleyball M/W.

Standardized Tests *Required for some:* ACT (for admission).

Costs (2006–07) *Tuition:* state resident $1920 full-time; nonresident $3528 full-time.

Financial Aid Of all full-time matriculated undergraduates, 100 Federal Work-Study jobs (averaging $1400). 100 state and other part-time jobs (averaging $1400).

Applying *Options:* deferred entrance. *Required:* high school transcript. *Application deadlines:* 7/27 (freshmen), 7/27 (transfers).

Director of Admissions Mr. Joseph F. Ray Jr., Vice President of Admissions, Mississippi Delta Community College, PO Box 668, Highway 3 and Cherry Street, Moorhead, MS 38761-0668. *Phone:* 662-246-6308.

MISSISSIPPI GULF COAST COMMUNITY COLLEGE

Perkinston, Mississippi www.mgccc.edu/

- **District-supported** 2-year, founded 1911, part of Mississippi State Board for Community and Junior Colleges
- **Small-town** 600-acre campus with easy access to New Orleans
- **Endowment** $3.0 million
- **Coed,** 8,822 undergraduate students, 63% full-time, 62% women, 38% men

Undergraduates 5,551 full-time, 3,271 part-time. Students come from 15 states and territories, 4% are from out of state, 20% African American, 2% Asian American or Pacific Islander, 2% Hispanic American, 0.5% Native American, 7% live on campus. *Retention:* 62% of 2003 full-time freshmen returned.

Freshmen *Admission:* 1,974 applied, 1,974 admitted, 1,974 enrolled.

Faculty *Total:* 624, 62% full-time. *Student/faculty ratio:* 26:1.

Majors Accounting; administrative assistant and secretarial science; advertising; agricultural business and management; art; art teacher education; automobile/automotive mechanics technology; biological and physical sciences; business administration and management; business teacher education; chemical engineering; clinical/medical laboratory technology; computer and information sciences related; computer engineering technology; computer graphics; computer programming related; computer science; computer systems networking and telecommunications; court reporting; criminal justice/law enforcement administration; criminal justice/police science; data entry/microcomputer applications; data entry/microcomputer applications related; drafting and design technology; education; electrical, electronic and communications engineering technology; elementary education; emergency medical technology (EMT paramedic); fashion merchandising; finance; horticultural science; hotel/motel administration; human services; industrial radiologic technology; information technology; kindergarten/preschool education; legal assistant/paralegal; liberal arts and sciences/liberal studies; marketing/marketing management; nursing (registered nurse training); ornamental horticulture; postal management; pre-engineering; respiratory care therapy; welding technology; word processing.

Academics *Calendar:* semesters. *Degree:* certificates, diplomas, and associate. *Special study options:* academic remediation for entering students, adult/continuing education programs, advanced placement credit, cooperative education, distance learning, English as a second language, honors programs, independent study, internships, part-time degree program, study abroad, summer session for credit.

Library Main Library plus 3 others with 100,472 titles, 933 serial subscriptions, an OPAC.

Student Life *Housing Options:* men-only, women-only. Campus housing is university owned. *Activities and Organizations:* drama/theater group, student-run newspaper, choral group, marching band, VICA, SIFE, Student Government Association. *Campus security:* 24-hour emergency response devices and patrols. *Student services:* personal/psychological counseling, women's center.

Athletics Member NJCAA. *Intercollegiate sports:* baseball M(s), basketball M(s)/W(s), football M(s), golf M(s), soccer M(s)/W(s), softball W(s), tennis M(s)/W(s), track and field M(s). *Intramural sports:* basketball M/W, football M, soccer M/W, softball M/W, volleyball M/W.

Costs (2007–08) *Tuition:* state resident $1602 full-time, $75 per semester hour part-time; nonresident $3548 full-time, $152 per semester hour part-time. *Required fees:* $520 full-time. *Room and board:* $2970.

Applying *Options:* electronic application, early admission. *Required:* high school transcript. *Application deadlines:* rolling (freshmen), rolling (transfers). *Notification:* continuous (freshmen), continuous (transfers).

Freshmen Application Contact Mr. Ladd Taylor, Director of Admissions, Mississippi Gulf Coast Community College, PO Box 548, Perkinston, MS 39573. *Phone:* 601-928-6264. *Fax:* 601-928-6299. *E-mail:* ladd.taylor@mgccc.edu.

NORTHEAST MISSISSIPPI COMMUNITY COLLEGE

Booneville, Mississippi www.nemcc.edu/

Freshmen Application Contact Office of Enrollment Services, Northeast Mississippi Community College, 101 Cunningham Boulevard, Booneville, MS 38829. *Phone:* 662-720-7239. *Toll-free phone:* 800-555-2154. *E-mail:* admitme@nemcc.edu.

NORTHWEST MISSISSIPPI COMMUNITY COLLEGE

Senatobia, Mississippi www.northwestms.edu/

- **State and locally supported** 2-year, founded 1927, part of Mississippi State Board for Community and Junior Colleges
- **Rural** 75-acre campus with easy access to Memphis
- **Coed,** 6,300 undergraduate students

Freshmen *Admission:* 2,000 applied, 2,000 admitted.

Faculty *Total:* 200. *Student/faculty ratio:* 20:1.

Majors Accounting; agricultural business and management; agricultural economics; agricultural mechanization; agriculture; animal sciences; art; business administration and management; civil engineering technology; commercial and advertising art; computer and information sciences; computer programming; computer programming (specific applications); court reporting; dairy science; data processing and data processing technology; drafting and design technology; education; electrical, electronic and communications engineering technology; elementary education; family and consumer sciences/home economics teacher education; fashion merchandising; foods, nutrition, and wellness; heating, air conditioning and refrigeration technology; heating, air conditioning, ventilation and refrigeration maintenance technology; hotel/motel administration; journalism; legal assistant/paralegal; liberal arts and sciences/liberal studies; machine tool technology; mathematics teacher education; medical administrative assistant and medical secretary; music teacher education; nursing (licensed practical/vocational nurse training); nursing (registered nurse training); office management; physical education teaching and coaching; plant sciences; poultry science; radio and television; radio and television broadcasting technology; respiratory care therapy; sales and marketing/marketing and distribution teacher education; science teacher education; social science teacher education; social studies teacher education; speech teacher education; telecommunications.

Academics *Calendar:* semesters. *Degree:* associate. *Special study options:* academic remediation for entering students, adult/continuing education programs, honors programs, part-time degree program, services for LD students, summer session for credit. *ROTC:* Air Force (b).

Library R. C. Pugh Library with 38,000 titles, 325 serial subscriptions.

Student Life *Activities and Organizations:* drama/theater group, student-run newspaper, radio station, choral group, marching band. *Campus security:* 24-hour emergency response devices, late-night transport/escort service, controlled dormitory access. *Student services:* health clinic.

Athletics Member NJCAA. *Intercollegiate sports:* baseball M, basketball M(s)/W(s), equestrian sports M(s)/W(s), football M(s), golf M, softball W(s), tennis M(s)/W(s). *Intramural sports:* basketball M/W, football M.

Standardized Tests *Required:* ACT (for placement).

Costs (2006–07) *Tuition:* state resident $1700 full-time; nonresident $3700 full-time.

Applying *Options:* early admission, deferred entrance. *Required:* high school transcript. *Application deadlines:* 9/7 (freshmen), 9/7 (transfers). *Notification:* continuous (freshmen), continuous (transfers).

Director of Admissions Ms. Deanna Ferguson, Director of Admissions and Recruiting, Northwest Mississippi Community College, 4975 Highway 51 North, Senatobia, MS 38668-1701. *Phone:* 662-562-3222.

PEARL RIVER COMMUNITY COLLEGE

Poplarville, Mississippi www.prcc.edu/

- **State and locally supported** 2-year, founded 1909, part of Mississippi State Board for Community and Junior Colleges
- **Rural** 240-acre campus with easy access to New Orleans
- **Coed,** 3,700 undergraduate students

Undergraduates Students come from 11 states and territories, 20% live on campus.

Faculty *Total:* 225, 71% full-time.

Pearl River Community College *(continued)*

Majors Administrative assistant and secretarial science; business administration and management; drafting and design technology; electrical, electronic and communications engineering technology; liberal arts and sciences/liberal studies; marketing/marketing management; medical administrative assistant and medical secretary; nursing (registered nurse training); respiratory care therapy.

Academics *Calendar:* semesters. *Degree:* certificates and associate. *Special study options:* academic remediation for entering students, adult/continuing education programs, advanced placement credit, cooperative education, part-time degree program, student-designed majors, summer session for credit.

Library Pearl River Community College Library with 40,000 titles, 340 serial subscriptions.

Student Life *Housing Options:* Campus housing is university owned. *Activities and Organizations:* drama/theater group, student-run newspaper, choral group, marching band. *Campus security:* 24-hour patrols. *Student services:* health clinic, personal/psychological counseling, women's center.

Athletics Member NJCAA. *Intercollegiate sports:* baseball M(s), basketball M(s)/W(s), football M(s), golf M/W, soccer M/W, softball W, tennis M/W. *Intramural sports:* badminton M/W, basketball M/W, football M/W, golf M, softball M/W, tennis M/W, volleyball M/W, weight lifting M/W.

Costs (2006–07) *Tuition:* state resident $1620 full-time, $86 per hour part-time; nonresident $3620 full-time, $186 per hour part-time. *Required fees:* $50 full-time, $50 per term part-time. *Room and board:* $3000.

Financial Aid Of all full-time matriculated undergraduates, 200 Federal Work-Study jobs (averaging $2000).

Applying *Options:* early admission, deferred entrance. *Required:* high school transcript. *Application deadlines:* rolling (freshmen), rolling (transfers). *Notification:* continuous until 8/15 (freshmen), continuous until 8/15 (transfers).

Freshmen Application Contact Mr. J. Dow Ford, Director of Admissions, Pearl River Community College, 101 Highway 11 North, Poplarville, MS 39470. *Phone:* 601-403-1000. *Toll-free phone:* 877-772-2338. *E-mail:* dford@prcc.edu.

SOUTHWEST MISSISSIPPI COMMUNITY COLLEGE

Summit, Mississippi   www.smcc.cc.ms.us/

- **State and locally supported** 2-year, founded 1918, part of Mississippi State Board for Community and Junior Colleges
- **Rural** 701-acre campus
- **Coed,** 1,752 undergraduate students, 79% full-time, 65% women, 35% men

Undergraduates 1,386 full-time, 366 part-time. Students come from 12 states and territories, 10% are from out of state, 39% African American, 0.4% Asian American or Pacific Islander, 0.7% Hispanic American, 0.1% Native American, 21% transferred in, 35% live on campus.

Freshmen *Admission:* 543 enrolled. *Test scores:* ACT scores over 18: 47%; ACT scores over 24: 11%; ACT scores over 30: 1%.

Faculty *Total:* 102, 88% full-time. *Student/faculty ratio:* 16:1.

Majors Accounting; administrative assistant and secretarial science; advertising; automobile/automotive mechanics technology; biological and physical sciences; biology/biological sciences; business administration and management; business teacher education; carpentry; chemistry; computer programming related; computer science; construction engineering technology; cosmetology; education; electrical, electronic and communications engineering technology; elementary education; emergency medical technology (EMT paramedic); engineering; English; fashion merchandising; finance; health science; history; humanities; information technology; legal administrative assistant/secretary; liberal arts and sciences/liberal studies; machine tool technology; marketing/marketing management; music; music teacher education; nursing (registered nurse training); physical education teaching and coaching; physical sciences; social sciences; system administration; welding technology.

Academics *Calendar:* semesters. *Degree:* certificates and associate. *Special study options:* academic remediation for entering students, adult/continuing education programs, distance learning, part-time degree program, summer session for credit.

Library Library Learning Resources Center (LLRC) with 34,000 titles, 150 serial subscriptions, an OPAC.

Student Life *Housing Options:* men-only, women-only. Campus housing is university owned. *Activities and Organizations:* student-run newspaper, choral group, marching band. *Campus security:* 24-hour patrols.

Athletics Member NJCAA. *Intercollegiate sports:* baseball M, basketball M(s)/W(s), football M(s), golf M, softball W, tennis M/W. *Intramural sports:* basketball M/W.

Costs (2007–08) *Tuition:* state resident $1700 full-time, $75 per hour part-time; nonresident $3900 full-time, $170 per hour part-time. *Required fees:* $100 full-time, $50 per term part-time. *Room and board:* $2180.

Financial Aid Of all full-time matriculated undergraduates, 85 Federal Work-Study jobs (averaging $698). 6 state and other part-time jobs (averaging $550).

Applying *Required:* high school transcript. *Application deadlines:* 8/1 (freshmen), 8/1 (transfers).

Freshmen Application Contact Mr. Matthew Calhoun, Dean of Admissions, Southwest Mississippi Community College, College Drive, Summit, MS 39666. *Phone:* 601-276-2001. *Fax:* 601-276-3888. *E-mail:* mattc@smcc.edu.

VIRGINIA COLLEGE AT JACKSON

Jackson, Mississippi   www.vc.edu/

Director of Admissions Mr. Bill Milstead, Vice President of Admissions, Virginia College at Jackson, Interstate 55 North, Jackson, MS 39211. *Phone:* 601-977-0960 Ext. 2704.

MISSOURI

ALLIED COLLEGE

Maryland Heights, Missouri   www.hightechinstitute.edu/

- **Proprietary** 2-year
- **Coed,** 732 undergraduate students

Majors Corrections and criminal justice related; dental assisting; massage therapy; medical/clinical assistant; medical insurance/medical billing; pharmacy technician; surgical technology.

Academics *Degree:* associate.

Costs (2006–07) *Tuition:* $21,350 per degree program part-time.

Applying *Application fee:* $50.

Freshmen Application Contact Admissions Office, Allied College, 13723 Riverport Drive, Maryland Heights, MO 63043. *Phone:* 314-595-3400. *Toll-free phone:* 866-501-1291.

AVIATION INSTITUTE OF MAINTENANCE—KANSAS CITY

Kansas City, Missouri   www.aviationmaintenance.edu/aviation-kansascity.asp

- **Proprietary** 2-year

Academics *Calendar:* quarters. *Degree:* certificates and associate.

Applying *Required:* High School Diploma or GED.

Freshmen Application Contact Kansas City School Director, Aviation Institute of Maintenance—Kansas City, 3130 Terrace Street, Kansas City, MO 64111. *Phone:* 816-753-9920. *Toll-free phone:* 877-538-5627. *Fax:* 816-753.-9941. *E-mail:* directoramk@tidetech.com.

COLORADO TECHNICAL UNIVERSITY - NORTH KANSAS CITY

North Kansas City, Missouri   kc.coloradotech.edu/

Director of Admissions Mr. Edward A. Beauchamp, Director of Admissions, Colorado Technical University - North Kansas City, 520 East 19th Avenue, North Kansas City, MO 64116. *Phone:* 816-472-0275. *Toll-free phone:* 800-456-7222. *Fax:* 816-472-0888. *E-mail:* edward.beauchamp@wix.net.

CONCORDE CAREER INSTITUTE

Kansas City, Missouri   www.concordecareercolleges.com/

- **Proprietary** 2-year, founded 1983
- **Coed,** 524 undergraduate students
- 100% of applicants were admitted

Freshmen *Admission:* 497 applied, 497 admitted.

Majors Respiratory care therapy.

Academics *Degree:* associate.

Costs (2006–07) *Tuition:* $20,036 per degree program part-time.

Applying *Required:* high school transcript.

Freshmen Application Contact Admissions Office, Concorde Career Institute, 3239 Broadway, Kansas City, MO 64111.

COTTEY COLLEGE

Nevada, Missouri   www.cottey.edu/

- **Independent** 2-year, founded 1884
- **Small-town** 51-acre campus
- **Endowment** $85,548
- **Women only,** 318 undergraduate students, 100% full-time

Undergraduates 318 full-time. Students come from 44 states and territories, 15 other countries, 90% are from out of state, 3% African American, 2% Asian American or Pacific Islander, 7% Hispanic American, 0.9% Native American, 8% international, 0.6% transferred in, 98% live on campus. *Retention:* 74% of 2003 full-time freshmen returned.

Freshmen *Admission:* 505 applied, 321 admitted, 171 enrolled. *Average high school GPA:* 3.4. *Test scores:* SAT verbal scores over 500: 62%; SAT math scores over 500: 55%; ACT scores over 18: 99%; SAT verbal scores over 600: 28%; SAT math scores over 600: 16%; ACT scores over 24: 48%; SAT verbal scores over 700: 4%; SAT math scores over 700: 1%; ACT scores over 30: 3%.

Faculty *Total:* 33. *Student/faculty ratio:* 10:1.

Majors Biological and physical sciences; liberal arts and sciences/liberal studies.

Academics *Calendar:* semesters. *Degree:* associate. *Special study options:* advanced placement credit, distance learning, independent study, internships, part-time degree program, services for LD students, study abroad.

Library Blanche Skiff Ross Memorial Library with 54,200 titles, 246 serial subscriptions, an OPAC.

Student Life *Housing:* on-campus residence required through sophomore year. *Options:* women-only. Campus housing is university owned. *Activities and Organizations:* drama/theater group, student-run newspaper, choral group, International Friendship Circle, Cottey Intramural Association, Ozarks Explorers Club, Inter-Varsity Club, Golden Keys. *Campus security:* 24-hour emergency response devices and patrols, late-night transport/escort service, controlled dormitory access. *Student services:* health clinic, personal/psychological counseling.

Athletics Member NAIA. *Intercollegiate sports:* basketball W, volleyball W. *Intramural sports:* badminton W, basketball W, fencing W, field hockey W, golf W, soccer W, softball W, swimming and diving W, tennis W, volleyball W, water polo W, weight lifting W.

Standardized Tests *Required:* SAT or ACT (for admission).

Costs (2007–08) *Comprehensive fee:* $18,710 includes full-time tuition ($12,800), mandatory fees ($710), and room and board ($5200). Part-time tuition: $150 per credit hour. *Required fees:* $11 per credit hour part-time, $25 per term part-time.

Financial Aid Of all full-time matriculated undergraduates, 26 Federal Work-Study jobs (averaging $1500). 131 state and other part-time jobs (averaging $1500).

Applying *Options:* electronic application, early admission, deferred entrance. *Application fee:* $20. *Required:* essay or personal statement, high school transcript, 1 letter of recommendation. *Recommended:* minimum 2.6 GPA, interview. *Application deadlines:* rolling (freshmen), rolling (out-of-state freshmen), rolling (transfers).

Freshmen Application Contact Ms. Judi Steege, Director of Admission, Cottey College, 1000 West Austin Boulevard, Nevada, MO 64772. *Phone:* 417-667-8181. *Toll-free phone:* 888-526-8839. *Fax:* 417-667-8103. *E-mail:* enrollmgt@cottey.edu.

▶**See page 536 for the College Close-Up.**

CROWDER COLLEGE

Neosho, Missouri   www.crowder.edu/

- **State and locally supported** 2-year, founded 1963, part of Missouri Coordinating Board for Higher Education
- **Rural** 608-acre campus
- **Coed,** 2,930 undergraduate students, 48% full-time, 63% women, 37% men

Undergraduates 1,403 full-time, 1,527 part-time. Students come from 25 states and territories, 16 other countries, 4% are from out of state, 0.8% African American, 1% Asian American or Pacific Islander, 6% Hispanic American, 2% Native American, 1% international, 11% transferred in, 10% live on campus.

Freshmen *Admission:* 1,307 applied, 1,307 admitted, 560 enrolled.

Faculty *Total:* 269, 25% full-time. *Student/faculty ratio:* 19:1.

Majors Administrative assistant and secretarial science; agribusiness; agriculture; art; biology/biological sciences; business administration and management; business automation/technology/data entry; computer systems networking and telecommunications; construction engineering technology; drafting and design technology; dramatic/theater arts; education; electrical, electronic and communications engineering technology; elementary education; environmental engineering technology; environmental health; executive assistant/executive secretary; farm and ranch management; fire science; general studies; industrial technology; legal administrative assistant/secretary; liberal arts and sciences/liberal studies; mass communication/media; mathematics; mathematics and computer science; medical administrative assistant and medical secretary; music; nursing (registered nurse training); physical education teaching and coaching; physical sciences; poultry science; pre-engineering; psychology; public relations/image management.

Academics *Calendar:* semesters. *Degree:* certificates and associate. *Special study options:* academic remediation for entering students, adult/continuing education programs, advanced placement credit, cooperative education, English as a second language, freshman honors college, honors programs, independent study, part-time degree program, student-designed majors, study abroad, summer session for credit.

Library Crowder College Learning Resources Center with 37,452 titles, 163 serial subscriptions, an OPAC, a Web page.

Student Life *Housing Options:* men-only, women-only. Campus housing is university owned. *Activities and Organizations:* drama/theater group, student-run newspaper, choral group, Phi Beta Lambda, Students in Free Enterprise, Baptist Student Union, Student Senate, Student Ambassadors. *Campus security:* 24-hour patrols. *Student services:* personal/psychological counseling.

Athletics Member NJCAA. *Intercollegiate sports:* baseball M(s), basketball W(s). *Intramural sports:* soccer M.

Costs (2007–08) *Tuition:* area resident $1950 full-time, $65 per credit hour part-time; state resident $2730 full-time, $91 per credit hour part-time; nonresident $3540 full-time, $118 per credit hour part-time. *Required fees:* $360 full-time. *Room and board:* $3870.

Financial Aid Of all full-time matriculated undergraduates, 150 Federal Work-Study jobs (averaging $1000).

Applying *Application fee:* $25. *Required:* high school transcript. *Application deadlines:* rolling (freshmen), rolling (transfers). *Notification:* continuous (freshmen).

Freshmen Application Contact Mr. Jim Riggs, Admissions Coordinator, Crowder College, 601 Laclede Avenue, Neosho, MO 64850. *Phone:* 417-451-3223 Ext. 5466. *Toll-free phone:* 866-238-7788. *Fax:* 417-455-5731. *E-mail:* jriggs@crowder.edu.

EAST CENTRAL COLLEGE

Union, Missouri   www.eastcentral.edu/

- **District-supported** 2-year, founded 1959
- **Rural** 207-acre campus with easy access to St. Louis
- **Endowment** $3.2 million
- **Coed,** 3,474 undergraduate students, 45% full-time, 61% women, 39% men

Undergraduates 1,560 full-time, 1,914 part-time. 0.9% African American, 0.8% Asian American or Pacific Islander, 1% Hispanic American, 0.4% Native American, 0.2% international.

Freshmen *Admission:* 811 admitted, 811 enrolled. *Average high school GPA:* 2.96. *Test scores:* ACT scores over 18: 77%; ACT scores over 24: 20%; ACT scores over 30: 1%.

Faculty *Total:* 187, 31% full-time, 11% with terminal degrees. *Student/faculty ratio:* 21:1.

Majors Accounting; accounting technology and bookkeeping; administrative assistant and secretarial science; automobile/automotive mechanics technology;

East Central College (continued)

biology/biological sciences; botany/plant biology; business administration and management; business, management, and marketing related; business operations support and secretarial services related; chemistry; commercial and advertising art; communications technologies and support services related; computer systems networking and telecommunications; construction engineering technology; construction trades; construction trades related; criminal justice/police science; culinary arts; drafting and design technology; early childhood education; education related; electrical, electronic and communications engineering technology; emergency medical technology (EMT paramedic); engineering; fire science; general studies; heating, air conditioning, ventilation and refrigeration maintenance technology; heavy/industrial equipment maintenance technologies related; industrial technology; legal administrative assistant/secretary; legal assistant/paralegal; machine tool technology; manufacturing technology; medical administrative assistant and medical secretary; nursing (registered nurse training); parks, recreation and leisure; philosophy; physical education teaching and coaching; physics; political science and government; pre-engineering; psychology; radiologic technology/science; religious studies; respiratory care therapy; sociology; special products marketing; speech and rhetoric; surgical technology; teacher assistant/aide; tourism and travel services management; wildlife and wildlands science and management; zoology/animal biology.

Academics *Calendar:* semesters. *Degree:* certificates and associate. *Special study options:* academic remediation for entering students, adult/continuing education programs, advanced placement credit, distance learning, English as a second language, honors programs, independent study, internships, part-time degree program, services for LD students, study abroad, summer session for credit.

Library East Central College Library with an OPAC, a Web page.

Student Life *Housing:* college housing not available. *Activities and Organizations:* drama/theater group, student-run newspaper, choral group, student government, Phi Theta Kappa, Amnesty International, Multicultural Club. *Campus security:* 24-hour emergency response devices, late-night transport/escort service.

Athletics Member NJCAA. *Intercollegiate sports:* soccer M(s), softball W(s).

Costs (2007–08) *Tuition:* area resident $1464 full-time, $61 per credit hour part-time; state resident $2088 full-time; nonresident $3144 full-time. *Required fees:* $240 full-time, $10 per credit hour part-time.

Financial Aid Of all full-time matriculated undergraduates, 35 Federal Work-Study jobs (averaging $1500). 35 state and other part-time jobs (averaging $1500).

Applying *Options:* early admission, deferred entrance. *Required:* high school transcript. *Application deadlines:* rolling (freshmen), rolling (transfers).

Freshmen Application Contact Ms. Ina "Cookie" Hays, Dean of Students, East Central College, 1964 Prairie Dell Road, Union, MO 63084. *Phone:* 636-583-5195. *Fax:* 636-583-6651. *E-mail:* haysir@eastcentral.edu.

EVEREST COLLEGE

Springfield, Missouri   www.everest.edu/campus/springfield

Director of Admissions Gerald F. Terrebrood, President, Everest College, 1010 West Sunshine Street, Springfield, MO 65807. *Phone:* 417-864-7220. *Toll-free phone:* 800-864-5697 (in-state); 800-475-2669 (out-of-state). *Fax:* 417-864-5697. *E-mail:* gterrebr@cci.edu.

EVEREST COLLEGE

Springfield, Missouri   www.everest.edu/campus/springfield

- **Proprietary** primarily 2-year
- **Coed,** 548 undergraduate students
- 95% of applicants were admitted

Freshmen *Admission:* 130 applied, 123 admitted.

Majors Accounting; business administration and management; computer and information sciences; legal assistant/paralegal.

Academics *Degrees:* certificates, associate, and bachelor's.

Costs (2006–07) *Tuition:* $9051 full-time.

Freshmen Application Contact Admissions Office, Everest College, 1010 West Sunshine Street, Springfield, MO 65807.

HERITAGE COLLEGE

Kansas City, Missouri   www.heritage-education.com/

Admissions Office Contact Heritage College, 534 East 99th Street, Kansas City, MO 64131-4203.

HICKEY COLLEGE

St. Louis, Missouri   www.hickeycollege.edu/

- **Proprietary** primarily 2-year, founded 1933
- **Suburban** campus
- **Coed**

Founded in 1933, Hickey College offers diploma, associate, and bachelor's degree programs. Eight- to sixteen-month programs include accounting, administrative assistant studies, computer programming, computer specialist studies, graphic design, legal administrative assistant studies, medical administrative assistant studies, network management, and paralegal studies. Tuition and fees vary by program. Financial assistance is available for those who qualify. Housing is offered. The College is an accredited member of ACICS. For more information, prospective students should call 314-434-2212 or 800-777-1544 (toll-free) or visit the College Web site at http://www.hickeycollege.edu.

Undergraduates 500 full-time, 110 part-time. 33% are from out of state.

Faculty *Student/faculty ratio:* 38:1.

Academics *Calendar:* semesters. *Degrees:* diplomas, associate, and bachelor's. *Special study options:* accelerated degree program.

Applying *Application fee:* $50. *Required:* high school transcript, interview.

Freshmen Application Contact Ms. Michelle Hayes, Director of Admissions, Hickey College, 940 West Port Plaza Drive, St. Louis, MO 63146. *Phone:* 314-434-2212 Ext. 136. *Toll-free phone:* 800-777-1544. *Fax:* 314-434-1974. *E-mail:* admin@hickeycollege.edu.

HIGH-TECH INSTITUTE

Kansas City, Missouri   www.high-techinstitute.com/

- **Proprietary** 2-year, founded 2003
- **Coed,** 687 undergraduate students

Majors Criminal justice/police science; dental assisting; massage therapy; medical/clinical assistant; medical insurance/medical billing; surgical technology.

Academics *Calendar:* semesters. *Degree:* associate.

Costs (2006–07) *Tuition:* $21,350 per degree program part-time.

Applying *Application fee:* $50.

Freshmen Application Contact Admissions Office, High-Tech Institute, 9001 State Line Road, Kansas City, MO 64114. *Phone:* 816-444-4300. *Toll-free phone:* 866-296-2110. *Fax:* 816-444-4494.

IHM HEALTH STUDIES CENTER

St. Louis, Missouri   www.ihmhealthstudies.com/

Director of Admissions Mr. Taz A. Meyer, Director of Education, IHM Health Studies Center, 2500 Abbott Place, St. Louis, MO 63143-2636. *Phone:* 314-768-1234 Ext. 1128. *E-mail:* meyer@abbottems.org.

ITT TECHNICAL INSTITUTE

Arnold, Missouri   www.itt-tech.edu/

- **Proprietary** primarily 2-year, founded 1997, part of ITT Educational Services, Inc
- **Coed**

Majors Accounting technology and bookkeeping; animation, interactive technology, video graphics and special effects; business administration and management; CAD/CADD drafting/design technology; communications technology; computer and information systems security; computer engineering technology; computer software engineering; computer software technology; computer systems networking and telecommunications; construction management; criminal justice/law enforcement administration; electrical, electronic and communications engineering technology; medical laboratory technology; web/multimedia management and webmaster; web page, digital/multimedia and information resources design.

Academics *Calendar:* quarters. *Degrees:* associate and bachelor's.

Library a Web page.

Student Life *Housing:* college housing not available.

Standardized Tests *Required:* Wonderlic aptitude test (for admission).

Costs (2006–07) *Tuition:* Contact school directly for program costs.

Applying *Options:* deferred entrance. *Application fee:* $100. *Required:* high school transcript, interview. *Recommended:* letters of recommendation. *Application deadlines:* rolling (freshmen), rolling (transfers). *Notification:* continuous (freshmen), continuous (transfers).

Freshmen Application Contact Mr. Brad Coleman, Director of Recruitment, ITT Technical Institute, 1930 Meyer Drury Drive, Arnold, MO 63010. *Phone:* 636-464-6600. *Toll-free phone:* 888-488-1082.

ITT TECHNICAL INSTITUTE
Earth City, Missouri www.itt-tech.edu/

- **Proprietary** primarily 2-year, founded 1936, part of ITT Educational Services, Inc
- **Suburban** 2-acre campus with easy access to St. Louis
- **Coed**

Majors Accounting technology and bookkeeping; animation, interactive technology, video graphics and special effects; business administration and management; CAD/CADD drafting/design technology; computer and information systems security; computer engineering technology; computer systems networking and telecommunications; construction management; criminal justice/law enforcement administration; electrical, electronic and communications engineering technology; health information/medical records technology; web/multimedia management and webmaster; web page, digital/multimedia and information resources design.

Academics *Calendar:* quarters. *Degrees:* associate and bachelor's.

Library a Web page.

Student Life *Housing:* college housing not available.

Standardized Tests *Required:* Wonderlic aptitude test (for admission).

Costs (2006–07) *Tuition:* Contact school for program costs.

Applying *Options:* deferred entrance. *Application fee:* $100. *Required:* high school transcript, interview. *Recommended:* letters of recommendation. *Application deadlines:* rolling (freshmen), rolling (transfers). *Notification:* continuous (freshmen), continuous (transfers).

Freshmen Application Contact Mr. Arlen K. Freeman, Director of Recruitment, ITT Technical Institute, 13505 Lakefront Drive, Earth City, MO 63045. *Phone:* 314-298-7800. *Toll-free phone:* 800-235-5488.

ITT TECHNICAL INSTITUTE
Kansas City, Missouri www.itt-tech.edu/

- **Proprietary** primarily 2-year, founded 2004, part of ITT Educational Services, Inc
- **Coed**

Majors Accounting and business/management; accounting technology and bookkeeping; business administration and management; CAD/CADD drafting/design technology; computer and information systems security; computer engineering technology; computer systems networking and telecommunications; criminal justice/law enforcement administration; health information/medical records technology.

Academics *Calendar:* quarters. *Degrees:* associate and bachelor's.

Standardized Tests *Required:* Wonderlic aptitude test (for admission).

Costs (2006–07) *Tuition:* Contact school for program costs.

Applying *Application fee:* $100. *Required:* high school transcript, interview. *Recommended:* letters of recommendation. *Application deadlines:* rolling (freshmen), rolling (transfers). *Notification:* continuous (freshmen), continuous (transfers).

Freshmen Application Contact Mr. William Vinson, Director of Recruitment, ITT Technical Institute, 9150 East 41st Terrace, Kansas City, MO 64133. *Phone:* 816-276-1400. *Toll-free phone:* 877-488-1442.

JEFFERSON COLLEGE
Hillsboro, Missouri www.jeffco.edu/

Freshmen Application Contact Ms. Julie Pierce, Director of Admissions and Financial Aid, Jefferson College, 1000 Viking Drive, Hillsboro, MO 63050. *Phone:* 636-797-3000. *Fax:* 636-789-5103. *E-mail:* admissions@jeffco.edu.

LINN STATE TECHNICAL COLLEGE
Linn, Missouri www.linnstate.edu/

- **State-supported** 2-year, founded 1961
- **Rural** 249-acre campus
- **Endowment** $48,958
- **Coed, primarily men,** 877 undergraduate students, 89% full-time, 9% women, 91% men

Undergraduates 783 full-time, 94 part-time. Students come from 5 states and territories, 1 other country, 1% are from out of state, 1% African American, 0.2% Asian American or Pacific Islander, 0.5% Hispanic American, 0.3% Native American, 0.2% international, 5% transferred in, 15% live on campus. *Retention:* 68% of 2003 full-time freshmen returned.

Freshmen *Admission:* 1,053 applied, 505 admitted, 418 enrolled. *Average high school GPA:* 2.91. *Test scores:* ACT scores over 18: 60%; ACT scores over 24: 9%.

Faculty *Total:* 88, 98% full-time. *Student/faculty ratio:* 10:1.

Majors Aircraft powerplant technology; autobody/collision and repair technology; automobile/automotive mechanics technology; civil engineering technology; computer programming; computer systems analysis; drafting and design technology; electrical, electronic and communications engineering technology; electrician; heating, air conditioning, ventilation and refrigeration maintenance technology; heavy equipment maintenance technology; laser and optical technology; lineworker; machine tool technology; physical therapist assistant; turf and turfgrass management.

Academics *Calendar:* semesters. *Degree:* certificates and associate. *Special study options:* academic remediation for entering students, accelerated degree program, adult/continuing education programs, advanced placement credit, cooperative education, distance learning, double majors, independent study, internships, off-campus study, part-time degree program, services for LD students, summer session for credit. *ROTC:* Army (c).

Library Linn State Technical College Library plus 2 others with 14,932 titles, 144 serial subscriptions, 1,707 audiovisual materials, an OPAC, a Web page.

Student Life *Housing Options:* coed, men-only, women-only, disabled students. Campus housing is university owned. *Activities and Organizations:* Skills USA-VICA, Phi Theta Kappa, Student Government Association, Aviation Club, Electricity Club. *Campus security:* 24-hour emergency response devices, student patrols, controlled dormitory access, indoor and outdoor surveillance cameras. *Student services:* personal/psychological counseling.

Athletics *Intercollegiate sports:* archery M/W, basketball M/W, bowling M/W, softball M/W, table tennis M/W, volleyball M/W. *Intramural sports:* archery M/W, basketball M/W, bowling M/W, golf M/W, riflery M/W, softball M/W, table tennis M/W, volleyball M/W.

Standardized Tests *Required:* ACT ASSET, ACT COMPASS (for admission). *Required for some:* ACT (for admission).

Costs (2007–08) *Tuition:* state resident $4200 full-time; nonresident $8400 full-time. *Required fees:* $990 full-time. *Room and board:* $1910; room only: $1485.

Financial Aid Of all full-time matriculated undergraduates, 70 Federal Work-Study jobs (averaging $769).

Applying *Options:* electronic application. *Required:* high school transcript. *Required for some:* essay or personal statement, letters of recommendation, interview, driving record, physical examination. *Notification:* continuous (freshmen), continuous (transfers).

Freshmen Application Contact Ms. Becky Dunn, Director of Admissions, Linn State Technical College, One Technology Drive, Linn, MO 65051. *Phone:* 573-897-5196. *Toll-free phone:* 800-743-TECH. *Fax:* 573-897-5026. *E-mail:* admissions@linnstate.edu.

METRO BUSINESS COLLEGE
Cape Girardeau, Missouri www.metrobusinesscollege.edu/

Director of Admissions Ms. Kyla Evans, Admissions Director, Metro Business College, 1732 North Kingshighway, Cape Girardeau, MO 63701. *Phone:* 573-334-9181. *Fax:* 573-334-0617.

METRO BUSINESS COLLEGE
Jefferson City, Missouri www.metrobusinesscollege.edu/

- **Proprietary** 2-year, founded 1979
- **Coed**
- 75% of applicants were admitted

Metro Business College (continued)

Undergraduates 140 full-time, 15 part-time. 1% are from out of state, 19% African American, 0.6% Hispanic American.

Faculty *Student/faculty ratio:* 14:1.

Academics *Calendar:* quarters. *Degree:* certificates, diplomas, and associate.

Standardized Tests *Required:* Wonderlic aptitude test (for admission).

Costs (2006–07) *Tuition:* $8385 full-time. No tuition increase for student's term of enrollment. *Required fees:* $125 full-time.

Applying *Application fee:* $25. *Required:* essay or personal statement, high school transcript, interview.

Freshmen Application Contact Ms. Cheri Chockley, Campus Director, Metro Business College, 1407 Southwest Boulevard, Jefferson City, MO 65109. *Phone:* 573-635-6600. *Toll-free phone:* 800-467-0786. *Fax:* 573-635-6999. *E-mail:* cheri@metrobusinesscollege.edu.

METRO BUSINESS COLLEGE
Rolla, Missouri   www.metrobusinesscollege.edu/

Freshmen Application Contact Admissions Office, Metro Business College, 1202 East Highway 72, Rolla, MO 65401. *Phone:* 314-364-8464. *Toll-free phone:* 800-978-7705.

METROPOLITAN COMMUNITY COLLEGE— BLUE RIVER
Independence, Missouri   www.mcckc.edu

- **State and locally supported** 2-year, founded 1997, part of Metropolitan Community Colleges System
- **Suburban** campus with easy access to Kansas City
- **Endowment** $2.4 million
- **Coed,** 2,662 undergraduate students, 40% full-time, 60% women, 40% men

Undergraduates 1,053 full-time, 1,609 part-time. Students come from 2 states and territories, 0.2% are from out of state, 2% African American, 0.7% Asian American or Pacific Islander, 2% Hispanic American, 0.8% Native American, 5% transferred in. *Retention:* 57% of 2003 full-time freshmen returned.

Freshmen *Admission:* 487 applied, 487 admitted, 487 enrolled.

Faculty *Total:* 304, 10% full-time. *Student/faculty ratio:* 13:1.

Majors Accounting technology and bookkeeping; administrative assistant and secretarial science; business administration and management; computer and information sciences related; computer science; criminal justice/police science; fire science; information science/studies; liberal arts and sciences/liberal studies.

Academics *Calendar:* semesters. *Degree:* certificates and associate. *Special study options:* academic remediation for entering students, accelerated degree program, adult/continuing education programs, advanced placement credit, cooperative education, distance learning, English as a second language, honors programs, independent study, internships, off-campus study, part-time degree program, study abroad.

Library Blue River Community College Library with 10,312 titles, 66 serial subscriptions, an OPAC, a Web page.

Student Life *Housing:* college housing not available. *Activities and Organizations:* choral group. *Campus security:* 24-hour emergency response devices and patrols.

Costs (2006–07) *Tuition:* area resident $2130 full-time, $73 per hour part-time; state resident $3870 full-time, $133 per hour part-time; nonresident $5250 full-time, $180 per hour part-time. *Required fees:* $150 full-time, $5 per hour part-time.

Applying *Options:* early admission, deferred entrance. *Application deadlines:* rolling (freshmen), rolling (transfers).

Freshmen Application Contact Mr. Jon Burke, Dean of Student Development, Metropolitan Community College–Blue River, 20301 East 78 Highway, Independence, MO 64057. *Phone:* 816-655-6118. *Fax:* 816-655-6014.

METROPOLITAN COMMUNITY COLLEGE— BUSINESS & TECHNOLOGY CAMPUS
Kansas City, Missouri   www.mcckc.edu

- **State and locally supported** 2-year, founded 1995, part of Metropolitan Community Colleges
- **Urban** 23-acre campus
- **Endowment** $2.4 million
- **Coed, primarily men,** 602 undergraduate students, 20% full-time, 10% women, 90% men
- **100%** of applicants were admitted

Undergraduates 118 full-time, 484 part-time. Students come from 2 states and territories, 2% are from out of state, 5% African American, 0.4% Asian American or Pacific Islander, 1% Hispanic American, 0.4% Native American, 2% transferred in. *Retention:* 26% of 2003 full-time freshmen returned.

Freshmen *Admission:* 68 applied, 68 admitted, 68 enrolled.

Faculty *Total:* 47, 21% full-time. *Student/faculty ratio:* 13:1.

Majors Accounting; accounting technology and bookkeeping; artificial intelligence and robotics; building/construction site management; business administration and management; business/commerce; carpentry; computer and information sciences; computer and information sciences and support services related; computer and information sciences related; computer and information systems security; computer graphics; computer/information technology services administration related; computer programming; computer programming related; computer programming (specific applications); computer programming (vendor/product certification); computer science; computer software and media applications related; computer systems analysis; computer systems networking and telecommunications; data entry/microcomputer applications; data entry/microcomputer applications related; data modeling/warehousing and database administration; data processing and data processing technology; drafting and design technology; electrical, electronic and communications engineering technology; engineering; engineering-related technologies; environmental engineering technology; glazier; information science/studies; information technology; liberal arts and sciences/liberal studies; machine shop technology; management information systems and services related; masonry; quality control technology; system administration; system, networking, and LAN/WAN management; web/multimedia management and webmaster; web page, digital/multimedia and information resources design; word processing.

Academics *Calendar:* semesters. *Degree:* certificates and associate.

Library Learning Resource Center/Library with an OPAC.

Student Life *Housing:* college housing not available. *Campus security:* 24-hour patrols, late-night transport/escort service.

Costs (2006–07) *Tuition:* area resident $2130 full-time, $73 per hour part-time; state resident $3870 full-time, $133 per hour part-time; nonresident $5250 full-time, $180 per hour part-time. *Required fees:* $150 full-time, $5 per hour part-time.

Freshmen Application Contact Ms. Debbie Goodall, Dean of Student Development, Metropolitan Community College–Business & Technology Campus, 1775 Universal Avenue, Kansas City, MO 64120. *Toll-free phone:* 800-841-7158.

METROPOLITAN COMMUNITY COLLEGE— LONGVIEW
Lee's Summit, Missouri   www.mcckc.edu

- **State and locally supported** 2-year, founded 1969, part of Metropolitan Community Colleges System
- **Suburban** 147-acre campus with easy access to Kansas City
- **Endowment** $2.4 million
- **Coed,** 5,667 undergraduate students, 43% full-time, 58% women, 42% men

Undergraduates 2,419 full-time, 3,248 part-time. Students come from 6 states and territories, 1 other country, 1% are from out of state, 11% African American, 0.6% Asian American or Pacific Islander, 2% Hispanic American, 0.2% Native American, 5% transferred in. *Retention:* 55% of 2003 full-time freshmen returned.

Freshmen *Admission:* 963 applied, 963 admitted, 963 enrolled.

Faculty *Total:* 380, 22% full-time. *Student/faculty ratio:* 19:1.

Majors Accounting; administrative assistant and secretarial science; agricultural mechanization; automobile/automotive mechanics technology; biological and physical sciences; biology/biological sciences; business administration and management; chemistry; computer and information sciences related; computer programming; computer science; computer typography and composition equipment operation; corrections; criminal justice/law enforcement administration;

criminal justice/police science; data processing and data processing technology; engineering; heavy equipment maintenance technology; human services; legal administrative assistant/secretary; liberal arts and sciences/liberal studies; marketing/marketing management; medical administrative assistant and medical secretary; postal management; pre-engineering.

Academics *Calendar:* semesters. *Degree:* certificates and associate. *Special study options:* academic remediation for entering students, accelerated degree program, adult/continuing education programs, advanced placement credit, cooperative education, distance learning, English as a second language, honors programs, independent study, internships, off-campus study, part-time degree program, study abroad.

Library Longview Community College Library with 56,266 titles, 288 serial subscriptions, an OPAC, a Web page.

Student Life *Housing:* college housing not available. *Activities and Organizations:* drama/theater group, student-run newspaper, choral group, student newspaper, student government, Phi Theta Kappa, Longview Mighty Voices Choir, Longview Broadcasting Network, national fraternities. *Campus security:* 24-hour patrols. *Student services:* personal/psychological counseling.

Athletics Member NJCAA. *Intercollegiate sports:* baseball M(s), cross-country running W(s), volleyball W(s). *Intramural sports:* basketball M/W, swimming and diving M/W, volleyball M/W.

Costs (2006–07) *Tuition:* area resident $2130 full-time, $73 per hour part-time; state resident $3870 full-time, $133 per hour part-time; nonresident $5250 full-time, $180 per hour part-time. *Required fees:* $150 full-time.

Applying *Options:* early admission, deferred entrance. *Application deadlines:* rolling (freshmen), rolling (transfers).

Freshmen Application Contact Ms. Janet Cline, Dean of Student Development, Metropolitan Community College–Longview, 500 Southwest Longview Road, Lee's Summit, MO 64081-2105. *Phone:* 816-672-2249. *Fax:* 816-672-2040.

METROPOLITAN COMMUNITY COLLEGE–MAPLE WOODS

Kansas City, Missouri www.mcckc.edu

- **State and locally supported** 2-year, founded 1969, part of Metropolitan Community Colleges System
- **Suburban** 205-acre campus
- **Endowment** $2.4 million
- **Coed,** 4,442 undergraduate students, 41% full-time, 60% women, 40% men

Undergraduates 1,817 full-time, 2,625 part-time. Students come from 4 states and territories, 1% are from out of state, 3% African American, 1% Asian American or Pacific Islander, 2% Hispanic American, 0.3% Native American, 5% transferred in. *Retention:* 59% of 2003 full-time freshmen returned.

Freshmen *Admission:* 856 applied, 856 admitted, 856 enrolled.

Faculty *Total:* 346, 15% full-time. *Student/faculty ratio:* 18:1.

Majors Accounting; administrative assistant and secretarial science; avionics maintenance technology; biological and physical sciences; biology/biological sciences; business administration and management; chemistry; computer and information sciences related; computer programming; computer science; criminal justice/law enforcement administration; criminal justice/police science; data processing and data processing technology; legal administrative assistant/secretary; liberal arts and sciences/liberal studies; marketing/marketing management; medical administrative assistant and medical secretary; pre-engineering; veterinary technology.

Academics *Calendar:* semesters. *Degree:* certificates and associate. *Special study options:* academic remediation for entering students, accelerated degree program, adult/continuing education programs, advanced placement credit, cooperative education, distance learning, English as a second language, honors programs, internships, off-campus study, part-time degree program, services for LD students, summer session for credit.

Library Maple Woods Community College Library with 32,906 titles, 250 serial subscriptions, an OPAC.

Student Life *Housing:* college housing not available. *Activities and Organizations:* drama/theater group, student-run newspaper, choral group, Student Activities Council, Art Club, Friends of All Cultures, Phi Theta Kappa, Engineering Club, national fraternities. *Campus security:* 24-hour patrols, late-night transport/escort service. *Student services:* personal/psychological counseling.

Athletics Member NJCAA. *Intercollegiate sports:* baseball M(s), softball W(s). *Intramural sports:* softball M/W, volleyball M/W.

Costs (2006–07) *Tuition:* area resident $2130 full-time, $73 per hour part-time; state resident $3870 full-time, $133 per hour part-time; nonresident $5250 full-time, $180 per hour part-time. *Required fees:* $150 full-time, $5 per hour part-time.

Applying *Options:* early admission, deferred entrance. *Application deadlines:* rolling (freshmen), rolling (transfers). *Notification:* continuous (freshmen), continuous (transfers).

Freshmen Application Contact Ms. Marilyn Donatello, Dean of Student Services, Metropolitan Community College–Maple Woods, 2601 Northeast Barry Road, Kansas City, MO 64156-1299. *Phone:* 816-437-3108. *Fax:* 816-437-3351.

METROPOLITAN COMMUNITY COLLEGE–PENN VALLEY

Kansas City, Missouri www.mcckc.edu

- **State and locally supported** 2-year, founded 1969, part of Metropolitan Community Colleges System
- **Urban** 25-acre campus
- **Endowment** $2.4 million
- **Coed,** 4,627 undergraduate students, 31% full-time, 72% women, 28% men

Undergraduates 1,457 full-time, 3,170 part-time. Students come from 6 states and territories, 1 other country, 5% are from out of state, 29% African American, 3% Asian American or Pacific Islander, 5% Hispanic American, 0.5% Native American, 5% transferred in. *Retention:* 52% of 2003 full-time freshmen returned.

Freshmen *Admission:* 785 applied, 785 admitted, 785 enrolled.

Faculty *Total:* 437, 23% full-time. *Student/faculty ratio:* 12:1.

Majors Accounting; administrative assistant and secretarial science; biological and physical sciences; biology/biological sciences; business administration and management; chemistry; child care provision; commercial and advertising art; computer and information sciences related; computer science; corrections; criminal justice/law enforcement administration; criminal justice/police science; data processing and data processing technology; emergency medical technology (EMT paramedic); engineering; family and consumer sciences/human sciences; fashion/apparel design; fashion merchandising; health information/medical records administration; kindergarten/preschool education; legal administrative assistant/secretary; legal assistant/paralegal; liberal arts and sciences/liberal studies; marketing/marketing management; medical administrative assistant and medical secretary; nursing (registered nurse training); occupational therapy; physical therapy; respiratory care therapy; special products marketing.

Academics *Calendar:* semesters. *Degree:* certificates and associate. *Special study options:* academic remediation for entering students, accelerated degree program, adult/continuing education programs, advanced placement credit, cooperative education, distance learning, English as a second language, honors programs, independent study, internships, off-campus study, part-time degree program, study abroad.

Library Penn Valley Community College Library with 91,428 titles, 89,242 serial subscriptions, an OPAC.

Student Life *Housing:* college housing not available. *Activities and Organizations:* drama/theater group, student-run newspaper, choral group, Black Student Association, Los Americanos, Phi Theta Kappa, Fashion Club, national fraternities. *Campus security:* 24-hour patrols. *Student services:* personal/psychological counseling.

Athletics Member NJCAA. *Intercollegiate sports:* basketball M(s)/W(s).

Costs (2006–07) *Tuition:* area resident $2130 full-time, $73 per hour part-time; state resident $3870 full-time, $133 per hour part-time; nonresident $5250 full-time, $180 per hour part-time. *Required fees:* $150 full-time, $5 per hour part-time.

Applying *Options:* early admission. *Required:* high school transcript. *Application deadlines:* rolling (freshmen), rolling (transfers).

Freshmen Application Contact Ms. Lisa Minis, Dean of Student Services, Metropolitan Community College–Penn Valley, 3201 Southwest Trafficway, Kansas City, MO 64111. *Phone:* 816-759-4101. *Fax:* 816-759-4478.

MIDWEST INSTITUTE

Earth City, Missouri www.midwestinstitute.com/

Admissions Office Contact Midwest Institute, 4260 Shoreline Drive, Earth City, MO 63045. *Toll-free phone:* 800-695-5550.

MIDWEST INSTITUTE

Kirkwood, Missouri www.midwestinstitute.com/

- **Proprietary** 2-year, founded 1963
- **Coed,** 162 undergraduate students
- 99% of applicants were admitted

Midwest Institute (continued)

Freshmen *Admission:* 150 applied, 148 admitted.
Majors Massage therapy; medical office management.
Academics *Degree:* associate.
Costs (2006–07) *Tuition:* $10,380 full-time.
Applying *Recommended:* high school transcript.
Freshmen Application Contact Admissions Office, Midwest Institute, 10910 Manchester Road, Kirkwood, MO 63122.

MINERAL AREA COLLEGE

Park Hills, Missouri   **www.mineralarea.edu/**

Freshmen Application Contact Mrs. Linda Huffman, Registrar, Mineral Area College, PO Box 1000, Park Hills, MO 63601-1000. *Phone:* 573-518-2130. *Fax:* 573-518-2166. *E-mail:* lhuffman@mineralarea.edu.

MISSOURI COLLEGE

St. Louis, Missouri   **www.mocollege.com/**

Director of Admissions Mr. Doug Brinker, Admissions Director, Missouri College, 10121 Manchester Road, St. Louis, MO 63122-1583. *Phone:* 314-821-7700. *Fax:* 314-821-0891.

MISSOURI STATE UNIVERSITY–WEST PLAINS

West Plains, Missouri   **www.wp.missouristate.edu/**

- **State-supported** 2-year, founded 1963, part of Missouri State University
- **Small-town** 11-acre campus
- **Endowment** $1.6 million
- **Coed,** 1,592 undergraduate students, 50% full-time, 65% women, 35% men

Undergraduates 795 full-time, 797 part-time. Students come from 15 states and territories, 6 other countries, 4% are from out of state, 0.8% African American, 0.9% Asian American or Pacific Islander, 1% Hispanic American, 0.9% Native American, 0.5% international, 3% transferred in, 6% live on campus. *Retention:* 56% of 2003 full-time freshmen returned.
Freshmen *Admission:* 435 applied, 435 admitted, 343 enrolled. *Test scores:* ACT scores over 18: 64%; ACT scores over 24: 13%.
Faculty *Total:* 112, 28% full-time. *Student/faculty ratio:* 17:1.
Majors Accounting; agriculture; business administration and management; business/commerce; computer and information sciences related; computer graphics; computer programming (specific applications); criminal justice/law enforcement administration; criminal justice/police science; engineering; entrepreneurship; fire science; general studies; industrial technology; information technology; legal assistant/paralegal; nursing (registered nurse training); respiratory therapy technician.
Academics *Calendar:* semesters. *Degree:* certificates and associate. *Special study options:* academic remediation for entering students, advanced placement credit, cooperative education, distance learning, honors programs, internships, part-time degree program, services for LD students, study abroad, summer session for credit.
Library Garnett Library with 21,210 titles, 189 serial subscriptions, an OPAC, a Web page.
Student Life *Housing Options:* coed. Campus housing is university owned. *Activities and Organizations:* drama/theater group, choral group, Student Government Association, Chi Alpha, Adult Students in Higher Education, Lambda Lambda Lambda, Programming Board. *Campus security:* late-night transport/escort service, controlled dormitory access. *Student services:* personal/psychological counseling.
Athletics Member NJCAA. *Intercollegiate sports:* basketball M(s), volleyball W(s).
Costs (2007–08) *Tuition:* state resident $3060 full-time, $102 per credit hour part-time; nonresident $6120 full-time, $204 per credit hour part-time. *Required fees:* $244 full-time, $52 per term part-time. *Room and board:* $4632.
Financial Aid Of all full-time matriculated undergraduates, 63 Federal Work-Study jobs (averaging $2000).
Applying *Application fee:* $15. *Required for some:* high school transcript. *Application deadlines:* rolling (freshmen), rolling (transfers).

Freshmen Application Contact Ms. Melissa Jett, Coordinator of Admissions, Missouri State University–West Plains, 128 Garfield, West Plains, MO 65775. *Phone:* 417-255-7955. *Fax:* 417-255-7959. *E-mail:* melissajett@missouristate.edu.

MOBERLY AREA COMMUNITY COLLEGE

Moberly, Missouri   **www.macc.edu/**

- **State and locally supported** 2-year, founded 1927
- **Small-town** 32-acre campus
- **Coed,** 3,710 undergraduate students, 51% full-time, 61% women, 39% men

Undergraduates 1,902 full-time, 1,808 part-time. Students come from 12 states and territories, 1% are from out of state, 6% African American, 1% Asian American or Pacific Islander, 1% Hispanic American, 0.4% Native American, 0.1% international, 3% transferred in, 1% live on campus. *Retention:* 44% of 2003 full-time freshmen returned.
Freshmen *Admission:* 3,878 admitted, 878 enrolled. *Average high school GPA:* 2.85. *Test scores:* ACT scores over 18: 61%; ACT scores over 24: 10%.
Faculty *Total:* 246, 27% full-time, 11% with terminal degrees. *Student/faculty ratio:* 20:1.
Majors Accounting technology and bookkeeping; administrative assistant and secretarial science; child guidance; clinical/medical laboratory technology; computer and information sciences; criminal justice/police science; drafting and design technology; electrical, electronic and communications engineering technology; graphic and printing equipment operation/production; industrial technology; liberal arts and sciences/liberal studies; marketing/marketing management; nursing (registered nurse training); pre-engineering; welding technology.
Academics *Calendar:* semesters. *Degree:* certificates and associate. *Special study options:* academic remediation for entering students, adult/continuing education programs, advanced placement credit, cooperative education, distance learning, honors programs, internships, part-time degree program, services for LD students, study abroad, summer session for credit.
Library Kate Stamper Wilhite Library with 23,027 titles, 88 serial subscriptions, an OPAC, a Web page.
Student Life *Housing Options:* men-only, women-only. Campus housing is university owned. *Activities and Organizations:* drama/theater group, student-run newspaper, choral group, Phi Theta Kappa, Student Nurses Association, Child Care Club, Delta Epsilon Chi, Brother Ox. *Campus security:* student patrols, controlled dormitory access, extensive surveillance.
Athletics Member NJCAA. *Intercollegiate sports:* basketball M(s)/W(s), cheerleading M(s)/W(s). *Intramural sports:* basketball M/W, volleyball M/W.
Standardized Tests *Required for some:* ACT (for admission), ACT ASSET. *Recommended:* ACT (for admission), ACT ASSET.
Costs (2007–08) *Tuition:* area resident $1830 full-time, $61 per credit hour part-time; state resident $2640 full-time, $88 per credit hour part-time; nonresident $4050 full-time, $235 per credit hour part-time. *Required fees:* $330 full-time, $11 per credit hour part-time. *Room and board:* room only: $2200.
Financial Aid Of all full-time matriculated undergraduates, 89 Federal Work-Study jobs (averaging $4193).
Applying *Options:* electronic application. *Required:* high school transcript. *Application deadlines:* rolling (freshmen), rolling (transfers). *Notification:* continuous until 9/1 (freshmen), continuous until 9/1 (transfers).
Freshmen Application Contact Ms. Michele McCall, Dean of Off-Campus Programs and Instructional Technology, Moberly Area Community College, 101 College Avenue, Moberly, MO 65270-1304. *Phone:* 660-263-4110 Ext. 235. *Toll-free phone:* 800-622-2070 Ext. 270. *Fax:* 660-263-2406. *E-mail:* info@macc.edu.

NORTH CENTRAL MISSOURI COLLEGE

Trenton, Missouri   **www.ncmissouri.edu/**

- **District-supported** 2-year, founded 1925
- **Small-town** 2-acre campus
- **Endowment** $443,875
- **Coed,** 1,458 undergraduate students, 52% full-time, 70% women, 30% men

Undergraduates 757 full-time, 701 part-time. Students come from 12 states and territories, 2% are from out of state, 2% African American, 0.4% Asian American or Pacific Islander, 1% Hispanic American, 0.8% Native American, 0.3% international, 5% transferred in, 9% live on campus.
Freshmen *Admission:* 531 applied, 312 admitted, 309 enrolled.
Faculty *Total:* 117, 26% full-time, 5% with terminal degrees. *Student/faculty ratio:* 13:1.

Majors Accounting; administrative assistant and secretarial science; agricultural business and management; automobile/automotive mechanics technology; business administration and management; carpentry; computer engineering technology; construction engineering technology; criminal justice/law enforcement administration; data processing and data processing technology; drafting and design technology; early childhood education; e-commerce; electrical, electronic and communications engineering technology; emergency medical technology (EMT paramedic); farm and ranch management; human services; liberal arts and sciences/liberal studies; marketing/marketing management; medical/clinical assistant; nursing (registered nurse training).

Academics *Calendar:* semesters. *Degree:* certificates and associate. *Special study options:* academic remediation for entering students, accelerated degree program, adult/continuing education programs, advanced placement credit, cooperative education, distance learning, internships, part-time degree program, services for LD students, summer session for credit.

Library North Central Missouri College Library with 34,748 titles, 6,122 serial subscriptions, 1,326 audiovisual materials, an OPAC, a Web page.

Student Life *Housing Options:* men-only, women-only. Campus housing is university owned. *Activities and Organizations:* drama/theater group. *Campus security:* controlled dormitory access. *Student services:* personal/psychological counseling.

Athletics Member NJCAA. *Intercollegiate sports:* baseball M(s), basketball M(s)/W(s), softball W(s).

Standardized Tests *Recommended:* SAT or ACT (for admission), COMPASS.

Costs (2007–08) *Tuition:* area resident $1890 full-time, $63 per credit part-time; state resident $2850 full-time, $95 per credit part-time; nonresident $3930 full-time, $131 per credit part-time. *Required fees:* $540 full-time, $18 per credit part-time. *Room and board:* $4506.

Financial Aid Of all full-time matriculated undergraduates, 40 Federal Work-Study jobs (averaging $1500). 25 state and other part-time jobs (averaging $1200).

Applying *Application fee:* $15. *Required:* high school transcript. *Application deadlines:* rolling (freshmen), rolling (transfers).

Freshmen Application Contact Ms. Susan Moffitt, Admissions Assistant, North Central Missouri College, 1301 Main Street, Trenton, MO 64683. *Phone:* 660-359-3948 Ext. 410. *Toll-free phone:* 800-880-6180 Ext. 401. *E-mail:* smoffitt@mail.ncmissouri.edu.

OZARKS TECHNICAL COMMUNITY COLLEGE

Springfield, Missouri　　　　　**www.otc.edu/**

- **District-supported** 2-year, founded 1990, part of Missouri Coordinating Board for Higher Education
- **Urban** 20-acre campus
- **Endowment** $3867
- **Coed,** 8,488 undergraduate students, 50% full-time, 53% women, 47% men

Undergraduates 4,232 full-time, 4,256 part-time. Students come from 37 states and territories, 2% are from out of state, 2% African American, 1% Asian American or Pacific Islander, 1% Hispanic American, 0.8% Native American, 0.1% international, 38% transferred in.

Freshmen *Admission:* 2,068 enrolled. *Average high school GPA:* 2.5.

Faculty *Total:* 393, 32% full-time.

Majors Accounting; administrative assistant and secretarial science; autobody/collision and repair technology; automobile/automotive mechanics technology; business administration and management; business machine repair; computer systems networking and telecommunications; construction engineering technology; culinary arts; diesel mechanics technology; electrical, electronic and communications engineering technology; emergency medical technology (EMT paramedic); fire science; graphic and printing equipment operation/production; health information/medical records technology; heating, air conditioning, ventilation and refrigeration maintenance technology; heavy equipment maintenance technology; hotel/motel administration; industrial technology; information science/studies; instrumentation technology; kindergarten/preschool education; liberal arts and sciences/liberal studies; machine tool technology; management information systems; mechanical drafting and CAD/CADD; occupational therapist assistant; occupational therapy; physical sciences; physical therapist assistant; radio and television broadcasting technology; respiratory care therapy; turf and turfgrass management; welding technology.

Academics *Calendar:* semesters. *Degree:* certificates, diplomas, and associate. *Special study options:* academic remediation for entering students, adult/continuing education programs, cooperative education, English as a second language, internships, off-campus study, part-time degree program, services for LD students, summer session for credit.

Library Learning Resource Center plus 1 other with 6,000 titles, 190 serial subscriptions, an OPAC.

Student Life *Housing:* college housing not available. *Activities and Organizations:* student-run newspaper, Phi Theta Kappa, Phi Beta Lambda. *Campus security:* 24-hour emergency response devices. *Student services:* personal/psychological counseling.

Athletics *Intramural sports:* cheerleading M/W.

Costs (2006–07) *Tuition:* area resident $2160 full-time; state resident $2640 full-time; nonresident $3360 full-time.

Financial Aid Of all full-time matriculated undergraduates, 168 Federal Work-Study jobs.

Applying *Options:* early admission. *Required:* high school transcript. *Notification:* continuous (freshmen), continuous (transfers).

Director of Admissions Mr. Jeff Jochems, Dean of Student Development, Ozarks Technical Community College, PO Box 5958, 1001 East Chestnut Expressway, Springfield, MO 65801. *Phone:* 417-895-7136.

PATRICIA STEVENS COLLEGE

St. Louis, Missouri　　　　　**www.patriciastevenscollege.edu/**

Freshmen Application Contact Mr. John Willmon, Director of Admissions, Patricia Stevens College, 330 North Fourth Street, Suite 306, St. Louis, MO 63102. *Phone:* 314-421-0949. *Toll-free phone:* 800-871-0949. *Fax:* 314-421-0304. *E-mail:* info@patriciastevenscollege.com.

PINNACLE CAREER INSTITUTE

Kansas City, Missouri　　　　　**www.pcitraining.edu/**

Director of Admissions Ms. Ruth Matous, Director of Admissions, Pinnacle Career Institute, 15329 Kensington Avenue, Kansas City, MO 64147-1212. *Phone:* 816-331-5700 Ext. 212.

RANKEN TECHNICAL COLLEGE

St. Louis, Missouri　　　　　**www.ranken.edu/**

Director of Admissions Ms. Elizabeth Keserauskis, Director of Admissions, Ranken Technical College, 4431 Finney Avenue, St. Louis, MO 63113. *Phone:* 314-371-0233 Ext. 4811. *Toll-free phone:* 866-4RANKEN.

SAINT CHARLES COMMUNITY COLLEGE

St. Peters, Missouri　　　　　**www.stchas.edu/**

- **State-supported** 2-year, founded 1986, part of Missouri Coordinating Board for Higher Education
- **Suburban** 234-acre campus with easy access to St. Louis
- **Endowment** $4.9 million
- **Coed,** 6,844 undergraduate students, 50% full-time, 60% women, 40% men

Undergraduates 3,391 full-time, 3,453 part-time. Students come from 13 states and territories, 31 other countries, 0.3% are from out of state, 4% African American, 2% Asian American or Pacific Islander, 2% Hispanic American, 0.4% Native American, 0.5% international, 5% transferred in.

Freshmen *Admission:* 1,611 applied, 1,611 admitted, 1,510 enrolled.

Faculty *Total:* 442, 19% full-time. *Student/faculty ratio:* 20:1.

Majors Accounting; administrative assistant and secretarial science; business administration and management; child development; commercial and advertising art; computer programming related; computer programming (specific applications); computer science; computer systems networking and telecommunications; criminal justice/law enforcement administration; criminal justice/police science; drafting and design technology; health information/medical records administration; human services; liberal arts and sciences/liberal studies; marketing/marketing management; medical transcription; nursing (registered nurse training); occupational therapy; office management; pre-engineering; web/multimedia management and webmaster.

Academics *Calendar:* semesters. *Degree:* certificates and associate. *Special study options:* academic remediation for entering students, adult/continuing education programs, advanced placement credit, cooperative education, distance learning, double majors, English as a second language, independent study, internships, part-time degree program, services for LD students, study abroad, summer session for credit.

Saint Charles Community College (continued)

Library Learning Resource Center with 89,165 titles, 295 serial subscriptions, 7,200 audiovisual materials, an OPAC, a Web page.

Student Life *Housing:* college housing not available. *Activities and Organizations:* drama/theater group, choral group, Phi Theta Kappa, SCCCC Roller Hockey Club, Student Senate, Criminal Justice Student Organization, Human Services Student Organization. *Campus security:* 24-hour emergency response devices and patrols, late-night transport/escort service. *Student services:* personal/psychological counseling.

Athletics Member NJCAA. *Intercollegiate sports:* baseball M(s), softball W(s). *Intramural sports:* basketball M/W, football M, soccer M/W, softball M/W, volleyball M/W.

Costs (2007–08) *Tuition:* area resident $2400 full-time; state resident $3540 full-time; nonresident $5250 full-time.

Financial Aid Of all full-time matriculated undergraduates, 21 Federal Work-Study jobs (averaging $1848).

Applying *Options:* early admission, deferred entrance. *Required for some:* high school transcript. *Recommended:* high school transcript. *Application deadlines:* rolling (freshmen), rolling (transfers). *Notification:* continuous (freshmen), continuous (transfers).

Freshmen Application Contact Ms. Kathy Brockgreitens, Director of Admissions/Registrar/Financial Assistance, Saint Charles Community College, 4601 Mid Rivers Mall Drive, St. Peters, MO 63376-0975. *Phone:* 636-922-8229. *Fax:* 636-922-8236. *E-mail:* regist@stchas.edu.

ST. LOUIS COLLEGE OF HEALTH CAREERS

St. Louis, Missouri www.slchc.com/

Admissions Office Contact St. Louis College of Health Careers, 909 South Taylor Avenue, St. Louis, MO 63110-1511. *Toll-free phone:* 866-529-7380.

ST. LOUIS COMMUNITY COLLEGE AT FLORISSANT VALLEY

St. Louis, Missouri www.stlcc.edu/

- **District-supported** 2-year, founded 1963, part of St. Louis Community College System
- **Suburban** 108-acre campus
- **Coed**

Undergraduates Students come from 31 other countries.

Majors Accounting; administrative assistant and secretarial science; art; broadcast journalism; business administration and management; chemical engineering; child development; cinematography and film/video production; civil engineering technology; commercial and advertising art; computer engineering technology; computer programming; computer science; construction engineering technology; corrections; criminal justice/law enforcement administration; criminal justice/police science; data processing and data processing technology; dietetics; dramatic/theater arts; electrical, electronic and communications engineering technology; elementary education; emergency medical technology (EMT paramedic); engineering; engineering science; engineering technology; fashion merchandising; finance; fire science; food science; food services technology; human services; information science/studies; journalism; legal studies; liberal arts and sciences/liberal studies; mass communication/media; mathematics; mechanical engineering/mechanical technology; music; nursing (registered nurse training); photography; pre-engineering; radio and television; real estate; sign language interpretation and translation; special products marketing; telecommunications.

Academics *Calendar:* semesters. *Degree:* certificates and associate. *Special study options:* academic remediation for entering students, adult/continuing education programs, advanced placement credit, cooperative education, English as a second language, honors programs, part-time degree program, services for LD students, study abroad, summer session for credit. *ROTC:* Army (c).

Library 90,021 titles, 655 serial subscriptions.

Student Life *Housing:* college housing not available. *Activities and Organizations:* drama/theater group, student-run newspaper, radio station, Phi Theta Kappa, Student Nurses Association, Women in New Goals, Florissant Valley Association of the Deaf, Student Government Association, national fraternities, national sororities. *Campus security:* 24-hour emergency response devices and patrols, late-night transport/escort service. *Student services:* health clinic, personal/psychological counseling.

Athletics Member NAIA, NJCAA. *Intercollegiate sports:* baseball M, basketball M(s)/W(s), cross-country running M(s)/W(s), soccer M(s)/W(s), softball W(s), track and field M(s)/W(s), volleyball W(s). *Intramural sports:* volleyball W.

Costs (2006–07) *Tuition:* $81 per credit hour part-time; state resident $118 per credit hour part-time; nonresident $148 per credit hour part-time.

Applying *Options:* electronic application, early admission. *Required:* high school transcript. *Application deadlines:* 8/19 (freshmen), 8/19 (transfers). *Notification:* continuous (freshmen), continuous (transfers).

Freshmen Application Contact Ms. Brenda Davenport, Manager of Admissions and Registration, St. Louis Community College at Florissant Valley, 3400 Pershall Road, St. Louis, MO 63135-1499. *Phone:* 314-513-4248. *Fax:* 314-513-4724.

ST. LOUIS COMMUNITY COLLEGE AT FOREST PARK

St. Louis, Missouri www.stlcc.edu/

Freshmen Application Contact Mr. Glenn Marshall, Coordinator of Enrollment Services, St. Louis Community College at Forest Park, 5600 Oakland Avenue, St. Louis, MO 63110. *Phone:* 314-644-9125.

ST. LOUIS COMMUNITY COLLEGE AT MERAMEC

Kirkwood, Missouri www.stlcc.edu/

Freshmen Application Contact Mr. Mike Cundiff, Coordinator of Admissions, St. Louis Community College at Meramec, 11333 Big Bend Boulevard, Kirkwood, MO 63122-5720. *Phone:* 314-984-7608.

SANFORD-BROWN COLLEGE

Fenton, Missouri www.sanford-brown.edu/

Director of Admissions Ms. Judy Wilga, Director of Admissions, Sanford-Brown College, 1203 Smizer Mill Road, Fenton, MO 63026. *Phone:* 636-349-4900 Ext. 102. *Toll-free phone:* 800-456-7222. *Fax:* 636-349-9170.

SANFORD-BROWN COLLEGE

Hazelwood, Missouri www.sanford-brown.edu/

Director of Admissions Sherri Bremer, Director of Admissions, Sanford-Brown College, 75 Village Square, Hazelwood, MO 63042. *Phone:* 314-731-5200 Ext. 201.

SANFORD-BROWN COLLEGE

St. Charles, Missouri www.sanford-brown.edu/

Director of Admissions Karl J. Petersen, Executive Director, Sanford-Brown College, 3555 Franks Drive, St. Charles, MO 63301. *Phone:* 636-949-2620. *Toll-free phone:* 800-456-7222. *Fax:* 636-949-5081. *E-mail:* karl.peterson@wix.net.

SOUTHEAST MISSOURI HOSPITAL COLLEGE OF NURSING AND HEALTH SCIENCES

Cape Girardeau, Missouri www.southeastmissourihospital.com/college/

- **Independent** 2-year, founded 1928
- **Rural** campus
- **Coed,** 221 undergraduate students, 93% full-time, 72% women, 28% men

Undergraduates 206 full-time, 15 part-time. Students come from 1 other country, 1% are from out of state, 2% African American, 0.8% international.

Freshmen *Admission:* 36 enrolled. *Test scores:* ACT scores over 18: 100%; ACT scores over 24: 25%; ACT scores over 30: 1%.

Majors Medical radiologic technology; nursing (registered nurse training).

Academics *Calendar:* six 7-week terms per year. *Degree:* associate. *Special study options:* advanced placement credit, study abroad.

Student Life *Housing:* college housing not available. *Campus security:* 24-hour emergency response devices and patrols, late-night transport/escort service.

Standardized Tests *Required:* SAT or ACT (for admission), ACT COMPASS (for admission).

Costs (2007–08) *Tuition:* $10,192 full-time, $300 per credit hour part-time. *Required fees:* $272 full-time, $8 per credit hour part-time.

Applying *Application fee:* $40. *Required:* high school transcript, minimum X GPA, letters of recommendation. *Application deadline:* rolling (freshmen). *Notification:* continuous (freshmen).

Director of Admissions Tonya L. Buttry, President, Southeast Missouri Hospital College of Nursing and Health Sciences, 2001 William Street, Cape Girardeau, MO 63701. *Phone:* 534-334-6825. *E-mail:* tbuttry@sehosp.org.

STATE FAIR COMMUNITY COLLEGE

Sedalia, Missouri   www.sfcc.cc.mo.us/

- **District-supported** 2-year, founded 1966, part of Missouri Coordinating Board for Higher Education
- **Small-town** 128-acre campus
- **Coed,** 3,391 undergraduate students, 50% full-time, 58% women, 42% men

Undergraduates 1,690 full-time, 1,701 part-time. Students come from 16 states and territories, 6% African American, 1% Asian American or Pacific Islander, 3% Hispanic American, 0.5% Native American. *Retention:* 55% of 2003 full-time freshmen returned.

Freshmen *Admission:* 1,215 admitted, 883 enrolled.

Faculty *Total:* 213, 36% full-time. *Student/faculty ratio:* 17:1.

Majors Accounting; administrative assistant and secretarial science; agricultural business and management; agricultural mechanization; agriculture; art; automobile/automotive mechanics technology; business administration and management; computer and information sciences related; computer engineering technology; computer programming (specific applications); computer systems networking and telecommunications; construction engineering technology; court reporting; criminal justice/law enforcement administration; electrical, electronic and communications engineering technology; finance; health information/medical records administration; horticultural science; industrial technology; information science/studies; legal administrative assistant/secretary; liberal arts and sciences/liberal studies; machine tool technology; marketing/marketing management; mass communication/media; medical administrative assistant and medical secretary; nursing (licensed practical/vocational nurse training); nursing (registered nurse training); special products marketing; welding technology.

Academics *Calendar:* semesters. *Degree:* certificates and associate. *Special study options:* academic remediation for entering students, accelerated degree program, adult/continuing education programs, advanced placement credit, distance learning, internships, off-campus study, part-time degree program, services for LD students, summer session for credit.

Library Learning Resources Center with 36,000 titles, 100 serial subscriptions.

Student Life *Housing Options:* coed, men-only, women-only. *Activities and Organizations:* drama/theater group, choral group. *Campus security:* security during evening class hours.

Athletics *Member NJCAA. Intercollegiate sports:* basketball M(s)/W(s), soccer M(s), volleyball W.

Costs (2006–07) *Tuition:* area resident $2190 full-time; state resident $2700 full-time; nonresident $4590 full-time.

Financial Aid Of all full-time matriculated undergraduates, 40 Federal Work-Study jobs (averaging $2600).

Applying *Options:* early admission. *Application fee:* $25. *Required:* high school transcript. *Application deadlines:* rolling (freshmen), rolling (transfers).

Director of Admissions Mrs. Sharon Peacock, Registrar, State Fair Community College, 3201 West 16th, Sedalia, MO 65301. *Phone:* 660-530-5800 Ext. 293. *Toll-free phone:* 877-311-7322 Ext. 217 (in-state); 877-311-7322 (out-of-state).

THREE RIVERS COMMUNITY COLLEGE

Poplar Bluff, Missouri   www.trcc.edu/

- **State and locally supported** 2-year, founded 1966, part of Missouri Coordinating Board for Higher Education
- **Rural** 70-acre campus
- **Endowment** $672,169
- **Coed,** 2,996 undergraduate students, 56% full-time, 69% women, 31% men

Undergraduates 1,691 full-time, 1,305 part-time. Students come from 9 states and territories, 2% are from out of state, 8% African American, 0.3% Asian American or Pacific Islander, 1% Hispanic American, 0.6% Native American, 6% live on campus.

Freshmen *Admission:* 658 applied, 658 admitted, 658 enrolled.

Faculty *Total:* 171, 36% full-time, 8% with terminal degrees. *Student/faculty ratio:* 22:1.

Majors Accounting; administrative assistant and secretarial science; agricultural business and management; agricultural mechanization; business administration and management; clinical/medical laboratory technology; computer and information sciences related; computer engineering technology; computer/technical support; construction engineering technology; criminal justice/law enforcement administration; criminal justice/police science; data entry/microcomputer applications; data entry/microcomputer applications related; education; elementary education; engineering technology; industrial technology; information technology; liberal arts and sciences/liberal studies; marketing/marketing management; music; nursing (registered nurse training); word processing.

Academics *Calendar:* semesters. *Degree:* certificates and associate. *Special study options:* academic remediation for entering students, accelerated degree program, adult/continuing education programs, advanced placement credit, distance learning, double majors, English as a second language, external degree program, honors programs, independent study, internships, part-time degree program, services for LD students, summer session for credit.

Library Rutland Library with 35,629 titles, 185 serial subscriptions, 1,095 audiovisual materials, an OPAC, a Web page.

Student Life *Housing Options:* coed. Campus housing is university owned. *Activities and Organizations:* student government, PTK, PBL, Alpha Beta Gamma, Lambda Alpha Epsilon. *Campus security:* 24-hour patrols.

Athletics Member NJCAA. *Intercollegiate sports:* baseball M(s), basketball M(s)/W(s), cheerleading M(s)/W(s), softball W(s), volleyball W(s).

Costs (2007–08) *Tuition:* area resident $1920 full-time, $64 per credit hour part-time; state resident $3090 full-time, $98 per credit hour part-time; nonresident $3840 full-time, $122 per credit hour part-time. *Required fees:* $575 full-time, $14 per credit hour part-time. *Room and board:* room only: $3114.

Applying *Options:* early admission. *Application fee:* $20. *Required:* high school transcript.

Freshmen Application Contact Ms. Marcia Fields, Director of Admissions and Recruiting, Three Rivers Community College, 2080 Three Rivers Boulevard, Poplar Bluff, MO 63901. *Phone:* 573-840-9675. *Toll-free phone:* 877-TRY-TRCC Ext. 605 (in-state); 877-TRY-TRCC (out-of-state). *E-mail:* trytrcc@trcc.edu.

VATTEROTT COLLEGE

Kansas City, Missouri   www.vatterott-college.edu/

- **Proprietary** 2-year
- **Coed,** 702 undergraduate students
- 84% of applicants were admitted

Freshmen *Admission:* 171 applied, 143 admitted.

Majors Administrative assistant and secretarial science; CAD/CADD drafting/design technology; computer programming; electrician; heating, air conditioning and refrigeration technology; medical/clinical assistant; pharmacy technician; plumbing technology; system administration; system, networking, and LAN/WAN management; web page, digital/multimedia and information resources design.

Academics *Calendar:* semesters. *Degree:* associate.

Costs (2006–07) *Tuition:* $10,168 full-time.

Admissions Office Contact Vatterott College, 8955 East 38th Terrace, Kansas City, MO 64129. *Toll-free phone:* 866-314-6454.

VATTEROTT COLLEGE

O'Fallon, Missouri   www.vatterott-college.edu/

Admissions Office Contact Vatterott College, 927 East Terra Lane, O'Fallon, MO 63366. *Toll-free phone:* 866-314-6454.

VATTEROTT COLLEGE

St. Ann, Missouri   www.vatterott-college.edu/

Director of Admissions Mrs. Shari H. Cobb, Director of Admissions, Vatterott College, 3925 Industrial Drive, St. Ann, MO 63074-1807. *Phone:* 314-428-5900 Ext. 215. *Toll-free phone:* 800-345-6018.

VATTEROTT COLLEGE

St. Joseph, Missouri   www.vatterott-college.edu/

Director of Admissions Ms. Sandra Wisdom, Director of Admissions, Vatterott College, 3131 Frederick Avenue, St. Joseph, MO 64506. *Phone:* 816-364-5399 Ext. 110. *Toll-free phone:* 800-282-5327.

VATTEROTT COLLEGE

Sunset Hills, Missouri   www.vatterott-college.edu/

Director of Admissions Ms. Michelle Tinsley, Director of Admission, Vatterott College, 12970 Maurer Industrial Drive, St. Louis, MO 63127. *Phone:* 314-843-4200.

VATTEROTT COLLEGE

Springfield, Missouri   www.vatterott-college.edu/

Freshmen Application Contact Ms. Abby Thornton, High School Relations Representative, Vatterott College, 3850 South Campbell, Springfield, MO 65807. *Phone:* 417-831-8116. *Toll-free phone:* 800-766-5829. *Fax:* 417-831-5099. *E-mail:* springfield@vatterott-college.edu.

WENTWORTH MILITARY ACADEMY AND JUNIOR COLLEGE

Lexington, Missouri   www.wma1880.org/

- **Independent** 2-year, founded 1880
- **Small-town** 130-acre campus with easy access to Kansas City
- **Coed**

Undergraduates 234 full-time, 327 part-time. Students come from 22 states and territories, 4 other countries, 18% are from out of state, 4% African American, 3% Asian American or Pacific Islander, 2% Hispanic American, 0.2% Native American, 0.4% international, 0.2% transferred in.

Faculty *Student/faculty ratio:* 10:1.

Academics *Calendar:* semesters. *Degree:* associate. *Special study options:* academic remediation for entering students, adult/continuing education programs, advanced placement credit, English as a second language, part-time degree program, student-designed majors, summer session for credit. *ROTC:* Army (b).

Student Life *Campus security:* 24-hour emergency response devices and patrols.

Athletics Member NJCAA.

Standardized Tests *Required for some:* SAT or ACT (for admission). *Recommended:* SAT or ACT (for admission).

Costs (2006–07) *One-time required fee:* $25. *Tuition:* $3480 full-time, $145 per hour part-time.

Applying *Application fee:* $100. *Required:* high school transcript.

Freshmen Application Contact Dr. Roger Hamilton, Vice President for Academic Affairs, Wentworth Military Academy and Junior College, 1880 Washington Avenue, Lexington, MO 64067. *Phone:* 660-259-2221. *Fax:* 660-259-2677. *E-mail:* admissions@wma1880.org.

MONTANA

BLACKFEET COMMUNITY COLLEGE

Browning, Montana   www.bfcc.org/

Freshmen Application Contact Ms. Deana M. McNabb, Registrar and Admissions Officer, Blackfeet Community College, PO Box 819, Browning, MT 59417. *Phone:* 406-338-5421. *Toll-free phone:* 800-549-7457. *Fax:* 406-338-3272. *E-mail:* helen_morris@bfcc.org.

CHIEF DULL KNIFE COLLEGE

Lame Deer, Montana   www.cdkc.edu/

- **Independent** 2-year, founded 1975
- **Rural** 3-acre campus
- **Coed,** 460 undergraduate students

Faculty *Total:* 30, 27% full-time.

Majors Administrative assistant and secretarial science; agriculture; business administration and management; health science; liberal arts and sciences/liberal studies; mental health/rehabilitation; natural resources management and policy; office management.

Academics *Calendar:* semesters. *Degree:* certificates and associate. *Special study options:* academic remediation for entering students, adult/continuing education programs, cooperative education, internships, off-campus study, part-time degree program, services for LD students, summer session for credit.

Library 10,000 titles, 128 serial subscriptions.

Student Life *Housing:* college housing not available. *Activities and Organizations:* student-run newspaper. *Student services:* personal/psychological counseling.

Athletics *Intramural sports:* basketball M/W, volleyball M/W.

Standardized Tests *Required:* ACT ASSET (for placement). *Recommended:* ACT (for placement).

Costs (2006–07) *Tuition:* state resident $2260 full-time.

Financial Aid Of all full-time matriculated undergraduates, 10 Federal Work-Study jobs (averaging $1000).

Applying *Options:* early admission. *Required:* high school transcript. *Application deadlines:* rolling (freshmen), rolling (transfers). *Notification:* continuous (freshmen), continuous (transfers).

Director of Admissions Mr. William L. Wertman, Registrar and Director of Admissions, Chief Dull Knife College, PO Box 98, 1 College Drive, Lame Deer, MT 59043-0098. *Phone:* 406-477-6215.

DAWSON COMMUNITY COLLEGE

Glendive, Montana   www.dawson.edu/

Director of Admissions Ms. Jolene Myers, Director of Admissions and Financial Aid, Dawson Community College, Box 421, Glendive, MT 59330-0421. *Phone:* 406-377-3396 Ext. 410. *Toll-free phone:* 800-821-8320.

FLATHEAD VALLEY COMMUNITY COLLEGE

Kalispell, Montana   www.fvcc.edu/

Freshmen Application Contact Ms. Marlene C. Stoltz, Admissions/Graduation Coordinator, Flathead Valley Community College, 777 Grandview Avenue, Kalispell, MT 59901-2622. *Phone:* 406-756-3846. *Toll-free phone:* 800-313-3822. *E-mail:* mstoltz@fvcc.cc.mt.us.

FORT BELKNAP COLLEGE

Harlem, Montana   www.fbcc.edu/

- **Federally supported** 2-year, founded 1984
- **Rural** 3-acre campus
- **Endowment** $291,263
- **Coed,** 158 undergraduate students, 74% full-time, 70% women, 30% men

Undergraduates 117 full-time, 41 part-time. Students come from 1 other state, 95% Native American.

Freshmen *Admission:* 43 enrolled. *Average high school GPA:* 2.0.

Faculty *Total:* 28, 29% full-time.

Majors Administrative assistant and secretarial science; American Indian/Native American studies; business/commerce; data processing and data processing technology; elementary education; kindergarten/preschool education; liberal arts and sciences/liberal studies; natural resources management and policy; pre-engineering.

Academics *Calendar:* quarters. *Degree:* certificates and associate. *Special study options:* academic remediation for entering students, cooperative education, part-time degree program.

Library Fort Belknap College Library with 16,000 titles, 95 serial subscriptions, an OPAC, a Web page.

Student Life *Housing:* college housing not available. *Activities and Organizations:* student-run radio station, student government, Red Nations Society Indian Club, American Indian Business Leaders, American Indians Society in Engineering and Science. *Campus security:* 24-hour patrols.

Athletics *Intercollegiate sports:* basketball M/W, cross-country running M/W, volleyball M/W. *Intramural sports:* basketball M/W, cross-country running M/W, volleyball M/W.

Standardized Tests *Required:* TABE (for placement).

Costs (2006–07) *Tuition:* state resident $3280 full-time.

Applying *Options:* early admission, deferred entrance. *Application fee:* $10. *Required:* high school transcript. *Application deadlines:* rolling (freshmen), rolling (transfers). *Notification:* continuous (freshmen), continuous (transfers).

Director of Admissions Ms. Dixie Brockie, Registrar and Admissions Officer, Fort Belknap College, PO Box 159, Harlem, MT 59526-0159. *Phone:* 406-353-2607 Ext. 219. *Fax:* 406-353-2898.

FORT PECK COMMUNITY COLLEGE

Poplar, Montana   www.fpcc.edu/

Director of Admissions Mr. Robert McAnally, Vice President for Student Services, Fort Peck Community College, PO Box 398, Poplar, MT 59255-0398. *Phone:* 406-768-6329.

LITTLE BIG HORN COLLEGE

Crow Agency, Montana   www.lbhc.cc.mt.us/

- **Independent** 2-year, founded 1980
- **Rural** 5-acre campus
- **Coed,** 317 undergraduate students

Undergraduates Students come from 1 other state.

Faculty *Total:* 12, 92% full-time. *Student/faculty ratio:* 25:1.

Majors Biological and physical sciences; business administration and management; carpentry; computer science; elementary education; liberal arts and sciences/liberal studies; mathematics.

Academics *Calendar:* quarters. *Degree:* certificates and associate. *Special study options:* off-campus study, part-time degree program.

Student Life *Housing:* college housing not available. *Activities and Organizations:* student-run newspaper.

Athletics *Intercollegiate sports:* basketball M/W. *Intramural sports:* basketball M/W.

Standardized Tests *Required:* ACT ASSET (for placement).

Costs (2006–07) *Tuition:* state resident $2780 full-time.

Applying *Required:* high school transcript. *Application deadlines:* rolling (freshmen), rolling (transfers). *Notification:* continuous (freshmen), continuous (transfers).

Freshmen Application Contact Ms. Ann Bullis, Dean of Student Services, Little Big Horn College, Box 370, 1 Forest Lane, Crow Agency, MT 59022-0370. *Phone:* 406-638-2228 Ext. 50.

MILES COMMUNITY COLLEGE

Miles City, Montana   www.milescc.edu/

Director of Admissions Ms. Laura J. Pierce, Chief Student Services Officer, Miles Community College, 2715 Dickinson, Miles City, MT 59301-4799. *Phone:* 406-874-6159. *Toll-free phone:* 800-541-9281.

MONTANA STATE UNIVERSITY–GREAT FALLS COLLEGE OF TECHNOLOGY

Great Falls, Montana   www.msugf.edu/

Freshmen Application Contact L. Gleason, Registrar, Montana State University–Great Falls College of Technology, 2100 16th Avenue South, Great Falls, MT 59405. *Phone:* 406-771-4300. *Toll-free phone:* 800-446-2698. *Fax:* 406-771-4317. *E-mail:* information@msugf.edu.

SALISH KOOTENAI COLLEGE

Pablo, Montana   www.skc.edu/

- **Independent** primarily 2-year, founded 1977
- **Rural** 4-acre campus
- **Coed,** 1,088 undergraduate students, 54% full-time, 61% women, 39% men

Undergraduates 585 full-time, 503 part-time. Students come from 3 states and territories, 0.2% African American, 0.3% Hispanic American, 79% Native American.

Freshmen *Admission:* 344 applied, 221 admitted, 108 enrolled.

Faculty *Total:* 80, 56% full-time.

Majors Administrative assistant and secretarial science; American Indian/Native American studies; carpentry; child development; computer science; dental hygiene; environmental studies; forestry; forestry technology; human services; kindergarten/preschool education; liberal arts and sciences/liberal studies; natural resources management and policy; natural sciences; nursing (registered nurse training).

Academics *Calendar:* quarters. *Degrees:* certificates, associate, and bachelor's. *Special study options:* academic remediation for entering students, adult/continuing education programs, cooperative education, off-campus study, part-time degree program, services for LD students, summer session for credit.

Library 24,000 titles, 200 serial subscriptions.

Student Life *Activities and Organizations:* drama/theater group. *Student services:* personal/psychological counseling.

Athletics *Intramural sports:* baseball M/W, basketball M/W, skiing (cross-country) M/W, skiing (downhill) M/W, softball M/W, tennis M/W, volleyball M/W, weight lifting M/W.

Standardized Tests *Required:* TABE (for placement).

Costs (2006–07) *Tuition:* area resident $2664 full-time, $74 per credit part-time; state resident $4572 full-time, $127 per credit part-time; nonresident $9144 full-time, $254 per credit part-time. Full-time tuition and fees vary according to course load. Part-time tuition and fees vary according to course load. *Required fees:* $789 full-time, $95 per credit part-time. *Room and board:* $6975. *Payment plan:* installment. *Waivers:* senior citizens.

Financial Aid Of all full-time matriculated undergraduates, 57 Federal Work-Study jobs (averaging $1327).

Applying *Options:* deferred entrance. *Required:* high school transcript, proof of immunization, tribal enrollment. *Application deadlines:* rolling (freshmen), rolling (transfers). *Notification:* continuous (freshmen), continuous (transfers).

Freshmen Application Contact Ms. Jackie Moran, Admissions Officer, Salish Kootenai College, 52000 Highway 93, PO Box 70, Pablo, MT 59855. *Phone:* 406-275-4866. *Fax:* 406-275-4810. *E-mail:* jackie_moran@skc.edu.

STONE CHILD COLLEGE

Box Elder, Montana   www.montana.edu/wwwscc/

- **Independent** 2-year, founded 1984
- **Rural** campus
- **Coed,** 240 undergraduate students

Freshmen *Admission:* 11 applied, 11 admitted.

Faculty *Total:* 22, 45% full-time.

Majors Administrative assistant and secretarial science; business administration and management; computer science; human services; liberal arts and sciences/liberal studies.

Academics *Calendar:* semesters. *Degree:* certificates and associate.

Costs (2006–07) *Tuition:* state resident $2370 full-time.

Applying *Application fee:* $10. *Required:* high school transcript.

Director of Admissions Mr. Ted Whitford, Director of Admissions/Registrar, Stone Child College, RR1, Box 1082, Box Elder, MT 59521. *Phone:* 406-395-4313 Ext. 110. *E-mail:* uanet337@quest.ocsc.montana.edu.

THE UNIVERSITY OF MONTANA-HELENA COLLEGE OF TECHNOLOGY

Helena, Montana   www.umhelena.edu/

- **State-supported** 2-year, founded 1939, part of Montana University System
- **Small-town** campus
- **Coed,** 850 undergraduate students

Faculty *Total:* 80, 63% full-time. *Student/faculty ratio:* 18:1.

Majors Accounting technology and bookkeeping; agricultural mechanization; airframe mechanics and aircraft maintenance technology; automobile/automotive mechanics technology; business automation/technology/data entry; carpentry; computer programming; diesel mechanics technology; electrical, electronic and communications engineering technology; executive assistant/executive secretary; fire science; general studies; legal administrative assistant/secretary; machine tool technology; medical administrative assistant and medical secretary; nursing (licensed practical/vocational nurse training); office occupations and clerical services; welding technology.

Academics *Calendar:* semesters. *Degree:* certificates and associate. *Special study options:* academic remediation for entering students, adult/continuing education programs, part-time degree program, services for LD students, summer session for credit.

Library 2,500 titles, 30 serial subscriptions.

Student Life *Housing:* college housing not available. *Activities and Organizations:* Student Senate.

Athletics *Intramural sports:* basketball M/W, volleyball M/W.

Standardized Tests *Required:* ACT ASSET (for placement).

Financial Aid Of all full-time matriculated undergraduates, 60 Federal Work-Study jobs (averaging $1500). 15 state and other part-time jobs (averaging $1500).

Applying *Options:* early admission, deferred entrance. *Application fee:* $30. *Application deadlines:* rolling (freshmen), rolling (transfers).

Director of Admissions Ms. Vicki Cavanaugh, Director of Admissions, The University of Montana-Helena College of Technology, 1115 North Roberts Street, Helena, MT 59601. *Phone:* 406-444-6800. *Toll-free phone:* 800-241-4882.

NEBRASKA

CENTRAL COMMUNITY COLLEGE— COLUMBUS CAMPUS

Columbus, Nebraska   www.cccneb.edu/

- **State and locally supported** 2-year, founded 1968, part of Central Community College
- **Small-town** 90-acre campus
- **Coed,** 2,091 undergraduate students, 21% full-time, 63% women, 37% men

Undergraduates 445 full-time, 1,646 part-time. Students come from 21 states and territories, 4% are from out of state, 0.8% African American, 1% Asian American or Pacific Islander, 6% Hispanic American, 0.4% Native American, 2% transferred in, 17% live on campus.

Freshmen *Admission:* 309 enrolled.

Faculty *Total:* 89, 43% full-time, 6% with terminal degrees. *Student/faculty ratio:* 15:1.

Majors Accounting; administrative assistant and secretarial science; agricultural business and management; automobile/automotive mechanics technology; business administration and management; commercial and advertising art; computer and information sciences; computer programming (specific applications); drafting and design technology; electrical, electronic and communications engineering technology; electromechanical technology; family and consumer sciences/human sciences; industrial technology; information technology; liberal arts and sciences/liberal studies; machine tool technology; marketing/marketing management; nursing (licensed practical/vocational nurse training); quality control technology; system administration; web/multimedia management and webmaster; welding technology.

Academics *Calendar:* semesters plus six-week summer session. *Degree:* certificates, diplomas, and associate. *Special study options:* academic remediation for entering students, accelerated degree program, adult/continuing education

programs, advanced placement credit, cooperative education, distance learning, English as a second language, external degree program, independent study, internships, off-campus study, part-time degree program, services for LD students, student-designed majors, summer session for credit.

Library Learning Resources Center with 22,000 titles, 118 serial subscriptions, an OPAC.

Student Life *Housing Options:* coed. Campus housing is university owned. *Activities and Organizations:* choral group, Phi Theta Kappa, Drama Club, Art Club, Cantari, Chorale. *Campus security:* 24-hour emergency response devices and patrols, controlled dormitory access, night security. *Student services:* personal/psychological counseling, women's center.

Athletics Member NJCAA. *Intercollegiate sports:* basketball M(s), volleyball W(s). *Intramural sports:* basketball M/W, football M, softball M/W, table tennis M/W, volleyball M/W.

Costs (2007–08) *Tuition:* state resident $1584 full-time, $66 per credit part-time; nonresident $2376 full-time, $99 per credit part-time. *Required fees:* $168 full-time, $7 per credit part-time. *Room and board:* $3944.

Applying *Options:* electronic application, early admission. *Required:* high school transcript. *Required for some:* 3 letters of recommendation, interview. *Application deadlines:* rolling (freshmen), rolling (transfers). *Notification:* continuous (freshmen), continuous (transfers).

Freshmen Application Contact Ms. Mary Young, Records Coordinator, Central Community College–Columbus Campus, PO Box 1027, Columbus, NE 68602-1027. *Phone:* 402-562-1296. *Toll-free phone:* 800-642-1083. *Fax:* 402-562-1201. *E-mail:* myoung@cccneb.edu.

CENTRAL COMMUNITY COLLEGE— GRAND ISLAND CAMPUS

Grand Island, Nebraska   www.cccneb.edu/

- **State and locally supported** 2-year, founded 1976, part of Central Community College
- **Small-town** 64-acre campus
- **Coed,** 2,890 undergraduate students, 16% full-time, 67% women, 33% men

Undergraduates 458 full-time, 2,432 part-time. Students come from 22 states and territories, 1 other country, 4% are from out of state, 0.8% African American, 2% Asian American or Pacific Islander, 8% Hispanic American, 0.4% Native American, 2% transferred in, 10% live on campus.

Freshmen *Admission:* 364 enrolled.

Faculty *Total:* 112, 38% full-time, 4% with terminal degrees. *Student/faculty ratio:* 15:1.

Majors Accounting; administrative assistant and secretarial science; automobile/automotive mechanics technology; business administration and management; child development; clinical/medical social work; computer and information sciences; computer programming (specific applications); criminal justice/safety; data processing and data processing technology; drafting and design technology; electrical, electronic and communications engineering technology; heating, air conditioning, ventilation and refrigeration maintenance technology; industrial technology; information technology; legal assistant/paralegal; liberal arts and sciences/liberal studies; nursing (licensed practical/vocational nurse training); nursing (registered nurse training); system administration; web/multimedia management and webmaster; welding technology.

Academics *Calendar:* semesters plus six-week summer session. *Degree:* certificates, diplomas, and associate. *Special study options:* academic remediation for entering students, accelerated degree program, adult/continuing education programs, advanced placement credit, cooperative education, distance learning, English as a second language, external degree program, independent study, internships, off-campus study, part-time degree program, services for LD students, student-designed majors, summer session for credit.

Library Central Community College–Grand Island Campus Library with 5,700 titles, 94 serial subscriptions, an OPAC, a Web page.

Student Life *Housing Options:* coed. Campus housing is provided by a third party. Freshman applicants given priority for college housing. *Activities and Organizations:* Mid-Nebraska Users of Computers, Student Activities Organization, intramurals. *Student services:* personal/psychological counseling.

Athletics *Intramural sports:* bowling M/W, table tennis M/W, volleyball M/W.

Costs (2007–08) *Tuition:* state resident $1584 full-time, $66 per credit part-time; nonresident $2376 full-time, $99 per credit part-time. *Required fees:* $168 full-time, $7 per credit part-time. *Room and board:* $3944.

Financial Aid Of all full-time matriculated undergraduates, 50 Federal Work-Study jobs (averaging $1000). 20 state and other part-time jobs (averaging $1000).

Applying *Options:* electronic application, early admission. *Required:* high school transcript. *Required for some:* 3 letters of recommendation, interview.

Application deadlines: rolling (freshmen), rolling (transfers). *Notification:* continuous (freshmen), continuous (transfers).

Freshmen Application Contact Ms. Liz Kohout, Admissions Director, Central Community College–Grand Island Campus, PO Box 4903, Grand Island, NE 68802-4903. *Phone:* 308-398-7406 Ext. 406. *Toll-free phone:* 800-652-9177. *Fax:* 308-398-7398. *E-mail:* lkohout@cccneb.edu.

CENTRAL COMMUNITY COLLEGE– HASTINGS CAMPUS

Hastings, Nebraska www.cccneb.edu/

- **State and locally supported** 2-year, founded 1966, part of Central Community College
- **Small-town** 600-acre campus
- **Coed,** 2,485 undergraduate students, 37% full-time, 56% women, 44% men

Undergraduates 928 full-time, 1,557 part-time. Students come from 36 states and territories, 4% are from out of state, 0.6% African American, 0.8% Asian American or Pacific Islander, 5% Hispanic American, 0.3% Native American, 0.1% international, 3% transferred in, 26% live on campus.

Freshmen *Admission:* 464 enrolled.

Faculty *Total:* 90, 68% full-time, 4% with terminal degrees. *Student/faculty ratio:* 15:1.

Majors Accounting; administrative assistant and secretarial science; agricultural business and management; applied horticulture; autobody/collision and repair technology; automobile/automotive mechanics technology; business administration and management; child development; clinical/medical social work; commercial and advertising art; computer and information sciences; computer programming (specific applications); construction engineering technology; dental assisting; dental hygiene; diesel mechanics technology; drafting and design technology; electrical, electronic and communications engineering technology; graphic and printing equipment operation/production; health information/medical records technology; heating, air conditioning, ventilation and refrigeration maintenance technology; hospital and health care facilities administration; hospitality administration; hotel/motel administration; industrial technology; information technology; liberal arts and sciences/liberal studies; machine tool technology; mass communication/media; medical administrative assistant and medical secretary; medical/clinical assistant; radio and television broadcasting technology; system administration; vehicle/petroleum products marketing; web/multimedia management and webmaster; welding technology.

Academics *Calendar:* semesters plus six-week summer session. *Degree:* certificates, diplomas, and associate. *Special study options:* academic remediation for entering students, accelerated degree program, adult/continuing education programs, advanced placement credit, cooperative education, distance learning, English as a second language, external degree program, independent study, internships, off-campus study, part-time degree program, services for LD students, student-designed majors, summer session for credit.

Library Nuckolls Library with 4,025 titles, 52 serial subscriptions, an OPAC.

Student Life *Housing Options:* coed, men-only, women-only. Campus housing is university owned. *Activities and Organizations:* student-run radio station, Student Senate, Central Dormitory Council, Judicial Board, Seeds and Soils, Young Farmers and Ranchers. *Campus security:* 24-hour emergency response devices and patrols, controlled dormitory access. *Student services:* personal/psychological counseling, women's center.

Athletics *Intramural sports:* basketball M/W, bowling M/W, golf M/W, softball M/W, volleyball M/W, weight lifting M/W.

Costs (2007–08) *Tuition:* state resident $1584 full-time, $66 per credit part-time; nonresident $2376 full-time, $99 per credit part-time. *Required fees:* $168 full-time, $7 per credit part-time. *Room and board:* $3944.

Financial Aid Of all full-time matriculated undergraduates, 70 Federal Work-Study jobs (averaging $1200). 12 state and other part-time jobs (averaging $1250).

Applying *Options:* electronic application, early admission. *Required:* high school transcript. *Required for some:* 3 letters of recommendation, interview. *Application deadlines:* rolling (freshmen), rolling (transfers). *Notification:* continuous (freshmen), continuous (transfers).

Freshmen Application Contact Mr. Robert Glenn, Admissions and Recruiting Director, Central Community College–Hastings Campus, PO Box 1024, East Highway 6, Hastings, NE 68902-1024. *Phone:* 402-461-2428. *Toll-free phone:* 800-742-7872. *E-mail:* rglenn@ccneb.edu.

THE CREATIVE CENTER

Omaha, Nebraska www.thecreativecenter.com/

- **Proprietary** 2-year, founded 1993
- **Urban** 1-acre campus
- **Coed,** 100 undergraduate students, 100% full-time, 42% women, 58% men

Undergraduates 100 full-time.

Faculty *Total:* 11, 36% full-time. *Student/faculty ratio:* 16:1.

Majors Computer graphics; design and visual communications; illustration.

Academics *Calendar:* semesters. *Degree:* associate. *Special study options:* distance learning, part-time degree program, services for LD students.

Library Student Library plus 1 other.

Student Life *Housing:* college housing not available.

Applying *Application fee:* $100. *Required:* essay or personal statement, high school transcript, 1 letter of recommendation, interview, portfolio.

Freshmen Application Contact Admissions and Placement Coordinator, The Creative Center, 10850 Emmet Street, Omaha, NE 68164. *Phone:* 402-898-1000. *Toll-free phone:* 888-898-1789. *Fax:* 402-898-1301. *E-mail:* admission@creativecenter.edu.

HAMILTON COLLEGE-LINCOLN

Lincoln, Nebraska www.hamiltonlincoln.com/

Director of Admissions Mr. Andy Bossler, Director of Admissions, Hamilton College-Lincoln, 1821 K Street, Lincoln, NE 68508. *Phone:* 402-474-5315. *Toll-free phone:* 800-742-7738. *Fax:* 402-474-5302. *E-mail:* losc@ix.netcom.com.

HAMILTON COLLEGE-OMAHA

Omaha, Nebraska www.hamiltonomaha.edu/

Director of Admissions Mr. Mark Stoltenberger, Director of Admissions, Hamilton College-Omaha, 3350 North 90 Street, Omaha, NE 68134. *Phone:* 402-572-8500. *Toll-free phone:* 800-642-1456.

ITT TECHNICAL INSTITUTE

Omaha, Nebraska www.itt-tech.edu/

- **Proprietary** primarily 2-year, founded 1991, part of ITT Educational Services, Inc
- **Urban** 1-acre campus
- **Coed**

Majors Accounting technology and bookkeeping; animation, interactive technology, video graphics and special effects; business administration and management; CAD/CADD drafting/design technology; communications technology; computer and information systems security; computer engineering technology; computer software engineering; computer software technology; computer systems networking and telecommunications; criminal justice/law enforcement administration; electrical, electronic and communications engineering technology; web/multimedia management and webmaster; web page, digital/multimedia and information resources design.

Academics *Calendar:* quarters. *Degrees:* associate and bachelor's.

Library a Web page.

Student Life *Housing:* college housing not available.

Standardized Tests *Required:* Wonderlic aptitude test (for admission).

Costs (2006–07) *Tuition:* Contact school for program costs.

Applying *Options:* deferred entrance. *Application fee:* $100. *Required:* high school transcript, interview. *Recommended:* letters of recommendation. *Application deadlines:* rolling (freshmen), rolling (transfers). *Notification:* continuous (freshmen), continuous (transfers).

Freshmen Application Contact Schon Nielson, Director of Recruitment, ITT Technical Institute, 9814 M Street, Omaha, NE 68127. *Phone:* 402-331-2900. *Toll-free phone:* 800-677-9260.

LITTLE PRIEST TRIBAL COLLEGE

Winnebago, Nebraska   **www.lptc.bia.edu/**

Director of Admissions Ms. Karen Kemling, Director of Admissions and Records, Little Priest Tribal College, PO Box 270, Winnebago, NE 68071. *Phone:* 402-878-2380.

METROPOLITAN COMMUNITY COLLEGE

Omaha, Nebraska   **www.mccneb.edu/**

- **State and locally supported** 2-year, founded 1974, part of Nebraska Coordinating Commission for Postsecondary Education
- **Urban** 172-acre campus
- **Endowment** $1.4 million
- **Coed,** 14,098 undergraduate students, 39% full-time, 56% women, 44% men

Metropolitan Community College (MCC) is a full-service, comprehensive public institution that serves more than 46,000 students annually. Located in Omaha, Nebraska, MCC provides personalized services and high-quality programs in business administration, computer and office technologies, culinary arts, industrial and construction technologies, nursing and allied health, social sciences and services, and visual and electronic technologies as well as academic transfer programs at seven convenient locations. In addition, the College provides education that accommodates many schedules with on-campus, online, weekend, and evening classes. Prospective students should call MCC at 800-228-9553 (toll-free) or visit the College's Web site at http://www.mccneb.edu. Student housing is now available on MCC's historic Fort Omaha campus, 30th and Fort Streets (http://www.mccneb.edu/studenthousing).

Undergraduates 5,472 full-time, 8,626 part-time. Students come from 31 states and territories, 3% are from out of state, 11% African American, 4% Asian American or Pacific Islander, 6% Hispanic American, 0.8% Native American, 0.1% international, 21% transferred in. *Retention:* 50% of 2003 full-time freshmen returned.

Freshmen *Admission:* 4,141 applied, 4,141 admitted, 1,588 enrolled.

Faculty *Total:* 877, 23% full-time, 6% with terminal degrees. *Student/faculty ratio:* 16:1.

Majors Accounting; administrative assistant and secretarial science; architectural engineering technology; automobile/automotive mechanics technology; business administration and management; child development; civil engineering technology; commercial and advertising art; computer programming; construction engineering technology; criminal justice/police science; culinary arts; drafting and design technology; electrical, electronic and communications engineering technology; graphic and printing equipment operation/production; heating, air conditioning, ventilation and refrigeration maintenance technology; heavy equipment maintenance technology; human services; interior design; kindergarten/preschool education; legal administrative assistant/secretary; legal assistant/paralegal; legal studies; liberal arts and sciences/liberal studies; mental health/rehabilitation; nursing (licensed practical/vocational nurse training); nursing (registered nurse training); ornamental horticulture; photography; pre-engineering; respiratory care therapy; surgical technology; welding technology.

Academics *Calendar:* quarters. *Degree:* certificates, diplomas, and associate. *Special study options:* academic remediation for entering students, adult/continuing education programs, advanced placement credit, cooperative education, distance learning, English as a second language, independent study, internships, part-time degree program, services for LD students, summer session for credit. *ROTC:* Army (c).

Library Metropolitan Community College plus 2 others with 43,788 titles, 453 serial subscriptions, 8,008 audiovisual materials, an OPAC, a Web page.

Student Life *Housing Options:* coed, men-only, women-only, disabled students. Campus housing is university owned. *Campus security:* 24-hour emergency response devices and patrols, late-night transport/escort service, controlled dormitory access, security on duty 9 pm to 6 am. *Student services:* personal/psychological counseling.

Costs (2007–08) *Tuition:* state resident $1845 full-time, $41 per credit part-time; nonresident $2768 full-time, $62 per credit part-time. *Required fees:* $225 full-time, $5 per credit part-time. *Room and board:* $3555.

Financial Aid Of all full-time matriculated undergraduates, 180 Federal Work-Study jobs (averaging $1339).

Applying *Options:* early admission. *Recommended:* high school transcript. *Application deadlines:* rolling (freshmen), rolling (transfers). *Notification:* continuous (freshmen), continuous (transfers).

Freshmen Application Contact Ms. Becky Nicks, Director of Admissions and Records, Metropolitan Community College, PO Box 3777, Omaha, NE 69103-0777. *Phone:* 402-457-2717. *Toll-free phone:* 800-228-9553. *Fax:* 402-457-2616. *E-mail:* bnicks@mccneb.edu.

MID-PLAINS COMMUNITY COLLEGE

North Platte, Nebraska   **www.mpcc.edu/**

- **District-supported** 2-year, founded 1973
- **Small-town** campus
- **Endowment** $509,000
- **Coed,** 3,030 undergraduate students, 35% full-time, 51% women, 49% men

Undergraduates 1,061 full-time, 1,969 part-time. Students come from 36 states and territories, 3 other countries, 2% are from out of state, 1% African American, 0.3% Asian American or Pacific Islander, 2% Hispanic American, 0.6% Native American, 0.1% international, 1% transferred in, 8% live on campus.

Freshmen *Admission:* 1,975 applied, 1,975 admitted, 271 enrolled. *Test scores:* ACT scores over 18: 73%; ACT scores over 24: 20%; ACT scores over 30: 1%.

Faculty *Total:* 302, 22% full-time, 2% with terminal degrees. *Student/faculty ratio:* 14:1.

Majors Administrative assistant and secretarial science; autobody/collision and repair technology; automobile/automotive mechanics technology; building/construction finishing, management, and inspection related; business administration and management; clinical/medical laboratory technology; computer and information sciences; construction engineering technology; dental assisting; diesel mechanics technology; electrical, electronic and communications engineering technology; fire science; heating, air conditioning, ventilation and refrigeration maintenance technology; liberal arts and sciences/liberal studies; nursing (licensed practical/vocational nurse training); nursing (registered nurse training); transportation and materials moving related; welding technology.

Academics *Calendar:* semesters. *Degree:* certificates, diplomas, and associate. *Special study options:* academic remediation for entering students, adult/continuing education programs, advanced placement credit, cooperative education, distance learning, external degree program, independent study, internships, part-time degree program, summer session for credit.

Library McDonald-Belton L R C plus 1 other with 65,352 titles, 4,697 serial subscriptions, 3,455 audiovisual materials, an OPAC, a Web page.

Student Life *Housing Options:* coed, disabled students. Campus housing is university owned. *Activities and Organizations:* drama/theater group, student-run newspaper, choral group, Student Senate, Phi Theta Kappa, Phi Beta Lamda, SEAN. *Campus security:* controlled dormitory access, patrols by trained security personnel.

Athletics Member NJCAA. *Intercollegiate sports:* baseball M(s), basketball M(s)/W(s), golf M(s), softball W(s), volleyball W(s). *Intramural sports:* baseball M, basketball M/W, softball W, volleyball W.

Standardized Tests *Required for some:* ACT COMPASS. *Recommended:* ACT (for admission).

Costs (2007–08) *Tuition:* state resident $1860 full-time, $62 per credit hour part-time; nonresident $2430 full-time, $81 per credit hour part-time. *Required fees:* $360 full-time, $12 per credit hour part-time. *Room and board:* $4500.

Applying *Required:* high school transcript. *Required for some:* letters of recommendation, interview. *Application deadlines:* rolling (freshmen), rolling (transfers). *Notification:* continuous (freshmen), continuous (transfers).

Freshmen Application Contact Ms. Sherry Mihel, Advisor, Mid-Plains Community College, 1101 Halligan Drive, North Platte, NE 69101. *Phone:* 308-535-3710. *Toll-free phone:* 800-658-4308 (in-state); 800-658-4348 (out-of-state). *E-mail:* mihels@mpcc.edu.

MYOTHERAPY INSTITUTE

Lincoln, Nebraska   **www.myotherapy.edu/**

- **Proprietary** 2-year
- **Coed,** 52 undergraduate students

Majors Massage therapy.

Academics *Degree:* associate.

Costs (2006–07) *Tuition:* $12,000 full-time.

Applying *Application fee:* $75.

Freshmen Application Contact Admissions Office, Myotherapy Institute, 6020 South 58th Street, Lincoln, NE 68516. *Phone:* 402-421-7410. *Toll-free phone:* 800-896-3363.

NEBRASKA COLLEGE OF TECHNICAL AGRICULTURE

Curtis, Nebraska   www.ncta.unl.edu/

- **State-supported** 2-year, founded 1965, part of University of Nebraska System
- **Small-town** campus
- **Endowment** $3.6 million
- **Coed,** 272 undergraduate students, 97% full-time, 49% women, 51% men

Undergraduates 265 full-time, 7 part-time. Students come from 8 states and territories, 17% are from out of state, 1% Hispanic American, 7% transferred in, 45% live on campus. *Retention:* 66% of 2003 full-time freshmen returned.

Freshmen *Admission:* 198 applied, 198 admitted, 198 enrolled. *Average high school GPA:* 2.2.

Faculty *Total:* 23, 48% full-time. *Student/faculty ratio:* 18:1.

Majors Agricultural business and management; agricultural mechanization; agronomy and crop science; animal sciences; heavy equipment maintenance technology; horticultural science; natural resources/conservation; natural resources management and policy; soil conservation; veterinary technology.

Academics *Calendar:* 8-week modular system. *Degree:* associate. *Special study options:* academic remediation for entering students, adult/continuing education programs, distance learning, double majors, external degree program, independent study, internships, part-time degree program, study abroad.

Library Nebraska College of Technical Agriculture Library with 6,000 titles, 230 serial subscriptions, an OPAC, a Web page.

Student Life *Housing:* on-campus residence required for freshman year. *Options:* men-only, women-only. Campus housing is university owned. *Activities and Organizations:* Aggie Livestock Association, Student Technicians Veterinary Medicine Association, Activities Without Alcohol and Drugs, Business Club, Phi Theta Kappa. *Campus security:* 24-hour emergency response devices, controlled dormitory access, night security. *Student services:* health clinic, personal/psychological counseling.

Athletics *Intercollegiate sports:* basketball M/W. *Intramural sports:* basketball M/W, football M/W, golf M/W, soccer M/W, softball M/W, volleyball M/W.

Standardized Tests *Recommended:* SAT or ACT (for admission).

Costs (2007–08) *Tuition:* state resident $3285 full-time; nonresident $6570 full-time. *Required fees:* $575 full-time. *Room and board:* $4481; room only: $2000.

Applying *Options:* early admission. *Application fee:* $10. *Required:* high school transcript. *Recommended:* interview. *Application deadline:* rolling (freshmen).

Director of Admissions Ms. Sue Shaner, Director of Instruction, Nebraska College of Technical Agriculture, RR3, Box 23A, Curtis, NE 69025-9205. *Phone:* 308-367-4124 Ext. 253. *Toll-free phone:* 800-3CURTIS. *E-mail:* sshaner3@unl.edu.

NEBRASKA INDIAN COMMUNITY COLLEGE

Macy, Nebraska   www.thenicc.edu/

- **Federally supported** 2-year, founded 1979
- **Rural** 2-acre campus with easy access to Omaha, NE
- **Endowment** $68,020
- **Coed,** 115 undergraduate students, 48% full-time, 57% women, 43% men

Undergraduates 55 full-time, 60 part-time. Students come from 2 states and territories, 7% are from out of state, 2% Hispanic American, 76% Native American.

Freshmen *Admission:* 44 enrolled.

Faculty *Total:* 12, 42% full-time, 8% with terminal degrees.

Majors American Indian/Native American studies; business administration and management; carpentry; corrections and criminal justice related; data entry/microcomputer applications; early childhood education; human services; information technology; liberal arts and sciences/liberal studies; natural resources/conservation; social work.

Academics *Calendar:* semesters. *Degree:* certificates and associate. *Special study options:* academic remediation for entering students, adult/continuing education programs, double majors, part-time degree program, study abroad.

Student Life *Housing:* college housing not available.

Applying *Options:* early admission, deferred entrance. *Application fee:* $50. *Required:* high school transcript, certificate of tribal enrollment if applicable.

Application deadlines: rolling (freshmen), rolling (transfers). *Notification:* continuous (freshmen), continuous (transfers).

Director of Admissions Ms. Theresa Henry, Admission Counselor, Nebraska Indian Community College, 2451 Saint Mary's Avenue, Omaha, NE 68105. *Phone:* 402-837-5078. *Toll-free phone:* 888-843-6432 Ext. 14.

NORTHEAST COMMUNITY COLLEGE

Norfolk, Nebraska   www.northeastcollege.com/

- **State and locally supported** 2-year, founded 1973, part of Nebraska Coordinating Commission for Postsecondary Education
- **Small-town** 205-acre campus
- **Endowment** $1.5 million
- **Coed,** 5,261 undergraduate students, 41% full-time, 47% women, 53% men

Undergraduates 2,156 full-time, 3,105 part-time. Students come from 15 states and territories, 24 other countries, 4% are from out of state, 0.8% African American, 0.4% Asian American or Pacific Islander, 3% Hispanic American, 0.9% Native American, 0.1% international, 11% live on campus.

Freshmen *Admission:* 791 enrolled.

Faculty *Total:* 376, 28% full-time, 0.8% with terminal degrees. *Student/faculty ratio:* 17:1.

Majors Accounting; administrative assistant and secretarial science; agricultural business and management; agricultural mechanization; agricultural production; agriculture; agronomy and crop science; animal sciences; applied horticulture; art; art teacher education; audio engineering; autobody/collision and repair technology; automobile/automotive mechanics technology; biological and physical sciences; biology/biological sciences; broadcast journalism; business administration and management; business teacher education; carpentry; chemistry; computer and information sciences; computer programming; computer programming (specific applications); computer science; corrections; criminal justice/law enforcement administration; criminal justice/police science; crop production; diesel mechanics technology; drafting and design technology; dramatic/theater arts; education; electrical, electronic and communications engineering technology; electrician; electromechanical technology; elementary education; emergency medical technology (EMT paramedic); engineering; English; entrepreneurship; farm and ranch management; general studies; health and physical education; heating, air conditioning, ventilation and refrigeration maintenance technology; horticultural science; journalism; legal administrative assistant/secretary; legal assistant/paralegal; liberal arts and sciences/liberal studies; lineworker; livestock management; marketing/marketing management; marketing related; mass communication/media; mathematics; medical administrative assistant and medical secretary; music; music management and merchandising; music performance; music teacher education; nursing (licensed practical/vocational nurse training); nursing (registered nurse training); physical education teaching and coaching; physical therapy; physics; pre-law studies; radio and television; real estate; retailing; social sciences; social work related; speech and rhetoric; surgical technology; veterinary technology; welding technology.

Academics *Calendar:* semesters. *Degree:* certificates, diplomas, and associate. *Special study options:* academic remediation for entering students, accelerated degree program, adult/continuing education programs, advanced placement credit, cooperative education, distance learning, English as a second language, independent study, internships, off-campus study, part-time degree program, services for LD students, summer session for credit.

Library Resource Center plus 1 other with 52,494 titles, 11,140 serial subscriptions, 1,805 audiovisual materials, an OPAC, a Web page.

Student Life *Housing Options:* coed, disabled students. Campus housing is university owned. *Activities and Organizations:* drama/theater group, student-run newspaper, radio and television station, choral group, Phi Theta Kappa, Campus Crusade for Christ, Diversified Ag Club, Electricians Club, Utility Line Club. *Campus security:* 24-hour patrols, controlled dormitory access. *Student services:* personal/psychological counseling.

Athletics Member NJCAA. *Intercollegiate sports:* basketball M(s)/W(s), cheerleading W(s). *Intramural sports:* basketball M/W, bowling M/W, football M/W, soccer M/W, softball M/W, table tennis M/W, volleyball M/W.

Costs (2007–08) *Tuition:* state resident $1984 full-time; nonresident $2480 full-time. *Required fees:* $352 full-time. *Room and board:* $3908.

Financial Aid Of all full-time matriculated undergraduates, 90 Federal Work-Study jobs (averaging $1700).

Applying *Options:* electronic application, early admission. *Recommended:* high school transcript. *Application deadlines:* rolling (freshmen), rolling (transfers). *Notification:* continuous (freshmen), continuous (transfers).

Freshmen Application Contact Ms. Maureen Baker, Dean of Enrollment Management, Northeast Community College, PO Box 469, Norfolk, NE 68702-0469. *Phone:* 402-844-7258. *Toll-free phone:* 800-348-9033 Ext. 7260. *Fax:* 402-844-7400. *E-mail:* admission@northeastcollege.com.

SOUTHEAST COMMUNITY COLLEGE, BEATRICE CAMPUS

Beatrice, Nebraska   www.southeast.edu/

Director of Admissions Ms. Mary Ann Harms, Admissions Technician, Southeast Community College, Beatrice Campus, 4771 W. Scott Road, Beatrice, NE 68310-7042. *Toll-free phone:* 800-233-5027 Ext. 214.

SOUTHEAST COMMUNITY COLLEGE, LINCOLN CAMPUS

Lincoln, Nebraska   www.southeast.edu/

Freshmen Application Contact Ms. Pat Frakes, Admissions Representative, Southeast Community College, Lincoln Campus, 8800 "O" Street, Lincoln, NE 68520. *Phone:* 402-437-2600 Ext. 2600. *Toll-free phone:* 800-642-4075 Ext. 2600.

SOUTHEAST COMMUNITY COLLEGE, MILFORD CAMPUS

Milford, Nebraska   www.southeast.edu/

Director of Admissions Mr. Larry E. Meyer, Dean of Students, Southeast Community College, Milford Campus, 600 State Street, Milford, NE 68405. *Phone:* 402-761-2131 Ext. 8270. *Toll-free phone:* 800-933-7223 Ext. 8243.

VATTEROTT COLLEGE

Omaha, Nebraska   www.vatterott-college.edu/

Director of Admissions Dr. James G. Hadley, Campus Director, Vatterott College, 225 North 80th Street, Omaha, NE 68114. *Phone:* 402-392-1300 Ext. 207. *Toll-free phone:* 800-865-8628.

VATTEROTT COLLEGE

Omaha, Nebraska   www.vatterott-college.edu/

Admissions Office Contact Vatterott College, 5318 South 136th Street, Omaha, NE 68137.

WESTERN NEBRASKA COMMUNITY COLLEGE

Sidney, Nebraska   www.wncc.net/

- **State and locally supported** 2-year, founded 1926, part of Western Community College Area System
- **Rural** 20-acre campus
- **Coed,** 3,151 undergraduate students

Undergraduates Students come from 18 states and territories, 10% are from out of state, 5% live on campus.

Freshmen *Admission:* 613 applied, 613 admitted. *Average high school GPA:* 2.17.

Faculty *Total:* 358, 18% full-time. *Student/faculty ratio:* 15:1.

Majors Agriculture; anthropology; art; art teacher education; biology/biological sciences; business administration and management; chemistry; clinical laboratory science/medical technology; community psychology; computer and information sciences; criminal justice/safety; dietetics; drama and dance teacher education; ecology; economics; elementary education; English; forest/forest resources management; French; general studies; geography; German; health and physical education; history; information technology; interdisciplinary studies; journalism; kindergarten/preschool education; liberal arts and sciences/liberal studies; mathematics; music teacher education; nursing (registered nurse training); physical therapist assistant; physical therapy; physics; political science and government; pre-dentistry studies; pre-engineering; pre-law studies; pre-medical

studies; pre-pharmacy studies; pre-veterinary studies; psychology; radiologic technology/science; secondary education; social work; sociology; Spanish.

Academics *Calendar:* semesters. *Degree:* certificates, diplomas, and associate. *Special study options:* academic remediation for entering students, accelerated degree program, adult/continuing education programs, advanced placement credit, cooperative education, distance learning, independent study, internships, part-time degree program, services for LD students, summer session for credit.

Library Western Nebraska Community College Library with 34,539 titles, 2,631 serial subscriptions, 2,631 audiovisual materials, an OPAC.

Student Life *Housing Options:* coed. Campus housing is university owned. *Activities and Organizations:* drama/theater group, student-run newspaper, choral group, Choices, Phi Theta Kappa, student government, SEAN, national sororities. *Campus security:* 24-hour emergency response devices and patrols, late-night transport/escort service, controlled dormitory access, patrols by trained security personnel from 12:30 a.m. to 6 a.m. *Student services:* personal/psychological counseling.

Athletics Member NJCAA. *Intercollegiate sports:* baseball M, basketball M(s)/W(s), soccer M/W, softball W, volleyball W(s). *Intramural sports:* basketball M/W, bowling M/W, football M/W, table tennis M/W, tennis M/W, volleyball M/W, weight lifting M/W.

Standardized Tests *Required:* ACT ASSET (for placement).

Costs (2006–07) *Tuition:* state resident $1620 full-time; nonresident $1950 full-time. *Required fees:* $12 per credit hour part-time.

Financial Aid Of all full-time matriculated undergraduates, 55 Federal Work-Study jobs (averaging $1800).

Applying *Options:* electronic application. *Recommended:* high school transcript. *Application deadlines:* rolling (freshmen), rolling (transfers). *Notification:* continuous until 8/21 (freshmen), continuous until 8/21 (transfers).

Director of Admissions Mr. Troy Archuleta, Admissions and Recruitment Director, Western Nebraska Community College, 371 College Drive, Sidney, NE 69162. *Phone:* 308-635-6015. *Toll-free phone:* 800-222-9682 (in-state); 800-348-4435 (out-of-state). *E-mail:* rhovey@wncc.net.

NEVADA

CAREER COLLEGE OF NORTHERN NEVADA

Reno, Nevada   www.ccnn.edu/

- **Proprietary** 2-year, founded 1984
- **Urban** 1-acre campus
- **Coed**

Undergraduates 283 full-time. Students come from 2 states and territories, 5% are from out of state, 8% African American, 6% Asian American or Pacific Islander, 17% Hispanic American, 6% Native American.

Faculty *Student/faculty ratio:* 20:1.

Academics *Calendar:* quarters six-week terms. *Degree:* diplomas and associate. *Special study options:* academic remediation for entering students, accelerated degree program, cooperative education, double majors, internships, summer session for credit.

Student Life *Campus security:* 24-hour emergency response devices.

Costs (2006–07) *Tuition:* $6600 full-time, $185 per credit hour part-time. No tuition increase for student's term of enrollment. *Required fees:* $285 full-time, $60 per term part-time. *Payment plans:* tuition prepayment, installment.

Financial Aid Of all full-time matriculated undergraduates, 6 Federal Work-Study jobs (averaging $3000).

Applying *Application fee:* $25. *Required:* essay or personal statement, high school transcript, interview.

Freshmen Application Contact Ms. Laura Goldhammer, Director of Admissions, Career College of Northern Nevada, 1195-A Corporate Boulevard, Reno, NV 89502. *Phone:* 775-856-2266 Ext. 11. *Fax:* 775-856-0935. *E-mail:* lgoldhammer@ccnn4u.com.

COMMUNITY COLLEGE OF SOUTHERN NEVADA

North Las Vegas, Nevada   www.ccsn.nevada.edu/

- **State-supported** 2-year, founded 1971, part of University and Community College System of Nevada
- **Suburban** 89-acre campus with easy access to Las Vegas
- **Endowment** $2.6 million
- **Coed,** 34,204 undergraduate students, 23% full-time, 57% women, 43% men

Undergraduates 7,850 full-time, 26,354 part-time. Students come from 55 states and territories, 13 other countries, 2% are from out of state, 0.8% transferred in.

Freshmen *Admission:* 1,592 enrolled.

Faculty *Total:* 2,280, 17% full-time.

Majors Accounting; administrative assistant and secretarial science; anthropology; art; automobile/automotive mechanics technology; behavioral sciences; biological and physical sciences; biology/biological sciences; business administration and management; chemistry; child development; clinical laboratory science/medical technology; clinical/medical laboratory technology; commercial and advertising art; computer engineering technology; computer programming; computer science; computer typography and composition equipment operation; construction engineering technology; construction management; consumer merchandising/retailing management; corrections; criminal justice/law enforcement administration; criminal justice/police science; culinary arts; data processing and data processing technology; dental hygiene; drafting and design technology; dramatic/theater arts; economics; electrical, electronic and communications engineering technology; emergency medical technology (EMT paramedic); English; environmental studies; finance; fire science; food services technology; graphic and printing equipment operation/production; health information/medical records administration; heating, air conditioning, ventilation and refrigeration maintenance technology; heavy equipment maintenance technology; history; horticultural science; hospitality administration; hotel/motel administration; industrial radiologic technology; information science/studies; kindergarten/preschool education; landscaping and groundskeeping; legal administrative assistant/secretary; legal assistant/paralegal; liberal arts and sciences/liberal studies; literature; marketing/marketing management; mass communication/media; mathematics; mechanical design technology; mechanical engineering/mechanical technology; medical administrative assistant and medical secretary; medical/clinical assistant; music; nursing (licensed practical/vocational nurse training); nursing (registered nurse training); occupational therapy; ornamental horticulture; parks, recreation and leisure; pharmacy; photography; radio and television; radiologic technology/science; real estate; respiratory care therapy; science teacher education; sign language interpretation and translation; social sciences; sociology; special products marketing; survey technology; teacher assistant/aide; veterinary technology; welding technology; wildlife and wildlands science and management.

Academics *Calendar:* semesters. *Degree:* certificates and associate. *Special study options:* academic remediation for entering students, accelerated degree program, adult/continuing education programs, advanced placement credit, cooperative education, distance learning, double majors, English as a second language, honors programs, independent study, internships, part-time degree program, services for LD students, summer session for credit. *ROTC:* Army (b).

Library Learning Assistance Center with 100,000 titles, 500 serial subscriptions, 5,400 audiovisual materials, an OPAC, a Web page.

Student Life *Housing:* college housing not available. *Activities and Organizations:* drama/theater group, student-run newspaper, choral group, Culinary Club, Art Club, Black Student Association, Student Organization of Latinos, Student Nurses Club. *Campus security:* 24-hour emergency response devices and patrols. *Student services:* health clinic, personal/psychological counseling, women's center, legal services.

Athletics Member NJCAA. *Intercollegiate sports:* baseball M. *Intramural sports:* basketball M/W, bowling M/W, racquetball M/W, tennis M/W, weight lifting M/W.

Costs (2006–07) *Tuition:* state resident $1575 full-time, $53 per credit part-time; nonresident $6218 full-time, $108 per credit part-time. *Required fees:* $120 full-time, $4 per credit part-time.

Financial Aid Of all full-time matriculated undergraduates, 355 Federal Work-Study jobs (averaging $2000).

Applying *Options:* early admission. *Application fee:* $5. *Required:* student data form. *Application deadline:* rolling (freshmen).

Director of Admissions Mr. Arlie J. Stops, Associate Vice President for Admissions and Records, Community College of Southern Nevada, 3200 East Cheyenne Avenue, North Las Vegas, NV 89030-4296. *Phone:* 702-651-4060. *Toll-free phone:* 800-492-5728. *E-mail:* stops@ccmail.ccsn.nevada.edu.

GREAT BASIN COLLEGE

Elko, Nevada www.gbcnv.edu/

- **State-supported** primarily 2-year, founded 1967, part of University and Community College System of Nevada
- **Small-town** 45-acre campus
- **Endowment** $150,000
- **Coed,** 3,349 undergraduate students, 25% full-time, 65% women, 35% men

Undergraduates 822 full-time, 2,527 part-time. Students come from 13 states and territories, 3% are from out of state, 0.9% African American, 1% Asian American or Pacific Islander, 10% Hispanic American, 4% Native American. *Retention:* 77% of 2003 full-time freshmen returned.

Freshmen *Admission:* 546 enrolled.

Faculty *Total:* 210, 32% full-time.

Majors Anthropology; art; business administration and management; business/commerce; chemistry; criminal justice/safety; data processing and data processing technology; diesel mechanics technology; electrical, electronic and communications engineering technology; elementary education; English; environmental studies; geology/earth science; history; industrial technology; interdisciplinary studies; kindergarten/preschool education; mathematics; nursing (registered nurse training); office management; operations management; physics; psychology; secondary education; social work; sociology; welding technology.

Academics *Calendar:* semesters. *Degrees:* certificates, associate, and bachelor's. *Special study options:* academic remediation for entering students, adult/continuing education programs, cooperative education, distance learning, English as a second language, external degree program, independent study, part-time degree program, services for LD students, summer session for credit.

Library Learning Resources Center with 38,765 titles, 2,635 audiovisual materials, an OPAC.

Student Life *Housing Options:* Campus housing is university owned. *Activities and Organizations:* drama/theater group, choral group. *Campus security:* evening patrols by trained security personnel. *Student services:* personal/psychological counseling.

Athletics *Intramural sports:* badminton M/W, basketball M/W, volleyball M/W, weight lifting M/W.

Costs (2007–08) *Tuition:* state resident $1643 full-time; nonresident $4335 full-time. *Room and board:* $4520; room only: $1900.

Financial Aid Of all full-time matriculated undergraduates, 35 Federal Work-Study jobs (averaging $1000). 50 state and other part-time jobs (averaging $1800).

Applying *Options:* electronic application, early admission, deferred entrance. *Application fee:* $5. *Required:* high school transcript. *Application deadlines:* rolling (freshmen), rolling (transfers). *Notification:* continuous (freshmen), continuous (transfers).

Freshmen Application Contact Ms. Julie Byrnes, Director of Enrollment Management, Great Basin College, 1500 College Parkway, Elko, NV 89801-3348. *Phone:* 775-753-2271. *Fax:* 775-753-2311. *E-mail:* stdsvc@gbcnv.edu.

HERITAGE COLLEGE

Las Vegas, Nevada www.heritagecollege.com/

- **Proprietary** 2-year, founded 1990
- **227 undergraduate students**

Majors Computer and information sciences related; criminal justice/law enforcement administration; data processing and data processing technology; legal assistant/paralegal; medical administrative assistant and medical secretary; medical/clinical assistant; medical insurance coding; pharmacy technician.

Academics *Degree:* associate.

Costs (2006–07) *Tuition:* $12,450 per degree program part-time.

Applying *Application fee:* $20.

Freshmen Application Contact Admissions Office, Heritage College, 3315 Spring Mountain Road, Las Vegas, NV 89102. *Toll-free phone:* 888-727-7863.

HIGH-TECH INSTITUTE

Las Vegas, Nevada www.high-techinstitute.com/

- **Proprietary** 2-year, founded 2002
- **Coed,** 589 undergraduate students

Majors Criminal justice/law enforcement administration; dental assisting; massage therapy; medical/clinical assistant; medical insurance/medical billing; pharmacy technician; surgical technology.

Academics *Calendar:* semesters. *Degree:* associate.

Costs (2006–07) *Tuition:* $24,791 per degree program part-time.

Applying *Application fee:* $50.

Freshmen Application Contact Admissions Office, High-Tech Institute, 2320 South Rancho Drive, Las Vegas, NV 89102. *Phone:* 702-385-6700. *Toll-free phone:* 866-385-6700.

ITT TECHNICAL INSTITUTE

Henderson, Nevada   **www.itt-tech.edu/**

- **Proprietary** primarily 2-year, founded 1997, part of ITT Educational Services, Inc
- **Coed**

Majors Animation, interactive technology, video graphics and special effects; business administration and management; CAD/CADD drafting/design technology; computer and information systems security; computer engineering technology; computer software technology; computer systems networking and telecommunications; construction management; criminal justice/law enforcement administration; electrical, electronic and communications engineering technology; medical laboratory technology; web/multimedia management and webmaster; web page, digital/multimedia and information resources design.

Academics *Degrees:* associate and bachelor's.

Library a Web page.

Student Life *Housing:* college housing not available.

Standardized Tests *Required:* Wonderlic aptitude test (for admission).

Costs (2006–07) *Tuition:* Contact school for program costs.

Financial Aid Of all full-time matriculated undergraduates, 6 Federal Work-Study jobs (averaging $5000).

Applying *Options:* deferred entrance. *Application fee:* $100. *Required:* high school transcript, interview. *Recommended:* letters of recommendation. *Application deadlines:* rolling (freshmen), rolling (transfers). *Notification:* continuous (freshmen), continuous (transfers).

Freshmen Application Contact Ms. Anne Buzak, Director of Recruitment, ITT Technical Institute, 168 North Gibson Road, Henderson, NV 89014. *Phone:* 702-558-5404. *Toll-free phone:* 800-488-8459.

LAS VEGAS COLLEGE

Las Vegas, Nevada   **www.lasvegas-college.com/**

Director of Admissions Mr. Bill Hall, Director of Admissions, Las Vegas College, 4100 West Flamingo Road, Suite 2100, Las Vegas, NV 89103-3926. *Phone:* 702-368-6200. *Toll-free phone:* 800-903-3101.

LE CORDON BLEU COLLEGE OF CULINARY ARTS, LAS VEGAS

Las Vegas, Nevada   **www.vegasculinary.com/**

- **Proprietary** 2-year, founded 2003
- **Coed,** 892 undergraduate students

Majors Cooking and related culinary arts.

Academics *Degree:* associate.

Costs (2006–07) *Tuition:* $19,000 full-time.

Applying *Application fee:* $50.

Freshmen Application Contact Admissions Office, Le Cordon Bleu College of Culinary Arts, Las Vegas, 1451 Center Crossing Road, Las Vegas, NV 89144. *Toll-free phone:* 888-551-8222.

PIMA MEDICAL INSTITUTE

Las Vegas, Nevada   **www.pmi.edu/**

Freshmen Application Contact Admissions Office, Pima Medical Institute, Pima Medical Institute, 3333 East Flamingo Road, Las Vegas, NV 89121. *Phone:* 702-458-9650 Ext. 202. *Toll-free phone:* 800-477-PIMA.

TRUCKEE MEADOWS COMMUNITY COLLEGE

Reno, Nevada   **www.tmcc.edu/**

Director of Admissions Mr. Dave Harbeck, Director of Admissions and Records, Truckee Meadows Community College, Mail Station #15, 7000 Dandini Boulevard, MS RDMT 319, Reno, NV 89512-3901. *Phone:* 775-674-7623. *Fax:* 775-673-7028. *E-mail:* dharbeck@tmcc.edu.

WESTERN NEVADA COMMUNITY COLLEGE

Carson City, Nevada   **www.wncc.edu/**

- **State-supported** 2-year, founded 1971, part of Nevada System of Higher Education
- **Small-town** 200-acre campus
- **Endowment** $189,740
- **Coed,** 5,531 undergraduate students, 18% full-time, 58% women, 42% men

Undergraduates 993 full-time, 4,538 part-time. Students come from 3 other countries, 4% are from out of state, 1% African American, 2% Asian American or Pacific Islander, 8% Hispanic American, 3% Native American, 5% transferred in.

Freshmen *Admission:* 760 applied, 760 admitted, 760 enrolled.

Faculty *Total:* 386, 20% full-time. *Student/faculty ratio:* 15:1.

Majors Accounting; accounting technology and bookkeeping; administrative assistant and secretarial science; automobile/automotive mechanics technology; biology/biological sciences; business administration and management; business automation/technology/data entry; business/commerce; carpentry; child care and support services management; clinical/medical laboratory technology; computer and information sciences; computer programming; construction management; corrections; criminal justice/law enforcement administration; criminal justice/police science; drafting and design technology; electrical and power transmission installation; electrical, electronic and communications engineering technology; engineering; environmental studies; fire protection and safety technology; general studies; heating, air conditioning, ventilation and refrigeration maintenance technology; industrial technology; legal assistant/paralegal; liberal arts and sciences/liberal studies; machine tool technology; management information systems; management science; marketing/marketing management; masonry; mathematics; nursing (registered nurse training); parks, recreation and leisure facilities management; physical sciences; pipefitting and sprinkler fitting; real estate; sheet metal technology; vehicle/equipment operation; welding technology.

Academics *Calendar:* semesters. *Degree:* certificates, diplomas, and associate. *Special study options:* academic remediation for entering students, adult/continuing education programs, advanced placement credit, cooperative education, distance learning, English as a second language, honors programs, independent study, internships, part-time degree program, services for LD students, summer session for credit.

Library Western Nevada Community College Library and Media Services plus 1 other with 50,612 titles, 197 serial subscriptions, 29,216 audiovisual materials, an OPAC, a Web page.

Student Life *Housing:* college housing not available. *Activities and Organizations:* drama/theater group, choral group, Phi Theta Kappa, writers group, Infinity Society, Golf Club, Physics and Engineering Club. *Campus security:* late-night transport/escort service. *Student services:* personal/psychological counseling.

Athletics *Intercollegiate sports:* baseball M, equestrian sports M/W, soccer W.

Costs (2007–08) *Tuition:* state resident $1643 full-time, $55 per credit part-time; nonresident $7028 full-time, $115 per credit part-time. *Required fees:* $120 full-time, $4 per credit part-time.

Financial Aid Of all full-time matriculated undergraduates, 24 Federal Work-Study jobs (averaging $4500). 48 state and other part-time jobs (averaging $4500).

Applying *Options:* early admission. *Application fee:* $15. *Required for some:* high school transcript. *Application deadlines:* rolling (freshmen), rolling (transfers).

Freshmen Application Contact Admissions and Records, Western Nevada Community College, 2201 West College Parkway, Carson City, NV 89703-7399. *Phone:* 775-445-2377. *Fax:* 775-445-3147. *E-mail:* wncc_aro@wncc.edu.

NEW HAMPSHIRE

HESSER COLLEGE

Manchester, New Hampshire   **www.hesser.edu/**

- **Proprietary** primarily 2-year, founded 1900, part of Quest Education Corporation
- **Urban** 1-acre campus with easy access to Boston
- **Coed,** 3,398 undergraduate students, 62% full-time, 71% women, 29% men

Undergraduates 2,104 full-time, 1,294 part-time. Students come from 12 states and territories, 50% live on campus.

Freshmen *Admission:* 1,725 applied, 1,562 admitted, 1,018 enrolled. *Average high school GPA:* 2.3.

Faculty *Total:* 215, 18% full-time.

Majors Accounting; business administration and management; business and personal/financial services marketing; child care and support services management; commercial and advertising art; computer and information sciences; computer engineering technology; computer management; computer programming; computer science; computer systems analysis; corrections; criminal justice/law enforcement administration; criminal justice/police science; criminal justice/safety; human services; information science/studies; interior design; kindergarten/preschool education; legal assistant/paralegal; liberal arts and sciences/liberal studies; management information systems; marketing/marketing management; mass communication/media; medical administrative assistant and medical secretary; medical/clinical assistant; physical therapist assistant; psychology; radio and television; sales, distribution and marketing; security and loss prevention; social work; sport and fitness administration/management.

Academics *Calendar:* semesters. *Degrees:* certificates, diplomas, associate, and bachelor's. *Special study options:* accelerated degree program, adult/continuing education programs, advanced placement credit, cooperative education, double majors, internships, part-time degree program, student-designed majors, summer session for credit.

Library Kenneth W. Galeucia Memorial Library with 38,000 titles, 200 serial subscriptions, 60 audiovisual materials, an OPAC, a Web page.

Student Life *Housing Options:* coed. Campus housing is university owned. Freshman campus housing is guaranteed. *Activities and Organizations:* student-run radio and television station, student government, Ski Club, Amnesty International, yearbook, student ambassadors. *Campus security:* 24-hour emergency response devices and patrols, student patrols, late-night transport/escort service, controlled dormitory access. *Student services:* health clinic, personal/psychological counseling.

Athletics *Intercollegiate sports:* basketball M(s)/W(s), soccer M(s)/W(s), volleyball M(s)/W(s). *Intramural sports:* baseball M, basketball M/W, bowling M/W, skiing (downhill) M/W, softball M/W, table tennis M/W, volleyball M/W.

Standardized Tests *Recommended:* SAT (for admission).

Costs (2006–07) *Tuition:* For more information please call Hesser at 888-234-4000 Dept. 266. Hesser College also offers financial aid and scholarships for those who qualify.

Financial Aid Of all full-time matriculated undergraduates, 700 Federal Work-Study jobs (averaging $1000).

Applying *Options:* electronic application, deferred entrance. *Application fee:* $10. *Required:* high school transcript, interview. *Required for some:* essay or personal statement, letters of recommendation. *Recommended:* minimum 2.0 GPA. *Application deadlines:* rolling (freshmen), rolling (transfers). *Notification:* continuous (freshmen), continuous (transfers).

Freshmen Application Contact Ms. Carey Boulanger, Director of Admissions, Hesser College, 3 Sundial Avenue, Manchester, NH 03103. *Phone:* 800-234-4000. *Toll-free phone:* 800-526-9231 Ext. 2110.

▶See page 546 for the College Close-Up.

McINTOSH COLLEGE

Dover, New Hampshire   www.mcintoshcollege.edu/

Freshmen Application Contact McIntosh College, 23 Cataract Avenue, Dover, NH 03820-3990. *Toll-free phone:* 800-McINTOSH.

▶See page 564 for the College Close-Up.

NEW HAMPSHIRE COMMUNITY TECHNICAL COLLEGE, BERLIN/LACONIA

Berlin, New Hampshire   www.berlin.nhctc.edu/

Freshmen Application Contact Ms. Chris Nicoletti, Program Assistant, New Hampshire Community Technical College, Berlin/Laconia, 2020 Riverside Drive, Berlin, NH 03570-3717. *Phone:* 603-752-1113 Ext. 1007. *Toll-free phone:* 800-445-4525. *Fax:* 603-752-6335. *E-mail:* cnicoletti@nhctc.edu.

NEW HAMPSHIRE COMMUNITY TECHNICAL COLLEGE, MANCHESTER/STRATHAM

Manchester, New Hampshire   www.manchester.nhctc.edu/

- **State-supported** 2-year, founded 1945, part of New Hampshire Community Technical College System
- **Urban** 60-acre campus with easy access to Boston
- **Coed,** 3,122 undergraduate students

Undergraduates Students come from 5 states and territories, 7% are from out of state, 2% African American, 1% Asian American or Pacific Islander, 3% Hispanic American, 1% Native American.

Faculty *Total:* 202, 26% full-time, 2% with terminal degrees. *Student/faculty ratio:* 14:1.

Majors Accounting; administrative assistant and secretarial science; athletic training; automobile/automotive mechanics technology; business administration and management; child development; commercial and advertising art; community organization and advocacy; construction engineering technology; drafting and design technology; heating, air conditioning, ventilation and refrigeration maintenance technology; human services; information science/studies; kindergarten/preschool education; kinesiology and exercise science; liberal arts and sciences/liberal studies; management information systems; marketing/marketing management; mechanical design technology; medical administrative assistant and medical secretary; nursing (registered nurse training); physical therapy; welding technology.

Academics *Calendar:* semesters. *Degree:* certificates, diplomas, and associate. *Special study options:* academic remediation for entering students, adult/continuing education programs, advanced placement credit, cooperative education, distance learning, double majors, English as a second language, external degree program, independent study, internships, part-time degree program, services for LD students, summer session for credit.

Library New Hampshire Community Technical College Library plus 1 other with 18,000 titles, 160 serial subscriptions, an OPAC.

Student Life *Housing:* college housing not available. *Activities and Organizations:* Student Senate, Phi Theta Kappa, American Society of Welders, Student Nurses Association. *Campus security:* trained security personnel. *Student services:* personal/psychological counseling.

Athletics *Intercollegiate sports:* baseball W, basketball M, skiing (downhill) M/W, soccer M/W, volleyball M/W. *Intramural sports:* basketball M/W, bowling M/W, ice hockey M, skiing (cross-country) M/W, skiing (downhill) M/W, volleyball M/W.

Costs (2007–08) *Tuition:* area resident $3936 full-time, $164 per credit part-time; state resident $5904 full-time, $246 per credit part-time; nonresident $9024 full-time, $376 per credit part-time. *Required fees:* $145 full-time, $5 per credit part-time.

Applying *Options:* early admission, deferred entrance. *Application fee:* $10. *Required:* high school transcript. *Required for some:* letters of recommendation, interview. *Application deadlines:* rolling (freshmen), rolling (transfers). *Notification:* continuous (freshmen), continuous (transfers).

Freshmen Application Contact Ms. Jacquie Poirier, Coordinator of Admissions, New Hampshire Community Technical College, Manchester/Stratham, 1066 Front Street, Manchester, NH 03102-8518. *Phone:* 603-668-6706 Ext. 283. *E-mail:* jpoirier@nhctc.edu.

NEW HAMPSHIRE COMMUNITY TECHNICAL COLLEGE, NASHUA/CLAREMONT

Nashua, New Hampshire   www.ncctc.edu/

- **State-supported** 2-year, founded 1967, part of New Hampshire Community Technical College System
- **Urban** 66-acre campus with easy access to Boston
- **Coed,** 1,725 undergraduate students, 37% full-time, 53% women, 47% men

Undergraduates 638 full-time, 1,087 part-time.

Faculty *Total:* 108, 39% full-time.

Majors Accounting; airframe mechanics and aircraft maintenance technology; artificial intelligence and robotics; autobody/collision and repair technology; automobile/automotive mechanics technology; avionics maintenance technology; business administration and management; child development; computer and information sciences; computer engineering technology; computer management; computer science; data processing and data processing technology; drafting and

New Hampshire Community Technical College, Nashua/Claremont (continued)

design technology; electrical, electronic and communications engineering technology; electromechanical technology; engineering technology; general studies; heavy equipment maintenance technology; human services; industrial technology; information science/studies; kindergarten/preschool education; legal assistant/paralegal; legal studies; liberal arts and sciences/liberal studies; machine tool technology; ophthalmic laboratory technology; quality control technology; social work; telecommunications.

Academics *Calendar:* semesters. *Degree:* certificates, diplomas, and associate. *Special study options:* academic remediation for entering students, adult/continuing education programs, cooperative education, distance learning, English as a second language, external degree program, internships, part-time degree program, services for LD students, student-designed majors, summer session for credit.

Library Walter B. Peterson Library and Media Center with 22,000 titles, 250 serial subscriptions, an OPAC.

Student Life *Housing:* college housing not available. *Activities and Organizations:* drama/theater group, student-run newspaper, Student Senate, Phi Theta Kappa, AmeriCorp, Paralegal Club, Ski Club. *Campus security:* 24-hour emergency response devices, late-night transport/escort service. *Student services:* personal/psychological counseling.

Athletics *Intercollegiate sports:* soccer M/W. *Intramural sports:* skiing (cross-country) M/W, skiing (downhill) M/W, soccer M/W, weight lifting M/W.

Costs (2006–07) *Tuition:* $164 per credit part-time; state resident $5248 full-time, $246 per credit part-time; nonresident $12,032 full-time, $376 per credit part-time. *Required fees:* $512 full-time, $16 per credit part-time.

Financial Aid Of all full-time matriculated undergraduates, 35 Federal Work-Study jobs (averaging $1000).

Applying *Options:* deferred entrance. *Application fee:* $10. *Required:* high school transcript, interview. *Required for some:* essay or personal statement, nursing exam. *Recommended:* letters of recommendation. *Application deadlines:* rolling (freshmen), rolling (transfers). *Notification:* continuous (freshmen), continuous (transfers).

Freshmen Application Contact Ms. Patricia Goodman, Vice President of Student Services, New Hampshire Community Technical College, Nashua/Claremont, 505 Amherst Street, Nashua, NH 03063. *Phone:* 603-882-6923. *Fax:* 603-882-8690. *E-mail:* nashua@nhctc.edu.

NEW HAMPSHIRE TECHNICAL INSTITUTE

Concord, New Hampshire   www.nhti.edu/

- **State-supported** 2-year, founded 1964, part of New Hampshire Community Technical College System
- **Small-town** 225-acre campus with easy access to Boston
- **Coed**, 3,700 undergraduate students

Undergraduates Students come from 12 states and territories, 24 other countries, 2% are from out of state, 1% African American, 1% Asian American or Pacific Islander, 2% Hispanic American, 0.3% Native American, 23% live on campus.

Freshmen *Admission:* 1,919 applied, 1,408 admitted. *Average high school GPA:* 2.5.

Faculty *Total:* 120, 9% with terminal degrees. *Student/faculty ratio:* 12:1.

Majors Accounting; animation, interactive technology, video graphics and special effects; architectural engineering technology; business administration and management; computer and information sciences; computer engineering technology; computer programming (specific applications); computer systems networking and telecommunications; criminal justice/law enforcement administration; dental assisting; dental hygiene; diagnostic medical sonography and ultrasound technology; electrical, electronic and communications engineering technology; emergency medical technology (EMT paramedic); engineering technology; general studies; hotel/motel administration; human resources management; human services; kindergarten/preschool education; legal assistant/paralegal; liberal arts and sciences/liberal studies; marketing/marketing management; mechanical engineering/mechanical technology; mental health/rehabilitation; nursing (registered nurse training); real estate; sport and fitness administration/management; substance abuse/addiction counseling; teacher assistant/aide; tourism and travel services management; visual and performing arts.

Academics *Calendar:* semesters. *Degree:* certificates, diplomas, and associate. *Special study options:* academic remediation for entering students, adult/continuing education programs, advanced placement credit, distance learning, double majors, English as a second language, external degree program, part-time degree program, services for LD students, summer session for credit.

Library Farnum Library plus 1 other with 32,000 titles, 500 serial subscriptions, 1,000 audiovisual materials, an OPAC, a Web page.

Student Life *Housing Options:* coed. *Activities and Organizations:* drama/theater group, Phi Theta Kappa, Student Senate, Student Nurses Association, Criminal Justice Club, Outing Club. *Campus security:* 24-hour patrols, late-night transport/escort service, controlled dormitory access. *Student services:* health clinic, personal/psychological counseling.

Athletics Member NSCAA. *Intercollegiate sports:* baseball M, basketball M/W, soccer M/W, softball W, volleyball M/W. *Intramural sports:* softball W, volleyball M/W.

Standardized Tests *Required for some:* National League of Nursing Exam. *Recommended:* SAT or ACT (for admission).

Costs (2006–07) *Tuition:* state resident $4920 full-time, $164 per credit part-time; nonresident $11,280 full-time, $376 per credit part-time. *Required fees:* $480 full-time, $16 per credit part-time. *Room and board:* $6110; room only: $4150.

Financial Aid Of all full-time matriculated undergraduates, 182 Federal Work-Study jobs (averaging $1000).

Applying *Options:* electronic application. *Application fee:* $10. *Required:* high school transcript. *Required for some:* essay or personal statement, letters of recommendation, interview. *Recommended:* minimum 2.0 GPA. *Application deadlines:* rolling (freshmen), rolling (transfers). *Notification:* continuous (freshmen), continuous (transfers).

Freshmen Application Contact Mr. Francis P. Meyer, Director of Admissions, New Hampshire Technical Institute, 11 Institute Drive, Concord, NH 03301-7412. *Phone:* 603-271-7131. *Toll-free phone:* 800-247-0179. *E-mail:* fmeyer@nhctc.edu.

NEW JERSEY

ASSUMPTION COLLEGE FOR SISTERS

Mendham, New Jersey   www.acscollegeforsisters.org/

- **Independent Roman Catholic** 2-year, founded 1953
- **Rural** 112-acre campus with easy access to New York City
- **Endowment** $86,392
- **Women only**

Undergraduates 30 full-time, 7 part-time. Students come from 3 states and territories, 5 other countries, 60% are from out of state, 84% international.

Faculty *Student/faculty ratio:* 5:1.

Academics *Calendar:* semesters. *Degree:* certificates, diplomas, and associate. *Special study options:* academic remediation for entering students, advanced placement credit, English as a second language, part-time degree program, services for LD students, summer session for credit.

Student Life *Campus security:* 24-hour emergency response devices.

Costs (2006–07) *Tuition:* $3300 full-time, $100 per credit part-time. *Required fees:* $50 full-time.

Applying *Required:* high school transcript, 1 letter of recommendation, women religious or women in religious formation. *Required for some:* essay or personal statement, interview.

Freshmen Application Contact Sr. Gerardine Tantsits, Academic Dean/Registrar, Assumption College for Sisters, 350 Bernardsville Road, Mendham, NJ 07945-2923. *Phone:* 973-543-6528 Ext. 228. *Fax:* 973-543-1738. *E-mail:* srgeraldine@scceat.org.

ATLANTIC CAPE COMMUNITY COLLEGE

Mays Landing, New Jersey   www.atlantic.edu/

- **County-supported** 2-year, founded 1964
- **Small-town** 537-acre campus with easy access to Philadelphia
- **Endowment** $673,167
- **Coed**

Undergraduates 3,074 full-time, 3,771 part-time. Students come from 3 states and territories, 17 other countries, 1% are from out of state, 14% African American, 8% Asian American or Pacific Islander, 10% Hispanic American, 0.3% Native American, 0.7% international, 3% transferred in.

Faculty *Student/faculty ratio:* 24:1.

Academics *Calendar:* semesters. *Degree:* certificates, diplomas, and associate. *Special study options:* academic remediation for entering students, adult/continuing education programs, advanced placement credit, cooperative education,

distance learning, double majors, English as a second language, independent study, internships, part-time degree program, services for LD students, summer session for credit.

Student Life *Campus security:* 24-hour emergency response devices and patrols.

Athletics Member NJCAA.

Costs (2006–07) *Tuition:* area resident $2370 full-time, $79 per credit part-time; state resident $4740 full-time, $158 per credit part-time; nonresident $9480 full-time, $316 per credit part-time. *Required fees:* $550 full-time, $18 per credit part-time, $3 per term part-time.

Financial Aid Of all full-time matriculated undergraduates, 90 Federal Work-Study jobs (averaging $2000). 1,800 state and other part-time jobs (averaging $1500).

Applying *Options:* electronic application, early admission, deferred entrance. *Application fee:* $35. *Recommended:* high school transcript.

Freshmen Application Contact Mrs. Linda McLeod, Assistant Director, Admissions and College Recruitment, Atlantic Cape Community College, 5100 Black Horse Pike, Mays Landing, NJ 08330-2699. *Phone:* 609-343-5000 Ext. 5009. *Toll-free phone:* 800-645-CHIEF. *Fax:* 609-343-4921. *E-mail:* accadmit@atlantic.edu.

BERGEN COMMUNITY COLLEGE

Paramus, New Jersey   www.bergen.edu/

- **County-supported** 2-year, founded 1965
- **Suburban** 167-acre campus with easy access to New York City
- **Coed,** 14,608 undergraduate students

Undergraduates Students come from 120 other countries, 7% African American, 11% Asian American or Pacific Islander, 23% Hispanic American, 0.2% Native American, 8% international.

Faculty *Total:* 799, 43% full-time. *Student/faculty ratio:* 22:1.

Majors Accounting; administrative assistant and secretarial science; automobile/automotive mechanics technology; biology/biological sciences; broadcast journalism; business administration and management; chemistry; clinical/medical laboratory technology; commercial and advertising art; computer engineering technology; computer programming; computer science; computer typography and composition equipment operation; consumer merchandising/retailing management; criminal justice/law enforcement administration; dance; dental hygiene; drafting and design technology; dramatic/theater arts; economics; education; electrical, electronic and communications engineering technology; engineering science; finance; health science; history; hotel/motel administration; industrial radiologic technology; industrial technology; kindergarten/preschool education; kinesiology and exercise science; legal administrative assistant/secretary; legal assistant/paralegal; liberal arts and sciences/liberal studies; literature; mass communication/media; mathematics; medical administrative assistant and medical secretary; medical/clinical assistant; music; nursing (registered nurse training); ornamental horticulture; parks, recreation and leisure; philosophy; photography; physics; political science and government; psychology; real estate; respiratory care therapy; sociology; special products marketing; tourism and travel services management; veterinary technology; women's studies.

Academics *Calendar:* semesters. *Degree:* certificates and associate. *Special study options:* academic remediation for entering students, adult/continuing education programs, cooperative education, distance learning, English as a second language, honors programs, internships, part-time degree program, services for LD students, study abroad, summer session for credit.

Library Sidney Silverman Library and Learning Resources Center plus 1 other with an OPAC.

Student Life *Housing:* college housing not available. *Activities and Organizations:* drama/theater group, student-run newspaper, choral group. *Campus security:* 24-hour patrols. *Student services:* health clinic, personal/psychological counseling.

Athletics Member NJCAA. *Intercollegiate sports:* baseball M, basketball M/W, cross-country running M/W, golf M, soccer M/W, softball W, tennis M/W, track and field M/W, volleyball W, wrestling M. *Intramural sports:* basketball M, soccer M, tennis M/W, volleyball M/W.

Costs (2007–08) *Tuition:* area resident $2362 full-time, $98 per credit part-time; state resident $4848 full-time, $202 per credit hour part-time; nonresident $5112 full-time, $213 per credit part-time. *Required fees:* $624 full-time, $13 per credit part-time, $8 per term part-time.

Financial Aid Of all full-time matriculated undergraduates, 159 Federal Work-Study jobs (averaging $1575).

Applying *Notification:* continuous (freshmen), continuous (transfers).

Freshmen Application Contact Director of Admissions and Recruitment, Bergen Community College, 400 Paramus Road, Paramus, NJ 07652-1595. *Phone:* 201-447-7193. *Fax:* 201-670-7973. *E-mail:* admsoffice@bergen.edu.

BERKELEY COLLEGE

West Paterson, New Jersey   www.berkeleycollege.edu/

- **Proprietary** primarily 2-year, founded 1931, administratively affiliated with Berkeley College
- **Suburban** 25-acre campus with easy access to New York City
- **Coed,** 2,729 undergraduate students, 85% full-time, 72% women, 28% men

Undergraduates 2,325 full-time, 404 part-time. Students come from 8 states and territories, 25 other countries, 4% are from out of state, 20% African American, 5% Asian American or Pacific Islander, 35% Hispanic American, 0.2% Native American, 1% international, 5% live on campus. *Retention:* 50% of 2003 full-time freshmen returned.

Freshmen *Admission:* 844 enrolled.

Faculty *Total:* 144, 35% full-time. *Student/faculty ratio:* 22:1.

Majors Accounting; business administration and management; business/commerce; computer management; fashion merchandising; interior design; international business/trade/commerce; legal assistant/paralegal; marketing/marketing management; system administration; web page, digital/multimedia and information resources design.

Academics *Calendar:* quarters. *Degrees:* certificates, associate, and bachelor's. *Special study options:* academic remediation for entering students, accelerated degree program, adult/continuing education programs, advanced placement credit, cooperative education, distance learning, English as a second language, independent study, internships, off-campus study, part-time degree program, summer session for credit.

Library Walter A. Brower Library with 49,584 titles, 224 serial subscriptions, an OPAC, a Web page.

Student Life *Housing Options:* coed. Campus housing is university owned. *Activities and Organizations:* student-run newspaper, Student Government Association, Athletics Club, Paralegal Student Association, International Club, Fashion and Marketing Club. *Campus security:* 24-hour emergency response devices, controlled dormitory access, security patrols. *Student services:* personal/psychological counseling.

Athletics *Intramural sports:* basketball M/W, football M/W, soccer M/W, softball M/W, volleyball M/W.

Standardized Tests *Required:* SAT or ACT (for admission).

Costs (2007–08) *Comprehensive fee:* $27,150 includes full-time tuition ($17,400), mandatory fees ($750), and room and board ($9000). Part-time tuition: $415 per credit.

Financial Aid Of all full-time matriculated undergraduates, 150 Federal Work-Study jobs (averaging $1200).

Applying *Options:* electronic application, deferred entrance. *Application fee:* $50. *Required:* high school transcript. *Recommended:* interview. *Application deadlines:* rolling (freshmen), rolling (transfers).

Freshmen Application Contact Mr. David Bertone, Senior Director of Enrollment, Berkeley College, 44 Rifle Camp Road, West Paterson, NJ 07424. *Phone:* 973-278-5400. *Toll-free phone:* 800-446-5400. *Fax:* 973-328-9141. *E-mail:* info@berkeleycollege.edu.

BROOKDALE COMMUNITY COLLEGE

Lincroft, New Jersey   www.brookdalecc.edu/

Director of Admissions Ms. Kim Toomey, Registrar, Brookdale Community College, 765 Newman Springs Road, Lincroft, NJ 07738. *Phone:* 732-224-2268.

BURLINGTON COUNTY COLLEGE

Pemberton, New Jersey   www.bcc.edu/

- **County-supported** 2-year, founded 1966
- **Suburban** 225-acre campus with easy access to Philadelphia
- **Coed,** 7,797 undergraduate students, 52% full-time, 60% women, 40% men

Undergraduates 4,029 full-time, 3,768 part-time. Students come from 7 states and territories, 1% are from out of state, 21% African American, 4% Asian American or Pacific Islander, 6% Hispanic American, 0.4% Native American.

Freshmen *Admission:* 2,902 applied, 2,902 admitted, 1,901 enrolled.

Faculty *Total:* 471, 13% full-time. *Student/faculty ratio:* 27:1.

Majors Accounting; American Sign Language (ASL); art; automobile/automotive mechanics technology; biological and physical sciences; biology/biological sciences; biotechnology; business administration and management; chemical engineering; chemical technology; chemistry; civil engineering tech-

Burlington County College *(continued)*

nology; commercial and advertising art; communications technology; computer graphics; computer science; drafting and design technology; dramatic/theater arts; education; electrical, electronic and communications engineering technology; engineering; English; environmental studies; fashion/apparel design; fire science; foodservice systems administration; graphic and printing equipment operation/production; health information/medical records technology; history; hotel/motel administration; human services; information technology; journalism; legal assistant/paralegal; liberal arts and sciences/liberal studies; management information systems; mathematics; medical radiologic technology; music; nursing (registered nurse training); philosophy; physics; political science and government; psychology; sales, distribution and marketing; sign language interpretation and translation; sociology; special products marketing; survey technology.

Academics *Calendar:* semesters plus 2 summer terms. *Degree:* certificates and associate. *Special study options:* academic remediation for entering students, adult/continuing education programs, advanced placement credit, cooperative education, distance learning, double majors, English as a second language, honors programs, independent study, internships, part-time degree program, services for LD students, summer session for credit.

Library Burlington County College Library plus 1 other with 92,400 titles, 1,750 serial subscriptions, an OPAC, a Web page.

Student Life *Housing:* college housing not available. *Activities and Organizations:* drama/theater group, student-run radio station, Student Government Association, Phi Theta Kappa, Creative Writing Guild. *Campus security:* 24-hour emergency response devices and patrols, late-night transport/escort service, electronic entrances to buildings and rooms, surveillance cameras. *Student services:* health clinic, personal/psychological counseling.

Athletics Member NJCAA. *Intercollegiate sports:* baseball M, basketball M/W, golf M, soccer M/W, softball W.

Costs (2007–08) *Tuition:* area resident $1752 full-time, $73 per credit part-time; state resident $2598 full-time, $92 per credit hour part-time; nonresident $4598 full-time, $157 per credit hour part-time. *Required fees:* $396 full-time, $17 per credit part-time.

Financial Aid Of all full-time matriculated undergraduates, 100 Federal Work-Study jobs (averaging $1200). 100 state and other part-time jobs (averaging $2000).

Applying *Options:* electronic application, early admission, deferred entrance. *Application fee:* $20. *Required:* high school transcript. *Application deadlines:* rolling (freshmen), rolling (transfers). *Notification:* continuous (freshmen), continuous (transfers).

Freshmen Application Contact Ms. Elva DeJesus-Lopez, Admissions Coordinator, Burlington County College, 601 Pemberton-Browns Mills Road, Pemberton, NJ 08068-1599. *Phone:* 609-894-9311.

CAMDEN COUNTY COLLEGE
Blackwood, New Jersey www.camdencc.edu/

As one of New Jersey's largest community colleges, Camden County College enrolls nearly 15,000 students in more than 150 degree and certificate programs at locations in Blackwood, Camden, and Cherry Hill. In addition to credit programs in allied health, business, education, liberal arts and sciences, and technology, the College offers cultural programming, customized training, and professional and personal development courses.

Freshmen Application Contact James Canonica, Student Services, Camden County College, PO Box 200, College Drive, Blackwood, NJ 08012-0200. *Phone:* 856-227-7200 Ext. 4371. *Toll-free phone:* 888-228-2466. *Fax:* 856-374-4916. *E-mail:* jcanonica@camdencc.edu.

COUNTY COLLEGE OF MORRIS
Randolph, New Jersey www.ccm.edu/

Director of Admissions Ms. Jessica Chambers, Director of Admissions, County College of Morris, 214 Center Grove Road, Randolph, NJ 07869-2086. *Phone:* 973-328-5100. *Toll-free phone:* 888-226-8001. *E-mail:* admiss@ccm.edu.

CUMBERLAND COUNTY COLLEGE
Vineland, New Jersey www.cccnj.edu/

Freshmen Application Contact Ms. Maud Fried-Goodnight, Executive Director of Enrollment Services, Cumberland County College, College Drive, Vineland, NJ 08362-1500. *Phone:* 856-691-8600.

ESSEX COUNTY COLLEGE
Newark, New Jersey www.essex.edu/

- **County-supported** 2-year, founded 1966, part of New Jersey Commission on Higher Education
- **Urban** 22-acre campus with easy access to New York City
- **Coed,** 10,972 undergraduate students, 57% full-time, 61% women, 39% men

Undergraduates 6,244 full-time, 4,728 part-time. Students come from 9 states and territories, 67 other countries, 1% are from out of state, 50% African American, 3% Asian American or Pacific Islander, 19% Hispanic American, 0.1% Native American, 8% international, 3% transferred in.

Freshmen *Admission:* 5,257 applied, 5,257 admitted, 2,838 enrolled.

Faculty *Total:* 654, 24% full-time. *Student/faculty ratio:* 28:1.

Majors Accounting; accounting technology and bookkeeping; administrative assistant and secretarial science; architectural engineering technology; art; biology/biological sciences; business administration and management; business teacher education; chemical technology; chemistry; civil engineering technology; communications technology; computer programming; computer programming (specific applications); computer science; criminal justice/law enforcement administration; criminal justice/police science; data processing and data processing technology; dental assisting; dental hygiene; electrical, electronic and communications engineering technology; elementary education; emergency medical technology (EMT paramedic); fire science; health/health care administration; health professions related; hotel/motel administration; human services; industrial production technologies related; information science/studies; kindergarten/preschool education; legal assistant/paralegal; legal professions and studies related; liberal arts and sciences/liberal studies; mathematics; medical administrative assistant and medical secretary; medical radiologic technology; music; nursing (registered nurse training); opticianry; physical education teaching and coaching; physical therapist assistant; physical therapy; pre-engineering; respiratory care therapy; secondary education; social sciences; social work.

Academics *Calendar:* semesters. *Degree:* certificates and associate. *Special study options:* academic remediation for entering students, accelerated degree program, adult/continuing education programs, advanced placement credit, cooperative education, distance learning, double majors, English as a second language, independent study, internships, off-campus study, part-time degree program, services for LD students, summer session for credit. *ROTC:* Army (c).

Library Martin Luther King, Jr. Library with 91,000 titles, 639 serial subscriptions, an OPAC, a Web page.

Student Life *Housing:* college housing not available. *Activities and Organizations:* drama/theater group, student-run newspaper, choral group, Fashion Entertainment Board, Phi Theta Kappa, Latin Student Union, DECA, Black Student Association. *Campus security:* 24-hour emergency response devices and patrols. *Student services:* health clinic, personal/psychological counseling, women's center.

Athletics Member NJCAA. *Intercollegiate sports:* basketball M(s)/W(s), cross-country running M(s)/W(s), soccer M, track and field M/W. *Intramural sports:* table tennis M, weight lifting M.

Costs (2007–08) *Tuition:* area resident $2625 full-time; state resident $5250 full-time, $88 per credit hour part-time; nonresident $5250 full-time, $175 per credit hour part-time. *Required fees:* $915 full-time, $30 per credit hour part-time.

Financial Aid Of all full-time matriculated undergraduates, 250 Federal Work-Study jobs (averaging $2880).

Applying *Options:* deferred entrance. *Application fee:* $25. *Required:* high school transcript. *Application deadlines:* 8/15 (freshmen), rolling (transfers). *Notification:* continuous (freshmen), continuous (transfers).

Freshmen Application Contact Ms. Marva Mack, Director of Admissions, Essex County College, 303 University Avenue, Newark, NJ 07102. *Phone:* 973-877-3119. *Fax:* 973-623-6449.

GIBBS COLLEGE
Livingston, New Jersey www.gibbsnj.edu/

Director of Admissions Mrs. Mary-Jo Greco, President, Gibbs College, 630 West Mount Pleasant Avenue, Route 10, Livingston, NJ 07039. *Phone:* 201-744-2010. *Toll-free phone:* 888-316-0444. *Fax:* 201-744-2298. *E-mail:* mgreco@njgibbscollege.net.

GLOUCESTER COUNTY COLLEGE

Sewell, New Jersey **www.gccnj.edu/**

- **County-supported** 2-year, founded 1967, part of New Jersey Commission on Higher Education
- **Rural** 270-acre campus with easy access to Philadelphia
- **Coed**, 5,863 undergraduate students

Undergraduates 9% African American, 2% Asian American or Pacific Islander, 2% Hispanic American, 0.4% Native American, 0.6% international.

Freshmen *Admission:* 2,219 applied, 2,219 admitted.

Faculty *Total:* 292, 22% full-time. *Student/faculty ratio:* 33:1.

Majors Accounting; accounting technology and bookkeeping; automobile/automotive mechanics technology; biology/biological sciences; business administration and management; chemical engineering; chemistry; civil engineering technology; communication/speech communication and rhetoric; computer graphics; computer science; consumer merchandising/retailing management; criminal justice/police science; data processing and data processing technology; diagnostic medical sonography and ultrasound technology; drafting and design technology; dramatic/theater arts; education; engineering science; English; environmental engineering technology; finance; fine/studio arts; health and physical education; history; hospitality and recreation marketing; human development and family studies; information science/studies; kinesiology and exercise science; legal administrative assistant/secretary; legal assistant/paralegal; legal studies; liberal arts and sciences/liberal studies; marketing/marketing management; mathematics; medical administrative assistant and medical secretary; nuclear medical technology; nursing (registered nurse training); political science and government; psychology; respiratory care therapy; social sciences; sociology.

Academics *Calendar:* semesters. *Degree:* certificates and associate. *Special study options:* academic remediation for entering students, advanced placement credit, cooperative education, distance learning, part-time degree program, services for LD students, summer session for credit.

Library Gloucester County College Library with 55,710 titles, 875 serial subscriptions, 13,407 audiovisual materials, an OPAC.

Student Life *Housing:* college housing not available. *Activities and Organizations:* drama/theater group, student-run newspaper, radio station, choral group, Student Activities Board, student government, Accounting Club, Student Nurses Club, student newspaper. *Campus security:* 24-hour emergency response devices and patrols, late-night transport/escort service. *Student services:* health clinic, personal/psychological counseling, women's center.

Athletics Member NJCAA. *Intercollegiate sports:* baseball M, basketball M/W, cross-country running M/W, soccer M/W, softball W, tennis M/W, track and field M/W, wrestling M. *Intramural sports:* volleyball M/W.

Standardized Tests *Required for some:* SAT or ACT (for admission).

Costs (2007–08) *Tuition:* area resident $1848 full-time, $77 per credit part-time; state resident $1872 full-time, $78 per credit part-time; nonresident $3720 full-time, $155 per credit part-time. *Required fees:* $456 full-time, $19 per credit part-time.

Financial Aid Of all full-time matriculated undergraduates, 25 Federal Work-Study jobs (averaging $1000). *Financial aid deadline:* 6/1.

Applying *Options:* electronic application, deferred entrance. *Application fee:* $10. *Required:* high school transcript. *Application deadlines:* rolling (freshmen), rolling (transfers).

Freshmen Application Contact Ms. Judy Apkinson, Admissions Supervisor, Gloucester County College, 1400 Tanyard Road, Sewell, NJ 08080. *Phone:* 856-468-5000. *E-mail:* japkinso@gccnj.edu.

HUDSON COUNTY COMMUNITY COLLEGE

Jersey City, New Jersey **www.hccc.edu/**

Director of Admissions Mr. Robert Martin, Assistant Dean of Admissions, Hudson County Community College, 162 Sip Avenue, Jersey City, NJ 07306. *Phone:* 201-714-2115.

MERCER COUNTY COMMUNITY COLLEGE

Trenton, New Jersey **www.mccc.edu/**

- **State and locally supported** 2-year, founded 1966
- **Suburban** 292-acre campus with easy access to New York City and Philadelphia
- **Coed**

Undergraduates 3,404 full-time, 5,524 part-time. Students come from 5 states and territories, 7% are from out of state, 24% African American, 5% Asian American or Pacific Islander, 8% Hispanic American, 0.2% Native American, 5% international, 4% transferred in.

Faculty *Student/faculty ratio:* 20:1.

Academics *Calendar:* semesters. *Degree:* certificates and associate. *Special study options:* academic remediation for entering students, accelerated degree program, adult/continuing education programs, advanced placement credit, cooperative education, distance learning, double majors, English as a second language, external degree program, independent study, internships, part-time degree program, services for LD students, student-designed majors, summer session for credit. *ROTC:* Army (c), Air Force (c).

Student Life *Campus security:* 24-hour emergency response devices and patrols.

Athletics Member NJCAA.

Costs (2006–07) *Tuition:* area resident $2940 full-time, $98 per credit part-time; state resident $3945 full-time, $132 per credit part-time; nonresident $6045 full-time, $202 per credit part-time. *Required fees:* $495 full-time, $17 per credit part-time.

Financial Aid Of all full-time matriculated undergraduates, 100 Federal Work-Study jobs (averaging $1500). 12 state and other part-time jobs (averaging $1500).

Applying *Options:* electronic application, deferred entrance. *Required:* high school transcript. *Recommended:* interview.

Freshmen Application Contact Dr. L. Campbell, Dean for Student and Academic Services, Mercer County Community College, 1200 Old Trenton Road, PO Box B, Trenton, NJ 08690-1004. *Phone:* 609-586-4800 Ext. 3222. *Toll-free phone:* 800-392-MCCC. *Fax:* 609-586-6944. *E-mail:* admiss@mccc.edu.

MIDDLESEX COUNTY COLLEGE

Edison, New Jersey **www.middlesexcc.edu/**

- **County-supported** 2-year, founded 1964
- **Suburban** 200-acre campus with easy access to New York City
- **Coed**

Undergraduates Students come from 4 states and territories.

Faculty *Student/faculty ratio:* 21:1.

Academics *Calendar:* semesters. *Degree:* certificates and associate. *Special study options:* academic remediation for entering students, adult/continuing education programs, advanced placement credit, cooperative education, distance learning, English as a second language, independent study, internships, off-campus study, part-time degree program, services for LD students, study abroad, summer session for credit. *ROTC:* Army (c).

Student Life *Campus security:* 24-hour emergency response devices and patrols.

Athletics Member NJCAA.

Standardized Tests *Required for some:* National League of Nursing Exam for most health-related programs.

Costs (2006–07) *Tuition:* area resident $1957 full-time, $82 per credit part-time; state resident $4526 full-time, $189 per credit part-time. *Required fees:* $612 full-time, $26 per credit part-time.

Financial Aid Of all full-time matriculated undergraduates, 69 Federal Work-Study jobs (averaging $3350).

Applying *Options:* early admission, deferred entrance. *Application fee:* $25. *Required:* high school transcript.

Director of Admissions Mr. Peter W. Rice, Director of Admissions and Recruitment, Middlesex County College, 2600 Woodbridge Avenue, PO Box 3050, Edison, NJ 08818-3050. *Phone:* 732-906-4243.

▶See page 568 for the College Close-Up.

OCEAN COUNTY COLLEGE

Toms River, New Jersey **www.ocean.edu/**

- **County-supported** 2-year, founded 1964, part of New Jersey Commission on Higher Education
- **Small-town** 275-acre campus with easy access to Philadelphia
- **Coed**

Undergraduates 4,023 full-time, 4,426 part-time. Students come from 6 other countries, 4% African American, 2% Asian American or Pacific Islander, 6% Hispanic American, 0.3% Native American, 0.4% international.

Academics *Calendar:* semesters. *Degree:* certificates, diplomas, and associate. *Special study options:* academic remediation for entering students, accelerated degree program, adult/continuing education programs, advanced placement

Ocean County College (continued)

credit, cooperative education, distance learning, English as a second language, freshman honors college, honors programs, part-time degree program, services for LD students, study abroad, summer session for credit.

Student Life *Campus security:* 24-hour emergency response devices and patrols, late-night transport/escort service.

Athletics Member NJCAA.

Costs (2006–07) *Tuition:* area resident $2460 full-time, $82 per credit part-time; state resident $3360 full-time, $112 per credit part-time; nonresident $5520 full-time, $184 per credit part-time. *Required fees:* $720 full-time, $24 per credit part-time.

Financial Aid Of all full-time matriculated undergraduates, 76 Federal Work-Study jobs (averaging $1300). 45 state and other part-time jobs (averaging $850).

Applying *Options:* early admission, deferred entrance. *Application fee:* $15. *Required for some:* high school transcript.

Freshmen Application Contact Ms. Mary Fennessy, Director of Admissions and Records, Ocean County College, College Drive, PO Box 2001, Toms River, NJ 08754-2001. *Phone:* 732-255-0304 Ext. 2423.

PASSAIC COUNTY COMMUNITY COLLEGE

Paterson, New Jersey   **www.pccc.cc.nj.us/**

- **County-supported** 2-year, founded 1968
- **Urban** 6-acre campus with easy access to New York City
- **Endowment** $78,695
- **Coed,** 6,308 undergraduate students

Undergraduates 1% are from out of state.

Freshmen *Admission:* 2,076 applied, 2,076 admitted.

Faculty *Total:* 357, 22% full-time, 11% with terminal degrees.

Majors Accounting; administrative assistant and secretarial science; biological and physical sciences; business administration and management; consumer merchandising/retailing management; criminal justice/law enforcement administration; electrical, electronic and communications engineering technology; English; finance; fire science; health information/medical records administration; hotel/motel administration; humanities; human services; industrial radiologic technology; industrial technology; information science/studies; kindergarten/preschool education; marketing/marketing management; mathematics; medical radiologic technology; natural sciences; nursing (registered nurse training); pre-engineering; psychology; public administration; respiratory care therapy.

Academics *Calendar:* semesters. *Degree:* certificates and associate. *Special study options:* academic remediation for entering students, advanced placement credit, cooperative education, distance learning, double majors, English as a second language, honors programs, independent study, internships, part-time degree program, study abroad, summer session for credit. *ROTC:* Army (c).

Library Passaic County Community College Learning Resource Center plus 1 other with 90,000 titles, 263 serial subscriptions, 2,000 audiovisual materials.

Student Life *Housing:* college housing not available. *Activities and Organizations:* student-run newspaper, choral group, Latin American Club, Christian Club, International Club, Soccer Club, Volleyball Club. *Campus security:* late-night transport/escort service. *Student services:* personal/psychological counseling.

Athletics Member NJCAA. *Intercollegiate sports:* basketball M/W, soccer M, volleyball W. *Intramural sports:* basketball M/W, soccer M/W(c), tennis M/W, volleyball M(c)/W(c).

Costs (2006–07) *Tuition:* state resident $2340 full-time, $78 per credit part-time; nonresident $4680 full-time, $156 per credit part-time. *Required fees:* $617 full-time, $21 per credit part-time. *Payment plan:* installment. *Waivers:* employees or children of employees.

Financial Aid Of all full-time matriculated undergraduates, 100 Federal Work-Study jobs (averaging $3000).

Applying *Options:* early admission, deferred entrance. *Application deadlines:* rolling (freshmen), rolling (transfers).

Freshmen Application Contact Mr. Patrick Noonan, Director of Admissions, Passaic County Community College, One College Boulevard, Paterson, NJ 07505. *Phone:* 973-684-6304.

RARITAN VALLEY COMMUNITY COLLEGE

Somerville, New Jersey   **www.raritanval.edu/**

- **County-supported** 2-year, founded 1965
- **Small-town** 225-acre campus with easy access to New York City and Philadelphia
- **Endowment** $674,354
- **Coed,** 6,408 undergraduate students, 43% full-time, 57% women, 43% men

Undergraduates 2,770 full-time, 3,638 part-time. 0.8% are from out of state, 8% African American, 7% Asian American or Pacific Islander, 9% Hispanic American, 0.2% Native American, 5% international. *Retention:* 64% of 2003 full-time freshmen returned.

Freshmen *Admission:* 2,433 applied, 1,646 admitted, 1,173 enrolled.

Faculty *Total:* 402, 29% full-time, 29% with terminal degrees. *Student/faculty ratio:* 19:1.

Majors Accounting; administrative assistant and secretarial science; aeronautics/aviation/aerospace science and technology; artificial intelligence and robotics; automobile/automotive mechanics technology; biology/biological sciences; business administration and management; chemistry; commercial and advertising art; computer programming; computer science; construction engineering technology; consumer merchandising/retailing management; criminal justice/law enforcement administration; data processing and data processing technology; diesel mechanics technology; dramatic/theater arts; education; electrical, electronic and communications engineering technology; electromechanical technology; elementary education; engineering; environmental studies; heating, air conditioning, ventilation and refrigeration maintenance technology; hospitality and recreation marketing; hotel/motel administration; human services; industrial technology; information science/studies; intermedia/multimedia; international business/trade/commerce; kindergarten/preschool education; legal assistant/paralegal; liberal arts and sciences/liberal studies; management information systems; marketing/marketing management; mathematics; mechanical design technology; music; nursing (registered nurse training); ophthalmic laboratory technology; real estate; respiratory care therapy; social sciences; tourism and travel services management; visual and performing arts.

Academics *Calendar:* semesters. *Degree:* certificates and associate. *Special study options:* academic remediation for entering students, adult/continuing education programs, advanced placement credit, cooperative education, distance learning, English as a second language, honors programs, independent study, internships, off-campus study, part-time degree program, services for LD students, summer session for credit. *ROTC:* Army (c), Air Force (c).

Library Evelyn S. Field Learning Resources Center with 82,975 titles, 335 serial subscriptions, 1,396 audiovisual materials, an OPAC, a Web page.

Student Life *Housing:* college housing not available. *Activities and Organizations:* drama/theater group, student-run newspaper, choral group, International Club, The Latin Pride Club, Student Nurses Association, The Record (student newspaper), Christian Fellowship Club. *Campus security:* 24-hour emergency response devices and patrols, 24-hour outdoor surveillance cameras. *Student services:* personal/psychological counseling.

Athletics Member NJCAA. *Intercollegiate sports:* baseball M, basketball M, softball W. *Intramural sports:* golf M/W.

Costs (2007–08) *Tuition:* state resident $2610 full-time, $87 per credit part-time; nonresident $2610 full-time, $87 per credit part-time. *Required fees:* $880 full-time, $24 per credit part-time, $80 per term part-time.

Financial Aid Of all full-time matriculated undergraduates, 12 Federal Work-Study jobs (averaging $2500).

Applying *Options:* electronic application, early admission. *Application fee:* $25. *Required:* high school transcript. *Application deadlines:* rolling (freshmen), rolling (transfers).

Freshmen Application Contact Mr. Richard Cole, Registrar, Enrollment Services, Raritan Valley Community College, PO Box 3300, Somerville, NJ 08876-1265. *Phone:* 908-526-1200 Ext. 8206. *Fax:* 908-704-3442. *E-mail:* rcole@raritanval.edu.

SALEM COMMUNITY COLLEGE

Carneys Point, New Jersey   **www.salemcc.org/**

- **County-supported** 2-year, founded 1972, part of New Jersey Commission on Higher Education
- **Small-town** campus with easy access to Philadelphia
- **Coed**

Undergraduates 598 full-time, 653 part-time. Students come from 6 states and territories, 15% are from out of state, 22% African American, 0.5% Asian American or Pacific Islander, 4% Hispanic American, 1% Native American, 5% international, 3% transferred in.

Faculty *Student/faculty ratio:* 19:1.

Academics *Calendar:* semesters. *Degree:* certificates and associate. *Special study options:* academic remediation for entering students, adult/continuing education programs, advanced placement credit, cooperative education, distance learning, double majors, English as a second language, independent study, off-campus study, part-time degree program, services for LD students, summer session for credit.

Student Life *Campus security:* 24-hour emergency response devices and patrols, late-night transport/escort service.

Athletics Member NJCAA.

Costs (2006–07) *Tuition:* area resident $2385 full-time, $80 per credit part-time; state resident $2685 full-time, $90 per credit part-time; nonresident $2685 full-time, $90 per credit part-time. Full-time tuition and fees vary according to course load and program. Part-time tuition and fees vary according to course load and program. *Required fees:* $920 full-time, $29 per credit part-time, $25 per term part-time. *Payment plans:* installment, deferred payment.

Financial Aid Of all full-time matriculated undergraduates, 63 Federal Work-Study jobs (averaging $1000).

Applying *Options:* early admission, deferred entrance. *Application fee:* $25. *Required:* essay or personal statement, high school transcript.

Freshmen Application Contact Dr. Reva Curry, Vice President of Student Services, Salem Community College, 460 Hollywood Avenue, Carney's Point, NJ 08069. *Phone:* 856-351-2707. *Fax:* 856-299-9193. *E-mail:* info@salemcc.edu.

SOMERSET CHRISTIAN COLLEGE

Zarephath, New Jersey　　　　　**www.somerset.edu/**

- **Independent religious** 2-year, founded 1908
- **Coed,** 142 undergraduate students, 8% full-time, 54% women, 46% men

Undergraduates 11 full-time, 131 part-time. Students come from 3 states and territories, 26% African American, 4% Asian American or Pacific Islander, 5% Hispanic American, 0.7% Native American. *Retention:* 13% of 2003 full-time freshmen returned.

Freshmen *Admission:* 70 applied, 62 admitted.

Faculty *Total:* 8, 38% full-time, 50% with terminal degrees. *Student/faculty ratio:* 12:1.

Majors Biblical studies.

Academics *Calendar:* semesters plus "FastTrack" semesters. *Degree:* associate. *Special study options:* adult/continuing education programs, part-time degree program.

Library Arthur K. White Library with 60,000 titles, 95 serial subscriptions, 150 audiovisual materials, an OPAC, a Web page.

Student Life *Housing:* college housing not available. *Activities and Organizations:* student-run newspaper, radio station, Nursing Home Visitation. *Student services:* personal/psychological counseling.

Standardized Tests *Required for some:* SAT or ACT (for admission).

Costs (2006–07) *Tuition:* $6000 full-time, $210 per credit part-time. *Required fees:* $200 full-time, $100 per term part-time. *Payment plan:* installment. *Waivers:* employees or children of employees.

Financial Aid *Financial aid deadline:* 8/1.

Applying *Options:* electronic application, deferred entrance. *Application fee:* $35. *Required:* essay or personal statement, letters of recommendation. *Required for some:* high school transcript, minimum 2.5 GPA, interview. *Application deadlines:* rolling (freshmen), 9/1 (transfers). *Notification:* continuous (freshmen), continuous (transfers).

Freshmen Application Contact Ms. Coleen Klein, Director of Recruitment, Somerset Christian College, 10 College Way, P. O. Box 9188, Zarephath, NJ 08890. *Phone:* 732-356-1595. *Toll-free phone:* 800-234-9305. *Fax:* 732-356-4846. *E-mail:* info@somerset.edu.

SUSSEX COUNTY COMMUNITY COLLEGE

Newton, New Jersey　　　　　**www.sussex.edu/**

- **State and locally supported** 2-year, founded 1981, part of New Jersey Commission on Higher Education
- **Small-town** 160-acre campus with easy access to New York City
- **Coed,** 3,566 undergraduate students

Undergraduates Students come from 3 states and territories, 12% are from out of state. *Retention:* 46% of 2003 full-time freshmen returned.

Freshmen *Admission:* 629 applied, 629 admitted.

Faculty *Total:* 233, 18% full-time, 15% with terminal degrees. *Student/faculty ratio:* 22:1.

Majors Accounting; administrative assistant and secretarial science; automotive engineering technology; biological and physical sciences; broadcast journalism; business administration and management; commercial and advertising art; computer and information sciences; consumer merchandising/retailing management; corrections and criminal justice related; English; environmental studies; fine/studio arts; fire protection related; health science; human services; journalism; legal assistant/paralegal; liberal arts and sciences/liberal studies; respiratory care therapy; veterinary/animal health technology.

Academics *Calendar:* semesters. *Degree:* certificates and associate. *Special study options:* academic remediation for entering students, advanced placement credit, distance learning, double majors, English as a second language, internships, part-time degree program, services for LD students, summer session for credit.

Library Sussex County Community College Library with 34,346 titles, 266 serial subscriptions, 602 audiovisual materials, an OPAC, a Web page.

Student Life *Housing:* college housing not available. *Activities and Organizations:* drama/theater group, student-run newspaper, choral group, Student Government Association, "The College Hill" (newspaper), Human Services Club, Arts Club, Returning Adult Support Group. *Campus security:* late-night transport/escort service, trained security personnel. *Student services:* personal/psychological counseling, women's center.

Athletics Member NJCAA. *Intercollegiate sports:* baseball M, basketball M, soccer M/W, softball W. *Intramural sports:* football M/W, volleyball M/W.

Costs (2007–08) *Tuition:* area resident $2460 full-time, $82 per credit part-time; state resident $4920 full-time, $164 per credit part-time; nonresident $4920 full-time, $164 per credit part-time. *Required fees:* $585 full-time, $17 per credit part-time, $45 per term part-time.

Financial Aid Of all full-time matriculated undergraduates, 29 Federal Work-Study jobs (averaging $1500).

Applying *Application fee:* $15. *Required:* high school transcript. *Application deadlines:* rolling (freshmen), rolling (transfers). *Notification:* continuous (freshmen), continuous (transfers).

Freshmen Application Contact Mr. James Donohue, Director of Admissions and Registrar, Sussex County Community College, 1 College Hill, Newton, NJ 07860. *Phone:* 973-300-2219. *Fax:* 973-579-5226. *E-mail:* jdonohue@sussex.edu.

UNION COUNTY COLLEGE

Cranford, New Jersey　　　　　**www.ucc.edu/**

- **State and locally supported** 2-year, founded 1933, part of New Jersey Commission on Higher Education
- **Urban** 48-acre campus with easy access to New York City
- **Endowment** $9.0 million
- **Coed,** 11,166 undergraduate students, 48% full-time, 64% women, 36% men

Undergraduates 5,341 full-time, 5,825 part-time. Students come from 14 states and territories, 79 other countries, 2% are from out of state, 24% African American, 6% Asian American or Pacific Islander, 26% Hispanic American, 0.7% Native American, 3% international, 6% transferred in. *Retention:* 58% of 2003 full-time freshmen returned.

Freshmen *Admission:* 7,087 applied, 5,949 admitted, 2,071 enrolled.

Faculty *Total:* 436, 41% full-time. *Student/faculty ratio:* 27:1.

Majors Accounting technology and bookkeeping; administrative assistant and secretarial science; allied health diagnostic, intervention, and treatment professions related; biology/biological sciences; business administration and management; business and personal/financial services marketing; business/commerce; chemistry; civil engineering technology; clinical/medical laboratory technology; communication/speech communication and rhetoric; criminal justice/police science; dental hygiene; electromechanical technology; engineering; fire protection and safety technology; gerontology; hotel/motel administration; industrial technology; information science/studies; language interpretation and translation; liberal arts and sciences/liberal studies; management information systems; mechanical engineering/mechanical technology; medical/clinical assistant; medical radiologic technology; nuclear medical technology; nursing (licensed practical/vocational nurse training); nursing (registered nurse training); occupational therapist assistant; physical sciences; physical therapist assistant; rehabilitation and therapeutic professions related; respiratory care therapy; sign language interpretation and translation.

Academics *Calendar:* semesters. *Degree:* certificates, diplomas, and associate. *Special study options:* academic remediation for entering students, accelerated degree program, adult/continuing education programs, advanced placement

Union County College *(continued)*

credit, distance learning, English as a second language, honors programs, independent study, internships, off-campus study, part-time degree program, services for LD students, student-designed majors, summer session for credit. *ROTC:* Air Force (c).

Library MacKay Library plus 2 others with 137,731 titles, 20,938 serial subscriptions, 3,610 audiovisual materials, an OPAC, a Web page.

Student Life *Housing:* college housing not available. *Activities and Organizations:* drama/theater group, student-run newspaper, radio and television station, SIGN, Spanish Club, Black Students Heritage Organization, Student Government Organization, International Cultural Exchange Students. *Campus security:* 24-hour emergency response devices and patrols, late-night transport/escort service. *Student services:* personal/psychological counseling.

Athletics Member NJCAA. *Intercollegiate sports:* baseball M, basketball M/W(s), golf M/W, soccer M, volleyball W. *Intramural sports:* cheerleading W.

Costs (2007–08) *Tuition:* area resident $2460 full-time, $87 per credit part-time; state resident $4920 full-time, $174 per credit part-time; nonresident $4920 full-time, $174 per credit part-time. *Required fees:* $780 full-time, $26 per credit part-time.

Financial Aid Of all full-time matriculated undergraduates, 150 Federal Work-Study jobs (averaging $1700).

Applying *Options:* electronic application, early admission, deferred entrance. *Application fee:* $30. *Required:* high school transcript. *Required for some:* interview. *Application deadlines:* rolling (freshmen), rolling (transfers). *Notification:* continuous (freshmen), continuous (transfers).

Freshmen Application Contact Ms. Jo Ann Davis-Wayne, Director of Admissions, Records, and Registration, Union County College, 1033 Springfield Avenue, Cranford, NJ 07016. *Phone:* 908-709-7127. *Fax:* 908-709-7125.

WARREN COUNTY COMMUNITY COLLEGE

Washington, New Jersey www.warren.edu/

- **State and locally supported** 2-year, founded 1981, part of New Jersey Commission on Higher Education
- **Rural** 77-acre campus
- **Coed,** 1,801 undergraduate students

Undergraduates Students come from 4 states and territories.

Freshmen *Admission:* 480 applied, 480 admitted.

Faculty *Total:* 70, 43% full-time. *Student/faculty ratio:* 13:1.

Majors Accounting; administrative assistant and secretarial science; biology/biological sciences; business administration and management; criminal justice/law enforcement administration; data processing and data processing technology; education; environmental studies; fine/studio arts; information science/studies; legal assistant/paralegal; liberal arts and sciences/liberal studies; social sciences.

Academics *Calendar:* semesters. *Degree:* certificates and associate. *Special study options:* academic remediation for entering students, advanced placement credit, cooperative education, distance learning, double majors, English as a second language, independent study, internships, off-campus study, part-time degree program, services for LD students, summer session for credit.

Library 23,143 titles, 375 serial subscriptions, 1,300 audiovisual materials.

Student Life *Housing:* college housing not available. *Activities and Organizations:* drama/theater group, student-run newspaper, national fraternities. *Campus security:* evening and weekend security.

Standardized Tests *Required:* New Jersey Basic Skills Exam (for placement).

Costs (2007–08) *Tuition:* area resident $2580 full-time, $86 per credit part-time; state resident $2880 full-time, $96 per credit part-time; nonresident $3180 full-time, $106 per credit part-time. *Required fees:* $683 full-time, $11 per credit part-time.

Financial Aid Of all full-time matriculated undergraduates, 20 Federal Work-Study jobs (averaging $2000).

Applying *Options:* early admission, deferred entrance. *Application fee:* $15. *Application deadlines:* rolling (freshmen), rolling (transfers).

Freshmen Application Contact Admissions Advisor, Warren County Community College, 475 Route 57 West, Washington, NJ 07882-9605. *Phone:* 908-835-2300.

NEW MEXICO

THE ART CENTER DESIGN COLLEGE

Albuquerque, New Mexico www.theartcenter.edu/

Director of Admissions Ms. Colleen Gimbel-Froebe, Associate Director of Admissions and Placement, The Art Center Design College, 5000 Marble NE, Albuquerque, NM 87110. *Phone:* 520-325-0123. *Toll-free phone:* 800-825-8753.

CENTRAL NEW MEXICO COMMUNITY COLLEGE

Albuquerque, New Mexico www.tvi.cc.nm.us/

- **State-supported** 2-year, founded 1965
- **Urban** 60-acre campus
- **Endowment** $1.2 million
- **Coed,** 22,615 undergraduate students, 30% full-time, 59% women, 41% men

Undergraduates 6,677 full-time, 15,938 part-time. 2% are from out of state, 3% African American, 2% Asian American or Pacific Islander, 42% Hispanic American, 7% Native American, 0.4% international, 5% transferred in.

Freshmen *Admission:* 4,558 applied, 4,558 admitted, 2,842 enrolled.

Faculty *Total:* 991, 34% full-time. *Student/faculty ratio:* 20:1.

Majors Accounting; administrative assistant and secretarial science; architectural drafting and CAD/CADD; banking and financial support services; biotechnology; building/construction finishing, management, and inspection related; business administration and management; child care and support services management; clinical/medical laboratory technology; computer systems analysis; construction trades related; cosmetology; court reporting; criminal justice/safety; culinary arts; data processing and data processing technology; diagnostic medical sonography and ultrasound technology; electrical, electronic and communications engineering technology; electrical/electronics drafting and CAD/CADD; elementary education; engineering; engineering technologies related; environmental/environmental health engineering; fire protection and safety technology; health information/medical records administration; hospitality administration; industrial technology; information science/studies; laser and optical technology; legal assistant/paralegal; liberal arts and sciences/liberal studies; nursing (registered nurse training); parks, recreation, and leisure related; respiratory care therapy; vehicle maintenance and repair technologies related.

Academics *Calendar:* trimesters. *Degree:* associate. *Special study options:* academic remediation for entering students, adult/continuing education programs, advanced placement credit, cooperative education, distance learning, double majors, English as a second language, internships, part-time degree program, services for LD students, summer session for credit. *ROTC:* Air Force (c).

Library Main Campus Library plus 1 other with an OPAC, a Web page.

Student Life *Housing:* college housing not available. *Activities and Organizations:* student-run newspaper, Phi Theta Kappa, student government, Hispanic Club, TVI Times (student newspaper). *Campus security:* 24-hour emergency response devices and patrols, late-night transport/escort service. *Student services:* health clinic, personal/psychological counseling.

Costs (2006–07) *Tuition:* area resident $1447 full-time, $41 per credit hour part-time; state resident $1717 full-time, $49 per credit hour part-time; nonresident $7730 full-time, $221 per credit hour part-time. *Required fees:* $90 full-time, $40 per term part-time. *Waivers:* senior citizens.

Financial Aid Of all full-time matriculated undergraduates, 175 Federal Work-Study jobs (averaging $6000). 225 state and other part-time jobs (averaging $6000).

Applying *Options:* electronic application, early admission. *Recommended:* high school transcript. *Application deadlines:* rolling (freshmen), rolling (transfers). *Notification:* continuous (freshmen).

Freshmen Application Contact Ms. Jane Campbell, Director, Enrollment Services, Central New Mexico Community College, 900 University, SE, Albuquerque, NM 87106-4096. *Phone:* 505-224-3160. *Fax:* 505-224-3237.

CLOVIS COMMUNITY COLLEGE

Clovis, New Mexico www.clovis.edu/

- **State-supported** 2-year, founded 1990
- **Small-town** 25-acre campus
- **Endowment** $600,000
- **Coed,** 3,522 undergraduate students, 26% full-time, 67% women, 33% men

Undergraduates 921 full-time, 2,601 part-time. Students come from 42 states and territories, 2 other countries, 26% are from out of state, 5% African American, 2% Asian American or Pacific Islander, 34% Hispanic American, 1% Native American, 5% transferred in. *Retention:* 33% of 2003 full-time freshmen returned.

Freshmen *Admission:* 612 applied, 612 admitted, 512 enrolled.

Faculty *Total:* 184, 27% full-time, 11% with terminal degrees. *Student/faculty ratio:* 15:1.

Majors Accounting; administrative assistant and secretarial science; automobile/automotive mechanics technology; bilingual and multilingual education; business administration and management; business automation/technology/data entry; commercial and advertising art; computer and information sciences; computer typography and composition equipment operation; corrections; cosmetology; criminal justice/police science; electromechanical technology; executive assistant/executive secretary; finance; fine/studio arts; health and physical education; heating, air conditioning, ventilation and refrigeration maintenance technology; legal administrative assistant/secretary; legal assistant/paralegal; liberal arts and sciences/liberal studies; library assistant; management information systems; mathematics; medical administrative assistant and medical secretary; medical office assistant; medical radiologic technology; nail technician and manicurist; nursing (registered nurse training); physical sciences; psychology; sign language interpretation and translation; teacher assistant/aide; technical and business writing; web/multimedia management and webmaster; web page, digital/multimedia and information resources design.

Academics *Calendar:* semesters. *Degree:* certificates and associate. *Special study options:* academic remediation for entering students, adult/continuing education programs, advanced placement credit, cooperative education, distance learning, double majors, English as a second language, independent study, internships, part-time degree program, services for LD students, summer session for credit.

Library Clovis Community College Library and Learning Resources Center with 52,000 titles, 370 serial subscriptions, an OPAC.

Student Life *Housing:* college housing not available. *Activities and Organizations:* drama/theater group, choral group, Student Senate, Student Nursing Association, Black Advisory Council, Hispanic Advisory Council, student ambassadors. *Campus security:* student patrols, late-night transport/escort service. *Student services:* personal/psychological counseling.

Athletics *Intramural sports:* basketball M/W, cross-country running M/W, racquetball M/W, tennis M/W, volleyball M/W.

Costs (2007–08) *Tuition:* area resident $736 full-time, $29 per credit hour part-time; state resident $784 full-time, $31 per credit hour part-time; nonresident $1480 full-time, $60 per credit hour part-time. *Required fees:* $36 full-time, $3 per credit part-time, $20 per term part-time.

Applying *Required:* high school transcript. *Required for some:* interview. *Notification:* continuous (transfers).

Freshmen Application Contact Ms. Rosie Corrie, Director of Admissions and Records/Registrar, Clovis Community College, 417 Schepps Boulevard, Clovis, NM 88101-8381. *Phone:* 505-769-4962. *Fax:* 505-769-4190. *E-mail:* admissions@clovis.edu.

CROWNPOINT INSTITUTE OF TECHNOLOGY

Crownpoint, New Mexico   www.citech.edu/academics.htm

Admissions Office Contact Crownpoint Institute of Technology, PO Box 849, Crownpoint, NM 87313.

DOÑA ANA BRANCH COMMUNITY COLLEGE

Las Cruces, New Mexico   dabcc-www.nmsu.edu/

Freshmen Application Contact Admissions Counselor, Doña Ana Branch Community College, MSC-3DA, Box 30001, Las Cruces, NM 88003-8001. *Phone:* 505-527-7532. *Toll-free phone:* 800-903-7503. *Fax:* 505-527-7515.

EASTERN NEW MEXICO UNIVERSITY–ROSWELL

Roswell, New Mexico   www.enmu.edu/

- **State-supported** 2-year, founded 1958, part of Eastern New Mexico University System
- **Small-town** 241-acre campus
- **Endowment** $494,460
- **Coed,** 3,522 undergraduate students

Undergraduates Students come from 6 states and territories, 3 other countries, 0.6% are from out of state, 2% African American, 0.3% Asian American or Pacific Islander, 47% Hispanic American, 2% Native American, 0.1% international, 5% live on campus.

Freshmen *Admission:* 860 applied, 473 admitted.

Faculty *Total:* 270, 23% full-time, 4% with terminal degrees. *Student/faculty ratio:* 16:1.

Majors Administrative assistant and secretarial science; airframe mechanics and aircraft maintenance technology; automobile/automotive mechanics technology; banking and financial support services; business administration and management; child care and support services management; computer and information sciences; criminal justice/safety; drafting and design technology; electromechanical technology; emergency medical technology (EMT paramedic); fire science; human services; industrial technology; legal assistant/paralegal; liberal arts and sciences/liberal studies; medical office management; nursing (registered nurse training); occupational therapist assistant; social work; welding technology.

Academics *Calendar:* semesters. *Degree:* certificates and associate. *Special study options:* academic remediation for entering students, adult/continuing education programs, advanced placement credit, cooperative education, distance learning, English as a second language, independent study, internships, off-campus study, part-time degree program, services for LD students, summer session for credit. *ROTC:* Army (c), Navy (c), Air Force (c).

Library Learning Resource Center with 327 serial subscriptions, 5,727 audiovisual materials, an OPAC.

Student Life *Housing Options:* coed. *Activities and Organizations:* drama/theater group, student-run newspaper, choral group, student government, Spanish Club, Drama Club, Phi Theta Kappa. *Campus security:* 24-hour emergency response devices, student patrols, late-night transport/escort service.

Athletics *Intramural sports:* basketball M, football M, golf M, racquetball M/W, skiing (cross-country) W, tennis M/W, volleyball M/W.

Standardized Tests *Recommended:* ACT (for admission).

Costs (2006–07) *Tuition:* area resident $1051 full-time; state resident $1090 full-time; nonresident $4320 full-time.

Financial Aid Of all full-time matriculated undergraduates, 100 Federal Work-Study jobs (averaging $4000). 60 state and other part-time jobs (averaging $4000).

Applying *Options:* early admission. *Required:* high school transcript. *Application deadlines:* rolling (freshmen), rolling (transfers).

Freshmen Application Contact Mr. James Mares, Assistant Director, Eastern New Mexico University–Roswell, PO Box 6000, Roswell, NM 88202-6000. *Phone:* 505-624-7149. *Toll-free phone:* 800-243-6687.

INSTITUTE OF AMERICAN INDIAN ARTS

Santa Fe, New Mexico   www.iaia.edu/

Director of Admissions Myra Garro, Manager of Enrollment and Admissions, Institute of American Indian Arts, 83 Avan Nu Po Road, Santa Fe, NM 87508. *Phone:* 505-424-2328.

INTERNATIONAL INSTITUTE OF THE AMERICAS

Albuquerque, New Mexico   www.iia-online.com/site/

- **Independent** primarily 2-year
- **Urban** campus
- **Coed,** 185 undergraduate students, 100% full-time, 89% women, 11% men

Undergraduates 185 full-time. 2% African American, 63% Hispanic American, 18% Native American.

Faculty *Total:* 15, 47% full-time, 27% with terminal degrees. *Student/faculty ratio:* 12:1.

Majors Accounting; business administration and management; criminal justice/law enforcement administration; health/health care administration; legal assistant/paralegal.

Academics *Calendar:* continuous. *Degrees:* diplomas, associate, and bachelor's. *Special study options:* distance learning, part-time degree program.

Library Learning Resource Center with an OPAC.

Student Life *Housing:* college housing not available. *Campus security:* 24-hour emergency response devices.

Costs (2007–08) *Tuition:* $9850 full-time. *Required fees:* $200 full-time.

Applying *Application fee:* $200. *Required:* interview. *Application deadlines:* rolling (freshmen), rolling (transfers). *Notification:* continuous (freshmen), continuous (transfers).

International Institute of the Americas (continued)

Freshmen Application Contact Campus Director, International Institute of the Americas, 4201 Central Avenue NW, Suite J, Albuquerque, NM 87105-1649. *Phone:* 505-880-2877. *Toll-free phone:* 888-660-2428. *Fax:* 505-352-0199. *E-mail:* esigman@iia.edu.

ITT TECHNICAL INSTITUTE

Albuquerque, New Mexico　　　　**www.itt-tech.edu/**

- **Proprietary** primarily 2-year, founded 1989, part of ITT Educational Services, Inc
- **Coed**

Majors Animation, interactive technology, video graphics and special effects; business administration and management; computer and information systems security; computer engineering technology; computer systems networking and telecommunications; construction management; criminal justice/law enforcement administration; electrical, electronic and communications engineering technology; medical laboratory technology; system, networking, and LAN/WAN management; web/multimedia management and webmaster; web page, digital/multimedia and information resources design.

Academics *Calendar:* quarters. *Degrees:* associate and bachelor's.

Library a Web page.

Student Life *Housing:* college housing not available.

Standardized Tests *Required:* Wonderlic aptitude test (for admission).

Costs (2006–07) *Tuition:* Contact school for program costs.

Applying *Options:* deferred entrance. *Application fee:* $100. *Required:* high school transcript, interview. *Recommended:* letters of recommendation. *Application deadlines:* rolling (freshmen), rolling (transfers). *Notification:* continuous (freshmen), continuous (transfers).

Freshmen Application Contact Mr. John Crooks, Director of Recruitment, ITT Technical Institute, 5100 Masthead Street NE, Albuquerque, NM 87109. *Phone:* 505-828-1114. *Toll-free phone:* 800-636-1114.

LUNA COMMUNITY COLLEGE

Las Vegas, New Mexico　　　　**www.luna.cc.nm.us/**

Freshmen Application Contact Ms. Henrietta Griego, Director of Admissions, Recruitment, and Retention, Luna Community College, 366 Luna Drive, Las Vegas, NM 87701. *Phone:* 505-454-2020. *Toll-free phone:* 800-588-7232 Ext. 1202. *Fax:* 505-454-2588. *E-mail:* hgriego@luna.cc.nm.us.

MESALANDS COMMUNITY COLLEGE

Tucumcari, New Mexico　　　　**www.mesalands.edu/**

Director of Admissions Mr. Ken Brashear, Director of Enrollment Management, Mesalands Community College, 911 South Tenth Street, Tucumcari, NM 88401. *Phone:* 505-461-4413.

NATIONAL AMERICAN UNIVERSITY

Rio Rancho, New Mexico　　　　**www.national.edu/**

- **Proprietary** 2-year
- **Coed,** 231 undergraduate students

Majors Accounting; business administration, management and operations related; computer and information sciences; education; engineering; general studies; health/health care administration; information technology; management science.

Academics *Degree:* associate.

Costs (2006–07) *Tuition:* $9302 full-time.

Applying *Application fee:* $25.

Freshmen Application Contact Admissions Office, National American University, 1601 Rio Rancho, Suite 200, Rio Rancho, NM 87124.

NEW MEXICO JUNIOR COLLEGE

Hobbs, New Mexico　　　　**www.nmjc.edu/**

- **State and locally supported** 2-year, founded 1965, part of New Mexico Commission on Higher Education
- **Small-town** 185-acre campus
- **Coed,** 3,222 undergraduate students

Undergraduates Students come from 17 states and territories, 7 other countries, 10% are from out of state, 4% African American, 0.5% Asian American or Pacific Islander, 32% Hispanic American, 0.9% Native American, 0.2% international, 15% live on campus.

Freshmen *Average high school GPA:* 2.75.

Faculty *Total:* 120, 54% full-time. *Student/faculty ratio:* 19:1.

Majors Accounting; administrative assistant and secretarial science; agriculture; art; art teacher education; athletic training; automobile/automotive mechanics technology; biological and physical sciences; biology/biological sciences; business administration and management; business teacher education; carpentry; chemistry; clinical/medical laboratory technology; commercial and advertising art; computer graphics; computer programming; computer science; computer typography and composition equipment operation; construction engineering technology; cosmetology; criminal justice/police science; data processing and data processing technology; drafting and design technology; dramatic/theater arts; education; elementary education; emergency medical technology (EMT paramedic); engineering; English; environmental education; environmental studies; finance; fire science; health science; history; industrial arts; legal administrative assistant/secretary; liberal arts and sciences/liberal studies; machine tool technology; marketing/marketing management; mathematics; medical administrative assistant and medical secretary; medical/clinical assistant; music; nursing (licensed practical/vocational nurse training); nursing (registered nurse training); parks, recreation and leisure; petroleum technology; physical education teaching and coaching; real estate; trade and industrial teacher education; welding technology.

Academics *Calendar:* semesters. *Degree:* certificates and associate. *Special study options:* academic remediation for entering students, adult/continuing education programs, advanced placement credit, cooperative education, distance learning, internships, part-time degree program, services for LD students, summer session for credit.

Library Pannell Library with 118,500 titles, 45 serial subscriptions, an OPAC, a Web page.

Student Life *Housing:* on-campus residence required for freshman year. *Options:* coed. Campus housing is university owned. *Activities and Organizations:* drama/theater group, choral group, Student Nurses Association, Phi Theta Kappa, Fellowship of Christian Athletes. *Campus security:* 24-hour emergency response devices and patrols, late-night transport/escort service, controlled dormitory access. *Student services:* health clinic, personal/psychological counseling.

Athletics Member NJCAA. *Intercollegiate sports:* baseball M(s), basketball M(s)/W(s), golf M(s). *Intramural sports:* badminton M/W, basketball M/W, cross-country running M/W, football M, racquetball M/W, table tennis M/W, volleyball M/W, weight lifting M/W.

Standardized Tests *Recommended:* ACT (for placement).

Costs (2006–07) *Tuition:* area resident $850 full-time; state resident $1258 full-time; nonresident $1378 full-time.

Applying *Options:* early admission, deferred entrance. *Application deadlines:* rolling (freshmen), rolling (transfers).

Director of Admissions Mr. Robert Bensing, Dean of Enrollment Management, New Mexico Junior College, 5317 Lovington Highway, Hobbs, NM 88240-9123. *Phone:* 505-392-5092. *Toll-free phone:* 800-657-6260.

NEW MEXICO MILITARY INSTITUTE

Roswell, New Mexico　　　　**www.nmmi.edu/**

- **State-supported** 2-year, founded 1891, part of New Mexico Commission on Higher Education
- **Small-town** 42-acre campus
- **Endowment** $370.9 million
- **Coed, primarily men,** 480 undergraduate students, 100% full-time, 15% women, 85% men

Undergraduates 480 full-time. Students come from 43 states and territories, 9 other countries, 59% are from out of state, 16% African American, 9% Asian American or Pacific Islander, 19% Hispanic American, 3% Native American, 7% international, 100% live on campus. *Retention:* 93% of 2003 full-time freshmen returned.

Freshmen *Admission:* 601 applied, 375 admitted.

Faculty *Total:* 65, 100% full-time. *Student/faculty ratio:* 17:1.

Majors Accounting; Army R.O.T.C./military science; art; biological and physical sciences; biology/biological sciences; business administration and management; chemistry; civil engineering technology; computer programming; computer science; criminal justice/law enforcement administration; criminal justice/police science; economics; engineering; English; finance; French; German; history; humanities; liberal arts and sciences/liberal studies; mathematics; physical education teaching and coaching; physics; pre-engineering; social sciences; Spanish; sport and fitness administration/management.

Academics *Calendar:* semesters. *Degree:* associate. *Special study options:* academic remediation for entering students, English as a second language, summer session for credit. *ROTC:* Army (b).

Library Paul Horgan Library plus 2 others with 65,000 titles, 200 serial subscriptions, an OPAC.

Student Life *Housing:* on-campus residence required through sophomore year. *Options:* coed. Campus housing is university owned. *Activities and Organizations:* drama/theater group, student-run newspaper, television station, choral group, marching band, band, chorus, drill teams, Officer's Club. *Campus security:* 24-hour emergency response devices and patrols, controlled dormitory access. *Student services:* health clinic, personal/psychological counseling.

Athletics Member NJCAA. *Intercollegiate sports:* baseball M(s), basketball M(s), fencing M/W, football M(s), golf M(s), riflery M/W, tennis M(s)/W(s), track and field M(s), volleyball W(s). *Intramural sports:* basketball M/W, bowling M/W, cross-country running M/W, fencing M/W, football M, golf M/W, racquetball M/W, riflery M/W, skiing (cross-country) M/W, skiing (downhill) M/W, soccer M/W, swimming and diving M/W, tennis M/W, track and field M/W, volleyball M/W, weight lifting M/W.

Standardized Tests *Required:* SAT or ACT (for admission).

Costs (2007–08) *One-time required fee:* $1800. *Tuition:* state resident $1337 full-time; nonresident $4577 full-time. *Required fees:* $1613 full-time. *Room and board:* $3736.

Financial Aid Of all full-time matriculated undergraduates, 15 Federal Work-Study jobs (averaging $181). 3 state and other part-time jobs (averaging $191).

Applying *Options:* early admission, deferred entrance. *Application fee:* $60. *Required:* high school transcript, minimum 2.0 GPA. *Application deadlines:* 8/1 (freshmen), 8/1 (transfers). *Notification:* continuous (freshmen), continuous (transfers).

Freshmen Application Contact New Mexico Military Institute, 101 West College Boulevard, Roswell, NM 88201-5173. *Phone:* 800-421-5376. *Toll-free phone:* 800-421-5376. *Fax:* 505-624-8058. *E-mail:* admissions@nmmi.edu.

NEW MEXICO STATE UNIVERSITY– ALAMOGORDO

Alamogordo, New Mexico alamo.nmsu.edu/

- **State-supported** 2-year, founded 1958, part of New Mexico State University System
- **Small-town** 540-acre campus
- **Coed,** 1,897 undergraduate students, 38% full-time, 65% women, 35% men

Undergraduates 712 full-time, 1,185 part-time. Students come from 3 other countries, 12% are from out of state, 4% African American, 3% Asian American or Pacific Islander, 28% Hispanic American, 4% Native American, 1% international, 5% transferred in. *Retention:* 45% of 2003 full-time freshmen returned.

Freshmen *Admission:* 270 applied, 270 admitted, 270 enrolled.

Faculty *Total:* 98, 54% full-time. *Student/faculty ratio:* 14:1.

Majors Administrative assistant and secretarial science; business/commerce; clinical/medical laboratory technology; commercial and advertising art; criminal justice/safety; data processing and data processing technology; education; electrical, electronic and communications engineering technology; engineering; fire science; legal assistant/paralegal; liberal arts and sciences/liberal studies; nursing (registered nurse training); office occupations and clerical services; social work; teacher assistant/aide.

Academics *Calendar:* semesters. *Degree:* certificates and associate. *Special study options:* academic remediation for entering students, adult/continuing education programs, advanced placement credit, distance learning, honors programs, independent study, internships, off-campus study, part-time degree program, services for LD students, study abroad, summer session for credit.

Library David H. Townsend Library with 39,000 titles, 350 serial subscriptions, an OPAC, a Web page.

Student Life *Housing:* college housing not available. *Activities and Organizations:* drama/theater group, choral group, Social Science Club, Phi Theta Kappa, Student/NEA, Christian Fellowship, Epsilon Tau Sigma. *Campus security:* 24-hour emergency response devices. *Student services:* personal/psychological counseling.

Athletics *Intramural sports:* basketball M/W, volleyball M/W.

Costs (2007–08) *Tuition:* area resident $1344 full-time, $56 per credit hour part-time; state resident $1512 full-time, $63 per credit hour part-time; nonresident $4008 full-time, $167 per credit hour part-time.

Financial Aid Of all full-time matriculated undergraduates, 10 Federal Work-Study jobs (averaging $3300). 60 state and other part-time jobs (averaging $3300). *Financial aid deadline:* 5/1.

Applying *Options:* electronic application, early admission, deferred entrance. *Application fee:* $15. *Required:* high school transcript, minimum 2.0 GPA. *Application deadlines:* rolling (freshmen), rolling (transfers). *Notification:* continuous (freshmen), continuous (transfers).

Freshmen Application Contact Ms. Kathy Fuller, Coordinator of Admissions and Records, New Mexico State University–Alamogordo, 2400 North Scenic Drive, Alamogordo, NM 88311-0477. *Phone:* 505-439-3700. *E-mail:* advisor@nmsua.nmsu.edu.

NEW MEXICO STATE UNIVERSITY– CARLSBAD

Carlsbad, New Mexico www.cavern.nmsu.edu/

Freshmen Application Contact Ms. Everal Shannon, Records Specialist, New Mexico State University–Carlsbad, 1500 University Drive, Carlsbad, NM 88220-3509. *Phone:* 505-234-9222.

NEW MEXICO STATE UNIVERSITY– GRANTS

Grants, New Mexico grants.nmsu.edu/

Director of Admissions Ms. Irene Lutz, Campus Student Services Officer, New Mexico State University–Grants, 1500 3rd Street, Grants, NM 87020-2025. *Phone:* 505-287-7981.

NORTHERN NEW MEXICO COLLEGE

Española, New Mexico www.nnmc.edu/

- **State-supported** primarily 2-year, founded 1909, part of New Mexico Commission on Higher Education
- **Rural** 35-acre campus
- **Endowment** $829,791
- **Coed,** 2,272 undergraduate students

Undergraduates Students come from 5 states and territories, 1% are from out of state, 1% live on campus.

Freshmen *Admission:* 320 applied, 320 admitted. *Average high school GPA:* 2.63.

Faculty *Total:* 253, 18% full-time, 8% with terminal degrees.

Majors Biotechnology; business/commerce; computer and information sciences; criminal justice/safety; electrical, electronic and communications engineering technology; elementary education; environmental studies; fine/studio arts; human services; industrial engineering; industrial radiologic technology; library assistant; medical radiologic technology.

Academics *Calendar:* semesters. *Degrees:* certificates, associate, and bachelor's. *Special study options:* academic remediation for entering students, advanced placement credit, distance learning, part-time degree program, services for LD students, summer session for credit.

Library Northern New Mexico Community College Library with 18,065 titles, 222 serial subscriptions.

Student Life *Housing Options:* coed. *Activities and Organizations:* nursing organization, radiography organization, AISES, Aikido, Phi Theta Kappa. *Campus security:* 24-hour emergency response devices and patrols.

Costs (2006–07) *Tuition:* state resident $1080 full-time, $36 per credit part-time; nonresident $2550 full-time, $85 per credit part-time. Full-time tuition and fees vary according to course level. Part-time tuition and fees vary according to course level. *Required fees:* $156 full-time, $7 per credit part-time. *Waivers:* senior citizens and employees or children of employees.

Financial Aid Of all full-time matriculated undergraduates, 150 Federal Work-Study jobs (averaging $3000). 140 state and other part-time jobs (averaging $3000).

Applying *Options:* early admission, deferred entrance. *Required:* high school transcript. *Application deadlines:* rolling (freshmen), rolling (transfers).

Northern New Mexico College (continued)
Freshmen Application Contact Mr. Mike L. Costello, Registrar, Northern New Mexico College, 921 Paseo de Oñate, Española, NM 87532. *Phone:* 505-747-2193. *Fax:* 505-747-2191. *E-mail:* dms@nnmc.edu.

PIMA MEDICAL INSTITUTE

Albuquerque, New Mexico
www.pmi.edu/

- **Proprietary** 2-year, founded 1985, part of Vocational Training Institutes, Inc
- **Urban** campus
- **Coed**

Undergraduates 420 full-time.
Faculty *Student/faculty ratio:* 20:1.
Academics *Calendar:* modular. *Degree:* certificates and associate. *Special study options:* academic remediation for entering students, cooperative education, internships, services for LD students.
Standardized Tests *Required:* Wonderlic Scholastic Level Exam (for admission).
Costs (2006–07) *Tuition:* Tuition varies depending on course.
Financial Aid Of all full-time matriculated undergraduates, 6 Federal Work-Study jobs.
Applying *Options:* early admission. *Required:* interview. *Required for some:* high school transcript.
Freshmen Application Contact Admissions Office, Pima Medical Institute, 2201 San Pedro NE, Building 3, Suite 100, Albuquerque, NM 87110. *Phone:* 505-881-1234. *Toll-free phone:* 888-898-9048. *Fax:* 505-881-5329.

SAN JUAN COLLEGE

Farmington, New Mexico
www.sanjuancollege.edu/

- **State-supported** 2-year, founded 1958, part of New Mexico Commission on Higher Education
- **Small-town** 698-acre campus
- **Endowment** $11.6 million
- **Coed,** 6,366 undergraduate students, 38% full-time, 48% women, 52% men

Undergraduates 2,441 full-time, 3,925 part-time. Students come from 17 states and territories, 2 other countries, 8% are from out of state, 0.7% African American, 0.5% Asian American or Pacific Islander, 12% Hispanic American, 35% Native American, 3% transferred in.
Freshmen *Admission:* 995 applied, 995 admitted, 584 enrolled.
Faculty *Total:* 374, 27% full-time. *Student/faculty ratio:* 20:1.
Majors Accounting technology and bookkeeping; administrative assistant and secretarial science; airline pilot and flight crew; anthropology; art; autobody/collision and repair technology; automobile/automotive mechanics technology; banking and financial support services; biology/biological sciences; business administration and management; carpentry; chemistry; commercial and advertising art; communication/speech communication and rhetoric; computer science; criminal justice/police science; criminal justice/safety; diesel mechanics technology; drafting and design technology; dramatic/theater arts; economics; education; engineering; English; fire protection and safety technology; foreign languages and literatures; general studies; geology/earth science; health information/medical records technology; history; human services; information science/studies; instrumentation technology; kindergarten/preschool education; legal assistant/paralegal; mathematics; music; nursing (registered nurse training); parks, recreation and leisure; philosophy; physical sciences; physical therapist assistant; physics; political science and government; pre-medical studies; psychology; public administration; real estate; social work; sociology; water quality and wastewater treatment management and recycling technology; welding technology.
Academics *Calendar:* semesters. *Degree:* certificates and associate. *Special study options:* academic remediation for entering students, adult/continuing education programs, advanced placement credit, cooperative education, distance learning, English as a second language, honors programs, independent study, internships, part-time degree program, services for LD students, summer session for credit.
Library San Juan College Library with 81,116 titles, 6,677 serial subscriptions, an OPAC, a Web page.
Student Life *Housing:* college housing not available. *Activities and Organizations:* drama/theater group, student-run newspaper, radio station, choral group, national fraternities, national sororities. *Campus security:* 24-hour patrols, late-night transport/escort service. *Student services:* personal/psychological counseling.

Athletics *Intramural sports:* archery M/W, badminton M/W, basketball M/W, bowling M/W, cross-country running M/W, football M/W, golf M/W, racquetball M/W, rock climbing M/W, skiing (cross-country) M/W, skiing (downhill) M/W, soccer M/W, softball M/W, table tennis M/W, tennis M/W, volleyball M/W.
Costs (2006–07) *Tuition:* state resident $720 full-time, $30 per credit hour part-time; nonresident $960 full-time, $40 per credit hour part-time. Full-time tuition and fees vary according to program and reciprocity agreements. Part-time tuition and fees vary according to program. *Payment plans:* tuition prepayment, installment. *Waivers:* senior citizens and employees or children of employees.
Financial Aid Of all full-time matriculated undergraduates, 150 Federal Work-Study jobs (averaging $2500). 175 state and other part-time jobs (averaging $2500).
Applying *Options:* electronic application, early admission, deferred entrance. *Required:* high school transcript. *Application deadlines:* rolling (freshmen), rolling (transfers). *Notification:* continuous (freshmen), continuous (transfers).
Freshmen Application Contact Admissions Specialist, San Juan College, 4601 College Boulevard, Farmington, NM 87402. *Phone:* 505-566-3318.

SANTA FE COMMUNITY COLLEGE

Santa Fe, New Mexico
www.sfccnm.edu/

Freshmen Application Contact Patty Armstrong, Admissions Counselor, Santa Fe Community College, 6401 Richards Avenue, Santa Fe, NM 87505. *Phone:* 505-428-1406. *Fax:* 505-428-1237. *E-mail:* parmstrong@sfccnm.edu.

SOUTHWESTERN INDIAN POLYTECHNIC INSTITUTE

Albuquerque, New Mexico
www.sipi.bia.edu/

- **Federally supported** 2-year, founded 1971
- **Suburban** 174-acre campus
- **Coed,** 818 undergraduate students

Undergraduates Students come from 33 states and territories.
Freshmen *Admission:* 337 applied, 320 admitted. *Average high school GPA:* 2.11.
Faculty *Total:* 98. *Student/faculty ratio:* 15:1.
Majors Accounting; administrative assistant and secretarial science; business administration and management; civil engineering technology; commercial and advertising art; computer science; culinary arts; data processing and data processing technology; drafting and design technology; electrical, electronic and communications engineering technology; engineering technology; laser and optical technology; liberal arts and sciences/liberal studies; marketing/marketing management; natural resources management and policy.
Academics *Calendar:* trimesters. *Degree:* certificates and associate. *Special study options:* academic remediation for entering students, advanced placement credit, cooperative education, double majors, internships, part-time degree program, services for LD students, summer session for credit.
Library 26,000 titles, 120 serial subscriptions.
Student Life *Housing:* college housing not available. *Campus security:* 24-hour emergency response devices, late-night transport/escort service. *Student services:* health clinic, personal/psychological counseling.
Athletics Member NJCAA. *Intercollegiate sports:* cross-country running M/W.
Standardized Tests *Required:* TABE or ACT COMPASS (for placement).
Costs (2006–07) *Tuition:* state resident $675 full-time; nonresident $675 full-time. *Payment plan:* deferred payment.
Financial Aid Of all full-time matriculated undergraduates, 25 Federal Work-Study jobs (averaging $300). 37 state and other part-time jobs (averaging $400). *Financial aid deadline:* 10/1.
Applying *Required:* high school transcript, certificate of Indian Blood form. *Application deadline:* rolling (freshmen). *Notification:* continuous (freshmen).
Director of Admissions Joseph Carpid, Director Admissions, Southwestern Indian Polytechnic Institute, 9169 Coors, NW, Box 10146, Albuquerque, NM 87120-3103. *Phone:* 505-346-2324. *Toll-free phone:* 800-586-7474. *Fax:* 505-346-2324. *E-mail:* jcarpid@sipi.bia.edu.

UNIVERSITY OF NEW MEXICO—GALLUP

Gallup, New Mexico
www.gallup.unm.edu/

- **State-supported** primarily 2-year, founded 1968, part of New Mexico Commission on Higher Education
- **Small-town** 80-acre campus
- **Coed,** 2,858 undergraduate students

Undergraduates Students come from 10 states and territories, 4 other countries, 0.3% African American, 0.5% Asian American or Pacific Islander, 10% Hispanic American, 76% Native American, 0.2% international.

Freshmen *Average high school GPA:* 2.25.

Faculty *Total:* 159, 47% full-time. *Student/faculty ratio:* 25:1.

Majors Accounting; administrative assistant and secretarial science; art; automobile/automotive mechanics technology; business administration and management; clinical/medical laboratory technology; communication/speech communication and rhetoric; community organization and advocacy; construction engineering technology; corrections; cosmetology; criminal justice/law enforcement administration; education; elementary education; entrepreneurship; general studies; graphic and printing equipment operation/production; health teacher education; kindergarten/preschool education; legal assistant/paralegal; liberal arts and sciences/liberal studies; marketing/marketing management; nursing (registered nurse training); physical education teaching and coaching; physical sciences; welding technology.

Academics *Calendar:* semesters. *Degrees:* certificates, diplomas, associate, and bachelor's. *Special study options:* academic remediation for entering students, adult/continuing education programs, advanced placement credit, cooperative education, honors programs, internships, part-time degree program, services for LD students, student-designed majors, summer session for credit.

Library Zollinger Library plus 1 other with 36,172 titles, 354 serial subscriptions.

Student Life *Housing:* college housing not available. *Activities and Organizations:* student-run newspaper. *Campus security:* late-night transport/escort service.

Standardized Tests *Required for some:* SAT (for admission), ACT (for admission).

Costs (2006–07) *Tuition:* state resident $1344 full-time; nonresident $3096 full-time.

Applying *Options:* early admission. *Application fee:* $15. *Required for some:* high school transcript. *Application deadlines:* rolling (freshmen), rolling (transfers). *Notification:* continuous (freshmen), continuous (transfers).

Director of Admissions Ms. Pearl A. Morris, Admissions Representative, University of New Mexico–Gallup, 200 College Road, Gallup, NM 87301-5603. *Phone:* 505-863-7576.

UNIVERSITY OF NEW MEXICO—LOS ALAMOS BRANCH

Los Alamos, New Mexico　　　　**www.la.unm.edu/**

- **State-supported** 2-year, founded 1980, part of New Mexico Commission on Higher Education
- **Small-town** 5-acre campus
- **Coed,** 890 undergraduate students

Undergraduates Students come from 12 states and territories, 3 other countries, 0.7% African American, 3% Asian American or Pacific Islander, 39% Hispanic American, 3% Native American, 1% international.

Freshmen *Admission:* 213 applied, 213 admitted.

Faculty *Total:* 96.

Majors Accounting; administrative assistant and secretarial science; applied art; biological and physical sciences; business administration and management; computer engineering technology; computer programming; computer science; electrical, electronic and communications engineering technology; engineering; environmental studies; fine/studio arts; liberal arts and sciences/liberal studies; pre-engineering.

Academics *Calendar:* semesters. *Degree:* certificates and associate. *Special study options:* academic remediation for entering students, adult/continuing education programs, advanced placement credit, cooperative education, English as a second language, internships, off-campus study, part-time degree program, services for LD students, summer session for credit.

Library 10,000 titles, 160 serial subscriptions.

Student Life *Housing Options:* Campus housing is university owned. *Activities and Organizations:* student-run newspaper, choral group.

Standardized Tests *Required for some:* SAT or ACT (for placement).

Costs (2006–07) *Tuition:* state resident $1176 full-time; nonresident $3228 full-time.

Financial Aid Of all full-time matriculated undergraduates, 15 Federal Work-Study jobs (averaging $5000). 10 state and other part-time jobs (averaging $7000).

Applying *Options:* early admission, deferred entrance. *Application fee:* $15. *Application deadlines:* 8/12 (freshmen), 8/12 (transfers). *Notification:* continuous (freshmen), continuous (transfers).

Director of Admissions Ms. Anna Mae Apodaca, Associate Campus Director for Student Services, University of New Mexico–Los Alamos Branch, 4000 University Drive, Los Alamos, NM 87544-2233. *Phone:* 505-661-4692. *Toll-free phone:* 800-894-5919. *E-mail:* aapodaca@la.unm.edu.

UNIVERSITY OF NEW MEXICO—TAOS

Taos, New Mexico　　　　**taos.unm.edu/**

- **State-supported** 2-year, founded 1923
- **Coed,** 1,186 undergraduate students

Majors Administrative assistant and secretarial science; art; behavioral sciences; business administration, management and operations related; communication and journalism related; construction trades; corrections and criminal justice related; crafts, folk art and artisanry; criminal justice/safety; early childhood education; education; general studies; human services; liberal arts and sciences/liberal studies; physical sciences.

Academics *Calendar:* semesters. *Degree:* associate.

Costs (2006–07) *Tuition:* state resident $1320 full-time; nonresident $3120 full-time.

Applying *Application fee:* $15.

Admissions Office Contact University of New Mexico–Taos, 115 Civic Plaza Drive, Taos, NM 87571.

UNIVERSITY OF NEW MEXICO— VALENCIA CAMPUS

Los Lunas, New Mexico　　　　**www.unm.edu/~unmvc/**

- **State-supported** 2-year, founded 1981, part of New Mexico Commission on Higher Education
- **Small-town** campus with easy access to Albuquerque
- **Coed,** 1,544 undergraduate students

Undergraduates Students come from 4 states and territories, 2 other countries.

Faculty *Total:* 93, 20% full-time.

Majors Administrative assistant and secretarial science; agriculture; business administration and management; computer science; computer typography and composition equipment operation; construction engineering technology; construction management; criminal justice/law enforcement administration; education; human services; information science/studies; liberal arts and sciences/liberal studies; pre-engineering; real estate.

Academics *Calendar:* semesters. *Degree:* certificates and associate. *Special study options:* academic remediation for entering students, adult/continuing education programs, English as a second language, honors programs, part-time degree program, services for LD students, summer session for credit.

Library 9,500 titles, 150 serial subscriptions.

Student Life *Housing:* college housing not available. *Campus security:* 24-hour emergency response devices and patrols, late-night transport/escort service. *Student services:* personal/psychological counseling.

Standardized Tests *Required for some:* SAT or ACT (for placement), ACT COMPASS. *Recommended:* ACT COMPASS.

Costs (2006–07) *Tuition:* state resident $1248 full-time; nonresident $3336 full-time.

Financial Aid *Financial aid deadline:* 3/1.

Applying *Options:* early admission, deferred entrance. *Application fee:* $15. *Required for some:* minimum 2.0 GPA. *Recommended:* high school transcript. *Application deadlines:* rolling (freshmen), rolling (transfers). *Notification:* continuous until 8/25 (freshmen).

Director of Admissions Ms. Lucy Sanchez, Registrar, University of New Mexico–Valencia Campus, 280 La Entrada, Los Lunas, NM 87031-7633. *Phone:* 505-925-8580.

NEW YORK

ADIRONDACK COMMUNITY COLLEGE

Queensbury, New York　　　　**www.sunyacc.edu/**

Freshmen Application Contact Office of Admissions, Adirondack Community College, 640 Bay Road, Queensbury, NY 12804. *Phone:* 518-743-2264. *Fax:* 518-743-2200.

AMERICAN ACADEMY MCALLISTER INSTITUTE OF FUNERAL SERVICE

New York, New York　　　　www.funeraleducation.org

- **Independent** 2-year, founded 1926
- **Urban** campus
- **Coed,** 130 undergraduate students, 100% full-time, 58% women, 42% men

Undergraduates 130 full-time. Students come from 9 states and territories, 4 other countries, 26% are from out of state, 44% African American, 5% Hispanic American, 7% international, 36% transferred in.

Freshmen *Admission:* 47 enrolled.

Faculty *Total:* 20, 10% full-time, 10% with terminal degrees. *Student/faculty ratio:* 25:1.

Majors Funeral service and mortuary science.

Academics *Calendar:* semesters. *Degree:* diplomas and associate.

Library American Academy MacAllister Institute Library with 1,672 titles, 78 serial subscriptions, 165 audiovisual materials.

Student Life *Housing:* college housing not available.

Costs (2006–07) *Tuition:* $11,040 full-time.

Applying *Options:* early admission, deferred entrance. *Application fee:* $35. *Required:* high school transcript, 2 letters of recommendation. *Recommended:* interview. *Application deadlines:* rolling (freshmen), 8/30 (transfers). *Notification:* continuous until 8/15 (freshmen).

Freshmen Application Contact Mr. Norman Provost, Registrar, American Academy McAllister Institute of Funeral Service, 619 West 54th Street, New York, NY 10019-3602. *Phone:* 212-757-1190. *Toll-free phone:* 866-932-2264.

AMERICAN ACADEMY OF DRAMATIC ARTS

New York, New York　　　　www.aada.org/

- **Independent** 2-year, founded 1884
- **Urban** campus
- **Endowment** $5.1 million
- **Coed,** 248 undergraduate students, 100% full-time, 65% women, 35% men

Undergraduates 248 full-time. Students come from 31 states and territories, 17 other countries, 88% are from out of state, 3% African American, 1% Asian American or Pacific Islander, 6% Hispanic American, 0.8% Native American, 19% international. *Retention:* 66% of 2003 full-time freshmen returned.

Freshmen *Admission:* 247 applied, 120 admitted, 61 enrolled. *Average high school GPA:* 2.86.

Faculty *Total:* 27, 26% full-time, 15% with terminal degrees. *Student/faculty ratio:* 16:1.

Majors Dramatic/theater arts.

Academics *Calendar:* continuous. *Degree:* certificates and associate.

Library Academy/CBS Library with 7,467 titles, 24 serial subscriptions, 570 audiovisual materials.

Student Life *Housing:* college housing not available. *Campus security:* 24-hour emergency response devices, trained security guard during hours of operation.

Costs (2006–07) *Tuition:* $16,900 full-time. *Required fees:* $500 full-time.

Financial Aid Of all full-time matriculated undergraduates, 40 Federal Work-Study jobs (averaging $3500). 10 state and other part-time jobs (averaging $2000). *Financial aid deadline:* 5/15.

Applying *Options:* deferred entrance. *Application fee:* $50. *Required:* essay or personal statement, high school transcript, minimum 2.00 GPA, 2 letters of recommendation, interview, audition. *Application deadlines:* rolling (freshmen), rolling (transfers). *Notification:* continuous (freshmen), continuous (transfers).

Freshmen Application Contact Ms. Karen Higginbotham, Director of Admissions, American Academy of Dramatic Arts, 120 Madison Avenue, New York, NY 10016. *Toll-free phone:* 800-463-8990. *Fax:* 212-696-1284. *E-mail:* admissions-ny@aada.org.

▶**See page 472 for the College Close-Up.**

THE ART INSTITUTE OF NEW YORK CITY

New York, New York　　　　www.ainyc.aii.edu/

- **Proprietary** 2-year, founded 1980, part of Education Management Corporation
- **Urban** campus
- **Coed,** 1,519 undergraduate students

Undergraduates Students come from 3 states and territories, 25% are from out of state, 30% African American, 7% Asian American or Pacific Islander, 30% Hispanic American, 2% Native American, 100% live on campus.

Freshmen *Average high school GPA:* 2.2.

Faculty *Total:* 99, 82% full-time, 4% with terminal degrees. *Student/faculty ratio:* 17:1.

Majors Animation, interactive technology, video graphics and special effects; cinematography and film/video production; fashion/apparel design; graphic design; restaurant, culinary, and catering management.

Academics *Calendar:* quarters. *Degree:* certificates, diplomas, and associate. *Special study options:* academic remediation for entering students, advanced placement credit, cooperative education, internships, part-time degree program, summer session for credit.

Library Metropolitan College of NYC with an OPAC, a Web page.

Student Life *Housing Options:* men-only, women-only. Campus housing is provided by a third party.

Costs (2007–08) *Tuition:* $21,150 full-time, $470 per credit part-time. *Required fees:* $697 full-time. *Room only:* $14,400.

Applying *Application fee:* $50. *Required:* essay or personal statement, high school transcript, interview. *Recommended:* minimum 2.0 GPA. *Application deadlines:* rolling (freshmen), rolling (out-of-state freshmen), rolling (transfers). *Notification:* continuous (freshmen), continuous (out-of-state freshmen), continuous (transfers).

Freshmen Application Contact Mr. Rick Henson, The Art Institute of New York City, 75 Varick Street, 16th Floor, New York, NY 10013. *Phone:* 212-226-5500 Ext. 6005. *Toll-free phone:* 800-654-2433. *Fax:* 212-226-5664. *E-mail:* rhenson@aii.edu.

▶**See page 480 for the College Close-Up.**

ASA INSTITUTE, THE COLLEGE OF ADVANCED TECHNOLOGY

Brooklyn, New York　　　　www.asa.edu/

Freshmen Application Contact Admissions Office, ASA Institute, The College of Advanced Technology, 151 Lawrence Street, Brooklyn, NY 11201. *Phone:* 718-522-9073.

BERKELEY COLLEGE–NEW YORK CITY CAMPUS

New York, New York　　　　www.berkeleycollege.edu/

- **Proprietary** primarily 2-year, founded 1936, administratively affiliated with Berkeley College
- **Urban** campus
- **Coed,** 2,412 undergraduate students, 91% full-time, 70% women, 30% men

Undergraduates 2,202 full-time, 210 part-time. Students come from 14 states and territories, 66 other countries, 9% are from out of state, 22% African American, 5% Asian American or Pacific Islander, 23% Hispanic American, 0.4% Native American, 15% international, 5% transferred in. *Retention:* 50% of 2003 full-time freshmen returned.

Freshmen *Admission:* 2,279 applied, 1,675 admitted, 458 enrolled.

Faculty *Total:* 140, 29% full-time. *Student/faculty ratio:* 26:1.

Majors Accounting; apparel marketing; business administration and management; business/commerce; entrepreneurship; fashion merchandising; international business/trade/commerce; legal assistant/paralegal; management information systems and services related; marketing/marketing management; office management; pre-law.

Academics *Calendar:* quarters. *Degrees:* certificates, associate, and bachelor's. *Special study options:* academic remediation for entering students, accelerated degree program, adult/continuing education programs, advanced

placement credit, cooperative education, distance learning, English as a second language, independent study, internships, off-campus study, part-time degree program, student-designed majors, study abroad, summer session for credit.

Library 13,164 titles, 138 serial subscriptions, an OPAC, a Web page.

Student Life *Housing:* college housing not available. *Activities and Organizations:* student-run newspaper, student government, International Club, Paralegal Club, Accounting Club. *Campus security:* 24-hour emergency response devices. *Student services:* personal/psychological counseling.

Standardized Tests *Required:* SAT or ACT (for admission).

Costs (2007–08) *Tuition:* $17,400 full-time, $425 per credit part-time. *Required fees:* $750 full-time.

Financial Aid Of all full-time matriculated undergraduates, 120 Federal Work-Study jobs (averaging $1500).

Applying *Options:* electronic application, deferred entrance. *Application fee:* $50. *Required:* high school transcript. *Recommended:* interview. *Application deadlines:* rolling (freshmen), rolling (transfers).

Freshmen Application Contact Ms. Linda Pinsky, Associate Vice President, Enrollment, Berkeley College-New York City Campus, 3 East 43rd Street, New York, NY 10017. *Phone:* 212-986-4343 Ext. 4117. *Toll-free phone:* 800-446-5400. *Fax:* 212-818-1079. *E-mail:* info@berkeleycollege.edu.

BERKELEY COLLEGE-WESTCHESTER CAMPUS

White Plains, New York   **www.berkeleycollege.edu/**

- **Proprietary** primarily 2-year, founded 1945
- **Suburban** campus with easy access to New York City
- **Coed,** 640 undergraduate students, 92% full-time, 70% women, 30% men

Undergraduates 591 full-time, 49 part-time. Students come from 9 states and territories, 28 other countries, 15% are from out of state, 23% African American, 4% Asian American or Pacific Islander, 24% Hispanic American, 0.3% Native American, 7% international, 10% live on campus. *Retention:* 55% of 2003 full-time freshmen returned.

Freshmen *Admission:* 167 enrolled.

Faculty *Total:* 42, 40% full-time. *Student/faculty ratio:* 22:1.

Majors Accounting; apparel marketing; business administration and management; business/commerce; fashion merchandising; international business/trade/commerce; legal assistant/paralegal; management information systems and services related; marketing/marketing management; office management; pre-law.

Academics *Calendar:* quarters. *Degrees:* certificates, associate, and bachelor's. *Special study options:* academic remediation for entering students, accelerated degree program, adult/continuing education programs, advanced placement credit, cooperative education, distance learning, English as a second language, independent study, internships, off-campus study, part-time degree program, student-designed majors, study abroad, summer session for credit.

Library 9,526 titles, 66 serial subscriptions, 777 audiovisual materials, an OPAC, a Web page.

Student Life *Housing Options:* coed. Campus housing is university owned. *Activities and Organizations:* student-run newspaper, student government, Paralegal Club, Fashion Club, Phi Theta Kappa. *Campus security:* 24-hour emergency response devices, controlled dormitory access, monitored entrance with front desk security guard. *Student services:* personal/psychological counseling.

Standardized Tests *Required:* SAT or ACT (for admission).

Costs (2007–08) *Comprehensive fee:* $27,150 includes full-time tuition ($17,400), mandatory fees ($750), and room and board ($9000). Part-time tuition: $415 per credit.

Financial Aid Of all full-time matriculated undergraduates, 40 Federal Work-Study jobs (averaging $1100).

Applying *Options:* electronic application, deferred entrance. *Application fee:* $50. *Required:* high school transcript. *Recommended:* interview. *Application deadlines:* rolling (freshmen), rolling (transfers).

Freshmen Application Contact Mr. John Wool, Assistant Director of Admissions, Berkeley College-Westchester Campus, 99 Church Street, White Plains, NY 10601. *Phone:* 914-694-1122 Ext. 3110. *Toll-free phone:* 800-446-5400. *Fax:* 914-328-9469. *E-mail:* info@berkeleycollege.edu.

BOROUGH OF MANHATTAN COMMUNITY COLLEGE OF THE CITY UNIVERSITY OF NEW YORK

New York, New York   **www.bmcc.cuny.edu/**

- **State and locally supported** 2-year, founded 1963, part of City University of New York System
- **Urban** 5-acre campus
- **Endowment** $3.3 million
- **Coed**

Undergraduates 10,809 full-time, 7,967 part-time. Students come from 3 states and territories, 100 other countries, 12% are from out of state, 36% African American, 10% Asian American or Pacific Islander, 29% Hispanic American, 0.1% Native American, 11% international, 10% transferred in.

Faculty *Student/faculty ratio:* 22:1.

Academics *Calendar:* semesters. *Degree:* certificates and associate. *Special study options:* academic remediation for entering students, adult/continuing education programs, advanced placement credit, cooperative education, distance learning, English as a second language, honors programs, independent study, internships, off-campus study, part-time degree program, services for LD students, study abroad, summer session for credit.

Student Life *Campus security:* 24-hour patrols.

Athletics Member NJCAA.

Costs (2006–07) *Tuition:* state resident $2800 full-time, $120 per credit hour part-time; nonresident $5700 full-time, $190 per credit hour part-time. Full-time tuition and fees vary according to course load. Part-time tuition and fees vary according to course load. *Required fees:* $268 full-time, $75 per term part-time.

Applying *Options:* electronic application, deferred entrance. *Application fee:* $65. *Required:* high school transcript.

Freshmen Application Contact Mr. Eugenio Barrios, Director of Admissions, Borough of Manhattan Community College of the City University of New York, 199 Chambers Street, Room S-300, New York, NY 10007. *Phone:* 212-220-1265. *Fax:* 212-220-2366. *E-mail:* admissions@bmcc.cuny.edu.

BRAMSON ORT COLLEGE

Forest Hills, New York   **www.bramsonort.edu/**

- **Independent** 2-year, founded 1977
- **Coed,** 600 undergraduate students

Undergraduates Students come from 3 states and territories, 5 other countries.

Faculty *Total:* 80, 40% full-time.

Majors Accounting; administrative assistant and secretarial science; business administration and management; business machine repair; business teacher education; computer engineering technology; computer management; computer programming; computer science; electrical, electronic and communications engineering technology; electromechanical technology; information science/studies; legal administrative assistant/secretary; marketing/marketing management.

Academics *Calendar:* semesters. *Degree:* certificates and associate. *Special study options:* academic remediation for entering students, advanced placement credit, English as a second language, internships, part-time degree program, summer session for credit.

Library 8,000 titles, 110 serial subscriptions.

Student Life *Housing:* college housing not available. *Activities and Organizations:* student-run newspaper. *Student services:* personal/psychological counseling, women's center.

Costs (2006–07) *Tuition:* $8760 full-time, $2190 per term part-time. Full-time tuition and fees vary according to course load. Part-time tuition and fees vary according to course load. No tuition increase for student's term of enrollment. *Required fees:* $330 full-time, $140 per term part-time. *Payment plans:* installment, deferred payment. *Waivers:* employees or children of employees.

Applying *Options:* early admission, deferred entrance. *Application fee:* $50. *Required:* high school transcript. *Application deadlines:* rolling (freshmen), rolling (transfers).

Freshmen Application Contact Admissions Office, Bramson ORT College, 69-30 Austin Street, Forest Hills, NY 11375-4239. *Phone:* 718-261-5800. *Fax:* 718-575-5119. *E-mail:* admission@bramsonort.edu.

BRONX COMMUNITY COLLEGE OF THE CITY UNIVERSITY OF NEW YORK

Bronx, New York　　　　　**www.bcc.cuny.edu/**

- **State and locally supported** 2-year, founded 1959, part of City University of New York System
- **Urban** 50-acre campus
- **Coed**

Undergraduates 5,088 full-time, 3,382 part-time. Students come from 16 states and territories, 100 other countries, 35% African American, 3% Asian American or Pacific Islander, 48% Hispanic American, 0.2% Native American, 11% international, 5% transferred in. *Retention:* 65% of 2003 full-time freshmen returned.

Faculty *Student/faculty ratio:* 15:1.

Academics *Calendar:* semesters. *Degree:* certificates and associate. *Special study options:* academic remediation for entering students, adult/continuing education programs, advanced placement credit, cooperative education, distance learning, English as a second language, honors programs, independent study, internships, part-time degree program, services for LD students, study abroad, summer session for credit.

Student Life *Campus security:* 24-hour patrols.

Athletics Member NJCAA.

Costs (2006–07) *Tuition:* state resident $2800 full-time; nonresident $4560 full-time. *Required fees:* $284 full-time.

Applying *Application fee:* $65. *Required:* high school transcript.

Freshmen Application Contact Ms. Alba N. Cancetty, Admissions Officer, Bronx Community College of the City University of New York, University Avenue and West 181st Street, Bronx, NY 10453. *Phone:* 718-289-5888. *E-mail:* admission@bcc.cuny.edu.

BROOME COMMUNITY COLLEGE

Binghamton, New York　　　　**www.sunybroome.edu/**

- **State and locally supported** 2-year, founded 1946, part of State University of New York System
- **Suburban** 223-acre campus
- **Endowment** $1.3 million
- **Coed**, 6,282 undergraduate students, 64% full-time, 56% women, 44% men

Undergraduates 3,993 full-time, 2,289 part-time. Students come from 32 states and territories, 33 other countries, 3% are from out of state, 4% African American, 1% Asian American or Pacific Islander, 2% Hispanic American, 0.4% Native American, 2% international, 6% transferred in. *Retention:* 64% of 2003 full-time freshmen returned.

Freshmen *Admission:* 1,398 enrolled.

Faculty *Total:* 406, 41% full-time. *Student/faculty ratio:* 19:1.

Majors Accounting technology and bookkeeping; business administration and management; child care and support services management; civil engineering technology; clinical/medical laboratory technology; communication/speech communication and rhetoric; communications systems installation and repair technology; computer and information sciences; computer engineering technology; corrections; criminal justice/police science; data processing and data processing technology; dental hygiene; electrical, electronic and communications engineering technology; emergency medical technology (EMT paramedic); engineering science; executive assistant/executive secretary; financial planning and services; fire science; health information/medical records technology; hotel/motel administration; industrial production technologies related; information science/studies; international finance; legal assistant/paralegal; liberal arts and sciences/liberal studies; mechanical engineering/mechanical technology; medical/clinical assistant; medical radiologic technology; mental and social health services and allied professions related; merchandising, sales, and marketing operations related (general); nursing (registered nurse training); physical therapist assistant; quality control technology; substance abuse/addiction counseling.

Academics *Calendar:* semesters. *Degree:* certificates and associate. *Special study options:* academic remediation for entering students, adult/continuing education programs, advanced placement credit, distance learning, English as a second language, external degree program, honors programs, independent study, internships, off-campus study, part-time degree program, services for LD students, student-designed majors, study abroad, summer session for credit.

Library Cecil C. Tyrrell Learning Resources Center with an OPAC, a Web page.

Student Life *Housing:* college housing not available. *Activities and Organizations:* student-run newspaper, choral group, Broome Early Childhood Organization, Differentially Disabled Student Association, Ecology Club, Phi Theta Kappa, Criminal Justice Club. *Campus security:* 24-hour emergency response devices and patrols. *Student services:* health clinic, personal/psychological counseling.

Athletics Member NJCAA. *Intercollegiate sports:* baseball M, basketball M/W, cross-country running M/W, golf M, ice hockey M, lacrosse M, soccer M/W, softball W, tennis M/W, volleyball W. *Intramural sports:* basketball M/W, volleyball M/W.

Costs (2006–07) *Tuition:* state resident $2914 full-time, $122 per credit hour part-time; nonresident $5828 full-time, $244 per credit hour part-time. Full-time tuition and fees vary according to course load. Part-time tuition and fees vary according to course load. *Required fees:* $405 full-time, $6 per credit hour part-time, $64 per term part-time. *Waivers:* senior citizens and employees or children of employees.

Applying *Options:* electronic application, early admission. *Required:* high school transcript. *Required for some:* interview. *Application deadlines:* rolling (freshmen), rolling (transfers). *Notification:* continuous (freshmen), continuous (transfers).

Freshmen Application Contact Mr. Anthony Fiorelli, Director of Admissions, Broome Community College, PO Box 1017, Upper Front Street, Binghamton, NY 13902. *Phone:* 607-778-5001. *Fax:* 607-778-5394. *E-mail:* admissions@sunybroome.edu.

BRYANT AND STRATTON COLLEGE

Albany, New York　　　　**www.bryantstratton.edu/**

- **Proprietary** 2-year, founded 1857, part of Bryant and Stratton College
- **Suburban** campus
- **Coed**

Undergraduates 354 full-time, 116 part-time. Students come from 1 other state, 48% African American, 2% Asian American or Pacific Islander, 7% Hispanic American, 1% Native American. *Retention:* 45% of 2003 full-time freshmen returned.

Academics *Calendar:* semesters. *Degree:* associate. *Special study options:* academic remediation for entering students, distance learning, double majors, independent study, internships, part-time degree program, services for LD students, summer session for credit.

Student Life *Campus security:* 24-hour emergency response devices.

Standardized Tests *Required:* CPAt, ACCUPLACER (for admission). *Recommended:* SAT or ACT (for admission).

Costs (2006–07) *Tuition:* $415 per credit hour part-time. Part-time tuition and fees vary according to course load. *Required fees:* $62 per term part-time.

Financial Aid Of all full-time matriculated undergraduates, 10 Federal Work-Study jobs (averaging $800).

Applying *Options:* deferred entrance. *Required:* high school transcript, interview, entrance and placement evaluations. *Required for some:* letters of recommendation.

Freshmen Application Contact Mr. Robert Ferrell, Director of Admissions, Bryant and Stratton College, 1259 Central Avenue, Albany, NY 12205. *Phone:* 518-437-1802 Ext. 205. *Fax:* 518-437-1048.

BRYANT AND STRATTON COLLEGE

Rochester, New York　　　　**www.bryantstratton.edu/**

- **Proprietary** 2-year, founded 1985, part of Bryant and Stratton College
- **Suburban** 1-acre campus
- **Coed**

Undergraduates 238 full-time, 59 part-time. Students come from 4 states and territories, 36% African American, 1% Asian American or Pacific Islander, 5% Hispanic American, 0.3% Native American, 6% transferred in.

Faculty *Student/faculty ratio:* 10:1.

Academics *Calendar:* semesters. *Degree:* associate. *Special study options:* academic remediation for entering students, adult/continuing education programs, distance learning, double majors, independent study, internships, part-time degree program, services for LD students, summer session for credit.

Student Life *Campus security:* late-night transport/escort service.

Standardized Tests *Required:* CPAt (for admission). *Recommended:* SAT or ACT (for admission).

Costs (2006–07) *Tuition:* $415 per credit hour part-time. *Required fees:* $62 per term part-time.

Financial Aid Of all full-time matriculated undergraduates, 44 Federal Work-Study jobs (averaging $630).

Applying *Options:* electronic application, deferred entrance. *Required:* high school transcript, interview, entrance evaluation and placement evaluation. *Required for some:* letters of recommendation. *Recommended:* minimum 2.0 GPA.

Freshmen Application Contact Ms. Maria Scalise, Market Director of Admissions, Bryant and Stratton College, 150 Bellwood Drive, Greece Campus, Rochester, NY 14606. *Phone:* 585-292-5627 Ext. 101. *Fax:* 716-292-6015.

BRYANT AND STRATTON COLLEGE

Rochester, New York   www.bryantstratton.edu/

- **Proprietary** 2-year, founded 1973, part of Bryant and Stratton College
- **Urban** campus
- **Coed**

Undergraduates 152 full-time, 42 part-time. Students come from 4 states and territories, 26% African American, 12% Hispanic American, 0.5% Native American, 14% transferred in.

Academics *Calendar:* semesters. *Degree:* associate. *Special study options:* academic remediation for entering students, adult/continuing education programs, distance learning, double majors, independent study, internships, part-time degree program, services for LD students, summer session for credit.

Student Life *Campus security:* 24-hour emergency response devices, late-night transport/escort service.

Standardized Tests *Required:* CPAt (for admission). *Recommended:* SAT or ACT (for admission).

Costs (2006–07) *Tuition:* $415 per credit hour part-time. *Required fees:* $62 per term part-time.

Financial Aid Of all full-time matriculated undergraduates, 40 Federal Work-Study jobs (averaging $600).

Applying *Options:* electronic application, deferred entrance. *Required:* high school transcript, interview, entrance evaluation and placement evaluation. *Required for some:* letters of recommendation.

Freshmen Application Contact Ms. Maria Scalise, Director of Admissions, Bryant and Stratton College, 1225 Jefferson Road, Henrietta Campus, Rochester, NY 14623. *Phone:* 585-720-0660 Ext. 201. *Fax:* 585-720-9226.

BRYANT AND STRATTON COLLEGE

Syracuse, New York   www.bryantstratton.edu/

- **Proprietary** 2-year, founded 1854, part of Bryant and Stratton Business Institute, Inc
- **Urban** campus
- **Coed**

Undergraduates 494 full-time, 142 part-time. Students come from 1 other state, 2 other countries, 1% are from out of state, 47% African American, 0.6% Asian American or Pacific Islander, 5% Hispanic American, 2% Native American, 0.6% international, 3% transferred in, 26% live on campus.

Academics *Calendar:* semesters. *Degree:* associate. *Special study options:* academic remediation for entering students, distance learning, double majors, internships, part-time degree program, services for LD students, summer session for credit.

Student Life *Campus security:* 24-hour emergency response devices, controlled dormitory access.

Athletics Member NJCAA.

Standardized Tests *Required:* CPAt (for admission). *Recommended:* SAT or ACT (for admission).

Costs (2006–07) *Tuition:* $415 per credit hour part-time. *Required fees:* $62 per term part-time.

Applying *Required:* high school transcript, interview, entrance, placement evaluations. *Required for some:* letters of recommendation.

Freshmen Application Contact Ms. Dawn Rajkowski, Director of Admissions, Bryant and Stratton College, 953 James Street, Syracuse, NY 13203-2502. *Phone:* 315-472-6603 Ext. 248. *Fax:* 315-474-4383.

BRYANT AND STRATTON COLLEGE, AMHERST CAMPUS

Clarence, New York   www.bryantstratton.edu/

- **Proprietary** primarily 2-year, founded 1977, part of Bryant and Stratton College
- **Suburban** 12-acre campus with easy access to Buffalo
- **Coed**

Undergraduates 240 full-time, 163 part-time. 15% African American, 0.5% Asian American or Pacific Islander, 2% Hispanic American, 0.7% Native American, 17% transferred in.

Academics *Calendar:* trimesters. *Degrees:* associate and bachelor's. *Special study options:* academic remediation for entering students, advanced placement credit, cooperative education, distance learning, double majors, independent study, internships, part-time degree program, summer session for credit.

Standardized Tests *Required:* TABE, CPAt or ACCUPLACER (for admission). *Recommended:* SAT or ACT (for admission).

Costs (2006–07) *Tuition:* $20,970 full-time, $436 per credit hour part-time. Full-time tuition and fees vary according to class time, course load, degree level, and program. Part-time tuition and fees vary according to course load and degree level. *Required fees:* $25 full-time.

Applying *Options:* deferred entrance. *Required:* high school transcript, interview, entrance evaluation and placement evaluation. *Required for some:* letters of recommendation.

Freshmen Application Contact Mr. Paul Kehr, WNY Market Admissions Director, Bryant and Stratton College, Amherst Campus, 40 Hazelwood Drive, Amherst, NY 14228. *Phone:* 716-677-9500. *Fax:* 716-677-9599. *E-mail:* jaweslowskiy@bryantstratton.edu.

BRYANT AND STRATTON COLLEGE, BUFFALO CAMPUS

Buffalo, New York   www.bryantstratton.edu/

- **Proprietary** 2-year, founded 1854, part of Bryant and Stratton College
- **Urban** 2-acre campus
- **Coed**

Undergraduates 495 full-time, 108 part-time. 65% African American, 0.2% Asian American or Pacific Islander, 5% Hispanic American, 0.7% Native American, 4% transferred in.

Academics *Calendar:* trimesters. *Degree:* associate. *Special study options:* academic remediation for entering students, advanced placement credit, cooperative education, distance learning, double majors, independent study, internships, part-time degree program, summer session for credit.

Standardized Tests *Required:* TABE, CPAt or ACCUPLACER (for admission). *Recommended:* SAT or ACT (for admission).

Costs (2006–07) *Tuition:* $20,970 full-time, $436 per credit hour part-time. *Required fees:* $25 full-time.

Applying *Options:* deferred entrance. *Required:* high school transcript, interview, entrance and placement evaluation. *Required for some:* letters of recommendation.

Freshmen Application Contact Mr. Phil Strubel, Director of Admissions, Bryant and Stratton College, Buffalo Campus, 465 Main Street, Suite 400, Buffalo, NY 14203-1713. *Phone:* 716-884-9120. *Fax:* 716-884-0091.

BRYANT AND STRATTON COLLEGE, LACKAWANNA CAMPUS

Lackawanna, New York   www.bryantstratton.edu/

- **Proprietary** 2-year, founded 1989, part of Bryant and Stratton College
- **Suburban** campus with easy access to Buffalo
- **Coed**

Undergraduates 189 full-time, 80 part-time. 4% African American, 2% Hispanic American, 1% Native American.

Academics *Calendar:* trimesters. *Degree:* associate. *Special study options:* academic remediation for entering students, advanced placement credit, cooperative education, distance learning, double majors, independent study, internships, part-time degree program, summer session for credit.

Student Life *Campus security:* 24-hour emergency response devices, late-night transport/escort service.

Standardized Tests *Required:* TABE, CPAt or ACCUPLACER (for admission). *Recommended:* SAT or ACT (for admission).

Costs (2006–07) *Tuition:* $20,970 full-time, $436 per credit hour part-time. Full-time tuition and fees vary according to class time, course load, degree level, and program. Part-time tuition and fees vary according to course load and degree level. *Required fees:* $25 full-time.

Applying *Options:* deferred entrance. *Required:* high school transcript, interview, entrance and placement evaluations. *Required for some:* letters of recommendation.

Bryant and Stratton College, Lackawanna Campus (continued)
Freshmen Application Contact Mr. Paul Kehr, WNY Market Admissions Director, Bryant and Stratton College, Lackawanna Campus, Sterling Park, 200 Redtail, Orchard Park, NY 14127. *Phone:* 716-677-9500. *Fax:* 716-677-9500. *E-mail:* jaweslowski@bryantstratton.edu.

BRYANT AND STRATTON COLLEGE, NORTH CAMPUS

Liverpool, New York   www.bryantstratton.edu/

Freshmen Application Contact Ms. Heather Macnik, Director of Admissions, Bryant and Stratton College, North Campus, 8687 Carling Road, Liverpool, NY 13090-1315. *Phone:* 315-652-6500.

BUSINESS INFORMATICS CENTER, INC.

Valley Stream, New York   www.thecollegeforbusiness.com/

- **Proprietary** 2-year, founded 1982
- **Coed,** 108 undergraduate students
- 78% of applicants were admitted

Freshmen *Admission:* 23 applied, 18 admitted.
Majors Business automation/technology/data entry; court reporting.
Academics *Degree:* associate.
Costs (2006–07) *Tuition:* $10,320 full-time.
Applying *Application fee:* $50. *Required:* high school transcript, Wonderlic.
Freshmen Application Contact Admissions Office, Business Informatics Center, Inc., 134 South Central Avenue, Valley Stream, NY 11580-5431.

CAYUGA COUNTY COMMUNITY COLLEGE

Auburn, New York   www.cayuga-cc.edu/

Director of Admissions Mr. Bruce M. Blodgett, Director of Admissions, Cayuga County Community College, 197 Franklin Street, Auburn, NY 13021-3099. *Phone:* 315-255-1743 Ext. 2244.

CLINTON COMMUNITY COLLEGE

Plattsburgh, New York   clintoncc.suny.edu/

Director of Admissions Mrs. Karen L. Burnam, Director of Admissions and Financial Aid, Clinton Community College, 136 Clinton Point Drive, Plattsburgh, NY 12901. *Phone:* 518-562-4170. *Toll-free phone:* 800-552-1160.

COCHRAN SCHOOL OF NURSING

Yonkers, New York   www.riversidehealth.org/

Freshmen Application Contact Ms. Maria Santiago, Registrar Coordinator, Cochran School of Nursing, 967 North Broadway, Yonkers, NY 10701. *Phone:* 914-964-4316. *Fax:* 914-964-4796. *E-mail:* msantiago@riversidehealth.org.

THE COLLEGE OF WESTCHESTER

White Plains, New York   www.cw.edu/

- **Proprietary** 2-year, founded 1915
- **Suburban** campus with easy access to New York City
- **Coed**

Undergraduates 829 full-time, 210 part-time. Students come from 3 states and territories, 4 other countries, 8% are from out of state, 28% African American, 2% Asian American or Pacific Islander, 30% Hispanic American, 0.4% Native American, 7% transferred in.
Faculty *Student/faculty ratio:* 15:1.
Academics *Calendar:* quarters for day division, semesters for evening and weekend divisions. *Degree:* certificates and associate. *Special study options:*

academic remediation for entering students, accelerated degree program, adult/continuing education programs, cooperative education, double majors, honors programs, internships, part-time degree program, summer session for credit.
Standardized Tests *Recommended:* SAT (for admission).
Costs (2006–07) *Tuition:* $18,315 full-time, $385 per credit part-time. Full-time tuition and fees vary according to class time, course load, and program. Part-time tuition and fees vary according to class time, course load, and program. *Required fees:* $810 full-time, $200 per term part-time.
Applying *Options:* electronic application, deferred entrance. *Application fee:* $40. *Required:* high school transcript, interview. *Required for some:* essay or personal statement.
Freshmen Application Contact Mr. Dale T. Smith, Vice President, The College of Westchester, 325 Central Avenue, PO Box 710, White Plains, NY 10602. *Phone:* 914-948-4442 Ext. 311. *Toll-free phone:* 800-333-4924 Ext. 318. *Fax:* 914-948-5441. *E-mail:* admissions@cw.edu.

▶See page 530 for the College Close-Up.

COLUMBIA-GREENE COMMUNITY COLLEGE

Hudson, New York   www.sunycgcc.edu/

- **State and locally supported** 2-year, founded 1969, part of State University of New York System
- **Rural** 143-acre campus
- **Endowment** $1.5 million
- **Coed,** 1,771 undergraduate students, 57% full-time, 60% women, 40% men

Undergraduates 1,001 full-time, 770 part-time. Students come from 3 states and territories, 5 other countries, 1% are from out of state, 4% African American, 1% Asian American or Pacific Islander, 4% Hispanic American, 0.6% Native American, 0.3% international, 7% transferred in.
Freshmen *Admission:* 444 applied, 440 admitted, 426 enrolled.
Faculty *Total:* 110, 45% full-time. *Student/faculty ratio:* 17:1.
Majors Accounting; administrative assistant and secretarial science; art; automobile/automotive mechanics technology; biological and physical sciences; business administration and management; computer and information sciences related; computer graphics; computer science; computer systems networking and telecommunications; criminal justice/law enforcement administration; data processing and data processing technology; humanities; human services; information science/studies; interdisciplinary studies; kinesiology and exercise science; liberal arts and sciences/liberal studies; mathematics; nursing (registered nurse training); real estate; social sciences; web/multimedia management and webmaster.
Academics *Calendar:* semesters. *Degree:* certificates and associate. *Special study options:* academic remediation for entering students, adult/continuing education programs, advanced placement credit, distance learning, double majors, honors programs, independent study, internships, part-time degree program, services for LD students, summer session for credit.
Library CGCC Library with 62,694 titles, 674 serial subscriptions, 25 audiovisual materials, an OPAC, a Web page.
Student Life *Housing:* college housing not available. *Activities and Organizations:* drama/theater group, student-run radio station, choral group, student council/government, Student Ambassadors, Nursing Club. *Campus security:* 24-hour patrols, late-night transport/escort service.
Athletics Member NJCAA. *Intercollegiate sports:* baseball M, basketball M, soccer M/W, softball W. *Intramural sports:* archery M/W, badminton M/W, baseball M, basketball M/W, fencing M/W, soccer M/W, table tennis M/W, tennis M/W, volleyball M/W, weight lifting M/W.
Costs (2006–07) *Tuition:* state resident $2976 full-time, $124 per credit hour part-time; nonresident $5952 full-time, $248 per credit hour part-time. *Required fees:* $280 full-time, $15 per credit hour part-time.
Applying *Options:* early admission, deferred entrance. *Application fee:* $40. *Required:* high school transcript. *Required for some:* interview. *Application deadlines:* rolling (freshmen), rolling (transfers). *Notification:* continuous (freshmen), continuous (transfers).
Freshmen Application Contact Admissions Counselors, Columbia-Greene Community College, 4400 Route 23, Hudson, NY 12534-0327. *Phone:* 518-828-4181 Ext. 5513. *E-mail:* info@mycommunitycollege.com.

CORNING COMMUNITY COLLEGE

Corning, New York   www.corning-cc.edu/

- **State and locally supported** 2-year, founded 1956, part of State University of New York System
- **Rural** 275-acre campus
- **Endowment** $2.3 million
- **Coed**

Undergraduates 2,638 full-time, 2,672 part-time. Students come from 13 states and territories, 5% are from out of state, 2% African American, 0.6% Asian American or Pacific Islander, 0.7% Hispanic American, 0.5% Native American, 0.1% international, 3% transferred in.

Faculty *Student/faculty ratio:* 18:1.

Academics *Calendar:* semesters. *Degree:* certificates and associate. *Special study options:* academic remediation for entering students, accelerated degree program, advanced placement credit, distance learning, double majors, honors programs, independent study, internships, part-time degree program, services for LD students, student-designed majors, summer session for credit. *ROTC:* Army (c), Navy (c), Air Force (c).

Student Life *Campus security:* 24-hour emergency response devices and patrols, late-night transport/escort service.

Athletics Member NJCAA.

Costs (2006–07) *Tuition:* state resident $3100 full-time, $128 per credit part-time; nonresident $6200 full-time, $258 per credit part-time.

Financial Aid Of all full-time matriculated undergraduates, 264 Federal Work-Study jobs (averaging $1128).

Applying *Options:* electronic application, early admission. *Application fee:* $25. *Required:* high school transcript. *Required for some:* interview.

Freshmen Application Contact Ms. Karen McCarthy, Director of Admissions, Corning Community College, 1 Academic Drive, Corning, NY 14830. *Phone:* 607-962-9221. *Toll-free phone:* 800-358-7171 Ext. 220. *Fax:* 607-962-9520. *E-mail:* admissions@corning-cc.edu.

CROUSE HOSPITAL SCHOOL OF NURSING
Syracuse, New York   www.crouse.org/nursing/

Freshmen Application Contact Ms. Amy Graham, Enrollment Management Supervisor, Crouse Hospital School of Nursing, 736 Irving Avenue, Syracuse, NY 13210. *Phone:* 315-470-7481. *Fax:* 315-470-7925. *E-mail:* amygraham@crouse.org.

DOROTHEA HOPFER SCHOOL OF NURSING AT THE MOUNT VERNON HOSPITAL
Mount Vernon, New York   www.ssmc.org/

- **Independent** 2-year
- 120 undergraduate students
- 33% of applicants were admitted

Freshmen *Admission:* 9 applied, 3 admitted.

Majors Nursing (registered nurse training).

Academics *Degree:* associate.

Costs (2006–07) *Tuition:* $5970 full-time.

Applying *Application fee:* $40.

Director of Admissions Office of Admissions, Dorothea Hopfer School of Nursing at The Mount Vernon Hospital, 53 Valentine Street, Mount Vernon, NY 10550. *Phone:* 914-664-8000 Ext. 3221.

DUTCHESS COMMUNITY COLLEGE
Poughkeepsie, New York   www.sunydutchess.edu/

Director of Admissions Ms. Rita Banner, Director of Admissions, Dutchess Community College, 53 Pendell Road, Poughkeepsie, NY 12601. *Phone:* 845-431-8010. *Toll-free phone:* 800-763-3933. *E-mail:* banner@sunydutchess.edu.

ELLIS HOSPITAL SCHOOL OF NURSING
Schenectady, New York   www.ehson.org/

- **Independent** 2-year, founded 1906
- **Coed, primarily women,** 69 undergraduate students, 51% full-time, 97% women, 3% men
- 50% of applicants were admitted

Undergraduates 35 full-time, 34 part-time. 3% African American, 1% Asian American or Pacific Islander, 1% Hispanic American.

Freshmen *Admission:* 101 applied, 50 admitted.

Faculty *Total:* 9, 100% full-time, 100% with terminal degrees. *Student/faculty ratio:* 8:1.

Majors Nursing (registered nurse training).

Academics *Degree:* associate.

Standardized Tests *Recommended:* SAT (for admission).

Costs (2006–07) *Tuition:* $4679 full-time, $160 per credit part-time. *Required fees:* $160 full-time, $80 per semester part-time.

Applying *Application fee:* $30. *Required:* essay or personal statement, high school transcript, 3 letters of recommendation. *Application deadlines:* rolling (freshmen), rolling (transfers).

Freshmen Application Contact Mary Lee Pollard, Director of School, Ellis Hospital School of Nursing, 1101 Nott Street, Schenectady, NY 12308. *Phone:* 518-243-4471. *Fax:* 518-243-4470.

ELMIRA BUSINESS INSTITUTE
Elmira, New York   www.ebi-college.com/

- **Private** 2-year, founded 1858
- **Urban** campus
- **Coed, primarily women,** 280 undergraduate students, 69% full-time, 85% women, 15% men
- 62% of applicants were admitted

Undergraduates 192 full-time, 88 part-time. Students come from 2 states and territories, 17% are from out of state, 9% African American, 0.4% Asian American or Pacific Islander, 0.7% Hispanic American.

Freshmen *Admission:* 151 applied, 94 admitted, 94 enrolled. *Average high school GPA:* 2.5.

Faculty *Total:* 27, 22% full-time. *Student/faculty ratio:* 11:1.

Majors Accounting; administrative assistant and secretarial science; legal administrative assistant/secretary; medical administrative assistant and medical secretary; tourism and travel services management.

Academics *Calendar:* semesters. *Degree:* certificates and associate. *Special study options:* academic remediation for entering students, advanced placement credit, internships, part-time degree program.

Library Elmira Business Institute Library with 800 titles, 14 serial subscriptions.

Student Life *Housing:* college housing not available.

Costs (2007–08) *Tuition:* $8250 full-time, $275 per credit hour part-time.

Applying *Options:* electronic application. *Required:* high school transcript, interview. *Application deadline:* rolling (freshmen).

Freshmen Application Contact Ms. Lisa Roan, Admissions Director, Elmira Business Institute, 303 North Main Street, Langdon Plaza, Elmira, NY 14901. *Phone:* 607-733-7178. *Toll-free phone:* 800-843-1812. *E-mail:* lroan@ebi-college.com.

ERIE COMMUNITY COLLEGE
Buffalo, New York   www.ecc.edu/

- **State and locally supported** 2-year, founded 1971, part of State University of New York System
- **Urban** 1-acre campus
- **Coed,** 2,993 undergraduate students, 72% full-time, 62% women, 38% men

Undergraduates 2,158 full-time, 835 part-time. Students come from 14 states and territories, 3 other countries, 0.5% are from out of state, 42% African American, 2% Asian American or Pacific Islander, 9% Hispanic American, 1% Native American, 0.2% international, 4% transferred in.

Freshmen *Admission:* 789 applied, 626 admitted, 617 enrolled. *Test scores:* SAT verbal scores over 500: 32%; SAT math scores over 500: 28%; SAT verbal scores over 600: 7%; SAT math scores over 600: 5%; SAT verbal scores over 700: 1%; SAT math scores over 700: 1%.

Faculty *Total:* 318, 25% full-time. *Student/faculty ratio:* 16:1.

Majors Administrative assistant and secretarial science; building/property maintenance and management; business administration and management; child care and support services management; community health services counseling; criminal justice/law enforcement administration; criminal justice/police science; culinary arts; humanities; industrial production technologies related; information science/studies; legal assistant/paralegal; liberal arts and sciences/liberal studies; medical radiologic technology; nursing (registered nurse training); office man-

Erie Community College (continued)

agement; physical education teaching and coaching; public administration and social service professions related; substance abuse/addiction counseling.

Academics *Calendar:* semesters. *Degree:* certificates, diplomas, and associate. *Special study options:* academic remediation for entering students, adult/continuing education programs, advanced placement credit, cooperative education, distance learning, double majors, English as a second language, honors programs, independent study, internships, part-time degree program, services for LD students, student-designed majors, study abroad, summer session for credit. *ROTC:* Army (c).

Library Leon E. Butler Library with 25,350 titles, 168 serial subscriptions, 1,800 audiovisual materials, an OPAC, a Web page.

Student Life *Housing:* college housing not available. *Activities and Organizations:* drama/theater group, student-run newspaper, radio station, choral group, Alpha Beta Gamma, Anthropology Club, Black Student Union, Business Club, Campus Ministry Club. *Campus security:* 24-hour emergency response devices and patrols, late-night transport/escort service. *Student services:* health clinic, personal/psychological counseling, women's center.

Athletics Member NJCAA. *Intercollegiate sports:* baseball M, basketball M/W, bowling M/W, cheerleading W, cross-country running M/W, football M, golf M/W, ice hockey M, lacrosse W, soccer M/W, softball W, swimming and diving M/W, track and field M/W, volleyball W.

Costs (2006–07) *Tuition:* area resident $2987 full-time, $125 per credit hour part-time; state resident $5974 full-time, $250 per credit hour part-time; nonresident $5974 full-time, $250 per credit hour part-time. *Required fees:* $320 full-time, $5 per credit hour part-time, $45 per term part-time. *Payment plans:* installment, deferred payment. *Waivers:* senior citizens and employees or children of employees.

Financial Aid Of all full-time matriculated undergraduates, 300 Federal Work-Study jobs (averaging $2000).

Applying *Options:* electronic application. *Required:* high school transcript. *Required for some:* interview. *Application deadlines:* rolling (freshmen), rolling (transfers). *Notification:* continuous (freshmen), continuous (transfers).

Freshmen Application Contact Ms. Petrina Hill-Cheatom, Director of Admissions, Erie Community College, 121 Ellicott Street, Buffalo, NY 14203-2698. *Phone:* 716-851-1588. *Fax:* 716-851-1129.

ERIE COMMUNITY COLLEGE, NORTH CAMPUS

Williamsville, New York   **www.ecc.edu**

- **State and locally supported** 2-year, founded 1946, part of State University of New York System
- **Suburban** 120-acre campus with easy access to Buffalo
- **Coed,** 5,859 undergraduate students, 66% full-time, 50% women, 50% men

Undergraduates 3,867 full-time, 1,992 part-time. Students come from 17 states and territories, 20 other countries, 0.5% are from out of state, 12% African American, 2% Asian American or Pacific Islander, 2% Hispanic American, 0.7% Native American, 1% international, 6% transferred in.

Freshmen *Admission:* 1,609 applied, 1,272 admitted, 1,272 enrolled. *Test scores:* SAT verbal scores over 500: 31%; SAT math scores over 500: 42%; SAT verbal scores over 600: 4%; SAT math scores over 600: 7%; SAT verbal scores over 700: 1%.

Faculty *Total:* 505, 32% full-time. *Student/faculty ratio:* 16:1.

Majors Business administration and management; civil engineering technology; clinical/medical laboratory technology; computer and information sciences; construction management; construction trades related; criminal justice/law enforcement administration; criminal justice/police science; culinary arts; dental hygiene; dietitian assistant; electrical, electronic and communications engineering technology; engineering; health information/medical records technology; humanities; information science/studies; liberal arts and sciences/liberal studies; mechanical engineering/mechanical technology; medical office management; nursing (registered nurse training); occupational therapist assistant; office management; opticianry; physical education teaching and coaching; respiratory care therapy; restaurant, culinary, and catering management.

Academics *Calendar:* semesters plus summer sessions. *Degree:* certificates, diplomas, and associate. *Special study options:* academic remediation for entering students, adult/continuing education programs, advanced placement credit, cooperative education, distance learning, double majors, English as a second language, honors programs, independent study, internships, part-time degree program, services for LD students, student-designed majors, study abroad, summer session for credit. *ROTC:* Army (c).

Library Richard R. Dry Memorial Library with 52,961 titles, 311 serial subscriptions, 5,315 audiovisual materials, an OPAC, a Web page.

Student Life *Housing:* college housing not available. *Activities and Organizations:* drama/theater group, student-run newspaper, radio station, choral group, APWA (American Public Works Association), Dental Hygiene Club, Environmental Awareness Club, Flame and Ice, Future Teachers. *Campus security:* 24-hour emergency response devices and patrols, late-night transport/escort service. *Student services:* health clinic, personal/psychological counseling, women's center.

Athletics Member NJCAA. *Intercollegiate sports:* baseball M, basketball M/W, bowling M/W, cheerleading W, cross-country running M/W, football M, golf M/W, ice hockey M, lacrosse W, soccer M/W, softball W, swimming and diving M/W, track and field M/W, volleyball W.

Costs (2006–07) *Tuition:* area resident $2987 full-time, $125 per credit hour part-time; state resident $5974 full-time, $250 per credit hour part-time; nonresident $5974 full-time, $250 per credit hour part-time. *Required fees:* $320 full-time, $5 per credit hour part-time, $45 per term part-time. *Payment plans:* installment, deferred payment. *Waivers:* senior citizens and employees or children of employees.

Financial Aid Of all full-time matriculated undergraduates, 300 Federal Work-Study jobs (averaging $2000).

Applying *Options:* electronic application. *Required:* high school transcript. *Required for some:* interview. *Application deadlines:* rolling (freshmen), rolling (transfers). *Notification:* continuous (freshmen), continuous (transfers).

Freshmen Application Contact Ms. Petrina Hill-Cheatom, Director of Admissions, Erie Community College, North Campus, 6205 Main Street, Williamsville, NY 14221-7095. *Phone:* 716-851-1588. *Fax:* 716-851-1429.

ERIE COMMUNITY COLLEGE, SOUTH CAMPUS

Orchard Park, New York   **www.ecc.edu/**

- **State and locally supported** 2-year, founded 1974, part of State University of New York System
- **Suburban** 110-acre campus with easy access to Buffalo
- **Coed,** 4,160 undergraduate students, 61% full-time, 44% women, 56% men

Undergraduates 2,519 full-time, 1,641 part-time. Students come from 19 states and territories, 4 other countries, 1% are from out of state, 6% African American, 0.7% Asian American or Pacific Islander, 3% Hispanic American, 1% Native American, 0.2% international, 4% transferred in.

Freshmen *Admission:* 1,128 applied, 942 admitted, 939 enrolled. *Test scores:* SAT verbal scores over 500: 32%; SAT math scores over 500: 42%; SAT verbal scores over 600: 5%; SAT math scores over 600: 6%.

Faculty *Total:* 486, 22% full-time. *Student/faculty ratio:* 16:1.

Majors Architectural engineering technology; autobody/collision and repair technology; automobile/automotive mechanics technology; biomedical technology; business administration and management; communication/speech communication and rhetoric; communications systems installation and repair technology; computer technology/computer systems technology; dental laboratory technology; fire services administration; graphic and printing equipment operation/production; humanities; industrial technology; information science/studies; liberal arts and sciences/liberal studies; mechanical drafting and CAD/CADD; office management; parks, recreation and leisure facilities management; physical education teaching and coaching; public administration and social service professions related.

Academics *Calendar:* semesters plus summer sessions. *Degree:* certificates, diplomas, and associate. *Special study options:* academic remediation for entering students, adult/continuing education programs, advanced placement credit, cooperative education, distance learning, double majors, English as a second language, honors programs, independent study, internships, part-time degree program, services for LD students, student-designed majors, study abroad, summer session for credit. *ROTC:* Army (c).

Library 63,844 titles, 204 serial subscriptions, 1,578 audiovisual materials, an OPAC, a Web page.

Student Life *Housing:* college housing not available. *Activities and Organizations:* drama/theater group, student-run newspaper, radio station, Habitat for Humanity, Honors Society, Phi Theta Kappa, Photo Club, Recreation Leadership Club. *Campus security:* 24-hour emergency response devices and patrols, late-night transport/escort service. *Student services:* health clinic, personal/psychological counseling, women's center.

Athletics Member NJCAA. *Intercollegiate sports:* baseball M, basketball M/W, bowling M/W, cheerleading W, cross-country running M/W, football M, golf M/W, ice hockey M, lacrosse W, soccer M/W, softball W, swimming and diving M/W, track and field M/W, volleyball W.

Costs (2006–07) *Tuition:* area resident $2987 full-time, $125 per credit hour part-time; state resident $5974 full-time, $250 per credit hour part-time; nonresident $5974 full-time, $250 per credit hour part-time. *Required fees:* $320

full-time, $5 per credit hour part-time, $45 per term part-time. *Payment plans:* installment, deferred payment. *Waivers:* senior citizens and employees or children of employees.

Financial Aid Of all full-time matriculated undergraduates, 300 Federal Work-Study jobs (averaging $2000).

Applying *Options:* electronic application. *Required:* high school transcript. *Required for some:* interview. *Application deadlines:* rolling (freshmen), rolling (transfers). *Notification:* continuous (freshmen), continuous (transfers).

Freshmen Application Contact Ms. Petrina Hill-Cheatom, Director of Admissions, Erie Community College, South Campus, 4041 Southwestern Boulevard, Orchard Park, NY 14127-2199. *Phone:* 716-851-1588. *Fax:* 716-851-1629.

EUGENIO MARÍA DE HOSTOS COMMUNITY COLLEGE OF THE CITY UNIVERSITY OF NEW YORK

Bronx, New York   **www.hostos.cuny.edu/**

- **State and locally supported** 2-year, founded 1968, part of City University of New York System
- **Urban** 8-acre campus
- **Endowment** $211,655
- **Coed,** 4,697 undergraduate students

Undergraduates Students come from 4 states and territories, 91 other countries, 1% are from out of state, 29% African American, 2% Asian American or Pacific Islander, 58% Hispanic American, 0.1% Native American, 8% international.

Freshmen *Admission:* 1,316 applied, 1,316 admitted.

Faculty *Total:* 324, 50% full-time. *Student/faculty ratio:* 14:1.

Majors Accounting; administrative assistant and secretarial science; business administration and management; clinical/medical laboratory technology; data entry/microcomputer applications related; data processing and data processing technology; dental hygiene; electrical and electronic engineering technologies related; gerontology; kindergarten/preschool education; legal assistant/paralegal; liberal arts and sciences/liberal studies; medical administrative assistant and medical secretary; medical radiologic technology; nursing (licensed practical/vocational nurse training); nursing (registered nurse training); public administration.

Academics *Calendar:* semesters. *Degree:* certificates and associate. *Special study options:* academic remediation for entering students, adult/continuing education programs, distance learning, double majors, English as a second language, internships, part-time degree program, services for LD students, study abroad, summer session for credit.

Library Hostos Community College Library with 56,100 titles, 846 serial subscriptions, 710 audiovisual materials, an OPAC, a Web page.

Student Life *Housing:* college housing not available. *Activities and Organizations:* student-run newspaper, Dominican Association, Puerto Rican Student Organization, Student Government Association, Black Student Union, Veterans Club. *Campus security:* 24-hour emergency response devices and patrols, late-night transport/escort service. *Student services:* health clinic, personal/psychological counseling, women's center, legal services.

Athletics Member NJCAA. *Intercollegiate sports:* baseball M, basketball M/W, volleyball W. *Intramural sports:* basketball M/W, soccer M/W, volleyball W.

Standardized Tests *Required:* CUNY Skills Assessment Tests (for placement). *Required for some:* SAT (for placement), ACT (for placement), SAT Subject Tests (for placement).

Costs (2007–08) *Tuition:* state resident $2500 full-time; nonresident $3076 full-time.

Financial Aid Of all full-time matriculated undergraduates, 1,482 Federal Work-Study jobs (averaging $1600).

Applying *Application fee:* $65. *Required:* high school transcript. *Application deadlines:* rolling (freshmen), rolling (transfers). *Notification:* continuous until 8/15 (freshmen), continuous until 8/15 (transfers).

Freshmen Application Contact Mr. Roland Velez, Director of Admissions, Eugenio María de Hostos Community College of the City University of New York, 120 149th Street, Room D-210, Bronx, NY 10451. *Phone:* 718-518-4406. *Fax:* 718-518-4256. *E-mail:* admissions2@hostos.cuny.edu.

FINGER LAKES COMMUNITY COLLEGE

Canandaigua, New York   **www.flcc.edu/**

- **State and locally supported** 2-year, founded 1965, part of State University of New York System
- **Small-town** 300-acre campus with easy access to Rochester
- **Coed,** 5,150 undergraduate students

Undergraduates Students come from 6 states and territories, 3 other countries, 1% are from out of state, 4% African American, 0.7% Asian American or Pacific Islander, 2% Hispanic American, 0.6% Native American.

Freshmen *Admission:* 4,023 applied.

Faculty *Total:* 280, 39% full-time. *Student/faculty ratio:* 20:1.

Majors Accounting; administrative assistant and secretarial science; architectural engineering technology; banking and financial support services; biological and physical sciences; biology/biological sciences; biology/biotechnology laboratory technician; broadcast journalism; business administration and management; chemistry; commercial and advertising art; computer and information sciences; computer science; consumer merchandising/retailing management; criminal justice/law enforcement administration; criminal justice/police science; data processing and data processing technology; drafting and design technology; dramatic/theater arts; engineering science; environmental studies; fine/studio arts; fish/game management; hotel/motel administration; humanities; human services; kindergarten/preschool education; legal assistant/paralegal; liberal arts and sciences/liberal studies; marketing/marketing management; mass communication/media; mathematics; mechanical engineering/mechanical technology; music; natural resources/conservation; natural resources management; natural resources management and policy; nursing (registered nurse training); ornamental horticulture; parks, recreation and leisure facilities management; physical education teaching and coaching; physics; political science and government; pre-engineering; psychology; social sciences; sociology; substance abuse/addiction counseling; tourism and travel services management.

Academics *Calendar:* semesters. *Degree:* certificates and associate. *Special study options:* academic remediation for entering students, advanced placement credit, distance learning, English as a second language, honors programs, internships, off-campus study, part-time degree program, services for LD students, summer session for credit. *ROTC:* Army (c).

Library Charles Meder Library with 73,305 titles, 464 serial subscriptions, an OPAC.

Student Life *Housing:* college housing not available. *Options:* Campus housing is provided by a third party. *Activities and Organizations:* drama/theater group, student-run newspaper, radio station, choral group, national fraternities, national sororities. *Campus security:* 24-hour emergency response devices and patrols, late-night transport/escort service. *Student services:* health clinic, personal/psychological counseling, legal services.

Athletics Member NJCAA. *Intercollegiate sports:* baseball M, basketball M/W, cross-country running M/W, lacrosse M/W, soccer M/W, softball W. *Intramural sports:* basketball M/W, tennis M/W, volleyball M/W.

Costs (2007–08) *Tuition:* state resident $3050 full-time, $117 per credit hour part-time; nonresident $6100 full-time, $234 per credit hour part-time. *Required fees:* $310 full-time, $8 per credit hour part-time.

Financial Aid Of all full-time matriculated undergraduates, 150 Federal Work-Study jobs (averaging $1800). 150 state and other part-time jobs (averaging $1800).

Applying *Options:* electronic application, early admission, deferred entrance. *Required:* high school transcript. *Recommended:* interview. *Application deadlines:* rolling (freshmen), rolling (transfers). *Notification:* continuous until 8/31 (freshmen), continuous until 8/31 (transfers).

Freshmen Application Contact Ms. Bonnie Ritts, Director of Admissions, Finger Lakes Community College, 4355 Lake Shore Drive, Canandaigua, NY 14424-8395. *Phone:* 585-394-3500 Ext. 7278. *Fax:* 585-394-5005. *E-mail:* admissions@flcc.edu.

FIORELLO H. LaGUARDIA COMMUNITY COLLEGE OF THE CITY UNIVERSITY OF NEW YORK

Long Island City, New York   **www.lagcc.cuny.edu/**

- **State and locally supported** 2-year, founded 1970, part of City University of New York System
- **Urban** 6-acre campus
- **Endowment** $1.2 million
- **Coed,** 14,185 undergraduate students, 55% full-time, 63% women, 37% men

LaGuardia Community College offers forty degree and certificate programs; day, evening, and weekend classes; world-renowned internship and honors programs; and strong support programs, including transfer services, that ensure student success. Recently named as one of the top-three large community colleges in the U.S., LaGuardia has the lowest college tuition in New York City. Based in western Queens, the College is 10 minutes from Manhattan and Brooklyn by subway or bus.

Undergraduates 7,817 full-time, 6,368 part-time. Students come from 5 states and territories, 160 other countries, 0.1% are from out of state, 17% African

Fiorello H. LaGuardia Community College of the City University of New York (continued)

American, 11% Asian American or Pacific Islander, 29% Hispanic American, 0.2% Native American, 22% international, 10% transferred in.

Freshmen *Admission:* 4,130 applied, 4,130 admitted, 2,423 enrolled. *Average high school GPA:* 2.4.

Faculty *Total:* 901, 33% full-time, 25% with terminal degrees. *Student/faculty ratio:* 21:1.

Majors Accounting; administrative assistant and secretarial science; business administration and management; computer and information sciences related; computer engineering technology; computer programming; computer programming related; computer programming (specific applications); computer programming (vendor/product certification); computer science; computer systems networking and telecommunications; data entry/microcomputer applications; dietetics; education; emergency medical technology (EMT paramedic); fine/studio arts; funeral service and mortuary science; gerontology; human services; information science/studies; kindergarten/preschool education; legal administrative assistant/secretary; legal assistant/paralegal; liberal arts and sciences/liberal studies; mental health/rehabilitation; nursing (registered nurse training); occupational therapy; photography; physical therapy; special products marketing; system administration; tourism and travel services management; veterinary technology.

Academics *Calendar:* modified semester. *Degree:* certificates and associate. *Special study options:* academic remediation for entering students, adult/continuing education programs, advanced placement credit, cooperative education, distance learning, double majors, English as a second language, honors programs, independent study, internships, off-campus study, part-time degree program, services for LD students, student-designed majors, study abroad, summer session for credit.

Library Fiorello H. LaGuardia Community College Library Media Resources Center plus 1 other with 134,200 titles, 1,130 serial subscriptions, 3,040 audiovisual materials, an OPAC.

Student Life *Housing:* college housing not available. *Activities and Organizations:* drama/theater group, student-run newspaper, radio station, Latinos Unidos Club, Bangladesh Club, Dominican Club, Law Club. *Campus security:* 24-hour emergency response devices and patrols, late-night transport/escort service. *Student services:* health clinic, personal/psychological counseling, women's center.

Athletics *Intramural sports:* basketball M/W, football M/W, golf M/W, soccer M/W, volleyball M/W, weight lifting M/W.

Costs (2007–08) *Tuition:* area resident $2800 full-time, $120 per credit part-time; state resident $2800 full-time, $120 per credit part-time; nonresident $6080 full-time, $190 per credit part-time. *Required fees:* $146 full-time, $73 per term part-time.

Financial Aid Of all full-time matriculated undergraduates, 1,425 Federal Work-Study jobs (averaging $1194).

Applying *Options:* electronic application, early admission, deferred entrance. *Application fee:* $65. *Required:* high school transcript. *Application deadlines:* rolling (freshmen), rolling (transfers). *Notification:* continuous (freshmen), continuous (transfers).

Freshmen Application Contact Ms. LaVora Desvigne, Director of Admissions, Fiorello H. LaGuardia Community College of the City University of New York, RM-147, 31-10 Thomson Avenue, Long Island City, NY 11101. *Phone:* 718-482-5114. *Fax:* 718-482-5112. *E-mail:* admissions@lagcc.cuny.edu.

FULTON-MONTGOMERY COMMUNITY COLLEGE

Johnstown, New York **www.fmcc.suny.edu/**

- **State and locally supported** 2-year, founded 1964, part of State University of New York System
- **Rural** 195-acre campus
- **Endowment** $1.5 million
- **Coed,** 2,157 undergraduate students, 65% full-time, 58% women, 42% men

Undergraduates 1,406 full-time, 751 part-time. Students come from 6 states and territories, 18 other countries, 5% are from out of state, 4% African American, 0.6% Asian American or Pacific Islander, 6% Hispanic American, 0.3% Native American, 6% international, 3% transferred in. *Retention:* 56% of 2003 full-time freshmen returned.

Freshmen *Admission:* 1,308 applied, 1,308 admitted, 562 enrolled.

Faculty *Total:* 98, 52% full-time. *Student/faculty ratio:* 23:1.

Majors Accounting; administrative assistant and secretarial science; art; automobile/automotive mechanics technology; behavioral sciences; biological and physical sciences; biology/biological sciences; business administration and management; carpentry; commercial and advertising art; computer engineering technology; computer science; computer typography and composition equip-

ment operation; construction engineering technology; criminal justice/law enforcement administration; data processing and data processing technology; developmental and child psychology; dramatic/theater arts; electrical, electronic and communications engineering technology; elementary education; engineering science; English; environmental studies; finance; fine/studio arts; graphic and printing equipment operation/production; health teacher education; history; humanities; human services; information science/studies; kindergarten/preschool education; legal administrative assistant/secretary; liberal arts and sciences/liberal studies; mass communication/media; mathematics; medical administrative assistant and medical secretary; natural resources/conservation; nursing (registered nurse training); physical education teaching and coaching; physical sciences; psychology; social sciences; teacher assistant/aide.

Academics *Calendar:* semesters plus winter session. *Degree:* certificates and associate. *Special study options:* academic remediation for entering students, accelerated degree program, adult/continuing education programs, advanced placement credit, cooperative education, distance learning, double majors, English as a second language, external degree program, honors programs, independent study, internships, off-campus study, part-time degree program, services for LD students, student-designed majors, study abroad, summer session for credit.

Library Evans Library with 51,642 titles, 139 serial subscriptions, 1,536 audiovisual materials, an OPAC, a Web page.

Student Life *Housing:* college housing not available. *Activities and Organizations:* drama/theater group, student-run newspaper, choral group, Business Students' Association, Criminal Justice Club, WAU (We Are United), Ski Club. *Campus security:* weekend and night security. *Student services:* personal/psychological counseling.

Athletics Member NJCAA. *Intercollegiate sports:* baseball M, basketball M/W, soccer M/W, softball W, volleyball W. *Intramural sports:* baseball M, basketball M/W, skiing (cross-country) M(c)/W(c), skiing (downhill) M(c)/W(c), volleyball M/W.

Costs (2006–07) *Tuition:* state resident $2975 full-time, $123 per credit part-time; nonresident $5950 full-time, $246 per credit part-time. *Required fees:* $290 full-time, $2 per credit hour part-time, $50 per term part-time.

Financial Aid Of all full-time matriculated undergraduates, 87 Federal Work-Study jobs (averaging $1000).

Applying *Options:* electronic application, early admission, deferred entrance. *Required:* high school transcript. *Application deadlines:* 9/10 (freshmen), 9/10 (transfers). *Notification:* continuous (freshmen), continuous (transfers).

Director of Admissions Ms. Jane Kelley, Associate Dean for Enrollment Management, Fulton-Montgomery Community College, 2805 State Highway 67, Johnstown, NY 12095-3790. *Phone:* 518-762-4651 Ext. 8301. *E-mail:* jkelley@fmcc.suny.edu.

GAMLA COLLEGE

Brooklyn, New York

Admissions Office Contact Gamla College, 1213 Elm Avenue, Brooklyn, NY 11230.

GENESEE COMMUNITY COLLEGE

Batavia, New York **www.genesee.edu/**

- **State and locally supported** 2-year, founded 1966, part of State University of New York System
- **Small-town** 256-acre campus with easy access to Buffalo
- **Endowment** $1.9 million
- **Coed,** 6,503 undergraduate students, 47% full-time, 64% women, 36% men

Undergraduates 3,035 full-time, 3,468 part-time. Students come from 15 states and territories, 18 other countries, 4% are from out of state, 4% African American, 0.7% Asian American or Pacific Islander, 2% Hispanic American, 0.7% Native American, 3% international, 5% transferred in.

Freshmen *Admission:* 2,682 applied, 2,682 admitted, 1,099 enrolled.

Faculty *Total:* 316, 24% full-time. *Student/faculty ratio:* 18:1.

Majors Accounting; administrative assistant and secretarial science; business administration and management; clinical/medical laboratory technology; commercial and advertising art; computer and information sciences related; computer engineering technology; computer graphics; computer software and media applications related; consumer merchandising/retailing management; criminal justice/law enforcement administration; drafting and design technology; dramatic/theater arts; education; electrical, electronic and communications engineering technology; elementary education; engineering science; fashion merchandising; gerontology; hotel/motel administration; human services; information science/studies; kindergarten/preschool education; legal assistant/paralegal; liberal arts

and sciences/liberal studies; marketing/marketing management; mass communication/media; mathematics; nursing (registered nurse training); occupational therapy; physical education teaching and coaching; physical therapy; psychology; respiratory care therapy; substance abuse/addiction counseling; system administration; tourism and travel services management.

Academics *Calendar:* semesters. *Degree:* certificates and associate. *Special study options:* academic remediation for entering students, adult/continuing education programs, advanced placement credit, cooperative education, distance learning, honors programs, independent study, internships, part-time degree program, services for LD students, summer session for credit.

Library Alfred C. O'Connell Library with 80,000 titles, 332 serial subscriptions, an OPAC, a Web page.

Student Life *Housing Options:* disabled students. Campus housing is university owned. *Activities and Organizations:* drama/theater group, student-run newspaper, radio station, choral group, Student Government Association, Phi Theta Kappa, DECA, Student Activities Council, Forum Players. *Campus security:* 24-hour emergency response devices and patrols, student patrols, late-night transport/escort service. *Student services:* health clinic, personal/psychological counseling.

Athletics Member NJCAA. *Intercollegiate sports:* baseball M, basketball M(s)/W(s), cross-country running M/W, soccer M/W(s), softball W, swimming and diving M/W, volleyball M/W(s). *Intramural sports:* badminton M/W, basketball M/W, football M/W, golf M/W, soccer M/W, softball M/W, swimming and diving M/W, table tennis M/W, tennis M/W, track and field M/W, volleyball M/W, water polo M/W, weight lifting M/W.

Standardized Tests *Recommended:* ACT (for admission).

Costs (2007–08) *Tuition:* state resident $3300 full-time; nonresident $3500 full-time. *Required fees:* $290 full-time. *Room and board:* room only: $5000.

Financial Aid Of all full-time matriculated undergraduates, 135 Federal Work-Study jobs (averaging $1450).

Applying *Options:* electronic application. *Required:* high school transcript. *Required for some:* 1 letter of recommendation. *Application deadlines:* rolling (freshmen), rolling (transfers). *Notification:* continuous (freshmen), continuous (transfers).

Freshmen Application Contact Mrs. Tanya Lane-Martin, Director of Admissions, Genesee Community College, 1 College Road, Batavia, NY 14020. *Phone:* 585-343-0055 Ext. 6413. *Toll-free phone:* 800-CALL GCC. *Fax:* 585-345-6892. *E-mail:* tmlanemartin@genesee.edu.

HELENE FULD COLLEGE OF NURSING OF NORTH GENERAL HOSPITAL
New York, New York   www.helenefuld.edu/

- **Independent** 2-year, founded 1945
- **Urban** campus
- **Coed, primarily women,** 363 undergraduate students

Undergraduates Students come from 3 states and territories, 3% are from out of state.

Freshmen *Admission:* 16 applied, 16 admitted.

Faculty *Total:* 26, 38% full-time, 12% with terminal degrees. *Student/faculty ratio:* 13:1.

Majors Nursing (registered nurse training).

Academics *Calendar:* quarters. *Degrees:* associate (program only open to licensed practical nurses). *Special study options:* accelerated degree program, part-time degree program, summer session for credit.

Library 6,200 titles, 82 serial subscriptions, 131 audiovisual materials.

Student Life *Housing:* college housing not available. *Campus security:* security guard during open hours. *Student services:* personal/psychological counseling.

Standardized Tests *Required:* nursing exam, Nelson Denny Reading Test, math exam (for admission).

Costs (2006–07) *Tuition:* $13,012 full-time.

Applying *Options:* deferred entrance. *Application fee:* $50. *Required:* essay or personal statement, high school transcript, 1 letter of recommendation, interview, must be Licensed Practical Nurse. *Application deadlines:* rolling (freshmen), rolling (transfers).

Freshmen Application Contact Mrs. Gladys Pineda, Student Services, Helene Fuld College of Nursing of North General Hospital, 1879 Madison Avenue, New York, NY 10035. *Phone:* 212-423-2768.

HERKIMER COUNTY COMMUNITY COLLEGE
Herkimer, New York   www.herkimer.edu

Director of Admissions Mr. Scott J. Hughes, Associate Dean for Enrollment Management, Herkimer County Community College, Herkimer, NY 13350. *Phone:* 315-866-0300 Ext. 278. *Toll-free phone:* 888-464-4222 Ext. 8278.

HUDSON VALLEY COMMUNITY COLLEGE
Troy, New York   www.hvcc.edu/

- **State and locally supported** 2-year, founded 1953, part of State University of New York System
- **Suburban** 135-acre campus
- **Endowment** $3.7 million
- **Coed**

Undergraduates Students come from 21 states and territories, 18 other countries, 5% are from out of state, 8% African American, 2% Asian American or Pacific Islander, 3% Hispanic American, 0.3% Native American, 0.6% international. *Retention:* 60% of 2003 full-time freshmen returned.

Faculty *Student/faculty ratio:* 19:1.

Academics *Calendar:* semesters. *Degree:* certificates and associate. *Special study options:* academic remediation for entering students, adult/continuing education programs, advanced placement credit, cooperative education, external degree program, internships, off-campus study, part-time degree program, services for LD students, student-designed majors, summer session for credit. *ROTC:* Army (b), Air Force (c).

Student Life *Campus security:* 24-hour emergency response devices and patrols, late-night transport/escort service.

Athletics Member NJCAA.

Costs (2006–07) *Tuition:* state resident $2700 full-time, $112 per credit hour part-time; nonresident $8100 full-time, $336 per credit hour part-time. *Required fees:* $480 full-time, $14 per credit hour part-time.

Financial Aid Of all full-time matriculated undergraduates, 100 Federal Work-Study jobs (averaging $2000).

Applying *Options:* early admission, deferred entrance. *Application fee:* $30. *Required:* high school transcript.

Freshmen Application Contact Ms. MaryClaire Bauer, Director of Admissions, Hudson Valley Community College, 80 Vandenburgh Avenue, Troy, NY 12180-6096. *Phone:* 518-629-4603. *E-mail:* panzajul@hvcc.edu.

INSTITUTE OF DESIGN AND CONSTRUCTION
Brooklyn, New York   www.idcbrooklyn.org/

- **Independent** 2-year, founded 1947
- **Urban** campus
- **Coed, primarily men,** 246 undergraduate students

Undergraduates Students come from 3 states and territories, 3% are from out of state, 36% African American, 8% Asian American or Pacific Islander, 21% Hispanic American, 2% international.

Freshmen *Admission:* 84 applied, 72 admitted.

Faculty *Total:* 32.

Majors Architectural engineering technology; construction engineering technology; drafting and design technology; interior architecture.

Academics *Calendar:* semesters. *Degree:* associate. *Special study options:* academic remediation for entering students, adult/continuing education programs, advanced placement credit, cooperative education, part-time degree program, summer session for credit.

Student Life *Housing:* college housing not available. *Student services:* personal/psychological counseling.

Costs (2006–07) *Tuition:* $6480 full-time.

Applying *Application fee:* $30. *Required:* high school transcript. *Recommended:* interview. *Application deadline:* rolling (freshmen). *Notification:* continuous until 9/30 (freshmen).

Director of Admissions Mr. Kevin Giannetti, Director of Admissions, Institute of Design and Construction, 141 Willoughby Street, Brooklyn, NY 11201-5317. *Phone:* 718-855-3661.

INTERBORO INSTITUTE

New York, New York   www.interboro.com/

Freshmen Application Contact Ms. Cheryl Ryan, Director of Admissions, Interboro Institute, 450 West 56th Street, New York, NY 10019. *Phone:* 212-399-0091 Ext. 6406. *E-mail:* ryan@interboro.com.

ISLAND DRAFTING AND TECHNICAL INSTITUTE

Amityville, New York   www.idti.edu/

- **Proprietary** 2-year, founded 1957
- **Suburban** campus
- **Coed, primarily men,** 143 undergraduate students, 100% full-time, 13% women, 87% men

Undergraduates 143 full-time. Students come from 1 other state, 16% African American, 3% Asian American or Pacific Islander, 15% Hispanic American, 0.7% Native American.

Freshmen *Admission:* 36 applied, 36 admitted, 34 enrolled. *Average high school GPA:* 3.5.

Faculty *Total:* 25, 20% full-time. *Student/faculty ratio:* 15:1.

Majors Architectural drafting and CAD/CADD; computer and information systems security; computer systems networking and telecommunications; computer/technical support; computer technology/computer systems technology; electrical, electronic and communications engineering technology; mechanical drafting and CAD/CADD; system administration.

Academics *Calendar:* semesters. *Degree:* certificates, diplomas, and associate. *Special study options:* accelerated degree program, adult/continuing education programs, summer session for credit.

Student Life *Housing:* college housing not available.

Costs (2007–08) *Tuition:* $12,450 full-time, $415 per credit part-time. *Required fees:* $350 full-time.

Applying *Options:* early admission. *Required:* interview. *Recommended:* high school transcript. *Notification:* continuous (freshmen).

Freshmen Application Contact Mr. Steven Rothenberg, Island Drafting and Technical Institute, 128 Broadway, Amityville, NY 11701. *Phone:* 631-691-8733. *Fax:* 631-691-8738. *E-mail:* info@idti.edu.

ITT TECHNICAL INSTITUTE

Albany, New York   www.itt-tech.edu/

- **Proprietary** 2-year, founded 1998, part of ITT Educational Services, Inc
- **Coed**

Majors Computer engineering technology; computer software technology; computer systems networking and telecommunications; web/multimedia management and webmaster; web page, digital/multimedia and information resources design.

Academics *Calendar:* quarters. *Degree:* associate.

Library a Web page.

Student Life *Housing:* college housing not available.

Standardized Tests *Required:* Wonderlic aptitude test (for admission).

Costs (2006–07) *Tuition:* Contact school for program costs.

Applying *Options:* deferred entrance. *Application fee:* $100. *Required:* high school transcript, interview. *Recommended:* letters of recommendation. *Application deadlines:* rolling (freshmen), rolling (transfers). *Notification:* continuous (freshmen), continuous (transfers).

Freshmen Application Contact Mr. David Hubbard, Director of Recruitment, ITT Technical Institute, 13 Airline Drive, Albany, NY 12205. *Phone:* 518-452-9300. *Toll-free phone:* 800-489-1191.

ITT TECHNICAL INSTITUTE

Getzville, New York   www.itt-tech.edu/

- **Proprietary** 2-year, part of ITT Educational Services, Inc
- **Coed**

Majors CAD/CADD drafting/design technology; computer engineering technology; computer software technology; computer systems networking and telecommunications; web/multimedia management and webmaster; web page, digital/multimedia and information resources design.

Academics *Degree:* associate.

Library a Web page.

Student Life *Housing:* college housing not available.

Standardized Tests *Required:* Wonderlic aptitude test (for admission).

Costs (2006–07) *Tuition:* Contact school for program costs.

Applying *Options:* deferred entrance. *Application fee:* $100. *Required:* high school transcript, interview. *Recommended:* letters of recommendation. *Application deadlines:* rolling (freshmen), rolling (transfers). *Notification:* continuous (freshmen), continuous (transfers).

Freshmen Application Contact Mr. Scott Jaskier, Director of Recruitment, ITT Technical Institute, 2295 Millersport Highway, PO Box 327, Getzville, NY 14068. *Phone:* 716-689-2200. *Toll-free phone:* 800-469-7593.

ITT TECHNICAL INSTITUTE

Liverpool, New York   www.itt-tech.edu/

- **Proprietary** 2-year, founded 1998, part of ITT Educational Services, Inc
- **Coed**

Majors Computer engineering technology; computer software technology; computer systems networking and telecommunications; web/multimedia management and webmaster; web page, digital/multimedia and information resources design.

Academics *Calendar:* semesters. *Degree:* associate.

Library a Web page.

Student Life *Housing:* college housing not available.

Standardized Tests *Required:* Wonderlic aptitude test (for admission).

Costs (2006–07) *Tuition:* Contact school for program costs.

Applying *Options:* deferred entrance. *Application fee:* $100. *Required:* high school transcript, interview. *Recommended:* letters of recommendation. *Application deadlines:* rolling (freshmen), rolling (transfers). *Notification:* continuous (freshmen), continuous (transfers).

Freshmen Application Contact Terry Riesel, Director of Recruitment, ITT Technical Institute, 235 Greenfield Parkway, Liverpool, NY 13088. *Phone:* 315-461-8000. *Toll-free phone:* 877-488-0011.

JAMESTOWN BUSINESS COLLEGE

Jamestown, New York   www.jbcny.org/

Freshmen Application Contact Mrs. Brenda Salemme, Director of Admissions and Placement, Jamestown Business College, 7 Fairmount Avenue, Jamestown, NY 14701. *Phone:* 716-664-5100. *Fax:* 716-664-3144. *E-mail:* admissions@jbcny.org.

JAMESTOWN COMMUNITY COLLEGE

Jamestown, New York   www.sunyjcc.edu/

- **State and locally supported** 2-year, founded 1950, part of State University of New York System
- **Small-town** 107-acre campus
- **Endowment** $5.7 million
- **Coed,** 3,721 undergraduate students, 66% full-time, 57% women, 43% men

Undergraduates 2,451 full-time, 1,270 part-time. Students come from 9 states and territories, 1 other country, 9% are from out of state, 2% African American, 0.7% Asian American or Pacific Islander, 2% Hispanic American, 2% Native American.

Freshmen *Admission:* 977 enrolled.

Faculty *Total:* 351, 23% full-time, 7% with terminal degrees. *Student/faculty ratio:* 18:1.

Majors Accounting; airline pilot and flight crew; business administration and management; clinical/medical laboratory technology; communication/speech communication and rhetoric; computer and information sciences; computer and information sciences related; computer and information systems security; computer engineering technology; computer science; criminal justice/police science; criminal justice/safety; electrical, electronic and communications engineering

technology; electrical, electronics and communications engineering; engineering; fine/studio arts; humanities; human services; mechanical engineering/ mechanical technology; nursing (registered nurse training); occupational therapist assistant; social sciences.

Academics *Calendar:* semesters. *Degree:* certificates and associate. *Special study options:* academic remediation for entering students, adult/continuing education programs, advanced placement credit, cooperative education, distance learning, honors programs, independent study, internships, part-time degree program, services for LD students, study abroad, summer session for credit.

Library Hultquist Library with 66,808 titles, 370 serial subscriptions, an OPAC, a Web page.

Student Life *Housing:* college housing not available. *Activities and Organizations:* drama/theater group, student-run radio station, choral group, Nursing Club, Inter-Varsity Christian Fellowship, Earth Awareness, Adult Student Network, Student Senate. *Student services:* health clinic, personal/psychological counseling.

Athletics Member NJCAA. *Intercollegiate sports:* baseball M, basketball M/W, golf M, soccer M(s)/W, softball W, swimming and diving M/W, volleyball W, wrestling M. *Intramural sports:* basketball M/W, bowling M/W, table tennis M/W, volleyball M/W.

Costs (2007–08) *Tuition:* state resident $3350 full-time, $140 per credit hour part-time; nonresident $6700 full-time, $253 per credit hour part-time.

Financial Aid Of all full-time matriculated undergraduates, 120 Federal Work-Study jobs (averaging $1000). 110 state and other part-time jobs (averaging $1000).

Applying *Options:* deferred entrance. *Application fee:* $40. *Required:* high school transcript. *Required for some:* standardized test scores. *Application deadlines:* rolling (freshmen), rolling (transfers). *Notification:* continuous (freshmen), continuous (transfers).

Freshmen Application Contact Ms. Wendy Present, Director of Admissions and Recruitment, Jamestown Community College, 525 Falconer Street, PO Box 20, Jamestown, NY 14702-0020. *Phone:* 716-665-5220 Ext. 2240. *Toll-free phone:* 800-388-8557. *Fax:* 716-338-1450. *E-mail:* admissions@mail.sunyjcc.edu.

JEFFERSON COMMUNITY COLLEGE
Watertown, New York   www.sunyjefferson.edu/

- **State and locally supported** 2-year, founded 1961, part of State University of New York System
- **Small-town** 90-acre campus with easy access to Syracuse
- **Endowment** $2.5 million
- **Coed**

Undergraduates 1,822 full-time, 1,723 part-time. Students come from 26 states and territories, 3 other countries, 1% are from out of state, 5% African American, 2% Asian American or Pacific Islander, 4% Hispanic American, 0.5% Native American, 0.2% international, 3% transferred in.

Faculty *Student/faculty ratio:* 18:1.

Academics *Calendar:* semesters. *Degree:* certificates and associate. *Special study options:* academic remediation for entering students, advanced placement credit, cooperative education, distance learning, double majors, honors programs, independent study, internships, part-time degree program, services for LD students, student-designed majors, summer session for credit.

Student Life *Campus security:* 24-hour emergency response devices and patrols.

Athletics Member NJCAA.

Standardized Tests *Recommended:* SAT or ACT (for admission).

Costs (2006–07) *Tuition:* state resident $3354 full-time, $122 per credit hour part-time; nonresident $5524 full-time, $212 per credit hour part-time. *Required fees:* $426 full-time, $15 per credit hour part-time, $21 per semester part-time.

Financial Aid Of all full-time matriculated undergraduates, 125 Federal Work-Study jobs (averaging $1200). 50 state and other part-time jobs (averaging $1000).

Applying *Options:* early admission, deferred entrance. *Required:* high school transcript. *Required for some:* letters of recommendation, interview.

Freshmen Application Contact Ms. Rosanne N. Weir, Director of Admissions, Jefferson Community College, 1220 Coffeen Street, Watertown, NY 13601. *Phone:* 315-786-2277. *Fax:* 315-786-2459. *E-mail:* admissions@ sunyjefferson.edu.

KATHARINE GIBBS SCHOOL
Melville, New York   www.gibbsmelville.com/

Director of Admissions Ms. Cynthia Gamache, Director of Admissions, Katharine Gibbs School, 320 South Service Road, Melville, NY 11747-3785. *Phone:* 631-370-3307.

KATHARINE GIBBS SCHOOL
New York, New York   www.katharinegibbs.com/

Director of Admissions Ms. Pat Martin, Admissions Director, Katharine Gibbs School, 50 West 40th Street, New York, NY 10018. *Phone:* 212-867-9300.

KINGSBOROUGH COMMUNITY COLLEGE OF THE CITY UNIVERSITY OF NEW YORK
Brooklyn, New York   www.kbcc.cuny.edu/

- **State and locally supported** 2-year, founded 1963, part of City University of New York System
- **Urban** 72-acre campus with easy access to New York City
- **Coed,** 14,687 undergraduate students, 53% full-time, 58% women, 42% men

Undergraduates 7,804 full-time, 6,883 part-time. 3% are from out of state, 31% African American, 9% Asian American or Pacific Islander, 13% Hispanic American, 0.1% Native American, 11% international, 9% transferred in.

Freshmen *Admission:* 1,977 admitted, 1,976 enrolled. *Average high school GPA:* 2.7. *Test scores:* SAT verbal scores over 500: 8%; SAT math scores over 500: 12%; SAT verbal scores over 600: 1%; SAT math scores over 600: 2%.

Faculty *Total:* 799, 38% full-time, 34% with terminal degrees. *Student/faculty ratio:* 23:1.

Majors Accounting; administrative assistant and secretarial science; applied art; art; biology/biological sciences; broadcast journalism; business administration and management; chemistry; commercial and advertising art; community health services counseling; computer and information sciences; computer science; data processing and data processing technology; dramatic/theater arts; early childhood education; education; elementary education; engineering science; fashion merchandising; health and physical education related; human services; journalism; labor and industrial relations; liberal arts and sciences/ liberal studies; marine technology; marketing/marketing management; mathematics; mental health/rehabilitation; music; nursing (registered nurse training); parks, recreation and leisure; physical therapist assistant; physical therapy; physics; psychiatric/mental health services technology; sport and fitness administration/management; teacher assistant/aide; tourism and travel services management.

Academics *Calendar:* semesters. *Degree:* associate. *Special study options:* academic remediation for entering students, adult/continuing education programs, advanced placement credit, distance learning, English as a second language, honors programs, independent study, internships, off-campus study, part-time degree program, services for LD students, summer session for credit.

Library Robert J. Kibbee Library with 185,912 titles, 458 serial subscriptions, an OPAC.

Student Life *Housing:* college housing not available. *Activities and Organizations:* drama/theater group, student-run newspaper, radio station, choral group, Peer Advisors, Caribbean Club, DECA. *Campus security:* 24-hour emergency response devices and patrols. *Student services:* health clinic, personal/ psychological counseling, women's center.

Athletics Member NJCAA. *Intercollegiate sports:* baseball M, basketball M/W, soccer M, softball W, tennis M/W, track and field M/W, volleyball W. *Intramural sports:* baseball M, basketball M/W, soccer M, softball W, tennis M/W, track and field M/W, volleyball W.

Costs (2006–07) *Tuition:* state resident $2800 full-time, $120 per credit part-time; nonresident $4580 full-time, $190 per credit part-time. *Required fees:* $300 full-time, $80 per term part-time. *Payment plan:* installment. *Waivers:* senior citizens.

Applying *Application fee:* $65. *Required:* high school transcript. *Application deadlines:* 8/15 (freshmen), rolling (transfers).

Freshmen Application Contact Mr. Robert Ingenito, Director of Admissions Information Center, Kingsborough Community College of the City University of New York, 2001 Oriental Boulevard, Brooklyn, NY 11235. *Phone:* 718-368-4600. *Fax:* 718-368-5356. *E-mail:* info@kbcc.cuny.edu.

LONG ISLAND BUSINESS INSTITUTE
Commack, New York   www.libi.edu/commack/index.html

- **Proprietary** 2-year, founded 1968
- **Urban** campus with easy access to New York City
- **Coed, primarily women,** 880 undergraduate students, 76% full-time, 75% women, 25% men

Long Island Business Institute (continued)

Undergraduates 666 full-time, 214 part-time. Students come from 2 states and territories, 1% are from out of state, 3% African American, 42% Asian American or Pacific Islander, 22% Hispanic American, 8% international, 4% transferred in.

Freshmen *Admission:* 265 applied, 265 admitted, 265 enrolled. *Average high school GPA:* 2.0.

Faculty *Total:* 88, 26% full-time, 3% with terminal degrees. *Student/faculty ratio:* 15:1.

Majors Accounting; administrative assistant and secretarial science; business administration and management; court reporting.

Academics *Calendar:* trimesters. *Degree:* certificates, diplomas, and associate. *Special study options:* academic remediation for entering students, adult/continuing education programs, advanced placement credit, cooperative education, English as a second language, independent study, internships, part-time degree program, summer session for credit.

Library Mendon W. Smith Memorial Library with 2,158 titles, 83 serial subscriptions, 645 audiovisual materials, an OPAC, a Web page.

Student Life *Housing:* college housing not available. *Campus security:* 24-hour emergency response devices.

Standardized Tests *Required:* CPAt; CELSA (for admission).

Costs (2007–08) *Tuition:* $9750 full-time, $325 per credit part-time. *Required fees:* $400 full-time.

Applying *Application fee:* $50. *Required:* essay or personal statement, high school transcript, interview. *Application deadlines:* rolling (freshmen), rolling (transfers).

Freshmen Application Contact Mr. Robert Nazar, Director of Admissions, Long Island Business Institute, 6500 Jericho Turnpike, Commack, NY 11725. *Phone:* 718-939-5100. *Fax:* 718-939-9235. *E-mail:* rnazar@libi.edu.

LONG ISLAND COLLEGE HOSPITAL SCHOOL OF NURSING

Brooklyn, New York   www.futurenurselich.org/

- **Independent** 2-year, founded 1883
- **Urban** campus
- **Coed, primarily women,** 140 undergraduate students, 51% full-time, 82% women, 18% men

Undergraduates 72 full-time, 68 part-time. Students come from 2 states and territories, 1% are from out of state, 44% African American, 11% Asian American or Pacific Islander, 12% Hispanic American, 51% transferred in.

Faculty *Total:* 17, 35% full-time. *Student/faculty ratio:* 12:1.

Majors Nursing (registered nurse training).

Academics *Calendar:* semesters. *Degree:* associate. *Special study options:* advanced placement credit, cooperative education, independent study, internships, summer session for credit.

Library E. King Morgan M.D. Health Sciences Library plus 1 other with 16,000 titles, 400 serial subscriptions.

Student Life *Housing:* college housing not available. *Activities and Organizations:* Student Government Association. *Campus security:* 24-hour emergency response devices. *Student services:* health clinic, personal/psychological counseling.

Costs (2006–07) *Tuition:* $24,030 full-time.

Financial Aid Of all full-time matriculated undergraduates, 5 Federal Work-Study jobs. *Financial aid deadline:* 6/30.

Applying *Application fee:* $50. *Required:* essay or personal statement, high school transcript, minimum 2.0 GPA, 2 letters of recommendation, interview, NLN Exam. *Application deadlines:* 4/13 (freshmen), 4/13 (transfers). *Notification:* continuous (freshmen), continuous (transfers).

Freshmen Application Contact Ms. Barbara J. Evans, Admissions Assistant, Long Island College Hospital School of Nursing, 340 Court Street, Brooklyn, NY 11231. *Phone:* 718-780-1071. *Fax:* 718-780-1936. *E-mail:* bevans@chpnet.org.

MARIA COLLEGE

Albany, New York   www.mariacollege.edu/

- **Independent** 2-year, founded 1958
- **Urban** 9-acre campus
- **Coed**

Undergraduates 277 full-time, 511 part-time. Students come from 5 states and territories, 4 other countries, 2% are from out of state, 20% African American,

2% Asian American or Pacific Islander, 3% Hispanic American, 0.5% Native American, 0.5% international, 30% transferred in.

Faculty *Student/faculty ratio:* 10:1.

Academics *Calendar:* semesters. *Degree:* certificates and associate. *Special study options:* academic remediation for entering students, adult/continuing education programs, advanced placement credit, independent study, off-campus study, part-time degree program, services for LD students, summer session for credit. *ROTC:* Air Force (c).

Student Life *Campus security:* late-night transport/escort service.

Standardized Tests *Required:* SAT or ACT (for admission).

Costs (2006–07) *Tuition:* $7800 full-time, $285 per credit part-time. *Required fees:* $200 full-time, $80 per term part-time.

Financial Aid Of all full-time matriculated undergraduates, 25 Federal Work-Study jobs (averaging $1000).

Applying *Options:* early admission. *Application fee:* $35. *Required:* essay or personal statement, high school transcript, minimum 2.0 GPA, 1 letter of recommendation, interview.

Freshmen Application Contact Ms. Laurie A. Gilmore, Director of Admissions, Maria College, 700 New Scotland Avenue, Albany, NY 12208. *Phone:* 518-438-3111. *Fax:* 518-453-1366. *E-mail:* admissions@mariacollege.edu.

MEMORIAL HOSPITAL SCHOOL OF NURSING

Albany, New York   www.nehealth.com/SON/

- **Independent** 2-year
- **Coed,** 113 undergraduate students

Majors Nursing (registered nurse training).

Academics *Calendar:* semesters. *Degree:* associate.

Costs (2006–07) *Tuition:* state resident $6650 full-time; nonresident $9960 full-time.

Applying *Recommended:* high school transcript.

Freshmen Application Contact Admissions Office, Memorial Hospital School of Nursing, 600 Northern Boulevard, Albany, NY 12204.

MILDRED ELLEY

Latham, New York   www.mildred-elley.edu/latham.htm

Director of Admissions Mr. Michael Cahalan, Enrollment Manager, Mildred Elley, 800 New Loudon Road, Suite 5120, Latham, NY 12110. *Phone:* 518-786-3171 Ext. 227. *Toll-free phone:* 800-622-6327.

MOHAWK VALLEY COMMUNITY COLLEGE

Utica, New York   www.mvcc.edu/

- **State and locally supported** 2-year, founded 1946, part of State University of New York System
- **Urban** 80-acre campus
- **Endowment** $3.2 million
- **Coed,** 5,895 undergraduate students, 63% full-time, 54% women, 46% men

Undergraduates 3,717 full-time, 2,178 part-time. Students come from 15 states and territories, 11 other countries, 2% are from out of state, 7% African American, 2% Asian American or Pacific Islander, 3% Hispanic American, 0.6% Native American, 1% international, 4% transferred in, 9% live on campus. *Retention:* 57% of 2003 full-time freshmen returned.

Freshmen *Admission:* 3,369 applied, 2,998 admitted, 1,488 enrolled.

Faculty *Total:* 292, 45% full-time, 51% with terminal degrees. *Student/faculty ratio:* 24:1.

Majors Accounting technology and bookkeeping; administrative assistant and secretarial science; advertising; airframe mechanics and aircraft maintenance technology; appliance installation and repair technology; architectural drafting and CAD/CADD; art; avionics maintenance technology; banking and financial support services; building/property maintenance and management; business administration and management; business and personal services marketing related; carpentry; chemical technology; civil engineering technology; commercial and advertising art; commercial photography; communications systems installation and repair technology; community organization and advocacy;

computer and information sciences; computer and information sciences and support services related; computer programming; criminal justice/law enforcement administration; culinary arts; design and applied arts related; drafting and design technology; dramatic/theater arts; electrical and electronic engineering technologies related; electrical, electronic and communications engineering technology; electrical/electronics maintenance and repair technology related; elementary education; emergency medical technology (EMT paramedic); engineering; English language and literature related; entrepreneurship; food services technology; foodservice systems administration; forensic science and technology; general studies; health information/medical records technology; heating, air conditioning and refrigeration technology; heating, air conditioning, ventilation and refrigeration maintenance technology; heavy equipment maintenance technology; hotel/motel administration; humanities; human services; industrial production technologies related; liberal arts and sciences/liberal studies; machine shop technology; management information systems and services related; mechanical design technology; mechanical drafting and CAD/CADD; mechanical engineering/mechanical technology; medical/clinical assistant; medical laboratory technology; medical radiologic technology; mental health/rehabilitation; metallurgical technology; nursing (registered nurse training); nutrition sciences; office management; office occupations and clerical services; parks, recreation and leisure facilities management; photographic and film/video technology; physical education teaching and coaching; public administration; respiratory care therapy; restaurant, culinary, and catering management; secondary education; substance abuse/addiction counseling; surgical technology; survey technology; tool and die technology.

Academics *Calendar:* semesters. *Degree:* certificates and associate. *Special study options:* academic remediation for entering students, adult/continuing education programs, advanced placement credit, distance learning, double majors, English as a second language, honors programs, independent study, internships, off-campus study, part-time degree program, services for LD students, student-designed majors, summer session for credit.

Library Mohawk Valley Community College Library plus 1 other with 94,200 titles, 628 serial subscriptions, 8,860 audiovisual materials, an OPAC, a Web page.

Student Life *Housing Options:* coed. Campus housing is university owned. Freshman campus housing is guaranteed. *Activities and Organizations:* drama/theater group, student-run newspaper, radio station, choral group, Drama Club, Student Congress, Returning Adult Student Association, Black Student Union, Program Board. *Campus security:* 24-hour emergency response devices and patrols, late-night transport/escort service, controlled dormitory access. *Student services:* health clinic, personal/psychological counseling.

Athletics Member NJCAA. *Intercollegiate sports:* baseball M, basketball M/W, bowling M/W, cross-country running M/W, golf M/W, ice hockey M, lacrosse M, soccer M/W, softball W, tennis M/W, track and field M/W, volleyball W. *Intramural sports:* basketball M/W, cheerleading W, football M, racquetball M/W, softball M/W, table tennis M/W, tennis M/W, volleyball M/W, weight lifting M.

Costs (2006–07) *Tuition:* state resident $3100 full-time, $120 per credit hour part-time; nonresident $6200 full-time, $240 per credit hour part-time. *Required fees:* $384 full-time, $2 per credit hour part-time, $35 per term part-time. *Room and board:* $6530; room only: $3710. *Payment plans:* installment, deferred payment. *Waivers:* employees or children of employees.

Financial Aid Of all full-time matriculated undergraduates, 229 Federal Work-Study jobs (averaging $1750).

Applying *Options:* electronic application, early admission, early decision, deferred entrance. *Required:* high school transcript. *Application deadlines:* rolling (freshmen), rolling (transfers).

Freshmen Application Contact Mrs. Sandra Fiebiger, Electronic Data Processing Clerk, Admissions, Mohawk Valley Community College, 1101 Sherman Drive, Utica, NY 13501. *Phone:* 315-792-5640. *Toll-free phone:* 800-SEE-MVCC. *Fax:* 315-792-5527. *E-mail:* sfiebiger@mvcc.edu.

▶See page 570 for the College Close-Up.

MONROE COMMUNITY COLLEGE
Rochester, New York   www.monroecc.edu/

- **State and locally supported** 2-year, founded 1961, part of State University of New York System
- **Suburban** 314-acre campus with easy access to Buffalo
- **Endowment** $3.6 million
- **Coed,** 16,596 undergraduate students, 57% full-time, 55% women, 45% men

Undergraduates 9,398 full-time, 7,198 part-time. Students come from 1 other state, 45 other countries, 17% African American, 3% Asian American or Pacific Islander, 5% Hispanic American, 0.6% Native American, 0.5% international, 6% transferred in.

Freshmen *Admission:* 3,710 enrolled.

Faculty *Total:* 1,192, 25% full-time, 4% with terminal degrees. *Student/faculty ratio:* 20:1.

Majors Accounting; administrative assistant and secretarial science; art; automobile/automotive mechanics technology; behavioral sciences; biological and physical sciences; biology/biological sciences; biology/biotechnology laboratory technician; business administration and management; chemical engineering; chemistry; civil engineering technology; commercial and advertising art; computer and information sciences related; computer engineering related; computer engineering technology; computer science; computer/technical support; construction engineering technology; consumer merchandising/retailing management; corrections; criminal justice/law enforcement administration; criminal justice/police science; data processing and data processing technology; dental hygiene; electrical, electronic and communications engineering technology; engineering science; environmental studies; fashion/apparel design; fashion merchandising; fire science; food services technology; forestry; graphic and printing equipment operation/production; health information/medical records administration; heating, air conditioning, ventilation and refrigeration maintenance technology; history; hotel/motel administration; human ecology; human services; industrial radiologic technology; industrial technology; information science/studies; information technology; instrumentation technology; interior design; international business/trade/commerce; landscape architecture; laser and optical technology; legal administrative assistant/secretary; liberal arts and sciences/liberal studies; marketing/marketing management; mass communication/media; mathematics; mechanical engineering/mechanical technology; music; nursing (registered nurse training); parks, recreation and leisure; physical education teaching and coaching; physics; political science and government; pre-pharmacy studies; quality control technology; social sciences; special products marketing; telecommunications; tourism and travel services management.

Academics *Calendar:* semesters. *Degree:* certificates and associate. *Special study options:* academic remediation for entering students, accelerated degree program, adult/continuing education programs, advanced placement credit, cooperative education, English as a second language, honors programs, internships, off-campus study, part-time degree program, services for LD students, summer session for credit. *ROTC:* Army (c), Air Force (c).

Library LeRoy V. Good Library plus 1 other with 110,748 titles, 745 serial subscriptions, 4,100 audiovisual materials, an OPAC.

Student Life *Activities and Organizations:* drama/theater group, student-run newspaper, radio station, choral group, student newspaper, Phi Theta Kappa, student government. *Campus security:* 24-hour emergency response devices, late-night transport/escort service. *Student services:* health clinic, personal/psychological counseling.

Athletics Member NJCAA. *Intercollegiate sports:* baseball M(s), basketball M(s)/W(s), golf M, ice hockey M(s), lacrosse M(s), soccer M(s)/W(s), softball W, swimming and diving M(s)/W(s), tennis M/W, volleyball W. *Intramural sports:* archery M/W, basketball M/W, bowling M/W, cross-country running M/W, lacrosse W, racquetball M/W, rugby M, skiing (cross-country) M/W, soccer M/W, softball M/W, swimming and diving M/W, tennis M/W, volleyball M/W.

Costs (2006–07) *Tuition:* state resident $3041 full-time; nonresident $5741 full-time.

Financial Aid Of all full-time matriculated undergraduates, 1,182 Federal Work-Study jobs (averaging $1450).

Applying *Options:* electronic application, early admission. *Application fee:* $20. *Required:* high school transcript. *Application deadlines:* rolling (freshmen), rolling (transfers). *Notification:* continuous (freshmen), continuous (transfers).

Freshmen Application Contact Mr. Andrew Freeman, Director of Admissions, Monroe Community College, 1000 East Henrietta Road, Rochester, NY 14623-5780. *Phone:* 585-292-2231. *Fax:* 585-292-3860. *E-mail:* admissions@monroecc.edu.

NASSAU COMMUNITY COLLEGE
Garden City, New York   www.ncc.edu/

- **State and locally supported** 2-year, founded 1959, part of State University of New York System
- **Suburban** 225-acre campus with easy access to New York City
- **Endowment** $825,000
- **Coed,** 21,229 undergraduate students, 65% full-time, 52% women, 48% men

Undergraduates 13,868 full-time, 7,361 part-time. Students come from 54 other countries, 20% African American, 6% Asian American or Pacific Islander, 13% Hispanic American, 0.3% Native American, 5% international, 9% transferred in.

Freshmen *Admission:* 10,205 applied, 9,499 admitted, 5,492 enrolled.

Faculty *Total:* 1,278, 42% full-time, 28% with terminal degrees. *Student/faculty ratio:* 18:1.

Majors Accounting; accounting technology and bookkeeping; administrative assistant and secretarial science; African-American/Black studies; art; business

Nassau Community College (continued)

administration and management; civil engineering technology; clinical/medical laboratory technology; commercial and advertising art; communication/speech communication and rhetoric; computer and information sciences; computer and information sciences related; computer graphics; computer science; computer systems networking and telecommunications; criminal justice/law enforcement administration; criminal justice/safety; dance; data processing and data processing technology; design and visual communications; dramatic/theater arts; engineering; entrepreneurship; fashion/apparel design; fashion merchandising; funeral service and mortuary science; general retailing/wholesaling; general studies; health science; hotel/motel administration; instrumentation technology; insurance; interior design; kindergarten/preschool education; legal administrative assistant/secretary; legal assistant/paralegal; liberal arts and sciences/liberal studies; management information systems; marketing/marketing management; mass communication/media; mathematics; medical administrative assistant and medical secretary; medical radiologic technology; music performance; nursing (registered nurse training); photography; physical therapist assistant; real estate; rehabilitation therapy; respiratory care therapy; security and loss prevention; surgical technology; theater design and technology; transportation technology; visual and performing arts.

Academics *Calendar:* semesters. *Degree:* certificates and associate. *Special study options:* academic remediation for entering students, adult/continuing education programs, advanced placement credit, cooperative education, distance learning, English as a second language, honors programs, internships, off-campus study, part-time degree program, services for LD students, summer session for credit.

Library A. Holly Patterson Library with 179,920 titles, 421 serial subscriptions, 20,253 audiovisual materials, an OPAC, a Web page.

Student Life *Housing:* college housing not available. *Activities and Organizations:* drama/theater group, student-run newspaper, radio station, choral group, Student Organization of Latinos, Student Government Association, Programming Board, Caribbean Student Organization, NYPIRG. *Campus security:* 24-hour emergency response devices and patrols, late-night transport/escort service. *Student services:* health clinic, personal/psychological counseling, women's center.

Athletics Member NJCAA. *Intercollegiate sports:* baseball M, basketball M/W, bowling M/W, cheerleading W, cross-country running M/W, equestrian sports M/W, football M, golf M/W, lacrosse M, soccer M/W, softball W, tennis M/W, track and field M/W, volleyball M/W, wrestling M. *Intramural sports:* badminton M/W, basketball M/W, cross-country running M/W, football M, ice hockey M, lacrosse M/W, racquetball M/W, soccer M/W, softball M/W, table tennis M/W, tennis M/W, volleyball M/W.

Standardized Tests *Recommended:* SAT or ACT (for admission).

Costs (2007–08) *Tuition:* state resident $3310 full-time, $138 per credit part-time; nonresident $6620 full-time, $276 per credit part-time. *Required fees:* $224 full-time, $22 per term part-time.

Financial Aid Of all full-time matriculated undergraduates, 400 Federal Work-Study jobs (averaging $3000).

Applying *Options:* deferred entrance. *Application fee:* $30. *Required:* high school transcript. *Required for some:* minimum 3.0 GPA, interview. *Recommended:* minimum 2.0 GPA. *Application deadlines:* 8/1 (freshmen), 8/1 (transfers). *Notification:* continuous (freshmen), continuous (transfers).

Freshmen Application Contact Mr. Craig Wright, Vice President of Enrollment Management, Nassau Community College, One Education Drive, Garden City, NY 11530. *Phone:* 516-572-7345. *E-mail:* admissions@sunynassau.edu.

NEW YORK CAREER INSTITUTE

New York, New York   www.nyci.com/

- **Proprietary** 2-year, founded 1942
- **Urban** campus
- **Coed,** 564 undergraduate students, 88% full-time, 87% women, 13% men

Undergraduates 498 full-time, 66 part-time. 27% African American, 1% Asian American or Pacific Islander, 17% Hispanic American.

Freshmen *Average high school GPA:* 3.0.

Faculty *Total:* 28, 14% full-time, 32% with terminal degrees.

Majors Court reporting; legal assistant/paralegal.

Academics *Calendar:* trimesters (semesters for evening division). *Degree:* associate. *Special study options:* academic remediation for entering students, advanced placement credit, cooperative education, internships, part-time degree program, summer session for credit.

Library 5,010 titles, 23 serial subscriptions.

Student Life *Housing:* college housing not available. *Activities and Organizations:* student-run newspaper.

Standardized Tests *Required:* CPAt (for admission).

Costs (2007–08) *Tuition:* $10,500 full-time, $350 per credit part-time. *Required fees:* $35 full-time, $35 per term part-time.

Applying *Application fee:* $50. *Required:* high school transcript, interview. *Application deadlines:* 9/21 (freshmen), 9/21 (transfers). *Notification:* continuous (freshmen), continuous (transfers).

Freshmen Application Contact Ms. Cindy McMahon, Director of Admissions, New York Career Institute, 11 Park Place- 4th Floor, New York, NY 10007. *Phone:* 212-962-0002 Ext. 101. *Fax:* 212-385-7574. *E-mail:* cmcmahon@nyci.edu.

NEW YORK CITY COLLEGE OF TECHNOLOGY OF THE CITY UNIVERSITY OF NEW YORK

Brooklyn, New York   www.citytech.cuny.edu/

- **State and locally supported** primarily 2-year, founded 1946, part of City University of New York System
- **Urban** campus
- **Endowment** $11.7 million
- **Coed,** 13,368 undergraduate students, 57% full-time, 50% women, 50% men

Undergraduates 7,641 full-time, 5,727 part-time. Students come from 10 states and territories, 59 other countries, 1% are from out of state, 38% African American, 13% Asian American or Pacific Islander, 26% Hispanic American, 0.2% Native American, 10% international, 8% transferred in. *Retention:* 78% of 2003 full-time freshmen returned.

Freshmen *Admission:* 11,118 applied, 9,641 admitted, 2,883 enrolled. *Average high school GPA:* 2.5. *Test scores:* SAT verbal scores over 500: 11%; SAT math scores over 500: 19%; SAT verbal scores over 600: 1%; SAT math scores over 600: 3%.

Faculty *Total:* 970, 33% full-time, 55% with terminal degrees. *Student/faculty ratio:* 18:1.

Majors Accounting; architectural drafting and CAD/CADD; chemical technology; civil engineering technology; commercial and advertising art; computer science; construction engineering technology; data processing and data processing technology; dental hygiene; dental laboratory technology; drafting and design technology; electrical, electronic and communications engineering technology; electromechanical technology; fashion merchandising; heating, air conditioning, ventilation and refrigeration maintenance technology; hospitality administration; human services; information science/studies; legal assistant/paralegal; liberal arts and sciences/liberal studies; marketing/marketing management; mechanical engineering/mechanical technology; medical radiologic technology; nursing (registered nurse training); ophthalmic laboratory technology; technical teacher education; telecommunications; theater design and technology; trade and industrial teacher education.

Academics *Calendar:* semesters. *Degrees:* certificates, associate, and bachelor's. *Special study options:* academic remediation for entering students, advanced placement credit, distance learning, English as a second language, freshman honors college, honors programs, independent study, internships, off-campus study, part-time degree program, services for LD students, student-designed majors, study abroad, summer session for credit. *ROTC:* Air Force (c).

Library Ursula C. Schwerin Library with 183,000 titles, 60,000 audiovisual materials, an OPAC, a Web page.

Student Life *Housing:* college housing not available. *Activities and Organizations:* drama/theater group, student-run newspaper, choral group, IBO, NUTREX, Human Services, Seekers Christian Fellowship Gospel Choir. *Campus security:* 24-hour emergency response devices and patrols. *Student services:* health clinic, personal/psychological counseling, women's center.

Athletics Member NCAA. All Division III. *Intercollegiate sports:* basketball M/W, cross-country running M/W, soccer M, track and field M/W, volleyball M/W. *Intramural sports:* basketball M/W, volleyball M/W.

Standardized Tests *Required for some:* SAT (for admission), ACT (for admission), SAT or ACT (for admission).

Costs (2006–07) *Tuition:* state resident $4000 full-time, $170 per credit part-time; nonresident $8640 full-time, $360 per credit part-time. *Required fees:* $269 full-time. *Payment plan:* deferred payment. *Waivers:* employees or children of employees.

Applying *Application fee:* $65. *Required:* high school transcript. *Application deadlines:* 3/15 (freshmen), 3/15 (transfers).

Freshmen Application Contact Alexis Chaconis, Director of Admissions, New York City College of Technology of the City University of New York, 300 Jay Street, Brooklyn, NY 11201-2983. *Phone:* 718-260-5500. *E-mail:* achaconis@citytech.cuny.edu.

NEW YORK COLLEGE OF HEALTH PROFESSIONS

Syosset, New York　　　　　**www.nycollege.edu/**

- **Independent** founded 1981
- **Suburban** campus with easy access to New York City
- **Coed,** 801 undergraduate students, 41% full-time, 76% women, 24% men

Undergraduates 332 full-time, 469 part-time. 11% African American, 8% Asian American or Pacific Islander, 12% Hispanic American, 0.3% Native American.

Freshmen *Admission:* 169 enrolled. *Average high school GPA:* 2.73.

Faculty *Total:* 93, 18% full-time. *Student/faculty ratio:* 19:1.

Majors Health services/allied health/health sciences; massage therapy.

Academics *Calendar:* trimesters. *Degrees:* associate, incidental bachelor's, and master's. *Special study options:* academic remediation for entering students, accelerated degree program, adult/continuing education programs, advanced placement credit, cooperative education, double majors, internships, part-time degree program, services for LD students, summer session for credit.

Library James and Lenore Jacobson Library at the Syosset Campus with 5,500 titles, 40 serial subscriptions, 200 audiovisual materials, an OPAC, a Web page.

Student Life *Housing:* college housing not available. *Campus security:* 24-hour emergency response devices and patrols, security guard evening and weekend hours. *Student services:* health clinic.

Costs (2007–08) *Tuition:* $9900 full-time, $275 per credit part-time. *Required fees:* $1000 full-time.

Financial Aid Of all full-time matriculated undergraduates, 15 Federal Work-Study jobs.

Applying *Options:* electronic application, deferred entrance. *Application fee:* $85. *Required:* essay or personal statement, high school transcript, minimum 2.0 GPA, interview. *Application deadlines:* rolling (freshmen), rolling (transfers). *Notification:* continuous (freshmen), continuous (transfers).

Director of Admissions Ms. Mary Rodas, Associate Director of Admissions, New York College of Health Professions, 6801 Jericho Turnpike, Syosset, NY 11791. *Toll-free phone:* 800-922-7337 Ext. 351. *E-mail:* rdodas@nycollege.edu.

▶**See page 574 for the College Close-Up.**

NIAGARA COUNTY COMMUNITY COLLEGE

Sanborn, New York　　　　**www.niagaracc.suny.edu/**

- **State and locally supported** 2-year, founded 1962, part of State University of New York System
- **Rural** 287-acre campus with easy access to Buffalo
- **Endowment** $2.5 million
- **Coed,** 5,944 undergraduate students, 60% full-time, 60% women, 40% men

Undergraduates 3,563 full-time, 2,381 part-time. Students come from 13 states and territories, 12 other countries, 1% are from out of state, 6% African American, 1% Asian American or Pacific Islander, 1% Hispanic American, 2% Native American, 1% international, 5% transferred in.

Freshmen *Admission:* 2,268 applied, 2,268 admitted, 1,036 enrolled. *Average high school GPA:* 2.48.

Faculty *Total:* 333, 35% full-time, 14% with terminal degrees. *Student/faculty ratio:* 17:1.

Majors Accounting; administrative assistant and secretarial science; animal sciences; biochemical technology; biological and physical sciences; business administration and management; computer science; consumer merchandising/retailing management; criminal justice/law enforcement administration; culinary arts; design and applied arts related; drafting and design technology; dramatic/theater arts; electrical, electronic and communications engineering technology; electroneurodiagnostic/electroencephalographic technology; fine/studio arts; general studies; hospitality administration; humanities; human services; information science/studies; liberal arts and sciences/liberal studies; mass communication/media; mathematics; mechanical design technology; medical/clinical assistant; music; natural resources/conservation; nursing (registered nurse training); occupational health and industrial hygiene; physical education teaching and coaching; physical therapist assistant; radiologic technology/science; social sciences; surgical technology; Web page, digital/multimedia and information resources design.

Academics *Calendar:* semesters. *Degree:* certificates and associate. *Special study options:* academic remediation for entering students, adult/continuing education programs, advanced placement credit, cooperative education, double

majors, honors programs, independent study, internships, off-campus study, part-time degree program, services for LD students, student-designed majors, study abroad, summer session for credit. *ROTC:* Army (c).

Library Library Learning Center with 93,055 titles, 524 serial subscriptions, an OPAC, a Web page.

Student Life *Housing:* college housing not available. *Activities and Organizations:* drama/theater group, student-run newspaper, radio station, choral group, student radio station, Student Nurses Association, Phi Theta Kappa, Alpha Beta Gamma, Physical Education Club. *Campus security:* student patrols, late-night transport/escort service, emergency telephones. *Student services:* health clinic, personal/psychological counseling.

Athletics Member NJCAA. *Intercollegiate sports:* baseball M, basketball M(s)/W, golf M/W, soccer M/W, softball W, volleyball W, wrestling M(s). *Intramural sports:* basketball M/W, bowling M/W, cheerleading W, skiing (cross-country) M(c)/W(c), volleyball M/W.

Costs (2006–07) *Tuition:* state resident $3168 full-time, $132 per credit hour part-time; nonresident $4752 full-time, $198 per credit hour part-time. Full-time tuition and fees vary according to program. Part-time tuition and fees vary according to program. *Required fees:* $302 full-time, $63 per term part-time. *Payment plan:* installment. *Waivers:* senior citizens and employees or children of employees.

Financial Aid Of all full-time matriculated undergraduates, 192 Federal Work-Study jobs (averaging $1925).

Applying *Options:* electronic application, early admission. *Required:* high school transcript. *Required for some:* minimum 2.0 GPA. *Notification:* continuous until 8/31 (freshmen), continuous until 8/31 (transfers).

Freshmen Application Contact Ms. Kathy Saunders, Director of Enrollment Services, Niagara County Community College, 3111 Saunders Settlement Road, Sanborn, NY 14132. *Phone:* 716-614-6200. *Fax:* 716-614-6820. *E-mail:* admissions@niagaracc.suny.edu.

NORTH COUNTRY COMMUNITY COLLEGE

Saranac Lake, New York　　　　**www.nccc.edu/**

- **State and locally supported** 2-year, founded 1967, part of State University of New York System
- **Rural** 100-acre campus
- **Coed,** 1,636 undergraduate students, 59% full-time, 66% women, 34% men

Undergraduates 973 full-time, 663 part-time. Students come from 8 states and territories, 6 other countries, 3% are from out of state, 1% African American, 0.6% Asian American or Pacific Islander, 0.6% Hispanic American, 3% Native American, 1% international, 6% transferred in, 7% live on campus.

Freshmen *Admission:* 1,897 applied, 1,829 admitted, 362 enrolled. *Average high school GPA:* 3.16.

Faculty *Total:* 151, 30% full-time, 10% with terminal degrees. *Student/faculty ratio:* 17:1.

Majors Biological and physical sciences; business administration and management; computer graphics; consumer merchandising/retailing management; criminal justice/safety; interdisciplinary studies; kinesiology and exercise science; liberal arts and sciences/liberal studies; mathematics; medical radiologic technology; mental health/rehabilitation; nursing (registered nurse training); office occupations and clerical services; parks, recreation and leisure facilities management.

Academics *Calendar:* semesters. *Degree:* certificates and associate. *Special study options:* academic remediation for entering students, advanced placement credit, distance learning, double majors, internships, part-time degree program, services for LD students, student-designed majors, summer session for credit.

Library North Country Community College Library plus 1 other with 58,556 titles, 177 serial subscriptions, a Web page.

Student Life *Housing Options:* coed. Campus housing is university owned. *Activities and Organizations:* drama/theater group, student-run newspaper, Student Government Association, Wilderness Recreation Club, Nursing Club, Radiology Club, Criminal Justice Club. *Campus security:* controlled dormitory access. *Student services:* personal/psychological counseling.

Athletics Member NJCAA. *Intercollegiate sports:* basketball M/W, ice hockey M, soccer M/W, softball W, volleyball W. *Intramural sports:* archery M/W, badminton M/W, basketball M/W, bowling M/W, football M/W, soccer M/W, softball M/W, swimming and diving M/W, tennis M/W, volleyball M/W, weight lifting M/W.

Standardized Tests *Recommended:* SAT or ACT (for admission).

Costs (2006–07) *Tuition:* state resident $3250 full-time, $160 per credit hour part-time; nonresident $6500 full-time, $320 per credit hour part-time. *Required fees:* $730 full-time, $40 per credit hour part-time. *Room and board:* $8150.

North Country Community College (continued)

Financial Aid Of all full-time matriculated undergraduates, 104 Federal Work-Study jobs (averaging $1164). 27 state and other part-time jobs (averaging $1600).

Applying *Options:* electronic application, early admission, early decision, deferred entrance. *Required:* high school transcript. *Recommended:* essay or personal statement, interview. *Application deadlines:* rolling (freshmen), rolling (transfers). *Notification:* continuous (freshmen), continuous (transfers).

Freshmen Application Contact Enrollment Management Assistant, North Country Community College, 23 Santanoni Avenue, PO Box 89, Saranac Lake, NY 12983-0089. *Phone:* 518-891-2915 Ext. 686. *Toll-free phone:* 888-TRY-NCCC Ext. 233. *Fax:* 518-891-0898. *E-mail:* info@nccc.edu.

OLEAN BUSINESS INSTITUTE

Olean, New York　　　　　　　**www.obi.edu/**

Director of Admissions Ms. Lori Kincaid, Director of Admissions, Olean Business Institute, 301 North Union Street, Olean, NY 14760-2691. *Phone:* 716-372-7978.

ONONDAGA COMMUNITY COLLEGE

Syracuse, New York　　　　　　**www.sunyocc.edu/**

- **State and locally supported** 2-year, founded 1962, part of State University of New York System
- **Suburban** 194-acre campus
- **Coed,** 9,394 undergraduate students, 56% full-time, 53% women, 47% men

Undergraduates 5,214 full-time, 4,180 part-time. Students come from 9 states and territories, 12 other countries, 1% are from out of state, 8% African American, 2% Asian American or Pacific Islander, 2% Hispanic American, 1% Native American, 0.1% international, 0.5% transferred in, 4% live on campus.

Freshmen *Admission:* 3,581 applied, 2,726 admitted, 1,333 enrolled.

Faculty *Total:* 546, 29% full-time. *Student/faculty ratio:* 16:1.

Majors Accounting; administrative assistant and secretarial science; architectural engineering technology; art; automobile/automotive mechanics technology; biological and physical sciences; business administration and management; chemical engineering; commercial and advertising art; computer and information sciences related; computer engineering related; computer engineering technology; computer/information technology services administration related; computer programming (specific applications); computer science; computer systems networking and telecommunications; computer/technical support; computer typography and composition equipment operation; construction engineering technology; criminal justice/law enforcement administration; culinary arts; data entry/microcomputer applications; data entry/microcomputer applications related; data processing and data processing technology; dental hygiene; drafting and design technology; electrical, electronic and communications engineering technology; engineering science; finance; fire science; health information/medical records administration; hotel/motel administration; humanities; human services; information science/studies; information technology; insurance; interior design; kindergarten/preschool education; labor and industrial relations; landscape architecture; liberal arts and sciences/liberal studies; machine tool technology; mathematics; mechanical engineering/mechanical technology; music; nursing (registered nurse training); parks, recreation and leisure; photography; physical therapy; quality control technology; radio and television; respiratory care therapy; special products marketing; system administration; telecommunications; web/multimedia management and webmaster; web page, digital/multimedia and information resources design.

Academics *Calendar:* semesters. *Degree:* certificates, diplomas, and associate. *Special study options:* academic remediation for entering students, accelerated degree program, adult/continuing education programs, advanced placement credit, cooperative education, distance learning, English as a second language, external degree program, honors programs, internships, part-time degree program, services for LD students, study abroad, summer session for credit. *ROTC:* Air Force (c).

Library Sidney B. Coulter Library with 96,611 titles, 802 serial subscriptions, an OPAC, a Web page.

Student Life *Housing Options:* coed. Campus housing is provided by a third party. *Activities and Organizations:* student-run newspaper, radio station, choral group, Jamal, Music Club, Photo Club, Outing Club, Veterans Club. *Campus security:* 24-hour patrols, controlled dormitory access. *Student services:* health clinic, personal/psychological counseling.

Athletics Member NJCAA. *Intercollegiate sports:* baseball M(s), basketball M/W, lacrosse M, soccer M, softball W, tennis M/W, volleyball W. *Intramural sports:* basketball M/W, tennis M/W, volleyball W.

Costs (2007–08) *Tuition:* area resident $3280 full-time, $129 per hour part-time; state resident $6560 full-time, $258 per hour part-time; nonresident $6560 full-time, $258 per hour part-time. *Required fees:* $361 full-time, $71 per term part-time. *Room and board:* $8500; room only: $5500.

Financial Aid Of all full-time matriculated undergraduates, 120 Federal Work-Study jobs (averaging $1850).

Applying *Options:* electronic application, early admission, deferred entrance. *Required:* high school transcript. *Required for some:* minimum 2.0 GPA, interview. *Application deadlines:* 9/1 (freshmen), 9/1 (transfers). *Notification:* continuous (freshmen), continuous (transfers).

Freshmen Application Contact Ms. Shari Piotrowski, Director of Admissions, Onondaga Community College, 4941 Onondaga Road, Syracuse, NY 13215. *Phone:* 315-488-2201. *Fax:* 315-488-2107. *E-mail:* admissions@sunyocc.edu.

ORANGE COUNTY COMMUNITY COLLEGE

Middletown, New York　　　　**www.orange.cc.ny.us/**

- **State and locally supported** 2-year, founded 1950, part of State University of New York System
- **Suburban** 37-acre campus with easy access to New York City
- **Coed**

Undergraduates 3,344 full-time, 3,097 part-time. Students come from 22 states and territories, 20 other countries, 1% are from out of state, 10% African American, 2% Asian American or Pacific Islander, 13% Hispanic American, 0.4% Native American, 2% transferred in.

Faculty *Student/faculty ratio:* 16:1.

Academics *Calendar:* semesters. *Degree:* certificates and associate. *Special study options:* academic remediation for entering students, accelerated degree program, adult/continuing education programs, English as a second language, external degree program, honors programs, internships, part-time degree program, services for LD students, summer session for credit.

Student Life *Campus security:* 24-hour emergency response devices, late-night transport/escort service.

Athletics Member NJCAA.

Costs (2006–07) *Tuition:* state resident $3000 full-time, $125 per credit part-time; nonresident $6000 full-time, $250 per credit part-time. *Required fees:* $350 full-time.

Financial Aid Of all full-time matriculated undergraduates, 70 Federal Work-Study jobs (averaging $2000). 25 state and other part-time jobs (averaging $2000).

Applying *Options:* early admission, deferred entrance. *Application fee:* $30. *Required:* high school transcript.

Freshmen Application Contact Ms. Margot St. Lawrence, Director of Admissions, Orange County Community College, 115 South Street, Middletown, NY 10940. *Phone:* 845-341-4030. *Fax:* 845-343-1228. *E-mail:* admssns@sunyorange.edu.

PHILLIPS BETH ISRAEL SCHOOL OF NURSING

New York, New York　　　　　**www.futurenursebi.org**

- **Independent** 2-year, founded 1904
- **Urban** campus
- **Endowment** $1.2 million
- **Coed, primarily women**

Undergraduates Students come from 8 states and territories, 5 other countries, 10% are from out of state, 15% African American, 22% Asian American or Pacific Islander, 14% Hispanic American, 4% international.

Faculty *Student/faculty ratio:* 9:1.

Academics *Calendar:* semesters. *Degree:* associate. *Special study options:* advanced placement credit, off-campus study, part-time degree program.

Student Life *Campus security:* 24-hour emergency response devices.

Standardized Tests *Required:* nursing exam (for admission). *Recommended:* SAT (for admission).

Costs (2006–07) *Tuition:* $14,380 full-time, $300 per credit part-time. Full-time tuition and fees vary according to course level. *Required fees:* $2180 full-time.

Financial Aid *Financial aid deadline:* 6/1.

Applying *Options:* deferred entrance. *Application fee:* $50. *Required:* essay or personal statement, high school transcript, minimum 2.5 GPA, 2 letters of recommendation, interview.

Freshmen Application Contact Mrs. Bernice Pass-Stern, Assistant Dean, Phillips Beth Israel School of Nursing, 310 East 22nd Street, 9th Floor, New York, NY 10010-5702. *Phone:* 212-614-6176. *Fax:* 212-6124-6109. *E-mail:* bstern@bethisraelny.org.

PLAZA COLLEGE

Jackson Heights, New York   www.plazacollege.edu/

Freshmen Application Contact Mr. Michael Talarico, Director of Admissions, Plaza College, 7409 37th Avenue, Jackson Heights, NY 11372-6300. *Phone:* 718-779-1430. *Toll-free phone:* 877-752-9233.

QUEENSBOROUGH COMMUNITY COLLEGE OF THE CITY UNIVERSITY OF NEW YORK

Bayside, New York   www.qcc.cuny.edu/

- **State and locally supported** 2-year, founded 1958, part of City University of New York System
- **Urban** 34-acre campus with easy access to New York City
- **Endowment** $1.0 million
- **Coed,** 13,008 undergraduate students

Undergraduates Students come from 2 states and territories, 132 other countries, 1% are from out of state, 27% African American, 20% Asian American or Pacific Islander, 22% Hispanic American, 0.2% Native American, 6% international.

Freshmen *Admission:* 3,485 applied, 3,485 admitted. *Average high school GPA:* 1.7. *Test scores:* SAT math scores over 500: 5%.

Faculty *Total:* 736, 40% full-time. *Student/faculty ratio:* 21:1.

Majors Accounting; business administration and management; business, management, and marketing related; clinical/medical laboratory technology; communication and journalism related; computer engineering technology; electrical, electronic and communications engineering technology; engineering science; environmental design/architecture; environmental health; fine/studio arts; health science; information science/studies; information technology; laser and optical technology; liberal arts and sciences/liberal studies; mechanical engineering/mechanical technology; musical instrument fabrication and repair; nursing (registered nurse training); telecommunications; visual and performing arts.

Academics *Calendar:* semesters. *Degree:* certificates and associate. *Special study options:* academic remediation for entering students, adult/continuing education programs, advanced placement credit, cooperative education, English as a second language, honors programs, internships, part-time degree program, services for LD students, student-designed majors, summer session for credit. *ROTC:* Army (c).

Library The Kurt R. Schmeller with 140,000 titles, 600 serial subscriptions.

Student Life *Housing:* college housing not available. *Activities and Organizations:* drama/theater group, student-run newspaper, radio station, choral group, Student Orientation Leaders, Student Nurses Association, Newman Club, Accounting Club, Flip Culture Society. *Campus security:* 24-hour patrols, late-night transport/escort service. *Student services:* health clinic, personal/psychological counseling.

Athletics Member NJCAA. *Intercollegiate sports:* baseball M, basketball M/W, cross-country running M/W, soccer M, softball W, tennis M/W, track and field M/W, volleyball M/W. *Intramural sports:* archery M/W, badminton M/W, basketball M/W, fencing M/W, soccer M/W, softball M/W, swimming and diving M/W, table tennis M/W, tennis M/W, track and field M/W, volleyball M/W, weight lifting M/W.

Costs (2007–08) *Tuition:* area resident $2880 full-time; state resident $4560 full-time, $120 per credit part-time; nonresident $4560 full-time, $190 per credit part-time. *Required fees:* $270 full-time, $75 per term part-time.

Applying *Options:* electronic application, deferred entrance. *Application fee:* $40. *Required:* high school transcript. *Application deadlines:* rolling (freshmen), rolling (transfers). *Notification:* continuous (freshmen), continuous (transfers).

Freshmen Application Contact Ms. Ann Tullio, Director of Registration, Queensborough Community College of the City University of New York, 222-05 56th Avenue, Bayside, NY 11364. *Phone:* 718-631-6307. *Fax:* 718-281-5189.

ROCHESTER BUSINESS INSTITUTE

Rochester, New York   www.rochester-institute.com/

Freshmen Application Contact Ms. Deanna Pfluke, Director of Admissions, Rochester Business Institute, 1630 Portland Avenue, Rochester, NY 14621. *Phone:* 585-266-0430. *Fax:* 585-266-8243. *E-mail:* csilvio@cci.edu.

ROCKLAND COMMUNITY COLLEGE

Suffern, New York   www.sunyrockland.edu/

Freshmen Application Contact Ms. Lucy Hirsch, Admissions Office Secretary, Rockland Community College, 145 College Road, Suffern, NY 10901-3699. *Phone:* 845-574-4237. *Toll-free phone:* 800-722-7666.

ST. ELIZABETH COLLEGE OF NURSING

Utica, New York   www.secon.edu/

- **Independent** 2-year, founded 1904
- **Coed,** 208 undergraduate students
- 69% of applicants were admitted

Freshmen *Admission:* 36 applied, 25 admitted.

Majors Nursing (registered nurse training).

Academics *Calendar:* semesters. *Degree:* associate.

Standardized Tests *Recommended:* SAT or ACT (for admission).

Costs (2006–07) *Tuition:* state resident $10,671 full-time; nonresident $16,962 full-time.

Applying *Application fee:* $35. *Required:* letters of recommendation.

Director of Admissions Marianne Monahan, Dean, St. Elizabeth College of Nursing, 2215 Genesee Street, Utica, NY 13501. *Phone:* 315-798-8253. *E-mail:* mmonahan@stemc.org.

ST. JOSEPH'S COLLEGE OF NURSING

Syracuse, New York   www.sjhsyr.org/nursing/

- **Independent** 2-year, founded 1898
- **Urban** campus
- **Coed, primarily women**

Undergraduates Students come from 2 states and territories, 3% African American, 1% Asian American or Pacific Islander, 2% Hispanic American, 2% Native American, 25% live on campus.

Faculty *Student/faculty ratio:* 9:1.

Academics *Calendar:* semesters. *Degree:* associate. *Special study options:* academic remediation for entering students, adult/continuing education programs, advanced placement credit, cooperative education, internships, part-time degree program, services for LD students.

Student Life *Campus security:* 24-hour patrols.

Standardized Tests *Required:* SAT or ACT (for admission).

Costs (2006–07) *Tuition:* $8735 full-time. *Required fees:* $1900 full-time. *Room only:* $3400.

Applying *Options:* deferred entrance. *Application fee:* $30. *Required:* essay or personal statement, high school transcript, minimum 3.0 GPA, 4 letters of recommendation, interview.

Freshmen Application Contact Ms. JoAnne Kiggins, Admissions and Recruitment Coordinator, St. Joseph's College of Nursing, 206 Prospect Avenue, Syracuse, NY 13203. *Phone:* 315-448-5040. *Fax:* 315-448-5745.

SAINT VINCENT CATHOLIC MEDICAL CENTERS SCHOOL OF NURSING

Fresh Meadows, New York   www.svcmcny.org/

- **Independent** 2-year, founded 1969
- **Suburban** 2-acre campus
- **Coed,** 106 undergraduate students, 8% full-time, 80% women, 20% men

Saint Vincent Catholic Medical Centers School of Nursing (continued)

Undergraduates 8 full-time, 98 part-time. Students come from 2 states and territories, 18% African American, 20% Asian American or Pacific Islander, 8% Hispanic American, 750% transferred in.

Freshmen *Admission:* 37 applied, 6 admitted, 5 enrolled.

Faculty *Total:* 10, 80% full-time. *Student/faculty ratio:* 10:1.

Majors Nursing (registered nurse training).

Academics *Calendar:* semesters. *Degree:* associate. *Special study options:* part-time degree program.

Library 2,326 titles, 42 serial subscriptions.

Student Life *Housing:* college housing not available.

Standardized Tests *Required:* nursing exam (for admission).

Costs (2007–08) *Tuition:* Contact School of Nursing directly for tuition information.

Financial Aid Of all full-time matriculated undergraduates, 11 Federal Work-Study jobs (averaging $900).

Applying *Options:* deferred entrance. *Application fee:* $45. *Required:* essay or personal statement, high school transcript, minimum X GPA, entrance exam, college transcript. *Application deadlines:* 4/1 (freshmen), 4/1 (transfers). *Notification:* continuous (freshmen), continuous (transfers).

Director of Admissions Nancy Wolinski, Chairperson of Admissions, Saint Vincent Catholic Medical Centers School of Nursing, 175-05 Horace Harding Expressway, Fresh Meadows, NY 11365. *Phone:* 718-357-0500 Ext. 131. *E-mail:* nwolinski@svcmcny.org.

SAMARITAN HOSPITAL SCHOOL OF NURSING

Troy, New York www.nehealth.com/

- **Independent** 2-year
- 70 undergraduate students
- 38% of applicants were admitted

Freshmen *Admission:* 65 applied, 25 admitted.

Faculty *Total:* 9, 56% full-time, 56% with terminal degrees.

Majors Nursing (registered nurse training).

Academics *Degree:* diplomas and associate.

Standardized Tests *Recommended:* SAT or ACT (for admission).

Costs (2006–07) *Tuition:* $6650 full-time.

Director of Admissions Ms. Jennifer DeBlois, Student Services Coordinator, Samaritan Hospital School of Nursing, 2215 Burdett Avenue, Troy, NY 12180. *Phone:* 518-271-3734. *Fax:* 518-271-3303. *E-mail:* deBlois@nehealth.com.

SCHENECTADY COUNTY COMMUNITY COLLEGE

Schenectady, New York www.sunysccc.edu/

Freshmen Application Contact Mr. David Sampson, Director of Admissions, Schenectady County Community College, 78 Washington Avenue, Schenectady, NY 12305. *Phone:* 518-381-1370. *E-mail:* sampsodg@gw.sunysccc.edu.

SIMMONS INSTITUTE OF FUNERAL SERVICE

Syracuse, New York www.simmonsinstitute.com/

Freshmen Application Contact Ms. Vera Wightman, Director of Admissions, Simmons Institute of Funeral Service, 1828 South Avenue, Syracuse, NY 13207. *Phone:* 315-475-5142. *Toll-free phone:* 800-727-3536. *Fax:* 315-475-3817. *E-mail:* wightman6@aol.com.

STATE UNIVERSITY OF NEW YORK COLLEGE OF AGRICULTURE AND TECHNOLOGY AT MORRISVILLE

Morrisville, New York www.morrisville.edu/

- **State-supported** primarily 2-year, founded 1908, part of State University of New York System
- **Rural** 185-acre campus with easy access to Syracuse
- **Endowment** $1.1 million
- **Coed,** 3,288 undergraduate students, 84% full-time, 41% women, 59% men

Undergraduates 2,767 full-time, 521 part-time. Students come from 25 states and territories, 8 other countries, 1% are from out of state, 10% African American, 0.7% Asian American or Pacific Islander, 4% Hispanic American, 0.6% Native American, 3% international, 6% transferred in, 73% live on campus.

Freshmen *Admission:* 3,540 applied, 2,671 admitted, 1,109 enrolled. *Average high school GPA:* 2.9. *Test scores:* SAT verbal scores over 500: 47%; SAT math scores over 500: 59%; SAT verbal scores over 600: 9%; SAT math scores over 600: 9%.

Faculty *Total:* 260, 50% full-time, 17% with terminal degrees. *Student/faculty ratio:* 13:1.

Majors Accounting; administrative assistant and secretarial science; agricultural business and management; agricultural mechanization; agriculture; agronomy and crop science; animal sciences; architectural engineering technology; automobile/automotive mechanics technology; biology/biological sciences; biology/biotechnology laboratory technician; business administration and management; chemistry; clinical/medical laboratory technology; computer engineering technology; computer programming; computer science; computer typography and composition equipment operation; construction engineering technology; dairy science; data processing and data processing technology; dietetics; drafting and design technology; electrical, electronic and communications engineering technology; engineering; engineering science; engineering technology; environmental studies; equestrian studies; fish/game management; food services technology; foods, nutrition, and wellness; forestry; forestry technology; horticultural science; hospitality administration; hotel/motel administration; humanities; information science/studies; journalism; landscape architecture; landscaping and groundskeeping; legal administrative assistant/secretary; liberal arts and sciences/liberal studies; marketing/marketing management; mathematics; mechanical engineering/mechanical technology; medical administrative assistant and medical secretary; natural resources/conservation; natural resources management and policy; nursing (registered nurse training); parks, recreation and leisure facilities management; physics; plastics engineering technology; pre-engineering; social sciences; special products marketing; technical and business writing; tourism and travel services management; wildlife and wildlands science and management; wood science and wood products/pulp and paper technology.

Academics *Calendar:* semesters. *Degrees:* certificates, associate, and bachelor's. *Special study options:* academic remediation for entering students, advanced placement credit, cooperative education, distance learning, double majors, honors programs, internships, off-campus study, part-time degree program, services for LD students, student-designed majors, summer session for credit. *ROTC:* Army (c).

Library Morrisville State Library plus 1 other with 100,000 titles, 2,500 serial subscriptions, 1,700 audiovisual materials, an OPAC, a Web page.

Student Life *Housing:* on-campus residence required for freshman year. *Options:* coed, disabled students. Campus housing is university owned. Freshman campus housing is guaranteed. *Activities and Organizations:* drama/theater group, student-run newspaper, radio station, choral group, African Student Union Black Alliance, Student Government Organization, Agriculture Club, Latino-American Student Association, WCVM (student radio station). *Campus security:* 24-hour emergency response devices and patrols, late-night transport/escort service, controlled dormitory access. *Student services:* health clinic, personal/psychological counseling.

Athletics Member NJCAA. *Intercollegiate sports:* baseball M, basketball M/W, cross-country running M/W, equestrian sports M/W, field hockey W, football M, ice hockey M, lacrosse M/W, skiing (downhill) M/W, soccer M/W, softball W, swimming and diving M/W, tennis W, track and field M/W, volleyball W, wrestling M. *Intramural sports:* basketball M/W, riflery M/W, skiing (cross-country) M/W, skiing (downhill) M/W, soccer M/W, softball M/W, swimming and diving M/W, tennis M/W, volleyball M/W, weight lifting M/W.

Standardized Tests *Required for some:* SAT (for admission), SAT or ACT (for admission), TOEFL.

Costs (2006–07) *Tuition:* state resident $4350 full-time, $181 per credit part-time; nonresident $10,610 full-time, $300 per credit part-time. *Required fees:* $925 full-time, $38 per credit part-time. *Room and board:* $7310; room only: $3920.

Financial Aid Of all full-time matriculated undergraduates, 300 Federal Work-Study jobs (averaging $1500).

Applying *Options:* electronic application, early admission, deferred entrance. *Application fee:* $40. *Required:* high school transcript. *Required for some:* essay or personal statement, letters of recommendation. *Recommended:* minimum 2.0 GPA, 2 letters of recommendation, interview. *Application deadlines:* rolling (freshmen), rolling (out-of-state freshmen), rolling (transfers). *Notification:* continuous (freshmen), continuous (out-of-state freshmen), continuous (transfers).

Director of Admissions Mr. Timothy Williams, Dean of Enrollment Management, State University of New York College of Agriculture and Technology at Morrisville, Box 901, Morrisville, NY 13408. *Phone:* 315-684-6046. *Toll-free phone:* 800-258-0111.

STATE UNIVERSITY OF NEW YORK COLLEGE OF ENVIRONMENTAL SCIENCE & FORESTRY, RANGER SCHOOL

Wanakena, New York   **www.esf.edu/**

- **State-supported** 2-year, founded 1912, part of State University of New York System
- **Rural** 2800-acre campus
- **Endowment** $524,891
- **Coed, primarily men,** 43 undergraduate students, 100% full-time, 12% women, 88% men

Undergraduates 43 full-time. Students come from 4 states and territories, 6% are from out of state, 100% transferred in, 100% live on campus.

Freshmen *Admission:* 72 applied, 55 admitted.

Faculty *Total:* 6, 100% full-time, 17% with terminal degrees. *Student/faculty ratio:* 7:1.

Majors Forestry technology; survey technology.

Academics *Calendar:* semesters. *Degree:* associate. *Special study options:* advanced placement credit, distance learning.

Library Ranger School Library with 5,000 titles, 60 serial subscriptions, an OPAC.

Student Life *Housing Options:* coed. Campus housing is university owned. *Campus security:* 24-hour emergency response devices. *Student services:* health clinic, personal/psychological counseling, legal services.

Athletics *Intramural sports:* basketball M/W, ice hockey M/W, skiing (cross-country) M/W, skiing (downhill) M/W, softball M/W, volleyball M/W, weight lifting M/W.

Standardized Tests *Required:* SAT or ACT (for admission).

Costs (2006–07) *Tuition:* state resident $4350 full-time, $181 per credit hour part-time; nonresident $10,610 full-time, $442 per credit hour part-time. *Required fees:* $1024 full-time, $49 per credit hour part-time. *Room and board:* $9700; room only: $3750.

Financial Aid Of all full-time matriculated undergraduates, 300 Federal Work-Study jobs (averaging $1500). 150 state and other part-time jobs (averaging $1200).

Applying *Options:* electronic application, deferred entrance. *Application fee:* $40. *Required:* minimum 2.00 GPA. *Recommended:* essay or personal statement, high school transcript, minimum 2.50 GPA, interview. *Application deadlines:* rolling (freshmen), rolling (transfers).

Freshmen Application Contact Ms. Susan Sanford, Director of Admissions, State University of New York College of Environmental Science & Forestry, Ranger School, Bray 106, Syracuse, NY 13210-2779. *Phone:* 315-470-6600. *Toll-free phone:* 800-777-7373. *Fax:* 315-470-6933. *E-mail:* esfinfo@esf.edu.

► See page 588 for the College Close-Up.

STATE UNIVERSITY OF NEW YORK COLLEGE OF TECHNOLOGY AT ALFRED

Alfred, New York   **www.alfredstate.edu/**

- **State-supported** primarily 2-year, founded 1908, part of State University of New York System
- **Rural** 175-acre campus
- **Endowment** $2.6 million
- **Coed,** 3,231 undergraduate students, 94% full-time, 36% women, 64% men

Undergraduates 3,035 full-time, 196 part-time. 8% are from out of state, 6% African American, 3% Asian American or Pacific Islander, 2% Hispanic American, 0.6% Native American, 21% transferred in, 75% live on campus.

Freshmen *Admission:* 4,414 applied, 2,864 admitted, 1,303 enrolled. *Average high school GPA:* 2.8.

Faculty *Total:* 191, 77% full-time. *Student/faculty ratio:* 20:1.

Majors Accounting; agricultural business and management; agriculture; animal sciences; architectural engineering technology; autobody/collision and repair technology; automobile/automotive mechanics technology; biological and physical sciences; biology/biotechnology laboratory technician; business administration and management; carpentry; civil engineering technology; computer and information sciences; computer engineering technology; computer graphics; computer hardware engineering; computer/information technology services administration related; computer installation and repair technology; computer science; computer/technical support; computer typography and composition equipment operation; construction engineering; construction engineering technology; court reporting; culinary arts; drafting and design technology; electrical, electronic and communications engineering technology; electrical/electronics equipment installation and repair; electromechanical technology; engineering science; environmental studies; finance; health information/medical records administration; heating, air conditioning and refrigeration technology; heating, air conditioning, ventilation and refrigeration maintenance technology; heavy equipment maintenance technology; humanities; human services; industrial electronics technology; landscaping and groundskeeping; liberal arts and sciences/liberal studies; machine tool technology; marketing/marketing management; masonry; mathematics; mechanical design technology; mechanical engineering/mechanical technology; nursing (registered nurse training); pipefitting and sprinkler fitting; restaurant, culinary, and catering management; sales, distribution and marketing; social sciences; sport and fitness administration/management; survey technology; system administration; veterinary sciences; welding technology.

Academics *Calendar:* semesters. *Degrees:* certificates, associate, and bachelor's. *Special study options:* academic remediation for entering students, adult/continuing education programs, advanced placement credit, cooperative education, distance learning, honors programs, independent study, internships, off-campus study, part-time degree program, services for LD students, student-designed majors, study abroad, summer session for credit. *ROTC:* Army (c).

Library Walter C. Hinkle Memorial Library plus 1 other with 71,243 titles, 594 serial subscriptions, an OPAC, a Web page.

Student Life *Housing Options:* coed, disabled students. Campus housing is university owned. Freshman campus housing is guaranteed. *Activities and Organizations:* drama/theater group, student-run newspaper, radio station, choral group, Outdoor Activity Club, BACCHUS, Sondai Society, Drama Club, choir. *Campus security:* 24-hour emergency response devices and patrols, late-night transport/escort service, residence hall entrance guards. *Student services:* health clinic, personal/psychological counseling.

Athletics Member NJCAA. *Intercollegiate sports:* baseball M, basketball M(s)/W(s), cheerleading M/W, cross-country running M(s)/W(s), football M(s), lacrosse M(s), soccer M(s)/W(s), softball W(s), swimming and diving M/W, track and field M(s)/W(s), volleyball W, wrestling M. *Intramural sports:* basketball M/W, bowling M/W, cross-country running M/W, football M, golf M/W, lacrosse M/W, racquetball M/W, rock climbing M/W, rugby M/W, skiing (cross-country) M/W, soccer M/W, softball M/W, table tennis M/W, tennis M/W, ultimate Frisbee M/W, volleyball M/W, water polo M/W.

Standardized Tests *Required for some:* SAT or ACT (for admission). *Recommended:* SAT or ACT (for admission).

Costs (2006–07) *Tuition:* state resident $4350 full-time; nonresident $7210 full-time. Full-time tuition and fees vary according to degree level. *Required fees:* $1056 full-time. *Room and board:* $8040; room only: $4570. Room and board charges vary according to board plan and housing facility. *Payment plan:* installment.

Financial Aid Of all full-time matriculated undergraduates, 350 Federal Work-Study jobs (averaging $1100).

Applying *Options:* electronic application, deferred entrance. *Application fee:* $40. *Required:* high school transcript. *Required for some:* minimum 2.0 GPA. *Recommended:* essay or personal statement, letters of recommendation, interview. *Application deadlines:* rolling (freshmen), rolling (transfers). *Notification:* continuous (freshmen), continuous (transfers).

Freshmen Application Contact Ms. Deborah Goodrich, Director of Admissions, State University of New York College of Technology at Alfred, Huntington Administration Building, 10 Upper College Drive, Alfred, NY 14802. *Phone:* 607-587-4215. *Toll-free phone:* 800-4-ALFRED. *Fax:* 607-587-4299. *E-mail:* admissions@alfredstate.edu.

STATE UNIVERSITY OF NEW YORK COLLEGE OF TECHNOLOGY AT CANTON

Canton, New York   www.canton.edu/

- **State-supported** primarily 2-year, founded 1906, part of State University of New York System
- **Small-town** 555-acre campus
- **Endowment** $310,031
- **Coed,** 2,584 undergraduate students, 84% full-time, 53% women, 47% men

Undergraduates 2,160 full-time, 424 part-time. Students come from 15 states and territories, 5 other countries, 2% are from out of state, 9% African American, 1% Asian American or Pacific Islander, 3% Hispanic American, 2% Native American, 0.4% international, 12% transferred in, 48% live on campus. *Retention:* 82% of 2003 full-time freshmen returned.

Freshmen *Admission:* 2,223 applied, 1,863 admitted, 778 enrolled. *Test scores:* SAT verbal scores over 500: 21%; SAT math scores over 500: 33%; ACT scores over 18: 65%; SAT verbal scores over 600: 3%; SAT math scores over 600: 6%; ACT scores over 24: 6%; ACT scores over 30: 1%.

Faculty *Total:* 168, 60% full-time, 20% with terminal degrees. *Student/faculty ratio:* 23:1.

Majors Accounting; automobile/automotive mechanics technology; banking and financial support services; biological and physical sciences; business administration and management; business/managerial economics; carpentry; civil engineering technology; clinical/medical laboratory technology; computer/information technology services administration related; construction engineering technology; corrections; criminal justice/law enforcement administration; criminal justice/police science; electrical, electronic and communications engineering technology; engineering science; engineering technology; environmental studies; forestry technology; funeral service and mortuary science; health/health care administration; heating, air conditioning, ventilation and refrigeration maintenance technology; humanities; industrial technology; information science/studies; interdisciplinary studies; kindergarten/preschool education; liberal arts and sciences/liberal studies; mechanical engineering/mechanical technology; nursing (registered nurse training); occupational therapist assistant; office management; physical therapist assistant; pipefitting and sprinkler fitting; social sciences; veterinary technology.

Academics *Calendar:* semesters. *Degrees:* certificates, associate, and bachelor's. *Special study options:* academic remediation for entering students, adult/continuing education programs, advanced placement credit, distance learning, independent study, internships, off-campus study, services for LD students, student-designed majors, summer session for credit. *ROTC:* Army (c), Air Force (c).

Library Southworth Library with 64,912 titles, 303 serial subscriptions, an OPAC, a Web page.

Student Life *Housing:* on-campus residence required through sophomore year. *Options:* coed, men-only, women-only. Campus housing is university owned. *Activities and Organizations:* drama/theater group, student-run newspaper, radio station, choral group, Karate Club, Automotive Club, Outing Club, WATC Radio, Afro-Latin Society, national fraternities, national sororities. *Campus security:* 24-hour emergency response devices and patrols, late-night transport/escort service, controlled dormitory access. *Student services:* health clinic, personal/psychological counseling.

Athletics Member NJCAA. *Intercollegiate sports:* baseball M, basketball M/W, ice hockey M, lacrosse M/W, soccer M/W, softball W, volleyball W. *Intramural sports:* badminton M/W, basketball M/W, cheerleading W, skiing (cross-country) M/W, soccer M/W, softball M/W, tennis M/W, volleyball M/W.

Standardized Tests *Required:* SAT or ACT (for admission). *Recommended:* SAT or ACT (for admission).

Costs (2007–08) *Tuition:* state resident $4350 full-time, $181 per credit hour part-time; nonresident $7210 full-time, $442 per credit hour part-time. *Required fees:* $1145 full-time, $5 per term part-time. *Room and board:* $8300; room only: $4750.

Financial Aid Of all full-time matriculated undergraduates, 200 Federal Work-Study jobs (averaging $1250). 10 state and other part-time jobs (averaging $1000).

Applying *Options:* electronic application, early admission, deferred entrance. *Application fee:* $40. *Required:* high school transcript. *Required for some:* interview. *Recommended:* minimum 2.0 GPA. *Application deadlines:* rolling (freshmen), rolling (transfers). *Notification:* continuous (freshmen), continuous (transfers).

Freshmen Application Contact Mr. Jonathan Kent, Director of Admissions, State University of New York College of Technology at Canton, 34 Cornell Drive, Canton, NY 13617. *Phone:* 315-386-7123. *Toll-free phone:* 800-388-7123. *Fax:* 315-386-7929. *E-mail:* admissions@canton.edu.

STATE UNIVERSITY OF NEW YORK COLLEGE OF TECHNOLOGY AT DELHI

Delhi, New York   www.delhi.edu/

- **State-supported** primarily 2-year, founded 1913, part of State University of New York System
- **Rural** 405-acre campus
- **Endowment** $1.2 million
- **Coed**

Undergraduates 2,206 full-time, 351 part-time. Students come from 7 states and territories, 3 other countries, 2% are from out of state, 12% African American, 2% Asian American or Pacific Islander, 6% Hispanic American, 0.2% Native American, 2% international, 61% live on campus.

Faculty *Student/faculty ratio:* 17:1.

Academics *Calendar:* semesters. *Degrees:* certificates, associate, and bachelor's. *Special study options:* academic remediation for entering students, adult/continuing education programs, advanced placement credit, distance learning, English as a second language, honors programs, internships, part-time degree program, services for LD students, student-designed majors, summer session for credit.

Student Life *Campus security:* 24-hour emergency response devices and patrols.

Athletics Member NAIA, NJCAA.

Costs (2006–07) *Tuition:* state resident $4350 full-time, $181 per credit hour part-time; nonresident $7210 full-time, $300 per credit hour part-time. *Required fees:* $1248 full-time, $42 per credit hour part-time, $5 per term part-time. *Room and board:* $7880.

Financial Aid Of all full-time matriculated undergraduates, 150 Federal Work-Study jobs (averaging $1050).

Applying *Options:* electronic application, early admission, deferred entrance. *Application fee:* $30. *Required:* high school transcript. *Required for some:* minimum 2.0 GPA.

Director of Admissions Mr. Larry Barrett, Dean of Enrollment, State University of New York College of Technology at Delhi, 2 Main Street, Delhi, NY 13753. *Phone:* 607-746-4000 Ext. 4856. *Toll-free phone:* 800-96-DELHI.

SUFFOLK COUNTY COMMUNITY COLLEGE

Selden, New York   www.sunysuffolk.edu/

- **State and locally supported** 2-year, founded 1959, part of State University of New York System
- **Small-town** 500-acre campus with easy access to New York City
- **Coed,** 20,280 undergraduate students, 54% full-time, 59% women, 41% men

Undergraduates 10,860 full-time, 9,420 part-time. Students come from 14 states and territories, 1% are from out of state, 7% African American, 2% Asian American or Pacific Islander, 10% Hispanic American, 0.4% Native American, 0.6% international, 3% transferred in.

Freshmen *Admission:* 6,095 applied, 5,507 admitted, 4,249 enrolled. *Average high school GPA:* 2.5. *Test scores:* SAT verbal scores over 500: 36%; SAT math scores over 500: 38%; ACT scores over 18: 30%; SAT verbal scores over 600: 8%; SAT math scores over 600: 8%; ACT scores over 24: 4%; SAT verbal scores over 700: 1%.

Faculty *Total:* 1,162, 27% full-time. *Student/faculty ratio:* 18:1.

Majors Accounting; art; automobile/automotive mechanics technology; biological and physical sciences; biology/biological sciences; business administration and management; chemistry; child development; civil engineering technology; clinical laboratory science/medical technology; commercial and advertising art; communications systems installation and repair technology; community organization and advocacy; computer engineering technology; computer programming; computer science; computer/technical support; construction engineering technology; consumer merchandising/retailing management; criminal justice/law enforcement administration; criminal justice/police science; culinary arts; data processing and data processing technology; dietetics; drafting and design technology; dramatic/theater arts; electrical, electronic and communications engineering technology; engineering; engineering science; English; horticultural science; humanities; human services; industrial technology; information science/studies; information technology; insurance; interior design; journalism; kindergarten/preschool education; legal assistant/paralegal; liberal arts and sciences/liberal studies; marketing/marketing management; mathematics; mechanical engineering/mechanical technology; medical/clinical assistant; music; nursing (registered nurse training); opticianry; parks, recreation and leisure; photographic and film/video technology; physical therapy; real estate; sign language interpretation

and translation; social sciences; substance abuse/addiction counseling; telecommunications; therapeutic recreation; veterinary sciences; women's studies.

Academics *Calendar:* semesters. *Degree:* certificates, diplomas, and associate. *Special study options:* academic remediation for entering students, adult/continuing education programs, advanced placement credit, cooperative education, distance learning, English as a second language, honors programs, independent study, internships, off-campus study, part-time degree program, services for LD students, summer session for credit. *ROTC:* Army (c).

Library 659 serial subscriptions, an OPAC, a Web page.

Student Life *Housing:* college housing not available. *Activities and Organizations:* drama/theater group, student-run newspaper, choral group. *Campus security:* 24-hour emergency response devices and patrols. *Student services:* health clinic, personal/psychological counseling, women's center.

Athletics Member NJCAA. *Intercollegiate sports:* baseball M, basketball M/W, cross-country running M/W, golf M/W, gymnastics M/W, lacrosse M, sailing M/W, soccer M, softball W, tennis M/W, volleyball W.

Standardized Tests *Required for some:* SAT or ACT (for placement). *Recommended:* SAT or ACT (for placement).

Costs (2006–07) *Tuition:* state resident $3454 full-time; nonresident $6554 full-time.

Financial Aid Of all full-time matriculated undergraduates, 109 Federal Work-Study jobs (averaging $1377).

Applying *Options:* deferred entrance. *Application fee:* $30. *Required:* high school transcript. *Application deadlines:* rolling (freshmen), rolling (transfers). *Notification:* continuous (freshmen), continuous (transfers).

Director of Admissions Executive Director of Admissions and Enrollment Management, Suffolk County Community College, 533 College Road, Selden, NY 11784-2899. *Phone:* 631-451-4000.

SULLIVAN COUNTY COMMUNITY COLLEGE

Loch Sheldrake, New York   www.sullivan.suny.edu/

- **State and locally supported** 2-year, founded 1962, part of State University of New York System
- **Rural** 405-acre campus
- **Endowment** $657,688
- **Coed**

Undergraduates 1,067 full-time, 617 part-time. Students come from 6 states and territories, 9 other countries, 1% are from out of state, 18% African American, 1% Asian American or Pacific Islander, 10% Hispanic American, 0.4% Native American, 0.6% international, 6% transferred in.

Faculty *Student/faculty ratio:* 18:1.

Academics *Calendar:* 4-1-4. *Degree:* certificates and associate. *Special study options:* academic remediation for entering students, adult/continuing education programs, advanced placement credit, distance learning, double majors, honors programs, internships, part-time degree program, services for LD students, summer session for credit.

Student Life *Campus security:* 24-hour emergency response devices and patrols.

Athletics Member NJCAA.

Costs (2006–07) *Tuition:* state resident $3200 full-time, $125 per credit part-time; nonresident $6400 full-time, $160 per credit part-time. *Required fees:* $306 full-time, $12 per credit part-time. *Room and board:* $6500; room only: $4080.

Financial Aid Of all full-time matriculated undergraduates, 105 Federal Work-Study jobs (averaging $800). 57 state and other part-time jobs (averaging $841).

Applying *Options:* electronic application, early admission, deferred entrance. *Required:* high school transcript.

Freshmen Application Contact Ms. Sari Rosenheck, Director of Admissions and Registration Services, Sullivan County Community College, 112 College Road, Loch Sheldrake, NY 12759. *Phone:* 845-434-5750 Ext. 4200. *Toll-free phone:* 800-577-5243. *Fax:* 845-434-4806. *E-mail:* sarir@sullivan.suny.edu.

TAYLOR BUSINESS INSTITUTE

New York, New York   www.tbiglobal.com/

Freshmen Application Contact Mr. Christopher Carbowell, Director of Admissions, Taylor Business Institute, 23 west 17th Street, 7th floor, New York, NY 10011. *Phone:* 212-229-1963. *Fax:* 212-229-2187.

TCI-THE COLLEGE OF TECHNOLOGY

New York, New York   www.tciedu.com/

Director of Admissions Ms. Sandra Germer, Director of Admission, TCI-The College of Technology, 320 West 31st Street, New York, NY 10001-2705. *Phone:* 212-594-4000 Ext. 437. *E-mail:* admissions@tciedu.com.

TOMPKINS CORTLAND COMMUNITY COLLEGE

Dryden, New York   www.sunytccc.edu/

- **State and locally supported** 2-year, founded 1968, part of State University of New York System
- **Rural** 250-acre campus with easy access to Syracuse
- **Endowment** $2.2 million
- **Coed,** 3,009 undergraduate students, 70% full-time, 58% women, 42% men

Undergraduates 2,105 full-time, 904 part-time. Students come from 21 states and territories, 22 other countries, 1% are from out of state, 7% African American, 2% Asian American or Pacific Islander, 3% Hispanic American, 0.5% Native American, 3% international, 9% transferred in, 18% live on campus.

Freshmen *Admission:* 748 enrolled. *Average high school GPA:* 2.48.

Faculty *Total:* 275, 24% full-time, 19% with terminal degrees. *Student/faculty ratio:* 18:1.

Majors Accounting; administrative assistant and secretarial science; aeronautics/aviation/aerospace science and technology; biological and physical sciences; business administration and management; child care provision; child development; commercial and advertising art; computer and information sciences related; computer and information systems security; computer graphics; computer hardware engineering; computer/information technology services administration related; computer programming related; computer science; computer software engineering; computer/technical support; construction engineering technology; criminal justice/law enforcement administration; data entry/microcomputer applications; electrical, electronic and communications engineering technology; engineering science; environmental studies; hotel/motel administration; humanities; human services; information science/studies; international business/trade/commerce; kindergarten/preschool education; legal assistant/paralegal; liberal arts and sciences/liberal studies; marketing/marketing management; mass communication/media; mathematics; nursing (registered nurse training); parks, recreation and leisure; radio and television; social sciences; sport and fitness administration/management; substance abuse/addiction counseling; system administration; tourism and travel services management; tourism and travel services marketing; web page, digital/multimedia and information resources design; women's studies.

Academics *Calendar:* semesters. *Degree:* certificates and associate. *Special study options:* academic remediation for entering students, adult/continuing education programs, advanced placement credit, cooperative education, double majors, English as a second language, honors programs, independent study, internships, off-campus study, part-time degree program, services for LD students, study abroad.

Library Gerald A. Barry Memorial Library plus 1 other with 53,897 titles, 537 serial subscriptions, 9,115 audiovisual materials, an OPAC, a Web page.

Student Life *Housing Options:* coed. Campus housing is provided by a third party. *Activities and Organizations:* drama/theater group, student-run newspaper, Art Works, Accounting Club, Nurse's Association. *Campus security:* 24-hour patrols, late-night transport/escort service, controlled dormitory access. *Student services:* personal/psychological counseling.

Athletics Member NJCAA. *Intercollegiate sports:* basketball M/W, cheerleading M/W, golf M/W, soccer M/W, softball W, volleyball W. *Intramural sports:* badminton M/W, basketball M/W, bowling M/W, football M/W, golf M/W, lacrosse M/W, racquetball M/W, skiing (cross-country) M/W, soccer M/W, softball M/W, swimming and diving M/W, table tennis M/W, tennis M/W, volleyball M/W, water polo M/W.

Costs (2007–08) *Tuition:* state resident $3325 full-time, $128 per credit part-time; nonresident $6950 full-time, $276 per credit part-time. *Required fees:* $588 full-time, $24 per credit part-time. *Room and board:* room only: $5200.

Financial Aid Of all full-time matriculated undergraduates, 150 Federal Work-Study jobs (averaging $1000). 150 state and other part-time jobs (averaging $1000).

Applying *Options:* early admission, deferred entrance. *Application fee:* $15. *Required:* high school transcript. *Required for some:* essay or personal statement, interview. *Application deadlines:* rolling (freshmen), rolling (transfers). *Notification:* continuous (freshmen), continuous (transfers).

Freshmen Application Contact Mr. Sandy Drumluk, Director of Admissions, Tompkins Cortland Community College, 170 North Street, PO Box 139, Dryden,

Tompkins Cortland Community College (continued)
NY 13053-0139. *Phone:* 607-844-8211. *Toll-free phone:* 888-567-8211. *Fax:* 607-844-6538. *E-mail:* admissions@tc3.edu.

TROCAIRE COLLEGE

Buffalo, New York　　　　　　　　　www.trocaire.edu/

- **Independent** 2-year, founded 1958
- **Urban** 1-acre campus
- **Endowment** $4.2 million
- **Coed, primarily women,** 780 undergraduate students

Undergraduates Students come from 3 states and territories, 4 other countries, 1% are from out of state, 23% African American, 0.8% Asian American or Pacific Islander, 2% Hispanic American, 0.4% Native American, 0.8% international.

Freshmen *Admission:* 526 applied, 490 admitted. *Test scores:* SAT verbal scores over 500: 37%; SAT math scores over 500: 31%; ACT scores over 18: 67%.

Faculty *Total:* 113, 34% full-time. *Student/faculty ratio:* 15:1.

Majors Administrative assistant and secretarial science; business administration and management; environmental studies; health information/medical records administration; hotel/motel administration; industrial radiologic technology; kindergarten/preschool education; legal administrative assistant/secretary; liberal arts and sciences/liberal studies; marketing/marketing management; medical administrative assistant and medical secretary; medical/clinical assistant; nursing (registered nurse training); radiologic technology/science; surgical technology.

Academics *Calendar:* semesters. *Degree:* certificates and associate. *Special study options:* academic remediation for entering students, adult/continuing education programs, advanced placement credit, external degree program, independent study, internships, off-campus study, part-time degree program, services for LD students, summer session for credit.

Library The Rachel R. Savarino Library with 15,403 titles, 93 serial subscriptions, an OPAC, a Web page.

Student Life *Activities and Organizations:* student-run newspaper, Student Government Association, student newspaper, Environmental Club, Ski Club, national fraternities. *Campus security:* 24-hour emergency response devices and patrols, late-night transport/escort service. *Student services:* health clinic, personal/psychological counseling.

Standardized Tests *Required for some:* SAT or ACT (for admission).

Costs (2006–07) *Tuition:* $10,146 full-time, $410 per credit hour part-time. *Required fees:* $160 full-time. *Payment plan:* installment. *Waivers:* children of alumni, senior citizens, and employees or children of employees.

Financial Aid Of all full-time matriculated undergraduates, 33 Federal Work-Study jobs (averaging $1500).

Applying *Options:* deferred entrance. *Application fee:* $25. *Required:* high school transcript. *Recommended:* interview. *Application deadlines:* rolling (freshmen), rolling (transfers).

Freshmen Application Contact Mrs. Theresa Horner, Director of Records, Trocaire College, 360 Choate Avenue, Buffalo, NY 14220. *Phone:* 716-827-2459. *Fax:* 716-828-6107. *E-mail:* info@trocaire.edu.

ULSTER COUNTY COMMUNITY COLLEGE

Stone Ridge, New York　　　　　www.sunyulster.edu/

- **State and locally supported** 2-year, founded 1961, part of State University of New York System
- **Rural** 165-acre campus
- **Endowment** $2.4 million
- **Coed,** 3,105 undergraduate students

Undergraduates Students come from 3 states and territories, 1 other country, 4% African American, 1% Asian American or Pacific Islander, 5% Hispanic American, 0.6% Native American, 1% international.

Faculty *Total:* 195, 33% full-time. *Student/faculty ratio:* 15:1.

Majors Accounting; administrative assistant and secretarial science; biological and physical sciences; business administration and management; commercial and advertising art; community organization and advocacy; computer science; consumer merchandising/retailing management; criminal justice/law enforcement administration; data processing and data processing technology; drafting and design technology; elementary education; engineering; engineering technology; environmental engineering technology; humanities; human services; industrial technology; information science/studies; journalism; liberal arts and sciences/liberal studies; marketing/marketing management; mass communication/media; mathematics; nursing (registered nurse training); parks, recreation and leisure; physical sciences; social sciences.

Academics *Calendar:* semesters. *Degree:* certificates, diplomas, and associate. *Special study options:* academic remediation for entering students, adult/continuing education programs, advanced placement credit, cooperative education, distance learning, double majors, English as a second language, honors programs, independent study, internships, off-campus study, part-time degree program, services for LD students, student-designed majors, summer session for credit.

Library McDonald Dewitt Library with 70,758 titles, 481 serial subscriptions, 3,880 audiovisual materials, an OPAC, a Web page.

Student Life *Housing:* college housing not available. *Activities and Organizations:* drama/theater group, student-run newspaper, radio station, choral group, Ski Club, Basic Club, Biology Club, Nursing Club. *Campus security:* 24-hour emergency response devices and patrols. *Student services:* health clinic, personal/psychological counseling.

Athletics Member NJCAA. *Intercollegiate sports:* baseball M, basketball M/W, golf M/W, soccer M, softball W, tennis M/W, volleyball W. *Intramural sports:* baseball M, basketball M, volleyball M/W.

Standardized Tests *Required for some:* ACT ASSET, ACT COMPASS.

Costs (2006–07) *Tuition:* state resident $3200 full-time; nonresident $6400 full-time.

Financial Aid Of all full-time matriculated undergraduates, 125 Federal Work-Study jobs (averaging $1000).

Applying *Options:* early admission, deferred entrance. *Application deadlines:* rolling (freshmen), rolling (transfers). *Notification:* continuous (freshmen), continuous (transfers).

Freshmen Application Contact Admissions Office, Ulster County Community College, Cottekill Road, Stone Ridge, NY. *Phone:* 914-687-5022. *Toll-free phone:* 800-724-0833.

UTICA SCHOOL OF COMMERCE

Utica, New York　　　　　　　　　www.uscny.edu/

Director of Admissions Chris Tacea, Dean of Enrollment Management, Utica School of Commerce, 201 Bleecker Street, Utica, NY 13501. *Phone:* 315-733-2300. *Toll-free phone:* 800-321-4USC.

VILLA MARIA COLLEGE OF BUFFALO

Buffalo, New York　　　　　　　　　www.villa.edu/

- **Independent** primarily 2-year, founded 1960, affiliated with Roman Catholic Church
- **Suburban** 9-acre campus
- **Endowment** $523,318
- **Coed,** 514 undergraduate students, 80% full-time, 69% women, 31% men

Undergraduates 411 full-time, 103 part-time. Students come from 2 states and territories, 2 other countries, 0.6% are from out of state, 27% African American, 0.8% Asian American or Pacific Islander, 3% Hispanic American, 0.8% Native American, 11% transferred in.

Freshmen *Admission:* 491 applied, 376 admitted, 151 enrolled. *Average high school GPA:* 2.5. *Test scores:* SAT verbal scores over 500: 22%; SAT math scores over 500: 22%; ACT scores over 18: 67%; SAT verbal scores over 600: 4%; SAT math scores over 600: 5%; ACT scores over 24: 33%.

Faculty *Total:* 74, 35% full-time, 39% with terminal degrees. *Student/faculty ratio:* 10:1.

Majors Business administration and management; education; fine/studio arts; graphic design; health science; interior design; jazz; kindergarten/preschool education; liberal arts and sciences/liberal studies; music; music management and merchandising; physical therapist assistant.

Academics *Calendar:* semesters. *Degrees:* associate and bachelor's. *Special study options:* academic remediation for entering students, advanced placement credit, cooperative education, double majors, independent study, internships, off-campus study, part-time degree program, services for LD students, study abroad, summer session for credit.

Library Villa Maria College Library with 37,000 titles, 130 serial subscriptions, an OPAC, a Web page.

Student Life *Housing:* college housing not available. *Activities and Organizations:* student-run newspaper, choral group, Design and Beyond, Teachers Love Children, Multicultural Club, Phi Theta Kappa, Helping Adults New Dreams Succeed. *Campus security:* late-night transport/escort service. *Student services:* health clinic, personal/psychological counseling.

Costs (2007–08) *Tuition:* $11,840 full-time, $400 per credit hour part-time. *Required fees:* $435 full-time, $85 per term part-time.

Financial Aid Of all full-time matriculated undergraduates, 159 Federal Work-Study jobs (averaging $320).

Applying *Options:* electronic application, deferred entrance. *Required:* essay or personal statement, high school transcript, interview, writing sample. *Application deadlines:* rolling (freshmen), rolling (transfers). *Notification:* continuous (freshmen), continuous (transfers).

Freshmen Application Contact Mr. Kevin Donovan, Director of Admissions, Villa Maria College of Buffalo, 240 Pine Ridge Road, Buffalo, NY 14225-3999. *Phone:* 716-896-0700 Ext. 1802. *Fax:* 716-896-0705. *E-mail:* admmissions@villa.edu.

WESTCHESTER COMMUNITY COLLEGE
Valhalla, New York www.sunywcc.edu/

- **State and locally supported** 2-year, founded 1946, part of State University of New York System
- **Suburban** 218-acre campus with easy access to New York City
- **Coed,** 11,579 undergraduate students, 48% full-time, 56% women, 44% men

Undergraduates 5,578 full-time, 6,001 part-time. Students come from 13 states and territories, 58 other countries, 0.5% are from out of state, 19% African American, 5% Asian American or Pacific Islander, 19% Hispanic American, 0.8% Native American, 2% international, 8% transferred in.

Freshmen *Admission:* 7,243 applied, 7,243 admitted, 2,218 enrolled.

Faculty *Total:* 497, 32% full-time. *Student/faculty ratio:* 17:1.

Majors Accounting; administrative assistant and secretarial science; applied art; automobile/automotive mechanics technology; biological and physical sciences; business administration and management; chemical engineering; child care provision; child development; civil engineering technology; clinical laboratory science/medical technology; clinical/medical laboratory technology; computer and information sciences; computer and information sciences related; computer science; computer systems networking and telecommunications; consumer merchandising/retailing management; corrections; criminal justice/law enforcement administration; criminal justice/police science; culinary arts; dance; data processing and data processing technology; dietetics; electrical, electronic and communications engineering technology; emergency medical technology (EMT paramedic); engineering science; engineering technology; environmental engineering technology; finance; fine/studio arts; food services technology; hotel/motel administration; humanities; human services; industrial radiologic technology; information science/studies; international business/trade/commerce; legal administrative assistant/secretary; legal assistant/paralegal; liberal arts and sciences/liberal studies; marketing/marketing management; mass communication/media; mechanical engineering/mechanical technology; nursing (registered nurse training); public administration; respiratory care therapy; social sciences; special products marketing; substance abuse/addiction counseling; tourism and travel services management; tourism promotion.

Academics *Calendar:* semesters. *Degree:* certificates and associate. *Special study options:* academic remediation for entering students, adult/continuing education programs, cooperative education, distance learning, double majors, English as a second language, honors programs, independent study, internships, off-campus study, part-time degree program, services for LD students, student-designed majors, study abroad, summer session for credit.

Library Harold L. Drimmer Library with 132,181 titles, 318 serial subscriptions, 9,434 audiovisual materials, an OPAC, a Web page.

Student Life *Housing:* college housing not available. *Activities and Organizations:* drama/theater group, student-run newspaper, radio station, choral group, Student Senate, African Culture Club, Italian Club, International Friendship Club, Alpha Beta Gamma. *Campus security:* 24-hour emergency response devices and patrols, late-night transport/escort service. *Student services:* health clinic, personal/psychological counseling, women's center.

Athletics Member NJCAA. *Intercollegiate sports:* baseball M, basketball M/W, bowling M/W, golf M, soccer M, softball W, volleyball W. *Intramural sports:* badminton M/W, basketball M/W, softball M/W, swimming and diving M/W, tennis M/W, volleyball M/W, weight lifting M/W.

Costs (2007–08) *Tuition:* state resident $3450 full-time, $144 per credit part-time; nonresident $8626 full-time, $360 per credit part-time. *Required fees:* $363 full-time, $83 per term part-time.

Financial Aid Of all full-time matriculated undergraduates, 200 Federal Work-Study jobs (averaging $1000).

Applying *Options:* electronic application, early admission. *Application fee:* $25. *Required:* high school transcript. *Recommended:* interview. *Application deadlines:* rolling (freshmen), rolling (transfers). *Notification:* continuous until 2/2 (freshmen), continuous (transfers).

Freshmen Application Contact Ms. Terre Wisell, Director of Admissions, Westchester Community College, 75 Grasslands Road, Administration Building, Valhalla, NY 10595-1698. *Phone:* 914-606-6735. *Fax:* 914-606-6540. *E-mail:* admissions@sunywcc.edu.

WOOD TOBE–COBURN SCHOOL
New York, New York www.woodtobecoburn.com/

- **Proprietary** 2-year, founded 1879, part of Bradford Schools, Inc
- **Urban** campus
- **Coed, primarily women**

Undergraduates 269 full-time. Students come from 3 states and territories, 5% are from out of state, 27% African American, 2% Asian American or Pacific Islander, 52% Hispanic American, 0.4% Native American, 2% international.

Faculty *Student/faculty ratio:* 27:1.

Academics *Calendar:* semesters. *Degree:* diplomas and associate. *Special study options:* academic remediation for entering students, cooperative education, internships, summer session for credit.

Student Life *Campus security:* 24-hour emergency response devices and patrols.

Costs (2006–07) *Tuition:* $14,400 full-time.

Applying *Application fee:* $50. *Required:* high school transcript, interview.

Director of Admissions Ms. Sandra L. Andujar, Director of Admissions, Wood Tobe–Coburn School, 8 East 40th Street, New York, NY 10016. *Phone:* 212-686-9040 Ext. 103.

NORTH CAROLINA

ALAMANCE COMMUNITY COLLEGE
Graham, North Carolina www.alamance.cc.nc.us/

- **State-supported** 2-year, founded 1959, part of North Carolina Community College System
- **Small-town** 48-acre campus
- **Endowment** $2.9 million
- **Coed,** 4,637 undergraduate students, 40% full-time, 66% women, 34% men

Undergraduates 1,836 full-time, 2,801 part-time. Students come from 6 states and territories, 1 other country, 1% are from out of state, 24% African American, 1% Asian American or Pacific Islander, 4% Hispanic American, 0.7% Native American, 17% transferred in.

Freshmen *Admission:* 650 applied, 650 admitted, 650 enrolled. *Average high school GPA:* 2.0.

Faculty *Total:* 381, 25% full-time, 6% with terminal degrees. *Student/faculty ratio:* 12:1.

Majors Accounting technology and bookkeeping; animal sciences; applied horticulture; automobile/automotive mechanics technology; banking and financial support services; biotechnology; business administration and management; carpentry; clinical/medical laboratory technology; commercial and advertising art; computer programming; criminal justice/safety; culinary arts; electrical, electronic and communications engineering technology; electromechanical technology; executive assistant/executive secretary; general retailing/wholesaling; heating, air conditioning and refrigeration technology; information science/studies; kindergarten/preschool education; legal administrative assistant/secretary; liberal arts and sciences/liberal studies; machine tool technology; mechanical engineering/mechanical technology; medical administrative assistant and medical secretary; medical/clinical assistant; nursing (registered nurse training); office occupations and clerical services; operations management; real estate; social work; teacher assistant/aide; welding technology.

Academics *Calendar:* semesters. *Degree:* certificates, diplomas, and associate. *Special study options:* academic remediation for entering students, adult/continuing education programs, cooperative education, distance learning, double majors, English as a second language, independent study, off-campus study, part-time degree program, services for LD students, summer session for credit.

Library Learning Resources Center with 22,114 titles, 185 serial subscriptions, an OPAC, a Web page.

Student Life *Housing:* college housing not available. *Campus security:* 24-hour emergency response devices and patrols, student patrols, late-night transport/escort service. *Student services:* personal/psychological counseling.

Athletics *Intramural sports:* basketball M/W, bowling M/W, tennis M/W, volleyball M/W.

Costs (2006–07) *Tuition:* state resident $1264 full-time, $40 per credit hour part-time; nonresident $7024 full-time, $220 per credit hour part-time. *Required fees:* $30 full-time, $5 per term part-time. *Waivers:* senior citizens.

Alamance Community College (continued)

Financial Aid Of all full-time matriculated undergraduates, 185 Federal Work-Study jobs (averaging $3000).

Applying *Options:* deferred entrance. *Required:* high school transcript. *Application deadlines:* rolling (freshmen), rolling (transfers). *Notification:* continuous (freshmen), continuous (transfers).

Freshmen Application Contact Ms. Beth Brehler, Director for Enrollment Management, Alamance Community College, Jimmy Kerr Road, Graham, NC 27253-8000. *Phone:* 336-506-4120. *Fax:* 336-506-4264. *E-mail:* aacadmissions@ alamance.cc.nc.us.

THE ART INSTITUTE OF CHARLOTTE

Charlotte, North Carolina   **www.aich.artinstitutes.edu/**

- **Proprietary** primarily 2-year, founded 1973, part of Education Management Corporation
- **Suburban** campus
- **Coed,** 880 undergraduate students, 71% full-time, 69% women, 31% men

Undergraduates 628 full-time, 252 part-time. Students come from 29 states and territories, 9 other countries, 26% are from out of state, 33% African American, 2% Asian American or Pacific Islander, 5% Hispanic American, 0.3% Native American, 26% live on campus. *Retention:* 54% of 2003 full-time freshmen returned.

Freshmen *Admission:* 697 applied, 225 enrolled. *Average high school GPA:* 2.62.

Faculty *Total:* 52, 40% full-time, 13% with terminal degrees. *Student/faculty ratio:* 19:1.

Academics *Calendar:* quarters. *Degrees:* certificates, associate, and bachelor's. *Special study options:* academic remediation for entering students, accelerated degree program, advanced placement credit, distance learning, independent study, internships, part-time degree program, services for LD students, study abroad, summer session for credit.

Library The Art Institute of Charlotte Library with 15,000 titles, 130 serial subscriptions, 825 audiovisual materials, an OPAC, a Web page.

Student Life *Housing Options:* Campus housing is leased by the school. Freshman campus housing is guaranteed. *Campus security:* 24-hour emergency response devices, late-night transport/escort service. *Student services:* personal/psychological counseling.

Standardized Tests *Required for some:* SAT (for admission). *Recommended:* SAT (for admission).

Costs (2007–08) *Tuition:* $18,576 full-time, $387 per credit part-time. *Required fees:* $200 full-time. *Room only:* $5780.

Applying *Options:* electronic application, deferred entrance. *Application fee:* $50. *Required:* essay or personal statement, high school transcript. *Required for some:* interview. *Application deadlines:* rolling (freshmen), rolling (out-of-state freshmen), rolling (transfers). *Notification:* continuous (freshmen), continuous (out-of-state freshmen), continuous (transfers).

Director of Admissions Mr. Gil Cendejas, Director of Admissions, The Art Institute of Charlotte, 2110 Water Ridge Parkway, Charlotte, NC 28217. *Phone:* 704-357-8020. *Fax:* 704-357-1133. *E-mail:* gcendejas@aii.edu.

▶See page 478 for the College Close-Up.

ASHEVILLE-BUNCOMBE TECHNICAL COMMUNITY COLLEGE

Asheville, North Carolina   **www.abtech.edu/**

- **State-supported** 2-year, founded 1959, part of North Carolina Community College System
- **Urban** 126-acre campus
- **Endowment** $98,442
- **Coed,** 6,449 undergraduate students

Undergraduates 2% are from out of state, 6% African American, 0.5% Asian American or Pacific Islander, 1% Hispanic American, 0.5% Native American, 0.6% international.

Freshmen *Admission:* 2,792 applied, 2,792 admitted.

Faculty *Total:* 636. *Student/faculty ratio:* 17:1.

Majors Accounting technology and bookkeeping; automobile/automotive mechanics technology; business administration and management; child care and support services management; civil engineering technology; clinical/medical laboratory technology; computer programming; computer systems networking and telecommunications; criminal justice/police science; culinary arts; dental

hygiene; emergency medical technology (EMT paramedic); executive assistant/executive secretary; general retailing/wholesaling; heating, air conditioning, ventilation and refrigeration maintenance technology; hotel/motel administration; institutional food workers; liberal arts and sciences/liberal studies; machine tool technology; mechanical design technology; mechanical engineering/mechanical technology; medical radiologic technology; nursing (registered nurse training); operations management; social work; survey technology; tool and die technology.

Academics *Calendar:* semesters. *Degree:* certificates, diplomas, and associate. *Special study options:* academic remediation for entering students, adult/continuing education programs, advanced placement credit, cooperative education, distance learning, double majors, independent study, internships, part-time degree program, services for LD students, summer session for credit.

Library Holly Learning Resources Center with 37,439 titles, 195 serial subscriptions, an OPAC.

Student Life *Housing:* college housing not available. *Activities and Organizations:* drama/theater group, student-run newspaper, Student Government Association, Phi Beta Lambda. *Campus security:* 24-hour emergency response devices and patrols. *Student services:* personal/psychological counseling.

Athletics *Intramural sports:* basketball M/W, softball M/W, volleyball M/W.

Standardized Tests *Required:* CPT, SAT, or ACT (for placement).

Costs (2007–08) *Tuition:* state resident $1264 full-time, $40 per credit hour part-time; nonresident $3512 full-time, $220 per credit hour part-time. *Required fees:* $28 full-time, $14 per term part-time.

Financial Aid Of all full-time matriculated undergraduates, 55 Federal Work-Study jobs (averaging $2000).

Applying *Options:* deferred entrance. *Required:* high school transcript. *Required for some:* letters of recommendation, interview. *Application deadlines:* rolling (freshmen), rolling (transfers). *Notification:* continuous (freshmen), continuous (transfers).

Freshmen Application Contact Ms. Lisa Bush, Director, Admissions, Asheville-Buncombe Technical Community College, 340 Victoria Road, Asheville, NC 28801. *Phone:* 828-254-1921 Ext. 202. *E-mail:* lbush@abtech.edu.

BEAUFORT COUNTY COMMUNITY COLLEGE

Washington, North Carolina   **www.beaufortccc.edu/**

- **State-supported** 2-year, founded 1967, part of North Carolina Community College System
- **Rural** 67-acre campus
- **Coed,** 1,433 undergraduate students, 100% full-time, 71% women, 29% men

Undergraduates 1,433 full-time. 1% are from out of state, 32% African American, 1% Hispanic American.

Faculty *Total:* 322, 49% full-time, 1% with terminal degrees.

Majors Accounting; administrative assistant and secretarial science; agricultural mechanization; automobile/automotive mechanics technology; business administration and management; clinical/medical laboratory technology; computer programming; computer systems networking and telecommunications; criminal justice/police science; drafting and design technology; electrical, electronic and communications engineering technology; heavy equipment maintenance technology; human resources management; information science/studies; kindergarten/preschool education; liberal arts and sciences/liberal studies; medical administrative assistant and medical secretary; medical office management; nursing (registered nurse training); social work; welding technology.

Academics *Calendar:* semesters. *Degree:* certificates, diplomas, and associate. *Special study options:* academic remediation for entering students, advanced placement credit, cooperative education, distance learning, English as a second language, off-campus study, part-time degree program, services for LD students, summer session for credit.

Library Beaufort Community College Library with 25,734 titles, 214 serial subscriptions, an OPAC, a Web page.

Student Life *Housing:* college housing not available. *Activities and Organizations:* Student Government Association, Gama Beta Phi, Phi Beta Lambda, Hope Club. *Campus security:* 24-hour emergency response devices and patrols, late-night transport/escort service. *Student services:* personal/psychological counseling.

Standardized Tests *Required:* CPT (for admission). *Recommended:* SAT or ACT (for admission).

Costs (2006–07) *Tuition:* state resident $1264 full-time, $40 per credit hour part-time; nonresident $7024 full-time, $220 per credit hour part-time. Part-time tuition and fees vary according to course load. *Required fees:* $64 full-time, $2 per credit hour part-time. *Waivers:* senior citizens and employees or children of employees.

Financial Aid Of all full-time matriculated undergraduates, 21 Federal Work-Study jobs (averaging $1600). *Financial aid deadline:* 7/15.

Applying *Options:* electronic application. *Required:* high school transcript. *Required for some:* essay or personal statement, letters of recommendation, interview. *Application deadlines:* 8/18 (freshmen), rolling (transfers). *Notification:* continuous (freshmen), continuous (transfers).

Freshmen Application Contact Mr. Gary Burbage, Director of Admissions, Beaufort County Community College, PO Box 1069, 5337 US Highway 264 East, Washington, NC 27889-1069. *Phone:* 252-940-6233. *Fax:* 252-940-6393. *E-mail:* garyb@beaufortccc.edu.

BLADEN COMMUNITY COLLEGE

Dublin, North Carolina　　　　　　**www.bladen.cc.nc.us/**

- **State and locally supported** 2-year, founded 1967, part of North Carolina Community College System
- **Rural** 45-acre campus
- **Endowment** $72,151
- **Coed,** 1,407 undergraduate students, 60% full-time, 77% women, 23% men

Undergraduates 838 full-time, 569 part-time. Students come from 3 states and territories, 48% African American, 0.2% Asian American or Pacific Islander, 0.6% Hispanic American, 10% Native American. *Retention:* 35% of 2003 full-time freshmen returned.

Freshmen *Admission:* 267 enrolled. *Average high school GPA:* 2.6.

Faculty *Total:* 85, 41% full-time, 5% with terminal degrees.

Majors Administrative assistant and secretarial science; biotechnology; business administration and management; child care provision; computer programming; computer programming (specific applications); cosmetology; criminal justice/police science; electrical, electronic and communications engineering technology; general studies; industrial technology; information technology; liberal arts and sciences/liberal studies; nursing (registered nurse training); welding technology.

Academics *Calendar:* semesters. *Degree:* certificates, diplomas, and associate. *Special study options:* academic remediation for entering students, adult/continuing education programs, advanced placement credit, distance learning, double majors, independent study, part-time degree program, services for LD students, summer session for credit.

Library Learning Resource Center with 19,881 titles, 52 serial subscriptions, 2,364 audiovisual materials, an OPAC, a Web page.

Student Life *Housing:* college housing not available. *Campus security:* 14-hour patrols. *Student services:* personal/psychological counseling.

Standardized Tests *Required:* ACT COMPASS (for admission).

Costs (2007–08) *Tuition:* state resident $1264 full-time, $40 per hour part-time; nonresident $7024 full-time, $220 per hour part-time. *Required fees:* $66 full-time, $26 per term part-time.

Financial Aid Of all full-time matriculated undergraduates, 30 Federal Work-Study jobs (averaging $1200).

Applying *Options:* electronic application, deferred entrance. *Required:* high school transcript. *Application deadlines:* 8/1 (freshmen), 8/1 (transfers). *Notification:* continuous until 8/15 (freshmen), continuous until 8/15 (transfers).

Freshmen Application Contact Ms. Yvonne Willoughby, Admissions Secretary, Bladen Community College, PO Box 266, Dublin, NC 28332. *Phone:* 910-879-5593. *Fax:* 910-879-5564. *E-mail:* ywilloughby@bladen.edu.

BLUE RIDGE COMMUNITY COLLEGE

Flat Rock, North Carolina　　　　**www.blueridge.edu/**

Freshmen Application Contact Ms. Sarah Jones, Registrar, Blue Ridge Community College, 180 West Campus Drive, Flat Rock, NC 28731. *Phone:* 828-694-1810. *E-mail:* sarahj@blueridge.cc.nc.us.

BRUNSWICK COMMUNITY COLLEGE

Supply, North Carolina　　　　　　**www.brunswickcc.edu/**

- **State-supported** 2-year, founded 1979, part of North Carolina Community College System
- **Rural** 266-acre campus
- **Endowment** $1.3 million
- **Coed,** 1,011 undergraduate students, 43% full-time, 71% women, 29% men

Undergraduates 433 full-time, 578 part-time. Students come from 5 states and territories, 1% are from out of state, 20% African American, 0.5% Asian American or Pacific Islander, 3% Hispanic American, 0.9% Native American, 4% transferred in.

Freshmen *Admission:* 350 enrolled.

Faculty *Total:* 105, 30% full-time, 12% with terminal degrees. *Student/faculty ratio:* 11:1.

Majors Administrative assistant and secretarial science; applied horticulture; aquaculture; business administration and management; child care provision; computer/information technology services administration related; computer programming; computer programming related; electrical, electronic and communications engineering technology; engineering technology; fishing and fisheries sciences and management; health information/medical records administration; industrial technology; liberal arts and sciences/liberal studies; nursing (registered nurse training); teacher assistant/aide; turf and turfgrass management.

Academics *Calendar:* semesters. *Degree:* certificates, diplomas, and associate. *Special study options:* academic remediation for entering students, advanced placement credit, cooperative education, distance learning, English as a second language, independent study, internships, part-time degree program, services for LD students, summer session for credit.

Library Brunswick Community College Library plus 1 other with 20,032 titles, 69 serial subscriptions, 986 audiovisual materials, an OPAC.

Student Life *Housing:* college housing not available. *Activities and Organizations:* Student Government Association, Phi Theta Kappa Honor Society, National Vocational-Technical Honor Society. *Campus security:* late-night transport/escort service, campus police. *Student services:* personal/psychological counseling.

Athletics Member NJCAA. *Intercollegiate sports:* basketball M/W, golf M, softball W. *Intramural sports:* volleyball M/W.

Standardized Tests *Required:* ACT ASSET (for placement).

Costs (2006–07) *Tuition:* state resident $1185 full-time, $40 per semester hour part-time; nonresident $6585 full-time, $220 per semester hour part-time. Part-time tuition and fees vary according to course load. *Required fees:* $73 full-time, $37 per term part-time. *Waivers:* senior citizens.

Applying *Options:* electronic application. *Required:* high school transcript. *Required for some:* letters of recommendation, interview. *Application deadlines:* rolling (freshmen), rolling (transfers). *Notification:* continuous (freshmen), continuous (transfers).

Freshmen Application Contact Ms. Julie Olsen, Admissions Counselor, Brunswick Community College, PO Box 30, Supply, NC 28462. *Phone:* 910-755-7324. *Toll-free phone:* 800-754-1050 Ext. 324. *Fax:* 910-754-9609. *E-mail:* olsenj@brunswickcc.edu.

CALDWELL COMMUNITY COLLEGE AND TECHNICAL INSTITUTE

Hudson, North Carolina　　　　　　**www.cccti.edu/**

- **State-supported** 2-year, founded 1964, part of North Carolina Community College System
- **Small-town** 50-acre campus
- **Coed,** 3,878 undergraduate students, 34% full-time, 56% women, 44% men

Undergraduates 1,320 full-time, 2,558 part-time. Students come from 17 states and territories, 15 other countries, 1% are from out of state, 6% African American, 0.8% Asian American or Pacific Islander, 1% Hispanic American, 0.3% Native American, 21% transferred in.

Freshmen *Admission:* 719 applied, 719 admitted, 719 enrolled.

Faculty *Total:* 432, 29% full-time, 8% with terminal degrees.

Majors Accounting; aeronautics/aviation/aerospace science and technology; art; biological and physical sciences; biomedical technology; business administration and management; business systems networking/ telecommunications; cardiovascular technology; child care/guidance; computer programming (specific applications); cosmetology; diagnostic medical sonography and ultrasound technology; drafting and design technology; electrical, electronic and communications engineering technology; health/health care administration; information technology; landscaping and groundskeeping; legal assistant/paralegal; liberal arts and sciences/liberal studies; medical radiologic technology; music; nuclear medical technology; nursing (registered nurse training); physical therapy; pre-engineering.

Academics *Calendar:* semesters. *Degree:* certificates, diplomas, and associate. *Special study options:* academic remediation for entering students, adult/continuing education programs, advanced placement credit, cooperative education, distance learning, double majors, independent study, part-time degree program, services for LD students, summer session for credit.

Library Broyhill Center for Learning Resources with 50,770 titles, 251 serial subscriptions, an OPAC, a Web page.

Caldwell Community College and Technical Institute (continued)

Student Life *Housing:* college housing not available. *Activities and Organizations:* drama/theater group, choral group. *Campus security:* trained security personnel during open hours.

Athletics Member NJCAA. *Intercollegiate sports:* basketball M/W, golf M, volleyball W. *Intramural sports:* basketball M/W, tennis M/W.

Costs (2006–07) *Tuition:* state resident $1185 full-time, $40 per credit hour part-time; nonresident $6585 full-time, $220 per credit hour part-time. Full-time tuition and fees vary according to course load. Part-time tuition and fees vary according to course load. *Required fees:* $4 per course part-time. *Payment plan:* installment. *Waivers:* senior citizens.

Financial Aid Of all full-time matriculated undergraduates, 69 Federal Work-Study jobs (averaging $960).

Applying *Options:* early admission. *Required:* high school transcript. *Application deadlines:* rolling (freshmen), rolling (transfers). *Notification:* continuous (freshmen), continuous (transfers).

Freshmen Application Contact Mrs. Carolyn Woodard, Director of Enrollment Management Services, Caldwell Community College and Technical Institute, 2855 Hickory Boulevard, Hudson, NC 28638. *Phone:* 828-726-2703. *Fax:* 828-726-2709. *E-mail:* cwoodard@cccti.edu.

CAPE FEAR COMMUNITY COLLEGE

Wilmington, North Carolina　　　**www.cfcc.edu/**

- **State-supported** 2-year, founded 1959, part of North Carolina Community College System
- **Urban** 150-acre campus
- **Endowment** $2.2 million
- **Coed,** 7,473 undergraduate students, 41% full-time, 55% women, 45% men

Undergraduates 3,081 full-time, 4,392 part-time. Students come from 39 states and territories, 7 other countries, 5% are from out of state, 14% African American, 0.8% Asian American or Pacific Islander, 2% Hispanic American, 1% Native American.

Freshmen *Admission:* 1,247 admitted, 1,088 enrolled.

Faculty *Total:* 586, 40% full-time, 6% with terminal degrees. *Student/faculty ratio:* 14:1.

Majors Accounting technology and bookkeeping; architectural engineering technology; automobile/automotive mechanics technology; business administration and management; chemical technology; child care and support services management; computer systems analysis; computer systems networking and telecommunications; computer technology/computer systems technology; criminal justice/police science; dental hygiene; diagnostic medical sonography and ultrasound technology; electrical, electronic and communications engineering technology; electrical/electronics equipment installation and repair; engineering/industrial management; environmental studies; executive assistant/executive secretary; hotel/motel administration; industrial production technologies related; institutional food workers; instrumentation technology; interior design; landscaping and groundskeeping; liberal arts and sciences/liberal studies; machine shop technology; marine maintenance and ship repair technology; marine technology; mechanical engineering/mechanical technology; medical radiologic technology; nursing (registered nurse training); occupational therapist assistant.

Academics *Calendar:* semesters. *Degree:* certificates, diplomas, and associate. *Special study options:* academic remediation for entering students, adult/continuing education programs, cooperative education, distance learning, English as a second language, part-time degree program, services for LD students, summer session for credit.

Library Cape Fear Community College Library with 45,633 titles, 656 serial subscriptions, 6,146 audiovisual materials, an OPAC, a Web page.

Student Life *Housing:* college housing not available. *Activities and Organizations:* student-run newspaper, choral group, Nursing Club, Dental Hygiene Club, Pineapple Guild. *Campus security:* 24-hour emergency response devices and patrols, late-night transport/escort service. *Student services:* personal/psychological counseling.

Athletics Member NJCAA. *Intercollegiate sports:* basketball M, cheerleading M/W, golf M, softball M/W, tennis M/W, volleyball M/W. *Intramural sports:* soccer M.

Costs (2006–07) *Tuition:* state resident $1264 full-time, $40 per credit part-time; nonresident $7024 full-time, $220 per credit part-time. Full-time tuition and fees vary according to course load. Part-time tuition and fees vary according to course load. *Required fees:* $70 full-time, $7 per credit part-time. *Payment plan:* deferred payment. *Waivers:* senior citizens and employees or children of employees.

Financial Aid Of all full-time matriculated undergraduates, 50 Federal Work-Study jobs.

Applying *Options:* electronic application, early admission, deferred entrance. *Required for some:* high school transcript, interview, placement testing. *Application deadlines:* 8/21 (freshmen), rolling (transfers). *Notification:* continuous (freshmen), continuous (transfers).

Freshmen Application Contact Ms. Linda Kasyan, Director of Enrollment Management, Cape Fear Community College, 411 North Front Street, Wilmington, NC 28401-3993. *Phone:* 910-362-7054. *Toll-free phone:* 910-362-7557. *Fax:* 910-362-7080. *E-mail:* admissions@cfcc.edu.

CAROLINAS COLLEGE OF HEALTH SCIENCES

Charlotte, North Carolina　　　**www.carolinascollege.edu/**

Freshmen Application Contact Ms. Elizabeth West, Admissions Officer, Carolinas College of Health Sciences, PO Box 32861, Charlotte, NC 28232-2861. *Phone:* 704-355-5043. *Fax:* 704-355-9336. *E-mail:* cchsinformation@carolinashealthcare.org.

CARTERET COMMUNITY COLLEGE

Morehead City, North Carolina　　　**www.carteret.edu/**

- **State-supported** 2-year, founded 1963, part of North Carolina Community College System
- **Small-town** 25-acre campus
- **Coed**

Undergraduates 639 full-time, 1,020 part-time. Students come from 24 states and territories, 5% African American, 0.2% Asian American or Pacific Islander, 3% Hispanic American, 0.4% Native American.

Academics *Calendar:* semesters. *Degree:* certificates, diplomas, and associate. *Special study options:* academic remediation for entering students, adult/continuing education programs, cooperative education, distance learning, double majors, internships, part-time degree program, services for LD students, summer session for credit.

Financial Aid Of all full-time matriculated undergraduates, 40 Federal Work-Study jobs (averaging $750).

Applying *Options:* electronic application, early admission. *Required:* high school transcript.

Freshmen Application Contact Mr. Rick Hill, Director of Student Enrollment Resources, Carteret Community College, 3505 Arendell Street, Morehead City, NC 28557-2989. *Phone:* 252-222-6153 Ext. 6153. *Fax:* 252-222-6265. *E-mail:* mhw@carteret.edu.

CATAWBA VALLEY COMMUNITY COLLEGE

Hickory, North Carolina　　　**www.cvcc.cc.nc.us/**

- **State and locally supported** 2-year, founded 1960, part of North Carolina Community College System
- **Small-town** 50-acre campus with easy access to Charlotte
- **Endowment** $591,181
- **Coed,** 4,869 undergraduate students, 41% full-time, 60% women, 40% men

Undergraduates 1,997 full-time, 2,872 part-time. Students come from 4 states and territories, 5 other countries, 10% African American, 7% Asian American or Pacific Islander, 4% Hispanic American, 0.3% Native American, 0.2% international, 28% transferred in.

Freshmen *Admission:* 2,713 applied, 1,926 admitted, 905 enrolled. *Average high school GPA:* 2.89.

Faculty *Total:* 466, 30% full-time. *Student/faculty ratio:* 11:1.

Majors Accounting technology and bookkeeping; administrative assistant and secretarial science; architectural engineering technology; automobile/automotive mechanics technology; banking and financial support services; business administration and management; business, management, and marketing related; commercial and advertising art; computer engineering related; computer engineering technology; computer programming; computer programming (specific applications); computer science; computer systems networking and telecommunications; criminal justice/police science; criminology; data processing and data processing technology; dental hygiene; electrical, electronic and communications engineering technology; emergency medical technology (EMT paramedic); engineering technologies related; fire protection and safety technology; funeral

service and mortuary science; furniture design and manufacturing; health and medical administrative services related; health information/medical records technology; industrial technology; information technology; legal assistant/paralegal; liberal arts and sciences/liberal studies; marketing/marketing management; mechanical engineering/mechanical technology; medical radiologic technology; nursing (registered nurse training); operations management; photographic and film/video technology; photography; real estate; respiratory care therapy; retailing; speech-language pathology; teacher assistant/aide.

Academics *Calendar:* semesters. *Degree:* certificates, diplomas, and associate. *Special study options:* academic remediation for entering students, adult/continuing education programs, advanced placement credit, cooperative education, distance learning, double majors, English as a second language, independent study, part-time degree program, services for LD students, student-designed majors, summer session for credit.

Library Learning Resource Center with 25,000 titles, 610 serial subscriptions, 700 audiovisual materials, an OPAC, a Web page.

Student Life *Housing:* college housing not available. *Activities and Organizations:* student-run newspaper, choral group, NCANS (Nursing), Phi Theta Kappa, Catawba Valley Outing Club, Respiratory Care Club, Rotoract. *Campus security:* 24-hour patrols. *Student services:* personal/psychological counseling.

Athletics Member NJCAA. *Intercollegiate sports:* golf M(s), volleyball W.

Costs (2006–07) *Tuition:* state resident $1185 full-time, $40 per credit hour part-time; nonresident $7024 full-time, $220 per credit hour part-time. *Required fees:* $24 full-time, $1 per credit hour part-time.

Applying *Options:* early admission, deferred entrance. *Required:* high school transcript. *Application deadlines:* rolling (freshmen), rolling (transfers). *Notification:* continuous (freshmen), continuous (transfers).

Director of Admissions Mrs. Caroline Farmer, Director of Admissions and Records, Catawba Valley Community College, 2550 Highway 70 SE, Hickory, NC 28602-9699. *Phone:* 828-327-7000 Ext. 4218.

CENTRAL CAROLINA COMMUNITY COLLEGE

Sanford, North Carolina   www.cccc.edu/

- **State and locally supported** 2-year, founded 1962, part of North Carolina Community College System
- **Small-town** 41-acre campus
- **Endowment** $1.0 million
- **Coed,** 4,857 undergraduate students, 38% full-time, 62% women, 38% men

Undergraduates 1,845 full-time, 3,012 part-time. Students come from 36 states and territories, 5 other countries, 6% are from out of state, 25% African American, 1% Asian American or Pacific Islander, 4% Hispanic American, 0.8% Native American, 0.2% international, 20% transferred in.

Freshmen *Admission:* 2,844 applied, 1,227 admitted, 1,100 enrolled. *Test scores:* SAT verbal scores over 500: 25%; SAT math scores over 500: 25%; ACT scores over 18: 25%.

Faculty *Total:* 425, 37% full-time, 4% with terminal degrees. *Student/faculty ratio:* 8:1.

Majors Accounting; administrative assistant and secretarial science; automobile/automotive mechanics technology; business administration and management; computer/information technology services administration related; computer programming; computer programming (specific applications); computer systems networking and telecommunications; criminal justice/law enforcement administration; drafting and design technology; electrical, electronic and communications engineering technology; information science/studies; information technology; instrumentation technology; kindergarten/preschool education; laser and optical technology; legal administrative assistant/secretary; legal assistant/paralegal; liberal arts and sciences/liberal studies; marketing/marketing management; medical administrative assistant and medical secretary; medical/clinical assistant; nursing (registered nurse training); operations management; quality control technology; radio and television; social work; telecommunications; veterinary technology.

Academics *Calendar:* semesters. *Degree:* certificates, diplomas, and associate. *Special study options:* academic remediation for entering students, adult/continuing education programs, advanced placement credit, distance learning, double majors, English as a second language, independent study, internships, part-time degree program, services for LD students, summer session for credit.

Library Library/Learning Resources Center plus 2 others with 50,479 titles, 240 serial subscriptions, 5,946 audiovisual materials, an OPAC, a Web page.

Student Life *Housing:* college housing not available. *Activities and Organizations:* student-run radio station. *Campus security:* patrols by trained security personnel during operating hours. *Student services:* personal/psychological counseling.

Athletics Member NJCAA. *Intercollegiate sports:* basketball M/W, golf M/W, softball W, volleyball W. *Intramural sports:* bowling M/W, golf M/W, softball W, volleyball W.

Standardized Tests *Required:* CPT, ACCUPLACER, ACT COMPASS, ACT ASSET (for placement). *Recommended:* SAT or ACT (for placement).

Costs (2007–08) *Tuition:* area resident $1344 full-time, $42 per hour part-time; nonresident $7466 full-time, $233 per hour part-time. *Required fees:* $34 full-time, $17 per term part-time.

Financial Aid Of all full-time matriculated undergraduates, 70 Federal Work-Study jobs (averaging $1361). *Financial aid deadline:* 5/4.

Applying *Options:* electronic application, early admission, deferred entrance. *Required:* high school transcript. *Application deadlines:* rolling (freshmen), rolling (transfers). *Notification:* continuous (freshmen), continuous (transfers).

Freshmen Application Contact Mr. Ken R. Hoyle, Dean of Student Services, Central Carolina Community College, 1105 Kelly Drive, Sanford, NC 27330. *Phone:* 919-775-5401. *Toll-free phone:* 800-682-8353 Ext. 7300. *Fax:* 919-718-7380.

CENTRAL PIEDMONT COMMUNITY COLLEGE

Charlotte, North Carolina   www.cpcc.edu/

- **State and locally supported** 2-year, founded 1963, part of North Carolina Community College System
- **Urban** 37-acre campus
- **Endowment** $16.1 million
- **Coed,** 16,631 undergraduate students, 37% full-time, 58% women, 42% men

Undergraduates 6,115 full-time, 10,516 part-time. Students come from 13 states and territories, 117 other countries, 3% are from out of state, 32% African American, 3% Asian American or Pacific Islander, 3% Hispanic American, 0.5% Native American, 9% international, 24% transferred in.

Freshmen *Admission:* 1,397 applied, 1,397 admitted, 1,397 enrolled.

Faculty *Total:* 2,034, 15% full-time. *Student/faculty ratio:* 16:1.

Majors Accounting; administrative assistant and secretarial science; advertising; applied art; architectural engineering technology; art; automobile/automotive mechanics technology; biology/biological sciences; business administration and management; business machine repair; child development; civil engineering technology; clinical laboratory science/medical technology; clinical/medical laboratory technology; commercial and advertising art; computer engineering technology; computer programming; computer programming (specific applications); computer science; consumer merchandising/retailing management; criminal justice/law enforcement administration; criminal justice/police science; culinary arts; dance; data processing and data processing technology; dental hygiene; drafting and design technology; electrical, electronic and communications engineering technology; electromechanical technology; engineering technology; environmental engineering technology; fashion merchandising; finance; fire science; food science; food services technology; graphic and printing equipment operation/production; health/health care administration; health information/medical records administration; horticultural science; hospitality administration; hotel/motel administration; human services; industrial technology; insurance; interior design; kindergarten/preschool education; legal administrative assistant/secretary; legal assistant/paralegal; liberal arts and sciences/liberal studies; machine tool technology; marketing/marketing management; mechanical engineering/mechanical technology; medical administrative assistant and medical secretary; medical/clinical assistant; music; nursing (licensed practical/vocational nurse training); nursing (registered nurse training); physical therapy; postal management; real estate; respiratory care therapy; sign language interpretation and translation; social work; special products marketing; survey technology; tourism and travel services management; transportation technology; welding technology.

Academics *Calendar:* semesters. *Degree:* certificates, diplomas, and associate. *Special study options:* academic remediation for entering students, accelerated degree program, advanced placement credit, cooperative education, distance learning, English as a second language, honors programs, off-campus study, part-time degree program, services for LD students, student-designed majors, summer session for credit.

Library Hagemeyer Learning Center plus 5 others with 102,649 titles, 750 serial subscriptions, 17,802 audiovisual materials, an OPAC, a Web page.

Student Life *Housing:* college housing not available. *Activities and Organizations:* drama/theater group, student-run newspaper, choral group, Phi Theta Kappa, Black Students Organization, Students for Environmental Sanity, Sierra Club, Nursing Club. *Campus security:* 24-hour emergency response devices and patrols. *Student services:* personal/psychological counseling, women's center.

Athletics Member NJCAA. *Intramural sports:* soccer M/W.

Costs (2006–07) *Tuition:* state resident $1264 full-time, $40 per semester hour part-time; nonresident $7024 full-time, $220 per semester hour part-time.

Central Piedmont Community College (continued)

Required fees: $170 full-time, $56 per term part-time. *Payment plan:* installment. *Waivers:* senior citizens and employees or children of employees.

Financial Aid Of all full-time matriculated undergraduates, 99 Federal Work-Study jobs (averaging $2988).

Applying *Required:* high school transcript. *Application deadlines:* rolling (freshmen), rolling (out-of-state freshmen), rolling (transfers). *Notification:* continuous (freshmen), continuous (out-of-state freshmen), continuous (transfers).

Freshmen Application Contact Ms. Linda McComb, Associate Dean, Central Piedmont Community College, PO Box 35009, Charlotte, NC 28235-5009. *Phone:* 704-330-6784. *Fax:* 704-330-6136.

CLEVELAND COMMUNITY COLLEGE

Shelby, North Carolina   www.clevelandcommunitycollege.edu/

- **State-supported** 2-year, founded 1965, part of North Carolina Community College System
- **Small-town** 43-acre campus with easy access to Charlotte
- **Coed,** 3,341 undergraduate students, 41% full-time, 67% women, 33% men

Undergraduates 1,379 full-time, 1,962 part-time. Students come from 3 states and territories, 1% are from out of state, 24% African American, 0.7% Asian American or Pacific Islander, 1% Hispanic American, 0.4% Native American, 0.1% international, 0.7% transferred in.

Freshmen *Admission:* 261 enrolled. *Average high school GPA:* 2.71.

Faculty *Total:* 391, 21% full-time, 1% with terminal degrees. *Student/faculty ratio:* 9:1.

Majors Accounting; administrative assistant and secretarial science; biological and physical sciences; business administration and management; communications technology; computer engineering technology; computer programming (specific applications); criminal justice/law enforcement administration; criminal justice/safety; data entry/microcomputer applications; electrical, electronic and communications engineering technology; electrician; engineering technologies related; executive assistant/executive secretary; fashion merchandising; fire protection and safety technology; industrial radiologic technology; information science/studies; information technology; liberal arts and sciences and humanities related; liberal arts and sciences/liberal studies; management information systems and services related; mechanical engineering/mechanical technology; medical administrative assistant and medical secretary; medical radiologic technology; nursing (registered nurse training); operations management; Spanish; special education; system administration; teacher assistant/aide.

Academics *Calendar:* semesters. *Degree:* certificates, diplomas, and associate. *Special study options:* academic remediation for entering students, adult/continuing education programs, advanced placement credit, distance learning, double majors, English as a second language, independent study, off-campus study, part-time degree program, summer session for credit.

Library Cleveland Community College Library with 34,000 titles, 280 serial subscriptions, an OPAC, a Web page.

Student Life *Housing:* college housing not available. *Activities and Organizations:* drama/theater group, student-run television station, choral group, Gamma Beta Phi Honor Society, Student Government Association, Lamplighters, Mu Epsilon Delta, Black Awareness Club. *Campus security:* security personnel during open hours. *Student services:* personal/psychological counseling.

Costs (2007–08) *Tuition:* area resident $1344 full-time, $42 per credit hour part-time; state resident $1344 full-time, $42 per credit hour part-time; nonresident $7465 full-time, $233 per credit hour part-time. *Required fees:* $38 full-time.

Financial Aid Of all full-time matriculated undergraduates, 20 Federal Work-Study jobs.

Applying *Options:* electronic application, deferred entrance. *Required:* high school transcript. *Application deadlines:* rolling (freshmen), rolling (transfers). *Notification:* continuous (freshmen), continuous (transfers).

Freshmen Application Contact Mr. Alan Price, Dean of Enrollment Management, Cleveland Community College, 137 South Post Road, Shelby, NC 28152. *Phone:* 704-484-4073. *Fax:* 704-484-5305. *E-mail:* price@cleveland.cc.nc.us.

COASTAL CAROLINA COMMUNITY COLLEGE

Jacksonville, North Carolina   www.coastalcarolina.edu/

- **State and locally supported** 2-year, founded 1964, part of North Carolina Community College System
- **Small-town** 98-acre campus
- **Endowment** $2.1 million
- **Coed,** 4,111 undergraduate students, 50% full-time, 65% women, 35% men

Undergraduates 2,072 full-time, 2,039 part-time. Students come from 48 states and territories, 5 other countries, 31% are from out of state, 19% African American, 3% Asian American or Pacific Islander, 9% Hispanic American, 1% Native American, 0.7% international, 13% transferred in.

Freshmen *Admission:* 3,451 applied, 2,695 admitted, 832 enrolled.

Faculty *Total:* 261, 51% full-time, 11% with terminal degrees. *Student/faculty ratio:* 16:1.

Majors Accounting; architectural engineering technology; business administration and management; child care provision; clinical/medical laboratory technology; computer/information technology services administration related; computer programming (specific applications); computer systems analysis; computer systems networking and telecommunications; criminal justice/law enforcement administration; dental hygiene; emergency medical technology (EMT paramedic); executive assistant/executive secretary; fire science; legal assistant/paralegal; liberal arts and sciences/liberal studies; medical administrative assistant and medical secretary; nursing (registered nurse training); surgical technology.

Academics *Calendar:* semesters. *Degree:* certificates, diplomas, and associate. *Special study options:* academic remediation for entering students, adult/continuing education programs, advanced placement credit, distance learning, double majors, English as a second language, independent study, internships, part-time degree program, services for LD students, summer session for credit.

Library C. Louis Shields Learning Resources Center with 44,062 titles, 266 serial subscriptions, an OPAC.

Student Life *Housing:* college housing not available. *Activities and Organizations:* drama/theater group, SHELL (environmental group), SPYS (social sciences group), student government, Star of Life, Association of Nursing Students. *Campus security:* 24-hour emergency response devices and patrols, late-night transport/escort service. *Student services:* personal/psychological counseling.

Costs (2007–08) *Tuition:* state resident $1264 full-time, $40 per credit hour part-time; nonresident $7024 full-time, $220 per credit hour part-time. *Required fees:* $30 full-time, $5 per term part-time.

Applying *Options:* deferred entrance. *Required:* high school transcript. *Required for some:* 2 letters of recommendation, interview. *Application deadlines:* rolling (freshmen), rolling (transfers). *Notification:* continuous (freshmen), continuous (transfers).

Freshmen Application Contact Mr. James B. Washington, Director of Admissions, Coastal Carolina Community College, 444 Western Boulevard, Jacksonville, NC 28546. *Phone:* 910-938-6246. *Fax:* 910-455-2767. *E-mail:* washingtonb@coastal.cc.nc.us.

COLLEGE OF THE ALBEMARLE

Elizabeth City, North Carolina   www.albemarle.edu/

- **State-supported** 2-year, founded 1960, part of North Carolina Community College System
- **Small-town** 40-acre campus
- **Coed,** 2,071 undergraduate students, 41% full-time, 66% women, 34% men

Undergraduates 854 full-time, 1,217 part-time. Students come from 17 states and territories, 4 other countries.

Freshmen *Admission:* 207 enrolled. *Test scores:* SAT verbal scores over 500: 8%; SAT math scores over 500: 20%; SAT verbal scores over 600: 1%; SAT math scores over 600: 5%.

Faculty *Total:* 122, 49% full-time.

Majors Administrative assistant and secretarial science; architectural engineering technology; art; biotechnology; business administration and management; computer engineering technology; computer programming; computer programming (specific applications); construction trades; crafts, folk art and artisanry; criminal justice/law enforcement administration; culinary arts; data entry/microcomputer applications; dramatic/theater arts; education; information science/studies; information technology; liberal arts and sciences/liberal studies; marine technology; mechanical design technology; medical administrative assistant and medical secretary; metal and jewelry arts; music; nursing (licensed practical/vocational nurse training); nursing (registered nurse training); teacher assistant/aide.

Academics *Calendar:* semesters. *Degree:* certificates, diplomas, and associate. *Special study options:* academic remediation for entering students, adult/continuing education programs, advanced placement credit, cooperative education, English as a second language, part-time degree program, services for LD students, summer session for credit.

Library Learning Resources Center with 48,400 titles, 280 serial subscriptions, an OPAC, a Web page.

Student Life *Housing:* college housing not available. *Activities and Organizations:* drama/theater group, choral group, Phi Beta Lambda, Phi Theta Kappa. *Campus security:* 24-hour patrols. *Student services:* personal/psychological counseling.

Athletics *Intercollegiate sports:* soccer M. *Intramural sports:* archery M/W, badminton M/W, baseball M/W, basketball M/W, football M/W, golf M/W, gymnastics M/W, sailing M/W, soccer M(c), softball M/W, swimming and diving M/W, table tennis M/W, tennis M/W, volleyball M/W.

Costs (2007–08) *Tuition:* state resident $1344 full-time, $42 per credit hour part-time; nonresident $7466 full-time, $233 per credit hour part-time. *Required fees:* $50 per term part-time.

Financial Aid Of all full-time matriculated undergraduates, 68 Federal Work-Study jobs (averaging $553).

Applying *Options:* early admission, deferred entrance. *Required:* high school transcript. *Application deadlines:* rolling (freshmen), rolling (transfers). *Notification:* continuous (freshmen), continuous (transfers).

Freshmen Application Contact Mr. Kenny Krentz, Director of Admissions and International Students, College of The Albemarle, PO Box 2327, 1208 North Road Street, Elizabeth City, NC 27909-2327. *Phone:* 252-335-0821. *Fax:* 252-335-2011. *E-mail:* kkrentz@albemarle.edu.

CRAVEN COMMUNITY COLLEGE

New Bern, North Carolina www.craven.cc.nc.us/

Freshmen Application Contact Ms. Millicent Fulford, Recruiter, Craven Community College, 800 College Court, New Bern, NC 28562-4984. *Phone:* 252-638-7232.

DAVIDSON COUNTY COMMUNITY COLLEGE

Lexington, North Carolina www.davidsonccc.edu/

- **State and locally supported** 2-year, founded 1958, part of North Carolina Community College System
- **Rural** 83-acre campus
- **Endowment** $8.5 million
- **Coed,** 2,303 undergraduate students, 36% full-time, 61% women, 39% men

Undergraduates 829 full-time, 1,474 part-time. Students come from 7 states and territories, 4 other countries, 1% are from out of state, 13% African American, 1% Asian American or Pacific Islander, 1% Hispanic American, 0.4% Native American.

Freshmen *Admission:* 692 applied, 692 admitted, 337 enrolled.

Faculty *Total:* 212, 34% full-time, 3% with terminal degrees. *Student/faculty ratio:* 11:1.

Majors Accounting; administrative assistant and secretarial science; business administration and management; clinical/medical laboratory technology; computer engineering technology; computer programming; criminal justice/law enforcement administration; criminal justice/police science; data processing and data processing technology; electrical, electronic and communications engineering technology; emergency medical technology (EMT paramedic); engineering technology; fire science; health information/medical records administration; legal assistant/paralegal; liberal arts and sciences/liberal studies; medical/clinical assistant; nursing (registered nurse training); plastics engineering technology; pre-engineering.

Academics *Calendar:* semesters. *Degree:* certificates, diplomas, and associate. *Special study options:* academic remediation for entering students, adult/continuing education programs, advanced placement credit, cooperative education, double majors, internships, off-campus study, part-time degree program, services for LD students, summer session for credit.

Library Grady E. Love Learning Resource Center plus 1 other with 56,445 titles, 454 serial subscriptions, an OPAC, a Web page.

Student Life *Housing:* college housing not available. *Activities and Organizations:* drama/theater group. *Campus security:* 24-hour patrols, late-night transport/escort service, security guards.

Costs (2007–08) *Tuition:* state resident $948 full-time, $40 per credit hour part-time; nonresident $5268 full-time, $220 per credit hour part-time. *Required fees:* $73 full-time, $36 per term part-time.

Financial Aid Of all full-time matriculated undergraduates, 20 Federal Work-Study jobs (averaging $1800).

Applying *Options:* early admission, deferred entrance. *Required:* high school transcript. *Required for some:* interview. *Application deadlines:* rolling (freshmen), rolling (transfers). *Notification:* continuous (freshmen), continuous (transfers).

Freshmen Application Contact Davidson County Community College, PO Box 1287, Lexington, NC 27293-1287. *Phone:* 336-249-8186 Ext. 6715. *Fax:* 336-224-0240. *E-mail:* admissions@davidsonccc.edu.

DURHAM TECHNICAL COMMUNITY COLLEGE

Durham, North Carolina www.durhamtech.edu/

Director of Admissions Ms. Penny Augustine, Director of Admissions and Testing, Durham Technical Community College, 1637 Lawson Street, Durham, NC 27703. *Phone:* 919-686-3619.

ECPI TECHNICAL COLLEGE

Raleigh, North Carolina www.ecpi.net/

- **Proprietary** 2-year, founded 1990
- **Coed**

Undergraduates Students come from 1 other state, 60% African American, 2% Asian American or Pacific Islander, 2% Hispanic American, 0.8% Native American.

Faculty *Student/faculty ratio:* 13:1.

Academics *Calendar:* trimesters. *Degree:* diplomas and associate. *Special study options:* academic remediation for entering students, accelerated degree program, adult/continuing education programs, cooperative education, distance learning, independent study, internships, study abroad.

Standardized Tests *Recommended:* SAT (for admission), SAT or ACT (for admission), SAT Subject Tests (for admission).

Costs (2006–07) *Tuition:* $9750 full-time.

Applying *Options:* electronic application. *Required:* high school transcript, interview.

Freshmen Application Contact Ms. Susan Wells, Campus President, ECPI Technical College, 4101 Doie Cope Road, Raleigh, NC 27613-7387. *Phone:* 919-571-0057. *Toll-free phone:* 800-986-1200. *Fax:* 919-571-0780. *E-mail:* swells@ecpi.edu.

EDGECOMBE COMMUNITY COLLEGE

Tarboro, North Carolina www.edgecombe.edu/

Freshmen Application Contact Ms. Jackie Heath, Admissions Officer, Edgecombe Community College, 2009 West Wilson Street, Tarboro, NC 27886. *Phone:* 252-823-5166 Ext. 254.

FAYETTEVILLE TECHNICAL COMMUNITY COLLEGE

Fayetteville, North Carolina www.faytechcc.edu/

- **State-supported** 2-year, founded 1961, part of North Carolina Community College System
- **Suburban** 135-acre campus with easy access to Raleigh
- **Endowment** $39,050
- **Coed,** 10,290 undergraduate students, 31% full-time, 70% women, 30% men

Undergraduates 3,228 full-time, 7,062 part-time. Students come from 37 states and territories, 9 other countries, 10% are from out of state, 42% African American, 2% Asian American or Pacific Islander, 7% Hispanic American, 3% Native American, 0.3% international, 19% transferred in.

Freshmen *Admission:* 3,363 applied, 3,363 admitted, 1,449 enrolled. *Average high school GPA:* 2.43.

Faculty *Total:* 842, 36% full-time. *Student/faculty ratio:* 16:1.

Majors Accounting; applied horticulture; architectural engineering technology; automobile/automotive mechanics technology; banking and financial support services; biology/biotechnology laboratory technician; building/construction finishing, management, and inspection related; business administration and management; business administration, management and operations related; civil engineering technology; commercial and advertising art; computer and information systems security; computer programming; corrections and criminal justice related; criminal justice/safety; culinary arts; dental hygiene; early childhood education; e-commerce; electrical, electronic and communications engineering technology; electrician; elementary education; emergency medical technology (EMT paramedic); fire protection and safety technology; fire protection related; forensic science and technology; funeral service and mortuary science; general studies; health information/medical records technology; heating, air condition-

Fayetteville Technical Community College (continued)

ing, ventilation and refrigeration maintenance technology; hotel/motel administration; human resources management; information science/studies; information technology; language interpretation and translation; legal assistant/paralegal; liberal arts and sciences and humanities related; liberal arts and sciences/liberal studies; machine shop technology; medical office management; nuclear medical technology; nursing (registered nurse training); office management; operations management; physical therapist assistant; public administration; radiologic technology/science; respiratory care therapy; special education; speech-language pathology; surgical technology; survey technology; system, networking, and LAN/WAN management.

Academics *Calendar:* semesters. *Degree:* certificates, diplomas, and associate. *Special study options:* academic remediation for entering students, adult/continuing education programs, advanced placement credit, cooperative education, distance learning, double majors, English as a second language, independent study, internships, off-campus study, part-time degree program, services for LD students, student-designed majors, summer session for credit.

Library Paul H. Thompson Library with 64,143 titles, 319 serial subscriptions, 7,797 audiovisual materials, an OPAC, a Web page.

Student Life *Housing:* college housing not available. *Activities and Organizations:* Criminal Justice Association, Early Childhood Club, Phi Beta Lambda, Student Nurses Club, Data Processing Management Association. *Campus security:* 24-hour emergency response devices and patrols, late-night transport/escort service. *Student services:* health clinic, personal/psychological counseling.

Athletics *Intramural sports:* basketball M/W, table tennis M/W, volleyball M/W.

Costs (2006–07) *Tuition:* state resident $1264 full-time, $40 per credit hour part-time; nonresident $7024 full-time, $220 per credit hour part-time. *Required fees:* $30 full-time, $30 per term part-time. *Waivers:* senior citizens and employees or children of employees.

Financial Aid Of all full-time matriculated undergraduates, 75 Federal Work-Study jobs (averaging $2000). *Financial aid deadline:* 6/1.

Applying *Options:* electronic application, deferred entrance. *Required for some:* high school transcript. *Application deadlines:* rolling (freshmen), rolling (transfers). *Notification:* continuous (freshmen), continuous (transfers).

Freshmen Application Contact Mr. James Kelley, Director of Admissions, Fayetteville Technical Community College, PO Box 35236, Fayetteville, NC 28303. *Phone:* 910-678-8274. *Fax:* 910-678-8407. *E-mail:* kelleyj@faytechcc.edu.

FORSYTH TECHNICAL COMMUNITY COLLEGE

Winston-Salem, North Carolina   **www.forsythtech.edu/**

- **State-supported** 2-year, founded 1964, part of North Carolina Community College System
- **Suburban** 38-acre campus
- **Endowment** $916,352
- **Coed,** 6,978 undergraduate students, 36% full-time, 64% women, 36% men

Undergraduates 2,509 full-time, 4,469 part-time. 23% African American, 1% Asian American or Pacific Islander, 2% Hispanic American, 0.6% Native American, 2% international.

Freshmen *Admission:* 932 applied, 932 admitted, 924 enrolled.

Faculty *Total:* 486, 36% full-time. *Student/faculty ratio:* 14:1.

Majors Accounting; administrative assistant and secretarial science; architectural engineering technology; automobile/automotive mechanics technology; business administration and management; carpentry; child development; commercial and advertising art; computer engineering technology; computer science; construction engineering technology; criminal justice/law enforcement administration; criminal justice/police science; data processing and data processing technology; drafting and design technology; electrical, electronic and communications engineering technology; electromechanical technology; engineering technology; finance; funeral service and mortuary science; graphic and printing equipment operation/production; heating, air conditioning, ventilation and refrigeration maintenance technology; horticultural science; industrial radiologic technology; industrial technology; kindergarten/preschool education; legal assistant/paralegal; machine tool technology; marketing/marketing management; mechanical design technology; medical/clinical assistant; nuclear medical technology; nursing (registered nurse training); ornamental horticulture; pipefitting and sprinkler fitting; real estate; respiratory care therapy; welding technology.

Academics *Calendar:* semesters. *Degree:* certificates, diplomas, and associate. *Special study options:* academic remediation for entering students, adult/continuing education programs, English as a second language, part-time degree program, services for LD students, summer session for credit.

Library Forsyth Technical Community College Library plus 1 other with 41,606 titles, 358 serial subscriptions.

Student Life *Housing:* college housing not available. *Activities and Organizations:* student-run newspaper. *Campus security:* 24-hour patrols. *Student services:* personal/psychological counseling, women's center.

Athletics *Intramural sports:* basketball M/W, bowling M/W, softball W, volleyball M/W.

Standardized Tests *Required for some:* SAT or ACT (for admission), TEAS, CPT, ASSET, COMPASS.

Costs (2007–08) *Tuition:* state resident $948 full-time, $40 per credit hour part-time; nonresident $5268 full-time, $220 per credit hour part-time. *Required fees:* $50 full-time, $24 per term part-time.

Financial Aid Of all full-time matriculated undergraduates, 42 Federal Work-Study jobs (averaging $2083).

Applying *Required:* high school transcript. *Application deadlines:* 8/25 (freshmen), 9/1 (transfers). *Notification:* continuous until 8/25 (freshmen), continuous until 9/8 (transfers).

Freshmen Application Contact Ms. Patrice Mitchell, Dean of Enrollment Services, Forsyth Technical Community College, 2100 Silas Creek Parkway, Winston-Salem, NC 27103-5197. *Phone:* 336-734-7331. *Fax:* 336-761-2098. *E-mail:* admissions@forsythtech.edu.

GASTON COLLEGE

Dallas, North Carolina   **www.gaston.edu/**

- **State and locally supported** 2-year, founded 1963, part of North Carolina Community College System
- **Small-town** 166-acre campus with easy access to Charlotte
- **Endowment** $716,546
- **Coed**

Undergraduates 2,449 full-time, 2,599 part-time. Students come from 10 states and territories, 15% African American, 1% Asian American or Pacific Islander, 3% Hispanic American, 0.4% Native American. *Retention:* 80% of 2003 full-time freshmen returned.

Faculty *Student/faculty ratio:* 18:1.

Academics *Calendar:* semesters. *Degree:* certificates, diplomas, and associate. *Special study options:* academic remediation for entering students, adult/continuing education programs, advanced placement credit, cooperative education, English as a second language, off-campus study, part-time degree program, services for LD students, summer session for credit.

Student Life *Campus security:* 24-hour patrols.

Financial Aid Of all full-time matriculated undergraduates, 50 Federal Work-Study jobs (averaging $1800). 30 state and other part-time jobs (averaging $1533).

Applying *Required for some:* high school transcript.

Freshmen Application Contact Ms. Alice D. Hopper, Admissions Specialist, Gaston College, 201 Highway 321 South, Dallas, NC 28034. *Phone:* 704-922-6214. *Fax:* 704-922-6443.

GUILFORD TECHNICAL COMMUNITY COLLEGE

Jamestown, North Carolina   **www.gtcc.edu/**

- **State and locally supported** 2-year, founded 1958, part of North Carolina Community College System
- **Suburban** 158-acre campus
- **Coed,** 9,802 undergraduate students, 51% full-time, 58% women, 42% men

Undergraduates 5,000 full-time, 4,802 part-time. Students come from 15 states and territories, 0.4% are from out of state, 36% African American, 3% Asian American or Pacific Islander, 3% Hispanic American, 0.5% Native American, 18% transferred in.

Freshmen *Admission:* 2,463 enrolled. *Average high school GPA:* 2.5.

Faculty *Total:* 941, 27% full-time, 5% with terminal degrees. *Student/faculty ratio:* 11:1.

Majors Accounting; airline pilot and flight crew; architectural engineering technology; automobile/automotive mechanics technology; aviation/airway management; avionics maintenance technology; biological and physical sciences; biology/biotechnology laboratory technician; building/construction finishing, management, and inspection related; business administration and management; business operations support and secretarial services related; chemistry related; cinematography and film/video production; civil engineering technology; clinical/medical laboratory technology; commercial and advertising art; computer/information technology services administration related; computer programming; computer systems networking and telecommunications; cosmetology; criminal

justice/law enforcement administration; criminal justice/police science; culinary arts; dental hygiene; drafting and design technology; dramatic/theater arts; education related; electrical, electronic and communications engineering technology; electrical/electronics equipment installation and repair; emergency medical technology (EMT paramedic); fire science; heating, air conditioning, ventilation and refrigeration maintenance technology; heavy equipment maintenance technology; human services; industrial arts; industrial mechanics and maintenance technology; industrial technology; information science/studies; kindergarten/preschool education; legal assistant/paralegal; liberal arts and sciences/liberal studies; machine tool technology; medical/clinical assistant; nursing (registered nurse training); occupational therapist assistant; physical therapist assistant; respiratory care therapy; speech-language pathology; surgical technology; survey technology; turf and turfgrass management; web page, digital/multimedia and information resources design.

Academics *Calendar:* semesters. *Degree:* certificates, diplomas, and associate. *Special study options:* academic remediation for entering students, adult/continuing education programs, advanced placement credit, cooperative education, distance learning, English as a second language, external degree program, independent study, internships, off-campus study, part-time degree program, services for LD students, student-designed majors, summer session for credit. *ROTC:* Army (c), Air Force (c).

Library M. W. Bell Library plus 2 others with 80,052 titles, 495 serial subscriptions, 7,701 audiovisual materials, an OPAC, a Web page.

Student Life *Housing:* college housing not available. *Activities and Organizations:* drama/theater group. *Campus security:* 24-hour emergency response devices and patrols, late-night transport/escort service.

Standardized Tests *Required:* ACT COMPASS (for placement).

Costs (2006–07) *Tuition:* state resident $1264 full-time, $40 per credit hour part-time; nonresident $7024 full-time, $220 per credit hour part-time. *Required fees:* $137 full-time, $37 per term part-time. *Payment plan:* installment. *Waivers:* senior citizens and employees or children of employees.

Financial Aid Of all full-time matriculated undergraduates, 84 Federal Work-Study jobs (averaging $3302).

Applying *Options:* early admission, deferred entrance. *Required:* high school transcript. *Required for some:* interview. *Application deadlines:* rolling (freshmen), rolling (transfers). *Notification:* continuous (freshmen), continuous (transfers).

Freshmen Application Contact Dr. Edward N. Knight, Director of Admissions, Guilford Technical Community College, PO Box 309, Jamestown, NC 27282. *Phone:* 336-334-4822 Ext. 2396. *E-mail:* enknight@gtcc.edu.

HALIFAX COMMUNITY COLLEGE
Weldon, North Carolina   www.hcc.cc.nc.us/

Director of Admissions Mrs. Scottie Dickens, Director of Admissions, Halifax Community College, PO Drawer 809, Weldon, NC 27890-0809. *Phone:* 252-536-7220.

HAYWOOD COMMUNITY COLLEGE
Clyde, North Carolina   www.haywood.edu/

Director of Admissions Ms. Debbie Rowland, Coordinator of Admissions, Haywood Community College, 185 Freedlander Drive, Clyde, NC 28721-9453. *Phone:* 828-627-4505.

ISOTHERMAL COMMUNITY COLLEGE
Spindale, North Carolina   www.isothermal.edu/

- **State-supported** 2-year, founded 1965, part of North Carolina Community College System
- **Rural** 120-acre campus
- **Coed,** 2,005 undergraduate students, 49% full-time, 65% women, 35% men

Undergraduates 988 full-time, 1,017 part-time. Students come from 40 states and territories, 3 other countries, 16% African American, 0.3% Asian American or Pacific Islander, 0.9% Hispanic American, 0.3% Native American, 0.3% international. *Retention:* 33% of 2003 full-time freshmen returned.

Freshmen *Admission:* 274 enrolled.

Faculty *Total:* 114, 53% full-time, 7% with terminal degrees. *Student/faculty ratio:* 17:1.

Majors Administrative assistant and secretarial science; automobile/automotive mechanics technology; biological and physical sciences; broadcast journalism;

business administration and management; business teacher education; commercial and advertising art; computer programming; computer science; cosmetology; criminal justice/law enforcement administration; criminal justice/police science; drafting and design technology; education; electrical, electronic and communications engineering technology; elementary education; insurance; kindergarten/preschool education; liberal arts and sciences/liberal studies; machine tool technology; marketing/marketing management; mechanical design technology; mechanical engineering/mechanical technology; music; nursing (licensed practical/vocational nurse training); pharmacy; plastics engineering technology; pre-engineering; radio and television; real estate; teacher assistant/aide; trade and industrial teacher education; veterinary sciences; welding technology.

Academics *Calendar:* semesters. *Degree:* certificates, diplomas, and associate. *Special study options:* academic remediation for entering students, adult/continuing education programs, advanced placement credit, cooperative education, English as a second language, external degree program, honors programs, part-time degree program, services for LD students, student-designed majors, summer session for credit.

Library 35,200 titles, 289 serial subscriptions, an OPAC, a Web page.

Student Life *Housing:* college housing not available. *Activities and Organizations:* student-run newspaper, radio station, choral group. *Student services:* personal/psychological counseling.

Athletics *Intramural sports:* basketball M/W, football M/W, volleyball M/W.

Standardized Tests *Required:* ACT ASSET (for placement).

Costs (2007–08) *Tuition:* state resident $1008 full-time, $42 per credit hour part-time; nonresident $5599 full-time, $233 per credit hour part-time. *Required fees:* $38 full-time, $19 per term part-time.

Financial Aid Of all full-time matriculated undergraduates, 21 Federal Work-Study jobs (averaging $2365).

Applying *Options:* early admission, deferred entrance. *Required:* high school transcript. *Application deadlines:* rolling (freshmen), rolling (transfers). *Notification:* continuous (freshmen), continuous (transfers).

Freshmen Application Contact Ms. Vickie Searcy, Enrollment Management Office, Isothermal Community College, PO Box 804, Spindale, NC 28160-0804. *Phone:* 828-286-3636 Ext. 251. *Fax:* 828-286-8109. *E-mail:* vsearcy@isothermal.edu.

JAMES SPRUNT COMMUNITY COLLEGE
Kenansville, North Carolina   www.sprunt.com/

- **State-supported** 2-year, founded 1964, part of North Carolina Community College System
- **Rural** 51-acre campus
- **Endowment** $993,945
- **Coed,** 1,192 undergraduate students, 50% full-time, 71% women, 29% men

Undergraduates 601 full-time, 591 part-time. Students come from 2 states and territories, 1% are from out of state, 40% African American, 0.7% Asian American or Pacific Islander, 4% Hispanic American, 0.4% Native American, 7% transferred in.

Freshmen *Admission:* 440 applied, 354 admitted, 354 enrolled.

Faculty *Total:* 128, 48% full-time, 2% with terminal degrees. *Student/faculty ratio:* 22:1.

Majors Accounting; administrative assistant and secretarial science; agribusiness; animal sciences; business administration and management; commercial and advertising art; computer systems analysis; cosmetology; criminal justice/police science; kindergarten/preschool education; liberal arts and sciences/liberal studies; medical/clinical assistant; nursing (registered nurse training).

Academics *Calendar:* semesters. *Degree:* certificates, diplomas, and associate. *Special study options:* academic remediation for entering students, accelerated degree program, advanced placement credit, cooperative education, distance learning, double majors, English as a second language, independent study, internships, part-time degree program, services for LD students, summer session for credit.

Library James Sprunt Community College Library with 27,000 titles, 141 serial subscriptions, 542 audiovisual materials, an OPAC.

Student Life *Housing:* college housing not available. *Activities and Organizations:* student-run newspaper, Student Nurses Association, Art Club, Alumni Association, National Technical-Vocational Honor Society, Phi Theta Kappa. *Campus security:* trained security personnel. *Student services:* personal/psychological counseling.

Athletics *Intercollegiate sports:* softball W, volleyball M/W.

Costs (2006–07) *Tuition:* state resident $1264 full-time, $40 per semester hour part-time; nonresident $7024 full-time, $220 per semester hour part-time. Full-time tuition and fees vary according to course load. Part-time tuition and fees vary according to course load. *Required fees:* $70 full-time, $35 per term part-time. *Waivers:* senior citizens and employees or children of employees.

James Sprunt Community College (continued)

Financial Aid Of all full-time matriculated undergraduates, 55 Federal Work-Study jobs (averaging $1387).

Applying *Options:* electronic application, early admission, deferred entrance. *Required:* high school transcript. *Application deadlines:* rolling (freshmen), rolling (transfers). *Notification:* continuous (freshmen), continuous (transfers).

Freshmen Application Contact Ms. Pat Norris, Registrar, James Sprunt Community College, Highway 11 South, 133 James Sprunt Drive, Kenansville, NC 28349. *Phone:* 910-296-2500. *Fax:* 910-296-1222. *E-mail:* pnorris@jamesprunt.edu.

JOHNSTON COMMUNITY COLLEGE

Smithfield, North Carolina   www.johnston.cc.nc.us/

- **State-supported** 2-year, founded 1969, part of North Carolina Community College System
- **Rural** 100-acre campus
- **Endowment** $2.2 million
- **Coed,** 4,011 undergraduate students, 32% full-time, 63% women, 37% men

Undergraduates 1,270 full-time, 2,741 part-time. Students come from 10 states and territories, 1 other country, 1% are from out of state, 18% African American, 0.6% Asian American or Pacific Islander, 5% Hispanic American, 0.7% Native American.

Freshmen *Admission:* 1,833 enrolled.

Faculty *Total:* 333, 37% full-time, 75% with terminal degrees. *Student/faculty ratio:* 18:1.

Majors Accounting technology and bookkeeping; administrative assistant and secretarial science; business administration and management; commercial and advertising art; computer programming; criminal justice/police science; diesel mechanics technology; electrical, electronic and communications engineering technology; heating, air conditioning, ventilation and refrigeration maintenance technology; kindergarten/preschool education; landscaping and groundskeeping; legal assistant/paralegal; liberal arts and sciences/liberal studies; machine tool technology; medical administrative assistant and medical secretary; medical/clinical assistant; medical radiologic technology; nursing (registered nurse training); operations management.

Academics *Calendar:* semesters. *Degree:* certificates, diplomas, and associate. *Special study options:* academic remediation for entering students, adult/continuing education programs, advanced placement credit, cooperative education, distance learning, double majors, honors programs, independent study, part-time degree program, services for LD students, summer session for credit.

Library Johnston Community College Library plus 1 other with 31,550 titles, 348 serial subscriptions, an OPAC, a Web page.

Student Life *Housing:* college housing not available. *Activities and Organizations:* choral group. *Campus security:* 24-hour patrols. *Student services:* personal/psychological counseling.

Athletics *Intercollegiate sports:* golf M/W, softball M/W, volleyball M/W. *Intramural sports:* basketball M/W.

Standardized Tests *Required:* ACCUPLACER (for admission). *Recommended:* SAT or ACT (for admission).

Costs (2006–07) *Tuition:* state resident $1264 full-time, $40 per credit hour part-time; nonresident $7024 full-time, $220 per credit hour part-time. *Required fees:* $70 full-time, $1 per credit hour part-time, $15 per term part-time.

Financial Aid Of all full-time matriculated undergraduates, 35 Federal Work-Study jobs (averaging $1853).

Applying *Options:* electronic application. *Required:* high school transcript, interview. *Application deadlines:* rolling (freshmen), rolling (transfers). *Notification:* continuous (freshmen), continuous (transfers).

Freshmen Application Contact Dr. Pam Harrell, Dean of Student Services, Johnston Community College, PO Box 2350, Smithfield, NC 27577-2350. *Phone:* 919-209-2048. *Fax:* 919-989-7662. *E-mail:* harrellp@johnstoncc.edu.

KING'S COLLEGE

Charlotte, North Carolina   www.kingscollegecharlotte.edu/

- **Proprietary** 2-year, founded 1901
- **Coed,** 515 undergraduate students
- **90%** of applicants were admitted

Freshmen *Admission:* 691 applied, 620 admitted.

Majors Accounting; administrative assistant and secretarial science; allied health and medical assisting services related; computer programming related; graphic design; legal administrative assistant; legal assistant/paralegal; tourism and travel services management.

Academics *Calendar:* quarters. *Degree:* associate.

Costs (2006–07) *Tuition:* $11,960 full-time.

Applying *Application fee:* $50. *Required:* high school transcript. *Recommended:* letters of recommendation.

Freshmen Application Contact Admissions Office, King's College, 322 Lamar Avenue, Charlotte, NC 28204-2436. *Phone:* 704-688-3613. *Toll-free phone:* 800-768-2255.

LENOIR COMMUNITY COLLEGE

Kinston, North Carolina   www.lenoircc.edu/

- **State-supported** 2-year, founded 1960, part of North Carolina Community College System
- **Small-town** 86-acre campus
- **Coed,** 3,771 undergraduate students

Faculty *Total:* 345, 28% full-time.

Majors Accounting; administrative assistant and secretarial science; agricultural business and management; agriculture; airline pilot and flight crew; art; aviation/airway management; avionics maintenance technology; business administration and management; commercial and advertising art; computer programming; consumer merchandising/retailing management; cosmetology; court reporting; criminal justice/law enforcement administration; criminal justice/police science; drafting and design technology; electrical, electronic and communications engineering technology; elementary education; finance; fire science; food services technology; graphic and printing equipment operation/production; heavy equipment maintenance technology; horticultural science; hydrology and water resources science; industrial technology; instrumentation technology; insurance; landscape architecture; legal administrative assistant/secretary; liberal arts and sciences/liberal studies; library science; marketing/marketing management; mechanical design technology; medical administrative assistant and medical secretary; medical/clinical assistant; mental health/rehabilitation; nursing (registered nurse training); ornamental horticulture; postal management; pre-engineering; trade and industrial teacher education; welding technology.

Academics *Calendar:* semesters. *Degree:* certificates, diplomas, and associate. *Special study options:* academic remediation for entering students, adult/continuing education programs, advanced placement credit, cooperative education, English as a second language, part-time degree program, summer session for credit.

Library Learning Resources Center plus 1 other with 55,053 titles, 381 serial subscriptions.

Student Life *Housing:* college housing not available. *Activities and Organizations:* student-run newspaper, choral group, Student Government Association, Automotive Club, Electronics Club, Drafting Club, Cosmetology Club. *Campus security:* 24-hour emergency response devices and patrols, student patrols. *Student services:* personal/psychological counseling.

Athletics Member NJCAA. *Intercollegiate sports:* baseball M, basketball M(s), volleyball M/W. *Intramural sports:* basketball M, softball W, volleyball M/W.

Standardized Tests *Required:* Assessment and Placement Services for Community Colleges (for placement). *Recommended:* SAT or ACT (for placement).

Costs (2007–08) *Tuition:* state resident $1000 full-time, $42 per credit hour part-time; nonresident $55,176 full-time, $216 per credit hour part-time.

Applying *Options:* early admission. *Required:* high school transcript. *Application deadlines:* rolling (freshmen), rolling (transfers). *Notification:* continuous (freshmen), continuous (transfers).

Freshmen Application Contact Ms. Tammy Buck, Director of Enrollment Management, Lenoir Community College, PO Box 188, Kinston, NC 28502-0188. *Phone:* 252-527-6223 Ext. 309. *Fax:* 252-526-5112. *E-mail:* tbuck@lenoircc.edu.

LOUISBURG COLLEGE

Louisburg, North Carolina   www.louisburg.edu/

- **Independent United Methodist** 2-year, founded 1787
- **Small-town** 75-acre campus with easy access to Raleigh
- **Endowment** $6.8 million
- **Coed,** 502 undergraduate students, 98% full-time, 42% women, 58% men

Undergraduates 494 full-time, 8 part-time. Students come from 21 states and territories, 4 other countries, 19% are from out of state, 46% African American,

0.4% Asian American or Pacific Islander, 3% Hispanic American, 1% international, 10% transferred in, 90% live on campus. *Retention:* 68% of 2003 full-time freshmen returned.

Freshmen *Admission:* 725 applied, 723 admitted, 321 enrolled. *Average high school GPA:* 2.34. *Test scores:* SAT verbal scores over 500: 10%; SAT math scores over 500: 10%; ACT scores over 18: 50%; SAT verbal scores over 600: 2%; SAT math scores over 600: 3%; SAT math scores over 700: 1%.

Faculty *Total:* 46, 59% full-time. *Student/faculty ratio:* 15:1.

Majors Athletic training; biological and physical sciences; biology/biological sciences; biology teacher education; business administration and management; business/commerce; business teacher education; chemistry; chemistry teacher education; clinical laboratory science/medical technology; computer science; dance; economics; education (multiple levels); elementary education; English; English/language arts teacher education; health and physical education; history; information science/studies; liberal arts and sciences/liberal studies; management science; mathematics; mathematics teacher education; nursing (registered nurse training); occupational therapy; physical therapy; physics; political science and government; pre-engineering; pre-law studies; pre-medical studies; pre-pharmacy studies; pre-veterinary studies; psychology; sales and marketing/marketing and distribution teacher education; social science teacher education; social work; sociology; special education; speech and rhetoric; sport and fitness administration/management.

Academics *Calendar:* semesters. *Degree:* associate. *Special study options:* academic remediation for entering students, adult/continuing education programs, advanced placement credit, English as a second language, part-time degree program, services for LD students, summer session for credit.

Library Robbins Library with 64,000 titles, 150 serial subscriptions.

Student Life *Housing:* on-campus residence required through sophomore year. *Options:* men-only, women-only. *Activities and Organizations:* drama/theater group, student-run newspaper, radio station, choral group, Student Government Association, Workers Actively Volunteering Energetic Services, Drama Club, Christian Life Council, Ecological Concerns Club. *Campus security:* 24-hour emergency response devices and patrols, controlled dormitory access. *Student services:* health clinic, personal/psychological counseling.

Athletics Member NJCAA. *Intercollegiate sports:* baseball M(s), basketball M(s)/W(s), golf M/W, soccer M(s)/W(s), softball W(s), volleyball M/W. *Intramural sports:* basketball M/W, football M/W, soccer M/W, softball M/W, table tennis M/W, tennis M, volleyball M/W.

Standardized Tests *Required:* SAT or ACT (for admission).

Costs (2006–07) *Comprehensive fee:* $18,540 includes full-time tuition ($10,540), mandatory fees ($1110), and room and board ($6890). Full-time tuition and fees vary according to course load. Part-time tuition: $440 per semester hour. Part-time tuition and fees vary according to course load. *Required fees:* $30 per semester hour part-time. *Room and board:* Room and board charges vary according to housing facility. *Waivers:* children of alumni and employees or children of employees.

Financial Aid Of all full-time matriculated undergraduates, 100 Federal Work-Study jobs (averaging $1200).

Applying *Options:* deferred entrance. *Application fee:* $25. *Required:* high school transcript. *Required for some:* letters of recommendation, interview. *Application deadlines:* rolling (freshmen), rolling (transfers). *Notification:* continuous (freshmen), continuous (transfers).

Freshmen Application Contact Ms. Stephanie Buchanan, Director of Admissions, Louisburg College, 501 North Main Street, Louisburg, NC 27549-2399. *Phone:* 919-497-3228. *Toll-free phone:* 800-775-0208. *Fax:* 919-496-1788. *E-mail:* admissions@louisburg.edu.

MARTIN COMMUNITY COLLEGE
Williamston, North Carolina   **www.martin.cc.nc.us/**

- **State-supported** 2-year, founded 1968, part of North Carolina Community College System
- **Rural** 65-acre campus
- **Endowment** $32,015
- **Coed**, 834 undergraduate students, 34% full-time, 73% women, 27% men

Undergraduates 281 full-time, 553 part-time. Students come from 1 other state, 1 other country, 1% are from out of state, 54% African American, 0.7% Hispanic American, 0.2% Native American, 11% transferred in.

Freshmen *Admission:* 134 applied, 134 admitted, 123 enrolled. *Average high school GPA:* 2.4.

Faculty *Total:* 59, 47% full-time. *Student/faculty ratio:* 14:1.

Majors Accounting; administrative assistant and secretarial science; automobile/automotive mechanics technology; business administration and management; cosmetology; dietitian assistant; electrical and power transmission installation related; electromechanical technology; equestrian studies; general studies; heating, air conditioning and refrigeration technology; heating, air conditioning,

ventilation and refrigeration maintenance technology; information science/studies; liberal arts and sciences and humanities related; liberal arts and sciences/liberal studies; management information systems; management information systems and services related; medical administrative assistant and medical secretary; medical/clinical assistant; physical therapist assistant.

Academics *Calendar:* semesters. *Degree:* certificates, diplomas, and associate. *Special study options:* academic remediation for entering students, advanced placement credit, distance learning, English as a second language, independent study, internships, off-campus study, part-time degree program, services for LD students, summer session for credit.

Library Martin Community College Learning Resources Center with 36,443 titles, 215 serial subscriptions, 10,809 audiovisual materials, an OPAC.

Student Life *Housing:* college housing not available. *Activities and Organizations:* Phi Theta Kappa, Student Government Association, Alpha Beta Gamma, Physical Therapy Club, Equine Club. *Campus security:* 24-hour emergency response devices, part-time patrols by trained security personnel. *Student services:* personal/psychological counseling.

Standardized Tests *Required for some:* ACT COMPASS.

Costs (2006–07) *Tuition:* state resident $1264 full-time; nonresident $7024 full-time.

Financial Aid Of all full-time matriculated undergraduates, 30 Federal Work-Study jobs (averaging $1200).

Applying *Required:* high school transcript. *Required for some:* interview. *Application deadlines:* rolling (freshmen), rolling (transfers). *Notification:* continuous until 8/17 (freshmen), continuous until 8/17 (transfers).

Director of Admissions Ms. Sonya C. Atkinson, Registrar and Admissions Officer, Martin Community College, 1161 Kehukee Park Road, Williamston, NC 27892. *Phone:* 252-792-1521 Ext. 243.

MAYLAND COMMUNITY COLLEGE
Spruce Pine, North Carolina   **www.mayland.edu**

Director of Admissions Ms. Cathy Morrison, Director of Admissions, Mayland Community College, PO Box 547, Spruce Pine, NC 28777. *Phone:* 828-765-7351 Ext. 224.

MCDOWELL TECHNICAL COMMUNITY COLLEGE
Marion, North Carolina   **www.mcdowelltech.cc.nc.us/**

Freshmen Application Contact Mr. Rick L. Wilson, Director of Admissions, McDowell Technical Community College, Route 1, Box 170, Marion, NC 28752-9724. *Phone:* 828-652-0632. *Fax:* 828-652-1014. *E-mail:* rickw@mcdowelltech.edu.

MITCHELL COMMUNITY COLLEGE
Statesville, North Carolina   **www.mitchell.cc.nc.us/**

Freshmen Application Contact Mr. Doug Rhoney, Counselor, Mitchell Community College, 500 West Broad, Statesville, NC 28677-5293. *Phone:* 704-878-3280.

MONTGOMERY COMMUNITY COLLEGE
Troy, North Carolina   **www.montgomery.edu/**

- **State-supported** 2-year, founded 1967, part of North Carolina Community College System
- **Rural** 159-acre campus
- **Coed**

Undergraduates 391 full-time, 459 part-time. Students come from 4 states and territories, 1% are from out of state, 24% African American, 2% Asian American or Pacific Islander, 4% Hispanic American, 0.7% Native American, 0.2% international, 14% transferred in.

Academics *Calendar:* semesters. *Degree:* certificates, diplomas, and associate. *Special study options:* academic remediation for entering students, advanced placement credit, cooperative education, distance learning, double majors, English as a second language, part-time degree program, services for LD students, summer session for credit.

Montgomery Community College (continued)

Financial Aid Of all full-time matriculated undergraduates, 24 Federal Work-Study jobs (averaging $500).

Applying *Options:* early admission, deferred entrance. *Required:* high school transcript.

Freshmen Application Contact Ms. Karen Frye, Admissions Officer, Montgomery Community College, 1011 Page Street, Troy, NC 27371. *Phone:* 910-576-6222 Ext. 240. *Toll-free phone:* 800-839-6222. *E-mail:* fryek@montgomery.edu.

NASH COMMUNITY COLLEGE
Rocky Mount, North Carolina   www.nash.cc.nc.us/

Freshmen Application Contact Ms. Dorothy Gardner, Admissions Officer, Nash Community College, PO Box 7488, Rocky Mount, NC 27804-0488. *Phone:* 252-451-8300. *E-mail:* dgardner@nashcc.edu.

PAMLICO COMMUNITY COLLEGE
Grantsboro, North Carolina   www.pamlico.cc.nc.us/

- **State-supported** 2-year, founded 1963, part of North Carolina Community College System
- **Rural** 44-acre campus
- **Coed,** 300 undergraduate students

Faculty *Total:* 10, 60% full-time.

Majors Accounting; administrative assistant and secretarial science; automobile/automotive mechanics technology; business administration and management; clinical/medical laboratory technology; computer engineering technology; electrical, electronic and communications engineering technology; environmental studies; liberal arts and sciences/liberal studies; medical/clinical assistant; neuroscience.

Academics *Calendar:* semesters. *Degree:* certificates, diplomas, and associate. *Special study options:* academic remediation for entering students, adult/continuing education programs, cooperative education, part-time degree program, services for LD students, summer session for credit.

Library Pamlico Community College Library plus 1 other with 19,500 titles, 202 serial subscriptions.

Student Life *Housing:* college housing not available. *Activities and Organizations:* student-run newspaper. *Campus security:* evening security guard. *Student services:* personal/psychological counseling.

Athletics *Intramural sports:* softball M/W, volleyball M/W.

Standardized Tests *Required:* ACT ASSET (for placement).

Costs (2006–07) *Tuition:* state resident $1264 full-time; nonresident $7024 full-time.

Financial Aid Of all full-time matriculated undergraduates, 15 Federal Work-Study jobs (averaging $4353).

Applying *Options:* early admission, deferred entrance. *Required:* high school transcript. *Application deadlines:* rolling (freshmen), rolling (transfers). *Notification:* continuous (freshmen), continuous (transfers).

Director of Admissions Mr. Floyd H. Hardison, Admissions Counselor, Pamlico Community College, PO Box 185, Grantsboro, NC 28529-0185. *Phone:* 252-249-1851 Ext. 28.

PIEDMONT COMMUNITY COLLEGE
Roxboro, North Carolina   www.piedmont.cc.nc.us/

Director of Admissions Ms. Sheila Williamson, Director of Admissions, Piedmont Community College, PO Box 1197, 1715 College Drive, Roxboro, NC 27573. *Phone:* 336-599-1181 Ext. 219.

PITT COMMUNITY COLLEGE
Greenville, North Carolina   www.pittcc.edu/

Freshmen Application Contact Ms. Mary Tate, Director of Counseling, Pitt Community College, PO Drawer 7007, 1986 Pitt Tech Road, Greenville, NC 27835-7007. *Phone:* 252-321-4217. *Fax:* 252-321-4612. *E-mail:* pittadm@pcc.pitt.cc.nc.us.

RANDOLPH COMMUNITY COLLEGE
Asheboro, North Carolina   www.randolph.edu/

Freshmen Application Contact Mrs. Carol M. Elmore, Director of Admissions and Registrar, Randolph Community College, PO Box 1009, Asheboro, NC 27204-1009. *Phone:* 336-633-0213. *Fax:* 336-629-4695. *E-mail:* info@randolph.edu.

RICHMOND COMMUNITY COLLEGE
Hamlet, North Carolina   www.richmondcc.edu/

- **State-supported** 2-year, founded 1964, part of North Carolina Community College System
- **Rural** 163-acre campus
- **Endowment** $1.0 million
- **Coed**

Undergraduates 691 full-time, 781 part-time. Students come from 3 states and territories, 0.5% are from out of state, 32% African American, 1% Asian American or Pacific Islander, 0.9% Hispanic American, 9% Native American, 7% transferred in.

Faculty *Student/faculty ratio:* 29:1.

Academics *Calendar:* semesters. *Degree:* diplomas and associate. *Special study options:* academic remediation for entering students, adult/continuing education programs, advanced placement credit, cooperative education, distance learning, double majors, English as a second language, independent study, internships, part-time degree program, student-designed majors, summer session for credit.

Student Life *Campus security:* 24-hour emergency response devices, security guard during evening hours.

Costs (2006–07) *Tuition:* state resident $1264 full-time, $40 per credit hour part-time; nonresident $7024 full-time, $220 per credit hour part-time. *Required fees:* $38 full-time, $12 per term part-time.

Financial Aid Of all full-time matriculated undergraduates, 35 Federal Work-Study jobs (averaging $2000).

Applying *Options:* deferred entrance. *Required:* high school transcript.

Freshmen Application Contact Ms. Wanda Watts, Director of Admissions/Registrar, Richmond Community College, PO Box 1189, Hamlet, NC 28345. *Phone:* 910-582-7113. *Fax:* 910-582-7102.

ROANOKE-CHOWAN COMMUNITY COLLEGE
Ahoskie, North Carolina   www.roanokechowan.edu/

Director of Admissions Miss Sandra Copeland, Director, Counseling Services, Roanoke-Chowan Community College, 109 Community College Road, Ahoskie, NC 27910. *Phone:* 252-862-1225.

ROBESON COMMUNITY COLLEGE
Lumberton, North Carolina   www.robeson.cc.nc.us/

- **State-supported** 2-year, founded 1965, part of North Carolina Community College System
- **Small-town** 78-acre campus
- **Coed,** 2,313 undergraduate students

Faculty *Total:* 114, 39% full-time.

Majors Administrative assistant and secretarial science; business administration and management; computer and information sciences; computer and information sciences and support services related; computer systems networking and telecommunications; criminal justice/law enforcement administration; early childhood education; electrical, electronic and communications engineering technology; food services technology; industrial technology; nursing (registered nurse training); respiratory care therapy.

Academics *Calendar:* semesters. *Degree:* associate. *Special study options:* adult/continuing education programs, services for LD students.

Library 39,000 titles, 225 serial subscriptions.

Student Life *Housing:* college housing not available. *Student services:* personal/psychological counseling.

Standardized Tests *Required:* ACT ASSET, ACT COMPASS (for placement).

Costs (2007–08) *Tuition:* state resident $1344 full-time, $42 per credit hour part-time; nonresident $7466 full-time, $233 per credit hour part-time. *Required fees:* $60 full-time, $30 per term part-time.

Applying *Options:* early admission. *Application deadlines:* rolling (freshmen), rolling (transfers). *Notification:* continuous (freshmen), continuous (transfers).

Freshmen Application Contact Ms. Judy Revels, Director of Admissions, Robeson Community College, PO Box 1420, 5160 Fayetteville Road, Lumberton, NC 28359. *Phone:* 910-618-5680 Ext. 251.

ROCKINGHAM COMMUNITY COLLEGE

Wentworth, North Carolina   www.rcc.cc.nc.us/

- **State-supported** 2-year, founded 1964, part of North Carolina Community College System
- **Rural** 257-acre campus
- **Coed**

Undergraduates 604 full-time, 1,432 part-time. Students come from 9 states and territories, 1 other country, 5% are from out of state, 21% African American, 0.6% Asian American or Pacific Islander, 1% Hispanic American, 0.5% Native American, 0.4% international.

Faculty *Student/faculty ratio:* 18:1.

Academics *Calendar:* semesters. *Degree:* certificates, diplomas, and associate. *Special study options:* academic remediation for entering students, adult/continuing education programs, advanced placement credit, cooperative education, part-time degree program, student-designed majors, summer session for credit.

Student Life *Campus security:* late-night transport/escort service.

Athletics Member NJCAA.

Costs (2006–07) *Tuition:* state resident $1264 full-time, $40 per credit hour part-time; nonresident $7024 full-time, $292 per credit hour part-time. Full-time tuition and fees vary according to course load. Part-time tuition and fees vary according to course load. *Required fees:* $69 full-time.

Financial Aid Of all full-time matriculated undergraduates, 37 Federal Work-Study jobs (averaging $2300).

Applying *Options:* early admission, deferred entrance.

Freshmen Application Contact Mrs. Leigh Hawkins, Director of Enrollment Services, Rockingham Community College, PO Box 38, Wentworth, NC 27375-0038. *Phone:* 336-342-4261 Ext. 2333. *Fax:* 336-342-1809.

ROWAN-CABARRUS COMMUNITY COLLEGE

Salisbury, North Carolina   www.rccc.cc.nc.us/

Freshmen Application Contact Mrs. Gail Cummins, Director of Admissions and Recruitment, Rowan-Cabarrus Community College, PO Box 1595, Salisbury, NC 28145. *Phone:* 704-637-0760. *Fax:* 704-633-6804.

SAMPSON COMMUNITY COLLEGE

Clinton, North Carolina   www.sampsoncc.edu/

- **State and locally supported** 2-year, founded 1965, part of North Carolina Community College System
- **Rural** 55-acre campus
- **Coed,** 1,579 undergraduate students, 43% full-time, 73% women, 27% men

Undergraduates 679 full-time, 900 part-time. Students come from 4 states and territories, 1% are from out of state, 37% African American, 3% Hispanic American, 2% Native American, 1% transferred in.

Freshmen *Admission:* 712 applied, 712 admitted, 447 enrolled.

Faculty *Total:* 95, 47% full-time, 1% with terminal degrees. *Student/faculty ratio:* 20:1.

Majors Accounting; administrative assistant and secretarial science; business administration and management; computer and information sciences; computer programming; criminal justice/law enforcement administration; horticultural science; industrial technology; information technology; liberal arts and sciences/liberal studies; nursing (licensed practical/vocational nurse training); nursing (registered nurse training); poultry science; system administration; word processing.

Academics *Calendar:* semesters. *Degree:* certificates, diplomas, and associate. *Special study options:* academic remediation for entering students, adult/continuing education programs, advanced placement credit, cooperative education, independent study, internships, part-time degree program, services for LD students, summer session for credit.

Library Sampson Community College Library with 25,000 titles, 250 serial subscriptions, an OPAC, a Web page.

Student Life *Housing:* college housing not available. *Activities and Organizations:* Student Government Association, Criminal Justice Club, Nursing Student Association, Cosmetology Alliance Club, Phi Beta Lambda. *Campus security:* local police patrol. *Student services:* personal/psychological counseling.

Athletics *Intramural sports:* basketball M, volleyball M/W.

Standardized Tests *Required:* ACT ASSET (for placement).

Costs (2006–07) *Tuition:* state resident $1332 full-time; nonresident $7092 full-time.

Financial Aid Of all full-time matriculated undergraduates, 37 Federal Work-Study jobs (averaging $1201). 8 state and other part-time jobs (averaging $463).

Applying *Options:* deferred entrance. *Required:* high school transcript, interview. *Recommended:* minimum 2.0 GPA. *Application deadlines:* rolling (freshmen), rolling (transfers). *Notification:* continuous (freshmen), continuous (transfers).

Director of Admissions Mr. William R. Jordan, Director of Admissions, Sampson Community College, PO Box 318, 1801 Sunset Avenue, Highway 24 West, Clinton, NC 28329. *Phone:* 910-592-8084 Ext. 2022.

SANDHILLS COMMUNITY COLLEGE

Pinehurst, North Carolina   www.sandhills.edu/

- **State and locally supported** 2-year, founded 1963, part of North Carolina Community College System
- **Small-town** campus
- **Endowment** $4.1 million
- **Coed,** 3,535 undergraduate students

Undergraduates Students come from 42 states and territories, 23 other countries, 1% are from out of state, 28% African American, 0.6% Asian American or Pacific Islander, 1% Hispanic American, 6% Native American.

Faculty *Total:* 178, 66% full-time. *Student/faculty ratio:* 18:1.

Majors Accounting; administrative assistant and secretarial science; architectural engineering technology; art; art teacher education; automobile/automotive mechanics technology; biological and physical sciences; business administration and management; business, management, and marketing related; child development; civil engineering technology; clinical/medical laboratory technology; computer engineering related; computer engineering technology; computer/information technology services administration related; computer programming; computer programming (specific applications); cosmetology; criminal justice/law enforcement administration; criminal justice/police science; culinary arts; fine/studio arts; gerontology; hotel/motel administration; human services; information science/studies; kindergarten/preschool education; landscaping and groundskeeping; liberal arts and sciences/liberal studies; mathematics; medical administrative assistant and medical secretary; mental health/rehabilitation; music; music teacher education; nursing assistant/aide and patient care assistant; nursing (licensed practical/vocational nurse training); nursing (registered nurse training); pre-engineering; radiologic technology/science; respiratory care therapy; science teacher education; substance abuse/addiction counseling; surgical technology; survey technology; system administration; teacher assistant/aide; turf and turfgrass management; web/multimedia management and webmaster.

Academics *Calendar:* semesters. *Degree:* certificates, diplomas, and associate. *Special study options:* academic remediation for entering students, advanced placement credit, cooperative education, distance learning, double majors, honors programs, independent study, internships, part-time degree program, services for LD students, summer session for credit.

Library Boyd Library with 76,080 titles, 286 serial subscriptions, 2,317 audiovisual materials, an OPAC, a Web page.

Student Life *Housing:* college housing not available. *Activities and Organizations:* student-run newspaper, choral group, Student Government Association, Minority Students for Academic and Cultural Enrichment, Circle K. *Campus security:* 24-hour emergency response devices, security on duty until 12 a.m. *Student services:* personal/psychological counseling.

Standardized Tests *Required:* ACT ASSET or ACT COMPASS (for placement).

Costs (2007–08) *Tuition:* state resident $1008 full-time, $42 per credit hour part-time; nonresident $5599 full-time, $233 per credit hour part-time. *Required fees:* $70 full-time, $35 per term part-time.

Financial Aid Of all full-time matriculated undergraduates, 59 Federal Work-Study jobs (averaging $1750).

Applying *Options:* deferred entrance. *Required:* high school transcript. *Application deadlines:* rolling (freshmen), rolling (transfers). *Notification:* continuous (freshmen), continuous (transfers).

Sandhills Community College (continued)

Freshmen Application Contact Ms. Rosa McAllister-McRae, Admissions Coordinator/Counselor, Sandhills Community College, 3395 Airport Road, Pinehurst, NC 28374. *Phone:* 910-695-3729. *Toll-free phone:* 800-338-3944. *E-mail:* mcallisterr@sandhills.edu.

SCHOOL OF COMMUNICATION ARTS
Raleigh, North Carolina   www.higherdigital.com/

- **Proprietary** 2-year, founded 1992
- **Coed,** 298 undergraduate students

Majors Animation, interactive technology, video graphics and special effects; digital communication and media/multimedia; Web page, digital/multimedia and information resources design.

Academics *Calendar:* quarters. *Degree:* associate.

Costs (2006–07) *Tuition:* $17,652 full-time.

Applying *Application fee:* $25.

Admissions Office Contact School of Communication Arts, 3000 Wakefield Crossing Drive, Raleigh, NC 27614. *Toll-free phone:* 800-288-7442.

SOUTH COLLEGE-ASHEVILLE
Asheville, North Carolina   www.southcollegenc.com/

Freshmen Application Contact Mr. Robert Hayden, Director of Admissions, South College-Asheville, 1567 Patton Avenue, Asheville, NC 28806. *Phone:* 828-277-5521. *Fax:* 828-277-6151.

SOUTHEASTERN COMMUNITY COLLEGE
Whiteville, North Carolina   www.sccnc.edu/

- **State-supported** 2-year, founded 1964, part of North Carolina Community College System
- **Rural** 106-acre campus
- **Coed,** 1,949 undergraduate students, 91% full-time, 65% women, 35% men

Undergraduates 1,780 full-time, 169 part-time. Students come from 2 states and territories, 2 other countries, 1% are from out of state, 26% African American, 4% Native American, 0.1% international. *Retention:* 33% of 2003 full-time freshmen returned.

Freshmen *Admission:* 890 applied, 890 admitted.

Faculty *Total:* 91, 82% full-time, 1% with terminal degrees. *Student/faculty ratio:* 20:1.

Majors Administrative assistant and secretarial science; art; biological and physical sciences; biotechnology; business administration and management; clinical/medical laboratory technology; computer engineering technology; cosmetology; criminal justice/law enforcement administration; electrical, electronic and communications engineering technology; environmental studies; forestry technology; industrial technology; kindergarten/preschool education; liberal arts and sciences/liberal studies; music; nursing (registered nurse training); parks, recreation and leisure; parks, recreation and leisure facilities management; teacher assistant/aide; welding technology.

Academics *Calendar:* semesters. *Degree:* certificates, diplomas, and associate. *Special study options:* academic remediation for entering students, adult/continuing education programs, advanced placement credit, cooperative education, distance learning, double majors, English as a second language, honors programs, independent study, internships, part-time degree program, services for LD students, summer session for credit.

Library Southeastern Community College Library with 50,297 titles, 192 serial subscriptions, an OPAC.

Student Life *Housing:* college housing not available. *Activities and Organizations:* drama/theater group, choral group, Student Government Association, Forestry Club, Nursing Club, Environmental Club. *Campus security:* 24-hour emergency response devices. *Student services:* personal/psychological counseling.

Athletics Member NJCAA. *Intercollegiate sports:* baseball M(s), softball W, squash W, volleyball W(s).

Costs (2006–07) *Tuition:* state resident $1264 full-time, $40 per credit part-time; nonresident $7024 full-time, $220 per credit part-time. *Required fees:* $65 full-time, $33 per term part-time. *Payment plan:* installment.

Financial Aid Of all full-time matriculated undergraduates, 80 Federal Work-Study jobs (averaging $1580).

Applying *Options:* electronic application, early admission, deferred entrance. *Required:* high school transcript. *Application deadlines:* rolling (freshmen), rolling (transfers).

Freshmen Application Contact Ms. Sylvia Tart, Registrar, Southeastern Community College, PO Box 151, Whiteville, NC 28472. *Phone:* 910-642-7141 Ext. 249. *Fax:* 910-642-5658. *E-mail:* start@sccnc.edu.

SOUTH PIEDMONT COMMUNITY COLLEGE
Polkton, North Carolina   www.spcc.edu/

- **State-supported** 2-year, founded 1962, part of North Carolina Community College System
- **Rural** 56-acre campus with easy access to Charlotte
- **Endowment** $27,818
- **Coed,** 2,075 undergraduate students

Undergraduates Students come from 3 states and territories, 1% are from out of state, 50% African American, 0.5% Asian American or Pacific Islander, 0.9% Hispanic American, 0.6% Native American, 0.3% international.

Freshmen *Admission:* 740 applied, 618 admitted.

Faculty *Total:* 106. *Student/faculty ratio:* 17:1.

Majors Accounting technology and bookkeeping; automobile/automotive mechanics technology; business administration and management; commercial and advertising art; computer programming (specific applications); computer systems analysis; computer systems networking and telecommunications; criminal justice/police science; drafting and design technology; electrical, electronic and communications engineering technology; electromechanical technology; executive assistant/executive secretary; health information/medical records technology; heating, air conditioning and refrigeration technology; legal administrative assistant/secretary; legal assistant/paralegal; liberal arts and sciences/liberal studies; machine tool technology; mechanical engineering/mechanical technology; medical administrative assistant and medical secretary; medical/clinical assistant; operations management; psychiatric/mental health services technology; social work.

Academics *Calendar:* semesters. *Degree:* certificates, diplomas, and associate. *Special study options:* academic remediation for entering students, accelerated degree program, adult/continuing education programs, cooperative education, English as a second language, independent study, internships, off-campus study, part-time degree program, services for LD students, summer session for credit.

Library Martin Learning Resource Center with 18,917 titles, 170 serial subscriptions, an OPAC.

Student Life *Activities and Organizations:* choral group, student association, Phi Beta Lambda, Phi Theta Kappa, Social Services Club, Criminal Justice Club. *Campus security:* 24-hour emergency response devices and patrols, evening security. *Student services:* personal/psychological counseling, women's center.

Standardized Tests *Required for some:* CAT, CPT. *Recommended:* CAT, CPT.

Costs (2007–08) *Tuition:* state resident $1185 full-time, $40 per semester hour part-time; nonresident $6585 full-time, $220 per semester hour part-time. *Required fees:* $66 full-time, $33 per term part-time.

Financial Aid Of all full-time matriculated undergraduates, 50 Federal Work-Study jobs (averaging $2500).

Applying *Options:* electronic application, early admission, deferred entrance. *Required:* high school transcript. *Application deadlines:* rolling (freshmen), rolling (transfers). *Notification:* continuous (freshmen), continuous (transfers).

Freshmen Application Contact Ms. Jeania Martin, Admissions Coordinator, South Piedmont Community College, PO Box 126, Polkton, NC 28135. *Phone:* 704-272-7635. *Toll-free phone:* 800-766-0319. *E-mail:* abaucom@vnet.net.

SOUTHWESTERN COMMUNITY COLLEGE
Sylva, North Carolina   www.southwest.cc.nc.us/

- **State-supported** 2-year, founded 1964, part of North Carolina Community College System
- **Small-town** 77-acre campus
- **Endowment** $2.2 million
- **Coed,** 2,065 undergraduate students, 41% full-time, 64% women, 36% men

Undergraduates 841 full-time, 1,224 part-time. Students come from 7 states and territories, 1 other country, 1% are from out of state, 1% African American, 0.6% Asian American or Pacific Islander, 2% Hispanic American, 8% Native American, 0.7% international, 21% transferred in.

Freshmen *Admission:* 279 enrolled. *Average high school GPA:* 2.9. *Test scores:* SAT verbal scores over 500: 5%; SAT math scores over 500: 5%; ACT scores over 18: 20%.

Faculty *Total:* 260, 28% full-time, 6% with terminal degrees. *Student/faculty ratio:* 11:1.

Majors Accounting; administrative assistant and secretarial science; automobile/automotive mechanics technology; business administration and management; child development; clinical/medical laboratory technology; commercial and advertising art; computer engineering technology; cosmetology; criminal justice/police science; culinary arts; electrical, electronic and communications engineering technology; emergency medical technology (EMT paramedic); environmental studies; health information/medical records administration; health information/medical records technology; information science/studies; legal assistant/paralegal; liberal arts and sciences/liberal studies; marketing/marketing management; massage therapy; medical radiologic technology; mental health/rehabilitation; nursing (licensed practical/vocational nurse training); nursing (registered nurse training); parks, recreation, and leisure related; physical therapist assistant; physical therapy; respiratory care therapy; substance abuse/addiction counseling; system, networking, and LAN/WAN management; trade and industrial teacher education.

Academics *Calendar:* semesters. *Degree:* certificates, diplomas, and associate. *Special study options:* academic remediation for entering students, adult/continuing education programs, cooperative education, distance learning, double majors, English as a second language, independent study, off-campus study, part-time degree program, services for LD students, summer session for credit.

Library Southwestern Community College Library with 37,860 titles, 166 serial subscriptions, 1,603 audiovisual materials, an OPAC, a Web page.

Student Life *Housing:* college housing not available. *Activities and Organizations:* Electronics Club, EMT Club, HIT Club, Cyber Crime Club, National Vocational-Technical Honor Society. *Campus security:* security during hours college is open. *Student services:* personal/psychological counseling.

Standardized Tests *Recommended:* SAT or ACT (for admission).

Costs (2006–07) *Tuition:* state resident $1106 full-time, $39 per credit hour part-time; nonresident $6146 full-time, $219 per credit hour part-time. *Required fees:* $65 full-time, $2 per credit hour part-time.

Financial Aid Of all full-time matriculated undergraduates, 55 Federal Work-Study jobs (averaging $900).

Applying *Options:* early admission, deferred entrance. *Required:* high school transcript. *Required for some:* minimum 2.0 GPA, letters of recommendation, interview. *Application deadlines:* rolling (freshmen), rolling (transfers). *Notification:* continuous (freshmen), continuous (transfers).

Freshmen Application Contact Mr. Delos Monteith, Institutional Research and Planning Officer, Southwestern Community College, 447 College Drive, Sylva, NC 28779. *Phone:* 828-586-4091 Ext. 236. *Toll-free phone:* 800-447-4091. *Fax:* 828-586-3129. *E-mail:* delos@southwesterncc.edu.

STANLY COMMUNITY COLLEGE

Albemarle, North Carolina　　　　　**www.stanly.edu/**

- **State-supported** 2-year, founded 1971, part of North Carolina Community College System
- **Small-town** 150-acre campus with easy access to Charlotte
- **Coed,** 2,000 undergraduate students

Undergraduates Students come from 13 states and territories, 3 other countries, 3% are from out of state.

Freshmen *Admission:* 642 applied, 642 admitted.

Faculty *Total:* 106, 50% full-time. *Student/faculty ratio:* 9:1.

Majors Accounting technology and bookkeeping; autobody/collision and repair technology; biomedical technology; business administration and management; child care and support services management; computer hardware engineering; computer/information technology services administration related; computer programming related; computer programming (specific applications); computer systems networking and telecommunications; computer/technical support; computer technology/computer systems technology; cosmetology; criminal justice/police science; electrical, electronic and communications engineering technology; executive assistant/executive secretary; human services; industrial technology; information science/studies; legal administrative assistant/secretary; mechanical drafting and CAD/CADD; medical administrative assistant and medical secretary; medical/clinical assistant; nursing (registered nurse training); occupational therapist assistant; physical therapist assistant; respiratory care therapy; system administration; web/multimedia management and webmaster; web page, digital/multimedia and information resources design; word processing.

Academics *Calendar:* semesters. *Degree:* certificates, diplomas, and associate. *Special study options:* academic remediation for entering students, adult/continuing education programs, advanced placement credit, cooperative education, distance learning, double majors, English as a second language, independent study, internships, part-time degree program, services for LD students, summer session for credit.

Library 23,966 titles, 200 serial subscriptions, 2,500 audiovisual materials, an OPAC, a Web page.

Student Life *Housing:* college housing not available. *Activities and Organizations:* student-run newspaper, television station. *Student services:* personal/psychological counseling.

Costs (2006–07) *Tuition:* state resident $1185 full-time, $40 per credit hour part-time; nonresident $6585 full-time, $220 per credit hour part-time. *Required fees:* $45 full-time, $45 per semester part-time. *Payment plan:* deferred payment. *Waivers:* senior citizens.

Financial Aid Of all full-time matriculated undergraduates, 20 Federal Work-Study jobs (averaging $1800).

Applying *Options:* early admission, deferred entrance. *Required:* high school transcript. *Application deadlines:* rolling (freshmen), rolling (transfers). *Notification:* continuous (freshmen), continuous (transfers).

Freshmen Application Contact Mr. Ronnie Hinson, Dean of Students, Stanly Community College, 141 College Drive, Albemarle, NC 28001. *Phone:* 704-982-0121. *Fax:* 704-982-0255.

SURRY COMMUNITY COLLEGE

Dobson, North Carolina　　　　　**www.surry.cc.nc.us/**

- **State-supported** 2-year, founded 1965, part of North Carolina Community College System
- **Rural** 100-acre campus
- **Coed,** 3,600 undergraduate students

Undergraduates Students come from 3 states and territories, 4% are from out of state, 5% African American, 0.3% Asian American or Pacific Islander, 2% Hispanic American, 0.3% Native American, 0.2% international.

Faculty *Total:* 450, 33% full-time. *Student/faculty ratio:* 27:1.

Majors Accounting; administrative assistant and secretarial science; advertising; agricultural business and management; automobile/automotive mechanics technology; business administration and management; child care provision; commercial and advertising art; computer engineering related; computer engineering technology; computer programming; computer programming related; computer systems networking and telecommunications; construction engineering technology; cosmetology; criminal justice/law enforcement administration; drafting and design technology; electrical, electronic and communications engineering technology; heating, air conditioning, ventilation and refrigeration maintenance technology; horticultural science; information science/studies; information technology; legal assistant/paralegal; liberal arts and sciences/liberal studies; machine tool technology; medical administrative assistant and medical secretary; nursing (licensed practical/vocational nurse training); nursing (registered nurse training); poultry science.

Academics *Calendar:* semesters. *Degree:* certificates, diplomas, and associate. *Special study options:* academic remediation for entering students, adult/continuing education programs, advanced placement credit, cooperative education, distance learning, double majors, English as a second language, independent study, internships, off-campus study, part-time degree program, services for LD students, summer session for credit.

Library Resource Center with 47,526 titles, 362 serial subscriptions, an OPAC, a Web page.

Student Life *Housing:* college housing not available. *Activities and Organizations:* drama/theater group, student-run radio station, choral group, Student Government Association, Phi Beta Lambda, Phi Theta Kappa, BSU. *Campus security:* late-night transport/escort service, security guard during day and evening hours.

Athletics Member NJCAA. *Intercollegiate sports:* baseball M, basketball M, volleyball W. *Intramural sports:* basketball M/W, softball M/W, volleyball M/W.

Standardized Tests *Required:* CPT (for admission).

Costs (2006–07) *Tuition:* state resident $1264 full-time, $40 per credit hour part-time; nonresident $7024 full-time, $220 per credit hour part-time. *Required fees:* $69 full-time, $2 per credit hour part-time, $5 per term part-time.

Financial Aid Of all full-time matriculated undergraduates, 35 Federal Work-Study jobs (averaging $2800).

Applying *Options:* electronic application, early admission, deferred entrance. *Required:* high school transcript.

Freshmen Application Contact Renita Hazelwood, Director of Admissions, Surry Community College, PO Box 304, Dobson, NC 27017-0304. *Phone:* 336-386-3392. *Fax:* 336-386-3690. *E-mail:* hazelwoodr@surry.edu.

TRI-COUNTY COMMUNITY COLLEGE

Murphy, North Carolina　　　　　**www.tricountycc.edu**

- **State-supported** 2-year, founded 1964
- **Rural** 40-acre campus
- **Coed,** 1,155 undergraduate students, 44% full-time, 67% women, 33% men

Tri-County Community College (continued)

Undergraduates 503 full-time, 652 part-time. Students come from 8 states and territories, 3% are from out of state, 0.9% African American, 1% Hispanic American, 2% Native American.

Freshmen *Admission:* 518 applied, 518 admitted. *Average high school GPA:* 2.9.

Faculty *Total:* 80, 58% full-time, 5% with terminal degrees. *Student/faculty ratio:* 21:1.

Majors Accounting; automobile/automotive mechanics technology; business administration and management; computer management; early childhood education; electrical, electronic and communications engineering technology; information technology; liberal arts and sciences/liberal studies; medical/clinical assistant; nursing (registered nurse training); welding technology.

Academics *Calendar:* semesters. *Degree:* certificates, diplomas, and associate. *Special study options:* academic remediation for entering students, adult/continuing education programs, distance learning, double majors, internships, part-time degree program, study abroad, summer session for credit.

Library 16,224 titles, 306 serial subscriptions.

Student Life *Housing:* college housing not available. *Student services:* personal/psychological counseling.

Costs (2007–08) *Tuition:* state resident $1006 full-time, $40 per credit hour part-time; nonresident $5268 full-time, $220 per credit hour part-time. *Required fees:* $60 full-time, $29 per term part-time.

Financial Aid Of all full-time matriculated undergraduates, 11 Federal Work-Study jobs.

Applying *Required:* high school transcript. *Application deadlines:* rolling (freshmen), rolling (transfers). *Notification:* continuous (freshmen), continuous (transfers).

Freshmen Application Contact Mr. Jason Chambers, Director of Admissions, Tri-County Community College, 4600 East US 64, Murphy, NC 28906-7919. *Phone:* 828-837-6810. *Fax:* 828-837-3266. *E-mail:* jchambers@tricountycc.edu.

VANCE-GRANVILLE COMMUNITY COLLEGE
Henderson, North Carolina www.vgcc.cc.nc.us/

- **State-supported** 2-year, founded 1969, part of North Carolina Community College System
- **Rural** 83-acre campus with easy access to Raleigh
- **Endowment** $3.0 million
- **Coed**

Undergraduates 1,718 full-time, 2,339 part-time. Students come from 10 states and territories, 15 other countries, 2% are from out of state, 43% African American, 0.2% Asian American or Pacific Islander, 2% Hispanic American, 0.7% Native American, 1% international, 2% transferred in.

Faculty *Student/faculty ratio:* 9:1.

Academics *Calendar:* semesters. *Degree:* certificates, diplomas, and associate. *Special study options:* academic remediation for entering students, accelerated degree program, adult/continuing education programs, advanced placement credit, cooperative education, distance learning, double majors, English as a second language, internships, part-time degree program, services for LD students, summer session for credit.

Student Life *Campus security:* 24-hour emergency response devices and patrols.

Financial Aid Of all full-time matriculated undergraduates, 38 Federal Work-Study jobs (averaging $1750).

Applying *Options:* early admission, deferred entrance. *Required:* high school transcript.

Freshmen Application Contact Ms. Kathy Kutl, Admissions Officer, Vance-Granville Community College, PO Box 917, State Road 1126, Henderson, NC 27536. *Phone:* 252-492-2061 Ext. 3265. *Fax:* 252-430-0460.

WAKE TECHNICAL COMMUNITY COLLEGE
Raleigh, North Carolina www.waketech.edu/

Director of Admissions Ms. Susan Bloomfield, Director of Admissions, Wake Technical Community College, 9101 Fayetteville Road, Raleigh, NC 27603-5696. *Phone:* 919-662-3357.

WAYNE COMMUNITY COLLEGE
Goldsboro, North Carolina www.waynecc.edu/

- **State and locally supported** 2-year, founded 1957, part of North Carolina Community College System
- **Small-town** 125-acre campus
- **Endowment** $45,924
- **Coed**, 3,181 undergraduate students

Undergraduates Students come from 47 states and territories, 16% are from out of state, 31% African American, 2% Asian American or Pacific Islander, 2% Hispanic American, 2% Native American.

Faculty *Total:* 215, 43% full-time, 3% with terminal degrees. *Student/faculty ratio:* 18:1.

Majors Accounting technology and bookkeeping; agribusiness; agricultural production; automobile/automotive mechanics technology; avionics maintenance technology; biological and physical sciences; business administration and management; clinical/medical social work; computer systems analysis; criminal justice/police science; dental hygiene; electrical, electronic and communications engineering technology; electromechanical technology; executive assistant/executive secretary; forestry technology; legal administrative assistant/secretary; liberal arts and sciences/liberal studies; machine tool technology; mechanical engineering/mechanical technology; medical administrative assistant and medical secretary; medical/clinical assistant; medical office management; nursing (registered nurse training); parks, recreation and leisure facilities management; poultry science; psychiatric/mental health services technology; rehabilitation therapy; retailing; turf and turfgrass management.

Academics *Calendar:* semesters. *Degree:* certificates, diplomas, and associate. *Special study options:* academic remediation for entering students, adult/continuing education programs, advanced placement credit, cooperative education, distance learning, double majors, English as a second language, part-time degree program, services for LD students, summer session for credit.

Library Wayne Community College Library with 42,133 titles, 427 serial subscriptions, 5,840 audiovisual materials, an OPAC, a Web page.

Student Life *Housing:* college housing not available. *Activities and Organizations:* student-run newspaper, choral group, Student Government Association, Phi Beta Lambda, Agriculture Club, Multicultural Association for Enrichment, Student American Dental Hygienist Association, national fraternities. *Campus security:* 24-hour emergency response devices and patrols, student patrols. *Student services:* health clinic, personal/psychological counseling.

Athletics *Intramural sports:* basketball M/W, bowling M/W, football M/W, golf M/W, softball M/W, table tennis M/W, tennis M/W, volleyball M/W.

Standardized Tests *Required:* ACT ASSET (for placement).

Costs (2006–07) *Tuition:* state resident $1296 full-time; nonresident $7056 full-time.

Financial Aid Of all full-time matriculated undergraduates, 100 Federal Work-Study jobs (averaging $2000).

Applying *Options:* deferred entrance. *Required:* high school transcript, interview. *Application deadlines:* rolling (freshmen), rolling (transfers). *Notification:* continuous (freshmen), continuous (transfers).

Director of Admissions Ms. Susan Mooring Sasser, Director of Admissions and Records, Wayne Community College, PO Box 8002, Goldsboro, NC 27533-8002. *Phone:* 919-735-5151 Ext. 216. *E-mail:* msm@wayne.cc.nc.us.

WESTERN PIEDMONT COMMUNITY COLLEGE
Morganton, North Carolina www.wpcc.edu/

- **State-supported** 2-year, founded 1964, part of North Carolina Community College System
- **Small-town** 130-acre campus
- **Coed**, 2,897 undergraduate students

Undergraduates Students come from 5 states and territories, 9% African American, 4% Asian American or Pacific Islander, 0.8% Hispanic American, 0.4% Native American, 0.6% international.

Freshmen *Admission:* 827 applied, 827 admitted.

Faculty *Total:* 133, 45% full-time.

Majors Accounting; administrative assistant and secretarial science; art; business administration and management; civil engineering technology; clinical/medical laboratory technology; computer engineering technology; computer programming; criminal justice/law enforcement administration; criminal justice/police science; drafting and design technology; electrical, electronic and communications engineering technology; finance; horticultural science; industrial arts; industrial technology; interior design; legal administrative assistant/secretary; legal assistant/paralegal; liberal arts and sciences/liberal studies;

marketing/marketing management; medical administrative assistant and medical secretary; medical/clinical assistant; nursing (registered nurse training); preengineering; therapeutic recreation.

Academics *Calendar:* semesters. *Degree:* certificates, diplomas, and associate. *Special study options:* academic remediation for entering students, adult/continuing education programs, advanced placement credit, cooperative education, part-time degree program, summer session for credit.

Library 31,195 titles, 200 serial subscriptions.

Student Life *Housing:* college housing not available. *Activities and Organizations:* drama/theater group, student-run newspaper. *Student services:* personal/psychological counseling, women's center.

Athletics *Intramural sports:* basketball M, volleyball M/W.

Standardized Tests *Required:* ACT ASSET (for placement).

Costs (2006–07) *Tuition:* area resident $948 full-time, $40 per semester hour part-time; nonresident $5268 full-time, $220 per semester hour part-time. *Required fees:* $13 full-time, $2 per semester hour part-time, $1 per term part-time. *Payment plan:* deferred payment. *Waivers:* senior citizens and employees or children of employees.

Financial Aid Of all full-time matriculated undergraduates, 35 Federal Work-Study jobs (averaging $2150).

Applying *Required:* high school transcript. *Application deadlines:* rolling (freshmen), rolling (transfers). *Notification:* continuous (freshmen), continuous (transfers).

Freshmen Application Contact Susan Williams, Director of Admissions, Western Piedmont Community College, 1001 Burkemont Avenue, Morganton, NC 28655-4511. *Phone:* 828-438-6051. *Fax:* 828-438-6065. *E-mail:* swilliams@wpcc.edu.

WILKES COMMUNITY COLLEGE
Wilkesboro, North Carolina   www.wilkescc.edu/

- **State-supported** 2-year, founded 1965, part of North Carolina Community College System
- **Small-town** 140-acre campus
- **Endowment** $2.7 million
- **Coed**

Undergraduates 1,347 full-time, 1,270 part-time. Students come from 13 states and territories, 15 other countries, 1% are from out of state, 5% African American, 0.5% Asian American or Pacific Islander, 2% Hispanic American, 0.5% Native American, 3% transferred in.

Faculty *Student/faculty ratio:* 10:1.

Academics *Calendar:* semesters. *Degree:* certificates, diplomas, and associate. *Special study options:* academic remediation for entering students, accelerated degree program, adult/continuing education programs, advanced placement credit, cooperative education, distance learning, double majors, English as a second language, independent study, internships, part-time degree program, services for LD students, summer session for credit.

Student Life *Campus security:* 24-hour emergency response devices, student patrols, late-night transport/escort service.

Athletics Member NJCAA.

Financial Aid Of all full-time matriculated undergraduates, 50 Federal Work-Study jobs (averaging $1800).

Applying *Options:* electronic application, deferred entrance. *Required:* high school transcript.

Freshmen Application Contact Mr. Mac Warren, Director of Admissions, Wilkes Community College, PO Box 120, Wilkesboro, NC 28697. *Phone:* 336-838-6141. *Fax:* 336-838-6547. *E-mail:* mac.warren@wilkescc.edu.

WILSON TECHNICAL COMMUNITY COLLEGE
Wilson, North Carolina   www.wilsontech.edu/

- **State-supported** 2-year, founded 1958, part of North Carolina Community College System
- **Small-town** 35-acre campus
- **Endowment** $837,822
- **Coed,** 1,849 undergraduate students, 46% full-time, 72% women, 28% men

Undergraduates 851 full-time, 998 part-time. Students come from 3 states and territories, 5 other countries, 0.5% are from out of state, 44% African American, 0.5% Asian American or Pacific Islander, 3% Hispanic American, 0.5% Native American, 14% transferred in.

Freshmen *Admission:* 92 admitted, 92 enrolled.

Faculty *Total:* 123, 47% full-time. *Student/faculty ratio:* 15:1.

Majors Accounting; administrative assistant and secretarial science; business administration and management; computer programming; criminal justice/law enforcement administration; electrical, electronic and communications engineering technology; fire science; general studies; industrial technology; information science/studies; kindergarten/preschool education; language interpretation and translation; legal assistant/paralegal; liberal arts and sciences/liberal studies; mechanical engineering/mechanical technology; nursing (registered nurse training); sign language interpretation and translation; tool and die technology.

Academics *Calendar:* semesters. *Degree:* certificates, diplomas, and associate. *Special study options:* academic remediation for entering students, advanced placement credit, cooperative education, distance learning, double majors, English as a second language, independent study, internships, part-time degree program, services for LD students, summer session for credit.

Library 38,466 titles, an OPAC.

Student Life *Housing:* college housing not available. *Campus security:* 11-hour patrols by trained security personnel.

Costs (2006–07) *Tuition:* state resident $1264 full-time, $40 per credit hour part-time; nonresident $7024 full-time, $220 per credit hour part-time. *Required fees:* $38 full-time, $1 per credit hour part-time, $7 per semester part-time.

Financial Aid Of all full-time matriculated undergraduates, 65 Federal Work-Study jobs (averaging $1500).

Applying *Options:* electronic application, deferred entrance. *Required:* high school transcript. *Application deadlines:* rolling (freshmen), rolling (transfers). *Notification:* continuous (freshmen), continuous (transfers).

Freshmen Application Contact Ms. Barbara Page, Admissions Technician, Wilson Technical Community College, PO Box 4305, Wilson, NC 27893-0305. *Phone:* 252-246-1275. *Fax:* 252-243-7148. *E-mail:* bpage@wilsontech.edu.

NORTH DAKOTA

AAKERS COLLEGE
Fargo, North Dakota   www.aakers-college.com/

- **Proprietary** primarily 2-year, founded 1902
- **Coed**

Undergraduates 320 full-time, 257 part-time. 24% are from out of state, 0.2% African American, 0.5% Asian American or Pacific Islander, 0.5% Hispanic American, 0.9% Native American.

Faculty *Student/faculty ratio:* 13:1.

Academics *Calendar:* quarters. *Degrees:* diplomas, associate, and bachelor's.

Costs (2006–07) *Tuition:* $5070 full-time, $845 per course part-time.

Applying *Application fee:* $60. *Required:* high school transcript.

Freshmen Application Contact Ms. Elizabeth Largent, Director, Aakers College, 4012 19th Avenue, SW, Fargo, ND 58103. *Phone:* 701-277-3889. *Toll-free phone:* 800-817-0009. *Fax:* 701-277-5604.

BISMARCK STATE COLLEGE
Bismarck, North Dakota   www.bismarckstate.edu/

- **State-supported** 2-year, founded 1939, part of North Dakota University System
- **Urban** 100-acre campus
- **Coed,** 3,477 undergraduate students, 63% full-time, 49% women, 51% men

Undergraduates 2,192 full-time, 1,285 part-time. Students come from 51 states and territories, 4 other countries, 16% are from out of state, 0.9% African American, 0.5% Asian American or Pacific Islander, 1% Hispanic American, 3% Native American, 0.3% international, 7% transferred in, 8% live on campus.

Freshmen *Admission:* 837 enrolled.

Faculty *Total:* 251, 43% full-time. *Student/faculty ratio:* 17:1.

Majors Administrative assistant and secretarial science; agricultural business and management; autobody/collision and repair technology; automobile/automotive mechanics technology; business automation/technology/data entry; business/commerce; carpentry; clinical/medical laboratory technology; commercial and advertising art; computer systems networking and telecommunications; construction engineering technology; emergency medical technology (EMT

Bismarck State College (continued)

paramedic); energy management and systems technology; heating, air conditioning, ventilation and refrigeration maintenance technology; hotel/motel administration; industrial technology; legal administrative assistant/secretary; liberal arts and sciences/liberal studies; lineworker; medical administrative assistant and medical secretary; nursing (licensed practical/vocational nurse training); surgical technology; welding technology.

Academics *Calendar:* semesters. *Degree:* certificates, diplomas, and associate. *Special study options:* academic remediation for entering students, adult/continuing education programs, advanced placement credit, cooperative education, distance learning, internships, part-time degree program, study abroad. *ROTC:* Army (c), Air Force (c).

Library Bismarck State College Library with 69,142 titles, 374 serial subscriptions, an OPAC, a Web page.

Student Life *Housing Options:* men-only, women-only. Campus housing is university owned. *Activities and Organizations:* drama/theater group, student-run newspaper, choral group, Phi Theta Kappa, Drama Club, Art Club, Anime Club. *Campus security:* 24-hour emergency response devices and patrols, controlled dormitory access.

Athletics Member NJCAA. *Intercollegiate sports:* baseball M, basketball M(s)/W(s), golf M/W, tennis M/W, volleyball W(s). *Intramural sports:* basketball M, softball M, volleyball M/W.

Standardized Tests *Required:* SAT or ACT (for admission).

Costs (2007–08) *Tuition:* $107 per credit part-time; state resident $3488 full-time; nonresident $8304 full-time. *Required fees:* $570 full-time.

Financial Aid Of all full-time matriculated undergraduates, 74 Federal Work-Study jobs (averaging $1012).

Applying *Options:* electronic application. *Application fee:* $35. *Required:* high school transcript. *Application deadlines:* rolling (freshmen), 8/1 (transfers). *Notification:* continuous (freshmen), continuous (transfers).

Freshmen Application Contact Ms. Karla Gabriel, Dean of Admissions and Enrollment Services, Bismarck State College, PO Box 5587, Bismarck, ND 58506-5587. *Phone:* 701-224-5426. *Toll-free phone:* 800-445-5073 Ext. 45429 (in-state); 800-445-5073 (out-of-state). *Fax:* 701-224-5643. *E-mail:* karla.gabriel@bsc.nodak.edu.

CANKDESKA CIKANA COMMUNITY COLLEGE

Fort Totten, North Dakota   www.littlehoop.edu/

- **Federally supported** 2-year, founded 1974
- **Small-town** 1-acre campus
- **Coed,** 168 undergraduate students

Undergraduates Students come from 5 states and territories.

Faculty *Total:* 15, 33% full-time. *Student/faculty ratio:* 12:1.

Majors Accounting; administrative assistant and secretarial science; art; art history, criticism and conservation; business administration and management; business teacher education; carpentry; chemistry; computer science; developmental and child psychology; English; geography; health teacher education; history; liberal arts and sciences/liberal studies; marketing/marketing management; mathematics; parks, recreation and leisure; trade and industrial teacher education.

Academics *Calendar:* semesters. *Degree:* certificates and associate. *Special study options:* academic remediation for entering students, adult/continuing education programs, cooperative education, off-campus study, part-time degree program, services for LD students, student-designed majors, summer session for credit.

Library 7,500 titles, 48 serial subscriptions.

Student Life *Housing:* college housing not available. *Activities and Organizations:* drama/theater group. *Campus security:* late-night transport/escort service. *Student services:* personal/psychological counseling.

Athletics *Intramural sports:* basketball M/W, bowling M/W, volleyball M/W, weight lifting M/W.

Standardized Tests *Required:* TABE (for placement).

Costs (2006–07) *Tuition:* state resident $2140 full-time.

Applying *Options:* early admission, deferred entrance. *Application deadlines:* 8/22 (freshmen), 8/22 (transfers). *Notification:* continuous (freshmen), continuous (transfers).

Director of Admissions Mr. Ermen Brown Jr., Registrar, Cankdeska Cikana Community College, PO Box 269, Fort Totten, ND 58335. *Phone:* 701-766-1342.

FORT BERTHOLD COMMUNITY COLLEGE

New Town, North Dakota   www.fbcc.bia.edu/

- **Independent** 2-year, founded 1973
- **Small-town** campus
- **Coed,** 416 undergraduate students

Faculty *Total:* 42, 29% full-time.

Majors Accounting; administrative assistant and secretarial science; biological and physical sciences; business administration and management; construction engineering technology; environmental studies; farm and ranch management; health information/medical records administration; human services; information science/studies; kindergarten/preschool education; liberal arts and sciences/liberal studies; marketing/marketing management; mathematics; nursing (licensed practical/vocational nurse training); public administration.

Academics *Calendar:* semesters. *Degree:* certificates and associate. *Special study options:* academic remediation for entering students, cooperative education, internships, off-campus study, part-time degree program, summer session for credit.

Library 10,000 titles, 300 serial subscriptions.

Student Life *Housing:* college housing not available. *Activities and Organizations:* drama/theater group, student-run newspaper. *Student services:* health clinic, personal/psychological counseling, legal services.

Athletics *Intercollegiate sports:* basketball M/W, cross-country running M/W. *Intramural sports:* basketball M/W, football M/W, golf M/W, softball M/W, volleyball M/W, weight lifting M/W.

Costs (2006–07) *Tuition:* $2640 full-time, $110 per credit part-time. Full-time tuition and fees vary according to course load. *Required fees:* $600 full-time, $25 per credit part-time, $25 per term part-time. *Payment plan:* installment. *Waivers:* employees or children of employees.

Financial Aid Of all full-time matriculated undergraduates, 11 Federal Work-Study jobs (averaging $1200).

Applying *Options:* deferred entrance. *Application fee:* $10. *Application deadline:* rolling (freshmen).

Freshmen Application Contact Twila Aulaumea, Registrar/Admissions Director, Fort Berthold Community College, PO Box 490, 220 8th Avenue North, New Town, ND 58763-0490. *Phone:* 701-627-4738 Ext. 286. *Fax:* 701-627-3609. *E-mail:* taulau@fbcc.bia.edu.

LAKE REGION STATE COLLEGE

Devils Lake, North Dakota   www.lrsc.nodak.edu/

- **State-supported** 2-year, founded 1941, part of North Dakota University System
- **Small-town** 120-acre campus
- **Endowment** $2.2 million
- **Coed**

Undergraduates 409 full-time, 1,062 part-time. Students come from 28 states and territories, 12 other countries, 10% are from out of state, 2% African American, 0.5% Asian American or Pacific Islander, 1% Hispanic American, 8% Native American, 2% international, 4% transferred in, 30% live on campus.

Faculty *Student/faculty ratio:* 15:1.

Academics *Calendar:* semesters. *Degree:* certificates, diplomas, and associate. *Special study options:* academic remediation for entering students, adult/continuing education programs, cooperative education, distance learning, double majors, English as a second language, freshman honors college, honors programs, internships, part-time degree program, summer session for credit.

Student Life *Campus security:* 24-hour emergency response devices, controlled dormitory access.

Athletics Member NJCAA.

Standardized Tests *Required:* SAT or ACT (for admission), COMPASS (for admission).

Costs (2006–07) *Tuition:* state resident $2780 full-time, $142 per credit part-time; nonresident $2780 full-time, $142 per credit part-time. *Required fees:* $783 full-time. *Room and board:* $4030. Room and board charges vary according to board plan.

Financial Aid Of all full-time matriculated undergraduates, 40 Federal Work-Study jobs (averaging $1600).

Applying *Options:* electronic application. *Application fee:* $35. *Required:* high school transcript, immunizations.

Freshmen Application Contact Ms. Diane Knodel, Administrative Assistant, Lake Region State College, 1801 College Drive North, Devils Lake, ND 58301. *Phone:* 701-662-1514. *Toll-free phone:* 800-443-1313 Ext. 514. *Fax:* 701-662-1581. *E-mail:* diane.knodel@lrsc.nodak.edu.

Minot State University—Bottineau Campus

Bottineau, North Dakota　　　**www.misu-b.nodak.edu/**

- **State-supported** 2-year, founded 1906, part of North Dakota University System
- **Rural** 35-acre campus
- **Endowment** $1.0 million
- **Coed,** 605 undergraduate students, 51% full-time, 58% women, 42% men

Undergraduates 311 full-time, 294 part-time. Students come from 25 states and territories, 5 other countries, 15% are from out of state, 1% African American, 0.3% Asian American or Pacific Islander, 1% Hispanic American, 6% Native American, 3% international, 45% live on campus.

Freshmen *Admission:* 422 applied, 422 admitted, 422 enrolled.

Faculty *Total:* 44, 59% full-time, 7% with terminal degrees. *Student/faculty ratio:* 12:1.

Majors Accounting technology and bookkeeping; administrative assistant and secretarial science; advertising; applied horticulture; applied horticulture/horticultural business services related; computer and information systems security; computer engineering technology; computer systems networking and telecommunications; computer technology/computer systems technology; data modeling/warehousing and database administration; environmental engineering technology; executive assistant/executive secretary; fish/game management; floriculture/floristry management; greenhouse management; horticultural science; hospitality/recreation marketing; information science/studies; information technology; landscaping and groundskeeping; marketing/marketing management; medical administrative assistant and medical secretary; medical/clinical assistant; medical insurance coding; medical transcription; natural resources/conservation; nursing (licensed practical/vocational nurse training); nursing (registered nurse training); office occupations and clerical services; ornamental horticulture; parks, recreation and leisure facilities management; receptionist; system administration; turf and turfgrass management; urban forestry; wildlife and wildlands science and management.

Academics *Calendar:* semesters. *Degree:* certificates, diplomas, and associate. *Special study options:* academic remediation for entering students, cooperative education, distance learning, double majors, internships, off-campus study, part-time degree program, services for LD students, summer session for credit.

Library Minot State University-Bottineau Library plus 1 other with 45,000 titles, 250 serial subscriptions, an OPAC, a Web page.

Student Life *Housing:* on-campus residence required through sophomore year. *Options:* men-only, women-only. Campus housing is university owned. Freshman campus housing is guaranteed. *Activities and Organizations:* drama/theater group, choral group, Student Senate, Wildlife Club, Paul Bunyan Club, Horticulture Club, DECA. *Campus security:* controlled dormitory access. *Student services:* personal/psychological counseling.

Athletics Member NJCAA. *Intercollegiate sports:* baseball M, basketball M(s)/W(s), ice hockey M(s), volleyball W(s). *Intramural sports:* archery M/W, badminton M/W, basketball M/W, skiing (downhill) M/W, softball M/W, volleyball M/W.

Costs (2007–08) *Tuition:* state resident $2972 full-time, $124 per credit part-time; nonresident $4458 full-time, $186 per credit part-time. *Required fees:* $331 full-time, $28 per credit part-time. *Room and board:* $3890; room only: $1523.

Financial Aid Of all full-time matriculated undergraduates, 50 Federal Work-Study jobs (averaging $1100).

Applying *Options:* electronic application, early admission, deferred entrance. *Application fee:* $35. *Required:* high school transcript. *Application deadlines:* rolling (freshmen), rolling (transfers).

Freshmen Application Contact Ms. Jessica Migler, Admissions Counselor, Minot State University–Bottineau Campus, 105 Simrall Boulevard, Bottineau, ND 58318. *Phone:* 701-228-5426. *Toll-free phone:* 800-542-6866. *Fax:* 701-228-5499. *E-mail:* jessica.migler@misu.nodak.edu.

North Dakota State College of Science

Wahpeton, North Dakota　　　**www.ndscs.nodak.edu/**

- **State-supported** 2-year, founded 1903, part of North Dakota University System
- **Rural** 125-acre campus
- **Endowment** $4000
- **Coed**

Undergraduates 1,954 full-time, 514 part-time. Students come from 54 states and territories, 11 other countries, 27% are from out of state, 2% African American, 0.4% Asian American or Pacific Islander, 0.5% Hispanic American, 2% Native American, 0.9% international, 9% transferred in, 56% live on campus.

Faculty *Student/faculty ratio:* 15:1.

Academics *Calendar:* semesters. *Degree:* certificates, diplomas, and associate. *Special study options:* academic remediation for entering students, adult/continuing education programs, cooperative education, distance learning, double majors, English as a second language, independent study, internships, part-time degree program, services for LD students, student-designed majors, summer session for credit.

Student Life *Campus security:* 24-hour emergency response devices and patrols, student patrols, late-night transport/escort service, controlled dormitory access.

Athletics Member NJCAA.

Costs (2006–07) *Tuition:* state resident $3757 full-time, $114 per credit part-time; nonresident $9197 full-time, $271 per credit part-time. *Room and board:* $4638.

Financial Aid Of all full-time matriculated undergraduates, 90 Federal Work-Study jobs (averaging $1500).

Applying *Options:* electronic application, early admission. *Application fee:* $35. *Required:* high school transcript.

Freshmen Application Contact Ms. Karen Reilly, Director of Enrollment Services, North Dakota State College of Science, 800 North 6th Street, Wahpeton, ND 58076. *Phone:* 701-671-2189. *Toll-free phone:* 800-342-4325 Ext. 2202. *Fax:* 701-671-2332.

Sitting Bull College

Fort Yates, North Dakota　　　**www.sittingbull.edu/**

- **Independent** 2-year, founded 1973
- **Rural** campus
- **Endowment** $541,000
- **Coed,** 214 undergraduate students

Undergraduates Students come from 2 states and territories.

Freshmen *Admission:* 63 applied, 63 admitted. *Average high school GPA:* 2.5.

Faculty *Total:* 32, 50% full-time, 9% with terminal degrees. *Student/faculty ratio:* 6:1.

Majors Administrative assistant and secretarial science; agribusiness; American Indian/Native American studies; business administration and management; carpentry; child care and support services management; education; environmental studies; farm and ranch management; human services; liberal arts and sciences/liberal studies; marketing/marketing management; office occupations and clerical services; social work; teacher assistant/aide.

Academics *Calendar:* semesters. *Degree:* certificates and associate. *Special study options:* academic remediation for entering students, adult/continuing education programs, off-campus study, part-time degree program.

Library Sitting Bull College Library with 10,000 titles, 130 serial subscriptions, an OPAC.

Student Life *Housing:* college housing not available. *Activities and Organizations:* student-run newspaper, student government, Future Teachers, Ikce Oyate Culture Club, Phi Beta Lambda, Ski Club. *Student services:* personal/psychological counseling.

Athletics *Intercollegiate sports:* basketball M/W. *Intramural sports:* basketball M/W.

Standardized Tests *Required:* TABE (for placement).

Costs (2006–07) *Tuition:* state resident $3540 full-time.

Financial Aid Of all full-time matriculated undergraduates, 20 Federal Work-Study jobs (averaging $2000).

Applying *Options:* early admission. *Application fee:* $10. *Required:* high school transcript, medical questionnaire. *Application deadlines:* 9/6 (freshmen), 9/6 (transfers). *Notification:* continuous (freshmen), continuous (transfers).

Director of Admissions Ms. Melody Silk, Director of Registration and Admissions, Sitting Bull College, 1341 92nd Street, Fort Yates, ND 58538-9701. *Phone:* 701-854-3864. *Fax:* 701-854-3403. *E-mail:* melodys@sbcl.edu.

Turtle Mountain Community College

Belcourt, North Dakota　　　**www.turtle-mountain.cc.nd.us/**

- **Independent** 2-year, founded 1972
- **Rural** 10-acre campus
- **Coed,** 579 undergraduate students, 65% full-time, 65% women, 35% men

Turtle Mountain Community College *(continued)*

Undergraduates 378 full-time, 201 part-time. Students come from 1 other state.

Freshmen *Admission:* 102 applied, 102 admitted, 102 enrolled.

Faculty *Total:* 42, 50% full-time.

Majors Accounting technology and bookkeeping; administrative assistant and secretarial science; art; biological and physical sciences; biology/biological sciences; business administration and management; carpentry; clinical laboratory science/medical technology; clinical/medical laboratory technology; computer science; elementary education; emergency medical technology (EMT paramedic); English; environmental studies; fish/game management; health information/medical records administration; history; human services; journalism; kindergarten/preschool education; liberal arts and sciences/liberal studies; marketing/marketing management; mathematics; natural resources management and policy; nursing (registered nurse training); pharmacy; physical therapy; pre-engineering; social sciences; social work; trade and industrial teacher education; veterinary technology; wildlife and wildlands science and management.

Academics *Calendar:* semesters. *Degree:* certificates and associate. *Special study options:* academic remediation for entering students, adult/continuing education programs, part-time degree program.

Library Turtle Mountain Community College Library with 20,500 titles, 150 serial subscriptions, an OPAC.

Student Life *Housing:* college housing not available. *Activities and Organizations:* student government. *Student services:* personal/psychological counseling.

Athletics *Intramural sports:* basketball M/W, softball M/W, tennis M/W, volleyball M/W.

Standardized Tests *Required:* ACT (for admission).

Costs (2006–07) *Tuition:* $2000 full-time.

Financial Aid *Financial aid deadline:* 6/30.

Applying *Options:* early admission, deferred entrance. *Required:* high school transcript. *Application deadlines:* rolling (freshmen), rolling (transfers).

Director of Admissions Ms. Joni LaFontaine, Admissions/Records Officer, Turtle Mountain Community College, Box 340, Belcourt, ND 58316-0340. *Phone:* 701-477-5605 Ext. 217. *E-mail:* jlafontaine@tm.edu.

UNITED TRIBES TECHNICAL COLLEGE
Bismarck, North Dakota   www.uttc.edu/

- **Federally supported** 2-year, founded 1969
- **Small-town** 105-acre campus
- **Coed**

Undergraduates 635 full-time, 250 part-time. Students come from 24 states and territories, 35% are from out of state, 0.5% African American, 0.2% Asian American or Pacific Islander, 89% Native American, 9% transferred in.

Faculty *Student/faculty ratio:* 8:1.

Academics *Calendar:* semesters. *Degree:* certificates and associate. *Special study options:* academic remediation for entering students, cooperative education, honors programs, independent study, part-time degree program, summer session for credit.

Student Life *Campus security:* 24-hour emergency response devices and patrols.

Athletics Member NJCAA.

Costs (2006–07) *One-time required fee:* $100. *Comprehensive fee:* $6580 includes full-time tuition ($2800), mandatory fees ($780), and room and board ($3000). Part-time tuition: $88 per credit.

Applying *Required:* high school transcript.

Freshmen Application Contact Ms. Vivian Gillette, Director of Admissions, United Tribes Technical College, 3315 University Drive, Bismarck, ND 58504. *Phone:* 701-255-3285 Ext. 1334. *Fax:* 701-530-0640. *E-mail:* vgillette@uttc.edu.

WILLISTON STATE COLLEGE
Williston, North Dakota   www.wsc.nodak.edu/

- **State-supported** 2-year, founded 1957, part of North Dakota University System
- **Small-town** 80-acre campus
- **Endowment** $52,200
- **Coed**

Undergraduates 557 full-time, 390 part-time. Students come from 9 states and territories, 3 other countries, 14% are from out of state, 1% African American, 0.3% Asian American or Pacific Islander, 2% Hispanic American, 5% Native American, 3% international, 84% transferred in, 13% live on campus.

Faculty *Student/faculty ratio:* 14:1.

Academics *Calendar:* semesters. *Degree:* certificates, diplomas, and associate. *Special study options:* academic remediation for entering students, advanced placement credit, cooperative education, distance learning, honors programs, independent study, off-campus study, part-time degree program, services for LD students, student-designed majors, summer session for credit.

Student Life *Campus security:* controlled dormitory access.

Athletics Member NJCAA.

Financial Aid Of all full-time matriculated undergraduates, 30 Federal Work-Study jobs (averaging $1500). 15 state and other part-time jobs (averaging $1000).

Applying *Options:* electronic application. *Application fee:* $35. *Required:* high school transcript.

Freshmen Application Contact Ms. Jan Solem, Director for Admission and Records, Williston State College, PO Box 1326, Williston, ND 58802-1326. *Phone:* 701-774-4554. *Toll-free phone:* 888-863-9455. *Fax:* 701-774-4211. *E-mail:* wsc.admission@wsc.nodak.edu.

NORTHERN MARIANA ISLANDS

NORTHERN MARIANAS COLLEGE
Saipan, Northern Mariana Islands   www.nmcnet.edu/

- **Territory-supported** primarily 2-year, founded 1981
- **Rural** 14-acre campus
- **Coed,** 1,299 undergraduate students, 60% full-time, 65% women, 35% men

Undergraduates 783 full-time, 516 part-time. Students come from 4 states and territories, 9 other countries, 0.2% African American, 76% Asian American or Pacific Islander, 0.1% Hispanic American, 17% international.

Freshmen *Admission:* 241 enrolled.

Faculty *Total:* 99, 49% full-time.

Majors Accounting; administrative assistant and secretarial science; agricultural business and management; agricultural mechanization; agriculture; business administration and management; data processing and data processing technology; education; liberal arts and sciences/liberal studies; marine technology; marketing/marketing management; nursing (registered nurse training); public administration.

Academics *Calendar:* semesters. *Degrees:* certificates, diplomas, associate, and bachelor's. *Special study options:* academic remediation for entering students, adult/continuing education programs, cooperative education, distance learning, English as a second language, internships, part-time degree program, services for LD students, summer session for credit.

Library Olympia T. Borja Library plus 1 other with 39,672 titles, 465 serial subscriptions, 1,928 audiovisual materials, an OPAC, a Web page.

Student Life *Housing:* college housing not available. *Activities and Organizations:* drama/theater group, Northern Marinas Academy, Korean Association, Micronesian Club, Learning Skills. *Campus security:* patrols by trained security personnel. *Student services:* personal/psychological counseling.

Athletics *Intramural sports:* basketball M/W, softball M/W, table tennis M/W, tennis M/W, volleyball M/W.

Costs (2006–07) *Tuition:* territory resident $2280 full-time, $95 per credit part-time; nonresident $4560 full-time, $190 per credit part-time. Full-time tuition and fees vary according to course level, course load, and program. Part-time tuition and fees vary according to course level, course load, and program. *Required fees:* $540 full-time, $25 per term part-time. *Payment plan:* installment. *Waivers:* senior citizens and employees or children of employees.

Applying *Options:* early admission, deferred entrance. *Application fee:* $25. *Required:* high school transcript. *Application deadlines:* rolling (freshmen), rolling (transfers).

Freshmen Application Contact Ms. Leilani M. Basa-Alam, Admission Specialist, Northern Marianas College, PO Box 501250, Saipan, MP 96950-1250. *Phone:* 670-234-3690 Ext. 1539. *Fax:* 670-235-4967. *E-mail:* leilanib@nmcnet.edu.

ACADEMY OF COURT REPORTING
Cleveland, Ohio — www.acr.edu/

- **Proprietary** 2-year, founded 1970
- **Coed,** 448 undergraduate students

Majors Court reporting; legal assistant/paralegal; security and loss prevention.
Academics *Degree:* associate.
Costs (2006–07) *Tuition:* $8195 full-time. Full-time tuition and fees vary according to program. Part-time tuition and fees vary according to program. No tuition increase for student's term of enrollment. *Payment plan:* installment.
Applying *Application fee:* $100.
Freshmen Application Contact Ms. Sheila Woods, Director of Admissions, Academy of Court Reporting, 2044 Euclid Avenue, Cleveland, OH 44115. *Phone:* 216-861-3222. *Fax:* 216-861-4517. *E-mail:* admissionaocr@hotmail.com.

ANTONELLI COLLEGE
Cincinnati, Ohio — www.antonellic.com/

Director of Admissions Ms. Connie D. Sharp, Director, Antonelli College, 124 East Seventh Street, Cincinnati, OH 45202. *Phone:* 513-241-4338. *Toll-free phone:* 800-505-4338.

THE ART INSTITUTE OF CINCINNATI
Cincinnati, Ohio — www.theartinstituteofcincinnati.com/

Director of Admissions Ms. Cyndi Mendell, Admissions, The Art Institute of Cincinnati, 1171 East Kemper Road, Cincinnati, OH 45246. *Phone:* 513-751-1206.

THE ART INSTITUTE OF OHIO—CINCINNATI
Cincinnati, Ohio — www.aiohc.aii.edu

- **Proprietary** 2-year, part of Education Management Corporation
- **Urban** campus
- **Coed,** 329 undergraduate students, 100% full-time, 68% women, 32% men

Undergraduates 329 full-time. Students come from 4 states and territories, 29% are from out of state, 23% African American, 1% Asian American or Pacific Islander, 0.6% Hispanic American, 0.9% Native American, 16% live on campus.
Freshmen *Admission:* 68 applied, 50 admitted.
Faculty *Total:* 36, 14% full-time, 17% with terminal degrees. *Student/faculty ratio:* 22:1.
Majors Graphic design; interior design.
Academics *Calendar:* continuous. *Degree:* associate. *Special study options:* accelerated degree program, cooperative education, distance learning, internships, part-time degree program, services for LD students.
Library Library with 7,018 titles, 75 serial subscriptions, 493 audiovisual materials.
Student Life *Housing Options:* Campus housing is leased by the school. *Campus security:* security guard.
Costs (2007–08) *Tuition:* $19,872 full-time, $414 per credit hour part-time.
Applying *Options:* early admission, early decision, early action, deferred entrance. *Application fee:* $50. *Required:* essay or personal statement, high school transcript, interview. *Application deadlines:* 10/8 (freshmen), rolling (transfers). *Notification:* continuous (freshmen), continuous (transfers).
Director of Admissions Mr. Maurice Lee, President, The Art Institute of Ohio–Cincinnati, 1011 Glendale-Milford Road, Cincinnati, OH 45215-1107. *Phone:* 513-833-2626. *Fax:* 877-477-8486. *E-mail:* mlee@aii.edu.

▶**See page 482 for the College Close-Up.**

ATS INSTITUTE OF TECHNOLOGY
Highland Heights, Ohio — www.atsinstitute.com/

- **Proprietary** 2-year
- **Coed,** 353 undergraduate students

Majors Nursing (licensed practical/vocational nurse training).
Academics *Degree:* associate.
Applying *Application fee:* $50.
Freshmen Application Contact Admissions Office, ATS Institute of Technology, 230 Alpha Park Drive, Highland Heights, OH 44143. *E-mail:* info@atsinstitute.com.

BELMONT TECHNICAL COLLEGE
St. Clairsville, Ohio — www.btc.edu/

Director of Admissions Mr. Gregory A. Fehr, Executive Director of Marketing and Advancement, Belmont Technical College, 120 Fox Shannon Place, St. Clairsville, OH 43950-9735. *Phone:* 740-695-9500 Ext. 1018. *Toll-free phone:* 800-423-1188. *E-mail:* gfehr@btc.edu.

BOHECKER'S BUSINESS COLLEGE
Ravenna, Ohio — www.boheckercollege.edu/

Freshmen Application Contact Admissions Office, Bohecker's Business College, 653 Enterprise Parkway, Ravenna, OH 44266. *Toll-free phone:* 800-794-2856.

BOWLING GREEN STATE UNIVERSITY—FIRELANDS COLLEGE
Huron, Ohio — www.firelands.bgsu.edu/

- **State-supported** primarily 2-year, founded 1968, part of Bowling Green State University System
- **Rural** 216-acre campus with easy access to Cleveland and Toledo
- **Endowment** $2.3 million
- **Coed,** 1,984 undergraduate students, 55% full-time, 65% women, 35% men

Undergraduates 1,092 full-time, 892 part-time. Students come from 3 states and territories, 0.4% are from out of state, 7% African American, 0.8% Asian American or Pacific Islander, 3% Hispanic American, 0.8% Native American, 21% transferred in.
Freshmen *Admission:* 542 applied, 505 admitted, 411 enrolled. *Average high school GPA:* 3.09. *Test scores:* SAT verbal scores over 500: 73%; SAT math scores over 500: 41%; ACT scores over 18: 71%; SAT verbal scores over 600: 18%; SAT math scores over 600: 8%; ACT scores over 24: 16%; ACT scores over 30: 1%.
Faculty *Total:* 121, 40% full-time, 35% with terminal degrees. *Student/faculty ratio:* 19:1.
Majors Accounting technology and bookkeeping; biological and physical sciences; business operations support and secretarial services related; communications technologies and support services related; computer engineering technology; computer programming; computer systems networking and telecommunications; computer/technical support; criminal justice/safety; design and visual communications; education; electrical, electronic and communications engineering technology; engineering technologies related; family and community services; health information/medical records administration; health professions related; humanities; human services; industrial technology; interdisciplinary studies; kindergarten/preschool education; liberal arts and sciences/liberal studies; mechanical design technology; nursing (registered nurse training); operations management; pre-engineering; respiratory care therapy; social sciences.
Academics *Calendar:* semesters. *Degrees:* certificates, associate, and bachelor's (also offers some upper-level and graduate courses). *Special study options:* academic remediation for entering students, adult/continuing education programs, advanced placement credit, distance learning, double majors, independent study, internships, part-time degree program, services for LD students, student-designed majors, summer session for credit. *ROTC:* Army (c), Air Force (c).
Library Firelands College Library with 31,262 titles, 223 serial subscriptions, an OPAC, a Web page.

Bowling Green State University–Firelands College (continued)

Student Life *Housing:* college housing not available. *Activities and Organizations:* drama/theater group, Speech Activities Organization, Allied Health Club, student government, Intramural Club, Campus Fellowship. *Campus security:* 24-hour emergency response devices, late-night transport/escort service, patrols by trained security personnel.

Athletics *Intramural sports:* basketball M/W, football M/W, skiing (downhill) M(c)/W(c), softball M/W, volleyball M/W, weight lifting M(c)/W(c).

Costs (2006–07) *Tuition:* state resident $4022 full-time, $196 per credit part-time; nonresident $11,330 full-time, $545 per credit part-time. Full-time tuition and fees vary according to course load and location. Part-time tuition and fees vary according to course load and location. *Required fees:* $206 full-time, $10 per credit part-time, $8 per term part-time. *Payment plans:* tuition prepayment, installment. *Waivers:* employees or children of employees.

Applying *Options:* electronic application, early admission, deferred entrance. *Application fee:* $35. *Required:* high school transcript. *Application deadlines:* 8/13 (freshmen), 8/13 (transfers). *Notification:* continuous until 8/13 (freshmen), continuous until 8/13 (transfers).

Freshmen Application Contact Ms. Debralee Divers, Director of Admissions and Financial Aid, Bowling Green State University–Firelands College, One University Drive, Huron, OH 44839. *Phone:* 419-433-5560. *Toll-free phone:* 800-322-4787. *Fax:* 419-372-0604. *E-mail:* divers@bgsu.edu.

BRADFORD SCHOOL

Columbus, Ohio   **www.bradfordschoolcolumbus.edu/**

Director of Admissions Ms. Raeann Lee, Director of Admissions, Bradford School, 2469 Stelzer Road, Columbus, OH 43219. *Phone:* 614-416-6200. *Toll-free phone:* 800-678-7981.

BROWN MACKIE COLLEGE–AKRON

Akron, Ohio   **www.socaec.com/**

- **Proprietary** 2-year, founded 1968, administratively affiliated with Southern Ohio College
- **Suburban** 3-acre campus with easy access to Cleveland
- **Coed,** 681 undergraduate students

Undergraduates Students come from 1 other state, 1 other country.

Faculty *Total:* 31, 45% full-time. *Student/faculty ratio:* 19:1.

Majors Accounting technology and bookkeeping; business administration and management; CAD/CADD drafting/design technology; computer programming (specific applications); computer systems networking and telecommunications; criminal justice/law enforcement administration; data modeling/warehousing and database administration; electrical, electronic and communications engineering technology; health/health care administration; information technology; medical/clinical assistant; paralegal/legal assistant; pharmacy technician.

Academics *Calendar:* quarters. *Degree:* certificates, diplomas, and associate. *Special study options:* academic remediation for entering students, advanced placement credit, cooperative education, internships, summer session for credit.

Library 3,725 titles, 56 serial subscriptions.

Student Life *Housing:* college housing not available. *Activities and Organizations:* student-run newspaper, Phi Beta Lambda, Student Advisory Board, Collegiate Secretaries International. *Campus security:* late-night transport/escort service. *Student services:* personal/psychological counseling.

Costs (2006–07) *Tuition:* $9072 full-time, $189 per credit part-time.

Applying *Options:* early admission, deferred entrance. *Recommended:* minimum 2.0 GPA. *Application deadlines:* rolling (freshmen), rolling (transfers). *Notification:* continuous (freshmen), continuous (transfers).

Freshmen Application Contact Director of Admissions, Brown Mackie College–Akron, 2791 Mogadore Road, Akron, OH 44312-1596. *Phone:* 330-869-3600. *Fax:* 330-869-3650. *E-mail:* jconte@brownmackie.edu.

▶**See page 496 for the College Close-Up.**

BROWN MACKIE COLLEGE–CINCINNATI

Cincinnati, Ohio   **www.brownmackie.edu/locations.asp?locid=6**

- **Proprietary** 2-year, founded 1927, part of American Education Centers, Inc
- **Suburban** 3-acre campus
- **Coed,** 1,322 undergraduate students

Undergraduates Students come from 3 states and territories, 1% are from out of state.

Faculty *Total:* 81, 38% full-time. *Student/faculty ratio:* 16:1.

Majors Accounting technology and bookkeeping; audiovisual communications technologies related; business administration and management; CAD/CADD drafting/design technology; computer programming (specific applications); computer software and media applications related; computer systems networking and telecommunications; electrical, electronic and communications engineering technology; gerontology; health/health care administration; legal assistant/paralegal; medical/clinical assistant; opticianry; pharmacy technician; surgical technology.

Academics *Calendar:* quarters. *Degree:* certificates, diplomas, and associate. *Special study options:* academic remediation for entering students, adult/continuing education programs, advanced placement credit, internships, summer session for credit.

Library 8,747 titles, 80 serial subscriptions, 437 audiovisual materials.

Student Life *Housing:* college housing not available. *Campus security:* 24-hour emergency response devices, night security guard on-campus.

Costs (2006–07) *Tuition:* $9072 full-time, $189 per credit hour part-time.

Financial Aid Of all full-time matriculated undergraduates, 4 Federal Work-Study jobs.

Applying *Options:* early admission, deferred entrance. *Application fee:* $20. *Required:* high school transcript, interview. *Application deadlines:* rolling (freshmen), rolling (transfers).

Freshmen Application Contact Director of Admissions, Brown Mackie College–Cincinnati, 1011 Glendale-Milford Road, Cincinnati, OH 45215. *Phone:* 512-771-2424. *Toll-free phone:* 800-888-1445. *E-mail:* awalker@brownmackie.edu.

▶**See page 500 for the College Close-Up.**

BROWN MACKIE COLLEGE–FINDLAY

Findlay, Ohio   **www.brownmackie.edu**

- **Proprietary** 2-year, founded 1929, administratively affiliated with Education Management Corporation
- **Rural** 1-acre campus
- **Coed,** 615 undergraduate students

Undergraduates Students come from 2 states and territories, 1% are from out of state.

Faculty *Total:* 51, 27% full-time. *Student/faculty ratio:* 16:1.

Majors Accounting technology and bookkeeping; business administration and management; CAD/CADD drafting/design technology; computer software technology; criminal justice/law enforcement administration; electrical, electronic and communications engineering technology; health/health care administration; medical/clinical assistant; paralegal/legal assistant; pharmacy technician.

Academics *Calendar:* continuous. *Degree:* diplomas and associate. *Special study options:* advanced placement credit, cooperative education, double majors, external degree program, independent study, internships.

Library 3,134 titles, 41 serial subscriptions, 26 audiovisual materials, an OPAC, a Web page.

Student Life *Housing:* college housing not available. *Campus security:* 24-hour emergency response devices.

Costs (2006–07) *Tuition:* $8592 full-time, $179 per credit hour part-time. *Required fees:* $460 full-time, $10 per credit hour part-time.

Financial Aid Of all full-time matriculated undergraduates, 14 Federal Work-Study jobs (averaging $1928).

Applying *Required:* high school transcript, interview. *Application deadlines:* rolling (freshmen), rolling (transfers). *Notification:* continuous (freshmen), continuous (transfers).

Freshmen Application Contact Director of Admissions, Brown Mackie College–Findlay, 1700 Fostoria Avenue, Suite 100, Findlay, OH 45840. *Phone:* 419-423-2211. *Toll-free phone:* 800-842-3687. *Fax:* 419-423-0725. *E-mail:* bmcfiadm@brownmackie.edu.

▶**See page 502 for the College Close-Up.**

BROWN MACKIE COLLEGE–NORTH CANTON

North Canton, Ohio   **www.socaec.com/**

- **Proprietary** 2-year, founded 1929, part of Education Management Corporation
- **Suburban** campus
- **Coed,** 930 undergraduate students

Undergraduates Students come from 1 other state.

Faculty *Total:* 29, 28% full-time. *Student/faculty ratio:* 21:1.

Majors Accounting technology and bookkeeping; business administration and management; CAD/CADD drafting/design technology; computer programming; computer software and media applications related; computer systems networking and telecommunications; criminal justice/law enforcement administration; electrical, electronic and communications engineering technology; health/health care administration; legal assistant/paralegal; medical/clinical assistant; pharmacy technician.

Academics *Calendar:* quarters. *Degree:* diplomas and associate. *Special study options:* adult/continuing education programs, advanced placement credit, independent study.

Student Life *Housing:* college housing not available. *Activities and Organizations:* student-run newspaper. *Student services:* personal/psychological counseling.

Standardized Tests *Required:* ASSET Evaluation (for admission).

Costs (2006–07) *Tuition:* $8592 full-time, $179 per credit part-time. *Required fees:* $480 full-time, $10 per credit part-time.

Applying *Required:* high school transcript, interview. *Required for some:* transcript of GED record. *Application deadlines:* rolling (freshmen), rolling (transfers). *Notification:* continuous (freshmen), continuous (transfers).

Freshmen Application Contact Director of Admissions, Brown Mackie College–North Canton, 1320 West Maple Street, NW, North Canton, OH 44720-2854. *Phone:* 330-494-1214. *Fax:* 330-494-8112. *E-mail:* bmcncadm@brownmackie.edu.

▶See page 520 for the College Close-Up.

BRYANT AND STRATTON COLLEGE
Parma, Ohio　　　　　　　　**www.bryantstratton.edu/**

- **Proprietary** primarily 2-year, founded 1981, part of Bryant and Stratton Business Institute, Inc
- **Suburban** 4-acre campus with easy access to Cleveland
- **Coed**

Undergraduates 183 full-time, 146 part-time. Students come from 1 other state, 25% African American, 0.3% Asian American or Pacific Islander, 13% Hispanic American, 2% transferred in. *Retention:* 33% of 2003 full-time freshmen returned.

Academics *Calendar:* semesters. *Degrees:* associate and bachelor's. *Special study options:* academic remediation for entering students, cooperative education, distance learning, double majors, independent study, internships, part-time degree program, summer session for credit.

Student Life *Campus security:* 24-hour emergency response devices.

Standardized Tests *Required:* CPAt (for admission). *Recommended:* SAT or ACT (for admission).

Costs (2006–07) *Tuition:* $415 per credit hour part-time. *Required fees:* $62 per term part-time.

Applying *Options:* deferred entrance. *Required:* high school transcript, interview, entrance evaluation and placement evaluation. *Required for some:* letters of recommendation.

Freshmen Application Contact Mr. F. Lee Nelly, Director of Admissions, Bryant and Stratton College, 12955 Snow Road, Parma, OH 44130. *Phone:* 216-265-3151 Ext. 229. *Toll-free phone:* 800-327-3151. *Fax:* 216-265-0325. *E-mail:* finelly@bryantstratton.edu.

BRYANT AND STRATTON COLLEGE
Willoughby Hills, Ohio　　　　　**www.bryantstratton.edu/**

Freshmen Application Contact Mr. James Pettit, Director of Admissions, Bryant and Stratton College, 27557 Chardon Road, Willoughby Hills, OH 44092. *Phone:* 440-944-6800.

CENTRAL OHIO TECHNICAL COLLEGE
Newark, Ohio　　　　　　　　**www.cotc.edu/**

- **State-supported** 2-year, founded 1971, part of Ohio Board of Regents
- **Small-town** 155-acre campus with easy access to Columbus
- **Coed,** 2,592 undergraduate students, 44% full-time, 72% women, 28% men

Undergraduates 1,149 full-time, 1,443 part-time. Students come from 3 states and territories, 1 other country, 1% are from out of state, 5% African American,

0.9% Asian American or Pacific Islander, 0.9% Hispanic American, 0.7% Native American, 5% transferred in, 1% live on campus. *Retention:* 52% of 2003 full-time freshmen returned.

Freshmen *Admission:* 1,171 applied, 1,171 admitted, 384 enrolled.

Faculty *Total:* 195, 32% full-time. *Student/faculty ratio:* 45:1.

Majors Accounting; administrative assistant and secretarial science; business administration and management; computer programming; corrections; criminal justice/law enforcement administration; criminal justice/police science; diagnostic medical sonography and ultrasound technology; drafting and design technology; electrical, electronic and communications engineering technology; electromechanical technology; human services; industrial technology; kindergarten/preschool education; mechanical engineering/mechanical technology; medical radiologic technology; nursing (registered nurse training); physical therapist assistant.

Academics *Calendar:* quarters. *Degree:* certificates and associate. *Special study options:* academic remediation for entering students, accelerated degree program, adult/continuing education programs, advanced placement credit, cooperative education, double majors, English as a second language, internships, off-campus study, part-time degree program, services for LD students, summer session for credit.

Library Newark Campus Library with 45,000 titles, 500 serial subscriptions, an OPAC.

Student Life *Housing Options:* coed. *Activities and Organizations:* drama/theater group, choral group, Student Senate, Phi Theta Kappa, Student Nurses Organization, Campus Chorus, Physical Therapy Assistants Organization. *Campus security:* 24-hour emergency response devices, student patrols, late-night transport/escort service. *Student services:* personal/psychological counseling.

Athletics *Intercollegiate sports:* baseball M, basketball M/W, golf M/W, soccer M, softball M, tennis M/W, volleyball W. *Intramural sports:* baseball M, basketball M/W, bowling M/W, cheerleading M/W, football M, golf M/W, skiing (downhill) M/W, soccer M, softball W, table tennis M/W, tennis M/W, volleyball M/W, weight lifting M/W.

Standardized Tests *Required:* ACT ASSET or ACT COMPASS (for placement).

Costs (2006–07) *Tuition:* state resident $3600 full-time, $100 per credit part-time; nonresident $6300 full-time, $175 per credit part-time. Full-time tuition and fees vary according to course load. Part-time tuition and fees vary according to course load. *Payment plan:* deferred payment. *Waivers:* senior citizens and employees or children of employees.

Financial Aid Of all full-time matriculated undergraduates, 68 Federal Work-Study jobs (averaging $4000).

Applying *Options:* electronic application, early admission, deferred entrance. *Application fee:* $15. *Required:* high school transcript. *Application deadlines:* rolling (freshmen), rolling (transfers).

Freshmen Application Contact Mr. John K. Merrin, Admissions Representative, Central Ohio Technical College, 1179 University Drive, Newark, OH 43055-1767. *Phone:* 740-366-9222. *Toll-free phone:* 800-9NEWARK. *Fax:* 740-366-5047. *E-mail:* jmerrin@cotc.edu.

CHATFIELD COLLEGE
St. Martin, Ohio　　　　　　　**www.chatfield.edu/**

- **Independent** 2-year, founded 1970, affiliated with Roman Catholic Church
- **Rural** 200-acre campus with easy access to Cincinnati and Dayton
- **Endowment** $700,000
- **Coed, primarily women**

Undergraduates Students come from 1 other state, 30% African American.

Faculty *Student/faculty ratio:* 12:1.

Academics *Calendar:* semesters. *Degree:* associate. *Special study options:* academic remediation for entering students, adult/continuing education programs, advanced placement credit, internships, off-campus study, part-time degree program, summer session for credit.

Student Life *Campus security:* 12-hour night patrols by security.

Costs (2006–07) *Tuition:* $3360 full-time, $280 per credit hour part-time. *Required fees:* $80 full-time.

Financial Aid Of all full-time matriculated undergraduates, 10 Federal Work-Study jobs (averaging $800). 4 state and other part-time jobs (averaging $600). *Financial aid deadline:* 8/1.

Applying *Options:* early admission, deferred entrance. *Application fee:* $10. *Required:* high school transcript.

Freshmen Application Contact Ms. Anna Jones, Director of Admissions, Chatfield College, St. Martin, OH 45118. *Phone:* 513-875-3344. *Fax:* 513-875-3912. *E-mail:* chatfield@chatfield.edu.

CINCINNATI COLLEGE OF MORTUARY SCIENCE

Cincinnati, Ohio

www.ccms.edu/

- **Independent** primarily 2-year, founded 1882
- **Urban** 10-acre campus
- **Coed**

Undergraduates 133 full-time. Students come from 17 states and territories, 7% African American, 0.8% Hispanic American, 68% transferred in.

Faculty *Student/faculty ratio:* 5:1.

Academics *Calendar:* quarters. *Degrees:* associate and bachelor's. *Special study options:* academic remediation for entering students, adult/continuing education programs, advanced placement credit, summer session for credit.

Costs (2006–07) *Tuition:* $13,500 full-time, $180 per credit part-time. *Required fees:* $610 full-time.

Applying *Options:* deferred entrance. *Application fee:* $25. *Required:* high school transcript. *Recommended:* letters of recommendation.

Freshmen Application Contact Ms. Pat Leon, Director of Financial Aid, Cincinnati College of Mortuary Science, 645 West North Bend Road, Cincinnati, OH 45224-1462. *Phone:* 513-761-2020. *Fax:* 513-761-3333.

CINCINNATI STATE TECHNICAL AND COMMUNITY COLLEGE

Cincinnati, Ohio

www.cincinnatistate.edu/

- **State-supported** 2-year, founded 1966, part of Ohio Board of Regents
- **Urban** 46-acre campus
- **Endowment** $1.7 million
- **Coed,** 8,277 undergraduate students, 40% full-time, 55% women, 45% men

Undergraduates 3,276 full-time, 5,001 part-time. Students come from 11 states and territories, 76 other countries, 11% are from out of state, 25% African American, 0.7% Asian American or Pacific Islander, 0.6% Hispanic American, 0.2% Native American, 3% international, 3% transferred in. *Retention:* 52% of 2003 full-time freshmen returned.

Freshmen *Admission:* 1,710 enrolled.

Faculty *Total:* 570, 31% full-time. *Student/faculty ratio:* 16:1.

Majors Accounting; administrative assistant and secretarial science; aeronautical/aerospace engineering technology; allied health and medical assisting services related; applied horticulture/horticultural business services related; architectural engineering technology; automotive engineering technology; biomedical technology; business administration and management; business, management, and marketing related; chemical technology; child care provision; cinematography and film/video production; civil engineering technology; clinical/medical laboratory technology; commercial and advertising art; computer and information sciences; computer engineering technology; computer programming; computer programming (specific applications); criminal justice/police science; culinary arts; diagnostic medical sonography and ultrasound technology; dietetics; electrical and electronic engineering technologies related; electrical, electronic and communications engineering technology; electromechanical technology; emergency medical technology (EMT paramedic); entrepreneurship; environmental engineering technology; executive assistant/executive secretary; fire science; general studies; health information/medical records technology; health professions related; heating, air conditioning and refrigeration technology; hotel/motel administration; information science/studies; international business/trade/commerce; landscaping and groundskeeping; laser and optical technology; liberal arts and sciences/liberal studies; management information systems; marketing/marketing management; mechanical engineering/mechanical technology; mechanic and repair technologies related; medical/clinical assistant; nursing (registered nurse training); nursing related; occupational therapist assistant; office management; parks, recreation, and leisure related; plastics engineering technology; purchasing, procurement/acquisitions and contracts management; real estate; respiratory care therapy; restaurant, culinary, and catering management; science technologies related; security and loss prevention; sign language interpretation and translation; surgical technology; survey technology; technical and business writing; telecommunications; turf and turfgrass management.

Academics *Calendar:* 5 ten-week terms. *Degree:* certificates and associate. *Special study options:* academic remediation for entering students, advanced placement credit, cooperative education, distance learning, double majors, English as a second language, honors programs, independent study, internships, off-campus study, part-time degree program, services for LD students, student-designed majors, summer session for credit.

Library Johnnie Mae Berry Library with 39,802 titles, 309 serial subscriptions, 3,570 audiovisual materials, an OPAC, a Web page.

Student Life *Housing:* college housing not available. *Activities and Organizations:* drama/theater group, student government, Nursing Student Association, Phi Theta Kappa, American Society of Civil Engineers, Students in Free Enterprise. *Campus security:* 24-hour emergency response devices and patrols, late-night transport/escort service. *Student services:* personal/psychological counseling.

Athletics Member NJCAA. *Intercollegiate sports:* basketball M/W, golf M/W, soccer M/W. *Intramural sports:* cheerleading W.

Costs (2006–07) *Tuition:* state resident $4411 full-time, $80 per credit hour part-time; nonresident $8822 full-time, $160 per credit hour part-time. Full-time tuition and fees vary according to reciprocity agreements. Part-time tuition and fees vary according to reciprocity agreements. *Required fees:* $258 full-time, $6 per credit hour part-time, $31 per term part-time. *Waivers:* senior citizens and employees or children of employees.

Financial Aid Of all full-time matriculated undergraduates, 100 Federal Work-Study jobs (averaging $3500).

Applying *Options:* electronic application. *Required:* high school transcript, ACT COMPASS. *Application deadlines:* rolling (freshmen), rolling (transfers). *Notification:* continuous (freshmen).

Freshmen Application Contact Ms. Gabriele Boeckermann, Director of Admission, Cincinnati State Technical and Community College, 3520 Central Parkway, Cincinnati, OH 45223-2690. *Phone:* 513-569-1550. *Fax:* 513-569-1562. *E-mail:* adm@cincinnatistate.edu.

CLARK STATE COMMUNITY COLLEGE

Springfield, Ohio

www.clarkstate.edu/

- **State-supported** 2-year, founded 1962, part of Ohio Board of Regents
- **Suburban** 60-acre campus with easy access to Columbus and Dayton
- **Coed,** 3,352 undergraduate students

Freshmen *Admission:* 1,743 applied, 1,743 admitted.

Faculty *Total:* 284, 18% full-time. *Student/faculty ratio:* 16:1.

Majors Accounting; administrative assistant and secretarial science; agricultural business and management; agricultural mechanization; agriculture; business administration and management; civil engineering technology; clinical/medical laboratory technology; commercial and advertising art; computer programming; computer programming related; computer systems networking and telecommunications; computer/technical support; corrections; court reporting; criminal justice/law enforcement administration; criminal justice/police science; drafting and design technology; dramatic/theater arts; electrical, electronic and communications engineering technology; emergency medical technology (EMT paramedic); horticultural science; human services; industrial technology; information science/studies; information technology; kindergarten/preschool education; kinesiology and exercise science; landscaping and groundskeeping; legal assistant/paralegal; liberal arts and sciences/liberal studies; mechanical engineering/mechanical technology; medical administrative assistant and medical secretary; nursing (licensed practical/vocational nurse training); nursing (registered nurse training); physical therapy; social work.

Academics *Calendar:* quarters. *Degree:* certificates and associate. *Special study options:* academic remediation for entering students, adult/continuing education programs, advanced placement credit, cooperative education, distance learning, off-campus study, part-time degree program, services for LD students, summer session for credit. *ROTC:* Army (c).

Library Clark State Community College Library with 31,988 titles, 378 serial subscriptions, an OPAC, a Web page.

Student Life *Housing:* college housing not available. *Activities and Organizations:* drama/theater group, student-run newspaper, choral group, Student Government Association, Minority Student Forum. *Campus security:* late-night transport/escort service. *Student services:* health clinic, personal/psychological counseling.

Athletics Member NJCAA. *Intercollegiate sports:* basketball M/W, softball W, volleyball W. *Intramural sports:* basketball M/W, tennis M/W, volleyball M/W.

Costs (2007–08) *Tuition:* state resident $3720 full-time, $78 per credit hour part-time; nonresident $7440 full-time, $155 per credit hour part-time. *Required fees:* $1500 full-time.

Applying *Options:* electronic application, early admission, deferred entrance. *Application fee:* $15. *Required:* high school transcript. *Application deadlines:* rolling (freshmen), rolling (transfers). *Notification:* continuous (freshmen), continuous (transfers).

Freshmen Application Contact Ms. Julie Schaid, Director, Enrollment and Precollege Program, Clark State Community College, PO Box 570, Springfield, OH 45501-0570. *Phone:* 937-328-6027. *Fax:* 937-328-3853. *E-mail:* admissions@clarkstate.edu.

CLEVELAND INSTITUTE OF ELECTRONICS

Cleveland, Ohio   www.cie-wc.edu/

- **Proprietary** 2-year, founded 1934
- **Coed, primarily men,** 2,317 undergraduate students

Undergraduates Students come from 52 states and territories, 70 other countries, 97% are from out of state.
Faculty *Total:* 6, 50% full-time.
Majors Electrical, electronic and communications engineering technology.
Academics *Calendar:* continuous. *Degrees:* associate (offers only external degree programs conducted through home study). *Special study options:* adult/continuing education programs, external degree program, part-time degree program.
Library 5,000 titles, 38 serial subscriptions.
Student Life *Housing:* college housing not available.
Costs (2006–07) *Tuition:* $1770 per term part-time. No tuition increase for student's term of enrollment. *Payment plans:* tuition prepayment, installment.
Applying *Options:* electronic application, early admission. *Required:* high school transcript. *Application deadlines:* rolling (freshmen), rolling (transfers). *Notification:* continuous (freshmen), continuous (transfers).
Freshmen Application Contact Mr. Scott Katzenmeyer, Registrar, Cleveland Institute of Electronics, 1776 East 17th Street, Cleveland, OH 44114. *Phone:* 216-781-9400. *Toll-free phone:* 800-243-6446. *Fax:* 216-781-0331. *E-mail:* instruct@cie-wc.edu.

COLLEGE OF ART ADVERTISING

Cincinnati, Ohio   artadvertisingoh.college-Info.net/

Director of Admissions Ms. Janet Bussberg, Director of Admissions, College of Art Advertising, 4343 Bridgetown Road, Cincinnati, OH 45211-4427. *Phone:* 937-294-0592. *E-mail:* janet.bussberg@fuse.net.

COLUMBUS STATE COMMUNITY COLLEGE

Columbus, Ohio   www.cscc.edu/

Freshmen Application Contact Ms. Tari Blaney, Director of Admissions, Columbus State Community College, 550 East Spring Street, Madison Hall, Columbus, OH 43215. *Phone:* 614-287-2669. *Toll-free phone:* 800-621-6407 Ext. 2669. *Fax:* 614-287-6019. *E-mail:* tblaney@cscc.edu.

CUYAHOGA COMMUNITY COLLEGE

Cleveland, Ohio   www.tri-c.edu/

- **State and locally supported** 2-year, founded 1963
- **Urban** campus
- **Endowment** $18.9 million
- **Coed,** 24,796 undergraduate students, 41% full-time, 62% women, 38% men

Undergraduates 10,120 full-time, 14,676 part-time. Students come from 21 states and territories, 78 other countries, 29% African American, 2% Asian American or Pacific Islander, 4% Hispanic American, 0.5% Native American, 2% international, 3% transferred in. *Retention:* 45% of 2003 full-time freshmen returned.
Freshmen *Admission:* 6,645 applied, 6,645 admitted, 2,204 enrolled.
Faculty *Total:* 1,440, 23% full-time, 11% with terminal degrees. *Student/faculty ratio:* 18:1.
Majors Accounting; administrative assistant and secretarial science; automobile/automotive mechanics technology; avionics maintenance technology; business administration and management; clinical laboratory science/medical technology; commercial and advertising art; computer engineering technology; computer typography and composition equipment operation; court reporting; criminal justice/police science; engineering technology; finance; fire science; industrial radiologic technology; kindergarten/preschool education; legal assistant/paralegal; liberal arts and sciences/liberal studies; marketing/marketing management; merchandising; nursing (registered nurse training); opticianry; photography; physician assistant; real estate; respiratory care therapy; restaurant, culinary, and

catering management; safety/security technology; sales, distribution and marketing; selling skills and sales; surgical technology; veterinary technology.
Academics *Calendar:* semesters. *Degree:* certificates and associate. *Special study options:* adult/continuing education programs, advanced placement credit, cooperative education, distance learning, English as a second language, external degree program, independent study, part-time degree program, services for LD students, summer session for credit.
Library Metro Library plus 3 others with 177,767 titles, 1,135 serial subscriptions, an OPAC, a Web page.
Student Life *Housing:* college housing not available. *Activities and Organizations:* drama/theater group, student-run newspaper, choral group, Student Senate, Student Nursing Organization, Business Focus, Phi Theta Kappa. *Campus security:* 24-hour emergency response devices and patrols, late-night transport/escort service. *Student services:* health clinic, personal/psychological counseling.
Athletics Member NJCAA. *Intercollegiate sports:* baseball M(s), basketball M(s), cross-country running M(s)/W(s), soccer M(s), softball W(s). *Intramural sports:* basketball M, tennis M/W, track and field M/W, volleyball M/W.
Costs (2006–07) *Tuition:* area resident $2416 full-time, $81 per credit hour part-time; state resident $3194 full-time, $106 per credit hour part-time; nonresident $6541 full-time, $218 per credit hour part-time.
Financial Aid Of all full-time matriculated undergraduates, 802 Federal Work-Study jobs (averaging $3300).
Applying *Options:* early admission, deferred entrance. *Required for some:* high school transcript. *Application deadlines:* rolling (freshmen), rolling (transfers). *Notification:* continuous (freshmen), continuous (transfers).
Freshmen Application Contact Mr. Kevin McDaniel, Director of Admissions and Records, Cuyahoga Community College, 2900 Community College Avenue, Cleveland, OH 44115. *Phone:* 216-987-4030. *Toll-free phone:* 800-954-8742. *Fax:* 216-696-2567.

DAVIS COLLEGE

Toledo, Ohio   daviscollege.edu/

- **Proprietary** 2-year, founded 1858
- **Urban** 1-acre campus with easy access to Detroit
- **Coed**

Undergraduates 225 full-time, 226 part-time. Students come from 2 states and territories, 5% are from out of state, 29% African American, 2% Hispanic American, 0.5% Native American, 26% transferred in.
Faculty *Student/faculty ratio:* 14:1.
Academics *Calendar:* quarters. *Degree:* diplomas and associate. *Special study options:* academic remediation for entering students, adult/continuing education programs, advanced placement credit, distance learning, internships, part-time degree program, summer session for credit.
Student Life *Campus security:* 24-hour emergency response devices, security cameras for parking lot.
Standardized Tests *Required:* CPAt (for admission).
Costs (2006–07) *Tuition:* $8100 full-time, $225 per credit hour part-time. *Required fees:* $480 full-time.
Financial Aid Of all full-time matriculated undergraduates, 10 Federal Work-Study jobs (averaging $3500).
Applying *Options:* electronic application, early admission, deferred entrance. *Application fee:* $30. *Required:* high school transcript, interview.
Freshmen Application Contact Ms. Dana Stern, Davis College, 4747 Monroe Street, Toledo, OH 43623-4307. *Phone:* 419-473-2700. *Toll-free phone:* 800-477-7021. *Fax:* 419-473-2472. *E-mail:* dstern@daviscollege.edu.

EDISON STATE COMMUNITY COLLEGE

Piqua, Ohio   www.edisonohio.edu/

Director of Admissions Ms. Beth Iams Culbertson, Director of Admissions, Edison State Community College, 1973 Edison Drive, Piqua, OH 45356. *Phone:* 937-778-8600 Ext. 317. *Toll-free phone:* 800-922-3722. *Fax:* 937-778-4692. *E-mail:* info@edison.cc.oh.us.

ETI TECHNICAL COLLEGE OF NILES

Niles, Ohio   www.eti-college.com/

Freshmen Application Contact Ms. Diane Marsteller, Director of Admissions, ETI Technical College of Niles, 2076 Youngstown-Warren Road, Niles, OH 44446-4398. *Phone:* 330-652-9919. *Fax:* 330-652-4399.

GALLIPOLIS CAREER COLLEGE

Gallipolis, Ohio   **www.gallipoliscareercollege.com/**

- **Independent** 2-year, founded 1962
- **Small-town** campus
- **Coed, primarily women**

Undergraduates 145 full-time, 9 part-time. Students come from 2 states and territories, 13% are from out of state, 9% African American.

Faculty *Student/faculty ratio:* 22:1.

Academics *Calendar:* quarters. *Degree:* certificates, diplomas, and associate. *Special study options:* academic remediation for entering students, adult/continuing education programs, double majors, independent study, internships, part-time degree program, summer session for credit.

Standardized Tests *Required:* Wonderlic aptitude test (for admission).

Costs (2006–07) *Tuition:* $8640 full-time, $180 per credit hour part-time. No tuition increase for student's term of enrollment. *Required fees:* $100 full-time.

Applying *Application fee:* $50. *Required:* high school transcript, interview.

Freshmen Application Contact Mr. Jack Henson, Director of Admissions, Gallipolis Career College, 1176 Jackson Pike, Suite 312, Gallipolis, OH 45631. *Phone:* 740-446-4367. *Toll-free phone:* 800-214-0452. *Fax:* 740-446-4124. *E-mail:* admissions@gallipoliscareercollege.com.

HOCKING COLLEGE

Nelsonville, Ohio   **www.hocking.edu/**

- **State-supported** 2-year, founded 1968, part of Ohio Board of Regents
- **Rural** 1600-acre campus with easy access to Columbus
- **Endowment** $2.3 million
- **Coed,** 5,250 undergraduate students

Undergraduates Students come from 28 states and territories, 3% are from out of state, 3% African American, 0.6% Asian American or Pacific Islander, 1% Hispanic American, 0.3% Native American, 9% live on campus.

Faculty *Total:* 236, 77% full-time.

Majors Accounting; administrative assistant and secretarial science; business administration and management; ceramic sciences and engineering; child development; computer engineering technology; computer programming; computer science; consumer merchandising/retailing management; corrections; criminal justice/law enforcement administration; criminal justice/police science; culinary arts; dietetics; drafting and design technology; ecology; electrical, electronic and communications engineering technology; emergency medical technology (EMT paramedic); equestrian studies; fire science; fish/game management; fishing and fisheries sciences and management; food science; forestry; forestry technology; health information/medical records administration; hospitality administration; hotel/motel administration; industrial technology; land use planning and management; marketing/marketing management; medical administrative assistant and medical secretary; medical/clinical assistant; natural resources/conservation; natural resources management; natural resources management and policy; nursing (licensed practical/vocational nurse training); nursing (registered nurse training); occupational therapist assistant; ophthalmic laboratory technology; parks, recreation and leisure facilities management; physical therapist assistant; special products marketing; tourism and travel services management; wildlife and wildlands science and management.

Academics *Calendar:* quarters. *Degree:* certificates, diplomas, and associate. *Special study options:* academic remediation for entering students, accelerated degree program, adult/continuing education programs, advanced placement credit, cooperative education, distance learning, double majors, English as a second language, internships, part-time degree program, services for LD students, student-designed majors, summer session for credit. *ROTC:* Army (c).

Library Hocking College Learning Resources Center plus 1 other with 19,663 titles, 223 serial subscriptions, 8,327 audiovisual materials, an OPAC, a Web page.

Student Life *Housing Options:* coed. Campus housing is university owned. *Activities and Organizations:* drama/theater group, choral group, Phi Theta Kappa, Recycling Club, Unity Board, Alpha Beta Gamma, Native American Club. *Campus security:* 24-hour emergency response devices and patrols, student patrols, late-night transport/escort service. *Student services:* health clinic, personal/psychological counseling, women's center.

Athletics *Intramural sports:* archery M/W, basketball M/W, cross-country running M/W, football M/W, golf M/W, soccer M/W, softball M/W, tennis M/W, volleyball M/W, weight lifting M/W.

Standardized Tests *Required for some:* nursing exam. *Recommended:* SAT or ACT (for placement).

Costs (2006–07) *Tuition:* state resident $3546 full-time; nonresident $7092 full-time.

Financial Aid Of all full-time matriculated undergraduates, 125 Federal Work-Study jobs (averaging $1700). 225 state and other part-time jobs (averaging $1700).

Applying *Options:* electronic application. *Application fee:* $15. *Required:* high school transcript. *Application deadlines:* rolling (freshmen), rolling (transfers). *Notification:* continuous (freshmen), continuous (transfers).

Director of Admissions Ms. Lyn Hull, Director of Admissions, Hocking College, 3301 Hocking Parkway, Nelsonville, OH 45764-9588. *Phone:* 740-753-3591 Ext. 2803. *Toll-free phone:* 877-462-5464. *E-mail:* hull_lyn@hocking.edu.

HONDROS COLLEGE

Westerville, Ohio   **www.hondroscollege.com/**

Director of Admissions Ms. Carol Thomas, Operations Manager, Hondros College, 4140 Executive Parkway, Westerville, OH 43081. *Phone:* 614-508-7244. *Toll-free phone:* 800-783-0095.

INTERNATIONAL COLLEGE OF BROADCASTING

Dayton, Ohio   **www.icbcollege.com/**

Director of Admissions Mr. Aan McIntosh, Director of Admissions, International College of Broadcasting, 6 South Smithville Road, Dayton, OH 45431. *Phone:* 937-258-8251. *Fax:* 937-258-8714.

ITT TECHNICAL INSTITUTE

Dayton, Ohio   **www.itt-tech.edu/**

- **Proprietary** 2-year, founded 1935, part of ITT Educational Services, Inc
- **Suburban** 7-acre campus
- **Coed**

Majors Accounting technology and bookkeeping; business administration and management; CAD/CADD drafting/design technology; computer engineering technology; computer systems networking and telecommunications; criminal justice/law enforcement administration; health information/medical records technology; web/multimedia management and webmaster; Web page, digital/multimedia and information resources design; web page, digital/multimedia and information resources design.

Academics *Calendar:* quarters. *Degree:* associate.

Library a Web page.

Student Life *Housing:* college housing not available.

Standardized Tests *Required:* Wonderlic aptitude test (for admission).

Costs (2006–07) *Tuition:* Contact school for program costs.

Applying *Options:* deferred entrance. *Application fee:* $100. *Required:* high school transcript, interview. *Recommended:* letters of recommendation. *Application deadlines:* rolling (freshmen), rolling (transfers). *Notification:* continuous (freshmen), continuous (transfers).

Freshmen Application Contact Mr. Darryl Dancy, Director of Recruitment, ITT Technical Institute, 3325 Stop 8 Road, Dayton, OH 45414. *Phone:* 937-454-2267. *Toll-free phone:* 800-568-3241.

ITT TECHNICAL INSTITUTE

Hilliard, Ohio   **www.itt-tech.edu/**

- **Proprietary** 2-year, founded 2003, part of ITT Educational Services, Inc
- **Coed**

Majors Accounting technology and bookkeeping; business administration and management; CAD/CADD drafting/design technology; computer engineering technology; computer systems networking and telecommunications; criminal justice/law enforcement administration; health information/medical records technology; web page, digital/multimedia and information resources design.

Academics *Calendar:* quarters. *Degree:* associate.

Standardized Tests *Required:* Wonderlic aptitude test (for admission).

Costs (2006–07) *Tuition:* Contact school for program costs.

Applying *Application fee:* $100. *Required:* high school transcript, interview. *Recommended:* letters of recommendation. *Application deadlines:* rolling (freshmen), rolling (transfers). *Notification:* continuous (freshmen), continuous (transfers).

Freshmen Application Contact Mr. Jim Tussing, Director of Recruitment, ITT Technical Institute, 3781 Park Mill Run Drive, Hilliard, OH 43026. *Phone:* 614-771-4888. *Toll-free phone:* 888-483-4888.

ITT TECHNICAL INSTITUTE
Norwood, Ohio   www.itt-tech.edu/

- **Proprietary** 2-year, founded 1995, part of ITT Educational Services, Inc
- **Coed**

Majors Accounting technology and bookkeeping; business administration and management; CAD/CADD drafting/design technology; computer engineering technology; computer systems networking and telecommunications; criminal justice/law enforcement administration; medical laboratory technology; web/multimedia management and webmaster; web page, digital/multimedia and information resources design.

Academics *Calendar:* quarters. *Degree:* associate.

Library a Web page.

Student Life *Housing:* college housing not available.

Standardized Tests *Required:* Wonderlic aptitude test (for admission).

Costs (2006–07) *Tuition:* Contact school for program costs.

Applying *Options:* deferred entrance. *Application fee:* $100. *Required:* high school transcript, interview. *Recommended:* letters of recommendation. *Application deadlines:* rolling (freshmen), rolling (transfers). *Notification:* continuous (freshmen), continuous (transfers).

Freshmen Application Contact Mr. Greg Hitt, Director of Recruitment, ITT Technical Institute, 4750 Wesley Avenue, Norwood, OH 45212. *Phone:* 513-531-8300. *Toll-free phone:* 800-314-8324.

ITT TECHNICAL INSTITUTE
Strongsville, Ohio   www.itt-tech.edu/

- **Proprietary** 2-year, founded 1994, part of ITT Educational Services, Inc
- **Coed**

Majors Accounting technology and bookkeeping; business administration and management; CAD/CADD drafting/design technology; computer engineering technology; computer software technology; computer systems networking and telecommunications; criminal justice/law enforcement administration; medical laboratory technology; web/multimedia management and webmaster; web page, digital/multimedia and information resources design.

Academics *Calendar:* quarters. *Degree:* associate.

Library a Web page.

Student Life *Housing:* college housing not available.

Standardized Tests *Required:* Wonderlic aptitude test (for admission).

Costs (2006–07) *Tuition:* Contact school for program costs.

Applying *Options:* deferred entrance. *Application fee:* $100. *Required:* high school transcript, interview. *Recommended:* letters of recommendation. *Application deadlines:* rolling (freshmen), rolling (transfers). *Notification:* continuous (freshmen), continuous (transfers).

Freshmen Application Contact Ms. Maggie Crum, Director of Recruitment, ITT Technical Institute, 14955 Sprague Road, Strongsville, OH 44136. *Phone:* 440-234-9091. *Toll-free phone:* 800-331-1488.

ITT TECHNICAL INSTITUTE
Warrensville Heights, Ohio   www.itt-tech.edu/

- **Proprietary** 2-year, founded 2005
- **Coed**

Majors Business administration and management; CAD/CADD drafting/design technology; computer engineering technology; computer systems networking and telecommunications; criminal justice/law enforcement administration; health information/medical records technology; web page, digital/multimedia and information resources design.

Academics *Calendar:* quarters. *Degree:* associate.

Standardized Tests *Required:* Wonderlic aptitude test (for admission).

Costs (2006–07) *Tuition:* Contact school for program costs.

Applying *Application fee:* $100. *Required:* high school transcript, interview. *Recommended:* letters of recommendation. *Application deadlines:* rolling (freshmen), rolling (transfers). *Notification:* continuous (freshmen), continuous (transfers).

Freshmen Application Contact Mr. Erik Andryszak, Director of Recruitment, ITT Technical Institute, 4700 Richmond Road, Warrensville Heights, OH 44128. *Phone:* 216-896-6500. *Toll-free phone:* 800-741-3494.

ITT TECHNICAL INSTITUTE
Youngstown, Ohio   www.itt-tech.edu/

- **Proprietary** 2-year, founded 1967, part of ITT Educational Services, Inc
- **Suburban** campus with easy access to Cleveland and Pittsburgh
- **Coed**

Majors Accounting technology and bookkeeping; business administration and management; CAD/CADD drafting/design technology; computer and information systems security; computer systems networking and telecommunications; criminal justice/law enforcement administration; health information/medical records technology; web/multimedia management and webmaster; web page, digital/multimedia and information resources design.

Academics *Calendar:* quarters. *Degree:* associate.

Library a Web page.

Student Life *Housing:* college housing not available. *Activities and Organizations:* student-run newspaper.

Standardized Tests *Required:* Wonderlic aptitude test (for admission).

Costs (2006–07) *Tuition:* Contact school for program costs.

Financial Aid Of all full-time matriculated undergraduates, 5 Federal Work-Study jobs (averaging $3979).

Applying *Options:* deferred entrance. *Application fee:* $100. *Required:* high school transcript, interview. *Recommended:* letters of recommendation. *Application deadlines:* rolling (freshmen), rolling (transfers). *Notification:* continuous (freshmen), continuous (transfers).

Freshmen Application Contact Mr. Mike Bishop, Director of Recruitment, ITT Technical Institute, 1030 North Meridian Road, Youngstown, OH 44509. *Phone:* 330-270-1600. *Toll-free phone:* 800-832-5001.

JAMES A. RHODES STATE COLLEGE
Lima, Ohio   www.rhodesstate.edu/

Freshmen Application Contact Mr. Scot Lingrell, Director, Student Advising and Development, James A. Rhodes State College, 4240 Campus Drive, Lima, OH 45804-3597. *Phone:* 419-995-8050. *E-mail:* peterl@ltc.tec.oh.us.

JEFFERSON COMMUNITY COLLEGE
Steubenville, Ohio   www.jcc.edu/

- **State and locally supported** 2-year, founded 1966, part of Ohio Board of Regents
- **Small-town** 83-acre campus with easy access to Pittsburgh
- **Endowment** $197,077
- **Coed,** 1,600 undergraduate students, 58% full-time, 62% women, 38% men

Undergraduates 927 full-time, 673 part-time. Students come from 23 states and territories, 16% are from out of state, 0.2% African American, 0.3% Asian American or Pacific Islander, 0.6% Hispanic American, 0.2% Native American.

Freshmen *Admission:* 838 applied, 838 admitted. *Average high school GPA:* 2.53.

Faculty *Total:* 124, 28% full-time, 6% with terminal degrees. *Student/faculty ratio:* 16:1.

Majors Accounting; administrative assistant and secretarial science; business administration and management; child care and support services management; computer engineering related; consumer merchandising/retailing management; corrections; criminal justice/police science; data processing and data processing technology; dental assisting; developmental and child psychology; drafting and design technology; electrical, electronic and communications engineering technology; emergency medical technology (EMT paramedic); finance; industrial radiologic technology; industrial technology; legal administrative assistant/secretary; mechanical engineering/mechanical technology; medical administra-

Jefferson Community College (continued)

tive assistant and medical secretary; medical/clinical assistant; nursing (licensed practical/vocational nurse training); real estate; respiratory care therapy; special products marketing.

Academics *Calendar:* semesters. *Degree:* certificates and associate. *Special study options:* academic remediation for entering students, adult/continuing education programs, internships, off-campus study, part-time degree program, services for LD students, summer session for credit.

Library Jefferson Community College Library with 12,500 titles, 180 serial subscriptions, an OPAC.

Student Life *Housing:* college housing not available. *Activities and Organizations:* Student Senate, SADD, AITP (Association for Information Technology Professionals), American Drafting and Design Association, Writers Club. *Campus security:* 24-hour emergency response devices, day and evening security.

Athletics *Intercollegiate sports:* basketball M/W. *Intramural sports:* basketball M/W, bowling M/W, football M/W, softball M/W, tennis M/W, volleyball M/W.

Standardized Tests *Required for some:* SAT or ACT (for admission).

Costs (2007–08) *Tuition:* area resident $2700 full-time; state resident $2880 full-time; nonresident $3690 full-time.

Financial Aid Of all full-time matriculated undergraduates, 30 Federal Work-Study jobs (averaging $1500).

Applying *Options:* early admission, deferred entrance. *Application fee:* $20. *Required for some:* high school transcript. *Application deadlines:* 8/20 (freshmen), 8/20 (transfers). *Notification:* continuous until 8/20 (freshmen), continuous until 8/20 (transfers).

Freshmen Application Contact Mr. Chuck Mascellino, Director of Admissions, Jefferson Community College, 4000 Sunset Boulevard, Steubenville, OH 43952. *Phone:* 740-264-5591. *Toll-free phone:* 800-68-COLLEGE Ext. 142. *Fax:* 740-266-2944. *E-mail:* cmascellino@jcc.edu.

KENT STATE UNIVERSITY, ASHTABULA CAMPUS

Ashtabula, Ohio　　　　　**www.ashtabula.kent.edu/**

- **State-supported** primarily 2-year, founded 1958, part of Kent State University System
- **Small-town** 120-acre campus with easy access to Cleveland
- **Coed,** 1,396 undergraduate students

Undergraduates 5% African American, 0.9% Asian American or Pacific Islander, 2% Hispanic American, 0.5% Native American, 0.4% international.

Faculty *Total:* 80, 45% full-time.

Majors Accounting; administrative assistant and secretarial science; business administration and management; computer engineering technology; criminal justice/police science; electrical, electronic and communications engineering technology; engineering technology; environmental studies; finance; human services; industrial technology; kindergarten/preschool education; legal administrative assistant/secretary; liberal arts and sciences/liberal studies; marketing/marketing management; materials science; mechanical engineering/mechanical technology; nursing (registered nurse training); physical therapy; real estate.

Academics *Calendar:* semesters. *Degrees:* certificates, associate, and bachelor's (also offers some upper-level and graduate courses). *Special study options:* academic remediation for entering students, advanced placement credit, freshman honors college, honors programs, internships, part-time degree program, student-designed majors, summer session for credit. *ROTC:* Army (c).

Library 51,884 titles, 225 serial subscriptions.

Student Life *Housing:* college housing not available. *Activities and Organizations:* drama/theater group, student-run newspaper, student government, student newspaper, Student Nurses Association. *Campus security:* 24-hour emergency response devices.

Standardized Tests *Recommended:* SAT or ACT (for placement).

Costs (2006–07) *Tuition:* state resident $4770 full-time; nonresident $12,202 full-time.

Financial Aid Of all full-time matriculated undergraduates, 1,042 Federal Work-Study jobs (averaging $2316).

Applying *Options:* early admission, deferred entrance. *Application fee:* $30. *Application deadlines:* 8/1 (freshmen), 7/15 (out-of-state freshmen), 7/15 (transfers). *Notification:* continuous until 8/1 (freshmen), continuous until 7/15 (out-of-state freshmen), continuous until 7/15 (transfers).

Director of Admissions Ms. Kelly Sanford, Director, Enrollment Management and Student Services, Kent State University, Ashtabula Campus, 3300 Lake Road West, Ashtabula, OH 44004-2299. *Phone:* 440-964-4217. *E-mail:* sanford@ashtabula.kent.edu.

KENT STATE UNIVERSITY, EAST LIVERPOOL CAMPUS

East Liverpool, Ohio　　　　　**www.kenteliv.kent.edu/**

- **State-supported** 2-year, founded 1967, part of Kent State University System
- **Small-town** 4-acre campus with easy access to Pittsburgh
- **Coed,** 657 undergraduate students

Undergraduates Students come from 3 states and territories, 6% are from out of state.

Freshmen *Admission:* 125 applied, 100 admitted. *Average high school GPA:* 3.18.

Faculty *Total:* 75, 27% full-time. *Student/faculty ratio:* 15:1.

Majors Accounting; business administration and management; computer and information sciences related; computer engineering technology; criminal justice/law enforcement administration; legal administrative assistant/secretary; liberal arts and sciences/liberal studies; nursing (registered nurse training); occupational therapy; physical therapy.

Academics *Calendar:* semesters. *Degrees:* certificates and associate (also offers some upper-level and graduate courses). *Special study options:* academic remediation for entering students, accelerated degree program, adult/continuing education programs, advanced placement credit, distance learning, internships, part-time degree program, services for LD students, student-designed majors, summer session for credit. *ROTC:* Army (c), Navy (c), Air Force (c).

Library East Liverpool Campus Library with 31,320 titles, 135 serial subscriptions, an OPAC, a Web page.

Student Life *Housing:* college housing not available. *Activities and Organizations:* student-run newspaper, Student Senate, Student Nurses Association, Alpha Beta Gamma, Occupational Therapist Assistant Club, Physical Therapist Assistant Club. *Campus security:* student patrols, late-night transport/escort service.

Standardized Tests *Recommended:* ACT (for placement).

Costs (2006–07) *Tuition:* area resident $4770 full-time, $217 per hour part-time; nonresident $12,202 full-time, $555 per hour part-time. Full-time tuition and fees vary according to course level. Part-time tuition and fees vary according to course level. *Payment plans:* tuition prepayment, installment. *Waivers:* employees or children of employees.

Financial Aid Of all full-time matriculated undergraduates, 16 Federal Work-Study jobs (averaging $2727).

Applying *Options:* early admission, deferred entrance. *Application fee:* $30. *Required:* high school transcript. *Application deadlines:* rolling (freshmen), rolling (transfers). *Notification:* continuous until 9/1 (freshmen), continuous until 9/1 (transfers).

Freshmen Application Contact Mr. Anthony M. Underwood, Director of Enrollment Management and Student Services, Kent State University, East Liverpool Campus, 400 East Fourth Street, East Liverpool, OH 43920. *Phone:* 330-382—7414. *E-mail:* admissions@eliv.kent.edu.

KENT STATE UNIVERSITY, GEAUGA CAMPUS

Burton, Ohio　　　　　**www.geauga.kent.edu/**

- **State-supported** founded 1964, part of Kent State University System
- **Rural** 87-acre campus with easy access to Cleveland
- **Coed,** 1,057 undergraduate students, 33% full-time, 58% women, 42% men

Undergraduates 344 full-time, 713 part-time. Students come from 8 states and territories, 1 other country, 1% are from out of state, 7% African American, 1% Asian American or Pacific Islander, 1% Hispanic American, 0.6% Native American, 0.2% international, 6% transferred in. *Retention:* 56% of 2003 full-time freshmen returned.

Freshmen *Admission:* 167 applied, 167 admitted, 124 enrolled. *Average high school GPA:* 2.5. *Test scores:* SAT verbal scores over 500: 17%; SAT math scores over 500: 17%; ACT scores over 18: 68%; ACT scores over 24: 7%.

Faculty *Total:* 87, 15% full-time, 15% with terminal degrees. *Student/faculty ratio:* 15:1.

Majors Accounting technology and bookkeeping; applied horticulture; business administration and management; emergency medical technology (EMT paramedic); industrial technology; information technology; liberal arts and sciences/liberal studies; nursing science.

Academics *Calendar:* semesters. *Degrees:* certificates, diplomas, associate, and bachelor's. *Special study options:* academic remediation for entering students, adult/continuing education programs, advanced placement credit, distance

learning, double majors, internships, part-time degree program, services for LD students, student-designed majors, summer session for credit. *ROTC:* Army (c), Air Force (c).

Library Kent State University Library with 8,300 titles, 6,600 serial subscriptions, an OPAC, a Web page.

Student Life *Housing:* college housing not available. *Activities and Organizations:* student-run newspaper, Computer Club, Student Senate, Accounting Club, student newspaper. *Campus security:* 24-hour emergency response devices.

Athletics *Intramural sports:* basketball M/W, skiing (downhill) M/W, table tennis M/W, volleyball M/W.

Standardized Tests *Required for some:* SAT or ACT (for admission). *Recommended:* SAT or ACT (for admission).

Costs (2006–07) *Tuition:* state resident $4770 full-time, $217 per credit hour part-time; nonresident $12,202 full-time, $555 per credit hour part-time. Full-time tuition and fees vary according to course level. Part-time tuition and fees vary according to course level. *Payment plans:* installment, deferred payment. *Waivers:* senior citizens and employees or children of employees.

Financial Aid Of all full-time matriculated undergraduates who enrolled in 2006, 257 applied for aid, 224 were judged to have need, 11 had their need fully met. 11 Federal Work-Study jobs (averaging $1554). In 2006, 2 non-need-based awards were made. *Average percent of need met:* 50%. *Average financial aid package:* $5960. *Average need-based loan:* $3380. *Average need-based gift aid:* $3519. *Average non-need-based aid:* $180. *Average indebtedness upon graduation:* $18,289.

Applying *Options:* early admission, deferred entrance. *Application fee:* $30. *Required:* high school transcript. *Application deadlines:* rolling (freshmen), rolling (transfers).

Freshmen Application Contact Ms. Betty Landrus, Kent State University, Geauga Campus, 14111 Claridon-Troy Road, Burton, OH 44021. *Phone:* 440-834-4187. *Fax:* 440-834-8846. *E-mail:* blandrus@kent.edu.

Kent State University, Salem Campus

Salem, Ohio   www.salem.kent.edu/

Freshmen Application Contact Mrs. Judy Heisler, Admissions Secretary, Kent State University, Salem Campus, 2491 State Route 45 South, Salem, OH 44460-9412. *Phone:* 330-332-0361 Ext. 74201. *E-mail:* ask-us@salem.kent.edu.

Kent State University, Stark Campus

Canton, Ohio   www.stark.kent.edu/

Freshmen Application Contact Ms. Deborah Ann Speck, Director of Admissions, Kent State University, Stark Campus, 6000 Frank Avenue NW, Canton, OH 44720-7599. *Phone:* 330-499-9600 Ext. 53259.

Kent State University, Trumbull Campus

Warren, Ohio   www.trumbull.kent.edu/

- **State-supported** primarily 2-year, founded 1954, part of Kent State University System
- **Suburban** 200-acre campus with easy access to Cleveland
- **Coed,** 1,996 undergraduate students, 46% full-time, 64% women, 36% men

Undergraduates 910 full-time, 1,086 part-time. Students come from 4 states and territories, 3 other countries, 1% are from out of state, 11% African American, 0.6% Asian American or Pacific Islander, 1% Hispanic American, 0.4% Native American, 0.2% international, 6% transferred in. *Retention:* 65% of 2003 full-time freshmen returned.

Freshmen *Admission:* 443 applied, 443 admitted, 309 enrolled. *Average high school GPA:* 2.8. *Test scores:* SAT math scores over 500: 50%; ACT scores over 18: 65%; SAT math scores over 600: 50%; ACT scores over 24: 15%.

Faculty *Total:* 123, 48% full-time, 33% with terminal degrees. *Student/faculty ratio:* 16:1.

Majors Automobile/automotive mechanics technology; business administration and management; computer engineering technology; criminal justice/law enforcement administration; electrical, electronic and communications engineering technology; English; environmental engineering technology; general studies;

industrial technology; liberal arts and sciences/liberal studies; mechanical engineering/mechanical technology; nursing science.

Academics *Calendar:* semesters. *Degrees:* certificates, associate, and bachelor's (also offers some upper-level and graduate courses). *Special study options:* academic remediation for entering students, adult/continuing education programs, advanced placement credit, cooperative education, distance learning, freshman honors college, honors programs, independent study, internships, part-time degree program, services for LD students, student-designed majors, summer session for credit. *ROTC:* Army (c), Air Force (c).

Library Trumbull Campus Library with 65,951 titles, 759 serial subscriptions, an OPAC, a Web page.

Student Life *Housing:* college housing not available. *Activities and Organizations:* drama/theater group, student-run newspaper, Student Senate, Trumbull Environmental Club, Union Activities Board, Gamemasters, Kent Christian Fellowship. *Campus security:* 24-hour emergency response devices, late-night transport/escort service, patrols by trained security personnel during open hours.

Athletics *Intramural sports:* basketball M/W, bowling M/W, skiing (downhill) M/W, volleyball M/W.

Standardized Tests *Required for some:* SAT or ACT (for admission). *Recommended:* SAT or ACT (for admission).

Costs (2006–07) *Tuition:* state resident $4586 full-time, $217 per credit hour part-time; nonresident $12,018 full-time, $555 per credit hour part-time. Full-time tuition and fees vary according to course level. Part-time tuition and fees vary according to course level. *Payment plans:* installment, deferred payment. *Waivers:* senior citizens and employees or children of employees.

Financial Aid Of all full-time matriculated undergraduates, 31 Federal Work-Study jobs (averaging $2708).

Applying *Options:* early admission, deferred entrance. *Application fee:* $30. *Required:* high school transcript. *Application deadlines:* 7/30 (freshmen), rolling (transfers). *Notification:* continuous until 8/30 (freshmen), continuous until 8/30 (transfers).

Freshmen Application Contact Ms. Patricia Davis, Clerical Specialist, Kent State University, Trumbull Campus, 4314 Mahoning Avenue, NW, Warren, OH 44483-1998. *Phone:* 330-675-888. *Fax:* 330-847-6571. *E-mail:* pdavis1@kent.edu.

Kent State University, Tuscarawas Campus

New Philadelphia, Ohio   www.tusc.kent.edu/

- **State-supported** primarily 2-year, founded 1962, part of Kent State University System
- **Small-town** 172-acre campus with easy access to Cleveland
- **Endowment** $1.6 million
- **Coed,** 1,977 undergraduate students, 51% full-time, 60% women, 40% men

Undergraduates 1,018 full-time, 959 part-time. 1% African American, 0.6% Asian American or Pacific Islander, 0.4% Hispanic American, 0.2% Native American, 0.2% international, 10% transferred in. *Retention:* 65% of 2003 full-time freshmen returned.

Freshmen *Admission:* 522 applied, 380 enrolled. *Average high school GPA:* 2.85. *Test scores:* ACT scores over 18: 76%; ACT scores over 24: 16%; ACT scores over 30: 1%.

Faculty *Total:* 115, 41% full-time, 25% with terminal degrees. *Student/faculty ratio:* 19:1.

Majors Accounting; administrative assistant and secretarial science; animation, interactive technology, video graphics and special effects; business administration and management; communications technology; computer engineering technology; criminal justice/police science; early childhood education; electrical, electronic and communications engineering technology; engineering technology; environmental studies; industrial technology; liberal arts and sciences/liberal studies; mechanical engineering/mechanical technology; nursing (registered nurse training); plastics engineering technology.

Academics *Calendar:* semesters. *Degrees:* certificates, diplomas, associate, bachelor's, and master's (also offers some upper-level and graduate courses). *Special study options:* academic remediation for entering students, accelerated degree program, adult/continuing education programs, advanced placement credit, distance learning, double majors, freshman honors college, honors programs, independent study, internships, part-time degree program, services for LD students, student-designed majors, summer session for credit. *ROTC:* Army (c), Air Force (c).

Library Tuscarawas Campus Library with 63,880 titles, 208 serial subscriptions, 1,179 audiovisual materials, an OPAC, a Web page.

Student Life *Housing:* college housing not available. *Activities and Organizations:* choral group, Society of Mechanical Engineers, IEEE, Imagineers, Criminal Justice Club, Salt and Light.

Kent State University, Tuscarawas Campus *(continued)*

Athletics *Intramural sports:* basketball M/W, volleyball M/W.

Standardized Tests *Recommended:* SAT or ACT (for admission).

Costs (2006–07) *Tuition:* $217 per credit hour part-time; state resident $5590 full-time; nonresident $12,202 full-time.

Financial Aid Of all full-time matriculated undergraduates, 26 Federal Work-Study jobs (averaging $2699).

Applying *Options:* early admission, deferred entrance. *Application fee:* $30. *Required:* high school transcript. *Application deadlines:* 9/1 (freshmen), 9/1 (transfers). *Notification:* continuous (freshmen), continuous (transfers).

Freshmen Application Contact Director of Admissions, Kent State University, Tuscarawas Campus, 330 University Drive NE, New Philadelphia, OH 44663-9403. *Phone:* 330-339-3391 Ext. 47425. *Fax:* 330-339-3321.

KETTERING COLLEGE OF MEDICAL ARTS

Kettering, Ohio   www.kcma.edu/

- **Independent Seventh-day Adventist** primarily 2-year, founded 1967
- **Suburban** 35-acre campus
- **Coed, primarily women,** 773 undergraduate students, 54% full-time, 80% women, 20% men

Undergraduates 414 full-time, 359 part-time. Students come from 18 states and territories, 10 other countries, 6% are from out of state, 6% African American, 1% Asian American or Pacific Islander, 2% Hispanic American, 0.2% Native American, 2% international, 22% transferred in, 20% live on campus. *Retention:* 78% of 2003 full-time freshmen returned.

Freshmen *Admission:* 69 enrolled. *Average high school GPA:* 3.35. *Test scores:* ACT scores over 18: 95%; ACT scores over 24: 17%.

Faculty *Total:* 61, 57% full-time, 39% with terminal degrees. *Student/faculty ratio:* 13:1.

Majors General studies; health science; nuclear medical technology; nursing (registered nurse training); physician assistant; radiologic technology/science; respiratory care therapy.

Academics *Calendar:* semesters. *Degrees:* certificates, associate, bachelor's, and postbachelor's certificates. *Special study options:* advanced placement credit, distance learning, honors programs, independent study, off-campus study, part-time degree program, study abroad, summer session for credit.

Library Learning Resources Center plus 1 other with 29,390 titles, 266 serial subscriptions, an OPAC, a Web page.

Student Life *Housing Options:* coed. Campus housing is university owned. *Activities and Organizations:* drama/theater group, choral group, student association/student life, campus ministries. *Campus security:* 24-hour emergency response devices and patrols, late-night transport/escort service. *Student services:* health clinic, personal/psychological counseling.

Athletics *Intramural sports:* basketball M/W, tennis M/W, volleyball M/W.

Standardized Tests *Required:* ACT (for admission).

Costs (2007–08) *Comprehensive fee:* $12,948 includes full-time tuition ($7008), mandatory fees ($540), and room and board ($5400). Part-time tuition: $292 per credit hour. *Required fees:* $220 per term part-time. *Room and board:* college room only: $2400.

Applying *Options:* early admission. *Application fee:* $25. *Required:* high school transcript, minimum 2.0 GPA, 3 letters of recommendation. *Recommended:* minimum 3.0 GPA, interview. *Application deadlines:* rolling (freshmen), rolling (transfers). *Notification:* continuous (freshmen), continuous (transfers).

Freshmen Application Contact Mrs. Becky McDonald, Associate Director of Enrollment Services, Kettering College of Medical Arts, 3737 Southern Boulevard, Kettering, OH 45429-1299. *Phone:* 937-395-8628. *Toll-free phone:* 800-433-5262. *Fax:* 937-296-4238.

LAKELAND COMMUNITY COLLEGE

Kirtland, Ohio   www.lakeland.cc.oh.us/

Director of Admissions Ms. Tracey Cooper, Director for Admissions/Registrar, Lakeland Community College, 7700 Clocktower Drive, Kirtland, OH 44094. *Phone:* 440-525-7230. *Toll-free phone:* 800-589-8520.

LORAIN COUNTY COMMUNITY COLLEGE

Elyria, Ohio   www.lorainccc.edu/

- **State and locally supported** 2-year, founded 1963, part of Ohio Board of Regents
- **Suburban** 280-acre campus with easy access to Cleveland
- **Coed,** 10,521 undergraduate students, 39% full-time, 65% women, 35% men

Undergraduates 4,089 full-time, 6,432 part-time. Students come from 14 states and territories, 28 other countries, 1% are from out of state, 8% African American, 1% Asian American or Pacific Islander, 6% Hispanic American, 0.8% Native American, 0.7% international.

Freshmen *Admission:* 3,966 applied, 3,966 admitted, 3,034 enrolled.

Faculty *Total:* 779, 16% full-time, 12% with terminal degrees. *Student/faculty ratio:* 18:1.

Majors Accounting; administrative assistant and secretarial science; art; artificial intelligence and robotics; athletic training; biological and physical sciences; biology/biological sciences; business administration and management; chemistry; civil engineering technology; clinical/medical laboratory technology; computer and information sciences related; computer engineering technology; computer programming; computer programming related; computer programming (specific applications); computer programming (vendor/product certification); computer science; computer systems networking and telecommunications; computer technology/computer systems technology; consumer merchandising/retailing management; corrections; cosmetology; cosmetology and personal grooming arts related; criminal justice/police science; data entry/microcomputer applications; data entry/microcomputer applications related; diagnostic medical sonography and ultrasound technology; drafting and design technology; dramatic/theater arts; education; electrical, electronic and communications engineering technology; elementary education; engineering; engineering technology; finance; fire science; history; human services; industrial radiologic technology; industrial technology; information science/studies; information technology; journalism; kindergarten/preschool education; liberal arts and sciences/liberal studies; machine tool technology; marketing/marketing management; mass communication/media; mathematics; mechanical design technology; music; nuclear medical technology; nursing (registered nurse training); personal/miscellaneous services; pharmacy; physical education teaching and coaching; physical therapist assistant; physics; plastics engineering technology; political science and government; pre-engineering; psychology; quality control technology; real estate; social sciences; social work; sociology; sport and fitness administration/management; surgical technology; tourism and travel services management; urban studies/affairs; veterinary sciences; word processing.

Academics *Calendar:* semesters. *Degree:* certificates and associate. *Special study options:* academic remediation for entering students, adult/continuing education programs, advanced placement credit, cooperative education, distance learning, English as a second language, external degree program, honors programs, independent study, part-time degree program, services for LD students, student-designed majors, summer session for credit.

Library Learning Resource Center with 198,984 titles, 3,289 audiovisual materials, an OPAC.

Student Life *Housing:* college housing not available. *Activities and Organizations:* drama/theater group, student-run newspaper, radio station, choral group, Phi Beta Kappa, Black Progressives, Hispanic Club, national fraternities, national sororities. *Campus security:* 24-hour emergency response devices and patrols, late-night transport/escort service. *Student services:* health clinic, personal/psychological counseling, women's center, legal services.

Athletics *Intramural sports:* archery M/W, basketball M/W, softball M/W, volleyball M/W, weight lifting M/W, wrestling M.

Costs (2007–08) *Tuition:* area resident $2400 full-time, $88 per credit hour part-time; state resident $2890 full-time, $106 per credit hour part-time; nonresident $5837 full-time, $220 per credit hour part-time. *Required fees:* $5 per credit hour part-time.

Financial Aid Of all full-time matriculated undergraduates, 100 Federal Work-Study jobs.

Applying *Options:* early admission, deferred entrance. *Required for some:* high school transcript. *Application deadlines:* rolling (freshmen), rolling (transfers). *Notification:* continuous (freshmen), continuous (transfers).

Director of Admissions Ms. Thalia Fountain, Interim Director of Enrollment Services, Lorain County Community College, 1005 Abbe Road, North, Elyria, OH 44035. *Phone:* 440-366-7683. *Toll-free phone:* 800-995-5222 Ext. 4032. *Fax:* 440-366-4150.

MARION TECHNICAL COLLEGE

Marion, Ohio   www.mtc.edu/

Freshmen Application Contact Mr. Joel O. Liles, Director of Admissions and Career Services, Marion Technical College, 1467 Mount Vernon Avenue, Marion, OH 43302. *Phone:* 740-389-4636. *E-mail:* enroll@mtc.edu.

MERCY COLLEGE OF NORTHWEST OHIO

Toledo, Ohio   www.mercycollege.edu/

- **Independent** primarily 2-year, founded 1993, affiliated with Roman Catholic Church
- **Urban** campus with easy access to Detroit
- **Endowment** $5.6 million
- **Coed, primarily women,** 780 undergraduate students, 53% full-time, 85% women, 15% men

Undergraduates 416 full-time, 364 part-time. Students come from 5 states and territories, 12% are from out of state, 7% African American, 0.4% Asian American or Pacific Islander, 3% Hispanic American, 0.5% Native American, 17% transferred in, 6% live on campus. *Retention:* 68% of 2003 full-time freshmen returned.

Freshmen *Admission:* 220 applied, 122 admitted, 72 enrolled.

Faculty *Total:* 100, 54% full-time, 16% with terminal degrees. *Student/faculty ratio:* 11:1.

Majors General studies; health/health care administration; health information/medical records technology; massage therapy; medical radiologic technology; nursing (registered nurse training).

Academics *Calendar:* semesters. *Degrees:* certificates, associate, and bachelor's. *Special study options:* academic remediation for entering students, advanced placement credit, distance learning, double majors, independent study, internships, part-time degree program, services for LD students, summer session for credit.

Library Mercy College of Northwest Ohio Library with 15,000 titles, 171 serial subscriptions, 352 audiovisual materials, an OPAC.

Student Life *Housing Options:* coed. Campus housing is provided by a third party. *Activities and Organizations:* student-run newspaper, Campus Ministry, Student Senate, Mercy College Musical Ensemble, Student Nurses Association, Stress Busters. *Campus security:* 24-hour patrols, late-night transport/escort service, controlled dormitory access. *Student services:* personal/psychological counseling.

Standardized Tests *Required for some:* SAT or ACT (for admission). *Recommended:* SAT or ACT (for admission).

Costs (2007–08) *Tuition:* $8896 full-time, $310 per credit hour part-time. *Required fees:* $650 full-time, $5 per credit hour part-time.

Financial Aid Of all full-time matriculated undergraduates, 18 Federal Work-Study jobs.

Applying *Application fee:* $25. *Required:* high school transcript. *Application deadlines:* rolling (freshmen), rolling (transfers). *Notification:* continuous (freshmen), continuous (transfers).

Freshmen Application Contact Admissions Counselor, Mercy College of Northwest Ohio, 2221 Madison Avenue, Toledo, OH 43624-1197. *Phone:* 419-251-1313. *Toll-free phone:* 888-80-Mercy. *Fax:* 419-251-1462. *E-mail:* admissions@mercycollege.edu.

MIAMI–JACOBS COLLEGE

Dayton, Ohio   www.miamijacobs.edu/

Director of Admissions Mary Percell, Vice President of Information Services, Miami–Jacobs College, 110 North Patterson Street, PO Box 1433, Dayton, OH 45402. *Phone:* 937-461-5174 Ext. 118.

MIAMI UNIVERSITY HAMILTON

Hamilton, Ohio   www.ham.muohio.edu/

- **State-supported** founded 1968, part of Miami University System
- **Suburban** 78-acre campus with easy access to Cincinnati
- **Coed,** 3,189 undergraduate students, 45% full-time, 56% women, 44% men

Undergraduates 1,450 full-time, 1,739 part-time. 7% African American, 2% Asian American or Pacific Islander, 1% Hispanic American, 0.5% Native American, 5% transferred in.

Freshmen *Admission:* 600 enrolled.

Faculty *Total:* 218, 40% full-time. *Student/faculty ratio:* 21:1.

Majors Accounting; American studies; anthropology; architectural history and criticism; architecture; art; art teacher education; athletic training; audiology and speech-language pathology; biochemistry; botany/plant biology related; business administration and management; business administration, management and operations related; business/commerce; business/managerial economics; chemistry; chemistry teacher education; city/urban, community and regional planning; classics and languages, literatures and linguistics; clinical laboratory science/medical technology; communication/speech communication and rhetoric; computer and information sciences related; computer engineering; computer science; computer systems analysis; computer technology/computer systems technology; creative writing; dietetics; early childhood education; econometrics and quantitative economics; economics; education (multiple levels); electrical and electronic engineering technologies related; electromechanical technology; engineering/industrial management; engineering physics; engineering technology; English; English composition; English/language arts teacher education; environmental science; environmental studies; ethnic, cultural minority, and gender studies related; exercise physiology; finance; French; French language teacher education; general studies; geography; geology/earth science; German; German language teacher education; gerontology; graphic design; health teacher education; history; human resources management and services related; interior design; international/global studies; journalism; Latin; Latin teacher education; linguistics; management information systems; marketing/marketing management; marketing related; mass communication/media; mathematics; mathematics and statistics related; mathematics teacher education; mechanical engineering/mechanical technology; microbiology; multi-/interdisciplinary studies related; music; music teacher education; office management; philosophy; physical education teaching and coaching; physics; physics teacher education; political science and government; psychology; public administration; purchasing, procurement/acquisitions and contracts management; real estate; Russian; science teacher education; social studies teacher education; social work related; sociology; Spanish; Spanish language teacher education; special education; speech-language pathology; statistics; technical and business writing; theater/theater arts management; work and family studies; zoology/animal biology.

Academics *Calendar:* semesters plus summer sessions. *Degrees:* certificates, associate, bachelor's, and master's (degrees awarded by Miami University main campus). *Special study options:* academic remediation for entering students, adult/continuing education programs, advanced placement credit, cooperative education, distance learning, double majors, English as a second language, honors programs, internships, part-time degree program, services for LD students, student-designed majors, study abroad, summer session for credit. *ROTC:* Navy (c), Air Force (c).

Library Rentschler Library with 68,000 titles, 400 serial subscriptions, an OPAC, a Web page.

Student Life *Housing:* college housing not available. *Activities and Organizations:* drama/theater group, choral group, student government, Campus Activities Committee, Ski Club, Student Nursing Association, Minority Action Committee. *Campus security:* 24-hour emergency response devices and patrols, late-night transport/escort service. *Student services:* personal/psychological counseling.

Athletics *Intercollegiate sports:* baseball M(c), basketball M(c)/W(c), cheerleading W, golf M(c), softball W(c), tennis M(c)/W(c), volleyball W(c). *Intramural sports:* basketball M/W, bowling M/W, skiing (cross-country) M/W, soccer M/W, softball M/W, tennis M/W, volleyball M/W, weight lifting M/W.

Costs (2006–07) *Tuition:* state resident $3954 full-time, $165 per credit part-time; nonresident $16,085 full-time, $670 per credit part-time. *Required fees:* $498 full-time, $15 per credit part-time, $22 per term part-time. *Payment plan:* installment. *Waivers:* employees or children of employees.

Applying *Options:* electronic application. *Application fee:* $35. *Required:* high school transcript. *Application deadline:* rolling (freshmen). *Notification:* continuous (freshmen), continuous (transfers).

Freshmen Application Contact Mr. Archie Nelson, Director of Admission and Financial Aid, Miami University Hamilton, 1601 University Boulevard, Hamilton, OH 45011-3399. *Phone:* 513-785-3111. *Fax:* 513-785-1807. *E-mail:* nelsona3@muohio.edu.

MIAMI UNIVERSITY–MIDDLETOWN CAMPUS

Middletown, Ohio   www.mid.muohio.edu/

- **State-supported** primarily 2-year, founded 1966, part of Miami University System
- **Small-town** 141-acre campus with easy access to Cincinnati and Dayton
- **Endowment** $779,742
- **Coed,** 2,660 undergraduate students

Undergraduates 1% are from out of state, 6% African American, 1% Asian American or Pacific Islander, 1% Hispanic American, 0.7% Native American. *Retention:* 71% of 2003 full-time freshmen returned.

Freshmen *Admission:* 763 applied, 731 admitted. *Test scores:* SAT verbal scores over 500: 49%; SAT math scores over 500: 49%; ACT scores over 18: 73%; SAT verbal scores over 600: 12%; SAT math scores over 600: 7%; ACT scores over 24: 16%; SAT verbal scores over 700: 1%; ACT scores over 30: 1%.

Faculty *Total:* 209, 38% full-time. *Student/faculty ratio:* 13:1.

Miami University–Middletown Campus (continued)

Majors Accounting; administrative assistant and secretarial science; anthropology; art; biological and physical sciences; botany/plant biology; business administration and management; business/commerce; business/managerial economics; chemical engineering; chemistry; communication/speech communication and rhetoric; computer and information sciences; computer engineering technology; computer science; economics; education; electrical, electronic and communications engineering technology; electromechanical technology; elementary education; engineering; engineering technology; English; geography; history; industrial technology; information science/studies; interdisciplinary studies; kindergarten/preschool education; legal administrative assistant/secretary; liberal arts and sciences/liberal studies; management information systems; marketing/marketing management; mass communication/media; mathematics; mechanical engineering/mechanical technology; medical administrative assistant and medical secretary; nursing (registered nurse training); office management; philosophy; physics; political science and government; pre-engineering; psychology; real estate; social sciences; social work; sociology; Spanish; systems science and theory; zoology/animal biology.

Academics *Calendar:* semesters. *Degrees:* certificates, diplomas, associate, and bachelor's (also offers up to 2 years of most bachelor's degree programs offered at Miami University main campus). *Special study options:* academic remediation for entering students, adult/continuing education programs, advanced placement credit, cooperative education, distance learning, double majors, independent study, internships, off-campus study, part-time degree program, services for LD students, student-designed majors, study abroad, summer session for credit. *ROTC:* Air Force (c).

Library Gardner-Harvey Library with 540 serial subscriptions, 4,857 audiovisual materials, an OPAC, a Web page.

Student Life *Housing:* college housing not available. *Activities and Organizations:* drama/theater group, student-run newspaper, radio station, choral group, student radio station, SEAL (Save Every Animal by Learning), Student Advisory Council, Model United Nations, Program Board. *Campus security:* 24-hour patrols, late-night transport/escort service. *Student services:* personal/psychological counseling, women's center.

Athletics *Intercollegiate sports:* baseball M(c), basketball M(c)/W(c), golf M(c)/W(c), softball W, tennis M(c)/W(c), volleyball W(c). *Intramural sports:* basketball W, football M/W, golf M/W, racquetball M/W, skiing (cross-country) M/W, skiing (downhill) M/W, soccer M/W, softball M/W, table tennis M/W, tennis M/W, volleyball M/W, weight lifting M/W.

Standardized Tests *Recommended:* SAT or ACT (for placement).

Costs (2006–07) *Tuition:* state resident $3954 full-time; nonresident $16,086 full-time. *Required fees:* $498 full-time. *Payment plan:* installment. *Waivers:* employees or children of employees.

Applying *Options:* electronic application, early admission, deferred entrance. *Application fee:* $25. *Required:* high school transcript. *Application deadlines:* rolling (freshmen), rolling (transfers). *Notification:* continuous (freshmen), continuous (transfers).

Freshmen Application Contact Mrs. Mary Lou Flynn, Director of Enrollment Services, Miami University–Middletown Campus, 4200 East University Boulevard, Middletown, OH 45042. *Phone:* 513-727-3346. *Toll-free phone:* 866-426-4643. *Fax:* 513-727-3223. *E-mail:* flynnml@muohio.edu.

NATIONAL INSTITUTE OF TECHNOLOGY
Cuyahoga Falls, Ohio www.nationalinstituteoftechnology.edu/

- **Proprietary** 2-year
- **Coed,** 375 undergraduate students

Majors Business administration, management and operations related; computer and information sciences and support services related; electrical and electronic engineering technologies related; medical/clinical assistant; medical office management; nursing (registered nurse training).

Academics *Degree:* associate.

Costs (2006–07) *Tuition:* $9900 full-time.

Applying *Application fee:* $55.

Freshmen Application Contact Admissions Office, National Institute of Technology, 2545 Bailey Road, Cuyahoga Falls, OH 44221. *Toll-free phone:* 888-519-4689.

NORTH CENTRAL STATE COLLEGE
Mansfield, Ohio www.ncstatecollege.edu/

Freshmen Application Contact Ms. Nikia L. Fletcher, Director of Admissions, North Central State College, PO Box 698, Mansfield, OH 44901-0698. *Phone:* 419-755-4813. *Toll-free phone:* 888-755-4899. *E-mail:* nfletcher@ncstatecollege.edu.

NORTHWEST STATE COMMUNITY COLLEGE
Archbold, Ohio www.northweststate.edu

Director of Admissions Mr. Jeffrey Ferezan, Dean of Student Success and Advocacy Center, Northwest State Community College, 22600 State Route 34, Archbold, OH 43502-9542. *Phone:* 419-267-1213.

OHIO BUSINESS COLLEGE
Lorain, Ohio www.ohiobusinesscollege.com/

Director of Admissions Mr. Jim Unger, Admissions Director, Ohio Business College, 1907 North Ridge Road, Lorain, OH 44055. *Toll-free phone:* 888-514-3126.

OHIO BUSINESS COLLEGE
Sandusky, Ohio www.ohiobusinesscollege.com/

- **Proprietary** 2-year, founded 1982
- **Suburban** 1-acre campus
- **Coed**
- **100%** of applicants were admitted

Undergraduates 157 full-time, 35 part-time.

Faculty *Student/faculty ratio:* 10:1.

Academics *Calendar:* quarters. *Degree:* diplomas and associate.

Costs (2006–07) *Tuition:* $7380 full-time, $195 per quarter hour part-time. Full-time tuition and fees vary according to course load. Part-time tuition and fees vary according to course load. *Required fees:* $360 full-time.

Applying *Application fee:* $25. *Required:* high school transcript.

Freshmen Application Contact Rohnda Pickering, Student Services Coordinator, Ohio Business College, 5202 Timber Commons Drive, Sandusky, OH 44870. *Phone:* 419-627-8345. *Toll-free phone:* 888-627-8345. *Fax:* 419-627-1958. *E-mail:* rpickering@ohiobusinesscollege.edu.

OHIO COLLEGE OF MASSOTHERAPY
Akron, Ohio www.ocm.edu/

- **Independent** 2-year, founded 1973
- **Coed,** 282 undergraduate students

Majors Massage therapy.

Academics *Calendar:* semesters. *Degree:* associate.

Costs (2006–07) *Tuition:* $8140 full-time.

Applying *Application fee:* $25.

Director of Admissions Mr. John Atkins, Director of Admissions and Marketing,, Ohio College of Massotherapy, 225 Heritage Woods Drive, Akron, OH 44321. *Phone:* 330-665-1084 Ext. 11. *Toll-free phone:* 888-888-4325. *E-mail:* johna@ocm.edu.

OHIO INSTITUTE OF PHOTOGRAPHY AND TECHNOLOGY
Dayton, Ohio www.oipt.com/

- **Proprietary** 2-year, founded 1971, part of Kaplan Higher Education
- **Urban** 2-acre campus with easy access to Cincinnati and Columbus
- **Coed**

Undergraduates 740 full-time. Students come from 20 states and territories, 19% are from out of state, 26% African American, 0.1% Asian American or Pacific Islander, 0.5% Hispanic American, 0.3% Native American.

Faculty *Student/faculty ratio:* 25:1.

Academics *Calendar:* quarters. *Degree:* diplomas and associate. *Special study options:* cooperative education, internships, part-time degree program, student-designed majors, summer session for credit.

Student Life *Campus security:* 24-hour emergency response devices.

Costs (2006–07) *Tuition:* $17,641 full-time. Full-time tuition and fees vary according to program. *Required fees:* $1248 full-time.

Applying *Options:* early admission, deferred entrance. *Application fee:* $100. *Required:* high school transcript, interview, entrance exam.

Freshmen Application Contact Ohio Institute of Photography and Technology, 2029 Edgefield Road, Dayton, OH 45439-1917. *Phone:* 937-294-6155. *Toll-free phone:* 800-932-9698. *Fax:* 937-294-2259. *E-mail:* info@oipt.com.

THE OHIO STATE UNIVERSITY AGRICULTURAL TECHNICAL INSTITUTE
Wooster, Ohio   www.ati.ohio-state.edu/

- **State-supported** 2-year, founded 1971, part of Ohio State University
- **Small-town** campus with easy access to Cleveland and Columbus
- **Endowment** $2.2 million
- **Coed,** 747 undergraduate students, 100% full-time, 35% women, 65% men

Undergraduates 747 full-time. Students come from 13 states and territories, 2 other countries, 2% are from out of state, 0.9% African American, 0.4% Hispanic American, 0.7% Native American, 0.4% international, 7% transferred in, 22% live on campus. *Retention:* 68% of 2003 full-time freshmen returned.

Freshmen *Admission:* 557 applied, 533 admitted, 348 enrolled. *Test scores:* SAT verbal scores over 500: 22%; SAT math scores over 500: 22%; ACT scores over 18: 57%; SAT verbal scores over 600: 11%; ACT scores over 24: 11%.

Faculty *Total:* 70, 47% full-time, 33% with terminal degrees. *Student/faculty ratio:* 16:1.

Majors Agribusiness; agricultural business and management; agricultural business technology; agricultural communication/journalism; agricultural economics; agricultural mechanization; agricultural power machinery operation; agricultural teacher education; agronomy and crop science; animal/livestock husbandry and production; animal sciences; biology/biotechnology laboratory technician; building/construction site management; clinical/medical laboratory technology; construction engineering technology; construction management; crop production; dairy husbandry and production; dairy science; environmental science; equestrian studies; floriculture/floristry management; greenhouse management; heavy equipment maintenance technology; horse husbandry/equine science and management; horticultural science; hydraulics and fluid power technology; industrial technology; landscaping and groundskeeping; livestock management; medical laboratory technology; natural resources management; natural resources management and policy; plant nursery management; soil conservation; turf and turfgrass management.

Academics *Calendar:* quarters. *Degree:* certificates, diplomas, and associate. *Special study options:* academic remediation for entering students, accelerated degree program, adult/continuing education programs, advanced placement credit, cooperative education, honors programs, internships, part-time degree program, services for LD students, student-designed majors, summer session for credit. *ROTC:* Army (c), Navy (c), Air Force (c).

Library Agricultural Technical Institute Library with 19,009 titles, 595 serial subscriptions, an OPAC.

Student Life *Housing:* on-campus residence required for freshman year. *Options:* coed. Campus housing is university owned. *Activities and Organizations:* Hoof-n-Hide Club, Horticulture Club, Campus Crusade for Christ, Phi Theta Kappa, Artist de Fleur Club. *Campus security:* 24-hour emergency response devices and patrols, controlled dormitory access. *Student services:* health clinic, personal/psychological counseling.

Athletics *Intramural sports:* basketball M/W, football M/W, racquetball M/W, softball M/W, volleyball M/W.

Standardized Tests *Required for some:* SAT or ACT (for admission).

Costs (2006–07) *Tuition:* state resident $5859 full-time; nonresident $17,754 full-time. Full-time tuition and fees vary according to course load. Part-time tuition and fees vary according to course load. *Required fees:* $38 full-time. *Room and board:* $5748; room only: $4803. Room and board charges vary according to board plan. *Payment plan:* installment. *Waivers:* employees or children of employees.

Applying *Options:* early admission. *Application fee:* $40. *Required:* high school transcript. *Application deadlines:* 7/1 (freshmen), 7/1 (transfers). *Notification:* continuous until 9/15 (freshmen).

Freshmen Application Contact Mr. Tim Kracker, Coordinator of Admissions, The Ohio State University Agricultural Technical Institute, 1328 Dover Road, Wooster, OH 44691. *Phone:* 800-647-8283 Ext. 1327. *Toll-free phone:* 800-647-8283 Ext. 1327. *Fax:* 330-287-1333. *E-mail:* kracker.7@osu.edu.

OHIO TECHNICAL COLLEGE
Cleveland, Ohio   www.ohiotechnicalcollege.com/

- **Proprietary** 2-year, founded 1969
- **Coed,** 654 undergraduate students

Majors Automobile/automotive mechanics technology; diesel mechanics technology; mechanic and repair technologies related.

Academics *Degree:* associate.

Costs (2006–07) *Tuition:* $18,520 full-time.

Applying *Application fee:* $100.

Director of Admissions Mr. Marc Brenner, President, Ohio Technical College, 1374 East 51st Street, Cleveland, OH 44103. *Phone:* 216-881-1700. *Toll-free phone:* 800-322-7000. *Fax:* 216-881-9145. *E-mail:* ohioauto@aol.com.

OHIO VALLEY COLLEGE OF TECHNOLOGY
East Liverpool, Ohio   www.ovct.edu/

Freshmen Application Contact Ms. Jessica M. Ewing, Director of Admissions, Ohio Valley College of Technology, PO Box 7000, East Liverpool, OH 43920. *Phone:* 330-385-1070. *Toll-free phone:* 877-777-8451. *E-mail:* info@ovct.edu.

OWENS COMMUNITY COLLEGE
Toledo, Ohio   www.owens.edu/

- **State-supported** 2-year, founded 1966
- **Suburban** 100-acre campus
- **Coed,** 19,141 undergraduate students, 37% full-time, 46% women, 54% men

Undergraduates 7,014 full-time, 12,127 part-time. Students come from 20 states and territories, 44 other countries, 4% are from out of state, 12% African American, 1% Asian American or Pacific Islander, 5% Hispanic American, 0.4% Native American, 0.1% international, 0.9% transferred in.

Freshmen *Admission:* 2,293 applied, 2,293 admitted, 1,785 enrolled. *Average high school GPA:* 2.65. *Test scores:* SAT verbal scores over 500: 17%; SAT math scores over 500: 17%; SAT writing scores over 500: 22; ACT scores over 18: 63%; ACT scores over 24: 7%.

Faculty *Total:* 1,302, 21% full-time, 9% with terminal degrees. *Student/faculty ratio:* 18:1.

Majors Accounting technology and bookkeeping; agricultural business and management; automotive engineering technology; business/commerce; CAD/CADD drafting/design technology; commercial and advertising art; criminal justice/law enforcement administration; criminal justice/police science; early childhood education; electrical, electronic and communications engineering technology; fashion merchandising; fire protection and safety technology; food services technology; general studies; health information/medical records technology; management information systems; manufacturing technology; marketing/marketing management; mechanical design technology; mechanical engineering/mechanical technology; nursing (registered nurse training); occupational therapist assistant; physical therapist assistant; survey technology; telecommunications.

Academics *Calendar:* semesters. *Degree:* certificates and associate. *Special study options:* academic remediation for entering students, adult/continuing education programs, advanced placement credit, cooperative education, distance learning, double majors, English as a second language, external degree program, freshman honors college, honors programs, independent study, internships, part-time degree program, services for LD students, summer session for credit. *ROTC:* Army (c), Air Force (b).

Library Owens Community College Library with 78,344 titles, 6,230 serial subscriptions, an OPAC, a Web page.

Student Life *Housing:* college housing not available. *Activities and Organizations:* drama/theater group, student-run newspaper, choral group, intramurals, Alpha Beta Gamma, Drama Club, Student Association for Young Children, Phi Theta Kappa. *Campus security:* 24-hour emergency response devices and patrols, student patrols. *Student services:* health clinic, personal/psychological counseling.

Athletics Member NJCAA. *Intercollegiate sports:* baseball M, basketball M(s)/W(s), soccer M, softball W, volleyball W. *Intramural sports:* basketball M/W, bowling M/W, football M/W, golf M/W, softball M/W, table tennis M/W, tennis M/W, volleyball M/W, weight lifting M/W.

Owens Community College (continued)

Costs (2007–08) *Tuition:* state resident $2952 full-time, $123 per credit part-time; nonresident $5532 full-time, $231 per credit part-time. *Required fees:* $400 full-time, $15 per credit part-time, $10 per term part-time.

Financial Aid Of all full-time matriculated undergraduates, 200 Federal Work-Study jobs (averaging $4500).

Applying *Options:* early admission. *Required for some:* minimum 2.0 GPA. *Recommended:* essay or personal statement, high school transcript, letters of recommendation. *Application deadlines:* rolling (freshmen), rolling (transfers). *Notification:* continuous (freshmen), continuous (transfers).

Freshmen Application Contact Ms. Donna Gruber, Director, Enrollment Services, Owens Community College, PO Box 1000, Toledo, OH 43699. *Phone:* 567-661-7575. *Toll-free phone:* 800-GO-OWENS. *E-mail:* donna_gruber@owens.edu.

PROFESSIONAL SKILLS INSTITUTE
Toledo, Ohio　　　　www.proskills.com/

Director of Admissions Ms. Hope Finch, Director of Marketing, Professional Skills Institute, 20 Arco Drive, Toledo, OH 43607. *Phone:* 419-531-9610.

REMINGTON COLLEGE–CLEVELAND CAMPUS
Cleveland, Ohio　　　www.remingtoncollege.edu/

Director of Admissions Mr. William Cassidy, Director of Recruitment, Remington College–Cleveland Campus, 14445 Broadway Avenue, Cleveland, OH 44125-1957. *Phone:* 216-475-7520.

REMINGTON COLLEGE–CLEVELAND WEST CAMPUS
North Olmstead, Ohio　　www.remingtoncollege.edu/

- **Proprietary** 2-year, founded 2003
- **Coed**

Undergraduates 399 full-time. 17% African American, 0.5% Asian American or Pacific Islander, 8% Hispanic American, 1% Native American.

Faculty *Student/faculty ratio:* 23:1.

Academics *Calendar:* quarters. *Degree:* diplomas and associate.

Applying *Required:* Wonderlic.

Freshmen Application Contact Mr. Gary Azotea, Campus President, Remington College–Cleveland West Campus, 26350 Brookpark Road, North Olmstead, OH 44070. *Phone:* 440-777-2560. *Fax:* 440-777-3238.

RETS TECH CENTER
Centerville, Ohio　　www.retstechcenter.com/

Freshmen Application Contact Mr. Rich Elkin, Director of Admissions, RETS Tech Center, 555 East Alex Bell Road, Centerville, OH 45459-2712. *Phone:* 937-433-3410. *Toll-free phone:* 800-837-7387.

ROSEDALE BIBLE COLLEGE
Irwin, Ohio　　　www.rosedalebible.org/

- **Independent Mennonite** 2-year, founded 1952
- **Coed,** 89 undergraduate students
- **94%** of applicants were admitted

Freshmen *Admission:* 81 applied, 76 admitted.

Majors Biblical studies.

Academics *Calendar:* five six-week terms. *Degree:* associate.

Student Life *Housing Options:* Campus housing is university owned.

Standardized Tests *Recommended:* SAT or ACT (for admission).

Costs (2006–07) *Tuition:* $5370 full-time.

Applying *Application fee:* $50. *Required:* letters of recommendation.

Director of Admissions Mr. John Showalter, Director of Enrollment Services, Rosedale Bible College, 2270 Rosedale Road, Irwin, OH 43029-9501. *Phone:* 740-857-1311. *Fax:* 740-857-1577. *E-mail:* pweber@rosedale.edu.

SCHOOL OF ADVERTISING ART
Kettering, Ohio　　　www.saacollege.com/

- **Proprietary** 2-year, founded 1983
- **Suburban** 5-acre campus with easy access to Dayton, Ohio; Cincinnati, Ohio
- **Coed**

Undergraduates 146 full-time. Students come from 4 states and territories, 2% are from out of state, 5% African American, 1% Asian American or Pacific Islander, 3% Hispanic American, 0.7% Native American, 0.7% international. *Retention:* 75% of 2003 full-time freshmen returned.

Faculty *Student/faculty ratio:* 12:1.

Academics *Calendar:* trimesters. *Degree:* diplomas and associate.

Costs (2006–07) *Tuition:* $17,775 full-time. *Required fees:* $210 full-time.

Applying *Required:* high school transcript, interview. *Required for some:* essay or personal statement, minimum 2.0 GPA, 1 letter of recommendation. *Recommended:* minimum 2.5 GPA.

Freshmen Application Contact Mr. Nathan Summers, Secretary, School of Advertising Art, 1725 East David Road, Kettering, OH 45440. *Phone:* 937-294-0592. *Toll-free phone:* 877-300-9866. *Fax:* 937-294-5869. *E-mail:* nathan@saacollege.com.

SINCLAIR COMMUNITY COLLEGE
Dayton, Ohio　　　www.sinclair.edu/

- **State and locally supported** 2-year, founded 1887, part of Ohio Board of Regents
- **Urban** 50-acre campus with easy access to Cincinnati
- **Endowment** $25.0 million
- **Coed**

Undergraduates 7,550 full-time, 12,013 part-time. Students come from 31 states and territories, 4% are from out of state, 16% African American, 1% Asian American or Pacific Islander, 1% Hispanic American, 0.4% Native American, 0.7% international, 6% transferred in. *Retention:* 56% of 2003 full-time freshmen returned.

Faculty *Student/faculty ratio:* 19:1.

Academics *Calendar:* quarters. *Degree:* certificates and associate. *Special study options:* academic remediation for entering students, adult/continuing education programs, cooperative education, distance learning, English as a second language, external degree program, honors programs, independent study, internships, off-campus study, part-time degree program, services for LD students, student-designed majors, summer session for credit. *ROTC:* Army (c), Air Force (c).

Student Life *Campus security:* 24-hour emergency response devices and patrols, student patrols, late-night transport/escort service.

Athletics Member NJCAA.

Costs (2006–07) *Tuition:* area resident $2025 full-time, $45 per credit hour part-time; state resident $3308 full-time, $74 per credit hour part-time; nonresident $6525 full-time, $145 per credit hour part-time. Full-time tuition and fees vary according to course load. Part-time tuition and fees vary according to course load.

Financial Aid Of all full-time matriculated undergraduates, 50 Federal Work-Study jobs (averaging $800). *Financial aid deadline:* 8/15.

Applying *Options:* electronic application, early admission, deferred entrance. *Application fee:* $10. *Required for some:* high school transcript, interview.

Freshmen Application Contact Ms. Sara Smith, Director and Systems Manager, Outreach Services, Sinclair Community College, 444 West Third Street, Dayton, OH 45402-1460. *Phone:* 937-512-3060. *Toll-free phone:* 800-315-3000. *Fax:* 937-512-2393. *E-mail:* ssmith@sinclair.edu.

SOUTHEASTERN BUSINESS COLLEGE
Chillicothe, Ohio　　　samuelstephencollege.edu/

Director of Admissions Ms. Elizabeth Scott, Admissions Representative, Southeastern Business College, 1855 Western Avenue, Chillicothe, OH 45601-1038. *Phone:* 740-774-6300.

SOUTHEASTERN BUSINESS COLLEGE

Jackson, Ohio   **www.careersohio.com/**

- **Proprietary** 2-year, founded 1976
- **Coed,** 76 undergraduate students

Majors Accounting; administrative assistant and secretarial science; business administration, management and operations related; computer and information sciences related; computer technology/computer systems technology; information technology; medical administrative assistant and medical secretary.

Academics *Calendar:* quarters. *Degree:* associate.

Costs (2006–07) *Tuition:* $9380 full-time.

Applying *Application fee:* $15.

Director of Admissions Mr. Todd A. Riegel, Director of Education, Southeastern Business College, 504 McCarty Lane, Jackson, OH 45640. *Phone:* 740-286-1554. *Fax:* 740-286-4476. *E-mail:* todd_sbc@yahoo.com.

SOUTHEASTERN BUSINESS COLLEGE

Lancaster, Ohio   **www.careersohio.com/**

- **Proprietary** 2-year, founded 1984
- **Coed,** 71 undergraduate students

Majors Accounting technology and bookkeeping; administrative assistant and secretarial science; business administration, management and operations related; computer/information technology services administration related; medical administrative assistant and medical secretary.

Academics *Calendar:* quarters. *Degree:* associate.

Costs (2006–07) *Tuition:* $9380 full-time.

Applying *Application fee:* $15.

Director of Admissions Mr. Ray Predmore, Director, Southeastern Business College, 1522 Sheridan Drive, Lancaster, OH 43130-1303. *Phone:* 740-687-6126. *Fax:* 740-687-0431. *E-mail:* rp_sbc@yahoo.com.

SOUTHEASTERN BUSINESS COLLEGE

New Boston, Ohio   **www.careersohio.com/**

- **Proprietary** 2-year
- **Coed,** 78 undergraduate students

Majors Accounting; administrative assistant and secretarial science; business administration, management and operations related; information technology; medical administrative assistant and medical secretary.

Academics *Degree:* associate.

Costs (2006–07) *Tuition:* $8880 full-time.

Applying *Application fee:* $15.

Admissions Office Contact Southeastern Business College, 3879 Rhodes Avenue, New Boston, OH 45662.

SOUTHERN STATE COMMUNITY COLLEGE

Hillsboro, Ohio   **www.sscc.edu/**

- **State-supported** 2-year, founded 1975
- **Rural** 60-acre campus
- **Endowment** $2.3 million
- **Coed,** 2,363 undergraduate students, 54% full-time, 72% women, 28% men

Undergraduates 1,274 full-time, 1,089 part-time. 1% African American, 0.6% Asian American or Pacific Islander, 0.6% Hispanic American, 0.4% Native American.

Freshmen *Admission:* 1,013 applied, 1,013 admitted.

Faculty *Total:* 144, 36% full-time, 8% with terminal degrees. *Student/faculty ratio:* 20:1.

Majors Accounting technology and bookkeeping; agricultural production; business/commerce; computer programming (specific applications); corrections; criminal justice/law enforcement administration; drafting and design technology; emergency medical technology (EMT paramedic); executive assistant/executive secretary; human services; kindergarten/preschool education; liberal arts and sciences/liberal studies; medical/clinical assistant; nursing (registered nurse training); real estate.

Academics *Calendar:* quarters. *Degree:* certificates and associate. *Special study options:* academic remediation for entering students, advanced placement credit, cooperative education, distance learning, double majors, independent study, internships, off-campus study, part-time degree program, services for LD students, student-designed majors, summer session for credit.

Library Learning Resources Center plus 3 others with 48,500 titles, 2,900 serial subscriptions, 8,950 audiovisual materials, an OPAC, a Web page.

Student Life *Housing:* college housing not available. *Activities and Organizations:* drama/theater group, choral group, Student Leadership, Student Nurses Association, Drama Club, Association of Medical Assistants, Phi Theta Kappa. *Student services:* personal/psychological counseling.

Athletics Member NJCAA. *Intercollegiate sports:* baseball M(c), basketball M(s)/W(s), soccer M(s), softball W(s), volleyball W(s).

Costs (2006–07) *Tuition:* state resident $3390 full-time; nonresident $6528 full-time. Full-time tuition and fees vary according to course load. Part-time tuition and fees vary according to course load. *Payment plan:* deferred payment. *Waivers:* senior citizens and employees or children of employees.

Applying *Options:* early admission, deferred entrance. *Recommended:* high school transcript. *Application deadlines:* rolling (freshmen), rolling (transfers). *Notification:* continuous (freshmen), continuous (transfers).

Freshmen Application Contact Ms. Wendy Johnson, Director of Admissions, Southern State Community College, 100 Hobart Drive, Hillsboro, OH 45133. *Phone:* 937-393-3431 Ext. 2720. *Toll-free phone:* 800-628-7722. *Fax:* 937-393-6682. *E-mail:* wjohnson@sscc.edu.

SOUTHWESTERN COLLEGE OF BUSINESS

Cincinnati, Ohio   **www.swcollege.net/**

Director of Admissions Mr. Greg Petree, Director of Admissions, Southwestern College of Business, 149 Northland Boulevard, Cincinnati, OH 45246-1122. *Phone:* 513-874-0432.

SOUTHWESTERN COLLEGE OF BUSINESS

Cincinnati, Ohio   **www.swcollege.net/**

Director of Admissions Ms. Betty Streber, Director of Admissions, Southwestern College of Business, 632 Vine Street, Suite 200, Cincinnati, OH 45202-4304. *Phone:* 513-421-3212.

SOUTHWESTERN COLLEGE OF BUSINESS

Dayton, Ohio   **www.swcollege.net/**

Director of Admissions Ms. Kathie Day, Director of Admissions, Southwestern College of Business, 111 West First Street, Dayton, OH 45402-3003. *Phone:* 937-224-0061 Ext. 17.

SOUTHWESTERN COLLEGE OF BUSINESS

Franklin, Ohio   **www.swcollege.net/**

Director of Admissions Ms. Susan Knodel, Director of Admissions, Southwestern College of Business, 201 East Second Street, Franklin, OH 45005. *Phone:* 937-746-6633. *Fax:* 937-746-6757.

STARK STATE COLLEGE OF TECHNOLOGY

North Canton, Ohio　　　www.starkstate.edu/

- **State and locally supported** 2-year, founded 1970, part of Ohio Board of Regents
- **Suburban** 34-acre campus with easy access to Cleveland
- **Endowment** $1.8 million
- **Coed,** 7,611 undergraduate students, 33% full-time, 57% women, 43% men

Undergraduates 2,528 full-time, 5,083 part-time. Students come from 12 states and territories, 0.1% are from out of state, 9% African American, 0.6% Asian American or Pacific Islander, 0.9% Hispanic American, 0.9% Native American, 0.1% international, 34% transferred in. *Retention:* 63% of 2003 full-time freshmen returned.

Freshmen *Admission:* 1,676 enrolled. *Test scores:* ACT scores over 18: 61%; ACT scores over 24: 6%; ACT scores over 30: 1%.

Faculty *Total:* 447, 32% full-time. *Student/faculty ratio:* 17:1.

Majors Accounting; administrative assistant and secretarial science; architectural engineering technology; automobile/automotive mechanics technology; biomedical technology; business administration and management; child development; civil engineering technology; clinical/medical laboratory technology; computer and information sciences related; computer engineering related; computer hardware engineering; computer/information technology services administration related; computer programming; computer programming related; computer programming (specific applications); computer programming (vendor/product certification); computer software and media applications related; computer software engineering; computer systems networking and telecommunications; computer/technical support; consumer merchandising/retailing management; court reporting; data entry/microcomputer applications; data entry/microcomputer applications related; dental hygiene; drafting and design technology; environmental studies; finance; fire science; food services technology; health information/medical records administration; human services; industrial technology; information technology; international business/trade/commerce; legal administrative assistant/secretary; marketing/marketing management; mechanical engineering/mechanical technology; medical/clinical assistant; nursing (registered nurse training); occupational therapy; operations management; physical therapy; respiratory care therapy; survey technology; web/multimedia management and webmaster; web page, digital/multimedia and information resources design; word processing.

Academics *Calendar:* semesters. *Degree:* certificates and associate. *Special study options:* academic remediation for entering students, adult/continuing education programs, distance learning, external degree program, independent study, off-campus study, part-time degree program, services for LD students, student-designed majors, summer session for credit.

Library Learning Resource Center with 70,000 titles, 425 serial subscriptions, an OPAC.

Student Life *Housing:* college housing not available. *Activities and Organizations:* student-run newspaper. *Campus security:* 24-hour emergency response devices, late-night transport/escort service. *Student services:* personal/psychological counseling.

Standardized Tests *Recommended:* SAT or ACT (for admission).

Costs (2007–08) *Tuition:* state resident $3810 full-time, $127 per credit hour part-time; nonresident $5610 full-time, $187 per credit hour part-time.

Financial Aid Of all full-time matriculated undergraduates, 194 Federal Work-Study jobs (averaging $2383).

Applying *Options:* electronic application, early admission, deferred entrance. *Application fee:* $65. *Required:* high school transcript. *Application deadlines:* rolling (freshmen), rolling (transfers).

Freshmen Application Contact Mr. Wallace Hoffer, Dean of Student Services, Stark State College of Technology, 6200 Frank Road, NW, Canton, OH 44720. *Phone:* 330-966-5450. *Toll-free phone:* 800-797-8275. *Fax:* 330-497-6313. *E-mail:* info@starkstate.edu.

STAUTZENBERGER COLLEGE

Toledo, Ohio　　　www.sctoday.com/

Director of Admissions Ms. Karen Fitzgerald, Director of Admissions and Marketing, Stautzenberger College, 5355 Southwyck Boulevard, Toledo, OH 43614. *Phone:* 419-866-0261. *Toll-free phone:* 800-552-5099. *Fax:* 419-867-9821. *E-mail:* klfitzgerald@stautzenberger.com.

TECHNOLOGY EDUCATION COLLEGE

Columbus, Ohio　　　www.tececducation.com/

- **Private** 2-year
- **Coed, primarily women,** 491 undergraduate students

Undergraduates 55% African American.

Faculty *Total:* 32, 53% full-time. *Student/faculty ratio:* 12:1.

Majors Accounting; architectural engineering technology; computer programming (specific applications); criminal justice/law enforcement administration; health/health care administration; medical/clinical assistant; system administration.

Academics *Calendar:* quarters. *Degree:* certificates and associate.

Costs (2006–07) *Tuition:* $11,634 full-time.

Director of Admissions Michael Mongomery, Executive Director, Technology Education College, 2745 Winchester Pike, Columbus, OH 43232. *Phone:* 614-456-4600. *Toll-free phone:* 800-838-3233. *Fax:* 614-456-4640. *E-mail:* mmontgomery@tececducation.com.

TERRA STATE COMMUNITY COLLEGE

Fremont, Ohio　　　www.terra.edu/

- **State-supported** 2-year, founded 1968, part of Ohio Board of Regents
- **Small-town** 100-acre campus with easy access to Toledo
- **Endowment** $864,654
- **Coed,** 2,314 undergraduate students, 35% full-time, 53% women, 47% men

Undergraduates 811 full-time, 1,503 part-time. Students come from 2 states and territories, 0.1% are from out of state, 3% African American, 0.5% Asian American or Pacific Islander, 5% Hispanic American, 0.4% Native American, 23% transferred in. *Retention:* 39% of 2003 full-time freshmen returned.

Freshmen *Admission:* 795 enrolled.

Faculty *Total:* 161, 25% full-time. *Student/faculty ratio:* 16:1.

Majors Accounting; administrative assistant and secretarial science; architectural engineering technology; automobile/automotive mechanics technology; automotive engineering technology; banking and financial support services; business administration and management; chemistry; commercial and advertising art; computer and information sciences; criminal justice/police science; electromechanical technology; engineering; engineering technology; English; entrepreneurship; finance; general studies; heating, air conditioning and refrigeration technology; heating, air conditioning, ventilation and refrigeration maintenance technology; industrial technology; information science/studies; kindergarten/preschool education; marketing/marketing management; mathematics; mechanical engineering/mechanical technology; medical administrative assistant and medical secretary; office occupations and clerical services; plastics engineering technology; psychology; quality control technology; robotics technology; sign language interpretation and translation; social work; technical and business writing; tool and die technology; welding technology.

Academics *Calendar:* quarters. *Degree:* certificates, diplomas, and associate. *Special study options:* academic remediation for entering students, accelerated degree program, adult/continuing education programs, advanced placement credit, cooperative education, distance learning, double majors, honors programs, independent study, internships, off-campus study, part-time degree program, services for LD students, student-designed majors, summer session for credit.

Library Learning Resource Center with 22,675 titles, 383 serial subscriptions, an OPAC, a Web page.

Student Life *Housing:* college housing not available. *Activities and Organizations:* choral group, Phi Theta Kappa, Student Activities Club, Society of Plastic Engineers, Koinonia, Student Senate, national fraternities. *Campus security:* 24-hour emergency response devices, late-night transport/escort service. *Student services:* personal/psychological counseling.

Athletics Member NJCAA. *Intercollegiate sports:* golf M, volleyball W(s). *Intramural sports:* basketball M/W, bowling M/W, football M, golf M/W, softball M/W, table tennis M/W, volleyball M/W.

Costs (2007–08) *Tuition:* state resident $3231 full-time, $108 per credit hour part-time; nonresident $5636 full-time, $176 per credit hour part-time. *Required fees:* $359 full-time, $12 per credit hour part-time.

Financial Aid Of all full-time matriculated undergraduates, 45 Federal Work-Study jobs (averaging $2000).

Applying *Options:* electronic application, early admission, deferred entrance. *Required:* high school transcript. *Application deadlines:* rolling (freshmen), rolling (transfers).

Freshmen Application Contact Mr. Dale Stearns, Dean of Student Services, Terra State Community College, 2830 Napoleon Road, Fremont, OH 43420. *Phone:* 419-559-2347. *Toll-free phone:* 800-334-3886. *Fax:* 419-334-9035. *E-mail:* dstearns@terra.edu.

TRUMBULL BUSINESS COLLEGE

Warren, Ohio   www.tbc-trumbullbusiness.com/

- **Proprietary** 2-year, founded 1972
- **Small-town** 6-acre campus
- **Coed, primarily women,** 321 undergraduate students, 91% full-time, 85% women, 15% men

Undergraduates 292 full-time, 29 part-time. Students come from 2 states and territories, 1% are from out of state.

Freshmen *Admission:* 62 applied, 62 admitted, 62 enrolled.

Faculty *Total:* 13, 69% full-time. *Student/faculty ratio:* 28:1.

Majors Accounting; administrative assistant and secretarial science; computer/information technology services administration related; legal administrative assistant/secretary; management information systems; medical administrative assistant and medical secretary; word processing.

Academics *Calendar:* quarters. *Degree:* diplomas and associate. *Special study options:* adult/continuing education programs, double majors, part-time degree program, study abroad.

Student Life *Housing:* college housing not available. *Activities and Organizations:* student-run newspaper, Student Senate, MADD/SADD.

Costs (2006–07) *Tuition:* $10,080 full-time, $210 per credit hour part-time. Full-time tuition and fees vary according to course load and program. Part-time tuition and fees vary according to course load and program. No tuition increase for student's term of enrollment. *Required fees:* $425 full-time. *Payment plan:* installment. *Waivers:* employees or children of employees.

Financial Aid Of all full-time matriculated undergraduates, 2 Federal Work-Study jobs. *Financial aid deadline:* 9/30.

Applying *Application fee:* $75. *Required:* high school transcript, interview. *Application deadline:* rolling (freshmen). *Notification:* continuous until 10/1 (freshmen).

Director of Admissions Admissions Office, Trumbull Business College, 3200 Ridge Road, Warren, OH 44484. *Phone:* 330-369-6792. *E-mail:* admissions@tbc-trumbullbusiness.com.

THE UNIVERSITY OF AKRON–WAYNE COLLEGE

Orrville, Ohio   www.wayne.uakron.edu/

- **State-supported** 2-year, founded 1972, part of The University of Akron
- **Rural** 157-acre campus
- **Coed,** 1,737 undergraduate students, 53% full-time, 63% women, 37% men

Undergraduates 924 full-time, 813 part-time. Students come from 1 other state, 3% African American, 0.7% Asian American or Pacific Islander, 0.5% Hispanic American, 0.4% Native American, 5% transferred in. *Retention:* 61% of 2003 full-time freshmen returned.

Freshmen *Admission:* 647 applied, 601 admitted, 320 enrolled. *Average high school GPA:* 2.93. *Test scores:* ACT scores over 18: 70%; ACT scores over 24: 15%; ACT scores over 30: 1%.

Faculty *Total:* 136, 20% full-time, 23% with terminal degrees. *Student/faculty ratio:* 17:1.

Majors Accounting; accounting technology and bookkeeping; administrative assistant and secretarial science; business administration and management; business automation/technology/data entry; computer science; computer systems networking and telecommunications; data processing and data processing technology; engineering; environmental health; executive assistant/executive secretary; general studies; interdisciplinary studies; legal administrative assistant/secretary; liberal arts and sciences/liberal studies; management information systems; medical administrative assistant and medical secretary; medical office management; occupational safety and health technology; social work.

Academics *Calendar:* semesters. *Degree:* certificates and associate. *Special study options:* academic remediation for entering students, adult/continuing education programs, advanced placement credit, cooperative education, distance learning, double majors, English as a second language, honors programs, independent study, internships, off-campus study, part-time degree program, services for LD students, summer session for credit. *ROTC:* Army (c), Air Force (c).

Library Wayne College Library with 23,450 titles, 219 serial subscriptions, an OPAC.

Student Life *Housing:* college housing not available. *Campus security:* 24-hour emergency response devices, late-night transport/escort service. *Student services:* personal/psychological counseling.

Athletics *Intercollegiate sports:* basketball M/W, cheerleading W, golf M, volleyball W. *Intramural sports:* basketball M/W, golf M, volleyball M/W.

Standardized Tests *Required for some:* SAT or ACT (for admission), ACT COMPASS. *Recommended:* SAT or ACT (for admission), ACT COMPASS.

Costs (2006–07) *Tuition:* state resident $4884 full-time, $216 per credit hour part-time; nonresident $13,202 full-time, $466 per credit hour part-time. Full-time tuition and fees vary according to course load. Part-time tuition and fees vary according to course load. *Required fees:* $146 full-time, $6 per credit hour part-time, $12 per term part-time.

Financial Aid Of all full-time matriculated undergraduates, 8 Federal Work-Study jobs (averaging $2200).

Applying *Options:* electronic application, early admission, deferred entrance. *Application fee:* $30. *Required for some:* high school transcript. *Application deadlines:* 8/30 (freshmen), 8/30 (transfers). *Notification:* continuous until 8/30 (freshmen), continuous until 8/30 (transfers).

Freshmen Application Contact Ms. Alicia Broadus, Student Services Counselor, The University of Akron–Wayne College, 1901 Smucker Road, Orrville, OH 44667. *Phone:* 800-221-8308 Ext. 8901. *Toll-free phone:* 800-221-8308 Ext. 8900. *Fax:* 330-684-8989. *E-mail:* wayneadmissions@uakron.edu.

UNIVERSITY OF CINCINNATI CLERMONT COLLEGE

Batavia, Ohio   www.clc.uc.edu/

- **State-supported** 2-year, founded 1972, part of University of Cincinnati System
- **Rural** 65-acre campus with easy access to Cincinnati
- **Endowment** $338,141
- **Coed,** 2,408 undergraduate students

Undergraduates Students come from 3 states and territories.

Freshmen *Test scores:* SAT verbal scores over 500: 45%; SAT math scores over 500: 30%; SAT verbal scores over 600: 15%.

Faculty *Total:* 163, 22% full-time.

Majors Accounting; administrative assistant and secretarial science; avionics maintenance technology; business administration and management; computer and information sciences; computer graphics; computer programming; court reporting; criminal justice/law enforcement administration; electrical, electronic and communications engineering technology; elementary education; hospitality administration; information science/studies; legal administrative assistant/secretary; legal assistant/paralegal; liberal arts and sciences/liberal studies; medical administrative assistant and medical secretary; pharmacy; social work.

Academics *Calendar:* quarters. *Degree:* certificates and associate. *Special study options:* academic remediation for entering students, adult/continuing education programs, advanced placement credit, cooperative education, internships, off-campus study, part-time degree program, student-designed majors, summer session for credit. *ROTC:* Air Force (c).

Library 19,235 titles, 174 serial subscriptions.

Student Life *Housing:* college housing not available. *Activities and Organizations:* drama/theater group, student-run newspaper. *Campus security:* 12-hour patrols by trained security personnel. *Student services:* personal/psychological counseling, women's center.

Athletics *Intramural sports:* basketball M, bowling M/W, table tennis M/W, tennis M/W, volleyball M/W.

Standardized Tests *Required for some:* SAT or ACT (for placement). *Recommended:* SAT or ACT (for placement).

Costs (2006–07) *Tuition:* state resident $4542 full-time; nonresident $11,394 full-time.

Applying *Options:* deferred entrance. *Application fee:* $35. *Required:* high school transcript. *Application deadlines:* rolling (freshmen), rolling (transfers). *Notification:* continuous (freshmen), continuous (transfers).

Freshmen Application Contact Ms. Tanya Bohart, Admissions Assistant, University of Cincinnati Clermont College, 4200 Clermont College Drive, Batavia, OH 45103-1785. *Phone:* 513-732-5202. *E-mail:* tanya.bohart@uc.edu.

UNIVERSITY OF CINCINNATI RAYMOND WALTERS COLLEGE

Cincinnati, Ohio   www.rwc.uc.edu/

Freshmen Application Contact Ms. Angelica Kennedy, Admission Counselor, University of Cincinnati Raymond Walters College, 9555 Plainfield Road, Cincinnati, OH 45236-1007. *Phone:* 513-745-5700.

UNIVERSITY OF NORTHWESTERN OHIO

Lima, Ohio   **www.unoh.edu/**

- **Independent** primarily 2-year, founded 1920
- **Small-town** 35-acre campus with easy access to Dayton and Toledo
- **Coed**

The University of Northwestern Ohio (UNOH) is a private, nonprofit university that was established in 1920. Located in Lima, Ohio, UNOH has a population of 3,200 students and offers associate degrees and diplomas in automotive, high performance, diesel, agriculture, alternative fuels, and HVAC/R. Associate degrees and diplomas are awarded in the College of Business for accounting, business, computers, and medical fields as well as various other majors.

Undergraduates 2,629 full-time, 286 part-time. Students come from 34 states and territories, 30% are from out of state, 0.5% African American, 0.1% Hispanic American, 2% transferred in, 45% live on campus. *Retention:* 70% of 2003 full-time freshmen returned.
Faculty *Student/faculty ratio:* 20:1.
Academics *Calendar:* quarters. *Degrees:* certificates, diplomas, associate, and bachelor's. *Special study options:* academic remediation for entering students, accelerated degree program, adult/continuing education programs, advanced placement credit, cooperative education, distance learning, double majors, part-time degree program, summer session for credit.
Student Life *Campus security:* 24-hour emergency response devices and patrols, late-night transport/escort service.
Financial Aid Of all full-time matriculated undergraduates, 40 Federal Work-Study jobs (averaging $2000).
Applying *Options:* electronic application, early admission, deferred entrance. *Application fee:* $50. *Required:* high school transcript.
Freshmen Application Contact Mr. Dan Klopp, Vice President for Enrollment Management, University of Northwestern Ohio, 1441 North Cable Road, Lima, OH 45805-1498. *Phone:* 419-227-3141. *Fax:* 419-229-6926. *E-mail:* info@nc.edu.

VATTEROTT COLLEGE

Broadview Heights, Ohio   **www.vatterott-college.edu/**

- **Proprietary** 2-year
- **Coed,** 236 undergraduate students
- 93% of applicants were admitted

Freshmen *Admission:* 46 applied, 43 admitted.
Majors Building/construction finishing, management, and inspection related; electrician; heating, air conditioning and refrigeration technology; information technology; system administration.
Academics *Calendar:* semesters. *Degree:* associate.
Costs (2006–07) *Tuition:* $9142 full-time.
Director of Admissions Mr. Jack Chalk, Director of Admissions, Vatterott College, 5025 East Royalton Road, Broadview Heights, OH 44147. *Phone:* 440-526-1660. *Toll-free phone:* 866-314-6454.

VIRGINIA MARTI COLLEGE OF ART AND DESIGN

Lakewood, Ohio   **www.vmcad.edu/**

Director of Admissions Quinn Marti, Head of Admissions, Virginia Marti College of Art and Design, 11724 Detroit Avenue, PO Box 580, Lakewood, OH 44107-3002. *Phone:* 216-221-8584.

WASHINGTON STATE COMMUNITY COLLEGE

Marietta, Ohio   **www.wscc.edu/**

- **State-supported** 2-year, founded 1971, part of Ohio Board of Regents
- **Small-town** campus
- **Coed,** 2,086 undergraduate students, 56% full-time, 62% women, 38% men

Undergraduates 1,174 full-time, 912 part-time. Students come from 5 states and territories, 1% African American, 0.4% Asian American or Pacific Islander, 0.5% Hispanic American, 0.6% Native American. *Retention:* 52% of 2003 full-time freshmen returned.
Freshmen *Admission:* 230 enrolled.
Faculty *Total:* 144, 40% full-time. *Student/faculty ratio:* 14:1.
Majors Accounting; administrative assistant and secretarial science; automobile/automotive mechanics technology; biological and physical sciences; biology/biological sciences; business administration and management; chemical engineering; clinical/medical laboratory technology; computer engineering technology; data processing and data processing technology; drafting and design technology; education; electrical, electronic and communications engineering technology; engineering; heating, air conditioning, ventilation and refrigeration maintenance technology; industrial technology; kindergarten/preschool education; liberal arts and sciences/liberal studies; marketing/marketing management; mathematics; mechanical engineering/mechanical technology; medical administrative assistant and medical secretary; nursing (licensed practical/vocational nurse training); nursing (registered nurse training); physical sciences; radio and television; social work.
Academics *Calendar:* quarters. *Degree:* certificates and associate. *Special study options:* academic remediation for entering students, adult/continuing education programs, double majors, independent study, internships, part-time degree program, services for LD students, student-designed majors, summer session for credit.
Library 15,000 titles, 200 serial subscriptions.
Student Life *Housing:* college housing not available. *Activities and Organizations:* choral group, Student Senate, Phi Theta Kappa, Practical Nursing Club, Business Lunch Club, Beta Club. *Student services:* personal/psychological counseling.
Athletics *Intramural sports:* basketball M, softball M/W, volleyball M/W.
Standardized Tests *Required:* ACT ASSET (for placement).
Costs (2006–07) *Tuition:* area resident $3420 full-time, $76 per credit hour part-time; nonresident $6840 full-time, $152 per credit hour part-time. Full-time tuition and fees vary according to course load and reciprocity agreements. Part-time tuition and fees vary according to course load and reciprocity agreements. *Payment plan:* installment. *Waivers:* senior citizens and employees or children of employees.
Financial Aid Of all full-time matriculated undergraduates, 50 Federal Work-Study jobs (averaging $2040).
Applying *Options:* early admission, deferred entrance. *Required for some:* high school transcript. *Recommended:* high school transcript. *Application deadlines:* rolling (freshmen), rolling (transfers). *Notification:* continuous (freshmen), continuous (transfers).
Freshmen Application Contact Ms. Rebecca Peroni, Director of Admissions, Washington State Community College, 710 Colegate Drive, Marietta, OH 45750-9225. *Phone:* 740-374-8716. *Fax:* 740-376-0257. *E-mail:* rperoni@wscc.edu.

WRIGHT STATE UNIVERSITY, LAKE CAMPUS

Celina, Ohio   **www.wright.edu/lake/**

- **State-supported** 2-year, founded 1969, part of Ohio Board of Regents
- **Rural** 173-acre campus
- **Coed,** 828 undergraduate students

Undergraduates Students come from 3 states and territories, 1 other country.
Freshmen *Admission:* 262 applied, 260 admitted.
Faculty *Total:* 48, 38% full-time. *Student/faculty ratio:* 15:1.
Majors Accounting; administrative assistant and secretarial science; biology/biological sciences; business administration and management; business/commerce; chemistry; communication/speech communication and rhetoric; computer typography and composition equipment operation; consumer merchandising/retailing management; drafting and design technology; electrical, electronic and communications engineering technology; elementary education; engineering; engineering related; engineering technology; English; finance; geography; graphic communications related; history; industrial technology; information science/studies; legal administrative assistant/secretary; liberal arts and sciences/liberal studies; management information systems; manufacturing technology; marketing/marketing management; mass communication/media; mechanical engineering/mechanical technology; medical administrative assistant and medical secretary; pre-engineering; psychology; social work; sociology.
Academics *Calendar:* quarters. *Degree:* certificates and associate. *Special study options:* academic remediation for entering students, adult/continuing

education programs, advanced placement credit, honors programs, off-campus study, part-time degree program, services for LD students, student-designed majors, summer session for credit.

Library Wright State University, Lake Campus Library with 26,000 titles, 347 serial subscriptions.

Student Life *Housing:* college housing not available. *Activities and Organizations:* drama/theater group, student-run newspaper, Business Professionals of America, Student Manufacturing Association. *Campus security:* 24-hour emergency response devices. *Student services:* personal/psychological counseling.

Athletics *Intercollegiate sports:* basketball M/W.

Standardized Tests *Required:* SAT or ACT (for placement).

Costs (2006–07) *Tuition:* state resident $4893 full-time, $148 per credit hour part-time; nonresident $11,619 full-time, $354 per credit hour part-time. Full-time tuition and fees vary according to course load and reciprocity agreements. *Payment plan:* installment. *Waivers:* senior citizens and employees or children of employees.

Applying *Options:* early admission, deferred entrance. *Application fee:* $40. *Required:* high school transcript. *Recommended:* minimum 2.0 GPA. *Application deadlines:* rolling (freshmen), rolling (transfers). *Notification:* continuous (freshmen), continuous (transfers).

Freshmen Application Contact Mrs. B.J. Hobler, Student Services Officer, Wright State University, Lake Campus, 7600 State Route 703, Celina, OH 45822-2921. *Phone:* 419-586-0324. *Toll-free phone:* 800-237-1477. *Fax:* 419-586-0358.

ZANE STATE COLLEGE

Zanesville, Ohio **www.zanestate.edu/**

- **State and locally supported** 2-year, founded 1969
- **Small-town** 170-acre campus with easy access to Columbus
- **Coed,** 1,915 undergraduate students

Undergraduates Students come from 1 other state, 2 other countries, 0.2% are from out of state.

Freshmen *Admission:* 722 applied, 593 admitted.

Faculty *Total:* 116, 43% full-time. *Student/faculty ratio:* 18:1.

Majors Accounting; administrative assistant and secretarial science; business administration and management; child care provision; clinical/medical laboratory assistant; computer programming (specific applications); criminal justice/law enforcement administration; culinary arts; data entry/microcomputer applications; drafting and design technology; electrical, electronic and communications engineering technology; environmental studies; human resources management; industrial radiologic technology; industrial technology; legal assistant/paralegal; marketing/marketing management; medical/clinical assistant; mental health/rehabilitation; natural resources management and policy; occupational therapy; parks, recreation and leisure; parks, recreation and leisure facilities management; physical therapist assistant; social work; tourism and travel services management; web page, digital/multimedia and information resources design.

Academics *Calendar:* quarters. *Degree:* certificates and associate. *Special study options:* academic remediation for entering students, adult/continuing education programs, cooperative education, honors programs, internships, off-campus study, part-time degree program, services for LD students, student-designed majors, summer session for credit.

Student Life *Housing:* college housing not available. *Activities and Organizations:* student-run newspaper. *Student services:* personal/psychological counseling.

Athletics *Intercollegiate sports:* baseball M/W, basketball M/W, golf M/W. *Intramural sports:* basketball M/W, golf M/W, volleyball M/W.

Standardized Tests *Recommended:* SAT or ACT (for admission).

Costs (2006–07) *Tuition:* state resident $3849 full-time; nonresident $7674 full-time.

Financial Aid Of all full-time matriculated undergraduates, 65 Federal Work-Study jobs (averaging $2010).

Applying *Options:* early admission. *Application fee:* $20. *Required:* high school transcript. *Required for some:* letters of recommendation, interview. *Application deadlines:* rolling (freshmen), rolling (transfers). *Notification:* continuous (freshmen), continuous (transfers).

Director of Admissions Mr. Paul Young, Director of Admissions, Zane State College, 1555 Newark Road, Zanesville, OH 43701-2626. *Phone:* 740-454-2501 Ext. 1225. *Toll-free phone:* 800-686-8324 Ext. 1225.

CARL ALBERT STATE COLLEGE

Poteau, Oklahoma **www.carlalbert.edu/**

- **State-supported** 2-year, founded 1934, part of Oklahoma State Regents for Higher Education
- **Small-town** 78-acre campus
- **Coed**

Undergraduates 1,484 full-time, 1,017 part-time. 11% are from out of state, 3% African American, 0.9% Asian American or Pacific Islander, 2% Hispanic American, 27% Native American, 0.6% international, 18% live on campus.

Faculty *Student/faculty ratio:* 16:1.

Academics *Calendar:* semesters. *Degree:* certificates and associate. *Special study options:* academic remediation for entering students, adult/continuing education programs, cooperative education, part-time degree program.

Student Life *Campus security:* security guards.

Athletics Member NJCAA.

Costs (2006–07) *Tuition:* state resident $2212 full-time, $71 per credit hour part-time; nonresident $4036 full-time, $168 per credit hour part-time. *Required fees:* $7 full-time, $2 per term part-time. *Room and board:* $2500. Room and board charges vary according to board plan.

Financial Aid Of all full-time matriculated undergraduates, 125 Federal Work-Study jobs (averaging $1751).

Applying *Required:* high school transcript.

Freshmen Application Contact Ms. Jennifer Williams, Admission Specialist, Carl Albert State College, 1507 South McKenna, Poteau, OK 74953-5208. *Phone:* 918-647-1300. *Fax:* 918-647-1306. *E-mail:* jwilliams@carlalbert.edu.

COMMUNITY CARE COLLEGE

Tulsa, Oklahoma **www.communitycarecollege.com/**

- **Proprietary** 2-year, founded 1995, part of Dental Directions, Inc
- **Coed**

Undergraduates 512 full-time, 13 part-time. 4% are from out of state, 17% African American, 0.6% Asian American or Pacific Islander, 3% Hispanic American, 12% Native American.

Academics *Calendar:* semesters. *Degree:* certificates, diplomas, and associate.

Costs (2006–07) *Tuition:* $9000 full-time. Full-time tuition and fees vary according to course load, degree level, and program. No tuition increase for student's term of enrollment. *Required fees:* $850 full-time.

Applying *Application fee:* $15. *Required:* high school transcript, interview, Assessment.

Freshmen Application Contact Ms. Teresa Knox, Chief Executive Officer, Community Care College, 4242 South Sheridan, Tulsa, OK 74145. *Phone:* 918-610-0027. *Fax:* 918-610-0029. *E-mail:* tknox@communitycarecollege.com.

CONNORS STATE COLLEGE

Warner, Oklahoma **www.connorsstate.edu/**

Freshmen Application Contact Ms. Sonya Baker, Registrar, Connors State College, Route 1 Box 1000 College Road, Warner, OK 74469. *Phone:* 918-463-6233. *Toll-free phone:* 918-463-2931 Ext. 6241.

EASTERN OKLAHOMA STATE COLLEGE

Wilburton, Oklahoma **www.eosc.edu/**

Freshmen Application Contact Ms. Leah McLaughlin, Director of Admissions, Eastern Oklahoma State College, 1301 West Main, Wilburton, OK 74578-4999. *Phone:* 918-465-1811. *Fax:* 918-465-2431. *E-mail:* lmiller@eosc.edu.

HERITAGE COLLEGE OF HAIR DESIGN
Oklahoma City, Oklahoma

Freshmen Application Contact Admissions Office, Heritage College of Hair Design, 7100 I-35 Services Road, Suite 7118, Oklahoma City, OK 73149.

ITT TECHNICAL INSTITUTE
Tulsa, Oklahoma   www.itt-tech.edu/

- **Proprietary** primarily 2-year, founded 2005
- **Coed**

Majors Business administration and management; CAD/CADD drafting/design technology; computer and information systems security; computer engineering technology; computer systems networking and telecommunications; construction management; criminal justice/law enforcement administration; electrical, electronic and communications engineering technology; web page, digital/multimedia and information resources design.

Academics *Calendar:* quarters. *Degrees:* associate and bachelor's.

Standardized Tests *Required:* Wonderlic aptitude test (for admission).

Costs (2006–07) *Tuition:* Contact school for program costs.

Applying *Application fee:* $100. *Required:* high school transcript, interview. *Recommended:* letters of recommendation. *Application deadlines:* rolling (freshmen), rolling (transfers). *Notification:* continuous (freshmen), continuous (transfers).

Freshmen Application Contact Gigi Braecklein, Director of Recruitment, ITT Technical Institute, 4943 South 78th East Avenue, Tulsa, OK 74145. *Phone:* 918-619-8700.

MURRAY STATE COLLEGE
Tishomingo, Oklahoma   www.mscok.edu/

- **State-supported** 2-year, founded 1908, part of Oklahoma State Regents for Higher Education
- **Rural** 120-acre campus
- **Coed,** 1,958 undergraduate students, 57% full-time, 64% women, 36% men

Undergraduates 1,115 full-time, 843 part-time. Students come from 16 states and territories, 4 other countries, 3% are from out of state, 6% African American, 0.5% Asian American or Pacific Islander, 2% Hispanic American, 15% Native American, 0.5% international, 6% live on campus.

Faculty *Total:* 73, 59% full-time. *Student/faculty ratio:* 27:1.

Majors Administrative assistant and secretarial science; agricultural teacher education; agriculture; animal sciences; art; biological and physical sciences; business administration and management; business teacher education; chemistry; child development; computer science; drafting and design technology; electrical, electronic and communications engineering technology; elementary education; engineering; engineering technology; English; equestrian studies; health science; history; information science/studies; liberal arts and sciences/liberal studies; mathematics; metallurgical technology; natural resources/conservation; nursing (registered nurse training); physical education teaching and coaching; physical therapy; pre-engineering; veterinary sciences; veterinary technology; wildlife and wildlands science and management.

Academics *Calendar:* semesters. *Degree:* associate. *Special study options:* academic remediation for entering students, advanced placement credit, distance learning, honors programs, internships, part-time degree program, services for LD students, summer session for credit.

Library Murray State College Library plus 1 other with 20,000 titles, 160 serial subscriptions.

Student Life *Housing Options:* coed. Campus housing is university owned. *Activities and Organizations:* drama/theater group, student-run newspaper, choral group. *Campus security:* 24-hour patrols. *Student services:* personal/psychological counseling.

Athletics Member NJCAA. *Intercollegiate sports:* baseball M, basketball M(s)/W(s), softball M. *Intramural sports:* basketball M/W, swimming and diving M/W, tennis M/W, volleyball M/W, weight lifting M/W.

Standardized Tests *Required:* ACT (for placement).

Costs (2006–07) *Tuition:* state resident $2040 full-time; nonresident $5190 full-time.

Financial Aid Of all full-time matriculated undergraduates, 81 Federal Work-Study jobs (averaging $2304). 15 state and other part-time jobs (averaging $2304).

Applying *Options:* early admission, deferred entrance. *Required:* high school transcript. *Application deadlines:* rolling (freshmen), rolling (transfers). *Notification:* continuous (freshmen), continuous (transfers).

Director of Admissions Mrs. Ann Beck, Registrar and Director of Admissions, Murray State College, One Murray Campus, Tishomingo, OK 73460. *Phone:* 580-371-2371 Ext. 171.

NORTHEASTERN OKLAHOMA AGRICULTURAL AND MECHANICAL COLLEGE
Miami, Oklahoma   www.neoam.cc.ok.us/

Freshmen Application Contact Amy Ishmael, Dean of Enrollment Management, Northeastern Oklahoma Agricultural and Mechanical College, PO Box 3842, 200 I Street NE, Miami, OK 74354. *Phone:* 918-540-6212. *Toll-free phone:* 800-464-6636. *Fax:* 918-540-6946. *E-mail:* neoadmission@neoam.edu.

NORTHERN OKLAHOMA COLLEGE
Tonkawa, Oklahoma   www.north-ok.edu/

- **State-supported** 2-year, founded 1901, part of Oklahoma State Regents for Higher Education
- **Rural** 10-acre campus
- **Coed,** 3,050 undergraduate students

Undergraduates Students come from 4 other countries, 20% live on campus.

Faculty *Total:* 80, 56% full-time. *Student/faculty ratio:* 35:1.

Majors Accounting; administrative assistant and secretarial science; agricultural business and management; biological and physical sciences; broadcast journalism; business administration and management; commercial and advertising art; computer science; construction engineering technology; criminal justice/law enforcement administration; drafting and design technology; elementary education; engineering; graphic and printing equipment operation/production; information science/studies; liberal arts and sciences/liberal studies; nursing (registered nurse training).

Academics *Calendar:* semesters. *Degree:* associate. *Special study options:* academic remediation for entering students, adult/continuing education programs, advanced placement credit, part-time degree program, services for LD students, summer session for credit.

Library Vineyard Library with 34,458 titles, 211 serial subscriptions.

Student Life *Housing:* on-campus residence required through sophomore year. *Options:* Campus housing is leased by the school. *Activities and Organizations:* drama/theater group, student-run newspaper, radio station, choral group, Phi Theta Kappa, Law Enforcement Club, Fellowship of Christian Athletes, Student Nurses Association, Young Republicans. *Campus security:* 24-hour emergency response devices and patrols. *Student services:* health clinic, personal/psychological counseling.

Athletics Member NJCAA. *Intercollegiate sports:* baseball W(s), basketball M(s)/W(s), soccer M/W, softball W, volleyball M/W. *Intramural sports:* badminton M/W, basketball M/W, football M/W, golf M/W, racquetball M/W, softball M/W, tennis M/W, volleyball M/W, water polo M/W.

Standardized Tests *Required:* ACT (for placement).

Costs (2006–07) *Tuition:* state resident $2060 full-time; nonresident $5083 full-time.

Financial Aid Of all full-time matriculated undergraduates, 73 Federal Work-Study jobs (averaging $1900). 240 state and other part-time jobs (averaging $1050).

Applying *Options:* early admission. *Application fee:* $25. *Required:* high school transcript. *Application deadline:* rolling (freshmen).

Freshmen Application Contact Ms. Sheri Snyder, Director of College Relations, Northern Oklahoma College, PO Box 310, Tonkawa, OK 74653. *Phone:* 580-628-6290. *Toll-free phone:* 800-429-5715.

OKLAHOMA CITY COMMUNITY COLLEGE
Oklahoma City, Oklahoma   www.okccc.edu/

- **State-supported** 2-year, founded 1969, part of Oklahoma State Regents for Higher Education
- **Urban** 143-acre campus
- **Coed,** 12,516 undergraduate students, 38% full-time, 57% women, 43% men

Undergraduates 4,714 full-time, 7,802 part-time. Students come from 18 states and territories, 58 other countries, 1% are from out of state, 9% African American, 4% Asian American or Pacific Islander, 6% Hispanic American, 6% Native American, 5% international, 8% transferred in.

Freshmen *Admission:* 2,966 enrolled. *Test scores:* ACT scores over 18: 70%; ACT scores over 24: 16%.

Faculty *Total:* 546, 25% full-time, 10% with terminal degrees. *Student/faculty ratio:* 23:1.

Majors Accounting; airframe mechanics and aircraft maintenance technology; applied art; area studies related; art; automobile/automotive mechanics technology; avionics maintenance technology; biology/biological sciences; biomedical technology; broadcast journalism; business administration and management; chemistry; child development; commercial and advertising art; computer engineering technology; computer science; drafting and design technology; dramatic/theater arts; electrical, electronic and communications engineering technology; emergency medical technology (EMT paramedic); finance; fine/studio arts; gerontology; health information/medical records administration; history; humanities; insurance; liberal arts and sciences/liberal studies; literature; mass communication/media; mathematics; modern languages; music; nursing (registered nurse training); occupational therapy; orthoptics; physical therapy; physics; political science and government; pre-engineering; psychology; respiratory care therapy; sociology; surgical technology.

Academics *Calendar:* semesters. *Degree:* certificates and associate. *Special study options:* academic remediation for entering students, accelerated degree program, advanced placement credit, cooperative education, distance learning, double majors, English as a second language, external degree program, honors programs, independent study, part-time degree program, student-designed majors, summer session for credit.

Library Keith Leftwich Memorial Library with an OPAC.

Student Life *Housing:* college housing not available. *Activities and Organizations:* drama/theater group, student-run newspaper, choral group, Phi Theta Kappa, College Republicans, Future Teachers, Hispanic Organization to Promote Education, Student Activities Board. *Campus security:* 24-hour emergency response devices and patrols, late-night transport/escort service. *Student services:* personal/psychological counseling.

Athletics *Intramural sports:* basketball M/W, football M, soccer M/W, softball M/W, swimming and diving M/W, volleyball M/W.

Costs (2006–07) *Tuition:* state resident $1577 full-time, $53 per credit hour part-time; nonresident $5222 full-time, $174 per credit hour part-time. Full-time tuition and fees vary according to location. Part-time tuition and fees vary according to location. *Required fees:* $614 full-time, $20 per credit hour part-time. *Payment plan:* installment. *Waivers:* senior citizens and employees or children of employees.

Financial Aid Of all full-time matriculated undergraduates, 305 Federal Work-Study jobs (averaging $2667).

Applying *Options:* early admission, deferred entrance. *Application fee:* $25. *Required:* high school transcript. *Application deadlines:* rolling (freshmen), rolling (transfers).

Freshmen Application Contact Ms. Susan Braun, Director of Admissions and Recruitment, Oklahoma City Community College, 7777 South May Avenue, Oklahoma City, OK 73159. *Phone:* 405-682-7515. *Fax:* 405-682-7521. *E-mail:* sbraun@occc.edu.

OKLAHOMA STATE UNIVERSITY, OKLAHOMA CITY

Oklahoma City, Oklahoma   **www.osuokc.edu/**

- **State-supported** 2-year, founded 1961, part of Oklahoma State University
- **Urban** 80-acre campus
- **Coed,** 5,704 undergraduate students, 31% full-time, 61% women, 39% men

Undergraduates 1,789 full-time, 3,915 part-time. Students come from 12 states and territories, 15 other countries, 1% are from out of state, 14% African American, 2% Asian American or Pacific Islander, 5% Hispanic American, 7% Native American, 1% international, 6% transferred in. *Retention:* 43% of 2003 full-time freshmen returned.

Freshmen *Admission:* 764 applied, 764 admitted, 764 enrolled.

Faculty *Total:* 250, 26% full-time. *Student/faculty ratio:* 18:1.

Majors Accounting; architectural engineering technology; business administration and management; business automation/technology/data entry; civil engineering technology; computer and information sciences; computer/technical support; construction engineering technology; criminal justice/police science; data entry/microcomputer applications; early childhood education; education; electrical and power transmission installation; electrical, electronic and communications engineering technology; engineering; fire science; floristry marketing; horticultural science; industrial design; landscape architecture; medical/health manage-

ment and clinical assistant; nursing (registered nurse training); occupational safety and health technology; quality control technology; sign language interpretation and translation; substance abuse/addiction counseling; survey technology; turf and turfgrass management; veterinary technology.

Academics *Calendar:* semesters. *Degree:* certificates and associate. *Special study options:* academic remediation for entering students, advanced placement credit, cooperative education, distance learning, double majors, honors programs, independent study, part-time degree program, services for LD students, study abroad, summer session for credit.

Library Oklahoma State University-Oklahoma City Campus with 11,973 titles, 244 serial subscriptions, an OPAC, a Web page.

Student Life *Housing:* college housing not available. *Activities and Organizations:* Phi Theta Kappa, Deaf/Hearing Social Club, American Criminal Justice Association, Horticulture Club, Vet-Tech Club. *Campus security:* 24-hour patrols, late-night transport/escort service.

Athletics *Intramural sports:* basketball M/W, volleyball M/W.

Costs (2007–08) *Tuition:* state resident $1584 full-time, $66 per hour part-time; nonresident $4848 full-time, $202 per hour part-time. *Required fees:* $452 full-time, $19 per hour part-time.

Financial Aid Of all full-time matriculated undergraduates, 75 Federal Work-Study jobs (averaging $2500).

Applying *Options:* early admission. *Required:* high school transcript. *Application deadlines:* rolling (freshmen), rolling (out-of-state freshmen), rolling (transfers). *Notification:* continuous (freshmen), continuous (out-of-state freshmen), continuous (transfers).

Director of Admissions Ms. Jeanne Kubier, Director of Admissions and Registrar, Oklahoma State University, Oklahoma City, 900 North Portland Avenue, Oklahoma City, OK 73107. *Phone:* 405-945-3287.

OKLAHOMA STATE UNIVERSITY, OKMULGEE

Okmulgee, Oklahoma   **www.osu-okmulgee.edu/**

- **State-supported** 2-year, founded 1946, part of Oklahoma State University
- **Small-town** 160-acre campus with easy access to Tulsa
- **Coed,** 2,329 undergraduate students, 74% full-time, 40% women, 60% men

Undergraduates 1,717 full-time, 612 part-time. Students come from 22 states and territories, 3 other countries, 25% live on campus.

Freshmen *Admission:* 825 enrolled.

Faculty *Total:* 129, 100% full-time, 3% with terminal degrees.

Majors Accounting; administrative assistant and secretarial science; architectural engineering technology; artificial intelligence and robotics; automobile/automotive mechanics technology; avionics maintenance technology; business administration and management; commercial and advertising art; computer graphics; construction engineering technology; culinary arts; dietetics; drafting and design technology; electrical, electronic and communications engineering technology; food services technology; graphic and printing equipment operation/production; heating, air conditioning, ventilation and refrigeration maintenance technology; heavy equipment maintenance technology; hospitality administration; industrial technology; information science/studies; legal administrative assistant/secretary; machine tool technology; marketing/marketing management; medical administrative assistant and medical secretary; metal and jewelry arts; photography; pipefitting and sprinkler fitting; special products marketing.

Academics *Calendar:* trimesters. *Degree:* associate. *Special study options:* academic remediation for entering students, adult/continuing education programs, advanced placement credit, internships, part-time degree program, services for LD students, summer session for credit.

Library Learning Resource Center with 9,965 titles, 484 serial subscriptions, an OPAC, a Web page.

Student Life *Housing:* on-campus residence required for freshman year. *Options:* coed. *Activities and Organizations:* drama/theater group, Student Senate, Junior Ambassadors, Phi Theta Kappa, departmental clubs, Drama Club. *Campus security:* 24-hour emergency response devices and patrols, late-night transport/escort service, controlled dormitory access. *Student services:* health clinic, personal/psychological counseling.

Athletics *Intramural sports:* basketball M/W, bowling M/W, football M, golf M, racquetball M/W, softball M/W, table tennis M/W, volleyball M/W.

Standardized Tests *Required:* SAT or ACT (for placement).

Costs (2006–07) *Tuition:* state resident $2340 full-time, $78 per credit hour part-time; nonresident $6690 full-time, $223 per credit hour part-time. Full-time tuition and fees vary according to course level and program. Part-time tuition and fees vary according to course level and program. *Required fees:* $945 full-time, $32 per credit hour part-time. *Room and board:* $4850. Room and board charges vary according to board plan. *Waivers:* employees or children of employees.

Oklahoma State University, Okmulgee (continued)

Applying *Options:* deferred entrance. *Application fee:* $15. *Required:* high school transcript. *Application deadlines:* rolling (freshmen), rolling (transfers).
Freshmen Application Contact Mary Graves, Director, Admissions, Oklahoma State University, Okmulgee, 1801 East Fourth Street, Okmulgee, OK 74447-3901. *Phone:* 918-293-5298. *Toll-free phone:* 800-722-4471. *Fax:* 918-293-4643. *E-mail:* mary.r.graves@okstate.edu.

PLATT COLLEGE

Moore, Oklahoma **www.plattcollege.org/campuses/moore.htm**

- **Proprietary** 2-year
- **Coed,** 71 undergraduate students
- 100% of applicants were admitted

Freshmen *Admission:* 178 applied, 178 admitted.
Majors Nursing (licensed practical/vocational nurse training).
Academics *Degree:* associate.
Costs (2006–07) *Tuition:* $19,945 per degree program part-time.
Applying *Application fee:* $100. *Required:* letters of recommendation.
Admissions Office Contact Platt College, 201 North Eastern Avenue, Moore, OK 73160.

PLATT COLLEGE

Oklahoma City, Oklahoma **www.plattcollege.org/**

Director of Admissions Ms. Jane Nowlin, Director, Platt College, 309 South Ann Arbor Avenue, Oklahoma City, OK 73128. *Phone:* 405-946-7799. *Fax:* 405-943-2150. *E-mail:* janen@plattcollege.org.

PLATT COLLEGE

Tulsa, Oklahoma **www.plattcollege.org/**

- **Proprietary** 2-year, founded 1979
- **Coed,** 415 undergraduate students

Majors Nursing (licensed practical/vocational nurse training); nursing science.
Academics *Calendar:* continuous. *Degree:* associate.
Costs (2006–07) *Tuition:* $19,945 per degree program part-time.
Applying *Application fee:* $100.
Director of Admissions Mrs. Susan Rone, Director, Platt College, 3801 South Sheridan Road, Tulsa, OK 74145-111. *Phone:* 918-663-9000. *Fax:* 918-622-1240. *E-mail:* susanr@plattcollege.org.

REDLANDS COMMUNITY COLLEGE

El Reno, Oklahoma **www.redlandscc.edu/**

- **State-supported** 2-year, founded 1938, part of Oklahoma State Regents for Higher Education
- **Suburban** 55-acre campus with easy access to Oklahoma City
- **Coed,** 2,323 undergraduate students, 25% full-time, 63% women, 37% men

Undergraduates 583 full-time, 1,740 part-time. Students come from 4 states and territories, 7 other countries, 6% African American, 2% Asian American or Pacific Islander, 3% Hispanic American, 8% Native American, 2% international, 15% transferred in.
Freshmen *Admission:* 1,066 enrolled.
Faculty *Total:* 125, 26% full-time, 7% with terminal degrees. *Student/faculty ratio:* 18:1.
Majors Administrative assistant and secretarial science; agricultural business and management; agricultural teacher education; agriculture; animal sciences; art; biological and physical sciences; biology/biological sciences; business administration and management; child development; commercial and advertising art; computer programming; computer science; construction engineering technology; corrections; criminal justice/law enforcement administration; criminal justice/police science; drafting and design technology; education; electrical, electronic and communications engineering technology; elementary education; emergency medical technology (EMT paramedic); English; equestrian studies; kindergarten/preschool education; liberal arts and sciences/liberal studies; math-

ematics; nursing (registered nurse training); physical education teaching and coaching; physical sciences; psychology; social sciences.
Academics *Calendar:* semesters. *Degree:* certificates and associate. *Special study options:* academic remediation for entering students, accelerated degree program, adult/continuing education programs, advanced placement credit, cooperative education, distance learning, double majors, external degree program, honors programs, internships, part-time degree program, services for LD students, summer session for credit.
Library Learning Resource Center with 14,810 titles, 292 serial subscriptions, 19,075 audiovisual materials, an OPAC.
Student Life *Housing:* college housing not available. *Activities and Organizations:* drama/theater group, choral group, Nursing Club, Aggie Club, Baptist Student Union, Phi Theta Kappa, Outdoors Club. *Campus security:* 24-hour patrols. *Student services:* personal/psychological counseling.
Athletics Member NJCAA. *Intercollegiate sports:* baseball M(s), basketball M(s)/W(s), volleyball W(s). *Intramural sports:* basketball M/W, volleyball W.
Standardized Tests *Required:* ACT (for placement).
Costs (2006–07) *Tuition:* state resident $2460 full-time; nonresident $5010 full-time.
Financial Aid Of all full-time matriculated undergraduates, 25 Federal Work-Study jobs (averaging $2000). 70 state and other part-time jobs (averaging $2000).
Applying *Options:* electronic application, early admission, deferred entrance. *Application fee:* $25. *Required:* high school transcript. *Application deadlines:* rolling (freshmen), rolling (transfers). *Notification:* continuous (freshmen), continuous (transfers).
Director of Admissions Vice President for Student Services, Redlands Community College, 1300 South Country Club Road, El Reno, OK 73036. *Phone:* 405-262-2552 Ext. 1282. *Toll-free phone:* 866-415-6367.

ROSE STATE COLLEGE

Midwest City, Oklahoma **www.rose.edu/**

- **State and locally supported** 2-year, founded 1968, part of Oklahoma State Regents for Higher Education
- **Suburban** 110-acre campus with easy access to Oklahoma City
- **Coed,** 7,000 undergraduate students

Undergraduates Students come from 18 states and territories, 33 other countries.
Faculty *Total:* 412, 35% full-time.
Majors Accounting; administrative assistant and secretarial science; art; avionics maintenance technology; biology/biological sciences; broadcast journalism; business administration and management; business/commerce; chemistry; clinical/medical laboratory technology; court reporting; criminal justice/law enforcement administration; dental assisting; dental hygiene; developmental and child psychology; drafting and design technology; dramatic/theater arts; electrical, electronic and communications engineering technology; elementary education; English; environmental engineering technology; family and consumer sciences/human sciences; history; industrial radiologic technology; information science/studies; journalism; kindergarten/preschool education; kinesiology and exercise science; legal administrative assistant/secretary; liberal arts and sciences/liberal studies; library science; management information systems; mathematics; medical laboratory technology; medical radiologic technology; modern languages; music; nursing (registered nurse training); parks, recreation and leisure facilities management; physical education teaching and coaching; physical therapy; physics; political science and government; pre-engineering; pre-pharmacy studies; psychology; respiratory care therapy; sociology; speech and rhetoric.
Academics *Calendar:* semesters. *Degree:* certificates and associate. *Special study options:* academic remediation for entering students, accelerated degree program, adult/continuing education programs, advanced placement credit, distance learning, honors programs, independent study, internships, off-campus study, part-time degree program, services for LD students, summer session for credit. *ROTC:* Army (c), Air Force (c).
Library Rose State College Learning Resources Center with 90,000 titles, 443 serial subscriptions, 9,620 audiovisual materials, an OPAC, a Web page.
Student Life *Housing:* college housing not available. *Activities and Organizations:* drama/theater group, student-run newspaper, choral group. *Campus security:* 24-hour patrols. *Student services:* health clinic, personal/psychological counseling, women's center.
Athletics Member NJCAA. *Intercollegiate sports:* baseball M(s), basketball M(s)/W(s), soccer W(s). *Intramural sports:* basketball M/W, bowling M/W, soccer M, tennis M/W, volleyball M/W, water polo M/W.
Costs (2006–07) *Tuition:* state resident $1607 full-time, $54 per credit hour part-time; nonresident $5977 full-time, $200 per credit hour part-time. *Required fees:* $540 full-time, $18 per credit hour part-time. *Waivers:* employees or children of employees.

Financial Aid Of all full-time matriculated undergraduates, 150 Federal Work-Study jobs (averaging $4000).

Applying *Options:* electronic application, early admission, deferred entrance. *Application fee:* $15. *Required:* high school transcript. *Application deadlines:* rolling (freshmen), rolling (transfers). *Notification:* continuous (freshmen), continuous (transfers).

Freshmen Application Contact Ms. Mechelle Aitson-Roessler, Registrar and Director of Admissions, Rose State College, 6420 Southeast 15th Street, Midwest City, OK 73110-2799. *Phone:* 405-733-7308. *Toll-free phone:* 866-621-0987. *Fax:* 405-736-0203. *E-mail:* maitson@ms.rose.cc.ok.us.

SEMINOLE STATE COLLEGE

Seminole, Oklahoma   **www.ssc.cc.ok.us/**

- **State-supported** 2-year, founded 1931, part of Oklahoma State Regents for Higher Education
- **Small-town** 40-acre campus with easy access to Oklahoma City
- **Coed,** 2,534 undergraduate students

Undergraduates Students come from 13 states and territories, 5 other countries, 2% are from out of state, 8% live on campus.

Freshmen *Test scores:* ACT scores over 18: 56%; ACT scores over 24: 6%.

Faculty *Total:* 101, 46% full-time, 4% with terminal degrees. *Student/faculty ratio:* 25:1.

Majors Accounting; administrative assistant and secretarial science; art; behavioral sciences; biology/biological sciences; business administration and management; clinical/medical laboratory technology; computer science; criminal justice/police science; elementary education; English; liberal arts and sciences/liberal studies; mathematics; nursing (registered nurse training); physical education teaching and coaching; physical sciences; pre-engineering; social sciences.

Academics *Calendar:* semesters. *Degree:* diplomas and associate. *Special study options:* academic remediation for entering students, accelerated degree program, adult/continuing education programs, advanced placement credit, cooperative education, distance learning, honors programs, independent study, off-campus study, part-time degree program, services for LD students, summer session for credit.

Library Boren Library with 27,507 titles, 200 serial subscriptions, an OPAC.

Student Life *Housing Options:* coed. Campus housing is university owned. *Activities and Organizations:* student-run newspaper, choral group, Student Government Association, Native American Student Association, Psi Beta Honor Society, Student Nurses Association, Phi Theta Kappa. *Campus security:* 24-hour patrols, student patrols, late-night transport/escort service, controlled dormitory access. *Student services:* personal/psychological counseling.

Athletics Member NJCAA. *Intercollegiate sports:* baseball M(s), basketball M(s)/W(s), golf M(s)/W(s), softball W(s), volleyball W(s).

Standardized Tests *Recommended:* ACT (for admission).

Costs (2006–07) *Tuition:* state resident $1116 full-time, $49 per credit hour part-time; nonresident $3589 full-time, $156 per credit hour part-time. *Required fees:* $719 full-time, $30 per credit hour part-time. *Room and board:* $4940.

Applying *Options:* early admission, deferred entrance. *Application fee:* $15. *Required:* high school transcript. *Application deadlines:* rolling (freshmen), rolling (transfers). *Notification:* continuous (freshmen), continuous (transfers).

Freshmen Application Contact Mr. Chris Lindley, Director of Enrollment Management, Seminole State College, PO Box 351, 2701 Boren Boulevard, Seminole, OK 74818-0351. *Phone:* 405-382-9272. *Fax:* 405-382-9524. *E-mail:* lindley_c@ssc.cc.ok.us.

SOUTHWESTERN OKLAHOMA STATE UNIVERSITY AT SAYRE

Sayre, Oklahoma   **www.swosu.edu/sayre/**

- **State and locally supported** 2-year, founded 1938, part of Southwestern Oklahoma State University
- **Rural** 6-acre campus
- **Coed**

Undergraduates 328 full-time, 221 part-time. Students come from 2 states and territories, 3% are from out of state, 1% African American, 0.4% Asian American or Pacific Islander, 5% Hispanic American, 5% Native American.

Faculty *Student/faculty ratio:* 18:1.

Academics *Calendar:* semesters. *Degree:* diplomas and associate. *Special study options:* academic remediation for entering students, adult/continuing education programs, advanced placement credit, cooperative education, distance learning, independent study, part-time degree program, services for LD students, summer session for credit.

Standardized Tests *Required for some:* ACT (for admission).

Costs (2006–07) *Tuition:* state resident $3680 full-time, $115 per credit hour part-time.

Applying *Options:* early admission, deferred entrance. *Application fee:* $15. *Required:* high school transcript.

Freshmen Application Contact Ms. Kim Seymour, Registrar, Southwestern Oklahoma State University at Sayre, 409 East Mississippi Street, Sayre, OK 73662-1236. *Phone:* 580-928-5533 Ext. 101. *Fax:* 580-928-1140. *E-mail:* kim.seymour@swosu.edu.

SPARTAN COLLEGE OF AERONAUTICS AND TECHNOLOGY

Tulsa, Oklahoma   **www.spartan.edu/**

Freshmen Application Contact Mr. Mark Fowler, Vice President of Student Records and Finance, Spartan College of Aeronautics and Technology, 8820 East Pine Street, PO Box 582833, Tulsa, OK 74158-2833. *Phone:* 918-836-6886.

TULSA COMMUNITY COLLEGE

Tulsa, Oklahoma   **www.tulsacc.edu/**

- **State-supported** 2-year, founded 1968, part of Oklahoma State Regents for Higher Education
- **Urban** 160-acre campus
- **Coed,** 16,632 undergraduate students, 36% full-time, 62% women, 38% men

Undergraduates 5,947 full-time, 10,685 part-time. Students come from 41 states and territories, 3 other countries, 0.6% are from out of state, 9% African American, 2% Asian American or Pacific Islander, 3% Hispanic American, 8% Native American, 50% transferred in.

Freshmen *Admission:* 1,671 applied, 1,671 admitted, 1,671 enrolled. *Average high school GPA:* 3.24. *Test scores:* ACT scores over 18: 69%; ACT scores over 24: 16%; ACT scores over 30: 1%.

Faculty *Total:* 1,001, 29% full-time. *Student/faculty ratio:* 20:1.

Majors Accounting; administrative assistant and secretarial science; advertising; aeronautics/aviation/aerospace science and technology; agriculture; airframe mechanics and aircraft maintenance technology; American studies; applied horticulture; architecture; art; artificial intelligence and robotics; astronomy; automobile/automotive mechanics technology; avionics maintenance technology; behavioral sciences; biology/biological sciences; biomedical technology; botany/plant biology; business administration and management; business and personal/financial services marketing; business teacher education; chemistry; child care and support services management; child development; child guidance; civil engineering technology; clinical/medical laboratory technology; computer and information sciences related; computer and information systems security; computer graphics; computer hardware engineering; computer/information technology services administration related; computer programming related; computer programming (specific applications); computer programming (vendor/product certification); computer science; computer software and media applications related; computer software engineering; computer systems networking and telecommunications; computer/technical support; construction engineering technology; corrections; creative writing; criminal justice/law enforcement administration; criminal justice/police science; data entry/microcomputer applications; data entry/microcomputer applications related; data modeling/warehousing and database administration; dental assisting; dental hygiene; desktop publishing and digital imaging design; drafting and design technology; dramatic/theater arts; ecology; economics; education; electrical, electronic and communications engineering technology; elementary and middle school administration/principalship; elementary education; emergency medical technology (EMT paramedic); engineering; English; environmental engineering technology; fashion/apparel design; fire protection and safety technology; fire science; forestry; French; geography; geology/earth science; German; health information/medical records administration; health science; health teacher education; heating, air conditioning, ventilation and refrigeration maintenance technology; history; horticultural science; hotel/motel administration; humanities; human resources management; human services; industrial radiologic technology; industrial technology; information science/studies; information technology; insurance; interior design; international business/trade/commerce; international relations and affairs; Italian; Japanese; journalism; kindergarten/preschool education; labor and industrial relations; landscape architecture; landscaping and groundskeeping; Latin; legal administrative assistant/secretary; legal assistant/paralegal; legal studies; liberal arts and sciences/liberal studies; library science; management science; marketing/marketing management; mass communication/media; materials science; mathematics; mechanical engineering/mechanical technology; medical administrative assistant and medical secretary; medical/clinical assistant; music; music teacher

Tulsa Community College (continued)

education; nursing (registered nurse training); occupational safety and health technology; occupational therapist assistant; occupational therapy; oceanography (chemical and physical); ornamental horticulture; petroleum technology; philosophy; physical education teaching and coaching; physical sciences; physical therapy; physician assistant; physics; plant protection and integrated pest management; political science and government; pre-dentistry studies; pre-engineering; pre-medical studies; pre-pharmacy studies; pre-veterinary studies; psychology; purchasing, procurement/acquisitions and contracts management; quality control technology; radio and television; radiologic technology/science; religious studies; respiratory care therapy; Russian; safety/security technology; sign language interpretation and translation; social sciences; social work; sociology; Spanish; speech and rhetoric; surgical technology; survey technology; system administration; telecommunications; therapeutic recreation; tourism and travel services management; veterinary technology; web/multimedia management and webmaster; web page, digital/multimedia and information resources design; word processing; zoology/animal biology.

Academics *Calendar:* semesters. *Degree:* certificates and associate. *Special study options:* academic remediation for entering students, accelerated degree program, adult/continuing education programs, advanced placement credit, cooperative education, distance learning, English as a second language, external degree program, freshman honors college, honors programs, independent study, internships, off-campus study, part-time degree program, services for LD students, student-designed majors, summer session for credit.

Library Learning Resource Center plus 1 other with 124,000 titles, 420 serial subscriptions, an OPAC, a Web page.

Student Life *Housing:* college housing not available. *Activities and Organizations:* drama/theater group, student-run newspaper. *Campus security:* 24-hour emergency response devices and patrols, student patrols, late-night transport/escort service. *Student services:* health clinic, personal/psychological counseling, women's center.

Athletics *Intramural sports:* basketball M/W, bowling M/W, cross-country running M/W, football M/W, golf M/W, racquetball M/W, soccer M/W, tennis M/W, track and field M/W, volleyball M/W.

Costs (2006–07) *Tuition:* state resident $1228 full-time, $51 per credit hour part-time; nonresident $4422 full-time, $184 per credit hour part-time. *Required fees:* $707 full-time, $29 per credit hour part-time. *Payment plan:* installment. *Waivers:* senior citizens and employees or children of employees.

Financial Aid Of all full-time matriculated undergraduates, 200 Federal Work-Study jobs (averaging $1500).

Applying *Options:* early admission. *Application fee:* $20. *Required:* high school transcript. *Application deadlines:* rolling (freshmen), rolling (transfers).

Freshmen Application Contact Ms. Leanne Brewer, Director of Admissions and Records, Tulsa Community College, 6111 East Skelly Drive, Tulsa, OK 74135. *Phone:* 918-595-7811. *Fax:* 918-595-7910. *E-mail:* lbrewer@tulsacc.edu.

TULSA WELDING SCHOOL

Tulsa, Oklahoma — www.weldingschool.com/

- **Proprietary** 2-year, founded 1949, administratively affiliated with Tulsa Welding School, Jacksonville Branch
- **Urban** 5-acre campus
- **Coed, primarily men,** 604 undergraduate students, 100% full-time, 4% women, 96% men

Undergraduates 604 full-time. Students come from 23 states and territories, 38% are from out of state, 7% African American, 0.8% Asian American or Pacific Islander, 3% Hispanic American, 10% Native American.

Faculty *Total:* 17, 100% full-time. *Student/faculty ratio:* 18:1.

Majors Welding technology.

Academics *Calendar:* continuous (phased start every 3 weeks). *Degree:* diplomas and associate.

Library Technical Resource Center with 403 titles, 3 serial subscriptions.

Student Life *Housing:* college housing not available. *Campus security:* 24-hour emergency response devices.

Costs (2007–08) *Tuition:* $11,860 full-time. *Required fees:* $2040 full-time.

Applying *Required:* high school diploma, GED, or ATB test.

Freshmen Application Contact Mr. Mike Thurber, Director of Admissions, Tulsa Welding School, 2545 East 11th Street, Tulsa, OK 74104. *Phone:* 800-331-2934. *Toll-free phone:* 800-WELD-PRO. *Fax:* 918-587-8170. *E-mail:* tws@ionet.net.

VATTEROTT COLLEGE

Oklahoma City, Oklahoma — www.vatterott-college.edu/

- **Proprietary** 2-year
- **Urban** campus
- **Coed,** 267 undergraduate students, 100% full-time, 61% women, 39% men

Undergraduates 267 full-time. 32% African American, 2% Asian American or Pacific Islander, 9% Hispanic American, 2% Native American.

Freshmen *Admission:* 157 applied, 124 admitted.

Faculty *Total:* 25, 88% full-time, 16% with terminal degrees. *Student/faculty ratio:* 11:1.

Majors Computer programming; electrical and electronic engineering technologies related; heating, air conditioning and refrigeration technology; information technology; medical office assistant.

Academics *Calendar:* semesters. *Degrees:* diplomas, associate, and first professional.

Student Life *Housing:* college housing not available. *Campus security:* 24-hour emergency response devices and patrols.

Costs (2007–08) *Tuition:* $21,000 full-time. *Required fees:* $975 full-time.

Applying *Required:* essay or personal statement, high school transcript, interview.

Freshmen Application Contact Mr. Mark Hybers, Director of Admissions, Vatterott College, 4629 Northwest 23rd Street, Oklahoma City, OK 73127. *Phone:* 405-945-0088 Ext. 4416. *Toll-free phone:* 888-948-0088. *Fax:* 405-945-0788. *E-mail:* mark.hybers@vatterott-college.edu.

VATTEROTT COLLEGE

Tulsa, Oklahoma — www.vatterott-college.edu/

- **Proprietary** 2-year
- **Urban** 3-acre campus
- **Coed, primarily women**
- 78% of applicants were admitted

Undergraduates 226 full-time. 28% African American, 4% Hispanic American, 11% Native American. *Retention:* 71% of 2003 full-time freshmen returned.

Faculty *Student/faculty ratio:* 12:1.

Academics *Calendar:* semesters. *Degree:* diplomas and associate.

Freshmen Application Contact Mr. Tim Maloukis, Director of Admissions, Vatterott College, 555 South Memorial Drive, Tulsa, OK 74112. *Phone:* 918-836-6656. *Toll-free phone:* 888-857-4016. *Fax:* 918-836-9698. *E-mail:* tulsa@vatterott-college.edu.

WESTERN OKLAHOMA STATE COLLEGE

Altus, Oklahoma — www.wosc.edu/

- **State-supported** 2-year, founded 1926, part of Oklahoma State Regents for Higher Education
- **Rural** 142-acre campus
- **Endowment** $2.5 million
- **Coed**

Undergraduates 859 full-time, 1,202 part-time. Students come from 30 states and territories, 1 other country, 13% African American, 2% Asian American or Pacific Islander, 11% Hispanic American, 4% Native American. *Retention:* 50% of 2003 full-time freshmen returned.

Faculty *Student/faculty ratio:* 20:1.

Academics *Calendar:* semesters. *Degree:* certificates and associate. *Special study options:* academic remediation for entering students, adult/continuing education programs, advanced placement credit, honors programs, off-campus study, part-time degree program, services for LD students, student-designed majors, summer session for credit.

Student Life *Campus security:* 24-hour emergency response devices.

Athletics Member NJCAA.

Standardized Tests *Required for some:* ACT (for admission).

Costs (2006–07) *Tuition:* state resident $2213 full-time, $74 per semester hour part-time; nonresident $5348 full-time, $178 per semester hour part-time. *Room and board:* $4400.

Financial Aid Of all full-time matriculated undergraduates, 85 Federal Work-Study jobs (averaging $1978).

Applying *Options:* electronic application, early admission. *Application fee:* $15. *Required:* high school transcript.

Freshmen Application Contact Dr. Larry W. Paxton, Director of Academic Services, Western Oklahoma State College, 2801 North Main Street, Altus, OK 73521-1397. *Phone:* 580-477-7720. *Fax:* 580-477-7723. *E-mail:* larry.paxton@wosc.edu.

OREGON

BLUE MOUNTAIN COMMUNITY COLLEGE

Pendleton, Oregon   www.bluecc.edu/

Director of Admissions Ms. Theresa Bosworth, Director of Admissions, Blue Mountain Community College, PO Box 100, Pendleton, OR 97801. *Phone:* 541-278-5774.

CENTRAL OREGON COMMUNITY COLLEGE

Bend, Oregon   www.cocc.edu/

- **District-supported** 2-year, founded 1949, part of Oregon Community College Association
- **Small-town** 193-acre campus
- **Endowment** $10.0 million
- **Coed,** 4,200 undergraduate students, 32% full-time, 59% women, 41% men

Located in Bend, Oregon, Central Oregon Community College (COCC) offers more than fifty certificate and degree options, affordable tuition, outstanding faculty members, small classes, and access to more than twenty bachelor's degree programs through Oregon State University's Cascades campus. COCC also features on-campus housing, intramural sports, and exceptional outdoor recreation opportunities.

Undergraduates 1,337 full-time, 2,863 part-time. Students come from 10 states and territories, 4% are from out of state, 0.4% African American, 2% Asian American or Pacific Islander, 5% Hispanic American, 2% Native American, 13% transferred in, 3% live on campus. *Retention:* 54% of 2003 full-time freshmen returned.

Freshmen *Admission:* 1,330 applied, 1,330 admitted, 859 enrolled.

Faculty *Total:* 230, 41% full-time. *Student/faculty ratio:* 23:1.

Majors Accounting; administrative assistant and secretarial science; art; automobile/automotive mechanics technology; biological and physical sciences; business administration and management; cartography; computer and information sciences related; computer science; criminal justice/law enforcement administration; culinary arts; dental assisting; early childhood education; education; emergency medical technology (EMT paramedic); fire science; fish/game management; forestry; forestry technology; health information/medical records technology; hospitality administration; hospitality and recreation marketing; hotel/motel administration; humanities; industrial technology; kinesiology and exercise science; liberal arts and sciences/liberal studies; marketing/marketing management; mathematics; medical/clinical assistant; nursing (licensed practical/vocational nurse training); nursing (registered nurse training); physical sciences; pre-engineering; social sciences; sport and fitness administration/management; tourism promotion; welding technology.

Academics *Calendar:* quarters. *Degree:* certificates and associate. *Special study options:* academic remediation for entering students, cooperative education, distance learning, double majors, English as a second language, independent study, internships, part-time degree program, student-designed majors, study abroad, summer session for credit.

Library COCC Library plus 1 other with 76,421 titles, 329 serial subscriptions, 3,570 audiovisual materials, an OPAC, a Web page.

Student Life *Housing Options:* coed. Campus housing is provided by a third party. *Activities and Organizations:* student-run newspaper, choral group, student government, club sports, Phi Theta Kappa, DEC, Science Learning Center. *Campus security:* 24-hour emergency response devices and patrols, late-night transport/escort service. *Student services:* health clinic, personal/psychological counseling.

Athletics *Intramural sports:* badminton M/W, baseball M/W, basketball M/W, cross-country running M/W, football M, soccer M/W, softball M/W, table tennis M/W, tennis M/W, track and field M/W, volleyball M/W, water polo M/W, weight lifting M/W.

Costs (2006–07) *Tuition:* area resident $2835 full-time, $63 per credit part-time; state resident $3870 full-time, $86 per credit part-time; nonresident $7920 full-time, $176 per credit part-time. *Required fees:* $123 full-time, $4 per credit part-time. *Room and board:* $6798.

Financial Aid Of all full-time matriculated undergraduates, 400 Federal Work-Study jobs (averaging $1900).

Applying *Options:* electronic application. *Application fee:* $25. *Application deadlines:* rolling (freshmen), rolling (transfers). *Notification:* continuous (freshmen), continuous (transfers).

Director of Admissions Ms. Alicia Moore, Director, Admissions, Central Oregon Community College, 2600 Northwest College Way, Bend, OR 97701-5998. *Phone:* 541-383-7211. *E-mail:* welcome@metolius.cocc.edu.

CHEMEKETA COMMUNITY COLLEGE

Salem, Oregon   www.chemeketa.edu/

- **State and locally supported** 2-year, founded 1955
- **Urban** 72-acre campus with easy access to Portland
- **Coed**

Undergraduates Students come from 5 states and territories, 1% are from out of state.

Academics *Calendar:* quarters. *Degree:* certificates, diplomas, and associate. *Special study options:* academic remediation for entering students, adult/continuing education programs, advanced placement credit, cooperative education, distance learning, double majors, English as a second language, independent study, internships, part-time degree program, services for LD students, summer session for credit.

Student Life *Campus security:* 24-hour emergency response devices and patrols, late-night transport/escort service.

Financial Aid Of all full-time matriculated undergraduates, 297 Federal Work-Study jobs (averaging $1502).

Applying *Options:* deferred entrance. *Required for some:* high school transcript.

Freshmen Application Contact Enrollment Center, Chemeketa Community College, 4000 Lancaster Drive, NE, Salem, OR 97305-7070. *Phone:* 503-399-5001. *Fax:* 503-399-3918. *E-mail:* registrar@chemeketa.edu.

CLACKAMAS COMMUNITY COLLEGE

Oregon City, Oregon   www.clackamas.edu/

- **District-supported** 2-year, founded 1966
- **Suburban** 175-acre campus with easy access to Portland
- **Endowment** $9.8 million
- **Coed,** 5,976 undergraduate students, 33% full-time, 52% women, 48% men

Undergraduates 1,960 full-time, 4,016 part-time. Students come from 11 states and territories, 3 other countries, 1% are from out of state, 1% African American, 4% Asian American or Pacific Islander, 6% Hispanic American, 1% Native American, 0.1% international, 33% transferred in.

Freshmen *Admission:* 1,749 applied, 1,749 admitted, 1,749 enrolled.

Faculty *Total:* 608, 27% full-time, 3% with terminal degrees. *Student/faculty ratio:* 12:1.

Majors Accounting; autobody/collision and repair technology; automobile/automotive mechanics technology; community organization and advocacy; computer technology/computer systems technology; corrections; criminal justice/police science; drafting and design technology; general studies; liberal arts and sciences/liberal studies; machine tool technology; nursing (registered nurse training); office management; ornamental horticulture; water quality and wastewater treatment management and recycling technology.

Academics *Calendar:* quarters. *Degree:* certificates, diplomas, and associate. *Special study options:* academic remediation for entering students, accelerated degree program, adult/continuing education programs, advanced placement credit, cooperative education, distance learning, double majors, English as a second language, honors programs, independent study, internships, part-time degree program, services for LD students, study abroad, summer session for credit. *ROTC:* Air Force (c).

Library Dye Learning Resource Center plus 1 other with 41,263 titles, 274 serial subscriptions, 1,141 audiovisual materials, an OPAC, a Web page.

Student Life *Housing:* college housing not available. *Activities and Organizations:* drama/theater group, student-run newspaper, choral group, Ski Club,

Clackamas Community College (continued)

Spanish Club, Phi Theta Kappa, Horticulture Club, Speech Club, national fraternities. *Campus security:* 24-hour emergency response devices and patrols, student patrols, late-night transport/escort service. *Student services:* personal/ psychological counseling, women's center.

Athletics Member NJCAA. *Intercollegiate sports:* baseball M(s), basketball M(s)/W(s), cross-country running M(s)/W(s), soccer W, softball W(s), track and field M(s)/W(s), volleyball W(s), wrestling M(s). *Intramural sports:* basketball M/W, football M, soccer M/W, tennis M/W.

Costs (2007–08) *Tuition:* state resident $2565 full-time, $57 per credit hour part-time; nonresident $8910 full-time, $198 per credit hour part-time. *Required fees:* $225 full-time, $75 per term part-time.

Financial Aid Of all full-time matriculated undergraduates, 115 Federal Work-Study jobs (averaging $1330).

Applying *Options:* early admission. *Application deadlines:* rolling (freshmen), rolling (transfers).

Freshmen Application Contact Ms. Tara Sprehe, Registrar, Clackamas Community College, 19600 South Molalla Avenue, Oregon City, OR 97045. *Phone:* 503-657-6958 Ext. 2742. *Fax:* 503-650-6654. *E-mail:* pattyw@clackamas.edu.

CLATSOP COMMUNITY COLLEGE

Astoria, Oregon www.clatsopcc.edu/

- **County-supported** 2-year, founded 1958
- **Small-town** 20-acre campus
- **Endowment** $2.0 million
- **Coed,** 3,002 undergraduate students

Undergraduates Students come from 28 states and territories, 1 other country, 15% are from out of state, 0.7% African American, 2% Asian American or Pacific Islander, 4% Hispanic American, 3% Native American, 0.9% international.

Freshmen *Admission:* 340 applied, 277 admitted.

Faculty *Total:* 113. *Student/faculty ratio:* 14:1.

Majors Accounting; administrative assistant and secretarial science; business administration and management; business automation/technology/data entry; computer engineering technology; computer systems networking and telecommunications; criminal justice/law enforcement administration; fire science; legal administrative assistant/secretary; liberal arts and sciences/liberal studies; medical administrative assistant and medical secretary; nursing (registered nurse training).

Academics *Calendar:* quarters. *Degree:* certificates and associate. *Special study options:* academic remediation for entering students, adult/continuing education programs, advanced placement credit, cooperative education, distance learning, English as a second language, external degree program, internships, part-time degree program, services for LD students, summer session for credit.

Library Dora Badollet Library plus 1 other with 48,517 titles, 180 serial subscriptions, 5,000 audiovisual materials, an OPAC, a Web page.

Student Life *Housing:* college housing not available. *Activities and Organizations:* Lives in Transition, Phi Theta Kappa, Nursing Club, Spanish Club, Fine Arts Club. *Campus security:* 24-hour emergency response devices, late-night transport/escort service. *Student services:* personal/psychological counseling.

Costs (2007–08) *Tuition:* state resident $3105 full-time, $69 per credit part-time; nonresident $5670 full-time, $126 per credit part-time.

Financial Aid Of all full-time matriculated undergraduates, 220 Federal Work-Study jobs (averaging $2175).

Applying *Options:* early admission. *Application fee:* $15. *Recommended:* high school transcript. *Application deadlines:* rolling (freshmen), 9/29 (transfers). *Notification:* continuous (freshmen), continuous (transfers).

Freshmen Application Contact Mr. Javier Ayala, Admissions Coordinator, Clatsop Community College, 1653 Jerome, Astoria, OR 97103-3698. *Phone:* 503-338-2325. *Toll-free phone:* 866-252-8767. *Fax:* 503-325-5738. *E-mail:* admissions@clatsopcc.edu.

COLUMBIA GORGE COMMUNITY COLLEGE

The Dalles, Oregon www.cgcc.cc.or.us/

Director of Admissions Ms. Karen Carter, Dean of Student Services, Columbia Gorge Community College, 400 East Scenic Drive, The Dalles, OR 97058. *Phone:* 541-298-3110. *E-mail:* kcarter@cgcc.cc.or.us.

EVEREST COLLEGE

Portland, Oregon www.western-college.com/

- **Proprietary** 2-year, founded 1955
- **Coed,** 827 undergraduate students
- 100% of applicants were admitted

Freshmen *Admission:* 205 applied, 205 admitted.

Majors Accounting.

Academics *Calendar:* quarters. *Degree:* associate.

Costs (2006–07) *Tuition:* $12,384 full-time, $258 per credit hour part-time. Full-time tuition and fees vary according to course load and program. Part-time tuition and fees vary according to course load and program. *Required fees:* $75 full-time. *Payment plans:* installment, deferred payment. *Waivers:* employees or children of employees.

Freshmen Application Contact Ms. Melanie Zea, Everest College, 425 Southwest Washington Street, Portland, OR 97204. *Phone:* 503-222-3225. *Fax:* 503-228-6926. *E-mail:* mzea@cci.edu.

HEALD COLLEGE-PORTLAND

Portland, Oregon www.heald.edu/

- **Independent** 2-year, founded 1863
- **Coed**

Undergraduates 149 full-time, 57 part-time. 7% African American, 4% Asian American or Pacific Islander, 5% Hispanic American, 0.5% Native American.

Faculty *Student/faculty ratio:* 10:1.

Academics *Calendar:* quarters. *Degree:* certificates, diplomas, and associate. *Special study options:* academic remediation for entering students, advanced placement credit, internships, part-time degree program, summer session for credit.

Standardized Tests *Required:* COMPASS (for admission).

Costs (2006–07) *Tuition:* $10,275 full-time.

Financial Aid Of all full-time matriculated undergraduates, 15 Federal Work-Study jobs.

Applying *Options:* electronic application, early admission, deferred entrance. *Application fee:* $40. *Required:* high school transcript, interview.

Freshmen Application Contact Director of Admissions, Heald College-Portland, 625 Southwest Broadway, 4th Floor, Portland, OR 97205. *Phone:* 503-229-0492. *Toll-free phone:* 800-755-3550. *Fax:* 503-229-0498. *E-mail:* info@heald.edu.

ITT TECHNICAL INSTITUTE

Portland, Oregon www.itt-tech.edu/

- **Proprietary** primarily 2-year, founded 1971, part of ITT Educational Services, Inc
- **Urban** 4-acre campus
- **Coed**

Majors Animation, interactive technology, video graphics and special effects; business administration and management; CAD/CADD drafting/design technology; communications technology; computer and information systems security; computer engineering technology; computer systems networking and telecommunications; construction management; criminal justice/law enforcement administration; electrical, electronic and communications engineering technology; health information/medical records technology; industrial technology; web/ multimedia management and webmaster; web page, digital/multimedia and information resources design.

Academics *Calendar:* quarters. *Degrees:* associate and bachelor's.

Library a Web page.

Student Life *Housing:* college housing not available. *Activities and Organizations:* student-run newspaper.

Standardized Tests *Required:* Wonderlic aptitude test (for admission).

Costs (2006–07) *Tuition:* Contact school for program costs.

Financial Aid Of all full-time matriculated undergraduates, 15 Federal Work-Study jobs (averaging $5000).

Applying *Options:* deferred entrance. *Application fee:* $100. *Required:* high school transcript, interview. *Recommended:* letters of recommendation. *Application deadlines:* rolling (freshmen), rolling (transfers). *Notification:* continuous (freshmen), continuous (transfers).

Freshmen Application Contact Mr. Greg Lester, Director of Recruitment, ITT Technical Institute, 6035 Northeast 78th Court, Portland, OR 97218. *Phone:* 503-255-6500. *Toll-free phone:* 800-234-5488.

KLAMATH COMMUNITY COLLEGE
Klamath Falls, Oregon   www.kcc.cc.or.us/

- **State-supported** 2-year, founded 1996
- **Coed,** 918 undergraduate students

Majors Accounting technology and bookkeeping; business administration, management and operations related; child care provider; corrections; criminal justice/police science; environmental science; liberal arts and sciences and humanities related; medical office management; science technologies related; system administration; system, networking, and LAN/WAN management; teacher assistant/aide.

Academics *Calendar:* quarters. *Degree:* certificates and associate.

Student Life *Housing:* college housing not available.

Costs (2006–07) *Tuition:* area resident $2550 full-time; state resident $5163 full-time.

Freshmen Application Contact Admissions Office, Klamath Community College, 7390 South 6th Street, Klamath Falls, OR 97603. *Phone:* 541-882-3521.

LANE COMMUNITY COLLEGE
Eugene, Oregon   www.lanecc.edu/

Director of Admissions Ms. Helen Garrett, Director of Admissions/Registrar, Lane Community College, 4000 East 30th Avenue, Eugene, OR 97405-0640. *Phone:* 541-747-4501 Ext. 2686.

LINN-BENTON COMMUNITY COLLEGE
Albany, Oregon   www.linnbenton.edu/

- **State and locally supported** 2-year, founded 1966
- **Small-town** 104-acre campus
- **Endowment** $2.1 million
- **Coed,** 4,983 undergraduate students, 53% full-time, 53% women, 47% men

Undergraduates 2,634 full-time, 2,349 part-time. 1% African American, 4% Asian American or Pacific Islander, 5% Hispanic American, 2% Native American, 0.1% international.

Freshmen *Admission:* 2,820 applied, 2,578 admitted, 1,191 enrolled.

Faculty *Total:* 483, 34% full-time.

Majors Accounting; administrative assistant and secretarial science; agricultural business and management; agricultural teacher education; agriculture; animal sciences; art; automobile/automotive mechanics technology; biological and physical sciences; biology/biological sciences; business administration and management; chemistry; child care and support services management; civil engineering technology; commercial and advertising art; computer and information sciences; computer programming (specific applications); computer/technical support; criminal justice/police science; criminal justice/safety; culinary arts; culinary arts related; dairy husbandry and production; desktop publishing and digital imaging design; diesel mechanics technology; drafting and design technology; dramatic/theater arts; economics; education; elementary education; engineering; English; family and consumer sciences/human sciences; foreign languages and literatures; graphic communications related; horse husbandry/equine science and management; horticultural science; industrial technology; journalism; juvenile corrections; legal administrative assistant/secretary; liberal arts and sciences/liberal studies; machine tool technology; mathematics; medical administrative assistant and medical secretary; medical/clinical assistant; metallurgical technology; multi-/interdisciplinary studies related; nursing (registered nurse training); photography; physical education teaching and coaching; physical sciences; physics; pre-engineering; restaurant, culinary, and catering management; speech and rhetoric; system administration; teacher assistant/aide; technical and business writing; water quality and wastewater treatment management and recycling technology; welding technology.

Academics *Calendar:* quarters. *Degree:* certificates and associate. *Special study options:* academic remediation for entering students, adult/continuing education programs, advanced placement credit, cooperative education, distance learning, English as a second language, independent study, internships, part-time degree program, services for LD students, student-designed majors, summer session for credit. *ROTC:* Army (c), Air Force (c).

Library Linn-Benton Community College Library with 42,561 titles, 91 serial subscriptions, 8,758 audiovisual materials, an OPAC, a Web page.

Student Life *Housing:* college housing not available. *Activities and Organizations:* drama/theater group, student-run newspaper, choral group, EBOP Club, Multicultural Club, Campus Family Co-op, Horticulture Club, Collegiate Secretary Club. *Campus security:* 24-hour emergency response devices and patrols, student patrols, late-night transport/escort service. *Student services:* personal/psychological counseling.

Athletics *Intercollegiate sports:* baseball M(s), basketball M(s)/W(s), volleyball W(s). *Intramural sports:* basketball M/W, tennis M/W, ultimate Frisbee M/W, volleyball M/W.

Costs (2006–07) *Tuition:* state resident $2925 full-time, $65 per credit hour part-time; nonresident $7470 full-time, $166 per credit hour part-time.

Financial Aid Of all full-time matriculated undergraduates, 290 Federal Work-Study jobs (averaging $1800).

Applying *Options:* deferred entrance. *Application fee:* $25. *Required for some:* high school transcript. *Application deadlines:* rolling (freshmen), rolling (transfers).

Freshmen Application Contact Ms. Christine Baker, Outreach Coordinator, Linn-Benton Community College, 6500 Pacific Boulevard, SW, Albany, OR 97321. *Phone:* 541-917-4813. *Fax:* 541-917-4838. *E-mail:* admissions@linnbenton.edu.

MT. HOOD COMMUNITY COLLEGE
Gresham, Oregon   www.mhcc.cc.or.us/

- **State and locally supported** 2-year, founded 1966
- **Suburban** 212-acre campus with easy access to Portland
- **Coed,** 8,771 undergraduate students, 36% full-time, 56% women, 44% men

Undergraduates 3,178 full-time, 5,593 part-time. Students come from 16 states and territories, 6 other countries.

Freshmen *Admission:* 2,441 enrolled.

Faculty *Total:* 638, 27% full-time. *Student/faculty ratio:* 25:1.

Majors Accounting; administrative assistant and secretarial science; architectural engineering technology; automobile/automotive mechanics technology; avionics maintenance technology; broadcast journalism; business administration and management; business teacher education; civil engineering technology; commercial and advertising art; computer engineering technology; cosmetology; dental hygiene; electrical, electronic and communications engineering technology; environmental health; fire science; fish/game management; food science; forestry technology; funeral service and mortuary science; horticultural science; hospitality administration; industrial technology; journalism; kindergarten/preschool education; legal administrative assistant/secretary; liberal arts and sciences/liberal studies; marketing/marketing management; mechanical engineering/mechanical technology; medical administrative assistant and medical secretary; medical/clinical assistant; mental health/rehabilitation; nursing (registered nurse training); occupational therapy; ornamental horticulture; physical therapy; radio and television; respiratory care therapy; surgical technology; tourism and travel services management.

Academics *Calendar:* quarters. *Degree:* certificates, diplomas, and associate. *Special study options:* academic remediation for entering students, adult/continuing education programs, advanced placement credit, cooperative education, English as a second language, internships, part-time degree program, services for LD students, study abroad, summer session for credit.

Library Library Resource Center with 64,000 titles, 412 serial subscriptions.

Student Life *Housing:* college housing not available. *Activities and Organizations:* drama/theater group, student-run newspaper, radio and television station, choral group. *Campus security:* 24-hour emergency response devices and patrols, student patrols, late-night transport/escort service. *Student services:* health clinic, personal/psychological counseling, women's center.

Athletics *Intercollegiate sports:* baseball M, basketball M(s)/W(s), cross-country running M(s)/W(s), softball W, track and field M(s)/W(s), volleyball W(s). *Intramural sports:* archery M/W, badminton M, basketball M/W, bowling M/W, cross-country running M/W, fencing M/W, field hockey M/W, football M/W, golf M, racquetball M/W, skiing (cross-country) M/W, skiing (downhill) M/W, soccer M/W, swimming and diving M/W, tennis M/W, track and field M/W, volleyball M/W.

Standardized Tests *Required for some:* CPT.

Costs (2006–07) *Tuition:* state resident $3240 full-time; nonresident $9675 full-time.

Financial Aid Of all full-time matriculated undergraduates, 202 Federal Work-Study jobs (averaging $1240).

Applying *Options:* early admission, deferred entrance. *Application fee:* $25. *Required for some:* high school transcript, minimum 2.0 GPA. *Application deadlines:* rolling (freshmen), rolling (transfers). *Notification:* continuous (freshmen), continuous (transfers).

Mt. Hood Community College (continued)

Director of Admissions Dr. Craig Kolins, Associate Vice President of Enrollment Services, Mt. Hood Community College, 26000 Southeast Stark Street, Gresham, OR 97030-3300. *Phone:* 503-491-7265.

OREGON COAST COMMUNITY COLLEGE

Newport, Oregon   www.occc.cc.or.us

- **Public** 2-year, founded 1987
- **Coed,** 479 undergraduate students, 25% full-time, 68% women, 32% men

Undergraduates 119 full-time, 360 part-time. Students come from 3 states and territories, 0.6% African American, 2% Asian American or Pacific Islander, 4% Hispanic American, 4% Native American, 40% transferred in.

Freshmen *Admission:* 57 applied, 57 admitted, 57 enrolled.

Faculty *Total:* 42, 14% full-time, 26% with terminal degrees. *Student/faculty ratio:* 12:1.

Majors General studies; liberal arts and sciences/liberal studies; marine biology and biological oceanography; nursing (registered nurse training).

Academics *Calendar:* quarters. *Degree:* certificates and associate. *Special study options:* academic remediation for entering students, cooperative education, distance learning, English as a second language, honors programs, internships, part-time degree program, services for LD students, summer session for credit.

Library Oregon Coast Community College Library with 10,029 titles, 50 serial subscriptions, 1,291 audiovisual materials, an OPAC, a Web page.

Student Life *Housing:* college housing not available.

Costs (2007–08) *Tuition:* state resident $2790 full-time, $62 per credit hour part-time; nonresident $7740 full-time, $172 per credit hour part-time. *Required fees:* $210 full-time, $5 per credit hour part-time, $70 per term part-time.

Freshmen Application Contact Student Services, Oregon Coast Community College, 332 Southwest Coast Highway, Newport, OR 97365. *Phone:* 541-574-7101. *Fax:* 541-574-7159. *E-mail:* webinfo@occc.cc.or.us.

PIONEER PACIFIC COLLEGE

Wilsonville, Oregon   www.pioneerpacific.edu/

- **Proprietary** primarily 2-year, founded 1981
- **Suburban** campus with easy access to Portland
- **Coed,** 986 undergraduate students, 73% full-time, 77% women, 23% men

Undergraduates 723 full-time, 263 part-time. 6% are from out of state, 2% African American, 3% Asian American or Pacific Islander, 5% Hispanic American, 0.2% Native American.

Freshmen *Admission:* 752 applied, 631 admitted, 94 enrolled.

Faculty *Total:* 119, 41% full-time, 8% with terminal degrees. *Student/faculty ratio:* 15:1.

Majors Accounting; business administration and management; criminal justice/police science; health/health care administration; information science/studies; information technology; legal assistant/paralegal; medical/clinical assistant; sales, distribution and marketing; web/multimedia management and webmaster.

Academics *Calendar:* continuous. *Degrees:* diplomas, associate, and bachelor's. *Special study options:* accelerated degree program, honors programs, internships.

Library Pioneer Pacific College Library with 2,500 titles.

Student Life *Housing:* college housing not available. *Activities and Organizations:* Phi Beta Lambda.

Standardized Tests *Required:* CPAt (for admission).

Costs (2007–08) *Tuition:* $9750 full-time, $228 per credit hour part-time. *Required fees:* $400 full-time.

Applying *Application fee:* $50. *Required:* high school transcript, interview. *Application deadline:* rolling (freshmen). *Notification:* continuous (transfers).

Freshmen Application Contact Ms. Kristin Lynn, Director of Admissions, Pioneer Pacific College, 27501 Southwest Parkway Avenue, Wilsonville, OR 97070. *Phone:* 866-772-4636. *Toll-free phone:* 866-PPC-INFO. *Fax:* 503-682-1514. *E-mail:* inquiries@pioneerpacific.edu.

▶See page 580 for the College Close-Up.

Director of Admissions Mr. Dennis Bailey-Fougnier, Director of Admissions, Portland Community College, PO Box 19000, Portland, OR 97280. *Phone:* 503-977-4519.

PORTLAND COMMUNITY COLLEGE

Portland, Oregon   www.pcc.edu/

Director of Admissions Mr. Dennis Bailey-Fougnier, Director of Admissions, Portland Community College, PO Box 19000, Portland, OR 97280. *Phone:* 503-977-4519.

ROGUE COMMUNITY COLLEGE

Grants Pass, Oregon   www.roguecc.edu/

- **State and locally supported** 2-year, founded 1970
- **Rural** 90-acre campus
- **Endowment** $6.4 million
- **Coed,** 4,341 undergraduate students, 35% full-time, 58% women, 42% men

Undergraduates 1,509 full-time, 2,832 part-time. Students come from 11 states and territories, 1 other country, 1% are from out of state, 1% African American, 2% Asian American or Pacific Islander, 6% Hispanic American, 3% Native American, 0.1% international, 32% transferred in.

Freshmen *Admission:* 316 applied, 316 admitted, 316 enrolled.

Faculty *Total:* 486, 20% full-time. *Student/faculty ratio:* 11:1.

Majors Automobile/automotive mechanics technology; business administration and management; child development; computer science; construction management; criminal justice/law enforcement administration; education related; electrical, electronic and communications engineering technology; fire science; heavy equipment maintenance technology; humanities; human services; industrial technology; liberal arts and sciences/liberal studies; manufacturing technology; nursing (registered nurse training); social sciences; substance abuse/addiction counseling; welding technology.

Academics *Calendar:* quarters. *Degree:* certificates, diplomas, and associate. *Special study options:* academic remediation for entering students, adult/continuing education programs, advanced placement credit, cooperative education, distance learning, double majors, English as a second language, independent study, internships, part-time degree program, services for LD students, study abroad, summer session for credit.

Library Rogue Community College Library with 33,000 titles, 275 serial subscriptions, an OPAC.

Student Life *Housing:* college housing not available. *Activities and Organizations:* drama/theater group, student-run newspaper, choral group. *Campus security:* 24-hour patrols, late-night transport/escort service. *Student services:* personal/psychological counseling, women's center.

Athletics *Intramural sports:* basketball M/W, soccer M/W, tennis M/W, volleyball M/W.

Costs (2007–08) *Tuition:* state resident $2376 full-time, $66 per credit hour part-time; nonresident $2880 full-time, $80 per credit hour part-time. *Required fees:* $294 full-time.

Financial Aid Of all full-time matriculated undergraduates, 210 Federal Work-Study jobs (averaging $3200). 300 state and other part-time jobs (averaging $3000).

Applying *Options:* early admission. *Application deadlines:* rolling (freshmen), rolling (transfers).

Freshmen Application Contact Ms. Claudia Sullivan, Director of Admissions, Rogue Community College, 3345 Redwood Highway, Grants Pass, OR 97527-9298. *Phone:* 541-956-7176. *Fax:* 541-471-3585. *E-mail:* csullivan@roguecc.edu.

SOUTHWESTERN OREGON COMMUNITY COLLEGE

Coos Bay, Oregon   www.socc.edu/

- **State and locally supported** 2-year, founded 1961
- **Small-town** 125-acre campus
- **Endowment** $769,894
- **Coed**

Undergraduates 976 full-time, 1,004 part-time. Students come from 4 other countries, 15% are from out of state, 2% African American, 1% Asian American or Pacific Islander, 3% Hispanic American, 5% Native American, 1% international.

Faculty *Student/faculty ratio:* 10:1.

Academics *Calendar:* quarters. *Degree:* certificates, diplomas, and associate. *Special study options:* academic remediation for entering students, adult/

continuing education programs, advanced placement credit, cooperative education, distance learning, English as a second language, internships, part-time degree program, services for LD students, summer session for credit.

Student Life *Campus security:* controlled dormitory access.

Athletics Member NJCAA.

Costs (2006–07) *Tuition:* state resident $3330 full-time, $62 per credit part-time; nonresident $3330 full-time, $62 per credit part-time. *Required fees:* $330 full-time, $12 per credit part-time, $22 per course part-time. *Room and board:* $6160.

Financial Aid Of all full-time matriculated undergraduates, 140 Federal Work-Study jobs (averaging $874). 42 state and other part-time jobs (averaging $545).

Applying *Options:* early admission. *Application fee:* $30. *Required for some:* high school transcript.

Freshmen Application Contact Miss Lela Wells, Southwestern Oregon Community College, Student First Stop, 1988 Newmark Avenue, Coos Bay, OR 97420. *Phone:* 541-888-7611. *Toll-free phone:* 800-962-2838. *E-mail:* lwells@socc.edu.

TILLAMOOK BAY COMMUNITY COLLEGE

Tillamook, Oregon www.tbcc.cc.or.us/

- **District-supported** 2-year, founded 1984, administratively affiliated with Portland Community College
- **Coed**
- 100% of applicants were admitted

Undergraduates 73 full-time, 226 part-time. Students come from 2 states and territories, 1 other country, 2% are from out of state, 1% African American, 2% Asian American or Pacific Islander, 1% Hispanic American, 2% Native American, 4% transferred in.

Faculty *Student/faculty ratio:* 8:1.

Academics *Calendar:* quarters. *Degree:* certificates, diplomas, and associate.

Student Life *Campus security:* evening security guard.

Costs (2006–07) *Tuition:* state resident $2976 full-time, $62 per credit part-time; nonresident $3936 full-time, $82 per credit part-time. *Required fees:* $530 full-time, $33 per course part-time.

Applying *Recommended:* high school transcript.

Freshmen Application Contact Lori Gates, Tillamook Bay Community College, 2510 First Street, Tillamook, OR 97141. *Phone:* 503-842-8222. *Fax:* 503-842-2214. *E-mail:* gates@tillamookbay.cc.

TREASURE VALLEY COMMUNITY COLLEGE

Ontario, Oregon www.tvcc.cc.or.us/

- **State and locally supported** 2-year, founded 1962
- **Small-town** 95-acre campus
- **Endowment** $2.0 million
- **Coed,** 1,912 undergraduate students, 53% full-time, 63% women, 37% men

Undergraduates 1,007 full-time, 905 part-time. Students come from 11 states and territories, 2 other countries, 67% are from out of state, 1% African American, 2% Asian American or Pacific Islander, 15% Hispanic American, 1% Native American, 0.2% international, 19% transferred in, 6% live on campus.

Freshmen *Admission:* 1,335 applied, 1,335 admitted, 540 enrolled.

Faculty *Total:* 140, 34% full-time. *Student/faculty ratio:* 11:1.

Majors Administrative assistant and secretarial science; agricultural business and management; agricultural mechanization; agriculture; agronomy and crop science; biological and physical sciences; biology/biological sciences; business administration and management; chemistry; commercial and advertising art; computer science; criminal justice/law enforcement administration; criminal justice/police science; drafting and design technology; dramatic/theater arts; economics; education; engineering; English; forestry; forestry technology; history; humanities; legal administrative assistant/secretary; liberal arts and sciences/liberal studies; mass communication/media; mathematics; medical administrative assistant and medical secretary; music; music teacher education; natural resources management and policy; nursing (registered nurse training); physical education teaching and coaching; political science and government; range science and management; social sciences; sociology; survey technology; welding technology; wildlife and wildlands science and management.

Academics *Calendar:* quarters. *Degree:* certificates and associate. *Special study options:* academic remediation for entering students, accelerated degree program, adult/continuing education programs, advanced placement credit, cooperative education, distance learning, English as a second language, external

degree program, honors programs, independent study, internships, part-time degree program, services for LD students, summer session for credit. *ROTC:* Army (c).

Library Treasure Valley Community College Library with 28,000 titles, 150 serial subscriptions, an OPAC.

Student Life *Housing Options:* coed. *Activities and Organizations:* drama/theater group, choral group, marching band. *Campus security:* student patrols, controlled dormitory access. *Student services:* health clinic, personal/psychological counseling.

Athletics Member NJCAA. *Intercollegiate sports:* baseball M(s), basketball M(s)/W(s), volleyball W(s). *Intramural sports:* basketball M/W, golf M/W, soccer M/W, softball M/W, volleyball M/W.

Costs (2007–08) *Tuition:* $66 per credit hour part-time; state resident $2925 full-time, $66 per credit hour part-time; nonresident $3375 full-time, $76 per credit hour part-time. *Required fees:* $405 full-time, $9 per credit hour part-time, $9 per credit hour part-time. *Room and board:* $4470; room only: $1680.

Financial Aid Of all full-time matriculated undergraduates, 90 Federal Work-Study jobs (averaging $1500).

Applying *Options:* early admission, deferred entrance. *Application deadlines:* rolling (freshmen), rolling (transfers). *Notification:* continuous (freshmen), continuous (transfers).

Freshmen Application Contact Ms. Candace Bell, Office of Admissions and Student Services, Treasure Valley Community College, 650 College Boulevard, Ontario, OR 97914. *Phone:* 541-881-8822 Ext. 239. *Fax:* 541-881-2721. *E-mail:* clbell@tvcc.cc.

UMPQUA COMMUNITY COLLEGE

Roseburg, Oregon www.umpqua.edu/

- **State and locally supported** 2-year, founded 1964
- **Rural** 100-acre campus
- **Endowment** $5.4 million
- **Coed,** 2,190 undergraduate students, 35% full-time, 58% women, 42% men

Undergraduates 760 full-time, 1,430 part-time. Students come from 5 states and territories, 3 other countries, 0.5% are from out of state, 0.7% African American, 2% Asian American or Pacific Islander, 4% Hispanic American, 2% Native American, 0.5% international, 11% transferred in.

Freshmen *Admission:* 112 applied, 112 admitted, 112 enrolled.

Faculty *Total:* 385, 16% full-time. *Student/faculty ratio:* 17:1.

Majors Accounting; administrative assistant and secretarial science; agriculture; anthropology; art; art history, criticism and conservation; art teacher education; automobile/automotive mechanics technology; behavioral sciences; biological and physical sciences; biology/biological sciences; business administration and management; chemistry; child development; civil engineering technology; computer engineering technology; computer science; cosmetology; criminal justice/law enforcement administration; desktop publishing and digital imaging design; dramatic/theater arts; economics; education; electrical, electronic and communications engineering technology; elementary education; emergency medical technology (EMT paramedic); engineering; English; fire science; forestry; health teacher education; history; humanities; human resources management; journalism; kindergarten/preschool education; legal administrative assistant/secretary; liberal arts and sciences/liberal studies; marketing/marketing management; mathematics; medical administrative assistant and medical secretary; music; music teacher education; natural sciences; nursing (registered nurse training); physical education teaching and coaching; physical sciences; political science and government; pre-engineering; psychology; social sciences; social work; sociology.

Academics *Calendar:* quarters. *Degree:* certificates and associate. *Special study options:* academic remediation for entering students, accelerated degree program, adult/continuing education programs, advanced placement credit, cooperative education, distance learning, English as a second language, honors programs, internships, part-time degree program, services for LD students, study abroad, summer session for credit.

Library Umpqua Community College Library with 41,000 titles, 350 serial subscriptions, an OPAC, a Web page.

Student Life *Housing:* college housing not available. *Activities and Organizations:* drama/theater group, student-run newspaper, choral group, Phi Theta Kappa, Computer Club, Phi Beta Lambda, Nursing Club, Umpqua Accounting Associates. *Student services:* personal/psychological counseling.

Athletics *Intercollegiate sports:* basketball M(s)/W(s). *Intramural sports:* basketball M/W.

Costs (2007–08) *Tuition:* state resident $3282 full-time, $64 per credit part-time. *Required fees:* $240 full-time, $7 per credit part-time, $15 per term part-time.

Financial Aid Of all full-time matriculated undergraduates, 120 Federal Work-Study jobs (averaging $3000).

Umpqua Community College *(continued)*

Applying *Options:* early admission, deferred entrance. *Application fee:* $25. *Recommended:* high school transcript. *Application deadlines:* rolling (freshmen), rolling (transfers).

Freshmen Application Contact Ms. Susan Taylor, Recruiter/Admissions Officer, Umpqua Community College, PO Box 967, 1140 College Road, Roseburg, OR 97470. *Phone:* 541-440-7784.

WESTERN CULINARY INSTITUTE
Portland, Oregon   **www.wci.edu/**

- **Proprietary** 2-year, founded 1983
- **Coed,** 1,025 undergraduate students

Majors Baking and pastry arts; culinary arts; hospitality administration related; restaurant/food services management.

Academics *Calendar:* continuous. *Degree:* associate.

Costs (2006–07) *Tuition:* $39,500 full-time.

Admissions Office Contact Western Culinary Institute, 921 SW Morrison Street Suite 400, Portland, OR 97205. *Toll-free phone:* 888-891-6222.

PENNSYLVANIA

ACADEMY OF MEDICAL ARTS AND BUSINESS
Harrisburg, Pennsylvania   **www.acadcampus.com/**

Freshmen Application Contact Tom Bogush, Director of Admissions, Academy of Medical Arts and Business, 2301 Academy Drive, Harrisburg, PA 17112. *Phone:* 717-545-4747. *Toll-free phone:* 800-400-3322. *Fax:* 717-901-9090. *E-mail:* info@acadcampus.com.

ALLIED MEDICAL AND TECHNICAL CAREERS
Forty Fort, Pennsylvania www.alliedteched.edu/forty_fort.htm

Freshmen Application Contact Admissions Office, Allied Medical and Technical Careers, 166 Slocum Street, Forty Fort, PA 18704. *Phone:* 570-288-8400.

ANTONELLI INSTITUTE
Erdenheim, Pennsylvania   **www.antonelli.edu/**

- **Proprietary** 2-year, founded 1938
- **Suburban** 15-acre campus with easy access to Philadelphia
- **Coed**

Undergraduates 183 full-time, 6 part-time. Students come from 9 states and territories, 22% are from out of state, 5% African American, 3% Hispanic American, 40% live on campus. *Retention:* 100% of 2003 full-time freshmen returned.

Faculty *Student/faculty ratio:* 13:1.

Academics *Calendar:* semesters. *Degree:* associate. *Special study options:* adult/continuing education programs, part-time degree program.

Student Life *Campus security:* 24-hour emergency response devices.

Costs (2006–07) *Tuition:* $16,300 full-time, $545 per credit part-time. Full-time tuition and fees vary according to program. *Required fees:* $25 full-time. *Room only:* $6100.

Financial Aid Of all full-time matriculated undergraduates, 5 Federal Work-Study jobs (averaging $2000).

Applying *Options:* deferred entrance. *Application fee:* $25. *Required:* high school transcript, interview.

Freshmen Application Contact Mr. Anthony Detore, Director of Admissions, Antonelli Institute, 300 Montgomery Avenue, Erdenheim, PA 19038. *Phone:* 215-836-2222. *Toll-free phone:* 800-722-7871. *Fax:* 215-836-2794.

THE ART INSTITUTE OF PHILADELPHIA
Philadelphia, Pennsylvania   **www.aiph.artinstitutes.edu/**

- **Proprietary** primarily 2-year, founded 1966, part of Education Management Corporation
- **Urban** campus
- **Coed,** 3,600 undergraduate students, 72% full-time, 54% women, 46% men

Undergraduates 2,589 full-time, 1,011 part-time. Students come from 30 states and territories, 18 other countries, 49% are from out of state, 19% African American, 4% Asian American or Pacific Islander, 5% Hispanic American, 0.3% Native American, 0.4% international, 27% live on campus.

Freshmen *Admission:* 3,070 applied, 2,640 admitted, 928 enrolled. *Average high school GPA:* 2.77. *Test scores:* SAT verbal scores over 500: 54%; SAT math scores over 500: 54%; SAT verbal scores over 600: 24%; SAT math scores over 600: 24%; SAT verbal scores over 700: 1%; SAT math scores over 700: 1%.

Faculty *Total:* 211, 48% full-time. *Student/faculty ratio:* 22:1.

Majors Animation, interactive technology, video graphics and special effects; cinematography and film/video production; culinary arts; desktop publishing and digital imaging design; fashion/apparel design; fashion merchandising; film/video and photographic arts related; graphic design; industrial design; interior design; intermedia/multimedia; photographic and film/video technology; photography.

Academics *Calendar:* quarters. *Degrees:* associate and bachelor's. *Special study options:* academic remediation for entering students, adult/continuing education programs, advanced placement credit, cooperative education, external degree program, independent study, internships, off-campus study, part-time degree program, services for LD students, summer session for credit.

Library The Art Institute of Philadelphia Library with 25,000 titles, 150 serial subscriptions, 2,000 audiovisual materials, an OPAC, a Web page.

Student Life *Housing Options:* coed, disabled students. Campus housing is university owned. Freshman campus housing is guaranteed. *Campus security:* student patrols, controlled dormitory access. *Student services:* personal/psychological counseling.

Athletics *Intramural sports:* basketball M/W, softball M/W.

Costs (2007–08) *Tuition:* $427 per credit part-time.

Financial Aid Of all full-time matriculated undergraduates, 230 Federal Work-Study jobs (averaging $3500).

Applying *Options:* electronic application, early admission, early decision, deferred entrance. *Application fee:* $50. *Required:* essay or personal statement, high school transcript, interview. *Recommended:* minimum 2.5 GPA, letters of recommendation. *Application deadlines:* rolling (freshmen), rolling (transfers). *Notification:* continuous (freshmen), continuous (transfers).

Freshmen Application Contact Admissions Office, The Art Institute of Philadelphia, 1622 Chestnut Street, Philadelphia, PA 19103. *Phone:* 800-567-7080. *Toll-free phone:* 800-275-2474. *Fax:* 215-405-6399. *E-mail:* aiphinfo@aii.edu.

BEREAN INSTITUTE
Philadelphia, Pennsylvania   **www.bereaninstitute.org/**

Director of Admissions Director of Recruitment, Berean Institute, 1901 West Girard Avenue, Philadelphia, PA 19130. *Phone:* 215-763-4833 Ext. 135.

BERKS TECHNICAL INSTITUTE
Wyomissing, Pennsylvania   **www.berkstech.com/**

- **Proprietary** 2-year, founded 1977, part of Fore Front Education, Inc
- **Small-town** 8-acre campus
- **Coed**

Undergraduates Students come from 1 other state, 6% African American, 0.8% Asian American or Pacific Islander, 10% Hispanic American, 0.2% Native American.

Faculty *Student/faculty ratio:* 12:1.

Academics *Calendar:* semesters. *Degree:* diplomas and associate. *Special study options:* advanced placement credit, part-time degree program.

Student Life *Campus security:* 24-hour emergency response devices.

Standardized Tests *Required for some:* SAT and SAT Subject Tests or ACT (for admission), CPat and COMPAS.

Costs (2006–07) *Tuition:* $23,405 full-time. *Required fees:* $300 full-time.

Applying *Options:* early admission. *Application fee:* $50. *Required:* high school transcript, letters of recommendation, interview.

Freshmen Application Contact Mr. Allan Brussolo, Academic Dean, Berks Technical Institute, 2205 Ridgewood Road, Wyomissing, PA 19610-1168. *Phone:* 610-372-1722. *Toll-free phone:* 800-284-4672 (in-state); 800-821-4662 (out-of-state). *Fax:* 610-376-4684. *E-mail:* abrussolo@berks.edu.

BIDWELL TRAINING CENTER

Pittsburgh, Pennsylvania www.bidwell-training.org/

- **Independent** 2-year, founded 1968
- **Coed,** 143 undergraduate students

Majors Chemical technology.

Academics *Degree:* certificates and associate.

Costs (2006–07) *Tuition:* $7360 per degree program part-time.

Freshmen Application Contact Admissions Office, Bidwell Training Center, 1815 Metropolitan Street, Pittsburgh, PA 15233. *E-mail:* admissions@mcg-btc.org.

BRADFORD SCHOOL

Pittsburgh, Pennsylvania www.bradfordpittsburgh.edu/

- **Private** 2-year, founded 1968
- 441 undergraduate students
- 91% of applicants were admitted

Freshmen *Admission:* 902 applied, 822 admitted.

Majors Accounting; administrative assistant and secretarial science; commercial and advertising art; computer and information sciences and support services related; hospitality/recreation marketing operations; medical/clinical assistant; paralegal/legal assistant; retailing operations; system, networking, and LAN/WAN management.

Academics *Degree:* associate.

Costs (2006–07) *Tuition:* $13,120 full-time.

Applying *Application fee:* $50. *Required:* high school transcript.

Freshmen Application Contact Admissions Office, Bradford School, 125 West Station Square Drive, Suite 129, Pittsburgh, PA 15219. *Phone:* 412-391-6710. *Toll-free phone:* 800-391-6810.

BRADLEY ACADEMY FOR THE VISUAL ARTS

York, Pennsylvania www.bradleyacademy.net/

- **Proprietary** 2-year, founded 1952, part of Education Management Corporation
- **Suburban** 7-acre campus with easy access to Baltimore
- **Endowment** $100,000
- **Coed,** 596 undergraduate students, 93% full-time, 60% women, 40% men

Undergraduates 552 full-time, 44 part-time. Students come from 4 states and territories, 8% are from out of state, 4% African American, 0.9% Asian American or Pacific Islander, 0.2% Native American.

Freshmen *Admission:* 302 applied, 197 admitted, 115 enrolled. *Average high school GPA:* 2.8.

Faculty *Total:* 48, 31% full-time, 6% with terminal degrees. *Student/faculty ratio:* 15:1.

Majors Advertising; animation, interactive technology, video graphics and special effects; clothing/textiles; commercial and advertising art; computer graphics; design and visual communications; fashion merchandising; interior design; web/multimedia management and webmaster; web page, digital/multimedia and information resources design.

Academics *Calendar:* quarters. *Degree:* associate. *Special study options:* academic remediation for entering students, adult/continuing education programs, internships, part-time degree program, services for LD students, summer session for credit.

Library Bradley Academy Library with 6,000 titles, 70 serial subscriptions, an OPAC, a Web page.

Student Life *Housing:* college housing not available. *Activities and Organizations:* student-run newspaper, ASID, Delta Epsilon Chi, AIGA. *Student services:* personal/psychological counseling.

Costs (2007–08) *Tuition:* $16,560 full-time, $460 per credit part-time. *Required fees:* $50 full-time.

Financial Aid Of all full-time matriculated undergraduates, 21 Federal Work-Study jobs (averaging $600).

Applying *Options:* deferred entrance. *Application fee:* $50. *Required:* essay or personal statement, high school transcript, interview. *Required for some:* portfolio. *Application deadlines:* rolling (freshmen), rolling (out-of-state freshmen), rolling (transfers). *Notification:* continuous (freshmen), continuous (out-of-state freshmen), continuous (transfers).

Freshmen Application Contact Diane Merino, Director of Admissions, Bradley Academy for the Visual Arts, 1409 Williams Road, York, PA 17402. *Phone:* 717-755-2300 Ext. 2511. *Toll-free phone:* 800-864-7725. *Fax:* 717-840-1951. *E-mail:* info@bradleyacademy.net.

►See page 492 for the College Close-Up.

BUCKS COUNTY COMMUNITY COLLEGE

Newtown, Pennsylvania www.bucks.edu/

- **County-supported** 2-year, founded 1964
- **Suburban** 200-acre campus with easy access to Philadelphia
- **Endowment** $2.4 million
- **Coed,** 9,572 undergraduate students, 43% full-time, 58% women, 42% men

Undergraduates 4,110 full-time, 5,462 part-time. Students come from 6 states and territories, 27 other countries, 1% are from out of state, 3% African American, 2% Asian American or Pacific Islander, 2% Hispanic American, 0.3% Native American, 6% international, 3% transferred in.

Freshmen *Admission:* 5,437 applied, 5,404 admitted, 2,731 enrolled.

Faculty *Total:* 568, 27% full-time. *Student/faculty ratio:* 24:1.

Majors Accounting; administrative assistant and secretarial science; American studies; art; biology/biological sciences; business administration and management; chemistry; cinematography and film/video production; commercial and advertising art; computer and information sciences; computer and information sciences related; computer engineering technology; computer/information technology services administration related; computer programming; computer programming related; computer programming (specific applications); computer science; consumer merchandising/retailing management; corrections; criminal justice/law enforcement administration; criminal justice/police science; culinary arts; data processing and data processing technology; dramatic/theater arts; education; engineering; entrepreneurship; environmental studies; health science; health teacher education; historic preservation and conservation; hospitality administration; hotel/motel administration; humanities; information science/studies; information technology; journalism; kindergarten/preschool education; legal assistant/paralegal; liberal arts and sciences/liberal studies; marketing/marketing management; mass communication/media; mathematics; medical/clinical assistant; music; nursing (registered nurse training); physical education teaching and coaching; psychology; radio and television; social sciences; social work; sport and fitness administration/management; teacher assistant/aide; visual and performing arts; woodworking.

Academics *Calendar:* semesters. *Degree:* certificates and associate. *Special study options:* academic remediation for entering students, adult/continuing education programs, advanced placement credit, cooperative education, distance learning, English as a second language, external degree program, independent study, internships, part-time degree program, services for LD students, student-designed majors, summer session for credit.

Library Bucks County Community College Library with 155,779 titles, 515 serial subscriptions, an OPAC, a Web page.

Student Life *Housing:* college housing not available. *Activities and Organizations:* drama/theater group, student-run newspaper, television station, choral group, Phi Theta Kappa, Students in Free Enterprise, student council, The Centurion (student newspaper). *Campus security:* 24-hour emergency response devices and patrols, late-night transport/escort service. *Student services:* personal/psychological counseling, women's center.

Athletics Member NJCAA. *Intercollegiate sports:* baseball M, basketball M, equestrian sports M/W, golf M/W, soccer M/W, tennis M/W, volleyball W. *Intramural sports:* basketball M/W, soccer M/W, softball M/W, tennis M/W, volleyball W.

Costs (2007–08) *Tuition:* $92 per credit part-time. *Required fees:* $644 full-time.

Financial Aid Of all full-time matriculated undergraduates, 200 Federal Work-Study jobs.

Bucks County Community College (continued)

Applying *Options:* electronic application, early admission. *Application fee:* $30. *Required:* high school transcript. *Required for some:* essay or personal statement, interview.

Freshmen Application Contact Ms. Amy Wilson, Director of Admissions, Bucks County Community College, 275 Swamp Road, Newtown, PA 18940. *Phone:* 215-968-8119. *Fax:* 215-968-8110. *E-mail:* wilsona@bucks.edu.

BUSINESS INSTITUTE OF PENNSYLVANIA

Meadville, Pennsylvania   **www.biop.edu/**

- **Proprietary** 2-year, founded 1987
- **Coed, primarily women**
- 82% of applicants were admitted

Undergraduates 68 full-time. 6% African American.

Faculty *Student/faculty ratio:* 17:1.

Academics *Calendar:* quarters. *Degree:* certificates, diplomas, and associate.

Costs (2006–07) *Tuition:* $7500 full-time, $250 per credit part-time. *Required fees:* $650 full-time.

Applying *Application fee:* $50. *Required:* high school transcript, interview, CPAt.

Freshmen Application Contact Ms. Cheryl Mever, Admissions Officer, Business Institute of Pennsylvania, 628 Arch Street, Suite B105, Meadville, PA 16335. *Phone:* 814-724-0700. *Fax:* 814-724-2777. *E-mail:* info@biop.edu.

BUSINESS INSTITUTE OF PENNSYLVANIA

Sharon, Pennsylvania   **www.biop.edu/**

- **Proprietary** 2-year, founded 1926
- **Small-town** 2-acre campus
- **Coed, primarily women,** 106 undergraduate students, 92% full-time, 93% women, 7% men
- 80% of applicants were admitted

Undergraduates 98 full-time, 8 part-time. 19% African American, 2% Hispanic American, 2% transferred in.

Freshmen *Admission:* 49 applied, 39 admitted, 39 enrolled. *Average high school GPA:* 3.1.

Faculty *Total:* 9, 56% full-time. *Student/faculty ratio:* 16:1.

Majors Administrative assistant and secretarial science; business administration and management; business automation/technology/data entry; computer programming; executive assistant/executive secretary; health information/medical records administration; legal administrative assistant/secretary; medical administrative assistant and medical secretary; medical/clinical assistant.

Academics *Calendar:* quarters. *Degree:* certificates, diplomas, and associate.

Student Life *Housing:* college housing not available.

Standardized Tests *Required:* ACT (for admission).

Costs (2006–07) *Tuition:* $7500 full-time, $250 per credit part-time. *Required fees:* $600 full-time. *Payment plan:* installment.

Applying *Required:* high school transcript, interview.

Freshmen Application Contact Irene Lewis, Business Institute of Pennsylvania, 335 Boyd Drive, Sharon, PA 16146. *Phone:* 724-983-0700. *Toll-free phone:* 800-289-2069. *Fax:* 724-983-8355. *E-mail:* info@biop.edu.

BUTLER COUNTY COMMUNITY COLLEGE

Butler, Pennsylvania   **www.bc3.edu/**

- **County-supported** 2-year, founded 1965
- **Rural** 300-acre campus with easy access to Pittsburgh
- **Coed**

Undergraduates 1,987 full-time, 1,822 part-time. Students come from 8 states and territories, 1 other country, 1% are from out of state, 2% African American, 0.7% Asian American or Pacific Islander, 0.8% Hispanic American, 0.1% Native American.

Faculty *Student/faculty ratio:* 20:1.

Academics *Calendar:* semesters. *Degree:* certificates, diplomas, and associate. *Special study options:* academic remediation for entering students, adult/

continuing education programs, advanced placement credit, cooperative education, English as a second language, internships, part-time degree program, services for LD students, summer session for credit.

Student Life *Campus security:* 24-hour emergency response devices, late-night transport/escort service.

Athletics Member NJCAA.

Costs (2006–07) *Tuition:* area resident $2190 full-time, $73 per credit part-time; state resident $4380 full-time, $146 per credit part-time; nonresident $6570 full-time, $219 per credit part-time. *Required fees:* $540 full-time, $18 per credit part-time.

Financial Aid Of all full-time matriculated undergraduates, 65 Federal Work-Study jobs (averaging $1545).

Applying *Options:* early admission, deferred entrance. *Application fee:* $25. *Required:* high school transcript. *Required for some:* letters of recommendation, interview.

Freshmen Application Contact Ms. Patricia Bajuszik, Director of Admissions, Butler County Community College, College Drive, PO Box 1203, Butler, PA 16003-1203. *Phone:* 724-287-8711 Ext. 344. *Toll-free phone:* 888-826-2829. *Fax:* 724-287-4961. *E-mail:* pattie.bajoszik@bc3.edu.

CAMBRIA-ROWE BUSINESS COLLEGE

Indiana, Pennsylvania   **www.crbc.net/**

Freshmen Application Contact Ms. Laurie Price, Representative at Indiana Campus, Cambria-Rowe Business College, 422 South 13th Street, Indiana, PA 15701. *Phone:* 724-483-0222. *Fax:* 724-463-7246. *E-mail:* lprice@crbc.net.

CAMBRIA-ROWE BUSINESS COLLEGE

Johnstown, Pennsylvania   **www.crbc.net/**

- **Proprietary** 2-year, founded 1891
- **Small-town** campus with easy access to Pittsburgh
- **Coed, primarily women,** 230 undergraduate students, 100% full-time, 89% women, 11% men

Undergraduates 230 full-time. Students come from 1 other state, 3% African American, 4% transferred in.

Freshmen *Admission:* 125 enrolled.

Faculty *Total:* 11, 100% full-time. *Student/faculty ratio:* 20:1.

Majors Accounting; administrative assistant and secretarial science; business administration and management; legal administrative assistant/secretary; medical administrative assistant and medical secretary.

Academics *Calendar:* quarters. *Degree:* diplomas and associate. *Special study options:* accelerated degree program, adult/continuing education programs, advanced placement credit, part-time degree program, summer session for credit.

Student Life *Housing:* college housing not available.

Costs (2007–08) *Tuition:* $15,600 full-time, $220 per credit part-time. *Required fees:* $1875 full-time, $300 per term part-time.

Financial Aid *Financial aid deadline:* 8/1.

Applying *Options:* electronic application, early admission. *Application fee:* $15. *Required:* high school transcript, entrance exam. *Recommended:* interview. *Application deadline:* rolling (freshmen). *Notification:* continuous (freshmen).

Freshmen Application Contact Mrs. Amanda Artim, Director of Admissions, Cambria-Rowe Business College, 221 Central Avenue, Johnstown, PA 15902-2494. *Phone:* 814-536-5168. *Fax:* 814-536-5160. *E-mail:* admissions@crbc.net.

CAREER TRAINING ACADEMY

Monroeville, Pennsylvania   **www.careerta.edu/**

- **Proprietary** 2-year, founded 1986
- **Coed,** 35 undergraduate students

Majors Massage therapy; medical/clinical assistant; medical insurance coding.

Academics *Calendar:* quarters. *Degree:* certificates and associate.

Costs (2006–07) *Tuition:* $7265 full-time.

Applying *Application fee:* $30.

Freshmen Application Contact Admissions Office, Career Training Academy, 4314 Old William Penn Highway, Suite 103, Monroeville, PA 15146. *E-mail:* director2@careerta.edu.

CAREER TRAINING ACADEMY

New Kensington, Pennsylvania   www.careerta.com/

- **Proprietary** 2-year, founded 1986
- **Coed**
- 85% of applicants were admitted

Undergraduates 12% African American, 0.3% Hispanic American, 0.6% Native American.
Faculty *Student/faculty ratio:* 20:1.
Academics *Calendar:* quarters. *Degrees:* diplomas and associate (profile includes branch campuses in Monroeville and Pittsburgh, PA).
Costs (2006–07) *Tuition:* $7000 full-time.
Applying *Application fee:* $30. *Required:* essay or personal statement, high school transcript, minimum 1.5 GPA, interview.
Freshmen Application Contact Ms. Anna Bartolini, Career Training Academy, 950 Fifth Avenue, New Kensington, PA 15068-6301. *Phone:* 412-367-4000. *Fax:* 412-369-7223. *E-mail:* director3@caveerta.edu.

CAREER TRAINING ACADEMY

Pittsburgh, Pennsylvania   www.careerta.edu/

- **Proprietary** 2-year
- **Coed,** 54 undergraduate students

Majors Massage therapy; medical/clinical assistant.
Academics *Calendar:* quarters. *Degree:* diplomas and associate.
Costs (2006–07) *Tuition:* $7535 full-time. Full-time tuition and fees vary according to program. No tuition increase for student's term of enrollment. *Payment plans:* tuition prepayment, installment.
Applying *Application fee:* $30.
Freshmen Application Contact Anna Bartolini, Career Training Academy, 1500 Northway Mall, Suite 200, Pittsburgh, PA 15237. *Phone:* 412-367-4000. *Fax:* 412-369-7223. *E-mail:* director3@careerta.edu.

CENTER FOR ADVANCED MANUFACTURING & TECHNOLOGY

Erie, Pennsylvania   www.erieit.edu/

Freshmen Application Contact Admissions Office, Center for Advanced Manufacturing & Technology, 5539 Peach Street, Erie, PA 16509. *Phone:* 814-897-0391 Ext. 226. *Toll-free phone:* 866-868-3743.

CHI INSTITUTE

Southampton, Pennsylvania   www.chitraining.com/

Director of Admissions Mr. Michael Herbert, Director of Admissions, CHI Institute, 520 Street Road, Southampton, PA 18966. *Phone:* 215-357-5100 Ext. 114. *Toll-free phone:* 800-336-7696.

CHI INSTITUTE, RETS CAMPUS

Broomall, Pennsylvania   www.chitraining.com/

Director of Admissions Mr. Stuart Kahn, Director of Admissions, CHI Institute, RETS Campus, Lawrence Park Shopping Center, Rt. 320 & Lawrence Road, Broomall, PA 19008. *Phone:* 610-353-7630.

COMMONWEALTH TECHNICAL INSTITUTE

Johnstown, Pennsylvania   www.hgac.org/

- **State-supported** 2-year
- **Suburban** 12-acre campus
- **Coed,** 275 undergraduate students, 100% full-time, 35% women, 65% men

Undergraduates 275 full-time. 1% are from out of state, 11% African American, 0.7% Asian American or Pacific Islander, 1% Hispanic American, 0.7% Native American. *Retention:* 64% of 2003 full-time freshmen returned.
Freshmen *Admission:* 113 applied, 101 admitted, 101 enrolled.
Faculty *Total:* 32, 100% full-time. *Student/faculty ratio:* 10:1.
Majors Accounting; architectural drafting and CAD/CADD; computer science; culinary arts; dental laboratory technology; mechanical drafting and CAD/CADD; medical office assistant.
Academics *Calendar:* trimesters. *Degree:* certificates, diplomas, and associate. *Special study options:* academic remediation for entering students.
Library Commonwealth Technical Institute at the Hiram G.Andrews Center Library with 4,294 titles, 62 serial subscriptions, 470 audiovisual materials.
Student Life *Housing Options:* disabled students. *Activities and Organizations:* choral group. *Campus security:* 24-hour patrols. *Student services:* health clinic, personal/psychological counseling.
Costs (2006–07) *Tuition:* state resident $16,836 full-time. *Room and board:* $14,274.
Financial Aid Of all full-time matriculated undergraduates, 20 Federal Work-Study jobs.
Applying *Required for some:* high school transcript. *Recommended:* high school transcript. *Application deadline:* rolling (freshmen). *Notification:* continuous (freshmen).
Freshmen Application Contact Ms. Rebecca Halza, Admissions Supervisor, Commonwealth Technical Institute, 727 Goucher Street, Johnstown, PA 15905-3092. *Phone:* 814-255-8200. *Toll-free phone:* 800-762-4211 Ext. 8237. *Fax:* 814-255-8283. *E-mail:* rhalza@state.pa.us.

COMMUNITY COLLEGE OF ALLEGHENY COUNTY

Pittsburgh, Pennsylvania   www.ccac.edu/

- **County-supported** 2-year, founded 1966
- **Urban** 242-acre campus
- **Coed,** 18,036 undergraduate students, 41% full-time, 58% women, 42% men

Undergraduates 7,328 full-time, 10,708 part-time. Students come from 17 states and territories, 79 other countries, 1% are from out of state, 17% African American, 1% Asian American or Pacific Islander, 0.8% Hispanic American, 0.6% Native American, 0.8% international, 5% transferred in.
Freshmen *Admission:* 4,063 applied, 4,034 admitted, 1,781 enrolled.
Faculty *Total:* 1,101, 18% full-time, 7% with terminal degrees. *Student/faculty ratio:* 22:1.
Majors Accounting technology and bookkeeping; administrative assistant and secretarial science; airline pilot and flight crew; applied horticulture; architectural drafting and CAD/CADD; art; athletic training; automotive engineering technology; aviation/airway management; banking and financial support services; biology/biological sciences; building/property maintenance and management; business administration and management; business automation/technology/data entry; business machine repair; carpentry; chemical technology; chemistry; child care provision; child development; civil drafting and CAD/CADD; civil engineering technology; clinical/medical laboratory technology; commercial and advertising art; communications technologies and support services related; community health services counseling; computer engineering technology; computer systems networking and telecommunications; computer technology/computer systems technology; construction engineering technology; construction trades related; corrections; cosmetology and personal grooming arts related; court reporting; criminal justice/police science; culinary arts; diagnostic medical sonography and ultrasound technology; dietitian assistant; drafting and design technology; drafting/design engineering technologies related; dramatic/theater arts; education (specific levels and methods) related; education (specific subject areas) related; electrical, electronic and communications engineering technology; electroneurodiagnostic/electroencephalographic technology; energy management and systems technology; engineering technologies related; English; entrepreneurship; environmental engineering technology; fire protection and safety technology; foodservice systems administration; foreign languages and literatures; general studies; greenhouse management; health and physical education; health information/medical records technology; health professions related; health unit coordinator/ward clerk; heating, air conditioning, ventilation and refrigeration maintenance technology; hotel/motel administration; housing and human environments related; human development and family studies related; humanities; human resources management; industrial technology; insurance; journalism; landscaping and groundskeeping; legal administrative assistant/secretary; legal assistant/paralegal; liberal arts and sciences/liberal studies; machine shop technology; management information systems; marketing/marketing management; mathematics; mechanical design technology; mechanical drafting and CAD/CADD; medical administrative assistant and medical secretary; medical/clinical assistant; medical radiologic technology; music; nuclear medical tech-

Community College of Allegheny County (*continued*)

nology; nursing assistant/aide and patient care assistant; nursing (licensed practical/vocational nurse training); nursing (registered nurse training); occupational therapist assistant; office management; ornamental horticulture; perioperative/operating room and surgical nursing; pharmacy technician; physical therapist assistant; physics; plant nursery management; psychiatric/mental health services technology; psychology; quality control technology; real estate; respiratory care therapy; restaurant, culinary, and catering management; retailing; robotics technology; science technologies related; sheet metal technology; sign language interpretation and translation; social sciences; social work; sociology; solar energy technology; substance abuse/addiction counseling; surgical technology; therapeutic recreation; tourism promotion; turf and turfgrass management; visual and performing arts related; welding technology.

Academics *Calendar:* semesters. *Degree:* certificates, diplomas, and associate. *Special study options:* academic remediation for entering students, advanced placement credit, distance learning, English as a second language, external degree program, honors programs, independent study, off-campus study, part-time degree program, services for LD students, study abroad, summer session for credit.

Library Community College of Allegheny County Library plus 4 others with 272,697 titles, 933 serial subscriptions, 13,165 audiovisual materials, an OPAC, a Web page.

Student Life *Housing:* college housing not available. *Activities and Organizations:* drama/theater group, student-run newspaper, choral group, Phi Theta Kappa. *Campus security:* 24-hour emergency response devices and patrols, late-night transport/escort service. *Student services:* health clinic, personal/psychological counseling, women's center.

Athletics Member NJCAA. *Intercollegiate sports:* baseball M, basketball M/W, bowling M/W, golf M/W, ice hockey M, softball W, table tennis M/W, tennis M/W, volleyball W. *Intramural sports:* badminton M/W, basketball M/W, bowling M/W, cross-country running M/W, football M, golf M/W, lacrosse M, racquetball M/W, softball M/W, table tennis M/W, tennis M/W, volleyball M/W, weight lifting M/W.

Costs (2007–08) *Tuition:* area resident $2240 full-time, $80 per credit part-time; state resident $4480 full-time, $160 per credit part-time; nonresident $6720 full-time, $240 per credit part-time. *Required fees:* $291 full-time, $11 per credit part-time.

Applying *Options:* deferred entrance. *Recommended:* high school transcript. *Application deadlines:* rolling (freshmen), rolling (transfers). *Notification:* continuous (freshmen), continuous (transfers).

Freshmen Application Contact Admissions, Community College of Allegheny County, 800 Allegheny Avenue, Pittsburgh, PA 15233. *Phone:* 412-237-4581.

COMMUNITY COLLEGE OF BEAVER COUNTY

Monaca, Pennsylvania
www.ccbc.edu/

- **State-supported** 2-year, founded 1966
- **Small-town** 75-acre campus with easy access to Pittsburgh
- **Coed,** 2,530 undergraduate students

Undergraduates Students come from 7 states and territories, 2 other countries, 3% are from out of state, 7% African American, 0.1% Asian American or Pacific Islander, 0.9% Hispanic American, 0.3% Native American.

Freshmen *Admission:* 850 applied, 850 admitted.

Faculty *Total:* 140, 34% full-time. *Student/faculty ratio:* 13:1.

Majors Accounting; administrative assistant and secretarial science; aeronautics/aviation/aerospace science and technology; airline pilot and flight crew; air traffic control; architectural engineering technology; avionics maintenance technology; biology/biological sciences; business administration and management; clinical/medical laboratory technology; communications technology; computer and information sciences; computer programming; computer typography and composition equipment operation; criminal justice/law enforcement administration; criminal justice/police science; culinary arts; data processing and data processing technology; drafting and design technology; education; electrical, electronic and communications engineering technology; industrial arts; information science/studies; liberal arts and sciences/liberal studies; marketing/marketing management; medical administrative assistant and medical secretary; nursing (licensed practical/vocational nurse training); nursing (registered nurse training); public relations/image management; telecommunications.

Academics *Calendar:* semesters. *Degree:* certificates, diplomas, and associate. *Special study options:* academic remediation for entering students, adult/continuing education programs, advanced placement credit, cooperative education, distance learning, double majors, independent study, internships, off-campus study, part-time degree program, services for LD students, summer session for credit.

Library Community College of Beaver County Library with 52,857 titles, 300 serial subscriptions.

Student Life *Housing:* college housing not available. *Campus security:* 24-hour emergency response devices and patrols, late-night transport/escort service.

Athletics Member NJCAA. *Intercollegiate sports:* baseball M, basketball M, softball W, tennis M/W, volleyball W. *Intramural sports:* basketball M, table tennis M/W, volleyball M/W.

Costs (2007–08) *Tuition:* area resident $2400 full-time, $83 per credit part-time; state resident $4800 full-time, $170 per credit part-time; nonresident $7200 full-time, $247 per credit part-time. *Required fees:* $525 full-time, $21 per credit part-time.

Financial Aid Of all full-time matriculated undergraduates, 50 Federal Work-Study jobs (averaging $1400).

Applying *Options:* early admission. *Application fee:* $25. *Required:* interview. *Recommended:* high school transcript. *Application deadlines:* rolling (freshmen), rolling (transfers). *Notification:* continuous (freshmen), continuous (transfers).

Freshmen Application Contact Mr. Michael Macon, Vice President for Enrollment Management, Community College of Beaver County, One Campus Drive, Monaca, PA 15061-2588. *Phone:* 724-775-8561. *Toll-free phone:* 800-335-0222. *Fax:* 724-775-4055. *E-mail:* mike.macon@ccbc.edu.

COMMUNITY COLLEGE OF PHILADELPHIA

Philadelphia, Pennsylvania
www.ccp.edu/

- **State and locally supported** 2-year, founded 1964
- **Urban** 14-acre campus
- **Coed,** 23,230 undergraduate students

Undergraduates Students come from 35 other countries.

Faculty *Total:* 1,329, 36% full-time.

Majors Accounting; administrative assistant and secretarial science; architectural engineering technology; art; automobile/automotive mechanics technology; biological and physical sciences; biomedical technology; business administration and management; business teacher education; chemical engineering; clinical/medical laboratory technology; communications technology; community organization and advocacy; computer engineering technology; computer science; construction engineering technology; consumer merchandising/retailing management; criminal justice/law enforcement administration; culinary arts; data processing and data processing technology; dental hygiene; dietetics; drafting and design technology; education; electrical, electronic and communications engineering technology; engineering; engineering technology; environmental engineering technology; fashion merchandising; finance; fire science; foods, nutrition, and wellness; gerontology; health information/medical records administration; hotel/motel administration; industrial radiologic technology; international business/trade/commerce; kindergarten/preschool education; legal administrative assistant/secretary; legal assistant/paralegal; liberal arts and sciences/liberal studies; library science; marketing/marketing management; medical administrative assistant and medical secretary; medical/clinical assistant; mental health/rehabilitation; music; nursing (registered nurse training); photography; pre-engineering; real estate; respiratory care therapy; sign language interpretation and translation; special products marketing.

Academics *Calendar:* semesters. *Degree:* certificates, diplomas, and associate. *Special study options:* academic remediation for entering students, accelerated degree program, adult/continuing education programs, distance learning, English as a second language, external degree program, honors programs, independent study, internships, part-time degree program, services for LD students, student-designed majors, study abroad, summer session for credit.

Library Main Campus Library with 110,000 titles, 420 serial subscriptions, a Web page.

Student Life *Housing:* college housing not available. *Activities and Organizations:* drama/theater group, student-run newspaper, radio station, choral group. *Campus security:* 24-hour emergency response devices and patrols. *Student services:* health clinic, personal/psychological counseling, women's center.

Athletics *Intercollegiate sports:* baseball M, basketball M/W, cross-country running M/W, soccer M, softball W, tennis M/W, volleyball W. *Intramural sports:* basketball M/W, soccer M/W, tennis M/W, track and field M/W, volleyball M/W.

Costs (2007–08) *Tuition:* area resident $2760 full-time, $115 per credit hour part-time; state resident $5520 full-time, $230 per credit hour part-time; nonresident $8280 full-time, $345 per credit hour part-time. *Required fees:* $30 per credit hour part-time.

Applying *Options:* early admission, deferred entrance. *Application fee:* $20. *Required for some:* high school transcript. *Application deadlines:* rolling (freshmen), rolling (transfers). *Notification:* continuous (freshmen), continuous (transfers).

Director of Admissions Ms. Pamela Gallimore, Interim Director of Admissions, Community College of Philadelphia, 1700 Spring Garden Street, Philadelphia, PA 19130-3991. *Phone:* 215-751-8010.

CONSOLIDATED SCHOOL OF BUSINESS

Lancaster, Pennsylvania   www.csb.edu/

- **Proprietary** 2-year, founded 1986
- **Suburban** campus with easy access to Philadelphia
- **Coed, primarily women**

Undergraduates 173 full-time. 7% African American, 19% Hispanic American.

Faculty *Student/faculty ratio:* 15:1.

Academics *Calendar:* continuous. *Degree:* diplomas and associate. *Special study options:* accelerated degree program, honors programs, independent study, internships, part-time degree program, services for LD students, student-designed majors.

Costs (2006–07) *Tuition:* $3500 full-time.

Applying *Application fee:* $25. *Required:* high school transcript, interview.

Freshmen Application Contact Mr. Jason McCue, Consolidated School of Business, 2124 Ambassador Circle, Lancaster, PA 17603. *Phone:* 717-764-9550. *Toll-free phone:* 800-541-8298. *Fax:* 717-394-6213. *E-mail:* jmccue@csb.edu.

CONSOLIDATED SCHOOL OF BUSINESS

York, Pennsylvania   www.csb.edu/

- **Proprietary** 2-year, founded 1981
- **Suburban** 6-acre campus with easy access to Baltimore
- **Coed, primarily women**

Undergraduates 176 full-time.

Faculty *Student/faculty ratio:* 15:1.

Academics *Calendar:* continuous. *Degree:* diplomas and associate. *Special study options:* accelerated degree program, honors programs, independent study, internships, part-time degree program, services for LD students, student-designed majors.

Costs (2006–07) *Tuition:* $7000 full-time, $292 per credit part-time. No tuition increase for student's term of enrollment. *Required fees:* $10 per course part-time.

Applying *Application fee:* $25. *Required:* high school transcript, interview.

Freshmen Application Contact Mr. Aaron Hoffman, Admissions Representative, Consolidated School of Business, 1605 Clugston Road, York, PA 17404. *Phone:* 717-764-9550. *Toll-free phone:* 800-520-0691. *Fax:* 717-764-9469. *E-mail:* ahoffman@csb.edu.

DEAN INSTITUTE OF TECHNOLOGY

Pittsburgh, Pennsylvania   home.earthlink.net/~deantech/

Director of Admissions Mr. Richard D. Ali, Admissions Director, Dean Institute of Technology, 1501 West Liberty Avenue, Pittsburgh, PA 15226-1103. *Phone:* 412-531-4433.

DELAWARE COUNTY COMMUNITY COLLEGE

Media, Pennsylvania   www.dccc.edu/

Freshmen Application Contact Ms. Hope Diehl, Director of Admissions and Enrollment Services, Delaware County Community College, Admissions Office, 901 South Media Line Road, Media, PA 19063-1094. *Phone:* 610-359-5333. *Toll-free phone:* 800-872-1102 (in-state); 800-543-0146 (out-of-state). *Fax:* 610-723-1530. *E-mail:* admis@dccc.edu.

DOUGLAS EDUCATION CENTER

Monessen, Pennsylvania   www.douglas-school.com/

Director of Admissions Ms. Linda Gambattista, Director of Admissions, Douglas Education Center, 130 Seventh Street, Monessen, PA 15062. *Phone:* 724-684-3684. *Fax:* 724-684-7463.

DUBOIS BUSINESS COLLEGE

DuBois, Pennsylvania   www.dbcollege.com/

Director of Admissions Mrs. Lisa Doty, Director of Admissions, DuBois Business College, 1 Beaver Drive, DuBois, PA 15801-2401. *Phone:* 814-371-6920. *Toll-free phone:* 800-692-6213. *Fax:* 814-371-3947. *E-mail:* dotylj@dbcollege.com.

ERIE BUSINESS CENTER, MAIN

Erie, Pennsylvania   www.eriebc.edu/

- **Proprietary** 2-year, founded 1884
- **Urban** 1-acre campus with easy access to Cleveland and Buffalo
- **Coed**

Undergraduates 279 full-time, 114 part-time. Students come from 3 states and territories, 2% are from out of state, 25% African American, 3% Hispanic American, 0.8% transferred in, 1% live on campus.

Faculty *Student/faculty ratio:* 14:1.

Academics *Calendar:* trimesters. *Degree:* certificates, diplomas, and associate. *Special study options:* adult/continuing education programs, advanced placement credit, independent study, part-time degree program, summer session for credit.

Student Life *Campus security:* 24-hour emergency response devices, security guard.

Standardized Tests *Required:* Wonderlic aptitude test (for admission).

Costs (2006–07) *Tuition:* $7290 full-time, $243 per credit part-time. *Required fees:* $850 full-time, $25 per credit part-time, $25 per term part-time.

Financial Aid Of all full-time matriculated undergraduates, 15 Federal Work-Study jobs (averaging $600).

Applying *Options:* deferred entrance. *Application fee:* $25. *Required:* essay or personal statement, high school transcript, interview, Wonderlic aptitude test.

Freshmen Application Contact Ms. Rose Mello, Academic Administrator, Erie Business Center, Main, 220 West Ninth Street, Erie, PA 16501-1392. *Phone:* 814-456-7504 Ext. 102. *Toll-free phone:* 800-352-3743. *Fax:* 814-456-4882. *E-mail:* mellor@eriebc.com.

ERIE BUSINESS CENTER SOUTH

New Castle, Pennsylvania   www.eriebc.edu/

Freshmen Application Contact Mr. Robert Landsberger, Administrative Representative, Erie Business Center South, 170 Cascade Galleria, New Castle, PA 16101-3950. *Phone:* 724-658-9066. *Toll-free phone:* 800-722-6227. *E-mail:* hallr@eriebcs.com.

ERIE INSTITUTE OF TECHNOLOGY

Erie, Pennsylvania   www.erieit.org/

Freshmen Application Contact Mr. Paul Fitzgerald, Admissions Representative, Erie Institute of Technology, 5539 Peach Street, Erie, PA 16509. *Phone:* 814-868-9900. *Toll-free phone:* 866-868-3743. *E-mail:* paulf@erieit.edu.

EVEREST INSTITUTE

Pittsburgh, Pennsylvania   www.everest-college.com/

Director of Admissions Ms. Lynn Fischer, Director of Admissions, Everest Institute, 100 Forbes Avenue, Suite 1200, Pittsburgh, PA 15222. *Phone:* 412-261-4520 Ext. 212. *Toll-free phone:* 888-279-3314.

HARCUM COLLEGE

Bryn Mawr, Pennsylvania   www.harcum.edu/

- **Independent** 2-year, founded 1915
- **Suburban** 12-acre campus with easy access to Philadelphia
- **Endowment** $9.0 million
- **Coed, primarily women**

Harcum College (continued)

Undergraduates 385 full-time, 188 part-time. Students come from 8 states and territories, 6 other countries, 10% are from out of state, 21% transferred in, 23% live on campus. *Retention:* 90% of 2003 full-time freshmen returned.

Faculty *Student/faculty ratio:* 9:1.

Academics *Calendar:* semesters. *Degree:* certificates and associate. *Special study options:* academic remediation for entering students, adult/continuing education programs, advanced placement credit, distance learning, double majors, English as a second language, honors programs, independent study, internships, off-campus study, part-time degree program, services for LD students, summer session for credit.

Student Life *Campus security:* 24-hour emergency response devices and patrols, controlled dormitory access.

Standardized Tests *Required:* SAT or ACT (for admission).

Costs (2006–07) *Comprehensive fee:* $22,596 includes full-time tuition ($15,250), mandatory fees ($100), and room and board ($7246). Part-time tuition: $508 per credit.

Financial Aid Of all full-time matriculated undergraduates, 161 Federal Work-Study jobs (averaging $1100).

Applying *Options:* electronic application, early admission, deferred entrance. *Application fee:* $25. *Required:* essay or personal statement, high school transcript, letters of recommendation. *Recommended:* interview.

Freshmen Application Contact Office of Enrollment Management, Harcum College, 750 Montgomery Avenue, Melville Hall, Bryn Mawr, PA 19010-3476. *Phone:* 610-526-6050. *Toll-free phone:* 800-345-2600.

▶See page 544 for the College Close-Up.

HARRISBURG AREA COMMUNITY COLLEGE

Harrisburg, Pennsylvania　　　　**www.hacc.edu/**

- **State and locally supported** 2-year, founded 1964
- **Urban** 212-acre campus
- **Endowment** $31.0 million
- **Coed,** 18,082 undergraduate students, 39% full-time, 66% women, 34% men

Undergraduates 6,967 full-time, 11,115 part-time. Students come from 15 states and territories, 65 other countries, 1% are from out of state, 9% African American, 3% Asian American or Pacific Islander, 6% Hispanic American, 0.3% Native American, 1% international, 7% transferred in.

Freshmen *Admission:* 8,327 applied, 8,276 admitted, 1,862 enrolled.

Faculty *Total:* 1,169, 26% full-time, 4% with terminal degrees. *Student/faculty ratio:* 18:1.

Majors Accounting; actuarial science; administrative assistant and secretarial science; agricultural business and management; architectural engineering technology; architecture; art; automobile/automotive mechanics technology; automotive engineering technology; banking and financial support services; biology/biological sciences; business administration and management; business/commerce; business, management, and marketing related; business teacher education; cardiovascular technology; chemistry; civil engineering technology; clinical/medical laboratory assistant; clinical/medical laboratory technology; commercial and advertising art; computer and information sciences; computer and information sciences and support services related; computer installation and repair technology; computer systems networking and telecommunications; construction engineering technology; consumer merchandising/retailing management; criminal justice/law enforcement administration; criminal justice/police science; culinary arts; dental hygiene; design and visual communications; dietetics; dramatic/theater arts; education; electrical, electronic and communications engineering technology; elementary education; emergency medical technology (EMT paramedic); engineering; engineering technologies related; engineering technology; environmental studies; fire science; foods, nutrition, and wellness; general retailing/wholesaling; health information/medical records administration; heating, air conditioning and refrigeration technology; hospital and health care facilities administration; hotel/motel administration; human services; industrial mechanics and maintenance technology; information technology; institutional food workers; international relations and affairs; journalism; kindergarten/preschool education; legal administrative assistant/secretary; legal assistant/paralegal; liberal arts and sciences/liberal studies; management information systems; management science; marketing/marketing management; mass communication/media; mathematics; mechanical engineering/mechanical technology; medical office assistant; medical radiologic technology; music; nuclear medical technology; nursing (registered nurse training); opticianry; pharmacy technician; photography; physical education teaching and coaching; physical sciences; psychology; real estate; respiratory care therapy; respiratory therapy technician; science teacher education; social sciences; social work; tourism and travel services management; tourism and travel services marketing; web/multimedia management and webmaster.

Academics *Calendar:* semesters. *Degree:* certificates, diplomas, and associate. *Special study options:* academic remediation for entering students, adult/continuing education programs, advanced placement credit, distance learning, double majors, English as a second language, honors programs, independent study, internships, part-time degree program, services for LD students, student-designed majors, study abroad, summer session for credit. *ROTC:* Army (b).

Library McCormick Library with 163,613 titles, 843 serial subscriptions, 9,510 audiovisual materials, an OPAC, a Web page.

Student Life *Housing:* college housing not available. *Activities and Organizations:* drama/theater group, student-run newspaper, radio station, Student Government Association, Phi Theta Kappa, African American Student Association, Mosiaco Club, Fourth Estate. *Campus security:* 24-hour emergency response devices and patrols, late-night transport/escort service. *Student services:* personal/psychological counseling.

Athletics *Intercollegiate sports:* basketball M/W, soccer M/W, swimming and diving M/W, tennis M/W, volleyball M/W. *Intramural sports:* basketball M/W, football M/W, golf M/W, racquetball M/W, skiing (downhill) M/W, soccer M, softball M/W, squash M/W, tennis M/W, volleyball W.

Costs (2006–07) *Tuition:* area resident $2925 full-time, $81 per credit hour part-time; state resident $5490 full-time, $161 per credit hour part-time; nonresident $8055 full-time, $242 per credit hour part-time. *Required fees:* $510 full-time, $17 per credit hour part-time. *Payment plan:* installment. *Waivers:* employees or children of employees.

Applying *Options:* electronic application, early admission. *Application fee:* $35. *Required:* high school transcript. *Application deadlines:* rolling (freshmen), rolling (transfers).

Freshmen Application Contact Mrs. Vanita L. Cowan, Administrative Clerk, Admissions, Harrisburg Area Community College, 1 HACC Drive, Harrisburg, PA 17110. *Phone:* 717-780-2406. *Toll-free phone:* 800-ABC-HACC. *Fax:* 717-231-7674. *E-mail:* admit@hacc.edu.

INFORMATION COMPUTER SYSTEMS INSTITUTE

Allentown, Pennsylvania　　　　**www.icsinstitute.com/**

Freshmen Application Contact Mr. Bill Barber, Director, Information Computer Systems Institute, 2201 Hangar Place, Allentown, PA 18103-9504. *Phone:* 610-841-3333. *Fax:* 610-841-3334. *E-mail:* wbarber@pennschoolofbusiness.edu.

INTERNATIONAL ACADEMY OF DESIGN & TECHNOLOGY

Pittsburgh, Pennsylvania　　　　**www.iadtpitt.com/**

Director of Admissions Ms. Debbie Love, Chief Admissions Officer, International Academy of Design & Technology, 555 Grant Street, Pittsburgh, PA 15219. *Phone:* 412-391-4197. *Toll-free phone:* 800-447-8324. *Fax:* 412-391-3912.

JNA INSTITUTE OF CULINARY ARTS

Philadelphia, Pennsylvania　　　　**www.culinaryarts.com/**

- **Proprietary** 2-year, founded 1988
- **Coed,** 65 undergraduate students

Majors Restaurant, culinary, and catering management.

Academics *Calendar:* continuous. *Degree:* associate.

Costs (2006–07) *Tuition:* $14,075 full-time.

Freshmen Application Contact Admissions Office, JNA Institute of Culinary Arts, 1212 South Broad Street, Philadelphia, PA 19146.

JOHNSON COLLEGE

Scranton, Pennsylvania　　　　**www.johnson.edu/**

- **Independent** 2-year, founded 1912
- **Urban** 65-acre campus
- **Coed**

Undergraduates Students come from 4 states and territories, 10% are from out of state, 17% live on campus.

Faculty *Student/faculty ratio:* 17:1.

Academics *Calendar:* semesters. *Degree:* associate. *Special study options:* academic remediation for entering students, adult/continuing education programs, internships, part-time degree program, services for LD students, summer session for credit.

Student Life *Campus security:* 24-hour emergency response devices.

Standardized Tests *Required for some:* SAT (for admission), ACCUPLACER. *Recommended:* SAT (for admission).

Costs (2006–07) *Tuition:* $12,248 full-time, $325 per credit part-time. Full-time tuition and fees vary according to program. Part-time tuition and fees vary according to course load and program. No tuition increase for student's term of enrollment. *Required fees:* $1000 full-time. *Room only:* $2975.

Financial Aid Of all full-time matriculated undergraduates, 40 Federal Work-Study jobs (averaging $800).

Applying *Options:* electronic application, deferred entrance. *Application fee:* $30. *Required:* essay or personal statement, high school transcript, letters of recommendation, interview.

Freshmen Application Contact Ms. Melissa Ide, Director of Enrollment Management, Johnson College, 3427 North Main Avenue, Scranton, PA 18508. *Phone:* 570-342-6404 Ext. 112. *Toll-free phone:* 800-2-WE-WORK Ext. 125. *Fax:* 570-348-2181. *E-mail:* admit@johnson.edu.

▶See page 552 for the College Close-Up.

KAPLAN CAREER INSTITUTE– HARRISBURG

Harrisburg, Pennsylvania **www.getinfokaplancareerinstitute.com/ KaplanInstitutePortal/KaplanInstituteCampuses/Pennsylvania/ Harrisburg**

Director of Admissions Mr. Charles Zimmerman, Admissions Director, Kaplan Career Institute–Harrisburg, 5650 Derry Street, Harrisburg, PA 17111. *Phone:* 717-564-4112. *Toll-free phone:* 800-431-1995.

KAPLAN CAREER INSTITUTE–ICM CAMPUS

Pittsburgh, Pennsylvania **www.icmschool.com/**

Director of Admissions Mrs. Marcia Rosenberg, Director of Admissions, Kaplan Career Institute–ICM Campus, 10 Wood Street, Pittsburgh, PA 15222. *Phone:* 412-261-2647 Ext. 229. *Toll-free phone:* 800-441-5222. *E-mail:* mrosenberg@icmschool.com.

KATHARINE GIBBS SCHOOL

Norristown, Pennsylvania **www.pagibbs.com/**

- **Proprietary** 2-year
- **Coed,** 386 undergraduate students

Majors Business administration, management and operations related; business systems networking/ telecommunications; computer technology/computer systems technology; criminal justice/law enforcement administration; design and visual communications; fashion merchandising; medical/clinical assistant.

Academics *Calendar:* quarters. *Degree:* associate.

Costs (2006–07) *Tuition:* $13,210 full-time.

Applying *Application fee:* $25.

Freshmen Application Contact Admissions Office, Katharine Gibbs School, 2501 Monroe Boulevard, Norristown, PA 19403. *Phone:* 610-676-0500. *Toll-free phone:* 866-PAGIBBS.

KEYSTONE COLLEGE

La Plume, Pennsylvania **www.keystone.edu/**

- **Independent** primarily 2-year, founded 1868
- **Rural** 270-acre campus
- **Endowment** $8.9 million
- **Coed,** 1,708 undergraduate students, 76% full-time, 62% women, 38% men

Undergraduates 1,306 full-time, 402 part-time. Students come from 12 states and territories, 7 other countries, 18% are from out of state, 3% African American, 0.7% Asian American or Pacific Islander, 2% Hispanic American, 0.3% Native American, 0.5% international, 9% transferred in, 24% live on campus. *Retention:* 63% of 2003 full-time freshmen returned.

Freshmen *Admission:* 945 applied, 749 admitted, 367 enrolled. *Average high school GPA:* 2.3. *Test scores:* SAT verbal scores over 500: 23%; SAT math scores over 500: 21%; SAT writing scores over 500: 19; ACT scores over 18: 44%; SAT verbal scores over 600: 3%; SAT math scores over 600: 1%; SAT writing scores over 600: 3; ACT scores over 24: 19%.

Faculty *Total:* 238, 27% full-time, 23% with terminal degrees. *Student/faculty ratio:* 12:1.

Majors Accounting; accounting and business/management; accounting related; art; art teacher education; biological and physical sciences; biology/biological sciences; business administration and management; business/commerce; communication and journalism related; communication and media related; communication/ speech communication and rhetoric; computer/information technology services administration related; computer programming; criminal justice/law enforcement administration; criminal justice/safety; culinary arts; culinary arts related; data processing and data processing technology; diagnostic medical sonography and ultrasound technology; drawing; early childhood education; education (K-12); elementary education; environmental biology; environmental science; environmental studies; family and community services; fine/studio arts; food preparation; forensic science and technology; forestry; forestry technology; graphic design; hotel/motel administration; human resources management; illustration; information technology; journalism; kindergarten/preschool education; landscape architecture; liberal arts and sciences/liberal studies; mathematics teacher education; medical radiologic technology; natural resources management; occupational therapy; painting; parks, recreation and leisure facilities management; photography; physical therapy; pre-nursing studies; printmaking; public relations, advertising, and applied communication related; radio and television; radiologic technology/science; radio, television, and digital communication related; restaurant, culinary, and catering management; restaurant/food services management; sculpture; social studies teacher education; sport and fitness administration/management; therapeutic recreation; water, wetlands, and marine resources management; wildlife and wildlands science and management; wildlife biology.

Academics *Calendar:* semesters. *Degrees:* certificates, associate, bachelor's, and postbachelor's certificates. *Special study options:* academic remediation for entering students, adult/continuing education programs, advanced placement credit, cooperative education, distance learning, external degree program, honors programs, independent study, internships, part-time degree program, services for LD students, student-designed majors, study abroad, summer session for credit. *ROTC:* Army (c), Air Force (c).

Library Miller Library with 65,000 titles, 309 serial subscriptions, an OPAC, a Web page.

Student Life *Housing:* on-campus residence required for freshman year. *Options:* coed, women-only, disabled students. Campus housing is university owned. Freshman campus housing is guaranteed. *Activities and Organizations:* drama/ theater group, student-run newspaper, radio station, choral group, Campus Activity Board, Student Senate, Art Society, Inter-Hall Council, Commuter Council. *Campus security:* 24-hour emergency response devices and patrols, student patrols, late-night transport/escort service, controlled dormitory access. *Student services:* health clinic, personal/psychological counseling, women's center.

Athletics Member NCAA. *Intercollegiate sports:* baseball M, basketball M/W, cross-country running M/W, golf M, soccer M/W, softball W, tennis M/W, track and field M/W, volleyball W. *Intramural sports:* basketball M/W, cheerleading M(c)/W(c), equestrian sports M(c)/W(c), football M/W, lacrosse M/W, skiing (downhill) M(c)/W(c), soccer M/W, softball M/W, table tennis M/W, tennis M/W, volleyball M/W, weight lifting M/W.

Standardized Tests *Required for some:* SAT or ACT (for admission). *Recommended:* SAT or ACT (for admission).

Costs (2007–08) *Comprehensive fee:* $25,440 includes full-time tuition ($15,990), mandatory fees ($1050), and room and board ($8400). Part-time tuition: $375 per credit. *Required fees:* $110 per term part-time.

Financial Aid Of all full-time matriculated undergraduates, 125 Federal Work-Study jobs (averaging $1000). 100 state and other part-time jobs (averaging $1000).

Applying *Options:* electronic application, early admission, deferred entrance. *Application fee:* $30. *Required:* high school transcript, 1 letter of recommendation. *Required for some:* interview, art portfolio. *Recommended:* essay or personal statement, interview. *Application deadlines:* 7/1 (freshmen), 8/1 (transfers).

Freshmen Application Contact Ms. Sarah Keating, Director of Admissions, Keystone College, One College Green, La Plume, PA 18440-1099. *Phone:* 570-945-8112. *Toll-free phone:* 877-4COLLEGE Ext. 1. *Fax:* 570-945-7916. *E-mail:* admissions@keystone.edu.

▶See page 554 for the College Close-Up.

LACKAWANNA COLLEGE

Scranton, Pennsylvania   www.lackawanna.edu/

- **Independent** 2-year, founded 1894
- **Urban** 4-acre campus
- **Endowment** $1.2 million
- **Coed**

Undergraduates 758 full-time, 439 part-time. Students come from 20 states and territories, 3% are from out of state, 11% African American, 0.5% Asian American or Pacific Islander, 2% Hispanic American, 0.3% Native American, 11% transferred in, 12% live on campus.

Faculty *Student/faculty ratio:* 13:1.

Academics *Calendar:* semesters. *Degree:* certificates, diplomas, and associate. *Special study options:* academic remediation for entering students, adult/continuing education programs, cooperative education, double majors, English as a second language, internships, part-time degree program, services for LD students, summer session for credit. *ROTC:* Army (c), Air Force (c).

Student Life *Campus security:* 24-hour emergency response devices, late-night transport/escort service, patrols by college liaison staff.

Athletics Member NJCAA.

Standardized Tests *Recommended:* SAT (for admission), ACT (for admission), SAT or ACT (for admission).

Costs (2006–07) *Comprehensive fee:* $16,105 includes full-time tuition ($9600), mandatory fees ($105), and room and board ($6400). Full-time tuition and fees vary according to course load. Part-time tuition: $320 per credit. Part-time tuition and fees vary according to course load. *Room and board:* college room only: $4200.

Financial Aid Of all full-time matriculated undergraduates, 101 Federal Work-Study jobs (averaging $1600).

Applying *Options:* electronic application, early admission, deferred entrance. *Application fee:* $30. *Required:* high school transcript, interview.

Freshmen Application Contact Mr. Brian Costanzo, Director of Admissions, Lackawanna College, 501 Vine Street, Scranton, PA 18509. *Phone:* 570-961-7841. *Toll-free phone:* 877-346-3552. *Fax:* 570-961-7843. *E-mail:* constanzob@lackawanna.edu.

LANCASTER GENERAL COLLEGE OF NURSING & HEALTH SCIENCES

Lancaster, Pennsylvania   www.lancastergeneral.org/content/LG_CollegeofNursing.htm

- **Independent** 2-year, founded 1903
- **Coed,** 299 undergraduate students

Majors Cardiovascular technology; diagnostic medical sonography and ultrasound technology; medical radiologic technology; nursing (registered nurse training); surgical technology.

Academics *Degree:* associate.

Standardized Tests *Recommended:* SAT or ACT (for admission).

Costs (2006–07) *Tuition:* $12,030 full-time.

Applying *Application fee:* $50. *Required:* high school transcript, letters of recommendation.

Freshmen Application Contact Admissions Office, Lancaster General College of Nursing & Health Sciences, 410 North Lime Street, Lancaster, PA 17602.

LANSDALE SCHOOL OF BUSINESS

North Wales, Pennsylvania   www.lsbonline.com/

Director of Admissions Ms. Marianne H. Johnson, Director of Admissions, Lansdale School of Business, 201 Church Road, North Wales, PA 19454-4148. *Phone:* 215-699-5700 Ext. 112. *Fax:* 215-699-8770. *E-mail:* mjohnson@lsb.edu.

LAUREL BUSINESS INSTITUTE

Uniontown, Pennsylvania   www.laurel.edu/

- **Proprietary** 2-year, founded 1985
- **Small-town** 10-acre campus with easy access to Pittsburgh
- **Coed,** 305 undergraduate students, 100% full-time, 77% women, 23% men

Undergraduates 305 full-time. Students come from 2 states and territories, 1 other country, 1% are from out of state, 4% African American, 0.3% Asian American or Pacific Islander, 0.3% international, 0.3% transferred in.

Freshmen *Admission:* 415 applied, 246 admitted, 166 enrolled. *Average high school GPA:* 2.75.

Faculty *Total:* 25, 64% full-time. *Student/faculty ratio:* 16:1.

Majors Accounting; administrative assistant and secretarial science; banking and financial support services; business administration and management; business automation/technology/data entry; child guidance; computer and information sciences related; computer and information systems security; computer/information technology services administration related; computer management; computer software and media applications related; computer systems networking and telecommunications; computer/technical support; consumer merchandising/retailing management; data entry/microcomputer applications; data entry/microcomputer applications related; executive assistant/executive secretary; home health aide/home attendant; information technology; insurance; legal administrative assistant/secretary; medical administrative assistant and medical secretary; medical/clinical assistant; medical transcription; office occupations and clerical services; system administration; web page, digital/multimedia and information resources design; word processing.

Academics *Calendar:* trimesters. *Degree:* certificates, diplomas, and associate. *Special study options:* adult/continuing education programs, advanced placement credit, cooperative education, double majors, honors programs, independent study, internships, part-time degree program.

Library Student Learning Center with 1,537 titles, 41 serial subscriptions.

Student Life *Housing:* college housing not available.

Standardized Tests *Required:* Wonderlic aptitude test (for admission).

Costs (2007–08) *Tuition:* $10,500 full-time, $225 per credit part-time. *Required fees:* $2940 full-time, $980 per term part-time.

Financial Aid Of all full-time matriculated undergraduates, 60 Federal Work-Study jobs (averaging $710).

Applying *Options:* electronic application, deferred entrance. *Application fee:* $55. *Required:* essay or personal statement, high school transcript, interview. *Application deadlines:* rolling (freshmen), rolling (transfers). *Notification:* continuous (freshmen), continuous (transfers).

Freshmen Application Contact Mrs. Lisa Dolan, Laurel Business Institute, 11-15 Penn Street, PO Box 877, Uniontown, PA 15401. *Phone:* 724-439-4900 Ext. 158. *Fax:* 724-439-3607. *E-mail:* ldolan@laurel.edu.

LEHIGH CARBON COMMUNITY COLLEGE

Schnecksville, Pennsylvania   www.lccc.edu/

- **State and locally supported** 2-year, founded 1967
- **Suburban** 153-acre campus with easy access to Philadelphia
- **Endowment** $589,575
- **Coed,** 7,076 undergraduate students, 38% full-time, 61% women, 39% men

Undergraduates 2,679 full-time, 4,397 part-time. Students come from 4 states and territories, 43 other countries, 1% are from out of state, 5% African American, 2% Asian American or Pacific Islander, 10% Hispanic American, 0.2% Native American, 0.3% international, 30% transferred in.

Freshmen *Admission:* 3,380 applied, 3,380 admitted, 1,851 enrolled.

Faculty *Total:* 531, 20% full-time, 6% with terminal degrees. *Student/faculty ratio:* 17:1.

Majors Accounting; accounting technology and bookkeeping; administrative assistant and secretarial science; adult development and aging; airline pilot and flight crew; art; aviation/airway management; avionics maintenance technology; biology/biological sciences; biomedical technology; biotechnology; business administration and management; chemical technology; child care provision; clinical/medical laboratory technology; commercial and advertising art; communication/speech communication and rhetoric; computer engineering technology; computer technology/computer systems technology; construction engineering technology; corrections; criminal justice/law enforcement administration; criminal justice/police science; culinary arts; digital communication and media/multimedia; drafting and design technology; education; electrical, electronic and communications engineering technology; electrical, electronics and communications engineering; engineering; executive assistant/executive secretary; forensic science and technology; general studies; health information/medical records technology; heating, air conditioning, ventilation and refrigeration maintenance technology; horticultural science; hotel/motel administration; humanities; human resources management; industrial technology; information science/studies; interior architecture; kindergarten/preschool education; legal administrative assistant/secretary; legal assistant/paralegal; liberal arts and sciences/liberal studies; lineworker; logistics and materials management; manufacturing technology; mathematics; mechanical engineering; mechanical engineering/mechanical technology; medical/clinical assistant; medical transcription; nursing (licensed

practical/vocational nurse training); nursing (registered nurse training); occupational therapist assistant; office occupations and clerical services; operations management; physical sciences; physical therapist assistant; real estate; respiratory care therapy; restaurant/food services management; social sciences; social work; special education; sport and fitness administration/management; tourism and travel services marketing; tourism promotion; veterinary/animal health technology.

Academics *Calendar:* semesters. *Degree:* certificates, diplomas, and associate. *Special study options:* academic remediation for entering students, adult/continuing education programs, advanced placement credit, cooperative education, distance learning, English as a second language, external degree program, honors programs, independent study, internships, part-time degree program, services for LD students, summer session for credit. *ROTC:* Army (c).

Library Learning Resource Center with 54,366 titles, 482 serial subscriptions, 6,078 audiovisual materials, an OPAC, a Web page.

Student Life *Housing:* college housing not available. *Activities and Organizations:* student-run newspaper, radio station, Phi Theta Kappa, STEP Student Association, student radio station, student government, College Activity Board. *Campus security:* 24-hour emergency response devices and patrols. *Student services:* personal/psychological counseling.

Athletics Member NJCAA. *Intercollegiate sports:* baseball M/W, basketball M/W, golf M/W, soccer M, softball W, volleyball W. *Intramural sports:* archery M/W, badminton M/W, baseball M, basketball M, bowling M/W, field hockey W, football M/W, golf M/W, racquetball M/W, skiing (downhill) M/W, soccer M/W, softball M/W, swimming and diving M/W, table tennis M/W, tennis M/W, track and field M, volleyball M/W, weight lifting M/W.

Costs (2007–08) *Tuition:* area resident $2400 full-time, $80 per credit part-time; state resident $5070 full-time, $169 per credit part-time; nonresident $7740 full-time, $258 per credit part-time. *Required fees:* $450 full-time, $15 per credit part-time.

Applying *Application fee:* $25. *Required for some:* essay or personal statement, high school transcript, interview. *Application deadlines:* rolling (freshmen), rolling (transfers). *Notification:* continuous (freshmen), continuous (transfers).

Freshmen Application Contact Mr. Rafael Limon, Associate Dean of Admissions, Lehigh Carbon Community College, 4525 Education Park Drive, Schnecksville, PA 18078-2598. *Phone:* 610-799-1575. *Fax:* 610-799-1527. *E-mail:* tellme@lccc.edu.

LEHIGH VALLEY COLLEGE

Center Valley, Pennsylvania   www.lehighvalley.edu/

- **Proprietary** 2-year, founded 1869, part of Career Education Corporation
- **Urban** 30-acre campus with easy access to Philadelphia
- **Endowment** $500,000
- **Coed,** 711 undergraduate students, 71% full-time, 66% women, 34% men

Undergraduates 502 full-time, 209 part-time. Students come from 9 states and territories, 6% are from out of state, 5% African American, 0.4% Asian American or Pacific Islander, 6% Hispanic American. *Retention:* 36% of 2003 full-time freshmen returned.

Freshmen *Admission:* 238 enrolled. *Average high school GPA:* 2.0.

Faculty *Total:* 56, 63% full-time, 16% with terminal degrees. *Student/faculty ratio:* 19:1.

Majors Accounting; business administration and management; computer and information sciences; computer programming; criminal justice/law enforcement administration; design and visual communications; hospitality administration related; information science/studies; legal assistant/paralegal; marketing/marketing management; massage therapy; medical administrative assistant and medical secretary; photography; tourism and travel services management.

Academics *Calendar:* quarters. *Degree:* associate. *Special study options:* academic remediation for entering students, adult/continuing education programs, advanced placement credit, cooperative education, independent study, internships, part-time degree program, services for LD students, study abroad.

Library Main Library plus 1 other.

Student Life *Housing:* college housing not available. *Options:* Campus housing is provided by a third party. *Activities and Organizations:* Student Government, Travel Club. *Campus security:* evening security guard.

Standardized Tests *Required:* ACCUPLACER (for admission).

Costs (2007–08) *Comprehensive fee:* $21,711 includes full-time tuition ($13,140), mandatory fees ($450), and room and board ($8121). Part-time tuition: $325 per credit. *Room and board:* college room only: $3939.

Financial Aid Of all full-time matriculated undergraduates, 30 Federal Work-Study jobs (averaging $2500).

Applying *Options:* electronic application, deferred entrance. *Application fee:* $50. *Required:* high school transcript. *Recommended:* interview. *Application deadlines:* rolling (freshmen), rolling (transfers). *Notification:* continuous (freshmen), continuous (transfers).

Freshmen Application Contact Alan Shikowitz, Lehigh Valley College, 2809 East Saucon Valley Road, Center Valley, PA 18034. *Phone:* 610-791-5100. *Toll-free phone:* 800-227-9109. *Fax:* 610-791-7810.

▶See page 558 for the College Close-Up.

LINCOLN TECHNICAL INSTITUTE

Allentown, Pennsylvania   www.lincolntech.com/

Freshmen Application Contact Admissions Office, Lincoln Technical Institute, 5151 Tilghman Street, Allentown, PA 18104-3298. *Phone:* 610-398-5301.

LINCOLN TECHNICAL INSTITUTE

Philadelphia, Pennsylvania   www.lincolntech.com/

Director of Admissions Mr. James Kuntz, Executive Director, Lincoln Technical Institute, 9191 Torresdale Avenue, Philadelphia, PA 19136-1595. *Phone:* 215-335-0800. *Toll-free phone:* 800-238-8381. *Fax:* 215-335-1443. *E-mail:* jkuntz@lincolntech.com.

LUZERNE COUNTY COMMUNITY COLLEGE

Nanticoke, Pennsylvania   www.luzerne.edu/

- **County-supported** 2-year, founded 1966
- **Suburban** 122-acre campus with easy access to Philadelphia
- **Coed**

Undergraduates 2,940 full-time, 3,230 part-time. Students come from 2 states and territories, 1 other country, 2% African American, 1% Asian American or Pacific Islander, 1% Hispanic American, 0.1% Native American, 0.1% international, 6% transferred in.

Faculty *Student/faculty ratio:* 19:1.

Academics *Calendar:* semesters. *Degree:* certificates, diplomas, and associate. *Special study options:* academic remediation for entering students, accelerated degree program, advanced placement credit, distance learning, external degree program, internships, part-time degree program, services for LD students, summer session for credit. *ROTC:* Air Force (c).

Student Life *Campus security:* 24-hour patrols.

Athletics Member NJCAA.

Costs (2006–07) *Tuition:* area resident $2310 full-time, $77 per credit part-time; state resident $4620 full-time, $154 per credit part-time; nonresident $6930 full-time, $231 per credit part-time. *Required fees:* $480 full-time, $16 per credit part-time.

Applying *Options:* early admission, deferred entrance. *Application fee:* $40. *Recommended:* high school transcript.

Freshmen Application Contact Mr. Francis Curry, Director of Admissions, Luzerne County Community College, 1333 South Prospect Street, Nanticoke, PA 18634. *Phone:* 570-740-0200. *Toll-free phone:* 800-377-5222 Ext. 337. *Fax:* 570-740-0238. *E-mail:* admissions@luzerne.edu.

MANOR COLLEGE

Jenkintown, Pennsylvania   www.manor.edu/

- **Independent Byzantine Catholic** 2-year, founded 1947
- **Small-town** 35-acre campus with easy access to Philadelphia
- **Coed**

Manor College, located in Jenkintown, a suburb of Philadelphia, offers associate degree and transfer programs in the allied health, business, and liberal arts fields. Areas of study include accounting, allied health, business administration, computer science, dental hygiene, early child care/elementary education, expanded functions dental assisting, human resource management, marketing, paralegal studies, psychology, and veterinary technology.

Manor College (continued)

Undergraduates 433 full-time, 432 part-time. Students come from 5 states and territories, 8 other countries, 7% are from out of state, 27% transferred in.

Faculty *Student/faculty ratio:* 14:1.

Academics *Calendar:* semesters. *Degrees:* certificates, diplomas, associate, and postbachelor's certificates. *Special study options:* academic remediation for entering students, adult/continuing education programs, advanced placement credit, distance learning, double majors, English as a second language, honors programs, independent study, internships, part-time degree program, summer session for credit.

Student Life *Campus security:* 24-hour emergency response devices and patrols.

Standardized Tests *Required:* SAT or ACT (for admission).

Costs (2006–07) *Comprehensive fee:* $16,514 includes full-time tuition ($10,868), mandatory fees ($350), and room and board ($5296). Part-time tuition: $235 per credit hour. *Required fees:* $25 per term part-time.

Financial Aid Of all full-time matriculated undergraduates, 45 Federal Work-Study jobs (averaging $1000). 11 state and other part-time jobs (averaging $2260). *Financial aid deadline:* 9/30.

Applying *Options:* electronic application, deferred entrance. *Application fee:* $20. *Required:* high school transcript, interview.

Director of Admissions Ms. I. Jerry Czenstuch, Vice President of Enrollment Management, Manor College, 700 Fox Chase Road, Jenkintown, PA 19046. *Phone:* 215-884-2216. *E-mail:* ftadmiss@manor.edu.

▶See page 560 for the College Close-Up.

McCANN SCHOOL OF BUSINESS & TECHNOLOGY

Pottsville, Pennsylvania   www.mccannschool.com/

Freshmen Application Contact Ms. Linda Walinsky, Director, Pottsville Campus, McCann School of Business & Technology, 2650 Woodglen Road, Pottsville, PA 17901. *Phone:* 570-622-7622. *Toll-free phone:* 888-622-2664. *Fax:* 570-622-7770.

MEDIAN SCHOOL OF ALLIED HEALTH CAREERS

Pittsburgh, Pennsylvania   www.medianschool.edu/

Director of Admissions Ms. Kris Jackson, Admission Coordinator, Median School of Allied Health Careers, 125 7th Street, Pittsburgh, PA 15222-3400. *Toll-free phone:* 800-570-0693.

METROPOLITAN CAREER CENTER

Philadelphia, Pennsylvania   www.careersinit.org/

Freshmen Application Contact Admissions Office, Metropolitan Career Center, 100 South Broad Street, Suite 830, Philadelphia, PA 19110. *Phone:* 215-843-6615. *E-mail:* vphillips@mcc2000.org.

MONTGOMERY COUNTY COMMUNITY COLLEGE

Blue Bell, Pennsylvania   www.mc3.edu

- **County-supported** 2-year, founded 1964
- **Suburban** 186-acre campus with easy access to Philadelphia
- **Coed,** 11,174 undergraduate students, 44% full-time, 59% women, 41% men

Undergraduates 4,883 full-time, 6,291 part-time. Students come from 6 states and territories, 73 other countries, 0.2% are from out of state, 10% African American, 6% Asian American or Pacific Islander, 3% Hispanic American, 0.3% Native American, 1% international. *Retention:* 58% of 2003 full-time freshmen returned.

Freshmen *Admission:* 4,321 applied, 4,321 admitted, 3,854 enrolled.

Faculty *Total:* 668, 26% full-time. *Student/faculty ratio:* 23:1.

Majors Accounting; accounting technology and bookkeeping; administrative assistant and secretarial science; architectural drafting and CAD/CADD; art; automotive engineering technology; baking and pastry arts; biology/biological sciences; biotechnology; business administration and management; business/commerce; business/corporate communications; child care and support services management; clinical/medical laboratory technology; commercial and advertising art; communication/speech communication and rhetoric; communications technologies and support services related; computer and information sciences; computer engineering technology; computer programming; computer systems networking and telecommunications; criminal justice/police science; culinary arts; dental hygiene; electrical, electronic and communications engineering technology; electromechanical technology; elementary education; engineering science; engineering technologies related; fire protection and safety technology; food sales operations; hospitality and recreation marketing; hotel/motel services marketing operations; humanities; information science/studies; liberal arts and sciences/liberal studies; management information systems and services related; mathematics; mechanical drafting and CAD/CADD; mechanical engineering/mechanical technology; medical radiologic technology; nursing (registered nurse training); physical education teaching and coaching; physical sciences; psychiatric/mental health services technology; radiologic technology/science; real estate; respiratory care therapy; sales, distribution and marketing; secondary education; social sciences; surgical technology; teacher assistant/aide.

Academics *Calendar:* semesters. *Degree:* certificates and associate. *Special study options:* academic remediation for entering students, accelerated degree program, adult/continuing education programs, advanced placement credit, distance learning, English as a second language, honors programs, independent study, internships, part-time degree program, services for LD students, student-designed majors, study abroad, summer session for credit.

Library The Brendlinger Library plus 1 other with 201,174 titles, 550 serial subscriptions, an OPAC, a Web page.

Student Life *Housing:* college housing not available. *Activities and Organizations:* drama/theater group, student-run newspaper, radio and television station, choral group, student government, Meridians Non-traditional Age Club, student radio station. *Campus security:* 24-hour emergency response devices and patrols, late-night transport/escort service, bicycle patrol. *Student services:* health clinic, personal/psychological counseling.

Athletics *Intramural sports:* badminton M/W, basketball M/W, bowling M/W, cross-country running M/W, football M, racquetball M/W, soccer M/W, softball M/W, table tennis M/W, tennis M/W, volleyball M/W, weight lifting M/W.

Costs (2007–08) *Tuition:* area resident $2580 full-time, $86 per credit hour part-time; state resident $5400 full-time, $170 per credit hour part-time; nonresident $8220 full-time, $254 per credit hour part-time. *Required fees:* $390 full-time, $14 per credit hour part-time.

Financial Aid Of all full-time matriculated undergraduates, 60 Federal Work-Study jobs (averaging $2500).

Applying *Options:* electronic application, early admission, deferred entrance. *Application fee:* $25. *Required for some:* high school transcript, interview. *Application deadlines:* 5/1 (freshmen), rolling (transfers). *Notification:* continuous (freshmen), continuous (transfers).

Freshmen Application Contact Ms. Penny Sawyer, Director of Admissions and Recruitment, Montgomery County Community College, Office of Admissions and Records, Blue Bell, PA 19422. *Phone:* 215-641-6551. *Fax:* 215-619-7188. *E-mail:* admrec@admin.mc3.edu.

NEW CASTLE SCHOOL OF TRADES

Pulaski, Pennsylvania   www.ncstrades.com/

Freshmen Application Contact Mr. James Catheline, Admissions Director, New Castle School of Trades, RD 1, Route 422, Pulaski, PA 16143. *Phone:* 724-964-8811. *Toll-free phone:* 800-837-8299 Ext. 12.

NEWPORT BUSINESS INSTITUTE

Lower Burrell, Pennsylvania   www.nbi.edu

- **Proprietary** 2-year, founded 1895
- **Small-town** 4-acre campus with easy access to Pittsburgh
- **Coed**

Undergraduates 79 full-time. Students come from 1 other state, 3% African American, 4% transferred in.

Faculty *Student/faculty ratio:* 14:1.

Academics *Calendar:* quarters. *Degree:* certificates, diplomas, and associate. *Special study options:* advanced placement credit, double majors, internships, student-designed majors.

Student Life *Campus security:* security system.

Costs (2006–07) *Tuition:* $7800 full-time, $655 per course part-time. *Required fees:* $1575 full-time.

Applying *Options:* early admission. *Application fee:* $25. *Required:* high school transcript. *Recommended:* interview.

Freshmen Application Contact Ms. Melissa Beck, Admissions Coordinator, Newport Business Institute, Lower Burrell, PA 15068. *Phone:* 724-339-7542. *Toll-free phone:* 800-752-7695. *Fax:* 724-339-2950.

NEWPORT BUSINESS INSTITUTE

Williamsport, Pennsylvania   www.nbi.edu

- **Proprietary** 2-year, founded 1955
- **Small-town** campus
- **Coed, primarily women**

Undergraduates 103 full-time, 1 part-time. Students come from 1 other state, 7% African American, 1% Asian American or Pacific Islander, 15% transferred in.

Faculty *Student/faculty ratio:* 15:1.

Academics *Calendar:* quarters. *Degree:* associate. *Special study options:* internships, part-time degree program, summer session for credit.

Costs (2006–07) *Tuition:* $8850 full-time, $738 per course part-time. *Required fees:* $475 full-time.

Financial Aid *Financial aid deadline:* 8/1.

Applying *Options:* deferred entrance. *Application fee:* $25. *Required:* high school transcript, interview.

Freshmen Application Contact Mr. David Andrus, Admissions Representative, Newport Business Institute, 941 West Third Street, Williamsport, PA 17701. *Phone:* 570-326-2869. *Toll-free phone:* 800-962-6971. *Fax:* 570-326-2136. *E-mail:* admissions_NBI@suscom.net.

NORTHAMPTON COUNTY AREA COMMUNITY COLLEGE

Bethlehem, Pennsylvania   www.northampton.edu/

- **State and locally supported** 2-year, founded 1967
- **Suburban** 165-acre campus with easy access to Philadelphia
- **Endowment** $17.4 million
- **Coed,** 9,488 undergraduate students, 43% full-time, 62% women, 38% men

Undergraduates 4,098 full-time, 5,390 part-time. Students come from 28 states and territories, 44 other countries, 3% are from out of state, 7% African American, 2% Asian American or Pacific Islander, 10% Hispanic American, 0.2% Native American, 1% international, 10% transferred in, 3% live on campus.

Freshmen *Admission:* 3,590 applied, 3,590 admitted, 2,937 enrolled.

Faculty *Total:* 575, 19% full-time, 21% with terminal degrees. *Student/faculty ratio:* 22:1.

Majors Accounting technology and bookkeeping; acting; administrative assistant and secretarial science; architectural engineering technology; automobile/automotive mechanics technology; biology/biological sciences; biotechnology; business administration and management; business/commerce; CAD/CADD drafting/design technology; chemical technology; chemistry; child care provision; communication disorders; communication/speech communication and rhetoric; computer and information systems security; computer installation and repair technology; computer programming; computer science; computer systems networking and telecommunications; criminal justice/safety; dental hygiene; diagnostic medical sonography and ultrasound technology; education; electrical, electronic and communications engineering technology; electrician; electromechanical technology; engineering; fine/studio arts; fire services administration; food preparation; funeral service and mortuary science; general studies; graphic design; heating, air conditioning, ventilation and refrigeration maintenance technology; hotel/motel administration; industrial electronics technology; interior design; journalism; legal administrative assistant/secretary; legal assistant/paralegal; liberal arts and sciences and humanities related; liberal arts and sciences/liberal studies; mathematics; medical administrative assistant and medical secretary; nursing (registered nurse training); physics; quality control technology; radio and television broadcasting technology; radiologic technology/science; restaurant/food services management; social work; sport and fitness administration/management; surgical technology; teacher assistant/aide; veterinary/animal health technology; web page, digital/multimedia and information resources design.

Academics *Calendar:* semesters. *Degree:* certificates, diplomas, and associate. *Special study options:* academic remediation for entering students, accelerated degree program, adult/continuing education programs, advanced placement credit, cooperative education, distance learning, double majors, English as a second language, honors programs, internships, part-time degree program, services for LD students, student-designed majors, study abroad, summer session for credit.

Library Paul & Harriett Mack Library with 69,805 titles, 311 serial subscriptions, 10,275 audiovisual materials, an OPAC, a Web page.

Student Life *Housing Options:* coed. Campus housing is university owned. *Activities and Organizations:* drama/theater group, student-run newspaper, radio station, choral group, Phi Theta Kappa, Nursing Student Organization, NAVTA (Veterinary Technology Club), Student American Dental Hygiene Association, Video Waves. *Campus security:* 24-hour emergency response devices and patrols, controlled dormitory access. *Student services:* health clinic, personal/psychological counseling.

Athletics *Intercollegiate sports:* baseball M, basketball M/W, bowling M/W, golf M/W, ice hockey M/W, soccer M/W, softball W, tennis M/W, volleyball M/W, wrestling M(c). *Intramural sports:* basketball M/W, bowling M/W, football M/W, golf M/W, racquetball M/W, soccer M/W, volleyball M/W.

Costs (2006–07) *Tuition:* area resident $2130 full-time, $71 per credit hour part-time; state resident $4260 full-time, $142 per credit hour part-time; nonresident $6390 full-time, $213 per credit hour part-time. Full-time tuition and fees vary according to course load. Part-time tuition and fees vary according to course load. *Required fees:* $780 full-time, $26 per credit hour part-time. *Room and board:* $6114; room only: $3536. Room and board charges vary according to board plan and housing facility. *Payment plan:* installment. *Waivers:* senior citizens and employees or children of employees.

Financial Aid Of all full-time matriculated undergraduates, 300 Federal Work-Study jobs (averaging $2400). 130 state and other part-time jobs (averaging $1500).

Applying *Options:* electronic application, deferred entrance. *Application fee:* $25. *Required:* high school transcript. *Required for some:* minimum X GPA, interview, interview required for radiography, veterinary technician, and diagnostic medical sonography programs; portfolio required for fine art programs; audition required for theatre program. *Application deadlines:* rolling (freshmen), rolling (transfers). *Notification:* continuous (freshmen), continuous (transfers).

Freshmen Application Contact Mr. James McCarthy, Director of Admissions, Northampton County Area Community College, 3835 Green Pond Road, Bethlehem, PA 18020-7599. *Phone:* 610-861-5506. *Fax:* 610-861-5551. *E-mail:* adminfo@northampton.edu.

NORTH CENTRAL INDUSTRIAL TECHNICAL EDUCATION CENTER

Ridgway, Pennsylvania   www.ncitec.edu/

- **Proprietary** 2-year, founded 1998
- **Coed,** 22 undergraduate students

Majors Machine tool technology; precision production trades.

Academics *Calendar:* trimesters. *Degree:* associate.

Costs (2006–07) *Tuition:* $20,000 full-time.

Applying *Application fee:* $50.

Director of Admissions Lugene Inzana, Director, North Central Industrial Technical Education Center, 653 Montmorenci Avenue, Ridgway, PA 15853. *Phone:* 814-772-1012. *Toll-free phone:* 800-242-5872. *Fax:* 814-772-1554. *E-mail:* linzana@ncentral.com.

OAKBRIDGE ACADEMY OF ARTS

Lower Burrell, Pennsylvania   www.akvalley.com/oakbridge/

- **Proprietary** 2-year, founded 1972
- **Small-town** 2-acre campus with easy access to Pittsburgh
- **Coed**

Undergraduates 66 full-time. Students come from 4 states and territories, 9% transferred in.

Faculty *Student/faculty ratio:* 16:1.

Academics *Calendar:* quarters. *Degree:* associate. *Special study options:* academic remediation for entering students, advanced placement credit, internships.

Student Life *Campus security:* 24-hour emergency response devices.

Costs (2006–07) *One-time required fee:* $30. *Tuition:* $11,200 full-time, $600 per course part-time. The tuition cost for the two-year program is $22,400. *Required fees:* $1000 full-time.

Financial Aid *Financial aid deadline:* 8/1.

Applying *Options:* electronic application. *Application fee:* $50. *Required:* high school transcript, portfolio.

Oakbridge Academy of Arts (continued)

Freshmen Application Contact Ms. Melissa Beck, Admissions Representative, Oakbridge Academy of Arts, 1250 Greensburg Road, Lower Burrell, PA 15068. *Phone:* 724-335-5336. *Toll-free phone:* 800-734-5601. *Fax:* 724-335-3367.

ORLEANS TECHNICAL INSTITUTE-CENTER CITY CAMPUS

Philadelphia, Pennsylvania www.jevs.org/schools_svs.asp

Director of Admissions Mr. Gary Bello, Admissions Representative, Orleans Technical Institute-Center City Campus, 1845 Walnut Street, 7th Floor, Philadelphia, PA 19103. *Phone:* 215-854-1853.

PACE INSTITUTE

Reading, Pennsylvania www.paceinstitute.com/

- **Private** 2-year, founded 1977
- **Coed,** 274 undergraduate students, 73% full-time, 62% women, 38% men

Undergraduates 201 full-time, 73 part-time.

Faculty *Total:* 14, 43% full-time, 7% with terminal degrees. *Student/faculty ratio:* 18:1.

Majors Accounting; administrative assistant and secretarial science; business administration and management; computer programming; computer systems networking and telecommunications; fashion merchandising; legal assistant/paralegal; medical/clinical assistant; tourism and travel services management.

Academics *Degree:* diplomas and associate.

Student Life *Housing:* college housing not available.

Costs (2006–07) *Tuition:* $6360 full-time.

Applying *Application fee:* $10.

Director of Admissions Mr. Ed Levandowski, Director of Enrollment Management, Pace Institute, 606 Court Street, Reading, PA 19601. *Phone:* 610-375-1212. *Fax:* 610-375-1924.

PENN COMMERCIAL BUSINESS AND TECHNICAL SCHOOL

Washington, Pennsylvania www.penncommercial.net/

Director of Admissions Mr. Michael John Joyce, Director of Admissions, Penn Commercial Business and Technical School, 242 Oak Spring Road, Washington, PA 15301. *Phone:* 724-222-5330 Ext. 1. *E-mail:* mjoyce@penncommercial.com.

PENNCO TECH

Bristol, Pennsylvania www.penncotech.com/

Director of Admissions Mr. Nate R. Aldsworth, Corporate Director of Admissions and Marketing, Pennco Tech, 3815 Otter Street, Bristol, PA 19007-3696. *Phone:* 215-824-3200. *Fax:* 215-785-1945. *E-mail:* admissions@penncotech.com.

PENN FOSTER CAREER SCHOOL

Scranton, Pennsylvania www.pennfoster.edu/

- **Proprietary** 2-year, founded 1975
- **Coed**

Undergraduates Students come from 52 states and territories, 15 other countries.

Academics *Calendar:* semesters. *Degrees:* associate (offers only external degree programs conducted through home study). *Special study options:* academic remediation for entering students, adult/continuing education programs, distance learning, external degree program, independent study, part-time degree program, summer session for credit.

Standardized Tests *Required:* Math/Reading (for admission).

Costs (2006–07) *Tuition:* $900 per term part-time. Full-time tuition and fees vary according to course load and program. No tuition increase for student's term of enrollment. *Required fees:* $60 per term part-time.

Applying *Required:* high school transcript.

Freshmen Application Contact Ms. Connie Dempsey, Director of Compliance and Academic Affairs, Penn Foster Career School, 925 Oak Street, Scranton, PA 18515. *Phone:* 570-342-7701 Ext. 4692. *Toll-free phone:* 800-233-4191.

PENN STATE BEAVER

Monaca, Pennsylvania www.br.psu.edu/

- **State-related** primarily 2-year, founded 1964, part of Pennsylvania State University
- **Small-town** 91-acre campus with easy access to Pittsburgh
- **Endowment** $1.2 billion
- **Coed,** 721 undergraduate students, 83% full-time, 40% women, 60% men

Undergraduates 600 full-time, 121 part-time. 4% are from out of state, 7% African American, 2% Asian American or Pacific Islander, 0.7% Hispanic American, 0.3% international, 5% transferred in, 25% live on campus. *Retention:* 73% of 2003 full-time freshmen returned.

Freshmen *Admission:* 677 applied, 616 admitted, 244 enrolled. *Average high school GPA:* 2.95. *Test scores:* SAT verbal scores over 500: 39%; SAT math scores over 500: 45%; SAT verbal scores over 600: 10%; SAT math scores over 600: 12%.

Faculty *Total:* 58, 55% full-time, 45% with terminal degrees. *Student/faculty ratio:* 16:1.

Majors Accounting; acting; actuarial science; adult and continuing education administration; advertising; aerospace, aeronautical and astronautical engineering; African-American/Black studies; agribusiness; agricultural and extension education; agricultural/biological engineering and bioengineering; agricultural business and management related; agricultural mechanization; agriculture; agronomy and crop science; animal sciences; animal sciences related; anthropology; applied economics; archeology; architectural engineering; art; art history, criticism and conservation; art teacher education; Asian studies (East); astronomy; atmospheric sciences and meteorology; biochemistry; biological and biomedical sciences related; biological and physical sciences; biology/biological sciences; biology/biotechnology laboratory technician; biomedical/medical engineering; business administration and management; business/commerce; business/managerial economics; chemical engineering; chemistry; civil engineering; classics and languages, literatures and linguistics; communication and journalism related; communication disorders; communication/speech communication and rhetoric; comparative literature; computer and information sciences; computer engineering; criminal justice/law enforcement administration; economics; electrical, electronics and communications engineering; elementary education; engineering science; English; environmental/environmental health engineering; film/cinema studies; finance; food science; foreign language teacher education; forestry technology; forest sciences and biology; French; geography; geological and earth sciences/geosciences related; geology/earth science; German; graphic design; health/health care administration; history; horticultural science; hospitality administration related; human development and family studies; human nutrition; industrial engineering; information science/studies; international relations and affairs; Italian; Japanese; Jewish/Judaic studies; journalism; kinesiology and exercise science; labor and industrial relations; landscaping and groundskeeping; Latin American studies; liberal arts and sciences/liberal studies; logistics and materials management; management information systems; marketing/marketing management; materials science; mathematics; mechanical engineering; medical microbiology and bacteriology; medieval and Renaissance studies; mining and mineral engineering; music; natural resources and conservation related; natural resources/conservation; nuclear engineering; nursing (registered nurse training); organizational behavior; parks, recreation and leisure facilities management; petroleum engineering; philosophy; physics; political science and government; pre-medical studies; psychology; rehabilitation and therapeutic professions related; religious studies; Russian; secondary education; sociology; soil science and agronomy; Spanish; special education; statistics; theater design and technology; toxicology; turf and turfgrass management; visual and performing arts; women's studies.

Academics *Calendar:* semesters. *Degrees:* associate and bachelor's. *Special study options:* academic remediation for entering students, accelerated degree program, adult/continuing education programs, advanced placement credit, distance learning, double majors, English as a second language, honors programs, independent study, internships, services for LD students, study abroad, summer session for credit.

Library 39,861 titles, 222 serial subscriptions.

Student Life *Housing Options:* coed. Campus housing is university owned. Freshman campus housing is guaranteed. *Activities and Organizations:* drama/theater group, student-run newspaper, radio station. *Campus security:* 24-hour patrols, controlled dormitory access. *Student services:* health clinic, personal/psychological counseling.

Athletics Member NJCAA. *Intercollegiate sports:* baseball M, basketball M, softball M/W, volleyball W. *Intramural sports:* basketball M/W, cheerleading M(c)/W(c), cross-country running M/W, football M, golf M/W, soccer M/W, softball M/W, table tennis M/W.

Standardized Tests *Required:* SAT or ACT (for admission).

Costs (2006–07) *Tuition:* state resident $10,008 full-time, $405 per credit hour part-time; nonresident $15,284 full-time, $637 per credit hour part-time. *Required fees:* $512 full-time. *Room and board:* $6850; room only: $3620.

Financial Aid Of all full-time matriculated undergraduates, 38 Federal Work-Study jobs (averaging $1495). 5 state and other part-time jobs (averaging $4655).

Applying *Options:* electronic application, early admission, deferred entrance. *Application fee:* $50. *Required:* high school transcript. *Required for some:* letters of recommendation, interview. *Recommended:* essay or personal statement. *Application deadlines:* rolling (freshmen), rolling (transfers). *Notification:* continuous (freshmen), continuous (transfers).

Director of Admissions Mr. Randall C. Deike, Assistant Vice President for Enrollment Management, Penn State Beaver, 100 University Drive, Suite 113, Monaca, PA 15061-2799. *Phone:* 814-865-5471. *E-mail:* admissions@psu.edu.

PENN STATE DELAWARE COUNTY

Media, Pennsylvania   www.de.psu.edu/

- **State-related** primarily 2-year, founded 1966, part of Pennsylvania State University
- **Small-town** 87-acre campus with easy access to Philadelphia
- **Endowment** $1.2 billion
- **Coed,** 1,631 undergraduate students, 85% full-time, 43% women, 57% men

Undergraduates 1,388 full-time, 243 part-time. 3% are from out of state, 16% African American, 7% Asian American or Pacific Islander, 2% Hispanic American, 0.1% Native American, 0.6% international, 4% transferred in. *Retention:* 69% of 2003 full-time freshmen returned.

Freshmen *Admission:* 1,724 applied, 1,295 admitted, 471 enrolled. *Average high school GPA:* 2.81. *Test scores:* SAT verbal scores over 500: 33%; SAT math scores over 500: 38%; SAT verbal scores over 600: 6%; SAT math scores over 600: 12%; SAT math scores over 700: 1%.

Faculty *Total:* 124, 50% full-time, 37% with terminal degrees. *Student/faculty ratio:* 18:1.

Majors Accounting; acting; actuarial science; adult and continuing education administration; advertising; aerospace, aeronautical and astronautical engineering; African-American/Black studies; agribusiness; agricultural and extension education; agricultural/biological engineering and bioengineering; agricultural business and management related; agricultural mechanization; agriculture; agronomy and crop science; American studies; animal sciences; animal sciences related; anthropology; applied economics; archeology; architectural engineering; art; art history, criticism and conservation; art teacher education; Asian studies (East); astronomy; atmospheric sciences and meteorology; biochemistry; biological and biomedical sciences related; biological and physical sciences; biology/biological sciences; biology/biotechnology laboratory technician; biomedical/medical engineering; business administration and management; business/commerce; business/managerial economics; chemical engineering; chemistry; civil engineering; classics and languages, literatures and linguistics; communication and journalism related; communication disorders; communication/speech communication and rhetoric; comparative literature; computer and information sciences; computer engineering; criminal justice/law enforcement administration; economics; electrical, electronic and communications engineering technology; electrical, electronics and communications engineering; elementary education; engineering science; English; environmental/environmental health engineering; film/cinema studies; finance; food science; foreign language teacher education; forestry technology; forest sciences and biology; French; geography; geological and earth sciences/geosciences related; geology/earth science; German; graphic design; health/health care administration; history; horticultural science; hospitality administration related; human development and family studies; human nutrition; industrial engineering; information science/studies; international relations and affairs; Italian; Japanese; Jewish/Judaic studies; journalism; kinesiology and exercise science; labor and industrial relations; landscape architecture; landscaping and groundskeeping; Latin American studies; liberal arts and sciences/liberal studies; logistics and materials management; management information systems; marketing/marketing management; materials science; mathematics; mechanical engineering; medical microbiology and bacteriology; medieval and Renaissance studies; mining and mineral engineering; music; natural resources and conservation related; natural resources/conservation; nuclear engineering; nursing (registered nurse training); organizational behavior; parks, recreation and leisure facilities management; petroleum engineering; philosophy; physics; political science and government; pre-medical studies; psychology; rehabilitation and therapeutic professions related; religious studies; Russian; secondary education; sociology; soil science and agronomy; Spanish; special education; statistics; theater design and technology; turf and turfgrass management; visual and performing arts; women's studies.

Academics *Calendar:* semesters. *Degrees:* associate and bachelor's. *Special study options:* academic remediation for entering students, adult/continuing education programs, advanced placement credit, distance learning, double majors, English as a second language, honors programs, independent study, internships, services for LD students, study abroad, summer session for credit. *ROTC:* Air Force (c).

Library 59,930 titles, 457 serial subscriptions.

Student Life *Housing:* college housing not available. *Activities and Organizations:* drama/theater group, student-run newspaper, choral group. *Campus security:* late-night transport/escort service, part-time trained security personnel. *Student services:* health clinic, personal/psychological counseling, women's center.

Athletics Member NJCAA. *Intercollegiate sports:* baseball M, basketball M/W, soccer M/W, tennis M/W, volleyball W. *Intramural sports:* basketball M/W, cheerleading M(c)/W(c), golf M/W, ice hockey M(c)/W(c), lacrosse M/W, soccer M/W, softball W(c), tennis M/W, volleyball M(c)/W.

Standardized Tests *Required:* SAT or ACT (for admission).

Costs (2006–07) *Tuition:* state resident $10,008 full-time, $405 per credit hour part-time; nonresident $15,284 full-time, $637 per credit hour part-time. *Required fees:* $512 full-time.

Financial Aid Of all full-time matriculated undergraduates, 58 Federal Work-Study jobs (averaging $1082).

Applying *Options:* electronic application, early admission, deferred entrance. *Application fee:* $50. *Required:* high school transcript. *Required for some:* letters of recommendation, interview. *Recommended:* essay or personal statement. *Application deadlines:* rolling (freshmen), rolling (transfers). *Notification:* continuous (freshmen), continuous (transfers).

Director of Admissions Mr. Randall C. Deike, Assistant Vice President for Enrollment Management, Penn State Delaware County, 25 Yearsley Mill Road, Media, PA 19063-5596. *Phone:* 814-865-5471. *E-mail:* admissions@psu.edu.

PENN STATE DUBOIS

DuBois, Pennsylvania   www.ds.psu.edu/

- **State-related** primarily 2-year, founded 1935, part of Pennsylvania State University
- **Small-town** 20-acre campus
- **Endowment** $1.2 billion
- **Coed,** 808 undergraduate students, 75% full-time, 53% women, 47% men

Undergraduates 604 full-time, 204 part-time. 1% are from out of state, 1% African American, 0.4% Asian American or Pacific Islander, 0.3% Hispanic American, 0.1% international, 3% transferred in. *Retention:* 82% of 2003 full-time freshmen returned.

Freshmen *Admission:* 424 applied, 376 admitted, 192 enrolled. *Average high school GPA:* 2.91. *Test scores:* SAT verbal scores over 500: 31%; SAT math scores over 500: 32%; SAT verbal scores over 600: 6%; SAT math scores over 600: 11%; SAT verbal scores over 700: 1%; SAT math scores over 700: 1%.

Faculty *Total:* 86, 49% full-time, 40% with terminal degrees. *Student/faculty ratio:* 12:1.

Majors Accounting; acting; actuarial science; adult and continuing education administration; advertising; aerospace, aeronautical and astronautical engineering; African-American/Black studies; agribusiness; agricultural and extension education; agricultural/biological engineering and bioengineering; agricultural business and management related; agricultural mechanization; agriculture; agronomy and crop science; animal sciences; animal sciences related; anthropology; applied economics; archeology; architectural engineering; art; art history, criticism and conservation; art teacher education; Asian studies (East); astronomy; atmospheric sciences and meteorology; biochemistry; biological and biomedical sciences related; biological and physical sciences; biology/biological sciences; biology/biotechnology laboratory technician; biomedical/medical engineering; biomedical technology; business administration and management; business/commerce; business/managerial economics; chemical engineering; chemistry; civil engineering; classics and languages, literatures and linguistics; clinical/medical laboratory technology; communication and journalism related; communication disorders; communication/speech communication and rhetoric; comparative literature; computer and information sciences; computer engineering; criminal justice/law enforcement administration; economics; electrical, electronic and communications engineering technology; electrical, electronics and communications engineering; elementary education; engineering science; English; environmental/environmental health engineering; film/cinema studies; finance; food science; foreign language teacher education; forestry technology; forest sciences and biology; French; geography; geological and earth sciences/geosciences related; geology/earth science; German; graphic design; health/health care administration; history; horticultural science; hospitality administration related; human development and family studies; human nutrition; industrial engineering; information science/studies; international business/trade/commerce; international relations and affairs; Italian; Japanese; Jewish/Judaic studies;

Penn State DuBois (continued)

journalism; kinesiology and exercise science; labor and industrial relations; landscaping and groundskeeping; Latin American studies; liberal arts and sciences/liberal studies; management information systems; marketing/marketing management; materials science; mathematics; mechanical engineering; mechanical engineering/mechanical technology; medical microbiology and bacteriology; medieval and Renaissance studies; metallurgical technology; mining and mineral engineering; music; natural resources and conservation related; natural resources/conservation; nuclear engineering; nursing (registered nurse training); occupational therapist assistant; organizational behavior; parks, recreation and leisure facilities management; petroleum engineering; philosophy; physical therapist assistant; physics; political science and government; pre-medical studies; psychology; rehabilitation and therapeutic professions related; religious studies; Russian; secondary education; sociology; soil science and agronomy; Spanish; special education; statistics; telecommunications technology; theater design and technology; toxicology; turf and turfgrass management; visual and performing arts; wildlife and wildlands science and management; women's studies.

Academics *Calendar:* semesters. *Degrees:* associate and bachelor's. *Special study options:* academic remediation for entering students, accelerated degree program, adult/continuing education programs, advanced placement credit, distance learning, double majors, honors programs, independent study, internships, services for LD students, student-designed majors, study abroad, summer session for credit.

Library 43,710 titles, 224 serial subscriptions, 1,091 audiovisual materials.

Student Life *Housing:* college housing not available. *Activities and Organizations:* drama/theater group, student-run newspaper, choral group. *Student services:* health clinic, personal/psychological counseling, women's center.

Athletics Member NJCAA. *Intercollegiate sports:* basketball M, cross-country running M/W, golf M/W, volleyball W. *Intramural sports:* basketball M/W, football M, soccer M/W, table tennis M/W, volleyball M/W.

Standardized Tests *Required:* SAT or ACT (for admission).

Costs (2006–07) *Tuition:* state resident $10,008 full-time, $405 per credit hour part-time; nonresident $15,284 full-time, $637 per credit hour part-time. *Required fees:* $502 full-time.

Financial Aid Of all full-time matriculated undergraduates, 94 Federal Work-Study jobs (averaging $1505). 4 state and other part-time jobs (averaging $1496).

Applying *Options:* electronic application, early admission, deferred entrance. *Application fee:* $50. *Required:* high school transcript. *Required for some:* letters of recommendation, interview. *Recommended:* essay or personal statement. *Application deadlines:* rolling (freshmen), rolling (transfers). *Notification:* continuous (freshmen), continuous (transfers).

Director of Admissions Mr. Randall C. Deike, Assistant Vice President for Enrollment Management, Penn State DuBois, 101 Hiller Building, College Place, DuBois, PA 15801-3199. *Phone:* 814-865-5471. *Toll-free phone:* 800-346-7627. *E-mail:* admissions@psu.edu.

PENN STATE FAYETTE, THE EBERLY CAMPUS

Uniontown, Pennsylvania   www.fe.psu.edu/

- **State-related** primarily 2-year, founded 1934, part of Pennsylvania State University
- **Small-town** 92-acre campus
- **Endowment** $1.2 billion
- **Coed,** 1,139 undergraduate students, 70% full-time, 60% women, 40% men

Undergraduates 794 full-time, 345 part-time. 1% are from out of state, 5% African American, 0.3% Asian American or Pacific Islander, 0.4% Hispanic American, 0.1% Native American, 4% transferred in. *Retention:* 78% of 2003 full-time freshmen returned.

Freshmen *Admission:* 537 applied, 456 admitted, 210 enrolled. *Average high school GPA:* 2.93. *Test scores:* SAT verbal scores over 500: 36%; SAT math scores over 500: 34%; SAT verbal scores over 600: 4%; SAT math scores over 600: 8%; SAT math scores over 700: 1%.

Faculty *Total:* 87, 61% full-time, 37% with terminal degrees. *Student/faculty ratio:* 14:1.

Majors Accounting; acting; actuarial science; adult and continuing education administration; advertising; aerospace, aeronautical and astronautical engineering; African-American/Black studies; agribusiness; agricultural and extension education; agricultural/biological engineering and bioengineering; agricultural business and management related; agricultural mechanization; agriculture; agronomy and crop science; animal sciences; animal sciences related; anthropology; applied economics; archeology; architectural engineering; architectural engineering technology; art; art history, criticism and conservation; art teacher education; Asian studies (East); astronomy; atmospheric sciences and meteorology; biochemistry; biological and biomedical sciences related; biological and physical sciences; biology/biological sciences; biology/biotechnology labora-

tory technician; biomedical/medical engineering; biomedical technology; business administration and management; business/commerce; business/managerial economics; chemical engineering; chemistry; civil engineering; classics and languages, literatures and linguistics; communication and journalism related; communication disorders; communication/speech communication and rhetoric; comparative literature; computer and information sciences; computer engineering; criminal justice/law enforcement administration; criminal justice/safety; economics; electrical, electronic and communications engineering technology; electrical, electronics and communications engineering; elementary education; engineering science; English; environmental/environmental health engineering; film/cinema studies; finance; food science; foreign language teacher education; forestry technology; forest sciences and biology; French; geography; geological and earth sciences/geosciences related; geology/earth science; German; graphic design; health/health care administration; history; horticultural science; hospitality administration related; human development and family studies; human nutrition; industrial engineering; information science/studies; international relations and affairs; Italian; Japanese; Jewish/Judaic studies; journalism; kinesiology and exercise science; labor and industrial relations; landscaping and groundskeeping; Latin American studies; liberal arts and sciences/liberal studies; logistics and materials management; management information systems; manufacturing engineering; marketing/marketing management; materials science; mathematics; mechanical engineering; medical microbiology and bacteriology; medieval and Renaissance studies; metallurgical technology; mining and mineral engineering; music; natural resources and conservation related; natural resources/conservation; nuclear engineering; nursing (registered nurse training); organizational behavior; parks, recreation and leisure facilities management; petroleum engineering; philosophy; physics; political science and government; pre-medical studies; psychology; rehabilitation and therapeutic professions related; religious studies; Russian; secondary education; sociology; soil science and agronomy; Spanish; special education; statistics; telecommunications technology; theater design and technology; toxicology; turf and turfgrass management; visual and performing arts; women's studies.

Academics *Calendar:* semesters. *Degrees:* associate and bachelor's. *Special study options:* academic remediation for entering students, accelerated degree program, adult/continuing education programs, advanced placement credit, distance learning, double majors, honors programs, independent study, internships, services for LD students, student-designed majors, study abroad, summer session for credit.

Library 54,610 titles, 187 serial subscriptions.

Student Life *Housing:* college housing not available. *Activities and Organizations:* drama/theater group, student-run newspaper, choral group. *Campus security:* student patrols, 8-hour patrols by trained security personnel. *Student services:* health clinic, personal/psychological counseling.

Athletics Member NJCAA. *Intercollegiate sports:* baseball M, basketball M, softball W, volleyball W. *Intramural sports:* badminton M/W, basketball M/W, cheerleading M(c)/W(c), equestrian sports M(c)/W(c), football M/W, golf M(c)/W(c), softball M/W, tennis M/W, volleyball M/W, weight lifting M/W.

Standardized Tests *Required:* SAT or ACT (for admission).

Costs (2006–07) *Tuition:* state resident $10,008 full-time, $405 per credit hour part-time; nonresident $15,284 full-time, $637 per credit hour part-time. *Required fees:* $502 full-time.

Financial Aid Of all full-time matriculated undergraduates, 76 Federal Work-Study jobs (averaging $1714).

Applying *Options:* electronic application, early admission, deferred entrance. *Application fee:* $50. *Required:* high school transcript. *Required for some:* letters of recommendation, interview. *Recommended:* essay or personal statement. *Application deadlines:* rolling (freshmen), rolling (transfers). *Notification:* continuous (freshmen), continuous (transfers).

Director of Admissions Mr. Randall C. Deike, Assistant Vice President for Enrollment Management, Penn State Fayette, The Eberly Campus, PO Box 519, Route 119 North, 108 Williams Building, Uniontown, PA 15401-0519. *Phone:* 814-865-5471. *Toll-free phone:* 877-568-4130. *E-mail:* admissions@psu.edu.

PENN STATE HAZLETON

Hazleton, Pennsylvania   www.hn.psu.edu/

- **State-related** primarily 2-year, founded 1934, part of Pennsylvania State University
- **Small-town** 98-acre campus
- **Endowment** $1.2 billion
- **Coed,** 1,142 undergraduate students, 95% full-time, 39% women, 61% men

Undergraduates 1,086 full-time, 56 part-time. 25% are from out of state, 8% African American, 6% Asian American or Pacific Islander, 7% Hispanic American, 0.3% Native American, 0.2% international, 3% transferred in, 42% live on campus. *Retention:* 80% of 2003 full-time freshmen returned.

Freshmen *Admission:* 1,296 applied, 1,150 admitted, 542 enrolled. *Average high school GPA:* 2.88. *Test scores:* SAT verbal scores over 500: 37%; SAT math

scores over 500: 42%; SAT verbal scores over 600: 5%; SAT math scores over 600: 12%; SAT math scores over 700: 1%.

Faculty *Total:* 81, 62% full-time, 46% with terminal degrees. *Student/faculty ratio:* 18:1.

Majors Accounting; acting; actuarial science; adult and continuing education administration; advertising; aerospace, aeronautical and astronautical engineering; African-American/Black studies; agribusiness; agricultural and extension education; agricultural/biological engineering and bioengineering; agricultural business and management related; agricultural mechanization; agriculture; agronomy and crop science; animal sciences; animal sciences related; anthropology; applied economics; archeology; architectural engineering; art; art history, criticism and conservation; art teacher education; Asian studies (East); astronomy; atmospheric sciences and meteorology; biochemistry; biological and biomedical sciences related; biological and physical sciences; biology/biological sciences; biology/biotechnology laboratory technician; biomedical/medical engineering; biomedical technology; business administration and management; business/commerce; business/managerial economics; chemical engineering; chemistry; civil engineering; classics and languages, literatures and linguistics; clinical/medical laboratory technology; communication and journalism related; communication disorders; communication/speech communication and rhetoric; comparative literature; computer and information sciences; computer engineering; criminal justice/law enforcement administration; economics; electrical, electronic and communications engineering technology; electrical, electronics and communications engineering; elementary education; engineering science; English; environmental/environmental health engineering; film/cinema studies; finance; food science; forestry technology; forest sciences and biology; French; geography; geological and earth sciences/geosciences related; geology/earth science; German; graphic design; health/health care administration; history; horticultural science; hospitality administration related; human development and family studies; human nutrition; industrial education; information science/studies; international relations and affairs; Italian; Japanese; Jewish/Judaic studies; journalism; kinesiology and exercise science; labor and industrial relations; landscaping and groundskeeping; Latin American studies; liberal arts and sciences/liberal studies; logistics and materials management; management information systems; manufacturing engineering; marketing/marketing management; materials science; mathematics; mechanical engineering; mechanical engineering/mechanical technology; medical microbiology and bacteriology; medieval and Renaissance studies; metallurgical technology; mining and mineral engineering; music; natural resources and conservation related; natural resources/conservation; nuclear engineering; nursing (registered nurse training); organizational behavior; parks, recreation and leisure facilities management; petroleum engineering; philosophy; physical therapist assistant; physics; political science and government; pre-medical studies; psychology; rehabilitation and therapeutic professions related; religious studies; Russian; secondary education; sociology; soil science and agronomy; Spanish; special education; statistics; telecommunications technology; theater design and technology; toxicology; turf and turfgrass management; visual and performing arts; women's studies.

Academics *Calendar:* semesters. *Degrees:* associate and bachelor's. *Special study options:* academic remediation for entering students, accelerated degree program, adult/continuing education programs, advanced placement credit, distance learning, double majors, English as a second language, honors programs, independent study, internships, services for LD students, student-designed majors, study abroad, summer session for credit. *ROTC:* Army (b), Air Force (c).

Library 83,266 titles, 996 serial subscriptions, 6,771 audiovisual materials.

Student Life *Housing Options:* coed. Campus housing is university owned. Freshman campus housing is guaranteed. *Activities and Organizations:* drama/theater group, student-run newspaper, radio station, choral group. *Campus security:* 24-hour patrols, late-night transport/escort service, controlled dormitory access. *Student services:* health clinic, personal/psychological counseling, women's center, legal services.

Athletics Member NJCAA. *Intercollegiate sports:* baseball M, basketball M/W, cheerleading M/W, soccer M, softball W(s), tennis M/W, volleyball M/W. *Intramural sports:* basketball M/W, skiing (downhill) M(c)/W(c), soccer M/W, volleyball M/W.

Standardized Tests *Required:* SAT or ACT (for admission).

Costs (2006–07) *Tuition:* state resident $10,008 full-time, $405 per credit hour part-time; nonresident $15,284 full-time, $637 per credit hour part-time. *Required fees:* $512 full-time. *Room and board:* $6850; room only: $3620.

Financial Aid Of all full-time matriculated undergraduates, 67 Federal Work-Study jobs (averaging $1524). 12 state and other part-time jobs (averaging $5850).

Applying *Options:* electronic application, early admission, deferred entrance. *Application fee:* $50. *Required:* high school transcript. *Required for some:* letters of recommendation, interview. *Recommended:* essay or personal statement. *Application deadlines:* rolling (freshmen), rolling (transfers). *Notification:* continuous (freshmen), continuous (transfers).

Director of Admissions Mr. Randall C. Deike, Assistant Vice President for Enrollment Management, Penn State Hazleton, 110 Administration Building, 76 University Drive, Hazleton, PA 18202-1291. *Phone:* 814-865-5471. *Toll-free phone:* 800-279-8495. *E-mail:* admissions@psu.edu.

PENN STATE LEHIGH VALLEY

Fogelsville, Pennsylvania   **www.lv.psu.edu/**

- **State-related** primarily 2-year, founded 1912, part of Pennsylvania State University
- **Small-town** 42-acre campus
- **Coed,** 730 undergraduate students, 76% full-time, 42% women, 58% men

Undergraduates 556 full-time, 174 part-time. 3% are from out of state, 4% African American, 4% Asian American or Pacific Islander, 8% Hispanic American, 0.3% Native American, 0.5% international, 5% transferred in. *Retention:* 72% of 2003 full-time freshmen returned.

Freshmen *Admission:* 982 applied, 769 admitted, 202 enrolled. *Average high school GPA:* 2.93. *Test scores:* SAT verbal scores over 500: 47%; SAT math scores over 500: 58%; SAT verbal scores over 600: 15%; SAT math scores over 600: 22%; SAT verbal scores over 700: 2%; SAT math scores over 700: 3%.

Faculty *Total:* 70, 40% full-time, 41% with terminal degrees. *Student/faculty ratio:* 15:1.

Majors Accounting; acting; actuarial science; adult and continuing education administration; advertising; aerospace, aeronautical and astronautical engineering; African-American/Black studies; agribusiness; agricultural and extension education; agricultural/biological engineering and bioengineering; agricultural business and management related; agricultural mechanization; agriculture; American studies; animal sciences; animal sciences related; anthropology; applied economics; archeology; architectural engineering; art; art history, criticism and conservation; art teacher education; Asian studies (East); astronomy; atmospheric sciences and meteorology; biochemistry; biological and biomedical sciences related; biological and physical sciences; biology/biological sciences; biology/biotechnology laboratory technician; biomedical/medical engineering; business/commerce; business/managerial economics; chemical engineering; chemistry; civil engineering; classics and languages, literatures and linguistics; communication and journalism related; communication disorders; communication/speech communication and rhetoric; comparative literature; computer and information sciences; computer engineering; criminal justice/law enforcement administration; economics; electrical, electronics and communications engineering; elementary education; engineering science; English; environmental/environmental health engineering; film/cinema studies; finance; food science; foreign languages and literatures; forestry technology; forest sciences and biology; French; geography; geological and earth sciences/geosciences related; geology/earth science; German; graphic design; health/health care administration; history; horticultural science; hospitality administration related; human development and family studies; human nutrition; industrial engineering; information science/studies; international business/trade/commerce; international relations and affairs; Italian; Japanese; Jewish/Judaic studies; journalism; kinesiology and exercise science; labor and industrial relations; landscape architecture; landscaping and groundskeeping; Latin American studies; liberal arts and sciences/liberal studies; logistics and materials management; management information systems; management sciences and quantitative methods related; marketing/marketing management; materials science; mathematics; mechanical engineering; medical microbiology and bacteriology; medieval and Renaissance studies; mining and mineral engineering; natural resources and conservation related; natural resources/conservation; nuclear engineering; nursing (registered nurse training); organizational behavior; parks, recreation and leisure facilities management; petroleum engineering; philosophy; physics; political science and government; pre-medical studies; psychology; rehabilitation and therapeutic professions related; religious studies; Russian; secondary education; sociology; soil science and agronomy; Spanish; special education; statistics; technical and business writing; theater design and technology; turf and turfgrass management; visual and performing arts; women's studies.

Academics *Calendar:* semesters. *Degrees:* associate and bachelor's. *Special study options:* academic remediation for entering students, accelerated degree program, adult/continuing education programs, advanced placement credit, cooperative education, distance learning, honors programs, independent study, internships, services for LD students, study abroad, summer session for credit.

Library 36,641 titles, 152 serial subscriptions.

Student Life *Housing:* college housing not available. *Activities and Organizations:* drama/theater group.

Athletics Member NJCAA. *Intercollegiate sports:* baseball M, basketball M/W, bowling M(c)/W(c), cheerleading M/W, cross-country running M/W, football M(c), golf M(c)/W(c), ice hockey M(c)/W(c), skiing (downhill) M(c)/W(c), soccer M(c)/W, tennis M/W, volleyball M(c)/W. *Intramural sports:* badminton M/W, basketball M/W, football M/W, golf M/W, soccer M/W, volleyball M/W.

Standardized Tests *Required:* SAT or ACT (for admission).

Costs (2006–07) *Tuition:* state resident $10,008 full-time, $405 per credit hour part-time; nonresident $15,284 full-time, $637 per credit hour part-time. *Required fees:* $512 full-time.

Financial Aid Of all full-time matriculated undergraduates who enrolled in 2003, 391 applied for aid, 301 were judged to have need, 21 had their need fully met. 23 Federal Work-Study jobs (averaging $1015). In 2003, 29 non-need-based

Penn State Lehigh Valley (continued)

awards were made. *Average percent of need met:* 67%. *Average financial aid package:* $9068. *Average need-based loan:* $3196. *Average need-based gift aid:* $4017. *Average non-need-based aid:* $1379. *Average indebtedness upon graduation:* $18,600.

Applying *Options:* electronic application, early admission, deferred entrance. *Application fee:* $50. *Required:* high school transcript. *Application deadlines:* rolling (freshmen), rolling (transfers). *Notification:* continuous (freshmen), continuous (transfers).

Director of Admissions Mr. Randall C. Deike, Assistant Vice President for Enrollment Management, Penn State Lehigh Valley, 8380 Mohr Lane, Academic Building, Fogelsville, PA 18051-9999. *Phone:* 814-865-5471.

PENN STATE MCKEESPORT

McKeesport, Pennsylvania   **www.mk.psu.edu/**

- **State-related** primarily 2-year, founded 1947, part of Pennsylvania State University
- **Small-town** 40-acre campus with easy access to Pittsburgh
- **Endowment** $1.2 billion
- **Coed,** 761 undergraduate students, 85% full-time, 43% women, 57% men

Undergraduates 645 full-time, 116 part-time. 6% are from out of state, 17% African American, 2% Asian American or Pacific Islander, 2% Hispanic American, 0.2% Native American, 0.5% international, 4% transferred in, 14% live on campus. *Retention:* 81% of 2003 full-time freshmen returned.

Freshmen *Admission:* 540 applied, 454 admitted, 230 enrolled. *Average high school GPA:* 2.82. *Test scores:* SAT verbal scores over 500: 38%; SAT math scores over 500: 37%; SAT verbal scores over 600: 8%; SAT math scores over 600: 11%; SAT math scores over 700: 1%.

Faculty *Total:* 72, 53% full-time, 47% with terminal degrees. *Student/faculty ratio:* 14:1.

Majors Accounting; acting; actuarial science; adult and continuing education administration; advertising; aerospace, aeronautical and astronautical engineering; African-American/Black studies; agribusiness; agricultural and extension education; agricultural/biological engineering and bioengineering; agricultural business and management related; agricultural mechanization; agriculture; agronomy and crop science; animal sciences; animal sciences related; anthropology; applied economics; archeology; architectural engineering; art; art history, criticism and conservation; art teacher education; Asian studies (East); astronomy; atmospheric sciences and meteorology; biochemistry; biological and biomedical sciences related; biological and physical sciences; biology/biological sciences; biology/biotechnology laboratory technician; biomedical/medical engineering; business administration and management; business/commerce; business/managerial economics; chemical engineering; chemistry; civil engineering; classics and languages, literatures and linguistics; communication and journalism related; communication disorders; communication/speech communication and rhetoric; comparative literature; computer and information sciences; computer engineering; criminal justice/law enforcement administration; economics; electrical, electronics and communications engineering; elementary education; engineering science; English; environmental/environmental health engineering; film/cinema studies; finance; food science; foreign language teacher education; forestry technology; forest sciences and biology; French; geography; geological and earth sciences/geosciences related; geology/earth science; German; graphic design; health/health care administration; history; horticultural science; hospitality administration related; human development and family studies; human nutrition; industrial engineering; information science/studies; international relations and affairs; Italian; Japanese; Jewish/Judaic studies; journalism; kinesiology and exercise science; labor and industrial relations; landscaping and groundskeeping; Latin American studies; liberal arts and sciences/liberal studies; logistics and materials management; management information systems; manufacturing engineering; marketing/marketing management; materials science; mathematics; mechanical engineering; medical microbiology and bacteriology; medieval and Renaissance studies; mining and mineral engineering; music; natural resources and conservation related; natural resources/conservation; nuclear engineering; nursing (registered nurse training); organizational behavior; parks, recreation and leisure facilities management; petroleum engineering; philosophy; physics; political science and government; pre-medical studies; psychology; rehabilitation and therapeutic professions related; religious studies; Russian; secondary education; sociology; soil science and agronomy; Spanish; special education; statistics; theater design and technology; toxicology; turf and turfgrass management; visual and performing arts; women's studies.

Academics *Calendar:* semesters. *Degrees:* associate and bachelor's. *Special study options:* academic remediation for entering students, accelerated degree program, adult/continuing education programs, advanced placement credit, distance learning, double majors, honors programs, independent study, internships, services for LD students, study abroad, summer session for credit.

Library 40,851 titles, 300 serial subscriptions, 2,783 audiovisual materials.

Student Life *Housing Options:* coed. Campus housing is university owned. Freshman campus housing is guaranteed. *Activities and Organizations:* drama/theater group, student-run newspaper, radio station, choral group. *Campus security:* 24-hour patrols, controlled dormitory access. *Student services:* health clinic, personal/psychological counseling, women's center.

Athletics Member NJCAA. *Intercollegiate sports:* baseball M, basketball M, softball W, volleyball W. *Intramural sports:* basketball M/W, cheerleading M(c)/W(c), football M/W, ice hockey M(c), racquetball M/W, skiing (cross-country) M(c)/W(c), skiing (downhill) M(c)/W(c), soccer M(c)/W(c), softball M/W, tennis M/W, volleyball M/W.

Standardized Tests *Required:* SAT or ACT (for admission).

Costs (2006–07) *Tuition:* state resident $10,008 full-time, $405 per credit hour part-time; nonresident $15,284 full-time, $637 per credit hour part-time. *Required fees:* $512 full-time. *Room and board:* $6850; room only: $3620.

Financial Aid Of all full-time matriculated undergraduates, 61 Federal Work-Study jobs (averaging $1321). 4 state and other part-time jobs (averaging $5929).

Applying *Options:* electronic application, early admission, deferred entrance. *Application fee:* $50. *Required:* high school transcript. *Required for some:* letters of recommendation, interview. *Recommended:* essay or personal statement. *Application deadlines:* rolling (freshmen), rolling (transfers). *Notification:* continuous (freshmen), continuous (transfers).

Director of Admissions Mr. Randall C. Deike, Assistant Vice President for Enrollment Management, Penn State McKeesport, 101 Frable Building, 4000 University Drive, McKeesport, PA 15132-7698. *Phone:* 814-865-5471. *E-mail:* admissions@psu.edu.

PENN STATE MONT ALTO

Mont Alto, Pennsylvania   **www.ma.psu.edu/**

- **State-related** primarily 2-year, founded 1929, part of Pennsylvania State University
- **Small-town** 64-acre campus
- **Endowment** $1.2 billion
- **Coed,** 1,032 undergraduate students, 75% full-time, 59% women, 41% men

Undergraduates 778 full-time, 254 part-time. 12% are from out of state, 14% African American, 3% Asian American or Pacific Islander, 3% Hispanic American, 0.1% Native American, 0.2% international, 5% transferred in, 44% live on campus. *Retention:* 74% of 2003 full-time freshmen returned.

Freshmen *Admission:* 827 applied, 713 admitted, 400 enrolled. *Average high school GPA:* 2.86. *Test scores:* SAT verbal scores over 500: 42%; SAT math scores over 500: 41%; SAT verbal scores over 600: 9%; SAT math scores over 600: 10%; SAT verbal scores over 700: 1%; SAT math scores over 700: 1%.

Faculty *Total:* 95, 56% full-time, 33% with terminal degrees. *Student/faculty ratio:* 13:1.

Majors Accounting; acting; actuarial science; adult and continuing education administration; advertising; aerospace, aeronautical and astronautical engineering; African-American/Black studies; agribusiness; agricultural and extension education; agricultural/biological engineering and bioengineering; agricultural business and management related; agricultural mechanization; agriculture; agronomy and crop science; animal sciences; animal sciences related; anthropology; applied economics; archeology; architectural engineering; art; art history, criticism and conservation; art teacher education; Asian studies (East); astronomy; atmospheric sciences and meteorology; biochemistry; biological and biomedical sciences related; biological and physical sciences; biology/biological sciences; biology/biotechnology laboratory technician; biomedical/medical engineering; business administration and management; business/commerce; business/managerial economics; chemical engineering; chemistry; civil engineering; classics and languages, literatures and linguistics; communication and journalism related; communication disorders; communication/speech communication and rhetoric; comparative literature; computer and information sciences; computer engineering; criminal justice/law enforcement administration; economics; electrical, electronics and communications engineering; elementary education; engineering science; English; environmental/environmental health engineering; film/cinema studies; finance; food science; foreign language teacher education; forestry technology; forest sciences and biology; French; geography; geological and earth sciences/geosciences related; geology/earth science; German; graphic design; health/health care administration; history; horticultural science; hospitality administration related; human development and family studies; human nutrition; industrial engineering; information science/studies; international relations and affairs; Italian; Japanese; Jewish/Judaic studies; journalism; kinesiology and exercise science; labor and industrial relations; landscaping and groundskeeping; Latin American studies; liberal arts and sciences/liberal studies; management information systems; marketing/marketing management; materials science; mathematics; mechanical engineering; medical microbiology and bacteriology; medieval and Renaissance studies; mining and mineral engineering; music; natural resources and conservation related; natural resources/conservation; nuclear engineering; nursing (registered nurse training); occupational therapist

assistant; occupational therapy; organizational behavior; parks, recreation and leisure facilities management; petroleum engineering; philosophy; physical therapist assistant; physics; political science and government; pre-medical studies; psychology; rehabilitation and therapeutic professions related; religious studies; Russian; secondary education; sociology; soil science and agronomy; Spanish; special education; statistics; theater design and technology; toxicology; turf and turfgrass management; visual and performing arts; women's studies.

Academics *Calendar:* semesters. *Degrees:* associate and bachelor's. *Special study options:* academic remediation for entering students, accelerated degree program, adult/continuing education programs, advanced placement credit, distance learning, double majors, honors programs, independent study, internships, services for LD students, study abroad, summer session for credit. *ROTC:* Army (c).

Library 38,962 titles, 273 serial subscriptions.

Student Life *Housing Options:* coed, disabled students. Campus housing is university owned. Freshman campus housing is guaranteed. *Activities and Organizations:* drama/theater group, student-run newspaper, radio station. *Campus security:* 24-hour patrols, controlled dormitory access. *Student services:* health clinic, women's center.

Athletics Member NJCAA. *Intercollegiate sports:* basketball M/W, cheerleading M/W, cross-country running M/W, golf M/W, soccer M/W, softball W, tennis M/W, volleyball W. *Intramural sports:* badminton M/W, basketball M/W, cheerleading M(c)/W(c), racquetball M/W, soccer M/W, softball W, volleyball M/W.

Standardized Tests *Required:* SAT or ACT (for admission).

Costs (2006–07) *Tuition:* state resident $10,008 full-time, $405 per credit hour part-time; nonresident $15,284 full-time, $637 per credit hour part-time. *Required fees:* $512 full-time. *Room and board:* $6850; room only: $3620.

Financial Aid Of all full-time matriculated undergraduates, 49 Federal Work-Study jobs (averaging $1165). 9 state and other part-time jobs (averaging $6156).

Applying *Options:* electronic application, early admission, deferred entrance. *Application fee:* $50. *Required:* high school transcript. *Required for some:* letters of recommendation, interview. *Recommended:* essay or personal statement. *Application deadlines:* rolling (freshmen), rolling (transfers). *Notification:* continuous (freshmen), continuous (transfers).

Director of Admissions Mr. Randall C. Deike, Assistant Vice President for Enrollment Management, Penn State Mont Alto, 1 Campus Drive, Mont Alto, PA 17237-9703. *Phone:* 814-865-5471. *Toll-free phone:* 800-392-6173. *E-mail:* admissions@psu.edu.

PENN STATE NEW KENSINGTON

New Kensington, Pennsylvania   www.nk.psu.edu/

- **State-related** primarily 2-year, founded 1958, part of Pennsylvania State University
- **Small-town** 71-acre campus with easy access to Pittsburgh
- **Endowment** $1.2 billion
- **Coed,** 840 undergraduate students, 74% full-time, 46% women, 54% men

Undergraduates 618 full-time, 222 part-time. 2% are from out of state, 3% African American, 0.6% Asian American or Pacific Islander, 1% Hispanic American, 0.3% Native American, 5% transferred in. *Retention:* 69% of 2003 full-time freshmen returned.

Freshmen *Admission:* 475 applied, 393 admitted, 204 enrolled. *Average high school GPA:* 2.97. *Test scores:* SAT verbal scores over 500: 43%; SAT math scores over 500: 50%; SAT verbal scores over 600: 9%; SAT math scores over 600: 12%; SAT verbal scores over 700: 1%; SAT math scores over 700: 1%.

Faculty *Total:* 84, 49% full-time, 42% with terminal degrees. *Student/faculty ratio:* 13:1.

Majors Accounting; acting; actuarial science; adult and continuing education administration; advertising; aerospace, aeronautical and astronautical engineering; African-American/Black studies; agribusiness; agricultural and extension education; agricultural/biological engineering and bioengineering; agricultural business and management related; agricultural mechanization; agriculture; agronomy and crop science; animal sciences; animal sciences related; anthropology; applied economics; archeology; architectural engineering; art; art history, criticism and conservation; art teacher education; Asian studies (East); astronomy; atmospheric sciences and meteorology; biochemistry; biological and biomedical sciences related; biological and physical sciences; biology/biological sciences; biology/biotechnology laboratory technician; biomedical/medical engineering; biomedical technology; business administration and management; business/commerce; business/managerial economics; chemical engineering; chemistry; civil engineering; classics and languages, literatures and linguistics; communication and journalism related; communication disorders; communication/speech communication and rhetoric; comparative literature; computer and information sciences; computer engineering; computer engineering technology; criminal justice/law enforcement administration; economics; electrical, electronic and communications engineering technology; electrical, electronics and communi-

cations engineering; elementary education; engineering science; English; environmental/environmental health engineering; film/cinema studies; finance; food science; foreign language teacher education; forestry technology; forest sciences and biology; French; geography; geological and earth sciences/geosciences related; geology/earth science; German; graphic design; health/health care administration; history; horticultural science; hospitality administration related; human development and family studies; human nutrition; industrial engineering; information science/studies; international relations and affairs; Italian; Japanese; Jewish/Judaic studies; journalism; kinesiology and exercise science; labor and industrial relations; landscaping and groundskeeping; Latin American studies; liberal arts and sciences/liberal studies; logistics and materials management; management information systems; marketing/marketing management; materials science; mathematics; mechanical engineering; mechanical engineering/mechanical technology; medical microbiology and bacteriology; medical radiologic technology; medieval and Renaissance studies; metallurgical technology; mining and mineral engineering; music; natural resources and conservation related; natural resources/conservation; nuclear engineering; nursing (registered nurse training); organizational behavior; parks, recreation and leisure facilities management; petroleum engineering; philosophy; physics; political science and government; pre-medical studies; psychology; rehabilitation and therapeutic professions related; religious studies; Russian; secondary education; sociology; soil science and agronomy; Spanish; special education; statistics; telecommunications technology; theater design and technology; toxicology; turf and turfgrass management; visual and performing arts; women's studies.

Academics *Calendar:* semesters. *Degrees:* associate and bachelor's. *Special study options:* academic remediation for entering students, adult/continuing education programs, advanced placement credit, distance learning, double majors, external degree program, honors programs, independent study, internships, services for LD students, study abroad, summer session for credit.

Library 28,897 titles, 404 serial subscriptions, 4,294 audiovisual materials.

Student Life *Housing:* college housing not available. *Activities and Organizations:* drama/theater group, student-run newspaper, choral group, marching band. *Campus security:* part-time trained security personnel. *Student services:* health clinic, women's center.

Athletics Member NJCAA. *Intercollegiate sports:* baseball M, basketball M/W, cheerleading M/W, golf M/W, softball W, volleyball W. *Intramural sports:* badminton M/W, basketball M/W, bowling M/W, cheerleading M(c)/W(c), football M/W, ice hockey M(c)/W(c), racquetball M/W, skiing (downhill) M(c)/W(c), soccer M/W, softball W, volleyball M/W.

Standardized Tests *Required:* SAT or ACT (for admission).

Costs (2006–07) *Tuition:* state resident $10,008 full-time, $405 per credit hour part-time; nonresident $15,284 full-time, $637 per credit hour part-time. *Required fees:* $512 full-time.

Financial Aid Of all full-time matriculated undergraduates, 40 Federal Work-Study jobs (averaging $1319). 1 state and other part-time job (averaging $1696).

Applying *Options:* electronic application, early admission, deferred entrance. *Application fee:* $50. *Required:* high school transcript. *Required for some:* letters of recommendation, interview. *Recommended:* essay or personal statement. *Application deadlines:* rolling (freshmen), rolling (transfers). *Notification:* continuous (freshmen), continuous (transfers).

Director of Admissions Mr. Randall C. Deike, Assistant Vice President for Enrollment Management, Penn State New Kensington, 3550 7th Street Road, Route 780, New Kensington, PA 15068-1765. *Phone:* 814-865-5471. *Toll-free phone:* 888-968-7297. *E-mail:* admissions@psu.edu.

PENN STATE SCHUYLKILL

Schuylkill Haven, Pennsylvania   www.sl.psu.edu/

- **State-related** primarily 2-year, founded 1934, part of Pennsylvania State University
- **Small-town** 42-acre campus
- **Coed,** 899 undergraduate students, 84% full-time, 55% women, 45% men

Undergraduates 751 full-time, 148 part-time. 12% are from out of state, 30% African American, 2% Asian American or Pacific Islander, 3% Hispanic American, 0.1% Native American, 0.1% international, 3% transferred in, 28% live on campus. *Retention:* 80% of 2003 full-time freshmen returned.

Freshmen *Admission:* 878 applied, 670 admitted, 298 enrolled. *Average high school GPA:* 2.69. *Test scores:* SAT verbal scores over 500: 29%; SAT math scores over 500: 29%; SAT verbal scores over 600: 4%; SAT math scores over 600: 7%.

Faculty *Total:* 62, 66% full-time, 56% with terminal degrees. *Student/faculty ratio:* 17:1.

Majors Accounting; acting; actuarial science; adult and continuing education administration; advertising; aerospace, aeronautical and astronautical engineering; African-American/Black studies; agribusiness; agricultural and extension education; agricultural/biological engineering and bioengineering; agricultural

Penn State Schuylkill (continued)

business and management related; agricultural mechanization; agriculture; American studies; animal sciences; animal sciences related; anthropology; applied economics; archeology; architectural engineering; art; art history, criticism and conservation; art teacher education; Asian studies (East); astronomy; atmospheric sciences and meteorology; biochemistry; biological and biomedical sciences related; biological and physical sciences; biology/biological sciences; biology/biotechnology laboratory technician; biomedical/medical engineering; biomedical technology; business/commerce; business/managerial economics; chemical engineering; chemistry; civil engineering; classics and languages, literatures and linguistics; clinical/medical laboratory technology; communication and journalism related; communication disorders; communication/speech communication and rhetoric; comparative literature; computer and information sciences; computer engineering; criminal justice/law enforcement administration; criminal justice/safety; economics; electrical, electronic and communications engineering technology; electrical, electronics and communications engineering; elementary education; engineering science; English; environmental/environmental health engineering; film/cinema studies; finance; food science; forestry technology; forest sciences and biology; French; geography; geological and earth sciences/geosciences related; geology/earth science; German; graphic design; health/health care administration; history; horticultural science; hospitality administration related; human development and family studies; human nutrition; industrial engineering; information science/studies; international business/trade/commerce; international relations and affairs; Italian; Japanese; Jewish/Judaic studies; journalism; kinesiology and exercise science; labor and industrial relations; landscape architecture; landscaping and groundskeeping; Latin American studies; liberal arts and sciences/liberal studies; logistics and materials management; management information systems; management sciences and quantitative methods related; marketing/marketing management; materials science; mathematics; mechanical engineering; medical microbiology and bacteriology; medical radiologic technology; medieval and Renaissance studies; metallurgical technology; mining and mineral engineering; natural resources and conservation related; natural resources/conservation; nuclear engineering; nursing (registered nurse training); organizational behavior; parks, recreation and leisure facilities management; petroleum engineering; philosophy; physics; political science and government; pre-medical studies; psychology; rehabilitation and therapeutic professions related; religious studies; Russian; secondary education; sociology; soil science and agronomy; Spanish; special education; statistics; telecommunications technology; theater design and technology; turf and turfgrass management; visual and performing arts; women's studies.

Academics *Calendar:* semesters. *Degrees:* associate and bachelor's (bachelor's degree programs completed at the Harrisburg campus). *Special study options:* academic remediation for entering students, accelerated degree program, adult/continuing education programs, advanced placement credit, cooperative education, distance learning, double majors, honors programs, independent study, internships, services for LD students, student-designed majors, study abroad, summer session for credit.

Library 39,289 titles, 518 serial subscriptions, 930 audiovisual materials.

Student Life *Housing Options:* Campus housing is provided by a third party. Freshman campus housing is guaranteed. *Activities and Organizations:* drama/theater group, student-run newspaper, choral group. *Campus security:* 24-hour patrols, controlled dormitory access.

Athletics Member NJCAA. *Intercollegiate sports:* basketball M, cross-country running M/W, golf M, soccer M, softball W, volleyball W. *Intramural sports:* basketball M/W, football M, soccer M/W, softball M/W, table tennis M/W, volleyball M/W.

Standardized Tests *Required:* SAT or ACT (for admission).

Costs (2006–07) *Tuition:* state resident $10,008 full-time, $405 per credit hour part-time; nonresident $15,284 full-time, $637 per credit hour part-time. *Required fees:* $492 full-time. *Room and board:* room only: $4336.

Financial Aid Of all full-time matriculated undergraduates who enrolled in 2003, 665 applied for aid, 563 were judged to have need, 39 had their need fully met. 86 Federal Work-Study jobs (averaging $1326). 7 state and other part-time jobs (averaging $3450). In 2003, 29 non-need-based awards were made. *Average percent of need met:* 68%. *Average financial aid package:* $11,204. *Average need-based loan:* $3285. *Average need-based gift aid:* $4384. *Average non-need-based aid:* $2087. *Average indebtedness upon graduation:* $18,600.

Applying *Options:* electronic application, early admission, deferred entrance. *Application fee:* $50. *Required:* high school transcript. *Application deadlines:* rolling (freshmen), rolling (transfers). *Notification:* continuous (freshmen), continuous (transfers).

Director of Admissions Mr. Randall C. Deike, Assistant Vice President for Enrollment Management, Penn State Schuylkill, 200 University Drive, A102 Administration Building, Schuylkill Haven, PA 17972-2208. *Phone:* 814-865-5471. *E-mail:* admissions@psu.edu.

PENN STATE SHENANGO
Sharon, Pennsylvania　　　　**www.shenango.psu.edu/**

- **State-related** primarily 2-year, founded 1965, part of Pennsylvania State University
- **Small-town** 14-acre campus
- **Endowment** $1.2 billion
- **Coed,** 893 undergraduate students, 55% full-time, 67% women, 33% men

Undergraduates 490 full-time, 403 part-time. 11% are from out of state, 9% African American, 0.2% Asian American or Pacific Islander, 0.9% Hispanic American, 0.3% Native American, 4% transferred in. *Retention:* 71% of 2003 full-time freshmen returned.

Freshmen *Admission:* 258 applied, 216 admitted, 134 enrolled. *Average high school GPA:* 2.86. *Test scores:* SAT verbal scores over 500: 25%; SAT math scores over 500: 24%; SAT verbal scores over 600: 2%; SAT math scores over 600: 5%.

Faculty *Total:* 73, 40% full-time, 32% with terminal degrees. *Student/faculty ratio:* 14:1.

Majors Accounting; acting; actuarial science; adult and continuing education administration; advertising; aerospace, aeronautical and astronautical engineering; African-American/Black studies; agribusiness; agricultural and extension education; agricultural/biological engineering and bioengineering; agricultural business and management related; agricultural mechanization; agriculture; agronomy and crop science; animal sciences; animal sciences related; anthropology; applied economics; archeology; architectural engineering; art; art history, criticism and conservation; art teacher education; Asian studies (East); astronomy; atmospheric sciences and meteorology; biochemistry; biological and biomedical sciences related; biological and physical sciences; biology/biological sciences; biology/biotechnology laboratory technician; biomedical/medical engineering; biomedical technology; business administration and management; business/commerce; business/managerial economics; chemical engineering; chemistry; civil engineering; classics and languages, literatures and linguistics; communication and journalism related; communication disorders; communication/speech communication and rhetoric; comparative literature; computer and information sciences; computer engineering; criminal justice/law enforcement administration; economics; electrical, electronic and communications engineering technology; electrical, electronics and communications engineering; elementary education; engineering science; English; environmental/environmental health engineering; film/cinema studies; finance; food science; foreign language teacher education; forestry technology; forest sciences and biology; French; geography; geological and earth sciences/geosciences related; geology/earth science; German; graphic design; health/health care administration; history; horticultural science; hospitality administration related; human development and family studies; human nutrition; industrial engineering; information science/studies; international relations and affairs; Italian; Japanese; Jewish/Judaic studies; journalism; kinesiology and exercise science; labor and industrial relations; landscaping and groundskeeping; Latin American studies; liberal arts and sciences/liberal studies; logistics and materials management; management information systems; marketing/marketing management; materials science; mathematics; mechanical engineering; mechanical engineering/mechanical technology; medical microbiology and bacteriology; medieval and Renaissance studies; metallurgical technology; mining and mineral engineering; music; natural resources and conservation related; natural resources/conservation; nuclear engineering; nursing (registered nurse training); organizational behavior; parks, recreation and leisure facilities management; petroleum engineering; philosophy; physical therapist assistant; physics; political science and government; pre-medical studies; psychology; rehabilitation and therapeutic professions related; religious studies; Russian; secondary education; sociology; soil science and agronomy; Spanish; special education; statistics; telecommunications technology; theater design and technology; toxicology; turf and turfgrass management; visual and performing arts; women's studies.

Academics *Calendar:* semesters. *Degrees:* associate and bachelor's. *Special study options:* academic remediation for entering students, accelerated degree program, adult/continuing education programs, advanced placement credit, distance learning, double majors, honors programs, independent study, internships, services for LD students, student-designed majors, study abroad, summer session for credit.

Library 25,273 titles, 346 serial subscriptions.

Student Life *Housing:* college housing not available. *Activities and Organizations:* drama/theater group. *Campus security:* part-time trained security personnel. *Student services:* health clinic, women's center.

Athletics *Intramural sports:* basketball M(c)/W, bowling M/W, football M(c), golf M/W, softball M/W, tennis M/W, volleyball M/W.

Standardized Tests *Required:* SAT or ACT (for admission).

Costs (2006–07) *Tuition:* state resident $10,008 full-time, $405 per credit hour part-time; nonresident $15,284 full-time, $637 per credit hour part-time. *Required fees:* $512 full-time.

Financial Aid Of all full-time matriculated undergraduates, 39 Federal Work-Study jobs (averaging $1790).

Applying *Options:* electronic application, early admission, deferred entrance. *Application fee:* $50. *Required:* high school transcript. *Required for some:* letters of recommendation, interview. *Recommended:* essay or personal statement. *Application deadlines:* rolling (freshmen), rolling (transfers). *Notification:* continuous (freshmen), continuous (transfers).

Director of Admissions Mr. Randall C. Deike, Assistant Vice President for Enrollment Management, Penn State Shenango, 147 Shenango Avenue, Sharon, PA 16146-1597. *Phone:* 814-865-5471. *E-mail:* admissions@psu.edu.

PENN STATE WILKES-BARRE

Lehman, Pennsylvania   www.wb.psu.edu/

- **State-related** primarily 2-year, founded 1916, part of Pennsylvania State University
- **Rural** 156-acre campus
- **Endowment** $1.2 billion
- **Coed,** 698 undergraduate students, 83% full-time, 34% women, 66% men

Undergraduates 576 full-time, 122 part-time. 4% are from out of state, 2% African American, 1% Asian American or Pacific Islander, 2% Hispanic American, 0.2% Native American, 6% transferred in. *Retention:* 75% of 2003 full-time freshmen returned.

Freshmen *Admission:* 540 applied, 451 admitted, 186 enrolled. *Average high school GPA:* 3.01. *Test scores:* SAT verbal scores over 500: 46%; SAT math scores over 500: 49%; SAT verbal scores over 600: 10%; SAT math scores over 600: 11%.

Faculty *Total:* 59, 59% full-time, 46% with terminal degrees. *Student/faculty ratio:* 15:1.

Majors Accounting; acting; actuarial science; adult and continuing education administration; advertising; aerospace, aeronautical and astronautical engineering; African-American/Black studies; agribusiness; agricultural and extension education; agricultural/biological engineering and bioengineering; agricultural business and management related; agricultural mechanization; agriculture; agronomy and crop science; animal sciences; animal sciences related; anthropology; applied economics; archeology; architectural engineering; art; art history, criticism and conservation; art teacher education; astronomy; atmospheric sciences and meteorology; biochemistry; biological and biomedical sciences related; biological and physical sciences; biology/biological sciences; biology/biotechnology laboratory technician; biomedical/medical engineering; business administration and management; business/commerce; business/managerial economics; chemical engineering; chemistry; civil engineering; classics and languages, literatures and linguistics; communication and journalism related; communication disorders; communication/speech communication and rhetoric; comparative literature; computer and information sciences; computer engineering; criminal justice/law enforcement administration; criminal justice/safety; economics; electrical, electronic and communications engineering technology; electrical, electronics and communications engineering; elementary education; engineering science; English; environmental/environmental health engineering; film/cinema studies; finance; food science; forestry technology; forest sciences and biology; French; geography; geological and earth sciences/geosciences related; geology/earth science; German; graphic design; health/health care administration; history; horticultural science; hospitality administration related; human development and family studies; human nutrition; industrial engineering; information science/studies; international relations and affairs; Italian; Japanese; Jewish/Judaic studies; journalism; kinesiology and exercise science; labor and industrial relations; landscape architecture; landscaping and groundskeeping; Latin American studies; liberal arts and sciences/liberal studies; management information systems; manufacturing engineering; marketing/marketing management; materials science; mathematics; mechanical engineering; medical microbiology and bacteriology; medieval and Renaissance studies; metallurgical technology; mining and mineral engineering; music; natural resources and conservation related; natural resources/conservation; nuclear engineering; nursing (registered nurse training); organizational behavior; parks, recreation and leisure facilities management; petroleum engineering; philosophy; physics; political science and government; pre-medical studies; psychology; rehabilitation and therapeutic professions related; religious studies; Russian; secondary education; sociology; soil science and agronomy; Spanish; special education; statistics; survey technology; telecommunications technology; theater design and technology; toxicology; turf and turfgrass management; visual and performing arts; women's studies.

Academics *Calendar:* semesters. *Degrees:* associate, bachelor's, and post-bachelor's certificates. *Special study options:* academic remediation for entering students, accelerated degree program, adult/continuing education programs, advanced placement credit, distance learning, double majors, honors programs, independent study, internships, services for LD students, student-designed majors, study abroad, summer session for credit. *ROTC:* Air Force (c).

Library 35,697 titles, 199 serial subscriptions.

Student Life *Housing:* college housing not available. *Activities and Organizations:* student-run newspaper, radio station. *Campus security:* part-time trained security personnel. *Student services:* health clinic, personal/psychological counseling.

Athletics Member NJCAA. *Intercollegiate sports:* baseball M, basketball M, cross-country running M/W, golf M/W, soccer M/W, volleyball W. *Intramural sports:* basketball M/W, bowling M(c)/W(c), cheerleading M(c)/W(c), football M, racquetball M/W, softball W, volleyball M(c)/W.

Standardized Tests *Required:* SAT or ACT (for admission).

Costs (2006–07) *Tuition:* state resident $10,008 full-time, $405 per credit hour part-time; nonresident $15,284 full-time, $637 per credit hour part-time. *Required fees:* $512 full-time.

Financial Aid Of all full-time matriculated undergraduates, 30 Federal Work-Study jobs (averaging $1172).

Applying *Options:* electronic application, early admission, deferred entrance. *Application fee:* $50. *Required:* high school transcript. *Required for some:* letters of recommendation, interview. *Recommended:* essay or personal statement. *Application deadlines:* rolling (freshmen), rolling (transfers). *Notification:* continuous (freshmen), continuous (transfers).

Director of Admissions Mr. Randall C. Deike, Assistant Vice President for Enrollment Management, Penn State Wilkes-Barre, PO Box PSU, Old Route 115, Lehman, PA 18627-9999. *Phone:* 814-865-5471. *Toll-free phone:* 800-966-6613. *E-mail:* admissions@psu.edu.

PENN STATE WORTHINGTON SCRANTON

Dunmore, Pennsylvania   www.sn.psu.edu/

- **State-related** primarily 2-year, founded 1923, part of Pennsylvania State University
- **Small-town** 43-acre campus
- **Endowment** $1.2 billion
- **Coed,** 1,291 undergraduate students, 81% full-time, 51% women, 49% men

Undergraduates 1,042 full-time, 249 part-time. 1% are from out of state, 1% African American, 2% Asian American or Pacific Islander, 2% Hispanic American, 0.1% Native American, 0.3% international, 5% transferred in. *Retention:* 76% of 2003 full-time freshmen returned.

Freshmen *Admission:* 785 applied, 663 admitted, 319 enrolled. *Average high school GPA:* 2.85. *Test scores:* SAT verbal scores over 500: 38%; SAT math scores over 500: 40%; SAT verbal scores over 600: 5%; SAT math scores over 600: 9%; SAT math scores over 700: 1%.

Faculty *Total:* 105, 50% full-time, 36% with terminal degrees. *Student/faculty ratio:* 16:1.

Majors Accounting; acting; actuarial science; adult and continuing education administration; advertising; aerospace, aeronautical and astronautical engineering; African-American/Black studies; agribusiness; agricultural and extension education; agricultural/biological engineering and bioengineering; agricultural business and management related; agricultural mechanization; agriculture; agronomy and crop science; American studies; animal sciences; animal sciences related; anthropology; applied economics; archeology; architectural engineering; architectural engineering technology; art; art history, criticism and conservation; art teacher education; Asian studies (East); astronomy; atmospheric sciences and meteorology; biochemistry; biological and biomedical sciences related; biological and physical sciences; biology/biological sciences; biology/biotechnology laboratory technician; biomedical/medical engineering; business administration and management; business/commerce; business/managerial economics; chemical engineering; chemistry; civil engineering; classics and languages, literatures and linguistics; communication and journalism related; communication disorders; communication/speech communication and rhetoric; comparative literature; computer and information sciences; computer engineering; criminal justice/law enforcement administration; economics; electrical, electronic and communications engineering technology; electrical, electronics and communications engineering; elementary education; engineering science; English; environmental/environmental health engineering; film/cinema studies; finance; food science; foreign language teacher education; forestry technology; forest sciences and biology; French; geography; geological and earth sciences/geosciences related; geology/earth science; German; graphic design; health/health care administration; history; horticultural science; hospitality administration related; human development and family studies; human nutrition; industrial engineering; information science/studies; international relations and affairs; Italian; Japanese; Jewish/Judaic studies; journalism; kinesiology and exercise science; labor and industrial relations; landscaping and groundskeeping; Latin American studies; liberal arts and sciences/liberal studies; management information systems; marketing/marketing management; materials science; mathematics; mechanical engineering; medical microbiology and bacteriology; medieval and Renaissance studies; mining and mineral engineering; music; natural resources and conservation related; natural resources/conservation; nuclear engineering; nursing (registered nurse training); organizational behavior; parks, recreation

Penn State Worthington Scranton (continued)

and leisure facilities management; petroleum engineering; philosophy; physics; political science and government; pre-medical studies; psychology; rehabilitation and therapeutic professions related; religious studies; Russian; secondary education; sociology; soil science and agronomy; Spanish; special education; statistics; theater design and technology; turf and turfgrass management; visual and performing arts; women's studies.

Academics *Calendar:* semesters. *Degrees:* associate and bachelor's. *Special study options:* academic remediation for entering students, accelerated degree program, adult/continuing education programs, advanced placement credit, cooperative education, distance learning, double majors, honors programs, independent study, internships, services for LD students, study abroad, summer session for credit. *ROTC:* Air Force (c).

Library 53,572 titles, 102 serial subscriptions.

Student Life *Housing:* college housing not available. *Activities and Organizations:* drama/theater group, student-run newspaper, choral group. *Campus security:* part-time trained security personnel. *Student services:* health clinic, personal/psychological counseling, women's center.

Athletics Member NJCAA. *Intercollegiate sports:* baseball M, basketball M/W, cheerleading M/W, cross-country running M/W, soccer M, softball W, volleyball W. *Intramural sports:* basketball M/W, bowling M(c)/W(c), skiing (downhill) M(c)/W(c), soccer M/W, softball M/W, volleyball M/W(c), weight lifting M(c)/W(c).

Standardized Tests *Required:* SAT or ACT (for admission).

Costs (2006–07) *Tuition:* state resident $10,008 full-time, $405 per credit hour part-time; nonresident $15,284 full-time, $637 per credit hour part-time. *Required fees:* $492 full-time.

Financial Aid Of all full-time matriculated undergraduates, 28 Federal Work-Study jobs (averaging $1120).

Applying *Options:* electronic application, early admission, deferred entrance. *Application fee:* $50. *Required:* high school transcript. *Required for some:* letters of recommendation, interview. *Recommended:* essay or personal statement. *Application deadlines:* rolling (freshmen), rolling (transfers). *Notification:* continuous (freshmen), continuous (transfers).

Director of Admissions Mr. Randall C. Deike, Assistant Vice President for Enrollment Management, Penn State Worthington Scranton, 120 Ridge View Drive, Dunmore, PA 18512-1699. *Phone:* 814-865-5471. *E-mail:* admissions@psu.edu.

PENN STATE YORK

York, Pennsylvania
www.yk.psu.edu/

- **State-related** primarily 2-year, founded 1926, part of Pennsylvania State University
- **Suburban** 53-acre campus
- **Endowment** $1.2 billion
- **Coed,** 1,437 undergraduate students, 57% full-time, 45% women, 55% men

Undergraduates 812 full-time, 625 part-time. 2% are from out of state, 5% African American, 6% Asian American or Pacific Islander, 4% Hispanic American, 0.3% Native American, 0.4% international, 3% transferred in. *Retention:* 71% of 2003 full-time freshmen returned.

Freshmen *Admission:* 1,039 applied, 836 admitted, 299 enrolled. *Average high school GPA:* 2.79. *Test scores:* SAT verbal scores over 500: 39%; SAT math scores over 500: 44%; SAT verbal scores over 600: 9%; SAT math scores over 600: 16%; SAT verbal scores over 700: 1%; SAT math scores over 700: 2%.

Faculty *Total:* 119, 52% full-time, 42% with terminal degrees. *Student/faculty ratio:* 14:1.

Majors Accounting; acting; actuarial science; adult and continuing education administration; advertising; aerospace, aeronautical and astronautical engineering; African-American/Black studies; agribusiness; agricultural and extension education; agricultural/biological engineering and bioengineering; agricultural business and management related; agricultural mechanization; agriculture; agronomy and crop science; American studies; animal sciences; animal sciences related; anthropology; applied economics; archeology; architectural engineering; art; art history, criticism and conservation; art teacher education; Asian studies (East); astronomy; atmospheric sciences and meteorology; biochemistry; biological and biomedical sciences related; biological and physical sciences; biology/biological sciences; biology/biotechnology laboratory technician; biomedical/medical engineering; biomedical technology; business administration and management; business/commerce; business/managerial economics; chemical engineering; chemistry; civil engineering; classics and languages, literatures and linguistics; communication and journalism related; communication disorders; communication/speech communication and rhetoric; comparative literature; computer and information sciences; computer engineering; criminal justice/law enforcement administration; economics; electrical, electronic and communications engineering technology; electrical, electronics and communications engi-

neering; elementary education; engineering science; English; environmental/environmental health engineering; film/cinema studies; finance; food science; foreign language teacher education; forestry technology; forest sciences and biology; French; geography; geological and earth sciences/geosciences related; geology/earth science; German; graphic design; health/health care administration; history; horticultural science; hospitality administration related; human development and family studies; human nutrition; industrial engineering; industrial technology; information science/studies; international relations and affairs; Italian; Japanese; Jewish/Judaic studies; journalism; kinesiology and exercise science; labor and industrial relations; landscaping and groundskeeping; Latin American studies; liberal arts and sciences/liberal studies; logistics and materials management; management information systems; manufacturing engineering; marketing/marketing management; materials science; mathematics; mechanical engineering; mechanical engineering/mechanical technology; medical microbiology and bacteriology; medieval and Renaissance studies; metallurgical technology; mining and mineral engineering; music; natural resources and conservation related; natural resources/conservation; nuclear engineering; nursing (registered nurse training); organizational behavior; parks, recreation and leisure facilities management; petroleum engineering; philosophy; physics; political science and government; pre-medical studies; psychology; rehabilitation and therapeutic professions related; religious studies; Russian; secondary education; sociology; soil science and agronomy; Spanish; special education; statistics; telecommunications technology; theater design and technology; toxicology; turf and turfgrass management; visual and performing arts; women's studies.

Academics *Calendar:* semesters. *Degrees:* associate and bachelor's (also offers up to 2 years of most bachelor's degree programs offered at University Park campus). *Special study options:* academic remediation for entering students, accelerated degree program, adult/continuing education programs, advanced placement credit, distance learning, double majors, English as a second language, honors programs, independent study, internships, services for LD students, student-designed majors, study abroad, summer session for credit.

Library 49,996 titles, 243 serial subscriptions.

Student Life *Housing:* college housing not available. *Activities and Organizations:* student-run newspaper. *Campus security:* part-time trained security personnel. *Student services:* health clinic, personal/psychological counseling, women's center.

Athletics Member NJCAA. *Intercollegiate sports:* basketball M/W, cross-country running M/W, soccer M, tennis M/W, volleyball W. *Intramural sports:* badminton M/W, basketball M/W, cheerleading M(c)/W(c), football M, soccer M/W, softball M/W, tennis M/W, ultimate Frisbee M/W, volleyball M/W.

Standardized Tests *Required:* SAT or ACT (for admission).

Costs (2006–07) *Tuition:* state resident $10,008 full-time, $405 per credit hour part-time; nonresident $15,284 full-time, $637 per credit hour part-time. *Required fees:* $492 full-time.

Financial Aid Of all full-time matriculated undergraduates, 40 Federal Work-Study jobs (averaging $1033).

Applying *Options:* electronic application, early admission, deferred entrance. *Application fee:* $50. *Required:* high school transcript. *Required for some:* letters of recommendation, interview. *Recommended:* essay or personal statement. *Application deadlines:* rolling (freshmen), rolling (transfers). *Notification:* continuous (freshmen), continuous (transfers).

Director of Admissions Mr. Randall C. Deike, Assistant Vice President for Enrollment Management, Penn State York, 1031 Edgecomb Avenue, York, PA 17403-3398. *Phone:* 814-865-5471. *Toll-free phone:* 800-778-6227. *E-mail:* admissions@psu.edu.

PENNSYLVANIA CULINARY INSTITUTE

Pittsburgh, Pennsylvania
www.paculinary.com/

Freshmen Application Contact Ms. Juliette Mariani, Dean of Students, Pennsylvania Culinary Institute, 717 Liberty Avenue, Pittsburgh, PA 15222-3500. *Phone:* 412-566-2433. *Toll-free phone:* 800-432-2433. *Fax:* 412-566-2434.

PENNSYLVANIA HIGHLAND COMMUNITY COLLEGE

Johnstown, Pennsylvania
www.pennhighlands.edu/

- **State and locally supported** 2-year, founded 1994
- **Small-town** campus
- **Coed,** 1,300 undergraduate students

Freshmen *Admission:* 459 applied, 459 admitted.

Faculty *Total:* 129, 19% full-time. *Student/faculty ratio:* 14:1.

Majors Accounting; banking and financial support services; computer and information sciences; computer/information technology services administration related; computer programming; computer programming related; computer programming (specific applications); computer/technical support; construction engineering technology; consumer merchandising/retailing management; court reporting; electrical, electronic and communications engineering technology; environmental engineering technology; geography; health/health care administration; heating, air conditioning and refrigeration technology; hospitality administration; human services; industrial technology; liberal arts and sciences/liberal studies; system administration; web/multimedia management and webmaster.

Academics *Calendar:* semesters. *Degree:* certificates, diplomas, and associate. *Special study options:* academic remediation for entering students, adult/continuing education programs, advanced placement credit, cooperative education, distance learning, honors programs, independent study, internships, part-time degree program, services for LD students.

Library Cambria County Area Community College Main Library plus 3 others with an OPAC.

Costs (2007–08) *Tuition:* area resident $2040 full-time, $85 per credit hour part-time; state resident $4080 full-time, $170 per credit hour part-time; nonresident $6120 full-time, $255 per credit hour part-time. *Required fees:* $510 full-time, $20 per credit hour part-time, $15 per term part-time.

Financial Aid Of all full-time matriculated undergraduates, 25 Federal Work-Study jobs (averaging $2500).

Applying *Application fee:* $20. *Recommended:* high school transcript, interview. *Application deadline:* 8/20 (freshmen).

Freshmen Application Contact Mr. Jeff Maul, Admissions Officer, Pennsylvania Highland Community College, PO Box 68, Johnstown, PA 15907. *Phone:* 814-262-6431. *E-mail:* jmaul@pennhighlands.edu.

PENNSYLVANIA INSTITUTE OF TECHNOLOGY
Media, Pennsylvania
www.pit.edu/

- **Independent** 2-year, founded 1953
- **Small-town** 12-acre campus with easy access to Philadelphia
- **Coed**

Undergraduates 270 full-time, 114 part-time. Students come from 3 states and territories, 3% are from out of state, 42% African American, 2% Asian American or Pacific Islander, 2% Hispanic American. *Retention:* 58% of 2003 full-time freshmen returned.

Faculty *Student/faculty ratio:* 10:1.

Academics *Calendar:* semesters. *Degree:* certificates and associate. *Special study options:* academic remediation for entering students, adult/continuing education programs, advanced placement credit, cooperative education, part-time degree program, summer session for credit.

Student Life *Campus security:* 24-hour emergency response devices.

Costs (2006–07) *Tuition:* $9000 full-time, $300 per credit part-time. *Required fees:* $330 full-time, $11 per credit part-time.

Financial Aid Of all full-time matriculated undergraduates, 15 Federal Work-Study jobs (averaging $1025). *Financial aid deadline:* 8/1.

Applying *Options:* electronic application, deferred entrance. *Application fee:* $25. *Required:* high school transcript, interview. *Required for some:* 2 letters of recommendation. *Recommended:* essay or personal statement.

Freshmen Application Contact Ms. Angela Cassetta, Dean of Enrollment Management, Pennsylvania Institute of Technology, 800 Manchester Avenue, Media, PA 19063-4036. *Phone:* 610-892-1550 Ext. 1553. *Toll-free phone:* 800-422-0025. *Fax:* 610-892-1510. *E-mail:* info@pit.edu.

PITTSBURGH INSTITUTE OF AERONAUTICS
Pittsburgh, Pennsylvania
www.pia.edu/

- **Independent** 2-year, founded 1929
- **Suburban** campus
- **Coed, primarily men,** 571 undergraduate students, 100% full-time, 4% women, 96% men

Undergraduates 571 full-time. Students come from 12 states and territories, 4 other countries, 35% are from out of state, 2% African American, 0.4% Asian American or Pacific Islander, 0.2% Hispanic American, 0.2% Native American, 2% international.

Freshmen *Admission:* 85 applied, 85 admitted, 85 enrolled.

Faculty *Total:* 37, 84% full-time. *Student/faculty ratio:* 17:1.

Majors Aeronautical/aerospace engineering technology; airframe mechanics and aircraft maintenance technology; avionics maintenance technology; electrical, electronic and communications engineering technology.

Academics *Calendar:* quarters. *Degree:* associate. *Special study options:* academic remediation for entering students, advanced placement credit.

Library Technical Library with 15,000 titles, 35 serial subscriptions.

Student Life *Housing:* college housing not available. *Student services:* personal/psychological counseling.

Costs (2006–07) *Tuition:* $10,155 full-time. No tuition increase for student's term of enrollment. *Required fees:* $180 full-time. *Room only:* Room and board charges vary according to housing facility. *Payment plans:* tuition prepayment, installment.

Applying *Options:* deferred entrance. *Application fee:* $150. *Recommended:* high school transcript, interview. *Application deadlines:* rolling (freshmen), rolling (transfers). *Notification:* continuous (freshmen), continuous (transfers).

Freshmen Application Contact Mr. Vincent J. Mezza, Director of Admissions, Pittsburgh Institute of Aeronautics, PO Box 10897, Pittsburgh, PA 15236. *Phone:* 412-346-2100. *Toll-free phone:* 800-444-1440. *Fax:* 412-466-5013. *E-mail:* admissions@pia.edu.

PITTSBURGH INSTITUTE OF MORTUARY SCIENCE, INCORPORATED
Pittsburgh, Pennsylvania
www.pims.edu/

- **Independent** 2-year, founded 1939
- **Urban** campus
- **Coed**

Undergraduates 181 full-time, 11 part-time. Students come from 10 states and territories, 23% are from out of state, 14% African American, 0.5% Hispanic American.

Faculty *Student/faculty ratio:* 13:1.

Academics *Calendar:* trimesters. *Degree:* diplomas and associate. *Special study options:* academic remediation for entering students, adult/continuing education programs, cooperative education, internships, part-time degree program, services for LD students.

Student Life *Campus security:* 24-hour emergency response devices.

Costs (2006–07) *Tuition:* $8000 full-time, $240 per credit part-time. *Required fees:* $170 full-time.

Applying *Application fee:* $40. *Required:* high school transcript, 2 letters of recommendation, interview, immunizations.

Freshmen Application Contact Ms. Karen Rocco, Registrar, Pittsburgh Institute of Mortuary Science, Incorporated, 5808 Baum Boulevard, Pittsburgh, PA 15206-3706. *Phone:* 412-362-8500 Ext. 101. *Toll-free phone:* 800-933-5808. *Fax:* 412-362-1684. *E-mail:* pims5808@aol.com.

PITTSBURGH TECHNICAL INSTITUTE
Oakdale, Pennsylvania
www.pti.edu/

Freshmen Application Contact Ms. Marylu Zuk, Vice President of Admissions, Pittsburgh Technical Institute, 1111 McKee Road, Oakdale, PA 15071. *Phone:* 412-809-5100. *Toll-free phone:* 800-784-9675.

THE PJA SCHOOL
Upper Darby, Pennsylvania
www.pjaschool.com/

- **Proprietary** 2-year, founded 1981, part of Prism Education Group
- **Suburban** campus
- **Coed,** 230 undergraduate students, 100% full-time, 83% women, 17% men

Undergraduates 230 full-time. Students come from 3 states and territories, 2% are from out of state, 64% African American, 4% Hispanic American.

Freshmen *Admission:* 140 applied, 73 admitted, 73 enrolled.

Faculty *Total:* 20, 25% full-time, 60% with terminal degrees.

Majors Accounting; accounting and business/management; legal assistant/paralegal.

Academics *Degree:* associate. *Special study options:* academic remediation for entering students, advanced placement credit, double majors, independent study, internships.

Library Ford Library plus 1 other with 2,350 titles, 7 serial subscriptions, 40 audiovisual materials.

The PJA School (continued)

Student Life *Housing:* college housing not available. *Campus security:* 24-hour emergency response devices.

Costs (2006–07) *Tuition:* $26,530 per degree program part-time.

Applying *Required:* essay or personal statement, interview, writing sample, high school diploma or equivalent. *Recommended:* 2 letters of recommendation.

Director of Admissions Ms. Dina Gentile, Director, The PJA School, 7900 West Chester Pike, Upper Darby, PA 19082-1926. *Phone:* 610-789-6700. *Toll-free phone:* 800-RING-PJA. *Fax:* 610-789-5208. *E-mail:* dgentile@ pjaschool.com.

READING AREA COMMUNITY COLLEGE

Reading, Pennsylvania www.racc.edu/

Director of Admissions Mr. David J. Adams, Director of Admissions, Reading Area Community College, PO Box 1706, Reading, PA 19603-1706. *Phone:* 610-607-6224. *Toll-free phone:* 800-626-1665.

THE RESTAURANT SCHOOL AT WALNUT HILL COLLEGE

Philadelphia, Pennsylvania www.walnuthillcollege.edu/

Freshmen Application Contact Mr. Karl D. Becker, Director of Admissions, The Restaurant School at Walnut Hill College, 4207 Walnut Street, Philadelphia, PA 19104. *Phone:* 267-295-2373. *Toll-free phone:* 877-925-6884 Ext. 3011. *Fax:* 215-222-4219. *E-mail:* kbecker@walnuthillcollege.edu.

▶**See page 582 for the College Close-Up.**

ROSEDALE TECHNICAL INSTITUTE

Pittsburgh, Pennsylvania www.rosedaletech.org/

- **Independent** 2-year, founded 1949
- **Suburban** 6-acre campus
- **Coed, primarily men**
- 65% of applicants were admitted

Undergraduates 200 full-time.

Faculty *Student/faculty ratio:* 13:1.

Academics *Calendar:* semesters. *Degree:* diplomas and associate.

Freshmen Application Contact Mr. Kevin Auld, Director, Rosedale Technical Institute, 215 Beecham Drive, Suite 2, Pittsburgh, PA 15205-9791. *Phone:* 412-521-6200. *Toll-free phone:* 800-521-6262. *Fax:* 412-521-2520. *E-mail:* admissions@rosedaletech.org.

SCHUYLKILL INSTITUTE OF BUSINESS AND TECHNOLOGY

Pottsville, Pennsylvania www.sibt.edu/

- **Proprietary** 2-year, part of Fore Front Education, Inc
- **Rural** campus
- **Coed**

Undergraduates 136 full-time. Students come from 1 other state, 0.7% African American, 0.7% Hispanic American, 0.7% Native American, 3% transferred in.

Faculty *Student/faculty ratio:* 6:1.

Academics *Calendar:* quarters. *Degree:* diplomas and associate. *Special study options:* academic remediation for entering students, advanced placement credit, cooperative education, independent study, internships, services for LD students.

Costs (2006–07) *Tuition:* $10,000 full-time. Full-time tuition and fees vary according to degree level and program. No tuition increase for student's term of enrollment. *Required fees:* $450 full-time. *Payment plans:* installment, deferred payment.

Applying *Application fee:* $50. *Required:* high school transcript, interview.

Freshmen Application Contact Michael Garcia, Director of Admissions, Schuylkill Institute of Business and Technology, 171 Red Horse Road, Pottsville, PA 17901. *Phone:* 570-622-4835. *Fax:* 570-622-6563. *E-mail:* mgarcia@ sibt.edu.

SOUTH HILLS SCHOOL OF BUSINESS & TECHNOLOGY

Atloona, Pennsylvania www.southhills.edu/

Freshmen Application Contact Ms. Marianne M. Beyer, Director, South Hills School of Business & Technology, 508 58th Street, Altoona, PA 16602. *Phone:* 814-944-6134.

SOUTH HILLS SCHOOL OF BUSINESS & TECHNOLOGY

State College, Pennsylvania www.southhills.edu/

- **Proprietary** 2-year, founded 1970
- **Small-town** 6-acre campus
- **Coed**

Undergraduates 611 full-time, 52 part-time. Students come from 1 other state, 1% are from out of state, 1% African American, 0.5% Asian American or Pacific Islander, 0.5% Hispanic American, 17% transferred in. *Retention:* 71% of 2003 full-time freshmen returned.

Faculty *Student/faculty ratio:* 15:1.

Academics *Calendar:* quarters. *Degrees:* certificates, diplomas, and associate (also includes Altoona campus). *Special study options:* advanced placement credit, distance learning, double majors, independent study, internships, part-time degree program.

Student Life *Campus security:* 24-hour emergency response devices.

Standardized Tests *Required:* CPAt (for admission). *Required for some:* CPAt.

Costs (2006–07) *Tuition:* $11,637 full-time, $323 per credit part-time. Full-time tuition and fees vary according to course load and program. Part-time tuition and fees vary according to course load and program. *Required fees:* $75 full-time, $25 per term part-time.

Applying *Options:* electronic application. *Application fee:* $25. *Required:* high school transcript, minimum 1.5 GPA, interview. *Required for some:* essay or personal statement, 2 letters of recommendation. *Recommended:* minimum 3.0 GPA.

Freshmen Application Contact Ms. Diane M. Brown, Director of Admissions, South Hills School of Business & Technology, 480 Waupelani Drive, State College, PA 16801-4516. *Phone:* 814-234-7755 Ext. 2020. *Toll-free phone:* 888-282-7427 Ext. 2020. *Fax:* 814-234-0926. *E-mail:* admissions@southhills.edu.

THADDEUS STEVENS COLLEGE OF TECHNOLOGY

Lancaster, Pennsylvania www.stevenscollege.edu/

Director of Admissions Ms. Erin Kate Nelsen, Director of Enrollment, Thaddeus Stevens College of Technology, Enrollment Services, 750 East King Street, Lancaster, PA 17602-3198. *Phone:* 717-299-7772. *Toll-free phone:* 800-842-3832.

TRIANGLE TECH, INC.—DuBOIS SCHOOL

DuBois, Pennsylvania www.triangle-tech.edu/

- **Proprietary** 2-year, founded 1944, part of Triangle Tech, Inc
- **Small-town** 5-acre campus
- **Coed, primarily men**

Undergraduates 246 full-time. Students come from 3 states and territories, 0.4% African American. *Retention:* 67% of 2003 full-time freshmen returned.

Faculty *Student/faculty ratio:* 11:1.

Academics *Calendar:* semesters. *Degree:* diplomas and associate. *Special study options:* academic remediation for entering students, advanced placement credit, off-campus study.

Costs (2006–07) *One-time required fee:* $75. *Tuition:* $11,978 full-time, $333 per credit part-time. Full-time tuition and fees vary according to course load and program. Part-time tuition and fees vary according to course load and program. *Required fees:* $470 full-time.

Applying *Options:* deferred entrance. *Required:* high school transcript, minimum 2.0 GPA, interview.

Freshmen Application Contact Jason Vallozzi, Director of Admissions, Triangle Tech, Inc.–DuBois School, PO Box 551, DuBois, PA 15801. *Phone:* 412-359-1000. *Toll-free phone:* 800-874-8324. *Fax:* 814-371-9227. *E-mail:* info@triangle-tech.com.

TRIANGLE TECH, INC.–ERIE SCHOOL
Erie, Pennsylvania　　　　**www.triangle-tech.com/**

Freshmen Application Contact Jennifer Provost, Admissions Representative, Triangle Tech, Inc.–Erie School, 2000 Liberty Street, Erie, PA 16502. *Phone:* 814-453-6016. *Toll-free phone:* 800-874-8324 (in-state); 800-TRI-TECH (out-of-state).

TRIANGLE TECH, INC.–GREENSBURG SCHOOL
Greensburg, Pennsylvania　　　　**www.triangle-tech.com/**

- **Proprietary** 2-year, founded 1944, part of Triangle Tech, Inc
- **Small-town** 1-acre campus with easy access to Pittsburgh
- **Coed, primarily men**

Undergraduates 271 full-time. Students come from 2 states and territories, 1% are from out of state, 0.7% African American, 0.4% Native American.

Faculty *Student/faculty ratio:* 12:1.

Academics *Calendar:* semesters. *Degree:* diplomas and associate. *Special study options:* academic remediation for entering students, adult/continuing education programs, advanced placement credit, summer session for credit.

Costs (2006–07) *Tuition:* $11,978 full-time, $333 per credit part-time. Full-time tuition and fees vary according to class time, program, and student level. Part-time tuition and fees vary according to class time, program, and student level. *Required fees:* $200 full-time.

Financial Aid Of all full-time matriculated undergraduates, 5 Federal Work-Study jobs (averaging $2000).

Applying *Options:* deferred entrance. *Application fee:* $75. *Required:* high school transcript.

Freshmen Application Contact Mr. John Mazzarese, Vice President of Admissions, Triangle Tech, Inc.–Greensburg School, 222 East Pittsburgh Street, Greensburg, PA 15601. *Phone:* 412-359-1000. *Toll-free phone:* 800-874-8324.

TRIANGLE TECH, INC.–PITTSBURGH SCHOOL
Pittsburgh, Pennsylvania　　　　**www.triangle-tech.edu/**

Freshmen Application Contact Mr. John A. Mazzarese, Vice President of Admissions, Triangle Tech, Inc.–Pittsburgh School, 1940 Perrysville Avenue, Pittsburgh, PA 15214. *Phone:* 412-359-1000. *Toll-free phone:* 800-874-8324. *Fax:* 412-359-1012. *E-mail:* info@triangle-tech.edu.

TRIANGLE TECH, INC.–SUNBURY SCHOOL
Sunbury, Pennsylvania　　　　**www.triangle-tech.com/**

- **Proprietary** 2-year
- **Coed,** 155 undergraduate students
- **100%** of applicants were admitted

Freshmen *Admission:* 28 applied, 28 admitted.

Majors Electrician.

Academics *Calendar:* semesters. *Degree:* associate.

Costs (2006–07) *Tuition:* $12,334 full-time.

Admissions Office Contact Triangle Tech, Inc.–Sunbury School, RR #1, Box 51, Sunbury, PA 17801.

TRI-STATE BUSINESS INSTITUTE
Erie, Pennsylvania　　　　**www.tsbi.org/**

- **Private** 2-year
- **475** undergraduate students
- **68%** of applicants were admitted

Freshmen *Admission:* 342 applied, 234 admitted.

Majors Accounting; administrative assistant and secretarial science; computer and information sciences and support services related; computer and information sciences related; computer programming related; computer science; legal assistant/paralegal; marketing/marketing management; medical transcription; nursing (registered nurse training).

Academics *Degree:* associate.

Costs (2006–07) *Tuition:* $13,970 full-time.

Applying *Application fee:* $50.

Director of Admissions Guy M. Euliano, President, Tri-State Business Institute, 5757 West 26th Street, Erie, PA 16506. *Phone:* 814-838-7673. *Fax:* 814-838-8642. *E-mail:* geuliano@tsbi.org.

UNIVERSITY OF PITTSBURGH AT TITUSVILLE
Titusville, Pennsylvania　　　　**www.upt.pitt.edu/**

- **State-related** 2-year, founded 1963, part of University of Pittsburgh System
- **Small-town** 10-acre campus
- **Endowment** $850,000
- **Coed,** 541 undergraduate students

Undergraduates Students come from 15 states and territories, 8% are from out of state.

Freshmen *Average high school GPA:* 3.09.

Majors Accounting; business/commerce; human services; liberal arts and sciences/liberal studies; management information systems; natural sciences; nursing (registered nurse training); physical therapist assistant.

Academics *Calendar:* semesters. *Degree:* certificates and associate. *Special study options:* academic remediation for entering students, advanced placement credit, distance learning, independent study, internships, part-time degree program, study abroad, summer session for credit.

Library Haskell Memorial Library with 49,256 titles, 126 serial subscriptions, an OPAC.

Student Life *Housing:* on-campus residence required through sophomore year. *Options:* coed, disabled students. Campus housing is university owned. Freshman campus housing is guaranteed. *Activities and Organizations:* drama/theater group, choral group, Phi Theta Kappa, Weight Club, SAB, SIFE, Diversity Club. *Campus security:* 24-hour emergency response devices and patrols, controlled dormitory access. *Student services:* health clinic, personal/psychological counseling.

Athletics Member NJCAA. *Intercollegiate sports:* basketball M(s)/W(s). *Intramural sports:* badminton M/W, basketball M/W, bowling M/W, football M/W, golf M/W, racquetball M/W, softball M/W, table tennis M/W, tennis M/W, volleyball M/W, weight lifting M/W.

Standardized Tests *Required:* SAT or ACT (for admission). *Recommended:* SAT (for admission).

Costs (2006–07) *Tuition:* state resident $8710 full-time, $373 per credit part-time; nonresident $17,610 full-time, $733 per credit part-time. Full-time tuition and fees vary according to program. Part-time tuition and fees vary according to program and student level. *Required fees:* $780 full-time, $113 per term part-time. *Room and board:* $7234. Room and board charges vary according to board plan. *Payment plan:* installment.

Applying *Options:* deferred entrance. *Application fee:* $35. *Required:* high school transcript, minimum 2.0 GPA. *Required for some:* essay or personal statement, 1 letter of recommendation. *Recommended:* interview. *Application deadlines:* rolling (freshmen), rolling (transfers). *Notification:* continuous (freshmen).

Freshmen Application Contact Mr. John Mumford, Executive Director of Enrollment Management, University of Pittsburgh at Titusville, PO Box 287, Titusville, PA 16354. *Phone:* 814-827-4409. *Toll-free phone:* 888-878-0462. *Fax:* 814-827-4519. *E-mail:* uptadm@pitt.edu.

VALLEY FORGE MILITARY COLLEGE

Wayne, Pennsylvania   **www.vfmac.edu/**

- **Independent** 2-year, founded 1928
- **Suburban** 120-acre campus with easy access to Philadelphia
- **Endowment** $7.2 million
- **Coed**

The Valley Forge Military College's (VFMC) primary goal is to prepare young men and women to transfer to and succeed at the four-year college or university of their choice. For more than 95 percent of the graduates, that goal is achieved through challenging academic programs, a structured environment that builds confidence and character and fosters academic success, and personal transfer counseling and transfer agreements with major universities. VFMC offers the only two-year Army ROTC commissioning program in the Northeast U.S., with full-tuition scholarships for qualified applicants.

Undergraduates 165 full-time. Students come from 6 other countries, 85% are from out of state, 13% African American, 6% Asian American or Pacific Islander, 7% Hispanic American, 2% international, 73% transferred in, 100% live on campus.

Faculty *Student/faculty ratio:* 10:1.

Academics *Calendar:* 4-1-4. *Degree:* associate. *Special study options:* academic remediation for entering students, advanced placement credit, English as a second language. *ROTC:* Army (b), Air Force (c).

Student Life *Campus security:* 24-hour patrols, student patrols.

Standardized Tests *Required:* SAT or ACT (for admission).

Costs (2006–07) *Comprehensive fee:* $30,977 includes full-time tuition ($19,693) and room and board ($11,284).

Financial Aid Of all full-time matriculated undergraduates, 20 Federal Work-Study jobs (averaging $1500).

Applying *Options:* early admission, deferred entrance. *Application fee:* $25. *Required:* high school transcript, guidance counselor/teacher evaluation form. *Recommended:* minimum 2.0 GPA, interview.

Freshmen Application Contact Maj. Greg Potts, Dean of Enrollment Management, Valley Forge Military College, 1001 Eagle Road, Wayne, PA 19087-3695. *Phone:* 610-989-1300. *Toll-free phone:* 800-234-8362. *Fax:* 610-688-1545. *E-mail:* admissions@vfmac.edu.

▶See page 590 for the College Close-Up.

WESTERN SCHOOL OF HEALTH AND BUSINESS CAREERS

Monroeville, Pennsylvania   **www.westernschool.com/**

Admissions Office Contact Western School of Health and Business Careers, 1 Monroeville Center, Suite 250, Route 22, 3824 Northern Pike, Monroeville, PA 15146-2142.

WESTERN SCHOOL OF HEALTH AND BUSINESS CAREERS

Pittsburgh, Pennsylvania   **www.westernschool.com/**

Director of Admissions Mr. Bruce E. Jones, Director of Admission, Western School of Health and Business Careers, 421 Seventh Avenue, Pittsburgh, PA 15219. *Phone:* 412-281-7083 Ext. 114. *Toll-free phone:* 800-333-6607.

WESTMORELAND COUNTY COMMUNITY COLLEGE

Youngwood, Pennsylvania   **www.wccc-pa.edu/**

- **County-supported** 2-year, founded 1970
- **Rural** 85-acre campus with easy access to Pittsburgh
- **Coed,** 5,986 undergraduate students, 44% full-time, 64% women, 36% men

Undergraduates 2,644 full-time, 3,342 part-time. Students come from 9 states and territories, 1% are from out of state, 3% African American, 0.4% Asian American or Pacific Islander, 0.5% Hispanic American, 0.2% Native American, 37% transferred in. *Retention:* 51% of 2003 full-time freshmen returned.

Freshmen *Admission:* 2,322 applied, 2,322 admitted, 1,687 enrolled.

Faculty *Total:* 430, 20% full-time. *Student/faculty ratio:* 17:1.

Majors Accounting; administrative assistant and secretarial science; architectural engineering technology; artificial intelligence and robotics; business administration and management; child development; commercial and advertising art; computer and information sciences; computer engineering technology; computer graphics; computer science; consumer merchandising/retailing management; criminal justice/law enforcement administration; criminal justice/police science; culinary arts; data processing and data processing technology; dental hygiene; dietetics; drafting and design technology; electrical, electronic and communications engineering technology; engineering; environmental engineering technology; fashion/apparel design; fashion merchandising; finance; fire science; graphic and printing equipment operation/production; health information/medical records administration; health teacher education; heating, air conditioning, ventilation and refrigeration maintenance technology; horticultural science; hospitality administration; hotel/motel administration; human services; information science/studies; legal administrative assistant/secretary; legal assistant/paralegal; liberal arts and sciences/liberal studies; marketing/marketing management; mechanical design technology; mechanical engineering/mechanical technology; medical administrative assistant and medical secretary; nuclear/nuclear power technology; nursing (licensed practical/vocational nurse training); nursing (registered nurse training); ophthalmic laboratory technology; photography; public administration; publishing; real estate; special products marketing; tourism and travel services management; welding technology.

Academics *Calendar:* semesters. *Degree:* certificates, diplomas, and associate. *Special study options:* academic remediation for entering students, adult/continuing education programs, advanced placement credit, cooperative education, distance learning, double majors, English as a second language, honors programs, independent study, internships, off-campus study, part-time degree program, services for LD students, summer session for credit.

Library Westmoreland County Community College Library with 64,000 titles, 400 serial subscriptions, 2,830 audiovisual materials, an OPAC, a Web page.

Student Life *Housing:* college housing not available. *Activities and Organizations:* student-run newspaper, radio station, choral group. *Campus security:* 24-hour emergency response devices and patrols. *Student services:* personal/psychological counseling.

Athletics Member NJCAA. *Intercollegiate sports:* baseball M, golf M/W, softball W, tennis M/W, volleyball W. *Intramural sports:* basketball M/W, bowling M/W, football M/W, racquetball M/W, skiing (downhill) M/W, softball M/W, table tennis M/W, volleyball M/W, weight lifting M/W.

Costs (2007–08) *Tuition:* area resident $2190 full-time, $73 per credit part-time; state resident $4380 full-time, $146 per credit part-time; nonresident $6570 full-time, $219 per credit part-time. *Required fees:* $240 full-time, $8 per credit part-time.

Applying *Options:* electronic application, early admission. *Application fee:* $10. *Application deadlines:* rolling (freshmen), rolling (transfers). *Notification:* continuous (freshmen), continuous (transfers).

Freshmen Application Contact Mr. Justin Tatar, Admissions Coordinator, Westmoreland County Community College, 400 Armbrust Road, Youngwood, PA 15697. *Phone:* 724-925-4064. *Toll-free phone:* 800-262-2103. *Fax:* 724-925-1150. *E-mail:* admission@wccc.edu.

THE WILLIAMSON FREE SCHOOL OF MECHANICAL TRADES

Media, Pennsylvania   **www.williamson.edu/**

- **Independent** 2-year, founded 1888
- **Small-town** 240-acre campus with easy access to Philadelphia
- **Men only,** 251 undergraduate students, 100% full-time

Undergraduates 251 full-time. Students come from 7 states and territories, 12% are from out of state, 10% African American, 5% Hispanic American, 100% live on campus.

Freshmen *Admission:* 409 applied, 95 admitted, 95 enrolled. *Average high school GPA:* 2.5.

Faculty *Total:* 29. *Student/faculty ratio:* 12:1.

Majors Carpentry; construction engineering technology; electrical, electronic and communications engineering technology; energy management and systems technology; horticultural science; landscaping and groundskeeping; machine tool technology; turf and turfgrass management.

Academics *Calendar:* semesters. *Degree:* diplomas and associate. *Special study options:* academic remediation for entering students, independent study, off-campus study.

Library Shrigley Library plus 3 others with 1,600 titles, 70 serial subscriptions.

Student Life *Activities and Organizations:* student-run newspaper, choral group, Campus Crusade for Christ, Vocational Industrial Clubs of America. *Campus security:* evening patrols, gate security. *Student services:* health clinic, personal/psychological counseling.

Athletics Member NJCAA. *Intercollegiate sports:* baseball M, basketball M, cross-country running M, football M, lacrosse M, soccer M, wrestling M. *Intramural sports:* archery M, badminton M, baseball M, basketball M, cross-country running M, football M, golf M, lacrosse M, racquetball M, soccer M, table tennis M, volleyball M, weight lifting M, wrestling M.

Standardized Tests *Required:* Armed Services Vocational Aptitude Battery (for admission).

Costs (2007–08) *Tuition:* All students attend on full scholarship which covers tuition, room and board, and textbooks.

Applying *Required:* essay or personal statement, high school transcript, minimum 2.0 GPA, interview. *Required for some:* 3 letters of recommendation. *Application deadline:* 2/15 (freshmen).

Freshmen Application Contact Mr. Edward D. Bailey, Director of Enrollments, The Williamson Free School of Mechanical Trades, 106 South New Middletown Road, Media, PA 19063. *Phone:* 610-566-1776 Ext. 235. *Fax:* 610-566-3854. *E-mail:* ebailey@williamson.edu.

WINNER INSTITUTE OF ARTS & SCIENCES

Transfer, Pennsylvania   www.winner-institute.edu/

- **Independent** 2-year
- **Coed,** 61 undergraduate students

Majors Culinary arts.

Academics *Calendar:* quarters. *Degree:* associate.

Costs (2006–07) *Tuition:* $9706 full-time.

Applying *Application fee:* $40.

Admissions Office Contact Winner Institute of Arts & Sciences, One Winner Place, Transfer, PA 16154. *Toll-free phone:* 888-414-2433.

WYOTECH

Blairsville, Pennsylvania   www.wyotech.com/

- **Proprietary** 2-year, founded 2002
- **Coed, primarily men**

Academics *Calendar:* 9-month program. *Degree:* diplomas and associate.

Applying *Application fee:* $100. *Required:* high school transcript.

Freshmen Application Contact Mr. Tim Smyers, WyoTech, 500 Innovation Drive, Blairsville, PA 15717. *Phone:* 724-459-2311. *Toll-free phone:* 800-822-8253. *Fax:* 724-459-6499. *E-mail:* tsmyers@wyotech.edu.

YORKTOWNE BUSINESS INSTITUTE

York, Pennsylvania   www.ybi.edu/

Director of Admissions Ms. Bonnie Gillespie, Director of Admissions, Yorktowne Business Institute, West Seventh Avenue, York, PA 17404. *Phone:* 717-846-5000 Ext. 124. *Toll-free phone:* 800-840-1004.

YTI CAREER INSTITUTE—YORK

York, Pennsylvania   www.yti.edu/

Freshmen Application Contact Ms. Sharon Mulligan, Associate Director of Admissions, YTI Career Institute–York, 1405 Williams Road, York, PA 17402. *Phone:* 717-757-1100 Ext. 318. *Toll-free phone:* 800-229-9675 (in-state); 800-227-9675 (out-of-state).

CENTRO DE ESTUDIOS MULTIDISCIPLINARIOS

San Juan, Puerto Rico   www.cempr.edu/

- **Independent** 2-year, founded 1980
- **Coed,** 1,687 undergraduate students
- 90% of applicants were admitted

Undergraduates 100% Hispanic American.

Freshmen *Admission:* 556 applied, 503 admitted.

Majors Nursing (registered nurse training); pharmacy technician; respiratory care therapy.

Academics *Degree:* certificates and associate.

Costs (2006–07) *Tuition:* $4481 full-time.

Applying *Application fee:* $30.

Director of Admissions Admissions Department, Centro de Estudios Multidisciplinarios, Calle 13 #1206, Ext. San Agustin, San Juan, PR 00926. *Phone:* 787-765-4210 Ext. 115.

COLEGIO UNIVERSITARIO DE SAN JUAN

San Juan, Puerto Rico   www.cunisanjuan.edu/

- **City-supported** 2-year, founded 1971
- **Coed,** 961 undergraduate students
- 94% of applicants were admitted

Freshmen *Admission:* 260 applied, 245 admitted.

Majors Accounting; administrative assistant and secretarial science; criminal justice/safety; electrical and electronic engineering technologies related; electrical/electronics equipment installation and repair; electrical/electronics maintenance and repair technology related; information science/studies; nursing (registered nurse training); office management; telecommunications.

Academics *Degree:* associate.

Costs (2006–07) *Tuition:* commonwealth resident $2950 full-time.

Applying *Application fee:* $15. *Recommended:* letters of recommendation.

Admissions Office Contact Colegio Universitario de San Juan, 180 Jose Oliver Avenue,, Tres Monjitas Industrial Park, San Juan, PR 00918.

COLEGIO UNIVERSITARIO DE SAN JUAN

San Juan, Puerto Rico   www.cunisanjuan.edu

- **City-supported** primarily 2-year, founded 1971
- **Urban** 5-acre campus
- **Endowment** $14.0 million
- **Coed,** 777 undergraduate students, 76% full-time, 47% women, 53% men

Undergraduates 592 full-time, 185 part-time. 100% Hispanic American, 4% transferred in.

Freshmen *Admission:* 257 applied, 254 admitted, 105 enrolled. *Average high school GPA:* 2.5.

Faculty *Total:* 70, 57% full-time, 3% with terminal degrees. *Student/faculty ratio:* 13:1.

Majors Accounting; administrative assistant and secretarial science; computer and information sciences related; computer programming; electrical, electronic and communications engineering technology; liberal arts and sciences/liberal studies; nursing (registered nurse training).

Academics *Calendar:* semesters. *Degrees:* certificates, diplomas, associate, and bachelor's. *Special study options:* academic remediation for entering students, cooperative education, English as a second language, independent study, internships, off-campus study, part-time degree program, services for LD students, summer session for credit.

Library Access to Information Center with 14,298 titles, 39 serial subscriptions, 199 audiovisual materials, an OPAC, a Web page.

Colegio Universitario de San Juan (continued)

Student Life *Activities and Organizations:* drama/theater group, student-run newspaper, student council. *Campus security:* 24-hour patrols. *Student services:* health clinic, personal/psychological counseling, women's center.

Athletics *Intercollegiate sports:* basketball M/W, cross-country running M/W, table tennis M/W, tennis M/W, track and field M/W, volleyball M/W, weight lifting M/W. *Intramural sports:* basketball M/W, cross-country running M/W, table tennis M/W, tennis M/W, track and field M/W, volleyball M/W, weight lifting M/W.

Standardized Tests *Required for some:* SAT (for admission), CEEB.

Costs (2006–07) *Tuition:* $85 per credit part-time; nonresident $2950 full-time. Full-time tuition and fees vary according to program. Part-time tuition and fees vary according to program. *Required fees:* $330 full-time. *Room and board:* $4850; room only: $1500. *Payment plan:* deferred payment. *Waivers:* employees or children of employees.

Financial Aid Of all full-time matriculated undergraduates, 127 Federal Work-Study jobs (averaging $618). 12 state and other part-time jobs (averaging $2991).

Applying *Application fee:* $15. *Required:* high school transcript, minimum 2.0 GPA, medical history. *Required for some:* letters of recommendation, interview. *Application deadlines:* 4/30 (freshmen), 4/30 (transfers). *Notification:* continuous until 7/31 (freshmen), continuous until 7/31 (transfers).

Freshmen Application Contact Mrs. Nilsa E. Rivera-Almenas, Director of Enrollment Management, Colegio Universitario de San Juan, 180 Jose R. Oliver Street, Tres Monjitas Industrial Park, San Juan, PR 00918. *Phone:* 787-250-7111. *Fax:* 787-250-7395.

COLUMBIA COLLEGE
Yauco, Puerto Rico   **www.columbiaco.edu/**

Director of Admissions Admissions Department, Columbia College, Box 3062, Yauco, PR 00698. *Phone:* 787-856-0845.

HUERTAS JUNIOR COLLEGE
Caguas, Puerto Rico   **www.huertas.edu/**

Director of Admissions Mrs. Barbara Hassim López, Director of Admissions, Huertas Junior College, PO Box 8429, Caguas, PR 00726. *Phone:* 787-743-1242. *Fax:* 787-743-0203. *E-mail:* huertas@huertas.org.

HUMACAO COMMUNITY COLLEGE
Humacao, Puerto Rico

Director of Admissions Ms. Xiomara Sanchez, Director of Admissions, Humacao Community College, PO Box 9139, Humacao, PR 00792. *Phone:* 787-852-2525.

ICPR JUNIOR COLLEGE–HATO REY CAMPUS
San Juan, Puerto Rico   **www.icprjc.edu/**

- **Proprietary** 2-year, founded 1946
- **Coed,** 371 undergraduate students

Majors Accounting related; computer and information sciences related; computer technology/computer systems technology; executive assistant/executive secretary; hotel/motel administration; marketing/marketing management; medical administrative assistant; office occupations and clerical services; tourism and travel services management.

Academics *Degree:* associate.

Costs (2006–07) *Tuition:* $5040 full-time.

Applying *Application fee:* $25.

Freshmen Application Contact Admissions Office, ICPR Junior College–Hato Rey Campus, San Juan, PR.

INSTITUTO COMERCIAL DE PUERTO RICO JUNIOR COLLEGE
San Juan, Puerto Rico   **www.icprjc.edu/**

Freshmen Application Contact Admissions Office, Instituto Comercial de Puerto Rico Junior College, PO Box 190304, San Juan, PR 00919-0304. *Phone:* 787-753-6335.

INTERNATIONAL JUNIOR COLLEGE
Santurce, Puerto Rico   **www.internationaljuniorcollege.com/**

- **Proprietary** 2-year
- 207 undergraduate students

Undergraduates 100% Hispanic American.

Majors Accounting and business/management; business administration, management and operations related; business automation/technology/data entry; computer science; tourism and travel services marketing.

Academics *Degree:* certificates and associate.

Costs (2006–07) *Tuition:* $7325 full-time.

Financial Aid Of all full-time matriculated undergraduates, 36 Federal Work-Study jobs. *Financial aid deadline:* 6/30.

Applying *Application fee:* $25.

Freshmen Application Contact Admissions Office, International Junior College, 1254 Avenue Ponce de Leon, pda. 18 1/2, Santurce, PR 00908. *Phone:* 787-723-3333 Ext. 223.

NATIONAL COLLEGE
Bayamon, Puerto Rico   **www.nationalcollegepr.edu/**

Freshmen Application Contact Mr. Ricardo Nieves, National College, National College Plaza Building, PO Box 2036, Bayamon, PR 00960. *Phone:* 787-780-5134. *Toll-free phone:* 800-780-5134. *E-mail:* rnieves@nationalcollegepr.edu.

PUERTO RICO TECHNICAL JUNIOR COLLEGE
Mayaguez, Puerto Rico

Director of Admissions Admissions Department, Puerto Rico Technical Junior College, Calle Santiago R. Palmer #15 Est, Mayaguez, PR 00680.

PUERTO RICO TECHNICAL JUNIOR COLLEGE
San Juan, Puerto Rico

- **Proprietary** 2-year
- **Coed,** 137 undergraduate students
- 91% of applicants were admitted

Undergraduates 100% Hispanic American.

Freshmen *Admission:* 233 applied, 211 admitted.

Majors Optical sciences.

Academics *Degree:* certificates and associate.

Costs (2006–07) *Tuition:* $10,090 per degree program part-time.

Applying *Application fee:* $25. *Required:* letters of recommendation.

Director of Admissions Admissions Department, Puerto Rico Technical Junior College, 703 Ponce De Leon Avenue, Hato Rey, San Juan, PR 00917. *Phone:* 787-751-0628 Ext. 28.

RAMÍREZ COLLEGE OF BUSINESS AND TECHNOLOGY

San Juan, Puerto Rico   www.galeon.com/ramirezcollege/

Director of Admissions Mr. Arnaldo Castro, Director of Admissions, Ramírez College of Business and Technology, Avenue Ponce de Leon #70, San Juan, PR 00918. *Phone:* 787-763-3120. *E-mail:* ramirezcollege@prtc.net.

UNIVERSIDAD CENTRAL DEL CARIBE

Bayamón, Puerto Rico   www.uccaribe.edu/

- **Independent** founded 1976
- **Coed,** 81 undergraduate students
- 67% of applicants were admitted

Undergraduates 100% Hispanic American.

Freshmen *Admission:* 30 applied, 20 admitted.

Majors Medical radiologic technology.

Academics *Calendar:* semesters. *Degrees:* certificates, associate, master's, first professional, and postbachelor's certificates.

Costs (2006–07) *Tuition:* $7265 full-time.

Applying *Application fee:* $25. *Required:* letters of recommendation.

Director of Admissions Admissions Department, Universidad Central del Caribe, PO Box 60-327, Bayamón, PR 00960-6032. *Phone:* 787-740-1611.

UNIVERSITY COLLEGE OF CRIMINAL JUSTICE OF PUERTO RICO

Gurabo, Puerto Rico

Director of Admissions Admissions Department, University College of Criminal Justice of Puerto Rico, HC 02 Box 12000, Gurabo, PR 00778-9601.

UNIVERSITY OF PUERTO RICO AT CAROLINA

Carolina, Puerto Rico   uprc.edu/

- **Commonwealth-supported** primarily 2-year, founded 1974, part of University of Puerto Rico System
- **Urban** 60-acre campus with easy access to San Juan
- **Coed,** 3,879 undergraduate students, 70% full-time, 65% women, 35% men

Undergraduates 2,710 full-time, 1,169 part-time. 100% Hispanic American.

Freshmen *Admission:* 2,025 applied, 1,042 admitted, 974 enrolled.

Faculty *Total:* 208, 60% full-time.

Majors Administrative assistant and secretarial science; advertising; automobile/automotive mechanics technology; commercial and advertising art; criminal justice/police science; education; finance; hotel/motel administration; humanities; interior design; mechanical engineering/mechanical technology; natural sciences; physical education teaching and coaching; public administration; social sciences.

Academics *Calendar:* quarters. *Degrees:* associate and bachelor's. *Special study options:* academic remediation for entering students, adult/continuing education programs, English as a second language, part-time degree program, services for LD students. *ROTC:* Army (c), Air Force (c).

Library Learning Resource Center, Prof. Jose Paulino Fernandez-Miranda with 37,958 titles, 216 serial subscriptions, 1,380 audiovisual materials, an OPAC, a Web page.

Student Life *Activities and Organizations:* drama/theater group, choral group, marching band. *Student services:* health clinic, personal/psychological counseling.

Athletics *Intercollegiate sports:* basketball M/W, cross-country running M/W, tennis M/W, track and field M(s)/W(s), volleyball M/W, weight lifting W. *Intramural sports:* basketball M/W, cross-country running M/W, tennis M/W, volleyball M/W.

Standardized Tests *Required:* SAT (for admission), ACT (for admission), SAT Subject Tests (for admission).

Costs (2006–07) *Tuition:* commonwealth resident $2263 full-time, $40 per credit part-time; nonresident $3192 full-time, $89 per credit part-time. Full-time tuition and fees vary according to class time. Part-time tuition and fees vary according to class time. *Required fees:* $74 per term part-time. *Room and board:* Room and board charges vary according to board plan, housing facility, and location. *Payment plan:* installment. *Waivers:* employees or children of employees.

Applying *Application fee:* $20. *Required:* high school transcript. *Application deadlines:* 12/6 (freshmen), 2/18 (transfers). *Notification:* continuous until 8/1 (freshmen), continuous until 5/26 (transfers).

Director of Admissions Ms. Celia Mendez, Admissions Officer, University of Puerto Rico at Carolina, PO Box 4800, Carolina, PR 00984-4800. *Phone:* 787-757-1485.

RHODE ISLAND

COMMUNITY COLLEGE OF RHODE ISLAND

Warwick, Rhode Island   www.ccri.edu/

- **State-supported** 2-year, founded 1964
- **Suburban** 205-acre campus with easy access to Boston
- **Endowment** $1.3 million
- **Coed,** 16,373 undergraduate students, 37% full-time, 62% women, 38% men

Undergraduates 6,127 full-time, 10,246 part-time. Students come from 16 states and territories, 35 other countries, 7% are from out of state, 8% African American, 3% Asian American or Pacific Islander, 11% Hispanic American, 0.6% Native American, 0.1% international.

Freshmen *Admission:* 6,721 applied, 5,783 admitted, 3,442 enrolled.

Faculty *Total:* 722, 41% full-time. *Student/faculty ratio:* 22:1.

Majors Accounting; administrative assistant and secretarial science; adult development and aging; art; banking and financial support services; biological and physical sciences; business administration and management; business/commerce; chemical technology; clinical/medical laboratory technology; computer engineering technology; computer programming; criminal justice/police science; dental hygiene; dramatic/theater arts; electrical, electronic and communications engineering technology; engineering; fashion merchandising; fire science; general retailing/wholesaling; general studies; instrumentation technology; kindergarten/preschool education; labor and industrial relations; legal administrative assistant/secretary; legal assistant/paralegal; liberal arts and sciences/liberal studies; marketing/marketing management; medical administrative assistant and medical secretary; medical radiologic technology; music; nursing (registered nurse training); occupational therapist assistant; physical therapist assistant; psychiatric/mental health services technology; rehabilitation and therapeutic professions related; respiratory care therapy; retailing; social work; special education; substance abuse/addiction counseling; theater design and technology; urban studies/affairs.

Academics *Calendar:* semesters. *Degree:* certificates and associate. *Special study options:* academic remediation for entering students, adult/continuing education programs, advanced placement credit, cooperative education, distance learning, double majors, English as a second language, external degree program, honors programs, independent study, internships, off-campus study, part-time degree program, services for LD students, study abroad, summer session for credit. *ROTC:* Army (c).

Library Community College of Rhode Island Learning Resources Center plus 3 others with 98,140 titles, 872 serial subscriptions, an OPAC, a Web page.

Student Life *Housing:* college housing not available. *Activities and Organizations:* drama/theater group, choral group, Distributive Education Clubs of America, theater group, ABLE, Phi Theta Kappa. *Campus security:* 24-hour emergency response devices and patrols. *Student services:* health clinic, personal/psychological counseling.

Athletics Member NJCAA. *Intercollegiate sports:* baseball M(s), basketball M(s)/W(s), cross-country running M/W, golf M/W, soccer M(s)/W(s), softball W(s), tennis M/W, track and field M/W, volleyball W(s). *Intramural sports:* basketball M/W, cross-country running M/W, volleyball M/W, water polo M/W.

Costs (2006–07) *Tuition:* $111 per credit part-time; state resident $2180 full-time, $111 per credit part-time; nonresident $6410 full-time, $336 per credit part-time. Part-time tuition and fees vary according to course load. *Required fees:* $290 full-time, $11 per credit part-time, $27 per semester part-time. *Payment plans:* installment, deferred payment. *Waivers:* senior citizens and employees or children of employees.

Community College of Rhode Island (continued)

Financial Aid Of all full-time matriculated undergraduates, 500 Federal Work-Study jobs (averaging $2500). 70 state and other part-time jobs (averaging $2000).

Applying *Options:* deferred entrance. *Application fee:* $20. *Application deadlines:* rolling (freshmen), rolling (transfers). *Notification:* continuous (freshmen).

Freshmen Application Contact Mr. Nick Figueroa, Assistant Dean of Enrollment Services, Community College of Rhode Island, 400 East Avenue, Warwick, RI 02886. *Phone:* 401-333-7490. *Fax:* 401-333-7122. *E-mail:* webadmission@ccri.edu.

NEW ENGLAND INSTITUTE OF TECHNOLOGY
Warwick, Rhode Island   www.neit.edu/

- **Independent** primarily 2-year, founded 1940
- **Suburban** 10-acre campus with easy access to Boston
- **Coed,** 3,009 undergraduate students, 87% full-time, 16% women, 84% men

Undergraduates 2,614 full-time, 395 part-time. Students come from 10 states and territories, 22 other countries, 6% African American, 2% Asian American or Pacific Islander, 6% Hispanic American, 0.6% Native American, 5% international.

Freshmen *Admission:* 668 enrolled.

Faculty *Total:* 230, 43% full-time.

Majors Architectural engineering technology; automobile/automotive mechanics technology; business administration and management; computer and information sciences; computer technology/computer systems technology; construction engineering technology; electrical, electronic and communications engineering technology; electrical, electronics and communications engineering; heating, air conditioning, ventilation and refrigeration maintenance technology; industrial technology; interior design; marine maintenance and ship repair technology; medical/clinical assistant; occupational therapist assistant; pipefitting and sprinkler fitting; radio and television broadcasting technology; surgical technology.

Academics *Calendar:* quarters. *Degrees:* associate and bachelor's. *Special study options:* academic remediation for entering students, adult/continuing education programs, advanced placement credit, distance learning, English as a second language, internships, part-time degree program, services for LD students, summer session for credit.

Library Library with 48,701 titles, 16,491 serial subscriptions, 1,470 audiovisual materials, an OPAC, a Web page.

Student Life *Housing:* college housing not available. *Campus security:* security personnel during open hours. *Student services:* personal/psychological counseling.

Costs (2007–08) *Tuition:* $15,300 full-time, $385 per credit part-time. *Required fees:* $1415 full-time.

Financial Aid Of all full-time matriculated undergraduates, 250 Federal Work-Study jobs (averaging $2290).

Applying *Options:* early admission, deferred entrance. *Application fee:* $25. *Required:* high school transcript, interview. *Application deadlines:* rolling (freshmen), rolling (transfers).

Freshmen Application Contact Mr. Michael Kwiatkowski, Director of Admissions, New England Institute of Technology, 2500 Post Road, Warwick, RI 02886-2266. *Phone:* 401-739-5000. *E-mail:* neit@ids.net.

SOUTH CAROLINA

AIKEN TECHNICAL COLLEGE
Aiken, South Carolina   www.aik.tec.sc.us/

- **State and locally supported** 2-year, founded 1972, part of South Carolina State Board for Technical and Comprehensive Education
- **Rural** 88-acre campus
- **Coed**

Undergraduates 1,397 full-time, 1,119 part-time. Students come from 6 states and territories, 2 other countries, 10% are from out of state, 2% African American, 88% Asian American or Pacific Islander, 4% Hispanic American, 3% Native American, 1% transferred in.

Academics *Calendar:* semesters. *Degree:* certificates, diplomas, and associate. *Special study options:* academic remediation for entering students, adult/continuing education programs, advanced placement credit, cooperative education, internships, off-campus study, part-time degree program, services for LD students, summer session for credit.

Student Life *Campus security:* 24-hour patrols, late-night transport/escort service.

Athletics Member NJCAA.

Costs (2006–07) *Tuition:* area resident $2920 full-time, $122 per credit hour part-time; state resident $3288 full-time, $137 per credit hour part-time; nonresident $8424 full-time, $351 per credit hour part-time. *Required fees:* $270 full-time, $5 per credit hour part-time, $75 per term part-time.

Financial Aid Of all full-time matriculated undergraduates, 48 Federal Work-Study jobs (averaging $3000).

Applying *Options:* deferred entrance. *Required:* high school transcript. *Required for some:* essay or personal statement.

Freshmen Application Contact Ms. Evelyn Pride Patterson, Director of Admissions and Records, Aiken Technical College, PO Drawer 696, Aiken, SC 29802-0696. *Phone:* 803-593-9231. *E-mail:* pridepae@atc.edu.

CENTRAL CAROLINA TECHNICAL COLLEGE
Sumter, South Carolina   www.cctech.edu/

- **State-supported** 2-year, founded 1963, part of South Carolina State Board for Technical and Comprehensive Education
- **Small-town** 70-acre campus
- **Coed,** 3,244 undergraduate students, 29% full-time, 70% women, 30% men

Undergraduates 945 full-time, 2,299 part-time. Students come from 2 states and territories, 1% are from out of state, 49% African American, 1% Asian American or Pacific Islander, 1% Hispanic American, 0.5% Native American, 0.2% international, 13% transferred in.

Freshmen *Admission:* 567 enrolled.

Faculty *Total:* 180, 46% full-time, 9% with terminal degrees. *Student/faculty ratio:* 19:1.

Majors Accounting; administrative assistant and secretarial science; business administration and management; child care and support services management; civil engineering technology; criminal justice/safety; data processing and data processing technology; environmental control technologies related; industrial electronics technology; legal assistant/paralegal; liberal arts and sciences/liberal studies; mechanical drafting and CAD/CADD; multi-/interdisciplinary studies related; natural resources management and policy; nursing (registered nurse training); sales, distribution and marketing; surgical technology.

Academics *Calendar:* semesters. *Degree:* certificates, diplomas, and associate. *Special study options:* academic remediation for entering students, adult/continuing education programs, advanced placement credit, cooperative education, distance learning, external degree program, independent study, internships, part-time degree program, summer session for credit.

Library Central Carolina Technical College Library with 20,356 titles, 245 serial subscriptions, an OPAC, a Web page.

Student Life *Housing:* college housing not available. *Activities and Organizations:* Creative Arts Society, Phi Theta Kappa, Computer Club, National Student Nurses Association (local chapter), Natural Resources Management Club. *Campus security:* 24-hour emergency response devices, security attendants for parking lots and halls during working hours. *Student services:* personal/psychological counseling.

Standardized Tests *Required:* COMPASS (for admission). *Required for some:* SAT (for admission), ACT (for admission), SAT or ACT (for admission).

Costs (2006–07) *Tuition:* area resident $2900 full-time, $121 per credit hour part-time; state resident $3400 full-time, $142 per credit hour part-time; nonresident $5156 full-time, $215 per credit hour part-time. *Required fees:* $25 full-time. *Payment plan:* installment. *Waivers:* senior citizens.

Applying *Options:* electronic application. *Application fee:* $25. *Required:* high school transcript. *Application deadlines:* rolling (freshmen), rolling (transfers).

Freshmen Application Contact Ms. Lisa M. Bracken, Director of Admissions and Counseling, Central Carolina Technical College, 506 North Guignard Drive, Sumter, SC 29150. *Phone:* 803-778-6652. *Toll-free phone:* 800-221-8711 Ext. 455. *Fax:* 803-778-6696. *E-mail:* brackenlm@cctech.edu.

CLINTON JUNIOR COLLEGE

Rock Hill, South Carolina   www.clintonjuniorcollege.edu/

- **Independent** 2-year, founded 1894, affiliated with African Methodist Episcopal Zion Church
- **Coed,** 123 undergraduate students

Majors Business/commerce; liberal arts and sciences/liberal studies.

Academics *Calendar:* semesters. *Degree:* associate.

Costs (2006–07) *Tuition:* $3635 full-time.

Applying *Application fee:* $25.

Director of Admissions Dr. Janis Pen, President, Clinton Junior College, 1029 Crawford Road, Rock Hill, SC 29730. *Phone:* 803-327-7402. *Toll-free phone:* 877-837-9645. *Fax:* 803-327-3261. *E-mail:* ecopeland@clintonjrcollege.org.

DENMARK TECHNICAL COLLEGE

Denmark, South Carolina   www.denmarktech.edu/

- **State-supported** 2-year, founded 1948, part of South Carolina State Board for Technical and Comprehensive Education
- **Rural** 53-acre campus
- **Coed**

Undergraduates 969 full-time, 439 part-time. Students come from 8 states and territories, 76% African American, 0.2% Native American.

Faculty *Student/faculty ratio:* 19:1.

Academics *Calendar:* semesters. *Degree:* certificates, diplomas, and associate. *Special study options:* academic remediation for entering students, adult/continuing education programs, advanced placement credit, cooperative education, internships, off-campus study, part-time degree program, summer session for credit. *ROTC:* Army (c).

Student Life *Campus security:* 24-hour patrols.

Standardized Tests *Required:* ACT ASSET (for admission).

Costs (2006–07) *Tuition:* state resident $5574 full-time, $87 per credit hour part-time; nonresident $7662 full-time, $174 per credit hour part-time. *Required fees:* $1189 full-time, $95 per term part-time. *Room and board:* $3096; room only: $711.

Financial Aid Of all full-time matriculated undergraduates, 250 Federal Work-Study jobs (averaging $2000).

Applying *Options:* early admission, deferred entrance. *Application fee:* $10. *Required:* high school transcript.

Freshmen Application Contact Mrs. Michelle McDowell, Director of Admissions and Records, Denmark Technical College, Solomon Blatt Boulevard, Box 327, Denmark, SC 29042-0327. *Phone:* 803-793-5176. *Fax:* 803-793-5942.

FLORENCE-DARLINGTON TECHNICAL COLLEGE

Florence, South Carolina   www.fdtc.edu/

- **State-supported** 2-year, founded 1963, part of South Carolina State Board for Technical and Comprehensive Education
- **Small-town** 100-acre campus with easy access to Columbia
- **Endowment** $1000
- **Coed,** 4,041 undergraduate students, 53% full-time, 71% women, 29% men

Undergraduates 2,147 full-time, 1,894 part-time. Students come from 4 states and territories, 46% African American, 0.4% Asian American or Pacific Islander, 0.4% Hispanic American, 0.5% Native American, 3% transferred in.

Freshmen *Admission:* 800 enrolled.

Faculty *Total:* 312, 35% full-time, 2% with terminal degrees. *Student/faculty ratio:* 17:1.

Majors Accounting; administrative assistant and secretarial science; automobile/automotive mechanics technology; biological and physical sciences; business administration and management; chemical engineering; civil engineering technology; clinical/medical laboratory technology; computer engineering technology; criminal justice/law enforcement administration; dental hygiene; drafting and design technology; electrical, electronic and communications engineering technology; electromechanical technology; engineering technology; funeral service and mortuary science; health information/medical records administration; heating, air conditioning, ventilation and refrigeration maintenance technology; human services; industrial radiologic technology; legal assistant/paralegal; liberal arts and sciences/liberal studies; machine tool technology; marketing/

marketing management; nursing (registered nurse training); occupational therapy; physical therapy; respiratory care therapy; trade and industrial teacher education.

Academics *Calendar:* semesters. *Degree:* certificates, diplomas, and associate. *Special study options:* academic remediation for entering students, adult/continuing education programs, advanced placement credit, English as a second language, internships, part-time degree program, study abroad, summer session for credit. *ROTC:* Army (c).

Library Florence-Darlington Technical College Library with 34,814 titles, 286 serial subscriptions.

Student Life *Housing:* college housing not available. *Activities and Organizations:* student-run newspaper, choral group, International Club, FDTC Outreach Choir, Student Ambassadors. *Campus security:* 24-hour emergency response devices and patrols, late-night transport/escort service. *Student services:* personal/psychological counseling.

Standardized Tests *Required for some:* SAT or ACT (for admission), CPT.

Costs (2006–07) *Tuition:* area resident $3074 full-time; state resident $3336 full-time; nonresident $5170 full-time.

Financial Aid Of all full-time matriculated undergraduates, 95 Federal Work-Study jobs (averaging $2500).

Applying *Options:* deferred entrance. *Application fee:* $15. *Required for some:* high school transcript. *Application deadlines:* 8/1 (freshmen), 8/1 (transfers).

Director of Admissions Mr. Kevin Qualls, Director of Enrollment Services, Florence-Darlington Technical College, 2715 West Lucas Street, PO Box 100548, Florence, SC 29501-0548. *Phone:* 843-661-8153. *Toll-free phone:* 800-228-5745. *E-mail:* kirvenp@flo.tec.sc.us.

FORREST JUNIOR COLLEGE

Anderson, South Carolina   www.forrestcollege.com/

- **Proprietary** 2-year, founded 1946
- **Rural** 3-acre campus
- **Coed, primarily women,** 231 undergraduate students, 100% full-time, 93% women, 7% men

Undergraduates 231 full-time. Students come from 2 states and territories, 10% are from out of state, 16% transferred in.

Freshmen *Admission:* 328 applied, 231 admitted, 231 enrolled.

Faculty *Total:* 51, 16% full-time, 59% with terminal degrees. *Student/faculty ratio:* 10:1.

Majors Accounting; business administration and management; child care services management; computer installation and repair technology; computer technology/computer systems technology; legal administrative assistant/secretary; medical/clinical assistant; medical office management; office management; paralegal/legal assistant.

Academics *Calendar:* quarters. *Degree:* certificates, diplomas, and associate. *Special study options:* advanced placement credit, cooperative education, distance learning, double majors, independent study, internships, part-time degree program, summer session for credit.

Library Forrest Junior College Library plus 1 other with 40,000 titles, 225 serial subscriptions, 2,200 audiovisual materials, an OPAC.

Student Life *Housing:* college housing not available. *Activities and Organizations:* student-run newspaper. *Campus security:* 24-hour emergency response devices, late-night transport/escort service. *Student services:* health clinic, legal services.

Standardized Tests *Required:* Gates-McGinnity (for admission).

Costs (2007–08) *Tuition:* $5328 full-time, $148 per quarter hour part-time. *Required fees:* $450 full-time.

Financial Aid Of all full-time matriculated undergraduates, 18 Federal Work-Study jobs (averaging $700).

Applying *Options:* deferred entrance. *Application fee:* $50. *Required:* essay or personal statement, high school transcript, minimum 2.0 GPA, interview. *Recommended:* minimum 2.5 GPA. *Application deadline:* 10/5 (freshmen).

Freshmen Application Contact Ms. Pamela Johnson, President, Forrest Junior College, 601 East River Street, Anderson, SC 29624. *Phone:* 864-225-7653. *Fax:* 864-261-7471. *E-mail:* pamelajohnson@forrestcollege.com.

GREENVILLE TECHNICAL COLLEGE

Greenville, South Carolina   www.greenvilletech.com/

- **State-supported** 2-year, founded 1962, part of South Carolina State Board for Technical and Comprehensive Education
- **Urban** 407-acre campus
- **Coed,** 13,000 undergraduate students

Undergraduates Students come from 6 other countries.

Greenville Technical College (continued)

Faculty *Total:* 478, 52% full-time.

Majors Accounting; administrative assistant and secretarial science; airframe mechanics and aircraft maintenance technology; architectural engineering technology; automobile/automotive mechanics technology; avionics maintenance technology; business administration and management; clinical/medical laboratory technology; computer programming; construction engineering technology; criminal justice/law enforcement administration; criminal justice/police science; dental hygiene; drafting and design technology; electrical, electronic and communications engineering technology; emergency medical technology (EMT paramedic); fire science; health science; heating, air conditioning, ventilation and refrigeration maintenance technology; hospitality administration; industrial radiologic technology; industrial technology; legal assistant/paralegal; liberal arts and sciences/liberal studies; machine tool technology; marketing/marketing management; materials science; mechanical engineering/mechanical technology; nursing (registered nurse training); physical therapy; pre-engineering; respiratory care therapy; special products marketing.

Academics *Calendar:* semesters. *Degree:* certificates, diplomas, and associate. *Special study options:* academic remediation for entering students, adult/continuing education programs, advanced placement credit, cooperative education, part-time degree program, summer session for credit.

Library Verne Smith Library/Technical Resource Center with 49,500 titles, 658 serial subscriptions.

Student Life *Housing:* college housing not available. *Activities and Organizations:* Student Government Association, Phi Theta Kappa, Student Nurses Association, Christians on Campus, International and Friends Organization. *Campus security:* 24-hour emergency response devices and patrols, student patrols, late-night transport/escort service.

Athletics *Intramural sports:* basketball M/W, bowling M/W, tennis M/W, volleyball M/W.

Standardized Tests *Recommended:* SAT, ACT ASSET, or ACT COMPASS.

Costs (2006–07) *Tuition:* area resident $3190 full-time; state resident $3458 full-time; nonresident $6490 full-time.

Financial Aid Of all full-time matriculated undergraduates, 120 Federal Work-Study jobs (averaging $3270). *Financial aid deadline:* 5/1.

Applying *Options:* early admission, deferred entrance. *Application fee:* $25. *Required:* high school transcript. *Application deadlines:* rolling (freshmen), rolling (transfers). *Notification:* continuous until 8/20 (freshmen), continuous until 8/20 (transfers).

Director of Admissions Ms. Martha S. White, Director of Admissions, Greenville Technical College, PO Box 5616, Greenville, SC 29606-5616. *Phone:* 864-250-8109. *Toll-free phone:* 800-922-1183 (in-state); 800-723-0673 (out-of-state).

HORRY-GEORGETOWN TECHNICAL COLLEGE

Conway, South Carolina   **www.hgtc.edu/**

- **State and locally supported** 2-year, founded 1966, part of South Carolina State Board for Technical and Comprehensive Education
- **Small-town** campus
- **Coed**

Undergraduates 2,446 full-time, 2,916 part-time. Students come from 10 states and territories, 22 other countries, 11% are from out of state, 24% African American, 0.8% Asian American or Pacific Islander, 1% Hispanic American, 0.6% Native American, 2% international. *Retention:* 51% of 2003 full-time freshmen returned.

Faculty *Student/faculty ratio:* 16:1.

Academics *Calendar:* semesters. *Degree:* certificates, diplomas, and associate. *Special study options:* academic remediation for entering students, adult/continuing education programs, advanced placement credit, cooperative education, internships, part-time degree program, services for LD students, summer session for credit.

Costs (2006–07) *Tuition:* area resident $2800 full-time, $117 per credit hour part-time; state resident $3544 full-time, $148 per credit hour part-time; nonresident $4264 full-time, $178 per credit hour part-time. *Required fees:* $144 full-time, $1 per credit hour part-time, $35 per term part-time.

Applying *Options:* early admission. *Application fee:* $25. *Required for some:* high school transcript.

Freshmen Application Contact Mr. George Swindoll, Vice President for Enrollment Development and Registration, Horry-Georgetown Technical College, 2050 Highway 501 East, PO Box 261966, Conway, SC 29528-6066. *Phone:* 843-349-5277. *Fax:* 843-349-7501. *E-mail:* george.swindoll@hgtc.edu.

ITT TECHNICAL INSTITUTE

Greenville, South Carolina   **www.itt-tech.edu/**

- **Proprietary** primarily 2-year, founded 1992, part of ITT Educational Services, Inc
- **Coed**

Majors Animation, interactive technology, video graphics and special effects; CAD/CADD drafting/design technology; computer and information systems security; computer engineering technology; computer software technology; computer systems networking and telecommunications; electrical, electronic and communications engineering technology; web/multimedia management and webmaster; web page, digital/multimedia and information resources design.

Academics *Calendar:* quarters. *Degrees:* associate and bachelor's.

Library a Web page.

Student Life *Housing:* college housing not available.

Standardized Tests *Required:* Wonderlic aptitude test (for admission).

Costs (2006–07) *Tuition:* Contact school for program costs.

Financial Aid Of all full-time matriculated undergraduates, 3 Federal Work-Study jobs.

Applying *Options:* deferred entrance. *Application fee:* $100. *Required:* high school transcript, interview. *Recommended:* letters of recommendation. *Application deadlines:* rolling (freshmen), rolling (transfers). *Notification:* continuous (freshmen), continuous (transfers).

Freshmen Application Contact Ms. Lynette Stucka, Director of Recruitment, ITT Technical Institute, Independence Corporate Park, Six Independence Point, Greenville, SC 29615. *Phone:* 864-288-0777. *Toll-free phone:* 800-932-4488.

MIDLANDS TECHNICAL COLLEGE

Columbia, South Carolina   **www.midlandstech.edu/**

- **State and locally supported** 2-year, founded 1974, part of South Carolina State Board for Technical and Comprehensive Education
- **Suburban** 113-acre campus
- **Endowment** $3.9 million
- **Coed,** 10,849 undergraduate students, 45% full-time, 64% women, 36% men

Undergraduates 4,869 full-time, 5,980 part-time. Students come from 31 states and territories, 5% are from out of state, 36% African American, 2% Asian American or Pacific Islander, 2% Hispanic American, 0.8% Native American, 0.2% international, 10% transferred in.

Freshmen *Admission:* 4,799 applied, 3,305 admitted, 2,265 enrolled.

Faculty *Total:* 692, 32% full-time. *Student/faculty ratio:* 18:1.

Majors Accounting; administrative assistant and secretarial science; architectural engineering technology; automobile/automotive mechanics technology; business administration and management; business/commerce; cartography; chemical technology; child care provision; civil engineering technology; clinical/medical laboratory technology; commercial and advertising art; computer and information sciences and support services related; computer installation and repair technology; computer systems networking and telecommunications; construction engineering technology; court reporting; criminal justice/safety; data processing and data processing technology; dental assisting; dental hygiene; electrical, electronic and communications engineering technology; engineering technology; fashion merchandising; gerontology; graphic and printing equipment operation/production; health information/medical records technology; health professions related; heating, air conditioning, ventilation and refrigeration maintenance technology; industrial electronics technology; industrial mechanics and maintenance technology; legal assistant/paralegal; liberal arts and sciences/liberal studies; mechanical drafting and CAD/CADD; mechanical engineering/mechanical technology; medical/clinical assistant; medical radiologic technology; multi-/interdisciplinary studies related; nuclear medical technology; nursing (licensed practical/vocational nurse training); nursing (registered nurse training); occupational therapist assistant; pharmacy technician; physical therapist assistant; precision production related; precision production trades; respiratory care therapy; sales, distribution and marketing; surgical technology; youth services.

Academics *Calendar:* semesters. *Degree:* certificates, diplomas, and associate. *Special study options:* academic remediation for entering students, adult/continuing education programs, advanced placement credit, cooperative education, distance learning, double majors, English as a second language, internships, part-time degree program, services for LD students, student-designed majors, summer session for credit.

Library 97,568 titles, 423 serial subscriptions, an OPAC, a Web page.

Student Life *Housing:* college housing not available. *Activities and Organizations:* student-run newspaper. *Campus security:* 24-hour emergency response devices and patrols, late-night transport/escort service.

Athletics *Intramural sports:* basketball M, football M, softball M/W, volleyball M/W.

Standardized Tests *Required:* ACT ASSET (for admission). *Recommended:* SAT or ACT (for admission).

Costs (2007–08) *Tuition:* area resident $3000 full-time, $125 per credit hour part-time; state resident $3744 full-time, $156 per credit hour part-time; nonresident $9000 full-time, $375 per credit hour part-time. *Required fees:* $100 full-time, $50 per term part-time.

Financial Aid Of all full-time matriculated undergraduates, 138 Federal Work-Study jobs (averaging $2496).

Applying *Options:* electronic application, early admission, deferred entrance. *Recommended:* high school transcript. *Application deadlines:* rolling (freshmen), rolling (transfers). *Notification:* continuous (freshmen), continuous (transfers).

Freshmen Application Contact Ms. Sylvia Littlejohn, Director of Admissions, Midlands Technical College, PO Box 2408, Columbia, SC 29202. *Phone:* 803-738-8324. *Fax:* 803-790-7524. *E-mail:* admissions@midlandstech.edu.

MILLER-MOTTE TECHNICAL COLLEGE

Charleston, South Carolina　　　　**www.miller-motte.com/**

Freshmen Application Contact Ms. Julie Corner, Campus President, Miller-Motte Technical College, 8085 Rivers Avenue, Suite E, Charleston, SC 29418. *Phone:* 843-574-0101. *Toll-free phone:* 877-617-4740. *Fax:* 843-266-3424. *E-mail:* juliasc@miller-mott.net.

NORTHEASTERN TECHNICAL COLLEGE

Cheraw, South Carolina　　　　**www.netc.edu/**

- **State and locally supported** 2-year, founded 1967, part of South Carolina State Board for Technical and Comprehensive Education
- **Rural** 59-acre campus
- **Endowment** $29,172
- **Coed,** 964 undergraduate students, 49% full-time, 73% women, 27% men

Undergraduates 472 full-time, 492 part-time. Students come from 2 states and territories, 1% are from out of state, 46% African American, 0.6% Asian American or Pacific Islander, 1% Hispanic American, 1% Native American, 4% transferred in.

Freshmen *Admission:* 468 applied, 468 admitted, 223 enrolled.

Faculty *Total:* 103, 27% full-time, 4% with terminal degrees. *Student/faculty ratio:* 25:1.

Majors Accounting; administrative assistant and secretarial science; business administration and management; computer programming; computer science; data processing and data processing technology; electrical, electronic and communications engineering technology; liberal arts and sciences/liberal studies; machine tool technology; marketing/marketing management; mechanical design technology.

Academics *Calendar:* semesters. *Degree:* certificates, diplomas, and associate. *Special study options:* academic remediation for entering students, adult/continuing education programs, advanced placement credit, distance learning, independent study, part-time degree program, study abroad.

Library Northeastern Technical College Library with 24,129 titles, 1,113 audiovisual materials, an OPAC, a Web page.

Student Life *Housing:* college housing not available. *Campus security:* 24-hour emergency response devices. *Student services:* personal/psychological counseling.

Standardized Tests *Required:* COMPASS (for admission). *Required for some:* SAT (for admission).

Costs (2006–07) *Tuition:* area resident $2616 full-time, $109 per credit hour part-time; state resident $2808 full-time, $117 per credit hour part-time; nonresident $5088 full-time, $212 per credit hour part-time. *Required fees:* $151 full-time, $4 per credit hour part-time, $15 per term part-time. *Waivers:* senior citizens.

Financial Aid Of all full-time matriculated undergraduates, 25 Federal Work-Study jobs (averaging $2700).

Applying *Options:* early admission. *Application fee:* $30. *Required:* high school transcript, interview. *Application deadlines:* 7/31 (freshmen), rolling (transfers). *Notification:* continuous (freshmen).

Freshmen Application Contact Mrs. Mary K. Newton, Dean of Students, Northeastern Technical College, PO Drawer 1007, Cheraw, SC 29520-1007. *Phone:* 843-921-6935. *Fax:* 843-921-1476. *E-mail:* mpace@netc.edu.

ORANGEBURG-CALHOUN TECHNICAL COLLEGE

Orangeburg, South Carolina　　　　**www.octech.edu/**

Freshmen Application Contact Dana Rickards, Director of Recruitment, Orangeburg-Calhoun Technical College, 3250 St. Matthews Road, Highway 601, Orangeburg, SC 29118. *Phone:* 803-535-1219. *Toll-free phone:* 800-813-6519.

PIEDMONT TECHNICAL COLLEGE

Greenwood, South Carolina　　　　**www.ptc.edu/**

- **State-supported** 2-year, founded 1966, part of South Carolina State Board for Technical and Comprehensive Education
- **Small-town** 60-acre campus
- **Endowment** $1.1 million
- **Coed,** 4,911 undergraduate students

Undergraduates Students come from 2 states and territories, 5 other countries, 1% are from out of state.

Freshmen *Admission:* 890 applied, 890 admitted.

Faculty *Total:* 233, 44% full-time. *Student/faculty ratio:* 18:1.

Majors Accounting; administrative assistant and secretarial science; automobile/automotive mechanics technology; biological and physical sciences; business administration and management; business/commerce; carpentry; child development; commercial and advertising art; computer programming; construction engineering technology; construction management; criminal justice/law enforcement administration; criminal justice/safety; data processing and data processing technology; drafting and design technology; electrical, electronic and communications engineering technology; engineering; engineering related; engineering technology; funeral service and mortuary science; heating, air conditioning, ventilation and refrigeration maintenance technology; human services; legal administrative assistant/secretary; liberal arts and sciences/liberal studies; machine tool technology; marketing/marketing management; mechanical drafting and CAD/CADD; mechanical engineering/mechanical technology; medical administrative assistant and medical secretary; medical radiologic technology; nursing (registered nurse training); office management; respiratory care therapy; social work.

Academics *Calendar:* semesters. *Degree:* certificates, diplomas, and associate. *Special study options:* academic remediation for entering students, adult/continuing education programs, advanced placement credit, cooperative education, distance learning, independent study, internships, part-time degree program, services for LD students, summer session for credit.

Library Piedmont Technical College Library with 27,497 titles, 345 serial subscriptions, 1,501 audiovisual materials, an OPAC, a Web page.

Student Life *Housing:* college housing not available. *Activities and Organizations:* choral group, National Honor Society, Career Peers (student volunteers), Student Nurses Association, Psychology Club, Ebony Club. *Campus security:* 24-hour emergency response devices and patrols, late-night transport/escort service. *Student services:* personal/psychological counseling, women's center.

Athletics *Intramural sports:* basketball M/W, football M/W, softball M/W, volleyball M/W.

Standardized Tests *Required:* ACT ACCESS, ACT COMPASS (for placement). *Recommended:* SAT (for placement).

Costs (2006–07) *Tuition:* area resident $2956 full-time; state resident $3364 full-time; nonresident $4564 full-time.

Financial Aid Of all full-time matriculated undergraduates, 98 Federal Work-Study jobs (averaging $3000).

Applying *Options:* electronic application, early admission, deferred entrance. *Application fee:* $25. *Required:* high school transcript. *Recommended:* interview. *Application deadlines:* rolling (freshmen), rolling (transfers). *Notification:* continuous until 8/20 (freshmen), continuous until 8/20 (transfers).

Director of Admissions Mr. Steve Coleman, Director of Admissions, Piedmont Technical College, 620 North Emerald Road, PO Box 1467, Greenwood, SC 29648. *Phone:* 864-941-8603. *Toll-free phone:* 800-868-5528.

SPARTANBURG METHODIST COLLEGE

Spartanburg, South Carolina　　　　**www.smcsc.edu/**

- **Independent Methodist** 2-year, founded 1911
- **Urban** 111-acre campus with easy access to Charlotte, NC
- **Endowment** $14.3 million
- **Coed**

Spartanburg Methodist College (continued)

Undergraduates 716 full-time, 63 part-time. Students come from 9 states and territories, 6 other countries, 6% are from out of state, 32% African American, 0.8% Asian American or Pacific Islander, 2% Hispanic American, 0.3% Native American, 2% international, 4% transferred in, 75% live on campus. *Retention:* 59% of 2003 full-time freshmen returned.

Faculty *Student/faculty ratio:* 23:1.

Academics *Calendar:* semesters. *Degree:* certificates, diplomas, and associate. *Special study options:* academic remediation for entering students, advanced placement credit, English as a second language, honors programs, independent study, part-time degree program, services for LD students, summer session for credit. *ROTC:* Army (c).

Student Life *Campus security:* 24-hour emergency response devices and patrols, student patrols, late-night transport/escort service, controlled dormitory access.

Athletics Member NJCAA.

Standardized Tests *Required:* SAT or ACT (for admission).

Financial Aid Of all full-time matriculated undergraduates, 80 Federal Work-Study jobs (averaging $1600). 90 state and other part-time jobs (averaging $1600). *Financial aid deadline:* 8/30.

Applying *Options:* electronic application, deferred entrance. *Application fee:* $20. *Required:* essay or personal statement, high school transcript, minimum 2.0 GPA, rank in upper 75% of high school class. *Required for some:* letters of recommendation, interview. *Recommended:* interview.

Freshmen Application Contact Daniel L. Philbeck, Vice President for Enrollment Management, Spartanburg Methodist College, 1000 Powell Mill Road, Spartanburg, SC 29301-5899. *Phone:* 864-587-4223. *Toll-free phone:* 800-772-7286. *Fax:* 864-587-4355. *E-mail:* admiss@smcsc.edu.

SPARTANBURG TECHNICAL COLLEGE

Spartanburg, South Carolina   www.stcsc.edu/

- **State-supported** 2-year, founded 1961, part of South Carolina State Board for Technical and Comprehensive Education
- **Suburban** 104-acre campus
- **Coed**

Undergraduates 2,435 full-time, 1,974 part-time. 2% are from out of state, 27% African American, 3% Asian American or Pacific Islander, 2% Hispanic American, 0.2% Native American.

Academics *Calendar:* semesters plus summer sessions. *Degree:* certificates, diplomas, and associate. *Special study options:* academic remediation for entering students, adult/continuing education programs, advanced placement credit, cooperative education, distance learning, part-time degree program, services for LD students, summer session for credit.

Student Life *Campus security:* 24-hour patrols.

Costs (2006–07) *Tuition:* area resident $3094 full-time, $130 per hour part-time; state resident $3860 full-time, $160 per hour part-time; nonresident $5490 full-time, $228 per hour part-time. *Required fees:* $20 full-time.

Financial Aid Of all full-time matriculated undergraduates, 75 Federal Work-Study jobs (averaging $2500).

Applying *Options:* early admission. *Required:* high school transcript.

Freshmen Application Contact Admissions Office, Spartanburg Technical College, PO Box 4386, Spartanburg, SC 29305. *Phone:* 864-592-4800. *Toll-free phone:* 866-591-3700. *Fax:* 864-592-4564. *E-mail:* admissions@stcsc.edu.

TECHNICAL COLLEGE OF THE LOWCOUNTRY

Beaufort, South Carolina   www.tclonline.org/

Director of Admissions Mr. Les Brediger, Director of Admissions, Technical College of the Lowcountry, 921 Ribaut Road, PO Box 1288, Beaufort, SC 29901-1288. *Phone:* 843-525-8307. *E-mail:* lbrediger@tcl.edu.

TRI-COUNTY TECHNICAL COLLEGE

Pendleton, South Carolina   www.tctc.edu/

Director of Admissions Ms. Rachel Campbell, Director, Admission and Counseling, Tri-County Technical College, PO Box 587, Highway 76, Pendleton, SC 29670-0587. *Phone:* 864-646-1500. *E-mail:* admstaff@tricty.tricounty.tec.sc.us.

TRIDENT TECHNICAL COLLEGE

Charleston, South Carolina   www.tridenttech.edu/

- **State and locally supported** 2-year, founded 1964, part of South Carolina State Board for Technical and Comprehensive Education
- **Urban** campus
- **Coed**, 11,808 undergraduate students, 44% full-time, 63% women, 37% men

Undergraduates 5,161 full-time, 6,647 part-time. 4% are from out of state, 26% African American, 2% Asian American or Pacific Islander, 2% Hispanic American, 0.5% Native American.

Freshmen *Admission:* 2,194 enrolled.

Faculty *Total:* 597, 45% full-time, 8% with terminal degrees. *Student/faculty ratio:* 19:1.

Majors Accounting; administrative assistant and secretarial science; airframe mechanics and aircraft maintenance technology; automobile/automotive mechanics technology; biological and physical sciences; broadcast journalism; business administration and management; child care provision; civil engineering technology; clinical/medical laboratory technology; commercial and advertising art; computer engineering technology; computer graphics; computer/information technology services administration related; computer programming (specific applications); computer systems networking and telecommunications; criminal justice/law enforcement administration; culinary arts; dental hygiene; electrical, electronic and communications engineering technology; engineering technology; horticultural science; hotel/motel administration; human services; industrial technology; legal assistant/paralegal; legal studies; liberal arts and sciences/liberal studies; machine tool technology; marketing/marketing management; mechanical engineering/mechanical technology; medical administrative assistant and medical secretary; nursing (registered nurse training); occupational therapy; physical therapy; respiratory care therapy; telecommunications; veterinary technology; web/multimedia management and webmaster; web page, digital/multimedia and information resources design.

Academics *Calendar:* semesters. *Degree:* certificates, diplomas, and associate. *Special study options:* academic remediation for entering students, advanced placement credit, cooperative education, English as a second language, part-time degree program, services for LD students, summer session for credit.

Library Learning Resources Center plus 3 others with 68,462 titles, 868 serial subscriptions.

Student Life *Housing:* college housing not available. *Activities and Organizations:* student-run newspaper. *Campus security:* 24-hour emergency response devices and patrols, late-night transport/escort service. *Student services:* personal/psychological counseling.

Costs (2006–07) *Tuition:* area resident $3014 full-time, $127 per credit hour part-time; state resident $3358 full-time, $141 per credit hour part-time; nonresident $5798 full-time, $243 per credit hour part-time. Full-time tuition and fees vary according to course load. Part-time tuition and fees vary according to course load. *Required fees:* $100 full-time, $5 per credit hour part-time.

Financial Aid Of all full-time matriculated undergraduates, 117 Federal Work-Study jobs (averaging $3000).

Applying *Options:* early admission. *Application fee:* $25. *Required for some:* high school transcript. *Application deadlines:* 8/6 (freshmen), 8/6 (transfers). *Notification:* continuous (freshmen), continuous (transfers).

Freshmen Application Contact Ms. Clara Martin, Admissions Director (Interim), Trident Technical College, 7000 Rivers Avenue, Charleston, SC 29423-8067. *Phone:* 843-574-6483. *Fax:* 843-574-6109. *E-mail:* Clara.Martin@tridenttech.edu.

UNIVERSITY OF SOUTH CAROLINA LANCASTER

Lancaster, South Carolina   usclancaster.sc.edu/

- **State-supported** 2-year, founded 1959, part of University of South Carolina System
- **Small-town** 17-acre campus with easy access to Charlotte
- **Coed**, 1,202 undergraduate students, 51% full-time, 65% women, 35% men

Undergraduates 611 full-time, 591 part-time. Students come from 1 other state, 1 other country, 1% are from out of state, 28% African American, 0.7% Asian American or Pacific Islander, 1% Hispanic American, 0.4% Native American.

Freshmen *Admission:* 448 applied, 284 admitted. *Average high school GPA:* 2.5. *Test scores:* SAT math scores over 500: 31%; SAT writing scores over 500: 22; SAT math scores over 600: 5%; SAT writing scores over 600: 5; SAT writing scores over 700: 1.

Faculty *Total:* 67, 48% full-time. *Student/faculty ratio:* 15:1.

Majors Administrative assistant and secretarial science; biological and physical sciences; business administration and management; criminal justice/law enforcement administration; liberal arts and sciences/liberal studies; nursing (registered nurse training).

Academics *Calendar:* semesters. *Degree:* associate. *Special study options:* academic remediation for entering students, adult/continuing education programs, advanced placement credit, distance learning, honors programs, part-time degree program.

Library Medford Library with 68,192 titles, 454 serial subscriptions.

Student Life *Housing:* college housing not available. *Activities and Organizations:* student-run newspaper, choral group. *Student services:* personal/psychological counseling, women's center.

Athletics *Intramural sports:* racquetball M/W, soccer M/W, tennis M/W, volleyball M/W, weight lifting M.

Standardized Tests *Required:* SAT or ACT (for admission).

Costs (2006–07) *One-time required fee:* $10. *Tuition:* state resident $2196 full-time, $183 per hour part-time; nonresident $5484 full-time, $457 per hour part-time. *Required fees:* $130 full-time, $10 per hour part-time.

Financial Aid Of all full-time matriculated undergraduates, 12 Federal Work-Study jobs (averaging $3000).

Applying *Options:* early admission. *Application fee:* $40. *Required:* high school transcript. *Application deadlines:* rolling (freshmen), rolling (transfers). *Notification:* continuous (freshmen), continuous (transfers).

Director of Admissions Ms. Karen Faile, Director of Enrollment Management, University of South Carolina Lancaster, PO Box 889, Lancaster, SC 29721-0889. *Phone:* 803-313-7000. *E-mail:* kfaile@gwm.sc.edu.

UNIVERSITY OF SOUTH CAROLINA SALKEHATCHIE

Allendale, South Carolina uscsalkehatchie.sc.edu/

Freshmen Application Contact Ms. Jane T. Brewer, Associate Dean for Student Services, University of South Carolina Salkehatchie, PO Box 617, Allendale, SC 29810-0617. *Phone:* 803-584-3446. *Toll-free phone:* 800-922-5500. *Fax:* 803-584-3884. *E-mail:* jtbrewer@gwm.sc.edu.

UNIVERSITY OF SOUTH CAROLINA SUMTER

Sumter, South Carolina www.uscsumter.edu/

- **State-supported** 2-year, founded 1966, part of University of South Carolina System
- **Urban** 50-acre campus
- **Endowment** $1.8 million
- **Coed**

Undergraduates 580 full-time, 440 part-time. Students come from 2 states and territories, 4 other countries, 1% are from out of state, 26% African American, 3% Asian American or Pacific Islander, 2% Hispanic American, 1% Native American, 0.1% international, 11% transferred in. *Retention:* 56% of 2003 full-time freshmen returned.

Faculty *Student/faculty ratio:* 19:1.

Academics *Calendar:* semesters. *Degree:* associate. *Special study options:* adult/continuing education programs, advanced placement credit, distance learning, honors programs, independent study, part-time degree program, services for LD students, summer session for credit. *ROTC:* Army (c), Air Force (c).

Student Life *Campus security:* late-night transport/escort service.

Athletics Member NSCAA.

Standardized Tests *Required:* SAT or ACT (for admission).

Costs (2006–07) *Tuition:* state resident $4392 full-time, $183 per semester hour part-time; nonresident $10,968 full-time, $457 per semester hour part-time. Full-time tuition and fees vary according to degree level. *Required fees:* $260 full-time, $10 per semester hour part-time.

Financial Aid Of all full-time matriculated undergraduates, 49 Federal Work-Study jobs (averaging $1428).

Applying *Options:* electronic application. *Application fee:* $40. *Required:* high school transcript, minimum 2.0 GPA.

Freshmen Application Contact Mr. Keith Britton, Director of Admissions, University of South Carolina Sumter, 200 Miller Road, Sumter, SC 29150-2498. *Phone:* 803-938-3882. *Fax:* 803-938-3901. *E-mail:* kbritton@usc.sumter.edu.

UNIVERSITY OF SOUTH CAROLINA UNION

Union, South Carolina uscunion.sc.edu/

- **State-supported** 2-year, founded 1965, part of University of South Carolina System
- **Small-town** campus with easy access to Charlotte
- **Coed**

Undergraduates 161 full-time, 160 part-time. Students come from 2 states and territories, 1% are from out of state, 27% African American, 0.6% Asian American or Pacific Islander, 0.6% Hispanic American, 0.3% Native American, 12% transferred in.

Faculty *Student/faculty ratio:* 14:1.

Academics *Calendar:* semesters. *Degree:* associate. *Special study options:* part-time degree program.

Standardized Tests *Required:* SAT or ACT (for admission).

Costs (2006–07) *Tuition:* state resident $4392 full-time, $182 per credit hour part-time; nonresident $10,968 full-time, $457 per hour part-time. *Required fees:* $100 full-time, $10 per hour part-time.

Financial Aid Of all full-time matriculated undergraduates, 16 Federal Work-Study jobs (averaging $3400).

Applying *Application fee:* $40. *Required:* high school transcript.

Freshmen Application Contact Mr. Terry Young, Director of Enrollment Services, University of South Carolina Union, PO Drawer 729, Union, SC 29379-0729. *Phone:* 864-429-8728.

WILLIAMSBURG TECHNICAL COLLEGE

Kingstree, South Carolina www.wiltech.edu/

Freshmen Application Contact Ms. Elaine M. Hanna, Director of Admissions, Williamsburg Technical College, 601 Martin Luther King Jr Avenue, Kingstree, SC 29556-4197. *Phone:* 843-355-4110 Ext. 4162. *Toll-free phone:* 800-768-2021 Ext. 4162. *E-mail:* admissions@witech.edu.

YORK TECHNICAL COLLEGE

Rock Hill, South Carolina www.yorktech.com/

- **State-supported** 2-year, founded 1961, part of South Carolina State Board for Technical and Comprehensive Education
- **Small-town** 110-acre campus with easy access to Charlotte
- **Coed,** 4,263 undergraduate students, 48% full-time, 63% women, 37% men

Undergraduates 2,040 full-time, 2,223 part-time. 2% are from out of state, 24% African American, 1% Asian American or Pacific Islander, 1% Hispanic American, 2% Native American.

Freshmen *Admission:* 1,032 admitted, 1,032 enrolled.

Faculty *Total:* 267, 48% full-time. *Student/faculty ratio:* 16:1.

Majors Accounting; administrative assistant and secretarial science; automobile/automotive mechanics technology; business administration and management; business/commerce; child care and support services management; child care provision; clinical/medical laboratory technology; commercial and advertising art; computer and information sciences and support services related; computer engineering technology; data processing and data processing technology; dental assisting; dental hygiene; electrical and electronic engineering technologies related; electrical, electronic and communications engineering technology; electrical/electronics equipment installation and repair; heating, air conditioning, ventilation and refrigeration maintenance technology; industrial electronics technology; industrial mechanics and maintenance technology; legal administrative assistant/secretary; liberal arts and sciences/liberal studies; machine tool technology; mechanical drafting and CAD/CADD; mechanical engineering/mechanical technology; medical administrative assistant and medical secretary; medical/clinical assistant; medical radiologic technology; multi-/interdisciplinary studies related; nursing (licensed practical/vocational nurse training); nursing (registered nurse training); office occupations and clerical services; radio and television broadcasting technology; surgical technology; welding technology.

Academics *Calendar:* semesters. *Degree:* certificates, diplomas, and associate. *Special study options:* academic remediation for entering students, adult/continuing education programs, advanced placement credit, cooperative education, distance learning, English as a second language, honors programs, internships, off-campus study, part-time degree program, services for LD students, summer session for credit.

York Technical College (continued)

Library Anne Springs Close Library with 26,947 titles, 475 serial subscriptions, an OPAC, a Web page.

Student Life *Housing:* college housing not available. *Activities and Organizations:* Jacobin Society, Phi Theta Kappa, Student Government Association, Phi Beta Lambda, Student Activities Board. *Campus security:* 24-hour patrols, late-night transport/escort service.

Standardized Tests *Required:* SAT, ACT, or ACT ASSET, ACT COMPASS (for admission).

Costs (2007–08) *Tuition:* area resident $2988 full-time; state resident $3312 full-time; nonresident $6864 full-time. *Required fees:* $136 full-time.

Financial Aid Of all full-time matriculated undergraduates, 56 Federal Work-Study jobs (averaging $3500).

Applying *Options:* electronic application. *Required for some:* high school transcript. *Application deadlines:* rolling (freshmen), rolling (transfers). *Notification:* continuous (freshmen), continuous (transfers).

Freshmen Application Contact Mr. Kenny Aldridge, Admissions Department Manager, York Technical College, 452 South Anderson Road, Rock Hill, SC 29730. *Phone:* 803-327-8008. *Toll-free phone:* 800-922-8324. *Fax:* 803-981-7237. *E-mail:* kaldridge@yorktech.com.

SOUTH DAKOTA

KILIAN COMMUNITY COLLEGE

Sioux Falls, South Dakota　　　　**www.kilian.edu/**

- **Independent** 2-year, founded 1977
- **Urban** 2-acre campus
- **Coed,** 477 undergraduate students, 19% full-time, 74% women, 26% men
- **100%** of applicants were admitted

Undergraduates 92 full-time, 385 part-time. Students come from 3 states and territories, 5% are from out of state, 7% African American, 1% Asian American or Pacific Islander, 1% Hispanic American, 10% Native American, 10% transferred in.

Freshmen *Admission:* 167 applied, 167 admitted, 64 enrolled.

Faculty *Total:* 55, 11% full-time, 5% with terminal degrees. *Student/faculty ratio:* 10:1.

Majors Accounting; administrative assistant and secretarial science; business administration and management; computer science; computer software and media applications related; counseling psychology; criminal justice/law enforcement administration; information technology; liberal arts and sciences/liberal studies; medical insurance coding; medical office management; medical transcription; social work.

Academics *Calendar:* trimesters. *Degree:* certificates and associate. *Special study options:* academic remediation for entering students, cooperative education, double majors, English as a second language, honors programs, independent study, internships, part-time degree program, services for LD students, summer session for credit.

Library University of Sioux Falls Mears Library with 78,000 titles, 395 serial subscriptions, an OPAC, a Web page.

Student Life *Housing:* college housing not available. *Campus security:* late-night transport/escort service. *Student services:* personal/psychological counseling.

Costs (2006–07) *Tuition:* $7416 full-time, $206 per credit hour part-time. *Required fees:* $180 full-time, $60 per term part-time. *Payment plan:* installment. *Waivers:* senior citizens.

Financial Aid Of all full-time matriculated undergraduates, 31 Federal Work-Study jobs (averaging $1200).

Applying *Options:* early admission, deferred entrance. *Application fee:* $25. *Required:* high school transcript. *Application deadlines:* rolling (freshmen), rolling (transfers).

Freshmen Application Contact Ms. Amy Modrell, Director of Admissions, Kilian Community College, 224 North Phillips Avenue, Sioux Falls, SD 57104-6014. *Phone:* 605-221-3100. *Toll-free phone:* 800-888-1147. *Fax:* 605-336-2606. *E-mail:* info@killian.edu.

LAKE AREA TECHNICAL INSTITUTE

Watertown, South Dakota　　　　**www.lati.tec.sd.us/**

Director of Admissions Ms. Debra Shephard, Assistant Director, Lake Area Technical Institute, 230 11th Street Northeast, Watertown, SD 57201. *Phone:* 605-882-5284. *Toll-free phone:* 800-657-4344. *E-mail:* latiinfo@lati.tec.sd.us.

MITCHELL TECHNICAL INSTITUTE

Mitchell, South Dakota　　　　**mti.tec.sd.us/**

Freshmen Application Contact Mr. Clayton Deuter, Admissions Representative, Mitchell Technical Institute, 821 North Capital, Mitchell, SD 57301. *Phone:* 605-995-3025. *Toll-free phone:* 800-952-0042.

NATIONAL AMERICAN UNIVERSITY

Ellsworth AFB, South Dakota　　　　**www.national.edu/**

- **Proprietary** 2-year
- **Coed,** 209 undergraduate students

Majors Business administration, management and operations related; computer and information sciences related.

Academics *Degree:* associate.

Costs (2006–07) *Tuition:* $6050 full-time.

Applying *Application fee:* $25.

Freshmen Application Contact Admissions Office, National American University, 1000 Ellsworth Street, Suite 2400B, Ellsworth AFB, SD 57706.

SISSETON-WAHPETON COMMUNITY COLLEGE

Sisseton, South Dakota　　　　**www.swc.tc/**

Director of Admissions Ms. Darlene Redday, Director of Admissions, Sisseton-Wahpeton Community College, Old Agency Box 689, Sisseton, SD 57262. *Phone:* 605-698-3966 Ext. 1110.

SOUTHEAST TECHNICAL INSTITUTE

Sioux Falls, South Dakota　　　　**www.southeasttech.com/**

- **State-supported** 2-year, founded 1968
- **Urban** 169-acre campus
- **Endowment** $423,589
- **Coed,** 2,115 undergraduate students, 83% full-time, 43% women, 57% men

Undergraduates 1,745 full-time, 370 part-time. Students come from 7 states and territories, 1 other country, 20% are from out of state, 0.9% African American, 1% Asian American or Pacific Islander, 0.3% Hispanic American, 1% Native American, 12% transferred in, 1% live on campus. *Retention:* 66% of 2003 full-time freshmen returned.

Freshmen *Admission:* 2,442 applied, 1,203 admitted, 583 enrolled. *Average high school GPA:* 2.73.

Faculty *Total:* 128, 59% full-time, 5% with terminal degrees. *Student/faculty ratio:* 18:1.

Majors Accounting; architectural engineering technology; artificial intelligence and robotics; autobody/collision and repair technology; automobile/automotive mechanics technology; biomedical technology; business administration and management; cardiovascular technology; civil engineering technology; clinical/medical laboratory technology; commercial and advertising art; computer and information sciences related; computer graphics; computer/information technology services administration related; computer programming; computer programming related; computer programming (specific applications); computer programming (vendor/product certification); computer software and media applications related; computer software engineering; computer systems networking and telecommunications; computer/technical support; computer technology/computer systems technology; diesel mechanics technology; drafting and design technology; electrical, electronic and communications engineering technology; electromechanical technology; engineering technology; finance; graphic and

printing equipment operation/production; health unit coordinator/ward clerk; heating, air conditioning, ventilation and refrigeration maintenance technology; horticultural science; industrial technology; information science/studies; information technology; laser and optical technology; machine tool technology; marketing/marketing management; mechanical engineering/mechanical technology; medical transcription; nuclear medical technology; nursing related; sign language interpretation and translation; surgical technology; survey technology; system administration; turf and turfgrass management; web/multimedia management and webmaster; web page, digital/multimedia and information resources design.

Academics *Calendar:* semesters. *Degree:* certificates, diplomas, and associate. *Special study options:* academic remediation for entering students, accelerated degree program, advanced placement credit, double majors, independent study, internships, part-time degree program, services for LD students, summer session for credit.

Library Southeast Library with 10,643 titles, 158 serial subscriptions, an OPAC.

Student Life *Housing Options:* coed. Campus housing is provided by a third party. *Activities and Organizations:* VICA, ICON, PBL, American Landscape Contractors Association, Silent Tones. *Campus security:* 24-hour emergency response devices and patrols, late-night transport/escort service. *Student services:* personal/psychological counseling.

Athletics *Intramural sports:* basketball M/W, volleyball M/W.

Standardized Tests *Recommended:* ACT (for admission).

Costs (2007–08) *Tuition:* state resident $2220 full-time, $74 per credit part-time; nonresident $2220 full-time, $74 per credit part-time. *Required fees:* $1372 full-time, $46 per credit part-time. *Room and board:* room only: $4140.

Financial Aid Of all full-time matriculated undergraduates, 35 Federal Work-Study jobs (averaging $2550).

Applying *Required:* high school transcript, minimum 2.2 GPA. *Required for some:* interview. *Application deadlines:* rolling (freshmen), rolling (out-of-state freshmen), rolling (transfers). *Notification:* continuous (freshmen), continuous (out-of-state freshmen), continuous (transfers).

Freshmen Application Contact Mr. Scott Dorman, Recruiter, Southeast Technical Institute, 2320 North Career Avenue, Sioux Falls, SD 57107. *Phone:* 605-367-7624. *Toll-free phone:* 800-247-0789. *Fax:* 605-367-8305. *E-mail:* scott.dorman@southeasttech.com.

WESTERN DAKOTA TECHNICAL INSTITUTE

Rapid City, South Dakota   www.westerndakotatech.org/

Freshmen Application Contact Jill Elder, Western Dakota Technical Institute, 800 Mickelson Drive, Rapid City, SD 57703. *Phone:* 605-718-2411 Ext. 111. *Toll-free phone:* 800-544-8765. *Fax:* 605-394-2204. *E-mail:* jill.elder@wdt.edu.

TENNESSEE

CHATTANOOGA STATE TECHNICAL COMMUNITY COLLEGE

Chattanooga, Tennessee   www.chattanoogastate.edu/

- **State-supported** 2-year, founded 1965, part of Tennessee Board of Regents
- **Urban** 100-acre campus
- **Coed,** 8,060 undergraduate students, 44% full-time, 62% women, 38% men

Undergraduates 3,560 full-time, 4,500 part-time. Students come from 22 states and territories, 24 other countries, 7% are from out of state, 19% African American, 1% Asian American or Pacific Islander, 1% Hispanic American, 0.4% Native American, 0.4% international, 8% transferred in.

Freshmen *Admission:* 1,349 applied, 1,349 admitted, 1,348 enrolled. *Average high school GPA:* 2.73. *Test scores:* ACT scores over 18: 56%; ACT scores over 24: 7%.

Faculty *Total:* 602, 35% full-time. *Student/faculty ratio:* 20:1.

Majors Accounting; administrative assistant and secretarial science; advertising; airline pilot and flight crew; applied art; artificial intelligence and robotics;

automobile/automotive mechanics technology; aviation/airway management; avionics maintenance technology; biology/biological sciences; broadcast journalism; business administration and management; chemical engineering; chemistry; child development; civil engineering technology; commercial and advertising art; computer engineering technology; computer programming; computer science; consumer merchandising/retailing management; criminal justice/law enforcement administration; data processing and data processing technology; dental hygiene; drafting and design technology; electrical, electronic and communications engineering technology; emergency medical technology (EMT paramedic); energy management and systems technology; engineering related; environmental engineering technology; finance; fire science; fish/game management; food services technology; forestry; forestry technology; graphic and printing equipment operation/production; health information/medical records administration; heating, air conditioning, ventilation and refrigeration maintenance technology; hotel/motel administration; industrial radiologic technology; information science/studies; instrumentation technology; kindergarten/preschool education; legal administrative assistant/secretary; liberal arts and sciences/liberal studies; machine tool technology; mass communication/media; mechanical design technology; mechanical engineering/mechanical technology; medical administrative assistant and medical secretary; nuclear medical technology; nuclear/nuclear power technology; nursing (registered nurse training); occupational therapy; physical therapy; radio and television; respiratory care therapy; sign language interpretation and translation; survey technology; transportation technology; welding technology; wildlife and wildlands science and management.

Academics *Calendar:* semesters. *Degree:* certificates, diplomas, and associate. *Special study options:* academic remediation for entering students, accelerated degree program, adult/continuing education programs, advanced placement credit, cooperative education, distance learning, English as a second language, honors programs, independent study, internships, part-time degree program, services for LD students, summer session for credit.

Library Augusta R. Kolwyck Library with 73,334 titles, 803 serial subscriptions, an OPAC, a Web page.

Student Life *Housing:* college housing not available. *Activities and Organizations:* student-run newspaper, radio station, choral group, Black Student Association, Adult Connections, Human Services Specialists, Student Government Association, Student Nurses Association. *Campus security:* 24-hour emergency response devices and patrols, late-night transport/escort service. *Student services:* personal/psychological counseling, women's center.

Athletics Member NJCAA. *Intercollegiate sports:* baseball M(s), basketball M(s)/W(s), softball W(s). *Intramural sports:* softball W.

Costs (2006–07) *Tuition:* state resident $2230 full-time, $95 per semester hour part-time; nonresident $8906 full-time, $384 per semester hour part-time.

Financial Aid Of all full-time matriculated undergraduates, 377 Federal Work-Study jobs (averaging $652).

Applying *Options:* early admission, deferred entrance. *Application fee:* $15. *Required:* high school transcript. *Application deadlines:* rolling (freshmen), rolling (transfers). *Notification:* continuous (freshmen), continuous (transfers).

Freshmen Application Contact Ms. Diane Norris, Director of Admissions, Chattanooga State Technical Community College, 4501 Amnicola Highway, Chattanooga, TN 37406-1097. *Phone:* 423-697-4401 Ext. 3107. *Fax:* 423-697-4709. *E-mail:* admsis@chattanoogastate.edu.

CLEVELAND STATE COMMUNITY COLLEGE

Cleveland, Tennessee   www.clevelandstatecc.edu/

- **State-supported** 2-year, founded 1967, part of Tennessee Board of Regents
- **Suburban** 83-acre campus
- **Endowment** $5.8 million
- **Coed,** 2,947 undergraduate students, 53% full-time, 61% women, 39% men

Undergraduates 1,559 full-time, 1,388 part-time. Students come from 9 states and territories, 19 other countries, 1% are from out of state, 5% African American, 2% Asian American or Pacific Islander, 2% Hispanic American, 0.5% Native American, 6% transferred in.

Freshmen *Admission:* 946 applied, 572 admitted, 572 enrolled. *Average high school GPA:* 2.0.

Faculty *Total:* 177, 39% full-time, 14% with terminal degrees. *Student/faculty ratio:* 19:1.

Majors Administrative assistant and secretarial science; business administration and management; child development; community organization and advocacy; general studies; industrial arts; industrial technology; kindergarten/preschool education; liberal arts and sciences/liberal studies; nursing (registered nurse training); public administration and social service professions related.

Cleveland State Community College (continued)

Academics *Calendar:* semesters. *Degree:* certificates and associate. *Special study options:* academic remediation for entering students, adult/continuing education programs, advanced placement credit, cooperative education, distance learning, double majors, external degree program, honors programs, independent study, internships, off-campus study, part-time degree program, services for LD students, summer session for credit.

Library Cleveland State Community College Library with 122,452 titles, 348 serial subscriptions, 4,531 audiovisual materials, an OPAC, a Web page.

Student Life *Housing:* college housing not available. *Activities and Organizations:* student-run newspaper, choral group, Student Senate, International Association of Administration Professionals, Phi Theta Kappa, Student Nursing Association. *Campus security:* 24-hour emergency response devices and patrols. *Student services:* personal/psychological counseling.

Athletics Member NJCAA. *Intercollegiate sports:* baseball M(s), basketball M(s)/W(s), softball W(s). *Intramural sports:* archery M/W, badminton M/W, basketball M/W, bowling M/W, golf M/W, softball M/W, table tennis M/W, tennis M/W, volleyball M/W.

Standardized Tests *Recommended:* SAT or ACT (for admission).

Costs (2007–08) *Tuition:* state resident $2405 full-time, $95 per credit hour part-time; nonresident $8819 full-time, $384 per credit hour part-time. *Required fees:* $263 full-time, $14 per credit hour part-time, $14 per term part-time.

Financial Aid Of all full-time matriculated undergraduates, 52 Federal Work-Study jobs (averaging $1025).

Applying *Options:* early admission, deferred entrance. *Application fee:* $10. *Required:* high school transcript. *Application deadlines:* rolling (freshmen), rolling (transfers). *Notification:* continuous (freshmen), continuous (transfers).

Freshmen Application Contact Ms. Midge Burnette, Director of Admissions and Recruitment, Cleveland State Community College, 3535 Adkisson Drive, Cleveland, TN 37320-3570. *Phone:* 423-478-6212. *Toll-free phone:* 800-604-2722. *Fax:* 423-478-6255. *E-mail:* mburnette@clevelandstatecc.edu.

COLUMBIA STATE COMMUNITY COLLEGE

Columbia, Tennessee — www.columbiastate.edu/

Freshmen Application Contact Mr. Joey Scruggs, Coordinator of Recruitment, Columbia State Community College, PO Box 1315, Columbia, TN 38402-1315. *Phone:* 931-540-2540. *E-mail:* scruggs@coscc.cc.tn.us.

CONCORDE CAREER COLLEGE

Memphis, Tennessee — www.concordecareercolleges.com/

- **Proprietary** 2-year, founded 1969
- **Coed,** 1,049 undergraduate students
- 100% of applicants were admitted

Freshmen *Admission:* 937 applied, 937 admitted.

Majors Respiratory care therapy.

Academics *Degree:* associate.

Applying *Required:* high school transcript.

Admissions Office Contact Concorde Career College, 5100 Poplar Avenue, Suite 132, Memphis, TN 38137.

DRAUGHONS JUNIOR COLLEGE

Clarksville, Tennessee — www.draughons.edu/

Director of Admissions Admissions Office, Draughons Junior College, 1860 Wilma Rudolph Boulevard, Clarksville, TN 37040.

DRAUGHONS JUNIOR COLLEGE

Nashville, Tennessee — www.draughons.edu/

Director of Admissions Admissions Office, Draughons Junior College, 340 Plus Park, Nashville, TN 37217. *Phone:* 615-361-7555. *Fax:* 615-367-2736.

DYERSBURG STATE COMMUNITY COLLEGE

Dyersburg, Tennessee — www.dscc.edu/

- **State-supported** 2-year, founded 1969, part of Tennessee Board of Regents
- **Small-town** 100-acre campus with easy access to Memphis
- **Endowment** $3.2 million
- **Coed,** 2,586 undergraduate students, 51% full-time, 71% women, 29% men

Undergraduates 1,315 full-time, 1,271 part-time. Students come from 10 states and territories, 1% are from out of state, 18% African American, 0.5% Asian American or Pacific Islander, 1% Hispanic American, 0.7% Native American, 6% transferred in. *Retention:* 55% of 2003 full-time freshmen returned.

Freshmen *Admission:* 953 applied, 947 admitted, 573 enrolled. *Average high school GPA:* 2.36. *Test scores:* ACT scores over 18: 55%; ACT scores over 24: 5%.

Faculty *Total:* 205, 28% full-time, 13% with terminal degrees. *Student/faculty ratio:* 17:1.

Majors Business administration and management; child development; computer/information technology services administration related; criminal justice/police science; electrical, electronic and communications engineering technology; health information/medical records technology; liberal arts and sciences/liberal studies; nursing (registered nurse training).

Academics *Calendar:* semesters. *Degree:* certificates and associate. *Special study options:* academic remediation for entering students, adult/continuing education programs, advanced placement credit, distance learning, double majors, honors programs, independent study, part-time degree program, services for LD students, summer session for credit.

Library Learning Resource Center with 44,355 titles, 87 serial subscriptions, 2,274 audiovisual materials, an OPAC, a Web page.

Student Life *Housing:* college housing not available. *Activities and Organizations:* drama/theater group, choral group, student government, Phi Theta Kappa, Minority Association for Successful Students, Video Club, Psychology Club. *Campus security:* 24-hour patrols. *Student services:* personal/psychological counseling.

Athletics Member NJCAA. *Intercollegiate sports:* baseball M(s), basketball M(s)/W(s), cheerleading W(s), softball W(s).

Standardized Tests *Required:* SAT or ACT (for admission).

Costs (2007–08) *Tuition:* state resident $2230 full-time, $95 per hour part-time; nonresident $9157 full-time, $384 per hour part-time. *Required fees:* $251 full-time, $126 per term part-time.

Financial Aid Of all full-time matriculated undergraduates, 84 Federal Work-Study jobs (averaging $997). 115 state and other part-time jobs (averaging $837).

Applying *Options:* early admission. *Application fee:* $10. *Required:* high school transcript. *Application deadlines:* rolling (freshmen), rolling (transfers). *Notification:* continuous (freshmen), continuous (transfers).

Freshmen Application Contact Mr. Dan Gullett, Assistant Vice President for Academic Affairs, Dyersburg State Community College, 1510 Lake Road, Dyersburg, TN 38024. *Phone:* 731-286-3327. *Fax:* 731-286-3325. *E-mail:* gulett@dscc.edu.

ELECTRONIC COMPUTER PROGRAMMING COLLEGE

Chattanooga, Tennessee — www.ecpconline.com/

Director of Admissions Toney McFadden, Admission Director, Electronic Computer Programming College, 3805 Brainerd Road, Chattanooga, TN 37411-3798. *Phone:* 423-624-0077. *Fax:* 423-624-1575.

FOUNTAINHEAD COLLEGE OF TECHNOLOGY

Knoxville, Tennessee — www.fountainheadcollege.edu/

- **Proprietary** primarily 2-year, founded 1947
- **Suburban** 1-acre campus
- **Coed,** 120 undergraduate students

Undergraduates Students come from 1 other state.

Faculty *Total:* 10, 90% full-time, 100% with terminal degrees. *Student/faculty ratio:* 13:1.

Majors Communications technology; computer and information systems security; computer engineering technology; electrical, electronic and communications engineering technology; industrial technology; information science/studies.

Academics *Calendar:* semesters. *Degrees:* associate and bachelor's. *Special study options:* summer session for credit.

Library 1,200 titles, 1,000 serial subscriptions, a Web page.

Student Life *Housing:* college housing not available. *Campus security:* 24-hour emergency response devices.

Applying *Application fee:* $100. *Recommended:* high school transcript. *Application deadlines:* rolling (freshmen), rolling (transfers). *Notification:* continuous (freshmen), continuous (transfers).

Freshmen Application Contact Mr. Todd Hill, Director of Administration, Fountainhead College of Technology, 3203 Tazewell Pike, Knoxville, TN 37918-2530. *Phone:* 865-688-9422. *Toll-free phone:* 888-218-7335. *Fax:* 865-688-2419.

HIGH-TECH INSTITUTE

Memphis, Tennessee www.high-techinstitute.com/

- **Proprietary** 2-year, founded 2003
- **Coed,** 1,101 undergraduate students

Majors Massage therapy; medical/clinical assistant; medical insurance/medical billing; pharmacy technician; surgical technology.

Academics *Calendar:* semesters. *Degree:* associate.

Costs (2006–07) *Tuition:* $21,350 per degree program part-time.

Applying *Application fee:* $50.

Freshmen Application Contact Admissions Office, High-Tech Institute, 5865 Shelby Oaks Circle, Suite 100, Memphis, TN 38134. *Toll-free phone:* 866-269-7251.

HIGH-TECH INSTITUTE

Nashville, Tennessee www.high-techinstitute.com/

- **Proprietary** 2-year, founded 1999
- **Coed,** 1,319 undergraduate students

Majors Computer and information systems security; dental assisting; massage therapy; medical/clinical assistant; medical insurance/medical billing; medical radiologic technology; surgical technology; web page, digital/multimedia and information resources design.

Academics *Calendar:* semesters. *Degree:* associate.

Costs (2006–07) *Tuition:* $22,134 per degree program part-time.

Applying *Application fee:* $50.

Freshmen Application Contact Admissions Office, High-Tech Institute, 560 Royal Parkway, Nashville, TN 37214. *Phone:* 615-902-9705. *Toll-free phone:* 888-616-6549.

ITT TECHNICAL INSTITUTE

Cordova, Tennessee www.itt-tech.edu/

- **Proprietary** primarily 2-year, founded 1994, part of ITT Educational Services, Inc
- **Suburban** 1-acre campus
- **Coed**

Majors Accounting and business/management; animation, interactive technology, video graphics and special effects; business administration and management; CAD/CADD drafting/design technology; communications technology; computer and information systems security; computer engineering technology; computer software engineering; computer systems networking and telecommunications; criminal justice/law enforcement administration; electrical, electronic and communications engineering technology; purchasing, procurement/acquisitions and contracts management; web page, digital/multimedia and information resources design.

Academics *Calendar:* quarters. *Degrees:* associate and bachelor's.

Library a Web page.

Student Life *Housing:* college housing not available. *Activities and Organizations:* student-run newspaper.

Standardized Tests *Required:* Wonderlic aptitude test (for admission).

Costs (2006–07) *Tuition:* Contact school for program costs.

Applying *Options:* deferred entrance. *Application fee:* $100. *Required:* high school transcript, interview. *Recommended:* letters of recommendation. *Application deadlines:* rolling (freshmen), rolling (transfers). *Notification:* continuous (freshmen), continuous (transfers).

Freshmen Application Contact Ms. Sharon Johnson, Director of Recruitment, ITT Technical Institute, 7260 Goodlett Farms Parkway, Cordova, TN 38016. *Phone:* 901-381-0200. *Toll-free phone:* 866-444-5141.

ITT TECHNICAL INSTITUTE

Knoxville, Tennessee www.itt-tech.edu/

- **Proprietary** primarily 2-year, founded 1988, part of ITT Educational Services, Inc
- **Suburban** 5-acre campus
- **Coed**

Majors Accounting technology and bookkeeping; animation, interactive technology, video graphics and special effects; business administration and management; CAD/CADD drafting/design technology; communications technology; computer and information systems security; computer engineering technology; computer software engineering; computer software technology; computer systems networking and telecommunications; construction management; criminal justice/law enforcement administration; electrical, electronic and communications engineering technology; web/multimedia management and webmaster; web page, digital/multimedia and information resources design.

Academics *Calendar:* quarters. *Degrees:* associate and bachelor's.

Library a Web page.

Student Life *Housing:* college housing not available.

Standardized Tests *Required:* Wonderlic aptitude test (for admission).

Costs (2006–07) *Tuition:* Contact school for program costs.

Applying *Options:* deferred entrance. *Application fee:* $100. *Required:* high school transcript, interview. *Recommended:* letters of recommendation. *Application deadlines:* rolling (freshmen), rolling (transfers). *Notification:* continuous (freshmen), continuous (transfers).

Freshmen Application Contact Mr. Dan Deck, Director of Recruitment, ITT Technical Institute, 10208 Technology Drive, Knoxville, TN 37932. *Phone:* 865-671-2800. *Toll-free phone:* 800-671-2801.

ITT TECHNICAL INSTITUTE

Nashville, Tennessee www.itt-tech.edu/

- **Proprietary** primarily 2-year, founded 1984, part of ITT Educational Services, Inc
- **Urban** 21-acre campus
- **Coed**

Majors Accounting technology and bookkeeping; animation, interactive technology, video graphics and special effects; business administration and management; CAD/CADD drafting/design technology; communications technology; computer and information systems security; computer engineering technology; computer software engineering; computer software technology; computer systems networking and telecommunications; construction management; criminal justice/law enforcement administration; electrical, electronic and communications engineering technology; web/multimedia management and webmaster; web page, digital/multimedia and information resources design.

Academics *Calendar:* quarters. *Degrees:* associate and bachelor's.

Library a Web page.

Student Life *Housing:* college housing not available.

Standardized Tests *Required:* Wonderlic aptitude test (for admission).

Costs (2006–07) *Tuition:* Contact school for program costs.

Applying *Options:* deferred entrance. *Application fee:* $100. *Required:* high school transcript, interview. *Recommended:* letters of recommendation. *Application deadlines:* rolling (freshmen), rolling (transfers). *Notification:* continuous (freshmen), continuous (transfers).

Freshmen Application Contact Mr. Glenn Wallace, Director of Recruitment, ITT Technical Institute, 2845 Elm Hill Pike, Nashville, TN 37214. *Phone:* 615-889-8700. *Toll-free phone:* 800-331-8386.

JACKSON STATE COMMUNITY COLLEGE

Jackson, Tennessee   www.jscc.edu/

- **State-supported** 2-year, founded 1967, part of Tennessee Board of Regents
- **Suburban** 104-acre campus
- **Endowment** $687,110
- **Coed,** 4,106 undergraduate students, 55% full-time, 68% women, 32% men

Undergraduates 2,266 full-time, 1,840 part-time. Students come from 3 states and territories, 5 other countries, 1% are from out of state, 19% African American, 0.4% Asian American or Pacific Islander, 1% Hispanic American, 0.3% Native American, 0.2% international, 7% transferred in. *Retention:* 51% of 2003 full-time freshmen returned.

Freshmen *Admission:* 1,416 applied, 1,003 admitted, 870 enrolled. *Average high school GPA:* 2.73. *Test scores:* ACT scores over 18: 56%; ACT scores over 24: 8%.

Faculty *Total:* 235, 49% full-time, 9% with terminal degrees. *Student/faculty ratio:* 18:1.

Majors Agricultural business and management; business administration and management; child development; clinical/medical laboratory technology; commercial and advertising art; computer science; electromechanical technology; industrial technology; liberal arts and sciences/liberal studies; management information systems; medical radiologic technology; nursing (registered nurse training); physical therapist assistant; respiratory care therapy; tool and die technology.

Academics *Calendar:* semesters. *Degree:* certificates and associate. *Special study options:* academic remediation for entering students, adult/continuing education programs, advanced placement credit, cooperative education, distance learning, external degree program, honors programs, internships, part-time degree program, services for LD students, summer session for credit.

Library Jackson State Community College Library with 62,500 titles, 178 serial subscriptions, 2,594 audiovisual materials, an OPAC, a Web page.

Student Life *Housing:* college housing not available. *Activities and Organizations:* drama/theater group, choral group, Student Government Organization, Spanish Club, Biology Club, Art Club, Black Student Association. *Campus security:* 24-hour patrols. *Student services:* health clinic, personal/psychological counseling.

Athletics Member NJCAA. *Intercollegiate sports:* baseball M(s), basketball M(s)/W(s), cheerleading W(s), softball W(s). *Intramural sports:* basketball M/W, football M, golf M, tennis M/W, volleyball W.

Standardized Tests *Required:* ACT (for admission), COMPASS (for admission).

Costs (2007–08) *Tuition:* state resident $2230 full-time, $95 per semester hour part-time; nonresident $8906 full-time, $384 per semester hour part-time. *Required fees:* $506 full-time, $9 per credit hour part-time, $14 per term part-time.

Financial Aid Of all full-time matriculated undergraduates, 60 Federal Work-Study jobs (averaging $3000). 10 state and other part-time jobs (averaging $3000).

Applying *Options:* electronic application, early admission, deferred entrance. *Application fee:* $10. *Required for some:* high school transcript. *Application deadlines:* 8/27 (freshmen), 8/27 (out-of-state freshmen), rolling (transfers). *Notification:* continuous (freshmen), continuous (out-of-state freshmen), continuous (transfers).

Freshmen Application Contact Ms. Monica Ray, Director of Admissions, Jackson State Community College, 2046 North Parkway, Jackson, TN 38301. *Phone:* 731-425-2644. *Toll-free phone:* 800-355-5722. *Fax:* 731-425-9559. *E-mail:* mray@jscc.edu.

JOHN A. GUPTON COLLEGE

Nashville, Tennessee   www.guptoncollege.edu/

- **Independent** 2-year, founded 1946
- **Urban** 1-acre campus
- **Endowment** $60,000
- **Coed,** 97 undergraduate students, 94% full-time, 44% women, 56% men

Undergraduates 91 full-time, 6 part-time. Students come from 8 states and territories, 25% are from out of state, 27% African American, 11% transferred in.

Freshmen *Admission:* 93 applied, 51 admitted, 51 enrolled.

Faculty *Total:* 18, 11% full-time. *Student/faculty ratio:* 13:1.

Majors Funeral service and mortuary science.

Academics *Calendar:* semesters. *Degree:* diplomas and associate. *Special study options:* part-time degree program.

Library Memorial Library with 4,000 titles, 54 serial subscriptions, a Web page.

Student Life *Housing Options:* coed. *Campus security:* controlled dormitory access, day patrols.

Standardized Tests *Required:* ACT (for admission).

Costs (2006–07) *Tuition:* $7200 full-time.

Financial Aid *Financial aid deadline:* 6/1.

Applying *Options:* deferred entrance. *Application fee:* $20. *Required:* essay or personal statement, high school transcript, 2 letters of recommendation, health forms. *Application deadlines:* rolling (freshmen), rolling (transfers).

Director of Admissions Ms. Lisa Bolin, Registrar, John A. Gupton College, 1616 Church Street, Nashville, TN 37203. *Phone:* 615-327-3927.

MEDVANCE INSTITUTE

Cookeville, Tennessee   www.medvance.org/

Director of Admissions Ms. Sharon Mellott, Director of Admissions, MedVance Institute, 1065 East 10th Street, Cookeville, TN 38501-1907. *Phone:* 931-526-3660. *Toll-free phone:* 800-259-3659 (in-state); 800-256-9085 (out-of-state).

MID-AMERICA BAPTIST THEOLOGICAL SEMINARY

Cordova, Tennessee   www.mabts.edu/

- **Independent Southern Baptist** founded 1972
- **Suburban** campus with easy access to Memphis
- **Endowment** $3.6 million
- **Coed, primarily men,** 51 undergraduate students, 57% full-time, 100% men

Undergraduates 29 full-time, 22 part-time. Students come from 26 states and territories, 8% African American, 2% international.

Faculty *Total:* 27, 100% full-time, 100% with terminal degrees. *Student/faculty ratio:* 15:1.

Majors Theology.

Academics *Calendar:* semesters. *Degrees:* associate, master's, doctoral, and first professional. *Special study options:* part-time degree program, summer session for credit.

Library Ora Byram Allison Memorial Library with 119,000 titles, 931 serial subscriptions, an OPAC, a Web page.

Student Life *Housing Options:* Campus housing is university owned. *Campus security:* 24-hour emergency response devices.

Costs (2007–08) *Tuition:* $3760 full-time, $310 per course part-time. *Required fees:* $40 full-time.

Applying *Application fee:* $25. *Required:* 2 letters of recommendation. *Required for some:* high school transcript. *Application deadline:* 8/4 (freshmen).

Freshmen Application Contact Mr. Duffy Guyton, Director of Admissions, Mid-America Baptist Theological Seminary, PO Box 2350, 2095 Appling Road, Cordova, TN 38016. *Phone:* 901-751-8453 Ext. 3066. *Toll-free phone:* 800-968-4508. *Fax:* 901-751-8454. *E-mail:* info@mabts.edu.

MILLER-MOTTE TECHNICAL COLLEGE

Clarksville, Tennessee   www.miller-motte.com/

- **Proprietary** 2-year, founded 1916
- **Coed,** 516 undergraduate students

Majors Accounting; accounting technology and bookkeeping; business, management, and marketing related; computer and information sciences and support services related; computer programming (specific applications); corrections and criminal justice related; drafting/design technology; executive assistant/executive secretary; massage therapy; medical/clinical assistant; paralegal/legal assistant; surgical technology.

Academics *Calendar:* quarters. *Degree:* associate.

Costs (2006–07) *Tuition:* $8020 full-time.

Financial Aid Of all full-time matriculated undergraduates, 5 Federal Work-Study jobs (averaging $1650).

Director of Admissions Ms. Lisa Teague, Director of Admissions, Miller-Motte Technical College, 1820 Business Park Drive, Clarksville, TN 37040. *Phone:* 800-558-0071. *E-mail:* lisateague@hotmail.com.

MOTLOW STATE COMMUNITY COLLEGE

Tullahoma, Tennessee   **www.mscc.cc.tn.us/**

- **State-supported** 2-year, founded 1969, part of Tennessee Board of Regents
- **Rural** 187-acre campus with easy access to Nashville
- **Endowment** $3.5 million
- **Coed,** 3,833 undergraduate students, 54% full-time, 65% women, 35% men

Undergraduates 2,087 full-time, 1,746 part-time. Students come from 15 states and territories, 5 other countries, 1% are from out of state, 8% African American, 1% Asian American or Pacific Islander, 2% Hispanic American, 0.4% Native American, 0.2% international, 9% transferred in.

Freshmen *Admission:* 1,268 applied, 1,033 admitted, 1,011 enrolled. *Average high school GPA:* 2.77. *Test scores:* SAT verbal scores over 500: 45%; SAT math scores over 500: 50%; ACT scores over 18: 60%; SAT verbal scores over 600: 5%; SAT math scores over 600: 15%; ACT scores over 24: 7%.

Faculty *Total:* 217, 35% full-time, 13% with terminal degrees. *Student/faculty ratio:* 22:1.

Majors Business administration and management; liberal arts and sciences/liberal studies; nursing (registered nurse training); special education (early childhood).

Academics *Calendar:* semesters. *Degree:* certificates and associate. *Special study options:* academic remediation for entering students, adult/continuing education programs, advanced placement credit, cooperative education, distance learning, double majors, honors programs, independent study, part-time degree program, services for LD students, summer session for credit.

Library Crouch Library with 116,049 titles, 211 serial subscriptions, 4,111 audiovisual materials, an OPAC, a Web page.

Student Life *Housing:* college housing not available. *Activities and Organizations:* drama/theater group, student-run newspaper, choral group, Photography Club, Psychology Club, Student Government Association, Outing Club, Baptist Student Union. *Campus security:* 24-hour patrols, late-night transport/escort service. *Student services:* health clinic, personal/psychological counseling.

Athletics Member NJCAA. *Intercollegiate sports:* baseball M(s), basketball M(s)/W(s), softball W(s). *Intramural sports:* archery M/W, badminton M/W, basketball M/W, bowling M/W, golf M/W, tennis M/W, volleyball M/W.

Costs (2006–07) *Tuition:* state resident $2142 full-time, $95 per credit hour part-time; nonresident $6414 full-time, $289 per credit hour part-time. Full-time tuition and fees vary according to program. Part-time tuition and fees vary according to course load and program. *Required fees:* $247 full-time, $15 per credit hour part-time. *Payment plans:* installment, deferred payment. *Waivers:* senior citizens and employees or children of employees.

Financial Aid Of all full-time matriculated undergraduates, 66 Federal Work-Study jobs (averaging $1285).

Applying *Options:* electronic application, early admission, deferred entrance. *Application fee:* $10. *Required:* high school transcript. *Application deadlines:* 8/13 (freshmen), 8/13 (transfers). *Notification:* continuous (freshmen), continuous (transfers).

Freshmen Application Contact Laura Monks, Assistant Director of Student Services, Motlow State Community College, PO Box 8500, Lynchburg, TN 37352. *Phone:* 931-393-1764. *Toll-free phone:* 800-654-4877. *Fax:* 931-393-1681. *E-mail:* lmonks@mscc.edu.

NASHVILLE AUTO DIESEL COLLEGE

Nashville, Tennessee   **www.nadcedu.com/**

- **Proprietary** 2-year, founded 1919
- **Urban** 13-acre campus
- **Coed, primarily men**

Undergraduates 1,306 full-time. Students come from 50 states and territories, 83% are from out of state, 30% African American, 0.8% Asian American or Pacific Islander, 0.8% Hispanic American, 1% Native American, 21% live on campus.

Faculty *Student/faculty ratio:* 30:1.

Academics *Calendar:* continuous. *Degree:* diplomas and associate. *Special study options:* advanced placement credit, cooperative education, honors programs.

Student Life *Campus security:* 24-hour emergency response devices and patrols.

Standardized Tests *Recommended:* SAT or ACT (for admission).

Applying *Options:* deferred entrance. *Application fee:* $100. *Required:* high school transcript. *Required for some:* interview.

Freshmen Application Contact Ms. Peggie Werrbach, Director of Admissions, Nashville Auto Diesel College, 1524 Gallatin Road, Nashville, TN 37206. *Phone:* 615-226-3990 Ext. 8465. *Toll-free phone:* 800-228-NADC. *Fax:* 615-262-8466. *E-mail:* wpruitt@nadcedu.com.

NASHVILLE STATE TECHNICAL COMMUNITY COLLEGE

Nashville, Tennessee   **www.nscc.edu/**

Freshmen Application Contact Ms. Laura Potter, Coordinator of Recruitment, Nashville State Technical Community College, 120 White Bridge Road, Nashville, TN 37209. *Phone:* 615-353-3265. *Toll-free phone:* 800-272-7363.

NATIONAL COLLEGE

Bristol, Tennessee   **www.national-college.edu/**

Freshmen Application Contact Ms. Angela Carrier, Campus Director, National College, 1328 Highway 11 West, Bristol, TN 37620. *Phone:* 423-878-4440. *Fax:* 540-669-4793. *E-mail:* adm@educorp.edu.

NATIONAL COLLEGE

Knoxville, Tennessee   **www.national-college.edu/**

Director of Admissions Mr. Andy W. Wills, Director, National College, 8415 Kingston Pike, Knoxville, TN 37919. *Phone:* 865-539-2011. *Toll-free phone:* 800-664-1886. *Fax:* 865-539-2049. *E-mail:* awills@ncbt.edu.

NATIONAL COLLEGE

Nashville, Tennessee   **www.national-college.edu/**

Director of Admissions Mr. Robert Leonard, Campus Director, National College, 3748 Nolensville Pike, Nashville, TN 37211. *Phone:* 615-333-3344. *Toll-free phone:* 800-664-1886.

NORTH CENTRAL INSTITUTE

Clarksville, Tennessee   **www.nci.edu/**

- **Proprietary** 2-year, founded 1988
- **Suburban** 14-acre campus
- **Coed, primarily men**

Undergraduates 52 full-time, 78 part-time. Students come from 50 states and territories, 90% are from out of state, 24% African American, 3% Asian American or Pacific Islander, 10% Hispanic American, 7% Native American.

Faculty *Student/faculty ratio:* 8:1.

Academics *Calendar:* continuous. *Degree:* associate. *Special study options:* advanced placement credit, external degree program, independent study, part-time degree program, summer session for credit.

Student Life *Campus security:* 24-hour emergency response devices.

Costs (2006–07) *Tuition:* $14,800 full-time. No tuition increase for student's term of enrollment. *Required fees:* $800 full-time.

Applying *Options:* electronic application, early admission. *Application fee:* $35. *Required:* proof of high school. *Recommended:* high school transcript.

Freshmen Application Contact Mrs. Sheri Nash-Kutch, Dean of Student Services, North Central Institute, 168 Jack Miller Boulevard, Clarksville, TN 37042. *Phone:* 931-431-9700 Ext. 247. *Fax:* 931-431-9771. *E-mail:* admissions@nci.edu.

NORTHEAST STATE TECHNICAL COMMUNITY COLLEGE

Blountville, Tennessee   **www.northeaststate.edu/**

- **State-supported** 2-year, founded 1966, part of Tennessee Board of Regents
- **Small-town** 100-acre campus
- **Endowment** $3.9 million
- **Coed,** 5,154 undergraduate students, 54% full-time, 54% women, 46% men

Undergraduates 2,793 full-time, 2,361 part-time. Students come from 3 states and territories, 3% are from out of state, 3% African American, 0.6% Asian American or Pacific Islander, 1% Hispanic American, 0.4% Native American, 5% transferred in. *Retention:* 58% of 2003 full-time freshmen returned.

Freshmen *Admission:* 3,286 applied, 3,286 admitted, 941 enrolled. *Average high school GPA:* 2.51. *Test scores:* ACT scores over 18: 57%; ACT scores over 24: 8%; ACT scores over 30: 1%.

Faculty *Total:* 243, 41% full-time, 12% with terminal degrees. *Student/faculty ratio:* 24:1.

Majors Accounting; administrative assistant and secretarial science; automobile/automotive mechanics technology; business administration and management; cardiovascular technology; chemistry; computer programming; computer programming related; computer systems networking and telecommunications; data processing and data processing technology; drafting and design technology; early childhood education; electrical, electronic and communications engineering technology; emergency medical technology (EMT paramedic); engineering technology; general studies; industrial technology; information technology; instrumentation technology; kindergarten/preschool education; liberal arts and sciences/liberal studies; machine tool technology; medical/clinical assistant; surgical technology; welding technology.

Academics *Calendar:* semesters. *Degree:* certificates and associate. *Special study options:* academic remediation for entering students, advanced placement credit, cooperative education, distance learning, double majors, honors programs, part-time degree program, services for LD students, summer session for credit.

Library Wayne G. Basler Library plus 1 other with 49,684 titles, 427 serial subscriptions, 9,061 audiovisual materials, an OPAC, a Web page.

Student Life *Housing:* college housing not available. *Activities and Organizations:* drama/theater group, student-run radio and television station, Phi Theta Kappa, Student Government Association, Student Tennessee Education Association, Students in Free Enterprise, Student Ambassadors. *Campus security:* 24-hour patrols, late-night transport/escort service. *Student services:* health clinic, personal/psychological counseling.

Athletics *Intramural sports:* basketball M/W, golf M/W, volleyball M/W.

Costs (2006–07) *Tuition:* state resident $2230 full-time, $95 per semester hour part-time; nonresident $8904 full-time, $414 per semester hour part-time. *Required fees:* $262 full-time, $30 per semester hour part-time. *Payment plan:* deferred payment. *Waivers:* senior citizens and employees or children of employees.

Financial Aid Of all full-time matriculated undergraduates, 109 Federal Work-Study jobs (averaging $1318). 35 state and other part-time jobs.

Applying *Options:* electronic application. *Application fee:* $10. *Required:* high school transcript, minimum 2.0 GPA. *Application deadlines:* rolling (freshmen), rolling (transfers). *Notification:* continuous (freshmen), continuous (transfers).

Freshmen Application Contact Dr. Jon P. Harr, Vice President for Student Affairs, Northeast State Technical Community College, PO Box 246, Blountville, TN 37617. *Phone:* 423-323-0231. *Toll-free phone:* 800-836-7822. *Fax:* 423-323-0215. *E-mail:* jpharr@northeaststate.edu.

NOSSI COLLEGE OF ART

Goodlettsville, Tennessee   **www.nossi.com/**

- **Independent** 2-year
- **Coed,** 250 undergraduate students, 100% full-time, 30% women, 70% men
- **64% of applicants were admitted**

Undergraduates 250 full-time.

Freshmen *Admission:* 260 applied, 167 admitted.

Faculty *Total:* 29, 14% full-time. *Student/faculty ratio:* 17:1.

Majors Commercial and advertising art; photography.

Academics *Calendar:* semesters. *Degree:* associate.

Costs (2006–07) *Tuition:* $9435 full-time.

Applying *Application fee:* $100. *Required:* portfolio.

Freshmen Application Contact Ms. Mary Alexander, Admissions Director, Nossi College of Art, 907 Rivergate Parkway, Goodlettsville, TN 37072. *Phone:* 615-851-1088. *Toll-free phone:* 877-860-1601. *E-mail:* admissions@nossi.com.

PELLISSIPPI STATE TECHNICAL COMMUNITY COLLEGE

Knoxville, Tennessee   **www.pstcc.edu/**

- **State-supported** 2-year, founded 1974, part of Tennessee Board of Regents
- **Suburban** 144-acre campus
- **Endowment** $2.8 million
- **Coed**

Undergraduates 3,882 full-time, 3,804 part-time. Students come from 23 states and territories, 7% African American, 2% Asian American or Pacific Islander, 2% Hispanic American, 0.5% Native American, 0.6% international.

Faculty *Student/faculty ratio:* 21:1.

Academics *Calendar:* semesters. *Degree:* certificates and associate. *Special study options:* academic remediation for entering students, adult/continuing education programs, advanced placement credit, cooperative education, distance learning, double majors, English as a second language, freshman honors college, honors programs, internships, part-time degree program, services for LD students, student-designed majors, summer session for credit.

Student Life *Campus security:* 24-hour patrols.

Applying *Options:* electronic application, early admission, deferred entrance. *Application fee:* $5. *Required:* high school transcript.

Freshmen Application Contact Ms. Leigh Touzeau, Director of Admissions and Records, Pellissippi State Technical Community College, PO Box 22990, Knoxville, TN 37933-0990. *Phone:* 865-694-6681. *E-mail:* latouzeau@pstcc.cc.tn.us.

REMINGTON COLLEGE—MEMPHIS CAMPUS

Memphis, Tennessee   **www.remingtoncollege.edu/**

Director of Admissions Dr. Lori May, Campus President, Remington College–Memphis Campus, 2731 Nonconnah Boulevard, Memphis, TN 38132-2131. *Phone:* 901-291-4225. *Fax:* 901-396-8310. *E-mail:* lori.may@remingtoncollege.edu.

REMINGTON COLLEGE—NASHVILLE CAMPUS

Nashville, Tennessee   **www.remingtoncollege.edu/**

- **Proprietary** 2-year, founded 2003
- **Coed,** 276 undergraduate students
- **100% of applicants were admitted**

Freshmen *Admission:* 266 applied, 266 admitted.

Majors Business administration, management and operations related; computer and information sciences related; computer systems networking and telecommunications; criminal justice/law enforcement administration.

Academics *Calendar:* quarters. *Degree:* associate.

Costs (2006–07) *Tuition:* $12,520 per degree program part-time.

Applying *Application fee:* $50.

Director of Admissions Mr. Frank Vivelo, Campus President, Remington College–Nashville Campus, 441 Donelson Pike, Suite 150, Nashville, TN 37214. *Phone:* 615-889-5520. *Fax:* 615-889-5528. *E-mail:* frank.vivelo@remingtoncollege.edu.

ROANE STATE COMMUNITY COLLEGE

Harriman, Tennessee   **www.roanestate.edu/**

- **State-supported** 2-year, founded 1971, part of Tennessee Board of Regents
- **Small-town** 104-acre campus with easy access to Knoxville
- **Endowment** $18,348
- **Coed,** 5,353 undergraduate students, 56% full-time, 67% women, 33% men

Undergraduates 2,987 full-time, 2,366 part-time. Students come from 12 states and territories, 15 other countries, 1% are from out of state, 2% African American, 0.9% Asian American or Pacific Islander, 0.7% Hispanic American, 0.3% Native American, 0.3% international, 7% transferred in. *Retention:* 55% of 2003 full-time freshmen returned.

Freshmen *Admission:* 2,389 applied, 2,386 admitted, 1,083 enrolled. *Average high school GPA:* 3.1. *Test scores:* ACT scores over 18: 70%; ACT scores over 24: 13%.

Faculty *Total:* 359, 38% full-time. *Student/faculty ratio:* 18:1.

Majors Accounting; administrative assistant and secretarial science; art; art teacher education; biology/biological sciences; business administration and management; business teacher education; chemistry; clinical/medical laboratory technology; computer engineering technology; computer science; corrections; criminal justice/law enforcement administration; criminal justice/police science; dental hygiene; early childhood education; education; elementary education; emergency medical technology (EMT paramedic); engineering; environmental health; general studies; health information/medical records administration; industrial radiologic technology; information technology; kindergarten/preschool education; laser and optical technology; legal administrative assistant/secretary; liberal arts and sciences/liberal studies; mathematics; medical administrative assistant and medical secretary; music teacher education; nursing (registered nurse training); occupational therapy; pharmacy technician; physical education teaching and coaching; physical sciences; physical therapy; pre-engineering; respiratory care therapy; social sciences; technology/industrial arts teacher education.

Academics *Calendar:* semesters. *Degree:* certificates and associate. *Special study options:* academic remediation for entering students, accelerated degree program, adult/continuing education programs, advanced placement credit, cooperative education, distance learning, double majors, freshman honors college, honors programs, independent study, internships, off-campus study, part-time degree program, services for LD students, summer session for credit. *ROTC:* Army (c), Air Force (c).

Library Roane State Community College Library plus 3 others with 103,404 titles, an OPAC, a Web page.

Student Life *Housing:* college housing not available. *Activities and Organizations:* drama/theater group, student-run newspaper, choral group, Baptist Student Union, American Chemical Society, Physical Therapy Student Association, Student Artists At Roane State (S.T.A.R.S.), Phi Theta Kappa. *Campus security:* 24-hour patrols. *Student services:* health clinic, personal/psychological counseling.

Athletics Member NJCAA. *Intercollegiate sports:* baseball M(s), basketball M(s)/W(s), cheerleading W(s), softball W(s). *Intramural sports:* basketball M/W, football M, golf M, soccer M, softball M/W, volleyball M/W, weight lifting M.

Costs (2007–08) *Tuition:* state resident $2142 full-time, $91 per credit hour part-time; nonresident $8556 full-time, $369 per credit hour part-time. *Required fees:* $265 full-time, $15 per credit hour part-time, $15 per term part-time.

Financial Aid Of all full-time matriculated undergraduates, 150 Federal Work-Study jobs (averaging $3000).

Applying *Options:* electronic application, early admission, deferred entrance. *Application fee:* $10. *Required:* high school transcript. *Application deadlines:* rolling (freshmen), rolling (transfers). *Notification:* continuous (freshmen), continuous (transfers).

Freshmen Application Contact Admissions Office, Roane State Community College, 276 Patton Lane, Harriman, TN 37748. *Phone:* 865-882-4523. *Toll-free phone:* 800-343-9104. *E-mail:* admissions@roanestate.edu.

SOUTH COLLEGE

Knoxville, Tennessee www.southcollegetn.edu/

Director of Admissions Mr. Walter Hosea, Director of Admissions, South College, 720 North Fifth Avenue, Knoxville, TN 37917. *Phone:* 865-524-3043 Ext. 1825.

SOUTHEASTERN CAREER COLLEGE

Nashville, Tennessee www.southeasterncareercollege.com/

Admissions Office Contact Southeastern Career College, 2416 South 21st Avenue, Suite 300, Nashville, TN 37212. *Toll-free phone:* 800-336-4457.

SOUTHWEST TENNESSEE COMMUNITY COLLEGE

Memphis, Tennessee www.southwest.tn.edu/

- **State-supported** 2-year, founded 2000, part of Tennessee Board of Regents
- **Urban** 100-acre campus
- **Endowment** $641,526
- **Coed**

Undergraduates 5,656 full-time, 5,900 part-time. Students come from 14 states and territories, 2% are from out of state, 59% African American, 1% Asian American or Pacific Islander, 2% Hispanic American, 0.7% Native American, 0.6% international, 4% transferred in.

Academics *Calendar:* semesters. *Degree:* certificates and associate. *Special study options:* academic remediation for entering students, accelerated degree program, adult/continuing education programs, advanced placement credit, cooperative education, distance learning, double majors, English as a second language, internships, part-time degree program, services for LD students, student-designed majors, summer session for credit. *ROTC:* Army (c), Air Force (c).

Student Life *Campus security:* 24-hour emergency response devices and patrols, late-night transport/escort service.

Athletics Member NJCAA.

Financial Aid Of all full-time matriculated undergraduates, 201 Federal Work-Study jobs (averaging $2600).

Applying *Options:* early admission, deferred entrance. *Application fee:* $5. *Required:* high school transcript.

Freshmen Application Contact Ms. Cindy Meziere, Assistant Director of Recruiting, Southwest Tennessee Community College, PO Box 780, Memphis, TN 38103-0780. *Phone:* 901-333-4195. *Toll-free phone:* 877-717-STCC. *Fax:* 901-333-4473. *E-mail:* cmeziere@southwest.tn.edu.

VATTEROTT COLLEGE

Memphis, Tennessee www.vatterott-college.edu/

- **Proprietary** 2-year, founded 2004
- **Coed,** 233 undergraduate students
- 45% of applicants were admitted

Freshmen *Admission:* 156 applied, 70 admitted.

Majors CAD/CADD drafting/design technology; computer technology/computer systems technology; heating, air conditioning and refrigeration technology; medical/clinical assistant; system administration.

Academics *Calendar:* semesters. *Degree:* associate.

Costs (2006–07) *Tuition:* $9436 full-time.

Admissions Office Contact Vatterott College, 2655 Dividend Drive, Memphis, TN 38132. *Toll-free phone:* 866-314-6454.

VOLUNTEER STATE COMMUNITY COLLEGE

Gallatin, Tennessee www.volstate.edu/

- **State-supported** 2-year, founded 1970, part of Tennessee Board of Regents
- **Small-town** 100-acre campus with easy access to Nashville
- **Endowment** $37,966
- **Coed,** 7,370 undergraduate students, 48% full-time, 64% women, 36% men

Undergraduates 3,542 full-time, 3,828 part-time. Students come from 15 states and territories, 29 other countries, 1% are from out of state, 10% African American, 1% Asian American or Pacific Islander, 2% Hispanic American, 0.5% Native American, 0.4% international, 10% transferred in.

Freshmen *Admission:* 1,942 applied, 1,942 admitted, 1,389 enrolled. *Average high school GPA:* 2.81. *Test scores:* SAT verbal scores over 500: 38%; SAT math scores over 500: 38%; SAT writing scores over 500: 29; ACT scores over 18: 63%; SAT math scores over 600: 8%; ACT scores over 24: 10%.

Faculty *Total:* 375, 39% full-time, 12% with terminal degrees. *Student/faculty ratio:* 22:1.

Majors Business administration and management; fire science; health information/medical records technology; health professions related; industrial arts; legal

Volunteer State Community College (continued)

assistant/paralegal; liberal arts and sciences/liberal studies; medical radiologic technology; ophthalmic technology; physical therapist assistant; respiratory care therapy.

Academics *Calendar:* semesters. *Degree:* certificates and associate. *Special study options:* academic remediation for entering students, accelerated degree program, adult/continuing education programs, advanced placement credit, distance learning, double majors, English as a second language, honors programs, independent study, part-time degree program, services for LD students, summer session for credit.

Library Thigpen Learning Resource Center with 53,000 titles, 275 serial subscriptions, an OPAC, a Web page.

Student Life *Housing:* college housing not available. *Activities and Organizations:* drama/theater group, student-run newspaper, radio station, choral group, Gamma Beta Phi, Returning Women's Organization, Phi Theta Kappa, Student Government Association, The Settler. *Campus security:* 24-hour emergency response devices and patrols, late-night transport/escort service. *Student services:* health clinic, personal/psychological counseling.

Athletics Member NJCAA. *Intercollegiate sports:* baseball M(s), basketball M(s)/W(s), softball W(s). *Intramural sports:* basketball M/W.

Standardized Tests *Required for some:* SAT or ACT (for admission).

Costs (2007–08) *Tuition:* state resident $2275 full-time, $97 per credit hour part-time; nonresident $9084 full-time, $392 per credit hour part-time. *Required fees:* $241 full-time, $9 per credit hour part-time, $8 per term part-time.

Financial Aid Of all full-time matriculated undergraduates, 37 Federal Work-Study jobs (averaging $1900). 21 state and other part-time jobs (averaging $2000).

Applying *Options:* electronic application, early admission, deferred entrance. *Application fee:* $10. *Required:* high school transcript. *Required for some:* essay or personal statement, minimum 2.0 GPA. *Application deadlines:* 8/28 (freshmen), 8/28 (transfers). *Notification:* continuous (freshmen), continuous (transfers).

Freshmen Application Contact Mr. Tim Amyx, Director of Admissions, Volunteer State Community College, 1480 Nashville Pike, Gallatin, TN 37066-3188. *Phone:* 615-452-8600 Ext. 3614. *Toll-free phone:* 888-335-8722. *Fax:* 615-230-4875. *E-mail:* admissions@volstate.edu.

WALTERS STATE COMMUNITY COLLEGE

Morristown, Tennessee   www.ws.edu/

Freshmen Application Contact Mr. Michael Campbell, Assistant Vice President for Student Affairs, Walters State Community College, 500 South Davy Crockett Parkway, Morristown, TN 37813-6899. *Phone:* 423-585-2682. *Toll-free phone:* 800-225-4770. *Fax:* 423-585-6876. *E-mail:* mary.hopper@ws.edu.

TEXAS

THE ACADEMY OF HEALTH CARE PROFESSIONS

Houston, Texas   www.academyofhealth.com/

Director of Admissions Ms. Wanda Federick, Director of Admissions, The Academy of Health Care Professions, 1900 North Loop West, Suite 100, Houston, TX 77018. *Phone:* 713-425-3111. *E-mail:* wfederick@academyofhealth.com.

ALVIN COMMUNITY COLLEGE

Alvin, Texas   www.alvincollege.edu/

Director of Admissions Ms. Stephanie Stockstill, Director of Admissions and Advising, Alvin Community College, 3110 Mustang Road, Alvin, TX 77511. *Phone:* 281-756-3531. *E-mail:* admiss.rec.acc@flipper.alvin.cc.tx.us.

AMARILLO COLLEGE

Amarillo, Texas   www.actx.edu/

- **State and locally supported** 2-year, founded 1929
- **Urban** 1542-acre campus
- **Endowment** $33.0 million
- **Coed,** 10,354 undergraduate students, 32% full-time, 62% women, 38% men

Undergraduates 3,315 full-time, 7,039 part-time. 4% are from out of state, 4% African American, 2% Asian American or Pacific Islander, 24% Hispanic American, 1% Native American, 1% live on campus.

Faculty *Total:* 234. *Student/faculty ratio:* 24:1.

Majors Accounting; administrative assistant and secretarial science; airframe mechanics and aircraft maintenance technology; architectural engineering technology; art; automobile/automotive mechanics technology; behavioral sciences; biblical studies; biology/biological sciences; broadcast journalism; business administration and management; business teacher education; chemical technology; chemistry; child development; clinical laboratory science/medical technology; commercial and advertising art; computer engineering technology; computer programming; computer science; computer systems analysis; corrections; criminal justice/law enforcement administration; criminal justice/police science; dental hygiene; drafting and design technology; dramatic/theater arts; electrical, electronic and communications engineering technology; elementary education; emergency medical technology (EMT paramedic); engineering; English; environmental health; fine/studio arts; fire science; funeral service and mortuary science; general studies; geology/earth science; health information/medical records administration; heating, air conditioning, ventilation and refrigeration maintenance technology; heavy equipment maintenance technology; history; industrial radiologic technology; information science/studies; instrumentation technology; interior design; journalism; laser and optical technology; legal administrative assistant/secretary; liberal arts and sciences/liberal studies; machine tool technology; mass communication/media; mathematics; medical administrative assistant and medical secretary; modern languages; music; music teacher education; natural sciences; nuclear medical technology; nursing (licensed practical/vocational nurse training); nursing (registered nurse training); occupational therapy; photography; physical education teaching and coaching; physical sciences; physical therapy; physics; pre-engineering; pre-pharmacy studies; psychology; public relations/image management; radio and television; radiologic technology/science; real estate; religious studies; respiratory care therapy; social sciences; social work; speech and rhetoric; substance abuse/addiction counseling; telecommunications; tourism and travel services management; visual and performing arts.

Academics *Calendar:* semesters. *Degree:* certificates and associate. *Special study options:* academic remediation for entering students, adult/continuing education programs, advanced placement credit, cooperative education, distance learning, English as a second language, freshman honors college, honors programs, part-time degree program, services for LD students, summer session for credit.

Library Lynn Library Learning Center plus 2 others with 80,000 titles, 110 serial subscriptions, an OPAC, a Web page.

Student Life *Housing Options:* Campus housing is provided by a third party. *Activities and Organizations:* drama/theater group, student-run newspaper, radio station, choral group, Student Government Association, College Republicans. *Campus security:* 24-hour patrols, late-night transport/escort service. *Student services:* personal/psychological counseling.

Athletics *Intramural sports:* basketball M/W, tennis M/W, volleyball M/W.

Costs (2006–07) *Tuition:* area resident $1182 full-time, $49 per hour part-time; state resident $1566 full-time, $65 per hour part-time; nonresident $2382 full-time, $99 per hour part-time. Full-time tuition and fees vary according to course load. Part-time tuition and fees vary according to course load. *Room and board:* room only: $2000. *Payment plan:* installment. *Waivers:* senior citizens and employees or children of employees.

Financial Aid Of all full-time matriculated undergraduates, 100 Federal Work-Study jobs (averaging $3000).

Applying *Options:* early admission, deferred entrance. *Required:* high school transcript. *Notification:* continuous (freshmen), continuous (transfers).

Freshmen Application Contact Amarillo College, PO Box 447, Amarillo, TX 79178-0001. *Phone:* 806-371-5000. *Fax:* 806-371-5497. *E-mail:* askac@actx.edu.

ANGELINA COLLEGE

Lufkin, Texas   www.angelina.cc.tx.us/

- **State and locally supported** 2-year, founded 1968
- **Small-town** 140-acre campus
- **Endowment** $2.6 million
- **Coed,** 4,976 undergraduate students

Undergraduates Students come from 15 states and territories, 2% are from out of state, 1% live on campus.

Freshmen *Average high school GPA:* 2.75.

Faculty *Total:* 121.

Majors Accounting; administrative assistant and secretarial science; art; art teacher education; automobile/automotive mechanics technology; biological and physical sciences; biology/biological sciences; business administration and management; child care and support services management; child care provision; child development; clinical laboratory science/medical technology; clinical/medical laboratory technology; computer engineering technology; computer programming; computer science; criminal justice/law enforcement administration; data processing and data processing technology; developmental and child psychology; drafting and design technology; education (K-12); electrical, electronic and communications engineering technology; electrical/electronics equipment installation and repair; electromechanical technology; elementary education; emergency medical technology (EMT paramedic); engineering; engineering technology; English; environmental engineering technology; health teacher education; history; humanities; human services; industrial radiologic technology; journalism; legal assistant/paralegal; liberal arts and sciences/liberal studies; mathematics; music; music teacher education; nursing (licensed practical/vocational nurse training); nursing (registered nurse training); physical education teaching and coaching; physical sciences; physical therapist assistant; piano and organ; pre-pharmacy studies; real estate; respiratory care therapy; science teacher education; social sciences; social work; speech/theater education; system administration; teacher assistant/aide; voice and opera; water quality and wastewater treatment management and recycling technology; welding technology.

Academics *Calendar:* semesters. *Degree:* certificates, diplomas, and associate. *Special study options:* academic remediation for entering students, adult/continuing education programs, advanced placement credit, cooperative education, distance learning, double majors, honors programs, internships, off-campus study, part-time degree program, services for LD students, student-designed majors, summer session for credit. *ROTC:* Army (c).

Library Angelina College Library with 37,000 titles, 270 serial subscriptions, an OPAC.

Student Life *Housing Options:* coed. *Activities and Organizations:* drama/theater group, student-run newspaper, choral group, Students in Free Enterprise, Phi Theta Kappa, Student Nurses Association, Rodeo Club. *Campus security:* 24-hour patrols. *Student services:* personal/psychological counseling.

Athletics Member NJCAA. *Intercollegiate sports:* baseball M(s), basketball M(s)/W(s). *Intramural sports:* basketball M/W, bowling M/W, golf M/W, racquetball M/W, tennis M/W, volleyball M/W, weight lifting M/W.

Standardized Tests *Required:* ACT COMPASS, THEA (for placement).

Costs (2006–07) *Tuition:* area resident $1200 full-time; state resident $1740 full-time; nonresident $2400 full-time.

Financial Aid Of all full-time matriculated undergraduates, 80 Federal Work-Study jobs (averaging $1400). 7 state and other part-time jobs (averaging $1000).

Applying *Options:* electronic application, early admission, deferred entrance. *Required:* high school transcript. *Application deadlines:* rolling (freshmen), rolling (transfers). *Notification:* continuous (freshmen), continuous (transfers).

Freshmen Application Contact Ms. Judith Cutting, Registrar/Enrollment Director, Angelina College, PO Box 1768, Lufkin, TX 75902-1768. *Phone:* 936-639-1301 Ext. 213.

ATI TECHNICAL TRAINING CENTER
Dallas, Texas   **www.aticareertraining.edu/**

Freshmen Application Contact Admissions Office, ATI Technical Training Center, 6627 Maple Ave, Dallas, TX 75235. *Phone:* 214-352-2222.

AUSTIN BUSINESS COLLEGE
Austin, Texas   **abctx.edu/**

Director of Admissions Ms. Pam Binns, Director of Admissions, Austin Business College, 2101 Interstate Highway 35, Suite 300, Austin, TX 78741. *Phone:* 512-447-9415. *E-mail:* pambinns@austinbusinesscollege.org.

AUSTIN COMMUNITY COLLEGE
Austin, Texas   **www.austincc.edu/**

- **District-supported** 2-year, founded 1972
- **Urban** campus
- **Coed**

Undergraduates 8,829 full-time, 23,079 part-time. Students come from 93 other countries, 2% are from out of state, 7% African American, 5% Asian American or Pacific Islander, 23% Hispanic American, 0.7% Native American, 2% international.

Faculty *Student/faculty ratio:* 20:1.

Academics *Calendar:* semesters. *Degree:* certificates and associate. *Special study options:* academic remediation for entering students, accelerated degree program, adult/continuing education programs, advanced placement credit, cooperative education, distance learning, English as a second language, external degree program, honors programs, independent study, internships, part-time degree program, services for LD students, summer session for credit. *ROTC:* Army (c), Air Force (c).

Costs (2006–07) *Tuition:* area resident $1170 full-time, $39 per credit hour part-time; state resident $3300 full-time, $110 per credit hour part-time; nonresident $7530 full-time, $251 per credit hour part-time. Full-time tuition and fees vary according to course load. Part-time tuition and fees vary according to course load. *Required fees:* $438 full-time, $15 per credit hour part-time.

Financial Aid Of all full-time matriculated undergraduates, 296 Federal Work-Study jobs (averaging $2000). 12 state and other part-time jobs (averaging $2000).

Applying *Options:* electronic application.

Freshmen Application Contact Ms. Linda Kluck, Director, Admissions and Records, Austin Community College, 5930 Middle Fiskville Road, Austin, TX 78752-4390. *Phone:* 512-223-7766. *Fax:* 512-223-7665. *E-mail:* outreach@austincc.edu.

BLINN COLLEGE
Brenham, Texas   **www.blinn.edu/**

- **State and locally supported** 2-year, founded 1883
- **Small-town** 100-acre campus with easy access to Houston
- **Endowment** $29.8 million
- **Coed,** 14,016 undergraduate students, 54% full-time, 51% women, 49% men

Undergraduates 7,505 full-time, 6,511 part-time. Students come from 36 states and territories, 42 other countries, 1% are from out of state, 8% African American, 1% Asian American or Pacific Islander, 12% Hispanic American, 0.7% Native American, 1% international, 32% transferred in, 9% live on campus.

Freshmen *Admission:* 3,825 applied, 3,825 admitted, 886 enrolled.

Faculty *Total:* 575, 37% full-time, 22% with terminal degrees. *Student/faculty ratio:* 24:1.

Majors Accounting; administrative assistant and secretarial science; agriculture; biology/biological sciences; business administration and management; chemistry; child guidance; computer science; computer systems networking and telecommunications; criminal justice/law enforcement administration; dental hygiene; dramatic/theater arts; English; fire science; French; German; health information/medical records technology; history; industrial radiologic technology; legal administrative assistant/secretary; literature; mass communication/media; mathematics; mental health/rehabilitation; music; nursing (registered nurse training); philosophy; physical education teaching and coaching; physical therapist assistant; physics; psychology; real estate; Spanish; speech and rhetoric.

Academics *Calendar:* semesters. *Degree:* certificates, diplomas, and associate. *Special study options:* academic remediation for entering students, adult/continuing education programs, advanced placement credit, distance learning, double majors, English as a second language, freshman honors college, part-time degree program, services for LD students, summer session for credit.

Library W. L. Moody, Jr. Library plus 1 other with 130,000 titles, 700 serial subscriptions, an OPAC, a Web page.

Student Life *Housing:* on-campus residence required through sophomore year. *Options:* men-only, women-only. Campus housing is university owned. *Activities and Organizations:* drama/theater group, student-run newspaper, choral group, marching band, Student Government Association, Phi Theta Kappa, Baptist student ministries, Blinn Ethnic Student Organization, Circle K. *Campus security:* 24-hour emergency response devices and patrols, controlled dormitory access. *Student services:* personal/psychological counseling.

Athletics Member NJCAA. *Intercollegiate sports:* baseball M(s), basketball M(s)/W(s), cheerleading M(s)/W(s), football M(s), softball W(s), volleyball W(s). *Intramural sports:* basketball M/W, bowling M/W, football M, golf M, softball W, table tennis M/W, volleyball M/W, weight lifting M/W.

Costs (2007–08) *Tuition:* area resident $1512 full-time, $63 per semester hour part-time; state resident $2208 full-time, $92 per semester hour part-time; nonresident $4032 full-time, $168 per semester hour part-time. *Room and board:* $6190; room only: $3800.

Applying *Options:* electronic application, early admission, deferred entrance. *Required:* high school transcript. *Application deadlines:* rolling (freshmen), rolling (transfers).

Blinn College (continued)

Freshmen Application Contact Mrs. Stephanie Wehring, Coordinator, Recruitment and Admissions, Blinn College, 902 College Avenue, Brenham, TX 77833-4049. *Phone:* 979-830-4152. *Fax:* 979-830-4110. *E-mail:* recruit@blinn.edu.

BORDER INSTITUTE OF TECHNOLOGY

El Paso, Texas   bitelp.edu/

Director of Admissions Mr. Miguel Gamino, Admissions Director, Border Institute of Technology, 9611 Acer Avenue, El Paso, TX 79925-6744. *Phone:* 915-593-7328 Ext. 24.

BRAZOSPORT COLLEGE

Lake Jackson, Texas   **www.brazosport.edu/**

- **State and locally supported** 2-year, founded 1968
- **Small-town** 160-acre campus with easy access to Houston
- **Endowment** $3.3 million
- **Coed**

Undergraduates 1,670 full-time, 1,833 part-time. Students come from 12 states and territories, 11 other countries, 1% are from out of state, 6% African American, 1% Asian American or Pacific Islander, 24% Hispanic American, 0.4% Native American, 0.5% international, 4% transferred in.

Faculty *Student/faculty ratio:* 18:1.

Academics *Calendar:* semesters. *Degree:* certificates and associate. *Special study options:* academic remediation for entering students, adult/continuing education programs, advanced placement credit, cooperative education, distance learning, honors programs, internships, part-time degree program, summer session for credit.

Student Life *Campus security:* 24-hour patrols.

Standardized Tests *Required for some:* THEA, ACT COMPASS.

Costs (2006–07) *Tuition:* area resident $840 full-time, $28 per hour part-time; state resident $1470 full-time, $49 per hour part-time; nonresident $2880 full-time, $96 per hour part-time. Full-time tuition and fees vary according to course load. Part-time tuition and fees vary according to course load. *Required fees:* $450 full-time, $14 per hour part-time, $15 per term part-time.

Applying *Options:* early admission, deferred entrance. *Required for some:* high school transcript.

Freshmen Application Contact Ms. Patricia S. Leyendecker, Director of Admissions/Registrar, Brazosport College, 500 College Drive, Lake Jackson, TX 77566. *Phone:* 979-230-3217. *Fax:* 979-230-3376. *E-mail:* pleyende@brazosport.edu.

BROOKHAVEN COLLEGE

Farmers Branch, Texas   **www.brookhavencollege.edu/**

- **County-supported** 2-year, founded 1978, part of Dallas County Community College District System
- **Suburban** 200-acre campus with easy access to Dallas–Fort Worth
- **Coed,** 10,269 undergraduate students, 9% full-time, 58% women, 42% men

Undergraduates 931 full-time, 9,338 part-time. Students come from 16 states and territories, 68 other countries, 9% are from out of state, 13% African American, 13% Asian American or Pacific Islander, 26% Hispanic American, 0.5% Native American, 2% international, 46% transferred in.

Freshmen *Admission:* 1,230 applied, 1,230 admitted, 1,230 enrolled.

Faculty *Total:* 702, 18% full-time, 9% with terminal degrees. *Student/faculty ratio:* 20:1.

Majors Accounting; automobile/automotive mechanics technology; business administration and management; child development; emergency medical technology (EMT paramedic); fashion merchandising; liberal arts and sciences/liberal studies; marketing/marketing management; nursing (registered nurse training); radiologic technology/science.

Academics *Calendar:* semesters. *Degree:* certificates and associate. *Special study options:* academic remediation for entering students, adult/continuing education programs, advanced placement credit, cooperative education, distance learning, English as a second language, honors programs, independent study, internships, off-campus study, part-time degree program, services for LD students, student-designed majors, study abroad, summer session for credit. *ROTC:* Army (c).

Library Brookhaven College Learning Resources Center with 58,225 titles, 117 serial subscriptions, 12,400 audiovisual materials, an OPAC, a Web page.

Student Life *Housing:* college housing not available. *Activities and Organizations:* drama/theater group, student-run newspaper, choral group, Brookhaven Nursing Students Association, Phi Theta Kappa, International Clubs, Brookhaven Student Government, Latin American Student Association. *Campus security:* 24-hour emergency response devices and patrols, late-night transport/escort service. *Student services:* health clinic, personal/psychological counseling.

Athletics Member NJCAA. *Intercollegiate sports:* tennis M/W, volleyball W. *Intramural sports:* archery M/W, basketball M/W, bowling M/W, gymnastics M/W, racquetball M/W, soccer M/W, weight lifting M/W.

Standardized Tests *Required for some:* THEA.

Costs (2007–08) *Tuition:* area resident $936 full-time, $117 per course part-time; state resident $1728 full-time, $216 per course part-time; nonresident $2760 full-time, $345 per course part-time.

Applying *Options:* early admission, deferred entrance. *Required:* high school transcript. *Application deadlines:* rolling (freshmen), rolling (transfers).

Freshmen Application Contact Marketing and Public Information Office, Brookhaven College, 3939 Valley View Lane, Farmers Branch, TX 75244-4997. *Phone:* 972-860-4883. *Fax:* 972-860-4886. *E-mail:* bhcinfo@dcccd.edu.

BROWN MACKIE COLLEGE—DALLAS

Garland, Texas www.brownmackie.edu/locations.asp?locid=5

Freshmen Application Contact Admissions Office, Brown Mackie College–Dallas, 1500 Eastgate Drive, Garland, TX 75041. *Toll-free phone:* 888-699-4446. *E-mail:* bmcdaadm@brownmackie.edu.

BROWN MACKIE COLLEGE—FORT WORTH

Hurst, Texas www.brownmackie.edu/locations.asp?locid=10

Admissions Office Contact Brown Mackie College–Fort Worth, 301 Northeast Loop 820, Hurst, TX 76053. *Toll-free phone:* 888-906-0505.

CEDAR VALLEY COLLEGE

Lancaster, Texas   **www.cedarvalleycollege.edu/cvc.htm**

- **State-supported** 2-year, founded 1977, part of Dallas County Community College District System
- **Suburban** 353-acre campus with easy access to Dallas–Fort Worth
- **Endowment** $17.2 million
- **Coed,** 4,504 undergraduate students, 33% full-time, 61% women, 39% men

Undergraduates 1,472 full-time, 3,032 part-time. Students come from 5 other countries, 2% are from out of state, 56% African American, 1% Asian American or Pacific Islander, 13% Hispanic American, 0.5% Native American, 0.2% international.

Freshmen *Admission:* 943 applied, 943 admitted.

Faculty *Total:* 174, 37% full-time. *Student/faculty ratio:* 26:1.

Majors Accounting; administrative assistant and secretarial science; automobile/automotive mechanics technology; business administration and management; computer programming; computer programming (specific applications); criminal justice/law enforcement administration; data processing and data processing technology; heating, air conditioning, ventilation and refrigeration maintenance technology; liberal arts and sciences/liberal studies; management information systems and services related; marketing/marketing management; music; radio and television broadcasting technology; real estate; veterinary/animal health technology.

Academics *Calendar:* semesters. *Degree:* certificates and associate. *Special study options:* academic remediation for entering students, advanced placement credit, cooperative education, distance learning, English as a second language, part-time degree program, services for LD students, summer session for credit. *ROTC:* Army (c).

Library Cedar Valley College Library with 43,788 titles, 217 serial subscriptions, an OPAC, a Web page.

Student Life *Housing:* college housing not available. *Activities and Organizations:* drama/theater group, choral group, African-American Student Organization, Latin-American Student Organization, Veterinary Technology Club, Phi Theta Kappa, Police Academy Club. *Campus security:* 24-hour emergency

response devices and patrols, late-night transport/escort service. *Student services:* health clinic, personal/psychological counseling.

Athletics Member NJCAA. *Intercollegiate sports:* baseball M, basketball M, soccer W, volleyball W. *Intramural sports:* cheerleading W.

Standardized Tests *Required:* THEA (for admission). *Recommended:* SAT or ACT (for admission).

Costs (2006–07) *Tuition:* area resident $990 full-time, $36 per credit part-time; state resident $1800 full-time, $66 per credit part-time; nonresident $2880 full-time, $200 per credit part-time. *Payment plan:* installment. *Waivers:* senior citizens.

Applying *Options:* electronic application, early admission. *Required for some:* letters of recommendation, interview. *Recommended:* high school transcript. *Application deadlines:* rolling (freshmen), rolling (transfers). *Notification:* continuous (freshmen), continuous (transfers).

Freshmen Application Contact Ms. Carolyn Ward, Director of Admissions/Registrar, Cedar Valley College, 3030 North Dallas Avenue, Lancaster, TX 75134-3799. *Phone:* 972-860-8201. *Fax:* 972-860-8207. *E-mail:* cboswell-ward@dcccd.edu.

CENTER FOR ADVANCED LEGAL STUDIES

Houston, Texas   www.paralegal.edu/

- **Proprietary** 2-year, founded 1987
- 53 undergraduate students
- 89% of applicants were admitted

Freshmen *Admission:* 19 applied, 17 admitted.

Majors Paralegal/legal assistant.

Academics *Degree:* diplomas and associate.

Costs (2006–07) *One-time required fee:* $100. *Tuition:* $8246 full-time. No tuition increase for student's term of enrollment. *Required fees:* $395 full-time. *Payment plans:* tuition prepayment, installment, deferred payment.

Applying *Application fee:* $100. *Required:* high school transcript.

Freshmen Application Contact Ms. Debra Garcia, Center for Advanced Legal Studies, 3910 Kirby Drive, Suite 200, Houston, TX 77098-4151. *Phone:* 713-529-2778. *Fax:* 713-523-2715. *E-mail:* debra@paralegal.edu.

CENTRAL TEXAS COLLEGE

Killeen, Texas   www.ctcd.edu/

- **State and locally supported** 2-year, founded 1967
- **Suburban** 500-acre campus with easy access to Austin
- **Endowment** $1.5 million
- **Coed,** 17,726 undergraduate students, 18% full-time, 48% women, 52% men

Undergraduates 3,158 full-time, 14,568 part-time. Students come from 50 states and territories, 19 other countries, 17% are from out of state, 30% African American, 5% Asian American or Pacific Islander, 16% Hispanic American, 1% Native American, 0.7% international, 1% live on campus.

Freshmen *Admission:* 4,129 enrolled.

Faculty *Total:* 1,970, 11% full-time, 12% with terminal degrees. *Student/faculty ratio:* 10:1.

Majors Administrative assistant and secretarial science; agriculture; aircraft powerplant technology; airline pilot and flight crew; automobile/automotive mechanics technology; biology/biological sciences; business administration and management; chemistry; child care and support services management; clinical/medical laboratory technology; commercial and advertising art; computer and information sciences; computer programming; computer programming related; computer programming (specific applications); computer programming (vendor/product certification); cosmetology; criminal justice/police science; criminal justice/safety; data processing and data processing technology; drafting and design technology; electrical, electronic and communications engineering technology; emergency medical technology (EMT paramedic); engineering; environmental studies; equestrian studies; farm and ranch management; geology/earth science; graphic and printing equipment operation/production; heating, air conditioning, ventilation and refrigeration maintenance technology; hotel/motel administration; interdisciplinary studies; journalism; legal assistant/paralegal; liberal arts and sciences/liberal studies; marketing/marketing management; mathematics; medical administrative assistant and medical secretary; medical radiologic technology; music; nursing (licensed practical/vocational nurse training); nursing (registered nurse training); office management; physical education teaching and coaching; radio and television; social sciences; substance abuse/addiction counseling; welding technology.

Academics *Calendar:* semesters. *Degree:* certificates and associate. *Special study options:* academic remediation for entering students, accelerated degree program, adult/continuing education programs, advanced placement credit, distance learning, English as a second language, external degree program, internships, part-time degree program, services for LD students, student-designed majors, summer session for credit. *ROTC:* Army (b).

Library Oveta Culp Hobby Memorial Library with 80,381 titles, 467 serial subscriptions, an OPAC, a Web page.

Student Life *Housing Options:* coed. *Activities and Organizations:* drama/theater group, student-run newspaper, International Student Association, We Can Do It Club, Students in Free Enterprise, Student Nurses Association, NAACP. *Campus security:* 24-hour emergency response devices and patrols.

Athletics *Intramural sports:* badminton M/W, basketball M/W, bowling M/W, football M/W, golf M/W, soccer M/W, softball M/W, table tennis M/W, tennis M/W, volleyball M/W.

Costs (2006–07) *Tuition:* area resident $960 full-time, $32 per hour part-time; state resident $1288 full-time, $46 per hour part-time; nonresident $3900 full-time, $130 per hour part-time. Full-time tuition and fees vary according to course load and location. Part-time tuition and fees vary according to course load and location. *Required fees:* $390 full-time, $8 per hour part-time. *Room and board:* $4550. *Payment plan:* installment. *Waivers:* senior citizens.

Financial Aid Of all full-time matriculated undergraduates, 68 Federal Work-Study jobs.

Applying *Options:* electronic application, early admission, deferred entrance. *Required:* high school transcript, minimum 2.0 GPA. *Application deadlines:* rolling (freshmen), rolling (transfers).

Freshmen Application Contact Admissions Office, Central Texas College, PO Box 1800, Killeen, TX 76540-1800. *Phone:* 254-526-1696. *Toll-free phone:* 800-792-3348 Ext. 1696. *Fax:* 254-526-1545. *E-mail:* admrec@ctcd.edu.

CISCO JUNIOR COLLEGE

Cisco, Texas   www.cisco.cc.tx.us/

- **State and locally supported** 2-year, founded 1940
- **Rural** 40-acre campus
- **Coed,** 3,525 undergraduate students

Undergraduates Students come from 21 states and territories, 12% live on campus.

Freshmen *Admission:* 1,227 applied, 1,227 admitted.

Faculty *Total:* 120. *Student/faculty ratio:* 18:1.

Majors Accounting; agricultural business and management; agriculture; automobile/automotive mechanics technology; biology/biological sciences; business administration and management; business teacher education; chemistry; child development; clinical laboratory science/medical technology; computer programming; computer science; construction engineering technology; consumer merchandising/retailing management; cosmetology; criminal justice/police science; dairy science; data processing and data processing technology; developmental and child psychology; drafting and design technology; education; electrical, electronic and communications engineering technology; finance; fire science; French; history; human services; kindergarten/preschool education; marketing/marketing management; mathematics; nursing (registered nurse training); physical education teaching and coaching; psychology; real estate; welding technology.

Academics *Calendar:* semesters. *Degree:* certificates and associate. *Special study options:* academic remediation for entering students, advanced placement credit, part-time degree program, summer session for credit. *ROTC:* Army (c).

Library Maner Library with 34,000 titles, 173 serial subscriptions, an OPAC, a Web page.

Student Life *Housing:* on-campus residence required through sophomore year. *Options:* Campus housing is university owned. *Activities and Organizations:* drama/theater group, marching band, Christian Athletes Association, Agricultural Club. *Campus security:* late-night transport/escort service.

Athletics Member NJCAA. *Intercollegiate sports:* basketball M(s)/W(s), football M(s), golf M(s), softball W, volleyball W. *Intramural sports:* badminton M/W, basketball M/W, bowling M/W, football M, golf M, volleyball M/W.

Standardized Tests *Required:* THEA (for placement).

Costs (2007–08) *Tuition:* area resident $1564 full-time, $111 per hour part-time; state resident $1756 full-time, $119 per hour part-time; nonresident $2062 full-time, $272 per hour part-time. *Room and board:* $3100; room only: $900.

Applying *Options:* early admission. *Application deadlines:* rolling (freshmen), rolling (transfers).

Freshmen Application Contact Mr. Olin O. Odom III, Dean of Admission/Registrar, Cisco Junior College, 101 College Heights, Cisco, TX 76437-9321. *Phone:* 254-442-2567 Ext. 5130. *E-mail:* oodom@cjc.edu.

CLARENDON COLLEGE

Clarendon, Texas　　　　　**www.clarendoncollege.edu/**

- **State and locally supported** 2-year, founded 1898
- **Rural** 88-acre campus
- **Endowment** $2.3 million
- **Coed,** 1,102 undergraduate students, 52% full-time, 47% women, 53% men

Undergraduates 571 full-time, 531 part-time. Students come from 14 states and territories, 6 other countries, 10% are from out of state, 10% African American, 1% Asian American or Pacific Islander, 18% Hispanic American, 0.7% Native American, 1% international, 18% transferred in, 26% live on campus.

Freshmen *Admission:* 550 applied, 550 admitted, 504 enrolled.

Faculty *Total:* 76, 42% full-time, 3% with terminal degrees. *Student/faculty ratio:* 15:1.

Majors Accounting; agribusiness; agricultural economics; agriculture; architecture; art; behavioral sciences; biology/biological sciences; business administration and management; chemistry; computer and information sciences; dramatic/theater arts; economics; education; elementary education; engineering; English; environmental science; farm and ranch management; finance; general studies; health services/allied health/health sciences; history; horse husbandry/equine science and management; kinesiology and exercise science; liberal arts and sciences/liberal studies; marketing/marketing management; mass communications; mathematics; music; nursing (registered nurse training); physical education teaching and coaching; physical therapy; pre-dentistry studies; pre-law studies; pre-medical studies; psychology; secondary education; social sciences; social work related; sociology; speech and rhetoric.

Academics *Calendar:* semesters. *Degree:* certificates and associate. *Special study options:* academic remediation for entering students, adult/continuing education programs, advanced placement credit, distance learning, double majors, independent study, part-time degree program, services for LD students, summer session for credit.

Library Vera Dial Dickey Library plus 1 other with 22,000 titles, 89 serial subscriptions, an OPAC, a Web page.

Student Life *Housing:* on-campus residence required through sophomore year. *Options:* coed, men-only, women-only. Campus housing is university owned. *Activities and Organizations:* drama/theater group, choral group. *Campus security:* 24-hour patrols, 8-hour patrols by trained security personnel.

Athletics Member NJCAA. *Intercollegiate sports:* baseball M(s), basketball M(s)/W(s), cheerleading M(s)/W(s), softball W(s), volleyball W(s). *Intramural sports:* basketball M/W, football M/W, volleyball M/W.

Costs (2006–07) *Tuition:* area resident $1140 full-time, $38 per credit hour part-time; state resident $1650 full-time, $55 per credit hour part-time; nonresident $2100 full-time, $70 per credit hour part-time. *Required fees:* $720 full-time, $24 per credit hour part-time, $72 per term part-time. *Room and board:* $3250; room only: $1190.

Financial Aid Of all full-time matriculated undergraduates, 41 Federal Work-Study jobs (averaging $985). 9 state and other part-time jobs (averaging $860).

Applying *Options:* early admission, deferred entrance. *Required:* high school transcript. *Required for some:* letters of recommendation, interview. *Application deadlines:* rolling (freshmen), rolling (transfers). *Notification:* continuous (freshmen), continuous (transfers).

Freshmen Application Contact Ms. Sharon Hannon, Admissions Director/Registrar, Clarendon College, PO Box 968, Clarendon, TX 79226-0968. *Phone:* 806-874-3571 Ext. 107. *Toll-free phone:* 800-687-9737. *Fax:* 806-874-3201. *E-mail:* Sharon.hannon@clarendoncollege.edu.

COASTAL BEND COLLEGE

Beeville, Texas　　　　　**www.cbc.cc.tx.us/**

- **County-supported** 2-year, founded 1965
- **Rural** 100-acre campus
- **Endowment** $630,026
- **Coed,** 3,267 undergraduate students, 37% full-time, 62% women, 38% men

Undergraduates 1,217 full-time, 2,050 part-time. Students come from 4 states and territories, 3 other countries, 1% are from out of state, 4% African American, 0.6% Asian American or Pacific Islander, 65% Hispanic American, 0.4% Native American, 0.6% international, 67% transferred in, 5% live on campus.

Freshmen *Admission:* 1,123 applied, 1,123 admitted, 1,123 enrolled.

Faculty *Total:* 165, 57% full-time, 4% with terminal degrees. *Student/faculty ratio:* 16:1.

Majors Accounting; administrative assistant and secretarial science; agriculture; applied art; art; art teacher education; automobile/automotive mechanics technology; biological and physical sciences; biology/biological sciences; business administration and management; chemistry; child development; commercial and advertising art; computer and information sciences related; computer engineering technology; computer programming; computer programming related; computer programming (specific applications); computer programming (vendor/product certification); computer science; computer systems networking and telecommunications; cosmetology; criminal justice/law enforcement administration; criminal justice/police science; data entry/microcomputer applications; data entry/microcomputer applications related; data processing and data processing technology; dental hygiene; developmental and child psychology; drafting and design technology; dramatic/theater arts; economics; education; elementary education; engineering; English; environmental engineering technology; finance; fine/studio arts; French; geology/earth science; German; health teacher education; history; information technology; journalism; legal administrative assistant/secretary; liberal arts and sciences/liberal studies; mathematics; music; music teacher education; nursing (licensed practical/vocational nurse training); nursing (registered nurse training); parks, recreation and leisure; petroleum technology; pharmacy; physical education teaching and coaching; physical sciences; physics; political science and government; psychology; public relations/image management; sociology; speech and rhetoric; system administration; voice and opera; welding technology; word processing.

Academics *Calendar:* semesters. *Degree:* certificates and associate. *Special study options:* academic remediation for entering students, adult/continuing education programs, advanced placement credit, cooperative education, distance learning, internships, part-time degree program, services for LD students, summer session for credit.

Library Grady C. Hogue Learning Resource Center with 43,004 titles, 1,341 serial subscriptions, 2,179 audiovisual materials, an OPAC, a Web page.

Student Life *Housing Options:* coed, disabled students. Campus housing is university owned. *Activities and Organizations:* student government, Computer Science Club, Creative Writing Club, Drama Club, Art Club. *Campus security:* 24-hour emergency response devices, night security. *Student services:* personal/psychological counseling.

Athletics *Intramural sports:* archery M/W, badminton M/W, basketball M/W, bowling M/W, cross-country running M/W, golf M/W, soccer M/W, softball M/W, table tennis M/W, tennis M/W, track and field M/W, volleyball M/W, weight lifting M/W.

Costs (2007–08) *Tuition:* area resident $1320 full-time, $55 per credit hour part-time; state resident $2736 full-time, $114 per credit hour part-time; nonresident $3096 full-time, $129 per credit hour part-time. *Required fees:* $80 full-time, $40 per term part-time. *Room and board:* room only: $1560.

Financial Aid Of all full-time matriculated undergraduates, 80 Federal Work-Study jobs (averaging $1484). 11 state and other part-time jobs (averaging $1159).

Applying *Options:* deferred entrance. *Required:* high school transcript. *Application deadlines:* rolling (freshmen), rolling (out-of-state freshmen), rolling (transfers). *Notification:* continuous (freshmen), continuous (out-of-state freshmen), continuous (transfers).

Freshmen Application Contact Ms. Alicia Ulloa, Director of Admissions/Registrar, Coastal Bend College, 3800 Charco Road, Beeville, TX 78102-2197. *Phone:* 361-354-2245. *Fax:* 361-354-2254. *E-mail:* register@coastalbend.edu.

COLLEGE OF THE MAINLAND

Texas City, Texas　　　　　**www.com.edu/**

- **State and locally supported** 2-year, founded 1967
- **Suburban** 120-acre campus with easy access to Houston
- **Coed,** 3,849 undergraduate students

Undergraduates Students come from 8 states and territories, 0.4% are from out of state. *Retention:* 48% of 2003 full-time freshmen returned.

Freshmen *Admission:* 517 admitted.

Faculty *Total:* 329, 36% full-time. *Student/faculty ratio:* 17:1.

Majors Accounting technology and bookkeeping; administrative assistant and secretarial science; business administration and management; chemical technology; child development; computer programming; computer systems networking and telecommunications; criminal justice/law enforcement administration; criminal justice/safety; criminology; dramatic/theater arts; emergency medical technology (EMT paramedic); fine/studio arts; fire protection and safety technology; general studies; liberal arts and sciences/liberal studies; mathematics; music; natural sciences; nursing (registered nurse training); pre-engineering; public administration and social service professions related; social work; sociology; web page, digital/multimedia and information resources design.

Academics *Calendar:* semesters. *Degree:* certificates, diplomas, and associate. *Special study options:* academic remediation for entering students, adult/continuing education programs, cooperative education, distance learning, English as a second language, honors programs, part-time degree program, services for LD students, summer session for credit.

Library Com Library plus 1 other with 84,128 titles, 19,000 serial subscriptions, 492 audiovisual materials, an OPAC, a Web page.

Student Life *Housing:* college housing not available. *Activities and Organizations:* drama/theater group, choral group, Student Activities Board, Student Government Association, COM Amigos, COM Soccer Club, Phi Theta Kappa. *Campus security:* 24-hour emergency response devices and patrols, student patrols. *Student services:* personal/psychological counseling, women's center.

Athletics *Intramural sports:* basketball M/W, football M/W, golf M/W, racquetball M/W, soccer M, softball M/W, swimming and diving M/W, table tennis M/W, tennis M/W, track and field M/W, volleyball M/W.

Costs (2007–08) *Tuition:* area resident $744 full-time, $31 per credit part-time; state resident $1560 full-time, $65 per credit part-time; nonresident $2328 full-time, $97 per credit part-time. *Required fees:* $167 full-time, $11 per credit part-time, $65 per term part-time.

Financial Aid Of all full-time matriculated undergraduates, 204 Federal Work-Study jobs (averaging $789). 234 state and other part-time jobs (averaging $949).

Applying *Options:* electronic application, early admission, deferred entrance. *Required for some:* high school transcript. *Application deadlines:* rolling (freshmen), rolling (transfers). *Notification:* continuous (freshmen), continuous (transfers).

Freshmen Application Contact Ms. Kelly Musick, Registrar/Director of Admissions, College of the Mainland, 1200 Amburn Road, Texas City, TX 77591. *Phone:* 409-938-1211 Ext. 469. *Toll-free phone:* 888-258-8859 Ext. 264. *Fax:* 409-938-3126. *E-mail:* sem@com.edu.

COLLIN COUNTY COMMUNITY COLLEGE DISTRICT

Plano, Texas   www.ccccd.edu/

- **State and locally supported** 2-year, founded 1985
- **Suburban** 333-acre campus with easy access to Dallas-Fort Worth
- **Endowment** $2.4 million
- **Coed,** 19,332 undergraduate students, 39% full-time, 56% women, 44% men

Undergraduates 7,598 full-time, 11,734 part-time. Students come from 48 states and territories, 86 other countries, 4% are from out of state, 9% African American, 9% Asian American or Pacific Islander, 11% Hispanic American, 0.7% Native American, 2% international, 10% transferred in. *Retention:* 59% of 2003 full-time freshmen returned.

Freshmen *Admission:* 3,259 admitted, 3,259 enrolled.

Faculty *Total:* 1,102, 24% full-time. *Student/faculty ratio:* 21:1.

Majors Biology/biotechnology laboratory technician; business administration and management; business automation/technology/data entry; commercial and advertising art; computer and information sciences; computer engineering technology; computer programming; computer systems networking and telecommunications; dental hygiene; drafting and design technology; educational/instructional media design; electrical, electronic and communications engineering technology; electrical/electronics drafting and CAD/CADD; electrical/electronics equipment installation and repair; emergency medical technology (EMT paramedic); environmental engineering technology; family and community services; fire protection and safety technology; hospitality administration; interior design; legal assistant/paralegal; liberal arts and sciences/liberal studies; music management and merchandising; nursing (registered nurse training); real estate; respiratory care therapy; sales, distribution and marketing; sign language interpretation and translation; telecommunications technology; water quality and wastewater treatment management and recycling technology; web page, digital/multimedia and information resources design.

Academics *Calendar:* semesters. *Degree:* certificates and associate. *Special study options:* academic remediation for entering students, adult/continuing education programs, advanced placement credit, cooperative education, distance learning, English as a second language, honors programs, internships, part-time degree program, services for LD students, study abroad, summer session for credit.

Library Main Library plus 3 others with 259,627 titles, 909 serial subscriptions, 24,981 audiovisual materials, an OPAC, a Web page.

Student Life *Housing:* college housing not available. *Activities and Organizations:* drama/theater group, choral group, Phi Theta Kappa, LULAC/BSN, Baptist Student Ministry, Psi Beta, Collin Nursing Student Association. *Campus security:* 24-hour emergency response devices and patrols, late-night transport/escort service, controlled dormitory access. *Student services:* personal/psychological counseling.

Athletics Member NJCAA. *Intercollegiate sports:* basketball M(s)/W(s), tennis M(s)/W(s), volleyball W(s).

Standardized Tests *Required:* THEA (for admission).

Costs (2006–07) *Tuition:* area resident $810 full-time, $27 per credit hour part-time; state resident $1020 full-time, $35 per credit hour part-time; nonresi-

dent $2550 full-time, $86 per credit hour part-time. *Required fees:* $306 full-time, $10 per credit hour part-time, $2 per term part-time. *Payment plan:* installment. *Waivers:* senior citizens.

Financial Aid Of all full-time matriculated undergraduates, 80 Federal Work-Study jobs (averaging $3490).

Applying *Options:* electronic application. *Required:* high school transcript. *Application deadline:* rolling (freshmen). *Notification:* continuous (freshmen), continuous (transfers).

Freshmen Application Contact Todd Fields, Registrar, Collin County Community College District, 2200 West University Drive, McKinney, TX 75070-8001. *Phone:* 972-881-5174. *Fax:* 972-881-5175. *E-mail:* tfields@ccccd.edu.

COMMONWEALTH INSTITUTE OF FUNERAL SERVICE

Houston, Texas   www.commonwealthinst.org/

Freshmen Application Contact Ms. Patricia Moreno, Registrar, Commonwealth Institute of Funeral Service, 415 Barren Springs Drive, Houston, TX 77090. *Phone:* 281-873-0262. *Toll-free phone:* 800-628-1580. *Fax:* 281-873-5232.

COMPUTER CAREER CENTER

El Paso, Texas   www.computercareercenter.com/

Director of Admissions Ms. Sarah Hernandez, Registrar, Computer Career Center, 6101 Montana Avenue, El Paso, TX 79925. *Phone:* 915-779-8031.

COURT REPORTING INSTITUTE OF DALLAS

Dallas, Texas   www.crid.com/

Director of Admissions Ms. Debra Smith-Armstrong, Director of Admissions, Court Reporting Institute of Dallas, 8585 North Stemmons, #200 North Tower, Dallas, TX 75247. *Phone:* 214-350-9722 Ext. 227. *Toll-free phone:* 800-880-9722.

COURT REPORTING INSTITUTE OF HOUSTON

Houston, Texas   www.crid.com/

Freshmen Application Contact Admissions Office, Court Reporting Institute of Houston, 13101 Northwest Freeway, Suite 100, Houston, TX 77040. *Toll-free phone:* 866-996-8300.

CULINARY INSTITUTE ALAIN & MARIE LENOTRE

Houston, Texas   www.ciaml.com

- **Proprietary** 2-year
- **Coed,** 22 undergraduate students

Majors Baking and pastry arts; culinary arts; restaurant, culinary, and catering management.

Academics *Degree:* associate.

Costs (2006–07) *Tuition:* $33,530 per degree program part-time.

Applying *Application fee:* $50.

Freshmen Application Contact Admissions Office, Culinary Institute Alain & Marie LeNotre, 7070 Allensby, Houston, TX 77022-4322.

CY-FAIR COLLEGE

Houston, Texas   www.cy-faircollege.com/

Freshmen Application Contact Dr. Earl Campa, Vice President of Student Success, Cy-Fair College, 9191 Barker Cypress Road, Cypress, TX 77433-1383. *Phone:* 281-290-3950.

DALLAS INSTITUTE OF FUNERAL SERVICE

Dallas, Texas   www.dallasinstitute.edu/

- **Independent** 2-year, founded 1945
- **Urban** 8-acre campus with easy access to Dallas/Ft. Worth
- **Coed**

Undergraduates 247 full-time. Students come from 12 states and territories, 10% are from out of state, 26% African American, 0.8% Asian American or Pacific Islander, 9% Hispanic American, 0.4% Native American, 10% transferred in.

Faculty *Student/faculty ratio:* 32:1.

Academics *Calendar:* quarters. *Degree:* certificates and associate.

Student Life *Campus security:* 24-hour emergency response devices.

Costs (2006–07) *Tuition:* $10,000 full-time, $200 per hour part-time. *Required fees:* $50 full-time.

Applying *Application fee:* $50. *Required:* high school transcript.

Freshmen Application Contact Terry Parrish, Director of Admissions, Dallas Institute of Funeral Service, 3909 South Buckner Boulevard, Dallas, TX 75227. *Phone:* 214-388-5466. *Toll-free phone:* 800-235-5444. *Fax:* 214-388-0316. *E-mail:* difs@dallasinstitute.edu.

DEL MAR COLLEGE

Corpus Christi, Texas   www.delmar.edu/

Freshmen Application Contact Ms. Frances P. Jordan, Assistant Dean of Enrollment Services, Del Mar College, 101 Baldwin Boulevard, Corpus Christi, TX 78404-3897. *Phone:* 361-698-1255. *Toll-free phone:* 800-652-3357. *Fax:* 361-698-1595. *E-mail:* fjordan@delmar.edu.

EASTFIELD COLLEGE

Mesquite, Texas   www.efc.dcccd.edu/

- **State and locally supported** 2-year, founded 1970, part of Dallas County Community College District System
- **Suburban** 244-acre campus with easy access to Dallas–Fort Worth
- **Coed**

Undergraduates 2,322 full-time, 9,789 part-time. Students come from 18 states and territories, 1% are from out of state, 21% African American, 4% Asian American or Pacific Islander, 23% Hispanic American, 0.6% Native American, 0.5% international, 3% transferred in. *Retention:* 39% of 2003 full-time freshmen returned.

Faculty *Student/faculty ratio:* 23:1.

Academics *Calendar:* semesters. *Degree:* certificates and associate. *Special study options:* academic remediation for entering students, adult/continuing education programs, advanced placement credit, cooperative education, distance learning, English as a second language, honors programs, part-time degree program, services for LD students, summer session for credit.

Student Life *Campus security:* 24-hour emergency response devices and patrols.

Athletics Member NJCAA.

Costs (2006–07) *Tuition:* area resident $1170 full-time, $39 per credit part-time; state resident $2160 full-time, $72 per credit part-time; nonresident $3450 full-time, $115 per credit part-time.

Applying *Options:* early admission, deferred entrance. *Recommended:* high school transcript.

Freshmen Application Contact Ms. Glynis Miller, Director of Admissions/ Registrar, Eastfield College, 3737 Motley Drive, Mesquite, TX 75150-2099. *Phone:* 972-860-7010. *Fax:* 972-860-8306. *E-mail:* efc@dcccd.edu.

EL CENTRO COLLEGE

Dallas, Texas   www.ecc.dcccd.edu/

- **County-supported** 2-year, founded 1966, part of Dallas County Community College District System
- **Urban** 2-acre campus
- **Coed,** 6,281 undergraduate students, 23% full-time, 70% women, 30% men

Undergraduates 1,439 full-time, 4,842 part-time. Students come from 16 states and territories, 62 other countries, 2% are from out of state, 36% African American, 4% Asian American or Pacific Islander, 28% Hispanic American, 0.5% Native American, 2% international, 55% transferred in.

Freshmen *Admission:* 890 applied, 890 admitted, 890 enrolled.

Faculty *Total:* 446, 25% full-time, 9% with terminal degrees. *Student/faculty ratio:* 14:1.

Majors Accounting; administrative assistant and secretarial science; baking and pastry arts; biotechnology research; business administration and management; business automation/technology/data entry; cardiovascular technology; clinical laboratory science/medical technology; clinical/medical laboratory technology; clothing/textiles; computer/information technology services administration related; computer programming; computer science; criminal justice/police science; criminal justice/safety; culinary arts; data processing and data processing technology; diagnostic medical sonography and ultrasound technology; drafting and design technology; emergency medical technology (EMT paramedic); fashion/apparel design; food science; food services technology; health information/medical records administration; hospitality administration; hotel/motel administration; information science/studies; information technology; interior design; legal administrative assistant/secretary; legal assistant/paralegal; legal studies; liberal arts and sciences/liberal studies; medical administrative assistant and medical secretary; medical/clinical assistant; medical radiologic technology; medical transcription; nursing (licensed practical/vocational nurse training); nursing (registered nurse training); office occupations and clerical services; radiologic technology/science; respiratory care therapy; special products marketing; surgical technology; teacher assistant/aide; web page, digital/multimedia and information resources design.

Academics *Calendar:* semesters. *Degree:* certificates and associate. *Special study options:* academic remediation for entering students, adult/continuing education programs, advanced placement credit, cooperative education, distance learning, double majors, English as a second language, freshman honors college, honors programs, internships, part-time degree program, services for LD students, summer session for credit. *ROTC:* Army (c).

Library El Centro College Library with 77,902 titles, 224 serial subscriptions, 585 audiovisual materials, an OPAC, a Web page.

Student Life *Housing:* college housing not available. *Activities and Organizations:* choral group, Phi Theta Kappa, Radiology Club, SPAR (Student Programs and Resources Office), Organization of Latin American Students. *Campus security:* 24-hour emergency response devices and patrols, late-night transport/ escort service. *Student services:* health clinic, personal/psychological counseling.

Athletics *Intramural sports:* basketball M/W, table tennis M/W, volleyball M/W, weight lifting M/W.

Costs (2006–07) *Tuition:* area resident $864 full-time, $36 per credit hour part-time; state resident $1584 full-time, $66 per credit hour part-time; nonresident $2544 full-time, $106 per credit hour part-time.

Applying *Options:* electronic application, early admission. *Required for some:* high school transcript, 1 letter of recommendation. *Application deadlines:* rolling (freshmen), rolling (transfers).

Freshmen Application Contact Ms. Rebecca Garza, Director of Admissions and Registrar, El Centro College, 801 Main Street, Dallas, TX 75202. *Phone:* 214-860-2618. *Fax:* 214-860-2233. *E-mail:* rgarza@dcccd.edu.

EL PASO COMMUNITY COLLEGE

El Paso, Texas   www.epcc.edu/

Freshmen Application Contact Daryle Hendry, Director of Admissions, El Paso Community College, PO Box 20500, El Paso, TX 79998-0500. *Phone:* 915-831-2580. *E-mail:* daryleh@epcc.edu.

EVEREST COLLEGE

Arlington, Texas   www.everest-college.com/

- **Proprietary** 2-year, founded 2003
- **Coed,** 838 undergraduate students
- 100% of applicants were admitted

Freshmen *Admission:* 225 applied, 225 admitted.
Majors Business administration and management.
Academics *Calendar:* 6 or 12 week terms. *Degree:* associate.
Costs (2006–07) *Tuition:* $13,865 full-time.
Applying *Application fee:* $25. *Required:* high school transcript.
Freshmen Application Contact Admissions Office, Everest College, 2801 East Division Street, Suite 250, Arlington, TX 76011.

EVEREST COLLEGE
Dallas, Texas www.everest-college.com/

- **Proprietary** 2-year, founded 2003
- **Coed,** 748 undergraduate students
- 88% of applicants were admitted

Freshmen *Admission:* 319 applied, 280 admitted.
Majors Business administration and management.
Academics *Calendar:* 6 or 12 week terms. *Degree:* associate.
Costs (2006–07) *Tuition:* $15,039 full-time.
Freshmen Application Contact Admissions Office, Everest College, 6080 North Central Expressway, Dallas, TX 75206.

EVEREST COLLEGE
Fort Worth, Texas www.everest-college.com/

- **Proprietary** 2-year, founded 2004
- **Coed,** 381 undergraduate students
- 100% of applicants were admitted

Freshmen *Admission:* 107 applied, 107 admitted.
Majors Business administration and management.
Academics *Degree:* associate.
Costs (2006–07) *Tuition:* $9327 full-time.
Applying *Application fee:* $25.
Freshmen Application Contact Admissions Office, Everest College, Suite 100, Fort Worth, TX 76137.

FRANK PHILLIPS COLLEGE
Borger, Texas www.fpc.cc.tx.us/

Director of Admissions Ms. Beth Raper, Director of Admissions, Frank Phillips College, Borger, TX 79008-5118. *Phone:* 806-457-4200 Ext. 741. *Toll-free phone:* 800-687-2056. *Fax:* 806-273-7642.

GALVESTON COLLEGE
Galveston, Texas www.gc.edu/

- **State and locally supported** 2-year, founded 1967
- **Urban** 11-acre campus with easy access to Houston
- **Coed**

Undergraduates 851 full-time, 1,379 part-time. Students come from 29 states and territories, 19 other countries, 4% are from out of state, 19% African American, 3% Asian American or Pacific Islander, 24% Hispanic American, 0.3% Native American, 1% international, 14% transferred in.
Faculty *Student/faculty ratio:* 16:1.
Academics *Calendar:* semesters. *Degree:* certificates and associate. *Special study options:* academic remediation for entering students, adult/continuing education programs, advanced placement credit, cooperative education, distance learning, English as a second language, internships, off-campus study, part-time degree program, services for LD students, summer session for credit.
Student Life *Campus security:* 24-hour emergency response devices, late-night transport/escort service.
Athletics Member NJCAA.
Costs (2006–07) *Tuition:* state resident $900 full-time, $30 per hour part-time; nonresident $1800 full-time, $60 per hour part-time. *Required fees:* $430 full-time, $12 per hour part-time, $30 per term part-time.
Financial Aid Of all full-time matriculated undergraduates, 36 Federal Work-Study jobs (averaging $2000).

Applying *Required for some:* high school transcript.
Freshmen Application Contact MaEsther Francis, Dean of Enrollment Management and Student Success, Galveston College, 4015 Avenue Q, Galveston, TX 77550. *Phone:* 409-944-1340. *Fax:* 409-944-1501. *E-mail:* mfrancis@gc.edu.

GRAYSON COUNTY COLLEGE
Denison, Texas www.grayson.edu/

- **State and locally supported** 2-year, founded 1964
- **Rural** 500-acre campus
- **Coed,** 3,344 undergraduate students, 51% full-time, 58% women, 42% men

Undergraduates 1,697 full-time, 1,647 part-time. Students come from 3 states and territories, 2 other countries. *Retention:* 54% of 2003 full-time freshmen returned.
Freshmen *Admission:* 3,344 applied, 3,344 admitted.
Faculty *Total:* 219, 43% full-time. *Student/faculty ratio:* 16:1.
Majors Accounting; administrative assistant and secretarial science; art; art teacher education; autobody/collision and repair technology; biology/biological sciences; business administration and management; chemistry; clinical laboratory science/medical technology; clinical/medical laboratory technology; computer engineering technology; computer science; cosmetology; criminal justice/law enforcement administration; criminal justice/police science; drafting and design technology; dramatic/theater arts; education; electrical, electronic and communications engineering technology; elementary education; geology/earth science; heating, air conditioning, ventilation and refrigeration maintenance technology; landscaping and groundskeeping; legal administrative assistant/secretary; liberal arts and sciences/liberal studies; machine tool technology; management information systems; mathematics; music; nursing (registered nurse training); physical education teaching and coaching; physics; pre-engineering; psychology; real estate; sociology; speech and rhetoric; veterinary sciences; welding technology.
Academics *Calendar:* semesters. *Degree:* certificates, diplomas, and associate. *Special study options:* academic remediation for entering students, adult/continuing education programs, advanced placement credit, English as a second language, honors programs, part-time degree program, summer session for credit.
Library 51,500 titles, 310 serial subscriptions.
Student Life *Housing Options:* Campus housing is university owned. *Activities and Organizations:* drama/theater group.
Athletics Member NJCAA. *Intercollegiate sports:* baseball M(s), basketball M(s)/W(s), softball W(s). *Intramural sports:* baseball M, basketball M/W, football M, soccer M, softball W.
Standardized Tests *Required:* THEA (for placement). *Recommended:* SAT or ACT (for placement).
Costs (2006–07) *Tuition:* area resident $1260 full-time, $42 per credit hour part-time; state resident $1470 full-time, $49 per credit hour part-time; nonresident $2940 full-time, $98 per credit hour part-time.
Applying *Options:* early admission, deferred entrance. *Application deadline:* 8/31 (freshmen). *Notification:* continuous (freshmen), continuous (transfers).
Director of Admissions Dr. Debbie Plyler, Associate Vice President for Admissions, Records and Institutional Research, Grayson County College, 6101 Grayson Drive, Denison, TX 75020. *Phone:* 903-463-8727.

HALLMARK INSTITUTE OF AERONAUTICS
San Antonio, Texas www.hallmarkinstitute.edu/Aviation/index.htm

- **Private** 2-year
- **Coed**

Majors Aircraft powerplant technology; airframe mechanics and aircraft maintenance technology.
Academics *Calendar:* continuous. *Degree:* diplomas and associate.
Director of Admissions Mr. David McSorley, Director, Hallmark Institute of Aeronautics, 8901 Wetmore Road, San Antonio, TX 78216. *Phone:* 210-690-9000. *Toll-free phone:* 888-656-9300.

HALLMARK INSTITUTE OF TECHNOLOGY

San Antonio, Texas　　　www.hallmarkinstitute.edu/

Director of Admissions Ms. Sonia Ross, Director of Admissions, Hallmark Institute of Technology, 10401 IH 10 West, San Antonio, TX 78230-1737. *Phone:* 210-690-9000 Ext. 212. *Toll-free phone:* 800-880-6600.

HIGH-TECH INSTITUTE

Irving, Texas　　　www.high-techinstitute.com/

Freshmen Application Contact Admissions Office, High-Tech Institute, 4250 North Beltline Road, Irving, TX 75038. *Phone:* 972-871-2824. *Toll-free phone:* 800-265-1825.

HILL COLLEGE OF THE HILL JUNIOR COLLEGE DISTRICT

Hillsboro, Texas　　　www.hillcollege.edu/

Freshmen Application Contact Ms. Diane Harvey, Director of Admissions/ Registrar, Hill College of the Hill Junior College District, PO Box 619, Hillsboro, TX 76645-0619. *Phone:* 254-582-2555. *Fax:* 254-582-7591. *E-mail:* diharvey@hill-college.cc.tx.us.

HOUSTON COMMUNITY COLLEGE SYSTEM

Houston, Texas　　　www.hccs.edu/

- **State and locally supported** 2-year, founded 1971
- **Urban** campus
- **Coed,** 42,526 undergraduate students, 31% full-time, 59% women, 41% men

Undergraduates 13,263 full-time, 29,263 part-time. 25% African American, 12% Asian American or Pacific Islander, 28% Hispanic American, 0.2% Native American, 10% international, 5% transferred in.

Freshmen *Admission:* 7,301 enrolled.

Faculty *Total:* 3,323, 24% full-time. *Student/faculty ratio:* 20:1.

Majors Accounting; administrative assistant and secretarial science; agriculture; automobile/automotive mechanics technology; business administration and management; business/corporate communications; cartography; child care and support services management; child development; civil engineering technology; clinical/medical laboratory technology; commercial and advertising art; commercial photography; computer and information sciences; computer engineering technology; computer science; construction engineering technology; court reporting; criminal justice/police science; drafting and design technology; dramatic/theater arts; electrical, electronic and communications engineering technology; emergency medical technology (EMT paramedic); engineering technology; family and consumer sciences/human sciences; fashion/apparel design; fashion merchandising; finance; fire science; graphic and printing equipment operation/production; health/health care administration; health information/medical records administration; health information/medical records technology; horticultural science; hotel/motel administration; human resources management; industrial radiologic technology; industrial technology; insurance; interior design; kinesiology and exercise science; legal assistant/paralegal; liberal arts and sciences/liberal studies; logistics and materials management; marketing/marketing management; mass communication/media; medical administrative assistant and medical secretary; medical radiologic technology; mental health/rehabilitation; music management and merchandising; music theory and composition; nuclear medical technology; nursing (registered nurse training); occupational safety and health technology; occupational therapist assistant; physical therapist assistant; psychiatric/mental health services technology; radio and television broadcasting technology; real estate; respiratory care therapy; sign language interpretation and translation; social sciences; technical and business writing; tourism and travel services management; transportation technology.

Academics *Calendar:* semesters. *Degree:* certificates and associate. *Special study options:* academic remediation for entering students, adult/continuing education programs, advanced placement credit, cooperative education, distance learning, English as a second language, honors programs, independent study, internships, part-time degree program, services for LD students, study abroad, summer session for credit. *ROTC:* Army (c).

Library Main Library plus 19 others with 140,674 titles, 2,012 serial subscriptions, 16,334 audiovisual materials, an OPAC, a Web page.

Student Life *Housing:* college housing not available. *Activities and Organizations:* drama/theater group, student-run newspaper, television station, Phi Theta Kappa, Eastwood Student Association, Eagle's Club, Society of Hispanic Professional Engineers, International Student Association. *Campus security:* 24-hour emergency response devices and patrols, late-night transport/escort service. *Student services:* personal/psychological counseling.

Costs (2007–08) *Tuition:* area resident $1314 full-time, $80 per credit hour part-time; state resident $2610 full-time, $134 per credit hour part-time; nonresident $3090 full-time, $293 per credit hour part-time.

Applying *Required for some:* high school transcript, interview. *Application deadline:* rolling (freshmen). *Notification:* continuous (transfers).

Freshmen Application Contact Ms. Mary Lemburg, Registrar, Houston Community College System, 3100 Main Street, PO Box 667517, Houston, TX 77266-7517. *Phone:* 713-718-8500. *Fax:* 713-718-2111.

HOWARD COLLEGE

Big Spring, Texas　　　www.howardcollege.edu/

- **State and locally supported** 2-year, founded 1945, part of Howard County Junior College District System
- **Small-town** 120-acre campus
- **Endowment** $1.2 million
- **Coed**

Undergraduates 1,174 full-time, 1,551 part-time. Students come from 10 states and territories, 2 other countries, 2% are from out of state, 5% African American, 0.9% Asian American or Pacific Islander, 31% Hispanic American, 0.5% Native American, 0.2% international, 0.4% transferred in, 18% live on campus.

Faculty *Student/faculty ratio:* 11:1.

Academics *Calendar:* semesters. *Degree:* certificates and associate. *Special study options:* academic remediation for entering students, adult/continuing education programs, advanced placement credit, cooperative education, distance learning, English as a second language, independent study, internships, part-time degree program, services for LD students, summer session for credit.

Student Life *Campus security:* 24-hour patrols.

Athletics Member NJCAA.

Applying *Options:* early admission. *Required:* high school transcript.

Freshmen Application Contact Ms. Dianah Collom, Outreach Coordinator, Howard College, 1001 Birdwell Lane, Big Spring, TX 79720-3702. *Phone:* 432-264-5105. *Toll-free phone:* 866-HC-HAWKS. *Fax:* 432-264-5082. *E-mail:* dcollom@howardcollege.edu.

ITT TECHNICAL INSTITUTE

Arlington, Texas　　　www.itt-tech.edu/

- **Proprietary** 2-year, founded 1982, part of ITT Educational Services, Inc
- **Suburban** campus with easy access to Dallas–Fort Worth
- **Coed**

Majors CAD/CADD drafting/design technology; computer engineering technology; computer systems networking and telecommunications; web page, digital/multimedia and information resources design.

Academics *Calendar:* quarters. *Degree:* associate.

Library a Web page.

Student Life *Housing:* college housing not available.

Standardized Tests *Required:* Wonderlic aptitude test (for admission).

Costs (2006–07) *Tuition:* Contact school for program costs.

Applying *Options:* deferred entrance. *Application fee:* $100. *Required:* high school transcript, interview. *Recommended:* letters of recommendation. *Application deadlines:* rolling (freshmen), rolling (transfers). *Notification:* continuous (freshmen), continuous (transfers).

Freshmen Application Contact Mr. Robert Perez Jr., Director of Recruitment, ITT Technical Institute, 551 Ryan Plaza Drive, Arlington, TX 76011. *Phone:* 817-794-5100. *Toll-free phone:* 888-288-4950. *Fax:* 817-275-8446.

ITT TECHNICAL INSTITUTE

Austin, Texas　　　www.itt-tech.edu/

- **Proprietary** 2-year, founded 1985, part of ITT Educational Services, Inc
- **Urban** campus
- **Coed**

Majors Accounting technology and bookkeeping; CAD/CADD drafting/design technology; computer engineering technology; computer systems networking and telecommunications; web page, digital/multimedia and information resources design.

Academics *Calendar:* quarters. *Degree:* associate.

Library a Web page.

Student Life *Housing:* college housing not available.

Standardized Tests *Required:* Wonderlic aptitude test (for admission).

Costs (2006–07) *Tuition:* Contact school for program costs.

Financial Aid Of all full-time matriculated undergraduates, 1 Federal Work-Study job.

Applying *Options:* deferred entrance. *Application fee:* $100. *Required:* high school transcript, interview. *Recommended:* letters of recommendation. *Application deadlines:* rolling (freshmen), rolling (transfers). *Notification:* continuous (freshmen), continuous (transfers).

Freshmen Application Contact Mr. Jim Branham, Director of Recruitment, ITT Technical Institute, 6330 Highway 290 East, Suite 150, Austin, TX 78723. *Phone:* 512-467-6800. *Toll-free phone:* 800-431-0677. *Fax:* 512-467-6677.

ITT TECHNICAL INSTITUTE
Houston, Texas
www.itt-tech.edu/

- **Proprietary** 2-year, founded 1985, part of ITT Educational Services, Inc
- **Suburban** 1-acre campus
- **Coed**

Majors CAD/CADD drafting/design technology; computer programming; electrical, electronic and communications engineering technology; system, networking, and LAN/WAN management; web/multimedia management and webmaster; web page, digital/multimedia and information resources design.

Academics *Calendar:* quarters. *Degree:* associate.

Library a Web page.

Student Life *Housing:* college housing not available.

Standardized Tests *Required:* Wonderlic aptitude test (for admission).

Costs (2006–07) *Tuition:* Contact school for program costs.

Applying *Options:* deferred entrance. *Application fee:* $100. *Required:* high school transcript, interview. *Recommended:* letters of recommendation. *Application deadlines:* rolling (freshmen), rolling (transfers). *Notification:* continuous (freshmen), continuous (transfers).

Freshmen Application Contact Valory Broussard, Director of Recruitment, ITT Technical Institute, 15621 Blue Ash Drive, Suite 160, Houston, TX 77090. *Phone:* 281-873-0512. *Toll-free phone:* 800-879-6486.

ITT TECHNICAL INSTITUTE
Houston, Texas
www.itt-tech.edu/

- **Proprietary** 2-year, founded 1983, part of ITT Educational Services, Inc
- **Urban** 4-acre campus
- **Coed**, 585 undergraduate students

Majors CAD/CADD drafting/design technology; computer engineering technology; computer systems networking and telecommunications.

Academics *Calendar:* quarters. *Degree:* associate.

Library a Web page.

Student Life *Housing:* college housing not available. *Activities and Organizations:* student-run newspaper.

Standardized Tests *Required:* Wonderlic aptitude test (for admission).

Costs (2006–07) *Tuition:* Contact school for program costs.

Applying *Options:* deferred entrance. *Application fee:* $100. *Required:* high school transcript, interview. *Recommended:* letters of recommendation. *Application deadlines:* rolling (freshmen), rolling (transfers). *Notification:* continuous (freshmen), continuous (transfers).

Freshmen Application Contact Ms. Jennifer Gomez, Director of Recruitment, ITT Technical Institute, 2950 South Gessner, Houston, TX 77063. *Phone:* 713-952-2294. *Toll-free phone:* 800-235-4787.

ITT TECHNICAL INSTITUTE
Richardson, Texas
www.itt-tech.edu/

- **Proprietary** 2-year, founded 1989, part of ITT Educational Services, Inc
- **Suburban** campus with easy access to Dallas–Fort Worth
- **Coed**

Majors CAD/CADD drafting/design technology; computer software technology; computer systems networking and telecommunications; data processing and data processing technology; web/multimedia management and webmaster; web page, digital/multimedia and information resources design.

Academics *Calendar:* quarters. *Degree:* associate.

Library a Web page.

Student Life *Housing:* college housing not available.

Standardized Tests *Required:* Wonderlic aptitude test (for admission).

Costs (2006–07) *Tuition:* Contact school for program costs.

Financial Aid Of all full-time matriculated undergraduates, 5 Federal Work-Study jobs (averaging $5000).

Applying *Options:* deferred entrance. *Application fee:* $100. *Required:* high school transcript, interview. *Recommended:* letters of recommendation. *Application deadlines:* rolling (freshmen), rolling (transfers). *Notification:* continuous (freshmen), continuous (transfers).

Freshmen Application Contact Ms. Carol Anderson, Director of Recruitment, ITT Technical Institute, 2101 Waterview Parkway, Richardson, TX 75080. *Phone:* 972-690-9100. *Toll-free phone:* 888-488-5761.

ITT TECHNICAL INSTITUTE
San Antonio, Texas
www.itt-tech.edu/

- **Proprietary** 2-year, founded 1988, part of ITT Educational Services, Inc
- **Urban** campus
- **Coed**

Majors Accounting technology and bookkeeping; CAD/CADD drafting/design technology; computer systems networking and telecommunications; web/multimedia management and webmaster; web page, digital/multimedia and information resources design.

Academics *Calendar:* quarters. *Degree:* associate.

Library a Web page.

Student Life *Housing:* college housing not available. *Activities and Organizations:* student-run newspaper.

Standardized Tests *Required:* Wonderlic aptitude test (for admission).

Costs (2006–07) *Tuition:* Contact school for program costs.

Applying *Options:* deferred entrance. *Application fee:* $100. *Required:* high school transcript, interview. *Recommended:* letters of recommendation. *Application deadlines:* rolling (freshmen), rolling (transfers). *Notification:* continuous (freshmen), continuous (transfers).

Freshmen Application Contact Mr. Jesus Perez, Director of Recruitment, ITT Technical Institute, 5700 Northwest Parkway, San Antonio, TX 78249. *Phone:* 210-694-4612. *Toll-free phone:* 800-880-0570.

ITT TECHNICAL INSTITUTE
Webster, Texas
www.itt-tech.edu/

- **Proprietary** 2-year, founded 1995, part of ITT Educational Services, Inc
- **Coed**

Majors CAD/CADD drafting/design technology; computer engineering technology; computer software technology; computer systems networking and telecommunications; web/multimedia management and webmaster; web page, digital/multimedia and information resources design.

Academics *Calendar:* quarters. *Degree:* associate.

Library a Web page.

Student Life *Housing:* college housing not available.

Standardized Tests *Required:* Wonderlic aptitude test (for admission).

Costs (2006–07) *Tuition:* Contact school for program costs.

Applying *Options:* deferred entrance. *Application fee:* $100. *Required:* high school transcript, interview. *Recommended:* letters of recommendation. *Application deadlines:* rolling (freshmen), rolling (transfers). *Notification:* continuous (freshmen), continuous (transfers).

ITT Technical Institute (continued)

Freshmen Application Contact Derrell Beck, Director of Recruitment, ITT Technical Institute, 1001 Magnolia Avenue, Webster, TX 77598. *Phone:* 281-486-2630. *Toll-free phone:* 888-488-9347.

JACKSONVILLE COLLEGE

Jacksonville, Texas www.jacksonville-college.edu/

- **Independent Baptist** 2-year, founded 1899
- **Small-town** 20-acre campus
- **Coed**

Undergraduates 220 full-time, 80 part-time. Students come from 16 states and territories, 15 other countries, 3% are from out of state, 16% African American, 0.3% Asian American or Pacific Islander, 12% Hispanic American, 3% international, 39% live on campus.

Faculty *Student/faculty ratio:* 16:1.

Academics *Calendar:* semesters. *Degree:* diplomas and associate. *Special study options:* academic remediation for entering students, adult/continuing education programs, advanced placement credit, part-time degree program, summer session for credit.

Student Life *Campus security:* 24-hour emergency response devices, evening security personnel.

Athletics Member NJCAA.

Standardized Tests *Required for some:* SAT (for admission), ACT (for admission), THEA.

Costs (2006–07) *Comprehensive fee:* $4480 includes full-time tuition ($2800), mandatory fees ($307), and room and board ($1373). Part-time tuition: $175 per credit hour.

Applying *Options:* electronic application, early admission. *Application fee:* $15.

Freshmen Application Contact Ms. Melissa Walles, Director of Admissions, Jacksonville College, 105 B.J. Albritton Drive, Jacksonville, TX 75766. *Phone:* 903-586-2518 Ext. 7134. *Toll-free phone:* 800-256-8522. *Fax:* 903-586-0743. *E-mail:* admissions@jacksonville-college.org.

KD STUDIO

Dallas, Texas www.kdstudio.com/

- **Proprietary** 2-year, founded 1979
- **Urban** campus
- **Coed**

Undergraduates 152 full-time. Students come from 10 states and territories, 4% are from out of state, 36% African American, 13% Hispanic American.

Faculty *Student/faculty ratio:* 7:1.

Academics *Calendar:* semesters. *Degree:* associate. *Special study options:* cooperative education.

Student Life *Campus security:* 24-hour emergency response devices and patrols.

Costs (2006–07) *Tuition:* Full-time tuition and fees vary according to program. No tuition increase for student's term of enrollment. Tuition varies by program. *Required fees:* $500 full-time.

Applying *Options:* deferred entrance. *Application fee:* $100. *Required:* essay or personal statement, high school transcript, interview, audition. *Required for some:* letters of recommendation.

Freshmen Application Contact Mr. T. Taylor, Director of Education, KD Studio, 2600 Stemmons Freeway, Suite 117, Dallas, TX 75207. *Phone:* 214-638-0484. *Fax:* 214-630-5140. *E-mail:* acting@onramp.net.

KILGORE COLLEGE

Kilgore, Texas www.kilgore.edu/

Freshmen Application Contact Ms. Jeanna Centers, Admissions Specialist, Kilgore College, 1100 Broadway, Kilgore, TX 75662. *Phone:* 903-983-8202. *Fax:* 903-983-8607. *E-mail:* register@kilgore.cc.tx.us.

KINGWOOD COLLEGE

Kingwood, Texas kcweb.nhmccd.edu/

- **State and locally supported** 2-year, founded 1984, part of North Harris Montgomery Community College District
- **Suburban** 264-acre campus with easy access to Houston
- **Coed**

Undergraduates 1,308 full-time, 5,534 part-time. Students come from 44 other countries, 0.6% are from out of state, 8% African American, 3% Asian American or Pacific Islander, 14% Hispanic American, 0.4% Native American, 2% international, 4% transferred in.

Faculty *Student/faculty ratio:* 16:1.

Academics *Calendar:* semesters. *Degree:* certificates and associate. *Special study options:* academic remediation for entering students, accelerated degree program, advanced placement credit, cooperative education, distance learning, double majors, English as a second language, external degree program, honors programs, independent study, internships, part-time degree program, services for LD students, summer session for credit.

Student Life *Campus security:* 24-hour emergency response devices and patrols, late-night transport/escort service.

Costs (2006–07) *Tuition:* area resident $984 full-time, $52 per credit part-time; state resident $1944 full-time, $92 per credit part-time; nonresident $2304 full-time, $220 per credit part-time.

Financial Aid *Financial aid deadline:* 5/15.

Applying *Options:* early admission. *Required:* high school transcript. *Required for some:* essay or personal statement.

Freshmen Application Contact Dr. Ike Williams, Director of Enrollment Management, Kingwood College, 20000 Kingwood Drive, Kingwood, TX 77339. *Phone:* 281-312-1562. *Fax:* 281-312-1477. *E-mail:* ronald.shade@nhmccd.edu.

LAMAR INSTITUTE OF TECHNOLOGY

Beaumont, Texas www.lit.edu/

- **State-supported** 2-year, founded 1995
- **Coed**, 2,711 undergraduate students

Majors Accounting technology and bookkeeping; administrative assistant and secretarial science; business administration, management and operations related; chemical technology; child care and support services management; child care provider; computer and information sciences related; computer technology/computer systems technology; dental hygiene; diagnostic medical sonography and ultrasound technology; diesel mechanics technology; drafting/design technology; emergency medical technology (EMT paramedic); fire protection and safety technology; health information/medical records technology; heating, air conditioning and refrigeration technology; industrial mechanics and maintenance technology; institutional food workers; instrumentation technology; machine tool technology; medical radiologic technology; occupational safety and health technology; public administration; real estate; respiratory care therapy; welding technology.

Academics *Calendar:* semesters. *Degree:* certificates and associate.

Costs (2006–07) *Tuition:* state resident $2720 full-time; nonresident $9344 full-time.

Financial Aid *Financial aid deadline:* 4/1.

Freshmen Application Contact Admissions Office, Lamar Institute of Technology, 855 East Lavaca, Beaumont, TX 77705. *Phone:* 409-880-8354. *Toll-free phone:* 800-950-6989.

LAMAR STATE COLLEGE—ORANGE

Orange, Texas www.lsco.edu/

- **State-supported** 2-year, founded 1969, part of The Texas State University System
- **Small-town** 21-acre campus
- **Endowment** $5524
- **Coed**

Undergraduates 920 full-time, 1,223 part-time. Students come from 1 other state, 10% are from out of state, 19% African American, 1% Asian American or Pacific Islander, 3% Hispanic American, 0.9% Native American, 6% transferred in.

Faculty *Student/faculty ratio:* 19:1.

Academics *Calendar:* semesters. *Degree:* certificates and associate. *Special study options:* academic remediation for entering students, distance learning, double majors, internships, part-time degree program, summer session for credit.

Student Life *Campus security:* 24-hour emergency response devices, late-night transport/escort service.

Costs (2006–07) *Tuition:* state resident $1872 full-time; nonresident $7800 full-time. *Required fees:* $1064 full-time.

Financial Aid Of all full-time matriculated undergraduates, 20 Federal Work-Study jobs (averaging $3000). 2 state and other part-time jobs (averaging $2000).

Applying *Options:* early admission, deferred entrance. *Required:* high school transcript.

Freshmen Application Contact Kerry Olson, Director of Admissions and Financial Aid, Lamar State College–Orange, 410 Front Street, Orange, TX 77632. *Phone:* 409-882-3362. *Fax:* 409-882-3374.

LAMAR STATE COLLEGE—PORT ARTHUR
Port Arthur, Texas www.lamarpa.edu/

- **State-supported** 2-year, founded 1909, part of The Texas State University System
- **Suburban** 34-acre campus with easy access to Houston
- **Coed**

Undergraduates 980 full-time, 1,550 part-time. 1% are from out of state, 28% African American, 6% Asian American or Pacific Islander, 12% Hispanic American, 0.4% Native American, 0.3% international, 9% transferred in.

Faculty *Student/faculty ratio:* 13:1.

Academics *Calendar:* semesters. *Degree:* certificates and associate. *Special study options:* academic remediation for entering students, accelerated degree program, adult/continuing education programs, advanced placement credit, cooperative education, distance learning, double majors, English as a second language, honors programs, independent study, internships, off-campus study, part-time degree program, services for LD students, summer session for credit. *ROTC:* Army (c).

Student Life *Campus security:* 24-hour emergency response devices, student patrols, late-night transport/escort service.

Costs (2006–07) *One-time required fee:* $10. *Tuition:* state resident $2340 full-time; nonresident $10,590 full-time. *Required fees:* $824 full-time.

Applying *Options:* early admission, deferred entrance. *Required:* high school transcript. *Required for some:* interview.

Freshmen Application Contact Ms. Connie Nicholas, Registrar, Lamar State College–Port Arthur, PO Box 310, Port Arthur, TX 77641-0310. *Phone:* 409-984-6165. *Toll-free phone:* 800-477-5872. *Fax:* 409-984-6025. *E-mail:* connie.nicholas@lamarpa.edu.

LAREDO COMMUNITY COLLEGE
Laredo, Texas www.laredo.edu/

- **State and locally supported** 2-year, founded 1946
- **Urban** 186-acre campus
- **Endowment** $2.0 million
- **Coed,** 8,152 undergraduate students, 37% full-time, 58% women, 42% men

Undergraduates 3,044 full-time, 5,108 part-time. Students come from 4 states and territories, 5 other countries, 8% are from out of state, 0.2% African American, 0.3% Asian American or Pacific Islander, 94% Hispanic American, 0.1% Native American, 3% international. *Retention:* 86% of 2003 full-time freshmen returned.

Freshmen *Admission:* 987 applied, 987 admitted, 987 enrolled.

Faculty *Total:* 343, 59% full-time, 13% with terminal degrees. *Student/faculty ratio:* 18:1.

Majors Administrative assistant and secretarial science; child development; clinical/medical laboratory technology; computer programming; computer programming related; computer software and media applications related; computer systems networking and telecommunications; construction engineering technology; criminal justice/police science; data entry/microcomputer applications; data entry/microcomputer applications related; data processing and data processing technology; electrical, electronic and communications engineering technology; emergency medical technology (EMT paramedic); fashion merchandising; fire science; hotel/motel administration; industrial radiologic technology; information science/studies; information technology; international business/trade/commerce; liberal arts and sciences/liberal studies; marketing/marketing management; medical/clinical assistant; nursing (registered nurse training); physical therapy; radiologic technology/science; real estate; social sciences.

Academics *Calendar:* semesters. *Degree:* certificates and associate. *Special study options:* academic remediation for entering students, adult/continuing education programs, advanced placement credit, distance learning, double majors, English as a second language, freshman honors college, honors programs, independent study, internships, part-time degree program, services for LD students, summer session for credit.

Library Yeary Library with 88,006 titles, 555 serial subscriptions, an OPAC.

Student Life *Housing Options:* coed. Campus housing is university owned. *Activities and Organizations:* drama/theater group, student-run newspaper, choral group. *Campus security:* 24-hour emergency response devices and patrols, student patrols. *Student services:* personal/psychological counseling, women's center.

Athletics Member NJCAA. *Intercollegiate sports:* baseball M(s), tennis M(s)/W(s), volleyball W(s). *Intramural sports:* cross-country running M/W, gymnastics M/W, swimming and diving M/W, tennis M/W, track and field M/W, volleyball M/W.

Standardized Tests *Recommended:* SAT (for admission), ACT (for admission).

Costs (2006–07) *Tuition:* area resident $840 full-time, $35 per credit hour part-time; state resident $1680 full-time, $70 per credit hour part-time; nonresident $2520 full-time, $105 per credit hour part-time. *Required fees:* $540 full-time, $24 per credit hour part-time, $28 per term part-time. *Room and board:* $4229; room only: $2600. *Payment plans:* installment, deferred payment. *Waivers:* senior citizens and employees or children of employees.

Financial Aid Of all full-time matriculated undergraduates, 282 Federal Work-Study jobs (averaging $1854). 127 state and other part-time jobs (averaging $1884).

Applying *Options:* early admission, deferred entrance. *Required:* high school transcript. *Application deadlines:* rolling (freshmen), rolling (transfers).

Freshmen Application Contact Ms. Josie Soliz, Admissions Records Supervisor, Laredo Community College, West End Washington Street, Laredo, TX 78040-4395. *Phone:* 956-721-5177. *Fax:* 956-721-5493.

LEE COLLEGE
Baytown, Texas www.lee.edu/

- **District-supported** 2-year, founded 1934
- **Suburban** 35-acre campus with easy access to Houston
- **Endowment** $5.2 million
- **Coed,** 5,347 undergraduate students, 34% full-time, 53% women, 47% men

Undergraduates 1,795 full-time, 3,552 part-time. Students come from 17 states and territories, 44 other countries, 5% are from out of state, 20% African American, 2% Asian American or Pacific Islander, 25% Hispanic American, 0.2% Native American, 2% international, 0.8% transferred in.

Freshmen *Admission:* 1,824 enrolled.

Faculty *Total:* 399, 46% full-time, 8% with terminal degrees. *Student/faculty ratio:* 14:1.

Majors Accounting technology and bookkeeping; administrative assistant and secretarial science; American studies; art; biology/biological sciences; business administration and management; chemistry; communication/speech communication and rhetoric; computer programming; computer systems analysis; criminal justice/police science; data processing and data processing technology; desktop publishing and digital imaging design; drafting and design technology; dramatic/theater arts; economics; education; electrical, electronic and communications engineering technology; emergency medical technology (EMT paramedic); English; environmental studies; executive assistant/executive secretary; fashion merchandising; French; geology/earth science; German; health information/medical records technology; heating, air conditioning, ventilation and refrigeration maintenance technology; history; humanities; information science/studies; instrumentation technology; international business/trade/commerce; journalism; kinesiology and exercise science; legal assistant/paralegal; liberal arts and sciences/liberal studies; logistics and materials management; machine tool technology; mathematics; music; natural sciences; nursing assistant/aide and patient care assistant; nursing (licensed practical/vocational nurse training); office management; operations management; photography; physical education teaching and coaching; physics; political science and government; pre-engineering; psychology; radio and television; sociology; Spanish; speech and rhetoric; substance abuse/addiction counseling; telecommunications; visual and performing arts; welding technology.

Academics *Calendar:* semesters. *Degree:* certificates and associate. *Special study options:* academic remediation for entering students, adult/continuing education programs, advanced placement credit, cooperative education, distance learning, English as a second language, honors programs, independent study, internships, part-time degree program, summer session for credit. *ROTC:* Army (c).

Library Erma Wood Carlson Learning Resource Center with 100,000 titles, 660 serial subscriptions, an OPAC, a Web page.

Lee College (continued)

Student Life *Housing:* college housing not available. *Activities and Organizations:* drama/theater group, student-run newspaper, choral group, Student Congress, Health Information Student Association, Lee College Awareness, Digital Information Society, ASHRAE - Air Conditioning Society of Heat and Refrigeration Engineers. *Campus security:* 24-hour patrols, late-night transport/escort service, emergency telephones. *Student services:* personal/psychological counseling.

Athletics Member NJCAA. *Intercollegiate sports:* basketball M(s), tennis W(s), volleyball W(s). *Intramural sports:* basketball M, bowling M/W, football M, racquetball M/W, table tennis M/W, volleyball W.

Costs (2006–07) *Tuition:* area resident $600 full-time; state resident $1200 full-time; nonresident $2040 full-time. *Required fees:* $237 full-time.

Financial Aid Of all full-time matriculated undergraduates, 30 Federal Work-Study jobs (averaging $3130).

Applying *Options:* early admission, deferred entrance. *Required for some:* high school transcript. *Application deadlines:* rolling (freshmen), rolling (transfers). *Notification:* continuous (freshmen), continuous (transfers).

Director of Admissions Ms. Becki Griffith, Registrar, Lee College, PO Box 818, Baytown, TX 77522-0818. *Phone:* 281-425-6399. *Toll-free phone:* 800-621-8724. *E-mail:* bgriffit@lee.edu.

LON MORRIS COLLEGE

Jacksonville, Texas   www.lonmorris.edu/

Freshmen Application Contact Ms. Pam Horton, Director of Enrollment Management, Lon Morris College, 800 College Avenue, Jacksonville, TX 75766-2923. *Phone:* 903-589-4063. *Toll-free phone:* 800-259-5753.

MCLENNAN COMMUNITY COLLEGE

Waco, Texas   www.mclennan.edu/

- **County-supported** 2-year, founded 1965
- **Urban** 200-acre campus
- **Coed,** 7,794 undergraduate students, 44% full-time, 67% women, 33% men

Undergraduates 3,467 full-time, 4,327 part-time. 2% are from out of state, 18% African American, 1% Asian American or Pacific Islander, 16% Hispanic American, 0.4% Native American, 0.4% international.

Freshmen *Admission:* 2,362 applied, 2,362 admitted, 1,247 enrolled.

Faculty *Total:* 389, 14% with terminal degrees.

Majors Accounting; administrative assistant and secretarial science; art teacher education; business administration and management; clinical/medical laboratory technology; computer engineering technology; criminal justice/law enforcement administration; criminal justice/police science; developmental and child psychology; finance; health information/medical records administration; industrial radiologic technology; information science/studies; kindergarten/preschool education; legal administrative assistant/secretary; legal assistant/paralegal; liberal arts and sciences/liberal studies; medical administrative assistant and medical secretary; mental health/rehabilitation; music; nursing (registered nurse training); physical education teaching and coaching; physical therapy; real estate; respiratory care therapy; sign language interpretation and translation.

Academics *Calendar:* semesters. *Degree:* certificates and associate. *Special study options:* academic remediation for entering students, adult/continuing education programs, advanced placement credit, cooperative education, distance learning, honors programs, internships, off-campus study, part-time degree program, services for LD students, study abroad, summer session for credit. *ROTC:* Air Force (c).

Library McLennan Community College Library with 93,000 titles, 400 serial subscriptions, an OPAC, a Web page.

Student Life *Housing:* college housing not available. *Activities and Organizations:* drama/theater group, student-run newspaper, choral group. *Campus security:* 24-hour emergency response devices and patrols. *Student services:* personal/psychological counseling.

Athletics Member NJCAA. *Intercollegiate sports:* baseball M(s), basketball M(s)/W(s), golf M(s)/W(s), softball W(s). *Intramural sports:* basketball M/W, football M, gymnastics M, volleyball M/W.

Standardized Tests *Required:* THEA (for admission).

Costs (2007–08) *Tuition:* area resident $1344 full-time, $56 per semester hour part-time; state resident $1632 full-time, $68 per semester hour part-time; nonresident $2784 full-time, $116 per semester hour part-time. *Required fees:* $216 full-time, $9 per semester hour part-time.

Financial Aid Of all full-time matriculated undergraduates, 265 Federal Work-Study jobs (averaging $850). 35 state and other part-time jobs (averaging $1000).

Applying *Options:* early admission. *Required:* high school transcript. *Application deadlines:* rolling (freshmen), rolling (transfers). *Notification:* continuous until 9/2 (freshmen), continuous until 9/2 (transfers).

Freshmen Application Contact Dr. Vivian G. Jefferson, Director, Admissions and Recruitment, McLennan Community College, 1400 College Drive, Waco, TX 76708-1499. *Phone:* 254-299-8689. *Fax:* 254-299-8694. *E-mail:* vjefferson@mclennan.edu.

MIDLAND COLLEGE

Midland, Texas   www.midland.edu/

- **State and locally supported** primarily 2-year, founded 1969
- **Suburban** 163-acre campus
- **Endowment** $3.3 million
- **Coed**

Undergraduates 2,027 full-time, 3,504 part-time. Students come from 22 states and territories, 31 other countries, 2% are from out of state, 5% African American, 1% Asian American or Pacific Islander, 29% Hispanic American, 0.5% Native American, 1% international, 5% transferred in, 5% live on campus.

Faculty *Student/faculty ratio:* 18:1.

Academics *Calendar:* semesters. *Degrees:* certificates, associate, and bachelor's. *Special study options:* academic remediation for entering students, adult/continuing education programs, advanced placement credit, distance learning, honors programs, services for LD students.

Student Life *Campus security:* 24-hour patrols.

Athletics Member NJCAA.

Costs (2006–07) *Tuition:* area resident $1204 full-time, $63 per credit hour part-time; state resident $1540 full-time, $105 per credit hour part-time; nonresident $2352 full-time. *Required fees:* $350 full-time. *Room and board:* $3600.

Financial Aid Of all full-time matriculated undergraduates, 75 Federal Work-Study jobs (averaging $2000). 5 state and other part-time jobs (averaging $2000).

Applying *Required:* high school transcript.

Freshmen Application Contact Mr. Trey Wetendorf, Admissions Director, Midland College, 3600 North Garfield, Midland, TX 79705-6399. *Phone:* 432-685-5502. *Toll-free phone:* 432-685-5502. *Fax:* 432-685-6401. *E-mail:* twetendorf@midland.edu.

MONTGOMERY COLLEGE

Conroe, Texas   www.woodstock.edu/

- **State and locally supported** 2-year, founded 1995, part of North Harris Montgomery Community College District
- **Suburban** 200-acre campus with easy access to Houston
- **Endowment** $500,000
- **Coed**

Undergraduates 2,970 full-time, 5,336 part-time. 0.5% are from out of state, 6% African American, 2% Asian American or Pacific Islander, 12% Hispanic American, 0.5% Native American, 1% international, 4% transferred in.

Faculty *Student/faculty ratio:* 20:1.

Academics *Calendar:* semesters. *Degree:* certificates and associate. *Special study options:* academic remediation for entering students, adult/continuing education programs, advanced placement credit, English as a second language, internships, part-time degree program, services for LD students, summer session for credit.

Student Life *Campus security:* 24-hour emergency response devices and patrols, late-night transport/escort service.

Costs (2006–07) *Tuition:* area resident $984 full-time, $32 per credit hour part-time; state resident $1944 full-time, $72 per credit hour part-time; nonresident $2304 full-time, $87 per credit hour part-time. *Required fees:* $20 full-time, $8 per credit hour part-time, $12 per term part-time.

Financial Aid Of all full-time matriculated undergraduates, 25 Federal Work-Study jobs (averaging $2500). 4 state and other part-time jobs.

Applying *Options:* early admission.

Freshmen Application Contact Ms. Cami Davey, Assistant Dean, Student Services, Montgomery College, 3200 College Park Drive, Conroe, TX 77384. *Phone:* 936-273-7236. *E-mail:* cami.davey@nhmccd.edu.

MOUNTAIN VIEW COLLEGE

Dallas, Texas   www.mvc.dcccd.edu/

- **State and locally supported** 2-year, founded 1970, part of Dallas County Community College District System
- **Urban** 200-acre campus
- **Coed**

Undergraduates 6,496 full-time. Students come from 9 states and territories, 36 other countries, 1% are from out of state, 29% African American, 3% Asian American or Pacific Islander, 44% Hispanic American, 0.6% Native American, 0.7% international.

Academics *Calendar:* semesters. *Degree:* certificates and associate. *Special study options:* academic remediation for entering students, adult/continuing education programs, advanced placement credit, cooperative education, distance learning, double majors, English as a second language, external degree program, freshman honors college, honors programs, independent study, internships, part-time degree program, services for LD students, summer session for credit. *ROTC:* Army (c).

Student Life *Campus security:* 24-hour patrols, late-night transport/escort service.

Athletics Member NJCAA.

Costs (2006–07) *Tuition:* area resident $1008 full-time; state resident $1848 full-time; nonresident $2968 full-time.

Financial Aid Of all full-time matriculated undergraduates, 145 Federal Work-Study jobs (averaging $2700).

Applying *Options:* electronic application, early admission, deferred entrance. *Required:* high school transcript.

Freshmen Application Contact Ms. Glenda Hall, Associate Dean of Student Support Services, Mountain View College, 4849 West Illinois Avenue, Dallas, TX 75211-6599. *Phone:* 214-860-8666. *Fax:* 214-860-8570. *E-mail:* ghall@dcccd.edu.

MTI COLLEGE OF BUSINESS & TECHNOLOGY
Houston, Texas
www.mti.edu/

Freshmen Application Contact Brenda Black, Director of eMarketing, MTI College of Business & Technology, 7277 Regency Square Boulevard, Houston, TX 77036-3163. *Phone:* 713-974-7181. *Toll-free phone:* 888-795-6888. *Fax:* 713-974-2090. *E-mail:* info@mti.edu.

NAVARRO COLLEGE
Corsicana, Texas
www.navarrocollege.edu/

- **State and locally supported** 2-year, founded 1946
- **Small-town** 275-acre campus with easy access to Dallas–Fort Worth
- **Coed,** 4,411 undergraduate students, 57% full-time, 58% women, 42% men

Undergraduates 2,516 full-time, 1,895 part-time. Students come from 22 states and territories, 30 other countries, 25% live on campus. *Retention:* 100% of 2003 full-time freshmen returned.

Freshmen *Admission:* 4,411 applied, 4,411 admitted, 1,885 enrolled.

Faculty *Total:* 380, 26% full-time, 6% with terminal degrees.

Majors Accounting; administrative assistant and secretarial science; agricultural mechanization; airline pilot and flight crew; art; avionics maintenance technology; biological and physical sciences; biology/biological sciences; broadcast journalism; business administration and management; chemistry; clinical/medical laboratory technology; commercial and advertising art; computer graphics; computer programming; computer science; consumer merchandising/retailing management; corrections; criminal justice/law enforcement administration; criminal justice/police science; dance; data processing and data processing technology; dental hygiene; developmental and child psychology; drafting and design technology; dramatic/theater arts; education; elementary education; engineering; English; fire science; industrial design; industrial technology; journalism; legal administrative assistant/secretary; legal assistant/paralegal; legal studies; marketing/marketing management; mathematics; music; nursing (licensed practical/vocational nurse training); nursing (registered nurse training); occupational therapy; pharmacy; physical education teaching and coaching; physical sciences; physics; pre-engineering; psychology; radio and television; real estate; social sciences; sociology; speech and rhetoric; veterinary sciences; voice and opera.

Academics *Calendar:* semesters. *Degree:* certificates, diplomas, and associate. *Special study options:* academic remediation for entering students, adult/continuing education programs, advanced placement credit, cooperative education, honors programs, part-time degree program, services for LD students, student-designed majors, summer session for credit.

Library Gaston T. Gooch Learning Resource Center with 40,000 titles, 250 serial subscriptions.

Student Life *Activities and Organizations:* drama/theater group, student-run television station, choral group, marching band, Student Government Association, Phi Theta Kappa, Ebony Club, Que Pasa. *Campus security:* 24-hour patrols. *Student services:* personal/psychological counseling.

Athletics Member NJCAA. *Intercollegiate sports:* baseball M(s), basketball M(s), football M(s), golf M(s), softball W, tennis M(s)/W(s), volleyball W(s). *Intramural sports:* basketball M/W, bowling M/W, football M, soccer M, softball M/W, volleyball M/W.

Costs (2006–07) *Tuition:* area resident $1048 full-time; state resident $1624 full-time; nonresident $2450 full-time. Full-time tuition and fees vary according to course load. Part-time tuition and fees vary according to course load. *Required fees:* $164 full-time. *Room and board:* $4063. Room and board charges vary according to board plan. *Payment plan:* installment. *Waivers:* employees or children of employees.

Financial Aid Of all full-time matriculated undergraduates, 75 Federal Work-Study jobs (averaging $1877).

Applying *Options:* early admission. *Required:* high school transcript. *Application deadlines:* 9/1 (freshmen), 9/1 (transfers). *Notification:* continuous until 9/1 (freshmen), continuous until 9/1 (transfers).

Freshmen Application Contact Judith Cutting, Registrar, Navarro College, 3200 West 7th Avenue, Corsicana, TX 75110-4899. *Toll-free phone:* 800-NAVARRO (in-state); 800-628-2776 (out-of-state). *Fax:* 903-875-7353.

NORTH CENTRAL TEXAS COLLEGE
Gainesville, Texas
www.nctc.edu/

- **County-supported** 2-year, founded 1924
- **Rural** 132-acre campus with easy access to Dallas–Fort Worth
- **Endowment** $2.4 million
- **Coed,** 6,183 undergraduate students

Undergraduates Students come from 14 states and territories, 21 other countries, 5% are from out of state, 6% African American, 2% Asian American or Pacific Islander, 7% Hispanic American, 0.8% Native American, 3% international, 2% live on campus. *Retention:* 68% of 2003 full-time freshmen returned.

Freshmen *Admission:* 1,964 applied, 1,964 admitted.

Faculty *Total:* 296, 29% full-time, 17% with terminal degrees.

Majors Administrative assistant and secretarial science; agricultural mechanization; animal/livestock husbandry and production; automobile/automotive mechanics technology; biological and physical sciences; business administration and management; business and personal/financial services marketing; computer engineering technology; computer graphics; computer/information technology services administration related; computer management; computer programming; computer programming related; computer programming (specific applications); computer programming (vendor/product certification); computer science; computer/technical support; criminal justice/law enforcement administration; criminal justice/police science; data processing and data processing technology; drafting and design technology; electrical, electronic and communications engineering technology; emergency medical technology (EMT paramedic); engineering technology; equestrian studies; farm and ranch management; health information/medical records administration; industrial mechanics and maintenance technology; information science/studies; legal administrative assistant/secretary; legal assistant/paralegal; liberal arts and sciences/liberal studies; machine shop technology; machine tool technology; merchandising; nursing (registered nurse training); occupational therapy; pre-engineering; real estate; retailing; sales, distribution and marketing; welding technology; word processing.

Academics *Calendar:* semesters. *Degree:* certificates, diplomas, and associate. *Special study options:* academic remediation for entering students, adult/continuing education programs, advanced placement credit, cooperative education, distance learning, internships, part-time degree program, services for LD students, summer session for credit.

Library North Central Texas College Library plus 1 other with 44,861 titles, 273 serial subscriptions, an OPAC.

Student Life *Housing Options:* coed. *Activities and Organizations:* drama/theater group, choral group, Baptist Student Ministry, Phi Theta Kappa, Nursing Student Association, Collegiate FFA. *Campus security:* late-night transport/escort service, late night security. *Student services:* personal/psychological counseling.

Athletics Member NJCAA. *Intercollegiate sports:* baseball M(s), equestrian sports M(s)/W(s), tennis W(s), volleyball W(s). *Intramural sports:* basketball M/W, bowling M/W, football M/W, golf M/W, tennis M/W, volleyball M/W.

Standardized Tests *Required:* THEA (for placement). *Recommended:* SAT or ACT (for placement).

Costs (2006–07) *Tuition:* area resident $1020 full-time, $34 per hour part-time; state resident $1890 full-time, $63 per hour part-time; nonresident $2940 full-time, $98 per hour part-time. *Required fees:* $270 full-time, $9 per hour part-time. *Room and board:* $3240. Room and board charges vary according to housing facility. *Payment plans:* installment, deferred payment. *Waivers:* employees or children of employees.

Financial Aid Of all full-time matriculated undergraduates, 108 Federal Work-Study jobs (averaging $1253). 29 state and other part-time jobs (averaging $392).

North Central Texas College (continued)

Applying *Options:* early admission. *Required:* high school transcript. *Application deadlines:* rolling (freshmen), rolling (transfers).

Freshmen Application Contact Michelle Winters, Director of Admissions/Registrar, North Central Texas College, 1525 West California Street, Gainesville, TX 76240-4699. *Phone:* 940-668-7731. *Fax:* 940-668-7075. *E-mail:* mwinters@actc.edu.

NORTHEAST TEXAS COMMUNITY COLLEGE

Mount Pleasant, Texas **www.ntcc.edu/**

Freshmen Application Contact Ms. Sherry Keys, Director of Admissions, Northeast Texas Community College, PO Box 1307, 1735 Farm to Market Road, Mount Pleasant, TX 75456-1307. *Phone:* 903-572-1911 Ext. 263.

NORTH HARRIS COLLEGE

Houston, Texas **www.nhmccd.edu/**

Freshmen Application Contact Mr. Michael Code, Assistant Dean, North Harris College, 2700 W.W. Thorne Drive, Houston, TX 77073. *Phone:* 281-618-5794.

NORTH LAKE COLLEGE

Irving, Texas **www.northlakecollege.edu/**

- **County-supported** 2-year, founded 1977, part of Dallas County Community College District System
- **Suburban** 250-acre campus with easy access to Dallas–Fort Worth
- **Coed,** 9,397 undergraduate students, 31% full-time, 53% women, 47% men

Undergraduates 2,951 full-time, 6,446 part-time. Students come from 16 states and territories, 21 other countries, 8% are from out of state, 15% African American, 10% Asian American or Pacific Islander, 22% Hispanic American, 0.4% Native American, 10% international. *Retention:* 52% of 2003 full-time freshmen returned.

Freshmen *Admission:* 1,048 enrolled.

Faculty *Total:* 537, 18% full-time, 7% with terminal degrees. *Student/faculty ratio:* 19:1.

Majors Accounting; administrative assistant and secretarial science; business administration and management; carpentry; communications technology; computer programming; construction engineering technology; data processing and data processing technology; electrical, electronic and communications engineering technology; heating, air conditioning, ventilation and refrigeration maintenance technology; information science/studies; kinesiology and exercise science; legal administrative assistant/secretary; liberal arts and sciences/liberal studies; real estate.

Academics *Calendar:* semesters. *Degree:* certificates, diplomas, and associate. *Special study options:* academic remediation for entering students, accelerated degree program, adult/continuing education programs, advanced placement credit, cooperative education, distance learning, double majors, English as a second language, external degree program, independent study, internships, off-campus study, part-time degree program, services for LD students, student-designed majors, summer session for credit.

Library North Lake College Library with 34,000 titles, 400 serial subscriptions, an OPAC, a Web page.

Student Life *Housing:* college housing not available. *Activities and Organizations:* drama/theater group, student-run newspaper, choral group. *Campus security:* 24-hour emergency response devices, late-night transport/escort service. *Student services:* health clinic, personal/psychological counseling, women's center.

Athletics Member NJCAA. *Intercollegiate sports:* baseball M, basketball M, softball W, volleyball W.

Costs (2006–07) *Tuition:* area resident $1170 full-time, $39 per credit hour part-time; state resident $2160 full-time, $72 per credit hour part-time; nonresident $3430 full-time, $115 per credit hour part-time.

Applying *Options:* early admission. *Recommended:* high school transcript. *Application deadlines:* rolling (freshmen), rolling (transfers). *Notification:* continuous (freshmen), continuous (transfers).

Freshmen Application Contact SPAR-A223, North Lake College, 5001 North MacArthur Boulevard, Irving, TX 75038-3899. *Phone:* 972-273-3020.

NORTHWEST VISTA COLLEGE

San Antonio, Texas **www.accd.edu/nvc/**

- **State and locally supported** 2-year, founded 1995, part of Alamo Community College District System
- **Urban** 137-acre campus
- **Coed,** 8,519 undergraduate students

Undergraduates 5% African American, 3% Asian American or Pacific Islander, 45% Hispanic American, 0.4% Native American, 0.2% international.

Faculty *Total:* 497, 17% full-time, 87% with terminal degrees. *Student/faculty ratio:* 12:1.

Majors Biology/biotechnology laboratory technician; business administration, management and operations related; community health and preventive medicine; computer and information sciences; computer and information systems security; computer/information technology services administration related; computer programming; computer science; computer/technical support; criminal justice/safety; international/global studies; liberal arts and sciences/liberal studies; pre-engineering; recording arts technology; water quality and wastewater treatment management and recycling technology; web page, digital/multimedia and information resources design.

Academics *Calendar:* semesters. *Degree:* associate. *Special study options:* academic remediation for entering students, advanced placement credit, cooperative education, distance learning, double majors, English as a second language, independent study, internships, off-campus study, part-time degree program, services for LD students, study abroad, summer session for credit.

Library Manzanillo Hall with a Web page.

Student Life *Housing:* college housing not available. *Activities and Organizations:* drama/theater group, student-run newspaper. *Campus security:* 24-hour emergency response devices, student patrols, late-night transport/escort service. *Student services:* health clinic, personal/psychological counseling.

Costs (2007–08) *Tuition:* area resident $1056 full-time, $44 per credit part-time; state resident $2112 full-time, $88 per credit part-time; nonresident $4224 full-time, $176 per credit part-time. *Required fees:* $318 full-time, $318 per term part-time.

Applying *Required:* high school transcript.

Freshmen Application Contact Dr. Elaine Lang, Interim Director of Enrollment Management, Northwest Vista College, 3535 North Ellison Drive, San Antonio, TX 78251. *Phone:* 210-348-2016. *E-mail:* elang@accd.edu.

ODESSA COLLEGE

Odessa, Texas **www.odessa.edu/**

- **State and locally supported** 2-year, founded 1946
- **Urban** 87-acre campus
- **Endowment** $2.5 million
- **Coed,** 4,647 undergraduate students, 34% full-time, 64% women, 36% men

Undergraduates 1,578 full-time, 3,069 part-time. Students come from 32 states and territories, 3% are from out of state, 4% African American, 0.9% Asian American or Pacific Islander, 47% Hispanic American, 0.7% Native American, 0.2% international, 4% live on campus.

Freshmen *Admission:* 743 applied, 743 admitted, 743 enrolled.

Faculty *Total:* 265, 45% full-time, 9% with terminal degrees. *Student/faculty ratio:* 12:1.

Majors Accounting; administrative assistant and secretarial science; agriculture; applied art; art; athletic training; automobile/automotive mechanics technology; biology/biological sciences; business administration and management; chemistry; child development; clinical/medical laboratory technology; computer and information sciences; computer science; computer systems networking and telecommunications; construction engineering technology; cosmetology; criminal justice/law enforcement administration; criminal justice/police science; culinary arts; data processing and data processing technology; drafting and design technology; education; electrical, electronic and communications engineering technology; emergency medical technology (EMT paramedic); English; fashion merchandising; fire science; geology/earth science; hazardous materials management and waste technology; heating, air conditioning, ventilation and refrigeration maintenance technology; history; human services; industrial radiologic technology; information science/studies; kindergarten/preschool education; legal administrative assistant/secretary; liberal arts and sciences/liberal studies; machine tool technology; mathematics; modern languages; music; nursing (registered nurse training); petroleum technology; photography; physical education teaching and coaching; physical therapy; physics; political science and government; pre-engineering; psychology; radio and television; respiratory care

therapy; social sciences; sociology; speech and rhetoric; substance abuse/addiction counseling; surgical technology; teacher assistant/aide; welding technology.

Academics *Calendar:* semesters. *Degree:* certificates and associate. *Special study options:* academic remediation for entering students, adult/continuing education programs, advanced placement credit, cooperative education, distance learning, independent study, internships, part-time degree program, services for LD students, study abroad.

Library Murray H. Fly Learning Resource Center with 79,882 titles, 496 serial subscriptions.

Student Life *Housing Options:* coed. Campus housing is provided by a third party. *Activities and Organizations:* choral group, Baptist Student Union, Student Government Association, Rodeo Club, Physical Therapy Assistant Club, American Chemical Society. *Campus security:* 24-hour emergency response devices and patrols, late-night transport/escort service, controlled dormitory access. *Student services:* personal/psychological counseling.

Athletics Member NJCAA. *Intercollegiate sports:* baseball M(s), basketball M(s)/W(s), golf M(s), softball W(s). *Intramural sports:* basketball M/W, bowling M/W, football M, racquetball M/W, softball M/W, table tennis M/W, volleyball M/W, weight lifting M/W.

Costs (2007–08) *Tuition:* area resident $1110 full-time, $126 per semester hour part-time; state resident $1410 full-time, $171 per semester hour part-time; nonresident $1860 full-time, $366 per semester hour part-time. *Required fees:* $330 full-time, $33 per semester hour part-time. *Room and board:* $4948; room only: $3500.

Financial Aid Of all full-time matriculated undergraduates, 114 Federal Work-Study jobs (averaging $1316). 15 state and other part-time jobs (averaging $965).

Applying *Options:* electronic application, early admission, deferred entrance. *Application deadlines:* rolling (freshmen), rolling (transfers). *Notification:* continuous (freshmen), continuous (transfers).

Freshmen Application Contact Ms. Norma Garcia, Director of Admissions, Odessa College, 201 West University Avenue, Odessa, TX 79764-7127. *Phone:* 432-335-6432. *Fax:* 432-335-6824. *E-mail:* ngarcia@odessa.edu.

PALO ALTO COLLEGE
San Antonio, Texas
www.accd.edu/pac/htm/

- **State and locally supported** 2-year, founded 1987, part of Alamo Community College District System
- **Urban** campus
- **Coed,** 8,038 undergraduate students

Undergraduates Students come from 50 states and territories, 1% are from out of state, 2% African American, 0.9% Asian American or Pacific Islander, 64% Hispanic American, 0.3% Native American, 0.4% international.

Freshmen *Admission:* 1,163 applied, 1,163 admitted.

Faculty *Total:* 402, 36% full-time. *Student/faculty ratio:* 18:1.

Majors Agriculture; architectural engineering technology; art; aviation/airway management; avionics maintenance technology; biology/biological sciences; business administration and management; chemistry; computer and information sciences related; computer engineering technology; computer management; computer science; economics; education; engineering; English; finance; geology/earth science; health science; history; horticultural science; information science/studies; information technology; journalism; legal studies; liberal arts and sciences/liberal studies; library science; mathematics; modern languages; music; philosophy; physical education teaching and coaching; physics; psychology; sociology; speech and rhetoric; trade and industrial teacher education; veterinary sciences.

Academics *Calendar:* semesters. *Degree:* certificates and associate. *Special study options:* academic remediation for entering students, adult/continuing education programs, cooperative education, English as a second language, part-time degree program, summer session for credit.

Library Ozuna Learning and Resource Center.

Student Life *Housing:* college housing not available. *Activities and Organizations:* drama/theater group, student-run newspaper, Catholic Campus Ministries, Veterinary Technician Association, Movimiento Estudiantil Chicano De Aztlan, Phi Theta Kappa. *Campus security:* 24-hour emergency response devices and patrols. *Student services:* health clinic, personal/psychological counseling.

Athletics Member NJCAA. *Intercollegiate sports:* cross-country running M/W, swimming and diving M/W, track and field M/W. *Intramural sports:* fencing M(c)/W(c).

Costs (2007–08) *Tuition:* area resident $1652 full-time; state resident $2972 full-time; nonresident $5736 full-time.

Financial Aid Of all full-time matriculated undergraduates, 272 Federal Work-Study jobs (averaging $2000).

Applying *Options:* early admission. *Required:* high school transcript. *Application deadline:* rolling (freshmen).

Freshmen Application Contact Ms. Rachel Montejano, Director of Enrollment Management, Palo Alto College, 1400 West Villaret Boulevard, San Antonio, TX 78224. *Phone:* 210-921-5279. *Fax:* 210-921-5310. *E-mail:* pacar@accd.edu.

PANOLA COLLEGE
Carthage, Texas
www.panola.edu/

- **State and locally supported** 2-year, founded 1947
- **Small-town** 35-acre campus
- **Endowment** $1.5 million
- **Coed,** 1,871 undergraduate students, 46% full-time, 67% women, 33% men

Undergraduates 861 full-time, 1,010 part-time. Students come from 22 states and territories, 7 other countries, 10% are from out of state, 17% African American, 0.8% Asian American or Pacific Islander, 4% Hispanic American, 0.5% Native American, 0.7% international, 8% transferred in, 11% live on campus. *Retention:* 50% of 2003 full-time freshmen returned.

Freshmen *Admission:* 354 applied, 354 admitted, 354 enrolled.

Faculty *Total:* 63, 100% full-time. *Student/faculty ratio:* 23:1.

Majors Business/commerce; health information/medical records technology; industrial technology; information science/studies; nursing (registered nurse training).

Academics *Calendar:* semesters. *Degree:* certificates and associate. *Special study options:* academic remediation for entering students, advanced placement credit, cooperative education, distance learning, English as a second language, part-time degree program, services for LD students, summer session for credit.

Library M. P. Baker Library with 104,086 titles, 347 serial subscriptions, 300 audiovisual materials, an OPAC, a Web page.

Student Life *Housing:* on-campus residence required through sophomore year. *Options:* coed, men-only, women-only. Campus housing is university owned. *Activities and Organizations:* drama/theater group, student-run newspaper, choral group, marching band, Student Senate, Excel Club, Baptist Student Union, Panola Pipers, Phi Theta Kappa. *Campus security:* controlled dormitory access.

Athletics Member NJCAA. *Intercollegiate sports:* baseball M(s), basketball M(s)/W(s), volleyball W(s). *Intramural sports:* basketball M/W, football M/W, racquetball M/W, table tennis M/W, volleyball M/W, weight lifting M/W.

Costs (2006–07) *Tuition:* area resident $1176 full-time, $49 per semester hour part-time; state resident $1776 full-time, $74 per semester hour part-time; nonresident $2256 full-time, $94 per semester hour part-time. *Room and board:* $3300.

Financial Aid Of all full-time matriculated undergraduates, 50 Federal Work-Study jobs (averaging $2472).

Applying *Options:* electronic application, early admission. *Required for some:* high school transcript. *Recommended:* high school transcript. *Application deadlines:* rolling (freshmen), rolling (transfers). *Notification:* continuous (freshmen), continuous (transfers).

Freshmen Application Contact Ms. Barbara Simpson, Registrar/Director of Admissions, Panola College, 1109 West Panola Street, Carthage, TX 75633-2397. *Phone:* 903-693-2009. *Fax:* 903-693-2031. *E-mail:* bsimpson@panola.edu.

PARIS JUNIOR COLLEGE
Paris, Texas
www.parisjc.edu/

- **State and locally supported** 2-year, founded 1924
- **Rural** 54-acre campus
- **Endowment** $7.4 million
- **Coed**

Undergraduates 1,457 full-time, 2,661 part-time. Students come from 16 states and territories, 11% African American, 1% Asian American or Pacific Islander, 6% Hispanic American, 2% Native American, 0.2% international.

Faculty *Student/faculty ratio:* 24:1.

Academics *Calendar:* semesters. *Degree:* certificates, diplomas, and associate. *Special study options:* academic remediation for entering students, adult/continuing education programs, English as a second language, external degree program, part-time degree program, summer session for credit.

Student Life *Campus security:* 24-hour emergency response devices and patrols, late-night transport/escort service.

Athletics Member NJCAA.

Costs (2006–07) *Tuition:* area resident $840 full-time, $35 per hour part-time; state resident $1560 full-time, $65 per hour part-time; nonresident $2520 full-time, $105 per hour part-time. *Required fees:* $228 full-time. *Room and board:* $1882; room only: $690.

Paris Junior College (continued)

Applying *Options:* early admission. *Required:* high school transcript.
Director of Admissions Ms. Sheila Reece, Director of Admissions, Paris Junior College, 2400 Clarksville Street, Paris, TX 75460-6298. *Phone:* 903-782-0425. *Toll-free phone:* 800-232-5804. *E-mail:* sreece@parisjc.edu.

RANGER COLLEGE

Ranger, Texas   www.ranger.cc.tx.us/

- **State-related** 2-year, founded 1926
- **Rural** 100-acre campus with easy access to Dallas–Fort Worth
- **Coed,** 843 undergraduate students

Undergraduates Students come from 7 states and territories, 4 other countries, 45% live on campus.
Faculty *Total:* 51, 55% full-time.
Majors Administrative assistant and secretarial science; automobile/automotive mechanics technology; computer engineering technology; liberal arts and sciences/liberal studies; science teacher education; welding technology.
Academics *Calendar:* semesters. *Degree:* associate. *Special study options:* academic remediation for entering students, adult/continuing education programs, advanced placement credit, freshman honors college, honors programs, part-time degree program, student-designed majors, summer session for credit.
Library Golemon Library with 24,211 titles, 133 serial subscriptions.
Student Life *Activities and Organizations:* choral group, marching band. *Campus security:* controlled dormitory access. *Student services:* health clinic, personal/psychological counseling.
Athletics Member NJCAA. *Intercollegiate sports:* baseball M(s), basketball M(s)/W(s), cross-country running M(s)/W(s), football M(s), golf M(s), softball W(s), track and field M(s)/W(s). *Intramural sports:* basketball M/W, football M/W, golf M/W, track and field M/W, volleyball M/W.
Costs (2006–07) *Tuition:* area resident $1622 full-time; state resident $1862 full-time; nonresident $1862 full-time.
Financial Aid Of all full-time matriculated undergraduates, 140 Federal Work-Study jobs (averaging $800). *Financial aid deadline:* 7/24.
Applying *Options:* early admission. *Application deadlines:* rolling (freshmen), rolling (transfers). *Notification:* continuous (freshmen), continuous (transfers).
Freshmen Application Contact Dr. Jim Davis, Dean of Students, Ranger College, 1100 College Circle, Ranger, TX 76470. *Phone:* 254-647-3234 Ext. 110.

REMINGTON COLLEGE–DALLAS CAMPUS

Garland, Texas   www.remingtoncollege.edu/

- **Proprietary** 2-year, founded 1987
- 861 undergraduate students
- 100% of applicants were admitted

Freshmen *Admission:* 540 applied, 540 admitted.
Majors Business administration and management; computer and information sciences related; computer systems networking and telecommunications; criminal justice/law enforcement administration; culinary arts; electrical and electronic engineering technologies related.
Academics *Degree:* associate.
Costs (2006–07) *Tuition:* $12,875 full-time.
Applying *Application fee:* $50.
Director of Admissions Mr. Skip Walls, Campus President, Remington College–Dallas Campus, 1800 Eastgate Drive, Garland, TX 75041-5513. *Phone:* 972-686-7878. *Fax:* 972-686-5116. *E-mail:* skip.walls@remingtoncollege.edu.

REMINGTON COLLEGE–FORT WORTH CAMPUS

Fort Worth, Texas   www.remingtoncollege.edu/

- **Proprietary** 2-year
- **Coed,** 922 undergraduate students
- 100% of applicants were admitted

Freshmen *Admission:* 316 applied, 316 admitted.

Majors Business administration and management; business/commerce; computer and information sciences related; computer systems networking and telecommunications; corrections and criminal justice related; criminal justice/law enforcement administration; electrical, electronic and communications engineering technology; graphic design.
Academics *Degree:* associate.
Costs (2006–07) *Tuition:* $12,520 per degree program part-time.
Applying *Application fee:* $50.
Director of Admissions Ms. Lynn Wey, Campus President, Remington College–Fort Worth Campus, 300 East Loop 820, Fort Worth, TX 76112. *Phone:* 817-451-0017. *Toll-free phone:* 800-336-6668. *Fax:* 817-496-1257. *E-mail:* lynn.wey@remingtoncollege.edu.

REMINGTON COLLEGE–HOUSTON CAMPUS

Houston, Texas   www.remingtoncollege.edu/houston/

Director of Admissions Mr. Lance Stribling, Director of Recruitment, Remington College–Houston Campus, 3110 Hayes Road, Suite 380, Houston, TX 77082. *Phone:* 281-89-1240.

RICHLAND COLLEGE

Dallas, Texas   www.rlc.dcccd.edu/

- **State and locally supported** 2-year, founded 1972, part of Dallas County Community College District System
- **Suburban** 250-acre campus
- **Coed,** 14,128 undergraduate students

Undergraduates Students come from 24 states and territories, 21 other countries.
Faculty *Total:* 665, 25% full-time.
Majors Accounting; administrative assistant and secretarial science; artificial intelligence and robotics; business administration and management; computer programming; data processing and data processing technology; electrical, electronic and communications engineering technology; engineering; horticultural science; industrial technology; international business/trade/commerce; liberal arts and sciences/liberal studies; mechanical design technology; mechanical engineering/mechanical technology; ornamental horticulture; real estate.
Academics *Calendar:* semesters. *Degree:* associate. *Special study options:* academic remediation for entering students, adult/continuing education programs, advanced placement credit, cooperative education, English as a second language, freshman honors college, honors programs, part-time degree program, services for LD students, study abroad, summer session for credit.
Library Richland College Library with 63,000 titles, 350 serial subscriptions.
Student Life *Housing:* college housing not available. *Activities and Organizations:* drama/theater group, student-run newspaper, choral group. *Campus security:* 24-hour emergency response devices and patrols, late-night transport/escort service, emergency call boxes. *Student services:* health clinic, personal/psychological counseling, women's center.
Athletics Member NJCAA. *Intercollegiate sports:* baseball M, basketball M, soccer M/W, volleyball W. *Intramural sports:* badminton M/W, basketball M/W, bowling M/W, cross-country running M/W, football M/W, golf M/W, soccer M/W, softball M/W, tennis M/W, track and field M/W, volleyball M/W, weight lifting M/W.
Standardized Tests *Recommended:* SAT or ACT (for placement).
Costs (2006–07) *Tuition:* area resident $1080 full-time; state resident $1980 full-time; nonresident $3180 full-time.
Financial Aid Of all full-time matriculated undergraduates, 123 Federal Work-Study jobs (averaging $2000).
Applying *Options:* early admission. *Required for some:* high school transcript. *Application deadlines:* rolling (freshmen), rolling (transfers). *Notification:* continuous (freshmen), continuous (transfers).
Freshmen Application Contact Ms. Carol McKinney, Department Assistant, Richland College, 12800 Abrams Road, Dallas, TX 75243-2199. *Phone:* 972-238-6100.

ST. PHILIP'S COLLEGE

San Antonio, Texas   www.accd.edu/spc/

- **District-supported** 2-year, founded 1898, part of Alamo Community College District System
- **Urban** 16-acre campus
- **Coed,** 9,264 undergraduate students, 42% full-time, 58% women, 42% men

Undergraduates 3,930 full-time, 5,334 part-time. Students come from 48 states and territories, 9 other countries, 1% are from out of state, 16% African American, 2% Asian American or Pacific Islander, 46% Hispanic American, 0.4% Native American, 0.2% international, 10% transferred in.

Freshmen *Admission:* 1,860 enrolled.

Faculty *Total:* 581, 38% full-time, 7% with terminal degrees. *Student/faculty ratio:* 17:1.

Majors Accounting; administrative assistant and secretarial science; aircraft powerplant technology; airframe mechanics and aircraft maintenance technology; art; autobody/collision and repair technology; automobile/automotive mechanics technology; biology/biological sciences; biomedical technology; business administration and management; CAD/CADD drafting/design technology; chemistry; clinical/medical laboratory technology; communications technology; computer and information systems security; computer maintenance technology; computer systems networking and telecommunications; construction engineering technology; construction management; criminal justice/law enforcement administration; culinary arts; data entry/microcomputer applications; diesel mechanics technology; dramatic/theater arts; dramatic/theater arts and stagecraft related; early childhood education; e-commerce; economics; education; electrical/electronics equipment installation and repair; electromechanical technology; English; environmental science; geology/earth science; health information/medical records technology; heating, air conditioning, ventilation and refrigeration maintenance technology; history; home furnishings and equipment installation; hotel/motel administration; interior architecture; interior design; kinesiology and exercise science; leatherworking/upholstery; legal administrative assistant/secretary; liberal arts and sciences/liberal studies; mathematics; medical administrative assistant and medical secretary; medical radiologic technology; music; nursing (licensed practical/vocational nurse training); occupational therapist assistant; philosophy; physical therapist assistant; political science and government; pre-dentistry studies; pre-engineering; pre-law studies; pre-medical studies; pre-nursing studies; pre-pharmacy studies; psychology; respiratory care therapy; restaurant/food services management; social work; sociology; Spanish; speech and rhetoric; system, networking, and LAN/WAN management; teacher assistant/aide; tourism and travel services management; urban studies/affairs; web/multimedia management and webmaster; welding technology.

Academics *Calendar:* semesters. *Degree:* certificates, diplomas, and associate. *Special study options:* academic remediation for entering students, adult/continuing education programs, advanced placement credit, cooperative education, distance learning, double majors, English as a second language, honors programs, independent study, internships, off-campus study, part-time degree program, services for LD students, study abroad, summer session for credit.

Library St. Philip's College Learning Resource Center plus 1 other with 121,173 titles, 623 serial subscriptions, 11,577 audiovisual materials, an OPAC, a Web page.

Student Life *Housing:* college housing not available. *Activities and Organizations:* drama/theater group, student-run newspaper, choral group, student government, Delta Epsilon Chi, Radiography Club, Respiratory Therapy Club, Diagnostic Imaging Club. *Campus security:* 24-hour emergency response devices and patrols, late-night transport/escort service. *Student services:* health clinic, women's center.

Athletics *Intramural sports:* basketball M/W, cheerleading M/W, table tennis M/W, tennis M/W, volleyball M/W, weight lifting M/W.

Costs (2007–08) *Tuition:* area resident $1320 full-time, $44 per hour part-time; state resident $2640 full-time, $88 per hour part-time; nonresident $5280 full-time, $176 per hour part-time. *Required fees:* $332 full-time.

Applying *Options:* electronic application, early admission. *Required:* high school transcript. *Application deadlines:* rolling (freshmen), rolling (transfers). *Notification:* continuous (freshmen), continuous (transfers).

Freshmen Application Contact Ms. Ana Lisa Garza, Recruiter, St. Philip's College, 1801 Martin Luther King Drive, San Antonio, TX 78203-2098. *Phone:* 210-531-4861. *Fax:* 210-531-4836. *E-mail:* angarza@accd.edu.

SAN ANTONIO COLLEGE

San Antonio, Texas www.accd.edu/

- **State and locally supported** 2-year, founded 1925, part of Alamo Community College District System
- **Urban** 45-acre campus
- **Coed,** 21,800 undergraduate students, 38% full-time, 60% women, 40% men

Undergraduates 8,375 full-time, 13,425 part-time. Students come from 54 states and territories, 112 other countries, 3% are from out of state, 5% African American, 3% Asian American or Pacific Islander, 47% Hispanic American, 0.4% Native American, 2% international, 8% transferred in.

Freshmen *Admission:* 4,053 enrolled.

Faculty *Total:* 1,000, 41% full-time. *Student/faculty ratio:* 22:1.

Majors Biological and physical sciences; business administration and management; business machine repair; child care and support services management; child care provision; child development; civil engineering technology; commercial and advertising art; computer engineering technology; computer graphics; computer/information technology services administration related; computer programming; computer programming related; computer programming (specific applications); computer programming (vendor/product certification); corrections; court reporting; criminal justice/law enforcement administration; criminal justice/police science; data entry/microcomputer applications; data processing and data processing technology; dental hygiene; developmental and child psychology; drafting and design technology; electrical, electronic and communications engineering technology; engineering technology; fire science; funeral service and mortuary science; industrial technology; legal administrative assistant/secretary; liberal arts and sciences/liberal studies; mechanical engineering/mechanical technology; medical/clinical assistant; metal and jewelry arts; nursing (registered nurse training); postal management; psychology; public administration; radio and television; real estate; speech/theater education; system administration; web page, digital/multimedia and information resources design; word processing.

Academics *Calendar:* semesters. *Degree:* certificates and associate. *Special study options:* academic remediation for entering students, adult/continuing education programs, advanced placement credit, cooperative education, distance learning, English as a second language, honors programs, independent study, internships, part-time degree program, services for LD students, summer session for credit. *ROTC:* Army (b), Air Force (c).

Library San Antonio College Library and Media Services with 233,714 titles, 1,498 serial subscriptions, an OPAC, a Web page.

Student Life *Housing:* college housing not available. *Activities and Organizations:* drama/theater group, student-run newspaper, radio station, choral group. *Campus security:* 24-hour emergency response devices and patrols, late-night transport/escort service. *Student services:* health clinic, personal/psychological counseling, women's center.

Athletics *Intramural sports:* basketball M(c)/W(c), football M/W, golf W(c), soccer W(c), volleyball W(c).

Standardized Tests *Required:* ACT ASSET, THEA, ACCUPLACER (for admission).

Costs (2007–08) *Tuition:* area resident $1056 full-time; state resident $2112 full-time; nonresident $4348 full-time. *Required fees:* $342 full-time.

Financial Aid Of all full-time matriculated undergraduates, 500 Federal Work-Study jobs (averaging $3000).

Applying *Options:* early admission. *Required for some:* high school transcript. *Recommended:* high school transcript. *Application deadlines:* rolling (freshmen), rolling (transfers). *Notification:* continuous (transfers).

Director of Admissions Mr. J. Martin Ortega, Director of Admissions and Records, San Antonio College, 1300 San Pedro Avenue, San Antonio, TX 78212-4299. *Phone:* 210-733-2582. *Toll-free phone:* 800-944-7575.

SAN JACINTO COLLEGE DISTRICT

Pasadena, Texas www.sanjac.edu

- **State and locally supported** 2-year, founded 1961
- **Suburban** campus
- **Endowment** $1.2 million
- **Coed,** 23,753 undergraduate students, 38% full-time, 58% women, 42% men

Undergraduates 8,931 full-time, 14,822 part-time. Students come from 17 states and territories, 12 other countries, 10% African American, 5% Asian American or Pacific Islander, 34% Hispanic American, 0.4% Native American, 4% international, 0.7% transferred in.

Freshmen *Admission:* 4,669 enrolled. *Average high school GPA:* 2.85.

Faculty *Total:* 1,127, 38% full-time.

Academics *Calendar:* semesters. *Special study options:* academic remediation for entering students, accelerated degree program, adult/continuing education programs, advanced placement credit, cooperative education, distance learning, double majors, English as a second language, honors programs, part-time degree program, services for LD students, student-designed majors, study abroad.

Library Lee Davis Library (Central) plus 2 others with an OPAC, a Web page.

Student Life *Housing:* college housing not available. *Campus security:* 24-hour emergency response devices and patrols, late-night transport/escort service.

Costs (2007–08) *Tuition:* area resident $960 full-time, $33 per credit hour part-time; state resident $1760 full-time, $58 per credit hour part-time; nonresident $2400 full-time, $108 per credit hour part-time. *Required fees:* $130 per term part-time.

Applying *Required:* high school transcript.

Freshmen Application Contact Brook Zemel, San Jacinto College District, 4624 Fairmont Parkway, Pasadena, TX 77504-3323. *Phone:* 281-998-6150. *Fax:* 281-929-4630. *E-mail:* brook.zemel@sicd.edu.

SOUTHEASTERN CAREER INSTITUTE

Dallas, Texas www.southeasterncareerinstitute.com/

Admissions Office Contact Southeastern Career Institute, 5440 Harvest Hill, Suite 200, Dallas, TX 75230-1600. *Toll-free phone:* 800-525-1446.

SOUTH PLAINS COLLEGE

Levelland, Texas www.southplainscollege.edu/

- **State and locally supported** 2-year, founded 1958
- **Small-town** 177-acre campus
- **Endowment** $3.0 million
- **Coed,** 9,045 undergraduate students, 48% full-time, 53% women, 47% men

Undergraduates 4,376 full-time, 4,669 part-time. Students come from 21 states and territories, 8 other countries, 4% are from out of state, 4% African American, 1% Asian American or Pacific Islander, 28% Hispanic American, 0.6% Native American, 0.6% international, 10% transferred in, 10% live on campus.

Freshmen *Admission:* 2,138 enrolled.

Faculty *Total:* 454, 60% full-time. *Student/faculty ratio:* 20:1.

Majors Accounting; administrative assistant and secretarial science; advertising; agricultural economics; agriculture; agronomy and crop science; art; audio engineering; automobile/automotive mechanics technology; biological and physical sciences; biology/biological sciences; business administration and management; carpentry; chemistry; child development; commercial and advertising art; computer engineering technology; computer programming; computer science; consumer merchandising/retailing management; cosmetology; criminal justice/law enforcement administration; criminal justice/police science; data processing and data processing technology; developmental and child psychology; dietetics; drafting and design technology; education; electrical, electronic and communications engineering technology; engineering; fashion merchandising; fire science; health/health care administration; health information/medical records administration; heating, air conditioning, ventilation and refrigeration maintenance technology; industrial radiologic technology; journalism; legal administrative assistant/secretary; liberal arts and sciences/liberal studies; machine tool technology; marketing/marketing management; mass communication/media; medical administrative assistant and medical secretary; mental health/rehabilitation; music; nursing (licensed practical/vocational nurse training); nursing (registered nurse training); petroleum technology; physical education teaching and coaching; physical therapy; postal management; pre-engineering; real estate; respiratory care therapy; social work; special products marketing; surgical technology; telecommunications; welding technology.

Academics *Calendar:* semesters. *Degree:* certificates and associate. *Special study options:* academic remediation for entering students, accelerated degree program, adult/continuing education programs, advanced placement credit, distance learning, internships, part-time degree program, services for LD students, study abroad, summer session for credit. *ROTC:* Army (c), Air Force (c).

Library South Plains College Library with 70,000 titles, 310 serial subscriptions, an OPAC.

Student Life *Housing:* on-campus residence required through sophomore year. *Options:* men-only, women-only. Campus housing is university owned. *Activities and Organizations:* drama/theater group, student-run newspaper, television station, choral group, student government, Phi Beta Kappa, Bleacher Bums, Law Enforcement Association. *Campus security:* 24-hour emergency response devices and patrols. *Student services:* health clinic.

Athletics Member NJCAA. *Intercollegiate sports:* basketball M(s)/W(s), cross-country running M(s)/W(s), track and field M(s)/W(s). *Intramural sports:* basketball M/W, cross-country running M/W, football M/W, golf M/W, racquetball M/W, softball M/W, table tennis M/W, tennis M/W, volleyball M/W.

Standardized Tests *Recommended:* ACT (for admission), SAT Subject Tests (for admission).

Costs (2007–08) *Tuition:* area resident $1484 full-time; state resident $2012 full-time; nonresident $2396 full-time. *Room and board:* $3300.

Financial Aid Of all full-time matriculated undergraduates, 80 Federal Work-Study jobs (averaging $2000). 22 state and other part-time jobs (averaging $2000).

Applying *Options:* early admission. *Required:* high school transcript. *Application deadlines:* rolling (freshmen), rolling (transfers).

Freshmen Application Contact Mrs. Andrea Rangel, Dean of Admissions and Records, South Plains College, 1401 College Avenue, Levelland, TX 78336. *Phone:* 806-894-9611 Ext. 2370. *Fax:* 806-897-3167. *E-mail:* arangel@southplainscollege.edu.

SOUTH TEXAS COLLEGE

McAllen, Texas www.southtexascollege.edu/

- **District-supported** primarily 2-year, founded 1993
- **Suburban** 20-acre campus
- **Endowment** $222,114
- **Coed,** 18,460 undergraduate students, 36% full-time, 59% women, 41% men

Undergraduates 6,712 full-time, 11,748 part-time. 0.2% African American, 1% Asian American or Pacific Islander, 94% Hispanic American, 0.1% Native American, 0.4% international. *Retention:* 55% of 2003 full-time freshmen returned.

Freshmen *Admission:* 2,412 enrolled.

Faculty *Total:* 598, 71% full-time. *Student/faculty ratio:* 22:1.

Majors Accounting; automobile/automotive mechanics technology; behavioral sciences; business administration and management; clinical laboratory science/medical technology; computer science; computer typography and composition equipment operation; developmental and child psychology; education; emergency medical technology (EMT paramedic); heating, air conditioning, ventilation and refrigeration maintenance technology; heavy equipment maintenance technology; hospitality administration; hotel/motel administration; human services; industrial radiologic technology; industrial technology; information science/studies; interdisciplinary studies; legal administrative assistant/secretary; legal assistant/paralegal; liberal arts and sciences/liberal studies; machine tool technology; nursing (registered nurse training); occupational therapy; plastics engineering technology.

Academics *Calendar:* semesters. *Degrees:* certificates, associate, and bachelor's. *Special study options:* academic remediation for entering students, accelerated degree program, adult/continuing education programs, cooperative education, off-campus study, part-time degree program, services for LD students, summer session for credit. *ROTC:* Army (c).

Library Learning Resources Center with 15,811 titles, 192 serial subscriptions, an OPAC, a Web page.

Student Life *Housing:* college housing not available. *Activities and Organizations:* Beta Epsilon Mu Honor Society, Automotive Technology Club, Child Care and Development Association Club, Heating, Air Conditioning, and Ventilation Club, Writing in Literary Discussion Club. *Campus security:* 24-hour emergency response devices and patrols, late-night transport/escort service. *Student services:* personal/psychological counseling.

Athletics *Intramural sports:* badminton M/W, basketball M/W, bowling M/W, football M/W, golf M/W, racquetball M/W, soccer M/W, softball M/W, table tennis M/W, volleyball M/W.

Standardized Tests *Required for some:* THEA.

Costs (2006–07) *Tuition:* area resident $1770 full-time, $127 per credit hour part-time; state resident $2283 full-time, $165 per credit hour part-time; nonresident $6060 full-time, $202 per credit hour part-time. *Required fees:* $350 full-time, $6 per credit hour part-time, $85 per term part-time. *Payment plan:* installment. *Waivers:* employees or children of employees.

Applying *Options:* early admission, deferred entrance. *Required:* high school transcript. *Application deadlines:* rolling (freshmen), rolling (transfers).

Freshmen Application Contact Mr. Matthew Hebbard, Director of Enrollment Services and Registrar, South Texas College, 3201 West Pecan, McAllen, TX 78501. *Phone:* 956-872-2147. *Toll-free phone:* 800-742-7822. *E-mail:* mshebbar@southtexascollege.edu.

SOUTHWEST INSTITUTE OF TECHNOLOGY

Austin, Texas www.swse.net/

Freshmen Application Contact Fredrico Garcia, Director of Admissions, Southwest Institute of Technology, 5424 Highway 290 West, Suite 200, Austin, TX 78735-8800. *Phone:* 512-892-2640. *Fax:* 512-892-1045.

SOUTHWEST TEXAS JUNIOR COLLEGE

Uvalde, Texas www.swtjc.net/

- **State and locally supported** 2-year, founded 1946
- **Small-town** 97-acre campus with easy access to San Antonio
- **Coed,** 4,350 undergraduate students

Undergraduates Students come from 2 states and territories, 4 other countries, 1% African American, 0.6% Asian American or Pacific Islander, 75% Hispanic American, 0.2% international, 9% live on campus.

Faculty *Total:* 166, 40% full-time.

Majors Agricultural mechanization; automobile/automotive mechanics technology; avionics maintenance technology; biological and physical sciences; business administration and management; computer engineering technology; cosmetology; criminal justice/law enforcement administration; data processing and data processing technology; education; engineering; farm and ranch management; liberal arts and sciences/liberal studies; teacher assistant/aide.

Academics *Calendar:* semesters. *Degree:* certificates and associate. *Special study options:* academic remediation for entering students, adult/continuing education programs, advanced placement credit, English as a second language, external degree program, honors programs, part-time degree program, summer session for credit.

Library Will C. Miller Memorial Library with 30,890 titles, 285 serial subscriptions.

Student Life *Housing Options:* coed, women-only. Campus housing is university owned. *Activities and Organizations:* drama/theater group, student-run newspaper, Catholic Students Club, Business Administration Club. *Campus security:* 24-hour patrols, controlled dormitory access. *Student services:* health clinic, personal/psychological counseling.

Athletics *Intercollegiate sports:* basketball M/W, equestrian sports M/W. *Intramural sports:* basketball M/W, equestrian sports M/W, football M, golf M/W, racquetball M/W, swimming and diving M/W, tennis M/W.

Standardized Tests *Required:* THEA (for placement). *Recommended:* SAT or ACT (for placement).

Costs (2006–07) *Tuition:* area resident $1285 full-time; state resident $1770 full-time; nonresident $2275 full-time.

Financial Aid Of all full-time matriculated undergraduates, 150 Federal Work-Study jobs (averaging $1250). 75 state and other part-time jobs (averaging $1250).

Applying *Options:* electronic application, early admission, deferred entrance. *Required:* high school transcript. *Application deadlines:* rolling (freshmen), rolling (transfers). *Notification:* continuous (freshmen), continuous (transfers).

Director of Admissions Mr. Joe C. Barker, Dean of Admissions and Student Services, Southwest Texas Junior College, 2401 Garner Field Road, Uvalde, TX 78801. *Phone:* 830-278-4401 Ext. 7284.

TARRANT COUNTY COLLEGE DISTRICT

Fort Worth, Texas   web.tccd.net/

- **County-supported** 2-year, founded 1967
- **Urban** 667-acre campus
- **Endowment** $1.5 million
- **Coed**

Undergraduates 12,259 full-time, 22,633 part-time. Students come from 6 states and territories, 14% African American, 5% Asian American or Pacific Islander, 17% Hispanic American, 0.6% Native American, 1% international.

Faculty *Student/faculty ratio:* 19:1.

Academics *Calendar:* semesters. *Degree:* certificates and associate. *Special study options:* academic remediation for entering students, adult/continuing education programs, advanced placement credit, distance learning, English as a second language, honors programs, part-time degree program, services for LD students, summer session for credit. *ROTC:* Army (c), Air Force (c).

Student Life *Campus security:* 24-hour emergency response devices and patrols.

Costs (2006–07) *Tuition:* area resident $1200 full-time, $50 per credit hour part-time; state resident $1512 full-time, $63 per credit hour part-time; nonresident $3600 full-time, $150 per credit hour part-time.

Financial Aid Of all full-time matriculated undergraduates, 372 Federal Work-Study jobs (averaging $1325). 39 state and other part-time jobs (averaging $927).

Applying *Options:* early admission.

Freshmen Application Contact Dr. Cathie Jackson, Director of Admissions and Records, Tarrant County College District, 1500 Houston Street, Fort Worth, TX 76102-6599. *Phone:* 817-515-5291. *Fax:* 817-515-5295.

TEMPLE COLLEGE

Temple, Texas   www.templejc.edu/

- **District-supported** 2-year, founded 1926
- **Suburban** 114-acre campus
- **Endowment** $615,090
- **Coed,** 4,279 undergraduate students, 39% full-time, 65% women, 35% men

Undergraduates 1,658 full-time, 2,621 part-time. Students come from 29 states and territories, 7 other countries, 2% are from out of state, 16% African American, 1% Asian American or Pacific Islander, 17% Hispanic American, 0.8% Native American, 0.2% international, 9% transferred in. *Retention:* 39% of 2003 full-time freshmen returned.

Freshmen *Admission:* 779 applied, 779 admitted, 779 enrolled.

Faculty *Total:* 229, 46% full-time, 15% with terminal degrees. *Student/faculty ratio:* 18:1.

Majors Administrative assistant and secretarial science; art; automobile/automotive mechanics technology; business administration and management; clinical laboratory science/medical technology; clinical/medical laboratory technology; computer programming; computer science; criminal justice/law enforcement administration; criminal justice/police science; data processing and data processing technology; dental hygiene; drafting and design technology; electrical, electronic and communications engineering technology; industrial technology; liberal arts and sciences/liberal studies; medical administrative assistant and medical secretary; nursing (licensed practical/vocational nurse training); nursing (registered nurse training); respiratory care therapy.

Academics *Calendar:* semesters. *Degree:* certificates and associate. *Special study options:* academic remediation for entering students, adult/continuing education programs, advanced placement credit, cooperative education, distance learning, English as a second language, internships, off-campus study, part-time degree program, services for LD students, study abroad, summer session for credit.

Library Hubert Dawson Library with 55,536 titles, 391 serial subscriptions, an OPAC, a Web page.

Student Life *Housing Options:* coed, disabled students. Campus housing is provided by a third party. *Activities and Organizations:* drama/theater group. *Campus security:* 24-hour emergency response devices and patrols. *Student services:* personal/psychological counseling.

Athletics Member NJCAA. *Intercollegiate sports:* baseball M(s), basketball M(s)/W(s), softball W(s), tennis M(s)/W(s). *Intramural sports:* basketball M/W, golf M/W, racquetball M/W, soccer M/W, tennis M/W, volleyball M/W.

Costs (2007–08) *Tuition:* area resident $2100 full-time, $70 per hour part-time; state resident $3300 full-time, $110 per hour part-time; nonresident $5280 full-time, $176 per hour part-time. *Required fees:* $72 full-time. *Room and board:* $6300.

Financial Aid Of all full-time matriculated undergraduates, 86 Federal Work-Study jobs (averaging $826). 7 state and other part-time jobs (averaging $951).

Applying *Options:* early admission. *Required for some:* high school transcript. *Application deadlines:* 8/10 (freshmen), 8/20 (transfers).

Freshmen Application Contact Ms. Toni Borras, Director of Admissions and Records, Temple College, 2600 South First Street, Temple, TX 76504-7435. *Phone:* 254-298-8308. *Toll-free phone:* 800-460-4636. *Fax:* 254-298-8288. *E-mail:* toni.borras@templejc.edu.

TEXARKANA COLLEGE

Texarkana, Texas   www.texarkanacollege.edu/

- **State and locally supported** 2-year, founded 1927
- **Urban** 88-acre campus
- **Coed,** 3,895 undergraduate students, 40% full-time, 62% women, 38% men

Undergraduates 1,550 full-time, 2,345 part-time. Students come from 7 states and territories, 5 other countries, 16% African American, 0.3% Asian American or Pacific Islander, 1% Hispanic American, 0.2% Native American, 0.2% international.

Freshmen *Admission:* 1,216 enrolled.

Faculty *Total:* 266, 32% full-time. *Student/faculty ratio:* 15:1.

Majors Administrative assistant and secretarial science; agriculture; art; automobile/automotive mechanics technology; biology/biological sciences; business administration and management; chemistry; computer programming; computer science; consumer merchandising/retailing management; cosmetology; criminal justice/law enforcement administration; criminal justice/police science; data entry/microcomputer applications related; data processing and data processing technology; drafting and design technology; dramatic/theater arts; electrical, electronic and communications engineering technology; emergency medical technology (EMT paramedic); engineering; finance; heating, air conditioning, ventilation and refrigeration maintenance technology; information technology; journalism; liberal arts and sciences/liberal studies; mathematics; music; nursing (licensed practical/vocational nurse training); nursing (registered nurse training); physics; real estate; substance abuse/addiction counseling; welding technology; wood science and wood products/pulp and paper technology.

Academics *Calendar:* semesters. *Degree:* certificates and associate. *Special study options:* academic remediation for entering students, adult/continuing education programs, advanced placement credit, cooperative education, part-time degree program, services for LD students, summer session for credit.

Texarkana College (continued)

Library Palmer Memorial Library with 46,700 titles, 646 serial subscriptions.

Student Life *Housing Options:* Campus housing is university owned. *Activities and Organizations:* drama/theater group, student-run newspaper, radio station, choral group, Black Student Association, Earth Club. *Campus security:* 24-hour patrols. *Student services:* personal/psychological counseling.

Athletics Member NJCAA. *Intercollegiate sports:* baseball M(s), softball W(s). *Intramural sports:* badminton M/W, basketball M, racquetball M/W, tennis M/W, volleyball M/W.

Standardized Tests *Required:* THEA (for placement).

Costs (2006–07) *Tuition:* area resident $1000 full-time, $29 per semester hour part-time; state resident $1400 full-time, $46 per semester hour part-time; nonresident $1900 full-time, $75 per semester hour part-time. Full-time tuition and fees vary according to course load. Part-time tuition and fees vary according to course load. *Required fees:* $100 full-time, $10 per semester hour part-time. *Room and board:* room only: $1300. *Payment plan:* installment. *Waivers:* employees or children of employees.

Financial Aid Of all full-time matriculated undergraduates, 30 Federal Work-Study jobs (averaging $3090).

Applying *Options:* early admission. *Required:* high school transcript. *Application deadlines:* rolling (freshmen), rolling (transfers).

Freshmen Application Contact Mr. Van Miller, Director of Admissions, Texarkana College, 2500 North Robison Road, Texarkana, TX 75599. *Phone:* 903-838-4541. *Fax:* 903-832-5030. *E-mail:* vmiller@texarkanacollege.edu.

TEXAS CULINARY ACADEMY

Austin, Texas   www.txca.com/

Director of Admissions Paula Paulette, Vice President of Marketing and Admissions, Texas Culinary Academy, 11400 Burnet Road, Austin, TX 78758. *Phone:* 512-837-2665. *Toll-free phone:* 888-553-2433. *E-mail:* ppaulette@txca.com.

TEXAS SOUTHMOST COLLEGE

Brownsville, Texas   www.utb.edu/

Director of Admissions Mr. Rene Villarreal, Director of Admissions, Texas Southmost College, 80 Fort Brown, Brownsville, TX 78520-4991. *Phone:* 956-544-8992. *E-mail:* rvillarreal@utb.edu.

TEXAS STATE TECHNICAL COLLEGE HARLINGEN

Harlingen, Texas   www.harlingen.tstc.edu/

Director of Admissions Mrs. Elva Short, Director of Admissions, Texas State Technical College Harlingen, 1902 North Loop 499, Harlingen, TX 78550-3697. *Phone:* 956-364-4100. *Toll-free phone:* 800-852-8784.

TEXAS STATE TECHNICAL COLLEGE— MARSHALL

Marshall, Texas   www.marshall.tstc.edu

- **State-supported** 2-year, founded 1991
- **565 undergraduate students**

Majors Computer science; diesel mechanics technology; e-commerce; electrical, electronic and communications engineering technology; industrial technology; information science/studies; instrumentation technology; mechanical engineering/mechanical technology; occupational safety and health technology; office management; robotics technology; system, networking, and LAN/WAN management.

Academics *Calendar:* semesters. *Degree:* associate.

Costs (2006–07) *Tuition:* state resident $3812 full-time; nonresident $7303 full-time.

Admissions Office Contact Texas State Technical College–Marshall, 2650 East End Blvd. South, Marshall, TX 75671. *Toll-free phone:* 888-382-8782.

TEXAS STATE TECHNICAL COLLEGE WACO

Waco, Texas   waco.tstc.edu/

- **State-supported** 2-year, founded 1965, part of Texas State Technical College System
- **Suburban** 200-acre campus
- **Coed**

Undergraduates 2,989 full-time, 1,463 part-time. Students come from 30 states and territories, 5 other countries, 2% are from out of state, 16% African American, 1% Asian American or Pacific Islander, 16% Hispanic American, 0.4% Native American, 2% international.

Faculty *Student/faculty ratio:* 16:1.

Academics *Calendar:* trimesters. *Degree:* certificates and associate. *Special study options:* academic remediation for entering students, adult/continuing education programs, cooperative education, distance learning, internships, part-time degree program, services for LD students, summer session for credit.

Student Life *Campus security:* 24-hour emergency response devices and patrols, late-night transport/escort service, controlled dormitory access.

Standardized Tests *Required:* ACCUPLACER (for admission).

Costs (2006–07) *Tuition:* state resident $1950 full-time, $65 per credit hour part-time; nonresident $5460 full-time, $182 per credit hour part-time. *Required fees:* $2000 full-time, $21 per credit hour part-time. *Room and board:* $4100; room only: $1860.

Financial Aid Of all full-time matriculated undergraduates, 125 Federal Work-Study jobs (averaging $2500). 150 state and other part-time jobs.

Applying *Options:* electronic application, early admission. *Required:* high school transcript. *Required for some:* interview.

Freshmen Application Contact Mr. Marcus Balch, Director, Recruiting Services, Texas State Technical College Waco, 3801 Campus Drive, Waco, TX 76705. *Phone:* 254-867-2026. *Toll-free phone:* 800-792-8784 Ext. 2362. *Fax:* 254-867-3827. *E-mail:* mrcus.balch@tstc.edu.

TEXAS STATE TECHNICAL COLLEGE WEST TEXAS

Sweetwater, Texas   www.sweetwater.tstc.edu/

- **State-supported** 2-year, founded 1970, part of Texas State Technical College System
- **Small-town** 115-acre campus
- **Endowment** $50,000
- **Coed,** 1,537 undergraduate students, 58% full-time, 50% women, 50% men

Undergraduates 892 full-time, 645 part-time. Students come from 20 states and territories, 1 other country, 3% are from out of state, 10% African American, 0.9% Asian American or Pacific Islander, 23% Hispanic American, 0.8% Native American, 0.2% international, 9% transferred in, 14% live on campus. *Retention:* 47% of 2003 full-time freshmen returned.

Freshmen *Admission:* 355 enrolled.

Faculty *Total:* 142, 65% full-time. *Student/faculty ratio:* 11:1.

Majors Airframe mechanics and aircraft maintenance technology; automobile/automotive mechanics technology; computer engineering technology; computer programming; computer systems networking and telecommunications; diesel mechanics technology; drafting and design technology; electrical, electronic and communications engineering technology; emergency medical technology (EMT paramedic); environmental engineering technology; health information/medical records technology; machine tool technology; robotics technology.

Academics *Calendar:* semesters. *Degree:* certificates and associate. *Special study options:* academic remediation for entering students, adult/continuing education programs, advanced placement credit, cooperative education, distance learning, internships, part-time degree program, services for LD students, summer session for credit.

Library Texas State Technical College West Texas Library with 59,711 titles, 212,050 serial subscriptions, 681 audiovisual materials, an OPAC, a Web page.

Student Life *Housing:* on-campus residence required through sophomore year. *Options:* coed, disabled students. Campus housing is university owned. Freshman campus housing is guaranteed. *Activities and Organizations:* Student Government Association, Vocational Industrial Clubs of America, Mexican-American Student Club, Auto Tech 2000, Vocational Nursing Club. *Campus security:* 24-hour patrols. *Student services:* health clinic, personal/psychological counseling.

Athletics *Intramural sports:* basketball M/W, bowling M/W, football M/W, golf M/W, racquetball M/W, soccer M/W, softball M/W, table tennis M/W, tennis M/W, volleyball M/W, weight lifting M/W.

Standardized Tests *Required:* THEA (for admission).

Costs (2007–08) *Tuition:* area resident $1950 full-time. *Required fees:* $118 full-time. *Room and board:* $6150.

Financial Aid Of all full-time matriculated undergraduates, 127 Federal Work-Study jobs (averaging $1350).

Applying *Options:* early admission, deferred entrance. *Required:* high school transcript. *Application deadlines:* rolling (freshmen), rolling (transfers). *Notification:* continuous (freshmen), continuous (transfers).

Freshmen Application Contact Ms. Maria Aguirre-Acuna, Texas State Technical College West Texas, 300 College Drive, Sweetwater, TX 79556-4108. *Phone:* 325-235-7349. *Toll-free phone:* 800-592-8784.

TOMBALL COLLEGE

Tomball, Texas wwwtc.nhmccd.edu/

- **State and locally supported** 2-year, founded 1988, part of North Harris Montgomery Community College District
- **Suburban** 210-acre campus with easy access to Houston
- **Coed,** 7,787 undergraduate students, 18% full-time, 61% women, 39% men

Undergraduates 1,399 full-time, 6,388 part-time. 0.6% are from out of state, 8% African American, 6% Asian American or Pacific Islander, 15% Hispanic American, 0.2% Native American, 3% international, 6% transferred in.

Freshmen *Admission:* 932 enrolled.

Faculty *Total:* 357, 31% full-time. *Student/faculty ratio:* 8:1.

Majors Accounting; business administration and management; computer programming; electrical, electronic and communications engineering technology; human services; legal administrative assistant/secretary; medical administrative assistant and medical secretary; nursing (registered nurse training); occupational therapy; veterinary technology.

Academics *Calendar:* semesters. *Degree:* certificates and associate. *Special study options:* academic remediation for entering students, adult/continuing education programs, advanced placement credit, cooperative education, English as a second language, honors programs, independent study, internships, part-time degree program, study abroad.

Library Library-Tomball College North Harris Community College with 24,063 titles, 385 serial subscriptions, an OPAC, a Web page.

Student Life *Housing:* college housing not available. *Activities and Organizations:* drama/theater group, student-run newspaper, Phi Theta Kappa, Culture Club, Veterinary Technicians Student Organization, Human Services Club, Student Nurses Association. *Campus security:* 24-hour emergency response devices and patrols, late-night transport/escort service, trained security personnel during open hours. *Student services:* personal/psychological counseling.

Standardized Tests *Recommended:* SAT or ACT (for admission), THEA, ACT COMPASS.

Costs (2007–08) *Tuition:* area resident $1080 full-time, $56 per credit hour part-time; state resident $2040 full-time, $96 per credit hour part-time; nonresident $2400 full-time, $220 per credit hour part-time.

Financial Aid Of all full-time matriculated undergraduates, 34 Federal Work-Study jobs (averaging $3000).

Applying *Options:* early admission. *Required for some:* high school transcript. *Recommended:* high school transcript.

Freshmen Application Contact Mr. Larry Rideaux, Dean of Enrollment Services, Tomball College, 30555 Tomball Parkway, Tomball, TX 77375-4036. *Phone:* 281-351-3334. *Fax:* 281-357-3773. *E-mail:* tc.advisors@nhmccd.edu.

TRINITY VALLEY COMMUNITY COLLEGE

Athens, Texas www.tvcc.edu/

- **State and locally supported** 2-year, founded 1946
- **Small-town** 65-acre campus with easy access to Dallas–Fort Worth
- **Endowment** $1.9 million
- **Coed**

Undergraduates 2,442 full-time, 3,379 part-time. Students come from 48 states and territories, 1% are from out of state, 13% African American, 0.3% Asian American or Pacific Islander, 6% Hispanic American, 0.3% Native American, 0.5% international.

Faculty *Student/faculty ratio:* 20:1.

Academics *Calendar:* semesters. *Degree:* certificates, diplomas, and associate. *Special study options:* academic remediation for entering students, adult/

continuing education programs, advanced placement credit, cooperative education, distance learning, honors programs, internships, part-time degree program, services for LD students, summer session for credit.

Student Life *Campus security:* 24-hour emergency response devices and patrols, controlled dormitory access.

Athletics Member NJCAA.

Costs (2006–07) *Tuition:* state resident $1200 full-time, $20 per semester hour part-time; nonresident $3900 full-time, $65 per semester hour part-time. *Required fees:* $900 full-time, $15 per semester hour part-time. *Room and board:* $3470.

Financial Aid Of all full-time matriculated undergraduates, 80 Federal Work-Study jobs (averaging $1544). 40 state and other part-time jobs (averaging $1544).

Applying *Options:* early admission. *Required:* high school transcript.

Freshmen Application Contact Dr. Colette Hilliard, Dean of Enrollment Management and Registrar, Trinity Valley Community College, 100 Cardinal Drive, Athens, TX 75751. *Phone:* 903-675-6209 Ext. 209.

TYLER JUNIOR COLLEGE

Tyler, Texas www.tjc.edu/

- **State and locally supported** 2-year, founded 1926
- **Suburban** 85-acre campus
- **Coed,** 9,591 undergraduate students

Undergraduates Students come from 30 states and territories, 25 other countries, 1% are from out of state, 19% African American, 1% Asian American or Pacific Islander, 8% Hispanic American, 0.5% Native American, 0.5% international, 8% live on campus.

Faculty *Total:* 456, 51% full-time. *Student/faculty ratio:* 21:1.

Majors Accounting; administrative assistant and secretarial science; agricultural business and management; agricultural economics; agricultural teacher education; agriculture; art; behavioral sciences; business administration and management; clinical/medical laboratory technology; commercial and advertising art; computer and information sciences related; computer engineering technology; computer graphics; computer programming related; computer science; computer systems networking and telecommunications; criminal justice/law enforcement administration; criminal justice/police science; data entry/microcomputer applications; dental hygiene; developmental and child psychology; drafting and design technology; electrical, electronic and communications engineering technology; environmental engineering technology; farm and ranch management; fashion merchandising; finance; fire science; graphic and printing equipment operation/production; health/health care administration; heating, air conditioning, ventilation and refrigeration maintenance technology; horticultural science; human resources management; industrial radiologic technology; information technology; legal administrative assistant/secretary; liberal arts and sciences/liberal studies; marketing/marketing management; medical administrative assistant and medical secretary; modern languages; music; nursing (licensed practical/vocational nurse training); nursing (registered nurse training); ophthalmic laboratory technology; ornamental horticulture; parks, recreation and leisure; petroleum technology; photography; plastics engineering technology; postal management; psychology; real estate; respiratory care therapy; sign language interpretation and translation; social sciences; speech and rhetoric; survey technology; welding technology.

Academics *Calendar:* semesters. *Degree:* certificates and associate. *Special study options:* academic remediation for entering students, accelerated degree program, adult/continuing education programs, advanced placement credit, distance learning, English as a second language, freshman honors college, honors programs, part-time degree program, services for LD students, summer session for credit.

Library Vaughn Library and Learning Resource Center with 569 serial subscriptions, 64,776 audiovisual materials, an OPAC.

Student Life *Housing Options:* men-only, women-only. *Activities and Organizations:* drama/theater group, student-run newspaper, choral group, marching band, student government, religious affiliation clubs, Phi Theta Kappa, national fraternities, national sororities. *Campus security:* 24-hour patrols, controlled dormitory access. *Student services:* health clinic, personal/psychological counseling.

Athletics Member NJCAA. *Intercollegiate sports:* baseball M, basketball M(s)/W(s), football M(s), golf M/W, soccer M(s), tennis M(s)/W(s), volleyball W. *Intramural sports:* basketball M/W, racquetball M/W, volleyball M/W, weight lifting M/W.

Standardized Tests *Required:* THEA (for placement).

Costs (2006–07) *Tuition:* area resident $1540 full-time; state resident $2500 full-time; nonresident $3340 full-time.

Financial Aid Of all full-time matriculated undergraduates, 39 Federal Work-Study jobs (averaging $1117). 23 state and other part-time jobs (averaging $992).

Applying *Options:* early admission. *Required:* high school transcript. *Application deadlines:* rolling (freshmen), rolling (transfers).

Tyler Junior College (continued)

Freshmen Application Contact Ms. Janna Chancey, Director of Enrollment Management, Tyler Junior College, PO Box 9020, Tyler, TX 75711. *Phone:* 903-510-2396. *Toll-free phone:* 800-687-5680.

UNIVERSAL TECHNICAL INSTITUTE

Houston, Texas www.uticorp.com/

Director of Admissions Randy Whitman, Director of Admissions, Universal Technical Institute, 721 Lockhaven Drive, Houston, TX 77073-5598. *Phone:* 281-443-6262 Ext. 261. *Fax:* 281-443-0610.

VERNON COLLEGE

Vernon, Texas www.vernoncollege.edu/

- **State and locally supported** 2-year, founded 1970
- **Small-town** 100-acre campus
- **Coed,** 2,270 undergraduate students

Undergraduates Students come from 32 states and territories, 4 other countries, 0.1% are from out of state, 7% African American, 1% Asian American or Pacific Islander, 12% Hispanic American, 1% Native American, 0.8% international.

Faculty *Total:* 128, 45% full-time. *Student/faculty ratio:* 17:1.

Majors Accounting; administrative assistant and secretarial science; automobile/automotive mechanics technology; business administration and management; child care and support services management; cosmetology; criminal justice/law enforcement administration; data processing and data processing technology; drafting and design technology; farm and ranch management; health information/medical records technology; legal studies; liberal arts and sciences/liberal studies; machine tool technology; nursing (licensed practical/vocational nurse training); nursing (registered nurse training).

Academics *Calendar:* semesters. *Degree:* certificates and associate. *Special study options:* academic remediation for entering students, adult/continuing education programs, advanced placement credit, cooperative education, distance learning, double majors, internships, part-time degree program, services for LD students, summer session for credit.

Library Wright Library with 29,000 titles, 200 serial subscriptions, an OPAC, a Web page.

Student Life *Housing Options:* men-only, women-only. *Activities and Organizations:* drama/theater group, choral group, Student Government Association, Baptist Student Union. *Campus security:* 24-hour patrols. *Student services:* health clinic, personal/psychological counseling.

Athletics Member NJCAA. *Intercollegiate sports:* baseball M(s), equestrian sports M(s)/W(s), softball W(s), volleyball W(s). *Intramural sports:* archery M/W, basketball M/W, football M/W, golf M/W, tennis M/W, volleyball M/W.

Standardized Tests *Required:* THEA (for placement).

Costs (2006–07) *Tuition:* area resident $1670 full-time; state resident $2405 full-time; nonresident $3590 full-time.

Financial Aid Of all full-time matriculated undergraduates, 50 Federal Work-Study jobs (averaging $3000). 2 state and other part-time jobs (averaging $3000).

Applying *Options:* electronic application, early admission. *Application fee:* $10. *Application deadlines:* rolling (freshmen), rolling (transfers).

Director of Admissions Mr. Joe Hite, Dean of Admissions/Registrar, Vernon College, 4400 College Drive, Vernon, TX 76384-4092. *Phone:* 940-552-6291 Ext. 2204.

VICTORIA COLLEGE

Victoria, Texas www.victoriacollege.edu/

- **County-supported** 2-year, founded 1925
- **Urban** 80-acre campus
- **Coed,** 4,244 undergraduate students

Undergraduates Students come from 4 states and territories, 2 other countries, 5% African American, 1% Asian American or Pacific Islander, 29% Hispanic American, 0.2% Native American, 0.2% international.

Freshmen *Admission:* 709 admitted.

Majors Accounting; administrative assistant and secretarial science; business administration and management; clinical/medical laboratory technology; computer programming; computer systems networking and telecommunications; criminal justice/police science; drafting and design technology; electrical, electronic and communications engineering technology; emergency medical technol-

ogy (EMT paramedic); industrial technology; information science/studies; legal assistant/paralegal; liberal arts and sciences/liberal studies; nursing (registered nurse training); respiratory care therapy.

Academics *Calendar:* semesters. *Degree:* certificates and associate. *Special study options:* academic remediation for entering students, adult/continuing education programs, advanced placement credit, distance learning, part-time degree program, services for LD students, summer session for credit.

Library Victoria College Library with 150,000 titles, 1,500 serial subscriptions.

Student Life *Housing:* college housing not available. *Activities and Organizations:* drama/theater group, choral group, Student Senate. *Campus security:* 24-hour emergency response devices. *Student services:* personal/psychological counseling.

Athletics *Intramural sports:* basketball M, softball M.

Standardized Tests *Required:* THEA (for placement). *Required for some:* SAT or ACT (for placement).

Costs (2006–07) *Tuition:* area resident $900 full-time, $30 per hour part-time; state resident $1500 full-time, $50 per hour part-time; nonresident $1650 full-time, $55 per hour part-time. Full-time tuition and fees vary according to course load and location. Part-time tuition and fees vary according to course load and location. *Required fees:* $440 full-time, $14 per hour part-time, $10 per term part-time. *Room and board:* Room and board charges vary according to housing facility. *Payment plan:* installment. *Waivers:* senior citizens and employees or children of employees.

Applying *Required:* high school transcript. *Application deadlines:* rolling (freshmen), rolling (transfers).

Freshmen Application Contact Lavern Dentler, Registrar, Victoria College, 2200 East Red River, Victoria, TX 77901-4494. *Phone:* 361-573-3291. *Toll-free phone:* 877-843-4369. *Fax:* 361-582-2525. *E-mail:* registrar@victoriacollege.edu.

VIRGINIA COLLEGE AT AUSTIN

Austin, Texas www.vc.edu/

- **Proprietary** 2-year, founded 2002
- **Coed,** 769 undergraduate students
- **69% of applicants were admitted**

Freshmen *Admission:* 186 applied, 128 admitted.

Majors Accounting; business administration and management; business operations support and secretarial services related; business systems networking/telecommunications; computer and information systems security; diagnostic medical sonography and ultrasound technology; entrepreneurial and small business related; hospitality administration; legal assistant/paralegal; medical insurance/medical billing; medical office assistant; office management; pre-law; resort management; surgical technology.

Academics *Calendar:* quarters. *Degree:* associate.

Costs (2006–07) *Tuition:* $11,780 full-time.

Applying *Application fee:* $100. *Recommended:* letters of recommendation.

Admissions Office Contact Virginia College at Austin, 6301 East Highway 290, Austin, TX 78723. *Toll-free phone:* 866-314-6324.

WADE COLLEGE

Dallas, Texas www.wadecollege.edu/

Freshmen Application Contact Ms. Suzan Wade, Admissions Director, Wade College, International Apparel Mart at Dallas Market Center, 2350 Stemmons Expressway, Suite M5120, PO Box 586343, Dallas, TX 75258. *Phone:* 214-637-3530. *Toll-free phone:* 800-624-4850.

WEATHERFORD COLLEGE

Weatherford, Texas www.wc.edu/

- **State and locally supported** 2-year, founded 1869
- **Small-town** 94-acre campus with easy access to Dallas–Fort Worth
- **Endowment** $42.5 million
- **Coed**

Undergraduates 2,287 full-time, 2,265 part-time. 8% are from out of state, 2% African American, 0.5% Asian American or Pacific Islander, 8% Hispanic American, 1% Native American, 1% international, 7% live on campus.

Faculty *Student/faculty ratio:* 22:1.

Academics *Calendar:* semesters. *Degree:* certificates, diplomas, and associate. *Special study options:* academic remediation for entering students, adult/continuing education programs, cooperative education, distance learning, freshman

---

honors college, honors programs, internships, part-time degree program, services for LD students, student-designed majors, summer session for credit. *ROTC:* Air Force (c).

Student Life *Campus security:* 24-hour emergency response devices and patrols, late-night transport/escort service.

Athletics Member NJCAA.

Costs (2006–07) *Tuition:* area resident $1456 full-time, $52 per hour part-time; state resident $1960 full-time, $70 per hour part-time; nonresident $3164 full-time, $113 per hour part-time. *Room and board:* $6500.

Applying *Options:* early admission.

Freshmen Application Contact Mr. Ralph Willingham, Dean of Admissions, Weatherford College, 225 College Park Drive, Weatherford, TX 76086-5699. *Phone:* 817-598-6248. *Toll-free phone:* 800-287-5471 Ext. 248. *Fax:* 817-598-6205. *E-mail:* willingham@wc.edu.

WESTERN TECHNICAL COLLEGE

El Paso, Texas
www.wtc-ep.edu/

- **Private** 2-year
- **Coed**

Undergraduates 600 full-time, 225 part-time. 3% African American, 85% Hispanic American.

Faculty *Student/faculty ratio:* 18:1.

Academics *Calendar:* continuous. *Degree:* certificates and associate.

Costs (2006–07) *Tuition:* $23,760 full-time. No tuition increase for student's term of enrollment. *Payment plans:* tuition prepayment, installment, deferred payment.

Applying *Options:* early admission, deferred entrance.

Freshmen Application Contact Mr. Bill Terrell, Chief Admissions Officer, Western Technical College, 1000 Texas Avenue, El Paso, TX 79901-1536. *Phone:* 915-532-3737 Ext. 117. *Fax:* 915-532-6946. *E-mail:* bterrell@wtc-ep.edu.

WESTERN TECHNICAL INSTITUTE

El Paso, Texas
www.wti-ep.com/

Director of Admissions Mr. Bill Terrell, Chief Admissions Officer, Western Technical Institute, 9451 Diana, El Paso, TX 79930-2610. *Phone:* 800-225-5984. *Toll-free phone:* 800-522-2072.

WESTERN TEXAS COLLEGE

Snyder, Texas
www.wtc.edu/

- **State and locally supported** 2-year, founded 1969
- **Small-town** 165-acre campus
- **Endowment** $653,379
- **Coed,** 1,685 undergraduate students

Undergraduates 20% live on campus.

Freshmen *Admission:* 1,775 applied, 1,685 admitted.

Faculty *Total:* 64, 75% full-time. *Student/faculty ratio:* 17:1.

Majors Accounting; administrative assistant and secretarial science; agricultural teacher education; agriculture; art; art teacher education; automobile/automotive mechanics technology; business administration and management; computer engineering technology; computer science; corrections; criminal justice/law enforcement administration; criminal justice/police science; education; journalism; landscape architecture; liberal arts and sciences/liberal studies; marketing/marketing management; mass communication/media; nursing (licensed practical/vocational nurse training); parks, recreation and leisure facilities management; welding technology.

Academics *Calendar:* semesters. *Degree:* certificates and associate. *Special study options:* academic remediation for entering students, adult/continuing education programs, advanced placement credit, internships, part-time degree program, services for LD students, student-designed majors, summer session for credit.

Library Western Texas College Resource Center with 43,000 titles, 127 serial subscriptions, a Web page.

Student Life *Housing:* on-campus residence required for freshman year. *Options:* coed. Campus housing is university owned. *Activities and Organizations:* drama/theater group, student-run newspaper, choral group. *Campus security:* 24-hour emergency response devices and patrols. *Student services:* personal/psychological counseling.

Athletics Member NJCAA. *Intercollegiate sports:* baseball M, softball W. *Intramural sports:* basketball M/W, bowling M/W, football M, racquetball M/W, soccer M, softball M/W, swimming and diving M/W, tennis M/W, volleyball M/W, weight lifting M/W.

Standardized Tests *Required:* THEA (for placement). *Required for some:* ACT (for placement).

Costs (2006–07) *Tuition:* area resident $1316 full-time; state resident $1460 full-time; nonresident $1676 full-time.

Financial Aid Of all full-time matriculated undergraduates, 30 Federal Work-Study jobs (averaging $1600).

Applying *Options:* early admission, deferred entrance. *Required:* high school transcript. *Application deadlines:* rolling (freshmen), rolling (transfers). *Notification:* continuous (freshmen), continuous (transfers).

Director of Admissions Dr. Jim Clifton, Dean of Student Services, Western Texas College, 6200 College Avenue, Snyder, TX 79549-6105. *Phone:* 325-573-8511 Ext. 204. *Toll-free phone:* 888-GO-TO-WTC. *E-mail:* jclifton@wtc.cc.tx.us.

WESTWOOD COLLEGE—DALLAS

Dallas, Texas
www.westwood.edu/

- **Proprietary** 2-year, founded 2002
- **Urban** campus with easy access to Dallas
- **Coed**

Undergraduates 397 full-time, 7 part-time. 30% African American, 4% Asian American or Pacific Islander, 31% Hispanic American, 0.5% Native American, 0.2% international.

Academics *Calendar:* continuous. *Degree:* associate.

Applying *Required:* interview, high school diploma or GED, and passing score on ACT/SAT or Accuplacer test.

Director of Admissions Eric Southwell, Director of Admissions, Westwood College–Dallas, 8390 LBJ Freeway, Executive Center I, Suite 100, Dallas, TX 75243. *Phone:* 800-803-3140. *Toll-free phone:* 800-281-2978.

▶**See page 610 for the College Close-Up.**

WESTWOOD COLLEGE—FORT WORTH

Euless, Texas
www.westwood.edu/

- **Proprietary** 2-year
- **Urban** campus with easy access to Dallas, TX
- **Coed**

Undergraduates 375 full-time, 97 part-time. 13% African American, 2% Asian American or Pacific Islander, 26% Hispanic American, 1% Native American.

Academics *Calendar:* continuous. *Degree:* associate.

Applying *Required:* interview, high school diploma/GED and passing scores on ACT/SAT or Accuplacer exam.

Director of Admissions Ms. Lisa Hecht, Director of Admissions, Westwood College–Fort Worth, 4232 North Freeway, Fort Worth, TX 76137. *Phone:* 817-685-9994. *Toll-free phone:* 866-533-9997.

▶**See page 616 for the College Close-Up.**

WESTWOOD COLLEGE—HOUSTON SOUTH CAMPUS

Houston, Texas
www.westwood.edu/

- **Proprietary** 2-year, founded 2003
- **Urban** campus with easy access to Houston, TX
- **Coed**
- 66% of applicants were admitted

Undergraduates 16 full-time. 56% African American, 13% Hispanic American.

Academics *Calendar:* continuous. *Degree:* associate.

Applying *Required:* interview, high school diploma/GED and passing ACT/SAT or Accuplacer scores.

Director of Admissions Admissions, Westwood College–Houston South Campus, One Arena Place, 7322 Southwest Freeway, Houston, TX 77074. *Phone:* 713-777-4433. *Toll-free phone:* 800-281-2978.

▶**See page 618 for the College Close-Up.**

WHARTON COUNTY JUNIOR COLLEGE
Wharton, Texas   www.wcjc.edu/

- **State and locally supported** 2-year, founded 1946
- **Rural** 90-acre campus with easy access to Houston
- **Coed**

Undergraduates Students come from 8 states and territories, 5 other countries, 9% African American, 4% Asian American or Pacific Islander, 24% Hispanic American, 0.2% Native American, 4% international, 5% live on campus.

Faculty *Student/faculty ratio:* 22:1.

Academics *Calendar:* semesters. *Degree:* certificates and associate. *Special study options:* academic remediation for entering students, adult/continuing education programs, advanced placement credit, part-time degree program, student-designed majors, summer session for credit.

Student Life *Campus security:* 24-hour patrols.

Athletics Member NJCAA.

Costs (2006–07) *Tuition:* area resident $1296 full-time, $54 per semester hour part-time; state resident $2160 full-time, $90 per semester hour part-time; nonresident $2928 full-time, $122 per semester hour part-time. *Room and board:* $2500; room only: $600.

Financial Aid Of all full-time matriculated undergraduates, 65 Federal Work-Study jobs (averaging $3000). 8 state and other part-time jobs (averaging $2000).

Applying *Application fee:* $10. *Required:* high school transcript, minimum 2.0 GPA.

Freshmen Application Contact Mr. Albert Barnes, Dean of Admissions and Registration, Wharton County Junior College, 911 Boling Highway, Wharton, TX 77488-3298. *Phone:* 979-532-6381. *E-mail:* albertb@wcjc.edu.

UTAH

COLLEGE OF EASTERN UTAH
Price, Utah   www.ceu.edu/

- **State-supported** 2-year, founded 1937, part of Utah System of Higher Education
- **Small-town** 15-acre campus
- **Coed**

Undergraduates 1,317 full-time, 977 part-time. Students come from 21 states and territories, 9% are from out of state, 0.9% African American, 1% Asian American or Pacific Islander, 3% Hispanic American, 15% Native American, 0.7% international, 10% transferred in, 15% live on campus.

Faculty *Student/faculty ratio:* 15:1.

Academics *Calendar:* semesters. *Degree:* certificates and associate. *Special study options:* academic remediation for entering students, adult/continuing education programs, advanced placement credit, cooperative education, distance learning, English as a second language, independent study, part-time degree program, services for LD students, summer session for credit.

Student Life *Campus security:* 24-hour emergency response devices and patrols, late-night transport/escort service.

Athletics Member NJCAA.

Standardized Tests *Recommended:* ACT (for admission).

Costs (2006–07) *Tuition:* state resident $2090 full-time, $88 per credit hour part-time; nonresident $7670 full-time, $339 per credit hour part-time. Full-time tuition and fees vary according to course load. Part-time tuition and fees vary according to course load. *Room and board:* $3820. Room and board charges vary according to board plan, housing facility, and location.

Financial Aid Of all full-time matriculated undergraduates, 66 Federal Work-Study jobs (averaging $1369). 27 state and other part-time jobs (averaging $773).

Applying *Options:* electronic application, early admission. *Application fee:* $25. *Recommended:* high school transcript.

Freshmen Application Contact Mr. Todd Olsen, Director of Admissions, High School Relations, College of Eastern Utah, 451 East 400 North, Price, UT 84501. *Phone:* 435-613-5217. *Fax:* 435-613-5814. *E-mail:* todd.olsen@ceu.edu.

DIXIE STATE COLLEGE OF UTAH
St. George, Utah   www.dixie.edu/

- **State-supported** primarily 2-year, founded 1911, part of Utah System of Higher Education
- **Small-town** 117-acre campus
- **Endowment** $10.5 million
- **Coed**, 5,704 undergraduate students, 57% full-time, 54% women, 46% men

Undergraduates 3,240 full-time, 2,464 part-time. Students come from 42 states and territories, 14 other countries, 7% are from out of state, 0.6% African American, 2% Asian American or Pacific Islander, 3% Hispanic American, 1% Native American, 0.5% international, 4% transferred in, 2% live on campus. *Retention:* 46% of 2003 full-time freshmen returned.

Freshmen *Admission:* 2,850 applied, 2,397 admitted, 1,329 enrolled. *Average high school GPA:* 3.34. *Test scores:* SAT math scores over 500: 37%; SAT writing scores over 500: 29; ACT scores over 18: 80%; SAT math scores over 600: 8%; ACT scores over 24: 22%; ACT scores over 30: 1%.

Faculty *Total:* 337, 34% full-time. *Student/faculty ratio:* 22:1.

Majors Accounting; administrative assistant and secretarial science; agriculture; airline pilot and flight crew; architectural drafting and CAD/CADD; art; art history, criticism and conservation; autobody/collision and repair technology; automobile/automotive mechanics technology; aviation/airway management; biology/biological sciences; biotechnology; botany/plant biology; broadcast journalism; business administration and management; cartography; ceramic arts and ceramics; chemistry; child care and support services management; commercial and advertising art; communication/speech communication and rhetoric; computer science; criminal justice/safety; dance; data processing and data processing technology; dental hygiene; diesel mechanics technology; dramatic/theater arts; drawing; ecology; economics; elementary education; emergency medical technology (EMT paramedic); engineering; English; environmental studies; foreign languages and literatures; forestry; general retailing/wholesaling; geology/earth science; health professions related; history; humanities; interior design; journalism; kindergarten/preschool education; liberal arts and sciences/liberal studies; marine biology and biological oceanography; mathematics; mechanical drafting and CAD/CADD; music; natural resources/conservation; natural resources management and policy; nursing (registered nurse training); painting; philosophy; photographic and film/video technology; photography; physical education teaching and coaching; physics; plant pathology/phytopathology; plant protection and integrated pest management; political science and government; pre-law studies; printmaking; psychology; radio and television; radio, television, and digital communication related; range science and management; sculpture; secondary education; social work; sociology; soil science and agronomy; tourism and travel services marketing; water resources engineering; web page, digital/multimedia and information resources design; wildlife and wildlands science and management; zoology/animal biology.

Academics *Calendar:* semesters. *Degrees:* certificates, diplomas, associate, and bachelor's. *Special study options:* academic remediation for entering students, adult/continuing education programs, advanced placement credit, cooperative education, distance learning, English as a second language, honors programs, independent study, off-campus study, part-time degree program, services for LD students, summer session for credit.

Library Val A. Browning Library with 94,747 titles, 263 serial subscriptions, an OPAC, a Web page.

Student Life *Housing Options:* coed, men-only. Campus housing is university owned. *Activities and Organizations:* drama/theater group, student-run newspaper, radio and television station, choral group, Dixie Spirit, Outdoor Club, Association of Women Students. *Campus security:* 24-hour emergency response devices and patrols. *Student services:* health clinic, personal/psychological counseling.

Athletics Member NJCAA. *Intercollegiate sports:* baseball M(s), basketball M(s)/W(s), football M(s), golf M(s), soccer W(s), softball W(s), volleyball W(s). *Intramural sports:* basketball M/W, football M, golf M/W, soccer M/W, softball M/W, tennis M/W, ultimate Frisbee M/W, volleyball M/W.

Costs (2007–08) *Tuition:* state resident $2292 full-time; nonresident $9024 full-time. *Required fees:* $442 full-time.

Financial Aid Of all full-time matriculated undergraduates, 100 Federal Work-Study jobs (averaging $2700). 20 state and other part-time jobs (averaging $2700).

Applying *Options:* electronic application, early admission, deferred entrance. *Application fee:* $35. *Required:* high school transcript. *Application deadline:* rolling (freshmen). *Notification:* continuous (transfers).

Freshmen Application Contact Ms. Darla Rollins, Admissions Coordinator, Dixie State College of Utah, 225 South 700 East Street, St. George, UT 84770-3876. *Phone:* 435-652-7702. *Toll-free phone:* 888-GO2DIXIE. *Fax:* 435-656-4005. *E-mail:* rollins@dixie.edu.

EVEREST COLLEGE

West Valley City, Utah   www.mwcollege.com/

Director of Admissions Mr. Jason Peterson, Director of Admissions, Everest College, 3280 West 3500 South, West Valley City, UT 84119. *Phone:* 801-840-4800. *Toll-free phone:* 888-741-4271. *Fax:* 801-485-0057. *E-mail:* jasonp@cci.edu.

ITT TECHNICAL INSTITUTE

Murray, Utah   www.itt-tech.edu/

- **Proprietary** primarily 2-year, founded 1984, part of ITT Educational Services, Inc
- **Suburban** 3-acre campus with easy access to Salt Lake City
- **Coed**

Majors Animation, interactive technology, video graphics and special effects; CAD/CADD drafting/design technology; computer and information systems security; computer engineering technology; computer software technology; computer systems networking and telecommunications; construction management; criminal justice/law enforcement administration; electrical, electronic and communications engineering technology; graphic design; health information/medical records technology; web/multimedia management and webmaster; web page, digital/multimedia and information resources design.

Academics *Calendar:* quarters. *Degrees:* associate and bachelor's.

Library a Web page.

Student Life *Housing:* college housing not available.

Standardized Tests *Required:* Wonderlic aptitude test (for admission).

Costs (2006–07) *Tuition:* Contact school for program costs.

Applying *Options:* deferred entrance. *Application fee:* $100. *Required:* high school transcript, interview. *Recommended:* letters of recommendation. *Application deadlines:* rolling (freshmen), rolling (transfers). *Notification:* continuous (freshmen), continuous (transfers).

Freshmen Application Contact Gabrielle Roh, Director of Recruitment, ITT Technical Institute, 920 West Levoy Drive, Murray, UT 84123. *Phone:* 801-263-3313. *Toll-free phone:* 800-365-2136.

LDS BUSINESS COLLEGE

Salt Lake City, Utah   www.ldsbc.edu/

- **Independent** 2-year, founded 1886, affiliated with The Church of Jesus Christ of Latter-day Saints, part of Latter-day Saints Church Educational System
- **Urban** campus
- **Coed,** 1,317 undergraduate students, 77% full-time, 54% women, 46% men

Undergraduates 1,015 full-time, 302 part-time. Students come from 40 states and territories, 50 other countries, 53% are from out of state, 0.5% African American, 1% Asian American or Pacific Islander, 5% Hispanic American, 0.3% Native American, 22% international, 13% live on campus.

Freshmen *Admission:* 650 applied, 550 admitted, 339 enrolled.

Faculty *Total:* 102, 21% full-time, 3% with terminal degrees. *Student/faculty ratio:* 20:1.

Majors Accounting; accounting and business/management; accounting technology and bookkeeping; administrative assistant and secretarial science; computer and information sciences and support services related; entrepreneurship; executive assistant/executive secretary; health information/medical records administration; information technology; interior design; legal administrative assistant/secretary; liberal arts and sciences/liberal studies; medical administrative assistant and medical secretary; medical/clinical assistant; medical insurance coding; medical office assistant; medical transcription; sales, distribution and marketing; system, networking, and LAN/WAN management; web page, digital/multimedia and information resources design.

Academics *Calendar:* semesters. *Degree:* certificates and associate. *Special study options:* academic remediation for entering students, adult/continuing education programs, advanced placement credit, internships, part-time degree program, summer session for credit. *ROTC:* Air Force (c).

Library LDS Business College Library with 24,000 titles, 130 serial subscriptions, an OPAC, a Web page.

Student Life *Housing Options:* men-only, women-only. Campus housing is university owned. *Activities and Organizations:* student-run newspaper, choral group, Institute Women's Association, Institute Men's Association. *Campus security:* 24-hour emergency response devices and patrols.

Standardized Tests *Recommended:* SAT or ACT (for admission).

Costs (2007–08) *Comprehensive fee:* $7180 includes full-time tuition ($2600) and room and board ($4580). Part-time tuition: $108 per credit hour.

Applying *Options:* electronic application, early admission, deferred entrance. *Application fee:* $25. *Required:* high school transcript, interview. *Application deadlines:* rolling (freshmen), rolling (transfers).

Freshmen Application Contact Mr. Matt D. Tittle, Assistant Dean of Students, LDS Business College, 411 East South Temple, Salt Lake City, UT 84111-1392. *Phone:* 801-524-8146. *Toll-free phone:* 800-999-5767. *Fax:* 801-524-1900. *E-mail:* md-tittle@ldsbc.edu.

PROVO COLLEGE

Provo, Utah   www.provocollege.edu/

- **Proprietary** 2-year, founded 1984
- **Coed,** 656 undergraduate students

Majors Accounting technology and bookkeeping; business administration, management and operations related; business operations support and secretarial services related; commercial and advertising art; computer and information sciences related; computer programming related; criminal justice/law enforcement administration; dental assisting; hospitality administration related; massage therapy; medical/clinical assistant; nursing (registered nurse training); physical therapist assistant.

Academics *Degree:* associate.

Costs (2006–07) *Tuition:* $8542 full-time.

Applying *Application fee:* $25.

Director of Admissions Mr. Gordon Peters, College Director, Provo College, 1450 West 820 North, Provo, UT 84601. *Phone:* 801-375-1861. *Toll-free phone:* 877-777-5886. *Fax:* 801-375-9728. *E-mail:* gordonp@provocollege.org.

SALT LAKE COMMUNITY COLLEGE

Salt Lake City, Utah   www.slcc.edu/

- **State-supported** 2-year, founded 1948, part of Utah System of Higher Education
- **Urban** 114-acre campus
- **Endowment** $5.8 million
- **Coed,** 24,241 undergraduate students, 33% full-time, 49% women, 51% men

Undergraduates 7,915 full-time, 16,326 part-time. 5% are from out of state, 2% African American, 4% Asian American or Pacific Islander, 8% Hispanic American, 1% Native American, 1% international, 6% transferred in.

Freshmen *Admission:* 8,665 applied, 8,665 admitted, 3,707 enrolled.

Faculty *Total:* 1,407, 25% full-time. *Student/faculty ratio:* 18:1.

Majors Accounting; airline pilot and flight crew; architectural engineering technology; autobody/collision and repair technology; avionics maintenance technology; biology/biological sciences; biology/biotechnology laboratory technician; business administration and management; chemistry; clinical/medical laboratory technology; computer and information sciences; computer science; construction management; cosmetology; criminal justice/law enforcement administration; dental hygiene; diesel mechanics technology; drafting and design technology; economics; electrical, electronic and communications engineering technology; engineering; engineering technology; English; environmental engineering technology; finance and financial management services related; general studies; graphic design; health science; heating, air conditioning, ventilation and refrigeration maintenance technology; heavy equipment maintenance technology; history; human development and family studies; humanities; industrial radiologic technology; information science/studies; information technology; instrumentation technology; international/global studies; international relations and affairs; kinesiology and exercise science; legal assistant/paralegal; marketing/marketing management; mass communication/media; medical/clinical assistant; music; nursing (registered nurse training); occupational therapist assistant; photographic and film/video technology; physical sciences; physical therapist assistant; physics; political science and government; psychology; quality control technology; radiologic technology/science; radio/television broadcasting technology; sign language interpretation and translation; social work; sociology; survey technology; teacher assistant/aide; telecommunications technology; welding technology.

Academics *Calendar:* semesters. *Degree:* certificates, diplomas, and associate. *Special study options:* academic remediation for entering students, advanced placement credit, cooperative education, distance learning, double majors, English as a second language, internships, part-time degree program, services for LD students, student-designed majors, study abroad, summer session for credit. *ROTC:* Army (c), Air Force (c).

Salt Lake Community College (continued)

Library Markosian Library plus 2 others with 96,470 titles, 781 serial subscriptions, 29,810 audiovisual materials, an OPAC, a Web page.

Student Life *Housing:* college housing not available. *Activities and Organizations:* drama/theater group, student-run newspaper, radio and television station, choral group, LDSSA, VICA, Phi Theta Kappa, PBL, Student Nurse Alliance. *Campus security:* 24-hour emergency response devices and patrols, late-night transport/escort service. *Student services:* health clinic, personal/psychological counseling.

Athletics Member NJCAA. *Intercollegiate sports:* baseball M(s), basketball M(s)/W(s), cheerleading M(s)/W(s), soccer M(c)/W(c), softball W(s), volleyball W(s).

Costs (2006–07) *Tuition:* state resident $2046 full-time; nonresident $7161 full-time. *Required fees:* $358 full-time.

Applying *Options:* electronic application, early admission, deferred entrance. *Application fee:* $35. *Application deadlines:* rolling (freshmen), rolling (transfers).

Freshmen Application Contact Mr. Andy Young, Director of Student Orientation, Salt Lake Community College, Salt Lake City, UT 84130. *Phone:* 801-957-4433. *E-mail:* andy.young@slcc.edu.

SNOW COLLEGE

Ephraim, Utah www.snow.edu/

- **State-supported** 2-year, founded 1888, part of Utah System of Higher Education
- **Rural** 50-acre campus
- **Endowment** $5.8 million
- **Coed**

Undergraduates 2,463 full-time, 870 part-time. Students come from 34 states and territories, 15 other countries, 8% are from out of state, 0.4% African American, 2% Asian American or Pacific Islander, 2% Hispanic American, 1% Native American, 2% international, 1% transferred in, 10% live on campus. *Retention:* 92% of 2003 full-time freshmen returned.

Faculty *Student/faculty ratio:* 13:1.

Academics *Calendar:* semesters. *Degree:* certificates, diplomas, and associate. *Special study options:* academic remediation for entering students, adult/continuing education programs, advanced placement credit, cooperative education, English as a second language, external degree program, honors programs, independent study, part-time degree program, services for LD students, summer session for credit.

Student Life *Campus security:* student patrols.

Athletics Member NJCAA.

Costs (2006–07) *Tuition:* state resident $1784 full-time, $73 per credit hour part-time; nonresident $7118 full-time, $297 per credit hour part-time. Full-time tuition and fees vary according to class time, course load, location, and program. Part-time tuition and fees vary according to class time, course load, location, and program. *Required fees:* $380 full-time, $380 per term part-time. *Room and board:* $4500; room only: $900. Room and board charges vary according to board plan and housing facility.

Financial Aid Of all full-time matriculated undergraduates, 127 Federal Work-Study jobs (averaging $1063).

Applying *Options:* early admission. *Application fee:* $30. *Required:* high school transcript.

Freshmen Application Contact Mr. Brach Schleuter, Dean of Students, Snow College, 150 East College Avenue, Ephraim, UT 84627. *Phone:* 435-283-7151. *Fax:* 435-283-6879. *E-mail:* snowcollege@snow.edu.

STEVENS-HENAGER COLLEGE

Ogden, Utah www.stevenshenager.edu/

Freshmen Application Contact Admissions Office, Stevens-Henager College, PO Box 9428, Ogden, UT 84409. *Phone:* 801-394-7791. *Toll-free phone:* 800-371-7791.

UTAH CAREER COLLEGE

West Jordan, Utah www.utahcollege.edu/

- **Proprietary** 2-year
- **Suburban** 1-acre campus with easy access to Salt Lake City
- **Coed**
- 100% of applicants were admitted

Undergraduates 152 full-time, 418 part-time. Students come from 2 states and territories, 1% are from out of state, 1% Asian American or Pacific Islander, 6% Hispanic American, 0.7% Native American.

Faculty *Student/faculty ratio:* 12:1.

Academics *Calendar:* quarters. *Degree:* certificates, diplomas, and associate.

Costs (2006–07) *Tuition:* $12,060 full-time, $335 per credit part-time.

Applying *Required:* high school transcript, interview.

Freshmen Application Contact Ms. Karma Cooper, Director of Admissions, Utah Career College, 1902 West 7800 South, West Jordan, UT 84088. *Phone:* 801-304-4224 Ext. 158. *Toll-free phone:* 866-304-4224. *Fax:* 801-304-4229. *E-mail:* kcooper@utahcollege.edu.

VERMONT

COMMUNITY COLLEGE OF VERMONT

Waterbury, Vermont www.ccv.edu/

- **State-supported** 2-year, founded 1970, part of Vermont State Colleges System
- **Rural** campus
- **Coed,** 6,048 undergraduate students, 17% full-time, 70% women, 30% men

Undergraduates 1,041 full-time, 5,007 part-time. Students come from 16 states and territories, 14 other countries, 3% are from out of state, 2% African American, 1% Asian American or Pacific Islander, 1% Hispanic American, 0.9% Native American, 0.5% international.

Freshmen *Admission:* 602 applied, 602 admitted.

Faculty *Total:* 635. *Student/faculty ratio:* 13:1.

Majors Accounting; administrative assistant and secretarial science; business administration and management; child development; community organization and advocacy; computer science; data entry/microcomputer applications; developmental and child psychology; education; human services; industrial technology; information technology; liberal arts and sciences/liberal studies; social sciences; teacher assistant/aide.

Academics *Calendar:* semesters. *Degree:* certificates, diplomas, and associate. *Special study options:* academic remediation for entering students, accelerated degree program, adult/continuing education programs, cooperative education, distance learning, double majors, English as a second language, external degree program, independent study, internships, part-time degree program, services for LD students, student-designed majors, summer session for credit.

Library Hartness Library with an OPAC.

Student Life *Housing:* college housing not available.

Costs (2007–08) *Tuition:* state resident $4420 full-time, $180 per course part-time; nonresident $8840 full-time, $360 per course part-time.

Financial Aid Of all full-time matriculated undergraduates, 35 Federal Work-Study jobs (averaging $2000).

Applying *Application deadlines:* rolling (freshmen), rolling (transfers).

Director of Admissions Ms. Susan Henry, Dean of Administration, Community College of Vermont, PO Box 120, Waterbury, VT 05676-0120. *Phone:* 802-865-4422.

LANDMARK COLLEGE

Putney, Vermont www.landmark.edu/

- **Independent** 2-year, founded 1983
- **Rural** 125-acre campus
- **Endowment** $10.3 million
- **Coed,** 460 undergraduate students, 67% full-time, 27% women, 73% men

Undergraduates 309 full-time, 151 part-time. Students come from 43 states and territories, 7 other countries, 96% are from out of state, 4% African American, 2% Asian American or Pacific Islander, 4% Hispanic American, 3% international, 15% transferred in, 97% live on campus.

Freshmen *Admission:* 310 applied, 224 admitted, 106 enrolled.

Faculty *Total:* 98, 97% full-time, 8% with terminal degrees. *Student/faculty ratio:* 5:1.

Majors Liberal arts and sciences/liberal studies.

Academics *Calendar:* semesters. *Degree:* associate. *Special study options:* academic remediation for entering students, adult/continuing education programs, advanced placement credit, services for LD students, study abroad, summer session for credit.

Library Landmark College Library with 31,371 titles, 174 serial subscriptions, 1,880 audiovisual materials, an OPAC, a Web page.

Student Life *Housing:* on-campus residence required for freshman year. *Options:* coed, disabled students. Campus housing is university owned. Freshman campus housing is guaranteed. *Activities and Organizations:* drama/theater group, choral group, Student Government Association, Campus Activities Board, Phi Theta Kappa Honor Society, Jazz Band Club, Cultural Diversity Club. *Campus security:* 24-hour emergency response devices and patrols, controlled dormitory access. *Student services:* health clinic, personal/psychological counseling, women's center.

Athletics *Intercollegiate sports:* baseball M(c), basketball M(c)/W(c), cross-country running M(c)/W(c), rock climbing M(c)/W(c), soccer M(c)/W(c), softball W(c). *Intramural sports:* badminton M/W, fencing M/W, golf M/W, ice hockey M/W, skiing (cross-country) M/W, soccer M/W, softball W, tennis M/W, volleyball M/W.

Standardized Tests *Required:* Wechsler Adult Intelligence Scale III and Nelson Denny Reading Test (for admission).

Costs (2007–08) *Comprehensive fee:* $48,860 includes full-time tuition ($40,500), mandatory fees ($860), and room and board ($7500). *Room and board:* college room only: $3750.

Financial Aid Of all full-time matriculated undergraduates, 80 Federal Work-Study jobs (averaging $1200).

Applying *Options:* deferred entrance. *Application fee:* $75. *Required:* essay or personal statement, high school transcript, 2 letters of recommendation, interview, diagnosis of LD and/or AD/HD. *Application deadlines:* rolling (freshmen), rolling (transfers). *Notification:* continuous (freshmen), continuous (transfers).

Freshmen Application Contact Admissions Main Desk, Landmark College, 1 River Road South, Putney, VT 05346. *Phone:* 802-387-6718. *Fax:* 802-387-6868. *E-mail:* admissions@landmark.edu.

▶**See page 556 for the College Close-Up.**

NEW ENGLAND CULINARY INSTITUTE

Montpelier, Vermont   www.neci.edu/

- **Proprietary** primarily 2-year, founded 1980
- **Small-town** campus
- **Endowment** $291,550
- **Coed,** 569 undergraduate students, 100% full-time, 38% women, 62% men

Undergraduates 569 full-time. 80% live on campus.

Freshmen *Admission:* 376 applied, 346 admitted.

Faculty *Total:* 85, 82% full-time. *Student/faculty ratio:* 8:1.

Majors Baking and pastry arts; culinary arts; hotel/motel administration; restaurant, culinary, and catering management.

Academics *Calendar:* quarters. *Degrees:* certificates, associate, and bachelor's. *Special study options:* accelerated degree program, advanced placement credit, cooperative education, distance learning, honors programs, independent study, internships, services for LD students.

Library New England Culinary Institute Library with 2,400 titles, 30 serial subscriptions, an OPAC.

Student Life *Housing Options:* coed, men-only, women-only. Campus housing is university owned and leased by the school. *Activities and Organizations:* student-run newspaper, American Culinary Federation, Toastmasters, Ice Carving Club. *Campus security:* 24-hour emergency response devices, student patrols, Mod patrols in the evening. *Student services:* personal/psychological counseling.

Costs (2007–08) *Comprehensive fee:* $32,017 includes full-time tuition ($24,788), mandatory fees ($664), and room and board ($6565).

Financial Aid Of all full-time matriculated undergraduates, 320 Federal Work-Study jobs (averaging $1000).

Applying *Options:* electronic application, early admission, deferred entrance. *Required:* essay or personal statement, high school transcript, 1 letter of recommendation, minimum TOEFL scores for foreign students. *Required for some:* letters of recommendation, interview. *Application deadline:* rolling (freshmen).

Freshmen Application Contact Dawn Hayward, Admissions Project Manager, New England Culinary Institute, 250 Main Street, Montpelier, VT 05602. *Toll-free phone:* 877-223-6324. *Fax:* 802-225-3280. *E-mail:* info@neci.edu.

NEW ENGLAND CULINARY INSTITUTE AT ESSEX

Essex Junction, Vermont   www.neci.edu/

- **Proprietary** primarily 2-year, founded 1989
- **Endowment** $336,943
- **Coed**
- 78% of applicants were admitted

Undergraduates 501 full-time. 72% are from out of state, 2% African American, 3% Asian American or Pacific Islander, 2% Hispanic American, 0.6% Native American.

Academics *Calendar:* quarters. *Degrees:* certificates, diplomas, associate, and bachelor's.

Costs (2006–07) *Comprehensive fee:* $31,750 includes full-time tuition ($23,835), mandatory fees ($1350), and room and board ($6565).

Applying *Required:* essay or personal statement, high school transcript, 1 letter of recommendation, interview, minimum TOEFL scores for foreign students. *Required for some:* 2 letters of recommendation.

Freshmen Application Contact Sherri Gilmore, Director of Admissions, New England Culinary Institute at Essex, 48 1/2 Park Street, Essex Junction, VT 05452. *Phone:* 802-223-6324. *Fax:* 802-225-3280. *E-mail:* sherrigilmore@neci.edu.

VIRGINIA

ACT COLLEGE

Arlington, Virginia   www.healthtraining.com/

- **Proprietary** 2-year, founded 1983
- **Coed,** 482 undergraduate students

Majors Allied health diagnostic, intervention, and treatment professions related; medical/clinical assistant; radiologic technology/science.

Academics *Degree:* diplomas and associate.

Costs (2006–07) *Tuition:* $11,200 per degree program part-time.

Applying *Application fee:* $50.

Freshmen Application Contact Admissions Office, ACT College, 1100 Wilson Boulevard, Suite M780, Arlington, VA 22209-2297.

ADVANCED TECHNOLOGY INSTITUTE

Virginia Beach, Virginia   www.auto.edu/

- **Proprietary** 2-year
- **Coed,** 697 undergraduate students
- 75% of applicants were admitted

Freshmen *Admission:* 403 applied, 302 admitted.

Majors Automobile/automotive mechanics technology; heating, air conditioning, ventilation and refrigeration maintenance technology.

Academics *Degree:* certificates and associate.

Costs (2006–07) *Tuition:* $10,425 full-time.

Applying *Application fee:* $50.

Freshmen Application Contact Admissions Office, Advanced Technology Institute, 5700 Southern Boulevard, Suite 100, Virginia Beach, VA 23462. *Phone:* 757-490-1241.

AVIATION INSTITUTE OF MAINTENANCE—MANASSAS

Manassas, Virginia   www.aviationmaintenance.edu/aviation-washington-dc.asp

- **Proprietary** 2-year

Academics *Calendar:* quarters. *Degree:* certificates and associate.

Aviation Institute of Maintenance–Manassas (continued)

Applying *Application fee:* $25. *Required:* High School Diploma or GED.

Freshmen Application Contact Washington, DC School Director, Aviation Institute of Maintenance–Manassas, 9821 Godwin Drive, Manassas, VA 20110. *Phone:* 703-257-5515. *Toll-free phone:* 877-604-2121. *Fax:* 703-257-5523. *E-mail:* directoramm@tidetech.com.

AVIATION INSTITUTE OF MAINTENANCE—VIRGINIA BEACH

Virginia Beach, Virginia   www.aviationmaintenance.edu/
aviation-norfolk.asp

- **Proprietary** 2-year

Academics *Calendar:* quarters. *Degree:* certificates and associate.

Applying *Application fee:* $25. *Required:* High school diploma or GED.

Freshmen Application Contact Virginia Beach School Director, Aviation Institute of Maintenance–Virginia Beach, 1429 Miller Store Road, Virginia Beach, VA 23455. *Phone:* 757-363-2121. *Toll-free phone:* 888-349-5387. *Fax:* 757-363-2044. *E-mail:* directoramn@tidetech.com.

BETA TECH

Richmond, Virginia   www.betatech.edu/

- **Proprietary** 2-year
- 306 undergraduate students

Majors Massage therapy; paralegal/legal assistant; system, networking, and LAN/WAN management.

Academics *Degree:* certificates and associate.

Costs (2006–07) *Tuition:* $19,910 per degree program part-time.

Applying *Application fee:* $25.

Freshmen Application Contact Admissions Office, Beta Tech, 7914 Midlothian Turnpike, Richmond, VA 23235-5230. *E-mail:* directorbtr@tidetech.com.

BLUE RIDGE COMMUNITY COLLEGE

Weyers Cave, Virginia   www.brcc.edu/

- **State-supported** 2-year, founded 1967, part of Virginia Community College System
- **Rural** 65-acre campus
- **Endowment** $2.1 million
- **Coed**

Undergraduates 1,513 full-time, 2,291 part-time. Students come from 29 states and territories, 2 other countries, 2% are from out of state, 4% African American, 2% Asian American or Pacific Islander, 2% Hispanic American, 0.4% Native American, 42% transferred in. *Retention:* 41% of 2003 full-time freshmen returned.

Faculty *Student/faculty ratio:* 22:1.

Academics *Calendar:* semesters. *Degree:* certificates, diplomas, and associate. *Special study options:* academic remediation for entering students, adult/continuing education programs, advanced placement credit, cooperative education, distance learning, double majors, English as a second language, honors programs, internships, off-campus study, part-time degree program, services for LD students, study abroad, summer session for credit.

Student Life *Campus security:* 24-hour emergency response devices and patrols, late-night transport/escort service.

Costs (2006–07) *Tuition:* state resident $2175 full-time, $71 per credit hour part-time; nonresident $7060 full-time, $235 per credit hour part-time. *Required fees:* $159 full-time, $5 per credit hour part-time.

Financial Aid Of all full-time matriculated undergraduates, 25 Federal Work-Study jobs (averaging $1582).

Applying *Options:* electronic application, early admission. *Required for some:* high school transcript, interview.

Freshmen Application Contact Ms. Mary Wayland, Dean of Admissions and Records, Blue Ridge Community College, PO Box 80, Weyers Cave, VA 24486-0080. *Phone:* 540-453-2332. *E-mail:* waylandm@brcc.edu.

BRYANT AND STRATTON COLLEGE, RICHMOND

Richmond, Virginia   www.bryantstratton.edu/

- **Proprietary** primarily 2-year, founded 1952, part of Bryant and Stratton Business Institute, Inc
- **Suburban** campus
- **Coed**

Undergraduates 137 full-time, 284 part-time. Students come from 1 other state, 71% African American, 0.5% Asian American or Pacific Islander, 3% Hispanic American, 1% Native American.

Faculty *Student/faculty ratio:* 10:1.

Academics *Calendar:* semesters. *Degrees:* associate and bachelor's. *Special study options:* academic remediation for entering students, adult/continuing education programs, advanced placement credit, distance learning, double majors, independent study, internships, part-time degree program, summer session for credit.

Student Life *Campus security:* late-night transport/escort service.

Standardized Tests *Required:* TABE, CPAt (for admission). *Recommended:* SAT or ACT (for admission).

Costs (2006–07) *Tuition:* $19,620 full-time, $436 per credit hour part-time. Full-time tuition and fees vary according to degree level. Part-time tuition and fees vary according to course load. *Required fees:* $25 full-time.

Applying *Options:* deferred entrance. *Required:* high school transcript, interview, entrance evaluation and placement evaluation. *Required for some:* letters of recommendation.

Freshmen Application Contact Mr. David K. Mayle, Director of Admissions, Bryant and Stratton College, Richmond, 8141 Hull Street Road, Richmond, VA 23235-6411. *Phone:* 804-745-2444. *Fax:* 804-745-6884. *E-mail:* tlawson@bryanstratton.edu.

BRYANT AND STRATTON COLLEGE, VIRGINIA BEACH

Virginia Beach, Virginia   www.bryantstratton.edu/

Director of Admissions Mr. Greg Smith, Director of Admissions, Bryant and Stratton College, Virginia Beach, 301 Centre Pointe Drive, Virginia Beach, VA 23462-4417. *Phone:* 757-499-7900.

CENTRAL VIRGINIA COMMUNITY COLLEGE

Lynchburg, Virginia   www.cvcc.vccs.edu/

- **State-supported** 2-year, founded 1966, part of Virginia Community College System
- **Suburban** 104-acre campus
- **Endowment** $1.7 million
- **Coed,** 4,741 undergraduate students

Undergraduates Students come from 11 states and territories, 1% are from out of state.

Faculty *Total:* 173, 33% full-time.

Majors Accounting; administrative assistant and secretarial science; architectural engineering technology; biological and physical sciences; business administration and management; civil engineering technology; clinical/medical laboratory technology; commercial and advertising art; consumer merchandising/retailing management; criminal justice/law enforcement administration; drafting and design technology; education; electrical, electronic and communications engineering technology; engineering technology; finance; general studies; information science/studies; liberal arts and sciences/liberal studies; management information systems; marketing/marketing management; mechanical engineering/mechanical technology; radiologic technology/science; respiratory care therapy.

Academics *Calendar:* semesters. *Degree:* certificates, diplomas, and associate. *Special study options:* academic remediation for entering students, advanced placement credit, cooperative education, distance learning, independent study, internships, part-time degree program, services for LD students, summer session for credit.

Library Bedford Learning Resources Center with 37,000 titles, 230 serial subscriptions, an OPAC, a Web page.

Student Life *Housing:* college housing not available. *Activities and Organizations:* drama/theater group, student-run newspaper, Black Student Union, Data

Processing Management Association, Radiology Club, Phi Theta Kappa, Respiratory Club. *Campus security:* 24-hour emergency response devices. *Student services:* personal/psychological counseling.

Costs (2007–08) *Tuition:* state resident $2448 full-time, $82 per credit hour part-time; nonresident $7704 full-time, $257 per credit hour part-time.

Financial Aid Of all full-time matriculated undergraduates, 65 Federal Work-Study jobs (averaging $2700).

Applying *Options:* early admission, deferred entrance. *Required for some:* high school transcript, interview. *Application deadlines:* rolling (freshmen), rolling (transfers). *Notification:* continuous (freshmen), continuous (transfers).

Freshmen Application Contact Ms. Judy Wilhelm, Admissions, Central Virginia Community College, 3506 Wards Road, Lynchburg, VA 24502-2498. *Phone:* 434-832-7633. *Toll-free phone:* 800-562-3060. *Fax:* 434-832-7793.

DABNEY S. LANCASTER COMMUNITY COLLEGE

Clifton Forge, Virginia
www.dl.vccs.edu/

- **State-supported** 2-year, founded 1964, part of Virginia Community College System
- **Rural** 117-acre campus
- **Endowment** $3.3 million
- **Coed,** 1,453 undergraduate students

Undergraduates Students come from 5 states and territories, 4% are from out of state, 5% African American, 0.5% Asian American or Pacific Islander, 0.7% Hispanic American, 0.3% Native American.

Faculty *Total:* 95, 22% full-time. *Student/faculty ratio:* 15:1.

Majors Administrative assistant and secretarial science; biological and physical sciences; business administration and management; computer programming; criminal justice/law enforcement administration; data processing and data processing technology; drafting and design technology; education; electrical, electronic and communications engineering technology; forestry technology; information science/studies; legal administrative assistant/secretary; liberal arts and sciences/liberal studies; mechanical design technology; medical administrative assistant and medical secretary; nursing (registered nurse training); wood science and wood products/pulp and paper technology.

Academics *Calendar:* semesters. *Degree:* certificates, diplomas, and associate. *Special study options:* academic remediation for entering students, adult/continuing education programs, advanced placement credit, cooperative education, distance learning, honors programs, independent study, internships, part-time degree program, study abroad, summer session for credit.

Library Scott Hall plus 1 other with 37,716 titles, 376 serial subscriptions, an OPAC.

Student Life *Housing:* college housing not available. *Activities and Organizations:* drama/theater group. *Campus security:* 24-hour emergency response devices. *Student services:* personal/psychological counseling.

Athletics *Intercollegiate sports:* basketball M. *Intramural sports:* basketball M/W, bowling M/W, equestrian sports M/W, football M/W, golf M/W, skiing (downhill) M/W, soccer M/W, tennis M/W, volleyball M/W.

Costs (2007–08) *Tuition:* state resident $73 per credit part-time; nonresident $235 per credit part-time. *Required fees:* $4 per credit part-time.

Applying *Options:* early admission, deferred entrance. *Recommended:* interview. *Application deadlines:* rolling (freshmen), rolling (transfers). *Notification:* continuous (freshmen), continuous (transfers).

Freshmen Application Contact Ms. Kathy Nicely, Registration Specialist, Dabney S. Lancaster Community College, 100 Dabney Drive, PO Box 1000, Clifton Forge, VA 24422. *Phone:* 540-863-2815. *E-mail:* knicely@dslcc.edu.

DANVILLE COMMUNITY COLLEGE

Danville, Virginia
www.dcc.vccs.edu/

- **State-supported** 2-year, founded 1967, part of Virginia Community College System
- **Urban** 76-acre campus
- **Coed,** 3,884 undergraduate students

Undergraduates Students come from 9 states and territories, 3 other countries, 2% are from out of state, 35% African American, 0.4% Asian American or Pacific Islander, 0.6% Hispanic American, 0.4% Native American. *Retention:* 100% of 2003 full-time freshmen returned.

Faculty *Total:* 201, 26% full-time. *Student/faculty ratio:* 19:1.

Majors Accounting; administrative assistant and secretarial science; biological and physical sciences; business administration and management; computer

programming; education; engineering technology; liberal arts and sciences/liberal studies; marketing/marketing management.

Academics *Calendar:* semesters. *Degree:* certificates, diplomas, and associate. *Special study options:* academic remediation for entering students, adult/continuing education programs, advanced placement credit, cooperative education, distance learning, honors programs, part-time degree program, summer session for credit.

Library Learning Resource Center with 41,600 titles, 345 serial subscriptions, an OPAC, a Web page.

Student Life *Housing:* college housing not available. *Campus security:* 24-hour patrols.

Athletics *Intramural sports:* basketball M/W, bowling M/W, football M, golf M, softball M/W, volleyball M/W.

Standardized Tests *Required for some:* ACT ASSET.

Costs (2006–07) *Tuition:* state resident $2300 full-time, $77 per credit hour part-time; nonresident $7251 full-time, $241 per credit hour part-time. *Required fees:* $249 full-time, $4 per credit hour part-time.

Financial Aid Of all full-time matriculated undergraduates, 40 Federal Work-Study jobs (averaging $1700).

Applying *Options:* early admission, deferred entrance. *Required:* high school transcript. *Application deadlines:* rolling (freshmen), rolling (transfers). *Notification:* continuous (freshmen), continuous (transfers).

Director of Admissions Mr. Peter Castiglione, Director of Student Development and Enrollment Management, Danville Community College, 1008 South Main Street, Danville, VA 24541-4088. *Phone:* 434-797-8490. *Toll-free phone:* 800-560-4291.

EASTERN SHORE COMMUNITY COLLEGE

Melfa, Virginia
www.es.cc.va.us/

- **State-supported** 2-year, founded 1971, part of Virginia Community College System
- **Rural** 117-acre campus
- **Coed,** 807 undergraduate students, 32% full-time, 72% women, 28% men

Undergraduates 260 full-time, 547 part-time. 44% African American, 0.7% Asian American or Pacific Islander, 1% Hispanic American. *Retention:* 36% of 2003 full-time freshmen returned.

Freshmen *Admission:* 390 applied, 322 admitted. *Average high school GPA:* 2.6.

Faculty *Total:* 57, 32% full-time, 7% with terminal degrees. *Student/faculty ratio:* 13:1.

Majors Administrative assistant and secretarial science; biological and physical sciences; business administration and management; computer/information technology services administration related; computer/technical support; education; electrical, electronic and communications engineering technology; liberal arts and sciences/liberal studies; nursing (registered nurse training).

Academics *Calendar:* semesters. *Degree:* certificates and associate. *Special study options:* academic remediation for entering students, adult/continuing education programs, advanced placement credit, cooperative education, distance learning, English as a second language, off-campus study, part-time degree program, services for LD students, summer session for credit.

Library Learning Resources Center with 20,479 titles, 95 serial subscriptions, an OPAC, a Web page.

Student Life *Housing:* college housing not available. *Campus security:* night security guard. *Student services:* personal/psychological counseling.

Standardized Tests *Required:* COMPASS (for admission).

Costs (2007–08) *Tuition:* state resident $2146 full-time; nonresident $6590 full-time. *Required fees:* $110 full-time.

Financial Aid Of all full-time matriculated undergraduates, 11 Federal Work-Study jobs.

Applying *Required:* high school transcript. *Application deadlines:* rolling (freshmen), rolling (transfers). *Notification:* continuous (freshmen), continuous (transfers).

Freshmen Application Contact P. Bryan Smith, Dean of Student Services, Eastern Shore Community College, 29300 Lankford Highway, Melfa, VA 23410. *Phone:* 757-789-1732. *Toll-free phone:* 877-871-8455. *Fax:* 757-789-1737. *E-mail:* bsmith@es.vccs.edu.

ECPI COLLEGE OF TECHNOLOGY

Virginia Beach, Virginia
www.ecpi.edu/

- **Proprietary** primarily 2-year, founded 1966
- **Suburban** 8-acre campus
- **Coed,** 6,501 undergraduate students, 97% full-time, 57% women, 43% men

ECPI College of Technology (continued)

Undergraduates 6,320 full-time, 181 part-time. Students come from 6 states and territories, 10% are from out of state, 44% African American, 3% Asian American or Pacific Islander, 4% Hispanic American, 0.4% Native American. *Retention:* 70% of 2003 full-time freshmen returned.

Freshmen *Admission:* 1,455 applied, 917 admitted, 917 enrolled.

Faculty *Total:* 460, 51% full-time. *Student/faculty ratio:* 15:1.

Majors Accounting; biomedical technology; business machine repair; communications technology; computer and information sciences; computer engineering technology; computer management; computer programming; computer science; computer typography and composition equipment operation; data processing and data processing technology; electrical, electronic and communications engineering technology; electromechanical technology; engineering technology; health/health care administration; health information/medical records administration; information science/studies; mechanical engineering/mechanical technology; medical administrative assistant and medical secretary; telecommunications.

Academics *Calendar:* trimesters. *Degrees:* certificates, diplomas, associate, and bachelor's. *Special study options:* academic remediation for entering students, accelerated degree program, adult/continuing education programs, advanced placement credit, distance learning, double majors, freshman honors college, honors programs, independent study, internships, off-campus study, part-time degree program, study abroad, summer session for credit.

Library ECPI-Virginia Beach Library with an OPAC, a Web page.

Student Life *Housing Options:* Campus housing is provided by a third party. *Activities and Organizations:* SETA, IEEE, NVTHS, ITE, Accounting Society, national fraternities, national sororities. *Campus security:* building and parking lot security. *Student services:* personal/psychological counseling.

Standardized Tests *Recommended:* SAT or ACT (for admission), SAT Subject Tests (for admission).

Costs (2006–07) *Tuition:* $9750 full-time.

Financial Aid Of all full-time matriculated undergraduates, 80 Federal Work-Study jobs (averaging $2000).

Applying *Options:* electronic application, deferred entrance. *Application fee:* $100. *Required:* high school transcript, interview. *Notification:* continuous (freshmen), continuous (transfers).

Freshmen Application Contact Mr. Ronald Ballance, Vice President, ECPI College of Technology, 5555 Greenwich Road, Suite 100, Virginia Beach, VA 23462. *Phone:* 757-671-7171. *Toll-free phone:* 800-986-1200. *Fax:* 757-671-8661. *E-mail:* rballance@ecpi.edu.

ECPI TECHNICAL COLLEGE

Richmond, Virginia www.ecpitech.edu/

- **Proprietary** primarily 2-year, founded 1966
- **Urban** campus
- **Coed,** 869 undergraduate students, 100% full-time, 33% women, 67% men

Undergraduates 869 full-time. Students come from 2 states and territories, 1% are from out of state. *Retention:* 75% of 2003 full-time freshmen returned.

Freshmen *Admission:* 182 applied, 146 admitted, 116 enrolled.

Faculty *Total:* 46, 80% full-time. *Student/faculty ratio:* 18:1.

Majors Accounting; business machine repair; communications technology; computer and information sciences; computer and information sciences related; computer and information systems security; computer management; computer programming; computer science; computer technology/computer systems technology; computer typography and composition equipment operation; data entry/microcomputer applications; data processing and data processing technology; electrical, electronic and communications engineering technology; electromechanical technology; engineering technology; health/health care administration; health information/medical records administration; information science/studies; mechanical engineering/mechanical technology; medical administrative assistant and medical secretary; telecommunications; telecommunications technology; trade and industrial teacher education; web page, digital/multimedia and information resources design.

Academics *Calendar:* semesters. *Degrees:* certificates, diplomas, associate, and bachelor's. *Special study options:* adult/continuing education programs, advanced placement credit, freshman honors college, honors programs, internships, part-time degree program, summer session for credit.

Library ECPI-Richmond Library with 3,165 titles, 81 serial subscriptions, an OPAC, a Web page.

Student Life *Housing:* college housing not available. *Activities and Organizations:* Collegiate Secretaries International, Data Processing Management Association, Student Electronics Technicians Association, Future Office Assistants, National Vocational-Technical Honor Society. *Campus security:* building and parking lot security.

Standardized Tests *Recommended:* SAT (for admission), SAT Subject Tests (for admission).

Costs (2006–07) *Tuition:* $9750 full-time.

Financial Aid Of all full-time matriculated undergraduates, 40 Federal Work-Study jobs (averaging $2000).

Applying *Options:* deferred entrance. *Application fee:* $100. *Required:* high school transcript, interview. *Application deadlines:* rolling (freshmen), rolling (transfers). *Notification:* continuous (freshmen), continuous (transfers).

Freshmen Application Contact Director, ECPI Technical College, 800 Moorefield Park Drive, Richmond, VA 23236. *Phone:* 804-330-5533. *Toll-free phone:* 800-986-1200. *Fax:* 804-330-5577. *E-mail:* agerard@ecpi.edu.

ECPI TECHNICAL COLLEGE

Roanoke, Virginia www.ecpi.net/

- **Proprietary** primarily 2-year, founded 1966
- **Suburban** 3-acre campus
- **Coed,** 358 undergraduate students, 100% full-time, 54% women, 46% men

Undergraduates 358 full-time. Students come from 4 states and territories, 2% are from out of state, 27% African American, 0.8% Hispanic American, 0.3% Native American. *Retention:* 75% of 2003 full-time freshmen returned.

Freshmen *Admission:* 102 applied, 82 admitted, 65 enrolled.

Faculty *Total:* 24, 46% full-time. *Student/faculty ratio:* 15:1.

Majors Accounting; communications technology; computer and information sciences; computer and information sciences related; computer and information systems security; computer engineering technology; computer science; computer technology/computer systems technology; computer typography and composition equipment operation; data entry/microcomputer applications; electrical, electronic and communications engineering technology; electromechanical technology; engineering technology; health/health care administration; health information/medical records administration; information science/studies; mechanical engineering/mechanical technology; medical administrative assistant and medical secretary; medical/clinical assistant; telecommunications; telecommunications technology.

Academics *Calendar:* semesters. *Degrees:* certificates, diplomas, associate, and bachelor's. *Special study options:* academic remediation for entering students, accelerated degree program, adult/continuing education programs, advanced placement credit, distance learning, double majors, honors programs, independent study, internships, off-campus study, part-time degree program, study abroad, summer session for credit.

Library ECPI-Roanoke Library plus 1 other with 1,703 titles, 43 serial subscriptions, a Web page.

Student Life *Housing:* college housing not available. *Activities and Organizations:* SETA, NVTHS, SAFA, FOAMA, ITE. *Campus security:* building and parking lot security.

Standardized Tests *Recommended:* SAT (for admission), SAT Subject Tests (for admission), SAT and SAT Subject Tests (for admission).

Costs (2006–07) *Tuition:* $9750 full-time.

Financial Aid Of all full-time matriculated undergraduates, 20 Federal Work-Study jobs (averaging $2000).

Applying *Options:* electronic application, deferred entrance. *Application fee:* $100. *Required:* high school transcript, interview. *Application deadlines:* rolling (freshmen), rolling (transfers). *Notification:* continuous (freshmen), continuous (transfers).

Freshmen Application Contact Ms. Carol Rouch, Director, ECPI Technical College, 5234 Airport Road, Roanoke, VA 24012. *Phone:* 540-563-8080. *Toll-free phone:* 800-986-1200. *Fax:* 540-362-5400. *E-mail:* crouch@ecpi.edu.

EVEREST COLLEGE

Arlington, Virginia www.parks-college.com/

Director of Admissions Lachelle Green, Director of Admissions, Everest College, 801 North Quincy Street, Arlington, VA 22203. *Phone:* 703-248-8887. *Fax:* 703-351-2202. *E-mail:* lgreen@cci.edu.

GERMANNA COMMUNITY COLLEGE

Locust Grove, Virginia www.gcc.vccs.edu/

- **State-supported** 2-year, founded 1970, part of Virginia Community College System
- **Suburban** 100-acre campus with easy access to Washington, DC
- **Coed,** 5,167 undergraduate students, 31% full-time, 64% women, 36% men

Undergraduates 1,597 full-time, 3,570 part-time. 14% African American, 3% Asian American or Pacific Islander, 4% Hispanic American, 0.5% Native American.
Freshmen *Admission:* 1,040 applied, 1,040 admitted, 1,040 enrolled.
Faculty *Total:* 371, 15% full-time. *Student/faculty ratio:* 17:1.
Majors Biological and physical sciences; business administration and management; criminal justice/police science; dental hygiene; education; general studies; information technology; liberal arts and sciences/liberal studies; nursing (registered nurse training).
Academics *Calendar:* semesters. *Degree:* certificates and associate. *Special study options:* academic remediation for entering students, advanced placement credit, distance learning, double majors, English as a second language, independent study, off-campus study, part-time degree program, services for LD students, study abroad, summer session for credit.
Library Locust Grove Campus Library plus 2 others with 124,808 titles, 208 serial subscriptions, 2,382 audiovisual materials, an OPAC, a Web page.
Student Life *Housing:* college housing not available. *Activities and Organizations:* student-run newspaper, Student Nurses Association, Student Government Association, Phi Theta Kappa, Students Against Substance Abuse. *Campus security:* 24-hour patrols. *Student services:* personal/psychological counseling.
Athletics *Intramural sports:* archery M/W, basketball M/W, bowling M/W, football M/W, golf M/W, tennis M/W, volleyball M/W.
Costs (2007–08) *Tuition:* state resident $2457 full-time, $82 per credit part-time; nonresident $7112 full-time, $257 per credit part-time.
Financial Aid Of all full-time matriculated undergraduates, 35 Federal Work-Study jobs (averaging $1212). 15 state and other part-time jobs (averaging $1667).
Applying *Options:* early admission. *Required for some:* high school transcript. *Application deadlines:* rolling (freshmen), rolling (transfers). *Notification:* continuous (freshmen), continuous (transfers).
Freshmen Application Contact Ms. Rita Dunston, Registrar, Germanna Community College, 10000 Germanna Point Drive, Fredericksburg, VA 22408. *Phone:* 540-891-3020. *Fax:* 540-891-3092.

ITT TECHNICAL INSTITUTE
Chantilly, Virginia   www.itt-tech.edu/
- **Proprietary** primarily 2-year, founded 2002, part of ITT Educational Services, Inc
- **Coed**

Majors Animation, interactive technology, video graphics and special effects; business administration and management; CAD/CADD drafting/design technology; communications technology; computer and information systems security; computer engineering technology; computer software engineering; computer software technology; computer systems networking and telecommunications; criminal justice/law enforcement administration; electrical, electronic and communications engineering technology; web/multimedia management and webmaster; web page, digital/multimedia and information resources design.
Academics *Calendar:* quarters. *Degrees:* associate and bachelor's.
Library a Web page.
Student Life *Housing:* college housing not available.
Standardized Tests *Required:* (for admission).
Costs (2006–07) *Tuition:* Contact institute directly for program costs.
Applying *Options:* deferred entrance. *Application fee:* $100. *Required:* high school transcript, interview. *Recommended:* letters of recommendation. *Application deadlines:* rolling (freshmen), rolling (transfers). *Notification:* continuous (freshmen), continuous (transfers).
Freshmen Application Contact Ms. Peggy T. Payne, Director of Recruitment, ITT Technical Institute, 14420 Albemarle Point Place, Chantilly, VA 20151. *Phone:* 703-263-2541. *Toll-free phone:* 888-895-8324.

ITT TECHNICAL INSTITUTE
Norfolk, Virginia   www.itt-tech.edu/
- **Proprietary** primarily 2-year, founded 1988, part of ITT Educational Services, Inc
- **Suburban** 2-acre campus
- **Coed**

Majors Accounting technology and bookkeeping; animation, interactive technology, video graphics and special effects; business administration and management; CAD/CADD drafting/design technology; communications technology; computer and information systems security; computer engineering technology; computer software technology; criminal justice/law enforcement administration;
electrical, electronic and communications engineering technology; web/multimedia management and webmaster; web page, digital/multimedia and information resources design.
Academics *Calendar:* quarters. *Degrees:* associate and bachelor's.
Library a Web page.
Student Life *Housing:* college housing not available. *Activities and Organizations:* student-run newspaper.
Standardized Tests *Required:* Wonderlic aptitude test (for admission).
Costs (2006–07) *Tuition:* Contact school for program costs.
Financial Aid Of all full-time matriculated undergraduates, 3 Federal Work-Study jobs (averaging $5000).
Applying *Options:* deferred entrance. *Application fee:* $100. *Required:* high school transcript, interview. *Recommended:* letters of recommendation. *Application deadlines:* rolling (freshmen), rolling (transfers). *Notification:* continuous (freshmen), continuous (transfers).
Freshmen Application Contact Mr. Jack Keesee, Director of Recruitment, ITT Technical Institute, 863 Glenrock Road, Norfolk, VA 23502. *Phone:* 757-466-1260. *Toll-free phone:* 888-253-8324.

ITT TECHNICAL INSTITUTE
Richmond, Virginia   www.itt-tech.edu/
- **Proprietary** primarily 2-year, founded 1999, part of ITT Educational Services, Inc
- **Coed**

Majors Animation, interactive technology, video graphics and special effects; business administration and management; CAD/CADD drafting/design technology; computer and information systems security; computer engineering technology; computer software technology; computer systems networking and telecommunications; criminal justice/law enforcement administration; electrical, electronic and communications engineering technology; web/multimedia management and webmaster; web page, digital/multimedia and information resources design.
Academics *Calendar:* quarters. *Degrees:* associate and bachelor's.
Library a Web page.
Student Life *Housing:* college housing not available.
Standardized Tests *Required:* Wonderlic aptitude test (for admission).
Costs (2006–07) *Tuition:* Contact school for program costs.
Applying *Options:* deferred entrance. *Application fee:* $100. *Required:* high school transcript, interview. *Recommended:* letters of recommendation. *Application deadlines:* rolling (freshmen), rolling (transfers). *Notification:* continuous (freshmen), continuous (transfers).
Freshmen Application Contact Director of Recruitment, ITT Technical Institute, 300 Gateway Centre Parkway, Richmond, VA 23235. *Phone:* 804-330-4992. *Toll-free phone:* 888-330-4888.

ITT TECHNICAL INSTITUTE
Springfield, Virginia   www.itt-tech.edu/
- **Proprietary** primarily 2-year, founded 2002, part of ITT Educational Services, Inc
- **Coed**

Majors Business administration and management; CAD/CADD drafting/design technology; computer and information systems security; computer engineering technology; computer software technology; computer systems networking and telecommunications; criminal justice/law enforcement administration; electrical, electronic and communications engineering technology; web/multimedia management and webmaster; web page, digital/multimedia and information resources design.
Academics *Calendar:* quarters. *Degrees:* associate and bachelor's.
Library a Web page.
Student Life *Housing:* college housing not available.
Standardized Tests *Required:* Wonderlic aptitude test (for admission).
Costs (2006–07) *Tuition:* Contact institute directly for program costs.
Applying *Options:* deferred entrance. *Application fee:* $100. *Required:* high school transcript, interview. *Recommended:* letters of recommendation. *Application deadlines:* rolling (freshmen), rolling (transfers). *Notification:* continuous (freshmen), continuous (transfers).
Freshmen Application Contact Ms. Cheryl Painter, Director of Recruitment, ITT Technical Institute, 7300 Boston Boulevard, Springfield, VA 22153. *Phone:* 703-440-9535. *Toll-free phone:* 866-817-8324.

JOHN TYLER COMMUNITY COLLEGE
Chester, Virginia   www.jtcc.edu/

- **State-supported** 2-year, founded 1967, part of Virginia Community College System
- **Suburban** 160-acre campus with easy access to Richmond
- **Endowment** $399,044
- **Coed,** 7,165 undergraduate students, 25% full-time, 62% women, 38% men

Undergraduates 1,824 full-time, 5,341 part-time. Students come from 7 states and territories, 2 other countries, 1% are from out of state, 25% African American, 3% Asian American or Pacific Islander, 3% Hispanic American, 0.6% Native American, 0.2% international, 27% transferred in.

Freshmen *Admission:* 3,042 applied, 3,042 admitted, 922 enrolled.

Faculty *Total:* 311, 23% full-time, 11% with terminal degrees. *Student/faculty ratio:* 23:1.

Majors Administrative assistant and secretarial science; architectural engineering technology; biology/biotechnology laboratory technician; business/commerce; electrical, electronics and communications engineering; environmental engineering technology; funeral service and mortuary science; human services; liberal arts and sciences/liberal studies; management information systems; mechanical engineering/mechanical technology; nursing (registered nurse training); physical therapy; safety/security technology.

Academics *Calendar:* semesters. *Degree:* certificates and associate. *Special study options:* academic remediation for entering students, adult/continuing education programs, advanced placement credit, distance learning, external degree program, honors programs, off-campus study, part-time degree program, services for LD students, study abroad, summer session for credit. *ROTC:* Army (c).

Library John Tyler Community College Learning Resource and Technology Center with 49,393 titles, 179 serial subscriptions, an OPAC, a Web page.

Student Life *Housing:* college housing not available. *Campus security:* 24-hour emergency response devices and patrols.

Athletics *Intramural sports:* golf M/W, softball M/W, tennis M/W, volleyball M/W.

Costs (2007–08) *Tuition:* state resident $2405 full-time, $80 per credit hour part-time; nonresident $7659 full-time, $255 per credit hour part-time. *Required fees:* $50 full-time, $25 per term part-time.

Applying *Options:* early admission, deferred entrance. *Recommended:* high school transcript. *Application deadline:* rolling (freshmen). *Notification:* continuous (freshmen).

Freshmen Application Contact Ms. Joy James, Registrar and Enrollment Services Coordinator, John Tyler Community College, 13101 Jefferson Davis Highway, Chester, VA 23831. *Phone:* 804-796-4150. *Toll-free phone:* 800-552-3490.

J. SARGEANT REYNOLDS COMMUNITY COLLEGE
Richmond, Virginia   www.reynolds.edu

Freshmen Application Contact Ms. Karen Pettis-Walden, Director of Admissions and Records, J. Sargeant Reynolds Community College, PO Box 85622, Richmond, VA 23285-5622. *Phone:* 804-523-5029. *Fax:* 804-371-3650. *E-mail:* kpettis-walden@reynolds.edu.

LORD FAIRFAX COMMUNITY COLLEGE
Middletown, Virginia   www.lfcc.edu/

- **State-supported** 2-year, founded 1969, part of Virginia Community College System
- **Rural** 100-acre campus with easy access to Washington, DC
- **Coed**

Undergraduates 1,535 full-time, 3,957 part-time. 2% are from out of state, 5% African American, 1% Asian American or Pacific Islander, 2% Hispanic American, 0.4% Native American. *Retention:* 52% of 2003 full-time freshmen returned.

Academics *Calendar:* semesters. *Degree:* certificates and associate. *Special study options:* academic remediation for entering students, adult/continuing education programs, advanced placement credit, cooperative education, distance learning, honors programs, part-time degree program, services for LD students, summer session for credit.

Student Life *Campus security:* late-night transport/escort service.

Costs (2006–07) *Tuition:* state resident $2175 full-time, $73 per credit hour part-time; nonresident $7061 full-time, $235 per credit hour part-time. *Required fees:* $143 full-time, $4 per credit hour part-time, $14 per term part-time.

Financial Aid Of all full-time matriculated undergraduates, 28 Federal Work-Study jobs (averaging $1600).

Applying *Options:* early admission. *Recommended:* high school transcript.

Freshmen Application Contact Ms. Cynthia Bambara, Vice President of Student Success, Lord Fairfax Community College, 173 Skirmisher Lane, Middletown, VA 22645. *Phone:* 540-868-7105. *Toll-free phone:* 800-906-5322 Ext. 7107. *Fax:* 540-868-7005. *E-mail:* lfsmitt@lfcc.edu.

MEDICAL CAREERS INSTITUTE
Newport News, Virginia   www.medical.edu/

- **Proprietary** 2-year, founded 1978
- **Coed,** 1,891 undergraduate students
- 64% of applicants were admitted

Freshmen *Admission:* 812 applied, 518 admitted.

Majors Health services administration; health services/allied health/health sciences; massage therapy; medical radiologic technology; nursing (registered nurse training); physical therapist assistant.

Academics *Calendar:* semesters. *Degree:* associate.

Costs (2006–07) *Tuition:* $9621 full-time.

Applying *Application fee:* $75.

Freshmen Application Contact Admissions Office, Medical Careers Institute, 1001 Omni Boulevard, Suite 200, Newport News, VA 23606.

MEDICAL CAREERS INSTITUTE
Richmond, Virginia   www.careers.edu/

Freshmen Application Contact Admissions Office, Medical Careers Institute, 800 Moorefield Park Drive, Suite 302, Richmond, VA 23236-3659. *Phone:* 804-521-0400.

MEDICAL CAREERS INSTITUTE
Virginia Beach, Virginia   www.medical.edu/

Freshmen Application Contact Admissions Office, Medical Careers Institute, 5501 Greenwich Road, #100, Virginia Beach, VA 23462.

MOUNTAIN EMPIRE COMMUNITY COLLEGE
Big Stone Gap, Virginia   www.me.vccs.edu/

Director of Admissions Mr. Perry Carroll, Director of Enrollment Services, Mountain Empire Community College, 3441 Mountain Empire Road, Big Stone Gap, VA 24219. *Phone:* 276-523-2400 Ext. 219.

NATIONAL COLLEGE
Bluefield, Virginia   www.national-college.edu/

Freshmen Application Contact Ms. Jennifer Hooper, Admissions Representative, National College, 100 Logan Street, Bluefield, VA 24605. *Phone:* 540-326-6321. *Toll-free phone:* 800-664-1886.

NATIONAL COLLEGE
Charlottesville, Virginia   www.national-college.edu/

Director of Admissions Ms. Adrienne D. Granitz, Campus Director, National College, 1819 Emmet Street, Charlottesville, VA 22903. *Phone:* 434-295-0136. *Toll-free phone:* 800-664-1886. *Fax:* 434-979-8061.

NATIONAL COLLEGE

Danville, Virginia   www.national-college.edu/

Director of Admissions Ms. Amy Bracey, Campus Director, National College, 734 Main Street, Danville, VA 24541. *Phone:* 434-793-6822. *Toll-free phone:* 800-664-1886.

NATIONAL COLLEGE

Harrisonburg, Virginia   www.national-college.edu/

Director of Admissions Jack Evey, Campus Director, National College, 51 B Burgess Road, Harrisonburg, VA 22801. *Phone:* 540-432-0943. *Toll-free phone:* 800-664-1886.

NATIONAL COLLEGE

Lynchburg, Virginia   www.national-college.edu/

Freshmen Application Contact Mr. George Wheelous, Admissions Representative, National College, 104 Candlewood Court, Lynchburg, VA 24502. *Phone:* 804-239-3500. *Toll-free phone:* 800-664-1886.

NATIONAL COLLEGE

Martinsville, Virginia   www.national-college.edu/

Director of Admissions Mr. John Scott, Campus Director, National College, 10 Church Street, Martinsville, VA 24114. *Phone:* 276-632-5621. *Toll-free phone:* 800-664-1886 (in-state); 800-664-1866 (out-of-state).

NATIONAL COLLEGE

Salem, Virginia   www.national-college.edu/

Freshmen Application Contact Ms. Bunnie Hancock, Admissions Representative, National College, PO Box 6400, Roanoke, VA 24017. *Phone:* 540-986-1800. *Toll-free phone:* 800-664-1886.

NEW RIVER COMMUNITY COLLEGE

Dublin, Virginia   www.nr.cc.va.us/

- **State-supported** 2-year, founded 1969, part of Virginia Community College System
- **Rural** 100-acre campus
- **Endowment** $1.9 million
- **Coed,** 4,345 undergraduate students, 46% full-time, 53% women, 47% men

Undergraduates 2,008 full-time, 2,337 part-time. Students come from 22 states and territories, 21 other countries, 3% are from out of state, 5% African American, 1% Asian American or Pacific Islander, 0.8% Hispanic American, 0.2% Native American, 5% transferred in.

Freshmen *Admission:* 850 enrolled.

Faculty *Total:* 206, 25% full-time. *Student/faculty ratio:* 22:1.

Majors Accounting; administrative assistant and secretarial science; architectural engineering technology; automobile/automotive mechanics technology; biological and physical sciences; business administration and management; child development; community organization and advocacy; computer engineering technology; computer graphics; computer typography and composition equipment operation; criminal justice/law enforcement administration; criminal justice/police science; drafting and design technology; education; electrical, electronic and communications engineering technology; engineering; forensic science and technology; general studies; gerontology; information science/studies; instrumentation technology; legal assistant/paralegal; liberal arts and sciences/liberal studies; machine tool technology; marketing/marketing management; medical administrative assistant and medical secretary; nursing (licensed practical/vocational nurse training); sign language interpretation and translation; welding technology.

Academics *Calendar:* semesters. *Degree:* certificates, diplomas, and associate. *Special study options:* academic remediation for entering students, adult/continuing education programs, advanced placement credit, cooperative education, distance learning, double majors, external degree program, internships, part-time degree program, services for LD students, summer session for credit.

Library New River Community College Library with 33,993 titles, 258 serial subscriptions, an OPAC.

Student Life *Housing:* college housing not available. *Activities and Organizations:* Student Government Association, Phi Beta Lambda, Instrument Society of America, Human Service Organization, Sign Language Club. *Campus security:* 24-hour patrols. *Student services:* personal/psychological counseling.

Athletics *Intramural sports:* archery M/W, basketball M/W, bowling M/W, football M, golf M, soccer M/W, table tennis M/W, tennis M/W, volleyball M/W, weight lifting M/W.

Costs (2007–08) *Tuition:* state resident $2299 full-time, $79 per semester hour part-time; nonresident $7569 full-time, $249 per semester hour part-time. *Required fees:* $6 per credit part-time.

Financial Aid Of all full-time matriculated undergraduates, 150 Federal Work-Study jobs (averaging $2000).

Applying *Options:* early admission, deferred entrance. *Required for some:* high school transcript. *Application deadlines:* rolling (freshmen), rolling (transfers). *Notification:* continuous (freshmen), continuous (transfers).

Freshmen Application Contact Ms. Margaret G. Taylor, Director of Student Services, New River Community College, PO Box 1127, 5251 College Drive, Dublin, VA 24084. *Phone:* 540-674-3600. *Fax:* 540-674-3644. *E-mail:* nrtaylm@nr.edu.

NORTHERN VIRGINIA COMMUNITY COLLEGE

Annandale, Virginia   www.nv.cc.va.us/

Director of Admissions Dr. Max L. Bassett, Dean of Academic and Student Services, Northern Virginia Community College, 4001 Wakefield Chapel Road, Annandale, VA 22003-3796. *Phone:* 703-323-3195.

PATRICK HENRY COMMUNITY COLLEGE

Martinsville, Virginia   www.ph.vccs.edu/

Director of Admissions Dr. Nolan Browning, Vice President of Academic and Student Development, Patrick Henry Community College, PO Box 5311, 645 Patriot Avenue, Martinsville, VA 24115. *Phone:* 276-656-0315. *Toll-free phone:* 800-232-7997.

PAUL D. CAMP COMMUNITY COLLEGE

Franklin, Virginia   www.pc.vccs.edu/

- **State-supported** 2-year, founded 1971, part of Virginia Community College System
- **Small-town** 99-acre campus
- **Endowment** $16,121
- **Coed,** 1,560 undergraduate students

Undergraduates Students come from 2 states and territories, 2 other countries, 0.5% are from out of state.

Freshmen *Admission:* 410 applied, 410 admitted. *Average high school GPA:* 2.2. *Test scores:* SAT verbal scores over 500: 27%; SAT math scores over 500: 19%; SAT verbal scores over 600: 2%.

Faculty *Total:* 113, 20% full-time. *Student/faculty ratio:* 17:1.

Majors Administrative assistant and secretarial science; business administration and management; criminal justice/law enforcement administration; data processing and data processing technology; education; liberal arts and sciences/liberal studies.

Academics *Calendar:* semesters. *Degree:* certificates and associate. *Special study options:* academic remediation for entering students, adult/continuing education programs, advanced placement credit, cooperative education, distance learning, honors programs, independent study, internships, off-campus study, part-time degree program, summer session for credit.

Library Paul D. Camp Community College Library with 22,000 titles, 200 serial subscriptions, an OPAC.

Paul D. Camp Community College (continued)

Student Life *Housing:* college housing not available. *Activities and Organizations:* student-run newspaper, African-American History Club, Phi Beta Lambda, Phi Theta Kappa, Student Government Association. *Campus security:* security staff until 7 p.m.

Standardized Tests *Required:* ACT COMPASS (for placement).

Costs (2007–08) *Tuition:* state resident $1816 full-time, $76 per credit hour part-time; nonresident $3392 full-time, $141 per credit hour part-time.

Financial Aid Of all full-time matriculated undergraduates, 30 Federal Work-Study jobs (averaging $2000).

Applying *Options:* deferred entrance. *Required:* high school transcript. *Application deadlines:* rolling (freshmen), rolling (transfers). *Notification:* continuous (freshmen), continuous (transfers).

Freshmen Application Contact Mr. Joe Edenfield, Director of Admissions and Records, Paul D. Camp Community College, PO Box 737, 100 North College Drive, Franklin, VA 23851-0737. *Phone:* 757-569-6744. *E-mail:* jedenfield@pc.vccs.edu.

PIEDMONT VIRGINIA COMMUNITY COLLEGE

Charlottesville, Virginia   **www.pvcc.edu/**

- **State-supported** 2-year, founded 1972, part of Virginia Community College System
- **Suburban** 114-acre campus with easy access to Richmond
- **Endowment** $1.3 million
- **Coed,** 4,451 undergraduate students, 23% full-time, 60% women, 40% men

Undergraduates 1,020 full-time, 3,431 part-time. Students come from 13 states and territories, 7% are from out of state, 14% African American, 3% Asian American or Pacific Islander, 2% Hispanic American, 0.3% Native American, 0.6% international.

Freshmen *Admission:* 721 enrolled.

Faculty *Total:* 216, 28% full-time. *Student/faculty ratio:* 19:1.

Majors Accounting; administrative assistant and secretarial science; biological and physical sciences; biotechnology; business administration and management; carpentry; clinical/medical laboratory technology; computer engineering technology; computer programming; computer programming (specific applications); computer science; computer systems networking and telecommunications; computer/technical support; criminal justice/police science; data processing and data processing technology; education; electrician; emergency medical technology (EMT paramedic); engineering; general studies; heating, air conditioning and refrigeration technology; liberal arts and sciences/liberal studies; marketing/marketing management; masonry; mechanical drafting and CAD/CADD; nursing (registered nurse training); plumbing technology; respiratory care therapy; visual and performing arts; web/multimedia management and webmaster.

Academics *Calendar:* semesters. *Degree:* certificates and associate. *Special study options:* academic remediation for entering students, adult/continuing education programs, advanced placement credit, cooperative education, distance learning, English as a second language, honors programs, independent study, internships, part-time degree program, services for LD students, summer session for credit. *ROTC:* Army (c).

Library Jessup Library with 39,117 titles, 163 serial subscriptions, 1,718 audiovisual materials, an OPAC, a Web page.

Student Life *Housing:* college housing not available. *Activities and Organizations:* drama/theater group, student-run newspaper, choral group, Phi Theta Kappa, Black Student Alliance, Science Club, Masquers, Christian Fellowship Club. *Campus security:* 24-hour patrols, late-night transport/escort service.

Athletics *Intramural sports:* basketball M/W, bowling M/W, football M/W, golf M/W, lacrosse M/W, skiing (cross-country) M/W, soccer M/W, softball M/W, tennis M/W, volleyball M/W, weight lifting M/W.

Costs (2007–08) *Tuition:* state resident $2300 full-time, $77 per credit hour part-time; nonresident $7814 full-time, $260 per credit hour part-time. *Required fees:* $170 full-time, $6 per credit hour part-time.

Financial Aid Of all full-time matriculated undergraduates, 50 Federal Work-Study jobs.

Applying *Options:* electronic application, early admission. *Required for some:* high school transcript, for nursing program: completion of any developmental studies; grade 'C' or better in high school or college developmental chemistry course; high school diploma/GED; and completion of nursing program application. *Application deadlines:* rolling (freshmen), rolling (transfers). *Notification:* continuous (freshmen), continuous (transfers).

Freshmen Application Contact Ms. Mary Lee Walsh, Dean of Student Services, Piedmont Virginia Community College, 501 College Drive, Charlottesville, VA 22902-7589. *Phone:* 434-961-6540. *Fax:* 434-961-5425. *E-mail:* mwalsh@pvcc.edu.

RAPPAHANNOCK COMMUNITY COLLEGE

Glenns, Virginia   **www.rcc.vccs.edu/**

- **State-related** 2-year, founded 1970, part of Virginia Community College System
- **Rural** 217-acre campus
- **Coed,** 2,824 undergraduate students

Undergraduates Students come from 1 other country, 18% African American, 1% Asian American or Pacific Islander, 1% Hispanic American, 0.5% Native American.

Majors Accounting; administrative assistant and secretarial science; biological and physical sciences; business administration and management; criminal justice/police science; engineering technology; information science/studies; liberal arts and sciences/liberal studies; nursing (registered nurse training).

Academics *Calendar:* semesters. *Degree:* certificates, diplomas, and associate. *Special study options:* academic remediation for entering students, adult/continuing education programs, distance learning, internships, off-campus study, part-time degree program, summer session for credit.

Library The College Library with 46,000 titles, 85 serial subscriptions, an OPAC.

Student Life *Housing:* college housing not available. *Activities and Organizations:* student-run newspaper, Phi Theta Kappa, Culture Club, Poetry Club, student government. *Campus security:* 24-hour emergency response devices. *Student services:* personal/psychological counseling, women's center.

Athletics *Intramural sports:* baseball M, table tennis M/W, tennis M/W, volleyball M/W.

Standardized Tests *Required:* CPT (for placement).

Costs (2006–07) *Tuition:* state resident $2300 full-time; nonresident $7251 full-time.

Financial Aid Of all full-time matriculated undergraduates, 40 Federal Work-Study jobs (averaging $1015).

Applying *Options:* early admission. *Application deadlines:* rolling (freshmen), rolling (transfers). *Notification:* continuous (freshmen), continuous (transfers).

Freshmen Application Contact Ms. Wilnet Willis, Admissions and Records Officer, Rappahannock Community College, Glenns Campus, 12745 College Drive, Glenns, VA 23149-2616. *Phone:* 804-758-6742. *Toll-free phone:* 800-836-9381.

RICHARD BLAND COLLEGE OF THE COLLEGE OF WILLIAM AND MARY

Petersburg, Virginia   **www.rbc.edu/**

- **State-supported** 2-year, founded 1961, part of College of William and Mary
- **Rural** 712-acre campus with easy access to Richmond
- **Coed**

Undergraduates 814 full-time, 623 part-time. Students come from 8 states and territories, 1% are from out of state, 19% African American, 2% Asian American or Pacific Islander, 2% Hispanic American, 0.5% Native American, 7% transferred in. *Retention:* 61% of 2003 full-time freshmen returned.

Faculty *Student/faculty ratio:* 23:1.

Academics *Calendar:* semesters. *Degree:* associate. *Special study options:* academic remediation for entering students, accelerated degree program, advanced placement credit, part-time degree program, services for LD students, summer session for credit. *ROTC:* Army (c).

Student Life *Campus security:* 24-hour patrols.

Standardized Tests *Required:* ACT COMPASS (for admission). *Recommended:* SAT or ACT (for admission).

Costs (2006–07) *Tuition:* state resident $2330 full-time, $93 per credit hour part-time; nonresident $10,050 full-time, $422 per credit hour part-time. Full-time tuition and fees vary according to course load and location. Part-time tuition and fees vary according to course load and location. *Required fees:* $190 full-time, $5 per credit hour part-time.

Financial Aid Of all full-time matriculated undergraduates, 10 Federal Work-Study jobs (averaging $2000).

Applying *Application fee:* $20. *Required:* essay or personal statement, high school transcript, minimum 2.0 GPA, In-State Residency Form. *Required for some:* letters of recommendation, interview.

Freshmen Application Contact Mr. Randy Dean, Director of Admissions and Student Services, Richard Bland College of The College of William and Mary, 11301 Johnson Road, Petersburg, VA 23805-7100. *Phone:* 804-862-6225. *Fax:* 804-862-6490. *E-mail:* admit@rbc.edu.

SOUTHSIDE VIRGINIA COMMUNITY COLLEGE

Alberta, Virginia   **www.sv.vccs.edu/**

- **State-supported** 2-year, founded 1970, part of Virginia Community College System
- **Rural** 207-acre campus
- **Endowment** $527,455
- **Coed,** 4,686 undergraduate students, 29% full-time, 65% women, 35% men

Undergraduates 1,359 full-time, 3,327 part-time. Students come from 3 states and territories, 2 other countries, 1% are from out of state, 46% African American, 0.7% Asian American or Pacific Islander, 0.5% Hispanic American, 0.2% Native American.

Freshmen *Admission:* 380 enrolled.

Faculty *Total:* 295, 24% full-time, 6% with terminal degrees. *Student/faculty ratio:* 17:1.

Majors Administrative assistant and secretarial science; biological and physical sciences; business administration and management; criminal justice/law enforcement administration; drafting and design technology; education; electrical, electronic and communications engineering technology; general studies; human services; information science/studies; information technology; liberal arts and sciences/liberal studies; nursing (registered nurse training); respiratory care therapy.

Academics *Calendar:* semesters. *Degree:* certificates, diplomas, and associate. *Special study options:* academic remediation for entering students, advanced placement credit, distance learning, honors programs, off-campus study, part-time degree program, services for LD students, study abroad, summer session for credit. *ROTC:* Army (c).

Library Julian M. Howell Library plus 1 other with 27,691 titles, 164 serial subscriptions, 1,307 audiovisual materials, an OPAC, a Web page.

Student Life *Housing:* college housing not available. *Activities and Organizations:* choral group, Student Forum, Phi Theta Kappa, Phi Beta Lambda, Alpha Delta Omega.

Athletics *Intramural sports:* basketball M, softball M/W, table tennis M/W, tennis M/W, volleyball M/W.

Costs (2007–08) *Tuition:* state resident $2300 full-time, $77 per credit part-time; nonresident $7554 full-time, $252 per credit part-time. *Required fees:* $165 full-time, $6 per credit part-time.

Applying *Options:* electronic application, deferred entrance. *Required:* high school transcript, interview. *Application deadlines:* rolling (freshmen), rolling (transfers). *Notification:* continuous (freshmen), continuous (transfers).

Freshmen Application Contact Dr. Ronald Mattox, Dean of Admissions, Records, and Institutional Research, Southside Virginia Community College, 109 Campus Drive, Alberta, VA 23821. *Phone:* 434-949-1012. *Fax:* 434-949-7863. *E-mail:* rhina.jones@sv.vccs.edu.

SOUTHWEST VIRGINIA COMMUNITY COLLEGE

Richlands, Virginia   **www.sw.edu/**

- **State-supported** 2-year, founded 1968, part of Virginia Community College System
- **Rural** 100-acre campus
- **Coed,** 3,580 undergraduate students, 36% full-time, 56% women, 44% men

Undergraduates 1,303 full-time, 2,277 part-time. Students come from 5 states and territories, 1 other country, 5% are from out of state, 2% African American, 0.3% Asian American or Pacific Islander, 0.4% Hispanic American, 0.3% Native American, 3% transferred in. *Retention:* 42% of 2003 full-time freshmen returned.

Freshmen *Admission:* 541 enrolled.

Faculty *Total:* 226, 31% full-time. *Student/faculty ratio:* 15:1.

Majors Accounting; administrative assistant and secretarial science; biological and physical sciences; business administration and management; criminal justice/police science; drafting and design technology; education; electrical, electronic and communications engineering technology; engineering; human services; industrial radiologic technology; information science/studies; land use planning and management; liberal arts and sciences/liberal studies; mining technology; music; nursing (registered nurse training); respiratory care therapy.

Academics *Calendar:* semesters. *Degree:* certificates, diplomas, and associate. *Special study options:* academic remediation for entering students, adult/

continuing education programs, advanced placement credit, distance learning, double majors, honors programs, internships, part-time degree program, summer session for credit.

Library 58,000 titles, 225 serial subscriptions, an OPAC, a Web page.

Student Life *Housing:* college housing not available. *Activities and Organizations:* drama/theater group, student-run newspaper, radio and television station, PTK, PBL, Intervoice, Black Student Union, Service Club. *Campus security:* 24-hour emergency response devices and patrols, student patrols. *Student services:* personal/psychological counseling, women's center.

Athletics *Intercollegiate sports:* baseball M, basketball M, golf M, rugby M. *Intramural sports:* basketball M/W, bowling M/W, football M, racquetball M/W, tennis M/W, volleyball M/W, weight lifting M/W.

Costs (2006–07) *Tuition:* state resident $2030 full-time, $73 per credit part-time; nonresident $6590 full-time, $235 per credit part-time. Full-time tuition and fees vary according to course load. Part-time tuition and fees vary according to course load. *Required fees:* $130 full-time, $5 per credit part-time. *Payment plan:* installment.

Financial Aid Of all full-time matriculated undergraduates, 150 Federal Work-Study jobs (averaging $1140).

Applying *Options:* early admission, deferred entrance. *Required:* high school transcript, interview. *Application deadlines:* rolling (freshmen), rolling (transfers).

Freshmen Application Contact Mr. Jim Farris, Director of Admissions, Records, and Counseling, Southwest Virginia Community College, Box SVCC, Richlands, VA 24641. *Phone:* 276-964-7300. *Toll-free phone:* 800-822-7822. *Fax:* 276-964-7716.

TESST COLLEGE OF TECHNOLOGY

Alexandria, Virginia   **www.tesst.com/**

- **Proprietary** 2-year, founded 1986
- **Coed,** 324 undergraduate students

Majors Criminal justice/law enforcement administration; electrical/electronics equipment installation and repair; system, networking, and LAN/WAN management.

Academics *Calendar:* quarters. *Degree:* associate.

Costs (2006–07) *Tuition:* $10,978 per degree program part-time.

Director of Admissions Mr. Bob Somers, Director, TESST College of Technology, 6315 Bren Mar Drive, Alexandria, VA 22312-6342. *Phone:* 703-548-4800. *Toll-free phone:* 800-833-0209. *Fax:* 703-683-2765. *E-mail:* tesstal@erols.com.

THOMAS NELSON COMMUNITY COLLEGE

Hampton, Virginia   **www.tncc.edu/**

- **State-supported** 2-year, founded 1968, part of Virginia Community College System
- **Suburban** 85-acre campus with easy access to Virginia Beach
- **Coed**

Undergraduates 2,658 full-time, 5,937 part-time. 34% African American, 4% Asian American or Pacific Islander, 4% Hispanic American, 0.6% Native American.

Academics *Calendar:* semesters. *Degree:* certificates, diplomas, and associate. *Special study options:* academic remediation for entering students, adult/continuing education programs, advanced placement credit, cooperative education, English as a second language, external degree program, honors programs, internships, off-campus study, part-time degree program, services for LD students, summer session for credit.

Student Life *Campus security:* 24-hour patrols.

Costs (2006–07) *Tuition:* state resident $2175 full-time, $73 per credit hour part-time; nonresident $7061 full-time, $235 per credit hour part-time. *Required fees:* $116 full-time, $3 per credit hour part-time, $11 per term part-time.

Financial Aid Of all full-time matriculated undergraduates, 110 Federal Work-Study jobs (averaging $3000).

Applying *Options:* early admission, deferred entrance. *Required:* high school transcript.

Freshmen Application Contact Ms. Jerri Newson, Admissions Office Manager, Thomas Nelson Community College, PO Box 9407, 99 Thomas Nelson Drive, Hampton, VA 23670. *Phone:* 757-825-2800. *Fax:* 757-825-2763. *E-mail:* admissions@tncc.edu.

TIDEWATER COMMUNITY COLLEGE

Norfolk, Virginia   www.tcc.edu/

- **State-supported** 2-year, founded 1968, part of Virginia Community College System
- **Suburban** 520-acre campus
- **Endowment** $7.1 million
- **Coed,** 24,938 undergraduate students, 34% full-time, 61% women, 39% men

Undergraduates 8,482 full-time, 16,456 part-time. Students come from 53 states and territories, 10% are from out of state, 31% African American, 5% Asian American or Pacific Islander, 4% Hispanic American, 0.6% Native American.

Faculty *Total:* 1,234, 28% full-time. *Student/faculty ratio:* 21:1.

Majors Accounting; administrative assistant and secretarial science; advertising; automobile/automotive mechanics technology; biological and physical sciences; business administration and management; civil engineering; commercial and advertising art; computer programming; drafting and design technology; education; electrical, electronic and communications engineering technology; engineering; finance; fine/studio arts; graphic design; horticultural science; information technology; interior design; kindergarten/preschool education; liberal arts and sciences/liberal studies; marketing/marketing management; music; nursing (registered nurse training); paralegal/legal assistant; real estate.

Academics *Calendar:* semesters. *Degree:* certificates, diplomas, and associate. *Special study options:* academic remediation for entering students, accelerated degree program, adult/continuing education programs, advanced placement credit, cooperative education, distance learning, English as a second language, honors programs, independent study, internships, off-campus study, part-time degree program, services for LD students, summer session for credit.

Library Main Library plus 5 others with 147,126 titles, 913 serial subscriptions, an OPAC, a Web page.

Student Life *Housing:* college housing not available. *Activities and Organizations:* drama/theater group, student-run newspaper. *Campus security:* 24-hour patrols. *Student services:* personal/psychological counseling, women's center.

Athletics *Intramural sports:* basketball M/W, soccer M, softball W, tennis M/W, volleyball W.

Costs (2007–08) *Tuition:* state resident $2300 full-time, $77 per credit hour part-time; nonresident $7464 full-time, $252 per credit hour part-time. *Required fees:* $255 full-time, $9 per credit hour part-time.

Financial Aid Of all full-time matriculated undergraduates, 64 Federal Work-Study jobs (averaging $2000).

Applying *Options:* early admission, deferred entrance. *Application deadlines:* rolling (freshmen), rolling (transfers). *Notification:* continuous (freshmen), continuous (transfers).

Freshmen Application Contact Ms. Tyjaun Lee, Associate Dean, Student Services, Tidewater Community College, 7000 College Drive, Portsmouth, VA 23703. *Phone:* 757-822-1068. *Fax:* 757-822-1060.

TIDEWATER TECH

Virginia Beach, Virginia   www.tidetech.com/

- **Proprietary** 2-year, founded 1969
- **Coed,** 1,192 undergraduate students

Majors Business administration, management and operations related; computer hardware technology; computer/information technology services administration related; computer systems networking and telecommunications; criminal justice/law enforcement administration; legal assistant/paralegal; massage therapy; medical/clinical assistant.

Academics *Degree:* associate.

Costs (2006–07) *Tuition:* $18,125 per degree program part-time.

Applying *Application fee:* $25.

Admissions Office Contact Tidewater Tech, 2697 Dean Drive, Suite 100, Virginia Beach, VA 23452. *Toll-free phone:* 877-604-2121.

VIRGINIA HIGHLANDS COMMUNITY COLLEGE

Abingdon, Virginia   www.vhcc.edu/

- **State-supported** 2-year, founded 1967, part of Virginia Community College System
- **Small-town** 100-acre campus
- **Coed,** 2,452 undergraduate students

Undergraduates Students come from 7 states and territories.

Faculty *Total:* 97, 60% full-time.

Majors Accounting; administrative assistant and secretarial science; biological and physical sciences; business administration and management; criminal justice/police science; data processing and data processing technology; drafting and design technology; dramatic/theater arts; education; electrical, electronic and communications engineering technology; engineering technology; heating, air conditioning, ventilation and refrigeration maintenance technology; human services; industrial radiologic technology; information science/studies; liberal arts and sciences/liberal studies; machine tool technology; nursing (registered nurse training); physical therapy.

Academics *Calendar:* semesters. *Degree:* certificates, diplomas, and associate. *Special study options:* academic remediation for entering students, adult/continuing education programs, advanced placement credit, cooperative education, part-time degree program, services for LD students, summer session for credit.

Library 29,683 titles, 174 serial subscriptions.

Student Life *Housing:* college housing not available. *Activities and Organizations:* drama/theater group, choral group. *Student services:* personal/psychological counseling.

Athletics *Intramural sports:* basketball M/W, football M/W, golf M/W, skiing (cross-country) M/W, skiing (downhill) M/W, tennis M/W, volleyball M/W.

Standardized Tests *Required for some:* SCAT, ACT ASSET. *Recommended:* SCAT, ACT ASSET.

Costs (2007–08) *Tuition:* state resident $1948 full-time, $81 per credit hour part-time; nonresident $6151 full-time, $256 per credit hour part-time.

Applying *Options:* early admission, deferred entrance. *Required:* high school transcript. *Application deadlines:* rolling (freshmen), rolling (transfers). *Notification:* continuous (freshmen), continuous (transfers).

Freshmen Application Contact Mr. David N. Matlock, Director of Admissions, Records, and Financial Aid, Virginia Highlands Community College, PO Box 828, 100 VHCC Drive Abingdon, Abingdon, VA 24210. *Phone:* 276-739-2414. *Toll-free phone:* 877-207-6115. *E-mail:* dmatlock@vhcc.edu.

VIRGINIA WESTERN COMMUNITY COLLEGE

Roanoke, Virginia   www.virginiawestern.edu/

- **State-supported** 2-year, founded 1966, part of Virginia Community College System
- **Suburban** 70-acre campus
- **Coed,** 7,636 undergraduate students, 25% full-time, 53% women, 47% men

Undergraduates 1,929 full-time, 5,707 part-time. 1% are from out of state, 9% African American, 2% Asian American or Pacific Islander, 1% Hispanic American, 0.5% Native American.

Freshmen *Average high school GPA:* 2.5.

Faculty *Total:* 406, 21% full-time. *Student/faculty ratio:* 25:1.

Majors Accounting; administrative assistant and secretarial science; art; automobile/automotive mechanics technology; biological and physical sciences; business administration and management; child development; civil engineering technology; commercial and advertising art; computer science; criminal justice/law enforcement administration; data processing and data processing technology; dental hygiene; education; electrical, electronic and communications engineering technology; engineering; industrial radiologic technology; kindergarten/preschool education; liberal arts and sciences/liberal studies; mechanical engineering/mechanical technology; mental health/rehabilitation; nursing (registered nurse training); pre-engineering; radio and television; radiologic technology/science.

Academics *Calendar:* semesters. *Degree:* certificates and associate. *Special study options:* academic remediation for entering students, advanced placement credit, cooperative education, distance learning, double majors, English as a second language, honors programs, independent study, internships, part-time degree program, services for LD students, summer session for credit.

Library Brown Library plus 1 other with 67,129 titles, 402 serial subscriptions, an OPAC, a Web page.

Student Life *Housing:* college housing not available. *Activities and Organizations:* drama/theater group, student-run newspaper. *Campus security:* 24-hour emergency response devices and patrols, late-night transport/escort service. *Student services:* personal/psychological counseling.

Athletics *Intramural sports:* baseball M, basketball M/W.

Costs (2007–08) *Tuition:* state resident $82 per credit part-time; nonresident $243 per credit part-time.

Applying *Options:* early admission, deferred entrance. *Required for some:* high school transcript. *Recommended:* high school transcript. *Application deadlines:* rolling (freshmen), rolling (transfers). *Notification:* continuous (freshmen), continuous (transfers).

Freshmen Application Contact Admissions Office, Virginia Western Community College, 3095 Colonial Avenue, Roanoke, VA 24038. *Phone:* 540-857-7231.

WYTHEVILLE COMMUNITY COLLEGE

Wytheville, Virginia   www.wcc.vccs.edu/

- **State-supported** 2-year, founded 1967, part of Virginia Community College System
- **Rural** 141-acre campus
- **Coed,** 2,450 undergraduate students

Undergraduates Students come from 22 states and territories, 1 other country.

Freshmen *Admission:* 794 applied, 794 admitted.

Faculty *Total:* 46. *Student/faculty ratio:* 16:1.

Majors Accounting; administrative assistant and secretarial science; biological and physical sciences; business administration and management; civil engineering technology; clinical/medical laboratory technology; corrections; criminal justice/law enforcement administration; criminal justice/police science; dental hygiene; drafting and design technology; education; electrical, electronic and communications engineering technology; information science/studies; liberal arts and sciences/liberal studies; machine tool technology; mass communication/media; mechanical engineering/mechanical technology; medical administrative assistant and medical secretary; nursing (registered nurse training); physical therapy; real estate.

Academics *Calendar:* semesters. *Degree:* certificates and associate. *Special study options:* academic remediation for entering students, adult/continuing education programs, advanced placement credit, distance learning, external degree program, part-time degree program, services for LD students, summer session for credit.

Library Wytheville Community College Library with 29,000 titles, 261 serial subscriptions.

Student Life *Housing:* college housing not available. *Activities and Organizations:* drama/theater group, student-run newspaper, national fraternities. *Campus security:* 24-hour emergency response devices and patrols.

Athletics *Intramural sports:* basketball M/W, golf M, softball M/W, table tennis M/W, tennis M/W, volleyball M/W.

Costs (2006–07) *Tuition:* state resident $2300 full-time; nonresident $7325 full-time.

Financial Aid Of all full-time matriculated undergraduates, 125 Federal Work-Study jobs (averaging $2592).

Applying *Options:* early admission. *Required:* high school transcript. *Required for some:* interview. *Application deadlines:* rolling (freshmen), rolling (transfers). *Notification:* continuous (freshmen), continuous (transfers).

Director of Admissions Ms. Sherry K. Dix, Registrar, Wytheville Community College, 1000 East Main Street, Wytheville, VA 24382-3308. *Phone:* 276-223-4755. *Toll-free phone:* 800-468-1195. *E-mail:* wcdixxs@wcc.vccs.edu.

WASHINGTON

APOLLO COLLEGE

Spokane, Washington   www.apollocollege.com/

Director of Admissions Deanna Baker, Campus Director, Apollo College, 10102 East Knox, Suite 200, Spokane, WA 99206. *Phone:* 509-532-8888. *Fax:* 509-533-5983.

BATES TECHNICAL COLLEGE

Tacoma, Washington   www.bates.ctc.edu/

Director of Admissions Ms. Gwen Sailer, Vice President for Student Services, Bates Technical College, 1101 South Yakima Avenue, Tacoma, WA 98405. *Phone:* 253-680-7000. *Toll-free phone:* 800-562-7099.

BELLEVUE COMMUNITY COLLEGE

Bellevue, Washington   www.bcc.ctc.edu/

Freshmen Application Contact Morenika Jacobs, Associate Dean of Enrollment Services, Bellevue Community College, 3000 Landerholm Circle SE, Bellerne, WA 98007. *Phone:* 425-564-2205. *Fax:* 425-564-4065.

BELLINGHAM TECHNICAL COLLEGE

Bellingham, Washington   www.btc.ctc.edu/

- **State-supported** 2-year, founded 1957
- **Coed,** 4,159 undergraduate students, 23% full-time, 51% women, 49% men

Undergraduates 968 full-time, 3,191 part-time. 0.7% African American, 2% Asian American or Pacific Islander, 4% Hispanic American, 2% Native American, 0.3% international.

Freshmen *Admission:* 656 applied, 575 admitted.

Faculty *Total:* 167, 34% full-time, 0.6% with terminal degrees. *Student/faculty ratio:* 20:1.

Majors Data entry/microcomputer applications; data entry/microcomputer applications related; information technology; system administration; web/multimedia management and webmaster; web page, digital/multimedia and information resources design.

Academics *Degree:* certificates and associate. *Special study options:* academic remediation for entering students, cooperative education, distance learning, English as a second language, independent study, internships, part-time degree program, services for LD students, summer session for credit.

Library Information Technology Resource Center with 9,537 titles, 5,023 serial subscriptions, 823 audiovisual materials, an OPAC, a Web page.

Standardized Tests *Required:* (for placement).

Costs (2006–07) *Tuition:* state resident $3500 full-time; nonresident $3500 full-time. Full-time tuition and fees vary according to program. Part-time tuition and fees vary according to program.

Financial Aid Of all full-time matriculated undergraduates, 40 state and other part-time jobs (averaging $2300).

Applying *Options:* early admission, deferred entrance. *Application fee:* $33. *Application deadline:* rolling (freshmen).

Freshmen Application Contact Ms. Erin Runestrand, Coordinator, Admissions, Bellingham Technical College, 3028 Lindbergh Avenue, Bellingham, WA 98225-1599. *Phone:* 360-752-8324. *Fax:* 360-676-2798. *E-mail:* beltcadm@beltc.ctc.edu.

BIG BEND COMMUNITY COLLEGE

Moses Lake, Washington   www.bigbend.edu/

- **State-supported** 2-year, founded 1962
- **Small-town** 159-acre campus
- **Endowment** $1.1 million
- **Coed,** 2,697 undergraduate students

Undergraduates Students come from 4 states and territories, 2 other countries, 5% are from out of state, 5% live on campus.

Freshmen *Admission:* 519 applied, 519 admitted.

Faculty *Total:* 132, 41% full-time, 3% with terminal degrees. *Student/faculty ratio:* 20:1.

Majors Accounting technology and bookkeeping; airline pilot and flight crew; automobile/automotive mechanics technology; aviation maintenance technology; civil engineering technology; heavy/industrial equipment maintenance technologies related; industrial electronics technology; information science/studies; liberal arts and sciences/liberal studies; nursing (licensed practical/vocational nurse training); nursing (registered nurse training); office management; teacher assistant/aide; welding technology.

Academics *Calendar:* quarters. *Degree:* certificates and associate. *Special study options:* academic remediation for entering students, advanced placement credit, cooperative education, distance learning, part-time degree program, services for LD students, summer session for credit.

Library Big Bend Community College Library with 41,900 titles, 3,700 serial subscriptions, 3,150 audiovisual materials, an OPAC, a Web page.

Student Life *Housing Options:* coed. Campus housing is university owned. *Activities and Organizations:* choral group. *Campus security:* 24-hour emergency response devices, student patrols. *Student services:* personal/psychological counseling.

Big Bend Community College (continued)

Athletics *Intercollegiate sports:* baseball M(s), basketball M(s)/W(s), softball W(s), volleyball W(s).

Costs (2007–08) *Tuition:* state resident $2676 full-time, $77 per credit part-time; nonresident $3076 full-time, $91 per credit part-time. *Required fees:* $90 full-time.

Financial Aid Of all full-time matriculated undergraduates, 50 Federal Work-Study jobs (averaging $2700). 100 state and other part-time jobs (averaging $3240).

Applying *Options:* early admission, deferred entrance. *Application fee:* $30. *Required for some:* high school transcript. *Application deadlines:* rolling (freshmen), rolling (transfers). *Notification:* continuous (freshmen), continuous (transfers).

Freshmen Application Contact Ms. Candis Lacher, Dean of Enrollment Services, Big Bend Community College, 7662 Chanute Street, Moses Lake, WA 98837. *Phone:* 509-793-2061. *Fax:* 509-782-6243. *E-mail:* admissions@bigbend.edu.

CASCADIA COMMUNITY COLLEGE

Bothell, Washington   www.cascadia.ctc.edu/

- **State-supported** 2-year, founded 1999
- **Suburban** 128-acre campus
- **Coed,** 1,950 undergraduate students, 48% full-time, 49% women, 51% men

Undergraduates 944 full-time, 1,006 part-time. Students come from 2 states and territories, 7 other countries, 1% are from out of state, 1% African American, 7% Asian American or Pacific Islander, 5% Hispanic American, 0.7% Native American, 0.6% international, 21% transferred in. *Retention:* 52% of 2003 full-time freshmen returned.

Freshmen *Admission:* 294 applied, 294 admitted, 294 enrolled.

Faculty *Total:* 94, 29% full-time, 23% with terminal degrees. *Student/faculty ratio:* 19:1.

Majors Liberal arts and sciences and humanities related; liberal arts and sciences/liberal studies; science technologies related.

Academics *Calendar:* quarters. *Degree:* certificates and associate. *Special study options:* academic remediation for entering students, accelerated degree program, adult/continuing education programs, advanced placement credit, cooperative education, distance learning, English as a second language, independent study, internships, off-campus study, part-time degree program, services for LD students, study abroad, summer session for credit.

Library UWB/CCC Campus Library with 73,749 titles, 850 serial subscriptions, 6,100 audiovisual materials, an OPAC, a Web page.

Student Life *Housing:* college housing not available. *Campus security:* 24-hour emergency response devices, late-night transport/escort service.

Costs (2006–07) *Tuition:* state resident $2372 full-time, $74 per credit part-time; nonresident $7545 full-time, $246 per credit part-time. *Required fees:* $270 full-time, $9 per credit part-time. *Waivers:* adult students, senior citizens, and employees or children of employees.

Applying *Application deadlines:* rolling (freshmen), rolling (out-of-state freshmen), rolling (transfers). *Notification:* continuous (freshmen), continuous (out-of-state freshmen), continuous (transfers).

Freshmen Application Contact Ms. Marla Coan, Dean for Student Success, Cascadia Community College, 18345 Campus Way, NE, Bothell, WA 98011. *Phone:* 425-352-8000. *Fax:* 425-352-8137. *E-mail:* admissions@cascadia.ctc.edu.

CENTRALIA COLLEGE

Centralia, Washington   www.centralia.edu/

- **State-supported** 2-year, founded 1925, part of Washington State Board for Community and Technical Colleges
- **Small-town** 31-acre campus
- **Endowment** $5.1 million
- **Coed,** 3,808 undergraduate students, 48% full-time, 64% women, 36% men

Undergraduates 1,827 full-time, 1,981 part-time. Students come from 9 states and territories, 12 other countries, 1% are from out of state, 0.8% African American, 2% Asian American or Pacific Islander, 11% Hispanic American, 2% Native American, 1% international. *Retention:* 72% of 2003 full-time freshmen returned.

Freshmen *Admission:* 2,602 applied, 2,602 admitted.

Faculty *Total:* 240, 24% full-time, 8% with terminal degrees. *Student/faculty ratio:* 25:1.

Majors Administrative assistant and secretarial science; applied art; art; biological and physical sciences; biology/biological sciences; botany/plant biology; broadcast journalism; business administration and management; business and personal/financial services marketing; business/commerce; chemistry; child care and support services management; child development; civil engineering technology; commercial and advertising art; computer and information sciences related; computer programming related; computer systems networking and telecommunications; consumer merchandising/retailing management; corrections; criminal justice/law enforcement administration; diesel mechanics technology; dramatic/theater arts; electrical, electronic and communications engineering technology; engineering; English; family living/parenthood; French; geology/earth science; German; heavy equipment maintenance technology; history; humanities; kindergarten/preschool education; legal administrative assistant/secretary; liberal arts and sciences/liberal studies; marketing/marketing management; mass communication/media; mathematics; medical administrative assistant and medical secretary; music; natural sciences; nursing (licensed practical/vocational nurse training); nursing (registered nurse training); parks, recreation and leisure; physical sciences; political science and government; pre-dentistry studies; pre-engineering; pre-law studies; pre-medical studies; pre-pharmacy studies; pre-veterinary studies; psychology; radio and television; receptionist; retailing; sales, distribution and marketing; social sciences; sociology; Spanish; survey technology; system administration; teacher assistant/aide; welding technology; zoology/animal biology.

Academics *Calendar:* quarters. *Degree:* certificates and associate. *Special study options:* academic remediation for entering students, adult/continuing education programs, advanced placement credit, cooperative education, distance learning, English as a second language, external degree program, freshman honors college, honors programs, independent study, part-time degree program, services for LD students, study abroad, summer session for credit.

Library Kirk Library with 38,000 titles, 225 serial subscriptions, 5,000 audiovisual materials, an OPAC, a Web page.

Student Life *Housing:* college housing not available. *Activities and Organizations:* drama/theater group, student-run newspaper, radio and television station, choral group, marching band, Phi Theta Kappa, Diesel Tech Club, Business Management Association, Student Activities/Admissions Team, International Club. *Campus security:* 24-hour patrols, student patrols, late-night transport/escort service. *Student services:* personal/psychological counseling.

Athletics Member NJCAA. *Intercollegiate sports:* baseball M(s), basketball M(s)/W(s), golf W(s), softball W(s), volleyball W(s).

Costs (2006–07) *Tuition:* state resident $2586 full-time, $74 per credit part-time; nonresident $2976 full-time, $88 per credit part-time. *Required fees:* $360 full-time, $4 per credit part-time, $5 per term part-time. *Waivers:* senior citizens.

Applying *Options:* electronic application. *Required:* high school transcript. *Application deadlines:* rolling (freshmen), rolling (transfers). *Notification:* continuous until 9/15 (freshmen), continuous until 9/15 (transfers).

Freshmen Application Contact Mr. Scott Copeland, Director of Enrollment Services and College Registrar, Centralia College, 600 West Locust, Centralia, WA 98531. *Phone:* 360-736-9391 Ext. 682. *Fax:* 360-330-7503. *E-mail:* admissions@centralia.edu.

CLARK COLLEGE

Vancouver, Washington   www.clark.edu/

- **State-supported** 2-year, founded 1933, part of Washington State Board for Community and Technical Colleges
- **Urban** 101-acre campus with easy access to Portland
- **Endowment** $51.0 million
- **Coed,** 9,906 undergraduate students, 43% full-time, 60% women, 40% men

Undergraduates 4,268 full-time, 5,638 part-time. Students come from 4 states and territories, 19 other countries, 4% are from out of state, 2% African American, 6% Asian American or Pacific Islander, 3% Hispanic American, 1% Native American, 0.6% international, 33% transferred in. *Retention:* 63% of 2003 full-time freshmen returned.

Freshmen *Admission:* 5,131 applied, 2,836 admitted, 924 enrolled.

Faculty *Total:* 591, 30% full-time, 10% with terminal degrees. *Student/faculty ratio:* 21:1.

Majors Accounting technology and bookkeeping; applied horticulture; automobile/automotive mechanics technology; baking and pastry arts; business administration and management; business automation/technology/data entry; computer programming; computer systems networking and telecommunications; construction engineering technology; culinary arts; data entry/microcomputer applications; dental hygiene; diesel mechanics technology; early childhood education; electrical, electronic and communications engineering technology; emergency medical technology (EMT paramedic); executive assistant/executive secretary; graphic communications; human resources management; landscaping and groundskeeping; legal assistant/paralegal; liberal arts and sciences/liberal studies; machine tool technology; manufacturing technology; medical administrative

assistant and medical secretary; medical/clinical assistant; nursing (registered nurse training); retailing; retailing operations; selling skills and sales; sport and fitness administration/management; substance abuse/addiction counseling; telecommunications technology; web/multimedia management and webmaster; welding technology.

Academics *Calendar:* quarters. *Degree:* certificates, diplomas, and associate. *Special study options:* academic remediation for entering students, accelerated degree program, adult/continuing education programs, advanced placement credit, cooperative education, distance learning, English as a second language, independent study, internships, part-time degree program, services for LD students, study abroad, summer session for credit. *ROTC:* Army (c), Air Force (c).

Library Lewis D. Cannell Library with 72,883 titles, 390 serial subscriptions, 2,246 audiovisual materials, an OPAC, a Web page.

Student Life *Housing:* college housing not available. *Activities and Organizations:* drama/theater group, student-run newspaper, choral group, Phi Theta Kappa, Baptist Student Ministries, Multicultural Students United, Peace Project, Students for Political Activism Now (SPAN). *Campus security:* 24-hour patrols, late-night transport/escort service, security staff during hours of operation. *Student services:* health clinic, personal/psychological counseling, legal services.

Athletics *Intercollegiate sports:* basketball M(s)/W(s), cross-country running M(s)/W(s), fencing M(c)/W(c), soccer M(s)/W(s), softball W, track and field M(s)/W(s), volleyball W(s). *Intramural sports:* basketball M/W, fencing M/W, football M/W, soccer M/W, softball M/W, table tennis M/W, volleyball M/W.

Costs (2006–07) *Tuition:* state resident $2327 full-time, $80 per credit hour part-time; nonresident $2327 full-time, $93 per credit hour part-time. Full-time tuition and fees vary according to course load and reciprocity agreements. Part-time tuition and fees vary according to course load and reciprocity agreements. *Waivers:* senior citizens and employees or children of employees.

Financial Aid Of all full-time matriculated undergraduates, 170 Federal Work-Study jobs (averaging $1900). 164 state and other part-time jobs (averaging $2150).

Applying *Options:* early admission, deferred entrance. *Required for some:* high school transcript, interview. *Application deadlines:* 8/6 (freshmen), 8/6 (transfers). *Notification:* continuous (freshmen), continuous (transfers).

Freshmen Application Contact Ms. Sheryl Anderson, Director of Admissions, Clark College, 1800 East McLoughlin Boulevard, Vancouver, WA 98663. *Phone:* 360-992-2308. *Toll-free phone:* 360-992-2107. *Fax:* 360-992-2867. *E-mail:* sanderson@clark.edu.

CLOVER PARK TECHNICAL COLLEGE

Lakewood, Washington · www.cptc.edu/

Director of Admissions Ms. Judy Richardson, Registrar, Clover Park Technical College, 4500 Steilacoom Boulevard Southwest, Lakewood, WA 98499. *Phone:* 253-589-5570.

COLUMBIA BASIN COLLEGE

Pasco, Washington · www.columbiabasin.edu

- **State-supported** 2-year, founded 1955, part of Washington State Board for Community and Technical Colleges
- **Small-town** 156-acre campus
- **Coed,** 5,837 undergraduate students, 42% full-time, 54% women, 46% men

Undergraduates 2,425 full-time, 3,412 part-time. Students come from 17 states and territories, 2 other countries, 2% are from out of state, 2% African American, 3% Asian American or Pacific Islander, 11% Hispanic American, 0.9% Native American, 0.3% international, 0.5% transferred in.

Freshmen *Admission:* 1,005 enrolled.

Faculty *Total:* 609, 19% full-time. *Student/faculty ratio:* 10:1.

Majors Administrative assistant and secretarial science; agricultural business and management; agricultural mechanization; automobile/automotive mechanics technology; carpentry; computer and information sciences related; computer programming related; computer science; computer software and media applications related; computer systems networking and telecommunications; criminal justice/police science; criminal justice/safety; electrical, electronic and communications engineering technology; engineering; environmental engineering technology; fire science; kindergarten/preschool education; legal assistant/paralegal; liberal arts and sciences/liberal studies; machine tool technology; marketing/marketing management; nuclear/nuclear power technology; nursing (registered nurse training); quality control technology; real estate; web page, digital/multimedia and information resources design; welding technology.

Academics *Calendar:* quarters. *Degree:* associate. *Special study options:* academic remediation for entering students, accelerated degree program, adult/continuing education programs, advanced placement credit, cooperative education, distance learning, English as a second language, internships, part-time degree program, services for LD students, summer session for credit.

Library Columbia Basin College Library with 54,331 titles, 363 serial subscriptions, 6,365 audiovisual materials, an OPAC, a Web page.

Student Life *Housing:* college housing not available. *Activities and Organizations:* drama/theater group, student-run newspaper, choral group, Phi Theta Kappa, Men's Athletic Club, Band Club, Women's Athletic Club, Drama Club. *Campus security:* 24-hour patrols. *Student services:* personal/psychological counseling, women's center.

Athletics *Intercollegiate sports:* baseball M(s), basketball M(s)/W(s), golf M(s)/W(s), soccer M(s)/W(s), volleyball W(s). *Intramural sports:* basketball M/W, bowling M/W, football M, skiing (downhill) M/W, soccer M/W, softball M/W.

Standardized Tests *Required:* ACT ASSET (for placement).

Costs (2006–07) *Tuition:* state resident $2754 full-time; nonresident $3752 full-time.

Financial Aid Of all full-time matriculated undergraduates, 123 Federal Work-Study jobs (averaging $858). 86 state and other part-time jobs (averaging $1441).

Applying *Options:* electronic application. *Application fee:* $26. *Required:* high school transcript. *Recommended:* high school transcript. *Application deadlines:* rolling (freshmen), rolling (transfers). *Notification:* continuous (freshmen), continuous (transfers).

Freshmen Application Contact Ms. Donna Korstad, Program Support Supervisor, Enrollment Management, Columbia Basin College, 2600 North 20th Avenue, Pasco, WA 99301. *Phone:* 509-547-0511 Ext. 2250. *Toll-free phone:* 509-547-0511 Ext. 2250.

CROWN COLLEGE

Tacoma, Washington · www.crowncollege.edu/

- **Proprietary** primarily 2-year, founded 1969, administratively affiliated with Killebrew Dalton, Inc
- **Urban** campus with easy access to Seattle
- **Coed**

Undergraduates Students come from 39 states and territories, 1 other country, 82% are from out of state.

Faculty *Student/faculty ratio:* 20:1.

Academics *Calendar:* continuous. *Degrees:* associate and bachelor's (bachelor's degree in public administration only). *Special study options:* academic remediation for entering students, cooperative education, distance learning, double majors, honors programs, internships, off-campus study, study abroad.

Student Life *Campus security:* 24-hour emergency response devices.

Costs (2006–07) *Tuition:* $7500 full-time. *Required fees:* $385 full-time.

Applying *Options:* electronic application. *Application fee:* $135. *Required:* high school transcript, interview. *Required for some:* essay or personal statement.

Freshmen Application Contact Mrs. Jesica McMullin, Crown College, 8739 South Hosmer, Tacoma, WA 98444. *Phone:* 253-531-3123. *Toll-free phone:* 800-755-9525 (in-state); 888-689-3688 (out-of-state). *Fax:* 253-531-3521. *E-mail:* admissions@crowncollege.edu.

EDMONDS COMMUNITY COLLEGE

Lynnwood, Washington · www.edcc.edu/

- **State and locally supported** 2-year, founded 1967, part of Washington State Board for Community and Technical Colleges
- **Suburban** 115-acre campus with easy access to Seattle
- **Endowment** $2.7 million
- **Coed**

Undergraduates 3,398 full-time, 4,183 part-time. Students come from 55 other countries, 2% are from out of state, 5% African American, 10% Asian American or Pacific Islander, 4% Hispanic American, 2% Native American, 11% international, 0.5% transferred in.

Faculty *Student/faculty ratio:* 21:1.

Academics *Calendar:* quarters. *Degree:* certificates and associate. *Special study options:* academic remediation for entering students, adult/continuing education programs, advanced placement credit, cooperative education, distance learning, English as a second language, honors programs, internships, off-campus study, part-time degree program, services for LD students, student-designed majors, study abroad, summer session for credit.

Edmonds Community College (continued)

Student Life *Campus security:* 24-hour emergency response devices and patrols, student patrols, late-night transport/escort service.

Costs (2006–07) *Tuition:* state resident $2586 full-time, $74 per credit hour part-time; nonresident $7794 full-time, $246 per credit hour part-time. Full-time tuition and fees vary according to course load. Part-time tuition and fees vary according to course load. *Required fees:* $145 full-time, $4 per credit hour part-time. *Room and board:* room only: $4500.

Financial Aid Of all full-time matriculated undergraduates, 125 Federal Work-Study jobs (averaging $7200). 100 state and other part-time jobs (averaging $7200).

Applying *Options:* electronic application, early admission, deferred entrance. *Application fee:* $17.

Freshmen Application Contact Ms. Nancy Froemming, Enrollment Services Office Manager, Edmonds Community College, 20000 68th Avenue West, Lynnwood, WA 98036-5999. *Phone:* 425-640-1853. *Fax:* 425-640-1159. *E-mail:* nanci.froemming@edcc.edu.

EVEREST COLLEGE

Vancouver, Washington www.western-college.com/

Director of Admissions Ms. Maryann Green, Director of Admission, Everest College, 120 Northeast 136th Avenue, Suite 300, Vancouver, WA 98684. *Phone:* 360-254-3282.

EVERETT COMMUNITY COLLEGE

Everett, Washington www.evcc.ctc.edu/

- **State-supported** 2-year, founded 1941, part of Washington State Board for Community and Technical Colleges
- **Suburban** 25-acre campus with easy access to Seattle
- **Endowment** $1.4 million
- **Coed,** 5,780 undergraduate students, 53% full-time, 63% women, 37% men

Undergraduates 3,049 full-time, 2,731 part-time. Students come from 37 states and territories, 15 other countries, 4% are from out of state, 3% African American, 5% Asian American or Pacific Islander, 5% Hispanic American, 2% Native American, 0.5% international, 2% transferred in. *Retention:* 47% of 2003 full-time freshmen returned.

Freshmen *Admission:* 600 admitted, 600 enrolled.

Faculty *Total:* 346, 39% full-time. *Student/faculty ratio:* 19:1.

Majors Accounting; animal sciences; anthropology; art; atmospheric sciences and meteorology; avionics maintenance technology; biology/biological sciences; botany/plant biology; business administration and management; chemistry; cinematography and film/video production; civil engineering technology; commercial and advertising art; computer science; consumer merchandising/retailing management; cosmetology; criminal justice/law enforcement administration; criminal justice/police science; data processing and data processing technology; dental hygiene; drafting and design technology; dramatic/theater arts; drawing; ecology; economics; education; elementary education; engineering; engineering science; engineering technology; English; environmental studies; fire science; funeral service and mortuary science; geology/earth science; German; history; human services; industrial arts; industrial technology; Japanese; journalism; kindergarten/preschool education; liberal arts and sciences/liberal studies; marketing/marketing management; mathematics; medical administrative assistant and medical secretary; medical/clinical assistant; modern languages; music; nursing (licensed practical/vocational nurse training); nursing (registered nurse training); occupational therapy; oceanography (chemical and physical); ophthalmic laboratory technology; pharmacy technician; philosophy; photography; physical education teaching and coaching; physical therapist assistant; physics; political science and government; pre-engineering; psychology; Russian; sociology; Spanish; speech and rhetoric; welding technology; wildlife biology; zoology/animal biology.

Academics *Calendar:* quarters. *Degree:* certificates, diplomas, and associate. *Special study options:* academic remediation for entering students, adult/continuing education programs, advanced placement credit, cooperative education, distance learning, English as a second language, independent study, internships, part-time degree program, services for LD students, study abroad, summer session for credit.

Library John Terrey Library/Media Center with 47,175 titles, 230 serial subscriptions, 7,750 audiovisual materials, an OPAC, a Web page.

Student Life *Housing:* college housing not available. *Activities and Organizations:* drama/theater group, student-run newspaper, choral group, United Native American Council, Nippon Friendship Club, Student Nurses Association, International Students Club, Math, Engineering and Science Student Organization.

Campus security: 24-hour emergency response devices and patrols, late-night transport/escort service. *Student services:* personal/psychological counseling, women's center.

Athletics Member NJCAA. *Intercollegiate sports:* baseball M(s), basketball M(s)/W(s), cross-country running M(s)/W(s), soccer M(s)/W(s), softball W(s), volleyball W(s). *Intramural sports:* basketball M/W, bowling M/W, crew M(c)/W(c), football M/W, golf M/W, soccer M/W, softball M/W, tennis M/W, volleyball M/W, weight lifting M/W.

Standardized Tests *Required:* ACT ASSET, ACT COMPASS (for admission).

Costs (2006–07) *Tuition:* state resident $2586 full-time, $74 per credit part-time; nonresident $7711 full-time, $246 per credit part-time. Full-time tuition and fees vary according to course load. Part-time tuition and fees vary according to course load. *Waivers:* senior citizens and employees or children of employees.

Financial Aid Of all full-time matriculated undergraduates, 152 Federal Work-Study jobs (averaging $3000). 48 state and other part-time jobs (averaging $3000).

Applying *Options:* electronic application, early admission, deferred entrance. *Recommended:* high school transcript. *Application deadlines:* rolling (freshmen), rolling (transfers). *Notification:* continuous (freshmen), continuous (transfers).

Freshmen Application Contact Ms. Linda Baca, Entry Services Manager, Everett Community College, 2000 Tower Street, Everett, WA 98201-1352. *Phone:* 425-388-9219. *Fax:* 425-388-9173. *E-mail:* admissions@everettcc.edu.

GRAYS HARBOR COLLEGE

Aberdeen, Washington www.ghc.ctc.edu/

- **State-supported** 2-year, founded 1930, part of Washington State Board for Community and Technical Colleges
- **Small-town** 125-acre campus
- **Endowment** $148,500
- **Coed,** 2,156 undergraduate students, 48% full-time, 57% women, 43% men

Undergraduates 1,039 full-time, 1,117 part-time. Students come from 4 states and territories, 0.6% are from out of state, 2% African American, 2% Asian American or Pacific Islander, 5% Hispanic American, 7% Native American, 0.2% international, 14% transferred in.

Freshmen *Admission:* 160 enrolled.

Faculty *Total:* 157, 36% full-time, 100% with terminal degrees. *Student/faculty ratio:* 17:1.

Majors Accounting technology and bookkeeping; agricultural business and management; automobile/automotive mechanics technology; business administration and management; carpentry; child care and support services management; corrections; criminal justice/police science; diesel mechanics technology; general studies; human services; industrial technology; information science/studies; liberal arts and sciences/liberal studies; machine tool technology; natural resources/conservation; nursing (registered nurse training); office management; welding technology.

Academics *Calendar:* quarters. *Degree:* certificates, diplomas, and associate. *Special study options:* academic remediation for entering students, accelerated degree program, adult/continuing education programs, advanced placement credit, cooperative education, distance learning, double majors, English as a second language, external degree program, honors programs, independent study, internships, part-time degree program, services for LD students, summer session for credit.

Library Spellman Library with 39,220 titles, 240 serial subscriptions, an OPAC, a Web page.

Student Life *Housing:* college housing not available. *Activities and Organizations:* drama/theater group, student-run newspaper, choral group, PTK, TYEE, Student Nurses Association, Human Services Student Association, student council. *Campus security:* 24-hour emergency response devices, late-night transport/escort service. *Student services:* personal/psychological counseling, women's center.

Athletics *Intercollegiate sports:* baseball M(s), basketball M(s)/W(s), golf M(s)/W(s), softball W(s), volleyball W(s).

Costs (2006–07) *Tuition:* state resident $2372 full-time, $74 per credit part-time; nonresident $2765 full-time, $88 per credit part-time. *Required fees:* $200 full-time, $6 per credit part-time.

Financial Aid Of all full-time matriculated undergraduates, 67 Federal Work-Study jobs (averaging $1064). 135 state and other part-time jobs (averaging $1693).

Applying *Options:* electronic application, early admission. *Recommended:* high school transcript. *Application deadlines:* rolling (freshmen), 9/1 (transfers). *Notification:* continuous (freshmen), continuous (transfers).

Freshmen Application Contact Ms. Brenda Dell, Admissions Officer, Grays Harbor College, 1620 Edward P. Smith Drive, Aberdeen, WA 98520-7599. *Phone:* 360-532-9020 Ext. 4026. *Toll-free phone:* 800-562-4830.

GREEN RIVER COMMUNITY COLLEGE
Auburn, Washington　　　www.greenriver.edu/

Freshmen Application Contact Ms. Peggy Morgan, Program Support Supervisor, Green River Community College, 12401 Southeast 320th Street, Auburn, WA 98092-3699. *Phone:* 253-833-9111. *Fax:* 253-288-3454.

HIGHLINE COMMUNITY COLLEGE
Des Moines, Washington　　　www.highline.edu/

- **State-supported** 2-year, founded 1961, part of Washington State Board for Community and Technical Colleges
- **Suburban** 81-acre campus with easy access to Seattle
- **Coed**

Highline Community College is one of the premier two-year schools in Washington State. The main 80-acre campus overlooks Puget Sound and the Olympic Mountains. Conveniently located between Seattle and Tacoma, Highline serves one of the most diverse student bodies in the region. Exceptional student services, outstanding staff and faculty members, high-quality transfer and professional/technical programs, and affordable cost combine to make Highline a great choice for a promising future.

Undergraduates 3,229 full-time, 3,143 part-time. 11% African American, 17% Asian American or Pacific Islander, 5% Hispanic American, 1% Native American, 0.2% international. *Retention:* 60% of 2003 full-time freshmen returned.

Academics *Calendar:* quarters. *Degree:* certificates, diplomas, and associate. *Special study options:* academic remediation for entering students, advanced placement credit, cooperative education, English as a second language, freshman honors college, honors programs, internships, part-time degree program, services for LD students, student-designed majors, study abroad, summer session for credit. *ROTC:* Army (c), Air Force (c).

Student Life *Campus security:* 24-hour patrols.

Athletics Member NJCAA.

Standardized Tests *Recommended:* ACT COMPASS.

Applying *Application fee:* $21.

Director of Admissions Ms. Debbie Faison, Assistant Registrar, Highline Community College, PO Box 98000, 2400 South 240th Street, Des Moines, WA 98198-9800. *Phone:* 206-878-3710 Ext. 3363.

ITT TECHNICAL INSTITUTE
Bothell, Washington　　　www.itt-tech.edu/

- **Proprietary** primarily 2-year, founded 1993, part of ITT Educational Services, Inc
- **Coed**

Majors Animation, interactive technology, video graphics and special effects; business administration and management; CAD/CADD drafting/design technology; communications technology; computer and information systems security; computer engineering technology; computer software technology; computer systems networking and telecommunications; construction management; criminal justice/law enforcement administration; electrical, electronic and communications engineering technology; medical laboratory technology; web/multimedia management and webmaster; web page, digital/multimedia and information resources design.

Academics *Calendar:* quarters. *Degrees:* associate and bachelor's.

Library a Web page.

Student Life *Housing:* college housing not available.

Standardized Tests *Required:* Wonderlic aptitude test (for admission).

Costs (2006–07) *Tuition:* Contact school for program costs.

Applying *Options:* deferred entrance. *Application fee:* $100. *Required:* high school transcript, interview. *Recommended:* letters of recommendation. *Application deadlines:* rolling (freshmen), rolling (transfers). *Notification:* continuous (freshmen), continuous (transfers).

Freshmen Application Contact Mr. Brad Tmavsky, Director of Recruitment, ITT Technical Institute, 1615 75th Street SW, Everett, WA 98203. *Phone:* 425-583-0200. *Toll-free phone:* 800-272-3791.

ITT TECHNICAL INSTITUTE
Seattle, Washington　　　www.itt-tech.edu/

- **Proprietary** primarily 2-year, founded 1932, part of ITT Educational Services, Inc
- **Urban** campus
- **Coed**

Majors Animation, interactive technology, video graphics and special effects; business administration and management; CAD/CADD drafting/design technology; computer and information systems security; computer engineering technology; computer software engineering; computer systems networking and telecommunications; construction management; criminal justice/law enforcement administration; electrical, electronic and communications engineering technology; health information/medical records technology; web/multimedia management and webmaster; web page, digital/multimedia and information resources design.

Academics *Calendar:* quarters. *Degrees:* associate and bachelor's.

Library a Web page.

Student Life *Housing:* college housing not available.

Standardized Tests *Required:* Wonderlic aptitude test (for admission).

Costs (2006–07) *Tuition:* Contact school for program costs.

Applying *Options:* deferred entrance. *Application fee:* $100. *Required:* high school transcript, interview. *Recommended:* letters of recommendation. *Application deadlines:* rolling (freshmen), rolling (transfers). *Notification:* continuous (freshmen), continuous (transfers).

Freshmen Application Contact Mr. David Thompson, Director of Recruitment, ITT Technical Institute, 12720 Gateway Drive, Seattle, WA 98168. *Phone:* 206-244-3300. *Toll-free phone:* 800-422-2029.

ITT TECHNICAL INSTITUTE
Spokane, Washington　　　www.itt-tech.edu/

- **Proprietary** primarily 2-year, founded 1985, part of ITT Educational Services, Inc
- **Suburban** 3-acre campus
- **Coed**

Majors Animation, interactive technology, video graphics and special effects; CAD/CADD drafting/design technology; computer and information systems security; computer software engineering; computer systems networking and telecommunications; construction management; criminal justice/law enforcement administration; electrical, electronic and communications engineering technology; medical laboratory technology; web/multimedia management and webmaster; web page, digital/multimedia and information resources design.

Academics *Calendar:* quarters. *Degrees:* associate and bachelor's.

Library a Web page.

Student Life *Housing:* college housing not available.

Standardized Tests *Required:* Wonderlic aptitude test (for admission).

Costs (2006–07) *Tuition:* Contact school for program costs.

Financial Aid Of all full-time matriculated undergraduates, 9 Federal Work-Study jobs (averaging $4000).

Applying *Options:* deferred entrance. *Application fee:* $100. *Required:* high school transcript, interview. *Recommended:* letters of recommendation. *Application deadlines:* rolling (freshmen), rolling (transfers). *Notification:* continuous (freshmen), continuous (transfers).

Freshmen Application Contact Mr. Gregory L. Alexander, Director of Recruitment, ITT Technical Institute, 13518 East Indiana Avenue, Spokane Valley, WA 99216. *Phone:* 509-926-2900. *Toll-free phone:* 800-777-8324.

LAKE WASHINGTON TECHNICAL COLLEGE
Kirkland, Washington　　　www.lwtc.ctc.edu/

Director of Admissions Mr. Jim West, Director of Admissions and Registration, Lake Washington Technical College, 11605 132nd Avenue NE, Kirkland, WA 98034-8506. *Phone:* 425-739-8233.

LOWER COLUMBIA COLLEGE

Longview, Washington   www.lcc.ctc.edu/

- **State-supported** 2-year, founded 1934, part of Washington State Board for Community and Technical Colleges
- **Small-town** 30-acre campus with easy access to Portland
- **Endowment** $2.9 million
- **Coed,** 3,268 undergraduate students, 54% full-time, 65% women, 35% men

Undergraduates 1,776 full-time, 1,492 part-time. Students come from 6 states and territories, 5 other countries, 9% are from out of state, 0.8% African American, 2% Asian American or Pacific Islander, 4% Hispanic American, 1% Native American, 0.1% international, 9% transferred in. *Retention:* 44% of 2003 full-time freshmen returned.

Freshmen *Admission:* 278 applied, 278 admitted, 278 enrolled.

Faculty *Total:* 182, 43% full-time. *Student/faculty ratio:* 20:1.

Majors Accounting; accounting technology and bookkeeping; administrative assistant and secretarial science; anthropology; art; automobile/automotive mechanics technology; biology/biological sciences; business administration and management; business/commerce; CAD/CADD drafting/design technology; computer and information sciences; computer engineering technology; computer programming; computer science; computer systems analysis; computer systems networking and telecommunications; computer technology/computer systems technology; corrections; criminal justice/law enforcement administration; criminal justice/police science; criminal justice/safety; data entry/microcomputer applications; data processing and data processing technology; diesel mechanics technology; dramatic/theater arts; early childhood education; economics; electrical, electronic and communications engineering technology; electrician; engineering; engineering technology; English; environmental studies; fire science; fire services administration; foreign languages and literatures; geography; geology/earth science; heavy equipment maintenance technology; history; industrial mechanics and maintenance technology; industrial technology; information science/studies; information technology; instrumentation technology; kindergarten/preschool education; legal administrative assistant/secretary; liberal arts and sciences/liberal studies; lineworker; machine tool technology; management information systems; mathematics; mechanical engineering/mechanical technology; medical administrative assistant and medical secretary; medical/clinical assistant; medical reception; medical transcription; music; nursing assistant/aide and patient care assistant; nursing (licensed practical/vocational nurse training); nursing (registered nurse training); office management; philosophy; photography; physical education teaching and coaching; physics; political science and government; pre-engineering; pre-law studies; psychology; receptionist; social sciences; sociology; speech and rhetoric; substance abuse/addiction counseling; teacher assistant/aide; welding technology; wood science and wood products/pulp and paper technology; word processing.

Academics *Calendar:* quarters. *Degree:* certificates, diplomas, and associate. *Special study options:* academic remediation for entering students, adult/continuing education programs, cooperative education, English as a second language, honors programs, internships, part-time degree program, services for LD students, study abroad, summer session for credit.

Library Allan Thompson Library plus 1 other with 41,991 titles, 217 serial subscriptions, an OPAC.

Student Life *Housing:* college housing not available. *Activities and Organizations:* drama/theater group, student-run newspaper, choral group, Campus Entertainment, Phi Theta Kappa, Services and Relations Club, Multicultural Students Club, Theater Club. *Campus security:* 24-hour emergency response devices and patrols. *Student services:* health clinic, personal/psychological counseling.

Athletics *Intercollegiate sports:* baseball M(s), basketball M(s)/W(s), soccer M(s)/W(s), softball W(s), volleyball W(s).

Costs (2006–07) *Tuition:* state resident $2793 full-time, $80 per credit part-time; nonresident $3495 full-time, $103 per credit part-time. Full-time tuition and fees vary according to reciprocity agreements. Part-time tuition and fees vary according to reciprocity agreements. *Required fees:* $6 per credit part-time. *Payment plan:* deferred payment. *Waivers:* senior citizens and employees or children of employees.

Financial Aid Of all full-time matriculated undergraduates, 440 Federal Work-Study jobs (averaging $708). 447 state and other part-time jobs (averaging $2415).

Applying *Options:* early admission, deferred entrance. *Application fee:* $13. *Recommended:* high school transcript. *Application deadlines:* rolling (freshmen), rolling (transfers). *Notification:* continuous (freshmen).

Freshmen Application Contact Ms. Mary Harding, Vice President for Student Success, Lower Columbia College, 1600 Maple Street, Longview, WA 98632. *Phone:* 360-442-2300. *Fax:* 360-442-2379. *E-mail:* registration@lcc.ctc.edu.

NORTH SEATTLE COMMUNITY COLLEGE

Seattle, Washington   www.northseattle.edu/

- **State-supported** 2-year, founded 1970, part of Seattle Community College District
- **Urban** 65-acre campus
- **Endowment** $4.4 million
- **Coed,** 6,210 undergraduate students, 30% full-time, 62% women, 38% men

Undergraduates 1,864 full-time, 4,346 part-time. Students come from 50 states and territories, 1% are from out of state, 8% African American, 15% Asian American or Pacific Islander, 6% Hispanic American, 1% Native American, 21% transferred in.

Freshmen *Admission:* 5,726 applied, 5,726 admitted, 747 enrolled.

Faculty *Total:* 280, 38% full-time, 18% with terminal degrees. *Student/faculty ratio:* 21:1.

Majors Accounting technology and bookkeeping; administrative assistant and secretarial science; allied health and medical assisting services related; architectural drafting; art; biomedical technology; business/corporate communications; civil drafting and CAD/CADD; communications systems installation and repair technology; computer and information systems security; computer systems networking and telecommunications; early childhood education; electrical, electronic and communications engineering technology; electrical/electronics drafting and CAD/CADD; heating, air conditioning, ventilation and refrigeration maintenance technology; industrial technology; liberal arts and sciences/liberal studies; mechanical drafting and CAD/CADD; medical/clinical assistant; music; nursing (licensed practical/vocational nurse training); nursing (registered nurse training); pharmacy technician; real estate; telecommunications technology; watchmaking and jewelrymaking; web page, digital/multimedia and information resources design.

Academics *Calendar:* quarters. *Degree:* certificates, diplomas, and associate. *Special study options:* academic remediation for entering students, adult/continuing education programs, advanced placement credit, cooperative education, distance learning, English as a second language, external degree program, independent study, internships, part-time degree program, services for LD students, summer session for credit. *ROTC:* Army (c).

Library North Seattle Community College Library with 52,496 titles, 594 serial subscriptions, an OPAC, a Web page.

Student Life *Housing:* college housing not available. *Activities and Organizations:* drama/theater group, student-run newspaper, television station, choral group, Muslim Students Association, Indonesian Community Club, Literary Guild, Phi Theta Kappa, Vietnamese Student Association. *Campus security:* 24-hour emergency response devices, late-night transport/escort service, patrols by security. *Student services:* personal/psychological counseling, women's center.

Athletics *Intercollegiate sports:* basketball M/W. *Intramural sports:* basketball M/W.

Costs (2006–07) *Tuition:* state resident $3213 full-time, $74 per credit part-time; nonresident $10,940 full-time, $246 per credit part-time. Full-time tuition and fees vary according to course load. Part-time tuition and fees vary according to course load. *Required fees:* $346 full-time, $90 per term part-time. *Waivers:* senior citizens and employees or children of employees.

Applying *Options:* electronic application, early admission, deferred entrance. *Required:* high school transcript. *Required for some:* essay or personal statement. *Application deadlines:* rolling (freshmen), rolling (transfers). *Notification:* continuous until 9/24 (freshmen), continuous until 9/24 (transfers).

Freshmen Application Contact Ms. Betsy Abts, Registrar, North Seattle Community College, 9600 College Way North, Seattle, WA 98103-3599. *Phone:* 206-527-3663. *Fax:* 206-527-3671. *E-mail:* arrc@sccd.ctc.edu.

NORTHWEST AVIATION COLLEGE

Auburn, Washington   www.afsnac.com/

- **Private** 2-year, founded 1992
- **Urban** campus
- **Coed,** 50 undergraduate students

Majors Aeronautics/aviation/aerospace science and technology.

Academics *Calendar:* quarters. *Degree:* certificates and associate. *Special study options:* summer session for credit.

Library Northwest Aviation College Library plus 1 other.

Costs (2006–07) *Tuition:* Full-time tuition and fees vary according to course load and program. Part-time tuition and fees vary according to course load and program. Contact college directly for full program costs. *Room and board:* Room and board charges vary according to housing facility.

Applying *Application fee:* $50. *Required:* high school transcript. *Application deadline:* rolling (freshmen).

Freshmen Application Contact Mr. Shawn Pratt, Assistant Director of Education, Northwest Aviation College, 506 23rd, NE, Auburn, WA 98002. *Phone:* 253-854-4960. *Toll-free phone:* 800-246-4960. *Fax:* 253-931-0768. *E-mail:* spratt@afsmac.com.

NORTHWEST INDIAN COLLEGE
Bellingham, Washington   www.nwic.edu/

- **Federally supported** 2-year, founded 1978
- **Rural** 5-acre campus
- **Endowment** $3.0 million
- **Coed**

Undergraduates Students come from 6 states and territories, 2 other countries, 1% African American, 0.9% Asian American or Pacific Islander, 1% Hispanic American, 78% Native American.

Academics *Calendar:* quarters. *Degrees:* certificates and associate (also offers bachelor's degree in elementary education in conjunction with Washington State University). *Special study options:* academic remediation for entering students, adult/continuing education programs, cooperative education, external degree program, internships, part-time degree program, student-designed majors, study abroad, summer session for credit.

Costs (2006–07) *Tuition:* state resident $2646 full-time, $74 per credit part-time; nonresident $7182 full-time, $200 per credit part-time. Part-time tuition and fees vary according to course load. *Required fees:* $150 full-time, $25 per credit part-time.

Applying *Application fee:* $25. *Required:* high school transcript.

Freshmen Application Contact Admissions, Northwest Indian College, 2522 Kwina Road, Bellingham, WA 98226. *Phone:* 360-676-2772 Ext. 4269. *Toll-free phone:* 866-676-2772 Ext. 4264. *Fax:* 360-392-4333. *E-mail:* cbogby@nwic.edu.

NORTHWEST SCHOOL OF WOODEN BOATBUILDING
Port Hadlock, Washington   www.nwboatschool.org/

Director of Admissions Ms. Gretchen Siegfried, Student Services Coordinator, Northwest School of Wooden Boatbuilding, 42 North Water Street, Port Hadlock, WA 98339. *Phone:* 360-385-4948. *Fax:* 360-385-5089. *E-mail:* info@nwboatschool.org.

OLYMPIC COLLEGE
Bremerton, Washington   www.olympic.edu/

- **State-supported** 2-year, founded 1946, part of Washington State Board for Community and Technical Colleges
- **Suburban** 32-acre campus with easy access to Seattle
- **Endowment** $3.9 million
- **Coed,** 6,765 undergraduate students, 51% full-time, 56% women, 44% men

Undergraduates 3,432 full-time, 3,333 part-time. Students come from 50 states and territories, 4 other countries, 3% African American, 7% Asian American or Pacific Islander, 11% Hispanic American, 2% Native American, 0.3% international, 13% transferred in.

Freshmen *Admission:* 6,765 applied, 6,765 admitted, 564 enrolled.

Faculty *Total:* 509, 22% full-time. *Student/faculty ratio:* 20:1.

Majors Accounting technology and bookkeeping; administrative assistant and secretarial science; aesthetician/esthetician and skin care; animation, interactive technology, video graphics and special effects; audiovisual communications technologies related; automobile/automotive mechanics technology; barbering; business administration and management; child care and support services management; computer and information sciences related; computer graphics; computer programming; computer programming related; computer software and media applications related; computer systems networking and telecommunications; cosmetology; cosmetology, barber/styling, and nail instruction; criminal justice/law enforcement administration; criminal justice/police science; culinary arts; culinary arts related; digital communication and media/multimedia; drafting and design technology; early childhood education; electrical, electronic and communications engineering technology; engineering; fire science; fire services administration; industrial technology; information science/studies; information technology; legal administrative assistant/secretary; liberal arts and sciences/

liberal studies; marine maintenance and ship repair technology; medical/clinical assistant; nail technician and manicurist; nursing (licensed practical/vocational nurse training); nursing (registered nurse training); office management; photographic and film/video technology; recording arts technology; special education (early childhood); system administration; system, networking, and LAN/WAN management; web/multimedia management and webmaster; welding technology.

Academics *Calendar:* quarters. *Degree:* certificates, diplomas, and associate. *Special study options:* academic remediation for entering students, adult/continuing education programs, advanced placement credit, cooperative education, distance learning, English as a second language, honors programs, independent study, off-campus study, part-time degree program, services for LD students, summer session for credit.

Library Haselwood Library with 60,000 titles, 541 serial subscriptions, an OPAC, a Web page.

Student Life *Housing:* college housing not available. *Activities and Organizations:* drama/theater group, student-run newspaper, choral group, Phi Theta Kappa, Aware, Oceans (Nursing), ASOC, ASAD. *Campus security:* 24-hour emergency response devices and patrols, student patrols, late-night transport/escort service. *Student services:* personal/psychological counseling, women's center.

Athletics *Intercollegiate sports:* baseball M(s), basketball M(s)/W(s), golf M/W, softball W(s), volleyball W(s). *Intramural sports:* basketball M/W, volleyball M/W.

Costs (2007–08) *Tuition:* state resident $2871 full-time, $74 per credit hour part-time; nonresident $4158 full-time, $117 per credit hour part-time. *Required fees:* $5 per credit hour part-time, $45 per term part-time.

Financial Aid Of all full-time matriculated undergraduates, 105 Federal Work-Study jobs (averaging $2380). 31 state and other part-time jobs (averaging $2880).

Applying *Options:* early admission. *Required for some:* high school transcript. *Application deadlines:* rolling (freshmen), rolling (transfers). *Notification:* continuous (freshmen), continuous (transfers).

Freshmen Application Contact Ms. Gerry Stamm, Director of Admissions and Outreach, Olympic College, 1600 Chester Avenue, Bremerton, WA 98337-1699. *Phone:* 360-475-7126. *Toll-free phone:* 800-259-6718. *Fax:* 360-475-7202. *E-mail:* gstamm@olympic.edu.

PENINSULA COLLEGE
Port Angeles, Washington   www.pc.ctc.edu/

- **State-supported** 2-year, founded 1961
- **Small-town** 75-acre campus
- **Endowment** $1.2 million
- **Coed,** 3,948 undergraduate students, 34% full-time, 58% women, 42% men

Undergraduates 1,362 full-time, 2,586 part-time. Students come from 3 states and territories, 11 other countries, 1% are from out of state, 2% African American, 1% Asian American or Pacific Islander, 2% Hispanic American, 2% Native American, 1% international.

Freshmen *Admission:* 101 applied, 101 admitted.

Faculty *Total:* 191, 34% full-time, 10% with terminal degrees. *Student/faculty ratio:* 20:1.

Majors Accounting; automobile/automotive mechanics technology; biological and physical sciences; business administration and management; child care and support services management; child development; civil engineering technology; commercial fishing; computer programming (vendor/product certification); criminal justice/law enforcement administration; data entry/microcomputer applications related; diesel mechanics technology; electrical, electronic and communications engineering technology; engineering technology; fishing and fisheries sciences and management; nursing (registered nurse training); office management; substance abuse/addiction counseling; web page, digital/multimedia and information resources design.

Academics *Calendar:* quarters. *Degree:* certificates and associate. *Special study options:* academic remediation for entering students, adult/continuing education programs, advanced placement credit, distance learning, English as a second language, honors programs, internships, part-time degree program, services for LD students, summer session for credit.

Library 33,736 titles, 383 serial subscriptions.

Student Life *Housing:* college housing not available. *Activities and Organizations:* drama/theater group, student-run newspaper, choral group, Phi Theta Kappa, SAGE (Students Advocating Global Environmentalism). *Campus security:* 8-hour patrols by trained security personnel. *Student services:* women's center.

Peninsula College (continued)

Athletics *Intercollegiate sports:* basketball M/W, soccer M, softball W. *Intramural sports:* badminton M/W, basketball M/W, bowling M/W, football M, golf M, skiing (cross-country) M/W, soccer M/W, softball M/W, table tennis M/W, tennis M/W, volleyball M/W.

Costs (2007–08) *Tuition:* state resident $2815 full-time, $77 per credit parttime; nonresident $3204 full-time, $90 per credit part-time. *Required fees:* $130 full-time, $28 per course part-time.

Financial Aid Of all full-time matriculated undergraduates, 30 Federal Work-Study jobs (averaging $3600). 25 state and other part-time jobs (averaging $3600).

Applying *Options:* electronic application, deferred entrance. *Required for some:* high school transcript. *Application deadlines:* rolling (freshmen), rolling (transfers). *Notification:* continuous (freshmen), continuous (transfers).

Freshmen Application Contact Ms. Pauline Marvin, Peninsula College, 1502 East Lauridsen Boulevard, Port Angeles, WA 98362-2779. *Phone:* 360-417-6596. *Fax:* 360-457-8100. *E-mail:* admissions@pcadmin.ctc.edu.

PIERCE COLLEGE

Puyallup, Washington   www.pierce.ctc.edu/

- **State-supported** 2-year, founded 1967, part of Washington State Board for Community and Technical Colleges
- **Suburban** 140-acre campus with easy access to Seattle
- **Endowment** $4540
- **Coed,** 13,294 undergraduate students

Undergraduates Students come from 12 other countries.

Faculty *Total:* 590, 41% full-time.

Majors Accounting; administrative assistant and secretarial science; business administration and management; clinical/medical laboratory technology; computer programming; computer typography and composition equipment operation; criminal justice/law enforcement administration; dental hygiene; electrical, electronic and communications engineering technology; fire science; industrial technology; information science/studies; kindergarten/preschool education; legal administrative assistant/secretary; legal assistant/paralegal; liberal arts and sciences/liberal studies; marketing/marketing management; mental health/rehabilitation; substance abuse/addiction counseling; veterinary technology.

Academics *Calendar:* quarters. *Degree:* certificates, diplomas, and associate. *Special study options:* academic remediation for entering students, adult/continuing education programs, advanced placement credit, cooperative education, English as a second language, internships, off-campus study, part-time degree program, services for LD students, summer session for credit. *ROTC:* Army (c).

Library 55,000 titles, 425 serial subscriptions.

Student Life *Housing:* college housing not available. *Activities and Organizations:* drama/theater group, student-run newspaper, choral group, Black Student Union, Phi Theta Kappa, Dental Hygiene Association, Veterinary Technology Association, Latino Student Union. *Campus security:* 24-hour emergency response devices and patrols, late-night transport/escort service. *Student services:* women's center.

Athletics *Intercollegiate sports:* baseball M(s), basketball M(s)/W(s), soccer M(s), softball W(s), volleyball W(s).

Standardized Tests *Required for some:* ACT ASSET. *Recommended:* ACT ASSET.

Costs (2006–07) *Tuition:* state resident $2787 full-time; nonresident $7665 full-time.

Financial Aid Of all full-time matriculated undergraduates, 18 Federal Work-Study jobs (averaging $1889). 55 state and other part-time jobs (averaging $3058).

Applying *Options:* early admission. *Application deadlines:* rolling (freshmen), rolling (transfers). *Notification:* continuous (freshmen).

Director of Admissions Ms. Cindy Burbank, Director of Admissions, Pierce College, 1601 39th Avenue Southeast, Puyallup, WA 98374-2222. *Phone:* 253-964-6686.

PIMA MEDICAL INSTITUTE

Seattle, Washington   www.pmi.edu/

Freshmen Application Contact Admissions Office, Pima Medical Institute, 1627 Eastlake Avenue East, Seattle, WA 98102. *Phone:* 206-322-6100. *Toll-free phone:* 888-898-9048.

RENTON TECHNICAL COLLEGE

Renton, Washington   www.rtc.edu/

- **State-supported** 2-year, founded 1942, part of Washington State Board for Community and Technical Colleges
- **Suburban** 30-acre campus with easy access to Seattle
- **Coed,** 9,301 undergraduate students, 43% full-time, 43% women, 57% men

Undergraduates 4,019 full-time, 5,282 part-time. Students come from 9 states and territories, 13 other countries, 8% African American, 12% Asian American or Pacific Islander, 5% Hispanic American, 1% Native American, 0.4% international.

Faculty *Total:* 282, 30% full-time. *Student/faculty ratio:* 15:1.

Majors Accounting; administrative assistant and secretarial science; automobile/automotive mechanics technology; business administration and management; civil engineering technology; clinical laboratory science/medical technology; communications technology; computer science; culinary arts; electrical, electronic and communications engineering technology; heating, air conditioning, ventilation and refrigeration maintenance technology; legal administrative assistant/secretary; machine tool technology; medical administrative assistant and medical secretary; medical/clinical assistant; musical instrument fabrication and repair; surgical technology; survey technology; teacher assistant/aide.

Academics *Calendar:* quarters. *Degree:* certificates, diplomas, and associate. *Special study options:* academic remediation for entering students, adult/continuing education programs, advanced placement credit, cooperative education, distance learning, English as a second language, internships, part-time degree program, services for LD students, student-designed majors, summer session for credit.

Library Renton Technical College Library with 12,876 titles, 2,316 serial subscriptions, 321 audiovisual materials, an OPAC.

Student Life *Housing:* college housing not available. *Campus security:* patrols by security, security system.

Standardized Tests *Required:* ACT ASSET, SLEP, COMPASS (for placement).

Costs (2006–07) *Tuition:* state resident $3324 full-time.

Financial Aid Of all full-time matriculated undergraduates, 20 Federal Work-Study jobs (averaging $1800). 100 state and other part-time jobs (averaging $2000).

Applying *Options:* early admission. *Application fee:* $25. *Required for some:* high school transcript. *Recommended:* interview. *Application deadline:* rolling (freshmen). *Notification:* continuous (freshmen).

Director of Admissions Mr. Jon Pozega, Vice President for Student Services, Renton Technical College, 3000 Fourth Street, NE, Renton, WA 98056. *Phone:* 425-235-2463.

SEATTLE CENTRAL COMMUNITY COLLEGE

Seattle, Washington   www.seattlecentral.edu/

- **State-supported** 2-year, founded 1966, part of Seattle Community College District System
- **Urban** 15-acre campus
- **Coed**

Undergraduates 10% African American, 14% Asian American or Pacific Islander, 5% Hispanic American, 0.9% Native American, 6% international.

Academics *Calendar:* quarters. *Degree:* certificates and associate. *Special study options:* academic remediation for entering students, adult/continuing education programs, cooperative education, English as a second language, external degree program, internships, part-time degree program, services for LD students, summer session for credit. *ROTC:* Army (c), Navy (c), Air Force (c).

Student Life *Campus security:* 24-hour emergency response devices.

Freshmen Application Contact Admissions Office, Seattle Central Community College, 1701 Broadway, Seattle, WA 98122-2400. *Phone:* 206-587-5450.

SHORELINE COMMUNITY COLLEGE

Shoreline, Washington   www.shore.ctc.edu/

Director of Admissions Ms. Robin Young, Registrar, Shoreline Community College, 16101 Greenwood Avenue North, Seattle, WA 98133. *Phone:* 206-546-4581.

SKAGIT VALLEY COLLEGE
Mount Vernon, Washington   www.skagit.edu/

- **State-supported** 2-year, founded 1926, part of Washington State Board for Community and Technical Colleges
- **Small-town** 85-acre campus with easy access to Seattle
- **Endowment** $3.2 million
- **Coed,** 6,858 undergraduate students

Undergraduates Students come from 4 states and territories, 23 other countries, 3% are from out of state, 1% live on campus.

Freshmen *Admission:* 3,321 applied, 1,994 admitted.

Faculty *Total:* 301. *Student/faculty ratio:* 22:1.

Majors Accounting; administrative assistant and secretarial science; agriculture; anthropology; applied horticulture; art; art history, criticism and conservation; automobile/automotive mechanics technology; biological and physical sciences; biology/biological sciences; business administration and management; chemistry; child development; commercial and advertising art; computer and information sciences; computer engineering technology; computer science; computer technology/computer systems technology; criminal justice/police science; culinary arts; cultural studies; diesel mechanics technology; economics; electrical, electronic and communications engineering technology; English; environmental engineering technology; family and community services; fire science; food services technology; foreign languages and literatures; geography; geology/earth science; heavy equipment maintenance technology; history; hotel/motel administration; humanities; human services; journalism; kindergarten/preschool education; legal assistant/paralegal; liberal arts and sciences/liberal studies; literature; marine technology; mathematics; medical administrative assistant and medical secretary; medical/clinical assistant; music; natural sciences; nursing (licensed practical/vocational nurse training); nursing (registered nurse training); office management; parks, recreation and leisure; parks, recreation and leisure facilities management; philosophy; physical education teaching and coaching; political science and government; pre-engineering; psychology; social sciences; sociology; Spanish; speech and rhetoric; telecommunications; vehicle/equipment operation; welding technology.

Academics *Calendar:* quarters. *Degree:* certificates, diplomas, and associate. *Special study options:* academic remediation for entering students, accelerated degree program, adult/continuing education programs, advanced placement credit, cooperative education, distance learning, English as a second language, external degree program, independent study, internships, part-time degree program, services for LD students, student-designed majors, study abroad, summer session for credit.

Library Norwood Cole Library with 78,631 titles, 359 serial subscriptions, 2,599 audiovisual materials, an OPAC, a Web page.

Student Life *Housing Options:* men-only, women-only, disabled students. *Activities and Organizations:* drama/theater group, student-run newspaper, radio station, choral group, Phi Theta Kappa, Calling All Colors, Business Management Training, Human Services, Paralegal Club. *Campus security:* 24-hour patrols, late-night transport/escort service, telephone/pager system. *Student services:* personal/psychological counseling, women's center.

Athletics *Intercollegiate sports:* baseball M(s), basketball M(s)/W(s), cross-country running M(s)/W(s), golf M(s)/W(s), soccer M(s)/W(s), softball W(s), tennis M(s)/W(s), volleyball W(s). *Intramural sports:* badminton M/W, basketball M/W, sailing M/W, skiing (cross-country) M/W, skiing (downhill) M/W, softball M/W, tennis M/W, volleyball M/W.

Costs (2006–07) *Tuition:* state resident $2712 full-time; nonresident $2850 full-time.

Financial Aid Of all full-time matriculated undergraduates, 100 Federal Work-Study jobs (averaging $2800).

Applying *Options:* electronic application, deferred entrance. *Required for some:* high school transcript, interview. *Application deadlines:* rolling (freshmen), rolling (transfers).

Freshmen Application Contact Ms. Karen Ackelson, Admissions and Recruitment Coordinator, Skagit Valley College, 2405 College Way, Mount Vernon, WA 98273-5899. *Phone:* 360-416-7620.

SOUTH PUGET SOUND COMMUNITY COLLEGE
Olympia, Washington   www.spscc.ctc.edu/

Director of Admissions Mr. Jerry Haynes, Dean of Enrollment Services, South Puget Sound Community College, 2011 Mottman Road, SW, Olympia, WA 98512. *Phone:* 360-754-7711 Ext. 5240.

SOUTH SEATTLE COMMUNITY COLLEGE
Seattle, Washington   southseattle.edu/

- **State-supported** 2-year, founded 1970, part of Seattle Community College District System
- **Urban** 65-acre campus
- **Coed,** 6,769 undergraduate students

Undergraduates Students come from 24 other countries.

Faculty *Total:* 285, 26% full-time.

Majors Accounting; administrative assistant and secretarial science; airframe mechanics and aircraft maintenance technology; artificial intelligence and robotics; automobile/automotive mechanics technology; avionics maintenance technology; biological and physical sciences; business administration and management; computer engineering technology; computer programming; cosmetology; culinary arts; drafting and design technology; engineering; engineering technology; food science; food services technology; heavy equipment maintenance technology; horticultural science; hospitality administration; landscape architecture; landscaping and groundskeeping; liberal arts and sciences/liberal studies; machine tool technology; quality control technology; special products marketing; trade and industrial teacher education; welding technology.

Academics *Calendar:* quarters. *Degree:* certificates, diplomas, and associate. *Special study options:* academic remediation for entering students, adult/continuing education programs, advanced placement credit, English as a second language, off-campus study, part-time degree program, services for LD students, summer session for credit.

Library South Seattle Community College Instructional Resource Center with 34,000 titles, 350 serial subscriptions, an OPAC, a Web page.

Student Life *Housing:* college housing not available. *Activities and Organizations:* drama/theater group, student-run newspaper, choral group, Phi Theta, Vietnamese Club, Afro-American Club, Delta Epsilon Chi, International Student Clubs. *Campus security:* 24-hour emergency response devices and patrols. *Student services:* personal/psychological counseling, women's center.

Athletics *Intramural sports:* basketball M/W, soccer M/W.

Standardized Tests *Required for some:* ACT ASSET.

Costs (2006–07) *Tuition:* state resident $2832 full-time; nonresident $8028 full-time.

Financial Aid Of all full-time matriculated undergraduates, 74 Federal Work-Study jobs (averaging $1925). 44 state and other part-time jobs (averaging $2350).

Applying *Options:* early admission. *Application deadlines:* rolling (freshmen), rolling (transfers).

Director of Admissions Ms. Kim Manderbach, Dean of Student Services/Registration, South Seattle Community College, 6000 16th Avenue, SW, Seattle, WA 98106-1499. *Phone:* 206-764-5378. *Fax:* 206-764-7947. *E-mail:* kimmanderb@sccd.ctc.edu.

SPOKANE COMMUNITY COLLEGE
Spokane, Washington   www.scc.spokane.edu/

- **State-supported** 2-year, founded 1963, part of Washington State Board for Community and Technical Colleges
- **Urban** 108-acre campus
- **Endowment** $33,508
- **Coed,** 5,874 undergraduate students, 73% full-time, 58% women, 42% men

Undergraduates 4,308 full-time, 1,566 part-time. 3% are from out of state, 33% transferred in.

Freshmen *Admission:* 2,081 enrolled.

Faculty *Total:* 509, 58% full-time. *Student/faculty ratio:* 18:1.

Majors Accounting technology and bookkeeping; administrative assistant and secretarial science; agricultural business and management; agronomy and crop science; applied horticulture; architectural engineering technology; artificial intelligence and robotics; automobile/automotive mechanics technology; avionics maintenance technology; biomedical technology; business administration and management; carpentry; civil engineering technology; computer programming; computer typography and composition equipment operation; construction engineering technology; corrections; cosmetology; criminal justice/police science; culinary arts; data processing and data processing technology; dental hygiene; dietetics; drafting and design technology; electrical, electronic and communications engineering technology; fire science; food services technology; forestry; health information/medical records administration; heating, air conditioning, ventilation and refrigeration maintenance technology; heavy equipment maintenance technology; hotel/motel administration; hydrology and water resources science; industrial technology; landscaping and groundskeeping; legal administrative assistant/secretary; legal assistant/paralegal; liberal arts and

Spokane Community College (continued)

sciences/liberal studies; machine tool technology; marketing/marketing management; mechanical design technology; mechanical engineering/mechanical technology; medical administrative assistant and medical secretary; natural resources management and policy; nursing (licensed practical/vocational nurse training); nursing (registered nurse training); ophthalmic laboratory technology; ornamental horticulture; parks, recreation and leisure facilities management; respiratory care therapy; surgical technology; welding technology; wildlife and wildlands science and management.

Academics *Calendar:* quarters. *Degree:* certificates, diplomas, and associate. *Special study options:* academic remediation for entering students, adult/continuing education programs, advanced placement credit, cooperative education, distance learning, English as a second language, independent study, internships, part-time degree program, services for LD students, student-designed majors, summer session for credit. *ROTC:* Army (c).

Library Learning Resources Center plus 1 other with 38,967 titles, 466 serial subscriptions, an OPAC.

Student Life *Housing:* college housing not available. *Activities and Organizations:* drama/theater group, student-run newspaper, VICA, Delta Epsilon Chi, Intercultural Student Organization, Rho Beta Psi, Student Awareness League. *Campus security:* 24-hour emergency response devices and patrols, student patrols, late-night transport/escort service.

Athletics Member NJCAA. *Intercollegiate sports:* baseball M(s), basketball M(s)/W(s), cross-country running M(s)/W(s), soccer M(s)/W(s), softball W(s), tennis M(s)/W(s), track and field M(s)/W(s), volleyball W(s). *Intramural sports:* badminton M/W, basketball M/W, bowling M/W, softball M/W, table tennis M/W, tennis M/W, volleyball M/W, water polo M/W.

Costs (2006–07) *Tuition:* state resident $2579 full-time, $74 per credit part-time; nonresident $3192 full-time, $100 per credit part-time. Full-time tuition and fees vary according to course load, program, and reciprocity agreements. Part-time tuition and fees vary according to course load. *Required fees:* $433 full-time. *Waivers:* senior citizens and employees or children of employees.

Financial Aid Of all full-time matriculated undergraduates, 291 Federal Work-Study jobs (averaging $3600). 250 state and other part-time jobs (averaging $3600).

Applying *Options:* early admission, deferred entrance. *Application fee:* $15. *Recommended:* high school transcript. *Application deadlines:* rolling (freshmen), rolling (transfers). *Notification:* continuous (freshmen).

Freshmen Application Contact Ms. Mary Lee, Researcher, District Institutional Research, Spokane Community College, North 1810 Greene Street, Spokane, WA 99217-5399. *Phone:* 509-434-5242. *Toll-free phone:* 800-248-5644. *Fax:* 509-434-5249. *E-mail:* mlee@ccs.spokane.edu.

SPOKANE FALLS COMMUNITY COLLEGE

Spokane, Washington   www.spokanefalls.edu/

- **State-supported** 2-year, founded 1967, part of State Board for Washington Community and Technical Colleges
- **Urban** 125-acre campus
- **Endowment** $33,407
- **Coed,** 5,445 undergraduate students, 70% full-time, 57% women, 43% men

Undergraduates 3,824 full-time, 1,621 part-time. 5% are from out of state, 2% African American, 4% Asian American or Pacific Islander, 5% Hispanic American, 3% Native American, 1% international, 66% transferred in. *Retention:* 15% of 2003 full-time freshmen returned.

Freshmen *Admission:* 1,729 enrolled.

Faculty *Total:* 545, 30% full-time. *Student/faculty ratio:* 27:1.

Majors Accounting technology and bookkeeping; administrative assistant and secretarial science; art; business administration and management; business and personal/financial services marketing; child care and support services management; commercial and advertising art; commercial photography; consumer merchandising/retailing management; fashion merchandising; gerontology; heavy equipment maintenance technology; information science/studies; interior design; international business/trade/commerce; leatherworking/upholstery; liberal arts and sciences/liberal studies; library assistant; marketing/marketing management; mass communication/media; music; office occupations and clerical services; orthotics/prosthetics; physical therapist assistant; real estate; sign language interpretation and translation; social work; sport and fitness administration/management; substance abuse/addiction counseling; vocational rehabilitation counseling; welding technology.

Academics *Calendar:* quarters. *Degree:* certificates, diplomas, and associate. *Special study options:* academic remediation for entering students, adult/continuing education programs, advanced placement credit, cooperative education, English as a second language, internships, part-time degree program, services for LD students, student-designed majors, summer session for credit. *ROTC:* Army (c).

Library Learning Resources Center plus 1 other with 58,000 titles, 705 serial subscriptions, an OPAC.

Student Life *Housing:* college housing not available. *Activities and Organizations:* drama/theater group, student-run newspaper, radio station, choral group, DECA, Associated Men Students, Associated Women Students, chorale, Forensics Club. *Campus security:* late-night transport/escort service, 24-hour emergency dispatch. *Student services:* personal/psychological counseling, women's center.

Athletics Member NJCAA. *Intercollegiate sports:* baseball M(s), basketball M(s)/W(s), cross-country running M(s)/W(s), soccer M(s)/W(s), softball W(s), tennis M(s)/W(s), track and field M(s)/W(s), volleyball W(s). *Intramural sports:* badminton M/W, basketball M/W, bowling M/W, soccer M/W, softball M/W, table tennis M/W, tennis M/W, volleyball M/W.

Costs (2006–07) *Tuition:* area resident $2579 full-time; state resident $74 per credit part-time; nonresident $3192 full-time, $100 per credit part-time. Full-time tuition and fees vary according to course load, program, and reciprocity agreements. Part-time tuition and fees vary according to course load, program, and reciprocity agreements. *Required fees:* $433 full-time, $4 per credit part-time, $6 per term part-time. *Payment plan:* deferred payment. *Waivers:* senior citizens.

Financial Aid Of all full-time matriculated undergraduates, 250 Federal Work-Study jobs (averaging $3600). 260 state and other part-time jobs (averaging $4500).

Applying *Options:* early admission, deferred entrance. *Application fee:* $15. *Recommended:* high school transcript. *Application deadlines:* rolling (freshmen), rolling (transfers). *Notification:* continuous (freshmen), continuous (transfers).

Freshmen Application Contact Admissions Office, Spokane Falls Community College, 3410 West Fort George Wright Drive, Spokane, WA 99224-5288. *Phone:* 509-533-3401. *Toll-free phone:* 888-509-7944. *Fax:* 509-533-3852.

TACOMA COMMUNITY COLLEGE

Tacoma, Washington   www.tacomacc.edu/

Freshmen Application Contact Ms. Annette Hayward, Admissions Officer, Tacoma Community College, 6501 South 19th Street, Tacoma, WA 98466. *Phone:* 253-566-5108. *E-mail:* ahayward@msmail.tacoma.ctc.edu.

WALLA WALLA COMMUNITY COLLEGE

Walla Walla, Washington   www.wwcc.edu/home/

Freshmen Application Contact Ms. Sally Wagoner, Director of Admissions and Records, Walla Walla Community College, 500 Tausick Way, Walla Walla, WA 99362-9267. *Phone:* 509-527-4283. *Toll-free phone:* 877-992-9282 (in-state); 877-992-9292 (out-of-state). *Fax:* 509-527-3361. *E-mail:* admissions@wccc.ctc.edu.

WENATCHEE VALLEY COLLEGE

Wenatchee, Washington   www.wvc.edu/

- **State and locally supported** 2-year, founded 1939, part of Washington State Board for Community and Technical Colleges
- **Rural** 56-acre campus
- **Endowment** $358,000
- **Coed,** 4,046 undergraduate students

Undergraduates Students come from 6 other countries.

Freshmen *Admission:* 843 applied, 843 admitted.

Faculty *Total:* 203, 33% full-time.

Majors Accounting; administrative assistant and secretarial science; agricultural mechanization; applied art; athletic training; automobile/automotive mechanics technology; biology/biological sciences; business administration and management; carpentry; chemistry; clinical/medical laboratory technology; commercial and advertising art; economics; education; fire science; heating, air conditioning, ventilation and refrigeration maintenance technology; history; industrial radiologic technology; kindergarten/preschool education; legal administrative assistant/secretary; liberal arts and sciences/liberal studies; mathematics; medical administrative assistant and medical secretary; medical/clinical assistant; music; music teacher education; nursing (licensed practical/vocational nurse training); nursing (registered nurse training); parks, recreation and leisure; physical education teaching and coaching; pre-engineering; sociology; substance abuse/addiction counseling; trade and industrial teacher education.

Academics *Calendar:* quarters. *Degree:* certificates, diplomas, and associate. *Special study options:* academic remediation for entering students, adult/continuing education programs, advanced placement credit, cooperative education, distance learning, English as a second language, external degree program, honors programs, independent study, part-time degree program, services for LD students, summer session for credit.

Library John Brown Library plus 1 other with 32,000 titles, 220 serial subscriptions, an OPAC, a Web page.

Student Life *Housing Options:* coed. *Activities and Organizations:* drama/theater group, student-run newspaper, choral group. *Campus security:* evening and late night security patrols.

Athletics *Intercollegiate sports:* baseball M, basketball M(s)/W(s), soccer M/W, softball W(s). *Intramural sports:* badminton M/W, basketball M/W, football M/W, golf M/W, racquetball M/W, skiing (cross-country) M/W, skiing (downhill) M/W, tennis M/W, volleyball M/W, weight lifting M/W.

Standardized Tests *Required:* ACT ASSET (for placement).

Costs (2006–07) *Tuition:* state resident $2486 full-time; nonresident $2879 full-time.

Applying *Options:* electronic application, early admission, deferred entrance. *Application fee:* $25. *Required for some:* high school transcript. *Application deadline:* rolling (freshmen).

Freshmen Application Contact Ms. Marlene Sinko, Registrar/Admissions Coordinator, Wenatchee Valley College, 1300 Fifth Street, Wenatchee, WA 98801-1799. *Phone:* 509-664-2564.

WHATCOM COMMUNITY COLLEGE

Bellingham, Washington   www.whatcom.ctc.edu/

Freshmen Application Contact Entry and Advising Center, Whatcom Community College, 237 West Kellogg Road, Bellingham, WA 98226. *Phone:* 360-650-5358.

YAKIMA VALLEY COMMUNITY COLLEGE

Yakima, Washington   www.yvcc.edu/

- **State-supported** 2-year, founded 1928, part of Washington State Board for Community and Technical Colleges
- **Small-town** 20-acre campus
- **Endowment** $5.4 million
- **Coed**

Undergraduates 3,755 full-time, 2,470 part-time. Students come from 10 other countries, 2% are from out of state, 1% African American, 2% Asian American or Pacific Islander, 37% Hispanic American, 3% Native American, 1% live on campus.

Faculty *Student/faculty ratio:* 20:1.

Academics *Calendar:* quarters. *Degree:* certificates and associate. *Special study options:* academic remediation for entering students, adult/continuing education programs, advanced placement credit, cooperative education, distance learning, English as a second language, internships, part-time degree program, services for LD students, summer session for credit.

Student Life *Campus security:* 24-hour emergency response devices, student patrols, late-night transport/escort service, controlled dormitory access.

Athletics Member NJCAA.

Financial Aid Of all full-time matriculated undergraduates, 133 Federal Work-Study jobs (averaging $1164). 156 state and other part-time jobs (averaging $2083).

Applying *Options:* electronic application, deferred entrance. *Application fee:* $20. *Required for some:* high school transcript, letters of recommendation, interview. *Recommended:* high school transcript.

Freshmen Application Contact Tessa Southards, Admissions Assistant, Yakima Valley Community College, PO Box 22520, Yakima, WA 98907-2520. *Phone:* 509-574-4713. *Fax:* 509-574-6860. *E-mail:* admis@yvcc.edu.

WEST VIRGINIA

BLUE RIDGE COMMUNITY AND TECHNICAL COLLEGE

Martinsburg, West Virginia   www.blueridgectc.edu/

- **County-supported** 2-year, founded 1974
- **Coed**

Undergraduates 427 full-time, 1,284 part-time. 40% are from out of state, 8% African American, 0.6% Asian American or Pacific Islander, 2% Hispanic American, 0.6% Native American, 0.2% international.

Faculty *Student/faculty ratio:* 29:1.

Academics *Degree:* certificates and associate.

Standardized Tests *Recommended:* SAT and SAT Subject Tests or ACT (for admission).

Costs (2006–07) *Tuition:* state resident $2944 full-time, $123 per credit part-time; nonresident $8542 full-time, $355 per credit part-time.

Applying *Application fee:* $35. *Required:* high school transcript. *Required for some:* interview.

Freshmen Application Contact Leslie C. See, Director of Enrollment Management, Blue Ridge Community and Technical College, 400 West Stephen Street, Martinsburg, WV 25401. *Phone:* 304-260-4380. *Fax:* 304-260-4376. *E-mail:* lseectc@shepherd.edu.

COMMUNITY & TECHNICAL COLLEGE AT WEST VIRGINIA UNIVERSITY INSTITUTE OF TECHNOLOGY

Montgomery, West Virginia   ctc.wvutech.edu/

Director of Admissions Ms. Lisa Graham, Director of Admissions, Community & Technical College at West Virginia University Institute of Technology, Box 10, Old Main, Montgomery, WV 25136. *Phone:* 304-442-3167. *Toll-free phone:* 888-554-8324.

EASTERN WEST VIRGINIA COMMUNITY AND TECHNICAL COLLEGE

Moorefield, West Virginia   www.eastern.wvnet.edu/

- **State-supported** 2-year, founded 1999
- **Rural** campus
- **Coed**, 786 undergraduate students, 9% full-time, 72% women, 28% men
- **100%** of applicants were admitted

Undergraduates 71 full-time, 715 part-time. 2% African American, 0.4% Hispanic American, 0.4% Native American, 4% transferred in.

Freshmen *Admission:* 85 applied, 85 admitted, 69 enrolled.

Faculty *Total:* 37, 3% full-time, 3% with terminal degrees. *Student/faculty ratio:* 24:1.

Majors Administrative assistant and secretarial science; child care provision; general studies; heavy/industrial equipment maintenance technologies related; liberal arts and sciences and humanities related; liberal arts and sciences/liberal studies; multi-/interdisciplinary studies related; science technologies related.

Academics *Calendar:* semesters. *Degree:* certificates and associate. *Special study options:* academic remediation for entering students, advanced placement credit, distance learning, double majors, external degree program, independent study, internships, part-time degree program, services for LD students, student-designed majors.

Student Life *Housing:* college housing not available.

Costs (2007–08) *Tuition:* state resident $1776 full-time, $74 per credit part-time; nonresident $6824 full-time, $284 per credit part-time.

Freshmen Application Contact Ms. Sharon Bungard, Dean for Learner Support Services, Eastern West Virginia Community and Technical College, 1929 State Road 55, Moorefield, WV 26836. *Phone:* 304-434-8000. *Toll-free phone:* 877-982-2322. *Fax:* 304-434-7001.

HUNTINGTON JUNIOR COLLEGE

Huntington, West Virginia www.huntingtonjuniorcollege.com/

Director of Admissions Mr. James Garrett, Educational Services Director, Huntington Junior College, 900 Fifth Avenue, Huntington, WV 25701-2004. *Phone:* 304-697-7550.

MARSHALL COMMUNITY AND TECHNICAL COLLEGE

Huntington, West Virginia **www.marshall.edu/ctc/**

- **County-supported** 2-year, part of Community and Technical College System of West Virginia, administratively affiliated with Marshall University
- **Urban** 70-acre campus
- **Endowment** $98,218
- **Coed,** 2,579 undergraduate students, 49% full-time, 39% women, 61% men

Undergraduates 1,274 full-time, 1,305 part-time. Students come from 29 states and territories, 4 other countries, 22% are from out of state, 7% African American, 0.7% Asian American or Pacific Islander, 1% Hispanic American, 0.4% Native American, 0.2% international, 8% transferred in. *Retention:* 53% of 2003 full-time freshmen returned.

Freshmen *Admission:* 772 applied, 772 admitted, 459 enrolled. *Average high school GPA:* 2.51. *Test scores:* ACT scores over 18: 27%; ACT scores over 24: 1%.

Faculty *Total:* 126, 29% full-time, 10% with terminal degrees. *Student/faculty ratio:* 25:1.

Majors Accounting technology and bookkeeping; administrative assistant and secretarial science; business/commerce; computer engineering technology; criminal justice/police science; dental laboratory technology; electrical, electronic and communications engineering technology; emergency medical technology (EMT paramedic); finance; health information/medical records technology; hospitality administration; interior design; legal assistant/paralegal; liberal arts and sciences/liberal studies; manufacturing technology; medical/clinical assistant; medical radiologic technology; medical transcription; multi-/interdisciplinary studies related; physical science technologies related; physical therapist assistant; respiratory care therapy; science technologies related.

Academics *Calendar:* semesters. *Degree:* certificates and associate. *Special study options:* academic remediation for entering students, accelerated degree program, cooperative education, distance learning, double majors, English as a second language, independent study, internships, off-campus study, part-time degree program, services for LD students, summer session for credit. *ROTC:* Army (b).

Library John Deaver Drinko Library plus 2 others with 1.6 million titles, 22,591 serial subscriptions, 209,391 audiovisual materials, an OPAC, a Web page.

Student Life *Housing:* on-campus residence required for freshman year. *Options:* coed, men-only, women-only, disabled students. Campus housing is university owned. Freshman campus housing is guaranteed. *Activities and Organizations:* drama/theater group, student-run newspaper, radio and television station, choral group, marching band, national fraternities, national sororities. *Campus security:* 24-hour emergency response devices and patrols, controlled dormitory access. *Student services:* health clinic, personal/psychological counseling, women's center, legal services.

Standardized Tests *Recommended:* SAT (for admission), ACT (for admission).

Costs (2006–07) *Tuition:* state resident $2898 full-time, $121 per credit hour part-time; nonresident $8142 full-time, $340 per credit hour part-time. Full-time tuition and fees vary according to degree level, location, program, and reciprocity agreements. Part-time tuition and fees vary according to course load, degree level, location, program, and reciprocity agreements. *Room and board:* $6492; room only: $3618. Room and board charges vary according to board plan and housing facility. *Payment plan:* installment. *Waivers:* children of alumni and senior citizens.

Applying *Options:* electronic application, early admission. *Application fee:* $30. *Required:* high school transcript, minimum 2.0 GPA. *Application deadlines:* rolling (freshmen), rolling (transfers). *Notification:* continuous (freshmen), continuous (transfers).

Freshmen Application Contact Dr. Tammy Johnson, Admissions Director, Marshall Community and Technical College, 1 John Marshall Drive, Huntington, WV 25755. *Phone:* 304-696-3160. *Toll-free phone:* 800-642-3499. *Fax:* 304-696-3135. *E-mail:* admissions@marshall.edu.

MOUNTAIN STATE COLLEGE

Parkersburg, West Virginia **www.mountainstate.org/**

- **Proprietary** 2-year, founded 1888
- **Small-town** campus
- **Coed, primarily women,** 166 undergraduate students, 100% full-time, 83% women, 17% men

Undergraduates 166 full-time. 1% African American, 0.6% Asian American or Pacific Islander, 0.6% Hispanic American. *Retention:* 70% of 2003 full-time freshmen returned.

Freshmen *Admission:* 27 enrolled.

Faculty *Total:* 11, 64% full-time, 36% with terminal degrees. *Student/faculty ratio:* 17:1.

Majors Accounting and business/management; administrative assistant and secretarial science; computer and information sciences; legal assistant/paralegal; medical/clinical assistant; medical transcription.

Academics *Calendar:* quarters. *Degree:* diplomas and associate.

Student Life *Housing:* college housing not available.

Standardized Tests *Required:* CPAt (for admission).

Costs (2006–07) *Tuition:* $7050 full-time. *Required fees:* $115 full-time.

Applying *Required:* interview.

Freshmen Application Contact Ms. Judith Sutton, Director, Student Services, Mountain State College, 1508 Spring Street, Parkersburg, WV 26101-3993. *Phone:* 304-485-5487. *Toll-free phone:* 800-841-0201. *Fax:* 304-485-3524. *E-mail:* jsutton@mountainstate.org.

NATIONAL INSTITUTE OF TECHNOLOGY

Cross Lanes, West Virginia **www.nitschools.com/**

Freshmen Application Contact Mrs. Karen Wilkinson, Director of Admissions, National Institute of Technology, 5514 Big Tyler Road, Cross Lanes, WV 25313. *Phone:* 304-776-6290. *Toll-free phone:* 888-741-4271. *Fax:* 304-776-6262.

NEW RIVER COMMUNITY AND TECHNICAL COLLEGE

Beckley, West Virginia **www.nrctc.org/**

Director of Admissions Mr. Michael Palm, Director of Student Services, New River Community and Technical College, 101 Church Street, Lewisburg, WV 24901. *Phone:* 304-647-6564.

PIERPONT COMMUNITY AND TECHNICAL COLLEGE OF FAIRMONT STATE UNIVERSITY

Fairmont, West Virginia **www.fairmontstate.edu/**

Freshmen Application Contact Mr. Steve Leadman, Director of Admissions and Recruiting, Pierpont Community and Technical College of Fairmont State University, 1201 Locust Avenue, Fairmont, WV 26554. *Phone:* 304-367-4892. *Toll-free phone:* 800-641-5678. *Fax:* 304-367-4789.

▶**See page 578 for the College Close-Up.**

POTOMAC STATE COLLEGE OF WEST VIRGINIA UNIVERSITY

Keyser, West Virginia **www.potomacstatecollege.edu/**

- **State-supported** 2-year, founded 1901, part of West Virginia Higher Education Policy Commission
- **Small-town** 616-acre campus
- **Endowment** $1.8 million
- **Coed,** 1,330 undergraduate students, 63% full-time, 52% women, 48% men

Undergraduates 842 full-time, 488 part-time. Students come from 17 states and territories, 2 other countries, 14% are from out of state, 35% live on campus.

Freshmen *Admission:* 1,006 admitted. *Average high school GPA:* 2.78. *Test scores:* SAT verbal scores over 500: 16%; SAT math scores over 500: 17%; ACT scores over 18: 60%; SAT verbal scores over 600: 3%; SAT math scores over 600: 5%; ACT scores over 24: 10%; ACT scores over 30: 1%.

Faculty *Total:* 95, 37% full-time, 17% with terminal degrees. *Student/faculty ratio:* 16:1.

Majors Accounting; administrative assistant and secretarial science; agricultural business and management; agricultural economics; agricultural mechanization; agricultural teacher education; agriculture; agronomy and crop science; animal sciences; biological and physical sciences; biology/biological sciences; business administration and management; business/managerial economics; chemistry; civil engineering technology; computer and information sciences related; computer engineering technology; computer programming; computer programming (specific applications); computer science; computer systems networking and telecommunications; criminal justice/safety; data processing and data processing technology; economics; education; electrical, electronic and communications engineering technology; elementary education; engineering; English; forestry; forestry technology; geology/earth science; history; horticultural science; information technology; journalism; kindergarten/preschool education; liberal arts and sciences/liberal studies; mathematics; mechanical engineering/mechanical technology; medical administrative assistant and medical secretary; music; music teacher education; parks, recreation and leisure facilities management; physical education teaching and coaching; political science and government; pre-engineering; psychology; social work; sociology; system administration; wildlife and wildlands science and management; wood science and wood products/pulp and paper technology.

Academics *Calendar:* semesters. *Degree:* certificates and associate. *Special study options:* academic remediation for entering students, adult/continuing education programs, advanced placement credit, honors programs, part-time degree program, services for LD students, summer session for credit.

Library Shipper Library with 44,197 titles, 304 serial subscriptions, 23,395 audiovisual materials, an OPAC, a Web page.

Student Life *Housing:* on-campus residence required through sophomore year. *Options:* men-only, women-only. *Activities and Organizations:* drama/theater group, student-run newspaper, choral group, student newspaper, Circle K Club, Agriculture and Forestry Club, Business Club, Community Chorus. *Campus security:* 24-hour emergency response devices and patrols, controlled dormitory access. *Student services:* health clinic, personal/psychological counseling.

Athletics Member NJCAA. *Intercollegiate sports:* baseball M(s), basketball M(s)/W(s), golf M(s)/W(s), soccer M/W, softball W, volleyball W(s). *Intramural sports:* basketball M/W, skiing (cross-country) M/W, skiing (downhill) M/W, tennis M/W, volleyball M/W.

Standardized Tests *Required for some:* SAT or ACT (for admission).

Costs (2006–07) *Tuition:* state resident $2474 full-time, $104 per credit hour part-time; nonresident $8066 full-time, $337 per credit hour part-time. Part-time tuition and fees vary according to course load. *Room and board:* $4962; room only: $2496. Room and board charges vary according to board plan and location. *Payment plan:* installment. *Waivers:* senior citizens.

Financial Aid Of all full-time matriculated undergraduates, 70 Federal Work-Study jobs (averaging $1300).

Applying *Options:* electronic application, early admission, deferred entrance. *Required:* high school transcript. *Application deadlines:* rolling (freshmen), rolling (transfers).

Freshmen Application Contact Ms. Beth Little, Director of Enrollment Services, Potomac State College of West Virginia University, One Grand Central Business Center, Suite 2090, Keyser, WV 26726. *Phone:* 304-788-6820. *Toll-free phone:* 800-262-7332 Ext. 6820. *Fax:* 304-788-6939. *E-mail:* go2psc@mail.wvu.edu.

SOUTHERN WEST VIRGINIA COMMUNITY AND TECHNICAL COLLEGE

Mount Gay, West Virginia   **www.southern.wvnet.edu/**

- **State-supported** 2-year, founded 1971, part of State College System of West Virginia
- **Rural** 23-acre campus
- **Coed**

Undergraduates 1,257 full-time, 725 part-time. Students come from 2 states and territories, 12% are from out of state, 2% African American, 0.3% Asian American or Pacific Islander, 0.2% Hispanic American, 0.2% Native American, 7% transferred in.

Faculty *Student/faculty ratio:* 20:1.

Academics *Calendar:* semesters. *Degree:* certificates and associate. *Special study options:* academic remediation for entering students, adult/continuing education programs, advanced placement credit, cooperative education, external degree program, part-time degree program, services for LD students, summer session for credit.

Costs (2006–07) *Tuition:* state resident $1634 full-time, $68 per credit hour part-time; nonresident $6486 full-time, $270 per credit hour part-time.

Financial Aid Of all full-time matriculated undergraduates, 45 Federal Work-Study jobs (averaging $1500). *Financial aid deadline:* 3/1.

Applying *Options:* early admission, deferred entrance. *Required:* high school transcript.

Freshmen Application Contact Mr. Roy Simmons, Registrar, Southern West Virginia Community and Technical College, PO Box 2900, Mt. Gay, WV 25637. *Phone:* 304-792-7160 Ext. 120. *Fax:* 304-792-7096. *E-mail:* admissions@southern.wvnet.edu.

VALLEY COLLEGE

Martinsburg, West Virginia   **www.valleycollege.com/**

- **Proprietary** 2-year, founded 1983
- **Suburban** campus
- **Coed, primarily women**

Undergraduates 47 full-time. 13% African American, 2% Hispanic American, 4% Native American.

Faculty *Student/faculty ratio:* 14:1.

Academics *Calendar:* continuous. *Degree:* certificates and associate.

Costs (2006–07) *Tuition:* $7200 full-time, $225 per credit part-time. Full-time tuition and fees vary according to course load and program. Part-time tuition and fees vary according to course load and program. *Required fees:* $100 full-time.

Applying *Required:* high school transcript, interview.

Freshmen Application Contact Ms. Gail Kennedy, Admissions Director, Valley College, 287 Aikens Center, Martinsburg, WV 25401. *Phone:* 304-263-0878. *Fax:* 304-263-2413. *E-mail:* gkennedy@vct.edu.

WEST VIRGINIA BUSINESS COLLEGE

Nutter Fort, West Virginia   **www.wvbc.edu/**

Admissions Office Contact West Virginia Business College, 116 Pennsylvania Avenue, Nutter Fort, WV 26301.

WEST VIRGINIA BUSINESS COLLEGE

Wheeling, West Virginia   **www.stratuswave.com/~wvbc/**

- **Proprietary** 2-year, founded 1881
- **Urban** 5-acre campus
- **Coed, primarily women**
- **100% of applicants were admitted**

Faculty *Student/faculty ratio:* 6:1.

Academics *Calendar:* quarters. *Degree:* diplomas and associate.

Costs (2006–07) *Tuition:* $15,999 full-time. *Required fees:* $200 full-time.

Freshmen Application Contact Ms. Karen D. Shaw, Director, West Virginia Business College, 1052 Main Street, Wheeling, WV 26003. *Phone:* 304-232-0361. *Fax:* 304-232-0363. *E-mail:* wvbcwheeling@stratuswave.net.

WEST VIRGINIA JUNIOR COLLEGE

Bridgeport, West Virginia   **www.wvjc.com/**

Freshmen Application Contact Ms. Cheryl Stickley, Executive Assistant, West Virginia Junior College, 176 Thompson Drive, Bridgeport, WV 26330. *Phone:* 304-363-8824.

WEST VIRGINIA JUNIOR COLLEGE

Charleston, West Virginia   **www.wvjc.com/**

Freshmen Application Contact Admission Department, West Virginia Junior College, 1000 Virginia Street East, Charleston, WV 25301-2817. *Phone:* 304-345-2820.

WEST VIRGINIA JUNIOR COLLEGE

Morgantown, West Virginia   **www.wvjc.com/**

Freshmen Application Contact Admissions Office, West Virginia Junior College, 148 Willey Street, Morgantown, WV 26505-5521. *Phone:* 304-296-8282.

WEST VIRGINIA NORTHERN COMMUNITY COLLEGE

Wheeling, West Virginia   www.northern.wvnet.edu/

- **State-supported** 2-year, founded 1972
- **Small-town** campus with easy access to Pittsburgh
- **Endowment** $700,706
- **Coed**

Undergraduates 1,421 full-time, 1,421 part-time. Students come from 5 states and territories, 17% are from out of state, 3% African American, 0.4% Asian American or Pacific Islander, 0.3% Hispanic American, 0.2% Native American, 0.1% international, 8% transferred in. *Retention:* 51% of 2003 full-time freshmen returned.

Faculty *Student/faculty ratio:* 19:1.

Academics *Calendar:* semesters. *Degree:* certificates and associate. *Special study options:* academic remediation for entering students, accelerated degree program, adult/continuing education programs, advanced placement credit, distance learning, double majors, honors programs, internships, part-time degree program, student-designed majors, summer session for credit.

Student Life *Campus security:* security personnel during evening and night classes.

Costs (2006–07) *Tuition:* state resident $1824 full-time, $76 per credit part-time; nonresident $5808 full-time, $242 per credit part-time. Full-time tuition and fees vary according to course load and reciprocity agreements. Part-time tuition and fees vary according to course load and reciprocity agreements.

Financial Aid Of all full-time matriculated undergraduates, 35 Federal Work-Study jobs (averaging $1650).

Applying *Options:* electronic application, early admission, deferred entrance. *Required for some:* high school transcript.

Freshmen Application Contact Ms. Janet Fike, Associate Dean of Enrollment Management, West Virginia Northern Community College, 1704 Market Street, Wheeling, WV 26003-3699. *Phone:* 304-233-5900 Ext. 4363. *E-mail:* jfike@northern.wvnet.edu.

WEST VIRGINIA STATE COMMUNITY AND TECHNICAL COLLEGE

Institute, West Virginia   www.wvsctc.edu/

- **County-supported** 2-year, part of WV Council for Community and Technical College Education
- **Suburban** 5219-acre campus
- **Coed,** 1,717 undergraduate students, 62% full-time, 65% women, 35% men
- 63% of applicants were admitted

Undergraduates 1,064 full-time, 653 part-time. 7% are from out of state, 16% African American, 0.6% Asian American or Pacific Islander, 0.7% Hispanic American, 0.3% Native American, 6% transferred in. *Retention:* 61% of 2003 full-time freshmen returned.

Freshmen *Admission:* 2,704 applied, 1,717 admitted, 348 enrolled. *Average high school GPA:* 2.52.

Faculty *Total:* 87, 40% full-time, 6% with terminal degrees.

Majors Accounting; architectural drafting; banking and financial support services; behavioral sciences; business administration, management and operations related; CAD/CADD drafting/design technology; chemical technology; computer science; criminal justice/safety; electrical and electronic engineering technologies related; electrical/electronics maintenance and repair technology related; general studies; gerontology; health services/allied health/health sciences; heating, air conditioning, ventilation and refrigeration maintenance technology; legal assistant/paralegal; marketing related; meteorology; nuclear medical technology; office occupations and clerical services.

Academics *Degree:* certificates and associate. *Special study options:* academic remediation for entering students, adult/continuing education programs, advanced placement credit, cooperative education, distance learning, double majors, English as a second language, external degree program, independent study, internships, services for LD students, student-designed majors, study abroad, summer session for credit.

Library Drain Jordan Library plus 1 other with 221,184 titles, 495 serial subscriptions, an OPAC, a Web page.

Student Life *Housing Options:* coed, men-only, women-only, cooperative, disabled students. Campus housing is university owned. *Campus security:* 24-hour emergency response devices and patrols, late-night transport/escort service, controlled dormitory access.

Standardized Tests *Required:* ACT (for admission).

Costs (2007–08) *Tuition:* state resident $2642 full-time, $110 per credit hour part-time; nonresident $7078 full-time, $282 per credit hour part-time. *Required fees:* $301 full-time. *Room and board:* $5600; room only: $2500.

Applying *Required:* high school transcript, minimum X GPA. *Recommended:* essay or personal statement.

Freshmen Application Contact Mr. Bryce Casto, Vice President Student Affairs, West Virginia State Community and Technical College, PO Box 1000, Institute, WV 25112-1000. *Phone:* 304-766-3140. *Toll-free phone:* 800-987-2112. *Fax:* 304-766-4158. *E-mail:* castosb@wvstateu.edu.

WEST VIRGINIA UNIVERSITY AT PARKERSBURG

Parkersburg, West Virginia   www.wvup.edu/

- **State-supported** primarily 2-year, founded 1961, administratively affiliated with West Virginia University
- **Small-town** 120-acre campus
- **Coed,** 3,884 undergraduate students, 57% full-time, 62% women, 38% men

Undergraduates 2,216 full-time, 1,668 part-time. Students come from 6 states and territories, 2% are from out of state, 0.8% African American, 0.5% Asian American or Pacific Islander, 0.7% Hispanic American, 0.3% Native American, 6% transferred in. *Retention:* 55% of 2003 full-time freshmen returned.

Freshmen *Admission:* 619 applied, 619 admitted, 619 enrolled. *Average high school GPA:* 2.93. *Test scores:* SAT verbal scores over 500: 50%; SAT math scores over 500: 30%; ACT scores over 18: 63%; SAT verbal scores over 600: 10%; ACT scores over 24: 10%.

Faculty *Total:* 233, 38% full-time, 9% with terminal degrees. *Student/faculty ratio:* 20:1.

Majors Accounting; administrative assistant and secretarial science; automobile/automotive mechanics technology; business administration and management; chemical engineering; criminal justice/law enforcement administration; data processing and data processing technology; drafting and design technology; education; electrical, electronic and communications engineering technology; electromechanical technology; elementary education; environmental engineering technology; finance; liberal arts and sciences/liberal studies; machine tool technology; marketing/marketing management; mechanical engineering/mechanical technology; nursing (registered nurse training); pre-engineering; social work; welding technology.

Academics *Calendar:* semesters. *Degrees:* certificates, associate, and bachelor's. *Special study options:* academic remediation for entering students, advanced placement credit, cooperative education, distance learning, English as a second language, independent study, internships, part-time degree program, services for LD students, study abroad, summer session for credit.

Library WVUP Library plus 1 other with 50,000 titles, 100 serial subscriptions, 800 audiovisual materials, an OPAC, a Web page.

Student Life *Housing:* college housing not available. *Activities and Organizations:* drama/theater group, student-run newspaper. *Student services:* health clinic, personal/psychological counseling.

Athletics *Intramural sports:* badminton M/W, basketball M/W, bowling M/W, cross-country running M/W, football M/W, golf M/W, table tennis M/W, tennis M/W, volleyball M/W, weight lifting M/W.

Costs (2006–07) *Tuition:* state resident $2388 full-time, $100 per credit hour part-time; nonresident $6306 full-time, $263 per credit hour part-time. Full-time tuition and fees vary according to degree level and reciprocity agreements. Part-time tuition and fees vary according to degree level and reciprocity agreements. *Payment plan:* installment.

Applying *Options:* electronic application, early admission, deferred entrance. *Required for some:* high school transcript. *Application deadlines:* rolling (freshmen), rolling (out-of-state freshmen), rolling (transfers). *Notification:* continuous (freshmen), continuous (out-of-state freshmen), continuous (transfers).

Freshmen Application Contact Ms. Violet Mosser, Senior Admissions Counselor, West Virginia University at Parkersburg, 300 Campus Drive, Parkersburg, WV 26101. *Phone:* 304-424-8223 Ext. 223. *Toll-free phone:* 800-WVA-WVUP. *Fax:* 304-424-8332. *E-mail:* violet.mosser@mail.wvu.edu.

WISCONSIN

BLACKHAWK TECHNICAL COLLEGE

Janesville, Wisconsin   www.blackhawk.edu/

Director of Admissions Ms. Barbara Erlandson, Student Services Manager, Blackhawk Technical College, PO Box 5009, Janesville, WI 53547-5009. *Phone:* 608-757-7713. *Toll-free phone:* 800-472-0024.

BRYANT AND STRATTON COLLEGE

Milwaukee, Wisconsin   **www.bryantstratton.edu/**

- **Proprietary** primarily 2-year, founded 1863, part of Bryant and Stratton Business Institute, Inc
- **Urban** 2-acre campus
- **Coed**

Undergraduates 351 full-time, 137 part-time. Students come from 1 other state, 84% African American, 0.6% Asian American or Pacific Islander, 4% Hispanic American, 0.2% Native American. *Retention:* 70% of 2003 full-time freshmen returned.

Faculty *Student/faculty ratio:* 10:1.

Academics *Calendar:* semesters. *Degrees:* associate and bachelor's. *Special study options:* academic remediation for entering students, adult/continuing education programs, advanced placement credit, cooperative education, distance learning, double majors, independent study, internships, part-time degree program, summer session for credit.

Student Life *Campus security:* 24-hour emergency response devices and patrols.

Standardized Tests *Required:* TABE (for admission). *Recommended:* SAT or ACT (for admission).

Costs (2006–07) *Tuition:* $415 per credit hour part-time. *Required fees:* $62 per term part-time.

Applying *Required:* high school transcript, interview, entrance and placement evaluations. *Required for some:* letters of recommendation.

Freshmen Application Contact Ms. Kathryn Cotey, Director of Admissions, Bryant and Stratton College, 310 West Wisconsin Avenue, Milwaukee, WI 53203-2214. *Phone:* 414-276-5200.

CHIPPEWA VALLEY TECHNICAL COLLEGE

Eau Claire, Wisconsin   **www.cvtc.edu/**

- **District-supported** 2-year, founded 1912, part of Wisconsin Technical College System
- **Urban** 160-acre campus
- **Coed,** 16,100 undergraduate students

Undergraduates Students come from 10 states and territories, 4 other countries, 5% are from out of state.

Faculty *Total:* 400, 88% full-time. *Student/faculty ratio:* 12:1.

Majors Accounting; administrative assistant and secretarial science; agricultural business and management; architectural engineering technology; automobile/automotive mechanics technology; child development; civil engineering technology; clinical/medical laboratory technology; computer and information sciences; construction engineering technology; criminal justice/police science; culinary arts; dairy science; data processing and data processing technology; dental hygiene; diagnostic medical sonography and ultrasound technology; drafting and design technology; electrical, electronic and communications engineering technology; electromechanical technology; fire science; health information/medical records administration; heating, air conditioning, ventilation and refrigeration maintenance technology; hospitality administration; legal assistant/paralegal; machine tool technology; marketing/marketing management; mechanical design technology; medical laboratory technology; medical radiologic technology; nursing (registered nurse training); quality control technology; real estate; substance abuse/addiction counseling; welding technology.

Academics *Calendar:* semesters. *Degree:* certificates, diplomas, and associate. *Special study options:* academic remediation for entering students, adult/continuing education programs, distance learning, double majors, English as a second language, internships, part-time degree program, services for LD students, summer session for credit.

Library Technical Resource Center with 34,000 titles, 750 serial subscriptions, an OPAC.

Student Life *Housing:* college housing not available. *Activities and Organizations:* student-run newspaper. *Campus security:* 24-hour emergency response devices, late-night transport/escort service. *Student services:* personal/psychological counseling.

Standardized Tests *Required:* ACT COMPASS (for placement). *Required for some:* ACT (for placement).

Costs (2006–07) *Tuition:* state resident $3913 full-time; nonresident $19,189 full-time.

Financial Aid Of all full-time matriculated undergraduates, 218 Federal Work-Study jobs (averaging $875).

Applying *Options:* early admission, deferred entrance. *Application fee:* $30. *Required:* high school transcript. *Required for some:* interview. *Application deadlines:* rolling (freshmen), rolling (transfers). *Notification:* continuous (freshmen), continuous (transfers).

Director of Admissions Mr. Timothy Shepardson, Director of Admissions, Chippewa Valley Technical College, 620 West Clairemont Avenue, Eau Claire, WI 54701-6162. *Phone:* 715-833-6245. *Toll-free phone:* 800-547-2882.

COLLEGE OF MENOMINEE NATION

Keshena, Wisconsin   **www.menominee.edu/**

- **Independent** 2-year, founded 1993
- **Coed,** 499 undergraduate students, 41% full-time, 76% women, 24% men

Undergraduates 206 full-time, 293 part-time. 0.4% African American, 0.6% Asian American or Pacific Islander, 0.2% Hispanic American, 77% Native American.

Faculty *Total:* 14.

Majors Business administration and management; computer science; education; liberal arts and sciences/liberal studies; natural resources/conservation; nursing (licensed practical/vocational nurse training); political science and government; social work.

Academics *Calendar:* semesters. *Degree:* certificates and associate.

Student Life *Housing:* college housing not available.

Standardized Tests *Required:* TABE (for placement).

Costs (2006–07) *Tuition:* $4524 full-time.

Financial Aid Of all full-time matriculated undergraduates, 10 Federal Work-Study jobs.

Applying *Application fee:* $10. *Application deadline:* 8/14 (freshmen).

Director of Admissions Ms. Cynthia Norton, Admissions Representative, College of Menominee Nation, PO Box 1179, Keshena, WI 54135. *Phone:* 715-799-5600 Ext. 3053. *Toll-free phone:* 800-567-2344.

FOX VALLEY TECHNICAL COLLEGE

Appleton, Wisconsin   **www.fvtc.edu/**

- **State and locally supported** 2-year, founded 1967, part of Wisconsin Technical College System
- **Suburban** 100-acre campus
- **Coed,** 7,462 undergraduate students, 29% full-time, 51% women, 49% men

Undergraduates 2,135 full-time, 5,327 part-time. Students come from 11 states and territories, 1% African American, 3% Asian American or Pacific Islander, 2% Hispanic American, 1% Native American, 0.1% international.

Freshmen *Admission:* 4,056 applied, 3,107 admitted, 832 enrolled.

Faculty *Total:* 1,059, 26% full-time. *Student/faculty ratio:* 7:1.

Majors Accounting; administrative assistant and secretarial science; agricultural business and management; airline pilot and flight crew; automobile/automotive mechanics technology; business administration and management; child development; commercial and advertising art; computer programming; computer typography and composition equipment operation; consumer merchandising/retailing management; criminal justice/law enforcement administration; criminal justice/police science; culinary arts; drafting and design technology; electrical, electronic and communications engineering technology; finance; fire science; fish/game management; forestry technology; graphic and printing equipment operation/production; hospitality administration; industrial technology; insurance; interior design; legal administrative assistant/secretary; marketing/marketing management; mechanical design technology; mechanical engineering/mechanical technology; natural resources/conservation; nursing (registered nurse training); occupational therapy; special products marketing; welding technology; wood science and wood products/pulp and paper technology.

Academics *Calendar:* semesters. *Degree:* certificates, diplomas, and associate. *Special study options:* academic remediation for entering students, accelerated degree program, adult/continuing education programs, advanced placement credit, cooperative education, distance learning, double majors, English as a second language, honors programs, independent study, internships, off-campus study, part-time degree program, services for LD students, student-designed majors, study abroad, summer session for credit.

Library William Sirek Educational Resource Center with 46,084 titles, 212 serial subscriptions, 8,526 audiovisual materials, an OPAC, a Web page.

Student Life *Housing:* college housing not available. *Activities and Organizations:* student-run newspaper, Business Professionals of America, Delta Epsilon Chi, Vocational Industrial Clubs of America. *Campus security:* late-night transport/

Fox Valley Technical College (continued)

escort service, 16-hour patrols by trained security personnel. *Student services:* health clinic, personal/psychological counseling, women's center.

Athletics *Intramural sports:* archery M/W, basketball M/W, bowling M/W, skiing (downhill) M/W, tennis M/W, volleyball M/W, weight lifting M/W.

Costs (2007–08) *Tuition:* state resident $2610 full-time, $92 per credit part-time; nonresident $15,309 full-time, $571 per credit part-time. *Required fees:* $407 full-time.

Financial Aid Of all full-time matriculated undergraduates, 165 Federal Work-Study jobs (averaging $2300).

Applying *Options:* electronic application, early admission, deferred entrance. *Application fee:* $30. *Required:* high school transcript. *Application deadlines:* rolling (freshmen), rolling (transfers).

Freshmen Application Contact Admissions Center, Fox Valley Technical College, 1825 North Bluemound Drive, PO Box 2277, Appleton, WI 54912-2277. *Phone:* 920-735-5643. *Toll-free phone:* 800-735-3882. *Fax:* 920-735-2582.

GATEWAY TECHNICAL COLLEGE

Kenosha, Wisconsin　　　　　　　　**www.gtc.edu/**

- **State and locally supported** 2-year, founded 1911, part of Wisconsin Technical College System
- **Urban** 10-acre campus with easy access to Chicago and Milwaukee
- **Coed,** 6,816 undergraduate students, 19% full-time, 62% women, 38% men

Undergraduates 1,304 full-time, 5,512 part-time. Students come from 7 states and territories, 10% African American, 1% Asian American or Pacific Islander, 7% Hispanic American, 0.3% Native American.

Freshmen *Admission:* 4,489 applied, 3,835 admitted, 2,801 enrolled.

Faculty *Total:* 582, 44% full-time.

Majors Accounting; administrative assistant and secretarial science; airline pilot and flight crew; applied horticulture; artificial intelligence and robotics; automobile/automotive mechanics technology; banking and financial support services; child development; civil engineering technology; communications technology; computer graphics; computer programming (specific applications); computer systems networking and telecommunications; corrections; court reporting; criminal justice/police science; dental hygiene; electrical, electronic and communications engineering technology; electromechanical technology; fire science; general retailing/wholesaling; health information/medical records administration; heating, air conditioning and refrigeration technology; human services; hydraulics and fluid power technology; industrial technology; interior design; legal administrative assistant/secretary; logistics and materials management; machine tool technology; management information systems; marketing/marketing management; mechanical design technology; nursing (registered nurse training); operations management; physical therapist assistant; physical therapy; quality control technology; radio and television broadcasting technology; surgical technology; technical and business writing.

Academics *Calendar:* semesters. *Degree:* certificates, diplomas, and associate. *Special study options:* academic remediation for entering students, advanced placement credit, cooperative education, distance learning, double majors, English as a second language, independent study, internships, part-time degree program, services for LD students, student-designed majors, summer session for credit.

Library Library/Learning Resources Center with 45,433 titles, 409 serial subscriptions, 12,400 audiovisual materials, an OPAC.

Student Life *Housing:* college housing not available. *Activities and Organizations:* student-run newspaper, radio station. *Campus security:* 24-hour emergency response devices and patrols, late-night transport/escort service. *Student services:* personal/psychological counseling.

Standardized Tests *Required:* ACT ASSET or ACT COMPASS (for placement). *Recommended:* ACT (for placement).

Costs (2006–07) *Tuition:* state resident $2610 full-time, $87 per credit part-time; nonresident $16,089 full-time, $537 per credit part-time. Full-time tuition and fees vary according to reciprocity agreements. Part-time tuition and fees vary according to reciprocity agreements. *Required fees:* $150 full-time, $8 per credit part-time. *Payment plan:* installment. *Waivers:* senior citizens.

Financial Aid Of all full-time matriculated undergraduates, 110 Federal Work-Study jobs (averaging $1500).

Applying *Options:* electronic application, early admission, deferred entrance. *Application fee:* $30. *Required for some:* high school transcript, minimum 2.0 GPA, interview. *Application deadlines:* rolling (freshmen), rolling (transfers). *Notification:* continuous (freshmen), continuous (transfers).

Freshmen Application Contact Ms. Susan Roberts, Director, Admissions and Testing, Gateway Technical College, 3520 30th Avenue, Kenosha, WI 53144-1690. *Phone:* 262-564-3224. *Toll-free phone:* 800-247-7122. *Fax:* 262-564-2301. *E-mail:* admissions@gtc.edu.

HERZING COLLEGE

Madison, Wisconsin　　　　　　**www.herzing.edu/madison**

- **Proprietary** primarily 2-year, founded 1948, part of Herzing Institutes, Inc
- **Suburban** campus with easy access to Milwaukee
- **Coed, primarily men,** 650 undergraduate students

Undergraduates Students come from 5 states and territories, 2 other countries, 33% are from out of state.

Freshmen *Average high school GPA:* 2.5.

Faculty *Total:* 46, 33% full-time, 15% with terminal degrees. *Student/faculty ratio:* 13:1.

Majors Computer and information sciences; computer programming related; computer systems networking and telecommunications; drafting and design technology; electrical, electronic and communications engineering technology.

Academics *Calendar:* semesters. *Degrees:* diplomas, associate, and bachelor's. *Special study options:* academic remediation for entering students, accelerated degree program, adult/continuing education programs, advanced placement credit, cooperative education, distance learning, double majors, honors programs, independent study, internships, part-time degree program, services for LD students.

Library Herzing College Library with 1,500 titles, 15 serial subscriptions, an OPAC, a Web page.

Student Life *Housing:* college housing not available. *Options:* Campus housing is provided by a third party. *Campus security:* 24-hour emergency response devices.

Costs (2006–07) *Tuition:* $10,720 full-time, $335 per credit hour part-time. Full-time tuition and fees vary according to course load, location, and program. Part-time tuition and fees vary according to course load, location, and program. *Required fees:* $48 full-time. *Payment plan:* installment. *Waivers:* employees or children of employees.

Financial Aid *Financial aid deadline:* 6/30.

Applying *Options:* electronic application, early admission. *Required:* high school transcript, interview. *Application deadlines:* rolling (freshmen), 10/10 (transfers).

Freshmen Application Contact Ms. Rebecca M. Abrams, Admissions Director, Herzing College, 5218 East Terrace Drive, Madison, WI 53718. *Phone:* 608-663-0804. *Toll-free phone:* 800-582-1227. *Fax:* 608-249-8593. *E-mail:* info@msn.herzing.edu.

ITT TECHNICAL INSTITUTE

Green Bay, Wisconsin　　　　　　**www.itt-tech.edu/**

- **Proprietary** primarily 2-year, founded 2000, part of ITT Educational Services, Inc
- **Coed**

Majors Animation, interactive technology, video graphics and special effects; business administration and management; CAD/CADD drafting/design technology; communications technology; computer and information systems security; computer engineering technology; computer software engineering; computer software technology; computer systems networking and telecommunications; criminal justice/law enforcement administration; electrical, electronic and communications engineering technology; health information/medical records technology; web/multimedia management and webmaster; web page, digital/multimedia and information resources design.

Academics *Calendar:* quarters. *Degrees:* associate and bachelor's.

Library a Web page.

Student Life *Housing:* college housing not available.

Standardized Tests *Required:* Wonderlic aptitude test (for admission).

Costs (2006–07) *Tuition:* Contact school for program costs.

Applying *Options:* deferred entrance. *Application fee:* $100. *Required:* high school transcript, interview. *Recommended:* letters of recommendation. *Application deadlines:* rolling (freshmen), rolling (transfers). *Notification:* continuous (freshmen), continuous (transfers).

Freshmen Application Contact Ms. Marnie Glanner, Director of Recruitment, ITT Technical Institute, 470 Security Boulevard, Green Bay, WI 54313. *Phone:* 920-662-9000. *Toll-free phone:* 888-884-3626. *Fax:* 920-662-9384.

ITT TECHNICAL INSTITUTE

Greenfield, Wisconsin　　　　　　**www.itt-tech.edu/**

- **Proprietary** primarily 2-year, founded 1968, part of ITT Educational Services, Inc
- **Suburban** campus with easy access to Milwaukee
- **Coed,** 548 undergraduate students

Majors Animation, interactive technology, video graphics and special effects; business administration and management; CAD/CADD drafting/design technology; computer and information systems security; computer engineering technology; computer software technology; computer systems networking and telecommunications; criminal justice/law enforcement administration; electrical, electronic and communications engineering technology; medical laboratory technology; web page, digital/multimedia and information resources design.

Academics *Calendar:* quarters. *Degrees:* associate and bachelor's.

Library a Web page.

Student Life *Housing:* college housing not available.

Standardized Tests *Required:* Wonderlic aptitude test (for admission).

Costs (2006–07) *Tuition:* Contact school for program costs.

Applying *Options:* deferred entrance. *Application fee:* $100. *Required:* high school transcript, interview. *Recommended:* letters of recommendation. *Application deadlines:* rolling (freshmen), rolling (transfers). *Notification:* continuous (freshmen), continuous (transfers).

Freshmen Application Contact Ms. Geraldine Purcell, Director of Recruitment, ITT Technical Institute, 6300 West Layton Avenue, Greenfield, WI 53220. *Phone:* 414-282-9494.

LAC COURTE OREILLES OJIBWA COMMUNITY COLLEGE

Hayward, Wisconsin www.lco-college.edu/

- **Federally supported** 2-year, founded 1982
- **Rural** 2-acre campus
- **Endowment** $950,616
- **Coed**

Undergraduates 294 full-time, 211 part-time. Students come from 1 other state, 3% are from out of state, 0.6% African American, 0.6% Hispanic American, 77% Native American.

Faculty *Student/faculty ratio:* 10:1.

Academics *Calendar:* semesters. *Degree:* certificates and associate. *Special study options:* academic remediation for entering students, adult/continuing education programs, distance learning, double majors, external degree program, honors programs, independent study, part-time degree program.

Student Life *Campus security:* 24-hour emergency response devices.

Standardized Tests *Required:* ACT COMPASS (for admission).

Costs (2006–07) *Tuition:* area resident $4050 full-time, $135 per credit part-time. *Required fees:* $25 full-time.

Financial Aid Of all full-time matriculated undergraduates, 15 Federal Work-Study jobs (averaging $1400).

Applying *Options:* early admission. *Application fee:* $10. *Required:* high school transcript.

Freshmen Application Contact Ms. Annette Wiggins, Registrar, Lac Courte Oreilles Ojibwa Community College, 13466 West Trepania Road, Hayward, WI 54843-2181. *Phone:* 715-634-4790 Ext. 104. *Toll-free phone:* 888-526-6221.

LAKESHORE TECHNICAL COLLEGE

Cleveland, Wisconsin www.gotoltc.com/

- **State and locally supported** 2-year, founded 1967, part of Wisconsin Technical College System
- **Rural** 160-acre campus with easy access to Milwaukee
- **Coed**, 2,789 undergraduate students, 25% full-time, 58% women, 42% men

Undergraduates 702 full-time, 2,087 part-time. Students come from 5 states and territories, 1% are from out of state, 0.7% African American, 2% Asian American or Pacific Islander, 2% Hispanic American, 0.4% Native American.

Freshmen *Admission:* 1,982 applied, 1,010 admitted, 448 enrolled.

Faculty *Total:* 229, 43% full-time. *Student/faculty ratio:* 14:1.

Majors Accounting; administrative assistant and secretarial science; computer and information sciences related; computer management; computer programming; computer programming related; computer systems analysis; court reporting; criminal justice/police science; dental hygiene; electrical, electronic and communications engineering technology; electromechanical technology; finance; legal assistant/paralegal; management science; marketing/marketing management; mechanical design technology; medical administrative assistant and medical secretary; nursing (registered nurse training); quality control technology; radiologic technology/science.

Academics *Calendar:* semesters. *Degree:* certificates, diplomas, and associate. *Special study options:* academic remediation for entering students, acceler-

ated degree program, adult/continuing education programs, advanced placement credit, cooperative education, distance learning, double majors, English as a second language, external degree program, independent study, internships, part-time degree program, services for LD students, student-designed majors, summer session for credit.

Library 15,749 titles, 220 serial subscriptions, an OPAC.

Student Life *Housing:* college housing not available. *Activities and Organizations:* student government, Business Professionals of America, Police Science Club, Lakeshore Student Nurse Association, Dairy Herd Club. *Campus security:* 24-hour patrols. *Student services:* health clinic, personal/psychological counseling.

Standardized Tests *Recommended:* SAT or ACT (for admission), ACCUPLACER/ ACT ASSET.

Costs (2006–07) *Tuition:* area resident $2610 full-time; state resident $16,089 full-time, $87 per credit part-time; nonresident $536 per credit part-time. Full-time tuition and fees vary according to reciprocity agreements. Part-time tuition and fees vary according to reciprocity agreements. *Payment plan:* installment. *Waivers:* senior citizens.

Financial Aid Of all full-time matriculated undergraduates, 37 Federal Work-Study jobs.

Applying *Options:* electronic application, early admission, deferred entrance. *Application fee:* $30. *Required for some:* high school transcript, interview. *Application deadlines:* rolling (freshmen), rolling (transfers). *Notification:* continuous (freshmen), continuous (transfers).

Freshmen Application Contact Lakeshore Technical College, 1290 North Avenue, Cleveland, WI 53015. *Phone:* 920-693-1339. *Toll-free phone:* 888-GO TO LTC. *Fax:* 920-693-3561.

MADISON AREA TECHNICAL COLLEGE

Madison, Wisconsin www.matcmadison.edu/matc/

- **District-supported** 2-year, founded 1911, part of Wisconsin Technical College System
- **Urban** 150-acre campus
- **Coed**, 13,479 undergraduate students

Undergraduates Students come from 9 states and territories.

Faculty *Total:* 1,881, 21% full-time.

Majors Accounting; administrative assistant and secretarial science; agricultural mechanization; architectural engineering technology; automobile/automotive mechanics technology; biology/biotechnology laboratory technician; business administration and management; business teacher education; child development; civil engineering technology; clinical/medical laboratory technology; commercial and advertising art; communications technology; computer engineering technology; computer programming; computer typography and composition equipment operation; court reporting; criminal justice/police science; culinary arts; data processing and data processing technology; dental hygiene; dietetics; electrical, electronic and communications engineering technology; emergency medical technology (EMT paramedic); fashion merchandising; finance; fire science; graphic and printing equipment operation/production; hospitality administration; human services; industrial radiologic technology; insurance; interior design; liberal arts and sciences/liberal studies; marketing/marketing management; mechanical design technology; medical administrative assistant and medical secretary; medical laboratory technology; nursing (registered nurse training); occupational therapy; parks, recreation and leisure; photography; real estate; respiratory care therapy; tourism and travel services management; veterinary technology; welding technology.

Academics *Calendar:* semesters. *Degree:* certificates, diplomas, and associate. *Special study options:* academic remediation for entering students, adult/continuing education programs, cooperative education, English as a second language, internships, off-campus study, part-time degree program, services for LD students, summer session for credit.

Library Truax-Information Resource Center with 66,000 titles, 657 serial subscriptions, an OPAC, a Web page.

Student Life *Housing:* college housing not available. *Activities and Organizations:* drama/theater group, student-run newspaper, choral group, Marketing Club, Minority Networking Groups, Data Processing Management Association, Student Nurses Association, Business Professionals of America. *Campus security:* 24-hour emergency response devices and patrols, late-night transport/escort service. *Student services:* health clinic, personal/psychological counseling, women's center.

Athletics Member NJCAA. *Intercollegiate sports:* baseball M, basketball M/W, bowling M/W, cross-country running M/W, softball W, tennis M/W, track and field M/W, volleyball M/W, wrestling M. *Intramural sports:* basketball M/W, bowling M/W, softball M/W, tennis M/W, volleyball M/W.

Standardized Tests *Required for some:* ACT (for admission).

Costs (2006–07) *Tuition:* state resident $2800 full-time; nonresident $16,279 full-time.

Madison Area Technical College (continued)

Financial Aid Of all full-time matriculated undergraduates, 180 Federal Work-Study jobs (averaging $1500). 150 state and other part-time jobs (averaging $1000).

Applying *Options:* early admission. *Application fee:* $25. *Required for some:* high school transcript. *Application deadlines:* 7/1 (freshmen), 7/1 (transfers). *Notification:* continuous (freshmen), continuous (transfers).

Director of Admissions Ms. Maureen Menendez, Interim Admissions Administrator, Madison Area Technical College, 3550 Anderson Street, Madison, WI 53704-2599. *Phone:* 608-246-6212. *Toll-free phone:* 800-322-6282.

MADISON MEDIA INSTITUTE

Madison, Wisconsin   **www.madisonmedia.edu/**

- **Proprietary** 2-year, founded 1969
- **Urban** campus
- **Coed,** 133 undergraduate students

Faculty *Total:* 22, 91% full-time.

Majors Animation, interactive technology, video graphics and special effects; music related; recording arts technology; web page, digital/multimedia and information resources design.

Academics *Degree:* associate.

Costs (2006–07) *Tuition:* $12,160 full-time.

Applying *Application fee:* $30. *Application deadline:* rolling (freshmen). *Notification:* continuous (freshmen).

Freshmen Application Contact Mr. Chris K. Hutchings, President/Director, Madison Media Institute, 2702 Agriculture Drive, Madison, WI 53718. *Phone:* 608-237-8301. *Toll-free phone:* 800-236-4997.

MID-STATE TECHNICAL COLLEGE

Wisconsin Rapids, Wisconsin   **www.mstc.edu/**

- **State and locally supported** 2-year, founded 1917, part of Wisconsin Technical College System
- **Small-town** 155-acre campus
- **Endowment** $1.2 million
- **Coed,** 10,737 undergraduate students

Undergraduates Students come from 2 states and territories, 1% are from out of state.

Freshmen *Admission:* 1,100 applied, 1,045 admitted.

Faculty *Total:* 300, 67% full-time.

Majors Accounting; administrative assistant and secretarial science; business administration and management; civil engineering technology; computer and information sciences related; computer engineering technology; computer programming related; computer programming (specific applications); corrections; criminal justice/police science; data entry/microcomputer applications; electrical, electronic and communications engineering technology; hotel/motel administration; industrial technology; information science/studies; instrumentation technology; marketing/marketing management; mechanical design technology; nursing (registered nurse training); quality control technology; respiratory care therapy.

Academics *Calendar:* semesters. *Degree:* certificates, diplomas, and associate. *Special study options:* academic remediation for entering students, adult/continuing education programs, cooperative education, distance learning, double majors, English as a second language, independent study, internships, part-time degree program, services for LD students, summer session for credit.

Library Mid-State Technical College Library with 20,148 titles, 539 serial subscriptions, 2,685 audiovisual materials, an OPAC.

Student Life *Housing:* college housing not available. *Activities and Organizations:* student-run newspaper, Business Professionals of America, Civil Tech Club, Barber and Cosmetology Club, Society of Hosteurs, UICA. *Student services:* health clinic, personal/psychological counseling, women's center.

Athletics Member NJCAA. *Intercollegiate sports:* basketball M/W, bowling M/W, golf M, volleyball W. *Intramural sports:* basketball M, bowling M/W, football M, golf M/W, volleyball M/W.

Standardized Tests *Required:* ACT ASSET (for placement). *Recommended:* SAT or ACT (for placement).

Costs (2006–07) *Tuition:* state resident $2852 full-time; nonresident $16,331 full-time.

Financial Aid Of all full-time matriculated undergraduates, 315 Federal Work-Study jobs (averaging $2000).

Applying *Options:* electronic application, early admission, deferred entrance. *Application fee:* $25. *Required:* high school transcript. *Application deadlines:* rolling (freshmen), rolling (transfers). *Notification:* continuous (freshmen), continuous (transfers).

Freshmen Application Contact Ms. Carole Prochnow, Admissions Assistant, Mid-State Technical College, 500 32nd Street North, Wisconsin Rapids, WI 54494-5599. *Phone:* 715-422-5444. *Toll-free phone:* 888-575-6782.

MILWAUKEE AREA TECHNICAL COLLEGE

Milwaukee, Wisconsin   **matc.edu**

Freshmen Application Contact Thomas Pilarzyk, Director, Enrollment Services, Milwaukee Area Technical College, 700 West State Street, Milwaukee, WI 53233. *Phone:* 414-297-6274. *Fax:* 414-297-7800. *E-mail:* apply@matc.edu.

MORAINE PARK TECHNICAL COLLEGE

Fond du Lac, Wisconsin   **www.morainepark.edu/**

- **State and locally supported** 2-year, founded 1967, part of Wisconsin Technical College System
- **Small-town** 40-acre campus with easy access to Milwaukee
- **Coed**

Undergraduates 1,197 full-time, 6,312 part-time. Students come from 5 states and territories, 1% are from out of state, 4% African American, 1% Asian American or Pacific Islander, 2% Hispanic American, 0.8% Native American, 0.4% transferred in.

Academics *Calendar:* semesters. *Degree:* certificates, diplomas, and associate. *Special study options:* academic remediation for entering students, accelerated degree program, adult/continuing education programs, advanced placement credit, distance learning, English as a second language, external degree program, independent study, internships, part-time degree program, summer session for credit.

Student Life *Campus security:* 24-hour emergency response devices.

Standardized Tests *Required:* ACT ASSET, ACCUPLACER (for admission). *Required for some:* ACT (for admission).

Costs (2006–07) *Tuition:* state resident $2610 full-time, $87 per credit part-time; nonresident $16,089 full-time, $536 per credit part-time. *Required fees:* $251 full-time, $8 per credit part-time.

Applying *Options:* electronic application, deferred entrance. *Application fee:* $30. *Required:* interview. *Recommended:* high school transcript.

Freshmen Application Contact Ms. Karen Jarvis, Student Services, Moraine Park Technical College, 235 North National Ave, PO Box 1940, Fond du Lac, WI 54936-1940. *Phone:* 920-924-3200. *Toll-free phone:* 800-472-4554. *Fax:* 920-924-3421. *E-mail:* kjarvis@morainepark.edu.

NICOLET AREA TECHNICAL COLLEGE

Rhinelander, Wisconsin   **www.nicoletcollege.edu/**

- **State and locally supported** 2-year, founded 1968, part of Wisconsin Technical College System
- **Rural** 280-acre campus
- **Coed,** 1,600 undergraduate students

Undergraduates Students come from 8 states and territories, 1% are from out of state.

Faculty *Total:* 100. *Student/faculty ratio:* 16:1.

Majors Accounting; administrative assistant and secretarial science; automobile/automotive mechanics technology; business administration and management; child development; computer and information sciences; computer science; criminal justice/police science; culinary arts; data processing and data processing technology; hotel/motel administration; kindergarten/preschool education; liberal arts and sciences/liberal studies; machine tool technology; marketing/marketing management; medical administrative assistant and medical secretary; nursing (registered nurse training); physical therapist assistant; real estate; survey technology; welding technology.

Academics *Calendar:* semesters. *Degree:* certificates, diplomas, and associate. *Special study options:* academic remediation for entering students, adult/continuing education programs, advanced placement credit, cooperative education, distance learning, double majors, English as a second language, independent study, internships, part-time degree program, services for LD students, student-designed majors, study abroad, summer session for credit.

Library Richard Brown Library with 38,369 titles, 598 serial subscriptions, an OPAC, a Web page.

Student Life *Housing:* college housing not available. *Activities and Organizations:* drama/theater group, student-run newspaper. *Campus security:* 24-hour emergency response devices. *Student services:* personal/psychological counseling, women's center.

Athletics Member NJCAA. *Intercollegiate sports:* golf M/W. *Intramural sports:* skiing (cross-country) M/W, skiing (downhill) M/W, soccer M/W, volleyball M/W, weight lifting M/W.

Standardized Tests *Recommended:* ACT (for admission).

Costs (2006–07) *Tuition:* state resident $3940 full-time, $124 per credit part-time; nonresident $11,296 full-time, $353 per credit part-time.

Applying *Options:* electronic application, early admission. *Application fee:* $30. *Required:* high school transcript, interview. *Application deadlines:* rolling (freshmen), rolling (transfers). *Notification:* continuous (freshmen), continuous (transfers).

Freshmen Application Contact Ms. Susan Kordula, Director of Enrollment Services, Nicolet Area Technical College, Box 518, Rhinelander, WI 54501-0518. *Phone:* 715-365-4451. *Toll-free phone:* 800-544-3039 Ext. 4451. *E-mail:* inquire@nicoletcollege.edu.

NORTHCENTRAL TECHNICAL COLLEGE
Wausau, Wisconsin www.ntc.edu/

Director of Admissions Ms. Carolyn Michalski, Team Leader, Student Services, Northcentral Technical College, 1000 West Campus Drive, Wausau, WI 54401-1899. *Phone:* 715-675-3331 Ext. 4285.

NORTHEAST WISCONSIN TECHNICAL COLLEGE
Green Bay, Wisconsin www.nwtc.edu/

Freshmen Application Contact Ms. Heather Hill, Director of Admission, Northeast Wisconsin Technical College, 2740 West Mason Street, PO Box 19042, Green Bay, WI 54307-9042. *Phone:* 920-498-5612. *Toll-free phone:* 800-498-5444 (in-state); 800-422-6982 (out-of-state). *Fax:* 920-498-6882. *E-mail:* heather.hill@nwtc.edu.

SOUTHWEST WISCONSIN TECHNICAL COLLEGE
Fennimore, Wisconsin www.swtc.edu/

Freshmen Application Contact Ms. Kathy Kreul, Admissions, Southwest Wisconsin Technical College, 1800 Bronson Boulevard, Fennimore, WI 53813. *Phone:* 608-822-3262 Ext. 2355. *Toll-free phone:* 800-362-3322 Ext. 2355.

UNIVERSITY OF WISCONSIN–BARABOO/ SAUK COUNTY
Baraboo, Wisconsin www.baraboo.uwc.edu/

- **State-supported** 2-year, founded 1968, part of University of Wisconsin System
- **Small-town** 68-acre campus
- **Coed,** 553 undergraduate students, 64% full-time, 56% women, 44% men

Undergraduates 354 full-time, 199 part-time. Students come from 2 states and territories, 3 other countries, 1% are from out of state, 0.5% African American, 0.9% Asian American or Pacific Islander, 2% Hispanic American, 1% Native American.

Faculty *Total:* 42, 36% full-time, 50% with terminal degrees. *Student/faculty ratio:* 13:1.

Majors Liberal arts and sciences/liberal studies.

Academics *Calendar:* semesters. *Degree:* certificates and associate. *Special study options:* academic remediation for entering students, advanced placement credit, distance learning, external degree program, honors programs, independent study, internships, off-campus study, part-time degree program, services for LD students, student-designed majors, study abroad, summer session for credit.

Library T. N. Savides Library with 45,000 titles, 300 serial subscriptions, an OPAC.

Student Life *Housing:* college housing not available. *Activities and Organizations:* drama/theater group, student-run newspaper, choral group, Student Government Association, chorus and band, dance team, Gaming Club, Business Club. *Student services:* personal/psychological counseling.

Athletics Member NJCAA. *Intercollegiate sports:* basketball M(s), golf M(s)/W(s), soccer M(s)/W(s), tennis M/W, volleyball W(s). *Intramural sports:* racquetball M/W, softball M/W, table tennis M/W, volleyball M/W, weight lifting M/W.

Standardized Tests *Required:* SAT or ACT (for admission). *Recommended:* ACT (for admission).

Costs (2006–07) *Tuition:* state resident $4605 full-time, $192 per semester hour part-time; nonresident $11,588 full-time, $483 per semester hour part-time. Part-time tuition and fees vary according to course load. *Payment plans:* installment, deferred payment. *Waivers:* senior citizens.

Financial Aid Of all full-time matriculated undergraduates, 650 Federal Work-Study jobs (averaging $2100).

Applying *Options:* electronic application, early admission, deferred entrance. *Application fee:* $35. *Required:* high school transcript. *Required for some:* interview. *Application deadlines:* rolling (freshmen), rolling (out-of-state freshmen), rolling (transfers). *Notification:* continuous until 8/31 (freshmen), continuous until 8/31 (out-of-state freshmen), continuous until 8/31 (transfers).

Freshmen Application Contact Ms. Jan Gerlach, Assistant Director of Student Services, University of Wisconsin–Baraboo/Sauk County, 1006 Connie Road, Baraboo, WI 53913-1015. *Phone:* 608-355-5270. *E-mail:* booinfo@uwc.edu.

UNIVERSITY OF WISCONSIN–BARRON COUNTY
Rice Lake, Wisconsin www.barron.uwc.edu/

Freshmen Application Contact Mr. Dale Fenton, Assistant Dean for Student Services, University of Wisconsin–Barron County, 1800 College Drive, Rice Lake, WI 54868. *Phone:* 715-234-8024. *Fax:* 715-234-8024. *E-mail:* dale.fenton@uwc.edu.

UNIVERSITY OF WISCONSIN– FOND DU LAC
Fond du Lac, Wisconsin www.fdl.uwc.edu/

- **State-supported** 2-year, founded 1968, part of University of Wisconsin System
- **Small-town** 182-acre campus with easy access to Milwaukee
- **Coed,** 716 undergraduate students, 63% full-time, 58% women, 42% men

Undergraduates 454 full-time, 262 part-time. Students come from 3 states and territories, 1% are from out of state, 0.6% African American, 2% Asian American or Pacific Islander, 0.6% Hispanic American, 0.6% Native American. *Retention:* 58% of 2003 full-time freshmen returned.

Freshmen *Admission:* 374 enrolled. *Average high school GPA:* 2.5. *Test scores:* ACT scores over 18: 93%; ACT scores over 24: 20%; ACT scores over 30: 1%.

Faculty *Total:* 37, 54% full-time, 59% with terminal degrees. *Student/faculty ratio:* 19:1.

Majors Liberal arts and sciences/liberal studies.

Academics *Calendar:* semesters. *Degree:* associate. *Special study options:* academic remediation for entering students, adult/continuing education programs, advanced placement credit, off-campus study, part-time degree program, summer session for credit. *ROTC:* Army (c).

Library 41,891 titles, 160 serial subscriptions.

Student Life *Housing:* college housing not available. *Activities and Organizations:* drama/theater group, choral group, student government, Campus Ambassadors, Phi Theta Kappa, drama. *Campus security:* 24-hour emergency response devices. *Student services:* personal/psychological counseling.

Athletics Member NJCAA. *Intercollegiate sports:* basketball M/W, golf M, soccer M/W, tennis M/W, volleyball W. *Intramural sports:* basketball M/W, bowling M/W, golf M/W, table tennis M/W, volleyball M/W.

Standardized Tests *Required:* ACT (for admission).

Financial Aid Of all full-time matriculated undergraduates, 650 Federal Work-Study jobs (averaging $2100).

University of Wisconsin–Fond du Lac (continued)

Applying *Options:* electronic application, deferred entrance. *Application fee:* $35. *Required:* high school transcript. *Application deadlines:* rolling (freshmen), rolling (transfers).

Director of Admissions Ms. Linda A. Reiss, Director of Student Services, University of Wisconsin–Fond du Lac, 400 University Drive, Fond du Lac, WI 54935-2950. *Phone:* 920-929-3606. *E-mail:* bstrande@uwcmail.uwc.edu.

UNIVERSITY OF WISCONSIN–FOX VALLEY

Menasha, Wisconsin   **www.uwfoxvalley.uwc.edu/**

- **State-supported** 2-year, founded 1933, part of University of Wisconsin System
- **Urban** 33-acre campus
- **Coed,** 1,797 undergraduate students, 51% full-time, 54% women, 46% men

Undergraduates 912 full-time, 885 part-time. Students come from 3 states and territories, 4 other countries, 1% are from out of state, 0.9% African American, 3% Asian American or Pacific Islander, 2% Hispanic American, 0.8% Native American, 0.8% international.

Freshmen *Admission:* 569 applied, 458 admitted. *Average high school GPA:* 2.5.

Faculty *Total:* 80, 39% full-time.

Majors Liberal arts and sciences/liberal studies.

Academics *Calendar:* semesters. *Degree:* associate. *Special study options:* academic remediation for entering students, adult/continuing education programs, advanced placement credit, cooperative education, distance learning, honors programs, independent study, off-campus study, part-time degree program, services for LD students, summer session for credit.

Library 29,000 titles, 230 serial subscriptions, an OPAC, a Web page.

Student Life *Housing:* college housing not available. *Activities and Organizations:* drama/theater group, student-run newspaper, radio and television station, choral group, Business Club, Education Club, Earth Science Club, Computer Science Club, Political Science Club. *Student services:* personal/psychological counseling.

Athletics Member NJCAA. *Intercollegiate sports:* basketball M/W, soccer M/W, tennis M/W, volleyball M/W. *Intramural sports:* basketball M/W, volleyball M/W.

Standardized Tests *Required:* ACT (for admission).

Financial Aid Of all full-time matriculated undergraduates, 650 Federal Work-Study jobs (averaging $2100).

Applying *Options:* early admission. *Required:* high school transcript. *Notification:* continuous (freshmen), continuous (transfers).

Director of Admissions Ms. Rhonda Uschan, Director of Student Services, University of Wisconsin–Fox Valley, 1478 Midway Road, Menasha, WI 54952. *Phone:* 920-832-2620. *Toll-free phone:* 888-INFOUWC. *E-mail:* foxinfo@uwc.edu.

UNIVERSITY OF WISCONSIN–MANITOWOC

Manitowoc, Wisconsin   **www.manitowoc.uwc.edu/**

- **State-supported** 2-year, founded 1935, part of University of Wisconsin System
- **Small-town** 50-acre campus with easy access to Milwaukee
- **Coed,** 588 undergraduate students, 100% full-time, 53% women, 47% men

Undergraduates 588 full-time. Students come from 3 states and territories, 0.5% African American, 5% Asian American or Pacific Islander, 1% Hispanic American, 0.7% Native American, 0.2% international, 5% transferred in.

Freshmen *Admission:* 320 applied, 290 admitted, 378 enrolled.

Faculty *Total:* 40, 53% full-time, 55% with terminal degrees. *Student/faculty ratio:* 24:1.

Majors Liberal arts and sciences/liberal studies.

Academics *Calendar:* semesters. *Degree:* certificates and associate. *Special study options:* academic remediation for entering students, adult/continuing education programs, advanced placement credit, cooperative education, distance learning, internships, off-campus study, services for LD students, student-designed majors, study abroad.

Library 25,750 titles, 150 serial subscriptions, an OPAC.

Student Life *Housing:* college housing not available. *Activities and Organizations:* drama/theater group, student-run newspaper, choral group, Business Club, Drama Club, Music Club, Phi Kappa Theta, Environmental Awareness.

Athletics *Intercollegiate sports:* basketball M/W, golf M, tennis M/W, volleyball W. *Intramural sports:* rock climbing M/W.

Standardized Tests *Required:* SAT or ACT (for admission).

Costs (2006–07) *Tuition:* state resident $4188 full-time, $178 per credit part-time; nonresident $12,888 full-time, $528 per credit part-time. *Required fees:* $211 full-time, $9 per credit part-time. *Payment plans:* installment, deferred payment.

Financial Aid Of all full-time matriculated undergraduates, 650 Federal Work-Study jobs (averaging $2100).

Applying *Options:* electronic application, early admission. *Application fee:* $35. *Required:* high school transcript, minimum X GPA. *Required for some:* essay or personal statement, interview. *Notification:* continuous until 9/1 (freshmen), continuous until 9/1 (transfers).

Freshmen Application Contact Dr. Christopher Lewis, Assistant Campus Dean for Student Services, University of Wisconsin–Manitowoc, 705 Viebahn Street, Manitowoc, WI 54220-6699. *Phone:* 920-683-4707. *Fax:* 920-683-4776. *E-mail:* christopher.lewis@uwc.edu.

UNIVERSITY OF WISCONSIN–MARATHON COUNTY

Wausau, Wisconsin   **www.uwmc.uwc.edu/**

Freshmen Application Contact Dr. Nolan Beck, Director of Student Services, University of Wisconsin–Marathon County, 518 South Seventh Avenue, Wausau, WI 54401-5396. *Phone:* 715-261-6238. *Toll-free phone:* 888-367-8962. *Fax:* 715-848-3568.

UNIVERSITY OF WISCONSIN–MARINETTE

Marinette, Wisconsin   **www.uwc.edu/**

Freshmen Application Contact Ms. Cynthia M. Bailey, Director of Student Services, University of Wisconsin–Marinette, 750 West Bay Shore, Marinette, WI 54143-4299. *Phone:* 715-735-4301. *E-mail:* cbailey@uwc.edu.

UNIVERSITY OF WISCONSIN–MARSHFIELD/WOOD COUNTY

Marshfield, Wisconsin   **marshfield.uwc.edu/**

- **State-supported** 2-year, founded 1964, part of University of Wisconsin System
- **Small-town** 71-acre campus
- **Endowment** $500,000
- **Coed,** 643 undergraduate students

Undergraduates Students come from 2 states and territories, 1 other country, 1% are from out of state, 0.9% African American, 0.5% Asian American or Pacific Islander, 0.2% Hispanic American, 2% Native American, 0.2% international. *Retention:* 99% of 2003 full-time freshmen returned.

Freshmen *Admission:* 322 applied, 301 admitted. *Average high school GPA:* 2.8. *Test scores:* ACT scores over 18: 95%; ACT scores over 24: 20%; ACT scores over 30: 5%.

Faculty *Total:* 36, 36% full-time. *Student/faculty ratio:* 17:1.

Majors Liberal arts and sciences/liberal studies.

Academics *Calendar:* semesters. *Degree:* associate. *Special study options:* academic remediation for entering students, accelerated degree program, adult/continuing education programs, advanced placement credit, distance learning, external degree program, independent study, off-campus study, part-time degree program, services for LD students, study abroad, summer session for credit. *ROTC:* Army (c).

Library Learning Resource Center with 35,000 titles, 185 serial subscriptions, an OPAC, a Web page.

Student Life *Housing:* college housing not available. *Activities and Organizations:* drama/theater group, student-run newspaper, choral group, Student Nurses Association, student newspaper, literary magazine, Student Education Association, Inter-Varsity Christian Fellowship. *Campus security:* 24-hour patrols, patrols by city police.

Athletics *Intercollegiate sports:* basketball M/W, golf M/W, tennis M/W, volleyball W. *Intramural sports:* basketball M/W, bowling M/W, football M/W, golf M/W, soccer M/W, table tennis M/W, tennis M/W, volleyball M/W, weight lifting M/W.

Standardized Tests *Required:* SAT or ACT (for admission).

Costs (2006–07) *Tuition:* state resident $4268 full-time, $178 per credit part-time; nonresident $11,252 full-time, $469 per credit part-time. Full-time tuition and fees vary according to reciprocity agreements. *Required fees:* $239 full-time, $10 per credit part-time. *Payment plan:* installment.

Financial Aid Of all full-time matriculated undergraduates, 650 Federal Work-Study jobs (averaging $2100).

Applying *Options:* electronic application, early admission, deferred entrance. *Application fee:* $35. *Required:* high school transcript. *Required for some:* essay or personal statement, letters of recommendation, interview. *Application deadlines:* rolling (freshmen), rolling (transfers).

Freshmen Application Contact Mr. Jeff Meece, Director of Student Services, University of Wisconsin–Marshfield/Wood County, 2000 West Fifth Street, Marshfield, WI 54449. *Phone:* 715-389-6500. *Fax:* 715-384-1718.

UNIVERSITY OF WISCONSIN—RICHLAND

Richland Center, Wisconsin　　　　**richland.uwc.edu/**

- **State-supported** 2-year, founded 1967, part of University of Wisconsin System
- **Rural** 135-acre campus
- **Coed**

Undergraduates 313 full-time, 151 part-time. Students come from 4 states and territories, 15 other countries, 1% are from out of state, 0.2% African American, 0.4% Asian American or Pacific Islander, 0.2% Hispanic American, 0.2% Native American, 4% international, 6% transferred in, 35% live on campus. *Retention:* 55% of 2003 full-time freshmen returned.

Faculty *Student/faculty ratio:* 18:1.

Academics *Calendar:* semesters. *Degree:* associate. *Special study options:* academic remediation for entering students, adult/continuing education programs, advanced placement credit, distance learning, external degree program, independent study, off-campus study, part-time degree program, services for LD students, study abroad, summer session for credit.

Standardized Tests *Required:* SAT or ACT (for admission). *Recommended:* ACT (for admission).

Costs (2006–07) *Tuition:* state resident $4674 full-time, $195 per credit part-time; nonresident $11,658 full-time, $486 per credit part-time. *Room and board:* $4730; room only: $2990. Room and board charges vary according to board plan.

Financial Aid Of all full-time matriculated undergraduates, 650 Federal Work-Study jobs (averaging $2100).

Applying *Options:* electronic application, early admission. *Application fee:* $35. *Required:* high school transcript. *Required for some:* letters of recommendation, interview.

Freshmen Application Contact Mr. John Poole, Assistant Campus Dean, University of Wisconsin–Richland, 1200 Highway 14 West, Richland Center, WI 53581. *Phone:* 608-647-8422. *Fax:* 608-647-6225. *E-mail:* john.poole@uwc.edu.

UNIVERSITY OF WISCONSIN—ROCK COUNTY

Janesville, Wisconsin　　　　**rock.uwc.edu/**

Freshmen Application Contact Ms. Donna Johnson, Program Manager, University of Wisconsin–Rock County, 2909 Kellogg Avenue, Janesville, WI 53456. *Phone:* 608-758-6523. *Toll-free phone:* 888-INFO-UWC.

UNIVERSITY OF WISCONSIN—SHEBOYGAN

Sheboygan, Wisconsin　　　　**www.sheboygan.uwc.edu/**

Director of Admissions Beth Raffaelli, Assistant Campus Dean for Student Services, University of Wisconsin–Sheboygan, One University Drive, Sheboygan, WI 53081-4789. *Phone:* 920-459-6633.

UNIVERSITY OF WISCONSIN— WASHINGTON COUNTY

West Bend, Wisconsin　　　　**www.washington.uwc.edu/**

- **State-supported** 2-year, founded 1968, part of University of Wisconsin System
- **Small-town** 87-acre campus with easy access to Milwaukee
- **Coed,** 951 undergraduate students, 70% full-time, 56% women, 44% men

Undergraduates 663 full-time, 288 part-time. Students come from 2 states and territories, 2 other countries, 1% are from out of state, 0.2% African American, 1% Hispanic American, 0.6% Native American, 7% transferred in. *Retention:* 63% of 2003 full-time freshmen returned.

Freshmen *Admission:* 708 applied, 477 admitted, 477 enrolled. *Average high school GPA:* 2.6. *Test scores:* ACT scores over 18: 65%; ACT scores over 24: 26%; ACT scores over 30: 6%.

Faculty *Total:* 52, 56% full-time, 63% with terminal degrees. *Student/faculty ratio:* 21:1.

Majors Liberal arts and sciences/liberal studies.

Academics *Calendar:* semesters. *Degree:* associate. *Special study options:* academic remediation for entering students, advanced placement credit, distance learning, double majors, honors programs, independent study, off-campus study, part-time degree program, services for LD students, summer session for credit.

Library University of Wisconsin-Washington County Library with 46,429 titles, 247 serial subscriptions, an OPAC, a Web page.

Student Life *Housing:* college housing not available. *Activities and Organizations:* drama/theater group, student-run newspaper, choral group, Student Government Association, Business Club, Phi Theta Kappa, Writers' Guild, Student Impact. *Student services:* personal/psychological counseling.

Athletics Member NAIA. *Intercollegiate sports:* basketball M/W, golf M/W, soccer M/W, tennis M/W, volleyball W. *Intramural sports:* basketball M/W, football M/W, softball M/W, volleyball M/W.

Standardized Tests *Recommended:* ACT (for admission).

Costs (2006–07) *Tuition:* state resident $4222 full-time, $190 per credit part-time; nonresident $12,922 full-time, $488 per credit part-time. *Required fees:* $244 full-time, $11 per credit part-time, $132 per term part-time.

Financial Aid Of all full-time matriculated undergraduates, 650 Federal Work-Study jobs (averaging $2100).

Applying *Options:* electronic application, deferred entrance. *Application fee:* $35. *Required:* high school transcript. *Required for some:* essay or personal statement, letters of recommendation, interview. *Application deadlines:* rolling (freshmen), rolling (transfers).

Freshmen Application Contact Mr. Dan Cebrario, Associate Director of Student Services, University of Wisconsin–Washington County, Student Services Office, 400 University Drive, West Bend, WI 53095. *Phone:* 262-335-5201. *Fax:* 262-335-5220. *E-mail:* dan.cibrario@uwc.edu.

UNIVERSITY OF WISCONSIN— WAUKESHA

Waukesha, Wisconsin　　　　**www.waukesha.uwc.edu/**

- **State-supported** 2-year, founded 1966, part of University of Wisconsin System
- **Suburban** 86-acre campus with easy access to Milwaukee
- **Coed,** 2,020 undergraduate students, 58% full-time, 49% women, 51% men

Undergraduates 1,169 full-time, 851 part-time. Students come from 5 states and territories, 1% are from out of state, 2% African American, 3% Asian American or Pacific Islander, 5% Hispanic American, 0.4% Native American, 0.1% international.

Freshmen *Admission:* 1,461 applied, 1,264 admitted.

Faculty *Total:* 88, 68% full-time, 56% with terminal degrees. *Student/faculty ratio:* 19:1.

Majors Liberal arts and sciences/liberal studies.

Academics *Calendar:* semesters. *Degree:* associate. *Special study options:* academic remediation for entering students, adult/continuing education programs, advanced placement credit, honors programs, internships, off-campus study, part-time degree program, services for LD students, study abroad, summer session for credit.

Library University of Wisconsin-Waukesha Library plus 1 other with 41,000 titles, 300 serial subscriptions.

Student Life *Housing:* college housing not available. *Activities and Organizations:* drama/theater group, student-run newspaper, radio station, choral group,

University of Wisconsin–Waukesha (continued)

student government, Student Activities Committee, Campus Crusade, Phi Theta Kappa, Circle K. *Campus security:* late-night transport/escort service, part-time patrols by trained security personnel.

Athletics Member NJCAA. *Intercollegiate sports:* basketball M/W, golf M/W, soccer M/W, tennis M/W, volleyball W. *Intramural sports:* basketball M, bowling M/W, football M/W, skiing (downhill) M/W, table tennis M/W, volleyball M(c).

Standardized Tests *Required:* SAT or ACT (for admission). *Required for some:* SAT (for admission).

Costs (2006–07) *Tuition:* state resident $5000 full-time, $190 per credit part-time; nonresident $11,500 full-time, $480 per credit part-time. Full-time tuition and fees vary according to course load and reciprocity agreements. Part-time tuition and fees vary according to course load and reciprocity agreements. *Payment plan:* installment.

Financial Aid Of all full-time matriculated undergraduates, 650 Federal Work-Study jobs (averaging $2100).

Applying *Options:* early admission, deferred entrance. *Application fee:* $35. *Required:* high school transcript. *Required for some:* letters of recommendation. *Recommended:* interview. *Application deadline:* rolling (freshmen). *Notification:* continuous (freshmen).

Freshmen Application Contact Admissions, University of Wisconsin–Waukesha, 1500 North University Drive, Waukesha, WI 53188. *Phone:* 262-521-5200. *Fax:* 262-521-5530. *E-mail:* becky.gill@uwc.edu.

WAUKESHA COUNTY TECHNICAL COLLEGE

Pewaukee, Wisconsin   www.wctc.edu/

- **State and locally supported** 2-year, founded 1923, part of Wisconsin Technical College System
- **Suburban** 137-acre campus with easy access to Milwaukee
- **Coed,** 7,123 undergraduate students, 25% full-time, 51% women, 49% men

Undergraduates 1,802 full-time, 5,321 part-time. Students come from 8 states and territories, 0.2% are from out of state, 4% African American, 2% Asian American or Pacific Islander, 4% Hispanic American, 0.6% Native American.

Freshmen *Admission:* 869 enrolled.

Faculty *Total:* 881, 21% full-time. *Student/faculty ratio:* 9:1.

Majors Accounting; administrative assistant and secretarial science; architectural drafting and CAD/CADD; autobody/collision and repair technology; automobile/automotive mechanics technology; computer and information sciences and support services related; computer installation and repair technology; computer programming; computer systems analysis; computer systems networking and telecommunications; criminal justice/police science; dental hygiene; early childhood education; electrical, electronic and communications engineering technology; electrical/electronics drafting and CAD/CADD; electromechanical and instrumentation and maintenance technologies related; financial planning and services; fire protection and safety technology; graphic communications; graphic design; hospitality administration; interior design; manufacturing technology; marketing/marketing management; mechanical drafting and CAD/CADD; mental and social health services and allied professions related; multi-/interdisciplinary studies related; nursing (registered nurse training); operations management; restaurant, culinary, and catering management; retailing; surgical technology; teacher assistant/aide; telecommunications technology.

Academics *Calendar:* semesters. *Degree:* certificates, diplomas, and associate. *Special study options:* academic remediation for entering students, adult/continuing education programs, advanced placement credit, cooperative education, distance learning, English as a second language, part-time degree program, services for LD students, student-designed majors, summer session for credit.

Student Life *Housing:* college housing not available. *Campus security:* patrols by police officers 8 a.m. to 10 p.m. *Student services:* health clinic.

Athletics Member NJCAA. *Intramural sports:* basketball M, bowling M/W, fencing W, football M, soccer M, tennis M/W(c), volleyball M.

Costs (2006–07) *Tuition:* state resident $2610 full-time, $87 per credit part-time; nonresident $16,089 full-time, $536 per credit part-time. Full-time tuition and fees vary according to program. Part-time tuition and fees vary according to program. *Required fees:* $160 full-time, $9 per credit part-time. *Payment plans:* installment, deferred payment. *Waivers:* senior citizens.

Financial Aid Of all full-time matriculated undergraduates, 67 Federal Work-Study jobs (averaging $4000).

Applying *Options:* early admission. *Application fee:* $30. *Required:* high school transcript. *Required for some:* interview, varies. *Application deadlines:* rolling (freshmen), rolling (transfers).

Freshmen Application Contact Ms. Susan Fenske, Director of Student Development, Waukesha County Technical College, 800 Main Street, Pewaukee, WI 53072-4601. *Phone:* 262-691-5295. *Toll-free phone:* 888-892-WCTC. *E-mail:* dfenske@wctc.edu.

WESTERN TECHNICAL COLLEGE

La Crosse, Wisconsin   www.wwtc.edu/

- **District-supported** 2-year, founded 1911, part of Wisconsin Technical College System
- **Urban** 10-acre campus
- **Coed**

Undergraduates 1,910 full-time, 2,855 part-time. Students come from 4 states and territories, 7% are from out of state, 2% African American, 3% Asian American or Pacific Islander, 1% Hispanic American, 1% Native American, 2% live on campus.

Faculty *Student/faculty ratio:* 7:1.

Academics *Calendar:* semesters. *Degree:* certificates, diplomas, and associate. *Special study options:* academic remediation for entering students, accelerated degree program, adult/continuing education programs, advanced placement credit, cooperative education, distance learning, English as a second language, external degree program, internships, off-campus study, part-time degree program, services for LD students, student-designed majors, summer session for credit.

Student Life *Campus security:* 24-hour emergency response devices and patrols, student patrols, late-night transport/escort service, controlled dormitory access.

Athletics Member NJCAA.

Standardized Tests *Required for some:* ACT ASSET. *Recommended:* ACT (for admission).

Costs (2006–07) *Tuition:* state resident $2610 full-time, $87 per credit part-time; nonresident $16,089 full-time, $536 per credit part-time. *Required fees:* $185 full-time, $185 per term part-time. *Room and board:* room only: $2312.

Financial Aid Of all full-time matriculated undergraduates, 102 Federal Work-Study jobs (averaging $1444).

Applying *Options:* electronic application, early admission. *Application fee:* $30. *Required:* high school transcript. *Recommended:* interview.

Freshmen Application Contact Ms. Jane Wells, Manager of Admissions, Registration and Records, Western Technical College, PO Box 908, La Crosse, WI 54602-0908. *Phone:* 608-785-9158. *Toll-free phone:* 800-322-9982 (in-state); 800-248-9982 (out-of-state). *Fax:* 608-785-9094. *E-mail:* mildes@wwtc.edu.

WISCONSIN INDIANHEAD TECHNICAL COLLEGE

Shell Lake, Wisconsin   www.witc.edu/

- **District-supported** 2-year, founded 1912, part of Wisconsin Technical College System
- **Urban** 113-acre campus
- **Endowment** $1.8 million
- **Coed**

Undergraduates 1,561 full-time, 1,972 part-time. 0.3% African American, 0.8% Asian American or Pacific Islander, 0.6% Hispanic American, 3% Native American.

Faculty *Student/faculty ratio:* 6:1.

Academics *Calendar:* semesters. *Degree:* certificates, diplomas, and associate.

Costs (2006–07) *Tuition:* state resident $3760 full-time, $87 per credit part-time. Full-time tuition and fees vary according to course level, course load, degree level, program, and reciprocity agreements. Part-time tuition and fees vary according to course level, course load, degree level, program, and reciprocity agreements.

Applying *Application fee:* $35.

Freshmen Application Contact Ms. Mimi Crandall, Dean, Student Services, Wisconsin Indianhead Technical College, 505 Pine Ridge Drive, Shell Lake, WI 54871. *Phone:* 715-468-2815 Ext. 2208. *Toll-free phone:* 800-243-9482. *Fax:* 715-468-2819. *E-mail:* mcrandal@witc.edu.

WYOMING

CASPER COLLEGE

Casper, Wyoming   **www.caspercollege.edu/**

- **District-supported** 2-year, founded 1945, part of Wyoming Community College Commission
- **Small-town** 125-acre campus
- **Coed**

Undergraduates 1,896 full-time, 2,389 part-time. Students come from 40 states and territories, 15 other countries, 8% are from out of state, 0.8% African American, 0.4% Asian American or Pacific Islander, 3% Hispanic American, 1% Native American, 0.9% international, 6% transferred in, 15% live on campus. *Retention:* 61% of 2003 full-time freshmen returned.

Faculty *Student/faculty ratio:* 14:1.

Academics *Calendar:* semesters. *Degree:* certificates and associate. *Special study options:* academic remediation for entering students, accelerated degree program, adult/continuing education programs, advanced placement credit, cooperative education, distance learning, English as a second language, independent study, internships, off-campus study, part-time degree program, services for LD students, summer session for credit. *ROTC:* Army (c).

Student Life *Campus security:* 24-hour patrols, late-night transport/escort service.

Athletics Member NJCAA.

Costs (2006–07) *Tuition:* state resident $1416 full-time, $59 per credit part-time; nonresident $4272 full-time, $178 per credit part-time. *Required fees:* $168 full-time, $7 per credit part-time. *Room and board:* $3590.

Financial Aid Of all full-time matriculated undergraduates, 104 Federal Work-Study jobs (averaging $1410).

Applying *Options:* electronic application, early admission. *Required:* high school transcript.

Freshmen Application Contact Ms. Donna Hoffman, Admission Specialist, Casper College, 125 College Drive, Casper, WY 82601. *Phone:* 307-268-2458. *Toll-free phone:* 800-442-2963. *Fax:* 307-268-2611. *E-mail:* dhoffman@ caspercollege.edu.

CENTRAL WYOMING COLLEGE

Riverton, Wyoming   **www.cwc.edu/**

- **State and locally supported** 2-year, founded 1966, part of Wyoming Community College Commission
- **Small-town** 200-acre campus
- **Endowment** $5.2 million
- **Coed,** 1,711 undergraduate students, 40% full-time, 66% women, 34% men

Undergraduates 681 full-time, 1,030 part-time. Students come from 26 states and territories, 8 other countries, 8% are from out of state, 0.6% African American, 1% Asian American or Pacific Islander, 4% Hispanic American, 19% Native American, 2% international, 7% transferred in, 9% live on campus. *Retention:* 46% of 2003 full-time freshmen returned.

Freshmen *Admission:* 366 applied, 366 admitted, 225 enrolled. *Average high school GPA:* 3.01. *Test scores:* SAT verbal scores over 500: 50%; SAT math scores over 500: 15%; ACT scores over 18: 74%; ACT scores over 24: 19%.

Faculty *Total:* 169, 28% full-time, 46% with terminal degrees. *Student/faculty ratio:* 14:1.

Majors Accounting; accounting technology and bookkeeping; acting; agribusiness; agricultural business and management; agriculture; American Indian/Native American studies; art; automobile/automotive mechanics technology; biology/biological sciences; business administration and management; business automation/technology/data entry; child care and support services management; computer science; computer systems networking and telecommunications; computer technology/computer systems technology; criminal justice/law enforcement administration; digital communication and media/multimedia; dramatic/theater arts; elementary education; English; environmental science; equestrian studies; general studies; horse husbandry/equine science and management; human services; management information systems; music; nursing (registered nurse training); parts, warehousing, and inventory management; physical sciences; pre-law studies; psychology; radio and television broadcasting technology; range science and management; secondary education; social sciences; surgical technology; theater design and technology; web page, digital/multimedia and information resources design; welding technology.

Academics *Calendar:* semesters. *Degree:* certificates and associate. *Special study options:* academic remediation for entering students, adult/continuing

education programs, advanced placement credit, cooperative education, distance learning, double majors, English as a second language, honors programs, independent study, off-campus study, part-time degree program, services for LD students, summer session for credit.

Library Central Wyoming College Library with 78,167 titles, 183 serial subscriptions, an OPAC, a Web page.

Student Life *Housing Options:* coed. Campus housing is university owned. *Activities and Organizations:* drama/theater group, student-run newspaper, radio and television station, choral group, Multi-Cultural Club, La Vida Nueva Club, Fellowship of College Christians, Quality Leaders, Science Club. *Campus security:* 24-hour emergency response devices and patrols, student patrols. *Student services:* personal/psychological counseling.

Athletics *Intercollegiate sports:* equestrian sports M(s)/W(s). *Intramural sports:* badminton M/W, basketball M/W, football M/W, skiing (downhill) M/W, soccer M/W, softball M/W, swimming and diving M/W, table tennis M/W, tennis M/W, volleyball M/W, weight lifting M/W.

Costs (2007–08) *Tuition:* state resident $1488 full-time, $62 per credit part-time; nonresident $4464 full-time, $186 per credit part-time. *Required fees:* $504 full-time, $21 per credit part-time. *Room and board:* $3280; room only: $1600.

Financial Aid Of all full-time matriculated undergraduates, 46 Federal Work-Study jobs (averaging $1337). *Financial aid deadline:* 6/30.

Applying *Options:* early admission, deferred entrance. *Recommended:* high school transcript. *Application deadlines:* rolling (freshmen), rolling (out-of-state freshmen), rolling (transfers).

Freshmen Application Contact Mrs. Brenda Barlow, Admissions Assistant, Central Wyoming College, 2660 Peck Avenue, Riverton, WY 82501-2273. *Phone:* 307-855-2119. *Toll-free phone:* 800-735-8418 Ext. 2119. *Fax:* 307-855-2093. *E-mail:* admit@cwc.edu.

EASTERN WYOMING COLLEGE

Torrington, Wyoming   **www.ewc.wy.edu/**

- **State and locally supported** 2-year, founded 1948, part of Wyoming Community College Commission
- **Rural** 40-acre campus
- **Coed**

Undergraduates 522 full-time, 824 part-time. Students come from 23 states and territories, 3 other countries, 26% are from out of state, 1% African American, 7% Hispanic American, 0.8% Native American, 0.8% international, 4% transferred in, 26% live on campus.

Faculty *Student/faculty ratio:* 13:1.

Academics *Calendar:* semesters. *Degree:* certificates, diplomas, and associate. *Special study options:* academic remediation for entering students, accelerated degree program, adult/continuing education programs, advanced placement credit, cooperative education, distance learning, English as a second language, independent study, internships, part-time degree program, services for LD students, student-designed majors, summer session for credit.

Student Life *Campus security:* 24-hour emergency response devices, controlled dormitory access.

Athletics Member NJCAA.

Costs (2006–07) *Tuition:* state resident $1416 full-time, $59 per credit hour part-time; nonresident $4272 full-time, $178 per credit hour part-time. *Required fees:* $384 full-time, $16 per credit hour part-time. *Room and board:* $3220; room only: $1364.

Financial Aid Of all full-time matriculated undergraduates, 100 Federal Work-Study jobs (averaging $700). 60 state and other part-time jobs (averaging $700).

Applying *Options:* electronic application, early admission. *Recommended:* high school transcript.

Freshmen Application Contact Mrs. Marilyn Cotant, Dean of Students, Eastern Wyoming College, 3200 West C Street, Torrington, WY 82240. *Phone:* 307-532-8257. *Toll-free phone:* 800-658-3195. *Fax:* 307-532-8222. *E-mail:* mcotant@ewc.wy.edu.

LARAMIE COUNTY COMMUNITY COLLEGE

Cheyenne, Wyoming   **www.lccc.wy.edu/**

- **State-supported** 2-year, founded 1968, part of Wyoming Community College Commission
- **Small-town** 270-acre campus
- **Endowment** $11.0 million
- **Coed,** 4,584 undergraduate students, 39% full-time, 60% women, 40% men

Laramie County Community College (continued)

Undergraduates 1,785 full-time, 2,799 part-time. Students come from 38 states and territories, 16 other countries, 12% are from out of state, 2% African American, 1% Asian American or Pacific Islander, 7% Hispanic American, 0.7% Native American, 0.5% international, 4% transferred in, 4% live on campus.

Freshmen *Admission:* 752 applied, 752 admitted, 373 enrolled.

Faculty *Total:* 279, 33% full-time. *Student/faculty ratio:* 20:1.

Majors Accounting; agribusiness; agricultural business technology; agricultural production; agriculture; anthropology; art; autobody/collision and repair technology; automobile/automotive mechanics technology; biological and physical sciences; biology/biological sciences; business administration and management; business/commerce; business operations support and secretarial services related; carpentry; chemistry; civil engineering technology; communication/speech communication and rhetoric; computer and information sciences; computer and information sciences and support services related; computer hardware technology; computer programming; computer science; computer systems analysis; construction engineering technology; construction trades; construction trades related; corrections; criminal justice/law enforcement administration; customer service support/call center/teleservice operation; data modeling/warehousing and database administration; dental assisting; dental hygiene; diagnostic medical sonography and ultrasound technology; diesel mechanics technology; digital communication and media/multimedia; dramatic/theater arts; early childhood education; economics; education; education (specific levels and methods) related; engineering; engineering technology; English; entrepreneurship; equestrian studies; health/medical preparatory programs related; history; humanities; industrial radiologic technology; information technology; journalism; mass communication/media; mathematics; multi-/interdisciplinary studies related; music; nursing assistant/aide and patient care assistant; nursing (registered nurse training); philosophy; physical education teaching and coaching; political science and government; pre-dentistry studies; pre-engineering; pre-law studies; pre-medical studies; pre-pharmacy studies; pre-veterinary studies; psychology; public administration; radiologic technology/science; religious studies; social sciences; sociology; Spanish; visual and performing arts; web/multimedia management and webmaster; web page, digital/multimedia and information resources design; wildlife and wildlands science and management.

Academics *Calendar:* semesters. *Degree:* certificates and associate. *Special study options:* academic remediation for entering students, adult/continuing education programs, advanced placement credit, cooperative education, distance learning, double majors, English as a second language, honors programs, independent study, internships, off-campus study, part-time degree program, services for LD students, summer session for credit. *ROTC:* Air Force (c).

Library Ludden Library plus 1 other with 54,396 titles, 243 serial subscriptions, 31,988 audiovisual materials, an OPAC, a Web page.

Student Life *Housing Options:* coed. Campus housing is university owned. *Activities and Organizations:* drama/theater group, student-run newspaper, choral group, Block and Bridle Club, Phi Theta Kappa, music, Student Nurses Association, STAR Club. *Campus security:* 24-hour patrols, controlled dormitory access. *Student services:* personal/psychological counseling.

Athletics Member NJCAA. *Intercollegiate sports:* basketball M(s), cheerleading M(s)/W(s), soccer M(s)/W(s), volleyball W(s). *Intramural sports:* basketball M/W, golf M/W, racquetball M/W, rock climbing M/W, skiing (cross-country) M/W, soccer M/W, table tennis M/W, ultimate Frisbee M/W, volleyball M/W.

Costs (2007–08) *Tuition:* state resident $1488 full-time, $62 per credit hour part-time; nonresident $4664 full-time, $186 per credit hour part-time. *Required fees:* $600 full-time, $25 per credit part-time. *Room and board:* $5690.

Applying *Options:* electronic application, early admission. *Application fee:* $20. *Required:* high school transcript. *Required for some:* interview. *Application deadlines:* rolling (freshmen), rolling (transfers). *Notification:* continuous until 8/31 (freshmen), continuous until 8/31 (transfers).

Freshmen Application Contact Ms. Holly Allison, Assistant Director of Enrollment Management/Admissions Coordinator, Laramie County Community College, 1400 East College Drive, Cheyenne, WY 82007. *Phone:* 307-778-1117. *Toll-free phone:* 800-522-2993 Ext. 1357. *Fax:* 307-778-1360. *E-mail:* learnmore@lccc.wy.edu.

NORTHWEST COLLEGE

Powell, Wyoming   www.northwestcollege.edu/

Freshmen Application Contact Assistant Director of Admissions, Northwest College, 231 West Sixth Street, Powell, WY 82435. *Phone:* 307-754-6043. *Toll-free phone:* 800-560-4692.

SHERIDAN COLLEGE–GILLETTE CAMPUS

Gillette, Wyoming   www.sheridan.edu/index_live.asp?id=2

Admissions Office Contact Sheridan College–Gillette Campus, 300 West Sinclair Street, Gillette, WY 82718.

SHERIDAN COLLEGE–SHERIDAN AND GILLETTE

Sheridan, Wyoming   www.sheridan.edu/

- **State and locally supported** 2-year, founded 1948, part of Wyoming Community College Commission
- **Small-town** 124-acre campus
- **Coed,** 3,136 undergraduate students, 33% full-time, 54% women, 46% men

Undergraduates 1,038 full-time, 2,098 part-time. Students come from 30 states and territories, 9 other countries, 17% are from out of state, 0.9% African American, 1% Asian American or Pacific Islander, 3% Hispanic American, 2% Native American, 1% international, 3% transferred in, 8% live on campus.

Freshmen *Admission:* 380 admitted, 380 enrolled.

Faculty *Total:* 164, 49% full-time, 12% with terminal degrees. *Student/faculty ratio:* 18:1.

Majors Administrative assistant and secretarial science; agricultural business and management; agriculture; art; biological and physical sciences; biology/biological sciences; business administration and management; business/commerce; computer programming (specific applications); computer software and media applications related; computer systems networking and telecommunications; criminal justice/law enforcement administration; criminal justice/police science; data entry/microcomputer applications; dental hygiene; diesel mechanics technology; drafting and design technology; education; elementary education; engineering; engineering technology; English; foreign languages and literatures; general studies; health and physical education; heavy equipment maintenance technology; history; hospitality administration; humanities; information science/studies; liberal arts and sciences/liberal studies; machine tool technology; mathematics; music; nursing (registered nurse training); respiratory care therapy; sign language interpretation and translation; social sciences; system administration; web/multimedia management and webmaster; web page, digital/multimedia and information resources design; welding technology.

Academics *Calendar:* semesters. *Degree:* certificates and associate. *Special study options:* academic remediation for entering students, advanced placement credit, cooperative education, distance learning, double majors, English as a second language, independent study, internships, off-campus study, part-time degree program, services for LD students, student-designed majors, summer session for credit.

Library Griffith Memorial Library plus 1 other with 65,221 titles, 581 serial subscriptions, an OPAC, a Web page.

Student Life *Housing Options:* coed, women-only, disabled students. Campus housing is university owned. *Activities and Organizations:* drama/theater group, choral group, student government, Phi Theta Kappa, Art Club, Nursing Club, Police Science Club. *Campus security:* 24-hour emergency response devices, student patrols, controlled dormitory access, night patrols by certified officers. *Student services:* personal/psychological counseling.

Athletics Member NJCAA. *Intercollegiate sports:* basketball M(s)/W(s), volleyball W(s). *Intramural sports:* basketball M/W, bowling M/W, soccer M/W, softball M/W, table tennis M/W, tennis M/W, ultimate Frisbee M/W, volleyball M/W.

Costs (2007–08) *Tuition:* state resident $1488 full-time, $62 per credit hour part-time; nonresident $4664 full-time, $186 per credit hour part-time. *Required fees:* $528 full-time, $22 per credit hour part-time. *Room and board:* $3920.

Financial Aid Of all full-time matriculated undergraduates, 59 Federal Work-Study jobs (averaging $912).

Applying *Options:* electronic application, early admission, deferred entrance. *Required for some:* high school transcript. *Recommended:* high school transcript. *Application deadlines:* rolling (freshmen), rolling (transfers). *Notification:* continuous (freshmen), continuous (transfers).

Freshmen Application Contact Mr. Zane Garstad, Director of Admissions, Sheridan College–Sheridan and Gillette, PO Box 1500, Sheridan, WY 82801-1500. *Phone:* 307-674-6446 Ext. 2002. *Toll-free phone:* 800-913-9139 Ext. 2002. *Fax:* 307-674-7205. *E-mail:* admissions@sheridan.edu.

WESTERN WYOMING COMMUNITY COLLEGE

Rock Springs, Wyoming   www.wwcc.wy.edu

- **State and locally supported** 2-year, founded 1959
- **Small-town** 10-acre campus
- **Endowment** $7.9 million
- **Coed,** 2,698 undergraduate students, 39% full-time, 57% women, 43% men

Undergraduates 1,052 full-time, 1,646 part-time. Students come from 33 states and territories, 24 other countries, 14% are from out of state, 0.8% African American, 0.6% Asian American or Pacific Islander, 6% Hispanic American, 1% Native American, 3% international, 3% transferred in, 14% live on campus. *Retention:* 58% of 2003 full-time freshmen returned.

Freshmen *Admission:* 694 applied, 485 admitted, 485 enrolled. *Average high school GPA:* 3.0. *Test scores:* ACT scores over 18: 90%; ACT scores over 24: 10%.

Faculty *Total:* 218, 32% full-time. *Student/faculty ratio:* 13:1.

Majors Accounting; administrative assistant and secretarial science; anthropology; archeology; art; automobile/automotive mechanics technology; biological and physical sciences; biology/biological sciences; business administration and management; chemistry; communication/speech communication and rhetoric; computer and information sciences; computer programming (specific applications); computer science; criminal justice/law enforcement administration; criminology; dance; data entry/microcomputer applications; data processing and data processing technology; diesel mechanics technology; dramatic/theater arts; early childhood education; economics; education; education (multiple levels); electrical, electronic and communications engineering technology; electrical/electronics equipment installation and repair; electrician; elementary education; engineering technology; English; environmental science; forestry; general studies; geography; geology/earth science; health/medical preparatory programs related; health services/allied health/health sciences; heavy equipment maintenance technology; history; humanities; human services; industrial electronics technology; industrial mechanics and maintenance technology; information science/studies; information technology; instrumentation technology; international relations and affairs; journalism; kinesiology and exercise science; legal administrative assistant/secretary; liberal arts and sciences/liberal studies; marketing/marketing management; mathematics; mechanics and repair; medical administrative assistant and medical secretary; medical/clinical assistant; medical office assistant; medical office computer specialist; mining technology; music; nursing assistant/aide and patient care assistant; nursing (licensed practical/vocational nurse training); photography; political science and government; pre-dentistry studies; pre-engineering; pre-law studies; pre-medical studies; pre-nursing studies; pre-pharmacy studies; pre-veterinary studies; psychology; secondary education; social sciences; social work; sociology; Spanish; special education; theater design and technology; visual and performing arts; web/multimedia management and webmaster; web page, digital/multimedia and information resources design; welding technology; wildlife and wildlands science and management; word processing.

Academics *Calendar:* semesters. *Degree:* certificates, diplomas, and associate. *Special study options:* academic remediation for entering students, adult/continuing education programs, advanced placement credit, cooperative education, distance learning, double majors, English as a second language, honors programs, independent study, internships, part-time degree program, services for LD students, summer session for credit.

Library Hay Library with 107,669 titles, 178 serial subscriptions, 3,596 audiovisual materials, an OPAC, a Web page.

Student Life *Housing Options:* coed, disabled students. Campus housing is university owned. *Activities and Organizations:* drama/theater group, student-run newspaper, choral group, Phi Theta Kappa, Students Without Borders (international club), Residence Hall Association, Associated Student Government, LDSSA. *Campus security:* 24-hour emergency response devices and patrols, late-night transport/escort service, controlled dormitory access, patrols by trained security personnel from 4 p.m. to 8 a.m., 24-hour patrols on weekends and holidays. *Student services:* personal/psychological counseling.

Athletics Member NJCAA. *Intercollegiate sports:* basketball M(s)/W(s), cheerleading M(s)/W(s), soccer M(s)(c)/W(s)(c), volleyball W(s), wrestling M(s). *Intramural sports:* badminton M/W, basketball M/W, bowling M/W, football M/W, rock climbing M/W, skiing (downhill) M/W, soccer M/W, softball M/W, table tennis M/W, tennis M/W, ultimate Frisbee M/W, volleyball M/W, water polo M/W.

Costs (2007–08) *Tuition:* state resident $1828 full-time, $78 per credit hour part-time; nonresident $4804 full-time, $202 per credit hour part-time. *Room and board:* $3394; room only: $1768.

Financial Aid Of all full-time matriculated undergraduates, 20 Federal Work-Study jobs (averaging $1500).

Applying *Options:* electronic application, early admission, deferred entrance. *Required:* high school transcript. *Application deadlines:* rolling (freshmen), rolling (transfers).

Freshmen Application Contact Ms. Laurie L. Watkins, Director of Admissions, Western Wyoming Community College, PO Box 428, 2500 College Drive, Rock Springs, WY 82902-0428. *Phone:* 307-382-1647. *Toll-free phone:* 800-226-1181. *Fax:* 307-382-1636. *E-mail:* admissions@wwcc.wy.edu.

WYOTECH

Laramie, Wyoming   www.wyotech.com/

Director of Admissions Mr. Troy Chaney, Director of Admissions, WyoTech, 4373 North Third Street, Laramie, WY 82072-9519. *Phone:* 307-742-3776. *Toll-free phone:* 800-521-7158.

INTERNATIONAL

MARSHALL ISLANDS

COLLEGE OF THE MARSHALL ISLANDS
Majuro, Marshall Islands   www.cmiedu.net/

- **State-supported** 2-year
- 604 undergraduate students
- 37% of applicants were admitted

Freshmen *Admission:* 404 applied, 150 admitted.
Majors Business administration, management and operations related; elementary education; health professions related; liberal arts and sciences/liberal studies; nursing (registered nurse training).
Academics *Degree:* associate.
Costs (2006–07) *Tuition:* state resident $2980 full-time.
Financial Aid Of all full-time matriculated undergraduates, 100 Federal Work-Study jobs (averaging $300). *Financial aid deadline:* 7/15.
Applying *Application fee:* $5.
Admissions Office Contact College of the Marshall Islands, PO Box 1258, Majuro 96960, Marshall Islands.

MEXICO

WESTHILL UNIVERSITY
Sante Fe, Mexico   www.westhill.edu.mx/

Admissions Office Contact Westhill University, 56 Domingo Garcia Ramos, Zona Escolar, Prados de la Montana I, Sante Fe, Mexico.

PALAU

PALAU COMMUNITY COLLEGE
Koror, Palau

- **Territory-supported** 2-year, founded 1969
- **Small-town** 30-acre campus
- **Endowment** $1.3 million
- **Coed,** 731 undergraduate students, 66% full-time, 59% women, 41% men

Undergraduates 479 full-time, 252 part-time. Students come from 1 other state, 32% are from out of state, 0.7% transferred in, 20% live on campus.
Freshmen *Admission:* 283 applied, 165 admitted, 134 enrolled. *Average high school GPA:* 2.82.
Faculty *Total:* 65, 54% full-time. *Student/faculty ratio:* 16:1.
Majors Accounting; administrative assistant and secretarial science; agriculture; automobile/automotive mechanics technology; business teacher education; carpentry; construction engineering technology; criminal justice/police science; education; electrical, electronic and communications engineering technology; hotel/motel administration; liberal arts and sciences/liberal studies; natural resources and conservation related; nursing (registered nurse training).
Academics *Calendar:* semesters. *Degree:* certificates and associate. *Special study options:* academic remediation for entering students, adult/continuing education programs, cooperative education, distance learning, double majors, English as a second language, internships, part-time degree program, summer session for credit.
Library Palau Community College Library with 28,458 titles, 1,888 serial subscriptions, 855 audiovisual materials, an OPAC.
Student Life *Housing Options:* coed, men-only. Campus housing is university owned. *Activities and Organizations:* Yapese Student Organization, Chuukes Student Organization, Palauans Student Organization, Environmental Club, Writing Club. *Campus security:* 24-hour emergency response devices and patrols, late-night transport/escort service, evening patrols by trained security personnel. *Student services:* health clinic, personal/psychological counseling, legal services.
Athletics *Intramural sports:* baseball M, basketball M, softball M/W, table tennis M/W, volleyball M/W, weight lifting M, wrestling M.
Costs (2007–08) *Tuition:* state resident $1680 full-time, $70 per credit part-time. *Required fees:* $460 full-time, $460 per term part-time. *Room and board:* $2352; room only: $588.
Financial Aid Of all full-time matriculated undergraduates, 200 Federal Work-Study jobs (averaging $200). *Financial aid deadline:* 6/30.
Applying *Options:* early admission, deferred entrance. *Application fee:* $10. *Required:* high school transcript, minimum 2.00 GPA. *Application deadlines:* 8/15 (freshmen), 8/15 (transfers). *Notification:* continuous (freshmen), continuous (transfers).
Freshmen Application Contact Ms. Dahlia Katosang, Director of Admissions and Financial Aid, Palau Community College, PO Box 9, Koror, PW 96940-0009, Palau. *Phone:* 680-488-2471 Ext. 233. *Fax:* 680-488-4468. *E-mail:* dahliapcc@palaunet.com.

SWITZERLAND

SCHILLER INTERNATIONAL UNIVERSITY
Engelberg, Switzerland   www.schiller-university.ch/

Freshmen Application Contact Ms. Annelies Muff, Administrative Assistant, Schiller International University, Hotel Europe, Dorfstrasse 40, Engelberg 6390, Switzerland. *Phone:* 41-41-639 74 74.

College
CLOSE-UPS

AMERICAN ACADEMY OF DRAMATIC ARTS
NEW YORK, NEW YORK, AND LOS ANGELES, CALIFORNIA

The American Academy of Dramatic Arts

The College and Its Mission

Founded in New York in 1884, the American Academy of Dramatic Arts (AADA) was the first school in the United States to provide a professional education for actors. Since 1974, the Academy has operated an additional campus in the Los Angeles area, making AADA the only degree granting conservatory for actors offering programs in both of the major centers of theatrical activity in the country. Now in its second century, the Academy remains dedicated to a single purpose: training actors. The love of acting, as an art and as an occupation, is the spirit that impels the school. For the serious, well-motivated student ready to make a commitment to acting and to concentrated professional training, the Academy offers more than a century of success; a well-balanced, carefully structured curriculum; and a vital, dedicated, and caring faculty. Academy training involves the student intellectually, physically, and emotionally. Designed for the individual, it stresses self-discovery and self-discipline. Underlying the training are the beliefs that an actor prepared to work on the stage has the best foundation for acting in any medium and that classroom learning must be put to the test in the practical arena of a theater. The soundness of this approach is reflected in the achievements of the alumni, a diverse body of professionals unmatched by the alumni of any other institution. (Performances by Academy alumni have received nominations for 72 Oscars, 58 Tonys, 205 Emmys, and 5 Kennedy Center Honorees.) The time spent at the Academy can be an important period of development for those who become professional actors as well as for those who eventually choose other paths. All students are expected to make a commitment to professionalism, excellence, and discipline while enrolled at the Academy. The American Academy of Dramatic Arts is a nonprofit educational institution, chartered in New York by the Board of Regents of the University of the State of New York. In New York the Academy is accredited by the Middle States Association of Colleges and Schools and in California by the Western Association of Schools and Colleges. Both schools are accredited by the National Association of Schools of Theatre.

Academic Programs

The Professional Training Program requires two years to complete. Students who meet the requirements of the program receive an associate degree. A third-year performance program is offered to selected graduates. Students who successfully complete this program earn the Certificate of Advanced Studies in Actor training. Through the Academy's articulation agreement with St. John's University, AADA students have the option of transferring their Academy credits to St. John's for a B.S. in film and television. Students may also transfer credits to one of Antioch University's six campuses through the Academy's agreement with Antioch University Los Angeles (AULA) for a B.A. degree.

The first year consists of two 12-week terms and one 6-week term, providing a total of 30 transferable college credits. Classes include acting, movement, voice and speech, vocal production, acting styles, and theater history. The primary goals of the first-year program are to achieve relaxed, free, and truthful use of oneself in imaginary circumstances; to gain awareness of the body in terms of alignment, flexibility, and strength; to develop an open, well-placed, and well-supported vocal tone; to acquire clearly articulated standard American speech; and to increase understanding of the historical and stylistic backgrounds of drama. Students may enter the first year in mid-September or late January for the course in Los Angeles; late October or early February for New York. Admission to the second year is by invitation. Selection is made on the basis of progress, potential, and readiness to benefit from advanced training, as evidenced by the quality of first-year classwork and examination play performances. The second year begins with advanced classwork designed to reinforce and build upon the learning experiences of the first year. Emphasis is gradually shifted to performance opportunities. Additional courses are given in fencing and stage makeup. The second-year course provides 30 transferable undergraduate credits. Workshops to deal with specific acting problems are set up as needed, and, toward the end of the second year, seminars are scheduled to familiarize students with basic procedures for attaining professional employment. Upon completion of the second year, students graduate from the Professional Training Program with associate degrees. Admission to the third-year program, which emphasizes performance, is also by invitation. Students who undertake a third year of study become members of the Academy Company, the school's performance ensemble. Selection is based on the individual's potential and the overall concept of a balanced acting company. The practical development of the actor is continued through study, rehearsal, and performance of fully-produced plays in Academy theaters over a thirty-week period from late summer to late winter. Agents, casting directors, and other professional personnel are invited to see Academy Company productions, and counseling is offered to assist third-year students in launching professional careers. Students completing the third-year program earn an additional 30 college credits and are awarded a certificate. Guest speakers, including Academy alumni, from the professional world are regularly invited to the Academy to share insights with the students at special assemblies.

The Academy also offers a six-week summer conservatory for those who would like to begin to study, to refresh basic skills, or to test interest and ability in an environment of professional training. Classes begin shortly after the Fourth of July and are open to anyone of high school age or older. Teaching standards are identical to those of the Academy's degree and certificate programs.

Costs

In 2007–08, the cost of the full-time program is $18,000 for tuition and $500 for the general fee. (The general fee covers the cost of accident insurance, costume and production costs, use of the library, and student identification.) Students need to budget an additional $600 for purchasing books and scripts, dance attire for movement class, a makeup kit, and other expenses related to the training. The cost of housing varies. On the average, housing, food, transportation, and personal expenses can amount to approximately $11,000 to $13,000.

Financial Aid

The Academy makes every effort to assist students in need of financial aid. The Academy participates in various financial aid programs, including government administered grants, loans, and college work-study. Grant awards are determined by financial need. (Only United States citizens and permanent residents are eligible for government-sponsored aid programs.) Payment plans (for those eligible) assist students by extending the payment of tuition over a period of time. Scholarships, awarded on the basis of both need and merit, are available to qualified students, including a limited number of Trustee Awards to first-year students. New York City and Los Angeles offer numerous job opportunities for students desiring part-time employment, including on-campus employment (work-study).

Faculty

To achieve its objectives, the Academy requires that its faculty members be well trained in the various performing arts disciplines; seasoned by professional experience; mature, objective, and sympathetic in their relations with students; and exemplars of the commitment to excellence that the Academy hopes to instill in its students. In their own training, the Academy's faculty members represent all of the master teachers and significant systems and philosophies of the performing arts of the past half-century. Their professional experience is diversified, encompassing a variety of positions in film, television, and theater. In selecting faculty members to support its specialized programs, the Academy places more importance on an instructor's professional training and experience and teaching ability than on traditional academic credentials. The student-faculty ratio ranges from 16:1 in classroom instruction, to 4:1 or 3:1 in some performance situations.

Student Body Profile

Academy students reflect a wide diversity of backgrounds and geographical origin; they come from every region of the United

States, from Canada, and from many other countries. Enrollment in 2005 was 310 in California and 302 in New York, with a combined average of 20 percent members of minority groups and 20 percent international students. Forty percent of the students are men. The average age of an entering Academy student is 22. Less than half of all first-year students come directly after high school; others enroll after a range of experiences, including college, military service, or other careers.

Student Activities

Students at the American Academy of Dramatic Arts are bonded by their love of acting. A common interest and the collaborative nature of the training contribute to genial social relations among the student body, and, accordingly, school-arranged activities are usually related to the performing arts. Academy students are frequently invited to attend all types of theatrical events for free or given the opportunity to purchase reduced-priced tickets. Every effort is made by the school to facilitate the cultural enrichment of the students.

Facilities and Resources

The Academy in New York is housed in a six-story building that is a registered New York City landmark. It includes classrooms, rehearsal studios, dance studios, a video studio, a student lounge, locker areas, and dressing rooms. A library, made possible by a grant from CBS, is a handsome facility, organized to serve the special research and study needs of the actor. Three theaters—a 160-seat proscenium theater, an intimate 160-seat thrust-stage theater, and a semi-arena theater that seats 103—are used for classes, rehearsals, and productions. Production facilities include a prop department, a costume department, a scene shop, and a sound room.

After housing its West Coast operation in leased space in Pasadena for more than twenty-five years, the Academy purchased a campus in the heart of Hollywood and took residence in 2000. Situated on 2.25 acres adjacent to the historic Charlie Chaplin Studios, the new campus includes a theater, ample parking, a library, and spacious classrooms and studios.

In place of on-campus housing, AADA offers a variety of attractive off-campus options through special arrangements with local housing resources.

Location

Located in midtown Manhattan, the New York home of the Academy is within walking distance of the Grand Central and Pennsylvania train stations, the Port Authority bus terminal, and Broadway and off-Broadway theaters.

AADA Los Angeles is located in the center of the motion picture and television production capital of the world. The new campus is a short walk from Hollywood Boulevard and is surrounded by film and television production companies. The California Freeway system affords access to beaches, deserts, and mountains.

At each location, the training at the Academy is enhanced by the exciting variety of nearby cultural and recreational opportunities afforded by New York and Los Angeles.

Admission Requirements

AADA seeks talented and highly motivated applicants. An audition/interview is the cornerstone of the admission process. The overall policy is to admit individuals who seem both artistically and academically qualified to undertake a rigorous conservatory program of professional training. Readiness to benefit fully from such training is assessed in the audition/interview. Auditions, whether for entrance into the program in New York City or Los Angeles, may be held at either school. In addition, regional auditions are held annually in major cities in the United States, Canada, and the United Kingdom. The audition requires the performance of two contrasting, memorized speeches (one comedic and one dramatic) from published plays (one period and one contemporary), the total performance time to be no more than 4 minutes. The audition appointment includes an interview. In the audition/interview, special attention is given to the quality of the applicant's instinctive emotional connection to the audition material. Since good listening is so fundamental to good acting, the auditioner notes how well the applicant listens in the "real world" context of the interview. Other criteria include sensitivity, sense of language, sense of humor, vitality, presence, vocal quality, cultural interests, a realistic sense of self, and the challenge involved in pursuing an acting career.

All entering students must hold a diploma from an accredited secondary school or its equivalent. Transcripts of all previous academic work must be submitted; previous college credits may not be transferred. High school seniors should submit SAT or ACT scores. Two letters of recommendation are required before an audition is scheduled. International students who are fluent in English are welcome to apply. AADA is approved for the training of veterans.

Application and Information

The Academy operates on a rolling admission basis, but early application is encouraged. There is a nonrefundable application fee of $50. Admission decisions are made within four weeks of the audition. Further information may be obtained from:

For AADA New York:
Karen Higginbotham
Director of Admissions
American Academy of Dramatic Arts
120 Madison Avenue
New York, New York 10016
Phone: 212-686-0620
       800-463-8990 (toll-free)
E-mail: admissions-ny@aada.org

For AADA Los Angeles:
Dan Justin
Director of Admissions
American Academy of Dramatic Arts
1336 North La Brea Avenue
Hollywood, California 90028
Phone: 800-222-2867 (toll-free)
E-mail: admissions-ca@aada.org
Web site: http://www.aada.org (both campuses)

Robert Redford presents fellow AADA alumnus Jason Robards with the Alumni Achievement Award at the Centennial Gala.

ANDREW COLLEGE
CUTHBERT, GEORGIA

The College and Its Mission

Founded in 1854, Andrew College is a small, two-year, residential college related to the United Methodist Church. Its mission is to provide an academically challenging liberal arts curriculum within a nurturing community. As a two-year, senior college–parallel, church-related college, Andrew exists to provide students with a better beginning to their college careers. Andrew specializes in the education of freshmen and sophomores.

For a quarter of a century, the Andrew College chapter of Phi Theta Kappa, the international honor society for two-year colleges, has won national recognition and was the number one chapter during five of those years. There are more than 1,000 chapters of Phi Theta Kappa, and no other chapter in public or private institutions has established a more impressive record.

Andrew College seeks to achieve its goals by providing several advantages, many of which are unique to a small campus with a church-related environment: the opportunity for intellectual, social, and spiritual development; a professionally competent faculty that is dedicated to teaching; individual attention to students at all levels of operation within the College; a two-year curriculum that parallels that of four-year colleges and universities; a cultural enrichment program that encourages students to appreciate the arts; the opportunity to learn leisure-time skills that lead to the development of a healthy body; remediation in the basic skills; orientation experiences for successful adjustment to college life; academic advising; a student community committed to the earning of a college education; and cultural and academic resources for the community and churches in the area.

Andrew College is accredited by the Commission on Colleges of the Southern Association of Colleges and Schools (1866 Southern Lane, Decatur, Georgia 30033-4097; telephone: 404-679-4501) to award associate degrees. Andrew College is listed by the University Senate of the United Methodist Church.

Academic Programs

The academic program at Andrew College is specifically designed for freshman and sophomore students. The faculty members serve at Andrew because they enjoy teaching freshmen and sophomores. This attitude and expertise contribute significantly to the quality of education that students receive.

Andrew College offers programs that lead to advanced degrees in the arts and sciences. The College offers the Associate of Arts degree, the Associate of Science degree, and the Associate of Music degree. To be eligible for graduation, a student must have earned at least a 2.0 cumulative grade point average on the work attempted at Andrew College. All associate degrees have a core curriculum of liberal studies, including a required curriculum of essential skills, humanities/fine arts, science/mathematics/technology, social science, and physical education. Each student must satisfactorily complete a course in religion or philosophy and satisfy Cultural Enrichment Program requirements. All students who graduate from Andrew College must demonstrate proficiency in computer and oral communication skills.

All students entering Andrew College are assigned a faculty adviser who assists students in all matters relating to their academic progress. Andrew College schedules free tutoring during each term for students who need extra help with their studies. Some students, including students on academic probation and those admitted on a conditional basis, are assigned to mandatory study and tutoring sessions. Enrichment seminars are offered in areas beyond those covered in regular class study. These courses provide students with a challenge to do in-depth study and carry institutional credit only. Andrew College offers a number of programs that assist students in reaching their educational potential. For a variety of reasons, some applicants to Andrew College may need to improve their academic skills in order to be successful in a full-time schedule of college-level courses. The Strategic Studies Program serves students who need to improve their academic skills before embarking on a full-time schedule of college-level courses. The program contains a selected schedule of college-level course work as well as other specially designed courses that provide intensive study and individual guidance at a pace that is compatible with the students' abilities. Tutorial assistance is provided.

Andrew College has established an intensive level of academic support services designed for and limited to specifically identified and accepted students with documented learning disabilities and/or attention deficit disorders. While the Focus Program supplements and complements the tutorial and advising services available to all students, it provides an additional level of professional assistance and monitoring to enhance the students' probability for success.

Andrew College offers an English as a Second Language (ESL) Program for students whose native language is not English and gives them a choice in the selection of the instructional program.

Through the Cultural Enrichment Program (CEP), Andrew College recognizes the fact that exposure to the cultural arts is an essential part of a liberal arts education. As a graduation requirement, all degree-seeking students must attend designated programs relating to the cultural arts during their enrollment.

Costs

Although Andrew College is a private college, an Andrew education is affordable. Tuition and fees for the 2006–07 academic year were $9814. Room and board were $6166 for the academic year. Books and supplies average $600 to $700 per academic year. Approximately $2300 per year should be allowed for other costs, including transportation and personal expenses.

Financial Aid

Approximately 90 percent of Andrew College students receive some type of federal or institutional aid. Students from Georgia are eligible for the Georgia Tuition Equalization Grant and may be eligible for the HOPE Scholarship. Scholarships are given for academic excellence, community service, intercollegiate sports, spiritual life, and programs such as chorus, art, drama, piano, photography, yearbook, and newspaper.

Every year, the Office of Admission holds a Scholarship Day program, where students who have a 3.0 GPA or above and at least a 1000 on the SAT are invited to compete for academic scholarships. Up to four Margaret A. Pitts Scholarships (full tuition, room, and board scholarships) are awarded at the competition, along with other academic awards. Scholarships or loans may be awarded to students who are members of the United Methodist Church. Other churches, religious and community organizations, and fraternal or business groups may also sponsor financial awards. Government programs at the federal and state levels provide a variety of grants, low-interest educational loans, and work-study employment opportunities for students. Eligibility for many of these programs is based on need.

Faculty

The faculty at Andrew College is committed to the education of freshmen and sophomores. The success of the students at the next level and beyond is the focus of the faculty and the academic program at Andrew.

The College employs 29 full-time and 5 part-time faculty members. The student-faculty ratio varies each year but is maintained at or below 15:1, resulting in lively discussions, teacher-student interaction, and individual attention. Eight members of the full-

time faculty hold doctoral degrees, 2 have terminal degrees in their field, and the rest hold master's degrees in their area of specialty.

Student Body Profile

Andrew College has a diverse population of students from all over the world. International students make up approximately 3 percent of the College population and come from such countries as Japan, Nigeria, Trinidad, Mexico, Guatemala, and Korea. Based on figures from fall 2006, 75 percent of students were from Georgia, 13 percent were from Florida, 4 percent were from Alabama, and 5 percent were from other states. The total student population in fall 2006 was 272 students. Ninety percent of Andrew College students live in a College residence hall.

While most students transfer to schools in Georgia, graduates have chosen to transfer to schools as far away as New England or California.

Student Activities

The student life program at Andrew College is designed to promote activities and programs that are supportive of the College's aims and purposes. The first two years of college are critical for academic success; therefore, programs that support and enhance students' lives are very important.

Andrew College is committed to the idea that total education involves more than academic pursuit. Activities, including intramural recreation, student activities, religious activities, career and transfer services, student government, and residential and commuter student programs, are among the many programs offered. All freshman students are required to complete a student orientation program.

Informal recreation opportunities available to students include basketball, indoor and outdoor volleyball, racquetball, tennis, walleyball, and weight training. Formalized recreational opportunities exist under the umbrella of intramurals and include team and individual sports and exercise programs. Off-campus recreational opportunities are promoted throughout the year.

A wide variety of student activities take place at Andrew. Many organizations and various offices of the College provide a diversity of programs. The Student Events and Activities (SEA) Board is the chief programming committee in the student life area and sponsors events such as Homecoming, major dances, movies, coffeehouse performers, speakers, and comedy acts. Student organizations at Andrew College offer many leadership opportunities and operate under the jurisdiction of the Student Development Committee. Such organizations include the Student Government Association, International Student Association, Phi Theta Kappa Honor Society, AndrewServes, and the Residence Hall Association.

Sports Andrew College maintains membership in the National Junior College Athletic Association and the Georgia Junior College Athletic Association. Andrew offers scholarships in all intercollegiate sports in which the College participates. Andrew participates competitively in men's baseball, cross-country, golf, and soccer and in women's basketball, cross-country, golf, soccer, and softball.

Facilities and Resources

Pitts Library subscribes to more than 100 periodicals, five daily newspapers, and three weekly newspapers. These publications supplement the library's holdings and provide reading and sources for the students and faculty members. Library computers provide students with access to holdings at other libraries and access to the World Wide Web through the Internet. A substantial collection of audiovisual and microfilm materials is maintained. An attractive main reading room provides areas for individual study, and a special reference section supplies ample space for research work.

The Andrew College Interactive Distance Learning Center is located adjacent to the main reading room and contains videoconferencing and Web-based instructional program development facilities.

In 1999, the College completed construction of an athletic complex, which contains baseball, soccer, and softball fields. The Fort Residence Building was completed and ready for occupancy by 142 students in fall 2000. The Phyllis and Jack Jones Chapel was completed in September 2001.

Location

Andrew College is located in southwest Georgia in the town of Cuthbert. Cuthbert is the county seat of Randolph County, which has a total population of 8,000 people. The Cuthbert area is a safe, friendly community located 40 miles east of Albany, Georgia; 161 miles southwest of Atlanta; 60 miles south of Columbus, Georgia; and 30 miles east of Eufaula, Alabama. The weather year-round is ideally suited to the many recreational opportunities in the region. A championship state park golf course is located 20 minutes from the campus of Andrew College. Lake George is also 20 minutes away and provides an ideal place for fishing, boating, and waterskiing. Large cities and shopping malls are within 1 hour's drive. Providence Canyon, for hiking, picnicking, and nature watching, is only a 20-minute drive from the campus.

Admission Requirements

Andrew College admits applicants who demonstrate abilities that are necessary for successful completion of the program. Admission decisions are based on the applicant's previous academic record, test scores, recommendations, and, in some cases, a personal interview. Equal educational opportunities are offered to students regardless of race, color, religion, disability, gender, age, creed, or national origin.

Applicants may be admitted for any term. In order to ensure proper processing, all credentials should be on file in the Office of Admission approximately thirty days prior to semester registration. All applicants must submit the following materials: a completed application for admission, a $20 application fee, transcripts of high school (or GED) and/or college course work attempted, and scores from either the SAT or ACT. Transfer students who have successfully completed college-level courses in English and math need not submit SAT/ACT scores. In addition, applicants whose native language is not English must submit scores from the Test of English as a Foreign Language (TOEFL) or an acceptable score on an equivalent English language examination.

Admission to Andrew College is gained through an individual selection process. The academic requirements for acceptance include a high school diploma and graduation from an accredited high school. Requirements for nonconditional full acceptance include an evaluated high school GPA of 2.0 or better on a 4.0 scale, and SAT scores of at least 460 on verbal and 430 on math or the ACT equivalent. Students not meeting the minimum academic requirements for nonconditional acceptance may be conditionally accepted but are required to take placement examinations prior to registering for their first semester.

Application and Information

A new student may enter Andrew College at the beginning of the fall, spring, and summer semesters. There is an application deadline set at two weeks prior to the registration date for each term.

For an application and further information about Andrew College, students should contact:

Office of Admission and Financial Aid
Andrew College
413 College Street
Cuthbert, Georgia 39840

Phone: 800-664-9250 (toll-free)
Fax: 229-732-2176
E-mail: admissions@andrewcollege.edu
Web site: http://www.andrewcollege.edu

ARGOSY UNIVERSITY, TWIN CITIES CAMPUS
College of Health Sciences
EAGAN, MINNESOTA

The University and Its Mission

Argosy University is a private institution of higher education dedicated to providing high-quality professional education programs at the doctoral, master's, bachelor's, and associate degree levels, as well as continuing education to individuals who seek to advance their professional and personal lives. The University emphasizes programs in the behavioral sciences, business, education, and the health-care professions. A limited number of preprofessional programs and general education offerings are provided to permit students to prepare for entry into these professional fields. The programs of Argosy University are designed to instill the knowledge, skills, and ethical values of professional practice and to foster values of social responsibility in a supportive, learning-centered environment of mutual respect and professional excellence.

With fifteen campuses and three approved degree sites nationwide, Argosy University's Twin Cities Campus provides students with a network of resources usually found at larger universities, including a career resources office, an academic resources center, and extensive information access for research.

Argosy University's innovative programs features dynamic, relevant, and practical curricula delivered in flexible class formats. Students enjoy scheduling options that make it easier to fit school into their busy lives. They choose from day and evening courses, on campus or online. Many students find a combination of both to be an ideal way of continuing their education while meeting family and professional demands.

Students typically live in apartments in the metropolitan area. Most students are full-time working professionals who live within driving distance of the campus. The University does not offer or operate student housing.

Argosy University is accredited by the Higher Learning Commission of the North Central Association (NCA; 30 North LaSalle Street, Suite 2400, Chicago, Illinois 60602; phone: 800-621-7440 (toll-free); Web site: http://www.ncahlc.org).

The Associate of Applied Science in diagnostic medical sonography degree program is accredited by the Commission on Accreditation of Allied Health Education Programs on the recommendation of the Joint Review Committee on Education in Diagnostic Medical Sonography (JRC-DMS; 1361 Park Street, Clearwater, Florida 33756; phone: 727-210-2350). The Commission on Accreditation of Allied Health Education Programs has awarded initial accreditation to the echocardiography concentration on the recommendation of the Joint Review Committee on Education in Diagnostic Medical Sonography.

The Associate of Applied Science in histotechnology and the Associate of Science in medical laboratory technology degree programs are accredited by the National Accrediting Agency for Clinical Laboratory Sciences (8410 West Bryn Mawr, Suite 670, Chicago, Illinois 60631; phone: 773-714-8880).

The Associate of Applied Science in medical assisting degree program is accredited by the Commission on Accreditation of Allied Health Education Programs on the recommendation of the Curriculum Review Board of the American Association of Medical Assistants Endowment (AAMAE; 1361 Park Street, Clearwater, Florida 33756; phone: 727-210-2350).

The Associate of Applied Science in radiologic technology and Associate of Science in radiation therapy degree programs are accredited by the Joint Review Committee on Education in Radiologic Technology (20 North Wacker Drive, Suite 900, Chicago, Illinois 60606; phone: 312-704-5300).

The Associate of Applied Science in veterinary technology degree program is accredited through the Council on Education of the American Veterinary Medical Association (AVMA) Committee on Veterinary Technician Education and Activities (CVTEA; 1931 North Meachum Road, Suite 100, Schaumburg, Illinois 60173; phone: 847-925-8070).

The Associate of Science in dental hygiene degree program is accredited by the Commission on Dental Accreditation (211 East Chicago Avenue, Chicago, Illinois 60611; phone: 312-440-4653.) The commission is a specialized accrediting body recognized by the United States Department of Education.

The Associate of Science in radiation therapy degree program is accredited by the Joint Review Committee on Education in Radiologic Technology (20 North Wacker Drive, Suite 900, Chicago, Illinois 60606; phone: 312-704-5300).

Academic Programs

The Argosy University, Twin Cities Campus, College of Health Sciences offers the Associate of Applied Science (A.A.S.) degree in diagnostic medical sonography, histotechnology, medical assisting, radiation therapy, radiologic technology, and veterinary technology and the Associate of Science (A.S.) degree in dental hygiene, medical laboratory technology, and radiation therapy. Typically, associate degree programs are completed in one to two years.

The A.A.S. in diagnostic medical sonography program prepares students to develop the best possible technical skills in sonography to work under the direction of a doctor using ultrasound imaging techniques for purposes of diagnosis. Students must choose a concentration in general sonography or echocardiography.

The A.A.S. in histotechnology program prepares students to provide health-care services and demonstrate the utmost respect and concern for the well-being of the patients they serve. Histotechnicians prepare tissue specimens for examination and diagnosis by pathologists.

The A.A.S. in medical assisting program is designed to train students to be multiskilled allied health–care professionals. Postgraduate professional responsibilities include patient care, laboratory testing, limited X-ray, office management, and assisting the physician.

The A.A.S. in radiologic technology program prepares students to become skilled professionals who are qualified to perform imaging examinations and accompanying responsibilities at the request of physicians who are qualified to prescribe and/or perform radiologic procedures.

The A.A.S. in veterinary technology program prepares students to work as health-care professionals who professionally interact

with veterinarians, other technicians, and animal owners. Veterinary technicians provide critical and ongoing assistance in the care of all types of animals.

The A.S. in dental hygiene program prepares students to provide effective and professional preventive dental services under the supervision of the dentist. The integrated curriculum provides opportunities to acquire assessment skills, cognitive skills, and technical skills.

The A.S. in medical laboratory technology program prepares students to perform extensive laboratory testing procedures. The program also emphasizes interaction with pathologists, technologists, other medical personnel, and patients in a professional and ethical manner.

The A.S. in radiation therapy program prepares students with the knowledge and technical skills required to assist cancer patients. Students learn to prepare patients for radiation treatment, position patients under a linear accelerator, and administer prescribed doses of ionizing radiation to specific parts of the body.

Costs

Tuition varies by program. Students should contact Argosy University's Twin Cities Campus for tuition information.

Financial Aid

A wide range of financial aid options is available to students who qualify. Argosy University, Twin Cities Campus, offers access to federal and state aid programs, merit-based awards, grants, loans, and a work-study program. As a first step, students should complete the Free Application for Federal Student Aid (FAFSA). Prospective students can apply electronically at http://www.fafsa.ed.gov or at the campus. To receive consideration for the maximum amount of aid and ensure timely receipt of funds, it is best to submit an application promptly.

Faculty

The Argosy University faculty is made up of working professionals who are eager to help students succeed. Members bring real-world experience and the latest practice innovations to the academic setting. Argosy's diverse faculty is widely recognized for contributions to the field. Most hold doctoral degrees. They provide a substantive education that combines comprehensive knowledge with critical skills and practical workplace relevance. Above all, faculty members of the College of Health Sciences are committed to their students' personal and professional development.

Student Activities

Argosy University, Twin Cities Campus, offers unique opportunities for student involvement beyond individual programs of study. Most faculty committees include a student representative. In addition, a student group meets with faculty members and administrators regularly to discuss pertinent campus-related issues.

Facilities and Resources

Argosy University libraries provide curriculum support and educational resources, including current text materials, diagnostic training documents, reference materials and databases, journals and dissertations, and major and current titles in program areas. The University provides an online public-access catalog of library resources throughout the Argosy University system. Students enjoy full remote access to their campus library database, enabling them to study and conduct research at home. Academic databases offer dissertation abstracts, academic journals, and professional periodicals. All library computers are Internet accessible. Software applications include Word, Excel, PowerPoint, SPSS, and various test-scoring programs.

Location

Argosy University's Twin Cities Campus offers rigorous academics in a supportive environment. The campus is nestled in a parklike suburban setting within 10 miles of the airport and the Mall of America. Students enjoy the convenience of nearby shops, restaurants, and housing and easy freeway access. The neighboring Eagan Community Center offers many amenities, including walking paths, a fitness center, meeting rooms, and an outdoor amphitheater. The Twin Cities of Minneapolis and St. Paul have been rated by popular magazines as one of the most livable metropolitan areas in the country. With a population of 2.5 million, the area offers an abundance of recreational activities. Year-round outdoor activities, nationally acclaimed venues for theater art and music, and professional sports teams attract residents and visitors alike. The Minneapolis–St. Paul metropolitan area offers a diversified economic base fueled by a broad array of companies. Among the numerous publicly traded companies headquartered in the area are Target, UnitedHealth Group, 3M, General Mills, and U.S. Bancorp.

Admission Requirements

Students who have successfully completed a program of secondary education or the equivalent (GED) are eligible for admission to the health sciences programs. Entrance requirements include either an ACT composite score of 18 or above, a combined math and verbal SAT score of 850 or above, a passing score on the Argosy University Entrance Exam, or a minimum TOEFL score of 500 (paper version), 173 (computer version), or 61 (Internet version) for all applicants whose native language is not English or who have not graduated from an institution in which English is the language of instruction.

All applicants must include a completed application form; proof of high school graduation or successful completion of the GED test; official postsecondary transcripts; SAT, ACT, Argosy University exam, or TOEFL scores; and the nonrefundable application fee. Additional materials are required prior to matriculation. Some programs have additional application requirements. An admissions representative can provide further detailed information.

Application and Information

Argosy University, Twin Cities Campus, accepts students on a rolling admissions basis year-round, depending on availability of required courses. Applications for admission are available online or by contacting the campus, using the information listed in this description.

Argosy University, Twin Cities Campus
1515 Central Parkway
Eagan, Minnesota 55121
Phone: 651-846-2882
　　　 888-844-2004 (toll-free)
E-mail: auadmissions@argosyu.edu
Web site: http://www.argosyu.edu/twincities

THE ART INSTITUTE OF CHARLOTTE
CHARLOTTE, NORTH CAROLINA

The Institute and Its Mission

The Art Institute of Charlotte prepares students for entry-level employment in the creative arts. Students learn through programs of study that reflect the needs of a changing job market. Courses are taught by faculty members who have professional experience in their fields of expertise. The school offers five associate degree programs and five bachelor's degree programs.

Student housing options include apartments that comfortably accommodate 4 students in two-bedroom, two-bath units complete with living room, dining area, and full kitchen. Students submit a roommate preference form and are assigned to apartments by the housing staff. The apartments are located close to The Art Institute of Charlotte and shopping, dining, and entertainment venues.

Services are available to assist students with resume writing, networking, and keeping aware of what employers are looking for in job applicants.

The school is accredited by the Accrediting Council for Independent Colleges and Schools (ACICS) and is licensed by the North Carolina Department of Community Colleges and the University of North Carolina Board of Governors.

Academic Programs

Associate degree programs are available in culinary arts, fashion marketing, graphic design, interactive media design, and interior design.

Bachelor's degree programs are available in culinary arts management, fashion marketing and management, graphic design, interactive media design, and interior design.

The Art Institute of Charlotte operates on a year-round, four-quarter system.

Costs

Tuition cost varies by program. Prospective students should contact the school for current tuition costs. Other charges include a starting kit for all first-quarter students. Kits vary in price, depending on the program of study.

Financial Aid

Financial aid is available for those who qualify. Students who require financial assistance should first complete and submit a Free Application for Federal Student Aid (FAFSA) and meet with a financial aid officer. The officer determines the level of need based on a required federal formula, the cost of education, and other factors. Gift aid is available in the form of Federal Pell Grants, Federal Supplemental Educational Opportunity Grants, and veterans' benefits. Loans include Federal Stafford Student Loans, Federal PLUS loans, and alternative loans. Other scholarships are available from the school and private sources. Application deadlines and eligibility requirements vary by program.

Faculty

Faculty members at The Art Institute of Charlotte are experienced instructors, many of whom have professional experience outside of the classroom. There are 52 full- and part-time faculty members at the school, and the student-faculty ratio is 19:1.

Student Body Profile

There are more than 800 students attending the school. Students come to The Art Institute of Charlotte from throughout the southeastern United States and abroad. The student population includes recent high school graduates, transfer students, and those who have left a previous employment situation to study and train for a new career. Students are creative, competitive, and open to new ideas. They place great value on an education that prepares them for an exciting entry-level position in the arts.

Student Activities

Students enrolled in The Art Institute of Charlotte can get involved in student-led activities through the Student Affairs Department. Activities stimulate cultural awareness, creativity, and social and professional development. Students enrolled in the Interior Design Program may join the Interior Design Student Association. In addition, academic departments regularly organize trips to the International Home Furnishing Market in High Point, North Carolina, as well as to local museums and galleries.

Facilities and Resources

The Art Institute of Charlotte facility has computer labs for student use. Additional computers are available in the library. Studios, classrooms, and meetings rooms are available for students and faculty members.

Location

Charlotte mixes the characteristics of a large urban center with the charm of suburban life. With a mild climate and central location, Charlotte residents are only 2 hours from the Blue Ridge Mountains and 3 hours from the Atlantic coast. Charlotte is known for its arts community, sports, shopping, and restaurants. More than 300 Fortune 500 companies have offices in Charlotte, the nation's second-largest banking center. The city is the nation's fifth-largest urban region, with 6.3 million people living within a 100-mile radius.

Admission Requirements

Applicants must be high school graduates or have a General Educational Development (GED) certificate. A 150-word written essay is required, as are high school transcripts and any records from other academic institutions attended. All interested students are interviewed in person or over the phone. Following this interview, prospective students complete an application for admission and submit the enrollment fee. Applicants who have taken the SAT or ACT are encouraged to submit their scores to the Admissions Office for evaluation. There is a $50 application fee.

Application and Information

To obtain an application or make arrangements for an interview or tour of the school, prospective students should contact:

The Art Institute of Charlotte
Three LakePointe Plaza
2110 Water Ridge Parkway
Charlotte, North Carolina 28217-4536
Phone: 704-357-8020
       800-872-4417 (toll-free)
Fax: 704-357-1133
E-mail: aichadm@aii.edu
Web site: http://www.artinstitutes.edu/charlotte

The Art Institute of Atlanta®, GA; The Art Institute of California^{SM}–Inland Empire; The Art Institute of California^{SM}–Los Angeles; The Art Institute of California^{SM}–Orange County; The Art Institute of California^{SM}–San Diego; The Art Institute of California^{SM}–San Francisco; The Art Institute of Charleston^{SM}, SC, A branch of The Art Institute of Atlanta, GA; The Art Institute of Charlotte®, NC; The Art Institute of Colorado® (Denver); The Art Institute of Dallas®, TX; The Art Institute of Fort Lauderdale®, FL; The Art Institute of Houston®, TX; The Art Institute of Indianapolis^{SM}, IN*; The Art Institute of Jacksonville^{SM}, A branch of Miami International University of Art & Design, FL; The Art Institute of Las Vegas®, NV; The Art Institute of New York City®, NY; The Art Institute of Ohio^{SM}–Cincinnati**; The Art Institute of Philadelphia®, PA; The Art Institute of Phoenix®, AZ; The Art Institute of Pittsburgh®, PA; The Art Institute of Portland®, OR; The Art Institute of Seattle®, WA; The Art Institute of Tampa^{SM}, FL, A branch of Miami International University of Art & Design; The Art Institute of Tennessee^{SM}–Nashville, A branch of The Art Institute of Atlanta, GA; The Art Institute of Toronto^{SM}, ON; The Art Institute of Vancouver^{SM}, BC (Burnaby location, Downtown location, Dubrulle Culinary Arts location); The Art Institute of Washington® (Arlington, VA), A branch of The Art Institute of Atlanta, GA; The Art Institute Online^{SM}, A division of The Art Institute of Pittsburgh, PA; The Art Institutes International Minnesota^{SM} (Minneapolis); Bradley Academy for the Visual Arts^{SM} (York, PA); California Design College^{SM} (Wilshire Boulevard, Los Angeles); The Illinois Institute of Art®–Chicago; The Illinois Institute of Art®–Schaumburg; Miami International University of Art & Design^{SM}, FL; The New England Institute of Art^{SM} (Boston, MA).

*The Art Institute of Indianapolis is licensed by the Indiana Commission on Proprietary Education, 302 West Washington Street, Room E201, Indianapolis, IN 46204, AC-0080.
**The Art Institute of Ohio–Cincinnati, 8845 Governors Hill Drive, Suite 100, Cincinnati, OH 45249-3317, Reg. #04-01-1698B.

THE ART INSTITUTE OF NEW YORK CITY
NEW YORK, NEW YORK

The Institute and Its Mission

The Art Institute of New York City prepares students for entry-level employment in the creative arts. Students learn through programs of study that reflect the needs of a changing job market. Courses are taught by faculty members who have knowledge and experience in their fields of expertise.

Individualized job search assistance is available to help students with resume writing, networking, and keeping aware of what employers are looking for in job candidates.

The Art Institute of New York City is accredited by the Accrediting Council for Independent Colleges and Schools (ACICS) to award associate degrees and certificates. ACICS is listed as a nationally recognized accrediting agency by the U.S. Department of Education. Its accreditation of degree-granting institutions is recognized by the Council for Higher Education Accreditation. ACICS can be contacted at 750 First Street, NE, Suite 980, Washington, D.C. 20002; telephone: 202-336-6780.

Academic Programs

The Art Institute of New York City offers associate degree programs in art and design technology (with concentrations in fashion design, graphic design, interactive media design, interior design, and video production) and culinary arts and restaurant management. Certificates are available in culinary arts, pastry arts, and restaurant management. Each academic program is offered on a year-round basis, allowing students to continue to work uninterrupted toward their degrees.

Costs

Tuition costs vary by program. Prospective students should contact the school for current tuition costs. Other charges include a starting kit for all first-quarter students. Kits vary in price, depending on the program of study.

Financial Aid

Financial aid is available to those who qualify. The Art Institute of New York City participates in federal, state, and other financial aid programs. Financial aid is divided into grants, loans, and work-study. Students may be eligible for several loans, including the Federal Stafford Student Loan, the Federal PLUS Program loan (parents), and the Creative Education Loan. Application deadlines and eligibility requirements vary.

Faculty

Faculty members at the The Art Institute of New York City are professionals, many of whom have experience in their respective fields. There are 98 full-time and part-time faculty members at the school. The student-faculty ratio is 16:1.

Student Body Profile

There are more than 1,470 students at the school. Students come to The Art Institute of New York City from throughout the United States and abroad. The student population includes recent high school graduates, transfer students, and those who have left a previous employment situation to study and train for a new career. Students are creative, competitive, and open to new ideas. They place great value on an education that prepares them for an exciting entry-level position in the arts.

Student Activities

There are several events for students throughout the year that celebrate culture, health, and holidays. The Student Activities Office also provides shape-up and wellness programs for students, along with The Art Institute of New York City Celebrates Women program. Students are offered many opportunities to volunteer throughout the year. Culinary students work at various events throughout the city as well as open-house programs at the school.

Facilities and Resources

The Art Institute of New York City occupies approximately 42,000 square feet of space at 75 Varick Street and 33,000 square feet at 11 Beach Street in the SoHo/Tribeca district of New York City.

Students study culinary techniques at the Varick Street location in nine kitchens that include ovens, broilers, food slicers, mixers, charcoal grills, stove tops, convection ovens, dishwashers, and refrigerators. The Art Institute of New York City restaurant, One Hudson Place, provides students with the opportunity to cook and serve in a professional setting. The Education Department is situated at the Varick Street location, as are library resources, facilities, and services that are shared with Metropolitan College.

The school's Beach Street location houses the Graphic Design, Interactive Media Design, Video Production, Interior Design, Advertising, and Fashion Design Departments. There are thirteen classrooms, four computer labs (two Macintosh computers and two PCs), two drawing studios (one for life drawing), and a dining room for wine seminars and service management classes. A large bookstore and an art gallery are located on the first floor. All lecture classes are housed at the Beach Street site, many in classrooms equipped with TV monitors, VCRs, and overhead projectors.

Location

The Art Institute of New York City is located in downtown Manhattan's SoHo/Tribeca area, a hub of contemporary style. SoHo is a focal point for individuals who appreciate and possess creative talents. West Broadway is the district's main thoroughfare, lined with avant-garde boutiques and trendsetting galleries, including a branch of the Guggenheim Museum, which exhibits both contemporary collections and selections from the museum's permanent collection. The New Museum of Contemporary Art is a major venue for innovative shows.

Admission Requirements

Applicants must complete an application form and complete a 150-word essay to apply for admission to The Art Institute of New York City. A personal interview with an admissions representative is required. Applicants must provide official high school transcripts, proof of successful completion of the General Educational Development (GED) test, or transcripts from any college previously attended. There is a $50 application fee.

Application and Information

To obtain an application or make arrangements for an interview or tour of the school, prospective students should contact:

The Art Institute of New York City
75 Varick Street, 16th Floor
New York, New York 10013-1917
Phone: 212-226-5500
          800-654-2433 (toll-free)
Fax: 212-966-0706
Web site: http://www.artinstitutes.edu/newyork

The Art Institute of Atlanta®, GA; The Art Institute of California^SM–Inland Empire; The Art Institute of California^SM–Los Angeles; The Art Institute of California^SM–Orange County; The Art Institute of California^SM–San Diego; The Art Institute of California^SM–San Francisco; The Art Institute of Charleston^SM, SC, A branch of The Art Institute of Atlanta, GA; The Art Institute of Charlotte®, NC; The Art Institute of Colorado® (Denver); The Art Institute of Dallas®, TX; The Art Institute of Fort Lauderdale®, FL; The Art Institute of Houston®, TX; The Art Institute of Indianapolis^SM, IN*; The Art Institute of Jacksonville^SM, A branch of Miami International University of Art & Design, FL; The Art Institute of Las Vegas®, NV; The Art Institute of New York City®, NY; The Art Institute of Ohio^SM–Cincinnati**; The Art Institute of Philadelphia®, PA; The Art Institute of Phoenix®, AZ; The Art Institute of Pittsburgh®, PA; The Art Institute of Portland®, OR; The Art Institute of Seattle®, WA; The Art Institute of Tampa^SM, FL, A branch of Miami International University of Art & Design; The Art Institute of Tennessee^SM–Nashville, A branch of The Art Institute of Atlanta, GA; The Art Institute of Toronto^SM, ON; The Art Institute of Vancouver^SM, BC (Burnaby location, Downtown location, Dubrulle Culinary Arts location); The Art Institute of Washington® (Arlington, VA), A branch of The Art Institute of Atlanta, GA; The Art Institute Online^SM, A division of The Art Institute of Pittsburgh, PA; The Art Institutes International Minnesota^SM (Minneapolis); Bradley Academy for the Visual Arts^SM (York, PA); California Design College^SM (Wilshire Boulevard, Los Angeles); The Illinois Institute of Art®–Chicago; The Illinois Institute of Art®–Schaumburg; Miami International University of Art & Design^SM, FL; The New England Institute of Art^SM (Boston, MA).
*The Art Institute of Indianapolis is licensed by the Indiana Commission on Proprietary Education, 302 West Washington Street, Room E201, Indianapolis, IN 46204, AC-0080.
**The Art Institute of Ohio–Cincinnati, 8845 Governors Hill Drive, Suite 100, Cincinnati, OH 45249-3317, Reg. #04-01-1698B.

THE ART INSTITUTE OF OHIO–CINCINNATI

CINCINNATI, OHIO

The Art Institute
of Ohio™-Cincinnati
One of The Art Institutes, America's Leader in Creative Education

The Institute and Its Mission

The Art Institute of Ohio–Cincinnati prepares students for entry-level employment in the creative arts. The school offers six associate degree programs.

The Art Institute of Ohio–Cincinnati includes more than 57,000 square feet of classroom, laboratory, and office space designed according to the school's specifications for its design programs. The school shares facility space with Brown Mackie College–Cincinnati.

The Art Institute of Ohio–Cincinnati provides students with convenient living accommodations. Students who choose school-sponsored housing share their living space with other students. The school is accessible by public transportation and provides ample student parking. Assistance is available to help students with resume writing, networking, and keeping aware of what employers are looking for in job candidates.

The Art Institute of Ohio–Cincinnati is accredited by the Accrediting Council for Independent Colleges and Schools (ACICS) to award associate degrees. ACICS is listed as a nationally recognized accrediting agency by the U.S. Department of Education. Its accreditation of degree-granting institutions also is recognized by the Council for Higher Education Accreditation. ACICS can be contacted at 750 First Street, NE, Suite 980, Washington, D.C. 20002; telephone: 202-336-6780.

Academic Programs

Students attending The Art Institute of Ohio–Cincinnati may pursue an Associate of Applied Science degree in culinary arts, fashion merchandising, graphic design, interactive media design, interior design, or video production. Each program requires the successful completion of 96 credits.

Costs

Tuition costs vary by program. Prospective students should contact the school for current tuition costs. Other charges include a starting kit for all first-quarter students. Kits vary in price, depending on the program of study.

Financial Aid

Financial aid is available for those who qualify. The Art Institute of Ohio–Cincinnati offers student financial planning. The goal of which is to structure affordable monthly payment plans so that students may concentrate on fulfilling their educational and career aspirations.

Available resources include federal and state aid, student loans from private lenders, and Federal Work-Study Program (FWS) opportunities, both on and off campus. Students seeking financial aid must complete the Free Application for Federal Student Aid (FAFSA). Application deadlines and eligibility requirements vary.

Faculty

The Art Institute of Ohio–Cincinnati's faculty members have experience in their fields and are committed to the academic and technical preparation of their students. The student-faculty ratio is 25:1.

Student Body Profile

Students come to The Art Institute of Ohio–Cincinnati from throughout the United States. The student population includes recent high school graduates, transfer students, and those who have left a previous employment situation to study and train for a new career. Students are creative, competitive, and open to new ideas. They place great value on an education that prepares them for an exciting entry-level position in the arts.

Student Activities

Student life is an integral part of The Art Institute of Ohio–Cincinnati experience. The Office of Student Affairs sponsors a variety of events, including intramural sports, dances, parties, lunch-and-learn sessions, and off-campus trips.

Facilities and Resources

The Art Institute of Ohio–Cincinnati provides easy access to the technology, tools, and facilities needed to complete

projects in all disciplines. Students may produce work in an environment that is appropriate for their chosen creative endeavors. The facilities include media presentation rooms for special instructional needs, libraries that provide instructional resources, and academic support for both faculty members and students.

Location

Cincinnati is home to major-league sporting events, concerts, a professional symphony, theater, Paramount's Kings Island, award-winning restaurants, and downtown entertainment districts that offer exciting nightlife.

The city is known for its great beauty, with steep hills, wooded suburbs, a picturesque downtown riverfront, and four distinct seasons. Cincinnati is an affordable city in which to live and has been designated by *Fortune* magazine as one of the top ten places to live and work in the United States.

Admission Requirements

Applicants to The Art Institute of Ohio–Cincinnati must demonstrate proof of high school graduation or its equivalent. An official copy of the high school transcript or General Educational Development (GED) certificate is required. Candidates are interviewed and must write an essay on how an education at The Art Institute of Ohio–Cincinnati can help them reach their career goals.

Each applicant's academic transcript and completed essay is evaluated by the Admissions Acceptance Committee. A separate application and enrollment form must be completed and signed by the applicant and then submitted to The Art Institute of Ohio–Cincinnati. There is an application fee of $50.

Application and Information

To obtain an application or make arrangements for an interview or tour of the school, prospective students should contact:

The Art Institute of Ohio–Cincinnati
8845 Governors Hill Drive, Suite 100
Cincinnati, Ohio 45249-3317
Phone: 513-833-2400
       866-613-5184 (toll-free)
Fax: 877-477-8486 (toll-free)
Web site: http://www.artinstitutes.edu/cincinnati

The Art Institute of Atlanta®, GA; The Art Institute of California^SM–Inland Empire; The Art Institute of California^SM–Los Angeles; The Art Institute of California^SM–Orange County; The Art Institute of California^SM–San Diego; The Art Institute of California^SM–San Francisco; The Art Institute of Charleston^SM, SC, A branch of The Art Institute of Atlanta, GA; The Art Institute of Charlotte®, NC; The Art Institute of Colorado® (Denver); The Art Institute of Dallas®, TX; The Art Institute of Fort Lauderdale®, FL; The Art Institute of Houston®, TX; The Art Institute of Indianapolis^SM, IN*; The Art Institute of Jacksonville^SM, A branch of Miami International University of Art & Design, FL; The Art Institute of Las Vegas®, NV; The Art Institute of New York City®, NY; The Art Institute of Ohio^SM–Cincinnati**; The Art Institute of Philadelphia®, PA; The Art Institute of Phoenix®, AZ; The Art Institute of Pittsburgh®, PA; The Art Institute of Portland®, OR; The Art Institute of Seattle®, WA; The Art Institute of Tampa^SM, FL, A branch of Miami International University of Art & Design; The Art Institute of Tennessee^SM–Nashville, A branch of The Art Institute of Atlanta, GA; The Art Institute of Toronto^SM, ON; The Art Institute of Vancouver^SM, BC (Burnaby location, Downtown location, Dubrulle Culinary Arts location); The Art Institute of Washington® (Arlington, VA), A branch of The Art Institute of Atlanta, GA; The Art Institute Online^SM, A division of The Art Institute of Pittsburgh, PA; The Art Institutes International Minnesota^SM (Minneapolis); Bradley Academy for the Visual Arts^SM (York, PA); California Design College^SM (Wilshire Boulevard, Los Angeles); The Illinois Institute of Art®–Chicago; The Illinois Institute of Art®–Schaumburg; Miami International University of Art & Design^SM, FL; The New England Institute of Art^SM (Boston, MA).
*The Art Institute of Indianapolis is licensed by the Indiana Commission on Proprietary Education, 302 West Washington Street, Room E201, Indianapolis, IN 46204, AC-0080.
**The Art Institute of Ohio–Cincinnati, 8845 Governors Hill Drive, Suite 100, Cincinnati, OH 45249-3317, Reg. #04-01-1698B.

THE ART INSTITUTE OF SEATTLE
SEATTLE, WASHINGTON

The Institute and Its Mission

The Art Institute of Seattle provides programs that prepare graduates for entry-level employment in the creative arts. Programs are developed with and taught by experienced educators. The Art Institute of Seattle has a proud history both as a part of the Seattle community and as a contributor to the Northwest's creative industries.

The Art Institute of Seattle offers twelve associate degree programs and six bachelor's degree programs.

The Career Services Department works with students to refine their presentations to potential employers. The department also helps provide student advisers with insight into each student's specialized skills and interests. Specific career advising occurs during the last two quarters of a student's education. Interviewing techniques and resume-writing skills are developed, and students receive portfolio advising from faculty members.

The Student Affairs Department offers a variety of services to students to help them make the most of their educational experience. These services include both school-sponsored and independent housing options.

The Art Institute of Seattle is accredited by the Northwest Commission on Colleges and Universities (NWCCU) and is licensed by the Washington Workforce Training and Education Coordinating Board. The Art Institute of Seattle is approved for the training of veterans and eligible veterans' dependents and is authorized to enroll nonimmigrant international students.

Academic Programs

Associate degrees are offered in animation art and design, audio production, baking and pastry, culinary arts, fashion design, fashion marketing, graphic design, industrial design technology, interactive media design, interior design, photography, and video production.

Bachelor's degree programs are available in fashion design, fashion marketing, game art and design, graphic design, interior design, and media arts and animation.

The Art Institute of Seattle operates on a year-round, quarterly basis. Each quarter totals eleven weeks. Bachelor's degree programs are twelve quarters in length.

Costs

Tuition costs vary by program. Prospective students should contact the school for current tuition costs. Other charges include a starting kit for all first-quarter students. Kits vary in price, depending on the program of study.

Financial Aid

Financial aid is available for those who qualify. The school's student financial aid officers take a holistic approach to developing a financial plan to assist the student in meeting projected education costs.

Eligible students may apply for financial assistance under various federal and state programs, including the Federal Pell Grant, Federal Supplemental Educational Opportunity Grant (FSEOG), Federal Perkins Loan, Federal Stafford Student Loan (subsidized and unsubsidized), Federal Work-Study Program (FWS), Alaska State Student Loan, Federal PLUS loan (for parents), Washington State Need Grant, Vocational Rehabilitation Assistance, Veterans Administration benefits, and Bureau of Indian Affairs awards. Awards are based on individual need, the availability of funds, and the individual student's eligibility.

The Art Institute of Seattle offers scholarships based on merit, motivation, and financial need. Scholarship awards and programs include the Advantage Grant Program, The Art Institute of Seattle Excellence Award, The Art Institute of Seattle Scholarship Competition, The Art Institute of Seattle Culinary Scholarship Competition, the National Art Honor Society Scholarship, the Evelyn Keedy Memorial Scholarship, VICA Skills USA Championship, Scholastic Arts Competition, HERO, IACP Foundation, C-Cap, ProStart, Technology Student Association Competition, and New York City Public Schools Scholarship Competition. Application deadlines and eligibility requirements vary.

Faculty

Faculty members at The Art Institute of Seattle are experienced professionals, many of whom bring real-world knowledge into the classroom. There are 174 full-time and part-time faculty members. The student-faculty ratio is 19:1.

Student Body Profile

There are more than 2,450 students at The Art Institute of Seattle. Students come to The Art Institute of Seattle from throughout the United States and abroad. The student population includes recent high school graduates, transfer students, and those who have left a previous employment situation to study and train for a new career. Students are creative, competitive, and open to new ideas. They place great value on an education that prepares them for an exciting entry-level position in the arts.

Student Activities

The Art Institute of Seattle places high importance on student life, both inside and outside the classroom. The school provides an environment that encourages involvement in a wide variety of activities, including clubs and organizations, community service opportunities, and various committees designed to enhance the quality of student life. Numerous all-school programs and events are planned throughout the year to meet students' needs.

Facilities and Resources

The Art Institute of Seattle is an urban campus that comprises three facilities. The school houses classrooms, audio and video studios, a student store, student lounges, copy centers, a gallery, a woodshop, a sculpture room, fashion display windows, a resource center, a technology center, and culinary facilities. The Art Institute of Seattle is also home to a public student-run restaurant.

Location

The Art Institute of Seattle is located in the city's Belltown district. Founded by Native Americans and traders, the city has retained respect for its different cultures and customs. People from all over the world come to study, work, and live in this city, known for its friendly people and beautiful natural surroundings.

World-class companies, such as Microsoft, Boeing, Starbucks, Amazon.com, and Nordstrom, make their global headquarters in Seattle. As a gateway to the Pacific Rim, Seattle is a crossroads where creativity, technology, and business meet.

Admission Requirements

A student seeking admission to The Art Institute of Seattle is required to interview with an admissions representative (in person or over the phone). Applicants are required to have a high school diploma or a General Educational Development (GED) certificate and to submit an admissions application and an essay describing how an education at The Art Institute of Seattle may help the student to achieve career goals. For advanced placement, additional information, including college transcripts, letters of recommendation, or portfolio work, may be required. Students may apply for admission online.

The Art Institute of Seattle follows a rolling admissions schedule. Students are encouraged to apply for their chosen quarter early so that they may take advantage of orientation activities. Students may also apply until the actual start date for any given quarter, depending on space availability. There is a $50 application fee.

Application and Information

To obtain an application, make arrangements for an interview, or tour the school, students should contact:

The Art Institute of Seattle
2323 Elliott Avenue
Seattle, Washington 98121-1642

Phone: 206-448-6600
        800-275-2471 (toll-free)
Fax: 206-269-0275
Web site: http://www.artinstitutes.edu/seattle

The Art Institute of Seattle's faculty members bring their professional experience into the classroom to create a collaborative, real-world learning environment.

BALTIMORE INTERNATIONAL COLLEGE
BALTIMORE, MARYLAND; VIRGINIA, COUNTY CAVAN, IRELAND

The College and Its Mission

Baltimore International College, a regionally accredited, private college, was founded in 1972 to provide students with the education and experience they need to pursue progressive careers within the international hospitality industry. The College is committed to providing students with the knowledge and ability necessary for employment and success in the hospitality industry.

In 1985, the College was authorized by the state of Maryland to grant associate degrees. In 1987, the Virginia Park Campus in Ireland was founded, enabling students to study under European chefs and hoteliers in a European environment. In 1996, the College was granted accreditation by the Commission on Higher Education of the Middle States Association of College and Schools. In 1998, the College was authorized by the state of Maryland to grant four-year baccalaureate degrees. In 2006, the State of Maryland and the Middle States Commission on Higher Education authorized the College to grant a master's degree in hospitality management.

In addition to classrooms, offices, and dorms, the College's campus in Baltimore includes a campus bookstore, a student union, a hotel, an inn, a restaurant, parking, student dining facilities, a Career Development Center, and a Learning Resource Center comprising a library, two academic computer labs, and an art gallery.

Academic Programs

The College provides a comprehensive curriculum, which includes an honors study abroad program at the Baltimore International College Virginia Park Campus near Dublin, Ireland.

The College's professional cooking program and the combined programs in professional cooking and baking and baking and pastry operate throughout the calendar year; new classes begin in the spring, summer, and fall. The College's hospitality management programs accept freshmen in the fall and spring semesters. The culinary arts certificate, which combines cooking and baking, and the certificate in professional marketing are available through evening classes and begin in the fall and spring semesters.

Associate Degree Programs Baltimore International College awards the associate degree in the following programs: professional baking and pastry, professional cooking, and professional cooking and baking. The associate degree is offered separately and as part of the 2+2 program at Baltimore International College. In the 2+2 program, students receive their two-year associate degree and then continue two additional years to complete the four-year bachelor's degree. Bachelor's degree programs require 125 to 133 credits.

To earn an associate degree in professional cooking, professional baking and pastry, or professional cooking and baking, the student must complete 62–66 credits. Certificate candidates must complete 54 credits. The certificate program concentrates on technical courses and is intended for students who already have a strong academic background. The associate degree program combines technical hands-on courses with general education courses such as nutrition, sanitation, psychology, English, and mathematics, as well as an internship or externship.

Off-Campus Programs

The Honors Program has been developed for qualified culinary arts and business and management majors. The Honors Program is taught at the College's historic, 100-acre Virginia Park campus in County Cavan, Ireland. Culinary students who are selected for the Honors Program further enhance their skills in and knowledge of European cuisine, baking and pastry, and a la carte service. Business and management students selected for the honors program have the opportunity to learn the day-to-day operation of a hotel and restaurant, from reception to housekeeping and from restaurant management to accounting. Students fully enjoy the cross-cultural experience of living in an English-speaking foreign country.

Costs

Tuition for 2006–07 was $7744. Fees ranged from $111 to $3165, depending on the student's major. Student housing costs ranged from $3418 to $5729 per semester for dormitory-style housing (includes meal plan).

Financial Aid

Students receive financial aid from federal, state, institutional, and private sources and may be employed during their attendance as full-time students. The forms of financial aid available at the College through federal sources include the Federal Pell Grant, the Federal Supplemental Educational Opportunity Grant, the Federal Work-Study Program, the Federal Subsidized and Unsubsidized Stafford Student Loans, FPLUS loans, and veterans' educational benefits. Students are encouraged to investigate the scholarship programs in their home state and apply for state scholarships if the grants can be used in Maryland. The College also offers its own series of scholarships and payment options. Students can request a financial aid application from the Student Financial Planning Office. The College employs the Federal Methodology of Need Analysis, approved by the U.S. Department of Education, as a fair and equitable means of determining the family's ability to contribute to the student's educational expenses, as well as eligibility for other financial aid programs.

Faculty

Baltimore International College faculty members include 29 chefs and academic instructors of high academic distinction. The student-faculty ratio averages 16:1 in culinary labs and 25:1 in academic classes. Each student is assigned a faculty adviser who oversees the student's progress and answers questions about academic and career concerns. Students are encouraged to discuss program-related issues with the Director of Student Counseling.

Student Body Profile

Current enrollment is 750 annually, with 52 percent men and 48 percent women. Approximately 17 percent of students are from out-of-state, representing twenty-four states and several other countries.

Student Activities

The College offers general academic counseling for all students, peer tutoring on request, and a variety of referrals for support services. In addition, student services provide many recreation and leisure activities, including the student union, a series of activities sponsored by the College, and information about cultural programs around the city. Student services also provides ongoing support to the College's alumni through surveys, mailings about the College's growth, and involvement in College-sponsored events such as open houses, resume referrals, and career fairs.

Facilities and Resources

The Baltimore campus includes the Culinary Arts Center, kitchens, storerooms, cooking demonstration theaters, academic classrooms, multipurpose rooms, a library, computer labs, a student union, and auxiliary services. Public operations that function as in-house training for students include the Mount Vernon Hotel, the Bay Atlantic Club Restaurant, and the Hopkins Inn.

The Virginia Park Campus is located on 100 acres, 50 miles from Dublin student housing, with laboratory kitchens and lecture facilities. The complex also includes the Park Hotel, with public operations that function as in-house training for students, including the Marquis Dining Room and the Marchioness Ballroom. The Park Hotel has thirty-six guest rooms. All students enjoy unlimited golf and fishing as well as hiking trails.

Career Planning/Placement Offices The College's Career Development Center offers students access to information about careers in food service and hospitality management. The College's career development services are located in the Career Information Center where coordinators organize on-campus recruiting and offer workshops and assistance in resume writing and interviewing skills.

Library The College's Learning Resource Center is a member of an interlibrary loan network that enables users to borrow from public, academic, and private libraries throughout Maryland. The library's current core collection has approximately 13,000 volumes, 200 periodicals, and almost 800 audiovisual selections. The library offers students access to the Internet, a worldwide network of electronic information. In-house services include two academic computer labs, electronic databases for research, and a photocopier.

The College's art gallery is part of the Learning Resource Center and features a permanent display of edible art. Student participation in all exhibits is encouraged.

Location

The College's main campus, located in downtown Baltimore, is just two blocks from the city's famous Inner Harbor, a location that puts the College in the midst of numerous hotels and restaurants. The city offers year-round cultural and entertainment opportunities, such as theater, opera, the Baltimore Symphony Orchestra, museums, sporting events, and festivals. Other attractions in Baltimore, within walking distance of the College, are the National Aquarium, Harborplace, Oriole Park at Camden Yards, Ravens Stadium, Maryland Science Center, and many historic sites, including Fort McHenry, Mount Vernon, and the Walters Art Museum. Baltimore also has parks and miles of waterfront for those who enjoy outdoor recreation. Washington, D.C., the nation's capital, is just 30 miles from downtown Baltimore. The city of Baltimore is easily accessed by major highways and bus, rail, and air service. Baltimore/Washington International Airport is a short drive from the campus.

Admission Requirements

Creativity and skill of students must be matched by dedication. The College seeks candidates who desire a professional career in the hospitality industry.

Individuals seeking admission to the College must have earned a high school diploma or have passed the GED. Applicants must either pass the College's Admissions Test, take developmental courses during their first semester, or have one of the following: minimum SAT scores of 430 verbal and 420 math, a minimum composite ACT score of 16, minimum CLEP scores in the 50th percentile in math and English composition with essay, a secondary degree, or 16 credit hours at the postsecondary level with a minimum average of C in math and English. Transfer students must submit an official college transcript as well as catalog course descriptions for credits they wish to transfer.

The College affords equally to all students the rights, privileges, programs, activities, scholarships and loan programs, and other programs administered by the College without regard to race, color, creed, sex, age, handicap, or national or ethnic origin.

Application and Information

Applicants are required to submit an application form along with a $40 nonrefundable fee. Requests by the College for additional information must be handled in a timely manner. An admission decision is made as soon as a file is complete. Upon acceptance, applicants are asked to submit a $100 tuition deposit.

For additional information, students should contact:

Office of Admissions
Baltimore International College
17 Commerce Street
Baltimore, Maryland 21202
Phone: 410-752-4710 Ext. 120
      800-624-9926 Ext. 120 (toll-free)
E-mail: admissions@bic.edu
Web site: http://www.bic.edu

Small classes at Baltimore International College enable students to receive individual instruction that helps them perfect their skills.

BAY STATE COLLEGE
BOSTON, MASSACHUSETTS

The College and Its Mission

Bay State College, a private, two-year, independent, coeducational institution, is located in Boston's historic Back Bay. Since 1946, Bay State College has been preparing young men and women with the skills necessary to attain outstanding careers in the business and allied health disciplines.

The College's goal is to prepare and educate students for successful and rewarding professional opportunities. Bay State College accomplishes this by providing the best possible education, which enables students to go out into the working world equipped with all the skills needed to succeed professionally. Bay State College assists, encourages, supports, and educates students in all their academic, professional, and personal goals and aspirations.

Bay State College is accredited by the New England Association of Schools and Colleges, is authorized to award the Bachelor of Science, Associate in Science, and Associate in Applied Science degrees by the Commonwealth of Massachusetts, and is a member of several professional educational associations.

Bay State College's medical assisting program is accredited by the Accrediting Bureau of Health Education Schools (ABHES). The Physical Therapist Assistant Program is accredited by the Commission on Accreditation in Physical Therapy Education (CAPTE) of the American Physical Therapy Association (APTA).

Academic Programs

Bay State College offers unique courses preparing students for careers in accounting, business, criminal justice, early childhood education, entertainment management, fashion design, fashion merchandising, medical assisting, and physical therapist assistant studies. In addition, students are exceptionally prepared to transfer to four-year colleges and universities.

The College's current programs include accounting (A.A.S.), business administration (A.A.S.), criminal justice (A.S.), early childhood education (A.S.), entertainment management (B.S., A.A.S.), fashion design (A.S.), fashion merchandising (B.S., A.A.S.), management (B.S.), medical assisting (A.S.), physical therapist assistant studies (A.S.), retail business management (A.A.S.), and travel and hospitality management (A.A.S.).

Bay State is now offering three baccalaureate degrees in entertainment management, fashion merchandising, and management.

Bay State College's Day and Continuing Education Divisions offer day and evening classes. Two satellite campuses for continuing education are located in Gloucester and Middleborough, Massachusetts.

Off-Campus Programs

The internship program, available in all major areas of study, provides practical field experience so that the students gain the skills and experience with the technologies used in the business and medical settings.

Students from Bay State College are among the 250 students participating in the Walt Disney World College Program. During their stay at Walt Disney World, students receive on-the-job training and classroom experience. This is just one of the many internship possibilities for students each year at Bay State College.

Costs

For the 2007–08 academic year, the College's Day Division charges a comprehensive fee between $27,350 and $28,700, which includes full-time tuition (between $16,500 and $17,850) and room and board ($10,500). There is an allied health lab fee of $475 per year (medical assisting and physical therapist assistant studies only) and a lab fee for fashion design students of $300 per year. Textbooks are estimated at $800 per year. Bay State College's Continuing Education Division, the Boston, Middleborough, and Gloucester campuses, charge $233 per credit. Tuition, dormitory charges, and fees are subject to change.

Financial Aid

Personal financial planning and counseling is completed with all students and families. Approximately 85 percent of students receive some form of financial assistance. Bay State College requires a completed Free Application for Federal Student Aid (FAFSA) form and signed federal tax forms. The College's institutional financial aid priority deadline is March 15. Financial aid is granted on a rolling basis.

Faculty

There are 50 faculty members, with 53 percent holding advanced degrees and 6 percent holding doctoral degrees. The student-faculty ratio is 14:1. In the Day Division, there are 57 faculty members, with 53 percent holding advanced degrees, and 6 percent holding doctoral degrees. In the Evening Division, there are 65 faculty members, with 77 percent holding advanced degrees and 14 percent holding doctoral degrees.

Student Body Profile

There are 740 students in degree programs. The average age is 18. The student body is ethnically and culturally diverse; 90 percent are state residents, 9 percent are transfer students, 4 percent are international students, 75 percent are women, 18 percent are African American, 11 percent are Hispanic, and 5 percent are Asian American. In the past year, 26 percent of Bay State College's graduating class continued on to a four-year college.

Bay State College's residence halls are located along Commonwealth Avenue. There are approximately 150 college housing spaces available. Each residence hall is designed to accommodate from 2 to 6 students per room. Housing is guaranteed on a first-come, first-served basis to students who complete and submit a residence hall agreement and deposit. The priority deadline for first-year students is May 1.

Each hall is staffed by professional live-in directors and a paraprofessional staff of resident assistants. The staff members strive to foster a living and learning environment that complements the academic mission. All residents have the opportunity to experience a wide variety of programs such as in-house educational, cultural, and awareness seminars; study breaks; discounts to area movies and theater productions; and holiday celebrations. Twenty-four-hour quiet hours are in effect during midterm and final periods. Students are also provided with wireless Internet access and cable television in every room. A campus dining facility is available, as are microwaves, laundry facilities, and cable-ready outlets, and computer labs are available in each residence hall as well.

Student Activities

Students participate in a multitude of activities offered by the College through student organizations. These include the Student Association, Entertainment Management Association, Justice Society, DEX, and the Early Childhood Education Club. Students also produce an annual talent show as well as an annual fashion show that showcases the original designs of the students in the College's Fashion Design program. A literary magazine is also published annually and features the work of students throughout the College. Students have access to a fitness facility for a discounted rate.

Facilities and Resources

Advisement/Counseling Trained staff members assist students in selecting courses and programs of study to satisfy their educational objectives. A counseling center is available to provide mental and physical health referrals to all Bay State students in need of such services. Referral networks are extensive, within a wide range of geographic areas, and provide access to a variety of public and private health agencies.

Specialized Services The Learning Center has been renamed the Center for Learning and Academic Support (CLAS). CLAS serves as a supplementary learning tool for those individuals wishing to improve their skills through self-paced individualized instruction. The center offers assistance through the use of peer and faculty tutors, individualized learning packets, and audio, visual, and other self-study resources. Introductory studies courses are designed for a diverse population of students, including workers returning to school, recent high school graduates seeking academic reinforcement, and ESL students. Their individual needs are met so they can be successful in the traditional course of study leading to an associate degree.

Career Planning/Placement Of the number of students seeking assistance from the Career Services Office, there was a 95 percent job placement rate. The primary purpose of the Career Services Office at Bay State College is to see that every graduating senior secures the best possible position in his or her chosen career. The process begins in the student's first year and continues throughout the student's time at the College through career development, one-on-one counseling, and internships. The Career Services Office, offering lifelong service to all alumni, continually posts job openings for current students and graduates. The annual Career Fair, offered in April, attracts a variety of employers from all majors. This provides students an opportunity to interact and network with employers to increase the likelihood of employment prior to graduation.

Library and Audiovisual Services The library is staffed with trained librarians who are available to guide students in their research process. The library's resources include 6,000 books, eighty-five periodical subscriptions, and access to 6 databases including ProQuest, InfoTrac, and LexisNexis. In addition, the library provides computer access and study space for students. The library catalog and databases are accessible from any Internet-ready terminal.

First-Year Experience The First-Year Experience (FYE) is a 1-credit course that is required of all first-year students and takes place during the first three days that students are on campus. FYE combines social activities with an academic syllabus that is designed to ease the transition into the college experience. Through FYE, students have the opportunity to connect with their academic advisers as well as with other students in their academic programs.

Location

The location of Bay State College makes it the perfect place to attend to get a complete education. While the academics are great, students are also within a mile of major-league sports, free concerts, museums, the Freedom Trail, Boston Symphony Hall, the Boston Public Library, the Boston Public Garden, and much more. The city is known for its college atmosphere. Tree-lined streets are mirrored in the skyscrapers of the Back Bay. Major shopping, cultural, and sporting events make College life an experience that students will always remember. The College's location is accessible by public transportation and in proximity to Boston Logan International Airport.

Admission Requirements

Students must be in pursuit of a high school diploma or GED certificate in order to apply and must receive it before the start of classes at Bay State College. A personal interview is strongly recommended for all students. Transcripts are requested once a student has applied. A decision is made by the Admissions Office upon completion and receipt of all documents. International students must complete an International Student Application and provide a transcript, a TOEFL score, and final documents in order to be considered for admission.

Application and Information

Bay State College accepts applications on a rolling basis, so students may apply at any time. A $40 fee is required at the time of application.

Applications should be submitted to:

Admissions Office
Bay State College
122 Commonwealth Avenue
Boston, Massachusetts 02116

Phone: 800-81-LEARN (toll-free)
Fax: 617-217-9195
Web site: http://www.baystate.edu

BENJAMIN FRANKLIN INSTITUTE OF TECHNOLOGY

BOSTON, MASSACHUSETTS

The Institute and Its Mission

Benjamin Franklin Institute of Technology (BFIT) is a small technical college offering a variety of instructional programs based on science, engineering, and technology. Programs of one, two, three, and four years' duration are provided for various levels of interest, abilities, and objectives. The aim of the Franklin Institute is to prepare the students in each program for immediate employment upon graduation in a chosen career field and at the same time to give students a technical education upon which they can continue to build. Because of the Institute's student-teacher ratio of 11:1, students receive a great deal of individual attention with a hands-on approach to learning.

The objectives of the Franklin Institute are threefold: to provide educational opportunities in science and technology for men and women in order that they may better themselves both economically and socially, to provide a sound educational foundation upon which the graduates of the Institute's programs may continue to grow both in personal terms as well as professional and educational terms, and to assess the present and future needs of industry and technology in order to anticipate and respond to those needs through curriculum revisions and the addition of new programs.

Academic Programs

Bachelor's Degree Programs Franklin Institute is one of the few colleges in the nation to offer a **Bachelor of Science** degree in automotive technology. The program follows completion of all requirements at the Franklin associate level. Its primary objective is to prepare students for middle management positions in the automotive industry and raise the standards for education industry-wide in an increasingly complex and technical profession. The curriculum is a combination of technical and business management courses. A total of eight semesters and 134 credit hours must be successfully completed for graduation.

Associate Degree Programs Franklin Institute grants the **Associate in Science** degree in automotive technology and opticianry. The **Associate in Engineering** degree is awarded in architectural technology, computer engineering technology, computer technology, electrical engineering technology, electronic engineering technology, mechanical engineering technology, and medical electronics engineering technology.

The engineering technology associate degree programs require four semesters for completion, with a total of 74 semester hours of credit. Half of the total curriculum in each engineering technology program is devoted to the technical specialty. One fourth of the total curriculum is devoted to physical science and mathematics, courses in college algebra and trigonometry, analytic geometry, calculus, and college physics. The remaining fourth of the curriculum includes English, humanities, and social studies. Most of the graduates of the engineering technology associate degree programs are employed by industry in various capacities in engineering and scientific fields. A high percentage of graduates continue their education at other colleges and universities.

The computer engineering technology program includes both fundamental and advanced courses in digital computer circuits, systems and languages, and electronic devices and circuit theory.

The electrical engineering technology program includes basic and advanced courses in the design and construction of electrical distribution systems for modern commercial and industrial buildings, commercial lighting design, and electrical estimating.

The electronic engineering technology program includes basic and advanced courses in electric and electronic circuit theory, semiconductor devices, principles and design of electrical and electronic equipment, and measurement techniques up to and including microwave frequencies.

The mechanical engineering technology program includes fundamental and advanced courses in applied mechanics, mechanics of materials, thermodynamics, heat transfer, machine design, fluid power, and instrumentation.

The medical electronics engineering technology curriculum incorporates basic and advanced courses in minicomputers and microcomputers, electronic devices, electric and electronic circuit theory, medical instrumentation, human physiology, medical instrument safety and grounding techniques, semiconductor circuitry, and principles and design of medical electronic instruments.

The industrial technology associate degree programs require four semesters for completion, with a total of 70 semester hours of credit. More than half of the total curriculum in each industrial technology program is devoted to the technical specialty. About one fourth of the total curriculum is devoted to basic science and mathematics, including algebra, trigonometry, and precalculus mathematics. The remainder of the curriculum includes English, humanities, and social studies.

More than half of the automotive technology two-year program is devoted to automotive technical specialties, including actual work on vehicles in the student instructional garage. About one third of the program is devoted to basic mathematics, physics, humanities, and social sciences, and the remaining time is devoted to basic mechanical technology studies.

The computer technology program prepares students to meet the rapidly growing demand for technicians who can install, maintain, and repair computer equipment and digital electronic systems.

The architectural technology program is designed to enable its graduates to become skilled and knowledgeable architectural draftspersons, capable of making important contributions to the architectural and/or engineering team that produces the complete working drawings from which buildings, residences, and other structures are erected.

Transfer Arrangements Transfer credit received for courses completed at Franklin Institute is dependent on the policies of the transferring institution. Many graduates receive a full two years' credit toward a baccalaureate degree.

Certificate Programs The BFIT certificate programs require two to three semesters for completion, with a total of 18 to 36

semester hours of credit. Instruction is concentrated in the student's main area of interest. The Institute currently offers certificate programs in heating, ventilation, and air conditioning (HVAC); marine technology; pharmacy technology; and practical electricity.

Costs

For the 2007–08 academic year, tuition is $12,750 per year. Books and supplies range from $600 to $2000, depending on program. While the Institute does not maintain its own residence halls, various housing options exist.

Financial Aid

Franklin Institute offers financial assistance to students on the basis of demonstrated financial need and satisfactory academic progress. All students are encouraged to file the Free Application for Federal Student Aid (FAFSA). The Institute participates in the Federal Pell Grant, Federal Supplemental Educational Opportunity Grant, Federal Family Education Loan, and Federal Work-Study programs and offers Franklin Institute grants and academic scholarships. State scholarships, VA assistance, rehabilitation funding, and payment plans are available for eligible students.

Faculty

The faculty at Franklin Institute consists of instructors with practical experience in their field of expertise and many years of instruction. Instructors meet annually with the Industrial Advisory Board for each program to review and update the curricula. There are 32 full-time and 9 part-time faculty members.

Student Body Profile

Ninety-two percent of students are state residents, 8 percent are transfer students, and 3 percent are international students. Fourteen percent of the student body are 25 years of age or older, and 8 percent are women. The student body is ethnically and culturally diverse: 30 percent are African American, 15 percent are Hispanic, and 14 percent are Asian American. Thirty-five percent of students work full-time.

Student Activities

All students are encouraged to participate in the campus environment. Activities include student government, Women's Support Group, engineering week competitions, yearbook, professional honor societies, and athletics. Franklin offers NJCAA Division III men's basketball and soccer.

Sports Franklin Institute offers outdoor recreation programs, including basketball and soccer. Indoor activities include table tennis.

Facilities and Resources

The Union building houses the library, which holds 10,000 bound volumes, 160 periodical subscriptions, eighty-five computer terminals, and a word processing lab for student use. Other labs associated with individual programs include digital and analog electronics, electrical wiring, computer systems, materials testing, machine tool, CAD, automotive engines, transmissions, drivability, and electrical as well as a full-service garage.

Location

The land on which the Institute stands, at the corner of Berkeley and Appleton Streets in the South End of Boston, was provided by the city in 1906. The Institute complex consists of three buildings, a plaza, a landscaped mall connecting the buildings on Berkeley and Appleton Streets, and a modern underground automotive technology shop. The facilities of the Kendall Administration Building and the Dunham Building are handicapped accessible. The Institute is readily accessible by public transportation and is within close walking distance of many cultural, social, and recreational activities offered in the city of Boston. Franklin Institute students have the opportunity to meet other college students from around the world, as there are more than seventy postsecondary institutions in the greater Boston area.

Admission Requirements

All applicants must possess a high school diploma or its equivalent and must have completed four full-year courses in high school English. For associate degrees in engineering technology, satisfactory completion of the following courses in mathematics and science is also required: algebra I, algebra II, and a laboratory science, preferably physics, although courses in chemistry or biology are acceptable. Additional courses in mathematics, such as trigonometry, math analysis, or precalculus, are helpful but not required.

Admission requirements for associate degree in industrial technology programs include a minimum of two high school courses in mathematics, including the study of elementary algebra, and one course in science.

Admission requirements for the Certificate of Proficiency include a minimum of two high school courses in mathematics and one course in science. The study of elementary algebra is recommended and in some cases required.

Application and Information

All applicants should complete a Franklin Institute Application for Admission and submit it with the required $25 processing fee to the Office of Admission. Official transcripts of high school records, including first-term senior-year grades, should be requested by the student and sent directly from the high school to the Office of Admission. Because applications are processed on a rolling basis, applicants are notified of their admission status shortly after all required documents have been received. International applicants are also required to demonstrate English language proficiency and provide a financial statement showing proof of ability to pay the first year's costs.

State and institutional financial aid resources can be exhausted early in the application process. For financial aid priority consideration, applicants should apply for admission and financial aid no later than April 15.

Requests for additional information and application forms should be addressed to:

Office of Admission
Benjamin Franklin Institute of Technology
41 Berkeley Street
Boston, Massachusetts 02116

Phone: 617-423-4630
Fax: 617-482-3706
E-mail: admissions@bfit.edu
Web site: http://www.bfit.edu

BRADLEY ACADEMY FOR THE VISUAL ARTS

YORK, PENNSYLVANIA

The Academy and Its Mission

Bradley Academy for the Visual Arts provides students with an educational environment and dedicated faculty members who are committed to preparing students for entry-level positions in the creative arts. Professional academic courses encourage the achievement of self-knowledge and the development of critical thinking. Under the guidance of industry professionals, students learn by doing the types of tasks they are likely to encounter in the workplace. In addition, assistance is available to help students with resume writing, networking, and keeping aware of what employers are looking for in job candidates.

Whenever possible and appropriate, courses are taught in a studio or lab setting. While at the school, students can access the wireless network to check mail, hand in assignments, and work on a project, anywhere on campus. The school offers six associate degree programs.

Bradley Academy for the Visual Arts is accredited by the Accrediting Commission of Career Schools and Colleges of Technology (ACCSCT), which is listed by the U.S. Department of Education as a nationally recognized accrediting agency. Bradley Academy for the Visual Arts is also licensed by the State Board of Private Licensed Schools (Pennsylvania Department of Education).

Academic Programs

Bradley Academy for the Visual Arts operates on a year-round, four-quarter system. Associate degrees are offered in animation, digital arts, fashion marketing, graphic design, interior design, and Web design.

Costs

Tuition costs vary by program. Prospective students should contact the school for current tuition costs. Other charges include a starting kit for all first-quarter students. Kits vary in price, depending on the program of study.

Financial Aid

Financial aid is available to those who qualify. Eligible students may apply for federal and state financial aid, including student loans, grants, and scholarships. Work-study programs are also available for qualifying students. Bradley Academy for the Visual Arts participates in the Imagine America Scholarship Program, which is sponsored by the Career Training Foundation. These scholarships are matched by the school and are awarded to qualifying high school seniors through the guidance offices at their high schools. Bradley Academy for the Visual Arts has committed to matching most Dollars for Scholars awards up to a maximum of $1000 per student, provided the student has demonstrated financial need. Application deadlines and eligibility requirements vary.

Faculty

Faculty members at Bradley Academy for the Visual Arts are professionals, many of whom have experience in their fields of expertise. The school has full-time and part-time faculty members, who provide their students with a unique, relevant educational experience.

Student Body Profile

Many of the school's students come from the York, Harrisburg, and Philadelphia, Pennsylvania, areas.

The student population includes recent high school graduates, transfer students, and those who have left a previous employment situation to study and train for a new career. Students are creative, competitive, and open to new ideas. They place great value on an education that prepares them for an exciting entry-level position in the arts.

Student Activities

In addition to a traditional student government association, many professional organizations exist on campus, including the American Society of Interior Designers (ASID), the National Kitchen and Bath Association (NKBA), the Baltimore chapter of the American Institute of Graphic Arts (AIGA), and DECA/Delta Epsilon Chi. Students maintaining a GPA of 3.5 or higher at the end of the fifth term are considered for induction into Alpha Beta Kappa, a national honor society. There is also a student-run newspaper.

Facilities and Resources

Bradley Academy for the Visual Arts is housed within a 38,000-square-foot building in suburban York, Pennsylvania. The new facility contains classrooms and studios, a student computer commons, a gallery, an art store, and a library.

Computer labs contain both Macintosh computers and PCs. All labs are equipped with color scanners and have access to more than 200 gigabytes of network storage. Each lab is supported by desktop and high-resolution printers. The school also has a graphics lab, display windows, and vignette space to allow students to apply skills learned in the classroom.

In association with the York Martin Memorial Library, Bradley Academy houses a 1,000-square-foot library on the first floor of the school. In addition to general reference books, the library houses titles specifically related to programs offered at the school. Eight Windows NT workstations with direct access to the Internet and to Martin Library's catalog are available for students. Open every weekday, the library features full-time staffing, interlibrary loan, CD-ROM–based reference materials, and PC business software for use by students and the public.

Location

Bradley Academy for the Visual Arts is located in York, a suburban area in south-central Pennsylvania. Surrounded by

sprawling hills and Amish farmlands, York offers visitors an abundance of shopping areas and museums and three centuries of American history, including the battle sites of the Revolutionary and Civil Wars. York is a 30-minute drive from Hershey and Harrisburg, Pennsylvania; approximately a 90-minute drive from Philadelphia; and a 1-hour drive from Baltimore, Maryland.

Admission Requirements

Bradley Academy for the Visual Arts encourages interested students to apply early. To apply, students must possess a high school diploma or General Educational Development (GED) certificate and a minimum SAT score of 800 (at least 400 math and 400 verbal) or a minimum ACT score of 16. A portfolio review is required for students majoring in graphic design and animation and is welcomed from students pursuing a degree in digital arts, interior design, or Web design. There is a $50 application fee.

Application and Information

To obtain an application or make arrangements for an interview or tour of the school, prospective students should contact:

Bradley Academy for the Visual Arts
1409 Williams Road
York, Pennsylvania 17402-9012
Phone: 717-755-2300
       800-864-7725 (toll-free)
Fax: 717-840-1951
Web site: http://www.artinstitutes.edu/york

The Art Institute of Atlanta®, GA; The Art Institute of California^{SM}–Inland Empire; The Art Institute of California^{SM}–Los Angeles; The Art Institute of California^{SM}–Orange County; The Art Institute of California^{SM}–San Diego; The Art Institute of California^{SM}–San Francisco; The Art Institute of Charleston^{SM}, SC, A branch of The Art Institute of Atlanta, GA; The Art Institute of Charlotte®, NC; The Art Institute of Colorado® (Denver); The Art Institute of Dallas®, TX; The Art Institute of Fort Lauderdale®, FL; The Art Institute of Houston®, TX; The Art Institute of Indianapolis^{SM}, IN*; The Art Institute of Jacksonville^{SM}, A branch of Miami International University of Art & Design, FL; The Art Institute of Las Vegas®, NV; The Art Institute of New York City®, NY; The Art Institute of Ohio^{SM}–Cincinnati**; The Art Institute of Philadelphia®, PA; The Art Institute of Phoenix®, AZ; The Art Institute of Pittsburgh®, PA; The Art Institute of Portland®, OR; The Art Institute of Seattle®, WA; The Art Institute of Tampa^{SM}, FL, A branch of Miami International University of Art & Design; The Art Institute of Tennessee^{SM}–Nashville, A branch of The Art Institute of Atlanta, GA; The Art Institute of Toronto^{SM}, ON; The Art Institute of Vancouver^{SM}, BC (Burnaby location, Downtown location, Dubrulle Culinary Arts location); The Art Institute of Washington® (Arlington, VA), A branch of The Art Institute of Atlanta, GA; The Art Institute Online^{SM}, A division of The Art Institute of Pittsburgh, PA; The Art Institutes International Minnesota^{SM} (Minneapolis); Bradley Academy for the Visual Arts^{SM} (York, PA); California Design College^{SM} (Wilshire Boulevard, Los Angeles); The Illinois Institute of Art®–Chicago; The Illinois Institute of Art®–Schaumburg; Miami International University of Art & Design^{SM}, FL; The New England Institute of Art^{SM} (Boston, MA).

*The Art Institute of Indianapolis is licensed by the Indiana Commission on Proprietary Education, 302 West Washington Street, Room E201, Indianapolis, IN 46204, AC-0080.
**The Art Institute of Ohio–Cincinnati, 8845 Governors Hill Drive, Suite 100, Cincinnati, OH 45249-3317, Reg. #04-01-1698B.

BRIARWOOD COLLEGE
SOUTHINGTON, CONNECTICUT

The College and Its Mission

Briarwood College is a student-centered private institution for men and women that fosters and encourages a commitment to learning throughout their lives.

The College is committed to the application of knowledge through a curriculum that is career and technically oriented, with an emphasis on the liberal arts and an awareness of the challenges and opportunities that a global economy offers.

The mission of the College is to provide an education that is practical in its application, yet stresses the need for students to use the resources of their own minds, with particular emphasis on the development of the self through discipline, responsibility, and strength of expression.

The College is committed to making a difference in the community of which it is a part. To this end, it encourages and allows faculty and staff members and students to participate in outreach and service programs designed to focus on the competitive challenges of diverse environments, both locally and globally.

Academic Programs

Briarwood College offers a variety of career-oriented programs, both full- and part-time, leading to a certificate, diploma, or associate degree. In general, an associate degree program requires two years of study and a certificate program, one year. Diploma programs may take up to one year.

Associate Degree Programs Briarwood College offers associate degrees in twenty-seven majors. The **Associate in Arts** (A.A.) degree is offered in general studies, with concentrations in ballet, biotechnology, computer information systems, English, environmental technology, fine arts, history, mathematics, psychology, and science. The **Associate in Applied Science** (A.A.S.) degree is offered in accounting, administrative technology (with concentrations in executive, legal, and management), broadcasting, business management, child development, communication, computer information systems, criminal justice, dental administrative assistant studies, dental hygiene, dietetic technician studies, executive medical assistant studies, fashion merchandising, fitness technician studies, health information technology, hospitality (with concentrations in hotel and restaurant management and travel and tourism management), marketing, medical office management, mortuary science, nuclear medicine technology, occupational therapy assistant studies, and paralegal studies.

Certificate Programs The following programs lead to a certificate after one year: administrative legal professional studies, administrative medical professional studies, child development assistant studies, dental chairside assistant studies, health information coding, health information processing, medical assistant studies, medical transcription, nuclear medicine technology, pharmacy technician studies, and word processing. Most of these programs may be applied toward an associate degree program. The College also offers noncredit certificate programs in acupuncture and court reporting.

Diploma Programs Briarwood also offers diploma courses in computer information systems, leading to certification in Microsoft certified systems engineer, Microsoft certified system administrator, certified Novell administrator, and Computer Technology Industry Association: A+ certification for hardware repair.

Education for Life® is a unique benefit offered to graduates of Briarwood College who complete associate degrees after at least three full-time semesters of study. Graduates are able to return to Briarwood for additional credit or noncredit courses tuition-free for the rest of their lives.

Costs

For the 2007–08 academic year, costs are as follows: tuition is $16,400 for resident and commuter students; part-time students pay $540 per credit. Resident students are also charged a $3600 residency fee. The nonrefundable registration and housing fees are $195 for resident students and $95 for commuter students; part-time students pay $95 per semester.

Financial Aid

The following types of financial aid are available individually or in combination with other resources: presidential scholarships, state scholarships, and the Capitol Scholarship Program. Briarwood College, in conjunction with outside professional associations, also awards several scholarships in the business, health, and office administration fields. As other scholarships become available in specific program fields, they are announced in Briarwood College publications and posted outside the Financial Aid Office. A number of scholarships are awarded annually to students by local civic groups, churches, and fraternal and union organizations. Students are encouraged to explore all outside possibilities, utilizing the assistance of high school guidance officers or the Briarwood College Financial Aid Office. Recipients are selected on the basis of their academic achievement, extracurricular activities, recommendation letters, and personal essays. Eligible students are encouraged to seek, and are assisted in obtaining, educational benefits from the Veterans Administration, G.I. Bill, and state agencies. There are also grants and loans available, including Connecticut Independent College Student Grants (CICS), Federal Pell Grants, Federal Stafford Student Loans, Federal PLUS loans, Federal Supplemental Educational Opportunity Grants, and Federal Perkins Loans. For more information, students should contact the Financial Aid Office at 860-628-4751 or 800-952-2444 (toll-free).

Faculty

The teaching experience among the faculty members at Briarwood College is distinct in its variety of professional, business, and years of teaching experience. There are several faculty members who remain active in their line of work. For example, the Allied Health Division has on its staff several faculty members who are currently active in their vocation who bring expertise to their students. The faculty members in this category include the Program Director of the Pharmacy Technician Program, who is a practicing pharmacist; the Program Director of Travel and Tourism, who has more than twenty years of experience in the travel industry and is still active in the field; and adjunct faculty members in the Mortuary Science Program, who are presently working in the funeral service business.

Student Body Profile

There were 647 full- and part-time students enrolled in fall 2006. Students come from eight states and two other countries. Approximately 33 percent (218 students) live on campus.

Student Activities

The Dean of Student Life and her staff coordinate a variety of recreational opportunities, including clubs, fitness activities, student organizations, volunteer opportunities, and special events. Popular events include an annual fashion show, international night, a formal dinner/dance, award ceremonies, trips, picnics, and noon-hour programs on a variety of topics.

Briarwood students participate in a number of community volunteer activities, including America Reads, food and toy drives, a soup kitchen, and a blood drive.

The College Culture Committee coordinates cultural and educational events with various academic departments. Recent events have included presentations by visiting authors, films, and panel discussions.

Sports Briarwood College is a member of the National Junior College Athletic Association and competes with other colleges in Region 21. The College currently offers men's basketball and women's soccer at the varsity level. Students may also become involved in a wide variety of outdoor/indoor recreational activities, such as softball, volleyball, and golf. Skiing is available locally at Mount Southington, only 1 mile from the College. Annual trips to area ski resorts are also planned.

Briarwood has an affiliation with a local gym, enabling students to use the facilities for a nominal fee. The gym is a 24,000-square-foot facility with large cardiovascular and free-weight areas, as well as areas for yoga, group cycling, pilates, and group exercise. Briarwood also has an affiliation with the Southington YMCA that allows students to use this facility during the academic year for a greatly reduced rate. This facility includes a gym and a pool as well as a complete line of cardiovascular and strength-training equipment.

Facilities and Resources

There are two residential facilities on campus: Eder Hall, with its town house–style apartments, and Palmisano Hall. All units have furnished bedrooms, kitchens, and living rooms as well as laundry facilities. The residence halls also have Internet and cable access. A student center provides recreation space, pool tables, lounge chairs, and a large-screen television. A softball/soccer field is located adjacent to the residence halls.

Career Services The Career Service Office at Briarwood College provides a comprehensive career development program designed to assist students in making appropriate career choices and in developing plans to achieve their goals. Both individual and group sessions are offered to assist students with resume writing, interviewing, and job search skills.

Counseling Services Students who experience academic, personal, learning, or study problems are urged to seek help as soon as the problem is recognized. Counselors provide academic intervention activities designed to assist students who are experiencing academic difficulties. These activities include Early Alert notices, midterm intervention sessions, and individual assistance. A counselor is available to assist students who are having academic difficulties by working with them individually or by referring them to the services of the College Learning Center.

College counselors are available to aid students in resolving many types of problems, including social, emotional, vocational, and personal concerns. All information is handled in a confidential setting. Services of the Counseling Center include short-term personal counseling, crisis intervention, career development, and administering and interpreting self-assessment inventories.

In some cases, a counselor determines that the needs of a student would be best met through a community agency off campus. Referrals are made when the student is in crisis; has a long-term, ongoing problem; or can otherwise benefit from the resources of an outside agency. Counselors assist students in obtaining such services when appropriate.

Disability Services The Disability Services Office is responsible for all disability-related concerns of Briarwood College students. Briarwood College encourages qualified students with disabilities to take advantage of its educational programs. The College is responsible for ensuring that courses, programs, services, activities, and facilities are available and usable in the most integrated and appropriate settings. Students with disabilities seeking accommodations must identify themselves as individuals with disabilities, request needed accommodations, and provide documentation from the appropriate professional as to how the disabilities limit their participation in courses, programs, activities, and use of facilities. Upon receipt of documentation of a disability, it is the responsibility of the Disability Services Office to explore and facilitate reasonable accommodations, academic adjustments,

and/or auxiliary aids and services for individuals with disabilities in courses, programs, services, activities, and facilities. Students anticipating the need for accommodations, both before and after enrollment, are encouraged to contact the Dean of Student Services, whose office is located in the lower level of Eder Hall Center.

Health and Wellness Services The Health Office provides basic first aid and health education information to Briarwood College students. In some cases, a nurse determines that the needs of a student would be best met through an off-campus community facility. All students are required by federal law to provide their medical history and documentation of illnesses and immunizations prior to matriculation at Briarwood College. This information is used by the nurse in providing routine and emergency care.

Library and Audiovisual Services The Dr. Anthony A. Pupillo Library, staffed by a professional librarian and knowledgeable library assistants, plays an integral part in the education process of the students. The library is committed to providing support for the various courses and programs of study offered by Briarwood College. Although the library's resources are richest in the curricula taught at the College, a wide variety of works for individual interest and personal growth are also offered. The library offers a wide variety of electronic resources to facilitate student research. Novice users quickly learn to utilize the capabilities of the library's computer technology. The library offers research-only computers for student use and one-on-one sessions with students to familiarize them with its resources. Interlibrary loan is available to the students.

Location

Briarwood College is located in Southington, Connecticut, only 2 hours from Boston and New York. Students find skiing and Connecticut beaches readily accessible, and the school is minutes from the Hartford and New Haven metropolitan areas. The picturesque 42-acre campus is nestled at the base of Mount Southington, next to an 18-hole golf course and close to Lake Compounce Amusement Park, the Mount Southington ski area, and ESPN. Hartford, Connecticut's capital city, is just 15 minutes from the campus and offers numerous restaurants, indoor and outdoor concert venues, theaters, museums, parks, and shopping centers. The greater Hartford area is also home to seven colleges and universities.

Admission Requirements

The College requires applicants for full-time and part-time study to submit a completed application form, a $25 application fee, and official high school transcripts or GED scores. A personal statement and one letter of recommendation should be submitted for scholarship opportunities. SAT scores are not required, but are also recommended for scholarship opportunities. International students for whom English is not the first language are required to show proof of English competency. Part-time and transfer applicants are ordinarily not required to submit a personal statement and recommendation letter. Transfer applicants are also required to submit transcripts from all colleges or universities previously attended. Interviews with the program directors are also required for applicants to the dental assisting and occupational therapy assisting programs. Applications are reviewed on a rolling basis and acceptances are mailed, usually within two weeks of receipt of all required documents. Applicants for fall semester are encouraged to apply by March 30 for priority scholarship consideration.

Application and Information

For more information, students should contact:

Admissions Department
Briarwood College
2279 Mt. Vernon Road
Southington, Connecticut 06489
Phone: 860-628-4751
      800-952-2444 (toll-free)
E-mail: admis@briarwood.edu
Web site: http://www.briarwood.edu

BROWN MACKIE COLLEGE–AKRON

AKRON, OHIO

The College and Its Mission

Brown Mackie College–Akron is dedicated to providing education programs that prepare students for entry-level positions in a competitive, rapidly changing workplace. The College provides associate degree and diploma programs in the areas of business and accounting, allied health sciences, legal studies, and computer-technology fields to approximately 680 students.

The College was founded in Cincinnati, Ohio, in February 1927, as a traditional business college. In March 1980, the College added a branch location in Akron, Ohio. This facility was extensively renovated, and a new classroom wing was added in the spring of 1986.

Brown Mackie College–Akron is accredited by the Accrediting Council for Independent Colleges and Schools (ACICS) to award associate degrees and diplomas. ACICS is listed as a nationally recognized accrediting agency by the United States Department of Education. Its accreditation of degree-granting institutions also is recognized by the Council for Higher Education Accreditation. ACICS can be contacted at 750 First Street, NE, Suite 980, Washington, D.C. 20002-4241; 202-336-6780. The College is licensed by the Ohio State Board of Career Colleges and Schools, 35 East Gay Street, Suite 403, Columbus, Ohio 43215 (OH registration #03-09-1685T).

The Medical Assisting degree program is accredited by the Commission on Accreditation of Allied Health Education Programs (CAAHEP), 35 East Wacker Drive, Suite 1970, Chicago, Illinois 60601-2208; 312-553-2208, on recommendation of the Curriculum Review Board of the American Association of Medical Assistants Endowment (AAMAE).

The College is a nonresidential, smoke-free institution and is owned and operated by Education Management Corporation, 210 Sixth Avenue, 33rd Floor, Pittsburgh, Pennsylvania 15222-2603; 800-275-2440 (toll-free); http://www.edmc.edu.

Academic Programs

Brown Mackie College–Akron provides higher education to traditional and nontraditional students through associate degree and diploma programs that assist them in enhancing their career opportunities, broadening their perspectives through appropriate general education courses, thinking independently and critically, and improving problem-solving abilities.

Each College quarter comprises twelve weeks. Associate degree programs require a minimum of eight quarters to complete. Programs are offered on a year-round basis, providing students with the ability to work uninterrupted toward their degree.

Associate Degree Programs The Associate of Applied Business degree (96 credits) is awarded in accounting technology, business management, computer software technology, criminal justice, and paralegal studies. The Associate of Applied Science

degree (96 credits) is awarded in database technology, health-care administration, information technology, medical assisting, and pharmacy technology.

Diploma Programs The College also offers diploma programs (48 credits) in accounting, business, computer software applications, criminal justice, medical assistant studies, paralegal assistant studies, and practical nursing.

Costs

Tuition for the 2006–07 academic year was $189 per credit hour. The cost of textbooks and other instructional materials varies by program.

Financial Aid

The College maintains a full-time staff of financial aid professionals to assist qualified students in obtaining financial assistance. The College participates in several student aid programs. Forms of financial aid available through federal resources include the Federal Pell Grant Program, Federal Supplemental Educational Opportunity Grant (FSEOG) Program, Federal Work-Study Program, Federal Perkins Loan Program, Federal Stafford Student Loan Program (subsidized and unsubsidized), and the Federal PLUS Loan Program. Through the Ohio Instructional Grant (OIG) program, Ohio residents enrolled in a degree program may receive an award to apply to their tuition costs. The amount of the award varies according to family income and other determining factors. Eligible students may also apply for veterans' educational benefits. Students with physical or mental disabilities that are a handicap to employment may be eligible for training services through the state Agency for Vocational Rehabilitation. For further information, students should contact the College Student Financial Services Office.

Each year, the College makes available scholarships of $1000 each to qualifying seniors from area high schools. Only one scholarship is awarded per high school. In order to qualify, a senior must be graduating from a participating high school, maintain a cumulative grade point average of at least 2.0, and submit a brief essay. The student's extracurricular activities and community service are also considered. The President's Scholarship is available only to students enrolling in one of the College's degree programs. Students awarded the scholarship must enroll at Brown Mackie College–Akron between June and September immediately following their high school graduation. Applications for these scholarships can be obtained from the guidance departments of participating high schools. These applications must be completed and returned to the College by March 31. Those who are awarded scholarships are notified by April 30.

Faculty

There are 14 full-time and 17 part-time faculty members. The student-faculty ratio is 19:1.

Facilities and Resources

Brown Mackie College–Akron provides media presentation rooms for special instructional needs, libraries that provide instructional resources and academic support for both faculty members and students, and qualified and experienced faculty members who are committed to the academic and technical preparation of their students. The College is nonresidential; students who are unable to commute daily from their homes may request assistance from the Office of Admissions in locating off-campus housing. The College is accessible by public transportation and provides ample parking, available at no charge.

Location

The College is located at 755 White Pond Drive in Akron, Ohio.

Admission Requirements

Each applicant for admission is assigned an Assistant Director of Admissions who directs the applicant through the steps of the admissions process, providing information on curriculum, policies, procedures, and services and assisting the applicant in setting necessary appointments and interviews.

To qualify for admission, each applicant must provide documentation of graduation from an accredited high school or from a state-approved secondary education curriculum or provide official documentation of high school graduation equivalency. All transcripts become the property of the College. Admission to the College is based upon the applicant's meeting the above requirements, a review of the applicant's previous education records, and a review of the applicant's career interests. If previous academic records indicate that the College's education and training would not benefit the applicant, the College reserves the right to advise the applicant not to enroll. Special requirements for enrollment into certain programs are discussed in the descriptions of those programs.

Application and Information

Applicants must complete and submit an application form along with documentation of graduation from an accredited high school or state-approved secondary education curriculum, or applicants must provide official documentation of high school graduation equivalency. For additional information, prospective students should contact:

Director of Admissions
Brown Mackie College–Akron
755 White Pond Drive
Akron, Ohio 44320

Phone: 330-869-3600
Fax: 330-869-3650
E-mail: jconte@brownmackie.edu
Web site: http://www.brownmackie.edu

BROWN MACKIE COLLEGE–ATLANTA
ATLANTA, GEORGIA

The College and Its Mission

Brown Mackie College–Atlanta is dedicated to providing education programs that prepare students for entry-level positions in a competitive, rapidly changing workplace. The College provides associate degree and diploma programs in the areas of business and accounting, allied health sciences, legal studies, and computer technology to approximately 150 students.

Brown Mackie College–Atlanta is accredited by the Accrediting Council for Independent Colleges and Schools (ACICS) to award associate degrees, diplomas, and certificates. The Accrediting Council for Independent Colleges and Schools is listed as a nationally recognized accrediting agency by the United States Department of Education. The Accrediting Council can be contacted at 750 First Street, NE, Suite 980, Washington, D.C. 20002-4241; 202-336-6780. Its accreditation of degree-granting institutions also is recognized by the Council for Higher Education Accreditation.

The College is a nonresidential, smoke-free institution and is owned and operated by Education Management Corporation, 210 Sixth Avenue, 33rd Floor, Pittsburgh, Pennsylvania 15222-2603; 800-275-2440 (toll-free); http://www.edmc.edu.

Academic Programs

Brown Mackie College–Atlanta provides higher education to traditional and nontraditional students through associate degree and diploma programs that assist them in enhancing their career opportunities, broadening their perspectives through appropriate general education courses, thinking independently and critically, and improving problem-solving abilities. The College strives to develop within its students the desire for lifelong and continued education.

Each College quarter comprises twelve weeks. Associate degree programs require a minimum of eight quarters to complete. Programs are offered on a year-round basis, providing students with the ability to work uninterrupted toward their degrees.

Associate Degree Programs The Associate of Applied Business degree (96 credits) is awarded in accounting technology, business management, computer programming and applications, computer software technology, criminal justice, and paralegal studies. The Associate of Applied Science degree (96 credits) is awarded in health-care administration, medical assisting, pharmacy technology, and surgical technology.

Diploma Programs The College also offers diploma programs (48 credits) in accounting, business, computer-aided design and drafting technician studies, computer applications, computer software applications, criminal justice, medical assistant studies, and paralegal assistant studies.

Costs

Tuition for the 2006–07 academic year was $189 per credit hour. Textbook fees were estimated at $425 per quarter.

Financial Aid

The College maintains a full-time staff of financial aid professionals to assist qualified students in obtaining financial assistance. The College participates in several student aid programs. Forms of financial aid available through federal resources include the Federal Pell Grant Program, Federal Supplemental Educational Opportunity Grant (FSEOG) Program, Federal Work-Study Program, Federal Perkins Loan Program, Federal Stafford Student Loan Program (subsidized and unsubsidized), and the Federal PLUS Loan Program. Eligible students may also apply for state awards and veterans' educational benefits. Students with physical or mental disabilities that are a handicap to employment may be eligible for training services through the state Agency for Vocational Rehabilitation. For further information, students should contact the College Student Financial Services Office.

Each year, the College makes available scholarships of $1000 each to qualifying seniors from area high schools. Only one scholarship is awarded per high school. In order to qualify, a senior must be graduating from a participating high school, maintain a cumulative grade point average of at least 2.0, and submit a brief essay. The student's extracurricular activities and community service are also considered. The President's Scholarship is available only to students enrolling in one of the College's degree programs. Students awarded the scholarship must enroll at Brown Mackie College–Atlanta between June and September immediately following their high school graduation. Applications for these scholarships can be obtained from the guidance departments of participating high schools. These applications must be completed and returned to the College by March 31. Those who are awarded scholarships are notified by April 30.

Faculty

There are 4 full-time and 5 part-time faculty members. The average student-faculty ratio is 19:1. Each student has a faculty and student adviser.

Facilities and Resources

The College comprises administrative offices, faculty and student lounges, a reception area, and spacious classrooms and laboratories. Instructional equipment includes personal computers, LANs, printers, and transcribers. The library provides support for the academic programs through volumes covering a broad range of subjects, as well as through Internet access. Vehicle parking is provided for both students and staff members.

Location

Brown Mackie College–Atlanta is located at 6600 Peachtree Dunwoody Road NE, 600 Embassy Row, Suite 130, in Atlanta, Georgia, and is easily accessible from interstate highway I-285 and the MARTA Sandy Springs rail station.

Admission Requirements

Each applicant for admission is assigned an Assistant Director of Admissions who directs the applicant through the steps of the admissions process, providing information on curriculum, policies, procedures, and services and assisting the applicant in setting necessary appointments and interviews.

To qualify for admission, each applicant must provide documentation of graduation from an accredited high school or from a state-approved secondary education curriculum or provide official documentation of high school graduation equivalency. All transcripts become the property of the College. Admission to the College is based upon the applicant's meeting the above requirements, a review of the applicant's previous education records, and a review of the applicant's career interests. If previous academic records indicate that the College's education and training would not benefit the applicant, the College reserves the right to advise the applicant not to enroll. Special requirements for enrollment into certain programs are discussed in the descriptions of those programs.

Application and Information

Applicants must complete and submit an application form along with documentation of graduation from an accredited high school or state-approved secondary education curriculum, or applicants must provide official documentation of high school graduation equivalency. For additional information, prospective students should contact:

Director of Admissions
Brown Mackie College–Atlanta
6600 Peachtree Dunwoody Road NE
600 Embassy Row
Suite 130
Atlanta, Georgia 30093
Phone: 770-510-2318
Fax: 770-638-0479
E-mail: jmtate@brownmackie.edu
Web site: http://www.brownmackie.edu

BROWN MACKIE COLLEGE–CINCINNATI

CINCINNATI, OHIO

The College and Its Mission

Brown Mackie College–Cincinnati is dedicated to providing education programs that prepare students for entry-level positions in a competitive, rapidly changing workplace. The College provides associate degree, diploma, and certificate programs in the areas of business and accounting, allied health sciences, legal studies, computer technology, and electronics fields to approximately 1,320 students.

The College was founded in February 1927 as Southern Ohio Business College. In 1978, the College's main location was relocated from downtown Cincinnati to the Bond Hill–Roselawn area and in 1995 to its current location at 1011 Glendale-Milford Road in the community of Woodlawn.

Brown Mackie College–Cincinnati is accredited by the Accrediting Council for Independent Colleges and Schools (ACICS) to award associate degrees, diplomas, and certificates. The Accrediting Council for Independent Colleges and Schools is listed as a nationally recognized accrediting agency by the United States Department of Education. Its accreditation of degree-granting institutions is also recognized by the Council for Higher Education Accreditation. ACICS can be contacted at 750 First Street, NE, Suite 980, Washington, D.C. 20002-4241; 202-336-6780. The medical assisting program is accredited by the Commission on Accreditation of Allied Health Education Programs (CAAHEP), on recommendation of the Committee on Accreditation for Medical Assistant Education. The College is licensed by the Ohio State Board of Career Colleges and Schools, 35 East Gay Street, Suite 403, Columbus, Ohio 43215 (OH registration #03-09-1686T).

The College is a nonresidential, smoke-free institution and is owned and operated by Education Management Corporation, 210 Sixth Avenue, 33rd Floor, Pittsburgh, Pennsylvania 15222-2603; http://www.edmc.edu.

Academic Programs

Brown Mackie College–Cincinnati provides higher education to traditional and nontraditional students through associate degree, diploma, and certificate programs that assist them in enhancing their career opportunities, broadening their perspectives through appropriate general education courses, thinking independently and critically, and improving problem-solving abilities. The College strives to develop within its students the desire for lifelong and continued education.

Each College quarter comprises twelve weeks. Associate degree programs require a minimum of eight quarters to complete. Programs are offered on a year-round basis, providing students with the ability to work uninterrupted toward their degrees.

Associate Degree Programs The Associate of Applied Business degree (96 credits) is awarded in accounting technology, business management, computer networking and applications, computer software technology, criminal justice, and paralegal studies. The Associate of Applied Science degree (96 credits) is awarded in audio/video production, computer-aided design and drafting technology, database technology, early childhood education, electronics, health-care administration, information technology, medical assisting, pharmacy technology, and surgical technology.

Diploma Programs The College offers diploma programs (48 credits) in accounting, audio/video technician studies, business, computer-aided design and drafting technician studies, computer software applications, criminal justice, medical assistant studies, paralegal assistant studies, and practical nursing studies (76 credits).

Certificate Program The College offers a certificate program (24 credits) in computer networking.

Costs

Tuition for the 2006–07 academic year was $189 per credit hour, with the exception of the practical nursing program at $250 per credit hour and Microsoft Certified Systems Engineer (MCSE) courses at $300 per credit hour. Textbook expenses were approximately $425 per quarter.

Financial Aid

The College maintains a full-time staff of financial aid professionals to assist qualified students in obtaining financial assistance. The College participates in several student aid programs. Forms of financial aid available to qualified students through federal resources include the Federal Pell Grant Program, Federal Supplemental Educational Opportunity Grant (FSEOG) Program, Federal Work-Study Program, Federal Perkins Loan Program, Federal Stafford Student Loan Program (subsidized and unsubsidized), and the Federal PLUS Loan Program. Eligible students may apply for state awards, such as the Ohio Instructional Grant (OIG), and veterans' educational benefits. Students with physical or mental disabilities that are a handicap to employment may be eligible for training services through the state Agency for Vocational Rehabilitation. For further information, students should contact the College Student Financial Services Office.

Each year, the College makes available President's Scholarships of $1000 each to qualifying seniors from area high schools. No more than one scholarship is awarded per high school. In order to qualify, a senior must be graduating from a participating high school, must be maintaining a cumulative grade point average of at least 2.0, and must submit a brief essay. The student's extracurricular activities and community service are also considered. The President's Scholarship is available only to students enrolling in one of the College's degree programs. Students awarded the scholarship must enroll at Brown Mackie College–Cincinnati between June and September immediately following their high school graduation. Applications for these scholarships can be obtained from the guidance departments of participating high schools. These applications must be completed and returned to the College by March 31. Those awarded scholarships are notified by April 30.

Faculty

There are 31 full-time and 50 part-time faculty members. The average student-faculty ratio is 16:1. Each student has a faculty and student adviser.

Academic Facilities

Brown Mackie College–Cincinnati consists of more than 57,000 square feet of classroom, laboratory, and office space designed to specifications of the College for its business, medical, and technical programs.

Location

Brown Mackie College–Cincinnati is located in the Woodlawn section of Cincinnati, Ohio. The College is accessible by public transportation and provides ample free parking. It shares its facility space with The Art Institute of Ohio–Cincinnati.

Admission Requirements

Each applicant for admission is assigned an Assistant Director of Admissions, who directs the applicant through the steps of the admissions process, providing information on curriculum, policies, procedures, and services and assisting the applicant in setting necessary appointments and interviews. To qualify for admission, each applicant must provide documentation of graduation from an accredited high school or from a state-approved secondary education curriculum or provide official documentation of high school graduation equivalency. All transcripts become the property of the College. Admission to the College is based on the applicant's meeting the above requirements, a review of the applicant's previous educational records, and a review of the applicant's career interests. If previous academic records indicate that the College's education and training would not benefit the applicant, the College reserves the right to advise the applicant not to enroll. Special requirements for enrollment into certain programs are discussed in the descriptions of those programs.

Application and Information

Applicants must complete and submit an application form, along with documentation of graduation from an accredited high school or state-approved secondary education curriculum or official documentation of high school graduation equivalency.

For additional information, prospective students should contact:

Director of Admissions
Brown Mackie College–Cincinnati
1011 Glendale-Milford Road
Cincinnati, Ohio 45215
Phone: 512-771-2424
          800-888-1445 (toll-free)
Fax: 513-771-3413
E-mail: awalker@brownmackie.edu
Web site: http://www.brownmackie.edu

BROWN MACKIE COLLEGE–FINDLAY

FINDLAY, OHIO

The College and Its Mission

Brown Mackie College–Findlay is dedicated to providing education programs that prepare students for entry-level positions in a competitive, rapidly changing workplace. The College provides associate degree and diploma programs in business and accounting, the allied health sciences, legal studies, electronics, and computer technology to approximately 615 students.

Brown Mackie College–Findlay was founded in 1926 by William H. Stautzenberger to provide solid business education at a reasonable cost. In 1960, the College was acquired by George R. Hawes, who served as its president until 1969. The College changed its name from Southern Ohio College–Findlay in 2001 to AEC Southern Ohio College; it was acquired by Education Management Corporation (EDMC) on September 2, 2003, and changed to Brown Mackie College–Findlay in November 2004.

Brown Mackie College–Findlay is accredited by the Accrediting Council for Independent Colleges and Schools (ACICS) to award associate degrees and diplomas. The Accrediting Council for Independent Colleges and Schools is listed as a nationally recognized accrediting agency by the United States Department of Education. Its accreditation of degree-granting institutions also is recognized by the Council for Higher Education Accreditation. The Accrediting Council's address is 750 First Street, NE, Suite 980, Washington, D.C. 20002-4241; 202-336-6780. The practical nursing program is approved by the Ohio Board of Nursing, 17 South High Street, Suite 400, Columbus, Ohio 43215-3413; 614-466-3947.

Brown Mackie College–Findlay is a nonresidential, smoke-free institution and is owned and operated by Education Management Corporation, 210 Sixth Avenue, 33rd Floor, Pittsburgh, Pennsylvania 15222-2603; http://www.edmc.edu. Although the College does not offer residential housing, students who are unable to commute daily from their homes may request assistance from the Admissions Office in locating housing. Ample parking is available at no additional cost.

Academic Programs

Brown Mackie College–Findlay provides higher education to traditional and nontraditional students through associate degree and diploma programs that assist them in enhancing their career opportunities, broadening their perspectives through appropriate general education courses, thinking independently and critically, and improving problem-solving abilities. The College strives to develop within its students the desire for lifelong and continued education.

Each College quarter comprises twelve weeks. Associate degree programs require a minimum of eight quarters to complete. Programs are offered on a year-round basis, providing students with the ability to work uninterrupted toward completion of their programs.

Associate Degree Programs The Associate of Applied Business degree (96 credits) is awarded in accounting technology, business management, computer software technology, criminal justice, and paralegal studies. The Associate of Applied Science degree (96 credits) is awarded in gerontology, health-care administration, medical assisting, pharmacy technology, and surgical technology.

Diploma Programs In addition to the associate degree programs, the College offers diploma programs (76 credits) in business, computer software applications, medical assistant studies, and practical nursing.

Costs

Tuition for programs in the 2005–06 academic year was $179 per credit hour, with the exception of the practical nursing diploma program, which was $250 per credit hour. The length of the program determines total cost. Textbooks per quarter for traditional programs were approximately $380; for the practical nursing program, they were approximately $435.

Financial Aid

The College maintains a full-time staff of financial aid professionals to assist qualified students in obtaining financial assistance. The College participates in several student aid programs. Forms of financial aid available through federal resources include the Federal Pell Grant Program, Federal Supplemental Educational Opportunity Grant (FSEOG) Program, Federal Work-Study Program, Federal Perkins Loan Program, Federal Stafford Student Loan Program (subsidized and unsubsidized), and the Federal PLUS Loan Program. Eligible students may apply for state awards, such as the Ohio Instructional Grant (OIG), and veterans' educational benefits. Students with physical or mental disabilities that are a handicap to employment may be eligible for training services through the state Agency for Vocational Rehabilitation. For further information, students should contact the College Student Financial Services Office.

Each year, the College makes available President's Scholarships of $1000 each to qualifying seniors from area high schools. No more than one scholarship is awarded per high school. In order to qualify, a senior must be graduating from a participating high school, must be maintaining a cumulative grade point average of at least 2.0, and must submit a brief essay. The student's extracurricular activities and community service are also considered. The President's Scholarship is available only to students enrolling in one of the College's degree programs. Students awarded the scholarship must enroll at Brown Mackie College–Findlay between June and September immediately following their high school graduation. Applications for these scholarships can be obtained from the guidance departments of participating high schools. These applications must be completed and returned to the College by March 31. Those awarded scholarships are notified by April 30.

Faculty

There are 14 full-time and 37 part-time instructors at the College. The average student-faculty ratio is 16:1. Each student is assigned a faculty adviser.

Academic Facilities

The College has 22,000 square feet of academic classrooms, laboratories, and offices.

Location

Located at 1700 Fostoria Avenue, Suite 100, in Findlay, Ohio, the College is easily accessible from Interstate 75.

Admission Requirements

Each applicant for admission is assigned an Assistant Director of Admissions, who directs the applicant through the steps of the admissions process, providing information on curriculum, policies, procedures, and services and assisting the applicant in setting necessary appointments and interviews. To qualify for admission, each applicant must provide documentation of graduation from an accredited high school or from a state-approved secondary education curriculum or provide official documentation of high school graduation equivalency. All transcripts become the property of the College. Admission to the College is based upon the applicant's meeting the above requirements, a review of the applicant's previous educational records, and a review of two applicant's career interests. If previous academic records indicate that the College's education and training would not benefit the applicant, the College reserves the right to advise the applicant not to enroll. Special requirements for enrollment into certain programs are discussed in the descriptions of those programs. For further information, students should contact the College Admissions Office.

Application and Information

Applicants must complete and submit an application form, along with documentation of graduation from an accredited high school or state-approved secondary education curriculum or official documentation of high school graduation equivalency.

For additional information, prospective students should contact:

Director of Admissions
Brown Mackie College–Findlay
1700 Fostoria Avenue, Suite 100
Findlay, Ohio 45840
Phone: 419-423-2211
       800-842-3687 (toll-free)
Fax: 419-423-0725
E-mail: bmcfiadm@brownmackie.edu
Web site: http://www.brownmackie.edu

BROWN MACKIE COLLEGE–FORT WAYNE

FORT WAYNE, INDIANA

The College and Its Mission

Brown Mackie College–Fort Wayne is dedicated to providing educational programs that prepare students for entry-level positions in a competitive, rapidly changing workplace. The College provides associate degree, diploma, and certificate programs in the areas of business and accounting, allied health sciences, legal studies, computer technology, and electronics to approximately 872 students.

Brown Mackie College–Fort Wayne is one of the oldest institutions of its kind in the country and the oldest in the state of Indiana. Established in 1882 as the South Bend Commercial College, the school later changed its name to Michiana College. In 1930, the College was incorporated under the laws of the state of Indiana and was authorized to confer associate degrees and certificates in business. In 1992, the College in South Bend added a branch location in Fort Wayne, Indiana. In 2004, Michiana College changed its name to Brown Mackie College–Fort Wayne.

Brown Mackie College–Fort Wayne is accredited by the Accrediting Council for Independent Colleges and Schools (ACICS) to award associate degrees, diplomas, and certificates. The Accrediting Council for Independent Colleges and Schools is listed as a nationally recognized accrediting agency by the United States Department of Education. Its accreditation of degree-granting institutions also is recognized by the Council for Higher Education Accreditation. ACICS can be contacted at 750 First Street, NE, Suite 980, Washington, D.C. 20002-4241; 202-336-6780.

Brown Mackie College–Fort Wayne is owned and operated by Education Management Corporation, 210 Sixth Avenue, 33rd Floor, Pittsburgh, Pennsylvania 15222-2603; http://www.edmc.edu. (AC 0109)

The College's medical assisting degree program is accredited by the Commission on Accreditation of Allied Health Education Programs (CAAHEP), on recommendation of the Curriculum Review Board of the American Association of Medical Assistants Endowment (AAMAE). The commission's address is 35 East Wacker Drive, Chicago, Illinois 60601; 312-553-9355. The College is licensed and regulated by the Indiana Commission on Proprietary Education, 302 West Washington Street, Indianapolis, Indiana 46204; 317-232-1320 or 800-227-5695 (toll-free). The College's occupational therapy assistant studies program is accredited by the Accreditation Council for Occupational Therapy Education (ACOTE) of the American Occupational Therapy Association (AOTA), 4720 Montgomery Lane, P.O. Box 31220, Bethesda, Maryland 20824-1220; 301-652-2682. The College's practical nursing program is accredited by the Indiana State Board of Nursing, 402 West Washington Street, Room W066, Indianapolis, Indiana 46204; 317-234-2043.

Brown Mackie College–Fort Wayne is a smoke-free institution.

Academic Programs

Brown Mackie College–Fort Wayne provides higher education to traditional and nontraditional students through associate degree, diploma, and certificate programs that assist them in enhancing their career opportunities, broadening their perspectives through appropriate general education courses, thinking independently and critically, and improving problem solving abilities. The College strives to develop within its students the desire for lifelong and continued education.

Each College quarter comprises twelve weeks. Associate degree programs require a minimum of eight quarters to complete. Programs are offered on a year-round basis, providing students with the ability to work uninterrupted toward their degrees.

Associate Degree Programs The Associate of Science degree (96 credits) is awarded in accounting technology, business management, computer software technology, criminal justice, health-care administration, medical assisting, paralegal studies, and surgical technology. The Associate of Applied Science degree (96 credits) is awarded in occupational therapy assistant studies.

Diploma Program A diploma (76 credits) is awarded in practical nursing.

Certificate Programs Certificates (48 credits) are awarded in accounting, business, computer software applications, criminal justice, medical assistant, medical coding and billing, and paralegal assistant studies.

Costs

Tuition in the 2006–07 academic year for all programs except practical nursing and occupational therapy assistant studies was $179 per credit hour; fees were $10 per credit hour. Textbook expenses were estimated at $372 per quarter. For the practical nursing program, tuition was $250 per credit hour; fees were $10 per credit hour. Textbook expenses were estimated at $400 for the first term, $600 for the second term, and $100 for the third, fourth, and fifth terms. For the occupational therapy assistant studies program, tuition was $179 per credit hour for general education courses and $300 per credit hour for occupational therapy courses; fees were $10 per credit hour. Textbook expenses were estimated at $372 per quarter for the first six terms and $458 for the seventh term.

Financial Aid

The College maintains a full-time staff of financial aid professionals to assist qualified students in obtaining financial assistance. The College participates in several student aid programs. Forms of financial aid available through federal resources include the Federal Pell Grant Program, Federal Supplemental Educational Opportunity Grant (FSEOG) Program, Federal Work-Study Program, Federal Perkins Loan Program, Federal Stafford Student Loan Program (subsidized and unsubsidized), and the Federal PLUS Loan Program. Eligible

students may apply for Indiana state awards, such as the Frank O'Bannon Grant Program (formerly the Indiana State Grant Program), the Higher Education Award, and Twenty-First Century Scholarships for high school students; for the Core 40 awards; and for veterans' educational benefits. Students with physical or mental disabilities that are a handicap to employment may be eligible for training services through the state Agency for Vocational Rehabilitation. For further information, students should contact the College Student Financial Services Office.

Each year, the College makes available President's Scholarships of $1000 each to qualifying seniors from area high schools. No more than one scholarship is awarded per high school. In order to qualify, a senior must be graduating from a participating high school, must be maintaining a cumulative grade point average of at least 2.0, and must submit a brief essay. The student's extracurricular activities and community service are also considered. The President's Scholarship is available only to students enrolling in one of the College's degree programs. Students awarded the scholarship must enroll at Brown Mackie College–Fort Wayne between June and September immediately following their high school graduation. Applications for these scholarships can be obtained from the guidance departments of participating high schools. These applications must be completed and returned to the College by March 31. Those awarded scholarships are notified by April 30.

Faculty

The College has 18 full-time and 35 part-time instructors, with a student-faculty ratio of 16.45:1. Each student is assigned a faculty adviser.

Academic Facilities

Brown Mackie College–Fort Wayne consists of 32,000 square feet of classrooms; medical, nursing, computer, and occupational therapy labs; a library; a bookstore; and office space.

Location

Brown Mackie College–Fort Wayne is located at 3000 East Coliseum Boulevard in Fort Wayne, Indiana. The College facility is accessible by public transportation. Ample parking is provided at no additional charge.

Admission Requirements

Each applicant for admission is assigned an Assistant Director of Admissions, who directs the applicant through the steps of the admissions process, providing information on curriculum, policies, procedures, and services and assisting the applicant in setting necessary appointments and interviews. To qualify for admission, each applicant must provide documentation of graduation from an accredited high school or from a state-approved secondary education curriculum or provide official documentation of high school graduation equivalency. All transcripts become the property of the College. Admission to the College is based upon the applicant's meeting the above requirements, a review of the applicant's previous educational records, and a review of the applicant's career interests. If previous academic records indicate that the College's education and training would not benefit the applicant, the College reserves the right to advise the applicant not to enroll. Special requirements for enrollment into certain programs are discussed in the descriptions of those programs.

As part of the admissions process, students are given an assessment of academic skills. Though the results of this assessment do not determine eligibility for admission, they provide the College with a means of determining the need for academic support, as well as a means by which the College can evaluate the effectiveness of its educational programs. All new students are required to complete this assessment, which is readministered at the end of the student's program so that results may be compared with those of the initial administration.

In addition to the College's general admission requirements, applicants enrolling in the practical nursing program must document the following, which must be completed and a record of proof must appear in the student's file prior to the start of the Nursing Fundamentals course. No student will be admitted to a clinical agency unless all paperwork is completed. The paperwork is a requirement of all contracted agencies. This paperwork includes records of (1) a complete physical, current to within six months of admission; (2) a two-step Mantoux test that is kept current throughout schooling; (3) a hepatitis B vaccination or signed refusal; (4) up-to-date immunizations, including tetanus and rubella; (5) a record of current CPR certification that is maintained throughout the student's clinical experience; and (6) hospitalization insurance or a signed waiver.

Application and Information

Applicants must complete and submit an application form, along with documentation of graduation from an accredited high school or state-approved secondary education curriculum or official documentation of high school graduation equivalency.

For additional information, prospective students should contact:

Director of Admissions
Brown Mackie College–Fort Wayne
3000 East Coliseum Boulevard
Fort Wayne, Indiana 46805
Phone: 260-484-4400
        866-433-2289 (toll-free)
Fax: 260-484-2678
E-mail: ktaboh@brownmackie.edu
Web site: http://www.brownmackie.edu

BROWN MACKIE COLLEGE–HOPKINSVILLE

HOPKINSVILLE, KENTUCKY

The College and Its Mission

Brown Mackie College–Hopkinsville is dedicated to providing education programs that prepare students for entry-level positions in a competitive, rapidly changing workplace. The College provides associate degree and diploma programs in the areas of business and accounting, allied health sciences, legal studies, and computer technology to approximately 150 students.

Brown Mackie College–Hopkinsville is accredited by the Accrediting Council for Independent Colleges and Schools (ACICS) to award associate degrees and diplomas. ACICS is listed as a nationally recognized accrediting agency by the United States Department of Education. Its accreditation of degree-granting institutions also is recognized by the Council for Higher Education Accreditation. ACICS may be contacted at 750 First Street, NE, Suite 980, Washington, D.C. 20002-4241; phone: 202-336-6780.

The College is a nonresidential, smoke-free institution and is owned and operated by Education Management Corporation, 210 Sixth Avenue, 33rd Floor, Pittsburgh, Pennsylvania 15222-2603; phone: 800-275-2440 (toll-free); Web site: http://www.edmc.edu.

Academic Programs

Brown Mackie College–Hopkinsville provides higher education to traditional and nontraditional students through associate degree and diploma programs that assist them in enhancing their career opportunities, broadening their perspectives through appropriate general education courses, thinking independently and critically, and improving problem-solving abilities. Each College quarter comprises ten to twelve weeks.

Associate Degree Programs Associate degree programs require a minimum of eight quarters to complete. Programs are offered on a year-round basis, providing students with the ability to work uninterrupted toward their degrees. The Associate of Applied Business degree (96 credits) is awarded in accounting technology, business management, computer programming and applications, computer software technology, criminal justice, and paralegal studies. The Associate of Applied Science degree (96 credits) is awarded in medical assisting and medical office management.

Diploma Programs The College also offers diploma programs (48 credits) in accounting, business, computer applications, computer software applications, criminal justice, medical assistant studies, medical coding and billing, and paralegal assistant studies.

Costs

Tuition is $169 per credit hour. A general fee of $10 per credit hour is charged and applied to the cost of institutional activities and services. The cost of textbooks and other instructional materials varies by program.

Financial Aid

The College maintains a full-time staff of financial aid professionals to assist qualified students in obtaining the financial assistance they require to meet their educational expenses. The College participates in several student aid programs. Forms of financial aid available through federal resources include Federal Pell Grants, Federal Supplemental Educational Opportunity Grants (FSEOG), the Federal Work-Study Program, Federal Perkins Loans, Federal Stafford Student Loans (subsidized and unsubsidized), and the Federal PLUS Program. Students may apply for the College Access Program (CAP) Grant Program and the Kentucky Education Excellence Award (KEES), a scholarship program based on their final high school grade point average. Eligible students may also apply for veterans' educational benefits. Students with physical or mental disabilities that are a handicap to employment may be eligible for training services through the State Vocational Rehabilitation Agency. For further information, students should contact the College Student Financial Services Office.

Each year, the College makes available President's Scholarships of $1000 each to qualifying seniors from area high schools. No more than one scholarship is awarded per high school. In order to qualify, a senior must be graduating from a participating high school, maintain a cumulative grade point average of at least 2.0, and submit a brief essay. The student's extracurricular activities and community service are also considered. The President's Scholarship is available only to students enrolling in one of the College's degree programs. Students awarded the scholarship must enroll at Brown Mackie College–Hopkinsville between June and September immediately following their high school graduation. Applications for these scholarships can be obtained from the guidance departments of participating high schools. These applications must be completed and returned to the College by March 31. Those awarded scholarships are notified by April 30.

Faculty

There are 3 full-time and 8 part-time faculty members. The student-faculty ratio is 12:1.

Facilities and Resources

Brown Mackie College–Hopkinsville occupies a spacious building that has been specifically designed to provide a comfortable and effective environment for learning. The facility comprises approximately 11,250 square feet, including six classrooms, a medical laboratory, an electronics laboratory, three computer laboratories, an academic resource center, administrative and faculty offices, a bookstore, and a student lounge. Computer equipment for hands-on learning includes three networked laboratories. Medical equipment includes monocular and binocular microscopes, electrocardiograph, autoclave, centrifuge, and other equipment appropriate to hands-on laboratory and clinical instruction. Convenient parking is available to all students.

Location

The College is located at 4001 Fort Campbell Boulevard in Hopkinsville, Kentucky.

Admission Requirements

Each applicant for admission is assigned an Assistant Director of Admissions who directs the applicant through the steps of the admissions process, providing information on curriculum, policies, procedures, and services and assisting the applicant in setting necessary appointments and interviews. To qualify for admission, each applicant must provide documentation of graduation from an accredited high school or from a state-approved secondary education curriculum or provide official documentation of high school graduation equivalency. All transcripts become the property of the College. Admission to the College is based upon the applicant's meeting the above requirements, a review of the applicant's previous education records, and a review of the applicant's career interests. If previous academic records indicate that the College's education and training would not benefit the applicant, the College reserves the right to advise the applicant not to enroll. Special requirements for enrollment into certain programs are discussed in the descriptions of those programs.

Application and Information

Applicants must complete and submit an application form, along with documentation of graduation from an accredited high school or state-approved secondary education curriculum or provide official documentation of high school graduation equivalency. For additional information, prospective students should contact:

Director of Admissions
Brown Mackie College–Hopkinsville
4001 Fort Campbell Boulevard
Hopkinsville, Kentucky 42240
Phone: 270-886-1302
     800-359-4753 (toll-free)
E-mail: bmchoadm@brownmackie.edu
Web site: http://www.brownmackie.edu

BROWN MACKIE COLLEGE–KANSAS CITY

LENEXA, KANSAS

The College and Its Mission

Brown Mackie College–Kansas City is dedicated to providing education programs that prepare students for entry-level positions in a competitive, rapidly changing workplace. The College provides associate degree, diploma, and certificate programs in the areas of business and accounting, allied health sciences, legal studies, and computer technology to approximately 370 students.

The College was originally founded in Salina, Kansas, in July 1892 as the Kansas Wesleyan School of Business. In 1938, the College was incorporated as the Brown Mackie School of Business under the ownership of former Kansas Wesleyan instructors Perry E. Brown and A. B. Mackie. It became Brown Mackie College in January 1975.

Brown Mackie College in Lenexa, Kansas, is a branch of Brown Mackie College in Salina, Kansas, which is accredited by the Higher Learning Commission and is a member of the North Central Association (NCA) of Colleges and Schools, 30 North LaSalle Street, Suite 2400, Chicago, Illinois 60602; 800-621-7440; http://www.ncahlc.org. The College, which operates in Salina and Lenexa, Kansas, is approved and authorized to grant the Associate of Applied Science degree by the Kansas Board of Regents, 1000 Southwest Jackson Street, Suite 520, Topeka, Kansas 66612-1368.

The College is a nonresidential, smoke-free institution and is owned by Education Management Corporation, 210 Sixth Avenue, 33rd Floor, Pittsburgh, Pennsylvania 15222-2603; 800-275-2440 (toll-free); http://www.edmc.edu.

Academic Programs

Brown Mackie College–Kansas City provides higher education to traditional and nontraditional students through associate degree, diploma, and certificate programs that assist them in enhancing their career opportunities, broadening their perspectives through appropriate general education courses, thinking independently and critically, and improving problem-solving abilities. The College strives to develop within its students the desire for lifelong and continued education. Each College quarter comprises twelve weeks.

Associate Degree Programs Associate degree programs require a minimum of ten quarters to complete. Programs are offered on a year-round basis, providing students with the ability to work uninterrupted toward their degrees. The Associate of Applied Science degree (96 credits) is awarded in accounting technology, business management, computer-aided design and drafting technology, computer software technology, criminal justice, medical assisting, medical office management, nursing, nursing-bridge studies, paralegal studies, and sales and marketing.

Diploma Programs The College also offers diploma programs (48 credits) in accounting, advertising, business, computer-aided design and drafting technician studies, computer applications, computer software applications, criminal justice, medical assistant studies, medical coding and billing, and paralegal assistant studies.

Certificate Program A certificate program (24 credits) is offered in practical nursing.

Costs

Tuition is $199 per credit hour. Textbook fees are estimated at $360 per quarter.

Financial Aid

The College maintains a full-time staff of financial aid professionals to assist qualified students in obtaining financial assistance. The College participates in several student aid programs. Forms of financial aid available to qualified students through federal resources include Federal Pell Grants, Federal Supplemental Educational Opportunity Grants (FSEOG), the Federal Work-Study Program, Federal Perkins Loans, Federal Stafford Student Loans (subsidized and unsubsidized), and the Federal PLUS Program. Eligible students may apply for veterans' educational benefits. Students with physical or mental disabilities that are a handicap to employment may be eligible for training services through the state Vocational Rehabilitation Agency. For further information, students should contact the College Student Financial Services Office.

Scholarship applications are reviewed by the College President, who is solely responsible for award decisions. Awards are disbursed to recipients in monthly increments over the academic year for which the scholarship has been awarded. All scholarship recipients must maintain full-time status and a minimum cumulative grade point average, or they must forfeit their awards. The total value of all college scholarships awarded to any one student shall not exceed the cost of one academic year (36 credits) of tuition.

Faculty

There are 7 full-time faculty members. The average classroom size is 14:1, with a student-faculty ratio of 50:1.

Facilities and Resources

In addition to classrooms and computer labs, the College maintains a library of curriculum-related resources, technical and general education materials, academic and professional periodicals, and audiovisual resources. Internet access also is available for research. The College has a bookstore that stocks texts, courseware, and other educational supplies required for courses and a variety of personal, recreational, and gift items,

including apparel, supplies, and general merchandise incorporating the College logo. Hours are posted at the bookstore entrance.

Location

Brown Mackie College–Kansas City is located at 9705 Lenexa Drive in Lenexa, Kansas, just off the I-435 loop at 95th Street in Johnson County.

Admission Requirements

Each applicant for admission is assigned an Assistant Director of Admissions, who directs the applicant through the steps of the admissions process, providing information on curriculum, policies, procedures, and services and assisting the applicant in setting necessary appointments and interviews. To qualify for admission, each applicant must provide documentation of graduation from an accredited high school or from a state-approved secondary education curriculum or provide official documentation of high school graduation equivalency. All transcripts become the property of the College. Admission to the College is based upon the applicant's meeting the above requirements, a review of the applicant's previous education records, and a review of the applicant's career interests. If previous academic records indicate that the College's education and training would not benefit the applicant, the College reserves the right to advise the applicant not to enroll. Special requirements for enrollment into certain programs are discussed in the descriptions of those programs.

Application and Information

Applicants must complete and submit an application form, along with documentation of graduation from an accredited high school or state-approved secondary education curriculum or official documentation of high school graduation equivalency. For additional information, prospective students should contact:

Director of Admissions
Brown Mackie College–Kansas City
9705 Lenexa Drive
Lenexa, Kansas 66215

Phone: 913-768-1900
Fax: 800-635-9101 (toll-free)
E-mail: dwhite@brownmackie.edu
Web site: http://www.brownmackie.edu

BROWN MACKIE COLLEGE–LOUISVILLE

LOUISVILLE, KENTUCKY

The College and Its Mission

Brown Mackie College–Louisville is dedicated to providing education programs that prepare students for entry-level positions in a competitive, rapidly changing workplace. The College provides associate degree, diploma programs, and certificate programs in the areas of business and accounting, the allied health sciences, legal studies, computer technology, graphic design, and electronics to approximately 300 students.

Brown Mackie College–Louisville opened in 1972 as RETS Institute of Technology. The first RETS school was founded in 1935 in Detroit in response to the rapid growth of radio broadcasting and the need for qualified radio technicians. The RETS Institute changed its name to Brown Mackie College–Louisville in 2004.

Brown Mackie College–Louisville is accredited by the Accrediting Council for Independent Colleges and Schools (ACICS) to award associate degrees, certificates, and diplomas. ACICS is listed as a nationally recognized accrediting agency by the U.S. Department of Education. Its accreditation of degree-granting institutions is recognized by the Council for Higher Education Accreditation. ACICS can be contacted at 750 First Street NE, Suite 980, Washington, D.C. 20002-4241; 202-336-6780.

The College is a nonresidential, smoke-free institution and is owned by Education Management Corporation (EDMC), 210 Sixth Avenue, 33rd floor, Pittsburgh, Pennsylvania 15222-2603; http://www.edmc.edu.

Academic Programs

Brown Mackie College–Louisville provides higher education to traditional and nontraditional students through associate degree, diploma, and certificate programs that assist them in enhancing their career opportunities, broadening their perspectives through appropriate general education courses, thinking independently and critically, and improving problem-solving abilities.

Each College quarter comprises ten to twelve weeks. Associate degree programs require a minimum of eight quarters to complete. Programs are offered on a year-round basis, providing students with the ability to work uninterrupted toward their degrees.

Associate Degree Programs The Associate of Applied Business degree (96 credits) is awarded in accounting technology, business management, computer networking and applications, criminal justice, graphic design, and paralegal studies. The Associate of Applied Science degree (96 credits) is awarded in early childhood education, electronics, gerontology, health-care administration, medical assisting, pharmacy technology, surgical technology, and veterinary technician studies.

Diploma Programs The College offers diploma programs (48 credits) in electronics, medical assistant studies, and paralegal assistant studies.

Certificate Program The College offers a certificate program (24 credits) in computer networking.

Costs

Tuition is $179 per credit hour. Textbook fees vary according to program.

Financial Aid

The College maintains a full-time staff of financial aid professionals to assist qualified students in obtaining financial assistance. The College participates in several student aid programs. Forms of financial aid available to qualified students through federal resources include the Federal Pell Grant Program, Federal Supplemental Educational Opportunity Grant (FSEOG) Program, Federal Work-Study Program, Federal Perkins Loan Program, Federal Stafford Student Loan Program (subsidized and unsubsidized), and the Federal PLUS Loan Program. Students may apply for state-based award programs, such as the College Access Program (CAP) Grant Program and the Kentucky Educational Excellence Award (KEES). Eligible students may also apply for veterans' benefits. Students with physical or mental disabilities that are a handicap to employment may be eligible for training services through the state Agency for Vocational Rehabilitation. For further information, students should contact the College Student Financial Services Office.

Each year, the College makes available scholarships of $1000 each to qualifying seniors from area high schools. No more than one scholarship is awarded per high school. In order to qualify, a senior must be graduating from a participating high school, must be maintaining a cumulative grade point average of at least 2.0, and must submit a brief essay. The student's extracurricular activities and community service are also considered. The President's Scholarship is available only to students enrolling in one of the College's degree programs. Students awarded the scholarship must enroll at Brown Mackie College–Louisville between June and September immediately following their high school graduation. Applications for these scholarships can be obtained from the guidance departments of participating high schools. These applications must be completed and returned to the College by March 31. Those awarded scholarships are notified by April 30.

Faculty

There are 6 full-time and 20 part-time faculty members at the College. The average student-faculty ratio is 11:1.

Facilities and Resources

Brown Mackie College–Louisville has more than 23,000 square feet of multipurpose classrooms, including networked computer laboratories, electronics laboratories, a resource center, and offices for administrative personnel as well as for student services such as admissions, student financial services, and career-services assistance.

Location

The College is at 3605 Fern Valley Road, Louisville, Kentucky, conveniently located at the intersection of Fern Valley and Preston Highway.

Admission Requirements

Each applicant for admission is assigned an Assistant Director of Admissions who directs the applicant through the steps of the admissions process, providing information on curriculum, policies, procedures, and services and assisting the applicant in setting necessary appointments and interviews. To qualify for admission, each applicant must provide documentation of graduation from an accredited high school or completion of a state-approved secondary education curriculum or provide official documentation of high school graduation equivalency. All transcripts become the property of the College. Admission to the College is based on the applicant's meeting the above requirements, a review of the applicant's previous educational records, and a review of the applicant's career interests. If previous academic records indicate that the College's education and training would not benefit the applicant, the College reserves the right to advise the applicant not to enroll. Special requirements for enrollment into certain programs are discussed in the descriptions of those programs.

Application and Information

Applicants must complete and submit an application form along with documentation of graduation from an accredited high school or completion of state-approved secondary education curriculum or provide official documentation of high school graduation equivalency. For additional information, prospective students should contact:

Director of Admissions
Brown Mackie College–Louisville
3605 Fern Valley Road
Louisville, Kentucky 40219
Phone: 502-968-7191
      800-999-7387 (toll-free)
Fax: 502-357-9956
E-mail: mdonahue@brownmackie.edu
Web site: http://www.brownmackie.edu

BROWN MACKIE COLLEGE–MERRILLVILLE

MERRILLVILLE, INDIANA

The College and Its Mission

Brown Mackie College–Merrillville is dedicated to providing educational programs that prepare students for entry-level positions in a competitive, rapidly changing workplace. The College provides associate degree, diploma, and certificate programs in business and accounting, allied health sciences, legal studies, computer technology, and electronics to approximately 615 students.

Founded in 1890 by A. N. Hirons as LaPorte Business College in LaPorte, Indiana, the institution later became known as Commonwealth Business College. In 1919, ownership was transferred to Grace and J. J. Moore, who successfully operated the College under the name of Reese School of Business for several decades. In 1975, the College came under the ownership of Steven C. Smith as Commonwealth Business College. A second location, now known as Brown Mackie College–Merrillville, was opened in 1984, in Merrillville, Indiana. The College changed ownership again in September 2003 when it was acquired by Education Management Corporation, and the College name was changed to Brown Mackie College–Merrillville in November 2004.

Brown Mackie College–Merrillville is accredited by the Accrediting Council for Independent Colleges and Schools (ACICS) to award associate degrees and certificates. ACICS is listed as a nationally recognized accrediting agency by the U.S. Department of Education. Its accreditation of degree-granting institutions also is recognized by the Council for Higher Education Accreditation. ACICS can be contacted at 750 First Street, NE, Suite 980, Washington, D.C. 20002-4241; 202-336-6780. Brown Mackie College–Merrillville has two branches: Brown Mackie College–Michigan City and Brown Mackie College–Moline.

The College's Medical Assisting degree program is accredited by the Accrediting Bureau of Health Education Schools (ABHES), 7777 Leesburg Pike, Suite 314N, Falls Church, Virginia 22403; 703-917-9503. The College's diploma program in practical nursing is accredited by the Health Professions Bureau (Attn: Indiana State Board of Nursing) 402 West Washington Street, Room W066, Indianapolis, Indiana 46204; 317-234-2043.

The College is a nonresidential, smoke-free institution and a subsidiary of Education Management Corporation, 210 Sixth Avenue, 33rd floor, Pittsburgh, Pennsylvania 15222-2603; http://www.edmc.edu.

Academic Programs

Brown Mackie College–Merrillville provides higher education to traditional and nontraditional students through associate degree, diploma, and certificate programs that assist them in enhancing their career opportunities, broadening their perspectives through appropriate general education courses, thinking independently and critically, and improving problem-solving abilities. The College strives to develop within its students the desire for lifelong and continued education.

Each College quarter comprises ten to twelve weeks. Associate degree programs require a minimum of eight quarters to complete. Programs are offered on a year-round basis, providing students with the ability to work uninterrupted toward completion of their programs.

Associate Degree Programs The Associate of Science degree (96 credits) is awarded in accounting technology, administration in gerontology, business management, computer software technology, criminal justice, medical assisting, medical office management, paralegal studies, and surgical technology.

Diploma Programs A diploma program (76 credits) in practical nursing is offered.

Certificate Programs The College offers certificate programs (48 credits) in accounting, business, computer software applications, criminal justice, medical assistant studies, and paralegal assistant studies.

Costs

Tuition for programs in the 2005–06 academic year was $179 per credit hour with the exception of the Practical Nursing Diploma program, which was $250 per credit hour. The length of the program determines total cost. Textbook fees vary according to program.

Financial Aid

The College maintains a full-time staff of financial aid professionals to assist qualified students in obtaining financial assistance. The College participates in several student aid programs. Forms of financial aid available through federal resources include the Federal Pell Grant Program, Federal Supplemental Educational Opportunity Grant (FSEOG) Program, Federal Work-Study Program, Federal Perkins Loan Program, Federal Stafford Student Loan Program (subsidized and unsubsidized), and the Federal PLUS Loan Program. Eligible students may apply for Indiana state awards such as the Higher Education Award and Twenty-First Century Scholarships for high school students, the Core 40 awards, and veterans' educational benefits. Students with physical or mental disabilities that are a handicap to employment may be eligible for training services through the state Agency for Vocational Rehabilitation.

For further information, students should contact the College Student Financial Services Office.

Each year, the College makes available scholarships of $1000 each to qualifying seniors from area high schools. No more than one scholarship is awarded per high school. In order to qualify, a senior must be graduating from a participating high school, must be maintaining a cumulative grade point average of at least 2.0, and must submit a brief essay. The student's extracurricular activities and community service are also considered. The President's Scholarship is available only to students enrolling in one of the College's degree programs. Students awarded the scholarship must enroll at Brown Mackie

College–Merrillville between June and September immediately following their high school graduation. Applications for these scholarships can be obtained from the guidance departments of participating high schools. These applications must be completed and returned to the College by March 31. Those awarded scholarships are notified by April 30.

Faculty

There are 11 full-time and 29 part-time faculty members at the College who are practitioners in their fields of expertise. The average student-faculty ratio is 17:1.

Facilities and Resources

Occupying 18,000 square feet, Brown Mackie College–Merrillville was opened to students in October 1998 in the Twin Towers complex of Merrillville and comprises several instructional rooms, including five computer labs with networked computers and four medical laboratories. The administrative offices, college library, and student lounge are all easily accessible to students. The college bookstore stocks texts, courseware, and other educational supplies required for courses at the College. Students also find a variety of personal, recreational, and gift items, including apparel, supplies, and general merchandise incorporating the College logo. Hours are posted at the bookstore entrance. A spacious parking lot provides ample parking at no additional charge.

Location

Brown Mackie College–Merrillville is located in northwest Indiana, in the Twin Towers business complex of Merrillville just west of the intersection of U.S. Route 30 and Interstate 65.

Admission Requirements

Each applicant for admission is assigned an Assistant Director of Admissions who directs the applicant through the steps of the admissions process, providing information on curriculum, policies, procedures, and services, and assisting the applicant in setting necessary appointments and interviews. To qualify for admission, each applicant must provide documentation of graduation from an accredited high school or completion of a state-approved secondary education curriculum or provide official documentation of high school graduation equivalency. All transcripts become the property of the College. Admission to the College is based upon the applicant's meeting the above requirements, a review of the applicant's previous educational records, and a review of the applicant's career interests. If previous academic records indicate that the College's education and training would not benefit the applicant, the College reserves the right to advise the applicant not to enroll. Special requirements for enrollment into certain programs are discussed in the descriptions of those programs.

Application and Information

Applicants must complete and submit an application form along with documentation of graduation from an accredited high school or completion of state-approved secondary education curriculum or provide official documentation of high school graduation equivalency. For additional information, prospective students should contact:

Director of Admissions
Brown Mackie College–Merrillville
1000 East 80th Place, Suite 101N
Merrillville, Indiana 46410
Phone: 219-769-3321
       800-258-3321 (toll-free)
Fax: 219-738-1076
E-mail: bmcmeadm@brownmackie.edu
Web site: http://www.brownmackie.edu

BROWN MACKIE COLLEGE–MIAMI

MIAMI, FLORIDA

BROWN MACKIE COLLEGE
MIAMI™

The College and Its Mission

Brown Mackie College–Miami is dedicated to providing education programs that prepare students for entry-level positions in a competitive, rapidly changing workplace. The College provides associate degree and diploma programs in the areas of business and accounting, allied health sciences, legal studies, and computer technology to 311 students.

Brown Mackie College–Miami was established as a branch of Brown Mackie College–Cincinnati in 2004. Brown Mackie College–Cincinnati was founded in Cincinnati, Ohio, in February 1927 as a traditional business college. In 1964, the College was granted accreditation as a business school by the Association of Independent Colleges and Schools (AICS) and as a junior college of business by the Accrediting Council of Independent Colleges and Schools (ACICS) in 1972. The school is accredited by ACICS to award associate degrees and diplomas. ACICS is listed as a nationally recognized accrediting agency by the United States Department of Education. ACICS can be contacted at 750 First Street, NE, Suite 980, Washington, D.C. 20002-4241; 202-336-6780. ACICS's accreditation of degree-granting institutions is also recognized by the Council for Higher Education Accreditation.

The College is a nonresidential, smoke-free institution. The College is owned and operated by Education Management Corporation, 210 Sixth Avenue, 33rd Floor, Pittsburgh, Pennsylvania 15222-2603; http://www.edmc.edu.

Students who are unable to commute daily from their homes may request housing assistance from the Housing Department.

Academic Programs

Brown Mackie College–Miami provides higher education to traditional and nontraditional students through associate degree and diploma programs that assist them in enhancing their career opportunities, broadening their perspectives through appropriate general education courses, thinking independently and critically, and improving problem-solving abilities. The College strives to develop within its students the desire for lifelong and continued education.

Each College quarter comprises twelve weeks. Associate degree programs require a minimum of eight quarters to complete. Programs are offered on a year-round basis, providing students with the ability to work uninterrupted toward their degree.

Associate Degree Programs: The Associate of Science degree (96 credits) is awarded in accounting technology, business management, computer software technology, criminal justice, medical assisting, and paralegal studies.

Diploma Programs: The College also offers diploma programs (48 credits) in accounting, criminal justice, medical assistant studies, and paralegal assistant studies.

Costs

Tuition is $239 per credit hour. Textbook fees vary according to the program.

Financial Aid

The College maintains a full-time staff of financial aid professionals to assist qualified students in obtaining financial assistance. The College participates in several student aid programs. Forms of financial aid available to qualified students through federal resources include the Federal Pell Grant Program, Federal Supplemental Educational Opportunity Grant (FSEOG) Program, Federal Work-Study Program, Federal Perkins Loan Program, Federal Stafford Student Loan Program (subsidized and unsubsidized), and Federal PLUS loan program. Eligible students may apply for veterans' educational benefits. Students with physical or mental disabilities that are a handicap to employment may be eligible for training services through the state Agency for Vocational Rehabilitation. For further information, students should contact the College Student Financial Services Office.

Faculty

There are 19 adjunct faculty members at the College. The average student-faculty ratio is 18:1.

Academic Facilities

Brown Mackie College–Miami co-locates with the Miami International University of Art & Design in 80,000 square feet of shared and dedicated space that includes computer labs, medical labs, lecture rooms, administrative offices, and a student lounge. The College facilities comprise media presentation rooms for special instructional needs and a library with more than 19,750 volumes, including books and visual aids and subscriptions to more than 200 periodicals specific to the academic programs offered. The College bookstore stocks texts, courseware, and other educational supplies required for courses at the College. Students also find a variety of personal, recreational, and gift items, including apparel, supplies, and general merchandise incorporating the College logo. Hours are posted at the bookstore entrance.

Location

Brown Mackie College–Miami occupies space within the newly renovated OMNI building at 1501 Biscayne Boulevard in Miami, Florida. It is conveniently located adjacent to the

OMNI Metro Mover and bus stop, with access to Metro Rail and Florida's regional Tri-Rail system. Ample parking is also available.

Admission Requirements

Each applicant for admission is assigned an Assistant Director of Admissions, who directs the applicant through the steps of the admissions process, providing information on curriculum, policies, procedures, and services and assisting the applicant in setting necessary appointments and interviews. To qualify for admission, each applicant must provide documentation of graduation from an accredited high school or from a state-approved secondary education curriculum or provide official documentation of high school graduation equivalency. All transcripts become the property of the College. Admission to the College is based on the applicant's meeting the above requirements, a review of the applicant's previous educational records, and a review of the applicant's career interests. If previous academic records indicate that the College's education and training would not benefit the applicant, the College reserves the right to advise the applicant not to enroll. Special requirements for enrollment into certain programs are discussed in the descriptions of those programs.

Application and Information

Applicants must complete and submit an application form, along with documentation of graduation from an accredited high school or state-approved secondary education curriculum or official documentation of high school graduation equivalency.

For additional information, prospective students should contact:

Director of Admissions
Brown Mackie College–Miami
1501 Biscayne Boulevard
Miami, Florida 33132-1418
Phone: 305-341-6600
       866-505-0335 (toll-free)
Fax: 305-373-8814
E-mail: mkoontz@brownmackie.edu
Web site: http://www.brownmackie.edu

BROWN MACKIE COLLEGE– MICHIGAN CITY

MICHIGAN CITY, INDIANA

BROWN MACKIE COLLEGE
MICHIGAN CITY™

The College and Its Mission

Brown Mackie College–Michigan City is dedicated to providing education programs that prepare students for entry-level positions in a competitive, rapidly changing workplace. The College provides associate degree and certificate programs in the areas of business and accounting, the allied health sciences, legal studies, electronics, and computer technology to 313 students.

Founded in 1890 by A. N. Hirons as LaPorte Business College in LaPorte, Indiana, the institution later became known as Commonwealth Business College. In 1919, ownership was transferred to Grace and J. J. Moore, who successfully operated the College under the name of Reese School of Business for several decades. In 1975, the College came under the ownership of Steven C. Smith as Commonwealth Business College. In 1997, the College site relocated to its present site in Michigan City, Indiana. The College was acquired by Education Management Corporation on September 2, 2003, and changed its name to Brown Mackie College–Michigan City in November 2004.

Brown Mackie College–Michigan City is accredited by the Accrediting Council for Independent Colleges and Schools (ACICS) to award associate degrees and certificates. ACICS is listed as a nationally recognized accrediting agency by the U.S. Department of Education. Its accreditation of degree-granting institutions is recognized by the Council for Higher Education Accreditation. ACICS can be reached at 750 First Street NE, Suite 980, Washington, D.C. 20002-4241; 202-336-6780. (AC 0138)

The College's medical assisting degree program is accredited by the Accrediting Bureau of Health Education Schools (ABHES), 803 West Broad Street, Suite 730, Falls Church, Virginia 22046; 703-533-2082.

The College is a nonresidential, smoke-free institution owned and operated by Education Management Corporation, 210 Sixth Avenue, 33rd floor, Pittsburgh, Pennsylvania 15222-2603; http://www.edmc.edu.

Academic Programs

Brown Mackie College–Michigan City provides higher education to traditional and nontraditional students through associate degree and certificate programs that assist them in enhancing their career opportunities, broadening their perspectives through appropriate general education courses, thinking independently and critically, and improving problem-solving abilities. The College strives to develop within its students the desire for lifelong and continued education.

Each College quarter comprises twelve weeks. Associate degree programs require a minimum of eight quarters to complete. Programs are offered on a year-round basis, providing students with the ability to work uninterrupted toward their degrees.

Associate Degree Programs: The Associate of Science degree (96 credits) is awarded in accounting technology, business management, computer software technology, criminal justice, early childhood education, medical assisting, medical office management, paralegal studies, and surgical technology.

Certificate Programs: The College offers certificate programs (48 credits) in accounting, business, computer software applications, criminal justice, medical assistant studies, and paralegal assistant studies.

Costs

Tuition is $189 per credit hour. Textbook fees vary according to program.

Financial Aid

The College maintains a full-time staff of financial aid professionals to assist qualified students in obtaining financial assistance. The College participates in several student aid programs. Forms of financial aid available to qualified students through federal resources include the Federal Pell Grant Program, Federal Supplemental Educational Opportunity Grant (FSEOG) Program, Federal Work-Study Program, Federal Stafford Student Loan Program (subsidized and unsubsidized), and Federal PLUS loan program. Eligible students may apply for Indiana state awards such as the Higher Education Award and Twenty-First Century Scholarships for high school students, the Core 40 awards, and veterans' educational benefits. Students with physical or mental disabilities that are a handicap to employment may be eligible for training services through the state Agency for Vocational Rehabilitation. For further information, students should contact the College Student Financial Services Office.

Faculty

There are 4 full-time and 18 part-time faculty members at the College. The average student-faculty ratio is 13:1. Each student is assigned a faculty adviser.

Facilities and Resources

In 2002, the College underwent a major renovation and completed the addition of 3,360 square feet, for a total of 10,338 square feet of occupancy. An additional medical laboratory, a larger library, new classrooms, and a bookstore were added. All classrooms and the library are equipped with new technology, including multimedia projectors, surround-sound audio systems, VCRs, and DVD players. Five of the ten new classrooms are equipped with networked computer systems. The two medical laboratories contain newly acquired medical equipment and instructional tools and supplies. Administrative offices are easily accessible to students. Additional parking spaces were added in 2002, providing students and employees with ample parking at no additional charge.

Location

Brown Mackie College–Michigan City is located in northwest Indiana, 1 mile north of Interstate 94, near the intersection of routes 20 and 421.

Admission Requirements

Each applicant for admission is assigned an Assistant Director of Admissions, who directs the applicant through the steps of the admissions process, providing information on curriculum, policies, procedures, and services and assisting the applicant in setting necessary appointments and interviews. To qualify for admission, each applicant must provide documentation of graduation from an accredited high school or completion of a state-approved secondary education curriculum or provide official documentation of high school graduation equivalency. All transcripts become the property of the College. Admission to the College is based on the applicant's meeting the above requirements, a review of the applicant's previous educational records, and a review of the applicant's career interests. If previous academic records indicate that the College's education and training would not benefit the applicant, the College reserves the right to advise the applicant not to enroll. Special requirements for enrollment into certain programs are discussed in the descriptions of those programs.

Application and Information

Applicants must complete and submit an application form along with documentation of graduation from an accredited high school or completion of a state-approved secondary education curriculum or provide official documentation of high school graduation equivalency. For additional information, prospective students should contact:

Director of Admissions
Brown Mackie College–Michigan City
325 East U.S. Highway 20
Michigan City, Indiana 46360
Phone: 219-877-3100
        800-519-2416 (toll-free)
Fax: 219-877-3110
E-mail: nspenny@brownmackie.edu
Web site: http://www.brownmackie.edu

BROWN MACKIE COLLEGE–MOLINE
MOLINE, ILLINOIS

The College and Its Mission

Brown Mackie College–Moline is dedicated to providing education programs that prepare students for entry-level positions in a competitive, rapidly changing workplace. The College provides diploma programs in business, health sciences, legal studies, information technology, and electronic fields to 153 students.

Founded in 1890 by A. N. Hirons as LaPorte Business College in LaPorte, Indiana, the institution later became known as Commonwealth Business College. In 1919, ownership was transferred to Grace and J. J. Moore, who successfully operated the College for almost thirty years. Following World War II, Harley and Stephanie Reese operated the College under the name of Reese School of Business for several decades.

In 1975, the College came under the ownership of Steven C. Smith as Commonwealth Business College. A second location, now known as Brown Mackie College–Merrillville, was opened in 1984 in Merrillville, Indiana, and a third location was opened a year later in Davenport, Iowa. In 1987, the Davenport location relocated to its present site in Moline, Illinois. In September 2003, the College changed ownership again when it was acquired by Education Management Corporation, and the College's name was changed to Brown Mackie College–Moline in November 2004.

Brown Mackie College–Moline is accredited by the Accrediting Council for Independent Colleges and Schools (ACICS) to award diplomas and certificates. The Accrediting Council for Independent Colleges and Schools is listed as a nationally recognized accrediting agency by the United States Department of Education. Its accreditation of degree-granting institutions also is recognized by the Council for Higher Education Accreditation. ACICS can be contacted at 750 First Street NE, Suite 980, Washington, D.C. 20002-4241; 202-336-6780.

The College is a nonresidential, smoke-free institution and is owned and operated by Education Management Corporation, 210 Sixth Avenue, 33rd floor, Pittsburgh, Pennsylvania 15222-2603; 800-275-2440 (toll-free); http://www.edmc.edu.

Academic Programs

Brown Mackie College–Moline provides higher education to traditional and nontraditional students through diploma programs that assist them in enhancing their career opportunities, broadening their perspectives through appropriate general education courses, thinking independently and critically, and improving problem-solving abilities. The College strives to develop within its students the desire for lifelong and continued education.

Each College quarter comprises twelve weeks. Programs are offered on a year-round basis, providing students with the ability to work uninterrupted toward the completion of their programs.

Diploma Programs: The College offers diploma programs (48 credits) in accounting, business, computer software applications, medical assistant studies, medical office management, and paralegal studies.

Costs

Tuition for the 2006–07 academic year was $179 per credit hour; fees were $10 per credit hour. Textbook costs vary by program.

Financial Aid

The College maintains a full-time staff of financial aid professionals to assist qualified students in obtaining the financial assistance they require to meet their educational expenses. The College participates in several student aid programs. Forms of financial aid available through federal resources include the Federal Pell Grant Program, Federal Supplemental Educational Opportunity Grant (FSEOG) Program, Federal Work-Study Program, Federal Perkins Loan Program, Federal Stafford Student Loan Program (subsidized and unsubsidized), and Federal PLUS loan program. Eligible students may apply for veterans' educational benefits. Students with physical or mental disabilities that are a handicap to employment may be eligible for training services through the state Agency for Vocational Rehabilitation. For further information, students should contact the College Student Financial Services Office.

Each year, the College makes available scholarships of $1000 each to qualifying seniors from area high schools. Only one scholarship is awarded per high school. In order to qualify, a senior must be graduating from a participating high school, maintain a cumulative grade point average of at least 2.0, and submit a brief essay. The student's extracurricular activities and community service are also considered. The President's Scholarship is available only to students enrolling in one of the College's diploma programs. Students awarded the scholarship must enroll at Brown Mackie College–Moline between June and September immediately following their high school graduation. Applications for these scholarships can be obtained from the guidance departments of participating high schools. These applications must be completed and returned to the College by March 31. Those who are awarded scholarships are notified by April 30.

Faculty

Brown Mackie College–Moline has 10 full- and part-time faculty members, with an average student-faculty ratio of 15:1.

Facilities and Resources

The College maintains a library of curriculum-related resources. Technical and general education materials, academic and professional periodicals, and audiovisual resources are available to both students and faculty members. Students have borrowing privileges at several local libraries. Internet access is available for research.

Location

Brown Mackie College–Moline is located at 1527 47th Avenue in Moline, Illinois. The College is easily accessible by public transportation, and ample parking is available at no charge.

Admission Requirements

Each applicant for admission is assigned an Assistant Director of Admissions, who directs the applicant through the steps of the admissions process, providing information on curriculum, policies, procedures, and services and assisting the applicant in setting necessary appointments and interviews.

To qualify for admission, each applicant must provide documentation of graduation from an accredited high school or from a state-approved secondary education curriculum or provide official documentation of high school graduation equivalency. All transcripts become the property of the College. Admission to the College is based on the applicant's meeting the above requirements, a review of the applicant's previous education records, and a review of the applicant's career interests. If previous academic records indicate that the College's education and training would not benefit the applicant, the College reserves the right to advise the applicant not to enroll. Special requirements for enrollment into certain programs are discussed in the descriptions of those programs.

Application and Information

Applicants must complete and submit an application form along with documentation of graduation from an accredited high school or state-approved secondary education curriculum, or applicants must provide official documentation of high school graduation equivalency. For further information, prospective students should contact:

Director of Admissions
Brown Mackie College–Moline
1527 47th Avenue
Moline, Illinois 61265

Phone: 309-762-2100
Fax: 309-762-2374
E-mail: asandoval@brownmackie.edu
Web site: http://www.brownmackie.edu

BROWN MACKIE COLLEGE–NORTH CANTON

NORTH CANTON, OHIO

BROWN MACKIE COLLEGE
NORTH CANTON™

The College and Its Mission

Brown Mackie College–North Canton is dedicated to providing educational programs that prepare students for entry-level positions in a competitive, rapidly changing workplace. The College provides associate degree and diploma programs in business and accounting, allied health sciences, legal studies, computer technology and electronics to approximately 930 students.

Brown Mackie College–North Canton opened its classroom doors in January 1984 as National Electronics Institute (NEI). In July 1985, the school was purchased by Electronics Technology Institute of Cleveland and became a branch facility, accredited by the Accrediting Commission of the National Association of Trade and Technical Schools (NATTS). The name was changed to Electronic Technology Institute. In June 2002, the College came under the ownership of Southern Ohio College LLC, and the College's name then changed to AEC Southern Ohio College. In September 2003, the College came under the ownership of Education Management Corporation (EDMC), and the name of the College was subsequently changed to Brown Mackie College in November 2004.

Brown Mackie College–North Canton is accredited by the Accrediting Council for Independent Colleges and Schools (ACICS) to award associate degrees and diplomas. ACICS is listed as a nationally recognized accrediting agency by the U.S. Department of Education. Its accreditation of degree-granting institutions also is recognized by the Council for Higher Education Accreditation. ACICS may be contacted at 750 First Street, NE, Suite 980, Washington, D.C. 20002-4241; phone: 202-336-6780.

The College is a nonresidential, smoke-free institution and is owned and operated by Education Management Corporation, 210 Sixth Avenue, 33rd Floor, Pittsburgh, Pennsylvania 15222-2603; Web site: http://www.edmc.edu.

Academic Programs

Brown Mackie College–North Canton provides higher education to traditional and nontraditional students through associate degree and diploma programs that assist them in enhancing their career opportunities, broadening their perspectives through appropriate general education courses, thinking independently and critically, and improving problem-solving abilities. The College strives to develop within its students the desire for lifelong and continued education. Each College quarter comprises twelve weeks.

Associate Degree Programs Associate degree programs require a minimum of eight quarters to complete. Programs are offered on a year-round basis, providing students with the ability to work uninterrupted toward completion of their programs. The Associate of Applied Business degree (96 credits) is awarded in accounting technology, business management, criminal justice, and paralegal studies. The Associate of Applied Science degree is awarded in computer-aided design and drafting technology, computer networking and applications, health-care administration, health-care assisting, medical assisting, and pharmacy technology.

Diploma Programs The College offers diploma programs (48 credits) in accounting, business, computer-aided design and drafting technician studies, criminal justice, medical assistant studies, paralegal assistant studies, and practical nursing.

Costs

Tuition for programs in the 2005–06 academic year was $179 per credit hour. Textbook fees were approximately $425 per quarter.

Financial Aid

The College maintains a full-time staff of financial aid professionals to assist qualified students in obtaining financial assistance. The College participates in several student aid programs. Forms of financial aid available through federal resources include Federal Pell Grants, Federal Supplemental Educational Opportunity Grants (FSEOG), the Federal Work-Study Program, Federal Perkins Loans, Federal Stafford Student Loans (subsidized and unsubsidized), and the Federal PLUS Program. Eligible students may apply for state awards such as the Ohio Instructional Grant (OIG) and veterans' educational benefits. Students with physical or mental disabilities that are a handicap to employment may be eligible for training services through the state Vocational Rehabilitation Agency. For further information, students should contact the College Student Financial Services Office.

Each year, the College makes available President's Scholarships of $1000 each to qualifying seniors from area high schools. No more than one scholarship is awarded per high school. In order to qualify, a senior must be graduating from a participating high school, maintain a cumulative grade point average of at least 2.0, and submit a brief essay. The student's extracurricular activities and community service are also considered. The President's Scholarship is available only to students enrolling in one of the College's degree programs. Students who receive the scholarship must enroll at Brown Mackie College–North Canton between June and September immediately following their high school graduation. Applications for these scholarships can be obtained from the guidance departments of participating high schools. These applications must be completed and returned to the College by March 31. Those awarded scholarships are notified by April 30.

Faculty

There are 8 full-time and 21 part-time faculty members. The average student-faculty ratio is 21:1. Each student has an adviser.

Facilities and Resources

In addition to classrooms and computer labs, the College maintains a library of curriculum-related resources, technical and general education materials, academic and professional periodicals, and audiovisual resources. Internet access also is available for research.

Location

Brown Mackie College–North Canton is located at 4300 Munson Street NW in North Canton, Ohio.

Admission Requirements

Each applicant for admission is assigned an Assistant Director of Admissions, who directs the applicant through the steps of the admissions process, providing information on curriculum, policies, procedures, and services and assisting the applicant in setting necessary appointments and interviews. To qualify for admission, each applicant must provide documentation of graduation from an accredited high school or from a state-approved secondary education curriculum or provide official documentation of high school graduation equivalency. All transcripts become the property of the College. Admission to the College is based upon the applicant's meeting the above requirements, a review of the applicant's previous educational records, and a review of the applicant's career interests. If previous academic records indicate that the College's education and training would not benefit the applicant, the College reserves the right to advise the applicant not to enroll. Special requirements for enrollment into certain programs are discussed in the descriptions of those programs.

Application and Information

Applicants must complete and submit an application form, along with documentation of graduation from an accredited high school or state-approved secondary education curriculum or official documentation of high school graduation equivalency. For further information, prospective students should contact:

Director of Admissions
Brown Mackie College–North Canton
4300 Munson Street NW
North Canton, Ohio 44718-3674

Phone: 330-494-1214
Fax: 330-494-8112
E-mail: bmcncadm@brownmackie.edu
Web site: http://www.brownmackie.edu

BROWN MACKIE COLLEGE–NORTHERN KENTUCKY

FORT MITCHELL, KENTUCKY

BROWN MACKIE COLLEGE
NORTHERN KENTUCKY™
Founded as AEC Southern Ohio College

The College and Its Mission

Brown Mackie College–Northern Kentucky is dedicated to providing education programs that prepare students for entry-level positions in a competitive, rapidly changing workplace. The College provides associate degree and diploma programs in the areas of business and accounting, allied health sciences, legal studies, and computer technology to approximately 500 students.

The College was founded in Cincinnati, Ohio, in February 1927 as a traditional business college. In 1964, the College was granted accreditation as a business school by the Association of Independent Colleges and Schools (ACICS); it was accredited as a junior college of business by ACICS in 1972. In May 1981, the College opened a branch location in northern Kentucky, which moved in 1986 to its current location in Fort Mitchell. ACICS is listed as a nationally recognized accrediting agency by the U.S. Department of Education. Its accreditation of degree-granting institutions also is recognized by the Council for Higher Education Accreditation. ACICS may be contacted at 750 First Street, NE, Suite 980, Washington, D.C. 20002-4241; 202-336-6780.

The College is a nonresidential, smoke-free institution and is owned and operated by Education Management Corporation, 210 Sixth Avenue, 33rd Floor, Pittsburgh, Pennsylvania 15222-2603; 800-275-2440 (toll-free); http://www.edmc.edu.

Academic Programs

Brown Mackie College–Northern Kentucky provides higher education to traditional and nontraditional students through associate degree and diploma programs that assist them in enhancing their career opportunities, broadening their perspectives through appropriate general education courses, thinking independently and critically, and improving problem-solving abilities. Each College quarter comprises ten to twelve weeks.

Associate Degree Programs Associate degree programs require a minimum of eight quarters to complete. Programs are offered on a year-round basis, providing students with the ability to work uninterrupted toward their degrees. The Associate of Applied Business degree (96 credits) is awarded in accounting technology, business management, computer networking and applications, computer programming and applications, computer software technology, criminal justice, health-care administration, and paralegal studies. The Associate of Applied Science degree (96 credits) is awarded in computer-aided design and drafting technology, medical assisting, pharmacy technology, and surgical technology.

Diploma Programs The College also offers diploma programs (48 credits) in accounting, business, computer applications, computer software applications, medical assistant studies, and practical nursing (76 credits).

Costs

Tuition for all programs, except practical nursing, is $189 per credit hour. Tuition for the practical nursing program is $250 per credit hour. Textbooks and other instructional materials vary by program.

Financial Aid

The College maintains a full-time staff of financial aid professionals to assist qualified students in obtaining financial assistance. The College participates in several student aid programs. Forms of financial aid available through federal resources include Federal Pell Grants, Federal Supplemental Educational Opportunity Grants (FSEOG), Federal Work-Study Program awards, Federal Perkins Loans, Federal Stafford Student Loans (subsidized and unsubsidized), and Federal PLUS loans. Eligible students may apply for veterans' educational benefits. Students with physical or mental disabilities that are a handicap to employment may be eligible for training services through the state Vocational Rehabilitation Agency. For further information, students should contact the College Student Financial Services Office.

Each year, the College makes available President's Scholarships of $1000 each to qualifying seniors from area high schools. No more than one scholarship is awarded per high school. In order to qualify, a senior must be graduating from a participating high school, maintain a cumulative grade point average of at least 2.0, and submit a brief essay. The student's extracurricular activities and community service are also considered. The President's Scholarship is available only to students enrolling in one of the College's degree programs. Students who receive the scholarship must enroll at Brown Mackie College–Northern Kentucky between June and September immediately following their high school graduation. Applications for these scholarships can be obtained from the guidance departments of participating high schools. These applications must be completed and returned to the College by March 31. Those awarded scholarships are notified by April 30.

Faculty

There are 9 full-time and 20 part-time faculty members. The student-faculty ratio is 17:1.

Facilities and Resources

Brown Mackie College–Northern Kentucky provides media presentation rooms for special instructional needs and a library that provides instructional resources and academic support for both faculty members and students. The College is nonresidential; students who are unable to commute daily from their homes may request assistance from the Office of Admissions in locating off-site housing. The College is accessible by public transportation and provides ample free parking.

Location

The College is located at 309 Buttermilk Pike in Fort Mitchell, Kentucky.

Admission Requirements

Each applicant for admission is assigned an Assistant Director of Admissions, who directs the applicant through the steps of the admissions process, providing information on curriculum, policies, procedures, and services and assisting the applicant in setting necessary appointments and interviews. To qualify for admission, each applicant must provide documentation of graduation from an accredited high school or from a state-approved secondary education curriculum or provide official documentation of high school graduation equivalency. All

transcripts become the property of the College. Admission to the College is based upon the applicant's meeting the above requirements, a review of the applicant's previous education records, and a review of the applicant's career interests. If previous academic records indicate that the College's education and training would not benefit the applicant, the College reserves the right to advise the applicant not to enroll. Special requirements for enrollment into certain programs are discussed in the descriptions of those programs.

Application and Information

Applicants must complete and submit an application form, along with documentation of graduation from an accredited high school or state-approved secondary education curriculum or official documentation of high school graduation equivalency. For additional information, prospective students should contact:

Director of Admissions
Brown Mackie College–Northern Kentucky
309 Buttermilk Pike
Fort Mitchell, Kentucky 41017
Phone: 859-341-5627
       800-888-1445 (toll-free)
Fax: 859-341-6483
E-mail: jdellefield@brownmackie.edu
Web site: http://www.brownmackie.edu

BROWN MACKIE COLLEGE–SALINA

SALINA, KANSAS

The College and Its Mission

Brown Mackie College–Salina is dedicated to providing education programs that prepare students for entry-level positions in a competitive, rapidly changing workplace. The College provides associate degree, diploma, and certificate programs in the areas of business and accounting, allied health sciences, legal studies, and computer technology to approximately 429 students.

The College was originally founded in July 1892 as the Kansas Wesleyan School of Business. In 1938, the College was incorporated as the Brown Mackie School of Business under the ownership of former Kansas Wesleyan instructors Perry E. Brown and A. B. Mackie; it became Brown Mackie College in January 1975.

Brown Mackie College is accredited by the Higher Learning Commission of the North Central Association of Colleges and Schools, 30 North LaSalle Street, Suite 2400, Chicago, Illinois 60602; phone: 800-621-7440 (toll-free). The College, which operates in Salina and Lenexa, Kansas, is approved and authorized to grant the Associate of Applied Science degree by the Kansas Board of Regents, 1000 Southwest Jackson Street, Suite 520, Topeka, Kansas 66612.

The College is a nonresidential, smoke-free institution owned and operated by of Education Management Corporation, 210 Sixth Avenue, 33rd Floor, Pittsburgh, Pennsylvania 15222-2603; 800-275-2440 (toll-free); http://www.edmc.edu.

Academic Programs

Brown Mackie College–Salina provides higher education to traditional and nontraditional students through associate degree, diploma, and certificate programs that assist them in enhancing their career opportunities, broadening their perspectives through appropriate general education courses, thinking independently and critically, and improving problem-solving abilities. The College strives to develop within its students the desire for lifelong and continued education.

In most programs, students can complete classes part-time or full-time, day or evening. Classes begin every month and programs are offered on a year-round basis, providing students with the ability to work uninterrupted toward their degrees. Students focus on and complete a single class every month.

Associate Degree Programs The Associate of Applied Science degree (96 credits) is awarded in accounting technology, business management, computer-aided design and drafting technology, computer networking and applications, computer software technology, criminal justice, medical assisting, medical office management, nursing, nursing-bridge program, paralegal studies, and sales and marketing.

Diploma Programs The College also offers diploma programs (48 credits) in accounting, advertising, business, computer-aided design and drafting technician studies, computer software applications, criminal justice, medical assistant studies, medical coding and billing, and paralegal assistant studies.

Certificate Programs Certificate programs (24 credits) are offered in computer networking, and practical nursing.

Costs

The cost of tuition for all programs, except computer networking and practical nursing, is $195 per quarter credit hour. Courses in the practical nursing program are $250 per quarter credit hour. Computer networking courses are $300 per quarter credit hour. Textbook fees for all programs are estimated at $500 per quarter.

Financial Aid

The College maintains a full-time staff of financial aid professionals to assist qualified students in obtaining financial assistance. The College participates in several student aid programs. Forms of financial aid that are available through federal resources include Federal Pell Grants, Federal Supplemental Educational Opportunity Grants (FSEOG), Federal Work-Study Program awards, Federal Perkins Loans, Federal Stafford Student Loans (subsidized and unsubsidized), and Federal PLUS loans. Eligible students may apply for veterans' educational benefits. Students with physical or mental disabilities that are a handicap to employment may be eligible for training services through the state Vocational Rehabilitation Agency. For further information, students should contact the College Student Financial Services Office.

The Merit Scholarship is a College-sponsored scholarship that may be awarded to students who demonstrate exceptional academic ability. To qualify for a Merit Scholarship, an applicant or student must have scored 21 or higher on the ACT or 900 or higher on the SAT. The maximum amount awarded by this scholarship to any student is $500.

Athletic scholarships may be awarded to students who participate in athletic programs that are sponsored by the College. Current sports are men's baseball, men's and women's basketball, and women's fast-pitch softball. Maximum awards for any applicant or student are determined by the College President. Further information is available from the Athletic Office. Recipients of athletic scholarships must achieve a cumulative grade point average of at least 2.0 by their graduation. Recipients who fail to maintain full-time status or the required grade point average forfeit their awards.

Faculty

There are 15 full-time and 19 part-time faculty members. The student-faculty ratio is 13:1.

Facilities and Resources

In addition to classrooms and computer labs, the College maintains a library of curriculum-related resources, technical and general education materials, academic and professional periodicals, and audiovisual resources. Internet access is also available for research. The College has a bookstore that stocks texts, courseware, and other educational supplies that are required for courses and a variety of personal, recreational, and gift items, including apparel, supplies, and general merchandise incorporating the College logo. Hours are posted at the bookstore entrance.

Location

Brown Mackie College–Salina is located at 2106 South Ninth Street in Salina, Kansas.

Admission Requirements

Each applicant for admission is assigned an Assistant Director of Admissions, who directs the applicant through the steps of the admissions process, providing information on curriculum, policies, procedures, and services and assisting the applicant in setting necessary appointments and interviews. To qualify for admission, each applicant must provide documentation of graduation from an accredited high school or from a state-approved secondary education curriculum or provide official documentation of high school graduation equivalency. All transcripts become the property of the College. Admission to the College is based upon the applicant's meeting the above requirements, a review of the applicant's previous education records, and a review of the applicant's career interests. If previous academic records indicate that the College's education and training would not benefit the applicant, the College reserves the right to advise the applicant not to enroll. Special requirements for enrollment into certain programs are discussed in the descriptions of those programs.

Application and Information

Applicants must complete and submit an application form, along with documentation of graduation from an accredited high school or state-approved secondary education curriculum or official documentation of high school graduation equivalency. For additional information, prospective students should contact:

Director of Admissions
Brown Mackie College–Salina
2106 South Ninth Street
Salina, Kansas 67401
Phone: 785-825-5422
        800-365-0433 (toll-free)
Fax: 785-827-7623
E-mail: dheath@brownmackie.edu
Web site: http://www.brownmackie.edu

BROWN MACKIE COLLEGE–SOUTH BEND

SOUTH BEND, INDIANA

The College and Its Mission

Brown Mackie College–South Bend is dedicated to providing education programs that prepare students for entry-level positions in a competitive, rapidly changing workplace. The College provides associate degree, diploma, and certificate programs in business and accounting, allied health sciences, legal studies, computer technology, and electronics to approximately 661 students.

The College is one of the oldest institutions of its kind in the country and the oldest in the state of Indiana. Established in 1882 as the South Bend Commercial College, the school later changed its name to Michiana College. In 1930, the school was incorporated under the laws of the state of Indiana and was authorized to confer associate degrees and certificates in business. The College relocated to its current location on East Jefferson Boulevard in 1987. Five years later it added a branch location in Fort Wayne, Indiana, now known as Brown Mackie College–Fort Wayne.

Brown Mackie College–South Bend is accredited by the Accrediting Council for Independent Colleges and Schools (ACICS) to award associate degrees, diplomas, and certificates. The Accrediting Council for Independent Colleges and Schools is listed as a nationally recognized accrediting agency by the United States Department of Education. Its accreditation of degree-granting institutions is also recognized by the Council for Higher Education Accreditation. ACICS can be contacted at 750 First Street, NE, Suite 980, Washington, D.C. 20002-4241; 202-336-6780.

The medical assisting program is accredited by the Commission on Accreditation of Allied Health Education Programs (CAAHEP), on recommendation of the Curriculum Review Board. The Commission's address is 35 East Wacker Drive, Chicago, Illinois 60601; 312-553-9355.

The occupational therapy assistant program is accredited by the Accreditation Council for Occupational Therapy Education (ACOTE) of the American Occupational Therapy Association (AOTA), 4720 Montgomery Lane, P.O. Box 31220, Bethesda, Maryland 20824-1220; 301-652-2682.

The physical therapist assistant program is accredited by the Commission on Accreditation in Physical Therapy Education (CAPTE) of the American Physical Therapy Association (APTA), 1111 North Fairfax Street, Alexandria, Virginia 22314; 703-706-3241.

The practical nursing program is accredited by the Indiana State Board of Nursing, 402 West Washington Street, Room W066, Indianapolis, Indiana 46204; 317-234-2043.

The College is a nonresidential, smoke-free institution and is owned and operated by Education Management Corporation, 210 Sixth Avenue, 33rd Floor, Pittsburgh, Pennsylvania 15222-2603; 800-275-2440 (toll-free); http://www.edmc.edu. (AC 0110)

Academic Programs

Brown Mackie College–South Bend provides higher education to traditional and nontraditional students through associate degree, diploma, and certificate programs that assist them in enhancing their career opportunities, broadening their perspectives through appropriate general education courses, thinking independently and critically, and improving problem-solving abilities.

Each College quarter comprises twelve weeks. Associate degree programs require a minimum of eight quarters to complete. Programs are offered on a year-round basis, providing students with the ability to work uninterrupted toward completion of their programs.

Associate Degree Programs The Associate of Science degree (96 credits) is awarded in accounting technology, business management, computer software technology, criminal justice, early childhood education, medical assisting, health-care administration, and paralegal studies. The Associate of Applied Science degree (96 credits) is awarded in physical therapist assistant studies.

Diploma Program The College offers a diploma program (76 credits) in practical nursing.

Certificate Programs The College offers the following certificate programs (48 credits): accounting, business, computer software applications, criminal justice, medical assistant studies, and paralegal assistant studies.

Costs

Tuition for programs in the 2006–07 academic year was $189 per credit hour, with a $10 per-credit-hour general fee applied to instructional costs for activities and services. Textbooks and other instructional materials varied by program. Tuition for all courses in the practical nursing program was $250 per credit hour. Tuition for the physical therapist assistant program was $300 per credit hour. Tuition for the occupational therapy assistant program was $300 per credit hour.

Financial Aid

The College maintains a full-time staff of financial aid professionals to assist qualified students in obtaining financial assistance. The College participates in several student aid programs. Forms of financial aid available through federal resources include the Federal Pell Grant Program, Federal Supplemental Educational Opportunity Grant (FSEOG) Program, Federal Work-Study Program, Federal Perkins Loan Program, Federal Stafford Student Loan Program (subsidized and unsubsidized), and the Federal PLUS Loan Program. Eligible students may apply for Indiana state awards such as the Frank O'Bannon Grant Program (formerly the Indiana Higher Education Grant) and Twenty-First Century Scholars Program for high school students, the Core 40 awards, and veterans' educational benefits. Students with physical or mental disabilities that are a

handicap to employment may be eligible for training services through the state Agency for Vocational Rehabilitation. For further information, students should contact the College Student Financial Services Office.

Each year, the College makes available President's Scholarships of $1000 each to qualifying seniors from area high schools. No more than one scholarship is awarded per high school. In order to qualify, a senior must be graduating from a participating high school, must be maintaining a cumulative grade point average of at least 2.0, and must submit a brief essay. The student's extracurricular activities and community service are also considered. The President's Scholarship is available only to students enrolling in one of the College's degree programs. Students awarded the scholarship must enroll at Brown Mackie College–South Bend between June and September immediately following their high school graduation. Applications for these scholarships can be obtained from the guidance departments of participating high schools. These applications must be completed and returned to the College by March 31. Those awarded scholarships are notified by April 30.

Faculty

There are 19 full-time and 23 part-time faculty members at the College. The average student-faculty ratio is 12:1. Each student is assigned a program director as an adviser.

Academic Facilities

Brown Mackie College–South Bend comprises 31,000 square feet of classrooms; medical, computer, occupational, and physical therapy laboratories; and a library, a bookstore, and office space.

Location

Brown Mackie College–South Bend is located in the Woodlawn section of Cincinnati, Ohio. The College is easily accessible by public transportation and provides ample parking at no charge.

Admission Requirements

Each applicant for admission is assigned an Assistant Director of Admissions, who directs the applicant through the steps of the admissions process, providing information on curriculum, policies, procedures, and services and assisting the applicant in setting necessary appointments and interviews. To qualify for admission, each applicant must provide documentation of graduation from an accredited high school or from a state-approved secondary education curriculum or provide official documentation of high school graduation equivalency. All transcripts become the property of the College. Admission to the College is based on the applicant's meeting the above

requirements, a review of the applicant's previous educational records, and a review of the applicant's career interests. If previous academic records indicate that the College's education and training would not benefit the applicant, the College reserves the right to advise the applicant not to enroll. Special requirements for enrollment into certain programs are discussed in the descriptions of those programs.

In addition to the College's general admission requirements, applicants enrolling in the occupational therapy assistant or physical therapist assistant programs must document one of the following: a high school cumulative grade point average of at least 2.5, a score on the GED examination of at least 57 (557 if taken on or after January 15, 2002), or completion of 12 quarter-credit hours or 8 semester-credit hours of collegiate course work with a grade point average of at least 2.5. Credit hours may not include Professional Development (CF 1100), the Brown Mackie College–South Bend course. Students entering either program must also have completed a biology course with a grade of at least a C (or an average of at least 2.0 on a 4.0 scale).

In addition to the College's general admission requirements, applicants enrolling in the practical nursing program must document the following: fulfillment of Brown Mackie College–South Bend general requirements; complete physical (must be current to within six months of admission); two-step Mantoux TB skin test (must be current throughout schooling); hepatitis B vaccination or signed refusal; up-to-date immunizations, including tetanus and rubella; record of current CPR certification (certification must be current throughout the clinical experience through health-care provider certification or the American Heart Association); and hospitalization insurance or a signed waiver.

Application and Information

Applicants must complete and submit an application form, along with documentation of graduation from an accredited high school or state-approved secondary education curriculum or official documentation of high school graduation equivalency.

For additional information, prospective students should contact:

Director of Admissions
Brown Mackie College–South Bend
1030 East Jefferson Boulevard
South Bend, Indiana 46617
Phone: 574-237-0774
        800-743-2447 (toll-free)
Fax: 574-237-3585
E-mail: phooks@brownmackie.edu
Web site: http://www.brownmackie.edu

BUNKER HILL COMMUNITY COLLEGE

BOSTON, MASSACHUSETTS

The College and Its Mission

A public institution of higher education, Bunker Hill Community College (BHCC) offers wide-ranging workforce education curricula interwoven throughout comprehensive programs and courses of study, including nursing and allied health, an extensive information technology program, criminal justice, hospitality and culinary arts, business, and early childhood development. Accredited by the Commission on Institutions of Higher Education of the New England Association of Schools and Colleges, BHCC supports open access to postsecondary education by providing a strong liberal arts foundation and a range of educational opportunities that include distance learning, self-directed learning, an honors program, and, for nonnative English-speaking students, a variety of levels of English as a second language (ESL) instruction.

BHCC graduates have gone on to continue their education at many four-year institutions, including Bentley College, Boston University, Cambridge College, Northeastern University, Salem State College, Smith College, Suffolk University, Tufts University, Wellesley College, and the University of Massachusetts. BHCC seeks to enhance its position as a primary educational and economic asset for the commonwealth through cooperative planning and program implementation involving neighboring institutions of higher education, the public schools, community organizations, and area businesses and industries.

Academic Programs

BHCC offers numerous programs of study. They include Associate in Arts (A.A.) degrees, Associate in Science (A.S.) degrees, and certificate programs. Associate in Arts concentrations are designed to permit the student to transfer smoothly to four-year colleges and universities. Although extreme care has been taken in fashioning these transfer-focused degrees, students are advised to consult the institution to which they wish to transfer to ensure the wisest choice of courses at BHCC. These students should also work with the BHCC transfer counselor and academic advisers in planning both the curriculum at BHCC and the transfer process.

Associate in Science programs are designed to develop the knowledge and skills required for employment at the conclusion of the associate degree. In addition to employment preparation, many Associate in Science programs have transfer options. To ensure smooth transfer to four-year programs, students are advised to consult the institution to which they wish to transfer.

A wide variety of certificate programs provide skills training and job-upgrade opportunities for students who successfully complete these programs.

The honors program offers students the opportunity to study and learn in an academically challenging and enriching learning environment.

Associate Degree Programs Associate in Arts degrees are available in biological science, business, chemical science, communication, computer information systems, computer science, education, English, fine arts, foreign language, general concentration, history and government, mathematics, music, physics/engineering, psychology, sociology, and theater. Students enrolling in any A.A. degree program can earn world-studies emphasis certification simultaneously.

Associate in Science degrees are offered in business administration (accounting, finance, international business, management), computer information technology (computer support specialist studies, database programming and administration, network technology and administration, Web development), criminal justice, culinary arts, early childhood

development, electric power utility, fire protection and safety, graphic arts, hotel/restaurant/travel (hotel/restaurant management, travel and tourism management), human services, media technology, medical imaging (cardiac sonography, general sonography, medical radiography, medical radiography–part-time evening), nursing (day, evening, or weekend), office and information management (administrative information management, medical information management), and pharmacy technology.

Certificate Programs Certificates are available in allied health (medical assistant studies, medical lab assistant studies, patient-care assistant studies, phlebotomy technician studies), business administration (accounting, e-commerce marketing management, international business, paralegal studies), computer information technology (computer support specialist studies, database programming and administration, network technology and administration, object-oriented computer programming and design), culinary arts, early childhood development, human services, law enforcement, medical coding, office and information management (information management specialist studies, medical information management assistant studies), surgical technology (central processing (sterile processing and distribution management), surgical technology), and travel and tourism management.

Off-Campus Programs

Bunker Hill Community College offers home study and online distance learning courses as a convenient alternative to the traditional classroom. These courses are designed for self-directed, motivated learners. The courses are equivalent in content and academic rigor to traditional classroom courses but offer students the flexibility and convenience of learning virtually anytime and anywhere. The College also offers hybrid courses. These courses incorporate both traditional classroom and online components. Hybrid courses generally meet on-site for 50 percent of the instructional time, with the remaining instruction conducted online.

BHCC offers a range of educational opportunities at its five satellite campuses, each intended to serve the distinct needs and interests of the host communities—Cambridge, Chinatown, Revere, Somerville, and Boston's South End. The curricula available at the satellites allow students to prepare for workforce advancement while earning credits toward an associate degree or certificate in several of the wide variety of fields offered by the College. Programs include foundation courses that fulfill general education requirements as well as courses in response to community interest, such as offerings in computer technology, business management, and hospitality.

Bunker Hill Community College has a comprehensive study-abroad program that allows students to experience different cultures. Each year, approximately twenty scholarships are awarded to assist BHCC students in realizing their dream of studying abroad. Faculty, staff, and interested community members are also invited to take part in the programs, although scholarships are available only to qualified BHCC students.

Credit for Nontraditional Learning Experiences

The Prior Learning Assessment Program provides an opportunity for students to condense their time of study by granting credits for college-level knowledge and skills. This program assists students in examining their outside learning experiences and identifying those that might be considered for college credits. Common

sources for this kind of learning are jobs, volunteer work, skills training, workshops or study groups, and community involvement.

Students can earn college credits in four ways: portfolio evaluation, the College-Level Examination Program (CLEP), military evaluation, and departmental challenge exams.

Costs

Tuition for Massachusetts residents is $106 per credit; for non-Massachusetts residents, it is $312 per credit. The New England Regional Student Program costs $118 per credit. The health course fee is $35 per credit (for health program courses only).

Financial Aid

The Financial Aid Office at Bunker Hill Community College assists students and their families in meeting the costs of a college education. Bunker Hill Community College participates in a wide variety of federal, state, and private financial aid programs. Students should be aware that all institutions, including Bunker Hill Community College, are subject to adjustments in funding allocations from both the commonwealth of Massachusetts and the United States Department of Education.

In order to be eligible for financial aid, an applicant must be a United States citizen or an eligible noncitizen enrolled or accepted for enrollment in an eligible program. In addition, the applicant must maintain satisfactory academic progress, comply with Federal Selective Service Law, and not be in default on any educational loans or owe a refund on any federal grants or loans to any institution. Students who have obtained a previous bachelor's degree at any U.S. or international institution are not eligible for financial aid.

Financial aid awards are subject to change if any of the factors used to calculate eligibility from the Free Application for Federal Student Aid (FAFSA) change after the date of original application. Other examples of factors that impact eligibility include increases in income and changes in family size and/or in the number of family members enrolled in college. Students are strongly advised to consult with the Financial Aid Office if they are contemplating a change in enrollment status.

Faculty

There are 123 full-time faculty members and 325 adjunct faculty members at BHCC. The average class size is 19.

Student Body Profile

The student body reflects the diversity of the urban community, and an essential part of the College's mission is to encourage this diversity. The average student age is 28. Nearly 60 percent of the students are women, more than half are members of minority groups, and most are employed while attending school.

Student Activities

Bunker Hill Community College has an active student life program. The activities coordinated through the Student Activities and Athletics Office provide students with the opportunity to have fun, meet people, and make a difference in campus life at the College. BHCC celebrates cultural diversity and encourages cultural interaction.

There are more than twenty-five student organizations and athletic teams at Bunker Hill Community College, which provide the campus with social, cultural, and educational programs as well as competitive sports, intramural/recreational programs, and leisure-time activities. New members are always welcome.

Athletic programs provide opportunities for students to participate in competitive or recreational activities on the intercollegiate and intramural levels. The Intercollegiate Athletic Program consists of men's baseball, basketball, and soccer; women's basketball, soccer, and softball; and coed golf. The Intramural Athletic Program includes basketball, table tennis, and tennis.

Student clubs and organizations include African-American Cultural Society; Alpha Kappa Mu Honor Society; Arab Students Association; Art Club; Asian Students Association; Brazilian Cultural Club; Business Club; Campus Activities Board; Cape Verdean Club; Criminal Justice Society; Evening Student Association; Gay, Lesbian, Bisexual, and Transgender Student Union; Gospel Choir; Haitian Club; Hillel Club; Hospitality Club; Islamic Students Association; Italian-American Society; Latinos Unidos Club; Multicultural Club; Parents' Association; Real Life Club; S.H.O.C.W.A.V.E.S. (Students Helping Our Communities with Active Volunteer Experiences and Services); Stage and Screen Club; Student Government Association; Upsidedown Club; Veterans of All Nations Club; and WBCC radio station.

Facilities and Resources

Facilities available at BHCC include the library and information center, advising and counseling center, center for self-directed learning, tutoring and academic support center, career center, international center, and technology support services center.

Location

All Bunker Hill Community College sites are located in urban communities within 5 miles of downtown Boston. The main campus is located in the historic Charlestown neighborhood of Boston. An annex campus is located in Bellingham Square in Chelsea. The satellites are in Cambridge, Chinatown, Revere, Somerville, and the South End. All locations are easily accessible via public transportation. A subway stop is located steps from the Charlestown Campus.

Admission Requirements

Bunker Hill Community College is committed to an open admission policy. This policy offers the opportunity to enroll to those who have earned a high school diploma, a GED certificate, or an associate degree or higher and who express a desire to pursue a college education. All students admitted to degree or certificate programs are required to take computerized placement tests (CPTs) in English, reading, and mathematics. Students whose first language is not English, and who have not earned a high school diploma or GED in the United States, must take the English Placement Test (EPT). International students must take the Levels of English Proficiency (LOEP) assessment if they have not scored at least 423 on the TOEFL paper test or 113 on the computerized version. The purpose of these tests is to determine the levels at which students begin their study. Based upon test results, the College may prescribe developmental courses or limit a student's enrollment, in an effort to enhance that student's ability to succeed. Applicants to health careers and technical programs must comply with program entrance requirements and application deadlines.

Application and Information

Although the College has a rolling admissions process, students should contact the Admissions and Transfer Counseling Office for program-specific application deadlines.

Admissions and Transfer Counseling
Charlestown Campus, Room B130
Bunker Hill Community College
250 New Rutherford Avenue
Boston, Massachusetts 02129
Phone: 617-228-2019
Fax: 617-228-3336
E-mail: admissions@bhcc.mass.edu
Web site: http://www.bhcc.mass.edu

THE COLLEGE OF WESTCHESTER

WHITE PLAINS, NEW YORK

The College and Its Mission

Founded in 1915, the College of Westchester (CW) has a rich history of providing the community with affordable, private education at the collegiate level. The beautiful, state-of-the-art campus in White Plains offers an environment that is conducive to learning. Programs are designed for college-bound students with an interest in a career-focused education leading to long-term security and financial success.

The College's mission is to offer high-quality, career-oriented programs that challenge both the traditional and returning student to advanced levels of intellectual and personal development. This commitment to educational excellence is reflected in a carefully constructed and distinctive curriculum that is designed to provide students with sophisticated, marketable skills and to promote in students those attributes that contribute to personal and career success and a desire for lifelong learning. In order to maximize student success, the College maintains a student-centered environment.

CW is accredited by the Commission on Higher Education (CHE) of the Middle States Association of Colleges and Schools (3624 Market Street, Philadelphia, Pennsylvania 19104; telephone: 215-662-5606). The CHE is an institutional accrediting agency recognized by the U.S. Department of Education and the Council for Higher Education Accreditation.

Academic Programs

The Associate in Applied Science (A.A.S.) degree or the Associate in Occupational Studies (A.O.S.) degree is awarded upon successful completion of a two-year program. The requirements include courses in basic college skills, courses pertaining to the student's major, and, for those students pursuing an A.A.S. degree, courses in general education.

The Business Administration–Management/Marketing program provides students with an opportunity to concentrate either in e-commerce marketing, entrepreneurial management, or information systems. Three new concentrations have been added to the day program: entertainment, music, and sports management; fashion/retail merchandising; and hotel and resort management. Graduates pursue management training, Internet marketing, and sales positions. The program also affords self-employment opportunities through an appropriate educational background.

The Accounting degree program provides students with the critical accounting, business, and software skills needed to enter the business world with confidence to compete for rewarding career positions. In today's increasingly complex, regulated, and competitive business environment, accounting skills are in demand, and accounting has become a dynamic career path.

The Computer Network Administration program provides students with a leading-edge career education for today's technical world. Students study administration, design, support, and maintenance of local area networks through lectures and by using Microsoft Windows 2000 systems and software. The program includes additional nontechnical courses to enhance the student's career opportunities.

The Multimedia Development and Management program provides students with the tools to design and develop multimedia applications for the general media, business, education, the Internet, and entertainment markets. The program utilizes the most current multimedia technologies that enable students to create portfolios of their work. Three new concentrations have been added: Web design and development, digital video and animation, and game design.

The Computer Applications Management program prepares students for various professional-level employment opportunities in the rapidly expanding information processing and office technology fields. Graduates of this program are qualified to seek office technology and information processing positions that require expert computer applications skills and knowledge of technical office procedures.

The Office Administration program prepares students for various professional-level employment opportunities. Graduates of the program are qualified to seek office administration, executive administrative assistant, executive assistant, or office management positions.

The Medical Assistant Management program provides students with the specific skills needed to seek careers as professionals in a medical or health-services setting. Graduates of the program have acquired the requisite skills to become employed in organizations ranging from large hospitals to physicians' offices. The program combines both administrative and clinical skills. The types of positions for which these graduates qualify include, but are not limited to, medical assistant, EKG technician, phlebotomist, patient-care assistant, medical biller, and medical coder.

The Medical Office Systems Management program prepares students for entry-level employment in such administrative positions as medical billers, coders, collectors, and office managers in organizations ranging from small medical practices to large health-care institutions.

Students in nondegree programs receive a certificate from CW if all courses are successfully completed. Credits may be transferred to the associate degree programs, providing a 2.0 or better cumulative grade point average has been achieved in addition to the successful completion of all required courses.

In a short certificate program, students can obtain specialized job skills to launch or upgrade their career. These programs are popular among students who already have some advanced skills or education as well as those who want to be employable and promotable in the shortest possible time.

Certificate programs include Computer Applications Specialist, Computer Networking Specialist, Intensive Accounting, Multimedia Technology, Word Processing Specialist, Medical Assistant Specialist, Medical Office Specialist, Microsoft Office Specialist, and Pharmacy Tech Specialist.

Costs

The cost of tuition and fees varies, depending on the student's program. Current costs are available from the CW admissions office.

Financial Aid

All students at CW are encouraged to apply for financial assistance and meet with a financial assistance counselor who conducts a confidential analysis detailing the funds available to finance their education. In addition to federal- and state-funded programs, the College offers a variety of institutional scholarships, grants, and payment plans each year.

Faculty

CW instructors are highly qualified, dedicated, and respected educators who are committed to excellence in teaching and service to students. Most faculty members have advanced degrees and all have extensive business experience. A comprehensive faculty development program ensures that all instructors remain current in their field of expertise and utilizes state-of-the-art technology and teaching methodologies.

Student Body Profile

Students come to CW from throughout the New York metropolitan area. The present student body represents 117 high schools, five states, and six countries. The breadth of racial, ethnic, and socioeconomic backgrounds represented in the student body creates a genuinely diverse institution. There are nearly equal numbers of women and men enrolled and a sizable population of mature, nontraditional students who primarily attend convenient evening and weekend classes.

Student Activities

CW offers an array of student activities and support services designed to help students achieve their fullest potential for growth. Activities include Student Government Association, Alpha Beta Kappa honor society, business- and technology-related clubs, field trips to businesses and corporations, and social events.

Academic Facilities

The College of Westchester is located in a beautiful five-story, 50,000-square-foot building. The College's academic facilities include nineteen classrooms; a library; a student life center that houses all student organizations and clubs; an academic advancement center, an open computer lab that also serves as a tutoring and study center; a student lounge; and faculty offices. The facility also includes the Admissions Office; the Academic Center, where the academic administrators, including academic advisers, are housed; the Financial Services Center; and Career Placement Services.

CW's Career Placement Services specializes in finding part-time work for currently enrolled students and full-time, career-related positions for graduates. The staff members work with students to secure internships, co-op opportunities, and work-study positions while they are attending the College and also carefully guide students through the many facets of planning and preparing for job searches. This may include guidance in areas such as properly completing resumes, writing letters of application, securing job interviews, researching companies, and conducting interviews.

At CW, leading-edge technology defines the teaching and learning environment. The computer classrooms feature Pentium-based personal computers, outfitted with an extensive selection of current software applications. The recent addition of a G5 Macintosh lab has enabled CW students to learn applications on both Macintosh and PC platforms.

Location

CW is located in White Plains, the county seat and hub of Westchester County. Many of the College's graduates work for area corporations, including IBM, Verizon, Kraft General Foods USA, the Bank of New York, PepsiCo, AT&T, the Reader's Digest Association, Philip Morris, MasterCard, Citibank, Con Ed, CIBA, Texaco, MCI, Bayer Corporation, MBIA, Lillian Vernon, Fuji Film USA, Sunburst Communications, Hitachi America, Ltd., MetLife Corporation, MTA, Nine West, Avon Products, Carolee Designs, Online Design, Pitney Bowes, American Express, Coca Cola Corporation, Dannon Corporation, Doral Arrowwood, FedEx, International Paper, *The Journal News*, KPMG Peat Marwick, Lincoln Center for the Performing Arts, MCS Cannon, Manulife Wood Logan, Marsh & McLennan, the United Way, Xerox, and Zurich Reinsurance.

The New York Metro North Railroad Station and the transportation center are both a short walk from CW.

Admission Requirements

To properly assist applicants in selecting the program that is best suited to their needs, a personal interview is conducted with an admissions associate. Prospective students should call the Admissions Office for an appointment. In addition to the interview, all applicants must be graduates of an accredited high school or its equivalent or have received a high school equivalency diploma (GED). In some cases, mature, non–high school graduates who have demonstrated an ability to benefit based upon an interview, counseling, and testing may be admitted. These individuals may qualify for a high school equivalency diploma through CW from the New York State Education Department by successfully completing 36 quarter hours of academic work with a minimum of a 2.0 GPA in one of the College programs.

Application and Information

CW has a rolling admissions policy. Students may apply at any time up to the beginning of the quarter; although, students are strongly encouraged to apply as early as possible. To be considered for admission, the following must be submitted: an application for admission, a $40 nonrefundable application fee, and an official high school transcript, its equivalent, or a GED equivalency diploma. If transferring credits from a prior college, students must submit an official college transcript. Students seeking to transfer credits from another institution of higher education should request that an official transcript be mailed to Transfer Credits, Office of Admissions. Students who have attended another accredited college or university may obtain credit toward graduation for courses taken at that institution. Credit is transferable for comparable courses in the student's selected curriculum in which the applicant has obtained a grade of C (2.0) or higher. A maximum of 50 percent of the credits required for program completion may be transferred. Official documentation of successful completion of high school or the equivalent must be received prior to the completion of the first quarter at the College.

For application materials and additional information, prospective students should contact:

Office of Admissions
The College of Westchester
325 Central Park Avenue
White Plains, New York 10606

Phone: 800-333-4924
E-mail: admissions@cw.edu
Web site: http://www.cw.edu

COLORADO MOUNTAIN COLLEGE
GLENWOOD SPRINGS, COLORADO

The College and Its Mission

There is a different view of the Rocky Mountains at each Colorado Mountain College campus. Learning is personal; classes are small; faculty members are friendly. Colorado Mountain College is a multicampus community college with three residential campuses and nine commuter locations. This coeducational public institution began operation in 1967. Colorado Mountain College operates on a semester system with a limited summer session and is accredited by the North Central Association of Colleges and Secondary Schools.

The three residential campuses include Alpine Campus in Steamboat Springs, Spring Valley Campus in Glenwood Springs, and Timberline Campus in Leadville. At these locations, students find a traditional college experience, including residence halls, cafeterias, extensive libraries, laboratories, and many opportunities to participate in residence life. The commuter campuses serve primarily local residents, and classes are scheduled for the convenience of working adults. Commuter sites are located in Aspen, Breckenridge, Buena Vista, Carbondale, Dillon, Edwards, Glenwood Springs, Rifle, and Salida.

Colorado Mountain College offers academic programs for transfer and for occupational training in several specialty areas. Students can begin their four-year degree because the State Guaranteed Transfer courses are guaranteed to satisfy general education requirements at all Colorado public higher-education institutions.

Students may also choose to start a career with occupational training programs. In one or two years, students can learn the skills for employment in some unique and exciting programs. The mountain environment gives students many opportunities to learn outside the classroom.

Academic Programs

Colorado Mountain College offers both occupational and transfer programs. Degrees awarded include the **Associate in Arts** degree, **Associate in Science** degree, **Associate in General Studies** degree, **Associate in Applied Science** degree, and a one-year Occupational Proficiency certificate. The Associate in Arts degree is available at all Colorado Mountain College campuses.

Degrees and programs vary by campus, with the residential campuses offering the fullest range of degrees and certificates. Alpine Campus offerings include the Associate in Arts (areas of specialization are business, fine arts, liberal arts, and wilderness studies), the Associate in Science (areas of specialization are biology, chemistry, geology, mathematics, and physics), and the Associate in Applied Science and Certificates of Occupational Proficiency (offerings include accounting, business, golf club management, pre-engineering, resort management, and ski and snowboard business).

Spring Valley Campus offerings include the Associate in Arts (areas of specialization are business, liberal arts, outdoor education, and theater), Associate in Science (areas of specialization are biology, chemistry, geology, mathematics, and nursing), and Associate in Applied Science and Certificates of Occupational Proficiency (offerings include accounting, business, graphic design, law enforcement, microcomputer support specialist studies, photography, practical nursing, and veterinary technology).

Timberline Campus offerings include the Associate in Arts (areas of specialization are business, liberal arts, and Outdoor Semester in the Rockies), the Associate in General Studies degree in outdoor recreational leadership, the Associate in Science (areas of specialization are biology, chemistry, geology, and mathematics), and the Associate in Applied Science and Certificates of Occupational Proficiency (offerings include accounting, business, historic

preservation, microcomputer support specialist studies, natural resources management, natural resources recreation management, and ski area operations).

Off-Campus Programs

One of the most popular off-campus programs is the Outdoor Semester in the Rockies. This program blends outdoor adventure with the disciplines of college classes such as science, history, and philosophy. Colorado Mountain College encourages students to take advantage of several study-abroad class tours. The College also offers exciting distance education opportunities to district and residential campus students through telecourses, an interactive video system, and some Internet courses.

Credit for Nontraditional Learning Experiences

Colorado Mountain College awards credit through national standardized exams, challenge exams, and credit for life experience. To be awarded credit, testing options are used if possible, and students must be enrolled in a degree or certificate program. Credits posted to a student's academic record through one of these nontraditional methods are noted, indicating the method by which they were awarded.

Costs

Colorado Mountain College's tuition for the academic year 2007–08 is $43 per credit hour for in-district students, $72 per credit hour for in-state students, and $231 per credit hour for out-of-state students. Residential campuses had student activity fees of $180 per academic year. Room and board costs average $6866 per year, and the housing reservation deposit is $300. Books average $650 per academic year.

Financial Aid

Colorado Mountain College is approved for participation in all major federal and state financial aid programs, including Federal Pell Grant, loan programs, and work-study. Financial assistance is awarded through a central district office for all Colorado Mountain College campuses and education centers. The application for financial assistance is the Free Application for Federal Student Aid (FAFSA). First priority is given to those students applying on or before March 31. Applications received after this date are processed pending availability of funds. Questions may be addressed to Student Financial Assistance, District Office, 831 Grand Avenue, Glenwood Springs, Colorado 81601. The College's financial aid code is 004506.

Faculty

Colorado Mountain College faculty members are accessible to students. They are at Colorado Mountain College because they believe in teaching and learning. There are 72 full-time faculty members and 144 part-time faculty members at the three residential campuses. The faculty members pride themselves on the high-quality education students receive in the classroom, with classes averaging 15 students. The student-faculty ratio is 12:1. Many faculty members have taught at colleges and universities and have chosen to teach at Colorado Mountain College.

Student Body Profile

Colorado Mountain College students are from the local area, forty-eight states, and six other countries. Undergraduate students at the residential campuses number approximately 500 full-time students at Alpine as well as Spring Valley, and Timberline has about 300 full-time students. The Alpine Campus can house about 236 students on campus, the Spring Valley Campus about 226 students, and the Timberline Campus about 136 students.

Student Activities

Each residential campus has active student government organizations. Each student government determines the student activity fee and how the funds are utilized on each campus. Student government helps to sponsor student activities, clubs and organizations, and guest speakers. Colorado Mountain College's Alpine ski team holds six national titles. A men's varsity soccer team is offered at the Spring Valley Campus, and there is a Nordic ski team at the Timberline campus. Every season brings new activities and celebrations to the mountain resort towns.

Facilities and Resources

The residential campuses offer a full college experience with residence halls, cafeterias, libraries, academic classrooms, learning labs, laboratories, and student center facilities.

The Alpine Campus offers residence halls and classroom buildings. At the Spring Valley Campus, students can enjoy the hot springs pool in Glenwood Springs, the charm of Carbondale, and the culture of Aspen. Spring Valley offers residence halls, a cafeteria, a gymnasium and climbing wall, a student center, a bookstore, classrooms, a working farm, laboratories, and an extensive library. An academic building, which opened in fall 1998, houses a theater, photography labs and studio, a graphic design computer lab, a student computer center, and classrooms. The faculty offices surround the classrooms so students can easily access their instructors and professors.

At the Timberline Campus, many students combine their environmental interests and their college education. Colorado's highest mountain peak is in the backyard, cross-country skiing begins at the edge of campus, and many of Colorado's big name slopes are no more than an hour away. The campus offers classroom facilities, a library and learning lab, a computer lab, and a bookstore. An academic building, which opened in fall 1999, houses classrooms, a computer center, laboratories, student services, and faculty offices. Students enjoy a relaxing student center and cafeteria and have access to Leadville's modern recreation complex.

Location

Like the Rockies that surround it, Colorado Mountain College is wide open and full of possibilities. There are miles of spruce and aspen, wildflowers, backroads, whitewater and bareback ranchland, three national forests, six wilderness areas, and most of Colorado's major ski resorts. There is a spirit among the teachers and students, an atmosphere of encouragement, and an attitude of confidence. **Alpine Campus** is situated above the downtown area on the west end of Steamboat Springs. In Leadville, **Timberline Campus** is less than an hour's drive from Vail and is surrounded by Colorado's highest peaks and the legends of a town built by silver. High above the Roaring Fork River, **Spring Valley Campus** is located 10 miles south of Glenwood Springs and within 40 miles of Aspen. All Colorado Mountain College locations are resort or mountain communities accessible by air, rail, or bus, and provide excellent outdoor opportunities.

Admission Requirements

Colorado Mountain College seeks, encourages, and assists all interested students beyond high-school age who demonstrate a desire to learn. With a few exceptions, admission follows an open-door policy. Even though Colorado Mountain College has open admission, certain occupational programs have selective admission. Programs with selection or testing requirements and admission deadlines include culinary arts, nursing, outdoor recreation leadership, paramedicine, professional photography, and veterinary technology.

To apply for admission, students must complete and return the Colorado Mountain College admissions application and official high school and/or college transcripts. There is no application fee. All entering students should submit ACT or SAT scores for scholarship, advising, and placement purposes. Some programs require testing for admission.

Transfer students are welcome and should have attained a cumulative grade point average of at least 2.0 on any college work attempted. Nongraduates may take the General Educational Development test (GED) to meet graduation equivalence. International students may be considered for admission to the residential campuses. International admission packets are available and must be completed and returned to apply for admission, and a minimum TOEFL score of 500 on the paper exam or a minimum score of 173 on the computerized exam is required for admission.

Students are encouraged to apply as soon as possible to secure on-campus housing. After applying for admission to a residential campus, students receive housing reservation information.

Application and Information

For more information, students should contact:

Central Admissions
Colorado Mountain College
831 Grand Avenue
Glenwood Springs, Colorado 81601
Phone: 970-945-8691
       800-621-8559 (toll-free)
Fax: 970-947-8324
E-mail: joinus@coloradomtn.edu
Web site: http://www.coloradomtn.edu

The Colorado Rockies are a classroom for Colorado Mountain College students.

THE COOKING AND HOSPITALITY INSTITUTE OF CHICAGO

CHICAGO, ILLINOIS

The Cooking and Hospitality
Institute of Chicago
Le Cordon Bleu Program

The Institute and Its Mission

The Cooking and Hospitality Institute of Chicago is a Le Cordon Bleu Program. Le Cordon Bleu is the famous cooking school founded in Paris in 1895. Thousands of graduates have become professional cooks, bakers, and chefs now staffing some of the most prestigious hospitality establishments in Chicago, the nation, and the world. The Institute is the only school in the Great Lakes Region offering the Le Cordon Bleu Program. The Institute awards Associate of Applied Science degrees as well as the Le Cordon Bleu Diplôme in culinary arts and pâtisserie and baking. By combining classical French cooking methods with modern American techniques, graduates are eagerly embraced by the hospitality industry.

The mission of the Cooking and Hospitality Institute of Chicago is to prepare students to fulfill their career aspirations and meet the needs of the food-service industry through high-quality culinary, pastry arts, hospitality, and general education curriculums of higher education.

The Cooking and Hospitality Institute of Chicago was established in 1983 to provide culinary education using the traditional European hands-on approach. As soon as the first students completed the Professional Cooking Program, most were employed at major hotels and restaurants. In 1989, the school undertook a major expansion into its present facility, and in 1991, it received degree-granting authority from the Illinois Board of Higher Education and began offering an Associate of Applied Science (AAS) degree in culinary arts. In June 2000, it became affiliated with Le Cordon Bleu. Le Cordon Bleu chefs evaluated the facilities and modified the curriculum to include exposure to an array of culinary proficiencies—skills taught in culinary arts programs. Le Cordon Bleu continues to monitor and train school faculty members to ensure not only that the curriculum is being delivered but also that the spirit of Le Cordon Bleu is communicated to the students. Through affiliation with Le Cordon Bleu, the school has been able to expand program offerings with the addition of an Associate of Applied Science in Pâtisserie and Baking degree.

In 2003, the Cooking and Hospitality Institute became a member of the North Central Association of Colleges and Schools and was accredited by the Higher Learning Commission. In 2004, due to demand for the Le Cordon Bleu Program, additional kitchen space was required. Five industry-current kitchens were built in a 20,000-square-foot space across the street from the main campus. The new campus also includes two classrooms and a modern computer lounge. By anticipating the dynamic changes in the food-service industry, the Cooking and Hospitality Institute of Chicago has developed an evolutionary set of programs that continually adapts to these needs.

Academic Programs

The Cooking and Hospitality Institute of Chicago offers accredited Associate of Applied Science (A.A.S.) degrees in Le Cordon Bleu Culinary Arts and Le Cordon Bleu Patisserie and Baking. The Cooking and Hospitality Institute of Chicago is devoted to fostering a lifelong love of learning and holding students to high academic standards. The Institute's premier Le Cordon Bleu A.A.S. program combines course work in three areas: culinary, baking and pastry, and restaurant management. Students at the Institute can complete the program in as little as fifteen months. There are currently eight start dates available per year. Morning, midmorning, and evening courses are offered to accommodate most students' schedules. Students enrolled in the Le Cordon Bleu programs show commitment to those programs as well as to the culinary profession by completing their education in a timely manner.

Associate Degree Programs The Cooking and Hospitality Institute of Chicago offers an Associate of Applied Science degree in Le Cordon Bleu Pâtisserie and Baking. This program teaches the principles and techniques of professional pastry and baking production and is intended for students who have an interest in large-quantity baking or who want to work for establishments that have in-house baking and pastry operations.

The Cooking and Hospitality Institute of Chicago also offers an Associate of Applied Science degree in Le Cordon Bleu culinary arts. The program includes professional cooking skills, baking and pastry skills, restaurant management skills, nutrition sciences, and general education. This well-rounded program is designed to give students the technical skills and theoretical expertise necessary for a career in the food service industry. Graduates can expect employment in entry-level to midlevel positions as well as rapid advancement into management and sous chef positions and further. Students with or without prior experience find that this program offers everything they need to begin a fast-track career in the fastest-growing industry in the United States.

Transfer Arrangements The Cooking and Hospitality Institute of Chicago may accept transfer credits from accredited colleges, provided that the credits are in courses comparable to the courses required under the student's program of study at the Institute. The school registrar determines if credits are transferable.

Off-Campus Programs

The Cooking and Hospitality Institute of Chicago has entered into cooperative agreements with three area colleges that allow students to transfer credits from the Institute toward a bachelor's degree. At Dominican University in River Forest, Illinois, students can continue on for a Bachelor of General Studies (B.G.S.) in culinary arts and management or a Bachelor of Science (B.S.) in nutrition and dietetics, food science management, or food science and nutrition. Students may opt to include in these programs elective courses for nursing home administrator licensure in Illinois. Students may also continue their studies at Robert Morris College, which has campuses in Chicago, Orland Park, Naperville, and Springfield, Illinois, to pursue a Bachelor of Business Administration (B.B.A.). Graduates of the Institute who transfer to Robert Morris with a GPA of at least 3.0 may also receive a tuition scholarship of up to $4800. Students also have the opportunity to continue their studies at Roosevelt University, which accepts 39 credits from the Cooking and Hospitality Institute of Chicago toward their B.S. in hospitality and tourism.

Credit for Nontraditional Learning Experiences

The Institute awards credit to students who have demonstrated proficiency through the Advanced Placement (AP) program and the College-Level Examination Program (CLEP).

Costs

As of January 2005, tuition for the entire culinary program was $39,950. The current tuition for the entire patisserie and baking program is $38,500. In addition, students can expect a one-time purchase of a supply kit. Books, uniforms, activity fees, application fee, and supplies can cost up to approximately $3600 for the full program (start through graduation).

Financial Aid

Tuition planning is provided free of charge to all applicants. The Institute participates in Federal Title IV assistance programs, such as Federal Stafford Student Loans, Federal PLUS loans, Federal Pell Grants, Federal Supplemental Educational Opportunity Grants, and the Federal Work-Study Program. Students may also receive funding from a variety of institutional and industry-related scholarships, which include the Nancy Abrams Academic Excellence Scholarship, the Educational Foundation's ProMgmt. Scholarship, and the Career College Association's Imagine America Scholarships for high school seniors as well as scholarships from the James Beard Foundation, the International Association of Culinary Professionals, the Illinois Restaurant Association, and the National Restaurant Association. Scholarships range from $500 to $10,000.

Nongovernmental loans are available through Sallie Mae. These loans may be used to supplement federal financial aid and in cases where students do not qualify for federal aid. The loan terms are similar to federal student loans, but the application procedure is greatly simplified.

Faculty

The best ingredient at the Institute is the faculty. Faculty members are selected for their professional backgrounds and academic experience. Students work closely with talented chefs and learn from their combined 400 years of industry experience.

Student Body Profile

The Cooking and Hospitality Institute of Chicago is both ethnically and culturally diverse, with international students representing more than fifteen different countries. Students range in age from 17 to 70. Twenty percent of the students are recent high school graduates, while more than half are career changers whose average age is about 30. In addition, 20 percent of the students are from out of state and have relocated to Chicago in order to participate in the Le Cordon Bleu programs.

Student Activities

The Cooking and Hospitality Institute of Chicago supports many student organizations that provide students with interesting networking and experiential opportunities. Under the advisement of the Dean of Education and faculty advisers, these organizations are the Student Recipe Development Association, the Alpha Beta Kappa Society, the Student Board, the Cellar Club, the Pastry Display Club, the Bread Guild, the Culinary Competition Team, and many more. The Culinary Competition Team has won medals and certificates throughout the country.

Facilities and Resources

The Cooking and Hospitality Institute occupies more than 85,000 square feet of space. The North Campus is located at 361 West Chestnut in a two-story red brick building, with easy access to both public transportation, the major expressways, and two international airports. The new South Campus is just across the parking lot at 820 North Orleans. All thirteen air-conditioned kitchens feature industry-current technology with complete cooking lines, automatic dishwashers, and several preparation areas. The Institute features multiple walk-in refrigerators, freezers, dry storage, and cleaning-supply areas. There are fourteen classrooms on campus as well as a library, computer lab, student lounge, tutoring center, and café. The café features a formal dining room with seating for up to 80 guests. The café is operated by students and is open to the public for breakfast, lunch, and dinner.

Student Housing A student housing program is available to students through a real estate firm. Apartments (shared housing) are competitively priced and accessible to the campus via public transportation.

Learning Resource Center Students and faculty members have full access to a collection of more than 5,000 volumes, forty related periodicals and newsletters, and reference materials in hospitality-related areas, as well as CD-ROMs and numerous online resources. Online services include a reference catalog, Internet access, ProQuest, and Infotrac. In addition to the current holdings, the library has cooperative arrangements with various local libraries and professional associations. Interlibrary loan service is available through Illinet (Illinois Library and Information Network). The LRC also maintains a staffed computer laboratory for student use, with access to the Internet, various hospitality and purchasing software, word processing, and scanners.

Career Planning/Placement Offices Whether a current student or alumni, Career Services is the first stop for career and employment information and guidance. The Cooking and Hospitality Institute of Chicago encourages current students to participate in networking opportunities available through Career Services for exposure to a variety of professionals in the culinary and hospitality industries. In addition, the Career Services Department offers workshops, tutoring, and personal career coaching. Students and alumni wishing to meet with a representative of the office to discuss career planning or to gain access to current job openings should contact the Career Services Office.

Career Services recognizes that many students may require employment during their tenure at the Cooking and Hospitality Institute of Chicago, so it provides assistance to these students in their search for part-time employment. In order to maximize the benefits of this program, Career Services recommends that students work a maximum of 25 hours a week. The Cooking and Hospitality Institute of Chicago has formed partnerships with employers so students may gain practical experience in the culinary/hospitality industry both during and after their attendance at the Institute. The student captures the opportunity to apply classroom theory to real-world practice and develops speed, efficiency, and food-production skills. Career Services is committed to the success of the students and works hard to assist with employment for all interested students; however, the Institute cannot guarantee employment placement. Career Services provides information on the student portal on temporary, part-time, and full-time positions; volunteer opportunities; and upcoming site visits.

Location

The Institute is located in the River North area of Chicago, within walking distance of some of the finest restaurants and art galleries in the city. It is eight blocks west of Chicago's famed shopping district, the Magnificent Mile, and only a few blocks north of Chicago's business district, the Loop. It is easily accessible by public transportation, two major expressways, and two international airports.

Admission Requirements

All applicants must be beyond compulsory school age and must furnish documentation of at least a high school diploma or a GED diploma. In addition, applicants must demonstrate their math and English abilities by providing high school or college transcripts or ACT or SAT scores, or they may take the Institute's math and/or English placement exams. International students may submit TOEFL scores for initial acceptance and issuance of an I-20 visa, but they must take the Institute's placement tests upon arrival for course determination.

Application and Information

Applications are accepted on an ongoing basis. Prospective students should contact:

Director of Admissions
Cooking and Hospitality Institute of Chicago
361 West Chestnut
Chicago, Illinois 60610
Phone: 312-944-0882
          877-828-7772 (toll-free)
Fax: 312-944-8557
E-mail: chic@chicnet.org
Web site: http://www.chic.edu

Students receive personalized, hands-on instruction from Le Cordon Bleu instructors.

COTTEY COLLEGE

NEVADA, MISSOURI

The College and Its Mission

Cottey College is a two-year independent, residential, liberal arts and sciences college for women. Virginia Alice Cottey founded the College in 1884 with the firm belief that women deserved the same quality of education as men. When the founder became a member of the P.E.O. Sisterhood—a philanthropic educational organization of more than 250,000 members dedicated to providing educational opportunities for women—she realized the organization paralleled her own goals and ideas about higher education for women. The P.E.O. Sisterhood accepted the College as a gift from the founder in 1927, which made it the only nonsectarian college owned and supported by women.

Cottey College concentrates on what it does best—providing two years of very focused and rigorous academics to move students closer to earning a four-year degree. A Cottey education emphasizes high academic standards with unique opportunities for personal growth through residential, cultural, and intellectual experiences. Cottey College educates qualified women in the arts and sciences to prepare them to transfer to programs beyond the associate degree by enhancing their intellectual ability, their store of knowledge, their personal skills, and, thereby, their capacity for contribution to society and their chosen fields.

Cottey is a member of the Missouri American Council on Education (ACE) Network for the Office of Women in Higher Education (OWHE) and hosts the state Web site on its server.

Academic Programs

The academic tradition at Cottey College is firmly established in the liberal arts. Because its mission is, in part, "to educate qualified women in arts and sciences to prepare them for transfer to programs beyond the associate degree," Cottey emphasizes general education. Fields of study are, in effect, prospective majors for Cottey students, allowing them to focus on specialized personal interests growing out of a general education in the liberal arts and sciences. A Cottey education in a chosen field of study permits students to start learning and working toward careers that interest them and prepares them to enter a major or preprofessional program when they transfer to another institution to complete their bachelor's degree.

Cottey College grants the Associate in Arts (A.A.) and the Associate in Science (A.S.) degrees. Both associate degrees require the completion of 62 credit hours with a cumulative grade point average (GPA) of 2.0 or higher. Thirty-two credit hours must be completed at Cottey College. All students must complete a 24-credit common core curriculum. The core includes 11 credits in basic skills, such as English composition (writing), mathematics, and physical activities. The other 13 credits are distribution requirements in the fine arts, humanities, natural sciences, and social sciences. Depending on their interests and prospective majors, Cottey graduates earn either the A.A. or A.S. degree by meeting additional degree requirements beyond the core curriculum. The A.A. degree requires 12 additional credits focusing on the humanities, foreign languages, and fine arts. The A.S. degree requires 11 additional credits focusing on the sciences and mathematics.

More than 95 percent of graduates transfer to four-year institutions, including such top schools as MIT, Smith, Grinnell, Pepperdine, and the University of Washington, to name a few. As a two-year college, Cottey does not pressure students to declare a major, but they are prepared to declare one at their next college or university.

Off-Campus Programs

In March 2000, for the first time in the College's history, second-year Cottey students spent the first week of the spring break in London, England. The Cottey College Board of Trustees approved a three-year pilot program that sends students to a European city during the spring break of their second year. The program continues to receive approval from the Board and in the last six years, the College has traveled to London, Paris, and Madrid. In 2006, the second-year class returned to London. There are no additional costs in terms of tuition increases or program or transportation fees placed upon students to participate in this program. Members of the Cottey faculty and staff are involved in the planning of this program and integrate on-campus instruction and activities with the trip preparations. Professors selected for the international trip create educational modules related to their disciplines or interests that they present during two days of the trip. Students have ample time for individual sight-seeing and group-touring opportunities, and all participants attend a farewell dinner at a first-class restaurant.

Costs

For the 2007–08 academic year, the total cost is $18,710. This includes tuition, room and board, and all fees.

Financial Aid

Approximately 97 percent of the students receive some form of need- or merit-based aid. Assistance programs include P.E.O. and Cottey scholarships, grants, campus employment, and loans. Amounts depend on financial need, talents, high school GPA, and ACT and/or SAT scores. More information can be obtained from the financial aid office.

Faculty

There are 35 full-time faculty members, of whom more than 94 percent hold doctoral degrees or the terminal degrees in their fields. Twenty-two hold a Ph.D. degree. The student-faculty ratio is 10:1, and the average class size is 13 students. The faculty members are first and foremost teachers. Their subject areas are obvious and inspiring, and their primary interest is in teaching and mentoring young women of promise. All classes are taught by Cottey professors, not teaching assistants. Students know their professors, and this access to faculty members allows students to ask questions and get the answers they need. Many faculty members accept calls at home, and some are known to regularly visit campus study groups on nights or weekends for last-minute tutoring sessions before a test.

Student Body Profile

Cottey students come from everywhere. Generally, no more than 10 percent of students come from any one state, and approximately 10 percent come from outside the United States.

Cottey's residential student population of 350 women typically represents forty states, Canada, and ten to fourteen countries.

Student Activities

Many outstanding cultural events, performances, lectures, workshops, and recreational activities are offered without charge to students. More than thirty-five clubs and organizations at Cottey represent varying student interests in academics, culture, recreation, social concerns, religion, and volunteerism. The clubs and organizations also offer many leadership positions for students each year, enabling women to gain valuable leadership experiences that can help shape their future, their education, and their career paths. Many students become involved in the programs at Cottey's Helen and George Washburn Center for Women's Leadership (CWL), which was established to build girls' and women's lives through enrichment, education, and leadership development. The CWL offers special guest lecturers and notable speakers, and Cottey students can obtain leadership certification through its Leadership, Education, Opportunities (LEO) program, which provides student leaders with an opportunity to document and receive recognition for their experiences inside and outside the classroom and to further develop leadership skills. The LEO program offers four levels of certification.

Cottey's regular slate of national and international guests and performers makes Nevada seem like a larger city. The CLASS series brings to campus such artists, experts, and entertainers as the National Theatre for the Deaf, a Japanese storyteller, the Preservation Hall Jazz Band, Alvin Ailey II Dance Company, Tibetan monks performing sacred music and dance, the Kansas City Symphony, State Ballet, and folk singer Karla Bonhoff. Cottey students take the lead in celebrating International Focus Week, during which they share the food, stories, artifacts, and artistry of their native or ancestral cultures.

Cottey College offers volleyball and basketball in its intercollegiate sports program. Cottey is a member of the National Junior College Athletic Association (NJCAA) Division II, Region XVI. The NJCAA is the athletic association for all two-year colleges. Division II is a mix of small and large two-year colleges. Region XVI is the state of Missouri. There are six colleges that are Division II in Missouri, and those colleges compete in the Regional Tournament.

Facilities and Resources

Completed in 1963, the Blanche Skiff Ross Memorial Library was named in honor of Mrs. Frank Ross of Oak Park, Illinois, niece of Alice Virginia Coffin, one of the 7 founders of the P.E.O. Sisterhood. Browsing the shelves of more than 50,000 volumes of books, videos, DVDs, CDs, slides, maps, and music scores can lead to exploring a broad range of subjects, viewpoints, and cultures. More than 180 current periodical subscriptions reflect the variety of today's interests; some titles extend to 150 years of history. On campus, the library Web site links to databases with full texts of more than 2,000 periodicals as well as news services, government documents, and scholarly databases. The library is a member of the Missouri Bibliographic Information User System (MOBIUS), a group of more than fifty libraries in Missouri, as well as SouthWest Academic Libraries (SWAN),

which is a regional branch of the MOBIUS system. MOBIUS and SWAN allow a Cottey student to request a book from libraries within this system. Items requested from MOBIUS and SWAN are delivered to Cottey's library usually within three to four days. This gives students access to resources and information beyond what Cottey can offer.

Location

A community of about 9,000 people, Nevada, Missouri, is approximately 100 miles south of Kansas City. The campus occupies fourteen buildings on eleven city blocks and a 33-acre wooded recreational area with a lodge. Nevada is a fairly self-sufficient town, with grocery stores, restaurants, local shops, and a Wal-Mart. In addition, there are several large cities and recreational areas within a 90-minute drive of the Cottey campus.

Admission Requirements

All applicants for admission to Cottey College should take a college preparatory sequence. The minimum required high school curriculum includes 4 years of study in English composition and literature, 3 years of math (algebra I and II and geometry), 2 years of history and government, 2 years of a laboratory science, and 2 years of the same foreign language. Acceptance to Cottey is based on prior performance, academic aptitude, and the student's likelihood for success.

Students can apply online or by mail. If applying by mail, there is a $20 nonrefundable application fee. Along with a completed application, students must submit an evaluation form completed by a high school teacher or guidance counselor, an official copy of the high school transcript (showing the completion of at least six semesters of course work), and official ACT or SAT scores. All international students must complete the international application for admission, even if they are currently living in the United States.

Application and Information

The application for admission should be on file with the Office of Enrollment Management as early as possible. The College accepts students for admission only until it reaches its capacity of 350 residential students. If a student has a high school GPA of at least 2.6 and standardized test results that meet the current eligibility requirements (ACT composite of 21 or better or an SAT total of 970 or better on the critical thinking and math sections), she is notified of an admission decision within two to four weeks after completing the application process. Cottey College does not require the Writing section of the SAT at this time.

Office of Enrollment Management
Cottey College
1000 West Austin Boulevard
Nevada, Missouri 64772
Phone: 417-667-8181
      888-5-COTTEY (toll-free)
Fax: 417-667-8103
E-mail: enrollmgt@cottey.edu
Web site: http://www.cottey.edu

FASHION INSTITUTE OF TECHNOLOGY
State University of New York
NEW YORK, NEW YORK

The Institute and Its Mission

The Fashion Institute of Technology (FIT) is a selective, State University of New York (SUNY) college of art and design, business, and technology, offering more than forty programs of study leading to the A.A.S., B.F.A., B.S., M.A., and M.P.S. degrees. Known worldwide as the premier educational institution for fashion and its related fields, FIT provides students an unmatched combination of specialized curricula, an in-depth liberal arts education, and an extraordinary location in the center of New York City, world capital of the arts, business, and media.

FIT serves nearly 10,000 full-time, part-time, and evening/weekend students from the New York metropolitan area, across the country, and around the world. For the Associate in Applied Science (A.A.S.) degree, FIT offers eleven majors through its School of Art and Design, and four through its Jay and Patty Baker School of Business and Technology. Each program is built upon a core of traditional liberal arts courses, providing students with a global perspective, critical thinking skills, and the ability to communicate effectively. *Community College Week* has ranked FIT as second in the nation for awarding A.A.S. degrees in communications, journalism, and related programs, and fifth in the nation for awarding A.A.S. degrees in business, management, marketing, and related support services.

For those students who have completed their A.A.S. and are interested in continuing their education at FIT, the college offers twenty-two baccalaureate-level programs—thirteen Bachelor of Fine Arts (B.F.A.) programs through the School of Art and Design, eight Bachelor of Science (B.S.) programs through the Jay and Patty Baker School of Business and Technology, and one B.S. program through the School of Liberal Arts. These programs may be completed in two years, provided the student holds an appropriate A.A.S. degree from FIT or an equivalent college degree. For those seeking postgraduate degrees, the School of Graduate Studies offers six programs leading to either a Master of Arts (M.A.) or Master of Professional Studies (M.P.S.).

FIT maintains close ties with the industries it serves, working in tandem with business to offer an education unmatched in professional preparation. Academic departments keep advisory boards of noted experts in their fields, who ensure that the course work and classroom technology adapt apace with industry practices. FIT's faculty is composed of successful professionals, who bring their experience to the classroom. Field trips, guest lectures, and sponsored competitions introduce students to the real-life opportunities and challenges of their disciplines. Internships are a required element of most programs, and available to all students. And the college's Career Services offers lifetime placement, with a graduation employment rate of nearly ninety percent.

FIT is an accredited institutional member of the Middle States Association of Colleges and Schools, the National Association of Schools of Art and Design, and the Foundation for Interior Design Education Research. And as a SUNY institution, tuition is affordable for both New York State residents and nonresidents.

Academic Programs

All students complete a two-year A.A.S. program in their major area of study and the liberal arts. They may then either choose to go on to a related, two-year B.F.A. or B.S. program, or begin their careers with the A.A.S. degree, which qualifies them for entry-level positions in a wide range of creative and/or business professions.

Associate Degree Programs There are fifteen programs leading to the A.A.S. degree: accessories design*, advertising and marketing communications*, communication design*, display and exhibit design, fashion design*, fashion merchandising management*, fine arts (with a career-exploration component), illustration, interior design, jewelry design*, menswear, photography, production management: fashion and related industries, textile development and marketing*, and textile/surface design*. Programs with an (*) are also available in a one-year format for those students with acceptable transferable credits or who already hold a bachelor's degree.

Bachelor's Degree Programs Upon completing their A.A.S. program, many students opt to pursue a related, two-year, baccalaureate-level program of study. There are thirteen programs leading to the B.F.A. degree: accessories design and fabrication, advertising design, computer animation and interactive media, fabric styling, fashion design (with specializations in children's wear, fashion design, intimate apparel, and knitting), fine arts, graphic design, illustration, interior design, packaging design, photography and the digital image, textile/surface design, and toy design. There are nine programs leading to the B.S. degree: advertising and marketing communications, cosmetics and fragrance marketing, direct marketing, fashion merchandising management, home products development, international trade and marketing for the fashion industries, production management: fashion and related industries, textile development and marketing, and visual art management.

Continuing Education FIT's School of Continuing Education and Professional Studies provides evening and weekend classes to students and working professionals alike who are interested in pursuing a degree or in furthering their knowledge of a particular industry. For those students looking to balance the demands of career or family with their education, there are nine degrees available through evening/weekend programs: advertising and marketing communications (A.A.S. and B.S.), communication design (A.A.S.), fashion design (A.A.S.), fashion merchandising management (A.A.S. and B.S.), graphic design (B.F.A.), illustration (B.F.A.), and international trade and marketing for the fashion industries (B.S.).

Honors Program The Presidential Scholars Program, available to academically exceptional students in all disciplines, offers special liberal arts courses, projects, colloquia, and off-campus visits designed to broaden horizons and stimulate discourse. Presidential Scholars are also afforded priority course registration, given an annual merit stipend, and guaranteed on-campus residence.

Internships FIT student internships provide real-world learning experience. In many programs, internships are required and credit-bearing. In others, students may take internships on a supplemental-credit or noncredit basis. Sponsor organizations have included American Eagle, Bloomingdale's, Calvin Klein, Estée Lauder, Fairchild Publications, MTV, and Saatchi & Saatchi.

Precollege Programs Precollege Programs (Saturday/Summer Live) are available to high school students during the fall, spring, and summer. More than forty-five courses provide the chance to learn in an innovative environment, develop art and design portfolios, explore the business and technological sides of a wide range of creative careers, and discover natural talents and abilities. Courses for middle school students are also available in the summer.

Off-Campus Programs

FIT believes in the value of the study-abroad experience, which provides students with the opportunity to immerse themselves in diverse cultures and prepares them to live and work in a global community. FIT offers students, chosen on a competitive basis, the option of studying abroad for a year, a semester, or in the summer or winter sessions, in countries such as Australia, China, England, France, Israel, and Mexico. Full-time students enrolled in fashion design or fashion merchandising management have the option of a full academic year in Italy, through programs in Florence (fashion design A.A.S. and fashion merchandising management B.S.) and Milan (fashion design B.F.A.). International Programs maintains up-to-date program listings on its Web site.

Costs

The 2006–07 associate-level tuition was $1614 per semester for New York state residents; $4842 for out-of-state residents. Baccalaureate-level tuition per semester was $2175 for state residents, $5305 for out-of-state. For fall 2007, per semester housing rates are $3051–$3190 for traditional (meal plan required) accommodations, and $3819–$7250 for apartment-style. A $325 annual fee, for technology services and the Student Resident Association, is required of all

residence hall students. Meal plans range from $2790 to $3590. Textbook costs and other nominal fees, such as locker rental or laboratory use, vary per program of study. All costs are subject to change.

Financial Aid

FIT offers scholarships, grants, loans, and work-study employment for students in financial need. Nearly all full-time undergraduate students who apply for financial aid receive some type of assistance. The college directly administers its own institutional grants and scholarships, which are provided by the Educational Foundation for the Fashion Industries.

College-administered federal funding includes Federal Pell Grants, Federal Supplemental Educational Opportunity Grants, Federal Perkins Loans, Federal Work-Study Program awards, and the Federal Family Educational Loan Program, which includes student and parent loans. New York state residents who meet state guidelines for eligibility may also receive Tuition Assistance Program (TAP) and/or Educational Opportunity Program (EOP) grants. Financial aid applicants must file the Free Application for Federal Student Aid (FAFSA), on which they apply for the Federal Pell Grant, and should also apply to all available outside sources of aid. Other documentation may be requested by the Financial Aid Office. Applications for financial aid should be completed prior to February 15 for fall admission, or prior to November 1 for spring admission.

Faculty

FIT's faculty is drawn from top professionals in academia and the marketplace. Together, they offer a curriculum rich in real-world experience and the traditional educational values of the liberal arts. Professors are often highly successful business and design professionals, regularly sought out as experts in their respective fields. Student-instructor interaction is encouraged, with a maximum class size of 25, and courses are structured to foster participation, independent thinking, and self-expression.

Student Body Profile

Fall 2006 enrollment was approximately 10,000, with nearly 7,500 students enrolled in degree programs. Fifty-one percent of degree-seeking students are enrolled in the School of Art and Design; 49 percent are in the Jay and Patty Baker School of Business and Technology. The average age of the student population is 23. Sixty-five percent of FIT's students are New York State residents; 35 percent are out-of-state or international. The ethnic/racial makeup of the student body is approximately 12 percent Asian/Pacific Islander; 8 percent black, non-Hispanic; 11 percent Hispanic; and 43 percent white, non-Hispanic. Twenty-six percent chose not to identify with any of the listed groups. There are more than 750 international students from over sixty different countries.

Student Activities

Participation in campus life is encouraged, and the college is home to more than sixty clubs, societies, and athletic teams. Each organization is open to all students who have paid their activity fee.

Student Government The Student Council, the governing body of the Student Association, grants all students the privileges and responsibilities of citizens in a self-governing college community. Faculty committees often include student representatives, and the president of the student government sits on FIT's Board of Trustees.

Athletics FIT has intercollegiate teams in basketball, bowling, cross-country track, dance, table tennis, tennis, and volleyball. Athletics and Recreation sponsors group fitness classes each semester, available at no extra cost to students. Classes include body toning, boxing, dance, soccer, tennis, and yoga. Intramural sports allow students to participate in team and individual sports.

Events Concerts, dances, field trips, films, flea markets, and other events are planned by the Student Association and Programming Board and the various FIT clubs throughout the year. Student-run publications include a campus newspaper, a literary and art magazine, and the annual FIT yearbook.

Facilities and Resources

FIT provides its students with an urban campus of classrooms, laboratories, and studios that reflect the most advanced educational and industry practices. The Fred P. Pomerantz Art and Design Center houses drawing, painting, photography, printmaking, and sculpture studios; display and exhibit design rooms; a model-making workshop;

and a graphics printing service bureau. The Peter G. Scotese Computer-Aided Design and Communications Facility provides the latest technology in computer graphics, photography, and the design of advertising, fashion, interiors, textiles, and toys. Other facilities include a professionally equipped fragrance development laboratory, cutting and sewing labs, a design/research lighting laboratory, a knitting lab, broadcasting studio, multimedia foreign languages laboratory, and twenty-three computer labs containing nearly 700 Mac and PC workstations in addition to several additional labs with computers reserved for students in specific programs.

The Museum at FIT contains one of the most important collections of fashion and textiles in the world, with an emphasis on twentieth-century apparel. The museum operates year-round and its exhibitions are free and open to the public. The Gladys Marcus Library provides more than 300,000 volumes of print, non-print, and electronic materials. The periodical collection includes over 500 current subscriptions, with a specialization in international design and trade publications, and the Digital Library contains over ninety searchable databases.

Throughout the David Dubinsky Student Center are lounges, a game room, a student radio station, the Style Shop (the student-run boutique), student government and club offices, a comprehensive health center, two gyms, a dance studio, a weight room, and a counseling center.

Four residence halls house approximately 2,500 students in fully furnished single-, double-, triple-, and quad-occupancy rooms. Each residence hall has lounges and laundry facilities; the West 31st Street residence hall also provides an onsite fitness center. Students have the option of either traditional (meal plan included) or apartment-style accommodations. Counselors and student staff live in the halls, helping students adjust to college life and living in New York City.

Location

FIT's campus comprises an entire block in Manhattan's Chelsea neighborhood, and the college makes extensive use of the city's creative, commercial, and cultural resources, providing students with unrivaled internship opportunities and professional connections. A wide range of cultural and entertainment options—from dining to galleries to theater—are available within a short walking distance from campus, as is easy and convenient access to several subway and bus routes and the city's major rail and bus transportation hubs.

Admission Requirements

Applicants for admission must be either candidates for or recipients of a high school diploma or the General Educational Development (GED) certificate. Candidates are judged on class rank, grades in college-preparatory course work, and the student essay. Letters of recommendation are not required. A portfolio evaluation is required for art and design majors only. Specific portfolio requirements are explained on FIT's Web site.

Transfer students must submit official transcripts for credit evaluation. Students may qualify for the one-year A.A.S. option if they hold a bachelor's degree or if they have a minimum of 30 transferable credits, including 24 credits equivalent to FIT's liberal arts requirements, and at least one semester of physical education.

Students seeking admission to a B.F.A. or B.S. program must hold an A.A.S. degree from FIT or an equivalent college degree and must meet the prerequisites as required by the major. Further requirements may include an interview with a departmental committee, review of academic standing, and portfolio review for all applicants to B.F.A. programs. Any student who applies for transfer to FIT from a four-year program must have completed a minimum of 60 credits, including the requisite art or technical courses and the liberal arts requirements.

Application and Information

Interested candidates may apply online, at http://www.fitnyc.edu/admissions. More information is available by contacting:

Admissions
Fashion Institute of Technology
Seventh Avenue at 27th Street
New York, New York 10001-5992

Phone: 212-217-7675
        800-GO-TO-FIT (toll-free)
E-mail: fitinfo@fitnyc.edu
Web site: http://www.fitnyc.edu

FIDM/THE FASHION INSTITUTE OF DESIGN & MERCHANDISING

LOS ANGELES, CALIFORNIA

The Institute and Its Mission

FIDM/The Fashion Institute of Design and Merchandising provides a dynamic and exciting community of learning in the fashion, graphics, interior design, digital media, and entertainment industries. The purpose of the Institute is to provide an educational environment designed to combine student goals with industry needs.

FIDM has a reputation for graduating professionally competent and confident men and women capable of creative thought. It has graduated more than 30,000 students in its thirty-eight-year history.

In addition to its associate degree programs, FIDM is currently offering a Bachelor of Science degree in business management (candidacy status WASC-ACSCU).

FIDM is accredited by the Accrediting Commission for Community and Junior Colleges of the Western Association of Schools and Colleges (WASC) and the National Association of Schools of Art and Design (NASAD).

Academic Programs

FIDM operates on a four-quarter academic calendar. New students may begin their studies any quarter throughout the year. The requirement for a two-year Associate of Arts degree is the completion of 90 units.

Associate Degree Programs FIDM offers Associate of Arts degrees in apparel manufacturing management, beauty industry merchandising and marketing, digital media, fashion design, footwear design, graphic design, interior design, international manufacturing and product development, jewelry design, merchandise marketing (fashion merchandising or product development), textile design, theater costume design, TV and film costume design, and visual communication. All of these programs offer the highly specialized curriculum of a specific major combined with a core general education/liberal arts foundation.

Transfer Arrangements FIDM accepts course work from other accredited colleges if there is an equivalent course at FIDM and the grade is a C or better. FIDM courses at the 100, 200, and 300 levels are certified by FIDM to be baccalaureate level. FIDM maintains articulation agreements with selected colleges with the intent of enhancing a student's transfer opportunities. Academic counselors will provide assistance to students interested in transferring to other institutions to attain a four-year degree.

Internship and Co-op Programs Internships are available within each of the various majors. Paid and volunteer positions provide work experience for students to gain practical application of classroom skills.

Special Programs and Services FIDM offers Associate of Arts professional designation degrees for individuals with substantial academic and professional experience who wish to add a new field of specialization. These are nine- or twelve-month programs of intensive study in one of the Institute's specialized majors. Students from other regionally accredited programs have the opportunity to complement their previous education by enrolling in a professional designation program. Requirements

for completion range from 45 to 66 units, depending on the field of study. FIDM also offers Associate of Arts Advanced Study Programs that develop specialized expertise in the student's unique area of study. These programs are open to students who possess extensive prior academic and professional experience within the discipline area. These areas include fashion design–advanced study, interior design–advanced study, theater costume–advanced study, and international manufacturing and product development. Completion requirements for these programs are 45 units. Some classes are offered online.

In response to student needs, FIDM has established an evening program in addition to the regular daytime courses. The program has been designed to accommodate the time requirements of working students. The entire evening program for the Associate in Arts degree can be completed in 2½ years.

FIDM offers English as a second language (ESL) for students requiring English development to complete their major field of study. The program is concurrent and within FIDM's existing college-level course work. These classes focus on the special needs of students in the areas of oral communication, reading comprehension, and English composition.

Community Programs Community service programs are offered both independently and in cooperation with various community groups. General studies course credit may be awarded to participating students. Each FIDM campus identifies community projects that allow students to support local service agencies.

Off-Campus Programs

FIDM provides the opportunity for students to participate in academic study tours in Europe, Asia, and New York. These tours are specifically designed to broaden and enhance the specialized education offered at the Institute. Study tour participants may earn academic credit under faculty-supervised directed studies. Exchange programs are also available with Esmod, Paris; Instituto Artictico dell' Abbigliamento Marangoni, Milan; Accademia Internazionale d'Alta Mode e d'Arte del Costume Koefia, Rome; St. Martins School of Art, London; College of Distributive Trades, London; and Janette Klein Design School, Mexico City.

Credit for Nontraditional Learning Experiences

The Institute may give credit for demonstrated proficiency in areas related to college-level courses. Sources used to determine proficiency are the College-Level Examination Program (CLEP) and Credit for Academically Relevant Experience (CARE), an Institute-sponsored program.

Costs

For the 2007–08 academic year, tuition and fees start at $18,285, depending on the major selected by the student. Textbooks and supplies start at $1900 per year, depending on the major. First-year application fees start at $225 for California residents and range up to $525 for international students.

Financial Aid

There are several sources of financial funding available to the student, including federal financial aid and education loan

programs, California state aid programs, institutional loan programs, and FIDM awards and scholarships.

Faculty

FIDM faculty members are selected as specialists in their fields. Many are actively employed in their respective fields of expertise. They bring daily exposure to their industry into the classroom for the benefit of the students. In pursuit of the best faculty members, consideration is given to both academic excellence as well as practical experience. FIDM has a 16:1 student-instructor ratio.

Student Body Profile

FIDM's ethnically and culturally diverse student body is one of the attractions to the Institute. Fifteen percent of the current student body are international students from more than thirty different countries. Twenty percent of the students are more than 25 years of age. More than 90 percent find career positions within one year of graduation.

Student Activities

The Student Activities Committee plans and coordinates social activities, cultural events, and community projects, including the ASID Student Chapter, International Club, Delta Epsilon Chi (DEX), Association of Manufacturing Students, Honor Society, and the Alumni Association. The students also produce their own trend newsletter, *The Mode.*

Facilities and Resources

Advisement/Counseling Department Chairs and other trained staff members provide assistance to students in selecting the correct sequence of courses to allow each student to complete degree requirements. The counseling department provides personal guidance and referral to outside counseling services as well as matching peer tutors to specific students' needs. Individual Development and Education Assistance (IDEA) centers at each campus provide students with additional educational assistance to supplement classroom instruction. Services are available in the areas of writing, mathematics, computer competency, study skills, research skills, and reading comprehension.

Career Planning/Placement Offices Career planning and job placement are among the most important services offered by the Institute. Career assistance includes job search techniques, preparation for employment interviews, resume preparation, and job adjustment assistance. Services provided by the center include undergraduate placement, graduate placement, alumni placement, internships, and industry work/study programs.

Library and Audiovisual Services FIDM's library goes beyond the traditional sources of information. In addition to more than 12,000 books and reference materials, FIDM also features an international video library, subscriptions to major predictive services, international and domestic periodicals, interior design workrooms, textile samples, a trimmings/findings collection, and access to the Internet. FIDM's Costume Museum houses more than 4,500 garments from the seventeenth century to present day. The collection includes items from the California Historical Society (First Families), the Hollywood Collection, and the Rudi Gernreich Collection.

State-of-the-art computer labs support and enhance the educational programs of the Institute. Specialized labs offer computerized cutting and marking, graphic and textile design, word processing, and database management.

Location

Established in 1969, FIDM is a private college that is proud to enroll more than 6,000 students a year. The main campus is in the heart of downtown Los Angeles near the famed California Mart and Garment District. This campus is adjacent to the beautiful Grand Hope Park. There are additional California branch campuses located in San Francisco, San Diego, and Orange County.

Admission Requirements

The Institute provides educational opportunities to high school graduates or applicants that meet the Institute's Ability to Benefit (ATB) criteria to pursue a two-year Associate of Arts degree. Qualifications for professional designation programs include students that meet the general education core requirements or who have a U.S. accredited degree. All applicants must have an initial interview with an admissions representative. In addition, students must submit references and specific portfolio projects if applicable to the chosen major. The Institute is on the approved list of the U.S. Department of Justice for nonimmigrant students and is authorized to issue Certificates of Eligibility (Form I-20).

Application and Information

Applications are accepted on an ongoing basis. All prospective students should contact:

Director of Admissions
FIDM/The Fashion Institute of Design & Merchandising,
    Los Angeles Campus
919 South Grand Avenue
Los Angeles, California 90015

Phone: 800-624-1200 (toll-free)
Fax: 213-624-4799
Web site: http://www.fidm.edu/

Debut. Student designer: Kim Yen Cao.

FULL SAIL REAL WORLD EDUCATION
WINTER PARK, FLORIDA

The College and Its Mission

Established in 1979, Full Sail Real World Education is a private, coeducational college offering extensive training and education in the entertainment media production industry and entertainment technology. Hands-on experience and solid practical knowledge combine to provide an education where learning meets the real world. Students receive an introduction to many job opportunities in each career field and an overview of what each position requires. Full Sail's campus facilities include recording consoles, digital video editing workstations, cameras, concert sound systems, computerized moving lights, and computer/graphic workstations that are used to create Web sites, animation sequences, 3-D graphics, computer generated models, characters, visual effects, and interactive games. Full Sail provides extensive instruction in all of these areas and more, offering a unique style of training that gets students hands-on and right in the middle of the entertainment and media production industry while in school.

Traditional learning techniques have their place at Full Sail, but the technology-intensive field of creative media demands a more rigorous pace than that offered by books, lectures, and seminars. As helpful as those are, their effectiveness is severely limited without practical, hands-on experience inside the school environment. Full Sail takes students' education beyond the confines of the classroom into real-world situations and puts them to work on the same kind of equipment encountered in media production facilities throughout the world.

Instructors and guest lecturers are professionals in their fields, and the low student-faculty ratio in labs allows students to interact with their mentors. Students come to Full Sail from around the world, and musicians, artists, and technicians come for the training and business savvy needed to further their careers.

With more than 23,000 alumni, graduate credits include work on Oscar- and GRAMMY®-winning projects, best-selling video games, and the top-grossing U.S. concert tour six out of the last six years. Students experience a "real world" education, with a professional class structure of 8–12 hours per day, and a 24-hour 'round-the-clock schedule that earned Full Sail the "Most Innovative Program" award by the Florida Association of Postsecondary Schools and Colleges. *Shift Magazine* called the school the "third-best new media school in the world," behind the Massachusetts Institute of Technology (MIT) and New York University (NYU). *Electronic Gaming Monthly* named Full Sail one of the top five game-degree programs in the world. *Rolling Stone* magazine recently named Full Sail one of the five best music programs in the country, in addition to naming it one of the best music business departments in the *Schools That Rock: The Rolling Stone College Guide. UNleashed Magazine* has named Full Sail one of the five best film programs in the country.

The school is fully accredited by the Accrediting Commission of Career Schools and Colleges of Technology (ACCSCT).

Academic Programs

Full Sail offers Associate of Science degrees in recording arts and show production and touring. Bachelor of Science degrees are also offered in computer animation, digital arts and design, film, game development, and entertainment business.

Full Sail runs on a modular schedule, with new classes beginning every month. Schedules vary depending on the degree programs. Once enrolled, students attend classes and labs five to six days, 35 to 40 hours each week. By doing so, students typically earn a bachelor's degree in less than twenty-one months. Lectures are scheduled during daytime hours, but some labs occur during evening and early morning hours. Full Sail recently won a Florida statewide award for the school with the "Most Innovative Program," due in part to this type of scheduling. It benefits students by ensuring a low student-teacher ratio and by representing the realistic demands of the entertainment and media production industry.

Full Sail's Recording Arts Program is an intensive audio education that covers every facet of music and audio production—from tracking and overdubs to mixing and mastering—in a college environment unlike any other. Full Sail's professional recording studios allow students to record bands using the same microphones, mixing boards, and digital audio workstations used in studios all over the world. Students learn from the best: Full Sail's instructors are studio professionals, and they bring years of audio engineering experience into the classroom as they show how to run a professional recording session. In addition, students explore techniques for the growing world of audio for video games and dive headfirst into the challenges of audio postproduction for movies and television shows.

Full Sail's Show Production and Touring Program covers everything from the rigors of life on the road to lighting design for live production—all in the space of only thirteen months. Students learn the ropes at Full Sail Live, a custom-designed theater environment outfitted with the same gear that is installed in live-sound venues and that travels the world with top touring acts. Students learn every aspect of live-event production from experienced instructors who have spent much of their lives on tour. At the time of graduation, students are ready to start careers in event production.

The curriculum for the Entertainment Business Program may be taken in addition to either the Show Production and Touring Program or the Recording Arts Program to receive a Bachelor of Science in entertainment business.

Costs

Tuition costs vary depending on the program. Tuition ranges from $40,005 to $61,775 per degree program. At Full Sail, these tuition costs include books, lab fees, course materials, career-development assistance, and lifetime auditing.

Financial Aid

Everyone's financial aid package is unique to them. The type of package that works best is determined by the important decisions made during this process as well as specific needs. Financial advisers work to ensure that students have all the information needed to make financial aid decisions that allow them the opportunity to attend Full Sail. Full Sail wants to assist every financial aid applicant in obtaining the financial aid assistance they are legally entitled to receive. The student's eligibility, the school's packaging criteria, and the amount and types of financial aid available determine this. Since Full Sail is an accredited school, the Financial Aid Department has a number of packages consisting of grants and loans available to those who qualify. These packages are tailored to each student's financial need.

Faculty

Full Sail has 482 full-time instructors, and the student-faculty ratio is 10:1. The typical Full Sail teacher has spent years working in the entertainment and media production industry doing the type of work that he or she now teaches at Full Sail. Instructors have earned hundreds of movie, record, game, television show, and Web credits, including GRAMMY and EMMY awards. These dedicated professionals come to Full Sail because of the school's reputation in the industry as one of the best colleges in entertainment media education. The majority of the instructors continue to be active in their professional field, which allows them to bring current product knowledge and examples to their students.

Student Body Profile

Full Sail is home to more than 5,000 students representing fifty states and thirty-five countries worldwide. The student body is primarily men (89 percent). Approximately 70 percent of the student population is white (non-Hispanic), 10 percent black, 10 percent Hispanic, and 2 percent Asian or Pacific Islander.

Academic Facilities

The 178-acre Full Sail campus houses more than 100 studios, production suites, soundstages, and computer labs as well as over fifty advanced college classrooms. Full Sail is a production facility that rivals any professional multimedia studio in the world.

Student advisers are available to assist students with questions about academics and referrals, and the Student Services Desk is open 24 hours a day for emergencies. Full Sail students and alumni can also utilize the school's Career Development Center. This center assists students with finding internships and entry-level employment, educates students on how to successfully market themselves, and promotes networking and professional relationships among students, alumni, and industry professionals.

Full Sail does not feature on-campus living arrangements, but does employ a Housing Manager who is dedicated to providing information about affordable accommodations in the many apartment complexes near the school. The Housing Manager can also help with information about roommates (other incoming Full Sail students), power, phones, furniture, and helpful community programs in the central Florida area.

Location

Full Sail's college campus is situated in a beautiful area of central Florida in Winter Park, a city that plays host to residential communities and light commerce. Thanks to tourism being Central Florida's primary business, entertainment, restaurants, and shopping are plentiful. The school is 20 minutes from downtown Orlando, 35 minutes from Disney and Universal Studios, 1 hour from Cape Canaveral and the Atlantic beaches, and 2 hours from the Gulf of Mexico.

Admission Requirements

There are only two things necessary for applicants to be ready to attend school at Full Sail—a sincere passion for a career in the entertainment and media production industry and a high school diploma or GED.

Application and Information

For details concerning applications and deadlines, students should contact a Full Sail Admissions Representative.

Full Sail Real World Education
3300 University Boulevard
Winter Park, Florida 39792-7429
    800-226-7625 (toll-free)
Fax: 407-678-0070
E-mail: admissions@fullsail.com
Web site: http://www.fullsail.com

Entrance to Full Sail Real World Education.

HARCUM COLLEGE
BRYN MAWR, PENNSYLVANIA

The College and Its Mission

Harcum College seeks to provide men and women with outstanding career preparation that meets or exceeds the standards of their chosen professions. At Harcum, self-realization and preparation for participative citizenship are also of great importance. Intent upon remaining among the foremost independent two-year colleges in America, Harcum aims to provide every student with the opportunity not only for a rewarding career but also for a fulfilling life.

Academic Programs

Harcum's academic programs are diverse and fall under four centers: the Center for Allied Health, the Center for Business and Professional Studies, the Center for Legal Studies, and the Center for Liberal Studies and Education. In addition, there are the School of Continuing and Professional Studies, which includes an evening/weekend college, and the Center for International Studies, which includes the English Language Academy. The four centers offer associate degrees and certificates.

Transfer Arrangements The Career and Transfer Services staff assists students in preparing for transfer to a four-year institution. Harcum students have been accepted by more than 200 colleges and universities nationwide and abroad. Harcum has close relationships with many colleges. The College has a number of articulation agreements with four-year colleges, whereby credit is seamlessly transferred to the four-year institution.

Internship and Co-op Programs All of Harcum's programs require an internship as part of the curriculum. Students spend a period of time gaining valuable work experience in a workplace appropriate to their program, where they apply the knowledge they have acquired in the classroom. Many students subsequently receive job offers from their internship sponsors.

Special Programs and Services The College offers a number of special programs to assist students in succeeding at college. Summer Advance is a five-week summer program that gives students an opportunity to adjust to college life while strengthening their academic preparation in reading, writing, math, and other areas. Achieving Individual Motivation for Success (AIM) develops academic and personal skills, cultural awareness, career plans, and lifelong learning tools for students who have disabilities, are economically disadvantaged, or are first-generation college attendees. The English Language Academy offers full- and part-time instruction in English as a second language. The Developmental Program provides courses to strengthen skills in English, math, and reading. Independent study is offered for students who want to study a topic that deeply interests them. A qualified, conscientious instructor guides students in their study, independent of regular classroom attendance. Periodic meetings and discussion seminars are held. The Center for Student Development and Counseling offers personal and individualized career and academic counseling.

Continuing Education Programs The College's School of Continuing and Professional Studies offers programs year-round. Courses are offered for professional development and personal enrichment. Continuing Education Units (CEUs) may be earned in the dental and veterinary fields and in many other fields related to the College's degree programs. Other popular programs include the pharmacy technician training course and the phlebotomy technician training course. For adult students looking to further their education in the evenings and on weekends, Harcum College offers flexible scheduling, a large selection of Internet courses, and an accelerated core curriculum to make the associate degree attainable. The College also offers a full schedule of evening and weekend classes for credit at a reduced tuition that is approximately one half the regular undergraduate studies rate.

Credit for Nontraditional Learning Experiences

The College awards credit for knowledge acquired outside the usual educational setting by accepting College-Level Examination Program (CLEP) scores for credit toward a degree. The College accepts general and subject examination CLEP scores based on the American Council on Education's recommended cut scores. Students working toward an associate degree may earn a total of 30 credits through CLEP, challenge exams, portfolio-assisted assessment, or traditional transfer.

Costs

The 2007–08 annual tuition for full-time students is $8000 per semester. There are additional miscellaneous fees and deposits. Annual room and board charges are $3740 per semester. All fees and tuition are subject to change. In addition, tuition for classes in the evening/weekend college is $192 per credit.

Financial Aid

More than 90 percent of students at Harcum receive some form of financial aid. Available aid includes Harcum grants-in-aid, scholarships, Federal Pell Grants, Federal Supplemental Educational Opportunity Grants, state grants, Federal Perkins Loans, and Federal Work-Study Program awards. The priority deadline for financial aid applications is May 1 for fall enrollment.

Faculty

All of Harcum's programs are led by full-time directors and have full-time professors. Their expertise is augmented by part-time adjunct instructors who usually are practicing professionals in their fields. There are 26 full-time faculty members. Eighty percent of full-time faculty members have advanced degrees, including 13 percent who hold doctorates. The student-faculty ratio is 9:1.

Student Body Profile

The student body is 75 percent women. The largest age group is between 18 and 26, but nearly as many are between 26 and 39 years of age. Seventy percent of the students are white, 16 percent are African American, and 3 percent are Asian. Full-time students make up 68 percent of the total. Commuters account for 83 percent. Eighty-nine percent of the students are from Pennsylvania, primarily from the five-county Philadelphia region. The next-largest group (4 percent) is from New Jersey. International students make up 2 percent. Sixty percent of those accepted to Harcum College enroll. Of those who enroll, 60 percent graduate.

Student Activities

It is easy to get involved on campus. Harcum has clubs and organizations for students with many different interests. Students make their mark on campus by joining one of more than twenty clubs, such as the student newspaper, the yearbook, the Organization for Animal Technician Students, or the Student

American Dental Hygienists Association. The College has a chapter of Phi Theta Kappa, the national honor society for two-year colleges, and Chi Alpha Epsilon, a national honor society for AIM students. The College also organizes many community service activities and events. Students participate in volunteer projects on and off campus, such as peer tutoring, clothing drives, and Earth Day.

Facilities and Resources

Harcum gives students full support throughout their time at the College and after graduation. At the Center for Student Development and Counseling, counselors give a hand with everything from advice on balancing a schedule to resolving a personal problem. The College also has academic tutors to help students with course work.

Students at Harcum have the option of living on campus in the residence halls, which is a great way to make friends and be in the middle of everything that is happening on campus. The residence hall staff plans programs and events, including seminars and discussion groups on topics ranging from study skills to current events, and stress-buster pizza parties.

Students feel at home at Harcum College. Even the students who commute say they do not feel like outsiders. Harcum is a small community, and students quickly find that they recognize friendly faces all over the campus.

Library and Audiovisual Services The library collection has 39,000 volumes, 300 periodicals, and more than 1,000 audiovisual items. It is a member of the Tri-State College Library Cooperative, a forty-two-college consortium, which provides access to more than 6 million volumes. Harcum's library also provides connections to the Internet and FirstSearch, an online database, and it is networked with 20 CD-ROM databases.

Location

Harcum is located in Bryn Mawr, Pennsylvania, 12 miles west of Philadelphia, in the heart of the Main Line, a string of attractive, safe, friendly suburban communities. The College is in the midst of one of the largest concentrations of educational institutions in the country. There are fifty-five colleges and universities in the Philadelphia area. The campus is on a parklike 12-acre site next to a commuter railroad station, which makes travel to Philadelphia and throughout the area easy. Available in Philadelphia are the world-renowned Philadelphia Orchestra, the Pennsylvania Ballet, the Opera Company of Philadelphia, and the world-famous Philadelphia Museum of Art. The city has major-league teams in baseball, football, ice hockey, and basketball. There are numerous historic sites in and around Philadelphia to visit, including Independence Hall, the Liberty Bell, and Valley Forge National Park.

Admission Requirements

All applicants are required to submit official academic transcripts, results of any standardized tests taken, a written essay, and a letter of recommendation. An interview is recommended. The dental hygiene application deadline is February 15. All other programs follow a rolling admission policy. Prospective students should consult the enrollment office for additional requirements specific to each program.

Application and Information

For more information, students should contact:

Office of Enrollment Management
Harcum College
750 Montgomery Avenue
Bryn Mawr, Pennsylvania 19010-3476
Phone: 610-526-6050
        800-345-2600 (toll-free)
Fax: 610-526-6147
E-mail: enroll@harcum.edu
Web site: http://www.harcum.edu

Library and Academic Center.

HESSER COLLEGE
MANCHESTER, NEW HAMPSHIRE

The College and Its Mission

The primary purpose of Hesser College is to provide a high-quality education that is personalized and employment oriented. Hesser College's innovative approach to higher education provides students with increased flexibility. After two years of college, students can earn an associate degree and are prepared to enter the workplace, or, if they prefer, students can continue on in one of Hesser College's bachelor's degree programs.

Hesser College was established in 1900 as Hesser Business College, a private, nonsectarian college. Since 1972, Hesser College has expanded and enriched its curriculum in keeping with its tradition of providing an affordable career education of high quality.

Hesser College is accredited by the New England Association of Schools and Colleges. Students who choose Hesser College receive a high-quality education.

Academic Programs

The primary goal of the curricula is to prepare students for success in specific career areas. The general education requirements are designed to provide the skills necessary for career growth and lifelong learning. Internships, practicums, and opportunities for part-time work experience are available in all majors. An education from Hesser College provides a solid career foundation. The College's goal is quite simple: to prepare people for careers and career advancement.

Many of the Hesser College programs are for the career-minded student who wants to concentrate on the skills required to be successful in the workplace. Seventy-five percent of the courses that students take are directly related to their career choices. Upon completion of the associate degree program, a student may pursue a four-year degree by enrolling in one of Hesser's bachelor's degree programs.

Associate Degree Programs Hesser offers a wide range of programs that prepare students for high-demand careers. They include accounting, business administration, communications and public relations, criminal justice, early childhood education, graphic design, interior design, liberal studies, medical assistant studies, paralegal studies, physical therapist assistant studies, psychology, and radio and video production and broadcasting.

Bachelor's Degree Programs Hesser College offers bachelor's degree programs in accounting, business administration, criminal justice, and psychology.

Off-Campus Programs

The College offers opportunities for cooperative education and externships in most of its academic programs. The early childhood education program includes practicums and supervised fieldwork in the freshman and senior years, utilizing a variety of child-care facilities. In addition, the curricula of several programs incorporate short-term study trips to such places as Walt Disney World and Washington, D.C.

Costs

Costs vary by program. Interested students should contact Hesser College for more information.

Financial Aid

Hesser College offers financial assistance to students who qualify. Many students receive some form of aid. Scholarships are awarded each year to students based on academic and financial standing. Hesser College also offers loans and grants.

Faculty

The faculty members of Hesser College consistently receive high student evaluations for their interest in each student's success and for the high quality of their teaching. The majority of the faculty members have completed programs of advanced study, many hold doctoral degrees, and all have practical experience in business or other career fields.

Student Body Profile

Most students work in the afternoons, evenings, or weekends while attending Hesser. The men and women currently enrolled represent several states and more than fifteen countries. A large part of the student population is from the New England region.

Student Activities

Hesser College offers intercollegiate sports teams in men's and women's basketball, soccer, and volleyball; men's baseball; and women's softball. The basketball and volleyball teams have consistently been a major power in the Northern New England Small College Conference. Students also participate in a number of intramural sports programs. Extracurricular activities are varied and include social activities, clubs, trips, and programs in the residence halls.

Facilities and Resources

The College includes dormitories for many students. A wide range of resources are located on campus. Academic advising is coordinated through department chairpersons and the Center for Teaching, Learning, and Assessment. The size of the College allows for individual attention to the financial and career counseling needs of each student.

The academic facilities include five computer labs, a Mac-based graphic design lab, medical assistant labs, a physical therapist assistant lab, and a radio/video production lab. Hesser College's library contains more than 30,000 titles. The Center for Teaching, Learning, and Assessment provides special tutoring and programs in study skills, reading, writing, math, and computer skills.

Hesser College has also developed a number of learning assistance programs to help students succeed in their studies. Tutoring and special classes are provided by the faculty throughout each semester. In addition, several departments offer honor programs and special opportunities for independent study. The College also sponsors an active chapter of the national honor society Phi Theta Kappa, which promotes scholarship and service to the College and the community.

Location

Hesser College is located in Manchester, New Hampshire. With a population of more than 100,000, Manchester is a medium-sized city that offers many cultural, historical, and social events. Hesser College's central location provides easy access to entertainment, shopping, and a variety of part-time jobs and academic work experiences.

Manchester was recently named by *Money* magazine as the number one small city in the northeast United States. In addition, Manchester was recently named as one of the best cities in the United States for business. According to *U.S. News & World Report*, Manchester is "at the hub of things" in the fast-growing, high-technology, financial, and information-oriented businesses of southern New Hampshire. Manchester has been called the "Gateway to Northern New England," and several major carriers serve the Manchester Airport.

Manchester is within 1 hour of Boston, and the mountains and major ski resorts are within 1–2 hours of Hesser's campus.

Admission Requirements

Hesser College has a rolling admissions policy. Students may apply for admission at any time.

Advisers are available to talk with students about their education and career goals, and interested students should contact Hesser College for more information.

Application and Information

Applicants must submit an application form with a $10 nonrefundable fee. Applications are reviewed on a first-come, first-served basis and normally take seven to fourteen days to be fully reviewed upon receipt of all required information.

Requests for additional information and application forms should be addressed to:

Director of Admissions
Hesser College
3 Sundial Avenue
Manchester, New Hampshire 03103
Phone: 603-668-6660 Ext. 2110
        800-526-9231 Ext. 2110 (toll-free)
Fax: 603-666-4722
E-mail: admissions@hesser.edu
Web site: http://www.hesser.edu

Students at Hesser College's main campus.

INDIANA BUSINESS COLLEGE
INDIANAPOLIS, INDIANA

INDIANA BUSINESS COLLEGE
WE CHANGE LIVES. ONE STUDENT AT A TIME℠

The College and Its Mission

Indiana Business College (IBC) was founded in 1902 to serve the specific education and career needs and interests of students planning to enter the business community. Indiana Business College consists of eleven campuses at convenient locations across the state. Full- and part-time programs, online classes, and day and evening classes are available at all locations. The philosophy behind the curriculum at the College is one of individual attention, allowing for flexibility and higher achievement in the classroom. The career-oriented emphasis enables course work to be highly specialized. Indiana Business College has a commitment to providing career-related education; students are trained by practical application and hands-on experience. This commitment, coupled with a reputation for offering a high-quality education, contributes to the employment opportunities for graduates. The College offers lifetime career assistance to its graduates and is continually updating the curriculum to meet the demands of today's business world. Indiana Business College is accredited by the Accrediting Council for Independent Colleges and Schools and is regulated by the Indiana Commission on Proprietary Education. The medical assisting programs at the Evansville, Fort Wayne, Medical (Indianapolis), and Terre Haute campuses are accredited by the Commission on Accreditation of Allied Health Education Programs on the recommendation of the Committee on Accreditation for Medical Assistant Education.

Academic Programs

Indiana Business College offers Associate of Applied Science degrees in accounting, administrative assistant studies, business administration, business administration/network technology, business and information technology, Cisco Network Associate studies, criminal justice, culinary arts, fashion merchandising, home technology integrator studies, health claims examiner studies, human resources, medical assisting, medical coding technology, medical laboratory technician studies, organizational management, and therapeutic massage and bodyworks.

Indiana Business College also offers diplomas in the areas of accounting assistant studies, medical office assistant studies, medical transcription, and office assistant studies.

Certificates are available in computer network technician studies and therapeutic massage practitioner studies.

Indiana Business College operates throughout the calendar year; classes begin quarterly in January, April, June, and September. To be awarded a degree, diploma, or certificate, students must maintain a minimum cumulative GPA of 2.0 (on a 4.0 scale).

The computer programs at Indiana Business College include courses in Cisco network administration, A+ computer technology, and Network+. The College has some of the state's top information technology programs available, including MCSE and MCSA. IBC is an associate member of CompTIA, offering A+ and Network+ certifications. The College is also a Microsoft IT Academy and one of the only Transcender Training partners in Indianapolis offering on-site testing for all IT certification programs.

The associate degree program in home technology integrator studies provides training in the automation of technology that is related to homes and businesses. The prospective student is involved in wiring, networking, lighting, HVAC, water, security, audio/video, and integration of services.

The organizational management degree is designed to prepare individuals for careers in project management, where sound business principles and state-of-the-art computer skills are essential for success in today's high-speed, high-technology marketplace. Topics include project integration, human and material resource allocation, risk analysis, cost engineering, procurement management, information technology topics, and e-business. Project managers are employed in every aspect of the business community.

The accounting programs offered at Indiana Business College include courses in intermediate and cost accounting, income tax, and payroll. Both diploma and Associate of Applied Science degree accounting programs incorporate the courses necessary to prepare students for excellent positions in private business, public accounting, and departments within the government.

The Associate of Applied Science degree program in business administration includes courses in the areas of computers, accounting, marketing, management, and sales. This program helps students to develop the creativity and the supervisory skills needed for managerial positions.

Indiana Business College's administrative support programs include administrative assistant studies and office assistant studies. These programs provide students with the necessary foundation in keyboarding, information processing, and computer technology.

The Associate of Applied Science degree program in criminal justice provides students with a broad spectrum of course work in corrections, law enforcement, private security, and investigation. This program is designed to prepare students for a variety of careers in the criminal justice field in both the public and private sectors.

The Associate of Applied Science degree program in fashion merchandising prepares the graduate for a career in the fashion industry. Combining business classes with fashion studies prepares the student to succeed in this competitive field. Included in this curriculum are courses such as textiles, display and design, marketing, and apparel merchandising.

The Associate of Applied Science degree program in culinary arts is part of the Chef's Academy—a division of Indiana Business College. This program is designed to provide hands-on training in practical food-preparation skills, preparation and presentation of classic and international cuisine, storeroom operations, nutrition, safety, sanitation, food selection, and purchasing. Upon successful completion of the program, graduates can pursue entry-level positions as cooks, line cooks, and assistant pastry chefs.

The Associate of Applied Science degree program in human resources trains individuals to maintain the personnel records of an organization's employees, assist with internal and external notification of position openings, assist in the hiring process, answer employee questions, prepare reports for managers, administer aptitude tests, and screen applicants.

Indiana Business College's medical programs include health claims examiner studies, medical assistant studies, medical coding technology, medical laboratory technician studies, medical office assistant studies, medical transcription, surgical technology, and therapeutic massage studies. The medical assistant studies

degree program provides students with skills to be competent in both front and back office procedures. The medical assistant may assist the physician in minor surgery, perform laboratory tests, assess vital signs, administer medication, operate an EKG machine, or perform other therapeutic modalities prescribed by the physician. The Associate of Applied Science degree program in surgical technology is designed to provide students with an academic and clinical background in the field of surgical technology. Students in this program develop the skills necessary to be a knowledgeable, professional, and responsible member of the surgical team. Programs in medical coding technology provide training to analyze medical records, to assign codes to index diagnoses and procedures, and to provide information for reimbursement purposes. Courses in medical science, medical terminology, medical office administration, and medical insurance processing are offered to help students meet the needs of the industry. The therapeutic massage and bodyworks studies program at Indiana Business College allows graduates to possess the necessary skills for applications and treatment goals of muscular and general relaxation, stress reduction, pain management, recovery from injury, health promotion, education, and body awareness. The successful practitioner must therefore be proficient at more than a simple massage; he or she must understand the body and its functions, master a variety of techniques, and hone such skills as client assessment, communication, and self-evaluation.

Costs

For 2005–06, the cost per credit hour ranged from $162 to $231. Tuition varies according to the program chosen and does not include books or fees.

Financial Aid

Many Indiana Business College students qualify for some form of financial aid. The College participates in the Federal Pell Grant, Federal Supplemental Educational Opportunity Grant, Federal Stafford Student Loan, Federal PLUS loan programs, Federal Work-Study Program, Twenty-first Century Scholars Program, and state grants. Students' eligibility to participate in these programs is contingent upon demonstration of financial need. In addition, the College offers scholarships to both graduating high school seniors and nontraditional students.

Financial planning and financial aid personnel are available to assist the student in the application process.

Students are also encouraged to investigate possibilities for private scholarships.

Faculty

The faculty at Indiana Business College is composed of dedicated professionals who are committed to giving personal attention to every student. The selection of instructors is based not only on their academic credentials, professional training, and business experience, but also on their capacity to develop students' abilities in preparation for the world of work.

Student Body Profile

The student body consists of approximately 3,500 students.

Student Activities

Students may join independent student groups and student councils. Coordinating activities with an executive director or department head, student groups organize a variety of on-campus and off-campus events. Professional organizations are also available for student participation. Intramural sports and group functions vary by campus.

Facilities and Resources

Indiana Business College offers resource centers and computer labs for its students. These facilities provide access to up-to-date information and programs.

Career Planning/Placement Offices The Career Services Department at Indiana Business College assists graduates in securing employment. The Career Services Department offers lifetime career assistance to all alumni and posts job openings for current students and graduates. Students are assisted in all aspects of the job search through career development classes focusing on goal setting, resumes, interviewing, and networking.

Location

Indiana Business College has three convenient Indianapolis locations (northwest, downtown, and southeast) as well as eight other statewide locations. Situated in the heart of Indianapolis, the downtown campus of Indiana Business College houses the Corporate Office for all branches of the College. The excitement of urban living, combined with the cultural and historical sites, makes Indiana Business College's locations ideal. Indianapolis' Children's Museum, Indiana Repertory Theater, and White River Park Zoo provide a variety of educational and recreational activities. The College is within walking distance of downtown shopping centers and major sports centers, such as Circle Centre Mall, Conseco Fieldhouse, and the RCA Dome. It is also readily accessible from many different transportation systems.

In addition to the three Indianapolis locations, Indiana Business College has campuses in Anderson, Columbus, Evansville, Fort Wayne, Lafayette, Marion, Muncie, and Terre Haute.

Students may earn credits toward the completion of a program at more than one location. The convenience of having eleven locations, online classes, and the Chef's Academy significantly lessens the cost of an education by eliminating additional housing and transportation expenses.

Admission Requirements

Applicants must be high school graduates or have obtained a General Educational Development (GED) certificate to be considered for admission to Indiana Business College. The College reviews each application for admission and bases the admission decision on a personal interview and scores from the Wonderlic Scholastic Level Exam.

The College is open to men and women of any race, faith, or national origin. All students are given equal opportunity to pursue their educational and career goals through the programs offered at Indiana Business College.

Application and Information

All applications must be accompanied by a $50 application fee. High school transcripts are requested directly from the student's school by Indiana Business College. Applicants are notified within two weeks of the completion of all application requirements.

All inquiries should be directed to:

Admissions Office
Indiana Business College
550 East Washington Street
Indianapolis, Indiana 46204
Phone: 800-IBC-GRAD (toll-free)
Fax: 317-264-5650
Web site: http://www.ibcschools.edu

INTERNATIONAL COLLEGE OF HOSPITALITY MANAGEMENT

SUFFIELD, CONNECTICUT

The College and Its Mission

The International College of Hospitality Management (ICHM) is located in the town of Suffield in northwest Connecticut. The mission of ICHM is to prepare students for successful careers in the hospitality industry by combining the renowned Swiss art of hotel management with American business techniques.

ICHM is located on a 56-acre residential campus set among woods and rolling lawns. Hospitality faculty members have extensive professional experience and instruct alongside liberal studies teachers of the highest caliber. Students receive intensive course training over four 11-week terms. This training is reinforced by a paid internship in prestigious hotels of the U.S.

The internship is an essential component in the program at ICHM. The resulting combination of professional, academic, and practical training provides graduates with a firm base for managing their careers. The internship also supplies ICHM students with a competitive edge in finding employment when they leave the College. The College's Director of Internships and Placements helps guide students in their career development. In addition, the College organizes career fairs twice each year. The College has a 100 percent placement rate, a record of which it is very proud.

ICHM students are encouraged to actively participate in the social and recreational life of the College, in much the same way that they assume significant responsibilities in managing their academic progress and professional comportment. Because students are very involved in many aspects of College life, a great sense of community has developed at ICHM.

Academic Programs

Associate of Science Degree in Hospitality Management This is a two-academic-year program, taught in eighteen months, that educates students in hotel, restaurant, and tourism management. The program emphasizes professionalism, develops students' practical skills and management techniques, and offers a solid foundation in general education. Four 11-week terms are followed by a paid 810-hour internship in a prestigious hospitality operation.

Associate of Science Degree in Culinary Arts Management This is an eighteen-month comprehensive culinary arts program that also includes skills used by entrepreneurs. The program emphasizes professionalism, develops students' technical skills and management techniques, and offers a solid foundation in liberal studies. The program is enhanced by a 675-clock-hour paid internship.

The first year of the program (two terms, each eleven weeks), includes theoretical and practical courses in the professional kitchen. In the second year of the program (two terms, each eleven weeks), students develop enhanced skills in culinary arts, professional management, operations, and planning and financial control. Students also study a foreign language. Upon the completion of the fourth term, students have the skills and professional knowledge to begin their paid internships in prestigious casinos, hotels, restaurants, or spas.

Certificate in Hospitality Management Candidates holding an associate degree or bachelor's degree in a different discipline may choose to enroll in the certificate program in hospitality management. This one-year program consists of two 11-week terms followed by an internship of at least 810 hours. It is designed to provide graduates with the skills and experience necessary to enter the hospitality industry with confidence.

Special Program Services Career fairs are held twice each year, wherein students and alumni are selected for 810-hour paid internships and positions of longer duration. The fairs are attended by recruiters from approximately thirty leading hotel and resort properties, typically five-star hospitality establishments. Many students receive multiple internship offers. In addition, individual hotel and resort properties often recruit directly on campus.

Transfer Arrangements Course-credit transfers must be comparable to ICHM courses and must have been awarded by an accredited institution. The student must have earned a minimum C grade (2.0 GPA) for transfer credits to be considered. This information must be provided on official sealed transcripts mailed directly to ICHM's Office of Admissions.

Credit for Nontraditional Learning Experiences

Credit may be awarded for prior professional experience in the hospitality industry. For details, applicants should consult the Registrar.

Costs

Expenses for the 2007–08 academic year include tuition and fees of $19,970 and room and board of $5000. An academic year is defined as two terms of eleven weeks each.

Financial Aid

To help eligible students meet their educational expense, the College participates in Federal Title IV financial assistance programs. Many students supplement Title IV aid with other financial assistance programs, such as employer reimbursement, veterans' benefits, agency sponsorship, and other educational funding sources. The College's Financial Aid Officer is happy to work with families on an individual basis to help them plan the cost of education.

Faculty

The student-faculty ratio at the College is 10:1. All full-time faculty members have student advising responsibilities and are involved in the administration of the College. The faculty members have a wide range of international hospitality experience, a diversity that supports the College's mission of offering students an intellectually challenging education in a multicultural environment.

Student Body Profile

The College attracts students from the United States and nearly thirty different countries each year, representing many different cultures. Most students are in their early twenties and, for many, English is a second language. Some are seeking a change of career, others have already obtained advanced qualifications in a different discipline, and all are drawn to the dynamics of international hospitality.

Student Activities

The Student Committee organizes sports, activities, theme nights, and excursions and serves as a representative of all students. Officers of the Student Committee are elected by a democratic vote and arrange meetings and activities with the Coordinator of Student Services. In addition, within the College is a voluntary organization called the Ritz Guild. Its members plan and coordinate events to benefit the local community, often with the help of civic organizations such as the Lions Club and the House of Bread. Each year, Ritz Guild members are given official recognition for their contributions. The College maintains several vans for student activities around the region.

Facilities and Resources

Students can enjoy an excellent regulation-size gymnasium and a modern exercise facility. There are also sports fields and hiking trails on campus. The area has many fine theaters, music venues, restaurants, clubs, and dancing. There are also many well-regarded museums and historic sites within a short distance.

ICHM's spacious library offers more than 10,000 volumes plus numerous industry periodicals and videotapes. The College's computer labs are all connected to broadband Internet services, and the entire building is a wireless broadband environment as well.

Location

The College is situated on 56 wooded acres in Suffield, Connecticut, a charming New England town. Next door to the campus is Six Flags New England Amusement Park, with a $140-million water park. The 135,000-square-foot building is located minutes from Springfield, Massachusetts, and Hartford, Connecticut. It is a short drive to Boston and New York City and only 10 minutes from Bradley International Airport.

Admission Requirements

The College seeks applications from both U.S. and international citizens and welcomes motivated students who have a desire to succeed in international hospitality management. The College requires U.S. applicants to submit a completed application form, $40 application fee, official high school transcripts or GED scores, and two letters of recommendation. SAT scores are not required but are recommended. International students must provide proof of high school or college transcripts. International students for whom English is a second language are required to show proof of English competency. The cultural mix of ICHM benefits students as they move towards their chosen profession. Because of the unique nature of the College and its program, applicants are strongly encouraged to schedule an on-campus interview.

Application and Information

The College accepts applications throughout the year for its August, November, February, and May starting dates. Applicants are notified of their admission status shortly after their forms are received, usually within two weeks. For application materials and additional information, students should contact:

Office of Admissions
International College of Hospitality Management
1760 Mapleton Avenue
Suffield, Connecticut 06078

Phone: 860-668-3515
Fax: 860-668-7369
E-mail: admissions@ichm.edu
Web site: http://www.ichm.edu

The elegant grounds of the International College of Hospitality Management.

JOHNSON COLLEGE
SCRANTON, PENNSYLVANIA

The College and Its Mission

Johnson College, a two-year technical college, was founded by Orlando S. Johnson, a wealthy coal baron in the Scranton area who died in 1912. Mr. Johnson left the bulk of his estate to establish and maintain a trade school, and his purpose became the mission of the College as an institution "where young men and women can be taught useful arts and trades that may enable them to make an honorable living and become contributing members of society."

A board of directors was created and a 65-acre tract in Scranton known as the William H. Richmond estate was selected as the site for the new enterprise. Opening in 1918, the school admitted young men and women who had completed a minimum of eight years of school and were at least 14 years old.

In 1964, the school became a postsecondary institution, requiring applicants to be high school graduates or to have equivalency certificates. The name of the institution changed from the Johnson Trade School to the Johnson School of Technology in 1966. The school was incorporated as a nonprofit corporation in 1967, and in 1968, it was licensed by the Commonwealth of Pennsylvania Bureau of Private Trade Schools. Approval to award an Associate in Specialized Technology degree came in 1974, with accreditation by the National Association of Trade and Technical Schools (NATTS) following in 1979.

In 1985, the name of the school was changed to Johnson Technical Institute, and the three-year Associate in Specialized Technology degree programs were changed to two-year programs in 1987.

Responding to the continuing technological changes in society, students along with members of the board, administration, faculty, and staff conducted an intense two-year self-study, beginning in 1994, to assess the institution's strengths and weaknesses. The study led to a formal application to the Commission on Higher Education for status as a two-year college. The Pennsylvania Department of Education approved the application of Johnson Technical Institute as a two-year college in 1997; the change of name to Johnson College was instituted in 2001. The State Board of Education has also approved Johnson College as a two-year college, as has the Accrediting Commission of Career Schools and Colleges of Technology (ACCSCT.

The graduating class of 1998 was the first class to receive either an Associate in Applied Science (A.A.S.) degree or an Associate in Science (A.S.) degree.

Continuing the expansion of the technology programs, a Veterinary Technology program was introduced in 1994. Clinical classes were held off campus until the completion of a 6,500-square-foot Science Center on campus. The program received full accreditation from the American Veterinary Medical Association (AVMA) for the fall semester of 2000. In January 2004, the College opened the Animal Care Center as a teaching facility to enhance the Veterinary Technology educational experience. In 1995, Electrical Construction and Maintenance Technology was added to the curriculum, and the Bureau of Private Licensed Schools approved the Diesel Truck Technology program in November 1996. A Computer Information Technology program that specializes in enterprise computer networking was approved by the Commission on Higher Education in 2000, and a curriculum in Radiologic Technology received the Commission's approval for the fall 2002 semester. The Radiologic Technology program received accreditation by the Joint Review Committee on Education in Radiologic Technology (JRCERT) in May 2005.

Today, approximately 400 students pursue careers in twelve different trade, technical, and clinical programs. The College's eight buildings include a library, a bookstore, a gymnasium, a physical fitness center, classrooms, shops, laboratories, administrative offices, and a student apartment complex for on-campus living.

Over the years, the College has served the region by providing technical education programs, and it continually evaluates its programs to meet the technology needs of society. This evaluation process is assisted by the Program Advisory Committees of each program area, which consist of regional business and community leaders who meet several times during the year to advise the College on curriculum content, length of programs, and current materials and equipment. They also review placement and retention statistics. The College has maintained the initial intent of Mr. Johnson with a professional and dedicated staff to ensure up-to-date training that prepares graduates to readily step into entry-level positions in business and industry.

The current student body is approximately 72 percent men. Students spend 70 percent of their time in technology courses and the remainder in general education classes. The College has an extensive program of internships, cooperative education, and practicums with a variety of businesses and professional organizations. One of the important success factors of Johnson College is a consistently high employment rate of students within a short time after graduation.

Today, Johnson College is a valuable resource for society's changing technological needs. The mission of Johnson College is to provide a foundation of education and skills necessary for specialized employment, career advancement, and lifelong learning.

Academic Programs

Johnson College offers twelve trade, technical, and clinical programs, awarding Associate in Applied Science and Associate in Science degrees.

The technology programs include Architectural Drafting and Design Technology, Automotive Technology, Biomedical Equipment Technology, Carpentry and Cabinetmaking Technology, Diesel Truck Technology, Distribution and Supply Logistics Technology, Electrical Construction and Maintenance Technology, Electronic Technology, and Precision Machining Technology.

The science programs include Computer Information Technology, Radiologic Technology, and Veterinary Technology.

Transfer Arrangements The College maintains articulation agreements with the State University of New York Institute of Technology at Utica/Rome for the following programs: Architectural Drafting and Design Technology, Biomedical

Equipment Technology, and Electronic Technology. Johnson College also has an articulation agreement with Marywood University in Scranton for the Veterinary Technology program.

Costs

The tuition for full-time attendance for 2006–07 (12 to 21 credit hours) was $6123 per semester for all programs. Books and supplies were approximately $1500 per school year; however, this amount varied by program. Program fees vary by department. On-campus housing is available in double-occupancy apartments at a rate of $350 per month per student. Students should consult the current College catalog for additional and recent financial information.

Financial Aid

Johnson College provides financial support through the Financial Aid Office, with several programs and opportunities available for students from all income categories. Scholarships are available and are awarded on the basis of merit, academic performance, and extracurricular involvement. The College also participates in the following federally sponsored programs: Federal Pell Grants, Federal Supplemental Educational Opportunity Grants (FSEOG), Federal PLUS loans, and Federal Stafford Student Loans. Other opportunities include employment programs and alternative loans at the College and state and College grants. For consideration for any financial assistance program, students must complete the Free Application for Federal Student Aid (FAFSA). In addition, the College offers $30,000 in merit scholarships for those who are eligible.

Faculty

There are 26 faculty members at the College, and the student-faculty ratio is 17:1. Counseling is available for academic, personal, and vocational issues. The College maintains strong interpersonal relationships among its students and faculty and staff members.

Student Activities

There are a variety of activities available for students on campus, including a Student Government Association, which consists of a student from each technical, trade, and clinical program. The Social Force Club, funded by Act 101, is a community service organization that involves students in on- and off-campus activities, including field trips. Students participate in an active intramural sports program, social functions, holiday parties, talent shows, clubs, and other events and functions.

Facilities and Resources

The Library Resource Center at the College is a technology-based library and is a participating member of the Northeastern Pennsylvania Library Network Consortium. Located in the Moffat Building, the collection consists of more than 4,000 volumes of books and more than 100 current periodical subscriptions. The library complements the curriculum of the academic and technical, trade, and clinical programs. This unique collection offers students the resources necessary to research issues that pertain to their fields of study and for which students should keep abreast of new technological developments. The library also offers online computer services and CD-ROM searching. A professionally staffed cafeteria is available for breakfast, lunch, and snacks. The Moffat Building contains two fitness centers that offer a variety of exercise equipment. A campus bookstore is available for student supplies, clothing items, and a variety of other items. Limited on-campus housing is available in fully furnished, two-story apartment-style units.

Location

Johnson College is conveniently located in Scranton, Pennsylvania, at Exit 190 on Interstate 81. Highway exit ramps clearly indicate the location of the campus. The College is just under 2 hours from New York City and Philadelphia. It is minutes from great skiing and other recreational activities, along with a variety of sports, arts, music, cultural, and historical events at places like Lackawanna County Stadium (home of the Triple-A Red Barons baseball team), Montage Amphitheater, and the Steamtown National Park and Mall.

Admission Requirements

Johnson College accepts qualified students regardless of race, religion, handicap, or national origin, and admissions are on a rolling basis. Applicants should be secondary school seniors, secondary school graduates, or recipients of a secondary school equivalency certificate. Successful completion of one year of algebra and two years of English with a grade of C or higher is required for all programs. Veterinary Technology applicants must have successfully completed 1 unit of biology and chemistry; Radiologic Technology applicants must have either 1 unit of biology or chemistry (a grade of C or better is considered successful completion). Each applicant is encouraged to arrange for a campus visit and a personal interview with an admissions representative, and appointments may be made for meeting with appropriate faculty members and current students.

Application and Information

Applications may be submitted in person, by mail, or online at http://www.johnson.edu. Accompanying information must include an official secondary school or equivalency transcript, satisfactory SAT or ACT test scores, one letter of recommendation, and a $30 nonrefundable processing fee. Applicants for the Veterinary Technology program and the Radiologic Technology program are also required to submit a questionnaire and observation hours. The deadline date for applicants for the Veterinary Technology and the Radiologic Technology programs is February 15.

Additional information may be obtained by contacting:

Office of Admissions
Johnson College
3427 North Main Avenue
Scranton, Pennsylvania 18508
Phone: 800-293-9675 (toll-free)
Web site: http://www.johnson.edu

KEYSTONE COLLEGE

LA PLUME, PENNSYLVANIA

The College and Its Mission

Keystone College was founded in 1868 as Keystone Academy in La Plume, Pennsylvania. Initially opened as the only high school between Binghamton, New York, and Scranton, Pennsylvania, Keystone flourished as a secondary school for more than sixty-five years. Rechartered as Scranton-Keystone Junior College in 1934 and then Keystone Junior College in 1944, the College served as one of the premier two-year institutions in the Northeast until 1995. In this year the school was again renamed, as Keystone College, and began its tenure as an "ideal" four-year degree-granting college. Keystone College has a current enrollment of 1,600, including students from fourteen states and seven other countries. Students can choose from sixteen different four-year majors and more than twenty-five different two-year degree and certificate programs.

Academic Programs

Associate Degree Programs Associate of Applied Science degrees are offered in accounting, culinary arts, hotel and restaurant management, and information technology. The Associate in Fine Arts is offered in art. The Associate in Arts is offered in communications, forest/resource management, landscape architecture, liberal studies, liberal studies–education emphasis, and wildlife biology. The Associate in Science is offered in biology; business; criminal justice; early childhood education; health sciences with emphasis in medical technology, nursing/cytotechnology, occupational therapy/respiratory care, and radiotherapy/medical imaging/cardiac perfusion; and sport and recreation management. In addition, there are one-year programs in Cisco, forestry technology, Microsoft Certified Systems Administrator, Microsoft Certified Systems Engineer, and pre–major studies (undeclared major).

Bachelor's Degree Programs The Bachelor of Arts degree is offered in communications and visual arts. The Bachelor of Science degree is offered in accounting, biology with tracks in the medical professions, business, criminal justice with a track in prelaw, early childhood education, elementary education, environmental biology, environmental resource management, forensic biology, information technology, sport and recreation management, teaching: art education, teaching: child and society, teaching: math education, and teaching: social studies education.

Postbaccalaureate certification is available in elementary education, early childhood education, and teaching–art education (K–12).

The College runs on a two-semester schedule (fall and spring) and has night and weekend classes available. The number of credit hours required to earn a degree is dependent on the field of study chosen, and students must have attained a minimum cumulative GPA of 2.0. Every student must complete a set of general core curriculum requirements as well as the courses specific to his or her major course of study. Depending on their course of study, students may be required to complete an internship or co-op before graduation.

Students have the opportunity to participate in both the Army and Navy ROTC programs in conjunction with other local participating institutions. There are opportunities for double majors as well as minors in various fields of study.

Off-Campus Programs

The College maintains articulation agreements with Thomas Jefferson University, College Misericordia, and SUNY Upstate Medical for students enrolling in the health science curriculums. Students enrolled in the environmental programs may opt to pursue Keystone's articulation with State University of New York College of Environmental Science and Forestry (SUNY-ESF) in Syracuse. Other transfer opportunities exist with Marywood University, University of Scranton, Bloomsburg University, Wilkes University, Temple University, University of the Arts, Parson's School of Design, Penn State University, and many others.

Costs

Tuition and fees for Keystone College for 2006–07 were $15,916 per year, while room and board costs were $8110 per year. Books and general supplies average $500 per semester and vary according to major.

Financial Aid

The Financial Aid Office provides adequate funds and resources to meet the financial needs of students from all income categories. In fact, 88 percent of incoming freshmen receive financial aid. Scholarships are awarded based on merit, academic performance, and extracurricular involvement. Keystone College also participates in the following federally sponsored programs: Federal Perkins Loan, Federal Pell Grant, Federal Supplemental Educational Opportunity Grant (FSEOG), Federal PLUS Loan, and Federal Stafford Student Loan. The College also offers college employment programs to students and alternative loans as well as state grants and Keystone grants. In order to be considered for financial aid, students must complete the Free Application for Federal Student Aid (FAFSA). Keystone's financial aid code is 003280.

Faculty

The student-faculty ratio is 12:1, and the average class size is 22 students. Counseling is available for academic, personal, and vocational issues. Keystone College is supported by strong interpersonal relationships among its students and faculty and staff members. All faculty members post regular office hours and are generally available outside of these hours.

Student Activities

Student Senate is the central governing body of all student government organizations on the campus. It serves as the liaison between the student body and the College administration. Members of Student Senate are chosen by their peers and are responsible for improving and maintaining student life both on

and off campus. Students may choose from more than twenty-five different clubs and organizations, including those with academic, service-oriented, and social interests.

Facilities and Resources

The Harry K. Miller Library is available on campus to all students. This facility offers standard print and online research opportunities. The Hibbard Campus Center is the setting for the student cafeteria, a full-service restaurant, and The Chef's Table (a student-run restaurant), as well as a U.S. post office, a print shop, a student-run radio station (WKCV), and reception halls. The campus also includes an art gallery, a celestial observatory, early childhood center, career development center, theater, and the Poinsard Greenhouse. Keystone College also serves as the home for the Urban Forestry Center, Willary Water Discovery Center, and the Countryside Conservancy.

There are more than 120 computers available on campus for general student use, and both the Internet and campus network can be accessed from all residence halls and most buildings on campus.

Location

Located at the foot of the Endless Mountains in northeastern Pennsylvania, the 270-acre campus is both scenic and historic, with buildings dating back to 1870. Located 13 miles from Scranton, Pennsylvania, the campus offers easy access to major East Coast cities, including New York, Philadelphia, and Baltimore.

Admission Requirements

Keystone accepts qualified students regardless of race, religion, handicap, or national origin, and admissions are on a rolling basis. Admission is based on prior academic performance and the ability of the applicant to profit from and contribute to the academic, interpersonal, and extracurricular life of the College. Keystone considers applicants who meet the following criteria:

graduation from an approved secondary school or the equivalent (with official transcripts), satisfactory scores on the SAT or ACT, one letter of recommendation, essay, and evidence of potential for successful college achievement. All students are strongly encouraged to visit the campus for a personal interview with the admissions staff and a member of the faculty from the student's area of interest. Students applying to the art and teaching–art education programs are required to participate in a portfolio interview.

Transfer students in good academic and financial standing at their current institution are also encouraged to apply to Keystone. Transfer students should contact the Office of Admissions and may be required to submit either high school transcripts or transcripts from each college attended, or both.

Admissions decisions are made within two weeks from the day all required materials are received in the Office of Admissions.

Application and Information

Students wishing to be considered for admission must submit an application and a $25 processing fee, along with official high school transcripts, college transcripts (if applicable), a letter of recommendation from someone other than a friend or relative, essay, and scores from either the SAT or ACT (submitted directly to the Office of Admissions; Keystone's CEEB code numbers are 2351 for the SAT, 2602 for the ACT).

Applications and any additional information about Keystone College may be obtained by contacting:

Office of Admissions
Keystone College
One College Green
La Plume, Pennsylvania 18440
Phone: 570-945-8111
       800-824-2764 Option 1 (toll-free)
E-mail: admissions@keystone.edu
Web site: http://www.keystone.edu

Students on the campus of Keystone College.

LANDMARK COLLEGE

PUTNEY, VERMONT

The College and Its Mission

Landmark College is one of only two accredited colleges in the country designed exclusively for students of average to superior intellectual potential with LD or AD/HD or other specific learning disabilities. Life-changing experiences are commonplace at Landmark College.

Landmark's beautiful campus offers all the resources students expect at a high-quality higher education institution, including an athletics center, a student center, a dining facility, a café, residence halls, and a Center for Academic Support. The College has also invested substantially in technology and offers a wireless network in all of its classrooms, along with LAN, telephone, and cable connections in all of the residence rooms. Notebook computers are required and are used in nearly every class session. The College's programs extensively integrate assistive technologies, such as Dragon Naturally Speaking, Kurzweil text-to-speech software, and Inspiration.

Landmark's faculty and staff members make it unique. The College's more than 100 full-time faculty members are all highly experienced in serving students with learning disabilities and attention deficit disorders. More than 100 staff members provide an array of support services that are unusually comprehensive for a student population of slightly more than 460 students.

Academic Programs

Students can earn an associate degree in either general studies or business studies. Landmark College builds strong literacy, organizational, study, and other skills—positioning students to successfully pursue a baccalaureate or advanced degree and to be successful in their professional careers. More than 80 percent of Landmark College graduates go on to a four-year college or university.

With more than 100 faculty members and slightly more than 460 students, Landmark College's small classes and personalized instruction provide a uniquely challenging, yet supportive, academic program. At Landmark College, students learn how to learn.

The College's diverse curriculum includes English, communications, the humanities, math, science, foreign language, theater, video, music, art, physical education, and other classes taught in a multimodal, multimedia environment that is highly interactive. There is no "back of the room" in a Landmark College classroom, and all students participate in class discussions while building strong academic skills.

Landmark College has articulation agreements with a number of other colleges. These colleges have agreed to admit Landmark College graduates as juniors and transfer their credits if they attain a specific grade point average upon graduation from Landmark.

Through a carefully sequenced, integrated curriculum, students develop the confidence and independence needed to meet the demands of college work. When students graduate with an associate degree from Landmark College, they are ready to succeed in a four-year college, a technical or professional program, or the workforce.

Off-Campus Programs

The Landmark Study Abroad Program has developed programs with students' diverse learning styles in mind. Landmark College's faculty members design and teach experiential courses in their specific disciplines that fulfill Landmark core requirements while helping students gain confidence and independence in new academic structures. College faculty members accompany students abroad, providing them with the Landmark College academic experience in an international setting. The College offers summer credit programs in England, Ireland, Italy, and Spain; in January, a two-week program in Costa Rica is offered.

Costs

Landmark College's tuition for the 2007–08 academic year is $37,000. Room and board costs are $6800. Single rooms or suites are available at an added cost of between $1000 and $1500. A damage deposit of $300 is required.

Since admission to Landmark College requires a diagnosis of a learning disability or attention deficit disorder, in most cases, the entire cost of a Landmark College education may be tax deductible as a medical expense. For more information, parents are advised to consult a tax attorney.

Financial Aid

Landmark College participates in all major federal and state financial aid programs, including the Federal Pell Grant, Federal Family Education Loans, and work-study. Institutional scholarships are available. To apply for financial assistance, students should submit the Free Application for Federal Student Aid (FAFSA), the Landmark College Financial Aid Application, and federal tax returns.

Faculty

With the College's low student-faculty ratio, Landmark College faculty members are unusually accessible to students. There are more than 100 full-time faculty members, who provide classroom teaching, professional advising, and office hours to students. In addition, faculty members provide individualized instruction throughout the day and into the evening at the Charles Drake Center for Academic Support. Landmark College does not typically employ adjunct faculty members or student teaching assistants. Regular faculty members deliver all instruction and advising. Their depth of experience in serving students with learning differences ensures that students receive the individualized education that is most appropriate to their learning style.

Student Body Profile

Landmark College students come from thirty-eight states, two U.S. territories, and thirteen other countries. Approximately two thirds of the student body are men. Ninety percent of all students are residential students living on campus in one of twelve residence facilities. Representatives of multicultural groups make up approximately 14 percent of Landmark College students.

Student Activities

Landmark College closely integrates academics and student life. Academic deans, advisers, and faculty members work

closely with student life deans and directors to provide a comprehensive program that serves the whole student. The goal is not simply to support academic success but also to guide and challenge students in their personal and social development. Each student has access to a comprehensive support team, including an academic adviser, classroom instructors, and a resident dean; an extensive program of athletics, adventure education, and activities; and a highly trained and experienced counseling department.

For a college its size, Landmark College has an extraordinary range of student-development resources, providing general educational, social, and recreational opportunities. Clubs at Landmark are active. In the past, they have included the Running Club, Monday Night Art, the Multicultural Awareness Club, the Gay/Lesbian/Bisexual/Transgender Alliance, the Mountain Biking Club, the Jazz Ensemble, *Impressions Literary Magazine,* the Coffee House Writers Group, the International Club, the Small Business Management Club, Choral Singing, the Weight Lifting Group, and the Spirituality Group.

Landmark College outdoor programs provide students with a diverse range of outdoor and experiential learning opportunities, including wilderness first-aid training, a ropes course, rock-climbing instruction, an indoor climbing wall, and a full inventory of camping equipment, cross-country skis, snowshoes, and mountain bikes. The College has an active intercollegiate and intramural athletics program that is supported by a well-equipped athletics center that opened in 2001.

Facilities and Resources

Landmark College's residence halls, academic buildings, athletics center, and student center provide a rich array of resources and educational, recreational, and social opportunities. The traditional brick campus, which was designed by noted architect Edward Durell Stone in the 1960s and entirely renovated beginning in the mid-1980s, includes such amenities as a 400-seat theater, an NCAA regulation basketball court, an exercise pool, three fitness centers, a tennis court, science laboratories, an infirmary, a Center for Academic Support, a bookstore, a café, a game room, an indoor climbing wall, and a ropes course.

Location

Located in scenic southeastern Vermont, Landmark College overlooks the Connecticut River Valley, with sweeping views of the mountains and valleys of southern Vermont and northern Massachusetts. Wilderness areas, national forests, ski areas, lakes and streams, and other natural attractions abound. Nearby Brattleboro, Vermont, and the five-college region in the Amherst, Massachusetts, area offer opportunities for culture, the arts, fine dining, and more. Putney is a picturesque Vermont village with several shops, stores, restaurants, a bakery/coffeehouse, a bookstore, and other resources.

The College is located just off Exit 4 on Interstate 91. The most convenient airport is Bradley International Airport in Hartford, Connecticut, which is about 1½ hours away by car. Metropolitan areas within a 4-hour driving radius include Boston, New York, and Providence.

Admission Requirements

Applicants to Landmark College must have a diagnosis of dyslexia, attention deficit disorder, or another specific learning disability. Diagnostic testing within the last three years is required, along with a diagnosis of a learning disability or

AD/HD. One of the Wechsler Scales (WAIS-III or WISC-III) administered within three years of application is required. Scores and subtest scores and their analysis are required to be submitted as well. Alternately, the Woodcock Johnson Cognitive Assessment may be substituted if administered within three years of application. Other criteria for admission include average to superior intellectual potential and high motivation to undertake the program.

The College offers rolling admission and enrolls students for fall and spring semesters. Students may begin in August (for the fall semester) or January (for the spring semester). The College offers credit-bearing courses each summer in addition to programs for students from other colleges, high school students, and students entering other colleges in the fall.

Application and Information

For more information, students should contact:

Office of Admissions
Landmark College
River Road South
Putney, Vermont 05346-0820

Phone: 802-387-6718
Fax: 802-387-6868
E-mail: admissions@landmark.edu
Web site: http://www.landmark.edu

Students on the campus of Landmark College.

LEHIGH VALLEY COLLEGE
CENTER VALLEY, PENNSYLVANIA

The College and Its Mission

Lehigh Valley College's vision is to provide student-centered career-focused higher education that prepares students to develop and achieve their personal and career potentials.

Lehigh Valley College (LVC) welcomes students, faculty members, and staff members from diverse nationalities, ethnic groups, and traditions. The College strives to be an instrument of growth for students of all ages. Through its curriculum, the College affirms the values of a broad range of study to enhance career opportunities and develop a sense of vocation. Through its services, the College provides students with the academic and personal support they need to promote student success. The College collaborates with community stakeholders to develop and maintain relevant educational pathways that are designed to enhance each graduate's potential.

Lehigh Valley College is committed to making an important difference in the lives of its stakeholders by creating and supporting an environment of quality education; offering degree programs within the context of a well-designed framework of liberal arts and sciences; developing each student's intellectual, analytical, and critical thinking abilities; offering degree programs that include both theoretical and practical components in order to prepare graduates to advance in their chosen careers; providing students with the educational foundation for more advanced study; providing an educational environment that imparts the attitudes and skills that will enable students to continue learning throughout their lives; and helping students become productive, creative, ethical, and engaged citizens.

Academic Programs

LVC provides career training leading to a diploma or specialized associate degree in business or technology. Programs follow a quarterly schedule and are eighteen to twenty-four months long. Associate degree programs consist of prescribed subjects that are divided into periods of instruction approximately twelve weeks in length and offered every twelve weeks.

Associate Degree Programs Business Administration–Fashion Merchandising: Business, marketing, management, and sales principles are presented as a means of developing concepts and refining merchandising skills. Students develop competent multitasking skills, integrating conceptual and creative abilities with technical and sound business practices for the fashion merchandising and retail industries.

Business Administration–Management/Marketing: Students gain strong managerial knowledge and skills as well as the marketing and sales-skills training needed to be an effective leader. Students are introduced to accounting, computer applications, and communication skills.

Criminal Justice: To prepare students to enter a variety of first-tier protective services positions, students are exposed to the culture of the criminal justice system, the foundational areas of the discipline (investigation and law enforcement, law and courts, and corrections and parole), and juvenile delinquency and the juvenile justice system. Additional education or testing may be required for employment in some positions.

Health Information Technology: Students develop an understanding and knowledge of the importance of medical records and how to apply information technologies to health-care and medical information operations. The curriculum combines general education, health-care statistics, and health-care management.

Massage Therapy: Students receive a solid educational foundation in the holistic approach of massage therapy. Students gain extensive hands-on practice and skills in a variety of techniques applicable to the clinical setting. This program provides key business knowledge that helps graduates build individual massage therapy practices while emphasizing client-centered services and the highest professional standards.

Medical Assisting: The curriculum provides training on the essential support areas of patient care, medical and lab procedures, records management, and office administration and introduces students to practical, administrative, interpersonal, and clinical skills that lead to the technical ability and versatility needed in allied health services.

Network Support: The course exposes students to the integration of multiple hardware and operating system configurations, helps them to troubleshoot multiplatform operating systems, and provides exposure to network configuration, administration, hardware, maintenance, and security.

Visual Communications: Students develop basic drawing, design, and typographical skills to create graphic solutions while gaining knowledge and developing their talents in digital imaging, computer illustration, Web design, interactive media, and prepress.

Certificate Programs Graphic Design: Students who are currently employed but need to attain or upgrade their graphic and Web-design skills benefit from this program. The program provides hands-on experience while introducing students to the most industry-current computer applications, current advertising strategies, typography, and conceptual solutions to design problems. The program exposes students to custom graphics creation and illustrations, photo manipulations, and design and page layouts that provide creative, effective solutions to Web- and print-based visual communication problems.

Network Technology: Students who are currently employed but need to attain or upgrade computer networking skills are provided with hands-on experience constructing and troubleshooting the latest PC hardware components. The program exposes students to the installation and administration of multiple computer operating systems as well as major network server software installation and administration. The curriculum addresses network topology, peripherals, and security in detail.

Costs

The costs for tuition, fees, books, and supplies vary by program and by each student's credit load. The following tuition information is based on a full-time course load of 15 credits per term for day students and 12 credits per term for evening students; costs for books and supplies are estimated.

Tuition for day students in Associate in Science (A.S.) programs: Business Administration–Fashion Merchandising, $4380 (books and supplies, $2500); Business Administration–Management/Marketing, $4380 (books and supplies, $2200); Criminal Justice, $4380 (books and supplies, $2200); Health Information Technology, $3600 (books and supplies, $2200); Massage Therapy, $4200 (books and supplies, $2200); Medical Assisting, $4380 (books and supplies, $2200); Network Support, $4920 (books and supplies, $3500); and Visual Communication, $4920 (books and supplies, $3400).

Tuition for evening students in Associate in Science (A.S.) programs: Business Administration-Management/Marketing, $3504 (books and supplies, $2200); Criminal Justice, $3504 (books and supplies, $2200); Health Information Technology, $2820 (books and supplies, $1200); Massage Therapy, $3360 (books and supplies, $2200); Medical Assisting, $3504 (books and supplies, $2200); Network Support, $3936 (books and supplies, $3500); and Visual Communication, $3936 (books and supplies, $3400).

Tuition for the graphic design and network technology certificate programs is $1920 per term. Books and supplies are estimated at $1450 for Graphic Design and $1400 for Network Technology.

All programs have a $50 per quarter technology fee. Three programs charge an administrative fee: Criminal Justice ($25 in the last quarter), Massage Therapy ($150 per quarter), and Medical Assisting ($50 in the last quarter). All new students pay a $150 graduation fee.

The Education Department evaluates any previous education and training that may be applicable to an educational program. If the education and/or training meets the standards for transfer of credit, the program may be shortened and the tuition reduced accordingly. Students who request credit for previous education or training are

required to provide the Registrar's Office with an official transcript from the educational institution for review and approval.

Financial Aid

The Financial Aid Department devotes personal attention to every student by individually mapping out financial options. Federal grants and loans, including Pell Grants, Stafford Student Loans, Supplemental Educational Opportunity Grants, and Parent Loans for Undergraduate Students; the Federal Work-Study Program; and alternative funding are available to those who qualify. More than $100,000 in scholarships, including those from Lehigh Valley College and Future Business Leaders of America for graduating high school seniors, are also available. Applicants must complete financial aid forms if they wish to apply for financial aid.

Faculty

Lehigh Valley College has more than 70 full- and part-time instructors with bachelor's, master's, or doctoral degrees in addition to their occupational qualifications.

Student Body Profile

There are currently more than 400 students enrolled at the College. The students who attend Lehigh Valley College come from a number of areas within a 50-mile radius. All students reside off campus; however, LVC assists with housing when necessary.

Student Activities

LVC has a number of activities and organizations for the students to participate in, such as SIFE, Student Government Association, and various organizations in the program specialties. The students are also encouraged to participate in community events and help raise money for worthy causes.

Throughout the academic year, activities that encourage college spirit and develop student leadership may be offered. The College believes that participation in these activities is an important part of the educational process, and student involvement is encouraged.

Facilities and Resources

Students are provided with facilities that have the latest industry-standard equipment. LVC's new facility houses a variety of teaching and resource tools, including a library, bookstore, student lounges, six PC labs, three Mac labs, two art studios, and a photography studio. The wireless environment allows students to work freely throughout the campus with access to the network at all times.

Career Services The College assists students in finding part-time employment while they attend College. Assistance includes advice in preparing for an interview, aid in securing an interview, and a list of available jobs. Some programs may require additional education, licensure, and/or certification for employment in some positions. Potential employers and agencies and institutions that seek LVC students may conduct a criminal and/or personal background check. Students with criminal records that include felonies or misdemeanors (including those that are drug-related) or personal background issues such as bankruptcy might not be accepted by these agencies for internship placement or employment following completion of the program. Some agencies and employers may require candidates to submit to a drug test. Employment and internship decisions are outside the control of the College.

The College encourages student to maintain satisfactory attendance, conduct, and academic progress so they may be viewed favorably by prospective employers. While the College cannot guarantee employment, it has been successful in assisting its graduates with obtaining employment in their field of training.

All graduating students can participate in career planning activities that help with the preparation of resumes and letters of introduction, an important step in a well-planned job search; learning interviewing techniques and acquiring effective interviewing skills through practice exercises; job referrals through the Career Services Department, which compiles job openings from employers in the area; and on-campus interviews by companies that visit the College to interview graduates. All students are expected to participate in the career-planning program, and failure to do so may jeopardize their employment opportunities.

Alumni may continue to utilize the College's career-planning program at no additional cost.

Location

Lehigh Valley College is located at 2809 East Saucon Valley Road, Center Valley, Pennsylvania. Its new 97,000-square foot building is easily accessible from I-78 and the Pennsylvania Turnpike. It is on a local bus route and within a short driving distance of the Poconos, Philadelphia, and New York. Nearby are Blue Mountain Ski Area, Doe Mountain Ski Area, Dorney Park and Wildwater Kingdom, and the Lehigh County Velodrome. Year-round activities include Musikfest, the Celtic Classic, the Great Allentown Fair, Mayfair, and the Pennsylvania Shakespeare Festival.

Admission Requirements

Students should apply for admission as soon as possible to be officially accepted for a specific program and starting date. To apply, students should complete the Student Data Sheet and return it to the College or call for a priority appointment to visit the College, receive a tour of its facilities, and discuss career options with an Admissions Representative.

All applicants are encouraged to have a personal interview with an Admissions Representative. Parents and/or spouses are also encouraged to see the College's equipment and facilities and ask questions relating to College's curriculum and career objectives. Personal interviews also enable college administrators to determine whether an applicant is acceptable for enrollment.

All students pay the $50 application fee. A fee waiver may be granted in certain cases.

In order to complete the application process, all students must complete an Enrollment Agreement. If the applicant is under 18 years of age, the agreement must be signed by parent or guardian. Prospective students are required to request an official high school transcript or GED certificate. In lieu of official documents, students may provide an original high school transcript, high school diploma, GED scores, or GED diploma to be photocopied at the College. Extensions to the documentation deadline may be granted on an individual basis as approved by the President and Registrar. Prospective students should check to see if their intended program of study has other application requirements.

A committee of three faculty members and/or administrative representatives will review each applicant's work history to determine if the experience is sufficient to meet the needs of the proposed program.

All students will be required to take the Accuplacer Test for course placement. To remain in college, all students attending Lehigh Valley College are required to provide proof of high school graduation or its equivalency by the last day of the drop/add period of the first quarter.

International students are encouraged to apply for admission. Applicants must meet the same admission requirements as U.S. citizens. All documents should be accompanied by an English translation. Students whose native language is not English may be required to take the Test of English as Foreign Language (TOEFL) or demonstrate English proficiency through other measures established by the school. International students who graduate from high school outside of the United States must have successfully completed the TOEFL with a minimum score of 450, paper-based exam; 133, computer-based exam; or 45, Internet-based exam. An affidavit of financial support should be submitted. Detailed information will be provided through the Admissions Office. The school is authorized under federal law to enroll nonimmigrant students.

The College reserves the right to reject students if the requirements listed above are not successfully completed.

Application and Information

Lehigh Valley College follows an open enrollment system; applications to the College are accepted at all times. To meet with one of the Admissions Representatives, tour the College, or get additional information, interested students should contact the Admissions Department:

Admissions Department
Lehigh Valley College
2809 East Saucon Valley Road
Center Valley, Pennsylvania 18034
Phone: 610-791-5100
      800-227-9109 (toll-free)
Fax: 610-791-7810
Web site: http://www.lehighvalley.edu

MANOR COLLEGE
JENKINTOWN, PENNSYLVANIA

The College and Its Mission

Manor College is a private, coed Catholic college founded in 1947 by the Ukrainian Sisters of Saint Basil the Great. The College is characterized by its dedication to the education, growth, and self-actualization of the whole person through its personalized and nurturing atmosphere. Upon graduation, 40 percent of Manor's students are employed in their chosen fields; the remaining 60 percent of students transfer to four-year institutions to earn baccalaureate degrees.

There are approximately 800 full- and part-time students enrolled at Manor. Extracurricular activities include honor societies and men's and women's intercollegiate soccer and basketball as well as the yearbook and special interest and cultural clubs. Manor provides free counseling and tutoring services through an on-campus learning center. Trained counselors are available to assist students on an individual and confidential basis for academic, career, and personal concerns. Upon entering Manor, students are assigned an academic adviser, who provides guidance and support throughout their Manor experience. Transfer counseling is available for students interested in pursuing a four-year degree.

The College's 35-acre campus includes a modern three-story dormitory, a library/administration building, and an academic building that also houses the bookstore, dining hall, an auditorium/gymnasium, and a student lounge. The Ukrainian Heritage Studies Center and the Manor Dental Health Center are also located on the campus grounds. Manor is accredited by the Middle States Association of Colleges and Schools.

Academic Programs

Manor offers career-oriented, two-year associate degrees, as well as transfer programs for the purpose of pursuing a bachelor's degree. Internships provide theory with practice, enhancing employment opportunities. The liberal arts core ensures a common breadth of knowledge along with mobility and future advancement. Manor College offers eleven programs with twenty-two majors/concentrations leading to associate degrees and transfer programs through its three divisions: Liberal Arts, Allied Health/Science/Mathematics, and Business.

The Liberal Arts Division offers **Associate in Arts** degrees in early childhood education, psychology, and liberal arts. In addition, the Liberal Arts Division provides a liberal arts transfer major as well as an elementary education transfer major, an early child-care major, a three-year English as a second language (ESL) concentration, a concentration in catechetical education, and a concentration in communications.

The Allied Health/Science/Mathematics Division offers **Associate in Science** degrees in dental hygiene, expanded functions dental assisting, and veterinary technology. This division also includes allied health and science transfer programs for students who seek preprofessional programs in biotechnology, chiropractic, cytotechnology, general sciences, medical technology, nursing, occupational therapy, pharmacy, physical therapy, radiologic science, and veterinary animal science.

The Business Division offers **Associate in Science** degrees in accounting, business administration, business administration/computer science, business administration/human resource management, business administration/international business, business administration/management, business administration/marketing, and paralegal studies. There are five certificate programs. There are a PC technician/computer support specialist studies certificate and a certificate program in paralegal studies for students who have a bachelor's degree, as well as a legal nurse consultant certificate. A certificate program in catechist/educator development is offered for both Roman and Byzantine rites. Manor

also offers selected courses through two modes of distance learning: online Web-based learning and teleconferencing.

The Office of Continuing Education serves adult learners by providing educational options for those who want to attend college on a part-time basis. The office also supports the needs of the community and business and industry by offering noncredit classes and workshops, as well as on- and off-site corporate training programs, throughout the year. Approved as an authorized provider by the International Association for Continuing Education and Training, the office also grants continuing education units (CEUs) for selected professional development courses each semester.

Off-Campus Programs

Externships are incorporated into various academic studies programs. Students earn credits as they gain practical experience under the supervision of professionals in a specific field of study. Externships are offered in the career-oriented programs of study and in some transfer programs. Manor's affiliation with several area hospitals, as well as Manor College's on-campus Dental Health Center, enables the allied health program student to fulfill clinical requirements at these sites. Students in other programs serve externships in law offices, courtrooms, day-care centers, businesses, and veterinary facilities. Manor has dual admissions, 2+2, and 2+3 articulation agreements with major allied health universities, hospitals, and local universities.

Credit for Nontraditional Learning Experiences

Manor College awards credit by examination for college-level learning through the College-Level Examination Program (CLEP). Manor administers exemption tests for courses not available through CLEP. Adults may also receive college credit for military experience and education through the Army/American Council on Education Registry Transcript System (AARTS), by submitting a transcript to Manor for evaluation of credits, and by requesting assessment of previous life and job experiences through nontraditional means.

Costs

Tuition for the 2006–07 academic year was $10,868 for full-time studies. Part-time study was $235 per credit hour. Students in certain allied health programs paid an additional $530 per year for full-time study or an additional $95 per credit hour for part-time study. On-campus room and board are available for men and women and cost $5296 per year. There is an additional $800 fee for a private room. Other fees included a $350 general fee per year and a $100 graduation fee.

Financial Aid

Manor College offers need-based financial aid to eligible applicants in the form of grants, loans, and campus employment. Scholarships are awarded on the basis of academic promise. Approximately 85 percent of Manor's students receive some form of financial aid. Federally funded sources include the Federal Pell Grant, Federal Supplemental Educational Opportunity Grant, Federal Perkins Loan, Federal Stafford Student Loan, Federal PLUS loan, and Federal Work-Study Program. State-funded programs offered are the PHEAA State Grant and State Work-Study programs. The institutionally funded sources are the Manor Grant and the Resident Grant. Scholarships available for attendance at Manor include the following: Manor Presidential Scholarship; Joseph and Rose Wawriw Scholarships; Henry Lewandowski Memorial Scholarship; Elizabeth A. Stahlecker Memorial Scholarship; Mary Wolchonsky Scholarship; John Woloschuk Memorial Scholarship; Lorraine Osinski Keating Memorial Scholarship; Yuri and Jaroslava Rybak Scholarship; Dr. and Mrs. Volodymyr and Lydia Bazarko Scholarship; Heritage Foundation Scholarship of First Securities Federal Savings Bank;

Father Chlystun Scholarship; Sesok Family Memorial Scholarship; Eileen Freedman Memorial Scholarship; Manor Allied Health, Science, and Math Division Scholarship; Business Division Scholarship; Liberal Arts Division Scholarship; Basilian Scholarships; Scholar Athlete Award; St. Basil Academy Scholarship; Wasyl and Jozefa Soroka Scholarships; and International Scholarships. Scholarship eligibility requirements vary; details are available from the Admissions Office.

Faculty

There are 24 full-time and 100 part-time faculty members at Manor. Forty-seven percent of the faculty members have master's degrees and 35 percent possess doctorates in their field. Faculty members spend three fourths of their time teaching and the remainder counseling and advising students. The overall faculty-student ratio is 1:13. Small class size allows for personal attention in an environment conducive to learning.

Student Body Profile

Of the approximately 900 full- and part-time students enrolled at Manor, 174 entered the College as full-time freshman students in fall 2006. Twenty-six percent of the recent freshman class lived in the on-campus residence hall. Twenty-six percent of the recent freshman class were members of minority groups. This included international students from Albania, Ecuador, Guatemala, Haiti, India, Korea, Pakistan, Philippines, Sierra Leone, Russia, Ukraine, and Uzbekistan.

Student Activities

Manor encourages students to develop leadership skills through active participation in all aspects of College life. A variety of options for extracurricular participation fall under the umbrella of Manor's student life department, including the Student Senate, athletic teams, and clubs. The Student Senate forms an important part of the College community. The Senate, representing the student population, responds to student interests and concerns and acts as a liaison between the administration and the student body. Other extracurricular activities include intercollegiate men's and women's basketball and soccer. Manor's sports teams compete in the Eastern Pennsylvania Collegiate Conference. Additional extracurricular activities include the honor societies, intramural sports, the yearbook, and various special interest and cultural clubs. Student services is also responsible for the campus ministry, the counseling center, the residence hall, and the on-campus security force.

Facilities and Resources

The Academic Building (also called Mother of Perpetual Help Hall) includes classrooms, lecture rooms, laboratories, the chapel, and the Offices of Student Services, Campus Ministry, and Counseling. The Academic Building is equipped with up-to-date facilities, including biology, chemistry, and clinical laboratories, as well as modern IBM-compatible microsystems network labs. The Learning Center provides professional and student tutors in all College subjects and conducts workshops in study and research skills. Courses in English as a second language are also offered at the center.

The Basileiad Library has the capacity for 60,000 books, journals, multimedia materials, and periodicals. The library offers study areas, a multimedia room, a special collections and rare book archive, and computer access. The current library collection contains 50,000 volumes, including a special law collection and a Ukrainian Language collection.

An on-campus community Manor Dental Health Center was established in 1979 as an adjunct to the Expanded Functions Dental Assisting (EFDA) Program. Located on the lower level of St. Josaphat Hall, the center provides students enrolled in the EFDA Program or the Dental Hygiene Program at Manor with training under the direct supervision of faculty dentists. Currently, more than 2,000 patients receive care, including the following services: general dentistry, oral hygiene, orthodontics, prosthodontics, endodontics, and cosmetic dentistry. Because Manor Dental Health Center is a teaching facility, the fees charged for services are lower than those charged by private practitioners. Community residents are welcome as patients.

The Ukrainian Heritage Studies Center, located on the campus, preserves and promotes Ukrainian heritage, arts, and culture through four areas: academic programs, a museum collection, a library, and archives. Special events, exhibits, workshops, and seminars are offered throughout the year. The center is open to the public for tours and educational presentations by appointment.

Location

Manor is located in Jenkintown, Pennsylvania, 15 miles north of Center City Philadelphia. Manor is accessible via public transportation and is located near the Pennsylvania Turnpike, Route 611, U.S. 1, and Route 232. Centers of cultural and historic interest are found in nearby Philadelphia, Valley Forge, and beautiful Bucks County. Manor's suburban campus is within walking distance of a large shopping mall, medical offices, and a township park.

Admission Requirements

Manor is open to qualified applicants of all races, creeds, and national origins. Candidates are required to have a high school diploma or its equivalent. Admission is based on the applicant's scholastic record, test scores, and interviews. The application procedure involves submission of a completed application form, a high school transcript, SAT or ACT scores (required for students less than 21 years old), an interview, and Manor's entrance/placement test (waived for candidates who hold the baccalaureate degree). Transfer students must submit transcripts of all college work completed. International students must also submit results of the Test of English as a Foreign Language (TOEFL) or, for the Liberal Arts/ESL program, must have completed two years of English language study at the high school or college level in their native country.

Application and Information

Manor has a rolling admission policy. Students may apply for admission in either the fall or the spring semester. Interested students are invited to visit the campus and meet with admissions staff, faculty members, program directors, and students. Open houses, career days and nights, and classroom visits are scheduled throughout the year. The Admissions Office is open Monday through Friday, 8:30 a.m. to 6 p.m. (Saturday hours are by appointment). Admissions staff members can schedule visits and answer questions concerning admission, careers, programs, special features, and student life. For application forms, program-of-study bulletins, and catalogs, students should write to:

I. Jerry Czenstuch
Vice President of Enrollment Management
Manor College
700 Fox Chase Road
Jenkintown, Pennsylvania 19046

Phone: 215-884-2216
E-mail: ftadmiss@manor.edu
Web site: http://www.manor.edu

Manor College students relax between classes on the steps outside Mother of Perpetual Help Hall.

MASSACHUSETTS BAY COMMUNITY COLLEGE

WELLESLEY HILLS, FRAMINGHAM, AND ASHLAND, MASSACHUSETTS

The College and Its Mission

Massachusetts Bay Community College (MassBay) provides a student-centered learning environment in which a diverse student body explores, develops, and achieves educational goals. MassBay is committed to academic excellence and student success. The College is a comprehensive, two-year public institution offering career programs for immediate employability and programs paralleling the first two years of a bachelor's degree. MassBay emphasizes technology and health-care programs and has strong transfer programs in the liberal arts and business. While the majority of the students hail from the Metro West and Boston areas, its reputation has attracted students from throughout the United States and worldwide. It has been serving the academic needs of the community since it was founded in 1961.

The student body at MassBay comprises a diverse group of individuals, all with various goals and educational needs. Some may be working toward an associate degree or certificate program by taking day or evening classes. Others may have plans to transfer to a four-year college or university to continue their education. Still others may have some college experience but want to broaden their professional skills. MassBay's programs are geared to meet the needs of this diverse population, ensuring access to education and flexibility to students by offering a variety of instructional delivery systems, including day and night schedules and online courses.

Each of MassBay's programs of study belongs to one of its specialized Centers of Excellence—the Business, Engineering, Science and Technology Institute (BEST), the Health, Human Services, and Education Institute (HHSEI), and the Liberal Arts Institute (LAI). Whether a student's level of study is undergraduate, professional training, or continuing education, the goal of the Centers of Excellence is to provide students with a seamless learning and training experience. In addition, the Centers of Excellence enable students to easily plan their education to meet their career goals and at a pace that fits their lifestyle. For example, they can decide to complete a degree or certificate program to obtain an entry-level position and then return to the Center for more advanced training as they prepare for the next step of their career ladder. Because MassBay is committed to the success of its students, the Centers of Excellence are designed to provide open and enriching dialogue among faculty members and fellow students in similar programs of study. This allows for students to share experiences, compare similarities in career fields, or mentor each other in a particular project. Through the Centers of Excellence, students experience an innovative way of learning that provides a rewarding college experience and prepares them to excel in meeting the ever-changing demands of today's workforce.

MassBay students perform better than the state average on the registered nurse licensing exam (NCLEX-RN) and the practical nurse licensing exam (NCLEX-PN). All of MassBay's automotive-technician training programs have received Automotive Service Excellence (ASE) MASTER certification, the highest level of achievement recognized by the National Institute for Automotive Service Excellence. MassBay students have received the prestigious and world-recognized Barry M. Goldwater Scholarship Award for mathematics, natural science, or engineering excellence. MassBay students regularly receive several Elizabeth Davis Scholarships from Wellesley College. MassBay's athletic teams routinely contend for state, regional, and national honors and championships.

MassBay is accredited by the New England Association of Schools and Colleges (NEASC), the Commission on Accreditation of Allied Health Education Programs (CAAHEP), the Joint Review Committee on Education in Radiologic Technology (JRCERT), the National League for Nursing Accrediting Commission (NLNAC), Commission on Accreditation in Physical Therapy Education (CAPTE), and the National Automotive Technician Educational Foundation (NATEF).

Academic Programs

MassBay Community College offers two-year professional and liberal arts programs and certificate programs. From automotive technology, business, education, engineering, health, information systems and computer technology, liberal arts, and physical sciences, MassBay students have a wide range of choices. Many of the College's professional programs give students the opportunity to learn not only in the classroom but also in the field, with hands-on experience and state-of-the-art labs simulating the real experiences faced on the job. MassBay's liberal arts program provides the foundation for further learning and career advancement. Certificates can help students enter a new field or advance their current one. MassBay recommends that students work with an adviser in designing their specific course of study and planning for further college study or employment.

Students who complete a MassBay degree program may receive an Associate of Arts or an Associate of Science degree and are fully prepared for further study at four-year institutions for a baccalaureate degree. Students may be eligible for transfer status as a junior to many colleges and universities. Many of these programs also qualify students for immediate employment in their chosen field.

MassBay also participates in the Joint Admissions Program for students to transfer from MassBay to one of the four University of Massachusetts campuses or seven state colleges. The program is open to students who receive an associate degree in an approved major with a 2.5 or higher grade point average. In addition, the Tuition Advantage Plan may help transferring graduates lower their tuition costs.

The associate degree programs offered are accounting, automotive technology, biotechnology, business administration, communication, computer information systems, computer science, criminal justice, early childhood education, electrical and computer engineering, electronics technology, engineering, engineering design, environmental science and occupational safety, forensic science, general business, general studies, hospitality management, human services, information systems technology and management, liberal arts, liberal arts: early childhood education, liberal arts: elementary education, liberal arts: global studies, life sciences, mechanical engineering, nursing, paralegal studies, physical therapist assistant, psychology/sociology/anthropology, and radiologic technology.

The certificate programs offered are accounting, automotive technology, central processing technology, central services and material management, communication, computer-aided design (CAD), CAD with Web option, early childhood education, early childhood education: infant-toddler teacher, emergency medical technician, hospitality management, human services, information technology, interior design, liberal arts, management, medical coding, medical interpreter, medical office administrative assistant, paralegal studies, paramedicine, personal fitness trainer, phlebotomy, practical nursing, surgical technology, and therapeutic massage.

Internships, clinicals, and co-ops play a critical role in the MassBay learning experience. Counselors in the Office of Career Development can assist students in finding internship opportunities that fit into their career paths. Internships are valuable experiences that allow students to gain experience in the field of their interest and develop professional contacts.

Costs

For January 2007, the cost per credit hour for Massachusetts residents was $119. For out-of-state/nonresidents, the cost was $325 per credit hour. Fees for health insurance, student parking, lab, or material costs may be added. Continuing education is $136 per credit hour for Massachusetts residents. For out-of-state/nonresidents, the cost per credit hour is $325. All evening AD nursing courses are $283 per credit hour plus additional fees. All evening practical nursing courses (CE, PN) are $245 per credit hour plus additional fees. Under the New England Regional Student Program, some New England students may attend MassBay for 150 percent of the in-state tuition rate, which is less than the out-of-state tuition rate.

Financial Aid

Financial assistance is available to all qualified students. Such aid is designed to help students meet basic college expenses. Financial assistance may be in the form of a grant, a scholarship, a loan, work-study employment, or any combination of these. MassBay's resources are obtained from federal, state, local, or private sources. Applicant eligibility and program guidelines are defined by the funding source. Grants and scholarships generally do not need to be paid back to MassBay or the sponsor. Loans can be made to the student or a student's parent and must be paid back. Loans can be need-based or non-need-based depending upon the individual circumstances of the student. A monthly payment plan through Academic Management Services (AMS) is also available.

Faculty

The faculty members at MassBay totaled 342, with 78 full-time and 264 part-time as of November 2006. Many members of the faculty are affiliated with other colleges and universities in the state, providing MassBay students with a valuable resource.

Student Body Profile

The student body at MassBay comprises a diverse group of individuals, all with various goals and educational needs. There are more than 5,000 students enrolled at MassBay. While the majority of students hail from the Metro West and the Boston vicinity, there are many international students as well, representing countries such as Brazil, Haiti, India, Russia, and Uganda. Fifty percent of MassBay students are between 17 and 22 years of age.

Student Activities

The College supports intercollegiate athletic programs, including men's baseball; women's softball; and men's and women's basketball, cross-country, golf, soccer, tennis, and volleyball.

Some other student clubs and organizations offered by MassBay are the Student Senate and Student Government; honor societies, such as Alpha Beta Gamma, the National Business Honor Society, Alpha Kappa Lamda, Psi Beta, Sigma Delta Mus, and Silver Key; the student-run theater group, the MassBay Players; concert/lecture series; the International and Multicultural Student Development program; and the student newspaper, *The Beacon*.

For students interested in a healthy lifestyle, the Recreation Center, built in 2003, offers a variety of activities, such as exercising, weight training, and pickup basketball.

Facilities and Resources

MassBay provides the College community with resources and facilities that support the academic programs and courses offered, including a Student Development Office; Advising Center, where students can speak with an academic adviser; an Academic Achievement Center that supplements classroom instruction with one-on-one support while accommodating MassBay students' diverse learning styles; the Reading and Writing Centers, which offer one-on-one help in completing a reading or writing assignment for any college course; smart classrooms, used by faculty members and students to enhance the classroom learning experience; a library with more than 49,000 volumes; wireless technologies; and computer labs with more than 400 computers for student use.

Location

MassBay serves students from three convenient locations. The Wellesley Hills Campus is located on Route 9 approximately 10 miles west of Boston. The Framingham Campus is near Routes 9 and 126. The Technology Center in Ashland is approximately 4 miles south of the Framingham Campus off Route 126.

Admission Requirements

MassBay maintains an open-door admissions policy, and there is no application deadline. If students have proof of a GED, high school graduation, or an associate degree or higher, they will be admitted to MassBay on a first-come, first-served basis, provided there is a vacancy in the program to which they have applied.

Application and Information

MassBay enrollment is open to Massachusetts residents at the in-state tuition rate. A Massachusetts resident is currently defined as a U.S. citizen or permanent resident having a minimum of six consecutive months of verifiable domicile in the Commonwealth. Others may attend MassBay at the out-of-state tuition rate.

All applicants must include a nonrefundable application fee of $20 with their application. Credit card payment is accepted for the online application. For an application and information, students should contact the Office of Admissions.

Office of Admissions
Massachusetts Bay Community College
50 Oakland Street
Wellesley Hills, Massachusetts 02481
Phone: 781-239-2500
Web site: http://www.massbay.edu

The MassBay Wellesley Hills campus.

McINTOSH COLLEGE
DOVER, NEW HAMPSHIRE

The College and Its Mission

For the residential or commuting student seeking the intimate personal experience of a small college and the training in practical skills needed to compete in today's job market, McIntosh College is the answer. For more than 110 years, McIntosh has provided an exciting variety of business and professional opportunities to recent high school graduates and adults seeking career changes or re-entry into the job market. McIntosh is a two-year degree-granting institution accredited by the New England Association of Schools and Colleges. The College currently enrolls more than 1,000 students at its campus in Dover, New Hampshire.

The mission of McIntosh College, a private provider of quality education since 1896, is to embrace the ideal of career education for all, preparing students to become involved, successful graduates in their chosen fields. The student-oriented environment provides the framework for student success. This integration allows the College to enhance the quality of personal and professional life of the business and academic communities that it serves.

McIntosh is a career-oriented institution dedicated to the personal, intellectual, and professional growth of its students. The College has a century-long tradition of providing academic programs that integrate the acquisition of job-related skills with the development of clear, critical thinking and effective reasoning. While McIntosh recognizes its obligation to provide the specific skills necessary for the student to function in a contemporary work environment, it operates under the philosophy that a college is more than a training facility. Students must leave the college experience with a sense of competence in their chosen fields, a belief in themselves as individuals, and an enhanced critical awareness of the world around them.

Academic Programs

McIntosh College offers a unique blend of courses and programs of study designed to prepare students for careers in allied health, business, Le Cordon Bleu culinary arts, design, legal, and law enforcement. All degree programs of study provide students with academic credit, which allows them to continue their studies at four-year institutions.

Associate Degree Programs McIntosh College is authorized by the Postsecondary Education Commission of the state of New Hampshire to offer associate degree programs with major areas of concentration in business management, criminal justice, criminal justice with a concentration in crime scene technology, Le Cordon Bleu culinary arts, fashion merchandising, graphic design, medical assisting, paralegal studies, and professional photography as well as a certificate program in massage therapy.

Honors Programs The McIntosh College Beta Gamma Gamma Chapter of the Phi Theta Kappa Honor Society supports a number of scholarship opportunities and activities for honor students.

Transfer Arrangements Academic counseling is available and full support is provided for students wishing to continue their education at other institutions of higher learning.

Internship and Co-op Programs All academic departments supporting degree programs support for-credit internship opportunities for qualified students. The Office of Career Services assists students in finding appropriate internships in business management, criminal justice, Le Cordon Bleu culinary arts, fashion merchandising, graphic design, massage therapy, medical assisting, paralegal studies, and professional photography.

Credit for Nontraditional Learning Experiences

The College grants credit to students who have passed authorized advanced placement courses in high school with grades of B or better or who present evidence of having received scores of 460 or better on CLEP examinations in subject areas that directly correspond to the content of individual McIntosh courses.

Costs

The 2006–07 annual tuition for a full-time degree candidate was $15,600. Tuition and costs are subject to change.

Financial Aid

The Office of Student Finance provides information and personal counseling with respect to the various federal grant and loan programs and institutional scholarships available to students attending McIntosh College. McIntosh College believes that every student should have access to the financial resources needed to pursue academic or career interests. Pell Grants, Supplemental Educational Opportunity Grants, Federal Work-Study, Stafford Student Loans, Plus Loans, State Incentive Programs, direct loans, scholarships, and family discounts are all available to students attending McIntosh College.

Faculty

There are 45 full-time faculty members at McIntosh College. Of these, 70 percent hold advanced degrees and specialized certifications.

Student Body Profile

McIntosh College attracts students from a wide age spectrum. Because the College offers parallel day and evening programs, there is a substantial mix of recent high school graduates and adult students returning to school. The average age of a McIntosh student is 24, slightly higher at night and slightly lower during the day program. Students are generally career oriented. More than 50 percent of graduates continue their studies at the bachelor's-degree level.

Student Activities

The College supports a variety of social clubs, organizations, and other extracurricular activities designed to enhance and enrich the student's educational experience at McIntosh. The Student Activities Committee provides a forum for students interested in planning and implementing social and cultural events at the College. There is a chapter of Delta Epsilon Chi on campus. Departmental associations include the McIntosh Paralegal Association and the Criminal Justice Association.

Facilities and Resources

In recent years, McIntosh has anticipated changes in the business environment and the need for a newly oriented work force by establishing a superior computer facility consisting of four computer labs housing more than 100 individual and networked stations. An integrated curriculum provides specific computer instruction related to each major field of study. In addition, McIntosh students can roam the Internet, explore online services such as LexisNexis, or browse through an extensive CD-ROM collection in the McIntosh academic and paralegal library facilities. A fully equipped medical lab and a real-world operative teaching kitchen provide hands-on working environments for medical assisting and culinary arts majors. At McIntosh, emphasis is placed on the practical aspects of career development. Internships are available in all departments.

On-campus student housing facilities at McIntosh College have been carefully designed to provide a warm, supportive living and

learning environment that serves to nurture students' personal development and to enhance their opportunities for academic and professional success. The residential facility includes spacious furnished living units that are cable-ready and have air-conditioning, a full bath, and access to a computer lab. Residential students may choose from a variety of meal plans. Initial inquiries about eligibility requirements and the availability of on-campus housing should be directed to the Office of Admissions. Room assignments are made on a first-come, first-served basis, depending on eligibility.

Advisement/Counseling The faculty and administration of the College are committed to the principle that students should be given every possible opportunity to achieve academic and professional success. For this reason, the College offers extensive academic and career counseling to its students. Free study skills workshops are regularly available. In addition, the College provides free tutorial assistance in accounting, computer applications, English, and math.

Office of Career Services The McIntosh College Office of Career Services provides students and graduates the opportunity to receive individualized career guidance and employment assistance. McIntosh graduates can be secure in the fact that if they ever need assistance in finding employment, career services representatives are available to assist them. These services include: career counseling, full-time employment opportunities for graduates, a worldwide job database, part-time job postings/assistance for students, internship opportunities/assistance, resume and letter writing assistance, interviewing techniques/coaching, online job searches, career fairs/networking opportunities, federal work-study positions (available for those who qualify), volunteer and community service opportunities, and an alumni section of Career Services on the student portal. The Career Services staff is located in the main building, and is open to serve students from 8 a.m. to 8 p.m., Monday through Thursday, and 8 a.m. to 5 p.m. on Fridays.

Location

McIntosh College is centrally located in scenic Dover, New Hampshire, in the heart of the seacoast region—not far from the Maine and Massachusetts borders. Road trips home to visit old friends and enjoy home cooking (and free laundry) are a breeze. New England has a lot to offer. From snowboarding to beach going, nature walks to city hops, mountain biking to seaside dining—it's all just a stone's throw away.

The McIntosh College experience extends beyond the campus. For those who like the great outdoors, the quaint city of Dover is located between the Bellamy and Cochecho Rivers, just minutes from unspoiled woodlands, Audubon trails, scenic river walks and boat tours, lakes, and the Atlantic Ocean. Downtown Dover has shops, restaurants, and a thriving arts community. And that's just the start. Dover is within a short drive of some of the East Coast's best recreation spots, tax free shopping in New Hampshire, and bargain hunting at the Kittery Maine Outlets. Dover is located within an hour's driving distance of three diverse cities: Portsmouth, Portland, and Boston. Portsmouth, New Hampshire, is a nearby seaside community with an eclectic downtown combining old New England charm with contemporary hipness. Portland, Maine, is a working port city with a touristy shopping area, plenty of casual dining, a Civic Center for concerts and sporting events, and a wonderful art museum. Then there is Boston, Massachusetts, home of the 2004 world series champions (the Boston Red Sox), Fenway Park, Faneuil Hall Marketplace, the shops of Copley Square, the New England Aquarium, the new Boston Garden for concerts and sporting events, and world-class museums, theaters, and restaurants.

Admission Requirements

Students should apply for admission as soon as possible in order to be accepted for a specific program and starting date. All applicants are required to complete a personal interview with an admissions representative, either in person or by telephone (depending upon the distance from the school), and parents and/or significant others are encouraged to attend. This gives applicants and their families an opportunity to see and learn about the school's equipment and facilities and to ask questions relating to the school's curriculum and career objectives. Personal interviews also enable school administrators to determine whether an applicant is a strong candidate for enrollment in the program.

Application and Information

Applications for admission are accepted on an ongoing basis. Most students may begin classes at the start of any term scheduled throughout the year. For application materials, students should contact:

Office of Admissions
McIntosh College
23 Cataract Avenue
Dover, New Hampshire 03820

Phone: 888-303-4999 (toll-free)
Fax: 603-742-0060
E-mail: admissions@mcintoshcollege.com
Web site: http://www.mcintoshcollege.edu

McIntosh has small-school charm with students' careers in mind.

MIAMI DADE COLLEGE
MIAMI, FLORIDA

The College and Its Mission

Miami Dade College (MDC) is recognized as one of the most outstanding community colleges in the nation. With more than 155,000 students, it is also the largest institution of higher learning in the United States. At Miami Dade, student success is the priority. The mission of the College is to provide accessible, affordable, high-quality education that keeps the learner's needs at the center of the decision-making process. The College is accredited by the Southern Association of Colleges and Schools.

Academic Programs

The College offers more than 200 undergraduate areas of study. An Associate in Arts (A.A.) prepares students to transfer to upper-division colleges and universities. An Associate in Science (A.S.) degree is designed for students seeking immediate job placement after graduation. In addition, the College offers bachelor's degree programs leading to teacher certification in exceptional student education (K–12), secondary mathematics (6–12), and secondary science education (6–12) with concentrations in biology, chemistry, earth and space science, and physics. As of fall 2006, the College offers a Bachelor of Applied Science degree with a major in public safety management, with concentrations in basic police academy, basic corrections academy, corrections, crime scene investigation, emergency management, field internship, law enforcement, probation and parole, security/loss prevention, and criminal justice, which is housed at the School of Justice.

The A.A. degree, which is offered for students planning to transfer to a university, can be earned in 60 credits, including 36 credits of required general education and 24 credits of electives. A variety of A.S. and Associate in Applied Science (A.A.S.) degrees, College Credit Certificate programs (CCC), Vocational Credit Certificate programs (VCC), and supplemental courses are offered to prepare students to enter the job market or upgrade skills. These programs vary in length. The A.S. degree includes a minimum of 15 credits of general education requirements. The Medical Center Campus offers a wide range of allied health and nursing programs, with clinicals in major local hospitals and health-care centers. Courses are offered year-round in two major terms of sixteen weeks each and summer terms consisting of two 6-week terms or one 12-week term.

The following A.S. degree programs, which prepare students for employment and may transfer to a four-year institution, are available: accounting technology; air conditioning; architectural design and construction technology; automotive service management technology; aviation administration; aviation maintenance management; banking; biomedical engineering technology; building construction technology; business administration; business application programming; business management; civil engineering technology; computer engineering technology; computer information technology; conservation ecology; court reporting technology; creative performance; creative production; criminal justice technology: BLE; criminal justice technology: corrections; criminal justice technology: generic; design and installation specialization; dietetic technician studies; drafting and design technology; early childhood education; electronics engineering technology; environmental science technology; film production technology; financial management; fire science technology; funeral service education; game development; graphic arts technology; graphic design technology; graphic Internet technology; hospitality and tourism management; human services–generalist studies; industrial management technology; interior design technology; international business; international trade marketing; Internet services technology; legal assisting; legal office specialist studies; maintenance technician studies; Microsoft Cisco; Microsoft database administrator studies; Microsoft solutions developer studies; mortgage finance; nonprofit management; office management specialist studies; Oracle database administration; Oracle database developer studies; photographic technology; professional pilot technology; radio and television broadcasting programming; real estate marketing; refrigeration and heating systems technology; sign language interpretation; software applications specialist studies; telecommunications engineering technology; theater and entertainment technology; translation interpretation studies, with tracks in English/Spanish and Haitian/Creole; travel industry management; and watershed management.

Allied health A.S. degree programs offered at the Medical Center Campus include dental hygiene, diagnostic medical sonography technology, emergency medical services, health information management, histologic technology, medical laboratory technology, midwifery, nuclear medicine technology, nursing-RN, opticianry, physical therapist assistant and physician assistant studies, radiation therapy technology, respiratory care, and veterinary technology. In addition, an A.A.S. degree is offered in radiography.

College credit certificates are offered in accounting applications, air cargo agent studies, airline/aviation management, airline reservation and ticketing agent studies, business management, Cisco network associate studies, computer-aided design assistant or operator studies, computer programming, computer specialist studies, embalming, emergency medical technician studies, information technology support, interpretation studies: English/Spanish, marketing operations, microcomputer repairer/installer studies, Microsoft database administrator studies, Microsoft solutions developer studies, mortgage finance, network systems developer studies, nuclear medicine technology specialist studies, office systems specialist studies, Oracle database administrator or database developer studies, paramedic studies, passenger service agent studies, translation studies: English/Spanish, and Web development specialist studies.

The **Honors College** at Miami Dade College provides a rigorous and comprehensive curriculum in a supportive environment where goal-oriented, academically gifted students explore new ideas, discuss global and environmental concerns, engage in inspired creativity and intellectual collaborations with experienced faculty members, and participate in study-travel and culturally enriching experiences. Graduates of the Honors College transfer into some of the nation's finest schools.

Launched in fall 2006, the Honors Dual Language Program is offered at the InterAmerican Campus, where, each semester, some courses are taught entirely in English and some, entirely in Spanish. In response to industry demands, the Honors Dual Language Program ensures that students are truly bi-literate and are able to function in writing, reading, and speaking in both languages. Colloquia and leadership courses are also taught in Spanish.

Distance Education Through the Virtual College, high-quality online academic and vocational programs are offered to meet the needs of nontraditional and out-of-area students as well as students who find it difficult to attend classes during scheduled hours and at specific locations. The array of instructional activities in the Web courses is designed to engage students in interactive and collaborative learning and cover the established competencies. Entire programs as well as more than ninety different courses are available online. Students should visit the Virtual College at http://virtual.mdc.edu for more information.

Transfer Arrangements A statewide articulation agreement among all Florida institutions of higher education facilitates transfers and ensures that a student who is awarded the Associate in Arts degree at Miami Dade College has met general education requirements for admission to the upper division in public and some private colleges and universities in Florida as well as out of state. In all, MDC has established matriculation agreements with sixty-one prestigious colleges and universities.

Certificate Programs Vocational Credit Certificates are offered in the Academy of International Marketing, accounting operations, administrative assistant studies, architectural drafting, bail bonding, business computer programming, business supervision and management, commercial art technology, community service officer/police service aide studies, correctional officer and correctional probation officer studies, customer assistance, early childhood education, electronic technology, firefighting, insurance marketing, law enforcement officer studies, legal secretary studies, massage

therapy, mechanical drafting, medical assisting, medical coder/biller studies, medical record transcribing, medical secretary studies, network support services, PC support services, pharmacy technician studies, phlebotomy, practical nursing, private security officer studies, public safety telecommunications, real estate marketing, television production, teller operations, and travel and tourism. Applied technology diplomas are offered in medical coder/biller studies and medical record transcribing.

Internship and Co-op Programs Miami Dade College is committed to giving students a competitive edge in the marketplace. Through its co-op and internship programs, students are given the opportunity to work with professionals in the field, obtaining valuable real-life employment skills while earning college credit, work experience, and/or compensation.

Special Programs and Services New World School of the Arts (NWSA) is a unique educational partnership of Miami-Dade County Public Schools, Miami Dade College, and the University of Florida. Through its sponsoring institutions, NWSA awards high school diplomas, A.A. degrees, and Bachelor of Music and Bachelor of Fine Arts degrees. Students are admitted through audition or portfolio presentation. Other special programs include academic remediation for entering students, English as a second language, services for disabled students (including learning disabled), study abroad, and advanced placement.

The College is a leader in working proactively to assist students with disabilities. Each campus has a ground-floor ACCESS office to provide the guidance and technological accommodations required. Computers equipped with voice synthesizer programs are available, as are note-takers to help physically challenged students. Sign-language interpreters are also available for deaf and hearing-impaired students. The College has more than 2,600 documented disabled students receiving services from its departments.

Miami Dade College provides students the opportunity to obtain Continuing Education Units (CEUs) for certain courses. Transcripts designating CEUs are provided.

Off-Campus Programs

Study-abroad programs, both short-term and full semester, are available in nearly thirty countries around the world. Faculty-led study-abroad programs are also available.

Credit for Nontraditional Learning Experiences

The College may award credit for demonstrated proficiency in areas related to college-level courses. Sources used to determine such proficiency are the College-Level Examination Program, the Advanced Placement Program, the Proficiency Examination Program, the International Baccalaureate Program, Dual Enrollment, Tech Prep Matriculation, the Defense Activity for Non-Traditional Educational Support, the United States Armed Forces Institute, the Institutional Credit by Exam, and the internal MDC procedures for awarding credit related to specific programs for approval licensures.

Costs

For the 2005–06 academic year, tuition was $68.94 per college credit for Florida residents; it was $228.76 per college credit for nonresidents. Textbooks and supplies for full-time students were estimated at $1500. Although housing is not available on campus, there are numerous housing options near the College at varying costs.

Financial Aid

Financial aid is determined through federal, state, and institutional guidelines and is offered to students in packages that may consist of grants, loans, employment, and scholarships. Most financial aid programs are based on financial need. The College also offers merit-based aid to qualified students as funds are available. Assistance includes Federal Pell Grants, Federal Supplemental Educational Opportunity Grants, the Florida Student Assistance Grant, the Florida Bright Futures Scholarship, the Federal Work-Study Program, the Florida Work Experience Program (FWEP), Federal Perkins Loans, Federal Stafford Student Loans, and Federal PLUS loans. The College also offers Foundation and Institutional Grants, scholarships, short-term tuition loans, and employment to students as well as funding for the purchase of special equipment for disabled students. About 53 percent of the student body receives some form of financial aid. In 2005–06, 33,000 students received Pell Grants.

Faculty

There are 2,108 faculty members, 726 full-time and 1,382 part-time. Of the full-time faculty members, 93 percent hold advanced degrees.

Student Body Profile

Of the 155,595 credit and noncredit students enrolled at Miami Dade College, almost 1,800 are international. Eighty-one percent of students with an A.A. degree continue their education at a four-year college. The average age of students is 27, although about 30 percent of MDC credit students are the "traditional" college age of 18 to 20 years old. Sixty-six percent attend on a part-time basis, and 61 percent are women. The student body is ethnically and culturally diverse. More information regarding admission and services for international students is available at http://www.mdc.edu/internationalstudents.

Student Activities

More than 100 organizations offer opportunities to participate in student government, student publications, music ensembles, drama productions (in English and Spanish), religious activities, service and political clubs, professional organizations, and honor societies. Intercollegiate and intramural athletics play an important role at Miami Dade College, which is a member of NJCAA and competes at the Division I level. Intercollegiate teams include women's basketball, softball, and volleyball and men's baseball and basketball. Sports facilities include racquetball, tennis, and handball courts; wellness centers; swimming pools; and a track.

Academic Facilities

The mission of Career Services at Miami Dade College is to assist students with their career planning, transfer, and employment needs. Career Services serves students who are undecided about their academic programs as well as those seeking career direction and vocational counseling. It also provides information on transfer options and transfer assistance to students wishing to continue their education upon completion of their programs at the College. Career Services assists students and alumni with job readiness through a comprehensive employability skills program that includes workshops, seminars, job-shadowing opportunities, annual job fairs, on-campus recruitment, and the MDC Employment and Internship Opportunities Online system, which is available through the Career Services Web site (http://www.mdc.edu/careerservices).

Library and Audiovisual Services The campus libraries have a combined book collection of more than 350,000 and more than 1,400 periodicals. There are approximately 25,000 audiovisual materials, and online databases are available. Computers for student use are available in computer labs, learning resource centers, labs, classrooms, and the library.

Location

Blessed with a sunny, subtropical climate; beautiful beaches; and an international flavor, Miami offers a rich variety of exciting cultural, sporting, and intellectual activities. Opportunities abound to explore unique settings, such as the historic Art Deco District of Miami Beach and Miami's colorful Little Havana or the nearby Everglades National Park. Eight campuses and numerous outreach centers are located throughout the greater Miami area.

Admission Requirements

Miami Dade has an open-door admission policy. The College provides educational opportunities to all high school graduates, including those who have a state high school equivalency diploma, and to transfer students from other colleges and universities. In addition to the College's application and the $20 application fee, students must have official transcripts from high school, college, university, or other postsecondary educational institutions sent directly to the Office of Admissions from the institutions. High school equivalency diploma or certificate holders must provide the original document and score report (which are returned) or an exact copy of the documents. Florida residents must complete a Florida residency statement. SAT, ACT, or TOEFL scores should be sent directly to the Office of Admissions by the testing board. Students not presenting test scores are tested for placement purposes upon acceptance.

Application and Information

Applications are accepted on an ongoing basis. All prospective students should contact:

District Office of Admissions and Registration Services
Miami Dade College
300 Northeast Second Avenue
Miami, Florida 33132

Phone: 305-237-8888
Fax: 305-237-2964
Web site: http://www.mdc.edu

MIDDLESEX COUNTY COLLEGE

EDISON, NEW JERSEY

The College and Its Mission

More students are choosing community colleges for their educational needs than ever before. Middlesex County College, with its diverse programs and specialized services, is the college of choice for more than 13,000 students in 2006–07. More students than ever are enrolled in full-time degree programs and are preparing to transfer as juniors to four-year colleges and universities.

Middlesex County College is one of the largest and among the oldest county colleges in New Jersey. The College, a two-year publicly supported coeducational institution, is committed to serving all those who can benefit from postsecondary learning, and the student body reflects this belief. More than 550 courses are offered during the day, evening, and on weekends. Students have the opportunity to prepare academically and through cooperative work placements, clinical experience, and laboratory work for careers in business, health, social science, and science technologies.

Middlesex County College offers modern, well-equipped facilities located on a beautiful 200-acre campus, together with excellent learning resources and dedicated faculty members. Most students commute to the College from Middlesex County. Each year, more and more students from outside the United States enroll as international students. All students have the opportunity to add to their collegiate experience through participation in a variety of student activities and clubs. The College has a recreational facility with a 25-meter pool, dance studio, wrestling and weight rooms, and racquetball courts. The College philosophy is directed toward assisting each individual in reaching his or her maximum potential, and counselors work with students to ensure this goal.

Academic Programs

More than seventy different degree and certificate programs, either transfer or career oriented, may be taken full-time or part-time during the day, evening, and on weekends. Courses are offered during the fall and spring semesters, a winter session, and summer sessions. The College offers **Associate in Arts (A.A.)** and **Associate in Science (A.S.)** degree programs designed specifically to transfer to four-year colleges and universities in the fields of arts, business education, engineering, and sciences. Students interested in preparing for careers in medicine or law begin their studies at Middlesex County College with courses in science and liberal arts.

Middlesex offers formal credit articulation transfer agreements and/or dual-degree admissions programs with more than 50 four-year institutions, including Rutgers, Montclair State, Kean, and NYU. It has always been the largest "feeder" school to the New Jersey Institute of Technology (NJIT), where its graduates are continually recognized for their outstanding academic achievements.

Students who complete the requirements of a transfer curriculum earn an associate degree and are accepted into the receiving college or university as members of the junior class. Working closely with their faculty and advisers assures this seamless transition, and students find that the cost of their undergraduate education is substantially lower because of their work at Middlesex.

Many challenging programs and options designed to prepare students for entry into the job market are available in business education, engineering technologies, health technologies, and science. Graduates of career programs receive an **Associate in Applied Science (A.A.S.)** degree. Many graduates holding the A.A.S. degree transfer to four-year colleges, which may accept all or part of the credits earned at Middlesex. Certificate programs are also available.

In addition to associate degree and certificate curricula, the College offers students the opportunity to enroll in a plan of study through the Open College Program. Open College serves students who want to try out an individualized academic program prior to formally enrolling in a specific degree or certificate program. The College offers Project Connections, a nationally recognized program for students with learning disabilities. Students interested in military education may participate in the Army or Air Force ROTC program through cross-registration at Rutgers University.

Degree and certificate programs are offered in accounting, biology transfer program, biotechnology, business administration, chemical technology, chemistry transfer program, civil construction engineering technology, computer-aided drafting, computer and information systems, computer programming, computer science transfer program, criminal justice, culinary arts certificate, dental hygiene, dietetic technology, education practitioner, electronic and computer engineering technology, energy utility technology, engineering science, English as a second language, environmental technology, fashion merchandising, fine arts (options in art, music, and theater), fire science technology, graphics for digital media, health science, help desk administration, hotel restaurant and institution management, information systems security, land surveying technology, liberal arts (options in business, communications, dance, English, general, health and physical education, history, journalism, media arts and design, modern languages, music, political science, psychology, sociology, social rehabilitation services, social science, theater, visual arts, and writing), management, marketing, mathematics transfer program, mechanical manufacturing technology, medical laboratory technology, nursing, paralegal studies, pharmacy assistant studies, physics transfer program, process technology, psychosocial rehabilitation and treatment, radiography education, respiratory care, small business management, and teacher aide studies.

Off-Campus Programs

In addition to the main campus in Edison, Middlesex offers outreach centers in New Brunswick and Perth Amboy. Both centers offer credit-level classes as well as classes in English as a second language. Credit and noncredit courses are also offered at selected locations throughout the county.

Credit for Nontraditional Learning Experiences

There are several programs at the College through which applicants may earn credit for knowledge learned in nontraditional ways. Both Credit by Examination and the College-Level Examination Program (CLEP) are available.

Costs

Tuition for the summer 2007 semester is $85.55 per credit for a Middlesex County resident and $171.10 per credit for an

out-of-county resident. There is a $14.50-per-credit general service fee, a $3.50-per-credit student service fee and an $9.50-per-credit technology fee for Middlesex residents. The fees for out-of-county residents are $29 per credit for general service, $7 per credit for student service, and $19 per credit for technology. There are also mandatory accident and health insurance fees. Some classes require special laboratory, material, or other fees.

Financial Aid

Through its financial aid programs, Middlesex County College makes every effort to overcome economic barriers. Funds from federal, state, and private sources are available to those who have need and meet the eligibility requirements. To be considered for financial aid, a student must complete the Free Application for Federal Student Aid (FAFSA) and the Middlesex County College Financial Aid Form. The priority deadline for the fall semester is April 1 and November 1 for the spring semester. Before a financial aid application can be reviewed, the student must be accepted to a degree program and be matriculated for a minimum of 6 credits.

Students who graduate from a New Jersey high school and finish in the top 20 percent of their graduating class may qualify for the NJSTARS free tuition program. Students must also apply for federal financial aid, be a U.S. citizen or permanent resident, be admitted to a degree program, and register for at least 12 college-level credits to be eligible for the program. NJSTARS II allows NJSTARS students who maintain eligibility and graduate with an associate degree and a minimum 3.0 grade point average to attend a public New Jersey college or university with tuition and fees covered.

Faculty

There are 200 full-time and 450 part-time members of the faculty. The student-faculty ratio is 21:1. Of the full-time faculty members, nearly 90 percent are teaching faculty members and serve as academic advisers. Middlesex faculty members have impressive resumes, outstanding accomplishments, and degrees from some of the country's finest colleges and universities. Many bring to the classroom years of workplace experience in their field. However, most important is the faculty's commitment to help students reach their potential and gain the confidence to achieve their life goals.

Student Body Profile

There are about 12,500 students on campus; about half attend on a full-time basis. The campus population is diverse, with students from more than sixty countries in attendance. Approximately half of the students come directly from high school, with an average age of 24 for the entire student body.

Student Activities

There are more than sixty chartered clubs and organizations, a College Center Program Board, College Assembly, national honor societies, special minority student activities, and a College newspaper, radio station, and literary magazine. The College offers intercollegiate competition through membership in Region XIX of the National Junior College Athletic Association and the Garden State Athletic Conference.

Facilities and Resources

The campus features twenty-five buildings, including a state-of-the-art Technical Services Center, a fully equipped Recreation Center, and a 440-seat Performing Arts Center. The Counseling and Career Services Center provides students with assistance in making decisions about career choices, education programs, college transfer, job placement, and other personal concerns. Bilingual counseling is available to Spanish-speaking students.

Location

The College is located just 15 minutes from New Brunswick, New Jersey. The College is conveniently located near numerous restaurants and shopping centers. The New Jersey shore is less than 30 minutes away. Mass transit to the College is available from many surrounding areas.

Admission Requirements

The admission policy is based on the premise that the College should provide an opportunity for further education to all citizens of the community. Enrollment is open to anyone who holds a high school diploma or any non–high school graduates 18 years of age or older who can demonstrate an ability to benefit from a college education. SAT scores are optional. Applicants to most programs are not required to submit any standardized test scores.

Admission to programs that specify additional selective criteria may require a review of prior educational performance, standardized test scores, the completion of an appropriate developmental program, or, when suitable, an assessment of an applicant's aptitude and interest, as determined during an admission counseling interview.

Application and Information

Completed applications are reviewed on a continuous basis, with the exception of the limited-seat programs in dental hygiene, medical laboratory technology, nursing, psychosocial rehabilitation, radiography education, and respiratory care. Automotive technology is offered every other year. A completed application form, a required $25 nonrefundable application fee, and all supporting materials should be sent to the Office of Admissions.

For further information or to schedule a campus visit, students should contact:

Office of Admissions
Middlesex County College
2600 Woodbridge Avenue, P.O. Box 3050
Edison, New Jersey 08818-3050
Phone: 732-906-4243
      888-YOU-4MCC (toll-free)
Fax: 732-906-7728
E-mail: admissions@middlesexcc.edu
Web site: http://www.middlesexcc.edu

MOHAWK VALLEY COMMUNITY COLLEGE

UTICA AND ROME, NEW YORK

The College and Its Mission

Mohawk Valley Community College (MVCC) offers choice, opportunity, and hope by providing accessible and affordable higher education, training, and services that emphasize academic excellence, diversity, and a global view.

Mohawk Valley Community College strives to be a college of choice through innovative educational leadership, programs, and services that address the current and future needs of rapidly changing local, regional, and global communities.

The College was founded in 1946 as the New York State Institute of Applied Arts and Sciences at Utica. One of five postsecondary institutions established on an experimental basis after World War II, the public institute offered programs leading to technical and semiprofessional employment in business and industry. After name changes in the 1950s, redefining its mission, the College moved to its current 80-acre campus location in Utica in 1960. In 1961, the College was renamed Mohawk Valley Community College. Today, the College offers a full range of academic programs.

The College is accredited by the Middle States Association of Colleges and Schools. Individual program accreditations are as follows: airframe and powerplant technology by the Federal Aviation Administration (FAA); civil, electrical, and mechanical engineering technology and surveying technology by the Commission for Technology Accreditation of the Accreditation Board for Engineering and Technology, Inc. (ABET); nursing by the National League for Nursing Accrediting Commission (NLNAC); and respiratory care and health information technology–medical records by the Commission on Accreditation of Allied Health Education Programs, in cooperation with the Committee on Accreditation for Respiratory Care and the American Health Information Management Association's Council on Accreditation, respectively.

Academic Programs

The College has been authorized to offer the following degrees and certificates: Associate in Arts (A.A.) degree, Associate in Science (A.S.) degree, Associate in Applied Science (A.A.S.) degree, Associate in Occupational Studies (A.O.S.) degree, and the MVCC Certificate.

The structure and goals of academic programming at MVCC have two main purposes. Certificate, A.O.S., and A.A.S. programs emphasize the development of employable skills through a combination of classroom and laboratory instruction. Some programs also include internship experiences. A.A. and A.S. programs provide students with the liberal arts, science, mathematics, business, engineering, or computer course work necessary for transfer into the junior year of a preprofessional program at a four-year public or private college or university upon the completion of their associate degree.

The minimum number of credits needed to earn an associate degree is 62. The maximum credits required for a degree differ by program and degree type.

Opportunities for specialization include the honors program, independent study, internships, study abroad, and ROTC (Army and Air Force).

The College operates on a semester calendar. Fall classes begin before Labor Day and end before Christmas. Spring classes begin in mid-January and end in mid-May.

Career and transfer programs are available. Majors offered include accounting (A.A.S.); administrative assistant (A.A.S.); air conditioning technology (A.O.S.); building management and maintenance (A.A.S.); business administration (A.S.); business management (A.A.S.); chemical dependency practitioner studies (A.A.S.); civil engineering technology (A.A.S.); computer-aided drafting (A.O.S.); computer information systems (A.A.S.); computer science (A.S.); criminal

justice (A.A.S.); culinary arts management (A.O.S.), also with baking and pastry emphasis; digital animation (A.A.S.); electrical engineering technology (A.A.S.); electrical service technician studies (A.O.S.), with options in electrical maintenance, fiber optics, and robotics; emergency medical services/paramedic studies (A.A.S.); engineering science (A.S.); environmental analysis–chemical technology (A.A.S.); financial services management (A.A.S.); fine arts (A.S.); fire protection technology (A.A.S.); general studies (A.S.); general studies–childhood education (A.S., joint admission with the State University of New York (SUNY) College at Oneonta); graphic arts technology (A.A.S.); graphic design (A.A.S.); health information technology (A.A.S.); hotel technology–meeting services (A.A.S.); human services (A.A.S.); illustration (A.A.S.); individual studies (A.A., A.A.S., A.S., and A.O.S.); international studies (A.A.); liberal arts–adolescence education (teacher transfer) (A.S.); liberal arts–childhood education (teacher transfer) (A.S.); liberal arts–humanities and social science (A.A.); liberal arts–psychology (A.S.); liberal arts–public policy (A.S.); liberal arts–theater (A.A.); manufacturing technology (A.O.S.); mathematics (A.S.); mechanical engineering technology (A.A.S.); mechanical technology–aircraft maintenance (A.A.S.); media marketing and management (A.A.S.); medical assisting (A.A.S.); nursing (A.A.S.); nutrition and dietetics (A.S.); photography (A.A.S.); pre–environmental science (A.S.); programming and systems (A.A.S.); radiologic technology (A.S.); recreation and leisure services (A.A.S.); respiratory care (A.A.S.); restaurant management (A.A.S.); science (A.S.), with emphasis areas in biology, chemistry, physical education, physics, and sports medicine; semiconductor manufacturing technology (A.A.S.); surveying technology (A.A.S.); telecommunications technology (A.A.S.); telecommunications technology–Verizon Next Step (A.A.S.); Web site design and management (A.A.S.); and welding technology (A.O.S.).

Certificate programs include airframe and powerplant technology; allied health care: options in health-unit coordinator, medical claims, medical coding, and medical transcription; appliance repair, refrigeration, and air conditioning; architectural-civil drafting; carpentry and masonry; chef training; CNC machinist technology; coaching; electronic technician studies; engineering drawing; English as a second language; finance; forensic photography; graphic communication; heating and air conditioning; individual studies: business and industry; individual studies: facilities management emphasis; industrial and commercial electricity; industrial engineering technician studies; insurance; machinist technology; managerial accounting; mechanical drafting; media marketing and management; medical assistant studies; metallurgy lab technician studies; office practices; photography; production planning; refrigeration; small-business management; supervisory management; surveying; tool design; transportation management; Web site design and management; and welding.

A jointly registered degree program with SUNY College at Oneonta offers applicants the opportunity to complete a bachelor's degree in childhood education (grades 1–6) at MVCC.

Credit for Nontraditional Learning Experiences

MVCC offers adult students the opportunity to earn credits through the CLEP examination, MVCC-administered examinations, life experience, and course work completed in a noncollegiate setting. The accumulated credit earned cannot exceed 75 percent of the student's degree program.

Costs

Tuition for New York State residents is $1550 per semester for full-time students and $120 per credit hour for part-time students; for out-of-state and international students, it is $3100 per semester for full-time students and $240 per credit hour for part-time

students. Student fees are $85 per semester for full-time students and $2 per credit hour for part-time students. Books and supplies range from $300 to $500 per semester, depending on the student's major. Residence hall occupants must purchase one of the available room and board packages each semester. Costs are approximately $3500 per semester, depending on type of accommodations and number of meals chosen. The residence hall technology fee is $100 per semester for Internet and phone access. The residence hall social fee is $10 per semester. The residence hall orientation fee is $40 and covers new-resident orientation programming and meals.

Financial Aid

One of MVCC's major objectives is to make college affordable for all. Approximately 90 percent of MVCC students receive some form of state or federal financial aid. The College offers a comprehensive financial assistance program of scholarships, loans, and grants. Most of the financial assistance received by MVCC students is need based. Non-need-based scholarships include the Presidential Scholarship Program for the top 10 percent of Oneida County (the College's sponsoring county) graduates, two similar Exceptional Student Scholarships for those not from Oneida County, and the Sodexho/MVCC Meal Plan Scholarships, which consider exceptional citizenship. Students eligible for non-need-based scholarships are expected to apply for state and federal financial assistance as applicable.

Faculty

The full-time faculty numbers 149, and the part-time faculty numbers 130. Approximately 8 percent of all faculty members have doctoral degrees. The student-faculty ratio is approximately 21:1.

Student Body Profile

MVCC enrolls approximately 5,300 students each year. Enrollment is divided between the main campus in Utica, New York, and the branch campus in Rome, New York, with approximately 80 percent of the student population enrolled on the main campus.

The College is designed to be predominantly commuter based; 85 percent of the students live within 60 miles of the campus in central New York State. The College has added an additional residence hall on the main campus in Utica, increasing housing capacity to approximately 550 students. The Residence Life Office provides a link on its Web site (http://www.mvcc.edu/students/housing/offcampus.cfm) to local resources in Utica and Rome for apartment-style housing listings.

The international student population is currently 80 students. Nineteen different countries are represented on campus.

The average age of students is about 22, with approximately 35 percent of the population being over the age of 25. Approximately 52 percent of the enrolled students are women. The racial/ethnic makeup of the campus is currently 80 percent white, non-Hispanic; 7 percent black, non-Hispanic; 1 percent American Indian/Alaskan native; 1 percent Asian/Pacific Islander; and 3 percent Hispanic. Of the total student body, 8 percent chose not to identify with any of the listed groups.

Enrolling students typically exhibit a 75 percent grade average in high school and a rank in the top 50 percent of their high school class.

Student Activities

The Student Activities program offers a wide variety of experiences for students through clubs, Student Congress, and other activities. On each campus, the staff assists students with the planning of events and programs. There are seventeen professional, curriculum-related clubs. In addition, there are thirty service/interest clubs that provide students with the opportunity to participate in a wide range of social, cultural, theatrical, athletic, and international activities to broaden their experiences.

MVCC participates in Division III of the National Junior College Athletic Association. Men's teams include baseball, basketball, bowling, cross-country, golf, ice hockey, indoor track, lacrosse, tennis, track and field, and soccer. Women's teams include basketball, bowling, cross-country, golf, indoor track, softball, soccer, tennis, track and field, and volleyball.

Throughout the last decade, MVCC's athletic teams have won an impressive ..700+ percent of their contests. This past year, MVCC had three teams that captured regional championships: women's basketball, women's soccer, and women's bowling.

Facilities and Resources

The main campus in Utica is composed of five residence halls; the Alumni College Center, which includes dining facilities, a bookstore, and the health center; the Gymnasium; the Academic Building; the Science and Technology building; the Information Technology and Performing Arts Conference Center (open computer labs and a handicap-accessible, state-of-the-art theater), and Payne Hall (library, administrative offices, and a comprehensive Student Services Center).

The branch campus in Rome consists of the Rome Academic Building, including a bookstore and dining room facilities for the hospitality programs, and the John D. Plumley Science and Technology Complex that includes a library, classrooms, and labs.

The goal of MVCC's libraries is to link students to the information they need. With more than 86,000 volumes and over 500 periodical titles, MVCC offers a comprehensive collection to support the College's curricula; library holdings also include popular best-sellers and feature film collections. MVCC students as well as faculty and staff members may request materials outside the collection through the College's comprehensive interlibrary loan service. The online resources include catalogs and periodical indexes with full-text articles. Coin-operated photocopiers and microfilm reader/printers are also available.

Academic tutoring is available at no cost to students in the Learning Centers on both campuses. The centers offer instructional support in mathematics, writing, reading, study skills, life sciences, and computer and social sciences.

Location

The main campus is in Utica, New York, a small city of 50,000 people. The branch campus in Rome, New York, is located in a community of 30,000 people. The small-city atmosphere, coupled with a wide range of cultural activities, museums, access to the Adirondack Mountains, good public transportation, and sports venues, provides an excellent location for student growth and development.

Admission Requirements

The College is an open-admission, full-opportunity college. The College does not require applicants to complete standardized admissions tests such as the ACT or SAT.

Application and Information

Students can apply in a variety of ways. MVCC provides its own admission application; no processing fee is required. It is available from the Admissions Office or from selected high schools in central New York State. The application can also be printed out from the College's Web site. An online application on the MVCC Web site will be available by fall 2007. MVCC also participates in the SUNY application process. Students can use the SUNY application—hard copy or online version; SUNY processing fees apply.

For further information, interested students should contact:

Admissions Office
Mohawk Valley Community College
1101 Sherman Drive
Utica, New York 13501

Phone: 315-792-5354
Fax: 315-792-5527
E-mail: admissions@mvcc.edu (U.S.)
        international_admissions@mvcc.edu (international)
Web site: http://www.mvcc.edu

MORRISON INSTITUTE OF TECHNOLOGY

MORRISON, ILLINOIS

The Institute and Its Mission

Morrison Institute of Technology is an independent, coeducational, not-for-profit, two-year college that specializes in engineering technology. Founded in 1973, the college provides a cost-effective educational program that leads to a professional career in engineering technology. While many graduates go directly into industry, some transfer to four-year colleges offering a continuation of studies in the engineering technology fields.

All classes are day classes offered at the campus in Morrison, Illinois. Courses are offered on a semester basis, with semesters starting in January and August.

Morrison has an open admissions policy. Anyone with a valid high school diploma or equivalent may enroll. It has been found from experience that some students who have had an otherwise undistinguished high school career often thrive and blossom when challenged by a college program that specializes in the area in which they are interested. Many students who have found their niche at Morrison have gone on to earn advanced technical degrees and some have even founded thriving technical businesses.

The college is authorized to operate and grant degrees in the state of Illinois under the applicable state statutes administered by the Illinois Board of Higher Education. The Engineering Technology program is accredited by the Technology Accreditation Commission (TAC) of the Accreditation Board for Engineering and Technology (ABET), 111 Market Place, Suite 1050, Baltimore, Maryland 21201; telephone: 410-347-7700. In addition, the drafting design program at Morrison Institute of Technology is certified by the American Drafting Design Association, P.O. Box 11937, Columbia, South Carolina 29211 (telephone: 803-771-0008), at the design/drafter level. The college is also fully accredited by the Council on Occupational Education, 41 Perimeter Center, NE Suite 640, Atlanta, Georgia 30346; telephone: 800-917-2081 (toll-free). The state of Illinois, Department of Veterans Affairs, State Approving Agency, has approved Morrison Institute of Technology for veteran's training under Chapter 36 of Title #38, U.S. Code. The Division of Rehabilitation Services (DORS) and the Job Training Partnership Act (JTPA) both refer clients to the college for training. The college is listed in the Educational Directory, U.S. Department of Education, as a legally authorized institution of higher learning, allowing qualified students to participate in a number of federally funded student financial aid and grant programs. The college is also a member of the Service Members Opportunity Colleges (SOC), thus extending educational opportunities to service personnel while on active duty. The college is also a member of the Better Business Bureau.

Student housing facilities are available on campus in Odey Residence Hall. This facility has been designed to provide housing for students in an efficiency apartment arrangement. The residence hall is coeducational, but individual rooms are not coeducational and accommodations for married couples are not available.

Academic Programs

The engineering technology program has been developed and is kept current in accordance with suggested guidelines provided by nationally recognized technical education groups, accrediting organizations, and the college Industrial Advisory Board.

The curriculum for the engineering technology program has been designed with an appropriate balance of study in the areas of engineering and construction technology and manual drafting. In addition, to ensure that a student is prepared to assume a productive and contributing role as a citizen locally, nationally, and worldwide, a core of general education courses, including basic sciences, humanities, written and oral communications, mathematics, and computer literacy, are required to provide that academic foundation which the student must acquire to continue a lifelong learning process on a formal or informal basis. Extensive exposure to computer usage in computer-aided drafting (CAD) is also provided to all students.

The program has a very open architecture to permit students to concentrate their technical electives in the construction area or the design drafting area. A student may also elect to choose technical electives from both concentrations, if he or she desires a more general background. The minimum total number of technical elective credit hours required is 21 in order to meet the minimum total number of credit hours required to receive the Associate in Applied Science (A.A.S.) degree in engineering technology.

The college also has an associate degree program in systems and network administration. This program gives students hands-on learning experiences in computer hardware and network wiring and equipment. It provides the student with the fundamentals required to gain industry-recognized certifications such as Microsoft MCP, Microsoft MCP + Internet, CompTIA A+, Microsoft MCSE, and CCNP.

Costs

The tuition for 2006–07 was $6050 per semester, based upon taking a typical academic load of 12 to 19 semester credit hours. The computer account fee was $100 per semester. Campus housing costs were $1300 per semester (not required if the student lives off campus). An additional $100 housing security deposit is required for first-time residents. The housing cost figure does not include food, laundry, or general living expenses. Parking fees were $25 per semester (not required if the student does not park a car on campus). The recreation center/activity fee was $30 per semester, and the technology fee was $150.

Financial Aid

The curricula offered at Morrison Institute of Technology have been accredited by a nationally recognized accrediting agency. Qualified students, therefore, may take advantage of a number of federally funded student financial aid programs.

Grant programs at Morrison include the Federal Pell Grant, the Illinois Student Assistance Commission Monetary Award Program Grant, the Federal Supplemental Educational Opportunity Grant (FSEOG), the Federal Work-Study Program (FWS), tutorial and lab supervisors, the Department of Rehabilitation Services, the Job Training Partnership Act and the Veterans Educational Program.

Morrison Institute of Technology has available a limited number of scholarships for students now attending high school or the associated area vocational technical school, who wish to pursue engineering technology studies at Morrison Institute of Technology. These scholarships are independent of, and in addition to, any other financial aid a student may obtain. There are three areas in which a student can qualify for a Morrison Institute of Technology sponsored scholarship: the Morrison Institute of Technology Academic Scholarships, the Morrison Institute of Technology Performance Scholarships, or the Morrison Institute of Technology Parent Scholarships.

Loan programs at Morrison include the Subsidized Federal Family Education Loan Program (student loan), the Unsubsidized Federal Family Education Loan Program (student loan), and the Federal PLUS loan.

All prospective students are encouraged to complete the Free Application for Federal Student Aid (FAFSA). Applications may be obtained from student's high school or the college Federal Aid Office or by downloading the FAFSA Express Software from the Web at http://www.ed.gov/offices/OPE/express.html.

Faculty

Morrison's faculty members are full-time employees. The student-faculty ratio is about 15:1, which means that students at Morrison receive a lot of personal attention. The faculty members are experienced in the areas they teach, and many are sought out by businesses to provide private consultative services; therefore, students learn what the profession is all about from persons who actually do the work. Approximately 30 percent of the faculty members are licensed professional engineers or surveyors. Approximately 23 percent have earned graduate-level degrees.

Student Body Profile

Morrison is a small college. The total full-time enrollment is about 200 students. The majority of the students attending are from the Midwest, mostly Illinois, Iowa, Wisconsin, and Indiana, with a few from the Eastern and Western states. Approximately 8–12 percent of the student enrollment is female, Hispanics make up 2–6 percent, African Americans number 6–10 percent, and Asians compose 1–2 percent. Approximately 75 percent of the students receive financial aid of some kind. About 60 percent are enrolled in the construction option while the remaining 40 percent are enrolled in the design drafting CAD option.

Student Activities

A student recreation center is provided for all students. The recreation center provides a place for students to relax; play pool, video games, Ping-Pong, card games, or chess; or watch TV. The facility also has a fitness room and Laundromat. Vending machines are also available in the recreation center. Morrison Institute of Technology sponsors a student chapter of the Society of Manufacturing Engineers (SME). Activities associated with SME include attending regional meetings, field trips, and SME-sponsored exhibitions and seminars.

Facilities and Resources

The college has two main educational facilities, the A. E. Rambo Center, which also houses the administrative offices and student learning center, and the Technical Center, which houses mainly the computer laboratories, survey, soils laboratory, and multimedia lecture halls. The college also has the student recreation center complex and Odey Residence Hall.

Location

The campus is located on 17 acres on the south side of Morrison, Illinois. Morrison is about 45 minutes by car from the Quad-Cities area and about 2¼ hours by car from Chicago. Morrison is a picturesque small town with a population of 4,300. It is a neat, clean, and friendly town with tree-lined streets, neighborhood churches, and a small but busy business district. The college took its mascot emblem, "The Thoroughbreds," because there are many horse ranches in the area. The town is considered very safe: children play on the streets after dark here, and many people don't bother to lock their doors. Nearby is Rockwood State Park, several wildlife sanctuaries along the Mississippi River, and several park areas featuring Native American pre-Columbian settlements.

Admission Requirements

Admission to Morrison Institute of Technology is considered if the applicant has graduated from high school or has completed GED testing with scores that can be accepted as meeting high school requirements. It is recommended, but not required, that an applicant's educational background include at least one semester each of high school algebra and geometry. ACT or SAT test scores are not required but, if available, are used for academic counseling. Those students who do not have either test score are administered an institutional placement test to assist in academic placement.

All applicants are encouraged to schedule a tour of the campus. Tours are conducted during any of the formal open houses held by the college. If an applicant is unable to attend an open house, tours can be arranged on an individual basis by appointment. To complete the application process the following items are to be mailed to the college: a completed application for enrollment; the appropriate fees; an official high school transcript; if transfer analysis is requested, an official transcript from the institution granting the credit, mailed directly from the institution to Morrison Institute of Technology; a copy of the applicant's immunization record; and ACT, SAT, or placement test scores.

Application and Information

Students who wish to attend Morrison Institute of Technology may obtain the required admission application material and additional information by contacting:

Admissions Office
Morrison Institute of Technology
701 Portland Avenue
Morrison, Illinois 61270

Phone: 815-772-7218
Fax: 815-772-7584
E-mail: admissions@morrison.tec.il.us
Web site: http://www.morrison.tec.il.us

NEW YORK COLLEGE OF HEALTH PROFESSIONS
School of Massage Therapy
SYOSSET, NEW YORK

The College and Its Mission

New York College of Health Professions, a private nonprofit institution, is one of the nation's premier centers of holistic medicine. The College educates students, treats patients, and conducts research. Founded in 1981, New York College has been a leader in holistic education and care for more than twenty-five years. It is firmly rooted in the principles of blending Western and Eastern practices, or Integrative medicine.

New York College offers approved degree programs in the field of complementary medicine. Undergraduate programs include an associate degree in massage therapy and a bachelor's degree in advanced Asian bodywork. Graduate programs include combined bachelor's and master's degrees in acupuncture or Oriental medicine (the combined study of acupuncture and Chinese herbology). All programs lead to New York State licensing and/or national certification.

The College also offers a 495-clock-hour continuing education program in holistic nursing for RNs and a selection of other continuing education courses and workshops for both health-care professionals and the general public. New York College was awarded a grant from New York State to train all the RNs at Bellevue Hospital in New York City in an Introduction to Holistic Nursing course and receives grants from SEIU 1199, the health-care workers' union, for RNs from Flushing Hospital and Beth Israel Hospital Center to also participate in the College's holistic nursing programs.

New York College is chartered by the Board of Regents of the University of the State of New York, and all programs are registered by the New York State Education Department. The Acupuncture and Oriental Medicine programs are accredited by the Accrediting Commission for Acupuncture and Oriental Medicine (ACAOM). The Oriental Medicine program is also approved by the California Acupuncture Board. The College is approved as a provider of Continuing Education by the New York State Nurses Association Council on Continuing Education and the National Certification Board for Therapeutic Massage and Bodywork. The College is a member of numerous professional organizations related to the fields of oriental medicine and massage therapy.

Academic Programs

The Massage Therapy program at New York College began in 1981 and was the School's first educational program. It has since become nationally recognized and was cited for academic excellence in 1997 by the National Certification Board for Therapeutic Massage and Bodywork. In 1996, New York College became the first college in the United States to award an associate degree in massage therapy. The program exceeds national certification and state licensing requirements. First-time candidates from New York College rank competitively in pass rates on the New York State Massage Therapy Licensing Examination for all first-time takers.

The benefits of massage therapy have become widely recognized. Documentation on the effects of massage shows that it improves circulation and lymph drainage and can help treat sports injuries and alleviate stress, headaches, and other aches and pains. When practiced in conjunction with Western medical treatment, massage can also be used to treat arthritis, hypertension, diabetes, asthma, bronchitis, and neuromuscular diseases, among others. Massage therapy most commonly falls into two categories: Western (Swedish), which focuses on the musculoskeletal system and is based on standard Western anatomy and physiology, and Eastern, or Oriental, which is based on the movement of energy through various channels in the body. At New York College, students learn both of these modalities as well as the specific techniques for sports massage, chair massage, shiatsu, hot stone massage, reflexology,

and more. Career opportunities in the field of massage therapy continue to grow and range from owning one's own business to working in spas, health clubs, resorts, Wellness Centers, hospitals, or doctors' offices or with sports teams.

New York College's Massage Therapy program is a 72-credit program. Upon completion, graduates receive an Associate of Occupational Studies (A.O.S.) degree in massage therapy. They are eligible to sit for the New York State Licensing Exam in Massage Therapy, the National Certification Exam for Therapeutic Massage and Bodywork, and the NCCAOM National Certification Exam for Oriental Bodywork Therapy. Course work for the Massage Therapy program includes in-depth study of both Western and Eastern health sciences, Western and Oriental bodywork techniques, and tai chi chuan, qi gong, or yoga. Courses are also offered in ethics, professional development, and business practice. The culmination of the program is the intensive clinical internship that students undergo in the College's on-site teaching clinic.

New York College operates on a fifteen-week trimester system. New students are admitted to the College for the September, January, and May trimesters. Ten-week, second-cycle trimester admissions may be added when there is sufficient demand. The program can be completed in twenty months, twenty-four months, or thirty-six months on a part-time basis.

Off-Campus Programs

New York College offers travel/life-experience trips abroad to its Luo Yang Medical Center facility in the People's Republic of China. Programs are three-week immersion trips to China that include visits to hospitals as well as attendance at lectures and demonstrations at medical centers and visits to historic sites throughout the country.

Costs

Tuition is based on a per-credit charge of $275 and is paid each trimester. The application fee is $85. Students should expect to incur an additional $2000 in expenses for texts and supplies throughout their course of study.

Financial Aid

New York College is an eligible institution approved by the United States Department of Education and the New York State Education Department to participate in the following programs: Federal Pell Grant, Federal Supplemental Educational Opportunity Grant (FSEOG), Tuition Assistance Program (TAP), Aid for Part-Time Study, Federal Work-Study Program, Veterans Administration, Vocational Rehabilitation, Federal Stafford Student Loan, Federal PLUS loan, and alternative financing. For additional information, students should contact the College's Financial Aid Office (800-922-7337 Ext. 244).

Faculty

New York College has a total of 98 faculty members, 17 of whom are full-time. The faculty-student ratio is 1:16 for technique classes, 1:40 for didactic classes, and up to 1:6 for clinical internships.

Student Body Profile

Total current enrollment at New York College is about 900 students, most of whom are enrolled in the Massage Therapy program. New York College does not have student housing; therefore, the majority of students are from the local area, with the largest group coming from Long Island, Brooklyn, and Queens. However, the College attracts a percentage of both international and out-of-state students.

Facilities and Resources

The Syosset, Long Island, campus occupies 70,000 square feet in a modern facility on three levels. Within the facility are the

administrative offices, classrooms for all College educational programs, a physical arts deck, the Integrative Health Center, Academic Health Care Teaching Clinics, the Herbal Dispensary, the James and Lenore Jacobson Library, the café, the bookstore, and student lounges. Classrooms are designed and used specifically for lecture or technique work and contain the most recent instructional materials. The physical arts deck for the practice of tai chi, hatha yoga, and qi gong is specifically designed with space, light, and quiet.

The James and Lenore Jacobson Library contains the most extensive collection of materials about complementary and alternative medicine available on Long Island. The library houses a collection of books and journals specializing in Oriental medicine, complementary and alternative therapies, acupuncture, herbs, massage therapy, and holistic nursing. The library belongs to a consortium of special and medical libraries that provide interloans of additional books and journal articles. Several networked workstations provide access to the computerized book collection catalog and magazine subject index, various software and CD-ROM programs, the Internet, and various online professional databases

The Academic Health Care Teaching Clinics are an integral part of a student's educational experience through this internship. The clinics provide affordable holistic health care to members of the community, treating more than 17,000 patients annually. Supervised student treatments include Swedish massage, Amma massage, acupuncture, herbal consultations, and holistic nursing.

The Integrative Health Center is the professional clinic of the College and offers the skills and services of licensed holistic practitioners to patients of all ages. For more than twenty-five years, this fully integrated clinic has provided patients with minimally invasive therapies, including acupuncture; herbal medicine; many modalities of massage therapy, such as Swedish, sports, Amma, shiatsu, reflexology, and pregnancy massage; and holistic nursing. Special patient programs exist for smoking cessation, weight loss, and cancer support.

The Office of Student Services is responsible for special-needs students, academic progress advisement, the organization of study groups, and tutoring services. New York College's Career Services Office offers graduates assistance with job placement. Currently, the College lists more than 300 employment and rental opportunities for its licensed graduates. Sponsorship opportunities for graduates waiting to sit for licensure are also available.

Location

Long Island The campus of New York College is located in Syosset, on the North Shore of Long Island, approximately 30 miles from Manhattan. Its proximity to all major parkways and railroad service provides easy access to one of the world's most exciting cities, while capturing the serenity, beauty, and open space of the suburbs. Long Island stretches for 110 miles and is a wealth of natural, cultural, and historic treasures. Some of the world's most beautiful sandy beaches surround the island—from the popular Jones Beach to the chic Hamptons and the barrier isle of Fire Island with its pristine beaches and absence of automobiles. The island's fifteen state parks also offer an abundance of recreational opportunities and even include a polo field. There are nearly 100 museums on the island.

China New York College owns the Luo Yang Medical Center in the People's Republic of China. Situated in the ancient capital of China, the 35-acre site is surrounded by historic and important attractions. Modern buildings are fully equipped with Western fixtures.

Admission Requirements

New York College is deeply committed to recruiting the highest qualified and motivated candidates for admission. The College is particularly proud of its diverse population, comprising individuals from a variety of cultural backgrounds with many unique strengths. New York College students contribute to the friendly and supportive atmosphere at the College.

Applicants who have graduated from high school must have achieved a minimum GPA of 2.0 or have equivalent qualifications. Students may earn their GED certificate while enrolled in a massage therapy degree program by successfully completing 24 credits of specified credit courses in six subject areas. Candidates must be at least 17 years of age and, in accordance with New York State guidelines, must hold U.S. citizenship, be an alien lawfully admitted for permanent residence in the U.S., or hold a valid visa. The College is authorized under federal law to enroll nonimmigrant alien students.

Candidates must complete and submit an application along with an $85 application fee and arrange for the submission of an official high school transcript (or proof of equivalency) and official transcripts from all previously attended higher educational institutions. Candidates are notified promptly of the receipt of their application and advised which, if any, of the required documents have not been received by the Admissions Office. An admissions interview is required. The College offers on-the-spot enrollment: a student can be interviewed and conditionally admitted and enrolled in one visit.

Application and Information

New students are admitted to New York College for the September, January, and May trimesters. Additional second-cycle trimesters in October, February, and June may be added if there is sufficient demand. It is recommended that applications be submitted three to four months prior to the desired entrance date.

Admissions Office
New York College of Health Professions
6801 Jericho Turnpike
Syosset, New York 11791

Phone: 800-9-CAREER Ext. 351 (toll-free)
Fax: 516-364-0989
E-mail: admissions@nycollege.edu
Web site: http://www.nycollege.edu

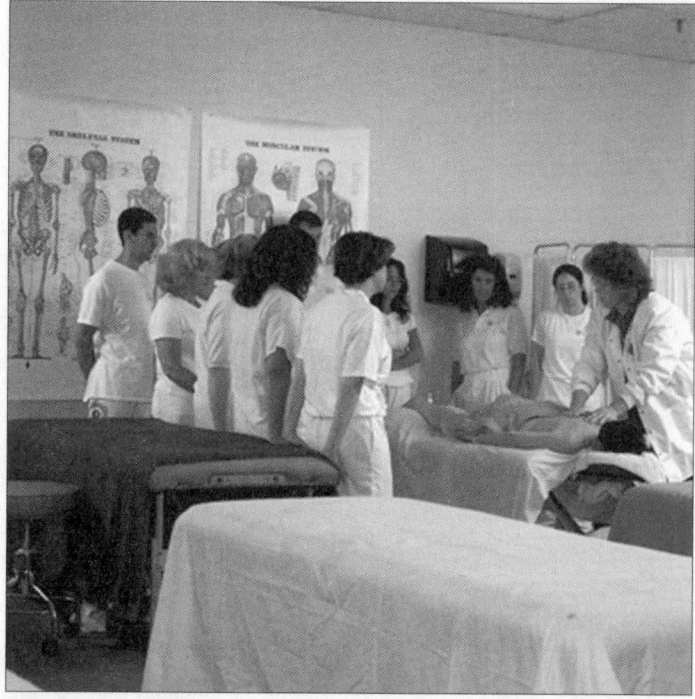

The Academic Health Care Teaching Clinics are an integral part of a student's education.

PENNSYLVANIA COLLEGE OF TECHNOLOGY
An Affiliate of The Pennsylvania State University
WILLIAMSPORT, PENNSYLVANIA

Pennsylvania
College of
Technology

PENNSTATE

The College and Its Mission

Pennsylvania College of Technology (Penn College) is a special mission affiliate of Penn State, committed to applied technology education. The College has a national reputation for the high quality and diversity of its "degrees that work" in traditional and advanced technology majors. Partnerships with industry leaders, including Honda, Ford, Mack Trucks, and Caterpillar, provide students unique opportunities to advance their careers. Excellent placement rates exceed 95 percent annually (100 percent in some majors). Among the keys to graduate success are Penn College's emphasis on small classes, personal attention, and hands-on experience using the latest technology. Student projects reflect real working situations. A number of campus buildings were designed and constructed by students—including a conference center, a Victorian guest house, an athletic field house, and a rustic retreat used for professional gatherings—and are maintained by students. The facilities stand as testimony to the quality of a Penn College education. State-of-the-art classrooms and laboratories on the ultramodern campus located in Williamsport, Pennsylvania, reflect the expectations of the modern workforce.

Academic Programs

Associate Degree Majors Associate degrees (A.A.S., A.A.A., or A.A.) are offered in accounting; advertising art; architectural technology; automated manufacturing technology; automotive service sales and marketing; automotive technology (including Ford ASSET and Honda industry-sponsored majors); aviation technology; baking and pastry arts; building construction technology; building construction technology/masonry; business management; civil engineering technology; collision repair technology; computer-aided drafting technology; culinary arts technology; dental hygiene; diesel technology (including a Mack Trucks industry-sponsored major); early childhood education; electric power generation technology; electrical technology; electromechanical maintenance technology; electronics and computer engineering technology (emphases in Cisco systems, communications and fiber optics, nanofabrication technology, and robotics and automation); emergency medical services; forest technology; general studies; graphic communications technology; health arts; health arts/practical nursing; health information technology; heating, ventilation, and air conditioning (HVAC) technology; heavy construction equipment technology (emphases in Caterpillar industry-sponsored, operator, and technician); hospitality management; human services; individual studies; information technology (emphases in Cisco technology, network technology, technical support technology, and Web and applications technology); legal assistant/paralegal studies; mass media communication; nursing; occupational therapy assistant studies; office information technology (medical office information and specialized office information emphases); ornamental horticulture (emphases in horticulture retail management, landscape technology, and plant productions); physical fitness specialist studies; plastics and polymer technology; radiography; studio arts; surgical technology; surveying technology; toolmaking technology; transmission and distribution technology; and welding technology.

Bachelor's Degree Majors Many associate degree graduates choose to continue their education with unique **Bachelor of Science (B.S.) degrees** that focus on applied technology in traditional and emerging career fields. Majors include accounting; applied health studies; applied human services; automotive technology management; aviation maintenance technology; building automation technology; business administration (concentrations in banking and finance, human resources management, management, management information systems, marketing, and small business and entrepreneurship); civil engineering technology; computer-

aided product design; construction management; culinary arts and systems; dental hygiene (concentrations in health policy and administration and special-population care); electronics and computer engineering technology; graphic communications management; graphic design; heating, ventilation, and air conditioning (HVAC) technology; information technology (concentrations in IT security specialist, network specialist, and Web and applications development); legal assistant/paralegal studies; manufacturing engineering technology; nursing; physician assistant studies; plastics and polymer engineering technology; residential construction technology and management; technology management; and welding and fabrication engineering technology.

Certificate Majors Certificates are offered in automotive service technician, aviation maintenance technician, collision repair technician, construction carpentry, diesel technician, electrical occupations, health information coding specialist, machinist general, nurse/health-care paralegal studies, paramedic technician, plumbing, practical nursing, and welding.

Off-Campus Programs

Cooperative education and internships give students the opportunity to gain workforce experience. Penn College students have worked throughout Pennsylvania, the United States, and around the world.

Costs

Tuition and related fees are based on a per-credit-hour charge. Pennsylvania residents attending Penn College in 2006–07 paid approximately $18,620 per year, and out-of-state students paid approximately $21,350 per year. These estimated costs were based on tuition and fees for an average 15 credits per semester, plus estimated expenses for housing, meals, books, and supplies. Rates vary according to specific choices for classes, housing, and meal plans.

All on-campus housing is apartment-style (kitchen, living room, bedrooms, and bathroom). On-campus housing is alcohol-free, drug-free, noise-controlled, and secure. Resident and nonresident students may purchase meal plans, which are accepted in the College's dining facilities, including the main dining hall, an all-you-can-eat buffet, a gourmet restaurant, a convenience store, snack areas, and on-campus pizza delivery.

Financial Aid

Approximately 4 out of 5 Penn College students receive some form of financial assistance. Types of aid available include Federal Pell Grants, Pennsylvania Higher Education Assistance Agency grants, Federal Supplemental Educational Opportunity Grants, Federal Work-Study Program awards, Federal Stafford Student Loans, Federal PLUS loans, veterans' benefits, and Bureau of Vocational Rehabilitation benefits. A deferred-payment plan allows students to spread their tuition cost over two payments each semester. Penn College offers academic, need-based, and technical scholarships to qualified students. For detailed information on scholarships, students should contact the Financial Aid Office or visit the Web at http://www.pct.edu/scholarships.

Faculty

Penn College's faculty members (299 full-time and 210 part-time) provide individual attention that students need to be successful in the classroom and the workplace. Faculty members are experienced in their fields. Each year, Penn College recognizes excellence among the faculty members through distinguished faculty award programs. Small class sizes (fewer than 20 students in most classes) promote student success. Advisory committees of faculty members and business and industry leaders work together to ensure that programs meet current workplace needs.

Student Body Profile

More than 6,500 students attend Penn College. More than 2,000 additional men and women take part in noncredit classes, including customized business and industry courses offered through Workforce Development and Continuing Education.

Student Activities

Penn College is a place where future technicians and designers mingle easily with chefs, health-care personnel, and business students. It is a place where students actually construct campus buildings, cater important campus functions, compute strategies for engineering technology problems, and care for children in an on-campus day-care center. The magnificent Campus Center provides an opportunity to eat, shop, work out, and spend time with friends. A modern fitness center, College Store, convenience store, art gallery, TV lounge, Internet lounge, video rental and game room, and an all-you-can-eat restaurant are among the features of the Campus Center. Impressive cultural activities are available both on the main campus and at Penn College's Community Arts Center, a restored 1920s-era theater in downtown Williamsport. Student ticket rates are available for performances that include Broadway shows, opera, ballet, symphony orchestras, and popular entertainers.

Student Government Association (SGA) and Wildcat Events Board (WEB) represent the student body in matters related to College policy and activities. Participation offers students the opportunity to develop leadership skills while contributing to the well-being of the College and the student body. In addition, more than forty student organizations, including the Residence Hall Association that represents all on-campus student residents, offer opportunities for organized campus activity and leadership experiences.

The Penn College Wildcats compete in Penn State's University Athletic Conference. Varsity sports include archery, baseball, basketball, bowling, cross-country, dance team, golf, soccer, softball, team tennis, and volleyball. Penn College's men's compound-bow archery team is a former two-time national champion in the National Archery Association (NAA).

Facilities and Resources

The hands-on experience offered at Penn College creates a need for a variety of special academic facilities. Campus computers are very accessible. Wireless zones and networked on-campus residences make study across the campus very convenient. Besides extensive, accessible computer labs, the main campus has an automated manufacturing center, plastics manufacturing center, printing and publishing facility, dental hygiene clinic, automotive repair center, machine shop, welding shop, building trades center, architectural studio, computer-aided drafting labs, broadcast studio, modern science laboratories, fine-dining restaurant, campus guest house, aviation and avionics instructional facility located at the regional airport, greenhouses, working sawmill, diesel center, and heavy-equipment training site.

Library Services The new Madigan Library on the main campus is open every day during the academic semesters and offers an impressive selection of print and electronic resources. Services available include a professional reference staff, a well-developed instructional program, reciprocal borrowing with regional libraries, interlibrary loans, and paper and electronic reserves. The library also houses fourteen study areas, two computer laboratories, a 100-seat open computer lab complex, the Student Help Desk, a café, and an art gallery.

Location

Penn College is located in north-central Pennsylvania. The main campus is in Williamsport, a city known around the world as the home of the Little League Baseball World Series. Penn College also offers classes at three other locations: the Advanced Automotive Technology Center at Wahoo Drive Industrial Park in Williamsport, the Aviation Center at the Williamsport Regional Airport in Montoursville, and the Earth Science Center, 10 miles south of Williamsport near Allenwood. Noncredit classes are offered from locations in Williamsport and Wellsboro.

Admission Requirements

Penn College offers educational opportunities to anyone who has the interest, desire, and ability to pursue advanced study. Due to the wide variety of majors, admission criteria vary according to the major. At a minimum, applicants must have a high school diploma or its equivalent. Some majors are restricted to persons who meet certain academic skill levels and prerequisites, have attained certain levels of academic achievement, and have earned an acceptable score on the SAT or ACT. Questions regarding the admission standards for specific majors should be directed to the Admissions Office. To ensure that applicants have the entry-level skills needed for success in college majors, all students are required to take placement examinations, which are used to assess skills in math, English, and reading. The College provides opportunities for students to develop the basic skills necessary for enrollment in associate degree and certificate majors when the placement tests indicate that such help is needed. International students whose native language is not English are required to take the TOEFL, submit an affidavit of support, and comply with test regulations of the Immigration and Naturalization Service, along with meeting all other admission requirements. The College offers equal opportunity for admission without regard to age, race, color, creed, sex, national origin, disability, veteran status, or political affiliation.

Penn College offers opportunities for students to transfer the following course credits: credit earned at other institutions, college credit earned before high school graduation, service credit, DANTES credit, and credit earned through the College-Level Examination Program (CLEP).

Application and Information

College catalogs, viewbooks, financial aid information, and other informative brochures, along with applications for admission, are available from the Admissions Office. Prospective students and their families should contact the Admissions Office to arrange a personal interview or campus tour. Fall and spring open-house events are held annually.

All inquiries should be addressed to:

Admissions Office, DIF 119
Pennsylvania College of Technology
One College Avenue
Williamsport, Pennsylvania 17701-5799

Phone: 570-327-4761
      800-367-9222 (toll-free)
E-mail: admissions@pct.edu
Web site: http://www.pct.edu/peter2

Banners representing each of the eight academic schools at Penn College adorn lampposts leading from the main entrance to the heart of the campus.

PIERPONT COMMUNITY AND TECHNICAL COLLEGE OF FAIRMONT STATE UNIVERSITY

FAIRMONT, WEST VIRGINIA

The College and Its Mission

Pierpont Community and Technical College of Fairmont State University (Pierpont C&TC) has an enrollment of approximately 3,500 students. Founded in 1974, the College is located in Fairmont, West Virginia.

Pierpont C&TC enhances the quality of life for the people of north-central West Virginia through accessible, affordable, comprehensive, responsive, workforce-related training and high-quality higher education opportunities.

Pierpont C&TC offers a variety of courses at more than twenty-five sites each semester in its thirteen-county service area through its Off-Campus Programs and provides job training for the region through its Center for Workforce Education in downtown Fairmont. The Weekend College program allows adults the opportunity to earn degrees by attending classes on Saturdays on the main campus in Fairmont and at the Gaston Caperton Center in Clarksburg, West Virginia. The Televised Classes Program offers adult students the opportunity to earn College credits from home. The Community Education Program has been developed to meet the needs of the community by offering noncredit classes as an introduction to lifelong learning.

Academic Programs

Pierpont C&TC offers more than fifty associate degrees, certificates, skill-set certificates, and occupational development classes. A complete list of majors and programs offered is available on the College's Web site at http://www.fairmontstate.edu.

Associate degree programs offered include accounting, airframe and aerospace electronics maintenance, aviation maintenance technology, business technology, criminal justice, culinary arts, emergency medical services, fashion design, graphics, health information technology, homeland security, information systems, interior design, interpreter training program, medical laboratory technology, nursing, paralegal studies, physical therapist assistant studies, radiologic technology, resort and hotel management, and veterinary technology.

Certificates are available in emergency medical technician–paramedic studies, laboratory assistant studies, paraprofessional education studies, and sign language communications. Skill-set certificates include accounting, administrative assistant studies, ballroom dancing, classroom teacher's aide and assistant studies, computer-aided design, computer forensics, early childhood teaching aide and assistant studies, intelligence research and analysis, office technician studies, ProMgmt®, and ServSafe®.

Occupational-development classes are offered for those in certain trades. These work-based programs include building and construction trades, correctional officer, early childhood practitioner, EMS specialist, food service specialist, highway technician, water and wastewater treatment, and wood production technology.

Costs

During the 2005–06 academic year, per-semester charges for Fairmont State students from West Virginia were $1639 for tuition and fees, $3310 for room and board, and $600 for books and supplies, for a total of $5549. Out-of-state students paid $3649 for tuition and fees, $3310 for room and board, and $600 for books and supplies each semester, for a total of $7559.

Financial Aid

About 86 percent of Fairmont State students receive some form of aid. Guidelines and forms for West Virginia and out-of-state residents are available from high school guidance counselors or the Fairmont State Financial Aid Office. Fairmont State awards more than $36 million in financial assistance each year.

Faculty

Pierpont C&TC employs 50 full-time faculty members, ensuring a low student-teacher ratio. Dedicated academic advisers and faculty members work one-on-one with students to meet their individual needs.

Student Activities

Fairmont State is a member of the NCAA Division II and the West Virginia Intercollegiate Athletic Conference. Varsity programs for men are offered in baseball, basketball, cross-country, football, golf, swimming, and tennis. Intercollegiate athletic programs for women include basketball, cross-country, golf, softball, swimming, tennis, and volleyball.

Fairmont State offers more than eighty clubs, organizations, student publications, honoraries, sororities, and fraternities as well as a wide range of intramural sports. Many fine arts performances and exhibits are planned each semester. Nationally prominent speakers are invited to the campus.

Student Government actively seeks to supplement the academic atmosphere with intellectual, cultural, and social activities. Student Government members are involved in all aspects of life on campus and work cooperatively with the administration.

The new student activity center, the Falcon Center, features 7,000 square feet of fitness equipment; five versatile courts for indoor sports; space for fitness classes; a four-lane pool with a whirlpool, sauna, and outdoor sunning deck; a four-lane cushioned jogging/walking track; game rooms; dining facilities; and more.

Academic Facilities

The Ruth Ann Musick Library has a collection of more than 200,000 books and more than 15,000 bound periodicals, microfilms, and other materials, including a large collection of audiotapes and videotapes. The library also has sites at the Caperton Center and the National Aerospace Education Center.

Fairmont State's state-of-the-art technology infrastructure includes thirty computer labs and high-speed network connections that are accessible from the library, classrooms, and every residence hall room, as well as the most up-to-date teaching software.

Location

Fairmont, a city of more than 19,000 in north-central West Virginia, is the county seat of Marion County. Located along Interstate 79 approximately 90 miles south of Pittsburgh, the city and the College are easily accessible to all travelers.

Shopping malls, restaurants, cultural entertainment, and nightlife are easily found throughout the area.

West Virginia's natural treasures—mountains, rivers, waterfalls, wildlife, wildflowers, clean air, and vast tracts of national forest—are all close at hand. In and near Fairmont are popular trails for hiking and biking; rivers for white-water rafting; excellent spots for rock and mountain climbing, camping, and fishing; and some of the best skiing in the East.

Pierpont C&TC shares a main campus with Fairmont State University. The campus features fifteen buildings on more than 90 acres. From the historic administration building, Hardway Hall, to the brand-new residence hall, Bryant Place, the facilities are a blend of tradition and technology. Facilities also include the Robert C. Byrd National Aerospace Education Center in Bridgeport, West Virginia, and the Gaston Caperton Center in Clarksburg, West Virginia.

Admission Requirements

First-time freshmen who are applying to Pierpont Community and Technical College must submit the following: (1) application for admission; (2) an official high school transcript from an accredited high school (partial or complete) or a GED certificate (for home-schooled students or for students who do not have a high school diploma) or placement test results (administered by the College to all students without ACT or SAT scores; ACT or SAT scores are required for admission into most health career, selective, and competitive programs); (3) immunization records (for students born after January 1, 1957); and (4) statement of activities (for students out of high school six months or longer).

Transfer students must submit an application for admission, college transcripts from accredited institutions (ACT, SAT, or COMPASS scores are also required if there are fewer than 15 earned credit hours), a statement of activities, and immunization records. Transient students (those enrolled at another school who are returning to that institution) must submit an application for admission and a course approval form (from the Registrar's office). Non-degree-seeking students (those with fewer than 15 hours who are not seeking a degree) must submit an application. Current high school students must submit an application for admission, have completed their junior year of high school with a GPA of at least 3.0, and submit a letter of recommendation from their high school principal.

Application and Information

On a Saturday each spring and fall, Fairmont State schedules a Campus Visitation Day so potential students and their family members and friends can visit the campus and attend information sessions on admissions, financial aid, and living on campus. An Academic Fair is also scheduled so students can meet with faculty members about the academic schools and departments.

Campus tours through the Office of Admissions are available Mondays through Fridays. To set up a tour, students should call 800-641-5678 Ext. 2 (toll-free) or 304-367-4855. Tours can also be scheduled online at Fairmont State's Web site at http://www.fairmontstate.edu.

Office of Admissions
Pierpont Community and Technical College
1201 Locust Avenue
Fairmont, West Virginia 26554

Phone: 304-367-4892
        800-641-5678 (toll-free)
        304-367-4213 (financial aid)
        304-367-4216 (residence life)
        304-367-4000 (campus operator)
        304-367-4026 (Gaston Caperton Center)
        304-842-8300 (Robert C. Byrd National Aerospace Education Center)
        304-367-4200 (TDD)
Fax: 304-367-4789
E-mail: admit@fairmontstate.edu
Web site: http://www.fairmontstate.edu

Pierpont Community and Technical College students explore airframe and aerospace electronics, aviation maintenance, and more at the Robert C. Byrd National Aerospace Education Center in Bridgeport, West Virginia.

PIONEER PACIFIC COLLEGE
WILSONVILLE, OREGON

The College and Its Mission

Pioneer Pacific College is a for-profit college that is uncompromisingly dedicated to helping people improve their lives through high-quality, college-level career education. To accomplish this mission, the College offers a curriculum that teaches students the skills necessary for employment; maintains an environment that encourages the ethical standards, self-discipline, and professionalism necessary to function in society; and cultivates an appreciation for lifelong learning in students.

Founded in 1981 as Skilltronics, Inc. in Corvallis, Oregon, the school began as a unique training program for students interested in entering the growing electronics industry. Over the years, the school has added programs in business, culinary arts, health care, and legal studies, and its programs have evolved to better meet the employment needs of industries in demand. Today, the school offers certificate, associate, and bachelor's degree programs, with locations in Clackamas, Eugene/Springfield, and Portland and two sites in Wilsonville.

Externships are available in some programs. In addition to career training, the College helps students and graduates with resume preparation, interviewing skills, portfolio preparation, and job search. Valuable community connections help students with their job search.

Pioneer Pacific College has articulation agreements with Warner Pacific College, the University of Phoenix, Concordia University, Remington College, City University, and American InterContinental University.

The College is accredited by the Accrediting Council for Independent Colleges and Schools and is authorized to grant degrees by the Oregon Department of Degree Authorization.

Academic Programs

Classes are offered year round in day or evening schedules, and programs begin every ten weeks. Bachelor's degrees can be earned in three years, associate degree programs can be completed in about seventeen months, and diploma programs can be completed in ten months.

Pioneer Pacific College offers the Bachelor of Science degree in business management, criminal justice, health-care administration, and information technology.

The College offers the Associate of Applied Science degree in business, with an emphasis in accounting, administration, or marketing; criminal justice; computer and network technology; legal assistant/paralegal studies program; medical assisting; medical assisting with limited X-ray; health-care administration; and Web design and administration.

Diplomas are available in massage therapy, medical assisting, medical assisting with limited X-ray, medical claims and billing, pharmacy technician, and practical nursing studies.

Credit for Nontraditional Learning Experiences

Up to one third of the total credit requirement may be awarded through transfer credit, challenge credit, or a combination of the two.

Costs

Tuition per credit ranges between $170 and $240 depending on the program.

Financial Aid

Financial aid is available for those who qualify. Financial aid officers are available to assist students in finding the right financial aid options that fit their need. Aid is available through Federal Pell Grants, Federal Stafford Student Loans, Federal Direct Plus Student Loans, high school scholarships, and the NAFTA Scholarship Program.

Faculty

The faculty at Pioneer Pacific College is made up of professionals with real-world working experience in the subjects they teach. Classes are small so instructors have more time to offer one-on-one help to students.

Student Body Profile

The median age of the students is between 18 and 34. Some students are just beginning their education, while others are returning to school for further training.

Student Activities

Some of Pioneer Pacific College's campuses offer membership in the Phi Beta Lambda association, and some campuses offer student-run activities based on programs of interest.

Academic Facilities

Pioneer Pacific College maintains industry-current equipment that enables students to learn using the tools and techniques of professionals working in their desired career field. The school offers access to a number of online academic resources, including the Westlaw library and the e-Global Library.

Location

The main campus in Wilsonville, Oregon, is nestled between Portland, the state's largest city, and Salem, its capital. Once a small farming community, Wilsonville now has a population of approximately 16,000. Some of the corporations doing business in Wilsonville are Xerox, Mentor Graphics, Hollywood Entertainment, and Nike. Residents have numerous recreational opportunities at Memorial Park, Boones Ferry Park, and other public facilities as well as sports, music, and community programs for every interest. Pioneer has a learning site in Clackamas, a campus in Springfield, and the Oregon Culinary Institute in Portland.

Admission Requirements

To be considered for admission, prospective students must hold a high school diploma or equivalent, such as a General Educational Development (GED) credential or an accredited home study course. Applicants must first complete an application form. Next they schedule a campus tour and meet with an admission representative who assists students with the application process. This is followed by an acceptance interview, when applicants are notified of their acceptance and a start date is confirmed. New students are also invited at that time to meet with a financial aid officer.

Application and Information

Prospective students should apply before the start of the next ten-week term. Application forms and information can be requested from the Admissions Department by e-mailing inquiries@pioneerpacific.edu or calling 866-772-4636 (toll-free).

Admissions Department
Wilsonville Main Campus
Pioneer Pacific College
27501 Southwest Parkway Avenue
Wilsonville, Oregon 97070
Phone: 503-682-3903
      866-772-4636 (toll-free)
E-mail: inquiries@pioneerpacific.edu
Web site: http://www.pioneerpacific.edu

THE RESTAURANT SCHOOL
AT WALNUT HILL COLLEGE

PHILADELPHIA, PENNSYLVANIA

The College and Its Mission

The Restaurant School at Walnut Hill College, *Philadelphia's Home of Hospitality Excellence*, was established in 1974 and is dedicated to inspiring the future of the restaurant and hotel industry through training that is dynamic, timely, and insightful, with a commitment of service to its students. The Restaurant School at Walnut Hill College combines both intensive classroom training and practical experience; students use their knowledge while they learn. Within eighteen months, graduates are working in the field, earning an income, building a resume, and gaining practical and professional experience.

A student's education is cultivated by the College's philosophy that hands-on training is an essential part of education. This approach has multiple benefits—it enhances learning abilities, creates marketable skills and experience for a resume, brings education to life, and, most importantly, puts the student at the center of it all.

The Restaurant School at Walnut Hill College is licensed by the Pennsylvania Department of Education State Board of Private License Schools, is a member of the Pennsylvania Association of Private School Administrators, is accredited by the Accrediting Commission of Career Schools and Colleges of Technology, is certified for veteran's training by the Veterans Administration, is approved by the United States Department of Justice to grant student visas, and is recognized as a Professional Management Development Partner of the Educational Foundation of the National Restaurant Association.

Academic Programs

Associate and Bachelor's Degree Programs There are four majors at the Restaurant School at Walnut Hill College: hotel management, restaurant management, culinary arts, and pastry arts. Each major provides the student with a broad-based knowledge of the overall workings of a fine restaurant or hotel. Beyond that, the programs prepare the student with the day-to-day skills and specific knowledge that are required as he or she develops a career as a restaurant manager, chef, pastry chef, hotel manager, or restaurateur. In partnership with the Educational Foundation of the National Restaurant Association, the College's curriculum includes up to twelve nationally recognized food service and hospitality management courses. Upon successful completion of the courses and the certification exam, students receive national certification.

All students must successfully complete four 15-week semesters to be awarded an Associate of Science degree or eight 15-week semesters to be awarded a Bachelor of Science degree.

Off-Campus Programs

The Restaurant School at Walnut Hill College was one of the first schools in the country to offer a travel experience as part of a curriculum. Culinary and pastry students participate in an eight-day tour of France, while hotel and restaurant management students participate in an eight-day Orlando resort and cruise tour. This travel experience enhances both training and resumes.

A study-abroad program to France and England is currently being formulated. Students may contact the College for detailed information.

Costs

Tuition for the two-year program for students who start September 2007 is $37,050 ($18,525 per academic year for the two-year Associate of Science degree program) or $74,100 ($18,525 per academic year for the four-year Bachelor of Science degree program). Equipment, books, activity fees, culinary whites, and management dining room attire cost approximately $1200. Students may contact the College for information on on-campus housing.

Financial Aid

Financial aid programs are available to those who qualify. It is recommended that students apply early. The College participates in the Federal Pell Grant, the Pennsylvania PHEAA State Grant, the Subsidized Federal Stafford Student Loan, the Unsubsidized Federal Stafford Student Loan, and the parents' Federal PLUS loan programs. The financial aid officers assist students and their families with the creation of a personal plan that outlines expenses and identifies financial resources that are available to students. Scholarships and grants are available to incoming students; for more specific information, students may contact the College.

Faculty

Learning comes to life under the guiding hands and encouragement of the highly trained, technically skilled faculty; the Restaurant School at Walnut Hill College has on staff 1 of only 20 Certified Master Pastry Chefs in the country. The faculty members are seasoned professionals, having logged many years of experience in restaurants and food service. Through their instruction, students gain professional insight, which gives them a competitive edge upon entering the hospitality field. The chefs and instructors are committed to helping students achieve success. As professionals, they continuously keep pace with current trends in the hospitality industry and convey their professional dedication and work ethic to their students.

Student Body Profile

There is a diverse population at the Restaurant School at Walnut Hill College, with students coming from throughout the United States and abroad and ranging in age from the high school graduate to the adult who wants to change careers.

Student Activities

Whether it is a celebrity chef's cooking demonstration, dinner and a tour at a notable restaurant or hotel, or a winery tour and tasting, students at the Restaurant School at Walnut Hill College are exposed to the very best Philadelphia has to offer. There are activities and weekly special events that are sponsored by student clubs. The Student Culinary Team has been the winner of several major competitions in recent years—both nationally and internationally. Activities are both educational and fun, combining opportunities to learn and to establish camaraderie and professional development. Events are listed in the student newsletter and monthly calendar.

Facilities and Resources

Recently completing a yearlong renovation, the Restaurant School at Walnut Hill College is poised to offer one of the most dynamic hands-on learning opportunities in the country. The

dining experience, situated in the breathtakingly restored 1853 Allison Mansion, turns into a dining event with the addition of three theme restaurants, including The Italian Trattoria, a casual Italian restaurant that features classic pasta presentations set amidst an Italian terrace. Guests are invited to sit inside the restaurant, where they can enjoy homemade pasta or dine amongst the twinkling lights in the European Courtyard.

American cuisine is presented in an innovative new style in the American Heartland. Depicting a country farm with a painted blue sky and cornfields, this restaurant allows students to explore some of America's best cooking while guests enjoy the comfort of a country dining or veranda setting.

Most notable is the elegant Great Chefs of Philadelphia restaurant. Amidst glittering crystal chandeliers and a rich tapestry motif, guests enjoy wonderful cuisine and service designed by some of Philadelphia's and America's top chefs.

Also in the mansion is the student resource center, featuring state-of-the-art computer lab stations as well as the Alumni Library, which encompasses thousands of books, magazines, and videotapes on cooking, management, and wines. The building also houses a student conference room and a wines and bartending training salon.

The Pastry Shop and Café is filled each morning with buttery croissants, crisp French baguettes, and glistening pastries that are prepared by the pastry arts students. Also available is a selection of pastas, salads, soups, and entrées for an informal café lunch, prepared by the culinary arts students.

The education building is the focal point of a student's training. It houses four modern classroom kitchens, two lecture halls, and the College's purchasing center.

Hunter Hall is a turn-of-the-century masterpiece that features magnificent carved mahogany, marble, and fireplaces. The College's Office of Admissions, Financial Aid, and Independent Student Housing is located in this building.

Career Development and Job Placement Assistance at the Restaurant School at Walnut Hill College begins on the first day of school with training that is thorough and realistic. In the classroom, students learn how to develop effective resumes and portfolios as well as various interviewing techniques. Career development never ends—graduates can always contact the College for assistance with employment possibilities and resume updates. The College regularly invites personnel directors and proprietors of successful restaurants, hotels, and other food businesses to visit the College. Placement of Restaurant School at Walnut Hill College graduates averages at approximately 97 percent.

Location

Philadelphia is a great place to live and learn. As the fourth-largest city in the United States, Philadelphia has much to offer and is a city of firsts—the first public library, the first college, the first zoo—all in a first-class city.

The Restaurant School at Walnut Hill College is located in the University City section of Philadelphia, neighboring both the University of Pennsylvania and Drexel University. Located just across the Schuylkill River from Center City, University City has a wonderful college-town ambiance. Restaurants, museums, shops, and theaters abound, with local merchants offering discounts to students. The Amtrak train station is within walking distance of the campus, and the airport is 20 minutes away by car.

Center City is located just minutes from campus. Here, students find a bustling shopping and business district, complete with award-winning restaurant row, luxury hotels, and exclusive boutiques.

Ethnic diversity abounds in this city of neighborhoods, including Chinatown, complete with exotic restaurants and shops; South Philadelphia, with its famed Italian Market; and the ever-eclectic South Street, with blocks of restaurants, galleries, shops, and entertainment. There are also the historic district, which was the birthplace of the nation, and a waterfront that features exciting nightlife.

Philadelphia is rich in culture and heritage. Students find world-class art and science museums, theaters that feature major Broadway shows and renowned regional productions, and music, including everything from jazz to pop to the internationally acclaimed Philadelphia Orchestra.

Admission Requirements

Typically, the admissions procedure begins with a visit to the College. At that time, prospective students and their families tour the College, watch hands-on classes in action, and get a feel for campus life. Application for admission to the College is available to any individual with a high school diploma or its equivalent and an interest in developing a career or ownership options in fine restaurants, food service, or hospitality. Applicants are evaluated on their educational background and demonstrated or stated interest in their chosen field. Two references are required, as are high school transcripts.

Students may contact the College for information on the early decision program for high school juniors and seniors.

Application and Information

The Restaurant School at Walnut Hill College practices rolling admission; qualified applicants are accepted at any time. Applications for admission are submitted with a $50 application fee and a $150 registration fee. Prospective students should contact:

Office of Admissions
The Restaurant School at Walnut Hill College
4207 Walnut Street
Philadelphia, Pennsylvania 19104
Phone: 215-222-4200 Ext. 3011
   877-925-6884 Ext. 3011 (toll-free)
Fax: 215-222-4219
E-mail: info@walnuthillcollege.com
Web site: http://www.walnuthillcollege.com

The Restaurant School at Walnut Hill College.

SANTA MONICA COLLEGE
SANTA MONICA, CALIFORNIA

The College and Its Mission

Santa Monica College is a two-year community college, founded in 1929. The College is supported by the state of California and is accredited by the Western Association of Schools and Colleges. It has an enrollment of 27,700 students, including 2,628 students from 105 other countries.

Santa Monica College welcomes students from all countries in the world and provides special assistance to them through the International Student Center. New incoming students are given an orientation that includes an introduction to the College and its services. In addition, information on immigration issues, housing, and registration are also covered in these sessions.

Santa Monica College ranks first among the 109 community colleges in California in transferring students to the University of California. The College also has articulation agreements with the California State Universities as well as with outstanding private universities, including the University of Southern California and Pepperdine and Loyola Marymount Universities.

To a great extent, the reputation of Santa Monica as one of the leading community colleges in America is based on the quality of its teaching faculty. Unlike some universities that place more emphasis on research, Santa Monica College chooses its professors for their ability to teach as well as their expertise in their fields.

A high priority is placed on individual interaction between instructors and students. Smaller classes give students the opportunity to receive more personal attention than they would in introductory courses at large universities.

The College radio station, KCRW, is the leading public radio station in southern California, providing both local and national news and entertainment programs. The Santa Monica Associates, a community-based foundation, enables the College to bring some of the world's outstanding scientists, writers, and artists to the campus for lectures and interaction with students. Santa Monica College students also present symphony concerts, plays, and operas.

Academic Programs

Graduation from Santa Monica College with the **Associate in Arts** degree is granted upon successful completion of a program of studies that includes the mastery of minimum skill requirements in English and mathematics; a selection of courses from the natural sciences, social sciences, and humanities; and prescribed courses in the major field. Graduating students are required to complete a minimum of 60 units with at least a C (2.0) average. A unit is based on the number of hours of classroom instruction. Most courses offer 3 units of credit for classes that meet 3 hours a week for a semester. Full-time students take a minimum of 12 units per semester.

Santa Monica College offers programs of courses that parallel the lower division, or the first two years, of four-year universities and colleges. Students wishing to transfer must complete a minimum of 56 transfer-level units in fields including English, mathematics, humanities, the physical sciences, and the social sciences. Requirements vary among universities, and it is to the student's advantage to choose the university to which he or she plans to transfer as soon as possible.

All nine campuses of the University of California, including UCLA and Berkeley, give preference to California's community college students over all other applicants for third-year transfer; however, students must complete the required courses with at least a 2.8 grade point average. In some majors, such as engineering and economics, a higher grade point average may be necessary for acceptance at high-demand campuses such as UCLA.

The twenty-three campuses of the California State University also give preference to community college students who have completed a prescribed program of lower-division courses with 56 transfer-level units and a minimum grade point average of 2.5. Campuses and majors in high demand by students may require higher grade point averages.

Associate Degree Programs Santa Monica College offers courses in sixty academic major fields of study, including accounting, anatomy, anthropology, art, astronomy, bilingual education, biological sciences, botany, broadcasting, business administration, chemistry, child development, Chinese, cinema, communication, computer information systems, economics, electronics, engineering, English, fashion merchandising, French, geography, geology, German, graphic design, history, interior design, Italian, Japanese, journalism, management, mathematics, merchandising, philosophy, photography, physical education, physics, physiology, political science, respiratory therapy, Russian, sociology, Spanish, speech, theater arts, and zoology. Courses for preprofessional study in such fields as chiropractic studies, medicine, optometry, pharmacy, physical therapy, and veterinary science are also offered.

Students who complete their first two years of undergraduate requirements may receive an Associate in Arts degree before transferring to a four-year university to complete their bachelor's degree. Occupational certificates are also granted in certain two-year programs including accounting, automotive technology, child development, computer information systems, cosmetology, electronics, fashion design, management, office information systems, photography, printing, real estate, recreational leadership, and supervision.

Credit for Nontraditional Learning Experiences

The cooperative work experience program at Santa Monica College makes it possible for students to earn College credit for work experience in technical, business, or professional settings. The program is a joint effort of the College and the community to combine on-the-job training with classroom instruction, enabling the student to acquire knowledge, skills, and attitudes necessary to enter into or progress in a chosen occupation.

Costs

For the 2006–07 academic year, California residents paid an enrollment fee of $26 per unit. Nonresidents paid an enrollment fee of $26 per unit plus $180 per unit in tuition. It is estimated that room and board in a homestay or apartment for this period cost $9832. Other costs include mandatory health insurance for F-1 international students ($684 per year) and textbooks and supplies ($1500). International students should have a minimum of $17,000 available to them to cover all of their costs for the year.

Financial Aid

U.S. students receive government support in the form of grants and loans based on their financial need. International students do not qualify for government support, but they are eligible to compete for 200 non-need scholarships (averaging $500) given by private donors.

Faculty

Santa Monica has 321 full-time faculty members and 581 part-time faculty members. All hold the equivalent of a master's degree or higher and are certified by the state of California. Although faculty members are chosen on the basis of their

teaching ability, many of the professors hold doctoral degrees, particularly in the sciences. The student-faculty ratio is 40:1, although some classes are larger or smaller than 40, depending on the subject. Many faculty members maintain office hours to advise students on an individual basis. In addition, counselors on the faculty help students plan their schedules and provide special assistance for personal learning problems.

Student Body Profile

Santa Monica College has a total enrollment of 27,700 students, of whom 44 percent are men and 56 percent are women. The average age is 29. The racial breakdown of the student group includes Asian, 23 percent; African American, 9 percent; Hispanic, 24 percent; Native American, 1 percent; Pacific Islander, 1 percent; other (nonwhites), 2 percent; and white (non-Hispanic), 40 percent. Of the full-time students enrolled, 65 percent plan to transfer to a four-year college or university, 13 percent are undecided, 6 percent are taking classes for personal interest, 4 percent enroll for professional development, 3 percent enroll for a vocational certificate or an associate degree, and 9 percent enroll for other reasons. The international student population numbers 2,628.

Student Activities

All students are encouraged to join a variety of clubs supported by the Associated Students. The clubs are organized by students with special interests such as ecology, geology, biology, skiing, karate, dance, music, and drama. There is also an international club and clubs organized by students from Hong Kong, Indonesia, and India. The clubs normally meet once a week and conduct activities on and off campus throughout the year.

Sports Sports facilities at the College include off-site tennis courts, a gymnasium, an Olympic-size swimming pool, and the track built for the 1984 Olympics in Los Angeles. The College competes on the varsity level in men's football and men's and women's basketball, tennis, track, and volleyball. All students have access to the sports facilities for classes and individual training.

Facilities and Resources

Santa Monica College has excellent teaching facilities, including laboratories for science, electronics, computers, and nursing. It also has a new state-of the-art library with 103,392 bound volumes, and a learning resources center provides media-assisted individual instruction and free tutoring. There are 160 terminals/PCs available for student use at various locations throughout the campus. Other facilities include an amphitheater, a music room and auditorium, a little theater, an art gallery, a planetarium, a media center, and a student activities building.

The Associated Student Center provides study areas and a computer laboratory with free use of Macintosh computers to all students. The Student Center also includes a cafeteria, conference center, and bookstore.

The Santa Monica College Transfer Center assists students who are seeking to continue their studies at a four-year college or university. Its services include workshops on the application process, opportunities to meet with representatives from the four-year institutions, and tours of the campuses throughout California.

A Mentor Program in the arts gives exceptionally talented students in the performing and applied arts an opportunity to further develop their abilities through individual instruction. Mentor programs exist in architecture, art, dance, fashion design, music, photography, and theater arts. Students wishing to be part of the Mentor Program must demonstrate exceptional abilities and commitment. The program of study is tailored to the goals of the individual and often results in a 1-person show of the student's work or a public performance.

Location

Santa Monica College is located on the beautiful coast of Southern California in the city of Santa Monica. Because of the nearness to the ocean, Santa Monica has clean air and a mild climate throughout the year. It is just to the west of Los Angeles, one of the most cosmopolitan cities in the world. The campus provides easy access to outstanding theater, music, and museum facilities in Los Angeles as well as to Universal Studios and other centers of the entertainment industry. Santa Monica College is less than 10 miles from UCLA, USC, Pepperdine University, Loyola Marymount University, and other fine institutions of higher education in the Los Angeles area.

Admission Requirements

Santa Monica College has an open admission policy. Math and English tests are given upon entry in order to counsel students and place them at the proper course levels. International students who are below the university level in English are able to take preuniversity courses in ESL while they are taking university transfer-level courses, such as mathematics, that are not as dependent on English skills. International students are required to have an English level equivalent to a TOEFL score of 450 (133 CBT/45–46 iBT) in order to enroll in academic courses. Students who do not have the required English proficiency (TOEFL score) can enroll in the Intensive ESL Program at Santa Monica College.

Application and Information

Applications are accepted on an ongoing basis prior to the beginning of each semester. For the 2007–08 academic year, the fall semester begins August 27, the winter session begins January 3, the spring semester begins February 11, and the summer session begins June 16. All students should apply two months prior to the beginning of each semester or session in order to have the best selection of classes. International students must submit the documents required by the U.S. government for issuing I-20 student visas two months in advance. These documents include transcripts from high school and other colleges or universities attended, verification of financial support, and a certification of the minimum English level. International student applications are processed within one week, and notification of acceptance can be made by fax or express mail when necessary.

For more information, students should contact:

Teresita Rodriguez
Dean of Admissions
Santa Monica College
1900 Pico Boulevard
Santa Monica, California 90405-1628

Phone: 310-434-4380
E-mail: admissions@smc.edu
Web site: http://www.smc.edu

International students should contact:

Dr. Elena M. Garate
Dean, International Education
International Student Center
Santa Monica College
1900 Pico Boulevard
Santa Monica, California 90405-1628

Phone: 310-434-4217
Fax: 310-434-3651
E-mail: intled@smc.edu
Web site: http://www.smc.edu/international/default.html

SANTA ROSA JUNIOR COLLEGE

SANTA ROSA, CALIFORNIA

The College and Its Mission

Santa Rosa Junior College (SRJC), founded in 1918, is the tenth oldest of California's publicly funded, two-year community colleges. Widely regarded as one of the finest community colleges in the state, it is known for its academic rigor, its outstanding vocational training programs, superb faculty, comprehensive student services, and excellent facilities. Sonoma County Junior College District's mission is to promote student learning throughout its diverse communities by increasing the knowledge, improving the skills, and enhancing the lives of those who participate in its programs and enroll in its courses. Its programs and courses instill an intellectual curiosity and respect for learning while preparing students for personal and professional fulfillment.

From its initial freshman class of 19 students in 1918, SRJC has grown into the Sonoma County Junior College District, one of the largest single-college districts in the country, with more than 35,000 students enrolled each semester and encompassing fourteen major high school districts.

The College's 100-acre main campus is characterized by ivy-covered brick buildings, towering oak trees, and gardens. In addition to excellent classroom and laboratory facilities, the campus includes a planetarium, art gallery, summer repertory theater, and Native American museum. The culinary arts program operates a full-service restaurant and bakery run by students. The College has a 300-acre farm and vineyard for students in its agriculture and viticulture programs and a Public Safety Training Center in Windsor for the law enforcement, EMT, and firefighter programs. The College has a second campus and technology center in the nearby city of Petaluma.

SRJC offers a strong general education program for students planning to transfer to four-year colleges and universities, as well as more than 140 occupational programs designed to prepare students for the workforce. The College grants both Associate of Arts (A.A.) and Associate of Sciences (A.S.) degrees, and it has developed a number of certificate programs that enable students to receive brief but intense learning experiences.

The College is accredited by the Western Association of Schools and Colleges.

Academic Programs

Santa Rosa's many programs of study provide students with a strong foundation for transfer, training for an occupational field, or sufficient depth in a field of knowledge to contribute to a lifelong interest. At least 18 units must be taken within the student's major. Each academic year begins in late August, when classes begin, and ends after the close of the subsequent summer session. Career Certificates require completion of 18 units. These certificates, which typically take one to two years to complete, demonstrate that students are prepared to enter careers in their designated fields. Achievement Certificate programs, which require less than 18 units, provide a brief but intense education in a particular area of study.

In order to receive an A.A. or an A.S. degree, students must complete 60 units, including at least 12 units in residence at the College, with a minimum GPA of 2.0. General education requirements can be met by completing 23 units of the associate degree's general education course requirements and the math competency requirement; by completing California State University's General Education Course Requirements; or by completing the Intersegmental General Education Transfer Curriculum.

The College awards associate degrees in more than seventy programs of study. Students should visit the Colleges Web site for a complete list of programs.

The new Weekend College program is designed for students who are unable to attend classes during the week. Classes meet Friday evenings and Saturday mornings or afternoons for twelve weeks each semester. Students are able to complete their degrees over five semesters.

The Community Education Program offers noncredit courses to members of the Santa Rosa community. Programs include the arts and lectures, the Chamber Concert Series, and College for Kids.

Off-Campus Programs

The College offers several study-abroad and work-abroad options. Locations include Australia, China, England, France, Italy, Mexico, and Spain.

Costs

California residents pay an enrollment fee of $26 per unit. Nonresident students pay $177 per unit plus the $26-per-unit enrollment fee. International students pay an additional $29 per unit. All students pay a student representation fee of $1 and a Health Services Fee of $13 per semester.

Financial Aid

The College's extensive scholarship and financial aid program provides more than $17 million annually to students. More than one third of the students receive federal or state financial aid. Federal grants and loans are available for students who demonstrate financial need, and some students work part-time through the Federal Work-Study Program. The Doyle Scholarship Program awards scholarships ranging from $1000 to $1600 per year, regardless of need. CalGrants are available for students who plan to transfer to a four-year college, students from disadvantaged backgrounds, and students who complete a two-year degree. Other scholarships may be available through the College or other sources, based on both merit and need; amounts and eligibility requirements vary. Veterans and their dependents may be eligible for benefits, and the CalWORKS program awards aid for room and board, books, and other expenses. Priority is given to students who apply for aid before March 2.

Faculty

More than 300 full-time professors and 1,000 adjunct instructors teach at the College. All have degrees in their respective fields of study.

Student Body Profile

The Sonoma County Junior College District serves more than 35,000 students each semester at all of its locations and attracts students of diverse backgrounds from throughout the state and from more than forty countries around the world. Most students

are in credit-earning programs, taking courses in the day and evening. The average age is 38, and the average course load is 5 credits per semester. The College enjoys a completion rate of 71 percent.

Student Activities

Many students take part in extracurricular activities at the College. Dozens of clubs and organizations are dedicated to the personal, academic, and professional interests of students. The Department of Physical Education, Dance, and Athletics schedules a wide variety of activity classes, including aerobics, Pilates, and dance, which emphasize physical fitness. The department hosts more than twenty sports teams, such as badminton, basketball, football, soccer, volleyball, and water polo. The College also hosts a summer repertory theater that stages productions for audiences of all ages.

Academic Facilities

The newly built Doyle Library and Media Center houses a large number of media and research tools, including an extensive book collection, 280 computer workstations, study spaces, an art gallery, a TV studio, and two technology-enhanced classrooms.

Media Services is located in the library and has a collection of compact discs, records, cassettes, and materials used in instruction, such as video cassettes, slides, and filmstrips. Librarians at both libraries teach introductory and advanced courses on information competency and research skills.

The Career Resources and Services Department assists students in choosing a major, developing career plans, and making a career change. Resources include career counseling, career guidance classes, an up-to-date career library, and employer information files.

Location

The city of Santa Rosa is located in northern California, one hour north of San Francisco. Santa Rosa has a population of approximately 153,000 and offers a relaxed suburban appeal. Sonoma County is a major wine producing area, with vineyards throughout the county. Santa Rosa has more than 400 acres of public parks and 58 miles of beach and coastal access along the Pacific Ocean and is just a few hours away from the resort areas of Lake Tahoe, Yosemite National Park, and Monterey Bay. The area has a moderate climate year-round, with average rainfall of about 30 inches per year.

Admission Requirements

The College accepts students who hold a high school diploma or its equivalent. In the admission process, prospective students submit an application for admission and transcripts from their high school or college. Placement tests are required for English, math, or chemistry courses at the College. Students may attend an orientation session and meet with a counselor to design a suitable program of study. International students must follow specific admission procedures as indicated in the College catalog.

High school students may apply for concurrent enrollment with the approval of a high school counselor.

Application and Information

Students may enroll at any time of the year and begin classes in the fall, spring, or summer. Prospective students may request application materials from the Office of Admissions.

Office of Admissions
Santa Rosa Junior College
1501 Mendocino Avenue
Santa Rosa, California 95401
Phone: 707-527-4685
Fax: 707-527-4798
Web site: http://www.santarosa.edu

STATE UNIVERSITY OF NEW YORK COLLEGE OF ENVIRONMENTAL SCIENCE AND FORESTRY, RANGER SCHOOL

WANAKENA, NEW YORK

The College and Its Mission

The forest technology and land surveying technology programs are offered through the State University of New York College of Environmental Science and Forestry (ESF) at the Ranger School campus. Throughout its history, the College has focused on the environmental issues of the time in each of its three mission areas: instruction, research, and public service. The College is dedicated to educating future scientists and managers who, through specialized skills, will be able to use a holistic approach to solving the environmental and resource problems facing society.

More than 3,200 students have graduated from the program over the past ninety-five years, including more than 180 women since 1974. Established in 1912 with the gift of 1,800 acres of land in the Adirondack Mountains, the ESF forest technology program is the oldest in the nation. The Ranger School's managed forest includes both hardwood and coniferous trees and is bounded on two sides by the New York State Forest Preserve. It is also adjacent to several acres of virgin timber in the Adirondack Forest preserve.

The main campus building houses the central academic, dining, and recreational facilities. Dormitory wings are located on either side of the main campus building. Dorm rooms are designed to accommodate 1 or 2 people. All second-year students live on campus, with the exception of married students accompanied by their families. These students should arrange for rental accommodations well before the start of the academic year.

A $6-million renovation and expansion of the Ranger School was completed in 2003. This project included renovations and an addition to the main campus building, a new dining hall, distance learning classrooms, additional residence hall facilities, and a new student recreational area.

Academic Programs

Associate Degree Programs Students who complete the program earn an **Associate in Applied Science (A.A.S.)** degree in forest technology or land surveying technology.

Both degree programs at the Ranger School are 1+1 programs, meaning they require 30 credit hours of course work in general studies to fulfill the program's freshman liberal arts requirements. Students who are considering later transfer to a four-year program should follow the suggestions for freshman-year selections outlined in the ESF catalog. The 30 credits taken in the freshman year may be taken at the college's Syracuse campus or any other accredited college a student chooses to attend. These are followed by an additional 48 credit hours at the Wanakena campus in the second year of the program. The sophomore year takes place at the Ranger School, where time is equally divided between classroom and laboratory work, and experience in the field. Fieldwork is a large component of the curriculum. Students take several short field trips during the second year of study, at no additional expense to them. These trips enhance courses in dendrology, silviculture, forest management, recreation, wildlife, ecology, and surveying. On weekends and evenings, students devote much of their time to studying, but there is time for recreation as well, when students can take advantage of the College's beautiful setting in the Adirondacks.

Transfer Arrangements Counseling is available for students interested in pursuing a four-year degree on the main campus in Syracuse. Students should contact the ESF admissions office.

Costs

The cost of the first year varies according to the institution attended. Estimated tuition and fees for the 2007–08 academic year at the Wanakena campus total $5325 for residents of New York State and $11,585 for out-of-state residents. Room and board at the Wanakena campus are $8050 and the estimated cost of books, personal expenses, and travel is $3050. (Books and supplies are sold on campus.)

Financial Aid

More than 80 percent of Ranger School students receive some form of financial aid, including grants and scholarships, low-interest loans, and student employment. All students are encouraged to apply for financial aid by completing the Free Application for Federal Student Aid.

Faculty

Five full-time faculty members and 1 part-time instructor teach at the Wanakena campus. The student-faculty ratio is approximately 10:1. Students have ready access to faculty members for consultations. Faculty members are housed on campus, and faculty offices are located near student living quarters. There is close contact between students and faculty members in the classroom and at fieldwork sites.

Student Body Profile

Ninety percent of all students complete the forest technology or land surveying technology program. About 50 percent go on to careers as forest technicians or aides with private companies or government agencies; some 30 percent become surveyors. Many graduates of the forest technology program or land surveying technology program go on to receive Bachelor of Science and even graduate-level degrees at ESF's main campus in Syracuse or at other colleges and universities.

Student Activities

Students have a variety of activities available to them at the Wanakena campus. Many recreational activities are readily available, including hiking, camping, canoeing, cross-country skiing, and ice-skating. Students are assigned a canoe for their use during the year. Each class forms a student government, which plans a number of class activities. A new recreational facility is available for student use. Students at the Ranger

School follow the ESF code of student conduct and follow the house rules of the Wanakena campus.

Location

The 2,800-acre campus is situated on the banks of the Oswegatchie River near the Adirondack Mountain hamlet of Wanakena, approximately 65 miles east of Watertown, New York, and 35 miles west of Tupper Lake on New York State's Route 3. At the Wanakena campus, social and recreational activities utilize the area's year-round opportunities for outdoor enjoyment. An excellent hospital, located in Star Lake, New York, serves the community.

Admission Requirements

Students may apply to ESF for admission to the Ranger School's programs during their senior year in high school for guaranteed transfer admission or during their freshman year of college for transfer admission. Prospective students should consult the current catalog for specific information concerning the application process. ESF cooperates with more than fifty colleges in cooperative transfer programs. Acceptance to the Ranger School is contingent upon satisfactory completion of first-year courses. While in high school, applicants should successfully complete a college-preparatory program with an emphasis in mathematics and science. Electives in such areas as computer applications and mechanical drawing are recommended. Transfer students are considered on the basis of college course work and interest in the program. In addition to academic requirements, applicants must be able to meet the physical requirements of the Ranger School program and must submit a full medical report. Parents of applicants under 18 years old should be aware of the field nature of the program and its rigorous study-work regimen.

Application and Information

The Ranger School accepts students for fall admission only. Fall admission decisions are made beginning around the middle of January and continue on a rolling basis until the class is filled. Application forms for New York State residents are available at all high schools in the state and at all colleges in the state university system. Out-of-state students should request application forms from the Office of Undergraduate Admissions at the address below. Prospective students who wish to visit the 2,800-acre campus can do so by contacting the Director, New York State Ranger School, Wanakena, New York 13695-0106 (telephone: 315-848-2566 or fax: 315-848-3249).

The Admissions office at the Syracuse campus also serves as the Admissions Office for the Ranger School. Students may request an application or information about course or college selection for the freshman year from the address listed below.

Office of Undergraduate Admissions
106 Bray Hall
State University of New York College of Environmental
    Science and Forestry
1 Forestry Drive
Syracuse, New York 13210-2779
Phone: 315-470-6600
       800-777-7373 (toll-free)
Fax: 315-470-6933
E-mail: esfinfo@esf.edu
Web site: http://rangerschool.esf.edu

VALLEY FORGE MILITARY COLLEGE
WAYNE, PENNSYLVANIA

The College and Its Mission

Valley Forge Military College (VFMC) is a private, coeducational residential college that offers the freshman and sophomore years of college. The primary mission of the College is to prepare students for transfer to competitive four-year colleges and universities. Established in 1935, the College has a long tradition of fostering personal growth through a comprehensive system built on the five cornerstones that make Valley Forge unique: academic excellence, character development, leadership, personal motivation, and physical development to all students regardless of race, creed, or national origin. The diverse student body represents more than nineteen states and four countries. The College has an excellent transfer record, with 95 percent of cadets accepted to their first- or second-choice schools. More than 63 percent were admitted to the top-tier schools in the country.

Valley Forge Military College is the only college in the northeastern United States that offers qualified freshmen the opportunity to participate in an Early Commissioning Program, leading to a commission as a second lieutenant in the U.S. Army Reserves or Army National Guard at the end of their sophomore year. The U.S. Air Force Academy, the U.S. Coast Guard Academy, the U.S. Military Academy, and the U.S. Naval Academy have all sponsored cadets through their Foundation Scholarship Programs and other programs to attend Valley Forge Military College.

The College is accredited by the Middle States Association of Colleges and Schools and is approved by the Pennsylvania State Council of Education and the Commission on Higher Education of the Pennsylvania State Department of Education. The College is a member of the National Association of Independent Colleges and Universities, the Association of Independent Colleges/Universities of Pennsylvania, the Pennsylvania Association of Two-Year Colleges, and the Association of Military Colleges and Schools in the United States.

Academic Programs

All students are required to complete an academic program of 60 credits, including a core program of approximately 45 credits that is designed to establish the essential competencies that are necessary for continued intellectual development and to facilitate the transfer process. Included in the core program are one semester of computer science, two semesters of English, one semester of literature, two semesters of mathematics, one semester of science, and one semester of Western civilization. Qualified cadets must also complete a minimum of two semesters of military science. To satisfy the requirement for the associate degree, cadets must complete at least 15 additional credits in courses related to their selected area of concentration. Associate degrees are awarded upon satisfactory completion of the degree requirements with a quality point average of 2.0 or higher.

Associate Degree Programs Valley Forge Military College offers concentrations in the business, criminal justice, general studies, leadership, and liberal arts, leading to an Associate of Arts degree, as well as concentrations in general studies, life sciences, physical sciences, and pre-engineering, leading to an Associate of Science degree.

Transfer Arrangements Transfer of academic credits and completion of the baccalaureate degree is facilitated by established relationships with a number of outstanding colleges and universities, including articulation agreements with the neighboring institutions of Cabrini College, Eastern University, and Rosemont College.

Credit for Nontraditional Learning Experiences

Valley Forge Military College may give credit for demonstrated proficiency in areas related to college-level courses. Sources used to determine such proficiency are the College-Level Examination Program (CLEP), Advanced Placement (AP) examinations, Defense Activity for Nontraditional Education Support (DANTES), and the Office of Education Credit and Credentials of the American Council on Education (ACE). All such requests must be approved by the Office of the Dean.

Costs

The annual charge for 2006–07 was $30,977. This charge included haircuts, maintenance, room and board, tuition, uniforms, and other fees. Optional expenses may include fee-based courses, such as aviation, driver's education, membership in the cavalry troop or artillery battery, or scuba. A fee is charged for Health Center confinement over 24 hours' duration. For information on the payment plan, students should contact the Business Office.

Financial Aid

The College offers a combination of merit- and need-based scholarships and grants as well as endowed scholarships based on donor specifications to help VFMC cadets finance their education. The academic scholarships reward incoming and returning cadets for demonstrated academic excellence. Performance scholarships are awarded to eligible cadets who participate in the athletic teams, band, or choir. To qualify for federal, state, and VFMC grants, students must file the Free Application for Federal Student Aid (FAFSA) by the published priority deadlines. In addition, qualified cadets in the advanced ROTC commissioning program are eligible for two-year, full-tuition scholarships. These scholarships are supplemented by assistance for room and board provided by the College. The FAFSA is also required for ROTC scholarship applications.

Valley Forge Military College offers federal student aid to eligible cadets in the form of Federal Pell Grants, Federal Supplemental Educational Opportunity Grants (FSEOG), Federal Work-Study (FWS) Program positions, Federal Stafford Student Loans, and Parent Loans for Undergraduate Students (PLUS) through the Federal Family Education Loan Program. Applicants must file the FAFSA and the VFMC financial aid application for consideration for all student aid.

Faculty

There are 12 full-time and 11 part-time faculty members holding the academic rank of assistant professor, associate professor, instructor, or professor. These faculty members are selected for their professional ability and strong personal leadership qualities; 50 percent of the full-time staff members hold doctorates in their field. Faculty members perform additional duties as advisers and athletic coaches of extracurricular activities. The Military Science Department has 5 active-duty Army officers and 4 noncommissioned officers assigned as full-time faculty members for the ROTC program. The faculty-student ratio is approximately 1:14. Classes are small, and the classroom atmosphere contributes to a harmonious relationship between faculty members and the students.

Student Body Profile

The military structure of Valley Forge provides extraordinary opportunities for cadets to develop and exercise leadership abilities. The Corps of Cadets is a self-administering body organized in nine company units along military lines, with a cadet officer and noncommissioned officer organization for cadet

control and administration. The College's cadets are appointed to major command positions in the Corps. The First Captain is generally a sophomore in the College. Cadet leadership and positive peer pressure within this structured setting result in a unique camaraderie among cadets. Cadets, through their student representatives, cooperate with the administration in enforcing regulations regarding student conduct. A Student Advisory Council represents the cadets in the school administration. The Dean's Council meets regularly to discuss aspects of academic life.

Student Activities

The proximity to many colleges and universities ensures a full schedule of local college-oriented events in addition to Valley Forge's own activities. Cadets are encouraged to become involved in community-service activities. The scholarship-supported Regimental Band has performed for U.S. presidents, royalty, and countless military and social events. The Regimental Chorus has performed at the Capitol Building in Washington, D.C.; New York's Carnegie Hall; and the Philadelphia Academy of Music. In addition, eligible students can participate in VFMC honor societies: Alpha Beta Gamma, Lambda Alpha Epsilon, or Phi Theta Kappa. Other available activities include Black Student Union, business and political clubs, flight training, French Club, participation in the local Radnor Fire Company, and Rotoract.

Sports Athletics and physical well-being are important elements in a Valley Forge education. The aim of the program is to develop alertness, all-around fitness, character, competitive spirit, courage, esprit de corps, leadership, and genuine desire for physical and mental achievement. For students aspiring to compete at the Division I-A or Division I-AA level, Valley Forge's residential college football and basketball programs offer a distinctive opportunity that combines such a strong academic transfer program with a highly successful athletic program that has habitually placed players at the national level. Continuing a legacy that began with its high school program, in only eight years, the College has placed 40 players on national-level teams in basketball and football. In the last seven years, the Valley Forge wrestling program has also produced 3 National Champions and 7 All-Americans in the National Collegiate Wrestling Association. Students may also compete at the collegiate level in cross-country, lacrosse, soccer, and tennis. Club and interscholastic teams are available in golf, polo, and riflery. The Valley Forge polo team is consistently among the top-ranked polo teams in the nation, regularly competing against nationally ranked teams.

Facilities and Resources

Campus buildings are equipped to meet student needs. A fiber-optic, Internet-capable computer network connects all campus classrooms, dormitory rooms, laboratories, and the library. All rooms are computer accessible and provide access to CadetNET, the institutional local area network. This network provides access to the library and the Internet. College classrooms are located in two buildings and contain biology, chemistry, and physics laboratories. A computer laboratory supports the computer science curriculum and student requirements through a local area network.

Library and Audiovisual Services The May H. Baker Memorial Library is a learning resource center for independent study and research. The library has more than 100,000 volumes and audiovisual materials, microfilm, and periodicals and houses the Cadet Achievement Center. It provides online database access, membership in the Tri-State Library Consortium, and computer links to ACCESS Pennsylvania and other databases to support the College requirements.

Location

Valley Forge Military College is situated on a beautifully landscaped 120-acre campus in the Main Line community of Wayne, 15 miles west of Philadelphia and close to Valley Forge National Historic Park. Ample opportunities exist for cadets to enjoy cultural and entertainment resources and activities in the Philadelphia area.

Admission Requirements

Admission to the College is based upon review of an applicant's SAT or ACT scores, high school transcript, recommendations from a guidance counselor, and personal interview. Students may be accepted for midyear admission. Minimum requirements for admission on a nonprobation status are a high school diploma or equivalency diploma with a minimum 2.0 average, rank in the upper half of the class, and minimum combined SAT score of 850 or ACT score of 17. The College reviews the new SAT standards and scores on a case-by-case basis. An international student for whom English is a second language must have a minimum score of 550 on the Test of English as a Foreign Language (TOEFL). Up to 20 percent of an entering class may be admitted on a conditional or probationary status, and individual entrance requirements may be waived by the Dean of the College for students who display a sincere commitment to pursuing a college degree.

Application and Information

Valley Forge Military College follows a program of rolling admissions. Applicants are notified of the admission decision as soon as their files are complete. A nonrefundable registration fee of $25 is required of all applicants.

For application forms and further information, students should contact:

College Admissions Officer
Valley Forge Military College
1001 Eagle Road
Wayne, Pennsylvania 19087

Phone: 800-234-VFMC (toll-free)
E-mail: admissions@vfmac.edu
Web site: http://www.vfmac.edu

A Valley Forge Military College cadet rappels down the Rappel Tower.

WESTWOOD COLLEGE–ANAHEIM

ANAHEIM, CALIFORNIA

The College and Its Mission

Today, the variables that define career success are ever changing. In order to get ahead and stay ahead, students need the right kind of preparation. To prepare them for the working world, students need a career-focused education program that teaches the skills employers demand and offers hands-on practical experience with real-world applications, and the right kind of job-placement assistance to help them get started in their new careers.

Students also need a fast-track learning program that shortens the time from education to career, with an academic schedule that fits their lifestyle. They need a high level of student services to help them reach their goals and the right financial package to make it all possible.

All of these are the focus at Westwood, which operates seventeen campuses, with locations in Anaheim, Inland Empire (Upland), Long Beach, and Los Angeles, California; Atlanta, Georgia; Chicago Loop, DuPage, O'Hare Airport, and River Oaks, Illinois; Denver North and Denver South, Colorado; Dallas, Fort Worth, and Houston, Texas; and the Washington, D.C., area.

Westwood College offers degree programs in business, design, justice, and technology. Degree programs in high-technology fields are also offered at two aviation campuses, Redstone College of Aviation Technology–Denver and Redstone College of Aviation Technology–Los Angeles.

The Anaheim campus is accredited by the Accrediting Commission of Career Schools and Colleges of Technology (ACCSCT).

Westwood College–Anaheim is a branch of Westwood College–Denver North.

Academic Programs

The Anaheim campus focuses on computer-based technology programs that prepare graduates to take advantage of southern California's unique, high-tech career opportunities. Programs are offered in computer-aided design/architectural drafting, computer network engineering, computer network management, criminal justice, e-business management, game art and design, graphic design and multimedia, information systems security, interior design, visual communications, and Web design and multimedia, to name a few.

The programs, which feature hands-on learning experience, are designed to prepare students for entry-level positions in their chosen careers.

Costs

Standard program costs can be found in the Westwood College academic catalog. They can also be accessed through the Web at http://www.westwood.edu/pdf/catalogs/default.asp.

Financial Aid

Tuition assistance is available for those who qualify. Scholarships include the Westwood High School Scholarship Program, which offers two scholarships to every high school in the United States; the Colorado Undergraduate Merit State Scholarships for Colorado residents; and several loan programs.

Student Activities

In addition to on-campus activities, the Anaheim area offers many cultural and recreational opportunities for students.

Facilities and Resources

The campus includes a primary building with approximately 25,000 square feet dedicated to classrooms, labs, and administrative offices. A nearby campus annex houses additional classroom space.

Location

The Anaheim campus is in Orange County, minutes from attractions such as Disneyland, Knott's Berry Farm, and Edison International Park. The area offers students an active lifestyle and is rich in career opportunities. Located directly across the street from Anaheim's arena, the Arrowhead Pond, the campus is easily accessible from I-5 at Katella.

Admission Requirements

Applicants must have either a diploma from an accredited high school or a GED certificate and passing scores on the College entrance exam (or qualifying ACT/SAT scores).

Application and Information

Westwood College–Anaheim
1551 South Douglass Road
Anaheim, California 92806

Phone: 714-704-2721
       877-650-6050 (toll-free)
Fax: 714-456-9971
E-mail: info@westwood.edu
Web site: http://www.westwood.edu

Westwood College–Anaheim campus.

WESTWOOD COLLEGE–ANNANDALE SATELLITE

ANNANDALE, VIRGINIA

The College and Its Mission

Today, the variables that define career success are ever changing. In order to get ahead and stay ahead, students need the right kind of preparation. To prepare for the working world, they need a career-focused education program that teaches the skills employers demand and offers hands-on, practical experience with real-world applications and the right kind of job-placement assistance to help students get started in their new careers.

Students also need a fast-track learning program that shortens the time from education to career, with an academic schedule that fits their lifestyle. They need a high level of student services to help them reach their goals and the right financial package to make it all possible.

All of these are the focus at Westwood, which operates seventeen campuses, with locations in Anaheim, Inland Empire (Upland), Long Beach, and Los Angeles, California; Atlanta, Georgia; Chicago Loop, DuPage, O'Hare Airport, and River Oaks, Illinois; Denver North and Denver South, Colorado; Dallas, Fort Worth, and Houston, Texas; and the Washington, D.C., area.

Westwood College offers degree programs in design, technology, and justice. Degree programs in high-technology fields are also offered at two aviation campuses, Redstone College of Aviation Technology–Denver and Redstone College of Aviation Technology–Los Angeles.

The Annandale campus, a satellite campus of Westwood College–Arlington Ballston, is accredited by the Accrediting Commission of Career Schools and Colleges of Technology (ACCSCT).

Academic Programs

The Annandale Satellite campus offers programs that prepare graduates to take advantage of the area's unique career opportunities. Degree programs are offered in animation, computer-aided design/architectural drafting, construction management, graphic design and multimedia, and interior design, to name a few.

Costs

Standard program costs can be found in the Westwood College academic catalog or accessed online through http://www.westwood.edu/pdf/catalogs/default.asp.

Financial Aid

Tuition assistance is available for those who qualify. Scholarships include the Westwood High School Scholarship Program, in which two scholarships are offered to every high school in the United States. In addition, several loan programs are available.

Faculty

Westwood has 528 faculty members in all. Half are employed on a full-time basis. Forty percent hold master's degrees, and 5 percent have doctorates.

Student Body Profile

Westwood College recruits recent high school graduates, young adults, and working adults who want to acquire new skills to take advantage of growing opportunities in the professional workplace. Students come to Westwood from all across the United States and from many countries around the world. Westwood's students are highly motivated, hardworking, and committed to preparing for rewarding careers.

Student Activities

In addition to on-campus activities, the northern Virginia–Washington, D.C., area offers many cultural and recreational opportunities for students.

Facilities and Resources

Westwood offers a variety of information and research resources, including on-campus Resource Centers, links to Internet-based information services, and a bookstore at each campus. The Campus Resource Centers offer a library of program-specific materials that have been

carefully selected to aid that school's career-focused educational mission. The Education Department at each campus collaborates closely with the campus' Resource Center staff to ensure that materials support the school's hands-on curriculum. Typical learning aids include books, periodicals, and Internet access. A virtual library, providing remote access to several selected databases, is also offered. Staff members are available to assist students during regular library hours and can provide instruction on how to conduct research in the library and online.

Location

The region offers an array of sporting and cultural events, famous exhibits and museums, and a variety of outdoor activities to keep students busy when not in class.

Admission Requirements

A diploma from an accredited high school or a GED certificate and passing scores on the college entrance exam (or qualifying ACT/SAT scores) are required. In addition, international students must submit TOEFL, IELTS, or MELAB scores. To apply, students must first contact the campus to schedule a personal career assessment.

Application and Information

Westwood College–Annandale Satellite Campus
7619 Little River Turnpike, Suite 500
Annandale, Virginia 22003
Phone: 703-642-3770
Fax: 703-642-3772
E-mail: info@westwood.edu
Web site: http://www.westwood.edu/locations/virginia-colleges/annandale-college.asp

WESTWOOD COLLEGE–ARLINGTON BALLSTON

ARLINGTON, VIRGINIA

The College and Its Mission

Today, the variables that define career success are ever changing. In order to get ahead and stay ahead, students need the right kind of preparation. To prepare for the working world, they need a career-focused education program that teaches the skills employers demand and offers hands-on, practical experience with real-world applications and the right kind of job-placement assistance to help students get started in their new careers.

Students also need a fast-track learning program that shortens the time from education to career, with an academic schedule that fits their lifestyle. They need a high level of student services to help them reach their goals and the right financial package to make it all possible.

All of these are the focus at Westwood, which operates seventeen campuses, with locations in Anaheim, Inland Empire (Upland), Long Beach, and Los Angeles, California; Atlanta, Georgia; Chicago Loop, DuPage, O'Hare Airport, and River Oaks, Illinois; Denver North and Denver South, Colorado; Dallas, Fort Worth, and Houston, Texas; and the Washington, D.C., area.

Westwood College offers degree programs in design, business, and justice. Degree programs in high-technology fields are also offered at two aviation campuses, Redstone College of Aviation Technology–Denver and Redstone College of Aviation Technology–Los Angeles.

The Arlington Ballston campus is accredited by the Accrediting Commission of Career Schools and Colleges of Technology (ACCSCT).

Academic Programs

The Arlington Ballston campus offers programs that prepare graduates to take advantage of the area's unique career opportunities. Degree programs are offered in animation, computer-aided design/architectural drafting, construction management, criminal justice, graphic design and multimedia, and interior design, to name a few.

Costs

Standard program costs can be found in the Westwood College academic catalog or accessed online through http://www.westwood.edu/pdf/catalogs/default.asp.

Financial Aid

Tuition assistance is available for those who qualify. Scholarships include the Westwood High School Scholarship Program, in which two scholarships are offered to every high school in the United States. In addition, several loan programs are available.

Faculty

Westwood has 528 faculty members in all. Half are employed on a full-time basis. Forty percent hold master's degrees, and 5 percent have doctorates.

Student Body Profile

Westwood College recruits recent high school graduates, young adults, and working adults who want to acquire new skills to take advantage of growing opportunities in the professional workplace. Students come to Westwood from all across the United States and from many countries around the world. Westwood's students are highly motivated, hardworking, and committed to preparing for rewarding careers.

Student Activities

In addition to on-campus activities, the northern Virginia–Washington, D.C., area offers many cultural and recreational opportunities for students.

Facilities and Resources

Westwood offers a variety of information and research resources, including on-campus Resource Centers, links to Internet-based information services, and a bookstore at each campus. The Campus Resource Centers offer a library of program-specific materials that have been

carefully selected to aid that school's career-focused educational mission. The Education Department at each campus collaborates closely with the campus' Resource Center staff to ensure that materials support the school's hands-on curriculum. Typical learning aids include books, periodicals, and Internet access. A virtual library, providing remote access to several selected databases, is also offered. Staff members are available to assist students during regular library hours and can provide instruction on how to conduct research in the library and online.

Location

The region offers an array of sporting and cultural events, famous exhibits and museums, and a variety of outdoor activities to keep students busy when not in class.

Admission Requirements

A diploma from an accredited high school or a GED certificate and passing scores on the college entrance exam (or qualifying ACT/SAT scores) are required. In addition, international students must submit TOEFL, IELTS, or MELAB scores. To apply, students must first contact the campus to schedule a personal career assessment.

Application and Information

Director of Admissions
Westwood College–Arlington Ballston Campus
4300 Wilson Boulevard, Suite 200
Arlington, Virginia 22203
Phone: 703-243-3900
Fax: 703-243-3990
E-mail: info@westwood.edu
Web site: http://www.westwood.edu

WESTWOOD COLLEGE–ATLANTA MIDTOWN

ATLANTA, GEORGIA

The College and Its Mission

Today, the variables that define career success are ever changing. In order to get ahead and stay ahead, students need the right kind of preparation. To prepare for the working world, they need a career-focused education program that teaches the skills employers demand and offers hands-on, practical experience with real-world applications and the right kind of job-placement assistance to help students get started in their new careers.

Students also need a fast-track learning program that shortens the time from education to career, with an academic schedule that fits their lifestyle. They need a high level of student services to help them reach their goals and the right financial package to make it all possible.

All of these are the focus at Westwood College, which operates seventeen campuses, with locations in Anaheim, Inland Empire (Upland), Long Beach, and Los Angeles, California; Atlanta, Georgia; Chicago Loop, DuPage, O'Hare Airport, and River Oaks, Illinois; Denver North and Denver South, Colorado; Dallas, Fort Worth, and Houston, Texas; and the Washington, D.C., area.

Westwood College offers degree programs in design, technology, business, justice, and health care. Degree programs in high-technology fields are also offered at two aviation campuses, Redstone College of Aviation Technology–Denver and Redstone College of Aviation Technology–Los Angeles.

The Atlanta Midtown campus is a branch of Westwood College–DuPage and is accredited by the Accrediting Council for Independent Colleges and Schools (ACICS).

Academic Programs

The Atlanta Midtown campus offers degree programs in computer-aided design/architectural drafting, computer network engineering, game art and design, graphic design and multimedia, information systems security, interior design, and visual communications, to name a few.

Costs

Standard program costs can be found in the Westwood College academic catalog or accessed online through http://www.westwood.edu/pdf/catalogs/default.asp.

Financial Aid

Tuition assistance is available for those who qualify. Scholarships include the Westwood High School Scholarship Program, in which two scholarships are offered to every high school in the United States. In addition, several loan programs are available.

Student Activities

In addition to on-campus activities, many cultural and recreational activities are available in the greater Atlanta area.

Facilities and Resources

Westwood offers a variety of information and research resources, including on-campus Resource Centers, links to Internet-based information services, and a bookstore at each campus. The Campus Resource Centers offer a library of program-specific materials that have been carefully selected to aid that school's career-focused educational mission. The Education Department at each campus collaborates closely with the campus' Resource Center staff to ensure that materials support the school's hands-on curriculum. Typical learning aids include books, periodicals, and Internet access. A virtual library, providing remote access to several selected databases, is also offered. Staff members are available to assist students during regular library hours and can provide instruction on how to conduct research in the library and online.

Location

Westwood College–Atlanta Midtown's convenient campus location just off I-85 and north of I-20 in midtown Atlanta is in the cultural heart of the city. Metropolitan Atlanta's population is more than 4 million, and the community offers all the entertainment advantages of a large city, including scores of galleries and alternative spaces that exhibit a broad variety of artwork; a ballet and opera; numerous movie houses showing new releases and foreign and classic films; a growing number of theater companies; and many opportunities for rock, jazz, avant-garde music, and outdoor performances. In addition, Atlanta has myriad natural areas and parks, restaurants and coffeehouses of every description, and four professional sports teams. The Arts Center Station of MARTA, Atlanta's clean, safe, and efficient rapid-transit system, is located just around the corner and offers easy access to many points of interest. The Georgia Institute of Technology and the Atlanta College of Design are only blocks away. Atlanta is a city full of life with a job market that values career-ready individuals such as Westwood College graduates.

Admission Requirements

A diploma from an accredited high school or a GED certificate and passing scores on the college entrance exam (or qualifying ACT/SAT scores) are required.

Application and Information

Westwood College–Atlanta Midtown
1100 Spring Street, Suite 102
Atlanta, Georgia 30309
Phone: 404-745-9862
         800-613-4515 (toll-free)
Fax: 404-892-7253
E-mail: info@westwood.edu
Web site: http://www.westwood.edu

WESTWOOD COLLEGE–ATLANTA NORTHLAKE

ATLANTA, GEORGIA

WESTWOOD COLLEGE

The College and Its Mission

Today, the variables that define career success are ever changing. In order to get ahead and stay ahead, students need the right kind of preparation. To prepare for the working world, they need a career-focused education program that teaches the skills employers demand and offers hands-on, practical experience with real-world applications and the right kind of job-placement assistance to help students get started in their new careers.

Students also need a fast-track learning program that shortens the time from education to career, with an academic schedule that fits their lifestyle. They need a high level of student services to help them reach their goals and the right financial package to make it all possible.

All of these are the focus at Westwood College, which operates seventeen campuses, with locations in Anaheim, Upland (Inland Empire), Long Beach, and Los Angeles, California; Atlanta, Georgia; DuPage, O'Hare Airport, River Oaks, and Chicago Loop, Illinois; Denver North, and Denver South, Colorado; Dallas, Fort Worth, and Houston, Texas; and the Washington, D.C., area.

Westwood College offers degree programs in business, design, health care, justice, and technology. Degree programs in high-technology fields are also offered at two aviation campuses, Redstone College of Aviation Technology–Denver and Redstone College of Aviation Technology–Los Angeles.

The Atlanta Northlake campus is a branch of Westwood College–O'Hare Airport and is accredited by the Accrediting Council for Independent Colleges and Schools (ACICS).

Academic Programs

The Atlanta Northlake campus offers degree programs in business administration (with a concentration in sales and marketing), computer-aided design/architectural drafting, computer networking engineering, interior design, and visual communications, to name a few.

Costs

Standard program costs can be found in the Westwood College academic catalog. They can also be accessed through the Web at http://www.westwood.edu/pdf/catalogs/default.asp.

Financial Aid

Tuition assistance is available for those who qualify. Scholarships include the Westwood High School Scholarship Program, in which two scholarships are offered to every high school in the United States. In addition, several loan programs are available.

Student Activities

In addition to on-campus activities, many cultural and recreational activities are available in the greater Atlanta area.

Facilities and Resources

Westwood offers a variety of information and research resources, including on-campus Resource Centers, links to Internet-based information services, and a bookstore at each campus. The Campus Resource Centers offer a library of program-specific materials that have been carefully selected to aid that school's career-focused educational mission. The Education Department at each campus collaborates closely with the campus Resource Center staff members to ensure that materials support the school's hands-on curriculum. Typical learning aids include books, periodicals, and Internet access. A virtual library, providing remote access to several selected databases, is also offered. Staff members are available to assist students during regular library hours and can provide instruction on how to conduct research in the library and online.

Location

Westwood College–Atlanta Northlake's convenient campus location is just off I-285 northeast of downtown Atlanta. Metropolitan Atlanta's population is more than 4 million, and the community offers all the entertainment advantages of a large city, including scores of galleries and alternative spaces that exhibit a broad variety of artwork; a ballet and opera; numerous movie houses showing new releases and foreign and classic films; a growing number of theater companies; and many opportunities for rock, jazz, avant-garde music, and outdoor performances. In addition, Atlanta has myriad natural areas and parks, restaurants and coffee houses of every description, and four professional sports teams. The Arts Center Station of MARTA, Atlanta's clean, safe, and efficient rapid transit system, is located just around the corner and offers easy access to many points of interest. The Georgia Institute of Technology and the Atlanta College of Design are only blocks away. Atlanta is a city full of life with a job market that values career-ready individuals such as Westwood College graduates.

Admission Requirements

A diploma from an accredited high school or a GED certificate and passing scores on the college entrance exam (or qualifying ACT/SAT scores) are required.

Application and Information

Director of Admissions
Westwood College–Atlanta Northlake
2309 Parklake Drive, NE
Atlanta, Georgia 30345
Phone: 404-962-2998
Fax: 770-934-9539
E-mail: info@westwood.edu
Web site: http://www.westwood.edu

WESTWOOD COLLEGE–CHICAGO DUPAGE

WOODRIDGE, ILLINOIS

The College and Its Mission

Today, the variables that define career success are ever changing. In order to get ahead and stay ahead, students need the right kind of preparation. To prepare for the working world, they need a career-focused education program that teaches the skills employers demand and offers hands-on, practical experience with real-world applications and the right kind of job-placement assistance to help students get started in their new careers.

Students also need a fast-track learning program that shortens the time from education to career, with an academic schedule that fits their lifestyle. They need a high level of student services to help them reach their goals and the right financial package to make it all possible.

All of these are the focus at Westwood College, which operates seventeen campuses, with locations in Anaheim, Inland Empire (Upland), Long Beach, and Los Angeles, California; Atlanta, Georgia; Chicago Loop, DuPage, O'Hare Airport, and River Oaks, Illinois; Denver North and Denver South, Colorado; Dallas, Fort Worth, and Houston, Texas; and the Washington, D.C., area.

Westwood College offers degree programs in design, technology, business, justice, and health care. Degree programs in high-technology fields are also offered at two aviation campuses, Redstone College of Aviation Technology–Denver and Redstone College of Aviation Technology–Los Angeles.

The DuPage campus is accredited by the Accrediting Council for Independent Colleges and Schools (ACICS) for Associate of Applied Science and bachelor's degrees.

Academic Programs

The DuPage campus focuses on computer-based technology programs that prepare graduates to take advantage of high-technology career opportunities. Both the faculty and campus have been designed specifically to meet the unique needs of Westwood's students. Degree programs are offered in computer-aided design/architectural drafting, construction management, game art and design, interior design, and visual communications, to name a few.

Costs

Standard program costs can be found in the Westwood College academic catalog or accessed online through http://www.westwood.edu/pdf/catalogs/default.asp.

Financial Aid

Tuition assistance is available for those who qualify. Scholarships include the Westwood High School Scholarship Program, in which two scholarships are offered to every high school in the United States, and the Colorado Undergraduate Merit State Scholarships for Colorado residents. In addition, several loan programs are available.

Student Activities

The greater Chicago area offers many cultural and recreational activities.

Facilities and Resources

The campus occupies 25,000 square feet of classroom, lab, and administrative space.

Location

One of three Westwood campuses in the greater Chicago area, the DuPage campus is located an hour's drive southwest of Chicago in Woodridge, Illinois.

Admission Requirements

A diploma from an accredited four-year high school or a GED certificate is required.

Application and Information

Director of Admissions
Westwood College–Chicago DuPage
7155 Janes Avenue
Woodridge, Illinois 60517-2321
Phone: 630-434-8244
      888-721-7646 (toll-free)
Fax: 630-434-8255
E-mail: info@westwood.edu
Web site: http://www.westwood.edu

Westwood College–Chicago DuPage campus.

WESTWOOD COLLEGE–CHICAGO LOOP

CHICAGO, ILLINOIS

The College and Its Mission

Today, the variables that define career success are ever changing. In order to get ahead and stay ahead, students need the right kind of preparation. To prepare for the working world, they need a career-focused education program that teaches the skills employers demand. The curriculum should include hands-on, practical experience and real-world applications to help graduates get started in their new careers.

Students also need a fast-track learning program that shortens the time from education to career, with an academic schedule that fits their lifestyle. They need a high level of student services to help them reach their goals and the right financial package to make it all possible.

All of these are the focus at Westwood College, which operates seventeen campuses, with locations in Anaheim, Upland (Inland Empire), Long Beach, and Los Angeles, California; Atlanta, Georgia; DuPage, O'Hare Airport, River Oaks, and Chicago Loop, Illinois; Denver North and Denver South, Colorado; Dallas, Fort Worth, and Houston, Texas; and the Washington, D.C., area.

Westwood College offers degree programs in business, design, health care, and technology. Degree programs in high-technology fields are also offered at two aviation campuses, Redstone College of Aviation Technology–Denver and Redstone College of Aviation Technology–Los Angeles.

Westwood College–Chicago Loop is a branch of Westwood College–Los Angeles and is accredited by the Accrediting Council for Independent Colleges and Schools (ACICS).

Academic Programs

At the Westwood College–Chicago Loop campus, the programs are designed to help adults move quickly into the high-technology world of work. Classes provide hands-on skills and career-focused training. Skilled technology workers with fine-tuned critical-thinking skills graduate from Westwood ready to succeed. Westwood College's career development services match students with employers to get graduates started on the right career path.

The Chicago Loop campus offers programs in animation, computer-aided design/architectural drafting, computer network engineering, computer network management, criminal justice, graphic design and multimedia, information systems security, interior design, and visual communications, to name a few.

Costs

Standard program costs can be found in the Westwood College academic catalog. They can also be accessed through the Web at http://www.westwood.edu/pdf/catalogs/default.asp.

Financial Aid

Tuition assistance is available for those who qualify. Scholarships include the Westwood High School Scholarship Program, in which two scholarships are offered to every high school in the United States. In addition, several loan programs are available.

Student Body Profile

Westwood College recruits recent high school graduates, young adults, and working adults who want to acquire new skills to take advantage of growing opportunities in the professional workplace. Students come to Westwood from all across the U.S. and many other countries.

Student Activities

In addition to the many on-campus activities available at Westwood College, the greater Chicago area abounds in cultural and recreational opportunities.

Facilities and Resources

Campus Resource Centers located on each Westwood campus contain a library of program-specific materials, books, and periodicals and Internet access. A virtual library provides remote access to several selected databases and links to Internet-based information that is specific to technology study. The Resource Center also contains the campus bookstore. Resource Center staff members can assist students in navigating all the research materials that are available.

Location

Westwood College's Chicago Loop campus is located on North State Street, in the heart of downtown Chicago, one of the nation's major urban hubs. Students find plenty of diversity and activity in Chicago's Loop area, the hub of central Chicago's shopping, dining, and commerce district. Arts and theater, nightlife, and city activities abound—all within easy access by foot, trolley, or public transit. Chicago is situated on Lake Michigan, providing plenty of outdoor recreational choices as well.

Admission Requirements

Admission requirements include a diploma from an accredited four-year high school or a GED certificate and passing scores on the College placement exam or qualifying SAT/ACT scores.

Application and Information

Director of Admissions
Westwood College–Chicago Loop
17 North State Street, Suite 300
Chicago, Illinois 60602
Phone: 312-739-0850
        800-693-5415 (toll-free)
Fax: 312-739-1004
E-mail: info@westwood.edu
Web site: http://www.westwood.edu

WESTWOOD COLLEGE–
CHICAGO O'HARE AIRPORT
CHICAGO, ILLINOIS

The College and Its Mission

Today, the variables that define career success are ever changing. In order to get ahead and stay ahead, students need the right kind of preparation. To prepare for the working world, students need a programmed, career-focused education that teaches the skills employers demand—that is, hands-on, practical experience with real-world applications and the right kind of job-placement assistance to help them get started in their new career.

Students also need a fast-track learning program that shortens the time from education to career, with an academic schedule that fits their lifestyle. Students need a high level of student services to help them reach their goals and the right financial package to make it all possible.

All of these are the focus at Westwood College, which operates seventeen campuses, with locations in Anaheim, Inland Empire (Upland), Long Beach, and Los Angeles, California; Atlanta, Georgia; Chicago Loop, DuPage, O'Hare Airport, and River Oaks, Illinois; Denver North and Denver South, Colorado; Dallas, Fort Worth, and Houston, Texas; and the Washington, D.C., area.

Westwood College offers degree programs in design, technology, business, justice, and health care. Degree programs in high-technology fields are also offered at two aviation campuses, Redstone College of Aviation Technology–Denver and Redstone College of Aviation Technology–Los Angeles.

The Westwood–O'Hare Airport campus is accredited by the Accrediting Council for Independent Colleges and Schools (ACICS).

Academic Programs

The Westwood College–O'Hare Airport campus focuses on computer-based technology programs that prepare graduates to take advantage of their high-technology career opportunities. Degree programs are offered in computer-aided design/architectural drafting, computer networking engineering, construction management, game software development, and interior design, to name a few.

Costs

Standard program costs can be found in the Westwood College academic catalog or accessed online through http://www.westwood.edu/pdf/catalogs/default.asp.

Financial Aid

Tuition assistance is available for those who qualify. Scholarships include the Westwood High School Scholarship Program, in which two scholarships are offered to every high school in the United States. In addition, several loan programs are available.

Student Activities

In addition to on-campus activities, the greater Chicago area offers many cultural and recreational opportunities.

Facilities and Resources

The campus includes 27,000 square feet of classrooms, labs, and administrative offices. In addition to an on-campus Resource Center, students benefit through cooperation with the suburban Inter-Library Loan Consortium and Illinet.

Location

The campus is located in Schiller Park, close to major highways and O'Hare International Airport.

Admission Requirements

A diploma from an accredited high school or GED certificate is required, as are passing scores on the college entrance exam (or qualifying ACT/SAT scores).

Application and Information

Director of Admissions
Westwood College–Chicago O'Hare Airport
8501 West Higgins Road, Suite 100
Chicago, Illinois 60631
Phone: 847-928-0200
        877-877-8857 (toll-free)
Fax: 847-928-2120
E-mail: info@westwood.edu
Web site: http://www.westwood.edu

Westwood College–Chicago O'Hare Airport campus.

WESTWOOD COLLEGE–CHICAGO RIVER OAKS
CALUMET CITY, ILLINOIS

The College and Its Mission

Today, the variables that define career success are ever changing. In order to get ahead and stay ahead, students need the right kind of preparation. To prepare for the working world, students need a career-focused education program that teaches the skills employers demand and offers hands-on, practical experience with real-world applications and the right kind of job-placement assistance to help them get started in their new careers.

Students also need a fast-track learning program that shortens the time from education to career, with an academic schedule that fits their lifestyle. They need a high level of student services to help them reach their goals and the right financial package to make it all possible.

All of these are the focus at Westwood College, which operates seventeen campuses, with locations in Anaheim, Upland (Inland Empire), Long Beach, and Los Angeles, California; Atlanta, Georgia; DuPage, O'Hare Airport, River Oaks, and Chicago Loop, Illinois; Denver North, and Denver South, Colorado; Dallas, Fort Worth, and Houston, Texas; and the Washington, D.C., area.

Westwood College offers degree programs in business, design, health care, justice, and technology. Degree programs in high-technology fields are also offered at two aviation campuses, Redstone College of Aviation Technology–Denver and Redstone College of Aviation Technology–Los Angeles.

The River Oaks campus is accredited by the Accrediting Council for Independent Colleges and Schools (ACICS).

Westwood College–River Oaks is a branch of Westwood College–Los Angeles.

Academic Programs

The River Oaks Campus focuses on computer-based technology programs that prepare students to take advantage of high-tech careers. Degree programs are offered in animation, computer-aided design/architectural drafting (CAD), computer network engineering, computer network management, e-business management, graphic design and multimedia, and visual communications, to name a few.

Costs

Standard program costs can be found in the Westwood College academic catalog. They can also be accessed through the Web at http://www.westwood.edu/pdf/catalogs/default.asp.

Financial Aid

Tuition assistance is available for those who qualify. Scholarships include the Westwood High School Scholarship Program, through which two scholarships are offered to every high school in the United States; the Colorado Undergraduate Merit State Scholarships for Colorado residents; and several loan programs.

Student Activities

In addition to on-campus activities, many cultural and recreational opportunities are available in the Greater Chicago area.

Facilities and Resources

The campus includes 25,000 square feet of classrooms, labs, and administrative offices. In addition to an on-campus resource center, students benefit from cooperation with the suburban Inter-Library Loan Consortium and Illinet.

Location

The campus is located an hour south of Chicago at 80 River Oaks Center in Calumet City. It is easily reached by several major freeways.

Admission Requirements

A diploma from an accredited high school or a GED certificate and passing scores on the college entrance exam (or qualifying ACT/SAT scores) are required.

Application and Information

Westwood College–Chicago River Oaks
80 River Oaks Drive, Suite D-49
Calumet City, Illinois 60409-5802
Phone: 708-832-1988
        888-549-6873 (toll-free)
Fax: 708-832-9617
E-mail: info@westwood.edu
Web site: http://www.westwood.edu

Westwood College–Chicago River Oaks campus.

WESTWOOD COLLEGE–DALLAS

DALLAS, TEXAS

The College and Its Mission

Today, the variables that define career success are ever changing. In order to get ahead and stay ahead, students need the right kind of preparation. To prepare for the working world, they need a career-focused education program that teaches the skills employers demand. The curriculum should include hands-on, practical experience and real-world applications to help graduates get started in their new career.

Students also need a fast-track learning program that shortens the time from education to career, with an academic schedule that fits their lifestyle. They need a high level of student services to help them reach their goals and the right financial package to make it all possible.

All of these are the focus at Westwood College, which operates seventeen campuses, with locations in Anaheim, Inland Empire (Upland), Long Beach, and Los Angeles, California; Atlanta, Georgia; Chicago Loop, DuPage, O'Hare Airport, and River Oaks, Illinois; Denver North and Denver South, Colorado; Dallas, Fort Worth, and Houston, Texas; and the Washington, D.C., area.

Westwood College offers degree programs in design, technology, and health care. Degree programs in high-technology fields are also offered at two aviation campuses, Redstone College of Aviation Technology–Denver and Redstone College of Aviation Technology–Los Angeles.

Westwood College–Dallas is a branch of Westwood College–O'Hare Airport and is accredited by the Accrediting Council for Independent Colleges and Schools (ACICS).

Academic Programs

At the Westwood College–Dallas campus, the programs are designed to help adults move into the high-tech world of work quickly. Classes provide hands-on skills and career-focused training. Skilled technology workers with fine-tuned critical-thinking skills graduate from Westwood ready to succeed. Westwood College's career development services work to match students with employers to get graduates started on the right career path.

The Dallas campus offers degree programs in computer-aided design/architectural drafting, computer network engineering, graphic design and multimedia, and medical assisting. Degrees from the computer network engineering program are not accepted toward licensure as a professional engineer.

Costs

Standard program costs can be found in the Westwood College academic catalog or accessed online through http://www.westwood.edu/pdf/catalogs/default.asp.

Financial Aid

Tuition assistance is available for those who qualify. Scholarships include the Westwood High School Scholarship Program, in which two scholarships are offered to every high school in the United States. In addition, several loan programs are available.

Student Body Profile

Westwood College recruits recent high school graduates, young adults, and working adults who want to acquire new skills to take advantage of growing opportunities in the professional workplace. Students come to Westwood from all across the U.S. and many other countries.

Student Activities

In addition to the on-campus activities available at the College, the greater Dallas area offers unlimited recreational opportunities for students.

Facilities and Resources

Campus Resource Centers located on each Westwood campus contain a library of program-specific materials, books, and periodicals and Internet access. A virtual library provides remote access to several selected databases and links to Internet-based information that is specific to technology study. The Resource Center also contains the campus bookstore. Resource Center staff members can assist students in navigating all the research materials that are available.

Location

Westwood's Dallas campus is located on LBJ Freeway in the heart of Dallas, Texas. One of the largest cities in the southern United States, Dallas offers a wide range of cultural and recreational activities in an urban setting. A 60-acre arts district is home to theater, dance, music, sculpture, and museums. The city maintains more than 20,000 acres of lake and park space within its borders.

Admission Requirements

Admission requirements include a diploma from an accredited four-year high school or a GED certificate and passing scores on the College placement exam or qualifying SAT or ACT scores.

Application and Information

Admissions Office
Westwood College–Dallas
Executive Center One, Suite 100
8390 LBJ Freeway
Dallas, Texas 75243

Phone: 214-570-0100
       800-803-3140 (toll-free)
Fax: 214-570-8502
E-mail: info@westwood.edu
Web site: http://www.westwood.edu

Westwood College–Dallas campus.

WESTWOOD COLLEGE–DENVER NORTH

DENVER, COLORADO

The College and Its Mission

Today, the variables that define career success are ever changing. In order to get ahead and stay ahead, students need the right kind of preparation. To prepare for the working world, they need a career-focused education program that teaches the skills employers demand and offers hands-on, practical experience with real-world applications and the right kind of job-placement assistance to help students get started in their new careers.

Students also need a fast-track learning program that shortens the time from education to career, with an academic schedule that fits their lifestyle. They need a high level of student services to help them reach their goals and the right financial package to make it all possible.

All of these are the focus at Westwood College, which operates seventeen campuses, with locations in Anaheim, Inland Empire (Upland), Long Beach, and Los Angeles, California; Atlanta, Georgia; Chicago Loop, DuPage, O'Hare Airport, and River Oaks, Illinois; Denver North and Denver South, Colorado; Dallas, Fort Worth, and Houston, Texas; and the Washington, D.C., area.

Westwood College offers degree programs in design, technology, business, justice, health care, and industrial services. Degree programs in high-technology fields are also offered at two aviation campuses, Redstone College of Aviation Technology–Denver and Redstone College of Aviation Technology–Los Angeles.

The Denver North campus is accredited by the Accrediting Commission of Career Schools and Colleges of Technology (ACCSCT).

Academic Programs

Denver North offers the largest variety of Westwood's bachelor's and associate degree programs. The campus, in addition to featuring high-technology opportunities, offers programs in high-demand industrial and medical fields. Degree programs include animation, computer network management, criminal justice, e-business management, game art and design, game software development, information systems security, interior design, visual communications, and Web design and multimedia, to name a few.

Westwood College welcomes students to the exciting world of fashion with the introduction of a new program in fashion merchandising. The Westwood College fashion merchandising degree program gives students exposure to all of the important areas in fashion, with courses that include Apparel Analysis, Trend Forecasting, Consumer Behavior, Retail Management, Retail Buying, Visual Merchandising, and Fashion Product Development. This new program explores all aspects of the clothing industry, such as product buying, retailing, visual merchandising, and promotion. The program is available only at the Denver campuses.

Off-Campus Programs

Many of the College's degree programs are also available online. This offers students the chance to obtain a degree at any time and location through a virtual campus. Students should call 800-992-5050 Ext. 244 (toll-free) for information.

Costs

Standard program costs can be found in the Westwood College academic catalog or accessed online through http://www.westwood.edu/pdf/catalogs/default.asp.

Financial Aid

Tuition assistance is available for those who qualify. Scholarships include the Westwood High School Scholarship Program, through which two scholarships are offered to every high school in the United States; the Colorado Undergraduate Merit State Scholarships for Colorado residents; and several loan programs.

Student Activities

With a diverse population of nearly 2 million and proximity to the Rocky Mountains, Denver offers students a unique opportunity to combine advanced learning with a healthy, active lifestyle. Skiing, snowboarding, mountain climbing, and other outdoor, recreational, and cultural activities abound.

Facilities and Resources

The Denver North campus is the largest of Westwood's campuses and recently underwent a $4-million renovation. The campus provides industry-standard classrooms and labs, providing a completely functional learning environment that complements Westwood's mission.

Location

The campus is located at 7350 North Broadway in Denver, near the intersection of Interstate 25 and the Boulder Turnpike. Students have easy access to the downtown business districts, LoDo cultural activities, and the I-36 High-Tech Corridor.

Admission Requirements

A diploma from an accredited high school or a GED certificate and passing scores on the college placement exam (or qualifying SAT/ACT scores) are required.

Application and Information

Westwood College–Denver North
7350 North Broadway
Denver, Colorado 80221-3653
Phone: 303-426-7000
       800-992-5050 (toll-free)
Fax: 303-487-0214
E-mail: info@westwood.edu
Web site: http://www.westwood.edu

Westwood College–Denver North campus.

WESTWOOD COLLEGE– DENVER SOUTH

DENVER, COLORADO

The College and Its Mission

Today, the variables that define career success are ever changing. In order to get ahead and stay ahead, students need the right kind of preparation. To prepare for the working world, they need a program of career-focused education that teaches the skills employers demand and offers hands-on, practical experience with real-world applications, and the right kind of job-placement assistance to help students get started in their new careers.

Students also need a fast-track learning program that shortens the time from education to career, with an academic schedule that fits their lifestyle. They need a high level of student services to help reach their goals and the right financial package to make it all possible.

All of these are the focus at Westwood College, which operates seventeen campuses, with locations in Anaheim, Upland (Inland Empire), Long Beach, and Los Angeles, California; Atlanta, Georgia; DuPage, O'Hare Airport, River Oaks, and Chicago Loop, Illinois; Denver North and Denver South, Colorado; Dallas, Fort Worth, and Houston, Texas; and the Washington, D.C., area.

Westwood College offers degree programs in business, design, health care, justice, and technology. Degree programs in high-technology fields are also offered at two aviation campuses, Redstone College of Aviation Technology–Denver and Redstone College of Aviation Technology–Los Angeles.

The Denver South campus is accredited by the Accrediting Commission of Career Schools and Colleges of Technology (ACCSCT).

Academic Programs

Denver South concentrates on computer-based high technology. It offers daytime, evening, and weekend class schedules in order to serve as many students as possible. Programs are offered in animation, computer-aided design/architectural drafting (CAD), computer network engineering, criminal justice, e-business management, game art and design, graphic design and multimedia, information systems security, interior design, medical assisting, and visual communications, to name a few.

Costs

Standard program costs can be found in the Westwood College academic catalog. They can also be accessed through the Web at http://www.westwood.edu/pdf/catalogs/default.asp.

Financial Aid

Tuition assistance is available for those who qualify. Scholarships include the Westwood High School Scholarship Program, through which two scholarships are offered to every high school in the United States; the Colorado Undergraduate Merit State Scholarships for Colorado residents; and several loan programs.

Student Activities

With a diverse population of nearly 2 million and proximity to the Rocky Mountains, students have a unique opportunity to combine advanced learning with a healthy, active lifestyle. Skiing, snowboarding, mountain climbing, and other outdoor, recreational, and cultural activities abound.

Facilities and Resources

The campus includes two dedicated buildings totaling more than 30,000 square feet of classrooms, labs, and administrative offices. There is also an annex containing classroom space.

Location

The campus is located at 3150 South Sheridan Boulevard in Denver, at the intersection of South Sheridan Boulevard and Hampden Avenue (Highway 285). It is easily accessible from Lakewood, Englewood, Littleton, and Denver's entire southwest metro area.

Admission Requirements

A diploma from an accredited high school or a GED certificate and passing scores on the college entrance exam (or qualifying ACT/SAT scores) are required.

Application and Information

Westwood College–Denver South
3150 South Sheridan Boulevard
Denver, Colorado 80227-5548

Phone: 303-934-2790
Fax: 303-934-2583
E-mail: info@westwood.edu
Web site: http://www.westwood.edu

Westwood College–Denver South campus.

WESTWOOD COLLEGE–FORT WORTH

FORT WORTH, TEXAS

The College and Its Mission

Today, the variables that define career success are ever changing. In order to get ahead and stay ahead, students need the right kind of preparation. To prepare for the working world, students need a programmed, career-focused education that teaches the skills employers demand—that is, hands-on, practical experience with real-world applications and the right kind of job-placement assistance to help them get started in their new career.

Students also need a fast-track learning program that shortens the time from education to career, with an academic schedule that fits their lifestyle. Students need a high level of student services to help them reach their goals and the right financial package to make it all possible.

All of these are the focus at Westwood College, which operates seventeen campuses, with locations in Anaheim, Inland Empire (Upland), Long Beach, and Los Angeles, California; Atlanta, Georgia; Chicago Loop, DuPage, O'Hare Airport, and River Oaks, Illinois; Denver North and Denver South, Colorado; Dallas, Fort Worth, and Houston, Texas; and the Washington, D.C., area.

Westwood College offers degree programs in design, technology, business, justice, and health care. Degree programs in high-technology fields are also offered at two aviation campuses, Redstone College of Aviation Technology–Denver and Redstone College of Aviation Technology–Los Angeles.

The Fort Worth campus is accredited by the Accrediting Council for Independent Colleges and Schools (ACICS).

Westwood College–Fort Worth is a branch of Westwood College–DuPage (Woodridge, Illinois).

Academic Programs

The Fort Worth campus focuses on computer-based technology programs that prepare graduates to take advantage of the high-technology career opportunities that exist in the Dallas–Fort Worth metroplex. Degree programs are offered in computer-aided design/architectural drafting, computer network engineering, graphic design and multimedia, medical assisting, and medical insurance coding and billing. Degrees from the computer network engineering program are not accepted toward licensure as a professional engineer.

Costs

Standard program costs can be found in the Westwood College academic catalog or accessed online through http://www.westwood.edu/pdf/catalogs/default.asp.

Financial Aid

Tuition assistance is available for those who qualify. Scholarships include the Westwood High School Scholarship Program, in which two scholarships are offered to every high school in the United States. In addition, several loan programs are available.

Student Activities

In addition to on-campus activities, students can take advantage of a vast array of recreational and cultural activities in this dynamic area, which offers a Southwestern flavor.

Facilities and Resources

Westwood College–Fort Worth currently occupies 12,000 square feet of administrative and instructional space. Also available is a Resource Center, with occupation-related reference materials and a number of resources that link students to library assets nationwide.

Location

The Fort Worth campus is located in Fort Worth, Texas.

Admission Requirements

A diploma from an accredited high school or GED certificate and passing scores on the college entrance exam (or qualifying ACT/SAT scores) are required.

Application and Information

Westwood College–Fort Worth
4232 North Freeway
Fort Worth, Texas 76137
Phone: 817-547-9600
       866-533-9997 (toll-free)
Fax: 817-685-8929
E-mail: info@westwood.edu
Web site: http://www.westwood.edu

Westwood College–Fort Worth campus.

WESTWOOD COLLEGE–HOUSTON SOUTH

HOUSTON, TEXAS

The College and Its Mission

Today, the variables that define career success are ever changing. In order to get ahead and stay ahead, students need the right kind of preparation. To prepare for the working world, they need a career-focused education program that teaches the skills employers demand. The curriculum should include hands-on, practical experience and real-world applications to help graduates get started in their new careers.

Students also need a fast-track learning program that shortens the time from education to career, with an academic schedule that fits their lifestyle. They need a high level of student services to help them reach their goals and the right financial package to make it all possible.

All of these are the focus at Westwood College, which operates seventeen campuses, with locations in Anaheim, Inland Empire (Upland), Long Beach, and Los Angeles, California; Atlanta, Georgia; Chicago Loop, DuPage, O'Hare Airport, and River Oaks, Illinois; Denver North and Denver South, Colorado; Dallas, Fort Worth, and Houston, Texas; and the Washington, D.C., area.

Westwood College offers degree programs in design, technology, and health care. Degree programs in high-technology fields are also offered at two aviation campuses, Redstone College of Aviation Technology–Denver and Redstone College of Aviation Technology–Los Angeles.

Westwood College–Houston South is accredited by the Accrediting Commission of Career Schools and Colleges of Technology (ACCSCT) and is a branch of Westwood College–Denver North.

Academic Programs

At the Westwood College–Houston South campus, the programs are designed to help adults move into the high-tech world of work quickly. Classes provide hands-on skills and career-focused training. Skilled technology workers with fine-tuned critical-thinking skills graduate from Westwood ready to succeed. Westwood College's career development services work to match students with employers to get graduates started on the right career path.

The Houston South campus focuses on computer-based programs that prepare graduates to take advantage of the high-tech career opportunities available in Houston. Programs include computer-aided design/architectural drafting, computer network engineering, and graphic design and multimedia. Houston South also offers programs in medical assisting and medical insurance coding and billing.

Costs

Standard program costs can be found in the Westwood College academic catalog or accessed online through http://www.westwood.edu/pdf/catalogs/default.asp.

Financial Aid

Tuition assistance is available for those who qualify. Scholarships include the Westwood High School Scholarship Program, in which two scholarships are offered to every high school in the United States. In addition, several loan programs are available.

Student Activities

In addition to on-campus activities, students can take advantage of the many cultural and recreational activities of the city and surrounding communities.

Facilities and Resources

The Campus Resource Center offers a library of program-specific materials that have been carefully selected to aid that school's career-focused educational mission. Typical learning aids include books, periodicals, and Internet access. A virtual library provides remote access to several selected databases, and staff members are available to assist with research and provide instruction on how to conduct research. Westwood offers tutoring at no charge, and specialized Student Success Workshops help students improve skills in areas such as test taking, time management, resume preparation, and general study skills.

Location

With the campus located in the nation's fourth-largest city, cultural and recreational opportunities abound for students. A cosmopolitan city of many cultures and world-class theater, music, museums, architecture, dance, art, sports, and shopping, Houston also offers nearby beaches, rivers, and outdoor activities.

Admission Requirements

Admission requirements include a diploma from an accredited high school or a GED certificate and passing scores on the College placement exam or qualifying SAT/ACT scores.

Application and Information

Westwood College–Houston South
One Arena Place
7322 Southwest Freeway, Suite 110
Houston, Texas 77074
Phone: 713-777-4433
E-mail: info@westwood.edu
Web site: http://www.westwood.edu

WESTWOOD COLLEGE–INLAND EMPIRE

UPLAND, CALIFORNIA

The College and Its Mission

Today, the variables that define career success are ever changing. In order to get ahead and stay ahead, students need the right kind of preparation. To prepare for the working world, students need a career-focused education program that teaches the skills employers demand and offers hands-on, practical experience with real-world applications, and the right kind of job-placement assistance to help them get started in their new careers.

Students also need a fast-track learning program that shortens the time from education to career, with an academic schedule that fits their lifestyle. They need a high level of student services to help them reach their goals and the right financial package to make it all possible.

All of these are the focus at Westwood College, which operates seventeen campuses, with locations in Anaheim, Upland (Inland Empire), Long Beach, and Los Angeles, California; Atlanta, Georgia; DuPage, O'Hare Airport, River Oaks, and Chicago–Loop, Illinois; Denver–North and Denver–South, Colorado; Dallas, Fort Worth, and Houston, Texas; and the Washington, D.C., area.

Such fields as computer-aided design, computer networking, e-business, and graphic design are featured at the Westwood College campuses located in Anaheim. Westwood College offers degree programs in business, design, justice, and technology. Degree programs in high-technology fields are also offered at two aviation campuses, Redstone College of Aviation Technology–Denver and Redstone College of Aviation Technology–Los Angeles.

The Inland Empire campus is accredited by the Accrediting Commission of Career Schools and Colleges of Technology (ACCSCT).

Westwood College–Inland Empire is a branch of Westwood College–Denver North.

Academic Programs

The Inland Empire campus focuses on computer-based programs that prepare graduates to take advantage of southern California's high-tech career opportunities. Programs include computer network management, criminal justice, e-business management, game art and design, game software development, information systems security, interior design, and visual communications, to name a few.

Costs

Standard program costs can be found in the Westwood College academic catalog. They can also be accessed through the Web at http://www.westwood.edu/pdf/catalogs/default.asp.

Financial Aid

Tuition assistance is available to those students who qualify. Scholarships include the Westwood High School Scholarship Program, which offers two scholarships to every high school in the United States; the Colorado Undergraduate Merit State Scholarships for Colorado residents; and several loan programs.

Student Activities

In addition to on-campus activities, students can take advantage of many outdoor recreational activities. Several minor-league baseball teams play in the area. Many cultural opportunities are available as well.

Facilities and Resources

The campus features an all-new facility that was designed and built specifically for Westwood College. The design, layout, and features of the facility are the product of an extensive research project that evaluated the unique requirements of Westwood's students, faculty, and staff.

Location

The campus is located on the western edge of southern California's Inland Empire, just minutes from the Ontario International Airport. It is easily reached by Interstate 10 and Interstate 15 from surrounding communities such as Covina, Ontario, Pomona, Rancho Cucamonga, Redlands, and San Bernardino.

Admission Requirements

A diploma from an accredited high school or a GED certificate and passing scores on the college entrance exam (or qualifying ACT/SAT scores) are required.

Application and Information

Westwood College–Inland Empire
20 West 7th Street
Upland, California 91786-7148

Phone: 909-931-7550
        866-288-9488 (toll-free)
Fax: 909-931-9195
E-mail: info@westwood.edu
Web site: http://www.westwood.edu

Westwood College–Inland Empire campus.

WESTWOOD COLLEGE–
LOS ANGELES

LOS ANGELES, CALIFORNIA

The College and Its Mission

Today, the variables that define career success are ever changing. In order to get ahead and stay ahead, students need the right kind of preparation. To prepare for the working world, they need a career-focused education program that teaches the skills employers demand and offers hands-on, practical experience with real-world applications, and the right kind of job-placement assistance to help students get started in their new careers.

Students also need a fast-track learning program that shortens the time from education to career, with an academic schedule that fits their lifestyle. They need a high level of student services to help them reach their goals and the right financial package to make it all possible.

All of these are the focus at Westwood College, which operates seventeen campuses, with locations in Anaheim, Upland (Inland Empire), Long Beach, and Los Angeles, California; Atlanta, Georgia; DuPage, O'Hare Airport, River Oaks, and Chicago Loop, Illinois; Denver North and Denver South, Colorado; Dallas, Fort Worth, and Houston, Texas; and the Washington, D.C., area.

Westwood College offers degree programs in business, design, justice, and technology. Degree programs in high-technology fields are also offered at two aviation campuses, Redstone College of Aviation Technology–Denver and Redstone College of Aviation Technology–Los Angeles.

The Los Angeles campus is accredited by the Accrediting Council for Independent Colleges and Schools (ACICS).

Academic Programs

The Los Angeles campus focuses on computer-based technologies that prepare graduates to take advantage of southern California's unique career opportunities. Degree programs offered are animation, computer network engineering, computer network management, criminal justice, game art and design, graphic design and multimedia, information systems security, visual communications, and Web design and multimedia, to name a few.

Costs

Standard program costs can be found in the Westwood College academic catalog. They can also be accessed through the Web at http://www.westwood.edu/pdf/catalogs/default.asp.

Financial Aid

Tuition assistance is available for those who qualify. Scholarships include the Westwood High School Scholarship Program, through which two scholarships are offered to every high school in the United States; the Colorado Undergraduate Merit State Scholarships for Colorado residents; and several loan programs.

Student Activities

The Los Angeles area, given its climate and recreational and cultural diversity, offers unlimited opportunities for students.

Facilities and Resources

The campus includes computer labs, featuring both PC and Macintosh machines running the most popular software applications used throughout industry, to give students the hands-on experience that employers demand. The campus offers both day and evening classes.

Location

The campus is located at 3460 Wilshire Boulevard, Suite 700, in the Central Plaza Complex, just minutes from downtown Los Angeles in an urban environment.

Admission Requirements

A diploma from an accredited high school or a GED certificate as well as passing scores on the college's entrance exam (or qualifying ACT/SAT scores) are required.

Application and Information

Westwood College–Los Angeles
3250 Wilshire Boulevard, Suite 400
Los Angeles, California 90010-2210
Phone: 213-739-9999
       877-377-4600 (toll-free)
Fax: 213-382-2468
E-mail: info@westwood.edu
Web site: http://www.westwood.edu

Westwood College–Los Angeles campus.

WESTWOOD COLLEGE–SOUTH BAY

SOUTH BAY, CALIFORNIA

 WESTWOOD COLLEGE

The College and Its Mission

Today, the variables that define career success are ever changing. In order to get ahead and stay ahead, students need the right kind of preparation. To prepare for the working world, they need a career-focused education program that teaches the skills employers demand. The curriculum should include hands-on, practical experience and real-world applications to help graduates get started in their new careers.

Students also need a fast-track learning program that shortens the time from education to career, with an academic schedule that fits their lifestyle. They need a high level of student services to help them reach their goals and the right financial package to make it all possible.

All of these are the focus at Westwood College, which operates seventeen campuses, with locations in Anaheim, Inland Empire (Upland), South Bay, and Los Angeles, California; Atlanta, Georgia; DuPage, O'Hare Airport, River Oaks, and Chicago–Loop, Illinois; Denver–North and Denver–South, Colorado; Dallas, Fort Worth, and Houston, Texas; and the Washington, D.C., area.

Westwood College offers degree programs in design, technology, and justice. Degree programs in high-technology fields are also offered at two aviation campuses, Redstone College of Aviation Technology–Denver and Redstone College of Aviation Technology–Los Angeles.

Westwood College–South Bay is accredited by the Accrediting Commission of Career Schools and Colleges of Technology (ACCSCT) and has received temporary approval from the Bureau for Private Postsecondary and Vocational Education.

Academic Programs

At the Westwood College–South Bay campus, the programs are designed to help adults move into the high-tech world of work quickly. Classes provide hands-on skills and career-focused training. Skilled technology workers with fine-tuned critical-thinking skills graduate from Westwood ready to succeed. Westwood College's career development services match students with employers to get graduates started on the right career path.

The South Bay campus offers programs in animation, computer-aided design/architectural drafting, computer network engineering, computer network management, criminal justice, graphic design and multimedia, information systems security, and visual communications, to name a few.

Costs

Standard program costs can be found in the Westwood College academic catalog or can be accessed through the Web site, http://www.westwood.edu/pdf/catalogs/default.asp.

Financial Aid

Tuition assistance is available for those who qualify. Scholarships include the Westwood High School Scholarship Program, in which two scholarships are offered to every high school in the United States. In addition, several loan programs are available.

Student Body Profile

Westwood College recruits recent high school graduates, young adults, and working adults who want to acquire new skills to take advantage of growing opportunities in the professional workplace. Students come to Westwood from all across the U.S. and many other countries.

Student Activities

In addition to the many on-campus activities available at Westwood College, the greater South Bay area abounds in cultural and recreational opportunities.

Facilities and Resources

Campus Resource Centers located on each Westwood campus contain a library of program-specific materials, books, and periodicals and Internet access. A virtual library provides remote access to several selected databases and links to Internet-based information that is specific to technology study. The Resource Center also contains the campus bookstore. Resource Center staff members can assist students in navigating all the research materials that are available.

Location

South Bay is located in southern California, on the Pacific coast. Outstanding cultural arts and music festivals, plus a short boat ride to Catalina Island and gorgeous weather year-round make South Bay a paradise. Shopping, dining, sporting events, endless beaches, and an array of cultural diversity and nightlife make South Bay a terrific place to begin a visitor's California adventure. Nearby Los Angeles as well as the many diverse towns and cities along the edge of the Pacific Ocean supply visitors with limitless opportunities for recreation, culture, and arts.

Admission Requirements

Admission requirements include a diploma from an accredited four-year high school or a GED certificate and passing scores on the College placement exam or qualifying SAT or ACT scores.

Application and Information

Westwood College–South Bay Campus
19700 South Vermont Avenue #100
Torrance, California 90502

Phone: 310-965-0888
Fax: 310-965-0881
E-mail: info@westwood.edu
Web site: http://www.westwood.edu

Westwood College–South Bay campus.

Appendix

2006–07 Changes in Institutions

Following is an alphabetical listing of institutions that have recently closed, merged with other institutions, or changed their name or status. In the case of a name change, the former name appears first, followed by the new name.

Aakers Business College (Fargo, ND): name changed to Aakers College.

Albuquerque Technical Vocational Institute (Albuquerque, NM): name changed to Central New Mexico Community College.

Bessemer State Technical College (Bessemer, AL): closed.

Blair College (Colorado Springs, CO): name changed to Everest College.

Blue River Community College (Independence, MO): name changed to Metropolitan Community College–Blue River.

Bryman College (New Orleans, LA): closed.

Bryman College (San Bernardino, CA): closed.

Butler County Community College (El Dorado, KS): name changed to Butler Community College.

Career Colleges of Chicago (Chicago, IL): closed.

Central Kentucky Technical College (Lexington, KY): closed.

Colorado Mountain College, Spring Valley Campus (Glenwood Springs, CO): name changed to Colorado Mountain College.

Community and Technical College of Shepherd (Martinsburg, WV): name changed to Blue Ridge Community and Technical College.

Compton Community College (Compton, CA): closed.

Cosumnes River College (Sacramento, CA): closed.

Duff's Business Institute (Pittsburgh, PA): name changed to Everest Institute.

Education Direct Center for Degree Studies (Scranton, PA): name changed to Penn Foster Career School.

Fairmont State Community & Technical College (Fairmont, WV): name changed to Pierpont Community and Technical College of Fairmont State University.

Gadsden State Community College-Ayers Campus (Anniston, AL): closed.

ICM School of Business & Medical Careers (Pittsburgh, PA): name changed to Kaplan Career Institute–ICM Campus.

International Institute of the Americas (Phoenix, AZ): closed.

Keiser College (Daytona Beach, FL): name changed to Keiser University.

Keiser College (Lakeland, FL): name changed to Keiser University.

Keiser College (Melbourne, FL): name changed to Keiser University.

Keiser College (Miami, FL): name changed to Keiser University.

Keiser College (Orlando, FL): name changed to Keiser University.

Keiser College (Pembroke Pines, FL): name changed to Keiser University.

Keiser College (Port St. Lucie, FL): name changed to Keiser University.

Keiser College (Sarasota, FL): name changed to Keiser University.

Keiser College (Tallahassee, FL): name changed to Keiser University.

Keiser College (West Palm Beach, FL): name changed to Keiser University.

Longview Community College (Lee's Summit, MO): name changed to Metropolitan Community College–Longview.

Maple Woods Community College (Kansas City, MO): name changed to Metropolitan Community College–Maple Woods.

Mountain West College (West Valley City, UT): name changed to Everest College.

MTI College of Business and Technology (Houston, TX): closed.

National College of Business & Technology (Bluefield, VA): name changed to National College.

National College of Business & Technology (Bristol, TN): name changed to National College.

National College of Business & Technology (Charlottesville, VA): name changed to National College.

National College of Business & Technology (Danville, KY): name changed to National College.

National College of Business & Technology (Danville, VA): name changed to National College.

National College of Business & Technology (Florence, KY): name changed to National College.

National College of Business & Technology (Harrisonburg, VA): name changed to National College.

National College of Business & Technology (Knoxville, TN): name changed to National College.

National College of Business & Technology (Lexington, KY): name changed to National College.

National College of Business & Technology (Louisville, KY): name changed to National College.

National College of Business & Technology (Lynchburg, VA): name changed to National College.

National College of Business & Technology (Martinsville, VA): name changed to National College.

National College of Business & Technology (Nashville, TN): name changed to National College.

National College of Business & Technology (Pikeville, KY): name changed to National College.

National College of Business & Technology (Richmond, KY): name changed to National College.

National College of Business & Technology (Salem, VA): name changed to National College.

Northern New Mexico Community College (Española, NM): name changed to Northern New Mexico College.

Northwestern Technical College (Sacramento, CA): name changed to Bryan College.

Parks College (Aurora, CO): name changed to Everest College.

Parks College (Denver, CO): name changed to Everest College.

Parks College (Arlington, VA): name changed to Everest College.

Penn Valley Community College (Kansas City, MO): name changed to Metropolitan Community College–Penn Valley.

The Pennsylvania State University Beaver Campus of the Commonwealth College (Monaca, PA): name changed to Penn State Beaver.

The Pennsylvania State University Delaware County Campus of the Commonwealth College (Media, PA): name changed to Penn State Delaware County.

The Pennsylvania State University DuBois Campus of the Commonwealth College (DuBois, PA): name changed to Penn State DuBois.

The Pennsylvania State University Fayette Campus of the Commonwealth College (Uniontown, PA): name changed to Penn State Fayette, The Eberly Campus.

The Pennsylvania State University Hazleton Campus of the Commonwealth College (Hazleton, PA): name changed to Penn State Hazleton.

The Pennsylvania State University, Lehigh Valley Campus of the Berks-Lehigh Valley College (Fogelsville, PA): name changed to Penn State Lehigh Valley.

The Pennsylvania State University McKeesport Campus of the Commonwealth College (McKeesport, PA): name changed to Penn State McKeesport.

The Pennsylvania State University Mont Alto Campus of the Commonwealth College (Mont Alto, PA): name changed to Penn State Mont Alto.

The Pennsylvania State University New Kensington Campus of the Commonwealth College (New Kensington, PA): name changed to Penn State New Kensington.

The Pennsylvania State University Schuylkill Campus of the Capital College (Schuylkill Haven, PA): name changed to Penn State Schuylkill.

The Pennsylvania State University Shenango Campus of the Commonwealth College (Sharon, PA): name changed to Penn State Shenango.

The Pennsylvania State University Wilkes-Barre Campus of the Commonwealth College (Lehman, PA): name changed to Penn State Wilkes-Barre.

The Pennsylvania State University Worthington Scranton Campus of the Commonwealth College (Dunmore, PA): name changed to Penn State Worthington Scranton.

The Pennsylvania State University York Campus of the Commonwealth College (York, PA): name changed to Penn State York.

Professional Careers Institute (Indianapolis, IN): name changed to Kaplan College–Indianapolis.

Rasmussen College Minnetonka (Minnetonka, MN): name changed to Rasmussen College Eden Prairie.

Saint Joseph's Hospital Health Center School of Nursing (Syracuse, NY): name changed to St. Joseph's College of Nursing.

Sanford-Brown College (North Kansas City, MO): name changed to Colorado Technical University - North Kansas City.

South Central Technical College (North Mankato, MN): name changed to South Central College.

Springfield College (Springfield, MO): name changed to Everest College.

Technological College of San Juan (San Juan, PR): name changed to Colegio Universitario de San Juan.

Thompson Institute (Harrisburg, PA): name changed to Kaplan Career Institute–Harrisburg.

VC Tech (Pelham, AL): closed.

Western Business College (Portland, OR): name changed to Everest College.

Western Business College (Vancouver, WA): name changed to Everest College.

Western Wisconsin Technical College (La Crosse, WI): name changed to Western Technical College.

William Rainey Harper College (Palatine, IL): name changed to Harper College.

York Technical Institute (York, PA): name changed to YTI Career Institute–York.

Indexes

Associate Degree Programs at Two-Year Colleges

Accounting

Academy Coll (MN)
AIB Coll of Business (IA)
Aims Comm Coll (CO)
Albany Tech Coll (GA)
Alexandria Tech Coll (MN)
Allen County Comm
  Coll (KS)
Alpena Comm Coll (MI)
Amarillo Coll (TX)
Angelina Coll (TX)
Anne Arundel Comm
  Coll (MD)
Anoka-Ramsey Comm
  Coll (MN)
Anoka-Ramsey Comm
  Coll, Cambridge
  Campus (MN)
Appalachian Tech
  Coll (GA)
Ashland Comm and Tech
  Coll (KY)
Asnuntuck Comm
  Coll (CT)
Athens Tech Coll (GA)
Atlanta Tech Coll (GA)
Augusta Tech Coll (GA)
Bainbridge Coll (GA)
Bakersfield Coll (CA)
Baltimore City Comm
  Coll (MD)
Barstow Coll (CA)
Barton County Comm
  Coll (KS)
Beaufort County Comm
  Coll (NC)
Bergen Comm Coll (NJ)
Berkeley City Coll (CA)
Berkeley Coll, West
  Paterson (NJ)
Berkeley Coll-New York
  City Campus (NY)
Berkeley Coll-Westchester
  Campus (NY)
Black Hawk Coll,
  Moline (IL)
Blinn Coll (TX)
Bradford School (PA)
Bramson ORT Coll (NY)
Brevard Comm Coll (FL)
Briarwood Coll (CT)
Brigham Young U –
  Idaho (ID)
Brookhaven Coll (TX)
Broward Comm Coll (FL)
Bucks County Comm
  Coll (PA)
Burlington County
  Coll (NJ)
Cabrillo Coll (CA)
Caldwell Comm Coll and
  Tech Inst (NC)
Calhoun Comm Coll (AL)
Cambria-Rowe Business
  Coll, Johnstown (PA)
Cankdeska Cikana Comm
  Coll (ND)
Cañada Coll (CA)
Cape Cod Comm
  Coll (MA)
Capital Comm Coll (CT)
Carroll Comm Coll (MD)
Cecil Comm Coll (MD)
Cedar Valley Coll (TX)
Central Arizona Coll (AZ)
Central Carolina Comm
  Coll (NC)
Central Carolina Tech
  Coll (SC)
Central Comm Coll–
  Columbus
  Campus (NE)
Central Comm Coll–Grand
  Island Campus (NE)

Central Comm Coll–
  Hastings Campus (NE)
Central Georgia Tech
  Coll (GA)
Central Lakes Coll (MN)
Central Maine Comm
  Coll (ME)
Central New Mexico
  Comm Coll (NM)
Central Ohio Tech
  Coll (OH)
Central Oregon Comm
  Coll (OR)
Central Piedmont Comm
  Coll (NC)
Central Virginia Comm
  Coll (VA)
Central Wyoming
  Coll (WY)
Century Coll (MN)
Cerritos Coll (CA)
Chaffey Coll (CA)
Chandler-Gilbert Comm
  Coll (AZ)
Chattahoochee Tech
  Coll (GA)
Chattanooga State Tech
  Comm Coll (TN)
Chesapeake Coll (MD)
Chipola Coll (FL)
Chippewa Valley Tech
  Coll (WI)
Cincinnati State Tech and
  Comm Coll (OH)
Cisco Jr Coll (TX)
City Coll, Fort
  Lauderdale (FL)
City Coll, Gainesville (FL)
City Coll, Miami (FL)
City Coll of San
  Francisco (CA)
City Colls of Chicago,
  Harold Washington
  College (IL)
City Colls of Chicago,
  Harry S. Truman
  College (IL)
City Colls of Chicago,
  Kennedy-King
  College (IL)
City Colls of Chicago,
  Olive-Harvey
  College (IL)
City Colls of Chicago,
  Richard J. Daley
  College (IL)
City Colls of Chicago,
  Wilbur Wright
  College (IL)
Clackamas Comm
  Coll (OR)
Clarendon Coll (TX)
Clark State Comm
  Coll (OH)
Clatsop Comm Coll (OR)
Cleveland Comm Coll (NC)
Clovis Comm Coll (NM)
Coahoma Comm Coll (MS)
Coastal Bend Coll (TX)
Coastal Carolina Comm
  Coll (NC)
Coconino Comm Coll (AZ)
Colby Comm Coll (KS)
Colegio Universitario de
  San Juan, San
  Juan (PR)
Colegio Universitario de
  San Juan, San
  Juan (PR)
CollAmerica–Colorado
  Springs (CO)
CollAmerica–Denver (CO)
Coll of Alameda (CA)
Coll of DuPage (IL)

Coll of Marin (CA)
Coll of Micronesia–
  FSM (FM)
Coll of San Mateo (CA)
Coll of Southern Idaho (ID)
Coll of Southern
  Maryland (MD)
Coll of the Canyons (CA)
Coll of the Siskiyous (CA)
Colorado Mountain
  Coll (CO)
Colorado Mountain Coll,
  Alpine Campus (CO)
Colorado Mountain Coll,
  Timberline
  Campus (CO)
Columbia-Greene Comm
  Coll (NY)
Columbus Tech Coll (GA)
Commonwealth Tech
  Inst (PA)
Comm Coll of Beaver
  County (PA)
Comm Coll of
  Philadelphia (PA)
Comm Coll of Rhode
  Island (RI)
Comm Coll of Southern
  Nevada (NV)
Comm Coll of
  Vermont (VT)
Coosa Valley Tech
  Coll (GA)
Cosumnes River Coll,
  Sacramento (CA)
Crafton Hills Coll (CA)
Cuyahoga Comm
  Coll (OH)
Cypress Coll (CA)
Danville Comm Coll (VA)
Davidson County Comm
  Coll (NC)
De Anza Coll (CA)
DeKalb Tech Coll (GA)
Delta School of Business
  & Technology (LA)
Dixie State Coll of
  Utah (UT)
Dodge City Comm
  Coll (KS)
Draughons Jr Coll (KY)
East Central Coll (MO)
ECPI Coll of
  Technology (VA)
ECPI Tech Coll (VA)
ECPI Tech Coll (VA)
Elaine P. Nunez Comm
  Coll (LA)
El Camino Coll (CA)
El Centro Coll (TX)
Elgin Comm Coll (IL)
Elmira Business Inst (NY)
Essex County Coll (NJ)
Eugenio María de Hostos
  Comm Coll of the City
  U of New York (NY)
Everest Coll, Phoenix (AZ)
Everest Coll,
  Springfield (MO)
Everest Coll (OR)
Everett Comm Coll (WA)
Fayetteville Tech Comm
  Coll (NC)
Finger Lakes Comm
  Coll (NY)
Fiorello H. LaGuardia
  Comm Coll of the City
  U of New York (NY)
Fisher Coll (MA)
Flint River Tech Coll (GA)
Florence-Darlington Tech
  Coll (SC)
Florida National Coll (FL)
Folsom Lake Coll (CA)

Foothill Coll (CA)
Forrest Jr Coll (SC)
Forsyth Tech Comm
  Coll (NC)
Fort Berthold Comm
  Coll (ND)
Fox Valley Tech Coll (WI)
Frederick Comm Coll (MD)
Front Range Comm
  Coll (CO)
Fullerton Coll (CA)
Fulton-Montgomery Comm
  Coll (NY)
Gateway Comm Coll (CT)
Gateway Tech Coll (WI)
Genesee Comm Coll (NY)
George C. Wallace Comm
  Coll (AL)
Georgia Highlands
  Coll (GA)
Gloucester County
  Coll (NJ)
Golden West Coll (CA)
Grayson County Coll (TX)
Greenville Tech Coll (SC)
Griffin Tech Coll (GA)
Grossmont Coll (CA)
Guilford Tech Comm
  Coll (NC)
Gwinnett Tech Coll (GA)
Harper Coll (IL)
Harrisburg Area Comm
  Coll (PA)
Hawkeye Comm Coll (IA)
Henry Ford Comm
  Coll (MI)
Hesser Coll (NH)
Hillsborough Comm
  Coll (FL)
Hocking Coll (OH)
Holyoke Comm Coll (MA)
Housatonic Comm
  Coll (CT)
Houston Comm Coll
  System (TX)
Howard Comm Coll (MD)
Illinois Eastern Comm
  Colls, Olney Central
  College (IL)
Illinois Valley Comm
  Coll (IL)
Imperial Valley Coll (CA)
Indiana Business Coll,
  Anderson (IN)
Indiana Business Coll,
  Columbus (IN)
Indiana Business Coll,
  Evansville (IN)
Indiana Business Coll, Fort
  Wayne (IN)
Indiana Business Coll,
  Indianapolis (IN)
Indiana Business Coll,
  Lafayette (IN)
Indiana Business Coll,
  Marion (IN)
Indiana Business Coll,
  Muncie (IN)
Indiana Business Coll,
  Terre Haute (IN)
International Business Coll,
  Fort Wayne (IN)
International Inst of the
  Americas, Mesa (AZ)
International Inst of the
  Americas, Phoenix (AZ)
International Inst of the
  Americas, Tucson (AZ)
International Inst of the
  Americas (NM)
Inver Hills Comm
  Coll (MN)
Iowa Lakes Comm
  Coll (IA)

Irvine Valley Coll (CA)
Itasca Comm Coll (MN)
James Sprunt Comm
  Coll (NC)
Jamestown Comm
  Coll (NY)
Jefferson Comm and Tech
  Coll (KY)
Jefferson Comm Coll (OH)
J. F. Drake State Tech
  Coll (AL)
John Wood Comm Coll (IL)
Joliet Jr Coll (IL)
Jones County Jr Coll (MS)
Kankakee Comm Coll (IL)
Kaplan U (IA)
Keiser U, Miami (FL)
Kellogg Comm Coll (MI)
Kennebec Valley Comm
  Coll (ME)
Kent State U, Ashtabula
  Campus (OH)
Kent State U, East
  Liverpool Campus (OH)
Kent State U, Tuscarawas
  Campus (OH)
Keystone Coll (PA)
Kilian Comm Coll (SD)
Kingsborough Comm Coll
  of the City U of New
  York (NY)
King's Coll (NC)
Kirkwood Comm Coll (IA)
Kirtland Comm Coll (MI)
Labette Comm Coll (KS)
Lakeshore Tech Coll (WI)
Lake Tahoe Comm
  Coll (CA)
Lamar Comm Coll (CO)
Laney Coll (CA)
Lanier Tech Coll (GA)
Lansing Comm Coll (MI)
Laramie County Comm
  Coll (WY)
Las Positas Coll (CA)
Lassen Comm Coll
  District (CA)
Laurel Business Inst (PA)
Lawson State Comm
  Coll (AL)
LDS Business Coll (UT)
Leeward Comm Coll (HI)
Lehigh Carbon Comm
  Coll (PA)
Lehigh Valley Coll (PA)
Lenoir Comm Coll (NC)
Lewis Coll of
  Business (MI)
Linn-Benton Comm
  Coll (OR)
Long Island Business
  Inst (NY)
Lorain County Comm
  Coll (OH)
Los Angeles City Coll (CA)
Los Angeles Harbor
  Coll (CA)
Los Angeles Mission
  Coll (CA)
Los Angeles Pierce
  Coll (CA)
Los Angeles Southwest
  Coll (CA)
Los Medanos Coll (CA)
Lower Columbia Coll (WA)
Macomb Comm Coll (MI)
Madison Area Tech
  Coll (WI)
Madisonville Comm
  Coll (KY)
Manatee Comm Coll (FL)
Marian Court Coll (MA)
Martin Comm Coll (NC)

Massachusetts Bay Comm
  Coll (MA)
Massasoit Comm
  Coll (MA)
Maui Comm Coll (HI)
McLennan Comm
  Coll (TX)
Mendocino Coll (CA)
Merced Coll (CA)
Mesa Comm Coll (AZ)
Metropolitan Comm
  Coll (NE)
Metropolitan Comm
  Coll–Business &
  Technology
  Campus (MO)
Metropolitan Comm
  Coll–Longview (MO)
Metropolitan Comm
  Coll–Maple
  Woods (MO)
Metropolitan Comm
  Coll–Penn Valley (MO)
Miami U–Middletown
  Campus (OH)
Middle Georgia Tech
  Coll (GA)
Middlesex Comm Coll (CT)
Midlands Tech Coll (SC)
Mid-State Tech Coll (WI)
Miller-Motte Tech Coll,
  Clarksville (TN)
Minnesota School of
  Business–Brooklyn
  Center (MN)
Minnesota School of
  Business–Plymouth (MN)
Minnesota School of
  Business–Richfield (MN)
Minnesota School of
  Business–St.
  Cloud (MN)
Minnesota School of
  Business–Shakopee (MN)
Minnesota State Coll–
  Southeast Tech (MN)
Minnesota State Comm
  and Tech Coll–Fergus
  Falls (MN)
Mission Coll (CA)
Mississippi Delta Comm
  Coll (MS)
Mississippi Gulf Coast
  Comm Coll (MS)
Missouri State U–West
  Plains (MO)
Mohave Comm Coll (AZ)
Monroe Comm Coll (NY)
Montcalm Comm Coll (MI)
Monterey Peninsula
  Coll (CA)
Montgomery County
  Comm Coll (PA)
Moorpark Coll (CA)
Morgan Comm Coll (CO)
Morton Coll (IL)
Moultrie Tech Coll (GA)
Mt. Hood Comm Coll (OR)
Mt. San Antonio Coll (CA)
Mount Wachusett Comm
  Coll (MA)
Muscatine Comm Coll (IA)
Muskegon Comm Coll (MI)
Napa Valley Coll (CA)
Nassau Comm Coll (NY)
National American U,
  Bloomington (MN)
National American U, Rio
  Rancho (NM)
National Park Comm
  Coll (AR)
Naugatuck Valley Comm
  Coll (CT)
Navarro Coll (TX)

Neosho County Comm Coll (KS)
New Hampshire Comm Tech Coll, Manchester/ Stratham (NH)
New Hampshire Comm Tech Coll, Nashua/ Claremont (NH)
New Hampshire Tech Inst (NH)
New Mexico Jr Coll (NM)
New Mexico Military Inst (NM)
New River Comm Coll (VA)
New York City Coll of Technology of the City U of New York (NY)
Niagara County Comm Coll (NY)
Nicolet Area Tech Coll (WI)
North Central Michigan Coll (MI)
North Central Missouri Coll (MO)
Northeast Comm Coll (NE)
Northeastern Jr Coll (CO)
Northeastern Tech Coll (SC)
Northeast Iowa Comm Coll (IA)
Northeast State Tech Comm Coll (TN)
Northern Essex Comm Coll (MA)
Northern Maine Comm Coll (ME)
Northern Marianas Coll (MP)
Northern Oklahoma Coll (OK)
North Hennepin Comm Coll (MN)
North Iowa Area Comm Coll (IA)
North Lake Coll (TX)
Northland Comm and Tech Coll–Thief River Falls (MN)
North Metro Tech Coll (GA)
North Shore Comm Coll (MA)
NorthWest Arkansas Comm Coll (AR)
Northwestern Connecticut Comm Coll (CT)
Northwestern Tech Coll (GA)
Northwest Iowa Comm Coll (IA)
Northwest Mississippi Comm Coll (MS)
Northwest-Shoals Comm Coll (AL)
Oakland Comm Coll (MI)
Odessa Coll (TX)
Ogeechee Tech Coll (GA)
Ohlone Coll (CA)
Oklahoma City Comm Coll (OK)
Oklahoma State U, Oklahoma City (OK)
Oklahoma State U, Okmulgee (OK)
Onondaga Comm Coll (NY)
Orange Coast Coll (CA)
Ouachita Tech Coll (AR)
Oxnard Coll (CA)
Ozarks Tech Comm Coll (MO)
Pace Inst (PA)
Palau Comm Coll (Palau)
Palm Beach Comm Coll (FL)
Pamlico Comm Coll (NC)
Paradise Valley Comm Coll (AZ)
Pasadena City Coll (CA)
Passaic County Comm Coll (NJ)
Peninsula Coll (WA)
Pennsylvania Highland Comm Coll (PA)
Piedmont Tech Coll (SC)
Piedmont Virginia Comm Coll (VA)
Pierce Coll (WA)
Pima Comm Coll (AZ)
Pioneer Pacific Coll, Wilsonville (OR)
The PJA School (PA)
Potomac State Coll of West Virginia U (WV)
Pueblo Comm Coll (CO)
Queensborough Comm Coll of the City U of New York (NY)
Quincy Coll (MA)

Quinebaug Valley Comm Coll (CT)
Rappahannock Comm Coll (VA)
Raritan Valley Comm Coll (NJ)
Rasmussen Coll Brooklyn Park (MN)
Red Rocks Comm Coll (CO)
Reedley Coll (CA)
Renton Tech Coll (WA)
Richland Coll (TX)
Richland Comm Coll (IL)
Ridgewater Coll (MN)
Roane State Comm Coll (TN)
Rockford Business Coll (IL)
Rose State Coll (OK)
Roxbury Comm Coll (MA)
Sacramento City Coll (CA)
St. Catharine Coll (KY)
Saint Charles Comm Coll (MO)
St. Cloud Tech Coll (MN)
St. Louis Comm Coll at Florissant Valley (MO)
Saint Paul Coll–A Comm & Tech College (MN)
St. Philip's Coll (TX)
Salt Lake Comm Coll (UT)
Sampson Comm Coll (NC)
San Bernardino Valley Coll (CA)
Sandersville Tech Coll (GA)
Sandhills Comm Coll (NC)
San Diego City Coll (CA)
San Joaquin Delta Coll (CA)
Santa Ana Coll (CA)
Santa Barbara City Coll (CA)
Santiago Canyon Coll (CA)
Savannah Tech Coll (GA)
Schoolcraft Coll (MI)
Scott Comm Coll (IA)
Scottsdale Comm Coll (AZ)
Seminole Comm Coll (FL)
Seminole State Coll (OK)
Shasta Coll (CA)
Skagit Valley Coll (WA)
Southeastern Business Coll, Jackson (OH)
Southeastern Business Coll, New Boston (OH)
Southeastern Comm Coll, North Campus (IA)
Southeastern Tech Coll (GA)
Southeast Tech Inst (SD)
Southern U at Shreveport (LA)
South Florida Comm Coll (FL)
South Georgia Coll (GA)
South Georgia Tech Coll (GA)
South Plains Coll (TX)
South Seattle Comm Coll (WA)
South Texas Coll (TX)
Southwestern Comm Coll (NC)
Southwestern Indian Polytechnic Inst (NM)
Southwest Georgia Tech Coll (GA)
Southwest Mississippi Comm Coll (MS)
Southwest Virginia Comm Coll (VA)
Spencerian Coll (KY)
Springfield Tech Comm Coll (MA)
Stark State Coll of Technology (OH)
State Fair Comm Coll (MO)
State U of New York Coll of Agriculture and Technology at Morrisville (NY)
State U of New York Coll of Technology at Alfred (NY)
State U of New York Coll of Technology at Canton (NY)
Suffolk County Comm Coll (NY)
Surry Comm Coll (NC)
Sussex County Comm Coll (NJ)
Swainsboro Tech Coll (GA)
Taft Coll (CA)

Technology Education Coll (OH)
Terra State Comm Coll (OH)
Three Rivers Comm Coll (CT)
Three Rivers Comm Coll (MO)
Tidewater Comm Coll (VA)
Tomball Coll (TX)
Tompkins Cortland Comm Coll (NY)
Tri-County Comm Coll (NC)
Trident Tech Coll (SC)
Trinidad State Jr Coll (CO)
Tri-State Business Inst (PA)
Trumbull Business Coll (OH)
Tulsa Comm Coll (OK)
Tunxis Comm Coll (CT)
Tyler Jr Coll (TX)
Ulster County Comm Coll (NY)
Umpqua Comm Coll (OR)
The U of Akron–Wayne Coll (OH)
U of Cincinnati Clermont Coll (OH)
U of New Mexico–Gallup (NM)
U of New Mexico–Los Alamos Branch (NM)
U of Pittsburgh at Titusville (PA)
Valdosta Tech Coll (GA)
Valencia Comm Coll (FL)
Ventura Coll (CA)
Vernon Coll (TX)
Victoria Coll (TX)
Vincennes U Jasper Campus (IN)
Virginia Coll at Austin (TX)
Virginia Highlands Comm Coll (VA)
Virginia Western Comm Coll (VA)
Wallace State Comm Coll (AL)
Warren County Comm Coll (NJ)
Washington State Comm Coll (OH)
Waukesha County Tech Coll (WI)
Wenatchee Valley Coll (WA)
West Central Tech Coll (GA)
Westchester Comm Coll (NY)
Western Nevada Comm Coll (NV)
Western Piedmont Comm Coll (NC)
Western Texas Coll (TX)
Western Wyoming Comm Coll (WY)
West Georgia Tech Coll (GA)
West Hills Comm Coll (CA)
West Los Angeles Coll (CA)
Westmoreland County Comm Coll (PA)
West Shore Comm Coll (MI)
West Valley Coll (CA)
West Virginia State Comm and Tech Coll (WV)
West Virginia U at Parkersburg (WV)
Wilson Tech Comm Coll (NC)
Wright State U, Lake Campus (OH)
Wytheville Comm Coll (VA)
York County Comm Coll (ME)
York Tech Coll (SC)
Yuba Coll (CA)
Zane State Coll (OH)

Accounting and Business/Management
International Jr Coll (PR)
LDS Business Coll (UT)
Mountain State Coll (WV)
The PJA School (PA)

Accounting Related
ICPR Jr Coll–Hato Rey Campus (PR)

Accounting Technology and Bookkeeping
Alamance Comm Coll (NC)

Allegany Coll of Maryland (MD)
Antonelli Coll, Hattiesburg (MS)
Asheville-Buncombe Tech Comm Coll (NC)
Big Bend Comm Coll (WA)
Bishop State Comm Coll (AL)
Bowling Green State U–Firelands Coll (OH)
Broome Comm Coll (NY)
Brown Mackie Coll–Akron (OH)
Brown Mackie Coll–Atlanta (GA)
Brown Mackie Coll–Cincinnati (OH)
Brown Mackie Coll–Findlay (OH)
Brown Mackie Coll–Fort Wayne (IN)
Brown Mackie Coll–Hopkinsville (KY)
Brown Mackie Coll–Kansas City (KS)
Brown Mackie Coll–Louisville (KY)
Brown Mackie Coll–Merrillville (IN)
Brown Mackie Coll–Miami (FL)
Brown Mackie Coll–North Canton (OH)
Brown Mackie Coll–Northern Kentucky (KY)
Brown Mackie Coll–Salina (KS)
Brown Mackie Coll–South Bend (IN)
Cape Fear Comm Coll (NC)
Catawba Valley Comm Coll (NC)
Central Florida Comm Coll (FL)
Central Wyoming Coll (WY)
Clark Coll (WA)
Coll of Lake County (IL)
Coll of the Mainland (TX)
Comm Coll of Allegheny County (PA)
Elgin Comm Coll (IL)
Essex County Coll (NJ)
Gloucester County Coll (NJ)
Grays Harbor Coll (WA)
Hagerstown Comm Coll (MD)
H. Councill Trenholm State Tech Coll (AL)
Iowa Lakes Comm Coll (IA)
ITT Tech Inst, Dayton (OH)
ITT Tech Inst, Hilliard (OH)
ITT Tech Inst, Norwood (OH)
ITT Tech Inst, Strongsville (OH)
ITT Tech Inst, Youngstown (OH)
ITT Tech Inst, Austin (TX)
ITT Tech Inst, San Antonio (TX)
Johnston Comm Coll (NC)
John Wood Comm Coll (IL)
Kellogg Comm Coll (MI)
Kent State U, Geauga Campus (OH)
Klamath Comm Coll (OR)
Lake Land Coll (IL)
Lamar Inst of Technology (TX)
LDS Business Coll (UT)
Lee Coll (TX)
Lehigh Carbon Comm Coll (PA)
Lower Columbia Coll (WA)
Madisonville Comm Coll (KY)
Marshall Comm and Tech Coll (WV)
Metropolitan Comm Coll–Blue River (MO)
Metropolitan Comm Coll–Business & Technology Campus (MO)
Miami Dade Coll (FL)
Miller-Motte Tech Coll, Clarksville (TN)
Minneapolis Comm and Tech Coll (MN)
Minot State U–Bottineau Campus (ND)
Moberly Area Comm Coll (MO)

Mohawk Valley Comm Coll (NY)
Montgomery Coll (MD)
Montgomery County Comm Coll (PA)
Mott Comm Coll (MI)
Nassau Comm Coll (NY)
Northampton County Area Comm Coll (PA)
North Iowa Area Comm Coll (IA)
North Seattle Comm Coll (WA)
Olympic Coll (WA)
Owens Comm Coll, Toledo (OH)
Parkland Coll (IL)
Polk Comm Coll (FL)
Provo Coll (UT)
St. Cloud Tech Coll (MN)
San Juan Coll (NM)
Southeastern Business Coll, Lancaster (OH)
Southern State Comm Coll (OH)
South Piedmont Comm Coll (NC)
Southwestern Michigan Coll (MI)
Spokane Comm Coll (WA)
Spokane Falls Comm Coll (WA)
Stanly Comm Coll (NC)
Tallahassee Comm Coll (FL)
Taylor Business Inst (IL)
Turtle Mountain Comm Coll (ND)
Union County Coll (NJ)
The U of Akron–Wayne Coll (OH)
The U of Montana-Helena Coll of Technology (MT)
Wayne Comm Coll (NC)
Western Nevada Comm Coll (NV)
Wor-Wic Comm Coll (MD)

Acting
Central Wyoming Coll (WY)
Northampton County Area Comm Coll (PA)
Santa Barbara City Coll (CA)

Actuarial Science
Harrisburg Area Comm Coll (PA)

Administrative Assistant and Secretarial Science
AIB Coll of Business (IA)
Aims Comm Coll (CO)
Alexandria Tech Coll (MN)
Allegany Coll of Maryland (MD)
Allen County Comm Coll (KS)
Alpena Comm Coll (MI)
Altamaha Tech Coll (GA)
Amarillo Coll (TX)
Angelina Coll (TX)
Anne Arundel Comm Coll (MD)
Anoka-Ramsey Comm Coll (MN)
Anoka-Ramsey Comm Coll, Cambridge Campus (MN)
Antelope Valley Coll (CA)
Antonelli Coll, Hattiesburg (MS)
Appalachian Tech Coll (GA)
Arizona Western Coll (AZ)
Ashland Comm and Tech Coll (KY)
Asnuntuck Comm Coll (CT)
Athens Tech Coll (GA)
Augusta Tech Coll (GA)
Bainbridge Coll (GA)
Bakersfield Coll (CA)
Baltimore City Comm Coll (MD)
Barstow Coll (CA)
Barton County Comm Coll (KS)
Beaufort County Comm Coll (NC)
Bergen Comm Coll (NJ)
Bishop State Comm Coll (AL)
Bismarck State Coll (ND)
Black Hawk Coll, Moline (IL)
Bladen Comm Coll (NC)

Blinn Coll (TX)
Bradford School (PA)
Bramson ORT Coll (NY)
Briarwood Coll (CT)
Brigham Young U – Idaho (ID)
Broward Comm Coll (FL)
Brunswick Comm Coll (NC)
Bucks County Comm Coll (PA)
Business Inst of Pennsylvania, Sharon (PA)
Cambria-Rowe Business Coll, Johnstown (PA)
Cankdeska Cikana Comm Coll (ND)
Cañada Coll (CA)
Cape Cod Comm Coll (MA)
Capital Comm Coll (CT)
Catawba Valley Comm Coll (NC)
Cecil Comm Coll (MD)
Cedar Valley Coll (TX)
Central Arizona Coll (AZ)
Central Carolina Comm Coll (NC)
Central Carolina Tech Coll (SC)
Central Comm Coll–Columbus Campus (NE)
Central Comm Coll–Grand Island Campus (NE)
Central Comm Coll–Hastings Campus (NE)
Central Georgia Tech Coll (GA)
Centralia Coll (WA)
Central Lakes Coll (MN)
Central Maine Comm Coll (ME)
Central New Mexico Comm Coll (NM)
Central Ohio Tech Coll (OH)
Central Oregon Comm Coll (OR)
Central Piedmont Comm Coll (NC)
Central Texas Coll (TX)
Central Virginia Comm Coll (VA)
Century Coll (MN)
Cerritos Coll (CA)
Chaffey Coll (CA)
Chattahoochee Tech Coll (GA)
Chattanooga State Tech Comm Coll (TN)
Chesapeake Coll (MD)
Chief Dull Knife Coll (MT)
Chippewa Valley Tech Coll (WI)
Cincinnati State Tech and Comm Coll (OH)
Citrus Coll (CA)
City Colls of Chicago, Harold Washington College (IL)
City Colls of Chicago, Kennedy-King College (IL)
City Colls of Chicago, Richard J. Daley College (IL)
Clark State Comm Coll (OH)
Clatsop Comm Coll (OR)
Cleveland Comm Coll (NC)
Cleveland State Comm Coll (TN)
Clinton Comm Coll (IA)
Clovis Comm Coll (NM)
Coahoma Comm Coll (MS)
Coastal Bend Coll (TX)
Cochise Coll, Douglas (AZ)
Cochise Coll, Sierra Vista (AZ)
Colegio Universitario de San Juan, San Juan (PR)
Colegio Universitario de San Juan, San Juan (PR)
Coll of Alameda (CA)
Coll of DuPage (IL)
Coll of Lake County (IL)
Coll of Marin (CA)
Coll of San Mateo (CA)
Coll of The Albemarle (NC)
Coll of the Canyons (CA)
Coll of the Desert (CA)
Coll of the Mainland (TX)
Coll of the Redwoods (CA)
Columbia Basin Coll (WA)

Columbia Coll (CA)
Columbia-Greene Comm Coll (NY)
Columbus Tech Coll (GA)
Comm Coll of Allegheny County (PA)
Comm Coll of Beaver County (PA)
Comm Coll of Philadelphia (PA)
Comm Coll of Rhode Island (RI)
Comm Coll of Southern Nevada (NV)
Comm Coll of Vermont (VT)
Contra Costa Coll (CA)
Crafton Hills Coll (CA)
Crowder Coll (MO)
Cuesta Coll (CA)
Cuyahoga Comm Coll (OH)
Cypress Coll (CA)
Dabney S. Lancaster Comm Coll (VA)
Danville Comm Coll (VA)
Davidson County Comm Coll (NC)
De Anza Coll (CA)
DeKalb Tech Coll (GA)
Delta School of Business & Technology (LA)
Dixie State Coll of Utah (UT)
Dodge City Comm Coll (KS)
Draughons Jr Coll (KY)
East Central Coll (MO)
East Central Tech Coll (GA)
Eastern New Mexico U–Roswell (NM)
Eastern Shore Comm Coll (VA)
Eastern West Virginia Comm and Tech Coll (WV)
Elaine P. Nunez Comm Coll (LA)
El Camino Coll (CA)
El Centro Coll (TX)
Elgin Comm Coll (IL)
Elmira Business Inst (NY)
Erie Comm Coll (NY)
Essex County Coll (NJ)
Eugenio María de Hostos Comm Coll of the City U of New York (NY)
Finger Lakes Comm Coll (NY)
Fiorello H. LaGuardia Comm Coll of the City U of New York (NY)
Flint Hills Tech Coll (KS)
Flint River Tech Coll (GA)
Florence-Darlington Tech Coll (SC)
Florida National Coll (FL)
Forsyth Tech Comm Coll (NC)
Fort Belknap Coll (MT)
Fort Berthold Comm Coll (ND)
Fox Valley Tech Coll (WI)
Fresno City Coll (CA)
Fulton-Montgomery Comm Coll (NY)
Gadsden State Comm Coll (AL)
Garrett Coll (MD)
Gateway Tech Coll (WI)
Genesee Comm Coll (NY)
George C. Wallace Comm Coll (AL)
Golden West Coll (CA)
Gordon Coll (GA)
Grand Rapids Comm Coll (MI)
Grayson County Coll (TX)
Greenville Tech Coll (SC)
Griffin Tech Coll (GA)
Grossmont Coll (CA)
Gwinnett Tech Coll (GA)
Harper Coll (IL)
Harrisburg Area Comm Coll (PA)
Hartnell Coll (CA)
Hawkeye Comm Coll (IA)
H. Councill Trenholm State Tech Coll (AL)
Henry Ford Comm Coll (MI)
Hillsborough Comm Coll (FL)
Hocking Coll (OH)
Holyoke Comm Coll (MA)
Hopkinsville Comm Coll (KY)

Housatonic Comm Coll (CT)
Houston Comm Coll System (TX)
Howard Comm Coll (MD)
Hutchinson Comm Coll and Area Vocational School (KS)
Illinois Eastern Comm Colls, Frontier Community College (IL)
Illinois Eastern Comm Colls, Olney Central College (IL)
Illinois Eastern Comm Colls, Wabash Valley College (IL)
Illinois Valley Comm Coll (IL)
Imperial Valley Coll (CA)
Indiana Business Coll, Anderson (IN)
Indiana Business Coll, Columbus (IN)
Indiana Business Coll, Evansville (IN)
Indiana Business Coll, Fort Wayne (IN)
Indiana Business Coll, Indianapolis (IN)
Indiana Business Coll, Lafayette (IN)
Indiana Business Coll, Marion (IN)
Indiana Business Coll, Muncie (IN)
Indiana Business Coll, Terre Haute (IN)
International Business Coll, Fort Wayne (IN)
Inver Hills Comm Coll (MN)
Iowa Lakes Comm Coll (IA)
Irvine Valley Coll (CA)
Isothermal Comm Coll (NC)
James H. Faulkner State Comm Coll (AL)
James Sprunt Comm Coll (NC)
Jefferson Comm Coll (OH)
J. F. Drake State Tech Coll (AL)
Johnston Comm Coll (NC)
John Tyler Comm Coll (VA)
John Wood Comm Coll (IL)
Joliet Jr Coll (IL)
Kankakee Comm Coll (IL)
Kansas City Kansas Comm Coll (KS)
Kellogg Comm Coll (MI)
Kennebec Valley Comm Coll (ME)
Kent State U, Ashtabula Campus (OH)
Kent State U, Tuscarawas Campus (OH)
Kilian Comm Coll (SD)
Kingsborough Comm Coll of the City U of New York (NY)
King's Coll (NC)
Kirkwood Comm Coll (IA)
Kirtland Comm Coll (MI)
Labette Comm Coll (KS)
Lake Land Coll (IL)
Lakeshore Tech Coll (WI)
Lake Tahoe Comm Coll (CA)
Lamar Comm Coll (CO)
Lamar Inst of Technology (TX)
Laney Coll (CA)
Lanier Tech Coll (GA)
Lansing Comm Coll (MI)
Laredo Comm Coll (TX)
Las Positas Coll (CA)
Lassen Comm Coll District (CA)
Laurel Business Inst (PA)
Lawson State Comm Coll (AL)
LDS Business Coll (UT)
Lee Coll (TX)
Leeward Comm Coll (HI)
Lehigh Carbon Comm Coll (PA)
Lenoir Comm Coll (NC)
Lewis Coll of Business (MI)
Lincoln Land Comm Coll (IL)
Linn-Benton Comm Coll (OR)
Long Island Business Inst (NY)

Lorain County Comm Coll (OH)
Los Angeles City Coll (CA)
Los Angeles Harbor Coll (CA)
Los Angeles Mission Coll (CA)
Los Angeles Southwest Coll (CA)
Los Medanos Coll (CA)
Louisiana State U at Eunice (LA)
Lower Columbia Coll (WA)
Macomb Comm Coll (MI)
Madison Area Tech Coll (WI)
Madisonville Comm Coll (KY)
Manatee Comm Coll (FL)
Marian Court Coll (MA)
Marshall Comm and Tech Coll (WV)
Martin Comm Coll (NC)
Massasoit Comm Coll (MA)
Maui Comm Coll (HI)
McLennan Comm Coll (TX)
Mendocino Coll (CA)
Merced Coll (CA)
Meridian Comm Coll (MS)
Mesabi Range Comm and Tech Coll (MN)
Mesa Comm Coll (AZ)
Metropolitan Comm Coll (NE)
Metropolitan Comm Coll–Blue River (MO)
Metropolitan Comm Coll–Longview (MO)
Metropolitan Comm Coll–Maple Woods (MO)
Metropolitan Comm Coll–Penn Valley (MO)
Miami Dade Coll (FL)
Miami U–Middletown Campus (OH)
Middle Georgia Tech Coll (GA)
Middlesex Comm Coll (CT)
Midlands Tech Coll (SC)
Mid-Plains Comm Coll, North Platte (NE)
Mid-State Tech Coll (WI)
Minneapolis Comm and Tech Coll (MN)
Minnesota School of Business–Brooklyn Center (MN)
Minnesota School of Business–Plymouth (MN)
Minnesota School of Business–Richfield (MN)
Minnesota School of Business–St. Cloud (MN)
Minnesota State Coll–Southeast Tech (MN)
Minnesota State Comm and Tech Coll–Fergus Falls (MN)
Minot State U–Bottineau Campus (ND)
Mission Coll (CA)
Mississippi Delta Comm Coll (MS)
Mississippi Gulf Coast Comm Coll (MS)
Moberly Area Comm Coll (MO)
Mohawk Valley Comm Coll (NY)
Monroe Comm Coll (NY)
Montcalm Comm Coll (MI)
Monterey Peninsula Coll (CA)
Montgomery County Comm Coll (PA)
Moraine Valley Comm Coll (IL)
Morgan Comm Coll (CO)
Morton Coll (IL)
Mott Comm Coll (MI)
Moultrie Tech Coll (GA)
Mountain State Coll (WV)
Mt. Hood Comm Coll (OR)
Mt. San Antonio Coll (CA)
Murray State Coll (OK)
Muscatine Comm Coll (IA)
Muskegon Comm Coll (MI)
Napa Valley Coll (CA)
Nassau Comm Coll (NY)
National Park Comm Coll (AR)
Naugatuck Valley Comm Coll (CT)
Navarro Coll (TX)

Neosho County Comm Coll (KS)
New Hampshire Comm Tech Coll, Manchester/Stratham (NH)
New Mexico Jr Coll (NM)
New Mexico State U–Alamogordo (NM)
New River Comm Coll (VA)
Niagara County Comm Coll (NY)
Nicolet Area Tech Coll (WI)
Northampton County Area Comm Coll (PA)
North Arkansas Coll (AR)
North Central Kansas Tech Coll (KS)
North Central Michigan Coll (MI)
North Central Missouri Coll (MO)
North Central Texas Coll (TX)
Northeast Comm Coll (NE)
Northeastern Jr Coll (CO)
Northeastern Tech Coll (SC)
Northeast State Tech Comm Coll (TN)
Northern Essex Comm Coll (MA)
Northern Maine Comm Coll (ME)
Northern Marianas Coll (MP)
Northern Oklahoma Coll (OK)
North Georgia Tech Coll (GA)
North Idaho Coll (ID)
North Iowa Area Comm Coll (IA)
North Lake Coll (TX)
Northland Comm and Tech Coll–Thief River Falls (MN)
North Metro Tech Coll (GA)
North Seattle Comm Coll (WA)
North Shore Comm Coll (MA)
NorthWest Arkansas Comm Coll (AR)
Northwestern Connecticut Comm Coll (CT)
Northwestern Tech Coll (GA)
Northwest Iowa Comm Coll (IA)
Northwest KansasTech Coll (KS)
Northwest-Shoals Comm Coll (AL)
Odessa Coll (TX)
Ogeechee Tech Coll (GA)
Ohlone Coll (CA)
Okefenokee Tech Coll (GA)
Oklahoma State U, Okmulgee (OK)
Olympic Coll (WA)
Onondaga Comm Coll (NY)
Orange Coast Coll (CA)
Ouachita Tech Coll (AR)
Oxnard Coll (CA)
Ozarka Coll (AR)
Ozarks Tech Comm Coll (MO)
Pace Inst (PA)
Palau Comm Coll (Palau)
Palm Beach Comm Coll (FL)
Pamlico Comm Coll (NC)
Paradise Valley Comm Coll (AZ)
Parkland Coll (IL)
Pasadena City Coll (CA)
Passaic County Comm Coll (NJ)
Paul D. Camp Comm Coll (VA)
Pearl River Comm Coll (MS)
Piedmont Tech Coll (SC)
Piedmont Virginia Comm Coll (VA)
Pierce Coll (WA)
Pima Comm Coll (AZ)
Pine Tech Coll (MN)
Porterville Coll (CA)
Potomac State Coll of West Virginia U (WV)
Pueblo Comm Coll (CO)
Pulaski Tech Coll (AR)
Quinebaug Valley Comm Coll (CT)

Rainy River Comm Coll (MN)
Ranger Coll (TX)
Rappahannock Comm Coll (VA)
Raritan Valley Comm Coll (NJ)
Rasmussen Coll Brooklyn Park (MN)
Redlands Comm Coll (OK)
Red Rocks Comm Coll (CO)
Reedley Coll (CA)
Reid State Tech Coll (AL)
Renton Tech Coll (WA)
Richland Coll (TX)
Richland Comm Coll (IL)
Ridgewater Coll (MN)
Riverland Comm Coll (MN)
Roane State Comm Coll (TN)
Robeson Comm Coll (NC)
Rose State Coll (OK)
Roxbury Comm Coll (MA)
Sacramento City Coll (CA)
St. Catharine Coll (KY)
Saint Charles Comm Coll (MO)
St. Cloud Tech Coll (MN)
St. Louis Comm Coll at Florissant Valley (MO)
Saint Paul Coll–A Comm & Tech College (MN)
St. Philip's Coll (TX)
Salish Kootenai Coll (MT)
Sampson Comm Coll (NC)
San Bernardino Valley Coll (CA)
Sandersville Tech Coll (GA)
Sandhills Comm Coll (NC)
San Diego City Coll (CA)
San Juan Coll (NM)
Santa Ana Coll (CA)
Santa Barbara City Coll (CA)
Savannah Tech Coll (GA)
Schoolcraft Coll (MI)
Scott Comm Coll (IA)
Scottsdale Comm Coll (AZ)
Seminole Comm Coll (FL)
Seminole State Coll (OK)
Shasta Coll (CA)
Sheridan Coll–Sheridan and Gillette (WY)
Sitting Bull Coll (ND)
Skagit Valley Coll (WA)
Southeastern Business Coll, Jackson (OH)
Southeastern Business Coll, Lancaster (OH)
Southeastern Business Coll, New Boston (OH)
Southeastern Comm Coll (NC)
Southeastern Comm Coll, North Campus (IA)
Southeastern Comm Coll, South Campus (IA)
Southeastern Tech Coll (GA)
Southeast Kentucky Comm and Tech Coll (KY)
South Florida Comm Coll (FL)
South Georgia Coll (GA)
South Georgia Tech Coll (GA)
South Plains Coll (TX)
South Seattle Comm Coll (WA)
Southside Virginia Comm Coll (VA)
Southwestern Comm Coll (NC)
Southwestern Indian Polytechnic Inst (NM)
Southwestern Michigan Coll (MI)
Southwest Georgia Tech Coll (GA)
Southwest Mississippi Comm Coll (MS)
Southwest Virginia Comm Coll (VA)
Spokane Comm Coll (WA)
Spokane Falls Comm Coll (WA)
Springfield Tech Comm Coll (MA)
Stark State Coll of Technology (OH)
State Fair Comm Coll (MO)

State U of New York Coll of Agriculture and Technology at Morrisville (NY)
Stone Child Coll (MT)
Surry Comm Coll (NC)
Sussex County Comm Coll (NJ)
Swainsboro Tech Coll (GA)
Taft Coll (CA)
Tallahassee Comm Coll (FL)
Temple Coll (TX)
Terra State Comm Coll (OH)
Texarkana Coll (TX)
Three Rivers Comm Coll (CT)
Three Rivers Comm Coll (MO)
Tidewater Comm Coll (VA)
Tompkins Cortland Comm Coll (NY)
Treasure Valley Comm Coll (OR)
Trident Tech Coll (SC)
Trinidad State Jr Coll (CO)
Tri-State Business Inst (PA)
Trocaire Coll (NY)
Trumbull Business Coll (OH)
Tulsa Comm Coll (OK)
Tunxis Comm Coll (CT)
Turtle Mountain Comm Coll (ND)
Tyler Jr Coll (TX)
Ulster County Comm Coll (NY)
Umpqua Comm Coll (OR)
Union County Coll (NJ)
The U of Akron–Wayne Coll (OH)
U of Alaska Anchorage, Kodiak Coll (AK)
U of Alaska, Prince William Sound Comm Coll (AK)
U of Arkansas Comm Coll at Morrilton (AR)
U of Cincinnati Clermont Coll (OH)
U of New Mexico–Gallup (NM)
U of New Mexico–Los Alamos Branch (NM)
U of New Mexico–Taos (NM)
U of New Mexico–Valencia Campus (NM)
U of Puerto Rico at Carolina (PR)
U of South Carolina Lancaster (SC)
Valdosta Tech Coll (GA)
Valencia Comm Coll (FL)
Vatterott Coll, Kansas City (MO)
Vernon Coll (TX)
Victoria Coll (TX)
Victor Valley Coll (CA)
Vincennes U Jasper Campus (IN)
Virginia Highlands Comm Coll (VA)
Virginia Western Comm Coll (VA)
Wallace State Comm Coll (AL)
Warren County Comm Coll (NJ)
Washington State Comm Coll (OH)
Waukesha County Tech Coll (WI)
Wenatchee Valley Coll (WA)
West Central Tech Coll (GA)
Westchester Comm Coll (NY)
Western Nevada Comm Coll (NV)
Western Piedmont Comm Coll (NC)
Western Texas Coll (TX)
Western Wyoming Comm Coll (WY)
West Georgia Tech Coll (GA)
West Hills Comm Coll (CA)
West Los Angeles Coll (CA)
Westmoreland County Comm Coll (PA)
West Valley Coll (CA)
West Virginia U at Parkersburg (WV)

Wilson Tech Comm
  Coll (NC)
Wor-Wic Comm Coll (MD)
Wright State U, Lake
  Campus (OH)
Wytheville Comm Coll (VA)
York Tech Coll (SC)
Yuba Coll (CA)
Zane State Coll (OH)

Adult Development and Aging
Comm Coll of Rhode
  Island (RI)
Lehigh Carbon Comm
  Coll (PA)

Advertising
Bradley Academy for the
  Visual Arts (PA)
Brigham Young U –
  Idaho (ID)
Central Piedmont Comm
  Coll (NC)
Chattanooga State Tech
  Comm Coll (TN)
Cosumnes River Coll,
  Sacramento (CA)
Cypress Coll (CA)
El Camino Coll (CA)
Grossmont Coll (CA)
Los Angeles City Coll (CA)
Manatee Comm Coll (FL)
Minot State U–Bottineau
  Campus (ND)
Mississippi Delta Comm
  Coll (MS)
Mississippi Gulf Coast
  Comm Coll (MS)
Mohawk Valley Comm
  Coll (NY)
Mt. San Antonio Coll (CA)
Muskegon Comm Coll (MI)
Parkland Coll (IL)
Pasadena City Coll (CA)
Sacramento City Coll (CA)
St. Cloud Tech Coll (MN)
Santa Rosa Jr Coll (CA)
South Plains Coll (TX)
Southwest Mississippi
  Comm Coll (MS)
Surry Comm Coll (NC)
Tidewater Comm Coll (VA)
Tulsa Comm Coll (OK)
U of Puerto Rico at
  Carolina (PR)
Yuba Coll (CA)

Aeronautical/ Aerospace Engineering Technology
Calhoun Comm Coll (AL)
Cincinnati State Tech and
  Comm Coll (OH)
Pittsburgh Inst of
  Aeronautics (PA)
Santa Rosa Jr Coll (CA)

Aeronautics/Aviation/ Aerospace Science and Technology
Caldwell Comm Coll and
  Tech Inst (NC)
Comm Coll of Beaver
  County (PA)
Hesston Coll (KS)
Miami Dade Coll (FL)
Northland Comm and Tech
  Coll–Thief River
  Falls (MN)
Northwest Aviation
  Coll (WA)
Orange Coast Coll (CA)
Raritan Valley Comm
  Coll (NJ)
San Bernardino Valley
  Coll (CA)
Tompkins Cortland Comm
  Coll (NY)
Tulsa Comm Coll (OK)

Aesthetician/Esthetician and Skin Care
Florida Coll of Natural
  Health, Bradenton (FL)
Florida Coll of Natural
  Health, Maitland (FL)
Florida Coll of Natural
  Health, Miami (FL)
Florida Coll of Natural
  Health, Pompano
  Beach (FL)
Keiser Career Coll -
  Greenacres (FL)
Olympic Coll (WA)

African-American/ Black Studies
City Coll of San
  Francisco (CA)

City Colls of Chicago,
  Olive-Harvey
  College (IL)
Coll of Alameda (CA)
Contra Costa Coll (CA)
El Camino Coll (CA)
Fresno City Coll (CA)
Laney Coll (CA)
Los Angeles City Coll (CA)
Manatee Comm Coll (FL)
Nassau Comm Coll (NY)
Pasadena City Coll (CA)
San Diego City Coll (CA)
Santa Ana Coll (CA)
Santa Barbara City
  Coll (CA)
Yuba Coll (CA)

African Studies
Los Angeles Southwest
  Coll (CA)
Pasadena City Coll (CA)

Agribusiness
Black Hawk Coll,
  Moline (IL)
Central Wyoming
  Coll (WY)
Clarendon Coll (TX)
Coll of Southern
  Maryland (MD)
Crowder Coll (MO)
Eastern Arizona Coll (AZ)
Iowa Lakes Comm
  Coll (IA)
James Sprunt Comm
  Coll (NC)
Laramie County Comm
  Coll (WY)
Ogeechee Tech Coll (GA)
The Ohio State U Ag Tech
  Inst (OH)
Sitting Bull Coll (ND)
Wayne Comm Coll (NC)

Agricultural Business and Management
Arizona Western Coll (AZ)
Bakersfield Coll (CA)
Barton County Comm
  Coll (KS)
Bismarck State Coll (ND)
Brigham Young U –
  Idaho (ID)
Central Comm Coll–
  Columbus
  Campus (NE)
Central Comm Coll–
  Hastings Campus (NE)
Central Wyoming
  Coll (WY)
Chippewa Valley Tech
  Coll (WI)
Cisco Jr Coll (TX)
City Coll of San
  Francisco (CA)
Clark State Comm
  Coll (OH)
Coastal Georgia Comm
  Coll (GA)
Cochise Coll, Douglas (AZ)
Colby Comm Coll (KS)
Coll of Southern Idaho (ID)
Coll of the Desert (CA)
Coll of the Redwoods (CA)
Columbia Basin Coll (WA)
Cosumnes River Coll,
  Sacramento (CA)
Dodge City Comm
  Coll (KS)
Fox Valley Tech Coll (WI)
Harrisburg Area Comm
  Coll (PA)
Hartnell Coll (CA)
Hawkeye Comm Coll (IA)
Illinois Eastern Comm
  Colls, Wabash Valley
  College (IL)
Illinois Valley Comm
  Coll (IL)
Imperial Valley Coll (CA)
Iowa Lakes Comm
  Coll (IA)
Jackson State Comm
  Coll (TN)
John Wood Comm Coll (IL)
Joliet Jr Coll (IL)
Kirkwood Comm Coll (IA)
Lake Land Coll (IL)
Lamar Comm Coll (CO)
Lassen Comm Coll
  District (CA)
Lenoir Comm Coll (NC)
Linn-Benton Comm
  Coll (OR)
Merced Coll (CA)
Mesa Comm Coll (AZ)
Mississippi Delta Comm
  Coll (MS)

Mississippi Gulf Coast
  Comm Coll (MS)
Mt. San Antonio Coll (CA)
Nebraska Coll of Tech
  Agriculture (NE)
North Arkansas Coll (AR)
North Central Missouri
  Coll (MO)
Northeast Comm Coll (NE)
Northeastern Jr Coll (CO)
Northeast Iowa Comm
  Coll (IA)
Northern Marianas
  Coll (MP)
Northern Oklahoma
  Coll (OK)
Northwest Mississippi
  Comm Coll (MS)
The Ohio State U Ag Tech
  Inst (OH)
Owens Comm Coll,
  Toledo (OH)
Oxnard Coll (CA)
Parkland Coll (IL)
Porterville Coll (CA)
Potomac State Coll of
  West Virginia U (WV)
Redlands Comm Coll (OK)
Reedley Coll (CA)
Richland Comm Coll (IL)
Ridgewater Coll (MN)
St. Catharine Coll (KY)
San Joaquin Delta
  Coll (CA)
Santa Rosa Jr Coll (CA)
Shasta Coll (CA)
Sheridan Coll–Sheridan
  and Gillette (WY)
Southeastern Comm Coll,
  North Campus (IA)
South Florida Comm
  Coll (FL)
South Georgia Coll (GA)
Spokane Comm Coll (WA)
State Fair Comm
  Coll (MO)
State U of New York Coll
  of Agriculture and
  Technology at
  Morrisville (NY)
State U of New York Coll
  of Technology at
  Alfred (NY)
Surry Comm Coll (NC)
Three Rivers Comm
  Coll (MO)
Treasure Valley Comm
  Coll (OR)
Tyler Jr Coll (TX)
West Hills Comm Coll (CA)
Yuba Coll (CA)

Agricultural Business and Management Related
Iowa Lakes Comm
  Coll (IA)
Penn State Beaver (PA)
Penn State Delaware
  County (PA)
Penn State DuBois (PA)
Penn State Fayette, The
  Eberly Campus (PA)
Penn State Hazleton (PA)
Penn State Lehigh
  Valley (PA)
Penn State
  McKeesport (PA)
Penn State Mont Alto (PA)
Penn State New
  Kensington (PA)
Penn State Schuylkill (PA)
Penn State Shenango (PA)
Penn State Wilkes-
  Barre (PA)
Penn State Worthington
  Scranton (PA)
Penn State York (PA)

Agricultural Business Technology
Iowa Lakes Comm
  Coll (IA)
Laramie County Comm
  Coll (WY)
North Iowa Area Comm
  Coll (IA)
The Ohio State U Ag Tech
  Inst (OH)

Agricultural Communication/ Journalism
The Ohio State U Ag Tech
  Inst (OH)

Agricultural Economics
Brigham Young U –
  Idaho (ID)

Clarendon Coll (TX)
Colby Comm Coll (KS)
Dodge City Comm
  Coll (KS)
Iowa Lakes Comm
  Coll (IA)
James H. Faulkner State
  Comm Coll (AL)
Lassen Comm Coll
  District (CA)
Mississippi Delta Comm
  Coll (MS)
Northeastern Jr Coll (CO)
North Iowa Area Comm
  Coll (IA)
Northwest Mississippi
  Comm Coll (MS)
The Ohio State U Ag Tech
  Inst (OH)
Potomac State Coll of
  West Virginia U (WV)
South Plains Coll (TX)
Tyler Jr Coll (TX)

Agricultural/Farm Supplies Retailing and Wholesaling
Iowa Lakes Comm
  Coll (IA)
Muscatine Comm Coll (IA)

Agricultural Mechanics and Equipment Technology
Black Hawk Coll,
  Moline (IL)
Iowa Lakes Comm
  Coll (IA)

Agricultural Mechanization
Aims Comm Coll (CO)
Beaufort County Comm
  Coll (NC)
Black Hawk Coll,
  Moline (IL)
Clark State Comm
  Coll (OH)
Columbia Basin Coll (WA)
Cosumnes River Coll,
  Sacramento (CA)
Cuesta Coll (CA)
Dodge City Comm
  Coll (KS)
Garrett Coll (MD)
Hawkeye Comm Coll (IA)
Hutchinson Comm Coll
  and Area Vocational
  School (KS)
Imperial Valley Coll (CA)
Iowa Lakes Comm
  Coll (IA)
Lake Land Coll (IL)
Lassen Comm Coll
  District (CA)
Madison Area Tech
  Coll (WI)
Maui Comm Coll (HI)
Mesa Comm Coll (AZ)
Metropolitan Comm
  Coll–Longview (MO)
Mt. San Antonio Coll (CA)
Navarro Coll (TX)
Nebraska Coll of Tech
  Agriculture (NE)
North Central Texas
  Coll (TX)
Northeast Comm Coll (NE)
Northeastern Jr Coll (CO)
Northern Marianas
  Coll (MP)
Northwest Mississippi
  Comm Coll (MS)
The Ohio State U Ag Tech
  Inst (OH)
Oxnard Coll (CA)
Parkland Coll (IL)
Potomac State Coll of
  West Virginia U (WV)
Ridgewater Coll (MN)
San Joaquin Delta
  Coll (CA)
Santa Rosa Jr Coll (CA)
South Florida Comm
  Coll (FL)
Southwest Georgia Tech
  Coll (GA)
Southwest Texas Jr
  Coll (TX)
State Fair Comm
  Coll (MO)
State U of New York Coll
  of Agriculture and
  Technology at
  Morrisville (NY)
Three Rivers Comm
  Coll (MO)

Treasure Valley Comm
  Coll (OR)
The U of Montana-Helena
  Coll of Technology (MT)
Wenatchee Valley
  Coll (WA)
West Hills Comm Coll (CA)
Yuba Coll (CA)

Agricultural Mechanization Related
Reedley Coll (CA)

Agricultural Power Machinery Operation
Iowa Lakes Comm
  Coll (IA)
North Central Kansas Tech
  Coll (KS)
The Ohio State U Ag Tech
  Inst (OH)

Agricultural Production
Allen County Comm
  Coll (KS)
Hillsborough Comm
  Coll (FL)
Illinois Eastern Comm
  Colls, Wabash Valley
  College (IL)
Iowa Lakes Comm
  Coll (IA)
John Wood Comm Coll (IL)
Lake Land Coll (IL)
Laramie County Comm
  Coll (WY)
Lincoln Land Comm
  Coll (IL)
Muscatine Comm Coll (IA)
Northeast Comm Coll (NE)
North Iowa Area Comm
  Coll (IA)
Southern State Comm
  Coll (OH)
Wayne Comm Coll (NC)

Agricultural Production Related
Black Hawk Coll,
  Moline (IL)
Iowa Lakes Comm
  Coll (IA)

Agricultural Teacher Education
Colby Comm Coll (KS)
Iowa Lakes Comm
  Coll (IA)
Kirkwood Comm Coll (IA)
Lamar Comm Coll (CO)
Linn-Benton Comm
  Coll (OR)
Murray State Coll (OK)
Northeastern Jr Coll (CO)
Northwest-Shoals Comm
  Coll (AL)
The Ohio State U Ag Tech
  Inst (OH)
Potomac State Coll of
  West Virginia U (WV)
Redlands Comm Coll (OK)
South Georgia Coll (GA)
Tyler Jr Coll (TX)
Victor Valley Coll (CA)
Western Texas Coll (TX)

Agriculture
Arizona Western Coll (AZ)
Bainbridge Coll (GA)
Bakersfield Coll (CA)
Barton County Comm
  Coll (KS)
Blinn Coll (TX)
Brigham Young U –
  Idaho (ID)
Calhoun Comm Coll (AL)
Central Arizona Coll (AZ)
Central Texas Coll (TX)
Central Wyoming
  Coll (WY)
Cerritos Coll (CA)
Chief Dull Knife Coll (MT)
Chipola Coll (FL)
Cisco Jr Coll (TX)
Clarendon Coll (TX)
Clark State Comm
  Coll (OH)
Coastal Bend Coll (TX)
Colby Comm Coll (KS)
Coll of Micronesia–
  FSM (FM)
Coll of Southern Idaho (ID)
Crowder Coll (MO)
Dixie State Coll of
  Utah (UT)
Eastern Arizona Coll (AZ)
East Georgia Coll (GA)
Fullerton Coll (CA)

Georgia Highlands
  Coll (GA)
Gordon Coll (GA)
Houston Comm Coll
  System (TX)
Hutchinson Comm Coll
  and Area Vocational
  School (KS)
Illinois Valley Comm
  Coll (IL)
Imperial Valley Coll (CA)
Iowa Lakes Comm
  Coll (IA)
Jones County Jr Coll (MS)
Kirkwood Comm Coll (IA)
Lamar Comm Coll (CO)
Laramie County Comm
  Coll (WY)
Lassen Comm Coll
  District (CA)
Lenoir Comm Coll (NC)
Linn-Benton Comm
  Coll (OR)
Los Angeles Pierce
  Coll (CA)
Macomb Comm Coll (MI)
Mendocino Coll (CA)
Merced Coll (CA)
Miami Dade Coll (FL)
Missouri State U–West
  Plains (MO)
Mt. San Antonio Coll (CA)
Murray State Coll (OK)
Napa Valley Coll (CA)
New Mexico Jr Coll (NM)
North Arkansas Coll (AR)
Northeast Comm Coll (NE)
Northeastern Jr Coll (CO)
Northern Marianas
  Coll (MP)
North Idaho Coll (ID)
Northwest Mississippi
  Comm Coll (MS)
Odessa Coll (TX)
Owensboro Comm and
  Tech Coll (KY)
Palau Comm Coll (Palau)
Palo Alto Coll (TX)
Potomac State Coll of
  West Virginia U (WV)
Redlands Comm Coll (OK)
Reedley Coll (CA)
St. Catharine Coll (KY)
San Joaquin Delta
  Coll (CA)
Santa Rosa Jr Coll (CA)
Sheridan Coll–Sheridan
  and Gillette (WY)
Skagit Valley Coll (WA)
South Georgia Coll (GA)
South Plains Coll (TX)
State Fair Comm
  Coll (MO)
State U of New York Coll
  of Agriculture and
  Technology at
  Morrisville (NY)
State U of New York Coll
  of Technology at
  Alfred (NY)
Texarkana Coll (TX)
Treasure Valley Comm
  Coll (OR)
Tulsa Comm Coll (OK)
Tyler Jr Coll (TX)
Umpqua Comm Coll (OR)
U of New Mexico–Valencia
  Campus (NM)
Ventura Coll (CA)
Wallace State Comm
  Coll (AL)
Western Nebraska Comm
  Coll (NE)
Western Texas Coll (TX)
Young Harris Coll (GA)
Yuba Coll (CA)

Agronomy and Crop Science
Brigham Young U –
  Idaho (ID)
Chipola Coll (FL)
Colby Comm Coll (KS)
Coll of the Redwoods (CA)
Cosumnes River Coll,
  Sacramento (CA)
Dodge City Comm
  Coll (KS)
Hartnell Coll (CA)
Hawkeye Comm Coll (IA)
Iowa Lakes Comm
  Coll (IA)
Kirkwood Comm Coll (IA)
Lamar Comm Coll (CO)
Lassen Comm Coll
  District (CA)
Merced Coll (CA)
Mesa Comm Coll (AZ)
Mt. San Antonio Coll (CA)

Nebraska Coll of Tech
Agriculture (NE)
Northeast Comm Coll (NE)
Northeastern Jr Coll (CO)
The Ohio State U Ag Tech
Inst (OH)
Potomac State Coll of
West Virginia U (WV)
Southeastern Comm Coll,
North Campus (IA)
Southern Maine Comm
Coll (ME)
South Plains Coll (TX)
Spokane Comm Coll (WA)
State U of New York Coll
of Agriculture and
Technology at
Morrisville (NY)
Treasure Valley Comm
Coll (OR)
West Hills Comm Coll (CA)
Yuba Coll (CA)

**Aircraft Powerplant
Technology**
Antelope Valley Coll (CA)
Central Texas Coll (TX)
Hallmark Inst of
Aeronautics (TX)
Linn State Tech Coll (MO)
Minneapolis Comm and
Tech Coll (MN)
Pima Comm Coll (AZ)
St. Philip's Coll (TX)

**Airframe Mechanics
and Aircraft
Maintenance
Technology**
Amarillo Coll (TX)
Antelope Valley Coll (CA)
Chandler-Gilbert Comm
Coll (AZ)
City Coll of San
Francisco (CA)
Cochise Coll, Douglas (AZ)
Coll of San Mateo (CA)
Eastern New Mexico
U–Roswell (NM)
Greenville Tech Coll (SC)
Hallmark Inst of
Aeronautics (TX)
Merced Coll (CA)
Middle Georgia Tech
Coll (GA)
Minneapolis Comm and
Tech Coll (MN)
Mohawk Valley Comm
Coll (NY)
Mt. San Antonio Coll (CA)
New Hampshire Comm
Tech Coll, Nashua/
Claremont (NH)
Oklahoma City Comm
Coll (OK)
Pittsburgh Inst of
Aeronautics (PA)
Sacramento City Coll (CA)
St. Philip's Coll (TX)
South Seattle Comm
Coll (WA)
Southwestern Michigan
Coll (MI)
Texas State Tech Coll
West Texas (TX)
Trident Tech Coll (SC)
Tulsa Comm Coll (OK)
The U of Montana–Helena
Coll of Technology (MT)
West Los Angeles
Coll (CA)

**Airline Flight
Attendant**
Cypress Coll (CA)

**Airline Pilot and Flight
Crew**
Academy Coll (MN)
Big Bend Comm Coll (WA)
Broward Comm Coll (FL)
Central Texas Coll (TX)
Chattanooga State Tech
Comm Coll (TN)
Cochise Coll, Douglas (AZ)
Coll of San Mateo (CA)
Comm Coll of Allegheny
County (PA)
Cypress Coll (CA)
Dixie State Coll of
Utah (UT)
Fox Valley Tech Coll (WI)
Gateway Tech Coll (WI)
Georgia Aviation & Tech
Coll (GA)
Guilford Tech Comm
Coll (NC)

Inver Hills Comm
Coll (MN)
Iowa Lakes Comm
Coll (IA)
Jamestown Comm
Coll (NY)
Lansing Comm Coll (MI)
Lehigh Carbon Comm
Coll (PA)
Lenoir Comm Coll (NC)
Miami Dade Coll (FL)
Mt. San Antonio Coll (CA)
Navarro Coll (TX)
North Shore Comm
Coll (MA)
Orange Coast Coll (CA)
Palm Beach Comm
Coll (FL)
Pasadena City Coll (CA)
Salt Lake Comm Coll (UT)
San Juan Coll (NM)
Scott Comm Coll (IA)
Wallace State Comm
Coll (AL)

Air Traffic Control
Cecil Comm Coll (MD)
Comm Coll of Beaver
County (PA)
Georgia Aviation & Tech
Coll (GA)
Inver Hills Comm
Coll (MN)
Miami Dade Coll (FL)
Mt. San Antonio Coll (CA)

**Allied Health and
Medical Assisting
Services Related**
Antonelli Coll,
Hattiesburg (MS)
Arizona Coll of Allied
Health (AZ)
Cincinnati State Tech and
Comm Coll (OH)
Florida National Coll (FL)
Heritage Coll (CO)
King's Coll (NC)
North Seattle Comm
Coll (WA)

**Allied Health
Diagnostic,
Intervention, and
Treatment
Professions Related**
ACT Coll, Arlington (VA)
Oakland Comm Coll (MI)
Union County Coll (NJ)

**Alternative and
Complementary
Medical Support
Services Related**
Southwest Inst of Healing
Arts (AZ)

**American Government
and Politics**
Manatee Comm Coll (FL)
Quincy Coll (MA)

**American Indian/
Native American
Studies**
Central Wyoming
Coll (WY)
Fond du Lac Tribal and
Comm Coll (MN)
Fort Belknap Coll (MT)
Fresno City Coll (CA)
Itasca Comm Coll (MN)
Nebraska Indian Comm
Coll (NE)
North Idaho Coll (ID)
Pima Comm Coll (AZ)
Saginaw Chippewa Tribal
Coll (MI)
Salish Kootenai Coll (MT)
Santa Barbara City
Coll (CA)
Sitting Bull Coll (ND)

**American Sign
Language (ASL)**
Burlington County
Coll (NJ)

American Studies
Anne Arundel Comm
Coll (MD)
Bucks County Comm
Coll (PA)
Cosumnes River Coll,
Sacramento (CA)
El Camino Coll (CA)
Foothill Coll (CA)
Holyoke Comm Coll (MA)
Lee Coll (TX)
Los Angeles City Coll (CA)

Manatee Comm Coll (FL)
Miami Dade Coll (FL)
Mississippi Delta Comm
Coll (MS)
Naugatuck Valley Comm
Coll (CT)
Tulsa Comm Coll (OK)

Anatomy
Cañada Coll (CA)
Northeastern Jr Coll (CO)

Animal Health
Santa Rosa Jr Coll (CA)

**Animal/Livestock
Husbandry and
Production**
Black Hawk Coll,
Moline (IL)
Hopkinsville Comm
Coll (KY)
Iowa Lakes Comm
Coll (IA)
John Wood Comm Coll (IL)
North Central Texas
Coll (TX)
The Ohio State U Ag Tech
Inst (OH)
Ridgewater Coll (MN)

Animal Physiology
Joliet Jr Coll (IL)
Santa Rosa Jr Coll (CA)

Animal Sciences
Alamance Comm Coll (NC)
Bakersfield Coll (CA)
Black Hawk Coll,
Moline (IL)
Brigham Young U –
Idaho (ID)
Colby Comm Coll (KS)
Cosumnes River Coll,
Sacramento (CA)
Dodge City Comm
Coll (KS)
Everett Comm Coll (WA)
Hartnell Coll (CA)
Hawkeye Comm Coll (IA)
Iowa Lakes Comm
Coll (IA)
James Sprunt Comm
Coll (NC)
Kirkwood Comm Coll (IA)
Lamar Comm Coll (CO)
Linn-Benton Comm
Coll (OR)
Los Angeles Pierce
Coll (CA)
Mendocino Coll (CA)
Merced Coll (CA)
Moorpark Coll (CA)
Mt. San Antonio Coll (CA)
Murray State Coll (OK)
Nebraska Coll of Tech
Agriculture (NE)
Niagara County Comm
Coll (NY)
Northeast Comm Coll (NE)
Northeastern Jr Coll (CO)
Northwest Mississippi
Comm Coll (MS)
The Ohio State U Ag Tech
Inst (OH)
Potomac State Coll of
West Virginia U (WV)
Redlands Comm Coll (OK)
Reedley Coll (CA)
St. Catharine Coll (KY)
San Joaquin Delta
Coll (CA)
Santa Rosa Jr Coll (CA)
Shasta Coll (CA)
South Georgia Coll (GA)
State U of New York Coll
of Agriculture and
Technology at
Morrisville (NY)
State U of New York Coll
of Technology at
Alfred (NY)
West Hills Comm Coll (CA)
Yuba Coll (CA)

**Animation, Interactive
Technology, Video
Graphics and Special
Effects**
The Art Inst of New York
City (NY)
The Art Inst of
Philadelphia (PA)
Bradley Academy for the
Visual Arts (PA)
Brooks Coll,
Sunnyvale (CA)
Hagerstown Comm
Coll (MD)

Kent State U, Tuscarawas
Campus (OH)
Madison Media Inst (WI)
New Hampshire Tech
Inst (NH)
Olympic Coll (WA)
Platt Coll San Diego (CA)
School of Communication
Arts (NC)

Anthropology
Bakersfield Coll (CA)
Barton County Comm
Coll (KS)
Cañada Coll (CA)
Cerritos Coll (CA)
Chaffey Coll (CA)
Cochise Coll, Douglas (AZ)
Cochise Coll, Sierra
Vista (AZ)
Coll of Alameda (CA)
Coll of Southern Idaho (ID)
Coll of the Desert (CA)
Columbia Coll (CA)
Comm Coll of Southern
Nevada (NV)
Contra Costa Coll (CA)
Crafton Hills Coll (CA)
Cypress Coll (CA)
Eastern Arizona Coll (AZ)
East Georgia Coll (GA)
El Camino Coll (CA)
Everett Comm Coll (WA)
Foothill Coll (CA)
Fresno City Coll (CA)
Fullerton Coll (CA)
Great Basin Coll (NV)
Hartnell Coll (CA)
Imperial Valley Coll (CA)
Kellogg Comm Coll (MI)
Laramie County Comm
Coll (WY)
Los Angeles Southwest
Coll (CA)
Los Medanos Coll (CA)
Lower Columbia Coll (WA)
Miami Dade Coll (FL)
Miami U–Middletown
Campus (OH)
Monterey Peninsula
Coll (CA)
Moorpark Coll (CA)
Muskegon Comm Coll (MI)
North Idaho Coll (ID)
Orange Coast Coll (CA)
Oxnard Coll (CA)
Pasadena City Coll (CA)
Pima Comm Coll (AZ)
San Bernardino Valley
Coll (CA)
San Diego City Coll (CA)
San Joaquin Delta
Coll (CA)
San Juan Coll (NM)
Santa Ana Coll (CA)
Santa Barbara City
Coll (CA)
Santa Rosa Jr Coll (CA)
Santiago Canyon Coll (CA)
Skagit Valley Coll (WA)
Umpqua Comm Coll (OR)
Western Nebraska Comm
Coll (NE)
Western Wyoming Comm
Coll (WY)
West Los Angeles
Coll (CA)

**Apparel and
Accessories
Marketing**
FIDM/The Fashion Inst of
Design &
Merchandising, Los
Angeles Campus (CA)
FIDM/The Fashion Inst of
Design &
Merchandising, San
Diego Campus (CA)
FIDM/The Fashion Inst of
Design &
Merchandising, San
Francisco
Campus (CA)

Apparel and Textiles
FIDM/The Fashion Inst of
Design &
Merchandising, Los
Angeles Campus (CA)
FIDM/The Fashion Inst of
Design &
Merchandising, San
Francisco
Campus (CA)
Mt. San Antonio Coll (CA)

Apparel Marketing
Berkeley Coll–New York
City Campus (NY)

Berkeley Coll–Westchester
Campus (NY)

**Appliance Installation
and Repair
Technology**
Mohawk Valley Comm
Coll (NY)

Applied Art
Anne Arundel Comm
Coll (MD)
Centralia Coll (WA)
Central Piedmont Comm
Coll (NC)
Chattanooga State Tech
Comm Coll (TN)
Coastal Bend Coll (TX)
Coll of Marin (CA)
Cosumnes River Coll,
Sacramento (CA)
Cuesta Coll (CA)
Cypress Coll (CA)
Henry Ford Comm
Coll (MI)
Howard Comm Coll (MD)
Iowa Lakes Comm
Coll (IA)
Jones County Jr Coll (MS)
Kingsborough Comm Coll
of the City U of New
York (NY)
Kirkwood Comm Coll (IA)
Lassen Comm Coll
District (CA)
Los Angeles City Coll (CA)
Merced Coll (CA)
Mississippi Delta Comm
Coll (MS)
Muskegon Comm Coll (MI)
Odessa Coll (TX)
Oklahoma City Comm
Coll (OK)
Porterville Coll (CA)
Ridgewater Coll (MN)
Tunxis Comm Coll (CT)
U of New Mexico–Los
Alamos Branch (NM)
Wenatchee Valley
Coll (WA)
Westchester Comm
Coll (NY)

Applied Horticulture
Alamance Comm Coll (NC)
Brunswick Comm
Coll (NC)
Central Comm Coll–
Hastings Campus (NE)
Clark Coll (WA)
Comm Coll of Allegheny
County (PA)
Fayetteville Tech Comm
Coll (NC)
Gateway Tech Coll (WI)
John Wood Comm Coll (IL)
Kent State U, Geauga
Campus (OH)
Minot State U–Bottineau
Campus (ND)
Montgomery Coll (MD)
Northeast Comm Coll (NE)
North Shore Comm
Coll (MA)
Oakland Comm Coll (MI)
Santa Barbara City
Coll (CA)
Skagit Valley Coll (WA)
Spokane Comm Coll (WA)
Tulsa Comm Coll (OK)

**Applied Horticulture/
Horticultural Business
Services Related**
Cincinnati State Tech and
Comm Coll (OH)
Minot State U–Bottineau
Campus (ND)

Applied Mathematics
Muskegon Comm Coll (MI)
Northeastern Jr Coll (CO)
South Georgia Coll (GA)

Aquaculture
Brunswick Comm
Coll (NC)
Hillsborough Comm
Coll (FL)
Trinidad State Jr Coll (CO)

Archeology
Western Wyoming Comm
Coll (WY)

Architectural Drafting
Coll of Lake County (IL)
North Seattle Comm
Coll (WA)
West Virginia State Comm
and Tech Coll (WV)

**Architectural Drafting
and Cad/Cadd**
Central New Mexico
Comm Coll (NM)
Clinton Comm Coll (IA)
Commonwealth Tech
Inst (PA)
Comm Coll of Allegheny
County (PA)
Dixie State Coll of
Utah (UT)
Hennepin Tech Coll (MN)
Island Drafting and Tech
Inst (NY)
Lincoln Land Comm
Coll (IL)
Macomb Comm Coll (MI)
Miami Dade Coll (FL)
Mohawk Valley Comm
Coll (NY)
Montgomery Coll (MD)
Montgomery County
Comm Coll (PA)
New York City Coll of
Technology of the City
U of New York (NY)
Pima Comm Coll (AZ)
St. Cloud Tech Coll (MN)
Waukesha County Tech
Coll (WI)

**Architectural
Engineering
Technology**
Amarillo Coll (TX)
Anne Arundel Comm
Coll (MD)
Bakersfield Coll (CA)
Brigham Young U –
Idaho (ID)
Broward Comm Coll (FL)
Cape Fear Comm
Coll (NC)
Catawba Valley Comm
Coll (NC)
Central Piedmont Comm
Coll (NC)
Central Virginia Comm
Coll (VA)
Cerritos Coll (CA)
Chesapeake Coll (MD)
Chippewa Valley Tech
Coll (WI)
Cincinnati State Tech and
Comm Coll (OH)
City Colls of Chicago,
Harold Washington
College (IL)
City Colls of Chicago,
Kennedy-King
College (IL)
City Colls of Chicago,
Richard J. Daley
College (IL)
City Colls of Chicago,
Wilbur Wright
College (IL)
Coastal Carolina Comm
Coll (NC)
Coll of Marin (CA)
Coll of San Mateo (CA)
Coll of The Albemarle (NC)
Coll of the Desert (CA)
Coll of the Redwoods (CA)
Comm Coll of Beaver
County (PA)
Comm Coll of
Philadelphia (PA)
Cosumnes River Coll,
Sacramento (CA)
El Camino Coll (CA)
Erie Comm Coll, South
Campus (NY)
Essex County Coll (NJ)
Fayetteville Tech Comm
Coll (NC)
Finger Lakes Comm
Coll (NY)
Forsyth Tech Comm
Coll (NC)
Front Range Comm
Coll (CO)
Fullerton Coll (CA)
Golden West Coll (CA)
Grand Rapids Comm
Coll (MI)
Greenville Tech Coll (SC)
Guilford Tech Comm
Coll (NC)
Harper Coll (IL)
Harrisburg Area Comm
Coll (PA)
Hartnell Coll (CA)
Hawkeye Comm Coll (IA)
Hillsborough Comm
Coll (FL)
Inst of Design and
Construction (NY)

John Tyler Comm Coll (VA)
Lake Land Coll (IL)
Laney Coll (CA)
Lansing Comm Coll (MI)
Los Angeles City Coll (CA)
Los Angeles Harbor Coll (CA)
Los Angeles Pierce Coll (CA)
Madison Area Tech Coll (WI)
Massasoit Comm Coll (MA)
Metropolitan Comm Coll (NE)
Miami Dade Coll (FL)
Midlands Tech Coll (SC)
Minnesota State Comm and Tech Coll–Fergus Falls (MN)
Mississippi Delta Comm Coll (MS)
Mott Comm Coll (MI)
Mt. Hood Comm Coll (OR)
Mt. San Antonio Coll (CA)
New England Inst of Technology (RI)
New Hampshire Tech Inst (NH)
New River Comm Coll (VA)
Northampton County Area Comm Coll (PA)
Northland Comm and Tech Coll–Thief River Falls (MN)
Oakland Comm Coll (MI)
Oklahoma State U, Oklahoma City (OK)
Oklahoma State U, Okmulgee (OK)
Onondaga Comm Coll (NY)
Orange Coast Coll (CA)
Palo Alto Coll (TX)
Pasadena City Coll (CA)
Penn State Fayette, The Eberly Campus (PA)
Penn State Worthington Scranton (PA)
St. Cloud Tech Coll (MN)
Salt Lake Comm Coll (UT)
San Bernardino Valley Coll (CA)
Sandhills Comm Coll (NC)
Seminole Comm Coll (FL)
Southeast Tech Inst (SD)
Southern Maine Comm Coll (ME)
Spokane Comm Coll (WA)
Springfield Tech Comm Coll (MA)
Stark State Coll of Technology (OH)
State U of New York Coll of Agriculture and Technology at Morrisville (NY)
State U of New York Coll of Technology at Alfred (NY)
Technology Education Coll (OH)
Terra State Comm Coll (OH)
Three Rivers Comm Coll (CT)
Westmoreland County Comm Coll (PA)

Architectural Technology
City Colls of Chicago, Wilbur Wright College (IL)

Architecture
Allen County Comm Coll (KS)
Barton County Comm Coll (KS)
Central Maine Comm Coll (ME)
Clarendon Coll (TX)
Harrisburg Area Comm Coll (PA)
Howard Comm Coll (MD)
Oakland Comm Coll (MI)
Tulsa Comm Coll (OK)

Area Studies Related
Oklahoma City Comm Coll (OK)

Army ROTC/Military Science
Brigham Young U – Idaho (ID)
Georgia Military Coll (GA)
New Mexico Military Inst (NM)

Sacramento City Coll (CA)

Art
Allen County Comm Coll (KS)
Amarillo Coll (TX)
Angelina Coll (TX)
Anne Arundel Comm Coll (MD)
Anoka-Ramsey Comm Coll (MN)
Anoka-Ramsey Comm Coll, Cambridge Campus (MN)
Arizona Western Coll (AZ)
Bainbridge Coll (GA)
Bakersfield Coll (CA)
Barton County Comm Coll (KS)
Berkeley City Coll (CA)
Brigham Young U – Idaho (ID)
Bucks County Comm Coll (PA)
Burlington County Coll (NJ)
Caldwell Comm Coll and Tech Inst (NC)
Cankdeska Cikana Comm Coll (ND)
Cañada Coll (CA)
Cape Cod Comm Coll (MA)
Cecil Comm Coll (MD)
Centralia Coll (WA)
Central Oregon Comm Coll (OR)
Central Piedmont Comm Coll (NC)
Central Wyoming Coll (WY)
Cerritos Coll (CA)
Chaffey Coll (CA)
Chesapeake Coll (MD)
Chipola Coll (FL)
Citrus Coll (CA)
City Coll of San Francisco (CA)
City Colls of Chicago, Harold Washington College (IL)
City Colls of Chicago, Harry S. Truman College (IL)
City Colls of Chicago, Olive-Harvey College (IL)
City Colls of Chicago, Richard J. Daley College (IL)
City Colls of Chicago, Wilbur Wright College (IL)
Clarendon Coll (TX)
Coahoma Comm Coll (MS)
Coastal Bend Coll (TX)
Coastal Georgia Comm Coll (GA)
Cochise Coll, Douglas (AZ)
Cochise Coll, Sierra Vista (AZ)
Coll of Alameda (CA)
Coll of Lake County (IL)
Coll of Marin (CA)
Coll of San Mateo (CA)
Coll of Southern Idaho (ID)
Coll of Southern Maryland (MD)
Coll of The Albemarle (NC)
Coll of the Canyons (CA)
Coll of the Desert (CA)
Columbia Coll (CA)
Columbia-Greene Comm Coll (NY)
Comm Coll of Allegheny County (PA)
Comm Coll of Philadelphia (PA)
Comm Coll of Rhode Island (RI)
Comm Coll of Southern Nevada (NV)
Contra Costa Coll (CA)
Cosumnes River Coll, Sacramento (CA)
Crafton Hills Coll (CA)
Crowder Coll (MO)
Cuesta Coll (CA)
Cypress Coll (CA)
De Anza Coll (CA)
Dixie State Coll of Utah (UT)
Dodge City Comm Coll (KS)
Eastern Arizona Coll (AZ)
East Georgia Coll (GA)
El Camino Coll (CA)
Elgin Comm Coll (IL)
Essex County Coll (NJ)

Everett Comm Coll (WA)
Folsom Lake Coll (CA)
Foothill Coll (CA)
Frederick Comm Coll (MD)
Fresno City Coll (CA)
Fullerton Coll (CA)
Fulton-Montgomery Comm Coll (NY)
Garrett Coll (MD)
Georgia Highlands Coll (GA)
Golden West Coll (CA)
Gordon Coll (GA)
Grand Rapids Comm Coll (MI)
Grayson County Coll (TX)
Great Basin Coll (NV)
Grossmont Coll (CA)
Harper Coll (IL)
Harrisburg Area Comm Coll (PA)
Hartnell Coll (CA)
Henry Ford Comm Coll (MI)
Hillsborough Comm Coll (FL)
Housatonic Comm Coll (CT)
Howard Comm Coll (MD)
Imperial Valley Coll (CA)
Iowa Lakes Comm Coll (IA)
Irvine Valley Coll (CA)
Joliet Jr Coll (IL)
Kellogg Comm Coll (MI)
Keystone Coll (PA)
Kingsborough Comm Coll of the City U of New York (NY)
Kirkwood Comm Coll (IA)
Kirtland Comm Coll (MI)
Labette Comm Coll (KS)
Lake Tahoe Comm Coll (CA)
Lamar Comm Coll (CO)
Laney Coll (CA)
Lansing Comm Coll (MI)
Laramie County Comm Coll (WY)
Lassen Comm Coll District (CA)
Lawson State Comm Coll (AL)
Lee Coll (TX)
Lehigh Carbon Comm Coll (PA)
Lenoir Comm Coll (NC)
Lincoln Land Comm Coll (IL)
Linn-Benton Comm Coll (OR)
Lorain County Comm Coll (OH)
Los Angeles City Coll (CA)
Los Angeles Pierce Coll (CA)
Los Medanos Coll (CA)
Lower Columbia Coll (WA)
Manatee Comm Coll (FL)
Mendocino Coll (CA)
Merced Coll (CA)
Mesa Comm Coll (AZ)
Miami Dade Coll (FL)
Miami U–Middletown Campus (OH)
Mission Coll (CA)
Mississippi Gulf Coast Comm Coll (MS)
Mohave Comm Coll (AZ)
Mohawk Valley Comm Coll (NY)
Monroe Comm Coll (NY)
Monterey Peninsula Coll (CA)
Montgomery County Comm Coll (PA)
Moorpark Coll (CA)
Morton Coll (IL)
Mount Wachusett Comm Coll (MA)
Murray State Coll (OK)
Muskegon Comm Coll (MI)
Napa Valley Coll (CA)
Nassau Comm Coll (NY)
National Park Comm Coll (AR)
Navarro Coll (TX)
New Mexico Jr Coll (NM)
New Mexico Military Inst (NM)
Northeast Comm Coll (NE)
Northeastern Jr Coll (CO)
North Idaho Coll (ID)
North Seattle Comm Coll (WA)
Northwestern Connecticut Comm Coll (CT)

Northwest Mississippi Comm Coll (MS)
Northwest-Shoals Comm Coll (AL)
Odessa Coll (TX)
Ohlone Coll (CA)
Oklahoma City Comm Coll (OK)
Onondaga Comm Coll (NY)
Orange Coast Coll (CA)
Palm Beach Comm Coll (FL)
Palo Alto Coll (TX)
Parkland Coll (IL)
Pasadena City Coll (CA)
Porterville Coll (CA)
Quinebaug Valley Comm Coll (CT)
Redlands Comm Coll (OK)
Red Rocks Comm Coll (CO)
Reedley Coll (CA)
Ridgewater Coll (MN)
Roane State Comm Coll (TN)
Rose State Coll (OK)
Sacramento City Coll (CA)
St. Catharine Coll (KY)
St. Louis Comm Coll at Florissant Valley (MO)
St. Philip's Coll (TX)
San Bernardino Valley Coll (CA)
Sandhills Comm Coll (NC)
San Diego City Coll (CA)
San Joaquin Delta Coll (CA)
San Juan Coll (NM)
Santa Ana Coll (CA)
Santa Rosa Jr Coll (CA)
Santiago Canyon Coll (CA)
Seminole State Coll (OK)
Shasta Coll (CA)
Sheridan Coll–Sheridan and Gillette (WY)
Skagit Valley Coll (WA)
Southeastern Comm Coll (NC)
South Plains Coll (TX)
Spokane Falls Comm Coll (WA)
State Fair Comm Coll (MO)
Suffolk County Comm Coll (NY)
Taft Coll (CA)
Temple Coll (TX)
Texarkana Coll (TX)
Tulsa Comm Coll (OK)
Tunxis Comm Coll (CT)
Turtle Mountain Comm Coll (ND)
Tyler Jr Coll (TX)
Umpqua Comm Coll (OR)
U of New Mexico–Gallup (NM)
U of New Mexico–Taos (NM)
Victor Valley Coll (CA)
Virginia Western Comm Coll (VA)
Western Nebraska Comm Coll (NE)
Western Piedmont Comm Coll (NC)
Western Texas Coll (TX)
Western Wyoming Comm Coll (WY)
West Hills Comm Coll (CA)
West Los Angeles Coll (CA)
West Valley Coll (CA)
Young Harris Coll (GA)
Yuba Coll (CA)

Art History, Criticism and Conservation
Cankdeska Cikana Comm Coll (ND)
Cañada Coll (CA)
De Anza Coll (CA)
Dixie State Coll of Utah (UT)
El Camino Coll (CA)
Foothill Coll (CA)
Grossmont Coll (CA)
Iowa Lakes Comm Coll (IA)
Manatee Comm Coll (FL)
Monterey Peninsula Coll (CA)
Muskegon Comm Coll (MI)
Palm Beach Comm Coll (FL)
Pasadena City Coll (CA)
St. Catharine Coll (KY)
Santa Barbara City Coll (CA)

Skagit Valley Coll (WA)
Umpqua Comm Coll (OR)

Artificial Intelligence and Robotics
Cecil Comm Coll (MD)
Chattanooga State Tech Comm Coll (TN)
Cuesta Coll (CA)
Gateway Tech Coll (WI)
Henry Ford Comm Coll (MI)
Kirkwood Comm Coll (IA)
Lorain County Comm Coll (OH)
Metropolitan Comm Coll–Business & Technology Campus (MO)
New Hampshire Comm Tech Coll, Nashua/Claremont (NH)
Oklahoma State U, Okmulgee (OK)
Raritan Valley Comm Coll (NJ)
Richland Coll (TX)
San Diego City Coll (CA)
Southeastern Comm Coll, North Campus (IA)
Southeast Tech Inst (SD)
South Seattle Comm Coll (WA)
Spokane Comm Coll (WA)
Tulsa Comm Coll (OK)
Westmoreland County Comm Coll (PA)

Arts Management
Cuesta Coll (CA)

Art Teacher Education
Angelina Coll (TX)
Bakersfield Coll (CA)
Coastal Bend Coll (TX)
Eastern Arizona Coll (AZ)
Grayson County Coll (TX)
Iowa Lakes Comm Coll (IA)
Jones County Jr Coll (MS)
Kellogg Comm Coll (MI)
Kirkwood Comm Coll (IA)
Los Angeles Mission Coll (CA)
McLennan Comm Coll (TX)
Mississippi Delta Comm Coll (MS)
Mississippi Gulf Coast Comm Coll (MS)
Muskegon Comm Coll (MI)
New Mexico Jr Coll (NM)
Northeast Comm Coll (NE)
Northeastern Jr Coll (CO)
Oxnard Coll (CA)
Parkland Coll (IL)
Roane State Comm Coll (TN)
St. Catharine Coll (KY)
Sandhills Comm Coll (NC)
Trinidad State Jr Coll (CO)
Umpqua Comm Coll (OR)
Wallace State Comm Coll (AL)
Western Nebraska Comm Coll (NE)
Western Texas Coll (TX)
Young Harris Coll (GA)

Asian Studies
City Coll of San Francisco (CA)
El Camino Coll (CA)
Laney Coll (CA)
Manatee Comm Coll (FL)
Miami Dade Coll (FL)

Astronomy
Anne Arundel Comm Coll (MD)
Crafton Hills Coll (CA)
El Camino Coll (CA)
Fullerton Coll (CA)
Iowa Lakes Comm Coll (IA)
Manatee Comm Coll (FL)
North Idaho Coll (ID)
Pasadena City Coll (CA)
San Bernardino Valley Coll (CA)
Santa Rosa Jr Coll (CA)
Tulsa Comm Coll (OK)

Athletic Training
Allen County Comm Coll (KS)
Barton County Comm Coll (KS)
Brigham Young U – Idaho (ID)

Comm Coll of Allegheny County (PA)
Dean Coll (MA)
Dodge City Comm Coll (KS)
Foothill Coll (CA)
Iowa Lakes Comm Coll (IA)
Lorain County Comm Coll (OH)
Louisburg Coll (NC)
Meridian Comm Coll (MS)
Neosho County Comm Coll (KS)
New Hampshire Comm Tech Coll, Manchester/Stratham (NH)
New Mexico Jr Coll (NM)
North Idaho Coll (ID)
Northland Comm and Tech Coll–Thief River Falls (MN)
Odessa Coll (TX)
Orange Coast Coll (CA)
Santa Barbara City Coll (CA)
Santa Rosa Jr Coll (CA)
Wenatchee Valley Coll (WA)

Atmospheric Sciences and Meteorology
City Coll of San Francisco (CA)
Everett Comm Coll (WA)
Santa Rosa Jr Coll (CA)

Audio Engineering
Northeast Comm Coll (NE)
Ridgewater Coll (MN)
South Plains Coll (TX)

Audiology and Hearing Sciences
Arkansas State U–Mountain Home (AR)

Audiology and Speech-Language Pathology
Miami Dade Coll (FL)

Audiovisual Communications Technologies Related
Brown Mackie Coll–Cincinnati (OH)
Olympic Coll (WA)

Autobody/Collision and Repair Technology
Antelope Valley Coll (CA)
Bismarck State Coll (ND)
Black Hawk Coll, Moline (IL)
Central Comm Coll–Hastings Campus (NE)
Century Coll (MN)
Clackamas Comm Coll (OR)
Coahoma Comm Coll (MS)
Coll of Southern Idaho (ID)
Cypress Coll (CA)
Dixie State Coll of Utah (UT)
Erie Comm Coll, South Campus (NY)
Fresno City Coll (CA)
Grayson County Coll (TX)
Hawkeye Comm Coll (IA)
Hutchinson Comm Coll and Area Vocational School (KS)
Illinois Eastern Comm Colls, Olney Central College (IL)
Iowa Lakes Comm Coll (IA)
Laramie County Comm Coll (WY)
Linn State Tech Coll (MO)
Mid-Plains Comm Coll, North Platte (NE)
Mott Comm Coll (MI)
New Hampshire Comm Tech Coll, Nashua/Claremont (NH)
Northeast Comm Coll (NE)
Northwest Iowa Comm Coll (IA)
Northwest KansasTech Coll (KS)
Ozarks Tech Comm Coll (MO)
Parkland Coll (IL)
Pueblo Comm Coll (CO)
Riverland Comm Coll (MN)

Riverside Comm Coll District (CA)
St. Cloud Tech Coll (MN)
St. Philip's Coll (TX)
Salt Lake Comm Coll (UT)
San Juan Coll (NM)
Scott Comm Coll (IA)
Southeast Tech Inst (SD)
Stanly Comm Coll (NC)
State U of New York Coll of Technology at Alfred (NY)
Waukesha County Tech Coll (WI)

Automobile/ Automotive Mechanics Technology

Advanced Technology Inst (VA)
Aims Comm Coll (CO)
Alamance Comm Coll (NC)
Allegany Coll of Maryland (MD)
Alpena Comm Coll (MI)
Amarillo Coll (TX)
Angelina Coll (TX)
Antelope Valley Coll (CA)
Arizona Western Coll (AZ)
Asheville-Buncombe Tech Comm Coll (NC)
ATI Career Training Center, Oakland Park (FL)
Bainbridge Coll (GA)
Bakersfield Coll (CA)
Barstow Coll (CA)
Barton County Comm Coll (KS)
Beaufort County Comm Coll (NC)
Bergen Comm Coll (NJ)
Big Bend Comm Coll (WA)
Bismarck State Coll (ND)
Brigham Young U – Idaho (ID)
Brookhaven Coll (TX)
Broward Comm Coll (FL)
Burlington County Coll (NJ)
Cape Fear Comm Coll (NC)
Catawba Valley Comm Coll (NC)
Cedar Valley Coll (TX)
Central Arizona Coll (AZ)
Central Carolina Comm Coll (NC)
Central Comm Coll– Columbus Campus (NE)
Central Comm Coll–Grand Island Campus (NE)
Central Comm Coll– Hastings Campus (NE)
Central Florida Comm Coll (FL)
Central Maine Comm Coll (ME)
Central Oregon Comm Coll (OR)
Central Piedmont Comm Coll (NC)
Central Texas Coll (TX)
Central Wyoming Coll (WY)
Century Coll (MN)
Cerritos Coll (CA)
Chaffey Coll (CA)
Chattahoochee Tech Coll (GA)
Chattanooga State Tech Comm Coll (TN)
Chippewa Valley Tech Coll (WI)
Cisco Jr Coll (TX)
Citrus Coll (CA)
City Coll of San Francisco (CA)
City Colls of Chicago, Kennedy-King College (IL)
Clackamas Comm Coll (OR)
Clark Coll (WA)
Clovis Comm Coll (NM)
Coastal Bend Coll (TX)
Coll of Alameda (CA)
Coll of DuPage (IL)
Coll of Lake County (IL)
Coll of Marin (CA)
Coll of Southern Idaho (ID)
Coll of the Desert (CA)
Coll of the Redwoods (CA)
Columbia Basin Coll (WA)
Columbia Coll (CA)
Columbia-Greene Comm Coll (NY)

Columbus Tech Coll (GA)
Comm Coll of Philadelphia (PA)
Comm Coll of Southern Nevada (NV)
Contra Costa Coll (CA)
Cossatot Comm Coll of the U of Arkansas (AR)
Cosumnes River Coll, Sacramento (CA)
Cuesta Coll (CA)
Cuyahoga Comm Coll (OH)
Cypress Coll (CA)
De Anza Coll (CA)
DeKalb Tech Coll (GA)
Dixie State Coll of Utah (UT)
Dodge City Comm Coll (KS)
Don Bosco Tech Inst (CA)
East Central Coll (MO)
Eastern Arizona Coll (AZ)
Eastern New Mexico U–Roswell (NM)
El Camino Coll (CA)
Elgin Comm Coll (IL)
Elizabethtown Tech Coll (KY)
Erie Comm Coll, South Campus (NY)
Fayetteville Tech Comm Coll (NC)
Flint Hills Tech Coll (KS)
Florence-Darlington Tech Coll (SC)
Forsyth Tech Comm Coll (NC)
Fox Valley Tech Coll (WI)
Fresno City Coll (CA)
Fullerton Coll (CA)
Fulton-Montgomery Comm Coll (NY)
Gateway Comm Coll (CT)
Gateway Tech Coll (WI)
George C. Wallace Comm Coll (AL)
Georgia Highlands Coll (GA)
Gloucester County Coll (NJ)
Golden West Coll (CA)
Grand Rapids Comm Coll (MI)
Grays Harbor Coll (WA)
Greenville Tech Coll (SC)
Griffin Tech Coll (GA)
Guilford Tech Comm Coll (NC)
Gwinnett Tech Coll (GA)
Harrisburg Area Comm Coll (PA)
Hartnell Coll (CA)
Hawkeye Comm Coll (IA)
H. Councill Trenholm State Tech Coll (AL)
Hennepin Tech Coll (MN)
Henry Ford Comm Coll (MI)
Houston Comm Coll System (TX)
Hutchinson Comm Coll and Area Vocational School (KS)
Illinois Eastern Comm Colls, Olney Central College (IL)
Illinois Valley Comm Coll (IL)
Imperial Valley Coll (CA)
Iowa Lakes Comm Coll (IA)
Isothermal Comm Coll (NC)
Joliet Jr Coll (IL)
Kankakee Comm Coll (IL)
Kent State U, Trumbull Campus (OH)
Kirkwood Comm Coll (IA)
Kirtland Comm Coll (MI)
Lake Land Coll (IL)
Lansing Comm Coll (MI)
Laramie County Comm Coll (WY)
Las Positas Coll (CA)
Lassen Comm Coll District (CA)
Leeward Comm Coll (HI)
Lincoln Land Comm Coll (IL)
Linn-Benton Comm Coll (OR)
Linn State Tech Coll (MO)
Los Angeles Harbor Coll (CA)
Los Angeles Pierce Coll (CA)
Los Medanos Coll (CA)

Lower Columbia Coll (WA)
Macomb Comm Coll (MI)
Madison Area Tech Coll (WI)
Martin Comm Coll (NC)
Maui Comm Coll (HI)
Mendocino Coll (CA)
Merced Coll (CA)
Mesa Comm Coll (AZ)
Metropolitan Comm Coll (NE)
Metropolitan Comm Coll–Longview (MO)
Midlands Tech Coll (SC)
Mid-Plains Comm Coll, North Platte (NE)
Minneapolis Comm and Tech Coll (MN)
Minnesota State Coll– Southeast Tech (MN)
Mississippi Gulf Coast Comm Coll (MS)
Mohave Comm Coll (AZ)
Monroe Comm Coll (NY)
Monterey Peninsula Coll (CA)
Montgomery Coll (MD)
Moraine Valley Comm Coll (IL)
Morgan Comm Coll (CO)
Morton Coll (IL)
Mott Comm Coll (MI)
Mt. Hood Comm Coll (OR)
Mount Wachusett Comm Coll (MA)
Muskegon Comm Coll (MI)
Naugatuck Valley Comm Coll (CT)
New England Inst of Technology (RI)
New Hampshire Comm Tech Coll, Manchester/ Stratham (NH)
New Hampshire Comm Tech Coll, Nashua/ Claremont (NH)
New Mexico Jr Coll (NM)
New River Comm Coll (VA)
Nicolet Area Tech Coll (WI)
Northampton County Area Comm Coll (PA)
North Arkansas Coll (AR)
North Central Kansas Tech Coll (KS)
North Central Missouri Coll (MO)
North Central Texas Coll (TX)
Northeast Comm Coll (NE)
Northeastern Jr Coll (CO)
Northeast State Tech Comm Coll (TN)
Northern Maine Comm Coll (ME)
North Idaho Coll (ID)
North Iowa Area Comm Coll (IA)
Northland Comm and Tech Coll–Thief River Falls (MN)
Northwestern Tech Coll (GA)
Northwest Iowa Comm Coll (IA)
Northwest KansasTech Coll (KS)
Oakland Comm Coll (MI)
Odessa Coll (TX)
Ogeechee Tech Coll (GA)
Ohio Tech Coll (OH)
Oklahoma City Comm Coll (OK)
Oklahoma State U, Okmulgee (OK)
Olympic Coll (WA)
Onondaga Comm Coll (NY)
Ouachita Tech Coll (AR)
Oxnard Coll (CA)
Ozarka Coll (AR)
Ozarks Tech Comm Coll (MO)
Palau Comm Coll (Palau)
Pamlico Comm Coll (NC)
Parkland Coll (IL)
Pasadena City Coll (CA)
Peninsula Coll (WA)
Piedmont Tech Coll (SC)
Pima Comm Coll (AZ)
Pine Tech Coll (MN)
Porterville Coll (CA)
Pueblo Comm Coll (CO)
Ranger Coll (TX)
Raritan Valley Comm Coll (NJ)
Reedley Coll (CA)
Renton Tech Coll (WA)
Richland Comm Coll (IL)

Riverside Comm Coll District (CA)
Rogue Comm Coll (OR)
St. Cloud Tech Coll (MN)
St. Philip's Coll (TX)
San Bernardino Valley Coll (CA)
Sandhills Comm Coll (NC)
San Diego City Coll (CA)
San Joaquin Delta Coll (CA)
San Juan Coll (NM)
Santa Ana Coll (CA)
Santa Barbara City Coll (CA)
Savannah Tech Coll (GA)
Scott Comm Coll (IA)
Seminole Comm Coll (FL)
Shasta Coll (CA)
Skagit Valley Coll (WA)
Southeastern Comm Coll, North Campus (IA)
Southeast Tech Inst (SD)
Southern Maine Comm Coll (ME)
South Piedmont Comm Coll (NC)
South Plains Coll (TX)
South Seattle Comm Coll (WA)
South Texas Coll (TX)
Southwestern Comm Coll (NC)
Southwestern Michigan Coll (MI)
Southwest Mississippi Comm Coll (MS)
Southwest Texas Jr Coll (TX)
Spokane Comm Coll (WA)
Stark State Coll of Technology (OH)
State Fair Comm Coll (MO)
State U of New York Coll of Agriculture and Technology at Morrisville (NY)
State U of New York Coll of Technology at Alfred (NY)
State U of New York Coll of Technology at Canton (NY)
Suffolk County Comm Coll (NY)
Surry Comm Coll (NC)
Taft Coll (CA)
Temple Coll (TX)
Terra State Comm Coll (OH)
Texarkana Coll (TX)
Texas State Tech Coll West Texas (TX)
Tidewater Comm Coll (VA)
Tri-County Comm Coll (NC)
Trident Tech Coll (SC)
Trinidad State Jr Coll (CO)
Tulsa Comm Coll (OK)
Umpqua Comm Coll (OR)
U of Arkansas Comm Coll at Morrilton (AR)
The U of Montana-Helena Coll of Technology (MT)
U of New Mexico–Gallup (NM)
U of Puerto Rico at Carolina (PR)
Ventura Coll (CA)
Vernon Coll (TX)
Victor Valley Coll (CA)
Virginia Western Comm Coll (VA)
Wallace State Comm Coll (AL)
Washington County Comm Coll (ME)
Washington State Comm Coll (OH)
Waukesha County Tech Coll (WI)
Wayne Comm Coll (NC)
Wenatchee Valley Coll (WA)
Westchester Comm Coll (NY)
Western Nevada Comm Coll (NV)
Western Texas Coll (TX)
Western Wyoming Comm Coll (WY)
West Georgia Tech Coll (GA)
West Hills Comm Coll (CA)
West Virginia U at Parkersburg (WV)

Wichita Area Tech Coll (KS)
WyoTech, Fremont (CA)
York Tech Coll (SC)
Yuba Coll (CA)

Automotive Engineering Technology

Cincinnati State Tech and Comm Coll (OH)
Comm Coll of Allegheny County (PA)
Front Range Comm Coll (CO)
Harrisburg Area Comm Coll (PA)
H. Councill Trenholm State Tech Coll (AL)
Macomb Comm Coll (MI)
Massachusetts Bay Comm Coll (MA)
Minnesota State Comm and Tech Coll–Fergus Falls (MN)
Montgomery County Comm Coll (PA)
Owens Comm Coll, Toledo (OH)
Springfield Tech Comm Coll (MA)
Sussex County Comm Coll (NJ)
Terra State Comm Coll (OH)
WyoTech, Fremont (CA)

Aviation/Airway Management

Academy Coll (MN)
Broward Comm Coll (FL)
Chattanooga State Tech Comm Coll (TN)
Comm Coll of Allegheny County (PA)
Cypress Coll (CA)
Dixie State Coll of Utah (UT)
Georgia Aviation & Tech Coll (GA)
Guilford Tech Comm Coll (NC)
Inver Hills Comm Coll (MN)
Iowa Lakes Comm Coll (IA)
Lehigh Carbon Comm Coll (PA)
Lenoir Comm Coll (NC)
Miami Dade Coll (FL)
Northland Comm and Tech Coll–Thief River Falls (MN)
Oakland Comm Coll (MI)
Palo Alto Coll (TX)
Pasadena City Coll (CA)

Avionics Maintenance Technology

Aims Comm Coll (CO)
Antelope Valley Coll (CA)
Big Bend Comm Coll (WA)
Broward Comm Coll (FL)
Chandler-Gilbert Comm Coll (AZ)
Chattanooga State Tech Comm Coll (TN)
City Coll of San Francisco (CA)
City Colls of Chicago, Richard J. Daley College (IL)
Cochise Coll, Douglas (AZ)
Coll of Alameda (CA)
Coll of San Mateo (CA)
Comm Coll of Beaver County (PA)
Cuyahoga Comm Coll (OH)
Everett Comm Coll (WA)
Foothill Coll (CA)
Gateway Comm Coll (CT)
Greenville Tech Coll (SC)
Guilford Tech Comm Coll (NC)
Hawkeye Comm Coll (IA)
Housatonic Comm Coll (CT)
Kankakee Comm Coll (IL)
Lansing Comm Coll (MI)
Lehigh Carbon Comm Coll (PA)
Lenoir Comm Coll (NC)
Los Angeles Mission Coll (CA)
Metropolitan Comm Coll–Maple Woods (MO)
Minneapolis Comm and Tech Coll (MN)

Minnesota State Coll– Southeast Tech (MN)
Mohawk Valley Comm Coll (NY)
Mt. Hood Comm Coll (OR)
Mt. San Antonio Coll (CA)
Navarro Coll (TX)
New Hampshire Comm Tech Coll, Nashua/ Claremont (NH)
Northland Comm and Tech Coll–Thief River Falls (MN)
Oklahoma City Comm Coll (OK)
Oklahoma State U, Okmulgee (OK)
Orange Coast Coll (CA)
Palo Alto Coll (TX)
Pasadena City Coll (CA)
Pittsburgh Inst of Aeronautics (PA)
Quinebaug Valley Comm Coll (CT)
Reedley Coll (CA)
Rose State Coll (OK)
Sacramento City Coll (CA)
Salt Lake Comm Coll (UT)
Shasta Coll (CA)
Southern U at Shreveport (LA)
South Seattle Comm Coll (WA)
Southwest Texas Jr Coll (TX)
Spokane Comm Coll (WA)
Three Rivers Comm Coll (CT)
Tulsa Comm Coll (OK)
U of Cincinnati Clermont Coll (OH)
Wallace State Comm Coll (AL)
Wayne Comm Coll (NC)
West Los Angeles Coll (CA)

Baking and Pastry Arts

Clark Coll (WA)
Coll of DuPage (IL)
The Cooking and Hospitality Inst of Chicago (IL)
Culinary Inst Alain & Marie LeNotre (TX)
El Centro Coll (TX)
Montgomery County Comm Coll (PA)
New England Culinary Inst (VT)
Orlando Culinary Academy (FL)
Quality Coll of Culinary Careers (AZ)
Western Culinary Inst (OR)

Banking and Financial Support Services

Alamance Comm Coll (NC)
Alexandria Tech Coll (MN)
Allen County Comm Coll (KS)
Asnuntuck Comm Coll (CT)
Barton County Comm Coll (KS)
Berkshire Comm Coll (MA)
Black Hawk Coll, Moline (IL)
Catawba Valley Comm Coll (NC)
Central Georgia Tech Coll (GA)
Central New Mexico Comm Coll (NM)
Comm Coll of Allegheny County (PA)
Comm Coll of Rhode Island (RI)
Eastern New Mexico U–Roswell (NM)
Fayetteville Tech Comm Coll (NC)
Finger Lakes Comm Coll (NY)
Gateway Tech Coll (WI)
Harrisburg Area Comm Coll (PA)
Lanier Tech Coll (GA)
Laurel Business Inst (PA)
Madisonville Comm Coll (KY)
Mohawk Valley Comm Coll (NY)
Ogeechee Tech Coll (GA)
Ozarka Coll (AR)
Pennsylvania Highland Comm Coll (PA)

St. Cloud Tech Coll (MN)
San Juan Coll (NM)
Seminole Comm Coll (FL)
Southern U at
Shreveport (LA)
Terra State Comm
Coll (OH)
Valdosta Tech Coll (GA)
West Virginia State Comm
and Tech Coll (WV)

Barbering
Coahoma Comm Coll (MS)
Olympic Coll (WA)

Behavioral Sciences
Amarillo Coll (TX)
Anne Arundel Comm
Coll (MD)
Citrus Coll (CA)
Clarendon Coll (TX)
Cochise Coll, Sierra
Vista (AZ)
Colby Comm Coll (KS)
Coll of Marin (CA)
Colorado Mountain
Coll (CO)
Colorado Mountain Coll,
Alpine Campus (CO)
Comm Coll of Southern
Nevada (NV)
De Anza Coll (CA)
Dodge City Comm
Coll (KS)
Fulton-Montgomery Comm
Coll (NY)
Garrett Coll (MD)
Gordon Coll (GA)
Hartnell Coll (CA)
Imperial Valley Coll (CA)
Iowa Lakes Comm
Coll (IA)
Irvine Valley Coll (CA)
Labette Comm Coll (KS)
Lamar Comm Coll (CO)
Los Angeles Southwest
Coll (CA)
Los Medanos Coll (CA)
Miami Dade Coll (FL)
Mississippi Delta Comm
Coll (MS)
Monroe Comm Coll (NY)
Moorpark Coll (CA)
Napa Valley Coll (CA)
Northwestern Connecticut
Comm Coll (CT)
Orange Coast Coll (CA)
Oxnard Coll (CA)
Quincy Coll (MA)
San Diego City Coll (CA)
San Joaquin Delta
Coll (CA)
Santa Rosa Jr Coll (CA)
Seminole State Coll (OK)
South Texas Coll (TX)
Tulsa Comm Coll (OK)
Tyler Jr Coll (TX)
Umpqua Comm Coll (OR)
U of New
Mexico–Taos (NM)
Vincennes U Jasper
Campus (IN)
West Virginia State Comm
and Tech Coll (WV)

Biblical Studies
Amarillo Coll (TX)
Hesston Coll (KS)
Rosedale Bible Coll (OH)
St. Catharine Coll (KY)
Somerset Christian
Coll (NJ)

Bilingual and Multilingual Education
Clovis Comm Coll (NM)

Biochemical Technology
Niagara County Comm
Coll (NY)

Biological and Physical Sciences
Angelina Coll (TX)
Anne Arundel Comm
Coll (MD)
Arizona Western Coll (AZ)
Baltimore City Comm
Coll (MD)
Bowling Green State
U–Firelands Coll (OH)
Burlington County
Coll (NJ)
Cabrillo Coll (CA)
Caldwell Comm Coll and
Tech Inst (NC)
Cañada Coll (CA)
Cape Cod Comm
Coll (MA)
Centralia Coll (WA)

Central Oregon Comm
Coll (OR)
Central Virginia Comm
Coll (VA)
Chesapeake Coll (MD)
Chipola Coll (FL)
City Colls of Chicago,
Wilbur Wright
College (IL)
Cleveland Comm Coll (NC)
Coastal Bend Coll (TX)
Coconino Comm Coll (AZ)
Colby Comm Coll (KS)
Coll of Alameda (CA)
Coll of DuPage (IL)
Coll of Lake County (IL)
Coll of the Canyons (CA)
Colorado Mountain
Coll (CO)
Colorado Mountain Coll,
Alpine Campus (CO)
Columbia-Greene Comm
Coll (NY)
Comm Coll of
Philadelphia (PA)
Comm Coll of Rhode
Island (RI)
Comm Coll of Southern
Nevada (NV)
Cosumnes River Coll,
Sacramento (CA)
Cottey Coll (MO)
Crafton Hills Coll (CA)
Cypress Coll (CA)
Dabney S. Lancaster
Comm Coll (VA)
Danville Comm Coll (VA)
Dodge City Comm
Coll (KS)
Eastern Shore Comm
Coll (VA)
Elgin Comm Coll (IL)
Finger Lakes Comm
Coll (NY)
Florence-Darlington Tech
Coll (SC)
Fort Berthold Comm
Coll (ND)
Fulton-Montgomery Comm
Coll (NY)
Georgia Highlands
Coll (GA)
Georgia Military Coll (GA)
Germanna Comm
Coll (VA)
Golden West Coll (CA)
Gordon Coll (GA)
Guilford Tech Comm
Coll (NC)
Harper Coll (IL)
Howard Comm Coll (MD)
Illinois Eastern Comm
Colls, Frontier
Community College (IL)
Illinois Eastern Comm
Colls, Lincoln Trail
College (IL)
Illinois Eastern Comm
Colls, Olney Central
College (IL)
Illinois Eastern Comm
Colls, Wabash Valley
College (IL)
Imperial Valley Coll (CA)
Iowa Lakes Comm
Coll (IA)
Irvine Valley Coll (CA)
Isothermal Comm
Coll (NC)
John Wood Comm Coll (IL)
Jones County Jr Coll (MS)
Kankakee Comm Coll (IL)
Kirkwood Comm Coll (IA)
Kirtland Comm Coll (MI)
Lake Land Coll (IL)
Lake Tahoe Comm
Coll (CA)
Lamar Comm Coll (CO)
Laney Coll (CA)
Lansing Comm Coll (MI)
Laramie County Comm
Coll (WY)
Lassen Comm Coll
District (CA)
Lincoln Land Comm
Coll (IL)
Linn-Benton Comm
Coll (OR)
Little Big Horn Coll (MT)
Lorain County Comm
Coll (OH)
Los Angeles City Coll (CA)
Louisburg Coll (NC)
Marion Military Inst (AL)
Massachusetts Bay Comm
Coll (MA)
Merced Coll (CA)

Metropolitan Comm
Coll–Longview (MO)
Metropolitan Comm
Coll–Maple
Woods (MO)
Metropolitan Comm
Coll–Penn Valley (MO)
Miami U–Middletown
Campus (OH)
Middlesex Comm Coll (CT)
Minnesota State Comm
and Tech Coll–Fergus
Falls (MN)
Mississippi Gulf Coast
Comm Coll (MS)
Monroe Comm Coll (NY)
Moraine Valley Comm
Coll (IL)
Morgan Comm Coll (CO)
Morton Coll (IL)
Murray State Coll (OK)
Napa Valley Coll (CA)
Naugatuck Valley Comm
Coll (CT)
Navarro Coll (TX)
Neosho County Comm
Coll (KS)
New Mexico Jr Coll (NM)
New Mexico Military
Inst (NM)
New River Comm Coll (VA)
Niagara County Comm
Coll (NY)
North Central Texas
Coll (TX)
North Country Comm
Coll (NY)
Northeast Comm Coll (NE)
Northeastern Jr Coll (CO)
Northern Essex Comm
Coll (MA)
Northern Oklahoma
Coll (OK)
North Idaho Coll (ID)
Onondaga Comm
Coll (NY)
Parkland Coll (IL)
Pasadena City Coll (CA)
Passaic County Comm
Coll (NJ)
Peninsula Coll (WA)
Penn State Beaver (PA)
Penn State DuBois (PA)
Penn State Fayette, The
Eberly Campus (PA)
Penn State
McKeesport (PA)
Penn State New
Kensington (PA)
Penn State Schuylkill (PA)
Penn State Shenango (PA)
Piedmont Tech Coll (SC)
Piedmont Virginia Comm
Coll (VA)
Porterville Coll (CA)
Potomac State Coll of
West Virginia U (WV)
Rainy River Comm
Coll (MN)
Rappahannock Comm
Coll (VA)
Redlands Comm Coll (OK)
Red Rocks Comm
Coll (CO)
Richland Comm Coll (IL)
Ridgewater Coll (MN)
Sacramento City Coll (CA)
St. Catharine Coll (KY)
San Antonio Coll (TX)
Sandhills Comm Coll (NC)
Santa Ana Coll (CA)
Sheridan Coll–Sheridan
and Gillette (WY)
Skagit Valley Coll (WA)
Southeastern Comm
Coll (NC)
South Georgia Coll (GA)
South Plains Coll (TX)
South Seattle Comm
Coll (WA)
Southside Virginia Comm
Coll (VA)
Southwest Mississippi
Comm Coll (MS)
Southwest Texas Jr
Coll (TX)
Southwest Virginia Comm
Coll (VA)
State U of New York Coll
of Technology at
Alfred (NY)
State U of New York Coll
of Technology at
Canton (NY)
Suffolk County Comm
Coll (NY)
Sussex County Comm
Coll (NJ)

Tidewater Comm Coll (VA)
Tompkins Cortland Comm
Coll (NY)
Treasure Valley Comm
Coll (OR)
Trident Tech Coll (SC)
Trinidad State Jr Coll (CO)
Turtle Mountain Comm
Coll (ND)
Ulster County Comm
Coll (NY)
Umpqua Comm Coll (OR)
U of New Mexico–Los
Alamos Branch (NM)
U of South Carolina
Lancaster (SC)
Victor Valley Coll (CA)
Virginia Highlands Comm
Coll (VA)
Virginia Western Comm
Coll (VA)
Washington State Comm
Coll (OH)
Wayne Comm Coll (NC)
Westchester Comm
Coll (NY)
Western Wyoming Comm
Coll (WY)
Wytheville Comm Coll (VA)
Young Harris Coll (GA)
Yuba Coll (CA)

Biology/Biological Sciences
Allen County Comm
Coll (KS)
Alpena Comm Coll (MI)
Amarillo Coll (TX)
Angelina Coll (TX)
Anne Arundel Comm
Coll (MD)
Antelope Valley Coll (CA)
Arizona Western Coll (AZ)
Bainbridge Coll (GA)
Bakersfield Coll (CA)
Barton County Comm
Coll (KS)
Bergen Comm Coll (NJ)
Berkshire Comm Coll (MA)
Blinn Coll (TX)
Brigham Young U –
Idaho (ID)
Bucks County Comm
Coll (PA)
Burlington County
Coll (NJ)
Calhoun Comm Coll (AL)
Cañada Coll (CA)
Cecil Comm Coll (MD)
Centralia Coll (WA)
Central Piedmont Comm
Coll (NC)
Central Texas Coll (TX)
Central Wyoming
Coll (WY)
Cerritos Coll (CA)
Chaffey Coll (CA)
Chattanooga State Tech
Comm Coll (TN)
Cisco Jr Coll (TX)
Citrus Coll (CA)
City Colls of Chicago,
Harold Washington
College (IL)
City Colls of Chicago,
Kennedy-King
College (IL)
City Colls of Chicago,
Olive-Harvey
College (IL)
Clarendon Coll (TX)
Coahoma Comm Coll (MS)
Coastal Bend Coll (TX)
Coastal Georgia Comm
Coll (GA)
Cochise Coll, Douglas (AZ)
Cochise Coll, Sierra
Vista (AZ)
Colby Comm Coll (KS)
Coll of Alameda (CA)
Coll of Marin (CA)
Coll of San Mateo (CA)
Coll of Southern Idaho (ID)
Coll of Southern
Maryland (MD)
Coll of the Canyons (CA)
Coll of the Desert (CA)
Coll of the Siskiyous (CA)
Colorado Mountain
Coll (CO)
Colorado Mountain Coll,
Alpine Campus (CO)
Columbia Coll (CA)
Comm Coll of Allegheny
County (PA)
Comm Coll of Beaver
County (PA)
Comm Coll of Southern
Nevada (NV)

Contra Costa Coll (CA)
Cosumnes River Coll,
Sacramento (CA)
Crafton Hills Coll (CA)
Crowder Coll (MO)
Cuesta Coll (CA)
Cypress Coll (CA)
De Anza Coll (CA)
Dixie State Coll of
Utah (UT)
Dodge City Comm
Coll (KS)
East Central Coll (MO)
Eastern Arizona Coll (AZ)
East Georgia Coll (GA)
El Camino Coll (CA)
Essex County Coll (NJ)
Everett Comm Coll (WA)
Finger Lakes Comm
Coll (NY)
Folsom Lake Coll (CA)
Foothill Coll (CA)
Frederick Comm Coll (MD)
Fullerton Coll (CA)
Fulton-Montgomery Comm
Coll (NY)
Garrett Coll (MD)
Gloucester County
Coll (NJ)
Golden West Coll (CA)
Gordon Coll (GA)
Grayson County Coll (TX)
Grossmont Coll (CA)
Harper Coll (IL)
Harrisburg Area Comm
Coll (PA)
Hawkeye Comm Coll (IA)
Holyoke Comm Coll (MA)
Hutchinson Comm Coll
and Area Vocational
School (KS)
Iowa Lakes Comm
Coll (IA)
Irvine Valley Coll (CA)
Joliet Jr Coll (IL)
Jones County Jr Coll (MS)
Kellogg Comm Coll (MI)
Kennebec Valley Comm
Coll (ME)
Keystone Coll (PA)
Kingsborough Comm Coll
of the City U of New
York (NY)
Kirkwood Comm Coll (IA)
Labette Comm Coll (KS)
Lamar Comm Coll (CO)
Lansing Comm Coll (MI)
Laramie County Comm
Coll (WY)
Lassen Comm Coll
District (CA)
Lawson State Comm
Coll (AL)
Lee Coll (TX)
Lehigh Carbon Comm
Coll (PA)
Linn-Benton Comm
Coll (OR)
Lorain County Comm
Coll (OH)
Los Angeles City Coll (CA)
Los Angeles Harbor
Coll (CA)
Los Angeles Mission
Coll (CA)
Los Angeles Southwest
Coll (CA)
Los Medanos Coll (CA)
Louisburg Coll (NC)
Lower Columbia Coll (WA)
Macomb Comm Coll (MI)
Manatee Comm Coll (FL)
Mendocino Coll (CA)
Mesa Comm Coll (AZ)
Metropolitan Comm
Coll–Longview (MO)
Metropolitan Comm
Coll–Maple
Woods (MO)
Metropolitan Comm
Coll–Penn Valley (MO)
Miami Dade Coll (FL)
Mississippi Delta Comm
Coll (MS)
Monroe Comm Coll (NY)
Monterey Peninsula
Coll (CA)
Montgomery County
Comm Coll (PA)
Moorpark Coll (CA)
Navarro Coll (TX)
New Mexico Jr Coll (NM)
New Mexico Military
Inst (NM)
Northampton County Area
Comm Coll (PA)
Northeast Comm Coll (NE)
Northeastern Jr Coll (CO)

North Hennepin Comm
Coll (MN)
North Idaho Coll (ID)
Northwestern Connecticut
Comm Coll (CT)
Odessa Coll (TX)
Ohlone Coll (CA)
Oklahoma City Comm
Coll (OK)
Orange Coast Coll (CA)
Oxnard Coll (CA)
Palm Beach Comm
Coll (FL)
Palo Alto Coll (TX)
Pasadena City Coll (CA)
Porterville Coll (CA)
Potomac State Coll of
West Virginia U (WV)
Raritan Valley Comm
Coll (NJ)
Redlands Comm Coll (OK)
Red Rocks Comm
Coll (CO)
Reedley Coll (CA)
Roane State Comm
Coll (TN)
Rose State Coll (OK)
Roxbury Comm Coll (MA)
St. Catharine Coll (KY)
St. Philip's Coll (TX)
Salt Lake Comm Coll (UT)
San Bernardino Valley
Coll (CA)
San Diego City Coll (CA)
San Joaquin Delta
Coll (CA)
San Juan Coll (NM)
Santa Ana Coll (CA)
Santa Barbara City
Coll (CA)
Santa Rosa Jr Coll (CA)
Santiago Canyon Coll (CA)
Seminole State Coll (OK)
Sheridan Coll–Sheridan
and Gillette (WY)
Skagit Valley Coll (WA)
Southern U at
Shreveport (LA)
South Georgia Coll (GA)
South Plains Coll (TX)
Southwest Mississippi
Comm Coll (MS)
Springfield Tech Comm
Coll (MA)
State U of New York Coll
of Agriculture and
Technology at
Morrisville (NY)
Suffolk County Comm
Coll (NY)
Taft Coll (CA)
Texarkana Coll (TX)
Treasure Valley Comm
Coll (OR)
Trinidad State Jr Coll (CO)
Tulsa Comm Coll (OK)
Turtle Mountain Comm
Coll (ND)
Umpqua Comm Coll (OR)
Union County Coll (NJ)
Ventura Coll (CA)
Victor Valley Coll (CA)
Warren County Comm
Coll (NJ)
Washington State Comm
Coll (OH)
Wenatchee Valley
Coll (WA)
Western Nebraska Comm
Coll (NE)
Western Nevada Comm
Coll (NV)
Western Wyoming Comm
Coll (WY)
West Hills Comm Coll (CA)
West Los Angeles
Coll (CA)
West Valley Coll (CA)
Wright State U, Lake
Campus (OH)
Young Harris Coll (GA)
Yuba Coll (CA)

Biology/ Biotechnology Laboratory Technician
Athens Tech Coll (GA)
Berkeley City Coll (CA)
Coll of San Mateo (CA)
Collin County Comm Coll
District (TX)
Contra Costa Coll (CA)
Fayetteville Tech Comm
Coll (NC)
Finger Lakes Comm
Coll (NY)
Foothill Coll (CA)
Guilford Tech Comm
Coll (NC)

John Tyler Comm Coll (VA)
Kirkwood Comm Coll (IA)
Lansing Comm Coll (MI)
Madison Area Tech
　Coll (WI)
Massachusetts Bay Comm
　Coll (MA)
Middlesex Comm Coll (CT)
Monroe Comm Coll (NY)
Muskegon Comm Coll (MI)
North Shore Comm
　Coll (MA)
Northwest Vista Coll (TX)
The Ohio State U Ag Tech
　Inst (OH)
Salt Lake Comm Coll (UT)
State U of New York Coll
　of Agriculture and
　Technology at
　Morrisville (NY)
State U of New York Coll
　of Technology at
　Alfred (NY)

**Biology Teacher
Education**
Coll of the Siskiyous (CA)
Louisburg Coll (NC)
Manatee Comm Coll (FL)

Biomedical Science
Anoka-Ramsey Comm
　Coll (MN)
Anoka-Ramsey Comm
　Coll, Cambridge
　Campus (MN)

**Biomedical
Technology**
Caldwell Comm Coll and
　Tech Inst (NC)
Cerritos Coll (CA)
Chattahoochee Tech
　Coll (GA)
Cincinnati State Tech and
　Comm Coll (OH)
Comm Coll of
　Philadelphia (PA)
ECPI Coll of
　Technology (VA)
Erie Comm Coll, South
　Campus (NY)
Gateway Comm Coll (CT)
Hillsborough Comm
　Coll (FL)
Howard Comm Coll (MD)
Lehigh Carbon Comm
　Coll (PA)
Madisonville Comm
　Coll (KY)
Miami Dade Coll (FL)
Muskegon Comm Coll (MI)
Napa Valley Coll (CA)
North Arkansas Coll (AR)
North Seattle Comm
　Coll (WA)
Oklahoma City Comm
　Coll (OK)
Parkland Coll (IL)
Penn State DuBois (PA)
Penn State Fayette, The
　Eberly Campus (PA)
Penn State Hazleton (PA)
Penn State New
　Kensington (PA)
Penn State Schuylkill (PA)
Penn State Shenango (PA)
Penn State York (PA)
St. Philip's Coll (TX)
Santa Barbara City
　Coll (CA)
Schoolcraft Coll (MI)
Southeastern Comm Coll,
　North Campus (IA)
Southeast Tech Inst (SD)
Spokane Comm Coll (WA)
Stanly Comm Coll (NC)
Stark State Coll of
　Technology (OH)
Tulsa Comm Coll (OK)

Biotechnology
Alamance Comm Coll (NC)
Augusta Tech Coll (GA)
Bladen Comm Coll (NC)
Briarwood Coll (CT)
Burlington County
　Coll (NJ)
Central New Mexico
　Comm Coll (NM)
Coll of Southern
　Maryland (MD)
Coll of The Albemarle (NC)
Dixie State Coll of
　Utah (UT)
Howard Comm Coll (MD)
Lehigh Carbon Comm
　Coll (PA)
Montgomery County
　Comm Coll (PA)

Northampton County Area
　Comm Coll (PA)
Northern New Mexico
　Coll (NM)
Piedmont Virginia Comm
　Coll (VA)
Santa Barbara City
　Coll (CA)
Southeastern Comm
　Coll (NC)
Springfield Tech Comm
　Coll (MA)

**Biotechnology
Research**
El Centro Coll (TX)

Botany/Plant Biology
Anne Arundel Comm
　Coll (MD)
Brigham Young U –
　Idaho (ID)
Centralia Coll (WA)
Cerritos Coll (CA)
City Coll of San
　Francisco (CA)
Coll of Southern Idaho (ID)
Dixie State Coll of
　Utah (UT)
East Central Coll (MO)
El Camino Coll (CA)
Everett Comm Coll (WA)
Harper Coll (IL)
Iowa Lakes Comm
　Coll (IA)
Lassen Comm Coll
　District (CA)
Miami U–Middletown
　Campus (OH)
North Idaho Coll (ID)
Palm Beach Comm
　Coll (FL)
San Bernardino Valley
　Coll (CA)
San Joaquin Delta
　Coll (CA)
Santa Rosa Jr Coll (CA)
Southern Maine Comm
　Coll (ME)
Tulsa Comm Coll (OK)

Broadcast Journalism
Amarillo Coll (TX)
Anne Arundel Comm
　Coll (MD)
Arizona Western Coll (AZ)
Bakersfield Coll (CA)
Bergen Comm Coll (NJ)
Brigham Young U –
　Idaho (ID)
Centralia Coll (WA)
Chaffey Coll (CA)
Chattanooga State Tech
　Comm Coll (TN)
City Coll of San
　Francisco (CA)
City Colls of Chicago,
　Kennedy-King
　College (IL)
Colby Comm Coll (KS)
Coll of San Mateo (CA)
Cosumnes River Coll,
　Sacramento (CA)
Dixie State Coll of
　Utah (UT)
Dodge City Comm
　Coll (KS)
Finger Lakes Comm
　Coll (NY)
Iowa Lakes Comm
　Coll (IA)
Isothermal Comm
　Coll (NC)
Kingsborough Comm Coll
　of the City U of New
　York (NY)
Kirkwood Comm Coll (IA)
Laney Coll (CA)
Lansing Comm Coll (MI)
Los Angeles City Coll (CA)
Meridian Comm Coll (MS)
Middlesex Comm Coll (CT)
Moorpark Coll (CA)
Mt. Hood Comm Coll (OR)
Navarro Coll (TX)
Northeast Comm Coll (NE)
Northern Oklahoma
　Coll (OK)
Northland Comm and Tech
　Coll–Thief River
　Falls (MN)
Ohlone Coll (CA)
Oklahoma City Comm
　Coll (OK)
Pasadena City Coll (CA)
Ridgewater Coll (MN)
Rose State Coll (OK)
St. Louis Comm Coll at
　Florissant Valley (MO)

San Joaquin Delta
　Coll (CA)
Sussex County Comm
　Coll (NJ)
Trident Tech Coll (SC)
U of Alaska, Prince William
　Sound Comm Coll (AK)

**Building/Construction
Finishing,
Management, and
Inspection Related**
Central New Mexico
　Comm Coll (NM)
Fayetteville Tech Comm
　Coll (NC)
Guilford Tech Comm
　Coll (NC)
Mid-Plains Comm Coll,
　North Platte (NE)
Pima Comm Coll (AZ)
Vatterott Coll (OH)

**Building/Construction
Site Management**
Metropolitan Comm
　Coll–Business &
　Technology
　Campus (MO)
The Ohio State U Ag Tech
　Inst (OH)

**Building/Home/
Construction
Inspection**
Orange Coast Coll (CA)

**Building/Property
Maintenance and
Management**
Coll of DuPage (IL)
Comm Coll of Allegheny
　County (PA)
Erie Comm Coll (NY)
Flint Hills Tech Coll (KS)
Illinois Eastern Comm
　Colls, Lincoln Trail
　College (IL)
Mohawk Valley Comm
　Coll (NY)
Pima Comm Coll (AZ)

**Business
Administration and
Management**
Academy Coll (MN)
AIB Coll of Business (IA)
Alamance Comm Coll (NC)
Alexandria Tech Coll (MN)
Allegany Coll of
　Maryland (MD)
Allen County Comm
　Coll (KS)
Alpena Comm Coll (MI)
Amarillo Coll (TX)
Angelina Coll (TX)
Anne Arundel Comm
　Coll (MD)
Anoka-Ramsey Comm
　Coll (MN)
Anoka-Ramsey Comm
　Coll, Cambridge
　Campus (MN)
Antelope Valley Coll (CA)
Appalachian Tech
　Coll (GA)
Arizona Western Coll (AZ)
Asheville-Buncombe Tech
　Comm Coll (NC)
Ashland Comm and Tech
　Coll (KY)
Asnuntuck Comm
　Coll (CT)
Augusta Tech Coll (GA)
Bainbridge Coll (GA)
Bakersfield Coll (CA)
Baltimore City Comm
　Coll (MD)
Barstow Coll (CA)
Barton County Comm
　Coll (KS)
Beaufort County Comm
　Coll (NC)
Bergen Comm Coll (NJ)
Berkeley City Coll (CA)
Berkeley Coll, West
　Paterson (NJ)
Berkeley Coll-New York
　City Campus (NY)
Berkeley Coll-Westchester
　Campus (NY)
Berkshire Comm Coll (MA)
Black Hawk Coll,
　Moline (IL)
Bladen Comm Coll (NC)
Blinn Coll (TX)
Bramson ORT Coll (NY)
Brevard Comm Coll (FL)
Briarwood Coll (CT)

Brigham Young U –
　Idaho (ID)
Brookhaven Coll (TX)
Broome Comm Coll (NY)
Broward Comm Coll (FL)
Brown Mackie Coll–
　Akron (OH)
Brown Mackie Coll–
　Atlanta (GA)
Brown Mackie Coll–
　Cincinnati (OH)
Brown Mackie Coll–
　Findlay (OH)
Brown Mackie Coll–Fort
　Wayne (IN)
Brown Mackie Coll–
　Hopkinsville (KY)
Brown Mackie Coll–
　Kansas City (KS)
Brown Mackie Coll–
　Louisville (KY)
Brown Mackie Coll–
　Merrillville (IN)
Brown Mackie Coll–
　Miami (FL)
Brown Mackie Coll–North
　Canton (OH)
Brown Mackie Coll–
　Northern Kentucky (KY)
Brown Mackie Coll–
　Salina (KS)
Brown Mackie Coll–South
　Bend (IN)
Brunswick Comm
　Coll (NC)
Bucks County Comm
　Coll (PA)
Burlington County
　Coll (NJ)
Business Inst of
　Pennsylvania,
　Sharon (PA)
Cabrillo Coll (CA)
Caldwell Comm Coll and
　Tech Inst (NC)
Calhoun Comm Coll (AL)
Cambria-Rowe Business
　Coll, Johnstown (PA)
Cankdeska Cikana Comm
　Coll (ND)
Cañada Coll (CA)
Cape Cod Comm
　Coll (MA)
Cape Fear Comm
　Coll (NC)
Capital Comm Coll (CT)
Carroll Comm Coll (MD)
Catawba Valley Comm
　Coll (NC)
Cecil Comm Coll (MD)
Cedar Valley Coll (TX)
Central Arizona Coll (AZ)
Central Carolina Comm
　Coll (NC)
Central Carolina Tech
　Coll (SC)
Central Comm Coll–
　Columbus
　Campus (NE)
Central Comm Coll–Grand
　Island Campus (NE)
Central Comm Coll–
　Hastings Campus (NE)
Central Georgia Tech
　Coll (GA)
Centralia Coll (WA)
Central Lakes Coll (MN)
Central Maine Comm
　Coll (ME)
Central New Mexico
　Comm Coll (NM)
Central Ohio Tech
　Coll (OH)
Central Oregon Comm
　Coll (OR)
Central Piedmont Comm
　Coll (NC)
Central Texas Coll (TX)
Central Virginia Comm
　Coll (VA)
Central Wyoming
　Coll (WY)
Century Coll (MN)
Cerritos Coll (CA)
Chaffey Coll (CA)
Chandler-Gilbert Comm
　Coll (AZ)
Chattahoochee Tech
　Coll (GA)
Chattanooga State Tech
　Comm Coll (TN)
Chesapeake Coll (MD)
Chief Dull Knife Coll (MT)
Chipola Coll (FL)
Cincinnati State Tech and
　Comm Coll (OH)
Cisco Jr Coll (TX)
Citrus Coll (CA)

City Coll of San
　Francisco (CA)
City Colls of Chicago,
　Harold Washington
　College (IL)
City Colls of Chicago,
　Harry S. Truman
　College (IL)
City Colls of Chicago,
　Kennedy-King
　College (IL)
City Colls of Chicago,
　Olive-Harvey
　College (IL)
City Colls of Chicago,
　Richard J. Daley
　College (IL)
City Colls of Chicago,
　Wilbur Wright
　College (IL)
Clarendon Coll (TX)
Clark Coll (WA)
Clark State Comm
　Coll (OH)
Clatsop Comm Coll (OR)
Cleveland Comm Coll (NC)
Cleveland State Comm
　Coll (TN)
Clinton Comm Coll (IA)
Clovis Comm Coll (NM)
Coahoma Comm Coll (MS)
Coastal Bend Coll (TX)
Coastal Carolina Comm
　Coll (NC)
Coastal Georgia Comm
　Coll (GA)
Cochise Coll, Douglas (AZ)
Cochise Coll, Sierra
　Vista (AZ)
Coconino Comm Coll (AZ)
Colby Comm Coll (KS)
CollAmerica–Colorado
　Springs (CO)
CollAmerica–Denver (CO)
Coll of Alameda (CA)
Coll of DuPage (IL)
Coll of Lake County (IL)
Coll of Marin (CA)
Coll of Menominee
　Nation (WI)
Coll of Micronesia–
　FSM (FM)
Coll of San Mateo (CA)
Coll of Southern Idaho (ID)
Coll of Southern
　Maryland (MD)
Coll of The Albemarle (NC)
Coll of the Canyons (CA)
Coll of the Desert (CA)
Coll of the Mainland (TX)
Coll of the Redwoods (CA)
Coll of the Siskiyous (CA)
Collin County Comm Coll
　District (TX)
Colorado Mountain
　Coll (CO)
Colorado Mountain Coll,
　Alpine Campus (CO)
Columbia Coll (CA)
Columbia-Greene Comm
　Coll (NY)
Comm Coll of Allegheny
　County (PA)
Comm Coll of Beaver
　County (PA)
Comm Coll of
　Philadelphia (PA)
Comm Coll of Rhode
　Island (RI)
Comm Coll of Southern
　Nevada (NV)
Comm Coll of
　Vermont (VT)
Contra Costa Coll (CA)
Cossatot Comm Coll of the
　U of Arkansas (AR)
Cosumnes River Coll,
　Sacramento (CA)
Crafton Hills Coll (CA)
Crowder Coll (MO)
Cuesta Coll (CA)
Cuyahoga Comm
　Coll (OH)
Cypress Coll (CA)
Dabney S. Lancaster
　Comm Coll (VA)
Danville Comm Coll (VA)
Davidson County Comm
　Coll (NC)
Dean Coll (MA)
De Anza Coll (CA)
Delta School of Business
　& Technology (LA)
Dixie State Coll of
　Utah (UT)
Dodge City Comm
　Coll (KS)
Draughons Jr Coll (KY)

Dyersburg State Comm
　Coll (TN)
East Central Coll (MO)
Eastern Arizona Coll (AZ)
Eastern New Mexico
　U–Roswell (NM)
Eastern Shore Comm
　Coll (VA)
East Georgia Coll (GA)
El Camino Coll (CA)
El Centro Coll (TX)
Elgin Comm Coll (IL)
Elizabethtown Tech
　Coll (KY)
Erie Comm Coll (NY)
Erie Comm Coll, North
　Campus (NY)
Erie Comm Coll, South
　Campus (NY)
Essex County Coll (NJ)
Eugenio María de Hostos
　Comm Coll of the City
　U of New York (NY)
Everest Coll, Arlington (TX)
Everest Coll, Dallas (TX)
Everest Coll, Fort
　Worth (TX)
Everett Comm Coll (WA)
Fayetteville Tech Comm
　Coll (NC)
Finger Lakes Comm
　Coll (NY)
Fiorello H. LaGuardia
　Comm Coll of the City
　U of New York (NY)
Fisher Coll (MA)
Florence-Darlington Tech
　Coll (SC)
Florida Metropolitan
　U–Orange Park
　Campus (FL)
Florida National Coll (FL)
Folsom Lake Coll (CA)
Foothill Coll (CA)
Forrest Jr Coll (SC)
Forsyth Tech Comm
　Coll (NC)
Fort Berthold Comm
　Coll (ND)
Fox Valley Tech Coll (WI)
Frederick Comm Coll (MD)
Fresno City Coll (CA)
Front Range Comm
　Coll (CO)
Fullerton Coll (CA)
Fulton-Montgomery Comm
　Coll (NY)
Garrett Coll (MD)
Gateway Comm Coll (CT)
Genesee Comm Coll (NY)
George C. Wallace Comm
　Coll (AL)
Georgia Highlands
　Coll (GA)
Georgia Military Coll (GA)
Germanna Comm
　Coll (VA)
Gloucester County
　Coll (NJ)
Golden West Coll (CA)
Gordon Coll (GA)
Grand Rapids Comm
　Coll (MI)
Grays Harbor Coll (WA)
Grayson County Coll (TX)
Great Basin Coll (NV)
Greenville Tech Coll (SC)
Griffin Tech Coll (GA)
Grossmont Coll (CA)
Guilford Tech Comm
　Coll (NC)
Gwinnett Tech Coll (GA)
Hagerstown Comm
　Coll (MD)
Hamilton Coll, Council
　Bluffs (IA)
Harper Coll (IL)
Harrisburg Area Comm
　Coll (PA)
Hartnell Coll (CA)
Hawkeye Comm Coll (IA)
Henry Ford Comm
　Coll (MI)
Hesser Coll (NH)
Hesston Coll (KS)
Hillsborough Comm
　Coll (FL)
Hocking Coll (OH)
Holyoke Comm Coll (MA)
Hopkinsville Comm
　Coll (KY)
Housatonic Comm
　Coll (CT)
Houston Comm Coll
　System (TX)
Howard Comm Coll (MD)

Illinois Eastern Comm Colls, Wabash Valley College (IL)
Illinois Valley Comm Coll (IL)
Imperial Valley Coll (CA)
Indiana Business Coll, Anderson (IN)
Indiana Business Coll, Columbus (IN)
Indiana Business Coll, Evansville (IN)
Indiana Business Coll, Fort Wayne (IN)
Indiana Business Coll, Indianapolis (IN)
Indiana Business Coll, Lafayette (IN)
Indiana Business Coll, Marion (IN)
Indiana Business Coll, Muncie (IN)
Indiana Business Coll, Terre Haute (IN)
International Business Coll, Fort Wayne (IN)
International Inst of the Americas, Mesa (AZ)
International Inst of the Americas, Phoenix (AZ)
International Inst of the Americas, Tucson (AZ)
International Inst of the Americas (NM)
Inver Hills Comm Coll (MN)
Iowa Lakes Comm Coll (IA)
Irvine Valley Coll (CA)
Isothermal Comm Coll (NC)
Itasca Comm Coll (MN)
ITT Tech Inst, Canton (MI)
ITT Tech Inst, Flint (MI)
ITT Tech Inst, Grand Rapids (MI)
ITT Tech Inst, Troy (MI)
ITT Tech Inst, Dayton (OH)
ITT Tech Inst, Hilliard (OH)
ITT Tech Inst, Norwood (OH)
ITT Tech Inst, Strongsville (OH)
ITT Tech Inst, Warrensville Heights (OH)
ITT Tech Inst, Youngstown (OH)
Jackson State Comm Coll (TN)
James H. Faulkner State Comm Coll (AL)
James Sprunt Comm Coll (NC)
Jamestown Comm Coll (NY)
Jefferson Comm and Tech Coll (KY)
Jefferson Comm Coll (NC)
Johnston Comm Coll (NC)
John Wood Comm Coll (IL)
Joliet Jr Coll (IL)
Jones County Jr Coll (MS)
Kansas City Kansas Comm Coll (KS)
Kaplan U (IA)
Keiser U, Miami (FL)
Kellogg Comm Coll (MI)
Kennebec Valley Comm Coll (ME)
Kent State U, Ashtabula Campus (OH)
Kent State U, East Liverpool Campus (OH)
Kent State U, Geauga Campus (OH)
Kent State U, Trumbull Campus (OH)
Kent State U, Tuscarawas Campus (OH)
Keystone Coll (PA)
Kilian Comm Coll (SD)
Kingsborough Comm Coll of the City U of New York (NY)
Kirkwood Comm Coll (IA)
Kirtland Comm Coll (MI)
Labette Comm Coll (KS)
Lake Land Coll (IL)
Lake-Sumter Comm Coll (FL)
Lake Tahoe Comm Coll (CA)
Lamar Comm Coll (CO)
Laney Coll (CA)
Lansing Comm Coll (MI)
Laramie County Comm Coll (WY)
Las Positas Coll (CA)

Lassen Comm Coll District (CA)
Laurel Business Inst (PA)
Lawson State Comm Coll (AL)
Lee Coll (TX)
Leeward Comm Coll (HI)
Lehigh Carbon Comm Coll (PA)
Lehigh Valley Coll (PA)
Lenoir Comm Coll (NC)
Lewis Coll of Business (MI)
Lincoln Land Comm Coll (IL)
Linn-Benton Comm Coll (OR)
Little Big Horn Coll (MT)
Long Island Business Inst (NY)
Lorain County Comm Coll (OH)
Los Angeles City Coll (CA)
Los Angeles Harbor Coll (CA)
Los Angeles Mission Coll (CA)
Los Angeles Southwest Coll (CA)
Los Medanos Coll (CA)
Louisburg Coll (NC)
Louisiana State U at Eunice (LA)
Lower Columbia Coll (WA)
Macomb Comm Coll (MI)
Madison Area Tech Coll (WI)
Madisonville Comm Coll (KY)
Manatee Comm Coll (FL)
Marian Court Coll (MA)
Martin Comm Coll (NC)
Massachusetts Bay Comm Coll (MA)
Massasoit Comm Coll (MA)
McLennan Comm Coll (TX)
Mendocino Coll (CA)
Merced Coll (CA)
Mesa Comm Coll (AZ)
Metropolitan Comm Coll (NE)
Metropolitan Comm Coll–Blue River (MO)
Metropolitan Comm Coll–Business & Technology Campus (MO)
Metropolitan Comm Coll–Longview (MO)
Metropolitan Comm Coll–Maple Woods (MO)
Metropolitan Comm Coll–Penn Valley (MO)
Miami Dade Coll (FL)
Miami U Hamilton (OH)
Miami U–Middletown Campus (OH)
Middle Georgia Coll (GA)
Middlesex Comm Coll (CT)
Midlands Tech Coll (SC)
Mid-Plains Comm Coll, North Platte (NE)
Mid-State Tech Coll (WI)
Minneapolis Comm and Tech Coll (MN)
Minnesota School of Business–Brooklyn Center (MN)
Minnesota School of Business–Plymouth (MN)
Minnesota School of Business–Richfield (MN)
Minnesota School of Business–St. Cloud (MN)
Minnesota School of Business–Shakopee (MN)
Minnesota State Comm and Tech Coll–Fergus Falls (MN)
Mission Coll (CA)
Mississippi Gulf Coast Comm Coll (MS)
Missouri State U–West Plains (MO)
Mohave Comm Coll (AZ)
Mohawk Valley Comm Coll (NY)
Monroe Comm Coll (NY)
Montcalm Comm Coll (MI)
Monterey Peninsula Coll (CA)
Montgomery Coll (MD)
Montgomery County Comm Coll (PA)

Moorpark Coll (CA)
Moraine Valley Comm Coll (IL)
Morgan Comm Coll (CO)
Morton Coll (IL)
Motlow State Comm Coll (TN)
Mott Comm Coll (MI)
Mt. Hood Comm Coll (OR)
Mt. San Antonio Coll (CA)
Mount Wachusett Comm Coll (MA)
Murray State Coll (OK)
Muscatine Comm Coll (IA)
Muskegon Comm Coll (MI)
Napa Valley Coll (CA)
Nassau Comm Coll (NY)
National American U, Bloomington (MN)
National Park Comm Coll (AR)
Naugatuck Valley Comm Coll (CT)
Navarro Coll (TX)
Nebraska Indian Comm Coll (NE)
Neosho County Comm Coll (KS)
New England Inst of Technology (RI)
New Hampshire Comm Tech Coll, Manchester/Stratham (NH)
New Hampshire Comm Tech Coll, Nashua/Claremont (NH)
New Hampshire Tech Inst (NH)
New Mexico Jr Coll (NM)
New Mexico Military Inst (NM)
New River Comm Coll (VA)
Niagara County Comm Coll (NY)
Nicolet Area Tech Coll (WI)
Northampton County Area Comm Coll (PA)
North Central Michigan Coll (MI)
North Central Missouri Coll (MO)
North Central Texas Coll (TX)
North Country Comm Coll (NY)
Northeast Comm Coll (NE)
Northeastern Jr Coll (CO)
Northeastern Tech Coll (SC)
Northeast State Tech Comm Coll (TN)
Northern Essex Comm Coll (MA)
Northern Maine Comm Coll (ME)
Northern Marianas Coll (MP)
Northern Oklahoma Coll (OK)
North Idaho Coll (ID)
North Iowa Area Comm Coll (IA)
North Lake Coll (TX)
Northland Comm and Tech Coll–Thief River Falls (MN)
North Shore Comm Coll (MA)
NorthWest Arkansas Comm Coll (AR)
Northwestern Connecticut Comm Coll (CT)
Northwest Iowa Comm Coll (IA)
Northwest Mississippi Comm Coll (MS)
Northwest-Shoals Comm Coll (AL)
Oakland Comm Coll (MI)
Odessa Coll (TX)
Ohlone Coll (CA)
Oklahoma City Comm Coll (OK)
Oklahoma State U, Oklahoma City (OK)
Oklahoma State U, Okmulgee (OK)
Olympic Coll (WA)
Onondaga Comm Coll (NY)
Orange Coast Coll (CA)
Ouachita Tech Coll (AR)
Owensboro Comm and Tech Coll (KY)
Oxnard Coll (CA)
Ozarka Coll (AR)
Ozarks Tech Comm Coll (MO)

Pace Inst (PA)
Palm Beach Comm Coll (FL)
Palo Alto Coll (TX)
Pamlico Comm Coll (NC)
Paradise Valley Comm Coll (AZ)
Parkland Coll (IL)
Pasadena City Coll (CA)
Pasco-Hernando Comm Coll (FL)
Passaic County Comm Coll (NJ)
Paul D. Camp Comm Coll (VA)
Pearl River Comm Coll (MS)
Peninsula Coll (WA)
Piedmont Tech Coll (SC)
Piedmont Virginia Comm Coll (VA)
Pierce Coll (WA)
Pima Comm Coll (AZ)
Pioneer Pacific Coll, Wilsonville (OR)
Polk Comm Coll (FL)
Porterville Coll (CA)
Potomac State Coll of West Virginia U (WV)
Pueblo Comm Coll (CO)
Queensborough Comm Coll of the City U of New York (NY)
Quincy Coll (MA)
Quinebaug Valley Comm Coll (CT)
Rainy River Comm Coll (MN)
Rappahannock Comm Coll (VA)
Raritan Valley Comm Coll (NJ)
Rasmussen Coll Brooklyn Park (MN)
Redlands Comm Coll (OK)
Red Rocks Comm Coll (CO)
Remington Coll–Baton Rouge Campus (LA)
Remington Coll–Dallas Campus (TX)
Remington Coll–Fort Worth Campus (TX)
Renton Tech Coll (WA)
Richland Coll (TX)
Richland Comm Coll (IL)
Ridgewater Coll (MN)
Rio Salado Coll (AZ)
Riverland Comm Coll (MN)
Riverside Comm Coll District (CA)
Roane State Comm Coll (TN)
Robeson Comm Coll (NC)
Rockford Business Coll (IL)
Rogue Comm Coll (OR)
Rose State Coll (OK)
Roxbury Comm Coll (MA)
Sacramento City Coll (CA)
St. Catharine Coll (KY)
Saint Charles Comm Coll (MO)
St. Cloud Tech Coll (MN)
St. Louis Comm Coll at Florissant Valley (MO)
St. Philip's Coll (TX)
Salt Lake Comm Coll (UT)
Sampson Comm Coll (NC)
San Antonio Coll (TX)
San Bernardino Valley Coll (CA)
Sandhills Comm Coll (NC)
San Diego City Coll (CA)
San Joaquin Delta Coll (CA)
San Juan Coll (NM)
Santa Ana Coll (CA)
Santa Barbara City Coll (CA)
Santa Rosa Jr Coll (CA)
Santiago Canyon Coll (CA)
Schoolcraft Coll (MI)
Scott Comm Coll (IA)
Scottsdale Comm Coll (AZ)
Seminole Comm Coll (FL)
Seminole State Coll (OK)
Shasta Coll (CA)
Sheridan Coll–Sheridan and Gillette (WY)
Sitting Bull Coll (ND)
Skagit Valley Coll (WA)
Southeastern Comm Coll (NC)
Southeastern Comm Coll, North Campus (IA)

Southeastern Comm Coll, South Campus (IA)
Southeast Kentucky Comm and Tech Coll (KY)
Southeast Tech Inst (SD)
Southern Maine Comm Coll (ME)
Southern U at Shreveport (LA)
South Florida Comm Coll (FL)
South Georgia Coll (GA)
South Piedmont Comm Coll (NC)
South Plains Coll (TX)
South Seattle Comm Coll (WA)
Southside Virginia Comm Coll (VA)
South Texas Coll (TX)
Southwestern Comm Coll (NC)
Southwestern Indian Polytechnic Inst (NM)
Southwestern Michigan Coll (MI)
Southwest Mississippi Comm Coll (MS)
Southwest Texas Jr Coll (TX)
Southwest Virginia Comm Coll (VA)
Spencerian Coll (KY)
Spokane Comm Coll (WA)
Spokane Falls Comm Coll (WA)
Springfield Tech Comm Coll (MA)
Stanly Comm Coll (NC)
Stark State Coll of Technology (OH)
State Fair Comm Coll (MO)
State U of New York Coll of Agriculture and Technology at Morrisville (NY)
State U of New York Coll of Technology at Alfred (NY)
State U of New York Coll of Technology at Canton (NY)
Stone Child Coll (MT)
Suffolk County Comm Coll (NY)
Surry Comm Coll (NC)
Sussex County Comm Coll (NJ)
Taft Coll (CA)
Tallahassee Comm Coll (FL)
Temple Coll (TX)
Terra State Comm Coll (OH)
Texarkana Coll (TX)
Three Rivers Comm Coll (CT)
Three Rivers Comm Coll (MO)
Tidewater Comm Coll (VA)
Tomball Coll (TX)
Tompkins Cortland Comm Coll (NY)
Treasure Valley Comm Coll (OR)
Tri-County Comm Coll (NC)
Trident Tech Coll (SC)
Trinidad State Jr Coll (CO)
Trocaire Coll (NY)
Tulsa Comm Coll (OK)
Tunxis Comm Coll (CT)
Turtle Mountain Comm Coll (ND)
Tyler Jr Coll (TX)
Ulster County Comm Coll (NY)
Umpqua Comm Coll (OR)
Union County Coll (NJ)
The U of Akron–Wayne Coll (OH)
U of Alaska Anchorage, Kodiak Coll (AK)
U of Alaska, Prince William Sound Comm Coll (AK)
U of Alaska Southeast, Sitka Campus (AK)
U of Cincinnati Clermont Coll (OH)
U of New Mexico–Gallup (NM)
U of New Mexico–Los Alamos Branch (NM)
U of New Mexico–Valencia Campus (NM)
U of South Carolina Lancaster (SC)

Valencia Comm Coll (FL)
Ventura Coll (CA)
Vernon Coll (TX)
Victoria Coll (TX)
Victor Valley Coll (CA)
Villa Maria Coll of Buffalo (NY)
Vincennes U Jasper Campus (IN)
Virginia Coll at Austin (TX)
Virginia Highlands Comm Coll (VA)
Virginia Western Comm Coll (VA)
Volunteer State Comm Coll (TN)
Wallace State Comm Coll (AL)
Warren County Comm Coll (NJ)
Washington State Comm Coll (OH)
Wayne Comm Coll (NC)
Wenatchee Valley Coll (WA)
West Central Tech Coll (GA)
Westchester Comm Coll (NY)
Western Nebraska Comm Coll (NE)
Western Nevada Comm Coll (NV)
Western Piedmont Comm Coll (NC)
Western Texas Coll (TX)
Western Wyoming Comm Coll (WY)
West Hills Comm Coll (CA)
West Los Angeles Coll (CA)
Westmoreland County Comm Coll (PA)
West Valley Coll (CA)
West Virginia U at Parkersburg (WV)
Wilson Tech Comm Coll (NC)
Wor-Wic Comm Coll (MD)
Wright State U, Lake Campus (OH)
Wytheville Comm Coll (VA)
York County Comm Coll (ME)
York Tech Coll (SC)
Young Harris Coll (GA)
Yuba Coll (CA)
Zane State Coll (OH)

Business Administration, Management and Operations Related

City Coll, Fort Lauderdale (FL)
City Coll, Gainesville (FL)
City Coll, Miami (FL)
Coll of the Marshall Islands (Marshall Islands)
Fayetteville Tech Comm Coll (NC)
Indiana Business Coll, Anderson (IN)
Indiana Business Coll, Columbus (IN)
Indiana Business Coll, Indianapolis (IN)
Indiana Business Coll, Lafayette (IN)
Indiana Business Coll, Muncie (IN)
Indiana Business Coll, Terre Haute (IN)
International Jr Coll (PR)
Katharine Gibbs School (PA)
Klamath Comm Coll (OR)
Lamar Inst of Technology (TX)
Leech Lake Tribal Coll (MN)
Maric Coll, Panorama City (CA)
Massasoit Comm Coll (MA)
National American U (KS)
National American U, Rio Rancho (NM)
National American U, Ellsworth AFB (SD)
National Inst of Technology (OH)
Northwest Vista Coll (TX)
Provo Coll (UT)
Remington Coll–Jacksonville Campus (FL)
Remington Coll–Little Rock Campus (AR)

Remington Coll–Nashville Campus (TN)
Santiago Canyon Coll (CA)
Savannah River Coll (GA)
Southeastern Business Coll, Jackson (OH)
Southeastern Business Coll, Lancaster (OH)
Southeastern Business Coll, New Boston (OH)
Tidewater Tech (VA)
U of New Mexico–Taos (NM)
West Virginia State Comm and Tech Coll (WV)

Business and Personal/Financial Services Marketing
Centralia Coll (WA)
Hesser Coll (NH)
Hutchinson Comm Coll and Area Vocational School (KS)
North Central Texas Coll (TX)
Spokane Falls Comm Coll (WA)
Tulsa Comm Coll (OK)
Union County Coll (NJ)

Business and Personal Services Marketing Related
Mohawk Valley Comm Coll (NY)

Business Automation/ Technology/Data Entry
Alpena Comm Coll (MI)
Antonelli Coll, Hattiesburg (MS)
Arkansas State U–Mountain Home (AR)
Asnuntuck Comm Coll (CT)
Berkshire Comm Coll (MA)
Bismarck State Coll (ND)
Business Informatics Center, Inc. (NY)
Business Inst of Pennsylvania, Sharon (PA)
Central Wyoming Coll (WY)
Clark Coll (WA)
Clatsop Comm Coll (OR)
Clovis Comm Coll (NM)
Coll of Lake County (IL)
Collin County Comm Coll District (TX)
Comm Coll of Allegheny County (PA)
Crowder Coll (MO)
El Centro Coll (TX)
Front Range Comm Coll (CO)
Illinois Eastern Comm Colls, Frontier Community College (IL)
Illinois Eastern Comm Colls, Lincoln Trail College (IL)
Illinois Eastern Comm Colls, Olney Central College (IL)
Illinois Eastern Comm Colls, Wabash Valley College (IL)
International Jr Coll (PR)
Iowa Lakes Comm Coll (IA)
Joliet Jr Coll (IL)
Laurel Business Inst (PA)
Lincoln Land Comm Coll (IL)
Macomb Comm Coll (MI)
Oakland Comm Coll (MI)
Oklahoma State U, Oklahoma City (OK)
Parkland Coll (IL)
Santiago Canyon Coll (CA)
The U of Akron–Wayne Coll (OH)
The U of Montana-Helena Coll of Technology (MT)
Western Nevada Comm Coll (NV)

Business/Commerce
Academy Coll (MN)
Allen County Comm Coll (KS)
Antelope Valley Coll (CA)
Arkansas State U–Newport (AR)
Berkeley City Coll (CA)

Berkeley Coll, West Paterson (NJ)
Berkshire Comm Coll (MA)
Bismarck State Coll (ND)
Central Florida Comm Coll (FL)
Centralia Coll (WA)
Clinton Jr Coll (SC)
Coll of Southern Idaho (ID)
Colorado Mountain Coll, Timberline Campus (CO)
Comm Coll of Rhode Island (RI)
DeKalb Tech Coll (GA)
Everest Coll, Phoenix (AZ)
Everest Coll, Ontario (CA)
Fond du Lac Tribal and Comm Coll (MN)
Fort Belknap Coll (MT)
Great Basin Coll (NV)
Hagerstown Comm Coll (MD)
Harrisburg Area Comm Coll (PA)
Hawkeye Comm Coll (IA)
Hutchinson Comm Coll and Area Vocational School (KS)
John Tyler Comm Coll (VA)
John Wood Comm Coll (IL)
Kankakee Comm Coll (IL)
Keystone Coll (PA)
Laramie County Comm Coll (WY)
Louisburg Coll (NC)
Lower Columbia Coll (WA)
Macomb Comm Coll (MI)
Manatee Comm Coll (FL)
Marshall Comm and Tech Coll (WV)
Massachusetts Bay Comm Coll (MA)
Mesabi Range Comm and Tech Coll (MN)
Metropolitan Comm Coll–Business & Technology Campus (MO)
Miami U–Middletown Campus (OH)
Midlands Tech Coll (SC)
Minneapolis Comm and Tech Coll (MN)
Missouri State U–West Plains (MO)
Montgomery Coll (MD)
Montgomery County Comm Coll (PA)
Moraine Valley Comm Coll (IL)
Mott Comm Coll (MI)
New Mexico State U–Alamogordo (NM)
Northampton County Area Comm Coll (PA)
North Arkansas Coll (AR)
Northern New Mexico Coll (NM)
Owens Comm Coll, Toledo (OH)
Panola Coll (TX)
Penn State Beaver (PA)
Penn State Delaware County (PA)
Penn State DuBois (PA)
Penn State Fayette, The Eberly Campus (PA)
Penn State Hazleton (PA)
Penn State Lehigh Valley (PA)
Penn State McKeesport (PA)
Penn State Mont Alto (PA)
Penn State New Kensington (PA)
Penn State Schuylkill (PA)
Penn State Shenango (PA)
Penn State Wilkes-Barre (PA)
Penn State Worthington Scranton (PA)
Penn State York (PA)
Piedmont Tech Coll (SC)
Reedley Coll (CA)
Remington Coll–Fort Worth Campus (TX)
Rose State Coll (OK)
Saginaw Chippewa Tribal Coll (MI)
Sheridan Coll–Sheridan and Gillette (WY)
Southern State Comm Coll (OH)
South Florida Comm Coll (FL)
Springfield Tech Comm Coll (MA)

Union County Coll (NJ)
U of Arkansas Comm Coll at Batesville (AR)
U of Pittsburgh at Titusville (PA)
Victor Valley Coll (CA)
Western Nevada Comm Coll (NV)
Wor-Wic Comm Coll (MD)
Wright State U, Lake Campus (OH)
York Tech Coll (SC)

Business Computer Programming
Barton County Comm Coll (KS)
Coll of Lake County (IL)

Business/Corporate Communications
Houston Comm Coll System (TX)
Montgomery County Comm Coll (PA)
North Seattle Comm Coll (WA)

Business Machine Repair
Bramson ORT Coll (NY)
Cabrillo Coll (CA)
Cañada Coll (CA)
Central Piedmont Comm Coll (NC)
Coahoma Comm Coll (MS)
Comm Coll of Allegheny County (PA)
De Anza Coll (CA)
ECPI Coll of Technology (VA)
ECPI Tech Coll (VA)
Hartnell Coll (CA)
Henry Ford Comm Coll (MI)
Iowa Lakes Comm Coll (IA)
Irvine Valley Coll (CA)
Lassen Comm Coll District (CA)
Minnesota State Coll–Southeast Tech (MN)
Mississippi Delta Comm Coll (MS)
Moorpark Coll (CA)
Muskegon Comm Coll (MI)
Neosho County Comm Coll (KS)
Ozarks Tech Comm Coll (MO)
St. Catharine Coll (KY)
San Antonio Coll (TX)
Southern Maine Comm Coll (ME)

Business, Management, and Marketing Related
Catawba Valley Comm Coll (NC)
Cincinnati State Tech and Comm Coll (OH)
Eastern Arizona Coll (AZ)
Everest Coll, Ontario (CA)
Harrisburg Area Comm Coll (PA)
Heart of Georgia Tech Coll (GA)
Keiser Career Coll - Greenacres (FL)
Miller-Motte Tech Coll, Clarksville (TN)
Queensborough Comm Coll of the City U of New York (NY)
Sandhills Comm Coll (NC)
Southwestern Michigan Coll (MI)

Business/Managerial Economics
Anne Arundel Comm Coll (MD)
Colby Comm Coll (KS)
Coll of the Desert (CA)
Joliet Jr Coll (IL)
Los Medanos Coll (CA)
Manatee Comm Coll (FL)
Miami U–Middletown Campus (OH)
Morgan Comm Coll (CO)
Potomac State Coll of West Virginia U (WV)
St. Catharine Coll (KY)
San Joaquin Delta Coll (CA)
South Georgia Coll (GA)
State U of New York Coll of Technology at Canton (NY)

Business Operations Support and Secretarial Services Related
Angley Coll (FL)
Bowling Green State U–Firelands Coll (OH)
East Central Comm Coll (MO)
Eastern Arizona Coll (AZ)
Guilford Tech Comm Coll (NC)
Hillsborough Comm Coll (FL)
Laramie County Comm Coll (WY)
Provo Coll (UT)
Virginia Coll at Austin (TX)

Business Systems Networking/ Telecommunications
Caldwell Comm Coll and Tech Inst (NC)
Coll of Lake County (IL)
Katharine Gibbs School (PA)
Virginia Coll at Austin (TX)

Business Teacher Education
Allen County Comm Coll (KS)
Amarillo Coll (TX)
Bainbridge Coll (GA)
Bramson ORT Coll (NY)
Brigham Young U – Idaho (ID)
Cankdeska Cikana Comm Coll (ND)
Chaffey Coll (CA)
Cisco Jr Coll (TX)
Colby Comm Coll (KS)
Coll of Alameda (CA)
Comm Coll of Philadelphia (PA)
Eastern Arizona Coll (AZ)
East Georgia Coll (GA)
Essex County Coll (NJ)
Harrisburg Area Comm Coll (PA)
Holyoke Comm Coll (MA)
Iowa Lakes Comm Coll (IA)
Isothermal Comm Coll (NC)
Kirkwood Comm Coll (IA)
Lamar Comm Coll (CO)
Lawson State Comm Coll (AL)
Louisburg Coll (NC)
Madison Area Tech Coll (WI)
Mississippi Gulf Coast Comm Coll (MS)
Morgan Comm Coll (CO)
Mt. Hood Comm Coll (OR)
Mt. San Antonio Coll (CA)
Murray State Coll (OK)
New Mexico Jr Coll (NM)
Northeast Comm Coll (NE)
Northeastern Jr Coll (CO)
Northern Essex Comm Coll (MA)
North Idaho Coll (ID)
Palau Comm Coll (Palau)
Pasadena City Coll (CA)
Pine Tech Coll (MN)
Porterville Coll (CA)
Rio Hondo Coll (CA)
Roane State Comm Coll (TN)
St. Catharine Coll (KY)
South Georgia Coll (GA)
Southwest Mississippi Comm Coll (MS)
Tulsa Comm Coll (OK)
Vincennes U Jasper Campus (IN)
Wallace State Comm Coll (AL)

Cabinetmaking and Millwork
Central Georgia Tech Coll (GA)
Coll of Southern Idaho (ID)
Illinois Eastern Comm Colls, Olney Central College (IL)
Macomb Comm Coll (MI)
Oakland Comm Coll (MI)

Cad/Cadd Drafting/ Design Technology
Alexandria Tech Coll (MN)
Black Hawk Coll, Moline (IL)
Brown Mackie Coll–Akron (OH)

Brown Mackie Coll–Atlanta (GA)
Brown Mackie Coll–Cincinnati (OH)
Brown Mackie Coll–Findlay (OH)
Brown Mackie Coll–Fort Wayne (IN)
Brown Mackie Coll–Kansas City (KS)
Brown Mackie Coll–North Canton (OH)
Brown Mackie Coll–Northern Kentucky (KY)
Brown Mackie Coll–Salina (KS)
Brown Mackie Coll–South Bend (IN)
Delta School of Business & Technology (LA)
ITT Tech Inst (AL)
ITT Tech Inst, Tucson (AZ)
ITT Tech Inst (AR)
ITT Tech Inst, Lathrop (CA)
ITT Tech Inst, Oxnard (CA)
ITT Tech Inst, Rancho Cordova (CA)
ITT Tech Inst, San Bernardino (CA)
ITT Tech Inst, San Diego (CA)
ITT Tech Inst, San Dimas (CA)
ITT Tech Inst, Sylmar (CA)
ITT Tech Inst, Torrance (CA)
ITT Tech Inst (CO)
ITT Tech Inst, Fort Lauderdale (FL)
ITT Tech Inst, Jacksonville (FL)
ITT Tech Inst, Lake Mary (FL)
ITT Tech Inst, Tampa (FL)
ITT Tech Inst, Duluth (GA)
ITT Tech Inst, Kennesaw (GA)
ITT Tech Inst (ID)
ITT Tech Inst, Mount Prospect (IL)
ITT Tech Inst, Orland Park (IL)
ITT Tech Inst, Fort Wayne (IN)
ITT Tech Inst, Indianapolis (IN)
ITT Tech Inst, Newburgh (IN)
ITT Tech Inst, Louisville (KY)
ITT Tech Inst (LA)
ITT Tech Inst (MD)
ITT Tech Inst, Norwood (MA)
ITT Tech Inst, Woburn (MA)
ITT Tech Inst, Canton (MI)
ITT Tech Inst, Flint (MI)
ITT Tech Inst, Grand Rapids (MI)
ITT Tech Inst, Troy (MI)
ITT Tech Inst (MN)
ITT Tech Inst, Arnold (MO)
ITT Tech Inst, Earth City (MO)
ITT Tech Inst, Kansas City (MO)
ITT Tech Inst (NE)
ITT Tech Inst (NV)
ITT Tech Inst, Getzville (NY)
ITT Tech Inst, Dayton (OH)
ITT Tech Inst, Hilliard (OH)
ITT Tech Inst, Norwood (OH)
ITT Tech Inst, Strongsville (OH)
ITT Tech Inst, Warrensville Heights (OH)
ITT Tech Inst, Youngstown (OH)
ITT Tech Inst, Tulsa (OK)
ITT Tech Inst (OR)
ITT Tech Inst (SC)
ITT Tech Inst, Cordova (TN)
ITT Tech Inst, Knoxville (TN)
ITT Tech Inst, Nashville (TN)
ITT Tech Inst, Arlington (TX)
ITT Tech Inst, Austin (TX)
ITT Tech Inst, Houston (TX)
ITT Tech Inst, Houston (TX)

ITT Tech Inst, Richardson (TX)
ITT Tech Inst, San Antonio (TX)
ITT Tech Inst, Webster (TX)
ITT Tech Inst (UT)
ITT Tech Inst, Chantilly (VA)
ITT Tech Inst, Norfolk (VA)
ITT Tech Inst, Richmond (VA)
ITT Tech Inst, Springfield (VA)
ITT Tech Inst, Bothell (WA)
ITT Tech Inst, Seattle (WA)
ITT Tech Inst, Spokane (WA)
ITT Tech Inst, Green Bay (WI)
ITT Tech Inst, Greenfield (WI)
Lower Columbia Coll (WA)
Northampton County Area Comm Coll (PA)
Owens Comm Coll, Toledo (OH)
St. Philip's Coll (TX)
Springfield Tech Comm Coll (MA)
Vatterott Coll, Kansas City (MO)
Vatterott Coll (TN)
West Virginia State Comm and Tech Coll (WV)

Cardiovascular Technology
Augusta Tech Coll (GA)
Caldwell Comm Coll and Tech Inst (NC)
Central Georgia Tech Coll (GA)
El Centro Coll (TX)
Harrisburg Area Comm Coll (PA)
Howard Comm Coll (MD)
Lancaster General Coll of Nursing & Health Sciences (PA)
Northeast State Tech Comm Coll (TN)
Northwestern Tech Coll (GA)
Orange Coast Coll (CA)
St. Cloud Tech Coll (MN)
Sanford-Brown Inst, Tampa (FL)
Southeast Tech Inst (SD)
Southern Maine Comm Coll (ME)
Southern U at Shreveport (LA)
Valencia Comm Coll (FL)

Carpentry
Alamance Comm Coll (NC)
Alexandria Tech Coll (MN)
Bakersfield Coll (CA)
Bismarck State Coll (ND)
Black Hawk Coll, Moline (IL)
Brigham Young U – Idaho (ID)
Cankdeska Cikana Comm Coll (ND)
Cecil Comm Coll (MD)
Central Georgia Tech Coll (GA)
Coahoma Comm Coll (MS)
Columbia Basin Coll (WA)
Comm Coll of Allegheny County (PA)
Cossatot Comm Coll of the U of Arkansas (AR)
Flint Hills Tech Coll (KS)
Forsyth Tech Comm Coll (NC)
Fresno City Coll (CA)
Fullerton Coll (CA)
Fulton-Montgomery Comm Coll (NY)
George C. Wallace Comm Coll (AL)
Grays Harbor Coll (WA)
Hartnell Coll (CA)
H. Councill Trenholm State Tech Coll (AL)
Hennepin Tech Coll (MN)
Hutchinson Comm Coll and Area Vocational School (KS)
Illinois Valley Comm Coll (IL)
Iowa Lakes Comm Coll (IA)
Laney Coll (CA)
Lansing Comm Coll (MI)

Laramie County Comm
 Coll (WY)
Lassen Comm Coll
 District (CA)
Lawson State Comm
 Coll (AL)
Little Big Horn Coll (MT)
Maui Comm Coll (HI)
Merced Coll (CA)
Metropolitan Comm
 Coll–Business &
 Technology
 Campus (MO)
Minnesota State Coll–
 Southeast Tech (MN)
Mohawk Valley Comm
 Coll (NY)
Nebraska Indian Comm
 Coll (NE)
Neosho County Comm
 Coll (KS)
New Mexico Jr Coll (NM)
North Central Missouri
 Coll (MO)
Northeast Comm Coll (NE)
Northern Maine Comm
 Coll (ME)
North Idaho Coll (ID)
North Iowa Area Comm
 Coll (IA)
North Lake Coll (TX)
Northwest KansasTech
 Coll (KS)
Oakland Comm Coll (MI)
Palau Comm Coll (Palau)
Pasadena City Coll (CA)
Piedmont Tech Coll (SC)
Piedmont Virginia Comm
 Coll (VA)
Porterville Coll (CA)
Red Rocks Comm
 Coll (CO)
St. Cloud Tech Coll (MN)
Salish Kootenai Coll (MT)
San Diego City Coll (CA)
San Joaquin Delta
 Coll (CA)
San Juan Coll (NM)
Santiago Canyon Coll (CA)
Sitting Bull Coll (ND)
Southern Maine Comm
 Coll (ME)
South Plains Coll (TX)
Southwest Mississippi
 Comm Coll (MS)
Spokane Comm Coll (WA)
State U of New York Coll
 of Technology at
 Alfred (NY)
State U of New York Coll
 of Technology at
 Canton (NY)
Trinidad State Jr Coll (CO)
Turtle Mountain Comm
 Coll (ND)
The U of Montana-Helena
 Coll of Technology (MT)
Wallace State Comm
 Coll (AL)
Wenatchee Valley
 Coll (WA)
Western Nevada Comm
 Coll (NV)
The Williamson Free
 School of Mecha
 Trades (PA)

Cartography
Alexandria Tech Coll (MN)
Anoka-Ramsey Comm
 Coll (MN)
Anoka-Ramsey Comm
 Coll, Cambridge
 Campus (MN)
Cabrillo Coll (CA)
Central Oregon Comm
 Coll (OR)
Dixie State Coll of
 Utah (UT)
Houston Comm Coll
 System (TX)
Midlands Tech Coll (SC)
Santiago Canyon Coll (CA)

**Ceramic Arts and
Ceramics**
Cabrillo Coll (CA)
Chaffey Coll (CA)
De Anza Coll (CA)
Dixie State Coll of
 Utah (UT)
Grossmont Coll (CA)
Henry Ford Comm
 Coll (MI)
Iowa Lakes Comm
 Coll (IA)
Kirkwood Comm Coll (IA)
Laney Coll (CA)

Lassen Comm Coll
 District (CA)
Los Angeles City Coll (CA)
Mohave Comm Coll (AZ)
Monterey Peninsula
 Coll (CA)
Oakland Comm Coll (MI)
Palm Beach Comm
 Coll (FL)
Pasadena City Coll (CA)
St. Catharine Coll (KY)
Ventura Coll (CA)

**Ceramic Sciences and
Engineering**
Hocking Coll (OH)
Pasadena City Coll (CA)

Chemical Engineering
Alpena Comm Coll (MI)
Brevard Comm Coll (FL)
Brigham Young U –
 Idaho (ID)
Burlington County
 Coll (NJ)
Chattanooga State Tech
 Comm Coll (TN)
City Coll of San
 Francisco (CA)
City Colls of Chicago,
 Harry S. Truman
 College (IL)
Comm Coll of
 Philadelphia (PA)
Florence-Darlington Tech
 Coll (SC)
Gloucester County
 Coll (NJ)
Itasca Comm Coll (MN)
Lansing Comm Coll (MI)
Miami U–Middletown
 Campus (OH)
Mississippi Gulf Coast
 Comm Coll (MS)
Monroe Comm Coll (NY)
Muskegon Comm Coll (MI)
Naugatuck Valley Comm
 Coll (CT)
Onondaga Comm
 Coll (NY)
St. Louis Comm Coll at
 Florissant Valley (MO)
San Bernardino Valley
 Coll (CA)
Washington State Comm
 Coll (OH)
Westchester Comm
 Coll (NY)
West Virginia U at
 Parkersburg (WV)

Chemical Technology
Amarillo Coll (TX)
Bidwell Training
 Center (PA)
Burlington County
 Coll (NJ)
Cape Fear Comm
 Coll (NC)
Cincinnati State Tech and
 Comm Coll (OH)
Coll of Lake County (IL)
Coll of the Mainland (TX)
Comm Coll of Allegheny
 County (PA)
Comm Coll of Rhode
 Island (RI)
Essex County Coll (NJ)
Kellogg Comm Coll (MI)
Lamar Inst of
 Technology (TX)
Lehigh Carbon Comm
 Coll (PA)
Massachusetts Bay Comm
 Coll (MA)
Midlands Tech Coll (SC)
Mohawk Valley Comm
 Coll (NY)
New York City Coll of
 Technology of the City
 U of New York (NY)
Northampton County Area
 Comm Coll (PA)
West Virginia State Comm
 and Tech Coll (WV)

Chemistry
Allen County Comm
 Coll (KS)
Alpena Comm Coll (MI)
Amarillo Coll (TX)
Anne Arundel Comm
 Coll (MD)
Arizona Western Coll (AZ)
Bainbridge Coll (GA)
Bakersfield Coll (CA)
Barton County Comm
 Coll (KS)
Bergen Comm Coll (NJ)
Blinn Coll (TX)

Brigham Young U –
 Idaho (ID)
Bucks County Comm
 Coll (PA)
Burlington County
 Coll (NJ)
Cankdeska Cikana Comm
 Coll (ND)
Cañada Coll (CA)
Centralia Coll (WA)
Central Texas Coll (TX)
Cerritos Coll (CA)
Chaffey Coll (CA)
Chattanooga State Tech
 Comm Coll (TN)
Cisco Jr Coll (TX)
City Coll of San
 Francisco (CA)
City Colls of Chicago,
 Harold Washington
 College (IL)
City Colls of Chicago,
 Kennedy-King
 College (IL)
City Colls of Chicago,
 Olive-Harvey
 College (IL)
Clarendon Coll (TX)
Coahoma Comm Coll (MS)
Coastal Bend Coll (TX)
Coastal Georgia Comm
 Coll (GA)
Cochise Coll, Douglas (AZ)
Cochise Coll, Sierra
 Vista (AZ)
Colby Comm Coll (KS)
Coll of Marin (CA)
Coll of San Mateo (CA)
Coll of Southern Idaho (ID)
Coll of the Canyons (CA)
Coll of the Desert (CA)
Coll of the Siskiyous (CA)
Columbia Coll (CA)
Comm Coll of Allegheny
 County (PA)
Comm Coll of Southern
 Nevada (NV)
Contra Costa Coll (CA)
Crafton Hills Coll (CA)
Cuesta Coll (CA)
Cypress Coll (CA)
Dixie State Coll of
 Utah (UT)
Dodge City Comm
 Coll (KS)
East Central Coll (MO)
Eastern Arizona Coll (AZ)
East Georgia Coll (GA)
El Camino Coll (CA)
Essex County Coll (NJ)
Everett Comm Coll (WA)
Finger Lakes Comm
 Coll (NY)
Foothill Coll (CA)
Frederick Comm Coll (MD)
Fullerton Coll (CA)
Gloucester County
 Coll (NJ)
Grayson County Coll (TX)
Great Basin Coll (NV)
Grossmont Coll (CA)
Harrisburg Area Comm
 Coll (PA)
Holyoke Comm Coll (MA)
Iowa Lakes Comm
 Coll (IA)
Joliet Jr Coll (IL)
Jones County Jr Coll (MS)
Kellogg Comm Coll (MI)
Kingsborough Comm Coll
 of the City U of New
 York (NY)
Labette Comm Coll (KS)
Lansing Comm Coll (MI)
Laramie County Comm
 Coll (WY)
Lassen Comm Coll
 District (CA)
Lawson State Comm
 Coll (AL)
Lee Coll (TX)
Linn-Benton Comm
 Coll (OR)
Lorain County Comm
 Coll (OH)
Los Angeles City Coll (CA)
Los Angeles Mission
 Coll (CA)
Los Medanos Coll (CA)
Louisburg Coll (NC)
Macomb Comm Coll (MI)
Manatee Comm Coll (FL)
Mendocino Coll (CA)
Metropolitan Comm
 Coll–Longview (MO)
Metropolitan Comm
 Coll–Maple
 Woods (MO)

Metropolitan Comm
 Coll–Penn Valley (MO)
Miami Dade Coll (FL)
Miami U–Middletown
 Campus (OH)
Monroe Comm Coll (NY)
Monterey Peninsula
 Coll (CA)
Moorpark Coll (CA)
Murray State Coll (OK)
Navarro Coll (TX)
New Mexico Jr Coll (NM)
New Mexico Military
 Inst (NM)
Northampton County Area
 Comm Coll (PA)
Northeast Comm Coll (NE)
Northeast State Tech
 Comm Coll (TN)
North Hennepin Comm
 Coll (MN)
North Idaho Coll (ID)
Odessa Coll (TX)
Oklahoma City Comm
 Coll (OK)
Orange Coast Coll (CA)
Palm Beach Comm
 Coll (FL)
Palo Alto Coll (TX)
Pasadena City Coll (CA)
Potomac State Coll of
 West Virginia U (WV)
Raritan Valley Comm
 Coll (NJ)
Red Rocks Comm
 Coll (CO)
Roane State Comm
 Coll (TN)
Rose State Coll (OK)
St. Catharine Coll (KY)
St. Philip's Coll (TX)
Salt Lake Comm Coll (UT)
San Bernardino Valley
 Coll (CA)
San Joaquin Delta
 Coll (CA)
San Juan Coll (NM)
Santa Ana Coll (CA)
Santa Barbara City
 Coll (CA)
Santa Rosa Jr Coll (CA)
Santiago Canyon Coll (CA)
Skagit Valley Coll (WA)
Southern U at
 Shreveport (LA)
South Georgia Coll (GA)
South Plains Coll (TX)
Southwest Mississippi
 Comm Coll (MS)
Springfield Tech Comm
 Coll (MA)
State U of New York Coll
 of Agriculture and
 Technology at
 Morrisville (NY)
Suffolk County Comm
 Coll (NY)
Terra State Comm
 Coll (OH)
Texarkana Coll (TX)
Treasure Valley Comm
 Coll (OR)
Trinidad State Jr Coll (CO)
Tulsa Comm Coll (OK)
Umpqua Comm Coll (OR)
Union County Coll (NJ)
Wenatchee Valley
 Coll (WA)
Western Nebraska Comm
 Coll (NE)
Western Wyoming Comm
 Coll (WY)
West Hills Comm Coll (CA)
West Los Angeles
 Coll (CA)
West Valley Coll (CA)
Wright State U, Lake
 Campus (OH)
Young Harris Coll (GA)
Yuba Coll (CA)

Chemistry Related
Guilford Tech Comm
 Coll (NC)

**Chemistry Teacher
Education**
Coll of the Siskiyous (CA)
Louisburg Coll (NC)
Manatee Comm Coll (FL)

**Child Care and
Guidance Related**
Albany Tech Coll (GA)

**Child Care and
Support Services
Management**
Alexandria Tech Coll (MN)
Angelina Coll (TX)

Antelope Valley Coll (CA)
Asheville-Buncombe Tech
 Comm Coll (NC)
Barton County Comm
 Coll (KS)
Broome Comm Coll (NY)
Calhoun Comm Coll (AL)
Cape Fear Comm
 Coll (NC)
Central Carolina Tech
 Coll (SC)
Central Georgia Tech
 Coll (GA)
Centralia Coll (WA)
Central New Mexico
 Comm Coll (NM)
Central Texas Coll (TX)
Central Wyoming
 Coll (WY)
Coll of DuPage (IL)
Dixie State Coll of
 Utah (UT)
Eastern New Mexico
 U–Roswell (NM)
Erie Comm Coll (NY)
Gadsden State Comm
 Coll (AL)
Grays Harbor Coll (WA)
Hagerstown Comm
 Coll (MD)
H. Councill Trenholm State
 Tech Coll (AL)
Hesser Coll (NH)
Hopkinsville Comm
 Coll (KY)
Houston Comm Coll
 System (TX)
Hutchinson Comm Coll
 and Area Vocational
 School (KS)
Jefferson Comm Coll (OH)
Kansas City Kansas
 Comm Coll (KS)
Kennebec Valley Comm
 Coll (ME)
Lake Land Coll (IL)
Lamar Inst of
 Technology (TX)
Linn-Benton Comm
 Coll (OR)
Macomb Comm Coll (MI)
Massachusetts Bay Comm
 Coll (MA)
Massasoit Comm
 Coll (MA)
Montcalm Comm Coll (MI)
Montgomery Coll (MD)
Montgomery County
 Comm Coll (PA)
Muscatine Comm Coll (IA)
Oakland Comm Coll (MI)
Olympic Coll (WA)
Orange Coast Coll (CA)
Ouachita Tech Coll (AR)
Peninsula Coll (WA)
Pima Comm Coll (AZ)
Rasmussen Coll Brooklyn
 Park (MN)
Reedley Coll (CA)
St. Cloud Tech Coll (MN)
San Antonio Coll (TX)
Santa Barbara City
 Coll (CA)
Schoolcraft Coll (MI)
Scott Comm Coll (IA)
Sitting Bull Coll (ND)
Southwestern Michigan
 Coll (MI)
Spokane Falls Comm
 Coll (WA)
Stanly Comm Coll (NC)
Tulsa Comm Coll (OK)
Vernon Coll (TX)
Victor Valley Coll (CA)
Western Nevada Comm
 Coll (NV)
Wor-Wic Comm Coll (MD)
York Tech Coll (SC)

Child Care/Guidance
Caldwell Comm Coll and
 Tech Inst (NC)

Child Care Provider
Elizabethtown Tech
 Coll (KY)
Klamath Comm Coll (OR)
Lamar Inst of
 Technology (TX)

Child Care Provision
Alexandria Tech Coll (MN)
Angelina Coll (TX)
Bladen Comm Coll (NC)
Brunswick Comm
 Coll (NC)
Cincinnati State Tech and
 Comm Coll (OH)
Coastal Carolina Comm
 Coll (NC)

Coll of DuPage (IL)
Coll of Lake County (IL)
Coll of the Redwoods (CA)
Comm Coll of Allegheny
 County (PA)
Crafton Hills Coll (CA)
Eastern Arizona Coll (AZ)
Eastern West Virginia
 Comm and Tech
 Coll (WV)
Iowa Lakes Comm
 Coll (IA)
Kennebec Valley Comm
 Coll (ME)
Lehigh Carbon Comm
 Coll (PA)
Lincoln Land Comm
 Coll (IL)
Massasoit Comm
 Coll (MA)
Metropolitan Comm
 Coll–Penn Valley (MO)
Midlands Tech Coll (SC)
Montcalm Comm Coll (MI)
Moraine Valley Comm
 Coll (IL)
Northampton County Area
 Comm Coll (PA)
Northland Comm and Tech
 Coll–Thief River
 Falls (MN)
Orange Coast Coll (CA)
Parkland Coll (IL)
Pima Comm Coll (AZ)
San Antonio Coll (TX)
Surry Comm Coll (NC)
Tompkins Cortland Comm
 Coll (NY)
Trident Tech Coll (SC)
Westchester Comm
 Coll (NY)
York Tech Coll (SC)
Zane State Coll (OH)

**Child Care Services
Management**
Forrest Jr Coll (SC)

Child Development
Aims Comm Coll (CO)
Albany Tech Coll (GA)
Allen County Comm
 Coll (KS)
Altamaha Tech Coll (GA)
Amarillo Coll (TX)
Angelina Coll (TX)
Appalachian Tech
 Coll (GA)
Athens Tech Coll (GA)
Atlanta Tech Coll (GA)
Augusta Tech Coll (GA)
Bakersfield Coll (CA)
Barstow Coll (CA)
Black Hawk Coll,
 Moline (IL)
Briarwood Coll (CT)
Brigham Young U –
 Idaho (ID)
Brookhaven Coll (TX)
Broward Comm Coll (FL)
Cabrillo Coll (CA)
Central Arizona Coll (AZ)
Central Comm Coll–Grand
 Island Campus (NE)
Central Comm Coll–
 Hastings Campus (NE)
Central Georgia Tech
 Coll (GA)
Centralia Coll (WA)
Central Piedmont Comm
 Coll (NC)
Chaffey Coll (CA)
Chattahoochee Tech
 Coll (GA)
Chattanooga State Tech
 Comm Coll (TN)
Chippewa Valley Tech
 Coll (WI)
Cisco Jr Coll (TX)
City Colls of Chicago,
 Harold Washington
 College (IL)
City Colls of Chicago,
 Kennedy-King
 College (IL)
City Colls of Chicago,
 Richard J. Daley
 College (IL)
Cleveland State Comm
 Coll (TN)
Coastal Bend Coll (TX)
Colby Comm Coll (KS)
Coll of DuPage (IL)
Coll of Southern Idaho (ID)
Coll of the Canyons (CA)
Coll of the Mainland (TX)
Columbus Tech Coll (GA)
Comm Coll of Allegheny
 County (PA)

Comm Coll of Southern
Nevada (NV)
Comm Coll of
Vermont (VT)
Coosa Valley Tech
Coll (GA)
Cosumnes River Coll,
Sacramento (CA)
Crafton Hills Coll (CA)
Cuesta Coll (CA)
De Anza Coll (CA)
Dodge City Comm
Coll (KS)
Dyersburg State Comm
Coll (TN)
East Central Tech
Coll (GA)
Flint River Tech Coll (GA)
Foothill Coll (CA)
Forsyth Tech Comm
Coll (NC)
Fox Valley Tech Coll (WI)
Frederick Comm Coll (MD)
Gateway Tech Coll (WI)
Griffin Tech Coll (GA)
Grossmont Coll (CA)
Harper Coll (IL)
Hartnell Coll (CA)
Hawkeye Comm Coll (IA)
Heart of Georgia Tech
Coll (GA)
Hillsborough Comm
Coll (FL)
Hocking Coll (OH)
Housatonic Comm
Coll (CT)
Houston Comm Coll
System (TX)
Howard Comm Coll (MD)
Illinois Eastern Comm
Colls, Wabash Valley
College (IL)
Illinois Valley Comm
Coll (IL)
Iowa Lakes Comm
Coll (IA)
Jackson State Comm
Coll (TN)
Jefferson Comm and Tech
Coll (KY)
Jones County Jr Coll (MS)
Kankakee Comm Coll (IL)
Kirkwood Comm Coll (IA)
Labette Comm Coll (KS)
Lanier Tech Coll (GA)
Lansing Comm Coll (MI)
Laredo Comm Coll (TX)
Los Angeles City Coll (CA)
Los Angeles Southwest
Coll (CA)
Madison Area Tech
Coll (WI)
Mendocino Coll (CA)
Mesa Comm Coll (AZ)
Metropolitan Comm
Coll (NE)
Miami Dade Coll (FL)
Middle Georgia Tech
Coll (GA)
Minnesota State Coll–
Southeast Tech (MN)
Monterey Peninsula
Coll (CA)
Moultrie Tech Coll (GA)
Mt. San Antonio Coll (CA)
Mount Wachusett Comm
Coll (MA)
Murray State Coll (OK)
Muskegon Comm Coll (MI)
Napa Valley Coll (CA)
National Park Comm
Coll (AR)
New Hampshire Comm
Tech Coll, Manchester/
Stratham (NH)
New Hampshire Comm
Tech Coll, Nashua/
Claremont (NH)
New River Comm Coll (VA)
Nicolet Area Tech Coll (WI)
Northeastern Jr Coll (CO)
Northland Comm and Tech
Coll–Thief River
Falls (MN)
North Metro Tech Coll (GA)
North Shore Comm
Coll (MA)
Northwestern Connecticut
Comm Coll (CT)
Northwestern Tech
Coll (GA)
Northwest-Shoals Comm
Coll (AL)
Odessa Coll (TX)
Ogeechee Tech Coll (GA)
Ohlone Coll (CA)
Okefenokee Tech
Coll (GA)

Oklahoma City Comm
Coll (OK)
Oxnard Coll (CA)
Peninsula Coll (WA)
Piedmont Tech Coll (SC)
Polk Comm Coll (FL)
Porterville Coll (CA)
Rasmussen Coll Brooklyn
Park (MN)
Redlands Comm Coll (OK)
Richland Comm Coll (IL)
Ridgewater Coll (MN)
Rogue Comm Coll (OR)
Saint Charles Comm
Coll (MO)
St. Cloud Tech Coll (MN)
St. Louis Comm Coll at
Florissant Valley (MO)
Saint Paul Coll–A Comm &
Tech College (MN)
Salish Kootenai Coll (MT)
San Antonio Coll (TX)
Sandersville Tech
Coll (GA)
Sandhills Comm Coll (NC)
San Joaquin Delta
Coll (CA)
Savannah Tech Coll (GA)
Seminole Comm Coll (FL)
Skagit Valley Coll (WA)
Southeastern Comm Coll,
North Campus (IA)
Southeastern Tech
Coll (GA)
Southern Maine Comm
Coll (ME)
South Florida Comm
Coll (FL)
South Georgia Tech
Coll (GA)
South Plains Coll (TX)
Southwestern Comm
Coll (NC)
Southwest Georgia Tech
Coll (GA)
Stark State Coll of
Technology (OH)
Suffolk County Comm
Coll (NY)
Swainsboro Tech Coll (GA)
Tompkins Cortland Comm
Coll (NY)
Tulsa Comm Coll (OK)
Umpqua Comm Coll (OR)
U of Arkansas Comm Coll
at Morrilton (AR)
Valdosta Tech Coll (GA)
Victor Valley Coll (CA)
Virginia Western Comm
Coll (VA)
Wallace State Comm
Coll (AL)
West Central Tech
Coll (GA)
Westchester Comm
Coll (NY)
West Georgia Tech
Coll (GA)
West Hills Comm Coll (CA)
Westmoreland County
Comm Coll (PA)
Yuba Coll (CA)

Child Guidance
Antelope Valley Coll (CA)
Blinn Coll (TX)
Hennepin Tech Coll (MN)
John Wood Comm Coll (IL)
Lassen Comm Coll
District (CA)
Laurel Business Inst (PA)
Lincoln Land Comm
Coll (IL)
Manatee Comm Coll (FL)
Minneapolis Comm and
Tech Coll (MN)
Moberly Area Comm
Coll (MO)
North Central Michigan
Coll (MI)
Santa Rosa Jr Coll (CA)
Tulsa Comm Coll (OK)

Chinese
Brigham Young U –
Idaho (ID)

Chiropractic Assistant
Barton County Comm
Coll (KS)
Iowa Lakes Comm
Coll (IA)

Cinematography and Film/Video Production
Anne Arundel Comm
Coll (MD)
Antelope Valley Coll (CA)
The Art Inst of New York
City (NY)

The Art Inst of
Philadelphia (PA)
Bucks County Comm
Coll (PA)
Cincinnati State Tech and
Comm Coll (OH)
City Coll of San
Francisco (CA)
Coll of DuPage (IL)
Coll of San Mateo (CA)
Coll of the Canyons (CA)
Everett Comm Coll (WA)
Guilford Tech Comm
Coll (NC)
Holyoke Comm Coll (MA)
Lansing Comm Coll (MI)
Miami Dade Coll (FL)
Minneapolis Comm and
Tech Coll (MN)
Orange Coast Coll (CA)
Riverside Comm Coll
District (CA)
St. Louis Comm Coll at
Florissant Valley (MO)
Southern Maine Comm
Coll (ME)
Valencia Comm Coll (FL)

Civil Drafting and Cad/Cadd
Comm Coll of Allegheny
County (PA)
North Seattle Comm
Coll (WA)

Civil Engineering
Itasca Comm Coll (MN)
Santa Rosa Jr Coll (CA)
Tidewater Comm Coll (VA)

Civil Engineering Technology
Asheville-Buncombe Tech
Comm Coll (NC)
Big Bend Comm Coll (WA)
Bishop State Comm
Coll (AL)
Black Hawk Coll,
Moline (IL)
Brigham Young U –
Idaho (ID)
Broome Comm Coll (NY)
Broward Comm Coll (FL)
Burlington County
Coll (NJ)
Central Arizona Coll (AZ)
Central Carolina Tech
Coll (SC)
Centralia Coll (WA)
Central Maine Comm
Coll (ME)
Central Piedmont Comm
Coll (NC)
Central Virginia Comm
Coll (VA)
Chattahoochee Tech
Coll (GA)
Chattanooga State Tech
Comm Coll (TN)
Chippewa Valley Tech
Coll (WI)
Cincinnati State Tech and
Comm Coll (OH)
City Coll of San
Francisco (CA)
Clark State Comm
Coll (OH)
Coll of Lake County (IL)
Comm Coll of Allegheny
County (PA)
Eastern Arizona Coll (AZ)
Erie Comm Coll, North
Campus (NY)
Essex County Coll (NJ)
Everett Comm Coll (WA)
Fayetteville Tech Comm
Coll (NC)
Florence-Darlington Tech
Coll (SC)
Fullerton Coll (CA)
Gadsden State Comm
Coll (AL)
Gateway Tech Coll (WI)
Gloucester County
Coll (NJ)
Guilford Tech Comm
Coll (NC)
Harrisburg Area Comm
Coll (PA)
Hawkeye Comm Coll (IA)
Houston Comm Coll
System (TX)
Lake Land Coll (IL)
Lansing Comm Coll (MI)
Laramie County Comm
Coll (WY)
Linn-Benton Comm
Coll (OR)
Linn State Tech Coll (MO)

Lorain County Comm
Coll (OH)
Macomb Comm Coll (MI)
Madison Area Tech
Coll (WI)
Manatee Comm Coll (FL)
Metropolitan Comm
Coll (NE)
Miami Dade Coll (FL)
Midlands Tech Coll (SC)
Mid-State Tech Coll (WI)
Mississippi Delta Comm
Coll (MS)
Mohawk Valley Comm
Coll (NY)
Monroe Comm Coll (NY)
Montgomery Coll (MD)
Moultrie Tech Coll (GA)
Mt. Hood Comm Coll (OR)
Mt. San Antonio Coll (CA)
Nassau Comm Coll (NY)
New Mexico Military
Inst (NM)
New York City Coll of
Technology of the City
U of New York (NY)
Northern Essex Comm
Coll (MA)
Northwest KansasTech
Coll (KS)
Northwest Mississippi
Comm Coll (MS)
Oklahoma State U,
Oklahoma City (OK)
Pasadena City Coll (CA)
Peninsula Coll (WA)
Potomac State Coll of
West Virginia U (WV)
Pueblo Comm Coll (CO)
Renton Tech Coll (WA)
St. Cloud Tech Coll (MN)
St. Louis Comm Coll at
Florissant Valley (MO)
Saint Paul Coll–A Comm &
Tech College (MN)
San Antonio Coll (TX)
San Bernardino Valley
Coll (CA)
Sandhills Comm Coll (NC)
San Joaquin Delta
Coll (CA)
Seminole Comm Coll (FL)
Shasta Coll (CA)
Southeast Tech Inst (SD)
Southwestern Indian
Polytechnic Inst (NM)
Spokane Comm Coll (WA)
Springfield Tech Comm
Coll (MA)
Stark State Coll of
Technology (OH)
State U of New York Coll
of Technology at
Alfred (NY)
State U of New York Coll
of Technology at
Canton (NY)
Suffolk County Comm
Coll (NY)
Tallahassee Comm
Coll (FL)
Three Rivers Comm
Coll (CT)
Trident Tech Coll (SC)
Trinidad State Jr Coll (CO)
Tulsa Comm Coll (OK)
Umpqua Comm Coll (OR)
Union County Coll (NJ)
Valencia Comm Coll (FL)
Virginia Western Comm
Coll (VA)
Westchester Comm
Coll (NY)
Western Piedmont Comm
Coll (NC)
Wytheville Comm Coll (VA)

Classics and Languages, Literatures And Linguistics
Foothill Coll (CA)

Clinical Laboratory Science/Medical Technology
Amarillo Coll (TX)
Angelina Coll (TX)
Anne Arundel Comm
Coll (MD)
Anoka-Ramsey Comm
Coll (MN)
Athens Tech Coll (GA)
Broward Comm Coll (FL)
Central Piedmont Comm
Coll (NC)
Chipola Coll (FL)
Cisco Jr Coll (TX)

City Colls of Chicago,
Harry S. Truman
College (IL)
City Colls of Chicago,
Kennedy-King
College (IL)
City Colls of Chicago,
Richard J. Daley
College (IL)
Coahoma Comm Coll (MS)
Coll of Southern Idaho (ID)
Comm Coll of Southern
Nevada (NV)
Cuyahoga Comm
Coll (OH)
Dodge City Comm
Coll (KS)
El Centro Coll (TX)
Georgia Highlands
Coll (GA)
Grayson County Coll (TX)
Grossmont Coll (CA)
Holyoke Comm Coll (MA)
Howard Comm Coll (MD)
Joliet Jr Coll (IL)
Lansing Comm Coll (MI)
Lawson State Comm
Coll (AL)
Louisburg Coll (NC)
Marian Court Coll (MA)
National Park Comm
Coll (AR)
Northeastern Jr Coll (CO)
North Idaho Coll (ID)
Northwest-Shoals Comm
Coll (AL)
Orange Coast Coll (CA)
Renton Tech Coll (WA)
South Texas Coll (TX)
Suffolk County Comm
Coll (NY)
Temple Coll (TX)
Turtle Mountain Comm
Coll (ND)
Westchester Comm
Coll (NY)
Western Nebraska Comm
Coll (NE)
Young Harris Coll (GA)

Clinical/Medical Laboratory Assistant
Allegany Coll of
Maryland (MD)
Harrisburg Area Comm
Coll (PA)
Minnesota State Comm
and Tech Coll–Fergus
Falls (MN)
North Arkansas Coll (AR)
Zane State Coll (OH)

Clinical/Medical Laboratory Science and Allied Professions Related
Oakland Comm Coll (MI)

Clinical/Medical Laboratory Technology
Alamance Comm Coll (NC)
Alexandria Tech Coll (MN)
Allegany Coll of
Maryland (MD)
Angelina Coll (TX)
Asheville-Buncombe Tech
Comm Coll (NC)
Barton County Comm
Coll (KS)
Beaufort County Comm
Coll (NC)
Bergen Comm Coll (NJ)
Bismarck State Coll (ND)
Brevard Comm Coll (FL)
Brigham Young U –
Idaho (ID)
Broome Comm Coll (NY)
Broward Comm Coll (FL)
Central Georgia Tech
Coll (GA)
Central Maine Comm
Coll (ME)
Central New Mexico
Comm Coll (NM)
Central Piedmont Comm
Coll (NC)
Central Texas Coll (TX)
Central Virginia Comm
Coll (VA)
Chippewa Valley Tech
Coll (WI)
Cincinnati State Tech and
Comm Coll (OH)
Clark State Comm
Coll (OH)
Coastal Carolina Comm
Coll (NC)

Coastal Georgia Comm
Coll (GA)
Comm Coll of Allegheny
County (PA)
Comm Coll of Beaver
County (PA)
Comm Coll of
Philadelphia (PA)
Comm Coll of Rhode
Island (RI)
Comm Coll of Southern
Nevada (NV)
Davidson County Comm
Coll (NC)
DeKalb Tech Coll (GA)
El Centro Coll (TX)
Elgin Comm Coll (IL)
Erie Comm Coll, North
Campus (NY)
Eugenio María de Hostos
Comm Coll of the City
U of New York (NY)
Florence-Darlington Tech
Coll (SC)
Gadsden State Comm
Coll (AL)
Genesee Comm Coll (NY)
George C. Wallace Comm
Coll (AL)
Grayson County Coll (TX)
Greenville Tech Coll (SC)
Guilford Tech Comm
Coll (NC)
Harrisburg Area Comm
Coll (PA)
Hawkeye Comm Coll (IA)
Housatonic Comm
Coll (CT)
Houston Comm Coll
System (TX)
Indiana Business Coll-
Medical (IN)
Jackson State Comm
Coll (TN)
Jamestown Comm
Coll (NY)
John Wood Comm Coll (IL)
Kankakee Comm Coll (IL)
Kellogg Comm Coll (MI)
Laredo Comm Coll (TX)
Lehigh Carbon Comm
Coll (PA)
Lorain County Comm
Coll (OH)
Madison Area Tech
Coll (WI)
McLennan Comm
Coll (TX)
Meridian Comm Coll (MS)
Miami Dade Coll (FL)
Midlands Tech Coll (SC)
Mid-Plains Comm Coll,
North Platte (NE)
Minnesota State Comm
and Tech Coll–Fergus
Falls (MN)
Mississippi Delta Comm
Coll (MS)
Mississippi Gulf Coast
Comm Coll (MS)
Moberly Area Comm
Coll (MO)
Montgomery County
Comm Coll (PA)
Nassau Comm Coll (NY)
National Park Comm
Coll (AR)
Navarro Coll (TX)
New Mexico Jr Coll (NM)
New Mexico State U–
Alamogordo (NM)
North Arkansas Coll (AR)
Northeast Iowa Comm
Coll (IA)
North Iowa Area Comm
Coll (IA)
Odessa Coll (TX)
The Ohio State U Ag Tech
Inst (OH)
Okefenokee Tech
Coll (GA)
Pamlico Comm Coll (NC)
Penn State Hazleton (PA)
Penn State Schuylkill (PA)
Piedmont Virginia Comm
Coll (VA)
Pierce Coll (WA)
Queensborough Comm
Coll of the City U of
New York (NY)
Roane State Comm
Coll (TN)
Rose State Coll (OK)
Saint Paul Coll–A Comm &
Tech College (MN)
St. Philip's Coll (TX)
Salt Lake Comm Coll (UT)

San Bernardino Valley Coll (CA)
Sandhills Comm Coll (NC)
Scott Comm Coll (IA)
Seminole State Coll (OK)
Southeastern Comm Coll (NC)
Southeast Kentucky Comm and Tech Coll (KY)
Southeast Tech Inst (SD)
Southern U at Shreveport (LA)
Southwestern Comm Coll (NC)
Springfield Tech Comm Coll (MA)
Stark State Coll of Technology (OH)
State U of New York Coll of Agriculture and Technology at Morrisville (NY)
State U of New York Coll of Technology at Canton (NY)
Temple Coll (TX)
Three Rivers Comm Coll (MO)
Trident Tech Coll (SC)
Tulsa Comm Coll (OK)
Turtle Mountain Comm Coll (ND)
Tyler Jr Coll (TX)
Union County Coll (NJ)
U of New Mexico–Gallup (NM)
Victoria Coll (TX)
Wallace State Comm Coll (AL)
Washington State Comm Coll (OH)
Wenatchee Valley Coll (WA)
Westchester Comm Coll (NY)
Western Nevada Comm Coll (NV)
Western Piedmont Comm Coll (NC)
Wichita Area Tech Coll (KS)
Wytheville Comm Coll (VA)
York Tech Coll (SC)

Clinical/Medical Social Work
Central Comm Coll–Grand Island Campus (NE)
Central Comm Coll–Hastings Campus (NE)
Wayne Comm Coll (NC)

Clothing/Textiles
Antelope Valley Coll (CA)
Bradley Academy for the Visual Arts (PA)
Brigham Young U – Idaho (ID)
El Centro Coll (TX)
H. Councill Trenholm State Tech Coll (AL)
Lawson State Comm Coll (AL)
Los Angeles City Coll (CA)
Monterey Peninsula Coll (CA)
Palm Beach Comm Coll (FL)

Commercial and Advertising Art
Academy Coll (MN)
Aims Comm Coll (CO)
Alamance Comm Coll (NC)
Alexandria Tech Coll (MN)
Amarillo Coll (TX)
Baltimore City Comm Coll (MD)
Bergen Comm Coll (NJ)
Bismarck State Coll (ND)
Bradford Scool (NC)
Bradley Academy for the Visual Arts (PA)
Brigham Young U – Idaho (ID)
Bucks County Comm Coll (PA)
Burlington County Coll (NJ)
Catawba Valley Comm Coll (NC)
Central Comm Coll– Columbus Campus (NE)
Central Comm Coll– Hastings Campus (NE)
Centralia Coll (WA)
Central Maine Comm Coll (ME)

Central Piedmont Comm Coll (NC)
Central Texas Coll (TX)
Central Virginia Comm Coll (VA)
Chattanooga State Tech Comm Coll (TN)
Cincinnati State Tech and Comm Coll (OH)
City Colls of Chicago, Harold Washington College (IL)
City Colls of Chicago, Kennedy-King College (IL)
Clark State Comm Coll (OH)
Clovis Comm Coll (NM)
Coastal Bend Coll (TX)
Colby Comm Coll (KS)
Coll of DuPage (IL)
Coll of San Mateo (CA)
Coll of Southern Idaho (ID)
Coll of the Redwoods (CA)
Collin County Comm Coll District (TX)
Colorado Mountain Coll (CO)
Comm Coll of Allegheny County (PA)
Comm Coll of Southern Nevada (NV)
Cuyahoga Comm Coll (OH)
De Anza Coll (CA)
Dixie State Coll of Utah (UT)
Don Bosco Tech Inst (CA)
East Central Coll (MO)
Eastern Arizona Coll (AZ)
Elgin Comm Coll (IL)
Everett Comm Coll (WA)
Fayetteville Tech Comm Coll (NC)
FIDM/The Fashion Inst of Design & Merchandising, Los Angeles Campus (CA)
FIDM/The Fashion Inst of Design & Merchandising, San Diego Campus (CA)
FIDM/The Fashion Inst of Design & Merchandising, San Francisco Campus (CA)
Finger Lakes Comm Coll (NY)
Flint Hills Tech Coll (KS)
Forsyth Tech Comm Coll (NC)
Fox Valley Tech Coll (WI)
Fresno City Coll (CA)
Fulton-Montgomery Comm Coll (NY)
Genesee Comm Coll (NY)
George C. Wallace Comm Coll (AL)
Golden West Coll (CA)
Guilford Tech Comm Coll (NC)
Hagerstown Comm Coll (MD)
Harrisburg Area Comm Coll (PA)
Hartnell Coll (CA)
Hawkeye Comm Coll (IA)
Henry Ford Comm Coll (MI)
Hesser Coll (NH)
Hillsborough Comm Coll (FL)
Holyoke Comm Coll (MA)
Housatonic Comm Coll (CT)
Houston Comm Coll System (TX)
International Business Coll, Fort Wayne (IN)
Iowa Lakes Comm Coll (IA)
Isothermal Comm Coll (NC)
Jackson State Comm Coll (TN)
James H. Faulkner State Comm Coll (AL)
James Sprunt Comm Coll (NC)
Jefferson Comm and Tech Coll (KY)
J. F. Drake State Tech Coll (AL)
Johnston Comm Coll (NC)
Kellogg Comm Coll (MI)

Kingsborough Comm Coll of the City U of New York (NY)
Labette Comm Coll (KS)
Lake-Sumter Comm Coll (FL)
Laney Coll (CA)
Lansing Comm Coll (MI)
Lassen Comm Coll District (CA)
Leeward Comm Coll (HI)
Lehigh Carbon Comm Coll (PA)
Lenoir Comm Coll (NC)
Linn-Benton Comm Coll (OR)
Los Medanos Coll (CA)
Macomb Comm Coll (MI)
Madison Area Tech Coll (WI)
Manatee Comm Coll (FL)
Metropolitan Comm Coll (NE)
Metropolitan Comm Coll–Penn Valley (MO)
Miami Dade Coll (FL)
Middlesex Comm Coll (CT)
Midlands Tech Coll (SC)
Minneapolis Comm and Tech Coll (MN)
Mission Coll (CA)
Mohawk Valley Comm Coll (NY)
Monroe Comm Coll (NY)
Monterey Peninsula Coll (CA)
Montgomery Coll (MD)
Montgomery County Comm Coll (PA)
Moorpark Coll (CA)
Mt. Hood Comm Coll (OR)
Mt. San Antonio Coll (CA)
Muskegon Comm Coll (MI)
Nassau Comm Coll (NY)
National Park Comm Coll (AR)
Navarro Coll (TX)
New Hampshire Comm Tech Coll, Manchester/ Stratham (NH)
New Mexico Jr Coll (NM)
New Mexico State U– Alamogordo (NM)
New York City Coll of Technology of the City U of New York (NY)
Northern Essex Comm Coll (MA)
Northern Oklahoma Coll (OK)
North Idaho Coll (ID)
Northwestern Connecticut Comm Coll (CT)
Northwest Mississippi Comm Coll (MS)
Nossi Coll of Art (TN)
Ohlone Coll (CA)
Oklahoma City Comm Coll (OK)
Oklahoma State U, Okmulgee (OK)
Onondaga Comm Coll (NY)
Orange Coast Coll (CA)
Owens Comm Coll, Toledo (OH)
Palm Beach Comm Coll (FL)
Piedmont Tech Coll (SC)
Platt Coll San Diego (CA)
Porterville Coll (CA)
Provo Coll (UT)
Raritan Valley Comm Coll (NJ)
Rasmussen Coll Brooklyn Park (MN)
Redlands Comm Coll (OK)
Reedley Coll (CA)
Saint Charles Comm Coll (MO)
St. Louis Comm Coll at Florissant Valley (MO)
San Antonio Coll (TX)
San Bernardino Valley Coll (CA)
San Diego City Coll (CA)
San Joaquin Delta Coll (CA)
San Juan Coll (NM)
Santa Ana Coll (CA)
Santa Barbara City Coll (CA)
Schoolcraft Coll (MI)
Skagit Valley Coll (WA)
Southeast Tech Inst (SD)
South Piedmont Comm Coll (NC)
South Plains Coll (TX)

Southwestern Comm Coll (NC)
Southwestern Indian Polytechnic Inst (NM)
Spokane Falls Comm Coll (WA)
Springfield Tech Comm Coll (MA)
Suffolk County Comm Coll (NY)
Surry Comm Coll (NC)
Sussex County Comm Coll (NJ)
Terra State Comm Coll (OH)
Tidewater Comm Coll (VA)
Tompkins Cortland Comm Coll (NY)
Treasure Valley Comm Coll (OR)
Trident Tech Coll (SC)
Trinidad State Jr Coll (CO)
Tunxis Comm Coll (CT)
Tyler Jr Coll (TX)
Ulster County Comm Coll (NY)
U of Arkansas Comm Coll at Morrilton (AR)
U of Puerto Rico at Carolina (PR)
Valencia Comm Coll (FL)
Ventura Coll (CA)
Virginia Western Comm Coll (VA)
Wenatchee Valley Coll (WA)
Westmoreland County Comm Coll (PA)
York Tech Coll (SC)

Commercial Fishing
Peninsula Coll (WA)

Commercial Photography
Houston Comm Coll System (TX)
Mohawk Valley Comm Coll (NY)
Montgomery Coll (MD)
Spokane Falls Comm Coll (WA)

Communication and Journalism Related
Folsom Lake Coll (CA)
Iowa Lakes Comm Coll (IA)
Keystone Coll (PA)
Queensborough Comm Coll of the City U of New York (NY)
U of New Mexico–Taos (NM)

Communication and Media Related
Asnuntuck Comm Coll (CT)
Coll of Micronesia– FSM (FM)
Keystone Coll (PA)

Communication Disorders
Northampton County Area Comm Coll (PA)

Communication/ Speech Communication and Rhetoric
Barton County Comm Coll (KS)
Briarwood Coll (CT)
Broome Comm Coll (NY)
Cochise Coll, Douglas (AZ)
Coll of Southern Idaho (ID)
Coll of Southern Maryland (MD)
Dean Coll (MA)
Dixie State Coll of Utah (UT)
Erie Comm Coll, South Campus (NY)
Gloucester County Coll (NJ)
Hutchinson Comm Coll and Area Vocational School (KS)
Jamestown Comm Coll (NY)
Kellogg Comm Coll (MI)
Keystone Coll (PA)
Laramie County Comm Coll (WY)
Lee Coll (TX)
Lehigh Carbon Comm Coll (PA)
Macomb Comm Coll (MI)

Massachusetts Bay Comm Coll (MA)
Miami U–Middletown Campus (OH)
Montgomery County Comm Coll (PA)
Nassau Comm Coll (NY)
Northampton County Area Comm Coll (PA)
San Juan Coll (NM)
Santa Ana Coll (CA)
Santa Barbara City Coll (CA)
Santa Rosa Jr Coll (CA)
Santiago Canyon Coll (CA)
Union County Coll (NJ)
U of New Mexico–Gallup (NM)
Western Wyoming Comm Coll (WY)
Wright State U, Lake Campus (OH)
Yuba Coll (CA)

Communications Systems Installation and Repair Technology
Broome Comm Coll (NY)
Coll of DuPage (IL)
Erie Comm Coll, South Campus (NY)
Kennebec Valley Comm Coll (ME)
Mohawk Valley Comm Coll (NY)
North Central Kansas Tech Coll (KS)
North Seattle Comm Coll (WA)
Northwest KansasTech Coll (KS)
Suffolk County Comm Coll (NY)

Communications Technologies and Support Services Related
Bowling Green State U–Firelands Coll (OH)
Comm Coll of Allegheny County (PA)
Montgomery County Comm Coll (PA)
Springfield Tech Comm Coll (MA)

Communications Technology
Allegany Coll of Maryland (MD)
Anne Arundel Comm Coll (MD)
Athens Tech Coll (GA)
Black Hawk Coll, Moline (IL)
Burlington County Coll (NJ)
Cleveland Comm Coll (NC)
Coll of DuPage (IL)
Comm Coll of Beaver County (PA)
Comm Coll of Philadelphia (PA)
Dodge City Comm Coll (KS)
ECPI Coll of Technology (VA)
ECPI Tech Coll (VA)
ECPI Tech Coll (VA)
Essex County Coll (NJ)
Fountainhead Coll of Technology (TN)
Gateway Tech Coll (WI)
Hutchinson Comm Coll and Area Vocational School (KS)
ITT Tech Inst, Tucson (AZ)
ITT Tech Inst, Woburn (MA)
ITT Tech Inst (OR)
ITT Tech Inst, Cordova (TN)
ITT Tech Inst, Chantilly (VA)
ITT Tech Inst, Norfolk (VA)
Kent State U, Tuscarawas Campus (OH)
Kirkwood Comm Coll (IA)
Lassen Comm Coll District (CA)
Madison Area Tech Coll (WI)
Mott Comm Coll (MI)
Napa Valley Coll (CA)
North Lake Coll (TX)
Northwestern Connecticut Comm Coll (CT)

Orange Coast Coll (CA)
Pasadena City Coll (CA)
Renton Tech Coll (WA)
St. Philip's Coll (TX)
Southern Maine Comm Coll (ME)

Community Health and Preventive Medicine
Northwest Vista Coll (TX)

Community Health Services Counseling
Comm Coll of Allegheny County (PA)
Erie Comm Coll (NY)
Kingsborough Comm Coll of the City U of New York (NY)
Manatee Comm Coll (FL)
Mott Comm Coll (MI)

Community Organization and Advocacy
Clackamas Comm Coll (OR)
Cleveland State Comm Coll (TN)
Comm Coll of Philadelphia (PA)
Comm Coll of Vermont (VT)
Crafton Hills Coll (CA)
Lamar Comm Coll (CO)
Mohawk Valley Comm Coll (NY)
New Hampshire Comm Tech Coll, Manchester/ Stratham (NH)
New River Comm Coll (VA)
Ridgewater Coll (MN)
Suffolk County Comm Coll (NY)
Ulster County Comm Coll (NY)
U of New Mexico–Gallup (NM)

Community Psychology
Western Nebraska Comm Coll (NE)

Computer and Information Sciences
Academy Coll (MN)
Albany Tech Coll (GA)
Alexandria Tech Coll (MN)
Alpena Comm Coll (MI)
Antelope Valley Coll (CA)
Asnuntuck Comm Coll (CT)
Berkeley City Coll (CA)
Berkshire Comm Coll (MA)
Bishop State Comm Coll (AL)
Broome Comm Coll (NY)
Brown Mackie Coll– Salina (KS)
Bryan Coll (CA)
Bucks County Comm Coll (PA)
Calhoun Comm Coll (AL)
Capital Comm Coll (CT)
Carroll Comm Coll (MD)
Central Arizona Coll (AZ)
Central Comm Coll– Columbus Campus (NE)
Central Comm Coll–Grand Island Campus (NE)
Central Comm Coll– Hastings Campus (NE)
Central Texas Coll (TX)
Chippewa Valley Tech Coll (WI)
Cincinnati State Tech and Comm Coll (OH)
City Colls of Chicago, Wilbur Wright College (IL)
Clarendon Coll (TX)
Clovis Comm Coll (NM)
Coll of Micronesia– FSM (FM)
Coll of the Redwoods (CA)
Collin County Comm Coll District (TX)
Comm Coll of Beaver County (PA)
Eastern New Mexico U–Roswell (NM)
ECPI Coll of Technology (VA)
ECPI Tech Coll (VA)
ECPI Tech Coll (VA)
Elizabethtown Tech Coll (KY)

Erie Comm Coll, North
Campus (NY)
Finger Lakes Comm
Coll (NY)
Folsom Lake Coll (CA)
Front Range Comm
Coll (CO)
Gadsden State Comm
Coll (AL)
Hagerstown Comm
Coll (MD)
Harper Coll (IL)
Harrisburg Area Comm
Coll (PA)
H. Council Trenholm State
Tech Coll (AL)
Henry Ford Comm
Coll (MI)
Herzing Coll (MN)
Herzing Coll (WI)
Hesser Coll (NH)
Houston Comm Coll
System (TX)
Hutchinson Comm Coll
and Area Vocational
School (KS)
Indiana Business Coll,
Indianapolis (IN)
James H. Faulkner State
Comm Coll (AL)
Jamestown Comm
Coll (NY)
Joliet Jr Coll (IL)
Kaplan U (IA)
Kingsborough Comm Coll
of the City U of New
York (NY)
Laramie County Comm
Coll (WY)
Lehigh Valley Coll (PA)
Linn-Benton Comm
Coll (OR)
Lower Columbia Coll (WA)
Manatee Comm Coll (FL)
Massachusetts Bay Comm
Coll (MA)
Massasoit Comm
Coll (MA)
Metropolitan Comm
Coll–Business &
Technology
Campus (MO)
Miami U–Middletown
Campus (OH)
Mid-Plains Comm Coll,
North Platte (NE)
Moberly Area Comm
Coll (MO)
Mohawk Valley Comm
Coll (NY)
Montgomery Coll (MD)
Montgomery County
Comm Coll (PA)
Mountain State Coll (WV)
Nassau Comm Coll (NY)
National American U,
Bloomington (MN)
National American U, Rio
Rancho (NM)
New England Inst of
Technology (RI)
New Hampshire Comm
Tech Coll, Nashua/
Claremont (NH)
New Hampshire Tech
Inst (NH)
Nicolet Area Tech Coll (WI)
North Arkansas Coll (AR)
Northeast Comm Coll (NE)
Northern Essex Comm
Coll (MA)
Northern New Mexico
Coll (NM)
North Iowa Area Comm
Coll (IA)
Northwest Mississippi
Comm Coll (MS)
Northwest-Shoals Comm
Coll (AL)
Northwest Vista Coll (TX)
Oakland Comm Coll (MI)
Odessa Coll (TX)
Oklahoma State U,
Oklahoma City (OK)
Ouachita Tech Coll (AR)
Owensboro Comm and
Tech Coll (KY)
Parkland Coll (IL)
Penn State Schuylkill (PA)
Pennsylvania Highland
Comm Coll (PA)
Pima Comm Coll (AZ)
Reedley Coll (CA)
Robeson Comm Coll (NC)
Rockford Business
Coll (IL)
Salt Lake Comm Coll (UT)
Sampson Comm Coll (NC)

Santiago Canyon Coll (CA)
Scott Comm Coll (IA)
Skagit Valley Coll (WA)
South Georgia Coll (GA)
State U of New York Coll
of Technology at
Alfred (NY)
Sussex County Comm
Coll (NJ)
Tallahassee Comm
Coll (FL)
Terra State Comm
Coll (OH)
U of Alaska Southeast,
Sitka Campus (AK)
U of Cincinnati Clermont
Coll (OH)
Ventura Coll (CA)
Victor Valley Coll (CA)
Westchester Comm
Coll (NY)
Western Nebraska Comm
Coll (NE)
Western Nevada Comm
Coll (NV)
Western Wyoming Comm
Coll (WY)
Westmoreland County
Comm Coll (PA)
Wor-Wic Comm Coll (MD)

Computer and Information Sciences And Support Services Related

Academy Coll (MN)
Baton Rouge School of
Computers (LA)
Bradford School (PA)
Gretna Career Coll (LA)
Harrisburg Area Comm
Coll (PA)
Indiana Business Coll,
Indianapolis (IN)
Indiana Business Coll,
Lafayette (IN)
Indiana Business Coll,
Muncie (IN)
Keiser Career Coll -
Greenacres (FL)
Laramie County Comm
Coll (WY)
LDS Business Coll (UT)
Massasoit Comm
Coll (MA)
Metropolitan Comm
Coll–Business &
Technology
Campus (MO)
Midlands Tech Coll (SC)
Miller-Motte Tech Coll,
Clarksville (TN)
Mohawk Valley Comm
Coll (NY)
Mott Comm Coll (MI)
National Inst of
Technology (OH)
Remington Coll–Baton
Rouge Campus (LA)
Remington
Coll–Jacksonville
Campus (FL)
Robeson Comm Coll (NC)
Springfield Tech Comm
Coll (MA)
Tri-State Business
Inst (PA)
Waukesha County Tech
Coll (WI)
York Tech Coll (SC)

Computer and Information Sciences Related

Anne Arundel Comm
Coll (MD)
Berkeley City Coll (CA)
Bucks County Comm
Coll (PA)
Cape Cod Comm
Coll (MA)
Capital Comm Coll (CT)
Centralia Coll (WA)
Central Oregon Comm
Coll (OR)
Chipola Coll (FL)
Citrus Coll (CA)
Coastal Bend Coll (TX)
Colby Comm Coll (KS)
Colegio Universitario de
San Juan, San
Juan (PR)
Coll of the Canyons (CA)
Coll of the Desert (CA)
Columbia Basin Coll (WA)
Columbia-Greene Comm
Coll (NY)
Cypress Coll (CA)
ECPI Tech Coll (VA)

ECPI Tech Coll (VA)
Elaine P. Nunez Comm
Coll (LA)
Fiorello H. LaGuardia
Comm Coll of the City
U of New York (NY)
Gateway Comm Coll (CT)
Genesee Comm Coll (NY)
Gordon Coll (GA)
Heritage Coll (NV)
High-Tech Inst (CA)
Howard Comm Coll (MD)
ICPR Jr Coll–Hato Rey
Campus (PR)
Iowa Lakes Comm
Coll (IA)
Jamestown Comm
Coll (NY)
Kent State U, East
Liverpool Campus (OH)
Lakeshore Tech Coll (WI)
Lake-Sumter Comm
Coll (FL)
Lamar Inst of
Technology (TX)
Laurel Business Inst (PA)
Lawson State Comm
Coll (AL)
Lorain County Comm
Coll (OH)
Los Angeles City Coll (CA)
Manatee Comm Coll (FL)
Maric Coll, Panorama
City (CA)
Massasoit Comm
Coll (MA)
Metropolitan Comm
Coll–Blue River (MO)
Metropolitan Comm
Coll–Business &
Technology
Campus (MO)
Metropolitan Comm
Coll–Longview (MO)
Metropolitan Comm
Coll–Maple
Woods (MO)
Metropolitan Comm
Coll–Penn Valley (MO)
Middle Georgia Coll (GA)
Mid-State Tech Coll (WI)
Minneapolis Comm and
Tech Coll (MN)
Mississippi Gulf Coast
Comm Coll (MS)
Missouri State U–West
Plains (MO)
Mohave Comm Coll (AZ)
Monroe Comm Coll (NY)
Nassau Comm Coll (NY)
National American U (KS)
National American U,
Ellsworth AFB (SD)
North Central Michigan
Coll (MI)
North Idaho Coll (ID)
Northland Comm and Tech
Coll–Thief River
Falls (MN)
North Shore Comm
Coll (MA)
Olympic Coll (WA)
Onondaga Comm
Coll (NY)
Palo Alto Coll (TX)
Potomac State Coll of
West Virginia U (WV)
Provo Coll (UT)
Quinebaug Valley Comm
Coll (CT)
Remington Coll–Dallas
Campus (TX)
Remington Coll–Fort Worth
Campus (TX)
Remington
Coll–Jacksonville
Campus (FL)
Remington Coll–Little Rock
Campus (AR)
Remington Coll–Nashville
Campus (TN)
Richland Comm Coll (IL)
Ridgewater Coll (MN)
Rio Salado Coll (AZ)
Santa Ana Coll (CA)
Seminole Comm Coll (FL)
Southeastern Business
Coll, Jackson (OH)
Southeast Tech Inst (SD)
Southwestern Michigan
Coll (MI)
Stark State Coll of
Technology (OH)
State Fair Comm
Coll (MO)
Three Rivers Comm
Coll (MO)

Tompkins Cortland Comm
Coll (NY)
Trinidad State Jr Coll (CO)
Tri-State Business
Inst (PA)
Tulsa Comm Coll (OK)
Tyler Jr Coll (TX)
West Central Tech
Coll (GA)
Westchester Comm
Coll (NY)
Yuba Coll (CA)

Computer and Information Systems Security

Academy Coll (MN)
Berkeley City Coll (CA)
Chattahoochee Tech
Coll (GA)
City Colls of Chicago,
Wilbur Wright
College (IL)
Cochise Coll, Douglas (AZ)
ECPI Tech Coll (VA)
ECPI Tech Coll (VA)
Fayetteville Tech Comm
Coll (NC)
Flint River Tech Coll (GA)
Florida National Coll (FL)
Griffin Tech Coll (GA)
High-Tech Inst (FL)
High-Tech Inst (MN)
High-Tech Inst,
Nashville (TN)
Island Drafting and Tech
Inst (NY)
ITT Tech Inst,
Youngstown (OH)
Jamestown Comm
Coll (NY)
Lanier Tech Coll (GA)
Laurel Business Inst (PA)
Los Angeles City Coll (CA)
Metropolitan Comm
Coll–Business &
Technology
Campus (MO)
Minnesota State Comm
and Tech Coll–Fergus
Falls (MN)
Minot State U–Bottineau
Campus (ND)
Northampton County Area
Comm Coll (PA)
North Seattle Comm
Coll (WA)
Northwest Vista Coll (TX)
Rasmussen Coll Brooklyn
Park (MN)
Riverland Comm Coll (MN)
St. Philip's Coll (TX)
Seminole Comm Coll (FL)
Stanbridge Coll (CA)
Tompkins Cortland Comm
Coll (NY)
Tulsa Comm Coll (OK)
Valdosta Tech Coll (GA)
Virginia Coll at Austin (TX)

Computer Engineering

Itasca Comm Coll (MN)
Santa Barbara City
Coll (CA)

Computer Engineering Related

Catawba Valley Comm
Coll (NC)
Coll of the Canyons (CA)
Columbus Tech Coll (GA)
Gateway Comm Coll (CT)
Itasca Comm Coll (MN)
Jefferson Comm Coll (OH)
Middle Georgia Coll (GA)
Monroe Comm Coll (NY)
Onondaga Comm
Coll (NY)
Sandhills Comm Coll (NC)
Seminole Comm Coll (FL)
Stark State Coll of
Technology (OH)
Surry Comm Coll (NC)

Computer Engineering Technology

Allegany Coll of
Maryland (MD)
Amarillo Coll (TX)
Angelina Coll (TX)
Anne Arundel Comm
Coll (MD)
Bergen Comm Coll (NJ)
Bowling Green State
U–Firelands Coll (OH)
Bramson ORT Coll (NY)
Brevard Comm Coll (FL)

Broome Comm Coll (NY)
Broward Comm Coll (FL)
Bucks County Comm
Coll (PA)
Cañada Coll (CA)
Capital Comm Coll (CT)
Catawba Valley Comm
Coll (NC)
Cecil Comm Coll (MD)
Central Piedmont Comm
Coll (NC)
Century Coll (MN)
Chandler-Gilbert Comm
Coll (AZ)
Chattanooga State Tech
Comm Coll (TN)
Chesapeake Coll (MD)
Cincinnati State Tech and
Comm Coll (OH)
City Colls of Chicago,
Olive-Harvey
College (IL)
Clatsop Comm Coll (OR)
Cleveland Comm Coll (NC)
Coastal Bend Coll (TX)
Coll of The Albemarle (NC)
Coll of the Redwoods (CA)
Collin County Comm Coll
District (TX)
Colorado Mountain
Coll (CO)
Colorado Mountain Coll,
Alpine Campus (CO)
Comm Coll of Allegheny
County (PA)
Comm Coll of
Philadelphia (PA)
Comm Coll of Rhode
Island (RI)
Comm Coll of Southern
Nevada (NV)
Cuesta Coll (CA)
Cuyahoga Comm
Coll (OH)
Davidson County Comm
Coll (NC)
DeKalb Tech Coll (GA)
ECPI Coll of
Technology (VA)
ECPI Tech Coll (VA)
Elaine P. Nunez Comm
Coll (LA)
Fiorello H. LaGuardia
Comm Coll of the City
U of New York (NY)
Florence-Darlington Tech
Coll (SC)
Forsyth Tech Comm
Coll (NC)
Fountainhead Coll of
Technology (TN)
Frederick Comm Coll (MD)
Fulton-Montgomery Comm
Coll (NY)
Gateway Comm Coll (CT)
Genesee Comm Coll (NY)
Grand Rapids Comm
Coll (MI)
Grayson County Coll (TX)
Harper Coll (IL)
Hawkeye Comm Coll (IA)
Hesser Coll (NH)
Hillsborough Comm
Coll (FL)
Hocking Coll (OH)
Houston Comm Coll
System (TX)
International Business Coll,
Fort Wayne (IN)
Irvine Valley Coll (CA)
ITT Tech Inst (AL)
ITT Tech Inst, Tucson (AZ)
ITT Tech Inst (AR)
ITT Tech Inst,
Anaheim (CA)
ITT Tech Inst, Lathrop (CA)
ITT Tech Inst, Oxnard (CA)
ITT Tech Inst, Rancho
Cordova (CA)
ITT Tech Inst, San
Bernardino (CA)
ITT Tech Inst, San
Diego (CA)
ITT Tech Inst, San
Dimas (CA)
ITT Tech Inst, Sylmar (CA)
ITT Tech Inst,
Torrance (CA)
ITT Tech Inst (CO)
ITT Tech Inst, Fort
Lauderdale (FL)
ITT Tech Inst,
Jacksonville (FL)
ITT Tech Inst, Lake
Mary (FL)
ITT Tech Inst, Miami (FL)
ITT Tech Inst, Tampa (FL)
ITT Tech Inst, Duluth (GA)

ITT Tech Inst,
Kennesaw (GA)
ITT Tech Inst (ID)
ITT Tech Inst, Burr
Ridge (IL)
ITT Tech Inst, Orland
Park (IL)
ITT Tech Inst, Fort
Wayne (IN)
ITT Tech Inst,
Indianapolis (IN)
ITT Tech Inst,
Newburgh (IN)
ITT Tech Inst, Louisville (KY)
ITT Tech Inst (LA)
ITT Tech Inst (MD)
ITT Tech Inst,
Norwood (MA)
ITT Tech Inst,
Woburn (MA)
ITT Tech Inst, Canton (MI)
ITT Tech Inst, Flint (MI)
ITT Tech Inst, Grand
Rapids (MI)
ITT Tech Inst, Troy (MI)
ITT Tech Inst (MN)
ITT Tech Inst, Arnold (MO)
ITT Tech Inst, Earth
City (MO)
ITT Tech Inst, Kansas
City (MO)
ITT Tech Inst (NE)
ITT Tech Inst (NV)
ITT Tech Inst (NM)
ITT Tech Inst, Albany (NY)
ITT Tech Inst,
Getzville (NY)
ITT Tech Inst,
Liverpool (NY)
ITT Tech Inst, Dayton (OH)
ITT Tech Inst, Hilliard (OH)
ITT Tech Inst,
Norwood (OH)
ITT Tech Inst,
Strongsville (OH)
ITT Tech Inst, Warrensville
Heights (OH)
ITT Tech Inst, Tulsa (OK)
ITT Tech Inst (OR)
ITT Tech Inst (SC)
ITT Tech Inst,
Cordova (TN)
ITT Tech Inst,
Knoxville (TN)
ITT Tech Inst,
Nashville (TN)
ITT Tech Inst,
Arlington (TX)
ITT Tech Inst, Austin (TX)
ITT Tech Inst,
Houston (TX)
ITT Tech Inst,
Webster (TX)
ITT Tech Inst (UT)
ITT Tech Inst,
Chantilly (VA)
ITT Tech Inst, Norfolk (VA)
ITT Tech Inst,
Richmond (VA)
ITT Tech Inst,
Springfield (VA)
ITT Tech Inst, Bothell (WA)
ITT Tech Inst, Seattle (WA)
ITT Tech Inst, Green
Bay (WI)
ITT Tech Inst,
Greenfield (WI)
Jamestown Comm
Coll (NY)
Kansas City Kansas
Comm Coll (KS)
Kellogg Comm Coll (MI)
Kent State U, Ashtabula
Campus (OH)
Kent State U, East
Liverpool Campus (OH)
Kent State U, Trumbull
Campus (OH)
Kent State U, Tuscarawas
Campus (OH)
Lamar Comm Coll (CO)
Lansing Comm Coll (MI)
Lehigh Carbon Comm
Coll (PA)
Lorain County Comm
Coll (OH)
Los Angeles City Coll (CA)
Los Angeles Harbor
Coll (CA)
Los Angeles Pierce
Coll (CA)
Lower Columbia Coll (WA)
Madison Area Tech
Coll (WI)
Manatee Comm Coll (FL)
Marshall Comm and Tech
Coll (WV)

Massachusetts Bay Comm Coll (MA)
McLennan Comm Coll (TX)
Merced Coll (CA)
Meridian Comm Coll (MS)
Miami Dade Coll (FL)
Miami U–Middletown Campus (OH)
Mid-State Tech Coll (WI)
Minnesota State Coll–Southeast Tech (MN)
Minot State U–Bottineau Campus (ND)
Mission Coll (CA)
Mississippi Delta Comm Coll (MS)
Mississippi Gulf Coast Comm Coll (MS)
Monroe Comm Coll (NY)
Monterey Peninsula Coll (CA)
Montgomery County Comm Coll (PA)
Mt. Hood Comm Coll (OR)
Mt. San Antonio Coll (CA)
New Hampshire Comm Tech Coll, Nashua/Claremont (NH)
New Hampshire Tech Inst (NH)
New River Comm Coll (VA)
North Central Missouri Coll (MO)
North Central Texas Coll (TX)
Northeastern Jr Coll (CO)
Northeast Iowa Comm Coll (IA)
Northern Essex Comm Coll (MA)
Northern Maine Comm Coll (ME)
North Shore Comm Coll (MA)
Northwestern Connecticut Comm Coll (CT)
Northwest-Shoals Comm Coll (AL)
Oklahoma City Comm Coll (OK)
Onondaga Comm Coll (NY)
Orange Coast Coll (CA)
Palo Alto Coll (TX)
Pamlico Comm Coll (NC)
Pasadena City Coll (CA)
Penn State New Kensington (PA)
Piedmont Virginia Comm Coll (VA)
Pima Comm Coll (AZ)
Potomac State Coll of West Virginia U (WV)
Pulaski Tech Coll (AR)
Queensborough Comm Coll of the City U of New York (NY)
Ranger Coll (TX)
Red Rocks Comm Coll (CO)
Ridgewater Coll (MN)
Roane State Comm Coll (TN)
St. Catharine Coll (KY)
St. Louis Comm Coll at Florissant Valley (MO)
San Antonio Coll (TX)
San Bernardino Valley Coll (CA)
Sandhills Comm Coll (NC)
San Diego City Coll (CA)
San Joaquin Delta Coll (CA)
Seminole Comm Coll (FL)
Skagit Valley Coll (WA)
Southeastern Comm Coll (NC)
Southeast Kentucky Comm and Tech Coll (KY)
Southern Maine Comm Coll (ME)
South Plains Coll (TX)
South Seattle Comm Coll (WA)
Southwestern Comm Coll (NC)
Southwest Texas Jr Coll (TX)
Springfield Tech Comm Coll (MA)
State Fair Comm Coll (MO)
State U of New York Coll of Agriculture and Technology at Morrisville (NY)

State U of New York Coll of Technology at Alfred (NY)
Suffolk County Comm Coll (NY)
Surry Comm Coll (NC)
Texas State Tech Coll West Texas (TX)
Three Rivers Comm Coll (CT)
Three Rivers Comm Coll (MO)
Trident Tech Coll (SC)
Tyler Jr Coll (TX)
Umpqua Comm Coll (OR)
U of Alaska Southeast, Sitka Campus (AK)
U of New Mexico–Los Alamos Branch (NM)
Washington State Comm Coll (OH)
Western Piedmont Comm Coll (NC)
Western Texas Coll (TX)
Westmoreland County Comm Coll (PA)
York County Comm Coll (ME)
York Tech Coll (SC)

Computer Graphics
Academy Coll (MN)
Antelope Valley Coll (CA)
Baltimore City Comm Coll (MD)
Berkeley City Coll (CA)
Bradley Academy for the Visual Arts (PA)
Burlington County Coll (NJ)
Calhoun Comm Coll (AL)
Cape Cod Comm Coll (MA)
Carroll Comm Coll (MD)
Cecil Comm Coll (MD)
Coll of the Desert (CA)
Coll of the Siskiyous (CA)
Columbia-Greene Comm Coll (NY)
The Creative Center (NE)
Cypress Coll (CA)
De Anza Coll (CA)
Elgin Comm Coll (IL)
Florida National Coll (FL)
Gateway Comm Coll (CT)
Gateway Tech Coll (WI)
Genesee Comm Coll (NY)
Gloucester County Coll (NJ)
Hartnell Coll (CA)
Howard Comm Coll (MD)
Iowa Lakes Comm Coll (IA)
Kellogg Comm Coll (MI)
Lansing Comm Coll (MI)
Manatee Comm Coll (FL)
Meridian Comm Coll (MS)
Mesabi Range Comm and Tech Coll (MN)
Metropolitan Comm Coll–Business & Technology Campus (MO)
Miami Dade Coll (FL)
Mississippi Gulf Coast Comm Coll (MS)
Missouri State U–West Plains (MO)
Mt. San Antonio Coll (CA)
Mount Wachusett Comm Coll (MA)
Nassau Comm Coll (NY)
National Park Comm Coll (AR)
Navarro Coll (TX)
New Mexico Jr Coll (NM)
New River Comm Coll (VA)
North Central Texas Coll (TX)
North Country Comm Coll (NY)
Northern Essex Comm Coll (MA)
Northland Comm and Tech Coll–Thief River Falls (MN)
North Shore Comm Coll (MA)
Northwestern Connecticut Comm Coll (CT)
Oklahoma State U, Okmulgee (OK)
Olympic Coll (WA)
Orange Coast Coll (CA)
Parkland Coll (IL)
Platt Coll San Diego (CA)
Pueblo Comm Coll (CO)
Quinebaug Valley Comm Coll (CT)

Richland Comm Coll (IL)
Ridgewater Coll (MN)
San Antonio Coll (TX)
Seminole Comm Coll (FL)
Southeast Tech Inst (SD)
State U of New York Coll of Technology at Alfred (NY)
Tallahassee Comm Coll (FL)
Tompkins Cortland Comm Coll (NY)
Trident Tech Coll (SC)
Tulsa Comm Coll (OK)
Tyler Jr Coll (TX)
U of Cincinnati Clermont Coll (OH)
Westmoreland County Comm Coll (PA)

Computer Hardware Engineering
Cuesta Coll (CA)
Seminole Comm Coll (FL)
Stanly Comm Coll (NC)
Stark State Coll of Technology (OH)
Tompkins Cortland Comm Coll (NY)
Tulsa Comm Coll (OK)

Computer Hardware Technology
Laramie County Comm Coll (WY)
Tidewater Tech (VA)

Computer/Information Technology Services Administration Related
Alpena Comm Coll (MI)
Barton County Comm Coll (KS)
Black Hawk Coll, Moline (IL)
Brevard Comm Coll (FL)
Brunswick Comm Coll (NC)
Bucks County Comm Coll (PA)
Central Carolina Comm Coll (NC)
Clinton Comm Coll (IA)
Coastal Carolina Comm Coll (NC)
Cypress Coll (CA)
Dyersburg State Comm Coll (TN)
Eastern Shore Comm Coll (VA)
Elaine P. Nunez Comm Coll (LA)
El Centro Coll (TX)
Guilford Tech Comm Coll (NC)
Hawkeye Comm Coll (IA)
Hesston Coll (KS)
Howard Comm Coll (MD)
Iowa Lakes Comm Coll (IA)
Kennebec Valley Comm Coll (ME)
Keystone Coll (PA)
Laurel Business Inst (PA)
Los Angeles City Coll (CA)
Mesabi Range Comm and Tech Coll (MN)
Metropolitan Comm Coll–Business & Technology Campus (MO)
Middle Georgia Coll (GA)
Muscatine Comm Coll (IA)
National American U, Bloomington (MN)
Naugatuck Valley Comm Coll (CT)
North Central Texas Coll (TX)
Northwest Vista Coll (TX)
Onondaga Comm Coll (NY)
Owensboro Comm and Tech Coll (KY)
Parkland Coll (IL)
Pennsylvania Highland Comm Coll (PA)
Ridgewater Coll (MN)
St. Cloud Tech Coll (MN)
San Antonio Coll (TX)
Sandhills Comm Coll (NC)
Seminole Comm Coll (FL)
Southeastern Business Coll, Lancaster (OH)
Southeast Kentucky Comm and Tech Coll (KY)
Southeast Tech Inst (SD)
Stanly Comm Coll (NC)

Stark State Coll of Technology (OH)
State U of New York Coll of Technology at Canton (NY)
Tidewater Tech (VA)
Tompkins Cortland Comm Coll (NY)
Trident Tech Coll (SC)
Trumbull Business Coll (OH)
Tulsa Comm Coll (OK)
York County Comm Coll (ME)

Computer Installation and Repair Technology
Black Hawk Coll, Moline (IL)
Coahoma Comm Coll (MS)
Coll of DuPage (IL)
Coll of Lake County (IL)
Forrest Jr Coll (SC)
Harrisburg Area Comm Coll (PA)
Kennebec Valley Comm Coll (ME)
Midlands Tech Coll (SC)
Montcalm Comm Coll (MI)
Northampton County Area Comm Coll (PA)
Ridgewater Coll (MN)
Riverland Comm Coll (MN)
State U of New York Coll of Technology at Alfred (NY)
Waukesha County Tech Coll (WI)

Computer Maintenance Technology
St. Philip's Coll (TX)

Computer Management
AIB Coll of Business (IA)
Anne Arundel Comm Coll (MD)
Berkeley Coll, West Paterson (NJ)
Bramson ORT Coll (NY)
Cossatot Comm Coll of the U of Arkansas (AR)
Cosumnes River Coll, Sacramento (CA)
De Anza Coll (CA)
ECPI Coll of Technology (VA)
ECPI Tech Coll (VA)
Grossmont Coll (CA)
Harper Coll (IL)
Hesser Coll (NH)
Kennebec Valley Comm Coll (ME)
Lakeshore Tech Coll (WI)
Lamar Comm Coll (CO)
Lansing Comm Coll (MI)
Laurel Business Inst (PA)
Lewis Coll of Business (MI)
New Hampshire Comm Tech Coll, Nashua/Claremont (NH)
North Central Texas Coll (TX)
Palo Alto Coll (TX)
Ridgewater Coll (MN)
Shasta Coll (CA)
Southern Maine Comm Coll (ME)
Tri-County Comm Coll (NC)

Computer Programming
Academy Coll (MN)
Alamance Comm Coll (NC)
Altamaha Tech Coll (GA)
Amarillo Coll (TX)
Angelina Coll (TX)
Anne Arundel Comm Coll (MD)
Antelope Valley Coll (CA)
Asheville-Buncombe Tech Comm Coll (NC)
Athens Tech Coll (GA)
Atlanta Tech Coll (GA)
Augusta Tech Coll (GA)
Beaufort County Comm Coll (NC)
Bergen Comm Coll (NJ)
Black Hawk Coll, Moline (IL)
Bladen Comm Coll (NC)
Bowling Green State U–Firelands Coll (OH)
Bramson ORT Coll (NY)

Brevard Comm Coll (FL)
Brigham Young U – Idaho (ID)
Broward Comm Coll (FL)
Brown Mackie Coll–Hopkinsville (KY)
Brown Mackie Coll–North Canton (OH)
Brown Mackie Coll–South Bend (IN)
Brunswick Comm Coll (NC)
Bucks County Comm Coll (PA)
Business Inst of Pennsylvania, Sharon (PA)
Cabrillo Coll (CA)
Cañada Coll (CA)
Catawba Valley Comm Coll (NC)
Cecil Comm Coll (MD)
Cedar Valley Coll (TX)
Central Carolina Comm Coll (NC)
Central Georgia Tech Coll (GA)
Central Ohio Tech Coll (OH)
Central Piedmont Comm Coll (NC)
Central Texas Coll (TX)
Cerritos Coll (CA)
Chattahoochee Tech Coll (GA)
Chattanooga State Tech Comm Coll (TN)
Chesapeake Coll (MD)
Cincinnati State Tech and Comm Coll (OH)
Cisco Jr Coll (TX)
City Coll of San Francisco (CA)
Clark Coll (WA)
Clark State Comm Coll (OH)
Cochise Coll, Douglas (AZ)
Cochise Coll, Sierra Vista (AZ)
Colegio Universitario de San Juan, San Juan (PR)
CollAmerica–Colorado Springs (CO)
CollAmerica–Denver (CO)
Coll of Southern Maryland (MD)
Coll of The Albemarle (NC)
Coll of the Mainland (TX)
Coll of the Redwoods (CA)
Coll of the Siskiyous (CA)
Collin County Comm Coll District (TX)
Comm Coll of Beaver County (PA)
Comm Coll of Rhode Island (RI)
Comm Coll of Southern Nevada (NV)
Contra Costa Coll (CA)
Coosa Valley Tech Coll (GA)
Cosumnes River Coll, Sacramento (CA)
Dabney S. Lancaster Comm Coll (VA)
Danville Comm Coll (VA)
Davidson County Comm Coll (NC)
De Anza Coll (CA)
DeKalb Tech Coll (GA)
Dodge City Comm Coll (KS)
ECPI Coll of Technology (VA)
ECPI Tech Coll (VA)
El Centro Coll (TX)
Essex County Coll (NJ)
Fayetteville Tech Comm Coll (NC)
Fiorello H. LaGuardia Comm Coll of the City U of New York (NY)
Flint Hills Tech Coll (KS)
Florida National Coll (FL)
Fox Valley Tech Coll (WI)
Georgia Highlands Coll (GA)
Grand Rapids Comm Coll (MI)
Greenville Tech Coll (SC)
Griffin Tech Coll (GA)
Grossmont Coll (CA)
Guilford Tech Comm Coll (NC)
Gwinnett Tech Coll (GA)
Harper Coll (IL)
Hennepin Tech Coll (MN)

Hesser Coll (NH)
Hillsborough Comm Coll (FL)
Hocking Coll (OH)
Illinois Valley Comm Coll (IL)
Indiana Business Coll, Indianapolis (IN)
International Business Coll, Fort Wayne (IN)
Iowa Lakes Comm Coll (IA)
Isothermal Comm Coll (NC)
ITT Tech Inst (CO)
ITT Tech Inst, Mount Prospect (IL)
ITT Tech Inst, Orland Park (IL)
ITT Tech Inst, Houston (TX)
Johnston Comm Coll (NC)
Joliet Jr Coll (IL)
Kellogg Comm Coll (MI)
Keystone Coll (PA)
Kirkwood Comm Coll (IA)
Lakeshore Tech Coll (WI)
Lamar Comm Coll (CO)
Laney Coll (CA)
Lanier Tech Coll (GA)
Lansing Comm Coll (MI)
Laramie County Comm Coll (WY)
Laredo Comm Coll (TX)
Lee Coll (TX)
Lehigh Valley Coll (PA)
Lenoir Comm Coll (NC)
Lewis Coll of Business (MI)
Linn State Tech Coll (MO)
Lorain County Comm Coll (OH)
Los Angeles City Coll (CA)
Los Angeles Mission Coll (CA)
Los Angeles Pierce Coll (CA)
Louisiana State U at Eunice (LA)
Lower Columbia Coll (WA)
Macomb Comm Coll (MI)
Madison Area Tech Coll (WI)
Manatee Comm Coll (FL)
Massasoit Comm Coll (NE)
Metropolitan Comm Coll–Business & Technology Campus (MO)
Metropolitan Comm Coll–Longview (MO)
Metropolitan Comm Coll–Maple Woods (MO)
Miami Dade Coll (FL)
Middlesex Comm Coll (CT)
Minneapolis Comm and Tech Coll (MN)
Minnesota State Coll–Southeast Tech (MN)
Minnesota State Comm and Tech Coll–Fergus Falls (MN)
Mission Coll (CA)
Mohawk Valley Comm Coll (NY)
Montgomery County Comm Coll (PA)
Naugatuck Valley Comm Coll (CT)
Navarro Coll (TX)
New Mexico Jr Coll (NM)
New Mexico Military Inst (NM)
Northampton County Area Comm Coll (PA)
North Central Michigan Coll (MI)
North Central Texas Coll (TX)
Northeast Comm Coll (NE)
Northeastern Tech Coll (SC)
Northeast State Tech Comm Coll (TN)
Northern Essex Comm Coll (MA)
Northern Maine Comm Coll (ME)
North Idaho Coll (ID)
North Lake Coll (TX)
North Shore Comm Coll (MA)
NorthWest Arkansas Comm Coll (AR)

Northwestern Connecticut Comm Coll (CT)
Northwest Iowa Comm Coll (IA)
Northwest Mississippi Comm Coll (MS)
Northwest-Shoals Comm Coll (AL)
Oakland Comm Coll (MI)
Ohlone Coll (WA)
Olympic Coll (WA)
Orange Coast Coll (CA)
Pace Inst (PA)
Palm Beach Comm Coll (FL)
Parkland Coll (IL)
Pasadena City Coll (CA)
Pennsylvania Highland Comm Coll (PA)
Piedmont Tech Coll (SC)
Piedmont Virginia Comm Coll (VA)
Pierce Coll (WA)
Potomac State Coll of West Virginia U (WV)
Raritan Valley Comm Coll (NJ)
Redlands Comm Coll (OK)
Red Rocks Comm Coll (CO)
Richland Coll (TX)
Riverside Comm Coll District (CA)
St. Cloud Tech Coll (MN)
St. Louis Comm Coll at Florissant Valley (MO)
Saint Paul Coll—A Comm & Tech College (MN)
Sampson Comm Coll (NC)
San Antonio Coll (TX)
Sandhills Comm Coll (NC)
San Joaquin Delta Coll (CA)
Schoolcraft Coll (MI)
Seminole Comm Coll (FL)
Southeastern Comm Coll, North Campus (IA)
Southeast Tech Inst (SD)
South Florida Comm Coll (FL)
South Georgia Coll (GA)
South Plains Coll (TX)
South Seattle Comm Coll (WA)
Southwestern Michigan Coll (MI)
Spokane Comm Coll (WA)
Stark State Coll of Technology (OH)
State U of New York Coll of Agriculture and Technology at Morrisville (NY)
Suffolk County Comm Coll (NY)
Surry Comm Coll (NC)
Tallahassee Comm Coll (FL)
Temple Coll (TX)
Texarkana Coll (TX)
Texas State Tech Coll West Texas (TX)
Three Rivers Comm Coll (CT)
Tidewater Comm Coll (VA)
Tomball Coll (TX)
U of Cincinnati Clermont Coll (OH)
The U of Montana-Helena Coll of Technology (MT)
U of New Mexico—Los Alamos Branch (NM)
Valdosta Tech Coll (GA)
Valencia Comm Coll (FL)
Vatterott Coll, Kansas City (MO)
Vatterott Coll, Oklahoma City (OK)
Victoria Coll (TX)
Vincennes U Jasper Campus (IN)
Wallace State Comm Coll (AL)
Waukesha County Tech Coll (WI)
Western Nevada Comm Coll (NV)
Western Piedmont Comm Coll (NC)
West Los Angeles Coll (CA)
Wilson Tech Comm Coll (NC)

Computer Programming Related

Brunswick Comm Coll (NC)

Bucks County Comm Coll (PA)
Centralia Coll (WA)
Central Texas Coll (TX)
Clark State Comm Coll (OH)
Coastal Bend Coll (TX)
Coll of the Desert (CA)
Columbia Basin Coll (WA)
Cypress Coll (CA)
Fiorello H. LaGuardia Comm Coll of the City U of New York (NY)
Florida National Coll (FL)
Herzing Coll (WI)
Kennebec Valley Comm Coll (ME)
King's Coll (NC)
Lakeshore Tech Coll (WI)
Laredo Comm Coll (TX)
Lorain County Comm Coll (OH)
Los Angeles City Coll (CA)
Manatee Comm Coll (FL)
Mesabi Range Comm and Tech Coll (MN)
Metropolitan Comm Coll—Business & Technology Campus (MO)
Mid-State Tech Coll (WI)
Mississippi Gulf Coast Comm Coll (MS)
North Central Texas Coll (TX)
Northeast State Tech Comm Coll (TN)
Northern Essex Comm Coll (MA)
Northwest Iowa Comm Coll (IA)
Olympic Coll (WA)
Pasco-Hernando Comm Coll (FL)
Pennsylvania Highland Comm Coll (PA)
Provo Coll (UT)
Rio Salado Coll (AZ)
Riverside Comm Coll District (CA)
Saint Charles Comm Coll (MO)
St. Cloud Tech Coll (MN)
San Antonio Coll (TX)
Santa Ana Coll (CA)
Savannah River Coll (GA)
Seminole Comm Coll (FL)
Southeast Tech Inst (SD)
Southwest Mississippi Comm Coll (MS)
Stanly Comm Coll (NC)
Stark State Coll of Technology (OH)
Surry Comm Coll (NC)
Tompkins Cortland Comm Coll (NY)
Tri-State Business Inst (PA)
Tulsa Comm Coll (OK)
Tyler Jr Coll (TX)
Valencia Comm Coll (FL)
Vincennes U Jasper Campus (IN)

Computer Programming (Specific Applications)

AIB Coll of Business (IA)
Alexandria Tech Coll (MN)
Bladen Comm Coll (NC)
Brevard Comm Coll (FL)
Brown Mackie Coll—Akron (OH)
Brown Mackie Coll—Atlanta (GA)
Brown Mackie Coll—Cincinnati (OH)
Brown Mackie Coll—Hopkinsville (KY)
Brown Mackie Coll—Northern Kentucky (KY)
Bucks County Comm Coll (PA)
Caldwell Comm Coll and Tech Inst (NC)
Catawba Valley Comm Coll (NC)
Cedar Valley Coll (TX)
Central Carolina Comm Coll (NC)
Central Comm Coll—Columbus Campus (NE)
Central Comm Coll—Grand Island Campus (NE)
Central Comm Coll—Hastings Campus (NE)
Central Piedmont Comm Coll (NC)

Central Texas Coll (TX)
Cincinnati State Tech and Comm Coll (OH)
City Coll, Fort Lauderdale (FL)
City Coll, Gainesville (FL)
City Coll, Miami (FL)
Cleveland Comm Coll (NC)
Coastal Bend Coll (TX)
Coastal Carolina Comm Coll (NC)
Coll of DuPage (IL)
Coll of The Albemarle (NC)
Cypress Coll (CA)
Elgin Comm Coll (IL)
Essex County Coll (NJ)
Fiorello H. LaGuardia Comm Coll of the City U of New York (NY)
Florida National Coll (FL)
Gateway Tech Coll (WI)
Indiana Business Coll, Indianapolis (IN)
Indiana Business Coll, Muncie (IN)
Inver Hills Comm Coll (MN)
John Wood Comm Coll (IL)
Joliet Jr Coll (IL)
Kaplan Coll—Indianapolis (IN)
Kellogg Comm Coll (MI)
Lake Land Coll (IL)
Lincoln Land Comm Coll (IL)
Linn-Benton Comm Coll (OR)
Lorain County Comm Coll (OH)
Los Angeles City Coll (CA)
Macomb Comm Coll (MI)
Mesabi Range Comm and Tech Coll (MN)
Metropolitan Comm Coll—Business & Technology Campus (MO)
Mid-State Tech Coll (WI)
Miller-Motte Tech Coll, Clarksville (TN)
Missouri State U—West Plains (MO)
Mohave Comm Coll (AZ)
Moraine Valley Comm Coll (IL)
Naugatuck Valley Comm Coll (CT)
New Hampshire Tech Inst (NH)
North Central Texas Coll (TX)
Northeast Comm Coll (NE)
Northern Essex Comm Coll (MA)
North Shore Comm Coll (MA)
Northwest Mississippi Comm Coll (MS)
Onondaga Comm Coll (NY)
Orange Coast Coll (CA)
Palm Beach Comm Coll (FL)
Parkland Coll (IL)
Pasco-Hernando Comm Coll (FL)
Pennsylvania Highland Comm Coll (PA)
Piedmont Virginia Comm Coll (VA)
Potomac State Coll of West Virginia U (WV)
Richland Comm Coll (IL)
Ridgewater Coll (MN)
Riverland Comm Coll (MN)
Saint Charles Comm Coll (MO)
St. Cloud Tech Coll (MN)
San Antonio Coll (TX)
Sandhills Comm Coll (NC)
Seminole Comm Coll (FL)
Sheridan Coll—Sheridan and Gillette (WY)
Southeast Tech Inst (SD)
Southern State Comm Coll (OH)
South Piedmont Comm Coll (NC)
Stanly Comm Coll (NC)
Stark State Coll of Technology (OH)
State Fair Comm Coll (MO)
Tallahassee Comm Coll (FL)
Technology Education Coll (OH)
Trident Tech Coll (SC)

Tulsa Comm Coll (OK)
Valencia Comm Coll (FL)
Victor Valley Coll (CA)
West Central Tech Coll (GA)
Western Wyoming Comm Coll (WY)
Zane State Coll (OH)

Computer Programming (Vendor/Product Certification)

Central Texas Coll (TX)
Coastal Bend Coll (TX)
Fiorello H. LaGuardia Comm Coll of the City U of New York (NY)
Inver Hills Comm Coll (MN)
Lorain County Comm Coll (OH)
Los Angeles City Coll (CA)
Metropolitan Comm Coll—Business & Technology Campus (MO)
North Central Texas Coll (TX)
Parkland Coll (IL)
Peninsula Coll (WA)
Riverland Comm Coll (MN)
San Antonio Coll (TX)
Seminole Comm Coll (FL)
Southeast Tech Inst (SD)
Stark State Coll of Technology (OH)
Tulsa Comm Coll (OK)

Computer Science

Allen County Comm Coll (KS)
Amarillo Coll (TX)
Angelina Coll (TX)
Anne Arundel Comm Coll (MD)
Anoka-Ramsey Comm Coll (MN)
Anoka-Ramsey Comm Coll, Cambridge Campus (MN)
Arizona Western Coll (AZ)
Aviation & Electronic Schools of America (CA)
Bakersfield Coll (CA)
Baltimore City Comm Coll (MD)
Barstow Coll (CA)
Barton County Comm Coll (KS)
Bergen Comm Coll (NJ)
Blinn Coll (TX)
Bramson ORT Coll (NY)
Brigham Young U – Idaho (ID)
Broward Comm Coll (FL)
Bucks County Comm Coll (PA)
Burlington County Coll (NJ)
Cabrillo Coll (CA)
Cankdeska Cikana Comm Coll (ND)
Cañada Coll (CA)
Cape Cod Comm Coll (MA)
Catawba Valley Comm Coll (NC)
Central Arizona Coll (AZ)
Central Maine Comm Coll (ME)
Central Oregon Comm Coll (OR)
Central Piedmont Comm Coll (NC)
Central Wyoming Coll (WY)
Cerritos Coll (CA)
Chattanooga State Tech Comm Coll (TN)
Chesapeake Coll (MD)
Chipola Coll (FL)
Cisco Jr Coll (TX)
Citrus Coll (CA)
City Coll of San Francisco (CA)
Coahoma Comm Coll (MS)
Coastal Bend Coll (TX)
Coastal Georgia Coll (GA)
Cochise Coll, Douglas (AZ)
Cochise Coll, Sierra Vista (AZ)
Colby Comm Coll (KS)
CollAmerica—Colorado Springs (CO)
CollAmerica—Denver (CO)
Coll of Marin (CA)

Coll of Menominee Nation (WI)
Coll of San Mateo (CA)
Coll of Southern Idaho (ID)
Coll of the Canyons (CA)
Coll of the Desert (CA)
Coll of the Siskiyous (CA)
Columbia Basin Coll (WA)
Columbia Coll (CA)
Columbia-Greene Comm Coll (NY)
Commonwealth Tech Inst (PA)
Comm Coll of Philadelphia (PA)
Comm Coll of Southern Nevada (NV)
Comm Coll of Vermont (VT)
Contra Costa Coll (CA)
Crafton Hills Coll (CA)
Cuesta Coll (CA)
Cypress Coll (CA)
De Anza Coll (CA)
Dixie State Coll of Utah (UT)
Dodge City Comm Coll (KS)
ECPI Coll of Technology (VA)
ECPI Tech Coll (VA)
ECPI Tech Coll (VA)
Elaine P. Nunez Comm Coll (LA)
El Centro Coll (TX)
Essex County Coll (NJ)
Everett Comm Coll (WA)
Finger Lakes Comm Coll (NY)
Fiorello H. LaGuardia Comm Coll of the City U of New York (NY)
Florida National Coll (FL)
Forsyth Tech Comm Coll (NC)
Frederick Comm Coll (MD)
Fullerton Coll (CA)
Fulton-Montgomery Comm Coll (NY)
George C. Wallace Comm Coll (AL)
Gloucester County Coll (NJ)
Gordon Coll (GA)
Grand Rapids Comm Coll (MI)
Grayson County Coll (TX)
Grossmont Coll (CA)
Gulf Coast Coll (FL)
Gwinnett Tech Coll (GA)
Harper Coll (IL)
Hartnell Coll (CA)
Henry Ford Comm Coll (MI)
Hesser Coll (NH)
Hocking Coll (OH)
Houston Comm Coll System (TX)
Howard Comm Coll (MD)
International Jr Coll (PR)
Iowa Lakes Comm Coll (IA)
Isothermal Comm Coll (NC)
Jackson State Comm Coll (TN)
Jamestown Comm Coll (NY)
Kilian Comm Coll (SD)
Kingsborough Comm Coll of the City U of New York (NY)
Kirkwood Comm Coll (IA)
Labette Comm Coll (KS)
Lake-Sumter Comm Coll (FL)
Lake Tahoe Comm Coll (CA)
Lamar Comm Coll (CO)
Lanier Tech Coll (GA)
Laramie County Comm Coll (WY)
Las Positas Coll (CA)
Lassen Comm Coll District (CA)
Leeward Comm Coll (HI)
Lewis Coll of Business (MI)
Little Big Horn Coll (MT)
Lorain County Comm Coll (OH)
Los Angeles Pierce Coll (CA)
Los Angeles Southwest Coll (CA)
Louisburg Coll (NC)
Lower Columbia Coll (WA)

Massachusetts Bay Comm Coll (MA)
Merced Coll (CA)
Metropolitan Comm Coll—Blue River (MO)
Metropolitan Comm Coll—Business & Technology Campus (MO)
Metropolitan Comm Coll—Longview (MO)
Metropolitan Comm Coll—Maple Woods (MO)
Metropolitan Comm Coll—Penn Valley (MO)
Miami Dade Coll (FL)
Miami U—Middletown Campus (OH)
Middle Georgia Coll (GA)
Mississippi Gulf Coast Comm Coll (MS)
Mohave Comm Coll (AZ)
Monroe Comm Coll (NY)
Monterey Peninsula Coll (CA)
Moorpark Coll (CA)
Mt. San Antonio Coll (CA)
Murray State Coll (OK)
Napa Valley Coll (CA)
Nassau Comm Coll (NY)
Navarro Coll (TX)
Neosho County Comm Coll (KS)
New Hampshire Comm Tech Coll, Nashua/Claremont (NH)
New Mexico Jr Coll (NM)
New Mexico Military Inst (NM)
New York City Coll of Technology of the City U of New York (NY)
Niagara County Comm Coll (NY)
Nicolet Area Tech Coll (WI)
Northampton County Area Comm Coll (PA)
North Central Texas Coll (TX)
Northeast Comm Coll (NE)
Northeastern Jr Coll (CO)
Northeastern Tech Coll (SC)
Northern Essex Comm Coll (MA)
Northern Oklahoma Coll (OK)
North Hennepin Comm Coll (MN)
North Idaho Coll (ID)
Northland Comm and Tech Coll—Thief River Falls (MN)
North Shore Comm Coll (MA)
Northwestern Connecticut Comm Coll (CT)
Northwest-Shoals Comm Coll (AL)
Northwest Vista Coll (TX)
Odessa Coll (TX)
Ohlone Coll (CA)
Oklahoma City Comm Coll (OK)
Onondaga Comm Coll (NY)
Palm Beach Comm Coll (FL)
Palo Alto Coll (TX)
Parkland Coll (IL)
Pasadena City Coll (CA)
Piedmont Virginia Comm Coll (VA)
Porterville Coll (CA)
Potomac State Coll of West Virginia U (WV)
Raritan Valley Comm Coll (NJ)
Redlands Comm Coll (OK)
Red Rocks Comm Coll (CO)
Renton Tech Coll (WA)
Rio Salado Coll (AZ)
Roane State Comm Coll (TN)
Rogue Comm Coll (OR)
Sacramento City Coll (CA)
Saint Charles Comm Coll (MO)
St. Louis Comm Coll at Florissant Valley (MO)
Salish Kootenai Coll (MT)
Salt Lake Comm Coll (UT)
San Bernardino Valley Coll (CA)
San Joaquin Delta Coll (CA)

San Juan Coll (NM)
Santa Ana Coll (CA)
Santa Barbara City Coll (CA)
Santa Rosa Jr Coll (CA)
Santiago Canyon Coll (CA)
Seminole State Coll (OK)
Skagit Valley Coll (WA)
Southern U at Shreveport (LA)
South Georgia Coll (GA)
South Plains Coll (TX)
South Texas Coll (TX)
Southwestern Indian Polytechnic Inst (NM)
Southwest Mississippi Comm Coll (MS)
Springfield Tech Comm Coll (MA)
State U of New York Coll of Agriculture and Technology at Morrisville (NY)
State U of New York Coll of Technology at Alfred (NY)
Stone Child Coll (MT)
Suffolk County Comm Coll (NY)
Taft Coll (CA)
Temple Coll (TX)
Texarkana Coll (TX)
Texas State Tech Coll–Marshall (TX)
Tompkins Cortland Comm Coll (NY)
Treasure Valley Comm Coll (OR)
Trinidad State Jr Coll (CO)
Tri-State Business Inst (PA)
Tulsa Comm Coll (OK)
Turtle Mountain Comm Coll (ND)
Tyler Jr Coll (TX)
Ulster County Comm Coll (NY)
Umpqua Comm Coll (OR)
The U of Akron–Wayne Coll (OH)
U of New Mexico–Los Alamos Branch (NM)
U of New Mexico–Valencia Campus (NM)
Victor Valley Coll (CA)
Virginia Western Comm Coll (VA)
Wallace State Comm Coll (AL)
Westchester Comm Coll (NY)
Western Texas Coll (TX)
Western Wyoming Comm Coll (WY)
Westmoreland County Comm Coll (PA)
West Virginia State Comm and Tech Coll (WV)
Young Harris Coll (GA)
Yuba Coll (CA)

Computer Software and Media Applications Related
AIB Coll of Business (IA)
Berkeley City Coll (CA)
Brevard Comm Coll (FL)
Brown Mackie Coll–Cincinnati (OH)
Brown Mackie Coll–Kansas City (KS)
Brown Mackie Coll–Louisville (KY)
Brown Mackie Coll–North Canton (OH)
Brown Mackie Coll–Salina (KS)
Columbia Basin Coll (WA)
Cypress Coll (CA)
Genesee Comm Coll (NY)
Kaplan Coll–Indianapolis (IN)
Kellogg Comm Coll (MI)
Kennebec Valley Comm Coll (ME)
Kilian Comm Coll (SD)
Laredo Comm Coll (TX)
Laurel Business Inst (PA)
Los Angeles City Coll (CA)
Mesabi Range Comm and Tech Coll (MN)
Metropolitan Comm Coll–Business & Technology Campus (MO)
Northland Comm and Tech Coll–Thief River Falls (MN)
Olympic Coll (WA)

Parkland Coll (IL)
Platt Coll San Diego (CA)
Riverland Comm Coll (MN)
Seminole Comm Coll (FL)
Sheridan Coll–Sheridan and Gillette (WY)
Southeast Tech Inst (SD)
Stark State Coll of Technology (OH)
Tulsa Comm Coll (OK)

Computer Software Engineering
ITT Tech Inst (CO)
ITT Tech Inst, Newburgh (IN)
ITT Tech Inst, Norwood (MA)
ITT Tech Inst, Cordova (TN)
ITT Tech Inst, Knoxville (TN)
ITT Tech Inst, Spokane (WA)
Seminole Comm Coll (FL)
Southeast Tech Inst (SD)
Stark State Coll of Technology (OH)
Tompkins Cortland Comm Coll (NY)
Tulsa Comm Coll (OK)

Computer Software Technology
Brown Mackie Coll–Atlanta (GA)
Brown Mackie Coll–Findlay (OH)
Brown Mackie Coll–Fort Wayne (IN)
Brown Mackie Coll–Merrillville (IN)
Brown Mackie Coll–Miami (FL)
Brown Mackie Coll–Northern Kentucky (KY)
Brown Mackie Coll–South Bend (IN)
Iowa Lakes Comm Coll (IA)
ITT Tech Inst (AL)
ITT Tech Inst, Lathrop (CA)
ITT Tech Inst, Oxnard (CA)
ITT Tech Inst, Fort Lauderdale (FL)
ITT Tech Inst, Jacksonville (FL)
ITT Tech Inst, Burr Ridge (IL)
ITT Tech Inst, Louisville (KY)
ITT Tech Inst (LA)
ITT Tech Inst, Canton (MI)
ITT Tech Inst, Flint (MI)
ITT Tech Inst (NV)
ITT Tech Inst, Albany (NY)
ITT Tech Inst, Getzville (NY)
ITT Tech Inst, Liverpool (NY)
ITT Tech Inst, Strongsville (OH)
ITT Tech Inst (SC)
ITT Tech Inst, Nashville (TN)
ITT Tech Inst, Richardson (TX)
ITT Tech Inst, Webster (TX)
ITT Tech Inst, Chantilly (VA)
ITT Tech Inst, Norfolk (VA)
ITT Tech Inst, Richmond (VA)
ITT Tech Inst, Bothell (WA)
ITT Tech Inst, Greenfield (WI)
Miami Dade Coll (FL)

Computer Systems Analysis
Amarillo Coll (TX)
Brevard Comm Coll (FL)
Cape Fear Comm Coll (NC)
Central New Mexico Comm Coll (NM)
Coastal Carolina Comm Coll (NC)
Gulf Coast Coll (FL)
Hesser Coll (NH)
James Sprunt Comm Coll (NC)
Lakeshore Tech Coll (WI)
Laramie County Comm Coll (WY)
Lee Coll (TX)
Linn State Tech Coll (MO)
Lower Columbia Coll (WA)

Metropolitan Comm Coll–Business & Technology Campus (MO)
Pima Comm Coll (AZ)
South Piedmont Comm Coll (NC)
U of Alaska Southeast, Sitka Campus (AK)
Waukesha County Tech Coll (WI)
Wayne Comm Coll (NC)
Wor-Wic Comm Coll (MD)

Computer Systems Networking and Telecommunications
Academy Coll (MN)
AIB Coll of Business (IA)
Alexandria Tech Coll (MN)
Allen County Comm Coll (KS)
Alpena Comm Coll (MI)
Altamaha Tech Coll (GA)
Anoka-Ramsey Comm Coll (MN)
Anoka-Ramsey Comm Coll, Cambridge Campus (MN)
Appalachian Tech Coll (GA)
Asheville-Buncombe Tech Comm Coll (NC)
Athens Tech Coll (GA)
Augusta Tech Coll (GA)
Barton County Comm Coll (KS)
Baton Rouge School of Computers (LA)
Beaufort County Comm Coll (NC)
Bismarck State Coll (ND)
Black Hawk Coll, Moline (IL)
Blinn Coll (TX)
Bowling Green State U–Firelands Coll (OH)
Brevard Comm Coll (FL)
Brown Mackie Coll–Akron (OH)
Brown Mackie Coll–Cincinnati (OH)
Brown Mackie Coll–Kansas City (KS)
Brown Mackie Coll–Louisville (KY)
Brown Mackie Coll–North Canton (OH)
Brown Mackie Coll–Northern Kentucky (KY)
Brown Mackie Coll–Salina (KS)
Brown Mackie Coll–South Bend (IN)
Cape Cod Comm Coll (MA)
Cape Fear Comm Coll (NC)
Catawba Valley Comm Coll (NC)
Central Carolina Comm Coll (NC)
Central Georgia Tech Coll (GA)
Centralia Coll (WA)
Central Wyoming Coll (WY)
Chattahoochee Tech Coll (GA)
Clark Coll (WA)
Clark State Comm Coll (OH)
Clatsop Comm Coll (OR)
Coastal Bend Coll (TX)
Coastal Carolina Comm Coll (NC)
Cochise Coll, Douglas (AZ)
CollAmerica–Colorado Springs (CO)
CollAmerica–Denver (CO)
Coll of the Mainland (TX)
Collin County Comm Coll District (TX)
Colorado Mountain Coll (CO)
Columbia Basin Coll (WA)
Columbia-Greene Comm Coll (NY)
Columbus Tech Coll (GA)
Comm Coll of Allegheny County (PA)
Crowder Coll (MO)
Cuesta Coll (CA)
Cypress Coll (CA)
DeKalb Tech Coll (GA)
East Central Coll (MO)
East Central Tech Coll (GA)

Fiorello H. LaGuardia Comm Coll of the City U of New York (NY)
Flint Hills Tech Coll (KS)
Flint River Tech Coll (GA)
Florida National Coll (FL)
Gateway Tech Coll (WI)
Griffin Tech Coll (GA)
Guilford Tech Comm Coll (NC)
Gwinnett Tech Coll (GA)
Harrisburg Area Comm Coll (PA)
Hawkeye Comm Coll (IA)
Hennepin Tech Coll (MN)
Herzing Coll (MN)
Herzing Coll (WI)
Hillsborough Comm Coll (FL)
Howard Comm Coll (MD)
Illinois Valley Comm Coll (IL)
Iowa Lakes Comm Coll (IA)
Island Drafting and Tech Inst (NY)
ITT Tech Inst (AL)
ITT Tech Inst, Anaheim (CA)
ITT Tech Inst, Oxnard (CA)
ITT Tech Inst, Rancho Cordova (CA)
ITT Tech Inst, San Bernardino (CA)
ITT Tech Inst, San Diego (CA)
ITT Tech Inst, Sylmar (CA)
ITT Tech Inst, Torrance (CA)
ITT Tech Inst (CO)
ITT Tech Inst, Fort Lauderdale (FL)
ITT Tech Inst, Lake Mary (FL)
ITT Tech Inst, Tampa (FL)
ITT Tech Inst, Duluth (GA)
ITT Tech Inst, Kennesaw (GA)
ITT Tech Inst (ID)
ITT Tech Inst, Orland Park (IL)
ITT Tech Inst, Fort Wayne (IN)
ITT Tech Inst, Indianapolis (IN)
ITT Tech Inst, Newburgh (IN)
ITT Tech Inst (LA)
ITT Tech Inst (MD)
ITT Tech Inst, Norwood (MA)
ITT Tech Inst, Canton (MI)
ITT Tech Inst, Flint (MI)
ITT Tech Inst, Grand Rapids (MI)
ITT Tech Inst (MN)
ITT Tech Inst, Earth City (MO)
ITT Tech Inst, Kansas City (MO)
ITT Tech Inst (NV)
ITT Tech Inst (NM)
ITT Tech Inst, Albany (NY)
ITT Tech Inst, Getzville (NY)
ITT Tech Inst, Liverpool (NY)
ITT Tech Inst, Dayton (OH)
ITT Tech Inst, Hilliard (OH)
ITT Tech Inst, Norwood (OH)
ITT Tech Inst, Strongsville (OH)
ITT Tech Inst, Warrensville Heights (OH)
ITT Tech Inst, Youngstown (OH)
ITT Tech Inst, Tulsa (OK)
ITT Tech Inst (OR)
ITT Tech Inst (SC)
ITT Tech Inst, Cordova (TN)
ITT Tech Inst, Arlington (TX)
ITT Tech Inst, Austin (TX)
ITT Tech Inst, Houston (TX)
ITT Tech Inst, Richardson (TX)
ITT Tech Inst, San Antonio (TX)
ITT Tech Inst, Webster (TX)
ITT Tech Inst (UT)
ITT Tech Inst, Chantilly (VA)
ITT Tech Inst, Richmond (VA)

ITT Tech Inst, Springfield (VA)
ITT Tech Inst, Seattle (WA)
ITT Tech Inst, Spokane (WA)
ITT Tech Inst, Green Bay (WI)
ITT Tech Inst, Greenfield (WI)
Joliet Jr Coll (IL)
Keiser Career Coll - Greenacres (FL)
Kennebec Valley Comm Coll (ME)
Lake Land Coll (IL)
Lanier Tech Coll (GA)
Laredo Comm Coll (TX)
Laurel Business Inst (PA)
Lincoln Land Comm Coll (IL)
Lorain County Comm Coll (OH)
Los Angeles City Coll (CA)
Lower Columbia Coll (WA)
Mesabi Range Comm and Tech Coll (MN)
Metropolitan Comm Coll–Business & Technology Campus (MO)
Middle Georgia Tech Coll (GA)
Midlands Tech Coll (SC)
Minnesota School of Business–Brooklyn Center (MN)
Minnesota School of Business–Plymouth (MN)
Minnesota School of Business–Richfield (MN)
Minnesota School of Business–St. Cloud (MN)
Minnesota School of Business–Shakopee (MN)
Minnesota State Comm and Tech Coll–Fergus Falls (MN)
Minot State U–Bottineau Campus (ND)
Mississippi Gulf Coast Comm Coll (MS)
Montgomery County Comm Coll (PA)
Moraine Valley Comm Coll (IL)
Mott Comm Coll (MI)
Moultrie Tech Coll (GA)
Nassau Comm Coll (NY)
New Hampshire Tech Inst (NH)
Northampton County Area Comm Coll (PA)
North Central Michigan Coll (MI)
Northeast State Tech Comm Coll (TN)
Northern Essex Comm Coll (MA)
North Georgia Tech Coll (GA)
Northland Comm and Tech Coll–Thief River Falls (MN)
North Metro Tech Coll (GA)
North Seattle Comm Coll (WA)
Northwestern Tech Coll (GA)
Northwest Iowa Comm Coll (IA)
Odessa Coll (TX)
Ogeechee Tech Coll (GA)
Okefenokee Tech Coll (GA)
Olympic Coll (WA)
Onondaga Comm Coll (NY)
Ozarks Tech Comm Coll (MO)
Pace Inst (PA)
Parkland Coll (IL)
Pasco-Hernando Comm Coll (FL)
Piedmont Virginia Comm Coll (VA)
Pima Comm Coll (AZ)
Potomac State Coll of West Virginia U (WV)
Quinebaug Valley Comm Coll (CT)
Rasmussen Coll Brooklyn Park (MN)
Remington Coll–Baton Rouge Campus (LA)
Remington Coll–Dallas Campus (TX)

Remington Coll–Fort Worth Campus (TX)
Remington Coll–Little Rock Campus (AR)
Remington Coll–Nashville Campus (TN)
Ridgewater Coll (MN)
Riverland Comm Coll (MN)
Robeson Comm Coll (NC)
Saint Charles Comm Coll (MO)
St. Cloud Tech Coll (MN)
St. Philip's Coll (TX)
Sandersville Tech Coll (GA)
Savannah Tech Coll (GA)
Seminole Comm Coll (FL)
Sheridan Coll–Sheridan and Gillette (WY)
Southeastern Tech Coll (GA)
Southeast Tech Inst (SD)
South Georgia Tech Coll (GA)
South Piedmont Comm Coll (NC)
Southwest Georgia Tech Coll (NC)
Stanly Comm Coll (NC)
Stark State Coll of Technology (OH)
State Fair Comm Coll (MO)
Surry Comm Coll (NC)
Swainsboro Tech Coll (GA)
Tallahassee Comm Coll (FL)
TESST Coll of Technology, Baltimore (MD)
TESST Coll of Technology, Beltsville (MD)
Texas State Tech Coll West Texas (TX)
Tidewater Tech (VA)
Trident Tech Coll (SC)
Trinidad State Jr Coll (CO)
Tulsa Comm Coll (OK)
Tyler Jr Coll (TX)
The U of Akron–Wayne Coll (OH)
U of Arkansas Comm Coll at Batesville (AR)
U of Arkansas Comm Coll at Morrilton (AR)
Valdosta Tech Coll (GA)
Victoria Coll (TX)
Vincennes U Jasper Campus (IN)
Waukesha County Tech Coll (WI)
West Central Tech Coll (GA)
Westchester Comm Coll (NY)
West Georgia Tech Coll (GA)
York County Comm Coll (ME)

Computer/Technical Support
Anne Arundel Comm Coll (MD)
Anoka-Ramsey Comm Coll (MN)
Baltimore City Comm Coll (MD)
Black Hawk Coll, Moline (IL)
Bowling Green State U–Firelands Coll (OH)
Clark State Comm Coll (OH)
Coll of the Desert (CA)
Coll of the Siskiyous (CA)
Colorado Mountain Coll (CO)
Cuesta Coll (CA)
Eastern Shore Comm Coll (VA)
Elaine P. Nunez Comm Coll (LA)
Florida National Coll (FL)
Hawkeye Comm Coll (IA)
Inver Hills Comm Coll (MN)
Island Drafting and Tech Inst (NY)
Joliet Jr Coll (IL)
Laurel Business Inst (PA)
Linn-Benton Comm Coll (OR)
Los Angeles City Coll (CA)
Massasoit Comm Coll (MA)
Monroe Comm Coll (NY)
North Central Texas Coll (TX)
North Idaho Coll (ID)

Northland Comm and Tech
  Coll–Thief River
  Falls (MN)
Northwest Vista Coll (TX)
Oklahoma State U,
  Oklahoma City (OK)
Onondaga Comm
  Coll (NY)
Palm Beach Comm
  Coll (FL)
Parkland Coll (IL)
Pennsylvania Highland
  Comm Coll (PA)
Piedmont Virginia Comm
  Coll (VA)
Quincy Coll (MA)
Rio Salado Coll (AZ)
Riverland Comm Coll (MN)
St. Cloud Tech Coll (MN)
Seminole Comm Coll (FL)
Southeast Tech Inst (SD)
Stanly Comm Coll (NC)
Stark State Coll of
  Technology (OH)
Suffolk County Comm
  Coll (NY)
Three Rivers Comm
  Coll (MO)
Tompkins Cortland Comm
  Coll (NY)
Tulsa Comm Coll (OK)

**Computer
Technology/Computer
Systems Technology**
Alexandria Tech Coll (MN)
Arkansas State
  U–Newport (AR)
Cape Fear Comm
  Coll (NC)
Central Wyoming
  Coll (WY)
Clackamas Comm
  Coll (OR)
Comm Coll of Allegheny
  County (PA)
ECPI Tech Coll (VA)
ECPI Tech Coll (VA)
Erie Comm Coll, South
  Campus (NY)
Forrest Jr Coll (SC)
ICPR Jr Coll–Hato Rey
  Campus (PR)
Island Drafting and Tech
  Inst (NY)
Katharine Gibbs
  School (PA)
Lamar Inst of
  Technology (TX)
Lehigh Carbon Comm
  Coll (PA)
Lorain County Comm
  Coll (OH)
Lower Columbia Coll (WA)
Madisonville Comm
  Coll (KY)
Miami Dade Coll (FL)
Miami U Hamilton (OH)
Minot State U–Bottineau
  Campus (ND)
Montgomery Coll (MD)
Mount Wachusett Comm
  Coll (MA)
New England Inst of
  Technology (RI)
Oakland Comm Coll (MI)
Okefenokee Tech
  Coll (GA)
Pasco-Hernando Comm
  Coll (FL)
Pima Comm Coll (AZ)
Schoolcraft Coll (MI)
Skagit Valley Coll (WA)
Southeastern Business
  Coll, Jackson (OH)
Southeast Tech Inst (SD)
Stanly Comm Coll (NC)
Vatterott Coll (TN)

**Computer Typography
and Composition
Equipment Operation**
Bergen Comm Coll (NJ)
Chaffey Coll (CA)
Clovis Comm Coll (NM)
Coll of DuPage (IL)
Coll of the Desert (CA)
Coll of the Redwoods (CA)
Comm Coll of Beaver
  County (PA)
Comm Coll of Southern
  Nevada (NV)
Cuyahoga Comm
  Coll (OH)
ECPI Coll of
  Technology (VA)
ECPI Tech Coll (VA)
ECPI Tech Coll (VA)
Elgin Comm Coll (IL)

Fox Valley Tech Coll (WI)
Fresno City Coll (CA)
Fulton-Montgomery Comm
  Coll (NY)
Gateway Comm Coll (CT)
Harper Coll (IL)
Holyoke Comm Coll (MA)
Housatonic Comm
  Coll (CT)
Lamar Comm Coll (CO)
Laney Coll (CA)
Lansing Comm Coll (MI)
Madison Area Tech
  Coll (WI)
Metropolitan Comm
  Coll–Longview (MO)
Minnesota State Coll–
  Southeast Tech (MN)
Monterey Peninsula
  Coll (CA)
New Mexico Jr Coll (NM)
New River Comm Coll (VA)
Northern Essex Comm
  Coll (MA)
Northwest-Shoals Comm
  Coll (AL)
Ohlone Coll (CA)
Onondaga Comm
  Coll (NY)
Orange Coast Coll (CA)
Paradise Valley Comm
  Coll (AZ)
Pasadena City Coll (CA)
Pierce Coll (WA)
South Texas Coll (TX)
Spokane Comm Coll (WA)
State U of New York Coll
  of Agriculture and
  Technology at
  Morrisville (NY)
State U of New York Coll
  of Technology at
  Alfred (NY)
Three Rivers Comm
  Coll (CT)
U of Arkansas Comm Coll
  at Morrilton (AR)
U of New Mexico–Valencia
  Campus (NM)
Wright State U, Lake
  Campus (OH)

**Construction
Engineering**
State U of New York Coll
  of Technology at
  Alfred (NY)

**Construction
Engineering
Technology**
Antelope Valley Coll (CA)
Bismarck State Coll (ND)
Brigham Young U –
  Idaho (ID)
Cecil Comm Coll (MD)
Central Comm Coll–
  Hastings Campus (NE)
Central Maine Comm
  Coll (ME)
Chippewa Valley Tech
  Coll (WI)
Cisco Jr Coll (TX)
Clark Coll (WA)
Coll of Lake County (IL)
Coll of San Mateo (CA)
Coll of the Redwoods (CA)
Comm Coll of Allegheny
  County (PA)
Comm Coll of
  Philadelphia (PA)
Comm Coll of Southern
  Nevada (NV)
Cosumnes River Coll,
  Sacramento (CA)
Crowder Coll (MO)
Cuesta Coll (CA)
De Anza Coll (CA)
Dodge City Comm
  Coll (KS)
Don Bosco Tech Inst (CA)
East Central Coll (MO)
El Camino Coll (CA)
Forsyth Tech Comm
  Coll (NC)
Fort Berthold Comm
  Coll (ND)
Fresno City Coll (CA)
Fullerton Coll (CA)
Fulton-Montgomery Comm
  Coll (NY)
Greenville Tech Coll (SC)
Harrisburg Area Comm
  Coll (PA)
Hartnell Coll (CA)
H. Councill Trenholm State
  Tech Coll (AL)
Henry Ford Comm
  Coll (MI)

Hillsborough Comm
  Coll (FL)
Houston Comm Coll
  System (TX)
Inst of Design and
  Construction (NY)
Inver Hills Comm
  Coll (MN)
Iowa Lakes Comm
  Coll (IA)
Joliet Jr Coll (IL)
Kirkwood Comm Coll (IA)
Lansing Comm Coll (MI)
Laramie County Comm
  Coll (WY)
Laredo Comm Coll (TX)
Lassen Comm Coll
  District (CA)
Lehigh Carbon Comm
  Coll (PA)
Los Angeles Pierce
  Coll (CA)
Macomb Comm Coll (MI)
Manatee Comm Coll (FL)
Maui Comm Coll (HI)
Merced Coll (CA)
Metropolitan Comm
  Coll (NE)
Miami Dade Coll (FL)
Midlands Tech Coll (SC)
Mid-Plains Comm Coll,
  North Platte (NE)
Monroe Comm Coll (NY)
Neosho County Comm
  Coll (KS)
New England Inst of
  Technology (RI)
New Hampshire Comm
  Tech Coll, Manchester/
  Stratham (NH)
New Mexico Jr Coll (NM)
New York City Coll of
  Technology of the City
  U of New York (NY)
North Central Missouri
  Coll (MO)
Northeast Iowa Comm
  Coll (IA)
Northern Oklahoma
  Coll (OK)
North Lake Coll (TX)
Odessa Coll (TX)
The Ohio State U Ag Tech
  Inst (OH)
Oklahoma State U,
  Oklahoma City (OK)
Oklahoma State U,
  Okmulgee (OK)
Onondaga Comm
  Coll (NY)
Orange Coast Coll (CA)
Ozarks Tech Comm
  Coll (MO)
Palau Comm Coll (Palau)
Pasadena City Coll (CA)
Pennsylvania Highland
  Comm Coll (PA)
Piedmont Tech Coll (SC)
Pima Comm Coll (AZ)
Raritan Valley Comm
  Coll (NJ)
Redlands Comm Coll (OK)
Richland Comm Coll (IL)
Riverside Comm Coll
  District (CA)
St. Cloud Tech Coll (MN)
St. Louis Comm Coll at
  Florissant Valley (MO)
St. Philip's Coll (TX)
San Joaquin Delta
  Coll (CA)
Seminole Comm Coll (FL)
Shasta Coll (CA)
Southeastern Comm Coll,
  North Campus (IA)
Southern Maine Comm
  Coll (ME)
South Florida Comm
  Coll (FL)
Southwest Mississippi
  Comm Coll (MS)
Spokane Comm Coll (WA)
State Fair Comm
  Coll (MO)
State U of New York Coll
  of Agriculture and
  Technology at
  Morrisville (NY)
State U of New York Coll
  of Technology at
  Alfred (NY)
State U of New York Coll
  of Technology at
  Canton (NY)
Suffolk County Comm
  Coll (NY)
Surry Comm Coll (NC)

Tallahassee Comm
  Coll (FL)
Three Rivers Comm
  Coll (MO)
Tompkins Cortland Comm
  Coll (NY)
Trinidad State Jr Coll (CO)
Tulsa Comm Coll (OK)
U of New
  Mexico–Gallup (NM)
U of New Mexico–Valencia
  Campus (NM)
Valencia Comm Coll (FL)
Ventura Coll (CA)
Victor Valley Coll (CA)
Wallace State Comm
  Coll (AL)
Washington County Comm
  Coll (ME)
The Williamson Free
  School of Mecha
  Trades (PA)

**Construction/Heavy
Equipment/Earthmoving
Equipment Operation**
Northwest Iowa Comm
  Coll (IA)

**Construction
Management**
Broward Comm Coll (FL)
Cabrillo Coll (CA)
City Coll of San
  Francisco (CA)
Coll of the Desert (CA)
Comm Coll of Southern
  Nevada (NV)
Cosumnes River Coll,
  Sacramento (CA)
Erie Comm Coll, North
  Campus (NY)
Frederick Comm Coll (MD)
Fresno City Coll (CA)
Gwinnett Tech Coll (GA)
Inver Hills Comm
  Coll (MN)
Iowa Lakes Comm
  Coll (IA)
Laney Coll (CA)
Montgomery Coll (MD)
Mt. San Antonio Coll (CA)
North Hennepin Comm
  Coll (MN)
Oakland Comm Coll (MI)
The Ohio State U Ag Tech
  Inst (OH)
Palm Beach Comm
  Coll (FL)
Parkland Coll (IL)
Piedmont Tech Coll (SC)
Rogue Comm Coll (OR)
St. Philip's Coll (TX)
Salt Lake Comm Coll (UT)
Santa Rosa Jr Coll (CA)
Seminole Comm Coll (FL)
U of New Mexico–Valencia
  Campus (NM)
Victor Valley Coll (CA)
Western Nevada Comm
  Coll (NV)

Construction Trades
Coll of The Albemarle (NC)
East Central Coll (MO)
Front Range Comm
  Coll (CO)
Iowa Lakes Comm
  Coll (IA)
Laramie County Comm
  Coll (WY)
Lassen Comm Coll
  District (CA)
Ogeechee Tech Coll (GA)
U of New
  Mexico–Taos (NM)

**Construction Trades
Related**
Central New Mexico
  Comm Coll (NM)
Comm Coll of Allegheny
  County (PA)
East Central Coll (MO)
Erie Comm Coll, North
  Campus (NY)
Laramie County Comm
  Coll (WY)

Consumer Education
Antelope Valley Coll (CA)

**Consumer
Merchandising/
Retailing Management**
Anne Arundel Comm
  Coll (MD)
Bergen Comm Coll (NJ)
Bucks County Comm
  Coll (PA)

Cabrillo Coll (CA)
Centralia Coll (WA)
Central Piedmont Comm
  Coll (NC)
Central Virginia Comm
  Coll (VA)
Chattanooga State Tech
  Comm Coll (TN)
Cisco Jr Coll (TX)
Coll of Marin (CA)
Coll of San Mateo (CA)
Colorado Mountain Coll,
  Alpine Campus (CO)
Comm Coll of
  Philadelphia (PA)
Comm Coll of Southern
  Nevada (NV)
Elgin Comm Coll (IL)
Everett Comm Coll (WA)
FIDM/The Fashion Inst of
  Design &
  Merchandising, Los
  Angeles Campus (CA)
FIDM/The Fashion Inst of
  Design &
  Merchandising, San
  Diego Campus (CA)
FIDM/The Fashion Inst of
  Design &
  Merchandising, San
  Francisco
  Campus (CA)
Finger Lakes Comm
  Coll (NY)
Fox Valley Tech Coll (WI)
Gateway Comm Coll (CT)
Genesee Comm Coll (NY)
Gloucester County
  Coll (NJ)
Golden West Coll (CA)
Grossmont Coll (CA)
Harrisburg Area Comm
  Coll (PA)
Hocking Coll (OH)
Holyoke Comm Coll (MA)
Howard Comm Coll (MD)
International Business Coll,
  Fort Wayne (IN)
Iowa Lakes Comm
  Coll (IA)
Jefferson Comm Coll (OH)
Kirkwood Comm Coll (IA)
Lansing Comm Coll (MI)
Laurel Business Inst (PA)
Leeward Comm Coll (HI)
Lenoir Comm Coll (NC)
Lorain County Comm
  Coll (OH)
Los Angeles City Coll (CA)
Madisonville Comm
  Coll (KY)
Merced Coll (CA)
Minnesota State Coll–
  Southeast Tech (MN)
Monroe Comm Coll (NY)
Navarro Coll (TX)
Niagara County Comm
  Coll (NY)
North Country Comm
  Coll (NY)
Northland Comm and Tech
  Coll–Thief River
  Falls (MN)
Oakland Comm Coll (MI)
Parkland Coll (IL)
Passaic County Comm
  Coll (NJ)
Pennsylvania Highland
  Comm Coll (PA)
Raritan Valley Comm
  Coll (NJ)
Ridgewater Coll (MN)
St. Cloud Tech Coll (MN)
South Plains Coll (TX)
Spokane Falls Comm
  Coll (WA)
Stark State Coll of
  Technology (OH)
Suffolk County Comm
  Coll (NY)
Sussex County Comm
  Coll (NJ)
Texarkana Coll (TX)
Three Rivers Comm
  Coll (CT)
Ulster County Comm
  Coll (NY)
Westchester Comm
  Coll (NY)
West Los Angeles
  Coll (CA)
Westmoreland County
  Comm Coll (PA)
Wright State U, Lake
  Campus (OH)

**Consumer Services
and Advocacy**
City Coll of San
  Francisco (CA)
Los Angeles Mission
  Coll (CA)
Ohlone Coll (CA)
Rio Salado Coll (AZ)
San Diego City Coll (CA)

**Cooking and Related
Culinary Arts**
Iowa Lakes Comm
  Coll (IA)
Le Cordon Bleu Coll of
  Culinary Arts,
  Atlanta (GA)
Le Cordon Bleu Coll of
  Culinary Arts, Las
  Vegas (NV)
Orlando Culinary
  Academy (FL)

Corrections
Alpena Comm Coll (MI)
Amarillo Coll (TX)
Anne Arundel Comm
  Coll (MD)
Antelope Valley Coll (CA)
Bakersfield Coll (CA)
Baltimore City Comm
  Coll (MD)
Brevard Comm Coll (FL)
Broome Comm Coll (NY)
Broward Comm Coll (FL)
Bucks County Comm
  Coll (PA)
Central Arizona Coll (AZ)
Centralia Coll (WA)
Central Ohio Tech
  Coll (OH)
Chaffey Coll (CA)
Chesapeake Coll (MD)
City Colls of Chicago,
  Harold Washington
  College (IL)
Clackamas Comm
  Coll (OR)
Clark State Comm
  Coll (OH)
Clovis Comm Coll (NM)
Coll of DuPage (IL)
Coll of Marin (CA)
Colorado Mountain Coll,
  Timberline
  Campus (CO)
Comm Coll of Allegheny
  County (PA)
Comm Coll of Southern
  Nevada (NV)
De Anza Coll (CA)
Eastern Arizona Coll (AZ)
Elgin Comm Coll (IL)
Fond du Lac Tribal and
  Comm Coll (MN)
Fresno City Coll (CA)
Gateway Tech Coll (WI)
Grand Rapids Comm
  Coll (MI)
Grays Harbor Coll (WA)
Grossmont Coll (CA)
Hartnell Coll (CA)
Hawkeye Comm Coll (IA)
Henry Ford Comm
  Coll (MI)
Hesser Coll (NH)
Hillsborough Comm
  Coll (FL)
Hocking Coll (OH)
Illinois Eastern Comm
  Colls, Frontier
  Community College (IL)
Illinois Eastern Comm
  Colls, Lincoln Trail
  College (IL)
Illinois Eastern Comm
  Colls, Olney Central
  College (IL)
Illinois Eastern Comm
  Colls, Wabash Valley
  College (IL)
Iowa Lakes Comm
  Coll (IA)
Jefferson Comm Coll (OH)
Joliet Jr Coll (IL)
Kellogg Comm Coll (MI)
Kirkwood Comm Coll (IA)
Kirtland Comm Coll (MI)
Klamath Comm Coll (OR)
Lake Land Coll (IL)
Lansing Comm Coll (MI)
Laramie County Comm
  Coll (WY)
Lassen Comm Coll
  District (CA)
Lehigh Carbon Comm
  Coll (PA)
Lorain County Comm
  Coll (OH)

Los Angeles City Coll (CA)
Lower Columbia Coll (WA)
Metropolitan Comm
Coll–Longview (MO)
Metropolitan Comm
Coll–Penn Valley (MO)
Mid-State Tech Coll (WI)
Minnesota State Comm
and Tech Coll–Fergus
Falls (MN)
Monroe Comm Coll (NY)
Montcalm Comm Coll (MI)
Moorpark Coll (CA)
Moraine Valley Comm
Coll (IL)
Mt. San Antonio Coll (CA)
Napa Valley Coll (CA)
Navarro Coll (TX)
Northeast Comm Coll (NE)
Northeastern Jr Coll (CO)
Polk Comm Coll (FL)
Pueblo Comm Coll (CO)
Redlands Comm Coll (OK)
Riverland Comm Coll (MN)
Roane State Comm
Coll (TN)
St. Louis Comm Coll at
Florissant Valley (MO)
San Antonio Coll (TX)
San Bernardino Valley
Coll (CA)
San Joaquin Delta
Coll (CA)
Schoolcraft Coll (MI)
Southern State Comm
Coll (OH)
Spokane Comm Coll (WA)
State U of New York Coll
of Technology at
Canton (NY)
Three Rivers Comm
Coll (CT)
Trinidad State Jr Coll (CO)
Tulsa Comm Coll (OK)
Tunxis Comm Coll (CT)
U of New
Mexico–Gallup (NM)
Westchester Comm
Coll (NY)
Western Nevada Comm
Coll (NV)
Western Texas Coll (TX)
West Shore Comm
Coll (MI)
Wytheville Comm Coll (VA)
Yuba Coll (CA)

**Corrections and
Criminal Justice
Related**
Albany Tech Coll (GA)
Allied Coll (MO)
Fayetteville Tech Comm
Coll (NC)
Miller-Motte Tech Coll,
Clarksville (TN)
Nebraska Indian Comm
Coll (NE)
Oakland Comm Coll (MI)
Reedley Coll (CA)
Remington Coll–Fort Worth
Campus (TX)
Remington
Coll–Jacksonville
Campus (FL)
U of New
Mexico–Taos (NM)

Cosmetology
Bakersfield Coll (CA)
Barstow Coll (CA)
Bladen Comm Coll (NC)
Caldwell Comm Coll and
Tech Inst (NC)
Central New Mexico
Comm Coll (NM)
Central Texas Coll (TX)
Century Coll (MN)
Cerritos Coll (CA)
Cisco Jr Coll (TX)
Citrus Coll (CA)
Clovis Comm Coll (NM)
Coahoma Comm Coll (MS)
Coastal Bend Coll (TX)
Coll of San Mateo (CA)
Dodge City Comm
Coll (KS)
El Camino Coll (CA)
Everett Comm Coll (WA)
Fullerton Coll (CA)
Golden West Coll (CA)
Grayson County Coll (TX)
Guilford Tech Comm
Coll (NC)
H. Councill Trenholm State
Tech Coll (AL)
Isothermal Comm
Coll (NC)

James Sprunt Comm
Coll (NC)
Kirtland Comm Coll (MI)
Lamar Comm Coll (CO)
Laney Coll (CA)
Lassen Comm Coll
District (CA)
Lawson State Comm
Coll (AL)
Lenoir Comm Coll (NC)
Lorain County Comm
Coll (OH)
Martin Comm Coll (NC)
Minnesota State Coll–
Southeast Tech (MN)
Minnesota State Comm
and Tech Coll–Fergus
Falls (MN)
Montcalm Comm Coll (MI)
Mt. Hood Comm Coll (OR)
Napa Valley Coll (CA)
New Mexico Jr Coll (NM)
Northeastern Jr Coll (CO)
Northland Comm and Tech
Coll–Thief River
Falls (MN)
Northwest KansasTech
Coll (KS)
Oakland Comm Coll (MI)
Odessa Coll (TX)
Olympic Coll (WA)
Pasadena City Coll (CA)
Riverside Comm Coll
District (CA)
Sacramento City Coll (CA)
Salt Lake Comm Coll (UT)
Sandhills Comm Coll (NC)
San Diego City Coll (CA)
Santa Ana Coll (CA)
Santa Barbara City
Coll (CA)
Santiago Canyon Coll (CA)
Southeastern Comm
Coll (NC)
Southeastern Comm Coll,
North Campus (IA)
Southeastern Comm Coll,
South Campus (IA)
South Plains Coll (TX)
South Seattle Comm
Coll (WA)
Southwestern Comm
Coll (NC)
Southwest Mississippi
Comm Coll (MS)
Southwest Texas Jr
Coll (TX)
Spokane Comm Coll (WA)
Springfield Tech Comm
Coll (MA)
Stanly Comm Coll (NC)
Surry Comm Coll (NC)
Texarkana Coll (TX)
Trinidad State Jr Coll (CO)
Umpqua Comm Coll (OR)
U of New
Mexico–Gallup (NM)
Vernon Coll (TX)
Wallace State Comm
Coll (AL)
Yuba Coll (CA)

**Cosmetology and
Personal Grooming
Arts Related**
Allegany Coll of
Maryland (MD)
Comm Coll of Allegheny
County (PA)
Lorain County Comm
Coll (OH)

**Cosmetology, Barber/
Styling, and Nail
Instruction**
Olympic Coll (WA)

**Counseling
Psychology**
Kilian Comm Coll (SD)

Court Reporting
Academy of Court
Reporting (OH)
AIB Coll of Business (IA)
Business Informatics
Center, Inc. (NY)
Central New Mexico
Comm Coll (NM)
Cerritos Coll (CA)
Chaffey Coll (CA)
City Coll of San
Francisco (CA)
Clark State Comm
Coll (OH)
Coll of Court
Reporting (IN)
Coll of Marin (CA)
Comm Coll of Allegheny
County (PA)

Cuyahoga Comm
Coll (OH)
Cypress Coll (CA)
Gadsden State Comm
Coll (AL)
Gateway Tech Coll (WI)
Houston Comm Coll
System (TX)
Illinois Eastern Comm
Colls, Wabash Valley
College (IL)
Kaplan U (IA)
Lakeshore Tech Coll (WI)
Lansing Comm Coll (MI)
Lenoir Comm Coll (NC)
Long Island Business
Inst (NY)
Madison Area Tech
Coll (WI)
Maric Coll, Panorama
City (CA)
Miami Dade Coll (FL)
Midlands Tech Coll (SC)
Mississippi Gulf Coast
Comm Coll (MS)
New York Career Inst (NY)
Northwest Mississippi
Comm Coll (MS)
Oakland Comm Coll (MI)
Pennsylvania Highland
Comm Coll (PA)
Rose State Coll (OK)
Sage Coll (CA)
San Antonio Coll (TX)
San Diego City Coll (CA)
Stark State Coll of
Technology (OH)
State Fair Comm
Coll (MO)
State U of New York Coll
of Technology at
Alfred (NY)
U of Cincinnati Clermont
Coll (OH)
West Valley Coll (CA)

**Crafts, Folk Art and
Artisanry**
Coll of The Albemarle (NC)
Lawson State Comm
Coll (AL)
U of New
Mexico–Taos (NM)

Creative Writing
Berkeley City Coll (CA)
Foothill Coll (CA)
Grossmont Coll (CA)
Irvine Valley Coll (CA)
Kirtland Comm Coll (MI)
South Georgia Coll (GA)
Tulsa Comm Coll (OK)

**Criminalistics and
Criminal Science**
Florida Metropolitan
U–Orange Park
Campus (FL)

**Criminal Justice/Law
Enforcement
Administration**
Aims Comm Coll (CO)
Allen County Comm
Coll (KS)
Amarillo Coll (TX)
Angelina Coll (TX)
Anne Arundel Comm
Coll (MD)
Antelope Valley Coll (CA)
Arizona Western Coll (AZ)
Arkansas State
U–Mountain
Home (AR)
Arkansas State
U–Newport (AR)
Athens Tech Coll (GA)
Bainbridge Coll (GA)
Bakersfield Coll (CA)
Bergen Comm Coll (NJ)
Black Hawk Coll,
Moline (IL)
Blinn Coll (TX)
Brevard Comm Coll (FL)
Briarwood Coll (CT)
Brigham Young U –
Idaho (ID)
Broward Comm Coll (FL)
Brown Mackie Coll–
Akron (OH)
Brown Mackie Coll–
Atlanta (GA)
Brown Mackie Coll–
Findlay (OH)
Brown Mackie Coll–Fort
Wayne (IN)
Brown Mackie Coll–
Hopkinsville (KY)
Brown Mackie Coll–
Louisville (KY)

Brown Mackie Coll–
Miami (FL)
Brown Mackie Coll–North
Canton (OH)
Brown Mackie Coll–
Northern Kentucky (KY)
Brown Mackie Coll–
Salina (KS)
Brown Mackie Coll–South
Bend (IN)
Bucks County Comm
Coll (PA)
Cape Cod Comm
Coll (MA)
Cecil Comm Coll (MD)
Cedar Valley Coll (TX)
Central Arizona Coll (AZ)
Central Carolina Comm
Coll (NC)
Centralia Coll (WA)
Central Ohio Tech
Coll (OH)
Central Oregon Comm
Coll (OR)
Central Piedmont Comm
Coll (NC)
Central Virginia Comm
Coll (VA)
Central Wyoming
Coll (WY)
Chattanooga State Tech
Comm Coll (TN)
Chesapeake Coll (MD)
Citrus Coll (CA)
City Coll of San
Francisco (CA)
City Colls of Chicago,
Harold Washington
College (IL)
Clark State Comm
Coll (OH)
Clatsop Comm Coll (OR)
Cleveland Comm Coll (NC)
Coahoma Comm Coll (MS)
Coastal Bend Coll (TX)
Coastal Carolina Comm
Coll (NC)
Coastal Georgia Comm
Coll (GA)
Cochise Coll, Sierra
Vista (AZ)
Coconino Comm Coll (AZ)
Colby Comm Coll (KS)
Coll of DuPage (IL)
Coll of Southern Idaho (ID)
Coll of The Albemarle (NC)
Coll of the Canyons (CA)
Coll of the Desert (CA)
Coll of the Mainland (TX)
Coll of the Redwoods (CA)
Coll of the Siskiyous (CA)
Colorado Mountain
Coll (CO)
Colorado Mountain Coll,
Timberline
Campus (CO)
Columbia-Greene Comm
Coll (NY)
Comm Coll of Beaver
County (PA)
Comm Coll of
Philadelphia (PA)
Comm Coll of Southern
Nevada (NV)
Contra Costa Coll (CA)
Cosumnes River Coll,
Sacramento (CA)
Crafton Hills Coll (CA)
Dabney S. Lancaster
Comm Coll (VA)
Davidson County Comm
Coll (NC)
Dean Coll (MA)
De Anza Coll (CA)
Dodge City Comm
Coll (KS)
Eastern Arizona Coll (AZ)
East Georgia Coll (GA)
Elgin Comm Coll (IL)
Elizabethtown Tech
Coll (KY)
Erie Comm Coll (NY)
Erie Comm Coll, North
Campus (NY)
Essex County Coll (NJ)
Everest Coll, Ontario (CA)
Everett Comm Coll (WA)
Finger Lakes Comm
Coll (NY)
Florence-Darlington Tech
Coll (SC)
Florida Metropolitan
U–Orange Park
Campus (FL)
Folsom Lake Coll (CA)
Forsyth Tech Comm
Coll (NC)
Fox Valley Tech Coll (WI)

Frederick Comm Coll (MD)
Fresno City Coll (CA)
Fulton-Montgomery Comm
Coll (NY)
Genesee Comm Coll (NY)
Georgia Military Coll (GA)
Golden West Coll (CA)
Grand Rapids Comm
Coll (MI)
Grayson County Coll (TX)
Greenville Tech Coll (SC)
Grossmont Coll (CA)
Guilford Tech Comm
Coll (NC)
Hamilton Coll, Council
Bluffs (IA)
Harper Coll (IL)
Harrisburg Area Comm
Coll (PA)
Hartnell Coll (CA)
Hawkeye Comm Coll (IA)
Henry Ford Comm
Coll (MI)
Heritage Coll (NV)
Hesser Coll (NH)
High-Tech Inst (FL)
High-Tech Inst (NV)
Hillsborough Comm
Coll (FL)
Hocking Coll (OH)
Housatonic Comm
Coll (CT)
Howard Comm Coll (MD)
Illinois Valley Comm
Coll (IL)
Imperial Valley Coll (CA)
International Inst of the
Americas, Mesa (AZ)
International Inst of the
Americas, Tucson (AZ)
International Inst of the
Americas (NM)
Iowa Lakes Comm
Coll (IA)
Irvine Valley Coll (CA)
Isothermal Comm
Coll (NC)
ITT Tech Inst, Fort
Lauderdale (FL)
ITT Tech Inst,
Jacksonville (FL)
ITT Tech Inst, Lake
Mary (FL)
ITT Tech Inst, Tampa (FL)
ITT Tech Inst,
Kennesaw (GA)
ITT Tech Inst, Canton (MI)
ITT Tech Inst, Flint (MI)
ITT Tech Inst, Grand
Rapids (MI)
ITT Tech Inst, Troy (MI)
ITT Tech Inst (NE)
ITT Tech Inst, Dayton (OH)
ITT Tech Inst, Hilliard (OH)
ITT Tech Inst,
Norwood (OH)
ITT Tech Inst,
Strongsville (OH)
ITT Tech Inst, Warrensville
Heights (OH)
ITT Tech Inst,
Youngstown (OH)
James H. Faulkner State
Comm Coll (AL)
Joliet Jr Coll (IL)
Kankakee Comm Coll (IL)
Katharine Gibbs
School (PA)
Kent State U, East
Liverpool Campus (OH)
Kent State U, Trumbull
Campus (OH)
Kilian Comm Coll (SD)
Kirkwood Comm Coll (IA)
Kirtland Comm Coll (MI)
Labette Comm Coll (KS)
Lake-Sumter Comm
Coll (FL)
Lake Tahoe Comm
Coll (CA)
Lansing Comm Coll (MI)
Laramie County Comm
Coll (WY)
Lawson State Comm
Coll (AL)
Lehigh Carbon Comm
Coll (PA)
Lehigh Valley Coll (PA)
Lenoir Comm Coll (NC)
Los Angeles City Coll (CA)
Los Angeles Southwest
Coll (CA)
Lower Columbia Coll (WA)
Macomb Comm Coll (MI)
Massachusetts Bay Comm
Coll (MA)
Maui Comm Coll (HI)

McLennan Comm
Coll (TX)
Mendocino Coll (CA)
Mesa Comm Coll (AZ)
Metropolitan Comm
Coll–Longview (MO)
Metropolitan Comm
Coll–Maple
Woods (MO)
Metropolitan Comm
Coll–Penn Valley (MO)
Miami Dade Coll (FL)
Mississippi Delta Comm
Coll (MS)
Mississippi Gulf Coast
Comm Coll (MS)
Missouri State U–West
Plains (MO)
Mohawk Valley Comm
Coll (NY)
Monroe Comm Coll (NY)
Montcalm Comm Coll (MI)
Monterey Peninsula
Coll (CA)
Moorpark Coll (CA)
Mount Wachusett Comm
Coll (MA)
Muskegon Comm Coll (MI)
Napa Valley Coll (CA)
Nassau Comm Coll (NY)
National Park Comm
Coll (AR)
National School of
Technology, Inc.,
Hialeah (FL)
Naugatuck Valley Comm
Coll (CT)
Navarro Coll (TX)
Neosho County Comm
Coll (KS)
New Hampshire Tech
Inst (NH)
New Mexico Military
Inst (NM)
New River Comm Coll (VA)
Niagara County Comm
Coll (NY)
North Arkansas Coll (AR)
North Central Michigan
Coll (MI)
North Central Missouri
Coll (MO)
North Central Texas
Coll (TX)
Northeast Comm Coll (NE)
Northern Essex Comm
Coll (MA)
Northern Oklahoma
Coll (OK)
North Hennepin Comm
Coll (MN)
North Idaho Coll (ID)
Northland Comm and Tech
Coll–Thief River
Falls (MN)
North Shore Comm
Coll (MA)
NorthWest Arkansas
Comm Coll (AR)
Northwestern Connecticut
Comm Coll (CT)
Northwest-Shoals Comm
Coll (AL)
Oakland Comm Coll (MI)
Odessa Coll (TX)
Ohlone Coll (CA)
Olympic Coll (WA)
Onondaga Comm
Coll (NY)
Owens Comm Coll,
Toledo (OH)
Ozarka Coll (AR)
Palm Beach Comm
Coll (FL)
Pasadena City Coll (CA)
Pasco-Hernando Comm
Coll (FL)
Passaic County Comm
Coll (NJ)
Paul D. Camp Comm
Coll (VA)
Peninsula Coll (WA)
Piedmont Tech Coll (SC)
Pierce Coll (WA)
Polk Comm Coll (FL)
Porterville Coll (CA)
Provo Coll (UT)
Pueblo Comm Coll (CO)
Quincy Coll (MA)
Raritan Valley Comm
Coll (NJ)
Rasmussen Coll Brooklyn
Park (MN)
Redlands Comm Coll (OK)
Red Rocks Comm
Coll (CO)
Remington Coll–Baton
Rouge Campus (LA)

Remington Coll–Dallas Campus (TX)
Remington Coll–Fort Worth Campus (TX)
Remington Coll–Little Rock Campus (AR)
Remington Coll–Nashville Campus (TN)
Ridgewater Coll (MN)
Rio Hondo Coll (CA)
Riverside Comm Coll District (CA)
Roane State Comm Coll (TN)
Robeson Comm Coll (NC)
Rogue Comm Coll (OR)
Rose State Coll (OK)
Roxbury Comm Coll (MA)
Sacramento City Coll (CA)
St. Catharine Coll (KY)
Saint Charles Comm Coll (MO)
St. Louis Comm Coll at Florissant Valley (MO)
St. Philip's Coll (TX)
Salt Lake Comm Coll (UT)
Sampson Comm Coll (NC)
San Antonio Coll (TX)
Sandhills Comm Coll (NC)
Santa Ana Coll (CA)
Santa Barbara City Coll (CA)
Santa Rosa Jr Coll (CA)
Scottsdale Comm Coll (AZ)
Seminole Comm Coll (FL)
Shasta Coll (CA)
Sheridan Coll–Sheridan and Gillette (WY)
Southeastern Comm Coll (NC)
Southeastern Comm Coll, North Campus (IA)
Southern Maine Comm Coll (ME)
Southern State Comm Coll (OH)
Southern U at Shreveport (LA)
South Florida Comm Coll (FL)
South Georgia Coll (GA)
South Plains Coll (TX)
Southside Virginia Comm Coll (VA)
Southwest Texas Jr Coll (TX)
State Fair Comm Coll (MO)
State U of New York Coll of Technology at Canton (NY)
Suffolk County Comm Coll (NY)
Surry Comm Coll (NC)
Taft Coll (CA)
Tallahassee Comm Coll (FL)
Taylor Business Inst (IL)
Technology Education Coll (OH)
Temple Coll (TX)
TESST Coll of Technology (VA)
Texarkana Coll (TX)
Three Rivers Comm Coll (CT)
Three Rivers Comm Coll (MO)
Tidewater Tech (VA)
Tompkins Cortland Comm Coll (NY)
Treasure Valley Comm Coll (OR)
Trident Tech Coll (SC)
Tulsa Comm Coll (OK)
Tunxis Comm Coll (CT)
Tyler Jr Coll (TX)
Ulster County Comm Coll (NY)
Umpqua Comm Coll (OR)
U of Cincinnati Clermont Coll (OH)
U of New Mexico–Gallup (NM)
U of New Mexico–Valencia Campus (NM)
U of South Carolina Lancaster (SC)
Valencia Comm Coll (FL)
Ventura Coll (CA)
Vernon Coll (TX)
Virginia Western Comm Coll (VA)
Wallace State Comm Coll (AL)
Warren County Comm Coll (NJ)

Westchester Comm Coll (NY)
Western Nevada Comm Coll (NV)
Western Piedmont Comm Coll (NC)
Western Texas Coll (TX)
Western Wyoming Comm Coll (WY)
West Hills Comm Coll (CA)
West Los Angeles Coll (CA)
Westmoreland County Comm Coll (PA)
West Valley Coll (CA)
West Virginia U at Parkersburg (WV)
Wilson Tech Comm Coll (NC)
Wytheville Comm Coll (VA)
Young Harris Coll (GA)
Yuba Coll (CA)
Zane State Coll (OH)

Criminal Justice/ Police Science

Aims Comm Coll (CO)
Alexandria Tech Coll (MN)
Allegany Coll of Maryland (MD)
Alpena Comm Coll (MI)
Amarillo Coll (TX)
Anne Arundel Comm Coll (MD)
Antelope Valley Coll (CA)
Arizona Western Coll (AZ)
Asheville-Buncombe Tech Comm Coll (NC)
Ashland Comm and Tech Coll (KY)
Bakersfield Coll (CA)
Baltimore City Comm Coll (MD)
Barton County Comm Coll (KS)
Beaufort County Comm Coll (NC)
Bladen Comm Coll (NC)
Brevard Comm Coll (FL)
Brigham Young U – Idaho (ID)
Broome Comm Coll (NY)
Broward Comm Coll (FL)
Bucks County Comm Coll (PA)
Calhoun Comm Coll (AL)
Cape Fear Comm Coll (NC)
Catawba Valley Comm Coll (NC)
Central Ohio Tech Coll (OH)
Central Piedmont Comm Coll (NC)
Central Texas Coll (TX)
Century Coll (MN)
Cerritos Coll (CA)
Chippewa Valley Tech Coll (WI)
Cincinnati State Tech and Comm Coll (OH)
Cisco Jr Coll (TX)
Citrus Coll (CA)
City Coll of San Francisco (CA)
City Colls of Chicago, Harold Washington College (IL)
City Colls of Chicago, Harry S. Truman College (IL)
City Colls of Chicago, Richard J. Daley College (IL)
City Colls of Chicago, Wilbur Wright College (IL)
Clackamas Comm Coll (OR)
Clark State Comm Coll (OH)
Clovis Comm Coll (NM)
Coastal Bend Coll (TX)
Cochise Coll, Douglas (AZ)
Cochise Coll, Sierra Vista (AZ)
Coll of DuPage (IL)
Coll of Lake County (IL)
Coll of Marin (CA)
Coll of San Mateo (CA)
Coll of Southern Idaho (ID)
Coll of the Canyons (CA)
Coll of the Desert (CA)
Columbia Basin Coll (WA)
Comm Coll of Allegheny County (PA)
Comm Coll of Beaver County (PA)

Comm Coll of Rhode Island (RI)
Comm Coll of Southern Nevada (NV)
Contra Costa Coll (CA)
Cuyahoga Comm Coll (OH)
Davidson County Comm Coll (NC)
Dean Coll (MA)
De Anza Coll (CA)
Dyersburg State Comm Coll (TN)
East Central Coll (MO)
Eastern Arizona Coll (AZ)
El Camino Coll (CA)
El Centro Coll (TX)
Elgin Comm Coll (IL)
Erie Comm Coll (NY)
Erie Comm Coll, North Campus (NY)
Essex County Coll (NJ)
Everest Coll, Phoenix (AZ)
Everett Comm Coll (WA)
Finger Lakes Comm Coll (NY)
Fond du Lac Tribal and Comm Coll (MN)
Forsyth Tech Comm Coll (NC)
Fox Valley Tech Coll (WI)
Fresno City Coll (CA)
Fullerton Coll (CA)
Gadsden State Comm Coll (AL)
Gateway Tech Coll (WI)
George C. Wallace Comm Coll (AL)
Georgia Highlands Coll (GA)
Germanna Comm Coll (VA)
Gloucester County Coll (NJ)
Golden West Coll (CA)
Grand Rapids Comm Coll (MI)
Grays Harbor Coll (WA)
Grayson County Coll (TX)
Greenville Tech Coll (SC)
Grossmont Coll (CA)
Guilford Tech Comm Coll (NC)
Hagerstown Comm Coll (MD)
Harper Coll (IL)
Harrisburg Area Comm Coll (PA)
Hawkeye Comm Coll (IA)
Henry Ford Comm Coll (MI)
Hesser Coll (NH)
High-Tech Inst (MO)
Hillsborough Comm Coll (FL)
Hocking Coll (OH)
Holyoke Comm Coll (MA)
Hopkinsville Comm Coll (KY)
Houston Comm Coll System (TX)
Hutchinson Comm Coll and Area Vocational School (KS)
Illinois Eastern Comm Colls, Olney Central College (IL)
Illinois Valley Comm Coll (IL)
Inver Hills Comm Coll (MN)
Iowa Lakes Comm Coll (IA)
Isothermal Comm Coll (NC)
James Sprunt Comm Coll (NC)
Jamestown Comm Coll (NY)
Jefferson Comm Coll (OH)
Johnston Comm Coll (NC)
John Wood Comm Coll (IL)
Joliet Jr Coll (IL)
Jones County Jr Coll (MS)
Kankakee Comm Coll (IL)
Kansas City Kansas Comm Coll (KS)
Kellogg Comm Coll (MI)
Kent State U, Ashtabula Campus (OH)
Kent State U, Tuscarawas Campus (OH)
Kirkwood Comm Coll (IA)
Klamath Comm Coll (OR)
Labette Comm Coll (KS)
Lake Land Coll (IL)
Lakeshore Tech Coll (WI)

Lake Tahoe Comm Coll (CA)
Lansing Comm Coll (MI)
Laredo Comm Coll (TX)
Las Positas Coll (CA)
Lassen Comm Coll District (CA)
Lawson State Comm Coll (AL)
Lee Coll (TX)
Lehigh Carbon Comm Coll (PA)
Lenoir Comm Coll (NC)
Lincoln Land Comm Coll (IL)
Linn-Benton Comm Coll (OR)
Lorain County Comm Coll (OH)
Los Angeles City Coll (CA)
Los Angeles Harbor Coll (CA)
Los Angeles Mission Coll (CA)
Los Angeles Southwest Coll (CA)
Louisiana State U at Eunice (LA)
Lower Columbia Coll (WA)
Macomb Comm Coll (MI)
Madison Area Tech Coll (WI)
Madisonville Comm Coll (KY)
Marshall Comm and Tech Coll (WV)
Massasoit Comm Coll (MA)
McLennan Comm Coll (TX)
Mendocino Coll (CA)
Merced Coll (CA)
Metropolitan Comm Coll (NE)
Metropolitan Comm Coll–Blue River (MO)
Metropolitan Comm Coll–Longview (MO)
Metropolitan Comm Coll–Maple Woods (MO)
Metropolitan Comm Coll–Penn Valley (MO)
Miami Dade Coll (FL)
Middle Georgia Coll (GA)
Mid-State Tech Coll (WI)
Minneapolis Comm and Tech Coll (MN)
Minnesota State Comm and Tech Coll–Fergus Falls (MN)
Mississippi Gulf Coast Comm Coll (MS)
Missouri State U–West Plains (MO)
Moberly Area Comm Coll (MO)
Mohave Comm Coll (AZ)
Monroe Comm Coll (NY)
Monterey Peninsula Coll (CA)
Montgomery Coll (MD)
Montgomery County Comm Coll (PA)
Moorpark Coll (CA)
Moraine Valley Comm Coll (IL)
Morton Coll (IL)
Mott Comm Coll (MI)
Mt. San Antonio Coll (CA)
Napa Valley Coll (CA)
Navarro Coll (TX)
Neosho County Comm Coll (KS)
New Mexico Jr Coll (NM)
New Mexico Military Inst (NM)
New River Comm Coll (VA)
Nicolet Area Tech Coll (WI)
North Arkansas Coll (AR)
North Central Michigan Coll (MI)
North Central Texas Coll (TX)
Northeast Comm Coll (NE)
Northeastern Jr Coll (CO)
North Idaho Coll (ID)
North Iowa Area Comm Coll (IA)
Northland Comm and Tech Coll–Thief River Falls (MN)
Northwestern Connecticut Comm Coll (CT)
Northwest-Shoals Comm Coll (AL)
Oakland Comm Coll (MI)
Odessa Coll (TX)

Ohlone Coll (CA)
Okefenokee Tech Coll (GA)
Oklahoma State U, Oklahoma City (OK)
Olympic Coll (WA)
Owensboro Comm and Tech Coll (KY)
Owens Comm Coll, Toledo (OH)
Palau Comm Coll (Palau)
Palm Beach Comm Coll (FL)
Piedmont Virginia Comm Coll (VA)
Pima Comm Coll (AZ)
Pioneer Pacific Coll, Wilsonville (OR)
Porterville Coll (CA)
Pueblo Comm Coll (CO)
Quincy Coll (MA)
Rappahannock Comm Coll (VA)
Redlands Comm Coll (OK)
Reedley Coll (CA)
Richland Comm Coll (IL)
Ridgewater Coll (MN)
Riverland Comm Coll (MN)
Roane State Comm Coll (TN)
Saint Charles Comm Coll (MO)
St. Louis Comm Coll at Florissant Valley (MO)
San Antonio Coll (TX)
San Bernardino Valley Coll (CA)
Sandhills Comm Coll (NC)
San Joaquin Delta Coll (CA)
San Juan Coll (NM)
Santa Ana Coll (CA)
Schoolcraft Coll (MI)
Scott Comm Coll (IA)
Seminole State Coll (OK)
Sheridan Coll–Sheridan and Gillette (WY)
Skagit Valley Coll (WA)
Southeast Kentucky Comm and Tech Coll (KY)
Southern Maine Comm Coll (ME)
South Piedmont Comm Coll (NC)
South Plains Coll (TX)
Southwestern Comm Coll (NC)
Southwest Virginia Comm Coll (VA)
Spokane Comm Coll (WA)
Springfield Tech Comm Coll (MA)
Stanly Comm Coll (NC)
State U of New York Coll of Technology at Canton (NY)
Suffolk County Comm Coll (NY)
Temple Coll (TX)
Terra State Comm Coll (OH)
TESST Coll of Technology, Beltsville (MD)
Texarkana Coll (TX)
Three Rivers Comm Coll (MO)
Treasure Valley Comm Coll (OR)
Trinidad State Jr Coll (CO)
Tulsa Comm Coll (OK)
Tyler Jr Coll (TX)
Union County Coll (NJ)
U of Puerto Rico at Carolina (PR)
Victoria Coll (TX)
Victor Valley Coll (CA)
Vincennes U Jasper Campus (IN)
Virginia Highlands Comm Coll (VA)
Wallace State Comm Coll (AL)
Waukesha County Tech Coll (WI)
Wayne Comm Coll (NC)
Westchester Comm Coll (NY)
Western Nevada Comm Coll (NV)
Western Piedmont Comm Coll (NC)
Western Texas Coll (TX)
West Los Angeles Coll (CA)
Westmoreland County Comm Coll (PA)
West Shore Comm Coll (MI)

West Valley Coll (CA)
Wor-Wic Comm Coll (MD)
Wytheville Comm Coll (VA)
Yuba Coll (CA)

Criminal Justice/ Safety

Alamance Comm Coll (NC)
Altamaha Tech Coll (GA)
Appalachian Tech Coll (GA)
Arkansas State U–Mountain Home (AR)
Asnuntuck Comm Coll (CT)
Augusta Tech Coll (GA)
Berkshire Comm Coll (MA)
Bowling Green State U–Firelands Coll (OH)
Brown Mackie Coll–Merrillville (IN)
Cambridge Coll (CO)
Career Tech Coll (LA)
Central Carolina Tech Coll (SC)
Central Comm Coll–Grand Island Campus (NE)
Central Georgia Tech Coll (GA)
Central New Mexico Comm Coll (NM)
Central Texas Coll (TX)
Chattahoochee Tech Coll (GA)
Cleveland Comm Coll (NC)
Colegio Universitario de San Juan, San Juan (PR)
Coll of the Mainland (TX)
Columbia Basin Coll (WA)
Coosa Valley Tech Coll (GA)
DeKalb Tech Coll (GA)
Dixie State Coll of Utah (UT)
East Central Tech Coll (GA)
Eastern New Mexico U–Roswell (NM)
El Centro Coll (TX)
Fayetteville Tech Comm Coll (NC)
Flint River Tech Coll (GA)
Garrett Coll (MD)
Georgia Highlands Coll (GA)
Great Basin Coll (NV)
Griffin Tech Coll (GA)
Heart of Georgia Tech Coll (GA)
Indiana Business Coll, Anderson (IN)
Indiana Business Coll, Columbus (IN)
Indiana Business Coll, Muncie (IN)
Indiana Business Coll, Terre Haute (IN)
Inver Hills Comm Coll (MN)
Jamestown Comm Coll (NY)
Kaplan U (IA)
Kellogg Comm Coll (MI)
Keystone Coll (PA)
Lamar Comm Coll (CO)
Lanier Tech Coll (GA)
Linn-Benton Comm Coll (OR)
Louisiana State U at Eunice (LA)
Lower Columbia Coll (WA)
Manatee Comm Coll (FL)
Marian Court Coll (MA)
Midlands Tech Coll (SC)
Minneapolis Comm and Tech Coll (MN)
Moultrie Tech Coll (GA)
Nassau Comm Coll (NY)
New Mexico State U–Alamogordo (NM)
Northampton County Area Comm Coll (PA)
North Country Comm Coll (NY)
Northern New Mexico Coll (NM)
North Georgia Tech Coll (GA)
North Hennepin Comm Coll (MN)
Northwestern Tech Coll (GA)
Northwest Vista Coll (TX)
Parkland Coll (IL)
Piedmont Tech Coll (SC)
Pima Comm Coll (AZ)

Potomac State Coll of West Virginia U (WV)
Remington Coll–Little Rock Campus (AR)
San Juan Coll (NM)
Savannah Tech Coll (GA)
Southeastern Comm Coll, South Campus (IA)
Southeastern Tech Coll (GA)
South Georgia Tech Coll (GA)
Southwest Georgia Tech Coll (GA)
Swainsboro Tech Coll (GA)
U of Arkansas Comm Coll at Batesville (AR)
U of New Mexico–Taos (NM)
Valdosta Tech Coll (GA)
West Central Tech Coll (GA)
Western Nebraska Comm Coll (NE)
West Georgia Tech Coll (GA)
West Virginia State Comm and Tech Coll (WV)

Criminology
Catawba Valley Comm Coll (NC)
Coll of the Mainland (TX)
Hartnell Coll (CA)
Northland Comm and Tech Coll–Thief River Falls (MN)
South Georgia Coll (GA)
Western Wyoming Comm Coll (WY)

Crop Production
Barton County Comm Coll (KS)
Iowa Lakes Comm Coll (IA)
Northeast Comm Coll (NE)
The Ohio State U Ag Tech Inst (OH)

Culinary Arts
Alamance Comm Coll (NC)
Albany Tech Coll (GA)
Allegany Coll of Maryland (MD)
The Art Inst of Philadelphia (PA)
Asheville-Buncombe Tech Comm Coll (NC)
Atlanta Tech Coll (GA)
Augusta Tech Coll (GA)
Bakersfield Coll (CA)
Black Hawk Coll, Moline (IL)
Brevard Comm Coll (FL)
Bucks County Comm Coll (PA)
California School of Culinary Arts (CA)
Central New Mexico Comm Coll (NM)
Central Oregon Comm Coll (OR)
Central Piedmont Comm Coll (NC)
Chattahoochee Tech Coll (GA)
Chippewa Valley Tech Coll (WI)
Cincinnati State Tech and Comm Coll (OH)
Clark Coll (WA)
Cochise Coll, Douglas (AZ)
Coll of DuPage (IL)
Coll of Southern Idaho (ID)
Coll of The Albemarle (NC)
Coll of the Desert (CA)
Columbia Coll (CA)
Commonwealth Tech Inst (PA)
Comm Coll of Allegheny County (PA)
Comm Coll of Beaver County (PA)
Comm Coll of Philadelphia (PA)
Comm Coll of Southern Nevada (NV)
Contra Costa Coll (CA)
The Cooking and Hospitality Inst of Chicago (IL)
Culinary Inst Alain & Marie LeNotre (TX)
Cypress Coll (CA)
East Central Coll (MO)
El Camino Coll (CA)
El Centro Coll (TX)
Elgin Comm Coll (IL)
Erie Comm Coll (NY)

Erie Comm Coll, North Campus (NY)
Fayetteville Tech Comm Coll (NC)
Fox Valley Tech Coll (WI)
Grand Rapids Comm Coll (MI)
Guilford Tech Comm Coll (NC)
Harper Coll (IL)
Harrisburg Area Comm Coll (PA)
H. Councill Trenholm State Tech Coll (AL)
Henry Ford Comm Coll (MI)
Hillsborough Comm Coll (FL)
Hocking Coll (OH)
Illinois Eastern Comm Colls, Lincoln Trail College (IL)
Jefferson Comm and Tech Coll (KY)
Joliet Jr Coll (IL)
Keystone Coll (PA)
Kirkwood Comm Coll (IA)
Laney Coll (CA)
Lehigh Carbon Comm Coll (PA)
Linn-Benton Comm Coll (OR)
Los Angeles Mission Coll (CA)
Macomb Comm Coll (MI)
Madison Area Tech Coll (WI)
Massasoit Comm Coll (MA)
Metropolitan Comm Coll (NE)
Minneapolis Comm and Tech Coll (MN)
Mohawk Valley Comm Coll (NY)
Montgomery County Comm Coll (PA)
Mott Comm Coll (MI)
New England Culinary Inst (VT)
Niagara County Comm Coll (NY)
Nicolet Area Tech Coll (WI)
North Georgia Tech Coll (GA)
North Idaho Coll (ID)
North Shore Comm Coll (MA)
Oakland Comm Coll (MI)
Odessa Coll (TX)
Ogeechee Tech Coll (GA)
Oklahoma State U, Okmulgee (OK)
Olympic Coll (WA)
Onondaga Comm Coll (NY)
Orange Coast Coll (CA)
Oxnard Coll (CA)
Ozarka Coll (AR)
Ozarks Tech Coll (MO)
Pueblo Comm Coll (CO)
Quality Coll of Culinary Careers (TX)
Remington Coll–Dallas Campus (TX)
Renton Tech Coll (WA)
Riverside Comm Coll District (CA)
St. Philip's Coll (TX)
Sandhills Comm Coll (NC)
San Joaquin Delta Coll (CA)
Santa Rosa Jr Coll (CA)
Savannah Tech Coll (GA)
Schoolcraft Coll (MI)
Scott Comm Coll (IA)
Scottsdale Comm Coll (AZ)
Shasta Coll (CA)
Skagit Valley Coll (WA)
Southern Maine Comm Coll (ME)
South Georgia Tech Coll (GA)
South Seattle Comm Coll (WA)
Southwestern Comm Coll (NC)
Southwestern Indian Polytechnic Inst (NM)
Spokane Comm Coll (WA)
State U of New York Coll of Technology at Alfred (NY)
Suffolk County Comm Coll (NY)
Trident Tech Coll (SC)

Valencia Comm Coll (FL)
Westchester Comm Coll (NY)
Western Culinary Inst (OR)
Westmoreland County Comm Coll (PA)
Winner Inst of Arts & Sciences (PA)
York County Comm Coll (ME)
Zane State Coll (OH)

Culinary Arts Related
Hillsborough Comm Coll (FL)
Iowa Lakes Comm Coll (IA)
Keystone Coll (PA)
Linn-Benton Comm Coll (OR)
Olympic Coll (WA)
Santa Barbara City Coll (CA)

Cultural Studies
Coll of Marin (CA)
Coll of San Mateo (CA)
Cosumnes River Coll, Sacramento (CA)
De Anza Coll (CA)
Foothill Coll (CA)
Fresno City Coll (CA)
Fullerton Coll (CA)
Grossmont Coll (CA)
Laney Coll (CA)
Mendocino Coll (CA)
Monterey Peninsula Coll (CA)
Orange Coast Coll (CA)
Pasadena City Coll (CA)
Sacramento City Coll (CA)
Santa Ana Coll (CA)
Santa Barbara City Coll (CA)
Santa Rosa Jr Coll (CA)
Santiago Canyon Coll (CA)
Skagit Valley Coll (WA)
Yuba Coll (CA)

Customer Service Support/Call Center/Teleservice Operation
Laramie County Comm Coll (WY)

Cytotechnology
Barton County Comm Coll (KS)

Dairy Husbandry and Production
Linn-Benton Comm Coll (OR)
The Ohio State U Ag Tech Inst (OH)

Dairy Science
Brigham Young U – Idaho (ID)
Chippewa Valley Tech Coll (WI)
Cisco Jr Coll (TX)
Mt. San Antonio Coll (CA)
Northeast Iowa Comm Coll (IA)
Northwest Mississippi Comm Coll (MS)
The Ohio State U Ag Tech Inst (OH)
State U of New York Coll of Agriculture and Technology at Morrisville (NY)

Dance
Barton County Comm Coll (KS)
Bergen Comm Coll (NJ)
Brigham Young U – Idaho (ID)
Cañada Coll (CA)
Central Piedmont Comm Coll (NC)
Chaffey Coll (CA)
Citrus Coll (CA)
Coll of Marin (CA)
Cypress Coll (CA)
Dean Coll (MA)
Dixie State Coll of Utah (UT)
Fullerton Coll (CA)
Grossmont Coll (CA)
Henry Ford Comm Coll (MI)
Hillsborough Comm Coll (FL)
Lake Tahoe Comm Coll (CA)
Laney Coll (CA)
Lansing Comm Coll (MI)
Louisburg Coll (NC)

Miami Dade Coll (FL)
Monterey Peninsula Coll (CA)
Nassau Comm Coll (NY)
Navarro Coll (TX)
Northern Essex Comm Coll (MA)
Orange Coast Coll (CA)
St. Catharine Coll (KY)
San Joaquin Delta Coll (CA)
Santa Ana Coll (CA)
Santa Rosa Jr Coll (CA)
Westchester Comm Coll (NY)
Western Wyoming Comm Coll (WY)

Data Entry/Microcomputer Applications
Anne Arundel Comm Coll (MD)
Bellingham Tech Coll (WA)
Clark Coll (WA)
Cleveland Comm Coll (NC)
Coastal Bend Coll (TX)
Coll of The Albemarle (NC)
Comm Coll of Vermont (VT)
Cypress Coll (CA)
Eastern Arizona Coll (AZ)
ECPI Tech Coll (VA)
ECPI Tech Coll (VA)
Fiorello H. LaGuardia Comm Coll of the City U of New York (NY)
Florida National Coll (FL)
Gateway Comm Coll (CT)
Howard Comm Coll (MD)
Iowa Lakes Comm Coll (IA)
Laredo Comm Coll (TX)
Laurel Business Inst (PA)
Lorain County Comm Coll (OH)
Los Angeles City Coll (CA)
Lower Columbia Coll (WA)
Metropolitan Comm Coll–Business & Technology Campus (MO)
Mid-State Tech Coll (WI)
Mississippi Gulf Coast Comm Coll (MS)
Nebraska Indian Comm Coll (NE)
Northland Comm and Tech Coll–Thief River Falls (MN)
North Shore Comm Coll (MA)
Oklahoma State U, Oklahoma City (OK)
Onondaga Comm Coll (NY)
Owensboro Comm and Tech Coll (KY)
Parkland Coll (IL)
Quinebaug Valley Comm Coll (CT)
Richland Comm Coll (IL)
Rio Salado Coll (AZ)
Riverland Comm Coll (MN)
Roxbury Comm Coll (MA)
St. Philip's Coll (TX)
San Antonio Coll (TX)
Santa Ana Coll (CA)
Seminole Comm Coll (FL)
Sheridan Coll–Sheridan and Gillette (WY)
Stark State Coll of Technology (OH)
Three Rivers Comm Coll (MO)
Tompkins Cortland Comm Coll (NY)
Tulsa Comm Coll (OK)
Tyler Jr Coll (TX)
U of Arkansas Comm Coll at Batesville (AR)
Valencia Comm Coll (FL)
West Central Tech Coll (GA)
Western Wyoming Comm Coll (WY)
Zane State Coll (OH)

Data Entry/Microcomputer Applications Related
AIB Coll of Business (IA)
Bellingham Tech Coll (WA)
Berkeley City Coll (CA)
Capital Comm Coll (CT)
Coastal Bend Coll (TX)
Coll of DuPage (IL)
The Coll of Office Technology (IL)

Colorado Mountain Coll (CO)
Colorado Mountain Coll, Alpine Campus (CO)
Cypress Coll (CA)
Eugenio María de Hostos Comm Coll of the City U of New York (NY)
Florida National Coll (FL)
Hawkeye Comm Coll (IA)
Kellogg Comm Coll (MI)
Laredo Comm Coll (TX)
Laurel Business Inst (PA)
Lorain County Comm Coll (OH)
Los Angeles City Coll (CA)
Metropolitan Comm Coll–Business & Technology Campus (MO)
Mississippi Gulf Coast Comm Coll (MS)
Northland Comm and Tech Coll–Thief River Falls (MN)
Onondaga Comm Coll (NY)
Orange Coast Coll (CA)
Peninsula Coll (WA)
Richland Comm Coll (IL)
Riverland Comm Coll (MN)
Santa Ana Coll (CA)
Seminole Comm Coll (FL)
Southwestern Michigan Coll (MI)
Stark State Coll of Technology (OH)
Texarkana Coll (TX)
Three Rivers Comm Coll (MO)
Tulsa Comm Coll (OK)
West Shore Comm Coll (MI)

Data Modeling/Warehousing and Database Administration
Brown Mackie Coll–Akron (OH)
Kennebec Valley Comm Coll (ME)
Laramie County Comm Coll (WY)
Metropolitan Comm Coll–Business & Technology Campus (MO)
Minot State U–Bottineau Campus (ND)
Northland Comm and Tech Coll–Thief River Falls (MN)
Seminole Comm Coll (FL)
Tulsa Comm Coll (OK)

Data Processing and Data Processing Technology
Academy Coll (MN)
Allen County Comm Coll (KS)
Alpena Comm Coll (MI)
Angelina Coll (TX)
Anne Arundel Comm Coll (MD)
Antelope Valley Coll (CA)
Bainbridge Coll (GA)
Bakersfield Coll (CA)
Baltimore City Comm Coll (MD)
Black Hawk Coll, Moline (IL)
Brigham Young U – Idaho (ID)
Broome Comm Coll (NY)
Broward Comm Coll (FL)
Bucks County Comm Coll (PA)
Cabrillo Coll (CA)
Cañada Coll (CA)
Career Tech Coll (LA)
Carroll Comm Coll (MD)
Catawba Valley Comm Coll (NC)
Cecil Comm Coll (MD)
Cedar Valley Coll (TX)
Central Carolina Tech Coll (SC)
Central Comm Coll–Grand Island Campus (NE)
Central New Mexico Comm Coll (NM)
Central Piedmont Comm Coll (NC)
Central Texas Coll (TX)
Cerritos Coll (CA)
Chattanooga State Tech Comm Coll (TN)

Chesapeake Coll (MD)
Chippewa Valley Tech Coll (WI)
Cisco Jr Coll (TX)
Citrus Coll (CA)
City Colls of Chicago, Harold Washington College (IL)
City Colls of Chicago, Kennedy-King College (IL)
City Colls of Chicago, Richard J. Daley College (IL)
City Colls of Chicago, Wilbur Wright College (IL)
Coastal Bend Coll (TX)
Cochise Coll, Douglas (AZ)
Coll of Marin (CA)
Columbia-Greene Comm Coll (NY)
Comm Coll of Beaver County (PA)
Comm Coll of Philadelphia (PA)
Comm Coll of Southern Nevada (NV)
Cuesta Coll (CA)
Dabney S. Lancaster Comm Coll (VA)
Davidson County Comm Coll (NC)
Dixie State Coll of Utah (UT)
Dodge City Comm Coll (KS)
ECPI Coll of Technology (VA)
ECPI Tech Coll (VA)
El Camino Coll (CA)
El Centro Coll (TX)
Elizabethtown Tech Coll (KY)
Essex County Coll (NJ)
Eugenio María de Hostos Comm Coll of the City U of New York (NY)
Everett Comm Coll (WA)
Finger Lakes Comm Coll (NY)
Florida National Coll (FL)
Forsyth Tech Comm Coll (NC)
Fort Belknap Coll (MT)
Frederick Comm Coll (MD)
Fullerton Coll (CA)
Fulton-Montgomery Comm Coll (NY)
Gateway Comm Coll (CT)
George C. Wallace Comm Coll (AL)
Gloucester County Coll (NJ)
Great Basin Coll (NV)
Harper Coll (IL)
Hartnell Coll (CA)
Henry Ford Comm Coll (MI)
Heritage Coll (NV)
Housatonic Comm Coll (CT)
Illinois Valley Comm Coll (IL)
Iowa Lakes Comm Coll (IA)
Irvine Valley Coll (CA)
ITT Tech Inst, Richardson (TX)
Jefferson Comm and Tech Coll (KY)
Jefferson Comm Coll (OH)
Jones County Jr Coll (MS)
Kansas City Kansas Comm Coll (KS)
Keystone Coll (PA)
Kingsborough Comm Coll of the City U of New York (NY)
Kirkwood Comm Coll (IA)
Labette Comm Coll (KS)
Lamar Comm Coll (CO)
Laredo Comm Coll (TX)
Lee Coll (TX)
Lewis Coll of Business (MI)
Los Angeles City Coll (CA)
Los Angeles Harbor Coll (CA)
Los Angeles Pierce Coll (CA)
Los Angeles Southwest Coll (CA)
Lower Columbia Coll (WA)
Madison Area Tech Coll (WI)
Marian Court Coll (MA)
Mendocino Coll (CA)

Merced Coll (CA)
Mesa Comm Coll (AZ)
Metropolitan Comm
 Coll–Business &
 Technology
 Campus (MO)
Metropolitan Comm
 Coll–Longview (MO)
Metropolitan Comm
 Coll–Maple
 Woods (MO)
Metropolitan Comm
 Coll–Penn Valley (MO)
Miami Dade Coll (FL)
Middle Georgia Coll (GA)
Midlands Tech Coll (SC)
Mission Coll (CA)
Monroe Comm Coll (NY)
Montcalm Comm Coll (MI)
Monterey Peninsula
 Coll (CA)
Moorpark Coll (CA)
Morton Coll (IL)
Mt. San Antonio Coll (CA)
Muskegon Comm Coll (MI)
Napa Valley Coll (CA)
Nassau Comm Coll (NY)
National Park Comm
 Coll (AR)
Navarro Coll (TX)
New Hampshire Comm
 Tech Coll, Nashua/
 Claremont (NH)
New Mexico Jr Coll (NM)
New Mexico State U–
 Alamogordo (NM)
New York City Coll of
 Technology of the City
 U of New York (NY)
Nicolet Area Tech Coll (WI)
North Central Michigan
 Coll (MI)
North Central Missouri
 Coll (MO)
North Central Texas
 Coll (TX)
Northeastern Jr Coll (CO)
Northeastern Tech
 Coll (SC)
Northeast State Tech
 Comm Coll (TN)
Northern Essex Comm
 Coll (MA)
Northern Maine Comm
 Coll (ME)
Northern Marianas
 Coll (MP)
North Lake Coll (TX)
NorthWest Arkansas
 Comm Coll (AR)
Northwest Mississippi
 Comm Coll (MS)
Odessa Coll (TX)
Onondaga Comm
 Coll (NY)
Orange Coast Coll (CA)
Palm Beach Comm
 Coll (FL)
Pasadena City Coll (CA)
Paul D. Camp Comm
 Coll (VA)
Piedmont Tech Coll (SC)
Piedmont Virginia Comm
 Coll (VA)
Polk Comm Coll (FL)
Potomac State Coll of
 West Virginia U (WV)
Raritan Valley Comm
 Coll (NJ)
Richland Coll (TX)
Ridgewater Coll (MN)
Sacramento City Coll (CA)
St. Louis Comm Coll at
 Florissant Valley (MO)
San Antonio Coll (TX)
San Bernardino Valley
 Coll (CA)
San Diego City Coll (CA)
Schoolcraft Coll (MI)
Seminole Comm Coll (FL)
Southeast Kentucky Comm
 and Tech Coll (KY)
South Plains Coll (TX)
Southwestern Indian
 Polytechnic Inst (NM)
Southwest Texas Jr
 Coll (TX)
Spokane Comm Coll (WA)
State U of New York Coll
 of Agriculture and
 Technology at
 Morrisville (NY)
Suffolk County Comm
 Coll (NY)
Taft Coll (CA)
Tallahassee Comm
 Coll (FL)
Temple Coll (TX)

Texarkana Coll (TX)
Three Rivers Comm
 Coll (CT)
Trinidad State Jr Coll (CO)
Tunxis Comm Coll (CT)
Ulster County Comm
 Coll (NY)
The U of Akron–Wayne
 Coll (OH)
Vernon Coll (TX)
Virginia Highlands Comm
 Coll (VA)
Virginia Western Comm
 Coll (VA)
Warren County Comm
 Coll (NJ)
Washington State Comm
 Coll (OH)
Westchester Comm
 Coll (NY)
Western Wyoming Comm
 Coll (WY)
West Los Angeles
 Coll (CA)
Westmoreland County
 Comm Coll (PA)
West Shore Comm
 Coll (MI)
West Valley Coll (CA)
West Virginia U at
 Parkersburg (WV)
York Tech Coll (SC)

Dental Assisting
Allied Coll (MO)
Athens Tech Coll (GA)
Black Hawk Coll,
 Moline (IL)
Briarwood Coll (CT)
Calhoun Comm Coll (AL)
Central Comm Coll–
 Hastings Campus (NE)
Central Oregon Comm
 Coll (OR)
Century Coll (MN)
Citrus Coll (CA)
Coll of Southern Idaho (ID)
Coll of the Redwoods (CA)
Cypress Coll (CA)
Essex County Coll (NJ)
Flint Hills Tech Coll (KS)
Foothill Coll (CA)
H. Councill Trenholm State
 Tech Coll (AL)
Hennepin Tech Coll (MN)
Herzing Coll (MN)
High-Tech Inst (FL)
High-Tech Inst (MO)
High-Tech Inst (NV)
High-Tech Inst,
 Nashville (TN)
James H. Faulkner State
 Comm Coll (AL)
Jefferson Comm Coll (OH)
Laramie County Comm
 Coll (WY)
Massasoit Comm
 Coll (MA)
Midlands Tech Coll (SC)
Mid-Plains Comm Coll,
 North Platte (NE)
Mott Comm Coll (MI)
New Hampshire Tech
 Inst (NH)
Northern Essex Comm
 Coll (MA)
Oxnard Coll (CA)
Provo Coll (UT)
Pueblo Comm Coll (CO)
Reedley Coll (CA)
Rose State Coll (OK)
Sacramento City Coll (CA)
St. Cloud Tech Coll (MN)
Tulsa Comm Coll (OK)
Wallace State Comm
 Coll (AL)
Western Career Coll,
 Pleasant Hill (CA)
Western Career Coll,
 Sacramento (CA)
York Tech Coll (SC)

Dental Hygiene
Allegany Coll of
 Maryland (MD)
Amarillo Coll (TX)
Asheville-Buncombe Tech
 Comm Coll (NC)
Athens Tech Coll (GA)
Atlanta Tech Coll (GA)
Bakersfield Coll (CA)
Baltimore City Comm
 Coll (MD)
Barton County Comm
 Coll (KS)
Bergen Comm Coll (NJ)
Blinn Coll (TX)
Brevard Comm Coll (FL)
Brigham Young U –
 Idaho (ID)

Broome Comm Coll (NY)
Broward Comm Coll (FL)
Cabrillo Coll (CA)
Cape Cod Comm
 Coll (MA)
Cape Fear Comm
 Coll (NC)
Catawba Valley Comm
 Coll (NC)
Central Comm Coll–
 Hastings Campus (NE)
Central Georgia Tech
 Coll (GA)
Central Piedmont Comm
 Coll (NC)
Century Coll (MN)
Cerritos Coll (CA)
Chattanooga State Tech
 Comm Coll (TN)
Chippewa Valley Tech
 Coll (WI)
City Coll of San
 Francisco (CA)
City Colls of Chicago,
 Richard J. Daley
 College (IL)
Clark Coll (WA)
Coastal Bend Coll (TX)
Coastal Carolina Comm
 Coll (NC)
Coastal Georgia Comm
 Coll (GA)
Colby Comm Coll (KS)
Coll of Alameda (CA)
Coll of DuPage (IL)
Coll of Lake County (IL)
Coll of Marin (CA)
Coll of San Mateo (CA)
Coll of Southern Idaho (ID)
Collin County Comm Coll
 District (TX)
Columbus Tech Coll (GA)
Comm Coll of
 Philadelphia (PA)
Comm Coll of Rhode
 Island (RI)
Comm Coll of Southern
 Nevada (NV)
Contra Costa Coll (CA)
Cypress Coll (CA)
Dixie State Coll of
 Utah (UT)
Erie Comm Coll, North
 Campus (NY)
Essex County Coll (NJ)
Eugenio María de Hostos
 Comm Coll of the City
 U of New York (NY)
Everett Comm Coll (WA)
Fayetteville Tech Comm
 Coll (NC)
Florence-Darlington Tech
 Coll (SC)
Florida National Coll (FL)
Foothill Coll (CA)
Fresno City Coll (CA)
Gateway Tech Coll (WI)
Georgia Highlands
 Coll (GA)
Germanna Comm
 Coll (VA)
Grand Rapids Comm
 Coll (MI)
Greenville Tech Coll (SC)
Guilford Tech Comm
 Coll (NC)
Harper Coll (IL)
Harrisburg Area Comm
 Coll (PA)
Hawkeye Comm Coll (IA)
Herzing Coll (MN)
Hillsborough Comm
 Coll (FL)
Kellogg Comm Coll (MI)
Lake Land Coll (IL)
Lakeshore Tech Coll (WI)
Lamar Inst of
 Technology (TX)
Lansing Comm Coll (MI)
Laramie County Comm
 Coll (WY)
Los Angeles City Coll (CA)
Madison Area Tech
 Coll (WI)
Merced Coll (CA)
Meridian Comm Coll (MS)
Miami Dade Coll (FL)
Middle Georgia Tech
 Coll (GA)
Midlands Tech Coll (SC)
Minnesota State Comm
 and Tech Coll–Fergus
 Falls (MN)
Mississippi Delta Comm
 Coll (MS)
Monroe Comm Coll (NY)
Monterey Peninsula
 Coll (CA)

Montgomery County
 Comm Coll (PA)
Mott Comm Coll (MI)
Mt. Hood Comm Coll (OR)
Mount Wachusett Comm
 Coll (MA)
Navarro Coll (TX)
New Hampshire Tech
 Inst (NH)
New York City Coll of
 Technology of the City
 U of New York (NY)
Northampton County Area
 Comm Coll (PA)
Oakland Comm Coll (MI)
Ogeechee Tech Coll (GA)
Onondaga Comm
 Coll (NY)
Orange Coast Coll (CA)
Oxnard Coll (CA)
Palm Beach Comm
 Coll (FL)
Parkland Coll (IL)
Pasadena City Coll (CA)
Pasco-Hernando Comm
 Coll (FL)
Pierce Coll (WA)
Pima Comm Coll (AZ)
Pueblo Comm Coll (CO)
Rio Salado Coll (AZ)
Roane State Comm
 Coll (TN)
Rose State Coll (OK)
Sacramento City Coll (CA)
St. Cloud Tech Coll (MN)
Salish Kootenai Coll (MT)
Salt Lake Comm Coll (UT)
San Antonio Coll (TX)
San Bernardino Valley
 Coll (CA)
Santa Rosa Jr Coll (CA)
Shasta Coll (CA)
Sheridan Coll–Sheridan
 and Gillette (WY)
Southeastern Tech
 Coll (GA)
Southern U at
 Shreveport (LA)
Spokane Comm Coll (WA)
Springfield Tech Comm
 Coll (MA)
Stark State Coll of
 Technology (OH)
Taft Coll (CA)
Tallahassee Comm
 Coll (FL)
Temple Coll (TX)
Trident Tech Coll (SC)
Tulsa Comm Coll (OK)
Tunxis Comm Coll (CT)
Tyler Jr Coll (TX)
Union County Coll (NJ)
Valencia Comm Coll (FL)
Virginia Western Comm
 Coll (VA)
Wallace State Comm
 Coll (AL)
Waukesha County Tech
 Coll (WI)
Wayne Comm Coll (NC)
West Central Tech
 Coll (GA)
West Los Angeles
 Coll (CA)
Westmoreland County
 Comm Coll (PA)
Wytheville Comm Coll (VA)
York Tech Coll (SC)

**Dental Laboratory
Technology**
Century Coll (MN)
Commonwealth Tech
 Inst (PA)
Erie Comm Coll, South
 Campus (NY)
H. Councill Trenholm State
 Tech Coll (AL)
Marshall Comm and Tech
 Coll (WV)
New York City Coll of
 Technology of the City
 U of New York (NY)
Pima Comm Coll (AZ)

**Design and Applied
Arts Related**
Mohawk Valley Comm
 Coll (NY)
Niagara County Comm
 Coll (NY)

**Design and Visual
Communications**
Academy Coll (MN)
Black Hawk Coll,
 Moline (IL)
Bradley Academy for the
 Visual Arts (PA)

Brooks Coll,
 Sunnyvale (CA)
Coll of DuPage (IL)
The Creative Center (NE)
Elgin Comm Coll (IL)
FIDM/The Fashion Inst of
 Design &
 Merchandising, Los
 Angeles Campus (CA)
FIDM/The Fashion Inst of
 Design &
 Merchandising, San
 Diego Campus (CA)
FIDM/The Fashion Inst of
 Design &
 Merchandising, San
 Francisco
 Campus (CA)
Fresno City Coll (CA)
Harrisburg Area Comm
 Coll (PA)
Katharine Gibbs
 School (PA)
Lehigh Valley Coll (PA)
Moraine Valley Comm
 Coll (IL)
Nassau Comm Coll (NY)
North Metro Tech Coll (GA)
Parkland Coll (IL)
Pima Comm Coll (AZ)
Pueblo Comm Coll (CO)
Shasta Coll (CA)
Southeastern Tech
 Coll (GA)
Trinidad State Jr Coll (CO)

**Desktop Publishing
and Digital Imaging
Design**
The Art Inst of
 Philadelphia (PA)
Coll of DuPage (IL)
Hennepin Tech Coll (MN)
Iowa Lakes Comm
 Coll (IA)
Lake Land Coll (IL)
Lee Coll (TX)
Linn-Benton Comm
 Coll (OR)
Northwest KansasTech
 Coll (KS)
Springfield Tech Comm
 Coll (MA)
Tulsa Comm Coll (OK)
Umpqua Comm Coll (OR)

**Developmental and
Child Psychology**
Angelina Coll (TX)
Arizona Western Coll (AZ)
Bakersfield Coll (CA)
Cankdeska Cikana Comm
 Coll (ND)
Central Lakes Coll (MN)
Chaffey Coll (CA)
Cisco Jr Coll (TX)
City Coll of San
 Francisco (CA)
City Colls of Chicago,
 Harold Washington
 College (IL)
City Colls of Chicago,
 Harry S. Truman
 College (IL)
City Colls of Chicago,
 Olive-Harvey
 College (IL)
City Colls of Chicago,
 Richard J. Daley
 College (IL)
Coastal Bend Coll (TX)
Coll of the Canyons (CA)
Columbia Coll (CA)
Comm Coll of
 Vermont (VT)
De Anza Coll (CA)
Fullerton Coll (CA)
Fulton-Montgomery Comm
 Coll (NY)
Grossmont Coll (CA)
Hartnell Coll (CA)
Iowa Lakes Comm
 Coll (IA)
Jefferson Comm Coll (OH)
Kirkwood Comm Coll (IA)
Lansing Comm Coll (MI)
Los Angeles City Coll (CA)
Los Angeles Harbor
 Coll (CA)
Los Angeles Mission
 Coll (CA)
Los Angeles Southwest
 Coll (CA)
Los Medanos Coll (CA)
McLennan Comm
 Coll (TX)
Mendocino Coll (CA)
Merced Coll (CA)

Mississippi Delta Comm
 Coll (MS)
Muskegon Comm Coll (MI)
Navarro Coll (TX)
North Idaho Coll (ID)
Pasadena City Coll (CA)
Ridgewater Coll (MN)
Rose State Coll (OK)
San Antonio Coll (TX)
San Bernardino Valley
 Coll (CA)
San Diego City Coll (CA)
San Joaquin Delta
 Coll (CA)
South Plains Coll (TX)
South Texas Coll (TX)
Tyler Jr Coll (TX)
West Los Angeles
 Coll (CA)

**Diagnostic Medical
Sonography and
Ultrasound
Technology**
Athens Tech Coll (GA)
Caldwell Comm Coll and
 Tech Inst (NC)
Cape Fear Comm
 Coll (NC)
Central New Mexico
 Comm Coll (NM)
Central Ohio Tech
 Coll (OH)
Chippewa Valley Tech
 Coll (WI)
Cincinnati State Tech and
 Comm Coll (OH)
Columbus Tech Coll (GA)
Comm Coll of Allegheny
 County (PA)
El Centro Coll (TX)
Florida National Coll (FL)
Foothill Coll (CA)
Gloucester County
 Coll (NJ)
Hillsborough Comm
 Coll (FL)
Keystone Coll (PA)
Lamar Inst of
 Technology (TX)
Lancaster General Coll of
 Nursing & Health
 Sciences (PA)
Lansing Comm Coll (MI)
Laramie County Comm
 Coll (WY)
Lorain County Comm
 Coll (OH)
Miami Dade Coll (FL)
Montgomery Coll (MD)
New Hampshire Tech
 Inst (NH)
Northampton County Area
 Comm Coll (PA)
Oakland Comm Coll (MI)
St. Cloud Tech Coll (MN)
Springfield Tech Comm
 Coll (MA)
Valencia Comm Coll (FL)
Virginia Coll at Austin (TX)

**Diesel Mechanics
Technology**
Alexandria Tech Coll (MN)
Black Hawk Coll,
 Moline (IL)
Central Comm Coll–
 Hastings Campus (NE)
Centralia Coll (WA)
Century Coll (MN)
Clark Coll (WA)
Coll of Southern Idaho (ID)
Coll of the Redwoods (CA)
Dixie State Coll of
 Utah (UT)
Elizabethtown Tech
 Coll (KY)
Grays Harbor Coll (WA)
Great Basin Coll (NV)
Illinois Eastern Comm
 Colls, Wabash Valley
 College (IL)
Johnston Comm Coll (NC)
Lamar Inst of
 Technology (TX)
Laramie County Comm
 Coll (WY)
Linn-Benton Comm
 Coll (OR)
Lower Columbia Coll (WA)
Massasoit Comm
 Coll (MA)
Mid-Plains Comm Coll,
 North Platte (NE)
North Central Kansas Tech
 Coll (KS)
Northeast Comm Coll (NE)
Northwest Iowa Comm
 Coll (IA)

Northwest KansasTech
Coll (KS)
Ohio Tech Coll (OH)
Ozarks Tech Comm
Coll (MO)
Peninsula Coll (WA)
Raritan Valley Comm
Coll (NJ)
Riverland Comm Coll (MN)
St. Cloud Tech Coll (MN)
St. Philip's Coll (TX)
Salt Lake Comm Coll (UT)
San Juan Coll (NM)
Santa Ana Coll (CA)
Scott Comm Coll (IA)
Shasta Coll (CA)
Sheridan Coll–Sheridan
and Gillette (WY)
Skagit Valley Coll (WA)
Southeast Tech Inst (SD)
Texas State Tech Coll–
Marshall (TX)
Texas State Tech Coll
West Texas (TX)
The U of Montana-Helena
Coll of Technology (MT)
Western Wyoming Comm
Coll (WY)

Dietetics
Bakersfield Coll (CA)
Baltimore City Comm
Coll (MD)
Briarwood Coll (CT)
Brigham Young U –
Idaho (ID)
Central Arizona Coll (AZ)
Chaffey Coll (CA)
Cincinnati State Tech and
Comm Coll (OH)
City Coll of San
Francisco (CA)
Coll of Southern Idaho (ID)
Comm Coll of
Philadelphia (PA)
Fiorello H. LaGuardia
Comm Coll of the City
U of New York (NY)
Fresno City Coll (CA)
Gateway Comm Coll (CT)
Grossmont Coll (CA)
Harper Coll (IL)
Harrisburg Area Comm
Coll (PA)
Hocking Coll (OH)
Lawson State Comm
Coll (AL)
Los Angeles City Coll (CA)
Madison Area Tech
Coll (WI)
Manatee Comm Coll (FL)
Merced Coll (CA)
Miami Dade Coll (FL)
Oklahoma State U,
Okmulgee (OK)
Orange Coast Coll (CA)
St. Louis Comm Coll at
Florissant Valley (MO)
Santa Rosa Jr Coll (CA)
Southern Maine Comm
Coll (ME)
South Plains Coll (TX)
Spokane Comm Coll (WA)
State U of New York Coll
of Agriculture and
Technology at
Morrisville (NY)
Suffolk County Comm
Coll (NY)
Westchester Comm
Coll (NY)
Western Nebraska Comm
Coll (NE)
Westmoreland County
Comm Coll (PA)

Dietetic Technician
Front Range Comm
Coll (CO)
Miami Dade Coll (FL)

Dietitian Assistant
Barton County Comm
Coll (KS)
Comm Coll of Allegheny
County (PA)
Erie Comm Coll, North
Campus (NY)
Martin Comm Coll (NC)

**Digital
Communication and
Media/Multimedia**
Brevard Comm Coll (FL)
Central Wyoming
Coll (WY)
Hillsborough Comm
Coll (FL)
Laramie County Comm
Coll (WY)

Lehigh Carbon Comm
Coll (PA)
Olympic Coll (WA)
Platt Coll San Diego (CA)
School of Communication
Arts (NC)
Trinidad State Jr Coll (CO)

**Drafting and Design
Technology**
Albany Tech Coll (GA)
Allen County Comm
Coll (KS)
Alpena Comm Coll (MI)
Amarillo Coll (TX)
Antelope Valley Coll (CA)
Arizona Western Coll (AZ)
Bainbridge Coll (GA)
Bakersfield Coll (CA)
Baltimore City Comm
Coll (MD)
Barstow Coll (CA)
Beaufort County Comm
Coll (NC)
Bergen Comm Coll (NJ)
Bishop State Comm
Coll (AL)
Brevard Comm Coll (FL)
Brigham Young U –
Idaho (ID)
Burlington County
Coll (NJ)
Cabrillo Coll (CA)
Caldwell Comm Coll and
Tech Inst (NC)
Calhoun Cornm Coll (AL)
Central Carolina Comm
Coll (NC)
Central Comm Coll–
Columbus
Campus (NE)
Central Comm Coll–Grand
Island Campus (NE)
Central Comm Coll–
Hastings Campus (NE)
Central Florida Comm
Coll (FL)
Central Georgia Tech
Coll (GA)
Central Ohio Tech
Coll (OH)
Central Piedmont Comm
Coll (NC)
Central Texas Coll (TX)
Central Virginia Comm
Coll (VA)
Cerritos Coll (CA)
Chaffey Coll (CA)
Chattahoochee Tech
Coll (GA)
Chattanooga State Tech
Comm Coll (TN)
Chippewa Valley Tech
Coll (WI)
Cisco Jr Coll (TX)
Citrus Coll (CA)
City Colls of Chicago,
Harry S. Truman
College (IL)
City Colls of Chicago,
Richard J. Daley
College (IL)
Clackamas Comm
Coll (OR)
Clark State Comm
Coll (OH)
Coastal Bend Coll (TX)
Cochise Coll, Sierra
Vista (AZ)
Coll of DuPage (IL)
Coll of San Mateo (CA)
Coll of Southern Idaho (ID)
Coll of the Canyons (CA)
Coll of the Desert (CA)
Coll of the Redwoods (CA)
Collin County Comm Coll
District (TX)
Columbus Tech Coll (GA)
Comm Coll of Allegheny
County (PA)
Comm Coll of Beaver
County (PA)
Comm Coll of
Philadelphia (PA)
Comm Coll of Southern
Nevada (NV)
Contra Costa Coll (CA)
Cosumnes River Coll,
Sacramento (CA)
Crowder Coll (MO)
Dabney S. Lancaster
Comm Coll (VA)
DeKalb Tech Coll (GA)
Don Bosco Tech Inst (CA)
East Central Coll (MO)
Eastern Arizona Coll (AZ)
Eastern New Mexico
U–Roswell (NM)

Elaine P. Nunez Comm
Coll (LA)
El Camino Coll (CA)
El Centro Coll (TX)
Elgin Comm Coll (IL)
Everett Comm Coll (WA)
Finger Lakes Comm
Coll (NY)
Florence-Darlington Tech
Coll (SC)
Forsyth Tech Comm
Coll (NC)
Fox Valley Tech Coll (WI)
Frederick Comm Coll (MD)
Fresno City Coll (CA)
Fullerton Coll (CA)
Genesee Comm Coll (NY)
George C. Wallace Comm
Coll (AL)
Gloucester County
Coll (NJ)
Golden West Coll (CA)
Grand Rapids Comm
Coll (MI)
Grayson County Coll (TX)
Greenville Tech Coll (SC)
Griffin Tech Coll (GA)
Guilford Tech Comm
Coll (NC)
Gwinnett Tech Coll (GA)
Harper Coll (IL)
Hartnell Coll (CA)
Hawkeye Comm Coll (IA)
H. Councill Trenholm State
Tech Coll (AL)
Henry Ford Comm
Coll (MI)
Herzing Coll (WI)
Hocking Coll (OH)
Houston Comm Coll
System (TX)
Hutchinson Comm Coll
and Area Vocational
School (KS)
Illinois Valley Comm
Coll (IL)
Inst of Design and
Construction (NY)
Iowa Lakes Comm
Coll (IA)
Isothermal Comm
Coll (NC)
Jefferson Comm Coll (OH)
J. F. Drake State Tech
Coll (AL)
Jones County Jr Coll (MS)
Kankakee Comm Coll (IL)
Kansas City Kansas
Comm Coll (KS)
Kellogg Comm Coll (MI)
Kennebec Valley Comm
Coll (ME)
Kirkwood Comm Coll (IA)
Kirtland Comm Coll (MI)
Labette Comm Coll (KS)
Lake Land Coll (IL)
Lanier Tech Coll (GA)
Lansing Comm Coll (MI)
Las Positas Coll (CA)
Lassen Comm Coll
District (CA)
Lawson State Comm
Coll (AL)
Lee Coll (TX)
Leeward Comm Coll (HI)
Lehigh Carbon Comm
Coll (PA)
Lenoir Comm Coll (NC)
Linn-Benton Comm
Coll (OR)
Linn State Tech Coll (MO)
Lorain County Comm
Coll (OH)
Los Angeles City Coll (CA)
Los Angeles Harbor
Coll (CA)
Los Angeles Pierce
Coll (CA)
Los Angeles Southwest
Coll (CA)
Los Medanos Coll (CA)
Macomb Comm Coll (MI)
Manatee Comm Coll (FL)
Massachusetts Bay Comm
Coll (MA)
Meridian Comm Coll (MS)
Mesa Comm Coll (AZ)
Metropolitan Comm
Coll (NE)
Metropolitan Comm
Coll–Business &
Technology
Campus (MO)
Miami Dade Coll (FL)
Middle Georgia Tech
Coll (GA)
Minnesota State Coll–
Southeast Tech (MN)

Mission Coll (CA)
Mississippi Gulf Coast
Comm Coll (MS)
Moberly Area Comm
Coll (MO)
Mohawk Valley Comm
Coll (NY)
Montcalm Comm Coll (MI)
Morton Coll (IL)
Mott Comm Coll (MI)
Mt. San Antonio Coll (CA)
Murray State Coll (OK)
Muskegon Comm Coll (MI)
Napa Valley Coll (CA)
Naugatuck Valley Comm
Coll (CT)
Navarro Coll (TX)
New Hampshire Comm
Tech Coll, Manchester/
Stratham (NH)
New Hampshire Comm
Tech Coll, Nashua/
Claremont (NH)
New Mexico Jr Coll (NM)
New River Comm Coll (VA)
New York City Coll of
Technology of the City
U of New York (NY)
Niagara County Comm
Coll (NY)
North Central Michigan
Coll (MI)
North Central Missouri
Coll (MO)
North Central Texas
Coll (TX)
Northeast Comm Coll (NE)
Northeast State Tech
Comm Coll (TN)
Northern Maine Comm
Coll (ME)
Northern Oklahoma
Coll (OK)
North Idaho Coll (ID)
Northland Comm and Tech
Coll–Thief River
Falls (MN)
NorthWest Arkansas
Comm Coll (AR)
Northwestern Tech
Coll (GA)
Northwest Mississippi
Comm Coll (MS)
Northwest-Shoals Comm
Coll (AL)
Odessa Coll (TX)
Ohlone Coll (CA)
Oklahoma City Comm
Coll (OK)
Oklahoma State U,
Okmulgee (OK)
Olympic Coll (WA)
Onondaga Comm
Coll (NY)
Orange Coast Coll (CA)
Palm Beach Comm
Coll (FL)
Pasadena City Coll (CA)
Pasco-Hernando Comm
Coll (FL)
Pearl River Comm
Coll (MS)
Piedmont Tech Coll (SC)
Porterville Coll (CA)
Pulaski Tech Coll (AR)
Redlands Comm Coll (OK)
Red Rocks Comm
Coll (CO)
Richland Comm Coll (IL)
Ridgewater Coll (MN)
Rose State Coll (OK)
Sacramento City Coll (CA)
Saint Charles Comm
Coll (MO)
Salt Lake Comm Coll (UT)
San Antonio Coll (TX)
San Bernardino Valley
Coll (CA)
San Diego City Coll (CA)
San Joaquin Delta
Coll (CA)
San Juan Coll (NM)
Santa Ana Coll (CA)
Santa Barbara City
Coll (CA)
Schoolcraft Coll (MI)
Seminole Comm Coll (FL)
Shasta Coll (CA)
Sheridan Coll–Sheridan
and Gillette (WY)
Southeastern Comm Coll,
North Campus (IA)
Southeast Tech Inst (SD)
Southern Maine Comm
Coll (ME)
Southern State Comm
Coll (OH)

South Florida Comm
Coll (FL)
South Georgia Tech
Coll (GA)
South Piedmont Comm
Coll (NC)
South Plains Coll (TX)
South Seattle Comm
Coll (WA)
Southside Virginia Comm
Coll (VA)
Southwestern Indian
Polytechnic Inst (NM)
Southwestern Michigan
Coll (MI)
Southwest Virginia Comm
Coll (VA)
Spokane Comm Coll (WA)
Stark State Coll of
Technology (OH)
State U of New York Coll
of Agriculture and
Technology at
Morrisville (NY)
State U of New York Coll
of Technology at
Alfred (NY)
Suffolk County Comm
Coll (NY)
Surry Comm Coll (NC)
Swainsboro Tech Coll (GA)
Taft Coll (CA)
Temple Coll (TX)
Texarkana Coll (TX)
Texas State Tech Coll
West Texas (TX)
Three Rivers Comm
Coll (CT)
Tidewater Comm Coll (VA)
Treasure Valley Comm
Coll (OR)
Trinidad State Jr Coll (CO)
Tulsa Comm Coll (OK)
Tyler Jr Coll (TX)
Ulster County Comm
Coll (NY)
U of Arkansas Comm Coll
at Morrilton (AR)
Valdosta Tech Coll (GA)
Valencia Comm Coll (FL)
Vernon Coll (TX)
Victoria Coll (TX)
Vincennes U Jasper
Campus (IN)
Virginia Highlands Comm
Coll (VA)
Wallace State Comm
Coll (AL)
Washington State Comm
Coll (OH)
Western Nevada Comm
Coll (NV)
Western Piedmont Comm
Coll (NC)
West Los Angeles
Coll (CA)
Westmoreland County
Comm Coll (PA)
West Valley Coll (CA)
West Virginia U at
Parkersburg (WV)
Wright State U, Lake
Campus (OH)
Wytheville Comm Coll (VA)
York County Comm
Coll (ME)
Zane State Coll (OH)

**Drafting/Design
Engineering
Technologies Related**
Comm Coll of Allegheny
County (PA)
Front Range Comm
Coll (CO)

**Drafting/Design
Technology**
Flint Hills Tech Coll (KS)
Lamar Inst of
Technology (TX)
Miller-Motte Tech Coll,
Clarksville (TN)
North Arkansas Coll (AR)

**Drama and Dance
Teacher Education**
Western Nebraska Comm
Coll (NE)

Dramatic/Theater Arts
Allen County Comm
Coll (KS)
Amarillo Coll (TX)
American Academy of
Dramatic Arts (NY)
Arizona Western Coll (AZ)
Bainbridge Coll (GA)
Bakersfield Coll (CA)

Barton County Comm
Coll (KS)
Bergen Comm Coll (NJ)
Berkshire Comm Coll (MA)
Blinn Coll (TX)
Brigham Young U –
Idaho (ID)
Bucks County Comm
Coll (PA)
Burlington County
Coll (NJ)
Calhoun Comm Coll (AL)
Cañada Coll (CA)
Cape Cod Comm
Coll (MA)
Centralia Coll (WA)
Central Wyoming
Coll (WY)
Cerritos Coll (CA)
Chaffey Coll (CA)
Citrus Coll (CA)
City Colls of Chicago,
Harold Washington
College (IL)
City Colls of Chicago,
Richard J. Daley
College (IL)
Clarendon Coll (TX)
Clark State Comm
Coll (OH)
Coastal Bend Coll (TX)
Colby Comm Coll (KS)
Coll of Marin (CA)
Coll of Southern Idaho (ID)
Coll of Southern
Maryland (MD)
Coll of The Albemarle (NC)
Coll of the Desert (CA)
Coll of the Mainland (TX)
Colorado Mountain
Coll (CO)
Columbia Coll (CA)
Comm Coll of Allegheny
County (PA)
Comm Coll of Rhode
Island (RI)
Comm Coll of Southern
Nevada (NV)
Cosumnes River Coll,
Sacramento (CA)
Crafton Hills Coll (CA)
Crowder Coll (MO)
Cypress Coll (CA)
Dean Coll (MA)
De Anza Coll (CA)
Dixie State Coll of
Utah (UT)
Dodge City Comm
Coll (KS)
Eastern Arizona Coll (AZ)
El Camino Coll (CA)
Everett Comm Coll (WA)
Finger Lakes Comm
Coll (NY)
Fresno City Coll (CA)
Fullerton Coll (CA)
Fulton-Montgomery Comm
Coll (NY)
Genesee Comm Coll (NY)
Gloucester County
Coll (NJ)
Gordon Coll (GA)
Grayson County Coll (TX)
Grossmont Coll (CA)
Guilford Tech Comm
Coll (NC)
Harrisburg Area Comm
Coll (PA)
Henry Ford Comm
Coll (MI)
Hillsborough Comm
Coll (FL)
Holyoke Comm Coll (MA)
Houston Comm Coll
System (TX)
Howard Comm Coll (MD)
Kellogg Comm Coll (MI)
Kingsborough Comm Coll
of the City U of New
York (NY)
Kirkwood Comm Coll (IA)
Lake Tahoe Comm
Coll (CA)
Laney Coll (CA)
Lansing Comm Coll (MI)
Laramie County Comm
Coll (WY)
Lee Coll (TX)
Linn-Benton Comm
Coll (OR)
Lorain County Comm
Coll (OH)
Los Angeles City Coll (CA)
Los Angeles Mission
Coll (CA)
Los Angeles Pierce
Coll (CA)

Los Angeles Southwest Coll (CA)
Lower Columbia Coll (WA)
Manatee Comm Coll (FL)
Massasoit Comm Coll (MA)
Mendocino Coll (CA)
Merced Coll (CA)
Miami Dade Coll (FL)
Mississippi Delta Comm Coll (MS)
Mohawk Valley Comm Coll (NY)
Monterey Peninsula Coll (CA)
Moorpark Coll (CA)
Nassau Comm Coll (NY)
Navarro Coll (TX)
New Mexico Jr Coll (NM)
Niagara County Comm Coll (NY)
Northeast Comm Coll (NE)
Northeastern Jr Coll (CO)
Northern Essex Comm Coll (MA)
North Idaho Coll (ID)
Oklahoma City Comm Coll (OK)
Orange Coast Coll (CA)
Oxnard Coll (CA)
Palm Beach Comm Coll (FL)
Pasadena City Coll (CA)
Pima Comm Coll (AZ)
Quincy Coll (MA)
Raritan Valley Comm Coll (NJ)
Ridgewater Coll (MN)
Rose State Coll (OK)
Sacramento City Coll (CA)
St. Louis Comm Coll at Florissant Valley (MO)
St. Philip's Coll (TX)
San Diego City Coll (CA)
San Joaquin Delta Coll (CA)
San Juan Coll (NM)
Santa Ana Coll (CA)
Santa Barbara City Coll (CA)
Santa Rosa Jr Coll (CA)
Santiago Canyon Coll (CA)
Scottsdale Comm Coll (AZ)
Shasta Coll (CA)
South Georgia Coll (GA)
Suffolk County Comm Coll (NY)
Texarkana Coll (TX)
Three Rivers Comm Coll (CT)
Treasure Valley Comm Coll (OR)
Trinidad State Jr Coll (CO)
Tulsa Comm Coll (OK)
Umpqua Comm Coll (OR)
Valencia Comm Coll (FL)
Ventura Coll (CA)
Victor Valley Coll (CA)
Virginia Highlands Comm Coll (VA)
Western Wyoming Comm Coll (WY)
West Valley Coll (CA)
Young Harris Coll (GA)
Yuba Coll (CA)

Dramatic/Theater Arts and Stagecraft Related
St. Philip's Coll (TX)

Drawing
Cañada Coll (CA)
Coll of San Mateo (CA)
De Anza Coll (CA)
Dixie State Coll of Utah (UT)
Everett Comm Coll (WA)
Grossmont Coll (CA)
Henry Ford Comm Coll (MI)
Iowa Lakes Comm Coll (IA)
Keystone Coll (PA)
Lassen Comm Coll District (CA)
Monterey Peninsula Coll (CA)
Northeastern Jr Coll (CO)
Pasadena City Coll (CA)
San Joaquin Delta Coll (CA)

Early Childhood Education
Arkansas State U–Newport (AR)
Asnuntuck Comm Coll (CT)

Barton County Comm Coll (KS)
Berkshire Comm Coll (MA)
Brevard Comm Coll (FL)
Central Florida Comm Coll (FL)
Central Oregon Comm Coll (OR)
Clark Coll (WA)
Cochise Coll, Douglas (AZ)
Coll of Micronesia–FSM (FM)
Coll of Southern Maryland (MD)
Colorado Mountain Coll, Timberline Campus (CO)
Dean Coll (MA)
Fayetteville Tech Comm Coll (NC)
Folsom Lake Coll (CA)
Front Range Comm Coll (CO)
Hagerstown Comm Coll (MD)
Hopkinsville Comm Coll (KY)
Iowa Lakes Comm Coll (IA)
John Wood Comm Coll (IL)
Kent State U, Tuscarawas Campus (OH)
Keystone Coll (PA)
Kingsborough Comm Coll of the City U of New York (NY)
Laramie County Comm Coll (WY)
Leech Lake Tribal Coll (MN)
Lower Columbia Coll (WA)
Minnesota State Comm and Tech Coll–Fergus Falls (MN)
Mott Comm Coll (MI)
Nebraska Indian Comm Coll (NE)
North Central Missouri Coll (MO)
North Seattle Comm Coll (WA)
Oklahoma State U, Oklahoma City (OK)
Olympic Coll (WA)
Owens Comm Coll, Toledo (OH)
Parkland Coll (IL)
Quincy Coll (MA)
Robeson Comm Coll (NC)
St. Philip's Coll (TX)
Tri-County Comm Coll (NC)
U of New Mexico–Taos (NM)
Waukesha County Tech Coll (WI)
Western Wyoming Comm Coll (WY)

Ecology
Brigham Young U–Idaho (ID)
Coll of Marin (CA)
Dixie State Coll of Utah (UT)
Everett Comm Coll (WA)
Hocking Coll (OH)
Iowa Lakes Comm Coll (IA)
Joliet Jr Coll (IL)
Tulsa Comm Coll (OK)
Western Nebraska Comm Coll (NE)

E-Commerce
Augusta Tech Coll (GA)
Central Georgia Tech Coll (GA)
Fayetteville Tech Comm Coll (NC)
North Central Missouri Coll (MO)
Pasco-Hernando Comm Coll (FL)
St. Philip's Coll (TX)
Texas State Tech Coll–Marshall (TX)
Valdosta Tech Coll (GA)

Economics
Allen County Comm Coll (KS)
Anne Arundel Comm Coll (MD)
Bakersfield Coll (CA)
Barton County Comm Coll (KS)
Bergen Comm Coll (NJ)
Brigham Young U–Idaho (ID)

Cañada Coll (CA)
Cerritos Coll (CA)
Chaffey Coll (CA)
Clarendon Coll (TX)
Coastal Bend Coll (TX)
Coll of the Desert (CA)
Comm Coll of Southern Nevada (NV)
Crafton Hills Coll (CA)
Cypress Coll (CA)
De Anza Coll (CA)
Dixie State Coll of Utah (UT)
El Camino Coll (CA)
Everett Comm Coll (WA)
Foothill Coll (CA)
Fullerton Coll (CA)
Georgia Highlands Coll (GA)
Grossmont Coll (CA)
Hartnell Coll (CA)
Iowa Lakes Comm Coll (IA)
Jones County Jr Coll (MS)
Laramie County Comm Coll (WY)
Lee Coll (TX)
Linn-Benton Comm Coll (OR)
Los Angeles Mission Coll (CA)
Los Angeles Southwest Coll (CA)
Louisburg Coll (NC)
Lower Columbia Coll (WA)
Manatee Comm Coll (FL)
Miami Dade Coll (FL)
Miami U–Middletown Campus (OH)
Mississippi Delta Comm Coll (MS)
Monterey Peninsula Coll (CA)
Muskegon Comm Coll (MI)
New Mexico Military Inst (NM)
Northeastern Jr Coll (CO)
Orange Coast Coll (CA)
Oxnard Coll (CA)
Palm Beach Comm Coll (FL)
Palo Alto Coll (TX)
Pasadena City Coll (CA)
Potomac State Coll of West Virginia U (WV)
Red Rocks Comm Coll (CO)
St. Philip's Coll (TX)
Salt Lake Comm Coll (UT)
San Bernardino Valley Coll (CA)
San Joaquin Delta Coll (CA)
San Juan Coll (NM)
Santa Ana Coll (CA)
Santa Barbara City Coll (CA)
Santa Rosa Jr Coll (CA)
Santiago Canyon Coll (CA)
Skagit Valley Coll (WA)
South Georgia Coll (GA)
Treasure Valley Comm Coll (OR)
Tulsa Comm Coll (OK)
Umpqua Comm Coll (OR)
Wenatchee Valley Coll (WA)
Western Nebraska Comm Coll (NE)
Western Wyoming Comm Coll (WY)
West Los Angeles Coll (CA)
West Valley Coll (CA)

Education
Anne Arundel Comm Coll (MD)
Arizona Western Coll (AZ)
Bainbridge Coll (GA)
Barstow Coll (CA)
Bergen Comm Coll (NJ)
Bowling Green State U–Firelands Coll (OH)
Brigham Young U–Idaho (ID)
Bucks County Comm Coll (PA)
Burlington County Coll (NJ)
Calhoun Comm Coll (AL)
Cape Cod Comm Coll (MA)
Cecil Comm Coll (MD)
Central Oregon Comm Coll (OR)
Central Virginia Comm Coll (VA)

Chipola Coll (FL)
Cisco Jr Coll (TX)
City Colls of Chicago, Harry S. Truman College (IL)
City Colls of Chicago, Kennedy-King College (IL)
City Colls of Chicago, Richard J. Daley College (IL)
Clarendon Coll (TX)
Coastal Bend Coll (TX)
Cochise Coll, Douglas (AZ)
Cochise Coll, Sierra Vista (AZ)
Colby Comm Coll (KS)
Coll of Menominee Nation (WI)
Coll of Micronesia–FSM (FM)
Coll of Southern Idaho (ID)
Coll of Southern Maryland (MD)
Coll of The Albemarle (NC)
Coll of the Desert (CA)
Comm Coll of Beaver County (PA)
Comm Coll of Philadelphia (PA)
Comm Coll of Vermont (VT)
Crowder Coll (MO)
Dabney S. Lancaster Comm Coll (VA)
Danville Comm Coll (VA)
Dodge City Comm Coll (KS)
Eastern Shore Comm Coll (VA)
East Georgia Coll (GA)
Everett Comm Coll (WA)
Fiorello H. LaGuardia Comm Coll of the City U of New York (NY)
Florida National Coll (FL)
Folsom Lake Coll (CA)
Frederick Comm Coll (MD)
Garrett Coll (MD)
Genesee Comm Coll (NY)
Germanna Comm Coll (VA)
Gloucester County Coll (NJ)
Gordon Coll (GA)
Grayson County Coll (TX)
Hagerstown Comm Coll (MD)
Harrisburg Area Comm Coll (PA)
Hawkeye Comm Coll (IA)
Hillsborough Comm Coll (FL)
Hutchinson Comm Coll and Area Vocational School (KS)
Illinois Valley Comm Coll (IL)
Iowa Lakes Comm Coll (IA)
Isothermal Comm Coll (NC)
Itasca Comm Coll (MN)
Joliet Jr Coll (IL)
Jones County Jr Coll (MS)
Kennebec Valley Comm Coll (ME)
Kingsborough Comm Coll of the City U of New York (NY)
Kirkwood Comm Coll (IA)
Labette Comm Coll (KS)
Lansing Comm Coll (MI)
Laramie County Comm Coll (WY)
Las Positas Coll (CA)
Lawson State Comm Coll (AL)
Lee Coll (TX)
Lehigh Carbon Comm Coll (PA)
Linn-Benton Comm Coll (OR)
Lorain County Comm Coll (OH)
Los Angeles Southwest Coll (CA)
Miami Dade Coll (FL)
Miami U–Middletown Campus (OH)
Mississippi Delta Comm Coll (MS)
Mississippi Gulf Coast Comm Coll (MS)
Montgomery Coll (MD)
Muskegon Comm Coll (MI)
National American U, Rio Rancho (NM)

National Park Comm Coll (AR)
Navarro Coll (TX)
New Mexico Jr Coll (NM)
New Mexico State U–Alamogordo (NM)
New River Comm Coll (VA)
Northampton County Area Comm Coll (PA)
Northeast Comm Coll (NE)
Northeastern Jr Coll (CO)
Northern Essex Comm Coll (MA)
Northern Marianas Coll (MP)
North Idaho Coll (ID)
NorthWest Arkansas Comm Coll (AR)
Northwest Mississippi Comm Coll (MS)
Northwest-Shoals Comm Coll (AL)
Odessa Coll (TX)
Oklahoma State U, Oklahoma City (OK)
Palau Comm Coll (Palau)
Palm Beach Comm Coll (FL)
Palo Alto Coll (TX)
Paul D. Camp Comm Coll (VA)
Piedmont Virginia Comm Coll (VA)
Porterville Coll (CA)
Potomac State Coll of West Virginia U (WV)
Raritan Valley Comm Coll (NJ)
Redlands Comm Coll (OK)
Roane State Comm Coll (TN)
St. Catharine Coll (KY)
St. Philip's Coll (TX)
San Juan Coll (NM)
Santa Rosa Jr Coll (CA)
Schoolcraft Coll (MI)
Sheridan Coll–Sheridan and Gillette (WY)
Sitting Bull Coll (ND)
South Florida Comm Coll (FL)
South Georgia Coll (GA)
South Plains Coll (TX)
Southside Virginia Comm Coll (VA)
South Texas Coll (TX)
Southwest Mississippi Comm Coll (MS)
Southwest Texas Jr Coll (TX)
Southwest Virginia Comm Coll (VA)
Three Rivers Comm Coll (MO)
Tidewater Comm Coll (VA)
Treasure Valley Comm Coll (OR)
Trinidad State Jr Coll (CO)
Tulsa Comm Coll (OK)
Umpqua Comm Coll (OR)
U of Arkansas Comm Coll at Batesville (AR)
U of New Mexico–Gallup (NM)
U of New Mexico–Taos (NM)
U of New Mexico–Valencia Campus (NM)
U of Puerto Rico at Carolina (PR)
Villa Maria Coll of Buffalo (NY)
Vincennes U Jasper Campus (IN)
Virginia Highlands Comm Coll (VA)
Virginia Western Comm Coll (VA)
Wallace State Comm Coll (AL)
Warren County Comm Coll (NJ)
Washington State Comm Coll (OH)
Wenatchee Valley Coll (WA)
Western Texas Coll (TX)
Western Wyoming Comm Coll (WY)
West Los Angeles Coll (CA)
West Virginia U at Parkersburg (WV)
Wytheville Comm Coll (VA)
Young Harris Coll (GA)
Yuba Coll (CA)

Educational/Instructional Media Design
Century Coll (MN)
City Coll of San Francisco (CA)
Collin County Comm Coll District (TX)
Hutchinson Comm Coll and Area Vocational School (KS)

Education (K-12)
Angelina Coll (TX)
Cecil Comm Coll (MD)
Itasca Comm Coll (MN)
Keystone Coll (PA)
Vincennes U Jasper Campus (IN)

Education (Multiple Levels)
Carroll Comm Coll (MD)
Coastal Georgia Comm Coll (GA)
Louisburg Coll (NC)
Western Wyoming Comm Coll (WY)

Education Related
Guilford Tech Comm Coll (NC)
Rogue Comm Coll (OR)

Education (Specific Levels and Methods) Related
Comm Coll of Allegheny County (PA)
Laramie County Comm Coll (WY)

Education (Specific Subject Areas) Related
Comm Coll of Allegheny County (PA)

Electrical and Electronic Engineering Technologies Related
Albany Tech Coll (GA)
Cincinnati State Tech and Comm Coll (OH)
Colegio Universitario de San Juan, San Juan (PR)
Eugenio María de Hostos Comm Coll of the City U of New York (NY)
Massasoit Comm Coll (MA)
Miami Dade Coll (FL)
Miami U Hamilton (OH)
Minnesota State Comm and Tech Coll–Fergus Falls (MN)
Mohawk Valley Comm Coll (NY)
National Inst of Technology (OH)
Remington Coll–Dallas Campus (TX)
Southwestern Michigan Coll (MI)
Springfield Tech Comm Coll (MA)
Vatterott Coll, Oklahoma City (OK)
West Virginia State Comm and Tech Coll (WV)
York Tech Coll (SC)

Electrical and Power Transmission Installation
Oklahoma State U, Oklahoma City (OK)
Orange Coast Coll (CA)
St. Cloud Tech Coll (MN)
Western Nevada Comm Coll (NV)

Electrical and Power Transmission Installation Related
Calhoun Comm Coll (AL)
Martin Comm Coll (NC)

Electrical, Electronic and Communications Engineering Technology
Aims Comm Coll (CO)
Alamance Comm Coll (NC)
Allen County Comm Coll (KS)
Amarillo Coll (TX)
Angelina Coll (TX)

Anne Arundel Comm Coll (MD)
Antelope Valley Coll (CA)
Arizona Western Coll (AZ)
Athens Tech Coll (GA)
Augusta Tech Coll (GA)
Bainbridge Coll (GA)
Bakersfield Coll (CA)
Baltimore City Comm Coll (MD)
Barstow Coll (CA)
Beaufort County Comm Coll (NC)
Bergen Comm Coll (NJ)
Berkshire Comm Coll (MA)
Bishop State Comm Coll (AL)
Bladen Comm Coll (NC)
Bowling Green State U–Firelands Coll (OH)
Bramson ORT Coll (NY)
Brevard Comm Coll (FL)
Brigham Young U – Idaho (ID)
Broome Comm Coll (NY)
Broward Comm Coll (FL)
Brown Mackie Coll–Akron (OH)
Brown Mackie Coll–Atlanta (GA)
Brown Mackie Coll–Cincinnati (OH)
Brown Mackie Coll–Findlay (OH)
Brown Mackie Coll–Fort Wayne (IN)
Brown Mackie Coll–Hopkinsville (KY)
Brown Mackie Coll–Kansas City (KS)
Brown Mackie Coll–Louisville (KY)
Brown Mackie Coll–North Canton (OH)
Brown Mackie Coll–Salina (KS)
Brown Mackie Coll–South Bend (IN)
Brunswick Comm Coll (NC)
Burlington County Coll (NJ)
Cabrillo Coll (CA)
Caldwell Comm Coll and Tech Inst (NC)
Calhoun Comm Coll (AL)
Cape Fear Comm Coll (NC)
Capital Comm Coll (CT)
Catawba Valley Comm Coll (NC)
Cecil Comm Coll (MD)
Central Carolina Comm Coll (NC)
Central Comm Coll–Columbus Campus (NE)
Central Comm Coll–Grand Island Campus (NE)
Central Comm Coll–Hastings Campus (NE)
Central Georgia Tech Coll (GA)
Centralia Coll (WA)
Central New Mexico Comm Coll (NM)
Central Ohio Tech Coll (OH)
Central Piedmont Comm Coll (NC)
Central Texas Coll (TX)
Central Virginia Comm Coll (VA)
Cerritos Coll (CA)
Chaffey Coll (CA)
Chattahoochee Tech Coll (GA)
Chattanooga State Tech Comm Coll (TN)
Chesapeake Coll (MD)
Chippewa Valley Tech Coll (WI)
Cincinnati State Tech and Comm Coll (OH)
Cisco Jr Coll (TX)
Citrus Coll (CA)
City Coll of San Francisco (CA)
City Colls of Chicago, Olive-Harvey College (IL)
City Colls of Chicago, Richard J. Daley College (IL)
Clark Coll (WA)
Clark State Comm Coll (OH)
Cleveland Comm Coll (NC)

Clinton Comm Coll (IA)
Cochise Coll, Douglas (AZ)
Cochise Coll, Sierra Vista (AZ)
Colegio Universitario de San Juan, San Juan (PR)
Coll of DuPage (IL)
Coll of Lake County (IL)
Coll of Marin (CA)
Coll of San Mateo (CA)
Coll of Southern Idaho (ID)
Coll of Southern Maryland (MD)
Coll of the Canyons (CA)
Coll of the Redwoods (CA)
Collin County Comm Coll District (TX)
Columbia Basin Coll (WA)
Columbus Tech Coll (GA)
Comm Coll of Allegheny County (PA)
Comm Coll of Beaver County (PA)
Comm Coll of Philadelphia (PA)
Comm Coll of Rhode Island (RI)
Comm Coll of Southern Nevada (NV)
Contra Costa Coll (CA)
Cosumnes River Coll, Sacramento (CA)
Crowder Coll (MO)
Cuesta Coll (CA)
Dabney S. Lancaster Comm Coll (NY)
Davidson County Comm Coll (NC)
DeKalb Tech Coll (GA)
Dodge City Comm Coll (KS)
Don Bosco Tech Inst (CA)
Dyersburg State Comm Coll (TN)
East Central Coll (MO)
Eastern Shore Comm Coll (VA)
ECPI Coll of Technology (VA)
ECPI Tech Coll (VA)
ECPI Tech Coll (VA)
Elaine P. Nunez Comm Coll (LA)
El Camino Coll (CA)
Elgin Comm Coll (IL)
Erie Comm Coll, North Campus (NY)
Essex County Coll (NJ)
Fayetteville Tech Comm Coll (NC)
Flint River Tech Coll (GA)
Florence-Darlington Tech Coll (SC)
Foothill Coll (CA)
Forsyth Tech Comm Coll (NC)
Fountainhead Coll of Technology (TN)
Fox Valley Tech Coll (WI)
Frederick Comm Coll (MD)
Fulton-Montgomery Comm Coll (NY)
Gateway Comm Coll (CT)
Gateway Tech Coll (WI)
Genesee Comm Coll (NY)
George C. Wallace Comm Coll (AL)
Georgia Highlands Coll (GA)
Golden West Coll (CA)
Grand Rapids Comm Coll (MI)
Grayson County Coll (TX)
Great Basin Coll (NV)
Greenville Tech Coll (SC)
Griffin Tech Coll (GA)
Guilford Tech Comm Coll (NC)
Gwinnett Tech Coll (GA)
Harper Coll (IL)
Harrisburg Area Comm Coll (PA)
Hartnell Coll (CA)
H. Councill Trenholm State Tech Coll (AL)
Heart of Georgia Tech Coll (GA)
Hennepin Tech Coll (MN)
Henry Ford Comm Coll (MI)
Herzing Coll (WI)
Hillsborough Comm Coll (FL)
Hocking Coll (OH)
Hopkinsville Comm Coll (KY)

Houston Comm Coll System (TX)
Howard Comm Coll (MD)
Illinois Eastern Comm Colls, Wabash Valley College (IL)
Illinois Valley Comm Coll (IL)
Island Drafting and Tech Inst (NY)
Isothermal Comm Coll (NC)
ITT Tech Inst, Tucson (AZ)
ITT Tech Inst, Lathrop (CA)
ITT Tech Inst, Oxnard (CA)
ITT Tech Inst, San Dimas (CA)
ITT Tech Inst (CO)
ITT Tech Inst, Fort Lauderdale (FL)
ITT Tech Inst, Jacksonville (FL)
ITT Tech Inst, Mount Prospect (IL)
ITT Tech Inst, Orland Park (IL)
ITT Tech Inst (NE)
ITT Tech Inst, Houston (TX)
ITT Tech Inst, Chantilly (VA)
ITT Tech Inst, Spokane (WA)
ITT Tech Inst, Greenfield (WI)
Jamestown Comm Coll (NY)
Jefferson Comm and Tech Coll (KY)
Jefferson Comm Coll (OH)
J. F. Drake State Tech Coll (AL)
Johnston Comm Coll (NC)
John Wood Comm Coll (IL)
Joliet Jr Coll (IL)
Jones County Jr Coll (MS)
Kankakee Comm Coll (IL)
Kent State U, Ashtabula Campus (OH)
Kent State U, Trumbull Campus (OH)
Kent State U, Tuscarawas Campus (OH)
Kirkwood Comm Coll (IA)
Lake Land Coll (IL)
Lakeshore Tech Coll (WI)
Lanier Tech Coll (GA)
Lansing Comm Coll (MI)
Laredo Comm Coll (TX)
Las Positas Coll (CA)
Lawson State Comm Coll (AL)
Lee Coll (TX)
Lehigh Carbon Comm Coll (PA)
Lenoir Comm Coll (NC)
Lincoln Land Comm Coll (IL)
Linn State Tech Coll (MO)
Lorain County Comm Coll (OH)
Los Angeles City Coll (CA)
Los Angeles Harbor Coll (CA)
Los Angeles Pierce Coll (CA)
Los Angeles Southwest Coll (CA)
Los Medanos Coll (CA)
Lower Columbia Coll (WA)
Macomb Comm Coll (MI)
Madison Area Tech Coll (WI)
Madisonville Comm Coll (KY)
Manatee Comm Coll (FL)
Marshall Comm and Tech Coll (WV)
Massasoit Comm Coll (MA)
Mendocino Coll (CA)
Merced Coll (CA)
Meridian Comm Coll (MS)
Mesa Comm Coll (AZ)
Metropolitan Comm Coll (NE)
Metropolitan Comm Coll–Business & Technology Campus (MO)
Miami Dade Coll (FL)
Miami U–Middletown Campus (OH)
Midlands Tech Coll (SC)
Mid-Plains Comm Coll, North Platte (NE)
Mid-State Tech Coll (WI)

Minnesota State Coll–Southeast Tech (MN)
Minnesota State Comm and Tech Coll–Fergus Falls (MN)
Mission Coll (CA)
Mississippi Delta Comm Coll (MS)
Mississippi Gulf Coast Comm Coll (MS)
Moberly Area Comm Coll (MO)
Mohawk Valley Comm Coll (NY)
Monroe Comm Coll (NY)
Montcalm Comm Coll (MI)
Montgomery Coll (MD)
Montgomery County Comm Coll (PA)
Moorpark Coll (CA)
Mott Comm Coll (MI)
Moultrie Tech Coll (GA)
Mt. Hood Comm Coll (OR)
Mt. San Antonio Coll (CA)
Mount Wachusett Comm Coll (MA)
Murray State Coll (OK)
Muskegon Comm Coll (MI)
Napa Valley Coll (CA)
National Park Comm Coll (AR)
Naugatuck Valley Comm Coll (CT)
Neosho County Comm Coll (KS)
New England Inst of Technology (RI)
New Hampshire Comm Tech Coll, Nashua/Claremont (NH)
New Hampshire Tech Inst (NH)
New Mexico State U–Alamogordo (NM)
New River Comm Coll (VA)
New York City Coll of Technology of the City U of New York (NY)
Niagara County Comm Coll (NY)
Northampton County Area Comm Coll (PA)
North Arkansas Coll (AR)
North Central Kansas Tech Coll (KS)
North Central Missouri Coll (MO)
North Central Texas Coll (TX)
Northeast Comm Coll (NE)
Northeastern Tech Coll (SC)
Northeast Iowa Comm Coll (IA)
Northeast State Tech Comm Coll (TN)
Northern Essex Comm Coll (MA)
Northern Maine Comm Coll (ME)
Northern New Mexico Coll (NM)
North Idaho Coll (ID)
North Iowa Area Comm Coll (IA)
North Lake Coll (TX)
Northland Comm and Tech Coll–Thief River Falls (MN)
North Metro Tech Coll (GA)
North Seattle Comm Coll (WA)
NorthWest Arkansas Comm Coll (AR)
Northwestern Connecticut Comm Coll (CT)
Northwestern Tech Coll (GA)
Northwest Iowa Comm Coll (IA)
Northwest Mississippi Comm Coll (MS)
Northwest-Shoals Comm Coll (AL)
Oakland Comm Coll (MI)
Odessa Coll (TX)
Ohlone Coll (CA)
Oklahoma City Comm Coll (OK)
Oklahoma State U, Oklahoma City (OK)
Oklahoma State U, Okmulgee (OK)
Olympic Coll (WA)
Onondaga Comm Coll (NY)
Orange Coast Coll (CA)

Owensboro Comm and Tech Coll (KY)
Owens Comm Coll, Toledo (OH)
Oxnard Coll (CA)
Ozarks Tech Comm Coll (MO)
Palau Comm Coll (Palau)
Palm Beach Comm Coll (FL)
Pamlico Comm Coll (NC)
Pasadena City Coll (CA)
Passaic County Comm Coll (NJ)
Pearl River Comm Coll (MS)
Peninsula Coll (WA)
Penn State Delaware County (PA)
Penn State DuBois (PA)
Penn State Fayette, The Eberly Campus (PA)
Penn State Hazleton (PA)
Penn State New Kensington (PA)
Penn State Schuylkill (PA)
Penn State Shenango (PA)
Penn State Wilkes-Barre (PA)
Penn State Worthington Scranton (PA)
Penn State York (PA)
Pennsylvania Highland Comm Coll (PA)
Piedmont Tech Coll (SC)
Pierce Coll (WA)
Pima Comm Coll (AZ)
Pittsburgh Inst of Aeronautics (PA)
Potomac State Coll of West Virginia U (WV)
Pueblo Comm Coll (CO)
Queensborough Comm Coll of the City U of New York (NY)
Raritan Valley Comm Coll (NJ)
Redlands Comm Coll (OK)
Red Rocks Comm Coll (CO)
Reid State Tech Coll (AL)
Remington Coll–Fort Worth Campus (TX)
Renton Tech Coll (WA)
Richland Coll (TX)
Richland Comm Coll (IL)
Ridgewater Coll (MN)
Robeson Comm Coll (NC)
Rogue Comm Coll (OR)
Rose State Coll (OK)
Sacramento City Coll (CA)
St. Cloud Tech Coll (MN)
St. Louis Comm Coll at Florissant Valley (MO)
Saint Paul Coll–A Comm & Tech College (MN)
Salt Lake Comm Coll (UT)
San Antonio Coll (TX)
San Bernardino Valley Coll (CA)
San Diego City Coll (CA)
San Joaquin Delta Coll (CA)
Santa Ana Coll (CA)
Santa Barbara City Coll (CA)
Santa Rosa Jr Coll (CA)
Savannah Tech Coll (GA)
Schoolcraft Coll (MI)
Scottsdale Comm Coll (AZ)
Seminole Comm Coll (FL)
Shasta Coll (CA)
Skagit Valley Coll (WA)
Southeastern Comm Coll (NC)
Southeastern Comm Coll, North Campus (IA)
Southeastern Tech Coll (GA)
Southeast Tech Inst (SD)
Southern Maine Comm Coll (ME)
Southern U at Shreveport (LA)
South Florida Comm Coll (FL)
South Georgia Tech Coll (GA)
South Piedmont Comm Coll (NC)
South Plains Coll (TX)
Southside Virginia Comm Coll (VA)
Southwestern Comm Coll (NC)
Southwestern Indian Polytechnic Inst (NM)

Southwest Mississippi Comm Coll (MS)
Southwest Virginia Comm Coll (VA)
Spokane Comm Coll (WA)
Springfield Tech Comm Coll (MA)
Stanly Comm Coll (NC)
State Fair Comm Coll (MO)
State U of New York Coll of Agriculture and Technology at Morrisville (NY)
State U of New York Coll of Technology at Alfred (NY)
State U of New York Coll of Technology at Canton (NY)
Suffolk County Comm Coll (NY)
Surry Comm Coll (NC)
Swainsboro Tech Coll (GA)
Taft Coll (CA)
Taylor Business Inst (IL)
Temple Coll (TX)
TESST Coll of Technology, Baltimore (MD)
TESST Coll of Technology, Beltsville (MD)
Texarkana Coll (TX)
Texas State Tech Coll–Marshall (TX)
Texas State Tech Coll West Texas (TX)
Three Rivers Comm Coll (CT)
Tidewater Comm Coll (VA)
Tomball Coll (TX)
Tompkins Cortland Comm Coll (NY)
Tri-County Comm Coll (NC)
Trident Tech Coll (SC)
Tulsa Comm Coll (OK)
Tyler Jr Coll (TX)
Umpqua Comm Coll (OR)
U of Cincinnati Clermont Coll (OH)
The U of Montana-Helena Coll of Technology (MT)
U of New Mexico–Los Alamos Branch (NM)
Valencia Comm Coll (FL)
Victoria Coll (TX)
Victor Valley Coll (CA)
Virginia Highlands Comm Coll (VA)
Virginia Western Comm Coll (VA)
Wallace State Comm Coll (AL)
Washington State Comm Coll (OH)
Waukesha County Tech Coll (WI)
Wayne Comm Coll (NC)
West Central Tech Coll (GA)
Westchester Comm Coll (NY)
Western Nevada Comm Coll (NV)
Western Piedmont Comm Coll (NC)
Western Wyoming Comm Coll (WY)
West Georgia Tech Coll (GA)
West Los Angeles Coll (CA)
Westmoreland County Comm Coll (PA)
West Shore Comm Coll (MI)
West Virginia U at Parkersburg (WV)
The Williamson Free School of Mecha Trades (PA)
Wilson Tech Comm Coll (NC)
Wor-Wic Comm Coll (MD)
Wright State U, Lake Campus (OH)
Wytheville Comm Coll (VA)
York Tech Coll (SC)
Yuba Coll (CA)
Zane State Coll (OH)

Electrical, Electronics and Communications Engineering
Allen County Comm Coll (KS)
Black Hawk Coll, Moline (IL)

Jamestown Comm
Coll (NY)
John Tyler Comm Coll (VA)
Lehigh Carbon Comm
Coll (PA)
Remington Coll–Baton
Rouge Campus (LA)

**Electrical/Electronics
Drafting and Cad/
Cadd**
Brevard Comm Coll (FL)
Central New Mexico
Comm Coll (NM)
Collin County Comm Coll
District (TX)
Joliet Jr Coll (IL)
Mission Coll (CA)
North Seattle Comm
Coll (WA)
Waukesha County Tech
Coll (WI)

**Electrical/Electronics
Equipment Installation
and Repair**
Angelina Coll (TX)
Cape Fear Comm
Coll (NC)
Colegio Universitario de
San Juan, San
Juan (PR)
Coll of DuPage (IL)
Collin County Comm Coll
District (TX)
Guilford Tech Comm
Coll (NC)
Hutchinson Comm Coll
and Area Vocational
School (KS)
Kennebec Valley Comm
Coll (ME)
Macomb Comm Coll (MI)
Mesabi Range Comm and
Tech Coll (MN)
Northwest KansasTech
Coll (KS)
Orange Coast Coll (CA)
Ridgewater Coll (MN)
Riverland Comm Coll (MN)
St. Philip's Coll (TX)
Santa Barbara City
Coll (CA)
State U of New York Coll
of Technology at
Alfred (NY)
TESST Coll of
Technology (VA)
Western Wyoming Comm
Coll (WY)
York Tech Coll (SC)

**Electrical/Electronics
Maintenance and
Repair Technology
Related**
Colegio Universitario de
San Juan, San
Juan (PR)
Front Range Comm
Coll (CO)
Mohawk Valley Comm
Coll (NY)
National Inst of
Technology (CA)
West Virginia State Comm
and Tech Coll (WV)

Electrician
Black Hawk Coll,
Moline (IL)
Cleveland Comm Coll (NC)
Coll of Lake County (IL)
Elizabethtown Tech
Coll (KY)
Fayetteville Tech Comm
Coll (NC)
H. Councill Trenholm State
Tech Coll (AL)
John Wood Comm Coll (IL)
Linn State Tech Coll (MO)
Lower Columbia Coll (WA)
National Inst of
Technology (CA)
Northampton County Area
Comm Coll (PA)
North Central Kansas Tech
Coll (KS)
Northeast Comm Coll (NE)
Northwest KansasTech
Coll (KS)
Piedmont Virginia Comm
Coll (VA)
Santiago Canyon Coll (CA)
Triangle Tech, Inc.–
Sunbury School (PA)
Vatterott Coll, Kansas
City (MO)
Vatterott Coll (OH)

Western Wyoming Comm
Coll (WY)

**Electrocardiograph
Technology**
St. Cloud Tech Coll (MN)

**Electromechanical
and Instrumentation
And Maintenance
Technologies Related**
Calhoun Comm Coll (AL)
North Arkansas Coll (AR)
Waukesha County Tech
Coll (WI)

**Electromechanical
Technology**
Alamance Comm Coll (NC)
Angelina Coll (TX)
Black Hawk Coll,
Moline (IL)
Bramson ORT Coll (NY)
Central Comm Coll–
Columbus
Campus (NE)
Central Maine Comm
Coll (ME)
Central Ohio Tech
Coll (OH)
Central Piedmont Comm
Coll (NC)
Chippewa Valley Tech
Coll (WI)
Cincinnati State Tech and
Comm Coll (OH)
Clovis Comm Coll (NM)
Coll of DuPage (IL)
DeKalb Tech Coll (GA)
Eastern New Mexico
U–Roswell (NM)
ECPI Coll of
Technology (VA)
ECPI Tech Coll (VA)
ECPI Tech Coll (VA)
Florence-Darlington Tech
Coll (SC)
Forsyth Tech Comm
Coll (NC)
Gateway Tech Coll (WI)
Hagerstown Comm
Coll (MD)
Irvine Valley Coll (CA)
Jackson State Comm
Coll (TN)
Kirkwood Comm Coll (IA)
Lake Land Coll (IL)
Lakeshore Tech Coll (WI)
Lansing Comm Coll (MI)
Los Angeles Harbor
Coll (CA)
Macomb Comm Coll (MI)
Martin Comm Coll (NC)
Miami U–Middletown
Campus (OH)
Montgomery Coll (MD)
Montgomery County
Comm Coll (PA)
Muskegon Comm Coll (MI)
New Hampshire Comm
Tech Coll, Nashua/
Claremont (NH)
New York City Coll of
Technology of the City
U of New York (NY)
Northampton County Area
Comm Coll (PA)
North Arkansas Coll (AR)
Northeast Comm Coll (NE)
Oakland Comm Coll (MI)
Pulaski Tech Coll (AR)
Raritan Valley Comm
Coll (NJ)
St. Philip's Coll (TX)
Schoolcraft Coll (MI)
Southeast Tech Inst (SD)
South Piedmont Comm
Coll (NC)
Springfield Tech Comm
Coll (MA)
State U of New York Coll
of Technology at
Alfred (NY)
Terra State Comm
Coll (OH)
Union County Coll (NJ)
Wayne Comm Coll (NC)
West Virginia U at
Parkersburg (WV)

**Electroneurodiagnostic/
Electroencephalo-
graphic Technology**
Black Hawk Coll,
Moline (IL)
Comm Coll of Allegheny
County (PA)
Niagara County Comm
Coll (NY)

Oakland Comm Coll (MI)
Parkland Coll (IL)
Scott Comm Coll (IA)

**Elementary and
Middle School
Administration/
Principalship**
Tulsa Comm Coll (OK)

Elementary Education
Allen County Comm
Coll (KS)
Alpena Comm Coll (MI)
Amarillo Coll (TX)
Angelina Coll (TX)
Anne Arundel Comm
Coll (MD)
Bainbridge Coll (GA)
Barton County Comm
Coll (KS)
Brigham Young U –
Idaho (ID)
Broward Comm Coll (FL)
Calhoun Comm Coll (AL)
Cecil Comm Coll (MD)
Central New Mexico
Comm Coll (NM)
Central Wyoming
Coll (WY)
Chesapeake Coll (MD)
City Colls of Chicago,
Harold Washington
College (IL)
City Colls of Chicago,
Harry S. Truman
College (IL)
City Colls of Chicago,
Richard J. Daley
College (IL)
City Colls of Chicago,
Wilbur Wright
College (IL)
Clarendon Coll (TX)
Coahoma Comm Coll (MS)
Coastal Bend Coll (TX)
Coll of Micronesia–
FSM (FM)
Coll of Southern Idaho (ID)
Coll of Southern
Maryland (MD)
Coll of the Marshall Islands
(Marshall Islands)
Crowder Coll (MO)
Dixie State Coll of
Utah (UT)
Dodge City Comm
Coll (KS)
Eastern Arizona Coll (AZ)
East Georgia Coll (GA)
Essex County Coll (NJ)
Everett Comm Coll (WA)
Fayetteville Tech Comm
Coll (NC)
Fort Belknap Coll (MT)
Frederick Comm Coll (MD)
Fulton-Montgomery Comm
Coll (NY)
Garrett Coll (MD)
Genesee Comm Coll (NY)
Grayson County Coll (TX)
Great Basin Coll (NV)
Hagerstown Comm
Coll (MD)
Harrisburg Area Comm
Coll (PA)
Hillsborough Comm
Coll (FL)
Holyoke Comm Coll (MA)
Howard Comm Coll (MD)
Illinois Valley Comm
Coll (IL)
Iowa Lakes Comm
Coll (IA)
Isothermal Comm
Coll (NC)
Kankakee Comm Coll (IL)
Kellogg Comm Coll (MI)
Kingsborough Comm Coll
of the City U of New
York (NY)
Kirkwood Comm Coll (IA)
Labette Comm Coll (KS)
Lansing Comm Coll (MI)
Lenoir Comm Coll (NC)
Linn-Benton Comm
Coll (OR)
Little Big Horn Coll (MT)
Lorain County Comm
Coll (OH)
Louisburg Coll (NC)
Miami Dade Coll (FL)
Miami U–Middletown
Campus (OH)
Mississippi Delta Comm
Coll (MS)
Mississippi Gulf Coast
Comm Coll (MS)

Mohawk Valley Comm
Coll (NY)
Montgomery County
Comm Coll (PA)
Murray State Coll (OK)
Muskegon Comm Coll (MI)
National Park Comm
Coll (AR)
Navarro Coll (TX)
New Mexico Jr Coll (NM)
Northeast Comm Coll (NE)
Northeastern Jr Coll (CO)
Northern Essex Comm
Coll (MA)
Northern New Mexico
Coll (NM)
Northern Oklahoma
Coll (OK)
North Idaho Coll (ID)
Northwest Mississippi
Comm Coll (MS)
Northwest-Shoals Comm
Coll (AL)
Palm Beach Comm
Coll (FL)
Parkland Coll (IL)
Pima Comm Coll (AZ)
Potomac State Coll of
West Virginia U (WV)
Quincy Coll (MA)
Raritan Valley Comm
Coll (NJ)
Redlands Comm Coll (OK)
Roane State Comm
Coll (TN)
Rose State Coll (OK)
St. Catharine Coll (KY)
St. Louis Comm Coll at
Florissant Valley (MO)
Seminole State Coll (OK)
Sheridan Coll–Sheridan
and Gillette (WY)
South Georgia Coll (GA)
Southwest Mississippi
Comm Coll (MS)
Springfield Tech Comm
Coll (MA)
Three Rivers Comm
Coll (MO)
Tulsa Comm Coll (OK)
Turtle Mountain Comm
Coll (ND)
Ulster County Comm
Coll (NY)
Umpqua Comm Coll (OR)
U of Cincinnati Clermont
Coll (OH)
U of New
Mexico–Gallup (NM)
Vincennes U Jasper
Campus (IN)
Wallace State Comm
Coll (AL)
Western Nebraska Comm
Coll (NE)
Western Wyoming Comm
Coll (WY)
Wor-Wic Comm Coll (MD)
Wright State U, Lake
Campus (OH)
Yuba Coll (CA)

**Emergency Care
Attendant (Emt
Ambulance)**
Iowa Lakes Comm
Coll (IA)

**Emergency Medical
Technology (Emt
Paramedic)**
Allen County Comm
Coll (KS)
Amarillo Coll (TX)
Angelina Coll (TX)
Anne Arundel Comm
Coll (MD)
Arkansas State
U–Mountain
Home (AR)
Arkansas State
U–Newport (AR)
Asheville-Buncombe Tech
Comm Coll (NC)
Athens Tech Coll (GA)
Augusta Tech Coll (GA)
Bakersfield Coll (CA)
Baltimore City Comm
Coll (MD)
Barton County Comm
Coll (KS)
Bismarck State Coll (ND)
Brevard Comm Coll (FL)
Brigham Young U –
Idaho (ID)
Brookhaven Coll (TX)
Broome Comm Coll (NY)
Broward Comm Coll (FL)
Calhoun Comm Coll (AL)

Capital Comm Coll (CT)
Catawba Valley Comm
Coll (NC)
Central Arizona Coll (AZ)
Central Florida Comm
Coll (FL)
Central Oregon Comm
Coll (OR)
Central Texas Coll (TX)
Century Coll (MN)
Chattanooga State Tech
Comm Coll (TN)
Cincinnati State Tech and
Comm Coll (OH)
City Coll, Fort
Lauderdale (FL)
City Coll, Gainesville (FL)
City Coll, Miami (FL)
City Colls of Chicago,
Harold Washington
College (IL)
Clark Coll (WA)
Clark State Comm
Coll (OH)
Clinton Comm Coll (IA)
Coastal Carolina Comm
Coll (NC)
Cochise Coll, Douglas (AZ)
Coll of DuPage (IL)
Coll of Southern
Maryland (MD)
Coll of the Mainland (TX)
Collin County Comm Coll
District (TX)
Columbus Tech Coll (GA)
Comm Coll of Southern
Nevada (NV)
Contra Costa Coll (CA)
Cossatot Comm Coll of the
U of Arkansas (AR)
Cosumnes River Coll,
Sacramento (CA)
Crafton Hills Coll (CA)
Davidson County Comm
Coll (NC)
Dixie State Coll of
Utah (UT)
East Central Coll (MO)
Eastern Arizona Coll (AZ)
Eastern New Mexico
U–Roswell (NM)
Elaine P. Nunez Comm
Coll (LA)
El Centro Coll (TX)
Elgin Comm Coll (IL)
Essex County Coll (NJ)
Fayetteville Tech Comm
Coll (NC)
Fiorello H. LaGuardia
Comm Coll of the City
U of New York (NY)
Flint Hills Tech Coll (KS)
Foothill Coll (CA)
Frederick Comm Coll (MD)
Gadsden State Comm
Coll (AL)
George C. Wallace Comm
Coll (AL)
Georgia Highlands
Coll (GA)
Greenville Tech Coll (SC)
Griffin Tech Coll (GA)
Guilford Tech Comm
Coll (NC)
Gwinnett Tech Coll (GA)
Hagerstown Comm
Coll (MD)
Harrisburg Area Comm
Coll (PA)
H. Councill Trenholm State
Tech Coll (AL)
Henry Ford Comm
Coll (MI)
Hillsborough Comm
Coll (FL)
Hocking Coll (OH)
Houston Comm Coll
System (TX)
Howard Comm Coll (MD)
Hutchinson Comm Coll
and Area Vocational
School (KS)
Inver Hills Comm
Coll (MN)
Iowa Lakes Comm
Coll (IA)
Jefferson Comm Coll (OH)
John Wood Comm Coll (IL)
Joliet Jr Coll (IL)
Jones County Jr Coll (MS)
Kankakee Comm Coll (IL)
Kansas City Kansas
Comm Coll (KS)
Keiser Career Coll -
Greenacres (FL)
Kellogg Comm Coll (MI)
Kennebec Valley Comm
Coll (ME)

Kent State U, Geauga
Campus (OH)
Lake-Sumter Comm
Coll (FL)
Lamar Comm Coll (CO)
Lamar Inst of
Technology (TX)
Lansing Comm Coll (MI)
Laredo Comm Coll (TX)
Lee Coll (TX)
Los Medanos Coll (CA)
Macomb Comm Coll (MI)
Madison Area Tech
Coll (WI)
Marshall Comm and Tech
Coll (WV)
Meridian Comm Coll (MS)
Metropolitan Comm
Coll–Penn Valley (MO)
Miami Dade Coll (FL)
Minnesota State Coll–
Southeast Tech (MN)
Mississippi Gulf Coast
Comm Coll (MS)
Mohawk Valley Comm
Coll (NY)
Montcalm Comm Coll (MI)
Mott Comm Coll (MI)
Mt. San Antonio Coll (CA)
Muscatine Comm Coll (IA)
Muskegon Comm Coll (MI)
Napa Valley Coll (CA)
National Park Comm
Coll (AR)
New Hampshire Tech
Inst (NH)
New Mexico Jr Coll (NM)
North Arkansas Coll (AR)
North Central Michigan
Coll (MI)
North Central Missouri
Coll (MO)
North Central Texas
Coll (TX)
Northeast Comm Coll (NE)
Northeastern Jr Coll (CO)
Northeast State Tech
Comm Coll (TN)
Northern Maine Comm
Coll (ME)
North Iowa Area Comm
Coll (IA)
NorthWest Arkansas
Comm Coll (AR)
Northwest Iowa Comm
Coll (IA)
Oakland Comm Coll (MI)
Odessa Coll (TX)
Oklahoma City Comm
Coll (OK)
Orange Coast Coll (CA)
Ozarks Tech Comm
Coll (MO)
Pasco-Hernando Comm
Coll (FL)
Piedmont Virginia Comm
Coll (VA)
Pima Comm Coll (AZ)
Polk Comm Coll (FL)
Redlands Comm Coll (OK)
Roane State Comm
Coll (TN)
St. Cloud Tech Coll (MN)
St. Louis Comm Coll at
Florissant Valley (MO)
San Diego City Coll (CA)
San Joaquin Delta
Coll (CA)
Santa Rosa Jr Coll (CA)
Schoolcraft Coll (MI)
Scott Comm Coll (IA)
Scottsdale Comm
Coll (AZ)
Seminole Comm Coll (FL)
Southeastern Comm Coll,
North Campus (IA)
Southeastern Comm Coll,
South Campus (IA)
Southern State Comm
Coll (OH)
South Texas Coll (TX)
Southwestern Comm
Coll (NC)
Southwest Mississippi
Comm Coll (MS)
Tallahassee Comm
Coll (FL)
Texarkana Coll (TX)
Texas State Tech Coll
West Texas (TX)
Tulsa Comm Coll (OK)
Turtle Mountain Comm
Coll (ND)
Umpqua Comm Coll (OR)
U of Arkansas Comm Coll
at Batesville (AR)
Valencia Comm Coll (FL)

Victoria Coll (TX)
Wallace State Comm Coll (AL)
Westchester Comm Coll (NY)
West Shore Comm Coll (MI)
Wor-Wic Comm Coll (MD)

Energy Management and Systems Technology
Bismarck State Coll (ND)
Cabrillo Coll (CA)
Chattanooga State Tech Comm Coll (TN)
Comm Coll of Allegheny County (PA)
Henry Ford Comm Coll (MI)
Iowa Lakes Comm Coll (IA)
Lassen Comm Coll District (CA)
Macomb Comm Coll (MI)
The Williamson Free School of Mecha Trades (PA)

Engineering
Allen County Comm Coll (KS)
Amarillo Coll (TX)
Angelina Coll (TX)
Antelope Valley Coll (CA)
Bakersfield Coll (CA)
Baltimore City Comm Coll (MD)
Berkshire Comm Coll (MA)
Brigham Young U – Idaho (ID)
Bucks County Comm Coll (PA)
Burlington County Coll (NJ)
Cañada Coll (CA)
Central Arizona Coll (AZ)
Centralia Coll (WA)
Central New Mexico Comm Coll (NM)
Central Texas Coll (TX)
Chaffey Coll (CA)
Citrus Coll (CA)
City Colls of Chicago, Harold Washington College (IL)
City Colls of Chicago, Kennedy-King College (IL)
City Colls of Chicago, Olive-Harvey College (IL)
City Colls of Chicago, Wilbur Wright College (IL)
Clarendon Coll (TX)
Coastal Bend Coll (TX)
Coll of DuPage (IL)
Coll of Lake County (IL)
Coll of Marin (CA)
Coll of San Mateo (CA)
Coll of Southern Idaho (ID)
Columbia Basin Coll (WA)
Comm Coll of Philadelphia (PA)
Comm Coll of Rhode Island (RI)
Contra Costa Coll (CA)
Cuesta Coll (CA)
Cypress Coll (CA)
De Anza Coll (CA)
Dixie State Coll of Utah (UT)
Dodge City Comm Coll (KS)
East Central Coll (MO)
El Camino Coll (CA)
Erie Comm Coll, North Campus (NY)
Everett Comm Coll (WA)
Frederick Comm Coll (MD)
Fresno City Coll (CA)
Georgia Military Coll (GA)
Hagerstown Comm Coll (MD)
Harper Coll (IL)
Harrisburg Area Comm Coll (PA)
Hillsborough Comm Coll (FL)
Howard Comm Coll (MD)
Hutchinson Comm Coll and Area Vocational School (KS)
Iowa Lakes Comm Coll (IA)
Itasca Comm Coll (MN)
Jamestown Comm Coll (NY)

Kankakee Comm Coll (IL)
Kellogg Comm Coll (MI)
Kirkwood Comm Coll (IA)
Lamar Comm Coll (CO)
Laney Coll (CA)
Lansing Comm Coll (MI)
Laramie County Comm Coll (WY)
Lehigh Carbon Comm Coll (PA)
Linn-Benton Comm Coll (OR)
Lorain County Comm Coll (OH)
Los Angeles City Coll (CA)
Los Angeles Southwest Coll (CA)
Lower Columbia Coll (WA)
Manatee Comm Coll (FL)
Marion Military Inst (AL)
Metropolitan Comm Coll–Business & Technology Campus (MO)
Metropolitan Comm Coll–Longview (MO)
Metropolitan Comm Coll–Penn Valley (MO)
Miami Dade Coll (FL)
Miami U–Middletown Campus (OH)
Missouri State U–West Plains (MO)
Mohawk Valley Comm Coll (NY)
Monterey Peninsula Coll (CA)
Montgomery Coll (MD)
Moorpark Coll (CA)
Murray State Coll (OK)
Napa Valley Coll (CA)
Nassau Comm Coll (NY)
National American U, Rio Rancho (NM)
Navarro Coll (TX)
New Mexico Jr Coll (NM)
New Mexico Military Inst (NM)
New Mexico State U–Alamogordo (NM)
New River Comm Coll (VA)
Northampton County Area Comm Coll (PA)
Northeast Comm Coll (NE)
Northern Oklahoma Coll (OK)
North Idaho Coll (ID)
Northwestern Connecticut Comm Coll (CT)
Oakland Comm Coll (MI)
Oklahoma State U, Oklahoma City (OK)
Olympic Coll (WA)
Orange Coast Coll (CA)
Palo Alto Coll (TX)
Pasadena City Coll (CA)
Piedmont Tech Coll (SC)
Piedmont Virginia Comm Coll (VA)
Potomac State Coll of West Virginia U (WV)
Raritan Valley Comm Coll (NJ)
Richland Coll (TX)
Ridgewater Coll (MN)
Roane State Comm Coll (TN)
Sacramento City Coll (CA)
St. Louis Comm Coll at Florissant Valley (MO)
Salt Lake Comm Coll (UT)
San Joaquin Delta Coll (CA)
San Juan Coll (NM)
Santa Ana Coll (CA)
Santa Barbara City Coll (CA)
Santa Rosa Jr Coll (CA)
Schoolcraft Coll (MI)
Sheridan Coll–Sheridan and Gillette (WY)
South Plains Coll (TX)
South Seattle Comm Coll (WA)
Southwest Mississippi Comm Coll (MS)
Southwest Texas Jr Coll (TX)
Southwest Virginia Comm Coll (VA)
Springfield Tech Comm Coll (MA)
State U of New York Coll of Agriculture and Technology at Morrisville (NY)
Suffolk County Comm Coll (NY)

Tallahassee Comm Coll (FL)
Terra State Comm Coll (OH)
Texarkana Coll (TX)
Three Rivers Comm Coll (CT)
Tidewater Comm Coll (VA)
Treasure Valley Comm Coll (OR)
Trinidad State Jr Coll (CO)
Tulsa Comm Coll (OK)
Tunxis Comm Coll (CT)
Ulster County Comm Coll (NY)
Umpqua Comm Coll (OR)
Union County Coll (NJ)
The U of Akron–Wayne Coll (OH)
U of New Mexico–Los Alamos Branch (NM)
Ventura Coll (CA)
Virginia Western Comm Coll (VA)
Wallace State Comm Coll (AL)
Washington State Comm Coll (OH)
Western Nevada Comm Coll (NV)
West Los Angeles Coll (CA)
Westmoreland County Comm Coll (PA)
Wright State U, Lake Campus (OH)

Engineering/Industrial Management
Cape Fear Comm Coll (NC)
International Business Coll, Fort Wayne (IN)

Engineering Related
Brigham Young U – Idaho (ID)
Chattanooga State Tech Comm Coll (TN)
Itasca Comm Coll (MN)
Macomb Comm Coll (MI)
Miami Dade Coll (FL)
Piedmont Tech Coll (SC)
San Joaquin Delta Coll (CA)
Southeastern Comm Coll, North Campus (IA)
Southern Maine Comm Coll (ME)
Wright State U, Lake Campus (OH)

Engineering-Related Technologies
Metropolitan Comm Coll–Business & Technology Campus (MO)

Engineering Science
Asnuntuck Comm Coll (CT)
Bergen Comm Coll (NJ)
Broome Comm Coll (NY)
Broward Comm Coll (FL)
Everett Comm Coll (WA)
Finger Lakes Comm Coll (NY)
Fulton-Montgomery Comm Coll (NY)
Genesee Comm Coll (NY)
Gloucester County Coll (NJ)
Holyoke Comm Coll (MA)
Itasca Comm Coll (MN)
Jones County Jr Coll (MS)
Kingsborough Comm Coll of the City U of New York (NY)
Middlesex Comm Coll (CT)
Monroe Comm Coll (NY)
Montgomery County Comm Coll (PA)
Northern Essex Comm Coll (MA)
North Shore Comm Coll (MA)
Onondaga Comm Coll (NY)
Parkland Coll (IL)
Queensborough Comm Coll of the City U of New York (NY)
St. Louis Comm Coll at Florissant Valley (MO)
State U of New York Coll of Agriculture and Technology at Morrisville (NY)

State U of New York Coll of Technology at Alfred (NY)
State U of New York Coll of Technology at Canton (NY)
Suffolk County Comm Coll (NY)
Three Rivers Comm Coll (CT)
Tompkins Cortland Comm Coll (NY)
Westchester Comm Coll (NY)

Engineering Technologies Related
Bowling Green State U–Firelands Coll (OH)
Catawba Valley Comm Coll (NC)
Central New Mexico Comm Coll (NM)
Cleveland Comm Coll (NC)
Comm Coll of Allegheny County (PA)
Harrisburg Area Comm Coll (PA)
Massasoit Comm Coll (MA)
McNally Smith Coll of Music (MN)
Montgomery County Comm Coll (PA)
Mott Comm Coll (MI)
Wor-Wic Comm Coll (MD)

Engineering Technology
Aims Comm Coll (CO)
Allen County Comm Coll (KS)
Angelina Coll (TX)
Anne Arundel Comm Coll (MD)
Antelope Valley Coll (CA)
Arizona Western Coll (AZ)
Ashland Comm and Tech Coll (KY)
Barton County Comm Coll (KS)
Berkshire Comm Coll (MA)
Bishop State Comm Coll (AL)
Brigham Young U – Idaho (ID)
Brunswick Comm Coll (NC)
Central Piedmont Comm Coll (NC)
Central Virginia Comm Coll (VA)
Citrus Coll (CA)
City Colls of Chicago, Harold Washington College (IL)
Coll of Marin (CA)
Coll of San Mateo (CA)
Coll of the Desert (CA)
Comm Coll of Philadelphia (PA)
Cuyahoga Comm Coll (OH)
Danville Comm Coll (VA)
Davidson County Comm Coll (NC)
De Anza Coll (CA)
DeKalb Tech Coll (GA)
Dodge City Comm Coll (KS)
ECPI Coll of Technology (VA)
ECPI Tech Coll (VA)
ECPI Tech Coll (VA)
Elizabethtown Tech Coll (KY)
Everett Comm Coll (WA)
Florence-Darlington Tech Coll (SC)
Forsyth Tech Comm Coll (NC)
Gateway Comm Coll (CT)
Golden West Coll (CA)
Harrisburg Area Comm Coll (PA)
Hawkeye Comm Coll (IA)
Houston Comm Coll System (TX)
Itasca Comm Coll (MN)
Kent State U, Ashtabula Campus (OH)
Kent State U, Tuscarawas Campus (OH)
Laney Coll (CA)
Lansing Comm Coll (MI)
Laramie County Comm Coll (WY)
Lassen Comm Coll District (CA)

Lorain County Comm Coll (OH)
Los Angeles Harbor Coll (CA)
Lower Columbia Coll (WA)
Massachusetts Bay Comm Coll (MA)
Mesa Comm Coll (AZ)
Miami Dade Coll (FL)
Miami U–Middletown Campus (OH)
Middlesex Comm Coll (CT)
Midlands Tech Coll (SC)
Moorpark Coll (CA)
Mt. San Antonio Coll (CA)
Murray State Coll (OK)
Muskegon Comm Coll (MI)
Naugatuck Valley Comm Coll (CT)
New Hampshire Comm Tech Coll, Nashua/Claremont (NH)
New Hampshire Tech Inst (NH)
North Central Michigan Coll (MI)
North Central Texas Coll (TX)
Northeast State Tech Comm Coll (TN)
Pasadena City Coll (CA)
Peninsula Coll (WA)
Piedmont Tech Coll (SC)
Pueblo Comm Coll (CO)
Quinebaug Valley Comm Coll (CT)
Rappahannock Comm Coll (VA)
St. Louis Comm Coll at Florissant Valley (MO)
Salt Lake Comm Coll (UT)
San Antonio Coll (TX)
San Diego City Coll (CA)
San Joaquin Delta Coll (CA)
Santa Ana Coll (CA)
Santa Barbara City Coll (CA)
Santa Rosa Jr Coll (CA)
Sheridan Coll–Sheridan and Gillette (WY)
Southeast Tech Inst (SD)
South Seattle Comm Coll (WA)
Southwestern Indian Polytechnic Inst (NM)
Southwestern Michigan Coll (MI)
State U of New York Coll of Agriculture and Technology at Morrisville (NY)
State U of New York Coll of Technology at Canton (NY)
Terra State Comm Coll (OH)
Three Rivers Comm Coll (CT)
Three Rivers Comm Coll (MO)
Trident Tech Coll (SC)
Tunxis Comm Coll (CT)
Ulster County Comm Coll (NY)
Virginia Highlands Comm Coll (VA)
Washington County Comm Coll (ME)
Westchester Comm Coll (NY)
Western Wyoming Comm Coll (WY)
Wright State U, Lake Campus (OH)

Engine Machinist
Black Hawk Coll, Moline (IL)

English
Alpena Comm Coll (MI)
Amarillo Coll (TX)
Angelina Coll (TX)
Anne Arundel Comm Coll (MD)
Arizona Western Coll (AZ)
Bainbridge Coll (GA)
Bakersfield Coll (CA)
Barton County Comm Coll (KS)
Berkeley City Coll (CA)
Blinn Coll (TX)
Brigham Young U – Idaho (ID)
Burlington County Coll (NJ)
Calhoun Comm Coll (AL)
Cankdeska Cikana Comm Coll (ND)

Cañada Coll (CA)
Centralia Coll (WA)
Central Wyoming Coll (WY)
Cerritos Coll (CA)
Chaffey Coll (CA)
Citrus Coll (CA)
City Coll of San Francisco (CA)
City Colls of Chicago, Harold Washington College (IL)
City Colls of Chicago, Wilbur Wright College (IL)
Clarendon Coll (TX)
Coahoma Comm Coll (MS)
Coastal Bend Coll (TX)
Coastal Georgia Comm Coll (GA)
Cochise Coll, Douglas (AZ)
Cochise Coll, Sierra Vista (AZ)
Colby Comm Coll (KS)
Coll of Alameda (CA)
Coll of San Mateo (CA)
Coll of Southern Idaho (ID)
Coll of Southern Maryland (MD)
Coll of the Canyons (CA)
Coll of the Desert (CA)
Coll of the Siskiyous (CA)
Colorado Mountain Coll (CO)
Colorado Mountain Coll, Alpine Campus (CO)
Columbia Coll (CA)
Comm Coll of Allegheny County (PA)
Comm Coll of Southern Nevada (NV)
Contra Costa Coll (CA)
Crafton Hills Coll (CA)
Cypress Coll (CA)
De Anza Coll (CA)
Dixie State Coll of Utah (UT)
Dodge City Comm Coll (KS)
Eastern Arizona Coll (AZ)
East Georgia Coll (GA)
El Camino Coll (CA)
Everett Comm Coll (WA)
Folsom Lake Coll (CA)
Foothill Coll (CA)
Frederick Comm Coll (MD)
Fullerton Coll (CA)
Fulton-Montgomery Comm Coll (NY)
Georgia Highlands Coll (GA)
Gloucester County Coll (NJ)
Gordon Coll (GA)
Great Basin Coll (NV)
Grossmont Coll (CA)
Hartnell Coll (CA)
Hutchinson Comm Coll and Area Vocational School (KS)
Illinois Valley Comm Coll (IL)
Imperial Valley Coll (CA)
Iowa Lakes Comm Coll (IA)
Irvine Valley Coll (CA)
Jones County Jr Coll (MS)
Kellogg Comm Coll (MI)
Kirkwood Comm Coll (IA)
Labette Comm Coll (KS)
Lamar Comm Coll (CO)
Lansing Comm Coll (MI)
Laramie County Comm Coll (WY)
Lawson State Comm Coll (AL)
Lee Coll (TX)
Linn-Benton Comm Coll (OR)
Los Angeles City Coll (CA)
Los Angeles Mission Coll (CA)
Los Angeles Southwest Coll (CA)
Louisburg Coll (NC)
Lower Columbia Coll (WA)
Manatee Comm Coll (FL)
Mendocino Coll (CA)
Miami Dade Coll (FL)
Miami U–Middletown Campus (OH)
Mississippi Delta Comm Coll (MS)
Mohave Comm Coll (AZ)
Monterey Peninsula Coll (CA)
Murray State Coll (OK)
Navarro Coll (TX)

New Mexico Jr Coll (NM)
New Mexico Military Inst (NM)
Northeast Comm Coll (NE)
Northeastern Jr Coll (CO)
North Idaho Coll (ID)
Northwestern Connecticut Comm Coll (CT)
Odessa Coll (TX)
Orange Coast Coll (CA)
Oxnard Coll (CA)
Palm Beach Comm Coll (FL)
Palo Alto Coll (TX)
Parkland Coll (IL)
Pasadena City Coll (CA)
Passaic County Comm Coll (NJ)
Porterville Coll (CA)
Potomac State Coll of West Virginia U (WV)
Quincy Coll (MA)
Redlands Comm Coll (OK)
Red Rocks Comm Coll (CO)
Reedley Coll (CA)
Rose State Coll (OK)
Roxbury Comm Coll (MA)
St. Philip's Coll (TX)
Salt Lake Comm Coll (UT)
San Bernardino Valley Coll (CA)
San Diego City Coll (CA)
San Joaquin Delta Coll (CA)
San Juan Coll (NM)
Santa Ana Coll (CA)
Santa Barbara City Coll (CA)
Santa Rosa Jr Coll (CA)
Santiago Canyon Coll (CA)
Seminole State Coll (OK)
Sheridan Coll–Sheridan and Gillette (WY)
Skagit Valley Coll (WA)
South Georgia Coll (GA)
Southwest Mississippi Comm Coll (MS)
Suffolk County Comm Coll (NY)
Sussex County Comm Coll (NJ)
Taft Coll (CA)
Terra State Comm Coll (OH)
Treasure Valley Comm Coll (OR)
Trinidad State Jr Coll (CO)
Tulsa Comm Coll (OK)
Turtle Mountain Comm Coll (ND)
Umpqua Comm Coll (OR)
Western Nebraska Comm Coll (NE)
Western Wyoming Comm Coll (WY)
West Los Angeles Coll (CA)
West Valley Coll (CA)
Wright State U, Lake Campus (OH)
Young Harris Coll (GA)
Yuba Coll (CA)

English Composition
Allen County Comm Coll (KS)
Berkeley City Coll (CA)

English Language and Literature Related
Coll of the Siskiyous (CA)
Mohawk Valley Comm Coll (NY)

English/Language Arts Teacher Education
Coll of the Siskiyous (CA)
Louisburg Coll (NC)
Manatee Comm Coll (FL)

Entrepreneurial and Small Business Related
Virginia Coll at Austin (TX)

Entrepreneurship
Berkeley Coll–New York City Campus (NY)
Bucks County Comm Coll (PA)
Calhoun Comm Coll (AL)
Cincinnati State Tech and Comm Coll (OH)
Comm Coll of Allegheny County (PA)
Eastern Arizona Coll (AZ)
Laramie County Comm Coll (WY)

LDS Business Coll (UT)
Missouri State U–West Plains (MO)
Mohawk Valley Comm Coll (NY)
Montcalm Comm Coll (MI)
Moraine Valley Comm Coll (IL)
Mott Comm Coll (MI)
Mount Wachusett Comm Coll (MA)
Nassau Comm Coll (NY)
Northeast Comm Coll (NE)
North Iowa Area Comm Coll (IA)
Oakland Comm Coll (MI)
Reedley Coll (CA)
Schoolcraft Coll (MI)
Springfield Tech Comm Coll (MA)
Terra State Comm Coll (OH)
U of New Mexico–Gallup (NM)

Environmental Biology
Northwest-Shoals Comm Coll (AL)

Environmental Control Technologies Related
Black Hawk Coll, Moline (IL)
Central Carolina Tech Coll (SC)
Oakland Comm Coll (MI)

Environmental Design/Architecture
Cosumnes River Coll, Sacramento (CA)
Iowa Lakes Comm Coll (IA)
Queensborough Comm Coll of the City U of New York (NY)
Scottsdale Comm Coll (AZ)

Environmental Education
Iowa Lakes Comm Coll (IA)
New Mexico Jr Coll (NM)

Environmental Engineering Technology
Angelina Coll (TX)
Bakersfield Coll (CA)
Broward Comm Coll (FL)
Cape Cod Comm Coll (MA)
Central Piedmont Comm Coll (NC)
Chaffey Coll (CA)
Chattanooga State Tech Comm Coll (TN)
Cincinnati State Tech and Comm Coll (OH)
City Colls of Chicago, Wilbur Wright College (IL)
Clinton Comm Coll (IA)
Coastal Bend Coll (TX)
Collin County Comm Coll District (TX)
Columbia Basin Coll (WA)
Comm Coll of Allegheny County (PA)
Comm Coll of Philadelphia (PA)
Coosa Valley Tech Coll (GA)
Cosumnes River Coll, Sacramento (CA)
Crowder Coll (MO)
Elaine P. Nunez Comm Coll (LA)
Gloucester County Coll (NJ)
Iowa Lakes Comm Coll (IA)
James H. Faulkner State Comm Coll (AL)
John Tyler Comm Coll (VA)
Kent State U, Trumbull Campus (OH)
Massachusetts Bay Comm Coll (MA)
Merced Coll (CA)
Metropolitan Comm Coll–Business & Technology Campus (MO)
Miami Dade Coll (FL)
Minot State U–Bottineau Campus (ND)

Muscatine Comm Coll (IA)
Napa Valley Coll (CA)
Pennsylvania Highland Comm Coll (PA)
Pima Comm Coll (AZ)
Rose State Coll (OK)
Roxbury Comm Coll (MA)
Salt Lake Comm Coll (UT)
San Diego City Coll (CA)
Schoolcraft Coll (MI)
Scott Comm Coll (IA)
Skagit Valley Coll (WA)
Southern Maine Comm Coll (ME)
Texas State Tech Coll West Texas (TX)
Three Rivers Comm Coll (CT)
Tulsa Comm Coll (OK)
Tyler Jr Coll (TX)
Ulster County Comm Coll (NY)
U of Alaska Southeast, Sitka Campus (AK)
Valencia Comm Coll (FL)
Westchester Comm Coll (NY)
Westmoreland County Comm Coll (PA)
West Virginia U at Parkersburg (WV)

Environmental/ Environmental Health Engineering
Central New Mexico Comm Coll (NM)
Santa Barbara City Coll (CA)

Environmental Health
Amarillo Coll (TX)
Black Hawk Coll, Moline (IL)
Crowder Coll (MO)
Mt. Hood Comm Coll (OR)
North Idaho Coll (ID)
Queensborough Comm Coll of the City U of New York (NY)
Roane State Comm Coll (TN)
The U of Akron–Wayne Coll (OH)

Environmental Science
Berkshire Comm Coll (MA)
Central Wyoming Coll (WY)
City Colls of Chicago, Wilbur Wright College (IL)
Clarendon Coll (TX)
Klamath Comm Coll (OR)
Northwest-Shoals Comm Coll (AL)
The Ohio State U Ag Tech Inst (OH)
St. Philip's Coll (TX)
Santa Rosa Jr Coll (CA)
Western Wyoming Comm Coll (WY)

Environmental Studies
Anne Arundel Comm Coll (MD)
Arizona Western Coll (AZ)
Bucks County Comm Coll (PA)
Burlington County Coll (NJ)
Cañada Coll (CA)
Cape Cod Comm Coll (MA)
Cape Fear Comm Coll (NC)
Central Texas Coll (TX)
Century Coll (MN)
Coll of San Mateo (CA)
Coll of Southern Idaho (ID)
Coll of the Desert (CA)
Colorado Mountain Coll, Timberline Campus (CO)
Columbia Coll (CA)
Comm Coll of Southern Nevada (NV)
Cossatot Comm Coll of the U of Arkansas (AR)
Cosumnes River Coll, Sacramento (CA)
De Anza Coll (CA)
Dixie State Coll of Utah (UT)
Everett Comm Coll (WA)
Finger Lakes Comm Coll (NY)

Fond du Lac Tribal and Comm Coll (MN)
Fort Berthold Comm Coll (ND)
Fullerton Coll (CA)
Fulton-Montgomery Comm Coll (NY)
Great Basin Coll (NV)
Harrisburg Area Comm Coll (PA)
Hillsborough Comm Coll (FL)
Holyoke Comm Coll (MA)
Housatonic Comm Coll (CT)
Howard Comm Coll (MD)
Iowa Lakes Comm Coll (IA)
Itasca Comm Coll (MN)
Kent State U, Ashtabula Campus (OH)
Kent State U, Tuscarawas Campus (OH)
Keystone Coll (PA)
Las Positas Coll (CA)
Lee Coll (TX)
Lower Columbia Coll (WA)
Middlesex Comm Coll (CT)
Monroe Comm Coll (NY)
Mount Wachusett Comm Coll (MA)
Napa Valley Coll (CA)
Naugatuck Valley Comm Coll (CT)
New Mexico Jr Coll (NM)
Northern New Mexico Coll (NM)
Pamlico Comm Coll (NC)
Raritan Valley Comm Coll (NJ)
St. Catharine Coll (KY)
Salish Kootenai Coll (MT)
San Bernardino Valley Coll (CA)
Santa Ana Coll (CA)
Santa Barbara City Coll (CA)
Santa Rosa Jr Coll (CA)
Sitting Bull Coll (ND)
Southeastern Comm Coll (NC)
Southwestern Comm Coll (NC)
Stark State Coll of Technology (OH)
State U of New York Coll of Agriculture and Technology at Morrisville (NY)
State U of New York Coll of Technology at Alfred (NY)
State U of New York Coll of Technology at Canton (NY)
Sussex County Comm Coll (NJ)
Tompkins Cortland Comm Coll (NY)
Trocaire Coll (NY)
Turtle Mountain Comm Coll (ND)
U of New Mexico–Los Alamos Branch (NM)
Warren County Comm Coll (NJ)
Western Nevada Comm Coll (NV)
Zane State Coll (OH)

Equestrian Studies
Allen County Comm Coll (KS)
Black Hawk Coll, Moline (IL)
Central Texas Coll (TX)
Central Wyoming Coll (WY)
Coll of Southern Idaho (ID)
Dodge City Comm Coll (KS)
Hocking Coll (OH)
Kirkwood Comm Coll (IA)
Lamar Comm Coll (CO)
Laramie County Comm Coll (WY)
Los Angeles Pierce Coll (CA)
Martin Comm Coll (NC)
Murray State Coll (OK)
North Central Texas Coll (TX)
Northeastern Jr Coll (CO)
The Ohio State U Ag Tech Inst (OH)
Redlands Comm Coll (OK)
Scott Comm Coll (IA)
Scottsdale Comm Coll (AZ)

State U of New York Coll of Agriculture and Technology at Morrisville (NY)
West Hills Comm Coll (CA)

Ethnic, Cultural Minority, and Gender Studies Related
Santa Rosa Jr Coll (CA)

European Studies
Anne Arundel Comm Coll (MD)

European Studies (Central and Eastern)
Manatee Comm Coll (FL)

Executive Assistant/ Executive Secretary
Alamance Comm Coll (NC)
Asheville-Buncombe Tech Comm Coll (NC)
Broome Comm Coll (NY)
Business Inst of Pennsylvania, Sharon (PA)
Cape Cod Comm Coll (MA)
Cape Fear Comm Coll (NC)
Cincinnati State Tech and Comm Coll (OH)
Clark Coll (WA)
Cleveland Comm Coll (NC)
Clovis Comm Coll (NM)
Coastal Carolina Comm Coll (NC)
Crowder Coll (MO)
Elgin Comm Coll (IL)
Elizabethtown Tech Coll (KY)
ICPR Jr Coll–Hato Rey Campus (PR)
John Wood Comm Coll (IL)
Kellogg Comm Coll (MI)
Kennebec Valley Comm Coll (ME)
Lake Land Coll (IL)
Laurel Business Inst (PA)
LDS Business Coll (UT)
Lee Coll (TX)
Lehigh Carbon Comm Coll (PA)
Miller-Motte Tech Coll, Clarksville (TN)
Minot State U–Bottineau Campus (ND)
Montcalm Comm Coll (MI)
Owensboro Comm and Tech Coll (KY)
Rockford Business Coll (IL)
Savannah River Coll (GA)
Southern State Comm Coll (OH)
South Piedmont Comm Coll (NC)
Stanly Comm Coll (NC)
The U of Akron–Wayne Coll (OH)
The U of Montana-Helena Coll of Technology (MT)
Wayne Comm Coll (NC)

Family and Community Services
Bowling Green State U–Firelands Coll (OH)
Brigham Young U – Idaho (ID)
Collin County Comm Coll District (TX)
Oxnard Coll (CA)
Ridgewater Coll (MN)
Skagit Valley Coll (WA)

Family and Consumer Economics Related
Arizona Western Coll (AZ)
Bakersfield Coll (CA)
Cosumnes River Coll, Sacramento (CA)
Cuesta Coll (CA)
Grossmont Coll (CA)
Hartnell Coll (CA)
Los Angeles City Coll (CA)
Los Angeles Mission Coll (CA)
Los Angeles Southwest Coll (CA)
Monterey Peninsula Coll (CA)
Orange Coast Coll (CA)
Sacramento City Coll (CA)
San Bernardino Valley Coll (CA)
Santa Ana Coll (CA)

West Los Angeles Coll (CA)
Yuba Coll (CA)

Family and Consumer Sciences/Home Economics Teacher Education
Brigham Young U – Idaho (ID)
East Georgia Coll (GA)
Jones County Jr Coll (MS)
Los Angeles Mission Coll (CA)
Manatee Comm Coll (FL)
Northwest Mississippi Comm Coll (MS)

Family and Consumer Sciences/Human Sciences
Allen County Comm Coll (KS)
Bainbridge Coll (GA)
Brigham Young U – Idaho (ID)
Central Comm Coll–Columbus Campus (NE)
Cerritos Coll (CA)
Chaffey Coll (CA)
City Colls of Chicago, Kennedy-King College (IL)
Colby Comm Coll (KS)
Contra Costa Coll (CA)
El Camino Coll (CA)
Fresno City Coll (CA)
Fullerton Coll (CA)
Holyoke Comm Coll (MA)
Houston Comm Coll System (TX)
Hutchinson Comm Coll and Area Vocational School (KS)
Iowa Lakes Comm Coll (IA)
Jones County Jr Coll (MS)
Linn-Benton Comm Coll (OR)
Los Angeles City Coll (CA)
Merced Coll (CA)
Mesa Comm Coll (AZ)
Metropolitan Comm Coll–Penn Valley (MO)
Mississippi Delta Comm Coll (MS)
Mt. San Antonio Coll (CA)
Northeastern Jr Coll (CO)
Ohlone Coll (CA)
Orange Coast Coll (CA)
Oxnard Coll (CA)
Palm Beach Comm Coll (FL)
Rose State Coll (OK)
San Joaquin Delta Coll (CA)
Santa Rosa Jr Coll (CA)
Shasta Coll (CA)
Yuba Coll (CA)

Family Living/Parenthood
Antelope Valley Coll (CA)
Centralia Coll (WA)

Family Psychology
Cochise Coll, Douglas (AZ)

Family Resource Management
Calhoun Comm Coll (AL)

Farm and Ranch Management
Alexandria Tech Coll (MN)
Allen County Comm Coll (KS)
Brigham Young U – Idaho (ID)
Central Texas Coll (TX)
Clarendon Coll (TX)
Colby Comm Coll (KS)
Cosumnes River Coll, Sacramento (CA)
Crowder Coll (MO)
Dodge City Comm Coll (KS)
Fort Berthold Comm Coll (ND)
Hawkeye Comm Coll (IA)
Hutchinson Comm Coll and Area Vocational School (KS)
Iowa Lakes Comm Coll (IA)
Kirkwood Comm Coll (IA)
Lamar Comm Coll (CO)
Lassen Comm Coll District (CA)

North Central Missouri
Coll (MO)
North Central Texas
Coll (TX)
Northeast Comm Coll (NE)
Northeastern Jr Coll (CO)
Northland Comm and Tech
Coll–Thief River
Falls (MN)
Ridgewater Coll (MN)
St. Catharine Coll (KY)
Sitting Bull Coll (ND)
Southwest Texas Jr
Coll (TX)
Trinidad State Jr Coll (CO)
Tyler Jr Coll (TX)
Vernon Coll (TX)
Wallace State Comm
Coll (AL)

**Fashion and Fabric
Consulting**
Coll of DuPage (IL)

**Fashion/Apparel
Design**
The Art Inst of New York
City (NY)
The Art Inst of
Philadelphia (PA)
Baltimore City Comm
Coll (MD)
Brigham Young U –
Idaho (ID)
Brooks Coll,
Sunnyvale (CA)
Burlington County
Coll (NJ)
Cañada Coll (CA)
Cerritos Coll (CA)
Chaffey Coll (CA)
Coll of Alameda (CA)
Coll of DuPage (IL)
El Camino Coll (CA)
El Centro Coll (TX)
FIDM/The Fashion Inst of
Design &
Merchandising, Los
Angeles Campus (CA)
FIDM/The Fashion Inst of
Design &
Merchandising, San
Diego Campus (CA)
FIDM/The Fashion Inst of
Design &
Merchandising, San
Francisco
Campus (CA)
Fisher Coll (MA)
Fullerton Coll (CA)
Harper Coll (IL)
Houston Comm Coll
System (TX)
Kirkwood Comm Coll (IA)
Maui Comm Coll (HI)
Merced Coll (CA)
Metropolitan Comm
Coll–Penn Valley (MO)
Monroe Comm Coll (NY)
Moorpark Coll (CA)
Nassau Comm Coll (NY)
Palm Beach Comm
Coll (FL)
Santa Ana Coll (CA)
Tulsa Comm Coll (OK)
Ventura Coll (CA)
Westmoreland County
Comm Coll (PA)
West Valley Coll (CA)

**Fashion
Merchandising**
Alexandria Tech Coll (MN)
The Art Inst of
Philadelphia (PA)
Baltimore City Comm
Coll (MD)
Berkeley Coll, West
Paterson (NJ)
Berkeley Coll-New York
City Campus (NY)
Berkeley Coll-Westchester
Campus (NY)
Bradley Academy for the
Visual Arts (PA)
Briarwood Coll (CT)
Brigham Young U –
Idaho (ID)
Brookhaven Coll (TX)
Brooks Coll,
Sunnyvale (CA)
Central Piedmont Comm
Coll (NC)
Century Coll (MN)
City Coll of San
Francisco (CA)
Cleveland Comm Coll (NC)
Coll of Alameda (CA)
Coll of DuPage (IL)

Comm Coll of
Philadelphia (PA)
Comm Coll of Rhode
Island (RI)
Cuesta Coll (CA)
FIDM/The Fashion Inst of
Design &
Merchandising, Los
Angeles Campus (CA)
FIDM/The Fashion Inst of
Design &
Merchandising, San
Diego Campus (CA)
FIDM/The Fashion Inst of
Design &
Merchandising, San
Francisco
Campus (CA)
Fisher Coll (MA)
Fresno City Coll (CA)
Fullerton Coll (CA)
Gateway Comm Coll (CT)
Genesee Comm Coll (NY)
Grand Rapids Comm
Coll (MI)
Harper Coll (IL)
Houston Comm Coll
System (TX)
Howard Comm Coll (MD)
Indiana Business Coll,
Indianapolis (IN)
Iowa Lakes Comm
Coll (IA)
Joliet Jr Coll (IL)
Katharine Gibbs
School (PA)
Kingsborough Comm Coll
of the City U of New
York (NY)
Kirkwood Comm Coll (IA)
Laredo Comm Coll (TX)
Las Positas Coll (CA)
Lee Coll (TX)
Madison Area Tech
Coll (WI)
Merced Coll (CA)
Mesa Comm Coll (AZ)
Metropolitan Comm
Coll–Penn Valley (MO)
Middle Georgia Coll (GA)
Midlands Tech Coll (SC)
Mississippi Gulf Coast
Comm Coll (MS)
Monroe Comm Coll (NY)
Monterey Peninsula
Coll (CA)
Mt. San Antonio Coll (CA)
Nassau Comm Coll (NY)
New York City Coll of
Technology of the City
U of New York (NY)
Northeastern Jr Coll (CO)
Northwest Mississippi
Comm Coll (MS)
Oakland Comm Coll (MI)
Odessa Coll (TX)
Ohlone Coll (CA)
Orange Coast Coll (CA)
Owens Comm Coll,
Toledo (OH)
Oxnard Coll (CA)
Pace Inst (PA)
Palm Beach Comm
Coll (FL)
Pasadena City Coll (CA)
St. Louis Comm Coll at
Florissant Valley (MO)
San Diego City Coll (CA)
San Joaquin Delta
Coll (CA)
Santa Ana Coll (CA)
Scottsdale Comm
Coll (AZ)
South Plains Coll (TX)
Southwest Mississippi
Comm Coll (MS)
Spokane Falls Comm
Coll (WA)
Tunxis Comm Coll (CT)
Tyler Jr Coll (TX)
Wallace State Comm
Coll (AL)
Westmoreland County
Comm Coll (PA)

**Fiber, Textile and
Weaving Arts**
Antelope Valley Coll (CA)
Mendocino Coll (CA)
Monterey Peninsula
Coll (CA)
Pasadena City Coll (CA)

Film/Cinema Studies
Cochise Coll, Sierra
Vista (AZ)
De Anza Coll (CA)
Lansing Comm Coll (MI)
Moorpark Coll (CA)

Orange Coast Coll (CA)
Santa Barbara City
Coll (CA)
Santa Rosa Jr Coll (CA)
Tallahassee Comm
Coll (FL)

Finance
Academy Coll (MN)
AIB Coll of Business (IA)
Bakersfield Coll (CA)
Bergen Comm Coll (NJ)
Black Hawk Coll,
Moline (IL)
Brigham Young U –
Idaho (ID)
Broward Comm Coll (FL)
Central Piedmont Comm
Coll (NC)
Central Virginia Comm
Coll (VA)
Chattanooga State Tech
Comm Coll (TN)
Chipola Coll (FL)
Cisco Jr Coll (TX)
City Coll of San
Francisco (CA)
City Colls of Chicago,
Harold Washington
College (IL)
Clarendon Coll (TX)
Clovis Comm Coll (NM)
Coastal Bend Coll (TX)
Coll of Southern Idaho (ID)
Comm Coll of
Philadelphia (PA)
Comm Coll of Southern
Nevada (NV)
Cosumnes River Coll,
Sacramento (CA)
Cuyahoga Comm
Coll (OH)
Dodge City Comm
Coll (KS)
El Camino Coll (CA)
Folsom Lake Coll (CA)
Fond du Lac Tribal and
Comm Coll (MN)
Forsyth Tech Comm
Coll (NC)
Fox Valley Tech Coll (WI)
Frederick Comm Coll (MD)
Fulton-Montgomery Comm
Coll (NY)
Gloucester County
Coll (NJ)
Harper Coll (IL)
Hillsborough Comm
Coll (FL)
Hopkinsville Comm
Coll (KY)
Houston Comm Coll
System (TX)
International Business Coll,
Fort Wayne (IN)
Iowa Lakes Comm
Coll (IA)
Jefferson Comm Coll (OH)
Kent State U, Ashtabula
Campus (OH)
Kirkwood Comm Coll (IA)
Lakeshore Tech Coll (WI)
Lake Tahoe Comm
Coll (CA)
Laney Coll (CA)
Lansing Comm Coll (MI)
Lenoir Comm Coll (NC)
Lorain County Comm
Coll (OH)
Los Angeles City Coll (CA)
Los Angeles Mission
Coll (CA)
Los Angeles Southwest
Coll (CA)
Macomb Comm Coll (MI)
Madison Area Tech
Coll (WI)
Manatee Comm Coll (FL)
Marshall Comm and Tech
Coll (WV)
McLennan Comm
Coll (TX)
Mendocino Coll (CA)
Merced Coll (CA)
Mesa Comm Coll (AZ)
Miami Dade Coll (FL)
Mississippi Gulf Coast
Comm Coll (MS)
Morton Coll (IL)
Mt. San Antonio Coll (CA)
Muskegon Comm Coll (MI)
National Park Comm
Coll (AR)
Naugatuck Valley Comm
Coll (CT)
Neosho County Comm
Coll (KS)
New Mexico Jr Coll (NM)

New Mexico Military
Inst (NM)
North Central Michigan
Coll (MI)
Northern Essex Comm
Coll (MA)
North Hennepin Comm
Coll (MN)
NorthWest Arkansas
Comm Coll (AR)
Oklahoma City Comm
Coll (OK)
Onondaga Comm
Coll (NY)
Palm Beach Comm
Coll (FL)
Palo Alto Coll (TX)
Pasadena City Coll (CA)
Passaic County Comm
Coll (NJ)
Polk Comm Coll (FL)
Porterville Coll (CA)
St. Cloud Tech Coll (MN)
St. Louis Comm Coll at
Florissant Valley (MO)
San Bernardino Valley
Coll (CA)
San Diego City Coll (CA)
Santa Barbara City
Coll (CA)
Scottsdale Comm
Coll (AZ)
Seminole Comm Coll (FL)
Southeast Tech Inst (SD)
South Florida Comm
Coll (FL)
South Georgia Coll (GA)
Southwest Mississippi
Comm Coll (MS)
Springfield Tech Comm
Coll (MA)
Stark State Coll of
Technology (OH)
State Fair Comm
Coll (MO)
State U of New York Coll
of Technology at
Alfred (NY)
Tallahassee Comm
Coll (FL)
Terra State Comm
Coll (OH)
Texarkana Coll (TX)
Tidewater Comm Coll (VA)
Tyler Jr Coll (TX)
U of Puerto Rico at
Carolina (PR)
Vincennes U Jasper
Campus (IN)
Wallace State Comm
Coll (AL)
Westchester Comm
Coll (NY)
Western Piedmont Comm
Coll (NC)
Westmoreland County
Comm Coll (PA)
West Virginia U at
Parkersburg (WV)
Wright State U, Lake
Campus (OH)

**Finance and Financial
Management Services
Related**
Black Hawk Coll,
Moline (IL)
National American U,
Bloomington (MN)
Salt Lake Comm Coll (UT)

**Financial Planning
and Services**
Broome Comm Coll (NY)
Howard Comm Coll (MD)
Minnesota State Comm
and Tech Coll–Fergus
Falls (MN)
Waukesha County Tech
Coll (WI)

Fine Arts Related
Oakland Comm Coll (MI)
Reedley Coll (CA)

Fine/Studio Arts
Amarillo Coll (TX)
Asnuntuck Comm
Coll (CT)
Berkeley City Coll (CA)
Clovis Comm Coll (NM)
Coastal Bend Coll (TX)
Coll of the Mainland (TX)
Colorado Mountain Coll,
Alpine Campus (CO)
Finger Lakes Comm
Coll (NY)
Fiorello H. LaGuardia
Comm Coll of the City
U of New York (NY)

Foothill Coll (CA)
Fulton-Montgomery Comm
Coll (NY)
Gloucester County
Coll (NJ)
Holyoke Comm Coll (MA)
Iowa Lakes Comm
Coll (IA)
Jamestown Comm
Coll (NY)
Kankakee Comm Coll (IL)
Lansing Comm Coll (MI)
Manatee Comm Coll (FL)
Massasoit Comm
Coll (MA)
Middlesex Comm Coll (CT)
Monterey Peninsula
Coll (CA)
Morton Coll (IL)
Mount Wachusett Comm
Coll (MA)
Niagara County Comm
Coll (NY)
Northampton County Area
Comm Coll (PA)
Northeastern Jr Coll (CO)
Northern New Mexico
Coll (NM)
North Hennepin Comm
Coll (MN)
Oklahoma City Comm
Coll (OK)
Queensborough Comm
Coll of the City U of
New York (NY)
Sandhills Comm Coll (NC)
Santa Barbara City
Coll (CA)
Springfield Tech Comm
Coll (MA)
Sussex County Comm
Coll (NJ)
Tidewater Comm Coll (VA)
U of New Mexico–Los
Alamos Branch (NM)
Ventura Coll (CA)
Villa Maria Coll of
Buffalo (NY)
Warren County Comm
Coll (NJ)
Westchester Comm
Coll (NY)

**Fire Protection and
Safety Technology**
Antelope Valley Coll (CA)
Capital Comm Coll (CT)
Catawba Valley Comm
Coll (NC)
Central New Mexico
Comm Coll (NM)
Cleveland Comm Coll (NC)
Coll of Lake County (IL)
Coll of Southern
Maryland (MD)
Coll of the Mainland (TX)
Collin County Comm Coll
District (TX)
Comm Coll of Allegheny
County (PA)
Elgin Comm Coll (IL)
Fayetteville Tech Comm
Coll (NC)
John Wood Comm Coll (IL)
Kellogg Comm Coll (MI)
Lamar Inst of
Technology (TX)
Lincoln Land Comm
Coll (IL)
Macomb Comm Coll (MI)
Montgomery Coll (MD)
Montgomery County
Comm Coll (PA)
Moraine Valley Comm
Coll (IL)
Mott Comm Coll (MI)
Owens Comm Coll,
Toledo (OH)
San Juan Coll (NM)
Tulsa Comm Coll (OK)
Union County Coll (NJ)
Victor Valley Coll (CA)
Waukesha County Tech
Coll (WI)
Western Nevada Comm
Coll (NV)

**Fire Protection
Related**
Fayetteville Tech Comm
Coll (NC)
Sussex County Comm
Coll (NJ)

Fire Science
Aims Comm Coll (CO)
Amarillo Coll (TX)
Arizona Western Coll (AZ)
Augusta Tech Coll (GA)

Bakersfield Coll (CA)
Barton County Comm
Coll (KS)
Berkshire Comm Coll (MA)
Blinn Coll (TX)
Brevard Comm Coll (FL)
Broome Comm Coll (NY)
Broward Comm Coll (FL)
Burlington County
Coll (NJ)
Cabrillo Coll (CA)
Cape Cod Comm
Coll (MA)
Central Florida Comm
Coll (FL)
Central Oregon Comm
Coll (OR)
Central Piedmont Comm
Coll (NC)
Chattahoochee Tech
Coll (GA)
Chattanooga State Tech
Comm Coll (TN)
Chippewa Valley Tech
Coll (WI)
Cincinnati State Tech and
Comm Coll (OH)
Cisco Jr Coll (TX)
City Coll of San
Francisco (CA)
City Colls of Chicago,
Harold Washington
College (IL)
City Colls of Chicago,
Richard J. Daley
College (IL)
Clatsop Comm Coll (OR)
Coastal Carolina Comm
Coll (NC)
Cochise Coll, Douglas (AZ)
Cochise Coll, Sierra
Vista (AZ)
Coconino Comm Coll (AZ)
Coll of DuPage (IL)
Coll of Marin (CA)
Coll of San Mateo (CA)
Coll of the Desert (CA)
Coll of the Siskiyous (CA)
Columbia Basin Coll (WA)
Columbia Coll (CA)
Comm Coll of
Philadelphia (PA)
Comm Coll of Rhode
Island (RI)
Comm Coll of Southern
Nevada (NV)
Coosa Valley Tech
Coll (GA)
Cosumnes River Coll,
Sacramento (CA)
Crafton Hills Coll (CA)
Crowder Coll (MO)
Cuyahoga Comm
Coll (OH)
Davidson County Comm
Coll (NC)
Dodge City Comm
Coll (KS)
East Central Coll (MO)
Eastern New Mexico
U–Roswell (NM)
El Camino Coll (CA)
Elgin Comm Coll (IL)
Essex County Coll (NJ)
Everett Comm Coll (WA)
Fox Valley Tech Coll (WI)
Frederick Comm Coll (MD)
Fresno City Coll (CA)
Gateway Comm Coll (CT)
Gateway Tech Coll (WI)
Georgia Military Coll (GA)
Greenville Tech Coll (SC)
Guilford Tech Comm
Coll (NC)
Harper Coll (IL)
Harrisburg Area Comm
Coll (PA)
Hartnell Coll (CA)
Hawkeye Comm Coll (IA)
Hennepin Tech Coll (MN)
Henry Ford Comm
Coll (MI)
Hillsborough Comm
Coll (FL)
Hocking Coll (OH)
Houston Comm Coll
System (TX)
Hutchinson Comm Coll
and Area Vocational
School (KS)
Imperial Valley Coll (CA)
Joliet Jr Coll (IL)
Kansas City Kansas
Comm Coll (KS)
Kirkwood Comm Coll (IA)
Labette Comm Coll (KS)
Lake-Sumter Comm
Coll (FL)

Lake Tahoe Comm
Coll (CA)
Lanier Tech Coll (GA)
Lansing Comm Coll (MI)
Laredo Comm Coll (TX)
Las Positas Coll (CA)
Lawson State Comm
Coll (AL)
Lenoir Comm Coll (NC)
Lorain County Comm
Coll (OH)
Los Angeles Harbor
Coll (CA)
Los Medanos Coll (CA)
Louisiana State U at
Eunice (LA)
Lower Columbia Coll (WA)
Madison Area Tech
Coll (WI)
Manatee Comm Coll (FL)
Massasoit Comm
Coll (MA)
Maui Comm Coll (HI)
Merced Coll (CA)
Meridian Comm Coll (MS)
Mesa Comm Coll (AZ)
Metropolitan Comm
Coll–Blue River (MO)
Miami Dade Coll (FL)
Mid-Plains Comm Coll,
North Platte (NE)
Mission Coll (CA)
Missouri State U–West
Plains (MO)
Mohave Comm Coll (AZ)
Monroe Comm Coll (NY)
Monterey Peninsula
Coll (CA)
Mt. Hood Comm Coll (OR)
Mt. San Antonio Coll (CA)
Mount Wachusett Comm
Coll (MA)
National Park Comm
Coll (AR)
Naugatuck Valley Comm
Coll (CT)
Navarro Coll (TX)
New Mexico Jr Coll (NM)
New Mexico State U–
Alamogordo (NM)
North Shore Comm
Coll (MA)
Northwest-Shoals Comm
Coll (AL)
Oakland Comm Coll (MI)
Odessa Coll (TX)
Oklahoma State U,
Oklahoma City (OK)
Olympic Coll (WA)
Onondaga Comm
Coll (NY)
Oxnard Coll (CA)
Ozarks Tech Comm
Coll (MO)
Palm Beach Comm
Coll (FL)
Pasadena City Coll (CA)
Passaic County Comm
Coll (NJ)
Pierce Coll (WA)
Pima Comm Coll (AZ)
Polk Comm Coll (FL)
Porterville Coll (CA)
Quincy Coll (MA)
Red Rocks Comm
Coll (CO)
Richland Comm Coll (IL)
Riverside Comm Coll
District (CA)
Rogue Comm Coll (OR)
St. Louis Comm Coll at
Florissant Valley (MO)
San Antonio Coll (TX)
San Joaquin Delta
Coll (CA)
Santa Ana Coll (CA)
Santa Rosa Jr Coll (CA)
Savannah Tech Coll (GA)
Schoolcraft Coll (MI)
Scottsdale Comm
Coll (AZ)
Seminole Comm Coll (FL)
Shasta Coll (CA)
Skagit Valley Coll (WA)
Southern Maine Comm
Coll (ME)
South Plains Coll (TX)
Spokane Comm Coll (WA)
Springfield Tech Comm
Coll (MA)
Stark State Coll of
Technology (OH)
Three Rivers Comm
Coll (CT)
Tulsa Comm Coll (OK)
Tyler Jr Coll (TX)
Umpqua Comm Coll (OR)

The U of Montana-Helena
Coll of Technology (MT)
Valdosta Tech Coll (GA)
Valencia Comm Coll (FL)
Victor Valley Coll (CA)
Volunteer State Comm
Coll (TN)
Wallace State Comm
Coll (AL)
Wenatchee Valley
Coll (WA)
West Georgia Tech
Coll (GA)
Westmoreland County
Comm Coll (PA)
Wilson Tech Comm
Coll (NC)
Yuba Coll (CA)

Fire Services Administration

Black Hawk Coll,
Moline (IL)
Calhoun Comm Coll (AL)
Capital Comm Coll (CT)
Erie Comm Coll, South
Campus (NY)
Lower Columbia Coll (WA)
Minnesota State Comm
and Tech Coll–Fergus
Falls (MN)
Northampton County Area
Comm Coll (PA)
North Iowa Area Comm
Coll (IA)
Olympic Coll (WA)

Fish/Game Management

Central Oregon Comm
Coll (OR)
Chattanooga State Tech
Comm Coll (TN)
Coll of Southern Idaho (ID)
Finger Lakes Comm
Coll (NY)
Fox Valley Tech Coll (WI)
Fullerton Coll (CA)
Garrett Coll (MD)
Hocking Coll (OH)
Iowa Lakes Comm
Coll (IA)
Itasca Comm Coll (MN)
Kirkwood Comm Coll (IA)
Minot State U–Bottineau
Campus (ND)
Monterey Peninsula
Coll (CA)
Mt. Hood Comm Coll (OR)
North Idaho Coll (ID)
State U of New York Coll
of Agriculture and
Technology at
Morrisville (NY)
Swainsboro Tech Coll (GA)
Turtle Mountain Comm
Coll (ND)

Fishing and Fisheries Sciences And Management

Brunswick Comm
Coll (NC)
Hocking Coll (OH)
Iowa Lakes Comm
Coll (IA)
Peninsula Coll (WA)
Santa Rosa Jr Coll (CA)

Flight Instruction

Iowa Lakes Comm
Coll (IA)

Floriculture/Floristry Management

Minot State U–Bottineau
Campus (ND)
The Ohio State U Ag Tech
Inst (OH)
Santa Rosa Jr Coll (CA)

Floristry Marketing

Oklahoma State U,
Oklahoma City (OK)

Food Preparation

Iowa Lakes Comm
Coll (IA)
Keystone Coll (PA)
Northampton County Area
Comm Coll (PA)

Food Sales Operations

Montgomery County
Comm Coll (PA)

Foods and Nutrition Related

Iowa Lakes Comm
Coll (IA)

Food Science

Cabrillo Coll (CA)
Central Piedmont Comm
Coll (NC)
El Centro Coll (TX)
Hawkeye Comm Coll (IA)
Hocking Coll (OH)
Los Angeles City Coll (CA)
Miami Dade Coll (FL)
Mt. Hood Comm Coll (OR)
Ohlone Coll (CA)
Orange Coast Coll (CA)
St. Louis Comm Coll at
Florissant Valley (MO)
South Seattle Comm
Coll (WA)

Food Service and Dining Room Management

Iowa Lakes Comm
Coll (IA)

Food Services Technology

Anne Arundel Comm
Coll (MD)
Cabrillo Coll (CA)
Central Piedmont Comm
Coll (NC)
Cerritos Coll (CA)
Chattanooga State Tech
Comm Coll (TN)
Columbia Coll (CA)
Comm Coll of Southern
Nevada (NV)
El Centro Coll (TX)
Fresno City Coll (CA)
Henry Ford Comm
Coll (MI)
Kirkwood Comm Coll (IA)
Leeward Comm Coll (HI)
Lenoir Comm Coll (NC)
Los Angeles City Coll (CA)
Maui Comm Coll (HI)
Mission Coll (CA)
Mohawk Valley Comm
Coll (NY)
Monroe Comm Coll (NY)
Oklahoma State U,
Okmulgee (OK)
Orange Coast Coll (CA)
Owens Comm Coll,
Toledo (OH)
Richland Comm Coll (IL)
Robeson Comm Coll (NC)
St. Louis Comm Coll at
Florissant Valley (MO)
San Joaquin Delta
Coll (CA)
Skagit Valley Coll (WA)
Southern Maine Comm
Coll (ME)
South Seattle Comm
Coll (WA)
Spokane Comm Coll (WA)
Stark State Coll of
Technology (OH)
State U of New York Coll
of Agriculture and
Technology at
Morrisville (NY)
Victor Valley Coll (CA)
Westchester Comm
Coll (NY)

Foodservice Systems Administration

Burlington County
Coll (NJ)
Comm Coll of Allegheny
County (PA)
Flint Hills Tech Coll (KS)
Mohawk Valley Comm
Coll (NY)
Mott Comm Coll (MI)
Oakland Comm Coll (MI)
Santa Barbara City
Coll (CA)

Foods, Nutrition, and Wellness

Antelope Valley Coll (CA)
Bakersfield Coll (CA)
Brigham Young U –
Idaho (ID)
Colby Comm Coll (KS)
Comm Coll of
Philadelphia (PA)
Cuesta Coll (CA)
Harrisburg Area Comm
Coll (PA)
Holyoke Comm Coll (MA)
Leech Lake Tribal
Coll (MN)
North Shore Comm
Coll (MA)
Northwest Mississippi
Comm Coll (MS)

Ohlone Coll (CA)
Orange Coast Coll (CA)
Palm Beach Comm
Coll (FL)
Santa Ana Coll (CA)
State U of New York Coll
of Agriculture and
Technology at
Morrisville (NY)

Foreign Languages and Literatures

Coastal Georgia Comm
Coll (GA)
Cochise Coll, Douglas (AZ)
Coll of Southern Idaho (ID)
Comm Coll of Allegheny
County (PA)
Dixie State Coll of
Utah (UT)
Eastern Arizona Coll (AZ)
Georgia Highlands
Coll (GA)
Hutchinson Comm Coll
and Area Vocational
School (KS)
Iowa Lakes Comm
Coll (IA)
Linn-Benton Comm
Coll (OR)
Lower Columbia Coll (WA)
Reedley Coll (CA)
San Juan Coll (NM)
Sheridan Coll–Sheridan
and Gillette (WY)
Skagit Valley Coll (WA)

Foreign Language Teacher Education

Manatee Comm Coll (FL)

Forensic Science and Technology

Appalachian Tech
Coll (GA)
Arkansas State
U–Mountain
Home (AR)
Arkansas State
U–Newport (AR)
Fayetteville Tech Comm
Coll (NC)
Lehigh Carbon Comm
Coll (PA)
Macomb Comm Coll (MI)
Massachusetts Bay Comm
Coll (MA)
Minnesota State Comm
and Tech Coll–Fergus
Falls (MN)
Mohawk Valley Comm
Coll (NY)
New River Comm Coll (VA)
North Arkansas Coll (AR)
Oakland Comm Coll (MI)
Tunxis Comm Coll (CT)

Forest/Forest Resources Management

Allegany Coll of
Maryland (MD)
Western Nebraska Comm
Coll (NE)

Forestry

Allen County Comm
Coll (KS)
Bainbridge Coll (GA)
Bakersfield Coll (CA)
Barton County Comm
Coll (KS)
Brigham Young U –
Idaho (ID)
Central Oregon Comm
Coll (OR)
Cerritos Coll (CA)
Chattanooga State Tech
Comm Coll (TN)
City Coll of San
Francisco (CA)
Coastal Georgia Comm
Coll (GA)
Colby Comm Coll (KS)
Coll of Southern Idaho (ID)
Coll of the Redwoods (CA)
Dixie State Coll of
Utah (UT)
Dodge City Comm
Coll (KS)
Eastern Arizona Coll (AZ)
Fullerton Coll (CA)
Georgia Highlands
Coll (GA)
Grand Rapids Comm
Coll (MI)
Hocking Coll (OH)
Iowa Lakes Comm
Coll (IA)
Itasca Comm Coll (MN)

Ohlone Coll (CA)
Orange Coast Coll (CA)
Palm Beach Comm
Coll (FL)
Santa Ana Coll (CA)
State U of New York Coll
of Agriculture and
Technology at
Morrisville (NY)

Foreign Languages and Literatures

Keystone Coll (PA)
Kirkwood Comm Coll (IA)
Miami Dade Coll (FL)
Monroe Comm Coll (NY)
Northeastern Jr Coll (CO)
North Idaho Coll (ID)
North Shore Comm
Coll (MA)
Northwest-Shoals Comm
Coll (AL)
Potomac State Coll of
West Virginia U (WV)
Salish Kootenai Coll (MT)
Spokane Comm Coll (WA)
State U of New York Coll
of Agriculture and
Technology at
Morrisville (NY)
Treasure Valley Comm
Coll (OR)
Trinidad State Jr Coll (CO)
Tulsa Comm Coll (OK)
Umpqua Comm Coll (OR)
Western Wyoming Comm
Coll (WY)

Forestry Technology

Albany Tech Coll (GA)
Central Oregon Comm
Coll (OR)
Chattanooga State Tech
Comm Coll (TN)
Columbia Coll (CA)
Dabney S. Lancaster
Comm Coll (VA)
El Camino Coll (CA)
Fox Valley Tech Coll (WI)
Hartnell Coll (CA)
Hocking Coll (OH)
Itasca Comm Coll (MN)
Jones County Jr Coll (MS)
Keystone Coll (PA)
Mt. Hood Comm Coll (OR)
Mt. San Antonio Coll (CA)
Ogeechee Tech Coll (GA)
Okefenokee Tech
Coll (GA)
Pasadena City Coll (CA)
Penn State Mont Alto (PA)
Potomac State Coll of
West Virginia U (WV)
Salish Kootenai Coll (MT)
Southeastern Comm
Coll (NC)
State U of New York Coll
of Agriculture and
Technology at
Morrisville (NY)
State U of New York Coll
of Environmental
Science & Forestry,
Ranger School (NY)
State U of New York Coll
of Technology at
Canton (NY)
Swainsboro Tech Coll (GA)
Treasure Valley Comm
Coll (OR)
Wayne Comm Coll (NC)

French

Bakersfield Coll (CA)
Blinn Coll (TX)
Brigham Young U –
Idaho (ID)
Cañada Coll (CA)
Centralia Coll (WA)
Cerritos Coll (CA)
Chaffey Coll (CA)
Cisco Jr Coll (TX)
Citrus Coll (CA)
City Colls of Chicago,
Harold Washington
College (IL)
Coastal Bend Coll (TX)
Coll of Marin (CA)
Coll of San Mateo (CA)
Coll of the Canyons (CA)
Coll of the Desert (CA)
Contra Costa Coll (CA)
Crafton Hills Coll (CA)
Grossmont Coll (CA)
Imperial Valley Coll (CA)
Kirkwood Comm Coll (IA)
Lee Coll (TX)
Los Angeles City Coll (CA)
Los Angeles Mission
Coll (CA)
Manatee Comm Coll (FL)
Mendocino Coll (CA)
Miami Dade Coll (FL)
Monterey Peninsula
Coll (CA)
New Mexico Military
Inst (NM)
North Idaho Coll (ID)
Orange Coast Coll (CA)
Pasadena City Coll (CA)
Red Rocks Comm
Coll (CO)

San Bernardino Valley
Coll (CA)
San Joaquin Delta
Coll (CA)
Santa Barbara City
Coll (CA)
South Georgia Coll (GA)
Tulsa Comm Coll (OK)
Western Nebraska Comm
Coll (NE)
West Los Angeles
Coll (CA)
West Valley Coll (CA)
Young Harris Coll (GA)

Funeral Service and Mortuary Science

Allen County Comm
Coll (KS)
Amarillo Coll (TX)
American Academy
McAllister Inst of
Funeral Service (NY)
Arkansas State
U–Mountain
Home (AR)
Barton County Comm
Coll (KS)
Bishop State Comm
Coll (AL)
Briarwood Coll (CT)
Catawba Valley Comm
Coll (NC)
Cypress Coll (CA)
Everett Comm Coll (WA)
Fayetteville Tech Comm
Coll (NC)
FINE Mortuary Coll,
LLC (MA)
Fiorello H. LaGuardia
Comm Coll of the City
U of New York (NY)
Florence-Darlington Tech
Coll (SC)
Forsyth Tech Comm
Coll (NC)
John A. Gupton Coll (TN)
John Tyler Comm Coll (VA)
Kansas City Kansas
Comm Coll (KS)
Miami Dade Coll (FL)
Mid-America Coll of
Funeral Service (IN)
Mt. Hood Comm Coll (OR)
Nassau Comm Coll (NY)
Northampton County Area
Comm Coll (PA)
Ogeechee Tech Coll (GA)
Piedmont Tech Coll (SC)
San Antonio Coll (TX)
State U of New York Coll
of Technology at
Canton (NY)

Furniture Design and Manufacturing

Catawba Valley Comm
Coll (NC)
Vincennes U Jasper
Campus (IN)

General Retailing/Wholesaling

Alamance Comm Coll (NC)
Asheville-Buncombe Tech
Comm Coll (NC)
Century Coll (MN)
Comm Coll of Rhode
Island (RI)
Dixie State Coll of
Utah (UT)
Elgin Comm Coll (IL)
Gadsden State Comm
Coll (AL)
Gateway Tech Coll (WI)
Harrisburg Area Comm
Coll (PA)
Nassau Comm Coll (NY)
Orange Coast Coll (CA)
St. Cloud Tech Coll (MN)

General Studies

Allen County Comm
Coll (KS)
Alpena Comm Coll (MI)
Amarillo Coll (TX)
Arkansas State
U–Newport (AR)
Asnuntuck Comm
Coll (CT)
Barton County Comm
Coll (KS)
Berkeley City Coll (CA)
Bishop State Comm
Coll (AL)
Bladen Comm Coll (NC)
Briarwood Coll (CT)
Calhoun Comm Coll (AL)
Career Tech Coll (LA)
Carroll Comm Coll (MD)

Cecil Comm Coll (MD)
Central Maine Comm Coll (ME)
Central Virginia Comm Coll (VA)
Central Wyoming Coll (WY)
Cincinnati State Tech and Comm Coll (OH)
City Colls of Chicago, Wilbur Wright College (IL)
Clackamas Comm Coll (OR)
Clarendon Coll (TX)
Cleveland State Comm Coll (TN)
Cochise Coll, Douglas (AZ)
Coll of Alameda (CA)
Coll of the Mainland (TX)
Colorado Mountain Coll, Timberline Campus (CO)
Comm Coll of Allegheny County (PA)
Comm Coll of Rhode Island (RI)
Crowder Coll (MO)
East Central Coll (MO)
Eastern West Virginia Comm and Tech Coll (WV)
Fayetteville Tech Comm Coll (NC)
Frederick Comm Coll (MD)
Front Range Comm Coll (CO)
Gadsden State Comm Coll (AL)
Garrett Coll (MD)
Germanna Comm Coll (VA)
Gordon Coll (GA)
Grays Harbor Coll (WA)
Howard Comm Coll (MD)
Illinois Eastern Comm Colls, Frontier Community College (IL)
Illinois Eastern Comm Colls, Lincoln Trail College (IL)
Illinois Eastern Comm Colls, Olney Central College (IL)
Illinois Eastern Comm Colls, Wabash Valley College (IL)
Iowa Lakes Comm Coll (IA)
Itasca Comm Coll (MN)
James H. Faulkner State Comm Coll (AL)
John Wood Comm Coll (IL)
Kellogg Comm Coll (MI)
Kennebec Valley Comm Coll (ME)
Kettering Coll of Medical Arts (OH)
Lake Land Coll (IL)
Lehigh Carbon Comm Coll (PA)
Lincoln Land Comm Coll (IL)
Louisiana State U at Eunice (LA)
Macomb Comm Coll (MI)
Martin Comm Coll (NC)
Massachusetts Bay Comm Coll (MA)
Mercy Coll of Northwest Ohio (OH)
Miami Dade Coll (FL)
Miami U Hamilton (OH)
Missouri State U–West Plains (MO)
Mohawk Valley Comm Coll (NY)
Montgomery Coll (MD)
Mott Comm Coll (MI)
Mount Wachusett Comm Coll (MA)
Nassau Comm Coll (NY)
National American U, Rio Rancho (NM)
New Hampshire Comm Tech Coll, Nashua/Claremont (NH)
New Hampshire Tech Inst (NH)
New River Comm Coll (VA)
Niagara County Comm Coll (NY)
Northampton County Area Comm Coll (PA)
Northeast Comm Coll (NE)
Northern Essex Comm Coll (MA)

Northwest-Shoals Comm Coll (AL)
Oakland Comm Coll (MI)
Oregon Coast Comm Coll (OR)
Owens Comm Coll, Toledo (OH)
Parkland Coll (IL)
Piedmont Virginia Comm Coll (VA)
Pima Comm Coll (AZ)
Pueblo Comm Coll (CO)
Reedley Coll (CA)
Roxbury Comm Coll (MA)
Salt Lake Comm Coll (UT)
San Juan Coll (NM)
Sheridan Coll–Sheridan and Gillette (WY)
Southern Maine Comm Coll (ME)
Southern U at Shreveport (LA)
Southside Virginia Comm Coll (VA)
Southwestern Michigan Coll (MI)
Springfield Tech Comm Coll (MA)
Taft Coll (CA)
Terra State Comm Coll (OH)
The U of Akron–Wayne Coll (OH)
The U of Montana-Helena Coll of Technology (MT)
U of New Mexico–Gallup (NM)
U of New Mexico–Taos (NM)
Western Nebraska Comm Coll (NE)
Western Nevada Comm Coll (NV)
Western Wyoming Comm Coll (WY)
West Virginia State Comm and Tech Coll (WV)
Wilson Tech Comm Coll (NC)
York County Comm Coll (ME)

Geography
Allen County Comm Coll (KS)
Bakersfield Coll (CA)
Brigham Young U – Idaho (ID)
Cankdeska Cikana Comm Coll (ND)
Cañada Coll (CA)
Cerritos Coll (CA)
Coll of Alameda (CA)
Coll of Southern Idaho (ID)
Coll of the Canyons (CA)
Coll of the Desert (CA)
Contra Costa Coll (CA)
Cypress Coll (CA)
El Camino Coll (CA)
Grossmont Coll (CA)
Itasca Comm Coll (MN)
Joliet Jr Coll (IL)
Lansing Comm Coll (MI)
Los Angeles Mission Coll (CA)
Lower Columbia Coll (WA)
Miami U–Middletown Campus (OH)
Mississippi Delta Comm Coll (MS)
Orange Coast Coll (CA)
Pasadena City Coll (CA)
Pennsylvania Highland Comm Coll (PA)
San Bernardino Valley Coll (CA)
Santa Ana Coll (CA)
Santa Barbara City Coll (CA)
Santa Rosa Jr Coll (CA)
Santiago Canyon Coll (CA)
Skagit Valley Coll (WA)
Tulsa Comm Coll (OK)
Western Nebraska Comm Coll (NE)
Western Wyoming Comm Coll (WY)
West Hills Comm Coll (CA)
West Los Angeles Coll (CA)
Wright State U, Lake Campus (OH)

Geology/Earth Science
Amarillo Coll (TX)
Arizona Western Coll (AZ)
Bakersfield Coll (CA)

Barton County Comm Coll (KS)
Brigham Young U – Idaho (ID)
Cañada Coll (CA)
Centralia Coll (WA)
Central Texas Coll (TX)
Cerritos Coll (CA)
Chaffey Coll (CA)
City Coll of San Francisco (CA)
City Colls of Chicago, Olive-Harvey College (IL)
Coastal Bend Coll (TX)
Coastal Georgia Comm Coll (GA)
Colby Comm Coll (KS)
Coll of Marin (CA)
Coll of San Mateo (CA)
Coll of Southern Idaho (ID)
Coll of the Canyons (CA)
Coll of the Desert (CA)
Coll of the Siskiyous (CA)
Colorado Mountain Coll, Alpine Campus (CO)
Columbia Coll (CA)
Contra Costa Coll (CA)
Cosumnes River Coll, Sacramento (CA)
Crafton Hills Coll (CA)
Cuesta Coll (CA)
Cypress Coll (CA)
Dixie State Coll of Utah (UT)
Eastern Arizona Coll (AZ)
East Georgia Coll (GA)
El Camino Coll (CA)
Everett Comm Coll (WA)
Folsom Lake Coll (CA)
Fullerton Coll (CA)
Georgia Highlands Coll (GA)
Grand Rapids Comm Coll (MI)
Grayson County Coll (TX)
Great Basin Coll (NV)
Grossmont Coll (CA)
Iowa Lakes Comm Coll (IA)
Lansing Comm Coll (MI)
Lee Coll (TX)
Lower Columbia Coll (WA)
Miami Dade Coll (FL)
Monterey Peninsula Coll (CA)
Moorpark Coll (CA)
North Idaho Coll (ID)
Odessa Coll (TX)
Orange Coast Coll (CA)
Palo Alto Coll (TX)
Pasadena City Coll (CA)
Potomac State Coll of West Virginia U (WV)
Red Rocks Comm Coll (CO)
St. Philip's Coll (TX)
San Bernardino Valley Coll (CA)
San Joaquin Delta Coll (CA)
San Juan Coll (NM)
Santa Ana Coll (CA)
Santa Barbara City Coll (CA)
Santa Rosa Jr Coll (CA)
Santiago Canyon Coll (CA)
Skagit Valley Coll (WA)
Tulsa Comm Coll (OK)
Western Wyoming Comm Coll (WY)
West Hills Comm Coll (CA)
West Los Angeles Coll (CA)
Young Harris Coll (GA)

German
Bakersfield Coll (CA)
Blinn Coll (TX)
Brigham Young U – Idaho (ID)
Cañada Coll (CA)
Centralia Coll (WA)
Cerritos Coll (CA)
Chaffey Coll (CA)
Citrus Coll (CA)
City Colls of Chicago, Harold Washington College (IL)
Coastal Bend Coll (TX)
Coll of Marin (CA)
Coll of San Mateo (CA)
Coll of the Canyons (CA)
Contra Costa Coll (CA)
El Camino Coll (CA)
Everett Comm Coll (WA)
Grossmont Coll (CA)
Lee Coll (TX)
Los Angeles City Coll (CA)

Manatee Comm Coll (FL)
Miami Dade Coll (FL)
Monterey Peninsula Coll (CA)
New Mexico Military Inst (NM)
North Idaho Coll (ID)
Orange Coast Coll (CA)
Pasadena City Coll (CA)
Red Rocks Comm Coll (CO)
San Bernardino Valley Coll (CA)
San Joaquin Delta Coll (CA)
South Georgia Coll (GA)
Tulsa Comm Coll (OK)
Western Nebraska Comm Coll (NE)
West Valley Coll (CA)

Gerontological Services
Albany Tech Coll (GA)
Central Georgia Tech Coll (GA)
Santa Rosa Jr Coll (CA)

Gerontology
Baltimore City Comm Coll (MD)
Brown Mackie Coll–Cincinnati (OH)
Brown Mackie Coll–Louisville (KY)
Brown Mackie Coll–Merrillville (IN)
Chaffey Coll (CA)
City Colls of Chicago, Wilbur Wright College (IL)
Comm Coll of Philadelphia (PA)
Cosumnes River Coll, Sacramento (CA)
El Camino Coll (CA)
Elgin Comm Coll (IL)
Eugenio María de Hostos Comm Coll of the City U of New York (NY)
Fiorello H. LaGuardia Comm Coll of the City U of New York (NY)
Gateway Comm Coll (CT)
Genesee Comm Coll (NY)
Lansing Comm Coll (MI)
Midlands Tech Coll (SC)
Naugatuck Valley Comm Coll (CT)
New River Comm Coll (VA)
North Shore Comm Coll (MA)
Oakland Comm Coll (MI)
Oklahoma City Comm Coll (OK)
Ridgewater Coll (MN)
Sandhills Comm Coll (NC)
Spokane Falls Comm Coll (WA)
Union County Coll (NJ)
West Virginia State Comm and Tech Coll (WV)

Glazier
Metropolitan Comm Coll–Business & Technology Campus (MO)

Graphic and Printing Equipment Operation/Production
Bishop State Comm Coll (AL)
Burlington County Coll (NJ)
Central Comm Coll–Hastings Campus (NE)
Central Maine Comm Coll (ME)
Central Piedmont Comm Coll (NC)
Central Texas Coll (TX)
Chattanooga State Tech Comm Coll (TN)
City Coll of San Francisco (CA)
City Colls of Chicago, Kennedy-King College (IL)
Clinton Comm Coll (IA)
Coll of DuPage (IL)
Comm Coll of Southern Nevada (NV)
Don Bosco Tech Inst (CA)
Erie Comm Coll, South Campus (NY)
Flint Hills Tech Coll (KS)
Forsyth Tech Comm Coll (NC)

Fox Valley Tech Coll (WI)
Fresno City Coll (CA)
Fullerton Coll (CA)
Fulton-Montgomery Comm Coll (NY)
Golden West Coll (CA)
H. Councill Trenholm State Tech Coll (AL)
Houston Comm Coll System (TX)
Iowa Lakes Comm Coll (IA)
Kirkwood Comm Coll (IA)
Lake Land Coll (IL)
Laney Coll (CA)
Lenoir Comm Coll (NC)
Macomb Comm Coll (MI)
Madison Area Tech Coll (WI)
Metropolitan Comm Coll (NE)
Midlands Tech Coll (SC)
Mission Coll (CA)
Mississippi Delta Comm Coll (MS)
Moberly Area Comm Coll (MO)
Monroe Comm Coll (NY)
Montgomery Coll (MD)
Moorpark Coll (CA)
Northern Oklahoma Coll (OK)
Oklahoma State U, Okmulgee (OK)
Ozarks Tech Comm Coll (MO)
Riverside Comm Coll District (CA)
Sacramento City Coll (CA)
San Diego City Coll (CA)
San Joaquin Delta Coll (CA)
Southeast Tech Inst (SD)
Southwestern Michigan Coll (MI)
Tyler Jr Coll (TX)
U of New Mexico–Gallup (NM)
Westmoreland County Comm Coll (PA)

Graphic Communications
Clark Coll (WA)
Iowa Lakes Comm Coll (IA)
Waukesha County Tech Coll (WI)

Graphic Communications Related
H. Councill Trenholm State Tech Coll (AL)
Linn-Benton Comm Coll (OR)
Western Career Coll, Pleasant Hill (CA)
Wright State U, Lake Campus (OH)

Graphic Design
Academy Coll (MN)
The Art Inst of New York City (NY)
The Art Inst of Ohio–Cincinnati (OH)
The Art Inst of Philadelphia (PA)
Barton County Comm Coll (KS)
Brown Mackie Coll–Louisville (KY)
Calhoun Comm Coll (AL)
CollAmerica–Colorado Springs (CO)
CollAmerica–Denver (CO)
Iowa Lakes Comm Coll (IA)
Keystone Coll (PA)
King's Coll (NC)
Massasoit Comm Coll (MA)
Mott Comm Coll (MI)
Northampton County Area Comm Coll (PA)
North Hennepin Comm Coll (MN)
Oakland Comm Coll (MI)
Parkland Coll (IL)
Platt Coll San Diego (CA)
Remington Coll–Fort Worth Campus (TX)
Salt Lake Comm Coll (UT)
Santa Rosa Jr Coll (CA)
Springfield Tech Comm Coll (MA)
Tidewater Comm Coll (VA)
Villa Maria Coll of Buffalo (NY)

Waukesha County Tech Coll (WI)

Greenhouse Management
Comm Coll of Allegheny County (PA)
Joliet Jr Coll (IL)
Minot State U–Bottineau Campus (ND)
The Ohio State U Ag Tech Inst (OH)

Gunsmithing
Trinidad State Jr Coll (CO)

Hazardous Materials Management and Waste Technology
Barton County Comm Coll (KS)
Kansas City Kansas Comm Coll (KS)
Odessa Coll (TX)

Health Aide
Allen County Comm Coll (KS)
Central Arizona Coll (AZ)
Springfield Tech Comm Coll (MA)

Health and Medical Administrative Services Related
Catawba Valley Comm Coll (NC)
Keiser U, Miami (FL)
Western Career Coll, Pleasant Hill (CA)
Western Career Coll, San Leandro (CA)

Health and Physical Education
Alexandria Tech Coll (MN)
Allen County Comm Coll (KS)
Antelope Valley Coll (CA)
Citrus Coll (CA)
Clovis Comm Coll (NM)
Coastal Georgia Comm Coll (GA)
Cochise Coll, Douglas (AZ)
Comm Coll of Allegheny County (PA)
Eastern Arizona Coll (AZ)
Gloucester County Coll (NJ)
Iowa Lakes Comm Coll (IA)
John Wood Comm Coll (IL)
Lassen Comm Coll District (CA)
Lawson State Comm Coll (AL)
Louisburg Coll (NC)
Northeast Comm Coll (NE)
Reedley Coll (CA)
Sheridan Coll–Sheridan and Gillette (WY)
Western Nebraska Comm Coll (NE)

Health and Physical Education Related
Bryan Coll (CA)
Kingsborough Comm Coll of the City U of New York (NY)
Oakland Comm Coll (MI)
Santa Rosa Jr Coll (CA)

Health/Health Care Administration
Brown Mackie Coll–Akron (OH)
Brown Mackie Coll–Cincinnati (OH)
Brown Mackie Coll–Findlay (OH)
Brown Mackie Coll–Louisville (KY)
Brown Mackie Coll–North Canton (OH)
Brown Mackie Coll–Northern Kentucky (KY)
Brown Mackie Coll–South Bend (IN)
Caldwell Comm Coll and Tech Inst (NC)
Central Piedmont Comm Coll (NC)
CollAmerica–Colorado Springs (CO)
CollAmerica–Denver (CO)
Coll of DuPage (IL)
Coll of Southern Idaho (ID)
ECPI Coll of Technology (VA)
ECPI Tech Coll (VA)

ECPI Tech Coll (VA)
Essex County Coll (NJ)
Houston Comm Coll System (TX)
International Inst of the Americas, Mesa (AZ)
International Inst of the Americas, Phoenix (AZ)
International Inst of the Americas, Tucson (AZ)
International Inst of the Americas (NM)
Inver Hills Comm Coll (MN)
Iowa Lakes Comm Coll (IA)
Manatee Comm Coll (FL)
National American U, Bloomington (MN)
National American U, Rio Rancho (NM)
National Park Comm Coll (AR)
North Idaho Coll (ID)
Oakland Comm Coll (MI)
Pennsylvania Highland Comm Coll (PA)
Pioneer Pacific Coll, Wilsonville (OR)
Rasmussen Coll Brooklyn Park (MN)
South Plains Coll (TX)
Technology Education Coll (OH)
Tyler Jr Coll (TX)
U of Alaska Southeast, Sitka Campus (AK)

Health Information/ Medical Records Administration
Amarillo Coll (TX)
Baltimore City Comm Coll (MD)
Barton County Comm Coll (KS)
Black Hawk Coll, Moline (IL)
Bowling Green State U–Firelands Coll (OH)
Briarwood Coll (CT)
Brunswick Comm Coll (NC)
Business Inst of Pennsylvania, Sharon (PA)
Cabrillo Coll (CA)
Central New Mexico Comm Coll (NM)
Central Piedmont Comm Coll (NC)
Chattanooga State Tech Comm Coll (TN)
Chippewa Valley Tech Coll (WI)
City Coll of San Francisco (CA)
City Colls of Chicago, Harry S. Truman College (IL)
Coll of DuPage (IL)
Comm Coll of Philadelphia (PA)
Comm Coll of Southern Nevada (NV)
Cosumnes River Coll, Sacramento (CA)
Cypress Coll (CA)
Davidson County Comm Coll (NC)
Dodge City Comm Coll (KS)
Draughons Jr Coll (KY)
ECPI Coll of Technology (VA)
ECPI Tech Coll (VA)
ECPI Tech Coll (VA)
Elaine P. Nunez Comm Coll (LA)
El Centro Coll (TX)
Elgin Comm Coll (IL)
Florence-Darlington Tech Coll (SC)
Fort Berthold Comm Coll (ND)
Fresno City Coll (CA)
Gateway Tech Coll (WI)
Hagerstown Comm Coll (MD)
Harrisburg Area Comm Coll (PA)
Henry Ford Comm Coll (MI)
Hocking Coll (OH)
Holyoke Comm Coll (MA)
Houston Comm Coll System (TX)
Kennebec Valley Comm Coll (ME)

Kirkwood Comm Coll (IA)
Lake-Sumter Comm Coll (FL)
LDS Business Coll (UT)
McLennan Comm Coll (TX)
Meridian Comm Coll (MS)
Metropolitan Comm Coll–Penn Valley (MO)
Miami Dade Coll (FL)
Mississippi Delta Comm Coll (MS)
Monroe Comm Coll (NY)
National Park Comm Coll (AR)
North Central Texas Coll (TX)
Northeast Iowa Comm Coll (IA)
Northern Essex Comm Coll (MA)
Oklahoma City Comm Coll (OK)
Onondaga Comm Coll (NY)
Passaic County Comm Coll (NJ)
Polk Comm Coll (FL)
Pueblo Comm Coll (CO)
Ridgewater Coll (MN)
Roane State Comm Coll (TN)
Saint Charles Comm Coll (MO)
Southern U at Shreveport (LA)
South Plains Coll (TX)
Southwestern Comm Coll (NC)
Spokane Comm Coll (WA)
Stark State Coll of Technology (OH)
State Fair Comm Coll (MO)
State U of New York Coll of Technology at Alfred (NY)
Trocaire Coll (NY)
Tulsa Comm Coll (OK)
Turtle Mountain Comm Coll (ND)
Wallace State Comm Coll (AL)
Westmoreland County Comm Coll (PA)
West Valley Coll (CA)

Health Information/ Medical Records Technology
Arizona Coll of Allied Health (AZ)
Atlanta Tech Coll (GA)
Bishop State Comm Coll (AL)
Blinn Coll (TX)
Broome Comm Coll (NY)
Burlington County Coll (NJ)
Catawba Valley Comm Coll (NC)
Central Comm Coll–Hastings Campus (NE)
Central Florida Comm Coll (FL)
Central Oregon Comm Coll (OR)
Cincinnati State Tech and Comm Coll (OH)
Coll of DuPage (IL)
Columbus Tech Coll (GA)
Comm Coll of Allegheny County (PA)
Dyersburg State Comm Coll (TN)
Erie Comm Coll, North Campus (NY)
Fayetteville Tech Comm Coll (NC)
Heart of Georgia Tech Coll (GA)
Houston Comm Coll System (TX)
Hutchinson Comm Coll and Area Vocational School (KS)
Indiana Business Coll, Anderson (IN)
Indiana Business Coll, Muncie (IN)
ITT Tech Inst, Rancho Cordova (CA)
ITT Tech Inst, San Bernardino (CA)
ITT Tech Inst, San Diego (CA)
ITT Tech Inst, San Dimas (CA)
ITT Tech Inst, Sylmar (CA)

ITT Tech Inst, Torrance (CA)
ITT Tech Inst, Lake Mary (FL)
ITT Tech Inst, Tampa (FL)
ITT Tech Inst (ID)
ITT Tech Inst, Indianapolis (IN)
ITT Tech Inst, Newburgh (IN)
ITT Tech Inst, Earth City (MO)
ITT Tech Inst, Dayton (OH)
ITT Tech Inst, Hilliard (OH)
ITT Tech Inst, Warrensville Heights (OH)
ITT Tech Inst, Youngstown (OH)
ITT Tech Inst (OR)
ITT Tech Inst (UT)
ITT Tech Inst, Seattle (WA)
ITT Tech Inst, Green Bay (WI)
Jefferson Comm and Tech Coll (KY)
Lamar Inst of Technology (TX)
Lee Coll (TX)
Lehigh Carbon Comm Coll (PA)
Marshall Comm and Tech Coll (WV)
Mercy Coll of Northwest Ohio (OH)
Midlands Tech Coll (SC)
Mohawk Valley Comm Coll (NY)
Montgomery Coll (MD)
Moraine Valley Comm Coll (IL)
Northwestern Tech Coll (GA)
Northwest Iowa Comm Coll (IA)
Ogeechee Tech Coll (GA)
Owens Comm Coll, Toledo (OH)
Ozarka Coll (AR)
Ozarks Tech Comm Coll (MO)
Panola Coll (TX)
Rasmussen Coll Brooklyn Park (MN)
St. Philip's Coll (TX)
San Juan Coll (NM)
Santa Barbara City Coll (CA)
Schoolcraft Coll (MI)
South Piedmont Comm Coll (NC)
Southwestern Comm Coll (NC)
Tallahassee Comm Coll (FL)
Taylor Business Inst (IL)
Texas State Tech Coll West Texas (TX)
Vernon Coll (TX)
Volunteer State Comm Coll (TN)
West Georgia Tech Coll (GA)

Health/Medical Preparatory Programs Related
Arkansas State U–Newport (AR)
Eastern Arizona Coll (AZ)
Laramie County Comm Coll (WY)
Miami Dade Coll (FL)
Western Wyoming Comm Coll (WY)

Health Professions Related
Allegany Coll of Maryland (MD)
Berkshire Comm Coll (MA)
Bowling Green State U–Firelands Coll (OH)
Cincinnati State Tech and Comm Coll (OH)
Coll of Micronesia–FSM (FM)
Coll of the Marshall Islands (Marshall Islands)
Comm Coll of Allegheny County (PA)
Dixie State Coll of Utah (UT)
Essex County Coll (NJ)
Keiser Career Coll - Greenacres (FL)
Lanier Tech Coll (GA)
Miami Dade Coll (FL)
Midlands Tech Coll (SC)
Oakland Comm Coll (MI)

Southwestern Michigan Coll (MI)
Volunteer State Comm Coll (TN)

Health Science
Arizona Western Coll (AZ)
Bergen Comm Coll (NJ)
Brigham Young U – Idaho (ID)
Bucks County Comm Coll (PA)
Cabrillo Coll (CA)
Cañada Coll (CA)
Carroll Comm Coll (MD)
Chief Dull Knife Coll (MT)
City Colls of Chicago, Kennedy-King College (IL)
Coll of the Canyons (CA)
Cypress Coll (CA)
Fisher Coll (MA)
Greenville Tech Coll (SC)
Mendocino Coll (CA)
Mission Coll (CA)
Mohave Comm Coll (AZ)
Murray State Coll (OK)
Nassau Comm Coll (NY)
National Park Comm Coll (AR)
New Mexico Jr Coll (NM)
Northeastern Jr Coll (CO)
North Shore Comm Coll (MA)
Northwestern Connecticut Comm Coll (CT)
Ohlone Coll (CA)
Orange Coast Coll (CA)
Palo Alto Coll (TX)
Queensborough Comm Coll of the City U of New York (NY)
Salt Lake Comm Coll (UT)
San Joaquin Delta Coll (CA)
Southwest Mississippi Comm Coll (MS)
Sussex County Comm Coll (NJ)
Tulsa Comm Coll (OK)
Villa Maria Coll of Buffalo (NY)
West Hills Comm Coll (CA)

Health Services Administration
Brown Mackie Coll–Merrillville (IN)
Medical Careers Inst, Newport News (VA)

Health Services/Allied Health/Health Sciences
Clarendon Coll (TX)
Cochise Coll, Douglas (AZ)
Florida National Coll (FL)
Keiser U, Miami (FL)
Medical Careers Inst, Newport News (VA)
New York Coll of Health Professions (NY)
Western Wyoming Comm Coll (WY)
West Virginia State Comm and Tech Coll (WV)

Health Teacher Education
Angelina Coll (TX)
Anne Arundel Comm Coll (MD)
Bainbridge Coll (GA)
Bucks County Comm Coll (PA)
Cankdeska Cikana Comm Coll (ND)
Cañada Coll (CA)
Chesapeake Coll (MD)
Coahoma Comm Coll (MS)
Coastal Bend Coll (TX)
Columbia Coll (CA)
East Georgia Coll (GA)
Fulton-Montgomery Comm Coll (NY)
Harper Coll (IL)
Hartnell Coll (CA)
Howard Comm Coll (MD)
Los Angeles Mission Coll (CA)
Manatee Comm Coll (FL)
Mississippi Delta Comm Coll (MS)
Palm Beach Comm Coll (FL)
St. Catharine Coll (KY)
South Georgia Coll (GA)
Tulsa Comm Coll (OK)
Umpqua Comm Coll (OR)

U of New Mexico–Gallup (NM)
Westmoreland County Comm Coll (PA)
Young Harris Coll (GA)
Yuba Coll (CA)

Health Unit Coordinator/Ward Clerk
Comm Coll of Allegheny County (PA)
Riverland Comm Coll (MN)
Southeast Tech Inst (SD)

Health Unit Management/Ward Supervision
Ridgewater Coll (MN)

Heating, Air Conditioning and Refrigeration Technology
Alamance Comm Coll (NC)
Calhoun Comm Coll (AL)
Cincinnati State Tech and Comm Coll (OH)
DeKalb Tech Coll (GA)
Front Range Comm Coll (CO)
Gadsden State Comm Coll (AL)
Gateway Tech Coll (WI)
Griffin Tech Coll (GA)
Harrisburg Area Comm Coll (PA)
Lamar Inst of Technology (TX)
Macomb Comm Coll (MI)
Martin Comm Coll (NC)
Massasoit Comm Coll (MA)
Miami Dade Coll (FL)
Minnesota State Comm and Tech Coll–Fergus Falls (MN)
Mohawk Valley Comm Coll (NY)
Mott Comm Coll (MI)
North Georgia Tech Coll (GA)
Northwest Mississippi Comm Coll (MS)
Oakland Comm Coll (MI)
Pennsylvania Highland Comm Coll (PA)
Piedmont Virginia Comm Coll (VA)
Riverside Comm Coll District (CA)
St. Cloud Tech Coll (MN)
Savannah Tech Coll (GA)
South Georgia Tech Coll (GA)
South Piedmont Comm Coll (NC)
Springfield Tech Comm Coll (MA)
State U of New York Coll of Technology at Alfred (NY)
Terra State Comm Coll (OH)
Vatterott Coll, Kansas City (MO)
Vatterott Coll (OH)
Vatterott Coll, Oklahoma City (OK)
Vatterott Coll (TN)

Heating, Air Conditioning, Ventilation and Refrigeration Maintenance Technology
Advanced Technology Inst (VA)
Amarillo Coll (TX)
Antelope Valley Coll (CA)
Arizona Western Coll (AZ)
Asheville-Buncombe Tech Comm Coll (NC)
ATI Career Training Center, Oakland Park (FL)
Bismarck State Coll (ND)
Black Hawk Coll, Moline (IL)
Calhoun Comm Coll (AL)
Cedar Valley Coll (TX)
Central Comm Coll–Grand Island Campus (NE)
Central Comm Coll–Hastings Campus (NE)
Central Texas Coll (TX)
Century Coll (MN)

Chattanooga State Tech Comm Coll (TN)
Chippewa Valley Tech Coll (WI)
City Colls of Chicago, Kennedy-King College (IL)
Clovis Comm Coll (NM)
Coll of DuPage (IL)
Coll of Lake County (IL)
Coll of Southern Idaho (ID)
Coll of the Desert (CA)
Comm Coll of Allegheny County (PA)
Comm Coll of Southern Nevada (NV)
Cypress Coll (CA)
East Central Coll (MO)
Elaine P. Nunez Comm Coll (LA)
El Camino Coll (CA)
Elgin Comm Coll (IL)
Fayetteville Tech Comm Coll (NC)
Florence-Darlington Tech Coll (SC)
Forsyth Tech Comm Coll (NC)
Fresno City Coll (CA)
George C. Wallace Comm Coll (AL)
Grand Rapids Comm Coll (MI)
Grayson County Coll (TX)
Greenville Tech Coll (SC)
Guilford Tech Comm Coll (NC)
Harper Coll (IL)
H. Councill Trenholm State Tech Coll (AL)
Henry Ford Comm Coll (MI)
Illinois Eastern Comm Colls, Lincoln Trail College (IL)
Johnston Comm Coll (NC)
Kankakee Comm Coll (IL)
Kellogg Comm Coll (MI)
Kirkwood Comm Coll (IA)
Labette Comm Coll (KS)
Laney Coll (CA)
Lansing Comm Coll (MI)
Lee Coll (TX)
Lehigh Carbon Comm Coll (PA)
Linn State Tech Coll (MO)
Los Medanos Coll (CA)
Macomb Comm Coll (MI)
Martin Comm Coll (NC)
Metropolitan Comm Coll (NE)
Miami Dade Coll (FL)
Midlands Tech Coll (SC)
Mid-Plains Comm Coll, North Platte (NE)
Minnesota State Coll–Southeast Tech (MN)
Mohawk Valley Comm Coll (NY)
Monroe Comm Coll (NY)
Morton Coll (IL)
Mt. San Antonio Coll (CA)
New England Inst of Technology (RI)
New Hampshire Comm Tech Coll, Manchester/Stratham (NH)
New York City Coll of Technology of the City U of New York (NY)
Northampton County Area Comm Coll (PA)
Northeast Comm Coll (NE)
Northern Maine Comm Coll (ME)
North Idaho Coll (ID)
North Iowa Area Comm Coll (IA)
North Lake Coll (TX)
North Seattle Comm Coll (WA)
Northwest KansasTech Coll (KS)
Northwest Mississippi Comm Coll (MS)
Odessa Coll (TX)
Oklahoma State U, Okmulgee (OK)
Orange Coast Coll (CA)
Oxnard Coll (CA)
Ozarks Tech Comm Coll (MO)
Piedmont Tech Coll (SC)
Raritan Valley Comm Coll (NJ)
Renton Tech Coll (WA)
St. Cloud Tech Coll (MN)
St. Philip's Coll (TX)

Salt Lake Comm Coll (UT)
San Bernardino Valley
  Coll (CA)
San Joaquin Delta
  Coll (CA)
Scott Comm Coll (IA)
Southeast Tech Inst (SD)
Southern Maine Comm
  Coll (ME)
South Plains Coll (TX)
South Texas Coll (TX)
Spokane Comm Coll (WA)
State U of New York Coll
  of Technology at
  Alfred (NY)
State U of New York Coll
  of Technology at
  Canton (NY)
Surry Comm Coll (NC)
Terra State Comm
  Coll (OH)
Texarkana Coll (TX)
Tulsa Comm Coll (OK)
Tyler Jr Coll (TX)
U of Arkansas Comm Coll
  at Morrilton (AR)
Virginia Highlands Comm
  Coll (VA)
Wallace State Comm
  Coll (AL)
Washington State Comm
  Coll (OH)
Wenatchee Valley
  Coll (WA)
Western Nevada Comm
  Coll (NV)
Westmoreland County
  Comm Coll (PA)
West Virginia State Comm
  and Tech Coll (WV)
WyoTech, Fremont (CA)
York Tech Coll (SC)

**Heavy Equipment
Maintenance
Technology**
Amarillo Coll (TX)
Beaufort County Comm
  Coll (NC)
Centralia Coll (WA)
Comm Coll of Southern
  Nevada (NV)
Guilford Tech Comm
  Coll (NC)
Hawkeye Comm Coll (IA)
H. Councill Trenholm State
  Tech Coll (AL)
Illinois Eastern Comm
  Colls, Olney Central
  College (IL)
Lansing Comm Coll (MI)
Lawson State Comm
  Coll (AL)
Lenoir Comm Coll (NC)
Linn State Tech Coll (MO)
Lower Columbia Coll (WA)
Mesa Comm Coll (AZ)
Metropolitan Comm
  Coll (NE)
Metropolitan Comm
  Coll–Longview (MO)
Mohawk Valley Comm
  Coll (NY)
Nebraska Coll of Tech
  Agriculture (NE)
New Hampshire Comm
  Tech Coll, Nashua/
  Claremont (NH)
Northern Maine Comm
  Coll (ME)
North Idaho Coll (ID)
The Ohio State U Ag Tech
  Inst (OH)
Oklahoma State U,
  Okmulgee (OK)
Ozarks Tech Comm
  Coll (MO)
Red Rocks Comm
  Coll (CO)
Rogue Comm Coll (OR)
Salt Lake Comm Coll (UT)
Sheridan Coll–Sheridan
  and Gillette (WY)
Skagit Valley Coll (WA)
South Seattle Comm
  Coll (WA)
South Texas Coll (TX)
Spokane Comm Coll (WA)
Spokane Falls Comm
  Coll (WA)
State U of New York Coll
  of Technology at
  Alfred (NY)
Trinidad State Jr Coll (CO)
West Central Tech
  Coll (GA)
Western Wyoming Comm
  Coll (WY)

**Heavy/Industrial
Equipment
Maintenance
Technologies Related**
Big Bend Comm Coll (WA)
Eastern West Virginia
  Comm and Tech
  Coll (WV)
Southwestern Michigan
  Coll (MI)

**Hispanic-American,
Puerto Rican, and
Mexican-American/
Chicano Studies**
Cerritos Coll (CA)
City Colls of Chicago,
  Wilbur Wright
  College (IL)
Coll of Alameda (CA)
Contra Costa Coll (CA)
Fresno City Coll (CA)
Laney Coll (CA)
Los Angeles City Coll (CA)
Pasadena City Coll (CA)
San Diego City Coll (CA)
Santa Ana Coll (CA)
Santa Barbara City
  Coll (CA)
Yuba Coll (CA)

Histologic Technician
Miami Dade Coll (FL)
Mott Comm Coll (MI)
Oakland Comm Coll (MI)

**Histologic
Technology/
Histotechnologist**
North Hennepin Comm
  Coll (MN)

**Historic Preservation
and Conservation**
Bucks County Comm
  Coll (PA)
Colorado Mountain Coll,
  Timberline
  Campus (CO)

History
Allen County Comm
  Coll (KS)
Amarillo Coll (TX)
Angelina Coll (TX)
Bainbridge Coll (GA)
Bakersfield Coll (CA)
Barton County Comm
  Coll (KS)
Bergen Comm Coll (NJ)
Blinn Coll (TX)
Brigham Young U –
  Idaho (ID)
Burlington County
  Coll (NJ)
Cankdeska Cikana Comm
  Coll (ND)
Cañada Coll (CA)
Cape Cod Comm
  Coll (MA)
Centralia Coll (WA)
Cerritos Coll (CA)
Chaffey Coll (CA)
Cisco Jr Coll (TX)
Clarendon Coll (TX)
Coastal Bend Coll (TX)
Coastal Georgia Comm
  Coll (GA)
Cochise Coll, Douglas (AZ)
Cochise Coll, Sierra
  Vista (AZ)
Colby Comm Coll (KS)
Coll of Alameda (CA)
Coll of Marin (CA)
Coll of Southern Idaho (ID)
Coll of Southern
  Maryland (MD)
Coll of the Canyons (CA)
Coll of the Desert (CA)
Coll of the Siskiyous (CA)
Columbia Coll (CA)
Comm Coll of Southern
  Nevada (NV)
Contra Costa Coll (CA)
Crafton Hills Coll (CA)
Cypress Coll (CA)
De Anza Coll (CA)
Dixie State Coll of
  Utah (UT)
Dodge City Comm
  Coll (KS)
Eastern Arizona Coll (AZ)
East Georgia Coll (GA)
El Camino Coll (CA)
Everett Comm Coll (WA)
Foothill Coll (CA)
Fullerton Coll (CA)
Fulton-Montgomery Comm
  Coll (NY)

Georgia Highlands
  Coll (GA)
Gloucester County
  Coll (NJ)
Gordon Coll (GA)
Great Basin Coll (NV)
Grossmont Coll (CA)
Hartnell Coll (CA)
Iowa Lakes Comm
  Coll (IA)
Irvine Valley Coll (CA)
Kellogg Comm Coll (MI)
Kirkwood Comm Coll (IA)
Labette Comm Coll (KS)
Lamar Comm Coll (CO)
Laramie County Comm
  Coll (WY)
Lassen Comm Coll
  District (CA)
Lawson State Comm
  Coll (AL)
Lee Coll (TX)
Lorain County Comm
  Coll (OH)
Los Angeles City Coll (CA)
Los Angeles Mission
  Coll (CA)
Louisburg Coll (NC)
Lower Columbia Coll (WA)
Manatee Comm Coll (FL)
Miami Dade Coll (FL)
Miami U–Middletown
  Campus (OH)
Mississippi Delta Comm
  Coll (MS)
Mohave Comm Coll (AZ)
Monroe Comm Coll (NY)
Monterey Peninsula
  Coll (CA)
Murray State Coll (OK)
Naugatuck Valley Comm
  Coll (CT)
New Mexico Jr Coll (NM)
New Mexico Military
  Inst (NM)
Northeastern Jr Coll (CO)
Northern Essex Comm
  Coll (MA)
North Idaho Coll (ID)
Odessa Coll (TX)
Oklahoma City Comm
  Coll (OK)
Orange Coast Coll (CA)
Oxnard Coll (CA)
Palm Beach Comm
  Coll (FL)
Palo Alto Coll (TX)
Parkland Coll (IL)
Pasadena City Coll (CA)
Porterville Coll (CA)
Potomac State Coll of
  West Virginia U (WV)
Quincy Coll (MA)
Red Rocks Comm
  Coll (CO)
Ridgewater Coll (MN)
Rose State Coll (OK)
St. Catharine Coll (KY)
St. Philip's Coll (TX)
Salt Lake Comm Coll (UT)
San Bernardino Valley
  Coll (CA)
San Joaquin Delta
  Coll (CA)
San Juan Coll (NM)
Santa Ana Coll (CA)
Santa Barbara City
  Coll (CA)
Santa Rosa Jr Coll (CA)
Santiago Canyon Coll (CA)
Sheridan Coll–Sheridan
  and Gillette (WY)
Skagit Valley Coll (WA)
South Georgia Coll (GA)
Southwest Mississippi
  Comm Coll (MS)
Treasure Valley Comm
  Coll (OR)
Tulsa Comm Coll (OK)
Turtle Mountain Comm
  Coll (ND)
Umpqua Comm Coll (OR)
Wenatchee Valley
  Coll (WA)
Western Nebraska Comm
  Coll (NE)
Western Wyoming Comm
  Coll (WY)
West Los Angeles
  Coll (CA)
West Valley Coll (CA)
Wright State U, Lake
  Campus (OH)
Young Harris Coll (GA)
Yuba Coll (CA)

History Related
Coll of the Siskiyous (CA)

**Home Furnishings
and Equipment
Installation**
St. Philip's Coll (TX)

Home Health Aide
Barton County Comm
  Coll (KS)

**Home Health Aide/
Home Attendant**
Allen County Comm
  Coll (KS)
Laurel Business Inst (PA)

**Horse Husbandry/
Equine Science and
Management**
Black Hawk Coll,
  Moline (IL)
Central Wyoming
  Coll (WY)
Clarendon Coll (TX)
Linn-Benton Comm
  Coll (OR)
The Ohio State U Ag Tech
  Inst (OH)
Santa Rosa Jr Coll (CA)

Horticultural Science
Anne Arundel Comm
  Coll (MD)
Bakersfield Coll (CA)
Black Hawk Coll,
  Moline (IL)
Brigham Young U –
  Idaho (ID)
Cabrillo Coll (CA)
Central Lakes Coll (MN)
Central Piedmont Comm
  Coll (NC)
Chattahoochee Tech
  Coll (GA)
City Coll of San
  Francisco (CA)
City Colls of Chicago,
  Richard J. Daley
  College (IL)
Clark State Comm
  Coll (OH)
Coll of San Mateo (CA)
Coll of the Desert (CA)
Columbus Tech Coll (GA)
Comm Coll of Southern
  Nevada (NV)
Cosumnes River Coll,
  Sacramento (CA)
El Camino Coll (CA)
Forsyth Tech Comm
  Coll (NC)
Fullerton Coll (CA)
Georgia Highlands
  Coll (GA)
Griffin Tech Coll (GA)
Gwinnett Tech Coll (GA)
Harper Coll (IL)
Hartnell Coll (CA)
Hawkeye Comm Coll (IA)
Houston Comm Coll
  System (TX)
Joliet Jr Coll (IL)
Jones County Jr Coll (MS)
Kirkwood Comm Coll (IA)
Lansing Comm Coll (MI)
Las Positas Coll (CA)
Lehigh Carbon Comm
  Coll (PA)
Lenoir Comm Coll (NC)
Linn-Benton Comm
  Coll (OR)
Los Angeles Pierce
  Coll (CA)
Maui Comm Coll (HI)
Meridian Comm Coll (MS)
Mesa Comm Coll (AZ)
Miami Dade Coll (FL)
Minot State U–Bottineau
  Campus (ND)
Mississippi Delta Comm
  Coll (MS)
Mississippi Gulf Coast
  Comm Coll (MS)
Mt. Hood Comm Coll (OR)
Mt. San Antonio Coll (CA)
Naugatuck Valley Comm
  Coll (CT)
Nebraska Coll of Tech
  Agriculture (NE)
Northeast Comm Coll (NE)
Northeastern Jr Coll (CO)
North Georgia Tech
  Coll (GA)
North Metro Tech Coll (GA)
The Ohio State U Ag Tech
  Inst (OH)
Oklahoma State U,
  Oklahoma City (OK)
Orange Coast Coll (CA)
Palo Alto Coll (TX)

Potomac State Coll of
  West Virginia U (WV)
Reedley Coll (CA)
Richland Coll (TX)
St. Catharine Coll (KY)
Sampson Comm Coll (NC)
Shasta Coll (CA)
Southeast Tech Inst (SD)
Southern Maine Comm
  Coll (ME)
South Georgia Tech
  Coll (GA)
South Seattle Comm
  Coll (WA)
State Fair Comm
  Coll (MO)
State U of New York Coll
  of Agriculture and
  Technology at
  Morrisville (NY)
Suffolk County Comm
  Coll (NY)
Surry Comm Coll (NC)
Tidewater Comm Coll (VA)
Trident Tech Coll (SC)
Tulsa Comm Coll (OK)
Tyler Jr Coll (TX)
U of Arkansas Comm Coll
  at Morrilton (AR)
Victor Valley Coll (CA)
Wallace State Comm
  Coll (AL)
Western Piedmont Comm
  Coll (NC)
Westmoreland County
  Comm Coll (PA)
The Williamson Free
  School of Mecha
  Trades (PA)

**Hospital and Health
Care Facilities
Administration**
Allen County Comm
  Coll (KS)
Central Comm Coll–
  Hastings Campus (NE)
Coll of DuPage (IL)
Harrisburg Area Comm
  Coll (PA)
Manatee Comm Coll (FL)

**Hospitality
Administration**
Alexandria Tech Coll (MN)
Allegany Coll of
  Maryland (MD)
Arizona Western Coll (AZ)
Baltimore City Comm
  Coll (MD)
Berkshire Comm Coll (MA)
Bucks County Comm
  Coll (PA)
Central Comm Coll–
  Hastings Campus (NE)
Central Maine Comm
  Coll (ME)
Central New Mexico
  Comm Coll (NM)
Central Oregon Comm
  Coll (OR)
Central Piedmont Comm
  Coll (NC)
Chippewa Valley Tech
  Coll (WI)
City Colls of Chicago,
  Harold Washington
  College (IL)
Cochise Coll, Douglas (AZ)
Coll of DuPage (IL)
Collin County Comm Coll
  District (TX)
Colorado Mountain Coll,
  Alpine Campus (CO)
Comm Coll of Southern
  Nevada (NV)
El Centro Coll (TX)
Fisher Coll (MA)
Florida National Coll (FL)
Fox Valley Tech Coll (WI)
Greenville Tech Coll (SC)
Harper Coll (IL)
Henry Ford Comm
  Coll (MI)
Hillsborough Comm
  Coll (FL)
Hocking Coll (OH)
Holyoke Comm Coll (MA)
International Business Coll,
  Fort Wayne (IN)
Iowa Lakes Comm
  Coll (IA)
James H. Faulkner State
  Comm Coll (AL)
Joliet Jr Coll (IL)
Lansing Comm Coll (MI)
Madison Area Tech
  Coll (WI)
Marian Court Coll (MA)

Marshall Comm and Tech
  Coll (WV)
Massachusetts Bay Comm
  Coll (MA)
Miami Dade Coll (FL)
Monterey Peninsula
  Coll (CA)
Mt. Hood Comm Coll (OR)
Muskegon Comm Coll (MI)
Naugatuck Valley Comm
  Coll (CT)
New York City Coll of
  Technology of the City
  U of New York (NY)
Niagara County Comm
  Coll (NY)
North Idaho Coll (ID)
North Shore Comm
  Coll (MA)
Oklahoma State U,
  Okmulgee (OK)
Pennsylvania Highland
  Comm Coll (PA)
Pima Comm Coll (AZ)
Reedley Coll (CA)
San Diego City Coll (CA)
Scottsdale Comm
  Coll (AZ)
Sheridan Coll–Sheridan
  and Gillette (WY)
Southern Maine Comm
  Coll (ME)
Southern U at
  Shreveport (LA)
South Florida Comm
  Coll (FL)
South Seattle Comm
  Coll (WA)
South Texas Coll (TX)
State U of New York Coll
  of Agriculture and
  Technology at
  Morrisville (NY)
Three Rivers Comm
  Coll (CT)
U of Cincinnati Clermont
  Coll (OH)
Valencia Comm Coll (FL)
Virginia Coll at Austin (TX)
Waukesha County Tech
  Coll (WI)
Westmoreland County
  Comm Coll (PA)
Wor-Wic Comm Coll (MD)
Young Harris Coll (GA)

**Hospitality
Administration
Related**
Arizona Western Coll (AZ)
City Coll, Fort
  Lauderdale (FL)
City Coll, Gainesville (FL)
City Coll, Miami (FL)
Coll of Micronesia–
  FSM (FM)
Lehigh Valley Coll (PA)
Orlando Culinary
  Academy (FL)
Penn State Beaver (PA)
Provo Coll (UT)
Western Culinary Inst (OR)

**Hospitality and
Recreation Marketing**
AIB Coll of Business (IA)
Central Oregon Comm
  Coll (OR)
Gloucester County
  Coll (NJ)
Kirkwood Comm Coll (IA)
Montgomery County
  Comm Coll (PA)
Muskegon Comm Coll (MI)
Raritan Valley Comm
  Coll (NJ)

**Hospitality/Recreation
Marketing**
Minot State U–Bottineau
  Campus (ND)

**Hospitality/Recreation
Marketing Operations**
Bradford School (PA)

**Hotel and Restaurant
Management**
Albany Tech Coll (GA)
Athens Tech Coll (GA)
Atlanta Tech Coll (GA)
Central Georgia Tech
  Coll (GA)
Coll of Micronesia–
  FSM (FM)
Ogeechee Tech Coll (GA)
Orlando Culinary
  Academy (FL)
Savannah Tech Coll (GA)

Hotel/Motel Administration

Alexandria Tech Coll (MN)
Anne Arundel Comm Coll (MD)
Asheville-Buncombe Tech Comm Coll (NC)
Bakersfield Coll (CA)
Bergen Comm Coll (NJ)
Bismarck State Coll (ND)
Briarwood Coll (CT)
Broome Comm Coll (NY)
Broward Comm Coll (FL)
Bucks County Comm Coll (PA)
Burlington County Coll (NJ)
Cape Cod Comm Coll (MA)
Cape Fear Comm Coll (NC)
Central Arizona Coll (AZ)
Central Comm Coll–Hastings Campus (NE)
Central Oregon Comm Coll (OR)
Central Piedmont Comm Coll (NC)
Central Texas Coll (TX)
Chaffey Coll (CA)
Chattanooga State Tech Comm Coll (TN)
Cincinnati State Tech and Comm Coll (OH)
City Coll of San Francisco (CA)
City Colls of Chicago, Harold Washington College (IL)
Cochise Coll, Sierra Vista (AZ)
Coll of DuPage (IL)
Coll of Southern Idaho (ID)
Coll of the Canyons (CA)
Colorado Mountain Coll, Alpine Campus (CO)
Columbia Coll (CA)
Comm Coll of Allegheny County (PA)
Comm Coll of Philadelphia (PA)
Comm Coll of Southern Nevada (NV)
Cypress Coll (CA)
El Centro Coll (TX)
Elgin Comm Coll (IL)
Essex County Coll (NJ)
Fayetteville Tech Comm Coll (NC)
Finger Lakes Comm Coll (NY)
Garrett Coll (MD)
Gateway Comm Coll (CT)
Genesee Comm Coll (NY)
Georgia Highlands Coll (GA)
Gwinnett Tech Coll (GA)
Harper Coll (IL)
Harrisburg Area Comm Coll (PA)
Henry Ford Comm Coll (MI)
Hillsborough Comm Coll (FL)
Hocking Coll (OH)
Holyoke Comm Coll (MA)
Houston Comm Coll System (TX)
ICPR Jr Coll–Hato Rey Campus (PR)
Iowa Lakes Comm Coll (IA)
John Wood Comm Coll (IL)
Keystone Coll (PA)
Kirkwood Comm Coll (IA)
Lake Tahoe Comm Coll (CA)
Lansing Comm Coll (MI)
Laredo Comm Coll (TX)
Lehigh Carbon Comm Coll (PA)
Lincoln Land Comm Coll (IL)
Massasoit Comm Coll (MA)
Maui Comm Coll (HI)
Meridian Comm Coll (MS)
Mid-State Tech Coll (WI)
Mississippi Gulf Coast Comm Coll (MS)
Mohawk Valley Comm Coll (NY)
Monroe Comm Coll (NY)
Monterey Peninsula Coll (CA)
Montgomery Coll (MD)
Mt. San Antonio Coll (CA)
Muskegon Comm Coll (MI)

Nassau Comm Coll (NY)
Naugatuck Valley Comm Coll (CT)
New Hampshire Tech Inst (NH)
Nicolet Area Tech Coll (WI)
Northampton County Area Comm Coll (PA)
Northern Essex Comm Coll (MA)
Northwest Mississippi Comm Coll (MS)
Oakland Comm Coll (MI)
Onondaga Comm Coll (NY)
Orange Coast Coll (CA)
Oxnard Coll (CA)
Ozarks Tech Comm Coll (MO)
Palau Comm Coll (Palau)
Palm Beach Comm Coll (FL)
Passaic County Comm Coll (NJ)
Raritan Valley Comm Coll (NJ)
St. Philip's Coll (TX)
San Bernardino Valley Coll (CA)
Sandhills Comm Coll (NC)
Santa Barbara City Coll (CA)
Santa Rosa Jr Coll (CA)
Scottsdale Comm Coll (AZ)
Skagit Valley Coll (WA)
Southern Maine Comm Coll (ME)
Southern U at Shreveport (LA)
South Texas Coll (TX)
Spokane Comm Coll (WA)
State U of New York Coll of Agriculture and Technology at Morrisville (NY)
Three Rivers Comm Coll (CT)
Tompkins Cortland Comm Coll (NY)
Trident Tech Coll (SC)
Trocaire Coll (NY)
Tulsa Comm Coll (OK)
Union County Coll (NJ)
U of Puerto Rico at Carolina (PR)
Westchester Comm Coll (NY)
Westmoreland County Comm Coll (PA)
York County Comm Coll (ME)

Hotel/Motel Services Marketing Operations

Montgomery County Comm Coll (PA)

Housing and Human Environments

Orange Coast Coll (CA)

Housing and Human Environments Related

Comm Coll of Allegheny County (PA)

Human Development and Family Studies

Coll of Alameda (CA)
Cuesta Coll (CA)
Gloucester County Coll (NJ)
Imperial Valley Coll (CA)
Orange Coast Coll (CA)
Penn State Delaware County (PA)
Penn State DuBois (PA)
Penn State Fayette, The Eberly Campus (PA)
Penn State Mont Alto (PA)
Penn State New Kensington (PA)
Penn State Schuylkill (PA)
Penn State Shenango (PA)
Penn State Worthington Scranton (PA)
Penn State York (PA)
Salt Lake Comm Coll (UT)
Santiago Canyon Coll (CA)

Human Development and Family Studies Related

Comm Coll of Allegheny County (PA)

Human Ecology

Monroe Comm Coll (NY)

Humanities

Allen County Comm Coll (KS)
Angelina Coll (TX)
Anne Arundel Comm Coll (MD)
Barstow Coll (CA)
Bowling Green State U–Firelands Coll (OH)
Brigham Young U – Idaho (ID)
Bucks County Comm Coll (PA)
Cañada Coll (CA)
Centralia Coll (WA)
Central Oregon Comm Coll (OR)
Chaffey Coll (CA)
Chesapeake Coll (MD)
City Colls of Chicago, Harold Washington College (IL)
City Colls of Chicago, Richard J. Daley College (IL)
Cochise Coll, Douglas (AZ)
Colby Comm Coll (KS)
Coll of Alameda (CA)
Coll of Marin (CA)
Coll of San Mateo (CA)
Coll of the Canyons (CA)
Colorado Mountain Coll (CO)
Colorado Mountain Coll, Alpine Campus (CO)
Columbia Coll (CA)
Columbia-Greene Comm Coll (NY)
Comm Coll of Allegheny County (PA)
Contra Costa Coll (CA)
Cosumnes River Coll, Sacramento (CA)
Crafton Hills Coll (CA)
De Anza Coll (CA)
Dixie State Coll of Utah (UT)
Dodge City Comm Coll (KS)
Erie Comm Coll (NY)
Erie Comm Coll, North Campus (NY)
Erie Comm Coll, South Campus (NY)
Finger Lakes Comm Coll (NY)
Fisher Coll (MA)
Fresno City Coll (CA)
Fulton-Montgomery Comm Coll (NY)
Golden West Coll (CA)
Harper Coll (IL)
Housatonic Comm Coll (CT)
Imperial Valley Coll (CA)
Iowa Lakes Comm Coll (IA)
Irvine Valley Coll (CA)
Jamestown Comm Coll (NY)
Kirkwood Comm Coll (IA)
Lake Tahoe Comm Coll (CA)
Lamar Comm Coll (CO)
Laney Coll (CA)
Laramie County Comm Coll (WY)
Lassen Comm Coll District (CA)
Lee Coll (TX)
Lehigh Carbon Comm Coll (PA)
Los Angeles Mission Coll (CA)
Los Angeles Southwest Coll (CA)
Manatee Comm Coll (FL)
Merced Coll (CA)
Miami Dade Coll (FL)
Mohawk Valley Comm Coll (NY)
Montgomery County Comm Coll (PA)
Napa Valley Coll (CA)
New Mexico Military Inst (NM)
Niagara County Comm Coll (NY)
Northeastern Jr Coll (CO)
Oklahoma City Comm Coll (OK)
Onondaga Comm Coll (NY)
Orange Coast Coll (CA)
Passaic County Comm Coll (NJ)
Quincy Coll (MA)

Red Rocks Comm Coll (CO)
Ridgewater Coll (MN)
Rogue Comm Coll (OR)
Roxbury Comm Coll (MA)
Sacramento City Coll (CA)
St. Catharine Coll (KY)
Salt Lake Comm Coll (UT)
San Joaquin Delta Coll (CA)
Sheridan Coll–Sheridan and Gillette (WY)
Skagit Valley Coll (WA)
South Georgia Coll (GA)
Southwest Mississippi Comm Coll (MS)
State U of New York Coll of Agriculture and Technology at Morrisville (NY)
State U of New York Coll of Technology at Alfred (NY)
State U of New York Coll of Technology at Canton (NY)
Suffolk County Comm Coll (NY)
Tompkins Cortland Comm Coll (NY)
Treasure Valley Comm Coll (OR)
Tulsa Comm Coll (OK)
Ulster County Comm Coll (NY)
Umpqua Comm Coll (OR)
U of Puerto Rico at Carolina (PR)
Victor Valley Coll (CA)
Westchester Comm Coll (NY)
Western Wyoming Comm Coll (WY)
West Hills Comm Coll (CA)

Human Resources Management

Beaufort County Comm Coll (NC)
Clark Coll (WA)
Comm Coll of Allegheny County (PA)
Fayetteville Tech Comm Coll (NC)
Harper Coll (IL)
Houston Comm Coll System (TX)
Indiana Business Coll, Anderson (IN)
Indiana Business Coll, Columbus (IN)
Indiana Business Coll, Indianapolis (IN)
Indiana Business Coll, Terre Haute (IN)
Keystone Coll (PA)
Lansing Comm Coll (MI)
Lehigh Carbon Comm Coll (PA)
Marian Court Coll (MA)
Minnesota State Comm and Tech Coll–Fergus Falls (MN)
Moraine Valley Comm Coll (IL)
New Hampshire Tech Inst (NH)
Saint Paul Coll–A Comm & Tech College (MN)
Tulsa Comm Coll (OK)
Tyler Jr Coll (TX)
Umpqua Comm Coll (OR)
Valencia Comm Coll (FL)
Zane State Coll (OH)

Human Resources Management and Services Related

Barton County Comm Coll (KS)
Iowa Lakes Comm Coll (IA)

Human Services

Alexandria Tech Coll (MN)
Angelina Coll (TX)
Anne Arundel Comm Coll (MD)
Arizona Western Coll (AZ)
Asnuntuck Comm Coll (CT)
Bakersfield Coll (CA)
Baltimore City Comm Coll (MD)
Berkshire Comm Coll (MA)
Bowling Green State U–Firelands Coll (OH)
Burlington County Coll (NJ)

Carroll Comm Coll (MD)
Central Florida Comm Coll (FL)
Central Ohio Tech Coll (OH)
Central Piedmont Comm Coll (NC)
Central Wyoming Coll (WY)
Chesapeake Coll (MD)
Cisco Jr Coll (TX)
Clark State Comm Coll (OH)
Cochise Coll, Douglas (AZ)
Coll of DuPage (IL)
Coll of Southern Idaho (ID)
Coll of Southern Maryland (MD)
Columbia-Greene Comm Coll (NY)
Comm Coll of Vermont (VT)
Cosumnes River Coll, Sacramento (CA)
Crafton Hills Coll (CA)
Cuesta Coll (CA)
Cypress Coll (CA)
Eastern New Mexico U–Roswell (NM)
Elgin Comm Coll (IL)
Essex County Coll (NJ)
Everett Comm Coll (WA)
Finger Lakes Comm Coll (NY)
Fiorello H. LaGuardia Comm Coll of the City U of New York (NY)
Florence-Darlington Tech Coll (SC)
Folsom Lake Coll (CA)
Fond du Lac Tribal and Comm Coll (MN)
Fort Berthold Comm Coll (ND)
Frederick Comm Coll (MD)
Fresno City Coll (CA)
Fulton-Montgomery Comm Coll (NY)
Gateway Comm Coll (CT)
Gateway Tech Coll (WI)
Genesee Comm Coll (NY)
Georgia Highlands Coll (GA)
Grays Harbor Coll (WA)
Guilford Tech Comm Coll (NC)
Harrisburg Area Comm Coll (PA)
Hartnell Coll (CA)
Hesser Coll (NH)
Hillsborough Comm Coll (FL)
Holyoke Comm Coll (MA)
Hopkinsville Comm Coll (KY)
Housatonic Comm Coll (CT)
Inver Hills Comm Coll (MN)
Itasca Comm Coll (MN)
Jamestown Comm Coll (NY)
John Tyler Comm Coll (VA)
Kellogg Comm Coll (MI)
Kent State U, Ashtabula Campus (OH)
Kingsborough Comm Coll of the City U of New York (NY)
Kirkwood Comm Coll (IA)
Lake Land Coll (IL)
Lansing Comm Coll (MI)
Lassen Comm Coll District (CA)
Leeward Comm Coll (HI)
Lorain County Comm Coll (OH)
Los Angeles City Coll (CA)
Madison Area Tech Coll (WI)
Massachusetts Bay Comm Coll (MA)
Massasoit Comm Coll (MA)
Maui Comm Coll (HI)
Mendocino Coll (CA)
Merced Coll (CA)
Mesabi Range Comm and Tech Coll (MN)
Metropolitan Comm Coll (NE)
Metropolitan Comm Coll–Longview (MO)
Miami Dade Coll (FL)
Middlesex Comm Coll (CT)
Minneapolis Comm and Tech Coll (MN)

Mississippi Gulf Coast Comm Coll (MS)
Mohawk Valley Comm Coll (NY)
Monroe Comm Coll (NY)
Mount Wachusett Comm Coll (MA)
Naugatuck Valley Comm Coll (CT)
Nebraska Indian Comm Coll (NE)
New Hampshire Comm Tech Coll, Manchester/Stratham (NH)
New Hampshire Comm Tech Coll, Nashua/Claremont (NH)
New Hampshire Tech Inst (NH)
New York City Coll of Technology of the City U of New York (NY)
Niagara County Comm Coll (NY)
North Central Missouri Coll (MO)
Northern Essex Comm Coll (MA)
Northern New Mexico Coll (NM)
North Idaho Coll (ID)
Northwestern Connecticut Comm Coll (CT)
Odessa Coll (TX)
Onondaga Comm Coll (NY)
Owensboro Comm and Tech Coll (KY)
Parkland Coll (IL)
Pasadena City Coll (CA)
Pasco-Hernando Comm Coll (FL)
Passaic County Comm Coll (NJ)
Pennsylvania Highland Comm Coll (PA)
Piedmont Tech Coll (SC)
Pine Tech Coll (MN)
Porterville Coll (CA)
Quincy Coll (MA)
Quinebaug Valley Comm Coll (CT)
Raritan Valley Comm Coll (NJ)
Ridgewater Coll (MN)
Riverland Comm Coll (MN)
Rogue Comm Coll (OR)
Sacramento City Coll (CA)
Saint Charles Comm Coll (MO)
St. Louis Comm Coll at Florissant Valley (MO)
Salish Kootenai Coll (MT)
San Bernardino Valley Coll (CA)
Sandhills Comm Coll (NC)
San Juan Coll (NM)
Santa Rosa Jr Coll (CA)
Sitting Bull Coll (ND)
Skagit Valley Coll (WA)
Southern State Comm Coll (OH)
Southern U at Shreveport (LA)
Southside Virginia Comm Coll (VA)
South Texas Coll (TX)
Southwest Virginia Comm Coll (VA)
Stanly Comm Coll (NC)
Stark State Coll of Technology (OH)
State U of New York Coll of Technology at Alfred (NY)
Stone Child Coll (MT)
Suffolk County Comm Coll (NY)
Sussex County Comm Coll (NJ)
Three Rivers Comm Coll (CT)
Tomball Coll (TX)
Tompkins Cortland Comm Coll (NY)
Trident Tech Coll (SC)
Tulsa Comm Coll (OK)
Tunxis Comm Coll (CT)
Turtle Mountain Comm Coll (ND)
Ulster County Comm Coll (NY)
U of New Mexico–Taos (NM)
U of New Mexico–Valencia Campus (NM)
U of Pittsburgh at Titusville (PA)

Virginia Highlands Comm
Coll (VA)
Westchester Comm
Coll (NY)
Western Wyoming Comm
Coll (WY)
Westmoreland County
Comm Coll (PA)
Yuba Coll (CA)

Hydraulics and Fluid Power Technology
Alexandria Tech Coll (MN)
Gateway Tech Coll (WI)
Hennepin Tech Coll (MN)
The Ohio State U Ag Tech
Inst (OH)

Hydrology and Water Resources Science
Cecil Comm Coll (MD)
Citrus Coll (CA)
Coll of Southern Idaho (ID)
Coll of the Canyons (CA)
Dodge City Comm
Coll (KS)
Hartnell Coll (CA)
Imperial Valley Coll (CA)
Iowa Lakes Comm
Coll (IA)
Kirkwood Comm Coll (IA)
Lawson State Comm
Coll (AL)
Lenoir Comm Coll (NC)
Red Rocks Comm
Coll (CO)
Spokane Comm Coll (WA)
Three Rivers Comm
Coll (CT)
Ventura Coll (CA)

Illustration
The Creative Center (NE)
Keystone Coll (PA)

Industrial Arts
Allen County Comm
Coll (KS)
Bakersfield Coll (CA)
Brigham Young U –
Idaho (ID)
Cerritos Coll (CA)
Cleveland State Comm
Coll (TN)
Comm Coll of Beaver
County (PA)
Contra Costa Coll (CA)
Dodge City Comm
Coll (KS)
El Camino Coll (CA)
Everett Comm Coll (WA)
Fresno City Coll (CA)
Fullerton Coll (CA)
Guilford Tech Comm
Coll (NC)
Los Angeles Pierce
Coll (CA)
Merced Coll (CA)
Mt. San Antonio Coll (CA)
Muskegon Comm Coll (MI)
New Mexico Jr Coll (NM)
Northern Maine Comm
Coll (ME)
Ouachita Tech Coll (AR)
Porterville Coll (CA)
San Diego City Coll (CA)
Taft Coll (CA)
Volunteer State Comm
Coll (TN)
Western Piedmont Comm
Coll (NC)

Industrial Design
Brigham Young U –
Idaho (ID)
Cabrillo Coll (CA)
Chaffey Coll (CA)
Las Positas Coll (CA)
Mt. San Antonio Coll (CA)
Navarro Coll (TX)
Oklahoma State U,
Oklahoma City (OK)
Orange Coast Coll (CA)
Santa Rosa Jr Coll (CA)

Industrial Electronics Technology
Big Bend Comm Coll (WA)
Central Carolina Tech
Coll (SC)
Coll of DuPage (IL)
Elizabethtown Tech
Coll (KY)
H. Councill Trenholm State
Tech Coll (AL)
John Wood Comm Coll (IL)
Kennebec Valley Comm
Coll (ME)
Midlands Tech Coll (SC)
Northampton County Area
Comm Coll (PA)

North Iowa Area Comm
Coll (IA)
Northland Comm and Tech
Coll–Thief River
Falls (MN)
Northwest Iowa Comm
Coll (IA)
Northwest KansasTech
Coll (KS)
Northwest-Shoals Comm
Coll (AL)
Oakland Comm Coll (MI)
State U of New York Coll
of Technology at
Alfred (NY)
Western Wyoming Comm
Coll (WY)
York Tech Coll (SC)

Industrial Engineering
Mount Wachusett Comm
Coll (MA)
Northern New Mexico
Coll (NM)
Santa Barbara City
Coll (CA)

Industrial Mechanics and Maintenance Technology
Calhoun Comm Coll (AL)
Coahoma Comm Coll (MS)
Coll of Lake County (IL)
Elizabethtown Tech
Coll (KY)
George C. Wallace Comm
Coll (AL)
Guilford Tech Comm
Coll (NC)
Harrisburg Area Comm
Coll (PA)
H. Councill Trenholm State
Tech Coll (AL)
Illinois Eastern Comm
Colls, Olney Central
College (IL)
John Wood Comm Coll (IL)
Kennebec Valley Comm
Coll (ME)
Lamar Inst of
Technology (TX)
Lower Columbia Coll (WA)
Macomb Comm Coll (MI)
Midlands Tech Coll (SC)
North Central Texas
Coll (TX)
Northwest-Shoals Comm
Coll (AL)
Riverland Comm Coll (MN)
Southwestern Michigan
Coll (MI)
Western Wyoming Comm
Coll (WY)
York Tech Coll (SC)

Industrial Production Technologies Related
Broome Comm Coll (NY)
Cape Fear Comm
Coll (NC)
Erie Comm Coll (NY)
Essex County Coll (NJ)
Mohawk Valley Comm
Coll (NY)

Industrial Radiologic Technology
Aims Comm Coll (CO)
Amarillo Coll (TX)
Angelina Coll (TX)
Anne Arundel Comm
Coll (MD)
Bakersfield Coll (CA)
Bergen Comm Coll (NJ)
Blinn Coll (TX)
Broward Comm Coll (FL)
Cañada Coll (CA)
Central Maine Comm
Coll (ME)
Chattanooga State Tech
Comm Coll (TN)
City Coll of San
Francisco (CA)
Cleveland Comm Coll (NC)
Comm Coll of
Philadelphia (PA)
Comm Coll of Southern
Nevada (NV)
Crafton Hills Coll (CA)
Cuyahoga Comm
Coll (OH)
Cypress Coll (CA)
Florence-Darlington Tech
Coll (SC)
Forsyth Tech Comm
Coll (NC)
Fresno City Coll (CA)
Gateway Comm Coll (CT)
Greenville Tech Coll (SC)

Henry Ford Comm
Coll (MI)
Hillsborough Comm
Coll (FL)
Houston Comm Coll
System (TX)
Jefferson Comm Coll (OH)
Kankakee Comm Coll (IL)
Labette Comm Coll (KS)
Laramie County Comm
Coll (WY)
Laredo Comm Coll (TX)
Las Positas Coll (CA)
Lorain County Comm
Coll (OH)
Los Angeles City Coll (CA)
Madison Area Tech
Coll (WI)
McLennan Comm
Coll (TX)
Merced Coll (CA)
Middlesex Comm Coll (CT)
Mississippi Gulf Coast
Comm Coll (MS)
Monroe Comm Coll (NY)
Montcalm Comm Coll (MI)
Mt. San Antonio Coll (CA)
National Park Comm
Coll (AR)
Naugatuck Valley Comm
Coll (CT)
Northern Essex Comm
Coll (MA)
Northern New Mexico
Coll (NM)
NorthWest Arkansas
Comm Coll (AR)
Odessa Coll (TX)
Orange Coast Coll (CA)
Palm Beach Comm
Coll (FL)
Pasadena City Coll (CA)
Passaic County Comm
Coll (NJ)
Ridgewater Coll (MN)
Roane State Comm
Coll (TN)
Rose State Coll (OK)
Salt Lake Comm Coll (UT)
San Joaquin Delta
Coll (CA)
Southeastern Comm Coll,
North Campus (IA)
Southern Maine Comm
Coll (ME)
South Plains Coll (TX)
South Texas Coll (TX)
Southwest Virginia Comm
Coll (VA)
Trocaire Coll (NY)
Tulsa Comm Coll (OK)
Tyler Jr Coll (TX)
Virginia Highlands Comm
Coll (VA)
Virginia Western Comm
Coll (VA)
Wallace State Comm
Coll (AL)
Wenatchee Valley
Coll (WA)
West Central Tech
Coll (GA)
Westchester Comm
Coll (NY)
Yuba Coll (CA)
Zane State Coll (OH)

Industrial Technology
Albany Tech Coll (GA)
Alexandria Tech Coll (MN)
Allen County Comm
Coll (KS)
Anne Arundel Comm
Coll (MD)
Asnuntuck Comm
Coll (CT)
Bakersfield Coll (CA)
Bergen Comm Coll (NJ)
Bismarck State Coll (ND)
Bladen Comm Coll (NC)
Bowling Green State
U–Firelands Coll (OH)
Brigham Young U –
Idaho (ID)
Brunswick Comm
Coll (NC)
Catawba Valley Comm
Coll (NC)
Central Arizona Coll (AZ)
Central Comm Coll–
Columbus
Campus (NE)
Central Comm Coll–Grand
Island Campus (NE)
Central Comm Coll–
Hastings Campus (NE)
Central Georgia Tech
Coll (GA)

Central New Mexico
Comm Coll (NM)
Central Ohio Tech
Coll (OH)
Central Oregon Comm
Coll (OR)
Central Piedmont Comm
Coll (NC)
Century Coll (MN)
Cerritos Coll (CA)
City Coll of San
Francisco (CA)
Clark State Comm
Coll (OH)
Cleveland State Comm
Coll (TN)
Coll of DuPage (IL)
Columbus Tech Coll (GA)
Comm Coll of Allegheny
County (PA)
Comm Coll of
Vermont (VT)
Cossatot Comm Coll of the
U of Arkansas (AR)
Crowder Coll (MO)
Cuesta Coll (CA)
De Anza Coll (CA)
DeKalb Tech Coll (GA)
Dodge City Comm
Coll (KS)
Don Bosco Tech Inst (CA)
East Central Coll (MO)
Eastern New Mexico
U–Roswell (NM)
Elgin Comm Coll (IL)
Erie Comm Coll, South
Campus (NY)
Everett Comm Coll (WA)
Forsyth Tech Comm
Coll (NC)
Fountainhead Coll of
Technology (TN)
Fox Valley Tech Coll (WI)
Fresno City Coll (CA)
Fullerton Coll (CA)
Gateway Comm Coll (CT)
Gateway Tech Coll (WI)
Grand Rapids Comm
Coll (MI)
Grays Harbor Coll (WA)
Great Basin Coll (NV)
Greenville Tech Coll (SC)
Griffin Tech Coll (GA)
Guilford Tech Comm
Coll (NC)
Hagerstown Comm
Coll (MD)
Harper Coll (IL)
Hartnell Coll (CA)
Henry Ford Comm
Coll (MI)
Hocking Coll (OH)
Hopkinsville Comm
Coll (KY)
Houston Comm Coll
System (TX)
Illinois Eastern Comm
Colls, Wabash Valley
College (IL)
Illinois Valley Comm
Coll (IL)
Jackson State Comm
Coll (TN)
Jefferson Comm Coll (OH)
Joliet Jr Coll (IL)
Kellogg Comm Coll (MI)
Kent State U, Ashtabula
Campus (OH)
Kent State U, Geauga
Campus (OH)
Kent State U, Trumbull
Campus (OH)
Kent State U, Tuscarawas
Campus (OH)
Kirkwood Comm Coll (IA)
Kirtland Comm Coll (MI)
Labette Comm Coll (KS)
Lake Land Coll (IL)
Lanier Tech Coll (GA)
Lansing Comm Coll (MI)
Lehigh Carbon Comm
Coll (PA)
Lenoir Comm Coll (NC)
Linn-Benton Comm
Coll (OR)
Lorain County Comm
Coll (OH)
Los Angeles Pierce
Coll (CA)
Lower Columbia Coll (WA)
Macomb Comm Coll (MI)
Mesa Comm Coll (AZ)
Miami Dade Coll (FL)
Miami U–Middletown
Campus (OH)
Mid-State Tech Coll (WI)
Minnesota State Coll–
Southeast Tech (MN)

Minnesota State Comm
and Tech Coll–Fergus
Falls (MN)
Missouri State U–West
Plains (MO)
Moberly Area Comm
Coll (MO)
Monroe Comm Coll (NY)
Montcalm Comm Coll (MI)
Mt. Hood Comm Coll (OR)
Mount Wachusett Comm
Coll (MA)
Muskegon Comm Coll (MI)
Naugatuck Valley Comm
Coll (CT)
Navarro Coll (TX)
New England Inst of
Technology (RI)
New Hampshire Comm
Tech Coll, Nashua/
Claremont (NH)
North Arkansas Coll (AR)
Northeast State Tech
Comm Coll (TN)
North Georgia Tech
Coll (GA)
North Seattle Comm
Coll (WA)
Oakland Comm Coll (MI)
The Ohio State U Ag Tech
Inst (OH)
Oklahoma State U,
Okmulgee (OK)
Olympic Coll (WA)
Ouachita Tech Coll (AR)
Ozarks Tech Comm
Coll (MO)
Panola Coll (TX)
Parkland Coll (IL)
Passaic County Comm
Coll (NJ)
Penn State York (PA)
Pennsylvania Highland
Comm Coll (PA)
Pierce Coll (WA)
Pulaski Tech Coll (AR)
Raritan Valley Comm
Coll (NJ)
Richland Coll (TX)
Richland Comm Coll (IL)
Robeson Comm Coll (NC)
Rogue Comm Coll (OR)
Saint Paul Coll–A Comm &
Tech College (MN)
Sampson Comm Coll (NC)
San Antonio Coll (TX)
San Diego City Coll (CA)
Santa Ana Coll (CA)
Santa Barbara City
Coll (CA)
Savannah Tech Coll (GA)
Schoolcraft Coll (MI)
Seminole Comm Coll (FL)
Southeastern Comm
Coll (NC)
Southeast Tech Inst (SD)
South Georgia Tech
Coll (GA)
South Texas Coll (TX)
Spokane Comm Coll (WA)
Stanly Comm Coll (NC)
Stark State Coll of
Technology (OH)
State Fair Comm
Coll (MO)
State U of New York Coll
of Technology at
Canton (NY)
Suffolk County Comm
Coll (NY)
Temple Coll (TX)
Terra State Comm
Coll (OH)
Texas State Tech Coll–
Marshall (TX)
Three Rivers Comm
Coll (CT)
Three Rivers Comm
Coll (MO)
Trident Tech Coll (SC)
Trinidad State Jr Coll (CO)
Tulsa Comm Coll (OK)
Ulster County Comm
Coll (NY)
Union County Coll (NJ)
U of Arkansas Comm Coll
at Batesville (AR)
Valencia Comm Coll (FL)
Victoria Coll (TX)
Vincennes U Jasper
Campus (IN)
Washington State Comm
Coll (OH)
Western Nevada Comm
Coll (NV)
Western Piedmont Comm
Coll (NC)

West Georgia Tech
Coll (GA)
Wilson Tech Comm
Coll (NC)
Wright State U, Lake
Campus (OH)
Yuba Coll (CA)
Zane State Coll (OH)

Information Resources Management
Mott Comm Coll (MI)

Information Science/Studies
Aims Comm Coll (CO)
Alamance Comm Coll (NC)
Allen County Comm
Coll (KS)
Alpena Comm Coll (MI)
Altamaha Tech Coll (GA)
Amarillo Coll (TX)
Anne Arundel Comm
Coll (MD)
Appalachian Tech
Coll (GA)
Arizona Western Coll (AZ)
Arkansas State
U–Mountain
Home (AR)
Ashland Comm and Tech
Coll (KY)
Athens Tech Coll (GA)
Augusta Tech Coll (GA)
Bainbridge Coll (GA)
Bakersfield Coll (CA)
Baltimore City Comm
Coll (MD)
Barton County Comm
Coll (KS)
Beaufort County Comm
Coll (NC)
Big Bend Comm Coll (WA)
Bramson ORT Coll (NY)
Brigham Young U –
Idaho (ID)
Broome Comm Coll (NY)
Broward Comm Coll (FL)
Bucks County Comm
Coll (PA)
Cambridge Coll (CO)
Cañada Coll (CA)
Cape Cod Comm
Coll (MA)
Cecil Comm Coll (MD)
Central Carolina Comm
Coll (NC)
Central Georgia Tech
Coll (GA)
Central New Mexico
Comm Coll (NM)
Central Virginia Comm
Coll (VA)
Chaffey Coll (CA)
Chattahoochee Tech
Coll (GA)
Chattanooga State Tech
Comm Coll (TN)
Cincinnati State Tech and
Comm Coll (OH)
City Colls of Chicago,
Harold Washington
College (IL)
City Colls of Chicago,
Harry S. Truman
College (IL)
Clark State Comm
Coll (OH)
Cleveland Comm Coll (NC)
Cochise Coll, Douglas (AZ)
Cochise Coll, Sierra
Vista (AZ)
Coconino Comm Coll (AZ)
Colegio Universitario de
San Juan, San
Juan (PR)
Coll of Alameda (CA)
Coll of Marin (CA)
Coll of San Mateo (CA)
Coll of Southern
Maryland (MD)
Coll of The Albemarle (NC)
Coll of the Canyons (CA)
Columbia-Greene Comm
Coll (NY)
Columbus Tech Coll (GA)
Comm Coll of Beaver
County (PA)
Comm Coll of Southern
Nevada (NV)
Coosa Valley Tech
Coll (GA)
Cosumnes River Coll,
Sacramento (CA)
Cypress Coll (CA)
Dabney S. Lancaster
Comm Coll (VA)
De Anza Coll (CA)

DeKalb Tech Coll (GA)
Dodge City Comm
 Coll (KS)
Draughons Jr Coll (KY)
East Central Tech
 Coll (GA)
Eastern Arizona Coll (AZ)
ECPI Coll of
 Technology (VA)
ECPI Tech Coll (VA)
ECPI Tech Coll (VA)
Elaine P. Nunez Comm
 Coll (LA)
El Centro Coll (TX)
Elgin Comm Coll (IL)
Erie Comm Coll (NY)
Erie Comm Coll, North
 Campus (NY)
Erie Comm Coll, South
 Campus (NY)
Essex County Coll (NJ)
Fayetteville Tech Comm
 Coll (NC)
Fiorello H. LaGuardia
 Comm Coll of the City
 U of New York (NY)
Flint River Tech Coll (GA)
Fort Berthold Comm
 Coll (ND)
Fountainhead Coll of
 Technology (TN)
Fullerton Coll (CA)
Fulton-Montgomery Comm
 Coll (NY)
Genesee Comm Coll (NY)
Georgia Highlands
 Coll (GA)
Gloucester County
 Coll (NJ)
Grays Harbor Coll (WA)
Grossmont Coll (CA)
Guilford Tech Comm
 Coll (NC)
Gwinnett Tech Coll (GA)
Harper Coll (IL)
H. Councill Trenholm State
 Tech Coll (AL)
Henry Ford Comm
 Coll (MI)
Hesser Coll (NH)
Hillsborough Comm
 Coll (FL)
Holyoke Comm Coll (MA)
Howard Comm Coll (MD)
Imperial Valley Coll (CA)
J. F. Drake State Tech
 Coll (AL)
Kankakee Comm Coll (IL)
Kirtland Comm Coll (MI)
Lamar Comm Coll (CO)
Laney Coll (CA)
Lanier Tech Coll (GA)
Lansing Comm Coll (MI)
Laredo Comm Coll (TX)
Las Positas Coll (CA)
Lawson State Comm
 Coll (AL)
Lee Coll (TX)
Lehigh Carbon Comm
 Coll (PA)
Lehigh Valley Coll (PA)
Lewis Coll of
 Business (MI)
Lorain County Comm
 Coll (OH)
Los Angeles Harbor
 Coll (CA)
Louisburg Coll (NC)
Lower Columbia Coll (WA)
Madisonville Comm
 Coll (KY)
Manatee Comm Coll (FL)
Martin Comm Coll (NC)
Massachusetts Bay Comm
 Coll (MA)
McLennan Comm
 Coll (TX)
Mendocino Coll (CA)
Metropolitan Comm
 Coll–Blue River (MO)
Metropolitan Comm
 Coll–Business &
 Technology
 Campus (MO)
Miami Dade Coll (FL)
Miami U–Middletown
 Campus (OH)
Middle Georgia Coll (GA)
Middle Georgia Tech
 Coll (GA)
Mid-State Tech Coll (WI)
Minneapolis Comm and
 Tech Coll (MN)
Minot State U–Bottineau
 Campus (ND)
Mission Coll (CA)
Monroe Comm Coll (NY)

Monterey Peninsula
 Coll (CA)
Montgomery County
 Comm Coll (PA)
Moorpark Coll (CA)
Moultrie Tech Coll (GA)
Mount Wachusett Comm
 Coll (MA)
Murray State Coll (OK)
Muskegon Comm Coll (MI)
National Park Comm
 Coll (AR)
Naugatuck Valley Comm
 Coll (CT)
Neosho County Comm
 Coll (KS)
New Hampshire Comm
 Tech Coll, Manchester/
 Stratham (NH)
New Hampshire Comm
 Tech Coll, Nashua/
 Claremont (NH)
New River Comm Coll (VA)
New York City Coll of
 Technology of the City
 U of New York (NY)
Niagara County Comm
 Coll (NY)
North Central Texas
 Coll (TX)
Northern Oklahoma
 Coll (OK)
North Lake Coll (TX)
North Shore Comm
 Coll (MA)
Northwestern Connecticut
 Comm Coll (CT)
Northwestern Tech
 Coll (GA)
Northwest-Shoals Comm
 Coll (AL)
Odessa Coll (TX)
Ogeechee Tech Coll (GA)
Okefenokee Tech
 Coll (GA)
Oklahoma State U,
 Okmulgee (OK)
Olympic Coll (WA)
Onondaga Comm
 Coll (NY)
Orange Coast Coll (CA)
Oxnard Coll (CA)
Ozarka Coll (AR)
Ozarks Tech Comm
 Coll (MO)
Palo Alto Coll (TX)
Panola Coll (TX)
Parkland Coll (IL)
Pasadena City Coll (CA)
Passaic County Comm
 Coll (NJ)
Penn State DuBois (PA)
Penn State Hazleton (PA)
Penn State Lehigh
 Valley (PA)
Penn State New
 Kensington (PA)
Penn State Schuylkill (PA)
Pierce Coll (WA)
Pioneer Pacific Coll,
 Wilsonville (OR)
Polk Comm Coll (FL)
Pueblo Comm Coll (CO)
Pulaski Tech Coll (AR)
Queensborough Comm
 Coll of the City U of
 New York (NY)
Rappahannock Comm
 Coll (VA)
Raritan Valley Comm
 Coll (NJ)
Reedley Coll (CA)
Richland Comm Coll (IL)
Ridgewater Coll (MN)
Rio Salado Coll (AZ)
Rose State Coll (OK)
Roxbury Comm Coll (MA)
St. Catharine Coll (KY)
St. Louis Comm Coll at
 Florissant Valley (MO)
Salt Lake Comm Coll (UT)
Sandersville Tech
 Coll (GA)
Sandhills Comm Coll (NC)
San Juan Coll (NM)
Santa Ana Coll (CA)
Santa Barbara City
 Coll (CA)
Scottsdale Comm
 Coll (AZ)
Seminole Comm Coll (FL)
Sheridan Coll–Sheridan
 and Gillette (WY)
Southeastern Comm Coll,
 North Campus (IA)
Southeastern Comm Coll,
 South Campus (IA)

Southeastern Tech
 Coll (GA)
Southeast Tech Inst (SD)
Southern Maine Comm
 Coll (ME)
South Georgia Coll (GA)
South Georgia Tech
 Coll (GA)
Southside Virginia Comm
 Coll (VA)
South Texas Coll (TX)
Southwestern Comm
 Coll (NC)
Southwest Georgia Tech
 Coll (GA)
Southwest Virginia Comm
 Coll (VA)
Spokane Falls Comm
 Coll (WA)
Stanly Comm Coll (NC)
State Fair Comm
 Coll (MO)
State U of New York Coll
 of Agriculture and
 Technology at
 Morrisville (NY)
State U of New York Coll
 of Technology at
 Canton (NY)
Suffolk County Comm
 Coll (NY)
Surry Comm Coll (NC)
Swainsboro Tech Coll (GA)
Terra State Comm
 Coll (OH)
Texas State Tech Coll–
 Marshall (TX)
Tompkins Cortland Comm
 Coll (NY)
Trinidad State Jr Coll (CO)
Tulsa Comm Coll (OK)
Tunxis Comm Coll (CT)
Ulster County Comm
 Coll (NY)
Union County Coll (NJ)
U of Arkansas Comm Coll
 at Morrilton (AR)
U of Cincinnati Clermont
 Coll (OH)
U of New Mexico–Valencia
 Campus (NM)
Victoria Coll (TX)
Victor Valley Coll (CA)
Virginia Highlands Comm
 Coll (VA)
Warren County Comm
 Coll (NJ)
West Central Tech
 Coll (GA)
Westchester Comm
 Coll (NY)
Western Wyoming Comm
 Coll (WY)
West Georgia Tech
 Coll (GA)
West Hills Comm Coll (CA)
Westmoreland County
 Comm Coll (PA)
West Valley Coll (CA)
Wilson Tech Comm
 Coll (NC)
Wright State U, Lake
 Campus (OH)
Wytheville Comm Coll (VA)

Information Technology

Antonelli Coll,
 Hattiesburg (MS)
Atlanta Tech Coll (GA)
Bellingham Tech Coll (WA)
Black Hawk Coll,
 Moline (IL)
Bladen Comm Coll (NC)
Brown Mackie Coll–
 Akron (OH)
Bucks County Comm
 Coll (PA)
Burlington County
 Coll (NJ)
Caldwell Comm Coll and
 Tech Inst (NC)
Cape Cod Comm
 Coll (MA)
Capital Comm Coll (CT)
Catawba Valley Comm
 Coll (NC)
Cecil Comm Coll (MD)
Central Carolina Comm
 Coll (NC)
Central Comm Coll–
 Columbus
 Campus (NE)
Central Comm Coll–Grand
 Island Campus (NE)
Central Comm Coll–
 Hastings Campus (NE)
Central Florida Comm
 Coll (FL)

Clark State Comm
 Coll (OH)
Cleveland Comm Coll (NC)
Coastal Bend Coll (TX)
Coll of The Albemarle (NC)
Coll of the Siskiyous (CA)
Comm Coll of
 Vermont (VT)
Cuesta Coll (CA)
Delta School of Business
 & Technology (LA)
Draughons Jr Coll (KY)
El Centro Coll (TX)
Fayetteville Tech Comm
 Coll (NC)
Frederick Comm Coll (MD)
Germanna Comm
 Coll (VA)
Gordon Coll (GA)
Gulf Coast Coll (FL)
Harrisburg Area Comm
 Coll (PA)
Hawkeye Comm Coll (IA)
Howard Comm Coll (MD)
Indiana Business Coll,
 Evansville (IN)
Indiana Business Coll,
 Indianapolis (IN)
Indiana Business Coll,
 Lafayette (IN)
Indiana Business Coll,
 Muncie (IN)
Iowa Lakes Comm
 Coll (IA)
ITT Tech Inst,
 Indianapolis (IN)
Kaplan U (IA)
Kent State U, Geauga
 Campus (OH)
Keystone Coll (PA)
Kilian Comm Coll (SD)
Lake Land Coll (IL)
Laramie County Comm
 Coll (WY)
Laredo Comm Coll (TX)
Lassen Comm Coll
 District (CA)
Laurel Business Inst (PA)
LDS Business Coll (UT)
Lorain County Comm
 Coll (OH)
Los Angeles City Coll (CA)
Lower Columbia Coll (WA)
Mesabi Range Comm and
 Tech Coll (MN)
Metropolitan Comm
 Coll–Business &
 Technology
 Campus (MO)
Minnesota School of
 Business–Brooklyn
 Center (MN)
Minnesota School of
 Business–Plymouth (MN)
Minnesota School of
 Business–Richfield (MN)
Minnesota School of
 Business–St.
 Cloud (MN)
Minnesota School of
 Business–Shakopee (MN)
Minot State U–Bottineau
 Campus (ND)
Mississippi Gulf Coast
 Comm Coll (MS)
Missouri State U–West
 Plains (MO)
Mohave Comm Coll (AZ)
Monroe Comm Coll (NY)
National American U (KS)
National American U, Rio
 Rancho (NM)
Naugatuck Valley Comm
 Coll (CT)
Nebraska Indian Comm
 Coll (NE)
North Central Michigan
 Coll (MI)
Northland Comm and Tech
 Coll–Thief River
 Falls (MN)
Olympic Coll (WA)
Onondaga Comm
 Coll (NY)
Owensboro Comm and
 Tech Coll (KY)
Palo Alto Coll (TX)
Pasco-Hernando Comm
 Coll (FL)
Potomac State Coll of
 West Virginia U (WV)
Queensborough Comm
 Coll of the City U of
 New York (NY)
Rio Salado Coll (AZ)
St. Cloud Tech Coll (MN)
Salt Lake Comm Coll (UT)
Sampson Comm Coll (NC)

Santa Ana Coll (CA)
Santa Barbara City
 Coll (CA)
Savannah Tech Coll (GA)
Seminole Comm Coll (FL)
Southeastern Business
 Coll, Jackson (OH)
Southeastern Business
 Coll, New Boston (OH)
Southeast Kentucky Comm
 and Tech Coll (KY)
Southeast Tech Inst (SD)
Southside Virginia Comm
 Coll (VA)
Southwest Mississippi
 Comm Coll (MS)
Stark State Coll of
 Technology (OH)
Suffolk County Comm
 Coll (NY)
Surry Comm Coll (NC)
Texarkana Coll (TX)
Three Rivers Comm
 Coll (MO)
Tidewater Comm Coll (VA)
Tri-County Comm
 Coll (NC)
Trinidad State Jr Coll (CO)
Tulsa Comm Coll (OK)
Tyler Jr Coll (TX)
U of Arkansas Comm Coll
 at Batesville (AR)
Valencia Comm Coll (FL)
Vatterott Coll (OH)
Vatterott Coll, Oklahoma
 City (OK)
Western Nebraska Comm
 Coll (NE)
Western Wyoming Comm
 Coll (WY)
West Shore Comm
 Coll (MI)

Institutional Food Workers

Asheville-Buncombe Tech
 Comm Coll (NC)
Cape Fear Comm
 Coll (NC)
Elaine P. Nunez Comm
 Coll (LA)
Harrisburg Area Comm
 Coll (PA)
Iowa Lakes Comm
 Coll (IA)
Lamar Inst of
 Technology (TX)
North Arkansas Coll (AR)
Santa Barbara City
 Coll (CA)

Instrumentation Technology

Amarillo Coll (TX)
Bishop State Comm
 Coll (AL)
Cape Fear Comm
 Coll (NC)
Central Carolina Comm
 Coll (NC)
Chattanooga State Tech
 Comm Coll (TN)
Comm Coll of Rhode
 Island (RI)
DeKalb Tech Coll (GA)
H. Councill Trenholm State
 Tech Coll (AL)
Henry Ford Comm
 Coll (MI)
Lamar Inst of
 Technology (TX)
Lee Coll (TX)
Lenoir Comm Coll (NC)
Lower Columbia Coll (WA)
Mesabi Range Comm and
 Tech Coll (MN)
Mid-State Tech Coll (WI)
Monroe Comm Coll (NY)
Moraine Valley Comm
 Coll (IL)
Nassau Comm Coll (NY)
New River Comm Coll (VA)
Northeast State Tech
 Comm Coll (TN)
Northern Maine Comm
 Coll (ME)
Ozarks Tech Comm
 Coll (MO)
Ridgewater Coll (MN)
St. Cloud Tech Coll (MN)
Salt Lake Comm Coll (UT)
San Juan Coll (NM)
Texas State Tech Coll–
 Marshall (TX)
Western Wyoming Comm
 Coll (WY)

Insurance

Broward Comm Coll (FL)

Central Piedmont Comm
 Coll (NC)
City Coll of San
 Francisco (CA)
Comm Coll of Allegheny
 County (PA)
Fond du Lac Tribal and
 Comm Coll (MN)
Fox Valley Tech Coll (WI)
Harper Coll (IL)
Houston Comm Coll
 System (TX)
Isothermal Comm
 Coll (NC)
Laurel Business Inst (PA)
Lenoir Comm Coll (NC)
Madison Area Tech
 Coll (WI)
Merced Coll (CA)
Mesa Comm Coll (AZ)
Nassau Comm Coll (NY)
Oklahoma City Comm
 Coll (OK)
Onondaga Comm
 Coll (NY)
Richland Comm Coll (IL)
St. Catharine Coll (KY)
San Diego City Coll (CA)
Suffolk County Comm
 Coll (NY)
Tulsa Comm Coll (OK)

Interdisciplinary Studies

Bowling Green State
 U–Firelands Coll (OH)
Central Texas Coll (TX)
Columbia-Greene Comm
 Coll (NY)
Elizabethtown Tech
 Coll (KY)
Folsom Lake Coll (CA)
Great Basin Coll (NV)
Hawkeye Comm Coll (IA)
Miami U–Middletown
 Campus (OH)
North Country Comm
 Coll (NY)
North Shore Comm
 Coll (MA)
Pasadena City Coll (CA)
Ridgewater Coll (MN)
South Texas Coll (TX)
State U of New York Coll
 of Technology at
 Canton (NY)
The U of Akron–Wayne
 Coll (OH)
Western Nebraska Comm
 Coll (NE)

Interior Architecture

Inst of Design and
 Construction (NY)
Lehigh Carbon Comm
 Coll (PA)
St. Philip's Coll (TX)

Interior Design

Alexandria Tech Coll (MN)
Amarillo Coll (TX)
Antelope Valley Coll (CA)
Antonelli Coll,
 Hattiesburg (MS)
The Art Inst of Ohio–
 Cincinnati (OH)
The Art Inst of
 Philadelphia (PA)
Bakersfield Coll (CA)
Berkeley Coll, West
 Paterson (NJ)
Black Hawk Coll,
 Moline (IL)
Bradley Academy for the
 Visual Arts (PA)
Brigham Young U –
 Idaho (ID)
Broward Comm Coll (FL)
Cañada Coll (CA)
Cape Fear Comm
 Coll (NC)
Central Piedmont Comm
 Coll (NC)
Century Coll (MN)
Chaffey Coll (CA)
City Coll of San
 Francisco (CA)
Coll of DuPage (IL)
Coll of Marin (CA)
Coll of the Canyons (CA)
Coll of the Desert (CA)
Collin County Comm Coll
 District (TX)
Cosumnes River Coll,
 Sacramento (CA)
Cuesta Coll (CA)
Dixie State Coll of
 Utah (UT)
El Camino Coll (CA)
El Centro Coll (TX)

FIDM/The Fashion Inst of Design & Merchandising, Los Angeles Campus (CA)
FIDM/The Fashion Inst of Design & Merchandising, San Diego Campus (CA)
FIDM/The Fashion Inst of Design & Merchandising, San Francisco Campus (CA)
Fox Valley Tech Coll (WI)
Fullerton Coll (CA)
Gateway Tech Coll (WI)
Gwinnett Tech Coll (GA)
Harper Coll (IL)
Hawkeye Comm Coll (IA)
Henry Ford Comm Coll (MI)
Hesser Coll (NH)
Hillsborough Comm Coll (FL)
Houston Comm Coll System (TX)
Joliet Jr Coll (IL)
Kirkwood Comm Coll (IA)
Lanier Tech Coll (GA)
Las Positas Coll (CA)
LDS Business Coll (UT)
Madison Area Tech Coll (WI)
Marshall Comm and Tech Coll (WV)
Mesa Comm Coll (AZ)
Metropolitan Comm Coll (NE)
Miami Dade Coll (FL)
Monroe Comm Coll (NY)
Monterey Peninsula Coll (CA)
Mt. San Antonio Coll (CA)
Nassau Comm Coll (NY)
New England Inst of Technology (RI)
Northampton County Area Comm Coll (PA)
Oakland Comm Coll (MI)
Ogeechee Tech Coll (GA)
Ohlone Coll (CA)
Onondaga Comm Coll (NY)
Orange Coast Coll (CA)
Palm Beach Comm Coll (FL)
Pasadena City Coll (CA)
St. Philip's Coll (TX)
San Bernardino Valley Coll (CA)
San Diego City Coll (CA)
San Joaquin Delta Coll (CA)
Santa Barbara City Coll (CA)
Santa Rosa Jr Coll (CA)
Scott Comm Coll (IA)
Scottsdale Comm Coll (AZ)
Seminole Comm Coll (FL)
Spokane Falls Comm Coll (WA)
Suffolk County Comm Coll (NY)
Tidewater Comm Coll (VA)
Tulsa Comm Coll (OK)
U of Puerto Rico at Carolina (PR)
Villa Maria Coll of Buffalo (NY)
Wallace State Comm Coll (AL)
Waukesha County Tech Coll (WI)
Western Piedmont Comm Coll (NC)
West Valley Coll (CA)
Wichita Area Tech Coll (KS)

Intermedia/Multimedia
Academy Coll (MN)
The Art Inst of Philadelphia (PA)
Coll of the Siskiyous (CA)
Front Range Comm Coll (CO)
Hillsborough Comm Coll (FL)
Middlesex Comm Coll (CT)
Minnesota School of Business–Brooklyn Center (MN)
Minnesota School of Business–Plymouth (MN)
Minnesota School of Business–Richfield (MN)
Minnesota School of Business–St. Cloud (MN)
Minnesota School of Business–Shakopee (MN)
Platt Coll San Diego (CA)
Raritan Valley Comm Coll (NJ)

International Business/Trade/Commerce
Berkeley Coll, West Paterson (NJ)
Berkeley Coll–New York City Campus (NY)
Berkeley Coll–Westchester Campus (NY)
Black Hawk Coll, Moline (IL)
Brevard Comm Coll (FL)
Cincinnati State Tech and Comm Coll (OH)
City Colls of Chicago, Harold Washington College (IL)
Comm Coll of Philadelphia (PA)
Foothill Coll (CA)
Frederick Comm Coll (MD)
Fullerton Coll (CA)
Grossmont Coll (CA)
Harper Coll (IL)
Kansas City Kansas Comm Coll (KS)
Kirkwood Comm Coll (IA)
Lansing Comm Coll (MI)
Laredo Comm Coll (TX)
Lee Coll (TX)
Monroe Comm Coll (NY)
Monterey Peninsula Coll (CA)
Mott Comm Coll (MI)
National American U, Bloomington (MN)
Northland Comm and Tech Coll–Thief River Falls (MN)
Oakland Comm Coll (MI)
Paradise Valley Comm Coll (AZ)
Pima Comm Coll (AZ)
Raritan Valley Comm Coll (NJ)
Richland Coll (TX)
Roxbury Comm Coll (MA)
Saint Paul Coll–A Comm & Tech College (MN)
Spokane Falls Comm Coll (WA)
Stark State Coll of Technology (OH)
Tompkins Cortland Comm Coll (NY)
Tulsa Comm Coll (OK)
Westchester Comm Coll (NY)
Young Harris Coll (GA)

International Finance
Broome Comm Coll (NY)

International/Global Studies
Berkshire Comm Coll (MA)
Macomb Comm Coll (MI)
Northwest Vista Coll (TX)
Salt Lake Comm Coll (UT)

International Relations and Affairs
Cochise Coll, Sierra Vista (AZ)
De Anza Coll (CA)
Harrisburg Area Comm Coll (PA)
Kellogg Comm Coll (MI)
Massachusetts Bay Comm Coll (MA)
Miami Dade Coll (FL)
Naugatuck Valley Comm Coll (CT)
Northern Essex Comm Coll (MA)
Salt Lake Comm Coll (UT)
Santa Barbara City Coll (CA)
Tulsa Comm Coll (OK)
Western Wyoming Comm Coll (WY)

Italian
City Colls of Chicago, Harold Washington College (IL)
Coll of the Desert (CA)
Contra Costa Coll (CA)
El Camino Coll (CA)
Los Angeles Mission Coll (CA)

Miami Dade Coll (FL)
San Joaquin Delta Coll (CA)
Tulsa Comm Coll (OK)
West Valley Coll (CA)

Japanese
Citrus Coll (CA)
City Colls of Chicago, Harold Washington College (IL)
El Camino Coll (CA)
Everett Comm Coll (WA)
St. Catharine Coll (KY)
San Joaquin Delta Coll (CA)
Tulsa Comm Coll (OK)

Jazz
Villa Maria Coll of Buffalo (NY)

Jazz/Jazz Studies
Iowa Lakes Comm Coll (IA)
Kirkwood Comm Coll (IA)
Manatee Comm Coll (FL)

Jewish/Judaic Studies
Manatee Comm Coll (FL)

Journalism
Allen County Comm Coll (KS)
Amarillo Coll (TX)
Angelina Coll (TX)
Bainbridge Coll (GA)
Bakersfield Coll (CA)
Barton County Comm Coll (KS)
Brigham Young U – Idaho (ID)
Bucks County Comm Coll (PA)
Burlington County Coll (NJ)
Cañada Coll (CA)
Central Texas Coll (TX)
Cerritos Coll (CA)
Chaffey Coll (CA)
Citrus Coll (CA)
City Coll of San Francisco (CA)
City Colls of Chicago, Harold Washington College (IL)
City Colls of Chicago, Harry S. Truman College (IL)
City Colls of Chicago, Richard J. Daley College (IL)
City Colls of Chicago, Wilbur Wright College (IL)
Coastal Bend Coll (TX)
Cochise Coll, Douglas (AZ)
Cochise Coll, Sierra Vista (AZ)
Colby Comm Coll (KS)
Coll of Marin (CA)
Coll of San Mateo (CA)
Coll of Southern Maryland (MD)
Coll of the Canyons (CA)
Coll of the Desert (CA)
Comm Coll of Allegheny County (PA)
Contra Costa Coll (CA)
Cosumnes River Coll, Sacramento (CA)
Cuesta Coll (CA)
De Anza Coll (CA)
Dixie State Coll of Utah (UT)
Dodge City Comm Coll (KS)
El Camino Coll (CA)
Everett Comm Coll (WA)
Fresno City Coll (CA)
Fullerton Coll (CA)
Georgia Highlands Coll (GA)
Golden West Coll (CA)
Gordon Coll (GA)
Harper Coll (IL)
Harrisburg Area Comm Coll (PA)
Housatonic Comm Coll (CT)
Illinois Valley Comm Coll (IL)
Imperial Valley Coll (CA)
Iowa Lakes Comm Coll (IA)
Kellogg Comm Coll (MI)
Keystone Coll (PA)
Kingsborough Comm Coll of the City U of New York (NY)
Kirkwood Comm Coll (IA)

Laney Coll (CA)
Lansing Comm Coll (MI)
Laramie County Comm Coll (WY)
Lassen Comm Coll District (CA)
Lee Coll (TX)
Linn-Benton Comm Coll (OR)
Lorain County Comm Coll (OH)
Los Angeles City Coll (CA)
Los Angeles Mission Coll (CA)
Los Angeles Pierce Coll (CA)
Los Medanos Coll (CA)
Manatee Comm Coll (FL)
Miami Dade Coll (FL)
Moorpark Coll (CA)
Mt. Hood Comm Coll (OR)
Mt. San Antonio Coll (CA)
Navarro Coll (TX)
Northampton County Area Comm Coll (PA)
Northeast Comm Coll (NE)
Northeastern Jr Coll (CO)
Northern Essex Comm Coll (MA)
North Idaho Coll (ID)
Northwest Mississippi Comm Coll (MS)
Ohlone Coll (CA)
Orange Coast Coll (CA)
Oxnard Coll (CA)
Palm Beach Comm Coll (FL)
Palo Alto Coll (TX)
Pasadena City Coll (CA)
Potomac State Coll of West Virginia U (WV)
Ridgewater Coll (MN)
Rose State Coll (OK)
St. Catharine Coll (KY)
St. Louis Comm Coll at Florissant Valley (MO)
San Bernardino Valley Coll (CA)
San Diego City Coll (CA)
San Joaquin Delta Coll (CA)
Santa Ana Coll (CA)
Santa Rosa Jr Coll (CA)
Shasta Coll (CA)
Skagit Valley Coll (WA)
South Georgia Coll (GA)
South Plains Coll (TX)
State U of New York Coll of Agriculture and Technology at Morrisville (NY)
Suffolk County Comm Coll (NY)
Sussex County Comm Coll (NJ)
Taft Coll (CA)
Texarkana Coll (TX)
Tulsa Comm Coll (OK)
Turtle Mountain Comm Coll (ND)
Ulster County Comm Coll (NY)
Umpqua Comm Coll (OR)
Ventura Coll (CA)
Western Nebraska Comm Coll (NE)
Western Texas Coll (TX)
Western Wyoming Comm Coll (WY)
West Los Angeles Coll (CA)
Young Harris Coll (GA)

Juvenile Corrections
Linn-Benton Comm Coll (OR)

Kindergarten/Preschool Education
Aims Comm Coll (CO)
Alamance Comm Coll (NC)
Anne Arundel Comm Coll (MD)
Bainbridge Coll (GA)
Baltimore City Comm Coll (MD)
Barstow Coll (CA)
Beaufort County Comm Coll (NC)
Bergen Comm Coll (NJ)
Brigham Young U – Idaho (ID)
Broward Comm Coll (FL)
Bucks County Comm Coll (PA)
Cabrillo Coll (CA)
Cañada Coll (CA)
Cape Cod Comm Coll (MA)

Capital Comm Coll (CT)
Carroll Comm Coll (MD)
Cecil Comm Coll (MD)
Central Arizona Coll (AZ)
Central Carolina Comm Coll (NC)
Centralia Coll (WA)
Central Maine Comm Coll (ME)
Central Ohio Tech Coll (OH)
Central Piedmont Comm Coll (NC)
Cerritos Coll (CA)
Chaffey Coll (CA)
Chattanooga State Tech Comm Coll (TN)
Chesapeake Coll (MD)
Cisco Jr Coll (TX)
City Colls of Chicago, Harold Washington College (IL)
City Colls of Chicago, Kennedy-King College (IL)
City Colls of Chicago, Olive-Harvey College (IL)
Clark State Comm Coll (OH)
Cleveland State Comm Coll (TN)
Coahoma Comm Coll (MS)
Colby Comm Coll (KS)
Coll of Marin (CA)
Coll of the Canyons (CA)
Coll of the Desert (CA)
Coll of the Redwoods (CA)
Coll of the Siskiyous (CA)
Columbia Basin Coll (WA)
Comm Coll of Philadelphia (PA)
Comm Coll of Rhode Island (RI)
Comm Coll of Southern Nevada (NV)
Contra Costa Coll (CA)
Cosumnes River Coll, Sacramento (CA)
Cuesta Coll (CA)
Cuyahoga Comm Coll (OH)
Dixie State Coll of Utah (UT)
Elaine P. Nunez Comm Coll (LA)
El Camino Coll (CA)
Elgin Comm Coll (IL)
Essex County Coll (NJ)
Eugenio María de Hostos Comm Coll of the City U of New York (NY)
Everett Comm Coll (WA)
Finger Lakes Comm Coll (NY)
Fiorello H. LaGuardia Comm Coll of the City U of New York (NY)
Fisher Coll (MA)
Forsyth Tech Comm Coll (NC)
Fort Belknap Coll (MT)
Fort Berthold Comm Coll (ND)
Frederick Comm Coll (MD)
Fullerton Coll (CA)
Fulton-Montgomery Comm Coll (NY)
Gateway Comm Coll (CT)
Genesee Comm Coll (NY)
Georgia Highlands Coll (GA)
Great Basin Coll (NV)
Guilford Tech Comm Coll (NC)
Harper Coll (IL)
Harrisburg Area Comm Coll (PA)
Hartnell Coll (CA)
Hesser Coll (NH)
Hesston Coll (KS)
Holyoke Comm Coll (MA)
Hopkinsville Comm Coll (KY)
Howard Comm Coll (MD)
Imperial Valley Coll (CA)
Iowa Lakes Comm Coll (IA)
Isothermal Comm Coll (NC)
James Sprunt Comm Coll (NC)
Johnston Comm Coll (NC)
Kellogg Comm Coll (MI)
Kent State U, Ashtabula Campus (OH)
Keystone Coll (PA)
Kirkwood Comm Coll (IA)

Labette Comm Coll (KS)
Lake Tahoe Comm Coll (CA)
Lansing Comm Coll (MI)
Las Positas Coll (CA)
Lassen Comm Coll District (CA)
Lehigh Carbon Comm Coll (PA)
Lorain County Comm Coll (OH)
Los Angeles Southwest Coll (CA)
Lower Columbia Coll (WA)
Manatee Comm Coll (FL)
McLennan Comm Coll (TX)
Mendocino Coll (CA)
Merced Coll (CA)
Metropolitan Comm Coll (NE)
Metropolitan Comm Coll–Penn Valley (MO)
Miami Dade Coll (FL)
Miami U–Middletown Campus (OH)
Minnesota State Coll–Southeast Tech (MN)
Mississippi Gulf Coast Comm Coll (MS)
Monterey Peninsula Coll (CA)
Moorpark Coll (CA)
Mt. Hood Comm Coll (OR)
Mt. San Antonio Coll (CA)
Napa Valley Coll (CA)
Nassau Comm Coll (NY)
Naugatuck Valley Comm Coll (CT)
New Hampshire Comm Tech Coll, Manchester/Stratham (NH)
New Hampshire Comm Tech Coll, Nashua/Claremont (NH)
New Hampshire Tech Inst (NH)
Nicolet Area Tech Coll (WI)
Northeastern Jr Coll (CO)
Northeast State Tech Comm Coll (TN)
Northern Essex Comm Coll (MA)
Northern Maine Comm Coll (ME)
North Shore Comm Coll (MA)
Northwestern Connecticut Comm Coll (CT)
Odessa Coll (TX)
Ohlone Coll (CA)
Onondaga Comm Coll (NY)
Orange Coast Coll (CA)
Owensboro Comm and Tech Coll (KY)
Oxnard Coll (CA)
Ozarks Tech Comm Coll (MO)
Palm Beach Comm Coll (FL)
Pasadena City Coll (CA)
Passaic County Comm Coll (NJ)
Pierce Coll (WA)
Potomac State Coll of West Virginia U (WV)
Pueblo Comm Coll (CO)
Raritan Valley Comm Coll (NJ)
Redlands Comm Coll (OK)
Roane State Comm Coll (TN)
Rose State Coll (OK)
Roxbury Comm Coll (MA)
Sacramento City Coll (CA)
St. Catharine Coll (KY)
St. Cloud Tech Coll (MN)
Salish Kootenai Coll (MT)
Sandhills Comm Coll (NC)
San Joaquin Delta Coll (CA)
San Juan Coll (NM)
Santa Ana Coll (CA)
Santa Barbara City Coll (CA)
Scottsdale Comm Coll (AZ)
Shasta Coll (CA)
Skagit Valley Coll (WA)
Southeastern Comm Coll (NC)
Southern Maine Comm Coll (ME)
Southern State Comm Coll (OH)
Southern U at Shreveport (LA)

South Georgia Coll (GA)
Springfield Tech Comm
Coll (MA)
State U of New York Coll
of Technology at
Canton (NY)
Suffolk County Comm
Coll (NY)
Taft Coll (CA)
Tallahassee Comm
Coll (FL)
Terra State Comm
Coll (OH)
Three Rivers Comm
Coll (CT)
Tidewater Comm Coll (VA)
Tompkins Cortland Comm
Coll (NY)
Trinidad State Jr Coll (CO)
Trocaire Coll (NY)
Tulsa Comm Coll (OK)
Tunxis Comm Coll (CT)
Turtle Mountain Comm
Coll (ND)
Umpqua Comm Coll (OR)
U of Arkansas Comm Coll
at Batesville (AR)
U of New
Mexico–Gallup (NM)
Victor Valley Coll (CA)
Villa Maria Coll of
Buffalo (NY)
Virginia Western Comm
Coll (VA)
Wallace State Comm
Coll (AL)
Washington State Comm
Coll (OH)
Wenatchee Valley
Coll (WA)
Western Nebraska Comm
Coll (NE)
West Hills Comm Coll (CA)
West Valley Coll (CA)
Wilson Tech Comm
Coll (NC)
York County Comm
Coll (ME)
Yuba Coll (CA)

**Kinesiology and
Exercise Science**
Barton County Comm
Coll (KS)
Bergen Comm Coll (NJ)
Cañada Coll (CA)
Central Oregon Comm
Coll (OR)
Clarendon Coll (TX)
Clark State Comm
Coll (OH)
Columbia-Greene Comm
Coll (NY)
Gloucester County
Coll (NJ)
Harper Coll (IL)
Henry Ford Comm
Coll (MI)
Houston Comm Coll
System (TX)
Lee Coll (TX)
Monterey Peninsula
Coll (CA)
Mount Wachusett Comm
Coll (MA)
Naugatuck Valley Comm
Coll (CT)
New Hampshire Comm
Tech Coll, Manchester/
Stratham (NH)
North Country Comm
Coll (NY)
North Lake Coll (TX)
Oakland Comm Coll (MI)
Orange Coast Coll (CA)
Rose State Coll (OK)
St. Philip's Coll (TX)
Salt Lake Comm Coll (UT)
Santa Ana Coll (CA)
Santa Barbara City
Coll (CA)
Santiago Canyon Coll (CA)
South Georgia Coll (GA)
Western Wyoming Comm
Coll (WY)

**Labor and Industrial
Relations**
City Coll of San
Francisco (CA)
Comm Coll of Rhode
Island (RI)
El Camino Coll (CA)
Kingsborough Comm Coll
of the City U of New
York (NY)
Laney Coll (CA)
Lansing Comm Coll (MI)

Onondaga Comm
Coll (NY)
San Diego City Coll (CA)
Tulsa Comm Coll (OK)
Wallace State Comm
Coll (AL)

**Landscape
Architecture**
Anne Arundel Comm
Coll (MD)
Brigham Young U –
Idaho (ID)
City Coll of San
Francisco (CA)
Coll of Marin (CA)
Coll of San Mateo (CA)
Foothill Coll (CA)
Harper Coll (IL)
Keystone Coll (PA)
Kirkwood Comm Coll (IA)
Lansing Comm Coll (MI)
Lenoir Comm Coll (NC)
Los Angeles Pierce
Coll (CA)
Merced Coll (CA)
Monroe Comm Coll (NY)
Mt. San Antonio Coll (CA)
Oakland Comm Coll (MI)
Oklahoma State U,
Oklahoma City (OK)
Onondaga Comm
Coll (NY)
Pasadena City Coll (CA)
St. Catharine Coll (KY)
Santa Rosa Jr Coll (CA)
South Seattle Comm
Coll (WA)
State U of New York Coll
of Agriculture and
Technology at
Morrisville (NY)
Tulsa Comm Coll (OK)
Western Texas Coll (TX)
West Valley Coll (CA)

**Landscaping and
Groundskeeping**
Caldwell Comm Coll and
Tech Inst (NC)
Cape Fear Comm
Coll (NC)
Central Florida Comm
Coll (FL)
Cincinnati State Tech and
Comm Coll (OH)
Clark Coll (WA)
Clark State Comm
Coll (OH)
Coll of DuPage (IL)
Coll of Lake County (IL)
Coll of Marin (CA)
Coll of San Mateo (CA)
Comm Coll of Allegheny
County (PA)
Comm Coll of Southern
Nevada (NV)
Cosumnes River Coll,
Sacramento (CA)
Front Range Comm
Coll (CO)
Grayson County Coll (TX)
Harper Coll (IL)
Iowa Lakes Comm
Coll (IA)
James H. Faulkner State
Comm Coll (AL)
Johnston Comm Coll (NC)
Joliet Jr Coll (IL)
Lincoln Land Comm
Coll (IL)
Los Angeles Pierce
Coll (CA)
Miami Dade Coll (FL)
Minot State U–Bottineau
Campus (ND)
Northeastern Jr Coll (CO)
North Shore Comm
Coll (MA)
Oakland Comm Coll (MI)
The Ohio State U Ag Tech
Inst (OH)
Parkland Coll (IL)
St. Catharine Coll (KY)
Sandhills Comm Coll (NC)
Santa Barbara City
Coll (CA)
Southern Maine Comm
Coll (ME)
South Seattle Comm
Coll (WA)
Spokane Comm Coll (WA)
Springfield Tech Comm
Coll (MA)
State U of New York Coll
of Agriculture and
Technology at
Morrisville (NY)

State U of New York Coll
of Technology at
Alfred (NY)
Tulsa Comm Coll (OK)
The Williamson Free
School of Mecha
Trades (PA)

**Land Use Planning
and Management**
Colorado Mountain Coll,
Timberline
Campus (CO)
Fullerton Coll (CA)
Hocking Coll (OH)
St. Catharine Coll (KY)
Southwest Virginia Comm
Coll (VA)

**Language
Interpretation and
Translation**
Allen County Comm
Coll (KS)
Cochise Coll, Douglas (AZ)
Fayetteville Tech Comm
Coll (NC)
Front Range Comm
Coll (CO)
Union County Coll (NJ)
Wilson Tech Comm
Coll (NC)

**Laser and Optical
Technology**
Amarillo Coll (TX)
Central Carolina Comm
Coll (NC)
Central New Mexico
Comm Coll (NM)
Cincinnati State Tech and
Comm Coll (OH)
Elaine P. Nunez Comm
Coll (LA)
George C. Wallace Comm
Coll (AL)
Linn State Tech Coll (MO)
Monroe Comm Coll (NY)
Moorpark Coll (CA)
Queensborough Comm
Coll of the City U of
New York (NY)
Roane State Comm
Coll (TN)
Schoolcraft Coll (MI)
Southeast Tech Inst (SD)
Southwestern Indian
Polytechnic Inst (NM)
Springfield Tech Comm
Coll (MA)
Three Rivers Comm
Coll (CT)

Latin
Tulsa Comm Coll (OK)

**Latin American
Studies**
City Coll of San
Francisco (CA)
Fullerton Coll (CA)
Manatee Comm Coll (FL)
Miami Dade Coll (FL)
Pasadena City Coll (CA)
San Diego City Coll (CA)
Santa Rosa Jr Coll (CA)

**Leatherworking/
Upholstery**
St. Philip's Coll (TX)
Spokane Falls Comm
Coll (WA)

**Legal Administrative
Assistant**
Antonelli Coll,
Hattiesburg (MS)
Asnuntuck Comm
Coll (CT)
King's Coll (NC)
Minnesota State Comm
and Tech Coll–Fergus
Falls (MN)
Sage Coll (CA)

**Legal Administrative
Assistant/Secretary**
AIB Coll of Business (IA)
Alamance Comm Coll (NC)
Alexandria Tech Coll (MN)
Amarillo Coll (TX)
Bakersfield Coll (CA)
Baltimore City Comm
Coll (MD)
Bergen Comm Coll (NJ)
Bismarck State Coll (ND)
Black Hawk Coll,
Moline (IL)
Blinn Coll (TX)
Bramson ORT Coll (NY)
Briarwood Coll (CT)

Broward Comm Coll (FL)
Business Inst of
Pennsylvania,
Sharon (PA)
Cambria-Rowe Business
Coll, Johnstown (PA)
Cape Cod Comm
Coll (MA)
Central Arizona Coll (AZ)
Central Carolina Comm
Coll (NC)
Centralia Coll (WA)
Central Lakes Coll (MN)
Central Piedmont Comm
Coll (NC)
Century Coll (MN)
Cerritos Coll (CA)
Chaffey Coll (CA)
Chattanooga State Tech
Comm Coll (TN)
Chesapeake Coll (MD)
City Coll of San
Francisco (CA)
Clatsop Comm Coll (OR)
Clovis Comm Coll (NM)
Coastal Bend Coll (TX)
Cochise Coll, Sierra
Vista (AZ)
Coll of DuPage (IL)
Coll of the Redwoods (CA)
Comm Coll of Allegheny
County (PA)
Comm Coll of
Philadelphia (PA)
Comm Coll of Rhode
Island (RI)
Comm Coll of Southern
Nevada (NV)
Crowder Coll (MO)
Cypress Coll (CA)
Dabney S. Lancaster
Comm Coll (VA)
DeKalb Tech Coll (GA)
Dodge City Comm
Coll (KS)
Draughons Jr Coll (KY)
East Central Coll (MO)
El Centro Coll (TX)
Elgin Comm Coll (IL)
Elmira Business Inst (NY)
Fiorello H. LaGuardia
Comm Coll of the City
U of New York (NY)
Florida National Coll (FL)
Forrest Jr Coll (SC)
Fox Valley Tech Coll (WI)
Frederick Comm Coll (MD)
Fresno City Coll (CA)
Fullerton Coll (CA)
Fulton-Montgomery Comm
Coll (NY)
Gateway Comm Coll (CT)
Gateway Tech Coll (WI)
Gloucester County
Coll (NJ)
Golden West Coll (CA)
Grand Rapids Comm
Coll (MI)
Grayson County Coll (TX)
Grossmont Coll (CA)
Harper Coll (IL)
Harrisburg Area Comm
Coll (PA)
Hennepin Tech Coll (MN)
Henry Ford Comm
Coll (MI)
Hillsborough Comm
Coll (FL)
Holyoke Comm Coll (MA)
Howard Comm Coll (MD)
Indiana Business Coll,
Indianapolis (IN)
International Business Coll,
Fort Wayne (IN)
Inver Hills Comm
Coll (MN)
Iowa Lakes Comm
Coll (IA)
Jefferson Comm Coll (OH)
John Wood Comm Coll (IL)
Kellogg Comm Coll (MI)
Kennebec Valley Comm
Coll (ME)
Kent State U, Ashtabula
Campus (OH)
Kent State U, East
Liverpool Campus (OH)
Kirkwood Comm Coll (IA)
Kirtland Comm Coll (MI)
Labette Comm Coll (KS)
Lake Land Coll (IL)
Lamar Comm Coll (CO)
Lansing Comm Coll (MI)
Lassen Comm Coll
District (CA)
Laurel Business Inst (PA)
Lawson State Comm
Coll (AL)

LDS Business Coll (UT)
Lehigh Carbon Comm
Coll (PA)
Lenoir Comm Coll (NC)
Lewis Coll of
Business (MI)
Lincoln Land Comm
Coll (IL)
Linn-Benton Comm
Coll (OR)
Los Angeles City Coll (CA)
Los Angeles Harbor
Coll (CA)
Lower Columbia Coll (WA)
Marian Court Coll (MA)
McLennan Comm
Coll (TX)
Merced Coll (CA)
Metropolitan Comm
Coll (NE)
Metropolitan Comm
Coll–Longview (MO)
Metropolitan Comm
Coll–Maple
Woods (MO)
Metropolitan Comm
Coll–Penn Valley (MO)
Miami Dade Coll (FL)
Miami U–Middletown
Campus (OH)
Middlesex Comm Coll (CT)
Minneapolis Comm and
Tech Coll (MN)
Minnesota School of
Business–Brooklyn
Center (MN)
Minnesota State Coll–
Southeast Tech (MN)
Minnesota State Comm
and Tech Coll–Fergus
Falls (MN)
Monroe Comm Coll (NY)
Monterey Peninsula
Coll (CA)
Morton Coll (IL)
Mott Comm Coll (MI)
Mt. Hood Comm Coll (OR)
Mt. San Antonio Coll (CA)
Muskegon Comm Coll (MI)
Napa Valley Coll (CA)
Nassau Comm Coll (NY)
Naugatuck Valley Comm
Coll (CT)
Navarro Coll (TX)
New Mexico Jr Coll (NM)
Northampton County Area
Comm Coll (PA)
North Central Michigan
Coll (MI)
North Central Texas
Coll (TX)
Northeast Comm Coll (NE)
Northeastern Jr Coll (CO)
Northern Maine Comm
Coll (ME)
North Idaho Coll (ID)
North Lake Coll (TX)
Northland Comm and Tech
Coll–Thief River
Falls (MN)
North Shore Comm
Coll (MA)
Odessa Coll (TX)
Oklahoma State U,
Okmulgee (OK)
Olympic Coll (WA)
Orange Coast Coll (CA)
Ouachita Tech Coll (AR)
Palm Beach Comm
Coll (FL)
Pasadena City Coll (CA)
Piedmont Tech Coll (SC)
Pierce Coll (WA)
Polk Comm Coll (FL)
Pueblo Comm Coll (CO)
Renton Tech Coll (WA)
Richland Comm Coll (IL)
Ridgewater Coll (MN)
Riverland Comm Coll (MN)
Roane State Comm
Coll (TN)
Rockford Business
Coll (IL)
Rose State Coll (OK)
Roxbury Comm Coll (MA)
Sacramento City Coll (CA)
St. Catharine Coll (KY)
St. Cloud Tech Coll (MN)
St. Philip's Coll (TX)
San Antonio Coll (TX)
San Diego City Coll (CA)
Shasta Coll (CA)
South Piedmont Comm
Coll (NC)
South Plains Coll (TX)
South Texas Coll (TX)
Southwest Mississippi
Comm Coll (MS)

Spokane Comm Coll (WA)
Stanly Comm Coll (NC)
Stark State Coll of
Technology (OH)
State Fair Comm
Coll (MO)
State U of New York Coll
of Agriculture and
Technology at
Morrisville (NY)
Tallahassee Comm
Coll (FL)
Three Rivers Comm
Coll (CT)
Tomball Coll (TX)
Treasure Valley Comm
Coll (OR)
Trocaire Coll (NY)
Trumbull Business
Coll (OH)
Tulsa Comm Coll (OK)
Tunxis Comm Coll (CT)
Tyler Jr Coll (TX)
Umpqua Comm Coll (OR)
The U of Akron–Wayne
Coll (OH)
U of Cincinnati Clermont
Coll (OH)
The U of Montana-Helena
Coll of Technology (MT)
Valencia Comm Coll (FL)
Vincennes U Jasper
Campus (IN)
Wallace State Comm
Coll (AL)
Wayne Comm Coll (NC)
Wenatchee Valley
Coll (WA)
Westchester Comm
Coll (NY)
Western Piedmont Comm
Coll (NC)
Western Wyoming Comm
Coll (WY)
West Los Angeles
Coll (CA)
Westmoreland County
Comm Coll (PA)
West Valley Coll (CA)
Wright State U, Lake
Campus (OH)
York Tech Coll (SC)

**Legal Assistant/
Paralegal**
Academy of Court
Reporting (OH)
Alexandria Tech Coll (MN)
Allegany Coll of
Maryland (MD)
Angelina Coll (TX)
Anne Arundel Comm
Coll (MD)
Athens Tech Coll (GA)
Baltimore City Comm
Coll (MD)
Bergen Comm Coll (NJ)
Berkeley Coll, West
Paterson (NJ)
Berkeley Coll-New York
City Campus (NY)
Berkeley Coll-Westchester
Campus (NY)
Black Hawk Coll,
Moline (IL)
Brevard Comm Coll (FL)
Briarwood Coll (CT)
Broome Comm Coll (NY)
Broward Comm Coll (FL)
Brown Mackie Coll–
Cincinnati (OH)
Brown Mackie Coll–Fort
Wayne (IN)
Brown Mackie Coll–
Kansas City (KS)
Brown Mackie Coll–
Merrillville (IN)
Brown Mackie Coll–North
Canton (OH)
Brown Mackie Coll–
Salina (KS)
Brown Mackie Coll–South
Bend (IN)
Bucks County Comm
Coll (PA)
Burlington County
Coll (NJ)
Caldwell Comm Coll and
Tech Inst (NC)
Calhoun Comm Coll (AL)
Cañada Coll (CA)
Cape Cod Comm
Coll (MA)
Catawba Valley Comm
Coll (NC)
Central Carolina Comm
Coll (NC)
Central Carolina Tech
Coll (SC)

Central Comm Coll–Grand Island Campus (NE)
Central New Mexico Comm Coll (NM)
Central Piedmont Comm Coll (NC)
Central Texas Coll (TX)
Chippewa Valley Tech Coll (WI)
Clark Coll (WA)
Clark State Comm Coll (OH)
Clovis Comm Coll (NM)
Coastal Carolina Comm Coll (NC)
Coll of Southern Maryland (MD)
Coll of the Redwoods (CA)
Coll of the Siskiyous (CA)
Collin County Comm Coll District (TX)
Columbia Basin Coll (WA)
Comm Coll of Allegheny County (PA)
Comm Coll of Philadelphia (PA)
Comm Coll of Rhode Island (RI)
Comm Coll of Southern Nevada (NV)
Cuyahoga Comm Coll (OH)
Davidson County Comm Coll (NC)
De Anza Coll (CA)
East Central Coll (MO)
Eastern New Mexico U–Roswell (NM)
Elaine P. Nunez Comm Coll (LA)
El Camino Coll (CA)
El Centro Coll (TX)
Elgin Comm Coll (IL)
Erie Comm Coll (NY)
Essex County Coll (NJ)
Eugenio María de Hostos Comm Coll of the City U of New York (NY)
Everest Coll, Phoenix (AZ)
Fayetteville Tech Comm Coll (NC)
Finger Lakes Comm Coll (NY)
Fiorello H. LaGuardia Comm Coll of the City U of New York (NY)
Florence-Darlington Tech Coll (SC)
Florida National Coll (FL)
Forsyth Tech Comm Coll (NC)
Frederick Comm Coll (MD)
Fresno City Coll (CA)
Fullerton Coll (CA)
Gadsden State Comm Coll (AL)
Genesee Comm Coll (NY)
Georgia Highlands Coll (GA)
Gloucester County Coll (NJ)
Greenville Tech Coll (SC)
Guilford Tech Comm Coll (NC)
Harper Coll (IL)
Harrisburg Area Comm Coll (PA)
Henry Ford Comm Coll (MI)
Heritage Coll (NV)
Hesser Coll (NH)
Houston Comm Coll System (TX)
Hutchinson Comm Coll and Area Vocational School (KS)
International Business Coll, Fort Wayne (IN)
International Inst of the Americas, Mesa (AZ)
International Inst of the Americas, Phoenix (AZ)
International Inst of the Americas, Tucson (AZ)
Inver Hills Comm Coll (MN)
Iowa Lakes Comm Coll (IA)
James H. Faulkner State Comm Coll (AL)
Johnston Comm Coll (NC)
Kansas City Kansas Comm Coll (KS)
Kaplan U (IA)
Keiser U, Miami (FL)
Kellogg Comm Coll (MI)
King's Coll (NC)
Kirkwood Comm Coll (IA)

Lakeshore Tech Coll (WI)
Lake-Sumter Comm Coll (FL)
Lansing Comm Coll (MI)
Lee Coll (TX)
Lehigh Carbon Comm Coll (PA)
Lehigh Valley Coll (PA)
Louisiana State U at Eunice (LA)
Macomb Comm Coll (MI)
Manatee Comm Coll (FL)
Maric Coll, Panorama City (CA)
Marshall Comm and Tech Coll (WV)
Massachusetts Bay Comm Coll (MA)
McLennan Comm Coll (TX)
Metropolitan Comm Coll (NE)
Metropolitan Comm Coll–Penn Valley (MO)
Miami Dade Coll (FL)
Midlands Tech Coll (SC)
Minnesota School of Business–Richfield (MN)
Mississippi Gulf Coast Comm Coll (MS)
Missouri State U–West Plains (MO)
Montgomery Coll (MD)
Mountain State Coll (WV)
Mt. San Antonio Coll (CA)
Mount Wachusett Comm Coll (MA)
Napa Valley Coll (CA)
Nassau Comm Coll (NY)
National American U (KS)
Naugatuck Valley Comm Coll (CT)
Navarro Coll (TX)
New Hampshire Comm Tech Coll, Nashua/Claremont (NH)
New Hampshire Tech Inst (NH)
New Mexico State U–Alamogordo (NM)
New River Comm Coll (VA)
New York Career Inst (NY)
New York City Coll of Technology of the City U of New York (NY)
Northampton County Area Comm Coll (PA)
North Central Michigan Coll (MI)
North Central Texas Coll (TX)
Northeast Comm Coll (NE)
Northern Essex Comm Coll (MA)
North Idaho Coll (ID)
Northland Comm and Tech Coll–Thief River Falls (MN)
North Shore Comm Coll (MA)
Northwestern Connecticut Comm Coll (CT)
Northwest Mississippi Comm Coll (MS)
Oakland Comm Coll (MI)
Ouachita Tech Coll (AR)
Pace Inst (PA)
Pasco-Hernando Comm Coll (FL)
Pierce Coll (WA)
Pima Comm Coll (AZ)
Pioneer Pacific Coll, Wilsonville (OR)
The PJA School (PA)
Pueblo Comm Coll (CO)
Raritan Valley Comm Coll (NJ)
Rockford Business Coll (IL)
Salt Lake Comm Coll (UT)
San Diego City Coll (CA)
San Juan Coll (NM)
Seminole Comm Coll (FL)
Shasta Coll (CA)
Skagit Valley Coll (WA)
Southern U at Shreveport (LA)
South Texas Coll (TX)
Southwestern Comm Coll (NC)
Southwestern Michigan Coll (MI)
Spokane Comm Coll (WA)
Suffolk County Comm Coll (NY)
Surry Comm Coll (NC)
Sussex County Comm Coll (NJ)

Tallahassee Comm Coll (FL)
Tidewater Tech (VA)
Tompkins Cortland Comm Coll (NY)
Trident Tech Coll (SC)
Tri-State Business Inst (PA)
Tulsa Comm Coll (OK)
U of Cincinnati Clermont Coll (OH)
U of New Mexico–Gallup (NM)
Valencia Comm Coll (FL)
Victoria Coll (TX)
Virginia Coll at Austin (TX)
Volunteer State Comm Coll (TN)
Wallace State Comm Coll (AL)
Warren County Comm Coll (NJ)
Westchester Comm Coll (NY)
Western Nevada Comm Coll (NV)
Western Piedmont Comm Coll (NC)
West Los Angeles Coll (CA)
Westmoreland County Comm Coll (PA)
West Virginia State Comm and Tech Coll (WV)
Wilson Tech Comm Coll (NC)
Zane State Coll (OH)

Legal Professions and Studies Related
Essex County Coll (NJ)
Florida National Coll (FL)

Legal Studies
City Colls of Chicago, Harold Washington College (IL)
City Colls of Chicago, Harry S. Truman College (IL)
City Colls of Chicago, Kennedy-King College (IL)
City Colls of Chicago, Richard J. Daley College (IL)
Coll of the Siskiyous (CA)
El Centro Coll (TX)
Florida National Coll (FL)
Foothill Coll (CA)
Gloucester County Coll (NJ)
Hillsborough Comm Coll (FL)
Iowa Lakes Comm Coll (IA)
Kirkwood Comm Coll (IA)
Macomb Comm Coll (MI)
Metropolitan Comm Coll (NE)
Navarro Coll (TX)
New Hampshire Comm Tech Coll, Nashua/Claremont (NH)
Northland Comm and Tech Coll–Thief River Falls (MN)
Oxnard Coll (CA)
Palo Alto Coll (TX)
Pasadena City Coll (CA)
Quincy Coll (MA)
St. Louis Comm Coll at Florissant Valley (MO)
Santa Ana Coll (CA)
Santa Barbara City Coll (CA)
Trident Tech Coll (SC)
Tulsa Comm Coll (OK)
Vernon Coll (TX)

Liberal Arts and Sciences And Humanities Related
Cascadia Comm Coll (WA)
Cleveland Comm Coll (NC)
Eastern West Virginia Comm and Tech Coll (WV)
Fayetteville Tech Comm Coll (NC)
Hagerstown Comm Coll (MD)
Iowa Lakes Comm Coll (IA)
Kansas City Kansas Comm Coll (KS)
Klamath Comm Coll (OR)
Martin Comm Coll (NC)
Massasoit Comm Coll (MA)

Northampton County Area Comm Coll (PA)
Oakland Comm Coll (MI)
Southwestern Michigan Coll (MI)
Wor-Wic Comm Coll (MD)

Liberal Arts and Sciences/Liberal Studies
Aims Comm Coll (CO)
Alamance Comm Coll (NC)
Allegany Coll of Maryland (MD)
Alpena Comm Coll (MI)
Amarillo Coll (TX)
Angelina Coll (TX)
Anne Arundel Comm Coll (MD)
Anoka-Ramsey Comm Coll (MN)
Anoka-Ramsey Comm Coll, Cambridge Campus (MN)
Antelope Valley Coll (CA)
Arkansas State U–Mountain Home (AR)
Arkansas State U–Newport (AR)
Asheville-Buncombe Tech Comm Coll (NC)
Ashland Comm and Tech Coll (KY)
Asnuntuck Comm Coll (CT)
Bainbridge Coll (GA)
Bakersfield Coll (CA)
Baltimore City Comm Coll (MD)
Barstow Coll (CA)
Barton County Comm Coll (KS)
Beaufort County Comm Coll (NC)
Bergen Comm Coll (NJ)
Berkeley City Coll (CA)
Berkshire Comm Coll (MA)
Big Bend Comm Coll (WA)
Bishop State Comm Coll (AL)
Bismarck State Coll (ND)
Bladen Comm Coll (NC)
Bowling Green State U–Firelands Coll (OH)
Brevard Comm Coll (FL)
Brigham Young U–Idaho (ID)
Brookhaven Coll (TX)
Broome Comm Coll (NY)
Broward Comm Coll (FL)
Brunswick Comm Coll (NC)
Bucks County Comm Coll (PA)
Burlington County Coll (NJ)
Cabrillo Coll (CA)
Caldwell Comm Coll and Tech Inst (NC)
Calhoun Comm Coll (AL)
Cankdeska Cikana Comm Coll (ND)
Cañada Coll (CA)
Cape Cod Comm Coll (MA)
Cape Fear Comm Coll (NC)
Capital Comm Coll (CT)
Carroll Comm Coll (MD)
Cascadia Comm Coll (WA)
Catawba Valley Comm Coll (NC)
Cecil Comm Coll (MD)
Cedar Valley Coll (TX)
Central Arizona Coll (AZ)
Central Carolina Comm Coll (NC)
Central Carolina Tech Coll (SC)
Central Comm Coll–Columbus Campus (NE)
Central Comm Coll–Grand Island Campus (NE)
Central Comm Coll–Hastings Campus (NE)
Central Florida Comm Coll (FL)
Centralia Coll (WA)
Central Lakes Coll (MN)
Central New Mexico Comm Coll (NM)
Central Oregon Comm Coll (OR)
Central Piedmont Comm Coll (NC)
Central Texas Coll (TX)

Central Virginia Comm Coll (VA)
Century Coll (MN)
Cerritos Coll (CA)
Chaffey Coll (CA)
Chandler-Gilbert Comm Coll (AZ)
Chattanooga State Tech Comm Coll (TN)
Chesapeake Coll (MD)
Chief Dull Knife Coll (MT)
Chipola Coll (FL)
Cincinnati State Tech and Comm Coll (OH)
Citrus Coll (CA)
City Colls of Chicago, Harold Washington College (IL)
City Colls of Chicago, Harry S. Truman College (IL)
City Colls of Chicago, Kennedy-King College (IL)
City Colls of Chicago, Olive-Harvey College (IL)
City Colls of Chicago, Richard J. Daley College (IL)
City Colls of Chicago, Wilbur Wright College (IL)
Clackamas Comm Coll (OR)
Clarendon Coll (TX)
Clark Coll (WA)
Clark State Comm Coll (OH)
Clatsop Comm Coll (OR)
Cleveland Comm Coll (NC)
Cleveland State Comm Coll (TN)
Clinton Comm Coll (IA)
Clinton Jr Coll (SC)
Clovis Comm Coll (NM)
Coahoma Comm Coll (MS)
Coastal Bend Coll (TX)
Coastal Carolina Comm Coll (NC)
Coastal Georgia Comm Coll (GA)
Cochise Coll, Douglas (AZ)
Cochise Coll, Sierra Vista (AZ)
Coconino Comm Coll (AZ)
Colby Comm Coll (KS)
Colegio Universitario de San Juan, San Juan (PR)
Coll of Alameda (CA)
Coll of DuPage (IL)
Coll of Lake County (IL)
Coll of Marin (CA)
Coll of Menominee Nation (WI)
Coll of Micronesia–FSM (FM)
Coll of San Mateo (CA)
Coll of Southern Idaho (ID)
Coll of Southern Maryland (MD)
Coll of The Albemarle (NC)
Coll of the Canyons (CA)
Coll of the Desert (CA)
Coll of the Mainland (TX)
Coll of the Marshall Islands (Marshall Islands)
Collin County Comm Coll District (TX)
Colorado Mountain Coll (CO)
Colorado Mountain Coll, Alpine Campus (CO)
Colorado Mountain Coll, Timberline Campus (CO)
Columbia Basin Coll (WA)
Columbia Coll (CA)
Columbia-Greene Comm Coll (NY)
Comm Coll of Allegheny County (PA)
Comm Coll of Beaver County (PA)
Comm Coll of Philadelphia (PA)
Comm Coll of Rhode Island (RI)
Comm Coll of Southern Nevada (NV)
Comm Coll of Vermont (VT)
Contra Costa Coll (CA)
Cossatot Comm Coll of the U of Arkansas (AR)
Cosumnes River Coll, Sacramento (CA)

Cottey Coll (MO)
Crafton Hills Coll (CA)
Crowder Coll (MO)
Cuesta Coll (CA)
Cuyahoga Comm Coll (OH)
Cypress Coll (CA)
Dabney S. Lancaster Comm Coll (VA)
Danville Comm Coll (VA)
Davidson County Comm Coll (NC)
Dean Coll (MA)
De Anza Coll (CA)
Diablo Valley Coll (CA)
Dixie State Coll of Utah (UT)
Dodge City Comm Coll (KS)
Dyersburg State Comm Coll (TN)
Eastern Arizona Coll (AZ)
Eastern New Mexico U–Roswell (NM)
Eastern Shore Comm Coll (VA)
Eastern West Virginia Comm and Tech Coll (WV)
East Georgia Coll (GA)
Elaine P. Nunez Comm Coll (LA)
El Camino Coll (CA)
El Centro Coll (TX)
Elgin Comm Coll (IL)
Elizabethtown Tech Coll (KY)
Emory U, Oxford Coll (GA)
Erie Comm Coll (NY)
Erie Comm Coll, North Campus (NY)
Erie Comm Coll, South Campus (NY)
Essex County Coll (NJ)
Eugenio María de Hostos Comm Coll of the City U of New York (NY)
Everett Comm Coll (WA)
Fayetteville Tech Comm Coll (NC)
Finger Lakes Comm Coll (NY)
Fiorello H. LaGuardia Comm Coll of the City U of New York (NY)
Fisher Coll (MA)
Florence-Darlington Tech Coll (SC)
Florida National Coll (FL)
Folsom Lake Coll (CA)
Fond du Lac Tribal and Comm Coll (MN)
Fort Belknap Coll (MT)
Fort Berthold Comm Coll (ND)
Frederick Comm Coll (MD)
Fresno City Coll (CA)
Front Range Comm Coll (CO)
Fullerton Coll (CA)
Fulton-Montgomery Comm Coll (NY)
Gadsden State Comm Coll (AL)
Garrett Coll (MD)
Gateway Comm Coll (CT)
Genesee Comm Coll (NY)
George C. Wallace Comm Coll (AL)
Georgia Highlands Coll (GA)
Georgia Military Coll (GA)
Germanna Comm Coll (VA)
Gloucester County Coll (NJ)
Golden West Coll (CA)
Grand Rapids Comm Coll (MI)
Grays Harbor Coll (WA)
Grayson County Coll (TX)
Greenville Tech Coll (SC)
Grossmont Coll (CA)
Guilford Tech Comm Coll (NC)
Hagerstown Comm Coll (MD)
Harper Coll (IL)
Harrisburg Area Comm Coll (PA)
Hartnell Coll (CA)
Hawkeye Comm Coll (IA)
Henry Ford Comm Coll (MI)
Hesser Coll (NH)
Hesston Coll (KS)
Hillsborough Comm Coll (FL)

Holy Cross Coll (IN)
Holyoke Comm Coll (MA)
Hopkinsville Comm Coll (KY)
Housatonic Comm Coll (CT)
Houston Comm Coll System (TX)
Howard Comm Coll (MD)
Hutchinson Comm Coll and Area Vocational School (KS)
Illinois Eastern Comm Colls, Frontier Community College (IL)
Illinois Eastern Comm Colls, Lincoln Trail College (IL)
Illinois Eastern Comm Colls, Olney Central College (IL)
Illinois Eastern Comm Colls, Wabash Valley College (IL)
Illinois Valley Comm Coll (IL)
Imperial Valley Coll (CA)
Inver Hills Comm Coll (MN)
Iowa Lakes Comm Coll (IA)
Irvine Valley Coll (CA)
Isothermal Comm Coll (NC)
Itasca Comm Coll (MN)
Jackson State Comm Coll (TN)
James H. Faulkner State Comm Coll (AL)
James Sprunt Comm Coll (NC)
Jefferson Comm and Tech Coll (KY)
Johnston Comm Coll (NC)
John Tyler Comm Coll (VA)
John Wood Comm Coll (IL)
Kankakee Comm Coll (IL)
Kansas City Kansas Comm Coll (KS)
Kellogg Comm Coll (MI)
Kennebec Valley Comm Coll (ME)
Kent State U, Ashtabula Campus (OH)
Kent State U, East Liverpool Campus (OH)
Kent State U, Geauga Campus (OH)
Kent State U, Trumbull Campus (OH)
Kent State U, Tuscarawas Campus (OH)
Keystone Coll (PA)
Kilian Comm Coll (SD)
Kingsborough Comm Coll of the City U of New York (NY)
Kirkwood Comm Coll (IA)
Kirtland Comm Coll (MI)
Labette Comm Coll (KS)
Lake Land Coll (IL)
Lake-Sumter Comm Coll (FL)
Lake Tahoe Comm Coll (CA)
Lamar Comm Coll (CO)
Landmark Coll (VT)
Laney Coll (CA)
Lansing Comm Coll (MI)
Laredo Comm Coll (TX)
Las Positas Coll (CA)
Lassen Comm Coll District (CA)
Lawson State Comm Coll (AL)
LDS Business Coll (UT)
Leech Lake Tribal Coll (MN)
Lee Coll (TX)
Leeward Comm Coll (HI)
Lehigh Carbon Comm Coll (PA)
Lenoir Comm Coll (NC)
Lewis Coll of Business (MI)
Lincoln Land Comm Coll (IL)
Linn-Benton Comm Coll (OR)
Little Big Horn Coll (MT)
Lorain County Comm Coll (OH)
Los Angeles City Coll (CA)
Los Angeles Harbor Coll (CA)
Los Angeles Mission Coll (CA)

Los Angeles Pierce Coll (CA)
Los Medanos Coll (CA)
Louisburg Coll (NC)
Lower Columbia Coll (WA)
Macomb Comm Coll (MI)
Madison Area Tech Coll (WI)
Manatee Comm Coll (FL)
Marian Court Coll (MA)
Marion Military Inst (AL)
Marshall Comm and Tech Coll (WV)
Martin Comm Coll (NC)
Marymount Coll, Palos Verdes, California (CA)
Massachusetts Bay Comm Coll (MA)
Massasoit Comm Coll (MA)
Maui Comm Coll (HI)
McLennan Comm Coll (TX)
Mendocino Coll (CA)
Merced Coll (CA)
Mesabi Range Comm and Tech Coll (MN)
Mesa Comm Coll (AZ)
Metropolitan Comm Coll (NE)
Metropolitan Comm Coll–Blue River (MO)
Metropolitan Comm Coll–Business & Technology Campus (MO)
Metropolitan Comm Coll–Longview (MO)
Metropolitan Comm Coll–Maple Woods (MO)
Metropolitan Comm Coll–Penn Valley (MO)
Miami U–Middletown Campus (OH)
Middle Georgia Coll (GA)
Middlesex Comm Coll (CT)
Midlands Tech Coll (SC)
Mid-Plains Comm Coll, North Platte (NE)
Minneapolis Comm and Tech Coll (MN)
Minnesota State Comm and Tech Coll–Fergus Falls (MN)
Mission Coll (CA)
Mississippi Delta Comm Coll (MS)
Mississippi Gulf Coast Comm Coll (MS)
Moberly Area Comm Coll (MO)
Mohave Comm Coll (AZ)
Mohawk Valley Comm Coll (NY)
Monroe Comm Coll (NY)
Montcalm Comm Coll (MI)
Monterey Peninsula Coll (CA)
Montgomery Coll (MD)
Montgomery County Comm Coll (PA)
Moorpark Coll (CA)
Moraine Valley Comm Coll (IL)
Morgan Comm Coll (CO)
Morton Coll (IL)
Motlow State Comm Coll (TN)
Mott Comm Coll (MI)
Mt. Hood Comm Coll (OR)
Mt. San Antonio Coll (CA)
Mount Wachusett Comm Coll (MA)
Murray State Coll (OK)
Muscatine Comm Coll (IA)
Muskegon Comm Coll (MI)
Nassau Comm Coll (NY)
National Park Comm Coll (AR)
Naugatuck Valley Comm Coll (CT)
Nebraska Indian Comm Coll (NE)
Neosho County Comm Coll (KS)
New Hampshire Comm Tech Coll, Manchester/Stratham (NH)
New Hampshire Comm Tech Coll, Nashua/Claremont (NH)
New Hampshire Tech Inst (NH)
New Mexico Jr Coll (NM)
New Mexico Military Inst (NM)

New Mexico State U–Alamogordo (NM)
New River Comm Coll (VA)
New York City Coll of Technology of the City U of New York (NY)
Niagara County Comm Coll (NY)
Nicolet Area Tech Coll (WI)
Northampton County Area Comm Coll (PA)
North Arkansas Coll (AR)
North Central Michigan Coll (MI)
North Central Missouri Coll (MO)
North Central Texas Coll (TX)
North Country Comm Coll (NY)
Northeast Comm Coll (NE)
Northeastern Jr Coll (CO)
Northeastern Tech Coll (SC)
Northeast Iowa Comm Coll (IA)
Northeast State Tech Comm Coll (TN)
Northern Essex Comm Coll (MA)
Northern Marianas Coll (MP)
Northern Oklahoma Coll (OK)
North Idaho Coll (ID)
North Iowa Area Comm Coll (IA)
North Lake Coll (TX)
Northland Comm and Tech Coll–Thief River Falls (MN)
North Seattle Comm Coll (WA)
North Shore Comm Coll (MA)
NorthWest Arkansas Comm Coll (AR)
Northwestern Connecticut Comm Coll (CT)
Northwest Iowa Comm Coll (IA)
Northwest Mississippi Comm Coll (MS)
Northwest-Shoals Comm Coll (AL)
Northwest Vista Coll (TX)
Oakland Comm Coll (MI)
Odessa Coll (TX)
Ohlone Coll (CA)
Oklahoma City Comm Coll (OK)
Olympic Coll (WA)
Onondaga Comm Coll (NY)
Orange Coast Coll (CA)
Oregon Coast Comm Coll (OR)
Ouachita Tech Coll (AR)
Owensboro Comm and Tech Coll (KY)
Oxnard Coll (CA)
Ozarka Coll (AR)
Ozarks Tech Comm Coll (MO)
Palau Comm Coll (Palau)
Palm Beach Comm Coll (FL)
Palo Alto Coll (TX)
Pamlico Comm Coll (NC)
Paradise Valley Comm Coll (AZ)
Parkland Coll (IL)
Pasadena City Coll (CA)
Pasco-Hernando Comm Coll (FL)
Paul D. Camp Comm Coll (VA)
Pearl River Comm Coll (MS)
Penn State Beaver (PA)
Penn State Delaware County (PA)
Penn State DuBois (PA)
Penn State Fayette, The Eberly Campus (PA)
Penn State Hazleton (PA)
Penn State Lehigh Valley (PA)
Penn State McKeesport (PA)
Penn State Mont Alto (PA)
Penn State New Kensington (PA)
Penn State Schuylkill (PA)
Penn State Shenango (PA)
Penn State Wilkes-Barre (PA)

Penn State Worthington Scranton (PA)
Penn State York (PA)
Pennsylvania Highland Comm Coll (PA)
Piedmont Tech Coll (SC)
Piedmont Virginia Comm Coll (VA)
Pierce Coll (WA)
Pima Comm Coll (AZ)
Polk Comm Coll (FL)
Porterville Coll (CA)
Potomac State Coll of West Virginia U (WV)
Pueblo Comm Coll (CO)
Queensborough Comm Coll of the City U of New York (NY)
Quincy Coll (MA)
Quinebaug Valley Comm Coll (CT)
Rainy River Comm Coll (MN)
Ranger Coll (TX)
Rappahannock Comm Coll (VA)
Raritan Valley Comm Coll (NJ)
Redlands Comm Coll (OK)
Red Rocks Comm Coll (CO)
Reedley Coll (CA)
Richland Coll (TX)
Richland Comm Coll (IL)
Ridgewater Coll (MN)
Rio Hondo Coll (CA)
Riverland Comm Coll (MN)
Riverside Comm Coll District (CA)
Roane State Comm Coll (TN)
Rogue Comm Coll (OR)
Rose State Coll (OK)
Sacramento City Coll (CA)
Saginaw Chippewa Tribal Coll (MI)
St. Catharine Coll (KY)
Saint Charles Comm Coll (MO)
St. Louis Comm Coll at Florissant Valley (MO)
St. Philip's Coll (TX)
Salish Kootenai Coll (MT)
Sampson Comm Coll (NC)
San Antonio Coll (TX)
San Bernardino Valley Coll (CA)
Sandhills Comm Coll (NC)
San Diego City Coll (CA)
San Joaquin Delta Coll (CA)
Santa Ana Coll (CA)
Santa Barbara City Coll (CA)
Santa Rosa Jr Coll (CA)
Santiago Canyon Coll (CA)
Schoolcraft Coll (MI)
Scott Comm Coll (IA)
Seminole Comm Coll (FL)
Seminole State Coll (OK)
Sheridan Coll–Sheridan and Gillette (WY)
Sitting Bull Coll (ND)
Skagit Valley Coll (WA)
Southeastern Comm Coll (NC)
Southeastern Comm Coll, North Campus (IA)
Southeastern Comm Coll, South Campus (IA)
Southeast Kentucky Comm and Tech Coll (KY)
Southern Maine Comm Coll (ME)
Southern State Comm Coll (OH)
South Florida Comm Coll (FL)
South Georgia Coll (GA)
South Piedmont Comm Coll (NC)
South Plains Coll (TX)
South Seattle Comm Coll (WA)
Southside Virginia Comm Coll (VA)
South Texas Coll (TX)
Southwestern Comm Coll (NC)
Southwestern Indian Polytechnic Inst (NM)
Southwestern Michigan Coll (MI)
Southwest Mississippi Comm Coll (MS)
Southwest Texas Jr Coll (TX)

Southwest Virginia Comm Coll (VA)
Spokane Comm Coll (WA)
Spokane Falls Comm Coll (WA)
Springfield Tech Comm Coll (MA)
State Fair Comm Coll (MO)
State U of New York Coll of Agriculture and Technology at Morrisville (NY)
State U of New York Coll of Technology at Alfred (NY)
State U of New York Coll of Technology at Canton (NY)
Stone Child Coll (MT)
Suffolk County Comm Coll (NY)
Surry Comm Coll (NC)
Sussex County Comm Coll (NJ)
Taft Coll (CA)
Tallahassee Comm Coll (FL)
Temple Coll (TX)
Texarkana Coll (TX)
Three Rivers Comm Coll (CT)
Three Rivers Comm Coll (MO)
Tidewater Comm Coll (VA)
Tompkins Cortland Comm Coll (NY)
Treasure Valley Comm Coll (OR)
Tri-County Comm Coll (NC)
Trident Tech Coll (SC)
Trinidad State Jr Coll (CO)
Trocaire Coll (NY)
Tulsa Comm Coll (OK)
Tunxis Comm Coll (CT)
Turtle Mountain Comm Coll (ND)
Tyler Jr Coll (TX)
Ulster County Comm Coll (NY)
Umpqua Comm Coll (OR)
Union County Coll (NJ)
The U of Akron–Wayne Coll (OH)
U of Alaska Anchorage, Kodiak Coll (AK)
U of Alaska, Prince William Sound Comm Coll (AK)
U of Alaska Southeast, Sitka Campus (AK)
U of Arkansas Comm Coll at Morrilton (AR)
U of Cincinnati Clermont Coll (OH)
U of New Mexico–Gallup (NM)
U of New Mexico–Los Alamos Branch (NM)
U of New Mexico–Taos (NM)
U of New Mexico–Valencia Campus (NM)
U of Pittsburgh at Titusville (PA)
U of South Carolina Lancaster (SC)
U of Wisconsin–Baraboo/Sauk County (WI)
U of Wisconsin–Fond du Lac (WI)
U of Wisconsin–Fox Valley (WI)
U of Wisconsin–Manitowoc (WI)
U of Wisconsin–Marshfield/Wood County (WI)
U of Wisconsin–Washington County (WI)
U of Wisconsin–Waukesha (WI)
Valencia Comm Coll (FL)
Ventura Coll (CA)
Vernon Coll (TX)
Victoria Coll (TX)
Victor Valley Coll (CA)
Villa Maria Coll of Buffalo (NY)
Vincennes U Jasper Campus (IN)
Virginia Highlands Comm Coll (VA)
Virginia Western Comm Coll (VA)
Volunteer State Comm Coll (TN)

Wallace State Comm Coll (AL)
Warren County Comm Coll (NJ)
Washington State Comm Coll (OH)
Wayne Comm Coll (NC)
Wenatchee Valley Coll (WA)
Westchester Comm Coll (NY)
Western Nebraska Comm Coll (NE)
Western Nevada Comm Coll (NV)
Western Piedmont Comm Coll (NC)
Western Texas Coll (TX)
Western Wyoming Comm Coll (WY)
West Hills Comm Coll (CA)
West Los Angeles Coll (CA)
Westmoreland County Comm Coll (PA)
West Shore Comm Coll (MI)
West Valley Coll (CA)
West Virginia U at Parkersburg (WV)
Wilson Tech Comm Coll (NC)
Wright State U, Lake Campus (OH)
Wytheville Comm Coll (VA)
York Tech Coll (SC)
Young Harris Coll (GA)

Library Assistant
Black Hawk Coll, Moline (IL)
Citrus Coll (CA)
Clovis Comm Coll (NM)
Coll of DuPage (IL)
Northern New Mexico Coll (NM)
Oakland Comm Coll (MI)
Spokane Falls Comm Coll (WA)

Library Science
Allen County Comm Coll (KS)
Citrus Coll (CA)
City Coll of San Francisco (CA)
City Colls of Chicago, Wilbur Wright College (IL)
Colby Comm Coll (KS)
Coll of DuPage (IL)
Coll of Southern Idaho (ID)
Comm Coll of Philadelphia (PA)
Cuesta Coll (CA)
Fresno City Coll (CA)
Fullerton Coll (CA)
Hartnell Coll (CA)
Lawson State Comm Coll (AL)
Lenoir Comm Coll (NC)
Merced Coll (CA)
Mesa Comm Coll (AZ)
Oxnard Coll (CA)
Palo Alto Coll (TX)
Pasadena City Coll (CA)
Rose State Coll (OK)
Sacramento City Coll (CA)
Santa Ana Coll (CA)
Tulsa Comm Coll (OK)
Wallace State Comm Coll (AL)

Lineworker
Bismarck State Coll (ND)
Lehigh Carbon Comm Coll (PA)
Linn State Tech Coll (MO)
Lower Columbia Coll (WA)
Northeast Comm Coll (NE)
Northwest Iowa Comm Coll (IA)

Linguistics
Foothill Coll (CA)

Literature
Bergen Comm Coll (NJ)
Blinn Coll (TX)
Comm Coll of Southern Nevada (NV)
Foothill Coll (CA)
Iowa Lakes Comm Coll (IA)
Irvine Valley Coll (CA)
Lamar Comm Coll (CO)
Lincoln Land Comm Coll (IL)
Miami Dade Coll (FL)
Oklahoma City Comm Coll (OK)

Palm Beach Comm
  Coll (FL)
Sacramento City Coll (CA)
San Joaquin Delta
  Coll (CA)
Skagit Valley Coll (WA)

Livestock Management
Barton County Comm
  Coll (KS)
Northeast Comm Coll (NE)
The Ohio State U Ag Tech
  Inst (OH)

Logistics and Materials Management
Athens Tech Coll (GA)
Chattahoochee Tech
  Coll (GA)
Gateway Tech Coll (WI)
Houston Comm Coll
  System (TX)
Lee Coll (TX)
Lehigh Carbon Comm
  Coll (PA)
Springfield Tech Comm
  Coll (MA)

Machine Shop Technology
Cape Fear Comm
  Coll (NC)
Coll of Lake County (IL)
Comm Coll of Allegheny
  County (PA)
Eastern Arizona Coll (AZ)
Fayetteville Tech Comm
  Coll (NC)
Illinois Eastern Comm
  Colls, Wabash Valley
  College (IL)
Metropolitan Comm
  Coll–Business &
  Technology
  Campus (MO)
Mohawk Valley Comm
  Coll (NY)
North Central Texas
  Coll (TX)
North Iowa Area Comm
  Coll (IA)
Northwest Iowa Comm
  Coll (IA)
Orange Coast Coll (CA)
Pima Comm Coll (AZ)
Ridgewater Coll (MN)
Riverland Comm Coll (MN)
Southwestern Michigan
  Coll (MI)

Machine Tool Technology
Alamance Comm Coll (NC)
Alexandria Tech Coll (MN)
Altamaha Tech Coll (GA)
Amarillo Coll (TX)
Asheville-Buncombe Tech
  Comm Coll (NC)
Asnuntuck Comm
  Coll (CT)
Bakersfield Coll (CA)
Black Hawk Coll,
  Moline (IL)
Brigham Young U –
  Idaho (ID)
Calhoun Comm Coll (AL)
Central Comm Coll–
  Columbus
  Campus (NE)
Central Comm Coll–
  Hastings Campus (NE)
Central Maine Comm
  Coll (ME)
Central Piedmont Comm
  Coll (NC)
Century Coll (MN)
Cerritos Coll (CA)
Chattanooga State Tech
  Comm Coll (TN)
Chippewa Valley Tech
  Coll (WI)
City Colls of Chicago,
  Richard J. Daley
  College (IL)
City Colls of Chicago,
  Wilbur Wright
  College (IL)
Clackamas Comm
  Coll (OR)
Clark Coll (WA)
Clinton Comm Coll (IA)
Coll of DuPage (IL)
Coll of Marin (CA)
Coll of San Mateo (CA)
Coll of the Redwoods (CA)
Columbia Basin Coll (WA)
Columbus Tech Coll (GA)
De Anza Coll (CA)
DeKalb Tech Coll (GA)

East Central Coll (MO)
Elgin Comm Coll (IL)
Florence-Darlington Tech
  Coll (SC)
Forsyth Tech Comm
  Coll (NC)
Fresno City Coll (CA)
Front Range Comm
  Coll (CO)
Gateway Tech Coll (WI)
George C. Wallace Comm
  Coll (AL)
Grays Harbor Coll (WA)
Grayson County Coll (TX)
Greenville Tech Coll (SC)
Guilford Tech Comm
  Coll (NC)
Gwinnett Tech Coll (GA)
Harper Coll (IL)
Hartnell Coll (CA)
Hawkeye Comm Coll (IA)
H. Councill Trenholm State
  Tech Coll (AL)
Heart of Georgia Tech
  Coll (GA)
Hennepin Tech Coll (MN)
Hutchinson Comm Coll
  and Area Vocational
  School (KS)
Isothermal Comm
  Coll (NC)
J. F. Drake State Tech
  Coll (AL)
Johnston Comm Coll (NC)
Kankakee Comm Coll (IL)
Kellogg Comm Coll (MI)
Kennebec Valley Comm
  Coll (ME)
Lamar Inst of
  Technology (TX)
Laney Coll (CA)
Lansing Comm Coll (MI)
Lee Coll (TX)
Linn-Benton Comm
  Coll (OR)
Linn State Tech Coll (MO)
Lorain County Comm
  Coll (OH)
Los Angeles Pierce
  Coll (CA)
Lower Columbia Coll (WA)
Macomb Comm Coll (MI)
Meridian Comm Coll (MS)
Minnesota State Coll–
  Southeast Tech (MN)
Mt. San Antonio Coll (CA)
Muscatine Comm Coll (IA)
Muskegon Comm Coll (MI)
Napa Valley Coll (CA)
New Hampshire Comm
  Tech Coll, Nashua/
  Claremont (NH)
New Mexico Jr Coll (NM)
New River Comm Coll (VA)
Nicolet Area Tech Coll (WI)
North Central Industrial
  Tech Education
  Center (PA)
North Central Texas
  Coll (TX)
Northeastern Tech
  Coll (SC)
Northeast State Tech
  Comm Coll (TN)
Northern Essex Comm
  Coll (MA)
North Idaho Coll (ID)
North Iowa Area Comm
  Coll (IA)
Northwest Mississippi
  Comm Coll (MS)
Oakland Comm Coll (MI)
Odessa Coll (TX)
Oklahoma State U,
  Okmulgee (OK)
Onondaga Comm
  Coll (NY)
Orange Coast Coll (CA)
Ouachita Tech Coll (AR)
Oxnard Coll (CA)
Ozarks Tech Comm
  Coll (MO)
Pasadena City Coll (CA)
Piedmont Tech Coll (SC)
Pine Tech Coll (MN)
Pueblo Comm Coll (CO)
Reedley Coll (CA)
Renton Tech Coll (WA)
St. Cloud Tech Coll (MN)
San Bernardino Valley
  Coll (CA)
San Diego City Coll (CA)
San Joaquin Delta
  Coll (CA)
Scott Comm Coll (IA)
Sheridan Coll–Sheridan
  and Gillette (WY)

Southeastern Comm Coll,
  North Campus (IA)
Southeast Tech Inst (SD)
Southern Maine Comm
  Coll (ME)
South Piedmont Comm
  Coll (NC)
South Plains Coll (TX)
South Seattle Comm
  Coll (WA)
South Texas Coll (TX)
Southwest Mississippi
  Comm Coll (MS)
Spokane Comm Coll (WA)
State Fair Comm
  Coll (MO)
State U of New York Coll
  of Technology at
  Alfred (NY)
Surry Comm Coll (NC)
Texas State Tech Coll
  West Texas (TX)
Trident Tech Coll (SC)
U of Arkansas Comm Coll
  at Morrilton (AR)
The U of Montana-Helena
  Coll of Technology (MT)
Valdosta Tech Coll (GA)
Ventura Coll (CA)
Vernon Coll (TX)
Virginia Highlands Comm
  Coll (VA)
Wallace State Comm
  Coll (AL)
Wayne Comm Coll (NC)
Western Nevada Comm
  Coll (NV)
West Shore Comm
  Coll (MI)
West Virginia U at
  Parkersburg (WV)
The Williamson Free
  School of Mecha
  Trades (PA)
Wytheville Comm Coll (VA)
York Tech Coll (SC)
Yuba Coll (CA)

Management Information Systems
Academy Coll (MN)
Allegany Coll of
  Maryland (MD)
Ashland Comm and Tech
  Coll (KY)
Burlington County
  Coll (NJ)
Central Virginia Comm
  Coll (VA)
Central Wyoming
  Coll (WY)
Century Coll (MN)
Chandler-Gilbert Comm
  Coll (AZ)
Cincinnati State Tech and
  Comm Coll (OH)
Clovis Comm Coll (NM)
Coll of San Mateo (CA)
Comm Coll of Allegheny
  County (PA)
Cosumnes River Coll,
  Sacramento (CA)
Gateway Tech Coll (WI)
Grayson County Coll (TX)
Gwinnett Tech Coll (GA)
Hagerstown Comm
  Coll (MD)
Harper Coll (IL)
Harrisburg Area Comm
  Coll (PA)
Hesser Coll (NH)
Hopkinsville Comm
  Coll (KY)
Hutchinson Comm Coll
  and Area Vocational
  School (KS)
Jackson State Comm
  Coll (TN)
John Tyler Comm Coll (VA)
Kirkwood Comm Coll (IA)
Lamar Comm Coll (CO)
Laney Coll (CA)
Lansing Comm Coll (MI)
Lower Columbia Coll (WA)
Martin Comm Coll (NC)
Merced Coll (CA)
Miami Dade Coll (FL)
Miami U Hamilton (OH)
Miami U–Middletown
  Campus (OH)
Mississippi Delta Comm
  Coll (MS)
Montcalm Comm Coll (MI)
Montgomery Coll (MD)
Mott Comm Coll (MI)
Mount Wachusett Comm
  Coll (MA)
Napa Valley Coll (CA)
Nassau Comm Coll (NY)

New Hampshire Comm
  Tech Coll, Manchester/
  Stratham (NH)
Ouachita Tech Coll (AR)
Owens Comm Coll,
  Toledo (OH)
Ozarks Tech Comm
  Coll (MO)
Pueblo Comm Coll (CO)
Raritan Valley Comm
  Coll (NJ)
Rose State Coll (OK)
Shasta Coll (CA)
Southeast Kentucky Comm
  and Tech Coll (KY)
Southern Maine Comm
  Coll (ME)
Tallahassee Comm
  Coll (FL)
Trinidad State Jr Coll (CO)
Trumbull Business
  Coll (OH)
Union County Coll (NJ)
The U of Akron–Wayne
  Coll (OH)
U of Pittsburgh at
  Titusville (PA)
Victor Valley Coll (CA)
Vincennes U Jasper
  Campus (IN)
Western Nevada Comm
  Coll (NV)
Wright State U, Lake
  Campus (OH)

Management Information Systems and Services Related
Arkansas State
  U–Newport (AR)
Berkeley Coll-New York
  City Campus (NY)
Berkeley Coll-Westchester
  Campus (NY)
Cedar Valley Coll (TX)
Cleveland Comm Coll (NC)
Eastern Arizona Coll (AZ)
Indiana Business Coll,
  Indianapolis (IN)
Indiana Business Coll,
  Muncie (IN)
Martin Comm Coll (NC)
Metropolitan Comm
  Coll–Business &
  Technology
  Campus (MO)
Mohawk Valley Comm
  Coll (NY)
Montgomery County
  Comm Coll (PA)
Oakland Comm Coll (MI)

Management Science
Black Hawk Coll,
  Moline (IL)
Cape Cod Comm
  Coll (MA)
Florida Metropolitan
  U–Orange Park
  Campus (FL)
Harrisburg Area Comm
  Coll (PA)
Lakeshore Tech Coll (WI)
Louisburg Coll (NC)
National American U,
  Bloomington (MN)
National American U, Rio
  Rancho (NM)
Oakland Comm Coll (MI)
Reedley Coll (CA)
Santa Ana Coll (CA)
Santiago Canyon Coll (CA)
Tulsa Comm Coll (OK)
Western Nevada Comm
  Coll (NV)

Manufacturing Engineering
Cochise Coll, Douglas (AZ)
Penn State Fayette, The
  Eberly Campus (PA)
Penn State Hazleton (PA)
Penn State
  McKeesport (PA)
Penn State Wilkes-
  Barre (PA)
Penn State York (PA)

Manufacturing Technology
Albany Tech Coll (GA)
Alpena Comm Coll (MI)
Altamaha Tech Coll (GA)
Black Hawk Coll,
  Moline (IL)
Brevard Comm Coll (FL)
Clark Coll (WA)
Coll of DuPage (IL)
East Central Coll (MO)
Flint Hills Tech Coll (KS)

Flint River Tech Coll (GA)
Griffin Tech Coll (GA)
Hopkinsville Comm
  Coll (KY)
Hutchinson Comm Coll
  and Area Vocational
  School (KS)
Illinois Eastern Comm
  Colls, Wabash Valley
  College (IL)
Lehigh Carbon Comm
  Coll (PA)
Macomb Comm Coll (MI)
Marshall Comm and Tech
  Coll (WV)
Minnesota State Comm
  and Tech Coll–Fergus
  Falls (MN)
Mott Comm Coll (MI)
Mount Wachusett Comm
  Coll (MA)
Oakland Comm Coll (MI)
Owens Comm Coll,
  Toledo (OH)
Rogue Comm Coll (OR)
South Georgia Tech
  Coll (GA)
Waukesha County Tech
  Coll (WI)
West Central Tech
  Coll (GA)
Wright State U, Lake
  Campus (OH)

Marine Biology and Biological Oceanography
Brigham Young U –
  Idaho (ID)
Dixie State Coll of
  Utah (UT)
Oregon Coast Comm
  Coll (OR)
Southern Maine Comm
  Coll (ME)

Marine Maintenance and Ship Repair Technology
Alexandria Tech Coll (MN)
Cape Fear Comm
  Coll (NC)
Iowa Lakes Comm
  Coll (IA)
New England Inst of
  Technology (RI)
Olympic Coll (WA)

Marine Science/ Merchant Marine Officer
Anne Arundel Comm
  Coll (MD)
Coll of Micronesia–
  FSM (FM)
Coll of the Redwoods (CA)

Marine Technology
Cape Fear Comm
  Coll (NC)
Coll of Marin (CA)
Coll of The Albemarle (NC)
Kingsborough Comm Coll
  of the City U of New
  York (NY)
Northeastern Jr Coll (CO)
Northern Marianas
  Coll (MP)
North Idaho Coll (ID)
Orange Coast Coll (CA)
Santa Barbara City
  Coll (CA)
Skagit Valley Coll (WA)
Washington County Comm
  Coll (ME)

Marketing/Marketing Management
AIB Coll of Business (IA)
Aims Comm Coll (CO)
Albany Tech Coll (GA)
Alexandria Tech Coll (MN)
Allegany Coll of
  Maryland (MD)
Altamaha Tech Coll (GA)
Anne Arundel Comm
  Coll (MD)
Anoka-Ramsey Comm
  Coll (MN)
Anoka-Ramsey Comm
  Coll, Cambridge
  Campus (MN)
Antelope Valley Coll (CA)
Arizona Western Coll (AZ)
Athens Tech Coll (GA)
Atlanta Tech Coll (GA)
Augusta Tech Coll (GA)
Bainbridge Coll (GA)
Bakersfield Coll (CA)

Baltimore City Comm
  Coll (MD)
Barton County Comm
  Coll (KS)
Berkeley Coll, West
  Paterson (NJ)
Berkeley Coll-New York
  City Campus (NY)
Berkeley Coll-Westchester
  Campus (NY)
Bramson ORT Coll (NY)
Brigham Young U –
  Idaho (ID)
Brookhaven Coll (TX)
Broward Comm Coll (FL)
Bucks County Comm
  Coll (PA)
Cankdeska Cikana Comm
  Coll (ND)
Catawba Valley Comm
  Coll (NC)
Cecil Comm Coll (MD)
Cedar Valley Coll (TX)
Central Arizona Coll (AZ)
Central Carolina Comm
  Coll (NC)
Central Comm Coll–
  Columbus
  Campus (NE)
Central Florida Comm
  Coll (FL)
Central Georgia Tech
  Coll (GA)
Centralia Coll (WA)
Central Lakes Coll (MN)
Central Oregon Comm
  Coll (OR)
Central Piedmont Comm
  Coll (NC)
Central Texas Coll (TX)
Central Virginia Comm
  Coll (VA)
Cerritos Coll (CA)
Chaffey Coll (CA)
Chattahoochee Tech
  Coll (CA)
Chippewa Valley Tech
  Coll (WI)
Cincinnati State Tech and
  Comm Coll (OH)
Cisco Jr Coll (TX)
City Coll of San
  Francisco (CA)
City Colls of Chicago,
  Harold Washington
  College (IL)
City Colls of Chicago,
  Harry S. Truman
  College (IL)
City Colls of Chicago,
  Kennedy-King
  College (IL)
City Colls of Chicago,
  Olive-Harvey
  College (IL)
City Colls of Chicago,
  Richard J. Daley
  College (IL)
City Colls of Chicago,
  Wilbur Wright
  College (IL)
Clarendon Coll (TX)
Colby Comm Coll (KS)
Coll of Alameda (CA)
Coll of DuPage (IL)
Coll of Marin (CA)
Coll of San Mateo (CA)
Coll of Southern Idaho (ID)
Coll of the Desert (CA)
Colorado Mountain Coll,
  Alpine Campus (CO)
Columbia Basin Coll (WA)
Comm Coll of Allegheny
  County (PA)
Comm Coll of Beaver
  County (PA)
Comm Coll of
  Philadelphia (PA)
Comm Coll of Rhode
  Island (RI)
Comm Coll of Southern
  Nevada (NV)
Coosa Valley Tech
  Coll (GA)
Cosumnes River Coll,
  Sacramento (CA)
Crafton Hills Coll (CA)
Cuesta Coll (CA)
Cuyahoga Comm
  Coll (OH)
Cypress Coll (CA)
Danville Comm Coll (VA)
De Anza Coll (CA)
DeKalb Tech Coll (GA)
Dodge City Comm
  Coll (KS)
El Camino Coll (CA)
Elgin Comm Coll (IL)

Everett Comm Coll (WA)
Finger Lakes Comm
  Coll (NY)
Florence-Darlington Tech
  Coll (SC)
Folsom Lake Coll (CA)
Forsyth Tech Comm
  Coll (NC)
Fort Berthold Comm
  Coll (ND)
Fox Valley Tech Coll (WI)
Frederick Comm Coll (MD)
Fullerton Coll (CA)
Gateway Tech Coll (WI)
Genesee Comm Coll (NY)
Georgia Highlands
  Coll (GA)
Gloucester County
  Coll (NJ)
Golden West Coll (CA)
Greenville Tech Coll (SC)
Griffin Tech Coll (GA)
Grossmont Coll (CA)
Gwinnett Tech Coll (GA)
Harper Coll (IL)
Harrisburg Area Comm
  Coll (PA)
Hartnell Coll (CA)
Hawkeye Comm Coll (IA)
Heart of Georgia Tech
  Coll (GA)
Henry Ford Comm
  Coll (MI)
Hesser Coll (NH)
Hillsborough Comm
  Coll (FL)
Hocking Coll (OH)
Houston Comm Coll
  System (TX)
ICPR Jr Coll–Hato Rey
  Campus (PR)
Illinois Valley Comm
  Coll (IL)
Imperial Valley Coll (CA)
Inver Hills Comm
  Coll (MN)
Iowa Lakes Comm
  Coll (IA)
Isothermal Comm
  Coll (NC)
Joliet Jr Coll (IL)
Kankakee Comm Coll (IL)
Kennebec Valley Comm
  Coll (ME)
Kent State U, Ashtabula
  Campus (OH)
Kingsborough Comm Coll
  of the City U of New
  York (NY)
Kirkwood Comm Coll (IA)
Kirtland Comm Coll (MI)
Lake Land Coll (IL)
Lakeshore Tech Coll (WI)
Lake Tahoe Comm
  Coll (CA)
Lamar Comm Coll (CO)
Laney Coll (CA)
Lanier Tech Coll (GA)
Lansing Comm Coll (MI)
Laredo Comm Coll (TX)
Las Positas Coll (CA)
Lehigh Valley Coll (PA)
Lenoir Comm Coll (NC)
Lorain County Comm
  Coll (OH)
Los Angeles City Coll (CA)
Los Angeles Southwest
  Coll (CA)
Macomb Comm Coll (MI)
Madison Area Tech
  Coll (WI)
Massasoit Comm
  Coll (MA)
Maui Comm Coll (HI)
Merced Coll (CA)
Meridian Comm Coll (MS)
Mesa Comm Coll (AZ)
Metropolitan Comm
  Coll–Longview (MO)
Metropolitan Comm
  Coll–Maple
  Woods (MO)
Metropolitan Comm
  Coll–Penn Valley (MO)
Miami Dade Coll (FL)
Miami U Hamilton (OH)
Miami U–Middletown
  Campus (OH)
Middle Georgia Tech
  Coll (GA)
Middlesex Comm Coll (CT)
Mid-State Tech Coll (WI)
Minnesota State Coll–
  Southeast Tech (MN)
Minnesota State Comm
  and Tech Coll–Fergus
  Falls (MN)

Minot State U–Bottineau
  Campus (ND)
Mission Coll (CA)
Mississippi Gulf Coast
  Comm Coll (MS)
Moberly Area Comm
  Coll (MO)
Mohave Comm Coll (AZ)
Monroe Comm Coll (NY)
Monterey Peninsula
  Coll (CA)
Moorpark Coll (CA)
Morton Coll (IL)
Mott Comm Coll (MI)
Moultrie Tech Coll (GA)
Mt. Hood Comm Coll (OR)
Mt. San Antonio Coll (CA)
Muskegon Comm Coll (MI)
Napa Valley Coll (CA)
Nassau Comm Coll (NY)
National American U,
  Bloomington (MN)
Naugatuck Valley Comm
  Coll (CT)
Navarro Coll (TX)
Neosho County Comm
  Coll (KS)
New Hampshire Comm
  Tech Coll, Manchester/
  Stratham (NH)
New Hampshire Tech
  Inst (NH)
New Mexico Jr Coll (NM)
New River Comm Coll (VA)
New York City Coll of
  Technology of the City
  U of New York (NY)
Nicolet Area Tech Coll (WI)
North Central Michigan
  Coll (MI)
North Central Missouri
  Coll (MO)
Northeast Comm Coll (NE)
Northeastern Jr Coll (CO)
Northeastern Tech
  Coll (SC)
Northeast Iowa Comm
  Coll (IA)
Northern Essex Comm
  Coll (MA)
Northern Marianas
  Coll (MP)
North Hennepin Comm
  Coll (MN)
Northland Comm and Tech
  Coll–Thief River
  Falls (MN)
North Metro Tech Coll (GA)
North Shore Comm
  Coll (MA)
Ogeechee Tech Coll (GA)
Ohlone Coll (CA)
Oklahoma State U,
  Okmulgee (OK)
Orange Coast Coll (CA)
Ouachita Tech Coll (AR)
Owens Comm Coll,
  Toledo (OH)
Oxnard Coll (CA)
Palm Beach Comm
  Coll (FL)
Pasadena City Coll (CA)
Pasco-Hernando Comm
  Coll (FL)
Passaic County Comm
  Coll (NJ)
Pearl River Comm
  Coll (MS)
Piedmont Tech Coll (SC)
Piedmont Virginia Comm
  Coll (VA)
Pierce Coll (WA)
Polk Comm Coll (FL)
Raritan Valley Comm
  Coll (NJ)
Red Rocks Comm
  Coll (CO)
Rockford Business
  Coll (IL)
Saint Charles Comm
  Coll (MO)
St. Cloud Tech Coll (MN)
Salt Lake Comm Coll (UT)
San Bernardino Valley
  Coll (CA)
San Diego City Coll (CA)
San Joaquin Delta
  Coll (CA)
Santa Ana Coll (CA)
Santa Barbara City
  Coll (CA)
Santiago Canyon Coll (CA)
Savannah Tech Coll (GA)
Schoolcraft Coll (MI)
Seminole Comm Coll (FL)
Sitting Bull Coll (ND)
Southeastern Tech
  Coll (GA)

Southeast Tech Inst (SD)
South Florida Comm
  Coll (FL)
South Georgia Tech
  Coll (GA)
South Plains Coll (TX)
Southwestern Comm
  Coll (NC)
Southwestern Indian
  Polytechnic Inst (NM)
Southwest Mississippi
  Comm Coll (MS)
Spokane Comm Coll (WA)
Spokane Falls Comm
  Coll (WA)
Springfield Tech Comm
  Coll (MA)
Stark State Coll of
  Technology (OH)
State Fair Comm
  Coll (MO)
State U of New York Coll
  of Agriculture and
  Technology at
  Morrisville (NY)
State U of New York Coll
  of Technology at
  Alfred (NY)
Suffolk County Comm
  Coll (NY)
Tallahassee Comm
  Coll (FL)
Terra State Comm
  Coll (OH)
Three Rivers Comm
  Coll (CT)
Three Rivers Comm
  Coll (MO)
Tidewater Comm Coll (VA)
Tompkins Cortland Comm
  Coll (NY)
Trident Tech Coll (SC)
Tri-State Business
  Inst (PA)
Trocaire Coll (NY)
Tulsa Comm Coll (OK)
Tunxis Comm Coll (CT)
Turtle Mountain Comm
  Coll (ND)
Tyler Jr Coll (TX)
Ulster County Comm
  Coll (NY)
Umpqua Comm Coll (OR)
U of Arkansas Comm Coll
  at Morrilton (AR)
U of New
  Mexico–Gallup (NM)
Valdosta Tech Coll (GA)
Valencia Comm Coll (FL)
Wallace State Comm
  Coll (AL)
Washington State Comm
  Coll (OH)
Waukesha County Tech
  Coll (WI)
West Central Tech
  Coll (GA)
Westchester Comm
  Coll (NY)
Western Nevada Comm
  Coll (NV)
Western Piedmont Comm
  Coll (NC)
Western Texas Coll (TX)
Western Wyoming Comm
  Coll (WY)
West Georgia Tech
  Coll (GA)
West Los Angeles
  Coll (CA)
Westmoreland County
  Comm Coll (PA)
West Shore Comm
  Coll (MI)
West Valley Coll (CA)
West Virginia U at
  Parkersburg (WV)
Wright State U, Lake
  Campus (OH)
Zane State Coll (OH)

Marketing Related

Black Hawk Coll,
  Moline (IL)
Northeast Comm Coll (NE)
Oakland Comm Coll (MI)
West Virginia State Comm
  and Tech Coll (WV)

Masonry

Alexandria Tech Coll (MN)
Metropolitan Comm
  Coll–Business &
  Technology
  Campus (MO)
Mississippi Delta Comm
  Coll (MS)
Piedmont Virginia Comm
  Coll (VA)

State U of New York Coll
  of Technology at
  Alfred (NY)
Western Nevada Comm
  Coll (NV)

Massage Therapy

Allied Coll (MO)
Antonelli Coll,
  Hattiesburg (MS)
Arizona Western Coll (AZ)
Beta Tech (VA)
Bryan Coll (CA)
Cambridge Coll (CO)
Career Tech Coll (LA)
Career Training Academy,
  Monroeville (PA)
Career Training Academy,
  Pittsburgh (PA)
Coll of DuPage (IL)
Coll of Southern
  Maryland (MD)
Florida Coll of Natural
  Health, Bradenton (FL)
Florida Coll of Natural
  Health, Maitland (FL)
Florida Coll of Natural
  Health, Miami (FL)
Florida Coll of Natural
  Health, Pompano
  Beach (FL)
H. Councill Trenholm State
  Tech Coll (AL)
Heritage Coll (CO)
Herzing Coll (MN)
High-Tech Inst (FL)
High-Tech Inst (MN)
High-Tech Inst (MO)
High-Tech Inst (NV)
High-Tech Inst,
  Memphis (TN)
High-Tech Inst,
  Nashville (TN)
Indiana Business Coll,
  Indianapolis (IN)
Indiana Business Coll-
  Medical (IN)
Iowa Lakes Comm
  Coll (IA)
Joliet Jr Coll (IL)
Keiser Career Coll -
  Greenacres (FL)
Lehigh Valley Coll (PA)
Medical Careers Inst,
  Newport News (VA)
Mercy Coll of Northwest
  Ohio (OH)
Midwest Inst,
  Kirkwood (MO)
Miller-Motte Tech Coll,
  Clarksville (TN)
Minnesota School of
  Business–Brooklyn
  Center (MN)
Minnesota School of
  Business–Plymouth (MN)
Minnesota School of
  Business–Richfield (MN)
Minnesota School of
  Business–St.
  Cloud (MN)
Minnesota School of
  Business–Shakopee (MN)
Mount Wachusett Comm
  Coll (MA)
Myotherapy Inst (NE)
New York Coll of Health
  Professions (NY)
Oakland Comm Coll (MI)
Ohio Coll of
  Massotherapy (OH)
Provo Coll (UT)
Rasmussen Coll Brooklyn
  Park (MN)
Southwestern Comm
  Coll (NC)
Springfield Tech Comm
  Coll (MA)
Tidewater Tech (VA)
Western Career Coll,
  Pleasant Hill (CA)
Western Career Coll,
  Sacramento (CA)

Mass Communication/ Media

Amarillo Coll (TX)
Anne Arundel Comm
  Coll (MD)
Asnuntuck Comm
  Coll (CT)
Bergen Comm Coll (NJ)
Blinn Coll (TX)
Brigham Young U –
  Idaho (ID)
Bucks County Comm
  Coll (PA)
Cape Cod Comm
  Coll (MA)

Central Comm Coll–
  Hastings Campus (NE)
Centralia Coll (WA)
Chattanooga State Tech
  Comm Coll (TN)
Chipola Coll (FL)
City Colls of Chicago,
  Richard J. Daley
  College (IL)
Cochise Coll, Sierra
  Vista (AZ)
Colby Comm Coll (KS)
Coll of Marin (CA)
Coll of the Desert (CA)
Comm Coll of Southern
  Nevada (NV)
Cosumnes River Coll,
  Sacramento (CA)
Crowder Coll (MO)
Cuesta Coll (CA)
De Anza Coll (CA)
Dodge City Comm
  Coll (KS)
Finger Lakes Comm
  Coll (NY)
Frederick Comm Coll (MD)
Fullerton Coll (CA)
Fulton-Montgomery Comm
  Coll (NY)
Genesee Comm Coll (NY)
Georgia Military Coll (GA)
Grand Rapids Comm
  Coll (MI)
Harrisburg Area Comm
  Coll (PA)
Henry Ford Comm
  Coll (MI)
Hesser Coll (NH)
Hillsborough Comm
  Coll (FL)
Holyoke Comm Coll (MA)
Houston Comm Coll
  System (TX)
Iowa Lakes Comm
  Coll (IA)
Kirkwood Comm Coll (IA)
Lamar Comm Coll (CO)
Lansing Comm Coll (MI)
Laramie County Comm
  Coll (WY)
Lassen Comm Coll
  District (CA)
Lorain County Comm
  Coll (OH)
Los Angeles City Coll (CA)
Manatee Comm Coll (FL)
Miami Dade Coll (FL)
Miami U–Middletown
  Campus (OH)
Middlesex Comm Coll (CT)
Monroe Comm Coll (NY)
Monterey Peninsula
  Coll (CA)
Nassau Comm Coll (NY)
Niagara County Comm
  Coll (NY)
Northeast Comm Coll (NE)
North Idaho Coll (ID)
Northland Comm and Tech
  Coll–Thief River
  Falls (MN)
Ohlone Coll (CA)
Oklahoma City Comm
  Coll (OK)
Orange Coast Coll (CA)
Palm Beach Comm
  Coll (FL)
Parkland Coll (IL)
Pasadena City Coll (CA)
Red Rocks Comm
  Coll (CO)
Ridgewater Coll (MN)
Sacramento City Coll (CA)
St. Louis Comm Coll at
  Florissant Valley (MO)
Salt Lake Comm Coll (UT)
South Georgia Coll (GA)
South Plains Coll (TX)
Spokane Falls Comm
  Coll (WA)
State Fair Comm
  Coll (MO)
Tompkins Cortland Comm
  Coll (NY)
Treasure Valley Comm
  Coll (OR)
Tulsa Comm Coll (OK)
Ulster County Comm
  Coll (NY)
Westchester Comm
  Coll (NY)
Western Texas Coll (TX)
Wright State U, Lake
  Campus (OH)
Wytheville Comm Coll (VA)
Yuba Coll (CA)

Mass Communications

Clarendon Coll (TX)
James H. Faulkner State
  Comm Coll (AL)

Materials Science

Central Arizona Coll (AZ)
Contra Costa Coll (CA)
Greenville Tech Coll (SC)
Harper Coll (IL)
Henry Ford Comm
  Coll (MI)
Kent State U, Ashtabula
  Campus (OH)
Mt. San Antonio Coll (CA)
Neosho County Comm
  Coll (KS)
Northern Essex Comm
  Coll (MA)
Tulsa Comm Coll (OK)

Mathematics

Allen County Comm
  Coll (KS)
Alpena Comm Coll (MI)
Amarillo Coll (TX)
Angelina Coll (TX)
Anne Arundel Comm
  Coll (MD)
Antelope Valley Coll (CA)
Arizona Western Coll (AZ)
Bainbridge Coll (GA)
Bakersfield Coll (CA)
Barstow Coll (CA)
Barton County Comm
  Coll (KS)
Bergen Comm Coll (NJ)
Blinn Coll (TX)
Brigham Young U –
  Idaho (ID)
Bucks County Comm
  Coll (PA)
Burlington County
  Coll (NJ)
Calhoun Comm Coll (AL)
Cankdeska Cikana Comm
  Coll (ND)
Cañada Coll (CA)
Cape Cod Comm
  Coll (MA)
Cecil Comm Coll (MD)
Centralia Coll (WA)
Central Oregon Comm
  Coll (OR)
Central Texas Coll (TX)
Cerritos Coll (CA)
Chaffey Coll (CA)
Chesapeake Coll (MD)
Cisco Jr Coll (TX)
Citrus Coll (CA)
City Coll of San
  Francisco (CA)
City Colls of Chicago,
  Harold Washington
  College (IL)
City Colls of Chicago,
  Kennedy-King
  College (IL)
City Colls of Chicago,
  Olive-Harvey
  College (IL)
Clarendon Coll (TX)
Clovis Comm Coll (NM)
Coastal Bend Coll (TX)
Coastal Georgia Comm
  Coll (GA)
Cochise Coll, Douglas (AZ)
Colby Comm Coll (KS)
Coll of Alameda (CA)
Coll of Marin (CA)
Coll of San Mateo (CA)
Coll of Southern Idaho (ID)
Coll of the Canyons (CA)
Coll of the Desert (CA)
Coll of the Mainland (TX)
Coll of the Siskiyous (CA)
Colorado Mountain
  Coll (CO)
Colorado Mountain Coll,
  Alpine Campus (CO)
Columbia Coll (CA)
Columbia-Greene Comm
  Coll (NY)
Comm Coll of Allegheny
  County (PA)
Comm Coll of Southern
  Nevada (NV)
Contra Costa Coll (CA)
Cosumnes River Coll,
  Sacramento (CA)
Crafton Hills Coll (CA)
Crowder Coll (MO)
Cuesta Coll (CA)
Cypress Coll (CA)
De Anza Coll (CA)
Dixie State Coll of
  Utah (UT)

Dodge City Comm
Coll (KS)
Eastern Arizona Coll (AZ)
East Georgia Coll (GA)
El Camino Coll (CA)
Essex County Coll (NJ)
Everett Comm Coll (WA)
Finger Lakes Comm
Coll (NY)
Folsom Lake Coll (CA)
Foothill Coll (CA)
Fort Berthold Comm
Coll (ND)
Frederick Comm Coll (MD)
Fullerton Coll (CA)
Fulton-Montgomery Comm
Coll (NY)
Garrett Coll (MD)
Genesee Comm Coll (NY)
Gloucester County
Coll (NJ)
Golden West Coll (CA)
Gordon Coll (GA)
Grayson County Coll (TX)
Great Basin Coll (NV)
Grossmont Coll (CA)
Harper Coll (IL)
Harrisburg Area Comm
Coll (PA)
Hartnell Coll (CA)
Housatonic Comm
Coll (CT)
Hutchinson Comm Coll
and Area Vocational
School (KS)
Imperial Valley Coll (CA)
Iowa Lakes Comm
Coll (IA)
Irvine Valley Coll (CA)
Joliet Jr Coll (IL)
Jones County Jr Coll (MS)
Kellogg Comm Coll (MI)
Kingsborough Comm Coll
of the City U of New
York (NY)
Kirkwood Comm Coll (IA)
Labette Comm Coll (KS)
Lake Tahoe Comm
Coll (CA)
Lamar Comm Coll (CO)
Laney Coll (CA)
Lansing Comm Coll (MI)
Laramie County Comm
Coll (WY)
Lassen Comm Coll
District (CA)
Lawson State Comm
Coll (AL)
Lee Coll (TX)
Lehigh Carbon Comm
Coll (PA)
Linn-Benton Comm
Coll (OR)
Little Big Horn Coll (MT)
Lorain County Comm
Coll (OH)
Los Angeles City Coll (CA)
Los Angeles Mission
Coll (CA)
Los Medanos Coll (CA)
Louisburg Coll (NC)
Lower Columbia Coll (WA)
Macomb Comm Coll (MI)
Mendocino Coll (CA)
Merced Coll (CA)
Mesa Comm Coll (AZ)
Miami Dade Coll (FL)
Miami U–Middletown
Campus (OH)
Mission Coll (CA)
Mississippi Delta Comm
Coll (MS)
Mohave Comm Coll (AZ)
Monroe Comm Coll (NY)
Monterey Peninsula
Coll (CA)
Montgomery County
Comm Coll (PA)
Moorpark Coll (CA)
Murray State Coll (OK)
Nassau Comm Coll (NY)
Naugatuck Valley Comm
Coll (CT)
Navarro Coll (TX)
New Mexico Jr Coll (NM)
New Mexico Military
Inst (NM)
Niagara County Comm
Coll (NY)
Northampton County Area
Comm Coll (PA)
North Country Comm
Coll (NY)
Northeast Comm Coll (NE)
Northeastern Jr Coll (CO)
North Idaho Coll (ID)
Northwestern Connecticut
Comm Coll (CT)

Odessa Coll (TX)
Oklahoma City Comm
Coll (OK)
Onondaga Comm
Coll (NY)
Orange Coast Coll (CA)
Oxnard Coll (CA)
Palm Beach Comm
Coll (FL)
Palo Alto Coll (TX)
Pasadena City Coll (CA)
Passaic County Comm
Coll (NJ)
Porterville Coll (CA)
Potomac State Coll of
West Virginia U (WV)
Quincy Coll (MA)
Raritan Valley Comm
Coll (NJ)
Redlands Comm Coll (OK)
Red Rocks Comm
Coll (CO)
Reedley Coll (CA)
Ridgewater Coll (MN)
Roane State Comm
Coll (TN)
Rose State Coll (OK)
Roxbury Comm Coll (MA)
Sacramento City Coll (CA)
St. Catharine Coll (KY)
St. Louis Comm Coll at
Florissant Valley (MO)
St. Philip's Coll (TX)
San Bernardino Valley
Coll (CA)
Sandhills Comm Coll (NC)
San Diego City Coll (CA)
San Joaquin Delta
Coll (CA)
San Juan Coll (NM)
Santa Ana Coll (CA)
Santa Barbara City
Coll (CA)
Santa Rosa Jr Coll (CA)
Santiago Canyon Coll (CA)
Scottsdale Comm
Coll (AZ)
Seminole State Coll (OK)
Sheridan Coll–Sheridan
and Gillette (WY)
Skagit Valley Coll (WA)
Southern U at
Shreveport (LA)
South Georgia Coll (GA)
Springfield Tech Comm
Coll (MA)
State U of New York Coll
of Agriculture and
Technology at
Morrisville (NY)
State U of New York Coll
of Technology at
Alfred (NY)
Suffolk County Comm
Coll (NY)
Taft Coll (CA)
Terra State Comm
Coll (OH)
Texarkana Coll (TX)
Tompkins Cortland Comm
Coll (NY)
Treasure Valley Comm
Coll (OR)
Tulsa Comm Coll (OK)
Turtle Mountain Comm
Coll (ND)
Ulster County Comm
Coll (NY)
Umpqua Comm Coll (OR)
Victor Valley Coll (CA)
Washington State Comm
Coll (OH)
Wenatchee Valley
Coll (WA)
Western Nebraska Comm
Coll (NE)
Western Nevada Comm
Coll (NV)
Western Wyoming Comm
Coll (WY)
West Hills Comm Coll (CA)
West Los Angeles
Coll (CA)
West Valley Coll (CA)
Young Harris Coll (GA)
Yuba Coll (CA)

Mathematics and Computer Science

Crowder Coll (MO)
Dean Coll (MA)
Fresno City Coll (CA)

Mathematics Related

Lassen Comm Coll
District (CA)

Mathematics Teacher Education

Frederick Comm Coll (MD)

Louisburg Coll (NC)
Manatee Comm Coll (FL)
Northwest Mississippi
Comm Coll (MS)

Mechanical Design Technology

Asheville-Buncombe Tech
Comm Coll (NC)
Bowling Green State
U–Firelands Coll (OH)
Brigham Young U –
Idaho (ID)
Carroll Comm Coll (MD)
Central Maine Comm
Coll (ME)
Chattanooga State Tech
Comm Coll (TN)
Chippewa Valley Tech
Coll (WI)
Coll of DuPage (IL)
Coll of The Albemarle (NC)
Comm Coll of Allegheny
County (PA)
Comm Coll of Southern
Nevada (NV)
Dabney S. Lancaster
Comm Coll (VA)
De Anza Coll (CA)
Forsyth Tech Comm
Coll (NC)
Fox Valley Tech Coll (WI)
Gateway Tech Coll (WI)
Harper Coll (IL)
Hartnell Coll (CA)
Hawkeye Comm Coll (IA)
Hennepin Tech Coll (MN)
Illinois Valley Comm
Coll (IL)
Isothermal Comm
Coll (NC)
Joliet Jr Coll (IL)
Kirkwood Comm Coll (IA)
Lakeshore Tech Coll (WI)
Lansing Comm Coll (MI)
Lenoir Comm Coll (NC)
Lorain County Comm
Coll (OH)
Macomb Comm Coll (MI)
Madison Area Tech
Coll (WI)
Mid-State Tech Coll (WI)
Minnesota State Coll–
Southeast Tech (MN)
Mohawk Valley Comm
Coll (NY)
Mt. San Antonio Coll (CA)
New Hampshire Comm
Tech Coll, Manchester/
Stratham (NH)
Niagara County Comm
Coll (NY)
Northeastern Tech
Coll (SC)
Northeast Iowa Comm
Coll (IA)
Northwest Iowa Comm
Coll (IA)
Owens Comm Coll,
Toledo (OH)
Raritan Valley Comm
Coll (NJ)
Richland Coll (TX)
St. Cloud Tech Coll (MN)
Spokane Comm Coll (WA)
State U of New York Coll
of Technology at
Alfred (NY)
Westmoreland County
Comm Coll (PA)

Mechanical Drafting and Cad/Cadd

Alexandria Tech Coll (MN)
Central Carolina Tech
Coll (SC)
Commonwealth Tech
Inst (PA)
Comm Coll of Allegheny
County (PA)
Dixie State Coll of
Utah (UT)
Erie Comm Coll, South
Campus (NY)
Island Drafting and Tech
Inst (NY)
John Wood Comm Coll (IL)
Macomb Comm Coll (MI)
Midlands Tech Coll (SC)
Mohawk Valley Comm
Coll (NY)
Montgomery County
Comm Coll (PA)
Mott Comm Coll (MI)
North Seattle Comm
Coll (WA)
Oakland Comm Coll (MI)
Ozarks Tech Comm
Coll (MO)

Piedmont Tech Coll (SC)
Piedmont Virginia Comm
Coll (VA)
St. Cloud Tech Coll (MN)
Stanly Comm Coll (NC)
Waukesha County Tech
Coll (WI)
York Tech Coll (SC)

Mechanical Engineering

Itasca Comm Coll (MN)
Lehigh Carbon Comm
Coll (PA)

Mechanical Engineering/ Mechanical Technology

Alamance Comm Coll (NC)
Anne Arundel Comm
Coll (MD)
Asheville-Buncombe Tech
Comm Coll (NC)
Augusta Tech Coll (GA)
Brigham Young U –
Idaho (ID)
Broome Comm Coll (NY)
Broward Comm Coll (FL)
Cape Fear Comm
Coll (NC)
Catawba Valley Comm
Coll (NC)
Central Ohio Tech
Coll (OH)
Central Piedmont Comm
Coll (NC)
Central Virginia Comm
Coll (VA)
Chattanooga State Tech
Comm Coll (TN)
Cincinnati State Tech and
Comm Coll (OH)
Citrus Coll (CA)
City Coll of San
Francisco (CA)
Clark State Comm
Coll (OH)
Cleveland Comm Coll (NC)
Coll of Lake County (IL)
Columbus Tech Coll (GA)
Comm Coll of Southern
Nevada (NV)
ECPI Coll of
Technology (VA)
ECPI Tech Coll (VA)
ECPI Tech Coll (VA)
Erie Comm Coll, North
Campus (NY)
Finger Lakes Comm
Coll (NY)
Fox Valley Tech Coll (WI)
Gadsden State Comm
Coll (AL)
Gateway Comm Coll (CT)
Greenville Tech Coll (SC)
Hagerstown Comm
Coll (MD)
Harper Coll (IL)
Harrisburg Area Comm
Coll (PA)
Hawkeye Comm Coll (IA)
Illinois Eastern Comm
Colls, Lincoln Trail
College (IL)
Illinois Valley Comm
Coll (IL)
Isothermal Comm
Coll (NC)
Jamestown Comm
Coll (NY)
Jefferson Comm and Tech
Coll (KY)
Jefferson Comm Coll (OH)
John Tyler Comm Coll (VA)
Kent State U, Ashtabula
Campus (OH)
Kent State U, Trumbull
Campus (OH)
Kent State U, Tuscarawas
Campus (OH)
Kirkwood Comm Coll (IA)
Lansing Comm Coll (MI)
Lassen Comm Coll
District (CA)
Lehigh Carbon Comm
Coll (PA)
Lower Columbia Coll (WA)
Macomb Comm Coll (MI)
Madisonville Comm
Coll (KY)
Massachusetts Bay Comm
Coll (MA)
Miami U Hamilton (OH)
Miami U–Middletown
Campus (OH)
Midlands Tech Coll (SC)

Minnesota State Comm
and Tech Coll–Fergus
Falls (MN)
Mohawk Valley Comm
Coll (NY)
Monroe Comm Coll (NY)
Montgomery County
Comm Coll (PA)
Moraine Valley Comm
Coll (IL)
Mott Comm Coll (MI)
Mt. Hood Comm Coll (OR)
Naugatuck Valley Comm
Coll (CT)
New Hampshire Tech
Inst (NH)
New York City Coll of
Technology of the City
U of New York (NY)
Onondaga Comm
Coll (NY)
Owens Comm Coll,
Toledo (OH)
Pasadena City Coll (CA)
Penn State DuBois (PA)
Penn State Hazleton (PA)
Penn State New
Kensington (PA)
Penn State Shenango (PA)
Penn State York (PA)
Piedmont Tech Coll (SC)
Potomac State Coll of
West Virginia U (WV)
Queensborough Comm
Coll of the City U of
New York (NY)
Red Rocks Comm
Coll (CO)
The Refrigeration
School (AZ)
Richland Coll (TX)
St. Louis Comm Coll at
Florissant Valley (MO)
San Antonio Coll (TX)
San Joaquin Delta
Coll (CA)
Schoolcraft Coll (MI)
Southeastern Comm Coll,
North Campus (IA)
Southeast Tech Inst (SD)
Southern U at
Shreveport (LA)
South Piedmont Comm
Coll (NC)
Spokane Comm Coll (WA)
Springfield Tech Comm
Coll (MA)
Stark State Coll of
Technology (OH)
State U of New York Coll
of Agriculture and
Technology at
Morrisville (NY)
State U of New York Coll
of Technology at
Alfred (NY)
State U of New York Coll
of Technology at
Canton (NY)
Suffolk County Comm
Coll (NY)
Terra State Comm
Coll (OH)
Texas State Tech Coll–
Marshall (TX)
Three Rivers Comm
Coll (CT)
Trident Tech Coll (SC)
Tulsa Comm Coll (OK)
Union County Coll (NJ)
U of Puerto Rico at
Carolina (PR)
Virginia Western Comm
Coll (VA)
Washington State Comm
Coll (OH)
Wayne Comm Coll (NC)
Westchester Comm
Coll (NY)
Westmoreland County
Comm Coll (PA)
West Virginia U at
Parkersburg (WV)
Wichita Area Tech
Coll (KS)
Wilson Tech Comm
Coll (NC)
Wright State U, Lake
Campus (OH)
Wytheville Comm Coll (VA)
York Tech Coll (SC)

Mechanic and Repair Technologies Related

Cincinnati State Tech and
Comm Coll (OH)
Macomb Comm Coll (MI)
Ohio Tech Coll (OH)

Mechanics and Repair

Black Hawk Coll,
Moline (IL)
Santa Rosa Jr Coll (CA)
Western Wyoming Comm
Coll (WY)

Medical Administrative Assistant

Elizabethtown Tech
Coll (KY)
ICPR Jr Coll–Hato Rey
Campus (PR)
Minnesota School of
Business–Brooklyn
Center (MN)
Minnesota School of
Business–Plymouth (MN)
Minnesota School of
Business–St.
Cloud (MN)

Medical Administrative Assistant and Medical Secretary

AIB Coll of Business (IA)
Alamance Comm Coll (NC)
Alexandria Tech Coll (MN)
Amarillo Coll (TX)
Angley Coll (FL)
Antelope Valley Coll (CA)
Baltimore City Comm
Coll (MD)
Barton County Comm
Coll (KS)
Beaufort County Comm
Coll (NC)
Bergen Comm Coll (NJ)
Berkeley City Coll (CA)
Bismarck State Coll (ND)
Brevard Comm Coll (FL)
Briarwood Coll (CT)
Broward Comm Coll (FL)
Business Inst of
Pennsylvania,
Sharon (PA)
Cabrillo Coll (CA)
Cambria-Rowe Business
Coll, Johnstown (PA)
Cape Cod Comm
Coll (MA)
Central Arizona Coll (AZ)
Central Carolina Comm
Coll (NC)
Central Comm Coll–
Hastings Campus (NE)
Central Florida Coll, Winter
Park (FL)
Centralia Coll (WA)
Central Lakes Coll (MN)
Central Maine Comm
Coll (ME)
Central Piedmont Comm
Coll (NC)
Central Texas Coll (TX)
Century Coll (MN)
Cerritos Coll (CA)
Chaffey Coll (CA)
Chattanooga State Tech
Comm Coll (TN)
Chesapeake Coll (MD)
City Coll, Fort
Lauderdale (FL)
City Coll, Gainesville (FL)
City Coll, Miami (FL)
City Colls of Chicago,
Harry S. Truman
College (IL)
City Colls of Chicago,
Richard J. Daley
College (IL)
Clark Coll (WA)
Clark State Comm
Coll (OH)
Clatsop Comm Coll (OR)
Cleveland Comm Coll (NC)
Clovis Comm Coll (NM)
Coastal Carolina Comm
Coll (NC)
Cochise Coll, Sierra
Vista (AZ)
Coll of Marin (CA)
Coll of San Mateo (CA)
Coll of The Albemarle (NC)
Comm Coll of Allegheny
County (PA)
Comm Coll of Beaver
County (PA)
Comm Coll of
Philadelphia (PA)
Comm Coll of Rhode
Island (RI)
Comm Coll of Southern
Nevada (NV)
Cosumnes River Coll,
Sacramento (CA)
Crafton Hills Coll (CA)

Crowder Coll (MO)
Cypress Coll (CA)
Dabney S. Lancaster
Comm Coll (VA)
Dodge City Comm
Coll (KS)
East Central Coll (MO)
ECPI Coll of
Technology (VA)
ECPI Tech Coll (VA)
ECPI Tech Coll (VA)
El Centro Coll (TX)
Elgin Comm Coll (IL)
Elmira Business Inst (NY)
Essex County Coll (NJ)
Eugenio María de Hostos
Comm Coll of the City
U of New York (NY)
Everett Comm Coll (WA)
Florida National Coll (FL)
Frederick Comm Coll (MD)
Fresno City Coll (CA)
Fulton-Montgomery Comm
Coll (NY)
Gateway Comm Coll (CT)
George C. Wallace Comm
Coll (AL)
Gloucester County
Coll (NJ)
Grand Rapids Comm
Coll (MI)
Gretna Career Coll (LA)
Grossmont Coll (CA)
Harper Coll (IL)
Hawkeye Comm Coll (IA)
Hennepin Tech Coll (MN)
Henry Ford Comm
Coll (MI)
Heritage Coll (NV)
Hesser Coll (NH)
Hillsborough Comm
Coll (FL)
Hocking Coll (OH)
Houston Comm Coll
System (TX)
Howard Comm Coll (MD)
Illinois Eastern Comm
Colls, Olney Central
College (IL)
Inver Hills Comm
Coll (MN)
Iowa Lakes Comm
Coll (IA)
Jefferson Comm Coll (OH)
Johnston Comm Coll (NC)
John Wood Comm Coll (IL)
Joliet Jr Coll (IL)
Kellogg Comm Coll (MI)
Kirkwood Comm Coll (IA)
Kirtland Comm Coll (MI)
Labette Comm Coll (KS)
Lake Land Coll (IL)
Lakeshore Tech Coll (WI)
Lake Tahoe Comm
Coll (CA)
Lamar Comm Coll (CO)
Lassen Comm Coll
District (CA)
Laurel Business Inst (PA)
LDS Business Coll (UT)
Lehigh Valley Coll (PA)
Lenoir Comm Coll (NC)
Lewis Coll of
Business (MI)
Linn-Benton Comm
Coll (OR)
Los Angeles City Coll (CA)
Los Angeles Harbor
Coll (CA)
Lower Columbia Coll (WA)
Madison Area Tech
Coll (WI)
Marian Court Coll (MA)
Martin Comm Coll (NC)
McLennan Comm
Coll (TX)
Merced Coll (CA)
Mesa Comm Coll (AZ)
Metropolitan Comm
Coll–Longview (MO)
Metropolitan Comm
Coll–Maple
Woods (MO)
Metropolitan Comm
Coll–Penn Valley (MO)
Miami U–Middletown
Campus (OH)
Middlesex Comm Coll (CT)
Minnesota State Coll–
Southeast Tech (MN)
Minnesota State Comm
and Tech Coll–Fergus
Falls (MN)
Minot State U–Bottineau
Campus (ND)
Montcalm Comm Coll (MI)
Monterey Peninsula
Coll (CA)

Morton Coll (IL)
Mott Comm Coll (MI)
Mt. Hood Comm Coll (OR)
Mt. San Antonio Coll (CA)
Muskegon Comm Coll (MI)
Nassau Comm Coll (NY)
National Park Comm
Coll (AR)
Naugatuck Valley Comm
Coll (CT)
New Hampshire Comm
Tech Coll, Manchester/
Stratham (NH)
New Mexico Jr Coll (NM)
New River Comm Coll (VA)
Nicolet Area Tech Coll (WI)
Northampton County Area
Comm Coll (PA)
Northeast Comm Coll (NE)
Northeastern Jr Coll (CO)
Northern Essex Comm
Coll (MA)
Northern Maine Comm
Coll (ME)
North Idaho Coll (ID)
North Shore Comm
Coll (MA)
Northwest Mississippi
Comm Coll (MS)
Ohlone Coll (CA)
Oklahoma State U,
Okmulgee (OK)
Orange Coast Coll (CA)
Ouachita Tech Coll (AR)
Pearl River Comm
Coll (MS)
Piedmont Tech Coll (SC)
Polk Comm Coll (FL)
Potomac State Coll of
West Virginia U (WV)
Pueblo Comm Coll (CO)
Rasmussen Coll Brooklyn
Park (MN)
Renton Tech Coll (WA)
Richland Comm Coll (IL)
Ridgewater Coll (MN)
Riverland Comm Coll (MN)
Roane State Comm
Coll (TN)
Roxbury Comm Coll (MA)
Sacramento City Coll (CA)
St. Catharine Coll (KY)
St. Cloud Tech Coll (MN)
Saint Paul Coll–A Comm &
Tech College (MN)
St. Philip's Coll (TX)
Sandhills Comm Coll (NC)
Scottsdale Comm
Coll (AZ)
Shasta Coll (CA)
Skagit Valley Coll (WA)
Southeastern Business
Coll, Jackson (OH)
Southeastern Business
Coll, Lancaster (OH)
Southeastern Business
Coll, New Boston (OH)
Southeastern Comm Coll,
South Campus (IA)
South Florida Comm
Coll (FL)
South Piedmont Comm
Coll (NC)
South Plains Coll (TX)
Spokane Comm Coll (WA)
Springfield Tech Comm
Coll (MA)
Stanly Comm Coll (NC)
State Fair Comm
Coll (MO)
State U of New York Coll
of Agriculture and
Technology at
Morrisville (NY)
Surry Comm Coll (NC)
Temple Coll (TX)
Terra State Comm
Coll (OH)
Three Rivers Comm
Coll (CT)
Tomball Coll (TX)
Treasure Valley Comm
Coll (OR)
Trident Tech Coll (SC)
Trocaire Coll (NY)
Trumbull Business
Coll (OH)
Tulsa Comm Coll (OK)
Tunxis Comm Coll (CT)
Tyler Jr Coll (TX)
Umpqua Comm Coll (OR)
The U of Akron–Wayne
Coll (OH)
U of Cincinnati Clermont
Coll (OH)
The U of Montana-Helena
Coll of Technology (MT)
Valencia Comm Coll (FL)

Vincennes U Jasper
Campus (IN)
Wallace State Comm
Coll (AL)
Washington State Comm
Coll (OH)
Wayne Comm Coll (NC)
Wenatchee Valley
Coll (WA)
Western Piedmont Comm
Coll (NC)
Western Wyoming Comm
Coll (WY)
West Los Angeles
Coll (CA)
Westmoreland County
Comm Coll (PA)
West Valley Coll (CA)
Wright State U, Lake
Campus (OH)
Wytheville Comm Coll (VA)
York Tech Coll (SC)

Medical/Clinical Assistant

ACT Coll, Arlington (VA)
Alamance Comm Coll (NC)
Allied Coll (MO)
Angley Coll (FL)
Anne Arundel Comm
Coll (MD)
Barstow Coll (CA)
Barton County Comm
Coll (KS)
Bergen Comm Coll (NJ)
Bradford School (PA)
Brevard Comm Coll (FL)
Briarwood Coll (CT)
Broome Comm Coll (NY)
Broward Comm Coll (FL)
Brown Mackie Coll–
Akron (OH)
Brown Mackie Coll–
Atlanta (GA)
Brown Mackie Coll–
Cincinnati (OH)
Brown Mackie Coll–
Findlay (OH)
Brown Mackie Coll–Fort
Wayne (IN)
Brown Mackie Coll–
Hopkinsville (KY)
Brown Mackie Coll–
Kansas City (KS)
Brown Mackie Coll–
Louisville (KY)
Brown Mackie Coll–
Miami (FL)
Brown Mackie Coll–North
Canton (OH)
Brown Mackie Coll–
Northern Kentucky (KY)
Brown Mackie Coll–
Salina (KS)
Brown Mackie Coll–South
Bend (IN)
Bucks County Comm
Coll (PA)
Business Inst of
Pennsylvania,
Sharon (PA)
Cambridge Coll (CO)
Capital Comm Coll (CT)
Career Tech Coll (LA)
Career Training Academy,
Monroeville (PA)
Career Training Academy,
Pittsburgh (PA)
Central Carolina Comm
Coll (NC)
Central Comm Coll–
Hastings Campus (NE)
Central Oregon Comm
Coll (OR)
Central Piedmont Comm
Coll (NC)
Century Coll (MN)
Cerritos Coll (CA)
Cincinnati State Tech and
Comm Coll (OH)
Clark Coll (WA)
Coll of Marin (CA)
Coll of San Mateo (CA)
Coll of the Desert (CA)
Coll of the Redwoods (CA)
Comm Coll of Allegheny
County (PA)
Comm Coll of
Philadelphia (PA)
Comm Coll of Southern
Nevada (NV)
Cossatot Comm Coll of the
U of Arkansas (AR)
Cosumnes River Coll,
Sacramento (CA)
Cuesta Coll (CA)
Davidson County Comm
Coll (NC)
De Anza Coll (CA)

DeKalb Tech Coll (GA)
Draughons Jr Coll (KY)
ECPI Tech Coll (VA)
El Camino Coll (CA)
El Centro Coll (TX)
Everest Coll, Phoenix (AZ)
Everett Comm Coll (WA)
Florida Metropolitan
U–Orange Park
Campus (FL)
Florida National Coll (FL)
Forrest Jr Coll (SC)
Forsyth Tech Comm
Coll (NC)
Fresno City Coll (CA)
George C. Wallace Comm
Coll (AL)
Gretna Career Coll (LA)
Grossmont Coll (CA)
Guilford Tech Comm
Coll (NC)
Gulf Coast Coll (FL)
Gwinnett Tech Coll (GA)
Hamilton Coll, Council
Bluffs (IA)
Harper Coll (IL)
H. Councill Trenholm State
Tech Coll (AL)
Henry Ford Comm
Coll (MI)
Heritage Coll (NV)
Herzing Coll (MN)
Hesser Coll (NH)
High-Tech Inst (FL)
High-Tech Inst (MN)
High-Tech Inst (MO)
High-Tech Inst (NV)
High-Tech Inst,
Memphis (TN)
High-Tech Inst,
Nashville (TN)
Hocking Coll (OH)
Indiana Business Coll,
Anderson (IN)
Indiana Business Coll,
Columbus (IN)
Indiana Business Coll,
Evansville (IN)
Indiana Business Coll, Fort
Wayne (IN)
Indiana Business Coll,
Indianapolis (IN)
Indiana Business Coll,
Indianapolis (IN)
Indiana Business Coll,
Lafayette (IN)
Indiana Business Coll,
Marion (IN)
Indiana Business Coll,
Terre Haute (IN)
Indiana Business Coll-
Medical (IN)
International Business Coll,
Fort Wayne (IN)
Iowa Lakes Comm
Coll (IA)
James Sprunt Comm
Coll (NC)
Jefferson Comm Coll (OH)
Johnston Comm Coll (NC)
Kaplan U (IA)
Katharine Gibbs
School (PA)
Keiser Career Coll -
Greenacres (FL)
Kennebec Valley Comm
Coll (ME)
Kirkwood Comm Coll (IA)
Lake Tahoe Comm
Coll (CA)
Lansing Comm Coll (MI)
Laredo Comm Coll (TX)
Laurel Business Inst (PA)
LDS Business Coll (UT)
Lehigh Carbon Comm
Coll (PA)
Lenoir Comm Coll (NC)
Linn-Benton Comm
Coll (OR)
Lower Columbia Coll (WA)
Macomb Comm Coll (MI)
Marshall Comm and Tech
Coll (WV)
Martin Comm Coll (NC)
Massasoit Comm
Coll (MA)
Merced Coll (CA)
Miami Dade Coll (FL)
Midlands Tech Coll (SC)
Miller-Motte Tech Coll,
Clarksville (TN)
Minnesota School of
Business–Richfield (MN)
Minot State U–Bottineau
Campus (ND)

Mohawk Valley Comm
Coll (NY)
Monterey Peninsula
Coll (CA)
Mountain State Coll (WV)
Mt. Hood Comm Coll (OR)
Mount Wachusett Comm
Coll (MA)
National Inst of
Technology (OH)
New England Inst of
Technology (RI)
New Mexico Jr Coll (NM)
Niagara County Comm
Coll (NY)
North Central Missouri
Coll (MO)
Northeast State Tech
Comm Coll (TN)
North Iowa Area Comm
Coll (IA)
North Seattle Comm
Coll (WA)
Northwestern Connecticut
Comm Coll (CT)
Northwest KansasTech
Coll (KS)
Oakland Comm Coll (MI)
Ohlone Coll (CA)
Olympic Coll (WA)
Orange Coast Coll (CA)
Pace Inst (PA)
Pamlico Comm Coll (NC)
Pasadena City Coll (CA)
Pioneer Pacific Coll,
Wilsonville (OR)
Provo Coll (UT)
Quinebaug Valley Comm
Coll (CT)
Renton Tech Coll (WA)
Rockford Business
Coll (IL)
Salt Lake Comm Coll (UT)
San Antonio Coll (TX)
Santa Ana Coll (CA)
Shasta Coll (CA)
Skagit Valley Coll (WA)
Southeastern Comm Coll,
North Campus (IA)
Southern Maine Comm
Coll (ME)
Southern State Comm
Coll (OH)
South Piedmont Comm
Coll (NC)
Springfield Tech Comm
Coll (MA)
Stanly Comm Coll (NC)
Stark State Coll of
Technology (OH)
Suffolk County Comm
Coll (NY)
Technology Education
Coll (OH)
Tidewater Tech (VA)
Tri-County Comm
Coll (NC)
Trocaire Coll (NY)
Tulsa Comm Coll (OK)
Union County Coll (NJ)
U of Alaska Southeast,
Sitka Campus (AK)
Vatterott Coll, Kansas
City (MO)
Vatterott Coll (TN)
Ventura Coll (CA)
Wallace State Comm
Coll (AL)
Wayne Comm Coll (NC)
Wenatchee Valley
Coll (WA)
Western Career Coll,
Pleasant Hill (CA)
Western Career Coll,
Sacramento (CA)
Western Career Coll, San
Leandro (CA)
Western Piedmont Comm
Coll (NC)
Western Wyoming Comm
Coll (WY)
West Valley Coll (CA)
York Tech Coll (SC)
Zane State Coll (OH)

Medical/Health Management and Clinical Assistant
Oklahoma State U,
Oklahoma City (OK)
Savannah River Coll (GA)

Medical Insurance Coding
Alexandria Tech Coll (MN)
Antonelli Coll,
Hattiesburg (MS)
Cambridge Coll (CO)

Career Training Academy,
Monroeville (PA)
Heritage Coll (NV)
Herzing Coll (MN)
Indiana Business Coll,
Evansville (IN)
Indiana Business Coll,
Indianapolis (IN)
Indiana Business Coll,
Indianapolis (IN)
Indiana Business Coll,
Lafayette (IN)
Indiana Business Coll,
Marion (IN)
Indiana Business Coll-
Medical (IN)
Keiser Career Coll -
Greenacres (FL)
Kilian Comm Coll (SD)
LDS Business Coll (UT)
Minot State U–Bottineau
Campus (ND)
Springfield Tech Comm
Coll (MA)

Medical Insurance/ Medical Billing
Allied Coll (MO)
Central Florida Coll, Winter
Park (FL)
Gretna Career Coll (LA)
High-Tech Inst (FL)
High-Tech Inst (MN)
High-Tech Inst (MO)
High-Tech Inst (NV)
High-Tech Inst,
Memphis (TN)
High-Tech Inst,
Nashville (TN)
Indiana Business Coll,
Anderson (IN)
Indiana Business Coll,
Columbus (IN)
Indiana Business Coll,
Evansville (IN)
Indiana Business Coll, Fort
Wayne (IN)
Indiana Business Coll,
Indianapolis (IN)
Indiana Business Coll,
Lafayette (IN)
Indiana Business Coll,
Terre Haute (IN)
Indiana Business Coll-
Medical (IN)
Keiser Career Coll -
Greenacres (FL)
Savannah River Coll (GA)
Taylor Business Inst (IL)
Virginia Coll at Austin (TX)
Western Career Coll,
Pleasant Hill (CA)

Medical Laboratory Technology
Athens Tech Coll (GA)
Cecil Comm Coll (MD)
Central Georgia Tech
Coll (GA)
Central Maine Comm
Coll (ME)
Chattahoochee Tech
Coll (GA)
Chippewa Valley Tech
Coll (WI)
DeKalb Tech Coll (GA)
Flint River Tech Coll (GA)
Frederick Comm Coll (MD)
Indiana Business Coll,
Indianapolis (IN)
Iowa Lakes Comm
Coll (IA)
ITT Tech Inst, Tucson (AZ)
ITT Tech Inst,
Anaheim (CA)
ITT Tech Inst, Lathrop (CA)
ITT Tech Inst, Oxnard (CA)
ITT Tech Inst (CO)
ITT Tech Inst, Fort
Lauderdale (FL)
ITT Tech Inst, Miami (FL)
ITT Tech Inst,
Louisville (KY)
ITT Tech Inst, Arnold (MO)
ITT Tech Inst (NV)
ITT Tech Inst (NM)
ITT Tech Inst,
Norwood (OH)
ITT Tech Inst,
Strongsville (OH)
ITT Tech Inst, Bothell (WA)
ITT Tech Inst,
Spokane (WA)
ITT Tech Inst,
Greenfield (WI)
Lanier Tech Coll (GA)

Madison Area Tech
Coll (WI)
Minnesota State Comm
and Tech Coll–Fergus
Falls (MN)
Mohawk Valley Comm
Coll (NY)
North Georgia Tech
Coll (GA)
North Hennepin Comm
Coll (MN)
Northwest-Shoals Comm
Coll (AL)
The Ohio State U Ag Tech
Inst (OH)
Rose State Coll (OK)
Schoolcraft Coll (MI)
Southeastern Tech
Coll (GA)
Southwest Georgia Tech
Coll (GA)
Valdosta Tech Coll (GA)
West Central Tech
Coll (GA)

Medical Office
Assistant
Alpena Comm Coll (MI)
Asnuntuck Comm
Coll (CT)
City Coll, Fort
Lauderdale (FL)
City Coll, Gainesville (FL)
City Coll, Miami (FL)
Clovis Comm Coll (NM)
Commonwealth Tech
Inst (PA)
Delta School of Business
& Technology (LA)
Harrisburg Area Comm
Coll (PA)
Indiana Business Coll,
Muncie (IN)
Iowa Lakes Comm
Coll (IA)
Keiser U, Miami (FL)
LDS Business Coll (UT)
Rasmussen Coll Brooklyn
Park (MN)
Vatterott Coll, Oklahoma
City (OK)
Virginia Coll at Austin (TX)
Western Wyoming Comm
Coll (WY)

Medical Office
Computer Specialist
Iowa Lakes Comm
Coll (IA)
Mississippi Delta Comm
Coll (MS)
Western Wyoming Comm
Coll (WY)

Medical Office
Management
Beaufort County Comm
Coll (NC)
Briarwood Coll (CT)
Brown Mackie Coll–
Hopkinsville (KY)
Brown Mackie Coll–
Kansas City (KS)
Brown Mackie Coll–
Merrillville (IN)
Brown Mackie Coll–
Salina (KS)
Career Tech Coll (LA)
Coll of Lake County (IL)
Columbus Tech Coll (GA)
Coosa Valley Tech
Coll (GA)
Eastern New Mexico
U–Roswell (NM)
Erie Comm Coll, North
Campus (NY)
Fayetteville Tech Comm
Coll (NC)
Forrest Jr Coll (SC)
Kilian Comm Coll (SD)
Klamath Comm Coll (OR)
Lamar Comm Coll (CO)
Midwest Inst,
Kirkwood (MO)
Minnesota School of
Business–Richfield (MN)
National Inst of
Technology (OH)
St. Cloud Tech Coll (MN)
Savannah River Coll (GA)
Spencerian Coll (KY)
The U of Akron–Wayne
Coll (OH)
U of Arkansas Comm Coll
at Batesville (AR)
Wayne Comm Coll (NC)
Western Career Coll,
Sacramento (CA)

Medical Radiologic
Technology
Albany Tech Coll (GA)
Allegany Coll of
Maryland (MD)
Asheville-Buncombe Tech
Comm Coll (NC)
Athens Tech Coll (GA)
Augusta Tech Coll (GA)
Broome Comm Coll (NY)
Burlington County
Coll (NJ)
Caldwell Comm Coll and
Tech Inst (NC)
Cambridge Coll (CO)
Cape Fear Comm
Coll (NC)
Capital Comm Coll (CT)
Catawba Valley Comm
Coll (NC)
Central Georgia Tech
Coll (GA)
Central Ohio Tech
Coll (OH)
Central Texas Coll (TX)
Century Coll (MN)
Chaffey Coll (CA)
Chattahoochee Tech
Coll (GA)
Chesapeake Coll (MD)
Chippewa Valley Tech
Coll (WI)
City Colls of Chicago,
Wilbur Wright
College (IL)
Cleveland Comm Coll (NC)
Clovis Comm Coll (NM)
Coastal Georgia Comm
Coll (GA)
Coll of DuPage (IL)
Coll of Lake County (IL)
Coll of Southern Idaho (ID)
Columbus Tech Coll (GA)
Comm Coll of Allegheny
County (PA)
Comm Coll of Rhode
Island (RI)
El Centro Coll (TX)
Elizabethtown Tech
Coll (KY)
Erie Comm Coll (NY)
Essex County Coll (NJ)
Eugenio María de Hostos
Comm Coll of the City
U of New York (NY)
Foothill Coll (CA)
Gadsden State Comm
Coll (AL)
Griffin Tech Coll (GA)
Gwinnett Tech Coll (GA)
Hagerstown Comm
Coll (MD)
Harrisburg Area Comm
Coll (PA)
Heart of Georgia Tech
Coll (GA)
High-Tech Inst (FL)
High-Tech Inst (MN)
High-Tech Inst,
Nashville (TN)
Houston Comm Coll
System (TX)
Hutchinson Comm Coll
and Area Vocational
School (KS)
Illinois Eastern Comm
Colls, Olney Central
College (IL)
Jackson State Comm
Coll (TN)
Jefferson Comm and Tech
Coll (KY)
Johnston Comm Coll (NC)
John Wood Comm Coll (IL)
Kellogg Comm Coll (MI)
Keystone Coll (PA)
Lamar Inst of
Technology (TX)
Lancaster General Coll of
Nursing & Health
Sciences (PA)
Lanier Tech Coll (GA)
Lansing Comm Coll (MI)
Lincoln Land Comm
Coll (IL)
Manatee Comm Coll (FL)
Marshall Comm and Tech
Coll (WV)
Massachusetts Bay Comm
Coll (MA)
Medical Careers Inst,
Newport News (VA)
Mercy Coll of Northwest
Ohio (OH)
Meridian Comm Coll (MS)
Middle Georgia Tech
Coll (GA)
Midlands Tech Coll (SC)

Mississippi Delta Comm
Coll (MS)
Mohawk Valley Comm
Coll (NY)
Montcalm Comm Coll (MI)
Montgomery Coll (MD)
Montgomery County
Comm Coll (PA)
Moraine Valley Comm
Coll (IL)
Mott Comm Coll (MI)
Nassau Comm Coll (NY)
New York City Coll of
Technology of the City
U of New York (NY)
North Arkansas Coll (AR)
North Country Comm
Coll (NY)
Northern New Mexico
Coll (NM)
North Metro Tech Coll (GA)
North Shore Comm
Coll (MA)
Oakland Comm Coll (MI)
Owensboro Comm and
Tech Coll (KY)
Parkland Coll (IL)
Passaic County Comm
Coll (NJ)
Penn State New
Kensington (PA)
Penn State Schuylkill (PA)
Piedmont Tech Coll (SC)
Pima Comm Coll (AZ)
Pueblo Comm Coll (CO)
Riverland Comm Coll (MN)
Rose State Coll (OK)
St. Philip's Coll (TX)
Santa Barbara City
Coll (CA)
Scott Comm Coll (IA)
Southeastern Tech
Coll (GA)
Southeast Kentucky Comm
and Tech Coll (KY)
Southeast Missouri
Hospital Coll of Nursing
and Health
Sciences (MO)
Southern U at
Shreveport (LA)
Southwestern Comm
Coll (NC)
Southwest Georgia Tech
Coll (GA)
Springfield Tech Comm
Coll (MA)
Union County Coll (NJ)
Universidad Central del
Caribe (PR)
Valdosta Tech Coll (GA)
Valencia Comm Coll (FL)
Volunteer State Comm
Coll (TN)
West Central Tech
Coll (GA)
West Georgia Tech
Coll (GA)
Wor-Wic Comm Coll (MD)
York Tech Coll (SC)

Medical Reception
Alexandria Tech Coll (MN)
Iowa Lakes Comm
Coll (IA)
Lower Columbia Coll (WA)

Medical Staff Services
Technology
Front Range Comm
Coll (CO)

Medical Transcription
Alexandria Tech Coll (MN)
Antonelli Coll,
Hattiesburg (MS)
Black Hawk Coll,
Moline (IL)
Central Arizona Coll (AZ)
El Centro Coll (TX)
Elgin Comm Coll (IL)
Iowa Lakes Comm
Coll (IA)
Kaplan U (IA)
Kilian Comm Coll (SD)
Laurel Business Inst (PA)
LDS Business Coll (UT)
Lehigh Carbon Comm
Coll (PA)
Lower Columbia Coll (WA)
Marshall Comm and Tech
Coll (WV)
Minot State U–Bottineau
Campus (ND)
Mountain State Coll (WV)
Northern Essex Comm
Coll (MA)
Oakland Comm Coll (MI)
Rasmussen Coll Brooklyn
Park (MN)

Rockford Business
Coll (IL)
Saint Charles Comm
Coll (MO)
South Coast Coll (CA)
Southeast Tech Inst (SD)
Tri-State Business
Inst (PA)
Ventura Coll (CA)

Mental and Social
Health Services And
Allied Professions
Related
Broome Comm Coll (NY)
Oakland Comm Coll (MI)
Waukesha County Tech
Coll (WI)

Mental
Health/Rehabilitation
Anne Arundel Comm
Coll (MD)
Blinn Coll (TX)
Chief Dull Knife Coll (MT)
City Coll, Gainesville (FL)
City Colls of Chicago,
Harold Washington
College (IL)
City Colls of Chicago,
Kennedy-King
College (IL)
Comm Coll of
Philadelphia (PA)
Elgin Comm Coll (IL)
Fiorello H. LaGuardia
Comm Coll of the City
U of New York (NY)
Gateway Comm Coll (CT)
Hopkinsville Comm
Coll (KY)
Housatonic Comm
Coll (CT)
Houston Comm Coll
System (TX)
Kingsborough Comm Coll
of the City U of New
York (NY)
Lenoir Comm Coll (NC)
Los Angeles City Coll (CA)
Macomb Comm Coll (MI)
McLennan Comm
Coll (TX)
Metropolitan Comm
Coll (NE)
Middlesex Comm Coll (CT)
Mohawk Valley Comm
Coll (NY)
Mt. Hood Comm Coll (OR)
Mt. San Antonio Coll (CA)
Naugatuck Valley Comm
Coll (CT)
New Hampshire Tech
Inst (NH)
North Country Comm
Coll (NY)
Northern Essex Comm
Coll (MA)
North Shore Comm
Coll (MA)
Oxnard Coll (CA)
Pierce Coll (WA)
Porterville Coll (CA)
Ridgewater Coll (MN)
San Bernardino Valley
Coll (CA)
Sandhills Comm Coll (NC)
Southern U at
Shreveport (LA)
South Plains Coll (TX)
Southwestern Comm
Coll (NC)
U of Alaska, Prince William
Sound Comm Coll (AK)
Virginia Western Comm
Coll (VA)
Wallace State Comm
Coll (AL)
Zane State Coll (OH)

Merchandising
Coll of DuPage (IL)
Cuyahoga Comm
Coll (OH)
North Central Texas
Coll (TX)

Merchandising, Sales,
and Marketing
Operations Related
(General)
Broome Comm Coll (NY)
Iowa Lakes Comm
Coll (IA)
Minnesota State Comm
and Tech Coll–Fergus
Falls (MN)
Southwestern Michigan
Coll (MI)

Metal and Jewelry
Arts
Coll of The Albemarle (NC)
Mohave Comm Coll (AZ)
Monterey Peninsula
Coll (CA)
Oklahoma State U,
Okmulgee (OK)
Pasadena City Coll (CA)
Pueblo Comm Coll (CO)
San Antonio Coll (TX)

Metallurgical
Technology
Brigham Young U –
Idaho (ID)
Don Bosco Tech Inst (CA)
Elgin Comm Coll (IL)
Linn-Benton Comm
Coll (OR)
Macomb Comm Coll (MI)
Mohawk Valley Comm
Coll (NY)
Murray State Coll (OK)
Penn State DuBois (PA)
Penn State Fayette, The
Eberly Campus (PA)
Penn State Hazleton (PA)
Penn State New
Kensington (PA)
Penn State Schuylkill (PA)
Penn State Shenango (PA)
Penn State Wilkes-
Barre (PA)
Penn State York (PA)
Ridgewater Coll (MN)
Schoolcraft Coll (MI)

Meteorology
West Virginia State Comm
and Tech Coll (WV)

Mexican-American
Studies
Pasadena City Coll (CA)

Middle School
Education
Arkansas State
U–Mountain
Home (AR)
Arkansas State
U–Newport (AR)
Miami Dade Coll (FL)
North Arkansas Coll (AR)
Ozarka Coll (AR)
South Georgia Coll (GA)

Military Studies
Barton County Comm
Coll (KS)

Military Technologies
Calhoun Comm Coll (AL)
Cochise Coll, Douglas (AZ)

Mining Technology
Eastern Arizona Coll (AZ)
Illinois Eastern Comm
Colls, Wabash Valley
College (IL)
Southwest Virginia Comm
Coll (VA)
Western Wyoming Comm
Coll (WY)

Modern Languages
Amarillo Coll (TX)
Barton County Comm
Coll (KS)
Cape Cod Comm
Coll (MA)
Citrus Coll (CA)
City Colls of Chicago,
Harry S. Truman
College (IL)
City Colls of Chicago,
Richard J. Daley
College (IL)
City Colls of Chicago,
Wilbur Wright
College (IL)
Everett Comm Coll (WA)
Imperial Valley Coll (CA)
Odessa Coll (TX)
Oklahoma City Comm
Coll (OK)
Palo Alto Coll (TX)
Pasadena City Coll (CA)
Rose State Coll (OK)
San Diego City Coll (CA)
Santa Ana Coll (CA)
Santiago Canyon Coll (CA)
Tyler Jr Coll (TX)

Motorcycle
Maintenance and
Repair Technology
Iowa Lakes Comm
Coll (IA)

Multi-/Interdisciplinary
Studies Related
Arkansas State
U–Newport (AR)
Central Carolina Tech
Coll (SC)
Eastern West Virginia
Comm and Tech
Coll (WV)
Kaplan U (IA)
Laramie County Comm
Coll (WY)
Linn-Benton Comm
Coll (OR)
Marshall Comm and Tech
Coll (WV)
Midlands Tech Coll (SC)
Northwest-Shoals Comm
Coll (AL)
Waukesha County Tech
Coll (WI)
York Tech Coll (SC)

Music
Allen County Comm
Coll (KS)
Amarillo Coll (TX)
Angelina Coll (TX)
Anne Arundel Comm
Coll (MD)
Anoka-Ramsey Comm
Coll (MN)
Anoka-Ramsey Comm
Coll, Cambridge
Campus (MN)
Antelope Valley Coll (CA)
Arizona Western Coll (AZ)
Bakersfield Coll (CA)
Barton County Comm
Coll (KS)
Bergen Comm Coll (NJ)
Berkshire Comm Coll (MA)
Blinn Coll (TX)
Brigham Young U –
Idaho (ID)
Bucks County Comm
Coll (PA)
Burlington County
Coll (NJ)
Caldwell Comm Coll and
Tech Inst (NC)
Calhoun Comm Coll (AL)
Cañada Coll (CA)
Cape Cod Comm
Coll (MA)
Carroll Comm Coll (MD)
Cedar Valley Coll (TX)
Centralia Coll (WA)
Central Piedmont Comm
Coll (NC)
Central Texas Coll (TX)
Central Wyoming
Coll (WY)
Cerritos Coll (CA)
Chaffey Coll (CA)
Chesapeake Coll (MD)
Citrus Coll (CA)
City Coll of San
Francisco (CA)
City Colls of Chicago,
Harold Washington
College (IL)
City Colls of Chicago,
Olive-Harvey
College (IL)
City Colls of Chicago,
Richard J. Daley
College (IL)
City Colls of Chicago,
Wilbur Wright
College (IL)
Clarendon Coll (TX)
Coastal Bend Coll (TX)
Colby Comm Coll (KS)
Coll of Lake County (IL)
Coll of Marin (CA)
Coll of San Mateo (CA)
Coll of Southern Idaho (ID)
Coll of Southern
Maryland (MD)
Coll of The Albemarle (NC)
Coll of the Desert (CA)
Coll of the Mainland (TX)
Columbia Coll (CA)
Comm Coll of Allegheny
County (PA)
Comm Coll of
Philadelphia (PA)
Comm Coll of Rhode
Island (RI)
Comm Coll of Southern
Nevada (NV)
Contra Costa Coll (CA)
Cosumnes River Coll,
Sacramento (CA)
Crafton Hills Coll (CA)
Crowder Coll (MO)
Cypress Coll (CA)
De Anza Coll (CA)

Dixie State Coll of Utah (UT)
Dodge City Comm Coll (KS)
Eastern Arizona Coll (AZ)
El Camino Coll (CA)
Essex County Coll (NJ)
Everett Comm Coll (WA)
Finger Lakes Comm Coll (NY)
Foothill Coll (CA)
Fullerton Coll (CA)
Garrett Coll (MD)
Golden West Coll (CA)
Grand Rapids Comm Coll (MI)
Grayson County Coll (TX)
Grossmont Coll (CA)
Harper Coll (IL)
Harrisburg Area Comm Coll (PA)
Hillsborough Comm Coll (FL)
Holyoke Comm Coll (MA)
Howard Comm Coll (MD)
Illinois Eastern Comm Colls, Lincoln Trail College (IL)
Illinois Eastern Comm Colls, Olney Central College (IL)
Imperial Valley Coll (CA)
Iowa Lakes Comm Coll (IA)
Isothermal Comm Coll (NC)
Jones County Jr Coll (MS)
Kellogg Comm Coll (MI)
Kingsborough Comm Coll of the City U of New York (NY)
Kirkwood Comm Coll (IA)
Labette Comm Coll (KS)
Lake Tahoe Comm Coll (CA)
Laney Coll (CA)
Lansing Comm Coll (MI)
Laramie County Comm Coll (WY)
Lawson State Comm Coll (AL)
Lee Coll (TX)
Lincoln Land Comm Coll (IL)
Lorain County Comm Coll (OH)
Los Angeles City Coll (CA)
Los Angeles Mission Coll (CA)
Los Angeles Pierce Coll (CA)
Los Angeles Southwest Coll (CA)
Los Medanos Coll (CA)
Lower Columbia Coll (WA)
Manatee Comm Coll (FL)
McLennan Comm Coll (TX)
McNally Smith Coll of Music (MN)
Mendocino Coll (CA)
Merced Coll (CA)
Mesa Comm Coll (AZ)
Miami Dade Coll (FL)
Mississippi Delta Comm Coll (MS)
Mohave Comm Coll (AZ)
Monroe Comm Coll (NY)
Monterey Peninsula Coll (CA)
Moorpark Coll (CA)
Morton Coll (IL)
Napa Valley Coll (CA)
Naugatuck Valley Comm Coll (CT)
Navarro Coll (TX)
New Mexico Jr Coll (NM)
Niagara County Comm Coll (NY)
Northeast Comm Coll (NE)
Northeastern Jr Coll (CO)
Northern Essex Comm Coll (MA)
North Idaho Coll (ID)
North Seattle Comm Coll (WA)
Odessa Coll (TX)
Oklahoma City Comm Coll (OK)
Onondaga Comm Coll (NY)
Orange Coast Coll (CA)
Palm Beach Comm Coll (FL)
Palo Alto Coll (TX)
Pasadena City Coll (CA)
Pima Comm Coll (AZ)
Porterville Coll (CA)

Potomac State Coll of West Virginia U (WV)
Quincy Coll (MA)
Raritan Valley Comm Coll (NJ)
Ridgewater Coll (MN)
Rose State Coll (OK)
Roxbury Comm Coll (MA)
Sacramento City Coll (CA)
St. Catharine Coll (KY)
St. Louis Comm Coll at Florissant Valley (MO)
St. Philip's Coll (TX)
Salt Lake Comm Coll (UT)
San Bernardino Valley Coll (CA)
Sandhills Comm Coll (NC)
San Diego City Coll (CA)
San Joaquin Delta Coll (CA)
San Juan Coll (NM)
Santa Ana Coll (CA)
Santa Barbara City Coll (CA)
Santa Rosa Jr Coll (CA)
Santiago Canyon Coll (CA)
Shasta Coll (CA)
Sheridan Coll–Sheridan and Gillette (WY)
Skagit Valley Coll (WA)
Southeastern Comm Coll (NC)
South Plains Coll (TX)
Southwest Mississippi Comm Coll (MS)
Southwest Virginia Comm Coll (VA)
Spokane Falls Comm Coll (WA)
Suffolk County Comm Coll (NY)
Texarkana Coll (TX)
Three Rivers Comm Coll (MO)
Tidewater Comm Coll (VA)
Treasure Valley Comm Coll (OR)
Trinidad State Jr Coll (CO)
Tulsa Comm Coll (OK)
Tyler Jr Coll (TX)
Umpqua Comm Coll (OR)
Ventura Coll (CA)
Victor Valley Coll (CA)
Villa Maria Coll of Buffalo (NY)
Wallace State Comm Coll (AL)
Wenatchee Valley Coll (WA)
Western Wyoming Comm Coll (WY)
West Los Angeles Coll (CA)
West Valley Coll (CA)
Young Harris Coll (GA)
Yuba Coll (CA)

Musical Instrument Fabrication and Repair
Hartnell Coll (CA)
Minnesota State Coll–Southeast Tech (MN)
Orange Coast Coll (CA)
Queensborough Comm Coll of the City U of New York (NY)
Renton Tech Coll (WA)

Music Management and Merchandising
Century Coll (MN)
Collin County Comm Coll District (TX)
Houston Comm Coll System (TX)
Los Medanos Coll (CA)
McNally Smith Coll of Music (MN)
Northeast Comm Coll (NE)
Orange Coast Coll (CA)
Villa Maria Coll of Buffalo (NY)

Music Performance
Fresno City Coll (CA)
Macomb Comm Coll (MI)
Manatee Comm Coll (FL)
McNally Smith Coll of Music (MN)
Miami Dade Coll (FL)
Nassau Comm Coll (NY)
Northeast Comm Coll (NE)
Parkland Coll (IL)
Reedley Coll (CA)

Music Related
Madison Media Inst (WI)
Minnesota School of Business–Brooklyn Center (MN)

Minnesota School of Business–Plymouth (MN)
Minnesota School of Business–Richfield (MN)
Minnesota School of Business–St. Cloud (MN)
Minnesota School of Business–Shakopee (MN)
Young Harris Coll (GA)

Music Teacher Education
Amarillo Coll (TX)
Angelina Coll (TX)
Brigham Young U – Idaho (ID)
Coastal Bend Coll (TX)
Colby Comm Coll (KS)
Coll of Lake County (IL)
Dodge City Comm Coll (KS)
Frederick Comm Coll (MD)
Illinois Eastern Comm Colls, Lincoln Trail College (IL)
Illinois Eastern Comm Colls, Olney Central College (IL)
Iowa Lakes Comm Coll (IA)
Jones County Jr Coll (MS)
Manatee Comm Coll (FL)
Miami Dade Coll (FL)
Mississippi Delta Comm Coll (MS)
Northeast Comm Coll (NE)
Northeastern Jr Coll (CO)
North Idaho Coll (ID)
Northwest Mississippi Comm Coll (MS)
Parkland Coll (IL)
Potomac State Coll of West Virginia U (WV)
Roane State Comm Coll (TN)
Sandhills Comm Coll (NC)
Schoolcraft Coll (MI)
Southwest Mississippi Comm Coll (MS)
Treasure Valley Comm Coll (OR)
Tulsa Comm Coll (OK)
Umpqua Comm Coll (OR)
Wenatchee Valley Coll (WA)
Western Nebraska Comm Coll (NE)
Young Harris Coll (GA)

Music Theory and Composition
Houston Comm Coll System (TX)
Manatee Comm Coll (FL)

Music Therapy
Pasadena City Coll (CA)

Nail Technician and Manicurist
Clovis Comm Coll (NM)
Olympic Coll (WA)

Natural Resources and Conservation Related
Palau Comm Coll (Palau)

Natural Resources/ Conservation
Coll of Menominee Nation (WI)
Dixie State Coll of Utah (UT)
Finger Lakes Comm Coll (NY)
Fox Valley Tech Coll (WI)
Fulton-Montgomery Comm Coll (NY)
Grays Harbor Coll (WA)
Hocking Coll (OH)
Iowa Lakes Comm Coll (IA)
Itasca Comm Coll (MN)
Kirkwood Comm Coll (IA)
Minot State U–Bottineau Campus (ND)
Murray State Coll (OK)
Muscatine Comm Coll (IA)
Nebraska Coll of Tech Agriculture (NE)
Nebraska Indian Comm Coll (NE)
Niagara County Comm Coll (NY)
Santa Rosa Jr Coll (CA)
State U of New York Coll of Agriculture and Technology at Morrisville (NY)

Natural Resources Management
Finger Lakes Comm Coll (NY)
Hocking Coll (OH)
The Ohio State U Ag Tech Inst (OH)
Reedley Coll (CA)

Natural Resources Management and Policy
Central Carolina Tech Coll (SC)
Chief Dull Knife Coll (MT)
Coll of Lake County (IL)
Coll of the Desert (CA)
Columbia Coll (CA)
Dixie State Coll of Utah (UT)
Finger Lakes Comm Coll (NY)
Fort Belknap Coll (MT)
Garrett Coll (MD)
Hawkeye Comm Coll (IA)
Hocking Coll (OH)
Itasca Comm Coll (MN)
Nebraska Coll of Tech Agriculture (NE)
The Ohio State U Ag Tech Inst (OH)
Sacramento City Coll (CA)
Salish Kootenai Coll (MT)
San Joaquin Delta Coll (CA)
Santa Rosa Jr Coll (CA)
Shasta Coll (CA)
Southwestern Indian Polytechnic Inst (NM)
Spokane Comm Coll (WA)
State U of New York Coll of Agriculture and Technology at Morrisville (NY)
Treasure Valley Comm Coll (OR)
Trinidad State Jr Coll (CO)
Turtle Mountain Comm Coll (ND)
Ventura Coll (CA)
Zane State Coll (OH)

Natural Sciences
Amarillo Coll (TX)
Cabrillo Coll (CA)
Centralia Coll (WA)
Citrus Coll (CA)
Coll of Marin (CA)
Coll of Southern Idaho (ID)
Coll of the Canyons (CA)
Coll of the Mainland (TX)
Colorado Mountain Coll (CO)
Cypress Coll (CA)
Golden West Coll (CA)
Iowa Lakes Comm Coll (IA)
Lake Tahoe Comm Coll (CA)
Lassen Comm Coll District (CA)
Lee Coll (TX)
Merced Coll (CA)
Miami Dade Coll (FL)
Moorpark Coll (CA)
Naugatuck Valley Comm Coll (CT)
Northeastern Jr Coll (CO)
Ohlone Coll (CA)
Orange Coast Coll (CA)
Passaic County Comm Coll (NJ)
Porterville Coll (CA)
Quincy Coll (MA)
Sacramento City Coll (CA)
Salish Kootenai Coll (MT)
San Joaquin Delta Coll (CA)
Santiago Canyon Coll (CA)
Skagit Valley Coll (WA)
Umpqua Comm Coll (OR)
U of Pittsburgh at Titusville (PA)
U of Puerto Rico at Carolina (PR)
Victor Valley Coll (CA)
Young Harris Coll (GA)

Neuroscience
Pamlico Comm Coll (NC)

Nonprofit Management
Miami Dade Coll (FL)

Nuclear Engineering
Itasca Comm Coll (MN)

Nuclear Engineering Technology
Flint Hills Tech Coll (KS)

Nuclear Medical Technology
Amarillo Coll (TX)
Broward Comm Coll (FL)
Caldwell Comm Coll and Tech Inst (NC)
Chattanooga State Tech Comm Coll (TN)
Coll of DuPage (IL)
Comm Coll of Allegheny County (PA)
Fayetteville Tech Comm Coll (NC)
Forsyth Tech Comm Coll (NC)
Frederick Comm Coll (MD)
Gateway Comm Coll (CT)
Gloucester County Coll (NJ)
Harrisburg Area Comm Coll (PA)
Hillsborough Comm Coll (FL)
Houston Comm Coll System (TX)
Howard Comm Coll (MD)
Jefferson Comm and Tech Coll (KY)
Keiser U, Miami (FL)
Kettering Coll of Medical Arts (OH)
Lorain County Comm Coll (OH)
Los Angeles City Coll (CA)
Miami Dade Coll (FL)
Midlands Tech Coll (SC)
Oakland Comm Coll (MI)
Orange Coast Coll (CA)
Southeast Tech Inst (SD)
Springfield Tech Comm Coll (MA)
Union County Coll (NJ)
West Virginia State Comm and Tech Coll (WV)

Nuclear/Nuclear Power Technology
Allen County Comm Coll (KS)
Chattanooga State Tech Comm Coll (TN)
Columbia Basin Coll (WA)
Georgia Military Coll (GA)
Joliet Jr Coll (IL)
Three Rivers Comm Coll (CT)
Westmoreland County Comm Coll (PA)

Nursing Assistant/ Aide and Patient Care Assistant
Alexandria Tech Coll (MN)
Allen County Comm Coll (KS)
Comm Coll of Allegheny County (PA)
Front Range Comm Coll (CO)
Gretna Career Coll (LA)
Laramie County Comm Coll (WY)
Lee Coll (TX)
Lower Columbia Coll (WA)
North Iowa Area Comm Coll (IA)
Sandhills Comm Coll (NC)
Trinidad State Jr Coll (CO)
Western Wyoming Comm Coll (WY)

Nursing (Licensed Practical/Vocational Nurse Training)
Alexandria Tech Coll (MN)
Alpena Comm Coll (MI)
Amarillo Coll (TX)
Angelina Coll (TX)
Arizona Western Coll (AZ)
Athens Tech Coll (GA)
ATS Inst of Technology (OH)
Bainbridge Coll (GA)
Big Bend Comm Coll (WA)
Bismarck State Coll (ND)
Black Hawk Coll, Moline (IL)
Central Arizona Coll (AZ)
Central Comm Coll–Columbus Campus (NE)
Central Comm Coll–Grand Island Campus (NE)
Centralia Coll (WA)
Central Oregon Comm Coll (OR)
Central Piedmont Comm Coll (NC)
Central Texas Coll (TX)

Citrus Coll (CA)
City Coll of San Francisco (CA)
Clark State Comm Coll (OH)
Clinton Comm Coll (IA)
Coahoma Comm Coll (MS)
Coastal Bend Coll (TX)
Colby Comm Coll (KS)
Coll of Menominee Nation (WI)
Coll of Southern Maryland (MD)
Coll of The Albemarle (NC)
Coll of the Canyons (CA)
Colorado Mountain Coll (CO)
Comm Coll of Allegheny County (PA)
Comm Coll of Beaver County (PA)
Comm Coll of Southern Nevada (NV)
Contra Costa Coll (CA)
De Anza Coll (CA)
Dodge City Comm Coll (KS)
Elaine P. Nunez Comm Coll (LA)
El Camino Coll (CA)
El Centro Coll (TX)
Elgin Comm Coll (IL)
Eugenio María de Hostos Comm Coll of the City U of New York (NY)
Everett Comm Coll (WA)
Flint Hills Tech Coll (KS)
Fort Berthold Comm Coll (ND)
Fresno City Coll (CA)
George C. Wallace Comm Coll (AL)
Gordon Coll (GA)
Grand Rapids Comm Coll (MI)
Gulf Coast Coll (FL)
Harper Coll (IL)
Hocking Coll (OH)
Hopkinsville Comm Coll (KY)
Howard Comm Coll (MD)
Illinois Eastern Comm Colls, Olney Central College (IL)
Imperial Valley Coll (CA)
Isothermal Comm Coll (NC)
Itasca Comm Coll (MN)
James H. Faulkner State Comm Coll (AL)
Jefferson Comm Coll (NY)
Jones County Jr Coll (MS)
Keiser Career Coll - Greenacres (FL)
Kellogg Comm Coll (MI)
Kirkwood Comm Coll (IA)
Kirtland Comm Coll (MI)
Lamar Comm Coll (CO)
Lansing Comm Coll (MI)
Lassen Comm Coll District (CA)
Lee Coll (TX)
Lehigh Carbon Comm Coll (PA)
Lower Columbia Coll (WA)
Merced Coll (CA)
Metropolitan Comm Coll (NE)
Midlands Tech Coll (SC)
Mid-Plains Comm Coll, North Platte (NE)
Minnesota State Coll–Southeast Tech (MN)
Minnesota State Comm and Tech Coll–Fergus Falls (MN)
Minot State U–Bottineau Campus (ND)
Mission Coll (CA)
Mount Wachusett Comm Coll (MA)
Muscatine Comm Coll (IA)
Navarro Coll (TX)
Neosho County Comm Coll (KS)
New Mexico Jr Coll (NM)
New River Comm Coll (VA)
Northeast Comm Coll (NE)
Northeastern Jr Coll (CO)
North Idaho Coll (ID)
North Iowa Area Comm Coll (IA)
Northland Comm and Tech Coll–Thief River Falls (MN)
North Seattle Comm Coll (WA)

Northwest Iowa Comm Coll (IA)
Northwest Mississippi Comm Coll (MS)
Northwest-Shoals Comm Coll (AL)
Oakland Comm Coll (MI)
Olympic Coll (WA)
Ouachita Tech Coll (AR)
Pasadena City Coll (CA)
Platt Coll, Moore (OK)
Platt Coll, Tulsa (OK)
Porterville Coll (CA)
Rasmussen Coll Brooklyn Park (MN)
Ridgewater Coll (MN)
Riverside Comm Coll District (CA)
Sacramento City Coll (CA)
St. Cloud Tech Coll (MN)
St. Philip's Coll (TX)
Sampson Comm Coll (NC)
Sandhills Comm Coll (NC)
San Diego City Coll (CA)
San Joaquin Delta Coll (CA)
Santa Barbara City Coll (CA)
Scott Comm Coll (IA)
Skagit Valley Coll (WA)
Southeastern Comm Coll, North Campus (IA)
Southeastern Comm Coll, South Campus (IA)
Southern Maine Comm Coll (ME)
South Plains Coll (TX)
Southwestern Comm Coll (NC)
Spokane Comm Coll (WA)
State Fair Comm Coll (MO)
Surry Comm Coll (NC)
Temple Coll (TX)
Texarkana Coll (TX)
Trinidad State Jr Coll (CO)
Tyler Jr Coll (TX)
Union County Coll (NJ)
U of Arkansas Comm Coll at Morrilton (AR)
The U of Montana-Helena Coll of Technology (MT)
Vernon Coll (TX)
Wallace State Comm Coll (AL)
Washington State Comm Coll (OH)
Wenatchee Valley Coll (WA)
Western Texas Coll (TX)
Western Wyoming Comm Coll (WY)
Westmoreland County Comm Coll (PA)
West Shore Comm Coll (MI)
York Tech Coll (SC)
Yuba Coll (CA)

Nursing (Registered Nurse Training)
Alamance Comm Coll (NC)
Allegany Coll of Maryland (MD)
Alpena Comm Coll (MI)
Amarillo Coll (TX)
Angelina Coll (TX)
Anne Arundel Comm Coll (MD)
Anoka-Ramsey Comm Coll (MN)
Anoka-Ramsey Comm Coll, Cambridge Campus (MN)
Antelope Valley Coll (CA)
Arizona Western Coll (AZ)
Arkansas State U–Newport (AR)
Asheville-Buncombe Tech Comm Coll (NC)
Ashland Comm and Tech Coll (KY)
Athens Tech Coll (GA)
Bainbridge Coll (GA)
Bakersfield Coll (CA)
Baltimore City Comm Coll (MD)
Barton County Comm Coll (KS)
Beaufort County Comm Coll (NC)
Bergen Comm Coll (NJ)
Berkshire Comm Coll (MA)
Big Bend Comm Coll (WA)
Bishop State Comm Coll (AL)
Black Hawk Coll, Moline (IL)
Bladen Comm Coll (NC)

Blinn Coll (TX)
Bowling Green State U–Firelands Coll (OH)
Brevard Comm Coll (FL)
Brigham Young U – Idaho (ID)
Brookhaven Coll (TX)
Broome Comm Coll (NY)
Broward Comm Coll (FL)
Brown Mackie Coll– Salina (KS)
Brunswick Comm Coll (NC)
Bucks County Comm Coll (PA)
Burlington County Coll (NJ)
Cabrillo Coll (CA)
Caldwell Comm Coll and Tech Inst (NC)
Calhoun Comm Coll (AL)
Cape Cod Comm Coll (MA)
Cape Fear Comm Coll (NC)
Capital Comm Coll (CT)
Carroll Comm Coll (MD)
Catawba Valley Comm Coll (NC)
Cecil Comm Coll (MD)
Central Arizona Coll (AZ)
Central Carolina Comm Coll (NC)
Central Carolina Tech Coll (SC)
Central Comm Coll–Grand Island Campus (NE)
Central Florida Comm Coll (FL)
Centralia Coll (WA)
Central Lakes Coll (MN)
Central Maine Comm Coll (ME)
Central New Mexico Comm Coll (NM)
Central Ohio Tech Coll (OH)
Central Oregon Comm Coll (OR)
Central Piedmont Comm Coll (NC)
Central Wyoming Coll (WY)
Centro de Estudios Multidisciplinarios (PR)
Century Coll (MN)
Cerritos Coll (CA)
Chaffey Coll (CA)
Chattanooga State Tech Comm Coll (TN)
Chipola Coll (FL)
Chippewa Valley Tech Coll (WI)
Cincinnati State Tech and Comm Coll (OH)
Cisco Jr Coll (TX)
City Coll of San Francisco (CA)
City Colls of Chicago, Harry S. Truman College (IL)
City Colls of Chicago, Kennedy-King College (IL)
City Colls of Chicago, Olive-Harvey College (IL)
City Colls of Chicago, Richard J. Daley College (IL)
Clackamas Comm Coll (OR)
Clarendon Coll (TX)
Clark Coll (WA)
Clark State Comm Coll (OH)
Clatsop Comm Coll (OR)
Cleveland Comm Coll (NC)
Cleveland State Comm Coll (TN)
Clinton Comm Coll (IA)
Clovis Comm Coll (NM)
Coastal Bend Coll (TX)
Coastal Carolina Comm Coll (NC)
Coastal Georgia Comm Coll (GA)
Cochise Coll, Douglas (AZ)
Cochise Coll, Sierra Vista (AZ)
Colby Comm Coll (KS)
Colegio Universitario de San Juan, San Juan (PR)
Colegio Universitario de San Juan, San Juan (PR)

Coll of DuPage (IL)
Coll of Lake County (IL)
Coll of Marin (CA)
Coll of Micronesia– FSM (FM)
Coll of San Mateo (CA)
Coll of Southern Idaho (ID)
Coll of Southern Maryland (MD)
Coll of The Albemarle (NC)
Coll of the Canyons (CA)
Coll of the Desert (CA)
Coll of the Mainland (TX)
Coll of the Marshall Islands (Marshall Islands)
Coll of the Redwoods (CA)
Collin County Comm Coll District (TX)
Colorado Mountain Coll (CO)
Columbia Basin Coll (WA)
Columbia-Greene Comm Coll (NY)
Columbus Tech Coll (GA)
Comm Coll of Allegheny County (PA)
Comm Coll of Beaver County (PA)
Comm Coll of Philadelphia (PA)
Comm Coll of Rhode Island (RI)
Comm Coll of Southern Nevada (NV)
Contra Costa Coll (CA)
Crowder Coll (MO)
Cuesta Coll (CA)
Cuyahoga Comm Coll (OH)
Cypress Coll (CA)
Dabney S. Lancaster Comm Coll (VA)
Davidson County Comm Coll (NC)
De Anza Coll (CA)
Dixie State Coll of Utah (UT)
Dodge City Comm Coll (KS)
Dorothea Hopfer School of Nursing at The Mount Vernon Hospital (NY)
Dyersburg State Comm Coll (TN)
East Central Coll (MO)
Eastern Arizona Coll (AZ)
Eastern New Mexico U–Roswell (NM)
Eastern Shore Comm Coll (VA)
East Georgia Coll (GA)
El Camino Coll (CA)
El Centro Coll (TX)
Elgin Comm Coll (IL)
Elizabethtown Tech Coll (KY)
Ellis Hospital School of Nursing (NY)
Erie Comm Coll (NY)
Erie Comm Coll, North Campus (NY)
Essex County Coll (NJ)
Eugenio María de Hostos Comm Coll of the City U of New York (NY)
Everett Comm Coll (WA)
Fayetteville Tech Comm Coll (NC)
Finger Lakes Comm Coll (NY)
Fiorello H. LaGuardia Comm Coll of the City U of New York (NY)
Florence-Darlington Tech Coll (SC)
Forsyth Tech Comm Coll (NC)
Fox Valley Tech Coll (WI)
Frederick Comm Coll (MD)
Fresno City Coll (CA)
Front Range Comm Coll (CO)
Fulton-Montgomery Comm Coll (NY)
Gadsden State Comm Coll (AL)
Gateway Tech Coll (WI)
Genesee Comm Coll (NY)
George C. Wallace Comm Coll (AL)
Georgia Highlands Coll (GA)
Germanna Comm Coll (VA)
Gloucester County Coll (NJ)
Golden West Coll (CA)
Gordon Coll (GA)

Grand Rapids Comm Coll (MI)
Grays Harbor Coll (WA)
Grayson County Coll (TX)
Great Basin Coll (NV)
Greenville Tech Coll (SC)
Grossmont Coll (CA)
Guilford Tech Comm Coll (NC)
Hagerstown Comm Coll (MD)
Harper Coll (IL)
Harrisburg Area Comm Coll (PA)
Hartnell Coll (CA)
Hawkeye Comm Coll (IA)
Helene Fuld Coll of Nursing of North General Hospital (NY)
Henry Ford Comm Coll (MI)
Hesston Coll (KS)
Hillsborough Comm Coll (FL)
Hocking Coll (OH)
Holyoke Comm Coll (MA)
Hopkinsville Comm Coll (KY)
Housatonic Comm Coll (CT)
Houston Comm Coll System (TX)
Howard Comm Coll (MD)
Hutchinson Comm Coll and Area Vocational School (KS)
Illinois Eastern Comm Colls, Frontier Community College (IL)
Illinois Eastern Comm Colls, Olney Central College (IL)
Illinois Valley Comm Coll (IL)
Imperial Valley Coll (CA)
International Inst of the Americas, Phoenix (AZ)
Inver Hills Comm Coll (MN)
Iowa Lakes Comm Coll (IA)
Jackson State Comm Coll (TN)
James H. Faulkner State Comm Coll (AL)
James Sprunt Comm Coll (NC)
Jamestown Comm Coll (NY)
Jefferson Comm and Tech Coll (KY)
Johnston Comm Coll (NC)
John Tyler Comm Coll (VA)
John Wood Comm Coll (IL)
Joliet Jr Coll (IL)
Jones County Jr Coll (MS)
Kankakee Comm Coll (IL)
Kansas City Kansas Comm Coll (KS)
Keiser U, Miami (FL)
Kellogg Comm Coll (MI)
Kennebec Valley Comm Coll (ME)
Kent State U, Ashtabula Campus (OH)
Kent State U, East Liverpool Campus (OH)
Kent State U, Tuscarawas Campus (OH)
Kettering Coll of Medical Arts (OH)
Kingsborough Comm Coll of the City U of New York (NY)
Kirkwood Comm Coll (IA)
Kirtland Comm Coll (MI)
Labette Comm Coll (KS)
Lake Land Coll (IL)
Lakeshore Tech Coll (WI)
Lake-Sumter Comm Coll (FL)
Lamar Comm Coll (CO)
Lancaster General Coll of Nursing & Health Sciences (PA)
Lansing Comm Coll (MI)
Laramie County Comm Coll (WY)
Laredo Comm Coll (TX)
Lassen Comm Coll District (CA)
Lawson State Comm Coll (AL)
Lehigh Carbon Comm Coll (PA)
Lenoir Comm Coll (NC)
Lincoln Land Comm Coll (IL)

Linn-Benton Comm Coll (OR)
Long Island Coll Hospital School of Nursing (NY)
Lorain County Comm Coll (OH)
Los Angeles Harbor Coll (CA)
Los Angeles Pierce Coll (CA)
Los Angeles Southwest Coll (CA)
Los Medanos Coll (CA)
Louisburg Coll (NC)
Louisiana State U at Eunice (LA)
Lower Columbia Coll (WA)
Macomb Comm Coll (MI)
Madison Area Tech Coll (WI)
Madisonville Comm Coll (KY)
Manatee Comm Coll (FL)
Maric Coll, San Diego (CA)
Massachusetts Bay Comm Coll (MA)
Massasoit Comm Coll (MA)
Maui Comm Coll (HI)
McLennan Comm Coll (TX)
Medical Careers Inst, Newport News (VA)
Memorial Hospital School of Nursing (NY)
Merced Coll (CA)
Mercy Coll of Northwest Ohio (OH)
Meridian Comm Coll (MS)
Mesa Comm Coll (AZ)
Metropolitan Comm Coll (NE)
Metropolitan Comm Coll–Penn Valley (MO)
Miami Dade Coll (FL)
Miami U–Middletown Campus (OH)
Middle Georgia Coll (GA)
Midlands Tech Coll (SC)
Mid-Plains Comm Coll, North Platte (NE)
Mid-State Tech Coll (WI)
Minneapolis Comm and Tech Coll (MN)
Minnesota State Coll– Southeast Tech (MN)
Minnesota State Comm and Tech Coll–Fergus Falls (MN)
Minot State U–Bottineau Campus (ND)
Mississippi Delta Comm Coll (MS)
Mississippi Gulf Coast Comm Coll (MS)
Missouri State U–West Plains (MO)
Moberly Area Comm Coll (MO)
Mohave Comm Coll (AZ)
Mohawk Valley Comm Coll (NY)
Monroe Comm Coll (NY)
Montcalm Comm Coll (MI)
Monterey Peninsula Coll (CA)
Montgomery Coll (MD)
Montgomery County Comm Coll (PA)
Moorpark Coll (CA)
Moraine Valley Comm Coll (IL)
Morton Coll (IL)
Motlow State Comm Coll (TN)
Mott Comm Coll (MI)
Mt. Hood Comm Coll (OR)
Mt. San Antonio Coll (CA)
Mount Wachusett Comm Coll (MA)
Murray State Coll (OK)
Muskegon Comm Coll (MI)
Napa Valley Coll (CA)
Nassau Comm Coll (NY)
National Inst of Technology (OH)
National Park Comm Coll (AR)
Naugatuck Valley Comm Coll (CT)
Navarro Coll (TX)
Neosho County Comm Coll (KS)
New Hampshire Comm Tech Coll, Manchester/ Stratham (NH)
New Hampshire Tech Inst (NH)

New Mexico Jr Coll (NM)
New Mexico State U– Alamogordo (NM)
New York City Coll of Technology of the City U of New York (NY)
Niagara County Comm Coll (NY)
Nicolet Area Tech Coll (WI)
Northampton County Area Comm Coll (PA)
North Arkansas Coll (AR)
North Central Kansas Tech Coll (KS)
North Central Michigan Coll (MI)
North Central Missouri Coll (MO)
North Central Texas Coll (TX)
North Country Comm Coll (NY)
Northeast Comm Coll (NE)
Northeastern Jr Coll (CO)
Northeast Iowa Comm Coll (IA)
Northern Essex Comm Coll (MA)
Northern Maine Comm Coll (ME)
Northern Marianas Coll (MP)
Northern Oklahoma Coll (OK)
North Hennepin Comm Coll (MN)
North Idaho Coll (ID)
North Iowa Area Comm Coll (IA)
Northland Comm and Tech Coll–Thief River Falls (MN)
North Seattle Comm Coll (WA)
North Shore Comm Coll (MA)
NorthWest Arkansas Comm Coll (AR)
Northwestern Tech Coll (GA)
Northwest Iowa Comm Coll (IA)
Northwest Mississippi Comm Coll (MS)
Northwest-Shoals Comm Coll (AL)
Oakland Comm Coll (MI)
Odessa Coll (TX)
Ohlone Coll (CA)
Oklahoma City Comm Coll (OK)
Oklahoma State U, Oklahoma City (OK)
Olympic Coll (WA)
Onondaga Comm Coll (NY)
Oregon Coast Comm Coll (OR)
Owensboro Comm and Tech Coll (KY)
Owens Comm Coll, Toledo (OH)
Palau Comm Coll (Palau)
Palm Beach Comm Coll (FL)
Panola Coll (TX)
Parkland Coll (IL)
Pasadena City Coll (CA)
Pasco-Hernando Comm Coll (FL)
Passaic County Comm Coll (NJ)
Pearl River Comm Coll (MS)
Peninsula Coll (WA)
Penn State Fayette, The Eberly Campus (PA)
Penn State Mont Alto (PA)
Penn State Worthington Scranton (PA)
Piedmont Tech Coll (SC)
Piedmont Virginia Comm Coll (VA)
Pima Comm Coll (AZ)
Polk Comm Coll (FL)
Provo Coll (UT)
Pueblo Comm Coll (CO)
Queensborough Comm Coll of the City U of New York (NY)
Quincy Coll (MA)
Rappahannock Comm Coll (VA)
Raritan Valley Comm Coll (NJ)
Redlands Comm Coll (OK)
Richland Comm Coll (IL)
Ridgewater Coll (MN)

Rio Hondo Coll (CA)
Riverland Comm Coll (MN)
Riverside Comm Coll District (CA)
Roane State Comm Coll (TN)
Robeson Comm Coll (NC)
Rogue Comm Coll (OR)
Rose State Coll (OK)
Roxbury Comm Coll (MA)
Sacramento City Coll (CA)
St. Catharine Coll (KY)
Saint Charles Comm Coll (MO)
St. Elizabeth Coll of Nursing (NY)
St. Louis Comm Coll at Florissant Valley (MO)
St. Luke's Coll (IA)
Saint Vincent Catholic Medical Centers School of Nursing (NY)
Salish Kootenai Coll (MT)
Salt Lake Comm Coll (UT)
Samaritan Hospital School of Nursing (NY)
Sampson Comm Coll (NC)
San Antonio Coll (TX)
San Bernardino Valley Coll (CA)
Sandhills Comm Coll (NC)
San Diego City Coll (CA)
San Joaquin Delta Coll (CA)
San Juan Coll (NM)
Santa Ana Coll (CA)
Santa Barbara City Coll (CA)
Santa Rosa Jr Coll (CA)
Schoolcraft Coll (MI)
Scott Comm Coll (IA)
Scottsdale Comm Coll (AZ)
Seminole Comm Coll (FL)
Seminole State Coll (OK)
Shasta Coll (CA)
Sheridan Coll–Sheridan and Gillette (WY)
Skagit Valley Coll (WA)
Southeastern Comm Coll (NC)
Southeastern Comm Coll, North Campus (IA)
Southeastern Comm Coll, South Campus (IA)
Southeast Kentucky Comm and Tech Coll (KY)
Southeast Missouri Hospital Coll of Nursing and Health Sciences (MO)
Southern Maine Comm Coll (ME)
Southern State Comm Coll (OH)
South Florida Comm Coll (FL)
South Georgia Coll (GA)
South Plains Coll (TX)
Southside Virginia Comm Coll (VA)
South Texas Coll (TX)
Southwestern Comm Coll (NC)
Southwestern Michigan Coll (MI)
Southwest Georgia Tech Coll (GA)
Southwest Mississippi Comm Coll (MS)
Southwest Virginia Comm Coll (VA)
Spokane Comm Coll (WA)
Springfield Tech Comm Coll (MA)
Stanly Comm Coll (NC)
Stark State Coll of Technology (OH)
State Fair Comm Coll (MO)
State U of New York Coll of Agriculture and Technology at Morrisville (NY)
State U of New York Coll of Technology at Alfred (NY)
State U of New York Coll of Technology at Canton (NY)
Suffolk County Comm Coll (NY)
Surry Comm Coll (NC)
Tallahassee Comm Coll (FL)
Temple Coll (TX)
Texarkana Coll (TX)

Three Rivers Comm Coll (CT)
Three Rivers Comm Coll (MO)
Tidewater Comm Coll (VA)
Tomball Coll (TX)
Tompkins Cortland Comm Coll (NY)
Treasure Valley Comm Coll (OR)
Tri-County Comm Coll (NC)
Trident Tech Coll (SC)
Trinidad State Jr Coll (CO)
Tri-State Business Inst (PA)
Trocaire Coll (NY)
Tulsa Comm Coll (OK)
Turtle Mountain Comm Coll (ND)
Tyler Jr Coll (TX)
Ulster County Comm Coll (NY)
Umpqua Comm Coll (OR)
Union County Coll (NJ)
U of Arkansas Comm Coll at Batesville (AR)
U of New Mexico–Gallup (NM)
U of Pittsburgh at Titusville (PA)
U of South Carolina Lancaster (SC)
Valencia Comm Coll (FL)
Ventura Coll (CA)
Vernon Coll (TX)
Victoria Coll (TX)
Victor Valley Coll (CA)
Virginia Highlands Comm Coll (VA)
Virginia Western Comm Coll (VA)
Wallace State Comm Coll (AL)
Washington State Comm Coll (OH)
Waukesha County Tech Coll (WI)
Wayne Comm Coll (NC)
Wenatchee Valley Coll (WA)
West Central Tech Coll (GA)
Westchester Comm Coll (NY)
Western Career Coll, Sacramento (CA)
Western Nebraska Comm Coll (NE)
Western Nevada Comm Coll (NV)
Western Piedmont Comm Coll (NC)
Westmoreland County Comm Coll (PA)
West Shore Comm Coll (MI)
West Virginia U at Parkersburg (WV)
Wilson Tech Comm Coll (NC)
Wor-Wic Comm Coll (MD)
Wytheville Comm Coll (VA)
York Tech Coll (SC)
Young Harris Coll (GA)
Yuba Coll (CA)

Nursing Related
Cincinnati State Tech and Comm Coll (OH)
Southeast Tech Inst (SD)
Western Career Coll, San Leandro (CA)

Nursing Science
Platt Coll, Tulsa (OK)

Nutrition Sciences
Mohawk Valley Comm Coll (NY)

Occupational Health and Industrial Hygiene
Niagara County Comm Coll (NY)

Occupational Safety and Health Technology
Central Maine Comm Coll (ME)
Clinton Comm Coll (IA)
Cossatot Comm Coll of the U of Arkansas (AR)
Houston Comm Coll System (TX)
Lamar Inst of Technology (TX)
Lanier Tech Coll (GA)

Las Positas Coll (CA)
Mt. San Antonio Coll (CA)
Muscatine Comm Coll (IA)
NorthWest Arkansas Comm Coll (AR)
Okefenokee Tech Coll (GA)
Oklahoma State U, Oklahoma City (OK)
Paradise Valley Comm Coll (AZ)
San Diego City Coll (CA)
Scott Comm Coll (IA)
Texas State Tech Coll–Marshall (TX)
Trinidad State Jr Coll (CO)
Tulsa Comm Coll (OK)
The U of Akron–Wayne Coll (OH)
Wallace State Comm Coll (AL)

Occupational Therapist Assistant
Allegany Coll of Maryland (MD)
Augusta Tech Coll (GA)
Briarwood Coll (CT)
Brown Mackie Coll–Fort Wayne (IN)
Brown Mackie Coll–South Bend (IN)
Cape Fear Comm Coll (NC)
Cincinnati State Tech and Comm Coll (OH)
Coll of DuPage (IL)
Comm Coll of Allegheny County (PA)
Comm Coll of Rhode Island (RI)
Eastern New Mexico U–Roswell (NM)
Erie Comm Coll, North Campus (NY)
Guilford Tech Comm Coll (NC)
Hocking Coll (OH)
Houston Comm Coll System (TX)
Jamestown Comm Coll (NY)
Keiser U, Miami (FL)
Kennebec Valley Comm Coll (ME)
Lehigh Carbon Comm Coll (PA)
Lincoln Land Comm Coll (IL)
Macomb Comm Coll (MI)
Madisonville Comm Coll (KY)
Manatee Comm Coll (FL)
Middle Georgia Coll (GA)
Midlands Tech Coll (SC)
Mott Comm Coll (MI)
New England Inst of Technology (RI)
Northwestern Tech Coll (GA)
Owens Comm Coll, Toledo (OH)
Ozarks Tech Comm Coll (MO)
Parkland Coll (IL)
Penn State DuBois (PA)
Penn State Mont Alto (PA)
Polk Comm Coll (FL)
Pueblo Comm Coll (CO)
Pulaski Tech Coll (AR)
St. Philip's Coll (TX)
Salt Lake Comm Coll (UT)
Schoolcraft Coll (MI)
Scott Comm Coll (IA)
Springfield Tech Comm Coll (MA)
Stanly Comm Coll (NC)
State U of New York Coll of Technology at Canton (NY)
Tulsa Comm Coll (OK)
Union County Coll (NJ)

Occupational Therapy
Allegany Coll of Maryland (MD)
Amarillo Coll (TX)
Barton County Comm Coll (KS)
Brigham Young U – Idaho (ID)
Chattanooga State Tech Comm Coll (TN)
City Colls of Chicago, Wilbur Wright College (IL)
Coastal Georgia Comm Coll (GA)
Coll of DuPage (IL)

Coll of Southern Idaho (ID)
Comm Coll of Southern Nevada (NV)
Everett Comm Coll (WA)
Fiorello H. LaGuardia Comm Coll of the City U of New York (NY)
Florence-Darlington Tech Coll (SC)
Fox Valley Tech Coll (WI)
Genesee Comm Coll (NY)
Georgia Highlands Coll (GA)
Grossmont Coll (CA)
Hillsborough Comm Coll (FL)
Kent State U, East Liverpool Campus (OH)
Keystone Coll (PA)
Kirkwood Comm Coll (IA)
Louisburg Coll (NC)
Madison Area Tech Coll (WI)
Manatee Comm Coll (FL)
Metropolitan Comm Coll–Penn Valley (MO)
Monterey Peninsula Coll (CA)
Morgan Comm Coll (CO)
Mt. Hood Comm Coll (OR)
Navarro Coll (TX)
North Central Texas Coll (TX)
North Shore Comm Coll (MA)
Oklahoma City Comm Coll (OK)
Ozarks Tech Comm Coll (MO)
Palm Beach Comm Coll (FL)
Pasadena City Coll (CA)
Pueblo Comm Coll (CO)
Roane State Comm Coll (TN)
Sacramento City Coll (CA)
Saint Charles Comm Coll (MO)
Santa Ana Coll (CA)
South Texas Coll (TX)
Stark State Coll of Technology (OH)
Tomball Coll (TX)
Trident Tech Coll (SC)
Tulsa Comm Coll (OK)
Wallace State Comm Coll (AL)
Zane State Coll (OH)

Oceanography (Chemical and Physical)
Everett Comm Coll (WA)
Fullerton Coll (CA)
Santa Rosa Jr Coll (CA)
Southern Maine Comm Coll (ME)
Tulsa Comm Coll (OK)

Office Management
Academy Coll (MN)
Alexandria Tech Coll (MN)
Alpena Comm Coll (MI)
Berkeley City Coll (CA)
Berkeley Coll-New York City Campus (NY)
Berkeley Coll-Westchester Campus (NY)
Big Bend Comm Coll (WA)
Calhoun Comm Coll (AL)
Career Tech Coll (LA)
Central Florida Comm Coll (FL)
Central Texas Coll (TX)
Chief Dull Knife Coll (MT)
Cincinnati State Tech and Comm Coll (OH)
Clackamas Comm Coll (OR)
Colegio Universitario de San Juan, San Juan (PR)
Coll of DuPage (IL)
Comm Coll of Allegheny County (PA)
Erie Comm Coll (NY)
Erie Comm Coll, North Campus (NY)
Erie Comm Coll, South Campus (NY)
Fayetteville Tech Comm Coll (NC)
Forrest Jr Coll (SC)
Grays Harbor Coll (WA)
Great Basin Coll (NV)
Howard Comm Coll (MD)
Iowa Lakes Comm Coll (IA)
Lake Land Coll (IL)

Lake-Sumter Comm Coll (FL)
Lee Coll (TX)
Lower Columbia Coll (WA)
Miami U–Middletown Campus (OH)
Mohawk Valley Comm Coll (NY)
Mott Comm Coll (MI)
Northwest Mississippi Comm Coll (MS)
Oakland Comm Coll (MI)
Olympic Coll (WA)
Peninsula Coll (WA)
Piedmont Tech Coll (SC)
Riverside Comm Coll District (CA)
Saint Charles Comm Coll (MO)
St. Cloud Tech Coll (MN)
Skagit Valley Coll (WA)
State U of New York Coll of Technology at Canton (NY)
Texas State Tech Coll–Marshall (TX)
Valencia Comm Coll (FL)
Virginia Coll at Austin (TX)

Office Occupations and Clerical Services
Alamance Comm Coll (NC)
Alexandria Tech Coll (MN)
El Centro Coll (TX)
Hillsborough Comm Coll (FL)
ICPR Jr Coll–Hato Rey Campus (PR)
Iowa Lakes Comm Coll (IA)
Laurel Business Inst (PA)
Lehigh Carbon Comm Coll (PA)
Minot State U–Bottineau Campus (ND)
Mohawk Valley Comm Coll (NY)
New Mexico State U–Alamogordo (NM)
North Country Comm Coll (NY)
Reedley Coll (CA)
Sitting Bull Coll (ND)
Spokane Falls Comm Coll (WA)
Terra State Comm Coll (OH)
The U of Montana-Helena Coll of Technology (MT)
West Virginia State Comm and Tech Coll (WV)
York Tech Coll (SC)

Operations Management
Alamance Comm Coll (NC)
Alexandria Tech Coll (MN)
Alpena Comm Coll (MI)
Asheville-Buncombe Tech Comm Coll (NC)
Bowling Green State U–Firelands Coll (OH)
Catawba Valley Comm Coll (NC)
Central Carolina Comm Coll (NC)
Cleveland Comm Coll (NC)
DeKalb Tech Coll (GA)
Fayetteville Tech Comm Coll (NC)
Gateway Tech Coll (WI)
Great Basin Coll (NV)
Johnston Comm Coll (NC)
Lee Coll (TX)
Lehigh Carbon Comm Coll (PA)
Macomb Comm Coll (MI)
Massasoit Comm Coll (MA)
Oakland Comm Coll (MI)
Remington Coll–Jacksonville Campus (FL)
South Piedmont Comm Coll (NC)
Stark State Coll of Technology (OH)
Waukesha County Tech Coll (WI)

Ophthalmic Laboratory Technology
DeKalb Tech Coll (GA)
Everett Comm Coll (WA)
Hillsborough Comm Coll (FL)
Hocking Coll (OH)
Los Angeles City Coll (CA)

Middlesex Comm Coll (CT)
New Hampshire Comm Tech Coll, Nashua/ Claremont (NH)
New York City Coll of Technology of the City U of New York (NY)
Pueblo Comm Coll (CO)
Raritan Valley Comm Coll (NJ)
Santa Rosa Jr Coll (CA)
Spokane Comm Coll (WA)
Tyler Jr Coll (TX)
Westmoreland County Comm Coll (PA)

Ophthalmic/Optometric Services
Howard Comm Coll (MD)

Ophthalmic Technology
Miami Dade Coll (FL)
Volunteer State Comm Coll (TN)

Optical Sciences
Puerto Rico Tech Jr Coll, San Juan (PR)

Opticianry
Arkansas State U–Mountain Home (AR)
Brown Mackie Coll–Cincinnati (OH)
Cuyahoga Comm Coll (OH)
DeKalb Tech Coll (GA)
Erie Comm Coll, North Campus (NY)
Essex County Coll (NJ)
Harrisburg Area Comm Coll (PA)
Ogeechee Tech Coll (GA)
Suffolk County Comm Coll (NY)

Optometric Technician
Barton County Comm Coll (KS)

Ornamental Horticulture
Antelope Valley Coll (CA)
Bakersfield Coll (CA)
Bergen Comm Coll (NJ)
Brigham Young U – Idaho (ID)
Cerritos Coll (CA)
City Coll of San Francisco (CA)
Clackamas Comm Coll (OR)
Coll of DuPage (IL)
Coll of Lake County (IL)
Coll of San Mateo (CA)
Coll of the Desert (CA)
Comm Coll of Allegheny County (PA)
Comm Coll of Southern Nevada (NV)
El Camino Coll (CA)
Finger Lakes Comm Coll (NY)
Foothill Coll (CA)
Forsyth Tech Comm Coll (NC)
Fullerton Coll (CA)
Golden West Coll (CA)
Gwinnett Tech Coll (GA)
Hawkeye Comm Coll (IA)
Hillsborough Comm Coll (FL)
Kirkwood Comm Coll (IA)
Lenoir Comm Coll (NC)
Los Angeles Pierce Coll (CA)
Mendocino Coll (CA)
Merced Coll (CA)
Mesa Comm Coll (AZ)
Metropolitan Comm Coll (NE)
Miami Dade Coll (FL)
Minot State U–Bottineau Campus (ND)
Mississippi Gulf Coast Comm Coll (MS)
Monterey Peninsula Coll (CA)
Mt. Hood Comm Coll (OR)
Mt. San Antonio Coll (CA)
Oakland Comm Coll (MI)
Orange Coast Coll (CA)
Richland Coll (TX)
San Joaquin Delta Coll (CA)
Santa Barbara City Coll (CA)
Shasta Coll (CA)

South Florida Comm
Coll (FL)
Spokane Comm Coll (WA)
Tulsa Comm Coll (OK)
Tyler Jr Coll (TX)
U of Arkansas Comm Coll
at Morrilton (AR)
Valencia Comm Coll (FL)
Victor Valley Coll (CA)

Orthoptics
Oklahoma City Comm
Coll (OK)

Orthotics/Prosthetics
Century Coll (MN)
Spokane Falls Comm
Coll (WA)

Painting
Dixie State Coll of
Utah (UT)
Keystone Coll (PA)

**Paralegal/Legal
Assistant**
Appalachian Tech
Coll (GA)
Atlanta Tech Coll (GA)
Beta Tech (VA)
Bradford School (PA)
Brown Mackie Coll–
Akron (OH)
Brown Mackie Coll–
Atlanta (GA)
Brown Mackie Coll–
Findlay (OH)
Brown Mackie Coll–
Hopkinsville (KY)
Brown Mackie Coll–
Louisville (KY)
Brown Mackie Coll–
Miami (FL)
Brown Mackie Coll–
Northern Kentucky (KY)
Camelot Coll (LA)
Center for Advanced Legal
Studies (TX)
Central Georgia Tech
Coll (GA)
City Coll, Fort
Lauderdale (FL)
City Coll, Gainesville (FL)
City Coll, Miami (FL)
Coosa Valley Tech
Coll (GA)
DeKalb Tech Coll (GA)
Forrest Jr Coll (SC)
Front Range Comm
Coll (CO)
Griffin Tech Coll (GA)
Miller-Motte Tech Coll,
Clarksville (TN)
Minnesota School of
Business–Brooklyn
Center (MN)
Minnesota School of
Business–Plymouth (MN)
Minnesota School of
Business–St.
Cloud (MN)
Minnesota School of
Business–Shakopee (MN)
National American U,
Bloomington (MN)
North Hennepin Comm
Coll (MN)
Ogeechee Tech Coll (GA)
Riverside Comm Coll
District (CA)
South Georgia Tech
Coll (GA)
Tidewater Comm Coll (VA)

**Parks, Recreation and
Leisure**
Bakersfield Coll (CA)
Bergen Comm Coll (NJ)
Brigham Young U –
Idaho (ID)
Cabrillo Coll (CA)
Cankdeska Cikana Comm
Coll (ND)
Cape Cod Comm
Coll (MA)
Central Florida Comm
Coll (FL)
Centralia Coll (WA)
Cerritos Coll (CA)
Chesapeake Coll (MD)
City Coll of San
Francisco (CA)
City Colls of Chicago,
Kennedy-King
College (IL)
Coastal Bend Coll (TX)
Coll of the Desert (CA)
Colorado Mountain Coll,
Timberline
Campus (CO)

Comm Coll of Southern
Nevada (NV)
East Central Coll (MO)
East Georgia Coll (GA)
Fresno City Coll (CA)
Fullerton Coll (CA)
Garrett Coll (MD)
Gordon Coll (GA)
Hartnell Coll (CA)
Iowa Lakes Comm
Coll (IA)
Kingsborough Comm Coll
of the City U of New
York (NY)
Kirkwood Comm Coll (IA)
Lawson State Comm
Coll (AL)
Leeward Comm Coll (HI)
Madison Area Tech
Coll (WI)
Miami Dade Coll (FL)
Minneapolis Comm and
Tech Coll (MN)
Monroe Comm Coll (NY)
Mt. San Antonio Coll (CA)
Muskegon Comm Coll (MI)
National Park Comm
Coll (AR)
New Mexico Jr Coll (NM)
Northern Essex Comm
Coll (MA)
Northwestern Connecticut
Comm Coll (CT)
Onondaga Comm
Coll (NY)
Pasadena City Coll (CA)
San Bernardino Valley
Coll (CA)
San Diego City Coll (CA)
San Juan Coll (NM)
Santa Barbara City
Coll (CA)
Skagit Valley Coll (WA)
Southeastern Comm
Coll (NC)
South Georgia Coll (GA)
Suffolk County Comm
Coll (NY)
Taft Coll (CA)
Tallahassee Comm
Coll (FL)
Tompkins Cortland Comm
Coll (NY)
Tyler Jr Coll (TX)
Ulster County Comm
Coll (NY)
Ventura Coll (CA)
Wenatchee Valley
Coll (WA)
Young Harris Coll (GA)
Zane State Coll (OH)

**Parks, Recreation and
Leisure Facilities
Management**
Allen County Comm
Coll (KS)
Augusta Tech Coll (GA)
Chattahoochee Tech
Coll (GA)
Coastal Georgia Comm
Coll (GA)
Coll of the Desert (CA)
Colorado Mountain Coll,
Alpine Campus (CO)
Colorado Mountain Coll,
Timberline
Campus (CO)
Cuesta Coll (CA)
Erie Comm Coll, South
Campus (NY)
Finger Lakes Comm
Coll (NY)
Garrett Coll (MD)
Harper Coll (IL)
Hawkeye Comm Coll (IA)
Hocking Coll (OH)
James H. Faulkner State
Comm Coll (AL)
Keiser Career Coll -
Greenacres (FL)
Keystone Coll (PA)
Kirkwood Comm Coll (IA)
Minot State U–Bottineau
Campus (ND)
Mohawk Valley Comm
Coll (NY)
Monterey Peninsula
Coll (CA)
Moraine Valley Comm
Coll (IL)
Mt. San Antonio Coll (CA)
National Park Comm
Coll (AR)
North Country Comm
Coll (NY)
North Georgia Tech
Coll (GA)

Northwestern Connecticut
Comm Coll (CT)
Potomac State Coll of
West Virginia U (WV)
Rose State Coll (OK)
Skagit Valley Coll (WA)
Southeastern Comm
Coll (NC)
South Georgia Coll (GA)
Spokane Comm Coll (WA)
State U of New York Coll
of Agriculture and
Technology at
Morrisville (NY)
Wayne Comm Coll (NC)
Western Nevada Comm
Coll (NV)
Western Texas Coll (TX)
West Valley Coll (CA)
Zane State Coll (OH)

**Parks, Recreation,
and Leisure Related**
Central New Mexico
Comm Coll (NM)
Cincinnati State Tech and
Comm Coll (OH)
Southwestern Comm
Coll (NC)

**Parts, Warehousing,
and Inventory
Management**
Central Wyoming
Coll (WY)

**Pastoral Studies/
Counseling**
Hesston Coll (KS)

**Peace Studies and
Conflict Resolution**
Berkshire Comm Coll (MA)

**Perioperative/Operating
Room and Surgical
Nursing**
Comm Coll of Allegheny
County (PA)

**Personal/Miscellaneous
Services**
Lorain County Comm
Coll (OH)

Petroleum Technology
Bakersfield Coll (CA)
Coastal Bend Coll (TX)
New Mexico Jr Coll (NM)
Odessa Coll (TX)
South Plains Coll (TX)
Tulsa Comm Coll (OK)
Tyler Jr Coll (TX)

Pharmacy
Barton County Comm
Coll (KS)
Cerritos Coll (CA)
City Colls of Chicago,
Kennedy-King
College (IL)
City Colls of Chicago,
Richard J. Daley
College (IL)
Coastal Bend Coll (TX)
Colby Comm Coll (KS)
Comm Coll of Southern
Nevada (NV)
Iowa Lakes Comm
Coll (IA)
Isothermal Comm
Coll (NC)
Lorain County Comm
Coll (OH)
Navarro Coll (TX)
Pasadena City Coll (CA)
Turtle Mountain Comm
Coll (ND)
U of Cincinnati Clermont
Coll (OH)

Pharmacy Technician
Albany Tech Coll (GA)
Allied Coll (MO)
Augusta Tech Coll (GA)
Brown Mackie Coll–
Akron (OH)
Brown Mackie Coll–
Cincinnati (OH)
Brown Mackie Coll–
Findlay (OH)
Brown Mackie Coll–
Louisville (KY)
Brown Mackie Coll–North
Canton (OH)
Brown Mackie Coll–
Northern Kentucky (KY)
Centro de Estudios
Multidisciplinarios (PR)
Century Coll (MN)
Clinton Comm Coll (IA)

Columbus Tech Coll (GA)
Comm Coll of Allegheny
County (PA)
Everett Comm Coll (WA)
Griffin Tech Coll (GA)
Harrisburg Area Comm
Coll (PA)
Heritage Coll (NV)
High-Tech Inst (FL)
High-Tech Inst (MN)
High-Tech Inst (NV)
High-Tech Inst,
Memphis (TN)
Hillsborough Comm
Coll (FL)
Keiser Career Coll -
Greenacres (FL)
Midlands Tech Coll (SC)
Minnesota State Comm
and Tech Coll–Fergus
Falls (MN)
Muscatine Comm Coll (IA)
North Seattle Comm
Coll (WA)
Northwestern Tech
Coll (GA)
Oakland Comm Coll (MI)
Pima Comm Coll (AZ)
Rasmussen Coll Brooklyn
Park (MN)
Roane State Comm
Coll (TN)
Santa Ana Coll (CA)
Scott Comm Coll (IA)
Vatterott Coll, Kansas
City (MO)
Western Career Coll,
Pleasant Hill (CA)
Western Career Coll,
Sacramento (CA)
Western Career Coll, San
Leandro (CA)
West Georgia Tech
Coll (GA)

Philosophy
Allen County Comm
Coll (KS)
Bakersfield Coll (CA)
Barton County Comm
Coll (KS)
Bergen Comm Coll (NJ)
Blinn Coll (TX)
Burlington County
Coll (NJ)
Cañada Coll (CA)
Cape Cod Comm
Coll (MA)
Cerritos Coll (CA)
Chaffey Coll (CA)
City Colls of Chicago,
Harold Washington
College (IL)
City Colls of Chicago,
Olive-Harvey
College (IL)
Coastal Georgia Comm
Coll (GA)
Coll of Alameda (CA)
Coll of Marin (CA)
Coll of the Desert (CA)
Coll of the Siskiyous (CA)
Contra Costa Coll (CA)
Crafton Hills Coll (CA)
Cypress Coll (CA)
De Anza Coll (CA)
Dixie State Coll of
Utah (UT)
East Central Coll (MO)
El Camino Coll (CA)
Everett Comm Coll (WA)
Foothill Coll (CA)
Fullerton Coll (CA)
Georgia Highlands
Coll (GA)
Grossmont Coll (CA)
Iowa Lakes Comm
Coll (IA)
Kellogg Comm Coll (MI)
Lansing Comm Coll (MI)
Laramie County Comm
Coll (WY)
Los Angeles Mission
Coll (CA)
Lower Columbia Coll (WA)
Manatee Comm Coll (FL)
Miami Dade Coll (FL)
Miami U–Middletown
Campus (OH)
Monterey Peninsula
Coll (CA)
Orange Coast Coll (CA)
Oxnard Coll (CA)
Palm Beach Comm
Coll (FL)
Palo Alto Coll (TX)
Pasadena City Coll (CA)
St. Philip's Coll (TX)

San Bernardino Valley
Coll (CA)
San Joaquin Delta
Coll (CA)
San Juan Coll (NM)
Santa Ana Coll (CA)
Santa Barbara City
Coll (CA)
Santa Rosa Jr Coll (CA)
Santiago Canyon Coll (CA)
Skagit Valley Coll (WA)
South Georgia Coll (GA)
Tulsa Comm Coll (OK)
West Los Angeles
Coll (CA)
Yuba Coll (CA)

Phlebotomy
Alexandria Tech Coll (MN)
City Coll, Gainesville (FL)

**Photographic and
Film/Video
Technology**
The Art Inst of
Philadelphia (PA)
Calhoun Comm Coll (AL)
Catawba Valley Comm
Coll (NC)
Dixie State Coll of
Utah (UT)
Miami Dade Coll (FL)
Mohawk Valley Comm
Coll (NY)
Olympic Coll (WA)
Salt Lake Comm Coll (UT)
Suffolk County Comm
Coll (NY)

Photography
Amarillo Coll (TX)
Anne Arundel Comm
Coll (MD)
Antelope Valley Coll (CA)
The Art Inst of
Philadelphia (PA)
Bakersfield Coll (CA)
Bergen Comm Coll (NJ)
Brigham Young U –
Idaho (ID)
Catawba Valley Comm
Coll (NC)
Cecil Comm Coll (MD)
Cerritos Coll (CA)
Chaffey Coll (CA)
Citrus Coll (CA)
City Coll of San
Francisco (CA)
City Colls of Chicago,
Olive-Harvey
College (IL)
City Colls of Chicago,
Richard J. Daley
College (IL)
Coll of DuPage (IL)
Coll of San Mateo (CA)
Coll of Southern Idaho (ID)
Colorado Mountain
Coll (CO)
Columbia Coll (CA)
Comm Coll of
Philadelphia (PA)
Comm Coll of Southern
Nevada (NV)
Cosumnes River Coll,
Sacramento (CA)
Cuyahoga Comm
Coll (OH)
Cypress Coll (CA)
De Anza Coll (CA)
Dixie State Coll of
Utah (UT)
El Camino Coll (CA)
Everett Comm Coll (WA)
Fiorello H. LaGuardia
Comm Coll of the City
U of New York (NY)
Foothill Coll (CA)
Fresno City Coll (CA)
Grossmont Coll (CA)
Gwinnett Tech Coll (GA)
Harrisburg Area Comm
Coll (PA)
Hartnell Coll (CA)
Hawkeye Comm Coll (IA)
Hennepin Tech Coll (MN)
Holyoke Comm Coll (MA)
Howard Comm Coll (MD)
Iowa Lakes Comm
Coll (IA)
Keystone Coll (PA)
Laney Coll (CA)
Lansing Comm Coll (MI)
Lassen Comm Coll
District (CA)
Lee Coll (TX)
Lehigh Valley Coll (PA)
Linn-Benton Comm
Coll (OR)

Los Angeles City Coll (CA)
Los Angeles Pierce
Coll (CA)
Lower Columbia Coll (WA)
Madison Area Tech
Coll (WI)
Metropolitan Comm
Coll (NE)
Miami Dade Coll (FL)
Monterey Peninsula
Coll (CA)
Moorpark Coll (CA)
Mott Comm Coll (MI)
Mt. San Antonio Coll (CA)
Napa Valley Coll (CA)
Nassau Comm Coll (NY)
Nossi Coll of Art (TN)
Oakland Comm Coll (MI)
Odessa Coll (TX)
Oklahoma State U,
Okmulgee (OK)
Onondaga Comm
Coll (NY)
Orange Coast Coll (CA)
Palm Beach Comm
Coll (FL)
Pasadena City Coll (CA)
Porterville Coll (CA)
Ridgewater Coll (MN)
Riverside Comm Coll
District (CA)
St. Louis Comm Coll at
Florissant Valley (MO)
San Bernardino Valley
Coll (CA)
San Diego City Coll (CA)
San Joaquin Delta
Coll (CA)
Santa Ana Coll (CA)
Scottsdale Comm
Coll (AZ)
Tyler Jr Coll (TX)
Western Wyoming Comm
Coll (WY)
Westmoreland County
Comm Coll (PA)
Yuba Coll (CA)

**Physical Education
Teaching and
Coaching**
Amarillo Coll (TX)
Angelina Coll (TX)
Anne Arundel Comm
Coll (MD)
Arizona Western Coll (AZ)
Bakersfield Coll (CA)
Barstow Coll (CA)
Barton County Comm
Coll (KS)
Blinn Coll (TX)
Brigham Young U –
Idaho (ID)
Bucks County Comm
Coll (PA)
Cabrillo Coll (CA)
Cañada Coll (CA)
Cape Cod Comm
Coll (MA)
Central Texas Coll (TX)
Cerritos Coll (CA)
Chaffey Coll (CA)
Chesapeake Coll (MD)
Cisco Jr Coll (TX)
Citrus Coll (CA)
City Colls of Chicago,
Harry S. Truman
College (IL)
Clarendon Coll (TX)
Coastal Bend Coll (TX)
Cochise Coll, Douglas (AZ)
Cochise Coll, Sierra
Vista (AZ)
Colby Comm Coll (KS)
Coll of Marin (CA)
Coll of Southern Idaho (ID)
Coll of the Canyons (CA)
Coll of the Desert (CA)
Columbia Coll (CA)
Crafton Hills Coll (CA)
Crowder Coll (MO)
Cuesta Coll (CA)
Cypress Coll (CA)
Dean Coll (MA)
De Anza Coll (CA)
Dixie State Coll of
Utah (UT)
Dodge City Comm
Coll (KS)
East Central Coll (MO)
East Georgia Coll (GA)
El Camino Coll (CA)
Erie Comm Coll (NY)
Erie Comm Coll, North
Campus (NY)
Erie Comm Coll, South
Campus (NY)
Essex County Coll (NJ)
Everett Comm Coll (WA)

Finger Lakes Comm
Coll (NY)
Foothill Coll (CA)
Frederick Comm Coll (MD)
Fullerton Coll (CA)
Fulton-Montgomery Comm
Coll (NY)
Gadsden State Comm
Coll (AL)
Garrett Coll (MD)
Genesee Comm Coll (NY)
Grayson County Coll (TX)
Harper Coll (IL)
Harrisburg Area Comm
Coll (PA)
Hartnell Coll (CA)
Hillsborough Comm
Coll (FL)
Imperial Valley Coll (CA)
Iowa Lakes Comm
Coll (IA)
Jones County Jr Coll (MS)
Kellogg Comm Coll (MI)
Kirkwood Comm Coll (IA)
Labette Comm Coll (KS)
Lake Tahoe Comm
Coll (CA)
Lansing Comm Coll (MI)
Laramie County Comm
Coll (WY)
Lassen Comm Coll
District (CA)
Lee Coll (TX)
Linn-Benton Comm
Coll (OR)
Lorain County Comm
Coll (OH)
Los Angeles Mission
Coll (CA)
Lower Columbia Coll (WA)
Manatee Comm Coll (FL)
McLennan Comm
Coll (TX)
Mendocino Coll (CA)
Merced Coll (CA)
Miami Dade Coll (FL)
Mississippi Delta Comm
Coll (MS)
Mohawk Valley Comm
Coll (NY)
Monroe Comm Coll (NY)
Monterey Peninsula
Coll (CA)
Montgomery County
Comm Coll (PA)
Murray State Coll (OK)
Navarro Coll (TX)
New Mexico Jr Coll (NM)
New Mexico Military
Inst (NM)
Niagara County Comm
Coll (NY)
Northeast Comm Coll (NE)
Northeastern Jr Coll (CO)
Northern Essex Comm
Coll (MA)
Northwest Mississippi
Comm Coll (MS)
Odessa Coll (TX)
Orange Coast Coll (CA)
Oxnard Coll (CA)
Palm Beach Comm
Coll (FL)
Palo Alto Coll (TX)
Pasadena City Coll (CA)
Porterville Coll (CA)
Potomac State Coll of
West Virginia U (WV)
Redlands Comm Coll (OK)
Ridgewater Coll (MN)
Roane State Comm
Coll (TN)
Rose State Coll (OK)
Sacramento City Coll (CA)
St. Catharine Coll (KY)
San Bernardino Valley
Coll (CA)
San Diego City Coll (CA)
San Joaquin Delta
Coll (CA)
Santa Barbara City
Coll (CA)
Santa Rosa Jr Coll (CA)
Seminole State Coll (OK)
Skagit Valley Coll (WA)
South Georgia Coll (GA)
South Plains Coll (TX)
Southwest Mississippi
Comm Coll (MS)
Taft Coll (CA)
Treasure Valley Comm
Coll (OR)
Trinidad State Jr Coll (CO)
Tulsa Comm Coll (OK)
Umpqua Comm Coll (OR)
U of New
Mexico–Gallup (NM)

U of Puerto Rico at
Carolina (PR)
Valencia Comm Coll (FL)
Wenatchee Valley
Coll (WA)
West Hills Comm Coll (CA)
West Los Angeles
Coll (CA)
West Valley Coll (CA)
Yuba Coll (CA)

Physical Sciences
Amarillo Coll (TX)
Angelina Coll (TX)
Antelope Valley Coll (CA)
Barton County Comm
Coll (KS)
Brigham Young U –
Idaho (ID)
Cecil Comm Coll (MD)
Centralia Coll (WA)
Central Oregon Comm
Coll (OR)
Central Wyoming
Coll (WY)
Chaffey Coll (CA)
Chesapeake Coll (MD)
Citrus Coll (CA)
City Colls of Chicago,
Harold Washington
College (IL)
City Colls of Chicago,
Wilbur Wright
College (IL)
Clovis Comm Coll (NM)
Coastal Bend Coll (TX)
Coll of San Mateo (CA)
Coll of the Canyons (CA)
Coll of the Siskiyous (CA)
Colorado Mountain Coll,
Alpine Campus (CO)
Columbia Coll (CA)
Crowder Coll (MO)
Dodge City Comm
Coll (KS)
El Camino Coll (CA)
Frederick Comm Coll (MD)
Fresno City Coll (CA)
Fulton-Montgomery Comm
Coll (NY)
Golden West Coll (CA)
Gordon Coll (GA)
Harper Coll (IL)
Harrisburg Area Comm
Coll (PA)
Howard Comm Coll (MD)
Hutchinson Comm Coll
and Area Vocational
School (KS)
Imperial Valley Coll (CA)
Iowa Lakes Comm
Coll (IA)
Jones County Jr Coll (MS)
Lamar Comm Coll (CO)
Lassen Comm Coll
District (CA)
Lawson State Comm
Coll (AL)
Lehigh Carbon Comm
Coll (PA)
Linn-Benton Comm
Coll (OR)
Los Angeles Mission
Coll (CA)
Mendocino Coll (CA)
Merced Coll (CA)
Miami Dade Coll (FL)
Montgomery County
Comm Coll (PA)
National Park Comm
Coll (AR)
Naugatuck Valley Comm
Coll (CT)
Navarro Coll (TX)
Neosho County Comm
Coll (KS)
Northeastern Jr Coll (CO)
North Idaho Coll (ID)
Northwestern Connecticut
Comm Coll (CT)
Ohlone Coll (CA)
Ozarks Tech Comm
Coll (MO)
Palm Beach Comm
Coll (FL)
Pasadena City Coll (CA)
Redlands Comm Coll (OK)
Reedley Coll (CA)
Ridgewater Coll (MN)
Roane State Comm
Coll (TN)
Roxbury Comm Coll (MA)
Sacramento City Coll (CA)
Salt Lake Comm Coll (UT)
San Bernardino Valley
Coll (CA)
San Diego City Coll (CA)
San Joaquin Delta
Coll (CA)

San Juan Coll (NM)
Santa Rosa Jr Coll (CA)
Seminole State Coll (OK)
South Georgia Coll (GA)
Southwest Mississippi
Comm Coll (MS)
Taft Coll (CA)
Tulsa Comm Coll (OK)
Ulster County Comm
Coll (NY)
Umpqua Comm Coll (OR)
Union County Coll (NJ)
U of New
Mexico–Gallup (NM)
U of New
Mexico–Taos (NM)
Ventura Coll (CA)
Victor Valley Coll (CA)
Washington State Comm
Coll (OH)
Western Nevada Comm
Coll (NV)

Physical Sciences
Related
Cerritos Coll (CA)
Folsom Lake Coll (CA)
Mt. San Antonio Coll (CA)
Schoolcraft Coll (MI)

Physical Science
Technologies Related
Marshall Comm and Tech
Coll (WV)

Physical Therapist
Assistant
Allegany Coll of
Maryland (MD)
Angelina Coll (TX)
Anoka-Ramsey Comm
Coll (MN)
Ashland Comm and Tech
Coll (KY)
Barton County Comm
Coll (KS)
Berkshire Comm Coll (MA)
Bishop State Comm
Coll (AL)
Black Hawk Coll,
Moline (IL)
Blinn Coll (TX)
Broome Comm Coll (NY)
Brown Mackie Coll–South
Bend (IN)
Cape Cod Comm
Coll (MA)
Capital Comm Coll (CT)
Carroll Comm Coll (MD)
Central Florida Comm
Coll (FL)
Central Ohio Tech
Coll (OH)
Colby Comm Coll (KS)
Coll of DuPage (IL)
Coll of Southern
Maryland (MD)
Comm Coll of Allegheny
County (PA)
Comm Coll of Rhode
Island (RI)
Essex County Coll (NJ)
Everett Comm Coll (WA)
Fayetteville Tech Comm
Coll (NC)
Gateway Tech Coll (WI)
George C. Wallace Comm
Coll (AL)
Georgia Highlands
Coll (GA)
Guilford Tech Comm
Coll (NC)
Gwinnett Tech Coll (GA)
Hesser Coll (NH)
Hocking Coll (OH)
Houston Comm Coll
System (TX)
Jackson State Comm
Coll (TN)
Kankakee Comm Coll (IL)
Kansas City Kansas
Comm Coll (KS)
Kellogg Comm Coll (MI)
Kennebec Valley Comm
Coll (ME)
Kingsborough Comm Coll
of the City U of New
York (NY)
Lake Land Coll (IL)
Lehigh Carbon Comm
Coll (PA)
Lincoln Land Comm
Coll (IL)
Linn State Tech Coll (MO)
Lorain County Comm
Coll (OH)
Macomb Comm Coll (MI)
Madisonville Comm
Coll (KY)

Manatee Comm Coll (FL)
Marshall Comm and Tech
Coll (WV)
Martin Comm Coll (NC)
Massachusetts Bay Comm
Coll (MA)
Medical Careers Inst,
Newport News (VA)
Miami Dade Coll (FL)
Middle Georgia Coll (GA)
Midlands Tech Coll (SC)
Montgomery Coll (MD)
Mott Comm Coll (MI)
Nassau Comm Coll (NY)
Naugatuck Valley Comm
Coll (CT)
Niagara County Comm
Coll (NY)
Nicolet Area Tech Coll (WI)
North Iowa Area Comm
Coll (IA)
North Shore Comm
Coll (MA)
Ohlone Coll (CA)
Owens Comm Coll,
Toledo (OH)
Ozarks Tech Comm
Coll (MO)
Pasco-Hernando Comm
Coll (FL)
Penn State DuBois (PA)
Penn State Hazleton (PA)
Penn State Mont Alto (PA)
Penn State Shenango (PA)
Polk Comm Coll (FL)
Provo Coll (UT)
Pueblo Comm Coll (CO)
Sacramento City Coll (CA)
St. Philip's Coll (TX)
Salt Lake Comm Coll (UT)
San Juan Coll (NM)
Southeast Kentucky Comm
and Tech Coll (KY)
Southern U at
Shreveport (LA)
Southwestern Comm
Coll (NC)
Spokane Falls Comm
Coll (WA)
Springfield Tech Comm
Coll (MA)
Stanly Comm Coll (NC)
State U of New York Coll
of Technology at
Canton (NY)
Union County Coll (NJ)
U of Pittsburgh at
Titusville (PA)
Villa Maria Coll of
Buffalo (NY)
Volunteer State Comm
Coll (TN)
Western Nebraska Comm
Coll (NE)
Zane State Coll (OH)

Physical Therapy
Allen County Comm
Coll (KS)
Amarillo Coll (TX)
Athens Tech Coll (GA)
Baltimore City Comm
Coll (MD)
Barton County Comm
Coll (KS)
Brigham Young U –
Idaho (ID)
Broward Comm Coll (FL)
Caldwell Comm Coll and
Tech Inst (NC)
Central Piedmont Comm
Coll (NC)
Cerritos Coll (CA)
Chattanooga State Tech
Comm Coll (TN)
City Coll of San
Francisco (CA)
Clarendon Coll (TX)
Clark State Comm
Coll (OH)
Coastal Georgia Comm
Coll (GA)
Colby Comm Coll (KS)
Coll of Southern Idaho (ID)
De Anza Coll (CA)
Dodge City Comm
Coll (KS)
Essex County Coll (NJ)
Fiorello H. LaGuardia
Comm Coll of the City
U of New York (NY)
Florence-Darlington Tech
Coll (SC)
Gateway Tech Coll (WI)
Genesee Comm Coll (NY)
Georgia Highlands
Coll (GA)
Greenville Tech Coll (SC)
Gwinnett Tech Coll (GA)

Hillsborough Comm
Coll (FL)
Housatonic Comm
Coll (CT)
Jefferson Comm and Tech
Coll (KY)
John Tyler Comm Coll (VA)
Kent State U, Ashtabula
Campus (OH)
Kent State U, East
Liverpool Campus (OH)
Kingsborough Comm Coll
of the City U of New
York (NY)
Laredo Comm Coll (TX)
Lawson State Comm
Coll (AL)
Louisburg Coll (NC)
Manatee Comm Coll (FL)
McLennan Comm
Coll (TX)
Meridian Comm Coll (MS)
Metropolitan Comm
Coll–Penn Valley (MO)
Monterey Peninsula
Coll (CA)
Morgan Comm Coll (CO)
Morton Coll (IL)
Mt. Hood Comm Coll (OR)
Mount Wachusett Comm
Coll (MA)
Murray State Coll (OK)
New Hampshire Comm
Tech Coll, Manchester/
Stratham (NH)
Northeast Comm Coll (NE)
NorthWest Arkansas
Comm Coll (AR)
Odessa Coll (TX)
Oklahoma City Comm
Coll (OK)
Onondaga Comm
Coll (NY)
Palm Beach Comm
Coll (FL)
Roane State Comm
Coll (TN)
Rose State Coll (OK)
Scott Comm Coll (IA)
Seminole Comm Coll (FL)
South Plains Coll (TX)
Southwestern Comm
Coll (NC)
Stark State Coll of
Technology (OH)
Suffolk County Comm
Coll (NY)
Trident Tech Coll (SC)
Tulsa Comm Coll (OK)
Tunxis Comm Coll (CT)
Turtle Mountain Comm
Coll (ND)
Virginia Highlands Comm
Coll (VA)
Wallace State Comm
Coll (AL)
Western Nebraska Comm
Coll (NE)
Wytheville Comm Coll (VA)
Young Harris Coll (GA)

Physician Assistant
Barton County Comm
Coll (KS)
Coastal Georgia Comm
Coll (GA)
Coll of Southern Idaho (ID)
Cuyahoga Comm
Coll (OH)
Foothill Coll (CA)
Georgia Highlands
Coll (GA)
Hartnell Coll (CA)
Kettering Coll of Medical
Arts (OH)
Manatee Comm Coll (FL)
Minnesota School of
Business–Brooklyn
Center (MN)
Minnesota School of
Business–Plymouth (MN)
Minnesota School of
Business–St.
Cloud (MN)
Minnesota School of
Business–Shakopee (MN)
Santa Rosa Jr Coll (CA)
Tulsa Comm Coll (OK)

Physics
Allen County Comm
Coll (KS)
Amarillo Coll (TX)
Arizona Western Coll (AZ)
Bakersfield Coll (CA)
Barton County Comm
Coll (KS)
Bergen Comm Coll (NJ)
Blinn Coll (TX)

Brigham Young U –
Idaho (ID)
Burlington County
Coll (NJ)
Cecil Comm Coll (MD)
Cerritos Coll (CA)
Chaffey Coll (CA)
City Colls of Chicago,
Harold Washington
College (IL)
City Colls of Chicago,
Kennedy-King
College (IL)
City Colls of Chicago,
Olive-Harvey
College (IL)
Coastal Bend Coll (TX)
Coastal Georgia Comm
Coll (GA)
Coll of Marin (CA)
Coll of San Mateo (CA)
Coll of Southern Idaho (ID)
Coll of the Desert (CA)
Coll of the Siskiyous (CA)
Columbia Coll (CA)
Comm Coll of Allegheny
County (PA)
Contra Costa Coll (CA)
Crafton Hills Coll (CA)
Cuesta Coll (CA)
Cypress Coll (CA)
De Anza Coll (CA)
Dixie State Coll of
Utah (UT)
Dodge City Comm
Coll (KS)
East Central Coll (MO)
Eastern Arizona Coll (AZ)
El Camino Coll (CA)
Everett Comm Coll (WA)
Finger Lakes Comm
Coll (NY)
Folsom Lake Coll (CA)
Foothill Coll (CA)
Fullerton Coll (CA)
Grayson County Coll (TX)
Great Basin Coll (NV)
Grossmont Coll (CA)
Holyoke Comm Coll (MA)
Kellogg Comm Coll (MI)
Kingsborough Comm Coll
of the City U of New
York (NY)
Lamar Comm Coll (CO)
Lee Coll (TX)
Linn-Benton Comm
Coll (OR)
Lorain County Comm
Coll (OH)
Los Angeles City Coll (CA)
Los Angeles Harbor
Coll (CA)
Louisburg Coll (NC)
Lower Columbia Coll (WA)
Manatee Comm Coll (FL)
Miami Dade Coll (FL)
Miami U–Middletown
Campus (OH)
Monroe Comm Coll (NY)
Monterey Peninsula
Coll (CA)
Navarro Coll (TX)
New Mexico Military
Inst (NM)
Northampton County Area
Comm Coll (PA)
Northeast Comm Coll (NE)
North Idaho Coll (ID)
Odessa Coll (TX)
Oklahoma City Comm
Coll (OK)
Orange Coast Coll (CA)
Palo Alto Coll (TX)
Pasadena City Coll (CA)
Red Rocks Comm
Coll (CO)
Rose State Coll (OK)
Salt Lake Comm Coll (UT)
San Bernardino Valley
Coll (CA)
San Juan Coll (NM)
Santa Ana Coll (CA)
Santa Barbara City
Coll (CA)
Santa Rosa Jr Coll (CA)
Santiago Canyon Coll (CA)
South Georgia Coll (GA)
State U of New York Coll
of Agriculture and
Technology at
Morrisville (NY)
Texarkana Coll (TX)
Tulsa Comm Coll (OK)
Western Nebraska Comm
Coll (NE)
West Hills Comm Coll (CA)
West Los Angeles
Coll (CA)

West Valley Coll (CA)
Young Harris Coll (GA)

Physics Teacher Education
Coll of the Siskiyous (CA)
Manatee Comm Coll (FL)

Piano and Organ
Angelina Coll (TX)
Brigham Young U – Idaho (ID)
Fresno City Coll (CA)
Iowa Lakes Comm Coll (IA)
St. Catharine Coll (KY)

Pipefitting and Sprinkler Fitting
Bakersfield Coll (CA)
Cecil Comm Coll (MD)
Coll of San Mateo (CA)
Forsyth Tech Comm Coll (NC)
H. Councill Trenholm State Tech Coll (AL)
Kellogg Comm Coll (MI)
New England Inst of Technology (RI)
Northern Maine Comm Coll (ME)
Oklahoma State U, Okmulgee (OK)
St. Cloud Tech Coll (MN)
Southern Maine Comm Coll (ME)
State U of New York Coll of Technology at Alfred (NY)
State U of New York Coll of Technology at Canton (NY)
Western Nevada Comm Coll (NV)

Plant Nursery Management
Comm Coll of Allegheny County (PA)
Foothill Coll (CA)
Joliet Jr Coll (IL)
Miami Dade Coll (FL)
The Ohio State U Ag Tech Inst (OH)

Plant Pathology/ Phytopathology
Dixie State Coll of Utah (UT)

Plant Protection and Integrated Pest Management
Dixie State Coll of Utah (UT)
Los Angeles Pierce Coll (CA)
Tulsa Comm Coll (OK)

Plant Sciences
Northwest Mississippi Comm Coll (MS)
Reedley Coll (CA)
Ventura Coll (CA)

Plastics Engineering Technology
Brigham Young U – Idaho (ID)
Cerritos Coll (CA)
Cincinnati State Tech and Comm Coll (OH)
Coll of DuPage (IL)
Davidson County Comm Coll (NC)
Elaine P. Nunez Comm Coll (LA)
Grand Rapids Comm Coll (MI)
Hennepin Tech Coll (MN)
Isothermal Comm Coll (NC)
Kellogg Comm Coll (MI)
Kent State U, Tuscarawas Campus (OH)
Lorain County Comm Coll (OH)
Macomb Comm Coll (MI)
Mount Wachusett Comm Coll (MA)
Quinebaug Valley Comm Coll (CT)
South Texas Coll (TX)
State U of New York Coll of Agriculture and Technology at Morrisville (NY)
Terra State Comm Coll (OH)
Tyler Jr Coll (TX)

West Georgia Tech Coll (GA)

Plumbing Technology
Macomb Comm Coll (MI)
Piedmont Virginia Comm Coll (VA)
Vatterott Coll, Kansas City (MO)

Political Science and Government
Allen County Comm Coll (KS)
Bainbridge Coll (GA)
Bakersfield Coll (CA)
Barton County Comm Coll (KS)
Bergen Comm Coll (NJ)
Brigham Young U – Idaho (ID)
Burlington County Coll (NJ)
Cañada Coll (CA)
Centralia Coll (WA)
Cerritos Coll (CA)
Chaffey Coll (CA)
Coastal Bend Coll (TX)
Coastal Georgia Comm Coll (GA)
Cochise Coll, Douglas (AZ)
Cochise Coll, Sierra Vista (AZ)
Colby Comm Coll (KS)
Coll of Alameda (CA)
Coll of Marin (CA)
Coll of Menominee Nation (WI)
Coll of Southern Idaho (ID)
Coll of the Canyons (CA)
Coll of the Desert (CA)
Contra Costa Coll (CA)
Crafton Hills Coll (CA)
Cypress Coll (CA)
De Anza Coll (CA)
Dixie State Coll of Utah (UT)
Dodge City Comm Coll (KS)
East Central Coll (MO)
Eastern Arizona Coll (AZ)
East Georgia Coll (GA)
El Camino Coll (CA)
Everett Comm Coll (WA)
Finger Lakes Comm Coll (NY)
Foothill Coll (CA)
Frederick Comm Coll (MD)
Fullerton Coll (CA)
Georgia Highlands Coll (GA)
Gloucester County Coll (NJ)
Gordon Coll (GA)
Grossmont Coll (CA)
Iowa Lakes Comm Coll (IA)
Kellogg Comm Coll (MI)
Kirkwood Comm Coll (IA)
Laramie County Comm Coll (WY)
Lawson State Comm Coll (AL)
Lee Coll (TX)
Lorain County Comm Coll (OH)
Louisburg Coll (NC)
Lower Columbia Coll (WA)
Merced Coll (CA)
Miami Dade Coll (FL)
Miami U–Middletown Campus (OH)
Mississippi Delta Comm Coll (MS)
Monroe Comm Coll (NY)
Monterey Peninsula Coll (CA)
Northern Essex Comm Coll (MA)
North Idaho Coll (ID)
Odessa Coll (TX)
Oklahoma City Comm Coll (OK)
Orange Coast Coll (CA)
Palm Beach Comm Coll (FL)
Pasadena City Coll (CA)
Pima Comm Coll (AZ)
Potomac State Coll of West Virginia U (WV)
Quincy Coll (MA)
Red Rocks Comm Coll (CO)
Rose State Coll (OK)
St. Philip's Coll (TX)
Salt Lake Comm Coll (UT)
San Bernardino Valley Coll (CA)
San Diego City Coll (CA)

San Joaquin Delta Coll (CA)
San Juan Coll (NM)
Santa Ana Coll (CA)
Santa Barbara City Coll (CA)
Santa Rosa Jr Coll (CA)
Santiago Canyon Coll (CA)
Skagit Valley Coll (WA)
South Georgia Coll (GA)
Treasure Valley Comm Coll (OR)
Tulsa Comm Coll (OK)
Umpqua Comm Coll (OR)
Western Nebraska Comm Coll (NE)
Western Wyoming Comm Coll (WY)
West Los Angeles Coll (CA)
Young Harris Coll (GA)

Portuguese
Miami Dade Coll (FL)

Postal Management
Allen County Comm Coll (KS)
Central Piedmont Comm Coll (NC)
Lenoir Comm Coll (NC)
Metropolitan Comm Coll–Longview (MO)
Mississippi Gulf Coast Comm Coll (MS)
San Antonio Coll (TX)
San Diego City Coll (CA)
South Plains Coll (TX)
Tyler Jr Coll (TX)
Wallace State Comm Coll (AL)

Poultry Science
Crowder Coll (MO)
Northwest Mississippi Comm Coll (MS)
Sampson Comm Coll (NC)
Surry Comm Coll (NC)
Wallace State Comm Coll (AL)
Wayne Comm Coll (NC)

Precision Metal Working Related
Oakland Comm Coll (MI)
Reedley Coll (CA)

Precision Production Related
Midlands Tech Coll (SC)
Mott Comm Coll (MI)
Southwestern Michigan Coll (MI)

Precision Production Trades
Coll of DuPage (IL)
North Central Industrial Tech Education Center (PA)
Santa Rosa Jr Coll (CA)

Precision Systems Maintenance and Repair Technologies Related
Southwestern Michigan Coll (MI)

Pre-Dentistry Studies
Allen County Comm Coll (KS)
Barton County Comm Coll (KS)
Calhoun Comm Coll (AL)
Centralia Coll (WA)
Clarendon Coll (TX)
Coastal Georgia Comm Coll (GA)
Howard Comm Coll (MD)
Iowa Lakes Comm Coll (IA)
Laramie County Comm Coll (WY)
Northwest-Shoals Comm Coll (AL)
St. Philip's Coll (TX)
Tulsa Comm Coll (OK)
Western Nebraska Comm Coll (NE)
Western Wyoming Comm Coll (WY)

Pre-Engineering
Alpena Comm Coll (MI)
Amarillo Coll (TX)
Anoka-Ramsey Comm Coll (MN)
Anoka-Ramsey Comm Coll, Cambridge Campus (MN)

Barton County Comm Coll (KS)
Bowling Green State U–Firelands Coll (OH)
Brigham Young U – Idaho (ID)
Broward Comm Coll (FL)
Cabrillo Coll (CA)
Caldwell Comm Coll and Tech Inst (NC)
Cape Cod Comm Coll (MA)
Centralia Coll (WA)
Central Oregon Comm Coll (OR)
Cerritos Coll (CA)
Chipola Coll (FL)
City Coll of San Francisco (CA)
City Colls of Chicago, Harold Washington College (IL)
City Colls of Chicago, Harry S. Truman College (IL)
City Colls of Chicago, Kennedy-King College (IL)
City Colls of Chicago, Richard J. Daley College (IL)
City Colls of Chicago, Wilbur Wright College (IL)
Coastal Georgia Comm Coll (GA)
Colby Comm Coll (KS)
Coll of the Canyons (CA)
Coll of the Desert (CA)
Coll of the Mainland (TX)
Colorado Mountain Coll, Alpine Campus (CO)
Comm Coll of Philadelphia (PA)
Cosumnes River Coll, Sacramento (CA)
Crafton Hills Coll (CA)
Crowder Coll (MO)
Cuesta Coll (CA)
Davidson County Comm Coll (NC)
De Anza Coll (CA)
Dodge City Comm Coll (KS)
East Central Coll (MO)
Elgin Comm Coll (IL)
Essex County Coll (NJ)
Everett Comm Coll (WA)
Finger Lakes Comm Coll (NY)
Fort Belknap Coll (MT)
Georgia Military Coll (GA)
Golden West Coll (CA)
Grayson County Coll (TX)
Greenville Tech Coll (SC)
Harper Coll (IL)
Henry Ford Comm Coll (MI)
Holyoke Comm Coll (MA)
Housatonic Comm Coll (CT)
Illinois Valley Comm Coll (IL)
Imperial Valley Coll (CA)
Iowa Lakes Comm Coll (IA)
Isothermal Comm Coll (NC)
Itasca Comm Coll (MN)
Kirkwood Comm Coll (IA)
Labette Comm Coll (KS)
Lamar Comm Coll (CO)
Lansing Comm Coll (MI)
Laramie County Comm Coll (WY)
Lassen Comm Coll District (CA)
Lawson State Comm Coll (AL)
Lee Coll (TX)
Lenoir Comm Coll (NC)
Lincoln Land Comm Coll (IL)
Linn-Benton Comm Coll (OR)
Lorain County Comm Coll (OH)
Los Angeles Harbor Coll (CA)
Los Angeles Pierce Coll (CA)
Louisburg Coll (NC)
Lower Columbia Coll (WA)
Macomb Comm Coll (MI)
Merced Coll (CA)
Mesabi Range Comm and Tech Coll (MN)
Mesa Comm Coll (AZ)

Metropolitan Comm Coll (NE)
Metropolitan Comm Coll–Longview (MO)
Metropolitan Comm Coll–Maple Woods (MO)
Miami Dade Coll (FL)
Miami U–Middletown Campus (OH)
Middlesex Comm Coll (CT)
Minnesota State Comm and Tech Coll–Fergus Falls (MN)
Mission Coll (CA)
Mississippi Gulf Coast Comm Coll (MS)
Moberly Area Comm Coll (MO)
Mt. San Antonio Coll (CA)
Murray State Coll (OK)
Naugatuck Valley Comm Coll (CT)
Navarro Coll (TX)
Neosho County Comm Coll (KS)
New Mexico Military Inst (NM)
North Central Michigan Coll (MI)
North Central Texas Coll (TX)
Northeastern Jr Coll (CO)
North Hennepin Comm Coll (MN)
North Shore Comm Coll (MA)
Northwestern Connecticut Comm Coll (CT)
Northwest-Shoals Comm Coll (AL)
Northwest Vista Coll (TX)
Oakland Comm Coll (MI)
Odessa Coll (TX)
Ohlone Coll (CA)
Oklahoma City Comm Coll (OK)
Palm Beach Comm Coll (FL)
Passaic County Comm Coll (NJ)
Polk Comm Coll (FL)
Porterville Coll (CA)
Potomac State Coll of West Virginia U (WV)
Quinebaug Valley Comm Coll (CT)
Rainy River Comm Coll (MN)
Richland Comm Coll (IL)
Ridgewater Coll (MN)
Roane State Comm Coll (TN)
Rose State Coll (OK)
Roxbury Comm Coll (MA)
Saint Charles Comm Coll (MO)
St. Louis Comm Coll at Florissant Valley (MO)
St. Philip's Coll (TX)
San Bernardino Valley Coll (CA)
Sandhills Comm Coll (NC)
San Diego City Coll (CA)
Seminole State Coll (OK)
Skagit Valley Coll (WA)
South Georgia Coll (GA)
South Plains Coll (TX)
State U of New York Coll of Agriculture and Technology at Morrisville (NY)
Taft Coll (CA)
Three Rivers Comm Coll (CT)
Trinidad State Jr Coll (CO)
Tulsa Comm Coll (OK)
Turtle Mountain Comm Coll (ND)
Umpqua Comm Coll (OR)
U of New Mexico–Los Alamos Branch (NM)
U of New Mexico–Valencia Campus (NM)
Valencia Comm Coll (FL)
Virginia Western Comm Coll (VA)
Wenatchee Valley Coll (WA)
Western Nebraska Comm Coll (NE)
Western Piedmont Comm Coll (NC)
Western Wyoming Comm Coll (WY)
West Hills Comm Coll (CA)
West Virginia U at Parkersburg (WV)

Wright State U, Lake Campus (OH)
Young Harris Coll (GA)
Yuba Coll (CA)

Pre-Law
Berkeley Coll-New York City Campus (NY)
Berkeley Coll-Westchester Campus (NY)
Virginia Coll at Austin (TX)

Pre-Law Studies
Allen County Comm Coll (KS)
Barton County Comm Coll (KS)
Calhoun Comm Coll (AL)
Centralia Coll (WA)
Central Wyoming Coll (WY)
Clarendon Coll (TX)
Dixie State Coll of Utah (UT)
Eastern Arizona Coll (AZ)
Iowa Lakes Comm Coll (IA)
Kellogg Comm Coll (MI)
Laramie County Comm Coll (WY)
Lawson State Comm Coll (AL)
Louisburg Coll (NC)
Lower Columbia Coll (WA)
Northeast Comm Coll (NE)
Northwest-Shoals Comm Coll (AL)
St. Philip's Coll (TX)
Western Nebraska Comm Coll (NE)
Western Wyoming Comm Coll (WY)

Pre-Medical Studies
Allen County Comm Coll (KS)
Barton County Comm Coll (KS)
Calhoun Comm Coll (AL)
Centralia Coll (WA)
Clarendon Coll (TX)
Coastal Georgia Comm Coll (GA)
Eastern Arizona Coll (AZ)
Howard Comm Coll (MD)
Iowa Lakes Comm Coll (IA)
Kellogg Comm Coll (MI)
Laramie County Comm Coll (WY)
Louisburg Coll (NC)
St. Philip's Coll (TX)
San Juan Coll (NM)
Tulsa Comm Coll (OK)
Western Nebraska Comm Coll (NE)
Western Wyoming Comm Coll (WY)

Pre-Nursing Studies
Cochise Coll, Douglas (AZ)
Iowa Lakes Comm Coll (IA)
Keystone Coll (PA)
Northwest-Shoals Comm Coll (AL)
St. Philip's Coll (TX)
Western Wyoming Comm Coll (WY)

Pre-Pharmacy Studies
Allen County Comm Coll (KS)
Amarillo Coll (TX)
Angelina Coll (TX)
Calhoun Comm Coll (AL)
Centralia Coll (WA)
Coastal Georgia Comm Coll (GA)
Coll of Southern Idaho (ID)
Dodge City Comm Coll (KS)
Eastern Arizona Coll (AZ)
Howard Comm Coll (MD)
Iowa Lakes Comm Coll (IA)
Kellogg Comm Coll (MI)
Laramie County Comm Coll (WY)
Louisburg Coll (NC)
Manatee Comm Coll (FL)
Monroe Comm Coll (NY)
Northwest-Shoals Comm Coll (AL)
Rose State Coll (OK)
St. Philip's Coll (TX)
Santa Rosa Jr Coll (CA)
Tulsa Comm Coll (OK)
Western Nebraska Comm Coll (NE)

Western Wyoming Comm
Coll (WY)

Pre-Theology/Pre-Ministerial Studies
Kellogg Comm Coll (MI)

Pre-Veterinary Studies
Allen County Comm
Coll (KS)
Barton County Comm
Coll (KS)
Calhoun Comm Coll (AL)
Centralia Coll (WA)
Coastal Georgia Comm
Coll (GA)
Howard Comm Coll (MD)
Iowa Lakes Comm
Coll (IA)
Kellogg Comm Coll (MI)
Laramie County Comm
Coll (WY)
Louisburg Coll (NC)
Northwest-Shoals Comm
Coll (AL)
Tulsa Comm Coll (OK)
Western Nebraska Comm
Coll (NE)
Western Wyoming Comm
Coll (WY)

Printing Press Operation
Iowa Lakes Comm
Coll (IA)
Lake Land Coll (IL)

Printmaking
Coll of San Mateo (CA)
De Anza Coll (CA)
Dixie State Coll of
Utah (UT)
Keystone Coll (PA)

Psychiatric/Mental Health Services Technology
Allegany Coll of
Maryland (MD)
Comm Coll of Allegheny
County (PA)
Comm Coll of Rhode
Island (RI)
Cypress Coll (CA)
Hagerstown Comm
Coll (MD)
Houston Comm Coll
System (TX)
Kingsborough Comm Coll
of the City U of New
York (NY)
Montgomery Coll (MD)
Montgomery County
Comm Coll (PA)
Pueblo Comm Coll (CO)
San Joaquin Delta
Coll (CA)
South Piedmont Comm
Coll (NC)
Wayne Comm Coll (NC)
Yuba Coll (CA)

Psychology
Allen County Comm
Coll (KS)
Amarillo Coll (TX)
Bainbridge Coll (GA)
Bakersfield Coll (CA)
Barton County Comm
Coll (KS)
Bergen Comm Coll (NJ)
Blinn Coll (TX)
Brigham Young U –
Idaho (ID)
Bucks County Comm
Coll (PA)
Burlington County
Coll (NJ)
Cañada Coll (CA)
Cape Cod Comm
Coll (MA)
Centralia Coll (WA)
Central Wyoming
Coll (WY)
Cerritos Coll (CA)
Chaffey Coll (CA)
Cisco Jr Coll (TX)
City Coll of San
Francisco (CA)
Clarendon Coll (TX)
Clovis Comm Coll (NM)
Coastal Bend Coll (TX)
Coastal Georgia Comm
Coll (GA)
Cochise Coll, Douglas (AZ)
Cochise Coll, Sierra
Vista (AZ)
Colby Comm Coll (KS)
Coll of Alameda (CA)
Coll of Marin (CA)
Coll of Southern Idaho (ID)

Coll of the Canyons (CA)
Coll of the Desert (CA)
Colorado Mountain
Coll (CO)
Columbia Coll (CA)
Comm Coll of Allegheny
County (PA)
Crafton Hills Coll (CA)
Crowder Coll (MO)
Cuesta Coll (CA)
Cypress Coll (CA)
De Anza Coll (CA)
Dixie State Coll of
Utah (UT)
Dodge City Comm
Coll (KS)
East Central Coll (MO)
Eastern Arizona Coll (AZ)
East Georgia Coll (GA)
El Camino Coll (CA)
Everett Comm Coll (WA)
Finger Lakes Comm
Coll (NY)
Fisher Coll (MA)
Folsom Lake Coll (CA)
Foothill Coll (CA)
Frederick Comm Coll (MD)
Fullerton Coll (CA)
Fulton-Montgomery Comm
Coll (NY)
Garrett Coll (MD)
Genesee Comm Coll (NY)
Georgia Highlands
Coll (GA)
Gloucester County
Coll (NJ)
Gordon Coll (GA)
Grayson County Coll (TX)
Great Basin Coll (NV)
Harrisburg Area Comm
Coll (PA)
Hesser Coll (NH)
Howard Comm Coll (MD)
Hutchinson Comm Coll
and Area Vocational
School (KS)
Imperial Valley Coll (CA)
Iowa Lakes Comm
Coll (IA)
Itasca Comm Coll (MN)
John Wood Comm Coll (IL)
Kankakee Comm Coll (IL)
Kellogg Comm Coll (MI)
Kirkwood Comm Coll (IA)
Lake Tahoe Comm
Coll (CA)
Laramie County Comm
Coll (WY)
Lassen Comm Coll
District (CA)
Lawson State Comm
Coll (AL)
Lee Coll (TX)
Lorain County Comm
Coll (OH)
Los Angeles City Coll (CA)
Los Angeles Mission
Coll (CA)
Los Medanos Coll (CA)
Louisburg Coll (NC)
Lower Columbia Coll (WA)
Manatee Comm Coll (FL)
Mendocino Coll (CA)
Miami Dade Coll (FL)
Miami U–Middletown
Campus (OH)
Mohave Comm Coll (AZ)
Monterey Peninsula
Coll (CA)
Navarro Coll (TX)
Northeastern Jr Coll (CO)
North Idaho Coll (ID)
Odessa Coll (TX)
Oklahoma City Comm
Coll (OK)
Palm Beach Comm
Coll (FL)
Palo Alto Coll (TX)
Pasadena City Coll (CA)
Passaic County Comm
Coll (NJ)
Potomac State Coll of
West Virginia U (WV)
Quincy Coll (MA)
Redlands Comm Coll (OK)
Red Rocks Comm
Coll (CO)
Ridgewater Coll (MN)
Rose State Coll (OK)
Sacramento City Coll (CA)
St. Philip's Coll (TX)
Salt Lake Comm Coll (UT)
San Antonio Coll (TX)
San Bernardino Valley
Coll (CA)
San Diego City Coll (CA)
San Joaquin Delta
Coll (CA)

San Juan Coll (NM)
Santa Ana Coll (CA)
Santa Barbara City
Coll (CA)
Santa Rosa Jr Coll (CA)
Santiago Canyon Coll (CA)
Skagit Valley Coll (WA)
South Georgia Coll (GA)
Terra State Comm
Coll (OH)
Trinidad State Jr Coll (CO)
Tulsa Comm Coll (OK)
Tyler Jr Coll (TX)
Umpqua Comm Coll (OR)
Vincennes U Jasper
Campus (IN)
Western Nebraska Comm
Coll (NE)
Western Wyoming Comm
Coll (WY)
West Hills Comm Coll (CA)
West Los Angeles
Coll (CA)
West Valley Coll (CA)
Wright State U, Lake
Campus (OH)
Young Harris Coll (GA)
Yuba Coll (CA)

Public Administration
Anne Arundel Comm
Coll (MD)
Barton County Comm
Coll (KS)
Citrus Coll (CA)
City Coll of San
Francisco (CA)
Eugenio María de Hostos
Comm Coll of the City
U of New York (NY)
Fayetteville Tech Comm
Coll (NC)
Fort Berthold Comm
Coll (ND)
Housatonic Comm
Coll (CT)
Lamar Inst of
Technology (TX)
Lansing Comm Coll (MI)
Laramie County Comm
Coll (WY)
Los Angeles City Coll (CA)
Manatee Comm Coll (FL)
Miami Dade Coll (FL)
Middle Georgia Coll (GA)
Mohawk Valley Comm
Coll (NY)
National Park Comm
Coll (AR)
Northern Marianas
Coll (MP)
Passaic County Comm
Coll (NJ)
Red Rocks Comm
Coll (CO)
Rio Salado Coll (AZ)
San Antonio Coll (TX)
San Joaquin Delta
Coll (CA)
San Juan Coll (NM)
Santiago Canyon Coll (CA)
Scottsdale Comm
Coll (AZ)
Southern U at
Shreveport (LA)
Tallahassee Comm
Coll (FL)
Three Rivers Comm
Coll (CT)
U of Puerto Rico at
Carolina (PR)
Westchester Comm
Coll (NY)
Westmoreland County
Comm Coll (PA)

Public Administration and Social Service Professions Related
Cleveland State Comm
Coll (TN)
Coll of the Mainland (TX)
Erie Comm Coll (NY)
Erie Comm Coll, South
Campus (NY)

Public Health
City Coll of San
Francisco (CA)

Public Health Education and Promotion
Coll of Southern Idaho (ID)

Public Policy Analysis
Anne Arundel Comm
Coll (MD)

Public Relations, Advertising, and Applied Communication Related
Keystone Coll (PA)

Public Relations/Image Management
Amarillo Coll (TX)
Coastal Bend Coll (TX)
Comm Coll of Beaver
County (PA)
Cosumnes River Coll,
Sacramento (CA)
Crowder Coll (MO)
Golden West Coll (CA)
Kellogg Comm Coll (MI)
Kirkwood Comm Coll (IA)
Lansing Comm Coll (MI)
Los Angeles City Coll (CA)

Publishing
Hennepin Tech Coll (MN)
Westmoreland County
Comm Coll (PA)

Purchasing, Procurement/Acquisitions and Contracts Management
Cincinnati State Tech and
Comm Coll (OH)
De Anza Coll (CA)
Fullerton Coll (CA)
Harper Coll (IL)
Miami U Hamilton (OH)
Tulsa Comm Coll (OK)

Quality Control and Safety Technologies Related
Elizabethtown Tech
Coll (KY)

Quality Control Technology
Broome Comm Coll (NY)
Central Carolina Comm
Coll (NC)
Central Comm Coll–
Columbus
Campus (NE)
Century Coll (MN)
Chaffey Coll (CA)
Chippewa Valley Tech
Coll (WI)
Coll of the Canyons (CA)
Columbia Basin Coll (WA)
Comm Coll of Allegheny
County (PA)
Contra Costa Coll (CA)
Gateway Tech Coll (WI)
Grand Rapids Comm
Coll (MI)
Harper Coll (IL)
Henry Ford Comm
Coll (MI)
Illinois Eastern Comm
Colls, Frontier
Community College (IL)
Illinois Eastern Comm
Colls, Lincoln Trail
College (IL)
Lakeshore Tech Coll (WI)
Lamar Comm Coll (CO)
Lansing Comm Coll (MI)
Lorain County Comm
Coll (OH)
Los Angeles Pierce
Coll (CA)
Los Angeles Southwest
Coll (CA)
Macomb Comm Coll (MI)
Mesa Comm Coll (AZ)
Metropolitan Comm
Coll–Business &
Technology
Campus (MO)
Mid-State Tech Coll (WI)
Monroe Comm Coll (NY)
Mott Comm Coll (MI)
Mt. San Antonio Coll (CA)
Naugatuck Valley Comm
Coll (CT)
New Hampshire Comm
Tech Coll, Nashua/
Claremont (NH)
Northampton County Area
Comm Coll (PA)
Oklahoma State U,
Oklahoma City (OK)
Onondaga Comm
Coll (NY)
Ridgewater Coll (MN)
Salt Lake Comm Coll (UT)
Santa Ana Coll (CA)

South Seattle Comm
Coll (WA)
Springfield Tech Comm
Coll (MA)
Terra State Comm
Coll (OH)
Tulsa Comm Coll (OK)

Radio and Television
Amarillo Coll (TX)
Asnuntuck Comm
Coll (CT)
Brevard Comm Coll (FL)
Brigham Young U –
Idaho (ID)
Bucks County Comm
Coll (PA)
Central Carolina Comm
Coll (NC)
Centralia Coll (WA)
Central Texas Coll (TX)
Chattanooga State Tech
Comm Coll (TN)
City Coll, Fort
Lauderdale (FL)
City Coll, Gainesville (FL)
City Coll, Miami (FL)
City Colls of Chicago,
Kennedy-King
College (IL)
Coahoma Comm Coll (MS)
Colby Comm Coll (KS)
Coll of San Mateo (CA)
Comm Coll of Southern
Nevada (NV)
Cosumnes River Coll,
Sacramento (CA)
Cuesta Coll (CA)
De Anza Coll (CA)
Dixie State Coll of
Utah (UT)
Dodge City Comm
Coll (KS)
Foothill Coll (CA)
Fullerton Coll (CA)
Golden West Coll (CA)
Grossmont Coll (CA)
Hesser Coll (NH)
Hillsborough Comm
Coll (FL)
Illinois Eastern Comm
Colls, Wabash Valley
College (IL)
Iowa Lakes Comm
Coll (IA)
Isothermal Comm
Coll (NC)
Keystone Coll (PA)
Kirkwood Comm Coll (IA)
Lake Land Coll (IL)
Laney Coll (CA)
Lansing Comm Coll (MI)
Lassen Comm Coll
District (CA)
Lawson State Comm
Coll (AL)
Lee Coll (TX)
Los Angeles City Coll (CA)
Los Angeles Southwest
Coll (CA)
Manatee Comm Coll (FL)
Miami Dade Coll (FL)
Middlesex Comm Coll (CT)
Mt. Hood Comm Coll (OR)
Mt. San Antonio Coll (CA)
Napa Valley Coll (CA)
Navarro Coll (TX)
Northeast Comm Coll (NE)
Northeastern Jr Coll (CO)
Northland Comm and Tech
Coll–Thief River
Falls (MN)
Northwest Mississippi
Comm Coll (MS)
Odessa Coll (TX)
Ohlone Coll (CA)
Onondaga Comm
Coll (NY)
Oxnard Coll (CA)
Parkland Coll (IL)
Pasadena City Coll (CA)
St. Louis Comm Coll at
Florissant Valley (MO)
San Antonio Coll (TX)
San Bernardino Valley
Coll (CA)
San Diego City Coll (CA)
Tompkins Cortland Comm
Coll (NY)
Tulsa Comm Coll (OK)
Virginia Western Comm
Coll (VA)
Washington State Comm
Coll (OH)

Radio and Television Broadcasting Technology
Black Hawk Coll,
Moline (IL)
Briarwood Coll (CT)
Cedar Valley Coll (TX)
Central Comm Coll–
Hastings Campus (NE)
Central Wyoming
Coll (WY)
Gadsden State Comm
Coll (AL)
Gateway Tech Coll (WI)
Hillsborough Comm
Coll (FL)
Houston Comm Coll
System (TX)
Iowa Lakes Comm
Coll (IA)
Kellogg Comm Coll (MI)
Manatee Comm Coll (FL)
Miami Dade Coll (FL)
New England Inst of
Technology (RI)
Northampton County Area
Comm Coll (PA)
Northwest Mississippi
Comm Coll (MS)
Oakland Comm Coll (MI)
Ozarks Tech Comm
Coll (MO)
Parkland Coll (IL)
Schoolcraft Coll (MI)
Scott Comm Coll (IA)
York Tech Coll (SC)

Radiologic Technology/Science
ACT Coll, Arlington (VA)
Amarillo Coll (TX)
Arizona Western Coll (AZ)
Barton County Comm
Coll (KS)
Black Hawk Coll,
Moline (IL)
Brevard Comm Coll (FL)
Brigham Young U –
Idaho (ID)
Brookhaven Coll (TX)
Career Tech Coll (LA)
Central Virginia Comm
Coll (VA)
Comm Coll of Southern
Nevada (NV)
East Central Coll (MO)
El Centro Coll (TX)
Fayetteville Tech Comm
Coll (NC)
Florida National Coll (FL)
Foothill Coll (CA)
George C. Wallace Comm
Coll (AL)
Georgia Highlands
Coll (GA)
Henry Ford Comm
Coll (MI)
Hillsborough Comm
Coll (FL)
Holyoke Comm Coll (MA)
Keiser U, Miami (FL)
Kettering Coll of Medical
Arts (OH)
Keystone Coll (PA)
Lakeshore Tech Coll (WI)
Laramie County Comm
Coll (WY)
Laredo Comm Coll (TX)
Los Angeles City Coll (CA)
Louisiana State U at
Eunice (LA)
Madisonville Comm
Coll (KY)
Manatee Comm Coll (FL)
Massasoit Comm
Coll (MA)
Miami Dade Coll (FL)
Minnesota State Comm
and Tech Coll–Fergus
Falls (MN)
Montgomery County
Comm Coll (PA)
National Park Comm
Coll (AR)
Niagara County Comm
Coll (NY)
Northampton County Area
Comm Coll (PA)
Northern Essex Comm
Coll (MA)
Pasco-Hernando Comm
Coll (FL)
Polk Comm Coll (FL)
St. Luke's Coll (IA)
Salt Lake Comm Coll (UT)
Sandhills Comm Coll (NC)
Southern Maine Comm
Coll (ME)

Trocaire Coll (NY)
Tulsa Comm Coll (OK)
Virginia Western Comm
Coll (VA)
Western Nebraska Comm
Coll (NE)

Radio, Television, and Digital Communication Related
Hillsborough Comm
Coll (FL)
Keystone Coll (PA)
Santiago Canyon Coll (CA)

Radio/Television Broadcasting Technology
Mount Wachusett Comm
Coll (MA)
Salt Lake Comm Coll (UT)

Range Science and Management
Brigham Young U –
Idaho (ID)
Central Wyoming
Coll (WY)
Colby Comm Coll (KS)
Coll of Southern Idaho (ID)
Dixie State Coll of
Utah (UT)
Lamar Comm Coll (CO)
St. Catharine Coll (KY)
Treasure Valley Comm
Coll (OR)

Reading Teacher Education
Laney Coll (CA)

Real Estate
Alamance Comm Coll (NC)
Amarillo Coll (TX)
Angelina Coll (TX)
Anne Arundel Comm
Coll (MD)
Antelope Valley Coll (CA)
Ashland Comm and Tech
Coll (KY)
Bakersfield Coll (CA)
Bergen Comm Coll (NJ)
Blinn Coll (TX)
Cabrillo Coll (CA)
Calhoun Comm Coll (AL)
Catawba Valley Comm
Coll (NC)
Cedar Valley Coll (TX)
Central Piedmont Comm
Coll (NC)
Cerritos Coll (CA)
Chaffey Coll (CA)
Chippewa Valley Tech
Coll (WI)
Cincinnati State Tech and
Comm Coll (OH)
Cisco Jr Coll (TX)
Citrus Coll (CA)
City Coll of San
Francisco (CA)
Coll of DuPage (IL)
Coll of Marin (CA)
Coll of San Mateo (CA)
Coll of Southern Idaho (ID)
Coll of the Canyons (CA)
Coll of the Desert (CA)
Coll of the Redwoods (CA)
Collin County Comm Coll
District (TX)
Columbia Basin Coll (WA)
Columbia-Greene Comm
Coll (NY)
Comm Coll of Allegheny
County (PA)
Comm Coll of
Philadelphia (PA)
Comm Coll of Southern
Nevada (NV)
Contra Costa Coll (CA)
Cosumnes River Coll,
Sacramento (CA)
Cuesta Coll (CA)
Cuyahoga Comm
Coll (OH)
De Anza Coll (CA)
Dodge City Comm
Coll (KS)
El Camino Coll (CA)
Folsom Lake Coll (CA)
Fond du Lac Tribal and
Comm Coll (MN)
Foothill Coll (CA)
Forsyth Tech Comm
Coll (NC)
Fresno City Coll (CA)
Fullerton Coll (CA)
Golden West Coll (CA)
Grayson County Coll (TX)
Harper Coll (IL)

Harrisburg Area Comm
Coll (PA)
Hartnell Coll (CA)
Henry Ford Comm
Coll (MI)
Houston Comm Coll
System (TX)
Iowa Lakes Comm
Coll (IA)
Isothermal Comm
Coll (NC)
Jefferson Comm and Tech
Coll (KY)
Jefferson Comm Coll (OH)
Joliet Jr Coll (IL)
Kankakee Comm Coll (IL)
Kent State U, Ashtabula
Campus (OH)
Lake Tahoe Comm
Coll (CA)
Lamar Inst of
Technology (TX)
Lansing Comm Coll (MI)
Laredo Comm Coll (TX)
Las Positas Coll (CA)
Lassen Comm Coll
District (CA)
Lehigh Carbon Comm
Coll (PA)
Lorain County Comm
Coll (OH)
Los Angeles City Coll (CA)
Los Angeles Harbor
Coll (CA)
Los Angeles Mission
Coll (CA)
Los Angeles Pierce
Coll (CA)
Los Angeles Southwest
Coll (CA)
Los Medanos Coll (CA)
Madison Area Tech
Coll (WI)
Madisonville Comm
Coll (KY)
McLennan Comm
Coll (TX)
Mendocino Coll (CA)
Merced Coll (CA)
Mesa Comm Coll (AZ)
Miami U Hamilton (OH)
Miami U–Middletown
Campus (OH)
Mission Coll (CA)
Monterey Peninsula
Coll (CA)
Montgomery County
Comm Coll (PA)
Morton Coll (IL)
Mt. San Antonio Coll (CA)
Napa Valley Coll (CA)
Nassau Comm Coll (NY)
Navarro Coll (TX)
New Hampshire Tech
Inst (NH)
New Mexico Jr Coll (NM)
Nicolet Area Tech Coll (WI)
North Central Texas
Coll (TX)
Northeast Comm Coll (NE)
Northern Essex Comm
Coll (MA)
North Lake Coll (TX)
North Seattle Comm
Coll (WA)
Ohlone Coll (CA)
Oxnard Coll (CA)
Pasadena City Coll (CA)
Pima Comm Coll (AZ)
Rainy River Comm
Coll (MN)
Raritan Valley Comm
Coll (NJ)
Red Rocks Comm
Coll (CO)
Richland Coll (TX)
Ridgewater Coll (MN)
Sacramento City Coll (CA)
St. Louis Comm Coll at
Florissant Valley (MO)
San Antonio Coll (TX)
San Bernardino Valley
Coll (CA)
San Diego City Coll (CA)
San Juan Coll (NM)
Santa Ana Coll (CA)
Santa Barbara City
Coll (CA)
Santiago Canyon Coll (CA)
Scottsdale Comm
Coll (AZ)
Shasta Coll (CA)
Southern State Comm
Coll (OH)
South Plains Coll (TX)
Spokane Falls Comm
Coll (WA)

Suffolk County Comm
Coll (NY)
Texarkana Coll (TX)
Tidewater Comm Coll (VA)
Tyler Jr Coll (TX)
U of New Mexico–Valencia
Campus (NM)
Ventura Coll (CA)
Victor Valley Coll (CA)
Wallace State Comm
Coll (AL)
Western Nevada Comm
Coll (NV)
West Los Angeles
Coll (CA)
Westmoreland County
Comm Coll (PA)
Wytheville Comm Coll (VA)

Receptionist
Alexandria Tech Coll (MN)
Centralia Coll (WA)
Iowa Lakes Comm
Coll (IA)
Lower Columbia Coll (WA)
Minot State U–Bottineau
Campus (ND)

Recording Arts Technology
Kansas City Kansas
Comm Coll (KS)
Madison Media Inst (WI)
Miami Dade Coll (FL)
Northwest Vista Coll (TX)
Olympic Coll (WA)

Rehabilitation and Therapeutic Professions Related
Comm Coll of Rhode
Island (RI)
Heritage Coll (CO)
Springfield Tech Comm
Coll (MA)
Union County Coll (NJ)

Rehabilitation Therapy
Harper Coll (IL)
Iowa Lakes Comm
Coll (IA)
Nassau Comm Coll (NY)
Wayne Comm Coll (NC)

Religious Studies
Allen County Comm
Coll (KS)
Amarillo Coll (TX)
Barton County Comm
Coll (KS)
Chaffey Coll (CA)
Crafton Hills Coll (CA)
East Central Coll (MO)
Fullerton Coll (CA)
Lansing Comm Coll (MI)
Laramie County Comm
Coll (WY)
Manatee Comm Coll (FL)
Orange Coast Coll (CA)
Palm Beach Comm
Coll (FL)
Pasadena City Coll (CA)
Queen of the Holy Rosary
Coll (CA)
San Bernardino Valley
Coll (CA)
San Joaquin Delta
Coll (CA)
Tulsa Comm Coll (OK)
Wallace State Comm
Coll (AL)
Young Harris Coll (GA)

Resort Management
Virginia Coll at Austin (TX)

Respiratory Care Therapy
Allegany Coll of
Maryland (MD)
Amarillo Coll (TX)
Angelina Coll (TX)
Ashland Comm and Tech
Coll (KY)
Athens Tech Coll (GA)
Augusta Tech Coll (GA)
Baltimore City Comm
Coll (MD)
Barton County Comm
Coll (KS)
Bergen Comm Coll (NJ)
Berkshire Comm Coll (MA)
Bowling Green State
U–Firelands Coll (OH)
Broward Comm Coll (FL)
Catawba Valley Comm
Coll (NC)
Central New Mexico
Comm Coll (NM)

Central Piedmont Comm
Coll (NC)
Central Virginia Comm
Coll (VA)
Centro de Estudios
Multidisciplinarios (PR)
Chattanooga State Tech
Comm Coll (TN)
Cincinnati State Tech and
Comm Coll (OH)
City Coll of San
Francisco (CA)
Coastal Georgia Comm
Coll (GA)
Coll of DuPage (IL)
Coll of Southern Idaho (ID)
Coll of the Desert (CA)
Collin County Comm Coll
District (TX)
Comm Coll of Allegheny
County (PA)
Comm Coll of
Philadelphia (PA)
Comm Coll of Rhode
Island (RI)
Comm Coll of Southern
Nevada (NV)
Concorde Career Coll (TN)
Concorde Career Colls,
Inc., Garden
Grove (CA)
Concorde Career Inst,
North Hollywood (CA)
Concorde Career
Inst (MO)
Crafton Hills Coll (CA)
Cuyahoga Comm
Coll (OH)
Dodge City Comm
Coll (KS)
El Camino Coll (CA)
El Centro Coll (TX)
Erie Comm Coll, North
Campus (NY)
Essex County Coll (NJ)
Fayetteville Tech Comm
Coll (NC)
Florence-Darlington Tech
Coll (SC)
Foothill Coll (CA)
Forsyth Tech Comm
Coll (NC)
Frederick Comm Coll (MD)
Fresno City Coll (CA)
Genesee Comm Coll (NY)
George C. Wallace Comm
Coll (AL)
Georgia Highlands
Coll (GA)
Gloucester County
Coll (NJ)
Greenville Tech Coll (SC)
Grossmont Coll (CA)
Guilford Tech Comm
Coll (NC)
Gwinnett Tech Coll (GA)
Harrisburg Area Comm
Coll (PA)
Hawkeye Comm Coll (IA)
Henry Ford Comm
Coll (MI)
Hillsborough Comm
Coll (FL)
Houston Comm Coll
System (TX)
Jackson State Comm
Coll (TN)
Jefferson Comm and Tech
Coll (KY)
Jefferson Comm Coll (OH)
Kankakee Comm Coll (IL)
Kansas City Kansas
Comm Coll (KS)
Kennebec Valley Comm
Coll (ME)
Kettering Coll of Medical
Arts (OH)
Kirkwood Comm Coll (IA)
Labette Comm Coll (KS)
Lamar Inst of
Technology (TX)
Lansing Comm Coll (MI)
Lehigh Carbon Comm
Coll (PA)
Lincoln Land Comm
Coll (IL)
Long Tech Coll (AZ)
Louisiana State U at
Eunice (LA)
Macomb Comm Coll (MI)
Madison Area Tech
Coll (WI)
Madisonville Comm
Coll (KY)
Manatee Comm Coll (FL)
Marshall Comm and Tech
Coll (WV)

Massachusetts Bay Comm
Coll (MA)
Massasoit Comm
Coll (MA)
McLennan Comm
Coll (TX)
Meridian Comm Coll (MS)
Metropolitan Comm
Coll (NE)
Metropolitan Comm
Coll–Penn Valley (MO)
Miami Dade Coll (FL)
Midlands Tech Coll (SC)
Mid-State Tech Coll (WI)
Mississippi Gulf Coast
Comm Coll (MS)
Mohawk Valley Comm
Coll (NY)
Montgomery County
Comm Coll (PA)
Moraine Valley Comm
Coll (IL)
Mott Comm Coll (MI)
Mt. Hood Comm Coll (OR)
Mt. San Antonio Coll (CA)
Napa Valley Coll (CA)
Nassau Comm Coll (NY)
Northern Essex Comm
Coll (MA)
North Shore Comm
Coll (MA)
NorthWest Arkansas
Comm Coll (AR)
Northwest Mississippi
Comm Coll (MS)
Oakland Comm Coll (MI)
Odessa Coll (TX)
Ohlone Coll (CA)
Oklahoma City Comm
Coll (OK)
Onondaga Comm
Coll (NY)
Orange Coast Coll (CA)
Ozarks Tech Comm
Coll (MO)
Parkland Coll (IL)
Passaic County Comm
Coll (NJ)
Pearl River Comm
Coll (MS)
Piedmont Tech Coll (SC)
Piedmont Virginia Comm
Coll (VA)
Pima Comm Coll (AZ)
Polk Comm Coll (FL)
Pueblo Comm Coll (CO)
Pulaski Tech Coll (AR)
Raritan Valley Comm
Coll (NJ)
Roane State Comm
Coll (TN)
Robeson Comm Coll (NC)
Rose State Coll (OK)
St. Luke's Coll (IA)
Saint Paul Coll–A Comm &
Tech College (MN)
St. Philip's Coll (TX)
Sandhills Comm Coll (NC)
Scott Comm Coll (IA)
Seminole Comm Coll (FL)
Sheridan Coll–Sheridan
and Gillette (WY)
Southeastern Comm Coll,
North Campus (IA)
Southeast Kentucky Comm
and Tech Coll (KY)
Southern Maine Comm
Coll (ME)
Southern U at
Shreveport (LA)
South Plains Coll (TX)
Southside Virginia Comm
Coll (VA)
Southwestern Comm
Coll (NC)
Southwest Georgia Tech
Coll (GA)
Southwest Virginia Comm
Coll (VA)
Spokane Comm Coll (WA)
Springfield Tech Comm
Coll (MA)
Stanly Comm Coll (NC)
Stark State Coll of
Technology (OH)
Sussex County Comm
Coll (NJ)
Tallahassee Comm
Coll (FL)
Temple Coll (TX)
Trident Tech Coll (SC)
Tulsa Comm Coll (OK)
Tyler Jr Coll (TX)
Union County Coll (NJ)
Valencia Comm Coll (FL)
Victoria Coll (TX)
Victor Valley Coll (CA)

Volunteer State Comm
Coll (TN)
Wallace State Comm
Coll (AL)
Westchester Comm
Coll (NY)

Respiratory Therapy Technician
Augusta Tech Coll (GA)
City Colls of Chicago,
Olive-Harvey
College (IL)
Coahoma Comm Coll (MS)
Columbus Tech Coll (GA)
Coosa Valley Tech
Coll (GA)
Griffin Tech Coll (GA)
Harrisburg Area Comm
Coll (PA)
Heart of Georgia Tech
Coll (GA)
Kansas City Kansas
Comm Coll (KS)
Massasoit Comm
Coll (MA)
Miami Dade Coll (FL)
Missouri State U–West
Plains (MO)
Northern Essex Comm
Coll (MA)
Okefenokee Tech
Coll (GA)
Southeastern Tech
Coll (GA)

Restaurant, Culinary, and Catering Management
The Art Inst of New York
City (NY)
Central Florida Comm
Coll (FL)
Cincinnati State Tech and
Comm Coll (OH)
Coahoma Comm Coll (MS)
Coll of DuPage (IL)
Coll of Lake County (IL)
Comm Coll of Allegheny
County (PA)
Culinary Inst Alain & Marie
LeNotre (TX)
Cuyahoga Comm
Coll (OH)
Erie Comm Coll, North
Campus (NY)
Hillsborough Comm
Coll (FL)
Iowa Lakes Comm
Coll (IA)
JNA Inst of Culinary
Arts (PA)
John Wood Comm Coll (IL)
Keystone Coll (PA)
Linn-Benton Comm
Coll (OR)
Mohawk Valley Comm
Coll (NY)
Moraine Valley Comm
Coll (IL)
New England Culinary
Inst (VT)
Orange Coast Coll (CA)
Pima Comm Coll (AZ)
State U of New York Coll
of Technology at
Alfred (NY)
Waukesha County Tech
Coll (WI)

Restaurant/Food Services Management
California School of
Culinary Arts (CA)
Front Range Comm
Coll (CO)
Iowa Lakes Comm
Coll (IA)
Keystone Coll (PA)
Lehigh Carbon Comm
Coll (PA)
Massasoit Comm
Coll (MA)
Northampton County Area
Comm Coll (PA)
Oakland Comm Coll (MI)
St. Philip's Coll (TX)
Western Culinary Inst (OR)

Retailing
Black Hawk Coll,
Moline (IL)
Catawba Valley Comm
Coll (NC)
Centralia Coll (WA)
Clark Coll (WA)
Coll of DuPage (IL)
Comm Coll of Allegheny
County (PA)

Comm Coll of Rhode
Island (RI)
Hutchinson Comm Coll
and Area Vocational
School (KS)
Iowa Lakes Comm
Coll (IA)
Moraine Valley Comm
Coll (IL)
North Central Texas
Coll (TX)
Northeast Comm Coll (NE)
Orange Coast Coll (CA)
Waukesha County Tech
Coll (WI)
Wayne Comm Coll (NC)

Retailing Operations
Bradford School (PA)
Clark Coll (WA)

Retail Management
Riverside Comm Coll
District (CA)

Robotics Technology
Coll of DuPage (IL)
Comm Coll of Allegheny
County (PA)
Kellogg Comm Coll (MI)
Macomb Comm Coll (MI)
Oakland Comm Coll (MI)
Schoolcraft Coll (MI)
Southern U at
Shreveport (LA)
Terra State Comm
Coll (OH)
Texas State Tech Coll–
Marshall (TX)
Texas State Tech Coll
West Texas (TX)
Yuba Coll (CA)

Romance Languages
Coll of the Desert (CA)

Russian
Brigham Young U –
Idaho (ID)
El Camino Coll (CA)
Everett Comm Coll (WA)
Tulsa Comm Coll (OK)

Russian Studies
Manatee Comm Coll (FL)

Safety/Security
Technology
Cuyahoga Comm
Coll (OH)
John Tyler Comm Coll (VA)
Macomb Comm Coll (MI)
Pine Tech Coll (MN)
Tulsa Comm Coll (OK)

Sales and Marketing/
Marketing And
Distribution Teacher
Education
Louisburg Coll (NC)
Northwest Mississippi
Comm Coll (MS)
Parkland Coll (IL)

Sales, Distribution
and Marketing
Academy Coll (MN)
Brown Mackie Coll–
Kansas City (KS)
Brown Mackie Coll–
Salina (KS)
Burlington County
Coll (NJ)
Central Carolina Tech
Coll (SC)
Centralia Coll (WA)
Coll of DuPage (IL)
Collin County Comm Coll
District (TX)
Cuyahoga Comm
Coll (OH)
Hesser Coll (NH)
Iowa Lakes Comm
Coll (IA)
John Wood Comm Coll (IL)
Kennebec Valley Comm
Coll (ME)
LDS Business Coll (UT)
Midlands Tech Coll (SC)
Montgomery County
Comm Coll (PA)
North Central Texas
Coll (TX)
Pioneer Pacific Coll,
Wilsonville (OR)
Ridgewater Coll (MN)
Santa Ana Coll (CA)
Santa Barbara City
Coll (CA)
State U of New York Coll
of Technology at
Alfred (NY)

Sales Operations
Coll of Lake County (IL)

Salon/Beauty Salon
Management
Keiser Career Coll -
Greenacres (FL)
Mott Comm Coll (MI)
Oakland Comm Coll (MI)

Sanitation Technology
Kirkwood Comm Coll (IA)
Red Rocks Comm
Coll (CO)

Science Teacher
Education
Angelina Coll (TX)
Colby Comm Coll (KS)
Comm Coll of Southern
Nevada (NV)
Harrisburg Area Comm
Coll (PA)
Iowa Lakes Comm
Coll (IA)
Jones County Jr Coll (MS)
Manatee Comm Coll (FL)
Miami Dade Coll (FL)
Mississippi Delta Comm
Coll (MS)
Northwest Mississippi
Comm Coll (MS)
Ranger Coll (TX)
Sandhills Comm Coll (NC)
South Georgia Coll (GA)

Science Technologies
Related
Cascadia Comm Coll (WA)
Cincinnati State Tech and
Comm Coll (OH)
Comm Coll of Allegheny
County (PA)
Eastern West Virginia
Comm and Tech
Coll (WV)
Klamath Comm Coll (OR)
Marshall Comm and Tech
Coll (WV)
Victor Valley Coll (CA)

Sculpture
De Anza Coll (CA)
Dixie State Coll of
Utah (UT)
Grossmont Coll (CA)
Keystone Coll (PA)
Monterey Peninsula
Coll (CA)

Secondary Education
Allen County Comm
Coll (KS)
Alpena Comm Coll (MI)
Barton County Comm
Coll (KS)
Calhoun Comm Coll (AL)
Central Wyoming
Coll (WY)
Clarendon Coll (TX)
Dixie State Coll of
Utah (UT)
Eastern Arizona Coll (AZ)
Essex County Coll (NJ)
Georgia Highlands
Coll (GA)
Howard Comm Coll (MD)
Kellogg Comm Coll (MI)
Mohawk Valley Comm
Coll (NY)
Montgomery County
Comm Coll (PA)
Northwest-Shoals Comm
Coll (AL)
Parkland Coll (IL)
Western Nebraska Comm
Coll (NE)
Western Wyoming Comm
Coll (WY)

Security and Loss
Prevention
Academy of Court
Reporting (OH)
Cincinnati State Tech and
Comm Coll (OH)
Hesser Coll (NH)
Nassau Comm Coll (NY)

Security and
Protective Services
Related
Black Hawk Coll,
Moline (IL)
Pima Comm Coll (AZ)

Selling Skills and
Sales
Alexandria Tech Coll (MN)
Century Coll (MN)
Clark Coll (WA)

Coll of DuPage (IL)
Cuyahoga Comm
Coll (OH)
Iowa Lakes Comm
Coll (IA)
Lincoln Land Comm
Coll (IL)
Moraine Valley Comm
Coll (IL)
Orange Coast Coll (CA)
Santa Barbara City
Coll (CA)

Sheet Metal
Technology
Black Hawk Coll,
Moline (IL)
Comm Coll of Allegheny
County (PA)
Kellogg Comm Coll (MI)
Macomb Comm Coll (MI)
Santiago Canyon Coll (CA)
Western Nevada Comm
Coll (NV)

Sign Language
Interpretation
Black Hawk Coll,
Moline (IL)

Sign Language
Interpretation and
Translation
Burlington County
Coll (NJ)
Central Piedmont Comm
Coll (NC)
Chattanooga State Tech
Comm Coll (TN)
Cincinnati State Tech and
Comm Coll (OH)
Clovis Comm Coll (NM)
Collin County Comm Coll
District (TX)
Comm Coll of Allegheny
County (PA)
Comm Coll of
Philadelphia (PA)
Comm Coll of Southern
Nevada (NV)
Golden West Coll (CA)
Harper Coll (IL)
Hillsborough Comm
Coll (FL)
Houston Comm Coll
System (TX)
Lansing Comm Coll (MI)
Los Angeles Pierce
Coll (CA)
Los Angeles Southwest
Coll (CA)
McLennan Comm
Coll (TX)
Miami Dade Coll (FL)
Mott Comm Coll (MI)
Mt. San Antonio Coll (CA)
Mount Wachusett Comm
Coll (MA)
New River Comm Coll (VA)
Northern Essex Comm
Coll (MA)
Northwestern Connecticut
Comm Coll (CT)
Ohlone Coll (CA)
Oklahoma State U,
Oklahoma City (OK)
Pasadena City Coll (CA)
Pima Comm Coll (AZ)
Riverside Comm Coll
District (CA)
St. Louis Comm Coll at
Florissant Valley (MO)
Saint Paul Coll–A Comm &
Tech College (MN)
Salt Lake Comm Coll (UT)
Scott Comm Coll (IA)
Sheridan Coll–Sheridan
and Gillette (WY)
Southeast Tech Inst (SD)
Spokane Falls Comm
Coll (WA)
Suffolk County Comm
Coll (NY)
Terra State Comm
Coll (OH)
Tulsa Comm Coll (OK)
Tyler Jr Coll (TX)
Union County Coll (NJ)
Wilson Tech Comm
Coll (NC)

Small Business
Administration
Alexandria Tech Coll (MN)
Black Hawk Coll,
Moline (IL)
Iowa Lakes Comm
Coll (IA)

Small Engine
Mechanics and Repair
Technology
Alexandria Tech Coll (MN)
Century Coll (MN)
Iowa Lakes Comm
Coll (IA)
Los Medanos Coll (CA)

Social Psychology
Macomb Comm Coll (MI)
Manatee Comm Coll (FL)

Social Sciences
Amarillo Coll (TX)
Angelina Coll (TX)
Anne Arundel Comm
Coll (MD)
Arizona Western Coll (AZ)
Barstow Coll (CA)
Bowling Green State
U–Firelands Coll (OH)
Bucks County Comm
Coll (PA)
Centralia Coll (WA)
Central Oregon Comm
Coll (OR)
Central Texas Coll (TX)
Central Wyoming
Coll (WY)
Chaffey Coll (CA)
Chesapeake Coll (MD)
Citrus Coll (CA)
City Coll of San
Francisco (CA)
City Colls of Chicago,
Harold Washington
College (IL)
City Colls of Chicago,
Olive-Harvey
College (IL)
Clarendon Coll (TX)
Cochise Coll, Sierra
Vista (AZ)
Coll of Alameda (CA)
Coll of Micronesia–
FSM (FM)
Coll of San Mateo (CA)
Coll of Southern
Maryland (MD)
Coll of the Canyons (CA)
Coll of the Desert (CA)
Colorado Mountain
Coll (CO)
Colorado Mountain Coll,
Alpine Campus (CO)
Columbia-Greene Comm
Coll (NY)
Comm Coll of Allegheny
County (PA)
Comm Coll of Southern
Nevada (NV)
Comm Coll of
Vermont (VT)
Cosumnes River Coll,
Sacramento (CA)
Cypress Coll (CA)
De Anza Coll (CA)
Dodge City Comm
Coll (KS)
Essex County Coll (NJ)
Finger Lakes Comm
Coll (NY)
Folsom Lake Coll (CA)
Foothill Coll (CA)
Fresno City Coll (CA)
Fulton-Montgomery Comm
Coll (NY)
Garrett Coll (MD)
Gloucester County
Coll (NJ)
Harper Coll (IL)
Harrisburg Area Comm
Coll (PA)
Housatonic Comm
Coll (CT)
Houston Comm Coll
System (TX)
Howard Comm Coll (MD)
Hutchinson Comm Coll
and Area Vocational
School (KS)
Imperial Valley Coll (CA)
Iowa Lakes Comm
Coll (IA)
Irvine Valley Coll (CA)
Jamestown Comm
Coll (NY)
Kirkwood Comm Coll (IA)
Labette Comm Coll (KS)
Lake Tahoe Comm
Coll (CA)
Lamar Comm Coll (CO)
Laney Coll (CA)
Laramie County Comm
Coll (WY)
Laredo Comm Coll (TX)
Lassen Comm Coll
District (CA)

Lawson State Comm
Coll (AL)
Lehigh Carbon Comm
Coll (PA)
Lorain County Comm
Coll (OH)
Los Angeles Mission
Coll (CA)
Los Angeles Southwest
Coll (CA)
Lower Columbia Coll (WA)
Manatee Comm Coll (FL)
Massachusetts Bay Comm
Coll (MA)
Mendocino Coll (CA)
Merced Coll (CA)
Miami Dade Coll (FL)
Miami U–Middletown
Campus (OH)
Mission Coll (CA)
Monroe Comm Coll (NY)
Montgomery County
Comm Coll (PA)
Navarro Coll (TX)
New Mexico Military
Inst (NM)
Niagara County Comm
Coll (NY)
Northeast Comm Coll (NE)
Northeastern Jr Coll (CO)
North Idaho Coll (ID)
Northwestern Connecticut
Comm Coll (CT)
Odessa Coll (TX)
Ohlone Coll (CA)
Orange Coast Coll (CA)
Palm Beach Comm
Coll (FL)
Pasadena City Coll (CA)
Porterville Coll (CA)
Quincy Coll (MA)
Raritan Valley Comm
Coll (NJ)
Redlands Comm Coll (OK)
Reedley Coll (CA)
Roane State Comm
Coll (TN)
Rogue Comm Coll (OR)
Roxbury Comm Coll (MA)
Sacramento City Coll (CA)
St. Catharine Coll (KY)
San Diego City Coll (CA)
San Joaquin Delta
Coll (CA)
Santa Ana Coll (CA)
Santa Rosa Jr Coll (CA)
Santiago Canyon Coll (CA)
Seminole State Coll (OK)
Sheridan Coll–Sheridan
and Gillette (WY)
Skagit Valley Coll (WA)
Southwest Mississippi
Comm Coll (MS)
State U of New York Coll
of Agriculture and
Technology at
Morrisville (NY)
State U of New York Coll
of Technology at
Alfred (NY)
State U of New York Coll
of Technology at
Canton (NY)
Suffolk County Comm
Coll (NY)
Taft Coll (CA)
Tompkins Cortland Comm
Coll (NY)
Treasure Valley Comm
Coll (OR)
Tulsa Comm Coll (OK)
Turtle Mountain Comm
Coll (ND)
Tyler Jr Coll (TX)
Ulster County Comm
Coll (NY)
Umpqua Comm Coll (OR)
U of Puerto Rico at
Carolina (PR)
Victor Valley Coll (CA)
Vincennes U Jasper
Campus (IN)
Warren County Comm
Coll (NJ)
Westchester Comm
Coll (NY)
Western Wyoming Comm
Coll (WY)
West Hills Comm Coll (CA)
West Valley Coll (CA)
Yuba Coll (CA)

Social Science
Teacher Education
Louisburg Coll (NC)
Northwest Mississippi
Comm Coll (MS)

Social Studies
Teacher Education
Manatee Comm Coll (FL)
Northwest Mississippi
Comm Coll (MS)

Social Work
Alamance Comm Coll (NC)
Allen County Comm
Coll (KS)
Amarillo Coll (TX)
Angelina Coll (TX)
Asheville-Buncombe Tech
Comm Coll (NC)
Barton County Comm
Coll (KS)
Beaufort County Comm
Coll (NC)
Berkshire Comm Coll (MA)
Brigham Young U –
Idaho (ID)
Bucks County Comm
Coll (PA)
Capital Comm Coll (CT)
Central Carolina Comm
Coll (NC)
Central Piedmont Comm
Coll (NC)
Century Coll (MN)
Chipola Coll (FL)
City Coll of San
Francisco (CA)
City Colls of Chicago,
Harold Washington
College (IL)
City Colls of Chicago,
Kennedy-King
College (IL)
City Colls of Chicago,
Richard J. Daley
College (IL)
Clark State Comm
Coll (OH)
Coahoma Comm Coll (MS)
Cochise Coll, Douglas (AZ)
Cochise Coll, Sierra
Vista (AZ)
Colby Comm Coll (KS)
Coll of Lake County (IL)
Coll of Menominee
Nation (WI)
Coll of the Mainland (TX)
Comm Coll of Allegheny
County (PA)
Comm Coll of Rhode
Island (RI)
Dixie State Coll of
Utah (UT)
Dodge City Comm
Coll (KS)
Eastern New Mexico
U–Roswell (NM)
El Camino Coll (CA)
Elgin Comm Coll (IL)
Elizabethtown Tech
Coll (KY)
Essex County Coll (NJ)
Harrisburg Area Comm
Coll (PA)
Hesser Coll (NH)
Illinois Eastern Comm
Colls, Wabash Valley
College (IL)
Iowa Lakes Comm
Coll (IA)
Jefferson Comm and Tech
Coll (KY)
Kellogg Comm Coll (MI)
Kilian Comm Coll (SD)
Kirkwood Comm Coll (IA)
Lake Land Coll (IL)
Lamar Comm Coll (CO)
Lansing Comm Coll (MI)
Lawson State Comm
Coll (AL)
Lehigh Carbon Comm
Coll (PA)
Lorain County Comm
Coll (OH)
Louisburg Coll (NC)
Manatee Comm Coll (FL)
Miami Dade Coll (FL)
Miami U–Middletown
Campus (OH)
Mississippi Delta Comm
Coll (MS)
Naugatuck Valley Comm
Coll (CT)
Nebraska Indian Comm
Coll (NE)
New Hampshire Comm
Tech Coll, Nashua/
Claremont (NH)
New Mexico State U–
Alamogordo (NM)
Northampton County Area
Comm Coll (PA)
Northeastern Jr Coll (CO)

Northwestern Tech Coll (GA)
Owensboro Comm and Tech Coll (KY)
Palm Beach Comm Coll (FL)
Piedmont Tech Coll (SC)
Potomac State Coll of West Virginia U (WV)
Quincy Coll (MA)
Ridgewater Coll (MN)
Sacramento City Coll (CA)
St. Catharine Coll (KY)
St. Philip's Coll (TX)
Salt Lake Comm Coll (UT)
San Diego City Coll (CA)
San Juan Coll (NM)
Sitting Bull Coll (ND)
South Piedmont Comm Coll (NC)
South Plains Coll (TX)
Spokane Falls Comm Coll (WA)
Terra State Comm Coll (OH)
Tulsa Comm Coll (OK)
Turtle Mountain Comm Coll (ND)
Umpqua Comm Coll (OR)
The U of Akron–Wayne Coll (OH)
U of Cincinnati Clermont Coll (OH)
Vincennes U Jasper Campus (IN)
Washington State Comm Coll (OH)
Western Nebraska Comm Coll (NE)
Western Wyoming Comm Coll (WY)
West Georgia Tech Coll (GA)
West Virginia U at Parkersburg (WV)
Wright State U, Lake Campus (OH)
Zane State Coll (OH)

Social Work Related
Clarendon Coll (TX)
Northeast Comm Coll (NE)

Sociology
Allen County Comm Coll (KS)
Bainbridge Coll (GA)
Bakersfield Coll (CA)
Barton County Comm Coll (KS)
Bergen Comm Coll (NJ)
Brigham Young U – Idaho (ID)
Burlington County Coll (NJ)
Cañada Coll (CA)
Centralia Coll (WA)
Cerritos Coll (CA)
Chaffey Coll (CA)
Chesapeake Coll (MD)
Clarendon Coll (TX)
Coastal Bend Coll (TX)
Coastal Georgia Comm Coll (GA)
Cochise Coll, Douglas (AZ)
Colby Comm Coll (KS)
Coll of Alameda (CA)
Coll of Marin (CA)
Coll of Southern Idaho (ID)
Coll of the Desert (CA)
Coll of the Mainland (TX)
Columbia Coll (CA)
Comm Coll of Allegheny County (PA)
Comm Coll of Southern Nevada (NV)
Contra Costa Coll (CA)
Crafton Hills Coll (CA)
Cypress Coll (CA)
De Anza Coll (CA)
Dixie State Coll of Utah (UT)
East Central Coll (MO)
Eastern Arizona Coll (AZ)
East Georgia Coll (GA)
El Camino Coll (CA)
Everett Comm Coll (WA)
Finger Lakes Comm Coll (NY)
Foothill Coll (CA)
Fullerton Coll (CA)
Garrett Coll (MD)
Georgia Highlands Coll (GA)
Gloucester County Coll (NJ)
Gordon Coll (GA)
Grayson County Coll (TX)
Great Basin Coll (NV)

Iowa Lakes Comm Coll (IA)
John Wood Comm Coll (IL)
Kellogg Comm Coll (MI)
Kirkwood Comm Coll (IA)
Laramie County Comm Coll (WY)
Lawson State Comm Coll (AL)
Lee Coll (TX)
Lorain County Comm Coll (OH)
Los Angeles City Coll (CA)
Los Angeles Mission Coll (CA)
Los Medanos Coll (CA)
Louisburg Coll (NC)
Lower Columbia Coll (WA)
Miami Dade Coll (FL)
Miami U–Middletown Campus (OH)
Mohave Comm Coll (AZ)
Monterey Peninsula Coll (CA)
Navarro Coll (TX)
North Idaho Coll (ID)
Odessa Coll (TX)
Oklahoma City Comm Coll (OK)
Orange Coast Coll (CA)
Oxnard Coll (CA)
Palo Alto Coll (TX)
Pasadena City Coll (CA)
Pima Comm Coll (AZ)
Potomac State Coll of West Virginia U (WV)
Quincy Coll (MA)
Red Rocks Comm Coll (CO)
Ridgewater Coll (MN)
Rose State Coll (OK)
St. Catharine Coll (KY)
St. Philip's Coll (TX)
Salt Lake Comm Coll (UT)
San Bernardino Valley Coll (CA)
San Diego City Coll (CA)
San Joaquin Delta Coll (CA)
San Juan Coll (NM)
Santa Ana Coll (CA)
Santa Barbara City Coll (CA)
Santa Rosa Jr Coll (CA)
Santiago Canyon Coll (CA)
Skagit Valley Coll (WA)
Southern U at Shreveport (LA)
South Georgia Coll (GA)
Treasure Valley Comm Coll (OR)
Tulsa Comm Coll (OK)
Umpqua Comm Coll (OR)
Vincennes U Jasper Campus (IN)
Wenatchee Valley Coll (WA)
Western Nebraska Comm Coll (NE)
Western Wyoming Comm Coll (WY)
West Los Angeles Coll (CA)
West Valley Coll (CA)
Wright State U, Lake Campus (OH)
Young Harris Coll (GA)

Soil Conservation
Nebraska Coll of Tech Agriculture (NE)
The Ohio State U Ag Tech Inst (OH)

Soil Science and Agronomy
Dixie State Coll of Utah (UT)
Iowa Lakes Comm Coll (IA)

Solar Energy Technology
Cabrillo Coll (CA)
Comm Coll of Allegheny County (PA)
Red Rocks Comm Coll (CO)

Spanish
Arizona Western Coll (AZ)
Bakersfield Coll (CA)
Berkeley City Coll (CA)
Blinn Coll (TX)
Brigham Young U – Idaho (ID)
Cabrillo Coll (CA)
Cañada Coll (CA)
Centralia Coll (WA)
Cerritos Coll (CA)

Chaffey Coll (CA)
Citrus Coll (CA)
City Colls of Chicago, Harold Washington College (IL)
Cleveland Comm Coll (NC)
Coll of Alameda (CA)
Coll of Marin (CA)
Coll of San Mateo (CA)
Coll of the Canyons (CA)
Contra Costa Coll (CA)
Crafton Hills Coll (CA)
De Anza Coll (CA)
El Camino Coll (CA)
Everett Comm Coll (WA)
Foothill Coll (CA)
Fresno City Coll (CA)
Gordon Coll (GA)
Grossmont Coll (CA)
Imperial Valley Coll (CA)
Iowa Lakes Comm Coll (IA)
Kirkwood Comm Coll (IA)
Lake Tahoe Comm Coll (CA)
Laramie County Comm Coll (WY)
Lee Coll (TX)
Los Angeles City Coll (CA)
Los Angeles Mission Coll (CA)
Los Angeles Southwest Coll (CA)
Manatee Comm Coll (FL)
Mendocino Coll (CA)
Miami Dade Coll (FL)
Miami U–Middletown Campus (OH)
Monterey Peninsula Coll (CA)
New Mexico Military Inst (NM)
North Idaho Coll (ID)
Orange Coast Coll (CA)
Oxnard Coll (CA)
Pasadena City Coll (CA)
Red Rocks Comm Coll (CO)
St. Catharine Coll (KY)
St. Philip's Coll (TX)
San Bernardino Valley Coll (CA)
San Joaquin Delta Coll (CA)
Santa Barbara City Coll (CA)
Skagit Valley Coll (WA)
South Georgia Coll (GA)
Tulsa Comm Coll (OK)
Western Nebraska Comm Coll (NE)
Western Wyoming Comm Coll (WY)
West Los Angeles Coll (CA)
West Valley Coll (CA)
Young Harris Coll (GA)

Spanish Language Teacher Education
Frederick Comm Coll (MD)

Special Education
Cleveland Comm Coll (NC)
Coll of Micronesia–FSM (FM)
Comm Coll of Rhode Island (RI)
Fayetteville Tech Comm Coll (NC)
Kellogg Comm Coll (MI)
Lehigh Carbon Comm Coll (PA)
Louisburg Coll (NC)
Western Wyoming Comm Coll (WY)

Special Education (Early Childhood)
Calhoun Comm Coll (AL)
Itasca Comm Coll (MN)
Motlow State Comm Coll (TN)
Olympic Coll (WA)

Special Education (Hearing Impaired)
Bishop State Comm Coll (AL)

Special Products Marketing
Asnuntuck Comm Coll (CT)
Bergen Comm Coll (NJ)
Brigham Young U – Idaho (ID)
Broward Comm Coll (FL)
Burlington County Coll (NJ)

Cabrillo Coll (CA)
Central Piedmont Comm Coll (NC)
Chaffey Coll (CA)
City Colls of Chicago, Kennedy-King College (IL)
Columbia Coll (CA)
Comm Coll of Philadelphia (PA)
Comm Coll of Southern Nevada (NV)
Cosumnes River Coll, Sacramento (CA)
Cypress Coll (CA)
East Central Coll (MO)
El Camino Coll (CA)
El Centro Coll (TX)
Fiorello H. LaGuardia Comm Coll of the City U of New York (NY)
Fox Valley Tech Coll (WI)
Gateway Comm Coll (CT)
Greenville Tech Coll (SC)
Henry Ford Comm Coll (MI)
Hocking Coll (OH)
Jefferson Comm Coll (OH)
Joliet Jr Coll (IL)
Kirkwood Comm Coll (IA)
Lansing Comm Coll (MI)
Los Angeles City Coll (CA)
Merced Coll (CA)
Metropolitan Comm Coll–Penn Valley (MO)
Mission Coll (CA)
Monroe Comm Coll (NY)
Muskegon Comm Coll (MI)
Naugatuck Valley Comm Coll (CT)
Oklahoma State U, Okmulgee (OK)
Onondaga Comm Coll (NY)
Orange Coast Coll (CA)
Palm Beach Comm Coll (FL)
St. Louis Comm Coll at Florissant Valley (MO)
San Diego City Coll (CA)
San Joaquin Delta Coll (CA)
Scottsdale Comm Coll (AZ)
Southern Maine Comm Coll (ME)
South Plains Coll (TX)
South Seattle Comm Coll (WA)
State Fair Comm Coll (MO)
State U of New York Coll of Agriculture and Technology at Morrisville (NY)
Three Rivers Comm Coll (CT)
Wallace State Comm Coll (AL)
Westchester Comm Coll (NY)
Westmoreland County Comm Coll (PA)

Speech and Rhetoric
Allen County Comm Coll (KS)
Amarillo Coll (TX)
Bainbridge Coll (GA)
Bakersfield Coll (CA)
Blinn Coll (TX)
Cañada Coll (CA)
Cerritos Coll (CA)
Chaffey Coll (CA)
City Colls of Chicago, Harold Washington College (IL)
City Colls of Chicago, Harry S. Truman College (IL)
City Colls of Chicago, Richard J. Daley College (IL)
City Colls of Chicago, Wilbur Wright College (IL)
Clarendon Coll (TX)
Coastal Bend Coll (TX)
Coll of Marin (CA)
Coll of San Mateo (CA)
Coll of the Desert (CA)
Crafton Hills Coll (CA)
Cypress Coll (CA)
De Anza Coll (CA)
Dodge City Comm Coll (KS)
East Central Coll (MO)
El Camino Coll (CA)
Everett Comm Coll (WA)

Foothill Coll (CA)
Fresno City Coll (CA)
Fullerton Coll (CA)
Grayson County Coll (TX)
Grossmont Coll (CA)
Iowa Lakes Comm Coll (IA)
Irvine Valley Coll (CA)
Lansing Comm Coll (MI)
Lee Coll (TX)
Linn-Benton Comm Coll (OR)
Los Angeles City Coll (CA)
Los Angeles Mission Coll (CA)
Louisburg Coll (NC)
Lower Columbia Coll (WA)
Manatee Comm Coll (FL)
Mendocino Coll (CA)
Navarro Coll (TX)
Northeast Comm Coll (NE)
Odessa Coll (TX)
Palo Alto Coll (TX)
Pasadena City Coll (CA)
Ridgewater Coll (MN)
Rose State Coll (OK)
Sacramento City Coll (CA)
St. Philip's Coll (TX)
San Diego City Coll (CA)
San Joaquin Delta Coll (CA)
Shasta Coll (CA)
Skagit Valley Coll (WA)
South Georgia Coll (GA)
Tulsa Comm Coll (OK)
Tyler Jr Coll (TX)
West Los Angeles Coll (CA)
West Valley Coll (CA)

Speech-Language Pathology
Catawba Valley Comm Coll (NC)
Coll of DuPage (IL)
Crafton Hills Coll (CA)
Fayetteville Tech Comm Coll (NC)
Guilford Tech Comm Coll (NC)
Parkland Coll (IL)
Santa Rosa Jr Coll (CA)

Speech Teacher Education
Northwest Mississippi Comm Coll (MS)

Speech/Theater Education
Angelina Coll (TX)
San Antonio Coll (TX)

Speech Therapy
Brigham Young U – Idaho (ID)
Mount Wachusett Comm Coll (MA)

Sport and Fitness Administration/ Management
Barton County Comm Coll (KS)
Bucks County Comm Coll (PA)
Central Oregon Comm Coll (OR)
Clark Coll (WA)
Coahoma Comm Coll (MS)
Dean Coll (MA)
Hesser Coll (NH)
Holyoke Comm Coll (MA)
Howard Comm Coll (MD)
Iowa Lakes Comm Coll (IA)
Keystone Coll (PA)
Kingsborough Comm Coll of the City U of New York (NY)
Lake-Sumter Comm Coll (FL)
Lehigh Carbon Comm Coll (PA)
Lorain County Comm Coll (OH)
Louisburg Coll (NC)
New Hampshire Tech Inst (NH)
New Mexico Military Inst (NM)
Northampton County Area Comm Coll (PA)
North Iowa Area Comm Coll (IA)
Oakland Comm Coll (MI)
South Georgia Coll (GA)
Spokane Falls Comm Coll (WA)

State U of New York Coll of Technology at Alfred (NY)
Tompkins Cortland Comm Coll (NY)

Statistics
Manatee Comm Coll (FL)
Pasadena City Coll (CA)

Substance Abuse/ Addiction Counseling
Amarillo Coll (TX)
Broome Comm Coll (NY)
Central Texas Coll (TX)
Century Coll (MN)
Chippewa Valley Tech Coll (WI)
City Colls of Chicago, Harold Washington College (IL)
Clark Coll (WA)
Coll of DuPage (IL)
Coll of Lake County (IL)
Coll of San Mateo (CA)
Comm Coll of Allegheny County (PA)
Comm Coll of Rhode Island (RI)
Elgin Comm Coll (IL)
Erie Comm Coll (NY)
Finger Lakes Comm Coll (NY)
Fresno City Coll (CA)
Gadsden State Comm Coll (AL)
Gateway Comm Coll (CT)
Genesee Comm Coll (NY)
Hartnell Coll (CA)
Housatonic Comm Coll (CT)
Howard Comm Coll (MD)
Kansas City Kansas Comm Coll (KS)
Lassen Comm Coll District (CA)
Lee Coll (TX)
Lower Columbia Coll (WA)
Mendocino Coll (CA)
Mesabi Range Comm and Tech Coll (MN)
Miami Dade Coll (FL)
Middlesex Comm Coll (CT)
Minneapolis Comm and Tech Coll (MN)
Mohawk Valley Comm Coll (NY)
Naugatuck Valley Comm Coll (CT)
New Hampshire Tech Inst (NH)
North Shore Comm Coll (MA)
Northwestern Connecticut Comm Coll (CT)
Odessa Coll (TX)
Oklahoma State U, Oklahoma City (OK)
Peninsula Coll (WA)
Pierce Coll (WA)
Quinebaug Valley Comm Coll (CT)
Ridgewater Coll (MN)
Rio Salado Coll (AZ)
Rogue Comm Coll (OR)
Sandhills Comm Coll (NC)
Southeastern Comm Coll, North Campus (IA)
Southeastern Comm Coll, South Campus (IA)
Southern U at Shreveport (LA)
Southwestern Comm Coll (NC)
Spokane Falls Comm Coll (WA)
Suffolk County Comm Coll (NY)
Texarkana Coll (TX)
Three Rivers Comm Coll (CT)
Tompkins Cortland Comm Coll (NY)
Tunxis Comm Coll (CT)
Wenatchee Valley Coll (WA)
Westchester Comm Coll (NY)
Wor-Wic Comm Coll (MD)
Yuba Coll (CA)

Surgical Technology
Allied Coll (MO)
Athens Tech Coll (GA)
Augusta Tech Coll (GA)
Baltimore City Comm Coll (MD)
Berkshire Comm Coll (MA)
Bismarck State Coll (ND)
Brevard Comm Coll (FL)

Brown Mackie Coll–
Cincinnati (OH)
Brown Mackie Coll–
Merrillville (IN)
Cambridge Coll (CO)
Career Tech Coll (LA)
Central Carolina Tech
Coll (SC)
Central Wyoming
Coll (WY)
Cincinnati State Tech and
Comm Coll (OH)
Coastal Carolina Comm
Coll (NC)
Coll of DuPage (IL)
Coll of Southern Idaho (ID)
Columbus Tech Coll (GA)
Comm Coll of Allegheny
County (PA)
Coosa Valley Tech
Coll (GA)
Cuyahoga Comm
Coll (OH)
DeKalb Tech Coll (GA)
East Central Coll (MO)
El Centro Coll (TX)
Fayetteville Tech Comm
Coll (NC)
Frederick Comm Coll (MD)
Gateway Tech Coll (WI)
Griffin Tech Coll (GA)
Guilford Tech Comm
Coll (NC)
High-Tech Inst (FL)
High-Tech Inst (MN)
High-Tech Inst (MO)
High-Tech Inst (NV)
High-Tech Inst,
Memphis (TN)
High-Tech Inst,
Nashville (TN)
Indiana Business Coll, Fort
Wayne (IN)
Indiana Business Coll,
Indianapolis (IN)
Indiana Business Coll–
Medical (IN)
Iowa Lakes Comm
Coll (IA)
James H. Faulkner State
Comm Coll (AL)
Keiser Career Coll -
Greenacres (FL)
Lancaster General Coll of
Nursing & Health
Sciences (PA)
Lanier Tech Coll (GA)
Lansing Comm Coll (MI)
Lorain County Comm
Coll (OH)
Macomb Comm Coll (MI)
Metropolitan Comm
Coll (NE)
Midlands Tech Coll (SC)
Miller-Motte Tech Coll,
Clarksville (TN)
Mohawk Valley Comm
Coll (NY)
Montgomery County
Comm Coll (PA)
Mt. Hood Comm Coll (OR)
Nassau Comm Coll (NY)
New England Inst of
Technology (RI)
Niagara County Comm
Coll (NY)
Northampton County Area
Comm Coll (PA)
North Arkansas Coll (AR)
Northeast Comm Coll (NE)
Northeast State Tech
Comm Coll (TN)
Northwestern Tech
Coll (GA)
Oakland Comm Coll (MI)
Odessa Coll (TX)
Okefenokee Tech
Coll (GA)
Oklahoma City Comm
Coll (OK)
Parkland Coll (IL)
Rasmussen Coll Brooklyn
Park (MN)
Renton Tech Coll (WA)
St. Cloud Tech Coll (MN)
Sandhills Comm Coll (NC)
Savannah Tech Coll (GA)
Southeast Tech Inst (SD)
Southern Maine Comm
Coll (ME)
Southern U at
Shreveport (LA)
South Plains Coll (TX)
Southwest Georgia Tech
Coll (GA)
Spokane Comm Coll (WA)

Springfield Tech Comm
Coll (MA)
Trocaire Coll (NY)
Tulsa Comm Coll (OK)
Virginia Coll at Austin (TX)
Waukesha County Tech
Coll (WI)
York Tech Coll (SC)

**Surveying
Engineering**
Santa Rosa Jr Coll (CA)

Survey Technology
Asheville-Buncombe Tech
Comm Coll (NC)
Bakersfield Coll (CA)
Burlington County
Coll (NJ)
Centralia Coll (WA)
Central Piedmont Comm
Coll (NC)
Chattanooga State Tech
Comm Coll (TN)
Cincinnati State Tech and
Comm Coll (OH)
Comm Coll of Southern
Nevada (NV)
Fayetteville Tech Comm
Coll (NC)
Guilford Tech Comm
Coll (NC)
Hawkeye Comm Coll (IA)
Lansing Comm Coll (MI)
Macomb Comm Coll (MI)
Middle Georgia Coll (GA)
Mohawk Valley Comm
Coll (NY)
Mott Comm Coll (MI)
Mt. San Antonio Coll (CA)
Nicolet Area Tech Coll (WI)
Oklahoma State U,
Oklahoma City (OK)
Owens Comm Coll,
Toledo (OH)
Palm Beach Comm
Coll (FL)
Penn State Wilkes-
Barre (PA)
Red Rocks Comm
Coll (CO)
Renton Tech Coll (WA)
Sacramento City Coll (CA)
Salt Lake Comm Coll (UT)
Sandhills Comm Coll (NC)
Santiago Canyon Coll (CA)
Southeast Tech Inst (SD)
Stark State Coll of
Technology (OH)
State U of New York Coll
of Environmental
Science & Forestry,
Ranger School (NY)
State U of New York Coll
of Technology at
Alfred (NY)
Treasure Valley Comm
Coll (OR)
Tulsa Comm Coll (OK)
Tyler Jr Coll (TX)
U of Arkansas Comm Coll
at Morrilton (AR)
Valencia Comm Coll (FL)

**System
Administration**
Academy Coll (MN)
AIB Coll of Business (IA)
Angelina Coll (TX)
Anne Arundel Comm
Coll (MD)
Bellingham Tech Coll (WA)
Berkeley Coll, West
Paterson (NJ)
Brevard Comm Coll (FL)
Brooks Coll,
Sunnyvale (CA)
Cape Cod Comm
Coll (MA)
Central Comm Coll–
Columbus
Campus (NE)
Central Comm Coll–Grand
Island Campus (NE)
Central Comm Coll–
Hastings Campus (NE)
Centralia Coll (WA)
Cleveland Comm Coll (NC)
Coastal Bend Coll (TX)
Cuesta Coll (CA)
Cypress Coll (CA)
Fiorello H. LaGuardia
Comm Coll of the City
U of New York (NY)
Florida National Coll (FL)
Genesee Comm Coll (NY)
Gulf Coast Coll (FL)
Hawkeye Comm Coll (IA)
Inver Hills Comm
Coll (MN)

Iowa Lakes Comm
Coll (IA)
Island Drafting and Tech
Inst (NY)
Klamath Comm Coll (OR)
Laurel Business Inst (PA)
Linn-Benton Comm
Coll (OR)
Los Angeles City Coll (CA)
Metropolitan Comm
Coll–Business &
Technology
Campus (MO)
Minot State U–Bottineau
Campus (ND)
Naugatuck Valley Comm
Coll (CT)
Northland Comm and Tech
Coll–Thief River
Falls (MN)
Olympic Coll (WA)
Onondaga Comm
Coll (NY)
Owensboro Comm and
Tech Coll (KY)
Palm Beach Comm
Coll (FL)
Parkland Coll (IL)
Pennsylvania Highland
Comm Coll (PA)
Potomac State Coll of
West Virginia U (WV)
Quinebaug Valley Comm
Coll (CT)
Ridgewater Coll (MN)
Rio Salado Coll (AZ)
Sampson Comm Coll (NC)
San Antonio Coll (TX)
Sandhills Comm Coll (NC)
Santa Barbara City
Coll (CA)
Seminole Comm Coll (FL)
Sheridan Coll–Sheridan
and Gillette (WY)
Southeast Tech Inst (SD)
Southwest Mississippi
Comm Coll (MS)
Stanly Comm Coll (NC)
Tallahassee Comm
Coll (FL)
Technology Education
Coll (OH)
Tompkins Cortland Comm
Coll (NY)
Tulsa Comm Coll (OK)
U of Arkansas Comm Coll
at Batesville (AR)
Vatterott Coll, Kansas
City (MO)
Vatterott Coll (OH)
Vatterott Coll (TN)

**System, Networking,
and Lan/Wan
Management**
Academy Coll (MN)
Berkshire Comm Coll (MA)
Beta Tech (VA)
Bradford School (PA)
Brevard Comm Coll (FL)
Fayetteville Tech Comm
Coll (NC)
Iowa Lakes Comm
Coll (IA)
ITT Tech Inst, Tucson (AZ)
ITT Tech Inst, San
Dimas (CA)
ITT Tech Inst (CO)
ITT Tech Inst, Burr
Ridge (IL)
ITT Tech Inst, Mount
Prospect (IL)
ITT Tech Inst, Orland
Park (IL)
ITT Tech Inst,
Louisville (KY)
ITT Tech Inst (MN)
ITT Tech Inst (NM)
ITT Tech Inst,
Houston (TX)
Klamath Comm Coll (OR)
LDS Business Coll (UT)
Metropolitan Comm
Coll–Business &
Technology
Campus (MO)
Olympic Coll (WA)
St. Philip's Coll (TX)
Southwestern Comm
Coll (NC)
TESST Coll of
Technology (VA)
Texas State Tech Coll–
Marshall (TX)
Vatterott Coll, Kansas
City (MO)

**Systems Science and
Theory**
Miami U–Middletown
Campus (OH)

Taxation
Minnesota School of
Business–Brooklyn
Center (MN)
Minnesota School of
Business–Plymouth (MN)
Minnesota School of
Business–Richfield (MN)
Minnesota School of
Business–St.
Cloud (MN)

**Teacher Assistant/
Aide**
Alamance Comm Coll (NC)
Angelina Coll (TX)
Antelope Valley Coll (CA)
Big Bend Comm Coll (WA)
Black Hawk Coll,
Moline (IL)
Brunswick Comm
Coll (NC)
Bucks County Comm
Coll (PA)
Catawba Valley Comm
Coll (NC)
Centralia Coll (WA)
City Colls of Chicago,
Harold Washington
College (IL)
City Colls of Chicago,
Harry S. Truman
College (IL)
City Colls of Chicago,
Kennedy-King
College (IL)
City Colls of Chicago,
Richard J. Daley
College (IL)
Cleveland Comm Coll (NC)
Clovis Comm Coll (NM)
Cochise Coll, Sierra
Vista (AZ)
Coll of Micronesia–
FSM (FM)
Coll of The Albemarle (NC)
Coll of the Desert (CA)
Comm Coll of Southern
Nevada (NV)
Comm Coll of
Vermont (VT)
East Central Coll (MO)
El Centro Coll (TX)
Elizabethtown Tech
Coll (KY)
Fresno City Coll (CA)
Fulton-Montgomery Comm
Coll (NY)
Illinois Eastern Comm
Colls, Lincoln Trail
College (IL)
Isothermal Comm
Coll (NC)
Joliet Jr Coll (IL)
Kingsborough Comm Coll
of the City U of New
York (NY)
Kirkwood Comm Coll (IA)
Klamath Comm Coll (OR)
Lamar Comm Coll (CO)
Lansing Comm Coll (MI)
Linn-Benton Comm
Coll (OR)
Los Angeles City Coll (CA)
Los Angeles Mission
Coll (CA)
Los Angeles Southwest
Coll (CA)
Lower Columbia Coll (WA)
Merced Coll (CA)
Mesa Comm Coll (AZ)
Miami Dade Coll (FL)
Montgomery County
Comm Coll (PA)
Moorpark Coll (CA)
Mott Comm Coll (MI)
Neosho County Comm
Coll (KS)
New Hampshire Tech
Inst (NH)
New Mexico State U–
Alamogordo (NM)
Northampton County Area
Comm Coll (PA)
Odessa Coll (TX)
Pasadena City Coll (CA)
Renton Tech Coll (WA)
Ridgewater Coll (MN)
St. Cloud Tech Coll (MN)
St. Philip's Coll (TX)
Salt Lake Comm Coll (UT)
Sandhills Comm Coll (NC)
San Diego City Coll (CA)
Sitting Bull Coll (ND)

Southeastern Comm
Coll (NC)
Southern U at
Shreveport (LA)
Southwest Texas Jr
Coll (TX)
Victor Valley Coll (CA)
Waukesha County Tech
Coll (WI)

**Technical and
Business Writing**
Cincinnati State Tech and
Comm Coll (OH)
Clovis Comm Coll (NM)
Coll of Lake County (IL)
De Anza Coll (CA)
El Camino Coll (CA)
Florida National Coll (FL)
Gateway Tech Coll (WI)
Golden West Coll (CA)
Houston Comm Coll
System (TX)
Linn-Benton Comm
Coll (OR)
State U of New York Coll
of Agriculture and
Technology at
Morrisville (NY)
Terra State Comm
Coll (OH)
Three Rivers Comm
Coll (CT)

**Technology/Industrial
Arts Teacher
Education**
Allen County Comm
Coll (KS)
Eastern Arizona Coll (AZ)
Iowa Lakes Comm
Coll (IA)
Kellogg Comm Coll (MI)
Manatee Comm Coll (FL)
Roane State Comm
Coll (TN)

Telecommunications
Amarillo Coll (TX)
Anne Arundel Comm
Coll (MD)
Central Carolina Comm
Coll (NC)
Central Maine Comm
Coll (ME)
Chaffey Coll (CA)
Cincinnati State Tech and
Comm Coll (OH)
City Colls of Chicago,
Richard J. Daley
College (IL)
Colegio Universitario de
San Juan, San
Juan (PR)
Comm Coll of Beaver
County (PA)
Cuesta Coll (CA)
DeKalb Tech Coll (GA)
ECPI Coll of
Technology (VA)
ECPI Tech Coll (VA)
ECPI Tech Coll (VA)
Gadsden State Comm
Coll (AL)
Golden West Coll (CA)
Grossmont Coll (CA)
Howard Comm Coll (MD)
Illinois Eastern Comm
Colls, Lincoln Trail
College (IL)
Kirkwood Comm Coll (IA)
Lake Land Coll (IL)
Lansing Comm Coll (MI)
Lee Coll (TX)
Los Angeles City Coll (CA)
Meridian Comm Coll (MS)
Monroe Comm Coll (NY)
Moorpark Coll (CA)
Mount Wachusett Comm
Coll (MA)
Napa Valley Coll (CA)
New Hampshire Comm
Tech Coll, Nashua/
Claremont (NH)
New York City Coll of
Technology of the City
U of New York (NY)
Northwest Mississippi
Comm Coll (MS)
Onondaga Comm
Coll (NY)
Owens Comm Coll,
Toledo (OH)
Oxnard Coll (CA)
Pasadena City Coll (CA)
Queensborough Comm
Coll of the City U of
New York (NY)
St. Louis Comm Coll at
Florissant Valley (MO)

San Bernardino Valley
Coll (CA)
San Diego City Coll (CA)
Santa Ana Coll (CA)
Seminole Comm Coll (FL)
Skagit Valley Coll (WA)
South Plains Coll (TX)
Suffolk County Comm
Coll (NY)
Trident Tech Coll (SC)
Tulsa Comm Coll (OK)

**Telecommunications
Technology**
Clark Coll (WA)
Coll of Micronesia–
FSM (FM)
Collin County Comm Coll
District (TX)
ECPI Tech Coll (VA)
ECPI Tech Coll (VA)
Miami Dade Coll (FL)
Minnesota State Comm
and Tech Coll–Fergus
Falls (MN)
Northern Essex Comm
Coll (MA)
North Seattle Comm
Coll (WA)
Penn State DuBois (PA)
Penn State Fayette, The
Eberly Campus (PA)
Penn State Hazleton (PA)
Penn State New
Kensington (PA)
Penn State Schuylkill (PA)
Penn State Shenango (PA)
Penn State Wilkes-
Barre (PA)
Penn State York (PA)
Salt Lake Comm Coll (UT)
Waukesha County Tech
Coll (WI)

**Theater Design and
Technology**
Central Wyoming
Coll (WY)
Comm Coll of Rhode
Island (RI)
Fresno City Coll (CA)
Howard Comm Coll (MD)
Lake-Sumter Comm
Coll (FL)
Nassau Comm Coll (NY)
Santa Barbara City
Coll (CA)
Western Wyoming Comm
Coll (WY)

**Theater/Theater Arts
Management**
Parkland Coll (IL)

Theology
Mid-America Baptist
Theological
Seminary (TN)

**Therapeutic
Recreation**
Colorado Mountain
Coll (CO)
Comm Coll of Allegheny
County (PA)
Cuesta Coll (CA)
Keystone Coll (PA)
Moraine Valley Comm
Coll (IL)
Northwestern Connecticut
Comm Coll (CT)
Santa Barbara City
Coll (CA)
Suffolk County Comm
Coll (NY)
Tulsa Comm Coll (OK)
Western Piedmont Comm
Coll (NC)

**Tool and Die
Technology**
Asheville-Buncombe Tech
Comm Coll (NC)
Black Hawk Coll,
Moline (IL)
Gadsden State Comm
Coll (AL)
Hawkeye Comm Coll (IA)
H. Councill Trenholm State
Tech Coll (AL)
Jackson State Comm
Coll (TN)
Macomb Comm Coll (MI)
Mohawk Valley Comm
Coll (NY)
North Iowa Area Comm
Coll (IA)
Northwest Iowa Comm
Coll (IA)
Oakland Comm Coll (MI)

- Terra State Comm Coll (OH)
- Ventura Coll (CA)
- Wilson Tech Comm Coll (NC)

Tourism and Travel Services Management
- AIB Coll of Business (IA)
- Albany Tech Coll (GA)
- Amarillo Coll (TX)
- Athens Tech Coll (GA)
- Atlanta Tech Coll (GA)
- Bergen Comm Coll (NJ)
- Briarwood Coll (CT)
- Broward Comm Coll (FL)
- Cañada Coll (CA)
- Central Georgia Tech Coll (GA)
- Central Piedmont Comm Coll (NC)
- City Colls of Chicago, Harold Washington College (IL)
- Coll of DuPage (IL)
- Cypress Coll (CA)
- East Central Coll (MO)
- Elgin Comm Coll (IL)
- Elmira Business Inst (NY)
- Finger Lakes Comm Coll (NY)
- Fiorello H. LaGuardia Comm Coll of the City U of New York (NY)
- Fisher Coll (MA)
- Florida National Coll (FL)
- Foothill Coll (CA)
- Fullerton Coll (CA)
- Genesee Comm Coll (NY)
- Gwinnett Tech Coll (GA)
- Harrisburg Area Comm Coll (PA)
- Hocking Coll (OH)
- Holyoke Comm Coll (MA)
- Houston Comm Coll System (TX)
- ICPR Jr Coll–Hato Rey Campus (PR)
- International Business Coll, Fort Wayne (IN)
- Iowa Lakes Comm Coll (IA)
- Kaplan U (IA)
- Kingsborough Comm Coll of the City U of New York (NY)
- King's Coll (NC)
- Lansing Comm Coll (MI)
- Lehigh Valley Coll (PA)
- Lorain County Comm Coll (OH)
- Los Angeles City Coll (CA)
- Los Medanos Coll (CA)
- Madison Area Tech Coll (WI)
- Marian Court Coll (MA)
- Massasoit Comm Coll (MA)
- Miami Dade Coll (FL)
- Monroe Comm Coll (NY)
- Mt. Hood Comm Coll (OR)
- New Hampshire Tech Inst (NH)
- Northern Essex Comm Coll (MA)
- North Shore Comm Coll (MA)
- Ogeechee Tech Coll (GA)
- Pace Inst (PA)
- Pasadena City Coll (CA)
- Raritan Valley Comm Coll (NJ)
- Ridgewater Coll (MN)
- St. Philip's Coll (TX)
- San Diego City Coll (CA)
- Santa Ana Coll (CA)
- Santiago Canyon Coll (CA)
- Savannah Tech Coll (GA)
- Southern U at Shreveport (LA)
- State U of New York Coll of Agriculture and Technology at Morrisville (NY)
- Three Rivers Comm Coll (CT)
- Tompkins Cortland Comm Coll (NY)
- Tulsa Comm Coll (OK)
- Valencia Comm Coll (FL)
- Westchester Comm Coll (NY)
- West Los Angeles Coll (CA)
- Westmoreland County Comm Coll (PA)
- Zane State Coll (OH)

Tourism and Travel Services Marketing
- AIB Coll of Business (IA)
- Coll of DuPage (IL)
- Dixie State Coll of Utah (UT)
- Harrisburg Area Comm Coll (PA)
- International Jr Coll (PR)
- Iowa Lakes Comm Coll (IA)
- Lehigh Carbon Comm Coll (PA)
- Moraine Valley Comm Coll (IL)
- Tompkins Cortland Comm Coll (NY)

Tourism Promotion
- AIB Coll of Business (IA)
- Central Oregon Comm Coll (OR)
- Coll of DuPage (IL)
- Comm Coll of Allegheny County (PA)
- Florida National Coll (FL)
- Iowa Lakes Comm Coll (IA)
- Lehigh Carbon Comm Coll (PA)
- Westchester Comm Coll (NY)

Trade and Industrial Teacher Education
- Brigham Young U–Idaho (ID)
- Cankdeska Cikana Comm Coll (ND)
- ECPI Tech Coll (VA)
- Florence-Darlington Tech Coll (SC)
- Iowa Lakes Comm Coll (IA)
- Isothermal Comm Coll (NC)
- Lenoir Comm Coll (NC)
- Manatee Comm Coll (FL)
- National Park Comm Coll (AR)
- Neosho County Comm Coll (KS)
- New Mexico Jr Coll (NM)
- Northeastern Jr Coll (CO)
- Northeast Iowa Comm Coll (IA)
- Palo Alto Coll (TX)
- Southeastern Comm Coll, North Campus (IA)
- South Seattle Comm Coll (WA)
- Southwestern Comm Coll (NC)
- Turtle Mountain Comm Coll (ND)
- Victor Valley Coll (CA)
- Wenatchee Valley Coll (WA)

Transportation and Materials Moving Related
- Cecil Comm Coll (MD)
- Mid-Plains Comm Coll, North Platte (NE)

Transportation Management
- Calhoun Comm Coll (AL)

Transportation Technology
- Central Piedmont Comm Coll (NC)
- Chattanooga State Tech Comm Coll (TN)
- City Coll of San Francisco (CA)
- City Colls of Chicago, Richard J. Daley College (IL)
- Coll of DuPage (IL)
- Henry Ford Comm Coll (MI)
- Houston Comm Coll System (TX)
- Mt. San Antonio Coll (CA)
- Muskegon Comm Coll (MI)
- Nassau Comm Coll (NY)
- Oxnard Coll (CA)
- Sacramento City Coll (CA)
- San Diego City Coll (CA)
- West Hills Comm Coll (CA)

Truck and Bus Driver/Commercial Vehicle Operation
- Alexandria Tech Coll (MN)
- Black Hawk Coll, Moline (IL)

Turf and Turfgrass Management
- Brunswick Comm Coll (NC)
- Cincinnati State Tech and Comm Coll (OH)
- Coll of Lake County (IL)
- Comm Coll of Allegheny County (PA)
- Guilford Tech Comm Coll (NC)
- Iowa Lakes Comm Coll (IA)
- Joliet Jr Coll (IL)
- Linn State Tech Coll (MO)
- Minot State U–Bottineau Campus (ND)
- North Georgia Tech Coll (GA)
- The Ohio State U Ag Tech Inst (OH)
- Oklahoma State U, Oklahoma City (OK)
- Ozarks Tech Comm Coll (MO)
- Sandhills Comm Coll (NC)
- Southeast Tech Inst (SD)
- Wayne Comm Coll (NC)
- The Williamson Free School of Mecha Trades (PA)

Urban Forestry
- Minot State U–Bottineau Campus (ND)

Urban Studies/Affairs
- Comm Coll of Rhode Island (RI)
- Lawson State Comm Coll (AL)
- Lorain County Comm Coll (OH)
- St. Philip's Coll (TX)

Vehicle/Equipment Operation
- Skagit Valley Coll (WA)
- Western Nevada Comm Coll (NV)

Vehicle Maintenance and Repair Technologies Related
- Black Hawk Coll, Moline (IL)
- Central New Mexico Comm Coll (NM)
- Massasoit Comm Coll (MA)
- Victor Valley Coll (CA)

Vehicle/Petroleum Products Marketing
- Central Comm Coll–Hastings Campus (NE)

Veterinary/Animal Health Technology
- Cedar Valley Coll (TX)
- Central Florida Comm Coll (FL)
- Gwinnett Tech Coll (GA)
- Joliet Jr Coll (IL)
- Lehigh Carbon Comm Coll (PA)
- Long Tech Coll (AZ)
- Macomb Comm Coll (MI)
- Northampton County Area Comm Coll (PA)
- Parkland Coll (IL)
- Pima Comm Coll (AZ)
- Sussex County Comm Coll (NJ)
- Western Career Coll, Pleasant Hill (CA)
- Western Career Coll, Sacramento (CA)
- Western Career Coll, San Leandro (CA)

Veterinary Sciences
- Colby Comm Coll (KS)
- Grayson County Coll (TX)
- Holyoke Comm Coll (MA)
- Isothermal Comm Coll (NC)
- Kirkwood Comm Coll (IA)
- Lorain County Comm Coll (OH)
- Macomb Comm Coll (MI)
- Murray State Coll (OK)
- Navarro Coll (TX)
- Northeastern Jr Coll (CO)
- Northwest-Shoals Comm Coll (AL)
- Palo Alto Coll (TX)
- Pasadena City Coll (CA)
- State U of New York Coll of Technology at Alfred (NY)

- Suffolk County Comm Coll (NY)

Veterinary Technology
- Athens Tech Coll (GA)
- Bergen Comm Coll (NJ)
- Brevard Comm Coll (FL)
- Central Carolina Comm Coll (NC)
- Central Georgia Tech Coll (GA)
- Colby Comm Coll (KS)
- Coll of Southern Idaho (ID)
- Colorado Mountain Coll (CO)
- Comm Coll of Southern Nevada (NV)
- Cosumnes River Coll, Sacramento (CA)
- Cuyahoga Comm Coll (OH)
- Fiorello H. LaGuardia Comm Coll of the City U of New York (NY)
- Foothill Coll (CA)
- Front Range Comm Coll (CO)
- Hartnell Coll (CA)
- Holyoke Comm Coll (MA)
- Kirkwood Comm Coll (IA)
- Lansing Comm Coll (MI)
- Long Tech Coll (AZ)
- Los Angeles Pierce Coll (CA)
- Madison Area Tech Coll (WI)
- Metropolitan Comm Coll–Maple Woods (MO)
- Minnesota School of Business–Brooklyn Center (MN)
- Minnesota School of Business–Plymouth (MN)
- Minnesota School of Business–Richfield (MN)
- Minnesota School of Business–St. Cloud (MN)
- Minnesota School of Business–Shakopee (MN)
- Murray State Coll (OK)
- Nebraska Coll of Tech Agriculture (NE)
- Northeast Comm Coll (NE)
- North Shore Comm Coll (MA)
- Northwestern Connecticut Comm Coll (CT)
- Ogeechee Tech Coll (GA)
- Oklahoma State U, Oklahoma City (OK)
- Pierce Coll (WA)
- Ridgewater Coll (MN)
- State U of New York Coll of Technology at Canton (NY)
- Tomball Coll (TX)
- Trident Tech Coll (SC)
- Tulsa Comm Coll (OK)
- Turtle Mountain Comm Coll (ND)
- Yuba Coll (CA)

Violin, Viola, Guitar and Other Stringed Instruments
- Minnesota State Coll–Southeast Tech (MN)

Visual and Performing Arts
- Amarillo Coll (TX)
- Berkshire Comm Coll (MA)
- Bucks County Comm Coll (PA)
- Calhoun Comm Coll (AL)
- Citrus Coll (CA)
- Holyoke Comm Coll (MA)
- Hutchinson Comm Coll and Area Vocational School (KS)
- Laramie County Comm Coll (WY)
- Lee Coll (TX)
- Moraine Valley Comm Coll (IL)
- Nassau Comm Coll (NY)
- New Hampshire Tech Inst (NH)
- Piedmont Virginia Comm Coll (VA)
- Queensborough Comm Coll of the City U of New York (NY)
- Quincy Coll (MA)
- Raritan Valley Comm Coll (NJ)
- Roxbury Comm Coll (MA)

- Western Wyoming Comm Coll (WY)

Visual and Performing Arts Related
- Comm Coll of Allegheny County (PA)

Vocational Rehabilitation Counseling
- Manatee Comm Coll (FL)
- Spokane Falls Comm Coll (WA)

Voice and Opera
- Angelina Coll (TX)
- Coastal Bend Coll (TX)
- Fresno City Coll (CA)
- Iowa Lakes Comm Coll (IA)
- Jones County Jr Coll (MS)
- Kirkwood Comm Coll (IA)
- Lansing Comm Coll (MI)
- Navarro Coll (TX)
- Reedley Coll (CA)

Watchmaking and Jewelrymaking
- North Seattle Comm Coll (WA)

Water Quality and Wastewater Treatment Management And Recycling Technology
- Angelina Coll (TX)
- Arizona Western Coll (AZ)
- Clackamas Comm Coll (OR)
- Collin County Comm Coll District (TX)
- Linn-Benton Comm Coll (OR)
- Northwest-Shoals Comm Coll (AL)
- Northwest Vista Coll (TX)
- Ogeechee Tech Coll (GA)
- St. Cloud Tech Coll (MN)
- San Juan Coll (NM)
- Santiago Canyon Coll (CA)
- U of Alaska Southeast, Sitka Campus (AK)

Water Resources Engineering
- Dixie State Coll of Utah (UT)
- Santa Ana Coll (CA)

Water, Wetlands, and Marine Resources Management
- Iowa Lakes Comm Coll (IA)
- Keystone Coll (PA)

Web/Multimedia Management and Webmaster
- Academy Coll (MN)
- Bellingham Tech Coll (WA)
- Black Hawk Coll, Moline (IL)
- Bradley Academy for the Visual Arts (PA)
- Cape Cod Comm Coll (MA)
- Central Comm Coll–Columbus Campus (NE)
- Central Comm Coll–Grand Island Campus (NE)
- Central Comm Coll–Hastings Campus (NE)
- Clark Coll (WA)
- Clovis Comm Coll (NM)
- Coll of the Siskiyous (CA)
- Columbia-Greene Comm Coll (NY)
- Harrisburg Area Comm Coll (PA)
- Hawkeye Comm Coll (IA)
- ITT Tech Inst (AL)
- ITT Tech Inst, Tucson (AZ)
- ITT Tech Inst (AR)
- ITT Tech Inst, Rancho Cordova (CA)
- ITT Tech Inst (CO)
- ITT Tech Inst, Fort Lauderdale (FL)
- ITT Tech Inst, Jacksonville (FL)
- ITT Tech Inst, Lake Mary (FL)
- ITT Tech Inst, Miami (FL)
- ITT Tech Inst, Tampa (FL)
- ITT Tech Inst (ID)
- ITT Tech Inst, Burr Ridge (IL)
- ITT Tech Inst, Orland Park (IL)
- ITT Tech Inst, Indianapolis (IN)
- ITT Tech Inst, Newburgh (IN)
- ITT Tech Inst (LA)
- ITT Tech Inst (MD)
- ITT Tech Inst, Norwood (MA)
- ITT Tech Inst, Woburn (MA)
- ITT Tech Inst, Canton (MI)
- ITT Tech Inst, Flint (MI)
- ITT Tech Inst, Grand Rapids (MI)
- ITT Tech Inst, Troy (MI)
- ITT Tech Inst, Arnold (MO)
- ITT Tech Inst, Earth City (MO)
- ITT Tech Inst (NE)
- ITT Tech Inst (NV)
- ITT Tech Inst (NM)
- ITT Tech Inst, Albany (NY)
- ITT Tech Inst, Getzville (NY)
- ITT Tech Inst, Liverpool (NY)
- ITT Tech Inst, Dayton (OH)
- ITT Tech Inst, Norwood (OH)
- ITT Tech Inst, Strongsville (OH)
- ITT Tech Inst, Youngstown (OH)
- ITT Tech Inst (OR)
- ITT Tech Inst (SC)
- ITT Tech Inst, Knoxville (TN)
- ITT Tech Inst, Nashville (TN)
- ITT Tech Inst, Houston (TX)
- ITT Tech Inst, Richardson (TX)
- ITT Tech Inst, San Antonio (TX)
- ITT Tech Inst, Webster (TX)
- ITT Tech Inst (UT)
- ITT Tech Inst, Chantilly (VA)
- ITT Tech Inst, Norfolk (VA)
- ITT Tech Inst, Richmond (VA)
- ITT Tech Inst, Springfield (VA)
- ITT Tech Inst, Bothell (WA)
- ITT Tech Inst, Seattle (WA)
- ITT Tech Inst, Spokane (WA)
- ITT Tech Inst, Green Bay (WI)
- Kennebec Valley Comm Coll (ME)
- Laramie County Comm Coll (WY)
- Los Angeles City Coll (CA)
- Metropolitan Comm Coll–Business & Technology Campus (MO)
- Minneapolis Comm and Tech Coll (MN)
- Northern Essex Comm Coll (MA)
- Northland Comm and Tech Coll–Thief River Falls (MN)
- Olympic Coll (WA)
- Onondaga Comm Coll (NY)
- Pennsylvania Highland Comm Coll (PA)
- Piedmont Virginia Comm Coll (VA)
- Pioneer Pacific Coll, Wilsonville (OR)
- Platt Coll San Diego (CA)
- Ridgewater Coll (MN)
- Rio Salado Coll (AZ)
- Riverland Comm Coll (MN)
- Saint Charles Comm Coll (MO)
- St. Philip's Coll (TX)
- Sandhills Comm Coll (NC)
- Seminole Comm Coll (FL)
- Sheridan Coll–Sheridan and Gillette (WY)
- Southeast Tech Inst (SD)
- Springfield Tech Comm Coll (MA)
- Stanly Comm Coll (NC)
- Stark State Coll of Technology (OH)
- Trident Tech Coll (SC)
- Tulsa Comm Coll (OK)

Western Wyoming Comm Coll (WY)

Web Page, Digital/Multimedia and Information Resources Design
Academy Coll (MN)
Alexandria Tech Coll (MN)
Bellingham Tech Coll (WA)
Berkeley City Coll (CA)
Berkeley Coll, West Paterson (NJ)
Bradley Academy for the Visual Arts (PA)
Brevard Comm Coll (FL)
Cape Cod Comm Coll (MA)
Capital Comm Coll (CT)
Central Georgia Tech Coll (GA)
Central Wyoming Coll (WY)
Chattahoochee Tech Coll (GA)
Clovis Comm Coll (NM)
Coll of the Mainland (TX)
Coll of the Redwoods (CA)
Coll of the Siskiyous (CA)
Collin County Comm Coll District (TX)
Columbia Basin Coll (WA)
Columbus Tech Coll (GA)
Coosa Valley Tech Coll (GA)
Cuesta Coll (CA)
Cypress Coll (CA)
Dixie State Coll of Utah (UT)
ECPI Tech Coll (VA)
El Centro Coll (TX)
Flint River Tech Coll (GA)
Florida National Coll (FL)
Griffin Tech Coll (GA)
Guilford Tech Comm Coll (NC)
Hagerstown Comm Coll (MD)
Hawkeye Comm Coll (IA)
High-Tech Inst (FL)
High-Tech Inst, Nashville (TN)
ITT Tech Inst (AL)
ITT Tech Inst, Tucson (AZ)
ITT Tech Inst (AR)
ITT Tech Inst, Anaheim (CA)
ITT Tech Inst, Lathrop (CA)
ITT Tech Inst, Oxnard (CA)
ITT Tech Inst, Rancho Cordova (CA)
ITT Tech Inst, San Bernardino (CA)
ITT Tech Inst, San Diego (CA)
ITT Tech Inst, San Dimas (CA)
ITT Tech Inst, Sylmar (CA)
ITT Tech Inst, Torrance (CA)
ITT Tech Inst (CO)
ITT Tech Inst, Fort Lauderdale (FL)
ITT Tech Inst, Jacksonville (FL)
ITT Tech Inst, Lake Mary (FL)
ITT Tech Inst, Miami (FL)
ITT Tech Inst, Tampa (FL)
ITT Tech Inst, Duluth (GA)
ITT Tech Inst, Kennesaw (GA)
ITT Tech Inst (ID)
ITT Tech Inst, Burr Ridge (IL)
ITT Tech Inst, Mount Prospect (IL)
ITT Tech Inst, Orland Park (IL)
ITT Tech Inst, Fort Wayne (IN)
ITT Tech Inst, Indianapolis (IN)
ITT Tech Inst, Newburgh (IN)
ITT Tech Inst, Newburgh (IN)
ITT Tech Inst, Louisville (KY)
ITT Tech Inst (LA)
ITT Tech Inst (MD)
ITT Tech Inst, Norwood (MA)
ITT Tech Inst, Woburn (MA)
ITT Tech Inst, Canton (MI)
ITT Tech Inst, Flint (MI)
ITT Tech Inst, Grand Rapids (MI)

ITT Tech Inst, Troy (MI)
ITT Tech Inst (MN)
ITT Tech Inst, Arnold (MO)
ITT Tech Inst, Earth City (MO)
ITT Tech Inst (NE)
ITT Tech Inst (NV)
ITT Tech Inst (NM)
ITT Tech Inst, Albany (NY)
ITT Tech Inst, Getzville (NY)
ITT Tech Inst, Liverpool (NY)
ITT Tech Inst, Dayton (OH)
ITT Tech Inst, Dayton (OH)
ITT Tech Inst, Hilliard (OH)
ITT Tech Inst, Norwood (OH)
ITT Tech Inst, Strongsville (OH)
ITT Tech Inst, Warrensville Heights (OH)
ITT Tech Inst, Youngstown (OH)
ITT Tech Inst, Tulsa (OK)
ITT Tech Inst (OR)
ITT Tech Inst (SC)
ITT Tech Inst, Cordova (TN)
ITT Tech Inst, Knoxville (TN)
ITT Tech Inst, Nashville (TN)
ITT Tech Inst, Arlington (TX)
ITT Tech Inst, Austin (TX)
ITT Tech Inst, Houston (TX)
ITT Tech Inst, Richardson (TX)
ITT Tech Inst, San Antonio (TX)
ITT Tech Inst, Webster (TX)
ITT Tech Inst (UT)
ITT Tech Inst, Chantilly (VA)
ITT Tech Inst, Norfolk (VA)
ITT Tech Inst, Richmond (VA)
ITT Tech Inst, Springfield (VA)
ITT Tech Inst, Bothell (WA)
ITT Tech Inst, Seattle (WA)
ITT Tech Inst, Spokane (WA)
ITT Tech Inst, Green Bay (WI)
ITT Tech Inst, Greenfield (WI)
Joliet Jr Coll (IL)
Kansas City Kansas Comm Coll (KS)
Kennebec Valley Comm Coll (ME)
Lanier Tech Coll (GA)
Laramie County Comm Coll (WY)
Laurel Business Inst (PA)
LDS Business Coll (UT)
Los Angeles City Coll (CA)
Madison Media Inst (WI)
Mesabi Range Comm and Tech Coll (MN)
Metropolitan Comm Coll–Business & Technology Campus (MO)
Middle Georgia Tech Coll (GA)
Minneapolis Comm and Tech Coll (MN)
Minnesota School of Business–Brooklyn Center (MN)
Minnesota School of Business–Plymouth (MN)
Minnesota School of Business–Richfield (MN)
Minnesota School of Business–St. Cloud (MN)
Minnesota School of Business–Shakopee (MN)
Minnesota State Comm and Tech Coll–Fergus Falls (MN)
Moultrie Tech Coll (GA)
Mount Wachusett Comm Coll (MA)
Niagara County Comm Coll (NY)
Northampton County Area Comm Coll (PA)
Northern Essex Comm Coll (MA)
North Georgia Tech Coll (GA)

Northland Comm and Tech Coll–Thief River Falls (MN)
North Metro Tech Coll (GA)
North Seattle Comm Coll (WA)
Northwestern Tech Coll (GA)
Northwest Vista Coll (TX)
Onondaga Comm Coll (NY)
Palm Beach Comm Coll (FL)
Parkland Coll (IL)
Pasco-Hernando Comm Coll (FL)
Peninsula Coll (WA)
Platt Coll San Diego (CA)
Rasmussen Coll Brooklyn Park (MN)
Ridgewater Coll (MN)
Rio Salado Coll (AZ)
Riverland Comm Coll (MN)
San Antonio Coll (TX)
School of Communication Arts (NC)
Seminole Comm Coll (FL)
Sheridan Coll–Sheridan and Gillette (WY)
Southeastern Tech Coll (GA)
Southeast Tech Inst (SD)
Stanly Comm Coll (NC)
Stark State Coll of Technology (OH)
Tompkins Cortland Comm Coll (NY)
Trident Tech Coll (SC)
Tulsa Comm Coll (OK)
U of Arkansas Comm Coll at Batesville (AR)
Valdosta Tech Coll (GA)
Vatterott Coll, Kansas City (MO)
West Central Tech Coll (GA)
Western Wyoming Comm Coll (WY)
West Georgia Tech Coll (GA)
York County Comm Coll (ME)
Zane State Coll (OH)

Welding Technology
Aims Comm Coll (CO)
Alamance Comm Coll (NC)
Alexandria Tech Coll (MN)
Angelina Coll (TX)
Antelope Valley Coll (CA)
Arizona Western Coll (AZ)
Bainbridge Coll (GA)
Bakersfield Coll (CA)
Beaufort County Comm Coll (NC)
Big Bend Comm Coll (WA)
Bismarck State Coll (ND)
Black Hawk Coll, Moline (IL)
Bladen Comm Coll (NC)
Brigham Young U–Idaho (ID)
Cabrillo Coll (CA)
Cecil Comm Coll (MD)
Central Comm Coll–Columbus Campus (NE)
Central Comm Coll–Grand Island Campus (NE)
Central Comm Coll–Hastings Campus (NE)
Centralia Coll (WA)
Central Oregon Comm Coll (OR)
Central Piedmont Comm Coll (NC)
Central Texas Coll (TX)
Central Wyoming Coll (WY)
Cerritos Coll (CA)
Chattanooga State Tech Comm Coll (TN)
Chippewa Valley Tech Coll (WI)
Cisco Jr Coll (TX)
Clark Coll (WA)
Coahoma Comm Coll (MS)
Coastal Bend Coll (TX)
Cochise Coll, Douglas (AZ)
Cochise Coll, Sierra Vista (AZ)
Coll of DuPage (IL)
Coll of San Mateo (CA)
Coll of Southern Idaho (ID)
Coll of the Canyons (CA)
Coll of the Desert (CA)
Coll of the Redwoods (CA)
Columbia Basin Coll (WA)

Comm Coll of Allegheny County (PA)
Comm Coll of Southern Nevada (NV)
Contra Costa Coll (CA)
Cossatot Comm Coll of the U of Arkansas (AR)
Cuesta Coll (CA)
Dodge City Comm Coll (KS)
Eastern Arizona Coll (AZ)
Eastern New Mexico U–Roswell (NM)
El Camino Coll (CA)
Elgin Comm Coll (IL)
Elizabethtown Tech Coll (KY)
Everett Comm Coll (WA)
Forsyth Tech Comm Coll (NC)
Fox Valley Tech Coll (WI)
Front Range Comm Coll (CO)
George C. Wallace Comm Coll (AL)
Grand Rapids Comm Coll (MI)
Grays Harbor Coll (WA)
Grayson County Coll (TX)
Great Basin Coll (NV)
Hartnell Coll (CA)
H. Councill Trenholm State Tech Coll (AL)
Hutchinson Comm Coll and Area Vocational School (KS)
Imperial Valley Coll (CA)
Iowa Lakes Comm Coll (IA)
Isothermal Comm Coll (NC)
Jefferson Comm and Tech Coll (KY)
Joliet Jr Coll (IL)
Kankakee Comm Coll (IL)
Kellogg Comm Coll (MI)
Kirkwood Comm Coll (IA)
Kirtland Comm Coll (MI)
Lamar Inst of Technology (TX)
Laney Coll (CA)
Lansing Comm Coll (MI)
Las Positas Coll (CA)
Lassen Comm Coll District (CA)
Lee Coll (TX)
Lenoir Comm Coll (NC)
Linn-Benton Comm Coll (OR)
Los Angeles Pierce Coll (CA)
Los Medanos Coll (CA)
Lower Columbia Coll (WA)
Macomb Comm Coll (MI)
Madison Area Tech Coll (WI)
Maui Comm Coll (HI)
Mendocino Coll (CA)
Metropolitan Comm Coll (NE)
Mid-Plains Comm Coll, North Platte (NE)
Minnesota State Coll–Southeast Tech (MN)
Mississippi Gulf Coast Comm Coll (MS)
Moberly Area Comm Coll (MO)
Mt. San Antonio Coll (CA)
Muskegon Comm Coll (MI)
Napa Valley Coll (CA)
Neosho County Comm Coll (KS)
New Hampshire Comm Tech Coll, Manchester/Stratham (NH)
New Mexico Jr Coll (NM)
New River Comm Coll (VA)
Nicolet Area Tech Coll (WI)
North Central Texas Coll (TX)
Northeast Comm Coll (NE)
Northeast State Tech Comm Coll (TN)
North Idaho Coll (ID)
North Iowa Area Comm Coll (IA)
Northland Comm and Tech Coll–Thief River Falls (MN)
Northwest Iowa Comm Coll (IA)
Northwest KansasTech Coll (KS)
Northwest-Shoals Comm Coll (AL)
Oakland Comm Coll (MI)
Odessa Coll (TX)

Olympic Coll (WA)
Orange Coast Coll (CA)
Oxnard Coll (CA)
Ozarks Tech Comm Coll (MO)
Pasadena City Coll (CA)
Pima Comm Coll (AZ)
Porterville Coll (CA)
Pueblo Comm Coll (CO)
Ranger Coll (TX)
Red Rocks Comm Coll (CO)
Reedley Coll (CA)
Riverside Comm Coll District (CA)
Rogue Comm Coll (OR)
St. Cloud Tech Coll (MN)
St. Philip's Coll (TX)
Salt Lake Comm Coll (UT)
San Bernardino Valley Coll (CA)
San Diego City Coll (CA)
San Juan Coll (NM)
Santa Ana Coll (CA)
Schoolcraft Coll (MI)
Shasta Coll (CA)
Sheridan Coll–Sheridan and Gillette (WY)
Skagit Valley Coll (WA)
Southeastern Comm Coll (NC)
Southeastern Comm Coll, North Campus (IA)
South Plains Coll (TX)
South Seattle Comm Coll (WA)
Southwestern Michigan Coll (MI)
Southwest Mississippi Comm Coll (MS)
Spokane Comm Coll (WA)
Spokane Falls Comm Coll (WA)
State Fair Comm Coll (MO)
State U of New York Coll of Technology at Alfred (NY)
Terra State Comm Coll (OH)
Texarkana Coll (TX)
Treasure Valley Comm Coll (OR)
Tri-County Comm Coll (NC)
Tulsa Welding School (OK)
Tyler Jr Coll (TX)
U of Arkansas Comm Coll at Morrilton (AR)
The U of Montana-Helena Coll of Technology (MT)
U of New Mexico–Gallup (NM)
Ventura Coll (CA)
Victor Valley Coll (CA)
Wallace State Comm Coll (AL)
Western Nevada Comm Coll (NV)
Western Texas Coll (TX)
Western Wyoming Comm Coll (WY)
West Hills Comm Coll (CA)
Westmoreland County Comm Coll (PA)
West Shore Comm Coll (MI)
West Virginia U at Parkersburg (WV)
York Tech Coll (SC)
Yuba Coll (CA)

Western Civilization
Lamar Comm Coll (CO)

Wildlife and Wildlands Science And Management
Barton County Comm Coll (KS)
Brigham Young U–Idaho (ID)
Cabrillo Coll (CA)
Cerritos Coll (CA)
Chattanooga State Tech Comm Coll (TN)
City Coll of San Francisco (CA)
Comm Coll of Southern Nevada (NV)
Dixie State Coll of Utah (UT)
East Central Coll (MO)
Fullerton Coll (CA)
Garrett Coll (MD)
Hocking Coll (OH)
Iowa Lakes Comm Coll (IA)

Itasca Comm Coll (MN)
Keystone Coll (PA)
Kirkwood Comm Coll (IA)
Laramie County Comm Coll (WY)
Minot State U–Bottineau Campus (ND)
Monterey Peninsula Coll (CA)
Moorpark Coll (CA)
Mt. San Antonio Coll (CA)
Murray State Coll (OK)
North Idaho Coll (ID)
Ogeechee Tech Coll (GA)
Penn State DuBois (PA)
Potomac State Coll of West Virginia U (WV)
Santa Rosa Jr Coll (CA)
Spokane Comm Coll (WA)
State U of New York Coll of Agriculture and Technology at Morrisville (NY)
Treasure Valley Comm Coll (OR)
Turtle Mountain Comm Coll (ND)
Western Wyoming Comm Coll (WY)

Wildlife Biology
Colby Comm Coll (KS)
Dodge City Comm Coll (KS)
Eastern Arizona Coll (AZ)
Everett Comm Coll (WA)
Garrett Coll (MD)
Iowa Lakes Comm Coll (IA)
Keystone Coll (PA)
Kirkwood Comm Coll (IA)
North Idaho Coll (ID)

Wind/Percussion Instruments
Iowa Lakes Comm Coll (IA)
Kirkwood Comm Coll (IA)

Women'S Studies
Bergen Comm Coll (NJ)
Cabrillo Coll (CA)
City Coll of San Francisco (CA)
Cosumnes River Coll, Sacramento (CA)
Foothill Coll (CA)
Fresno City Coll (CA)
Manatee Comm Coll (FL)
Monterey Peninsula Coll (CA)
Northern Essex Comm Coll (MA)
Sacramento City Coll (CA)
Santa Ana Coll (CA)
Santa Rosa Jr Coll (CA)
Santiago Canyon Coll (CA)
Suffolk County Comm Coll (NY)
Tompkins Cortland Comm Coll (NY)
West Valley Coll (CA)
Yuba Coll (CA)

Wood Science and Wood Products/Pulp And Paper Technology
Allen County Comm Coll (KS)
Bakersfield Coll (CA)
Cossatot Comm Coll of the U of Arkansas (AR)
Dabney S. Lancaster Comm Coll (VA)
Fox Valley Tech Coll (WI)
Kennebec Valley Comm Coll (ME)
Laney Coll (CA)
Lower Columbia Coll (WA)
Ogeechee Tech Coll (GA)
Potomac State Coll of West Virginia U (WV)
State U of New York Coll of Agriculture and Technology at Morrisville (NY)
Texarkana Coll (TX)

Woodworking
Bucks County Comm Coll (PA)
Coll of Southern Idaho (ID)

Woodworking Related
Oakland Comm Coll (MI)

Word Processing

Baltimore City Comm
Coll (MD)
Coastal Bend Coll (TX)
Coll of the Desert (CA)
Cypress Coll (CA)
Florida National Coll (FL)
Gateway Comm Coll (CT)
Hawkeye Comm Coll (IA)
Iowa Lakes Comm
Coll (IA)
Kellogg Comm Coll (MI)
Laurel Business Inst (PA)
Lorain County Comm
Coll (OH)
Los Angeles City Coll (CA)

Lower Columbia Coll (WA)
Metropolitan Comm
Coll–Business &
Technology
Campus (MO)
Mississippi Gulf Coast
Comm Coll (MS)
Mohave Comm Coll (AZ)
Naugatuck Valley Comm
Coll (CT)
North Central Texas
Coll (TX)
Northern Essex Comm
Coll (MA)

Northland Comm and Tech
Coll–Thief River
Falls (MN)
Orange Coast Coll (CA)
Owensboro Comm and
Tech Coll (KY)
Palm Beach Comm
Coll (FL)
Quinebaug Valley Comm
Coll (CT)
Richland Comm Coll (IL)
Riverland Comm Coll (MN)
Sampson Comm Coll (NC)
San Antonio Coll (TX)
Santa Ana Coll (CA)
Seminole Comm Coll (FL)

Stanly Comm Coll (NC)
Stark State Coll of
Technology (OH)
Tallahassee Comm
Coll (FL)
Three Rivers Comm
Coll (MO)
Trumbull Business
Coll (OH)
Tulsa Comm Coll (OK)
Valencia Comm Coll (FL)
Vincennes U Jasper
Campus (IN)
West Central Tech
Coll (GA)

Western Wyoming Comm
Coll (WY)
Yuba Coll (CA)

Youth Services

Midlands Tech Coll (SC)

Zoology/Animal Biology

Brigham Young U –
Idaho (ID)
Centralia Coll (WA)
Cerritos Coll (CA)
Colby Comm Coll (KS)
Coll of Southern Idaho (ID)

Dixie State Coll of
Utah (UT)
East Central Coll (MO)
El Camino Coll (CA)
Everett Comm Coll (WA)
Fullerton Coll (CA)
Miami U–Middletown
Campus (OH)
Northeastern Jr Coll (CO)
North Idaho Coll (ID)
Palm Beach Comm
Coll (FL)
San Bernardino Valley
Coll (CA)
Tulsa Comm Coll (OK)

Associate Degree Programs at Four-Year Colleges

Accounting
American Public U
System (WV)
Baker Coll of Allen
Park (MI)
Baker Coll of Auburn
Hills (MI)
Baker Coll of Cadillac (MI)
Baker Coll of Clinton
Township (MI)
Baker Coll of Flint (MI)
Baker Coll of Jackson (MI)
Baker Coll of
Muskegon (MI)
Baker Coll of Owosso (MI)
Baker Coll of Port
Huron (MI)
Becker Coll (MA)
Bluefield State Coll (WV)
Briarcliffe Coll (NY)
Brigham Young
U–Hawaii (HI)
British Columbia Inst of
Technology (BC,
Canada)
California U of
Pennsylvania (PA)
Calumet Coll of Saint
Joseph (IN)
Central Pennsylvania
Coll (PA)
Champlain Coll (VT)
Chestnut Hill Coll (PA)
Clayton State U (GA)
Coll of Mount St.
Joseph (OH)
Coll of St. Joseph (VT)
Coll of Saint Mary (NE)
Columbia Union Coll (MD)
Davenport U,
Dearborn (MI)
Evangel U (MO)
Fairmont State U (WV)
Faulkner U (AL)
Ferris State U (MI)
Florida Metropolitan
U–Brandon
Campus (FL)
Florida Metropolitan
U–Lakeland
Campus (FL)
Florida Metropolitan
U–Pompano Beach
Campus (FL)
Franciscan U of
Steubenville (OH)
Goldey-Beacom Coll (DE)
Gwynedd-Mercy Coll (PA)
Hawai'i Pacific U (HI)
Husson Coll (ME)
Immaculata U (PA)
Indiana Tech (IN)
Indiana Wesleyan U (IN)
Inter American U of Puerto
Rico, Aguadilla
Campus (PR)
Inter American U of Puerto
Rico, Barranquitas
Campus (PR)
Inter American U of Puerto
Rico, Bayamón
Campus (PR)
Inter American U of Puerto
Rico, Fajardo
Campus (PR)
Inter American U of Puerto
Rico, San Germán
Campus (PR)
International Coll (FL)
Johnson & Wales U (CO)
Johnson & Wales U (FL)
Johnson & Wales U (NC)
Johnson & Wales U (RI)
Johnson State Coll (VT)

Jones Coll,
Jacksonville (FL)
Lake Superior State U (MI)
Lebanon Valley Coll (PA)
Macon State Coll (GA)
Manchester Coll (IN)
Marian Coll (IN)
Marygrove Coll (MI)
Methodist U (NC)
Minnesota School of
Business (MN)
Missouri Southern State
U (MO)
Monroe Coll, Bronx (NY)
Morrison U (NV)
Mount Aloysius Coll (PA)
Mount Marty Coll (SD)
Mount Olive Coll (NC)
National American U,
Denver (CO)
National American U,
Rapid City (SD)
Northwood U (MI)
Northwood U, Florida
Campus (FL)
Northwood U, Texas
Campus (TX)
Oakwood Coll (AL)
Oglala Lakota Coll (SD)
Oklahoma Wesleyan
U (OK)
Peirce Coll (PA)
Point Park U (PA)
Purdue U North
Central (IN)
Rogers State U (OK)
Sacred Heart U (CT)
Saint Francis U (PA)
St. John's U (NY)
Saint Joseph's U (PA)
Shawnee State U (OH)
Southern Adventist U (TN)
Southern New Hampshire
U (NH)
South U (AL)
South U, West Palm
Beach (FL)
South U (GA)
South U (SC)
Southwest Baptist U (MO)
Southwest Minnesota
State U (MN)
State U of New York Coll
of Agriculture and
Technology at
Cobleskill (NY)
Sullivan U (KY)
Thiel Coll (PA)
Thomas Coll (ME)
Thomas More Coll (KY)
Tiffin U (OH)
Tri-State U (IN)
Union Coll (NE)
U of Alaska
Anchorage (AK)
U of Charleston (WV)
U of Cincinnati (OH)
The U of Findlay (OH)
U of Mary (ND)
U of Minnesota,
Crookston (MN)
U of Phoenix–Cleveland
Campus (OH)
U of Phoenix–Columbus
Ohio Campus (OH)
U of Phoenix–Houston
Campus (TX)
U of Phoenix–Indianapolis
Campus (IN)
U of Phoenix–Nevada
Campus (NV)
U of Phoenix–St. Louis
Campus (MO)

U of Phoenix–Springfield
Campus (MO)
U of Puerto Rico at
Humacao (PR)
U of Rio Grande (OH)
U of the District of
Columbia (DC)
U of the Virgin Islands (VI)
The U of Toledo (OH)
The U of West
Alabama (AL)
Utah Valley State Coll (UT)
Villa Julie Coll (MD)
Walsh U (OH)
Webber International
U (FL)
West Virginia State U (WV)
Wilson Coll (PA)
Youngstown State U (OH)

Accounting and Business/Management
Central Christian Coll of
Kansas (KS)
Chestnut Hill Coll (PA)
Davis & Elkins Coll (WV)
Mount Aloysius Coll (PA)
Peirce Coll (PA)

Accounting Related
Central Pennsylvania
Coll (PA)
Montana State
U–Billings (MT)
Park U (MO)
Peirce Coll (PA)

Accounting Technology and Bookkeeping
Baker Coll of Flint (MI)
British Columbia Inst of
Technology (BC,
Canada)
Cleary U (MI)
DeVry U, Fremont (CA)
DeVry U, Pomona (CA)
DeVry U,
Westminster (CO)
DeVry U, Miramar (FL)
DeVry U, Orlando (FL)
DeVry U, Decatur (GA)
DeVry U, Federal
Way (WA)
Gannon U (PA)
Georgia Southwestern
State U (GA)
Lewis-Clark State Coll (ID)
Montana State
U–Billings (MT)
New York Inst of
Technology (NY)
Ohio U (OH)
Peirce Coll (PA)
Pennsylvania Coll of
Technology (PA)
Robert Morris Coll (IL)
St. Augustine Coll (IL)
The U of Akron (OH)
U of Alaska Fairbanks (AK)
The U of Montana (MT)
U of Rio Grande (OH)
Wright State U (OH)

Acting
Central Christian Coll of
Kansas (KS)
New World School of the
Arts (FL)

Administrative Assistant and Secretarial Science
Alabama State U (AL)
Arkansas State U (AR)

Arkansas Tech U (AR)
Atlantic Union Coll (MA)
Baker Coll of Auburn
Hills (MI)
Baker Coll of Cadillac (MI)
Baker Coll of Clinton
Township (MI)
Baker Coll of Flint (MI)
Baker Coll of Jackson (MI)
Baker Coll of
Muskegon (MI)
Baker Coll of Owosso (MI)
Baker Coll of Port
Huron (MI)
Ball State U (IN)
Baptist Bible Coll (MO)
Black Hills State U (SD)
Bluefield State Coll (WV)
Briarcliffe Coll (NY)
British Columbia Inst of
Technology (BC,
Canada)
Bryant and Stratton Coll,
Cleveland (OH)
Campbellsville U (KY)
Clayton State U (GA)
Columbia Coll,
Caguas (PR)
Concordia Coll–New
York (NY)
Davenport U,
Dearborn (MI)
Dickinson State U (ND)
Dordt Coll (IA)
Eastern Kentucky U (KY)
Eastern Oregon U (OR)
Electronic Data Processing
Coll of Puerto
Rico (PR)
Evangel U (MO)
Fairmont State U (WV)
Faith Baptist Bible Coll and
Theological
Seminary (IA)
Faulkner U (AL)
Fort Hays State U (KS)
Free Will Baptist Bible
Coll (TN)
Georgia Southwestern
State U (GA)
God's Bible School and
Coll (OH)
Grace Coll (IN)
Henderson State U (AR)
Idaho State U (ID)
Inter American U of Puerto
Rico, Aguadilla
Campus (PR)
Inter American U of Puerto
Rico, Barranquitas
Campus (PR)
Inter American U of Puerto
Rico, Bayamón
Campus (PR)
Inter American U of Puerto
Rico, Fajardo
Campus (PR)
Inter American U of Puerto
Rico, San Germán
Campus (PR)
Jones Coll,
Jacksonville (FL)
Kentucky Christian U (KY)
Kuyper Coll (MI)
Lancaster Bible Coll (PA)
Lewis-Clark State Coll (ID)
Macon State Coll (GA)
Maranatha Baptist Bible
Coll (WI)
Mayville State U (ND)
Mercyhurst Coll (PA)
Mesa State Coll (CO)
Minnesota School of
Business (MN)

Montana State
U–Billings (MT)
Montana Tech of The U of
Montana (MT)
Morrison U (NV)
Mountain State U (WV)
Murray State U (KY)
New York Inst of
Technology (NY)
Northern State U (SD)
Northwestern State U of
Louisiana (LA)
Oakwood Coll (AL)
Oglala Lakota Coll (SD)
Ohio U (OH)
Oklahoma Wesleyan
U (OK)
Pennsylvania Coll of
Technology (PA)
Pontifical Catholic U of
Puerto Rico (PR)
Robert Morris Coll (IL)
Rogers State U (OK)
St. Augustine Coll (IL)
Southeastern Louisiana
U (LA)
Southern Arkansas
U–Magnolia (AR)
South U, West Palm
Beach (FL)
Sullivan U (KY)
Sul Ross State U (TX)
Tabor Coll (KS)
Tennessee State U (TN)
Trinity Baptist Coll (FL)
Universidad Adventista de
las Antillas (PR)
The U of Akron (OH)
U of Alaska Fairbanks (AK)
U of Alaska
Southeast (AK)
U of Arkansas at Fort
Smith (AR)
U of Central Missouri (MO)
U of Cincinnati (OH)
The U of Findlay (OH)
The U of Montana–
Western (MT)
U of Puerto Rico at
Humacao (PR)
U of Rio Grande (OH)
U of Sioux Falls (SD)
U of the District of
Columbia (DC)
U of the Virgin Islands (VI)
The U of Toledo (OH)
Utah State U (UT)
Washburn U (KS)
Weber State U (UT)
West Virginia State U (WV)
Wiley Coll (TX)
Williams Baptist Coll (AR)
Wright State U (OH)

Adult Development and Aging
Madonna U (MI)
Saint Mary-of-the-Woods
Coll (IN)
The U of Toledo (OH)

Advertising
Academy of Art U (CA)
The Art Inst of California–
San Diego (CA)
Fashion Inst of
Technology (NY)
Hussian School of Art (PA)
Johnson & Wales U (CO)
Johnson & Wales U (FL)
Johnson & Wales U (RI)
New England School of
Communications (ME)
Northwood U (MI)

Northwood U, Florida
Campus (FL)
Northwood U, Texas
Campus (TX)
U of the District of
Columbia (DC)
West Virginia State U (WV)
Xavier U (OH)

Aeronautical/ Aerospace Engineering Technology
British Columbia Inst of
Technology (BC,
Canada)
Pennsylvania Coll of
Technology (PA)
Purdue U (IN)

Aeronautics/Aviation/ Aerospace Science and Technology
Daniel Webster Coll (NH)
Embry-Riddle Aeronautical
U, Extended
Campus (FL)
Indiana State U (IN)
Purdue U (IN)
Vaughn Coll of Aeronautics
and Technology (NY)

Agribusiness
Morehead State U (KY)
Vermont Tech Coll (VT)

Agricultural and Domestic Animals Services Related
Sterling Coll (VT)

Agricultural and Food Products Processing
North Carolina State
U (NC)

Agricultural and Horticultural Plant Breeding
Sterling Coll (VT)

Agricultural Animal Breeding
Sterling Coll (VT)

Agricultural/Biological Engineering and Bioengineering
State U of New York Coll
of Agriculture and
Technology at
Cobleskill (NY)

Agricultural Business and Management
Andrews U (MI)
Central Christian Coll of
Kansas (KS)
Clayton State U (GA)
Dickinson State U (ND)
Dordt Coll (IA)
North Carolina State
U (NC)
Rogers State U (OK)
Southwest Minnesota
State U (MN)
State U of New York Coll
of Agriculture and
Technology at
Cobleskill (NY)
U of Minnesota,
Crookston (MN)
U of New Hampshire (NH)

Agricultural Business and Management Related
Penn State Abington (PA)

Penn State Altoona (PA)
Penn State Berks (PA)
Penn State Erie, The Behrend Coll (PA)
Penn State U Park (PA)

Agricultural Economics
The U of British Columbia (BC, Canada)

Agricultural Mechanization
Andrews U (MI)
Clayton State U (GA)
State U of New York Coll of Agriculture and Technology at Cobleskill (NY)

Agricultural Production
U of Arkansas at Monticello (AR)
U of Puerto Rico at Utuado (PR)
Western Kentucky U (KY)

Agricultural Production Related
Sterling Coll (VT)

Agricultural Public Services Related
Sterling Coll (VT)

Agriculture
Andrews U (MI)
Clayton State U (GA)
Dalton State Coll (GA)
Fort Lewis Coll (CO)
Lubbock Christian U (TX)
Macon State Coll (GA)
Murray State U (KY)
North Carolina State U (NC)
Oglala Lakota Coll (SD)
Oklahoma Panhandle State U (OK)
Purdue U (IN)
South Dakota State U (SD)
Southern Utah U (UT)
State U of New York Coll of Agriculture and Technology at Cobleskill (NY)
Sterling Coll (VT)
U of Delaware (DE)
U of Minnesota, Crookston (MN)

Agriculture and Agriculture Operations Related
Eastern Kentucky U (KY)
Sterling Coll (VT)

Agronomy and Crop Science
Andrews U (MI)
State U of New York Coll of Agriculture and Technology at Cobleskill (NY)
U of Minnesota, Crookston (MN)

Aircraft Powerplant Technology
British Columbia Inst of Technology (BC, Canada)
Embry-Riddle Aeronautical U, Extended Campus (FL)
Georgia Southwestern State U (GA)
Idaho State U (ID)
Pennsylvania Coll of Technology (PA)

Airframe Mechanics and Aircraft Maintenance Technology
British Columbia Inst of Technology (BC, Canada)
Clayton State U (GA)
Georgia Southwestern State U (GA)
Kansas State U (KS)
Lewis U (IL)
U of Alaska Anchorage (AK)
U of Alaska Fairbanks (AK)
Utah State U (UT)
Vaughn Coll of Aeronautics and Technology (NY)
Wentworth Inst of Technology (MA)

Airline Flight Attendant
The U of Akron (OH)

Airline Pilot and Flight Crew
Andrews U (MI)
Baker Coll of Flint (MI)
Baker Coll of Muskegon (MI)
Central Christian Coll of Kansas (KS)
Daniel Webster Coll (NH)
Kansas State U (KS)
Southern Illinois U Carbondale (IL)
U of Alaska Anchorage (AK)
Utah Valley State Coll (UT)
Vaughn Coll of Aeronautics and Technology (NY)

Air Traffic Control
U of Alaska Anchorage (AK)

Allied Health and Medical Assisting Services Related
Bloomsburg U of Pennsylvania (PA)
Washburn U (KS)

Allied Health Diagnostic, Intervention, and Treatment Professions Related
British Columbia Inst of Technology (BC, Canada)
Cameron U (OK)
Gwynedd-Mercy Coll (PA)
Pennsylvania Coll of Technology (PA)
The U of Akron (OH)

American Indian/Native American Studies
Oglala Lakota Coll (SD)
Rogers State U (OK)

American Native/Native American Languages
Idaho State U (ID)

American Sign Language (ASL)
Idaho State U (ID)
Madonna U (MI)
Rochester Inst of Technology (NY)

Ancient Near Eastern and Biblical Languages
Indiana Wesleyan U (IN)

Anesthesiologist Assistant
Thompson Rivers U (BC, Canada)

Animal Health
Sterling Coll (VT)

Animal/Livestock Husbandry and Production
Saint Mary-of-the-Woods Coll (IN)
Sterling Coll (VT)
Thompson Rivers U (BC, Canada)
U of Connecticut (CT)
U of New Hampshire (NH)

Animal Nutrition
Sterling Coll (VT)

Animal Sciences
Becker Coll (MA)
State U of New York Coll of Agriculture and Technology at Cobleskill (NY)
Sterling Coll (VT)
Sul Ross State U (TX)
U of Connecticut (CT)
U of Minnesota, Crookston (MN)
U of New Hampshire (NH)
U of Puerto Rico at Utuado (PR)

Animal Sciences Related
Sterling Coll (VT)

Animal Training
Becker Coll (MA)

Animation, Interactive Technology, Video Graphics and Special Effects
Academy of Art U (CA)
The Art Inst of Dallas (TX)
The Art Inst of Houston (TX)
The Art Inst of Seattle (WA)
The Art Inst of Tampa (FL)
Champlain Coll (VT)
The Illinois Inst of Art–Chicago (IL)
National U (CA)
New England School of Communications (ME)

Anthropology
Kwantlen U Coll (BC, Canada)
Université Laval (QC, Canada)

Apparel and Accessories Marketing
California Design Coll (CA)
Clayton State U (GA)
The U of Montana (MT)

Apparel and Textile Manufacturing
Fashion Inst of Technology (NY)

Apparel and Textiles
Academy of Art U (CA)
Fashion Inst of Technology (NY)
The Illinois Inst of Art–Chicago (IL)

Applied Art
Academy of Art U (CA)
The Art Inst of Fort Lauderdale (FL)
The Art Inst of Pittsburgh (PA)
New World School of the Arts (FL)
Rochester Inst of Technology (NY)
U of Maine at Presque Isle (ME)
The U of Montana–Western (MT)
Villa Julie Coll (MD)

Applied Horticulture
Bob Jones U (SC)
Georgia Southwestern State U (GA)
Sterling Coll (VT)
Temple U (PA)
U of Connecticut (CT)
The U of Maine at Augusta (ME)

Applied Horticulture/Horticultural Business Services Related
Pennsylvania Coll of Technology (PA)
U of Massachusetts Amherst (MA)

Applied Mathematics
Central Methodist U (MO)
Hawai'i Pacific U (HI)
Rochester Inst of Technology (NY)

Archeology
Weber State U (UT)

Architectural Drafting and Cad/Cadd
Baker Coll of Flint (MI)
Baker Coll of Muskegon (MI)
British Columbia Inst of Technology (BC, Canada)
Indiana State U (IN)
Indiana U–Purdue U Indianapolis (IN)
Montana Tech of The U of Montana (MT)
The U of Toledo (OH)
Western Kentucky U (KY)
Westwood Coll–Annandale Campus (VA)

Architectural Engineering Technology
Baker Coll of Cadillac (MI)
Baker Coll of Clinton Township (MI)
Baker Coll of Owosso (MI)
Baker Coll of Port Huron (MI)
Bluefield State Coll (WV)
British Columbia Inst of Technology (BC, Canada)
Clayton State U (GA)
Ferris State U (MI)
Indiana–Purdue U Fort Wayne (IN)
Northern Kentucky U (KY)
Pennsylvania Coll of Technology (PA)
Purdue U (IN)
Purdue U Calumet (IN)
Purdue U North Central (IN)
U of Alaska Anchorage (AK)
U of Cincinnati (OH)
U of the District of Columbia (DC)
Vermont Tech Coll (VT)
Wentworth Inst of Technology (MA)
West Virginia State U (WV)

Architectural Technology
The U of Maine at Augusta (ME)

Architecture
Central Christian Coll of Kansas (KS)
Coll of Staten Island of the City U of New York (NY)
New York Inst of Technology (NY)

Architecture Related
Abilene Christian U (TX)

Army ROTC/Military Science
American Public U System (WV)
Methodist U (NC)

Art
Adrian Coll (MI)
The Art Inst of Colorado (CO)
Ashland U (OH)
Burlington Coll (VT)
Central Christian Coll of Kansas (KS)
Clayton State U (GA)
Coll of Mount St. Joseph (OH)
Eastern New Mexico U (NM)
Felician Coll (NJ)
Idaho State U (ID)
Indiana Wesleyan U (IN)
Lindsey Wilson Coll (KY)
Lourdes Coll (OH)
Macon State Coll (GA)
Madonna U (MI)
Manchester Coll (IN)
Marian Coll (IN)
Mesa State Coll (CO)
Methodist U (NC)
Miami International U of Art & Design (FL)
Mount Olive Coll (NC)
North Greenville U (SC)
Parsons The New School for Design (NY)
Pontifical Catholic U of Puerto Rico (PR)
Rivier Coll (NH)
Rochester Inst of Technology (NY)
Rogers State U (OK)
St. Gregory's U, Shawnee (OK)
Shawnee State U (OH)
State U of New York Empire State Coll (NY)
Suffolk U (MA)
Union Coll (NE)
U of Rio Grande (OH)
The U of Toledo (OH)
U of Wisconsin–Green Bay (WI)
Villa Julie Coll (MD)
West Virginia State U (WV)

Art History, Criticism and Conservation
John Cabot U (Italy)
Lourdes Coll (OH)
Thomas More Coll (KY)
Université Laval (QC, Canada)

Artificial Intelligence and Robotics
Clayton State U (GA)

U of Cincinnati (OH)

Art Teacher Education
Central Christian Coll of Kansas (KS)
Clayton State U (GA)

Athletic Training
Central Christian Coll of Kansas (KS)

Audio Engineering
The Art Inst of Seattle (WA)
Five Towns Coll (NY)
New England School of Communications (ME)

Audiology and Hearing Sciences
Ohio U (OH)

Audiovisual Communications Technologies Related
The Art Inst of Tennessee–Nashville (TN)

Autobody/Collision and Repair Technology
British Columbia Inst of Technology (BC, Canada)
Georgia Southwestern State U (GA)
Idaho State U (ID)
Lewis-Clark State Coll (ID)
Montana State U–Billings (MT)
Montana Tech of The U of Montana (MT)
Pennsylvania Coll of Technology (PA)
Utah Valley State Coll (UT)
Weber State U (UT)

Automobile/Automotive Mechanics Technology
Arkansas State U (AR)
Baker Coll of Flint (MI)
Boise State U (ID)
British Columbia Inst of Technology (BC, Canada)
Ferris State U (MI)
Georgia Southwestern State U (GA)
Idaho State U (ID)
Lewis-Clark State Coll (ID)
Mesa State Coll (CO)
Montana State U–Billings (MT)
Montana Tech of The U of Montana (MT)
Northern Michigan U (MI)
Pittsburg State U (KS)
Southern Adventist U (TN)
Southern Utah U (UT)
U of Alaska Anchorage (AK)
Utah Valley State Coll (UT)
Walla Walla Coll (WA)
Weber State U (UT)

Automotive Engineering Technology
Farmingdale State Coll (NY)
Pennsylvania Coll of Technology (PA)
The U of Akron (OH)
Vermont Tech Coll (VT)

Aviation/Airway Management
Clayton State U (GA)
Daniel Webster Coll (NH)
Fairmont State U (WV)
Mountain State U (WV)
Northern Kentucky U (KY)
Park U (MO)
The U of Akron (OH)
U of Alaska Anchorage (AK)
U of Alaska Fairbanks (AK)
U of Minnesota, Crookston (MN)
U of the District of Columbia (DC)

Avionics Maintenance Technology
Andrews U (MI)
Baker Coll of Flint (MI)
British Columbia Inst of Technology (BC, Canada)
Clayton State U (GA)
Excelsior Coll (NY)
Fairmont State U (WV)
Georgia Southwestern State U (GA)
Hampton U (VA)
Lewis U (IL)
Northern Michigan U (MI)
Pennsylvania Coll of Technology (PA)
U of Alaska Anchorage (AK)
U of Minnesota, Crookston (MN)
U of the District of Columbia (DC)
Vaughn Coll of Aeronautics and Technology (NY)
Walla Walla Coll (WA)
Wentworth Inst of Technology (MA)

Baking and Pastry Arts
The Art Inst of California–San Diego (CA)
The Art Inst of Charleston (SC)
The Art Inst of Houston (TX)
The Art Inst of Pittsburgh (PA)
The Culinary Inst of America (NY)
Johnson & Wales U (CO)
Johnson & Wales U (FL)
Johnson & Wales U (NC)
Johnson & Wales U (RI)
Kendall Coll (IL)
Pennsylvania Coll of Technology (PA)
Southern New Hampshire U (NH)

Banking and Financial Support Services
Globe Inst of Technology (NY)
Hilbert Coll (NY)
Mercy Coll (NY)
Mountain State U (WV)
Northwood U (MI)
Northwood U, Florida Campus (FL)
Northwood U, Texas Campus (TX)
Pennsylvania Coll of Technology (PA)
The U of Akron (OH)
U of Indianapolis (IN)
Utah Valley State Coll (UT)
Washburn U (KS)

Behavioral Sciences
Felician Coll (NJ)
Granite State Coll (NH)
Lewis-Clark State Coll (ID)
Methodist U (NC)
Mount Aloysius Coll (PA)
Oklahoma Wesleyan U (OK)
Utah Valley State Coll (UT)

Biblical Studies
Alaska Bible Coll (AK)
American Baptist Coll of American Baptist Theological Seminary (TN)
Appalachian Bible Coll (WV)
Barclay Coll (KS)
Beacon U (GA)
Boise Bible Coll (ID)
Boston Baptist Coll (MA)
California Christian Coll (CA)
Calvary Bible Coll and Theological Seminary (MO)
Cincinnati Christian U (OH)
Clear Creek Baptist Bible Coll (KY)
Columbia International U (SC)
Corban Coll (OR)
Crown Coll (MN)
Dallas Baptist U (TX)
Davis Coll (NY)
Eastern Mennonite U (VA)
Faith Baptist Bible Coll and Theological Seminary (IA)
Faulkner U (AL)
Fresno Pacific U (CA)
Geneva Coll (PA)
God's Bible School and Coll (OH)
Grace Coll (IN)
Heritage Christian U (AL)

Hillsdale Free Will Baptist
Coll (OK)
Houghton Coll (NY)
Howard Payne U (TX)
John Brown U (AR)
Kuyper Coll (MI)
Lancaster Bible Coll (PA)
Nazarene Bible Coll (CO)
Oak Hills Christian
Coll (MN)
Oakwood Coll (AL)
Ohio Valley U (WV)
Ouachita Baptist U (AR)
Pacific Union Coll (CA)
Patten U (CA)
Roanoke Bible Coll (NC)
Shasta Bible Coll (CA)
Simpson U (CA)
Southeastern Bible
Coll (AL)
Tabor Coll (KS)
Trinity Coll of Florida (FL)
Trinity Lutheran Coll (WA)
Universidad Adventista de
las Antillas (PR)
Valley Forge Christian
Coll (PA)
Warner Pacific Coll (OR)
Washington Bible
Coll (MD)

Biochemistry
Saint Joseph's Coll (IN)

Biological and Biomedical Sciences Related
Gwynedd-Mercy Coll (PA)

Biological and Physical Sciences
Bluefield State Coll (WV)
Central Christian Coll of
Kansas (KS)
Clayton State U (GA)
Crown Coll (MN)
Dalton State Coll (GA)
Indiana U East (IN)
Madonna U (MI)
Medgar Evers Coll of the
City U of New
York (NY)
Montana Tech of The U of
Montana (MT)
Mount Olive Coll (NC)
Ohio U (OH)
Ohio U–Zanesville (OH)
Penn State Altoona (PA)
Sacred Heart U (CT)
State U of New York Coll
of Agriculture and
Technology at
Cobleskill (NY)
State U of New York
Empire State Coll (NY)
Sterling Coll (VT)
Tri-State U (IN)
U of Cincinnati (OH)
Valparaiso U (IN)
Villa Julie Coll (MD)

Biology/Biological Sciences
Adrian Coll (MI)
Brewton-Parker Coll (GA)
Canadian Mennonite U
(MB, Canada)
Chestnut Hill Coll (PA)
Cleveland Chiropractic
Coll-Kansas City
Campus (MO)
Cleveland Chiropractic
Coll-Los Angeles
Campus (CA)
Crown Coll (MN)
Cumberland U (TN)
Dalton State Coll (GA)
Felician Coll (NJ)
Fresno Pacific U (CA)
Idaho State U (ID)
Indiana U–Purdue U Fort
Wayne (IN)
Indiana U South Bend (IN)
Indiana Wesleyan U (IN)
Inter American U of Puerto
Rico, Barranquitas
Campus (PR)
Lourdes Coll (OH)
Macon State Coll (GA)
Mesa State Coll (CO)
Methodist U (NC)
Montana Tech of The U of
Montana (MT)
Mount Olive Coll (NC)
Oklahoma Wesleyan
U (OK)
Pennsylvania Coll of
Technology (PA)
Pine Manor Coll (MA)
Presentation Coll (SD)

Rochester Inst of
Technology (NY)
Rogers State U (OK)
Sacred Heart U (CT)
Saint Joseph's U (PA)
Shawnee State U (OH)
Thomas More Coll (KY)
The U of Maine at
Augusta (ME)
U of New Hampshire at
Manchester (NH)
U of Rio Grande (OH)
The U of Tampa (FL)
The U of Toledo (OH)
U of Wisconsin–Green
Bay (WI)
Utah Valley State Coll (UT)
Villa Julie Coll (MD)
Wright State U (OH)
York Coll of
Pennsylvania (PA)

Biology/ Biotechnology Laboratory Technician
British Columbia Inst of
Technology (BC,
Canada)
Ferris State U (MI)
State U of New York Coll
of Agriculture and
Technology at
Cobleskill (NY)
U of the District of
Columbia (DC)
Villa Julie Coll (MD)
Weber State U (UT)

Biology Teacher Education
Central Christian Coll of
Kansas (KS)

Biomedical Technology
Baker Coll of Flint (MI)
Faulkner U (AL)
Indiana U–Purdue U
Indianapolis (IN)
Penn State Altoona (PA)
Penn State Berks (PA)
Penn State Erie, The
Behrend Coll (PA)
Pennsylvania Coll of
Technology (PA)
Wentworth Inst of
Technology (MA)

Biotechnology
British Columbia Inst of
Technology (BC,
Canada)

Broadcast Journalism
Cornerstone U (MI)
Evangel U (MO)
Five Towns Coll (NY)
John Brown U (AR)
Manchester Coll (IN)
New England School of
Communications (ME)
Ohio U–Zanesville (OH)
Pennsylvania Coll of
Technology (PA)
Rogers State U (OK)
Trevecca Nazarene U (TN)

Buddhist Studies
Heritage Bible Coll (NC)

Building/Home/ Construction Inspection
Utah Valley State Coll (UT)

Building/Property Maintenance and Management
Park U (MO)

Business Administration and Management
Adrian Coll (MI)
Alabama State U (AL)
Alaska Pacific U (AK)
Alderson-Broaddus
Coll (WV)
American Public U
System (WV)
The American U in Dubai
(United Arab Emirates)
The American U of Rome
(Italy)
Andrews U (MI)
Anna Maria Coll (MA)
Argosy U, Orange
County (CA)
Austin Peay State U (TN)
Averett U (VA)

Baker Coll of Allen
Park (MI)
Baker Coll of Auburn
Hills (MI)
Baker Coll of Cadillac (MI)
Baker Coll of Clinton
Township (MI)
Baker Coll of Flint (MI)
Baker Coll of Jackson (MI)
Baker Coll of
Muskegon (MI)
Baker Coll of Owosso (MI)
Baker Coll of Port
Huron (MI)
Ball State U (IN)
Baptist Bible Coll (MO)
Becker Coll (MA)
Benedictine U (IL)
Bentley Coll (MA)
Briarcliffe Coll (NY)
British Columbia Inst of
Technology (BC,
Canada)
Bryan Coll (TN)
California U of
Pennsylvania (PA)
Calumet Coll of Saint
Joseph (IN)
Cameron U (OK)
Campbellsville U (KY)
Cardinal Stritch U (WI)
Cazenovia Coll (NY)
Central Baptist Coll (AR)
Central Christian Coll of
Kansas (KS)
Central Pennsylvania
Coll (PA)
Champlain Coll (VT)
Charleston Southern
U (SC)
Chestnut Hill Coll (PA)
Clarion U of
Pennsylvania (PA)
Clayton State U (GA)
Cleary U (MI)
Coll of Mount St.
Joseph (OH)
Coll of Mount Saint
Vincent (NY)
Coll of St. Joseph (VT)
Coll of Saint Mary (NE)
Coll of Santa Fe (NM)
Columbia Coll (MO)
Columbia Coll,
Caguas (PR)
Concordia Coll–New
York (NY)
Concordia U (OR)
Concord U (WV)
Corban U (OR)
Crown Coll (MN)
Dakota State U (SD)
Dakota Wesleyan U (SD)
Dallas Baptist U (TX)
Dalton State Coll (GA)
Daniel Webster Coll (NH)
Davenport U,
Dearborn (MI)
DeVry U (NJ)
East-West U (IL)
Edinboro U of
Pennsylvania (PA)
Electronic Data Processing
Coll of Puerto
Rico (PR)
Emmanuel Coll (GA)
Excelsior Coll (NY)
Fairmont State U (WV)
Farmingdale State
Coll (NY)
Faulkner U (AL)
Felician Coll (NJ)
Five Towns Coll (NY)
Florida Metropolitan
U–Brandon
Campus (FL)
Florida Metropolitan
U–Lakeland
Campus (FL)
Florida Metropolitan
U–Pompano Beach
Campus (FL)
Franciscan U of
Steubenville (OH)
Free Will Baptist Bible
Coll (TN)
Fresno Pacific U (CA)
Geneva Coll (PA)
Globe Inst of
Technology (NY)
Goldey-Beacom Coll (DE)
Grace Bible Coll (MI)
Granite State Coll (NH)
Grantham U (MO)
Gwynedd-Mercy Coll (PA)
Hawai'i Pacific U (HI)
Hilbert Coll (NY)
Husson Coll (ME)

Immaculata U (PA)
Indiana Tech (IN)
Indiana U Northwest (IN)
Indiana U of
Pennsylvania (PA)
Indiana U–Purdue U Fort
Wayne (IN)
Indiana Wesleyan U (IN)
Inter American U of Puerto
Rico, Aguadilla
Campus (PR)
Inter American U of Puerto
Rico, Barranquitas
Campus (PR)
Inter American U of Puerto
Rico, Bayamón
Campus (PR)
Inter American U of Puerto
Rico, Fajardo
Campus (PR)
Inter American U of Puerto
Rico, San Germán
Campus (PR)
International Coll (FL)
John Cabot U (Italy)
Johnson & Wales U (CO)
Johnson & Wales U (FL)
Johnson & Wales U (NC)
Johnson & Wales U (RI)
Johnson State Coll (VT)
Jones Coll,
Jacksonville (FL)
Kent State U (OH)
King's Coll (PA)
LA Coll International (CA)
Lake Superior State U (MI)
Lebanon Valley Coll (PA)
Limestone Coll (SC)
Lincoln Memorial U (TN)
Lindsey Wilson Coll (KY)
Lourdes Coll (OH)
Lyndon State Coll (VT)
MacMurray Coll (IL)
Macon State Coll (GA)
Madonna U (MI)
Manchester Coll (IN)
Marian Coll (IN)
Marietta Coll (OH)
Mayville State U (ND)
Medaille Coll (NY)
Medgar Evers Coll of the
City U of New
York (NY)
Mercy Coll (NY)
Mercyhurst Coll (PA)
Merrimack Coll (MA)
Mesa State Coll (CO)
Methodist U (NC)
Midway Coll (KY)
Minnesota School of
Business (MN)
Missouri Baptist U (MO)
Missouri Valley Coll (MO)
Missouri Western State
U (MO)
Monroe Coll, Bronx (NY)
Montana State
U–Billings (MT)
Montreat Coll,
Montreat (NC)
Morrison U (NV)
Mountain State U (WV)
Mount Aloysius Coll (PA)
Mount Ida Coll (MA)
Mount Marty Coll (SD)
Mount Olive Coll (NC)
Mount St. Mary's Coll (CA)
National American U,
Denver (CO)
National American U,
Rapid City (SD)
Newman U (KS)
New Mexico Inst of Mining
and Technology (NM)
New York Inst of
Technology (NY)
Niagara U (NY)
Nichols Coll (MA)
Northern Kentucky U (KY)
Northern Michigan U (MI)
Northern State U (SD)
Northwestern State U of
Louisiana (LA)
Northwood U (MI)
Northwood U, Florida
Campus (FL)
Northwood U, Texas
Campus (TX)
Notre Dame Coll (OH)
Nyack Coll (NY)
Oglala Lakota Coll (SD)
Ohio Dominican U (OH)
Ohio U (OH)
Oklahoma Panhandle
State U (OK)
Oklahoma Wesleyan
U (OK)
Park U (MO)

Paul Smith's Coll of Arts
and Sciences (NY)
Peirce Coll (PA)
Pennsylvania Coll of
Technology (PA)
Pikeville Coll (KY)
Pine Manor Coll (MA)
Point Park U (PA)
Pontifical Catholic U of
Puerto Rico (PR)
Presentation Coll (SD)
Purdue U North
Central (IN)
Reinhardt Coll (GA)
Rider U (NJ)
Rivier Coll (NH)
Robert Morris Coll (IL)
Rochester Inst of
Technology (NY)
Rogers State U (OK)
Roger Williams U (RI)
Rust Coll (MS)
Sacred Heart U (CT)
Sage Coll of Albany (NY)
St. Augustine Coll (IL)
St. Francis Coll (NY)
Saint Francis U (PA)
St. Gregory's U,
Shawnee (OK)
Saint Joseph's U (PA)
Saint Peter's Coll (NJ)
Salem International
U (WV)
Salve Regina U (RI)
Schiller International U
(France)
Schiller International U
(Spain)
Shawnee State U (OH)
Shaw U (NC)
Southeastern U (DC)
Southern New Hampshire
U (NH)
Southern Vermont
Coll (VT)
Southern Wesleyan U (SC)
South U (AL)
South U, West Palm
Beach (FL)
South U (GA)
South U (SC)
Southwest Minnesota
State U (MN)
Spring Hill Coll (AL)
State U of New York Coll
of Agriculture and
Technology at
Cobleskill (NY)
State U of New York
Empire State Coll (NY)
Sullivan U (KY)
Taylor U (IN)
Thomas Coll (ME)
Tiffin U (OH)
Tri-State U (IN)
Tulane U (LA)
Union Coll (NE)
Universidad Adventista de
las Antillas (PR)
U of Alaska
Anchorage (AK)
U of Alaska Fairbanks (AK)
U of Alaska
Southeast (AK)
U of Arkansas at Fort
Smith (AR)
U of Bridgeport (CT)
U of Charleston (WV)
U of Cincinnati (OH)
The U of Findlay (OH)
U of Indianapolis (IN)
The U of Maine at
Augusta (ME)
U of Management and
Technology (VA)
U of Mary (ND)
U of Minnesota,
Crookston (MN)
The U of Montana–
Western (MT)
U of New Hampshire (NH)
U of New Hampshire at
Manchester (NH)
U of Puerto Rico at
Humacao (PR)
U of Puerto Rico at
Utuado (PR)
U of Regina (SK, Canada)
U of Rio Grande (OH)
U of Saint Francis (IN)
The U of Scranton (PA)
U of Sioux Falls (SD)
U of the Virgin Islands (VI)
The U of Toledo (OH)
U of Wisconsin–Green
Bay (WI)
Upper Iowa U (IA)
Utah Valley State Coll (UT)

Vermont Tech Coll (VT)
Villa Julie Coll (MD)
Walla Walla Coll (WA)
Walsh U (OH)
Wayland Baptist U (TX)
Waynesburg Coll (PA)
Webber International
U (FL)
Wentworth Inst of
Technology (MA)
Western Kentucky U (KY)
West Virginia State U (WV)
Williams Baptist Coll (AR)
Williamson Christian
Coll (TN)
Wilson Coll (PA)
Xavier U (OH)
York Coll of
Pennsylvania (PA)
Youngstown State U (OH)

Business Administration, Management and Operations Related
Briarcliffe Coll (NY)
Embry-Riddle Aeronautical
U, Extended
Campus (FL)
Peirce Coll (PA)
St. Augustine Coll (IL)
U of Management and
Technology (VA)

Business and Personal/Financial Services Marketing
Southern New Hampshire
U (NH)

Business Automation/ Technology/Data Entry
Austin Peay State U (TN)
Baker Coll of Clinton
Township (MI)
Central Christian Coll of
Kansas (KS)
Montana State
U–Billings (MT)
Montana Tech of The U of
Montana (MT)
Pennsylvania Coll of
Technology (PA)
The U of Akron (OH)
The U of Montana–
Western (MT)
U of Rio Grande (OH)
The U of Toledo (OH)
Utah Valley State Coll (UT)

Business/Commerce
Anderson U (IN)
Andrew Jackson U (AL)
Baker Coll of Flint (MI)
Bluefield State Coll (WV)
Bryant and Stratton Coll,
Cleveland (OH)
California U of
Pennsylvania (PA)
Castleton State Coll (VT)
Champlain Coll (VT)
Coll of Staten Island of the
City U of New
York (NY)
Crown Coll (MN)
Cumberland U (TN)
Dalton State Coll (GA)
Delaware Valley Coll (PA)
Deree Coll, The American
College of Greece
(Greece)
Eastern Nazarene
Coll (MA)
Gannon U (PA)
Glenville State Coll (WV)
God's Bible School and
Coll (OH)
Hillsdale Free Will Baptist
Coll (OK)
Idaho State U (ID)
Indiana U East (IN)
Indiana U Kokomo (IN)
Indiana U South Bend (IN)
Indiana U Southeast (IN)
Limestone Coll (SC)
Macon State Coll (GA)
Marygrove Coll (MI)
Metropolitan Coll of New
York (NY)
Montana State
U–Billings (MT)
Mountain State U (WV)
Mount Vernon Nazarene
U (OH)
New Mexico State U (NM)
Nicholls State U (LA)
Northern Kentucky U (KY)
Northern Michigan U (MI)

Peirce Coll (PA)
Penn State Abington (PA)
Penn State Altoona (PA)
Penn State Berks (PA)
Penn State Erie, The
  Behrend Coll (PA)
Penn State Harrisburg (PA)
Penn State U Park (PA)
Southern Wesleyan U (SC)
Southwest Baptist U (MO)
Thomas More Coll (KY)
Thomas U (GA)
Troy U (AL)
Tulane U (LA)
U of Management and
  Technology (VA)
The U of Montana–
  Western (MT)
U of Phoenix–Cleveland
  Campus (OH)
U of Phoenix–Columbus
  Ohio Campus (OH)
U of Phoenix–Houston
  Campus (TX)
U of Phoenix–Indianapolis
  Campus (IN)
U of Phoenix–Nevada
  Campus (NV)
U of Phoenix–St. Louis
  Campus (MO)
U of Phoenix–Springfield
  Campus (MO)
The U of Toledo (OH)
Utah Valley State Coll (UT)
Webber International
  U (FL)
Youngstown State U (OH)

**Business/Corporate
Communications**
Central Christian Coll of
  Kansas (KS)
Chestnut Hill Coll (PA)

**Business Machine
Repair**
Boise State U (ID)
Idaho State U (ID)
U of Alaska
  Anchorage (AK)

**Business,
Management, and
Marketing Related**
The Art Inst of California–
  San Francisco (CA)
Taylor U Fort Wayne (IN)
The U of Akron (OH)
U of Southern Indiana (IN)

**Business/Managerial
Economics**
Central Christian Coll of
  Kansas (KS)
Hawai'i Pacific U (HI)
Northwood U (MI)
Saint Peter's Coll (NJ)

**Business Operations
Support and
Secretarial Services
Related**
The U of Akron (OH)

**Business Teacher
Education**
Central Christian Coll of
  Kansas (KS)
Clayton State U (GA)
Faulkner U (AL)
Inter American U of Puerto
  Rico, Fajardo
  Campus (PR)
Macon State Coll (GA)
U of the District of
  Columbia (DC)

**Cabinetmaking and
Millwork**
British Columbia Inst of
  Technology (BC,
  Canada)
Pennsylvania Coll of
  Technology (PA)
Utah Valley State Coll (UT)

**Cad/Cadd Drafting/
Design Technology**
The Art Inst of Las
  Vegas (NV)
ITT Tech Inst, Tempe (AZ)
ITT Tech Inst,
  Lexington (KY)
Johnson & Wales U (RI)
Shawnee State U (OH)

**Cardiopulmonary
Technology**
Nicholls State U (LA)

**Cardiovascular
Technology**
British Columbia Inst of
  Technology (BC,
  Canada)
Gwynedd-Mercy Coll (PA)
Molloy Coll (NY)
Nebraska Methodist
  Coll (NE)
Thompson Rivers U (BC,
  Canada)
The U of Toledo (OH)

Carpentry
Bob Jones U (SC)
British Columbia Inst of
  Technology (BC,
  Canada)
Idaho State U (ID)
Oglala Lakota Coll (SD)
Pennsylvania Coll of
  Technology (PA)
Southern Utah U (UT)
Thompson Rivers U (BC,
  Canada)

Celtic Languages
Sacred Heart U (CT)

**Ceramic Arts and
Ceramics**
Rochester Inst of
  Technology (NY)

Chemical Engineering
Ball State U (IN)
Excelsior Coll (NY)
Ferris State U (MI)
U of New Haven (CT)
U of the District of
  Columbia (DC)
West Virginia State U (WV)

Chemical Technology
British Columbia Inst of
  Technology (BC,
  Canada)
Indiana U–Purdue U Fort
  Wayne (IN)
Lawrence Technological
  U (MI)
Millersville U of
  Pennsylvania (PA)
Nicholls State U (LA)
State U of New York Coll
  of Agriculture and
  Technology at
  Cobleskill (NY)
The U of Akron (OH)
U of Puerto Rico at
  Humacao (PR)
The U of Toledo (OH)
Weber State U (UT)

Chemistry
Adrian Coll (MI)
Castleton State Coll (VT)
Central Methodist U (MO)
Chestnut Hill Coll (PA)
Clayton State U (GA)
Dalton State Coll (GA)
Hannibal-LaGrange
  Coll (MO)
Idaho State U (ID)
Indiana U South Bend (IN)
Indiana Wesleyan U (IN)
Keene State Coll (NH)
Lake Superior State U (MI)
Lindsey Wilson Coll (KY)
Lourdes Coll (OH)
Macon State Coll (GA)
Madonna U (MI)
Methodist U (NC)
Ohio Dominican U (OH)
Oklahoma Wesleyan
  U (OK)
Presentation Coll (SD)
Rochester Inst of
  Technology (NY)
Rogers State U (OK)
Sacred Heart U (CT)
Saint Joseph's U (PA)
Thomas More Coll (KY)
U of Indianapolis (IN)
U of Rio Grande (OH)
The U of Tampa (FL)
U of Wisconsin–Green
  Bay (WI)
Utah Valley State Coll (UT)
Villa Julie Coll (MD)
Wright State U (OH)
York Coll of
  Pennsylvania (PA)

Chemistry Related
U of the Incarnate
  Word (TX)

**Chemistry Teacher
Education**
Central Christian Coll of
  Kansas (KS)

**Child Care and
Support Services
Management**
The Baptist Coll of
  Florida (FL)
Bob Jones U (SC)
Cameron U (OK)
Chestnut Hill Coll (PA)
Eastern New Mexico
  U (NM)
Georgia Southwestern
  State U (GA)
Henderson State U (AR)
Idaho State U (ID)
Mount Aloysius Coll (PA)
Mount Vernon Nazarene
  U (OH)
Nicholls State U (LA)
Pennsylvania Coll of
  Technology (PA)
St. Augustine Coll (IL)
Southeast Missouri State
  U (MO)
Thompson Rivers U (BC,
  Canada)
U of Central
  Arkansas (AR)
Weber State U (UT)
Youngstown State U (OH)

Child Care/Guidance
American Public U
  System (WV)
Eastern Kentucky U (KY)

Child Care Provision
Eastern Kentucky U (KY)
Mayville State U (ND)
Murray State U (KY)
Pacific Union Coll (CA)
Pennsylvania Coll of
  Technology (PA)
Saint Mary-of-the-Woods
  Coll (IN)
U of Alaska Fairbanks (AK)

**Child Care Services
Management**
Cameron U (OK)
U of Louisiana at
  Monroe (LA)

Child Development
Alabama State U (AL)
Arkansas Tech U (AR)
Boise State U (ID)
Central Pennsylvania
  Coll (PA)
Eastern Kentucky U (KY)
Evangel U (MO)
Fairmont State U (WV)
Franciscan U of
  Steubenville (OH)
Grambling State U (LA)
Kuyper Coll (MI)
Lewis-Clark State Coll (ID)
Madonna U (MI)
Northern Michigan U (MI)
Ohio U (OH)
Purdue U Calumet (IN)
Southern Utah U (UT)
Southern Vermont
  Coll (VT)
Trevecca Nazarene U (TN)
U of Arkansas at Fort
  Smith (AR)
U of Cincinnati (OH)
U of the District of
  Columbia (DC)
Villa Julie Coll (MD)
Weber State U (UT)
Youngstown State U (OH)

Child Guidance
Tougaloo Coll (MS)

Christian Studies
God's Bible School and
  Coll (OH)
Heritage Bible Coll (NC)
Vennard Coll (IA)
Wayland Baptist U (TX)

**Cinematography and
Film/Video Production**
Academy of Art U (CA)
American InterContinental
  U, Atlanta (GA)
The Art Inst of Atlanta (GA)
The Art Inst of California–
  Los Angeles (CA)
The Art Inst of
  Colorado (CO)
The Art Inst of Dallas (TX)
The Art Inst of Fort
  Lauderdale (FL)
The Art Inst of
  Pittsburgh (PA)
The Art Inst of
  Seattle (WA)
Burlington Coll (VT)

Collins Coll: A School of
  Design and
  Technology (AZ)
Five Towns Coll (NY)
New England School of
  Communications (ME)
Rochester Inst of
  Technology (NY)
Southern Adventist U (TN)

**City/Urban,
Community and
Regional Planning**
U of the District of
  Columbia (DC)

**Civil Drafting and
Cad/Cadd**
British Columbia Inst of
  Technology (BC,
  Canada)
Montana Tech of The U of
  Montana (MT)

Civil Engineering
Macon State Coll (GA)

**Civil Engineering
Technology**
Bluefield State Coll (WV)
British Columbia Inst of
  Technology (BC,
  Canada)
Fairmont State U (WV)
Ferris State U (MI)
Idaho State U (ID)
Indiana U–Purdue U Fort
  Wayne (IN)
Indiana U–Purdue U
  Indianapolis (IN)
Michigan Technological
  U (MI)
Missouri Western State
  U (MO)
Murray State U (KY)
Pennsylvania Coll of
  Technology (PA)
Point Park U (PA)
Purdue U Calumet (IN)
Purdue U North
  Central (IN)
U of Cincinnati (OH)
U of Massachusetts
  Lowell (MA)
U of New Hampshire (NH)
U of the District of
  Columbia (DC)
The U of Toledo (OH)
Vermont Tech Coll (VT)
Wentworth Inst of
  Technology (MA)
Youngstown State U (OH)

**Clinical Laboratory
Science/Medical
Technology**
Arkansas State U (AR)
Clayton State U (GA)
Dalton State Coll (GA)
Faulkner U (AL)
Indiana U East (IN)
The U of Toledo (OH)
Villa Julie Coll (MD)
Weber State U (UT)

**Clinical/Medical
Laboratory Assistant**
Argosy U, Twin Cities,
  Eagan (MN)
Northern Michigan U (MI)
The U of Maine at
  Augusta (ME)

Child Guidance
Tougaloo Coll (MS)

**Clinical/Medical
Laboratory Science
and Allied
Professions Related**
The U of Akron (OH)

**Clinical/Medical
Laboratory
Technology**
Baker Coll of Owosso (MI)
British Columbia Inst of
  Technology (BC,
  Canada)
Clayton State U (GA)
Coll of Staten Island of the
  City U of New
  York (NY)
Dalton State Coll (GA)
Eastern Kentucky U (KY)
Fairmont State U (WV)
Farmingdale State
  Coll (NY)
Faulkner U (AL)
Felician Coll (NJ)
Ferris State U (MI)
The George Washington
  U (DC)

Indiana U Northwest (IN)
Macon State Coll (GA)
Madonna U (MI)
Marshall U (WV)
Our Lady of the Lake
  Coll (LA)
Presentation Coll (SD)
Shawnee State U (OH)
State U of New York Coll
  of Agriculture and
  Technology at
  Cobleskill (NY)
U of Alaska
  Anchorage (AK)
U of Cincinnati (OH)
U of Maine at Presque
  Isle (ME)
U of Rio Grande (OH)
U of the District of
  Columbia (DC)
Villa Julie Coll (MD)
Weber State U (UT)
Youngstown State U (OH)

Clothing/Textiles
The Art Inst of Fort
  Lauderdale (FL)
Indiana U Bloomington (IN)

**Commercial and
Advertising Art**
Academy of Art U (CA)
Andrews U (MI)
The Art Inst of Atlanta (GA)
The Art Inst of California–
  San Diego (CA)
The Art Inst of California–
  San Francisco (CA)
The Art Inst of
  Colorado (CO)
The Art Inst of Fort
  Lauderdale (FL)
The Art Inst of
  Pittsburgh (PA)
The Art Inst of
  Washington (VA)
The Art Insts International
  Minnesota (MN)
Baker Coll of Auburn
  Hills (MI)
Baker Coll of Clinton
  Township (MI)
Baker Coll of Flint (MI)
Baker Coll of
  Muskegon (MI)
Baker Coll of Owosso (MI)
Baker Coll of Port
  Huron (MI)
Becker Coll (MA)
Briarcliffe Coll (NY)
British Columbia Inst of
  Technology (BC,
  Canada)
Champlain Coll (VT)
Collins Coll: A School of
  Design and
  Technology (AZ)
Fairmont State U (WV)
Fashion Inst of
  Technology (NY)
Felician Coll (NJ)
Ferris State U (MI)
Hussian Coll of Art (PA)
The Illinois Inst of Art–
  Chicago (IL)
Indiana U–Purdue U Fort
  Wayne (IN)
International Academy of
  Design &
  Technology (IL)
Mercy Coll (NY)
Mesa State Coll (CO)
Miami International U of
  Art & Design (FL)
Mount Ida Coll (MA)
Northern Michigan U (MI)
Northern State U (SD)
Oakwood Coll (AL)
Pace U (NY)
Parsons The New School
  for Design (NY)
Pennsylvania Coll of
  Technology (PA)
Pratt Inst (NY)
Robert Morris Coll (IL)
Rogers State U (OK)
Sacred Heart U (CT)
Silver Lake Coll (WI)
Suffolk U (MA)
U of New Haven (CT)
U of Saint Francis (IN)
U of the District of
  Columbia (DC)
Utah Valley State Coll (UT)
Villa Julie Coll (MD)
Virginia Intermont Coll (VA)
Walla Walla Coll (WA)

**Commercial
Photography**
The Art Inst of Atlanta (GA)
The Art Inst of
  Pittsburgh (PA)
Fashion Inst of
  Technology (NY)
Harrington Coll of
  Design (IL)
Paier Coll of Art, Inc. (CT)
The U of Akron (OH)

**Communication and
Journalism Related**
Champlain Coll (VT)
New England School of
  Communications (ME)
Tulane U (LA)

**Communication and
Media Related**
Champlain Coll (VT)

**Communication/
Speech
Communication and
Rhetoric**
Andrew Jackson U (AL)
Baker Coll of Jackson (MI)
Brigham Young
  U–Hawaii (HI)
Cameron U (OK)
Central Christian Coll of
  Kansas (KS)
Coll of Mount St.
  Joseph (OH)
Idaho State U (ID)
Indiana Wesleyan U (IN)
Lyndon State Coll (VT)
The New England Inst of
  Art (MA)
Presentation Coll (SD)
Thomas More Coll (KY)
Tri-State U (IN)
Tulane U (LA)
U of New Haven (CT)
U of Rio Grande (OH)
Utah Valley State Coll (UT)
West Virginia State U (WV)
Wright State U (OH)

**Communications
Systems Installation
and Repair
Technology**
Idaho State U (ID)
Thompson Rivers U (BC,
  Canada)

**Communications
Technologies and
Support Services
Related**
New England School of
  Communications (ME)

**Communications
Technology**
Bluefield State Coll (WV)
East Stroudsburg U of
  Pennsylvania (PA)
Ferris State U (MI)
Vennard Coll (IA)

**Community Health
and Preventive
Medicine**
Utah Valley State Coll (UT)

**Community
Organization and
Advocacy**
Alabama State U (AL)
Fairmont State U (WV)
Samford U (AL)
State U of New York
  Empire State Coll (NY)
The U of Akron (OH)
The U of Findlay (OH)
U of New Hampshire (NH)
U of New Mexico (NM)

**Community
Psychology**
Kwantlen U Coll (BC,
  Canada)
Woodbury Coll (VT)

**Computer and
Information Sciences**
Baker Coll of Allen
  Park (MI)
Black Hills State U (SD)
Bluefield State Coll (WV)
Champlain Coll (VT)
Columbia Coll (MO)
Dalton State Coll (GA)
Davenport U,
  Dearborn (MI)
Delaware Valley Coll (PA)

Edinboro U of
Pennsylvania (PA)
Electronic Data Processing
Coll of Puerto
Rico (PR)
Florida Metropolitan
U–Brandon
Campus (FL)
Globe Inst of
Technology (NY)
Indiana Wesleyan U (IN)
Inter American U of Puerto
Rico, Barranquitas
Campus (PR)
Keene State Coll (NH)
Kentucky State U (KY)
King's Coll (PA)
Lewis-Clark State Coll (ID)
Lyndon State Coll (VT)
Madonna U (MI)
Midway Coll (KY)
Millersville U of
Pennsylvania (PA)
Montana State
U–Billings (MT)
National American U,
Denver (CO)
Oklahoma Panhandle
State U (OK)
Pennsylvania Coll of
Technology (PA)
Sacred Heart U (CT)
Sage Coll of Albany (NY)
St. Augustine Coll (IL)
Spring Hill Coll (AL)
Thomas Coll (ME)
Thomas More Coll (KY)
Tri-State U (IN)
Troy U (AL)
Tulane U (LA)
U of Alaska
Anchorage (AK)
U of Charleston (WV)
U of Cincinnati (OH)
The U of Maine at
Augusta (ME)
The U of Montana–
Western (MT)
U of Phoenix–Houston
Campus (TX)
Utah Valley State Coll (UT)
Villa Julie Coll (MD)
Weber State U (UT)
Wiley Coll (TX)

**Computer and
Information Sciences
And Support Services
Related**
Becker Coll (MA)
Cleary U (MI)
Florida Metropolitan
U–Brandon
Campus (FL)
Montana State
U–Billings (MT)
Pennsylvania Coll of
Technology (PA)
U of Arkansas at Fort
Smith (AR)

**Computer and
Information Sciences
Related**
Lindsey Wilson Coll (KY)
Madonna U (MI)
National American U,
Denver (CO)
Washburn U (KS)

**Computer and
Information Systems
Security**
Champlain Coll (VT)
ITT Tech Inst, Tempe (AZ)

**Computer
Engineering**
Missouri Western State
U (MO)
The U of Scranton (PA)

**Computer
Engineering Related**
Thompson Rivers U (BC,
Canada)

**Computer
Engineering
Technology**
Andrews U (MI)
Baker Coll of Owosso (MI)
Clayton State U (GA)
Dalton State Coll (GA)
Eastern Kentucky U (KY)
Excelsior Coll (NY)
Grantham U (MO)
ITT Tech Inst, Clovis (CA)
ITT Tech Inst,
Lexington (KY)

ITT Tech Inst, Oklahoma
City (OK)
Johnson & Wales U (RI)
Lake Superior State U (MI)
Madonna U (MI)
National American U,
Rapid City (SD)
Oregon Inst of
Technology (OR)
Peirce Coll (PA)
Purdue U Calumet (IN)
Purdue U North
Central (IN)
Rogers State U (OK)
U of Cincinnati (OH)
U of Hartford (CT)
U of the District of
Columbia (DC)
Vermont Tech Coll (VT)
Weber State U (UT)
Wentworth Inst of
Technology (MA)

Computer Graphics
Academy of Art U (CA)
The Art Inst of California–
Orange County (CA)
The Art Inst of California–
San Francisco (CA)
The Art Inst of
Colorado (CO)
The Art Inst of Dallas (TX)
The Art Inst of
Pittsburgh (PA)
The Art Inst of
Washington (VA)
Baker Coll of Cadillac (MI)
Champlain Coll (VT)
International Academy of
Design &
Technology (IL)
Johnson & Wales U (RI)
Miami International U of
Art & Design (FL)
New England School of
Communications (ME)
Thompson Rivers U (BC,
Canada)
U of Advancing
Technology (AZ)
Vaughn Coll of Aeronautics
and Technology (NY)
Villa Julie Coll (MD)

**Computer Hardware
Technology**
Inter American U of Puerto
Rico, Aguadilla
Campus (PR)

**Computer/Information
Technology Services
Administration
Related**
Champlain Coll (VT)
Dalton State Coll (GA)
Johnson & Wales U (RI)
Medgar Evers Coll of the
City U of New
York (NY)
Mercy Coll (NY)
National American U,
Denver (CO)
Pennsylvania Coll of
Technology (PA)
The U of Akron (OH)
Vennard Coll (IA)

**Computer Installation
and Repair
Technology**
Dalton State Coll (GA)
Inter American U of Puerto
Rico, Bayamón
Campus (PR)
Thompson Rivers U (BC,
Canada)

**Computer
Maintenance
Technology**
Eastern Kentucky U (KY)

**Computer
Management**
Champlain Coll (VT)
Daniel Webster Coll (NH)
Faulkner U (AL)
Five Towns Coll (NY)
Granite State Coll (NH)
Life U (GA)
Northwood U (MI)
Northwood U, Florida
Campus (FL)
Thomas Coll (ME)

**Computer
Programming**
Atlantic Union Coll (MA)
Baker Coll of Flint (MI)

Baker Coll of
Muskegon (MI)
Baker Coll of Owosso (MI)
Baker Coll of Port
Huron (MI)
Black Hills State U (SD)
Briarcliffe Coll (NY)
California U of
Pennsylvania (PA)
Castleton State Coll (VT)
Charleston Southern
U (SC)
Coll of Staten Island of the
City U of New
York (NY)
Dakota State U (SD)
Daniel Webster Coll (NH)
Delaware Valley Coll (PA)
Electronic Data Processing
Coll of Puerto
Rico (PR)
Farmingdale State
Coll (NY)
Florida Metropolitan
U–Lakeland
Campus (FL)
Florida Metropolitan
U–Pompano Beach
Campus (FL)
Gwynedd-Mercy Coll (PA)
Indiana U East (IN)
Johnson & Wales U (RI)
Kent State U (OH)
Limestone Coll (SC)
Lindsey Wilson Coll (KY)
Macon State Coll (GA)
National American U,
Rapid City (SD)
New York U (NY)
Oregon Inst of
Technology (OR)
Pontifical Catholic U of
Puerto Rico (PR)
Purdue U Calumet (IN)
Purdue U North
Central (IN)
Rogers State U (OK)
Saint Francis U (PA)
State U of New York Coll
of Agriculture and
Technology at
Cobleskill (NY)
Tiffin U (OH)
U of Advancing
Technology (AZ)
U of Arkansas at Little
Rock (AR)
U of Cincinnati (OH)
The U of Toledo (OH)
Villa Julie Coll (MD)
Walla Walla Coll (WA)
West Virginia State U (WV)
Youngstown State U (OH)

**Computer
Programming Related**
Central Pennsylvania
Coll (PA)
Inter American U of Puerto
Rico, Barranquitas
Campus (PR)
National American U,
Denver (CO)

**Computer
Programming
(Specific Applications)**
Georgia Southwestern
State U (GA)
Idaho State U (ID)
Kent State U (OH)
Macon State Coll (GA)
National American U,
Denver (CO)
Peirce Coll (PA)
Pennsylvania Coll of
Technology (PA)
Robert Morris Coll (IL)
The U of Toledo (OH)

Computer Science
Alderson-Broaddus
Coll (WV)
Baker Coll of Allen
Park (MI)
Baker Coll of Owosso (MI)
Black Hills State U (SD)
British Columbia Inst of
Technology (BC,
Canada)
Calumet Coll of Saint
Joseph (IN)
Central Christian Coll of
Kansas (KS)
Central Methodist U (MO)
Clayton State U (GA)
Columbia Union Coll (MD)

Columbus State U (GA)
Creighton U (NE)
Dalton State Coll (GA)
East-West U (IL)
Excelsior Coll (NY)
Farmingdale State
Coll (NY)
Felician Coll (NJ)
Florida Metropolitan
U–Lakeland
Campus (FL)
Grantham U (MO)
Indiana U–Purdue U Fort
Wayne (IN)
Indiana U South Bend (IN)
Indiana U Southeast (IN)
Inter American U of Puerto
Rico, Aguadilla
Campus (PR)
Inter American U of Puerto
Rico, Barranquitas
Campus (PR)
Inter American U of Puerto
Rico, Bayamón
Campus (PR)
Inter American U of Puerto
Rico, Fajardo
Campus (PR)
John Cabot U (Italy)
Keene State Coll (NH)
LA Coll International (CA)
Limestone Coll (SC)
Lincoln U (MO)
Lyndon State Coll (VT)
Macon State Coll (GA)
Madonna U (MI)
Manchester Coll (IN)
Medgar Evers Coll of the
City U of New
York (NY)
Merrimack Coll (MA)
Mesa State Coll (CO)
Methodist U (NC)
Millersville U of
Pennsylvania (PA)
Missouri Southern State
U (MO)
Monroe Coll, Bronx (NY)
Montana Tech of The U of
Montana (MT)
Morrison U (NV)
Mountain State U (WV)
Mount Aloysius Coll (PA)
Oglala Lakota Coll (SD)
Park U (MO)
Rivier Coll (NH)
Rochester Inst of
Technology (NY)
Rogers State U (OK)
Sacred Heart U (CT)
Sage Coll of Albany (NY)
Saint Joseph's U (PA)
Southeastern U (DC)
Southern Adventist U (TN)
Southwest Baptist U (MO)
State U of New York Coll
of Agriculture and
Technology at
Cobleskill (NY)
Sullivan U (KY)
Tabor Coll (KS)
Universidad Adventista de
las Antillas (PR)
The U of Findlay (OH)
U of New Haven (CT)
U of Rio Grande (OH)
U of the Virgin Islands (VI)
Utah Valley State Coll (UT)
Weber State U (UT)
Wentworth Inst of
Technology (MA)
West Virginia State U (WV)
Wiley Coll (TX)

**Computer Software
and Media
Applications Related**
Indiana U–Purdue U Fort
Wayne (IN)
New England School of
Communications (ME)

**Computer Software
Engineering**
Grantham U (MO)
Vermont Tech Coll (VT)

**Computer Software
Technology**
U of New Hampshire (NH)

**Computer Systems
Analysis**
Baker Coll of Flint (MI)
British Columbia Inst of
Technology (BC,
Canada)
Davenport U,
Dearborn (MI)

The U of Akron (OH)
The U of Toledo (OH)

**Computer Systems
Networking and
Telecommunications**
Baker Coll of Allen
Park (MI)
Baker Coll of Flint (MI)
Champlain Coll (VT)
DeVry Inst of
Technology (NY)
DeVry U, Fremont (CA)
DeVry U, Long Beach (CA)
DeVry U, Pomona (CA)
DeVry U, Sherman
Oaks (CA)
DeVry U, Miramar (FL)
DeVry U, Orlando (FL)
DeVry U, Alpharetta (GA)
DeVry U, Decatur (GA)
DeVry U, Addison (IL)
DeVry U, Chicago (IL)
DeVry U, Tinley Park (IL)
DeVry U, Indianapolis (IN)
DeVry U (MN)
DeVry U (NJ)
DeVry U, Columbus (OH)
DeVry U (OK)
DeVry U, Irving (TX)
DeVry U, Arlington (VA)
DeVry U, Federal
Way (WA)
ITT Tech Inst, Clovis (CA)
ITT Tech Inst,
Lexington (KY)
ITT Tech Inst, Oklahoma
City (OK)
Minnesota School of
Business (MN)
National American U,
Denver (CO)
Pennsylvania Coll of
Technology (PA)
Remington Coll–Colorado
Springs Campus (CO)
Robert Morris Coll (IL)
U of Phoenix–St. Louis
Campus (MO)

**Computer Teacher
Education**
Baker Coll of Flint (MI)
Central Christian Coll of
Kansas (KS)

**Computer/Technical
Support**
Davenport U,
Dearborn (MI)

**Computer
Technology/Computer
Systems Technology**
Collins Coll: A School of
Design and
Technology (AZ)
Dalton State Coll (GA)
DeVry U, Pomona (CA)
DeVry U,
Westminster (CO)
DeVry U, Kansas
City (MO)
DeVry U (NJ)
DeVry U, Fort
Washington (PA)
Eastern Kentucky U (KY)
Peirce Coll (PA)
Pennsylvania Coll of
Technology (PA)
Southeast Missouri State
U (MO)
State U of New York Coll
of Agriculture and
Technology at
Cobleskill (NY)
Thompson Rivers U (BC,
Canada)

**Computer Typography
and Composition
Equipment Operation**
Baker Coll of Auburn
Hills (MI)
Baker Coll of Cadillac (MI)
Baker Coll of Clinton
Township (MI)
Baker Coll of Flint (MI)
Baker Coll of Jackson (MI)
Calumet Coll of Saint
Joseph (IN)
Faulkner U (AL)
McNeese State U (LA)
The U of Toledo (OH)

**Construction
Engineering
Technology**
Baker Coll of Owosso (MI)

British Columbia Inst of
Technology (BC,
Canada)
Coll of Staten Island of the
City U of New
York (NY)
Fairmont State U (WV)
Ferris State U (MI)
Lake Superior State U (MI)
Lawrence Technological
U (MI)
Pennsylvania Coll of
Technology (PA)
Purdue U Calumet (IN)
Purdue U North
Central (IN)
The U of Akron (OH)
U of Cincinnati (OH)
U of New Hampshire (NH)
The U of Toledo (OH)
Vermont Tech Coll (VT)
Wentworth Inst of
Technology (MA)
Wright State U (OH)

**Construction
Management**
Baker Coll of Flint (MI)
British Columbia Inst of
Technology (BC,
Canada)
John Brown U (AR)
Pratt Inst (NY)
U of New Hampshire (NH)
Vermont Tech Coll (VT)
Wentworth Inst of
Technology (MA)

Construction Trades
Northern Michigan U (MI)
U of Alaska
Southeast (AK)
Utah Valley State Coll (UT)

**Construction Trades
Related**
British Columbia Inst of
Technology (BC,
Canada)

Consumer Economics
U of Alaska
Southeast (AK)

**Consumer
Merchandising/
Retailing Management**
Baker Coll of Owosso (MI)
Central Pennsylvania
Coll (PA)
Fairmont State U (WV)
Johnson & Wales U (RI)
Madonna U (MI)
Mount Ida Coll (MA)
Sullivan U (KY)
The U of Toledo (OH)

**Cooking and Related
Culinary Arts**
The Art Inst of California–
Los Angeles (CA)
The Art Inst of California–
Orange County (CA)
The Art Inst of California–
San Diego (CA)
The Art Inst of
Pittsburgh (PA)
Kendall Coll (IL)
Lexington Coll (IL)

Corrections
Baker Coll of
Muskegon (MI)
Bluefield State Coll (WV)
Eastern Kentucky U (KY)
Lake Superior State U (MI)
Macon State Coll (GA)
Marygrove Coll (MI)
Northern Michigan U (MI)
U of Indianapolis (IN)
U of the District of
Columbia (DC)
The U of Toledo (OH)
Washburn U (KS)
Weber State U (UT)
Xavier U (OH)

Cosmetology
Bob Jones U (SC)
Georgia Southwestern
State U (GA)

**Counselor Education/
School Counseling
and Guidance**
Oglala Lakota Coll (SD)

Court Reporting
U of Cincinnati (OH)
Villa Julie Coll (MD)

Creative Writing
Manchester Coll (IN)
U of Maine at Presque Isle (ME)
The U of Tampa (FL)

Criminal Justice/Law Enforcement Administration
Adrian Coll (MI)
Anderson U (IN)
Argosy U, Orange County (CA)
Arkansas State U (AR)
Ashland U (OH)
Ball State U (IN)
Becker Coll (MA)
Bemidji State U (MN)
Boise State U (ID)
Bryant and Stratton Coll, Cleveland (OH)
Calumet Coll of Saint Joseph (IN)
Campbellsville U (KY)
Castleton State Coll (VT)
Central Christian Coll of Kansas (KS)
Central Pennsylvania Coll (PA)
Champlain Coll (VT)
Chestnut Hill Coll (PA)
Clayton State U (GA)
Columbia Coll (MO)
Dakota Wesleyan U (SD)
Dalton State Coll (GA)
Eastern Kentucky U (KY)
Farmingdale State Coll (NY)
Faulkner U (AL)
Finlandia U (MI)
Georgia Southwestern State U (GA)
Glenville State Coll (WV)
Grambling State U (LA)
Grantham U (MO)
Hannibal-LaGrange Coll (MO)
Hilbert Coll (NY)
Indiana Tech (IN)
Indiana U Northwest (IN)
Indiana U South Bend (IN)
Johnson & Wales U (CO)
Johnson & Wales U (FL)
Johnson & Wales U (RI)
Lake Superior State U (MI)
Lincoln U (MO)
Lourdes Coll (OH)
MacMurray Coll (IL)
Macon State Coll (GA)
Mansfield U of Pennsylvania (PA)
Mercyhurst Coll (PA)
Mesa State Coll (CO)
Methodist U (NC)
Monroe Coll, Bronx (NY)
Mount Ida Coll (MA)
Northern Michigan U (MI)
Oglala Lakota Coll (SD)
Park U (MO)
Remington Coll–Colorado Springs Campus (CO)
Rogers State U (OK)
Roger Williams U (RI)
St. John's U (NY)
Saint Joseph's U (PA)
Southern Utah U (UT)
Southern Vermont Coll (VT)
Suffolk U (MA)
Thomas More Coll (KY)
Thomas U (GA)
Tri-State U (IN)
U of Arkansas at Fort Smith (AR)
U of Cincinnati (OH)
The U of Findlay (OH)
U of Indianapolis (IN)
U of Maine at Presque Isle (ME)
U of Phoenix–Columbus Ohio Campus (OH)
U of Phoenix–Houston Campus (TX)
U of Phoenix–Indianapolis Campus (IN)
U of Phoenix–St. Louis Campus (MO)
U of Phoenix–Springfield Campus (MO)
U of the District of Columbia (DC)
Utah Valley State Coll (UT)
Washburn (KS)
West Virginia State U (WV)

Criminal Justice/ Police Science
Arkansas State U (AR)

Armstrong Atlantic State U (GA)
Becker Coll (MA)
Bluefield State Coll (WV)
Cameron U (OK)
Dalton State Coll (GA)
Davis & Elkins Coll (WV)
Eastern Kentucky U (KY)
Edinboro U of Pennsylvania (PA)
Fairmont State U (WV)
Grantham U (MO)
Husson Coll (ME)
Idaho State U (ID)
Inter American U of Puerto Rico, Fajardo Campus (PR)
Lake Superior State U (MI)
MacMurray Coll (IL)
Macon State Coll (GA)
Mercyhurst Coll (PA)
Middle Tennessee State U (TN)
Missouri Southern State U (MO)
Monroe Coll, Bronx (NY)
Nicholls State U (LA)
Northern Kentucky U (KY)
Northern Michigan U (MI)
Northwestern State U of Louisiana (LA)
Ohio U (OH)
Rogers State U (OK)
Southeastern Louisiana U (LA)
Southern U and A&M Coll (LA)
Tiffin U (OH)
The U of Akron (OH)
U of Arkansas at Little Rock (AR)
U of Arkansas at Pine Bluff (AR)
U of Cincinnati (OH)
U of Louisiana at Monroe (LA)
U of New Haven (CT)
U of the District of Columbia (DC)
U of the Virgin Islands (VI)
The U of Toledo (OH)
Washburn (KS)
Weber State U (UT)
York Coll of Pennsylvania (PA)

Criminal Justice/ Safety
Andrew Jackson U (AL)
Arkansas Tech U (AR)
Augusta State U (GA)
Cazenovia Coll (NY)
Central Christian Coll of Kansas (KS)
Champlain Coll (VT)
Columbus State U (GA)
Florida Metropolitan U–Brandon Campus (FL)
Florida Metropolitan U–Lakeland Campus (FL)
Gannon U (PA)
Georgia Southwestern State U (GA)
Grantham U (MO)
Husson Coll (ME)
Idaho State U (ID)
Indiana U East (IN)
Indiana U Kokomo (IN)
Indiana U–Purdue U Fort Wayne (IN)
Indiana U–Purdue U Indianapolis (IN)
Indiana Wesleyan U (IN)
International Coll (FL)
King's Coll (PA)
Madonna U (MI)
Manchester Coll (IN)
Missouri Western State U (MO)
Mountain State U (WV)
Mount Aloysius Coll (PA)
Murray State U (KY)
New Mexico State U (NM)
Penn State Altoona (PA)
Pikeville Coll (KY)
St. Francis Coll (NY)
St. Gregory's U, Shawnee (OK)
Shaw U (NC)
Sullivan U (KY)
The U of Maine at Augusta (ME)
The U of Scranton (PA)
Weber State U (UT)
Xavier U (OH)
Youngstown State U (OH)

Criminology
Ball State U (IN)
Dalton State Coll (GA)
Faulkner U (AL)
Indiana State U (IN)
Indiana U of Pennsylvania (PA)
Kwantlen U Coll (BC, Canada)
Marquette U (WI)
U of the District of Columbia (DC)

Crop Production
Sterling Coll (VT)
U of Massachusetts Amherst (MA)

Culinary Arts
The Art Inst of Atlanta (GA)
The Art Inst of California–San Diego (CA)
The Art Inst of Charleston (SC)
The Art Inst of Colorado (CO)
The Art Inst of Dallas (TX)
The Art Inst of Fort Lauderdale (FL)
The Art Inst of Houston (TX)
The Art Inst of Jacksonville (FL)
The Art Inst of Phoenix (AZ)
The Art Inst of Pittsburgh (PA)
The Art Inst of Seattle (WA)
The Art Inst of Tampa (FL)
The Art Inst of Tennessee–Nashville (TN)
The Art Inst of Washington (VA)
The Art Insts International Minnesota (MN)
Baker Coll of Muskegon (MI)
Boise State U (ID)
The Culinary Inst of America (NY)
Georgia Southwestern State U (GA)
Idaho State U (ID)
The Illinois Inst of Art–Chicago (IL)
Johnson & Wales U (CO)
Johnson & Wales U (FL)
Johnson & Wales U (NC)
Johnson & Wales U (RI)
Kendall Coll (IL)
Lexington Coll (IL)
Mercyhurst Coll (PA)
Mesa State Coll (CO)
Mountain State U (WV)
Nicholls State U (LA)
Paul Smith's Coll of Arts and Sciences (NY)
Pennsylvania Coll of Technology (PA)
Purdue U Calumet (IN)
Robert Morris Coll (IL)
St. Augustine Coll (IL)
Saint Francis U (PA)
Southern New Hampshire U (NH)
State U of New York Coll of Agriculture and Technology at Cobleskill (NY)
Sullivan U (KY)
The U of Akron (OH)
U of Alaska Anchorage (AK)
U of Alaska Fairbanks (AK)
The U of Montana (MT)
U of New Hampshire (NH)
Utah Valley State Coll (UT)
Virginia Intermont Coll (VA)

Culinary Arts Related
The Art Inst of Pittsburgh (PA)
Delaware Valley Coll (PA)
Lexington Coll (IL)
New York Inst of Technology (NY)

Cultural Studies
Indiana Wesleyan U (IN)

Cytotechnology
Indiana U–Purdue U Indianapolis (IN)
Indiana U Southeast (IN)

Dairy Husbandry and Production
Sterling Coll (VT)

Dairy Science
State U of New York Coll of Agriculture and Technology at Cobleskill (NY)
U of New Hampshire (NH)
Vermont Tech Coll (VT)

Dance
New World School of the Arts (FL)
Utah Valley State Coll (UT)

Data Entry/Microcomputer Applications
Baker Coll of Allen Park (MI)
National American U, Denver (CO)

Data Entry/Microcomputer Applications Related
Baker Coll of Allen Park (MI)

Data Processing and Data Processing Technology
Austin Peay State U (TN)
Baker Coll of Auburn Hills (MI)
Baker Coll of Cadillac (MI)
Baker Coll of Clinton Township (MI)
Baker Coll of Flint (MI)
Baker Coll of Jackson (MI)
Baker Coll of Muskegon (MI)
Baker Coll of Owosso (MI)
Baker Coll of Port Huron (MI)
British Columbia Inst of Technology (BC, Canada)
Campbellsville U (KY)
Clayton State U (GA)
Dordt Coll (IA)
Farmingdale State Coll (NY)
Five Towns Coll (NY)
Florida Metropolitan U–Lakeland Campus (FL)
Hawai'i Pacific U (HI)
Macon State Coll (GA)
Missouri Southern State U (MO)
Montana State U–Billings (MT)
Montana Tech of The U of Montana (MT)
New York Inst of Technology (NY)
Northern State U (SD)
Sacred Heart U (CT)
St. Francis Coll (NY)
Saint Francis U (PA)
St. John's U (NY)
Saint Peter's Coll (NJ)
State U of New York Coll of Agriculture and Technology at Cobleskill (NY)
Thomas More Coll (KY)
The U of Akron (OH)
U of Cincinnati (OH)
The U of Montana–Western (MT)
U of the Virgin Islands (VI)
The U of Toledo (OH)
Utah Valley State Coll (UT)
Western Kentucky U (KY)
Wright State U (OH)
Youngstown State U (OH)

Data Warehousing/ Mining/Database Administration
Electronic Data Processing Coll of Puerto Rico (PR)

Dental Assisting
Georgia Southwestern State U (GA)
Robert Morris Coll (IL)
U of Alaska Anchorage (AK)
The U of Maine at Augusta (ME)
U of Southern Indiana (IN)

Dental Hygiene
Argosy U, Twin Cities, Eagan (MN)
Armstrong Atlantic State U (GA)

Baker Coll of Port Huron (MI)
Clayton State U (GA)
Dalton State Coll (GA)
Farmingdale State Coll (NY)
Ferris State U (MI)
Indiana U Northwest (IN)
Indiana U–Purdue U Fort Wayne (IN)
Indiana U–Purdue U Indianapolis (IN)
Indiana U South Bend (IN)
Minnesota State U Mankato (MN)
Missouri Southern State U (MO)
Montana State U–Billings (MT)
Mount Ida Coll (MA)
New York U (NY)
Pennsylvania Coll of Technology (PA)
Shawnee State U (OH)
Southern Adventist U (TN)
Tennessee State U (TN)
U of Alaska Anchorage (AK)
U of Arkansas at Fort Smith (AR)
U of Bridgeport (CT)
U of Louisville (KY)
The U of Maine at Augusta (ME)
U of New England (ME)
U of New Haven (CT)
U of New Mexico (NM)
The U of South Dakota (SD)
U of Southern Indiana (IN)
Utah Valley State Coll (UT)
Vermont Tech Coll (VT)
Weber State U (UT)
Western Kentucky U (KY)
West Liberty State Coll (WV)
Wichita State U (KS)
Youngstown State U (OH)

Dental Laboratory Technology
Idaho State U (ID)
Indiana U–Purdue U Fort Wayne (IN)
Southern Illinois U Carbondale (IL)

Design and Visual Communications
The American U in Dubai (United Arab Emirates)
The Art Inst of Pittsburgh (PA)
Champlain Coll (VT)
Collins Coll: A School of Design and Technology (AZ)
Pace U (NY)
Wilmington Coll (DE)

Desktop Publishing and Digital Imaging Design
Davenport U, Dearborn (MI)
Thompson Rivers U (BC, Canada)

Developmental and Child Psychology
Fresno Pacific U (CA)
U of Sioux Falls (SD)
Villa Julie Coll (MD)

Diagnostic Medical Sonography and Ultrasound Technology
Argosy U, Twin Cities, Eagan (MN)
Baker Coll of Auburn Hills (MI)
Baker Coll of Owosso (MI)
Baker Coll of Port Huron (MI)
Coll of St. Catherine (MN)
Ferris State U (MI)
Mountain State U (WV)
Nebraska Methodist Coll (NE)
New York U (NY)

Diesel Mechanics Technology
British Columbia Inst of Technology (BC, Canada)
Georgia Southwestern State U (GA)
Idaho State U (ID)

Lewis-Clark State Coll (ID)
Montana State U–Billings (MT)
Pennsylvania Coll of Technology (PA)
U of Alaska Anchorage (AK)
Utah Valley State Coll (UT)
Weber State U (UT)

Dietetics
Ball State U (IN)
Faulkner U (AL)
Loma Linda U (CA)
Oakwood Coll (AL)
Rochester Inst of Technology (NY)
U of Minnesota, Crookston (MN)
U of New Hampshire (NH)
U of Ottawa (ON, Canada)
Youngstown State U (OH)

Dietetic Technician
U of New Hampshire (NH)

Dietician Assistant
Eastern Kentucky U (KY)

Dietitian Assistant
Penn State U Park (PA)
Pennsylvania Coll of Technology (PA)
Youngstown State U (OH)

Digital Communication and Media/Multimedia
Academy of Art U (CA)
The Art Inst of Pittsburgh (PA)
The Art Insts International Minnesota (MN)
Cameron U (OK)
Champlain Coll (VT)
Corcoran Coll of Art and Design (DC)
Utah Valley State Coll (UT)

Divinity/Ministry
Atlantic Union Coll (MA)
Boise Bible Coll (ID)
Carson-Newman Coll (TN)
Clear Creek Baptist Bible Coll (KY)
Faith Baptist Bible Coll and Theological Seminary (IA)
Faulkner U (AL)
Mount Olive Coll (NC)
Warner Pacific Coll (OR)

Dog/Pet/Animal Grooming
Becker Coll (MA)

Drafting
Eastern Kentucky U (KY)

Drafting and Design Technology
Baker Coll of Auburn Hills (MI)
Baker Coll of Cadillac (MI)
Baker Coll of Clinton Township (MI)
Baker Coll of Flint (MI)
Baker Coll of Muskegon (MI)
Baker Coll of Owosso (MI)
Baker Coll of Port Huron (MI)
Black Hills State U (SD)
Boise State U (ID)
British Columbia Inst of Technology (BC, Canada)
California U of Pennsylvania (PA)
Clayton State U (GA)
Dalton State Coll (GA)
Eastern Kentucky U (KY)
Fairmont State U (WV)
Ferris State U (MI)
Georgia Southwestern State U (GA)
Idaho State U (ID)
Keene State Coll (NH)
Kentucky State U (KY)
Langston U (OK)
LeTourneau U (TX)
Lewis-Clark State Coll (ID)
Lincoln U (MO)
Missouri Southern State U (MO)
Montana State U–Billings (MT)
Montana Tech of The U of Montana (MT)
Murray State U (KY)
Northern Michigan U (MI)

Pennsylvania Coll of
Technology (PA)
Robert Morris Coll (IL)
Saint Francis U (PA)
Southern Utah U (UT)
Thompson Rivers U (BC,
Canada)
Tri-State U (IN)
The U of Akron (OH)
U of Alaska
Anchorage (AK)
U of Central Missouri (MO)
U of Cincinnati (OH)
U of Rio Grande (OH)
The U of Toledo (OH)
Utah State U (UT)
Utah Valley State Coll (UT)
Washburn (KS)
Weber State U (UT)
West Virginia State U (WV)
Wright State U (OH)
Youngstown State U (OH)

Drafting/Design Engineering Technologies Related
Idaho State U (ID)
Pennsylvania Coll of
Technology (PA)
The U of Akron (OH)

Drafting/Design Technology
ITT Tech Inst, Clovis (CA)
ITT Tech Inst, Oklahoma
City (OK)
U of Arkansas at Fort
Smith (AR)

Drama and Dance Teacher Education
Central Christian Coll of
Kansas (KS)

Dramatic/Theater Arts
Adrian Coll (MI)
Brigham Young
U–Hawaii (HI)
Clayton State U (GA)
Five Towns Coll (NY)
Indiana U Bloomington (IN)
Macon State Coll (GA)
Mesa State Coll (CO)
Methodist U (NC)
New World School of the
Arts (FL)
North Greenville U (SC)
Thomas More Coll (KY)
Université Laval (QC,
Canada)
U of Sioux Falls (SD)
U of Wisconsin–Green
Bay (WI)
Utah Valley State Coll (UT)
Villa Julie Coll (MD)

Drawing
Academy of Art U (CA)
New World School of the
Arts (FL)
Parsons The New School
for Design (NY)
Pratt Inst (NY)
Sacred Heart U (CT)

Early Childhood Education
Baker Coll of Allen
Park (MI)
Baker Coll of Jackson (MI)
Champlain Coll (VT)
Coll of Saint Mary (NE)
Columbia Union Coll (MD)
Crown Coll (MN)
Gannon U (PA)
Granite State Coll (NH)
Indiana U–Purdue U Fort
Wayne (IN)
Keene State Coll (NH)
Lake Superior State U (MI)
Lancaster Bible Coll (PA)
Lincoln U (MO)
Lindsey Wilson Coll (KY)
Mercyhurst Coll (PA)
Point Park U (PA)
Rust Coll (MS)
St. Augustine Coll (IL)
Taylor U Fort Wayne (IN)
Thompson Rivers U (BC,
Canada)
U of Great Falls (MT)
Utah Valley State Coll (UT)
Washburn U (KS)
Wheelock Coll (MA)
Wilmington Coll (DE)

Ecology
Paul Smith's Coll of Arts
and Sciences (NY)
Sterling Coll (VT)

E-Commerce
Champlain Coll (VT)

Economics
Adrian Coll (MI)
Central Christian Coll of
Kansas (KS)
Clayton State U (GA)
Dalton State Coll (GA)
John Cabot U (Italy)
Macon State Coll (GA)
Methodist U (NC)
Sacred Heart U (CT)
State U of New York
Empire State Coll (NY)
Thomas More Coll (KY)
U of Sioux Falls (SD)
The U of Tampa (FL)
U of Wisconsin–Green
Bay (WI)

Education
Alabama State U (AL)
Baker Coll of Auburn
Hills (MI)
Baker Coll of Cadillac (MI)
Central Baptist Coll (AR)
Cincinnati Christian U (OH)
Clayton State U (GA)
Cumberland U (TN)
Dalton State Coll (GA)
Evangel U (MO)
Inter American U of Puerto
Rico, Barranquitas
Campus (PR)
Kent State U (OH)
Macon State Coll (GA)
Medgar Evers Coll of the
City U of New
York (NY)
Montana State
U–Billings (MT)
Montreat Coll,
Montreat (NC)
National U (CA)
Pontifical Catholic U of
Puerto Rico (PR)
Reinhardt Coll (GA)
Saint Francis U (PA)
Spring Hill Coll (AL)
State U of New York
Empire State Coll (NY)
U of Puerto Rico at
Utuado (PR)
U of Southern Indiana (IN)

Educational Leadership and Administration
Shasta Bible Coll (CA)

Education Related
The U of Akron (OH)
Wayland Baptist U (TX)

Education (Specific Subject Areas) Related
Pennsylvania Coll of
Technology (PA)

Electrical and Electronic Engineering Technologies Related
Boise State U (ID)
Lawrence Technological
U (MI)
New York Inst of
Technology (NY)
Pennsylvania Coll of
Technology (PA)

Electrical and Power Transmission Installation
British Columbia Inst of
Technology (BC,
Canada)

Electrical, Electronic and Communications Engineering Technology
Andrews U (MI)
Arkansas State U (AR)
Baker Coll of Cadillac (MI)
Baker Coll of
Muskegon (MI)
Baker Coll of Owosso (MI)
Bluefield State Coll (WV)
Boise State U (ID)
Briarcliffe Coll (NY)
British Columbia Inst of
Technology (BC,
Canada)
Bryant and Stratton Coll,
Cleveland (OH)
Cameron U (OK)
Clayton State U (GA)

Columbia Coll,
Caguas (PR)
Dalton State Coll (GA)
Davenport U,
Dearborn (MI)
DeVry Inst of
Technology (NY)
DeVry U, Phoenix (AZ)
DeVry U, Fremont (CA)
DeVry U, Long Beach (CA)
DeVry U, Pomona (CA)
DeVry U, Sherman
Oaks (CA)
DeVry U,
Westminster (CO)
DeVry U, Miramar (FL)
DeVry U, Orlando (FL)
DeVry U, Alpharetta (GA)
DeVry U, Decatur (GA)
DeVry U, Addison (IL)
DeVry U, Chicago (IL)
DeVry U, Tinley Park (IL)
DeVry U, Indianapolis (IN)
DeVry U (MN)
DeVry U, Kansas
City (MO)
DeVry U (NV)
DeVry U (NJ)
DeVry U, Columbus (OH)
DeVry U (OR)
DeVry U, Fort
Washington (PA)
DeVry U, Houston (TX)
DeVry U, Irving (TX)
DeVry U, Arlington (VA)
DeVry U, Federal
Way (WA)
Eastern Kentucky U (KY)
Electronic Data Processing
Coll of Puerto
Rico (PR)
Excelsior Coll (NY)
Fairmont State U (WV)
Grantham U (MO)
Idaho State U (ID)
Indiana State U (IN)
Indiana U–Purdue U Fort
Wayne (IN)
Indiana U–Purdue U
Indianapolis (IN)
Johnson & Wales U (RI)
Keene State Coll (NH)
Kentucky State U (KY)
Lake Superior State U (MI)
Langston U (OK)
Lawrence Technological
U (MI)
McNeese State U (LA)
Merrimack Coll (MA)
Mesa State Coll (CO)
Michigan Technological
U (MI)
Missouri Western State
U (MO)
Northern Michigan U (MI)
Northern State U (SD)
Northwestern State U of
Louisiana (LA)
Oglala Lakota Coll (SD)
Ohio U (OH)
Oregon Inst of
Technology (OR)
Penn State Abington (PA)
Penn State Altoona (PA)
Penn State Berks (PA)
Penn State Erie, The
Behrend Coll (PA)
Pennsylvania Coll of
Technology (PA)
Pittsburg State U (KS)
Point Park U (PA)
Purdue U (IN)
Purdue U Calumet (IN)
Purdue U North
Central (IN)
Rochester Inst of
Technology (NY)
Southern Utah U (UT)
The U of Akron (OH)
U of Alaska
Anchorage (AK)
U of Arkansas at Little
Rock (AR)
U of Cincinnati (OH)
U of Hartford (CT)
U of Massachusetts
Lowell (MA)
The U of Montana (MT)
U of Puerto Rico at
Humacao (PR)
U of the District of
Columbia (DC)
The U of Toledo (OH)
Utah Valley State Coll (UT)
Vermont Tech Coll (VT)
Weber State U (UT)
Wentworth Inst of
Technology (MA)

West Virginia State U (WV)
Wright State U (OH)
Youngstown State U (OH)

Electrical, Electronics and Communications Engineering
Fairfield U (CT)
Macon State Coll (GA)
Thompson Rivers U (BC,
Canada)

Electrical/Electronics Equipment Installation and Repair
Georgia Southwestern
State U (GA)
Idaho State U (ID)
Lewis-Clark State Coll (ID)
Thompson Rivers U (BC,
Canada)
U of Arkansas at Fort
Smith (AR)

Electrician
Georgia Southwestern
State U (GA)
Pennsylvania Coll of
Technology (PA)
Thompson Rivers U (BC,
Canada)

Electromechanical and Instrumentation And Maintenance Technologies Related
Georgia Southwestern
State U (GA)

Electromechanical Technology
Clayton State U (GA)
Excelsior Coll (NY)
Idaho State U (ID)
Michigan Technological
U (MI)
Northern Michigan U (MI)
Shawnee State U (OH)
The U of Akron (OH)
U of the District of
Columbia (DC)
Utah Valley State Coll (UT)
Walla Walla Coll (WA)
Wright State U (OH)

Elementary and Middle School Administration/ Principalship
Inter American U of Puerto
Rico, Barranquitas
Campus (PR)

Elementary Education
Alaska Pacific U (AK)
Central Christian Coll of
Kansas (KS)
Clayton State U (GA)
Dalton State Coll (GA)
God's Bible School and
Coll (OH)
Hillsdale Free Will Baptist
Coll (OK)
Inter American U of Puerto
Rico, Barranquitas
Campus (PR)
Inter American U of Puerto
Rico, Fajardo
Campus (PR)
Macon State Coll (GA)
Mountain State U (WV)
New Mexico Highlands
U (NM)
Oglala Lakota Coll (SD)
Ozark Christian Coll (MO)
Rogers State U (OK)
Vennard Coll (IA)
Villa Julie Coll (MD)
Wilson Coll (PA)

Emergency Care Attendant (Emt Ambulance)
Trinity Coll of Nursing and
Health Sciences (IL)

Emergency Medical Technology (Emt Paramedic)
Arkansas State U (AR)
Baker Coll of Cadillac (MI)
Baker Coll of Clinton
Township (MI)
Baker Coll of
Muskegon (MI)
Ball State U (IN)
Clayton State U (GA)
Creighton U (NE)
Eastern Kentucky U (KY)
Faulkner U (AL)

Hannibal-LaGrange
Coll (MO)
Idaho State U (ID)
Indiana U–Purdue U
Indianapolis (IN)
Missouri Western State
U (MO)
Montana State
U–Billings (MT)
Mountain State U (WV)
Nebraska Methodist
Coll (NE)
Nicholls State U (LA)
Our Lady of the Lake
Coll (LA)
Pennsylvania Coll of
Technology (PA)
Rogers State U (OK)
Saint Francis U (PA)
Shawnee State U (OH)
Southwest Baptist U (MO)
U of Alaska
Anchorage (AK)
U of Pittsburgh at
Johnstown (PA)
U of Saint Francis (IN)
U of the District of
Columbia (DC)
The U of Toledo (OH)
Weber State U (UT)
Western Kentucky U (KY)
Youngstown State U (OH)

Energy Management and Systems Technology
Baker Coll of Flint (MI)
U of Cincinnati (OH)
U of Rio Grande (OH)

Engineering
Campbell U (NC)
Central Christian Coll of
Kansas (KS)
Clayton State U (GA)
Coll of Staten Island of the
City U of New
York (NY)
Columbia Union Coll (MD)
Daniel Webster Coll (NH)
Geneva Coll (PA)
Lake Superior State U (MI)
Macon State Coll (GA)
Mesa State Coll (CO)
Montana Tech of The U of
Montana (MT)
Mountain State U (WV)
Palm Beach Atlantic U (FL)
Southern Adventist U (TN)
Thompson Rivers U (BC,
Canada)
Union Coll (NE)
York Coll of
Pennsylvania (PA)

Engineering/Industrial Management
Grantham U (MO)

Engineering Related
British Columbia Inst of
Technology (BC,
Canada)
Eastern Kentucky U (KY)
Montana State
U–Billings (MT)

Engineering-Related Technologies
U of Alaska
Southeast (AK)

Engineering Science
Daniel Webster Coll (NH)
Merrimack Coll (MA)
Pennsylvania Coll of
Technology (PA)
Rochester Inst of
Technology (NY)
U of Cincinnati (OH)

Engineering Technologies Related
Cameron U (OK)
Keene State Coll (NH)
McNeese State U (LA)
Rogers State U (OK)
The U of Akron (OH)
Western Kentucky U (KY)

Engineering Technology
Andrews U (MI)
Arkansas State U (AR)
Clayton State U (GA)
Fairmont State U (WV)
John Brown U (AR)
Lake Superior State U (MI)
Macon State Coll (GA)
McNeese State U (LA)

Michigan Technological
U (MI)
Montana Tech of The U of
Montana (MT)
New Mexico State U (NM)
Pacific Union Coll (CA)
Rochester Inst of
Technology (NY)
State U of New York Coll
of Agriculture and
Technology at
Cobleskill (NY)
Tri-State U (IN)
U of Alaska
Anchorage (AK)
U of the District of
Columbia (DC)
Vaughn Coll of Aeronautics
and Technology (NY)
Wentworth Inst of
Technology (MA)
Youngstown State U (OH)

English
Adrian Coll (MI)
Calumet Coll of Saint
Joseph (IN)
Central Methodist U (MO)
Clayton State U (GA)
Coll of Santa Fe (NM)
Dalton State Coll (GA)
Felician Coll (NJ)
Fresno Pacific U (CA)
Hannibal-LaGrange
Coll (MO)
Hillsdale Free Will Baptist
Coll (OK)
Idaho State U (ID)
Indiana U–Purdue U Fort
Wayne (IN)
Indiana Wesleyan U (IN)
Kwantlen U Coll (BC,
Canada)
Lourdes Coll (OH)
Macon State Coll (GA)
Madonna U (MI)
Manchester Coll (IN)
Mesa State Coll (CO)
Methodist U (NC)
Pine Manor Coll (MA)
Presentation Coll (SD)
Sacred Heart U (CT)
Thomas More Coll (KY)
Université Laval (QC,
Canada)
U of Rio Grande (OH)
The U of Tampa (FL)
U of the District of
Columbia (DC)
U of Wisconsin–Green
Bay (WI)
Utah Valley State Coll (UT)
Xavier U (OH)

English Composition
Kwantlen U Coll (BC,
Canada)

English/Language Arts Teacher Education
Lyndon State Coll (VT)

Entrepreneurial and Small Business Related
Central Pennsylvania
Coll (PA)

Entrepreneurship
Baker Coll of Flint (MI)
British Columbia Inst of
Technology (BC,
Canada)
Davenport U,
Dearborn (MI)
Johnson & Wales U (CO)
Lyndon State Coll (VT)
Mountain State U (WV)
Northwood U (MI)
The U of Akron (OH)
U of the District of
Columbia (DC)

Environmental Control Technologies Related
Pennsylvania Coll of
Technology (PA)

Environmental Engineering Technology
Baker Coll of Flint (MI)
Baker Coll of Owosso (MI)
Baker Coll of Port
Huron (MI)
Mesa State Coll (CO)
New York Inst of
Technology (NY)
Ohio U (OH)

Pennsylvania Coll of
Technology (PA)
U of Cincinnati (OH)
U of the District of
Columbia (DC)
The U of Toledo (OH)
Utah Valley State Coll (UT)
Wentworth Inst of
Technology (MA)

**Environmental/
Environmental Health
Engineering**
British Columbia Inst of
Technology (BC,
Canada)
Ohio U (OH)

Environmental Health
British Columbia Inst of
Technology (BC,
Canada)
The U of Akron (OH)

**Environmental
Science**
U of Wisconsin–Green
Bay (WI)

**Environmental
Studies**
Central Christian Coll of
Kansas (KS)
Dickinson State U (ND)
Macon State Coll (GA)
Mountain State U (WV)
Paul Smith's Coll of Arts
and Sciences (NY)
Samford U (AL)
Southern Vermont
Coll (VT)
State U of New York Coll
of Agriculture and
Technology at
Cobleskill (NY)
Sterling Coll (VT)
U of Cincinnati (OH)
The U of Findlay (OH)
U of Ottawa (ON, Canada)
The U of Toledo (OH)
U of Wisconsin–Green
Bay (WI)

Equestrian Studies
Centenary Coll (NJ)
Johnson & Wales U (RI)
Midway Coll (KY)
National American U,
Rapid City (SD)
Ohio U (OH)
Rogers State U (OK)
Saint Mary-of-the-Woods
Coll (IN)
State U of New York Coll
of Agriculture and
Technology at
Cobleskill (NY)
The U of Findlay (OH)
U of Massachusetts
Amherst (MA)
U of Minnesota,
Crookston (MN)
The U of Montana–
Western (MT)
U of New Hampshire (NH)

European Studies
Sacred Heart U (CT)

**Executive Assistant/
Executive Secretary**
Baker Coll of Allen
Park (MI)
Baker Coll of Flint (MI)
Central Pennsylvania
Coll (PA)
Kentucky State U (KY)
Montana Tech of The U of
Montana (MT)
Murray State U (KY)
Robert Morris Coll (IL)
Thompson Rivers U (BC,
Canada)
The U of Akron (OH)
The U of Montana (MT)
Utah Valley State Coll (UT)
Western Kentucky U (KY)

**Family and
Community Services**
Baker Coll of Flint (MI)
Central Christian Coll of
Kansas (KS)
State U of New York Coll
of Agriculture and
Technology at
Cobleskill (NY)

**Family and Consumer
Economics Related**
Dalton State Coll (GA)
Fairmont State U (WV)

**Family and Consumer
Sciences/Human
Sciences**
Clayton State U (GA)
Mount Vernon Nazarene
U (OH)
Oglala Lakota Coll (SD)
U of Alaska
Anchorage (AK)

**Family and Consumer
Sciences/Human
Sciences Related**
Morehead State U (KY)

**Farm and Ranch
Management**
Idaho State U (ID)
Johnson & Wales U (RI)
Oklahoma Panhandle
State U (OK)
Rogers State U (OK)

**Fashion/Apparel
Design**
Academy of Art U (CA)
American InterContinental
U, Atlanta (GA)
The Art Inst of California–
San Francisco (CA)
The Art Inst of Dallas (TX)
The Art Inst of Fort
Lauderdale (FL)
The Art Inst of
Portland (OR)
The Art Inst of
Seattle (WA)
California Design Coll (CA)
Fashion Inst of
Technology (NY)
Indiana U Bloomington (IN)
International Academy of
Design &
Technology (IL)
Miami International U of
Art & Design (FL)
Mount Ida Coll (MA)
Parsons The New School
for Design (NY)
U of the Incarnate
Word (TX)

**Fashion
Merchandising**
Academy of Art U (CA)
American InterContinental
U, Atlanta (GA)
The Art Inst of
Seattle (WA)
California Design Coll (CA)
Clayton State U (GA)
Fairmont State U (WV)
Fashion Inst of
Technology (NY)
International Academy of
Design &
Technology (IL)
Johnson & Wales U (CO)
Johnson & Wales U (FL)
Johnson & Wales U (NC)
Johnson & Wales U (RI)
Laboratory Inst of ·
Merchandising (NY)
Miami International U of
Art & Design (FL)
Mount Ida Coll (MA)
Northwood U (MI)
Northwood U, Texas
Campus (TX)
Parsons The New School
for Design (NY)
Southern New Hampshire
U (NH)
The U of Akron (OH)
U of Bridgeport (CT)
U of the District of
Columbia (DC)
U of the Incarnate
Word (TX)
Weber State U (UT)
West Virginia State U (WV)

Fashion Modeling
Fashion Inst of
Technology (NY)

**Fiber, Textile and
Weaving Arts**
Academy of Art U (CA)

Film/Cinema Studies
Academy of Art U (CA)
Burlington Coll (VT)
Indiana U South Bend (IN)

**Film/Video and
Photographic Arts
Related**
The Art Inst of
Pittsburgh (PA)

New England School of
Communications (ME)

Finance
British Columbia Inst of
Technology (BC,
Canada)
Central Christian Coll of
Kansas (KS)
Central Pennsylvania
Coll (PA)
Clayton State U (GA)
Davenport U,
Dearborn (MI)
Fairmont State U (WV)
Hawai'i Pacific U (HI)
Indiana U South Bend (IN)
Indiana Wesleyan U (IN)
Marian Coll (IN)
Methodist U (NC)
Sacred Heart U (CT)
Saint Joseph's U (PA)
Saint Peter's Coll (NJ)
U of Cincinnati (OH)
U of Phoenix–Cleveland
Campus (OH)
Walsh U (OH)
Webber International
U (FL)
West Virginia State U (WV)
Youngstown State U (OH)

**Finance and Financial
Management Services
Related**
British Columbia Inst of
Technology (BC,
Canada)

**Financial Planning
and Services**
British Columbia Inst of
Technology (BC,
Canada)
The U of Maine at
Augusta (ME)

Fine Arts Related
Saint Francis U (PA)
York Coll of
Pennsylvania (PA)

Fine/Studio Arts
Academy of Art U (CA)
Corcoran Coll of Art and
Design (DC)
Fashion Inst of
Technology (NY)
Manchester Coll (IN)
Pace U (NY)
Pine Manor Coll (MA)
Pratt Inst (NY)
Rochester Inst of
Technology (NY)
Sage Coll of Albany (NY)
St. Gregory's U,
Shawnee (OK)
Thomas More Coll (KY)
The U of Maine at
Augusta (ME)
U of New Hampshire at
Manchester (NH)

**Fire Protection and
Safety Technology**
British Columbia Inst of
Technology (BC,
Canada)
Eastern Kentucky U (KY)
Montana State
U–Billings (MT)
The U of Akron (OH)
U of
Nebraska–Lincoln (NE)
U of New Haven (CT)
The U of Toledo (OH)

Fire Science
American Public U
System (WV)
Idaho State U (ID)
Lake Superior State U (MI)
Lewis-Clark State Coll (ID)
Madonna U (MI)
Mountain State U (WV)
U of Alaska
Anchorage (AK)
U of Alaska Fairbanks (AK)
U of Cincinnati (OH)
U of the District of
Columbia (DC)
Utah Valley State Coll (UT)

**Fish/Game
Management**
State U of New York Coll
of Agriculture and
Technology at
Cobleskill (NY)

**Fishing and Fisheries
Sciences And
Management**
Sterling Coll (VT)

**Floriculture/Floristry
Management**
Inter American U of Puerto
Rico, Barranquitas
Campus (PR)

Folklore
Université Laval (QC,
Canada)

Food Preparation
The Art Inst of
Pittsburgh (PA)
Lexington Coll (IL)

Food Science
Macon State Coll (GA)
U of Puerto Rico at
Utuado (PR)

**Food Service and
Dining Room
Management**
Johnson & Wales U (FL)
Johnson & Wales U (NC)
Lexington Coll (IL)

**Food Services
Technology**
Purdue U Calumet (IN)
State U of New York Coll
of Agriculture and
Technology at
Cobleskill (NY)
U of the District of
Columbia (DC)
Washburn U (KS)

**Foodservice Systems
Administration**
Murray State U (KY)
U of New Haven (CT)

**Foods, Nutrition, and
Wellness**
Cedar Crest Coll (PA)
Eastern Kentucky U (KY)
Madonna U (MI)
Southern Adventist U (TN)
U of Maine at Presque
Isle (ME)
U of New Hampshire (NH)
U of Ottawa (ON, Canada)

**Foreign Languages
and Literatures**
Dalton State Coll (GA)

**Foreign Languages
Related**
U of Alaska Fairbanks (AK)

**Forensic Science and
Technology**
Arkansas State U (AR)
British Columbia Inst of
Technology (BC,
Canada)
U of Arkansas at Fort
Smith (AR)

**Forest/Forest
Resources
Management**
British Columbia Inst of
Technology (BC,
Canada)
Sterling Coll (VT)

**Forest Products
Technology**
Pittsburg State U (KS)

**Forest Resources
Production and
Management**
Sterling Coll (VT)

Forestry
Clayton State U (GA)
Columbus State U (GA)
Dalton State Coll (GA)
Paul Smith's Coll of Arts
and Sciences (NY)
Sterling Coll (VT)

Forestry Related
Sterling Coll (VT)

Forestry Technology
British Columbia Inst of
Technology (BC,
Canada)
Georgia Southwestern
State U (GA)
Glenville State Coll (WV)
Michigan Technological
U (MI)

Paul Smith's Coll of Arts
and Sciences (NY)
Pennsylvania Coll of
Technology (PA)
U of New Hampshire (NH)

**Forest Sciences and
Biology**
Sterling Coll (VT)

French
Adrian Coll (MI)
Chestnut Hill Coll (PA)
Clayton State U (GA)
Idaho State U (ID)
Indiana U–Purdue U Fort
Wayne (IN)
Methodist U (NC)
Université Laval (QC,
Canada)
U of Wisconsin–Green
Bay (WI)
Xavier U (OH)

**Funeral Service and
Mortuary Science**
Mount Ida Coll (MA)
Point Park U (PA)

**Furniture Design and
Manufacturing**
Rochester Inst of
Technology (NY)

General Studies
Alderson-Broaddus
Coll (WV)
Anderson U (IN)
Arkansas State U (AR)
Arkansas Tech U (AR)
Averett U (VA)
Avila U (MO)
Barclay Coll (KS)
Black Hills State U (SD)
Brewton-Parker Coll (GA)
Calumet Coll of Saint
Joseph (IN)
Castleton State Coll (VT)
Central Baptist Coll (AR)
Columbia Union Coll (MD)
Concordia (MI)
Concordia U at Austin (TX)
Concordia U, St.
Paul (MN)
Crown Coll (MN)
Dakota State U (SD)
Dalton State Coll (GA)
Eastern Connecticut State
U (CT)
Eastern Mennonite U (VA)
Eastern Nazarene
Coll (MA)
Eastern New Mexico
U (NM)
Finlandia U (MI)
Franciscan U of
Steubenville (OH)
Granite State Coll (NH)
Grantham U (MO)
Hillsdale Free Will Baptist
Coll (OK)
Hope International U (CA)
Idaho State U (ID)
Indiana U Bloomington (IN)
Indiana U East (IN)
Indiana U Kokomo (IN)
Indiana U Northwest (IN)
Indiana U of
Pennsylvania (PA)
Indiana U–Purdue U Fort
Wayne (IN)
Indiana U–Purdue U
Indianapolis (IN)
Indiana U South Bend (IN)
Indiana U Southeast (IN)
Indiana Wesleyan U (IN)
Johnson State Coll (VT)
Lawrence Technological
U (MI)
Lebanon Valley Coll (PA)
Liberty U (VA)
Louisiana Tech U (LA)
Macon State Coll (GA)
McNeese State U (LA)
Messenger Coll (MO)
Monmouth U (NJ)
Montana State
U–Billings (MT)
Morehead State U (KY)
Mount Aloysius Coll (PA)
Mount Marty Coll (SD)
Mount Vernon Nazarene
U (OH)
New Mexico Inst of Mining
and Technology (NM)
New York U (NY)
Nicholls State U (LA)
Northern Michigan U (MI)

Northwestern State U of
Louisiana (LA)
Northwest U (WA)
Nyack Coll (NY)
Oak Hills Christian
Coll (MN)
Ohio Dominican U (OH)
Oklahoma Panhandle
State U (OK)
Our Lady of the Lake
Coll (LA)
Palm Beach Atlantic U (FL)
Pennsylvania Coll of
Technology (PA)
Presentation Coll (SD)
Rider U (NJ)
Rochester Inst of
Technology (NY)
St. Augustine Coll (IL)
Shawnee State U (OH)
Silver Lake Coll (WI)
Simpson U (CA)
South Dakota School of
Mines and
Technology (SD)
Southeastern Louisiana
U (LA)
Southern Adventist U (TN)
Southern Arkansas
U–Magnolia (AR)
Southwest Baptist U (MO)
Taylor U Fort Wayne (IN)
Temple U (PA)
Toccoa Falls Coll (GA)
Trevecca Nazarene U (TN)
U of Alaska
Southeast (AK)
U of Arkansas at Fort
Smith (AR)
U of Arkansas at Little
Rock (AR)
U of Central
Arkansas (AR)
U of Hartford (CT)
U of Louisiana at
Monroe (LA)
U of Mobile (AL)
U of New Hampshire (NH)
U of New Haven (CT)
U of North Florida (FL)
U of Phoenix–Cleveland
Campus (OH)
U of Phoenix–Columbus
Ohio Campus (OH)
U of Phoenix–Houston
Campus (TX)
U of Phoenix–Indianapolis
Campus (IN)
U of Phoenix–St. Louis
Campus (MO)
U of Phoenix–Springfield
Campus (MO)
U of Rio Grande (OH)
The U of South
Dakota (SD)
The U of Toledo (OH)
U of
Wisconsin–Superior (WI)
Utah State U (UT)
Utah Valley State Coll (UT)
Vennard Coll (IA)
Virginia Intermont Coll (VA)
Western Kentucky U (KY)
Wilmington Coll (DE)
Woodbury Coll (VT)

Geography
Dalton State Coll (GA)
Kwantlen U Coll (BC,
Canada)
Université Laval (QC,
Canada)
The U of Tampa (FL)
Wright State U (OH)

**Geological and Earth
Sciences/Geosciences
Related**
Kwantlen U Coll (BC,
Canada)

**Geology/Earth
Science**
Adrian Coll (MI)
Clayton State U (GA)
Dalton State Coll (GA)
Idaho State U (ID)
Indiana U East (IN)
Mesa State Coll (CO)
U of Wisconsin–Green
Bay (WI)
Utah Valley State Coll (UT)

**Geophysics and
Seismology**
U of Ottawa (ON, Canada)

German
Adrian Coll (MI)
Idaho State U (ID)

Indiana U–Purdue U Fort
Wayne (IN)
Methodist U (NC)
Xavier U (OH)

Germanic Languages
U of Wisconsin–Green
Bay (WI)

Gerontology
Madonna U (MI)
Manchester Coll (IN)
Millersville U of
Pennsylvania (PA)
Ohio Dominican U (OH)
Pontifical Catholic U of
Puerto Rico (PR)
Thomas More Coll (KY)
The U of Toledo (OH)
Washburn U (KS)
West Virginia State U (WV)

**Graphic and Printing
Equipment Operation/
Production**
Ball State U (IN)
Fairmont State U (WV)
Georgia Southwestern
State U (GA)
Idaho State U (ID)
Lewis-Clark State Coll (ID)
Pennsylvania Coll of
Technology (PA)
U of the District of
Columbia (DC)

**Graphic
Communications**
Academy of Art U (CA)
Indiana Tech (IN)
New England School of
Communications (ME)
Robert Morris Coll (IL)
U of Phoenix–Cleveland
Campus (OH)
U of Phoenix–Columbus
Ohio Campus (OH)
U of Phoenix–Houston
Campus (TX)
U of Phoenix–Indianapolis
Campus (IN)
U of Phoenix–St. Louis
Campus (MO)
U of Phoenix–Springfield
Campus (MO)

**Graphic
Communications
Related**
The Art Insts International
Minnesota (MN)

Graphic Design
Academy of Art U (CA)
Art Academy of
Cincinnati (OH)
The Art Inst of California–
Inland Empire (CA)
The Art Inst of California–
Los Angeles (CA)
The Art Inst of California–
Orange County (CA)
The Art Inst of California–
San Diego (CA)
The Art Inst of
Charleston (SC)
The Art Inst of Dallas (TX)
The Art Inst of
Houston (TX)
The Art Inst of
Jacksonville (FL)
The Art Inst of
Phoenix (AZ)
The Art Inst of
Pittsburgh (PA)
The Art Inst of
Portland (OR)
The Art Inst of
Seattle (WA)
The Art Inst of Tampa (FL)
The Art Inst of Tennessee–
Nashville (TN)
The Art Insts International
Minnesota (MN)
Becker Coll (MA)
Champlain Coll (VT)
Coll of Mount St.
Joseph (OH)
Corcoran Coll of Art and
Design (DC)
New World School of the
Arts (FL)
Pratt Inst (NY)
Rochester Inst of
Technology (NY)
Sage Coll of Albany (NY)
Thompson Rivers U (BC,
Canada)
Union Coll (NE)

U of Arkansas at Fort
Smith (AR)
Westwood Coll–Annandale
Campus (VA)

**Graphic/Printing
Equipment**
Eastern Kentucky U (KY)

**Greenhouse
Management**
Sterling Coll (VT)

**Hazardous Materials
Information Systems
Technology**
Ohio U (OH)

**Hazardous Materials
Management and
Waste Technology**
Ohio U (OH)

**Health and Medical
Administrative
Services Related**
British Columbia Inst of
Technology (BC,
Canada)
Kent State U (OH)
The U of Akron (OH)

**Health and Physical
Education**
Central Christian Coll of
Kansas (KS)
Mount Vernon Nazarene
U (OH)
Robert Morris Coll (IL)
Utah Valley State Coll (UT)

**Health and Physical
Education Related**
Pennsylvania Coll of
Technology (PA)
Utah Valley State Coll (UT)

**Health/Health Care
Administration**
American Public U
System (WV)
Baker Coll of Auburn
Hills (MI)
Baker Coll of Flint (MI)
Baker Coll of
Muskegon (MI)
British Columbia Inst of
Technology (BC,
Canada)
Cabarrus Coll of Health
Sciences (NC)
Chestnut Hill Coll (PA)
Madonna U (MI)
Methodist U (NC)
National American U,
Denver (CO)
New York U (NY)
Point Park U (PA)
Saint Joseph's U (PA)
Southeastern U (DC)
The U of Scranton (PA)

**Health Information/
Medical Records
Administration**
Baker Coll of Auburn
Hills (MI)
Baker Coll of Cadillac (MI)
Baker Coll of Clinton
Township (MI)
Baker Coll of Flint (MI)
Baker Coll of Jackson (MI)
Baker Coll of Port
Huron (MI)
Boise State U (ID)
Clayton State U (GA)
Coll of Saint Mary (NE)
Dalton State Coll (GA)
Eastern Kentucky U (KY)
Fairmont State U (WV)
Faulkner U (AL)
Ferris State U (MI)
Gwynedd-Mercy Coll (PA)
Indiana U Northwest (IN)
Inter American U of Puerto
Rico, San Germán
Campus (PR)
Montana State
U–Billings (MT)
Northern Michigan U (MI)
Park U (MO)
Pennsylvania Coll of
Technology (PA)
Universidad Adventista de
las Antillas (PR)

**Health Information/
Medical Records
Technology**
Baker Coll of Flint (MI)
Baker Coll of Jackson (MI)

Coll of St. Catherine (MN)
Dakota State U (SD)
Davenport U,
Dearborn (MI)
DeVry U, Fremont (CA)
DeVry U, Long Beach (CA)
DeVry U, Pomona (CA)
DeVry U, Sherman
Oaks (CA)
DeVry U,
Westminster (CO)
DeVry U, Miramar (FL)
DeVry U, Orlando (FL)
DeVry U, Alpharetta (GA)
DeVry U, Decatur (GA)
DeVry U, Chicago (IL)
DeVry U (MN)
DeVry U (NJ)
DeVry U, Columbus (OH)
DeVry U, Fort
Washington (PA)
DeVry U, Houston (TX)
DeVry U, Irving (TX)
Eastern Kentucky U (KY)
Gwynedd-Mercy Coll (PA)
Idaho State U (ID)
International Coll (FL)
Louisiana Tech U (LA)
Macon State Coll (GA)
Missouri Western State
U (MO)
Molloy Coll (NY)
New York U (NY)
Robert Morris Coll (IL)
Washburn U (KS)
Weber State U (UT)
Western Kentucky U (KY)

**Health/Medical
Preparatory Programs
Related**
Emmanuel Coll (GA)
Union Coll (NE)

**Health Professions
Related**
British Columbia Inst of
Technology (BC,
Canada)
East Tennessee State
U (TN)
Howard Payne U (TX)
Lock Haven U of
Pennsylvania (PA)
U of Alaska
Southeast (AK)

Health Science
Howard Payne U (TX)
Macon State Coll (GA)
National U (CA)
Newman U (KS)
Northwest U (WA)
South U (AL)
Union Coll (NE)
U of Hartford (CT)

**Health Services
Administration**
U of Phoenix–Cleveland
Campus (OH)
U of Phoenix–Columbus
Ohio Campus (OH)
U of Phoenix–Houston
Campus (TX)
U of Phoenix–Indianapolis
Campus (IN)
U of Phoenix–St. Louis
Campus (MO)
U of Phoenix–Springfield
Campus (MO)

**Health Services/Allied
Health/Health
Sciences**
Immaculata U (PA)
Lindsey Wilson Coll (KY)
National American U,
Denver (CO)
South U, West Palm
Beach (FL)

**Health Teacher
Education**
Central Christian Coll of
Kansas (KS)
Clayton State U (GA)

**Heating, Air
Conditioning and
Refrigeration
Technology**
Pennsylvania Coll of
Technology (PA)

**Heating, Air
Conditioning,
Ventilation and
Refrigeration
Maintenance
Technology**
Boise State U (ID)

British Columbia Inst of
Technology (BC,
Canada)
Ferris State U (MI)
Lewis-Clark State Coll (ID)
Montana State
U–Billings (MT)
Northern Michigan U (MI)
U of Alaska
Anchorage (AK)
U of Cincinnati (OH)
Utah Valley State Coll (UT)

**Heavy Equipment
Maintenance
Technology**
British Columbia Inst of
Technology (BC,
Canada)
Ferris State U (MI)
Georgia Southwestern
State U (GA)
Mesa State Coll (CO)
Pennsylvania Coll of
Technology (PA)
U of Alaska
Anchorage (AK)
The U of Montana (MT)

**Heavy/Industrial
Equipment
Maintenance
Technologies Related**
Pennsylvania Coll of
Technology (PA)

**Histologic
Technology/
Histotechnologist**
Argosy U, Twin Cities,
Eagan (MN)
Tarleton State U (TX)

History
Adrian Coll (MI)
American Public U
System (WV)
Central Christian Coll of
Kansas (KS)
Dalton State Coll (GA)
Felician Coll (NJ)
Fresno Pacific U (CA)
Idaho State U (ID)
Indiana U East (IN)
Indiana U–Purdue U Fort
Wayne (IN)
Indiana Wesleyan U (IN)
Kwantlen U Coll (BC,
Canada)
Lindsey Wilson Coll (KY)
Lourdes Coll (OH)
Macon State Coll (GA)
Marian Coll (IN)
Methodist U (NC)
Millersville U of
Pennsylvania (PA)
Pine Manor Coll (MA)
Rogers State U (OK)
Sacred Heart U (CT)
State U of New York
Empire State Coll (NY)
Thomas More Coll (KY)
U of Rio Grande (OH)
The U of Tampa (FL)
U of the District of
Columbia (DC)
U of Wisconsin–Green
Bay (WI)
Villa Julie Coll (MD)
Wright State U (OH)
Xavier U (OH)

**History Teacher
Education**
Central Christian Coll of
Kansas (KS)

Home Furnishings
Eastern Kentucky U (KY)

**Home Furnishings
and Equipment
Installation**
Eastern Kentucky U (KY)

Horticultural Science
Andrews U (MI)
Boise State U (ID)
Eastern Kentucky U (KY)
State U of New York Coll
of Agriculture and
Technology at
Cobleskill (NY)
U of Connecticut (CT)
U of Minnesota,
Crookston (MN)
U of New Hampshire (NH)
U of Puerto Rico at
Utuado (PR)

**Hospitality
Administration**
American Public U
System (WV)
The Art Inst of
Pittsburgh (PA)
Baker Coll of Flint (MI)
Baker Coll of Owosso (MI)
Bob Jones U (SC)
Champlain Coll (VT)
Davis & Elkins Coll (WV)
Indiana U–Purdue U Fort
Wayne (IN)
Johnson & Wales U (FL)
Kendall Coll (IL)
Lewis-Clark State Coll (ID)
Lexington Coll (IL)
Monroe Coll, Bronx (NY)
Mountain State U (WV)
Paul Smith's Coll of Arts
and Sciences (NY)
The U of Akron (OH)
U of Minnesota,
Crookston (MN)
U of the District of
Columbia (DC)
Utah Valley State Coll (UT)
Youngstown State U (OH)

**Hospitality
Administration
Related**
The Art Inst of
Pittsburgh (PA)
Champlain Coll (VT)
Lexington Coll (IL)
Mountain State U (WV)
Penn State Berks (PA)
Penn State U Park (PA)
Purdue U (IN)

**Hospitality and
Recreation Marketing**
Champlain Coll (VT)
Johnson & Wales U (RI)
Thompson Rivers U (BC,
Canada)
The U of Akron (OH)

**Hotel and Restaurant
Management**
Georgia Southwestern
State U (GA)
Johnson & Wales U (NC)

**Hotel/Motel
Administration**
The Art Inst of
Pittsburgh (PA)
Baker Coll of
Muskegon (MI)
Baker Coll of Owosso (MI)
Baker Coll of Port
Huron (MI)
Bluefield State Coll (WV)
Central Pennsylvania
Coll (PA)
Champlain Coll (VT)
Florida Metropolitan
U–Pompano Beach
Campus (FL)
Indiana U–Purdue U
Indianapolis (IN)
Johnson & Wales U (FL)
Johnson & Wales U (RI)
Kendall Coll (IL)
Lexington Coll (IL)
Mercyhurst Coll (PA)
Mesa State Coll (CO)
Mount Ida Coll (MA)
Northwood U (MI)
Northwood U, Florida
Campus (FL)
Northwood U, Texas
Campus (TX)
Paul Smith's Coll of Arts
and Sciences (NY)
Purdue U Calumet (IN)
Rochester Inst of
Technology (NY)
State U of New York Coll
of Agriculture and
Technology at
Cobleskill (NY)
Sullivan U (KY)
Thompson Rivers U (BC,
Canada)
The U of Akron (OH)
U of Minnesota,
Crookston (MN)
U of the Virgin Islands (VI)
Webber International
U (FL)
West Virginia State U (WV)

**Human Development
and Family Studies**
Penn State Altoona (PA)
Penn State U Park (PA)

State U of New York
Empire State Coll (NY)

**Human Development
and Family Studies
Related**
The U of Toledo (OH)
Utah State U (UT)

Human Ecology
Sterling Coll (VT)

Humanities
Burlington Coll (VT)
Faulkner U (AL)
Felician Coll (NJ)
John Cabot U (Italy)
Macon State Coll (GA)
Mesa State Coll (CO)
Michigan Technological
U (MI)
Ohio U (OH)
Rider U (NJ)
Sage Coll of Albany (NY)
St. Gregory's U,
Shawnee (OK)
Saint Peter's Coll (NJ)
Shawnee State U (OH)
State U of New York
Empire State Coll (NY)
Taylor U Fort Wayne (IN)
U of Alaska
Southeast (AK)
U of Cincinnati (OH)
The U of Findlay (OH)
U of Sioux Falls (SD)
U of Wisconsin–Green
Bay (WI)
Utah Valley State Coll (UT)
Washburn U (KS)

**Human Resources
Development**
Georgia Southwestern
State U (GA)

**Human Resources
Management**
Baker Coll of Owosso (MI)
British Columbia Inst of
Technology (BC,
Canada)
Central Christian Coll of
Kansas (KS)
Chestnut Hill Coll (PA)
King's Coll (PA)
Montana State
U–Billings (MT)
Montana Tech of The U of
Montana (MT)
The U of Findlay (OH)
The U of Montana–
Western (MT)
U of Richmond (VA)
U of Saint Francis (IN)

**Human Resources
Management and
Services Related**
Becker Coll (MA)
Bryant and Stratton Coll,
Cleveland (OH)
Concordia U Coll of
Alberta (AB, Canada)

Human Services
Adrian Coll (MI)
Baker Coll of Clinton
Township (MI)
Baker Coll of Flint (MI)
Baker Coll of
Muskegon (MI)
Beacon Coll (FL)
Burlington Coll (VT)
Cazenovia Coll (NY)
Champlain Coll (VT)
Chestnut Hill Coll (PA)
Hilbert Coll (NY)
Indiana U East (IN)
Indiana U–Purdue U Fort
Wayne (IN)
Kendall Coll (IL)
Mercy Coll (NY)
Merrimack Coll (MA)
Metropolitan Coll of New
York (NY)
Mount Vernon Nazarene
U (OH)
New York U (NY)
Northern Kentucky U (KY)
Oglala Lakota Coll (SD)
Ohio U (OH)
Southern Vermont
Coll (VT)
State U of New York
Empire State Coll (NY)
U of Alaska
Anchorage (AK)
U of Cincinnati (OH)
U of Great Falls (MT)

The U of Maine at Augusta (ME)
U of Saint Francis (IN)
The U of Scranton (PA)
Walsh U (OH)
Washburn U (KS)

Hydrology and Water Resources Science
Lake Superior State U (MI)
U of the District of Columbia (DC)

Illustration
Academy of Art U (CA)
The Art Inst of Pittsburgh (PA)
Fashion Inst of Technology (NY)
Pratt Inst (NY)

Industrial Arts
Austin Peay State U (TN)
Dalton State Coll (GA)
Eastern Kentucky U (KY)
U of Cincinnati (OH)
The U of Montana (MT)
Weber State U (UT)

Industrial Design
Academy of Art U (CA)
The Art Inst of Pittsburgh (PA)
The Art Inst of Seattle (WA)
Ferris State U (MI)
Rochester Inst of Technology (NY)
Wentworth Inst of Technology (MA)

Industrial Electronics Technology
Dalton State Coll (GA)
Lewis-Clark State Coll (ID)
Pennsylvania Coll of Technology (PA)
Thompson Rivers U (BC, Canada)

Industrial Engineering
The U of Toledo (OH)

Industrial Mechanics and Maintenance Technology
Arkansas Tech U (AR)
British Columbia Inst of Technology (BC, Canada)
Dalton State Coll (GA)
Pennsylvania Coll of Technology (PA)

Industrial Production Technologies Related
Ferris State U (MI)
Pennsylvania Coll of Technology (PA)
U of Nebraska–Lincoln (NE)

Industrial Radiologic Technology
Baker Coll of Owosso (MI)
Ball State U (IN)
Boise State U (ID)
Faulkner U (AL)
Ferris State U (MI)
Fort Hays State U (KS)
The George Washington U (DC)
Inter American U of Puerto Rico, San Germán Campus (PR)
Mesa State Coll (CO)
Northern Kentucky U (KY)
Our Lady of the Lake Coll (LA)
U of Cincinnati (OH)
U of the District of Columbia (DC)
Widener U (PA)

Industrial Technology
Baker Coll of Muskegon (MI)
Ball State U (IN)
British Columbia Inst of Technology (BC, Canada)
Cameron U (OK)
Dalton State Coll (GA)
Eastern Kentucky U (KY)
Edinboro U of Pennsylvania (PA)
Excelsior Coll (NY)
Fairmont State U (WV)
Ferris State U (MI)
Indiana U–Purdue U Fort Wayne (IN)
Keene State Coll (NH)
Kent State U (OH)
Mesa State Coll (CO)
Millersville U of Pennsylvania (PA)
Morehead State U (KY)
Murray State U (KY)
Oklahoma Panhandle State U (OK)
Pennsylvania Coll of Technology (PA)
Purdue U Calumet (IN)
Purdue U North Central (IN)
Southeastern Louisiana U (LA)
Southern Arkansas U–Magnolia (AR)
Tri-State U (IN)
The U of Akron (OH)
U of Alaska Fairbanks (AK)
U of Arkansas at Pine Bluff (AR)
U of Central Missouri (MO)
U of Cincinnati (OH)
U of Rio Grande (OH)
The U of Toledo (OH)
Washburn U (KS)
Weber State U (UT)
Wentworth Inst of Technology (MA)
Wright State U (OH)

Information Science/Studies
Albertus Magnus Coll (CT)
Arkansas Tech U (AR)
Baker Coll of Cadillac (MI)
Baker Coll of Clinton Township (MI)
Baker Coll of Flint (MI)
Baker Coll of Jackson (MI)
Baker Coll of Muskegon (MI)
Baker Coll of Owosso (MI)
Baker Coll of Port Huron (MI)
Ball State U (IN)
Beacon Coll (FL)
Briarcliffe Coll (NY)
British Columbia Inst of Technology (BC, Canada)
Calumet Coll of Saint Joseph (IN)
Campbellsville U (KY)
Central Pennsylvania Coll (PA)
Champlain Coll (VT)
Clayton State U (GA)
Coll of St. Joseph (VT)
Dakota State U (SD)
Dalton State Coll (GA)
Daniel Webster Coll (NH)
Fairmont State U (WV)
Farmingdale State Coll (NY)
Faulkner U (AL)
Goldey-Beacom Coll (DE)
Husson Coll (ME)
Immaculata U (PA)
Indiana Tech (IN)
Johnson State Coll (VT)
Jones Coll, Jacksonville (FL)
Limestone Coll (SC)
Macon State Coll (GA)
Mansfield U of Pennsylvania (PA)
Missouri Southern State U (MO)
Monroe Coll, Bronx (NY)
Morrison U (NV)
Mountain State U (WV)
Mount Olive Coll (NC)
Murray State U (KY)
National American U, Denver (CO)
National American U, Rapid City (SD)
Newman U (KS)
Oakwood Coll (AL)
Oklahoma Panhandle State U (OK)
Oklahoma Wesleyan U (OK)
Pacific Union Coll (CA)
Penn State Altoona (PA)
Penn State Berks (PA)
Purdue U North Central (IN)
Rivier Coll (NH)
Rogers State U (OK)
Sage Coll of Albany (NY)
Saint Peter's Coll (NJ)
Southeastern U (DC)
Southern Utah U (UT)
South U (AL)
South U, West Palm Beach (FL)
State U of New York Coll of Agriculture and Technology at Cobleskill (NY)
Trevecca Nazarene U (TN)
Tulane U (LA)
Union Coll (NE)
U of Alaska Anchorage (AK)
U of Cincinnati (OH)
U of Minnesota, Crookston (MN)
The U of Montana–Western (MT)
U of Pittsburgh at Bradford (PA)
The U of Scranton (PA)
The U of Tampa (FL)
The U of Toledo (OH)
U of Wisconsin–Green Bay (WI)
Villa Julie Coll (MD)
Weber State U (UT)

Information Technology
Bryant and Stratton Coll, Cleveland (OH)
Davenport U, Dearborn (MI)
Grantham U (MO)
Indiana Tech (IN)
International Academy of Design & Technology (IL)
International Coll (FL)
McNeese State U (LA)
Minnesota School of Business (MN)
Mountain State U (WV)
National American U, Denver (CO)
Pennsylvania Coll of Technology (PA)
Point Park U (PA)
Southern New Hampshire U (NH)
South U, West Palm Beach (FL)
South U (GA)
South U (SC)
U of Massachusetts Lowell (MA)
U of Phoenix–Cincinnati Campus (OH)
U of Phoenix–Columbus Ohio Campus (OH)
U of Phoenix–Houston Campus (TX)
U of Phoenix–Indianapolis Campus (IN)
U of Phoenix–St. Louis Campus (MO)
U of Phoenix–Springfield Campus (MO)
Utah Valley State Coll (UT)

Institutional Food Workers
The Art Inst of Pittsburgh (PA)
Fairmont State U (WV)
Kendall Coll (IL)
Lexington Coll (IL)
Pennsylvania Coll of Technology (PA)
State U of New York Coll of Agriculture and Technology at Cobleskill (NY)

Instrumentation Technology
Clayton State U (GA)
Excelsior Coll (NY)
Idaho State U (ID)
McNeese State U (LA)
Pennsylvania Coll of Technology (PA)

Insurance
Mercyhurst Coll (PA)
Université Laval (QC, Canada)
U of Cincinnati (OH)

Intercultural/Multicultural and Diversity Studies
Immaculata U (PA)

Interdisciplinary Studies
Bluefield State Coll (WV)
Burlington Coll (VT)
Cardinal Stritch U (WI)
Central Methodist U (MO)
Coll of Mount Saint Vincent (NY)
Grantham U (MO)
Hillsdale Free Will Baptist Coll (OK)
Kansas State U (KS)
Lesley U (MA)
Mountain State U (WV)
Ohio Dominican U (OH)
State U of New York Empire State Coll (NY)
Suffolk U (MA)
Tabor Coll (KS)
Unity Coll (ME)
The U of Akron (OH)
U of Sioux Falls (SD)
U of Wisconsin–Green Bay (WI)
Villa Julie Coll (MD)

Interior Architecture
U of New Haven (CT)

Interior Design
Academy of Art U (CA)
American InterContinental U, Atlanta (GA)
The American U in Dubai (United Arab Emirates)
The Art Inst of Dallas (TX)
The Art Inst of Las Vegas (NV)
The Art Inst of Pittsburgh (PA)
The Art Inst of Portland (OR)
The Art Inst of Seattle (WA)
The Art Insts International Minnesota (MN)
Baker Coll of Allen Park (MI)
Baker Coll of Auburn Hills (MI)
Baker Coll of Clinton Township (MI)
Baker Coll of Flint (MI)
Baker Coll of Muskegon (MI)
Baker Coll of Owosso (MI)
Baker Coll of Port Huron (MI)
British Columbia Inst of Technology (BC, Canada)
Coll of Mount St. Joseph (OH)
Eastern Kentucky U (KY)
Fairmont State U (WV)
Fashion Inst of Technology (NY)
Harrington Coll of Design (IL)
The Illinois Inst of Art–Chicago (IL)
Indiana U–Purdue U Fort Wayne (IN)
International Academy of Design & Technology (IL)
Marian Coll (IN)
Miami International U of Art & Design (FL)
New York School of Interior Design (NY)
Parsons The New School for Design (NY)
Robert Morris Coll (IL)
Rochester Inst of Technology (NY)
Sage Coll of Albany (NY)
Southern Utah U (UT)
U of the Incarnate Word (TX)
Watkins Coll of Art and Design (TN)
Weber State U (UT)
Wentworth Inst of Technology (MA)

Intermedia/Multimedia
The Art Inst of Atlanta (GA)
The Art Inst of Charleston (SC)
The Art Inst of Colorado (CO)
The Art Inst of Jacksonville (FL)
The Art Inst of Pittsburgh (PA)
The Art Inst of Portland (OR)
The Art Inst of Seattle (WA)
The Art Inst of Tennessee–Nashville (TN)
The Art Inst of Washington (VA)
The Art Insts International Minnesota (MN)
Champlain Coll (VT)
DigiPen Inst of Technology (WA)
International Academy of Design & Technology (IL)
Minnesota School of Business (MN)
New England School of Communications (ME)
New World School of the Arts (FL)
Robert Morris Coll (IL)
Westwood Coll–Annandale Campus (VA)

International Business/Trade/Commerce
The American U of Rome (Italy)
Bob Jones U (SC)
British Columbia Inst of Technology (BC, Canada)
Champlain Coll (VT)
Florida Metropolitan U–Pompano Beach Campus (FL)
Northwood U (MI)
Northwood U, Florida Campus (FL)
Saint Peter's Coll (NJ)
Schiller International U (FL)
Schiller International U (France)
Schiller International U (Germany)
Schiller International U (Spain)
Schiller International U (United Kingdom)
Southern New Hampshire U (NH)
State U of New York Coll of Agriculture and Technology at Cobleskill (NY)
Webber International U (FL)

International Relations and Affairs
John Cabot U (Italy)
Thomas More Coll (KY)

Italian Studies
John Cabot U (Italy)

Jazz/Jazz Studies
Five Towns Coll (NY)
Indiana U South Bend (IN)
Southern U and A&M Coll (LA)
Université Laval (QC, Canada)

Journalism
Ball State U (IN)
Clayton State U (GA)
Dalton State Coll (GA)
Evangel U (MO)
Indiana U Southeast (IN)
John Brown U (AR)
Macon State Coll (GA)
Madonna U (MI)
Manchester Coll (IN)
Villa Julie Coll (MD)

Kindergarten/Preschool Education
Atlantic Union Coll (MA)
Baker Coll of Clinton Township (MI)
Baker Coll of Muskegon (MI)
Baker Coll of Owosso (MI)
Bethany U (CA)
California U of Pennsylvania (PA)
Central Christian Coll of Kansas (KS)
Champlain Coll (VT)
Clayton State U (GA)
Coll of Mount St. Joseph (OH)
Crown Coll (MN)
Eastern Nazarene Coll (MA)
Edinboro U of Pennsylvania (PA)
Hope International U (CA)
Indiana U–Purdue U Indianapolis (IN)
Indiana U South Bend (IN)
Keene State Coll (NH)
Kendall Coll (IL)
Lourdes Coll (OH)
Manchester Coll (IN)
Maranatha Baptist Bible Coll (WI)
Marian Coll (IN)
Marygrove Coll (MI)
McNeese State U (LA)
Mesa State Coll (CO)
Mount Aloysius Coll (PA)
Mount Ida Coll (MA)
Mount St. Mary's Coll (CA)
Nova Southeastern U (FL)
Oglala Lakota Coll (SD)
Pacific Union Coll (CA)
Purdue U Calumet (IN)
Rivier Coll (NH)
State U of New York Coll of Agriculture and Technology at Cobleskill (NY)
Taylor U (IN)
Tennessee State U (TN)
Tougaloo Coll (MS)
U of Alaska Fairbanks (AK)
U of Arkansas at Pine Bluff (AR)
U of Great Falls (MT)
The U of Montana–Western (MT)
U of Rio Grande (OH)
U of Sioux Falls (SD)
Valley Forge Christian Coll (PA)
Villa Julie Coll (MD)
Western Kentucky U (KY)
Wilmington Coll (DE)

Kinesiology and Exercise Science
Atlantic Union Coll (MA)
Manchester Coll (IN)
Thomas More Coll (KY)

Labor and Industrial Relations
Indiana U Bloomington (IN)
Indiana U Kokomo (IN)
Indiana U Northwest (IN)
Indiana U–Purdue U Indianapolis (IN)
Indiana U South Bend (IN)
Indiana U Southeast (IN)
State U of New York Empire State Coll (NY)
Université Laval (QC, Canada)
The U of Akron (OH)
Youngstown State U (OH)

Labor Studies
Indiana U–Purdue U Fort Wayne (IN)

Landscape Architecture
Eastern Kentucky U (KY)
State U of New York Coll of Agriculture and Technology at Cobleskill (NY)
U of Arkansas at Little Rock (AR)
U of New Hampshire (NH)

Landscaping and Groundskeeping
Farmingdale State Coll (NY)
North Carolina State U (NC)
State U of New York Coll of Agriculture and Technology at Cobleskill (NY)
U of Massachusetts Amherst (MA)
U of New Hampshire (NH)
Vermont Tech Coll (VT)

Laser and Optical Technology
Excelsior Coll (NY)
Idaho State U (ID)
Indiana U Bloomington (IN)
Pennsylvania Coll of Technology (PA)

Latin
Idaho State U (ID)

Legal Administrative Assistant
Bryant and Stratton Coll, Cleveland (OH)

Legal Administrative Assistant/Secretary
Baker Coll of Auburn Hills (MI)
Baker Coll of Clinton Township (MI)
Baker Coll of Flint (MI)
Baker Coll of Jackson (MI)
Baker Coll of Muskegon (MI)
Baker Coll of Owosso (MI)
Baker Coll of Port Huron (MI)

Ball State U (IN)
Central Pennsylvania
Coll (PA)
Clarion U of
Pennsylvania (PA)
Clayton State U (GA)
Dordt Coll (IA)
Ferris State U (MI)
Lewis-Clark State Coll (ID)
Mesa State Coll (CO)
Minnesota School of
Business (MN)
Montana State
U–Billings (MT)
Montana Tech of The U of
Montana (MT)
Morrison U (NV)
Pacific Union Coll (CA)
Peirce Coll (PA)
Robert Morris Coll (IL)
Rogers State U (OK)
Shawnee State U (OH)
Sullivan U (KY)
The U of Akron (OH)
U of Cincinnati (OH)
The U of Montana (MT)
U of Richmond (VA)
U of Rio Grande (OH)
U of the District of
Columbia (DC)
The U of Toledo (OH)
Washburn U (KS)
Wright State U (OH)
Youngstown State U (OH)

**Legal Assistant/
Paralegal**
Anna Maria Coll (MA)
Atlantic Union Coll (MA)
Ball State U (IN)
Becker Coll (MA)
Bluefield State Coll (WV)
Boise State U (ID)
Briarcliffe Coll (NY)
Burlington Coll (VT)
Central Pennsylvania
Coll (PA)
Champlain Coll (VT)
Clayton State U (GA)
Coll of Mount St.
Joseph (OH)
Coll of Saint Mary (NE)
Eastern Kentucky U (KY)
Faulkner U (AL)
Ferris State U (MI)
Florida Metropolitan
U–Brandon
Campus (FL)
Florida Metropolitan
U–Lakeland
Campus (FL)
Florida Metropolitan
U–Pompano Beach
Campus (FL)
Gannon U (PA)
Grambling State U (LA)
Hilbert Coll (NY)
Husson Coll (ME)
Indiana U South Bend (IN)
International Coll (FL)
Johnson & Wales U (RI)
Jones Coll,
Jacksonville (FL)
Lake Superior State U (MI)
Lewis-Clark State Coll (ID)
Madonna U (MI)
Marywood U (PA)
McNeese State U (LA)
Merrimack Coll (MA)
Missouri Western State
U (MO)
Morrison U (NV)
Mountain State U (WV)
Mount Aloysius Coll (PA)
National American U,
Rapid City (SD)
Nicholls State U (LA)
Oglala Lakota Coll (SD)
Peirce Coll (PA)
Pennsylvania Coll of
Technology (PA)
Robert Morris Coll (IL)
Rogers State U (OK)
St. John's U (NY)
Saint Mary-of-the-Woods
Coll (IN)
Shawnee State U (OH)
South U (AL)
South U, West Palm
Beach (FL)
South U (GA)
South U (SC)
Suffolk U (MA)
Sullivan U (KY)
Tulane U (LA)
The U of Akron (OH)
U of Alaska
Anchorage (AK)
U of Alaska Fairbanks (AK)

U of Arkansas at Fort
Smith (AR)
U of Cincinnati (OH)
U of Great Falls (MT)
U of Louisville (KY)
The U of Montana (MT)
The U of Toledo (OH)
Utah Valley State Coll (UT)
Villa Julie Coll (MD)
Western Kentucky U (KY)
Widener U (PA)
William Woods U (MO)
Woodbury Coll (VT)

**Legal Professions and
Studies Related**
Peirce Coll (PA)

Legal Studies
Central Christian Coll of
Kansas (KS)
Clayton State U (GA)
Hilbert Coll (NY)
Lake Superior State U (MI)
Mountain State U (WV)
Ohio Dominican U (OH)
Sage Coll of Albany (NY)
Southeastern U (DC)
U of Alaska
Southeast (AK)
U of Hartford (CT)
The U of Montana (MT)
U of New Haven (CT)

**Liberal Arts and
Sciences And
Humanities Related**
Beacon Coll (FL)
Pennsylvania Coll of
Technology (PA)
The U of Akron (OH)

**Liberal Arts and
Sciences/Liberal
Studies**
Adams State Coll (CO)
Adelphi U (NY)
Alabama State U (AL)
Albertus Magnus Coll (CT)
Alverno Coll (WI)
The American U of Rome
(Italy)
Anderson U (SC)
Andrews U (MI)
Armstrong Atlantic State
U (GA)
Ashford U (IA)
Ashland U (OH)
Augusta State U (GA)
Austin Peay State U (TN)
Averett U (VA)
Ball State U (IN)
Beacon Coll (FL)
Becker Coll (MA)
Bemidji State U (MN)
Bethany Lutheran
Coll (MN)
Bethany U (CA)
Bethel U (MN)
Bluefield State Coll (WV)
Briar Cliff U (IA)
Bryan Coll (TN)
Bryn Athyn Coll of the New
Church (PA)
Burlington Coll (VT)
Butler U (IN)
Calumet Coll of Saint
Joseph (IN)
Campbell U (NC)
Cardinal Stritch U (WI)
Cazenovia Coll (NY)
Centenary Coll (NJ)
Champlain Coll (VT)
Charleston Southern
U (SC)
Charter Oak State
Coll (CT)
Christendom Coll (VA)
Clarion U of
Pennsylvania (PA)
Clarke Coll (IA)
Colby-Sawyer Coll (NH)
Coll of St. Catherine (MN)
Coll of St. Joseph (VT)
The Coll of Saint Thomas
More (TX)
Coll of Staten Island of the
City of New
York (NY)
Colorado Christian U (CO)
Columbia Coll (MO)
Columbus State U (GA)
Concordia Coll–New
York (NY)
Concordia U (OR)
Concordia U at Austin (TX)
Crossroads Coll (MN)
Crown Coll (MN)
Cumberland U (TN)

Dakota Wesleyan U (SD)
Dallas Baptist U (TX)
Daniel Webster Coll (NH)
Deree Coll, The American
College of Greece
(Greece)
Dickinson State U (ND)
Dominican Coll (NY)
Eastern U (PA)
East Texas Baptist U (TX)
East-West U (IL)
Edgewood Coll (WI)
Edinboro U of
Pennsylvania (PA)
Emmanuel Coll (MA)
Emory U (GA)
Endicott Coll (MA)
Excelsior Coll (NY)
Fairleigh Dickinson U,
Metropolitan
Campus (NJ)
Fairmont State U (WV)
Farmingdale State
Coll (NY)
Faulkner U (AL)
Felician Coll (NJ)
Ferris State U (MI)
Five Towns Coll (NY)
Florida Atlantic U (FL)
Florida Coll (FL)
Florida State U (FL)
Franklin Coll Switzerland
(Switzerland)
Fresno Pacific U (CA)
Gannon U (PA)
Glenville State Coll (WV)
Grace Bible Coll (MI)
Grand View Coll (IA)
Granite State Coll (NH)
Gwynedd-Mercy Coll (PA)
Hilbert Coll (NY)
Hillsdale Free Will Baptist
Coll (OK)
Houghton Coll (NY)
Indiana State U (IN)
John Brown U (AR)
Johnson State Coll (VT)
John Wesley Coll (NC)
Keene State Coll (NH)
Kent State U (OH)
Kentucky State U (KY)
Kuyper Coll (MI)
LaGrange Coll (GA)
Lake Superior State U (MI)
La Salle U (PA)
Lebanon Valley Coll (PA)
Lewis-Clark State Coll (ID)
Limestone Coll (SC)
Loras Coll (IA)
Lourdes Coll (OH)
Lyndon State Coll (VT)
Macon State Coll (GA)
Marian Coll (IN)
Marietta Coll (OH)
Marygrove Coll (MI)
Marymount U (VA)
Medaille Coll (NY)
Medgar Evers Coll of the
City U of New
York (NY)
Mercy Coll (NY)
Mercyhurst Coll (PA)
Merrimack Coll (MA)
Mesa State Coll (CO)
Methodist U (NC)
Midwestern State U (TX)
Millersville U of
Pennsylvania (PA)
Minnesota State U
Mankato (MN)
Missouri Valley Coll (MO)
Molloy Coll (NY)
Montana State
U–Billings (MT)
Montana Tech of The U of
Montana (MT)
Mountain State U (WV)
Mount Aloysius Coll (PA)
Mount Marty Coll (SD)
Mount Olive Coll (NC)
Mount St. Mary's Coll (CA)
Murray State U (KY)
National American U,
Rapid City (SD)
Neumann Coll (PA)
New England Coll (NH)
Newman U (KS)
New York U (NY)
Niagara U (NY)
Nicholls State U (LA)
Northern Michigan U (MI)
Northern State U (SD)
North Greenville U (SC)
Northwestern Coll (MN)
Nyack Coll (NY)
Oglala Lakota Coll (SD)
The Ohio State U at
Lima (OH)

The Ohio State U at
Marion (OH)
The Ohio State
U–Mansfield
Campus (OH)
The Ohio State U–Newark
Campus (OH)
Ohio U (OH)
Ohio U–Zanesville (OH)
Ohio Valley U (WV)
Oklahoma Wesleyan
U (OK)
Oregon Inst of
Technology (OR)
Pace U (NY)
Park U (MO)
Patten U (CA)
Paul Smith's Coll of Arts
and Sciences (NY)
Peace Coll (NC)
Penn State Abington (PA)
Penn State Altoona (PA)
Penn State Berks (PA)
Penn State Erie, The
Behrend Coll (PA)
Penn State Harrisburg (PA)
Penn State Park (PA)
Pennsylvania Coll of
Technology (PA)
Pine Manor Coll (MA)
Reinhardt Coll (GA)
Rider U (NJ)
Rivier Coll (NH)
Rochester Coll (MI)
Rocky Mountain Coll (MT)
Rogers State U (OK)
Roger Williams U (RI)
Sacred Heart U (CT)
Sage Coll of Albany (NY)
St. Augustine Coll (IL)
St. Cloud State U (MN)
St. Francis Coll (NY)
St. Gregory's U,
Shawnee (OK)
St. John's U (NY)
Saint Joseph's U (PA)
Saint Leo U (FL)
Saint Mary-of-the-Woods
Coll (IN)
Salem International
U (WV)
Salve Regina U (RI)
Schiller International
U (FL)
Schiller International U
(France)
Schiller International U
(Germany)
Schiller International U
(Spain)
Schiller International U
(United Kingdom)
Schiller International U,
American Coll of
Switzerland
(Switzerland)
Simon's Rock Coll of
Bard (MA)
Southern Connecticut
State U (CT)
Southern New Hampshire
U (NH)
Southern Polytechnic State
U (GA)
Southern Vermont
Coll (VT)
Spring Arbor U (MI)
State U of New York Coll
of Agriculture and
Technology at
Cobleskill (NY)
Stephens Coll (MO)
Sterling Coll (VT)
Taylor U Fort Wayne (IN)
Thiel Coll (PA)
Thomas Coll (ME)
Thomas More Coll (KY)
Thomas U (GA)
Tri-State U (IN)
Troy U (AL)
The U of Akron (OH)
U of Alaska Fairbanks (AK)
U of Alaska
Southeast (AK)
U of Arkansas at Fort
Smith (AR)
U of Arkansas at
Monticello (AR)
U of Bridgeport (CT)
U of Central Florida (FL)
U of Cincinnati (OH)
U of Delaware (DE)
U of Hartford (CT)
U of Indianapolis (IN)
U of La Verne (CA)
The U of Maine at
Augusta (ME)

U of Maine at Presque
Isle (ME)
U of New Hampshire (NH)
U of New Hampshire at
Manchester (NH)
U of Pittsburgh at
Bradford (PA)
U of Saint Francis (IN)
U of Saint Mary (KS)
U of South Carolina
Beaufort (SC)
U of South Florida (FL)
The U of Toledo (OH)
U of West Florida (FL)
U of Wisconsin–Eau
Claire (WI)
U of Wisconsin–
Oshkosh (WI)
U of Wisconsin–
Platteville (WI)
U of Wisconsin–Stevens
Point (WI)
U of
Wisconsin–Whitewater (WI)
Upper Iowa U (IA)
Valdosta State U (GA)
Villa Julie Coll (MD)
Villanova U (PA)
Virginia Intermont Coll (VA)
Walsh U (OH)
Washburn U (KS)
Waynesburg Coll (PA)
Weber State U (UT)
Western Connecticut State
U (CT)
Western International
U (AZ)
Western New England
Coll (MA)
Western Oregon U (OR)
West Virginia State U (WV)
Wichita State U (KS)
Williams Baptist Coll (AR)
Wilson Coll (PA)
Xavier U (OH)
York Coll (NE)
York Coll of
Pennsylvania (PA)
Youngstown State U (OH)

Library Assistant
Ohio Dominican U (OH)
The U of Maine at
Augusta (ME)

Library Science
Mountain State U (WV)
U of the District of
Columbia (DC)

Lineworker
Utah Valley State Coll (UT)

Linguistics
Oklahoma Wesleyan
U (OK)

Literature
John Cabot U (Italy)
Manchester Coll (IN)
Sacred Heart U (CT)
Université Laval (QC,
Canada)

**Livestock
Management**
Sterling Coll (VT)

**Logistics and
Materials Management**
Park U (MO)
The U of Akron (OH)
The U of Toledo (OH)

**Machine Shop
Technology**
Dalton State Coll (GA)
Georgia Southwestern
State U (GA)
Pennsylvania Coll of
Technology (PA)

**Machine Tool
Technology**
Boise State U (ID)
British Columbia Inst of
Technology (BC,
Canada)
Ferris State U (MI)
Georgia Southwestern
State U (GA)
Idaho State U (ID)
Mesa State Coll (CO)
Missouri Southern State
U (MO)
Utah Valley State Coll (UT)
Vaughn Coll of Aeronautics
and Technology (NY)
Weber State U (UT)

**Management
Information Systems**
Arkansas State U (AR)
Cameron U (OK)
Central Pennsylvania
Coll (PA)
Colorado Christian U (CO)
Columbia Coll,
Caguas (PR)
Daniel Webster Coll (NH)
Davenport U,
Dearborn (MI)
Florida Metropolitan
U–Pompano Beach
Campus (FL)
Georgia Southwestern
State U (GA)
Globe Inst of
Technology (NY)
Hilbert Coll (NY)
Husson Coll (ME)
Inter American U of Puerto
Rico, Bayamón
Campus (PR)
Johnson State Coll (VT)
Lake Superior State U (MI)
Lindsey Wilson Coll (KY)
Lock Haven U of
Pennsylvania (PA)
Morehead State U (KY)
Northern Michigan U (MI)
Northwood U (MI)
Northwood U, Texas
Campus (TX)
Peirce Coll (PA)
Robert Morris Coll (IL)
St. Augustine Coll (IL)
Saint Joseph's Coll (IN)
Saint Joseph's U (PA)
Shawnee State U (OH)
Southeastern U (DC)
Taylor U (IN)
Thiel Coll (PA)
U of Management and
Technology (VA)
Weber State U (UT)
Wilson Coll (PA)
Wright State U (OH)

**Management
Information Systems
and Services Related**
Coll of Mount St.
Joseph (OH)
Davis & Elkins Coll (WV)
Purdue U (IN)
U of Southern Indiana (IN)

Management Science
British Columbia Inst of
Technology (BC,
Canada)
Mountain State U (WV)

**Manufacturing
Technology**
Excelsior Coll (NY)
Lawrence Technological
U (MI)
Lewis-Clark State Coll (ID)
Missouri Western State
U (MO)
Penn State Erie, The
Behrend Coll (PA)
Pennsylvania Coll of
Technology (PA)
Thompson Rivers U (BC,
Canada)
Utah Valley State Coll (UT)

**Marine Science/
Merchant Marine
Officer**
State U of New York
Maritime Coll (NY)
U of the District of
Columbia (DC)

**Marketing/Marketing
Management**
Baker Coll of Allen
Park (MI)
Baker Coll of Auburn
Hills (MI)
Baker Coll of Cadillac (MI)
Baker Coll of Clinton
Township (MI)
Baker Coll of Flint (MI)
Baker Coll of Jackson (MI)
Baker Coll of
Muskegon (MI)
Baker Coll of Owosso (MI)
Baker Coll of Port
Huron (MI)
Ball State U (IN)
Bluefield State Coll (WV)
Boise State U (ID)
British Columbia Inst of
Technology (BC,
Canada)

Central Christian Coll of
  Kansas (KS)
Central Pennsylvania
  Coll (PA)
Champlain Coll (VT)
Chestnut Hill Coll (PA)
Clayton State U (GA)
Dalton State Coll (GA)
Daniel Webster Coll (NH)
Davenport U,
  Dearborn (MI)
Five Towns Coll (NY)
Florida Metropolitan
  U–Brandon
  Campus (FL)
Florida Metropolitan
  U–Lakeland
  Campus (FL)
Florida Metropolitan
  U–Pompano Beach
  Campus (FL)
Georgia Southwestern
  State U (GA)
Hawai'i Pacific U (HI)
Idaho State U (ID)
Inter American U of Puerto
  Rico, Fajardo
  Campus (PR)
Johnson & Wales U (CO)
Johnson & Wales U (FL)
Johnson & Wales U (RI)
Mountain State U (WV)
New England School of
  Communications (ME)
Peirce Coll (PA)
Purdue U North
  Central (IN)
Sage Coll of Albany (NY)
Saint Joseph's U (PA)
Saint Peter's Coll (NJ)
Southeastern U (DC)
Southern New Hampshire
  U (NH)
Southwest Minnesota
  State U (MN)
Sullivan U (KY)
Tulane U (LA)
U of Bridgeport (CT)
U of Cincinnati (OH)
U of Management and
  Technology (VA)
U of Sioux Falls (SD)
U of the District of
  Columbia (DC)
Walsh U (OH)
Webber International
  U (FL)
Weber State U (UT)
West Virginia State U (WV)
Wright State U (OH)
Youngstown State U (OH)

Marketing Related
Fashion Inst of
  Technology (NY)

Masonry
Pennsylvania Coll of
  Technology (PA)

Massage Therapy
Minnesota School of
  Business (MN)

**Mass Communication/
Media**
Adrian Coll (MI)
Black Hills State U (SD)
Central Pennsylvania
  Coll (PA)
Champlain Coll (VT)
Clayton State U (GA)
Cornerstone U (MI)
Evangel U (MO)
Five Towns Coll (NY)
Fresno Pacific U (CA)
Inter American U of Puerto
  Rico, Bayamón
  Campus (PR)
Macon State Coll (GA)
Madonna U (MI)
Methodist U (NC)
Oglala Lakota Coll (SD)
Pennsylvania Coll of
  Technology (PA)
Sacred Heart U (CT)
Sage Coll of Albany (NY)
Salem International
  U (WV)
U of Rio Grande (OH)
Villa Julie Coll (MD)
Wilson Coll (PA)

**Mass
Communications**
John Cabot U (Italy)

Materials Science
U of New Hampshire (NH)

Mathematics
Central Christian Coll of
  Kansas (KS)
Clayton State U (GA)
Creighton U (NE)
Dalton State Coll (GA)
Felician Coll (NJ)
Fresno Pacific U (CA)
Hillsdale Free Will Baptist
  Coll (OK)
Idaho State U (ID)
Indiana U East (IN)
Indiana U–Purdue U Fort
  Wayne (IN)
Indiana Wesleyan U (IN)
Lindsey Wilson Coll (KY)
Macon State Coll (GA)
Mesa State Coll (CO)
Methodist U (NC)
Rogers State U (OK)
Sacred Heart U (CT)
State U of New York
  Empire State Coll (NY)
Thomas More Coll (KY)
Thomas U (GA)
Tri-State U (IN)
U of Great Falls (MT)
U of Rio Grande (OH)
The U of Tampa (FL)
U of Wisconsin–Green
  Bay (WI)
Utah Valley State Coll (UT)
York Coll of
  Pennsylvania (PA)

**Mathematics and
Computer Science**
Immaculata U (PA)

**Mathematics Teacher
Education**
Central Christian Coll of
  Kansas (KS)

**Mechanical Design
Technology**
Clayton State U (GA)
Ferris State U (MI)

Mechanical Drafting
Cameron U (OK)

**Mechanical Drafting
and Cad/Cadd**
Baker Coll of Flint (MI)
British Columbia Inst of
  Technology (BC,
  Canada)
Cameron U (OK)
Indiana U–Purdue U
  Indianapolis (IN)
Montana Tech of The U of
  Montana (MT)
Purdue U (IN)

**Mechanical
Engineering**
Fairfield U (CT)
Macon State Coll (GA)

**Mechanical
Engineering/
Mechanical
Technology**
Andrews U (MI)
Baker Coll of Flint (MI)
Bluefield State Coll (WV)
British Columbia Inst of
  Technology (BC,
  Canada)
Fairmont State U (WV)
Farmingdale State
  Coll (NY)
Ferris State U (MI)
Indiana U–Purdue U Fort
  Wayne (IN)
Indiana U–Purdue U
  Indianapolis (IN)
Lake Superior State U (MI)
Lawrence Technological
  U (MI)
Michigan Technological
  U (MI)
Murray State U (KY)
New York Inst of
  Technology (NY)
Penn State Altoona (PA)
Penn State Berks (PA)
Penn State Erie, The
  Behrend Coll (PA)
Point Park U (PA)
Purdue U Calumet (IN)
Purdue U North
  Central (IN)
Rochester Inst of
  Technology (NY)
The U of Akron (OH)
U of Arkansas at Little
  Rock (AR)
U of Cincinnati (OH)

U of Massachusetts
  Lowell (MA)
U of Rio Grande (OH)
U of the District of
  Columbia (DC)
The U of Toledo (OH)
Vermont Tech Coll (VT)
Weber State U (UT)
Wentworth Inst of
  Technology (MA)
Youngstown State U (OH)

**Mechanical
Engineering
Technologies Related**
Purdue U (IN)

**Mechanic and Repair
Technologies Related**
Bob Jones U (SC)
Pennsylvania Coll of
  Technology (PA)

Mechanics and Repair
Idaho State U (ID)
Lewis-Clark State Coll (ID)

**Medical
Administrative
Assistant**
Minnesota School of
  Business (MN)

**Medical
Administrative
Assistant and Medical
Secretary**
Baker Coll of Auburn
  Hills (MI)
Baker Coll of Cadillac (MI)
Baker Coll of Clinton
  Township (MI)
Baker Coll of Flint (MI)
Baker Coll of Jackson (MI)
Baker Coll of
  Muskegon (MI)
Baker Coll of Owosso (MI)
Baker Coll of Port
  Huron (MI)
Boise State U (ID)
British Columbia Inst of
  Technology (BC,
  Canada)
Central Pennsylvania
  Coll (PA)
Dickinson State U (ND)
Hannibal-LaGrange
  Coll (MO)
Mesa State Coll (CO)
Monroe Coll, Bronx (NY)
Montana State
  U–Billings (MT)
Montana Tech of The U of
  Montana (MT)
Morrison U (NV)
Pacific Union Coll (CA)
Pennsylvania Coll of
  Technology (PA)
Sullivan U (KY)
Universidad Adventista de
  las Antillas (PR)
The U of Akron (OH)
U of Cincinnati (OH)
The U of Montana (MT)
U of Rio Grande (OH)
Wright State U (OH)

**Medical/Clinical
Assistant**
Argosy U, Orange
  County (CA)
Argosy U, Twin Cities,
  Eagan (MN)
Arkansas Tech U (AR)
Baker Coll of Allen
  Park (MI)
Baker Coll of Auburn
  Hills (MI)
Baker Coll of Cadillac (MI)
Baker Coll of Clinton
  Township (MI)
Baker Coll of Flint (MI)
Baker Coll of Jackson (MI)
Baker Coll of
  Muskegon (MI)
Baker Coll of Owosso (MI)
Baker Coll of Port
  Huron (MI)
Bluefield State Coll (WV)
Cabarrus Coll of Health
  Sciences (NC)
Central Pennsylvania
  Coll (PA)
Clayton State U (GA)
Davenport U,
  Dearborn (MI)
Eastern Kentucky U (KY)
Faulkner U (AL)

Florida Metropolitan
  U–Brandon
  Campus (FL)
Georgia Southwestern
  State U (GA)
Idaho State U (ID)
International Coll (FL)
Jones Coll,
  Jacksonville (FL)
Montana State
  U–Billings (MT)
Mountain State U (WV)
Mount Aloysius Coll (PA)
National American U,
  Denver (CO)
Ohio U (OH)
Palmer Coll of
  Chiropractic (IA)
Presentation Coll (SD)
Robert Morris Coll (IL)
South (AL)
South U, West Palm
  Beach (FL)
South U (GA)
South U (SC)
The U of Akron (OH)
U of Alaska
  Anchorage (AK)
U of Alaska Fairbanks (AK)
The U of Toledo (OH)
West Virginia State U (WV)
Youngstown State U (OH)

**Medical/Health
Management and
Clinical Assistant**
Lewis-Clark State Coll (ID)
National American U,
  Denver (CO)

Medical Illustration
Clayton State U (GA)

**Medical Insurance
Coding**
Baker Coll of Allen
  Park (MI)

**Medical Insurance/
Medical Billing**
Baker Coll of Allen
  Park (MI)

**Medical Laboratory
Technology**
Argosy U, Twin Cities,
  Eagan (MN)
British Columbia Inst of
  Technology (BC,
  Canada)
Evangel U (MO)
ITT Tech Inst, Tempe (AZ)
Villa Julie Coll (MD)

**Medical Office
Assistant**
Lewis-Clark State Coll (ID)
Mercy Coll of Health
  Sciences (IA)

**Medical Office
Computer Specialist**
Baker Coll of Allen
  Park (MI)

**Medical Office
Management**
Dalton State Coll (GA)
The U of Akron (OH)

**Medical Radiologic
Technology**
Argosy U, Twin Cities,
  Eagan (MN)
Arkansas State U (AR)
Bluefield State Coll (WV)
British Columbia Inst of
  Technology (BC,
  Canada)
Coll of St. Catherine (MN)
Fairleigh Dickinson U, Coll
  at Florham (NJ)
Fairleigh Dickinson U,
  Metropolitan
  Campus (NJ)
Gannon U (PA)
Georgia Southwestern
  State U (GA)
Idaho State U (ID)
Indiana U Northwest (IN)
Indiana U–Purdue U
  Indianapolis (IN)
Indiana U South Bend (IN)
La Roche Coll (PA)
Loma Linda U (CA)
Mercy Coll of Health
  Sciences (IA)
Missouri Southern State
  U (MO)
Morehead State U (KY)
Mountain State U (WV)

Northern Kentucky U (KY)
Pennsylvania Coll of
  Technology (PA)
Presentation Coll (SD)
Shawnee State U (OH)
Trinity Coll of Nursing and
  Health Sciences (IL)
The U of Akron (OH)
U of New Mexico (NM)
U of Saint Francis (IN)
U of Southern Indiana (IN)
Weber State U (UT)

Medical Transcription
Baker Coll of Flint (MI)
Baker Coll of Jackson (MI)
Dalton State Coll (GA)
Presentation Coll (SD)

**Mental and Social
Health Services And
Allied Professions
Related**
U of Alaska Fairbanks (AK)
The U of Maine at
  Augusta (ME)

**Mental Health
Counseling**
Washburn U (KS)

**Mental
Health/Rehabilitation**
Evangel U (MO)
Felician Coll (NJ)
Lake Superior State U (MI)
St. Augustine Coll (IL)
The U of Toledo (OH)

Merchandising
Clayton State U (GA)
The U of Akron (OH)

**Merchandising, Sales,
and Marketing
Operations Related
(General)**
Clayton State U (GA)

**Merchandising, Sales,
and Marketing
Operations Related
(Specialized)**
Clayton State U (GA)

**Metal and Jewelry
Arts**
Academy of Art U (CA)
Fashion Inst of
  Technology (NY)
Miami International U of
  Art & Design (FL)
Rochester Inst of
  Technology (NY)

**Metallurgical
Technology**
Penn State Altoona (PA)
Penn State Berks (PA)
Penn State Erie, The
  Behrend Coll (PA)
Purdue U Calumet (IN)

Microbiology
Canadian Mennonite U
  (MB, Canada)
Inter American U of Puerto
  Rico, Barranquitas
  Campus (PR)

**Middle School
Education**
Dalton State Coll (GA)
U of Arkansas at Fort
  Smith (AR)

Military Studies
American Public U
  System (WV)
Hawai'i Pacific U (HI)

Military Technologies
Murray State U (KY)

Mining Technology
British Columbia Inst of
  Technology (BC,
  Canada)

**Missionary Studies
and Missiology**
Bob Jones U (SC)
Central Christian Coll of
  Kansas (KS)
Faith Baptist Bible Coll and
  Theological
  Seminary (IA)
God's Bible School and
  Coll (OH)
Hillsdale Free Will Baptist
  Coll (OK)
Hope International U (CA)

Modern Languages
Macon State Coll (GA)
Sacred Heart U (CT)

**Molecular
Biochemistry**
Sacred Heart U (CT)

**Mortuary Science and
Embalming**
Ferris State U (MI)

**Multi-/Interdisciplinary
Studies Related**
Arkansas Tech U (AR)
International Coll (FL)
Ohio U (OH)
Pennsylvania Coll of
  Technology (PA)
Sterling Coll (VT)
The U of Akron (OH)
U of Alaska Fairbanks (AK)
U of Arkansas at Fort
  Smith (AR)
The U of Toledo (OH)

Music
Alverno Coll (WI)
Brigham Young
  U–Hawaii (HI)
Central Baptist Coll (AR)
Clayton State U (GA)
Crown Coll (MN)
Dallas Baptist U (TX)
Five Towns Coll (NY)
Fresno Pacific U (CA)
Hillsdale Free Will Baptist
  Coll (OK)
Indiana Wesleyan U (IN)
John Brown U (AR)
Kwantlen U Coll (BC,
  Canada)
Lourdes Coll (OH)
Macon State Coll (GA)
Marian Coll (IN)
Mesa State Coll (CO)
Methodist U (NC)
Mount Olive Coll (NC)
Mount Vernon Nazarene
  U (OH)
Peace Coll (NC)
Sacred Heart U (CT)
Shawnee State U (OH)
Thomas More Coll (KY)
The U of Maine at
  Augusta (ME)
U of Rio Grande (OH)
The U of Tampa (FL)
U of the District of
  Columbia (DC)
Utah Valley State Coll (UT)
Williams Baptist Coll (AR)
York Coll of
  Pennsylvania (PA)

**Musical Instrument
Fabrication and
Repair**
Indiana U Bloomington (IN)

**Music History,
Literature, and Theory**
Central Christian Coll of
  Kansas (KS)

**Music Management
and Merchandising**
Five Towns Coll (NY)
The New England Inst of
  Art (MA)

Music Performance
Central Christian Coll of
  Kansas (KS)
New World School of the
  Arts (FL)
Northwestern Coll (MN)

Music Related
Minnesota School of
  Business (MN)

**Music Teacher
Education**
Central Christian Coll of
  Kansas (KS)
Union Coll (NE)

**Music Theory and
Composition**
Kwantlen U Coll (BC,
  Canada)
New World School of the
  Arts (FL)

**Natural Resources
and Conservation
Related**
Sterling Coll (VT)

**Natural Resources/
Conservation**
Sterling Coll (VT)

U of Alaska
Southeast (AK)
U of Minnesota,
Crookston (MN)

**Natural Resources/
Conservation Related**
Sterling Coll (VT)

**Natural Resources
Management**
Sterling Coll (VT)

**Natural Resources
Management and
Policy**
Lake Superior State U (MI)
Oglala Lakota Coll (SD)
Sterling Coll (VT)
U of Alaska Fairbanks (AK)
U of Minnesota,
Crookston (MN)

Natural Sciences
Alderson-Broaddus
Coll (WV)
Charleston Southern
U (SC)
Felician Coll (NJ)
Fresno Pacific U (CA)
Lourdes Coll (OH)
Madonna U (MI)
Medgar Evers Coll of the
City U of New
York (NY)
Roberts Wesleyan
Coll (NY)
Shawnee State U (OH)
Sterling Coll (VT)
U of Cincinnati (OH)
U of Puerto Rico at
Utuado (PR)
The U of Toledo (OH)
Utah Valley State Coll (UT)
Villanova U (PA)
Washburn U (KS)

**Naval Architecture
and Marine
Engineering**
British Columbia Inst of
Technology (BC,
Canada)
Maine Maritime
Academy (ME)

**Nuclear Engineering
Technology**
Arkansas Tech U (AR)
Excelsior Coll (NY)

**Nuclear Medical
Technology**
Ball State U (IN)
British Columbia Inst of
Technology (BC,
Canada)
Dalton State Coll (GA)
Ferris State U (MI)
The George Washington
U (DC)
Molloy Coll (NY)
The U of Findlay (OH)
West Virginia State U (WV)

**Nursing
Administration**
British Columbia Inst of
Technology (BC,
Canada)

**Nursing Assistant/
Aide and Patient Care
Assistant**
Cabarrus Coll of Health
Sciences (NC)
Central Christian Coll of
Kansas (KS)
Montana Tech of The U of
Montana (MT)

**Nursing (Licensed
Practical/Vocational
Nurse Training)**
Central Christian Coll of
Kansas (KS)
Dickinson State U (ND)
Georgia Southwestern
State U (GA)
Lewis-Clark State Coll (ID)
Medgar Evers Coll of the
City U of New
York (NY)
Montana State
U–Billings (MT)
Pennsylvania Coll of
Technology (PA)
Thompson Rivers U (BC,
Canada)
The U of Montana (MT)

U of the District of
Columbia (DC)
Vermont Tech Coll (VT)
Virginia State U (VA)

**Nursing (Registered
Nurse Training)**
Alcorn State U (MS)
Angelo State U (TX)
Arkansas State U (AR)
Atlantic Union Coll (MA)
Augusta State U (GA)
Baker Coll of Clinton
Township (MI)
Baker Coll of Flint (MI)
Baker Coll of
Muskegon (MI)
Baker Coll of Owosso (MI)
Ball State U (IN)
Barnes-Jewish Coll of
Nursing and Allied
Health (MO)
Becker Coll (MA)
Bluefield State Coll (WV)
Boise State U (ID)
British Columbia Inst of
Technology (BC,
Canada)
Cabarrus Coll of Health
Sciences (NC)
Cardinal Stritch U (WI)
Castleton State Coll (VT)
Central Christian Coll of
Kansas (KS)
Clarion U of
Pennsylvania (PA)
Coll of Saint Mary (NE)
Coll of Staten Island of the
City U of New
York (NY)
Columbia Coll (MO)
Columbia Coll,
Caguas (PR)
Dakota Wesleyan U (SD)
Dalton State Coll (GA)
Davenport U,
Dearborn (MI)
Davis & Elkins Coll (WV)
Eastern Kentucky U (KY)
Excelsior Coll (NY)
Fairmont State U (WV)
Farmingdale State
Coll (NY)
Felician Coll (NJ)
Ferris State U (MI)
Gardner-Webb U (NC)
Gwynedd-Mercy Coll (PA)
Hannibal-LaGrange
Coll (MO)
Hillsdale Free Will Baptist
Coll (OK)
Houston Baptist U (TX)
Indiana U East (IN)
Indiana U Kokomo (IN)
Indiana U Northwest (IN)
Indiana U–Purdue U Fort
Wayne (IN)
Indiana U–Purdue U
Indianapolis (IN)
Indiana U South Bend (IN)
Inter American U of Puerto
Rico, Barranquitas
Campus (PR)
Inter American U of Puerto
Rico, Fajardo
Campus (PR)
Kent State U (OH)
Kentucky State U (KY)
Lincoln Memorial U (TN)
Lincoln U (MO)
Lock Haven U of
Pennsylvania (PA)
Loma Linda U (CA)
Louisiana Tech U (LA)
Macon State Coll (GA)
Marshall U (WV)
McNeese State U (LA)
Mercy Coll of Health
Sciences (IA)
Mercyhurst Coll (PA)
Mesa State Coll (CO)
Midway Coll (KY)
Montana Tech of The U of
Montana (MT)
Morehead State U (KY)
Mount Aloysius Coll (PA)
Mount St. Mary's Coll (CA)
Nebraska Methodist
Coll (NE)
Nicholls State U (LA)
Northern Kentucky U (KY)
North Georgia Coll & State
U (GA)
Northwestern State U of
Louisiana (LA)
Oakwood Coll (AL)
Oglala Lakota Coll (SD)
Ohio U–Zanesville (OH)

Oklahoma Panhandle
State U (OK)
Our Lady of the Lake
Coll (LA)
Pacific Union Coll (CA)
Park U (MO)
Penn State Altoona (PA)
Pennsylvania Coll of
Technology (PA)
Pikeville Coll (KY)
Presentation Coll (SD)
Purdue U Calumet (IN)
Purdue U North
Central (IN)
Regis Coll (MA)
Reinhardt Coll (GA)
Rivier Coll (NH)
Rogers State U (OK)
Shawnee State U (OH)
Southern Adventist U (TN)
Southern Arkansas
U–Magnolia (AR)
Southern Vermont
Coll (VT)
Southwest Baptist U (MO)
Sul Ross State U (TX)
Tennessee State U (TN)
Thomas U (GA)
Trinity Coll of Nursing and
Health Sciences (IL)
Troy U (AL)
Universidad Adventista de
las Antillas (PR)
U of Alaska
Anchorage (AK)
U of Arkansas at Fort
Smith (AR)
U of Arkansas at Little
Rock (AR)
U of Charleston (WV)
U of Cincinnati (OH)
U of Indianapolis (IN)
The U of Maine at
Augusta (ME)
U of Mobile (AL)
U of New England (ME)
U of Pittsburgh at
Bradford (PA)
U of Puerto Rico at
Humacao (PR)
U of Rio Grande (OH)
U of Saint Francis (IN)
U of South Carolina
Upstate (SC)
The U of South
Dakota (SD)
U of Southern Indiana (IN)
U of the District of
Columbia (DC)
U of the Virgin Islands (VI)
The U of Toledo (OH)
The U of West
Alabama (AL)
Utah Valley State Coll (UT)
Vermont Tech Coll (VT)
Walsh U (OH)
Warner Pacific Coll (OR)
Weber State U (UT)
Western Kentucky U (KY)

Nursing Related
British Columbia Inst of
Technology (BC,
Canada)
Inter American U of Puerto
Rico, Aguadilla
Campus (PR)
Madonna U (MI)
Rogers State U (OK)

Nursing Science
Davenport U,
Dearborn (MI)
La Roche Coll (PA)
National U (CA)
Trinity Coll of Nursing and
Health Sciences (IL)

**Occupational Health
and Industrial
Hygiene**
British Columbia Inst of
Technology (BC,
Canada)

**Occupational Safety
and Health
Technology**
Ferris State U (MI)
Indiana U Bloomington (IN)
Montana Tech of The U of
Montana (MT)
Southwest Baptist U (MO)
U of Cincinnati (OH)
U of New Haven (CT)
Wright State U (OH)

**Occupational
Therapist Assistant**
Baker Coll of
Muskegon (MI)

Cabarrus Coll of Health
Sciences (NC)
California U of
Pennsylvania (PA)
Clarion U of
Pennsylvania (PA)
Coll of St. Catherine (MN)
Idaho State U (ID)
Loma Linda U (CA)
Mercy Coll (NY)
Mountain State U (WV)
Mount Aloysius Coll (PA)
Mount St. Mary's Coll (CA)
Pennsylvania Coll of
Technology (PA)
U of Louisiana at
Monroe (LA)
U of Puerto Rico at
Humacao (PR)
U of Saint Francis (IN)
U of Southern Indiana (IN)

Occupational Therapy
Clayton State U (GA)
Dalton State Coll (GA)
Faulkner U (AL)
Oakwood Coll (AL)
Shawnee State U (OH)
Southern Adventist U (TN)

Office Management
Baker Coll of Flint (MI)
Baker Coll of Jackson (MI)
Dakota State U (SD)
Dalton State Coll (GA)
Emmanuel Coll (GA)
God's Bible School and
Coll (OH)
Lake Superior State U (MI)
Mercyhurst Coll (PA)
Mountain State U (WV)
Park U (MO)
Peirce Coll (PA)
Shawnee State U (OH)
Thompson Rivers U (BC,
Canada)
Washburn U (KS)

**Office Occupations
and Clerical Services**
Bob Jones U (SC)
Georgia Southwestern
State U (GA)
Pennsylvania Coll of
Technology (PA)
U of Alaska Fairbanks (AK)
U of Puerto Rico at
Utuado (PR)
Wright State U (OH)

**Operations
Management**
Baker Coll of Flint (MI)
British Columbia Inst of
Technology (BC,
Canada)
Indiana U–Purdue U Fort
Wayne (IN)
Indiana U–Purdue U
Indianapolis (IN)
Northern Kentucky U (KY)
Purdue U (IN)

**Ophthalmic
Laboratory
Technology**
Central Pennsylvania
Coll (PA)
Indiana U Bloomington (IN)
Rochester Inst of
Technology (NY)

Opticianry
Ferris State U (MI)
The U of Akron (OH)

Optometric Technician
Indiana U Bloomington (IN)

**Organizational
Communication**
Creighton U (NE)

**Ornamental
Horticulture**
Farmingdale State
Coll (NY)
Ferris State U (MI)
Pennsylvania Coll of
Technology (PA)
State U of New York Coll
of Agriculture and
Technology at
Cobleskill (NY)
U of Massachusetts
Amherst (MA)
Utah State U (UT)

Orthotics/Prosthetics
Baker Coll of Flint (MI)

Painting
Academy of Art U (CA)

The Art Inst of
Pittsburgh (PA)
New World School of the
Arts (FL)
Pratt Inst (NY)

**Paralegal/Legal
Assistant**
American Public U
System (WV)
Argosy U, Orange
County (CA)
Bryant and Stratton Coll,
Cleveland (OH)
Davenport U,
Dearborn (MI)
Minnesota School of
Business (MN)
Newman U (KS)
Utah Valley State Coll (UT)

**Parks, Recreation and
Leisure**
Central Christian Coll of
Kansas (KS)
Clayton State U (GA)
Johnson & Wales U (NC)
Johnson & Wales U (RI)
Mount Olive Coll (NC)
Oklahoma Panhandle
State U (OK)
U of Maine at Presque
Isle (ME)
U of the District of
Columbia (DC)
Utah Valley State Coll (UT)

**Parks, Recreation and
Leisure Facilities
Management**
Eastern Kentucky U (KY)
Indiana Tech (IN)
Johnson & Wales U (NC)
Johnson & Wales U (RI)
Paul Smith's Coll of Arts
and Sciences (NY)
State U of New York Coll
of Agriculture and
Technology at
Cobleskill (NY)

**Pastoral Studies/
Counseling**
Boise Bible Coll (ID)
Indiana Wesleyan U (IN)
Notre Dame Coll (OH)
Oakwood Coll (AL)

**Peace Studies and
Conflict Resolution**
Woodbury Coll (VT)

Pediatric Nursing
British Columbia Inst of
Technology (BC,
Canada)

Perfusion Technology
Boise State U (ID)
Thompson Rivers U (BC,
Canada)

**Perioperative/Operating
Room and Surgical
Nursing**
British Columbia Inst of
Technology (BC,
Canada)

**Personal and Culinary
Services Related**
The Art Inst of
Pittsburgh (PA)
Lexington Coll (IL)

Petroleum Technology
British Columbia Inst of
Technology (BC,
Canada)
McNeese State U (LA)
Montana State
U–Billings (MT)
Montana Tech of The U of
Montana (MT)
Nicholls State U (LA)
U of Alaska
Anchorage (AK)

Pharmacy
Clayton State U (GA)

Pharmacy Technician
Baker Coll of Flint (MI)
Baker Coll of Jackson (MI)
Baker Coll of
Muskegon (MI)
Florida Metropolitan
U–Brandon
Campus (FL)
Idaho State U (ID)
Inter American U of Puerto
Rico, Aguadilla
Campus (PR)

Mount Aloysius Coll (PA)

Philosophy
Clayton State U (GA)
Dalton State Coll (GA)
Felician Coll (NJ)
Kwantlen U Coll (BC,
Canada)
Methodist U (NC)
Sacred Heart U (CT)
Thomas More Coll (KY)
Université Laval (QC,
Canada)
The U of Tampa (FL)
U of the District of
Columbia (DC)
U of Wisconsin–Green
Bay (WI)
Utah Valley State Coll (UT)
York Coll of
Pennsylvania (PA)

**Photographic and
Film/Video
Technology**
Burlington Coll (VT)
New England School of
Communications (ME)

Photography
Academy of Art U (CA)
Andrews U (MI)
The Art Inst of
Colorado (CO)
The Art Inst of Fort
Lauderdale (FL)
The Art Inst of
Pittsburgh (PA)
The Art Inst of
Seattle (WA)
Central Christian Coll of
Kansas (KS)
Corcoran Coll of Art and
Design (DC)
New World School of the
Arts (FL)
Pacific Union Coll (CA)
Rochester Inst of
Technology (NY)
Sage Coll of Albany (NY)
The U of Maine at
Augusta (ME)
Villa Julie Coll (MD)

**Physical Education
Teaching and
Coaching**
Adrian Coll (MI)
Central Christian Coll of
Kansas (KS)
Clayton State U (GA)
Fresno Pacific U (CA)
Hillsdale Free Will Baptist
Coll (OK)
Macon State Coll (GA)
Methodist U (NC)
U of Rio Grande (OH)

Physical Sciences
Faulkner U (AL)
Pennsylvania Coll of
Technology (PA)
Roberts Wesleyan
Coll (NY)
Rogers State U (OK)
U of the District of
Columbia (DC)
Utah Valley State Coll (UT)
Villa Julie Coll (MD)

**Physical Science
Technologies Related**
The U of Akron (OH)
Western Kentucky U (KY)

**Physical Therapist
Assistant**
Arkansas State U (AR)
Baker Coll of Flint (MI)
Baker Coll of
Muskegon (MI)
Becker Coll (MA)
Central Pennsylvania
Coll (PA)
Coll of St. Catherine (MN)
Finlandia U (MI)
Idaho State U (ID)
Loma Linda U (CA)
Missouri Western State
U (MO)
Mountain State U (WV)
Mount Aloysius Coll (PA)
Mount St. Mary's Coll (CA)
New York U (NY)
Our Lady of the Lake
Coll (LA)
Southern Illinois U
Carbondale (IL)
South U (AL)
South U, West Palm
Beach (FL)

South U (GA)
U of Central
Arkansas (AR)
U of Evansville (IN)
U of Indianapolis (IN)
U of Puerto Rico at
Humacao (PR)
U of Saint Francis (IN)
Washburn U (KS)

Physical Therapy
Clayton State U (GA)
Dalton State Coll (GA)
Fairmont State U (WV)
Faulkner U (AL)
Macon State Coll (GA)
Mercyhurst Coll (PA)
Oakwood Coll (AL)
Shawnee State U (OH)
Southern Adventist U (TN)
U of Central
Arkansas (AR)
U of Cincinnati (OH)

Physician Assistant
Central Christian Coll of
Kansas (KS)
Dalton State Coll (GA)
Minnesota School of
Business (MN)
Southern Adventist U (TN)

Physics
Adrian Coll (MI)
Clayton State U (GA)
Dalton State Coll (GA)
Idaho State U (ID)
Macon State Coll (GA)
Mesa State Coll (CO)
Rochester Inst of
Technology (NY)
Thomas More Coll (KY)
U of the Virgin Islands (VI)
Utah Valley State Coll (UT)
York Coll of
Pennsylvania (PA)

Piano and Organ
Kwantlen U Coll (BC,
Canada)
New World School of the
Arts (FL)

**Pipefitting and
Sprinkler Fitting**
British Columbia Inst of
Technology (BC,
Canada)
Thompson Rivers U (BC,
Canada)

**Plant Nursery
Management**
Inter American U of Puerto
Rico, Barranquitas
Campus (PR)
Pennsylvania Coll of
Technology (PA)
State U of New York Coll
of Agriculture and
Technology at
Cobleskill (NY)

**Plant Protection and
Integrated Pest
Management**
North Carolina State
U (NC)
Sterling Coll (VT)
U of Puerto Rico at
Utuado (PR)

Plant Sciences
State U of New York Coll
of Agriculture and
Technology at
Cobleskill (NY)

**Plant Sciences
Related**
Sterling Coll (VT)

**Plastics Engineering
Technology**
British Columbia Inst of
Technology (BC,
Canada)
Ferris State U (MI)
Penn State Erie, The
Behrend Coll (PA)
Pennsylvania Coll of
Technology (PA)
Shawnee State U (OH)

Platemaking/Imaging
Pennsylvania Coll of
Technology (PA)

Plumbing Technology
Pennsylvania Coll of
Technology (PA)
Thompson Rivers U (BC,
Canada)

**Political Science and
Government**
Adrian Coll (MI)
Clayton State U (GA)
Dalton State Coll (GA)
Fresno Pacific U (CA)
Idaho State U (ID)
Indiana U–Purdue U Fort
Wayne (IN)
Indiana Wesleyan U (IN)
John Cabot U (Italy)
Kwantlen U Coll (BC,
Canada)
Macon State Coll (GA)
Methodist U (NC)
Rogers State U (OK)
Sacred Heart U (CT)
Thomas More Coll (KY)
Université Laval (QC,
Canada)
The U of Scranton (PA)
The U of Tampa (FL)
The U of Toledo (OH)
U of Wisconsin–Green
Bay (WI)
Villa Julie Coll (MD)
Xavier U (OH)
York Coll of
Pennsylvania (PA)

Postal Management
Macon State Coll (GA)

**Precision Systems
Maintenance and
Repair Technologies
Related**
British Columbia Inst of
Technology (BC,
Canada)

Pre-Dentistry Studies
Concordia U
Wisconsin (WI)

Pre-Engineering
Anderson U (IN)
Atlantic Union Coll (MA)
Boise State U (ID)
Campbell U (NC)
Charleston Southern
U (SC)
Clayton State U (GA)
Columbus State U (GA)
Deree Coll, The American
College of Greece
(Greece)
Eastern Kentucky U (KY)
Edgewood Coll (WI)
Faulkner U (AL)
Ferris State U (MI)
Hannibal-LaGrange
Coll (MO)
Keene State Coll (NH)
LaGrange Coll (GA)
Lincoln U (MO)
Macon State Coll (GA)
Marian Coll (IN)
Medgar Evers Coll of the
City U of New
York (NY)
Mesa State Coll (CO)
Methodist U (NC)
Minnesota State U
Mankato (MN)
Missouri Southern State
U (MO)
Montana State
U–Billings (MT)
Newman U (KS)
Niagara U (NY)
Northern State U (SD)
Purdue U North
Central (IN)
St. Gregory's U,
Shawnee (OK)
Shawnee State U (OH)
Southern Utah U (UT)
U of New Hampshire (NH)
U of Sioux Falls (SD)
Utah Valley State Coll (UT)
Vaughn Coll of Aeronautics
and Technology (NY)
West Virginia State U (WV)

Pre-Law Studies
Calumet Coll of Saint
Joseph (IN)
Ferris State U (MI)
Immaculata U (PA)
Peirce Coll (PA)
Thomas More Coll (KY)

Pre-Medical Studies
Concordia U
Wisconsin (WI)
Schiller International U
(Spain)
Schiller International U
(United Kingdom)

State U of New York Coll
of Agriculture and
Technology at
Cobleskill (NY)
U of Ottawa (ON, Canada)

Pre-Nursing Studies
Concordia U
Wisconsin (WI)
South U, West Palm
Beach (FL)
Trinity International U (IL)

Pre-Pharmacy Studies
Dalton State Coll (GA)
Emmanuel Coll (GA)
Ferris State U (MI)
Macon State Coll (GA)
Thompson Rivers U (BC,
Canada)

**Pre-Theology/Pre-
Ministerial Studies**
Manchester Coll (IN)
Nazarene Bible Coll (CO)
St. Gregory's U,
Shawnee (OK)

Pre-Veterinary Studies
Schiller International U
(Spain)
Schiller International U
(United Kingdom)
Shawnee State U (OH)

Printmaking
Academy of Art U (CA)
New World School of the
Arts (FL)

Professional Studies
Ohio Valley U (WV)

**Psychiatric/Mental
Health Services
Technology**
Lake Superior State U (MI)
Northern Kentucky U (KY)
Pennsylvania Coll of
Technology (PA)
The U of Toledo (OH)

Psychology
Adrian Coll (MI)
Bluefield State Coll (WV)
Central Methodist U (MO)
Chestnut Hill Coll (PA)
Crown Coll (MN)
Dalton State Coll (GA)
Eastern New Mexico
U (NM)
Felician Coll (NJ)
Fresno Pacific U (CA)
Hillsdale Free Will Baptist
Coll (OK)
Indiana U–Purdue U Fort
Wayne (IN)
Kwantlen U Coll (BC,
Canada)
Lourdes Coll (OH)
Macon State Coll (GA)
Marian Coll (IN)
Methodist U (NC)
Montana State
U–Billings (MT)
Mount Olive Coll (NC)
Sacred Heart U (CT)
Salem International
U (WV)
Thomas More Coll (KY)
U of Rio Grande (OH)
The U of Tampa (FL)
U of Wisconsin–Green
Bay (WI)
Villa Julie Coll (MD)
Wright State U (OH)
Xavier U (OH)

**Psychology Teacher
Education**
Central Christian Coll of
Kansas (KS)

Public Administration
Central Methodist U (MO)
Indiana U Bloomington (IN)
Indiana U Northwest (IN)
Indiana U–Purdue U Fort
Wayne (IN)
Indiana U–Purdue U
Indianapolis (IN)
Indiana U South Bend (IN)
Macon State Coll (GA)
Medgar Evers Coll of the
City U of New
York (NY)
Point Park U (PA)
The U of Maine at
Augusta (ME)
U of Regina (SK, Canada)
U of the District of
Columbia (DC)

**Public Administration
and Social Service
Professions Related**
Indiana U–Purdue U Fort
Wayne (IN)
The U of Akron (OH)
U of Saint Francis (IN)

Public Health
U of Alaska Fairbanks (AK)

Public Policy Analysis
Indiana U Bloomington (IN)
Saint Peter's Coll (NJ)

**Public Relations,
Advertising, and
Applied
Communication
Related**
Champlain Coll (VT)
John Brown U (AR)
Madonna U (MI)

**Public Relations/
Image Management**
Champlain Coll (VT)
John Brown U (AR)
Johnson & Wales U (NC)
Madonna U (MI)
New England School of
Communications (ME)
Xavier U (OH)

**Purchasing,
Procurement/
Acquisitions and
Contracts
Management**
Mercyhurst Coll (PA)
Saint Joseph's U (PA)
U of Management and
Technology (VA)
Washburn U (KS)

**Quality Control and
Safety Technologies
Related**
Madonna U (MI)

**Quality Control
Technology**
Baker Coll of Cadillac (MI)
Baker Coll of Flint (MI)
Baker Coll of
Muskegon (MI)
Eastern Kentucky U (KY)
Pennsylvania Coll of
Technology (PA)
U of Cincinnati (OH)

Rabbinical Studies
Université Laval (QC,
Canada)

Radiation Biology
Inter American U of Puerto
Rico, Barranquitas
Campus (PR)

Radio and Television
Academy of Art U (CA)
The Art Inst of Fort
Lauderdale (FL)
The Art Inst of
Pittsburgh (PA)
Ashland U (OH)
Lawrence Technological
U (MI)
New England School of
Communications (ME)
Northwestern Coll (MN)
Ohio U (OH)
Ohio U–Zanesville (OH)
Rogers State U (OK)
Salem International
U (WV)
Xavier U (OH)
York Coll of
Pennsylvania (PA)

**Radio and Television
Broadcasting
Technology**
British Columbia Inst of
Technology (BC,
Canada)
Lyndon State Coll (VT)
The New England Inst of
Art (MA)
New England School of
Communications (ME)
New York Inst of
Technology (NY)
Southern Adventist U (TN)

**Radiologic
Technology/Science**
Allen Coll (IA)
Baker Coll of Clinton
Township (MI)

Baker Coll of
Muskegon (MI)
Boise State U (ID)
Champlain Coll (VT)
Clayton State U (GA)
Dalton State Coll (GA)
Indiana U Northwest (IN)
Indiana U–Purdue U Fort
Wayne (IN)
Lewis-Clark State Coll (ID)
Mansfield U of
Pennsylvania (PA)
Mesa State Coll (CO)
Midwestern State U (TX)
Mountain State U (WV)
Mount Aloysius Coll (PA)
Nebraska Methodist
Coll (NE)
Newman U (KS)
U of Arkansas at Fort
Smith (AR)
The U of Montana (MT)
U of Rio Grande (OH)
Washburn U (KS)

**Range Science and
Management**
Sterling Coll (VT)

Real Estate
American Public U
System (WV)
British Columbia Inst of
Technology (BC,
Canada)
Fairmont State U (WV)
Ferris State U (MI)
Saint Francis U (PA)
U of Cincinnati (OH)

Receptionist
Baker Coll of Allen
Park (MI)
The U of Montana (MT)

**Recording Arts
Technology**
New England School of
Communications (ME)

Religious Education
Apex School of
Theology (NC)
The Baptist Coll of
Florida (FL)
Boise Bible Coll (ID)
Calvary Bible Coll and
Theological
Seminary (MO)
Cincinnati Christian U (OH)
Cornerstone U (MI)
Dallas Baptist U (TX)
Eastern Nazarene
Coll (MA)
Great Lakes Christian
Coll (MI)
Hillsdale Free Will Baptist
Coll (OK)
Houghton Coll (NY)
Indiana Wesleyan U (IN)
Kuyper Coll (MI)
Mercyhurst Coll (PA)
Methodist U (NC)
Nazarene Bible Coll (CO)
Warner Pacific Coll (OR)
Washington Bible
Coll (MD)

**Religious/Sacred
Music**
Aquinas Coll (MI)
The Baptist Coll of
Florida (FL)
Boise Bible Coll (ID)
Cincinnati Christian U (OH)
Hillsdale Free Will Baptist
Coll (OK)
Immaculata U (PA)
Indiana Wesleyan U (IN)
Mount Vernon Nazarene
U (OH)
Nazarene Bible Coll (CO)
Vennard Coll (IA)

Religious Studies
Adrian Coll (MI)
Atlantic Union Coll (MA)
Boise Bible Coll (ID)
Brewton-Parker Coll (GA)
Calumet Coll of Saint
Joseph (IN)
Central Christian Coll of
Kansas (KS)
Felician Coll (NJ)
Global U of the Assemblies
of God (MO)
Grace Bible Coll (MI)
Griggs U (MD)
Holy Apostles Coll and
Seminary (CT)
Howard Payne U (TX)

Liberty U (VA)
Lourdes Coll (OH)
Madonna U (MI)
Manchester Coll (IN)
Maranatha Baptist Bible
Coll (WI)
Missouri Baptist U (MO)
Mount Marty Coll (SD)
Mount Olive Coll (NC)
Oakwood Coll (AL)
Pacific Islands Bible
Coll (GU)
Presentation Coll (SD)
Sacred Heart U (CT)
Shaw U (NC)
Tabor Coll (KS)
Thomas More Coll (KY)
The U of Findlay (OH)
U of Sioux Falls (SD)
Vennard Coll (IA)
Washington Bible
Coll (MD)

**Religious Studies
Related**
Lindsey Wilson Coll (KY)

Resort Management
The Art Inst of
Pittsburgh (PA)
Rochester Inst of
Technology (NY)
Thompson Rivers U (BC,
Canada)

**Respiratory Care
Therapy**
Ball State U (IN)
Cameron U (OK)
Columbia Union Coll (MD)
Dakota State U (SD)
Dalton State Coll (GA)
Faulkner U (AL)
Ferris State U (MI)
Gannon U (PA)
Gwynedd-Mercy Coll (PA)
Indiana U Northwest (IN)
Indiana U–Purdue U
Indianapolis (IN)
Loma Linda U (CA)
Macon State Coll (GA)
Mansfield U of
Pennsylvania (PA)
Missouri Southern State
U (MO)
Molloy Coll (NY)
Morehead State U (KY)
Mountain State U (WV)
Nebraska Methodist
Coll (NE)
Newman U (KS)
Northern Kentucky U (KY)
Point Park U (PA)
St. Augustine Coll (IL)
Shawnee State U (OH)
Shenandoah U (VA)
Southern Adventist U (TN)
Southern Illinois U
Carbondale (IL)
Universidad Adventista de
las Antillas (PR)
The U of Akron (OH)
U of Arkansas at Fort
Smith (AR)
The U of Montana (MT)
U of Pittsburgh at
Johnstown (PA)
U of Southern Indiana (IN)
U of the District of
Columbia (DC)
The U of Toledo (OH)
Vermont Tech Coll (VT)
Washburn U (KS)
Weber State U (UT)
Western Kentucky U (KY)
York Coll of
Pennsylvania (PA)

**Respiratory Therapy
Technician**
Thompson Rivers U (BC,
Canada)

**Restaurant, Culinary,
and Catering
Management**
The Art Inst of Dallas (TX)
The Art Inst of
Houston (TX)
Bob Jones U (SC)
Ferris State U (MI)
Johnson & Wales U (FL)
Johnson & Wales U (NC)
Johnson & Wales U (RI)
Lexington Coll (IL)
The U of Akron (OH)
U of New Hampshire (NH)

Restaurant/Food Services Management
The Art Inst of Pittsburgh (PA)
Ferris State U (MI)
Johnson & Wales U (CO)
Lexington Coll (IL)
Rochester Inst of Technology (NY)
U of New Hampshire (NH)

Retailing
Johnson & Wales U (RI)

Robotics Technology
British Columbia Inst of Technology (BC, Canada)
Indiana U–Purdue U Indianapolis (IN)
Purdue U (IN)
U of Rio Grande (OH)

Safety/Security Technology
Keene State Coll (NH)
Madonna U (MI)
Ohio U (OH)
U of Cincinnati (OH)

Sales and Marketing/Marketing And Distribution Teacher Education
Central Christian Coll of Kansas (KS)

Sales, Distribution and Marketing
Baker Coll of Flint (MI)
Baker Coll of Jackson (MI)
Central Pennsylvania Coll (PA)
Champlain Coll (VT)
Dalton State Coll (GA)
Johnson & Wales U (NC)
Johnson & Wales U (RI)
Purdue U North Central (IN)
Thompson Rivers U (BC, Canada)
The U of Findlay (OH)

Science Teacher Education
Central Christian Coll of Kansas (KS)
U of Cincinnati (OH)

Science Technologies Related
British Columbia Inst of Technology (BC, Canada)
Madonna U (MI)
Ohio Valley U (WV)

Science, Technology and Society
Samford U (AL)

Sculpture
Academy of Art U (CA)
New World School of the Arts (FL)

Secondary Education
Central Christian Coll of Kansas (KS)
Dalton State Coll (GA)
Mountain State U (WV)
Rogers State U (OK)
Vennard Coll (IA)

Security and Protective Services Related
Ohio U (OH)

Selling Skills and Sales
The U of Akron (OH)

Sheet Metal Technology
British Columbia Inst of Technology (BC, Canada)
Montana State U–Billings (MT)

Sign Language Interpretation and Translation
Cincinnati Christian U (OH)
Coll of St. Catherine (MN)
Fairmont State U (WV)
Mount Aloysius Coll (PA)
Rochester Inst of Technology (NY)
U of Arkansas at Little Rock (AR)
U of Louisville (KY)

Slavic Languages
U of Ottawa (ON, Canada)

Small Business Administration
Central Christian Coll of Kansas (KS)
Lewis-Clark State Coll (ID)

Small Engine Mechanics and Repair Technology
British Columbia Inst of Technology (BC, Canada)
The U of Montana (MT)

Social Psychology
Central Christian Coll of Kansas (KS)
Kwantlen U Coll (BC, Canada)
Park U (MO)

Social Sciences
Adrian Coll (MI)
Campbellsville U (KY)
Clayton State U (GA)
Crown Coll (MN)
Evangel U (MO)
Faulkner U (AL)
Felician Coll (NJ)
Indiana Wesleyan U (IN)
Kwantlen U Coll (BC, Canada)
Lindsey Wilson Coll (KY)
Marymount Manhattan Coll (NY)
Mesa State Coll (CO)
Ohio U (OH)
Ohio U–Zanesville (OH)
Rogers State U (OK)
Sage Coll of Albany (NY)
Saint Peter's Coll (NJ)
Samford U (AL)
Shawnee State U (OH)
State U of New York Empire State Coll (NY)
Tri-State U (IN)
U of Cincinnati (OH)
The U of Findlay (OH)
The U of Maine at Augusta (ME)
U of Puerto Rico at Utuado (PR)
U of Sioux Falls (SD)
U of Southern Indiana (IN)
The U of Toledo (OH)
Valparaiso U (IN)
Villa Julie Coll (MD)
Warner Pacific Coll (OR)
Wayland Baptist U (TX)

Social Sciences Related
Concordia U at Austin (TX)

Social Science Teacher Education
Central Christian Coll of Kansas (KS)

Social Studies Teacher Education
Central Christian Coll of Kansas (KS)

Social Work
Central Christian Coll of Kansas (KS)
Champlain Coll (VT)
Dalton State Coll (GA)
Edinboro U of Pennsylvania (PA)
Indiana U East (IN)
Methodist U (NC)
Northern State U (SD)
Oglala Lakota Coll (SD)
Suffolk U (MA)
U of Cincinnati (OH)
U of Rio Grande (OH)
The U of Toledo (OH)
U of Wisconsin–Green Bay (WI)
Wright State U (OH)

Sociology
Adrian Coll (MI)
Central Christian Coll of Kansas (KS)
Clayton State U (GA)
Dalton State Coll (GA)
Felician Coll (NJ)
Fresno Pacific U (CA)
Grand View Coll (IA)
Kwantlen U Coll (BC, Canada)
Lourdes Coll (OH)
Macon State Coll (GA)
Methodist U (NC)
Montana State U–Billings (MT)

Penn State U Park (PA)
Sacred Heart U (CT)
Thomas More Coll (KY)
U of Rio Grande (OH)
The U of Scranton (PA)
The U of Tampa (FL)
Villa Julie Coll (MD)
Wright State U (OH)
Xavier U (OH)

Soil Conservation
U of Minnesota, Crookston (MN)

Soil Science and Agronomy
Sterling Coll (VT)

Soil Sciences Related
Sterling Coll (VT)

Solar Energy Technology
Pennsylvania Coll of Technology (PA)

Spanish
Adrian Coll (MI)
Chestnut Hill Coll (PA)
Clayton State U (GA)
Fresno Pacific U (CA)
Idaho State U (ID)
Indiana U–Purdue U Fort Wayne (IN)
Methodist U (NC)
Sacred Heart U (CT)
Thomas More Coll (KY)
The U of Tampa (FL)
U of Wisconsin–Green Bay (WI)
Xavier U (OH)

Special Education
Edinboro U of Pennsylvania (PA)
Montana State U–Billings (MT)
St. Augustine Coll (IL)

Special Education (Multiply Disabled)
Inter American U of Puerto Rico, Barranquitas Campus (PR)

Special Education Related
Minot State U (ND)

Special Education (Speech Or Language Impaired)
U of Nebraska at Omaha (NE)

Special Products Marketing
Ball State U (IN)
Ferris State U (MI)
Johnson & Wales U (FL)
Johnson & Wales U (RI)
U of Minnesota, Crookston (MN)

Speech and Rhetoric
Clayton State U (GA)
Dalton State Coll (GA)
Ferris State U (MI)
Macon State Coll (GA)
Madonna U (MI)

Speech-Language Pathology
Baker Coll of Muskegon (MI)
Southern Adventist U (TN)

Speech Teacher Education
Central Christian Coll of Kansas (KS)

Sport and Fitness Administration/Management
Lake Superior State U (MI)
Northwood U (MI)
Northwood U, Florida Campus (FL)
Northwood U, Texas Campus (TX)
Thompson Rivers U (BC, Canada)
Webber International U (FL)

Substance Abuse/Addiction Counseling
Indiana Wesleyan U (IN)
Keene State Coll (NH)
Newman U (KS)
Rogers State U (OK)
St. Augustine Coll (IL)
The U of Akron (OH)

U of Great Falls (MT)
The U of Toledo (OH)
Washburn U (KS)

Surgical Technology
Baker Coll of Clinton Township (MI)
Baker Coll of Flint (MI)
Baker Coll of Jackson (MI)
Baker Coll of Muskegon (MI)
Boise State U (ID)
Cabarrus Coll of Health Sciences (NC)
Florida Metropolitan U–Brandon
Georgia Southwestern State U (GA)
Loma Linda U (CA)
Mercy Coll of Health Sciences (IA)
Montana State U–Billings (MT)
Mount Aloysius Coll (PA)
Our Lady of the Lake Coll (LA)
Presentation Coll (SD)
Robert Morris Coll (IL)
Trinity Coll of Nursing and Health Sciences (IL)
The U of Akron (OH)
U of Arkansas at Fort Smith (AR)
The U of Montana (MT)
U of Pittsburgh at Johnstown (PA)
U of Saint Francis (IN)

Survey Technology
British Columbia Inst of Technology (BC, Canada)
Ferris State U (MI)
Glenville State Coll (WV)
Paul Smith's Coll of Arts and Sciences (NY)
Pennsylvania Coll of Technology (PA)
The U of Akron (OH)
U of Alaska Anchorage (AK)
U of New Hampshire (NH)

System Administration
National American U, Denver (CO)
Sage Coll of Albany (NY)
Thompson Rivers U (BC, Canada)

System, Networking, and Lan/Wan Management
Baker Coll of Auburn Hills (MI)
Champlain Coll (VT)
DeVry U, Phoenix (AZ)
DeVry U, Fremont (CA)
DeVry U, Long Beach (CA)
DeVry U, Pomona (CA)
DeVry U, Sherman Oaks (CA)
DeVry U, Westminster (CO)
DeVry U, Orlando (FL)
DeVry U, Alpharetta (GA)
DeVry U, Decatur (GA)
DeVry U, Chicago (IL)
DeVry U, Tinley Park (IL)
DeVry U, Kansas City (MO)
DeVry U (NJ)
DeVry U, Columbus (OH)
DeVry U, Fort Washington (PA)
DeVry U, Houston (TX)
DeVry U, Irving (TX)
DeVry U, Federal Way (WA)
National American U, Denver (CO)
Peirce Coll (PA)
Thompson Rivers U (BC, Canada)
U of Phoenix–Cleveland Campus (OH)
U of Phoenix–Columbus Ohio Campus (OH)
U of Phoenix–Indianapolis Campus (IN)
U of Phoenix–Springfield Campus (MO)

Taxation
British Columbia Inst of Technology (BC, Canada)

Minnesota School of Business (MN)

Teacher Assistant/Aide
Alabama State U (AL)
Alverno Coll (WI)
Boise State U (ID)
Dordt Coll (IA)
Mount Ida Coll (MA)
New Mexico Highlands U (NM)
New Mexico State U (NM)
The U of Akron (OH)
U of New Mexico (NM)
U of Phoenix–Cleveland Campus (OH)
U of Phoenix–Columbus Ohio Campus (OH)
U of Phoenix–Houston Campus (TX)
U of Phoenix–Indianapolis Campus (IN)
U of Phoenix–St. Louis Campus (MO)

Technical and Business Writing
Ferris State U (MI)
Murray State U (KY)

Technical Teacher Education
Eastern Kentucky U (KY)
New York Inst of Technology (NY)
Northern Kentucky U (KY)
Western Kentucky U (KY)

Technology/Industrial Arts Teacher Education
Arkansas State U (AR)

Telecommunications
Briarcliffe Coll (NY)
Champlain Coll (VT)
Clayton State U (GA)
Columbia Coll Hollywood (CA)
Inter American U of Puerto Rico, Bayamón Campus (PR)
Salem International U (WV)
State U of New York Coll of Agriculture and Technology at Cobleskill (NY)

Telecommunications Technology
Penn State Altoona (PA)
Penn State Berks (PA)
Penn State Erie, The Behrend Coll (PA)

Theater Design and Technology
Indiana U Bloomington (IN)
Johnson State Coll (VT)
U of Rio Grande (OH)

Theological and Ministerial Studies Related
Bob Jones U (SC)
U of Saint Francis (IN)

Theology
Appalachian Bible Coll (WV)
The Baptist Coll of Florida (FL)
Briar Cliff U (IA)
Central Christian Coll of Kansas (KS)
Creighton U (NE)
Franciscan U of Steubenville (OH)
Griggs U (MD)
Heritage Bible Coll (NC)
Marian Coll (IN)
Ohio Dominican U (OH)
Ozark Christian Coll (MO)
Sacred Heart Major Seminary (MI)
Université Laval (QC, Canada)
Washington Bible Coll (MD)
William Jessup U (CA)
Williams Baptist Coll (AR)
Xavier U (OH)

Therapeutic Recreation
Indiana Tech (IN)
U of Southern Maine (ME)

Tool and Die Technology
Pennsylvania Coll of Technology (PA)

Tourism and Travel Services Management
Baker Coll of Flint (MI)
Baker Coll of Muskegon (MI)
Black Hills State U (SD)
Brigham Young U–Hawaii (HI)
British Columbia Inst of Technology (BC, Canada)
Central Pennsylvania Coll (PA)
Champlain Coll (VT)
Johnson & Wales U (FL)
Johnson & Wales U (RI)
Mesa State Coll (CO)
Morrison U (NV)
Mountain State U (WV)
Ohio U (OH)
Paul Smith's Coll of Arts and Sciences (NY)
Pennsylvania Coll of Technology (PA)
Robert Morris Coll (IL)
Rochester Inst of Technology (NY)
Schiller International U (FL)
Sullivan U (KY)
The U of Akron (OH)
The U of Montana–Western (MT)
Webber International U (FL)

Tourism and Travel Services Marketing
Champlain Coll (VT)
Johnson & Wales U (RI)
Ohio U (OH)
Pontifical Catholic U of Puerto Rico (PR)
State U of New York Coll of Agriculture and Technology at Cobleskill (NY)
The U of Montana–Western (MT)

Tourism Promotion
Champlain Coll (VT)
Thompson Rivers U (BC, Canada)

Tourism/Travel Marketing
Mountain State U (WV)

Trade and Industrial Teacher Education
British Columbia Inst of Technology (BC, Canada)
Cincinnati Christian U (OH)
Indiana State U (IN)
Murray State U (KY)
Purdue U (IN)

Transportation and Highway Engineering
British Columbia Inst of Technology (BC, Canada)

Transportation Technology
Baker Coll of Flint (MI)
Maine Maritime Academy (ME)
U of Cincinnati (OH)
The U of Toledo (OH)

Turf and Turfgrass Management
North Carolina State U (NC)
Pennsylvania Coll of Technology (PA)
State U of New York Coll of Agriculture and Technology at Cobleskill (NY)
U of Massachusetts Amherst (MA)

Urban Studies/Affairs
Clayton State U (GA)
Mount St. Mary's Coll (CA)
Saint Peter's Coll (NJ)
U of the District of Columbia (DC)
U of Wisconsin–Green Bay (WI)

Vehicle and Vehicle Parts And Accessories Marketing
Northwood U (MI)
Northwood U, Florida Campus (FL)
Northwood U, Texas Campus (TX)
Pennsylvania Coll of Technology (PA)

Vehicle/Equipment Operation
Baker Coll of Flint (MI)
The U of Montana (MT)

Vehicle Maintenance and Repair Technologies Related
British Columbia Inst of Technology (BC, Canada)
Pennsylvania Coll of Technology (PA)
U of Alaska Fairbanks (AK)

Veterinary/Animal Health Technology
Baker Coll of Cadillac (MI)
Baker Coll of Jackson (MI)
Baker Coll of Muskegon (MI)
Medaille Coll (NY)
Morehead State U (KY)
Northwestern State U of Louisiana (LA)

Purdue U (IN)
Thompson Rivers U (BC, Canada)
The U of Maine at Augusta (ME)

Veterinary Sciences
Clayton State U (GA)

Veterinary Technology
Argosy U, Twin Cities, Eagan (MN)
Becker Coll (MA)
Fairmont State U (WV)
Lincoln Memorial U (TN)
Medaille Coll (NY)
Minnesota School of Business (MN)
Mount Ida Coll (MA)
National American U, Rapid City (SD)
Sul Ross State U (TX)
Vermont Tech Coll (VT)

Violin, Viola, Guitar and Other Stringed Instruments
Five Towns Coll (NY)
Kwantlen U Coll (BC, Canada)
New World School of the Arts (FL)

Visual and Performing Arts
Briarcliffe Coll (NY)
Indiana U East (IN)

Miami International U of Art & Design (FL)
Thomas More Coll (KY)
U of Arkansas at Fort Smith (AR)

Voice and Opera
Five Towns Coll (NY)
Kwantlen U Coll (BC, Canada)
New World School of the Arts (FL)

Water Quality and Wastewater Treatment Management And Recycling Technology
Lake Superior State U (MI)
Murray State U (KY)
U of the District of Columbia (DC)
Wright State U (OH)

Web/Multimedia Management and Webmaster
Academy of Art U (CA)
The Art Inst of Pittsburgh (PA)
Central Pennsylvania Coll (PA)
Champlain Coll (VT)
ITT Tech Inst, Tempe (AZ)
Lewis-Clark State Coll (ID)
Limestone Coll (SC)
New England School of Communications (ME)

Web Page, Digital/ Multimedia and Information Resources Design
The Art Inst of Atlanta (GA)
The Art Inst of California– Los Angeles (CA)
The Art Inst of Dallas (TX)
The Art Inst of Houston (TX)
The Art Inst of Pittsburgh (PA)
The Art Inst of Portland (OR)
The Art Insts International Minnesota (MN)
Baker Coll of Allen Park (MI)
Champlain Coll (VT)
Indiana Tech (IN)
ITT Tech Inst, Tempe (AZ)
ITT Tech Inst, Lexington (KY)
Minnesota School of Business (MN)
Mountain State U (WV)
National American U, Denver (CO)
New England School of Communications (ME)
Pennsylvania Coll of Technology (PA)
Robert Morris Coll (IL)
Thomas More Coll (KY)
Thompson Rivers U (BC, Canada)

Welding Technology
Boise State U (ID)
British Columbia Inst of Technology (BC, Canada)
Excelsior Coll (NY)
Ferris State U (MI)
Georgia Southwestern State U (GA)
Idaho State U (ID)
Lewis-Clark State Coll (ID)
Mesa State Coll (CO)
Pennsylvania Coll of Technology (PA)
U of Alaska Anchorage (AK)
The U of Montana (MT)
The U of Toledo (OH)
Utah Valley State Coll (UT)

Wildlife and Wildlands Science And Management
British Columbia Inst of Technology (BC, Canada)
State U of New York Coll of Agriculture and Technology at Cobleskill (NY)
Sterling Coll (VT)
U of Minnesota, Crookston (MN)
Winona State U (MN)

Wildlife Biology
Central Christian Coll of Kansas (KS)

Wind/Percussion Instruments
Five Towns Coll (NY)
New World School of the Arts (FL)

Women'S Studies
Indiana U–Purdue U Fort Wayne (IN)
Nazarene Bible Coll (CO)

Wood Science and Wood Products/Pulp And Paper Technology
U of Arkansas at Monticello (AR)

Woodworking Related
Pennsylvania Coll of Technology (PA)

Word Processing
Baker Coll of Allen Park (MI)

Zoology/Animal Biology
Central Christian Coll of Kansas (KS)

Alphabetical Listing of Two-Year Colleges

In this index, the page locations of profiles are printed in regular type, **Special Messages** in *italics*, and **Close-Ups** in **bold type.** When there is more than one number in **bold type,** it indicates that the institution has more than one **Close-Up;** in most such cases, the first of the series is a general institutional description.